OXFORD REF

The Concise
Australian
National
Dictionary

THE AUSTRALIAN NATIONAL DICTIONARY and THE CONCISE AUSTRALIAN NATIONAL DICTIONARY were researched and written at the Australian National Dictionary Centre, which is located on the campus of the Australian National University, Canberra. Funded by the University and by Oxford University Press, the Centre created and maintains a 250 000-entry database of Australian English. Dr W. S. Ramsom heads the Centre, which conducts research into language and language-use in Australia.

Joan Hughes is Associate Editor of the Australian National Dictionary Centre. She graduated with Honours in English from the Australian National University in 1976 and completed an M.A. in 1979. From 1978 until its completion, Miss Hughes was Associate Editor of THE AUSTRALIAN NATIONAL DICTIONARY, and was Editor of the recently published AUSTRALIAN REFERENCE DICTIONARY.

Australian National Dictionary Centre publications include:
- THE AUSTRALIAN NATIONAL DICTIONARY
- THE AUSTRALIAN REFERENCE DICTIONARY
- AUSTRALIAN ABORIGINAL WORDS IN ENGLISH
- AUSTRALIAN WORDS AND THEIR ORIGINS
- THE AUSTRALIAN WRITERS' AND EDITORS' GUIDE
- DIGGER DIALECTS

Forthcoming publications include:
- THE AUSTRALIAN CONCISE OXFORD DICTIONARY (SECOND EDITION)
- THE AUSTRALIAN POCKET OXFORD DICTIONARY (SEVENTH EDITION)
- MODERN AUSTRALIAN USAGE

OXFORD REFERENCE

The Concise Australian National Dictionary

Edited by Joan Hughes

Melbourne
OXFORD UNIVERSITY PRESS
Oxford   Auckland   New York

OXFORD UNIVERSITY PRESS AUSTRALIA

Oxford   New York   Toronto
Delhi   Bombay   Calcutta   Madras   Karachi
Kuala Lumpur   Singapore   Hong Kong   Tokyo
Nairobi   Dar es Salaam   Cape Town
Melbourne   Auckland

and associated companies in
Berlin   Ibadan

OXFORD is a trade mark of Oxford University Press

© Australian National University 1989
First published 1989
Reprinted as The Concise Australian National Dictionary 1992

This book is copyright. Apart from any fair
dealing for the purposes of private study,
research, criticism or review as permitted under
the Copyright Act, no part may be reproduced,
stored in a retrieval system, or transmitted, in
any form or by any means, electronic, mechanical,
photocopying, recording, or otherwise without
prior written permission. Inquiries to be made to
Oxford University Press.

Copying for educational purposes.
Where copies of part or whole of the book are
made under section 53B or section 53D of the Act,
the law requires that records of such copying be
kept. In such cases the copyright owner is
entitled to claim payment.

National Library of Australia
Cataloguing-in-Publication data:

[Australian words and their origins]. The Concise Australian national
dictionary.

ISBN 0 19 553433 6.

1. English language — Australia — Dictionaries. 2. Australianisms —
Dictionaries. I. Hughes, Joan. II. Title: Australian words and their origins.

423

Typeset by Abb-typesetting Pty Ltd
Printed in Hong Kong
Published by Oxford University Press,
253 Normanby Road, South Melbourne, Australia

CONTENTS

Preface   vii

Explanation of style   vii

List of Aboriginal languages   ix

Proprietary names   xi

List of abbreviations   xii

Pronunciation   xv

DICTIONARY   1

PREFACE

This Dictionary is an abridged version of the *Australian National Dictionary*. It preserves the entire word list, including combinations and collocations, with the definitions, etymologies, and pronunciations of the parent Dictionary. The illustrative material has been reduced: this Dictionary records the earliest citation and at least one other, with such additional citations as are required by particular entries. It is the purpose of this Dictionary to make more widely available the essence of the *Australian National Dictionary*.

EXPLANATION OF THE STYLE AND ARRANGEMENT OF ENTRIES

The entry. Each entry is designed to present the information it contains in the most illuminating, convenient, and economic form. Entries range from the simple, one word recorded as one part of speech and in one sense, to the complex, subdivided first according to part of speech and then according to sense. Combinations and collocations of which the headword is the main element are normally listed in a sub-section of the entry, with derivatives of minor importance at the end of the entry. In a sequence of combinations and collocations the main element is listed in the first instance but thereafter understood. Combinations which have coalesced into one, usually unhyphenated, compound, which require fuller treatment, or which are essentially independent of the bulk of the entry, are listed in their own alphabetical place. The elements of an entry (not all of which may be required) appear in the following order.

Headword. The headword, the word which is the subject of the entry, appears at its head in bold roman. Subordinate items – combinations, collocations, and phrases of which the headword is the main element, as well as derivatives, appear in their place in the entry in bold roman. Words which normally have an initial capital, as place-names used in a transferred sense and proprietary names, retain the capital, all other initial letters being in lower case. Superscript numerals are used to distinguish two or more headwords having the same spelling. If a word has separate entries according to its parts of speech these are arranged chronologically, the noun usually preceding the verb, unless the logic of the word's history demands otherwise.

Pronunciation. Words borrowed from Aboriginal languages, survivals from British dialects, and words which have been coined in Australia are supplied with pronunciations. Words from other varieties of English which have acquired new meanings in Australian English are given pronunciations only when there is a possible ambiguity; *station*, e.g., does not need a pronunciation but *lead* does. Where a pronunciation is given it follows the headword, marked off by slashes and in International Phonetic Alphabet notation (see table on p. 00), using the system established by A.G. Mitchell and A. Delbridge in *The Pronunciation of English in Australia*, revised edition (Sydney 1965).

Part of speech. If a word is recorded only as a noun, and there is no other noun in the same form, no part of speech is given. Otherwise the part of speech is given in abbreviated form in italics.

Subject or restrictive labels. Subject labels (designating an occupation, sport, etc.) and restrictive labels, such as *Obs.* (obsolete),

Hist. (now only in an historical context), and *N.S.W.* (used chiefly in New South Wales), are printed in italics and with an initial capital. In run-on entries, as sequences of special combinations and collocations, such labels (other than abbreviations of proper names) have a lower-case initial letter.

Variant spellings. The main variant spellings are given in bold roman after the headword (pronunciation, part of speech, label) and before the etymology. Spellings which are clearly aberrant or which do not help establish main directions are not listed. Some standard English spelling variants, as *color* for *colour, license* for *licence, parrakeet* for *parakeet, pigmy* for *pygmy* and *waggon* for *wagon,* are not remarked.

Etymology. The etymology is enclosed in square brackets. An etymology which informs all senses of a word precedes any numbered or lettered subdivision. An etymology which informs a specific sense follows that sense's number or (in the case of special combinations or collocations) the second element of the combination. The etymon, or primary word which is the basis of a derivative form or sense, is given in italics, unless it is a word for which there is a main entry in the dictionary, in which case it is in roman small capitals with initial full capital. Etymologies for borrowings from Aboriginal languages have been provided by R.M.W. Dixon. A standardized orthography, using letters of the Roman alphabet with the addition of ŋ,* is employed in most instances, the orthography being that used by R.M.W. Dixon and described in his book, *The Languages of Australia* (Cambridge 1980). The locations of Aboriginal languages are given in a table (p. 00) and on a map (p. 00). In many instances a cross-reference to the corresponding entry in OED(S is supplied.

Ordering of senses. Senses within an entry are arranged chronologically, first according to part of speech and then according to sense. If an entry is divided according to parts of speech more than one part of speech label will follow the headword (as *n.* and *attrib.,* or *n., a.,* and *adv.*).

Definition. The definition is either discrete, if there is no division, or subdivided according to the division. The definition may include cross-references to words which have main entries or are subordinate items. These are readily identified as follows:

a word printed in small capitals with an initial full capital, as BOBUCK, has a main entry in the dictionary (part of speech is given only if necessary to distinguish the main entry being referred to; a numbered sense is specified when appropriate);

a word printed in italics is either a subordinate item in the main entry in which it appears (so **sheep tobacco** is defined as *sheep-wash tobacco* which is in the same entry), or a subordinate item in a main entry indicated in capitals (so, for **sheep-shed,** the definition given is *shearing shed,* see SHEARING B. 3). A reference to a subordinate item in a main entry may vary in form as

---
*Where ŋ appears as the initial letter in the name of a language and is capitalized it is written as *Ng.*

required by its place in the text, as 'shortened form of *shearing shed* (see SHEARING B. 3)' or 'see also *shearing shed* SHEARING B. 3'.

Cross-references. There are two main forms of cross-reference:

if a word is defined by another in the dictionary, as **sorcerer** by KORADJI, or listed without qualification in the definition as, in the entry for **Major Mitchell cockatoo,** are LEADBEATER'S COCKATOO, *pink cockatoo,* see PINK *a.*, and WEE JUGGLER, the synonymy is exact;

if the cross-reference is introduced by 'see also' the synonymy is not exact but the information provided under the word referred to is complementary or in some other way useful.

Variant forms. Variant forms (as distinct from spellings) are listed at the end of the definition.

Citations. Every effort has been made to record the earliest written occurrence of a word and, where appropriate, to supply additional citations illustrating spelling, form, etymology, or meaning. A citation is preceded by a date (of utterance, when this can be established, or publication) and a short bibliographical reference which is in most instances sufficient to enable the reader to identify the text or edition used. The name of the author of an article published in a periodical or of a story in a collection is not normally given. Volume numbers are given in upper case roman, numbers of issues or parts in lower case roman. (Fuller information on sources which have been used heavily or which may be difficult to identify is contained in the select bibliography of the *Australian National Dictionary*.) Citations are given as they appear in the source except that, in the interests of elegance and economy, extraneous material has been omitted (medial ellipsis is indicated by .. and an ellipsis including a stop by ...). Care has been taken not to distort the author's intent.

ABORIGINAL LANGUAGES
See map page x.

39 Adnyamadhanha – in the vicinity of Lake Torrens, S.A.
41 Arabana Waŋgaŋuru – west of Lake Eyre and in the Simpson Desert, S.A.
43 Aranda – in the vicinity of Alice Springs, N.T.
3   Awabakal – on the coast from north of Sydney to Newcastle, N.S.W.
32 Bagandji – along the Darling River, N.S.W.
17 Bandjalang – in the Clarence and Richmond Rivers district in n.e. N.S.W. and s.e. Qld.
38 Baŋgala – south of Lake Torrens to the Gawler Ranges, S.A.
52 Bardi – north of Broome and on Sunday Island, in n. W.A.
5   Dharawal – on the coast from Jervis Bay to Port Hacking, N.S.W.
4   Dharuk – in the vicinity of Port Jackson, Sydney, N.S.W.
6   Dhurga – on the coast from Bermagui to Jervis Bay, N.S.W.
40 Diyari – in the Cooper Creek district, east of Lake Eyre, S.A.
1   Djaŋadi – in the Macleay River district, N.S.W.
23 Dyirbal – in the Tully River district, n. Qld.
19 Gabi – in the Mary River district from Redcliffe to Fraser Island, s.e. Qld.
8   Ganay – in Gippsland, Vic.
34 Gangubanud – on the coast at Portland Bay, Vic.
21 Gangulu – in the Dawson River district, s.e. Qld.
28 Garuwali – in the Ferrar Creek district, n.e. of Birdsville, s.w. Qld.
37 Gaurna – in the vicinity of Adelaide, S.A.
20 Goreng Goreng – in the vicinity of Bundaberg, s.e. Qld.
55 Gunwinygu – from upper Cooper Creek to the Liverpool River, Arnhem Land, N.T.
30 Gunya – between Charleville and Cunnamulla in s.w. Qld.
25 Guugu Yimidhirr – in the vicinity of Cooktown, n. Qld.
18 Jagara – in the Moreton Bay district, s.e. Qld.
46 Kalaaku – at Israelite Bay and inland around the Fraser Range and Norseman, W.A.
15 Kamilaroi – in the Namoi River district, n. N.S.W. (closely related to Wiradhuri and Ngiyambaa).
2   Kattaŋ – on the coast from Port Stephens to Port Macquarie, N.S.W.
24 Kuku-Yalanji – in the Bloomfield River district, n. Qld.
27 Majuli – in the upper Diamantina River district, s.w. Qld.
16 Manandjali – in s.e. Qld.
31 Margany – in the upper Paroo and Warrego Rivers district, s.e. Qld.

ABORIGINAL LANGUAGES

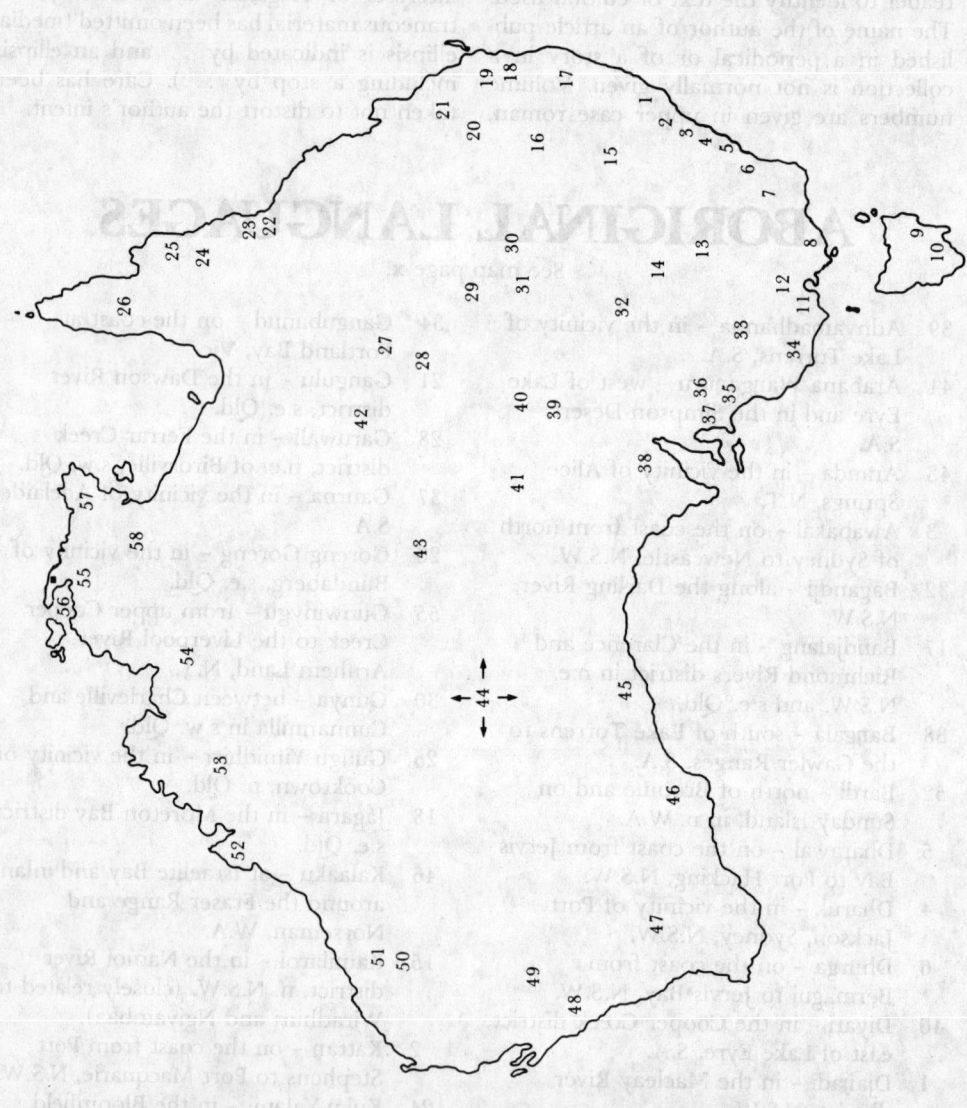

56 Margu – on Croker Is. and mainland.
45 Mirniny – along the coast of the Great Australian Bight, W.A. and S.A.
54 Ngaliwuru – in the upper Victoria River district, N.T.
7   Ngarigo – from Canberra across the Monaro tablelands to the Snowy Mountains and Omeo, N.S.W. (incl. A.C.T.) and Vic.
53 Ngarinjin – in the central Kimberley district, W.A.
36 Ngayawuŋ – in the lower Murray River district, S.A.
14 Ngiyambaa – in the Darling and Macquarie Rivers district, N.S.W. (very closely related to Wiradhuri, and closely related to Kamilaroi).
48 Nhanta-anmaŋu – on the coast from Dongara to the Murchison River, W.A.
47 Nyungar – over a wide area of s.w. W.A., including Perth and Albany.
9   Oyster Bay language of Tasmania – in the vicinity of Oyster Bay, east coast of Tasmania.
50 Panyjima – in the Pilbara region of n.w. W.A.
42 Pitta Pitta – in the Boulia district, n.w. central Qld.
29 Punthamara – in the Grey Range district, s.w. Qld.
10 South-eastern language of Tasmania – from Hobart south to Prion Bay, including Bruny Island.
58 Warndarang – on the west coast of Arnhem Land, N.T. from Roper River to Rose River.
22 Warrgamay – in the Herbert River district, n. Qld.
11 Wathawurung – in the vicinity of Geelong, Vic. (closely related to Wuywurung and Wemba).
49 Watjari – in the Murchison River district, W.A.
33 Wemba – in the Glenelg and Loddon Rivers district, Vic. (closely related to Wuywurung and Wathawurung). Has several dialects including Djadjala, Wemba Wemba and Wergaia.
44 Western Desert language – spoken in the Desert areas of S. and W. Australia, and in s.w. N.T. (has many dialects including Luritja, Mantjiltjara, Yulbaritja, Pitjantjatjara and Yankunytjatjara).
26 Wik Munkan – in the Archer River district, n. Qld.
13 Wiradhuri – over a wide area in central N.S.W. in the region of the Murrumbidgee River and Lachlan River districts (very closely related to Ngiyambaa and closely related to Kamilaroi).
12 Wuywurung – in the vicinity of Melbourne, Vic. (closely related to Wathawurung and Wemba).
35 Yaralde – on the coast at Encounter Bay and at Lake Alexandrina, S.A.
51 Yinjibarndi – in the Fortescue River district, W.A.
57 Yolŋu Sub-group – a group of closely related languages spoken in n.e. Arnhem Land, N.T.
15 Yuwaalaraay – near Lightning Ridge, n. N.S.W. (a dialect of the same language as Kamilaroi).

PROPRIETARY NAMES

This dictionary includes some words which are, or are asserted to be, proprietary names or trade marks. Their inclusion does not imply that they have acquired for legal purposes a non-proprietary or general significance, nor is any other judgement implied concerning their legal status. In cases where the editor has some evidence that a word is used as a proprietary name or trade mark this is indicated, but no judgement concerning the legal status of such words is made or implied thereby.

LIST OF ABBREVIATIONS

Abbreviations are listed in the form in which they most commonly occur: those printed in italics may in some contexts be in roman, and vice versa. Abbreviations may similarly be printed with or without an initial capital, as the context requires.

a.	adjective
a.	adaptation of, adoption of
a (before a date)	*ante*, before
A.A.O.	Australian Archives Office
abbrev.	abbreviated, abbreviation (of)
absol.	absolute, -ly
A.C.T.	Australian Capital Territory
adj. phr.	adjectival phrase
adj(s).	adjective(s)
adv. phr.	adverbial phrase
adv(s).	adverb(s)
Advt.	advertisement
AJCP	Australian Joint Copying Project
ALR	Australian Law Reports
Amer.	American
Ann. Rep.	annual report
app.	apparently
AR	Industrial Arbitration Reports
assoc.	association
attrib.	attributive, -ly
Aust.	Australia
Austral(s).	Australian(s)
Br.	British
Br. dial.	British dialect
Brit.	Britain, British
c (before a date)	*circa*, about
c. (as 19th c.)	century
CAR	Commonwealth Arbitration Reports
cf.	*confer*, compare
CLR	Commonwealth Law Reports
collect.	collective, -ly
colloq.	colloquial, -ly
Comb.	combination(s)
Comm.	commission
compar.	comparative
conj.	conjunction
const.	construed(with)
C.P.D.	Commonwealth of Australia Parliamentary debates
C.P.P.	Commonwealth of Australia Papers presented to Parliament
cv.	cultivar
Cwlth.	Commonwealth
DAE	*Dictionary of American English*
def.	definition
deriv.	derivative, -ation
dial.	dialect
Dict.	dictionary
dimin.	diminutive
DOST	*Dictionary of the Older Scottish Tongue*
Du.	Dutch
e.	east, eastern
ed.	edition, editor
EDD	*English Dialect Dictionary*
e.g.	*exempli gratia*, for example
ellipt.	elliptical, -ly
Eng.	English
esp.	especially
etc.	*et cetera*, and the rest
etym.	etymology
et al.	*et alii*, and others
euphem.	euphemism, euphemistically
exc.	except
excl.	exclusively
exclam.	exclamation
f.	formed on, from
fam.	family, families
Fed.	federal
fem.	feminine
fig.	figurative, -ly
fl.	*floruit*, flourished
Fr.	French
freq.	frequent, -ly
G.	German
G.B.P.P.	Great Britain Parliamentary papers
Gr.	Greek
Grose	F. Grose, *Dictionary of the Vulgar Tongue*
H.C.	House of Commons

LIST OF ABBREVIATIONS

Hist.	now only in an historical context	OED(S	(reference to) Dictionary and Supplement
Hist.	historical, history	orig.	originally
H. of R.	House of Representatives	p.	page
Hotten	J.C. Hotten, *Dictionary of Modern Slang*	*pa. pple.*	past participle
		past pple.	past participle
HRA	Historical Records of Australia	Parl.	parliament, -ary
Ibid.	*ibidem*, in the same book or passage	Partridge	E. Partridge, *Dictionary of Slang and Unconventional English*
i.e.	*id est*, that is		
imit.	imitative	*pass.*	passive, -ly
imp.	imperative	perh.	perhaps
incl.	including	Pg.	Portuguese
infl.	influenced (by)	phr.	phrase(s)
Inst.	Institute	*pl.*	plural
int.	interjection	Pl.	plate
intr.	intransitive	pop.	popular, -ly
Ir.	Irish	poss.	possibly
irreg.	irregular, -ly	*ppl. a.*	participial adjective
Is.	island	*pple.*	participle
It.	Italian	*pr.*	present
joc.	jocular, -ly	prec.	preceding (word or entry)
L.	Latin	predom.	predominantly
L.A.	Legislative Assembly	Pref.	preface
L.C.	Legislative Council	*pref.*	prefix
Let(t).	letter(s)	*prep.*	preposition
m.	metre(s)	*pres.*	present
masc.	masculine	*pres. pple.*	present participle
Mathews	M.M. Mathews, *Dictionary of Americanisms*	prob.	probably
		pron.	pronoun
ML	Mitchell Library	pronunc.	pronunciation
mod.	modern	Proc.	proceedings
Morris	E.E. Morris, *Austral English*	*pr. pple.*	present participle
n.	noun	pseud.	pseudonym
n.	north, northern	Qld.	Queensland
N. Amer.	North American	QPD	Queensland Parliamentary debates
N.G.	New Guinea		
NLA	National Library of Australia	quot(s).	quotation(s)
		q.v.	*quo vide*, which see
no.	number	R.	Royal (in names of periodicals, etc.)
n.p.	no place of publication		
N.S.W.	New South Wales	R. Comm.	Royal Commission
NSWPD	New South Wales Parliamentary debates	Rec.	records
		redupl.	reduplicating
N.T.	Northern Territory	ref.	reference
N.Z.	New Zealand	*refl., reflex.*	reflexive
obj.	object	Rep.	report(s)
Obs.	obsolete	repr.	representation, representing
occas.	occasional, -ly	s.	south, southern
OED	*Oxford English Dictionary* 13 vols.	S.A.	South Australia
		S. Afr.	South Africa, South African
OEDS	Supplement to the *Oxford English Dictionary* 4 vols.	SAPD	South Australian Parliamentary debates

S. Austral.	South Australian	tr.	translation (of), translator
sb.	substantive	*trans.*	transitive
sc.	*scilicet*, understand or supply	Trans.	transactions
Sched.	schedule	*transf.*	transferred (sense)
Scot.	Scottish	ult.	ultimate, -ly
Scot. dial.	Scottish dialect	U.S.	United States
Ser.	series	usu.	usually
Sess.	session	*v.*	verb, verbal
sing.	singular	V & P	Votes and Proceedings
SND	*Scottish National Dictionary*	var. (in scientific nomenclature)	variety
spec.	specific, -ally		
sp(p).	species (singular, plural)		
ssp.	subspecies	var(r).	variant(s) of
subfam.	subfamily	*vbl. n.*	verbal noun
subj.	subject	*vbl. phr.*	verbal phrase
subsp.	subspecies	*vbl. sb.*	verbal substantive
suff.	suffix	Vic.	Victoria
superl.	superlative	vol(s).	volume(s)
Suppl.	supplement	v.p.	various places
syn.	synonym	VPD	Victorian Parliamentary debates
t.	tense		
Tas.	Tasmania	w.	west, western
T.H.A.J.	Tasmania House of Assembly Journals	W.A.	Western Australia
		W. Austral.	Western Australian

PRONUNCIATION

List of symbols used.

Vowels

i	h<u>ea</u>t
ɪ	h<u>i</u>t
ɛ	b<u>e</u>t
æ	b<u>a</u>t
a	p<u>ar</u>t
ɒ	h<u>o</u>t
ɔ	s<u>or</u>t
ʊ	p<u>u</u>t
u	h<u>oo</u>t
ʌ	h<u>u</u>t
ɜ	h<u>ur</u>t
ə	<u>a</u>noth<u>er</u>

Diphthongs

eɪ	h<u>ay</u>
oʊ	h<u>oe</u>
aɪ	h<u>igh</u>
aʊ	h<u>ow</u>
ɔɪ	t<u>oy</u>
ɪə	t<u>ier</u>
ɛə	d<u>are</u>
ʊə	t<u>our</u>

Consonants

p	<u>p</u>at
b	<u>b</u>at
t	<u>t</u>ap
d	<u>d</u>ot
k	<u>c</u>at
g	<u>g</u>oat
f	<u>f</u>at
v	<u>v</u>at
θ	<u>th</u>in
ð	<u>th</u>at
s	<u>s</u>at
z	<u>z</u>ap
ʃ	<u>sh</u>ot
ʒ	mea<u>s</u>ure
tʃ	<u>ch</u>oke
dʒ	<u>j</u>oke
m	<u>m</u>at
n	<u>n</u>ot
ŋ	so<u>ng</u>
l	<u>l</u>ong
r	<u>r</u>ing
h	<u>h</u>ang
j	<u>y</u>oung
w	<u>w</u>ay

PRONUNCIATION

List of symbols used:

Vowels		Consonants	
ɑ	bar	p	pat
i	bit	b	bat
e	bet	t	tip
æ	bat	d	dot
ɑː	barn	k	cat
ɒ	hot	g	got
ɔ	son	f	fat
u	put	v	vat
uː	boot	θ	thin
ʌ	bud	ð	that
ə	but	s	sat
ɜ	another	z	zap
		ʃ	shoe
		ʒ	measure
Diphthongs		tʃ	choke
eɪ	hay	dʒ	joke
oʊ	hoe	m	mat
aɪ	high	n	not
aʊ	how	ŋ	song
ɔɪ	toy	l	long
ɪə	tier	r	rut
eə	dare	h	bang
ʊə	tour	j	young
		w	way

A

Abbott's booby. [f. the name of W.L. *Abbott* (1860–1936), U.S. naturalist, who collected the type specimen on Assumption Island in 1892.] The gannet *Sula abbotti*, which now breeds only on Christmas Island in the Indian Ocean.
1964 A.L. THOMSON *New Dict. Birds* 331 Abbott's Booby is a tree-nester. **1984** *Canberra Times* 13 Apr. 3/5 The Government knew Christmas Island was .. the only known breeding ground of the endangered Abbott's booby bird.

Abdul. *Hist.* [Transf. use of the proper name, common in Turkey.]
1. A nickname for a Turkish soldier, esp. during the war of 1914–18. Also collectively, the Turkish army.
1915 'LANCE-CORPORAL COBBER' *Anzac Pilgrim's Progress* (1918) 70 Here my thoughts have lost that goodly colour, An' I delight in strafing poor Abdulla. **1949** G. BERRIE *Morale* 92 I'd give a quid to be planted somewhere where I could watch some Abdul go in.
2. A nickname for an AFGHAN.
1919 R.J. CASSIDY *Gipsy Road* 57 Abdul and his inelegant 'hunchies' are an essentiality of life on the lone, level lands that stretch away back o' sunset.

Abo /'æboʊ/, *n.* and *a.* Pl. **Abos.** [An abbreviated form, perh. brought into written currency by its use in a column entitled 'Aboriginalities', appearing in the Sydney *Bulletin* from 15 Oct. 1887: see quots. 1904 and 1906. See also ABORIGINALITY.]
A. *n.*
1. Abbrev. of ABORIGINAL *n.* 1 a.
[**1904** *Bulletin* (Sydney) 8 Sept. 16/2 Have any 'Abo's' [*sc.* readers of 'Aboriginalities'] noticed that Willie is a one-man-one-job advocate? **1906** *Ibid.* 18 Oct. 17/3 Remarkable the number of 'Abo' writers who have been chased by snakes.] **1908** *Ibid.* 12 Mar. 14/3 At one time when a stranger approached a blacks' camp the juvenile King Billies .. would disappear into the gunyahs .. and the departing visitor was always well out of coo-ee before the little black nuts would bob out. .. The little abos. of the present day have not much trace of shyness. **1981** C. WALLACE-CRABBE *Splinters* 51 Not much of a place, Canberra. Sometimes I reckon it should be given back to the Abos.
2. Abbrev. of ABORIGINAL *n.* 2.
1918 *Bulletin* (Sydney) 9 May 22/2 A booly (abo. for whirlwind) visited our little mission-school. **1952** C. SIMPSON *Come away, Pearler* 229 He speaks three or four languages, not counting abo.
B. *adj.* Abbrev. of ABORIGINAL *a.* (in some cases of ABORIGINAL *n.* 1 a. used *attrib.*).
1911 *Bulletin* (Sydney) 2 Nov. 14/1 All the Abo. Protector crowd are being run down by Chow white-men. **1975** X. HERBERT *Poor Fellow my Country* 322 He's a beautiful child, isn't he .. despite the Abo features.

abolitionist. *Hist.* [f. the use of *abolition(ist)* with reference to slavery.] One who advocates the cessation of TRANSPORTATION. See also ANTI-TRANSPORTATION.
1847 (*title*) The abolitionists and transportationists. **1911** R.G.S. WILLIAMS *Austral. White Slaves* 72 The Fusionists were overthrown with great slaughter, and the leg-iron abolitionists reigned in their stead.

Aboriginal, *a., n.,* and *adv.* [Spec. use of *aboriginal* dwelling in a country before the arrival of (European) colonists: see OED *a.* 2 and *sb.*]

A. *adj.*
1. Of, pertaining to, or characteristic of the Aborigines; ABORIGINE *a.*
1820 [see *aboriginal native*]. **1829** *Colonial Times* (Hobart) 7 Mar., In furtherance of the Lieutenant Governor's anxious desire to ameliorate the condition of the Aboriginal inhabitants of this Territory, His Excellency will allow a Salary of Fifty Pounds per annum to a steady person of good character .. who will take an interest in effecting an intercourse with this unfortunate race. **1980** ANSELL & PERCY *To fight Wild* 134 The whole trip .. was as good an example as you could wish to see of Aboriginal bushcraft.
2. In collocations: **Aboriginal black, black man, black native, English, Establishment, Mission, native, police, reserve, school, settlement, station, trooper.**
1824 *Hobart Town Gaz.* 29 Oct., About twenty **Aboriginal blacks** approached the house and stock-yard. **1839** *Port Phillip Patriot* 26 Dec. 3 The whole country only a few short months ago was uninhabited, save by the **aboriginal black man**. **1827** *Australasian Almanack* 95 An **aboriginal black native** admitted within the pale of the Church, by the rites of baptism. **1883** E.M. CURR *Recoll. Squatting Vic.* 117 This was the party which the blackfellow had described as consisting of 'Towsan', which all the country over, is the **aboriginal English** for any number over half-a-dozen. **1841** *Geelong Advertiser* 7 Aug. 1/4 Strayed .. *two working bullocks*. .. Whoever will bring the same to the **Aboriginal Establishment** near Killembeet .. will receive the above reward. **1826** L.E. THRELKELD *Statement* (1828) 19, I was endeavouring to direct the conversation from other concerns to the concerns of the **Aboriginal Mission**. **1820** *N.S.W. Pocket Almanack* 74 Institution for the Children of the **aboriginal Natives** of this Colony, founded at Parramatta. **1842** *Portland Mercury* 19 Oct. 3/1 Captain Dana with his party of **aboriginal police** .. went in pursuit of the robbers. .. The sable corps showed much anxiety to overtake and capture the 'myalls', i.e. wild blackfellows. **1868** J.K. TUCKER *Aborigines & Chinese Question* 26 Another mission was established .. on the **aboriginal reserve** at Lake Condale. **1846** *Melbourne Argus* 23 Oct. 2/2 We regret extremely to learn that the fund for the support of the **Aboriginal School** at the Merrai Creek, has fallen so low. **1897** *Bulletin* (Sydney) 24 July 11/1 One of Meston's niggers at the White Cliffs **Aboriginal Settlement**. **1841** *Port Phillip Patriot* 31 May 2/4 No damage whatever was done to Mr Darlot's property by the temporary formation of the **aboriginal station** on the land claimed as his run. **1843** *Port Phillip Patriot* 19 Jan. 2/3 Captain Dana started on Tuesday evening with five of his **aboriginal troopers**.

B. *n.*
1. a. (For the pl.: see ABORIGINES.) One of the Aborigines; ABORIGINE *n.* 1.
1828 *Hobart Town Courier* 19 Apr. 1 Nothing herein contained shall authorize, or be taken to authorize, any Settler, or Settlers, Stockkeeper, or Stockkeepers, Sealer, or Sealers to make use of force (except for necessary self-defence) against any Aboriginal. **1985** *Canberra Times* 7 July 22/7 Many more Aboriginals are going into Years 11 and 12.
b. *Obs.* An early settler; an Australian-born colonist.
1837 *Perth Gaz.* 21 Jan. 838 As long as the noble and graceful Swan shall row her majestic 'state' to the ocean, so long will *the memorial* last of the attachment and gratitude of the first settlers to Sir James Stirling. I am, Sir, An Aboriginal. **1880** *Bulletin* (Sydney) 18 Sept. 1/1 The sensitive ears of our white aboriginals.

2. An (unspecified) Aboriginal language; ABORIGINE n. 2.

1845 J.O. BALFOUR *Sketch of N.S.W.* 8 You may see a *gin* (the aboriginal for a married woman). **1974** A. BUZO *Coralie Lansdowne says No* 18 The address is 18 Jacka Avenue. Jacka. The Aboriginal for bourgeois.

C. *adv.* In a manner characteristic of the Aborigines; cf. ABORIGINALLY.

1959 L. ROSE *Country of Dead* 112 He's begun to think aboriginal... He's been out here too long.

Aboriginality. [Spec. use of *aboriginality* the quality of being aboriginal: see OED and also ABO.] The quality of being Aboriginal; the culture of the Aboriginal people.

1897 J.J. MURIF *From Ocean to Ocean* 72 Physically the natives to be seen about are very good samples of aboriginality. **1985** *Canberra Times* 7 July 22/6 Consciously or unconsciously, the white population has suppressed Aboriginality.

Aboriginally, *adv.* In an Aboriginal language.

1863 J. MORRILL *Sketch of Residence* 19 The native small plum, aboriginally known as the Bolemo, botanically as the Ficus aspera. **1917** *Bulletin* (Sydney) 5 July 22/2 Leach's kingfisher is aboriginally known as kitticarrara.

Aborigine, *n.* and *a.* Formerly also **Aboriginee.** [A singular form derived analogically from ABORIGINES. ABORIGINAL is now preferred (see ABORIGINES quot. 1978).]

A. *n.*

1. ABORIGINAL *n.* 1 a.

1829 H. WIDOWSON *Present State Van Diemen's Land* 187 An aborigine has occasionally been seen in Hobart Town, but not of late years. **1978** P. PORTER *Cost of Seriousness* 28 A man and a boy are eating with an aborigine In a boat.

2. ABORIGINAL *n.* 2.

1879 'AUSTRALIAN' *Adventures Qld.* 39 Bony.. spoke a curious jargon—a mixture of bad English and aborigine—freely intermixed with snatches of profanity. **1893** *Bulletin* (Sydney) 18 Feb. 15/2 The word 'warrigal' was current aboriginee ere the British Lion deposited 'our forefathers' here.

B. *adj.* ABORIGINAL *a.* 1.

1835 G.C. INGLETON *True Patriots All* (1952) 163 Captain Pigeon, and his company, are placed on the 'Aborigine Establishment', which forms an item in an expenditure, of *only* £1899 per annum. **1969** R.A. GOULD *Yiwara* 15 Aborigine children are indulged to an extreme degree, and sometimes continue to suckle until they are four or five years old.

Aborigines, *pl.* Formerly also **Aboriginees.** [Spec. use of *aborigines* those believed to have been the inhabitants of a country *ab origine*, i.e. from the beginning. At first, in Aust. as earlier elsewhere, used only in the pl.: see OED. Now the preferred pl. (but see quot. 1978 and, for examples of *Aboriginals*, ABORIGINAL *n.* 1 a.).] The indigenous inhabitants of Australia; their descendants.

1803 Banks Papers VIII. 221 Nature not having furnished it with food sufficient to maintain any other race of men than the Aborigines. **1978** *Style Manual* (ed. 3) 11 When referring to the first inhabitants of Australia, prefer the forms *Aboriginal* (singular noun), *Aboriginals* (plural noun) and *Aboriginal* (adjective). While the form *Aborigine* is not acceptable as an alternative to *Aboriginal* for the singular noun, *Aborigines* may be used as an alternative plural form.

abscond, *v. Hist.* [Spec. use of *abscond* to depart (usu. to elude the law) secretly.]

a. *intr.* Of a convict: to escape from custody.

1788 D. COLLINS *Acct. Eng. Colony N.S.W.* (1798) I. 32 One of these [convicts] had absconded, and lived in the woods for nineteen days. **1863** C. GIBSON *Life among Convicts* II. 275 The condition of a convict, who takes to the backwoods, is a desperate one. It is thought that 75 of the 116 who absconded from Macquarie Harbour, perished in the woods.

b. In the phr. **to abscond into the woods, bush,** (of a convict) to escape into unsettled country.

1790 *Hist. Rec. N.S.W.* 391 If any person, male or female, shall desert or abscond into the woods, every such person or persons shall be deemed and held to be of the most dangerous and pernicious consequence to the community at large, and therefore be adjudged to suffer death. **1827** *Colonial Times* (Hobart) 21 July, The Lieutenant Governor has much pleasure to announce the Capture of the three remaining Convicts, who after attempting to surprise the Emma Kemp cutter, absconded into the bush.

Hence **absconder** *n.*

1840 *Tasmanian Weekly Dispatch* 27 Mar. 7/4 An unusual number of absconders have been dealt with.

absconding, *vbl. n. Hist.* The act of escaping from custody.

1804 *Sydney Gaz.* 15 July, *Wm. Cheshire,* for absconding from public labour at Castle Hill. **1852** J. MORGAN *Life & Adventures W. Buckley* 15 Four of us agreed to take to the bush, as absconding is called.

absent, *v. Hist. trans.* (usu. *refl.*) Of a convict: to remove (oneself) from custody.

1806 *Sydney Gaz.* 23 Nov., *Ralph Summer* was ordered 50 lashes and the gaol gang for absenting himself from Government labour. **1810** *Ibid.* 28 Jan., The following Prisoners have absented themselves from Public Labour in the Town and other Gangs at Sydney.

absentee.

1. a. *Hist.* A convict who has escaped from custody and remains at large.

1805 *Sydney Gaz.* 29 Dec., Wm. Page, an absentee into the woods. **1837** *Rep. Select Committee Transportation* 24 By the word 'absentee' which you have used just now, you mean a runaway convict?—I used it as it was used in the Committee-room; but my own term for such a person was an absconding person. 'Absentee' may be used as a word to express it.—Is it not a common word in the Colony?—It may be; it is a very proper word to use; I do not dispute that the word is very common in the colony.

b. In the phr. **absentee from public labour.**

1805 *Sydney Gaz.* 3 Nov., *Lee,* one of the absentees from public labor.

2. [Spec. use of *absentee* a landlord who lives abroad: see OED 2.] A non-resident landholder, esp. one who lives in the British Isles. Also *attrib.*

1831 *Sydney Herald* 15 Aug. 2/3 Immense absentee grants will be less frequently met with. **1911** V. DESMOND *Awful Austral.* 72 A squatter's son is a chip off the old blockhead. When he's about twenty he's sent to England for a brush up, and he either becomes an absentee or returns to help make Australian cities more vicious.

absenteeism. *Hist.* The practice of being an ABSENTEE (esp. sense 2).

1831 *Sydney Monitor* 7 May 3/4 A female assigned servant of Mr Whitaker was brought before the Police on a charge of *absenteeism.* **1892** 'E. KINGLAKE' *Austral. at Home* 85 All good Australians hope to go to England when they die. Not only does everybody, now-a-days, go 'home' when able to do so, but many stay there. Absenteeism is becoming common.

absolute emancipation. *Hist.* ABSOLUTE PARDON.

1799 D. COLLINS *Acct. Eng. Colony N.S.W.* (1802) II. 268 Absolute emancipation, with permission to quit the colony. **1805** *HRA* (1915) 1st Ser. V. 477 The enclosed are Twelve Counterparts of Absolute Emancipations, which I have granted to enable the objects thereof to enter on board His Majesty's Ship, Investigator.

absolute pardon. *Hist.* A complete remission of (a convict's) sentence, including restitution of the right of return to the British Isles; FREE PARDON.

1802 *N.S.W. Gen. Orders* 1 Oct. (1806) 1 To any convict, an Absolute Pardon, the Governor's Interest to get a Passage home. **1822** J.T. BIGGE *Rep. State Colony N.S.W.* 119 An absolute pardon of the governor of New South Wales contains a declaration under his hand, and the seal of the territory, that the unexpired term of transportation of the convict is absolutely remitted to him.

acacia. [Transf. use of *acacia* (fam. Mimosaceae), a genus of leguminous trees and shrubs (the most common sense in Aust.): see WATTLE.]

1. Any of several trees and shrubs of the genus *Cassia* (fam. Caesalpiniaceae) bearing some resemblance to species of *Acacia*.

1903 *Proc. Linnean Soc. N.S.W.* XXVIII. 764 *Cassia laevigata*... Known as 'Acacia'; a very bad weed.

2. Any of several trees of the genus *Albizia* (fam. Mimosaceae), perh. confused with *Acacia* because members of both genera rapidly colonize burnt ground.

1938 C.T. WHITE *Princ. Bot. Qld. Farmers* 182 The tree colloquially known as 'Acacia' in the Queensland sugar-belt is a species of *Albizzia* (*A. procera*). Another species extensively planted in the central-west and familiarly known as 'Acacia' is *A. Lebbek*, a native of India.

3. Special Comb. **acacia cedar**, the tree *Albizia toona* (fam. Mimosaceae) of Qld.

1926 *Qld. Agric. Jrnl.* XXV. 435 Albizzia toona.. Mackay Cedar, Acacia Cedar (Cairns). **1944** J. DEVANNY *By Tropic Sea & Jungle* 128 Acacia cedar is red striated with cream, with an open, wide grain.

acca /'ækə/. Also **acker**. Alteration of 'academic'.

1977 *Meanjin* 90 (*heading*) Accas and ockers: Australia's new dictionaries. **1984** *Age Weekender* (Melbourne) 2 Mar. 11/2 Ackers from the university.

accommodation house. [In Br. use freq. with reference to a house of ill repute: see OEDS.] A house providing board and lodging for travellers, and in which refreshments are served; HOUSE OF ACCOMMODATION.

1843 *Church in Aust.* (Soc. Propagation Gospel) (1845) ii. 39 We reached Mr Owen's accommodation-house. **1899** *Northern Tas.* (Northern Tasmanian Tourists' Assoc.) 57 An accommodation house, consisting of a living room and two sleeping apartments—one for the ladies and one for their escorts.

Hence **accommodation tent** *n.*

1861 T. M'COMBIE *Austral. Sketches* 90, I determined to endeavour to reach a station or accommodation-tent.

accommodation paddock. An enclosed area for the confinement and pasturing of travelling stock.

1843 *Colonial Observer* (Sydney) 22 Feb. 838/1 Four miles from town, near the accommodation paddocks. **1874** R.P. FALLA *Knocking About* (1976) 8 There is a very fine accommodation paddock attached to the above hotel.

accord. An agreement between the Australian Labor Party and the Australian Council of Trade Unions negotiated as part of a prices and income policy.

1983 *Sydney Morning Herald* 17 Feb. 12/4 As a result of the months of painstaking consultation, discussion and work, we, the representatives of the incoming Labor Government, have reached an historic accord with the trade union movement which will form the basis for a firm, genuine and workable prices and incomes policy for this nation. **1986** *Nat. Times* 18 Apr. 41/1 (*heading*) Accord begins to creak: major surgery advised.

ace. [Fig. use of *ace* a single dot or symbol on a die or playing-card.] In the phr. **on one's ace**, on one's own, using one's own resources; alone.

1904 *Truth* (Sydney) 2 Oct. 3/1 As a burglar bold, Kelly works strictly on his ace, believing that comradeship in crime is dangerous. **1934** A. RUSSELL *Tramp-Royal* 213 'They're capable of good work at times,' said a 'boss cattleman' to whom I had applied for his opinion of the merits and demerits of the aboriginal as a stockman, 'but you've got to be with them. Send 'em out "on their ace" and they'll probably "go camp" under the first shady tree they come to.'

acher, var. ACRE.

acid. [f. *acid test* a test in which gold is distinguished from other metals by its resistance to nitric acid.] In the phr. **to put (ply, try) the acid (on)**, to exert a pressure which is difficult to resist; to exert such pressure on (a person, etc.); to be successful in the exertion of such pressure. Hence **to take the acid off**.

1906 E. DYSON *Fact'ry 'Ands* 210 E's er hartist—got er touch like velvet. 'E put's ther acid on so't yeh think it's ther milk 'iv 'uman kindness. **1906** *Ibid.* 215 Evidently it was Mr Cato's intention to try the acid on Feathers again. **1910** L. ESSON *Three Short Plays* (1911) 9 Don' you worry. I'll come back orl rite... Take the acid orf. **1938** J. MOSES *Nine Miles from Gundagai* 10 The barber's shop's a witness-box (They ply the acid there).

acker, var. ACCA.

ack-willie. *a.* Also **ack-willy**. [f. a superseded military signalling code in which *a* was represented as *ack* and *w* as *William*, A.W. being a shortening of A.W.L. or A.W.O.L.] In Services' speech: absent without leave.

1943 *Signals* (Melbourne) Christmas 39 Is it Stylish to go Ackwilly so consistently at night? **1977** R. BEILBY *Gunner* 22 While he wore it he was merely 'ack-willie', A.W.L., Absent Without Leave.

Hence **ack-willie** *n.*, one absent without leave.

1951 E. LAMBERT *Twenty Thousand Thieves* 31 Another couple of ack-willies.

acre. Also **acher**. [Fig. use of *acre* an expanse.] A euphemism for 'arse'.

1965 J. O'GRADY *Aussie Eng.* 9 'A kick in the acre' does not mean a kick in four thousand eight hundred and forty square yards of earth. Female 'acres' are generally referred to as 'rears'. **1971** F. HARDY *Outcasts of Foolgarah* 94 I'll give you a free kick up the acher.

addle, var. ATTLE.

Adelaidean. Also **Adelaidian**. [f. the name of the capital city of S.A.] A resident of Adelaide. Also **Adelaider, Adelaidonian**, and *attrib.*

1839 *Port Phillip Patriot* 20 Mar. 3/2 Australia Felix.. is as *free* from being a *penal* settlement as the most Antipenal Adelaidian can wish. **1845** R. HOWITT *Impressions Aust. Felix* 210 Little short of a million of money passed from the Adelaiders into the old colonies, for cattle, sheep, and farm produce. *c* **1848** 'SICK MAN' *Voyage Sydney to S.A.* 10 The Adelaidonians would justly oppose the commentary. **1852** S. SIDNEY *Three Colonies* 206 New arrivals from England fortunate enough to be admitted to the delightful evening parties given by a lady of the 'highest ton', the leader of the Adelaidean fashion, were astonished.

Adelaide pheasant. *Obs.* See quot.

1881 J.C.F. JOHNSON *To Mount Browne & Back* 13, I was

met with the startling information that all Adelaide men were croweaters, and that the parson-coated birds were known on the border as 'Adelaide pheasants' because it was asserted that the early settlers of 'Farinaceous Village', when short of mutton, made a meal of the unwary crow.

Adelaide rosella. [f. *Adelaide* (see quot. 1900), first applied as the specific name *Adelaidae* by English zoologist J. Gould (*Proc. Zool. Soc. London* (1841) VIII. 161) + ROSELLA *n.*[1] 1.] The parrot *Platycercus elegans adelaidae*, a subspecies of the crimson rosella, restricted to wooded country in S.A. from the Flinders Ranges to the Fleurieu Peninsula; *pheasant parrot,* see PHEASANT 2.

1900 A.J. CAMPBELL *Nests & Eggs Austral. Birds* 631 The Adelaide Rosella or Pheasant Parrakeet is a beautiful species in radiant colouring... It was named *adelaidensis*, from the circumstance that Gould, in 1838, procured some of his first specimens in the very streets of Adelaide. 1969 J.M. FORSHAW *Austral. Parrots* 189 The Adelaide Rosella is very variable and.. no change in plumage can be adequately correlated with distribution.

adjigo /'ædʒɪgoʊ, 'ædʒɪkoʊ/. Also **adjiko, ijjecka**. [prob. a. Nhanta *ajuga.*] The native yam *Dioscorea hastifolia* (fam. Dioscoreaceae) of near-coastal s.w. W.A.; the edible underground part of this plant; WARRAN.

1863 *Jrnls. & Rep. Two Voyages Glenelg River* 1 Aug. (1864) 27/2 Edible roots.. identical with those of Champion Bay (warrein and adjiko). 1975 M.A. BAIN *Ancient Landmarks* 151 The people in the vicinity of the Bowes River lived mainly on the ijjecka root. 1979 E. SMITH *Saddle in Kitchen* 20 'Adjigo', a native creeper... Grandpa said the tuber.. was good to eat and tasted like sweet potato.

Adrian Quist, *a.* [The name of an Austral. tennis player, b. 1913.] Rhyming slang for 'pissed', inebriated. Also *ellipt.* as **Adrian**.

1978 *Austral.* (Sydney) 31 May 9/5 I'm on the turps again—got Adrian Quist somethin' terrible the other night. 1978 *Boozer's Diary* (1979) 80 Adrian (= drunk).

Advance Australia. A patriotic catch-phrase, used freq. in song and verse and, independently, as a slogan.

1832 *Sydney Herald* 21 June 1/3 (Advt.), Advance Australia! 1984 *Canberra Times* 8 Mar. 21/7 Legislation to prevent unauthorised use of the Advance Australia logo was introduced into the House of Representatives yesterday... Advance Australia was now a self-funding, private-sector project.

Adventure Bay pine. [f. the name of a bay and township in Tas.] CELERY-TOP PINE.

1821 *HRA* (1921) 3rd Ser. III. 507 Q. Did you observe any Turpentine in them? A. There may be in the Adventure Bay Pine. 1934 J.W. AUDAS *Native Trees Aust.* 102 *Phyllocladus rhomboidalis*.. the Adventure Bay Pine, is another fine tree of Tasmania, growing in dense forests and near rivers.

aerial ping-pong. [So called because the play is characterized by freq. exchanges of long and high kicks.] A jocular (freq. derisive) name for Australian National Football: see quots.

1964 *Footy Fan* (Melbourne) II. viii. 23 Sydney folk are generally curious about this religion or mania which they term 'aerial ping pong' or 'Aussie Rules'. 1985 *Bulletin* (Sydney) 24 Dec. 53/1 In Europe.. cycling is about the same mad preoccupation as aerial ping pong is to the Melbourne crowds.

Afghan. Formerly also **Affghan**. [Spec. use of *Afghan* an inhabitant of Afghanistan.] An Afghan immigrant to Australia, esp. one engaged in camel-driving or camel-breeding (but see quot. 1933); 'GHAN 1. Also *attrib.*

1869 *S. Austral. Register* (Adelaide) 2 Sept. 3/8 Sheep-dogs, the property of Lalloo, Eleme, and Pioo, three Afghan shepherds. 1933 R.B. PLOWMAN *Camel Pads* 4 All Mohammedan camel-drivers in the Inland are classed as Afghans.

agate. *Obs.* [Fig. use of *agate* playing marble: see OEDS 1 b.] In the phr. **to toss in one's agate,** *to throw one's alley,* (etc.) *in,* see ALLEY 1.

1906 E. DYSON *Fact'ry 'Ands* 152 They put th' steam on her, 'n' she tossed in her agate.

agile wallaby. [f. *agile*, first applied as the specific name *agilis* by English zoologist J. Gould (*Proc. Zool. Soc. London* (1841) IX. 81) + WALLABY 1.] The large sandy-brown wallaby *Macropus agilis* of W.A., N.T., Qld., and New Guinea.

1857 J. GOULD *Mammals of Aust.* II. Pl. 25, The Agile Wallaby appears to be abundant on all the low swampy lands of the northern coast of Australia. 1981 D. LEVITT *Plants & People* 20 The island's Agile Wallabies have very acute hearing.

agricultural, *a.* [Spec. use of *agricultural* pertaining to agriculture (including the rearing of animals): see OED.]

1. Of, pertaining to, or engaged in the cultivation of land for the production of crops, as distinct from the use of land for grazing. See PASTORAL.

1806 *HRA* (1915) 1st Ser. V. 711 Our principal Agricultural settlement at Hawkesbury. 1965 G.H. FEARNSIDE *Golden Ram* 160 Australia has the potential.. of being both a great agricultural-pastoral and industrial country.

2. In special collocations: **agricultural high school,** a secondary school offering a general education with special courses in agriculture; **reserve** *Qld., obs.,* land close to towns reserved for small farms.

1905 *Victorian Yr. Bk. of Agric.* 25 In a country centre where an attendance of 50 to 100 pupils could be guaranteed, the **Agricultural High School** should be worked in connexion with the local State school. 1855 W. CAMPBELL *Crown Lands Aust.* 9 The pastoral interest was the only interest beyond the settled district, and did not require either townships or **agricultural reserves**.

agriculturist. One engaged primarily in the production of crops. Also **agriculturalist**.

1820 C. JEFFREYS *Van Dieman's Land* 149 The agriculturist in Van Dieman's Land, always reckons upon at least thirty-five bushels [*sc.* of wheat per acre.]. 1880 *Bulletin* (Sydney) 21 Aug. 3 (Advt.) *Preliminary Notice.* To capitalists, graziers, agriculturalists, and others.

agro-politician. One politically active on behalf of the rural sector; a lobbyist.

1978 *Cattleman* (Rockhampton) Sept. 20/1 Mr Barry Cassell, national director of the Cattlemen's Union, does not beat about the bush... Men such as Mr Cassell prefer to be styled 'agro-politician', a reflection of the importance the union places on its role as a political lobbyist.

Hence **agro-politics** *n.*

1986 *Canberra Times* 5 Mar. 2/3 What Mr Kerin rather neatly referred to as 'agropolitics'.

alarm bird.

1. *Obs.* SPUR-WINGED PLOVER.

1827 *HRA* (1923) 3rd Ser. VI. 271 The 'Alarm Bird'.. is in the Body not so large as a Partridge... Flying round without Gun shot, and disappointing a person of his Game by alarming it; hence 'Alarm Bird' by Sealers. 1896 F.G. AFLALO *Sketch Nat. Hist. Aust.* 103 The Wattled Plover (*Lobivanellus*), or 'Spur Wing', spoils many a day's kangaroo stalking by its provoking habit of rising just in front of one and putting every living thing on the alert by its piercing cries—for which peculiarity colonials have dubbed it the 'Alarm Bird'.

2. (App. recorded only in Dicts.) The kookaburra *Dacelo novaeguinea*.
1943 S.J. BAKER *Pop. Dict. Austral. Slang* (ed. 3) 5 *Alarm bird*, the Kookaburra. Cf. 'Bushman's Clock'.

Albany doctor: see DOCTOR $n.^3$

Albany pitcher plant: see PITCHER PLANT.

Albert lyre-bird. [f. the name of Prince *Albert* (1819–61), Consort of Queen Victoria, first applied as the specific name *Alberti* by English zoologist J. Gould (*Proc. Linnean Soc. London* (1850) II. 67) + LYRE-BIRD 1.] The lyre-bird *Menura alberti*, restricted to a small area of rainforest in n. N.S.W. and s. Qld. Also **Albert's lyrebird**.
1851 J. GOULD *Birds of Aust. Suppl.* (1869) Pl. 19, Albert Lyre Bird... I have great pleasure in naming this species *M. Alberti*, in honour of His Royal Highness Prince Albert, as a slight token of respect for his personal virtues. 1975 *Ecos* vi. 7/1 The paradise rifle-bird, rufous scrub-bird, and Albert's lyrebird live only in subtropical rainforests.

Alberts. *Obs.* Shortened form of PRINCE ALBERTS.
c 1892 STEWART & KEESING *Old Bush Songs* (1957) 203 Through his boots his toes were shining And his feet looked very sore, I knew his feet were blistered From the Alberts that he wore. 1904 L. LAWSON *Lonely Crossing* 5 Alberts you are wearing?

alcheringa /ælt∫ə'rɪŋgə/. Also **alchuringa**. [a. Aranda *aljerre* dream + *nge, ablative suffix* from, meaning 'in the dreamtime'.] DREAMTIME 1. Also *attrib*.
1897 *Proc. R. Soc. Vic.* 23 All the ceremonies were concerned with mythical ancestors who lived in what the natives call the 'alcheringa' or dream times. 1944 A.W. UPFIELD *No Footprints in Bush* 196 Here were kept the tribe's churinga stones, the head of the sacred pole decorated with bird's down and hair alleged to have belonged to the tribe's Alchuringa ancestor, bull-roarers and other sacred objects.

alec. Also **aleck.** [Shortened f. (orig.) U.S. *smart alec* a conceited person or show-off: see OEDS.] A fool or simpleton.
1919 C.L. DREW *Doings of Dave* 161 Yes, Blind Alec could see that. 1962 A. SEYMOUR *One Day of Yr.* 64 He looked such a big aleck, marching along as though he'd won both wars single-handed.

Alexandra palm. [f. the name of *Alexandra* (1844–1925), Princess of Wales and later Queen-Consort of King Edward VII, first applied as the specific name *Alexandrae* by the botanist F. von Mueller (*Fragmenta Phytographiae Australiae* (1865–6) 47).] The palm *Archontophoenix alexandrae*, restricted to the e. coast of Qld. from near Cape York to just south of the Tropic of Capricorn.
1881 F. VON MUELLER *Select Extra-Tropical Plants* (ed. 2) 273 The Alexandra-Palm. The tallest of Australian Palms, and one of the noblest forms in the whole empire of vegetation. 1982 A. BLOMBERY *Palms* 48 The Alexandra Palm has a number of different geographical forms.

Alexandra parakeet. [f. *Alexandra* (see prec.), first applied as the specific name *Alexandrae* by English zoologist J. Gould (*Proc. Zool. Soc. London* (1863) 232).] PRINCESS PARROT. Also **Alexandra parrot**.
1900 A.J. CAMPBELL *Nests & Eggs Austral. Birds* 624 Mr A. Zeitz, Assistant Curator of the Adelaide Museum, was successful in getting the Alexandra Parrakeets to breed in captivity. 1921 *Bulletin* (Sydney) 29 Sept. 20/2 For the four most beautiful of Australian parrots I plump for the green leek (superb parrot), the Mallee and Alexandra parrots, and the yellow parrot or 'Murray smoker'.

Alf. [Abbrev. of the proper name *Alfred*.] A derogatory term for the type of the uneducated and unthinkingly conservative Australian. See also ROY. Also *attrib*. and as *adj*.
1960 *Encounter* (London) May 28 The Australian worker, the 'Alf' as we call him. 1971 *Bulletin* (Sydney) 31 July 45/3 The division now is not only between the extremes of the alf drinker and the mystic head. The earnest cerebral Left see the head scene as 'privatist, antirational, and male chauvinist'. 1980 *Weekend Austral. Mag.* (Sydney) 18 Oct. 7/1 To be gay could very easily become very Alf in a few years time.

Alfred, Royal: see ROYAL ALFRED.

all about, *adv., attrib.,* and *pron.* Orig. Austral. *pidgin*.
1. *adv.* Everywhere.
1848 H.W. HAYGARTH *Recoll. Bush Life* 25 All travellers are universally welcome throughout the far districts, literally stopping, as the blacks call it, 'all about'. 1863 *Adelaide Observer* 12 Dec. 6/5 The blacks up there say, 'Very good country this one, all about flour, sugar, tea, clothes, and sheep.'

2. *pron.* Everyone, all those present; esp. of Aboriginal employees on a rural property.
1908 MRS A. GUNN *We of Never-Never* 302 Cheon was announcing dinner in his own peculiar way. 'Dinner! Missus! Boss! All-about!' he chanted. 1976 C.D. MILLS *Hobble Chains & Greenhide* 9 'All about' employed as gate-openers, we took our first jaunt in the open.

3. *attrib.* In the phr. **all-about-gin**, a domestic servant. See GIN.
1962 C. GYE *Cockney & Crocodile* 75 And back to hot baths, the water heated over wood fires in kerosene tins and poured in by tousle-headed, cotton-frocked 'all-about-gins', the house-girls who arouse such envy in the servantless cities of the south.

all-Australian, *a.*
1. Exclusively or distinctively Australian in character or provenance.
1926 *Film Weekly* 4 Nov. 10 A new all-Australian movie. 1986 *Canberra Times* 13 June 8/6 It is possible to build the 'all-Australian house' in any price range.

2. Of, pertaining to, or representative of the whole, as distinguished from part, of Australia; ALL-STATE. Also **all-Australia**.
1927 R. *Comm. on Wireless* 2514 The cultivation of an All-Australian attitude that State consciousness shall gradually die out. 1965 L. WALKER *Other Girl* 157 Four.. hold State records and one is an all-Australia champion. 1973 P. MCKENNA *My World of Football* 94 My first All Australian Blazer.

all clear, *phr.,* also used as *n.* Australian National Football. See quot. 1968.
1925 *Laws of Football* (Australasian Football Council) 10 Field and goal umpires are not allowed to come to an understanding by signalling 'All Clear' by nodding of head, holding up fingers, etc. 1968 EAGLESON & MCKIE *Terminology Austral. Nat. Football* i. 9 *All-clear*, the signal given to the goal umpire by the field umpire to indicate that there was no breach of the rules just prior to an attempt at goal or behind and that the goal umpire is at liberty to give a decision on whether a goal or behind has been scored. (This is the standard term, used in all States.)

all day sucker. A large, long-lasting sweet, usually on a stick.
1935 K. TENNANT *Tiburon* 92 He's only fit for pickin' on Johns and takin' all-day suckers from kids. 1959 C. & E. CHAUVEL *Walkabout* 37 Children crowded in with pennies.. for ice-cream cones and 'all day suckers'.

alley. Also **ally.** [Fig. use of *alley* playing marble; cf. AGATE, MARBLE.]
1. In the phr. **to throw (chuck, pass, roll, sky, sling, toss) one's alley (in),** to die; to acknowledge defeat. See also AGATE, MARBLE 1.
1903 *Sporting News* (Launceston) 25 Apr. 2/8 Most of the cricketers have thrown in their 'ally' and the various clubs have stored away the paraphernalia until next spring. 1916 C.J. DENNIS *Moods Ginger Mick* 97 But if I dodge, an' keep out uv the rain, An' don't toss in me alley 'fore we wins. 1919 E. DYSON *Hello Soldier* 33 When Ulrich stopped a Port bookay he rolled his alley in. 1924 C.J. DENNIS *Rose of Spadgers* 23 When my pal, Ginger Mick, Chucked in 'is alley in this war we won, 'E left things tangled; fer 'e went too quick Fer makin' last requests uv anyone. 1927 F.C. BIGGERS *Bat-Eye* 18 'Is alley's skied. An' then yer reads: '*Killed by a fall uv coal.*' 1933 N. LINDSAY *Saturdee* (1936) 25 'This book says a bloke kicked the bucket,.. so what's it mean?' 'Means a bloke passed his alley in.' 1960 *Khaki Bush & Bigotry* (1968) 228 Don't sling in yer alley, missus. There's a good time comin'.
2. In the phr. **to make one's alley good,** to exploit a situation; to improve one's position. See also MARBLE 2.
1924 C.J. DENNIS *Rose of Spadgers* 160 'E 'ad swore to git me one uv those Fine days, an' make 'is alley good with Rose. 1964 *Sydney Morning Herald* 10 Aug. 2/6 The dark, knowing whisper.. 'Hey Tom! Joe is making his alley good with Nellie Bli down be th' crik!' carries its own significance.

alligator. [Transf. use of *alligator* a genus of the subfam. Alligatorinae, found chiefly in the Americas.] Either of the two species of crocodile *Crocodylus,* subfam. Crocodylinae, found in Aust.
1770 J. COOK *Jrnls.* 23 Aug. (1955) I. 395 In the Rivers and salt Creeks are some Aligators [*sic*]. 1931 'L. KAYE' *Tybal Men* 187 We went to the museum and.. found they were crocodiles—that there wasn't any alligators *anywhere in Australia.* It's just blasted ignorance calling them alligators.

alligator pike. [Cf. U.S. *alligator-gar:* see OEDS.] Any of several marine and estuarine carnivorous fish of the fam. Belonidae, having long jaws; LONG TOM 2.
1908 E.J. BANFIELD *Confessions of Beachcomber* 154 The 'long tom'.. or alligator-pike, which shoots from the water and skips along. 1935 DAVISON & NICHOLLS *Blue Coast Caravan* 236 We saw the alligator pike.. about eighteen inches long and shaped like torpedoes.

allotment. *Hist.* [Spec. use of *allotment* allotted portion of land: see OED 4.]
1. A piece of Crown land granted to a particular person or (see quots. 1821 and 1828) for a specified purpose.
1788 *HRA* (1914) 1st Ser. I. 48 The land will be granted with a clause that will ever prevent more than one house being built on the allotment. 1821 *Austral. Mag.* 29 The site of this building is in Macquarie-street, being a choice allotment which was handsomely presented by His Excellency the Governor. 1828 J.D. LANG *Narr. Settlement Scots Church* 67 The contemplated buildings were immediately commenced, partly on the allotment of the Scots Church.
2. A piece of land: in towns, a building block or section; in the country an area used for pasture or cultivation.

1811 *Sydney Gaz.* 12 Jan., Dwelling House.. with an extensive allotment of garden ground. 1880 R. ROSE *Vic. Guide* 7 He may obtain a lease of his allotment for seven years, at 2s. per acre.

all right: see RIGHT *a.* 1.

all-State, *a.* ALL-AUSTRALIAN 2.
1943 H.W. MALLOCH *Fellows All* 99 Christesen is a University 'blue' and State and all-State champion athlete and footballer. 1973 P. McKENNA *My World of Football* 144 Also a player worthy of leading an All State side such as this.

all-up, *a.* [Spec. use of *all-up* all-inclusive.] In the phr. **all-up bet,** a progressive bet, the stake and winnings from the first race being placed on the next, and so on, the sum accumulating for as long as the bet is successful; an accumulator.
[1933 R. SPARGO *Betting Systems Analysed* 24 All Up. The super optimist's method... For making sure of a losing day after picking a winner the all-up method is 'one hundred per cent. the goods'.] 1949 L. GLASSOP *Lucky Palmer* 15 'Does this bookie pay full odds?' 'No limit on all-up bets.'
Hence as *adv., v. intr.* and **all-upper** *n.*
1959 S.J. BAKER *Drum* 84 *All-upper,* a punter who bets 'all up' on a number of horse or greyhound races. 1978 D. STUART *Wedgetail View* 111 He.. practically all-upped all the way, so you can guess he'd made a killing.

alluvial, *a.* and *n.* [Spec. use of *alluvial* pertaining to alluvium.]
A. *adj.* Of or pertaining to gold-bearing alluvium, a sedimentary deposit of earth, sand, etc., found on flood-plains and in river-beds.
1892 T. BRACKEN *Dear Old Bendigo* 14 In the alluvial days the gold passed through the hands of a large number of persons.
B. *n.*
1. Gold-bearing alluvium; gold found in alluvium.
1871 *Austral. Town & Country Jrnl.* (Sydney) 18 Mar. 335/2 At the bottom of the ridge there is alluvial which has never been thoroughly tested for water. 1963 A. MOOREHEAD *Cooper's Creek* 5 Nearly all the surface alluvial was exhausted and now gold had to be mined.. in deep shafts.
2. *Obs.* Alluvial mining; an alluvial mine.
1871 *Austral. Town & Country Jrnl.* (Sydney) 7 June 15/4 In alluvial, things are quiet. 1891 *Braidwood Dispatch* 16 May 2/2 The chain of shafts that mapped the lead marked an alluvial of yore.
C. In Comb. and collocations: **alluvial claim, digger, digging, diggings, miner, mining, rush, working.**
1859 *Colonial Mining Jrnl.* June 79/1 Claims are divided into three sorts—**alluvial claims,** river claims, and quartz claims. 1893 A.F. CALVERT *W.A. & its Gold Fields* 32 The reefs are so rich at the surface that some of the **alluvial diggers** in slack times have earned fair wages by simply dollying the stone. 1858 T. McCOMBIE *Hist. Colony Vic.* 310 The gold had been obtained.. from **alluvial digging,** and by individual exertions. 1853 A. MACKAY *Great Gold Field* 16 As a considerable space of ground.. is granted to holders of quartz claims, on each side of the veins, their claims.. include the adjacent **alluvial diggings.** 1858 *Colonial Mining Jrnl.* Oct. 28/3 The reef was taken up by **'alluvial' miners**—men who had.. exhausted their little means in the deep wet sinking. 1867 R.L.M. KITTO *Goldfields of Vic.* 63 *Quartz* mining is a much more profitable speculation than *alluvial* **mining.** 1871 *Austral. Town & Country Jrnl.* (Sydney) 15 Apr. 454/1 The **alluvial rush** to Eurongilly, in the Wagga Wagga district, has not been turning out satisfactorily. 1865 *Rep. Mining Surveyors & Registrars* (Vic. Dept. Mines) Mar. 22 In the **alluvial workings**.. a strong leader has been cut.

Hence **alluvialist** n.
1956 J.E. WEBB *So much for Sydney* 24 Had the 'alluvialists' had their way Kalgoorlie might . . have become a deserted camp, the surface gold cut out and the English companies gone to other countries.

alpine ash. The tall tree *Eucalyptus delegatensis* (fam. Myrtaceae) of mountains in N.S.W., Vic., and Tas.; the wood of the tree.
1942 R.T. PATTON *Know your Own Trees* 31 Alpine Ash is found above an elevation of 3,000 feet. **1983** *Ecos* xxxvii. 7/3 For more than 50 years, natural stands of alpine ash . . in northern Tasmania have been . . declining in vigour.

alunqua /əˈlʌŋkwə/. [a. Aranda *alangkwe*.] The twining plant *Leichhardtia australis* (fam. Asclepiadaceae) of drier Aust., the young fruit of which is edible; the fruit itself; *bush cucumber*, see BUSH C. 3. See also *native pear* NATIVE *a.* 6 a.
1935 H.H. FINLAYSON *Red Centre* 84 The alunqua; a green cucumber-like fruit borne by a plant which climbs upon the mallee in the sand-hills. **1974** M. TERRY *War of Warramullas* 151 The alunqua, or bush cucumber, is an important source of food. . . The fruit looks rather like a large banana passionfruit . . is deep green in colour and tastes like fresh green peas.

amalgamated claim. Two or more originally discrete gold-mining titles which have been combined into one (see also quot. 1869).
[**1857** *Vic. Govt. Gaz.* 9 Jan. 58 *Amalgamation.* Claims may be permitted to be amalgamated.] **1864** *Ibid.* 22 Jan. 144/1 An amalgamated claim shall mean any number of claims . . the owners whereof have combined to facilitate the working thereof. **1869** R.B. SMYTH *Gold Fields & Mineral Districts* 602 *Amalgamated claim*, claims adjoining one another which have been thrown temporarily or permanently into one claim for more economical working.

amber, *a.* Used as a distinguishing epithet in collocations designating beer, esp. as **amber fluid.** Also *absol.* as *n.*
1906 *Truth* (Sydney) 22 July 1/3 The amber fluid is the cause why most men amble to the lock-up. **1918** *Ibid.* 3 Feb. 9/1 (*heading*) Rogue Reggie—runs amuck with a rug—but blames the amber beverage. **1943** H.M. MURPHY *Strictly for Soldiers* 30 Just a quart of amber liquid with a bonzer sort of smell, Like an angel's breath from heaven, as the poets often tell. **1962** A. SEYMOUR *One Day of Yr.* 9 It's too cold for beer anyway. . . Never too cold for the old amber, love. **1972** *Bulletin* (Sydney) 19 Aug. 6/2 Barry Crocker as Bazza is beautiful. He shows off remarkable cultural achievements, like being able to open a tube of the chilled article with one hand and give himself a swift amber transfusion. **1972** A. BUZO *Tom* (1975) 15 I'll stick with the old amber article.

ambit. *Industrial Relations.* [Spec. use of *ambit* extent or compass.] The definition of the limits of an industrial dispute: see quots. 1974 and 1980. See also LOG *n.*² Also *attrib.* and *transf.*
1972 SYKES & GLASBEEK *Labour Law in Aust.* 514 For practical purposes the log of claims sets out the ambit of the dispute. **1974** *MOA* (Melbourne) Sept. 1/5 Many years ago MOA made a claim on these employers which was designed mainly to do two things: 1. Give the association an 'ambit', 'bounds', 'compass' in which to make claims for some time in the future. 2. Create a dispute—because without a dispute being found you cannot bring a log of claims before the Australian Conciliation and Arbitration Commission. **1980** MCCALLUM & TRACEY *Cases & Materials Industr. Law* 174 An 'ambit' log of claims, that is, a log of claims designed to create a dispute with a very extensive coverage of both employers and matters and with extremely large claims for each of the individual items so as to provide an ambit of sufficient scope that the award, when made, would be capable of variation for a considerable time so reducing the need for further logs to be served. **1985** *Canberra Times* 20 Oct. 1/5 The hard-line ambit claim from Thatcher opponents was put by the Indian Prime Minister . . when he called . . for comprehensive mandatory sanctions.

American, *a.*
a. Applied to conveyances, constructions, etc., of American origin, or having characteristics believed to be American.
1828 *Hobart Town Courier* 12 July 4 Wanted, two or three Men . . to cut the timber, and put up 2 to 3000 rods of the American water fence. **1864** *Bell's Life in Sydney* 12 Mar. 3/4 *The Australian Buggy.* An improvement on the American Buggy.
b. In the collocation **American shout,** *Yankee shout*, see YANKEE.
1945 S.J. BAKER *Austral. Lang.* 170 We have versions of the shout, such as the *American shout.*

ampster. Also **amster.** [Perh. abbrev. of *Amsterdam* rhyming slang for RAM *n.* 2.] The accomplice of a sideshow operator or salesman, who dummies as the purchaser of a ticket or article with the intention of persuading others to do likewise.
1941 K. TENNANT *Battlers* 144 The ampster rushes eagerly up to the ticket-window and says: 'Right-o, mister, I'll have a ticket.' His brother-ampsters form into an impatient queue . . at the head of the multitude who, like sheep, will follow the leader. **1945** S.J. BAKER *Austral. Lang.* 138 An *amster* is a decoy who works with a sideshow operator to induce the public to spend its money.

Hence **ampster** *v. intr.*
1941 K. TENNANT *Battlers* 143 Mr Fosdick was agreeable, provided the busker would 'ampster' for him.

anabranch. [See quot. 1834.] An arm of a river which separates from and later re-joins the main stream. Also *attrib.* and *fig.*
[**1834** *Jrnl. R. Geogr. Soc. London* IV. 79 Such branches of a river as after separation re-unite, I would term anastomosing-branches; or, if a word might be coined, anabranches.] **1839** T.L. MITCHELL *Three Exped. Eastern Aust.* (rev. ed.) II. 40 We proceeded along the right bank of the Lachlan, crossing at five miles a small arm or ana-branch which had been seen higher up diverging from the river. **1913** H. LAWSON *Triangles of Life* 234 The station was not far away, but on a branch track of its own, an anabranch track, in fact.

Hence as *v. intr.*, to form an anabranch.
1956 T. RONAN *Moleskin Midas* 46 He swung away into the top of the bend and came to the end of a long, clear, claybanked billabong anabranching off the main creek channel.

Andersonian, *a.* and *n.* [f. the name of John *Anderson* (1893–1962), Challis Professor of Philosophy in the University of Sydney (1927–58).]
A. *adj.* Of, pertaining to, or characterized by the philosophy and attitudes of John Anderson and his followers.
1950 *Australasian Jrnl. Psych. & Philos.* XXVIII. 138, I am concerning myself not with the fate of inflationist doctrines which have been under fire for so long in both hemispheres, but with one position which is peculiarly Andersonian. **1976** *Quadrant* Jan. 8/3 Kamenka describes certain aspects of the earlier Marx, such as his hatred of censorship and of servility, and his advocacy of freedom of enquiry, and these are very Andersonian qualities.
B. *n.* A follower of the philosophical doctrines of John Anderson; one who founds on them a way of life and a set of moral, social, political, and anti-religious attitudes.

1958 *Austral. Highway* 72 It has always seemed to hostile critics that Andersonians have always followed a single line, opposing orthodoxy with an orthodoxy, repeating the master's arguments and even his phrases, in too narrow, sectarian and slavish a fashion. **1983** *Quadrant* Jan. 43/2 Not, of course, that even the most simple-minded Andersonian believed in anything but the continuance of conflict.

Hence **Andersonianism** *n.*

1958 *Observer* (Sydney) 653 Philosophically, nothing has yet come from Andersonianism other than Andersonianism.

angel stone. See quot. 1961. See also SHIN CRACKER.

1940 E. HILL *Great Austral. Loneliness* (ed. 2) 260 Holes in the ground . . fantastic with the gleam of potch and angelstone and fragments of opal itself. **1961** F. LEECHMAN *Opal Bk.* 132 Angel Stone has had two meanings; we now use it sometimes to describe a clay which has cracked in consequence of having been baked hard and dry; in these wavering and wandering cracks precious opal, often very brilliant, has formed making pretty pieces. . . The name was first used at White Cliffs . . to refer to the layer of intensely hard stone just above the opal level.

Anglo-Australian, *a.* and *n.*

A. *adj.*

1. a. *Obs.* Of British descent, but born in Australia.

1827 *Monitor* (Sydney) 19 Nov. 774/3 By shutting up the Convict women in the Factory, lest they should turn prostitutes or concubines, we add to the temptations by which our free Anglo-Australian female youth, of the lower orders, are daily and hourly beset in a Colony, where the sexes are so unnaturally disproportioned. **1881** *Macmillan's Mag.* (London) Apr. 114/2 Will the Anglo-Australian race degenerate?

b. *Obs.* Of British birth, but resident in Australia.

1888 *Plea for Separation* 26 An Anglo-Australian Bishop of the Anglican Church refused to administer the church sacraments to those Australians who had availed themselves of the Deceased Wife's Sister Act. **1899** *Austral. Tit-Bits* (Sydney) 6 May 199/3 William Caffyn, the old Anglo-Australian cricketer, is publishing his reminiscences.

c. *Obs.* Of Australian birth, but resident in Britain.

1894 *Bulletin* (Sydney) 17 Nov. 7/1 The Anglo-Australian officials in England. **1896** *Ibid.* 11 Jan. 16/1 In place of 'Anglo-Australian, absentee-parasite', etc., what's the complaint with 'Exhaustralian'?

d. Born (or resident) in Australia and of British, as distinct from European, Asian, etc., descent.

1984 *Canberra Times* 23 Feb. 1/2 It was asserted . . that Anglo-Australian students were rewarded for making their knowledge look natural.

2. Involving both British and Australian interests; of jointly British and Australian origin.

1848 J. FOWLES *Sydney* 6 There are four Banks of Issue— the Bank of New South Wales, and the Commercial Bank, both *Colonial*; and the Union Bank of Australia, and the Bank of Australasia, *Anglo-Australian*. **1962** I. SOUTHALL *Woomera* 48 Anglo-Australian rocketry . . has to solve its problems on tight budgets and ingenuity.

B. *n.*

a. *Obs.* A person born in Australia of British descent.

1836 J.F. O'CONNELL *Residence Eleven Yrs. New Holland* 100 Beside the transported population, there are growing generations of Anglo-Australians. **1893** F.W.L. ADAMS *Australs.* 5 The Anglo-Australian of Melbourne rushes away with the English 'new chum' whom he has generously engaged to 'show round', and proudly points out to him the second-rate imitations of the second-rate results of English contemporary civilization.

b. *Obs.* A person born in Britain but resident in Australia.

1894 E.H. CANNEY *Land of Dawning* 132 Excessive drinking is for the most part confined to the Anglo-Australian . . with the native born it is very uncommon.

c. *Obs.* A person born in Australia but resident in Britain.

1902 *Bulletin* (Sydney) 25 Oct. 25/1 A well-known Anglo-Australian now in London.

d. A person of British (as distinct from European, Asian, etc.) descent born or resident in Australia.

1979 J.J. SMOLICZ *Culture & Educ.* 273 We have used the term Anglo-Australian for people bred in the Anglo-Saxon-based 'core' or 'dominant' culture. The label 'Anglo-Australian' is designed to distinguish them from arrivals from continental Europe and their descendants to whom we refer as 'ethnic-Australians'. **1984** J. JUPP *Ethnic Politics in Aust.* 11 Are the methods and avenues used by ethnics the same as those used by comparable groups of Anglo-Australians?

Anglo-Celtic, *a.* Of or belonging to Great Britain or the Republic of Ireland; of British descent or provenance (see quot. 1977). Also as **Anglo-Celt** *n.*

1888 E.W. O'SULLIVAN IN *NSWPD* 1st Ser. XXXV. 597, I believe that the centre of power of the Anglo-Celtic race no longer lies in London. The majority are now to be found in the west, in America, and in the south, in Australasia. **1977** P. O'FARRELL *Catholic Church & Community in Aust.* 233 But fundamentally—Anglo-Celt—the self-description of the prominent layman E.W. O'Sullivan may also be applied to Moran; indeed he used the term himself. However elevated his estimate of the religion and culture of the Celt, he derived his political principles, his ideas of proper constitutional structure, his concepts of appropriate social behaviour, from Victorian England.

Anglo-colonial, *a. Obs.* Involving British and Australian interests; ANGLO-AUSTRALIAN *a.* 2. Also as *n.*

1843 *Colonial Observer* (Sydney) 1 Apr. 921/3 The selfishness and the griping and grasping policy of their Anglo-Colonial neighbours. **1844** *Sydney Morning Herald* 1 Aug. 2/2 As to the Anglo-Colonials, while in the Bank of Australasia, the deposits have *decreased* nearly 4 per cent, in the Union they have *increased* more than 5½ per cent.

Anglo-native. *Obs.* A person of British descent born in Australia; ANGLO-AUSTRALIAN *n.* a.

1827 *Monitor* (Sydney) 1 Nov. 736/2 The Captain, three mates, Carpenter, and boat-steerer, *are all native-born*. From the natural intrepidity of the Anglo-Natives, they seem peculiarly adapted for the adventurous calling of Mariners.

angophora /æŋ'gɒfərə/. Formerly also **angophera**. [f. Gr. ἄγγος jar + Φορός bearing, alluding to the vase-like fruits. The name was coined as the scientific name of the genus (see quot. 1797).] Any tree or shrub of the genus *Angophora* (fam. Myrtaceae) of e. mainland Aust. See also *apple tree* APPLE 3.

[**1797** A.J. CAVANILLES *Icon. et Descr. Plant.* IV. 21 *Angophora* . . quia fructus huius generis vasis formam referunt.] **1827** *HRA* (1923) 3rd Ser. VI. 580 Here is seen a magnificent specimen of Angophera. **1942** *Southerly* iii. 14 The angophora preaches on the hillsides With the gestures of Moses.

animated stick. *Obs.* The stick insect *Acrophylla titan* of e. coastal Aust., the female of which is one of the world's longest insects. Also **animated straw, twig.**

1805 J.H. TUCKEY *Acct. Voyage to establish Colony Port Philip* 164 The species of insects are almost innumerable: among them are . . several kinds of beetles, the animated straw, etc. **1833** G.R. GRAY *Ent. Aust.* 19 The *Titan tailed Spectre*, or *Diura Titan* . . is found on shrubs in the scrubby parts of the Colony . . and is locally termed 'Walking Straw', or

'Animated Stick'. **1839** J. STEPHENS *Land of Promise* 60 Mr Gouger mentions one very extraordinary insect, called the 'animated twig'. It somewhat resembles the mantis.

ankle-biter. A child.
1981 *Sun-Herald* (Sydney) 2 Aug. 167/4 The middle-aged Petula Clark does the Julie Andrews bit, skipping and trilling over the edelweiss with the Von Trapp ankle-biters. **1984** *People Mag.* 7 May 28/2 When he was still just an anklebiter his father got a posting in Sydney. At North Sydney High, Ian was a top athlete.

Annie's room. Orig. in Services' speech: see quot. 1919.
1919 W.H. DOWNING *Digger Dialects* 8 'In Annie's room'—an answer to questions as to the whereabouts of someone who cannot be found. **1945** *Newsreel* (Launceston) May 7 The curtain falls once more on the general jottings in and around 'Annie's Room'.

Anniversary Day. A name given formerly, in some States, to the anniversary of the beginning of British settlement at Sydney Cove. See AUSTRALIA DAY a.
1846 *Sydney Morning Herald* 27 Jan. 2/1 *Celebration of the fifty-eighth anniversary of the foundation of the colony.* The 'Anniversary Day', as it is pretty generally called, is now a regularly established holiday in Sydney. **1971** *Bulletin* (Sydney) 30 Jan. 11/2 The eastern States could learn from them and try to make Anniversary Day not a national day but a State day and celebrate their own communities modestly.

anothery. Also **anotherie.** Another one.
1963 X. HERBERT *Disturbing Element* 24 The pity was the dog could not talk, because when I got home and excitedly related my adventure, the family laughed. Mother said: 'Garn .. give us anothery!' **1979** B. HUMPHRIES *Bazza comes into his Own*, 'Scuse I, gotta go and shake hands with the unemployed! Line us up anotherie!

antarctic beech: see BEECH.

antbed.
1. a. An earth mound built by termites to house their nests.
1846 *Sydney Morning Herald* 22 June 2/5 They discovered five ant beds, which had been hollowed out to make ovens. **1975** X. HERBERT *Poor Fellow my Country* 12 Small spiked grey termites' nests, or Ant Beds, as called in these parts.
b. Earth from termite mounds, esp. used as a simple flooring material. Also *attrib.*, as **antbed floor**.
1913 *Bull. N.T.* vi. 6 The floors are of cement .. or are merely of rough earth or 'ant-bed'. **1930** J.S. LITCHFIELD *Far-North Memories* 20 The ant-bed floors needed only a daily damping and sweeping to be kept in perfect order.
2. The nest of any of various true ants (Formicidae), such as the *meat ant* (see MEAT).
1965 L. HAYLEN *Big Red* 164 Only for Johnny last night you'd have written your poetry on an ant bed with your arse bitten off by the bull joes.
3. Special Comb. **antbed parrot,** ANTHILL PARROT.
1964 M. SHARLAND *Territory of Birds* 206 The Golden-shouldered Parrot .. is sometimes called the 'ant-bed parrot'.

ant cap. A shield placed on top of a building support to discourage termites from entering the building from below.
1955 K. SHERROTT *Your House* 39 Fit termite-shields (ant-caps) to all foundation walls, piers and stumps. **1984** *N.S.W. Contract Reporter* 24 Jan., The presence of a correctly-designed and installed ant cap will not prevent a colony of termites from gaining access to a house... It will .. cause subterranean termites to form a visible bridge over the cap.
Hence **ant capping** *vbl. n.*
1973 *Sun-Herald* (Sydney) 26 Aug. 108/4 There should be no danger if effective ant-capping had been provided during construction of your house.

anteater.
1. ECHIDNA.
1817 J. O'HARA *Hist. N.S.W.* 432 A species of ant-eater is found in addition to the luxuries of the table. **1975** D. STUART *Walk, trot, canter & Die* 39 Here in the flat creek bed they found tracks of an anteater, and .. he marvelled at the casual ease with which one of the men followed the track to where the echidna was hiding under a spinifex.
2. NUMBAT.
1853 S. SIDNEY *Three Colonies* (ed. 2) 293 (*caption*) Bonded [*sic*] Myrmicobius, or ant-eater. **1952** J.F. HADDLETON *Katanning Pioneer* 101 The ant eater or numbat .. is a small animal, runs on four legs, part of the body light brown, back part dark brown with bands of white a quarter of an inch wide across his back.

ante-up, *n.* Also **anty-up.** [f. (orig.) U.S. *ante* the initial stake in the game of poker.] The game of poker.
1881 A.C. GRANT *Bush-Life Qld.* II. 169 Two or three men crawl out from underneath the tarpaulin of the nearest dray, where they have been playing 'Anty-up' (a favourite game with cards) for tobacco. **1954** T. RONAN *Vision Splendid* 305 Sit in at a small game of nap or ante-up.

ante-up, *v.* [Transf. use of *ante-up* to put up an *ante* (see prec.).] *trans.* To provide (money) in advance, often as a contribution to a collective expense. Also *absol.*
1878 'IRONBARK' *Southerly Busters* 181, I works a little 'on the cross', I never trusts to luck; I hates to have to 'ante-up', And likes to 'pass the buck'. **1890** *Quiz* (Adelaide) 11 Apr. 2/3 Subscription lists have been sent around... The Bank was going to ante-up £1,000.

anthill parrot. See quot. 1964; *antbed parrot*, see ANTBED 3.
1929 A.H. CHISHOLM *Birds & Green Places* 104 Bushmen of old had gazed wide-eyed at the male bird, resplendent in green, blue, red, brown and black, and knew him .. as the .. ant-hill parrot (because of the habit of nesting in termites' mounds). **1964** M. SHARLAND *Territory of Birds* 205 Three species of parrots use termites' mounds for nesting—the Hooded Parrot of the Northern Territory, the Golden-shouldered Parrot of north Queensland, and the rare Paradise Parrot of southern areas in Queensland. They are known by the common name of 'ant-hill parrots'.

Anti-Billite. *Hist.* One who opposes the terms of the Bill to constitute the Commonwealth of Australia, while supporting federation. Also *attrib.*
1898 *Argus* (Melbourne) 10 May 7/4 It completely destroys the arguments of the anti-billites that in the settlement of a deadlock the wishes of the majority of the people in the Commonwealth cannot prevail. **1931** H.L. HALL *Vic.'s Part in Austral. Federation Movt.* 141 There was a band of young men who went to the 'Anti-Billite' meetings and moved amendments to hostile motions against the Bill.

anti-convict, *a. Hist.* ANTI-TRANSPORTATION; esp. in the collocation **anti-convict league,** an organization opposed to the reintroduction of transportation.
1852 *Four Colonies Aust.* 16 Amongst other events which occurred between 1846 and 1850 were the attempt to reintroduce convicts into Australia, the consequent formation of the anti-convict league. **1855** W. HOWITT *Land, Labor & Gold* II. 404 The anti-convict league cut short his operations by depriving him of the labor he employed.

ANTIPODAL

antipodal, *a. Obs.* ANTIPODEAN *a.*
1849 A. HARRIS *Guide to Port Stephens* 11 If anything suggests the antipodal locality of the spot it is the timber, with which it takes some time for the eye to become familiar in Australia. **1924** LAWRENCE & SKINNER *Boy in Bush* 96 You were grilling under a fierce sun and the rush of the intense antipodal summer.

antipodeal, *a. Obs.* [Br. *antipodeal*, 'rare and erroneous form of prec.' (OED 1881).] ANTIPODEAN *a.*
1854 W. SHAW *Land of Promise* 21 The river Paramatta—the antipodeal Thames below bridge.

antipodean, *a.* and *n.* [Spec. use of *antipodean* of the opposite side of the world: see OED(S.)]
A. *adj.* Of or pertaining to the British antipodes; Australian.
1835 *Hist. Van Diemen's Land* 152 It remains to be decided whether the Colonists generally, or the Antipodean Princes, are of most consideration in the eyes of our Home Rulers. **1984** *Canberra Times* 12 Feb. 2/4 For my part, as the owner of many eucalypts of many sizes and habits, I take the view that they were here before us and that they have a perfect right to behave in an antipodean way.
B. *n.* An Australian.
1843 *Sydney Morning Herald* 25 May 4/3 Antipodeans here—I see them sit Before me in the middle of the pit. **1972** *Southerly* iv. 281 Brook always rose to dinner invitations for they represented to him that order and elegance and cultured society he felt should have been his, had he not been born an antipodean.

antipodes. [Restricted use of *antipodes* places on the earth's surface directly opposite each other: see OED 3.] Usu. with **the**: the British antipodes, spec. Australia, the calendar of the seasons and unusualness of the flora and fauna strengthening the sense of oppositeness (see quots., esp. 1857).
1833 *Sydney Herald* 12 Dec. 3/1 These are the Antipodes! 'The world is turned upside down!' **1857** W. WESTGARTH *Vic. & Austral. Gold Mines* 33 The trees without leaves, of which the native cherry tree and several species of the 'she-oak' are the most common. The former gives the standing instance of everything going by contraries at the antipodes, by producing a cherry with the stone on the outside.

anti-sosh, *a. Hist.* [See SOSH.] Opposed to socialism; anti-socialist.
1906 *Gadfly* (Adelaide) 18 July 20/1 The anti-sosh crowd wanted us to breakfast with them. **1908** *Bulletin* (Sydney) 17 Sept. 14/4 A great Anti-Sosh cry was 'Give us back our eleven days. You stole our eleven days.'

anti-squatter. *Hist.* [See SQUATTER.] One politically active in opposing the squatting interest.
1847 *Atlas* (Sydney) III. 222/2 'Dermid'.. appears to be an 'anti-squatter'. **1867** J. BONWICK *J. Batman* 38 One of the so-called party of anti-squatters, Mr Evans, assured me that he went with the avowed intention to run sheep.
Also **anti-squatterish, anti-squatting** *adjs.*
1853 J.R. GODLEY *Extracts Jrnl. Visit N.S.W.* 11 The Legislative Council of Victoria is decidedly '**anti-squatterish**' in its tendencies. **1848** *Maitland Mercury* 20 May 2/1 In the spirit of Hannibal, the leader of the **anti-squatting** party has sworn eternal hatred to the Land Orders.

anti-transportation. *Hist.* Used *attrib.* to designate an association, proposal, etc., opposed to the continuance of the convict system. See also TRANSPORTATIONIST.
1847 *Atlas* (Sydney) III. 122/3 The mean system of 'burking', or the petty expedient of attempting to 'damn with small sneers', is pursued towards those gentlemen who.. have the manliness to brave the hootings of an anti-transportation meeting. **1865** 'SPECIAL CORRESPONDENT' *Transportation* 49 The anti-transportation party is insignificant in numbers and influence.
Hence **anti-transportationist** *n.*
1847 *Port Phillip Herald* 23 Sept. 2/7 Mr McCombie.. attempted to charge the anti transportationists with inconsistency, and endeavouring to prevent the importation of convicts and Pentonvilles, and employ them after.

anvil-bird. [See quots.] *Noisy pitta*, see NOISY.
1918 *Bulletin* (Sydney) 21 Nov. 24/2 The anvil-bird.. is a very rare and exceedingly shy creature. Its clear metallic notes ring out 'Kling, kling, kling, kling', several times in measured tones. **1976** *Reader's Digest Compl. Bk. Austral. Birds* 330 Noisy pitta... Other names Anvil-bird... The pitta holds a snail in its bill and repeatedly strikes the shell against an 'anvil'.

Anzac, *n.* and *attrib.* [Acronym f. the initial letters of *Australian and New Zealand Army Corps* orig. used as a telegraphic code name for the Corps.]
A. *n.*
1. The Australian and New Zealand Army Corps.
1915 C.E.W. BEAN *Diary* 25 Apr. 67 *Col. Knox to Anzac.* 'Ammunition required at once.' **1920** *Aussie* (Sydney) May 13/1 The Army ceased to be officially known by the name Anzac some time after its arrival in France, and became the 'Australian Corps'.
2. Abbrev. of 'Anzac Cove': see quot. 1916.
1915 I. HAMILTON *Second Dispatch* 26 Aug., Lieut.-Gen. Sir W.R. Birdwood has been the soul of Anzac. Not for a single day has he ever quitted his post. Cheery and full of human sympathy, he has spent many hours of each twenty-four inspiring the defenders of the front trenches. **1916** 'MEN OF ANZAC' *Anzac Bk.* p. ix, I was asked by General Headquarters to suggest a name for the beach where we had made good our precarious footing, and then asked that this might be recorded as 'Anzac Cove'—a name which the bravery of our men has now made historical, while it will remain a geographical landmark for all time. Our eight months at 'Anzac' cannot help stamping on the memory of every one of us days of trial and anxiety, hopes, and perhaps occasional fears, rejoicings at success, and sorrow—very deep and sincere—for many a good comrade whom we can never see again.
3. The Gallipoli campaign.
1915 *Honk* x. 6/1 The whole Italian Press praises the valour of the Australasian troops in the Dardanelles at Anzac. **1984** *Canberra Times* 25 Apr. 2/2 Sixteen military commanders, from Anzac to 1970.
4. A member of the Australian and New Zealand Army Corps who served in the Gallipoli campaign.
1916 *Truth* (Sydney) 9 Apr. 8/4 Lord Mayor Dick Meagher has decided to entertain returned Anzacs at luncheon at the Town Hall. **1967** A. SEYMOUR *One Day of Yr.* 97 They put Australia on the map, they did, the Anzacs did. And bloody died, doin' it.
5. Used emblematically to reflect the traditional view of the virtues displayed by those who served in the Gallipoli campaign, esp. as these are seen as national characteristics.
1916 *Man. War Precautions* (Dept. of Defence) (1918) 158 No person shall, after the first day of July, One thousand nine hundred and sixteen, without the authority of the Governor-General or of a Minister of State.. assume or use in connexion with any trade, business, calling, or profession the word 'Anzac' or any word resembling the word 'Anzac', or any word notified by the Governor-General, by notice in the *Gazette*, to be for the purposes of this Regulation a prohibited word. **1976** K. CLIFT *Soldier who never grew Up* 88 Before I went to school, he would proclaim if I were hurt, 'never cry, be an Anzac'.
6. Generally, an Australian (or New Zealand) soldier or ex-soldier.

1917 T.E. Ruth *Mannixisms* 8 We are called, called by the Anzacs who have fallen, called by the Anzacs who are maimed. **1941** H. Percy *Here's H. Percy* 4 The exploits of the Anzacs are known in every land. Hitler knows 'em, to his sorrow—he's tackled 'em before, So he's sent his sidekick 'Musso' to face 'em in this war.

7. See quot. 1923; *Anzac biscuit*, see Anzac B. 2.

1923 Mrs H.W. Shaw *Six Hundred Tested Recipes* (ed. 9) 54 Anzacs: 2 breakfast cups John Bull oats, ½ breakfast cup sugar, 1 scant cup plain flour, ½ cup melted butter, 1 tablespoon golden syrup, 2 ditto. boiling water, 1 teaspoon carb. soda. Mix butter, golden syrup and soda together, pour boiling water on, then add dry ingredients. Put on oven sheet or scone tray with teaspoon. Slow oven till browned. **1980** McKenzie & Allen *Look at Yesteryear* 126 Cakes and biscuits, which became known as *Anzacs*, were sent to the soldiers to keep them in touch with home.

B. 1. *attrib.*

1915 C.E.W. Bean *Diary* 17 May 4 The beach was fairly clear but I could see men going about working careless of any fire, in the good old Anzac way. **1971** *Sydney Morning Herald* 20 Apr. 18/7 The Anzac campaign is regarded as having created the spirit and identity of Australia as a nation.

2. Comb. **Anzac biscuit, button, march, overcoat, parade, wafer.**

1943 *Austral. Home Cookery* 257 **Anzac biscuits**... These biscuits should be stored in an airtight tin, immediately they are cold. **1919** W.H. Downing *Digger Dialects* 8 **Anzac button**, a nail used in place of a trouser button. **1945** I.L. Idriess *Horrie Wog-Dog* 32 We're going home so you can lead the **Anzac march** through Melbourne. **1957** D. Niland *Call me when Cross turns Over* 157 He wore a dyed blue **Anzac overcoat** with the collar up. **1966** J. Aldridge *My Brother Tom* 164 As usual on the twenty-fifth of April the Australian activity nearest to God, the **Anzac parade**, was held in the town. **1918** C.L. Hartt *Diggerettes* 15 We were out for a spell, and from our billets could see the light railway crawling along laden with whizz-bangs and **Anzac wafers**.

Anzac Day. April 25, the anniversary of the landing at Gallipoli: a national public holiday commemorating all Australia's war dead. Also *attrib.*

1916 *Truth* (Sydney) 9 Apr. 1/8 What? We're going to have an Anzac Day, A night of Fireworks and Illumination, For which ratepayers they will have to pay To hold high revelry and jubilation, Strange conduct this is, truly be it said, To hold a picnic o'er Australia's dead. **1957** J.M. Hosking *Aust. First & Last* 32 The men of the original A.I.F. were far away the best, The chockoes throw their chests out on Anzac Day parades, But all those daffodils were fit for was putting on charades.

apostle bird. [See quot. 1928.] **a.** The predom. grey bird *Struthidea cinerea*, which builds its nest of mud and lives in family groups of about nine (twelve, according to tradition) in wooded parts of e. Aust.; Lousy Jack. **b.** Happy Jack. **c.** Rarely, Chough. See also Happy family, Twelve apostles. Also *ellipt.* as **apostles.**

1894 G. Boothby *On Wallaby* 291 The Apostle Bird's peculiarity is always to move about with eleven of his fellows. **1911** *Bulletin* (Sydney) 26 Jan. 15/2 The babbler or chatterer. In the bush.. these birds are variously known as 'the happy family', 'twelve apostles' or plain 'apostles' (sharing the appellation with the grey jumper). **1928** G.E. Wilkins *Undiscovered Aust.* 31 The Apostle-birds have gained their local name because of their habit of congregating together.. in groups of twelve.

appearance money. A payment made to employees presenting themselves for work irrespective of its availability: see quot. 1979. Also **attendance money.**

1947 *58 CAR* 20 App., Any waterside worker who refuses to accept work which he is capable of performing.. shall not be paid such attendance money in respect of any day or days upon which he so refuses. **1979** S. Moran *Reminisc. of Rebel* 29 During the struggle for the payment of appearance money, i.e. payment for the days on which the employers were not able to offer employment but on which the wharfies had to report for work, the Sydney Branch organised a march to the Sydney Domain.

apple.

1. Any of several fruits which in some way resembles the apple.

1770 J. Cook *Jrnls.* 23 Aug. (1955) I. 394 There are indeed found growing wild in the woods a few sorts of fruits.. which when ripe do not eat a miss, one sort especially which we call'd Apples. **1928** M.E. Fullerton *Austral. Bush* 130 The sheoak 'apple', as it is called, is armed with semi-pricks, placed like the covering of the pine-cones.

2. Abbrev. of *apple tree.*

1825 B. Field *Geogr. Mem. N.S.W.* 463 Excepting.. the wild apple (achras australis).. the wood-cutters had no names for the many trees of gigantic growth which cover this mountain. **1984** D.J. Boland et al. *Forest Trees Aust.* (rev. ed.) 186 'Apple' is believed to have originated from the apple-tree appearance of the first observed species, *A*[*ngophora*] *hispida.*

3. Special Comb. **apple berry,** any of several climbing plants of the Austral. genus *Billardiera* (fam. Pittosporaceae), some of which have edible fruits; **box,** any of several myrtaceous trees having a soft, fibrous bark and dull green leaves, as *Eucalyptus bridgesiana*; also *attrib.*; **bush,** a shrub with features reminiscent of the apple tree, as *Pterocaulon sphacelatum* (fam. Asteraceae) which emits a fruity aroma when crushed; **gum,** *apple box*; **isle (island, land),** Tasmania, so called because of its popular identification as an apple-growing region; also **islander** (or **lander**), a Tasmanian; **tree,** any of several trees thought to resemble the apple (*Malus*), esp. of the genera *Eucalyptus* and *Angophora* (fam. Myrtaceae); **tree flat,** see Flat *n.*[1] b.

1798 J.E. Smith *Specimen Bot. New Holland* 1 *Billardiera scandens*. Climbing **Apple-berry**. **1890** *Argus* (Melbourne) 9 Aug. 4/6 An ironstone hill.. with **apple-box** and ironbark dotted about. **1979** Douglas & Heathcote *Far Cry* 85 It was utterly wild, fairly open bush of stringy barks and grey apple-box trees. **1900** *Proc. Linnean Soc. N.S.W.* XXV. 710 *Heterodendron oleaefolium* (locally called **Apple Bush**, though in most places it is known as Rosewood). **1845** L. Leichhardt *Jrnl. Overland Exped. Aust.* 22 May (1847) 264 The rocky ridges were occupied by.. another Eucalyptus, with a scaly butt like the Moreton Bay ash, but with smooth upper trunk and cordate ovate leaves... We called it the **Apple-gum**. **1901** [**apple isle**] *Advocate* (Burnie) 3 Oct. 2/5 The term 'apple-land' and Tasmania grew to be synonymous. **1906** *Gadfly* (Adelaide) 7 Mar. 19/1 The apple isle still continues to *fête* Senator Keating and his bride. *Ibid.* 21 Mar. 17/3 The apple island still continues to attract a few stragglers from our city. **1914** [**apple islander**] *Truth* (Sydney) 15 Feb. 8/6 Three Applelanders arrived in Sydney this week. **1928** *Aussie* (Sydney) Apr. 15/3 The newly-arrived Apple Islander blinked his eyes nervously. 'Well, you're a disgrace to Tasmania!' he roared. **1801** *HRA* (1915) 1st Ser. III. 415 The timber on the low ground is principally blue-gum and **apple-tree**.

4. *pl.* Rhyming slang for 'apples and spice' (or 'rice'), nice. Used *ellipt.* (esp. as **she's apples**), to indicate general approbation; all right, in good order.

1943 J. Binning *Target Area* 140 If everything is running smoothly 'she's apples'. **1978** *Overland* lxxii. 16 'Is the fire safe..?' 'Yeah, she's apples.'

Arbitration. [Spec. use of *arbitration* settlement, with reference to industrial contexts.] Used *attrib.* in Special Comb. **arbitration award,** an award made by a court of industrial arbitration (see AWARD); **system,** the organization and method of the settling of industrial disputes, determining of awards, etc., federally and in the States.

1897 *Argus* (Melbourne) 7 Apr. 6/1 An unusual application was made to-day to the Chief Justice, sitting in Equity, that execution should issue against the Crown in respect to an unsettled **arbitration award. 1920** E.G. THEODORE *Some Industr. Problems* 5 The criticism I speak of was mostly directed against the Commonwealth Government **arbitration system.**

area school. A school formed by the amalgamation of several small rural schools, offering both primary and secondary education: see quot. 1974. Also *attrib.*

1940 *Educ. Studies & Investigations* (Austral. Council Educ. Research) 226 He paid two visits to Tasmania during 1939 in order to examine the working of the newly established Area Schools. **1942** *Tasmanian Area School* (Tas. Educ. Dept.) 28 The pupil who has satisfactorily completed the work of Grades VII and VIII is entitled to an Area School Certificate. **1974** J. MCLAREN *Dict. Austral. Educ.* 27 Area School. The name used in Tasmania and South Australia for schools formed by the consolidation of a number of small rural schools, and offering both primary and secondary courses... The first area schools were established in Tasmania in 1936.

Argyle apple. [f. the name of *Argyle* County in the Goulburn district of N.S.W.] The small tree *Eucalyptus cinerea* (fam. Myrtaceae), native to a small area of N.S.W. and Vic., and cultivated as an ornamental; (formerly) the similar *E. pulverulenta.*

1867 W. WOOLLS *Contribution to Flora Aust.* 236 *E. pulverulenta*, and .. *E. cinerea* seem to be two varieties of the small tree usually called 'Argyle Apple'. It is similar in appearance to *Angophora subvelutina* or the 'Apple' of the colonists, as the leaves are opposite, and the bark furrowed and wrinkled. **1956** T.Y. HARRIS *Naturecraft in Aust.* 142 Argyle Apple .. often picturesque in habit, occurring on poor sandy and shaley soil in the southern parts of New South Wales and in Victoria.

aristotle. Rhyming slang for 'bottle'. Also **Arrystottle.**

1897 *Bulletin* (Sydney) 7 Aug. (Red Page), Bottle (of anything)—'Aristotle'.. rarely used, and only of late. **1968** D. O'GRADY *Bottle of Sandwiches* 93 How about stickin' around till I knock off at seven, an' then we'll take a few Arrystottles out to your joint.

arm. *Obs.* A narrow tract of open land projecting into forested and mountainous country, as a tributary valley.

1834 J.D. LANG *Hist. & Statistical Acct. N.S.W.* II. 108 The valley of the Wollombi .. is bounded on either side by mountain-ranges .. and throws off numerous *arms*, as the settlers call them, to the right and left, some of them extending for a distance of twenty or thirty miles among the mountains. These arms, as well as the principal valley, abound in excellent pasture. **1874** R.W. MAYNE *Two Visions* 8 Inland in Australia 'arm' is used conversely to denote a continuation, or inlet as it were, of open land from a plain.

arse.

1. Dismissal (from employment). Also *fig.*

1955 *Overland* v. 4 We cleaned up that concreting before 9 a.m. only to get the arse just as Plugger had intended... He told us that if we cared to come back next week, there might be another couple of hours' work going. **1983** L. CLANCY *Perfect Love* 238 She's been playing around with half the town. So I went home and gave her the arse.

2. Insolence, effrontery, 'cheek'.

1958 F. HARDY *Four-Legged Lottery* 188 See all the snooker balls going into the pockets—he had more arse than a married cow playing snooker, I can tell yer. **1979** *Bulletin* (Sydney) 11 Sept. 86/3 Since the place was set up 25 years ago there have been less than 200 visitors in total and I only got there through sheer arse and lots of it.

arsehole, *v. trans.* To dismiss or get rid of (a person).

1965 W. DICK *Bunch of Ratbags* 153 It's orright when yuh young, but when yuh get a bit old and yuh can't keep up with the younger stickers .. they'll arsehole yuh. **1974** D. IRELAND *Burn* 125 They want to clear us right out. Arsehole us completely.

arsey, *a.* Also **arsie, arsy.** [Alteration of *tin arse* TIN *n.*² 2.] Lucky.

1953 S.J. BAKER *Aust. Speaks* 104 *Arsey*, lucky. **1960** J. WALKER *No Sunlight Singing* 23, I was real arsy to pick up a job here. **1978** T. DAVIES *More Austral. Nicknames* 25 *Arsie*, is very lucky at cards and raffles.

artesian. *a.* and *n.* [Spec. use of *artesian* of the type of well found in Artois.]

A. *adj.* In the collocation **artesian bore,** an artesian well; a well formed by drilling through impervious strata to tap water held under sufficient pressure to cause it to rise spontaneously to the surface. See BORE.

1897 R. NEWTON *Work & Wealth Qld.* 14 Artesian bores have been put down in numbers to tap these stores. **1977** W.A. WINTER-IRVING *Bush Stories* 7 We passed a couple of artesian bores belching up hot water that came from hundreds of metres underground.

B. *n. transf.* A name for beer: see quot. 1892.

1892 K. LENTZNER *Dict. Slang-Eng. Aust.* 1 *Artesian*, colonial beer. People in Gippsland, Victoria, use *artesian* just as Tasmanians use *cascade*, in the sense of 'beer', because the one is manufactured from the celebrated *artesian* well at Sale, Gippsland, and the other from the *cascade* water. **1948** R. RAVEN-HART *Canoe in Aust.* 166 Another .. tried to entrap me into tasting the sulphuretted-hydrogen-loaded water—it gave Australia one of the slang names for beer, 'artesian', apparently because the beer made with this water was .. good.

artist. [Orig. U.S.: see OEDS 10.] A person practised or habitually engaged in an activity which requires little skill or is reprehensible; now esp. as final element in Comb., as **booze, bullshit artist,** etc. See also *grog artist* GROG *n.* 3, *fang artist* FANG *n.*¹ b., *stoush artist* STOUSH *n.* 3.

1889 J.L. HUNT *Bk. of Bonanzas* 9 The twenty-seven artists on the roof spat on their hands .. and pulled away at the rope. **1938** X. HERBERT *Capricornia* 23 These men .. were what are called Booze Artists, fellows who can drink continuously without getting drunk. **1969** F. MOORHOUSE *Futility & Other Animals* 97, I was a bullshit artist and I wrote bullshit letters.

art union. [Spec. use of *art union* a union of persons for the purpose of promoting art, orig. by subscription to the purchase of works of art, which were then distributed among the subscribers by lottery: see OED(S *art* V, and also quots. 1841 and 1846.] A lottery organized to raise funds for a charity or public cause, with prizes in cash or kind. Also *attrib.*

[**1841** *Sydney Herald* 15 Dec. 3/3 The Subscribers to *Mr Felton's Art Union*, who have not paid their subscriptions, are respectfully requested to do so without delay, as the distribution of the Paintings will take place as soon as the above is complied with. **1846** *Sydney Morning Herald* 9 Jan. 2/5 *Art Union*—The first distribution of pictures in the colony by this, now in England, very popular medium, came off at the Court House on Monday. The Art Union had its origin in Mr Howard Bower, the artist, being desirous to proceed to England as early as possible, and finding it impossible to find eight-and-twenty purchasers for as many pictures at any thing like remunerating prices, hit on the present idea... Sixty subscribed at £1 1s. each, entered for the chances of the eight-and-twenty prizes.] **1849** *Ibid.* 27 Nov. 1/4 The undersigned guarantees the respective sums of £50 and £40 to the drawers of the 1st and 2nd Prizes, in his Art Union. **1897** *Bulletin* (Sydney) 7 Aug. 24/2 The one just past probably absorbed £7000 of public money, of which £1700 went to the charities, £1500 went in art-union prizes, the balance being swallowed up in bicycle prizes and expenses—chiefly expenses.

arvo /'avoʊ/. [Modified pronunc. of *af(ternoon* + *-O.*]
1. Afternoon. Esp. in the phr. **this arvo**. Also *attrib.* See SARVO.
1927 *Sunday Sun* (Sydney) 9 Oct. (Sunbeams Suppl.) 1, I told young 'Ocker' Stevens to come up and say that so I could go shooting with him with his new pea rifle this arvo. **1980** E. METCALFE *Garden Party* 98 You remember the time you popped out for *two* minutes—to get me cakes for 'arvo tea'—or whatever?
2. Afternoon tea (but see quot. 1972).
1950 A.W. UPFIELD *Widows of Broome* 42 He hoped the 'arvo' would soon be served. **1972** *Bulletin* (Sydney) 17 June 62/3 The watercress salad and cheeses came with a masked bottle, which was voted the top wine of the 'baked arvo'.

ash. [See quot. 1957.] Any of many trees, usu. of the genus *Eucalyptus* (fam. Myrtaceae), yielding a valuable timber; the timber, which is typically pale, strong, and straight-grained. Also *attrib.*, and with distinguishing epithet, as **alpine, mountain, red, white** (see under first element).
1801 *HRA* (1915) 1st Ser. III. 170 Here [*sc.* Ash Island] we found plenty of different sorts of wood, and the ash trees of considerable magnitude. **1957** *Forest Trees Aust.* (Cwlth. Forestry & Timber Bureau) 132 The ash group of eucalypts.. includes some of the most important timber trees of Australia... The name 'ash' was applied in the early days of settlement because of a superficial resemblance of the timber to that of the European ash (*Fraxinus* spp.) Botanically, however, there is no close relationship between the two groups of trees.

Ashes. *Cricket.* [See quot. 1882. Recorded earliest in Aust.] The symbolic trophy awarded to the winner of a series of test matches played periodically between Australia and England; the actual wooden urn containing the ashes of a cricket stump and remaining permanently at Lord's Cricket Ground, headquarters of the Marylebone Cricket Club. Chiefly in the phr. **the Ashes**. Also *transf.* (see quot. 1948).
[**1882** *Sporting Times* (London) 2 Sept., In Affectionate Remembrance of English Cricket Which died at the Oval on 29th August, 1882. Deeply lamented by a large circle of sorrowing friends and acquaintances. R.I.P. N.B.—The body will be cremated and the ashes taken to Australia.] **1883** BEESTON & MASSIE *St. Ivo & Ashes* 3 Mr Bligh humorously declared that he and his eleven had come to 'beard the kangaroo in his den, and try to recover *those* ashes.' **1948** *Australs.' Tour Official Souvenir* (Rugby Football League) 4, I am told that the Australian Rugby League side, the 'Kangaroos', hope to win back the 'Ashes' from England this year.

assign, *v. Hist. trans.* To make over the services (of a convict) to a private individual. Occas. with services as obj.
1789 *Hist. Rec. N.S.W.* I. ii. 258 It is Our Will and Pleasure, that in case there should be a prospect of their employing any of the said convicts to advantage, that you assign to each grantee the service of any number of them. **1791** P.G. KING Jrnl. Norfolk Island 12 Nov. 2 The service of convicts to be assigned them on its appearing that such Settlers can Maintain, Feed, Cloath, and Employ them to advantage.

assignable, *a. Hist.* Of a convict: eligible to be assigned to a private individual.
1829 Tas. Colonial Secretary's Office Rec. 1/32 198 It has to supply not only the Washerwomen belonging to the Assignable Class, but also those in the Crime Class with hot water. **1842** *Colonial Observer* (Sydney) 16 Feb. 159/2 There are at present a number of female servants in the factory assignable.

assigned, *ppl. a. Hist.*
1. Of a convict: made over into the service of a private individual. Also applied to convict service and with **out**.
1806 *Sydney Gaz.* 16 Mar., Any *assigned Prisoner* of the Stores with Individuals, who do not appear as above will.. be sentenced. **1845** *Southern Queen* (Sydney) 66/1 That the assigned labour of the convict in town and country has been most beneficial to the colony we have never heard disputed. **1879** C.P. WILLIAMS *Southern Sunbeams* 13 Do you wish to stay here, like this, and to die, nothing but an assigned-out lag?
2. In collocations: **assigned convict, convict servant, servant, service**.
1827 *HRA* (1920) 1st Ser. XIII. 137 The **Assigned Convicts** are on all occasions forwarded by the Government to the Persons, to whom they are assigned. **1824** E. CURR *Acct. Colony Van Diemen's Land* 160 Colonial regulations touching the summary jurisdiction of magistrates over the relation of master and **assigned convict servants**. **1817** *Regulations respecting Assigned Convict Servants* 28 Mar. (1821) 5 **Assigned Servants** will clearly understand, that the Settler or Inhabitant to whom they are appropriated by Government has a Right to their extra Time for the Wages above specified. **1818** *Hobart Town Gaz.* 28 Mar., The Lieutenant Governor makes known his intention of sending up to Port Jackson, to be placed in the Factory there, such Female Prisoners as.. cannot be continued in **Assigned Service**.

assignee. *Hist.* A person to whom the services of a convict are made over.
1825 *HRA* (1917) 1st Ser. XI. 496 His labor belongs to the Crown and the Crown's Assignees. **1848** *Sydney Morning Herald* 23 Aug. 3/5 No convict assigned under these regulations.. shall be permitted to remain within the limits of the town of Sydney for more than one week at any one time.. upon pain of such servants being withdrawn, and the assignee considered incapable of receiving convict servants in future.

assignment. *Hist.*
1. The making over to a private individual of the services of a convict; the state of being so placed.
1822 T. REID *Two Voyages N.S.W. & Van Diemen's Land* 252 The Superintendent of convicts is.. perfectly apprized of everything requisite for directing a just and satisfactory assignment of the prisoners. **1845** *HRA* (1845) 1st Ser. XXIV. 250 Of these Convicts, one half at least have been placed in what is called 'Assignment' (a species of domestic Slavery) as Servants to the Settlers.
2. Comb. **assignment system**.
1838 *Colonist* (Sydney) 10 Jan. 2/2 In regard to the Assignment System, *Dr Lang* gave it as his opinion that it ought to be discontinued forthwith.

assimilation.
1. The acceptance, by non-British immigrant minorities, of Australian cultural values; the integration of such minorities into Australian society.

1927 J. LYNG *Non-Britishers in Aust.* 105 The question of 'assimilation' has of late been raised in Australia, more frequently in connection with Italian immigrants than with any other foreign nationals. **1942** W.D. FORSYTH *Myth of Open Spaces* 190 Northern Europeans have a long tradition of assimilation into Australian life.

2. The integration of Aborigines into white Australian society: see quots. Also *attrib.*

1951 *CPD* (H. of R.) CCXIV. 875 Assimilation means, in practical terms, that, in the course of time, it is expected that all persons of Aboriginal blood or mixed blood in Australia will live as do white Australians. **1978** C.H. & R.M. BERNDT *Pioneers & Settlers* 125 The word 'assimilation' was interpreted in various ways, but in practice it was always intended to mean absorption. **1984** P. READ *Down there with me on Cowra Mission* 129 What did you make of the Assimilation policy? I think its a load of crap.

assisted, *ppl. a.* Of or pertaining to Government-subsidized immigration to Australia.

1848 *HRA* (1925) 1st Ser. XXVI. 578 We propose sending out Assisted Emigrants as they are passed, in the Ships we charter for the conveyance of the Free Emigrants. **1984** *Yr. Bk. Aust.* 112 From May 1981 the grant of assisted passage was restricted to refugees.

attendance money: see APPEARANCE MONEY.

attle. *S.A. Obs.* Also **addle**. [Cornish mining *attle* mine refuse: see EDD *attle* and *addle*.] Earth or rock which contains no ore; refuse from a mine; MULLOCK *n.* 1.

1850 *S. Austral. Register* (Adelaide) 2 July 2/5 And have spoiled to (many eyes) the appearance of these places, by putting in the addle, but they have nevertheless left ore in sight. **1962** O. PRYOR *Aust.'s Little Cornwall* 35 When the ore was brought up to the surface, it was sorted by 'pickey boys' under the supervision of a 'grass captain', or surface boss. They graded it into 'prill' (rich ore), 'alvins' (low grade), and 'attle' (waste).

aunty. *Aboriginal English.* Used as a mode of address: see quot. 1963.

1963 D.E. BARWICK *Little more than Kin* 287 'Aunty' . . and 'coz' are here significant terms of address. . . Aunty is used as a courtesy title of address and reference for older women belonging to the same regional population, regardless of their genealogical connection to the speaker. **1980** *N.S.W. Parl. Papers* (1980–81) 3rd Sess. IV. 1794 The teachers are not just their teachers; they are their aunties. They are part of the extended family process that Aborigines have always kept. All the teachers are called auntie. It was a bit awkward for the European teachers when they first came.

Aurora Australis. [mod. L. 'the southern lights' (OED 1741) by analogy with *aurora borealis* the northern lights.] An illumination of the night sky occurring in a belt about the southern magnetic pole and irregularly visible, esp. in southern parts of Australia.

1788 J. WHITE *Jrnl. Voyage N.S.W.* (1790) 214 About half after six in the evening, we saw an aurora australis, a phenomenon uncommon in the southern hemisphere. **1983** B. CORBETT *Fistful of Buttercups* 118 'It could be the aurora australis,' said my father. . . Sure enough, there was a faint flickering in the southern sky.

Aus, var. Oz.

Aussie /'ɒzi/, *n.* and *attrib.* Also **Ossie, Ozzie**. [f. AUS(TRALIA or AUS(TRALIAN + -Y.]

A. *n.*

1. Australia.

1915 G.F. MOBERLY *Experiences 'Dinki Di' R.R.C. Nurse* (1933) 30 A farewell dance for the boys going home to 'Aussie' tomorrow. **1965** G. MCINNES *Road to Gundagai* 35 People with complaints were so glad to be back in dear old Aussie that they forgot their troubles.

2. An Australian; orig. an Australian soldier serving in the war of 1914–18. Also *fig.*

1918 *Truth* (Sydney) 28 July 6/5 We consider the term Aussie or Ossie as evolved is a properly picturesque and delightfully descriptive designation of the boys who have gone forth from Australia. **1919** C.A. SMITH *New Words Self-Defined* 15 The fondness between the soldiers was mutual. There was nothing an Ozzie liked so much as fighting with a Yankee company. **1925** E. MCDONNELL *My Homeland* 68, I have often noticed Jacky in the Sydney parks, where the little Aussie has to battle with the pommy pest—the English house sparrow.

3. Australian English.

1945 'MASTER-SARG' *Yank discovers Aust.* 64 This one was dinkum (which is Aussie for O.K.) **1972** B. REED *Mr Siggie Morrison* 93 Oh, crayfish is Aussie for lobster. I think.

B. *attrib.* passing into *adj.* Australian.

[N.Z. *c* 1910 A.E. WOODHOUSE *N.Z. Farm & Station Verse* (1950) 49 We'd a bunch of Aussie shearers, and they come from New South Wales.] **1916** G.F. MOBERLY *Experiences 'Dinki Di' R.R.C. Nurse* (1933) 51 One of our Aussie officers. **1986** *Sydney Morning Herald* 8 Mar. 28/1 At the Adelaide Festival lurked that perennial ghost at every literary banquet, the starving Aussie writer.

Hence **Aussieism** *n.*, AUSTRALIANISM 1.

1966 *Sunday Truth* (Brisbane) 23 Dec. 22/7 We of the 'weird mob' are noted for the wealth of our idiomatic language and the sooner Aussieisms are coined for our new currency the better will people understand the decimal units of exchange.

Aussieland. Australia.

1920 *Aussie* (Sydney) Aug. 34/2 The girl he left in Aussieland Went nearly out her mind. **1969** *Kings Cross Whisper* (Sydney) lxxviii. 5/2 We want to make him into Knuckler Grogon, Aussieland's forthright, thrusting leader—the punchiest PM since Mauler Ming.

Hence **Aussielander** *n.*

1941 S.J. BAKER *Pop. Dict. Austral. Slang* 6 *Aussie . .* whence, 'Aussieland', 'Aussielander'.

Aussie rules. Shortened form of AUSTRALIAN RULES.

1941 S.J. BAKER *Pop. Dict. Austral. Slang* 6 *Aussie Rules*, Australian Rules football. **1983** *Nat. Times* (Sydney) 13 May 50/3 A lot of people will bag Aussie Rules, calling it a sheila's game, but the guys that are playing it are top class sportsmen, there's incredible skill involved.

Austral. *a.* and *n.* [Spec. use of *austral* belonging to the south, southern.]

A. *adj.*

1. Australian. Freq. poetic.

1823 W.C. WENTWORTH *Australasia* 21 Grant that yet an Austral Milton's song . . flow deep and rich along;—An Austral Shakspeare rise. **1922** J. LEWIS *Fought & Won* 144 Yes, we remember Anzac . . that dazzling and glorious concentration of Austral love and Austral courage.

2. Used as the first element in the names of some plants. See also AUSTRALIAN *a.* 2.

1833 J. BACKHOUSE *Narr. Visit Austral. Colonies* (1843) 166 This [*sc.* Bruny] island is nearly covered with wood like that of the main land, and has a few Austral Grass-trees interspersed among them. **1956** B. BEATTY *Beyond Aust.'s Cities* 198 A remarkable feature of the North-West landscape is the Austral baobab, Australia's most grotesque tree.

B. *n. Obs.*

1. Australia.

1868 *Colonial Soc.* (Sydney) 31 Dec. 3 That we're sons of old England we ne'er shall forget, And must think of our own native home with regret—But, aye let us remember in Austral's bright strand We live in a free,—perhaps a

happier, land. **1891** H. Nisbet *Colonial Tramp* I. 64 Fair daughters of sunny Austral.
2. A non-Aboriginal Australian.
1884 D.B.W. Sladen *Summer Christmas* 231 She was slim, As Australs are, of waist and limb at wrist and ankle.

Australasia. *Obs.* [a. Fr. *Australasie* the Australian continent and neighbouring islands; ult. f. L. *australis* southern + *Asia*.] The Australian mainland; Australia.

[**1756** C. de Brosses *Histoire des Navigations* I. 80 L'une dans l'océan des Indes au sud de l'Asie que j'appellerai par cette raison *australasie*. **1766** J. Callander *Terra Australis Cognita* I. 49 The first [division] in the *Indian Ocean* to the south of *Asia*, which, for this reason we shall call *Australasia*.] **1794** G. Shaw *Zool. New Holland* 2 The vast Island or rather Continent of Australia, Australasia, or New Holland, which has so lately attracted.. particular attention. **1890** H.A. White *Crime & Criminals* 68 No country in the world could offer such numerous facilities as Australasia.

Australasian, *a.* and *n. Obs.*

A. *adj.* Of, pertaining to, or characteristic of Australia.
1802 G. Shaw *Gen. Zool.* III. iii. 506 An extremely good general representation of this species.. as well as of some other Australasian snakes. **1903** *Truth* (Sydney) 19 Apr. 3/1 The annual session of the Australasian Natives' Association was opened.. on Tuesday.

B. *n.*

1. A non-Aboriginal Australian.
1819 *Edinburgh Rev.* XXXII. 40 The Australasians grow corn; and it is necessarily their staple. **1917** *Huon Times* (Franklin) 1 May 4/1 In remembrance of the Australasians who had counted their lives not their own as they went forth to suffer and to die.

2. An Aboriginal.
1845 P.E. de Strzelecki *Physical Descr. N.S.W.* 349 Since the time that the fate of the Australasian awoke the sympathies of the public, neither the efforts of the missionary, nor the enactments of the Government, and still less the protectorate of the 'Protectors', have effected any good.

Australasiatic, *n.* and *a. Obs.*

A. *n.*

1. A non-Aboriginal Australian.
1824 *Hobart Town Gaz.* 30 Apr., The mind of an Australasiatic is not formed to be bounded by the Blue Mountains, and a bullock's hide.

2. Australian English.
1890 *Cornhill Mag.* (London) July 98 It was neither Cockney nor Yankee, but a nasal blend of both... In a word, it was Australasiatic of the worst description.

B. *adj.* Australian.
1819 *Blackwood's Mag.* (Edinburgh) V. 96 Craf-callee, which is a kind of Australasiatic Delos. **1859** D. Bunce *Travels with Dr Leichhardt* 92 Sydney.. one of the most important cities in the Austral-Asiatic colonies.

Austral Felician. *Hist.* A resident of **Australia Felix.** Also as *adj.*
1839 *Port Phillip Patriot* 21 Oct. 3/1 The.. paragraph.. caused feelings of surprise to arise in our mind, and in the minds of the Austral-Felicians generally. **1843** *Colonial Observer* (Sydney) 25 Jan. 770/2 This is the first trial of Austral-felician beef in the English market.

Australia. [An anglicization of (*Terra*) *Australis* the southern land, a name used to designate the islands and supposed continent s. of Asia from the early sixteenth century. With spec. reference to the known continent it was preferred by Matthew Flinders (1774–1814), and popularized by Lachlan Macquarie (1762–1824): see quots. 1805, 1814, and 1817.]

1. The continent in the Southern Hemisphere bounded by the Indian, Southern, and Pacific Oceans (in early use often restricted to the mainland or to N.S.W. as the known part of the mainland); the federated States and Territories which together make up the Commonwealth of Australia.

[**1770** J. Cook *Jrnls.* 14 Aug. (1955) I. 376 The Islands discover'd by *Quiros* call'd by him Astralia [*sic*] del Espiritu Santo lays in this parallel. **1773** J. Hawkesworth *Acct. of Voyages Southern Hemisphere* III. 602 The islands which were discovered by Quiros and called Australia del Espiritu Santa, lie in this parallel.] **1794** G. Shaw *Zool. New Holland* 2 The vast Island or rather Continent of Australia, Australasia, or New Holland, which has so lately attracted.. particular attention. **1805** M. Flinders Memo. 14 May Adm. 55076 *AJCP* 1587/77, It is necessary, however, to geographical propriety, that the whole body of land should be designated under one general name; on this account, and under the circumstances of the discovery of the different parts, it seems best to refer back to the original Terra Australis, or Australia; which being descriptive of its situation, having antiquity to recommend it, and no reference to either of the two claiming nations, is perhaps the least objectionable that could have been chosen; for it is little to be apprehended, that any considerable body of land, in a more southern situation, will be hereafter discovered. **1814** —— *Voyages to Terra Australis* I. p. iii Introd., I have ventured upon the re-adoption of the *original* Terra Australis... Had I permitted myself any innovation upon the original term, it would have been to convert it into Australia; as being more agreeable to the ear, and an assimilation to the names of the other great portions of the earth. **1817** L. Macquarie in *HRA* (1917) 1st Ser. IX. 356, I beg leave to acknowledge the Receipt of Captn. Flinders' Chart of *Australia. Ibid.* 747 Lieut. King expects to be absent from Port Jackson between Eight and Nine Months, and I trust in that time will be able to make very important additions to the Geographical knowledge already acquired of the Coasts of the Continent of *Australia*, which I hope will be the Name given to this country in future, instead of the very erroneous and misapplied name, hitherto given it, of 'New Holland', which properly speaking only applies to a part of this immense Continent. **1976** R. Robinson *Shift of Sands* 117 My Australia. She is like a beautiful, mysterious woman.

2. *Obs.* In the collocation **the Australias**: the several Australian colonies considered collectively; regions of Australia so considered.
1846 *Sydney Morning Herald* 20 Apr. 2/2 It is a co-incidence somewhat out of the ordinary course of events, that all the Australias, Eastern, Western, and Southern, should have experienced a change in the person of their respective rulers within a few months of each other... There are at least two great interests in which the Australias have a common stake. **1910** *Huon Times* (Franklin) 3 Dec. 2/7 A panorama of mountain and valley opens out before the eye, the grandeur of which is not excelled anywhere in the Australias.

Australia Day. **a.** A name given to the day, 26 January, on which the anniversary of the beginning of British settlement, at Sydney Cove in 1788, is celebrated. Formerly (in some States) Anniversary Day. **b.** *Hist.* A name given in the Roman Catholic community to the day, 24 May, formerly celebrated as Empire Day, in protest at its allegedly Protestant character (see quots. 1911). **c.** *Hist.* The name given to a day, 30 July, so proclaimed in connection with an Australian Red Cross Society fund-raising campaign (see quots. 1915). Also *attrib.*

1911 *Sydney Morning Herald* 19 Jan. 5/7 And that, as a help to the cultivation of the patriotic spirit, May 24 should be formally set apart as 'Australia Day', under the auspices of Our Lady, Help of Christians. *Ibid.* 23 May 6/3 But in arrogantly setting up an Australia Day of its own, with no historical or other reference to our universal Australia Day,

January 26, that Church assumes a prerogative it has no right, human or divine, to exercise. The proper authority to proclaim an Australia Day, if one is wanted, is the Parliament of the Australian Commonwealth. **1915** *Sydney Morning Herald* 30 July 7/7 The object of Australia Day is to raise a fund of sufficient proportions to provide comforts and nursing assistance for our men who have fought so valiantly, and suffered so grievously. **1915** *Bulletin* (Sydney) 16 Sept. 18/1 Australia Day committee purred over the cream-puff at Government House. **1981** A.J. BURKE *Pommies & Patriots* 38 The name Australia Day is a tribute to Joe Lyons who died in office of Prime Minister in 1939 and he largely sponsored the change of name from Foundation Day to Australia Day in 1932.

Australia Felix. *Hist.* [f. L. *felix, felicis* happy, fertile, productive.] The name given by Thomas Mitchell in 1836 to the region south of the Murray River which, in 1851, was separated from New South Wales and named Victoria.

1836 *HRA* (1923) 1st Ser. XVIII. 590 He has also gone over .. rich and well watered Country deserving as he thinks the name of Australia Felix. **1852** *Murray's Guide to Gold Diggings* 28 The district not ill-named by Sir Thomas Mitchell, Australia Felix .. Phillipsland of Dr. Lang, Port Phillip of the masses and common parlance, and Victoria .. are all the same country.

Hence **Australia Felician, Australia Felixian** *n.*, AUSTRAL FELICIAN.

1839 *Port Phillip Patriot* 24 Apr. 4/1 Would not a standing committee be useful in our rising Capital? Could we not meet in such a committee, not as Vandemonians, or Sydneyites, but as Australia Felixians? *Ibid.* 17 June 4/2 The people of Adelaide .. are terribly hurt too, like many of the silly Australia Felicians, because, forsooth, the Protector cannot do impossibilities.

Australian, *n.* and *a.* [Spec. use of *Australian* inhabitant of *Terra Australis*, a. Fr. *australien* southern: see OED.]

A. *n.*

1. An Aboriginal.

1814 M. FLINDERS *Voyage Terra Australis* II. 205 Several natives were seen on the shore abreast of the ship and lieutenant Fowler was sent to communicate with them... They staid to receive him, without showing that timidity so usual with the Australians. **1960** D. MCLEAN *Roaring Days* 93 No other native people but Australians ever discovered the secret of the bent hardwood throwing-stick called the boomerang.

2. A non-Aboriginal person native to or resident in Australia.

1822 M. EDGEWORTH *Let.* 5 Jan. (1971) 307 Mr Rolfe has lately seen and questioned one of the men from new South-Wales—I should say an *Australian*—So they chuse to be called. **1960** D. MCLEAN *Roaring Days* 127 That pommy turned out to be one of the best Australians I ever met. He became a rich station-owner and married a squatter's daughter.

3. Australian English, esp. as it is popularly characterized.

1902 *Bulletin* (Sydney) 14 June (Red Page), The schoolboy reciting .. to the inspector in 'perfect English' and then calling for the inspector's horse in pure Australian. **1969** L. HADOW *Full Cycle* 101 The other women of her age still spoke the tongue of their native Jugoslavia .. but .. except in moments of excitement, of strain, of great joy, Australian was the currency.

B. *adj.*

1. Of, characteristic of, or belonging to Australia.

1814 R. BROWN *Gen. Remarks Bot. Terra Australis* 7 The existence of certain natural classes is already acknowledged, and I have, in treating of the Australian natural families, ventured to propose a few that are perhaps less obvious. **1971** *Bulletin* (Sydney) 9 Oct. 65/1 Once upon a time building a weekender for holidays—and eventual retirement—was an integral part of the Australian dream, like owning a Holden, a Victa lawnmower, and one's own home.

2. Used as the first element in the names of flora and fauna, esp. when the second element is a common English name: see quots. and cf. NATIVE *a.* 6.

1819 *First Fruits Austral. Poetry* 3 When first I landed on Australia's Shore .. A Flower gladden'd me above the rest .. The Australian 'fringed Violet' Shall henceforward be my pet! **1964** M. SHARLAND *Territory of Birds* 163 Beside the track a sprightly little Australian Dotterel, an inhabitant of inland places, dodged out of our way.

3. In collocations designating an Aboriginal: **Australian Aboriginal, Aborigine, black, savage.**

1861 W. WESTGARTH *Aust.* 17 Pickering has remarked the noble bust of a well-conditioned **Australian aboriginal.** **1843** *Arden's Sydney Mag.* Oct. 66 To arrive at any definite end in legislating for the existing races of the **Australian aborigine,** it is necessary to take a plain and truthful view of his character and state by nature. **1845** J.O. BALFOUR *Sketch of N.S.W.* 9 The **Australian blacks,** both male and female, are most expert swimmers. **1833** *Jrnls. Several Exped. W.A.* 197 To the **Australian savage** it is of little use.

4. In special collocations: **Australian adjective,** the epithet 'bloody'; also **great Australian adjective; ballot,** a form of secret ballot; also *attrib.*; **blue** *obs.*, light blue; **crawl,** CRAWL; *pl.* **feathers,** gum leaves; **football, game,** AUSTRALIAN NATIONAL FOOTBALL; **language, (a)** an Aboriginal language; **(b)** Australian English; **(c)** blasphemous language (see SLANGUAGE); **metropolis** *obs.*, Sydney; **salute,** see quot; **slanguage,** see SLANGUAGE; **terrier,** a small, sturdy breed of dog; *Sydney silky,* see SYDNEY 2; **ugliness,** see quot. 1960.

1894 *Bulletin* (Sydney) 18 Aug. 22 The 'Bulletin' calls it the **Australian adjective** simply because it is more used and used more exclusively by Australians than by any other allegedly civilised nation. **1897** A. HAYWARD *Along Road to Cue,* But round the push and in the bush They're not so strangely sensitive: Unmasked and bare it riots there, The Great Australian Adjective. **1888** *Nation* (N.Y.) 2 Aug. 91/2 By introducing the secret '**Australian ballot**' in Congressional elections .. the use of bribery in the choice of Congressmen might be discouraged to some extent. **1889** J.H. WIGMORE *Austral. Ballot System* 2 It is proposed in the following introductory pages to sketch the history of the measure known as the Australian ballot system, as it passed from state to state in Australasia, on to the mother country in Europe, thence westward to Canada and eastward to continental countries, and finally westward again to these United States. **1843** *Sydney Morning Herald* 26 June 4/1 The flag borne at the head of this procession, was **Australian blue,** fringed with true blue. **1906** TAYLOR & GIBSON *Extra Dry* 32 Arthur Haddock .. swam out with a rope in his teeth, using the **Australian crawl.** **1853** *Austral. Gold Digger's Monthly Mag.* iv. 123 '**Australian feathers**! What are they?' cried I. 'Gum leaves to be sure', said he. **1910** *Argus* (Melbourne) 11 Nov. 7/1 The **Australian Football** Council further discussed the proposal to co-operate in an oversea tour. **1903** *Sporting News* (Launceston) 30 May 3/7 Hon. treasurer of the Rugby union; on being asked his opinion of the **Australian game** said [etc.]. **1872** G.S. BADEN-POWELL *New Homes for Old Country* 402 **Australian language** is chiefly noticeable for the general absence of all dialect. .. Of course a certain number of peculiar words have crept in, among which may be noticed, *plant* for hide, *plum* for perfection, *bogie* for bath. **1886** E.M. CURR *Austral. Race* I. p. xv, The Australian languages have not unfrequently two words in the same sense. **1891** M. ROBERTS *Land-Travel & Sea-Faring* 69, I tried to back the bullocks, but they scorned me utterly, in spite of the Australian language I used. **1848** C. COZENS *Adventures of Guardsman* 130 The country immediately adjacent to Sidney .. the **Australian Metropolis.** **1972** I. MOFFITT *U-Jack Soc.* 65, I flopped a hand at the flies (the **Australian salute**). **1906** *R. Agric.*

Soc. N.S.W. Ann. 122 There were 17 rough-haired terriers, some of them possibly progenitors of our **Australian terriers**. **1960** R. BOYD (title) The **Australian ugliness**. Ibid. (1968) 251 The Australian Ugliness begins with fear of reality, denial of the need for the everyday environment to reflect the heart of the human problem, satisfaction with veneer and cosmetic effects. It ends in betrayal of the element of love and a chill near the root of national self-respect.

Australiana. [f. AUSTRALI(A 1 + -ana, L. suffix attaching to names to denote memorabilia relating to the subject.] Items relating to or characteristic of Australia.
1845 (title) The Australiana. A weekly paper. **1935** MUNN & PITT Austral. Libraries 43 This library, bequeathed by Mr David Scott Mitchell, is a magnificent collection of Australiana. **1982** Austral. Financial Rev. (Sydney) 5 Feb. 40/4 But there may not be much Australiana left in the cupboard. Then prices could soar.

Australian-born, a. Born in Australia (but not of Aboriginal descent). Also absol. as n.
1829 HRA (1922) 1st Ser. XIV. 594 Refused me pasture for my cattle, and the cattle of eight Australian born children. **1842** Colonial Observer (Sydney) 6 Apr. 212/3 For I am an Australian born, And want no praise of thine; Go herd, I say, with your own friends, And let me keep to mine.

Australianese. Obs. Australian English.
1902 Truth (Sydney) 19 Oct. 2/6 Several toadies, lickspittles, cringelings, crawlers and sneaks, or, in Australianese, 'smoodgers'. **1953** Advertiser (Adelaide) 2 Oct. 2/2 Australianese. 'The first scientific study of the Australian accent' has been embarked upon by Dr Franklin Hunt, a Fulbright scholar from the United States.

Australianism.
1. A distinctively Australian word or phrase.
1883 R.E.N. TWOPENY Town Life Aust. 245 There is room for a very interesting dictionary of Australianisms. **1981** Macquarie Dict. 12 Our dictionary is not merely a dictionary of Australianisms.
2. Pride in, or loyalty to, Australian nationalism; a character distinctively Australian.
1909 Bulletin (Sydney) 11 Nov. 14/2 Wherever Australian products go outside of Australia they make many converts to Australianism. **1956** J.T. LANG I Remember 6 Aggressive Australianism has been the keystone of Labor's real appeal to the people of this country.

Australianity. A character distinctively Australian.
1936 Publicist (Sydney) i. 3/1 Bunyip is the presiding god of Australianity, a religion scarcely yet born and therefore certainly not yet extinct. **1967** Southerly iv. 265 We take pleasure in the Australianity of our literature.

Australianize, v. trans. To render (a person, institution, etc.) Australian in character. Chiefly as pa. pple.
1883 St. James's Gaz. (London) 10 May 7/1 Are the latter wronged, then, in having to become, for instance, 'Australianized'? **1983** Age (Melbourne) 1 Oct. (Saturday Extra) 3/1 Werner Herzog has employed Bob Ellis to Australianise his script, but it is not peppered with jokes.

Australian National Football. The formal name of a game of football originating in the mid-nineteenth century in Victoria and played according to rules now determined by the Australian National Football Council. See also AUSTRALIAN RULES.
1927 Argus (Melbourne) 9 Aug. 10/6 The name of the council was altered to that of the Australian National Football Council, and all of the States will place before the word 'football' in the title of their organisations the words 'Australian National'. **1971** B. ANDREW Austral. Football Handbk. 12 The necessity of having a national controlling body was often expounded by State administrators until, in 1906, the Australian National Football Council was formed.

Australian native.
1. An Aboriginal. Also attrib.
1839 T.L. MITCHELL Three Exped. Eastern Aust. (rev. ed.) I. 34 The white man is known as yet only by name—or as the manufacturer of this most important of all implements to the Australian native. **1879** Native Tribes S.A. p. xi, All who have written upon the subject of the Australian native tribes acknowledge that they vanish before the white settler.
2. A non-Aboriginal Australian. Also attrib.
1872 Argus (Melbourne) 2 July 6/4 An entertainment was given by the Australian Natives' Association .. last night, in celebration of the first anniversary of that body. **1889** Illustr. Austral. News (Melbourne) July 2/3 A large percentage of the new House consists of young men returned on the Australian Native ticket.

Australianness. A quality or character distinctive of Australia or of Australians.
1954 Landfall (Christchurch) 27 An essential Australianness which is apt to recede when too deliberately pursued. **1960** Encounter (London) May 28/1 The migrant .. must not, of course, attack the country itself or its Australianness. **1981** P. SEKULESS Fred 5 More importantly, he acquired qualities of individualism and mateship, a distinctive Australianness.

Australian rules. The rules under which Australian National Football is played; the game itself. Also attrib., esp. as **Australian rules football**.
1903 Truth (Sydney) 19 Apr. 3/1 They had accorded their patronage to the Australian Football League and the game as played under Australian rules. **1904** Ibid. 4 Sept. 1/4 Another good man killed playing 'Australian rules' football. **1956** E. LAMBERT Watermen 173 In the fishing-ports of Western Victoria football meant Australian Rules, and soccer and rugby were distant aberrations.

Australienne. [f. AUSTRAL(IAN n. 2 + -ienne, Fr. feminine suffix.] A non-Aboriginal Australian woman.
1895 Bulletin (Sydney) 16 Feb. 14/3 The Australienne, having got her medical diploma, thought she would like to settle into a practice at Darstadt. **1934** Bulletin (Sydney) 18 Apr. 11/4, I have just been reading the complaint of an Australienne, now resident in India.

Australioid, var. AUSTRALOID.

australite. An Austral. tektite, a small glassy body considered to be of extra-terrestrial origin; blackfellow's button, see BLACKFELLOW n. 2, button stone, see BUTTON n.; OBSIDIANITE.
1909 Geol. Mag. (London) VI. 411 Occurrences of the related 'obsidianites' (referred to by Professor Weinschenck as Billitonite and Australite) in the Malay Peninsula. **1985** West Austral. (Perth) 25 June 30/5 Till about 20 years ago tectites—or australites—were thought to be glassy meteorites from the moon. But more recent studies showed that their composition was like clayey sandstone.

Australoid, a. Of, allied to, or resembling the ethnological type of the Aborigines. Also as n., and formerly **Australioid**.
1869 J. LUBBOCK Pre-Hist. Times 378 Prof. Huxley .. divides mankind into four groups, the Australoid, Negroid, Mongoloid, and Xanthochroid. . . The Australoid type contains all the inhabitants of Australia, and the native races of the Deccan, with whom he also associates the Ancient Egyptians. **1870** T.H. HUXLEY in Jrnl. Ethnol. Soc. London New Ser. II. 405 The chief representative [sic] of the

Australioid type is the Australian of Australia. **1913** H. JOHNSTON *Pioneers in Australasia* 49 When races of superior intellect and bodily strength were developed in Europe and northern Asia, the ancestors of the Tasmanians and the Australoids were driven forth into the forests of Africa and southern Asia.

Australorp. [f. AUSTRAL(IAN *a.* 1 + *Orp(ington)*, the name of a town in Kent, England.] An Australian fowl belonging to or descended from the Orpington breed; the name of the Australian breed developed from the Orpington and given distinct status in 1930. Also *attrib.*

1922 *Daily Mail* (London) 9 Dec. 14 (Advt.), Australorps imported. Australian Black Orpingtons. World's Record Layers—1,750 eggs 6 birds, 12 months. **1933** *Bulletin* (Sydney) 8 Feb. 21/1 A sinister and suspicious happening at Townsville .. has set the town by the ears... An Australorp hen entered for the N.Q. egg-laying competition .. was a comparative unknown on starting, .. rapidly forged to the front .. then .. was discovered in the pen at the Show Ground with the head missing and the body badly battered.

awake up, var. WAKE UP.

award.

1. A determination made by a State or Federal industrial court or commission regulating conditions of employment.

1886 *Arbitrations between Proprietors & Miners* 115 The award given on that occasion reads—'that an advance of 3d. per ton be given on the coal worked on No. 1 Heading'. **1984** *People Mag.* (Sydney) 7 May 40/3 All were unionists who denied working outside the award.

2. Comb. **award conditions, rates, wage, work.**

1983 *Bulletin* (Sydney) 4 Jan. 24/3 Wide combs will break down their **award conditions** and create unfair competition between shearers. **1919** *Smith's Weekly* (Sydney) 19 Apr. 10/6 Workers belonging to the Railway Workers' Branch of the A.W.U. are .. denouncing the Commissioners, who refuse to pay **award rates**. **1941** *Bulletin* (Sydney) 3 Sept. 15/1 He knew all about **award wages**, keep and economics in general. **1941** O. DE R. FOENANDER *Solving Labour Problems Aust.* 119 A respondent may in certain circumstances engage these persons to do **award work** outside the workshop or factory.

away back, var. WAYBACK.

axe-handle.

1. Used *attrib.* in Special Comb. **axe-handle wood,** any of several tree species producing wood suitable for axe handles, such as the native elm *Aphananthe philippinensis* (fam. Ulmaceae) of rainforests in N.S.W., Qld., and n. to the Philippine Islands, and *Planchonella myrsinoides* (fam. Sapotaceae) of n. N.S.W., s. Qld., and Lord Howe Island.

1898 *Proc. Linnean Soc. N.S.W.* XXIII. 130 'Axe-handle Wood' .. An ornamental small tree with foliage reminding one of that of a Camellia [Lord Howe Island] **1926** *Qld. Agric. Jrnl.* XXV. 438 *Aphananthe Philippinensis* .. Axehandle-wood.

2. A rough unit of measurement. Esp. in the fig. phr. (so many) **axe-handles across the arse.**

1958 R.G. HOWARTH et al. *Penguin Bk. Austral. Verse* 268 My arms are aching and I'm dripping sweat But the sun is three axe-handles in the sky And I must toss sheaves till dark. **1977** *Austral.* (Sydney) 11 Apr. 6/8 A big woman, but not a big man, would be described as being 'two axe handles across the arse'.

azure kingfisher. The kingfisher *Alcedo azurea* of n. and e. Aust., New Guinea, and adjacent regions, having deep blue plumage on the head, back, and wings. Formerly also **azure kingsfisher.**

1801 J. LATHAM *Gen. Synopsis Birds* Suppl. II. 372 Azure K[ingfisher]... Inhabits *Norfolk Island.* **1808** J.W. LEWIN *Birds of New Holland* 5 (*caption*) Azure Kingsfisher .. visits dead trees from whose branches it darts on its prey in the water beneath, and is sometimes completely immersed by the velocity of its descent. **1945** C. BARRETT *Austral. Bird Life* 143 The azure kingfisher .. darts past like 'a living flash of blue'.

B

baal /'bal/, *adv. Austral. pidgin. Obs.* Also **bael, bail.** [a. Dharuk *biyal*.] Used to express negation: cf. BORAK *adv.* Also as *adj.*
1790 D. SOUTHWELL Corresp. & Papers 149 *Bei-yăl* or *bey-ăl*, no. **1818** J. HOLT *Mem.* (1838) 154 He said 'Bail, bail', that is, never fear. **1830** R. DAWSON *Present State Aust.* 65 The word *bael* means no, not, or any negative. **1844** *Bee of Aust.* (Sydney) 2 Nov. 4/1 The learned member for Sydney: Who in baal gammon style of eloquence will no doubt, Let my Lord Stanley's mother know 'that he is out'.

bab. Abbrev. of BABBLING BROOK.
1936 *Bulletin* (Sydney) 22 July 21/1 Old 'Forty-Mile Tom' is the 'bab' on our station, But, though he is famed all along the Paroo, He sets little store by his great reputation For making a duff or concocting a stew. **1965** R. FAIR *Treasury Anzac Humour* 34 We have a tame Babbling Brook, who in civvy life was a parson... Fritz put up another salvo... The Bab. ducked.

babbler. BABBLING BROOK.
1904 *Worker* (Sydney) 6 Aug. 7/1 Ninety per cent of the cooks do their full share of work. The offsider gets a third and emerges for next season as a full-fledged Babbler— that is if he takes to the game. **1977** F.A. REEDER *Diary of Rat* 63 We came back to camp with the ute loaded down to the Plimsoll with jams, milk, beans, bully and tinned fruit. If that did not give the babblers encouragement nothing would.

babbling brook. Rhyming slang for 'cook', esp. one catering for a party of shearers or stockmen; an army cook.
1913 *Bulletin* (Sydney) 25 Sept. 24/1 I'll touch the babblin' brook here for .. scran today .. and work the other sheds down to Yanco. **1920** *Aussie* (Sydney) Apr. 20/3 Indignant Digger to Babbling Brook: 'Tea! Tea! D'yer call this tea? It's nothing but innocent water scalded to death!'
Hence **babble** *v. trans.*, to cook. Also as *vbl. n.*
1938 *Bulletin* (Sydney) 19 Jan. 20/1 I've bin babblin' for fifty-four years, Cookin' all sorts o' scran—yairs, from wombats to steers. **1962** *Sydney Morning Herald* 24 Nov. 12/1 Gaily aproned women do the 'babbling' (cooking).

bach, var. BATCH *n.* and *v.*

bachelor's buttons. Also **bachelors' buttons** and as sing. [Spec. use of *bachelor's buttons* any of various plants with button-like flowers: see OED *bachelor* 6.] BILLY BUTTONS.
1852 W. HOWITT *Land, Labor & Gold* 7 Nov. (1855) I. 109 In the grassy places, the Murnong of the natives, like a yellow hawkweed, and a yellow bachelor's button (*Craspedia Ridua*), are very gay. **1855** *Ibid.* II. 92 A sort of bachelor's buttons, or golden balls, different to the ordinary ones of this colony. These balls were round and firm as if of solid gold, and covered with little points. **1981** E. POTTER *Scone I Remember* 23 The silver-stemmed, silver-leaved yellow balls of a flower we used to call 'bachelors' buttons'.

bachelor's hall. *Obs.* Also **bachelors' hall.** [Transf. use of *bachelor's hall* a bachelor's establishment.] BACHELORS' QUARTERS.
1875 *Austral. Town & Country Jrnl.* (Sydney) 180/2 The five buildings shown in the engraving is the general manager's residence, then there are to the right and left, the bachelor's hall, overseer's, storekeepers, and accountant's cottages, the mens' quarters, &c. **1913** W.K. HARRIS *Outback in Aust.* 46 The 'Batchelors' Hall' was a better structure than is usually found so far outback, and consisted of eight separate rooms, with two entrances.

bachelors' quarters. *Obs.* Accommodation provided on a station for single men, esp. jackeroos and overseers; BARRACKS *n.*¹ 2.
1878 G. WALCH *Australasia* 19 The unconscious object of his threats was seated on the verandah of the bachelors' quarters. **1964** J.S. MANIFOLD *Who wrote Ballads?* 86 Next below the homestead socially comes the 'narangy barracks', 'bachelors' quarters' or 'jackaroos' quarters'... It would be rare indeed to find a piano in the bachelors' quarters, but in the '80s and '90s you might bet on finding the highly fashionable banjo.

back, *a., n.*¹, and *adv.* [Spec. use of *back* distant, outlying.]
A. *adj.*
1. Inland of settled districts.
1800 *HRA* (1914) 1st Ser. II. 411 Those of the back Farms and above the Creek in remote situations are exposed to great Danger from the Natives. **1900** *Bulletin* (Sydney) 19 May 14/3 One of the speakers complimented said tradesman upon having worked so hard to get a road opened to some back place.
2. Distant from a permanent watercourse.
1837 *Perth Gaz.* 14 Oct. 988 A party relinquishes 3,000 acres of his original back grant on the Swan, for which he receives a choice of selection elsewhere for 1000 in fee simple. **1956** T. RONAN *Moleskin Midas* 193 If ever we strike one of them droughts there'll be a big smash on this river. There ain't enough back water on any of these joints barring my place.
3. In the sparsely populated interior, remote from towns and settled districts. See also OUTBACK *a.*
1848 J.A. JACKSON *National Emigration* 7 The illimitable and easily accessible back-pastures of the Australian continent. **1975** G. PAGE *Smalltown Memorials* 1 Out on back-roads the churches are dying.
B. *n.* Chiefly in the phr. **at** (**out,** etc.) **the back of.**
1. The part of a station most distant from the homestead or from permanent water.
1878 'R. BOLDREWOOD' *Ups & Downs* 22 But the herd had spread by degrees over the wide plains of 'the back', as well as over the broad river flats and green reed-beds of 'the frontage'. **1884** —— *Old Melbourne Memories* 62 An expedition had been made to a .. desolate tract of country which lay at 'the back' of the run. **1930** V. PALMER *Passage* (1957) 172 Living out at the back of runs, too, on wells and potholes.
2. A part of the interior which is remote from towns and settled districts. See also OUTBACK *n.*
1897 *Bulletin* (Sydney) 4 Sept. 32/1 On a little old bush-racecourse at the back of No Man's Land. **1959** J. CLEARY *Strike me Lucky* 185, I could be out the back of Alice Springs, out on me own in the mulga, and there'd allus be some nosey parker shoving his nose in to complain.
C. *adv.* At or to the back of: see quots.
1878 'R. BOLDREWOOD' *Ups & Downs* 232 The well-marked but unfrequented track which led 'back'—that is, to the indifferently-watered, sparsely-stocked, and thinly-populated region which stretched endless at the rear of the great leading streams. **1911** *Huon Times* (Franklin) 4 Feb. 2/5 Do

you know the Upper Huon very well?—I have been back about 20 miles, and know the country pretty well.

D. In phr.

a. back of (or **o'**) (a town or place): behind; beyond. Freq. **back o' sunset.** See also SUNSET 1.

1891 J. FENTON *Bush Life Tas.* (1964) 127 This summer I have grown in pots and boxes .. the native indigo, the thorny acacia from the mountains back of Melbourne, and the glory pea from seeds out of your garden. 1912 L. ESSON *Red Gums* 30 Beyond the world—the track is never ended—Back o' the sunset, there the region splendid The Unknown, lures men ever. 1963 I.L. IDRIESS *Our Living Stone Age* p. ix Prospecting in that marvellous tableland back o' Cairns.

b. back of beyond: see BEYOND.

c. back of Bourke: see BOURKE.

back, $n.^2$ *Timber-getting.* [Spec. use of *back* the opposite to the front.] The side of a tree trunk opposite the BELLY. See quot. 1909. Also *attrib.* as **back-cut.**

1901 *Advocate* (Burnie) 28 Nov. 2/6 Bryan put in excellent work and was the first to turn to the back cut despite his handicap. 1909 R. KALESKI *Austral. Settler's Compl. Guide* 55 Standing timber is *chopped* through by cutting two scarfs or notches in it, which run out in the centre; the first one on the side the tree is to fall (the 'belly' scarf), the second on the reverse side or 'back'. The 'belly' scarf is cut first so that the tree won't fall on the cutter; if he wants to commit suicide he cuts the 'belly' last.

back, $n.^3$ [Spec. use of *back* situated to the rear.] That part of a gaol in which prisoners are kept in solitary confinement. Also *attrib.*

1896 M. HORNSBY *Old Time Echoes Tas.* 173 'Fourteen days in the back cells,' said Boyd. 1962 J. BROWN *Harpoon* 50 McLeod lost two stone in weight while he was in solitary confinement. When he was released, and appeared in the exercise yard, prisoners .. came up and asked him how he was. It was obvious that anyone who had done a stretch out 'the back' was treated with respect.

back, $v.^1$ [Poss. transf. use of *back* to mount (see OED(S *v.* 10), but prob. of independent development.] *intr.* Of a sheep dog: to run across the backs of yarded sheep and, by barking, cause the sheep to move in the required direction.

[N.Z. 1934 J.E. LILICO *Sheep-Dog Mem.* 26 Finest backing dogs .. any keen dog constantly forcing in yards can be trained to back .. but stockmen in Addington have evolved a race which take naturally to backing.] 1942 R.B. KELLEY *Animal Breeding* 142 In sheep yards the dog that will 'back' probably is the most specialized.

Hence **backing dog** *n.*

1934 [see BACK $v.^1$]. 1941 S.J. BAKER *Pop. Dict. Austral. Slang* 6 *Backing dog,* a sheepdog that will run across the backs of sheep to aid mustering or droving.

back, $v.^2$ *Timber-getting.* [Spec. use of *back, v.* to set back.] *trans.* With **off:** to trim (a post, sleeper, etc.) with a broad-axe.

1855 'RUSTICUS' *How to settle in Vic.* 10 If good sound timber be employed, and the posts split in the way the splitters term *backing off,* they will probably last for twenty years. 1908 *Bulletin* (Sydney) 27 Feb. 15/1 The sawn sleeper is inferior because it is cut across the grain, while the sleeper-chopper 'backs' his off with the grain.

back block, *n.* and *attrib.*

A. *n.*

1. A tract of land in the remote interior; in *pl.*, sparsely populated country beyond the closely settled districts.

1870 *Argus* (Melbourne) 22 Mar. 7/2 Fancy the change, the transition from a cis-Darling back block to Melbourne and the Theatre Royal! *c* 1872 J.C.F. JOHNSON *Over Island* 2 You'll have to go many miles out of your course, and perhaps get bushed altogether out in the back blocks.

2. Land behind that with a water frontage; land on which there is no permanent watercourse. Also *attrib.*

1871 *Austral. Town & Country Jrnl.* (Sydney) 29 Apr. 518/4 The feed on both frontage and back blocks looks splendid. 1980 P. FREEMAN *Woolshed* 132 Wargam was a 'back block' run—there were no permanent watercourses, and only the sinking of wells or the ownership of other riverside property could make such properties useful in the last century.

3. *transf.* and *fig.*

1944 F. BRUNO *Sa-eeda Wog!* 32 The fortunes of war .. deposited us thirstily in this back-block of the Balkans. 1972 *Bulletin* (Sydney) 26 Feb. 41/1 Ringside tables are all labelled 'reserved'. . . But the back blocks are full of wide open spaces and you can settle down to wait for curtains up at nine.

B. *attrib.* Located in a remote and sparsely populated inland district; characteristic of those who live in such a district. Also **backblocks.**

1868 *Adelaide Punch* 19 Dec. 11/1 And this is the daily city life of the hardy back-block pioneer. 1978 B. ST. A. SMITH *Spirit beyond Psyche* 97 No matter where the tiny backblocks pub in which they were drinking might be, people always seemed to know him, to recognise him.

backblocker. One who lives in the back blocks: see BACK BLOCK *n.* 1.

1870 *Argus* (Melbourne) 22 Mar. 7/2, I am a bushman, a back blocker, to whom it happens about once in two years to visit Melbourne. 1948 M. UREN *Glint of Gold* 155 Like most back-blockers he was prematurely grey, but possessed the keen eyes of the bushman, the easy walk of a man used to long trails.

back country, *n.* and *attrib.* [U.S. *back country* country at the rear of a settled district: see OEDS.]

A. *n.*

1. Country lying inland of settled districts.

1798 *Hist. Rec. N.S.W.* (1895) III. 820 A report which some artful villain in the colony had propagated amongst the Irish convicts lately arrived, 'That there was a colony of white people at no very great distance in the back country—150 or 200 miles—where there was abundance of every sort of provision without the necessity of so much labour.' 1968 K. WEATHERLY *Roo Shooter* 25 Ben .. had been a miner and knocked about all parts of the back country with his mate.

2. Land removed from a permanent watercourse; BACK GROUND 2; BACK LAND 1. See also BACK BLOCK *n.* 2.

1839 T.L. MITCHELL *Three Exped. Eastern Aust.* (rev. ed.) I. 302 Grass is only to be found on the banks of the river. . . None may appear in the back country. 1890 'R. BOLDREWOOD' *Colonial Reformer* III. 117 By degrees it began to be asserted that 'back country', *i.e.* the lands remote from all visible means of subsistence for flocks and herds, as far as water was concerned, paid the speculative pastoral occupier better than the 'frontage', or land in the neighbourhood of permanent creeks, and of the few well-known rivers.

3. The hinterland of a port; BACK LAND 2.

1849 *Belfast Gaz.* (Port Phillip) 14 Sept. 3/1 Melbourne boasts of itself as the capital, Geelong as the 'commercial emporium', Warrnambool as possessing a fine back-country, and snug little harbour. 1876 'EIGHT YRS.' RESIDENT' *Queen of Colonies* 167 There is no back country to the port.

4. Land immediately beyond settled districts, or adjacent to stations, used as supplementary grazing land.

BACK GROUND 21 **BACK STATION**

1876 'CAPRICORNUS' *Colonisation* 8 The unsold back country was left open in an easy way, so that the settlers might get the use of the grass. **1927** A. CROMBIE *After Sixty Yrs.* 74 Tarrawong Station .. had been the headquarters for Tyson's back country.

5. Land in the sparsely populated interior, remote from towns and closely settled districts.

1887 'OVERLANDER' *Austral. Sketches* 1 You want to know how I first took to the roads and the back country. **1979** D. LOCKWOOD *My Old Mates & I* 82 The beef roads had reached into the back country, bitumen to Wave Hill and beyond.

B. *attrib.*

1888 'R. BOLDREWOOD' *Robbery under Arms* 234 Dad was dressed up to look like a back-country squatter. **1968** E.M. NOBLET *Winds that Blew* 60 Her face was very thin and had what I called the 'uncooked look' of many of the back-country women.

back ground. *Obs.* [f. BACK *a.* + GROUND *n.*^{2} 1.]

1. Land immediately behind an allotment or settlement, used as grazing land; BACK LAND 3.

1804 *Sydney Gaz.* 11 Nov. A number of labourers had been employed in clearing and burning off a back ground contiguous to the cultivated lands. **1832** G.F. MOORE *Diary Ten Yrs. W.A.* 9 Aug. (1884) 127 The brook traverses my grant twice, and makes the back ground valuable.

2. *pl.* BACK COUNTRY *n.* 2.

1842 *Colonial Observer* (Sydney) 6 July 318/3 The Commissioner observes that an extended portion of water frontage is occupied, and the back grounds kept in a state of idleness. **1854** W. HOWITT *Land, Labor & Gold* 12 Mar. (1855) II. 183 In the unsettled district, where agricultural land is required, it may be accommodated with large backgrounds of mere barren ranges fit for the wandering over of flocks and cattle.

back land. *Obs.* Also in *pl.*

1. BACK COUNTRY *n.* 2.

1814 M. FLINDERS *Voyage Terra Australis* I. 127, I do not think that any stream, more considerable than perhaps a small rill from the back land, falls into it. **1881** W.E. ABBOTT *Notes Journey on Darling* 61 These back lands had little or no value in their natural state.

2. BACK COUNTRY *n.* 3.

1824 *HRA* (1921) 3rd Ser. IV. 148 The Back lands at Swan Port to the northward communicate through Tiers of Hills with an extensive Country.

3. BACK GROUND 1.

1846 *Sydney Morning Herald* 17 Feb. 3/1 He is *at least* entitled *freely* to the use of the detached pond in his back land, for which he is indebted to a casual and providential fall of rain, and which is for half the year as likely to be a mere 'water *hole*' as a hole of water.

4. Land in the sparsely populated interior. See BACK COUNTRY *n.* 5.

1850 J.W. MELVIN *Emigrant's Guide to Colonies* 22 As to marriage, however in the back lands or bush. **1891** J. FENTON *Bush Life Tas.* (1964) 172 Mr W.R. Bell knows perhaps more of the backlands of the western districts than any other man.

Hence **backlander** *n.*

1928 B. CRONIN *Dragonfly* 66 Too many canary-grass backlanders in these parts. They live on the land, not for it.

back-loading, *vbl. n.* Freight carried on a return journey, after delivery of the principal load. See LOADING *vbl. n.*^{1}

1925 M. TERRY *Across Unknown Aust.* 85 These long treks without back-loading (i.e. both ways). **1984** *N.T. News* (Darwin) 30 Oct. 25/5 Furniture pantec unloading Darwin .. require backloading Brisbane.

backman. *Australian National Football.* One who plays in a defensive back position.

1928 G. MORIARTY *Teaching Game of Football* xi. 2 A Backman's motto should be:- that '*no kicks to the Forwards mean no goals to their side*'. **1973** J. DUNN *How to play Football* 82 A backman, and especially a back pocket, should always remember that his job is to restrict scoring.

back paddock. A paddock distant from the main source of water on a station, or from the station homestead.

1898 A.S. MURRAY *Twelve Hundred Miles* 28 The most effectual plan, in the back paddocks, away from the river (the Murrumbidgee), was poisoned water in troughs. **1974** J. JOST *This is Harry Flynn* 17 One of his clearest recollections was the day she dropped dead in the back paddock and he had found her, an object of curiosity for a couple of poddy calves.

back pocket: see POCKET.

back run. *Obs.*

1. An area of Crown land immediately behind a holding and available to the landholder as supplementary grazing land: see quot. 1833.

1824 *Hobart Town Gaz.* 30 July, A Farm of 400 acres .. with a large back run. **1833** *HRA* (1923) 1st Ser. XVII. 112 On three fourths of the Grants on the Hunter River .. the Proprietors enjoy the advantages of what is called a 'back run' for their Cattle, etc., namely, Land not appropriated, nor ever likely to be appropriated, as separate Farms, *being only useful in connection with the Neighbouring Estates,* which latter must in a multitude of instances be passed through to arrive at the unappropriated land.

2. A run distant from a water frontage, or from a station homestead.

1876 'CAPRICORNUS' *Colonisation* 8 Of those inland pastures one acre was worth three of the poorer country to the eastward; and if water was scarce on the back runs, there were miles and miles of frontage to running rivers. **1891** W.B. DEAN *Notorious Bushrangers* 72 The unfortunate woman .. was discovered in one of the ravines on Barnes' back run.

back settlement. *Obs.* [U.S. *back settlement* a remote settlement: see Mathews *back, a.* 1.] An isolated settlement, inland from settled districts; freq. in *pl.*, the sparsely populated interior.

1791 G.C. INGLETON *True Patriots All* (1952) 10 We have four different settlements—viz. Sydney Cove—Rose-Hill—and two back settlements which are not yet named. **1817** *Hobart Town Gaz.* 9 Aug., Ticket of Leave Men, in the District of New Norfolk, the Back Settlement, & District of Melville. **1841** *Colonial Mag.* (London) IV. 63 The small rustic capitalist locates himself as squatter or proprietor in the back settlements of New Holland.

back settler. *Obs.* [U.S. *back settler:* see Mathews *back, a.* 2.] One who lives in a remote settlement, or in the interior.

1829 E.G. WAKEFIELD *Let. from Sydney* 103 Bush-ranging is a dreadful evil, being a kind of land piracy. None but back settlers, it is true, are exposed to its burnings, rapes, and massacres. **1891** J. FENTON *Bush Life Tas.* (1964) 136 The back settlers .. were the victims of indescribable torment, no provision having been made for roads.

back station. OUT-STATION 2 a.

c **1887** R.G. GALLOP In Never Never Land, Life on these back stations is necessarily rather rough. **1953** *Bulletin* (Sydney) 30 Sept. 12/2 When I was a nipper Top Hut was always known as an out-camp of Arumpo, which was itself a back-station of Tarcoola... Now Top Hut is a station in its own right.

back to, *adv.* [f. *back, adv.*, in the reverse direction + *to.*] Used with reference to a reunion of former residents or associates, with appropriate festivities. Also *n. phr.* and *attrib.*

1925 *S. Eastern Star* (Mount Gambier) 31 Dec. 3/2 The activities of the publicity committee of the 'Back-to-Mount Gambier' movement have brought many advantages other than the 'boosting' of the March celebrations. **1944** A.J. & J.J. MCINTYRE *Country Towns Vic.* 237 *'Back to's'* are . . infrequent . . usually occurring only every ten, or even fifteen to twenty years. Their chief aim is to give the town a financial boost. **1971** B. LESTER *Verses* 15 The clay bird shoot attracted many shooters Saturday night And the 'Back to' Ball was crowded, the music sweet and light.

back track. A little-frequented and often indirect road or track, away from the main route. Also *attrib.*

1867 G. WALCH *Fireflash* 10 So if you'll please say goodbye to the worthy owner of this delightful property, we'll start to-morrow morning on the back track. **1895** *Worker* (Sydney) 4 May 3/1 The back-track boys will engage the Walgett band, and go out and meet them with all honour and conduct them to Dungalear.

back up. A second helping of food. Also as *v. trans.* and *intr.*

1929 'F. BLAIR' *Digger Sea-Mates* 19 'Our first meal aboard.' . . 'Any 'buckshee', Boy?' he enquired. 'Yes, back up yer cart.' Tom's plate received another slice of beef. **1946** R.D. RIVETT *Behind Bamboo* 93 An exclusive monopoly of all 'back-ups' or 'gash', as the Perth boys called second helpings. **1966** S.J. BAKER *Austral. Lang.* (ed. 2) 217 *Back up,* to seek another helping or share.

back verandah: see VERANDAH.

back yard. Also *attrib.* (usu. as **backyard**).

1. An enclosure, usually including a garden in which fruit and vegetables are grown, at the back of a house.

1793 W. TENCH *Compl. Acct. Settlement* 44 Baneelon no sooner found himself in a back-yard, than he nimbly leaped over a slight paling. **1954** *Bulletin* (Sydney) 16 June 13/1, I had a bumper backyard tomato-crop.

2. *fig.* Used of a business conducted in domestic premises and often implying small-scale work that may be inferior or illegal. Usu. *attrib.*

1927 *R. Comm. Moving Picture Industry* 151 'The Sentimental Bloke' was also made in the back yard for something like £2,000. **1939** J. CAMPBELL *Babe is Wise* 214 'Backyard' factories, Mrs McDougall called them, denouncing them with all the righteous indignation of one whose own man's employers were beyond reproach.

backyarder. One who conducts a backyard business: see BACK YARD 2.

1948 C.B. MAXWELL *Cold Nose of Law* 19 Unfortunately the less admirable type of 'backyarder' got hold of the breed about 1930, after which it embarked on a period of major decline. **1984** *Open Road* Apr. 9/1 Be careful of the backyarder! The man who repairs cars from a shed behind his house . . the man who buys cars at auction and 'does them up' for resale from his home.

bacon-and-egg(s): see EGGS-AND-BACON.

bad, *a. Obs.*

1. [Ironic use of *bad* wicked.] Applied to a convict who dissociates himself from his fellows and cooperates with the prison officers.

1835 J. BACKHOUSE *Narr. Visit Austral. Colonies* (1843) 278 He [*sc.* a convict] could no longer join in many of the evil practices in which they indulged and he became in their estimation and language, 'a bad fellow'. Before when he ran with them into the depths of iniquity, he passed among them as a 'good fellow'; for thus, among this depraved portion of our race is good too generally called evil and evil good. **1838** W. MOLESWORTH *Rep. Select Committee Transportation* 17 Dr Ullathorne likewise said: 'I was very much struck with the peculiar language used by the convicts at Norfolk Island. . . A prisoner . . said, that it was the habitual language of the place . . that a bad man was called a good man; and that a man who was ready to perform his duty was generally called a bad man.'

2. [U.S. *bad* hostile, dangerous: see Mathews.] Of an Aboriginal: hostile, opposed to white settlement.

1910 *Bulletin* (Sydney) 20 Oct. 14/1 Although he had travelled through country infested with 'bad' niggers, he was never troubled by them. **1948** M. UREN *Glint of Gold* 246 All this country in the North-West was 'bad native' country. The natives resented the penetration of this alien men . . and . . tried to hold off the invaders.

badger. a. *Obs.* Any of several indigenous marsupial mammals. **b.** Chiefly *Tas.* WOMBAT *n.* 1.

1803 *Sydney Gaz.* 23 Oct. The Margaret's sealing party at King's Island, who have brought round a number of very fine Kangaroos and *badgers.* **1850** J.B. CLUTTERBUCK *Port Phillip* 37 The rock Wallaby, or Badger. **1852** F. LANCELOTT *Aust. as it Is* I. 35 The bandicoot, or pouched badger. **1920** B. CRONIN *Timber Wolves* 163 Here in Tassie we . . got names of our own for things this side the straits. . . For instance they ain't no wombats here; we call them badgers.

badger box. *Tas. Obs.* [f. BADGER + *box* shelter.] A makeshift hut or shelter.

1864 *Papers & Proc. R. Soc. Tas.* (1876) 100 Took rations to the Badger box. **1911** *Huon Times* (Franklin) 1 Mar. 2/7 It is interesting to watch the gradual development in houses here. First comes the bush hut or 'badger box', with the fire often outside.

bael, var. BAAL.

bag, *n.*¹ [Abbrev. of *bagging* sacking.]

1. Used *attrib.* in Comb. to distinguish a contrivance, structure, etc. made of (used) hessian sacks.

1903 *Bulletin* (Sydney) 6 June 17/1 He places a bag-swag and jam-tin billy outside his front gate so that travellers . . will pass . . on their way, thinking that *that* beat is occupied. **1972** C. DUGUID *Doctor & Aborigines* 140 The houses are no more than 'bag huts', with walls of hessian surrounding floors of earth or cement.

2. In the phr. **rough as bags,** lacking in refinement.

1919 *Ça ne fait Rien: 6th Battalion A.I.F.* 10 Jan. 1 As we've said before [Belgian girls]'re as rough as bags. **1984** M. ELDRIDGE *Walking Dog* 89 'Rough as bags', people said of Raelene, and in the same breath, 'heart of gold'.

bag, *n.*²

1. *Horse-racing.* [Fig. use of (bookmaker's) *bag.*] In the phr. **in the bag,** applied to a horse being run to lose. See also quot. 1982.

[N.Z. **1900** J. SCOTT *Tales of Colonial Turf* 3 The neddy was in the bag in the Cup; he was no trier.] **1903** *Sporting News* (Launceston) 6 June 3/3 Had I not known for certain she was a fair trier, would have thought she was 'in the bag'. **1982** J. ANDERSON *Winners can Laugh* 148 Sam rejected many offers from the smart bookmakers to put him in the bag, meaning that, in return for preventing a horse from winning, a rider received a percentage of the money the bookmaker won on the race as a result of the arrangement.

2. *pl.* [Abbrev. of *sand-bag.*] In the phr. **over the bags,** over the sand-bags protecting a trench, 'over the top'; also *fig.*

1918 *Aussie* (Sydney) Jan. 10/2 *Over the bags,* the intensive form of danger; denoting a test of fitness and experience for Billzac and his brethren. **1919** W.A. CULL *At All Costs* 36

On the Somme we were twice over the bags in something more imposing than trench fighting.

3. [Orig. U.S.] In the phr. **bag of fruit,** rhyming slang for 'suit'.

1924 *Truth* (Sydney) 27 Apr. 6, *Bag of fruit*, a suit. **1981** P. BARTON *Bastards I have Known* 92 She dressed me up fit to kill in my best 'bag of fruit'.

4. [Prob. abbrev. of *bag of tricks* stock of resources: see OEDS *bag*, *sb.* 17 and cf. Box *n.*⁶.] In the phr. **out of the bag,** unexpected, surprising.

1954 T.A.G. HUNGERFORD *Sowers of Wind* 44 The only difference is, it was all done with one bloody bomb—that's what makes it one out of the bag. One place that's been skittled is like any other, otherwise. **1980** ANSELL & PERCY *To fight Wild* 9 Anyway, that was out of the bag. Writing poetry.

bag, *v.*

1. [f. BAG *n.*² 1.] *trans.* See quot. 1958. Also as *vbl. n.*

1958 F. HARDY *Four-Legged Lottery* 174 'Don't back that horse, Paul. It's been bagged.' 'Bagged?' This can be done by the owner or the jockey, but more often it is done by the trainer... A trainer gets a horse 'in the market'. He approaches a bookmaker or a group of bookmakers through an intermediary. The horse will not win if they pay up; he is prepared to 'bag it', to run it for the bookmakers. **1983** HIBBERD & HUTCHINSON *Barracker's Bible* 19 'Bagging' may be arranged by owner, trainer, or jockey. The bookmaker will then guarantee a kickback.

2. [Fig. use of *bag* to sack, dismiss.] *trans.* To denigrate. Freq. as *vbl. n.*

1969 *Daily Tel.* (Sydney) 20 Mar. 6/6 In the last couple of decades the poor old Poms have taken such a bagging from the rest of the world.. that they'd relish any chance to get back to a bit of good, old-fashioned British sneering. **1986** *Bulletin* (Sydney) 22 Apr. 73/2 Telecom is a pretty suspect outfit, deserving of the consistent bagging it gets from exasperated subscribers.

bagman, *n.*¹ [Prob. orig. a facetious application of *bagman* commercial traveller.]

1. A swagman.

1866 H. SIMCOX *Rustic Rambles* 21 See the dummies and the mediums, Bagmen, swagmen, hastening down. **1977** J. DOUGHTY *Gold in Blood* 23 The swagman—or bagman, as he was always called in Queensland—scorning the trains and striding the roads like a free man.

2. *spec.* A mounted swagman.

1902 *Bulletin* (Sydney) 8 Feb. 32/3 Of 'bagmen', the slang W. Queensland word for mounted travellers, there are.. several grades. **1967** M. SELLARS *Carramar* 44 Itinerant bagmen, 'jes ridin' round'; and most colourful of all, the swaggie.

3. In the Depression of the 1930s: one of the itinerant unemployed, in search of work or sustenance. See TRAVELLER 1.

1935 K. TENNANT *Tiburon* 8 The shelter-shed on the travellers' reserve, unlike most of the structures erected by charitable town councils, actually did shelter.. and.. during the long rainy spells had saved many a bagman from lying stiff with rheumatism under a bridge. **1979** G. STEWART *Leveller* 20 A bagman was an unemployed person whose only possessions were bags: a water bag, a tucker bag, flour bags washed and sewn together called a Wogga; all carried in yet another bag.

4. In special collocations: **bagman's gazette, leg, Bagmen's Union,** see quots.

1936 K.L. SMITH *Sky Pilot's Last Flight* 210 Ned has been arrested. The aeroplane travels quicker than the '**bagman's gazette**', so of course you have not heard of it. **1970** W. FEARN-WANNAN *Austral. Folklore* 27 The *Bagman's Gazette* was an imaginary swagmen's newspaper; a mythical source of bush rumours, i.e. 'According to the Bagman's Gazette.' **1977** STIRLING & RICHARDSON *Memories of Aberfeldy* 27 There had been several accidents caused by 'taking her on the fly' (jumping on when the train was moving at speed). This resulted in a new addition to the language, '**bagman's leg**' (loss of limb by falling under the train). **1954** *Coast to Coast 1953–54* 77 'How'd you come to do a thing like that—it's against the **Bagmen's Union** rules.' 'Ah, the Bagmen's Union is a thing of the past,' says the sundowner, rattling the corks to chase the flies off his face. **1965** F. HARDY *Yarns of Billy Borker* 48 'What? Sundowners never pay fares. It's against the rules of the Bagmen's Union.' 'Bagmen's Union? Never heard of it.' 'Easy to see you weren't on the track during the Depression.'

bagman, *n.*² [f. BAG *n.*²]

1. A bookmaker's clerk.

1973 F. PARSONS *Man called Mo* 140 Having a brother who was a bookmaker, he knew the best bagmen to bet with—those who gave him the best odds. **1984** *Nat. Times* (Sydney) 21 Dec. 8/6 According to the transcripts of the illegal N.S.W. police tapes, Coombs had been 'a bagman for a major SP bookmaker'.

2. *transf.*

1972 *Sunday Sun* (Brisbane) 2 July 14/2 Now he [*sc.* the drug supplier] is called the connection, the bagman, the wingman, the dealer. **1981** *Canberra Times* 6 Nov. 3/7 The Leader of the NSW National Country Party, Mr Punch, told State Parliament yesterday that the Deputy Police Commissioner, Mr Bill Allen, was the 'bag man' for the Premier, Mr Wran.

bagpipes, *pl.* [f. the tubular appearance of sugar cane.] See quot. 1938.

1988 F. CLUNE *Free & Easy Land* 285 *Bagpipes*, an armful of cane picked up and carried on the shoulders. **1976** S. WELLER *Bastards I have Met* 7 One day I picked up the bundle wrong and was slipping and sliding on the tops... Keith burst out laughing and said, 'Give us a tune on your bagpipes Sam.'

bail, var. BAAL.

bail, *n.* [Spec. use of *bail* a bar used to confine an animal (see OED *sb.*³ 4). Prob. Br. dial. but recorded earliest in Aust. and N.Z. (see OED(S *sb.*³ 5 and EDD *sb.*²).] Orig. a frame to secure a cow's head during milking (see quot. 1876); now usu. a stall, or one of a number of stalls in a milking shed, in which a cow is confined during milking, the head being held steady in a frame. Also *attrib.*

1843 J.F. BENNETT *Hist. & Descr. Acct. S.A.* 101 In the yard 'bails' are erected, in which the cow is held while she is being milked. **1876** 'EIGHT YRS.' RESIDENT' *Queen of Colonies* 221 In one corner of the yard the 'milking bail' is put up, which consists of two strong posts with a cross-piece on the top, and a thin rail, fastened to a bottom cross-piece, and working on a pin... The cow puts her head inside this moveable piece against the post, and it is then pushed forth close to her neck behind the ears and secured by a peg running through it and the cross-piece. The cow is thus prevented from moving her head while being milked. She is in fact 'bailed up'. **1911** I.A. ROSENBLUM *Stella Sothern* 32 I'll just see if she is down the bail-yard.

bail, *v.* Also **bale.** [f. prec.] Usu. with **up.**

1. a. *trans.* To confine (a cow) in a bail for the purpose of milking. Also *intr.*, to accept such confinement (see quot. 1881). In quot. 1843 the part of speech is uncertain.

[N.Z. **1841** N.M. TAYLOR *Jrnl. Ensign Best* 6 Apr. (1966) 285, I saw a small herd of Cows driven into a little stockyard bailed up and milked all by a *mauri* lad.] **1843** *Port Phillip Patriot* 23 Feb. 3/5 Thirty cows, broken-in to bail. **1881** H.W. NESFIELD *Chequered Career* 251 When it came to the vicious cow's turn to be milked, I determined to try a soothing and gentle mode of proceeding. I was told that she objected to the 'leg-rope'. She baled up quietly enough.

b. *intr. imp.* A call with which a cow is encouraged into a bail. Also in fig. contexts.

1847 T. McCOMBIE *Austral. Sketches* 2 The women and children now get long branches of trees, and lay on with a will, crying 'bail up, Coffee', or whatever name she is known by, 'bail up'. **1876** J.A. EDWARDS *Gilbert Gogger* 154 It is customary to say of a man who cannot understand English, 'He cannot say bail up to a cow.'

2. a. *trans.* Orig. of bushrangers: to confront (a person or persons) usu. with intent to commit robbery, preventing resistance by threat, force, or some means of confinement. Also *intr.*, to submit to such treatment without offering resistance (see quots. 1845 and 1892). See also STICK *v.* 1 b.

1838 *Colonist* (Sydney) 20 Oct. 3/2 They '*bail up*' the inmates, and commence plundering. **1845** *Standard* (Melbourne) 19 Feb. 3/2 He said I have settled him. . . I said what for? 'Because he would not bail up,' was his reply. **1892** *Western Champion* (Barcaldine) 19 Apr. 1/2 Suddenly as he gained the 'drop' on them, he thundered out—'Bail up, you donkeys; throw up your arms. I'm Power!' They 'bailed'.

b. *Hist. intr. imp.* A bushranger's challenge, requiring those challenged to submit without resistance to being robbed.

1842 *Geelong Advertiser* 4 Apr. 3/2 *Bushranging at Sydney.* On Thursday evening, about ten o'clock, while Mr Grey of Balmain was sitting in his room, three bush-rangers, heavily armed, rushed in, presenting their muskets and calling on him and his family to 'bail up'. **1929** J.J. KENNEALLY *Compl. Inner Hist. Kelly Gang* 58 Suddenly Ned Kelly cried out, 'Bail up! Throw up your arms.'

3. a. *trans.* To bring (an animal) to bay.

1870 E.B. KENNEDY *Four Yrs. in Qld.* 93 Two Kangaroo hounds (they sometimes resemble coarse deer hounds) one day 'bailed up' a Kangaroo in a water-hole. **1973** R. ROBINSON *Drift of Things* 112 The greyhounds would overtake and 'bail up' a kangaroo.

b. *intr.* Of an animal: to stand at bay.

[N.Z. **1894** J.K. ARTHUR *Kangaroo & Kauri* II. 98 The pigs will oftentimes 'bale up', or stop, and with their backs to a rock, tree, or other obstacle, keep two or more dogs at bay.] **1934** 'S. RUDD' *Green Grey Homestead* 125 He stuck to a black sow, in and out, and over everything, till he ran her to a standstill. And when she bailed up she had a snout on her as long as the nose of the smithy's bellows. **1980** ANSELL & PERCY *To fight Wild* 102 Cows gallop too hard and fast, bulls get hot and bail up under trees.

4. *trans., transf.* and *fig.* Also (rarely) *intr.*

1841 *Geelong Advertiser* 14 Aug. 2/3 A 'barker' is a barefaced fellow who lays hold of you by the collar, drags you into a dark den . . bails you up in a corner, and holds you fast until you purchase some of his goods 'all as better as new'. **1916** *Truth* (Sydney) 26 Nov. 5/1 The wages board has stepped in with a heavy and ignorant hand, *bailing up* the pork trade. **1977** T. RONAN *Mighty Men on Horseback* 32, I reckoned it was about time I bailed up.

Hence **bailed-up** *ppl. a.*, **bailing (up)** *vbl. n..*

1963 X. HERBERT *Disturbing Element* 22, I grew up on tales of what a fearsome thing a **bailed-up** old man 'roo could be. **1841** *Sydney Herald* 17 Apr. 2/4 On the road from Goulburn upwards a single bushranger . . has been levying contributions, the most serious of which is the robbery of her Majesty's mail . . and the '**bailing up**' of the coachman.

bailer shell. Also **baler shell.** Any of several volutid molluscs of the genus *Melo*, used by Aborigines in n. Aust. for bailing out canoes, for digging, and as a cooking utensil; the shell of such a mollusc.

1908 E.J. BANFIELD *Confessions of Beachcomber* 148 The bailer shell (*Cymbium aethiopicum*) [is] the 'Ping-ah' of the blacks. . . The bailer shell alive is like an egg, in the fact that it is full of meat. **1978** N. COLEMAN *Look at Wildlife Great Barrier Reef* 69 Entirely carnivorous, baler shells feed almost exclusively on other molluscs.

baked, *ppl. a. Obs.* [Br. dial.: see EDD *bake, v.*[1] 4.] Exhausted.

1861 *Burke & Wills Exploring Exped.* 22 The horse, Billy, being completely baked, next morning we started at daybreak, leaving the horse short hobbled. **1888** 'R. BOLDREWOOD' *Robbery under Arms* (1937) 86 Pulled up before if I knowed your horses were getting baked.

baker. FLOURY BAKER.

1860 G. BENNETT *Gatherings of Naturalist* 271 Many of the species of this insect have various parts of the body covered with a whitish secretion; hence they are named *Millers* and *Bakers* by the colonial youth. **1903** *Agric. Gaz. N.S.W.* XIV. 418 A well-known 'locust', to the Sydney boys is popularly known as the 'Floury Miller', or the 'Baker', on account of the rich, silvery pubescence, which makes it look as if it had been dusted with flour.

bal /bæl/. [Cornish *bal* a mine or cluster of mines: see OED.] In Cornish mining settlements in S.A.: see quot. 1971. Freq. *attrib.*

1867 *Wallaroo Times* (Kadina) 28 Aug. 2/3 We have had several of the 'bal bills' from the Moonta Mines left at our office to show the actual earnings of a number of the tributers. **1971** *AUMLA* xxxvi. 167 *Wheal* and *bal* . . seem to have been widely used in South Australia. . . *Bal* seems to have been the word regularly used to describe a mine or group of mines together with the associated buildings, plant, and machinery, as . . in . . *scatterin' the bal* . . the closing down of a mine and disposal of the plant, . . *bal bill* 'statement of a miner's earnings', *bal friend*, and *balmaiden* . . a woman working on the surface, especially in the dressing of ore.

balander /bəˈlændə/. *Aboriginal English.* Also **balanda, ballanda.** [a. Maccasarese *balanda*, a. Malay *bĕlanda* (corruption of *Hollander*), a Dutchman, a white man.] A white man. Also as *adj.*

1845 L. LEICHHARDT *Jrnl. Overland Exped.* 2 Dec. (1847) 503 They knew the white people of Victoria, and called them Bálanda, which is nothing more than 'Hollanders'; a name used by the Malays, from whom they received it. **1915** E.R. MASSON *Untamed Territory* 112 The blacks rushed up to the house calling 'Ballanda, Ballanda'—white man—and the Boss and Missus ran out. **1976** C.C. MACKNIGHT *Voyage to Marege'* p. ix, Friends in the Northern Territory, both Aboriginal and Balanda . . trusted me to tell the story. **1978** *Austral.* (Sydney) 6 Oct. 7/2 Balander . . is an Aboriginal name for a white man—corruption of the word Hollander. The tribes of Arnhem Land knew the tough, phlegmatic Dutchmen of the East Indies before Cook was born. Now a balander means any white man.

baldcoot. [Transf. use of *baldcoot* the coot *Fulica atra.*] Swamp hen see SWAMP *n.*

1829 H. WIDOWSON *Present State Van Diemen's Land* 182 The baldcoot, and a large bird, called the native hen . . frequent the lakes and lagunes. **1953** A. RUSSELL *Murray Walkabout* 50 The bald-coot is . . among the loveliest of all the Australian swamp-dwellers; its red legs and bill, blue vest, and upright form give it a singular beauty.

baldy, *n.* and *a.* Also **bally.** [f. Br. dial. *bald* marked with white: see EDD *adj.* 1.]

A. *n.* A Hereford, so called from the white face of the breed; a white-faced beast (see quot. 1946).

1887 *Bungendore Mirror* 19 Oct. 3, 50 18-months old Heifers—nearly all ballies. **1946** *Bulletin* (Sydney) 24 July 28/3 The bullock team, a strung-out procession of baldies, brindles and blacks, plods slowly along. **1976** C.D. MILLS *Hobble Chains & Greenhide* 145 If I say Hereford, the

Shorthorn blokes'll gang up to prove that I'm wrong, and if I defend the 'baldies' against 'em, the Polled Angus champions will show me pictures provin' they've won the export body of beef.
B. *adj.* **a.** Hereford (cattle). **b.** Of other animals: white-faced or with a white marking on the face. Also applied to the face itself.
1890 *Braidwood Dispatch* 30 Apr. 4/1 Now Jack you take the bally mare And ride right round Gum Swamp today. 1914 C.H.S. MATTHEWS *Bill* 137 A nice-looking chestnut called Pink 'un, with four white legs and a 'baldy' face. 1981 A. WILKINSON *Up Country* 149 Good baldy (Hereford) cattle in the paddocks.

bale, var. BAIL *v.*

baler shell, var. BAILER SHELL.

ball. *Obs.* [Prob. metaphoric use of *ball* as fired by a musket (cf. *slug*). The slang use of *ball* glass of spirits, is attested by *ball of fire* glass of brandy (OEDS *ball, sb.*¹ 6 b. 1821), U.S. *highball* (OEDS 1898), and the chiefly Irish *ball (of malt)* glass of malt whisky (OEDS *sb.*⁴ 1925).] A glass of spirits.
1832 *Hill's Life N.S.W.* 3 Aug. 2 The party then adjourned to a *max*-house, and drowned their sorrows in a few *balls*. 1888 A. McLEAN *Harry Bloomfield* 13 'Sure ye know what a *ball* is?' 'For a gun?' . . 'Ye'd vex St. Patrick himself; sure ye ken undherstand a good glass of whiskey?'
Hence as *v. trans.*
1845 *Parramatta Chron.* 1 Feb. 3/3 At a public-house, near the police office . . they were apparently accidentally joined by a man named Adams—who also 'balled it' off— which done, they separated.

ballander, var. BALANDER.

Ballarat (seedling): see STEWART'S BALLARAT SEEDLING.

ballart /'bælat/. [a. Kuurn Kopan Noot *balad.*] **a.** Any of several shrubs or small trees of the partly-parasitic genus *Exocarpos* (fam. Santalaceae) having a swollen and often edible cherry-like pedicel. **b.** With distinguishing epithet, as **cherry ballart,** *native cherry* (a), see NATIVE *a.* 6 a. See also CHERRY 1.
1889 J.H. MAIDEN *Useful Native Plants Aust.* 30 'Oringorin' of the Queensland aboriginals; and 'Ballat' of those of Gippsland. The fruit is edible. 1967 V.G.C. NORWOOD *Long Haul* 79 A troop of green-wings quit the light-green foliage of a drooping cherry ballart. 1980 G.R. COCHRANE et al. *Flowers & Plants Vic. & Tas.* (rev. ed.) 111 The common name 'Ballart' is not used in Tasmania.

ball of muscle. [Cf. *ball of fire.*] A person of dynamic energy; one who is physically very fit.
1914 A.B. PATERSON in C. Semmler *World of Banjo Paterson* (1967) 321 The handicap king, Moonlighter, bounds along, a ball of muscle, in last place. 1963 D. ATTENBOROUGH *Quest under Capricorn* 26 'G'day,' we said, slipping into the vernacular. 'Yer right?' 'Ball o' muscle,' he replied with gusto. . . 'If I felt any better I couldn't stand it.'

ball-tearer. [Fig. use of *ball* testicle.] Something outstanding of its kind; a source of exasperation or dismay.
1971 J. McNEIL *Chocolate Frog* (1973) 25, I mean you bein' pinched for street fightin' . . yer must be a real little ball-tearer. 1984 *Sydney Morning Herald* 26 Mar. 2/6 He thought the Opposition might have done better in the country and not quite as well in the city. 'The result in the city shows that corruption is a ball-tearer in the city.'

ball-up. *Australian National Football.* The bouncing of the ball by the field umpire to start or restart play, at the beginning of a quarter or after certain interruptions of play. See BOUNCE. Also *attrib.*
1890 J. SADLER *Lyrics & Rhymes* 143 'Jump on him!' 'Kick it!' 'Ball up!' 1983 G. ATKINSON *Bk. Austral. Rules Finals* 202 Umpire Schwab blew his whistle for a puzzling 'ball-up' decision.

bally, var. BALDY.

Balmain bug. [f. *Balmain* the name of a Sydney suburb + *bug*: see quot. 1974.] The edible marine crustacean *Ibacus peronii* of s. Aust., having a dorso-ventrally flattened body. See also SHOVEL-NOSED LOBSTER.
1952 W.J. DAKIN *Austral. Seashores* 184 The flapjack, also known to trawlermen as the Balmain bug. 1974 J.M. THOMSON *Fish Ocean & Shore* 77 The Balmain bug owes its name to the trawlermen who pioneered the trawling industry in New South Wales. . . The trawlers were based at Balmain. . . Any jointed crawly thing was a bug to the locals.

Balt /bɔlt/. [Transf. use of *Balt* native or inhabitant of one of the Baltic states.] An immigrant to Australia from one of the Baltic countries in the period following the war of 1939–45; loosely, any non-British immigrant from Europe. Freq. in *pl.*
1945 *Queanbeyan Age* 28 Sept. 1/7 Officials believe it will be impossible to repatriate at least 300,000; while 25,000 refuse to be sent home. Of this number 170,000 Balts refuse to be returned to Russian controlled areas. 1979 B. SCOTT *Tough in Old Days* 77 There was a New Australian in the compartment, though they were called 'Balts' in those days.

ban: see *black ban* BLACK *a.*⁴ 2, GREEN BAN.

banana.
1. Used *attrib.* in Special Comb., chiefly with reference to Queensland.
a. Banana land, State, a name for the State of Queensland.
1880 *Bulletin* (Sydney) 26 June 3/1 (*heading*) Notes from **Banana Land** (From our Brisbane Correspondent). 1916 *Truth* (Sydney) 17 Dec. 10/4 He *was going to Roma,* in the **Banana State.**
b. Banana-bender, -lander, -skin, a nickname for a Queenslander.
1964 D. LOCKWOOD *Up Track* 110 We are so close to Queensland that I think we should hop over the border. What do you say to a quick look at the **banana-benders**? 1887 *Bulletin* (Sydney) 26 Feb. 6/4 He made all arrangements for being married on that day, and his friends rallied up to congratulate him, and see him through, after the custom of the simple **Bananalanders.** 1921 F. GROSE *Rough Y.M. Bloke* 148 Combat the pestilential attacks of 'Cornstalks', 'Croweaters' and '**Bananaskins**'.
c. Banana city, Brisbane; **curtain,** the Queensland border; **-man** *obs.*, **(a)** a Queenslander; **(b)** a (Queensland) drink.
1893 J.A. BARRY *Steve Brown's Bunyip* 181 He had, he flattered himself . . been making rapid progress with the damsels of the **Banana city.** 1979 *Austral.* (Sydney) 28 Dec. 1/1 We know the Fleet Street system, Henry. Even up here behind the **banana curtain.** 1868 *Wallaroo Times* (Kadina) 9 Sept. 6/2 The '**Bananah Men**' have struck some really splendid patches of gold. 1880 *Bulletin* (Sydney) 14 Feb. 4/3 When a Cooktown man arises he goes to the bar and takes what is variously known as a 'Queenslander' or a 'Bananaman'. To make this delectable beverage . . you mix in a lemonade tumbler, a big nobbler of gin, ditto of whiskey, some limejuice, curacoa, cloves, absinthe, and Hostetter's bitters together with a tea-

spoonful of cayenne, and a little of the grounds of a bottle of Worcestershire sauce.

2. In the names of animals: **banana bird,** any of several birds, esp. the blue-faced honeyeater *Entomyzon cyanotis*, Lewin honeyeater (see LEWIN), and FIGBIRD; **prawn,** the crustacean *Penaeus merguiensis* of warm waters from India to New Caledonia, including n. Aust., fished commercially in the Gulf of Carpentaria.

1931 N.W. CAYLEY *What Bird is That?* 9 Lewin Honeyeater *Meliphaga lewini*... Also called Yellow-eared Honeyeater and **Banana-bird**. **1953** *Fisheries Newsletter* XII. ii. 23/1 The King and Banana are 'summer' prawns. **Banana prawns** are not particularly common in Moreton Bay, but large catches of them are made in the Mary and neighbouring rivers.

band. *Opal-mining.* A layer of sandstone containing some opal, above and below which larger deposits are likely to occur.

1902 *Geol. Survey Rep.* (Qld. Dept. Mines) clxxvii. 10 The opal-bearing stratum 'band' in which the sandstone opal is found, occurs in the falsely-bedded series of sandstones and clays at the base of the sandstone, and at its junction with the underlying clay. **1960** D. MCLEAN *Roaring Days* 62 We gouged them from a white clay below the band, and the country round the ugly bush town was like a rabbit warren of shafts and white dumps left by the opal gougers.

banded stilt. The wading bird *Cladorhynchus leucocephalus* of s. Aust., which feeds and breeds in salt lakes: see quot. 1968.

1841 J. GOULD *Birds of Aust.* (1848) VI. Pl. 26, The Banded Stilt is an inhabitant of the southern and western coast of Australia. **1968** R. HILL *Bush Quest* 4 Even more shy were the banded stilts, handsome white birds with dark brown backs and a chestnut band on their breast.

bandicoot, n. Also **bandycoot.** [Transf. use of *bandicoot* (lit. 'pig-rat'), the Indian eutherian mammal *Bandicota indica*, to which the Austral. animals bear some resemblance.]

1. Any of several marsupial mammals of the fam. Peramelidae and Thylacomyidae of Aust., New Guinea, and nearby islands, having long, pointed heads, esp. *Isoodon macrourus* of n. and e. Aust., which frequents suburban gardens. Also with distinguishing epithet, as **pig-footed, rabbit, short-nosed:** see under first element. Rarely **bandicoot rat.**

1799 D. COLLINS *Acct. Eng. Colony N.S.W.* (1802) II. 188 The bones of small animals, such as opossums .. and bandicoots. **1832** J. BISCHOFF *Sketch Hist. Van Diemen's Land* 177 The only creatures inhabiting these large forests, appeared to be opossums and bandicoot rats [etc.].

2. *transf.* and *fig.* Used in various phrases as an emblem of deprivation or desolation.

1837 H. WATSON *Lecture on S.A.* 20 The land here is generally good; there is a small proportion that is actually good for nothing; to use a colonial phrase, 'a bandicoot (an animal between a rat and a rabbit) would starve upon it'. **1920** C.L. HART *More Diggerettes* 9 That's the worst of them French tabs. They look oright, but they're as ignorant as blanky bandycoots.

bandicoot, *v.* [f. prec.]

1. *Obs. intr.* To hunt the bandicoot.

1825 *London Mag.* May II. 59 You can always tell .. where the blacks have been bandy cooting.

2. *trans.* To remove (potatoes) surreptitiously from the ground, leaving the tops undisturbed.

1896 *Bulletin* (Sydney) 12 Dec. 26/4, I must 'bandicoot' spuds from the cockies—Or go on the track! **1978** W. LOWENSTEIN *Weevils in Flour* 326 We learnt to bandicoot spuds. We'd feel the drill where the potatoes were and take a good sized one. We'd fill the earth back so it wouldn't interfere with the rest of his crop.

3. *Mining. intr.* To fossick, esp. in previously worked ground.

1907 *Bulletin* (Sydney) 29 Aug. 15/3 Chows are the very worst botchers of mining work in the world. I've seen thousands of them bandicooting in Australia .. and not a miner in the whole yellow horde. **1940** *Ibid.* 29 May 17/4 Me an' cobber Bill 'ad bin doin' a bit o' bandicootin' on some old workin's on the Macquarie, but we slings it in after on'y gittin' about 18 'weights after three munce yakka.

Hence **bandicooted** *ppl. a.*, **bandicooter** *n.*

1916 J. FURPHY *Poems* 15 And trade away your pin and studs, To live on **bandicooted** spuds. **1899** *Bulletin* (Sydney) 2 Dec. 14/1 The **bandicooter** goes at night to a field of ripe potatoes.

bandicoot gunyah. *Obs.* A makeshift shelter. Cf. BADGER BOX.

1849 S. & J. SIDNEY *Emigrant's Jrnl.* 34 They will make a bandicoot gunya, that is to say, a house in the shape of a large dog kennel. **1867** F.J. BYERLEY *Narr. Overland Exped. Northern Qld.* 56 At night, on camping, a 'bandicoot gunyah' was erected, and covered with the broad pliable paper bark of melaleuca, which made a snug shelter for the night from the still pouring rain.

banditti. *Obs.* [Spec. use of *banditti* (It. *banditi*) pl. of *bandit*, also as a collect. sing. (see OED *bandit*).]

1. *pl.* Bushrangers.

1796 *HRA* (1914) 1st Ser. I. 554 We have now, my Lord, a band or two of banditti, who have armed themselves and infest the country all round, committing robberies upon defenceless people, and frequently joining the natives for that purpose. **1855** G.H. WATHEN *Golden Colony* 203 Their country is ruined, their houses pillaged, their roads infested by banditti.

2. *collect. sing.* Pl. **banditties.** A gang of bushrangers.

1803 *Sydney Gaz.* 5 Mar., We should here observe that this banditti is entirely composed of Irish prisoners. **1816** *Hobart Town Gaz.* 3 Aug., The Robbery committed upon Mr John Beamont by one of the Banditties of Bush Rangers .. was .. at his house near Jericho.

bandy. Abbrev. of BANDICOOT *n.*

1895 *Proc. Linnean Soc. N.S.W.* X. (note) 400 Mr Barry on one occasion noticed two bandicoots near a native grave and told some blacks of it... The natives were hard pressed for food, but they would not touch the 'bandies' because they believed them to be the dogs of the dead. **1945** *Bulletin* (Sydney) 5 Sept. 12/1 In my early days many of the windows cut in the prostrate trunks of trees by the abos. were intended to provide a draught for the very purpose of smoking out a bandy or kanga-rat.

bandy-bandy /'bændi-bændi/. [a. Kattaŋ *bandi bandi*.] Either of two small elapid snakes patterned with black and white bands around the body, *Vermicella annulata* of e. and central Aust. and *V. multifasciata* of n. W.A. and N.T. See also RING SNAKE. Also **bunda-bunda.**

1911 *Bulletin* (Sydney) 22 June 14/4 The small and slender coral snake of South America .. is no larger than our 'bandy-bandy'. **1918** *Ibid.* 22 Aug. 24/4, I have struck a great number of bunda-bunda snakes (commonly known as 'bandy-bandy').

bandycoot, var. BANDICOOT.

bang, *v. trans.* To cut (the tail of an animal), usually square across (but see quot. 1911).

1900 *Advocate* (Burnie) 15 Aug. 1/6 They are like yearlings or weedy two-year-olds of the hack breed, and have their tails 'banged' and manes 'hogged', which gives them the look of big foals. **1911** E.J. BRADY *King's Caravan* 241

Station hands were busy 'banging' the mob; which operation consists chiefly in cutting the hair of the animal's tail in different ways for different paddocks.
Hence **banged** *ppl. a.*
1905 *Bulletin* (Sydney) 19 Jan. 17/1 The 'broken' horses were commandeered by night, being known by their banged tails.

bangalay /'bæŋəleɪ, bæŋ'geɪli/. [Prob. f. a N.S.W. Aboriginal language.] The tree *Eucalyptus botryoides* (fam. Myrtaceae) of N.S.W. and Vic., commonly found on saline coastal soils; *bastard mahogany*, see BASTARD *a.*
1861 *Catal. Natural & Industr. Products N.S.W.* 28 Bang alay .. a crooked growing tree, the timber much valued for knees and crooked timbers of coasting vessels. **1962** N.C.W. BEADLE et. al. *Handbk. Vascular Plants Sydney & Blue Mountains* 278 Near the sea. Deep, usually wet and often saline soils .. Bangalay.

bangalow /'bæŋɡəloʊ/. Formerly also **bangally, bungalow**. [Poss. a. Dharawal *baŋgala*.] The tall palm *Archontophoenix cunninghamiana* (fam. Arecaceae) of N.S.W. and Qld., having arching, feather-like fronds; (occas.) a similar palm. See also PICCABEEN.
1826 J. ATKINSON *Acct. Agric. & Grazing N.S.W.* 4 To their other productions are then generally added the bangally, much resembling the cabbage tree in appearance, but having long and wide leaves of a thick and tenacious texture. **1887** H. GULLET *Tropical N.S.W.* 9 The tall slender stems of the graceful bungalow palms struggle upwards for air and light. **1980** C. KELEN *Punks Travels* 51 In the filtered sun of the rainforest floor .. bangalow palm at my shoulder.

bange /'bændʒi/, *v.* Also **banje**. [Of unknown origin; prob. f. Br. dial. *benge* to lounge lazily: see EDD.] *intr.* To rest; to sleep. Also with **off** and **to bange it**.
1845 D.G. BROCK *To Desert with Sturt* (1975) 142 Sullivan never has cared about getting birds—he prefers what is called here 'Banging it'—that is, ever lying under the dray. **1877** W. ARCHER in R. Stanley *Tourist to Antipodes* (1977) 65 Around the fire the men were 'banjing' (i.e., resting) in all sorts of different positions. **1976** C.D. MILLS *Hobble Chains & Greenhide* 7 'We'll 'bange off' for a few days, and let the big bloke settle down,' remarked the Boss, well pleased.

bange /'bændʒi/, *n. Obs.* [See prec.] A rest; a sleep.
1844 *Parramatta Chron.* 15 June 2/1 Michael Cahill .. was doomed to experience the fallacy of his conceptions by a four days' 'bange' in the cells. **1902** E.B. KENNEDY *Black Police Qld.* 184, I should follow their example .. and .. turn on to my bunk for a 'bange', *i.e.*, sleep, and in such manner get my one day of rest.

banger. [Of unknown origin. Cf. *bang-up* stylish: see OED(S but see also FLOGGER.] A morning-coat. Formerly also **fantail banger**.
1882 *Sydney Slang Dict.* 10 The Parson is on the highfly in a fantail banger. **1978** D. VAWR *Ratbag Mind* 17 He left three of his old morning-coats ('bangers' in the slang of the day) hanging in a bedroom.

bangtail, *n.* Abbrev. of BANGTAIL MUSTER. Usu. *attrib.*
1931 *Bulletin* (Sydney) 29 July 20/4 On the big cattle stations of western Queensland .. a general muster on such occasions as the sale of the run is necessary. . . There is nothing for it but the tedious 'bangtail' count through the races. **1974** D. STUART *Prince of my Country* 212 'Reckon we oughta have a muster, along our boundary with you? .. ' 'No, I can't see we need a bangtail.'

bangtail, *v. trans.* To bang the tails of (horses or cattle), esp. as a means of counting or identifying.

1908 MRS A. GUNN *We of Never-Never* 252 'Well I'm blest!' he said. 'If we didn't forget all about bangtailing that mob for her mattress.' **1976** C.D. MILLS *Hobble Chains & Greenhide* 164 We rode to the rail yards to 'bang-tail' our mob.
Hence **bang-tailed** *ppl. a.*, **bangtailing** *vbl. n.*
1933 R.B. PLOWMAN *Camel Pads* 291 A **bang-tailed** beast is as conspicuous among other cattle as a girl with a shingled head. **1922** *Bulletin* (Sydney) 26 Oct. 20/4 He had an outsize pocket-knife (as used for **'bangtailing'**), keen as the average barber's razor.

bangtail muster. A muster of the stock on a station during which the tail of each beast is banged, to distinguish it from those still to be counted.
1886 *S.A. Parl. Papers* III. no. 54 1 The manager of the station, Mr Lindsay Crawford, was instructed to make a bang-tail muster and classify the stock on the run. **1971** W.A. WINTER-IRVING *Beyond Bitumen* 47 A bang-tail muster turned up Father's estimated number of livestock.

banjo. [Fig. use of *banjo* musical instrument, as applied to objects similar in shape.]
1. A shoulder (of mutton).
1897 *Bulletin* (Sydney) 7 Aug. (Red Page), Shoulder of Mutton—'Banjo'. **1974** B. KIDMAN *On Wallaby* 32 What a 'hand-out' I received! A banjo (shoulder) of mutton .. a big piece of brownie.
2. A shovel.
1915 *Bulletin* (Sydney) 9 Dec. 22/1, I was wielding the pick and banjo in a gang on a big channel job once. **1983** *Sun-Herald* (Sydney) 9 Oct. 71/4 My dad and I laid our 80 to 90 yards of gravel a day, working with a banjo (shovel) and a two-horse dray.
3. *Mining*. A device for washing tin: see quot. 1932.
1932 I.L. IDRIESS *Prospecting for Gold* 17 A banjo is simply an open box, about four feet long. The 'head' of the box may be two feet high, with the sides sloping to six inches. The width is two feet at the head, tapering to eighteen inches at the end. . . The bottom is covered with bagging. **1985** M. KENNEDY *Born Half-Caste* 33 The men would get the banjo (sluice-box) ready for washing the tin.
4. FIDDLER. Also *attrib.* as **banjo ray**.
1969 J. POLLARD *Austral. & N.Z. Fishing* 573 The brown fiddler or banjo ray occurs along the Australian east coast from south Queensland to Tasmania and is common down the coast of New South Wales. **1986** *Canberra Chron.* 29 Jan. 19/1 There are a few cockies and a lot of banjos mixed in with them but they provide good fishing.

bank, $n.^1$ *Gold-mining*. [Cf. U.S. *bank-diggings*: see Mathews.] Used *attrib.* to designate a place being mined in the bank as opposed to the bed of a creek or river.
1851 *Empire* (Sydney) 7 Oct. 231/7 The bank or dry diggings are being worked in situations that excite astonishment in the visitor. **1944** M.W. PEACOCK *Dead Puppets Dance* 22 I've only got a creek claim. If I had a bank claim—including the bank as well as the bed of the creek—I'd sink a shaft.

bank, $n.^2$ [Prob. generalized use of *bank* as in gambling.] A sum of money; spec. one reserved for a particular purpose, i.e. for drinking, gambling, etc.
1919 C. DREW *Doings of Dave* 28 Did you have any bank to kick off with? **1978** D. STUART *Wedgetail View* 47 A few quiet bottles, just once a week. . . This way, a feller'll get a bank together in no time.

banker.
1. A creek or river swollen to the top of, or overflowing, its banks. Freq. in the phr. **to run** (or **come down**) **a banker**.

1848 H.W. Haygarth *Recoll. Bush Life* 129 Now that I take a second glance at the river, its waters look very muddy, which is a sure sign of its being high, not to say a 'banker'. **1867** 'S. McTavish' *Chowla* 4 Great, then, was the joy, when a telegram was received from Fort Bourke, announcing that the sluggish Darling was at length coming down 'a banker'. **1935** K.L. Smith *Sky Pilot Arnhem Land* 267 The thirsty ground was unable to absorb it all... Every creek and depression ran a banker.

2. *fig.*

1898 *Examiner* (Launceston) 11 Oct. 6/3 Feeling is running a banker at Devonport in reference to the coming election. **1966** P. Mathers *Trap* 95 Colin's arse-cleft ran a banker with sweat.

bank high, *a. Obs.* [Used elsewhere but recorded earliest in Aust.] Of a river in flood: swollen to the top of its banks.

1847 *Atlas* (Sydney) III. 3/1 Two creeks, now bank high, although probably dry in ordinary seasons. **1875** Campbell & Wilks *Early Settlement Qld.* 4 Upon arriving at the Condamine found it running bank high.

banksia. [f. the name of Joseph *Banks* (1743–1820), English botanist, given by J.R. and G. Forster in 1776 to a N.Z. plant genus now classified as *Pimelea.* The name was applied to the Australian plant genus by the younger Linnaeus (*Suppl. Plantarum* (1782) 15, 126).]

1. Any tree or shrub of the genus *Banksia* (fam. Proteaceae), usu. with leathery leaves and dense flower spikes forming thick woody cones as the fruits mature. Also *attrib.*

1788 J. White *Jrnl. Voyage N.S.W.* (1790) 221 (*heading*) The different species of Banksia. **1857** W. Howitt *Tallangetta* II. 143 But Dinah Slaughter sits alone Under the Banksia tree.

2. Special Comb. **banksia man,** a name for the large woody cone of any of several *Banksia* species; orig. applied to a type of character in a children's story (see quot.).

1918 M. Gibbs *Snugglepot & Cuddlepie* 74 She could see the glistening, wicked eyes of Mrs. Snake and the bushy heads of the bad Banksia men.

Banksian cockatoo. [See prec. and quot. 1822.] A black cockatoo, esp. the *red-tailed black cockatoo* (see Red *a.* 1 b.).

1787 J. Latham *Gen. Synopsis Birds* Suppl. 63 Bankian [*sic*] Cockatoo... The tail is pretty long... The two middle feathers are black; the others the same at the base and ends; the middle of them, for about one third, of a fine deep crimson... Inhabits *New Holland.* **1822** J. Latham *Gen Hist. Birds* II. 199 Banksian Cockatoo... Sir Jos. Banks first brought this with him into England, on his return from his Voyage round the World.

banyan. Formerly **banian.** [Transf. use of *banian* the Indian fig tree *Ficus benghalensis.* The name Banian (or Banians') Tree was orig. given by Europeans to an individual tree near the Persian Gulf under which the Banians (Hindu traders) had built a pagoda: see OED *banian* 5.] Freq. *attrib.*, esp. as **banyan tree.**

1. Any of several trees of the genus *Ficus* (fam. Moraceae), the adventitious roots of which form buttresses around the trunk, as *F. virens* of n. Aust. and Asia.

1845 J.O. Balfour *Sketch of N.S.W.* 40 The tree which has excited most interest in the colony is the banian tree lately discovered to the northward of Moreton Bay. **1896** J.W. Fawcett *Narr. Terrible Cyclone Townsville* 9 Mr Clayton had his kitchen verandah and out-buildings, as well as several trees in the garden, including a mango tree 18 years old, torn up by the roots, and a banyan three feet in circumference broken off short.

2. Special Comb. **banyan rum,** a spirituous drink: see quots. 1944 and 1977.

1938 F. Clune *Free & Easy Land* 252 Two bottles of banyan-rum. **1944** J. Devanny *By Tropic Sea & Jungle* 26 When they ran out of the real stuff, the grog-sellers would manufacture Banyan Rum while you waited—a mixture of boot black, Condy's crystals and methylated spirits. **1977** Lowenstein & Loh *Immigrants* 26 The traditional recipe for Banyan Rum was very simple. 'Two gallons of overproof rum, a pound of salt to keep you drinking, two tablespoons of water, an armful of leaves off a stinging tree and a pound plug of tobacco nailed to the bottom of the keg. Allow to mature for five minutes. If you're a fussy bastard you can strain it through a greasy horse blanket.'

baobab. [Transf. use of *baobab* the African tree *Adansonia digitata.*] **a.** The swollen-trunked tree *Adansonia gregorii* (fam. Bombacaceae) of n.w. Aust. **b.** Bottle tree. Also **baob, boab, boabab,** and *attrib.*

1863 *Jrnls. & Rep. Two Voyages Glenelg River* (1864) 17 Noticed some poor sandalwood, also acacia, baobab, and palms, and a rose-like vine. **1880** A. Forrest *N.-W. Exploration* 12 We saw a boab tree today, about ten feet in diameter. **1886** F. Cowan *Aust.* 17 The Boabab: the Gouty Stem, the Monkey-bread, Sour Gourd, or Cream-of-Tartar-tree:... a huge, aerial, arborescent [*sic*] yam! a bulb become a tree without a bole!... its gourd-like fruit filled with a mealy melting acid mass: a desert substitute for lemonade! **1946** *Bulletin* (Sydney) 21 Aug. 28/1, I suppose Binghi's pictorial efforts with the baob nut as a canvas should really be classed as engraving.

bar, *n.*[1] [Transf. use of *bar* bank of sand at the mouth of a river, applied to banks formed by currents upstream. Used elsewhere but recorded earliest in Aust.: see OED *sb.*[1] 15 b.] A bank of sand or silt formed by river currents, either mid-stream or on river bends. Also *attrib.*

1843 R.D. Murray *Summer at Port Phillip* 55 One of those bars, from which no river in Australia is wholly free. **1851** *Empire* (Sydney) 5 Aug. 15/1 The most successful were those who were working steadily on 'bars', or banks of sand and gravel formed on the many points along the winding river. *Ibid.* 7 Oct. 231/7 The water having subsided, bar diggings are again being worked, but the water still interferes to a great extent.

bar, *n.*[2] *Opal-mining.* [Spec. use of *bar* a stripe.] Banding within a layer of opal.

1932 I.L. Idriess *Prospecting for Gold* 241 Some opals are sand-pitted, others are milky, cloudy, smoky, broken barred, etc. Judge by the 'bar' and the brilliance of the colour. **1962** Whiting & Relph *Occurrence of Opal* 9 The seams are thick in comparison with the rest of the field and some large pieces of potch were found. Some bars of opal were up to one-half inch in thickness.

bar, *n.*[3] [Of unknown origin.] In the phr. **not to like (have, be able to stand) a bar of,** to be unable to tolerate (someone, etc.), to dislike intensely; to reject utterly (a course of action).

1933 J. McCarter *Love's Lunatic* 238, I didn't like a bar of him when he was alive—an' I'm not shook on lookin' at his dead chivvy. **1945** G. Casey *Downhill is Easier* 25 Reg wanted to have another drink.. but I wouldn't have a bar of it. **1972** A. Chipper *Aussie Swearers Guide* 75, I don't care if his mother's won *Tatts.* I can't stand a bar of him.

bar, *v.* [f. *to bar the dice* to declare the throw void.] *trans.* In the game of two-up: to disallow (a throw of the coins).

1897 *Worker* (Sydney) 18 Dec. 3/4 Hey, bar that toss! Heads it is! **1977** R. Beilby *Gunner* 299 Slight shock put Gunner off his toss so that the coins drifted up sedately, not turning. 'Floater,' several voices shouted. 'Barred,' shouted the ringie.

barb. [Prob. from the name of an individual dog: see quots. 1911 and 1914.] A black strain of KELPIE. Also attrib.

1898 *Sydney Morning Herald* 4 July 3/1 To sheepmen the dogs are known as kelpies, barbs, or Clydes, and the origin of the breed is said to be the smooth-haired 'coolie' [*sic*] and the English fox. 1908 W.H. OGILVIE *My Life in Open* 162 The barb dogs are all prick-eared and have a peculiar crouching and watchful carriage... They fight like Japs and resent a thrashing from their masters with tooth and nail. 1911 *Australasian* (Melbourne) 29 Apr. 1043/1 Mr King called his dog 'Barb', after the horse of that name that won the Melbourne Cup in the old days. 1914 R. KALESKI *Austral. Barkers & Biters* 47 There have been some awful fights and arguments as to where the barb originated; this is the truth about it. Kelpie was a bitch owned by C. King, of Woollongough. One of her pups.. had been called Barb. Barb turned out a great worker... Mr Edols bought him.. and kept him on Burrawang, where he got many fine pups. These all took after him, so they were called Barb's pups, and then, as the name spread, just barb.

barber, *n. Obs.* A nickname for a shearer; *jumbuck barber*, see JUMBUCK 2; *sheep barber*, see SHEEP 2.

1898 *Bulletin* (Sydney) 19 Nov. 14/1 When I took to dabbing tar, And 'picking up' on Blaringar, The cook when 'barbers' came at morn To get a snack, would say, with scorn: 'Tea on the left.' 1936 A.B. PATERSON *Shearer's Colt* 17 Wears a barber's delight (silk shirt) and jemimas (elastic-sided boots), but the dressier they are the hotter they are.

barber, *v. Obs. trans.* To shear (a sheep). Also *absol.*

1910 *Bulletin* (Sydney) 22 Dec. 13/2, I took a hand in the formation of the Shearers' Union in 1885, previous to which shearers had to barber the jumbucks at the sweet will of the shed bosses, whether wet or dry. 1929 C.H. WINTER *Story of 'Bidgee Queen* 94 But still they 'barbered' cheerfully—though roughly.

Hence **barbered** *ppl. a.*, **barbering** *vbl. n.*

1922 *Bulletin* (Sydney) 16 Mar. 22/1 The cocky gazed gloomily upon the **barbered** jumbucks in the ringer's pen. 1912 *Ibid.* 28 Nov. 16/4 The next most meagre **barbering** was that of the aforesaid Nugget, and my friend had wagered him a bottle of whisky he would disrobe more jumbucks than Nugget on the following day.

barbie /'babi/. [f. *barb(ecue* + -Y.] A barbecue; a meal cooked on a barbecue. Also *attrib.*, and *fig.*

1976 *Austral.* (Sydney) 14 Aug. 20/4 He propounded the natural and national virtues of the Aussie beach barbie with beer and prawns, and the big chunder. 1981 *Weekend Austral. Mag.* (Sydney) 11 July 6/8 A few tinnies and an impromptu barbie. 1984 *Overlander* June 52 Refuse to give some cove who's.. y' know.. a few snags short of a barbie—refuse to give him a job as a brain surgeon and.. you're up in front of the bloody Discrimination Board. 1986 *Austral. Geographic* Jan. 19/1 It.. like most barbie guests, enjoys a drink.

Barcoo /ba'ku/, *attrib.* and *n.* [The name of a river in w. Qld.; applied also to the surrounding country.]

A. 1. *attrib.* Of or pertaining to the district traversed by the Barcoo River; in some way characterizing the people or living conditions of that part of the country or of the remote inland generally.

1882 *Bulletin* (Sydney) 6 May 9/4 There were two young squatters and a Barcoo banker on the box seat. 1927 J. MATHIEU *Backblock Ballads* 44, I boiled me bloomin' billy and knocked up a 'Barcoo Bun'. [*Note*] Barcoo Bun—Small Damper. 1933 J. HAMILTON *Nights Ashore* 100 The parrot's language would have shamed the choicest repartee of a Blue-nosed bosun or a Barcoo bullocky. 1973 P. ADAM SMITH *Barcoo Salute*, 'I see you've learnt the Barcoo Salute,' said a Buln Buln Shire Councillor to the Duke of Edinburgh.

'What's that?' said His Royal Highness, waving his hand again to brush the flies off his face. 'That's it,' said the man from the bush.

2. Special Comb. **Barcoo dog,** see quots.; **grass,** FLINDERS GRASS; **rot,** scurvy (see quot. 1894); also **rotted** *a.*; **sandwich,** see quots.; **shout,** see quot. 1919; **sickness,** a condition characterized by attacks of vomiting; BELYANDO SPEW; **sore,** an ulcer on the skin symptomatic of Barcoo rot; **spew, vomit,** *Barcoo sickness.*

1936 *Bulletin* (Sydney) 9 Sept. 20/2 A winner among discordant bush noises is the **Barcoo dog**—an elaboration of a baby's rattle that some genius long ago invented for scaring sheep up into the forcing pens and down the drafting race. 1977 B. SCOTT *My Uncle Arch* 55 Now, a Barcoo Dog isn't a dog... It's a six inch circle of eight gauge fencing wire with seventeen tin lids on it that rattle like hell when you shake it. 1880 J. BONWICK *Resources Qld.* 45 The *A* [*nthistiria*] *membranacaea* is the brittle, dry **Barcoo grass**. 1870 E.B. KENNEDY *Four Yrs. in Qld.* 46 Land Scurvy.. is better known in Queensland by local names, which do not sound very pleasant, such as '**Barcoo rot**'.. according to the district it appears in. 1894 *Intercolonial Q. Jrnl. Med. & Surg.* I. 218 'Barcoo rot', in which the slightest scratches or abrasions of the skin pass speedily into rapidly spreading, freely suppurating, yet superficial and painless, circular ulcers, often of extraordinary persistence. 1927 *Bulletin* (Sydney) 24 Nov. 27/1 His hands were barcoo-rotted and his shoulders labor-bowed. 1968 W.N. SCOTT *Some People* 120 Before he went he taught the little bloke.. how to make a **Barcoo Sandwich**, which is a curlew between two sheets of bark. 1976 B. SCOTT *Compl. Bk. Austral. Folk Lore* 380 A Barcoo sandwich is a goanna between two sheets of bark, or a double rum between two beers. 1919 *Bulletin* (Sydney) 20 Mar. 22/1 West of Winton (Q.) a gargle costs a bob. A pound-note buys 20 drinks; but if three thirsts breast the bar and place thereon a half-crown, it buys the three drinks. This is the '**Barcoo shout**'. 1896 B. SPENCER *Horn Sci. Exped. Central Aust.* IV. 132 There is a complaint, from which those long resident in the distant bush frequently suffer severely, which has received the name of the '**Barcoo Sickness**' or simply 'Barcoo'... To Queenslanders it is known as the 'Belyando Spew'. 1898 D.W. CARNEGIE *Spinifex & Sand* 420 Sudden changes in temperature made any '**Barcoo**' **sores** most painful. 1901 P.D. LORIMER *Songs & Verses* 20 **Barcoo spew**, rot, and sandy blight, Dingoes howling all the night. 1881 J.C.F. JOHNSON *To Mount Browne & Back* 23 The '**Barcoo vomit**', which here usually accompanies dysentery, is a very distressing complaint.

B. *n.*

1. *Barcoo rot.*

1885 *Once a Month* (Melbourne) Jan. 55 In Queensland and all the pioneer stations.. every one is liable to have festering sores on his hands, and it is briefly designated as Barcoo. 1977 F.B. VICKERS *Stranger no Longer* 25 Onions and dried apricots. Best things in the world for keeping the barcoo away.

2. *Barcoo sickness.*

1891 *Adelaide Observer* 16 May 37/1 We were warned against 'barcoo'—an epidemic which is very prevalent when the Cooper is in flood. The popular antidote for the unpleasant sensation of vomiting immediately after a meal is Lea and Perrins' sauce. 1932 M.R. WHITE *No Roads go By* 191 Barcoo was rife among the kiddies and station-hands; vomiting attacks lasting for days laid each low in turn.

3. *fig.*

1920 *Bulletin* (Sydney) 24 June 20/2 The bloke who rode 100 'whistlers' in one day gives me the barcoo.

4. See quot.

1984 *Bulletin* (Sydney) 21 Nov. 21/2 So far as I know there are no sandstone ridges at Longreach (Q.), but the electrical storms.. there—called Barcoos—are terrific and take toll of both human and stock life.

5. Language characterized by profanity.

1875 R. THATCHER *Something to his Advantage* 18 Old Daddy objurgates and blesses their eyes and limbs in choicest Barcoo.

bardie /'badi/. Chiefly *W.A.* Also **barde, bardee, bardi.** [a. Nyungar *bardi.*] **a.** The edible larva or pupa of the cerambycid beetle *Bardistus cibarius*, found in the stems of grass-trees, eucalypts, and acacias. **b.** The edible larva or pupa of any of several species of hepialid moth, esp. *Trictena argentata*, found underground, feeding on roots of eucalypts and acacias. See also WITCHETTY. Also **bardie grub**.
1840 T.J. BUCKTON *W.A.* 97 The *Bar-de* (the native name for the white grub alluded to), has a fragrant, aromatic flavour; and is eaten either raw or roasted. 1841 G. GREY *Jrnls. Two Exped. N.-W. & W.A.* II. 289 If the top of the tree is observed to be dead, the native gives it a few sharp kicks with his foot, when, if it contains any *barde* or grubs, it begins to give. 1845 J. BRADY *Descr. Vocab. Native Lang. W.A.* 14 *Bardi*, the edible grub in the grass tree. 1890 *Trans. & Proc. R. Geogr. Soc. Australasia Vic.* 93 When hungry they simply go forth with a strong stick .. and dig for 'bardies' or large white grubs that attack the jam trees. 1926 R.J. TILLYARD *Insects Aust. & N.Z.* 233 The 'bardee' of Western Australia, *Bardistus cibarius* . . , ranges right across to New South Wales; its larvae are found in the stems of grass-trees and 'black-boys' (*Xanthorrhoea*) and are eaten. 1938 D. BATES *Passing of Aborigines* 217 For constipation a cooked iguana liver . . and a few bardie grubs.

bare-belly. See quot. 1965.
[N.Z. *c* 1875 G.L. MEREDITH in A.J. Harrop *Adventuring in Maoriland* (1935) 143 Naturally, the easiest-shorn sheep— 'bare-bellies' and 'bare-points'—are selected first.] 1897 *Worker* (Sydney) 11 Sept. 1/2 At a 'clean point' 'bare belly' he'd hardly ever scoff. 1965 J.S. GUNN *Terminol. Shearing Industry* i. 6 Barebelly, a sheep with defective wool growth caused by a break in the fibre structure. This causes the wool to fall off the belly and legs.
Hence **bare-bellied** *a.*
1912 J. BRADSHAW *Highway Robbery under Arms* (ed. 3) 23 In came the bare-bellied ewes. Then the pickers-up were bogged in wool, the penner-up was up to his rump in trouble, and the tarboys were almost blind from perspiration.

barilla. *Hist.* [Transf. use of *barilla* a maritime plant *Salsola soda* (fam. Chenopodiaceae); the alkali obtained by burning the plant.] Any of several coastal plants, esp. of the fam. Rhizophoraceae and Chenopodiaceae; the alkaline ashes, formerly used in soap-making, obtained by burning the plants.
1826 Tas. Colonial Secretary's Office Rec. 1/36 201 The most important production however, is the Vegetable from which Barilla is made:- and which is, itself, commonly called British Barilla;—from which that important article *soap* is principally manufactured. 1891 *Papers & Proc. R. Soc. Tas.* (1892) 1 These petrels choose islands where the soil is composed of a loose sand, covered in places by a bush with a blue flower called 'barilla'.

bark. [Used *attrib.* in Comb. not always excl. Austral. but of local importance.]
1. Applied to items made of bark by Aborigines: **bark canoe, shield.**
1830 R. DAWSON *Present State Aust.* 246 A fleet of small **bark-canoes**, belonging to the natives, was lying moored to some mangrove-trees. 1798 D. COLLINS *Acct. Eng. Colony N.S.W.* (1798) I. 328 One native of the tribe of Cammerray .. was suffered indeed to cover himself with a **bark shield**, and behaved with the greatest courage.
2. Used with reference to the gathering and processing of bark as a source of tannin: **bark chopper, cutter, -cutting, gatherer, getter, licence, mill, peeler, stripper, -stripping.**

1835 *True Colonist* (Hobart) 7 Feb. 3/2 They told us they were going to a **bark-chopper's** hut. 1848 *Arden's Sydney Mag.* Oct. 107 Many of the harbours which abound along the southern coast of the colony were frequented by sealers, whalers, and **bark cutters**. 1853 *Austral. Gold Digger's Monthly Mag.* v. 187 By begging or **bark cutting** they obtain money. 1848 *Adelaide Miscellany* 21 Oct. 183/1 The ruthless stripping knife of the **bark gatherer**, and the eager search of the gum collectors. 1849 A. HARRIS *Guide Port Stephens* 43 He had better, if possible, secure the services of a few blacks: they are capital **bark-getters**, but usually strip off merely the butt sheet from the tree as it stands. 1844 *Portland Mercury* 1 May 2/2 Monthly list of persons who have taken out **bark** and timber **licenses** for the District of Portland Bay. 1833 *Trumpeter* (Hobart) 15 Oct. 203 For Sale. A **Bark Mill**, complete, on the most improved principle. 1845 R. HOWITT *Impressions Aust. Felix* 148 These loiterers were the **bark-peelers**, their wives and children .. enjoying the sea-breeziness of a fine cheery Australian Sabbath. 1829 *Sydney Monitor* 23 May 1613/2 'The **barkstrippers**' may be numerous as a class in the Colony; but one thing we know, they do not strip enough bark to tan all the shoes that are consumed in the Colony. 1881 A.C. GRANT *Bush-Life Qld.* II. 156 Owing to the long dry season, the boys found **bark-stripping** exceedingly arduous work.
3. Applied to dwellings or buildings made of bark: **bark gunyah, humpy, school.**
1847 *Portland Guardian* 1 Mar. 4/4 Having erected a **bark gunnee** as token of possession, the squatter's next measure is to hasten away unto the Commissioner of Crown Lands, and put in his application for the run. 1851 *Empire* (Sydney) 3 May 2/4 The increased desire for squatters to make themselves contented, and the rumours of nice brick cottages which are superseding the 'bark gunyahs'. 1872 C.H. EDEN *My Wife & I in Qld.* 281 Every man has an innate desire to own some place .. even though that home may be only a **bark humpie**. 1895 *Worker* (Sydney) 20 July 4/1 Bill and Jim and Joe went to the old **bark school** through Long Gully and over the Gap.
4. Special Comb. **bark hut.**
a. *Obs.* A name given by colonists to a temporary shelter constructed by an Aboriginal.
1793 J. HUNTER *Hist. Jrnl. Trans. Port Jackson* 60 We sometimes met with a piece of the bark of a tree, bent in the middle, and set upon the ends, with a piece set up against that end on which the wind blows... These bark huts (if they deserve even the name of huts) are intended .. for those employed in hunting.
b. A dwelling of which the walls and roof are made of bark.
1810 E. BENT Let. 30 July II. 192, I mean to .. make the Stockmen build themselves a Bark Hut.

barking, *ppl. a.* Used in the names of various animals to describe the sounds they produce or are supposed to produce, esp. **barking bird** *obs.*, barking owl; **gecko, lizard,** any of several lizards, esp. the thick-tailed gecko *Underwoodisaurus milii* of s. Aust.; **owl,** the owl *Ninox connivens* of all exc. the arid parts of Aust.; SCREAMING-WOMAN BIRD; WINKING OWL; **spider,** see quot. 1976.
1844 L. LEICHHARDT *Jrnl. Overland Exped. Aust.* 25 Oct. (1847) 23 The stillness of the moonlight night is not interrupted by .. the monotonous note of the **barking-bird** and little owlet. 1962 B.W. LEAKE *Eastern Wheatbelt Wildlife* 105 The **barking gecko**, about four inches long, differs from other lizards and goannas by its habit of barking softly when disturbed. 1916 *Bulletin* (Sydney) 31 Aug. 24/3 Binghi will have nothing whatever to do with .. the 'weelitcha' or **barking lizard**. 1844 L. LEICHHARDT *Jrnl. Overland Exped. Aust.* 20 Nov. (1847) 47 The glucking-bird and the **barking-owl** were heard throughout the moonlight nights. 1896 B. SPENCER *Rep. Horn Sci. Exped. Central Aust.* I. 130, I was also especially anxious .. to watch the so-called '**barking spider**' in its natural state. 1976 B.Y. MAIN *Spiders* 78 *Selenocosmia* [*stirlingi*] is the legendary

barking spider or **whistling spider** of inland Australia... Although the spider does apparently produce a whistling sound its 'bark' was more likely attributable to .. quails which frequent the same localities.

bark painting. A picture painted on bark, traditionally that of the stringybark *Eucalyptus tetrodonta*, as part of the ceremonial of Arnhem Land Aborigines; now a widely practised Aboriginal art form. Also *attrib.*
1897 T. WORSNOP *Prehistoric Arts Aborigines* 37 A copy of a bark painting from Port Essington natives is figured in one of the volumes of the Linnean Society of New South Wales. **1983** *Canberra Chron.* 31 Aug. 5/1 Students demonstrated Aboriginal bark-painting techniques.

bark ringer. *Obs.* RING BARKER.
1894 J.K. ARTHUR *Kangaroo & Kauri* 24 A station of 100,000 acres may have for two or three months in the year 15 to 20 bark-ringers at work.

bark-ringing, *vbl. n. Obs.* See RING-BARK *v.*
1926 *Illustr. Tasmanian Mail* (Hobart) 6 Jan. 59/4 Early spring is the best season for wholesale bark-ringing.

barley grass. [Transf. use of U.S. *barley grass* meadow barley: see DAE.] Any of several annual grasses bearing seeds in awned spikelets, esp. naturalized species of *Hordeum.*
1846 *Sydney Morning Herald* 8 Dec. 2/6 Along the banks of the Narran, the grass is of the very best description, *Panicum laevinode* .. (barley-grass .. of the colonists) growing on plains or in open forests... The seeds of the *Panicum laevinode* constitute the chief food of the natives, who bruise these seeds between stones, and bake the dough into cakes. **1955** STEWART & KEESING *Austral. Bush Ballads* 204 There spear-grass grows, and barley-grass, And crow-foot green and high.

barmaid's blush. See quot. 1970.
1912 *Huon Times* (Franklin) 3 Apr. 6/2 The plaintiff urged that he could not have been drunk because he had swallowed nothing beyond 'barmaid's blush'. **1970** W. FEARN-WANNAN *Austral. Folklore* 32 Usually in old-time bushmen's meaning, a drink of rum and raspberry is a Barmaid's Blush.

barney, *n.* [Br. dial.: see OED(S and EDD.] A dispute or altercation; a fight.
1858 *Bell's Life in Sydney* 30 Jan. 2/4 After the usual bit of *barney* that follows a mistake. **1981** *Business Review* (Sydney) 11 Jan. 2/3 Andrew Peacock is planning to pull-on a barney with the unions. If he wins the face of industrial relations may never be the same again.

barney, *v.* [f. prec.] *intr.* To dispute or argue. Freq. as *vbl. n.*
1861 *Bell's Life in Sydney* 9 Nov. 2/4 After considerable 'barneying' the dusky darling was induced to retire. **1947** V. PALMER *Hail Tomorrow* 63 No more barneying with pannikin bosses about the length of a smoko or whether the sheep's wet or dry.

barra /'bærə/. Abbrev. of BARRAMUNDI.
1900 *Bulletin* (Sydney) 1 Sept. 15/1 When a 'barra' is hooked he strives hard to entangle the line. **1981** P. RICE-CHAPMAN *Food at Top End* 10 Probably the fish most associated with the Top End is barramundi, known colloquially as Barra.

barrack, *n.*[1] Freq. *pl.* [Spec. use of *barrack* a building for the accommodation of troops.]
1. *Hist.*
a. A building or set of buildings for the temporary accommodation of convicts; *convict barrack*, see CONVICT B. 3. Also *attrib.*
1826 *Colonial Times* (Hobart) 6 May, Malcolm Laing Smith, Esquire, to act as Barrack Master. **1842** *Austral. & N.Z. Monthly Mag.* 48 His rations and his lodgings are the same .. in the great barrack his bed either of wood or iron, a straw pallet under, and a common rug over him.
b. A building or set of buildings for the temporary accommodation of immigrants.
1841 *Hunter River Gaz.* 11 Dec. 3/4 Shortly before we left Sydney we happened to pass the Immigration Barrack yard, and overheard, in spite of ourselves, the conversation of a knot of these immigrants. **1852** S. SIDNEY *Three Colonies Aust.* 244 We were received in the Immigration Barracks.

2. BACHELORS' QUARTERS.
1876 *Austral. Town & Country Jrnl.* (Sydney) 9 Sept. 422/3 To the barracks also were relegated those just too exalted for the men's hut, while not eligible for the possibly distinguished company occasionally entertained at 'the cottage'. Such were cattle-dealers, sheep buyers, overseers of neighbouring stations, and generally unaccredited travellers whose manners or appearance rendered classification hazardous. **1942** J. DEVANNY *Killing Jacqueline Love* 3 A hundred yards from the house the low wooden barracks, the home of the overseer and jackeroo and occasional workmen.

barrack, *n.*[2] [f. BARRACK *v.*] Banter; provocative or derisive language.
1892 *Bulletin* (Sydney) 5 Nov. 17/2 While in her guileless presence he ceased to chew or swear, He knew the kind of barrack that can fetch a square affair. **1948** V. PALMER *Golconda* 60 His flood of good-humoured barrack made the newcomers feel at home.

barrack, *v.* [Prob. Br. dial. (N. Irel.) *barrack* to brag, to be boastful of one's fighting powers: see EDD and OEDS. It is unlikely that there is any connection with BORAK.]
1. *trans.* To ridicule, jeer at, verbally abuse (a person, etc.). Also *absol.*
1878 [see *barracking, vbl. n.*]. **1887** G. WALCH *Victorian Jubilee Bk.* 32 That's what I meant by actin' fair, not fightin' and barrackin' one another. **1892** A.B. PATERSON in C. Semmler *World of Banjo Paterson* (1967) 130 And if you want to get your two eyes knocked straight into one, go and 'barrack' against the land of Erin.

2. *intr.*
a. With **for**: to give support or encouragement to (a person, team, etc.), usu. by shouting names, slogans or exhortations. Also *trans.* (see quot. 1892).
1890 *Bull-Ant* (Melbourne) 8 May 14/1, I alwus barrack fer the club I put my stuff on, an' .. I'd backed the South for a tanner. **1892** A.B. PATERSON in C. Semmler *World of Banjo Paterson* (1967) 129 The Australians impartially barracked both sides.
b. *transf.* To argue or agitate for (a cause, etc.).
1897 A. HAYWARD *Along Road to Cue*, For the lawyer chaps to speak, The coves in wigs that barrack for the drunks. **1909** *Truth* (Sydney) 10 Jan. 1/5 Those barracking for a bridge across the harbor will have a walk-over when they get it.

Hence **barracking** *vbl. n.* and *ppl. a.*
1878 *Pilgrim* (Sydney) 2nd Ser. iv. 39 Douglass mumbled over a 'petition' .. for the edification of assembled roughs and larrikins; but was received with noisy insult and cries of 'cheese your barrickin' and 'shut up'. **1884** *Austral. Tit-Bits* (Melbourne) 26 June 14/2 The umpire .. was grossly insulted by some of the 'barracking' rowdies.

barracker. [f. BARRACK *v.*] One who barracks.
1889 *Bulletin* (Sydney) 6 July 8/2 (*caption*) Become a barracker in a Melbourne football club. **1979** K. DUNSTAN *Ratbags* 14 The barracker of the nineteen-seventies tended to be a bore.

barracouta. Also **barracoota.** [Transf. use of *barracuda, barracouta* a West Indian fish: see quot. 1843.] The sea fish *Leionura atun* of the fam. Gempylidae, widespread in southern waters, including those of s. Aust. and N.Z.; COOTA.

1835 J. BATMAN *Settlement in Port Phillip* 28 May (1856) 10 Two fine, long, bright, and well-tasted barracoutas, fish peculiar to the coast of Australia, were caught. **1837** J. BACKHOUSE *Extracts from Lett.* (1839) v. 3 Many barracootas were taken from the stern by large hooks baited with pieces of red rag. **1843** J.F. BENNETT *Hist. & Descr. Acct. S.A.* 47 Barracouta .. [*Note*] In Colonial parlance so called, from a supposed resemblance to that fish.

barramundi /bærə'mʌndi/. Also **barramunda**. [Prob. f. a Qld. Aboriginal language.] **a.** Any of several n. Austral. fish found in rivers, now chiefly *Lates calcarifer* of warm rivers and coastal waters from Japan to the Persian gulf and s. to W.A., N.T., and Qld., valued as food. **b.** LUNGFISH. **c.** Either of the osteoglossids *Scleropages leichhardti*, of n. N.T. and Qld., and *S. jardini*. Also abbrev. as BARRA.

1864 'E.S.H.' *Narr. Trip Sydney to Peak Downs* 28 There is also a fine large fish in the river, called by the aborigines 'Barramundi', which attains a weight of more than 20 lbs. **1880** A.C.L.G. GÜNTHER *Introd. Study Fishes* 357 The Barramunda is said to be in the habit of going on land, or at least on mud-flats; and this assertion appears to be borne out by the fact that it is provided with a lung. **1881** *Proc. Linnean Soc. N.S.W.* VI. 256 *Osteoglossum Leichardti* .. 'Burramundi' of the Aborigines of the Dawson River.

barrel, *v.* [Perh. f. (rifle-)*barrel* orig. in Austral. Services' speech.] *trans.* To kill, esp. by shooting; to knock down; to manhandle. Also *intr.*, and *fig.*

1966 S.J. BAKER *Austral. Lang.* (ed. 2) 169 *Barrel*, to shoot and kill. **1972** J. DE HOOG *Skid Row Dossier* 106 I'll barrel her... The only thing that stopped me shovin' her through the window was a charge of assault and breakin' and enterin'. **1977** *Cattleman* (Rockhampton) Mar. 2/3 Keep barrelling away at Government and get into every field of endeavour.

barrow, *v.* [Of unknown origin: perh. a Gaelic *bearradh* shearing, clipping.] *intr.* Of one learning to shear: to shear, or shear partially, a sheep (see quot. 1930). Freq. as *vbl. n.*

1887 *Gen. Rules* (Amalgam. Shearers' Union) 13 No 'barrowing' shall be permitted in any shed. [*Note*] 'Barrowing' means shearing done by persons other than those engaged to shear in the shed. **1930** *Aussie* (Sydney) May 27/3 In those blade days 'barrowing' was a most important institution. When the shearer knocked off for smoke-oh, a picker-up or other lad about the shed would take his shears over and learn to shear by taking the belly wool off the sheep in the pen, and perhaps trimming woolly legs. The shearer watched with good advice, and by the system of barrowing most youngsters turned into fine shearers.

Hence **barrower** *n.*

1911 5 *CAR* 107 None of the respondents shall permit 'barrowing' during 'smoke-ohs' or meal hours if it interfere in any way with the 'smoke-oh' or meal hour of any member of the claimant organization (other than the 'barrower').

bar-shouldered dove. The ground-feeding pigeon *Geopelia humeralis*, of n. and e. Aust. and New Guinea, having a brown back barred with black. Formerly **barred-shouldered dove.**

1844 J. GOULD *Birds of Aust.* (1848) V. Pl. 72, *Geopelia humeralis*. Barred-shouldered Ground-Dove .. Mangrove Pigeon. **1935** D. THOMSON *In Arnhem Land* 17 June (1983) 39 Shot a Bar-shouldered Dove—our only fresh meat for the day—a few mouthfuls each.

bart. *Obs.* Rhyming slang for TART.

1879 *Truth* (Sydney) 23 Dec. 5/4 Adores the fair sex... Lately spirited away Sol's 'bart'. **1900** *Western Champion* (Barcaldine) 26 June 16/1 He makes a dart ter see his 'bart', Goes on th' randy dan.

basement. *Obs.* [f. *basement* lowest storey, from the position of solitary confinement cells.] In prison speech: solitary confinement.

1919 V. MARSHALL *World of Living Dead* 33 He'd done lots o' basement, lots o' bread an' water, an' it hadn't killed him.

bash, *v.* [Transf. (often joc.) use of *bash* to strike.] *trans.* In various informal phrases, **to bash the spine** (**scrub**, etc.): see EAR-BASH, SCRUB-BASH, SPINE-BASH *v.*

1945 I.L. IDRIESS *Horrie Wog-Dog* 6 At our tent all the Rebels were 'bashing the spine', sprawled out in various attitudes of 'I don't care'. **1965** F. HARDY *Yarns of Billy Borker* 56 Always bashing their ear about how much money he was making, about having shares in the B.H.P., a barbecue in the backyard and a didee in the house. **1968** *Swag* (Sydney) i. 40/3 In temperatures around the 100 mark, the police shore the sheep, and bashed scrub to keep them alive.

Hence **bashing** *vbl. n.*

1920 *Land of Lyre Bird* (S. Gippsland Pioneers' Assoc.) 74 In the heavy blackbutt spar country a style of scrub-cutting, known as 'bashing' or 'wild-dog flash', was adopted after a few years.

basic wage. A standard minimum wage for an adult unskilled worker as determined by arbitration, orig. based on an assessment of living costs. Also *attrib.*

1911 5 *CAR* 14 There seems to be no doubt that the cost of living is increasing; but the evidence does not justify me in saying how much, or in altering the amount of what I may now call the basic wage by any definite sum. **1937** W. HATFIELD *I find Aust.* 205, I got a job painting, and was .. overjoyed to get on to something *supposed* to have a margin of skill in it and lift it above basic-wage labouring.

basket, *attrib.* and *n.*

A. Used *attrib.* in Special Comb. **basket fence**: see quot. 1890.

1872 G.S. BADEN-POWELL *New Homes for Old Country* 208 For sheep .. is made the 'basket fence'. Stakes are driven in, and then pliant 'stuff' interwoven, as in a stake hedge in England. **1890** A. MACKAY *Austral. Agriculturist* (ed. 2) 32 'Basket' Fence .. is made by driving five feet six inch stakes in the ground with mauls, to a depth of 9 to 12 inches, and four feet six inches apart; saplings from about two inches in diameter are then closely entwined with the stakes to a height of four feet six inches.

B. *n.* [Cf. U.S. *basket lunch, meeting, picnic*: see OEDS *sb.* B. 2.] PLATE. Also *attrib.*

1900 *Advocate* (Burnie) 3 Dec. 3/5 A Monster Picnic... Heads of families are requested to *provide 'baskets'*; the committee will find hot water and crockery. **1965** R.H. CONQUEST *Horses in Kitchen* 35 Bush dances were usually basket affairs. Married ladies brought baskets, in which were cakes and sandwiches.

bastard, *a.* and *n.* [Transf. use of *bastard* illegitimate child. The adjectival use is common elsewhere but produces some distinctively Austral. collocations. The weakened and generalized use of the noun is also widespread though often remarked on as characteristically Austral.]

A. *adj.* Incorporated in the names of some plants and animals which closely resemble their namesakes, as

bastard box, any of several rough-barked *Eucalyptus* trees; **dory,** any of several fish of Australian coastal waters (see quots.); **mahogany,** BANGALAY.
  1814 *HRA* (1916) 1st Ser. VIII. 222 The **Bastard Box** Bark No. 4 . . is very thick and hard.   **1896** F.G. AFLALO *Sketch Nat. Hist. Aust.* 225 The Old Wife of Port Jackson and elsewhere is a remarkable little member of the perch family. The names by which it is known in the Melbourne Market, 'Zebra-fish' or '**Bastard Dory**', are considerably more appropriate.   **1906** D.G. STEAD *Fishes of Aust.* 176 The Silver Dory (*Cyttus australis*) . . in Tasmania . . is known as 'Bastard Dory'.   **1827** *HRA* (1923) 3rd Ser. VI. 503 The Banks on both sides are covered with very large timber . . such as **Bastard Mahogany**.
  B. *n.*
  1. Used variously of a person; sometimes derogatory (but without any suggestion of illegitimacy), freq. good-humoured if sometimes edged. See quots.
  1892 *Bulletin* (Sydney) 26 Mar. 19/2 Here's the bleedin' push, me covey—here's a bastard from the bush!   **1918** C.E.W. BEAN *Official Hist. Aust. 1914–18* (1942) VI. 16 'Would yer, yer bastard!'—and you look out of the window and find that it is all spoken with a grin.   **1929** F. MANNING *Middle Parts of Fortune* I. 39 'Has anyone seen anything of Redmain?' 'Yes, sir,' cried Pike, with sullen anger in his voice. 'The poor bastard's dead, sir.'   **1961** L. GLASSOP *We were Rats* (ed. 3) 149 'G'day, ya old bastard,' said Jim, and I was amused again by the thought that the Tommies could never get used to our main term of endearment.   **1978** R.H. CONQUEST *Dusty Distances* 128 There are times when I even think the good bastards outnumber the bad bastards.
  2. Anything considered disagreeable or unpleasant.
  1919 V. MARSHALL *World of Living Dead* 12 Bastard, ain't it! Fer the love o' Gawd, give us a taste o' snout.   **1972** *Bulletin* (Sydney) 2 Sept. 50/1 A bastard of a Budget—for the next Treasurer.

bastardization. [f. *bastardize* to debase.] In some educational institutions: a college ritual of physical and psychological harassment, in which newly-enrolled students are required to perform certain (usu. humiliating) tasks.
  1964 *Bulletin* (Sydney) 6 June 22/2 Fourth Class cadets suffer what is known as 'bastardisation'. They have to listen to the 6.45 a.m. news and they may have to repeat this back at breakfast, item by item.   **1983** *Sydney Morning Herald* 13 Apr. 1/3 Bastardisation, or the systematic hazing of junior cadets, has been back at Duntroon for 10 years.

bastardry. Unpleasant treatment or activity: see quot. 1945.
  1945 S.J. BAKER *Austral. Lang.* 156 *Bastardry*, ill treatment, injustice, anything unpleasant, especially when done at the whim of a superior officer.   **1983** *Age* (Melbourne) 27 Oct. 13/3 People in the Kremlin . . will undoubtedly store up the Grenada episode as a good excuse for their future bastardry.

batch, *v.* Also **bach.** [f. U.S. *bach* to live as a bachelor: see OEDS *sb.* and *v.*] *intr.* To live on one's own, or provide for oneself, simply and without the usual domestic conveniences. Also **to batch it.**
  1882 W. SOWDEN *N.T. as it Is* 154 Supposing he lives in a hut and 'batches', this is the kind of bill he is confronted with.   **1892** G.L. JAMES *Shall I try Aust.?* 116 Boarding-houses soon spring up, where he can be very well fed at about 2s. daily; but, if he elects to 'batch' himself, I have heard many declare that they can live well for 7s. weekly.   **1914** C. MACKNESS *Gem of Flat* 11 Grandfather and child 'batched it' in the old house.   **1926** A.A.B. APSLEY *Amateur Settlers* 52 The farmer is 'baching'—that is to say, has no wife and is living, or rather camping on his block.
  Hence **batcher** *n.,* **batching** *vbl. n.* and *ppl. a.*
  1895 *Bulletin* (Sydney) 28 Sept. 27/1 The two Macks were the best '**batchers**' in the district; they were as neat and as careful of things as two old women.   **1931** *Bulletin* (Sydney) 1 Apr. 20/1, I think I'll sling this **batchin'** game, an' get meself a bride.   **1936** M. FRANKLIN *All that Swagger* (1980) 126 There was no such feast as at Wong's, but the baching was improved by rice and potatoes boiled in the one billy-can with the salt junk.

batch, *n.* Also **bach.** [f. prec. but prob. infl. by N.Z. *bach* a makeshift dwelling: see OEDS *sb.* 2 and quot. 1911.] A holiday house or WEEKENDER, often simple and freq. at the beach.
  [N.Z. **1911** *N.Z. Truth* (Wellington) 28 Jan. 6/1 A room in the 'batch' formerly occupied by Munn, whose belongings were still stored there.]   **1929** C.H. WINTER *Story of 'Bidgee Queen* 98 In seaside 'bach' or far-back pub.   **1978** *Overland* lvi. 19 They have what they call 'batches' (derived from bachelor and batching) which, in the main, are badly built weekenders.

bathers, *pl.* A swimming costume.
  1930 K.S. PRICHARD *Haxby's Circus* 230 If they went down the lakes to the coast perhaps they would find Mart and his mother there on the beach in bathers.   **1985** *Good Weekend* (Sydney) 7 Dec. 58/2 We fled through the gravelly school-yard down the back streets to snatch our bathers from home before mum knew what we were up to.

bathing togs: see TOGS.

Bathurst burr. [f. the name of a town in central N.S.W.] The S. American plant *Xanthium spinosum* (fam. Asteraceae), the spiny stems of which bear fruits covered with numerous slender hooked spines; the fruit of the plant.
  1853 *Moreton Bay Free Press* 1 Feb. 3/4 The Bathurst Burr is spreading widely in some stations on the Downs.   **1967** E. HUXLEY *Their Shining Eldorado* 191 Bathurst burr. It gets into the fleece and ruins the quality.

battery. *Mining.* A set of stamps used for crushing quartz. Also *attrib.*
  1858 *Colonial Mining Jrnl.* Sept. 11/3 The machinery used in crushing quartz consists of 3 batteries of 12 stamps each, and one of 8 stamps and a Chilian mill.   **1895** A.C. BICKNELL *Travel & Adventure Northern Qld.* 117, I hear the ring of the battery stamp, I guess I'm coming to a mining camp.

battery gang. *Hist.* [f. *battery* fortified gun emplacement + GANG.] A party of convicts assigned to labour in the construction of a (gun) battery.
  1801 *HRA* (1915) 1st Ser. III. 257 If a prisoner either makes the purchase or sells the article, he will be severely punished and work six months in the battery gang.   **1803** *Sydney Gaz.* 10 July, The Prisoner Dobson is to receive 100 Lashes, and to labour in the Battery-gang at George's Head.

battle, *v.*
  1. *intr.* Usu. of one with few natural advantages: to work doggedly and with little reward, to struggle for a livelihood, to display courage in so doing.
  1895 [see *battling, vbl. n.*].   **1896** H. LAWSON *In Days when World was Young* 40 But the men who never 'battle' always seem to travel aft.   **1978** D. STUART *Wedgetail View* 234 She battled on, poor, trapped, with a crook heart, and a mob of hungry kids to be fed and clothed and sheltered.
  2. Of an unemployed itinerant.
  a. *intr.* To seek to subsist, esp. while seeking employment.
  1897 *Worker* (Sydney) 11 Sept. 1/1 And while in search of shearing work he rides from hut to hut, He says he's merely 'battling' round and looking for a 'cut'.   **1965** R.H. CONQUEST *Horses in Kitchen* 113 We regarded giving

assistance to battlers as a sort of insurance, as there was always the chance we'd be battling ourselves some day.

b. *trans.* To obtain (sustenance or a means of subsistence) by the use of one's wits; to employ one's wits against (a person, etc.) to obtain sustenance. Also *intr.*

1902 H. LAWSON *Children of Bush* 88 They were tramping along the track towards Bourke; they were very hard-up and had to 'battle' for tucker and tobacco along the track. **1947** *Bulletin* (Sydney) 1 Oct. 28/3 A cove from the Marthaguy battled a hunk of corned beef from a Narromine butcher.

3. *intr.* To attempt to earn one's living at racecourses, esp. by punting (in a small way).

1895 [implied at BATTLER 3]. **1898** T. HAYDON *Sporting Reminisc.* 118, I don't believe there is another man living who can present such a healthy and youthful appearance after so many years of 'battling', and its attendant excitement. **1915** A. WRIGHT *Sport from Hollowlog Flat* 20 Battling on the pony courses for a living, soon began to pall.

4. *intr.* To work as a prostitute.

1898 [implied at BATTLER 4]. **1901** *Truth* (Sydney) 18 Aug. 5/3 After a few years of 'battling' in the Chow's baneful brothel, they were cast adrift to swell the ranks of the toe-rag crowd. **1912** L. ESSON *Red Gums* 37 All the tarts is waitin', Linin' Little Lon, In ther [*sic*] flashest clobber, Battlin' ter git on.

Hence **battling** *vbl. n.* and *ppl. a.*

1895 *Bulletin* (Sydney) 13 Nov. 27/2 Six long years' battling in the bush is not so very gay, And so I chucked the job and took once more the Sydney way. **1918** *Bulletin* (Sydney) 6 June 22/2 In the battling days I was operating a slaughter-yard for 'stags' and other game at an out-station on a Riverina squattage.

battle, *n.* [Back-formation from BATTLER 4.] In the phr. **to be on the battle,** to work as a prostitute.

1944 L. GLASSOP *We were Rats* 146 She tells me how she useter be on the battle... To think she'd been a chromo all the time! **1969** F.B. VICKERS *No Man is Himself* 17 She's charged with being on the battle.

battleaxe. *Obs.* [Fig. use of *battle-axe* weapon.] Rum.

1871 *Austral. Town & Country Jrnl.* (Sydney) 18 Mar. 335/2 To brace up his nerves with a drop of 'battle-axe', as the christening was conducted on strict temperance principles. **1899** P.W. MCNALLY *Life & Adventures* 30 Several good stockmen.. were made special constables... These 'specials' had a 'rare old time of it' in Roma, billiards and battleaxe being the game and the tipple.

battler. [f. BATTLE *v.*]

1. One who battles: see BATTLE *v.* 1. Also *attrib.*

1896 H. LAWSON *While Billy Boils* 26, I sat on him pretty hard for his pretensions, and paid him out for all the patronage he'd worked off on me.. and told him never to pretend to me again that he was a battler. **1970** *Bulletin* (Sydney) 14 Mar. 28/2 Battler pastoralists in the Northern Territory.. cannot see any cause to resist the Americans with bulging wallets.

Also *fig.*

1919 *Smith's Weekly* (Sydney) 15 Mar. 2/1 That remarkable battler, the sparrow, is to be met with in every part of the civilized world nowadays. **1968** D. O'GRADY *Bottle of Sandwiches* 128 But the chooks were really up against it... Real battlers.

2. Of an unemployed, or irregularly employed person.

a. In the country: a swagman or itinerant worker. See BATTLE *v.* 2 a.

1898 *Bulletin* (Sydney) 2 Apr. 14/3, I found patch after patch destroyed. Almost everyone I met blamed the unfortunate 'battler', and I put it down to some of the Sydney 'talent' until.. I caught two Chows vigorously destroying melon-vines. **1960** *N.T. News* (Darwin) 22 Jan. 6/3 Bella was a first-class bush cook and very generous in her handouts to many a battler travelling this district in the depression days.

b. In an urban context: an unemployed person who lives by opportunism. See BATTLE *v.* 2 b.

1946 F. CLUNE *Try Nothing Twice* 7 George was a great battler. His technique was to get us into a crowded tram, and wait until 'Mrs Fares-please' came. Then.. look pathetic, and tell the truth—'We haven't any money.' **1976** S. WELLER *Bastards I have Met* 100 He was a battler, into all the lurks about the place and just one jump ahead of the coppers all the time.

3. One who frequents racecourses in search of a living, esp. from punting. See BATTLE *v.* 3.

1895 C. CROWE *Austral. Slang Dict.* 7 Battlers, brokendown backers of horses still sticking to the game. **1936** A.B. PATERSON *Shearer's Colt* 8 The speaker was Dear Boy Dickson, turf urger, battler and general hanger-on at race-meetings.

4. A prostitute. See BATTLE *v.* 4.

1898 *Bulletin* (Sydney) 17 Dec. (Red Page), A *bludger* is about the lowest grade of human thing, and is a brothel bully... A *battler* is the feminine. **1978** R.J. RODDEWIG *Green Bans* 7 A battler was also the name given a woman who earned a few extra quid for her old man by sleeping around.

bauera /ˈbaʊərə/. [The plant genus *Bauera* was named by Joseph Banks (in Henry C. Andrews *Botanist's repository for new and rare plants* (1801) Pl. 198) after Austrian botanical artists Franz (1758–1840) and Ferdinand (1760–1826) *Bauer.*] Any shrub of the Austral. genus *Bauera* (fam. Saxifragaceae), of spreading habit and with wiry branches. Freq. *attrib.*

1801 H.C. ANDREWS *Botanist's Repository* III. Pl. 198, *Bauera rubioides.* Three-leaved Bauera. **1888** R.M. JOHNSTON *Systematic Acct. Geol. Tas.* 6 The Bauera scrub is met with in the wet flats along the stream courses. On open hill sides it is a tiny, beautiful shrub with soft verticillate leaf whorls and lovely pink and white blossoms.

bauple nut, var. BOPPLE NUT.

Bay. Usu. with **the.**

1. *Obs.*

a. BOTANY BAY 1.

1841 J. WARD *Diary of Convict* 113 The roll was called—and the gangs gone ashore; when we for Bay, as it is called were mustered into the Chapel, to wash... All the washing or wetting bustle is over; all the Bay men on Deck for inspection. **1857** *V & P* (Vic. L.A.) III. 86, I have scarcely more than one or two men to try at weekly visits out of my 1000 men; whereas in the Bay you see no end of it.

b. Special Comb. **bay ship,** a ship carrying convicts from England to Botany Bay.

1825 *London Mag.* May II. 49 When they first leave the hulks, every man pulls of [*sic*] his hulk dress, and has given him a fresh dress.. then goes on board the Bay ship.

2. Locally: an abbrev. of a place-name; a place by the sea.

a. Glenelg, S.A.

1883 *Adelaide Punch* 5 Jan. 422/1 At the Bay on the 28th... We went to commemorate the plantin' of the flagstaff by Capting Indmarsh. **1938** *South Australiana* (1963) Sept. 69 Recent shells were collected on the shores of St. Vincent Gulf at 'the Bay' as Glenelg was mostly called then, and at the Semaphore.

b. Port Phillip Bay, Vic.

1915 C.J. DENNIS *Songs of Sentimental Bloke* 81 We're honey-moonin' down beside the Bay. **1965** G. McINNES *Road to Gundagai* 115 In Melbourne.. a ship was.. just going 'down the Bay' to Queenscliff, Portarlington or Geelong.

c. Long Bay Gaol, Sydney.

1918 V. MARSHALL *Jail from Within* 16 'If yer lucky yer might get a bite at the Bay tonight,' said the officer with brutal unconcern. 1974 ADAMSON & HANFORD *Zimmer's Essay* 29 Long Bay Penitentiary is the largest prison in New South Wales... There are three reasons for the high turnover in The Bay.

Bay of Biscay, *attrib.* and *n.* [f. the popular association of stormy seas with the *Bay of Biscay*.]

A. *attrib.* Terrain of heavy clay soils forming mounds and depressions, often linear in form; lattice GILGAI. Freq. as **Bay of Biscay country, ground.**

1854 C.H. SPENCE *Clara Morison* II. 231 The occasional interruptions caused by a bad gully or an awkward piece of 'Bay of Biscay ground'. 1944 M.J. O'REILLY *Bouyangs & Boomerangs* 124 There were a number of mud springs in very dangerous country. This is known as 'Bay of Biscay country'. It is a soft springy tract of swelling soil .. soft and silky smooth to touch, resembling Fuller's earth in quality and consistency. It bears a rough appearance; to walk on it is soft and silent, leaving a clear imprint as in snow. The soil does not drift, wind has no influence on it.

B. Rarely, as *n.*

1901 O. OSBORNE *Golden Jubilee* 8 And in the Bay of Biscay bogged Some teamsters were delayed for weeks. 1933 *Bulletin* (Sydney) 20 Dec. 34/1 The alternation of wet seasons or floodings on the one hand and of droughts on the other induces characteristic alternations of depressions and rises in heavy soils. These have received various local names, of which melonhole, gilgai, Bay of Biscay, devil-devil and crab-hole are the most frequently met.

bay whale. *Hist.* The southern right whale *Eubalaena australis*.

1820 *HRA* (1921) 3rd Ser. III. 458 In June, July and August the Bay or Black Whale Fishery is best carried on. That is the season when the whales come into the Bays to Calve.

bay whaler. *Hist.* a. One engaged in bay whaling. b. A boat used for bay whaling.

1867 *Australasian* (Melbourne) 12 Jan. 37/3 My first acquaintance with the bay-whaler was made at St. Paul's Island, or Amsterdam Island. *Ibid.* 2 Feb. 132/3 The coasts of New Zealand presented great attractions to the bay whalers.

bay whaling, *vbl. n.* and *ppl. a. Hist.* Whaling from shore stations; engaging in this.

1837 W.B. RHODES *Whaling Jrnl.* 6 May (1954) 102 The season .. would be far advanced for Bay Whaling. 1838 T.H. JAMES *Six Months S.A.* 45 Men who have been discharged from the bay-whaling gangs, on the coast, and have come up to Adelaide to spend their wages.

beachcomber. *Pearling.* [Spec. use of *beachcomber* one who seeks a subsistence living on a beach: see OED(S.)] See quot. 1907.

1907 A. MACDONALD *In Land of Pearl & Gold* 289 The poorer class of pearlers are termed 'beachcombers' by their more fortunate fellows. 1940 E. HILL *Great Austral. Loneliness* (ed. 2) 242 Taking out a beach-comber's licence and a permit to employ native labour, you hire an old lugger at Broome for £1 a month .. and set out for where you fancy 'up east'.

beacher. *Surfing.* A wave which a body-surfer rides to the beach.

1930 *Surf: All about It* 10 The gentle art of scraping your nose .. on the sand of the beach itself, is in both senses of the word, the high-water mark of surfing. But don't, for this reason, imagine that the glory of the Beacher is reserved for a chosen race of experts alone. 1956 S. HOPE *Diggers' Paradise* 166 The beacher .. takes you from deep water right to the shallows.

beakie. [Cf. *half-beak* any of various garfish (see OED).] Any of several GARFISH, esp. *Hyporhamphus australis* of coastal waters in Qld. and N.S.W., *H. ardelio* of Qld., N.S.W., Vic., S.A., and W.A., and *H. melanochir* of s. Aust.

1924 LORD & SCOTT *Synopsis Vertebrate Animals Tas.* 42 The Sea Garfish .. is often referred to as the 'Beakie' in New South Wales. 1983 *Canberra Chron.* 14 Dec. 18/4 Best bet is that it was a .. yellowfin, but a beakie could not be ruled out at this time of the year.

beal, var. BULL *n.*[1]

bean tree. Any of several trees bearing podded seeds, esp. *black bean* (a) (see BLACK *a.*[2] 1 a.) and some species of *Erythrina* (fam. Fabaceae) incl. STUART'S BEAN TREE; the wood of these trees. Freq. *attrib.*

1861 J.M. STUART *Explorations in Aust.* 4 Apr. (1865) 265 After crossing the range, we found the bean-tree in blossom; it was magnificent. I have obtained a specimen of it; also some beans, a number of which were of a cream colour; we have roasted a few of them, and find that they make very good coffee. *c* 1960 C. MACKNESS *Clump Point & District* 5 Most roots and seeds were macerated in running water to free them of poisonous elements. The big beans from the bean-tree pod were treated thus, after a preliminary roasting.

bear. *Obs.* [Transf. use of *bear* any of several large mammals of the genus *Ursus*, to which the Austral. animal displays a fancied resemblance.] KOALA 1.

1827 *Monitor* (Sydney) 30 Mar. 363/1 A small paddock is enclosed .. for a menagerie, and we have in it .. the Bear found in the mountains. 1911 I.A. ROSENBLUM *Stella Sothern* 49 She heard the mopoke and the bear complaining against fate.

bearded dragon. The lizard *Amphibolurus barbatus* of e. Aust., having large spiny scales on the throat pouch and other parts of the body; JEW LIZARD 1. Also **bearded lizard.**

1861 *Catal. Natural & Industr. Products N.S.W.* 136 Lizards .. the Bearded ditto. 1909 LUCAS & LE SOUEF *Animals of Aust.* 228 The Bearded Dragon is usually found on the ground or fallen trees, or on fences.

beardie. *Hist.* Also **Beardy.** A nickname for a follower of John Wroe (1782–1863), founder of a sect called the Christian Israelites, who visited Australia several times between 1843 and his death in Melbourne in 1863. Chiefly in *pl.* Also *attrib.*

1851 *Empire* (Sydney) 9 Sept. 135/5 A party of Israelites, Beardies, Southcotarians or by whatever signification they may be known .. have just left for Sydney with 75 oz of clean gold. 1967 F.T. MACARTNEY *Proof against Failure* 13 Music was provided by a brass band, consisting of the male members of a sect who, as their religion prohibited them from cutting any of their hair, each had a coil of it on his head, surmounted by a large belltopper hat peculiar to themselves. They were known as the Israelites, but we boys called them the Beardy-bucks.

beaut, *n.* and *a.* [Abbrev. of BEAUTY. Recorded earliest in U.S.: see OEDS.]

A. *n.* Abbrev. of BEAUTY *n.*

1898 M. CANNON *That Damned Democrat* (1981) 13 He is known as a 'Beaut' by his scavenging, slabbering [*sic*], suckless face. 1978 SAW & MILBANK *Back to back Tango* 1 I'd be crazy to pretend that what I had going with National was anything but a marvellous job. It was a beaut.

B. *adj.* Exciting admiration; pleasing, satisfying. Also as *exclam.* (cf. BEAUTY *a.*).

1983 *Weekend Austral. Mag.* (Sydney) 29 Oct. 12/5 The rugged 'you beaut' oddities expected from this strange southern continent.

beauty, *n.* and *a.* Also **beaudy, bewdy.** [Generalized use of *beauty*: see OED(S (esp. 5 and 7).]

A. *n.* Anything outstanding of its kind.

1852 J. BONWICK *Notes of Gold Digger* 34 A bullock driver spied a nugget at the foot of a tree; he scratched up a handful of beauties. 1978 SAW & MILBANK *Back to Back Tango* 56 'Turn on the booze,' I said. 'And don't forget it's on the house.'. . 'You little bloody bewdy,' said the biggest bikie. 'Free piss.'

B. *adj.* Good, pleasing, esp. as an exclamation of approval or satisfaction.

[N.Z. 1960 N. HILLIARD *Maori Girl* 80 Beauty, boy! room to myself.] 1968 F.J. THWAITES *Sky full of Thunder* 100 'How's our tucker going?' 'Will be ready soon.' 'Beauty—'. 1972 *Bulletin* (Sydney) 3 June 17/2 That used car ad with Ron Frazer saying 'Beaudy'.

beaver rat. *Water rat*, see WATER.

1861 'OLD BUSHMAN' *Bush Wanderings* 51 We used to kill a large species of water rat, which we called the *Beaver Rat*. 1981 WATTS & ASLIN *Rodents of Aust.* 67 Water-rats from south-western Australia are dark.. and are commonly known as the 'sooty beaver rat'.

bed. *Tas. Obs.* A stand of trees.

1871 *Mercury* (Hobart) 5 Apr. 2 The piners have to go some 15 or 20 miles up the Davey River to the timber beds. 1911 *Huon Times* (Franklin) 14 Jan. 3/2 How much blue-gum is there? There are some fine beds back in the hills, and you can always get it down hill.

bed claim. *Mining. Hist.* [f. *bed* river bottom + CLAIM.] A claim, part or all of which is situated in the bed of a river or creek. Also *attrib.*

1851 *Empire* (Sydney) 8 Dec. 443/2 Heavy and continuous showers, with thunder, have again sunk the hopes of the bed-claim diggers, who are now flocking either to the mountains or the metropolis. 1867 *Illustr. Sydney News* 16 Feb. 123/3 Down among the bed claims and working ground fringing the river, diggers began to cluster like bees.

Hence **bed claimant** *n.*, one who works a bed claim.

1851 *Bell's Life in Sydney* 20 Dec. 2/3 The hopes of the bed-claimants.

Bedourie /bəˈduri/. [The name of a town in s.w. Qld.]

1. A dust storm: see quot. 1954.

1931 D.B. O'CONNOR *Black Velvet* 29 And the warm Bedouries blowing Stir the dust eternally? 1954 H.G. LAMOND *Manx Star* 257 *Bedourie*, a storm from the west which brings dust and sand, no rain.

2. A type of camp oven: see quot. 1960. Also *attrib.*, esp. as **Bedourie dish, (camp) oven.**

1936 C.T. MADIGAN *Central Aust.* 94 It is usual to carry a small, pressed steel, camp oven, the 'Bidourie'. 1946 — *Crossing Dead Heart* 19 Another item of camp equipment peculiar to Australia.. is the Bedourie camp oven, a flat round pressed-steel oven. 1960 B. HARNEY *Cook Bk.* Camp ovens.. have been largely supplanted by Bedourie ovens, which were first made in West Queensland. Bedourie ovens are made of steel, so that you could put a Bedourie on a packhorse and, if the horse bucked and threw its pack, the steel oven would not break as the old brittle cast-iron pots did. 1975 D. STUART *Walk, trot, canter & Die* 44 Joe brought out sugar and a yeast loaf that showed the shape of the Bedourie dish.

beech. [Transf. use of *beech* a forest tree of the genus *Fagus*, incl. *F. sylvatica.*] Any of several trees, esp. of the genus *Nothofagus* (fam. Fagaceae); the wood of these trees. Often with distinguishing epithet, as **antarctic beech,** *N. cunninghamii* and *N. moorei*; **deciduous beech,** *N. gunnii* (see TANGLEFOOT); **myrtle beech** (see MYRTLE 1); **negrohead** (or **niggerhead**) **beech,** *N. moorei* of n.e. N.S.W. and s.e. Qld.; **white beech,** any of several trees of the genus *Gmelina* (fam. Verbenaceae), esp. *G. leichhardtii*.

1790 J. HUNTER *Hist. Jrnl. Trans. Port Jackson* (1793) 390 The live-oak, yellow-wood, black-wood, and beech, are all of a close grain. 1884 A. NILSON *Timber Trees N.S.W.* 78 *Negrohead Beech.*—A beautiful tree, attaining a height of 150 feet and a diameter of 4 feet. 1892 W.H. WARREN *Austral. Timbers* 11 *Gmelina Leichhardtii*.. Beech, or White Beech, of New South Wales (found also in Queensland). *c* 1910 W.R. GUILFOYLE *Austral. Plants* 177 *Fagus* Gunnii.. 'Deciduous Beech' (shrub, 5 to 8 ft.)—Tas. 1933 H.J. CARTER *Gulliver in Bush* 88 The many rotten logs of the nigger-head beech (*Nothofagus*). 1938 C.T. WHITE *Princ. Bot. Qld. Farmers* 152 Nothofagus, the so-called Antarctic or southern beeches. They are of interest botanically, as representative of the so-called Antarctic element in the Australian flora.

beef. [Archaic in Br. Eng. but common in U.S.: see OED(S *sb.* 3 b.]

1. A bull, cow, or steer, esp. one reared for human consumption. Freq. *attrib.*

1873 *Illustr. Sydney News* 16 Apr. 4/1 The style of house.. is a common one at an out-station. To the left is the yard and that necessary appendage the beef gallows. 1977 *Caravan World* Jan. 63/2 On the beeves that were dried out, no good horns. Where there were good horns there was still too much meat attached to them.

2. Special Comb. **beef road,** an all-weather road built for trucking cattle from remote areas.

1962 *N.T. News* (Darwin) 1 Sept. 5/1 The Government's big road construction program since 1956–57 had included a special beef roads project to improve roads serving the higher-carrying country and so boost beef exports.

beefer. BEEF 1.

1945 *Bulletin* (Sydney) 27 June 14/1 We pass a paddock in which a few Angus beefers graze. 1964 B. WANNAN *Fair Go, Spinner* 67 Twenty 'beefers' were slaughtered for each meal.

beef tree. BEEFWOOD.

1845 J.O. BALFOUR *Sketch of N.S.W.* 40 To these may be added.. the tree named by the colonists, from a peculiarity in the grain, beef tree, Australian maple, and black wood. 1931 MRS E.P. HALFORD *Pioneers of Yesterday* 16 Good beeftree, saltbush, grass, and native geranium grow well in this jumble of hills.

beefwood. [See quot. 1885.] **a.** The tree *Grevillea striata* (fam. Proteaceae) of drier Australia; its timber. **b.** Any of several other trees having similar wood, esp. *Stenocarpus salignus* (fam. Proteaceae) and some species of the fam. Casuarinaceae. Also *attrib.*

1803 Banks Papers 9 May VII. 192, I have also sent a quantity of our Beefwood, or She-Oak to Sir E. Nepean. 1805 *Ibid.* 7 Jan. XX. 129 A species of Casurina [*sic*] different to that of Port Jackson (called the Beefwood) and I think equally beautiful. 1885 *Once a Month* (Melbourne) June 455 A tree, known as beefwood, is widely distributed. The wood is dark red, with a purple tinge, coarse-grained, and soft. 1976 C.D. MILLS *Hobble Chains & Greenhide* 40 Mick carried his swag over to a great, fallen beef-wood log this night.

beer-chewer. A heavy drinker of beer. Also **beer-eater (-guzzler, -sparrer, -sucker).** Also **beer-chewing** *vbl. n.* and *ppl. a.*
   1891 'SMILER' *Wanderings Simple Child* (ed. 3) 81, I called him a 'beer-eater', and thought him a mean-spirited cur. 1907 *Bulletin* (Sydney) 28 Feb. 15/3 Seventeen beer-chewers went into a Winton (Q.) bar the other day, and came out an hour later, having .. surrounded 28 drinks each. *Ibid.* 19 Sept. 39/1 There was not a solitary beer-sparrer to help him dissipate the cheque. 1912 *Truth* (Sydney) 28 Jan. 12/2 That foul, beer-chewing skunk I was speaking of. 1929 *Bulletin* (Sydney) 26 June 23/4 Here's my entry for the beer-chewing championship. . . Three swipers for a wager consumed respectively 45, 44 and 42 ordinary glasses of beer. 1965 *Kings Cross Whisper* (Sydney) Jan. 5/3 He has entered for Sydney's Best Beer-Guzzler title and is flat out to clinch a place in the finals. 1971 D. IRELAND *Unknown Industr. Prisoner* 231 Have you mob ever thought of the inhabitants of this pretty little earth before we started brewing beer on it? . . Just picture them, you beer-suckers.

beer-up. A beer-drinking party or session; a 'booze-up'.
   1919 W.H. DOWNING *Digger Dialects* 10 *Beer-up*, a drunken orgy. 1978 K. GARVEY *Tales of my Uncle Harry* 62 We had a good beer-up at the pub that night.

before, *prep. Obs.* In the phr. **before the gold** (or **diggings**), prior to the discovery of gold in Australia.
   1855 G.H. WATHEN *Golden Colony* 22 The discovery of gold in Victoria forms the great epoch in its history, to which all events are referred, as having happened 'before' or 'after the gold'. 1891 J. FENTON *Bush Life Tas.* (1964) 77 The circumference of a sovereign 'before the diggings' had a very much wider gauge than it has now.

beggar. [Prob. familiar or playful use of *beggar*: see OED *sb.* 6 b.] In the phr. **beggar on (the) coal(s),** a small damper (see DAMPER 1). Formerly also **beggar-in-the-pan.**
   1847 G.F. ANGAS *Savage Life & Scenes* I. 161 Our cook had not been idle: there were 'dampers', 'dough-boys', 'leather-jackets', 'johnny-cakes', and 'beggars-in-the-pan', awaiting our arrival, for in the Australian bush, flour and water are transformed into a variety of shapes, designated by as many colonial appellations. 1848 C. COZENS *Adventures of Guardsman* 141 There is another sort of bread made when in a hurry, called 'beggars on the coal', which is made very thin like our girdle-bread, and merely placed on the hot ashes, and afterwards turned. 1902 R.C. PRAED *My Austral. Girlhood* 45 If the ashes be not properly prepared, the Johnny-cake will be heavy and no longer a Johnny-cake; it is then a 'Leather-jacket', or it is a 'Beggar on coals', when little bits of the sticks are turned into charcoal and make black marks on the dough.

beg-pardon. [f. the phr. *to beg pardon* to excuse (oneself): see OED *v.* 3.] An expression of apology; esp. in the phr. **no beg-pardons,** without concern for the niceties.
   1906 E. DYSON *Fact'ry 'Ands* 137 'Twas quick business down below here, 'n' no beg-pardons with Bunyip. 1974 D. STUART *Prince of my Country* 122, I just want him to accept the fact that he's half blackfeller, half white feller and be a strong enough character to make everyone else accept it without any beg pardons.

behind. *Australian National Football.*
   1. a. *Hist.* The kicking of the ball over the *behind line*, a 'near miss' (see quot. 1876). **b.** A scoring kick that earns one point (see quot. 1925); the score itself.
   1866 *Australasian* (Melbourne) 28 July 523/2 The umpires are instructed to count the number of times the ball is driven behind goal; and in the event of no goal, or one goal by each being obtained, the side obtaining the greater number of 'behinds' should be declared the winners. 1876 T.P. POWER *Footballer* 9 A struggle for it results in it being seized by a nimble player, who kicks it forward, where a friend awaiting, if he can, kicks it towards the goal-posts, outside which it goes, and within the 20 yard posts, and the goal umpire calls 'Behind!' This is looked upon as an honor for the attacking team, though nothing counts in the game but goals. 1888 *Australasian* (Melbourne) 23 June 1373/4 M'Inerney .. added a behind just before the first bell sounded. The visitors had up to this scored only one behind to Carlton's 2 goals 5 behinds. 1925 *Laws of Football* (Australasian Football Council) 4 A behind shall be won when the ball passes over the line drawn between the goal posts after being touched by any player or touches either of the goal posts, or is kicked or forced over the line drawn between the goal posts and behind posts.
   2. Special Comb. **behind line,** the line between the goal post and the behind post; **post,** either of a pair of posts, in line with and flanking the goal posts.
   1930 W.S. SHARLAND *Sporting Globe Football Bk.* 24 The space occupied by the goal-line and the **behind lines** in all makes twenty-one yards. 1925 *Laws of Football* (Australasian Football Council) 4 Should the ball touch a **behind post** it shall be out of bounds.

belah /bəˈlɑː/. Also **belar, billar.** [a. Wiradhuri *bilaarr.*] Any of several trees or large shrubs of the fam. Casuarinaceae with slender jointed branchlets and woody cones, esp. *Casuarina cristata* of drier regions of Aust. Also *attrib.*
   [1798 D. COLLINS *Acct. Eng. Colony N.S.W.* I. 612 *Bil-larr*, a spear with one barb, cut from the wood. 1834 J.S.C. DUMONT D'URVILLE *Voyage de Découvertes: Philologie* 11 Casuarina. *Bela.*] 1862 H. KENDALL *Poems & Songs* 18 A voice in the beela grows wild in its wail. 1887 W.H. SUTTOR *Austral. Stories Retold* 117 On the low-lying, black, flooded land, the belar, a species of native oak or casuarina, is found, casting so dense a shade as to prevent all other vegetation from showing. 1986 *Trees & Natural Resources* Mar. 7 (caption) Belah woodland in sound condition.

bell, *n.* Used *attrib.* in the names of animals and birds having calls which resemble the sound of a bell: **bell frog,** a frog of the genus *Litoria,* esp. *L. aurea,* a green species with patches of brown or gold, found in or near water in coastal N.S.W.; **magpie,** any of the three species of CURRAWONG; **miner,** BELLBIRD 1.
   1834 G. BENNETT *Wanderings N.S.W.* I. 138 The peculiar sound uttered by that species known by the name of the '**bell frog**' is . . very similar to a sheep-bell. 1916 S.A. WHITE *In Far Northwest* 45 The liquid call of the **bell magpie** .. was heard far on ahead of us. 1900 A.J. CAMPBELL *Nests & Eggs Austral. Birds* 417 The **Bell Miner** is .. gregarious to an extent, living in companies in certain restricted areas.

bell, *v.* [See OED *v.*⁵ 1.] *trans.* To furnish (a grazing animal) with a bell, so that its whereabouts remain known.
   1882 A.J. BOYD *Old Colonials* 68 As soon as the animals were attended to, hobbled and belled, the billies were slung on the fire. 1942 W. GLASSON *Our Shepherds* 8 Six big wethers, all having shown some signs of independent leadership when the mob was let out to graze, would be 'belled'.
   Hence **belled** *ppl. a.*
   1959 C. & E. CHAUVEL *Walkabout* 12 The ringing of the bells is only intermittent and quite like the sound which 'belled' horses make when feeding.

bellbird. [Cf. BELL *n.*]
   1. The bird *Manorina melanophrys* (fam. Meliphagidae) of woodlands in s.e. Aust., typically living in

colonies and maintaining contact by frequent calls; *bell miner,* see BELL *n.*

1799 D. COLLINS *Acct. Eng. Colony N.S.W.* (1802) II. 91 The melancholy cry of the bell-bird (dil boong, after which Bennilong named his infant child). **1980** F. MOORHOUSE *Everlasting Secret Family* 43 Bellbirds could send you demented, too, the incessant single note.

2. *Crested bellbird,* see CRESTED.

1843 J. GOULD *Birds of Aust.* (1848) II. Pl. 81, *Oreoica gutturalis*.. Bell-bird, Colonists of Swan River. **1960** *Bulletin* (Sydney) 6 July 16/3 Next to cuckoos, the chief patron of hairy-caterpillars is the crested bellbird... Every self-respecting bellbird actually stocks its nest with 'stingarees' and other such larvae.

bellowser. *Obs.* [Br. dial. *bellowser* a violent blow or hard task which takes one's breath away: see EDD.] A sentence or term of transportation for life; one who serves this.

1812 J.H. VAUX *Mem.* (1819) II. 225 *Wind,* a man transported for his natural life, is said to be *lag'd for his wind,* or to have *knap'd a winder,* or *a bellowser,* according to the humour of the speaker. **1844** *Parramatta Chron.* 29 June 2/1 What is termed in colonial phraseology a 'Bellowser' vulgo, a transport for life.

bell sheep. A sheep secured by a shearer just before the bell rings to signal the end of a period of work.

1897 *Bulletin* (Sydney) 20 Feb. 3/2 And rip 'em through and yell for 'tar' and get the bell-sheep out. **1918** *Truth* (Sydney) 1 Dec. 10/2, I, together with thousands more of roussies, would like to see this whistle or bell sheep business knocked on the head.

belltopper. [f. *bell,* from the shape of the crown + *topper* top hat.] Any of various types of tall hat. Also **belltopper hat.**

1858 C.R. THATCHER *Colonial Songster* (rev. ed.) 64 Who can cut it jolly fat, Without a mag, on Ballarat, Wear a bad belltopper hat? **1872** Mrs E. MILLETT *Austral. Parsonage* 87, I was the only woman whom Isaac had ever seen in a black beaver riding-hat, of the shape commonly called in the colony a 'bell-topper'.

Hence **bell-toppered** *a.,* wearing a belltopper.

1874 *Adelaide Observer* 26 Dec. (Christmas Suppl.) 40/1 The now buttoned and bell-toppered page.

belly. *Timber-getting.* [Spec. use of *belly* the front, inner, or lower surface as opposed to the *back.*] A scarf or notch cut in that side of the trunk facing the direction in which the tree is intended to fall. Also *attrib.,* esp. as **belly cut, scarf.**

1848 *Maitland Mercury* 26 July 1/6 Making a 'belly' in the timber.. means cutting that side of the tree to which it leans and on which side it is calculated it will most likely fall. **1909** R. KALESKI *Austral. Settler's Compl. Guide* 55 The 'belly' scarf is cut first so that the tree won't fall on the cutter; if he wants to commit suicide he cuts the 'belly' last. **1916** *Bulletin* (Sydney) 8 June 24/3 When referring to the cut made by axe or saw, they spoke of it as the 'belly-cut' or the 'back-cut'.

belly board.

1. See quot.

1960 K. SMITH *Word from Children* 156 The soapbox has gone; in its place is a flat piece of something for lying on going down hills; this is called a 'belly board'.

2. *Surfing.* [Used elsewhere but recorded earliest in Aust.] A short surf-board, ridden in a prone or kneeling position. Also *attrib.*

1964 *Surfabout* (Sydney) I. vi. 17 Lee has been riding a belly board for many years. **1967** *Ibid.* IV. iii. 13 Though belly-board riding has reached a degree of sophistication, it is just entering a new phase of development in what the board and its rider are able to do.

belly-buster. A dive in which the front of the body strikes flatly on the water, a 'belly-flop'. Also **belly-thumper** and *fig.*

1941 S.J. BAKER *Pop. Dict. Austral. Slang* 9 *Belly-buster,* a bad fall, an ungainly dive into water. Also 'belly-flopper'. **1968** S. GORE *Holy Smoke* 51 You'll come a big belly-thumper if you don't watch out!

belly wool, *n.* Wool shorn from the belly of the sheep. Also *ellipt.* **belly** (chiefly in *pl.*).

[N.Z. **1851** F.A. WELD *Hints intending Sheep-Farmers* 10 Their mothers do not lose the belly-wool as they would do by lambing in spring.] **1871** *Austral. Town & Country Jrnl.* (Sydney) 18 Mar. 331/2 Sheep that strip at the points, and lose the belly-wool, having a clean head without topknot. **1928** C.E. COWLEY *Classing Clip* 45 The wool that has good length, is bulky and comparatively light in condition, will constitute the leading line. The balance will make up the bellies.

belly-wool, *v.* [f. prec.] *trans.* To shear the underside of (a sheep). Also *ellipt.* as **belly** (in quot. as *vbl. n.*).

1902 *Bulletin* (Sydney) 1 Feb. 16/2 The shearers had men belly-woolling their sheep. **1930** D. COTTRELL *Earth Battle* 123 Fifty rams and wethers.. had been flyblown, and needed shearing round the belly and horns—'wigging and bellying' as it was called.

belt. *Surf life-saving.* The wide canvas belt with line attached worn by the member of a surf life-saving team who swims to the rescue. Usu. in Comb., as **belt man, belt (and line) race.**

1914 *Newcastle Morning Herald* 14 Nov. 6/2 Another bather, whose name was not ascertained, and N. Mason, went to his assistance, the former putting on the belt. **1942** M.L. MACPHERSON *I heard Anzacs Singing* 21 First comes the belt-man whose task it is to swim out, carrying the line to the drowning person. *Ibid.* 23 There are boat races, belt-and-line races, 'chariot' races. **1964** *Austral. Surf Life Saving Competition Handbk.* (Surf Life Saving Assoc. Aust.) (ed. 4) 14 For dead-heats in belt races, the beltmen concerned shall be required to no-contest the event on the same day.

Belyando spew /bɛljændoʊ 'spju/. [f. the name of a river in central Qld.] *Barcoo sickness,* see BARCOO A. 2. Also *ellipt.*

1889 R.B. ANDERSON tr. Lumholtz's *Among Cannibals* 58 *Beliander* is also a common disease in Queensland; without the slightest apparent cause, a person is suddenly seized with vomiting, but is relieved just as suddenly. **1976** B. SCOTT *Compl. Bk. Austral. Folk Lore* 375 The worst of the lot Is the Bellyando Spew.

bencher. BENCHMAN.

1904 *Bulletin* (Sydney) 2 June 16/1 But the bencher jams the billets 'gainst the saw with all his might.

benchman. In a saw-mill: the employee responsible for feeding the log or length of timber being cut through the saw.

1895 *Bulletin* (Sydney) 3 Aug. 3/2 Few know the song—for the tailer-out, And the benchman swart and his underlings, and the truckerman, and the trammer stout, Have their souls in the flitch and in wooden things. **1984** *Canberra Times* 16 Jan. 9/1 Working as a top-line benchman at several mills.

bend, *n.* [U.S. *bend* a tract of land within a bend of a river: see DAE *n.* 1 b.] The land bordered by a curve in a river.

1860 *Trans. & Proc. R. Soc. Vic.* (1861) 142 Points of land or 'bends' of the river. **1905** H. LAWSON *When I was King* 85 She loved me! And why? Ask the she-oaks that sighed in the bends.

bend, *v.* [Spec. use of *bend* to turn from a straight line.] *trans.* To head off and turn back (a mob of stampeding cattle). Also as *n.* (see quot. 1923).
1923 *Six Austral. One-Act Plays* (1944) 9 By gum, tho', look at the old bloke putting a bend on them. He's got them... Wheeled 'em a treat... You should have seen him bending that mob. **1951** E. HILL *Territory* 293 Sometimes they ring in midstream, or scatter when they reach the bank, which makes adventurous riding, gallop and smash through the scrub to 'bend' them.

bendee /bɛn'di/. Also **bendi**. [Perh. f. a Qld. Aboriginal language.] The tree of Qld. and N.T. *Acacia catenulata* (fam. Mimosaceae), found on shallow stony soils and (usu.) having a deeply-fluted trunk; the wood of the tree.
1881 W. FEILDING *Austral. Trans-Continental Railway* 18 The road enters a scrub .. of 'bendee'. **1911** ST. C. GRONDONA *Collar & Cuffs* 69 Bendi, as a very thick scrub is called, is almost impenetrable... It is most awkward if the stock you are after take it into their heads to investigate the interior of a patch of bendi.

benjamin. *Obs.* [Prob. transf. use of the name of the patriarch Jacob's youngest son, hence a favourite son: see OEDS.] See quot. 1870.
1870 C.H. ALLEN *Visit to Qld.* 183 With the black people a husband is now called a 'benjamin'... All white men are called 'Willy', all white women 'Mary'. **1909** E. WALTHAM *Life & Labour in Aust.* 66 While these gins are occupied in searching for their daily food, the 'Warriors' and the 'Benjamins' are out hunting in the Bush.

Bennett's wallaby. [Applied as the specific epithet *Bennetti* by English naturalist G.R. Waterhouse (*Proc. Zool. Soc. London* (1837) 103) after E.T. Bennett (1797–1836), secretary of the Zool. Soc. London.] The brownish-grey wallaby *Macropus rufogriseus rufogriseus* of Tas. and Bass Strait islands. Formerly also **Bennett's kangaroo.**
1838 *Proc. Zool. Soc. London* 137 In Bennett's Kangaroo there are twenty-four caudal vertebrae. **1986** *Austral.* (Sydney) 18 Feb. 3/2, 18 animals—eastern grey and red kangaroos and bennett's wallabies—at the Barringo Wildlife Reserve near Gisborne, 85 km. north-west of Melbourne.

berdan. [Of unknown origin.] '*Berdan*, a circular revolving iron inclined pan in which concentrates are ground with mercury and water by an iron ball' (H.A. Gordon *Mining & Engineering* (1906), 576.). Also *attrib.*
1901 O. OSBORNE *Golden Jubilee* 5 Cornish buddles and berdan That saved sludge gold so fine. **1939** I.L. IDRIESS *Cyaniding for Gold* 200 The job can also be done in a Berdan pan.

berg. *Obs.* [a. G. *berg* mountain.] See quot. 1839.
1839 T.L. MITCHELL *Three Exped. Eastern Aust.* (rev. ed.) II. 90 Having experienced on this journey the inconvenient want of terms relative to rivers, I determined to use some of those recommended by Colonel Jackson in his able paper on the subject, in the Journal of the Royal Geographical Society for 1833, as I might find necessary. They are .. *Berg*—*bergs* heights now at some distance, once the immediate banks of a river or lake. **1867** F.J. BYERLEY *Narr. Overland Exped. Northern Qld.* 14 Leichhardt describes the stream .. as stony, and with conical hills .. near the river banks, 'Bergues' running into it on each side.

berley, *n.* Also **burley**. [Of unknown origin.]
1. Ground-bait.
1874 *N.S.W. Rep. R. Comm. Fisheries* (1880) 1292 The bait should be crabs. It is usual to wrench legs and shell off the back, and cast them out for berley. **1909** F.E. BIRTLES *Lonely Lands* 61 His mode of fishing was to camp near a homestead and at an opportune moment approach the fowl run, scatter a handful of breadcrumbs over the fence and drop his well-baited line among the 'burley'.
2. *fig.*
1903 *Truth* (Sydney) 30 Aug. 1/4 The public have already had more than a bellyful of this Bartonian bunkum; they're not taking any more Bartonian burley, thank you. **1972** J. FINGLETON *On Cricket* 24 Hall gave Favell a loose one outside the off-stump for 'burley' and to take his attention away from his leg trap.

berley, *v.* Also **burley**. [See prec.] *trans.* To scatter ground-bait on (the water), in order to attract fish. Also *absol.*, esp. as **berley-up.**
1852 G.C. MUNDY *Our Antipodes* I. 388 The first operation was the baiting of the spot—locally termed 'burley-ing'—with burnt fish. **1975** *Meanjin* 186 I'm not tempted, said Kit, By dry-fly or wet. And one never berleys a flood. **1978** J. ROWE *Warlords* 206 Let's burley-up on the reef here and see what comes sniffing about.

Berry blight. *Hist.* [f. the name of Graham *Berry* (1822–1904), Victorian politician.] A name given to a period of economic depression in the Colony of Victoria: see quot. 1886, and also *Black Wednesday* BLACK $a.^3$
1879 *Australasian* (Melbourne) 4 Jan. 16/4 The year that is gone .. will be painfully memorable hereafter as the sinister epoch of Black Wednesday and the 'Berry blight', and it has acquired an evil pre-eminence for acts of political turpitude in which we hope it will stand alone. **1886** R.C. SEATON *Six Lett. from Colonies* 36 Mr Berry is a well-known Radical politician. It is about six years ago since, in one day, he dismissed the greater number of Civil servants in consequence of a disagreement between the two Houses. Most of them had to be quickly restored to their places, but public confidence was so much shaken by this arbitrary act that a large amount of capital was transferred to New South Wales... This period is known as the Berry-blight.
Also **Berryism** *n.*, **Berryite** *n.* and *a.*
1878 *Australasian* (Melbourne) 9 Feb. 178/4 The Queensland papers had been unanimous in opposing **Berryism**. **1879** *Victorian Rev.* Nov. 45 The ruling principle of the **Berryite** system. **1905** J. FURPHY *Rigby's Romance* (1946) 70 I'm Berryite to the bone; and Binney's tarred with the same stick as yourself—with this difference, that he's a sound Conservative, and you're a rotten one.

best, to give (someone, something): see GIVE 2.

betcherrygah, var. BUDGERIGAR. Also **betshiregah.**

bettong /'betɒŋ/. [a. Dharuk *biduŋ*.] A rat-kangaroo, esp. either of two small species of the genus *Bettongia*, *B. penicillata* of drier regions of s. Aust., and *B. gaimardi* of s. and e. Aust.; SQUEAKER 3. See also WOYLIE.
1802 Banks Papers 1 June VIII. 103 Betong. I think this is the one with the slender tail. **1986** *New Scientist* (London) 6 Feb. 27 Lesser-known species such as the .. burrowing bettong are truly endangered, but are ignored.

betty. *Obs.* [Transf. use of *betty* bar used to force a door or window.] An instrument for picking locks; a skeleton key.
1812 J.H. VAUX *Mem.* (1819) 156 *Betty*, a picklock; to *unbetty*, or *betty* a lock, is to open or relock it, by means of the *betty*, so as to avoid subsequent detection. **1882** *Sydney Slang Dict.* 1 *Betty*, skeleton key, or picklock.

bewdy, var. BEAUTY.

beyond. [Spec. use of *the back of beyond* humorous phr. for a distant place: see OED *beyond* quasi-*sb.* b.] In the phr. **back of** (or **o'**) **beyond,** (country) far inland, remote from large towns or closely settled districts. Also used adverbially. See BACK COUNTRY *n.* 5.
 1888 'R. BOLDREWOOD' *Robbery under Arms* (1937) 149 You'll mostly find that these far-out-back-of-beyond places have got men and women to match 'em. 1974 P. ADAM SMITH *Desert Railway* 21 Port Augusta is Beyond. Anywhere beyond this is truly Back o' Beyond.

beyond the black stump: see BLACK STUMP.

beyond the boundaries: see BOUNDARY *n.*

beyond the limits: see LIMITS.

beyond the limits of location: see LOCATION 4.

bib. [Fig. use of *bib* upper garment.] In the phr. **to push (put, stick) one's bib in,** to interfere; **to keep one's bib out,** to refrain from interfering.
 1952 T.A.G. HUNGERFORD *Ridge & River* 57 Here was Wilder . . sticking in his bib. 1959 S.J. BAKER *Drum* 89 *Bib in,* any interference, any action of a busybody, esp. in the phrases stick one's bib in, put (or push) one's bib in. 1974 BLAZEY & CAMPBELL *Political Dice Men* 201 Askin 'thanked the pussy-footing Victorians to keep their bib out of New South Wales politics'.

Bible-basher. [Cf. *Bible-pounder:* see OEDS. Used elsewhere but recorded earliest in Aust.] A clergyman; a religious zealot. Also **Bible-banger.**
 1904 *Bulletin* (Sydney) 21 Jan. 16/3 The clerical calling gathered a rich store of opprobrious appellations from irreverent Australians. Some that I have heard: Sky-pilot, devil-dodger, gospel-puncher, snuffler, amen-snorter, bible-banger. 1958 R. STOW *To Islands* 74 They were Bible-bashers and humourless clods.
 Hence **Bible bash** *v. intr.,* **Bible-bashing** *ppl. a.*
 1944 L. GLASSOP *We were Rats* 124, I doan want any bible-bashing bastard who's never seen me before mumblin' any bull– over me. 1967 H. SAINT-THOMAS *Night of Long Shadows* 117 The cow, always Bible bashing.

biccies, bickies, varr. BIKKIES.

bidgee-widgee. [Altered form of N.Z. *biddy-biddy* burr of the piripiri, a. Maori *piripiri:* see OEDS *biddy-biddy.*] Any of several creeping perennial herbs of the genus *Acaena* (fam. Rosaceae) having a burr-like fruit, esp. the widespread *A. novae-zelandiae* and related species; BUZZY.
 c 1910 W.R. GUILFOYLE *Austral. Plants* 390 Bidgee-widgee *Acaena Sanguisorbae.* 1980 J. WOLFE *End of Pricklystick* 30 The bidgee-widgee plants threw their deep-green creepers over the land and a million little stems shot up from the creepers. Each stem carried a green, spiked ball that looked something like a sea-urchin.

big, *a.*
 1. a. *Austral. pidgin.* Great in size, quantity, duration, importance, or intensity, esp. in the collocations **big fellow, mob, one.**
 1840 J.P. JOHNSON *Plain Truths* 17 The natives appeared equally afraid of the horses and bullocks, which they called big dogs. 1867 W. MILTON *Victim Nineteenth Century* 23, I heard the blacks talking very much about '*big one emu*', meaning the camels, from which I inferred that Burke had crossed the Murray, and very likely the Darling by this time. 1870 C.H. ALLEN *Visit to Qld.* 182 'Big fellow waddy', a large quantity of wood. 1968 S. GORE *Holy Smoke* 16 God's make 'im all this one country longa you. Make 'im land, make 'im sea—big mob water.
 b. *Obs.* **big one** (used advb. with (*ppl.*) *a.*), very, extremely.
 1856 W.W. DOBIE *Recoll. Visit Port-Phillip* 91 The ground was *big one* hard, and his back was *big one* tired. 1872 'RESIDENT' *Glimpses Life Vic.* 191 'Me big one frightened.' [*Note*] 'Big one' signifies in the black's English 'very' or 'very much'.
 2. [Orig. *pidgin.*] **big smoke,** a town or city.
 1848 H.W. HAYGARTH *Recoll. Bush Life* 6 He gradually leaves behind him the 'big smoke' (as the aborigines picturesquely call the town). 1975 T. SCHURMANN *Shop!* 129 There were men from the city and the world outside, who returned to the big smoke every weekend and actually went to see the big games of football.
 3. [Prob. strongly influenced by sense 1.]
 a. In collocations implying (a person's) superiority: **big bloke, boss, cog, fellow, man, squatter,** a powerful or successful person.
 1916 *Bulletin* (Sydney) 6 July 24/1 Here are a few of the pet names given by the wielder of the pick and banjo to the ganger: 'The red light', 'the **big bloke**', [etc.]. 1964 P. ADAM SMITH *Hear Train Blow* 151 He . . said his father was no longer the '**big boss** cocky'. 1925 *Bulletin* (Sydney) 12 Mar. 22/3 In south-west Queensland many station managers are known as 'the **big cog**'. This title was originally earned by Clement Ladbury, of Milo, who explained to a station-hand that everyone working on the place was a 'cog in the machine'. 'And I,' he added, 'am the big cog.' 1907 *Ibid.* 14 Nov. 15/2 The managers of tin sluicing and dredging concerns . . are all called, irrespective of size, 'the **Big Feller**'. 1911 R.G.S. WILLIAMS *Austral. White Slaves* 99 But when those five million acres were abandoned by '**big men**' in the Western division of New South Wales how many small men took their places? 1845 *Port Phillip Gaz.* 4 June 2 We cannot see that the '**big**' **Squatters**—as the phrase goes—have any right to claim any more than is just sufficient for their stock.
 b. In collocations describing a tract of land or type of vegetation distinguished by extent or dimension: **big bush, country, paddock, sand, scrub, timber**.
 1909 *Bulletin* (Sydney) 8 Apr. 43/1 We was special settlers, an' we had a hundred acres of **big bush**. 1968 *TV Times* (Sydney) 28 Aug. 8/1 A new half-hour programme dealing with the big issues that confront people living outside the cities. Titled A **Big Country**. 1937 M. TERRY *Sand & Sun* 26 We would wander in the **Big Paddock** where Jackey, the black-fellow, is still King. 1899 *Bulletin* (Sydney) 9 Dec. 19/2 On the further edge of the **Big Sand** is a hut. 1881 R. CRAWFORD *Echoes from Bushland* 102 There's a **big scrub** right a-head! 1904 *Bulletin* (Sydney) 13 Oct. 18/2 Smith was a settler far out in mountainous **big-timber** country.
 c. In collocations denoting the duration or severity of seasonal phenomena: **big blow, dry, rain, wet**.
 1944 J. DEVANNY *By Tropic Sea & Jungle* 3 That's the **big blow** season. 1942 L. & K. HARRIS *Lost Hole Bingoola* 51 The long rainless season which the natives called the '**big dry**' had begun. 1903 *Bulletin* (Sydney) 3 Jan. 16/2 A **big rain** is magnified under glaring head-lines in the daily press. 1927 M. DORNEY *Adventurous Honeymoon* 95 We would never have got through before the '**big wet**'.
 d. In miscellaneous collocations denoting greatness of extent, dimension, or number: **big fence,** see quot.; **house** [orig. U.S.: see OEDS *big house* 1], the homestead on a sheep or cattle station; **mob,** a large number (of animals or people); a large quantity; **ring,** a game played with marbles; **spit,** the act of vomiting; esp. in the phr. **to go for the big spit,** to vomit; **stoush,** see STOUSH *n.* 2.
 1940 E. HILL *Great Austral. Loneliness* (ed. 2) 57 He is a rider of the **Big Fence,** the only fence in the world that cuts a continent into two mighty paddocks—the Number One Rabbit Proof. 1881 A.C. GRANT *Bush-Life Qld.* I. 57 'There,'

said Stone, pointing to the **big house**, 'nobody has lived in the *cawbawn humpy*—that is what the blacks call it—since Mr Cosgrove went away.' **1951** E. HILL *Territory* 328 A glass of beer and a counter-lunch at a 'billabong' nearby, and they are off . . to watch the **'big mobs'** galloping past like a bang-tail muster. **1947** M. RAYMOND *Smiley gets Gun* 44 Blue joined them and suggested a game of marbles. They chalked a rough circle on the wooden floor of the shed and started to play **big-ring**. **1959** *R.A.N. News* (Sydney) 20 Mar. 4 Down in the Strait The wave rolled high The waves rolled wide And the **'Big Spit'** starters lined the side. **1960** J. WYNNUM *Sailor Blushed* (1962) 85 He retired to the stern-sheet, and without any ceremony, 'went for the big spit' into the darkness in the lee of the launch.

e. *Australian National Football.* In collocations denoting height: **big man**, a tall player, esp. a FOLLOWER; **ones, sticks** *pl.*, the goal posts (see STICK *n.* 1).

1920 *Australasian* (Melbourne) 8 May 911/2 Hiskens, a **big man** and strong, a younger brother of a famous football family, hailed from Rutherglen. **1979** *Herald* (Melbourne) 7 Sept. 2 *It's through*: A score worth six points. . . Bisects the **big ones**—Right through the centre: Likewise. Bangs it through the **big sticks**: Ditto. **1981** L. MONEY *Footy Fan's Handbk.* 37 *Terms for a goal*: . . Bangs it through the big sticks!

Big Brother. [Fig. use of *big brother* elder brother.] A member of a voluntary organization founded in 1925 to provide foster-care for British youths emigrating to Australia. Also **Big Brother Movement** (or **Scheme**).

1925 *Youth* (Big Brother Movt.) 2 The Big Brother Movement is founded upon the belief that the outstanding need of Australia is more population. **1926** F.M. SKY *Our most Important Problem* 4 Mr Henry E. Budden . . gave . . an address on the Big Brother movement, and in response to his appeal . . readily signified, in writing, their willingness to become a 'Big Brother'. **1986** *Bulletin* (Sydney) 18 Feb. 58/3 The Hawke government's first Immigration and Ethnic Affairs Minister . . put a stop to the Big Brother scheme under which British youngsters were brought out to Australia as settlers.

big-note, *v. refl.* In the phr. **to big-note** (oneself), to display or boast of one's wealth; to exaggerate one's own importance.

[**1950** *Austral. Police Jrnl.* Apr. 111 *Big-note man*, wealthy.] **1953** K. TENNANT *Joyful Condemned* 23 'Morton the bustman!' Rene sneered. 'Listen to him big-note himself. He's going to do a bust.' **1983** *Age* (Melbourne) 2 June 1/2 He agreed that Mr Farquhar was egotistical, a name-dropper and frequently big-noted himself.

Hence **big-noter** *n.*, one who tries to impress others.

1967 *Kings Cross Whisper* (Sydney) xxxii. 6/3 *Big noter*, a braggart who uses money to impress birds.

bike. [Fig. use of *bike*, abbrev. of *bicycle*.]
1. See quot. 1945.
1945 S.J. BAKER *Austral. Lang.* 123 A willing girl is sometimes described as *an office bike, a town bike*, etc. **1981** *Nat. Times* (Sydney) 5 Apr. 38/3 Girls at school were called 'slut', 'dog', and 'bike' for sleeping with anyone.

2. In the phr. **to get off** (or occas. **on**) **one's bike,** to become angry.

1938 X. HERBERT *Capricornia* 565 Don't get off your bike, son. I know you're tellin' lies. **1986** *Sydney Morning Herald* 12 Apr. 45/1 Magistrate Blisset is a fair magistrate and a 'good bloke'. 'I've never heard anyone get on a bike about him.'

bikie. [Abbrev. of *motor-)bike* (rider + -Y.] See quot. 1967.

1967 *Kings Cross Whisper* xxxii. 6/3 *Bikie*, a member of a gang or a club of people interested in motor bikes. **1984** *Open Road* Oct. 10/5 All he asked was that the motorist remember he had been 'helped by a bikie'.

bikkies, *pl.* Also **biccies, bickies.** [Facetious use of *bicky* biscuit.] Money.

1966 *Kings Cross Whisper* (Sydney) xx. 8/1 Here in Kings Cross cabbage means money, and so does . . lolly, bikkies and fat. **1975** B. DAWE *Just Dugong at Twilight* 7, I reckon now I've got it made: My Earth Dynamics thesis in, There'll be more biccies in the tin! **1981** *Canberra Times* 30 Oct. 2/7 We reckon the presence of a highly qualified academic in a tutorial is worth something in its own right, regardless of whether he or she actually says anything. . . Just showing up is worth big bickies.

bilby /'bɪlbi/. [a. Yuwaalaraay *bilbi*.] **a.** The rabbit-eared bandicoot *Macrotis lagotis*, a small, burrowing marsupial of woodlands and plains of drier parts of mainland Aust.; DALGITE. **b.** (Occas.) the smaller *M. leucura*, now rare and poss. extinct. See also *rabbit bandicoot, rat* RABBIT A. 1. Also *attrib.*

1885 *Once a Month* (Melbourne) May 376 There are several kinds of burrowing animals . . everywhere. . . The most remarkable is the Bailby—some call it Billby—about the size of a rabbit. **1896** T. HENEY *Girl at Birrell's* 14 'Possum and bilby-skin rugs. **1984** *Austral.* (Sydney) 12 July 3/1 It might sound like something from Tolkien, but the bilby is real.

Biljim, var. BILLJIM.

billabong /'bɪləbɒŋ/. Also formerly **billibong, billybong.** [a. Wiradhuri *bila* river + -*baŋ*, signifying a watercourse which runs only after rain; said to be orig. a place-name, with reference to the Bell River in s.e. N.S.W., but this is improbable.]

1. An arm of a river, made by water flowing from the main stream, usu. only in time of flood, to form a backwater, blind creek, anabranch, or, when the water level falls, a pool or lagoon (often of considerable extent); the dry bed of such a formation. Also *attrib.*

[**1836** T.L. MITCHELL *Three Exped. Eastern Aust.* (1838) II. 21 The name this stream receives from the natives here, is Billibang. **1848** *Port Phillip Herald* 15 Feb. 3/1 The cattle station of W. O'Sullivan, Esq., at Billy Bong forest. **1851** *Britannia* (Hobart) 13 Feb. 4/5 In the Billebong country, water is an unknown treasure.] **1853** J. ALLEN *Jrnl. River Murray* 31 This station is situated about half-a-mile inland, over a 'billy-bong' (the native name for a small creek or backwater). **1861** *Burke & Wills Exploring Exped.* 27 At the end of a very long waterhole, it breaks into billibongs, which continue splitting into sandy channels until they are all lost in the earthy soil. **1927** R.S. BROWNE *Journalist's Memories* 76 In the shearers' huts in the West, on mustering camps and at these little meetings of 'billabong whalers' where two or three were gathered together the name of 'Billy' Lane was reverenced. **1986** *Sydney Morning Herald* 26 Apr. 6/3 Wetlands in the upper Lachlan were usually linked to the river with billabongs, the remnants of earlier river channels, which formed lagoons with moderate to high river flows.

2. *transf.* and *fig.*

1895 *Bulletin* (Sydney) 23 Nov. 3/2 And down the beds of dried-up creeks they wandered all day long Till life seemed, in a trooper's view, one endless billabong. **1930** J.S. LITCHFIELD *Far-North Memories* 6 Their amazement at the harbour, which they described as a 'whopping big billabong', was very funny.

Hence **billabong** *v. intr.*, to follow a circuitous route in leisurely fashion, to meander; **billabonger** *n.*, a swagman.

1908 MRS A. GUNN *We of Never-Never* 1 It [*sc.* the train] was out of town just then, up-country somewhere, **billabonging** in true bushwhacker style, but was expected to return in a day or two. **1886** *Illustr. Sydney News* Dec. 33/3

The shearers grinned, and Sam the **Billabonger,** Whose noted points were ribaldry and beer, Exclaimed, when, after a protracted laugh he Could speak, 'The super, to an ephigraphy!'

billar, var. BELAH.

billet. [Transf. use of *billet* soldier's lodging place: see OEDS *sb.*¹ 4 b.]

1. A job, employment; a particular task (see quot. 1911); a sinecure (see quot. 1909). Also *fig.*

1843 *Adelaide Observer* 9 Dec. 4/1 If men have to walk ten or twelve miles to their labour .. it is not to be wondered at that they should fly off at a tangent, or look out for what they not inaptly term *a better billet.* **1887** *Bulletin* (Sydney) 26 Feb. 6/4 Already Sir Henry Parkes has found that the Premiership is not the very rosiest of billets. **1896** *Ibid.* 14 Mar. 27/2 One Barrier speculator-squatter has £50,000 looking for a billet. **1909** W.G. SPENCE *Aust.'s Awakening* 267 One Premier after another retired to a good fat billet. **1911** ST. C. GRONDONA *Collar & Cuffs* 112 My billet for that day was to boundary ride the seven-mile spring paddock. **1980** BRENNAN & WHITE *Keep Billy Boiling* 82 Times being bad I had to take a billet of boundary rider.

2. Comb. **billet-hunter, -seeker.**

1894 *Bulletin* (Sydney) 16 June 8/3 He was constantly worried by **billet-hunters. 1876** 'CAPRICORNUS' *Colonisation* 4 The youth of the colony crowding into the towns to become stock-jobbers and **billet-seekers.**

billeted, *ppl. a.* Orig. of convicts: quartered (see quot. 1850); having certain privileges in return for service.

1848 R. MARSH *Seven Yrs. of My Life* 88 There were five or six old hands, billited men, about the station, that would steal our cloths, and often we were punished for loosing them. **1850** W. GATES *Recoll. Van Dieman's Land* 130 There are usually at every station what are termed billeted men, who are prisoners that can work at such trades as blacksmithing, carpentry, masonry, &c. It is the law that they can work only for government. **1895** *Bulletin* (Sydney) 24 Aug. 7/3 The food sent in is overhauled by a 'searcher'— not a warder, but a 'billeted' prisoner—and—well good care is taken by him that I shall not grow fat from overfeeding.

Hence **billeter** *n.*

1847 *Hobart Town Herald* 6 Mar. 2/2 With 112 prisoners, billiters, to clean the rooms.

billibong, var. BILLABONG.

Billite. *Hist.* A supporter of the Constitution Bill, enacted as the Commonwealth of Australia Constitution Act by the Parliament of the United Kingdom on 9 July 1900.

1898 *Riverine Grazier* (Hay) 7 June 2/6 A band of billites, wearing badges, marched up Lachlan-street, singing. **1975** R. NORRIS *Emergent Commonwealth* 22 As the Billites defeated their opponents one must assume that the majority were readier to believe in them than in the anti-billites.

Billjim. *Obs.* Also **Biljim.** [Blend of the proper names *Bill* and *Jim,* a coinage of popular journalism.]

1. The typical Australian, the 'man in the street'.

[**1893** *Bulletin* (Sydney) 18 Nov. 20/4 Half the bushmen are *not* called 'Bill', nor the other half 'Jim'. We knew a shearer whose name was Reginald! *Ibid.* 31 Oct. (Red Page), The harrowing tale of the lost Bill or Jim in the Australian desert whose eyes are picked out by the crow almost before his death-struggle ceases.] **1898** *Ibid.* 12 Mar. 14/3 Billjim saddled his favourite cuddy about tea-time, pushed on, and struck the Bushman's Rest at dawn next day. **1907** *Lone Hand* Nov. 17 A certain man from anywhere, call him Biljim, .. leaves a sick mate at the Half-way Pub.

2. The typical Australian soldier of the 1914–18 war. Cf. the British 'Tommy (Atkins)'.

1915 *Truth* (Sydney) 28 Feb. 3/6 These exemplary young gentlemen are still doing the 'Block', either too proud to consort with Billjim, or too cowardly to risk their precious skins in defence of the country. **1961** C. McKAY *This is Life* 132 When the parties took to the hustings Thomas Joseph Ryan jumped on to the Digger bandwagon. He acclaimed 'Billjim', so he called the Digger, as the saviour of his country.

billy, *n.*¹ [f. Scot. dial. *billy-pot* cooking utensil, cf. *bally, bally-cog* milk pail: see SND.]

1. A vessel for the boiling of water, making of tea, etc., over an open fire; a cylindrical container, usu. of tin, enamel ware, or aluminium, fitted with a lid and a wire handle.

[N.Z. **1839** J. HEBERLEY Autobiogr. 87 [We] boiled the Billy and made some Tea out of tawa bark.] **1849** G.B. WILKINSON *Working Man's Handbk. S.A.* 79 Singing, near the wooden fire, is what is called the *billy*, or tea kettle. **1980** BRENNAN & WHITE *Keep Billy Boiling* 86 The 'billy', of course was synonymous with the Swagman and lost opportunities or maybe of opportunities that were never really there.

2. Abbrev. of *billy tea.*

1900 *Albury Banner* 5 Jan. 16/3 Farmers, selectors, and halves-men seem to care very little about comfort in their small shantys, as long as they get plenty of black billy, tough burnt chops, and half-baked bread.

3. Comb. **billy boy, -can, -full, tea.**

1944 *Bulletin* (Sydney) 19 July 13/3 By noon 300-a-day sheep-barbers were only pickers-up, while brickies who couldn't put away their thousand in eight and three-quarters were only **billy-boys.** *c* **1870** H. BAYLIS *Reminisc. Bush-Ranging Days N.S.W.* 9 A small fire was burning, on which was a **billy-can** half-full of tea. **1861** *Bell's Life in Sydney* 16 Nov. 2/5 Fifty-four ounces .. out of only just a **billy-full.** **1890** MRS R.D. DOUGLAS *Romance at Antipodes* 83 We had a small fire on which to boil our oddly-shaped tin tea-kettles, or billy cans, in order to make '**billy tea**'.

4. In collocations with a qualifying term: **black billy,** a fire-blackened billy; **Christmas billy,** a billy containing donated Christmas gifts, as distributed to Australian service personnel during the war of 1914–18; **rugged billy** *obs.,* an insulated billy.

1862 C. MUNRO *Fern Vale* II. 24 **Black Billy** .. a name applied by the diggers to the tin pot in which they boil their water. **1916** I.L. IDRIESS *Diary* 22 Dec. vi. 15 We are back with the regiment again. . . The **Xmas billies** have arrived, one each to a man. **1902** *Bulletin* (Sydney) 1 Feb. 16/2 The process of swathing billies in bagging is called 'rugging' (horsey term). Hence '**rugged billy**'.

5. a. In the phr. **to boil the billy,** to brew tea.

1839 [see BILLY *n.*¹ 1]. **1867** G. WALCH *Fireflash* 13 Our noble selves are grouped 'waiting for the billy to boil'. **1979** D. LOCKWOOD *My Old Mates & I* 154 We stopped beside a crystal-clear creek to boil the billy.

b. **billy-boiled** *ppl. a.,* **billy-boiler** *n.,* **billy-boiling** *vbl. n.*

1898 G. GARNET *Barrier Bride* 77 He took his cup of **billy-boiled** tea, too, from her hands, and deemed it nectar. **1957** F. CLUNE *Fortune Hunters* 44, I acted as **billy-boiler** and steak-griller. **1934** C. MACKNESS *Young Beachcombers* 82 It's up to us to go and help with the **billy-boiling** and the lunch.

6. In the phr. **to sling** (or **swing**) **the billy (kettle, pot),** to prepare to make tea, esp. as an act of hospitality.

1848 *Bell's Life in Sydney* 4 Mar. 1/2 Jack Jones and his good wife made much of us, slung the pot in double quick time. **1862** G.T. LLOYD *Thirty-Three Yrs. Tas. & Vic.* 125 Four or five times in one day .. was the over-welcome command, 'Spell O, and sling kettles', responded to. **1879** W.J.

BARRY *Up & Down* 9 The proprietor immediately 'slung the billy' and you were made welcome to 'Damper, mutton and tea'. **1928** M.E. FULLERTON *Austral. Bush* 119 The cracking of stock-whips among the tree-ferns near may cause the lonely hut dweller to 'swing the billy' on hospitable thoughts intent, for the approaching stranger who, however, fails to materialise.

billy, *n.*² *Obs.* [Abbrev. of BILLYCOCK.] A low-crowned hard felt hat.

1862 C. MUNRO *Fern Vale* II. 40 On his head stood erect a black cylindrical deformity, designated in the vulgar parlance of the colony, a 'Billy'.. but which he.. called a hat. **1867** J.R. HOULDING *Austral. Capers* 227 Some of the 'cabbage-tree boys' were there too, indulging in their favourite holiday rollick of knocking all the 'black billies' from the heads of the wearers.

billy, *n.*³ Shortened form of GREY BILLY.

1967 R.O. CHALMERS *Austral. Rocks* 313 The sapphire occurs principally in a wash consisting of fragments of basalt, 'Billy', sand, and clay.

billybong, var. BILLABONG.

billy buttons. Also as sing. [f. *billy*, dim. of *William*, popular name of some plants + *button* button-like flower.] Any of several herbaceous plants of the fam. Asteraceae, esp. of the genus *Craspedia*, having button-shaped or globular flower-heads; BACHELOR'S BUTTONS. Also *attrib.*

1909 *Bulletin* (Sydney) 4 Nov. 13/2 A Mulga mate of mine writes to say that there are wonderful expanses made yellow with everlastings and 'billy-buttons'. **1940** E. HILL *Great Austral. Loneliness* 304 Across vast plains of buck-bush, through a Mohammedan paradise of Billy Button daisies, yellow and white.

billycart. [Perh. f. *billy*(*goat* male goat + *cart*.] A small handcart, sometimes drawn by a goat; a go-cart.

1923 Anthony Hordern *Catal.* 304 Very Strong 2-wheel Billy Cart, Iron Axle and Wheels, long handle.. 17s. **1984** *Canberra Times* 11 Nov. 6/4 He graphically described the screech of billy-carts sweeping down Sunbeam Avenue and scything to the ground every one of Mrs Branthwaite's poppies.

billycock. *Obs.* [Br. *billycock* low-crowned felt hat; app. rare: see OED.] Any of several styles of round, low-crowned hat worn by men. Also **billycock hat.** See BILLY *n.*²

[N.Z. **1865** B.L. FARJEON *Shadows on Snow* 61 All are alike attired in rough jackets, moleskin trousers, and billy-cock hats.] **1867** J.S. BORLASE *Night Fossickers* 54 Billy-cock or cabbage-tree hats, blue or red serge suits. **1892** *Braidwood Dispatch* 17 Dec. 6/1 'Two hundred fiddlesticks!' shouted the wretched digger.. throwing down his battered billycock.

Billzac. *Obs.* [Blend of BILL(JIM + AN)ZAC.] BILLJIM 2.

1918 *Aussie: Austral. Soldiers' Mag.* Jan. 10/2 Home, the place or places where Billzac would fain be when the job is done. **1926** 'DRYBLOWER' *Verses* 22 When Billzac and his mates Belted the Huns.

bim: see BIMBO.

bimble box. [a. Wiradhuri *bimbil*.] The tree *Eucalyptus populnea* (fam. Myrtaceae) of N.S.W. and Qld., having a fibrous, brownish-grey bark and glossy green leaves. Also **bimble,** and *attrib.*

1839 T.L. MITCHELL *Three Exped. Eastern Aust.* (ed. 2) II. 55 The 'bimbel' (or spear-wood) which grows on dry forest land. **1953** *Bulletin* (Sydney) 28 Jan. 13/4 The bimble-boxes seemed hung with leaves of glass. **1961** *Ibid.* 29 Mar. 42/1 A flock of Happy Jacks ran merrily and noisily up and down the bimble-box trees.

bimbo. [U.S. *bimbo* fellow, chap: see OEDS.] A male companion, esp. a homosexual. Also abbrev. **bim.**

1961 X. HERBERT *Soldiers' Women* 208 Got a Yank in tow too... Well, are you going anywhere particular with your bimbo? **1978** D. STUART *Wedgetail View* 243 He's just what's needed in a bimbo. Fresh and neat, dapper, a real well-dressed little bastard; he'll polish Piggy's boots, make his bed, do his washing; just a regular little handmaiden. *Ibid.* 242 You're a clown, even for a bimbo. Anyone knows a bim has to be stupid, but you're the world's expert at stupidity.

bin. Wool bin, see WOOL 2.

[N.Z. **1865** M.A. BARKER *Let.* 1 Dec. in *Station Life N.Z.* (1870) 32 Armfulls of rolled-up fleeces [were] laid on the tables before the wool-sorters who.. pronounced.. to which bin they belonged.] **1867** J.C. JORDON *Managem. Sheep & Stations* 92 When a fleece is folded and tied, the classer will place it in the proper bin or compartment, according to its class. **1970** HARMSWORTH & PAGE-SHARP *Sheep & Wool Classing* 60 The rolled fleece must be classed so that all fleeces in one bin are as similar as possible.

bindi-eye /'bɪndi-aɪ/. Also **bindy-eye** and formerly with much variety, as **bindei, bindiyi.** [a. Kamilaroi and Yuwaalaraay *bindayaa*.] Any of several plants bearing barbed fruits, esp. herbs of the widespread genus *Calotis* (fam. Asteraceae); the fruit of these plants. Also **blindy-eye.**

1896 K.L. PARKER *Austral. Legendary Tales* 7 In the country of the Galah are lizards coloured reddish brown, and covered with spikes like bindeah prickles. *Ibid.* 129 Bindeah, a prickle or small thorn. **1905** *Steele Rudd's Mag.* (Brisbane) Feb. 142 Tyres are now.. puncture proof against the Bindei, that little ball of spikes so plentiful on the ground in many parts of Australia. **1911** E.J. BRADY *King's Caravan* 115 That night I lay awake.. on my blankets, prickly with bindiyi burrs. **1920** J.H. MAIDEN *Weeds N.S.W.* 12 Everybody in the country knows the pest called Bindi-eye or Bogan flea. **1948** R. RAVEN-HART *Canoe in Aust.* 73 The prickly 'bindi-eye', the flowers looking like lavender daisies. **1959** H. LAMOND *Sheep Station* 35 He scraped the blindy-eye burrs from the soles.

Hence **bindi-eyed** *a.*

1984 K. LETTE *Hit & Ms* 95 Though you violently disagree with your host's economic, emotional and political persuasions, it's a long, bindi-eyed walk back to town.

bingey, var. BINGY.

Binghi /'bɪŋgi/. [a. Awabakal (and neighbouring languages) *biŋay* (elder) brother.]

1. An Aboriginal; the typical Aboriginal. Also *attrib.*

1830 R. DAWSON *Present State Aust.* 224 We were all bingeyes (brothers). **1940** E. HILL *Great Austral. Loneliness* (ed. 2) 63, I followed the flat simian footprints of the 'Binghi-pads' to the turtle-feasts and sing-abouts of the good Australian blackfellow. **1985** J. MILLER *Koori* 156 The popular Press of Australia makes a joke of us by presenting silly and out-of-date drawings and jokes of 'Jacky' or 'Binghi', which have educated city-dwellers and young Australians to look upon us as sub-human.

2. *transf.* See quot.

1918 R.H. KNYVETT *Over there with Australs.* 25 The 'Binghies' (natives of New Guinea).

bingie, var. BINGY.

bingle. [Prob. f. Br. dial. *bing* thump, blow: see EDD and OEDS *bing, sb.*³] A fight or skirmish; a collision. Also **bingle-bingle.**
   1945 'MASTER-SARG' *Yank discovers Aust.* 17 A 'bingle' is a fight, a 'do' is a battle.   1945 *Mud & Blood* 51 After a lapse, the old 'bingle-bingle' was going this morning with a vengeance. After watching those Stukas diving .. one was left with the impression that tremendous damage must have been caused.

bingy /'bɪndʒi/. Also **bingey, bingie, binjie.** [a. Dharuk *bindhi.*] The stomach; the belly. Also *fig.*
   1791 W. TENCH *Compl. Acct. Settlement* (1793) 122 Belly .. *Bin'-dee* [name at the Hawkesbury].   1859 H. KINGSLEY *Recoll. Geoffry Hamlyn* II. 94 Don't you fret your bingy, boss.   1892 *Truth* (Sydney) 19 June 5/7 And each small boy went home and told his parents that he warn't going to be a butcher or a baker, but to be a member of Parliament, have a big binjie, wear a gold chain, and cut about among the toffs!   1902 *Ibid.* 23 Mar. 3/5 If I could be a Pre-me-eer It's very likely I must say, I'd fill my bingie up with beer Some five and forty times a day.   1948 I.L. IDRIESS *Opium Smugglers* 149 My bingey was demanding whether my throat was cut.
   Hence **bingied** *a.*, **bingyful** *n.*
   1913 H. LAWSON *For Aust.* 159 They're patting their binjies with pride, old man, and I want you to understand, That a **binjied** bard is a bard indeed.   1907 *Ibid.* 7 Apr. 1/7 Daddy Hayseed, staggering homewards .. under a heavy **bingeyful** of purge, reckons that the 'Frisco and Valparaiso earthquakes were trivial affairs.

bird. Abbrev. of *dead bird* (see DEAD 2).
   1941 S.J. BAKER *Pop. Dict. Austral. Slang* 10 *Bird*, a certainty.   1980 A. HOPGOOD *And here comes Bucknuckle* 20 Let me give you a tip. Next race .. Bolivia. It's a bird. Look .. twenty five to one.

birdcage. [Transf. use of *birdcage* the paddock at the Newmarket racecourse, England, in which horses are saddled.] An enclosure at a racecourse, freq. surrounded by a high wire mesh fence, in which jockeys mount and dismount.
   1893 *Antipodean* (Melbourne) 48 The betting ring is at the far end of the grandstand, and then comes the 'bird cage', where an extra charge of five shillings is made to keep the crowd away from the horses.   1980 *Age* (Melbourne) 16 Sept. 3/1 You have a big serve on a bird and you are relaxing over a glass by the birdcage waiting for it to trot in. .. This means that you have a big bet on a certain winner and you are in a bar at the races waiting for the event which your chosen animal will win with ease.

birder.
   1. Abbrev. of BLACKBIRDER 1.
   1898 *Bulletin* (Sydney) 2 Apr. 29/2 'Harry Monck' .. I take to be an ex 'birder desirous of showing that his craft isn't quite as black as painted.
   2. Abbrev. of *mutton-birder* (see MUTTON-BIRD *v.*).
   1986 *Weekend Austral.* (Sydney) 29 Mar. 5/4 The cruel and insensitive killing methods used by many amateur birders often results [*sic*] in chicks not even being stunned when their head and entrails are wrenched from their bodies.

birding, *vbl. n.* See MUTTON-BIRD *v.*
   1896 *Papers & Proc. R. Soc. Tas.* (1897) p. vi, Mutton-birding, a unique industry, and only carried on in the Furneaux Islands as a regular one. .. The 'birding' begins on March 20.   1969 J. WOODBERRY *Garland of Gannets* 26 'Do you go birdin', Ben?' .. 'Me!' Ben was insulted. 'Me! Birdin'? I'm a respectable bloke. Work for the guvermint. Can't stand the things. Taste nothing like mutton, nor bird, neither.'

bird of paradise. [A name applied to birds of the fam. Paradisaeidae: see OED(S *bird, sb.* 7.] In sense 1 the name has been applied to an unrelated bird also having a long and beautiful tail.]
   1. *Obs.* LYRE-BIRD.
   1800 D. COLLINS *Acct. Eng. Colony N.S.W.* (1802) II. 300 The first bird of paradise ever seen in this country had been shot.   1837 J. BACKHOUSE *Narr. Visit Austral. Colonies* (1843) 506 The Blacks often bring in the splendid tails of the Lyre-bird, *Menura superba*, which is called in Australia, the Pheasant, or the Bird of Paradise.
   2. Any of several Austral. bird species in the fam. Paradisaeidae, esp. *Ptiloris victoriae* (see VICTORIA RIFLE-BIRD).
   1853 J. SHERER *Gold Finder Aust.* 26 The lyre-bird and the bird of Paradise, two of the most beautiful of the feathered species.   1889 R.B. ANDERSON tr. Lumholtz's *Among Cannibals* 171 It was an Australian bird of paradise, the celebrated Rifle-bird (*Ptiloris victoriae*), which, according to Gould, has the most brilliant plumage of all Australian birds.

bird of providence. *Obs.* MOUNT PITT BIRD.
   1790 J. HUNTER *Hist. Jrnl. Trans. Port Jackson* (1793) 182 This *bird of Providence*, which I may with great propriety call it, appeared to me to resemble that sea bird in England, called the puffin. .. We were highly indebted to Providence for this vast resource.

Birdsville. [The name of a town in s.w. Qld.] A condition of horses caused by eating the central Austral. plant *Indigofera linnaei* (fam. Fabaceae) and characterized by staggering and toe-dragging. Also **Birdsville disease.**
   1915 *Bulletin* (Sydney) 28 Jan. 22/2 The Birdsville horse disease is peculiar to the lower Diamantina country. .. A horse may .. be fit and well in the morning, and by midday may suddenly collapse, struggle in agony for perhaps half an hour, and then pass out. The victims may go through several fits before finally throwing a seven. .. It is easy to kill a horse that has had a touch of 'Birdsville'.   1976 C.D. MILLS *Hobble Chains & Greenhide* 1 'Walkabout' and Birdsville had taken heavy toll of our horses.

birdwing. [From the butterfly's appearance in flight; cf. *bird-winged butterfly* an Indonesian species of the genus *Ornithoptera*: see OEDS *bird, sb.* 8 c.] Any of several large colourful butterflies of the tropical genus *Ornithoptera*, occurring in n.e. coastal Aust. and elsewhere. Also **bird's wing butterfly.**
   1933 H.J. CARTER *Gulliver in Bush* 100 The splendid green butterfly that floats so serenely among the vines, commonly called the 'Bird's Wing' butterfly.   1972 COMMON & WATERHOUSE *Butterflies of Aust.* 189 *Ornithoptera priamus pronomus* .. Cape York birdwing.

birthstain. *Hist.* [See quots. 1892 and 1899; the lines written by Kipling with reference to Sydney were adapted and used by William Lygon, 7th Earl Beauchamp, on his arrival as Governor of N.S.W. in 1899.] The stigma attached to the convict period or to convict ancestry. See also STAIN.
   1892 R. KIPLING in *Eng. Illustr. Mag.* (1893) X. 537 Greeting! My birth-stain have I turned to good; Forcing strong wills perverse to steadfastness; The first flush of the tropics in my blood, And at my feet Success!   1899 *Sydney Morning Herald* 11 May 5/6 Greeting,—Your birthstain have you turned to good, Forcing strong wills perverse to steadfastness, The first flush of the tropics in your blood, And at your feet success.—Beauchamp.   1956 J.T. LANG *I Remember* 195 Beauchamp had started off badly by trying to add a literary flourish to one of his statements, when he declaimed, Your *birth stains, you have turned to good*. It didn't make him very popular in squatter society.
   Hence **birthstained** *a.*

Biscay. Abbrev. of BAY OF BISCAY.
1897 J.J. MURIF *From Ocean to Ocean* 163 'Devil-devil'.. is applied to clay.. similar to 'Biscay', but.. in contracting after rains, in the quick-drying rays of fierce tropical sun it cracks, while the 'Biscay' becomes distressingly bumpy.

biscuit bomber. An aircraft which used to drop supplies to troops in remote parts of New Guinea during the war of 1939-45.
1948 A. DAWES *Soldier Superb* 58 The biscuit bombers—the transport planes—had gone over. 1978 R. MACKLIN *Newsfront* 99 Above they could see old 'Biscuit Bombers', resurrected from war service, dropping supplies.

Bishop Barker. *Obs.* [f. the name of Frederic *Barker* (1808–1882), Anglican Bishop of Sydney: see quot. 1892.] A large glass of beer.
1886 F. COWAN *Aust.* 32 *Long-sleever, Bishop Barker,* and *Deep-sinker,* synonyms of Yankee Schooner. 1892 *Bulletin* (Sydney) 9 Jan. 14/1 Dr Barker.. was so abnormally tall that (incited thereto also by the fact that he was a teetotaller) the tavernites called the 'longest' drink of beer procurable at a public-house 'a Bishop Barker'.

bit. [Cf. *bit of muslin* woman: see OED *muslin, sb.* 2.] In the phr. **a bit of** (or **o'**) **skirt,** a woman, esp. a young woman (regarded sexually).
1898 *Truth* (Sydney) 17 Apr. 3/1 Demanded free admission for himself and his 'bit o' skirt'. 1965 J. WYNNUM *Jiggin' in Riggin'* 35 I'll lay even money she can line up a bit of skirt for me, too.

bite, *n.* [f. *bite* swindler (OED *sb.* 9 b.), prob. influenced by BITE *v.*]

1. A cadger.
1944 *Bulletin* (Sydney) 2 Aug. 14/1 Bush lawyers, cockies who insist they can help you make out your tax return,.. the tobacco 'bite', the chap who wants to borrow everything. 1982 J. MORRISON *North Wind* 54 Your old mates have had a win in Tatts.. and all the bots and bites in Victoria are on to them.

2. That which is cadged; the act of cadging.
1919 W.H. DOWNING *Digger Dialects* 10 Bite (n. or vb.), (1) a borrowing, to borrow; (2) an attempt to borrow. 1967 *Kings Cross Whisper* (Sydney) xxxiv. 4/5 Whereas a snip is only a small loan a fang is a large 'bite'.

3. In the collocation **good bite,** one who responds favourably to a cadger, a 'soft touch'.
1965 R.H. CONQUEST *Horses in Kitchen* 192 He was.. considered a good 'bite' by down-and-outs. 1966 D. NILAND *Pairs & Loners* 38 He was a good bite, and the men soon realised that.

4. In the phr. **to put the bite on** (someone), to cadge from; also **on the bite,** cadging, 'on the scrounge'.
1941 H. PERCY *Here's Hal Percy* 23 He used to dine on meat pies at Mother Bourke's Cafe, And was always on the bite for a few bob till next pay day. 1955 R. LAWLER *Summer of Seventeenth Doll* (1965) 98 Your money's runnin' out, you know you can't put the bite on me any more, and so here's the new champion, all loaded and ready.

bite, *v.* [Abbrev. of *to bite the ear* to borrow money from (someone): see OEDS *bite, v.* 16.] *trans.* To solicit money, etc., from; to 'touch' for; to scrounge (food). Also *intr.*
1912 *Truth* (Sydney) 8 Dec. 7/4 They 'bit' him not merely for 'tens' or 'twenties', but for hundreds and even thousands. 1922 C. DREW *Rogues & Ruses* 67 He'd been a member of the leadin' sportin' clubs, but he'd bitten his way out of all of them.

biter. BITE *n.* 1.
1955 *Bulletin* (Sydney) 26 Oct. 13/3 Ned looked the supplicant quizzically up and down and said, 'Hmnn, have you ever bit me before?' 'Nò,' beamed the biter confidently. 'Well,' replied the big bloke.. 'I ain't puttin' on no new customers!' 1967 *Kings Cross Whisper* (Sydney) xxxvi. 7/2 Outraged, biter leaps to his feet saying he couldn't possibly take her money—how much has she got by the way.

bitser, var. BITZER.

bitter bark. Any of several trees having a bitter bark, esp. *Alstonia constricta* (fam. Apocynaceae) of N.S.W. and Qld. See also QUININE TREE.
1881 *Proc. Linnean Soc. N.S.W.* VI. 742 The beautiful flowering shrub *Clerodendron floribundum*, which is here mistaken for the 'Bitter-bark' (*Alstonia constricta*). 1965 *Austral. Encycl.* II. 17 Bitter-bark.. is also called fever-bark or quinine bush. Its thick fissured bark is intensely bitter and contains a febrifugal tonic principle.

bitumen.

1. A road with a tarred surface; a sealed road.
1948 G. MEREDITH *Lawsons* 1 Wongalee is.. an impressive little one-horse town whose few hundred yards of bitumen, straggling at each end into dusty dirt roads, rouse no excess of enthusiasm. 1983 *Open Road* Feb. 17/3 Because of the difficult terrain and weather conditions in the shire that means about a kilometre and a half of new bitumen a year.

2. *spec.* The Stuart Highway between Darwin and Alice Springs.
1949 H.E. THONEMANN *Tell White Man* 149 There were the workmen who made a beautiful road now called the 'Bitumen'. 1977 T. RONAN *Mighty Men on Horseback* 74 If you are in Darwin you go 'up the bitumen' to get down to Alice Springs. If you are in the Alice you go 'down the bitumen' to get up to Darwin.

bitumenize, *v. trans.* To surface (a road, etc.), with bitumen.
1959 H. DRAKE-BROCKMAN *West Coast Stories* 194 The company told him they were going to bitumenize the pearlshell road. 1964 *Mount Isa Mail* 30 Jan. 1/3 The car bays have not been bitumenised.

bitzer. Also **bitser, bitza.** [f. abbrev. of *bits (and pieces.*]

1. A contraption made from previously unrelated parts.
1924 *Smith's Weekly* (Sydney) 6 Dec. 24/5 Toombes built.. the super Bitza.. and those who do not know that its ragged bonnet hides a Vauxhall engine ponder over the origin of its cheek. 1951 S. HICKEY *Travelled Roads* 27 George had a big 'bitza' clock with a powerful knock at each hour, but it struck one every time.

2. A mongrel dog. Also *attrib.*
1936 *Bulletin* (Sydney) 4 Mar. 21/4 The 'bitzer'-bred dog belonging to a resident of the Hawkesbury River. 1978 B. ST. A. SMITH *Spirit beyond Psyche* 10 Jim bent and scratched the dog's ears. Poor old Seidlitz, a bitzer if ever there was one! 1980 G.F. BREWER *On Breadline* 15 The.. 'bitser' dog plays on the adjoining balcony.

bizzo. [Abbrev. of *bus(iness* + -O.] Something to which the speaker does not wish to refer precisely; cf. 'thingummy'.
1969 A. BUZO *Front Room Boys* (1970) 27 Do the overall tallies in the squares provided on the bizzo. 1984 *Canberra Times* 6 May 6/6, I hear Jim was on to Parramatta the other day after fixing up the Michelle bizzo.

black, *n.*, *a.*¹, and *attrib*. [Spec. use of *black* dark-skinned (person).]

A. *n.*

1. An Aboriginal.

1795 D. COLLINS *Acct. Eng. Colony N.S.W.* (1798) I. 434 Samuel Chinnery (a black) servant to Mr Arndell. **1984** *Age* (Melbourne) 24 Aug. 4 *(heading)* Blacks may have arrived 130,000 years ago.

2. In the collocation **black's bread**, *native bread* NATIVE *a.* 6 a.

1904 *Bulletin* (Sydney) 13 Oct. 18/3 A 7lb. lump of 'black's bread' has been unearthed in the neighbourhood of Bathurst (N.S.W.)... According to the oldest and least reliable inhabitant, this bread was once plentiful in the Oberon district... It has a tough crust, but the inside is soft, resembling sago, and is not unpalatable. There is no visible root or germ about it, and its origin is a mystery.

B. *adj.* and *attrib.*

1. Aboriginal. See also BLACKBOY 1, BLACKFELLOW.

1788 [see *black man*]. **1820** *HRA* (1921) 3rd Ser. III. 363 Are the native Black Children, who have been Baptized, brought in by their Parents? **1974** M. GILLESPIE *Into Hollow Mountains* 53 The Builder's Arms is supposedly Melbourne's 'black-pub', although .. a black activist from Sydney says it doesn't deserve the title. 'A black pub is full of black people talking about black topics.'

2. In Comb. and collocations: **black camp, girl, -hunting, man, people, police, population, trooper, woman**.

1826 R. DAWSON *Private & Confidential* 15 He .. carried it a considerable way to the **black camp**, as they call it. **1815** *HRA* (1921) 3rd Ser. II. 95 The **Black Girl**.. is a Native of the Island. **1879** 'AUSTRALIAN' *Adventures Qld.* 25 They dared not call out loudly—that was against all rules on **black-hunting** expeditions—for the natives' ears are sharp as well as their eyes. **1788** R. CLARK Jrnl. 29 Feb. 129 Two **black men**.. received sentence of death. **1826** *HRA* (1919) 1st Ser. XII. 672 The advice you are supposed to have given in the cases of the **Black People** and Bushrangers. **1825** B. FIELD *Geogr. Mem. N.S.W.* 33 Should the runaways even escape the **black police**, they are almost sure to perish by hunger or the hostility of the other Indians. **1828** *Blossom* (Sydney) i. 43 Much .. has been said, as to the impracticability of ever civilizing the **black population** of Australia. **1843** *Portland Mercury* 25 Oct. 3/4 The serjeant with five of the **black troopers**.. returned back at full speed. **1845** L. LEICHHARDT *Jrnl. Overland Exped. Aust.* 12 Feb. (1847) 149 We soon came in sight of three **black women**.

3. Used tautologously to qualify nouns which themselves denote Aboriginality: **black Aboriginal, Aborigine, gin, lubra, native, piccaninny, tribe**.

1870 C.H. ALLEN *Visit to Qld.* 98 The **black aboriginals** lying in ambush. **1842** *Colonial Observer* (Sydney) 24 Aug. 421/2 His own views of the relation between the whites and the **black aborigines**. **1837** *Rep. Select Committee Transportation* 18 Apr. (1838) 27 What are the native women called by the assigned convicts?—**Black gins**. **1841** *Geelong Advertiser* 7 Aug. 2/3 Tender-hearted creatures would no doubt be wonderfully edified at the sight of a **black leubra** suckling a pup at her breast, while her own emaciated offspring was squalling at her back!! **1816** *Hobart Town Gaz.* 31 Aug., A few days ago a party of about twenty **Black Natives** pursued three of the Government Stock-keepers. **1923** T. HALL *Short Hist. Downs Blacks* 5 A lot of **black picaninnies** (children) clapping their hands. **1808** *Sydney Gaz.* 6 Nov., Your sage Correspondent affects to describe The Habits that grace Australia's **Black Tribe**.

4. Used in collocations to evoke, (often) ironically, the image of the 'noble savage', as **black gentleman, gentry, ladies, lords (of the soil), proprietors (of the soil)**. Cf. CHILD.

1839 W.H. LEIGH *Reconnoitering Voyages* 85, I .. saw .. two black gentlemen from whom the 'coo-ēē' proceeded. **1840** J.P. JOHNSON *Plain Truths* 55 The black gentlemen begin thrashing the black ladies. **1848** *Observer* (Melbourne) 25 May 75/4 The very loose and incorrect notions which these black gentry have of the rights of *meum* and *tuum* [*sic*]. **1851** H. MELVILLE *Present State Aust.* 52 The white population .. have always acted kindly towards these black proprietors of the soil. **1854** MRS C. CLACY *Lights & Shadows* II. 23 Their wives or lubras .. do all the disagreeable work, whilst their black lords recline lazily upon the grass. **1867** 'CLERGYMAN' *Aust. as it Is* 54 The territory .. they proposed taking possession of from the black proprietors. **1875** G.M. NEWMAN *N.T. & its Gold-Fields* 16 The black lords of the soil .. on all occasions show the utmost contempt for civilization and labor.

5. Used pejoratively in collocations, as **black animal, bastard, brother, crow, cur, game, savage, sister**.

1838 *Sydney Herald* 5 Oct. 3/1 The whole gang of black animals are not worth the money which the Colonists will have to pay for printing the silly documents. **1847** *Moreton Bay Courier* 6 Feb. 2/4 The circumstances attending the deaths of several of the white population who have been slaughtered by the black savages. **1857** F. GERSTAECKER *Two Convicts* 13 If I were certain .. I would make the black curs pay for it dearly enough. **1882** W. SOWDEN *N.T. as it Is* 20 Even now it is considered a joke all along the coast beyond Cooktown .. to shoot down black-fellows .. and some men pride themselves on the 'row of stiff 'uns' they have made in their time, and others talk pleasantly of 'black-crow shooting'. **1895** A.C. BICKNELL *Travel & Adventure Northern Qld.* 66, I might get a brace or two of black game before the morning. **1909** *Bulletin* (Sydney) 25 Nov. 14/4 Our black brother is soaking in education... The other day he was awarded two years for forging and uttering a cheque for £6. **1943** *Ibid.* 25 Aug. 12/2 Black sister of the Murchison and the Nullagine (W.A.) could do one quite remarkable thing with her coolamon or yandi. **1975** R.J. MERRITT *Cake Man* (1978) 27 Come back with my property! Black bastard! Mission Rat!

6. In special collocations: **black tracker,** TRACKER; **velvet,** Aboriginal women as the focus of a white man's sexual interest; sexual intercourse with an Aboriginal woman.

1862 *Leader* (Melbourne) 5 July, The **black trackers** could only discover the tracks of six horsemen. **1900** H. LAWSON *Verses Pop. & Humorous* 57, I know the track from Spencer's Gulf and north of Cooper's Creek—Where falls the half-caste to the strong, 'black velvet' to the weak.

7. Hist. In Special Comb. and collocations: **black line,** a dragnet operation in 1830 in which the military and police, aided by settlers and their convict servants, moved systematically across eastern Tasmania in an attempt to round up the Aboriginal population; **protector, protectorate,** PROTECTOR, PROTECTORATE; **string, war,** *black line*.

1835 H. MELVILLE *Hist. Van Diemen's Land* 99 In September, of 1830, the **black line** was projected, and proved a very innocent amusement for the various Government officers, as also for a very large portion of the settlers, and their convict servants. **1842** *Melbourne Times* 16 July 2/6 We have not for some weeks seen a **Black Protector** in town, which is indeed something new, as they may be generally seen sauntering about our streets as unconcernedly as if there was not a single black in the colony. **1844** *Portland Mercury* 31 Jan. 3/5 Such a rotten, dangerous system known as the **Black Protectorate**? **1870** J. BONWICK *Last Tasmanians* 163 Some good stories of the Line, or '**Black String**'. **1830** P.L. BROWN *Clyde Co. Papers* (1941) I. 110 The **Black War** ended here after 2 months' campaign of 3,000 men.

8. a. Of or pertaining to a KANAKA. Also used instrumentally.

1876 [see BLACK 8 b.]. **1896** N. GOULD *Town & Bush* 69 Black labour must be employed on the Queensland sugar plantations. **1904** *Advocate* (Burnie) 14 Nov. 2/4 Black-grown sugar enjoys a protection of £3 per ton, and white-grown sugar of £5 per ton.

b. Special Comb. **black-labour man, party,** a person or faction favouring the use of Kanaka labour in Queensland.

1876 'EIGHT YRS.' RESIDENT' *Queen of Colonies* 300 A very strong public opinion developed itself, yet the **black-labour men**, as they are called, had influence enough with Government to cause the matter to be hushed up. 1876 'EIGHT YRS.' RESIDENT' *Queen of Colonies* 301 So strong is the **black-labour party** in the colony—the premier himself being a large employer of Polynesians on his station.

black, $a.^2$ [Spec. use of *black* characterized by the colour.]

1. a. Used as a distinguishing epithet in the names of plants: **black apple,** any of several trees bearing a dark fruit, esp. *Planchonella australis* (fam. Sapotaceae) of N.S.W. and Qld., which also yields a fine-grained timber; *bush apple,* see BUSH C. 3; **bean, (a)** the large tree *Castanospermum australe* (fam. Fabaceae) of e. Qld. and n.e. N.S.W., having dark green leaves and a hard, heavy pod containing poisonous chestnut-like seeds; the dark brown, attractively figured wood of the tree; CHESTNUT *n.*; *Moreton Bay chestnut,* see MORETON BAY; see also BEAN TREE; **(b)** the tree *Erythrophleum chlorostachys* (see CAMEL POISON); **oak,** any of several trees of the genera *Allocasuarina* and *Casuarina* (fam. Casuarinaceae), incl. *C. cristata* (see BELAH); **sallee** (or **sally**), the small tree of s.e. Aust. *Eucalyptus stellulata* (fam. Myrtaceae), having a rough black lower trunk and smooth olive green to grey upper trunk; MUZZLEWOOD; **wattle, (a)** any of several dark-barked trees of the genus *Acacia* (fam. Mimosaceae), esp. *A. mearnsii*; **(b)** the shrub or small tree *Callicoma serratifolia* (fam. Cunoniaceae), which bears wattle-like heads of flowers.

1888 *Proc. Linnean Soc. N.S.W.* III. 485 *Achras australis*.. '**Black Apple**', 'Brush Apple', 'Wild' or 'Native Plum' of colonists. 1895 *Agric. Gaz. N.S.W.* V. 1 The **black bean** or Moreton Bay Chestnut... Because of the seeds, which are very large beans, this tree goes under the name of beantree; and because of the dark colour of the wood.. it is usually known by timber merchants as black bean. 1974 S.L. EVERIST *Poisonous Plants Aust.* 296 *Erythrophleum chlorostachys*... In Western Australia it is also known as *camel poison* and *black bean.* 1860 J.M. STUART *Exploration of Interior* 5/1 Alternate sandhills and grassy plains, consisting of mulga, malay, and **black oak.** 1889 J.H. MAIDEN *Useful Native Plants Aust.* 522 In Gippsland it [*sc. Eucalyptus stellulata*] is known by the names of '**Black Sallee**' and 'Muzzlewood'. 1968 C. BURGESS *Blue Mountain Gums* 48 '*Black Sally*' was named *Eucalyptus stellulata* by Sieber. 1797 D. COLLINS *Acct. Eng. Colony N.S.W.* (1802) II. 63 A similar timber was called the **Black Wattle.** 1881 *Proc. Linnean Soc. N.S.W.* VI. 771 In the early days of the colony.. *Callicoma serratifolia* was the Black Wattle.. but now the terms Black and Green Wattle are applied almost universally to the two varieties of *Acacia decurrens.*

b. In the names of animals: **black and white fantail,** WILLY WAGTAIL; **and white swallow,** *white-backed swallow*, see WHITE $a.^2$ 1 b.; **-backed wren,** the small bird *Malurus splendens*, a species of *fairy wren* (see FAIRY $n.^1$ 1) of inland s.e. Aust.; the breeding male is largely blue above, but the lower back and rump are black; **bream,** any of several dark-coloured fish, esp. the estuarine *Acanthopagrus australis*, ranging from Qld. to Vic., and *A. butcheri* of s. Aust.; **-breasted buzzard** (or **kite**), the large bird of prey *Hamirostra melanosternon* of central, n. and w. Aust., characterized in flight by its short, square-ended tail; **cap,** any of several honeyeaters with black crowns in the genus *Melithreptus*; **-capped sittella,** a common bird of woodlands in s. but not s.e. Aust., being one form of the SITTELLA, and having a black top and sides to the head; **-cheeked falcon,** the peregrine falcon *Falco peregrinus*, which swoops on prey at high speed and occurs throughout Aust. and in all exc. the polar continents; **cockatoo,** any of the five species of large crested parrot with predom. black plumage of the Austral. genus *Calyptorhynchus*; also with distinguishing epithet, as **red-tailed, white-tailed, yellow-tailed** (see under first element); **cormorant,** *black shag*; **currawong,** the predom. black bird *Strepera fuliginosa* of Tas.; see also *black magpie*; **duck,** the common water fowl and game bird *Anas superciliosa*, predom. brown and distinguished by a dark line from the bill to behind the eye, bordered by pale lines; **-eared cuckoo,** the pale brownish cuckoo *Chrysococcyx osculans*, typically occurring in drier parts of Aust., and on islands to the north, named for a dark line extending from the bill to the ear-covert feathers; **-faced cuckooshrike,** the mainly grey bird of woodland *Coracina novaehollandiae*, the adult having a black patch extending from the forehead to the throat and behind the eyes; *blue jay*, see BLUE *a.*; see also *summer bird* SUMMER; **-faced wood swallow,** the grey bird *Artamus cinereus*, with a black patch between the bill and eyes, occurring widely in relatively dry parts of Aust., and in Timor and New Guinea; **falcon,** the dark brown, fast-flying, Austral. bird of prey *Falco subniger*; **-fronted dotterel,** the wading bird *Elseyornis melanops*, having a black V-shaped mark on its white breast, of Aust. and N.Z.; **-gloved wallaby,** the wallaby *Macropus irma* of s.w. Aust., having black forefeet; **-headed honeyeater,** the brownish honeyeater *Melithreptus affinis* of Tas., having a black head; **jay,** CHOUGH; CURRAWONG; **magpie, (a)** CHOUGH; **(b)** *pied currawong,* see PIED; **(c)** *black currawong*; **prince,** the predom. black cicada *Psaltoda plaga* of e. Qld. and N.S.W.; **rock cod,** the fish *Epinephelus damelii* of rocky coasts and estuaries in the s.w. Pacific, including Qld. and N.S.W., the adult being almost uniformly black or dark grey; **shag,** a widely distributed water bird, the predom. black cormorant *Phalacrocorax carbo*; **-shouldered kite,** the widespread bird of prey *Elanus axillaris*, having a black area at the 'shoulder' or bend of the wing's leading edge; **snake,** either of two species of elapid snake, the red-bellied *Pseudechis porphyriacus* of s.e. Aust. and coastal e. Qld., and the spotted *P. guttatus* of s.e. Qld. and n.e. N.S.W.; **swan,** the large water bird *Cygnus atratus* of s. Aust., with plumage mainly black in adults, the faunal emblem of W.A.; SWAN; **trevally,** any of several marine fish, usu. of the fam. Siganidae, esp. *Siganus spinus.*

1900 A.J. CAMPBELL *Nests & Eggs Austral. Birds* 118 The **Black-and-white Fantail** is exceedingly persevering in nest-building. 1842 J. GOULD *Birds of Aust.* (1848) II. Pl. 12, *Atticora leucosternon*.. White-breasted Swallow.. **Black and White Swallow** of the Colonists. 1841 J. GOULD *Birds of Aust.* (1848) III. Pl. 20, *Malurus melanotus*.. **Black-backed Wren.** 1857 J. ASKEW *Voyage Aust. & N.Z.* 228 The harbour abounds with fish, of which the.. **black** and red **bream**.. are used for food. 1842 J. GOULD *Birds of Aust.* (1848) I. Pl. 20, The **Black-breasted Buzzard** generally flies high in the air, through which it soars in large circles. 1976 *Reader's Digest Compl. Bk. Austral. Birds* 120 Six or more black-breasted kites will gather to feed at ravaged emu nests. 1855 J. BONWICK *Geogr. Aust. & N.Z.* (ed. 3) 198 In the island [*sc.* Tas.].. are **Black Caps.** 1844 J. GOULD *Birds of Aust.* (1848) IV. Pl. 104, *Sittella pileata*.. **Black-capped Sittella.** 1849 C. STURT *Narr. Exped. Central Aust.* II. 35 App. *Black-capped Sittella.* A creeper, with a black head, and grey brown plumage. 1841 J. GOULD *Birds of Aust.* (1848) I. Pl. 8, **Black-cheeked Falcon**.. *Blue Hawk*, Colonists of Western Australia. 1770 S. PARKINSON *Jrnl. Voyage to South Seas* (1773) 144 We found.. large **black cocatoes**, with scarlet and orange-coloured feathers on their tails. 1864 *Papers & Proc. R. Soc. Tas.* 63 The **black cormorant** (*Phalacrocorax carboides*) will, I apprehend, prove a worse poacher than any other bird. 1945 C. BARRETT *Austral. Bird Life* 215 Of currawongs or bell-magpies (*Strepera*) there are six species, two—the **black currawong** (*S. fuliginosa*) and the hill strepera (*S. arguta*)—being restricted to Tasmania. 1820

C. JEFFREYS *Van Dieman's Land* 35 This lake abounds with black swans, **black ducks,** widgeons. **1847** J. GOULD *Birds of Aust.* (1848) IV. Pl. 88, *Chalcites osculans* . . **Black-eared Cuckoo,** Colonists of Swan River. **1900** A.J. CAMPBELL *Nests & Eggs Austral. Birds* 96 Under various trivial vernacular names, such as Blue Dove, Summer Bird, etc., the **Black-faced Cuckoo Shrike** is found through the length and breadth of Australia. **1896** B. SPENCER *Rep. Horn Sci. Exped. Central Aust.* II. 68 **Black-faced Wood Swallow** . . great variation in the size of this species. **1848** J. GOULD *Birds of Aust.* (1848) I. Pl. 9, *Falco subniger* . . **Black Falcon. 1845** J. GOULD *Birds of Aust.* (1848) VI. Pl. 20, *Hiaticula nigrifons*. **Black-fronted Dottrel. 1886** F. COWAN *Aust.* 36 Wallaby being a generic term of native origin for a number of kangaroo-like animals specifically distinguished as the rock-wallaby, **black-gloved-wallaby**, . . and the like. [**1801 black-headed honeyeater:** J. LATHAM *Gen. Synopsis Birds* Suppl. II. 167 Black-headed Cr[eeper] . . Inhabits *New South Wales.*] **1822** —— *Gen. Hist. Birds* IV. 175 Black-headed Honey-eater. **1900** *Tocsin* (Melbourne) 9 Aug. 6/1 For some days lived on an abundance of magpies and **black jays. 1832** J. BISCHOFF *Sketch Hist. Van Diemen's Land* 177 We also occasionally heard the trumpeter, or **black-magpie. 1836** J. BACKHOUSE *Narr. Visit Austral. Colonies* (1843) 438 Some of the birds of V.D. Land abound; such as . . the Jay or Black Magpie, *Coronica fuliginosa*. **1911** *Bulletin* (Sydney) 26 Jan. 15/2 The name 'black magpie' is given to both the white-winged chough and the pied crow-shrike, while the latter is called by various onomatopoeic renderings of its cry, such as charawack or corowong. **1951** CUSACK & JAMES *Come in Spinner* 106 'Mine's a Floury Baker . . and mine's a **Black Prince**!' Young Jack and Andrew held up their fists for her to peep at frosted fawn body and tan-and-black. **1880** *Proc. Linnean Soc. N.S.W.* V. 317 *Serranus Damelii* . . '**Black Rock Cod**' of the Sydney Fishermen. **1834** J. BACKHOUSE *Narr. Visit Austral. Colonies* (1843) 189 The pools of Jordan, in which, as well as in the other rivers of Tasmania, and on the sea-coast, **Black Shaggs** are often seen fishing. **1821** J. LATHAM *Gen. Hist. Birds* I. 231 **Black-shouldered Kite**. This is full two feet in length. **1795** D. COLLINS *Acct. Eng. Colony N.S.W.* (1798) I. 404 A convict, on entering the door of his hut, was bit in the foot by a **black snake**; the effect was, an immediate swelling of the foot, leg, and thigh, and a large tumour in the groin. **1698** *Philos. Trans. R. Soc. London* (1699) XX. 361 Here is returned a Ship, which by our *East India* Company, was sent to the South Land, called *Hollandia Nova*. . . **Black Swans,** Parrots, and many Sea-Cows were found there. **1874** *N.S.W. Rep. R. Comm. Fisheries* (1880) 1294 The **black trevally** is a very good eating fish when used at once.

2. In special collocations: **black billy,** see BILLY *n.*[1] 4; **book** *hist.*, a book in which the offences of a convict were recorded; also as *v. trans.*; **hat** *obs.* [from the unsuitability of dress], NEW CHUM *n.* 2; **money** *Austral. pidgin, obs.*, a copper coin; **peter,** a solitary confinement cell; see PETER 1.

1816 *N.S.W. Pocket Almanack* 43 Gaoler's Fees. . . From every person receiving a certificate of his or her term of transportation being expired (reference being always had to the **black book** in his possession). **1835** *True Colonist* (Hobart) 29 Jan. 2/4 Would have been tried for the offence, and, if not punished at least 'black-booked'. **1876** *Austral. Town & Country Jrnl.* (Sydney) 15 July 102/2 It is more a bush expression than a town one, and rather slangy. A '**black hat**', in Australia [*sic*] parlance, means a new arrival. **1899** W. MANN *Six Yrs.' Residence* 285 'De be no good—no money but **black money**'; by which they mean pence. **1953** K. TENNANT *Joyful Condemned* 259 The prison doctor was walking down from the gate. He had once got a girl two days in the **black peter** for saying good-day to him.

black, *a.*[3] [Spec. use of *black* malignant, disastrous.] In special collocations qualifying the name of a day of the week: **Black Thursday,** 6 Feb. 1851, a day on which devastating bushfires occurred in Victoria; **Wednesday,** 9 Jan. 1878, the day on which the Victorian Government, having failed to pass its Appropriation Bill, dismissed a large number of public servants; also *v. trans.*, to dismiss (a public servant); see BERRY BLIGHT.

1851 *Illustr. Austral. Mag.* (Melbourne) July 26 The 6th of February last, which received around Port Phillip the ominous designation of '**Black Thursday**', will be long remembered in Victoria for its intense heat and burning winds, and the extensive conflagrations that occurred over all the country. **1878** 'Y.O.-B.A.' *Proclamation!* 3 The Government announced . . on the celebrated **Black Wednesday**, that they had dispensed with the services of . . many of the civil servants. **1880** *Argus* (Melbourne) 7 Feb. 6/6 Mr Symonds is an official liable to be 'Black Wednesdayed' at any moment.

black, *a.*[4] [Spec. use of *black* incurring censure, as in *black list:* see OED(S *black, a.* 11 and *black list, sb.* 1 c. Sense 1 is used elsewhere but recorded earliest in Aust.]

1. Used to designate a category or place of work, person, piece of machinery, etc., declared subject to a boycott by a trade union during a dispute.

1911 ST. C. GRONDONA *Collar & Cuffs* 100 None of these gentlemen here is blacklegs. . . Anyone wantin' to prove who's black let him step out here, and I'll d–n quick settle the dispute by blackenin' his eyes for him. **1971** *Austral.* (Sydney) 19 Jan. 2/7 Any employer who calls in police against federation officials will be declared black and 'driven out of the industry'.

2. In the special collocation **black ban,** a prohibition (esp. as imposed by a trade union) which prevents work from proceeding: see quot. 1981. Also as *v. trans.* See also GREEN BAN.

1972 *Sydney Morning Herald* 11 Aug. 3/7 The Builders Labourers' Federation of N.S.W. lifted its eight-months-old black ban on restoration work in the $500-million East Rocks redevelopment scheme yesterday. **1976** *Bulletin* (Sydney) 7 Aug. 9/1 The Plumbers' Union has black-banned a number of private citizens who want to build homes in Pascoe Vale Road, Broadmeadows. The union's attitude is that the homesites are too close to Tullamarine. The land-owners, who bought the land three years ago, naturally agree that it's none of the union's business. **1981** SHEEHAN & WORLAND *Gloss. Industr. Relations Terms* (ed. 2) 9 *Ban*, an organised refusal by employees to undertake certain work, to use certain equipment or to work with certain people. They are generally known as 'black bans'.

blackbird, *n.*

1. *Obs.* An Aboriginal. Esp. in the phr. **blackbird shooting.**

1865 *London Soc.* Dec. 448/1 Men travelling up country used to provide themselves with . . a kind of 'licence to shoot blacks'. . . The sport-loving traveller would frequently indulge in what we should call a decidedly sensational pastime, which he called 'blackbird shooting'. But this sort of thing is all of the past now.

2. *Hist.* A Pacific islander brought to Australia as a labourer, a KANAKA. Also *attrib.*

1869 P.A. TAYLOR *Colony of Qld. & Alleged Slave Trade* 11 Polynesian labourers were employed, who had been taken from their homes by fraud. Ships went to the New Hebrides to 'catch blackbirds', and they caught them by utter deceit for three years' engagements. **1875** G.S. SEARLE *Mount & Morris Exonerated* 7 They were going to take a cruise round the islands 'blackbird' catching.

blackbird, *v. Hist.* [Back-formation from BLACKBIRDING.]

a. *intr.* To engage in blackbirding.

1894 J. MACDONALD *Thunderbolt* 304 I've been down to the islands, sir, with a schooner 'blackbirding', and the skipper felt it his business to get useful labour for the Queensland tropics, where a white man can't work all day in the sun. **1952** C. SIMPSON *Come away, Pearler* 7 They say his mother was a Rotuma woman Bully got hold of when he was blackbirding down Fiji way.

b. *trans.* To kidnap (a Pacific islander).

1901 *Tocsin* (Melbourne) 5 Sept. 4/4 Savages .. who can be blackbirded and whipped into working for nothing more than the cost of keeping them alive. **1979** A.J. BURKE *Bite Pineapple* 86 Kanakas were blackbirded as slaves for the Queensland sugar plantations, the cost to some cane farmers being as low as six shillings per head.

blackbirder. *Hist.*

1. One engaged in blackbirding.

1880 *Bulletin* (Sydney) 17 Apr. 4/3 Three well-known 'blackbirders', alias Government labour agents .. are known as 'The world, the flesh and the angel'. **1978** M. PAICE *Shadow of Wings* 74, I had read about the blackbirders, .. how they brought men—and women too—from the islands of the New Hebrides and New Guinea to work the plantations of Queensland.

2. A ship used for blackbirding.

1903 *Bulletin* (Sydney) 4 Apr. 17/1 Things happened pretty suddenly those days on board a black-birder.

blackbirding, *vbl. n. Hist.* The act or practice of kidnapping, or otherwise obtaining, Pacific islanders and trafficking in them as labour, mainly for the Queensland cotton and sugar plantations; RECRUITING. Also *fig.*

1871 G. PALMER *Kidnapping in South Seas* 120 Of late English traders find '*black-birding*' far more lucrative than bêche-de-mering. **1981** SANDERCOCK & TURNER *Up Where, Cazaly?* 58 There was acrimonious argument .. about Victoria's 'black-birding'. In 1911, a Tasmanian delegate .. urged that an interstate player should be required to establish two years' residence before he was permitted to transfer to a Melbourne club.

blackboy.

1. *Hist.* An adult Aboriginal male, esp. one accompanying explorers or employed on a station. See also BOY.

1810 *Sydney Gaz.* 1 Dec., My servant, Nussee, a black boy, has absconded from my Employ. **1855** H. HUME *Brief Statement* 3 A black boy, a native of Appin, started on an exploring journey. **1950** 'N. SHUTE' *Town like Alice* 82 Black boys—black stockmen.

2. Chiefly *W.A.* **a.** GRASS-TREE 1. **b.** The resin of the grass-tree; also **blackboy gum.**

1834 J. ROBERTS *Two Yrs. at Sea* 97 Near our encampment .. was a tree of a singular though not very ornamental form: it was called 'grass tree', from its grassy head, and 'black boy', from the dark colour of its stem. **1847** *Atlas* (Sydney) III. 111/2 Blackboy Gum... This very powerful gum is now in constant use by our boat and shipbuilders as a substitute for pitch. **1853** I. CHAMBERLAYNE *Austral. Captive* 107 Blackboy is the colonial name of a large growing herbaceous plant, as well as of the gutta percha-like substance which it furnishes.

blackbutt. Any of several trees of the genus *Eucalyptus* (fam. Myrtaceae) with a characteristic fire-charred fibrous bark on the lower trunk; esp. *Eucalyptus pilularis* an important source of hardwood timber in the coastal ranges of N.S.W. and s. Qld. Formerly also **black-butted gum.**

1801 *HRA* (1915) 1st Ser. III. 414 The finest stringybark and black-butted blue-gum trees I ever saw. **1847** A. HARRIS *Settlers & Convicts* (1953) 29 Fine tall black butts, even as a gun-barrel, and as straight in the grain as a skein of thread.

blackee, blackey, varr. BLACKIE.

blackfellow, *n., a.,* and *attrib.* Also **black fella, blackfeller.** [f. BLACK *a.*[1] + *fellow* familiar synonym for *man*, widespread in pidgin.]

A. *n.*

1. An Aboriginal.

1798 D. COLLINS *Acct. Eng. Colony N.S.W.* I. 590 Car-ru-ey strenuously urged him .. to shoot the Botany Bay black fellows. **1938** A. UPFIELD *Bone is Pointed* (1966) 52 I've known lots of fine blackfellers and more 'n one extra good half-caste. **1958** F.B. VICKERS *Mirage* 194 No matter how he dressed her up, she was a gin—a black fella.

2. In special collocations: **blackfellow's bread,** *native bread,* see NATIVE *a.* 6 a.; **blackfellow's button,** AUSTRALITE; **blackfellow's oven,** *native oven,* see NATIVE *a.* 5; **blackfellow's wash,** see quot. 1915; **blackfellow's well,** *native well,* see NATIVE *a.* 5.

1902 *Proc. Linnean Soc. N.S.W.* XXVII. 542 *Polyporus mylittae.* .. The sclerotium of this species is of common occurrence in the eastern States of Australia as well as in Tasmania under the name of '**Black Fellows' Bread**'. **1933** C. FENNER *Bunyips & Billabongs* 40 Most of us have seen an Australite... They are also known as '**blackfellows' buttons**', obsidianites, emu-stones, and 'trans-line' meteorites. **1883** *Jrnl. & Proc. R. Soc. N.S.W.* (1884) 37 **Blackfellows' ovens** or cooking-places have been a fertile source of argument for many years, some holding that they are not cooking places at all, but tumuli .. left by some race long since passed away. **1915** N. DUNCAN *Austral. Byways* 68 In outward aspect he was not by so much as a **black fellow's wash** (which is no wash at all) improved above his wretched neighbor. **1944** M.J. O'REILLY *Bouyangs & Boomerangs* 107 Such waterholes are known as 'enama holes' or **blackfellows' wells.**

B. 1. *adj.* and *attrib.* Aboriginal.

1829 D. BURN *Bushrangers* (1971) 30 Well, matta, how you like black fello corobbora? **1886** R. HENTY *Australiana* 244 There were very few red kangaroos of the old man species (old man, blackfellow for 'big').

2. In Comb. and collocations: **blackfellow country, doctor, fashion.**

1863 J. BONWICK *Wild White Man* 86 The white man .. 'take him everything **blackfellow country**'. **1884** A.W. HOWITT *On Some Austral. Ceremonies Initiation* 5 His father .. was a renowned '**blackfellow doctor**' of the Wiraijuri tribe. **1862** A. POLEHAMPTON *Kangaroo Land* 106 Our meat we .. threw .. on the ashes to cook itself—**black-fellow fashion.**

blackfish. Any of several dark-coloured marine and fresh-water fish, esp. the LUDERICK and *Gadopsis marmoratus,* of fresh water in s.e. Aust.

1790 R. CLARK *Jrnl.* 15 June 176 Four fish of which number there was a large black fish. **1985** *Canberra Times* 26 Jan. 23/3 When Dad caught a blackfish the little boys got very excited.

blackie. Formerly also **blackee, blackey, blacky.** [Transf. use of *blacky* a Black: see OED *sb.* 1.] An Aboriginal. Freq. used facetiously, and now uncommon.

1827 P. CUNNINGHAM *Two Yrs. in N.S.W.* II. 21 The instant *blacky* perceives *whity* beating a retreat, he vociferates after him—'Go along, you dam rascal.' **1834** G. BENNETT *Wanderings N.S.W.* I. 277 He took a piece of charcoal and sketched some figures upon a sheet of bark ..; blackee called them 'white fellers'. **1856** *Full & True Acct. Murder of P. Brown,* There's nothing looming in the distance, To cheer the heart or glad the eye; There's nothing certain for old blackey, But the doom that, he must die. **1977** T.A.G. HUNGERFORD *Wong Chu* 2 Scarecrow 'blackies' and their stick-insect children, whose tangled black hair and blazing black eyes I can still see.

black soil. [Not exclusively Austral. but of local importance.]

1. A black, cracking, clay soil characterizing natural grasslands, valued for its fertility but soft and hazardous to travel across in wet weather. Also *attrib*.

1874 J.J. HALCOMBE *Emigrant & Heathen* 57 In some places the road is deep with sand, in others it is a dry hard gravel; while the decomposed '*trap*' makes a rich black soil, which in wet weather is most tenacious. **1876** 'EIGHT YRS.' RESIDENT' *Queen of Colonies* 81 The Darling Downs squatters, often spoken of in colonial parlance as the Black Soil men, had no intention of foregoing the privileges they enjoyed as occupiers of this fruitful district.

2. Comb. **black soil country, flat, plain, plainsman**.

1882 G. RANDALL *Aust. for Industrious* 11 The Darling Downs—magnificent **black soil country**. **1894** *Bulletin* (Sydney) 10 Mar. 20/1 They may be at Mundooran now, or past the Overflow—Or tramping down the **black-soil flats** across by Waddiwong. **1867** A.J. RICHARDSON *Private Jrnl. Surveyor Exped. Cape York* 4/1 We encamped near some waterholes, on the western side of a small **black-soil plain**. **1977** C. MCCULLOUGH *Thorn Birds* 188 Let Sydney and Melbourne brides petition him for forecasts; the **black-soil plainsmen** would stick with that old sensation in their bones.

black stump. [Spec. use of *black* fire-blackened. From the use of the ubiquitous black stump as a marker when giving directions to travellers (see quot. 1900).]

1. An imaginary marker at the limits of settled and, by implication, civilized country. Also *attrib*.

[**1900** *Bulletin* (Sydney) 31 Mar. 31/1 A rigmarole of details concerning the turns and hollows, the big tree, the dog-leg fence, and the black stump.] **1957** J.M. HOSKING *Aust. First & Last* 16 There must be some of that Black Stump left, It's out near the Queensland border. **1978** R.H. CONQUEST *Dusty Distances* 142 Haven't you heard of the black stump court?

2. a. In the phr. **this side of the black stump,** in the world known to the speaker.

1954 T. RONAN *Vision Splendid* 264 You're looking .. at the best bloody station bookkeeper this side of the black stump. **1981** P. BARTON *Bastards I have Known* 63 Wolfy .. was a German and turned out to be one of the best bastards this side of the black stump.

b. In the phr. **beyond the black stump,** in the remote outback.

1965 G.H. FEARNSIDE *Golden Ram* 78 Fair go, mate, we're out beyond the black stump here. **1979** D. MAITLAND *Breaking Out* 83 Beyond the mythical Black Stump, where, as Hunt often joked, the crows flew backwards to keep the sun and the flies out of their eyes.

3. A local name for the State Office Block in Sydney. Also *attrib*.

1970 J. CLEARY *Helga's Web* 263 His office was in the State Government block, a beautiful dark grey tower that the citizens, with the local talent for belittling anything that embarrassed them with its pretensions, had dubbed the Black Stump. **1975** *Bulletin* (Sydney) 24 May 29/1 Legal & General Assurance fairly recently built a 17-storey 'black stump' type office on the North Shore.

blackwood. The tree *Acacia melanoxylon* (fam. Mimosaceae) of Qld., N.S.W., Vic., Tas., and S.A.; the reddish-brown wood of the tree; *Tasmanian blackwood*, see TASMANIAN *a*. **2.** Also *attrib*.

1790 J. HUNTER *Hist. Jrnl. Trans. Port Jackson* (1793) 390 The live-oak, yellow-wood, black-wood, and beech, are all of a close grain, and durable. **1910** *Huon Times* (Franklin) 30 Mar. 4/3 Bush fires have devastated the thickly-timbered Bridgetown blackwood districts in the southeast.

blacky, var. BLACKIE.

bladder saltbush. [f. *bladder*, referring to the appearance of the fruits + SALTBUSH 1.] Any of several small shrubs of the genus *Atriplex* (fam. Chenopodiaceae), the fruits of which have large inflated appendages, esp. *A. vesicaria* and *A. hymenotheca*.

1897 L. LINDLEY-COWEN *W. Austral. Settler's Guide* 426 (caption) *Atriplex vesicaria* .. 'Bladder salt-bush.' **1982** *Ecos* xxxiii. 19/1 One widespread type of pasture land, the bladder saltbush .. community.

blade. *Shearing. Hist.*

1. *pl*. Hand shears. Also (in *sing*.) *attrib*., and **blade shears**.

1897 *Worker* (Sydney) 11 Sept. 1/1 That's what he calls his shears at work; he calls them 'blades' in songs. **1965** R.H. CONQUEST *Horses in Kitchen* 193 His father had shorn at Isisford in the old blade days, as had Jacky Howe. **1980** P. FREEMAN *Woolshed* 20 Until the introduction of the mechanical handpiece in 1888, 'blade' shears were exclusively used.

2. Comb. **blade-man, -shearer, -shearing** *vbl*. *n*.

1918 *Huon Times* (Franklin) 29 Nov. 3/5 They got through upwards of 400,000 sheep per year there, and some of the champion **blade-men** gathered. **1937** *Bulletin* (Sydney) 14 July 20/1 No bladesmen sought For artificial aids to pace. **1924** *Ibid*. 10 Jan. 24/4 Howe proved himself to be absolutely the world's champion **blade-shearer**. **1945** *Bulletin* (Sydney) 14 Mar. 15/1 Sam was doing casual **blade-shearing**.

3. In the phr. **to go out with the blades,** to become obsolete.

1958 J.R. SPICER *Cry of Storm-Bird* 2 Others .. were still on the pedal-wireless system, but most wirelesses were up-to-date and pedalling had 'gone out with the blades'.

blady grass. Also **bladey grass**. [f. *blady* blade-like.] Any of several grasses (fam. Poaceae), esp. the perennial *Imperata cylindrica* var. *major*, the mature blades of which are stiff and fibrous, with sharp edges. Formerly also **blade of grass**.

1827 P. CUNNINGHAM *Two Yrs. in N.S.W*. I. 209 The blady grass grows often to the height of two or three feet, and from its broad strong leaf makes excellent thatch. **1847** A. HARRIS *Settlers & Convicts* (1953) 132 Here and there a little meadow-like spot covered with the coarse grass called 'blade of grass'. **1981** T. SHAPCOTT *Stump & Grape & Bopple-nut* 13 When they tugged at the bladeygrass they cut their fingers.

blank. Of a waterside worker: one who holds an unendorsed licence for casual work (see PREFERENCE 2).

1947 J. MORRISON *Sailors belong Ships* 32 Work on these ships sometimes trickles out to the Blanks, but to-day the Seconds rush it. **1982** LOWENSTEIN & HILLS *Under Hook* 78 About 1933 I went in for a licence. The First Preference was P and C and Federation men. The Second Preference was men that used to follow the wharf as much as they could and the Third Preference was the blanks. And when you first paid you were a blank.

blanket.

1. *Hist. Government blanket*, see GOVERNMENT B. **4.** Also *attrib*., as **blanket day** (see quot. 1857).

1857 *Moreton Bay Free Press* 29 Apr. 3/1 Blanket Day.—The blankets and articles of clothing usually distributed to the aborigines on the Queen's birth-day, were given out last Thursday (St. George's Day). **1880** *Bulletin* (Sydney) 19 June 21/9 Queen's Birthday (the annual 'blanket-day' of the Wide Bay blacks).

2. *Gold-mining. Obs*. A device for trapping particles of water-borne gold; a blanket-sluice (see quot. 1871). Also **blanket-table**.

1862 J.A. PATTERSON *Gold Fields Vic*. 260 If blanket-tables, or revolving blankets, are added only impalpable gold can escape. **1871** J. BALLANTYNE *Homes & Homesteads* 42 A table, or platform of wood, so laid as to have a gentle incline, and covered with what diggers call 'a blanket'—in other words, a cloth made of green baize or some other coarse material—is prepared as the bed over which the water with its precious freight is to flow.

3. Used *attrib.* in Special Comb. **blanket cheque,** a large cheque; **muster,** see MUSTER *n.* 5.

1905 *Bulletin* (Sydney) 16 Mar. 3/2 My cheque was not the size of shearing-cheques of long ago (The good old days of 'blanket' cheques were dead).

blanketing, *vbl. n. Obs.* See quot. 1825.

1825 *Colonial Times* (Hobart) 19 Nov., The common practice in the gaol called *blanketing*. When a prisoner receives a loaf or other provisions, before he has time to commence his repast, a blanket is thrown over him, he is wrested of his food, and held in durance until the whole is devoured out of sight. **1826** *Ibid.* 2 Sept., Disgraceful attempts to rob a fellow-prisoner by *blanketing*.

bleeders, *pl. Obs.* [Survival of Br. slang *bleeder* a spur: see F. Grose *Dict. Vulgar Tongue* (1811).] Spurs.

1812 J.H. VAUX *Mem.* (1819) II. 156 *Bleeders*, spurs. **1915** T. SKEYHILL *Soldier-Songs from Anzac* 14, I urged and forced him to his best, and plied the whip and bleeders, And truly well he stood the test, and rattled past the leaders.

blew, var. BLUE *v.*[1]

blight. SANDY BLIGHT.

1807 *Sydney Gaz.* 8 Feb., The blights which affect the eye perhaps in a much greater degree here than elsewhere are more severely felt this season than ever before remembered. **1929** K.S. PRICHARD *Coonardoo* (1961) 173 Phyllis went down to an attack of blight, which kept her to her room for days.

blind, *a.*

1. [Spec. use of *blind*, of a geographical feature that terminates abruptly: see OEDS *a*. 11 c.] In collocations: **blind creek, gully** (see CREEK, GULLY).

1834 *Sydney Herald* 1 Sept. 2/4 All those lagoons have, what they term here, '**blind creeks**', (or a hollow made by floods). [N.Z. **1848** C.J. PHARAZYN Jrnl. 15 Jan. 97 Teddy and W. to lambs to drive them to pen, smother'd 10 in a **blind gully**.] **1852** D. MACKENZIE *Ten Yrs. Aust.* 22 The best places to look for gold are .. along the sides of gullies (especially 'blind' gullies, as they are called, that lose themselves in the hills).

2. In the collocation **Blind Freddie** [poss. the nickname of a Sydney hawker], a most unperceptive person (as a type).

1946 D. STIVENS *Courtship of Uncle Henry* 188 He doesn't want to go on with tonight. Blind Freddie could see that. **1985** *Bulletin* (Sydney) 4 June 12/2 It was obvious to blind Freddie there was no real impediment to air safety.

blind, *n.* In the phr. **on the blind,** on chance, without prior information.

1917 *All abaht It* (London) (1919) Feb. 62 What about getting it—'one on the blind'? **1960** D. McLEAN *Roaring Days* 62 When you're on opal country .. you have to sink 'on the blind'.

blind grass. [See quot. 1926.] Either of the perennial plants *Stypandra grandiflora* and *S. imbricata* (fam. Liliaceae) of s.w. W.A.

1897 L. LINDLEY-COWEN *W. Austral. Settler's Guide* 589 The Candyup poison, or blind grass, has been identified with *Stypandra glauca*, a liliaceous plant met with from King George's Sound to the Swan and Murchison. **1926** *Poison Plants W.A.* (W.A. Dept. Agric.) 62 The Blind Grasses .. are reputed to cause blindness in stock.

blindy-eye, var. BINDI-EYE.

blind-your-eye. Also **blind-your-eyes.** Either of the trees *Excoecaria agallocha* (see *milky mangrove* MANGROVE) and *E. dallachyana* (fam. Euphorbiaceae), the milky sap of which can cause temporary blindness.

1888 *Proc. Linnean Soc. N.S.W.* III. 380 *Excaecaria agallocha* .. 'Blind-your-eyes'. **1974** S.L. EVERIST *Poisonous Plants Aust.* 199 Blind-your-eye .. is reputed to be capable of causing blistering and blindness in man.

blister, *n.*[1] [Abbrev. of *blister pearl* irregularly shaped pearly excrescence.]

1. See quot. 1919.

1913 *Cwlth. Parl. Papers* III. 640 Do the Japanese divers break up the shells to get the pearl blisters? **1919** *Smith's Weekly* (Sydney) 10 May 11/2 Seed pearl and 'blisters' (pearls of irregular shape attached to the oyster's inner shell) are fairly common.

2. An oyster shell having a protuberance which contains a pearl; the protuberance as distinct from the shell.

1937 J.M. HARCOURT *It never Fails* 130 The pearl-cleaner sat at a table working on a blister with a file. **1941** K.S. PRICHARD *Moon of Desire* 72 T.B. chuckled about the pearl, sold for one hundred pounds, he had found in a blister on some old shells used for a doorstep.

blister, *n.*[2] [f. *blister* summons: see OEDS *sb.* 6.] A debt.

1934 T. WOOD *Cobbers* 134 Men talked about their blister .. which means a mortgage, with complacency. **1951** E. HILL *Territory* 431 Never carry a 'blister', a bill or an account.

blithered, *ppl. a.* [f. *blither* to talk nonsense: see OEDS *v.*] Drunk.

1911 *Bulletin* (Sydney) 12 Oct. 14/2 Who ever hears .. of a man being 'drunk'? .. The staid and dignified citizen will say he is 'intoxicated' .., the average boy that he is 'shickered', 'blithered' or 'tonicked'. **1921** K.S. PRICHARD *Black Opal* 37 Old Ted! .. He's blithered!

blitz. [Transf. use of *blitz* attack.] **a.** An army sobriquet for an open truck, esp. a personnel carrier. **b.** Any modified heavy-duty ex-army vehicle. In full **blitz buggy (truck, wagon).**

1943 *Troppo Tribune* (Mataranka) 8 Feb. 3 The blitz-buggy in the vanguard of the returning Concert Troupe. **1950** G.M. FARWELL *Land of Mirage* 110 It turned out to be Ron Michell, whose Ford 'blitz' wagon had passed us. **1970** D. BAIRD *Incredible Gulf* 18 Just after dawn the rumble of the 'blitz' truck engine awakens me... Baker is backing the blitz up to the drums of fuel scattered in one corner. **1981** P. BARTON *Bastards I have Known* 55 A youth .. was on hand to .. assist with the transfer of supplies on to an old army 'blitz'... We were sitting on the back of the 'blitz' heading for the homestead .. up a winding, sandy track.

block, *n.*[1] [U.S. *block* each of the parcels of land in which a town is laid out for subdivision, orig. with reference to a mass of contiguous buildings wholly or mainly occupying an area bounded by four streets: see Mathews 1 b.]

1. One of the parcels into which a town site or other land made available for settlement and development is divided.

1833 *Sydney Herald* 4 Mar. 2/5 A large site of ground is occupied by the new arrangement... This is divided into sections, or what are professionally designated 'blocks', .. each block containing ten acres. **1952** J.F. HADDLETON *Katanning Pioneer* 9 The first block selected was 100 acres, Kojonup Location 66.

2. A parcel of land which is entire and of a piece, esp. one taken up for settlement.

1835 J. BATMAN *Settlement in Port Phillip* 6 June (1856) 20, I purchased two large blocks or tracts of land, about 600,000 acres, more or less, and, in consideration there for, I gave them blankets, knives, looking glasses, tomahawks, beads, scissors, flour, &c., and I also further agreed to pay them a tribute or rent yearly. **1979** W.D. JOYNT *Breaking Road for Rest* 45 When the time came to leave the station, I took on a contract with another fellow to clear and burn the mallee scrub on a six hundred acre block at a place in a newly developed district north of Ouyen.

3. A variously defined unit of measurement used to limit the size of a piece of land taken up for settlement or to determine the rent payable on it.

1843 *Adelaide Observer* 18 Nov. 7/1. *Waste Lands Bill*. On laying this Bill on the table, his Excellency stated that its object was chiefly, to lease runs in the neighbourhood of purchased land; the runs would be divided into blocks of a square mile, and be let at one pound for that quantity of land. **1937** *Bulletin* (Sydney) 30 June 21/4 For 25 years I've lived on the edge of a large block of tropical jungle.

4. A building allotment.

1874 J.J. HALCOMBE *Emigrant & Heathen* 16 The school.. was built by the Bishop in 1849, on a block of land. **1976** *Meanjin* 380 Trip overseas, holiday block, washing-machine, dishwasher, colour TV upstairs.

5. *Mining*. See quots. 1869 and 1870. Also *attrib*.

1858 *Colonial Mining Jrnl.* Oct. 28/3 The amount of litigation in connection with this lead is great, some of the claims being under the frontage, and others the block system. **1862** 'W.T.G.' *Quite Colonial* (c 1948) 7 With right good will he went about stripping the worthless soil off his 'block'; and before dinner time he had laid bare some couple of square yards of auriferous stratum. **1869** R.B. SMYTH *Gold Fields & Mineral Districts* 604 *Block-claim*, a claim bounded by right lines (except where in very rare cases a creek or river forms a boundary) which are fixed and defined by pegs, posts, or trenches at each angle of the claim; either at the time of taking possession, or within a prescribed time thereafter by survey, prior to registration. **1870** W.B. WITHERS *Hist. Ballarat* 126 The block claim is a fixed area, with bounds ascertained from the first.

6. A small holding; esp. an irrigated orchard or vineyard near Mildura, Vic.

1888 *Illustr. Austral. News* (Melbourne) 3 Mar. 35/1 The property.. will be cut up into small farms, orchard blocks and vineyards. **1968** J. BEGLEY *Block with One Holer* 18 They admired the miles of orange groves as they sped by. 'I was twenty-five years too late for one of those blocks,' mused Bluey.

block, *n.*² [Spec. use of BLOCK *n.*¹] Also *attrib*.

1. A street or block in which it is fashionable to promenade.

a. In Melbourne: Collins Street between Swanston and Elizabeth Streets.

1868 [see sense 2]. **1872** 'RESIDENT' *Glimpses Life Vic.* 349 A certain portion of Collins Street, lined by the best drapers' and jewellers' shops.. is known as 'The Block', and is the daily resort of the belles and beaux. **1928** *Melbourne Univ. Mag.* Oct. 14 We sell more buttons on the Block on Saturday morning than at any other time. **1947** *Ibid.* 31 The annual 'block parade' in Commencement Week.

b. In Sydney: see quot. 1872.

1872 BUNSTER & THATCHER *It runs in Blood* 60 *'The Block'* is supposed to extend down George-street, from King-street to Hunter-street, round Pitt-street, and up King-street into George-street again. But George-street is the 'subs'-walk' *par excellence*. **1945** H.M. MORAN *Beyond Hill lies China* 131 Challis's mind slipped back to the days when, as a student, he 'did the block' on Saturday mornings. Down George Street and around the Post Office, up Pitt Street, past King Street, and through the Arcade, then back to George Street again.

c. In Brisbane: the rectangle formed by Queen, Edward, Elizabeth, and Albert Streets.

1878 E. BRADDON *Lett. to India from Tas.* (1980) 15 We have done the block thoroughly; 'doing the block' being the local expression for wearing out one's shoe-leather on the Brisbane-street pavement. **1899** *Truth* (Sydney) 2 Apr. 2/6 Any quantity of Northerners have come and are coming to swell the gang who consider it *the* thing to do the wretched little block.

2. In the phr. **to do the block,** to promenade along 'the block'.

1868 *Australasian* (Melbourne) 6 June 721/4, I was slinking down the sunny side of Collins-street to avoid a bailiff.. and I was surprised to see so many people 'doing the block'. **1930** H. REDCLIFFE *Yellow Cygnet* 110 Here the fashionable lounger, lately of Collins Street, Melbourne, redolent in attar of roses and the scent of opoponax, 'doing the block' in spatted boots.

block, *n.*³ In the phr. **to do** (or **lose**) **one's block, (a)** to lose one's temper; **(b)** to lose one's heart (to someone).

1907 C. MACALISTER *Old Pioneering Days* 19 At this Mr Donovan 'lost his block' completely. **1915** C.J. DENNIS *Songs of Sentimental Bloke* 34 She knoo. I've done me block in on 'er, straight. A cove 'as got to think some time in life An' get some decent tart, ere it's too late, To be 'is wife. **1980** ANSELL & PERCY *To fight Wild* 112 Of course I did my block: 'Get off that fuckin' horse and come over here, you old bastard.'

block, *n.*⁴ *Obs*. A block of wood used in road-making: see quot. 1954. Freq. *attrib*.

1894 W.A. SMITH *On Austral. Hard Woods* 10 In Sydney, there are blocks which have been laid thirteen years in one of the busiest streets of the city, which are today in a perfect state of preservation. **1954** *Bulletin* (Sydney) 3 Nov. 12/2 Section of an old 'block' road, last of its kind in W.A., is to be preserved as a memorial to the pioneers who built it... The road was built by felling trees up to 3 ft. in diameter, sawing off rounds about 9 in. thick, and laying them side by side on a formed sand foundation.

block, *v.*¹ *Mining. Obs.* [Spec. use of *block* to cut out: see OED *v.* 10.] In the phr. **to block out,** to excavate (gold-bearing wash-dirt) in sections.

1862 J.A. PATTERSON *Gold Fields Vic.* 128 When the tunnel is driven.. and the drives are made, and the roof propped.. 'blocking out' the wash-dirt begins, and the stuff is.. piled at the bottom till the supply of water permits 'washing-up' to take place. **1877** G. WALCH *Hash* 61 We were *blocking out* near our western boundary, in a fair way to work out the claim in four days.

block, *v.*² *Obs.* [Spec. use of *block* to mark out: see OED *v.* 9.] In the phr. **to block off,** to place markers at the angles of (a mining claim), as required by law.

1871 *Austral. Town & Country Jrnl.* (Sydney) 4 Feb. 143/3 This claim is not yet lawfully blocked off. *Ibid.* 11 Feb. 166/4 No. 7 has blocked off, having defeated the 'jumpers'. **c 1882** T.F. DE C. BROWNE *Miners' Handy Bk.* (ed. 2) 11 On a frontage lead the block claim is exactly the same size that a frontage claim for the same number of miners is, when 'blocked off'—see Regulation 20.

block, *v.*³ *Obs.* [Spec. use of *block* to make with blocks of wood: see OED *v.* 11 and BLOCK *n.*⁴] *trans.* To surface (a road) with blocks.

1891 *Argus* (Melbourne) 25 Nov. 7/8 Only those streets in which the most traffic takes place will be blocked.

block and tackle. [Fig. use of *block and tackle* rope and pulley-block (also U.S.).] A watch and chain.

1899 *Western Champion* (Barcaldine) 25 Apr. 12/5 One of our own crowd had his 'block and tackle' (watch and chain) taken from him not so long ago. **1962** D. McLean *World turned upside Down* 105 Somewhere Arnot had a gold watch and chain, known in the 'Loo as a 'block and tackle'.

block boy. A street-cleaner.
1918 *Shire & Municipal Rec.* X. Feb. 275/2 *Log of the Federated Municipal and Shire Council Employees' Union of Australia.* Wages and Working Conditions... Block Boys.. £1 16 0. **1945** E.W. Campbell *Hist. Austral. Labour Movt.* 99 The block boys, employed by the City Council, objected to pursuing their usual calling while horses driven by free laborers remained on the streets, and.. struck work.

blocker. [f. Block $n.^1$ 2.]
1. *Obs.* One who occupies a small block of rural or semi-rural land.
1890 *Quiz* (Adelaide) 9 May 2/1 *Quiz* has never lost his mental balance in gushing on the subject of homestead blocks, but at the same time he heartily congratulates the blockers on the success of their show. **1910** *Huon Times* (Franklin) 16 Mar. 4/3 As the result of the rain-storms, the properties of many blockers near Murray-bridge were inundated.
2. *spec.* The proprietor of a small holding: see Block $n.^1$ 6.
1934 J.S. Neilson *Autobiogr.* (1978) 131 I reported the matter to the blocker's wife. **1968** J. Begley *Block with One Holer* 14 During late February and early March Bluey and Flo picked grapes for other blockers.
3. *Mining.* An occupant of a category of claim (see Block $n.^1$ 5).
1890 'R. Boldrewood' *Miner's Right* 76 Some of the impatient holders of claims on 'the line' frontages and others who were merely 'blockers' or occupants of ordinary chance claims anywhere in the vicinity, were more impatient.

blockie. Also **blocky.** [f. Block $n.^1$ 6 + -Y.] Blocker 2.
1944 A.J. & J.J. McIntyre *Country Towns of Vic.* 185 The irrigation districts, and particularly the Mildura district, present a contrast... Here the blockies' wives are in everything, and it is the town women who are in the minority. **1950** G. Farwell *Surf Music* 22 Don't bring him up to be a blockie, girl... Growing grapes, that's no life for a man. Send him out in the bush. **1979** C. Stone *Running Brumbies* 120 There we found a 'blocky', who owned one of the irrigation blocks, who gave us work but drove a pretty hard bargain.

bloke. A person in authority or of superior status.
1841 B. Wait *Lett. from Van Dieman's Land* (1843) 265 These removes are always made 'under the rose', (in secret) principally when the 'bloke' (proprietor) is out. **1966** T. Ronan *Once there was Bagman* 2 See if you can work me in for a yarn with the Bloke. I'll bite him if you won't.

blood. [Spec. use of *blood* red.] In the names of birds: **blood-bird,** either of two birds, the *scarlet honeyeater* (see Scarlet), and the *red-headed honeyeater* (see Red *a.* 1 b.); **-finch,** *crimson finch,* see Crimson.
1843 J. Gould *Birds of Aust.* (1848) IV. Pl. 63, *Sanguineous Honey-eater...* **Blood-bird** of the Colonists of New South Wales. **1928** G.H. Wilkins *Undiscovered Aust.* 143 **Blood-finches** passed through each year in migration.

blood house. [f. *blood* bloodshed + *(public) house.*] A disorderly public house; one with a reputation for violence.
[N.Z. **1951** *Evening Post* (Wellington) 13 Jan. 12 For many years its customers earned it the reputation of a 'blood house' and the licensee's job of keeping the peace was a hard one.] **1952** A.C.C. Lock *Travels across Aust.* 140 In Queensland it would have been called a 'blood house'; a

hotel whose management was interested only in getting the maximum number of people drunk in the minimum time. **1977** R. Beilby *Gunner* 128 You bloody booze hound!.. I've hauled you out of every boozer and blood house from here to Perth.

blood tree. *Obs.* Bloodwood.
1827 *Trans. Linnean Soc. London* XV. 271 *Mun'ning-trees,* or *Blood-trees* of the colonists (a species of *Eucalyptus*). **1892** *Proc. Linnean Soc. N.S.W.* VI. 412 That (kino) from a species called 'Blood-tree' is heated.. by the blacks of Lake Macquarie.. and applied to external wounds.

bloodwood.
1. Any of many trees of the genus *Eucalyptus* (fam. Myrtaceae), typically having a rough, tesselated, persistent bark and exuding a viscous reddish kino when damaged; the wood of these trees, usu. having abundant veins and pockets of kino; Blood tree. Also *attrib.*
1827 *HRA* (1923) 3rd Ser. VI. 503 The Banks on both sides are covered with very large Timber.. such as.. Blood Wood. **1938** R. Ingamells *Sun-Freedom* 38 Bleached bones tied to a bloodwood tree!
2. Special Comb. **bloodwood apple,** a rounded gall formed on the smaller branches of the tree in response to insect damage.
1903 H. Basedow *Jrnl. Govt. N.-W. Exped.* (1914) 108 Our natives have collected a bagful of what they call 'bloodwood apples'.

bloody, *a.* and *adv.* [Used as in general English but from its frequency and ubiquity often thought of as characteristically Austral.: see *Australian adjective* Australian *a.* 4.]
A. *adj.*
1. An intensive, ranging in force from 'mildly irritating' to 'execrable'.
1814 *HRA* (1916) 1st Ser. VIII. 363 He said Bloody Main at the Toll bar; he said that Main informed against some Bushrangers. **1980** Ansell & Percy *To fight Wild* 16 He might decide he doesn't want to go to bloody Hall's Creek after all and go home.
2. In the collocation **(my) blood(y) oath,** an intensive form of *my oath* (see Oath).
1848 R. Marsh *Seven Yrs. of my Life* 70 Come along you bloody crawlers, you'll have to walk faster than this tomorrow, with a cart load of stone—my bloody oath you will. **1967** M. & M. Leyland *Where Dead Men Lie* 20 Bloody oath... Most important part of any fishing trip is the ice box. **1968** K. Denton *Walk around my Cluttered Mind* 5 One of the blokes said to me, 'Y' gonna havanutha cuppa, digger?' And I said, 'Blood oath, mate!'
B. *adv.* An intensive: extremely, very.
1823 *HRA* (1917) 1st Ser. XI. 45, I know bloody well who the Captain meant to shoot. **1958** *Coast to Coast 1957–58* 51 Good day, missus. Bloody hot, ain't it? **1975** R.J. Merritt *Cake Man* (1978) 16 Know what happens when y' cross a black crow with a white rooster? Y' get a magpie. That's why we got so bloody many magpies in Australia and parts elsewhere.

blot. [Transf. use of *blot* dark patch.] The anus.
1945 S.J. Baker *Austral. Lang.* 156 [World War II slang.] *Blot,* the posterior or anus. **1974** D. Ireland *Burn* 146 Maybe he'll grab this last chance for some action after sitting on his blot all these years.

blotch, *v. Obs.* [Spec. use of *blotch* to mark, disfigure.] *trans.* To obscure (a brand on an animal).
1899 G.E. Boxall *Story Austral. Bushrangers* 355 The manner in which brands might be 'faked' was endless, and when it was impossible to 'fake' a brand it was 'blotched'

or burned over, so that the original design could not be recognised.

Hence **blotch-brand** n. Obs.

1880 'ERRO' *Squattermania* 111 Dan appeared with the well-heated blotch-brand, and clapping it over the letters I.R., previously stamped on the near side of the bullocks, soon rendered them . . illegible.

blow, n.[1] Obs. [Chiefly Br. dial. and U.S. *blow* boast: see OED sb.[2] 2 and EDD sb.[1] 6.] A boast; boasting.

1867 *Sydney Punch* 19 Oct. 169/2 Australia's hope and 'blow'. [*Note*] 'Blow', *Anglice*, Boast. 'Quite Colonial!'—Ed. **1871** *Austral. Town & Country Jrnl.* (Sydney) 25 Mar. 359/2 They are undoubtedly a very good lot of bullocks, but certainly do not deserve all the blow that has been bestowed upon them.

blow, n.[2] *Shearing.* [Spec. use of *blow* firm stroke, recorded in EDD Suppl. as meaning 'the mark left by the shears'.] A stroke of the shears.

1870 *Austral. Town & Country Jrnl.* (Sydney) 5 Nov. 11/2 Every 'blow' of the shears is acutely painful. **1979** HARMSWORTH & DAY *Wool & Mohair* 153 Sufficient wool must be removed over the tail . . so that the sheep will not have to be lifted for the last few blows.

blow, n.[3] [f. *blow* to erupt: see OED v.[1] 26.] A body, usu. outcropping, of quartz or other mineral substance.

1871 *Austral. Town & Country Jrnl.* (Sydney) 25 Mar. 367/4 And when 7 feet had been driven, the reef, or a kind of a 'blow' was met with. The holders then started to drive on this 'blow', but when 4 feet had been driven it changed into a well-defined reef of blue-looking quartz. **1976** *Tracks we Travel* 121 A lifetime of deserts and dried watercourses, of outcrops of reef beneath rotten granite and 'blows' of quartz among shale.

blow, n.[4] [f. *blow* to smoke (tobacco): see OED v.[1] 9 b.] A rest (from the association between smoking and relaxing).

[**1855** R. CARBONI *Eureka Stockade* 10 He must have a 'blow', but the d—d things—his matches—had got damp, and so in a rage he must hasten to his tent to light the pipe.] **1910** *Huon Times* (Franklin) 26 Feb. 2/3 We didn't even get time to have a blow before we were called on to get on with the job again. **1984** W.W. AMMON et al. *Working Lives* 24 Look, they've been in the scrub belting their guts out. . . Don't you think they're entitled to a bit of a blow.

blow, n.[5] A cyclone; a very strong wind.

1935 *Frontier News* July 6/1 The week before our arrival they had had a blow which lasted three days and three nights. Afterwards she took forty-two kerosene buckets of sand out of her two front rooms. **1979** T. ASTLEY *Hunting Wild Pineapple* 163 She was given to those underplay phrases so dear to our myth: 'After the blow,' she'd say, referring to our worst cyclone in years.

blow, v.[1] [Chiefly Br. dial. *blow* to deposit eggs: see OED v.[1] 28 c. and EDD v.[1] 10.] *trans.* Of a fly, to deposit eggs on (meat, etc.).

1827 P. CUNNINGHAM *Two Yrs. in N.S.W.* I. 270 Meat is blown here, as soon as killed, by our bottle-flies; nay, even the very meat roasting on the spit, or smoking on the table, not always escapes. **1975** A. MARSHALL *Hammers over Anvil* 32 I've never seen a woman take meat out of a safe without smelling it all over. If it had just been blown there was a little pile of maggots.

Hence **blown** ppl. a., fly-blown.

1910 *Bulletin* (Sydney) 7 July 7/4 The blowfly pest means big trouble. . . The sheep are continually 'blown', which means great suffering to the animals.

blow, v.[2] [Chiefly Br. dial. and U.S. *blow* to boast: see OED v.[1] 6 a.] *intr.* To boast; to exaggerate.

1858 C.R. THATCHER *Colonial Songster* (rev. ed.) 35 About your talents *blow*, Mind, that's the regular caper. **1952** J. CLEARY *Sundowners* 88 'It was no worse than a landslide I was in in the Himalayas.' 'Always blowing. . .'

Hence **blowing** vbl. n. and ppl. a.

1858 A. PENDRAGON *Queen of South* 55 Wilson, from his constant habit of romancing, peculiar to colonists, and colonially termed 'blowing'. **1882** *Sydney Mail* 23 Dec. 1123/3 Jonathan was a blowing, blatherskiting fool.

blow, v.[3] *Horse-racing. trans.* To lengthen the odds on (a horse, etc.) Also with 'odds' as obj., and *absol.* Freq. with **out**.

1911 A. WRIGHT *Gamblers' Gold* (1923) 93 'They'll have us up!' whined Nelson. 'I wish y'd never started th' bally horse. A nice thing to be blown out. **1949** L. GLASSOP *Lucky Palmer* 63 I've got the commission . . and I'm trying to blow the price out. **1968** J. ALARD *He who shoots Last* 86 'She's blown in the bettin',' said a suspicious Ragged.

blow, v.[4] [Phrasal use of *blow* to leave hurriedly: see OEDS v.[1] 12 e.] *intr.* With **through**: to leave, esp. in a hurry.

1950 *Austral. Police Jrnl.* Apr. 110 Blow through . . Go away, leave. **1981** A. MARSHALL *Aust.* 37 'When he is down, don't hang round, blow through,' a king-hit expert once told me. 'When he gets up you might find he can scrap.'

blow, v.[5] Obs. In the phr. **to blow the froth (off),** to drink beer. Also *fig.*

1910 L. ESSON *Three Short Plays* (1911) 17, I don' forget 'ow you stuck to me. . . Ah, blow ther froth orf. **1931** D.B. O'CONNOR *Black Velvet* 30 There's a pub around the corner You must blow the froth with me.

blower. Obs. [Br. dial. and U.S. *blower* boaster: see OED sb.[1] 5.] A boaster.

1864 J. SNODGRASS *N.S.W. as Is* 8 He was not only communicative, but talkative. . . He was, what is usually termed in colonial parlance, a 'blower' i.e., one who never ceases talking of himself in particular, and everything in general. **1899** J. BRADSHAW *Quirindi Bank Robbery* 24 He was the ringer at Hammond's, and not a blower.

blowey, n.[1] Also **blowie**. [f. *blow(fly* + -Y.] A blowfly, esp. *Lucilia cuprina*, introduced to Australia in the twentieth century.

1916 J.B. COOPER *Coo-oo-ee!* 84 A dead jumbuck is buzzing with blowies. **1972** K. DUNSTAN *Knockers* 14 Finally there was the blowfly, better known as the Blowey, which was unquestionably a native of this country.

blowey, n.[2] Chiefly *W.A.* Also **blowy**. [f. *blow(fish* + -Y.] A blowfish, esp. *Torquigener pleurogramma*, a marine fish with potentially poisonous flesh.

1916 *Bulletin* (Sydney) 24 Feb. 22/2 It has been stated that the toad fish is rarely found outside of Japanese waters. In the Swan River and in the waters surrounding Fremantle 'blowy', as he is named, abounds. **1945** *Ibid.* 24 Jan. 13/4 Fish were plentiful, and none more so than the 'blowey'.

blowfly. [Fig. use of *blow-fly*.] One who acts officiously.

1899 *Bulletin* (Sydney) 26 Aug. 16/2 Police are sometimes called 'blowflies'. On the Condamine (Q.) I heard— 'Going to kill the brindle steer today father?' 'No, Sonny; the blowflies are too bad. I asked Sonny what his father meant, and he explained that 'the old cove must have heard that the police are about'. **1977** J. O'GRADY *There was Kid* 68 The 'blow flies' [Army hygiene personnel] insisted that we construct a urinal.

Hence **blowflyism** n.
1918 *Truth* (Sydney) 28 July 7/1 The spurious form of One-Big-Unionism favoured by some of the A.W.U. officials (which has been aptly named 'Blowflyism').

blow-hole. [Transf. use of *blow-hole* hole through which a whale 'blows'.] **a.** In coastal rock, a hole through which air or water rushes in response to the action of waves. **b.** Inland, a vent through which air passes, often with some force, to or from an underground air reservoir in response to temperature variation.
1849 J. TOWNSEND *Rambles & Observations N.S.W.* 141 At Kiama is a cavern running horizontally into the cliffs on the sea-side, and open to the sea... A gigantic fountain spouts through the opening, or 'blow-hole', to the height of sixty feet. **1894** A.F. CALVERT *Coolgardie Goldfield* 51 Our route was .. through salt bush and cotton bush country... The formation is of a limestone character full of blow holes.

blowie, var. BLOWEY n.[1]

blow-in. [f. (orig. U.S.) *blow in* to turn up unexpectedly: see OEDS *blow* v.[1] 12 d.] A newcomer or recent arrival; an intruder.
1937 E. HILL *Great Austral. Loneliness* 32 They had been painted by a 'blow-in', an Englishman named Malcolmsen, said to have been a crack steeplechase rider in his day. **1986** *Sydney Morning Herald* 14 June 44/6 Some blow-ins to Canberra .. said recently that the 'board under Wilenski' had lost its once powerful position.

blow my (or **me**) **skull** (**off**), n. phr. An alcoholic drink: see quots. Also **blow-your-hat-off.**
1853 C.R. READ *What I heard, saw, & Did* 172 'Blow my skull off... Some of the ingredients .. were as follows:- 'Cocculus indicus, spirits of wine, Turkey opium, Cayenne pepper and rum'; to this was added about five times the quantity of water, and sold at 2s. 6d. per wine glass. **1864** *Colonial Cook Bk.* (1970) 152 Blow my skull. This was a colonial beverage in use in the earlier days of Tasmania, and was named and drank by an eccentric governor... It was made in the following proportions:- Two pints of boiling water, with 'quantum sufficit' of loaf sugar, and lime or lemon-juice, one pint of ale or porter, one pint of rum, and half a pint of brandy. **1888** G. ROCK *Colonists* 28 'Blow me skull off'. This expression .. is the popular name by which the most common decoctions sold at the diggings are known—a name too, which is well deserved. **1956** *Bulletin* (Sydney) 28 Nov. 13/3 Wine purveyed there graded from 'dynamite' and 'blow-your-hat-off' to 'belltopper' brand and was pretty potent.

blow-up. [f. BLOW n.[4] + *-up*.] The signal that a rest period is over, and work about to begin. Also as *exclam*.
1873 THOMSON & GREGG *Desperate Character* I. 63 As his watch marked six, he shouted, in stentorian tones, 'Blow up'; and all the men fell to. **1951** *Bulletin* (Sydney) 21 Feb. 12/2 When, at blow-up, the 'pannikin' succeeded in bringing him back to life he crawled back to work like a blue-tongued lizard.

blowy, var. BLOWEY n.[2]

blucher. [Br. *blucher* a type of boot, having local significance as part of the dress of the bushman: see quot. 1881.] A strong leather half-boot. Also *attrib*.
1839 *Southern Austral.* (Adelaide) 17 July 1/3 Just received .. Blucher boots and gents. half dress ditto. **1850** *Monthly Almanac* (Adelaide) 9 And in their place appear the sober Guernsey—the humble moleskin—the strong fossil shaped colonial Blucher. **1881** R. CRAWFORD *Echoes from Bushland* 77 Put him into the squatting costume of the period, namely, a twill shirt open at the neck, and a pair of moleskin trousers, a size too big, tucked over a pair of *blootcher* boots.

bludge /blʌdʒ/, v. [Back formation from BLUDGER.] Usu. with **on**.
1. *intr.* To evade one's own responsibilities and impose on, or prey upon, others; to live off the efforts of others.
1899 *Truth* (Sydney) 12 Mar. 1/7 What else could they expect from the gang who bludge on cricket in Sydney? **1978** R.H. CONQUEST *Dusty Distances* 128 A man has to eat. Bludge on the bastards, right and left.
2. *intr. Obs.* To live on the earnings of a prostitute.
1903 *Truth* (Sydney) 20 Dec. 5/3 The increasing number of these fellows .. togged up in fine linen and fashionable clothes, procured with sin-money wrung from the unfortunate females upon whom they bludge, is a disgrace. **1910** *Truth* (Sydney) 20 Feb. 7/4 *The brother 'bludges' on his sister...* A vile fellow who lives on the prostitution of *his own sister*.
3. *intr.* To idle, usually (by implication) at someone else's expense.
1942 *Ack Ack News* (Melbourne) Aug. 2 Three men knocked out, rest of instrument crew bludged. **1980** *Sunday Tel.* (Sydney) 20 Apr. 43/4 Ask him, for instance what he does to relax and he replies, 'Bludge.'
4. *trans.* To cadge or scrounge (food, etc.).
1954 T. RONAN *Vision Splendid* 98 It makes me a man in work again, not just a bloke bludging a lift. **1963** J. O'GRADY *Things they do to You* 129, I might be able to bludge a bit of raw potato from him to put in my tobacco tin.

Hence **bludging** *vbl. n.* and *ppl. a.*
1903 *Truth* (Sydney) 11 Oct. 3/3 She had called him a 'bludging bastard', to which he replied, 'Like your mother, who keeps a brothel.' *c* **1907** W.C. CHANDLER *Darkest Adelaide* 2/1 That bludging has been reduced to a fine art here in Adelaide cannot be gainsaid. Here the bludger is an institution.

bludge /blʌdʒ/, n. [f. prec.]
1. An undemanding job; a period of idleness, usually at someone else's expense.
1943 J. BINNING *Target Area* 24 They realised you had not come down there just for a joke or a 'bludge'. **1979** CAREY & LETTE *Puberty Blues* 48 Phew. The class sat back for a bludge.
2. An imposition or exaction.
1947 V.C. HALL *Bad Medicine* 160 The history of the Northern Territory is the story of one long bludge on the aboriginal. **1979** CAREY & LETTE *Puberty Blues* 89 We bought our ten cents worth of lollies. That was our daily bludge from Mr Knight.

bludger /ˈblʌdʒə/. [Survival of Br. slang *bludger*, shortened form of *bludgeoner*: see OED(S.)]
1. One who lives on the earnings of a prostitute.
[**1856** H. MAYHEW *Great World of London* 46 'Bludgers' or 'stick slingers', who rob in company with low women.] **1882** *Sydney Slang Dict.* 1 *Bludgers*, or *Stick Slingers*, plunderers in company with prostitutes. **1963** X. HERBERT *Disturbing Element* 96 Two other famous protectors of molls, Bludgers as they were called, were an Irishman .. and a negro.
2. a. A generalized term of abuse, esp. as applied to a person who appears to live off the efforts of others.
1900 *Truth* (Sydney) 28 Jan. 5/4 Lyttleton's battalion of Bludgers. **1977** *Bronze Swagman Bk. Bush Verse* 58, I charged him like a scrubber that's got murder in its mind, And when a roarin' shout, I donged the bludger from behind.
b. *spec.* A derogatory term for a person engaged in non-manual employment, a white-collar worker.
1910 *Truth* (Sydney) 27 Mar. 5/3 Blackguard band of blatant, bumptious bummers and bludgers, who bum and

bludge on Labor. **1979** *Canberra Times* 19 Sept. 2/2 It was when you came to analyse the reasons for the uncomplimentary stereotype of public servants as a pack of tea-swilling bludgers.

3. An idler, one who makes little effort.

1942 *Ack Ack News* (Melbourne) Apr. 3 By the way, who said our sappers are bludgers? **1980** *Sydney Morning Herald* 4 Jan. 7/8, I suspect there are far more bludgers in jobs than there are on the dole.

4. One who does not make a fair contribution (to a cost, enterprise, etc.); a cadger.

1955 D. NILAND *Shiralee* 46 Put the nips into me for tea and sugar and tobacco in his usual style. The biggest bludger in the country. **1978** J. ANDERSON *Tirra Lirra* 46 But you always say Les is a bludger. I'll do the swearing round here! He's a bludger all right, but naturally, he had to kick in *something*.

Hence **bludgerdom** *n.*, **bludgeress** *n.*

1903 *Truth* (Sydney) 19 July 3/5 Another case, savoring somewhat of **bludgerdom**, was heard at the same court. *c* **1907** C.W. CHANDLER *Darkest Adelaide* 12/1 In the face of this thriving state of affairs in Bludgerdom, the police don't seem over-anxious to swoop down on the carrion with a big swoop. **1908** *Truth* (Sydney) 27 Dec. 1/5 Latterly, bludgers, so the police say, are marrying **bludgeresses**.

blue, *n.*^{1} [Back formation f. BLUEY.]

1. *Obs.* BLUEY 1 a. Also as *adj.* in the collocation **blue one**.

1896 *Bulletin* (Sydney) 30 July 32/2 'Neddy' the tuckerbag is of more importance than the 'blue one', and by way of precedence dangles in front, mostly hanging to Matilda's apron-strings. **1918** 'LANCE-CORPORAL COBBER' *Anzac Pilgrim's Progress* 14 Coo-ee! Coo-ee-ee! Hump yer blue an' away.

2. BLUEY 4.

1939 K. TENNANT *Foveaux* 348 Before we get any more blues for obstructin' the traffic, there's something I want to tell you. **1980** B. HORNADGE *Austral. Slanguage* 267 A legal summons is a *blue* (or *bluey*) and the origins of this is not hard to fathom since summonses are printed on blue paper.

3. BLUEY 6.

1932 L. MANN *Flesh in Armour* 56 Blue McIntosh, No. 1, red in the head. **1978** H.C. BAKER *I was Listening* 141 In American a red-headed man is 'Red', in England 'Carrots' or 'Ginger'; only an Aussie could make him 'Blue'.

blue, *n.*^{2} [Poss. from *blue* characterized by swearing, as in *to make the air blue*: see OEDS *blue, a.* 9 b.]

1. A fight; an altercation; a disagreement.

1943 A. DAWES *Soldier Superb* 29, I heard the 'blue' (battle) was still on. **1978** D. STUART *Wedgetail View* 51 If a feller gets in a blue, he can talk his way out, or he can grab a pick handle and break a leg on the bastard that's tryin' to force a fight on him.

2. In the phr. **to smack a blue,** to run into trouble.

1939 K. TENNANT *Foveaux* 290 You can always get a bet 'cause there's sure to be some bloke wiv a life sentence an' a wireless. As long as you don't smack a bad blue, you ought to 'ave a 'appy time. **1968** J. ALARD *He who shoots Last* 24, I know the kid never had a chance. . . I did my best to stop him smacking a blue; but it wasn't enough.

3. A mistake, a faux pas.

1941 *Action Front: Jrnl. 2/2 Field Regiment* Sept. 8 Decided he'd made a 'blue'. **1983** *Sun-Herald* (Sydney) 4 Dec. 168/6 Labor Party chappies were quick to jump in last week and score off Nick Greiner's tactical blue in saying the Opposition wasn't ready to govern yet.

4. In the phr. **to bung (put, stack) on a blue,** to make a fuss, to create a disturbance.

1950 *Austral. Police Jrnl.* Apr. 118 If it is said that a particular mug 'sings' well, then it means that he pays well without 'bunging on a blue'. **1953** D. CUSACK *Southern Steel* 137 'Luke-bloody-warm. It's time we put on a bloody blue for a ziggin' refrigerator.' 'Union's got it in hand, Slap.' **1965** *Tracks we Travel* 76 When the publican refused to serve him a drink on the grounds that he was an Aborigine under the Act, the town-workers really stacked on a blue.

blue, *v.*^{1} Also **blew.** [Br. slang *blue* to spend lavishly (see OEDS *v.*^{2} 1). Not excl. Austral.] *trans.* To squander (money to hand, earnings for a period, etc.). Esp. in the phr. **to blue a cheque.**

1881 G.C. EVANS *Stories* 300 When the old fool found a piece of gold, instead of blueing it in a proper manner [etc.]. **1962** MARSHALL & DRYSDALE *Journey among Men* 56 Then they would enter the bar and hand over their cheque to the publican. Thus they would 'blue' their cheques.

blue, *v.*^{2} [Cf. BLUE *n.*^{2}] *intr.* To argue, fight.

1969 W. DICK *Naked Prodigal* 27 'I thought youse were still goin' together, Kenny, even though youse bin bluein' a bit,' Raincoat said. **1977** R. EDWARDS *Austral. Yarn* 82 We'd been blueing in Camooweal at the bottom pub.

blue, *a.* Used as a distinguishing epithet in the names of flora and fauna: **blue-billed duck,** the diving duck *Oxyura australis* of s.e. and s.w. Aust., so called because the bill of the male turns blue in summer; **bonnet, (a)** the parrot *Northiella haematogaster*, having a blue face and occurring in relatively dry areas of s. Aust.; **(b)** *red-collared lorikeet*, see RED *a.* 1 a.; **bush,** any of several shrubs of inland plains and arid shrublands esp. of the genus *Maireana* (formerly *Kochia*), fam. Chenopodiaceae, the hairy leaves of which give the low bushes a blue-green to grey-green appearance; **caladenia,** the slender orchid *Caladenia caerulea* (fam. Orchidaceae) which bears a blue flower on a stem less than 20 cm. high; **cap,** any of several fairy wrens, the males having blue crowns; **cattle dog,** *blue heeler*; **couch,** any of several grasses (fam. Poaceae) with couch-like creeping root-stocks and blue-green leaves, esp. the African *Cynodon incompletus*, widespread in N.S.W., and *Digitaria didactyla* of Qld. and n.e. N.S.W.; **crane,** *white-faced heron*, see WHITE *a.*^{2} 1 b.; **dog,** *blue heeler*; **eye,** the fish *Pseudomugil signifer* of N.S.W. and s. Qld., occurring mainly in brackish but also in fresh and salt water; **fig,** QUANDONG 1 c.; the wood or fruit of the tree; **fish,** the marine fish *Girella cyanea* of N.S.W., New Zealand, and nearby islands, having a blue back and sides with small golden spots; **flyer,** an adult female *red kangaroo* (a) (see RED *a.* 1 b.); **grass,** any of several perennial grasses (fam. Poaceae) having flower-head spikes of a blue or purple colour, esp. of the genera *Bothriochloa* and *Dichanthium*; **groper,** the blue or brown parrot fish *Achoerodus gouldii* (fam. Labridae) of rocky coasts of s. Aust.; **gum,** any of several trees of the genus *Eucalyptus* (fam. Myrtaceae) having a smooth bluish-grey bark or bluish-grey juvenile foliage; the wood of these trees; also with distinguishing epithet, as **southern, Sydney, Tasmanian** (see under first element); **heeler,** the blue, or Australian cattle dog, a breed having a blue or red flecked coat, developed in Australia in the nineteenth century by crossing dingo with merle collie from Scotland and subsequently with Dalmatian and black-and-tan kelpie; **jay,** *black-faced cuckoo-shrike*, see BLACK *a.*^{2} 1 b.; **mallee,** the bluish-leaved mallee tree *Eucalyptus polybractea* (fam. Myrtaceae) of central Vic. and N.S.W.; also **blue-leafed mallee; martin, (a)** *fairy martin*, see FAIRY *n.*^{1} 1; **(b)** a wood swallow, esp. the *masked wood swallow* (see MASKED); **mountain parrot (lorikeet, parakeet),** *rainbow lorikeet*, see RAINBOW 2; also **mountaineer;** **-ringed octopus,** the small venomous octopus *Hapalochlaena maculosa* of Austral. coasts; **swimmer (crab),** the edible blue crab *Portunus pelagicus*, widely distributed in sheltered estuaries and inlets; also **swimming crab; -tongue(d) lizard,** any of several lizards with a blue tongue, prominent when the animal is threatened, esp. BOBTAIL or certain species of the closely-related genus *Tiliqua* (see also SLEEPING LIZARD); **-winged kookaburra,** the large kingfisher *Dacelo leachii* of woodlands in n. Aust. and New Guinea, having conspicuous blue areas on the wing; LEACH'S KINGFISHER; **wren,** any of several Austral. wrens of the fam. Maluridae, the adult male having blue on the crown and other parts of the body, esp. the *superb blue wren* (see SUPERB).

1844 J. GOULD *Birds of Aust.* (1848) VII. Pl. 17, *Erismatura australis*... **Blue-billed Duck** of the Colonists. **1865** J. GOULD *Handbk. Birds Aust.* II. 62 Red-vented Parrakeet... **Blue bonnet** of the Colonists of New South Wales. **1964** M. SHARLAND *Territory of Birds* 36 The gaudy Red-collared Parrots, usually referred to around Darwin as 'blue bonnets', have .. heads of rich blue, fringed with a scarlet collar, and with vermilion beneath the wings. **1862** W.R.H. JESSOP *Flindersland and Sturtland* II. 37 Before we reached this, however, we passed through a couple of miles of **blue bush,** a sign of good feed... This curious bush, so plentiful in Sturtland, is about the size of a gooseberry or currant bush, of the colour of sage, and of a very saltish taste. **1835** *Hobart Town Almanack* 74 *Caladenia caerulea.* **Blue Caladenia.** Smells like honey or meadow-sweet. It derives its name from *kalos,* beautiful. [*c* **1872 blue cap:** J.C.F. JOHNSON *Over Island* 11 A tiny 'blue-capped wren'.] **1903** *Emu* III. 27 Long-tailed Blue Wren... Under various names, such as .. 'Blue-cap' .. is this beautiful little species known to us. [**1909 blue cattle dog:** R. KALESKI *Austral. Settler's Compl. Guide* 24 Cattle-Dog—The best to get is a pure-bred blue one.] **1935** DAVISON & NICHOLLS *Blue Coast Caravan* 148 With them came two blue-cattle dogs. **1923** *Bulletin* (Sydney) 27 Dec. 23/4 To .. **blue couch** .. and .. sweet potato vines .. I can add another common bush plant with generally unsuspected poisonous properties. **1814** M. FLINDERS *Voyage Terra Australis* II. 226 The aquatic birds were **blue** and white **cranes. 1949** *Bulletin* (Sydney) 26 Jan. 15/1 The visiting salesman was gingerly patting the **blue dog. 1906** D.G. STEAD *Fishes of Aust.* 71 The tiny, but beautiful, **Blue-eye** (*Pseudomugil signifer*). **1884** A. NILSON *Timber Trees N.S.W.* 55 **Blue Fig.**—A tall slender tree... Timber close-grained and soft, but little used. **1790** R. CLARK *Jrnl.* 19 Apr. 159, 16 fishes consisting of Snappers **Blue Fish** and one Rock Cod. **1851** J. HENDERSON *Excursions & Adventures N.S.W.* II. 170 The **blue-flyer** is the swiftest, and tries the speed of the best kangaroo-dogs. **1862** J.M. STUART *Explorations in Aust.* 5 June (1865) 359 At four o'clock arrived at the **blue-grass** swamp. **1874** *N.S.W. Rep. R. Comm. Fisheries* (1880) 1294 The gruper .. popularly called in this country **blue** or black **groper**—no doubt from the fact of these fishes groping in and out of the caverns and crevices of rocks in search of crustaceae. **1799** D. COLLINS *Acct. Eng. Colony N.S.W.* (1802) II. 145 A sort of gum tree .. its leaf, that of the **blue gum** tree. **1908** W.H. OGILVIE *My Life in Open* 52 The **blue 'heelers'** or cattle dogs. **1861** 'OLD BUSHMAN' *Bush Wanderings* 131 The bird that we called the **Blue Jay** resembled its British namesake in no one particular. **1901** *Proc. Linnean Soc. N.S.W.* XXV. 692 *Eucalyptus Polybractea,* sp. nov. '**Blue Mallee**'... A glaucous Mallee, with quadrangular branchlets. **1984** *Sun News-Pictorial* (Melbourne) 2 Aug. 3/4 The contraption, run on 'only the best of blue-leafed Mallee gums', brews 87-per-cent pure 'euky oil'. **1924** *Bulletin* (Sydney) 10 Jan. 22/2 The **blue martin**, or bottle-swallow, seems to stop his flight by gripping the landing-place with his claws. **1934** H.G. LAMOND *Aviary on Plains* 112 It is the blue martin (masked wood-swallow). **1804** G. CALEY in A.E.J. Andrews *Devil's Wilderness* (1984) 39 A deal of **Blue Mountain Parrots** (Psittacus haematotus novae Hollandia) on the road. **1845** L. LEICHHARDT *Jrnl. Overland Exped. Aust.* 31 Aug. (1847) 382 A strange mess was made of cockatoo, Blue Mountaineers, an eagle hawk, and dried emu. **1948** P.J. HURLEY *Red Cedar* 179 Loquat trees were loaded with Blue Mountain parakeets. **1956** A.C.C. LOCK *Tropical Tapestry* 177 The silence was disturbed by the screeches of blue mountain lorikeets flashing past us with a brilliant display of colours. **1933** *Victorian Naturalist* XLIX. 238, I have seen the small, **blue-ringed octopus** (*Octopus maculosus*), common in Sydney Harbour, sitting on about fifty small, white, pea-shaped eggs. [**1897 blue swimmer:** W. SAVILLE-KENT *Naturalist in Aust.* 238 The so-called Blue Crab, *Neptunus pelagicus*. It belongs to the group known as swimming crabs.] **1905** D.G. STEAD *Crustaceans* 28 Some crabs swim about freely in the waters, their legs being flattened, and the last pair turned into oars to enable them to propel themselves readily through the water. To this pelagic kind belongs our common Blue Swimming Crab. **1953** *Bulletin* (Sydney) 25 Mar. 12/2, I have a boyhood memory of catching 'blue-swimmer' crabs on a tuppenny fishing-line. **1984** *Canberra Chron.* 15 Aug. 23/3 Freshly boiled blue swimmers and mussels and pipis grilled alive in the shells. **1848** W. CARRON *Narr. Exped. Rockingham Bay & Cape York* (1849) 74 The natives .. gave us a **blue-tongued lizard,** which I opened and took out eleven young ones, which we roasted and ate. **1923** *Bulletin* (Sydney) 3 May 24/4 What's the proper tucker for blue-tongue or shingle-back lizards? **1945** C. BARRETT *Austral. Bird Life* 143 The **blue-winged kookaburra** (*Dacelo leachi*) is more brightly coloured than its cousin of Eastern and South Australia. **1841** J. GOULD *Birds of Aust.* (1848) III. Pl. 18, *Malurus Cyaneus* .. Superb Warbler, **Blue Wren**, etc., of the colonists.

bluebell. Any of several small herbs of the genus *Wahlenbergia* (fam. Campanulaceae) bearing blue flowers reminiscent of the related Scottish bluebell; *native bluebell*, see NATIVE *a.* 6 *a.*

1839 *Southern Austral.* (Adelaide) 16 Oct. 4/1 May... The blue bell is almost the only flower in bloom this month. **1975** A.B. & J.W. CRIBB *Wild Food in Aust.* 164 Flavour of the bluebells is very mild, but the attractive appearance makes them worth using in salads.

blue-blind, *a. Obs.* [U.S. *blue* intoxicated (see OEDS *a.* 3 b.) + *blind (drunk).*] (Extremely) drunk. Also **blue-blind paralytic**.

1911 *Bulletin* (Sydney) 12 Oct. 14/2 Who ever hears .. of a man being 'drunk'? .. The staid and dignified citizen will say he is 'intoxicated', .. the dustman that he is 'blue-blind paralytic'. **1913** *Ibid.* 25 Sept. 22/2 'Inebriated'... In the number, aptness and variety of its colloquial equivalents I consider it commanderes the pastry. For instance:-loaded, primed, beered, .. blind, blue-blind.

Also **blue-blinded** *ppl. a.*

1914 E. DYSON *Spats' Fact'ry* 65 'Well, I'm blue-blinded,' murmured Nippo O'Kieffe.

bluebottle. The Portuguese man o' war, the blue marine siphonophore *Physalia physalis*, having a floating jelly-like body bearing a crest and trailing tentacles that sting on contact and may be several metres in length.

1911 *Bulletin* (Sydney) 27 Apr. 13/4 The famous 'bluebottle', which at times infests the ocean beaches, and whose greeting resembles that of a much-magnified stinging nettle. **1986** *Canberra Times* 17 Jan. 9/1 A Batemans Bay doctor said he knew of one death recently in N.S.W. when a man had accidentally swallowed a bluebottle while swimming at Bondi Beach.

blue duck. [Of unknown origin, but cf. (orig. U.S.) *dead duck.*] A lost cause, a failure.

1895 C. CROWE *Austral. Slang Dict.* 10 *Blue duck,* no good; no money in it. **1978** R. MCKIE *Bitter Bread* 142 He had rung round the usual contacts. But this Saturday had, early, an unmistakable feeling of being a blue duck for news.

blue metal, *n.* [f. *blue metal* bluish stone used in roadmaking: see OEDS *blue, a.* 12 c.] Pieces of stone used as missiles, esp. in street fights. Also *attrib.* and *fig.*

1891 *Truth* (Sydney) 8 Mar. 4/6 Federalists, at the next polling-day, will get more 'blue metal' than Union votes. **1935** F. CLUNE *Rolling down Lachlan* 59 A large heap of blue metal being used by an imp and an urchin for duelling purposes. **1946** —— *Try Nothing Twice* 5 The streets of Woolloomooloo were paved with blue-metal stones, which came in quite handy for the larrikin 'pushes' in their frequent fights.

blue-metal, *v.* [f. prec.] *trans.* To attack (someone) by throwing stones; to pelt with stones.

1891 *Truth* (Sydney) 18 Jan. 1/4 A gentleman named Charles Durkin was painting the atmosphere of Cowper-Street blue when a constable remonstrated, whereupon Durkin blue-metalled *him.* **1946** F. CLUNE *Try Nothing Twice* 71 In Woolloomooloo . . larrikin pushes blue-metalled one another.

blue orchid. [From the colour of the uniform and with reference to its supposed smartness.] During the war of 1939–45: a member of the R.A.A.F. Chiefly in *pl.*

1940 *Ack Ack: Jrnl. 2nd Anti Aircraft Regiment* 17 Oct. 9 Gordon Orchard has joined the 'Blue Orchids'. **1968** G. MILL *Nobody dies but Me* 61 There's about as much love between the Army and the Air Force as there is between a pork chop and a Jew. They call us Blue Orchids, amongst other things. Menzies' Blue Orchids, in fact.

bluestone. [Spec. use of *bluestone* a building stone of a bluish grey colour.] In e. Aust., a basalt used for building, road making, etc.; in S.A., an argillite or quartzite. Also *attrib.*

1850 *Illustr. Austral. Mag.* (Melbourne) Dec. 389 It is constructed of blue-stone, with granite in the arch and parapet. **1969** MORGAN & GILBERT *Early Adelaide Arch.* p. viii, A greyish-blue young slate which in Adelaide is called bluestone; this is neither as black nor is it as hard as the basalt which was so individual to early Melbourne and which is also called, or miscalled, bluestone. **1975** L.H. CLARK *Rouseabout Reflections* 5 'Neath the ancient shade of the elms and birches Stands the last of the Outback's blue-stone churches.

blue-tongue.

1. Shortened form of *blue-tongue lizard* (see BLUE *a.*).

1882 F. MCCOY *Prodromus of Zool. Vic.* (1885) I. viii. 15 These Lizards are very sluggish, so that the popular name 'Sleepy Lizard' as well as 'Blue-tongue' comes to be applied to both. **1979** C. KLEIN *Women of Certain Age* 60 A blue-tongue opened a sudden mouth at her feet, almost catapulting her down the stairs.

2. *transf.* (Esp. in allusion to the supposed sleepiness of lizards.)

1900 *Bulletin* (Sydney) 18 Aug. 14/3 The shearer terms the rouseabout variously a 'loppy', 'bluetongue', 'wop-wop', 'leather-neck', 'crocodile', etc. **1975** L. RYAN *Shearers* 124 'Righto, you blue-tongues!' he bellowed out. 'Get stuck into it!'

bluey. [f. *blue* + -Y.]

1. a. A swag (so called because the outer covering was traditionally a blue blanket); BLUE *n.*[1] 1.

1878 *Squatter's Plum* 42 If a Minister wishes to gain information on anything connected with station-work, he need not go to a kangaroo-drive. . . Rather let him arm himself with a billy, and 'hump bluey' *incognito* in search of work. **1981** G. CROSS *George & Widda-Woman* 10 A swaggie suddenly appearing out of the bush, unshaven, with wild, haunted eyes, his bluey and billycan on his back.

b. *transf.* Luggage.

1959 *Overland* xv. 13 To get there I had to swim the Russell River with my bluey, a tin trunk. I had been carrying the trunk on my shoulder. **1963** J. DUFFY *Outsville Pub* 22 Where's yer bluey? No luggage?

2. A swagman's (usu. blue) blanket.

1888 J. POTTS *One Yr. Anti-Chinese Work in Qld.* 10 Then fancy hears a snake hissing as it glides along the ground—perhaps to curl with you in 'bluey'. **1965** B. JAMES *Collecting Austral. Gemstones* 83 Humping his water-bags and a few simple tools wrapped in his dusty bluey.

3. Orig. and in early use chiefly *Tas.* A heavy grey-blue woollen outer garment or coat, protective against cold and wet (see quots. 1899); *Tasmanian bluey,* see TASMANIAN *a.* 3. Also *attrib.*

1890 A.M. ANDREWS *Card Only* (1891) 6 The ordinary camp costume of a miner, moleskins and light 'bluey', with broad, slouched hat. **1899** *Bulletin* (Sydney) 11 Feb. 17/1 Term 'bluey' never applied to swag in Tasmania. The Tas. 'bluey' is a rough overcoat of blue-grey woollen, and never seen by writer in any other part of Australasia. **1899** *North-Western Advocate* (Devonport) 1 Sept. 4/1 The winter costume . . is incomplete without . . a 'bluey'. A bluey is a sort of smock such as is worn by carters in Great Britain, made of rough blue or grey serge, and will keep the water out for a whole long day's journey. **1953** K. GRAVES *Tasmanian Pastoral* 59 From the little farms high on the mountain walls above the men had gathered, wearing 'bluey' coats, oil-skin slickers, or even chaff-bags slung over their shoulders, since sudden squalls sweep across the highlands.

4. A summons; BLUE *n.*[1] 2.

[**1895** C. CROWE *Austral. Slang Dict.* 58 *Piece of blue paper,* a summons.] **1909** 'H. THOMPSON' *Ballads about Business* 13 I'll show you valls papered mit blueys. **1986** *Choice* Apr. 2/1 Imagine my shock upon returning to a bluey at the end of the day.

5. A familiar hypocoristic form of any of a number of popular names for birds, animals, etc., usu. beginning with 'blue'; a bird, animal, etc., predom. blue in colour.

1903 *Bulletin* (Sydney) 31 Jan. 36/1 We had no knowledge of scientific terms. To us they were . . bluies, diamonds, big and little silver-eyes. **1912** *Ibid.* 22 Aug. 13/1 Have no fear of the lick of the blue-tongued lizard. Have seen a terrier's ear torn in three strips by a bite from 'bluey' with no ill-effects. **1979** S.W. DUTHIE *Fidlers Creek* 32 We get . . red mullet, a bluey, a couple of flounder.

6. A nickname given to a red-haired person; BLUE *n.*[1] 3.

1906 *Truth* (Sydney) 28 Oct. 9/4 The Perilous Adventure of Red-headed 'Bluey', a Dealer in Greens. **1978** R.H. CONQUEST *Dusty Distances* 32, I found out later that he was a native of New South Wales, called 'Bluey' because of his red hair—typical Australian logic.

7. In *pl.* Denim working trousers or overalls.

1917 *Stretcher* (Melbourne) Mar. 15 Yes, combination blueys are still fashionable in France. **1950** J. MORRISON *Port of Call* 243 You'll be back in time to catch her, Jim, only you won't get home to change. How would it be if you turned up in the blueys? You could get a wash and brush-up at the station.

boab, boabab: see BAOBAB.

boang, var. BUNG.

board.

1. The part of the floor of a shearing shed upon which the sheep are shorn (see quot. 1893); *shearing board,* see SHEARING B. 3. Also *attrib.*

[N.Z. **1857** R.B. PAUL *Lett. from Canterbury* 90 One of these huts must serve for your first year's wool-shed, with the help of a few hurdles in front, and a tarpaulin or a few boards to shear on. **1867** J.C. JORDAN *Managem. Sheep & Stations* 90 The shearing boards should be kept constantly swept and clean from pieces and locks.] **1870** *Austral. Town & Country Jrnl.* (Sydney) 5 Nov. 11/3 So unreasonable are they, that an act of simple justice is often the signal for a strike, which includes a third or a half of the men 'on the board', as the shearing floor is by them termed. **1898** 'OLD CHUM' *Chips* 42 Down each side . . is a clear space about ten feet wide called the 'board'. Here the shearing is done by a long row of men on each side. In the middle is a large enclosure, or 'pen', into which the sheep are driven from outside, and there are smaller pens, called 'catching pens', on each side, which are fed from this large one. **1979** HARMSWORTH & DAY *Wool & Mohair* 150 The *board boy* picks up the fleece, carries it to the skirting table, throws it so that it spreads evenly over the table.

2. Used with reference to the employment of shearers at a shed, esp. in the phr. **on the board;** also **full board,** a full complement of shearers.

1879 S.W. SILVER *Austral. Grazier's Guide* 51 There are fifty or seventy of the smartest shearers in the land 'on the board'. **1912** T.E. SPENCER *Bindawalla* 65 There were men enough at the camp now to make a full board, and next week shearing would be in full swing.

3. In the phr. **over the board,** used to designate the overseer of a shearing gang, the contractor; esp. in the collocation **boss over** (or **of**) **the board**: see quots. 1908 and 1979. Also **man over the board.**

1893 H. LAWSON *Collected Prose* (1972) I. 105 The 'boss over the board' comes along to tell the men not to swear, 'there's ladies coming.' **1908** W.H. OGILVIE *My Life in Open* 39 The shearing-board is supervised by an overseer, commonly known as the Boss of the Board, whose duties are to keep the shearers in check, to see that the sheep are properly shorn, and to act generally as a middle man between shearers and owner. **1912** J. BRADSHAW *Highway Robbery under Arms* (ed. 3) 37 You could not leave the shed without the permission of the man over the board, or you would be fined the ensuing pen of sheep. **1979** HARMSWORTH & DAY *Wool & Mohair* 151 The *boss of the board* is generally in charge of the team. He supervises the shearers, seeing that they shear the sheep correctly, counts the sheep from the counting out pens, enters the number shorn to the credit of each individual shearer in a tally book and writes up the daily tally board.

Hence **boss of the boarding** *vbl. n.*

1944 A.E. MINNIS *And All Trees are Green* 97, I suppose he does the boss of the boarding himself?

bob-in. Shilling-in, see SHILLING 2.

[N.Z. **1889** W. DAVIDSON *Stories N.Z. Life* 5 From tricks at cards, the fun changed to 'a bob in' the winner shouting.] **1919** *Smith's Weekly* (Sydney) 15 Mar. 14/3 Forty of them gathered him up and made for the bar. 'A bob in' was suggested... After paying for the shout he salvaged a whole quid. **1961** *Bulletin* (Sydney) 15 Feb. 7/1 A 'bob-in' testimonial opened by the 'Courier-Mail'.. raised a total of over £500.

bobtail. [Transf. use of *bob-tail* animal with tail cut short.] The slow-moving lizard *Trachydosaurus rugosus* of s. mainland Aust., having large ridged scales on the back and a short rounded tail; SHINGLEBACK; STUMP LIZARD; STUMPY TAIL. See also *blue-tongue lizard* BLUE *a.*, SLEEPING LIZARD. Also **bob-tailed goanna** (or **lizard**).

1872 MRS E. MILLETT *Austral. Parsonage* 180 The lizard which the colonists call the 'bob-tailed' guana, or in colonial pronunciation 'gew-anna'. *Ibid.* 181 A lizard of exactly the same shape as that of the 'bob-tails'. **1937** R. FAIRBRIDGE *Pinjarra* 197 It was difficult to avoid running over bob-tailed lizards sleeping in the hot dust.

bobuck /ˈbɒbʌk/. [Prob. f. a N.S.W. Aboriginal language.] The possum *Trichosurus caninus* of mountain forests in s.e. mainland Aust.

1953 E. MITCHELL *Flow River, blow Wind* 75 'A young bobuck!' said Charlie... Joseph let the possum sit on his shoulder. **1970** W.D.L. RIDE *Guide Native Mammals Aust.* 70 In Victoria it and the Bobuck are destructive in plantations of introduced pine trees.

boco, var. BOKO.

bodger. *Obs.* [Prob. f. Br. dial. *bodge* to work clumsily: see OED *v.* and EDD *v.*¹, and cf. *botch*.] Something (occas. someone) which is fake, false, or worthless. Also *attrib.*

1945 *Biscuit Bomber Weekly: Mag. 1st Austral. Air Maintenance Co.* 18 Feb. 3 This when the Bodgers, or sly guys place themselves in the most concealed.. places in the line. **1950** F.J. HARDY *Power without Glory* 383 This entailed the addition of as many more 'bodger' votes as possible. **1966** S.J. BAKER *Austral. Lang.* (ed. 2) 292 An earlier underworld and Army use of *bodger* for something faked, worthless or shoddy. For example, a faked receipt or false name.. is a *bodger*; so is a shoddy piece of material sold by a door-to-door hawker.

bodgie, *n.*¹ [f. BODG(ER + -Y.] A male youth, esp. of the 1950s, distinguished by his conformity to certain fashions of dress and larrikin behaviour; analogous to the Br. 'teddy boy'. Also *attrib.*

1950 *Sunday Tel.* (Sydney) 7 May 47/3 The bizarre uniform of the 'bodgey'—belted velvet cord jacket, bright blue sports shirt without a tie, brown trousers narrowed at the ankle, shaggy Cornel Wilde haircut. **1986** *Canberra Times* 23 Feb. 8/7 Set in Brisbane in the bodgie and widgie era, the novel is the beautifully honed story of Lola and Brownie.

bodgie, *n.*² Altered form of BODGER, infl. by BODGIE *n.*¹: see quot. 1952. Freq. as *adj.*

1952 *Sun* (Sydney) 6 Mar. 1/7 An office in town has a mail file marked *bodgies*. It's for letters that don't seem to come under any of the regular classifications. The misfits, in other words. **1984** *Canberra Times* 27 Aug. 1/2 Allegations.. of branch-stacking and the use of hundreds of 'bodgie' members in the electorate.

Hence **bodgied up** *a.*

1972 A. CHIPPER *Aussie Swearers Guide* 31 'In he lobs, bodgied up and smelling like *dead horse gully*.' ('He arrived wearing a new suit and after shave lotion.')

body bullock. [Spec. use of *body* main part of a collection.] See quots. 1872 and 1959. Also *ellipt.* as **body.**

1872 C.H. EDEN *My Wife & I in Qld.* 36 Twelve bullocks is the usual number in a team, the two polers and the leaders being steady old stagers; the pair next to the pole are called the 'pointers'.. the remainder being called the 'body bullocks'. **1959** H.P. TRITTON *Time means Tucker* 36 A bullock-team is made up in four parts: polers, pin, body and leaders... The body is the bulk of the team, sometimes 20 of [sic] more, the labourers of the team, mainly noted for their strength.

body-line, *a.* *Cricket. Hist.* Usu. in the collocation **body-line bowling.** Fast, leg-theory (bowling), intimidatory in effect: see quots. 1933.

1932 *Australasian* (Melbourne) 10 Dec. 27/4 It has many names, such as bowling at the leg stump, the author's definition, a clever one, leg theory, or bodyline offensive. **1933** *Age* (Melbourne) 19 Jan. 11/1 The Australian Board of Control has forwarded the following cablegram to the Marylebone club:- Body-line bowling assumed such proportions as to menace best interests of game, making protection of the body by batsmen the main consideration... Unless stopped at once is likely to upset friendly relations existing between Australia and England. **1933** BLUNDELL & BRANSON *Bodywhine* 36 In a sincere effort to stamp out body-line bowling the Australian Board of Control suggested a new rule, enabling the umpire to call a no-ball if he thought the bowler intended to injure the batsman.

Hence **body-liner** *n.*

1933 BLUNDELL & BRANSON *Bodywhine* 27 (*caption*) A former body-liner plays bowls.

body surf, *v. trans.* To ride (a breaking wave) towards the beach, streamlining the body and holding it rigid like a board: see SURF *n.* and *v.* Also *absol.*, and **body shoot.**

1956 T.I. THOMPSON *Pop. Handbk. Swimming* Pref., It is surprising how little has been written on the technique of body surfing which is so popular on the ocean beaches. **1956** S. HOPE *Diggers' Paradise* 166, I can't remember seeing anyone 'body-shoot' a wave in the way the lads do it now. **1981** *Nat. Times* (Sydney) 20 Dec. 26/2 To body surf a big wave is to feel briefly like Superman or Superwoman.

Hence **body surfer** *n.*

1963 *Bulletin* (Sydney) 30 Mar. 10/3 The Surfies had only one real complaint. That was that while they were banned from swimming in the be-flagged area on beaches .. body-surfers were not prevented from swimming in the board area.

bog, *v.* [Prob. fig. use of *bog* to sink, 'to get stuck into'.]

1. In the phr. **bog in(to),** to engage (in a task or activity) with vigour or enthusiasm; esp. to begin eating.

1907 *Bulletin* (Sydney) 24 Oct. 14/3 As for 'Bog into it!' that expression is a good deal older than I am. I heard, a few days since, a little girl request her brother to 'bog his frame down here'. **1927** F.C. BIGGERS *Bat-Eye* 14 Nights fer bucks, 'Oo bog in straight, an' try their 'and at stoushin's arts. **1968** W.N. SCOTT *Some People* 120 He made it up that the two of them should each cook a feed and the contract men could bog into it.

2. *intr.* Chiefly *W.A. Mining.* To work underground, in a coal or gold mine, shovelling ore or mining refuse away from the workface, usu. into trucks for transport to the surface. Also *trans.*

1935 *Bulletin* (Sydney) 8 May 20/1 Back in the early days of the Golden Mile the writer, then a 'shoveller', was frequently urged to 'bog' his frame into a big heap of mullock or ore. Now, 35 years later, from the verb 'to bog' has descended the noun 'bogger'. **1982** M. WATTONE *Winning Gold in W.A.* 64, I then went back to Kalgoorlie... I got a job for the Croesus Proprietory [*sic*] Ltd, bogging (shovelling) down the mine.

Hence **bogging-out** *vbl. n.*, **bog-in** *n.*

1943 *Jest: Digestion Good Humor* 43 **Bogging out** is the use of a shovel, commonly known as a *banjo* to shovel ore or mullock (usually off flat sheets) into trucks. **1954** J. CLEARY *Climate of Courage* 58 Two suburban ladies .. sat toying with their food and wishing they had gone to Sargent's where they could have had a real **bog-in** for less than half the price.

Bogan /'boʊgən/. [The name of a river in w. N.S.W.] Used *attrib.* in Special Comb. **Bogan flea,** any of several prostrate annual plants of the genus *Calotis* (fam. Asteraceae) esp. *C. hispidula*, the seeds of which have small rigid spines; see also BINDI-EYE; **gate,** see quot. 1980; **shower,** a dust storm.

1905 *Proc. Linnean Soc. N.S.W.* XXX. 44 The 'burr'-like fruiting heads of several species of *Calotis* are regarded with disfavour by sheep-owners... The pappus surmounting each achene is composed of barbed bristles or sharp spines, and sometimes causes great irritation to those who camp out. Hence stockmen call these fruits '**Bogan Fleas**'. **1980** J. WRIGHT *Big Hearts & Gold Dust* 45 Don stopped at a **bogan gate**... Though I'd seen many of these intricate contraptions of barbed wire and sticks, I'd never had the pleasure of trying to open one. Usually bogan gates were erected as a temporary block but almost invariably remained to become a jigsaw puzzle of flesh devouring spikes. **1904** A.B. PATERSON *Rio Grande's Last Race* 29 We don't respect the clouds up there, they fill us with disgust, They mostly bring a **Bogan shower**—three rain-drops and some dust.

bogey /'boʊgi/, *n.* Also **bogie.** [f. BOGEY *v.*]

1. A swim or bathe; a bath.

1847 A. HARRIS *Settlers & Convicts* (1953) 132 In the cool of the evening had a 'bogie' (bathe) in the river. **1974** D. STUART *Prince of my Country* 110 Take a bogey .. there; keep an eye on your soap, the gins are always pinching mine.

2. Comb. **bogey hole.**

1918 *Newcastle Morning Herald* 31 Dec. 5/3 They .. went to Blackwood's Beach, a treacherous bogey-hole.

bogey /'boʊgi/, *v.* [a. Dharuk *bu-gi.*] *intr.* To swim; to bathe.

1788 *Hist. Rec. N.S.W.* (1893) II. 700, I have bathed, or have been bathing .. Bogie d'oway. These were Colby's words on coming out of the water. **1841** *HRA* (1924) 1st Ser. XXI. 472, I suppose you want your Boat, Sir; Yes, said Mr Dixon; well, said Crabb I suppose we must bogey for it. Yes, said Mr Dixon, any two of ye that can swim.

bog-eye, var. BOGGI.

boggabri /'bɒgəbraɪ/. [Perh. f. an Aboriginal language. Also the name of a town in n.e. N.S.W.] Any of several low herbs, esp. *Amaranthus mitchellii* (fam. Amaranthaceae), *Chenopodium pumilio* and *C. carinatum* (fam. Chenopodiaceae), and *Commelina cyanea* (see SCURVY GRASS).

1893 *Antipodean* (Melbourne) 95, I cud do a bit of doughboy, an' that theer boggabria'll eat like marrer, along of the salt junk. **1964** P. WHITE *Burnt Ones* 284 A smell of sink strayed out of grey, unpainted weatherboard, to oppose the stench of crushed boggabri and cotton pear.

bogger. Chiefly *W.A. Mining.* [f. BOG 2.] One who works underground shovelling mullock or ore. Also **bogger-out.**

1935 *Red Star* (Perth) 29 Nov. 3/4 The Ivanhoe uses a cunning method of making boggers stay on the shaft more than eight hours. **1943** *Jest: Digestion of Good Humor* 43 It was *necessity*—the italics emphasise the truth—which first sent me underground to earn my living as a *bogger-out*.

boggi /'bɒgaɪ/. Also **bog-eye, bogi,** etc. [Wiradhuri prob. *bugay.*]

1. SLEEPING LIZARD.

1911 *Bulletin* (Sydney) 28 Sept. 13/2 The blue-tongue ('bogi', 'bob-tailed gohanna', or 'sleepy lizard'). **1965** R. OTTLEY *By Sandhills* 29 A bog-eye ain't much. They seldom bite you.

2. The handpiece of a shearing machine: see quot. 1915.

1915 *Bulletin* (Sydney) 14 Oct. 24/2 The jumbuck barber has a vocabulary of his own... In a shed where the barbering is done by machinery he always alludes to his handpiece as 'a bog-eye'. This from the likeness to the lizard of that name. **1982** *Sydney Morning Herald* 23 Oct. 29/3 'I grabbed my boggi and I ran her down the whipping side.'... Which, translated, means that the shearer took up his handpiece—named after the boggi lizard of inland Australia which it is said to resemble—and ran the clippers down the last side to be shorn while the sheep is on its back.

boggins, *pl.* [Of unknown origin.] An abundance.

1849 A. HARRIS *Emigrant Family* (1967) 97 There must be very nigh a hundredweight of meat there: boggins for a whole week. **1927** 'S. RUDD' *Romance of Runnibede* 34 There was always boggins of rains and grass that he used to lose his horses in.

bogi, var. BOGGI.

bogie, var. BOGEY.

bogong /'boʊgɒŋ/. Formerly **bugong**. [a. Ngarigo *buguŋ*.] The brown noctuid moth *Agrotis infusa*, which breeds on plains in s. Aust. The adults, which migrate to hills where they aestivate in rock crevices, were formerly eaten by Aborigines. Now usu. **bogong moth**.
1834 G. Bennett *Wanderings N.S.W.* I. 265 It is named the 'Bugong Mountain', from the circumstance of multitudes of small moths, called Bugong by the aborigines, congregating at certain months of the year about masses of granite on this and other parts of the range. **1981** *Austral. Women's Weekly* (Sydney) 23 Sept. 5/3 We were driven crazy by the Bogong moths last year and nearly had to leave home.

boil, *n.* *S.A. Mining. Obs.* [f. *boil* to seethe, upheave.] A mineral outcrop, esp. one giving surface indications of the presence of a lode.
1850 *S. Austral. Register* (Adelaide) 11 July 3/1 There is apparently a great boil of copper ore—the whole surface, for many yards round, being covered with specimens of copper ore. **1882** *Yorke's Peninsula Advertiser* (Moonta) 13 Jan. 3/5 A valuable lode was reported... By some miners it was described as a 'big boil'.

boil, *v.*[1] [Spec. use of *boil down* to lessen the bulk of (anything) by boiling: see OED *v.* 8.]
1. *trans. Hist.* With **down.** In the preparation of tallow: to reduce (animal carcasses) by boiling. Also *absol.*
1843 M. Hindmarsh *Lett.* (1945) 43 Sheep are now being boiled down by thousands for to extract the tallow from their carcases. **1937** D. Gunn *Links with Past* 211 W.H. Walker of Tenterfield, had a boiling down place, where in 1892 I had some old ewes boiled down... My father seems to have been among the very first to boil down; he started in 1843.
2. *fig.* [So used elsewhere but seeming in Aust. to draw its connotations from the prec.]
1872 'Capricornus' *Bush Essays* 19 Bankers and merchants had stations on hand which they wanted to sell. One customer had got the length of his tether and it was time to 'boil him down' and get a new one into the concern. **1932** J.J. Hardie *Cattle Camp* (1944) 26 Boiled down, the reason seems to me that people here do more thinking than talking.

boil, *v.*[2] [Spec. use of *boil* to bring to boiling point.] *intr.* With **up**: to make tea (see also Billy *n.*[1] 5 and Quart pot 1).
1923 J. Armour *Spell of Inland* 30 Alex., accompanied by George and Robertson, rode in the direction of the Mulga Well, where they proposed to 'boil up'. **1960** R.S. Porteous *Cattleman* 41, I boil up and 'ave a bit of tucker down along the creek.
Hence **boil-up** *n.* Also *fig.*
[N.Z. **1934** *Canterbury Mountaineer* Aug. 52 We had a welcome boil up.] **1936** C.T. Madigan *Central Aust.* 210 We emptied our cans of the Glauber's-salt solution from Glen Helen, and filled up with this beautiful liquid, and had a boil-up and good tea for the first time in the last few days. **1975** M.B. Roberts *King of Con Men* 68 The main method of gold stealing was to palm rich 'tailings' and when enough had been stolen there would be a 'boil-up' in the scrub.

boiler. [f. Boil *v.*[1]]
1. *Hist.* A vessel in which animal carcasses are boiled down.
1843 *Sydney Morning Herald* 18 July 3/2 They have clearly shown that they will not be driven like sheep either to the shambles or to the boiler. **1844** *Ibid.* 11 Nov. 2/7 The 'boilers' will doubtless be in requisition to an immense extent after the clip is taken off.
2. a. *Hist.* An animal relegated to be boiled down.

1884 'R. Boldrewood' *Old Melbourne Memories* 109 Two hundred and seventy 'boilers' are safe in the small yard, the which will be started for their last drive on the following morning.
b. *fig.* [Prob. influenced latterly by *boiler* boiling fowl.]
1862 *Bell's Life in Sydney* 14 June 4/3 On asking a night guardian where a night's lodging is to be obtained, he tells you 'all the old boilers are full, the verandah at the post-office is overcrowded; and, mate, if you mean to sleep under a door-way why you will have to turn out somebody else'. **1967** A. Seymour *One Day of Yr.* 51 He.. patronized the old boilers.
3. *Hist.* With **down**: one who operates a boiling down establishment.
1848 *Maitland Mercury* 13 May 3/1 *Tallow Casks*... A loss of fifteen per cent. has lately been sustained by a settler, which has arisen solely from bad casks which were supplied by his 'boiler-down'.

boiling, *vbl. n. Hist.* [f. Boil *v.*[1] 1.] Usu. with **down**.
1. The process of separating fat from animal carcasses in the preparation of tallow: see quot. 1848. Also *attrib.*
1843 *Adelaide Observer* 15 July 5/3 When our Sydney friends trumpeted forth the boiling down of sheep as a discovery of their own, they found a mare's nest... Sheep boiling has been quietly going on in Adelaide from the commencement of the present year. **1848** H.W. Haygarth *Recoll. Bush Life* 71 'Boiling down' is a very simple and rapid process. The whole carcase, having been cut up into pieces, and thrown into large cast-iron pans.. is boiled to rags, during which operation the fat is skimmed off, until no more rises to the surface. The boiled meat is then taken out of the pans, and, after having been squeezed in a wooden press, which forces out the remaining particles of tallow, it is either thrown away, or used as food for pigs, vast numbers of which are sometimes kept in this manner, in the neighbourhood of a boiling establishment. **1882** W. Coote *Hist. Colony Qld.* 51 Another, and still more beneficial consequence, was the introduction of the 'boiling down' process, by which unsaleable sheep and cattle were converted into saleable tallow.
2. An establishment for boiling down; the site of a boiling-down operation.
1857 F. de B. Cooper *Wild Adventures* 66 Fletcher, the proprietor of the boiling-down. **1898** G. Dunderdale *Bk. of Bush* 236 On every station in New South Wales the paddocks still called 'the boiling down' were devoted to the destruction of sheep and cattle and to the production of tallow.
3. Comb. boiling (-down) establishment, house, pot, season, system, works.
1848 *Duncan's Weekly Register* (Sydney) 29 July 2/1 **Boiling establishments** are being erected on the Parramatta-road. **1844** *Guardian* (Sydney) 65/4 The great nuisance which was springing up in the city, in the shape of the boiling-down establishments. **1846** *Cumberland Times* (Parramatta) 28 Feb. 1/2 The Mayor of Sydney has commenced a crusade against those detestable nuisances, the small **boiling houses**, some of which are in the heart of the city, and in the chief thoroughfares—the stench arising from these receptacles of corrupt filth is beyond endurance, and most offensive to passengers. **1870** C.H. Allen *Visit to Qld.* 139 The killing-yards and boiling down houses are on a very extensive scale. **1844** *Bee of Aust.* (Sydney) 9 Nov. 2/6 To the **boiling pot** daily, I wend my sad way, And gaze on my flocks as they wither away. **1853** Mossman & Banister *Aust. Visited & Revisited* 71 Sending their surplus stock to the boiling-down pots. **1848** *Maitland Mercury* 8 Mar. 3/3 The squatters are making extensive preparations for the **boiling-down season** just beginning. **1853** *Moreton Bay Free Press* 1 Feb. 3/4 A quantity of tallow from the last boiling season—now five months over—is not shipped yet. **1843** *Sydney Morning Herald* 22 June 2/8

Stock-owners may with certainty avail themselves of the convenience held out by the **boiling system** to realize at all seasons from their herds and flocks. **1844** *Parramatta Chron.* 24 Feb. 2/3 *Effect of the late rains*... Feed and water are proportionably abundant, and fat cattle are likely to increase in consequence, despite the boiling-down system. **1901** *Bulletin* (Sydney) 7 Dec. 31/3 He smelt like a **boilin'-down works** an' had ernuff grog in him to cure all the toothache in the Commonwealth.

boilover. Orig. *Horse-racing.* [Fig. use of *boil over* to overflow: see HOT POT.]

a. A surprise result; the unexpected defeat of the favourite.

1871 *Austral. Town & Country Jrnl.* (Sydney) 18 Feb. 217/3 The sensation has this week been the Launceston Champion Race, with its boil over; and the knowing fraternity now begin to wonder if there be a possibility, no matter how remote, of a favourite pulling off this great event. **1986** *Canberra Times* 31 Mar. 19/3 St. Kilda provided a boil-over to win at Moorabbin when the two teams met last year.

b. *transf.*

1974 J. GABY *Restless Waterfront* 222 We got caught up in one senseless dispute, a demarcation issue, a most frustrating and hopeless affair... There was a boil-over for you.

boko /'boʊkoʊ/. Also **boco**. [Prob. f. a Qld. Aboriginal language.] An animal or person blind in one eye. Also as *adj.*

1847 C. DE BOOS *Congewoi Correspondence* 119 They useter call him Boco because he'd only got one eye, and I suppose boco is French for bein blinder one eye, for that's what they callser one eye man up the country. **1953** H.G. LAMOND *Big Red* 154 As horses, men and other animals, were liable to infection, it can be assumed 'roos also ran the risk. If they did, the curse never got beyond the initial stages—boko, scummy-eyed kangaroos were unknown.

bollocky /'bɒləki/, *a.* Also **bollicky**. [f. *bollock* naked (see OEDS 3) + -Y.] Of a person: naked. Also as *n.*

1952 T.A.G. HUNGERFORD *Ridge & River* 161 Remember that time .. we're all stark bollocky and that jeep-load of Yank nurses comes down. **1967** *Kings Cross Whisper* (Sydney) xxxii. 7/1 *Bollicky*, to be in the bollicky is to be completely nude.

bolly gum /'bɒli gʌm/. [f. *bolly* (prob. f. a N.S.W. Aboriginal language) + GUM *n.* 1.] Any of several trees esp. of the genera *Beilschmiedia*, *Litsea* and *Neolitsea* (fam. Lauraceae), and *Blepharocarya* (fam. Anacardiaceae); the wood of these trees. Also **bolly wood**.

1904 J.H. MAIDEN *Notes on Commercial Timbers N.S.W.* 29 *Bolly gum* .. yields a soft whitish timber valuable for boxes, meat casks, and for many other purposes. **1956** N.K. WALLIS *Austral. Timber Handbk.* 4 Other timbers have special uses, such as .. bollywood (aircraft construction).

bolt, *v.* [Spec. use of *bolt* to take flight.]

1. *intr. Obs.* To abscond, either abandoning one's debts or in possession of illicit gains.

1829 *Sydney Monitor* 24 Oct. 2/2 *The family* .. are now departed or departing, save *the scion.* His *darling has bolted.* **1871** *Austral. Town & Country Jrnl.* (Sydney) 4 Mar. 259/4 Samson, clerk of the National Marine Insurance Company, has bolted; his accounts are deficient.

2. *Hist.* Of a convict: to escape from custody.

1832 *Currency Lad* (Sydney) 13 Oct. 3 He hoped the Magistrate would excuse him, because it was *only* the second time of his bolting, and he went the three days he was absent to see the races. **1874** *Illustr. Sydney News* 19 Sept. 153 Taking advantage of the absence of his keepers, he quietly scaled the stockade and bolted.

Hence **bolt** *n.,* **bolting** *vbl. n.* and *ppl. a.*

1838 *Colonist* (Sydney) 21 Mar. 2/2 The facilities afforded for escape, or, in other words, for making a successful **bolt**. **1833** *Trumpeter General* (Hobart) 29 July 3 We are happy to find that some check is put to the **bolting** system, it has long been wanting (and highly commendable it is) that persons about leaving this colony must produce certificates from their employers before they can obtain the signature of our Assistant Police Magistrate. **1867** J. BONWICK *J. Batman* 11 These rough fellows were either runaway sailors or bolting convicts.

bolter. [f. BOLT *v.*]

1. *Hist.* A runaway convict.

1832 *Hill's Life N.S.W.* 17 Aug. 2 *Margaret Champion*, assigned to Mr Wood of George street, was brought in by a constable, who said, he had just *grabbed* her, and knowing her to be a *bolter*, took her under his *protection*. **1865** J.F. MORTLOCK *Experiences of Convict* 109 A damsel at the gold fields often received a 'nugget' for washing a shirt, so that feminine 'bolters' to the 'diggings' became pretty numerous.

2. *Hist.* An absconder.

1838 *Sydney Herald* 10 May 2/3 '*Bolters*'. This class of animals adds one or more to its number by every vessel that leaves the port... Several fellows (Jews and Gentiles) are making arrangements to defraud their creditors by leaving the Colony in a few days. **1897** H. HUSSEY *Colonial Life & Christian Experience* 59 Others, who had determined to defraud their creditors if possible, made a 'bolt' in any vessel that would take them away... One of the vessels that took away several .. had conferred upon her the .. designation of 'the bolters' clipper'.

3. One with only a remote chance of succeeding, an outsider; freq. in the phr. **a bolter's (chance)** (cf. BUCKLEY'S).

1941 S.J. BAKER *Pop. Dict. Austral. Slang* 35 *Haven't (hasn't) the bolter's*, used of a person or racehorse that has no chance at all in a contest or situation. **1964** H.P. TRITTON *Time means Tucker* (rev. ed.) 33 At the race game 'The Bolter' always won when the favourite 'Esmeralda' was well backed. **1970** *Matilda* (Winton Tourist Promotion Assoc.) 7 They never had a bolter's chance when Brumby went to war.

bomaring, var. BOOMERANG *n.* 1.

bomb. [Fig. use of *bomb* explosive projectile.] An old or unreliable motor vehicle; (by extension) anything in a dilapidated condition.

1950 *Austral. Police Jrnl.* Apr. 110 *Bomb*, .. a dud—usually refers to second-hand motor vehicles in poor mechanical shape. **1956** *Bulletin* (Sydney) 30 May 13/1 No longer is 'It's a bomb' restricted to senile cars; the word has become synonymous with worn-out or up-to-putty anything.

bombo /'bɒmboʊ/. [Prob. as prec. + -O, and independent of *bombo* or *bumbo* a spiced alcoholic drink (see OED *bumbo*).]

1. Cheap (often fortified) wine of inferior quality. Also *attrib.*

1942 *Sun* (Sydney) 26 Aug. 4/8 Bombo has replaced plonk as a term for cheap wine. **1980** HEPWORTH & HINDLE *Boozing out in Melbourne Pubs* 17 The men who ran the bombo bars seemed, by and large, to be chaps who had suffered, but who had become finer chaps because of it.

2. An habitual drinker of such wine.

1966 P. PINNEY *Restless Men* 69 Saves winos and bombos from drinkin' their selves mad.

bombora /bɒm'bɔrə/. Formerly also **bumbora**. [Perh. *a.* Dharuk *bumbora*.]

1. A wave which forms over a submerged offshore reef or rock, sometimes (in very calm weather or at high tide) merely swelling but in other conditions

breaking heavily and producing a dangerous stretch of broken water; the reef or rock itself.
1871 *Industr. Progress N.S.W.* 789 Some [fishing grounds] are on sunken rocks in about 8 fathoms water, 'Bumborers', as they are generally termed, from 1 to 3 miles distant from the shore others on rocky patches in deeper water. **1880** *V & P* (N.S.W. L.A.) III. 1132 A few 'Bumboras' are found in this bight, and they (like all 'Bumboras' on the coast) have been and still are the favourite resort of the schnapper-men during particular conditions of the currents. **1933** *Bulletin* (Sydney) 24 May 27/1 'Bombora' is an aboriginal word applied to the high-crested wave which breaks, even on windless days, over submerged rocks near the coastline and in some cases at entrances to coastal harbors and inlets.

2. *transf. and fig.*
1969 W. MOXHAM *Apprentice* 44 The trouble with Lenny was like a bombora. There was a commotion followed by an uneasy calm, a feeling it was likely to blow up again any old time, cause harm to someone. **1979** D. MAITLAND *Breaking Out* 73 He married Shirley and inherited her bitch of a mother at Coogee, the Eastern Suburbs beach community .. and got sucked into a deadly *bombora* of domesticity.

bomerang, bommerang, varr. BOOMERANG *n.* 1.

bommie. Also **bommy.** [f. BOM(BORA + -Y.] BOMBORA.
1949 C.B. MAXWELL *Surf* 112 Surfmen, swimmers and the 'surfboat happy' .. wondered what it might be like to 'crack the bommy' out there. **1963** J. POLLARD *Austral. Surfrider* 100, I had to break through a heavy sea before reaching the swell outside and then to where the 'bommie' was breaking a long way above normal sea level.

bomring, var. BOOMERANG *n.* 1.

bond, *a. Hist.* [Spec. use of *bond* not free.]
1. Of convict status.
1800 *Gen. Orders issued by Governor King* 26 Nov. (1802) 26 He strictly forbids all officers, and every other person, bond or free, from striking or ill using any other person in this colony. **1856** W.H.G. KINGSTON *Emigrant's Home* 6 Western Australians .. arranged to receive a certain proportion of free emigrants with the bond.

2. In collocations indicating convict status, as **bond labour, list, man, servant, stockman, population, woman.** Also **bondsman.**
1827 *Monitor* (Sydney) 30 Mar. 363/1 My bond-woman is offered as a prize to the best deserver or truest lover, and 30 acres in fee. **1830** *Ibid.* 12 May 2/2 The labour of this country, agricultural as well as commercial, is chiefly performed by bond-men. **1835** *Colonist* (Sydney) 30 July 243/3 Five of the persons convicted of cattle stealing were originally bond or freed stockmen. **1845** A. MACONOCHIE *On Managem. Transported Convicts* 3 The last Census of Bond Population that I took on Norfolk Island in September 1843. **1845** *Sydney Morning Herald* 30 Dec. 2/6 Not a single free case of drunkenness, and only three charges for such on the bond list, all ticket holders. **1847** J. LACKLAND *Common Sense* 16 Bond labour requires an extra oversight. **1848** C. COZENS *Adventures of Guardsman* 160 His master .. could not obtain another bond servant, and .. if he retained his services after he obtained his ticket, he would be compelled to pay him a free man's wages. **1850** *Irish Exile* (Hobart) 19 Oct. 2/1 The man of wealth and influence, the employer and the employed, the bondsman and the free, can once for all cooperate for the common good.

bondage. *Hist.* [Spec. use of *bondage* servitude.] The state or condition of being a convict; penal servitude.
1831 TYERMAN & BENNET *Jrnl. Voyages & Travels* II. 174 Those who were never in bondage are naturally jealous of those who bear the barbarous name of *emancipists*. **1851** 'FEMALE TRANSPORT' *Let.*, Here am I in bondage, in a foreign land.

bondi /'bɒndi, 'bʌndi, 'bɒndaɪ/, *n.*[1] Also **boondie, bundi, bundy.** [Prob. a. Wiradhuri and Kamilaroi *bundi.*]
1. A heavy Aboriginal club.
1844 C. WILKES *Narr. U.S. Exploring Exped.* II. 202 Their weapons are the spear, club, or nulla nulla, boomerang, dundumel and the bundi. **1846** *Cumberland Times* (Parramatta) 4 Apr. 4/1 Fishhook held his bundy over his head, saying, '*bail you saucy, or pie cobra belonging you*', meaning he would strike me on the head. **1851** *Empire* (Sydney) 30 Dec. 519/6 Jackey was found lying dead... A bondi, or club, was seen near him, with marks of blood on it. **1900** *Advocate* (Burnie) 24 July 3/4 Jimmy Governor pursued and overtook them, and felled Miss Kerz with his 'boondie'.

2. [Poss. of independent development and apparently infl. by the form and pronunc. of the place-name (see BONDI *n.*[2]).] In the phr. **to give** (someone) **bondi,** to attack savagely.
1890 *Truth* (Sydney) 19 Oct. 3/6 A live policeman is on the ground while the gay and festive members of a 'push' are 'giving him Bondi'. **1951** D. STIVENS *Jimmy Brockett* 67 Then Snowy got Maxie in a corner and began to give him Bondi.

Hence as *v. trans.*
1907 C. MACALISTER *Old Pioneering Days* 124 They were mercilessly speared and 'boondied' (beaten to death with nullas) by the blacks.

Bondi /'bɒndaɪ/, *n.*[2] [The name of a suburb in Sydney.] Used allusively to designate a hasty departure, esp. in the phr. **to shoot through like a Bondi tram.** See also *shoot through* SHOOT *v.* 3.
1945 D. ROBINSON *Pop's Blonde* 62 The Choco went through like a Bondi tram. **1976** B. SUTTON *Comrade George* 53 When she got her copy she shot through like a Bondi tram.

bone, *n.*
1. In Aboriginal ritual practice: a bone pointed at a person whose death is willed; DEATH BONE; *pointing bone,* see POINTING. Chiefly in the phr. **to point the bone.**
1884 A.W. STIRLING *Never Never Land* 89 The blacks in the neighbourhood of the Peake, a well-known region of South Australia, believe that if one of a tribe at a feast with evil intent 'points a bone' at a fellow black, the latter is doomed. **1963** I.L. IDRIESS *Our Living Stone Age* 89 Only one kind of fear could be shown without shame—fear of the supernatural. This might take the form of fear of the Bone from a malicious witch-doctor.

2. *transf. and fig.*
1943 D. FRIEND *Gunner's Diary* 21 The bone is pointed at myself and a few others. We are to be transferred to a draft battery. **1972** A. CHIPPER *Aussie Swearers Guide* 33 The greatest sin against the Australian spirit of mateship is to *point the bone* at a cobber, i.e. sneak on a friend or leave him in the lurch.

Hence **bone-pointer** *n.*, **bone-pointing** *vbl. n.*
1956 A. UPFIELD *Battling Prophet* 11 The quack's a **bone-pointer,** like. He wouldn't know. **1928** W. ROBERTSON *Coo-ee Talks* 80 The method of **bone-pointing** differed among the tribes.

bone, *v.* [f. prec.] *trans.* In Aboriginal ritual practice: to influence (a person at whom a bone is pointed), with the intention of causing the person's death.
1901 F.J. GILLEN *Diary* 21 Aug. (1968) 235 The Puntudia crept up and 'boned' him with their pointing sticks... He

became very ill and finally died. **1985** B. ROSSER *Dreamtime Nightmares* 47 They think the other tribes are out to kill them or bone them.

Hence **boning** *vbl. n.*

1925 M. TERRY *Across Unknown Aust.* 147 There is a custom, common to all Australian natives, whereby an enemy can be killed without violence. It is called 'boning', or 'singing'.

boneseed. [See quot. 1973.] The introduced South African shrub *Chrysanthemoides monilifera* (fam. Asteraceae), naturalized and regarded as a troublesome weed in s. Aust. incl. Tas.

1962 N.C.W. BEADLE et al. *Handbk. Vascular Plants Sydney & Blue Mountains* 387 *Osteospermum*. . . Ray flowers . . long, yellow. . . Sand dunes; roadsides. Fl. chiefly spring. Introd. from Africa. Boneseed. *O. moniliferum* L. **1973** W.T. PARSONS *Noxious Weeds Vic.* 100 'Boneseed' refers to the colour and hardness of the seed. . . Boneseed was first introduced to Victoria in 1858.

bong, var. BUNG A.

bong tong. *Obs.* [Altered form of *bon-ton* good style, breeding: see OED.] A term applied ironically to a supposed social elite. Also *attrib.*

1892 *Truth* (Sydney) 5 June 3/6 This is the latest in 'bong tong' circles. *c* **1907** C.W. CHANDLER *Darkest Adelaide* 63 A sycophantic licensee would receive her in the most obsequious fashion, bowing as he escorted her into the parlor kept specially for the bong tong of harlotry.

bontosher /bɒnˈtɒʃə/. [See quot. 1904 (2) and cf. BONZER.] BONZER *n.* Also as *adj.*

1904 *Bulletin* (Sydney) 14 Apr. 29/1 A bontosher is a real slasher, a fair hummer, virtually a past master . . but no female has yet achieved the dignity of a bontosherina. *Ibid.* 5 May 17/3 'Bonster' is a corruption of Bontojer, pronounced Bontodger; and Bontojer is a corruption of the two French words *bon* and *toujours*—'always good'. **1951** D. STIVENS *Jimmy Brockett* 141 It was a bontosher of a flat though.

bony bream. The fresh-water fish *Nematalosa erebi* (fam. Clupeidae), widespread in mainland Aust.

1882 J.E. TENISON-WOODS *Fish & Fisheries N.S.W.* 106 A fish of the herring tribe is also found in these rivers. . . By the white settlers it is sometimes known as the 'bony bream'. **1980** R.M. MCDOWALL *Freshwater Fishes S.-E. Aust.* 48 Bony bream *Nematalosa erebi*. . . Not a bream, but a herring.

bonz, *a. Obs.* Also **bonze.** Abbrev. of BONZER *a.*

1920 *Bulletin* (Sydney) 4 Nov. 20/1 'Struth! its bonz to be the skipper of a full-rigged racin' stripper. **1935** A. CROCKER *Aust. hops In* (1941) 54 'Wasn't that bonze, Alick?' he wanted to know, when he could speak; and Alick agreed between his own chuckles that it was bonze.

bonzarina /bɒnzəˈriːnə/. *Obs.* [f. BONZER + -*ina* L. fem. suffix.] A beautiful woman. Also *attrib.*

1906 *Bulletin* (Sydney) 22 Nov. 17/2 Bonzarina, feminine of bonza. **1934** T. WOOD *Cobbers* 212 She was a little bonzarina. **1950** F.J. HARDY *Power without Glory* 45 She's a bonzarina shiela, like a colleen from old Ireland.

bonzer /ˈbɒnzə/, *n., a.,* and *adv.* Also **bonza.** [Perh. formed in word-play on F. *bon* good, infl. by U.S. *bonanza*: see early quots. and BONTOSHER. See also BOSHTER and BOSKER which may have a similar origin.]

A. *n.* Something (or someone) which excites admiration by being surpassingly good of its kind.

1904 *Bulletin* (Sydney) 14 Apr. 29/1 *Re* that bulwark of Austral Slanguage—'Bonster'. . . A bonser or bonster is comparatively superior to a bons. **1972** B. FULLER *West of Bight* 18 A suitable caravan turned up at last. . . 'She's a bonzer. I guess you'll be lucky.'

B. *adj.* Surpassingly good.

1906 *Bulletin* (Sydney) 5 July 17/1 There's allers bits o' jobs about ther Farm; Doin' Polly, breakin' metal, keeps a bloke in bonza fettle. **1986** *Nat. Times* (Sydney) 10 Jan. 14/1 Should there be a national breast-beating . . over our lost reputation as a bonzer little nation of sportsmen?

C. *adv.* Beautifully, splendidly.

1914 'B. CABLE' *By Blow & Kiss* 246 Came back grinning widely, with the assurance that it [*sc.* the rain] was coming down 'Bonzer'. **1944** A.S. SMITH *Boys write Home* 215 It's a bonzer clear day, perhaps the Zeros think so, too.

boobialla /buˈbiːælə/. Also **boobyalla.** [a. Oyster Bay and s.e. Tas. *bubiala.*] **a.** The shrub or small tree of coastal sand dunes *Acacia longifolia* var. *sophorae* (fam. Mimosaceae). **b.** Any of several shrubs or small trees of the genus *Myoporum* (fam. Myoporaceae) with pale flowers and globular, often purplish, fruits. Also *attrib.*

1832 J. BACKHOUSE *Narr. Visit Austral. Colonies* (1843) 59 The sand-banks at the mouth of Macquarie Harbour are covered with Boobialla, a species of *Acacia*, the roots of which run far in the sand. **1861** L.A. MEREDITH *Over Straits* 62 Boobyalla bushes lay within the dash of the ceaseless spray. **1880** *Argus* (Melbourne) 2 Feb. 6/7 Now in bloom:-. . . a variety of myoporum serratum, called by the aborigines of the Western district the 'boobiala'.

boobook /ˈbuːbʊk/. [a. Dharuk *bug bug.*] The owl *Ninox boobook* of Aust. and elsewhere, having a characteristic two-note call; MOPOKE *n.* **1** a. Also **boobook owl.**

c **1790** W. DAWES *Grammatical Forms Lang.* N.S.W., *Bōk bōk*, an owl. **1801** J. LATHAM *Gen. Synopsis Birds* Suppl. II. 64 Boobook O. Description. Size of the Brown Owl. . . Place. This inhabits *New Holland*, where it is known by the name of Boobook. **1846** *Portland Gaz.* 18 Sept. 4/5 The boobook or barking bird, and the curlew called during the night. **1976** *Reader's Digest Compl. Bk. Austral. Birds* 303 The boobook owl . . is the smallest and most abundant of the Australian owls.

boodie /ˈbuːdi/. [a. Nyungar *burdi.*] A burrowing rat-kangaroo *Bettongia lesueur*, formerly widespread on mainland Aust. but now rare or extinct exc. on islands off the W.A. coast; LESUEUR'S RAT-KANGAROO. Also **boodie rat.**

1857 W.S. BRADSHAW *Voyages* 114 Many of the animals of the forest . . are very good for food, namely, the opossums, bandicoots, boodies. **1897** L. LINDLEY-COWEN *W. Austral. Settler's Guide* 33 Boodie rats . . do some damage among the fruit trees and cereal crops.

boofhead. [Prob. from *bufflehead* (lit. bullock head), fool: see quot. 1945.]

1. A fool or simpleton.

[**1941** *Daily Mirror* (Sydney) 12 May 15/1 (*caption*) Boof-head looks fishy.] **1945** S.J. BAKER *Austral. Lang.* 130 *Boofhead*, from the English *bufflehead*, a stupid person, or dialectal *boof*, stupid. *Boofhead* is the name of a cartoon strip character in the Sydney 'Mirror', since 1941. **1986** *Canberra Times* 15 Feb. 2/5 You bunch of boofheads.—The Special Minister of State, Mr Young, on the Opposition.

2. A person or animal having a big head.

1946 R.D. RIVETT *Behind Bamboo* 395 *Boof head*, one with a big head. **1981** A. MARSHALL *Aust.* 132 'What a boofhead of a foal,' he had thought—and so it was named. The foal did indeed have a large head, a hairy head, whiskered like a draught horse.

Hence **boofheaded** *a.,* **boofheadedness** *n.*

1965 J. BEEDE *They hosed them Out* 171 Tubby . . asked, 'Who's that **boofheaded** old bastard, anyway?' It was an apt description and from then on . . he was known as 'boofhead'. **1983** *Sun-Herald* (Sydney) 18 Sept. 143/4 It is a scandal that they have been allowed to get away with this **boofheadedness** for so long.

boojeree, var. BUDGEREE.

book. Abbrev. of 'bookmaker'.
1891 *Truth* (Sydney) 11 Jan. 5/7 It must be evident to those who are not blind that bona fide bookmakers must soon cease to attend pony meetings; and experience shows that when the 'books' begin to leave, the game is up. **1984** *Sun-Herald* (Sydney) 25 Nov. 152/6 A local rails book was abused by a professional punter.

book muster. An inventory based upon the evidence of the stockbook, rather than an inspection of the actual stock. Also *attrib.*
1880 J.B. STEVENSON *Seven Yrs. Austral. Bush* 108 A book muster, particularly upon an outside scrubby station is never to be depended upon. **1939** J.G. PATTISON *'Battler's' Tales Early Rockhampton* 125, I would not have liked to buy any properties the late Government bought on book muster. *Ibid.,* I have often heard controversy re the merits of buying a property on a walk-in, walk-out, or bookmuster delivery, and the bang-tail system.

bool, var. BULL $n.^1$

Booligal /'buligəl/. [The name of a town in w. N.S.W.] Used *fig.* to designate a place of the greatest imaginable discomfort, 'the last place on earth', esp. in the sequence **Hay, (and) Hell, and Booligal**.
1888 *Illustr. Austral. News* (Melbourne) 12 Jan. 10/1 The grass everywhere is gone, and, to use the expression of a landholder there, 'there was not enough to whip a mosquito with'. Added to this, both flies and mosquitos are more plentiful than anything else, so that, when the climate is taken into consideration, Booligal seems to fully earn its place in the comparison instituted by residents and visitors, who place it thus—Hay, Hell and Booligal. **1896** *Bulletin* (Sydney) 25 Apr. 7/4 And people have an awful down upon the district and the town—Which worse than hell itself they call; In fact, the saying far and wide Along the Riverina side Is 'Hay and Hell and Booligal'. **1898** *Ibid.* 2 July 32/1 Hot? Great Scot! [*sic*] It was Hell, with some improvements, worse than Booligal, a lot!

boomalli, /bu'mæli/, *v.* [Prob. f. an Aboriginal language.] *trans.* To beat (an animal); see also quot. 1876.
1876 *Austral. Town & Country Jrnl.* (Sydney) 2 Dec. 902/4 To-night yan longa camp; boomalli (shoot, slay) Hut-keeper. **1945** T. RONAN *Strangers on Ophir* 99 A thousand head of bullocks, hungry and mostly thirsty, boomallied and knocked about as these had been, are hard to hold. **1981** K. GARVEY *Slowly sweats Gun* 177 I'll tell yer what yer spoilt, pampered little Guardsman needs! A bloke with a good heavy whip to boom-alley him into a corner of the yard and flog the legs off him until he faces up and takes the bridle.

boomer, $n.^1$ Also **boomah**. [Br. dial. *boomer* anything very large of its kind: see EDD.] Also *attrib.*
1. Orig. *Tas.* A large kangaroo, esp. an adult male *Macropus giganteus* (see *grey kangaroo* (a), GREY *a.*) or *M. rufus* (see *red kangaroo* (a), RED *a.* 1 b.).
1830 *Hobart Town Almanack* 111 The fore-legs of a kangaroo are scarce one-third so long as the hind ones. For this reason, if a boomah attempts to run down a hill on all fours he is very apt to tumble head over heels. **1917** T.J. BRIGGS *Life & Experiences Successful W. Austral.* 126 The average weight of 'boomer' skins was about two and a half pounds when dry.
2. A large or otherwise remarkable specimen of its kind.

1843 C. ROWCROFT *Tales of Colonies* III. 96 'Wool! No Boomahs [*sc.* fleas]! I hope—Eh! Dick?,' beginning to scratch himself instinctively at the sight of the wool. **1892** 'MRS A. MACLEOD' *Silent Sea* II. 272 'A boomer nugget! a boomer nugget!' The cry flew like wildfire, and strange excitement ensued.

boomer, $n.^2$ [f. *boom* to call resonantly.] The Austral. bittern *Botaurus poiciloptilus,* a swamp bird with a booming call, occurring in s. Aust. and New Zealand; *brown bittern,* see BROWN *a.* 1; *bull bird,* see BULL $n.^3$; BUNYIP 4.
[**1857** *Australasian* (Melbourne) ii. 11 The boom-boom .. the bittern]. **1951** *Argus* (Melbourne) 14 Dec. (Suppl.) 2/5 The hollow boom so often heard on the margins of reedy swamps .. is the mythical bunyip. . . Our brown bittern is the culprit. He it is who cries at night from the depths of lonely swamps. Bushmen call him the 'Boomer'. **1953** A. RUSSELL *Murray Walkabout* 25 It was an Australian bittern, or boomer.

boomerang /'buməræŋ/, *n.* Formerly also with much variety, as **bomerang, bommerang, bomring, boomering, bumerang.** [a. Dharuk *bumariny*.]
1. An Aboriginal weapon: a crescent-shaped wooden implement used as a missile or club, in hunting or warfare, and for recreational purposes. The best-known type of boomerang can be made to circle in flight and return to the thrower. See also SWORD, THROWING STICK b., THROW-STICK 1, WADDY *n.* 1 a., WOMERA.
c **1790** W. DAWES *Grammatical Forms Lang.* N.S.W., *Boo-mer-rit,* the Scimiter. **1825** B. FIELD *Geogr. Mem. N.S.W.* 292 The spear is universal, as is also the throwing-stick; the *boomerang* or *woodah,*—a short crested weapon which the natives of Port Jackson project with accurate aim into a rotary motion, which gives a precalculated bias to its forcible fall,—was also seen at Port Bowen on the east coast, and at Goulburn Island on the north. **1832** *Hill's Life N.S.W.* (Sydney) 21 Sept. 4 Unerring his aim when his barbed spear flew, Nor less so, when wamrah, or bomring, he threw. **1834** G. BENNETT *Wanderings N.S.W.* I. 116 'Bomerang' .. is a peculiar weapon thrown by the hand, and possesses the apparent anomalous property of striking an object in the opposite direction from that in which it is at first propelled. **1846** *Portland Guardian* 22 Sept. 4/2 At the Macarthur we still saw the boomerang, which is unknown at the Alligator River or Port Essington, where the throwing stick and the goose spears are the means of obtaining game. **1861** T. M'COMBIE *Austral. Sketches* 158 They are equally expert in killing birds with the bumerang. **1923** T. HALL *Short Hist. Downs Blacks* 15 It will be noticed that I have always used the word 'Boomering', not 'Boomerang', because the latter word was a white man's 'Cockneyism'.

2. *transf.* and *fig.,* esp. with reference to something which returns to or recoils upon its author. Also *attrib.*
1846 *Boston Daily Advertiser* 5 May, Like the strange missile which the Australian throws, Your verbal *boomerang* slaps you on the nose. **1949** P.A. JACOBS *Lawyer Tells* 102 The circular did not disclose the name of the person who composed or authorised it. . . It probably acted as a boomerang and may have done me more harm than good. **1981** Q. WILD *Honey Wind* 109 'I believe there is a kind of boomerang law,' Galiali said to Harry. 'And that the way you treat the world around you .. will rebound and reflect like a mirror.'
3. Comb. **boomerang thrower, throwing;** also *fig.*, as **boomerang bill, cheque**.
1884 *Bulletin* (Sydney) 12 July 20/4 One of Barnum's troop of Australian **boomerang throwers** died recently. **1910** W.C. WALL *Sydney Stage Employee's Pictorial Ann.* 74 The blacks gave an exhibition of **boomerang throwing** and so on. **1961** *Bulletin* (Sydney) 21 Oct. 8/1 The delegates had

decided to go far beyond the issue of the '**boomerang**
bills and press for: a fully elected Legislative Council.
1951 E. HILL *Territory* 237 He had a notice put in the Northern Territory Times: Old hands still welcome at the Depot but . . **boomerang cheque** artists take another track.

4. Special Comb. **boomerang leg, (a)** a disease characterized by flattening and forward bowing of the shinbone; **(b)** a leg affected by the disease; also as **boomerang-legged**, *a*.

1894 *Intercolonial Q. Jrnl. Med. & Surg.* I. 223 The condition is well recognised by the residents who, not inaptly, describe the natives so affected as 'boomerang-legged'. **1899** SPENCER & GILLEN *Native Tribes Central Aust.* 44 Not infrequently platycnemia, or flattening of the tibial bones, is met with, and at times the curious condition to which Dr Stirling has given the name of Camptocnemia. The latter consists in an anterior curvature of the tibial bone and gives rise to what the white settlers have, for long, described by the very apt term 'boomerang-leg'. **1936** C. CHEWINGS *Back in Stone Age* 34 The legs of the natives thus affected are referred to by the whites as 'boomerang legs'.

boomerang /'buməræŋ/, *v*. [f. BOOMERANG *n*. 2.] *intr*. To return in the manner of a boomerang; to recoil (upon the author); to ricochet.

1891 *Worker* (Brisbane) 16 May 8 Australia's a big country An' Freedom's humping bluey And Freedom's on the wallaby Oh don't you hear her Cooee, She's just begun to boomerang She'll knock the tyrants silly. **1979** *Canberra Times* 13 Nov. 28/6 Greg Chappell's decision to send England in appeared to have boomeranged.

boomeranging, *vbl. n*. The throwing of a boomerang.

1880 J.B. STEPHENS *Misc. Poems* 26 No faint forhearing of the waddies banging, Of clubs and heelaman together clanging, War shouts, and universal boomeranging? **1899** *Longman's Mag.* (London) XXXIII. 475 Boomeranging is dangerous for on-lookers, till the thrower is a perfect master of his weapon.

boomerang propeller. *Hist*. A steamship propeller the design of which was inspired by the Aboriginal weapon; invented by the explorer Thomas Mitchell (1792–1855), but never developed commercially.

1849 T.L. MITCHELL *Let.* 22 Oct. in *Mechanic's Mag.* (London) (1850) LII. 448/2 A boomerang propeller, whose diameter was 22 inches. **1937** *Publicist* (Sydney) viii. 11/1 Mitchell was interested in a project for the formation of a company . . to exploit the 'Boomerang propeller', an invention of his own based on the aboriginal weapon.

boonaree /'bunəri/. Also **boonery**. [a. Kamilaroi *bunari*.] The plant *Heterodendrum oleifolium* (see ROSEWOOD).

1932 R.H. ANDERSON *Trees of N.S.W.* 7 Rosewood or boonery (*Heterodendron oleaefolium*). A small to medium-sized tree, but sometimes little more than a shrub. **1974** S.L. EVERIST *Poisonous Plants Aust.* 438 Boonaree is one of the most useful fodder trees in inland Australia and sheep and cattle often live on it during drought periods.

boondie, var. BONDI *n*.[1]

boondie /'bundi/. [Prob. f. a W.A. Aboriginal language.] A stone.

1952 T.A.G. HUNGERFORD *Ridge & River* 94 See that bastard, practising grenade-throwing with bits of boondies? **1986** A. WELLER *Going Home* 40 He could fight, chuck boondies . . and run better than anyone.

boonery, var. BOONAREE.

boong /buŋ/. [Perh. a. Jakarata dial. of Indonesian *bung* elder brother.]

1. A name for an Aboriginal (see also quot. 1933).

1924 *Smith's Weekly* (Sydney) 2 Aug. 16/2 The abos. or boongs around Cairns cure headaches by placing a grass plaited band, about two and a half inches wide, across the forehead. **1933** F.E. BAUME *Tragedy Track* 51 'So then our job is to catch 'em,' Simon says. He and George usually speak 'bung', or blackfellow 'pidgin'. It is the custom of the country. **1986** *Nat. Times* (Sydney) 10 Jan. 25/4, I get called 'wog' by the ethnics because I'm not an Aborigine. . . The girls who are Aborigines get called boongs or chocos. There's heaps of name-calling but it is mostly just fun.

2. *transf*. An indigenous inhabitant of New Guinea, Malaysia, etc.

1943 *Survey Sentinel: 2/1 Austral. Army Topogr. Survey Co.* 2 May, If near a native village, just follow the 'boongs'. **1946** *Southerly* iv. 208 In Malaya . . the chooks we had got from a boong's place.

3. Special Comb. **boong line**, a team of native bearers, as employed in New Guinea during the war of 1939–45.

1943 A. DAWES *Soldier Superb* 58 Suddenly there was a shout and a cheer, and in at the double burst the carriers—the 'boong line', as the Australian soldiers (much against the grain of Angau, for 'boong' is an Australian Aboriginal word) call them.

Hence **boongess** *n*.

1945 *Aust. Week-End Bk.* 153 Isn't there a fancy boongess somewhere around this joint? Classy bit of colour?

boongarry /'buŋgəri/. [a. Warrgamay *bulŋgari*.] The tree-kangaroo *Dendrolagus lumholtzi* of forests in n.e. Qld.; MAPI.

1889 R.B. ANDERSON tr. Lumholtz's *Among Cannibals* 102 According to the statement of the blacks, it was a tree-kangaroo. . . It had a very long tail . . and was called *boongary*. **1944** J. DEVANNY *By Tropic Sea & Jungle* 19 There are a lot of tree-kangaroos in the Cardwell Ranges. Boongarrie, the natives call them.

boorah, var. BORA.

boorie /'buri/. Also **burry**. [a. Wiradhuri (and neighbouring languages) *burraay* boy, child.] A name for an Aboriginal.

1955 N. PULLIAM *I traveled Lonely Land* 369 The abo is sometimes called a blackfellow or binghi, burry or blackman, etc. **1972** K. WILLEY *Tales Big Country* 170 Some Queenslanders still disparage Aborigines as 'abos' and 'boories'.

boot, *n*.[1]

1. [Now used elsewhere.] In the phr. **to put** (or **sink**) **the boot in, to put in the boot**.

a. To attack savagely, esp. when the opponent is disadvantaged, or in a manner which is otherwise conventionally unacceptable.

1915 C.J. DENNIS *Songs of Sentimental Bloke* 42 'It's me or you!' 'e 'owls, an' wiv a yell, Plunks Tyball through the gizzard wiv 'is sword, 'Ow I ongcored! 'Put in the boot!' I sez. 'Put in the boot!' **1932** J. TRURAN *Green Mallee* 18 Get on wi' the job, or I'll put the boot inter yer. **1962** E. LANE *Mad as Rabbits* 81 Father had a dreadful job stopping him from rushing after the offender, and without a word, 'sinking the boots in' as punishment.

b. *fig*.

1916 *West Austral.* (Perth) 11 Nov. 7/7 Don't scab on the unemployed. Slow work means more jobs, more jobs less competition, higher wages. Fast workers die young. Someone has to be slowest—let it be you. Get wise to the I.W.W. tactics. Organise on the job. Put in the boot. Sabotage. Kick like hell. **1968** S. GORE *Holy Smoke* 36 As per usual when things go crook, the first bloke they put the boots into is their own leader, Moses.

2. In the phr. **boots and all,** without reservation, with no holds barred.

[N.Z. **1947** O.M. Davin *Rest of our Lives* 96 The next thing he'll do is counter-attack, boots and all.] **1950** *Arna* (Sydney) 27 Their [*sc.* Marxists] historical science informs them that ruling classes in the period of their decline resort increasingly to violence and repression—'boots and all', to use the phrase of a Democratic Prime Minister, as he threw police and troops against striking mine-workers. **1985** *Weekend Austral.* (Sydney) 28 Sept. 4/4 Canberra's cabbies go in boots and all for a fair deal.

boot, *n.*² [Br. *boot* that which is given to make up a deficiency of value (*obs.* exc. Scot. dial.): see OED *sb.*¹ 2.] Something added in from one side to ensure the equality of an exchange.

1863 *Frank Gardiner, or Bushranging in 1863* 10 If I had known that the boot was only fifteen notes and a ticker, I wouldn't have started on such a wet night. **1903** J. Furphy *Such is Life* 10 'And how much boot are you going to give me?' I asked, with a feeling of shame which did honour to my heart.

booyong /ˈbujʊŋ/. [a. Bandjalang *buyaŋ*.] Any of several ornamental and timber trees of the genus *Argyrodendron* (fam. Sterculiaceae) of N.S.W. and Qld.; *crowsfoot elm*, see Crowsfoot; Tulip oak.

1908 *Emu* VII. 203, I arrived at the Booyong scrubs from Sydney on the 4th of October, 1899. **1981** A.B. & J.W. Cribb *Useful Wild Plants Aust.* 110 Buttressing of the trunk base . . is particularly noticeable in booyong, where the upper edge of the buttress is typically concave in outline.

booze bus. A police vehicle carrying equipment for the random breath-testing of motorists.

1982 *Sydney Morning Herald* 16 Dec. 2/1 (*heading*) Police 'booze buses' gear up for start of random breath tests. **1984** *Open Road* Dec. 3 (*caption*) Booze buses operating through the night.

bo-peep. A peep, a look.

1941 *Coast to Coast* 67 'I'll 'ave a bo-peep,' he said. 'You gotter watch 'er. We don't want no dead pups.' **1983** *Sydney Morning Herald* 21 May 35/4 Sister prowled in regularly for a bo-peep at my progress.

Hence *v. intr.*

1949 I.L. Idriess *One Wet Season* 24 'Bo-Peep at that bunch of pretty girls,' shouted Bunch.

bopple nut. Chiefly *Qld.* Also **bauple nut.** [See quot. 1975.] Macadamia. Also *ellipt.* as **bopple.**

1927 H.J. Rumsey *Austral. Nuts* 5 The Australian Nut . . has been variously known as 'Queensland Nut', 'Bush Nut', 'Mullumbimby Bush Nut', 'Bauple Nut', 'Popple Nut'. . . The term 'Poplar Nut' is absurd, and should be dropped, as the word is only a demoralised form of 'Bauple', from Mount Bauple, in Queensland. **1948** H.A. Lindsay *Bushman's Handbk.* 64 Queensland has two food plants not mentioned in the books; one of which is the Queensland nut or 'bopple' (*Macadamia ternifolia*). It grows in gullies and has leaves with serrated edges, quite like those of a banksia. The nut is an inch in diameter and has a remarkably hard shell. **1975** A.B. & J.W. Cribb *Wild Food in Aust.* 88 This species was once well known in the rainforests of the Mt Bauple [*sc.* s.e. Qld.] area, and for this reason was commonly called Bauple nut, a name sometimes corrupted to bopple or popple nut.

bora /ˈbɔrə/. Also **boorah, borah.** [a. Kamilaroi *buurr-a*.]

1. An initiation ceremony: a ceremony at which an Aboriginal youth is admitted to the privileges of manhood. Also *attrib.*

1851 *Colonial Intelligencer* (London) III. 316 They have to observe the difficult and unpleasant custom of 'borra', in order to make them *men*. **1870** E.B. Kennedy *Four Yrs. in Qld.* 79 A Boorah . . consists of the surrounding tribes congregating to perform a mysterious ceremony. **1925** *Smith's Weekly* (Sydney) 4 July 15/7 Attendance of whites at a native Borah dance was forbidden.

2. The site at which a bora is held.

1937 D. Gunn *Links with Past* 17 All the boras I know consist of two round patches of ground cleared of grass and sticks. **1971** K. Gilbert *End of Dreamtime* 24 Once again the tribe is gathered—on the bora—by the sea!

3. Comb. **bora ceremony, circle, ground, ring.**

1896 *Bulletin* (Sydney) 18 Apr. 27/2 The white quartz crystal used at the **bora ceremony**. **1896** *Bulletin* (Sydney) 18 Apr. 27/3 The small pathway from the large to the small **bora circles**. **1885** Mrs C. Praed *Austral. Life* 24 The **Bora ground** is usually in a retired spot, on a slight elevation, level at the top. **1923** T. Hall *Short Hist. Downs Blacks* 8 Knowing the object of the Bora ceremonies, and seeing the symbols on the trees at the **Bora ring**.

borak /ˈbɔræk/, *adv.* and *n.* Also **borack, borax.** [a. Wathawurung *burag*.]

A. *adv. Austral. pidgin. Obs.* Used to express negation: cf. Baal.

1839 *Port Phillip Gaz.* 13 Nov. 3 Constable—Plenty white man I got here—borack me give 'em anything to eat. **1903** J. Furphy *Such is Life* 176 'Borak this you paddock, John?' 'My plully paddock, all li.'

B. *n.*

1. Nonsense, rubbish; Gammon *n.* 2. Also *attrib.*

1845 T. McCombie *Adventures of Colonist* 273 Borack, gammon, nonsense. **1876** J.A. Edwards *Gilbert Gogger* 185 'O! Hume; that is all borack. . .' Borack: humbug. Thus it is a common saying amongst bushmen, when any person is attempting to make them believe something improbable. 'O! don't poke borack at me!' **1950** *Southerly* iii. 142 The borak-pokers, with grouch Against all lordship.

2. In the phr. **to poke borak** (at a person), to deride. See also Poke *v.*

1873 J.C.F. Johnson *Christmas at Carringa* 4 Oh! he's a [*sic*] awful cove for to poke borack at a feller, that old O'Niel. **1901** *Truth* (Sydney) 12 Jan. 1/6 Bloodyard Drippling's preposterous 'pome', which virtually pokes borak at England's helplessness. **1902** *Ibid.* 16 Mar. 4/3 This is the sort of 'light and airy persiflage' in which Elijah, the Prophet of the Lord, 'poked borax' at the poor prophets of Baal.

Hence **borak** *v. trans.*

1885 *Bulletin* (Sydney) 25 Apr. 10/1 And what had this young gentleman been doing to be so deprived of sweetness and light and the songs of birds and the innocent delights of expectorating on street corners and gaily 'borracking' the passers-by?

border. [Spec. use of (also U.S.) *border* frontier: see OED *sb.* 3 c.]

1. The outer limit of land surveyed and available for tenure; land at or beyond that boundary. See also Boundary *n.* and Location 4. Also *attrib.*

1827 *Tasmanian* (Hobart) 21 Dec. 3 [Signature to a letter.] A Border Settler. **1846** *Portland Gaz.* 2 June 3/5 We beg to caution newcomers into the district against a practice which has lately become very prevalent, especially about 'the borders' and in the 'new country', of men going to them and offering to point out runs for a certain fee.

2. The boundary between two Colonies; after Federation, between two States. Also *attrib.*

1847 *Port Phillip Herald* 29 July 2/3 The South Australian and Port Phillip boundary line offers no terrors to the 'border' thief. **1945** F. Cork *Tales from Cattle Country* 25 At the border the mob is met by the police and stock inspector who rides through the herd.

3. Special Comb. **border fence,** a vermin-proof

fence at the outer limit of a settled district or on a Colonial (later State) boundary; **police** *obs.*, a police force established to maintain law and order at or beyond the border (sense 1).

1895 *Bulletin* (Sydney) 5 Jan. 23/4 No grass this side the **Border-fence**! and all the mulga's dead. **1927** *Ibid.* 26 May 24/2, I can bear witness to the uselessness of Queensland's expensive vermin-proof border fence. **1839** *Sydney Standard* 11 Mar. 4/2, I object to settlers being obliged to supply the **Border police** with tea and sugar.

bore, *n.*

1. An artesian well. See also *government bore* GOVERNMENT B. 4. Also *attrib.*

1897 *Western Champion* (Barcaldine) 31 Aug. 3/3 It used to be a dry country out there in years gone by, but bores have changed all of it to a white man's land, carrying many sheep. **1986** *Canberra Times* 19 Feb. 14/3 Police were trying .. to determine the events that preceded the death of a group of six people .. on a lonely bore road on a Northern Territory pastoral station.

2. Special Comb. **bore drain,** a channel which carries water from a bore; **head,** the point at which the underground water surfaces; **stream,** *bore drain*; **water,** water from a bore.

1914 *Bulletin* (Sydney) 18 June 16/4 The sheep were still alive, and even had sufficient strength to make a frenzied dash for the **boredrain**. **1932** M.R. WHITE *No Roads go By* 157, I called loudly for a tub, mustard, and hot water from the **bore-head**. **1902** *Bulletin* (Sydney) 19 June 16/2 Dozens of **bore-streams** in W.Q. well adapted for irrigation. **1899** *Bulletin* (Sydney) 9 Sept. 17/1 *Re* quality of **bore-water**... The Richmond .. Govt. bore gives splendid water.

bore, *v.* [Fig. use of *bore* to push or thrust (esp. in sporting context).] *trans.* In the phr. **to bore it up** (or **into**) (someone), to attack with vigour, 'to let (someone) have it'.

1947 *Coast to Coast 1946* 76 He bored into Wally and chopped his face about—cut his eyes and ears and smashed his mouth. **1951** E. LAMBERT *Twenty Thousand Thieves* 178 A provost I got into a blue with in Tel Aviv was barkin' the orders. Christ! Did that bastard bore it up me?

boree /ˈbɔri, bɔˈri/, *n.* [a. Wiradhuri and Kamilaroi *burrii.*]

1. a. Any of several *Acacia* species (fam. Mimosaceae), esp. *A. tephrina*, the phyllodes of which are covered with short white hairs. **b.** *N.S.W. spec. A. pendula* (see MYALL *n.*²). Also *attrib.*

1845 D. MACKENZIE *Emigrant's Guide* 212 In the heart of the main root of a small sapling, called the *Myall* or *Boree*. **1921** 'J. O'BRIEN' *Around Boree Log* 11 Yet spend another night with me around the boree log. **1977** G.W. LILLEY *Lengthening Shadows* 171 Boree .. is confined to the western districts of Queensland north of Tambo. Myall (acacia pendula) is also called 'boree' in western N.S. Wales, but although the trees are closely related botanically acacia canae is the genuine boree.

2. Comb. **boree scrub**.

1864 J.G. MACDONALD *Jrnl. Exped. Port Denison to Gulf of Carpentaria* (1865) 17 Next through belts of boree scrub, one and a half mile.

boring, *vbl. n.* used *attrib.*

1. Of or relating to an artesian well, or the drilling thereof.

1901 *Bulletin* (Sydney) 28 Dec. 14/1 *Re* reported recent discovery of fish in 'boring'-water. **1954** T. RONAN *Vision Splendid* 112 He saw two of the lubras who had sought protection, coming back from the boring camp.

2. Special Comb. **boring plant,** equipment used to sink a bore.

1911 'S. RUDD' *Bk. of Dan* 1 Dan turned up one morning in possession of a boring plant and asked for a job.

boronia /bəˈroʊniə/. [The plant genus *Boronia* was named by English botanist J.E. Smith in honour of his former assistant, the Milanese botanist Francesco *Borone* (1769–1794).] Any shrub of the genus *Boronia* (fam. Rutaceae), the flowers of some species being highly aromatic.

1848 *Maitland Mercury* 6 Dec. 4/3 Boronia, the latter plant of such exceeding beauty that the aborigines, unpoetical as they are supposed to be in their composition, name their gins or women after it, in the same manner as we (their more cultivated brethren) do our wives and daughters from the rose and other favourite plants. **1985** *New Idea* (Melbourne) 7 Sept. 141 If you enjoy the perfume of boronias, most varieties are small growing but seem to prefer a moist soil and need to be trimmed when flowering is finished.

bosca, boscar, varr. BOSKER.

bosey, var. BOSIE.

boshter /ˈbɒʃtə/, *n.* and *a. Obs.* [Of unknown origin: see BONZER.] BONZER.

A. *n.*

1903 *Sporting News* (Launceston) 2 June 1/4 George, although within 10 yards of the last-named, escaped a penalty. With what result. This, a 'boshter' in the mile and a half at a great disadvantage, and an absolute 'nong' in this, under more favorable circumstances. **1916** *All abaht It* (London) Nov. 13 He's proved himself a boshter.

B. *adj.*

1908 *Bulletin* (Sydney) 10 Dec. 17/1 It was Sam's eye-drop taw! .. 'Me only boshter taw!' he roared. **1929** W.J. RESIDE *Golden Days* 377, I didn't mind our luck—'Twas bad, but then, I'd struck A boshter mate.

bosie /ˈboʊzi/. *Cricket.* Also **bosey.** [f. the name of the English cricketer, B.J.T. *Bos(anquet* (1877–1936) + -Y.] A googly, a ball which breaks in the direction opposite from that suggested by the action of its delivery. Also *attrib.*

[N.Z. **1909** *N.Z. Truth* (Wellington) 23 Oct. 3/2 Geo. Schmoll fell a victim to a 'bosie' delivery from Senior, the ball coming back from the opposite way in which the hand delivery indicated.] **1912** *Australasian* (Melbourne) 2 Mar. 481/2 Then he lifted the 'Bosie' bowler high to the on, the ball bouncing just inside the fence. **1954** A.G. MOYES *Austral. Batsmen* 190 One thing the 'bosey' did—it introduced a new touch of science into bowling, and nothing more beautiful has been seen on Australian cricket fields.

bosker /ˈbɒskə/, *n.*, *a.*, and *adv. Obs.* Also **bosca, boscar.** [Of unknown origin: see BONZER.] BONZER.

A. *n.*

1904 *Truth* (Sydney) 3 Apr. 6/1 The show is described as a 'bosker', the horses, cows, and pigs are in great condition. **1973** H. LEWIS *Crow on Barbed Wire Fence* 49 'If they'd been some beer in the town,' he muttered, 'it would have been a bosker.'

B. *adj.*

1905 *Steele Rudd's Mag.* (Brisbane) Oct. 835 Oh, she's a real bosker gal is Matildee. **1920** H.J. RUMSEY *Pommies* 66 My word, mum, this is a bosca place. I should like you to see it.

C. *adv.*

1923 J. MOSES *Beyond City Gates* 32 It's a bosker big river, the Clarence. **1943** G. McIVER *Bunyip & Other Verses* 31 But if I liked to buy some stores, My half was there for sure— And boscar rich whenever struck, In weighty nuggets pure.

boskerina. *Obs.* Var. of BONZARINA.
   1905 *Steele Rudd's Mag.* (Brisbane) July 701 Joe .. murmured in a tone of mingled admiration and endearment— 'You're a—boskerina.'

boss cocky. [See COCKY *n.*²]
   1. A small farmer who has achieved a degree of prosperity (esp. one able to employ labour to supplement his own).
   1879 'DOCTOR DORIC' *Unsophisticated Rhymes* 3 The iron heel you know; 'Tis Boss-Cokie Law Fit for an Indian squaw. **1958** G. CASEY *Snowball* 12 The chief stock-and-station agent, and the head officials of the local Road Board were often linked up with some of the boss-cockies from round about to form a clique.
   2. One who assumes or who is accorded, often grudgingly, authority or superior status.
   1902 *Truth* (Sydney) 19 Oct. 4/8 He might be the grand high boss cocky in Australia's political world, but he was no friend of Queensland's. **1979** D. MAITLAND *Breaking Out* 327 'Who're we going to negotiate with?'... 'The Governor, I guess .. whoever's the boss cocky in New South Wales.'

boss over (or **of**) **the board**: see BOARD 3.

bot, *n.* [Fig. use of *bot* parasitic worm or maggot, as in 'Had a situation .. near Cobargo (N.S.W.) what time the bot-fly was botting there with much vigor.' (1907 *Bulletin* (Sydney) 10 Jan. 14/2).]
   1. *Obs.* A scheme for illicit gain, a 'lurk'.
   1888 'R. BOLDREWOOD' *Robbery under Arms* (1937) 42 'You think you can't be tracked,' says I, 'but you must bear in mind you haven't got to do with the old-fashioned mounted police as was potterin' about when this 'bot' was first hit on.'
   2. A cadger.
   1916 *All abaht It* (London) Nov. 24 Lit in time for the 'Bot's fatigue'. **1982** J. MORRISON *North Wind* 54 Your old mates have had a win in Tatts... They're a bit scared of all the commotion it's stirred up. The track down from the township is worn bare, and all the bots and bites in Victoria are on to them.

bot, *v.* Also **bott.** [f. prec.]
   a. *trans.* To cadge.
   1921 F. GROSE *Rough Y.M. Bloke* 73 However, I had firmly made up my mind that the boys were not going to be disappointed, and I eventually 'botted' (the diggers' word for begged, borrowed or stolen) a lorry. **1986** *Nat. Times* (Sydney) 3 Jan. 11/1 Johnson botted a smoke and tried to let the conversation die.
   b. *intr.* Usu. with **on**: to borrow from, to impose upon.
   1934 *Bulletin* (Sydney) 7 Nov. 46/2 Settle up when I sell me next picture... Never did like botting on a bloke. **1965** K. TENNANT *Summer's Tales* 82 They'll bot on property owners or missions. That's where they're going.

Botany. *Obs.* Abbrev. of BOTANY BAY.
   1787 R. CLARK *Jrnl.* 27 Dec. 106, I wish to God that we had got to Botany that I might be able to get some greens. **1827** P. CUNNINGHAM *Two Yrs. in N.S.W.* I. 15 If you chance to .. burst forth perhaps in praise of the beauties of *Botany* .. he measures you over and over with a most suspicious eye.

Botany Bay. [The name given by James Cook to a bay south of Sydney, the site of his first landing in Australia.]
   1. *Obs.* A name used variously to refer to Port Jackson, to New South Wales, and to other Australian Colonies, individually and collectively. Also *attrib.*
   1787 J. WHITE *Jrnl. of Voyage N.S.W.* (1790) 1, I this day left London, charged with dispatches .. relative to the embarkation of that part of the marines and convicts intended for Botany Bay. **1820** C. JEFFREYS *Van Dieman's Land* 143 The term Botany Bay, has a very extensive signification, including, in the general acceptance of the word, all our Australian territories. **1835** *Colonist* (Sydney) 16 July 225/4 All we want is permission *to oil the wheels* of our own little Botany Bay state-carriage ourselves.
   2. *transf.* Penal servitude; a penal colony. Also *attrib.*
   1789 *Times* (London) 20 Nov. 3/3 Men of profligate principles empowered with empanelling of juries, may give away the lives of every honest Englishman, and send people to the New-drop, or Botany Bay, who ought to go to some better place. **1794** G. THOMPSON *Slavery & Famine* ii. 9 If guilty, he is taken to a cart wheel to receive a Botany Bay dozen, which is twenty-five lashes. **1890** J.E. RITCHIE *Austral. Ramble* 135 To talk of the taint of Botany Bay is the silliest of bunkum in the world. There is no trace of it now. Young Australia knows nothing of transportation.
   3. Special Comb. **Botany Bay aristocracy,** see quots.; **greens,** see quot. 1834.
   1832 *Colonial Times* (Hobart) 9 May, **Botany Bay Aristocracy;** or, Shop-boys and Groggy Dunderheads converted into Justices and Esquires, performing Works of Antiquity. **1838** 'A.L.F.' *Hist. S. Terry* 16 Some .. of the Botany Bay aristocracy possess fifty, seventy, one hundred, and three hundred convicts (gratuitously given away white slaves). **1802** M. FLINDERS *Voyage Terra Australis* (1814) I. 114 The soil .. was overspread with shrubs, mostly of one kind, a whitish velvety plant—(*artriplex* [sic] *reniformis* of Brown), nearly similar to what is called at Port Jackson, **Botany-Bay greens. 1834** *Hobart Town Almanack* 134 The Barilla shrubs (*Atriplex Halimus*, *Rhagodia Billardieri*, and *Salicornia arbuscula*) .. with some others, and under the promiscuous name of Botany Bay greens, were boiled and eaten along with some species of sea-weed, by the earliest settlers, when in a state of starvation.

bott, var. BOT *v.*

bottle, *n.*¹ *Obs.* [Abbrev. of *bottle jaw.*]
   1. A fluke infestation of sheep characterized by a swelling under the throat: see quot. 1871.
   1827 *Monitor* (Sydney) 3 Sept. 631 During a period of extreme drought .. all the finest sheep were dying of the bottle, and other diseases, for want of grass and water. **1871** *Austral. Town & Country Jrnl.* (Sydney) 27 May 647/4 This remedy, among his own lambs, caused the 'bottle' to disappear. The 'bottle'—a swelling under the throat from the point of the jaw to the throat—is a sure sign of worms in lambs.
   2. Special Comb. **bottle plant** (or **weed**) *obs.*, the plant *Drosera peltata* (fam. Droseraceae), the consumption of which was mistakenly believed to cause the disease in sheep.
   1876 *Jrnl. & Proc. R. Soc. N.S.W.* (1878) 24 With reference to the 'bottle' disease—a selector about two years ago pointed out to me a small plant which he called the bottle weed, and he assured me that sheep contracted the disease by eating it. The plant grows to a height of from four to six inches, bearing a small pink flower... It is botanically known as *Drosera peltata*. **1880** J. BONWICK *Resources Qld.* 47 The Bottle plant, three inches high, having a small pink flower, is carnivorous, and the cause of the Bottle disease in sheep; it is a Drosera, delighting in swamps of granite regions.
   Hence **bottled, bottley** *adjs.*
   1871 *Austral. Town & Country Jrnl.* (Sydney) 21 Jan. 74/4 Flukey ewes especially get '**bottled**' in the neck, and die off rapidly at six years of age. **1908** *Bulletin* (Sydney) 4 June 14/3 *Death* .. claims many an old ewe an hour or so before it is due, when the cocky has decided it is not possible to save her. She may be '**bottley**'.

bottle, *n.*² [Perh. by analogy with the phr. *no bottle no good.*] In the phr. **the** (or **a**) **full bottle,** (an) expert.
1968 S. GORE *Holy Smoke* 39 It wouldn't have entered their nuts that God .. just happened to be the real full-bottle on Natural Forces as well. 1976 *Bulletin* (Sydney) 28 Feb. 25/3 A consciousness that he is intellectually superior to most of his colleagues, 'a full bottle'.

bottle, *v. trans.* To attack, using a bottle as a weapon.
1917 *Advocate* (Burnie) 11 July 3/9 And moved down the street, because he had heard that some person was going to 'bottle' him. 1977 K. GILBERT *Living Black* 304 If you stand over .. the goomees you get bottled or kicked.

bottlebrush. a. Any shrub or small tree of the Australian genus *Callistemon* (fam. Myrtaceae), the flower spikes of which are shaped like a bottle brush. **b.** Any of several other plants with similar flowers esp. of the genera *Melaleuca* (fam. Myrtaceae) and *Banksia* (fam. Proteaceae).
1841 *Kerr's Melbourne Almanac* 134 Kalistemon, lopanthes and crestata (bottle brush). 1885 MRS C. PRAED *Austral. Life* 112 We composed jointly .. while we sat on a log that bridged the river, with the bottle-brush flowers of the ti-trees touching our shoulders.

bottle-oh. Also **bottle-o.** [f. *bottle* + -O.]
1. A dealer in used bottles. Also *attrib.*
1898 *Truth* (Sydney) 3 Apr. 5/2 The 'bottle-oh men' (*i.e.,* the dealers in bottles), a Sydney class corresponding in some degree to the London costers. 1901 *Ibid.* 6 Jan. 8/5 The crowd in this street was largely of the 'bottle-oh' variety, and mercilessly chaffed the procession. 1921 *Smith's Weekly* (Sydney) 1 Jan. 9/4, I know a lady Bottle-O.
2. A name for a marble: see quot. 1981. Also **bottley.**
1956 *Bulletin* (Sydney) 22 Aug. 13/1 Heard a couple of our old-timers reminiscing about marbles: 'Remember when we used to exchange chows for stonkers, knock over a commons or a bottley and trade conks for smokies?' said one old chap. 1959 *Ibid.* 22 July 18/3 I'm old enough to remember the small bottles of soft-drink that were corked with a built-in glass marble—known to us kids as a 'bottle-oh'. 1981 A. MARSHALL *Aust.* 74 Marble games seemed to vary in each State. Even the terms used were different... The glass marble obtained from the top of a soft drink bottle was called a 'bottley'.

bottler. [Of unknown origin.] Something (or someone) which excites admiration. Also as *adj.*
1855 *Bell's Life in Sydney* 19 May 2/4 He has proved himself, as the saying is, 'a bottler'. 1964 *Qld. Guardian* 8 Apr. 5/4 This bottler little booklet.

bottle-swallow. [See quot. 1898.] *Fairy martin,* see FAIRY *n.*¹ 1.
1898 E.E. MORRIS *Austral Eng.* 47 Bottle-Swallow, .. a popular name for the bird *Lagenoplastis ariel,* otherwise called the *Fairy Martin.* .. The name refers to the bird's peculiar retort-shaped nest. 1924 *Bulletin* (Sydney) 10 Jan. 22/2 The blue martin, or bottle-swallow, seems to stop his flight by gripping the landing-place with his claws.

bottle tick. [f. *bottle,* prob. alluding to the animal's shape when engorged + *tick* parasite.] *Scrub tick,* see SCRUB *n.* 5.
1876 'EIGHT YRS.' RESIDENT' *Queen of Colonies* 44 There are two kinds of these in the scrub, the black and the bottle tick. 1965 *Austral. Encycl.* VIII. 498 *I[xodes] holocyclus,* the dog, bush or bottle tick (this last name is merited only by the female in its fully engorged state).

bottle tree. Any of several trees having a swollen trunk, esp. of the genus *Brachychiton* (fam. Sterculiaceae); BAOBAB b. Also *attrib.*

1844 L. LEICHHARDT *Jrnl. Overland Exped. Aust.* 11 Oct. (1847) 13 The Bottle-tree (Sterculia, remarkable for an enlargement of the stem, about three feet above the ground) was observed within the scrub. 1902 *Bulletin* (Sydney) 8 Nov. 16/1 He was feeding his horse on a mixture of boiled prickly-pear and bottle-tree chaff in a trough.

bottley: see BOTTLE-OH 2.

bottling, *ppl. a.* [Prob. f. BOTTLER.] Excellent.
1894 A.B. BELL *Austral. Camp Fire Tales* 87 Full of gold nuggets—thick as plums in a bottlin' Christmas puddin'.
1976 C.D. MILLS *Hobble Chains & Greenhide* 180 Tumble-up found some bottlin' sugar-bags too.

bottom, *n.*¹ *Mining.* [See BOTTOM *v.*] A mineral-bearing stratum, esp. an auriferous stratum. Also *attrib.*
1853 *Austral. Gold Digger's Monthly Mag.* v. 192 Many a hole has now yielded two, three, and even four bottoms of treasure. 1864 J. ARMOUR *Diggings, Bush & Melbourne* 5 We have learnt how the diggers wash their bottom stuff, and hurry up for some of our tin dishes.

bottom, *n.*² In the phr. **bottom of the harbour,** the depths of a harbour (orig. Sydney Harbour), the fig. destination of a company stripped of its assets and sold off as a means of evading a taxation liability: see quot. 1984. Also *attrib.*
1980 *Austral. Financial Rev.* (Sydney) 11 Jan. 1/1 The tax schemes are jokingly referred to as 'Bottom of the Harbour Pty Ltd', by members of the Sydney tax avoidance fraternity, as many of the documents have gone to a watery grave. 1984 *Canberra Times* 11 Apr. 3/1 An example of a simple bottom-of-the-harbour scheme would begin with a 'target' company with large assets, say $1 million, and a large tax liability, say $400,000. Net value of shares would be $600,000. The shareholders sell the company to a promoter for that $600,000 (plus a commission). The promoter and his clients then convert the $1 million to cash and keep it (thus getting $1 million for about $600,000). The shares in the company are 'sold' to fictitious people and the company's office is transferred to a fictitious address, and the company can never meet its $400,000 tax liability—it has been sent to the bottom of the harbour.

bottom, *v.* [Spec. use of *bottom* to reach the bottom of: see OED *v.* 4.]
1. *Mining.* **a.** *trans.* To excavate (a hole, etc.) to the level of a mineral-bearing stratum. **b.** *absol.* To reach this stratum. Also with **on:** to strike (gold, etc.).
1852 F. TRELOAR *Extracts from Diary* 5 Apr., Went to our claim, Bottomed hole—a blank—about 24 feet deep.
1855 R. CARBONI *Eureka Stockade* 6, I had marked my claim in accordance with the run of the ranges, and safe as the Bank of England I bottomed on gold. 1862 J.A. PATTERSON *Gold Fields Vic.* 182 They bottomed on the 29th of June, 1861, having been five years in getting through the bluestone.
2. *fig.*
1861 L.A. MEREDITH *Over Straits* 250 Not unfrequently in danger of 'bottoming a shycer' by slipping into it. 1903 J. FURPHY *Such is Life* 209 Bottoming on gold this time, she buried the old man within eighteen months, and paid probate duty on £25,000.
Hence **bottoming** *vbl. n.*
1856 S.C. BREES *How to Farm & Settle in Aust.* 56 Deep-sinking was connected with the later practice of 'bottoming', in which the mass of the 'drift', that was previously wont to be washed in its entirety, was passed over, excepting a small quantity immediately adjacent to the rock or bottom on which it rested.

bottom end. In local use: the lower part of the Murray River and its surrounding country. See also TOP END 2. Also *attrib.*
1947 W. LAWSON *Paddle-Wheels Away* 16 'Bottom-end?' Dan Dalley asked. 'Where's that?' 'Down near the mouth—Goolwa, Murray Bridge, Mannum, Blanchetown, Morgan—they're all 'bottom-end' ports. This is the only 'top-end' one, and we're busy, I tell you.' 'What divides the two classes—'bottom-end' and 'top-end'?' Dan asked. 'The Darling. She comes in 500 miles down.' **1981** B.J. BROCK *Catharsis* 54 You came through clear tonight, mate, On the tape from Stenhouse Bay, Talking of shells and Bottom End lore Over a black and tan.

Hence **bottom-ender** *n.*, a member of the crew of a Murray River boat: see quot. 1953. See also TOP-ENDER 2.

1947 W. LAWSON *Paddle-Wheels Away* 103 There were about a dozen 'bottom-enders' in the brawl. **1953** A. MORRIS *Rich River* 53 The crew .. made merry in the Wilcannia hotels where top-enders (Echuca men) vied with bottom-enders, their rivals from South Australia.

bough. Used *attrib.* in Comb. to denote a type of structure: made in a rough and ready way from branches.
1848 *Maitland Mercury* 6 Dec. 4/4 The careful manner in which they appeared to manage their sheep—making very neat and substantial bough yards. **1983** *Yulngu* Dec. 9 Most of the kids will have seen the improvement in the bough shelter area.

boulder opal. See quot. 1974.
1928 R.M. MACDONALD *Opals & Gold* 35 The opal was a specimen of 'boulder opal' cut from a boulder. **1974** B. MYATT *Dict. Austral. Gemstones* 134 The term boulder opal or Queensland opal is commonly used by miners for some stones found in Queensland. These consist usually of brownish coloured iron stained sandstone containing scattered veins or coatings of opal or of opal coated concretions.

bounce, *v. Australian National Football. trans.* To bounce (the ball) in a BALL-UP, esp. with reference to the beginning of the game.
1900 B. KERR *Silliad* 35 The ball is bounced, the glorious game renewed. **1936** E.C.H. TAYLOR *Our Austral. Game Football* 43 The field umpire shall bounce the ball .. at the start of each quarter, and after each goal has been kicked.

Hence **bounce** *n.*
1910 *Huon Times* (Franklin) 18 May 4/3 Immediately on the bounce they swooped down on the leather.

bound. In the phr. **bounds of location:** see LOCATION 4.

boundary, *n.* and *attrib.* [Shortening of 'boundary of location': see LOCATION 4.]
A. *n. Hist.* The boundary defining that part of a Colony in which land is surveyed and available for legal tenure: see quot. 1845. See also BORDER 1. Freq. in the phr. **beyond** (or **within**) **the boundaries.**
1803 *Sydney Gaz.* 27 Nov., A Settler at the Northern Boundary .. on Monday last employed a thresher. **1835** *Sydney Times* 6 Jan. 2/5 We have the particulars of another dreadful outrage by bushrangers, at the remotest part of the county of Argyle, we believe beyond the boundaries. **1845** J.O. BALFOUR *Sketch of N.S.W.* 87 The settlers, properly speaking, are those who, either by purchases or grants, are possessed of landed property within the boundary; and the squatters those who live and depasture their sheep and cattle outside the boundary. By the boundary is meant a line that separates the land already surveyed .. from the lands in the interior, called in the colony 'bush', which are not surveyed.

B. *attrib.*
1. Of or pertaining to the perimeter of a rural property.
1808 *Sydney Gaz.* 5 June, Three allotments of 30 acres each: the boundary line continuing further as far as Burk's Farm. **1965** R.H. CONQUEST *Horses in Kitchen* 161 And there the fiction writers leave the squatter's daughter—up to her neck in happiness in a remote boundary hut, cooking, washing nappies and hanging up curtains.

2. Special Comb. **boundary rider,** an employee responsible for maintaining the (outer) fences on a station, or a publicly owned vermin-proof fence. Also *fig.* (see quot. 1919).
1864 H. JONES *New Valuations* 13 Fencing does not decrease the expenses of working a station. .. Instead of shepherds we have to get boundary riders. **1919** H.B. FLETCHER *Boundary Riders Egypt* 24 The supports are brought up and a very lively scrap takes place, almost inevitably in Billjim's favour, as the Turk has a holy fear of the 'Boundary Riders'. **1950** G.M. FARWELL *Land of Mirage* 24 Today the only men working camels are Australian; two boundary riders on the dog-fence north of Marree .. some brumby-shooter in the Diamantina sandhills.

boundary-ride, *v. trans.* and *intr.* To ride (round) the boundaries of a station: see prec. (sense 2). Also *transf. and fig.*
1889 W.R. THOMAS *In Early Days* 21 He used to boundary-ride the pegs [on a mining claim] once a day. **1894** *Bulletin* (Sydney) 6 Jan. 23/3 Whether boundary-riding, burr-cutting or droving he did not like being called Doctor. **1899** *Ibid.* 19 Aug. 15/1 Station-hand to injured mate in bed, as the priest leaves the room: 'What sorter cove's that? Looks like a cross atween a doc, an' a parson.' Mate: 'No, them ain't his lines; he's boundary-ridin' for the Pope.' **1980** R. BROPHO *Fringedweller* 77 His reply was not direct. He boundary-rided most of the important questions.

Hence **boundary-riding** *vbl. n.*
1878 *Squatters' Plum* 39 The wife is expected to cook, wash, make beds, and bake bread; and the husband to do boundary-riding, cut and cart wood, kill and dress sheep, and be always doing something.

boung, var. BUNG *a.*

bounty. *Hist.*
1. A sum of money paid by the government to an immigrant, or to an individual or company who sponsors certain categories of immigrant; an immigrant so sponsored.
1832 *Emigrant's Guide N.S.W.* 23 Females desirous to emigrate to New South Wales .. will be admitted as candidates for the bounty of £8. **1837** J. MACARTHUR *N.S.W.; its Present State & Future Prospects* 149 The offer of a bounty by the local government of the colony, for the importation of agricultural families from the continent of Europe, having excited remark in this country, it may be proper to explain the enlightened principles upon which His Excellency Sir Richard Bourke was led partially to adopt this provision. **1844** *Port Phillip Gaz.* 30 Nov. 3 Twenty probationers from the new model prison of Pentonville .. are the very best we could have, inasmuch as they cost us nothing, and are like a free supply of labour, while the 'bounties' were brought here at a cost of £8 to £12 to the Colony.

2. Comb. **bounty agent, emigrant, emigration, immigrant, immigration, order, ship, system, ticket.**
1841 *Port Phillip Patriot* 16 Aug. 2/6 He (Mr Arden) would attract the attention of his listeners to the manner in which the work of the **Bounty agents** had been performed. **1840** *S. Austral. Rec.* (London) 4 July 4 The *Arkwright*, from Liverpool, arrived at Sydney on the same day, having on board 172 **bounty emigrants.** **1840** *S. Austral. Rec.* (London) 21 Mar. 129 The materials of **bounty emigration,** from the very nature of the case,

must ever be superior to those of government emigration. Bounty emigrants are selected, with few exceptions, on behalf of capitalists in the colony, and good engagements are made with them. **1842** *Sydney Herald* 3 Feb. 2/3 (heading) **Bounty immigrants**. **1841** *Port Phillip Patriot* 5 Aug. 2/1 The danger which threatens this Province from the stoppage of **Bounty Immigration**. **1842** *Colonial Observer* (Sydney) 9 Feb. 145/3 His Excellency's **Bounty Orders** have been selling publicly, under the name of 'Botany Bay Emigration Scrip', we presume, in the Stock Exchanges of London, Liverpool and Glasgow. **1840** *S. Austral. Rec.* (London) 26 Dec. 409 Letters have been received from many .. emigrants .. urging all poor families who desire to emigrate to Australia to come out in the government ships, and not in the **bounty ships**. **1839** *HRA* (1924) 1st Ser. XX. 43 The comparative state of health which has existed on board the Government Ships and those sent out on the **Bounty System**. **1854** BACKHOUSE & TYLOR *Life & Labours G.W. Walker* (1862) 536 The Government furnishes **Bounty Tickets** for each adult emigrant.

Bourke /bɜk/. [The name of a town in n.w. N.S.W.] In the phr. **back of** (or **o'**) **Bourke**, the remote and sparsely populated inland. Also used adverbially.
1896 *Bulletin* (Sydney) 15 Feb. 3/2 Where the mulga paddocks are wild and wide, That's where the pick of the stockmen ride, At the Back o' Bourke. **1937** W.R. GLASSON *Musings in my Saddle* 42 The story of the child, born at the back of Bourke, who, on coming to Sydney, encountered rain for the first time and complained to his mother that some naughty person was throwing water on him, is a true one.

Bourke parrot. [f. the name of Richard *Bourke*, Governor of N.S.W. (1831- 1837).] The parrot *Neophema bourkii* of inland Australia, having pink on the underside of the body and blue areas on the wings. Formerly **Bourke parakeet**.
1934 *Bulletin* (Sydney) 18 Apr. 20/3 One of our most elusive birds is the Bourke parrakeet. **1937** R.H. CROLL *Wide Horizons* 51 An observant station owner .. pointed out the large eyes of the Bourke Parrots and said that these parrots assuredly fly by night.

Bourke-street, *attrib*. [The name of a street in Melbourne.] Citified; cf. PITT STREET.
1944 *Bulletin* (Sydney) 10 May 12/2 We've all heard Bourke-street pioneers giving tongue to the alleged Aussie call as they battled through the trackless wilds of the Sherbrooke Forest. **1946** *Ibid.* 4 Dec. 29/4 Bourke-street bushmen .. marvel at the tolerance of the wedgetail eagle.

bower. A structure, made by the male of certain species of bower-bird to attract a mate, consisting of an avenue of sticks or other vegetation and decorated with numerous natural or man-made objects collected by the bird.
1841 *Proc. Zool. Soc. London* VIII. 94 These constructions, Mr Gould states, are perfectly anomalous in the architecture of birds, and consist in a collection of pieces of stick and grass, formed into a bower... They are used by the birds as a playing-house, or 'run', as it is termed, and are used by the males to attract the females. **1976** *Reader's Digest Compl. Bk. Austral. Birds* 552 The smallest of the bower birds builds the biggest bower.

bower-bird.
1. Any of several species of bird in the fam. Paradisaeidae, occurring in Australia and New Guinea. (Most Austral. species build a bower.)
1841 J. GOULD *Birds of Aust.* (1848) IV. Pl. 9, *Chlamydera nuchalis*. Great Bower-bird. **1980** ANSELL & PERCY *To fight Wild* 75 Up in the fig trees there were bower-birds, looking for ripe figs.

2. *fig*. A person who collects objects, ideas, etc.; a hoarder; a thief. Also *attrib*.
1926 H.W. FOWLER *Dict. Mod. Eng. Usage* 193 Use of French words... Only fools will think it commends them to the English reader to decorate incongruously with such bower-birds' treasures as *au pied de la lettre*. *Ibid.* 194 Every writer .. who suspects himself of the bower-bird instinct should .. remember that acquisitiveness & indiscriminate display are pleasing to contemplate only in birds & savages & children. **1943** S.J. BAKER *Pop. Dict. Austral. Slang* (ed. 3) 13 *Bower bird*, a petty thief. **1981** *Sunday Mail* (Brisbane) 14 June 13/1 Brisbane State High School principal Mr Ray Fitzgerald admits to being a bit of a bower bird. Indicating his executive-size office he says: 'I don't know how I'm going to get this cleaned out by June 26.'

Hence as *v. trans.* and *absol*.
1941 K. TENNANT *Battlers* 301, I don't want him bowerbirding round this camp. **1948** W. HATFIELD *Barrier Reef Days* 66 What a mess-up things would be if we couldn't put a thing down and turn our backs without somebody bowerbirding it.

Bowser /'baʊzə/. Also **bowser**. [Proprietary name.]
1. A petrol pump; a petrol tanker used for refuelling aircraft, tanks, etc. Also *attrib*.
1918 *Austral. Official Jrnl. Patents* (Canberra) 31 *Bowser* 22,099... Pumps. *S.F. Bowser and Company, Incorporated*, Fort Wayne, Indiana, United States of America, oil storage engineers. **1930** *Bulletin* (Sydney) 7 May 20/2 Wallerbrith .. keeps the general store, the garage and the bowser palace in our village. **1963** D. IRVING *Destruction of Dresden* 139 The bowsers were waiting to top up the tanks once again.

2. *transf*. and *fig*.
1937 *Bulletin* (Sydney) 20 Oct. 20/2 Nature played a shabby trick on the dormouse-opossum... The first four to arrive are set, each having a teat to fasten to. The late arrivals find that there are no more bowsers available and quickly die. **1976** S. WELLER *Bastards I have Met* 25 In the days before bowsers, when beer was a zac and spirits a deener, it was customary to give the bloke the bottle and let him pour his own.

bowyang /'boʊjæŋ/. Also **boyang**. Usu. in *pl.* [f. Br. dial. *booyangs* straps buckled over trousers below the knees: see SND and also EDD *bowy-yanks* leather leggings.]
1. A string or narrow strap tied round the trouser-leg below the knee: see quot. 1893.
1893 *Warracknabeal Herald* 22 Sept., To those not in the cult of 'boyang worship', it may be necessary to explain that the two straps used to hitch the lower part of labourers' trousers are 'boyangs'. **1981** P. RADLEY *Jack Rivers & Me* 90 We're wearin' bowyangs... That's like when you tie a rope round the legs of your pants to stop snakes from crawling up. The boys call them shit-catchers.

2. *transf.* and *fig.* Used *attrib*. as a symbol of engagement in manual labour: limited in education and outlook.
1951 S. HICKEY *Travelled Roads* 48 His artistry and polish made him the foremost propagandist in Labour's early days, and helped counter the cry that it was a bowyang party. **1983** *Austral.* (Sydney) 18 Feb. 11/2, I think it has to do with the increasing conservatism of the electorate and the disappearance of the true-blue, boots and bowyangs Labor man.

Hence **bowyanged** *a*.
1915 J.P. BOURKE *Off Bluebush* 92 For the world wags fine with the bow-yanged blokes While they work for a miner's pay!

box, *n*.[1] [Transf. use of *box* the tree.]
1. Any of several trees of the fam. Myrtaceae, esp. of the genus *Eucalyptus*, having close-grained timber resembling that of the European *Buxus* and (usu.) a

fibrous bark; the wood of these trees. Also *attrib.*, and with distinguishing epithet, as **apple, brush, red, white, yellow** (see under first element).

1801 *HRA* (1915) 1st Ser. III. 177 The banks of the river covered with cedar, ash and what is called box. **1965** *Austral. Encycl.* III. 406 Box eucalypts also range from Victoria to the Northern Territory and are so named from their hard tough timbers (like European boxwood); the barks consist of finely matted fibrils .. tending to flake away in small pieces.

2. Comb. **box bark, creek, flats, forest.**

1827 P. CUNNINGHAM *Two Yrs. in N.S.W.* I. 206 The bark of the .. box and the stringy-bark makes good roofs for cattle, as also cart-sheds, and workmen's huts, the **box-bark** possessing considerable incombustible properties. **1847** *Moreton Bay Courier* 23 Oct. 4/1, I am inclined to believe that the open box country of the four last mentioned creeks extends in an easterly direction round the scrub we had crossed to the first **box creek**. **1844** L. LEICHHARDT *Jrnl. Overland Exped. Aust.* 23 Dec. (1847) 83 The country begins to open, with large **Box-flats** extending on both sides. **1847** E.B. KENNEDY *Extracts Jrnl. Exped. Central Aust.* 232 Continued our journey .. through a flooded **box-forest**.

3. Special Comb. **box poison,** the shrub poisonous to stock *Oxylobium parviflorum* (fam. Fabaceae) of s.w. W.A.

1872 Mrs E. MILLETT *Austral. Parsonage* 50 The 'box' poison (one of the *Gastrolobrum* [sic] tribe, I believe) takes its name from a fancied resemblance between the pernicious shrub and the well-known box-tree.

box, $n.^2$ *Hist.*

1. A moveable box-like shelter in which convicts were confined at night; CARAVAN.

1836 J. BACKHOUSE *Extracts from Lett.* (1839) iv. 5 At the quarries the men are lodged in 'boxes' or caravans, a little more than seven feet wide; four tiers of men, of five each, occupy one box. **1863** C. GIBSON *Life among Convicts* II. 228 They were locked up from sunrise to sunset, in caravans or boxes, which held from twenty to twenty-eight men each; but which were not high enough to allow of the men standing.

2. A moveable shelter in which a shepherd could sleep while remaining close by his flock.

1843 J.F. BENNETT *Hist. & Descr. Acct. S.A.* 97 The shepherd or hut-keeper, with his dog, sleeps in a moveable box placed close to the fold. **1909** H. BUTTON *Flotsam & Jetsam* 103 He followed his sheep over immense plains, sleeping in a portable 'box' fixed on wheels.

box, $n.^3$ [Prob. f. the phr. *to be in a (the same, wrong) box* to be in a fix: see OED $sb.^2$ 21.] A mixing of two flocks or herds. Also **box-up.**

1868 C.W. BROWNE *Overlanding in Aust.* 2 A. and B. represent two shepherds on a run. They live not far apart, and in consequence occasionally meet, each man having his flock with him. On such an occasion A. comes over to B. to have a chat and a smoke with him. The flocks meanwhile are left to take care of themselves, and in process of time come feeding closer and closer to each other. Suddenly the leading sheep in A.'s mob lifts up his head, gives a preparatory 'Bah!' and charges straight at B.'s followed by all his companions. The two thus become amalgamated. This is a box, and it has occurred through the negligence of both parties. **1917** A.L. BREWER *'Gators' Euchre* 97 'Have to go some to prevent a box-up,' he mutters. Now his whip flies round; his horse props and wheels in all directions; and the station cattle are turned after a determined resistance.

box, $n.^4$ *Mining.* Abbrev. of 'sluice box'; a compartment of a sluice box.

1870 *Sydney Morning Herald* 5 July 2/4 The Big Engine claim is the only fresh one that has started washing... They have, I am informed, come on to some payable dirt... The boxes are going, which will soon test its quality. **1931** W. BARAGWANATH et al. *Guide for Prospectors in Vic.* 12 A box sluice consists of a long wooden trough or series of troughs .. each length being called a 'box'.

Hence **box** *v. intr.*

1932 I.L. IDRIESS *Prospecting for Gold* 26 Now for a much faster method of gold working, 'boxing'. *Ibid.* 51 You can box in a running stream under conditions where it would not be advantageous to hand sluice your whole claim in a face.

box, $n.^5$ [Fig. use of *box* dice-box.] In the collocation **the whole box and dice:** everything, the whole lot.

1888 'R. BOLDREWOOD' *Robbery under Arms* (1937) 74, I could see him turn his head and keep watching me when I put on the whole box and dice of the telegraph business. **1985** J. CLANCHY *Lie of Land* 80 Everything's changed. The whole box and dice.

box, $n.^6$ [Var. of U.S. *to look as if one came out of a bandbox* to look very smart: see OEDS *bandbox* c.] In the phr. **out of the box:** unusually good.

1926 *Sun* (Sydney) 1 July 1/4 Two out of the box. These Siamese cats are just looking at the world from the box in which they travelled. **1975** *Sun-Herald* (Sydney) 9 Nov. 111/2 To be frank, the novel is nothing out of the box, and neither is the movie.

box, $v.^1$ [f. Box $n.^3$]

1. *trans.* To allow, either by accident or design, (discrete flocks or herds) to become mixed. Also with **up.**

[N.Z. **1864** Puketoi Diary 19 Apr., Lambs boxed.] **1870** J.C. WHITE *Qld. Progressive* 27 But if the sheep do get mixed, or 'boxed' as the saying is, you must yard them. **1884** 'R. BOLDREWOOD' *Old Melbourne Memories* 10 As his cattle were drawing into camp, I cheerfully 'boxed' mine therewith and relieved myself by the act of further anxiety. **1890** 'MRS A. MACLEOD' *Austral. Girl* (1894) 181 Some sheep got boxed up at the seven-mile hut, and we had a high old time of it drafting them.

2. *transf.* and *fig.*

c **1884** *Punchialities from Punch* 50 Squatter's daughter—We had such a jolly lark to day. In going out for a walk we got boxed with another school; we had to be mustered, and then drafted out. **1960** *Sydney Morning Herald* 19 July 1/10 Thurber's moral is: Those who live in grass houses shouldn't stow thrones. Emile boxed it.

Hence **boxing** *vbl. n.*

1868 C.W. BROWNE *Overlanding in Aust.* 62 He must be, moreover, constantly on the move, and on the alert to prevent boxing with other flocks, or those of the run he may be passing through.

box, $v.^2$ *intr.* With **on:** to fight, to persevere.

1919 W.H. DOWNING *Digger Dialects* 13 Box on, (1) continue; (2) fight. **1980** M. WILLIAMS *Dingo!* 76, I got five years' hard labour. Five years! .. The big shots said I was lucky. Box on with it, they said.

boxer, $n.^1$ [Prob. Br. dial. *boxer* tall (hard) hat: see OEDS 4.] A bowler hat. Also *attrib.*

1895 *Bulletin* (Sydney) 29 June 3/2 You might chance to meet a spectre on some God-forgotten track Wearing spectacles and boxer with a lib'ry on his back. **1981** A. MARSHALL *Aust.* 25 It was the days of boxer hats, ankle-choker pants, handlebar moustaches and Charlie Chaplin gallantry.

boxer, $n.^2$ *Two-up.* [Prob. fig. use of *boxer* one who boxes in the ring.] The person in charge of the game; a payment to this person, either as a percentage of some winnings or by contribution. See also *ring-keeper* RING $n.^2$ 2.

1911 L. STONE *Jonah* 216 The spinner threw down the kip, and took his winnings from the boxer. **1949** L. GLASSOP *Lucky Palmer* 169 In response to the fat man's appeal for a 'boxer', a few florins and shillings were tossed into the ring.

box jellyfish. [See quot. 1976.] Any of the jelly-like sea animals of the class Cubozoa of the phylum Cnidaria, having stinging tentacles; STINGER 3.
  1971 *Bulletin* (Sydney) 25 Sept. 26/1 The sea-wasp, or box-jelly fish, is said to have killed some 70 swimmers this century. **1976** E. WORRELL *Things that Sting* 56 Also called the Box Jellyfish, the Sea Wasp can be recognised from other less dangerous jellyfish by its box-shaped body, with long venomous tentacles suspended from the four corners.

box-on. [f. Box $v.^2$] See quot. 1919.
  1919 W.H. DOWNING *Digger Dialects* 13 *Box-on*, a fight; a battle; a tussle. **1968** S. GORE *Holy Smoke* 8 Yair, here we are—around the time of the Israel-Philistine box-on, in the Holy Land.

boy. [Spec. use of *boy* coloured servant or slave: see OED(S $sb.^1$ 3 c. and 3 e.] A non-white male employee (of any age). See also BLACKBOY 1. Also *attrib.*
  1864 R. HENNING *Lett.* (1952) 68 He takes with him Alick, one of the blackboys—they are always called 'boys' though the said Alick must be thirty-five at least. **1907** *Truth* (Sydney) 7 Apr. 10/6 The Chow boy is everywhere to be seen nursing and washing the baby .. making beds, and doing all domestic work. The boy institution is ruining the rising generation and Northern Territorians generally.

boylya /'bɔɪljə/. Also **bullya**. [a. Nyungar prob. *bulya*.] KORADJI. Also *attrib.*
  1841 G. GREY *Jrnls. Two Exped. N.-W. & W.A.* II. 84 The 'Boyl-yas' would acquire some mysterious influence over him, which would end in his death... The Boyl-ya is the native sorcerer. **1863** J. BONWICK *Wild White Man* 59 Venus .. that Boyl-ya dame now raised on high. **1929** W.J. RESIDE *Golden Days* 158 They also place faith in the powers of the 'bullya', or the sorcerer of the tribe.

bracken. [Transf. use of *bracken* a fern.] The perennial fern *Pteridium esculentum* (fam. Dennstaedtiaceae), sometimes divided into *P. esculentum, P. semihastatum,* and *P. revolutum*, and abundant in forests which are subject to frequent burning. Also **bracken fern**.
  1844 N.L. KENTISH *Work in Bush Van Diemen's Land* (1846) 12 Thicket of fern or braken, growing to the height frequently of 8 or 9 feet. **1931** B. CRONIN *Bracken* 53 Full of weeds, Martin. Full of bracken-fern. Get the fern-hook to work, man.

Braddon Blot. *Hist.* [f. the name of Edward *Braddon* (1829–1904), Premier of Tasmania and member of the first Federal Parliament.] See quot. 1936.
  1899 *North-Western Advocate* (Devonport) 6 Feb. 3/3 The so-called 'Braddon Blot' had been retained, but in a modified form. **1936** J. KIRWAN *My Life's Adventure* 179 He .. succeeded in embodying in the Constitution what is known as the Braddon Clause, by which for the first ten years after Federation the Commonwealth Government had one-fourth of the Customs and Excise revenue and the balance went to the States. Many called it 'The Braddon Blot'.

brain-fever bird. [Transf. use of *brain-fever bird* an Indian cuckoo which calls repeatedly.] PALLID CUCKOO.
  1924 *Bulletin* (Sydney) 14 Aug. 22/3 Several of our cuckoos—including .. the pallid cuckoo (brain-feverbird)—are migratory. **1970** J.V. MARSHALL *Walk to Hills of Dreamtime* 41 The cry of the brain-fever bird, a fluted long-drawn coo-ee, haunting as an invocation to the moon.

bramble. Any of several introduced or native prickly shrubs of the genus *Rubus* (fam. Rosaceae), incl. the naturalized blackberries *R. discolor* and *R. ulmifolius*.
  1827 *Hobart Town Courier* 29 Dec. 3 It may be acceptable to those who are disposed to attempt the culture of the silk worm to know, that the mulberry tree thrives here with astonishing luxuriance .. and that the leaves of the common wild bramble of Van Diemen's Land, form a very good substitute. **1912** *Huon Times* (Franklin) 27 Apr. 6/2 The tints of autumn amongst the orchards, the red and gold leaves of the bramble etc. make a pleasing sight to lovers of nature.

brand, *v. trans.* With **up:** to brand (an animal or animals) with an identifying mark. Also *absol.*
  1879 S.W. SILVER *Austral. Grazier's Guide* 21 It is usual for the stockmen and proprietors of the neighbouring runs to assemble at one another's homesteads .. for the purpose of aiding the owner to 'brand up'. **1929** 'OLD STOCKMAN' *Sensational Cattle-Stealing Case* 18, I stopped there some days spelling my horses. While I was loafing on him, I gave him a hand to muster and brand up his horses.
  Hence **branding-up** *vbl. n.*
  1919 *Bulletin* (Sydney) 25 Sept. 22/3 Owing to the rise in price of cattle and the difficulty stations have in branding-up, 'poddy-dodging' has become an established trade.

brand-fake, brand faker: see FAKE *v.*

branding, *vbl. n.* Used *attrib.* in various Comb.: of or pertaining to the branding of stock.
  1848 H.W. HAYGARTH *Recoll. Bush Life* 70 The fence of the branding-yard is more closely constructed than that of the other divisions, and is provided with what is called a 'branding panel', which is, in fact, a sort of screen, behind which the men take refuge, if suddenly charged by an infuriated animal. **1881** A.C. GRANT *Bush-Life Qld.* I. 227 The branding-pen is getting particularly lively now. **1934** W. HATFIELD *River Crossing* 152 Men were injured .. in their man-handling of grown beasts on the branding-camps. **1954** H.G. LAMOND *Manx Star* 118 The stock-camp was completing the final branding muster of the year.

brass razoo: see RAZOO.

breadcarter. An itinerant vendor of bread, etc.
  1908 *Truth* (Sydney) 12 Apr. 7/3 (*heading*) Breadcarter's battle against buns. **1956** *Bulletin* (Sydney) 14 Mar. 13/1 Our local breadcarter and his horse always struck me as a happy combination.

breadfruit. [Transf. use of *breadfruit* the farinaceous fruit of a tree, esp. that furnished by *Artocarpus altilis*, which is cultivated in Aust.] Any of several native plants bearing an edible fruit, esp. SCREW PINE; the fruits of these plants. Also *attrib.*
  1830 W.J. HOOKER *Bot. Miscellany* I. 250 On the beach were thickets of *Hibiscus tiliaceus*, and *Pandanus pedunculata*: the latter is called *Bread-fruit*, and eagerly eaten by the natives. **1930** M.M.J. COSTELLO *Life J. Costello* 229 Here the beautiful Breadfruit Palm, now in full bearing and utilised by the blacks in making a food which when pulverised, moulded into dough and baked in the ashes results in a product resembling a sodden damper in which no baking powder had been used.

break, *n.* [Spec. use of *break* an interruption of continuity.]
  1. A temporary barrier: see quot. 1876.
  1876 J.A. EDWARDS *Gilbert Gogger* 143 Breaks: Temporary brush fences, built by parties travelling with sheep, to count their sheep through, upon the road. **1934** A. RUSSELL *Tramp-Royal* 54 Rolled in our 'nap' with the break at our heads and the camp fire at our feet.

2. A fire-break.
1925 M. TERRY *Across Unknown Aust.* 244 To burn a break around it . . i.e. burn off the grass so as to leave the yards surrounded by cleared ground, over which the flames could not leap. **1965** G. McINNES *Road to Gundagai* 248 To see him burning a break, dipping sheep or leaning over a wire fence talking to a stockrider, was to recognize a grazier's hierarchy in which everyone was equal because everyone had his place.

3. The point at which the swell of a wave 'breaks'. Also with qualifying word, as **beach, reef, shore break.**
1963 J. POLLARD *Austral. Surfrider* 20 The next one you might take right to the 'shore break', the waves breaking on the very edge of the beach. *Ibid.* 27 The highlight of the Duke's performance came when he picked up a wave in the northern corner, stood erect and ran the board across the bay, continually beating the break. **1965** *Surfabout* (Sydney) II. ix. 25 There is a reef break which occasionally produces good right slides. **1967** *Ibid.* III. vii. 8 The other popular surf, the left beachbreak, works best at 3–4 feet on high tide.

break, *v.* [Spec. use of *break, v.* to escape from restraint; with *out* to burst out (as of fire); with *down* to demolish.]

1. *intr.* Of stock: to stampede. Also *transf.*
1888 'R. BOLDREWOOD' *Robbery under Arms* (1937) 35 Stop 'em from breaking or running clear away from the others. **1938** F. RATCLIFFE *Flying Fox & Drifting Sand* 124 The camp [of flying foxes] 'broke' at precisely 6 P.M . . first forming a packed wheeling mass above the trees.

2. *intr.* With **out.**
a. Of a goldfield: to become the centre of a rush; to burst into life. Also as *vbl. n.*
1855 G.H. WATHEN *Golden Colony* 43 When first the gold 'broke out' (to use the diggers' phrase), the general excitement . . almost put an end to private convivial meetings. **1879** *Kelly Gang* 13 Here . . the young couple resided until the breaking out of the diggings, the husband pursuing his adopted calling of splitter and fencer.

b. To go on a drinking bout: see BREAK OUT *n.*
[N.Z. **1899** J. BELL *In Shadow of Bush* 161 He had thought it best on the occasion in which Dan had 'broken out', to give him a wide berth.] **1965** F. HARDY *Yarns of Billy Borker* 126 The old Ragged was a good bloke, a good worker and a good unionist, but he was fond of the gargle, see. He'd break out now and then and when he did, you couldn't get him out of the cart to turn to. Cart? Bed.

3. In the imp. phr. **break it down,** 'desist!'
1941 *Coast to Coast* 127 Ah, break it down, feller. Everybody knew you had her on the town. **1972** D. MARTIN *Frank & Francesca* 16 Jeez, you talk exactly like my mum now. Break it down!

breakaway.
1. An animal that rushes free from a flock or herd. Also *attrib.*
1881 A.C. GRANT *Bush-Life Qld.* I. 223 After a good deal of shouting, cracking of whips, and galloping after odd breakaways, the cattle were yarded amid clouds of dust. **1955** H.G. LAMOND *Towser* 167 As soon as the sheep started to run odd ones gave the usual 'break-away' call.

2. Chiefly W.A. A low escarpment. Also *attrib.*
1896 D. STEWART *Thousand Miles & More* 54 The appearance and contour of this district is very picturesque—abrupt ironstone 'breakaways' and quartz hills and blows are passed through. **1973** *Meanjin* 253 My father's mine was about a quarter of a mile south. Rich, too, until they lost the lode. It's tricky here. Breakaway country.

3. A rush of floodwater bursting from its usual course; the channel thus eroded.
1926 A.A.B. APSLEY *Amateur Settlers* 98 'Washouts' and 'breakaways' as the run-offs made by the terrific rainfall in 'the wet' are called. **1935** I.L. IDRIESS *Man Tracks* 25 Then the desert face broke into chasm-like wrinkles that were 'breakaways', rocky cracks, enormous channels one after the other down into which and across the labouring camels had to be coaxed and driven.

break o' day bird. *Obs.* [See quot. 1872.] MAGPIE *n.* 1 a. Also **break o' day boy.**
1872 MRS E. MILLETT *Austral. Parsonage* 42 The business of the lark as harbinger of morning devolves in Australia upon the magpies, which on this account are commonly called 'break-of-day birds'. **1916** E. & M.S. GREW *Rambles in Aust.* 28 The magpies . . are called 'break o' day boys' in the country, because, like our cocks, they call the neighbourhood.

break out. *Obs.* A drinking bout.
1847 A. HARRIS *Settlers & Convicts* (1953) 142 The notion of a 'spree' gets into their head, they are never easy till they have their 'break out' over. **1888** 'R. BOLDREWOOD' *Robbery under Arms* (1937) 81 He saw him once in one of his break-outs.

breakweather. *Obs.* BREAKWIND 1.
1839 *Royal S. Austral. Almanack* 110 It being now sunset we formed a native 'breakweather' of boughs, and passed the night in this place. **1852** G.C. MUNDY *Our Antipodes* I. 331 The natives . . squatted before a fire and behind a sloping sheet of bark turned from the wind—in bush lingo, a break-weather.

breakwind.
1. An Aboriginal shelter.
1832 J. BACKHOUSE *Extracts from Lett.* (1838) i. 55 We went into their breakwinds (as their huts are called) and took leave of them. **1943** *Bulletin* (Sydney) 17 Nov. 12/2 Most times a breakwind of bark and boughs suffices the Kimberley abo. for a roof.

2. Any temporary shelter; a wind-break.
1840 *S. Austral. Rec.* (London) 17 Oct. 251 Arrived upon his estate, his [*sc.* the settler's] primary object is to erect a brush-hut or break-wind, which is formed of the boughs of trees, and sometimes thatched in a rude manner with long grass. This serves for a shelter until a log-hut can be constructed. **1938** D. BATES *Passing of Aborigines* 190, I built an enclosing breakwind of mulga bushes, and set up the little household that was to be my domain for 16 years.

bream /brɪm/. Also **brim.** [Transf. use of *bream* as applied to certain fish, either fresh-water (fam. Cyprinidae), or marine (various fam.)] Any of several fresh-water and marine fish, esp. *black bream* (see BLACK *a.*^{2} 1 b.); see quot. 1963. Also with distinguishing epithet, as **bony, red, silver** (see under first element).
1699 W. DAMPIER *New Voyage round World* (1703) III. 140 In the night while Calm we fish'd with Hook and line, and caught good store of Fish, *viz* Snappers, Breams, Old Wives, and Dog-Fish. **1963** B. CROPP *Handbk. for Skindivers* 116 There are two common species—black and southern bream. Bream are mainly found in New South Wales and Queensland. . . Southern bream (*Mylie butcheri*) are confined to the southern section of Australia.

breast, *v.* [Fig. use of *breast* to face.] Esp. in the phr. **to breast the bar,** to approach (a bar) purposefully. Also *transf.* and *fig.*
1909 E. WALTHAM *Life & Labour in Aust.* 31 No sooner do we 'breast the bar' than a huge rough-and-ready miner accosts us thusly 'Well mate, what's your poison?' **1909** F.E. BIRTLES *Lonely Lands* 75 Plucky little Burketown came up smiling every time to 'breast the bar' and 'face the music', as the local language so pithily expressed it. **1968** S. GORE *Holy Smoke* 26 Yair, he didn't even have the price of the fare home; let alone feeling too much of a crumb to breast the old man again and give him the score.

breezer. *Shearing.* In the phr. **from the breezer** (or **sneezer**) **to the sneezer** (or **breezer**), from nose to tail. Also *transf.*

c 1895 CLARK & WHITELAW *Golden Summers* (1986) 133 So I . . catches my bird, gives him two blows, from his sneezer to his breezer. **1899** J. BRADSHAW *Highway Robbery under Arms* (1912) 36 Cut the sheep from the breezer to the sneezer. **1978** J. DINGWALL *Sunday too far Away* 88, I hope you've got clean hands doctor—you've cut him from the sneezer to the breezer.

brewer. In special collocations: **brewers' asthma**, see quots. 1953 and 1967; **droop** [used elsewhere but recorded earliest in Aust.], alcohol-induced flaccidity of the penis; **goitre**, see quot. 1953.

1953 S.J. BAKER *Aust. Speaks* 137 **Brewer's asthma**, shortness of breath, allegedly due to habitual drinking of strong waters. **1967** *Kings Cross Whisper* (Sydney) xxxii. 7/1 *Brewers' asthma*, a very severe hangover. **1971** B. HUMPHRIES *Bazza pulls it Off*, I know you've had a few but don't tell me you've copped the **brewer's droop**! **1953** S.J. BAKER *Aust. Speaks* 137 **Brewer's goitre**, a paunch allegedly acquired by consuming beer in large quantities.

brick, *n.*¹ Chiefly *Tas. Obs.* [Prob. ironic use of *brick good fellow*: see OED *sb.*¹ 6.] A member of a street gang; a hooligan.

1840 *Tasmanian Weekly Dispatch* (Hobart) 31 July 7/1 Some of the vagabonds of the Town, who call themselves 'Bricks', had much annoyed Clark. **1866** *Sydney Punch* 13 Jan. 687/1 How very hard headed both Scotch and Colonial 'bricks' are.

Hence **brickism** *n.*

1841 *Geelong Advertiser* 14 Aug. 2/4 *Midnight Marauders.—* We had hopes that this gang of mischievous youths had been broken up. . . If the police would only keep a sharp eye upon them for a few nights, and lay a few of them fast by heels, the spirit of 'brickism' would soon be broken.

brick, *n.*² *Obs.* [From the colour of the note.]

1. In gambling: a ten-pound note; ten pounds.

1914 A.B. PATERSON in C. Semmler *World of Banjo Paterson* (1967) 324 Pop it down, gents, if you don't put down a brick you can't pick up a castle! **1967** A.E. DEBENHAM *All Manner of People* 89 The husband sold his new suit for £10 and put the 'brick' on the dead cert.

2. In the phr. **London to a brick,** see quot. 1972.

1965 F. HARDY *Yarns of Billy Borker* 108 'Close: but Magger by a head,' the course announcer Ken Howard says, 'London to a brick on Magger.' **1972** *Bulletin* (Sydney) 8 Apr. 53/1 *A well-known* Sydney race caller has been heard to utter the phrase 'London to a brick', to describe the seemingly indisputable chances of certain horses at Royal Randwick.

brick, *n.*³

1. *attrib.* In the collocation **brick area,** a residential area in which the houses are of brick or brick veneer, and which therefore has a certain social cachet.

1935 *Austral. Home Beautiful* July 28 The 'better class' suburbs have their brick areas in which no weatherboard may show its face. **1981** B. HUMPHRIES *Nice Night's Entertainment* 4 It's a brick area, of course, and our neighbours are all a very nice type of person.

2. In the collocation **brick veneer.** Usu. hyphenated as *adj.*

a. *adj.* Of a house (or other small building): having external walls which consist of a timber frame faced with a single, non-structural skin of bricks (see quot. 1937).

1935 *Austral. Home Beautiful* July 22 The construction is brick veneer on timber frame with the rear portion in timber. **1937** *Building* (Sydney) 24 Apr. 35/1 A brick veneer job consists wholly of timber frame walls with an outer 4½ in. brick veneer external wall which is tied to the studs at intervals either with 8 in. lengths of 20 gauge 1¼ galvanised hoop iron bent strapping or by special No. 8 gauge galvanised wire ties with ends bent to form eyes and double nailed to the stud. **1983** *Canberra Chron.* 7 Sept. 1/2 Some of the fibro houses . . have been replaced with attractive brick-veneer government houses and some have been bought by tenants.

b. *n.* A house built with brick-veneer walls.

1968 *Swag* (Sydney) iii. 22/1 Our new ranch-style brick veneer in a little court in outer suburban Melbourne. **1977** P. ADAMS *Unspeakable Adams* 1 It's 1944 and I'm five years old, living with my grandparents in an old weatherboard in what has become a middle-class suburb of brick veneers with flouncy curtains.

brickfielder. [f. the name of *Brickfield* Hill, a hill in what is now central Sydney where, until *c* 1850, there was a brickworks.]

1. *Hist.* In Sydney, a sudden squally wind from the south, bringing relief at the end of a hot day but sometimes characterized also by an accompanying duststorm: see quot. 1835.

1829 *Sydney Monitor* 10 Oct. 2/6 On Monday last His Excellency and family were placed in considerable danger whilst sailing in consequence of a *brickfielder* coming on, which nearly capsized the boat. **1835** J. BACKHOUSE *Narr. Visit Austral. Colonies* (1843) 236 The thermometer rose to 100° in the shade. About two o'clock the wind rose, with violence, from the south east, and the temperature fell to 70°. It rained in the evening. This kind of wind has occurred a few times before, since our arrival: it is frequent in the summer, and coming upon the town from the direction of some old brickfields, has obtained the name of a Brickfielder. It brings small pebbles pelting like rain, and clouds of red dust, formed, not however entirely from the brickfields, but also from the reddish sand and soil in the neighbourhood. This dust penetrates the houses, in spite of closed doors and windows, till it is seen upon everything, and may be felt grating between the teeth.

2. Elsewhere (but see quot. 1851) a hot wind, usu. from the north and accompanied by a dust-storm. Also *attrib.*

1840 A. RUSSELL *Tour through Austral. Colonies* 206 The hot winds are oppressive, particularly in the neighbourhood of the sandy districts so common here, and at Adelaide. These winds are generally termed *brickfielders*. **1851** H. MELVILLE *Present State Aust.* 27 At Sydney, the . . soil in the immediate neighbourhood, westward of the city, is of a red colour, and when the wind blows from the interior it is, in consequence, called a 'brick-fielder'. **1935** H.H. FINLAYSON *Red Centre* 21 'Brickfielder' dust-storms . . occasionally cloud the towns.

brickie. [f. *brick(layer* + -Y. Used elsewhere but recorded earliest in Aust.] A bricklayer.

1900 *Tocsin* (Melbourne) 6 Sept. 5/2 On Monday I went along, accompanied only by the 'brickolie'. **1986** *Good Weekend* (Sydney) 1 Mar. 36/2, I worked for two days recently as a brickie's labourer but it was too hard.

bricklow, var. BRIGALOW.

bridled nail-tailed wallaby: see NAIL-TAILED WALLABY.

brigalow /ˈbrɪɡəloʊ/. Formerly also **bricklow**. [Poss. a. Kamilaroi *burriigal*.] Any of several trees of the genus *Acacia* (fam. Mimosaceae), esp. the N.S.W. and Qld. tree *A. harpophylla*, having a dark furrowed bark and silver foliage. Also *attrib.*

1844 L. LEICHHARDT *Jrnl. Overland Exped. Aust.* 8 Oct. (1847) 9 The Bricklow scrub compelled us frequently to travel upon the flood-bed of the river. **1975** R. MACKLIN

brim, var. BREAM.

brindabella /ˌbrɪndəˈbɛlə/. [The name of a range of mountains, and (formerly) a sheep station, near Canberra.] See quot. 1959.
   1959 *Bulletin* (Sydney) 23 Dec. 16/1 Most sheep-barbers either drink one or two bottles of beer between knocking-off and going in to tea or slap a brace of rums down. The last 'run' of the day is traditionally called 'The Rum Run'. Some go for the 'brindabella'—rum with a beer-chaser. **1962** *Ibid.* 3 Feb. 43/3 We oldies .. hit ourselves first up with a Brindabella—OP rum with a beer chaser.

brindle. [f. *brindle(d* of two colours.] A person of part-Aboriginal, part-white descent. Also *attrib*.
   1934 C. SAYCE *Comboman* 20 There must have been fifty niggers all told at Kendal Station, counting the brindles. **1941** *Bulletin* (Sydney) 5 Nov. 14/1 At a church service at Alice Springs .. recently the white, black and brindle congregation didn't know at one stage of the service whether they should kneel or not.

bring, *v*. In the phr. **bring your own** (beer, wine, etc.), an intimation to patrons of an unlicensed restaurant that they may bring into the restaurant liquor purchased elsewhere. Also used adjectivally. See also B.Y.O.
   1967 *This Week in Melbourne* 28 Jan. 13/3 The only French seafood restaurant in Melbourne La Bouillabaisse 1455 Malvern Road Glen Iris—20 3685 (Closed Mondays) Bring your own liquor. **1976** *Melbourne BYO's* (Consumers' Assoc. Vic.) 2 Victoria is fortunate and somewhat unique in having a large number of restaurants which have a 'bring-your-own' liquor permit.

brinny. [Prob. f. an Aboriginal language.] A stone, esp. one used by children for throwing as a missile.
   1943 S.J. BAKER *Pop. Dict. Austral. Slang* (ed. 3) 14 *Brinny*, a stone. **1981** B. GREEN *Small Town Rising* 104 The copper's dog hadn't even been friendly though. 'How'd we kill him?' 'Toss a few brinnies at him, and when he comes out lay into him.'

Brisbane line. [f. the name of the capital city of Queensland.] See quot. 1943 (1).
   [**1943** *West Austral.* (Perth) 3 May 2/4 The defence plan of Australia provided for all of Australia north of a line north of Brisbane and following a diagonal course to a point north of Adelaide to be abandoned to the enemy.] **1943** *Ibid.* 4 May 2/7 A military plan to defend Australia south of the 'Brisbane line'. **1985** *Canberra Times* 5 Dec. 1/4 A new 'Brisbane Line' concept .. has been put up by the Australian Army.

bristlebird. Any of the three species of *Dasyornis*, brown ground birds having prominent bristles on the face, and restricted to certain coastal areas of mainland Aust. Also with distinguishing epithet, as **rufous, western** (see under first element).
   1827 *Trans. Linnean Soc. London* XV. 232 [*Dasyornis*] *Australis*... This bird Mr Caley procured in a scrubby place on the north side of Paramatta [*sic*]... He calls it in his notes 'Bristle Bird'. **1976** *Reader's Digest Compl. Bk. Austral. Birds* 422 The eastern bristlebird builds a dome-shaped nest close to the ground.

brittle gum. Any of several trees of the genus *Eucalyptus* (fam. Myrtaceae), having brittle timber, esp. *Eucalyptus mannifera* subsp. *maculosa* and *E. haemastoma* (see SNAPPY GUM).
   1896 *Proc. Linnean Soc. N.S.W.* XXI. 451 *E. viminalis* .. known under several vernacular names such as .. 'Brittle Gum'. **1983** *Canberra Chron.* 14 Sept. 18/1 The three species which form the canopy layer are .. brittle gum (*E. mannifera* ssp. *maculosa*) [etc.].

broad-leaved ironbark. The tree *Eucalyptus fibrosa* subsp. *fibrosa* (fam. Myrtaceae) of N.S.W. and Qld., bearing broad juvenile leaves. Also **broad-leaf ironbark** and *attrib*.
   1861 J.D. LANG *Qld., Aust.* 277 It is generally covered with the broad or silver-leaved iron-bark tree. **1899** *Proc. Linnean Soc. N.S.W.* XXIV. *E*[*ucalyptus*] *siderophloia* .. var. *glauca* var. nov. This is the glaucous interior form of the species, which goes under the names of 'Blue-leaf Ironbark' .. and 'Broad-leaf Ironbark', in allusion to its broad sucker-leaves.

broken, *ppl. a.* Of wool: see quot. 1950.
   1880 J. BONWICK *Resources Qld.* 43 The proportion of broken wool, pieces, and locks. **1950** H.G. BELSCHNER *Sheep Managem.* 692 *Broken*, a trade term applied to the best wool of the skirtings, having the characteristics of fleece wool.

broker. *Obs*. A bankrupt; one who is 'broke'.
   1882 *Sydney Slang Dict.* 9 Dick's a broker, and has gone out snow-dropping. **1915** 'ALPHA' *Reminisc. Goldfields* i. 73 Most of the boarders, who knew nothing about cards, would be found playing with others more skilful than themselves, and in due course became 'brokers'—their week's earnings gone and unable to pay their board and drink bill.

brolga /ˈbrɒlgə/. [a. Kamilaroi *burralga*.] A large bird, the crane *Grus rubicundus*, living near water in e. and n. Aust. and in New Guinea; *native companion*, see NATIVE *a*. 6 b. Also *attrib*.
   1896 *Westminster Gaz.* (London) 6 Oct. 2/1 The native companion crane, otherwise known as the brolga. **1922** *Smith's Weekly* (Sydney) 5 Aug. 19/4 The Brolga dance was Binghi's conception of the frolicksome movements of the native companion.

brome. *Obs*. [Transf. use of *brome* a grass of the genus *Bromus*.] Kangaroo grass (a), see KANGAROO *n*. 5.
   1827 *HRA* (1923) 3rd Ser. VI. 580 The brome or Kangaroo grass was here seen in great abundance. **1848** T.L. MITCHELL *Jrnl. Exped. Tropical Aust.* 61 There I also observed a brome grass, probably not distinct from the Bromus australis of Brown; it called to mind the squarrose brome grass of Europe.

broncho /ˈbrɒŋkoʊ/, *n.* used *attrib*. [See *v*.]
   1. Of or pertaining to the practice of roping cattle for branding, etc., while on horseback.
   1932 J.J. HARDIE *Cattle Camp* (1944) 47 That's old Belle—she used to be a great broncho-mare. **1946** W.E. HARNEY *North of 23°* 39 On Coorabulka, the bronco system was in vogue.
   2. Special Comb. **broncho bail, panel**, see quot. 1964; **yard**, a yard or set of yards in which a mob is held, esp. while calves are branded.
   1964 *N. Austral. Monthly* Nov. 11/2 A **broncho bail** .. is a panel of stout fence. . . The focal point is the actual bail itself .. two posts, about a foot apart, stoutly built and firm in the ground. When the calf is roped it is dragged .. to the bail. The lassoo rope slides over the panel and runs along on top of that to slot between the two main posts. **1968** D. O'GRADY *Bottle of Sandwiches* 26 'Hear yer want some yards built... How much, an' what size?' 'Seventy quid each, hundred yards square, with a **bronco panel** in the guts.' **1923** F.A.C. BISHOP *Rep. on Inspection Barkly Tableland* 3 The improvements on Newcastle are few, and consist of—Two paddocks containing 8 miles of fencing, with the addition of a check fence extending through the gap over the Ashburton Range, and continuing on into the Downs

broncho /'brɒŋkoʊ/, *v.* Also **bronco**. [f. *bronco* unbroken horse.] *trans.* To rope (a calf, etc.), usu. for branding, while on horseback. Chiefly as *vbl. n.* Also *absol.*
1914 Austral. Archives CRS A3 Item 14/2576, All our boarding and herding is done in wire yards, making a small yard to broncho in. **1927** M. TERRY *Through Land of Promise* 230 The man who does the 'bronco-ing' (the local term for this roping of cattle, only found in the most bushy out-Bush stations) rides amongst the mob. **1945** F. CORK *Tales from Cattle Country* 28 It takes two men to broncho a calf, and so rapidly and deftly is it done that to the onlooker it appears easy.

bronze. The anus; the backside. Also **bronza, bronzo.**
1953 S.J. BAKER *Aust. Speaks* 105 *Bronzo,* anus (a variation of *bronze,* used similarly). **1957** D. NILAND *Call me when Cross turns Over* 139, I know the one with the ugly face like a handful of bronzas. Who's the other? **1975** L. RYAN *Shearers* 104 Go and sit on your bronze while we give scabs your jobs.

bronze cuckoo. Any of several species of cuckoo in the genus *Chrysococcyx,* having more or less bronze-coloured feathers on various parts of the body and occurring in Aust. and nearby regions.
1841 J. GOULD *Birds of Aust.* (1848) III. Pl. 18, The female [Blue Wren] .. is also the foster-parent of the Bronze Cuckoo (*Chalcites lucidus*), a single egg of which species is frequently found deposited in her nest. **1976** *Reader's Digest Compl. Bk. Austral. Birds* 299 The little bronze cuckoo and the rufous-breasted bronze cuckoo are separated from other Australian bronze cuckoos by their small size and red around the male's eye.

bronze-wing. a. Any of several pigeons having bronze-coloured markings on the wings, esp. the common bronze-wing, *Phaps chalcoptera,* widespread in Aust., and the *brush bronze-wing* (see BRUSH *n.*[1] B. 2); also **bronze-wing(ed) pigeon. b.** *fig.* A person of part-Aboriginal, part-white descent (see quot. 1956).
1789 A. PHILLIP *Voyage to Botany Bay* 162 Bronze-winged Pigeon... The greater [*sc.* coverts].. have each of them a large oval spot of bronze. **1848** J. GOULD *Birds of Aust.* (1848) V. Pl. 64, Although .. the Bronze-wing is an excellent article of food, it must yield the palm in this respect to .. the Partridge Bronze-wing (*Geophaps scripta*), whose flesh is white and more delicate in flavour. **1935** DAVISON & NICHOLLS *Blue Coast Caravan* 271 A pair of bronzewing pigeons—cinnamon brown with wings of iridescent green. **1956** T. RONAN *Moleskin Midas* 161 If there is a few bronze-wings being born about my place there's nearly as much chance of your being their daddy as me. The blacks reckon that since your hoppy leg keeps you from riding colts you seem to make up for it with the fillies.

bronzo, var. BRONZE.

brook. Used as elsewhere of a stream. Now, exc. in W.A., generally superseded by CREEK. Also *attrib.*
1770 G.W. ANDERSON *New Collection Voyages* 22 Aug. (1784) 70 There are several salt creeks, running in many directions through the country, where there are also brooks of fresh water, but there are no rivers of any considerable extent. **1882** ARMSTRONG & CAMPBELL *Austral. Sheep Husbandry* 164 The rule that all wools shall be washed, or subjected to a deduction of one-third, to put them on a par with brook-washed wools, operates very unequally. **1940** *Bulletin* (Sydney) 17 July 17/2 In Eastern Australia a 'creek' is any stream too small to be called a river. In the West such streams are properly called brooks, and dozens of examples could be quoted.

broom. [Transf. use of *broom,* as applied to shrubs of the genera *Cytisus* and *Genista.*]
1. The name is used in Aust. both for several naturalized European species of broom and for any of several native broom-like shrubs, esp. *Viminaria juncea* (fam. Fabaceae), which has long, wiry, apparently leafless branchlets and yellow flowers.
1841 *S. Austral. Mag.* Oct. 123 The strata of the banks, through which it [*sc.* the Torrens] directs its course, are usually composed of a clayey or marlish substance, in many places ornamented with the native broom, and myrtle, or honeysuckle. **1955** 'M. HILL' *Land nearest Stars* 173 In addition to wattle there was the soft yellow broom in profusion.
2. Special Comb. **broom-bush,** any of several shrubs, esp. *Templetonia egena* (fam. Fabaceae) and *Melaleuca uncinata* (fam. Myrtaceae); also *attrib.*
1883 F. BONNEY *On Some Customs Aborigines* 5 The root of broom-bushes (*poontee*). **1911** *Emu* XI. 111 Patches of broom-bush country relieved the monotony.

broomie. *Shearing.* [f. *broom* + -Y.] One employed to sweep in a shearing shed: see quot. 1915.
1895 *Bulletin* (Sydney) 13 July 23/3 There's the flying hurry-scurry up and down the greasy floors Of the pickers and the broomies; there's the banging of the doors. **1915** *Ibid.* 28 Oct. 22/3 The 'broomie' is the 'blue-tongue' who sweeps the board free of locks, etc.

brother colonist. *Hist.* A resident of an Australian Colony other than that in which the speaker resides. Cf. SISTER.
1834 *Hobart Town Mag.* May 115 Why should not we be allowed the privilege of a ten years' purchase, like our brother-Colonists of New South Wales? **1845** *Atlas* (Sydney) I. 323/1 It seems a strange accusation to bring against our brother colonists of Port Phillip.

brown, *a.* and *n.* [Spec. use of *brown* the colour.]
A. *adj.*
1. Used as a distinguishing epithet in the names of flora and fauna: **brown barrel,** the timber tree of e. N.S.W. and n.e. Vic. *Eucalyptus fastigata* (fam. Myrtaceae) which has a brown fibrous bark on the trunk; see also CUT TAIL 1; **bittern,** BOOMER *n.*[2]; **flycatcher,** *Jacky Winter,* see JACKY *n.*[2]; **gannet,** the large seabird *Sula leucogaster* of n. Aust. and other tropical regions; **goshawk,** the hawk *Accipiter fasciatus,* found throughout Aust. and in neighbouring areas, having predominantly brown plumage; **hawk,** the falcon *Falco berigora,* having pale or dark brown upperparts, and found throughout Aust. and in New Guinea and nearby islands; *orange-speckled hawk,* see ORANGE; **-headed honeyeater,** the honeyeater *Melithreptus brevirostris* of s. Aust., having a grey-brown head and pale line across the nape; **honeyeater,** the honeyeater *Lichmera indistincta* of tropical woodland, a summer visitor to s.w. and s.e. Aust., having brown upperparts; **pigeon,** the pigeon *Macropygia amboinensis* of rainforests in coastal Aust., and n. to the Philippines, having brown upperparts; *pheasant-tailed pigeon,* see PHEASANT 2; **quail,** the plump bird *Coturnix ypsilophora* of grassland and swamps in Aust., New Guinea, and nearby islands; *swamp quail,* see SWAMP *n.*; see also PARTRIDGE; **snake,** any of several more or less brown snakes, esp. the venomous *Pseudonaja textilis* of e. Aust. and New Guinea and *P. nuchalis* of central and w. Aust.; see also *western brown snake* WESTERN; **songlark,** the widespread brown bird *Cinclorhamphus cruralis*; **thornbill** (or **tit**), the small bird *Acanthiza pusilla* of s.e. Aust., having a pale brown body with red-brown feathers on the head and tail; **treecreeper,** the grey-brown tree-climbing bird *Climacteris picumnus* of e. Aust.;

warbler, the small brown-backed bird *Gerygone mouki* of forests in coastal e. Aust.

1896 *Proc. Linnean Soc. N.S.W.* XXI. 810 '**Brown-barrel**' at Queanbeyan.   **1945** C. BARRETT *Austral. Bird Life* 55 'Bunyip-bird' and 'bull bird' are nicknames for the large **brown bittern**.   **1845** J. GOULD *Birds of Aust.* (1848) II. Pl. 94, *Microeca flavigaster*. . . **Brown Flycatcher,** Residents at Port Essington.   **1846** J. GOULD *Birds of Aust.* (1848) III. Pl. 78, *Sula fusca*. . . **Brown Gannet** . . Brown Booby . . *Booby,* of the Colonists.   **1968** R. HILL *Bush Quest* 81 Gos was a young **Brown goshawk**.   **1777** G.W. ANDERSON *New Collection Voyages* (1784) 426 The principal sorts of birds are **brown hawks** or eagles.   **1900** A.J. CAMPBELL *Nests & Eggs Austral. Birds* 365 *Melithreptus brevirostris*. . . We found **Brown-headed Honeyeaters** somewhat numerous. **1846** J. GOULD *Birds of Aust.* (1848) IV. Pl. 31, *Glyciphila ocularis*. . . **Brown Honey-eater**. . . Brown Honey-sucker of the Colonists.   **1917** *Bulletin* (Sydney) 9 Aug. 24/4 Guess he hasn't tasted the green-pigeon, which . . excels the wonga as the latter excels the **brown-pigeon**.   **1848** J. GOULD *Birds of Aust.* (1848) V. Pl. 89, *Synoicus australis.* Australian Partridge. . . New Holland Quail. . . **Brown Quail,** Colonists of Swan River and Van Diemen's Land. **1805** *Sydney Gaz.* 13 Jan., A **brown snake** was killed a few days ago on the Blackwattle Swamp.   **1898** E.E. MORRIS *Austral Eng.* 259 **Brown Song Lark**—*Cincloramphus cruralis.* [**1844 brown thornbill:** J. GOULD *Birds of Aust.* (1848) III. Pl. 54, *Acanthiza diemenensis*. . . Brown-tail, Colonists of Van Diemen's Land.]   **1900** A.J. CAMPBELL *Nests & Eggs Austral. Birds* 230 *Brown tit* . . is an active little bird. . . Some recent authors use the term Thornbill—a name already applied to a number of Humming Birds—as a vernacular name for the Acanthizas.   **1945** C. BARRETT *Austral. Bird Life* 186 The brown thornbill . . and the striated thornbill . . are common birds of the bush.   **1841** J. GOULD *Birds of Aust.* (1848) IV. Pl. 93, *Climacteris scandens*. . . **Brown Tree-Creeper**. **1929** A.H. CHISHOLM *Birds & Green Places* 32 When thinking of jungle choristers generally I think chiefly of scrub-wrens, shrike-thrushes, flycatchers and robins, golden-breasted whistlers and **brown warblers**.

2. In the collocation **brown bomber** *N.S.W.,* an officer employed to police parking regulations.

1953 *Sydney Morning Herald* 3 Jan. 6/2 The year produced many slang words. Some of them were inherited from previous years but acquired wide usage in the past 12 months. . . 'Brown bombers', Sydney parking police, probably derived from the colour of their uniforms and influenced by the use of 'bomb' for an old car.

B. *n. Obs.* A penny.

1845 *Parramatta Chron.* 15 Mar. 2/1 The charged was not only descanting most learnedly on the evolution and revolutions of 'three up' and with upturned eyes and outstretched body intently watching the fall of some 'Browns', but had just given tongue to an expressive predilection for *heads*, when Fox laid him by the *heels*.   **1946** F. CLUNE *Try Nothing Twice* 67 'Without a single brown' was the truth as far as I was concerned, as I had spent Mum's twopence on an apple.

brownie, *n.*[1] Also **browny**. [f. *brown* + -Y.]

1. A sweetened currant bread.

1883 J.E. PARTINGTON *Random Rot* 312 It was an amusing sight to see the three of us, each with a huge hunch of 'browny' (bread sweetened with brown sugar and currants) in one hand.   **1978** M. WALKER *Pioneer Crafts Early Aust.* 151 Cooking for shearers was testing work for the self-opinionated connoisseurs of damper, meat, 'dough boys', Johnnie cakes, brownies (simply damper with sugar and currants) were harsh critics.

2. Special Comb. **brownie gorger,** see quot. 1982.

1939 *Bulletin* (Sydney) 26 Apr. 20/4 We were shearing out Hungerford way. Joe was one of the 'browny gorgers'. **1982** P. ADAM SMITH *Shearers* 403 *Brownie gorger*, hungry shed-hands (usually young boys with big appetites).

brownie, *n.*[2] [f. BROWN *n.* + -Y.] A penny.

1899 *Western Champion* (Barcaldine) 13 June 7/4 To shoot at my 'headpiece' with ordinary, common, low-down 'brownies' (coppers) is a bit too stiff.   **1951** CUSACK & JAMES *Come in Spinner* 7 'Two-up.' . . 'It's the great Australian pastime . . just a matter of spinning a couple of brownies.'

bruce auction. [Prob. f. the name of John Vans Agnew *Bruce* (1822–1863), construction contractor and philanthropist.] An auction of donated goods, the proceeds which are dedicated to a charitable cause; used esp. in church fund-raising. Also *transf.* (see quot. 1959).

1868 *Yass Courier* 1 Dec. 2/4 Blessed be the name of Bruce—the Bruce of Victoria (now in his grave) who invented the description of auction to which his name is irrevocably linked. How many struggling communities have been relieved from embarrassment by his means that might otherwise have languished under a load of debt. How else could the Wagga Wagga Presbyterians have raised the magnificent sum of £700 to build a church, but by means of a Bruce auction. Honour to the memory of Bruce who discovered the secret of combining business with pleasure.   **1959** *Southern Mail* (Bowral) 14 May, A famous annual event was the 'Bruce Auction' . . held by the late George Lake at his barber and tobacconist shop every New Year's Eve. . . This auction did not require a licensed auctioneer. George himself offered the goods at a certain price which came down if there were no takers, until a price was reached satisfactory to both seller and buyer. He would offer a job lot comprising a cherrywood pipe, plug of tobacco and a box of matches, or such like bundle, and cleared off a lot of stock.

brum. Abbrev. of BRUMBY.

1936 J.C. DOWNIE *Galloping Hoofs* 102 This is goin' to be a 'dinkum nark' of a 'brum', and I reckon I'll take it out of 'im, and ride 'im till he quits.   **1955** STEWART & KEESING *Austral. Bush Ballads* 195 They stared to see him stick aloft— The brum. bucked fierce and free.

brumby /'brʌmbi/. Also **brummy**. [Of unknown origin.]

1. A wild horse.

1880 *Australasian* (Melbourne) 4 Dec. 712/3 Passing through a belt of mulga, we saw, on reaching its edge, a mob of horses grazing on the plains beyond. These our guide pronounced to be 'brumbies', the bush name here [*sc.* Qld.] for wild horses.   **1885** *Once a Month* (Melbourne) Jan. 53, I came to the conclusion that he was a 'Brummy'— the New South Wales name for wild horses.   **1947** *Bulletin* (Sydney) 13 Aug. 28/3 The word 'brumby' . . comes from Captain (or Major) Brumby, who had a reputation as a horsebreeder in the early part of last century. . . The other—and less-likely—origin is the abo. word booramby.

2. A (partially) tamed wild horse (see quot. 1948); a worn-out or ill-bred horse.

1891 T. BATEMAN *Valley Council* 4 Five of my station hands, a motley crew, horsed on brumbies, as we call our unbroken half-wild horses.   **1948** M. UREN *Glint of Gold* 105 They purchased a spring cart and two hardy brumbies. . . A bush horse of questionable breeding and ownership which, because of its hard life spent in the bush, was much in demand by prospecting parties.

3. *transf.* and *fig.* Also *attrib.,* passing into *adj.*

1890 *Truth* (Sydney) 16 Nov. 4/5 It is wonderful to witness the number of sky-pilots, devil-dodgers and brumby parsons who visit the House.   **1903** *Ibid.* 8 Mar. 4/2 A few flat-chested, flat-footed female brumbies can't supply the place of the splendid breed sprung from Eden's stock.   **1911** ST. C. GRONDONA *Collar & Cuffs* 98 They were a brumbie lot of rotters, all swagmen, and to all appearance at least, considerably down on their uppers.

4. Special Comb. **brumby hunter,** one who rounds

up wild horses; also **-hunting** *vbl. n.* and *pr. pple;* **runner, (a)** *brumby hunter;* **(b)** a horse used for brumby hunting; also **running** *vbl. n.*

1891 H.W. HARRIS *Shearers or Shorn* 26 One young Queenslander who has lived the greater portion of his life in the bush, has worked as a shearer, drover, **brumby hunter,** and scalp collector. **1892** *Western Champion* (Barcaldine) 26 Jan. 5/3 **Brumbie hunting** at Jericho... About half-a-dozen really smart horsemen left here.. with the object of running in wild horses. **1908** *Bulletin* (Sydney) 9 Jan. 39/1 They were brumby hunting on Taromeo. **1937** C. WARBURTON *White Poppies* 153 Mounted on one of the **brumby-runners,** Big Head thundered away in a swirl of dust. **1968** LINKLATER & TAPP *Gather No Moss* 97 It was during 1894 that men known as the brumby runners of the McDonnell [*sic*] Ranges began passing through Newcastle Waters. **1897** *Western Champion* (Barcaldine) 23 Nov. 10/3 In **'brumby' running** of the immediate future the.. 'Lord of the Hills' will at last be yarded by the station Platt-Betts astride his steel-rubber 'moke'.

brummy, var. BRUMBY.

brummy, *n.* and *a.* [f. *Brumm(agem* counterfeit coin + -Y.]

A. *n.* A counterfeit coin; a dud.

1921 *Bulletin* (Sydney) 11 Aug. 24/2 The decent cove rang true, in the same way as a dinkum coin rang true when thrown down, whereas the brummy fell with a thud. **1966** G. WYATT *Strip Jack Naked* 17 If I go around telling everyone they can buy a watch for seven pounds ten, they'll suspect it is a brummy.

B. *adj.* Counterfeit; sham and often showy; cheaply made.

1900 *Truth* (Sydney) 24 June 4/4 It is down on the 'brummy' parsons and shark lawyers. **1980** J. WRIGHT *Big Hearts & Gold Dust* 155 A claw-like hand.. glittered with jewelled rings—brummy jewels, I thought.

brush, *n.*[1] and *attrib.*

A. *n.* A tract of dense natural vegetation: orig. applied chiefly to the understorey, later to forest, esp. rainforest (see esp. quots. 1793, 1834, and 1843).

1789 D. COLLINS *Acct. Eng. Colony N.S.W.* (1798) I. 56 Lost their way in some of the thick and almost impenetrable brushes which were in the vicinity of Rose Hill. **1793** J. HUNTER *Hist. Jrnl. Trans. Port Jackson* 61 Those fires were intended to clear that part of the country through which they have frequent occasion to travel, of the brush or underwood, from which they, being naked, suffer very great inconvenience. **1834** G. BENNETT *Wanderings N.S.W.* I. 201 A rugged road led through 'Bargo Brush', which is a dense forest, small portions only being occasionally seen cleared. **1843** J.D. LANG *Cooksland* (1847) 84 After much pains I got into this brush, and here all lower vegetation ceases at once. Every thing strives to get to the light. The climbers ascend to the tops of the trees, and display there their rich foliage and blossoms. The trees themselves rarely form branches under forty to fifty feet high.

B. 1. *attrib.*

1821 T. GODWIN *Descr. Acct. Van Diemen's Island* 18 The ploughing will not stand him in more than 10s. the acre; which, added to the clearing makes £1 18s. per acre for preparing forest land for seed-corn, while the brush-land is £3 2s. **1956** N.K. WALLIS *Austral. Timber Handbk.* 2 In addition to the hardwood forests and the cypress pine belt, the coastal strip in Queensland and northern New South Wales provides 'rain' or 'brush' (scrubwood) forests.

2. In the names of flora and fauna: **brush apple,** *black apple,* see BLACK *a.*[2] 1 a.; **box,** any of several trees, esp. *Lophostemon confertus* (fam. Myrtaceae) of e. Qld. and n.e. N.S.W., with pinkish-grey scaly bark; the wood of these trees; **bronze-wing,** the pigeon *Phaps elegans* of dense vegetation in s. Aust.; **cherry,** any of several trees esp. *Syzygium australe* (fam. Myrtaceae) which bears succulent fruits; the wood of these trees; **kangaroo,** *brush wallaby;* **turkey,** the large, mound-building bird *Alectura lathami* of e. Aust., having a bare red head and neck, yellow wattles at the base of the neck, and otherwise mainly black plumage; *bush turkey,* see BUSH C. 3; *New Holland vulture,* see NEW HOLLAND 2; *scrub turkey* (a), see SCRUB *n.* 5; **wallaby,** any of several macropodids, usu. larger wallabies, of coastal scrubs and more open inland forest, as the *red-necked wallaby* (see RED *a.* 1 b.); *brush kangaroo;* **wattle bird,** the large honeyeater *Anthochaera chrysoptera* of s.e. Aust. incl. Tas.; see also *little wattle bird* LITTLE 2.

1888 *Proc. Linnean Soc. N.S.W.* III. 485 'Black Apple', '**Brush Apple'**. **1889** J.H. MAIDEN *Useful Native Plants Aust.* 608 '**Brush Box**'.. timber is much prized for its strength and durable qualities. It is used in ship-building. [**1801 brush bronze-wing:** J. LATHAM *Gen. Synopsis Birds* Suppl. II. 267 Bronze-winged P[igeon].. called by some also *Brush Pigeon.* **1843** J. GOULD *Birds of Aust.* (1848) V. Pl. 65, *Peristera elegans*... Brush Bronze-winged Pigeon... Little Bronze Pigeon, Colonists of Swan River.] **1902** *Emu* II. 75 Phaps elegans (Brush Bronze-wing)—I flushed many of these birds in the sage scrubs. **1888** *Proc. Linnean Soc. N.S.W.* III. 512 *Eugenia myrtifolia*.. '**Brush cherry'** or 'Native myrtle'. The fruit is acid, and makes a good preserve. **1802** Banks Papers 1 June VIII. 103 A **Brush Kangoroo** (Walaby) which is of a blackish colour. **1840** J. GOULD *Birds of Aust.* (1848) V. Pl. 77, *Talegalla lathami*... **Brush Turkey** of the Colonists. **1846** *Portland Guardian* 22 Sept. 4/1 At the Mitchell we met a **brush wallabi** of a brownish colour and very coarse hair, (halmaturus agilis gld.) which was common all round the Gulf of Carpentaria. **1841** J. GOULD *Birds of Aust.* (1848) IV. Pl. 56, The **Brush Wattle-bird**.. constantly resorts to the Banksias.

3. Special Comb. **brush hook,** a long-handled arcuate tool, used for cutting light scrub.

1904 *Bulletin* (Sydney) 15 Sept. 40/3 We have laid in a supply of brushhooks and axes.. for neither last long in chopping scrub.

brush, *n.*[2] [Abbrev. of *brushwood.*]

1. Brushwood, applied (chiefly *attrib.*) to dead or felled vegetation used for building purposes.

1840 *S. Austral. Rec.* (London) 17 Oct. 251 Arrived upon his estate, his [*sc.* the settler's] primary object is to erect a brush-hut or break-wind, which is formed of the boughs of trees, and sometimes thatched in a rude manner with long grass. **1961** *N. Austral. Monthly* Dec. 11 Gentlewomen.. braved the wilderness and lived under a brush shed that Australia should march with the older nations.

2. Comb. **brush fence, yard.**

1824 E. CURR *Acct. Colony Van Diemen's Land* 119 Those lands that are protected from depredations upon stock are generally surrounded.. with a **brush fence. 1835** J. BATMAN *Settlement in Port Phillip* 1 June (1856) 16 We have not yet met with timber fit for the saw or splitting. **Brush yards** might be made for sheep or cattle.

brush, *n.*[3] Abbrev. of *brush kangaroo, wallaby* (see BRUSH *n.*[1] B. 2). Also *attrib.*

1834 *Colonist* (Hobart) 15 Apr. 3/5 The Kangaroos in the neighbourhood are mostly of the brush kind, which, not being gregarious like the forest or boomah species, are not numerous. **1839** J. STEPHENS *Land of Promise* 57 Kangaroos are of five distinct kinds; namely, the forester, the brush, the wallaby, the kangaroo rat, and the kangaroo mouse. They are all in great abundance.

brush, *n.*[4] [Prob. spec. use of *brush* animal's tail; cf. slang uses of *arse* (*ass*), *tail,* etc., for a woman as a sexual object.] A woman, esp. one regarded sexually.

1941 S.J. BAKER *Pop. Dict. Austral. Slang* 14 *Brush,* a girl or young woman. **1984** *Sun-Herald* (Sydney) 24 June 82/3 He carefully rehearsed some of the smart talk at the track; intrigued by the younger men's comments about the beautiful 'brush' (women) eager to be entertained by visiting trainers.

brush, v.¹ [f. BRUSH n.¹] trans. To clear (land) of scrub. Also with **up.**
1914 *Bulletin* (Sydney) 10 Dec. 22/2 The old lady .. gazed at the fire-tortured timber... 'There's a bit of picking-up to be done over there this summer, and there's the gully to be 'brushed' again. It takes a lot of keeping down. 1981 *Bega District News* 27 Nov. 5/6 A track was brushed up with a tractor and the fire was allowed to burn itself out.

Hence **brushing** vbl. n.
1909 *Bulletin* (Sydney) 26 Aug. 15/2 You cut all the small undergrowth, vines, etc., with a slasher (or scrub-hook); this is 'vining' in N.S.W., 'brushing' in Queensland.

brush, v.² [f. BRUSH n.²] trans. To build (a fence, etc.) with dead or felled vegetation. Also intr. and with **up.**
1913 *Bulletin* (Sydney) 16 Jan. 14/2 'Sydney' was sent ahead and told to 'brush up' the wire at the back of the canvas... When we arrived Sydney was still hard at work 'brushing up' the fence. But not with timber and small boughs. He had a tin of polish. 1934 W. HATFIELD *River Crossing* 45 They set off into the scrub close by for loads of boughs, with which to brush in from the veranda to the hut. 1958 F.B. VICKERS *Mirage* 277 'How's things?' he asked. 'Not so bad.' 'Brushing Ritchie's dam, aren't you?' 'Yes. Just made a start on it.'

brusher, n.¹ *Obs.* [Perh. f. *brush, v.* to decamp.] In the phr. **to give** (someone) **brusher,** to defraud (someone); to abscond, avoid.
1878 *Pilgrim* (Sydney) 2nd Ser. x. 5 He subsequently victimised Mr Weber, Post Office Hotel; .. indeed anywhere this penniless Hebrew obtained admission he never failed to give 'brusher' to the confiding boniface. 1918 *Bulletin* (Sydney) 30 May 24/3 The animal with the bristly-haired tail .. was probably the 'brusher' or scrub-wallaby, whose celerity in leaving a vacancy when he felt his presence was superfluous gave rise to the expression of the bookie with an empty bag when he sees the wrong number go up—'Give 'em brusher!'

brusher, n.² *Obs.* [Transf. use of Br. dial. *brusher* 'a boy who is quick and active': see EDD *brush, v.²* and *sb.²*] See quot. 1916.
1882 *Freeman's Jrnl.* (Sydney) 30 Sept. 17/1, I have often thought how admirably that decidedly vulgar phrase 'fussy little brusher' defines you. 1916 *Bulletin* (Sydney) 21 Sept. 22/3 'Brusher' (rare), any nondescript old chap, like the English 'geezer'. Said to be in reference to an old station cook who always commenced brushing boots when he was annoyed. Or possibly from a likeness to a horse or bullock run wild in the 'brush' (scrub).

brush-tailed, ppl. a. Used as a distinguishing epithet in the names of flora and fauna: **brush-tailed phascogale,** the arboreal marsupial *Phascogale tapoatafa,* widespread in wooded country of mainland Aust., having a bushy, 'bottle-brush' tail; see also TUAN; **possum,** the common possum, the widespread arboreal marsupial *Trichosurus vulpecula,* cat-sized with a long prehensile tail; VULPINE OPOSSUM; also abbrev. as **brush-tail; rock wallaby,** the wallaby *Petrogale penicillata,* widespread in rocky places of mainland Aust. and having a bushy dark tail; also **brush-tailed wallaby.**

[1852 **brush-tailed phascogale:** *Austral. Gold Digger's Monthly Mag.* i. 21 In South Australia there is a brush-tailed Kangaroo Rat.] 1926 A.S. LE SOUEF et al. *Wild Animals Australasia* 335 The brush-tailed phascogale is widely spread over the continent. 1887 [**brush-tailed possum**] *Illustr. Austral. News* 21 (Melbourne) Dec. 218/1 Two varieties of opossum are found, the ring-tail and brush-tail. 1970 W.D.L. RIDE *Guide Native Mammals Aust.* 70 Most Australians dwell in suburbs and, under these conditions, they have more contact with the common Brush-tailed Possum .. than they have with any other native mammal. [1887 **brush-tailed rock-wallaby:** A. NICOLS *Wild Life & Adventure* 58 The agile brush-tailed rock kangaroos were springing over the broken surface with astonishing bounds.] 1926 A.S. LE SOUEF et al. *Wild Animals Australasia* 201 The eastern species (the brush-tailed rock-wallaby). 1978 M. DOUGLAS *Follow Sun* 115 Brush-tailed wallabies, startled by our presence, jumped up the almost perpendicular cliffs.

brushy, a. *Obs.* [f. BRUSH n.¹] Covered with dense natural vegetation.
1805 *HRA* (1915) 1st Ser. V. 583 For the Brushy and Rocky Land that prevails from the first M to the River Side. 1847 A. HARRIS *Settlers & Convicts* (1953) 134 Lost himself in the deep brushy Budawong gullies.

bubba. Also **bubby.** [Var. of *baby.*] A young child. Also **bub.**
1906 *Steele Rudd's Mag.* (Brisbane) Mar. 159 Why, in Australia, is every baby a 'bubba'? The word will be found in use from one end of the continent to the other. 1960 *Overland* xvii. 7 'All right. How's Bubby?' 'Fit as a Mallee bull! Got another tooth.' 1983 *Canberra Chron.* 5 Oct. 19/1 Wife and bub are well.

Bubble. *Obs.* [Spec. use of *bubble* something unsubstantial, delusive; often with reference to allegedly fraudulent commercial undertakings and so used of the South Australian Company's plan to finance immigration from land sales.] Used *attrib.* with reference to the South Australian Company or Colony.
1838 *Sydney Herald* 28 Nov. 2/1 *South Australia.* What a rot among the bubble Province officials! 1839 *Ibid.* 18 Jan. 2/1 (heading) The Bubble Company.

bubble-bubble. Austral. pidgin. *Obs.* See quot. 1888.
1888 E. FINN *Chron. Early Melbourne* I. 371 The 'wallaby trackers' would, on a certain evening, treat all the blacks that might cross the river to a big feast of 'bubble-bubble'—a mess of flour and water to which the Port Phillipian Aborigines were even more partial than to the squatters' rum or beef. 1923 H.C.A. HARRISON *Story of Athlete* 21 The lubras .. were also very fond of boiled flour, which they used to call 'bubble bubble'.

bubbler. A drinking fountain.
1970 J.S. GUNN in W.S. Ramson *Eng. Transported* 57 Over a long period we have picked up odd terms like bubbler. 1985 *Good Weekend* (Sydney) 24 Aug. 20/2 One wonders .. why the dedicatee's heirs weren't approached to discuss the alternative of a well-designed bubbler.

bubby, var. BUBBA.

buck, n.¹ [Spec. use of *buck* male animal; used also of humans and derog. of the U.S. Indian or Black.]

1. A large male kangaroo.
1845 *Atlas* (Sydney) I. 258/1 The large full-grown male is termed a Buck or Boomer, and attains a great size. 1926 A.S. LE SOUEF et al. *Wild Animals Australasia* 177 The bucks grow fairly large, in rare cases almost equal to the Grey.

2. **a.** An Aboriginal male.
1870 [see *buck nigger*]. 1896 W.H. WILLSHIRE *Land of Dawning* 57 We discovered about fifteen blacks, who upon hearing our approach made most desperate attempts to get away. One old buck met with a geographical accident by falling flop into a dry gully and breaking his crupper-bone. 1976 C.D. MILLS *Hobble Chains & Greenhide* 22 She had been betrothed from birth to a young buck. He had picked up another, and was crooked on the world because the old fellas made him take this one.

b. Comb. **buck nigger.**

1870 E.B. Kennedy *Four Yrs. in Qld.* 29 We .. waited .. for the big 'Buck nigger' (or niggers), whom we were certain were within a few yards of us.

3. A foreman.

1906 *Bulletin* (Sydney) 5 July 17/1 Accept 'is invitation to ther Farm, Fur away from biffs an' rossers, bucks an' bats an' 'ooks an' dossers. **1944** *Austral. New Writing* 34 'Does the buck know you've left?' 'I'm not worried. I wouldn't work to-night, not for King George.'

4. *attrib.* Exclusively male, esp. as **buck set**.

1898 D.W. Carnegie *Spinifex & Sand* 24 We .. had frequent sing-songs and 'buck dances'—that is dances in which there were no ladies to take part. **1900** *Western Champion* (Barcaldine) 12 June 13/2 Inside the dining room adjoining a 'buck set' had been formed waltzing indiscriminately to any tune.

5. In the collocation **buck(s') party** (or **night**), a party given for a bridegroom on the eve of his wedding by male friends.

1918 *Home Trail: Souvenir Issue Voyage H.M.T. 'A 30'* Dec. 5 It was a buck party. **1972** G. Morley *Jockey rides Honest Race* 261 Kon organized my bucks night, because he was going to be my best man. **1980** S. Thorne *I've met some Bloody Wags* 94 We had a buck's party for him at Toby's woolshed, and during the night old Mick was skiting that he was as fit as any of us.

buck, $n.^2$ [f. Buck *v.* 1.]

1. Buckjump *n.* 1.

1898 D.W. Carnegie *Spinifex & Sand* 98 Wait till you make your evening feed off mulga scrub and bark—that'll take the buck out of you! **1929** K.S. Prichard *Coonardoo* (1961) 49 He'd begin with a flying root and a couple of high bucks .. and go on buckin' and rootin' in a circle.

2. Buckjumper.

1944 *Bulletin* (Sydney) 20 Dec. 12/3 That phrase 'sit a buck' .. always brands its user, in my mind, as a cocky-country horseman. **1978** D. Stuart *Wedgetail View* 26 Davey's mount, a flashy chestnut .. was a willing buck but Davey made nothing of the hurried, flurried attempt at dislodging him.

Hence **buckrunner** *n.*, see quot.

1970 J.S. Gunn in W.S. Ramson *Eng. Transported* 59 Buckrunner, one who rounds up wild horses.

buck, *a. Mining.* [Of unknown origin.] Barren; not containing the mineral sought.

1875 G.M. Newman *N.T. & its Gold-Fields* 15 In this locality numerous barren or buck reefs are seen cropping above the surface. **1946** K.S. Prichard *Roaring Nineties* 455 He had left Jack beside a big outcrop of buck quartz. .. There was nothing more unpopular among the early prospectors than the cold, unkindly white stone which had betrayed their hopes so often in a likely looking outcrop.

buck, *v.* [Abbrev. of Buckjump *v.*]

1. *intr.* Buckjump *v.* Also *trans.*

1848 H.W. Haygarth *Recoll. Bush Life* 78 'Buckjumping', or as it is more familiarly called, 'bucking'. **1908** W.H. Ogilvie *My Life in Open* 82 Countess, in the parlance of the Bush, can 'buck a town down'.

2. *transf.* and *fig.* With **in**.

1900 J. Bufton *Tasmanians in Transvaal War* 3 Mar. (1905) 140 After tea had a grand game of football, our captain and doctor 'bucking in' well. **1903** *Sporting News* (Launceston) 2 May 3/6 The pluvial visitation did not stop the teams from 'bucking' in, as the barracker would say.

Hence **bucking** *vbl. n.*

1865 *London Soc.* Dec. 446/2 The horses of the bush are a native breed, and have a curious vice which the troopers call 'bucking'.

buckbush. Any of several shrubs, esp. *Salsola kali* (see Roly-poly).

1898 D.W. Carnegie *Spinifex & Sand* 191 The scrub in the trough of the ridges became more open with an undergrowth of coarse grass, buck-bush or 'Roly-Poly' (*Salsola Kali*) and low acacia. **1951** W. Hatfield *Wild Dog Frontier* 153 Like tufts of crackly buck-bush before a light dawn breeze.

bucker.

1. Buckjumper.

1853 H.B. Jones *Adventures in Aust.* 143 A 'bucker' is a vicious horse, to be found only in Australia. His peculiarity consists in curling his back upwards, till he wriggles saddle, girth, and rider over his head. **1918** *Bulletin* (Sydney) 6 June 22/1 P'raps I can't sit buckers, but b'gosh, I'm game to try.

2. One capable of riding a bucking horse.

1979 Carey & Lette *Puberty Blues* 22 'Ah, Kim's a good bucker!' cried Steve Strachan as Kim rode Conchise into the scene.

bucket, *n.* [Fig. use of *bucket* container.]

1. An ice-cream carton, now usu. small (see quot. 1972). See also Dandy, Dixie.

1945 S.J. Baker *Austral. Lang.* 195 An ice-cream carton is called a *dixie* in Melbourne .. and a *bucket* in Sydney. **1972** G.W. Turner *Eng. Lang. in Aust. & N.Z.* (rev. ed.) 124 Why should .. a pot or tub of icecream be a dandy in Adelaide, a dixie in Melbourne and elsewhere a *bucket*?

2. *fig.*

a. In the phr. **to drop (tip, turn) the bucket (on)**, to make damaging revelations (about someone, often a political opponent).

1950 *Austral. Police Jrnl.* Apr. 112 Drop the bucket. .. Drop the responsibility suddenly on to someone else. **1971** A. Reid *Gorton Experiment* 219 But the position as regards Gorton could not go on indefinitely. Labor or 'somebody else' sooner or later would 'turn a bucket'. **1983** *Austral. Weekend Mag.* (Sydney) 29 Oct. 12/3 Delivering the message to an English audience: 'I didn't come over here to tip the bucket on yas.'

b. A damaging revelation.

1986 *Nat. Times* (Sydney) 28 Feb. 7/4 In the Parliament under privilege .. where all skilled exponents of the bucket operate.

Hence **bucket-dropper** *n.*

1976 *Bulletin* (Sydney) 13 Nov. 25/1 In parliamentary parlance, 'bucket-droppers' are those who, under parliamentary privilege and hence free from any fear of legal action, raise subjects only marginally in the political arena which their more respectable and conventional parliamentary colleagues would not touch with a 40 ft bargepole.

bucket, *v.* [f. prec.] *trans.* To denigrate (a person, etc.).

1974 *Austral.* (Sydney) 1 Apr. 6/7 While it might be valid to find Brisbane lacking in Adelaide's grace or Sydney's vigor or Melbourne's dignity, it is not valid to bucket it in total. **1984** *Canberra Times* 20 June 16/6 Here is a Minister for *Education*, a graduate of this university, ready enough to 'bucket' (her word) the academic staff who are part of her responsibility.

buckjump, *v.* [f. *buck* male animal + *jump*, from the resemblance to the leap of a (startled) male animal, perh. esp. the kangaroo (see Buck $n.^1$ 1).]

1. *intr.* Of a horse: to leap with head down, legs drawn together, and back arched in an attempt to throw the rider. Freq. as *vbl. n.*

1838 S. Hack Let. 17 June, I bought a colt that had only been mounted a week to help him on the remaining journey to Portland Bay, I was vain enough to think I could ride him but in a week he convinced me of the fallacy of this idea by sending me up in the air like a skyrocket by buckjumping. **1848** H.W. HAYGARTH *Recoll. Bush Life* 78 Australian horses have a vicious habit known as 'buckjumping', or as it is more familiarly called, 'bucking'. This trick . . is peculiar to colts bred in the colony and in Van Diemen's Land, and is decidedly the most expeditious way that could be devised for emptying a saddle. **1852** G.C. MUNDY *Our Antipodes* I. 364 The 'Agitator' colt will buckjump a bit at starting.

2. *fig.*
1876 'EIGHT YRS.' RESIDENT' *Queen of Colonies* 343 One of the blacks . . on seeing him approaching, cried out, 'Here Missa —, you see 'em me Cabona (very much) me directly buck-jump!' referring to the convulsions directly caused by the poison, and which he called buck-jumping.

buckjump, *n.* [f. prec.]
1. The act of buckjumping. Also *attrib.*
1882 A.J. BOYD *Old Colonials* 200 It . . succeeded in making a succession of the most tremendous screwing buck-jumps I ever witnessed. **1919** *Bulletin* (Sydney) 16 Oct. 20/1 'The Cattle King', was the best buckjump rider I ever saw.
2. Abbrev. of *buckjumping event* (etc.).
1977 V. PRIDDLE *Larry & Jack* 157 He's won a novice buckjump and I'm sure he's not nominated for the Open. **1981** A. MARSHALL *Aust.* 24 A vivid, alert man . . stood in the ring of a buckjump show in a Queensland town telling tall stories to the crowd.

buckjumper. A horse which buckjumps (habitually).
1888 S. HACK Let. 1 Sept., I have bought the horse today for 65 guineas his name is Bucksfoot and he is rightly named for its my belief he is the worst buckjumper in South Australia. **1981** A. MARSHALL *Aust.* 24 The telling of these tales probably began as an impromptu, between-acts stunt to hold the audience while some refractory buckjumper was being brought in for riding.

buckle. [f. *buckle* to apply oneself vigorously (orig. from being buckled into armour).] In the phr. **in (good, great,** etc.) **buckle,** in good fettle.
1871 *Austral. Town & Country Jrnl.* (Sydney) 4 Feb. 153/4 We know little of how the New South Wales horses are getting on in Melbourne, but we hear from pretty good authority that Tim Whiffler is in good buckle. **1888** 'R. BOLDREWOOD' *Robbery under Arms* (1937) 216 The horses were in great buckle. **1891** *Truth* (Sydney) 26 Apr. 6/3 Joe . . was in town last Monday, and looked in superb buckle.

bucklee /'bʌkli/. [Prob. a. Yinjibarndi *bagarli*.] An Aboriginal initiation rite. Also *attrib.*
[**1929** K.S. PRICHARD *Coonardoo* (1961) 17 The older men took the boys off into the mulga thickets . . for the bucklegarroo ceremonies which no woman was allowed to see.] **1959** D. STUART *Yandy* 4 All the blackfellers had come together for a bucklee meeting, for the circumcision of two boys.
Also **bucklee** *v. trans.*
1969 F.B. VICKERS *No Man is Himself* 56 He went to give young Tommy . . the law before he's circumcised—*bucklee'd.*

Buckley's. [Poss. f. the name of William *Buckley* (1780-1856), an escaped convict who lived for 32 years with Aborigines in s. Vic.; but see also quot. 1953.] In full **Buckley's chance (choice, hope, show).** A forlorn hope; no prospect whatever.
1895 *Bulletin* (Sydney) 9 Nov. 13/1 'Buckley's chance'; the Maoriland Supreme Court vacant Judgeship. **1896** *Ibid.* 25 Jan. 25/2 Freemasonry and R.C.-ism . . are worked for all they are worth in Q'sland. . . Unless you are a 'child' of either party your chances of promotion are 'Buckley's'. **1897** *Worker* (Sydney) 30 Oct. 2/4 He has 'Buckley's show' of working the mine with them. **1908** E.G. MURPHY *Jarrahland Jingles* 16 You've 'done the rattler in to-day', you ain't got Buckley's 'ope, But there's one goes down at night-time when the stoney-brokers slope. **1940** *Sentry Go* (Keswick) Oct. 9/1 *Buckley's choice.* A new tunic was being issued to a recruit. 'We have two kinds, those too large and those too small. Which will you have?' **1953** H.M. EASTMAN *Mem. of Sheepman* 109 You may not have heard how this phrase, taken from the old firm 'Buckley and Nunn', came into the language some seventy years ago in dealing with one's chances. 'You have two chances, 'Buckley's and Nunn" only one really, or 50-50 (as it sounds).

buck scraper. See quot. 1890.
1890 W.H. BUNDEY *Winter Cruise* 14 After the land is cleared and ploughed . . comes the 'grading for irrigation'. For this three instruments are used, viz. the 'buck scraper', an ordinary 'earth scoop', and the 'smoother'. **1925** A.N. SHEPHERD *Irrigation Farming N.S.W.* 11 If there are many 'bumps' to take off or holes to fill, the buck-scraper may be employed to produce an even surface.
Hence as *v. trans.*
1920 H.S. TAYLOR *Pioneer Irrigationists' Man.* xxxvi. 1 When the whole of the land is contoured, run a plough round each row of pegs, then start buckscraping the banks, terracing the land.

buck-shot. [Transf. use of *buck-shot* coarse shot: see OED 2.] A stratum of ironstone concretions: see quot. 1855.
1855 G.H. WATHEN *Golden Colony* 14 While describing these plains, I ought to allude to what the settlers have named 'buck-shot'. This is a kind of black gravel, mingled with the soil to a depth of a few inches, and consisting of small, irregular-shaped stones, about the size of a pea or of a small bean. This, though not universally diffused, is found over large areas. It may perhaps be a volcanic ash. **1948** G.W. LEEPER *Introd. Soil Science* (rev. ed.) 19 The ironstone gravel, which is known in Victoria as 'buckshot', often appears on the surface after erosion.

buck spinifex. Any of several plants, esp. the grass *Triodia longiceps* (fam. Poaceae) which has rigid pointed blades; *old man spinifex* see OLD MAN B. 3.
1883 W.J. O'DONNELL *Diary Exploring Exped.* 8 Aug. (1884) 15 Following the valley of a small creek, which joined the Margaret near here, we steered easterly, and soon reached the foot of some rough sandstone ridges, covered with buck spinifex. **1977** J. DOUGHTY *Gold in Blood* 174 This was not stock country: this was a land of small buck-spinifex, needle sharp, growing porcupine-like on the hard red earth.

budda /'bʌdə/. Also **buddha, budtha.** [a. Wiradhuri and Yuwaalaraay *badah.*] Any of several shrubs or small trees of inland Aust. esp. *Eremophila mitchellii* (fam. Myoporaceae), the leaves and timber of which have a strong aroma resembling that of sandalwood; the wood of the plant. See also SANDALWOOD $n.^2$ Also *attrib.*
1890 *Sydney Mail* 14 June 1300/1, I would state that the tree known as sandalwood on the Darling and in the West generally, one of the 'Eremophylla', called 'Butha' by the natives, is not eaten by sheep, and is only attacked by rabbits when nothing better is to be had. **1895** *Worker* (Sydney) 26 June 4/1 The sun was just rising, and the dewdrops, still clinging to the drooping branches of the buddha scrub, were glittering like so many diamonds. **1899** *Truth* (Sydney) 31 Dec. 2/6 A Sahara tempered to the eye with clumps of budda-bush and ti-tree. **1901** K.L. PARKER in M. Muir *My Bush Bk.* (1982) 101 The bright shiny green budtha, with its nutty-scented white or pale heliotrope flowers, which every shower brings out so lavishly as almost to hide the leaves, should be near the homestead.

buddawong, var. BURRAWANG.

buddha, var. BUDDA.

budgeree /'bʌdʒəri, 'bʊdʒəri/, *a. Austral. pidgin.* Also with much variety, as **boojeree, budgeri**. [a. Dharuk *bujiri*.] Good.

1790 D. SOUTHWELL Corresp. & Papers *Boó-gĕ-reē* (boo-jē-ree), good, handsome, comely, pretty. 1830 R. DAWSON *Present State Aust.* 12 'Budgeree,' (very good,) he replied. 1944 C. FENNER *Mostly Austral.* 8 The approved spelling for this substance is 'pitjeri', but it is also commonly spelt 'pituri', a word that is said to be related to budgeri, which means 'good'.

budgerigar /'bʌdʒəriga/. Also **betcherrygah, betshiregah, budgerygar**. [Poss. mispronunciation of Kamilaroi *gijirrigaa*.] The small green and yellow parrot *Melopsittacus undulatus*, occurring in drier mainland areas, often in large flocks, and a popular cage bird; LOVE-BIRD; SHELL PARROT; WARBLING GRASS PARAKEET; *zebra parrot*, see ZEBRA.

1840 J. GOULD *Birds of Aust.*(1848) V. Pl. 44, *Melopsittacus undulatus*. Warbling Grass-Parrakeet... Undulated Parrot... Canary Parrot, Colonists. Betcherrygah, Natives of Liverpool Plains. 1845 L. LEICHHARDT *Jrnl. Overland Exped. Aust.* 20 June (1847) 297 The rose-breasted Cockatoo and the Betshiregah (Melopsittacus undulatus..) were very numerous. 1854 *Southern Cross & Antarctic Gaz.* 15 Mar. 3/2 Ah, no! 'tis but a little bird, The gentle Budgery Gar! 1877 C.W. GEDNEY *Foreign Cage Birds* 19 The budgerigars are Australian birds, congregating in large flocks upon the inland pastures.

budgie /'bʌdʒi/. [f. BUDG(ERIGAR + -Y. Used elsewhere but recorded earliest in Aust.] BUDGERIGAR.

1935 W. WATMOUGH *Cult of Budgerigar* 207 Although Budgies are so hardy.. reasonable care should at all times be exercised to protect them from chills. 1985 *Canberra Times* 11 Dec. 10/5 How do you degrease a budgie that has fallen into a pot of fat?

budtha, var. BUDDA.

buffalo grass. [U.S. *buffalo grass*, referring orig. to the low-growing perennial grass *Buchloë dactyloides* common on former buffalo ranges.] The introduced *Stenotaphrum secundatum* (fam. Poaceae), cultivated as a coarse lawn grass.

1875 *Illustr. Sydney News* 19 Jan. 18/2 It can be propagated either from seed or roots, the same as couch or buffalo grass. 1968 G. DUTTON *Andy* 229 Andy and Feline lay on a rug on the bumpy buffalo grass of Merv's ill-kept lawn.

buffel grass. [S. Afr. *buffel grass*, f. Du. *buffel* buffalo.] The tussocky perennial African grass *Cenchrus ciliaris* (fam. Poaceae), valued as a forage plant and soil stabilizer.

1931 M. TERRY *Hidden Wealth* 324 A marsh on Wallal sown with buffle grass gives a great body of feed. 1978 O. WHITE *Silent Reach* 122 A pair of hunting eagle hawks, soaring, dipping and wheeling above the expanse of bleached buffel grass.

bugeen /'bʌgin/. Also **buggeen**. [a. Wiradhuri *bagiinʸ*, but cf. Br. dial. *bugan* evil spirit (see EDD).] A devil or evil spirit. See also quot. 1980.

1834 G. BENNETT *Wanderings N.S.W.* I. 126 They were afraid, if they buried them, the *Buckee*, or devil devil would take them away. 1948 F. CLUNE *Wild Colonial Boys* 102 By night they.. protected their hut with a 'buggeen' or devil-on-a-stump. This was a pumpkin, scooped hollow, with three holes to represent eyes and mouth, and a lighted candle inside, placed on a tree-stump outside the hut. 1958 R. ROBINSON *Black-Feller White-Feller* 111 Someone, a *bugeen* perhaps, is sneaking up on me to kill me with his *guneena*, his devils' stones. 1980 P. PEPPER *You are what you make Yourself* 33 Their parents went to the *bugheen*, that's the clever bloke of the tribe and got him to sing the one who took the girls away.

bugle.

1. The nose.

1891 *Truth* (Sydney) 3 May 6/3 He got a good left flush home on George's mouth, and George met him full on the bugle, and drew first blood. 1904 M. WHITE *Shanty Entertainment* 15 It was never known as a nose. It was sheer insult to call it anything less than a bugle.

2. In the phr. **on the bugle,** smelly; hence 'a bit off', crooked.

1943 J. DEVINE *Rats of Tobruk* 111 Everything was 'on the bugle' to him. By this he meant that he disliked it. Bugle stood for nose, and saying a thing was on the nose meant that it smelt. 1973 J. O'GRADY *Survival in Doghouse* 80, I.. tell Ray things are all right, and ask him how they are with him. He says 'They're a bit on the bugle, mate.' I say, 'What seems to be the trouble?'

bugong, var. BOGONG.

build-up. *N.T.* [Spec. use of *build-up* gradual accumulation.] The period of gradually increasing heat and humidity which precedes the wet season.

1977 K. COLE *Winds of Fury* 12 The transition from the Dry to the Wet, known as the 'build-up', takes place from October to December. 1985 *Centralian Advocate* (Alice Springs) 18 Dec. 2/4 The Wet Season arrived dubiously, not bringing many of its promised merciful downpours.. and the build-up keeps building.

bulk, *a.* [Prob. by analogy with *bulk-buying*.] Many.

1977 *Surf Wacks* 2 Bulk people camped at Cactus, and Witzig was raking in bulk money. 1984 *Canberra Times* 14 Feb. 17/4 Bulk kisses and hugs, Marcus.

bull, $n.^1$ *Hist.* Also **beal, bool.** [Spec. use of *bull* a drink made from spirit or sugar residue: see OED $sb.^6$ and $v.^4$] A crudely sweetened or alcoholic drink formerly favoured by Aborigines: see quots. 1839 and 1840.

1821 Methodist Missionary Soc. Rec. 5 Oct., If they cut wood, or do any other trifling work, they are rewarded with what they call *bull*; sometimes this is composed of a mixture of spirituous liquors, and at others is the washing of liquor puncheons. 1838 T.L. MITCHELL *Three Exped. Eastern Aust.* II. 286 Piper explained the purpose for which these flowers had been gathered, by informing me that by steeping them a night in water the natives make a sweet beverage named 'bool'. 1839 W. MANN *Six Yrs.' Residence* 152 He asked for a vessel to mix the honey with some water, which mixture they call *bull*; the same term is applied if sugar be the substitute for honey. This they drank with great glee, which excited them almost as much as the same quantity of wine would affect Europeans. 1840 J.P. JOHNSON *Plain Truths* 55 Their grog, or bull, as it is termed, is a small quantity of boiling water put into a cask, out of which all the spirits have been drawn, or at any rate only leaving the dirt at the bottom. 1878 R.B. SMYTH *Aborigines of Vic.* I. 210 In the flowers of a dwarf species of Banksia (*B. ornata*) there is a good deal of honey, and this was got out of the flowers by immersing them in water. The water thus sweetened was greedily swallowed by the natives. The drink was named *Beal* by the natives of the west of Victoria.

bull, $n.^2$ *Obs.* [Transf. use of *bull*, former Br. slang for a five shilling coin.] Seventy-five strokes of the lash.

1859 J. LANG *Botany Bay* (1885) 30 There were slang terms applied to these doses of the lash: twenty five was called a 'tester', fifty, a 'bob',—seventy five, a 'bull' and a hundred a 'canary'.

bull, $n.^3$ Used *attrib.* in the names of flora and fauna: **bull bird**, BOOMER $n.^2$; **head**, any of several unrelated plants bearing spiny fruits, esp. DOUBLE-GEE; also **bull (head) burr; mallee, (a)** a form of growth of mallee eucalypts (see quots. 1956, 1962, and 1982); **(b)** any of several mallee eucalypts, esp. *Eucalyptus behriana* (fam. Myrtaceae) of N.S.W., Vic., and S.A.; **Mitchell**, see MITCHELL GRASS 2; **oak**, any of several trees, esp. of the genera *Casuarina* and *Allocasuarina* (fam. Casuarinaceae) and usu. *A. luehmanii* of inland Qld., N.S.W., Vic., and S.A.; the wood of these trees; also **buloke; rout**, any of several fish, esp. *Notesthes robusta*, a scorpion fish (fam. Scorpaenidae) of e. Aust. and Irian Jaya coastal waters, estuaries and fresh-water streams, having venomous spines on the head which can inflict painful wounds.

1857 *Moreton Bay Free Press* 15 Apr. 3/7 The **bull-bird** has only been seen three or four times in Australia. **1938** [**bull head**] *Qld. Agric. Jrnl.* L. 790 Cape spinach or prickly jack . . also called bull head burr. **1977** KLEINSCHMIDT & JOHNSON *Weeds Qld.* 178 In Queensland, spiny ernex is also known as . . bullhead. **1967** *Southerly* iii. 199 Weeds flourished, wait-a-whiles, bull-burrs, wild blackberries, Bathurst burrs. **1890** W.H. BUNDEY *Winter Cruise* 13 **Bull mallee** is a problem to the ordinary grubbing contractor. **1956** R.H. ANDERSON *Trees of N.S.W.* (ed. 3) 37 The larger Mallees which often become single-stemmed are called Bull Mallees. **1962** H.J. FRITH *Mallee-Fowl* 54 On heavy soils the eucalypts have only a few stems, perhaps six to eight inches thick, and are known as bull mallee. **1982** BARKER & GREENSLADE *Evol. Flora & Fauna* 153 In western New South Wales, most of the common mallee species . . can occur either as 1–3 stemmed trees known as 'bull' mallee up to 10 m in height or as multi-stemmed 'whipstick' mallee 1–3 m high. **1874** 'REV. F.T.P.' *Thirty-Shilling Horse* 40 'That wasn't she-oak you gave your horse, but **bull-oak**.' I had never heard of bull-oak before, so I asked the difference. He informed me that she-oak was sour, bull-oak was bitter. **1931** *Bulletin* (Sydney) 4 Feb. 20/3 'Sheoke' and 'buloke' are the names that have been adopted for two kinds of casuarinas. It was considered that 'she-oak' and 'bull-oak', the previous names, would suggest a relationship with the oak of Europe which the casuarinas cannot claim. **1851** J. HENDERSON *Excursions & Adventures N.S.W.* II. 207 There is a small fish, called the **Bull-rout**, which inhabits the rivers, and is capable of biting or stinging in a desperate manner.

bull, $n.^4$ [Prob. fig. use of *bull* the animal, as chosen by a buyer in a sale-yard: see quot. 1975.]

1. A wharf labourer who is given preferential treatment when work is allocated by the foreman. See also PINK-EYE $n.^3$

1957 T. NELSON *Hungry Mile* 80 The employers were often responsible for the undermining of the union's attempt to prevent wrongful movement of men from job to job by indulging in illegal trafficking of 'bulls' to suit their own ends, or meet the request of other companies for early release of 'bulls' for new jobs starting. **1975** V. WILLIAMS *Yrs. of Big Jim* 71 The compound, now known as the Waterside Labour Bureau, resembled the Newmarket cattle yards. Members of the Federation were herded into one pen.

2. Comb. **bull system**.

1957 T. NELSON *Hungry Mile* 77 The battle to end the bull system is unsurpassed in the history of Australian unionism.

bull, $v.^1$ Mining. [f. *bull* iron rod used in blasting: see OED $sb.^1$ 5.] *trans.* See quot. 1958.

1889 *Braidwood Dispatch* 30 Oct. 2/4 He was engaged in 'bulling' three drills, and was very unwisely carrying all lighted fuses with plugs of dynamite attached to his hand. **1958** *Prospector's Guide* (N.S.W. Mines Dept.) 191 *Bull*, to enlarge the bottom of a drilled hole to increase the explosive charge.

bull, $v.^2$ [Survival of Br. *bull* to adulterate: see OED $v.^4$ and BULL $n.^1$.] *trans.* To adulterate. Also as *ppl. a.*

1891 *Truth* (Sydney) 8 Mar. 7/3 Then the whisky comes. That is watered and 'bulled'. You may say that there is no profit in that. Don't you know that a 'tanner' saved is a sixpence gained? **1929** W.J. RESIDE *Golden Days* 277 'Bulled' water is the condensed brackish fluid to which a proportion of uncondensed has been added to make the measurement when the sale is by the gallon. The term is obsolete. There are no condensers, and *few prospectors* in W.A. now. **1959** *Bulletin* (Sydney) 23 Dec. 16/1 The most heinous crime in the shearing-shed—next to 'scabbing'—is to 'bull' your room-mate's rum after surreptitiously swiping some.

Bullamakanka /bʊləməˈkæŋkə/. Also **Bullabakanka**. [Perh. based on pidgin *bulla macow* bully beef: see OEDS.] An imaginary place, remote and supposedly backward. See also WOOP WOOP 1.

1953 T.A.G. HUNGERFORD *Riverslake* 230 Hitch out to Bullamakanka and live with the blacks. **1980** A.S. VEITCH *Run from Morning* 129 One of your original Aussie battlers. Started with a horse and dray at Bullabakanka.

bullan bullan /ˈbʊlən bʊlən/. *Obs.* Also **bullen bullen, buln buln**. [a. Wuywurung *bulen bulen*.] Superb lyre-bird, see SUPERB.

1848 *Port Phillip Mag.* Feb. (Advt.), Beautiful specimens of the 'Lyre Bird', 'Menura Superba', or 'Bullen Bullen'. **1896** F.G. AFLALO *Sketch Nat. Hist. Aust.* 132 Besides a mellow note of its own, from which the aboriginals know it as the Bullan-Bullan, the bird is a capital mimic. **1948** J. FURPHY *Buln-Buln & Brolga* 85 The Buln-buln and Brolga returned to their seat.

bull-ant. Shortened form of BULLDOG ANT. Also *attrib.*

1880 J. BALLANTYNE *Our Colony* 93 Ants are numerous, . . the bull-ant being of large size. **1942** C. BARRETT *From Bush Hut* 15 Goanna oil's best for a cold, and splendid for bullant stings.

bullbar. A strong metal bar or frame mounted at the front of a vehicle to reduce damage to the vehicle in the event of a collision with a stray beast, kangaroo, etc; *kangaroo bar*, see KANGAROO *n.* 6; *roo bar*, see ROO $n.^2$ c.

1967 J. YEOMANS *Scarce Australs.* 97 Most beasts had been killed by one blow from the bull bars (the heavy horizontal steel tubing mounted as cattle guards) on the front of a road train. **1985** *Canberra Times* 8 Feb. 2/7 'The roos are a bit of a risk aren't they?' . . 'Not since I got the bullbars fitted!'

bulldog ant. A large ant of any of several species of the genus *Myrmecia*, capable of inflicting a painful sting; BULL-ANT; BULLJOE. Also *ellipt.* as **bulldog**.

1851 W.B. CLARKE *Researches Southern Gold Fields N.S.W.* (1860) 120 It was difficult to find a spot on which to lay our blankets, on account of the 'Bull Dog Ants'. **1853** MRS C. CLACY *Lady's Visit to Gold Diggings* 134 The largest [ants] are called by the old colonists, 'bull-dogs', and formidable creatures they are . . about an inch and a half long, black, or rusty black, with a red tail. They bite like a little crab.

bulldust, *n.*

1. [Prob. with ref. to powdered dirt in e.g. a stock yard, etc., but see also quot. 1962.] A kind of fine powdery dirt or dust. Also *attrib.*

1932 I.L. IDRIESS *Flynn of Inland* (1965) 170 Crossing the Arthur River . . they came down on to the flat country and the 'bull dust' (finer than sand yet not quite dust), a greasy sort of dust in which, in wet or dry, beast and car can bog very easily if they break through the crust. **1962** C. GYE

Cockney & Crocodile 74 The track was full of deep holes, filled up flat with fine dust as yielding as water and apt to break axles or bog you down. It was called bull dust, not from any connection with bulls but from its ferocity. **1984** 4 × 4 July 30 A bulldust hole .. can just as easily trip up a 4WD.

2. [Orig. U.S.] Euphemistic var. of 'bullshit', *n.*

1951 'S. MACKENZIE' *Dead Men Rising* 70 He, while a soldier on active service—what bulldust .. did absent himself. **1978** B. ST. A. SMITH *Spirit beyond Psyche* 213 Nerves? *Nerves is all bull-dust.*

3. Comb. **bulldust artist.**

1965 I. HAMILTON *Persecutor* 189, I know you'll pass for an honest man, even if you are a bull-dust artist.

bulldust, *v.* [f. BULLDUST *n.* 2.] *intr.* Euphemistic var. of 'bullshit', *v.* Also *trans.*

1967 F. HARDY *Billy Borker yarns Again* 58 He bull-dusted and yak-yaked while the ex-warder paid for the beer. **1975** C. PERKINS *Bastard like Me* 166, I was sick and tired of .. getting bull-dusted by all the Yanks and the people from the Australian Embassies.

Hence **bullduster** *n.*

1963 R. STOW *Tourmaline* 93 'I say he's a bloody good prospector,' said Kestrel; 'and the best bullduster I'm likely to meet.'

bulldusted, *a.* [f. BULLDUST *n.* 1.] Of a (road) surface: covered in fine dust.

1975 *Bulletin* (Sydney) 20 Sept. 34/3 Until you get to Georgetown .. you are on corrugated, bull-dusted dirt. **1976** MULLALLY & SEXTON *Stir Possum* 11 I've travelled many a road in the outback And some which are no road at all, Pot-holed and stony, bull-dusted track.

bulldusty, *a.* Of or pertaining to BULLDUST *n.* 1.

1936 C.T. MADIGAN *Central Aust.* 172 At one cape we were forced close in to the shore, and tried a run on the land surface, but it was altogether too 'bull-dusty', and heavier than the lake surface. **1979** D. LOCKWOOD *My Old Mates & I* 5 Thousands of hooves had assisted wheels in grinding the ground to bulldusty talc.

bullen bullen, var. BULLAN BULLAN.

Bulli soil /ˈbʊlaɪ sɔɪl/. [f. the name of a coastal town s. of Sydney, N.S.W.] A clay-rich soil taken from coastal headlands at Bulli and formerly used extensively for cricket pitches and lawn tennis courts.

1912 P.F. WARNER *England v. Aust.* 53 The almost impervious Bulli soil. **1965** *Austral. Encycl.* II. 180 Bulli soil is valued for turf cricket pitches.

bulljoe /ˈbʊl dʒoʊ/. [f. BULL(DOG ANT + the proper name *Joe.*] BULLDOG ANT. Also **bulljoe ant.**

1952 C. SIMPSON *Come away, Pearler* 222 When Bulljoe got on a trail he hung on to it, never let go—'just like those inch-ants with the big nippers, the ones we call bulljoes.' **1958** *Bulletin* (Sydney) 16 July 18/1, I threw a lighted cigarette-butt on the ground and it landed near a bulljoe-ant. Game as Ned Kelly, Bulljoe charged.

bullo. [f. *bull* nonsense + -O.] Rubbish, nonsense.

1942 *Cheeriodical* (Rathmines) 5 Mar. 2 Believe me, that's no Bullo. **1974** M. PAICE *Dolan's Roost* 126 'Ah, bullo!' Dobbo decided at last. 'Who'd be mad enough to stick a bag of money in there?'

bullock, *n.*

1. Used *attrib.* in Comb. not necessarily excl. to Austral. but of local importance: **bullock cart, conductor, dray, driver, driving, paddock, persuader, team, track, train, wagon, watchman, whip.** See also Ox.

1805 *Sydney Gaz.* 3 Mar., Two stout able men, as labouring servants, whose work will mainly consist in attending a **bullock cart**. **1971** *Bulletin* (Sydney) 13 Nov. 27/1 There's a Cobb & Co. coach, a bullock cart with a white banner proclaiming 'Australia's living history'. **1915** *Ibid.* 1 Apr. 14/4 Don't let us miss the chance of securing a good, technical education to the coming generations of **bullock conductors**... The engineering of bullocks is a dying industry. **1847** L. LEICHHARDT *Jrnl. Overland Exped. Aust.* p. xvi, My friends had lent me a **bullock dray**. **1836** *Cornwall Chron.* (Launceston) 24 Dec. 1, I am, Sir, your obedient servant, a poor **bullock driver**. **1847** J. SIDNEY *Voice from Far Interior* 48 **Bullock-driving** in the bush being almost a science, we say, 'any man can knock bullocks about, but very few can drive them.' **1923** F.A.C. BISHOP *Rep. on Inspection Barkly Tableland* 5 The country traversed was through the **bullock paddock**. **1916** *Bulletin* (Sydney) 6 Jan. 24/3 **Bullock-persuaders** vary in their methods, like other artists. **1829** J. ATKINSON *Distilling & Brewing N.S.W.* 5 It occupies a **bullock team** 12 days, and very often more, to perform a journey from this place to Sydney and back. **1848** *Maitland Mercury* 21 Oct. 2/4 An acquaintance of his was travelling on the Lower Murray, and passing along a **bullock track** .. within about five miles of a certain public-house. **1855** W. HOWITT *Land, Labor & Gold* I. 72 The colonials plough their way with their ponderous **bullock trains**. **1909** *Bulletin* (Sydney) 26 Aug. 15/2 Two men on the Victoria 'sat down' on a billabong with a **bullock-waggon**. In two years they had 600 cattle. **1849** S. & J. SIDNEY *Emigrant's Jrnl.* 25 Bullock-driving is more of an art .. but any one can make a **bullock watchman**. **1846** G.H. HAYDON *Five Yrs. Experience Aust. Felix* 138 A large emu .. in consequence of the noise made by the **bullock-whip**, was off.

2. Special Comb. **bullock bell**, a bell worn by a bullock to indicate its whereabouts; **bush**, the plant *Heterodendrum oleifolium* (see ROSEWOOD).

1845 *Bell's Life in Sydney* 20 Dec. 1/3 The Undersigned has on sale .. **Bullock Bells**. **1915** *Bull. N.T.* xiv. 10 Boree (camel bush or **bullock bush**).

3. Austral. pidgin. *Obs.* BULLOCKY *n.* 1.

1847 A. HARRIS *Settlers & Convicts* (1953) 207 They soon began to ask for bread and 'bullock' (beef). **1879** 'AUSTRALIAN' *Adventures Qld.* 50 Salamanca [*sc.* a thieving pet emu] plagued the poor blacks terribly... They often went up to the store with whining requests for 'more flour and bullock—that fellow S'manker been *patter* altogether'.

4. *Obs.* See quot. 1881.

1881 H.W. NESFIELD *Chequered Career* 346 He calls them his *bullocks*, a term used up country for men who work hard for the benefit of the publican. **1895** *Worker* (Sydney) 30 Mar. 4/2 On settling day the publican gives each of his 'bullocks' any small sum he thinks fit.

5. *transf.* A working camel.

1893 D. LINDSAY *Jrnl. Elder Sci. Exploring Exped.* 18 Hadji was breaking in one of the young bullocks, which he says will make a very good riding camel. **1978** D. STUART *Wedgetail View* 65 He never used a ridin' camel, just led the two bullock camels on foot.

6. Brute force, brawn.

1936 E.C.H. TAYLOR *Our Austral. Game Football* 91 Football is not all 'bullock' and 'sheer stupidity'.

bullock, *v.* [f. prec.]

1. *intr.* To work tirelessly (like a bullock). Freq. as *pr. pple.* Also *trans.*

1875 *Austral. Town & Country Jrnl.* (Sydney) 28 Aug. 343/4, I don't believe in running after new country; let other fellows, if they're fools enough, do all that bullocking. Wise men buy their work afterwards—and cheap enough, too. **1980** R. BROPHO *Fringedweller* 23 Aboriginal people have dropped dead .. by standing in the heat of the sun and bullocking their guts out.

2. *fig.*

1930 V. PALMER *Passage* (1957) 5 Fred was tough as

tarred canvas, able to bullock his way anywhere. **1950** *Coast to Coast 1949–50* 141 It was a good thing the other kids ate like rabbits and bullocked and banged through life.
Hence **bullocking** *vbl. n.*
1888 'R. BOLDREWOOD' *Robbery under Arms* (1937) 57 It would have paid us better if we'd read a little more and put the bullocking on one side.

bullocker. *Obs.* A bullock driver.
1889 BARRÈRE & LELAND *Dict. Slang* I. 197 *Bullockirs* in Australia are as proverbial as bargees or Billingsgate fishwives in England for the forcibleness of their language. **1894** J.K. ARTHUR *Kangaroo & Kauri* 31 Men are employed to cut down shrubs and small trees for the sake of feeding the stock with the leaves. Roadmen, especially hawkers and bullockers have to do the same.

bullock puncher. [f. BULLOCK *n.* + PUNCH *v.* 1 + -*er*.] A bullock driver.
[N.Z. **1856** H. BEATTIE *Early Runholding Otago* (1947) 42 In the hands of an experienced 'bullock-puncher'.] **1859** W. KELLY *Life in Vic.* I. 172 The demon yells of the savage bullock puncher .. another sobriquet for the teamster, whose whip-shaft is always armed with a spike to punch an over-obdurate animal. **1956** R.G. EDWARDS *Overlander Songbk.* 121 And the hardy bullock-punchers throw Aside their occupation.

bullock punching, *vbl. n.* [See prec.] The activity of driving cattle. Also *attrib.*
[N.Z. **1868** H. PHILLIPS Jrnl. Rockwood & Point 10 Nov. (typescript), Heavy bullock punching—stone carting &c.] **1886** F. COWAN *Aust.* 29 Bullock-punching on the Cambridge downs of Kimberly. **1895** *Bulletin* (Sydney) 3 Aug. 6/3 The interests of the drought-stricken West were sacrificed to the teamster and bullock-punching vote of one constituency.

bullocky, *n.* [f. BULLOCK *n.* + -Y.]
1. Orig. *Austral. pidgin.* Beef; BULLOCK *n.* 3.
1839 *S. Austral. Rec.* (London) (1840) 1 Feb. 22 There was a public dinner given to the Adelaide tribe of Aborigines of roast beef and plum pudding, but they call it *bullocky*. **1952** A.M. DUNCAN-KEMP *Where Strange Paths go Down* 16 No pastoralist can afford to pay a pensioned stockman or his dependents, but he is ever willing to give them a home and 'bullocky' (fresh meat), blankets and tobacco in return for odd jobs done.
2. A bullock driver.
1869 *Australasian* (Melbourne) 17 July 72/5 *Cornstalk* and *gumsucker* are both of colonial growth, and so, I think, is .. *bullocky* (a teamster). **1986** *Bulletin* (Sydney) 11 Mar. 78/1 The garden is worked by Murray senior, a lithe man after years as a bullocky, dairyman and timber cutter.
3. An idiom or use of language supposedly characterizing bullock drivers. Also *attrib.* and quasi-*adv.*
1879 *Kelly Gang* 122 The perpetrators of the robbery were not known throughout to make use of a single 'bullocky' or colonially-emphasized expression. **1894** A.B. BELL *Oscar* 55 That made dad mad, he bounced out the house swearin' bullocky. **1916** 'MEN OF ANZAC' *Anzac Bk.* 103 Bang! bang! went a couple of bombs, followed by cries and shouts from Abdul, and above it all we were certain we heard fragments of language, or the category known in Australia as 'bullocky'.
4. In the collocation **bullocky's joy** (or **delight**), treacle or golden syrup.
1901 *Bulletin* (Sydney) 9 Mar. 31/3, I bitterly thought of .. the tin of 'bullocky's joy' reposing in a saucer of water to keep the ants out. **1911** *Ibid.* 13 July 14/4 How many aliases does treacle travel on through the bush? Here are some of them: 'Cockies'-Joy', 'Bullocky's-Delight', 'Oh-bejoyful', 'Wild honey'.
5. Comb. **bullocky bush**, *bullock bush*, see BULLOCK *n.* 2.

1963 A.E. FARRELL *Vengeance* 22 Their fringe was dotted with innumerable Callitris pines, quondongs and hardy bastard mulgas and bullocky bush.

bullocky, *a.* Of or pertaining to bullock driving or rural life generally. Also in the collocation **Bullocky Bill**, a nickname for a bullock driver.
1876 *Austral. Town & Country Jrnl.* (Sydney) 1 Apr. 544/4 Poor bullocky Bill! In the circles select Of the scholars he hasn't a place; But he walks like a *man*, with his forehead erect, And looks at God's day in the face. **1985** *Canberra Times* 23 Mar. 2/5 Every word of it is true .. except a few bullocky yarns.

bull puncher. Abbrev. of BULLOCK PUNCHER.
1871 *Illustr. Sydney News* 23 Dec. 211/2, I, a new chum—the imported new material, used to nothing save quill-driving, striving to compete with bull-punchers, who had taken their colonial experience degree in Macquarie's or Darling's time. **1924** J. NISBET *Scraps* 14 The fluent 'bull puncher'.
Also **bull punching** *vbl. n.*
1879 'AUSTRALIAN' *Adventures Qld.* 111 Old Ben used to let him take the whip, and instructed him in the noble art of 'bull-punching'.

bull-ring, *v. Obs. trans.* See quot. 1880. Also as *vbl. n.*
1880 *V & P* (N.S.W. L.A.) III. 1134 Inside the huge ring made by a mile or so of net, a boat from time to time throws off a small seine, which is 'bull-ringed', or drawn to the shore where practicable round as many fish as are required for the next trip of the steamer. **1906** D.G. STEAD *Fishes of Aust.* 66 When fish are in large schools at the surface of the water .. the process followed is what is termed 'Bull-ringing'; the net being thrown in a circle right round the school.

bullroarer. [So called because of a fancied resemblance to the child's toy.] A sacred object of Aboriginal ceremony and ritual: see quot. 1898.
1848 *Adelaide Miscellany* 2 Sept. 77 The assembled 'bull-roarers', as those rude and mysterious instruments are popularly called, were swung round more vehemently than ever. **1898** D.W. CARNEGIE *Spinifex & Sand* 333 They use flat carved sticks, some eight inches long, and of a pointed oval shape. Through a hole in one point they thread a string, with which the stick is rapidly swung round, making a booming noise—'Bull-roarers' is the general whitefellows' name for them.

bull run. Esp. in a country house, a wide passage dividing one part of the house from another and allowing free movement of air.
1935 DAVISON & NICHOLLS *Blue Coast Caravan* 112 The houses are mostly bungalows, that is a more or less four-square structure, with a 'bull run' passage through the centre. **1946** F. CLUNE *Try Nothing Twice* 78 He careered into the 'bull-run', an open corridor between the kitchen annexe and the house.

bullsh. Also **bulsh**. [Abbrev. of *bullshit*: see OEDS.] Rubbish, nonsense: see quot. 1919. Also *attrib.* as **bullsh artist**.
1919 W.H. DOWNING *Digger Dialects* 14 Bullsh .. (1) Insincerity; (2) an incorrect or insincere thing; (3) flattery; (4) praise. **1938** X. HERBERT *Capricornia* 377 This talk of invasion by the Japs is all plain bulsh. **1949** G. BERRIE *Morale* 125 When he told them what gallant fellows they were, they promptly put him down as one more 'bulsh' artist.

bullswool. Also **bull's wool**. [So called from the resemblance to coarse hair.]
1. Fibrous bark, esp. that of some stringybark trees; any kindling material.

1881 G. WALCH *Vic.* 73 A few matches and some frayed fibres of stringy-bark—called by experts 'bull's wool'. **1981** M. SHARLAND *Tracks of Morning* 65 Australian bark, easy to gather and quick to burn presents few problems, whether in strips or a handful of 'bull's wool' from a hoary stem.

2. A euphemism for 'bullshit'. Also *attrib*.
1933 R.D. TATE *Doughman* 20 The way you harp on Honesty, and you the bull's-wool artist from the Devil's Sunday School! **1948** I.L. IDRIESS *Opium Smugglers* 88 'Fiddlesticks!' I yawned. 'Bullswool!'

bullwaddy, var. BULWADDY.

bull wire. [So called because of its strength.] A heavy gauge fencing wire.
1945 *Coast to Coast 1944* 56 Sand, gibbers; and crazy bullwire fences staggering into infinity. **1968** A. D'OMBRAIN *Fish Tales* 11 For our fishing expedition he cut off two tenfoot lengths of what he termed 'Bull Wire', or heavy gauge fencing wire.

Bully. [f. *Bull(etin* + -Y.] *The Bulletin*, the name of an influential weekly journal published in Sydney from 1880; *bushman's bible*, see BUSHMAN 8.
1913 *Truth* (Sydney) 16 Nov. 5/8 The 'Bully' should be the last paper in the world to sneer at the advertisements other journals publish. **1981** L. McLEAN *Pumpkin Pie* 43 My father kept a rolled up copy of the 'Bulletin' at the back of his seat... Some of Dad's early articles were published in the 'Bully', as we affectionately called this magazine.

bullya, var. BOYLYA.

buln buln, var. BULLAN BULLAN.

buloke, var. *bull oak*, see BULL *n.*[3]

bulrush. [Transf. use of *bulrush* a tall rush of wet places, esp. *Typha latifolia*.] Any of several tall reed-like plants growing in or near water, esp. the native *Typha domingensis* and *T. orientalis* (fam. Typhaceae) of all States, Asia, and N.Z.; CUMBUNGI; WONGA.
1793 J. HUNTER *Hist. Jrnl. Trans. Port Jackson* 339 The huts were very soon built.. and thatched with bullrushes and flaggs. **1965** K. TENNANT *Summer's Tales* p. vi, As different from the native narrative as a beautiful hothouse tuberose is from a bulrush.

bulwaddy /bʊlˈwɒdi/. Also **bullwaddi, bullwaddie, bullwaddy.** [Prob. f. an Aboriginal language.] The tree of n. Aust. *Macropteranthes kekwickii* (fam. Combretaceae) which forms dense thickets.
1925 M. TERRY *Across Unknown Aust.* 194 Bull-waddi grows in.. thickets... It gives off greater heat than any other Australian wood... Gidgee is supposed to be one of the hottest, but it is cool compared with bull-waddi. **1936** 'L. KAYE' *Black Wilderness* 36 In a little patch of bulwaddy near the herd, Lex stopped and tethered his horse. **1945** T. RONAN *Strangers of Ophir* 111 He was in a tangle of lancewood and bullwaddy. **1959** D. LOCKWOOD *Crocodiles & Other People* 71 A few patches of the dreaded, low-slung bulwaddie, where wild cattle shelter from stockmen who dare not follow.

bum.
A. Used *attrib*. in Special Comb. **bum brusher,** a batman; **chum,** an intimate; **puncher,** a homosexual.
1941 S.J. BAKER *Pop. Dict. Austral. Slang* 15 **Bumbrusher,** an officer's servant. **1972** G. MORLEY *Jockey rides Honest Race* 254, I can go round saying I'm Kon Malouf's **bum chum.** Know him? I've shared a flat with the bastard. **1977** D. WHITTINGTON *Strive to be Fair* 31 There was no easy acceptance of homosexuals. They were still referred to scathingly as 'queans' [*sic*] and '**bum punchers**'.

B. *n.* In the phr. **bum to mum**: see quot. 1972.
1972 *Bulletin* (Sydney) 30 Sept. 45/1 Australian rules footballers in Melbourne, when forbidden sexual relations before an important match, are told: 'Bum to Mum'. The phrase is appealing, both for its conciseness and for its Melburnian assumption that the amorous activity of footballers is exclusively conjugal. **1980** B. HORNADGE *Austral. Slanguage* 241 Australian Rules has also given an amusing new phrase to the world in the form of *bum to mum*—this being another way of saying 'no sex with the wife'.

bumble tree. [a. Kamilaroi and Yuwaalaraay *bambul* + (Eng.) *tree.*] *Wild orange*, see WILD 1. Also **bumble.**
1846 C.P. HODGSON *Reminisc. Aust.* 150 The bumble (or *Capparis Mitchelii*) has three varieties. **1897** K.L. PARKER *Austral. Legendary Tales* (ed. 2) 15 Many and ripe are the bumbles hanging now on the bumble trees.

bumboat. [Transf. use of *bumboat* a boat carrying provisions for sale to ships.] A travelling sly grog shop; the proprietor or stock of such a shop. Also *attrib*.
1851 *Bell's Life in Sydney* 25 Oct. 1/1 Scarcely a station in the interior but has been visited by the 'bum-boat'.. of the Bathurst sly grog-sellers. **1905** D. REID *Reminisc.* 58 He was what was called a bum-boat man and had his cart and an immense puncheon of rum which he was selling at a good figure and intending to proceed to the diggings.

bumbora, var. BOMBORA.

bumerang, var. BOOMERANG *n.* 1.

bump, *v.*
1. *trans*. To encounter (a person, etc.).
1907 *Truth* (Sydney) 5 May 1/5 Bumped a tramguard the other day.. who did not know where Grosvenor-street was. **1957** D. WHITTINGTON *Treasure upon Earth* 115, I was pickin' up when I first bumped him. 'Tar, boy,' he'd yell and I'd rush up with the tar stick.

2. *trans*. To get the better of (someone).
1911 A. WRIGHT *Gamblers' Gold* (1923) 87 I'll bump you every time. You expect to win the Sydney Cup with the horse I have been robbed of, but let me tell you I'll down you if it costs me a thousand. **1956** T. RONAN *Moleskin Midas* 253 Ophir Downs always made sure it carried at least one man big enough and clever enough 'to bump Blake the half-caste' if he and his boss were caught with O.D.I. cattle.

bumper, *n.* [Of unknown origin.]
1. A cigarette butt. Also *attrib*.
1899 *Austral. Tit-Bits* (Sydney) 6 May 194/3 Bumper hunters.. are men and boys who, unable to buy tobacco, or in order to save money, make a practice of picking up and smoking all the 'butts'.. of cigars and cigarettes which they can find lying in the streets. **1916** 'MEN OF ANZAC' *Anzac Bk.* 47 Along comes the bloomin' officer, so 'Enessy sticks 'is lighted bumper down south into 'is overcoat pocket.

2. In the phr. **not worth a bumper,** worthless.
1947 M. TRIST *Daddy* 164 My old man's not going to be worth a bumper that day. **1974** D. IRELAND *Burn* 44 'Billy, you're not worth a bumper,' Joy says. 'You couldn't fight your way out of a paper bag.'

bumper, *v.* [f. prec.] *trans*. To make (a cigarette) from butts; to extinguish (a cigarette) and save the butt.
1968 D. O'GRADY *Bottle of Sandwiches* 30 Hope he brings the makin's we asked him to. Smokin' bumpers is all right when there's nothin' else, but by tomorrow we'll be bumperin' the bumpers. **1978** T. DAVIES *More Austral.*

BUMPY ASH 89 **BUNGARRA**

Nicknames 34 As soon as he came into the danger area they would have to bumper their cigarettes.

bumpy ash. [See quot. 1932.] The tree *Flindersia schottiana* (see CUDGERIE).

1925 *Bulletin* (Sydney) 15 Jan. 22/2 Another member of the family (*F*[*lindersia*] *schottiana*), bumpy ash or cudgery, might be put to better use. **1932** R.H. ANDERSON *Trees of N.S.W.* 138 Cudgerie (*Flindersia Schottiana*) is also known as Bumpy Ash owing to the presence of fairly large protuberances along the stem.

bunchy top. [See quot. 1921.] A viral disease afflicting banana trees and other crops, transmitted by the banana aphid *Pentalonia nigronervosa*.

1919 *Agric. Gaz. N.S.W.* XXX. 814 That Bunchy Top should occur in plants so widely separated botanically as the sugar cane and the banana, indicates that the disease is of physiological origin. **1921** *Bulletin* (Sydney) 10 Mar. 20/3 'Bunchy-top' in banana growth .. is caused by a white fungus that attacks the roots and eats away the covering thereof, leaving only a dried and dead fibre, which, of course fails to transmit the necessary food to the bulb of the plant—hence the dwarfed and unhealthy leaves, which 'bunch' together instead of spreading out, and so prevent the bananas from growing to fruition.

bunda-bunda, var. BANDY-BANDY.

bundi, var. BONDI *n.*[1]

bundle.

1. *Obs.* SWAG *n.* 1.
1853 [see BUNDLEMAN]. **1907** *Bulletin* (Sydney) 6 June 14/4 A swag is known .. as 'bundle', 'parcel', 'nap', 'matilda', 'drum'. **1920** *Smith's Weekly* (Sydney) 28 Aug. 9/4 No traveller likes to be on the road without a bluey of ordinary dimensions. A man might 'swamp his cheque' but he won't part with his bundle.

2. In the phr. **to drop one's bundle,** to go to pieces.
1897 *Antipodean* (Melbourne) 91 In the latest Colonial slang, a man who loses his nerve at a critical part of a game is said to 'drop his bundle', while a man who plays a determined game is called a 'battler'. **1980** S. HAZZARD *Transit of Venus* 40 'We could all give in,' she said, when told that Miss Garside the librarian had completely dropped her bundle.

bundleman. *Obs.* [a. G. *bündelmann,* tr. of SWAGMAN.] SWAGMAN. Also **bundler.**

1853 F. GERSTAECKER *Narr. Journey round World* III. 64, I did not look like a common bundleman with my gun and knife, and the way I carried my blanket. *c* **1856** —— *Life in Bush* 15 Not far off, beneath a tree, sate a foot passenger, one of the men known as bundlers, eating his breakfast very tranquilly in the open air.

bundy, var. BONDI *n.*[1]

bundy /'bʌndi/, *n.*[1] [a. Dharuk *bunda*.] Any of several trees of the genus *Eucalyptus* (fam. Myrtaceae), esp. the rough-barked *E. goniocalyx* of s.e. Aust.

1899 *Proc. Linnean Soc. N.S.W.* XXIV. 462 *E. goniocalyx, F.v.M.* .. In this colony this species is sometimes known as 'Yellow Gum'. .. It is known as 'Bundy' at Burraga and Rockley. **1981** A.B. & J.W. CRIBB *Useful Wild Plants Aust.* 28 The bundy or long-leaved box, *E. goniocalyx,* of the Dividing Range areas of New South Wales and Victoria, extending into some of the South Australian Ranges.

Bundy /'bʌndi/, *n.*[2] Also **bundy.** [The proprietary name of a make of time clock.] A machine which records the times at which employees start and finish work; a clock used to regulate the punctuality of public transport services; *transf.,* a signal for the beginning or end of work. Also **bundy clock.**

1912 *Truth* (Sydney) 29 Dec. 5/6 The Sydney car conductor .. reckons it the joy of his life to beat bundy, and he will whiz the old car along .. so that he can have a couple of minutes' spell while waiting to get his correct time at every bundy along the route. **1922** *Smith's Weekly* (Sydney) 1 Apr. 19/4 Out of 365 days this year, the average Australian workman will ring the Bundy clock on 251 days—the remaining 114 being swallowed up by Saturdays, Sundays, and holidays.

Hence **bundy-puncher** *n.*

1948 A. DAWES *Soldier Superb* 99 The rotten minority—the schemer, the job stealer, the non-co-Operating boss and the non-co-operating bundy-puncher.

Bundy /'bʌndi/, *n.*[3] [f. *Bundaberg* the name of a town in Qld. and proprietary name of a brand of rum + -Y.] Bundaberg rum. Also **Bundy rum.**

1972 D. SHEAHAN *Songs from Canefields* 85 And some to drown their sorrow tore into Bundy Rum. Old Bundy is the dinkum stuff that serves a fellow well—Whether heading for Paradise or going to 'Inverell'. **1980** S. THORNE *I've met some Bloody Wags* 83 We hadn't had any scran all day, and the 'Bundy' had made us reckless.

bung /bʌŋ/, (formerly) bʊŋ, bɒŋ/, *a.* Orig. Austral. pidgin. Also **boang, boung** and formerly **bong.** [a. Jagara *baŋ.*]

1. *Obs.* Dead. Also in the (orig. pidgin) phr. **to go bung,** to die.
1841 *Colonial Observer* (Sydney) 14 Oct. 10/3 To the right the path to Umpie Boang or Old Settlement. **1847** J.D. LANG *Cooksland* 65 The black natives, whose nomenclature is always distinctive and appropriate—not like that of the Colonial Office—call it Umpie Bong, the 'Dead Houses', or 'Deserted Village'. **1857** F. DE B. COOPER *Wild Adventures* 58 'Boung!' said he, making use of the Cameleroi term for dead. **1886** A.M. HUGHES *Idylls of Bush* 13 'Good Lord! he's a stiff un!' 'Gone right bung?' sez Tim. So I feel his heart; it warn't beatin'.

2. *fig.* **a.** Bankrupt, in financial ruin. **b.** Incapacitated, exhausted, broken. Esp. in the phr. **to go bung,** to fail, to collapse.
1885 *Australasian Printers' Keepsake* 40 He was importuned to desist, as his musical talent had 'gone bung' probably from over-indulgence in confectionery. **1891** *Bohemia* (Melbourne) 3 Dec. 4 If we ever start a building society, and there is a possibility of it going bung, we will secure the services of Alfred Deakin as chairman. **1954** J. CLEARY *Climate of Courage* 41 Even with that bung hand of his, he'd have knocked me arse-over-Bluey.

bung /bʌŋ/, *v.* [f. *bung* to throw, put forcibly.] *trans.* With **on:** to stage (an event); to assume (a style of speech or behaviour, usu. pretentious or ostentatious), esp. in the phr. **to bung it on.** See also **to bung on a blue,** BLUE *n.*[2] 4.

1942 A.J. MCINTYRE *Putting over Burst* 4 So we say 'Go to it, Sergeant, Bung it on real thick.' **1965** K. SMITH *OGF* 170 Lance Hogarty .. suggested that we should bung on a compulsory church parade next Sunday evening.

bungalow, var. BANGALOW.

bungarra /'bʌŋærə/. *W.A.* Also **bung-arrer, bung-arrow.** [a. Nhanta prob. *baŋarra.*] The widespread monitor lizard, *Varanus gouldii,* usu. having a dark horizontal stripe through the eye, bordered by pale lines; *sand goanna,* see SAND. Also *transf.*

1897 A. HAYWARD *Along Road to Cue,* Ah, me! It grieves me sore To hear the batteries roar Where only roamed of yore The mild bungarra. **1927** M. TERRY *Through Land of Promise* 120 A larger breed known as the 'bung-arrer' is found up to 12 feet long. **1962** MARSHALL & DRYSDALE

Journey among Men 170 Even the goannas, or bung-arrows, as the Western Australians call them, can be made into reasonable food. **1978** T. DAVIES *More Austral. Nicknames* 35 *Bungarra* (That's an Aboriginal word for Lazy Sun Lizard, I'm told.) He's not noted for overexertion.

bunged, *ppl. a.* Afflicted with BUNG EYE 1.
1912 SPENCER & GILLEN *Across Aust.* 50 If both eyes become 'bunged' at the same time, you are quite blind for so long as the 'bung' lasts. **1928** B. SPENCER *Wanderings in Wild Aust.* 355 Fortunately, you do not often get both 'bunged' completely at the same time.

bunger. [Var. of *banger*.] A kind of firework which explodes with a loud report.
1929 D.J. HOPKINS *Hop of 'Bulletin'* 17 A parcel of gay fireworks, consisting of big bungers, little bungers, and strings of smaller ammunition. **1979** DOUGLAS & HEATHCOTE *Far Cry* 56 There followed the most colourful explosion and Catherine wheels and Big Bungers and Flower Pots and Volcanoes exploded together.

bung eye.
1. An infection of the eye caused by the bite of the sandfly *Leptoconops stygius*, or transmitted by bush flies; an eye so affected; SWELLING BLIGHT. Also **bungey eye.**
1892 G.L. JAMES *Shall I try Aust.?* 242 [Sandy Blight] is also known as 'bung-eye', because, as an Irishman would say, when you open your eyes in the morning, the lids are tightly closed, and require no small amount of fomentation to get them open. **1901** K.L. PARKER in M. Muir *My Bush Bk.* (1982) 116 Sometimes they would only have swelling blight—'bungey eye' colloquially called—from a fly sting which the blacks used to cure by pressing on hot budtha twigs, and the whites with the blue-bag.
2. Comb. **bung-eye fly.**
1932 H. PRIEST *Call of Bush* 147, I was stung in the eye by a small fly that inhabits the river country. I have heard it spoken of as the 'bung eye' fly—and very appropriately too.

bunging, *vbl. n. Obs.* [Of unknown origin.] In the collocation **bunging the mill**: see quots.
1895 J.T. RYAN *Reminisc. Aust.* 258 'Bunging the mill' was a term used for grinding flour with a steel mill . . among the first settlers. **1907** C. MACALISTER *Old Pioneering Days* 122 'Bunging the Mill', as it was called, was largely practised on the stations. This was simply the grinding of wheat in a little steel grinding machine (or mill).

bungwall /'bʌŋwɔl/. [a. Yagara *bangwal*.] The fern of swampy land *Blechnum indicum* (fam. Blechnaceae), occurring in Qld., N.S.W., N.T., and elsewhere; the rhizome of the plant, an important traditional foodstuff.
1824 *Austral.* (Sydney) 21 Oct. 2 The natives . . shewed them where to find and how to use the bungwa, as they call it—a very nutritious root, something like *ferne*, but larger; it is found in swamps. **1978** K. MCARTHUR *Pumicestone Passage* 43 Their principal vegetable food was 'bungwall', the root of a fern (*Blechnum indicum*), which is still very common in the swamps along the coast.

bunji-man. /'bʌndʒə-mən/. [Poss. f. a W.A. Aboriginal language; or poss. f. Eng. *fancy-man*.] A white man with a predilection for Aboriginal women.
1975 R. BEILBY *Brown Land Crying* 4 'When you see one really crawling along you know it's a bunji-man.' A bunji-man, an adventurer in sex seeking something exotic. 'Black-velvet, that's what they call us Ab'rig'nes.' **1981** A. WELLER *Day of Dog* 54 Ya the cunning one, Val. But ya better not be givin' that ole bunji man a bit on the side.

bunny. A simpleton or innocent; a scapegoat. Freq. in *pl.*
1943 S.J. BAKER *Pop. Dict. Austral. Slang* (ed. 3) 16 *Bunny*, a simpleton or fool, an easy victim for exploitation. **1972** *Bulletin* (Sydney) 12 Aug. 16/3 Employers became increasingly fed up with being 'the bunnies' of the government.

bunya /'bʌnjə/. [a. Yagara *bunya-bunya*.] The Queensland tree *Araucaria bidwillii* (fam. Araucariaceae), the cones of which contain seeds which are eaten raw, roasted, or pounded to a flour; the seeds of the tree. Also **bunya bunya,** and *attrib.*
1842 *Colonial Observer* (Sydney) 7 Dec. 662/2 The fruit is at present as large as a pear, and resembles a pine-apple: it grows, however, about five or six times larger, and is then covered with nuts, which contain the proper bunya fruit. **1870** *Illustr. Sydney News* 6 July 3/1 The Government have proclaimed that the cutting and removal of certain timber named the 'Bunya Bunya' and the 'Queensland nut' is now absolutely prohibited. **1881** C.F. CHUBB *Fugitive Pieces* 18 Delighting the gins in their gunyahs, Grinning like wild cats, with pearly teeth chewing the bunya, Washing it down with a choogar-bag.

bunyip /'bʌnjəp/. [a. Wemba-wemba *banib*.]
1. A fabulous amphibious monster supposed to inhabit inland waterways. Also *attrib.*
1845 *Sydney Morning Herald* 12 July 2/5 On the bone being shown to an intelligent black, he at once recognised it as belonging to the 'Bunyip', which he declared he had seen. **1907** A. MACDONALD *In Land of Pearl & Gold* 83 The presence of some natives fantastically adorned with snake, kangaroo, and emu skins—bunyip-men, as they are called—was a sign that developments might take place later.
2. *fig.* See quot. 1852. Also *attrib.*, esp. as **bunyip aristocracy.**
1852 G.C. MUNDY *Our Antipodes* II. 19 A new and strong word was adopted into the Australian vocabulary: Bunyip became, and remains, a Sydney synonym for *imposter, pretender, humbug,* and the like. **1853** *Sydney Morning Herald* 16 Aug. 5/3 Here they all knew the common water mole was transferred into the duck-billed platypus, and in some dislocant emulation of this degeneration, he supposed they were to be favoured with a bunyip aristocracy.
3. *transf.* See quot. 1952.
1875 R. BRUCE *Dingoes* 123 Six horsemen urge with voice and whip The cattle in the rear, And teach each surly bunyip A little wholesome fear. **1952** A.C.C. LOCK *Travels across Aust.* 271 'Now and again we have a combined muster. . . Sometimes we strike a few bunyips.' A bunyip . . was a beast that had grown to full size without being branded.
4. *transf.* BOOMER *n.*² Also **bunyip bird.**
1909 E. ASH *Austral. Oracle* 31 The bittern is certainly what our early colonists called the 'swamp bull' or 'bunyip'. **1954** C. BARRETT *Wild Life Aust. & New Guinea* 112 Bitterns are sometimes called 'Bunyip-birds'. . . When a booming call breaks the silence of a lonely swamp, it is the voice of the 'Bunyip-bird', largest of the five kinds of bitterns found in Australia.
Hence **bunyipian** *a.*, fantastic.
1899 *Bulletin* (Sydney) 4 Feb. 14/4 His unique treasure utters small plaintive cries . . and was captured under bunyipian circumstances.

Burdekin /'bədəkən/. [The name of a river in n.e. Qld.] Used *attrib.* in Special Comb. **Burdekin duck, (a)** the shelduck *Tadorna radjah* of n. Aust., having a white head, neck, and underparts exc. for a chestnut band across the breast; RAJAH SHIELDRAKE; **(b)** a slice of meat, battered and fried; **plum,** the tree of Qld. and New Guinea *Pleiogynium timorense* (fam. Anacardiaceae) which yields both timber and a dark plum-like fruit, palatable when ripe; the fruit itself; *sweet plum*, see SWEET *a*.¹; **vine** *obs*., the vine of Qld. and N.S.W. *Cissus opaca* (fam. Vitaceae), the tubers of which are a traditional foodstuff; **vomit,** an attack of vomiting (see also *Barcoo sickness* BARCOO A. 2, BELYANDO SPEW).

1867 F.J. BYERLEY *Narr. Overland Exped. Northern Qld.* 6 The beautiful **Burdekin duck** (*Tadorna Radjah*). **1945** T. RONAN *Strangers on Ophir* 39 A meat fritter known in the Kimberleys as a 'Burdekin Duck', and on the Burdekin as a 'Kimberley Oyster'. **1889** J.H. MAIDEN *Useful Native Plants Aust.* 599 *Spondias pleiogyna* . . 'Sweet Plum', or '**Burdekin Plum**'. Wood hard, dark brown, with red markings, resembling American walnut. **1888** *Proc. Linnean Soc. N.S.W.* III. 553 *Vitis opaca*. . . '**Burdekin vine**'. . . The tubers . . are eaten after immersion in hot water. **1918** C. FETHERSTONHAUGH *After Many Days* 272 What I called the Belyando Spue was a most trying ailment. . . The Western fellows called it the 'Barcoo sickness', the Northern men termed it the '**Burdekin vomit**'.

burka /'bəkə/. *Obs.* [a. Gaurna *burga*.] See quot. 1858.

1841 C.G. TEICHELMANN *Aborigines S.A.* 6 The male sex is divided into several ages, the last of which is called *burka*, an old, full adult. **1858** W.A. CAWTHORNE *Legend of Kupirri* 30 'Burka.'—An aged man, the last stage through which men pass, and in whom the knowledge of all charms, ceremonies, &c., is deposited.

Burketown mosquito net. [f. the name of a town in Qld.] See quots. 1960 and 1976.

1960 B. HARNEY *Cook Bk.* 89 A Burketown Mosquito Net. Drink a bottle of O.P. rum with swamp-water. **1976** B. SCOTT *Compl. Bk. Austral. Folk Lore* 380 A Burketown mosquito net is a bottle of rum and a cowdung fire.

burl. [Br. dial. (esp. Scot.) *birl*, *v.* to spin, twirl.] A try or attempt; esp. in the phr. **to give it a burl,** to venture an attempt.

[N.Z. **1917** *Chrons. N.Z. Exped. Force* 16 May 137/2 So up they [*sc.* pennies] went and spinning well And betters cried 'Fair 'burl'!' **1924** *Truth* (Sydney) 27 Apr. 6/3 Burl, to try anything.] **1927** F.C. BIGGERS *Bat-Eye* 10 These dancin' stunts was jakeloo—a bloke Jist prats 'is frame in, an' selects a girl: A sorter joint wear blokes can sit an' smoke, W'ile waitin' round ter give the 'op a burl. **1981** C. JAMES *Charles Charming's Challenges* 37 We're real thrilled You're giving *Timbertop* a burl, Your Grace.

burley, var. BERLEY *n*. and *v*.

burn, *v*.

1. *trans.* With **off**: to clear (land) for agricultural purposes by burning the vegetation; to burn (timber, stubble, etc.). Also *intr*.

1798 D. COLLINS *Acct. Eng. Colony N.S.W.* (1798) I. 334 For cutting down the timber of an acre of ground, burning it off, and afterwards hoeing it for corn, the price was four Pounds. **1849** S. & J. SIDNEY *Emigrant's Jrnl.* 162 Other settlers do not burn off at all, but saw the logs into pieces and square chain them off the land.

Hence **burning off** *vbl. n.*

1827 *Monitor* (Sydney) 30 Aug. 619/3 When '*the burning off*' commenced, the spare time would vary from two or three days, to nine or ten, out of a month.

2. To drive a motor vehicle at high speed. Also as *n.*

1963 G. BAHNEMANN *Hoodlum* 155 He parked his bike at the kerb and waited. Soon the others burned around the corner as if hunted by the devil in person. **1967** J. HIBBERD *White with Wire Wheels* (1970) 164 He . . wants to know how the Valiant performs. I've promised to take him for a burn when I've driven it in.

burn, *n.* [U.S. *burn* burning of vegetation, in order to clear land.] In clearing land: the controlled burning of standing or felled vegetation; the area so burned; also, the burning of sugar cane prior to its being cut. Also **burn-off.**

1849 W. ARCHER Diary 14 Apr., Found that the threshers had finished . . and that the burn of rushes in Bull Pad[dock] was also at an end. **1910** *Emu* X. 127 Throwing together the branches and debris after the burn-off. **1981** *Woman's Day* (Sydney) 16 Sept. 27/3 An announcement that a big daytime burn of cane would be used in the film had farmers clamouring for their burn to be seen around the world.

Burnett salmon. Chiefly *Qld.* [f. the name of the *Burnett* River in s.e. Qld., from which the type specimens came.] LUNGFISH. See also *mud fish* MUD 1.

1886 F. COWAN *Aust.* 18 The Burnett Salmon of the Queensland streams: Ceratodus: nor fish, nor flesh, nor good red herring. **1928** M.E. FULLERTON *Austral. Bush* 222 Among the best table-fish native to the fresh-water rivers is the Burnet [*sic*] River salmon. **1951** T.C. ROUGHLEY *Fish & Fisheries Aust.* 159 This lungfish [*Ceratodus forsteri*], now referred to always as the 'Queensland lungfish' . . was often called by the local settlers 'Burnett salmon'.

burnt, *ppl. a.*

1. With **up**: burned dry, scorched.

1828 Tas. Colonial Secretary's Office Rec. 1/12 98, The Grass is so completely burnt up that the Oxen are dyeing [*sic*]—Two of them have died this week. *c* **1960** C. MACKNESS *Clump Point & District* 74 The memory of the bitter struggle on 'the bit of eaten-out, burnt-up bush that killed poor old Dad and his spuds and weedy cows' refused to die.

2. With **out**: destroyed by fire, esp. bushfire; (of people) afflicted by the loss of property so caused.

1851 *Empire* (Sydney) 13 Feb. 3/3 The flock masters . . are compelled to move their flocks, and such of them as have not runs in watered districts . . as are the unfortunate owners of the runs that are 'burnt out'. **1880** *Argus* (Melbourne) 13 Jan. 6/2 Extensive bush-fires are raging close to the town, and the heat has been excessive. Early in the afternoon it became rumoured that two people had been burnt out, but this proved subsequently to be incorrect. Only the fencing of the places was destroyed.

3. In the collocation **burnt feed,** new and succulent growth following a fire.

1837 *Colonist* (Sydney) 27 Apr. 134/3 The young grass was shooting up with the usual vivid green peculiar to 'burnt feed'. **1859** W. BURROWS *Adventures Mounted Trooper* 141 They can get a patch of 'burnt feed', as the young shoots are called, which spring up on a piece of land that has been on fire.

4. *Mining. Obs.* In the collocation **burnt stuff**: see quot. 1852.

1852 J. BONWICK *Notes of Gold Digger* 38 The burnt stuff, or burnt quartz of the miners, is a ferruginous cement binding quartz pebbles. . . In the Ballarat holes the 'Burnt quartz' has been found ten feet thick. **1853** MRS C. CLACY *Lady's Visit to Gold Diggings* (1963) 65 This was succeeded by a strata almost as hard as iron—technically called 'burnt-stuff'.

'burra. Also **burra.** Shortened form of KOOKABURRA.

1901 'A. FERRES' *Free Selector* 97 The burra laughs the rosy dawn Into the sweet spring day. **1904** E.S. EMERSON *Shanty Entertainment* (1910) 10 While 'burras, magpies and galahs jeered at them.

burrawang /'bʌrəwæŋ/. Also **buddawong, burrawong**. [a. Dharuk *buruwan*.] Any of several plants of the genera *Macrozamia* (fam. Zamiaceae) and *Cycas* (fam. Cycadaceae), esp. *M. communis*, having palm-like fronds and pineapple-like cones yielding nuts edible after treatment (see quot. 1901). Also *attrib.*

c 1790 W. DAWES *Grammatical Forms Lang. N.S.W., Names of fruit in N.S.W.*.. buruwang [etc.]. **1825** B. FIELD *Geogr. Mem. N.S.W.* 244 A kind of dwarf palm, called *burrawang* by the natives (zamia spiralis). **1901** *Bulletin* (Sydney) 21 Dec. 16/2 The buddawong nuts, when crushed and soaked in running water for about 10 hours, may with safety be boiled and eaten. They are very plentiful along N.S.W. South Coast. **1943** *Bulletin* (Sydney) 7 July 12/1 Tree-fern tops and squatty burrawongs.

burr-cutter. One employed (in the country) to cut burr-bearing plants.

1890 *Braidwood Dispatch* 30 Apr. 4/1, I know.. the edge of Little Plain.. by the burr-cutter's old camp. **1964** H.P. TRITTON *Time means Tucker* (rev. ed.) 15 We met a chap who wanted burr cutters for Pine Ridge.. and thought we would have a go at it... Wool infested with burr was almost worthless... The only method of control used then was to dig them out, rake them.. and burn them.

Hence **burr-cutting** *vbl. n.*

1894 *Bulletin* (Sydney) 6 Jan. 23/3 Whether boundary-riding, burr-cutting or droving he did not like being called Doctor.

burry, var. BOORIE.

bursaria /bɜ'sɛərɪə/. [The plant genus *Bursaria* was named by Spanish botanist A.J. Cavanilles (*Icon. et Descr. Plant.* (1797) IV. 30) f. L. *bursa* bag or satchel, referring to the pouch-like fruit capsules.] **a.** Any species of the Austral. genus of prickly shrubs and small trees *Bursaria* (fam. Pittosporaceae) which is cultivated in Aust. and w. Europe. **b.** With distinguishing epithet, as (*Vic.*) **sweet bursaria,** *B. spinosa,* bearing sweet-smelling flowers; *native box,* see NATIVE *a.* 6 a.; *prickly box,* see PRICKLY.

1814 R. BROWN *Gen. Remarks Bot. Terra Australis* 10 Both Pittosporum and Bursaria are found within the tropic. **1914** E.E. PESCOTT *Native Flowers Vic.* 33 'Sweet Bursaria'.. is called in many localities the 'Christmas Bush'.

burst, $n.^1$ [Br. dial. *burst* an outburst of drinking: see EDD.]

1. A drinking bout, esp. in the phr. **on the burst.** See also BUST *n.*

1852 *V & P* (N.S.W. L.A.) II. 769, I should say perhaps one-third of the miners are incorrigible drunkards, who are eternally at these houses; many of these are very lucky; they frequently fall into good claims, and make large hauls in the course of the week; then they go 'upon the burst', as they call it, and drink until all their earnings are 'knocked down', and they then go to work again. **1912** S. LOCKE *Dawsons' Uncle George* 79 They all have the idea that Sydney's a fair petunia of a place... So when they want a burst, they hails a steamer, an' over here they comes an' lets themselves go. Blows themselves right out. **1942** C. CASEY *It's Harder for Girls* 98 He was a real damn nuisance, allus in arguments an' stayin' on th' burst for as much as a fortnight at a time.

2. *fig.*

1912 E. FISHER *Kiss of Dolly Day* 57 Pure thoughts are borne to realms above. My soul is on the burst.

burst, $n.^2$ *Obs.* [Abbrev. of BURSTER $n.^2$] SOUTHERLY BUSTER.

[N.Z. **1851** C.O. TORLESSE *Canterbury Settlement* 9 The north-west wind.. somewhat resembling the 'hot winds' of Australia.. is almost invariably succeeded by one from the south-west, which in the summer time is a cool and pleasant guest, but in the winter season what is aptly denominated 'a burst', and sometimes lasts for two or three days, being generally accompanied by rain, if not snow and sleet.] **1894** *Jrnl. & Proc. R. Soc. N.S.W.* XXVIII. 140 In the early morning on the day of a 'burst' the sky is white and hazy of aspect.

burster, $n.^1$ *Obs.* [f. *burst* to break (in various contexts).] A heavy fall from a horse; BUSTER $n.^3$

1845 *Bell's Life in Sydney* 18 Jan. 2/2 In the first heat the rider of Rob Roy got a terrific burster, shortly after turning the sharper angle we have already complained of or rather on his way down the hill. **1886** R. HENTY *Australiana* 245 A gallop after wild horses over the plains, with the prospect of a 'burster' when crossing the crab-hole country, was exciting.

burster, $n.^2$ *Obs.* [Shortened form of SOUTHERLY BURSTER.] A strong sudden wind, esp. from the south.

1854 M.B. MOWLE *Diary* 16 May, The Cosmopolite sailed today for Hobarton... All the vessels left the Bay with a N.E. wind, they have been detained here three weeks in consequence of the late constant southerly gales, occasionally being lured out for a few hours, or a day by the promise of a north-easter & then sent flying back by a '*burster*' from the southward. **1903** W. CRAIG *My Adventures* 233 The intense heat and the clouds of dust raised by northerly 'bursters' during the summer season were hard to bear.

bursting, *vbl. n. Timber-getting.* The splitting of a log into four or more billets, out of each of which a sleeper is cut.

1882 A.J. BOYD *Old Colonials* 25 You want to be very particular in a tree for staves. They ain't split like palings or shingles. We run them off the 'bursting way', as it is called, across the grain. It isn't exactly across the grain, but that's the best way I can explain it. **1903** *Bulletin* (Sydney) 24 Dec. 36/3 Sleepers are split, 'on the flat', the 'boarding' way of the tree—i.e. if you can see in imagination, the sleepers in the log before they are cut out, they lie side by side round the bole. And herein is [the reason why sleepers are split and not sawn. If sawn the most would be made of the block and the sleepers sawn 'on the flat' the 'bursting' way of the tree and be no use.

bush, *n., a.,* and *attrib.* [a. Du. *bosch* woodland. Used earliest in S. Afr. and U.S.: see OED(S $sb.^1$ 9 and Mathews.]

A. *n.* Freq. with **the.**

1. Natural vegetation of any kind; a tract of land covered in such vegetation.

1790 R. CLARK *Jrnl.* 15 Feb. 133 They had run into the bush, on there [*sic*] seeing the Boat pulling towards them. **1978** 'B. WONGAR' *Track to Bralgu* 25 The settlers cleared the bush long ago and the country hereabouts looks like a skinned beast.

2. Country which remains in its natural state; country which has not been settled or which has resisted settlement.

1803 *Sydney Gaz.* 17 Apr., Upon perusing a paragraph in one of your Papers, which suggested the propriety of converting the Rocks into an Academy for *tumblers,* I rather conceived that you might, with an equal promise of success, recommend some parts of the *bush* for an improvement in the talent of *dancing,* as there much instruction might be expected from the assistance of the accomplished *kangaroo.* **1978** R.A.F. WEBB *Brothers in Sun* 9 Huge areas of grasslands, dense jungles of rainforest, Texas-size deserts and great tracts of arid semi-desert, lush wheat lands set amid lonely splendour—all have one thing in common. They are called 'the bush'.

3. The country as opposed to the town; rural as opposed to urban life; those who dwell in the country collectively (see quot. 1983).

1825 *Howe's Weekly Commercial Express* 23 May 3 There is at this moment many a poor settler living up the country, buried in the bush. **1972** *Bulletin* (Sydney) 2 Sept. 39/1 There is a strong counter-tradition that asserts that Lawson hated the bush and revelled in the city. **1983** *Ibid.* 22 Mar. 24/2 Labor found out in 1975 that it had alienated the entire rural electorate mainly because it had removed the petrol subsidy to the bush—a move of irrefutable economic responsibility. The coalition offered to restore the differential on petrol prices. It did not fully honor that promise, but it did win the bush.

4. In phr. with various verbs of motion, esp. **to take (to) the bush**.

a. Orig. of convicts: to escape from custody or justice; to run away; (of animals) to run wild. See also ABSCOND b.

1804 *Sydney Gaz.* 10 June, One of the ringleaders was apprehended, and two others escaped into the bush before they were accused. **1813** *HRA* (1921) 3rd Ser. II. 20 Betaken themselves to the Woods, *or Bush*. **1821** *Ibid.* IV. 22 To prevent Prisoners of the Crown from absconding from the former Town and running into the Bush. **1826** *Ibid.* (1922) 3rd Ser. V. 290 Prosecuting four other men, who had absconded from the Public Works and taken to the Bush. **1833** *Currency Lad* (Sydney) 23 Mar. 3 Mr B. . . gave the fellow sixteen shillings, who said, 'we would not take this only we are starving,' and jumping from the chaise, 'now you may hang us as soon as you please.' Then they took the bush. **1847** *Maitland Mercury* 10 July 2/4 The cart came in contact with a stump, and an overturn was the consequence, throwing out both men, and breaking off the shafts of the cart, with which the two horses immediately started, taking the bush. **1978** H.C. BAKER *I was Listening* 170 To disperse—take to the bush while the bombing was on.

b. To leave the town for the country. See *to go bush* BUSH *n.* 5c.

1829 E.G. WAKEFIELD *Let. from Sydney* 10, I bore my disappointment as well as could be expected; and, to use a colonial phrase, 'took boldly to the bush'. **1904** *Bulletin* (Sydney) 1 Sept. 36/2, I met an old schoolmate recently . . who had 'taken to the bush' sixteen years before. . . And their name is legion—the bright, capable young men who get the 'bagman' brain-twist and go out and waste their splendid forces carrying preposterous swags about the bush and running down the Government.

c. Of Aborigines: to return to traditional life.

1841 G. GREY *Jrnls. Two Exped. N.-W. & W.A.* II. 371 You see the taste for a savage life was strong in him, and he took to the bush again directly. **1847** E.W. LANDOR *Bushman* 187 Most . . betake themselves to the bush, and resume their hereditary pursuits.

5. Freq. passing into *adj.*. In the phr. **to go bush**. Also with other verbs of motion.

a. To escape, to disappear from one's usual haunts.

1908 MRS A. GUNN *We of Never-Never* 90 Considering ourselves homeless, the Maluka decided that we should 'go bush' for awhile. **1984** *Sydney Morning Herald* 24 Mar. 6/3 A farmer 'went bush' for nine days after shooting a neighbour in a dispute over water supplies and boundary gates. . . After the shooting Elford ran off and lived for nine days in the bush, surviving on bird's eggs and sour lemons.

b. Of Aborigines: to return to traditional life. See also quots. 1922 and 1956.

1908 MRS A. GUNN *We of Never-Never* 170 Maudie, discovering that the house was infested with debbil-debbils, had resigned and 'gone bush'. **1922** 'J. BUSHMAN' *In Musgrove Ranges* 247 It was a strange position for a white man to be in, and if Stobart had not had a stout heart he would have given way to despair, and either 'gone bush' entirely as some white men have done, and become a full member of the warragul tribe, or he would have committed suicide. **1956** A.C.C. LOCK *Tropical Tapestry* 120 That's where you see the 'white' black fellows—white men who have gone bush with the natives, like.

c. To leave the beaten track and travel cross-country.

1913 W.K. HARRIS *Outback in Aust.* 131 A little distance out we 'went Bush' (that is, left the track). **1976** E. BAIN *Ways of Life* 37 They left the road and started bush.

d. To leave urban life for that of the country; to visit the country.

1916 *Bulletin* (Sydney) 17 Aug. 6/4 It was good to 'go bush', even a paltry 250 miles from Sydney. **1986** *Nat. Times* (Sydney) 14 Feb. 3/4 Prime Minister Bob Hawke, who a few days earlier had been bush to talk with farmers in trouble . . reacted with considerable concern to the news.

e. Of flora and fauna: to become wild.

1921 *Bulletin* (Sydney) 13 Jan. 20/2 My dog put up a domestic cat 'gone bush' and chased it to twin saplings. **1965** R.H. CONQUEST *Horses in Kitchen* 148 The horses . . were mostly little short of the brumby class, descendants of horses that had gone bush earlier.

B. *adj.* and *attrib.*

1. a. Of or pertaining to natural vegetation or to a tract of land covered therein: cf. BUSH *n.* 1.

1828 *Tasmanian* (Hobart) 12 Dec. 4 Then give me still the bush-clad hill Where sweet the daisies blow. **1907** *Truth* (Sydney) 24 Feb. 3/1 They formed a lengthy chain, with a break at each crossing street or road. And there are not many breaks in a mile out in that bush suburb.

b. Of artefacts: made with branches, saplings, etc., as materials.

1839 D. MACKELLAR *Austral. Emigrant's Guide* 8 Great care ought to be taken that they are not folded in any of the bush folds that may be found by the road side, for fear of getting infected, *scab* and *catarrh* being very prevalent throughout the Colony. **1981** A.B. FACEY *Fortunate Life* 10 Aunt's place, which was only a hut, was built near a big hill. It consisted of bush poles for uprights with hessian pulled tight around the poles.

2. a. Of Aborigines: living outside white society. **b.** Of flora and fauna: indigenous; also used of these as a source of food. Cf. BUSH *n.* 2.

1827 P. CUNNINGHAM *Two Yrs. in N.S.W.* II. 30, I have now taken out upwards of six hundred convicts . . versed in every species of cunning, address, and plausibility, yet none of that number ever exceeded in these particulars a bush acquaintance of mine on Hunter's River. **1870** E.B. KENNEDY *Four Yrs. in Qld.* 99 Bush game is poor eating when cooked on a camp fire. **1911** *Bulletin* (Sydney) 13 July 14/4 What about the friendliest bush animal? I place them: (1) The W.A. boodie rat, (2) native cat, (3) carpet snake.

3. a. Of or pertaining to rural, as opposed to urban, life: cf. BUSH *n.* 3.

1845 T. MCCOMBIE *Adventures of Colonist* 185 The landlord . . was not by any means a good specimen of Bush publicans. **1964** *Bulletin* (Sydney) 14 Nov. 25/3, I feel half-way bush, half-way city.

b. By extension, and with connotations depending on whether the perception is urban or rural: of artefacts, constructions, etc., simple, (crudely, ingeniously, etc.) improvised; of people, lacking an urban sophistication; of domestic animals, useless, unmarketable, fit to be put 'out to grass'.

1835 J. LHOTSKY *Journey from Sydney to Austral. Alps* 36 There is . . no *artificial road* whatever, nothing than better or worse bush-ways, tracked and kept in order as far as they are so, by the working of the iron wheels. **1849** S. & J. SIDNEY *Emigrant's Jrnl.* 53 If you have seen navvies in a beer-shop after twenty-four hours' drinking, you will know what Bush-drinking is like. **1890** 'R. BOLDREWOOD' *Colonial Reformer* II. 114 Whenever this 'pound' holds cattle of *only one class* you hear the deciding shouts of the cockatoo stockmen, who are doing the 'reviewing' safely on the fence, of 'Fat', 'Bush', 'Stranger', or 'Calf-yard', as the case may be. **1982** *Open Road* (Sydney) v. 12/3 A bush retread—a tyre with good casing and tread which has blown at the beading, and which was fitted over the top of a worn tyre. They were often used as spares in the depression days.

C. 1. Comb. bush ballad, balladist, bed, biscuit, black, blanket, boy, -bred a., **camp, carpenter, carpentering, constable, cook, costume, dress, duty, experience, eye, fare, fashion, feed, fence, girl, hand, horse, hospitality, hotel, hut, inn, knife, labour, labourer, land, life, lore, mad, madness, mile, missionary, native, nurse, paddock, parson, picnic, poet, pub, races, rider, riding, road, school, servant, shanty, shower, song, sport, style, tea, timber, town, township, track, traveller, travelling, tucker, work, worker, yard.**

[**1888** bush ballad: D.B.W. SLADEN *Austral. Ballads & Rhymes* p. xxiv, Consequently the commonest types of Australian Poems are Bushman's Ballads à la Gordon, often very spirited, but often also very rugged.] **1895** A.B. PATERSON *Man from Snowy River* p. iii, In my opinion this collection comprises the best bush ballads written since the death of Lindsay Gordon. **1898** *Bulletin* (Sydney) 11 June (Red Page), One does not depreciate our prized **bush-balladists. 1846** C. ROWCROFT *Bushranger Van Diemen's Land* III. 199 He left his **bush-bed** and came out into the clear space. **1845** C. HODGKINSON *Aust., Port Macquarie to Moreton Bay* 28 Breakfasted on toasted bacon, and **bush biscuit**, (thin cakes of flour and water baked on hot embers). **1830** R. DAWSON *Present State Aust.* 123 Been see mandoehah (foot or footsteps) belonging to **bush black.** **1845** *S. Austral. Odd Fellows Mag.* Apr. 67 With the assistance of an old **bush blanket** we sluiced. **1856** J. BONWICK *Bushrangers* 48 All naughty **bush boys** who surrendered themselves before a certain day were to be forgiven. **1849** A. HARRIS *Guide Port Stephens* 115 In three cases out of four, the **bush-bred** youth possesses at least the virtues of innocence. **1846** N.L. KENTISH *Work in Bush Van Diemen's Land* 83 **Bush Camp** at the junction of the 'Wilmot' with the 'Forth'. **1841** G. ARDEN *Recent Information Port Phillip* 108 **Bush carpenters**, sawyers, splitters. **1859** F. SINNET *Acct.* '*Rush*' *Port Curtis* 43 A powerful Scotchman . . has developed . . a genius for **bush-carpentering**. **1826** Tas. Colonial Secretary's Office Rec. 1/34 113, Three persons in the shape of **Bush Constables** . . called here. [N.Z. **1873** ST. JOHN *Pakeha Rambles* in N.M. Taylor *Early Travellers* (1959) 554 The untutored paws of a **bush cook**.] **1887** *Bulletin* (Sydney) 19 Feb. 8/4, I, once a Guardsman, now a bush-cook, was comparatively virtuous. **1847** G.F. ANGAS *Savage Life & Scenes* I. 118 All in '**bush**' **costume**, with tether-ropes and pannikins slung to our saddles, jogged on through the winding paths. **1836** *Hobart Town Almanack* 165 Bushrangers were committing outrages in different parts of the country, and a tall athletic man in a **bush dress**, and armed, had been seen there four or three times. **1833** *Hill's Life N.S.W.* (Sydney) 28 Dec. 2 The Police, who were on **bush-duty**, had taken up their quarters at a hut belonging to Mr O'Loughlin. **1869** *Illustr. Sydney News* 29 Sept. 262/1 They even require advice in the laying out and clearing of their grants of land for building their houses or huts, and other matters learnt only by actual **bush experience**. **1878** *Austral.: Monthly Mag.* (Sydney) I. 491 'And I could not tell . . what were there—cows, or calves, or bullocks. I question if I could see them at all if I were not told where they were.' I had not got my **bush eyes. 1827** P. CUNNINGHAM *Two Yrs. in N.S.W.* II. 158 Your muskets will furnish you with birds of various kinds; and with a brace of good grayhounds you will never lack kangaroos and emus; so that your **bush-fare** is a true sportsman's feast. **1848** R.D. MURRAY *Summer at Port Phillip* 257 Cooked . . after the **bush fashion**—that is to say, in a very indifferent style. **1841** *Colonial Observer* (Sydney) 25 Nov. 59/1 **Bush feed** is abundant: we do not recollect since we knew the district having seen the Plains so truly verdant. **1828** Tas. Colonial Secretary's Office Rec. 1/47 33, About a quarter of a mile of Post and Railing fence has been put up, and there are now four to five acres of wheat growing within a **Bush fence. 1849** A. HARRIS *Emigrant Family* (1967) 221 The self-helpfulness of the **bush girl**. **1850** S. SIDNEY *Female Emigration* 35, I should also require two or three good **bush hands** (*prisoners*) from Hyde-Park Barracks. **1842** R.G. JAMESON *N.Z., S.A., & N.S.W.* 69 We should have been unable to continue our journey, but for the skilful piloting of an old **bush-horse** from Van Dieman's Land, whose rider gave him a loose rein. **1855** W. HOWITT *Land, Labor & Gold* I. 173 Is this, thought I, **bush hospitality? 1865** *Illustr. Sydney News* 15 July 3/3 The **bush hotel** is . . little better than a sort of aristocratic extensive gunyah: walls of slab and roof of bark. **1830** *Sydney Monitor* 2 June 2/2 Three hundred decent families . . will be blown and washed out of their **bush huts** (for of *timber* there is none). **1847** J.D. LANG *Phillipsland* 157 We halted at a respectable **Bush Inn. 1843** C. ROWCROFT *Tales of Colonies* III. 195, I took out my **bush-knife** and presented it to Musqueeto. **1846** *Port Phillip Gaz.* 11 Nov. 2 Very extensive employers of **bush labour** say that they find old convicts preferable to free or bound emigrants. **1832** *Colonist* (Hobart) 23 Nov. 2/3 Depriving . . every settler, stock-keeper and **bush-labourer** of the only means of warning. **1827** *Tasmanian* (Hobart) 3 Mar. 4 The report represents . . the maize as promising where it has been sown in rich alluvial soil—but a failure on **bush land**. **1831** *HRA* (1923) 1st Ser. XVI. 285 A **bush life** being attended with much less expense. **1862** G.T. LLOYD *Thirty-Three Yrs. Tas. & Vic.* 121 Accompanied by two companions learned in **Bush lore**. **1924** LAWRENCE & SKINNER *Boy in Bush* 221 'The man's potty!' '**Bush mad**,' supplemented Rackett. **1974** *Gayzette* (Sydney) 19 Sept. 19/4 **Bush madness** was a common phenomenon. Therefore men were employed to work in pairs. One male was the actual worker, the other was his 'mate'. **1862** A. POLEHAMPTON *Kangaroo Land* 252 **Bush miles** are long, and evening closed in ere I reached the desired goal. **1864** N. SHREEVE *Short Hist. S.A.* 37 There are both **missionaries**, who travel up the country for the purpose of preaching to the different shepherds. **1801** *Hist. Rec. N.S.W.* (1896) IV. 514, I mean to keep a **bush native** constant soon, as they can trace anything so well in the woods. **1909** *Truth* (Sydney) 17 Oct. 1/3 The ladies in the back-blocks are to receive the doubtful benefit of '**bush nurses**'. **1847** *Moreton Bay Courier* 17 July 3/2 What was once a bush **paddock** is now a well-appointed race-course. **1873** M. CLARKE *Holiday Peak* 19 It was considered a point of honour for all travelling clergymen ('**bush parsons**', the Bullocktowners called them) to give an evening at the 'brick edifice'. **1901** *Advocate* (Burnie) 8 June 4/2 The **bush picnic** arranged on the Darling Downs, Queensland, for the Duke and Duchess. **1846** N.L. KENTISH *Work in Bush Van Diemen's Land* 55 The **Bush-poet** blushes at the thought of . . great merit having been attributed to him. **1880** J.B. STEVENSON *Seven Yrs. Austral. Bush* 137 Dan . . kept a **bush pub** out on the River road. **1880** J.B. STEVENSON *Seven Yrs. Austral. Bush* 133, I think it would be a good idea for **bush races**, to give a prize for the best man and horse at camp work. **1850** *Bell's Life in Sydney* 22 June 3/2 Certainly the best **bush-rider** in this country. **1848** H.W. HAYGARTH *Recoll. Bush Life* 62 The native youths particularly excel in **bush-riding**. **1827** P. CUNNINGHAM *Two Yrs. in N.S.W.* I. 123 A made **bush-road** is one where the brushes have been cleared, banks of rivers and gullies levelled, and trees notched, on the route, and cuts made on the faces or tops of hills when necessary, the remainder being all left in a natural state; while a *natural* bush-road signifies one to which nothing has been done except notching the trees, the carts simply following each other's tracks. **1852** G.C. MUNDY *Our Antipodes* III. 61 There was a humble hedge-school—or rather **bush-school**, for there is hardly a mile of hedge in Australia. **1842** *Geelong Advertiser* 10 Jan. 3/2 The **bush servants** being in the interior for some time, come to town to spend their money. **1885** *Illustr. Austral. News* (Melbourne) 2 Jan. 10/3 The true haven of the sundowner is the **bush shanty**. **1981** *Austral. Women's Weekly* (Sydney) 18 Nov. 21/2 Good outback style: **bush shower** dangling from a gum tree, hessian-screened dunny (with reading material, of course) and even, a bath. **1846** N.L. KENTISH *Work in Bush Van Diemen's Land* 35 My **Bush song**, is much too long To need a peroration. **1858** T. MCCOMBIE *Hist. Colony Vic.* 22 Like most young men born in Australia, he was much addicted to **bush sports**. **1838**

Colonist (Sydney) 9 May 4/1, I proposed to Mr Hill .. to make an excursion in our **bush style** to the banks of the Murray. **1848** *Adelaide Miscellany* 2 Dec. 303 **Bush tea** .. is generally made excessively strong .. is seldom softened by milk, and always sweetened with very coarse, dark sugar. **1846** *Port Phillip Gaz.* 16 Sept. 3 (Advt.), Port Phillip **bush timber. 1874** A. TROLLOPE *Harry Heathcote* 18 Small towns, as they grow up, are called **bush towns**—as we talk of country towns. **1880** J.B. STEVENSON *Seven Yrs. Austral. Bush* 117 A good specimen of a **bush township**. One long straggling street upon the bank of a river, the backs of all the houses on the river side turned upon the splendid sheet of water, fringed with giant gums, which lay below them. **1837** *Tegg's N.S.W. Pocket Almanac* 46 **Bush track** leading across Kenyon's bush track into the great southern road. **1834** G. BENNETT *Wanderings N.S.W.* I. 113 Tea, sugar, a tin-pot, and a blanket, are the requisites for a **bush-traveller. 1844** *Sydney Morning Herald* 25 July 2/2 His supplies will be carried on pack-horses, it being evident that in **bush travelling** any sort of vehicle must cause great delay. **1895** W.H. WILLSHIRE *Thrilling Tale Real Life* 41 It is well known that after rain the natives want to wander about in search of **bush-tucker. 1846** *Port Phillip Gaz.* 11 Nov. 4 They have been accustomed to sheep, and **bush work** generally. **1891** M. ROBERTS *Land-Travel & Sea-Faring* 75 Like many **bush workers**, he had made quite enough money for a spree. **1846** C.P. HODGSON *Reminisc. Aust.* 41 The **bush-yard** .. received the herd from the run.

2. Special Comb. **bush bass,** an improvised musical instrument (see quot. 1979); **bellows,** see quot. 1856 (2); **bread,** DAMPER 1; **(-bred) cattle,** wild cattle; **Contingent,** *Bushmen's Contingent,* see BUSHMAN 8; **craft,** see quots. 1883 and 1963; **fever,** a sickness associated with bush living; a longing to return to the bush; **happy** *a.,* mentally disturbed; **-head,** BUSHY *n.* 1; **honey,** honey from the nests of wild bees; **house, (a)** a roughly-built dwelling in the country; **(b)** a garden shelter in which plants needing protection are cultivated (see quot. 1890, 1); **(c)** a dwelling occupied by a rural commune (see quot. 1981); **liar,** one who tells tall stories; **oysters,** see quot. 1971; **pickles,** see quot. 1962; **walk, (a)** of an Aboriginal, WALKABOUT *n.* 2; **(b)** a hike; also **-walker, -walking** (see quot. 1945); **week, (a)** a time in which people from the country come to, and are reputed to go 'on' the town; **(b)** a period of licence, esp. in the phr. **what do you think this is—bush week?**; **(c)** at some universities, a period of student festivity.

1966 R. MORLEY *Cool Change* 81 She gets a brumby and goes miles off looking for someone with a **bush-bass** who can raise some sort of a band. **1979** R. EDWARDS *Skills Austral. Bushman* 150 The standard bush bass is made by turning a tea chest upside down, boring a hole in the centre of the base, and passing a string from this hole to the top of the stick. .. The butt of the stick rests on the outer edge of the box, and varying tensions are applied to this to produce the changes in tone. **1856** J. BONWICK *Bushrangers* 52 While Michael stooped down to apply the **bush bellows**, his mate leaped upon him. **1856** G. WILLMER *Draper in Aust.* 155 But for our perseverance in puffing away with the bush bellows (our hats). **1840** S. *Austral. Rec.* (London) 7 Nov. 292 The mode of conversion to damper—the true **bush-bread**—is as unartificial as any other part of our unartificial repast. **1833** J. KING *Information Van Diemen's Land* 10 Dairy cows bred up by the hand, sell at about £15 each. .. **Bush bred cattle** .. varying from £3 to £6 each. **1842** *Tasmanian Jrnl. Nat. Sci.* I. 319 A stock-yard, made and used for collecting bush cattle. **1900** *Advocate* (Burnie) 2 Jan. 2/8 The fund for the **Bush contingent** now amounts to £12,000. **1851** C.P. FORD *Emigrant Family* 54 The early age at which he had begun, had given him an opportunity of acquiring **bush-craft. 1883** E.M. CURR *Recoll. Squatting Vic.* 428 By the term *a good man in the bush* .. is meant a man well versed in bush craft; one who can find his way fairly; track, shoot, and swim well; who can bear hunger, thirst and fatigue; is able to look after his horses under circumstances of every sort; understands the Blacks and their ways; has a good idea of where to look for water, and so on. **1963** I.L. IDRIESS *Our Living Stone Age* 16 Soon she will be following in mother's footsteps, using all her inborn and taught bushcraft to find her quota of the small game and particularly the plant foods for the tribe. **1854** W. HOWITT *Boy's Adventures* 135 He was attacked by a fever which the men called the **bush-fever. 1944** *Aust. Week-End Bk.* 104 'Troppo' is a new disease—or rather an old disease with a new name—sometimes known as **'bush happy'**, 'mulga mania', 'Darwin dementia', 'Moresby Madness' .. or just plain 'nuttiness'. **1950** J. MORRISON *Port of Call* 66 That ain't no reason for 'er to go pokin' mullick at the **bush-'eads**. These city sheilas are all the same. **1907** *Bulletin* (Sydney) 15 Aug. 44/2 Going for **bush honey** is sometimes called beehunting. **1837** *Perth Gaz.* 21 Oct. 994 All he had to provide for in the first instance, was the erection of a **bush-house**, and the clearing and cultivating of a few acres of land. **1890** A. MACKAY *Austral. Agriculturist* (ed. 2) 228 The Bush-House .. is becoming, and deservedly so, a special feature of the Australian garden. .. The principle is .. to get shade, and shelter, without shutting out the air. .. The roof should be as high as convenient, say eight feet at least. Then the sides and roof are covered with bush material, laid as evenly and neatly as possible. The brushwood of young tee tree answers admirably; laths are also used; also Chinese matting, and close-mesh wire netting .. and at no great outlay, the bush house may be ornamental as well as useful. *Ibid.* 229 Nurserymen and gardeners are taking more advantage of the opportunities the bush-house offers for raising seedlings of all kinds. **1981** *Nimbin Newsletter* 19 Nov. 1 'Bush houses', those communal dwellings which have aroused much controversy on the North Coast, are now sanctioned—if they meet minimum standards—and multiple occupancy is recognised as an acceptable lifestyle. **1892** *Bulletin* (Sydney) 5 Nov. 20/2 We met the **bush liar** in all his glory. He was dressed like—like a bush larrikin. .. He had been to a ball where some blank had 'touched' his blanky overcoat. **1971** *Bulletin* (Sydney) 27 Nov. 48/3 Mick Hunter attributes his 'morbid, unbalanced lust for the opposite sex to over-indulgence in **bush oysters**'. He describes the taste this way: 'Testicles are to meat as monstera deliciosa are to fruit.' **1962** MARSHALL & DRYSDALE *Journey among Men* 170 **Bush pickles**, according to the old recipe, are made by stirring a bottle of Worcester sauce into a large tin of plum jam. This can be varied to suit individual tastes. **1846** J.L. STOKES *Discoveries in Aust.* II. 184 Malay boy, work, have house; Swan River boy, no work, **bush walk. 1892** MRS F. HUGHES *My Childhood in Aust.* 83 Now let me tell you of some of our bush walks. **1948** H.A. LINDSAY *Bushman's Handbk.* 137 For **bushwalkers**, who carry all their gear on their backs and are on the move most of the time, we have not yet worked out a method for killing the flies. **1930** *Bulletin* (Sydney) 15 Jan. 23/2 Dave was busy scuffling corn when one of those **bush walking** enthusiasts shouted out to him. **1945** A. RUSSELL *Bush Ways* 57 Bush-walking is something more than tramping along a well-worn road by day, and sleeping at inns and lodging houses. It is something more than making a mountain traverse under the comfortable guidance of a compass. These things are .. only correlated parts of a transcending purpose—the search for the spiritual meaning of the hills. **1919** *Lone Hand* Feb. 10 **Bush week**. .. An excellent movement was started some time ago in a quiet way to organise a Bush festival in the City of Sydney. It is proposed that it should last a week, and thoroughly represent every phase of primary and secondary production. **1945** S.J. BAKER *Austral. Lang.* 76 The time-honoured chant of derision *What's this, bush week?* **1948** *Bulletin* (Sydney) 11 Aug. 22/2 It was bush week or something in Murrayville, and when we blew off the train into the pub there was nothing between us and several long cool beers except most of the local cockies, townsmen, shophands, their friends, relatives and acquaintances. **1972** *Bulletin* (Sydney) 12 Aug. 17 *(caption)* In Canberra, forestry students provided their commentary on the strike in the Bush Week procession.

3. In the names of flora and fauna: **bush apple,** *black apple,* see BLACK *a.*[2] 1 a.; **canary,** *white-throated warbler,*

see WHITE $a.^2$ 1 b.; **cat,** a wild cat; **cucumber,** ALUNQUA; **devil,** *Tasmanian devil,* see TASMANIAN *a.* 2; **fly,** the fly *Musca vetustissima* (fam. Muscidae), which settles persistently on the eyes, mouth, and other moist parts of the body; **grass,** any of several native grasses used as fodder on uncultivated land; **hay,** hay made from native grasses; **kangaroo,** a medium-sized kangaroo; **lark,** the small bird *Mirafra javanica* (fam. Alaudidae) of n. and e. Aust., resembling the introduced skylark in plumage and song; **mouse,** any of many small native mammals, esp. the marsupial hopping mouse, *Notomys,* and the *marsupial mouse* (see MARSUPIAL 1); perh. also native rodents of the genus *Pseudomys;* **rat,** any of several rat-sized native marsupials and rodents, esp. native species of *Rattus;* **tick,** *scrub tick,* see SCRUB *n.* 5; **turkey,** *brush turkey,* see BRUSH $n.^1$ B. 2.

1935 DAVISON & NICHOLLS *Blue Coast Caravan* 40 Valleys dotted with dark clumps of **bush apple** and turpentine. **1918** *Bulletin* (Sydney) 14 Feb. (Red Page), *White-throated Flyeater* (**Bush Canary**) and other members of the genus *Gerygone*. **1933** J. MCCARTER *Love's Lunatic* 124 He had seen the same crazy look in **bush cats** inadvertently caught in rabbit traps. **1937** M. TERRY *Sand & Sun* 213 Another common bush delicacy was the alunqua, some call it the **bush cucumber. 1833** J. BACKHOUSE *Narr. Visit Austral. Colonies* (1843) 123 Another animal, .. black, with a few irregular white spots, .. is commonly known by the name of the Devil, or the **Bush-Devil. 1838** T.H. JAMES *Six Months S.A.* 71 The large **bush flies** had settled on him by thousands. **1827** *Monitor* (Sydney) 24 July 534/3 The discord of *3d. an acre rent* for the use of His Majesty's **bush-grass,** soon put an end to the *country* portion of this national chorus. **1827** *Monitor* (Sydney) 1 Nov. 781/3 **Bush Hay** from £6 to £9 per ton. **1832** BACKHOUSE & TYLOR *Life & Labours G.W. Walker* (1862) 45 The Forest and the **Bush Kangaroo,** and the Wallaby. **1865** J. GOULD *Handbk. Birds Aust.* I. 404 Horsefield's **Bush-Lark. 1872** G.S. BADEN-POWELL *New Homes for Old Country* 321 The '**bush-mouse**', a perfect kangaroo of.. diminutive proportions. **1855** *Trans. Philos. Soc. Vic.* I. 70 The **bush rat** (*P*[*erameles*] *Gunnii*). **1872** A. MCFARLAND *Illawarra & Manaro* 43 A former proprietor stocked it with hogs... The **bush-tick**.. settled upon, and killed every one of them. **1836** J. BACKHOUSE *Narr. Visit Austral. Colonies* (1843) 425 The **Bush Turkey,** *Allectura Lathami,* inhabits these forests.

bush, $v.^1$ [f. prec.]

1. *intr. Obs.* Freq. with **it**: to camp, often involuntarily, in the bush. Also as *vbl. n.*

1825 *Austral.* (Sydney) 5 May 2 One of those fathers of the Colony.. recollects when it was a common thing for people to lose themselves in the bush at Wooloomooloo— and after walking about in the woods a whole day, lay themselves down in despair and 'bush it' within 10 minutes walk of the camp! **1838** T.H. JAMES *Six Months S.A.* 289 We bushed for the night under a low scrubby tree with nothing for the horses to eat, and *no water.* **1842** E. IRBY *Mem.* (1908) 60 A smart shower or two came on in the night, but on the whole we passed our first night's regular bushing pretty well.

2. *intr. Obs.* With **it**: to go into the bush; to make an expedition into unknown country.

1828 *Tasmanian* (Hobart) 15 Aug. 4 The bullocks bolted, and I had to *bush it* after them. **1846** *Bell's Life in Sydney* 27 June 1/4 Since the successful termination of Leichardt's expedition from this place to Port Essington, I, in common with many others, have felt an inkling to bush it in search of something wonderful and new.

3. *intr. Obs.* With **it**: to live, usu. under conditions of hardship, in the bush.

1839 *Port Phillip Patriot* 26 Aug. 3 For a young man, not afraid of bushing it, and determined to look after his shop himself, I am inclined to think that he would make more of £1000 at Port Phillip in five years, than he could at South Australia. **1874** R.P. FALLA *Knocking About* (1976) 20 Can you feast upon mutton, drink gallons of tea? Then come o'er the waves and bush it with me.

4. *trans.* To turn (cattle) out into open country. Also *fig.*

1959 *Bulletin* (Sydney) 16 Sept. 18/3 The cream-carter.. took one look at the cow and said positively: 'She ain't got brucellosis!' whereupon Daisy's owner said, 'Well, if the carter says she hasn't got the disease, we won't waste time testing her!' and he promptly bushed the cow. **1980** ANSELL & PERCY *To fight Wild* 118 I'd smelt the rib bones hanging up the night before, and reckoned I'd get one more feed off them before I had to bush the rest—throw them out.

Hence **bushing (it)** *vbl. n.*

1839 W.H. LEIGH *Reconnoitering Voyages* 105 'Bushing it', was the only thing to be done; and, for this purpose, we struck into the woods. **1846** S. DAVENPORT *Lett.* 18 Feb. in *S. Australiana* (1971) Sept. 69 Bushing is the best life.. a man sleeps with the sun and rises with it too.

bush, $v.^2$ [Back-formation from BUSHED.] *trans.* To disorient (a person), to cause 'to lose one's bearings'.

1916 *Bulletin* (Sydney) 27 Apr. 22/3 A man I knew could find his way anywhere. You couldn't 'bush' *him.* **1950** G. FARWELL *Surf Music* 216 'Takes more'n that to bush me, son'... 'If you'd not shown up by dark, I was sending Quartpot after you.'

bush-bash, *v.* [f. BUSH *n.* 1 + *bash* to strike.] *intr.* SCRUB-BASH 2. Also *trans.*

1967 L. BEADELL *Blast Bush* p. ix, Short cuts through mulga scrub (known as 'bush-bashing') can be an interesting experience but is attended with real dangers. **1972** R. ERICKSEN *West of Centre* 41 He had spent.. a large part of the preceding fifteen years bush-bashing new tracks and patrolling old ones.

Hence **bush basher** *n.*

1971 L. BEADELL *Bush Bashers* 1 Several hundred miles north was the road my little camp of six bush bashers had made, extending for nearly a thousand miles east to west.

Bush Brother. A member of the BUSH BROTHERHOOD.

1908 C.H.S. MATTHEWS *Parson in Austral. Bush* 213 Bush christenings are a constant source of delight to the Bush brother. **1978** R.A.F. WEBB *Brothers in Sun* 9 Their title is expressive of their relationship with the people of the bush over the last three-quarters of a century—that of Bush Brothers.

Bush Brotherhood. [f. BUSH *n.* 3 + *brotherhood* a fraternity.] An Anglican missionary organization founded to provide a peripatetic ministry in remote areas.

1897 *Theology* (London) (1947) May 165 Bishop Dawes himself spoke. Half-humorously he called the venture a 'Bush Brotherhood'. **1962** *N.T. News* (Darwin) 9 Jan. 5/6 Changes in the administration of the Darwin Church of England parish will follow a reunion of the Bush Brotherhood.

bush capital. [f. BUSH *n.* 3 + *capital.*] A (derisive) name for Canberra, the capital city of the Commonwealth of Australia. (See also quot. 1911.)

1906 *Truth* (Sydney) 19 Aug. 1/3 The search for a Bush Capital has already cost Australia £14,406. **1911** A. MARSHALL *Sunny Aust.* 68 It is all very well to laugh at the 'Bush Capital'; but Washington was laughed at in just the same way before it grew to be the fine city it is.

bushed, *ppl. a.* [f. BUSH $v.^1$]

1. Lost in the bush.

1844 H. MCCRAE *Georgiana's Jrnl.* 6 Feb. (1934) 107 Even with the aid of his compass, Captain Reid thinks we run the risk of being bushed for the night. **1981** A. WILKINSON *Up*

Country 49 After all .. we didn't find our cliff, and it was only John's sharp eyes which prevented us from being 'bushed' for the night.
  2. *transf.* and *fig.*
  1885 MRS C. PRAED *Austral. Life* 29 He added with true Australian simplicity, 'I get quite bushed in these streets. London is an awful place.' **1978** M.J. BURTON *Bush Pub* 126 'That's got 'im completely bushed,' the Fanatic whispered to me. 'It would be all bloody Eskimo talk to 'im.'

bushfire.
  1. A fire which burns through (freq. extensive) areas of natural vegetation, often causing loss of life and property. Also *attrib.*
  1832 *Sydney Monitor* 1 Dec. 2/6 Another large bush fire has been very destructive in the neighbourhood of Windsor. **1956** A. MARSHALL *How's Andy Going?* 160 February—the bushfire month.
  2. *Obs.* A camp-fire; occas., a fire indoors (in the bush).
  1832 *Currency Lad* (Sydney) 1 Sept. 3 She was sitting about an hour before daylight near a bush fire contiguous to the house. **1903** M. MOORE-BENTLEY *Sketched from Life* 43 The fire blazed and crackled as only Australian bush fires can, the blue smoke, escaping the chimney, filling the room with incense of eucalyptus fragrance.
  3. *Obs.* A controlled burning of natural vegetation for a particular purpose: see quots. 1845 and 1865.
  1844 L. LEICHHARDT *Jrnl. Overland Exped. Aust.* 29 Nov. (1847) 54 Recent bush fires and still smoking trees betokened the presence of natives. **1845** R. HOWITT *Impressions Aust. Felix* 70 The convicts, busily employed at their bushfires, burning off and clearing the land. **1865** G.F. ANGAS *Aust.* 41 Many of these bush fires are caused by the blacks burning the scrub to drive out game.
  4. *fig.*
  1888 H.S. RUSSELL *Genesis Qld.* 163 Active, energetic, prince of 'bushmen' and good fellows, full of 'bush-fire', he was a man not likely to sit down satisfied with the first thing he happened to meet with. **1898** W. DOLLMAN *Bush Fancies* 59 A drop of whisky, or 'bush fire', used to get into the hut.
  5. Special Comb. **bushfire blonde,** see quot. 1943; **brigade,** a volunteer fire-fighting organization; **fighter,** a member of a bushfire brigade.
  1943 S.J. BAKER *Pop. Dict. Austral. Slang* (ed. 3) 17 **Bushfire blonde,** a red-haired girl. **1904** *Truth* (Sydney) 3 Jan. 2/6 A **bush fire brigade** has been formed at Brown's Creek. **1980** *Sydney Morning Herald* 4 Nov. 1/1 **Bushfire fighters** at Waterfall took advantage early today of a drop in wind to start back-burning operations.

bushie, var. BUSHY.

bush lawyer.
  1. One who parades an only fancied knowledge of the law; one who 'lays down the law'.
  1835 *True Colonist* (Hobart) 4 Sept. 7/4 The able oratory of the bush lawyer, whose time of servitude, in one of the worst of Mr O'Connor's gangs, expired last week. **1985** *Daily Mirror* (Sydney) 25 July 41/2 (*heading*) Bush lawyer fires off telling shots.
  2. A member of the legal profession who has a rural practice.
  1976 N.V. WALLACE *Bush Lawyer* 181 A bush lawyer is perhaps in an even better position to study humanity in all its aspects than parson, priest, or doctor.
  3. LAWYER VINE.
  [N.Z. **1853** C.W. ADAMS *Spring in Canterbury Settlement* 44 Hour after hour we toiled on, sometimes making our way through masses of thorn, and the long and clinging bramble, called by colonists the 'bush-lawyer', sometimes scrambling down steep banks.] **1878** *Austral.: Monthly Mag.* I. 36 The 'bush lawyer' twists and twines, half strangling the eucalypti. **1905** A. SEARCY *In Northern Seas* 15 There is another pet plant, known as the 'waitawhile' or 'bush lawyer', both very appropriate names.

bushman.
  1. One skilled and experienced in travelling through bush country and able to do so without getting lost or into difficulty.
  1825 B. FIELD *Geogr. Mem. N.S.W.* 369 Set out .. from Bong Bong .. taking with us Joseph Wild (a constable of the district of Argyle, well known as a bushman on similar excursions to the one we were about to take). **1979** DOUGLAS & HEATHCOTE *Far Cry* 107 My infallible bushman's experience at finding my way through trackless bush was no help to me here.
  2. *Obs.* BUSHRANGER n. 1.
  1827 'OFFICER OF LINE' *Military Sketch-Bk.* II. 322 She pointed to a man lying in the long grass, and bleeding profusely—it was a desperate Bushman of the name of Collyer. **1897** M. CLARKE *Stories Aust.* 104 The bushranger, in high glee, filled a 'goblet'... 'There!' cried Howe; 'these fires have cost a pretty penny. Here's success to the bushman's tinder-box, and a blazing fire to his enemies!'
  3. One who lives in the country as opposed to the town; one who displays the manners, practical skills, etc., of a country-dweller, with connotations often depending on whether the perception of the user is urban or rural; cf. BUSH B. 3 b.
  1832 *Colonial Times* (Hobart) 21 Mar., What! go to Swan River and be sea-sick all the passage, and die before you get there; and, perhaps, not get a husband after all, or only get a bushman? **1842** *Melbourne Times* 18 June 4/1 His flocks encrease, and the wool pays all, While his generous board's at the traveller's call; By the clear river side he improves his time—Oh, the Bushman's the stay of Australia's clime. **1982** R. HALL *Just Relations* 336 Course I'm only an old bushman sittin up on my little mountain like Jacky; and you've travelled the world.
  4. A rural employee, esp. an (unskilled) labourer able to work in a range of capacities.
  1843 J.F. BENNETT *Hist. & Descr. Acct. S.A.* 101 Stockmen .. searching for stray cattle .. are often in the 'Bush' for days... When night comes, the horse is unsaddled and .. the bushman .. covers himself with his blanket. **1943** H.G. LAMOND *From Tariaro to Ross Roy* 27 Shearers then were bushmen, all round men, who did all classes of station work.
  5. *Timber-getter,* see TIMBER.
  1847 A. HARRIS *Settlers & Convicts* (1953) 86 If I wanted employment as a bushman I could not miss it here; as there were sawyers, splitters, squarers, firewood getters scattered through the bush hereabouts in all directions. **1980** *Sydney Morning Herald* 30 May 7/2 A bushman out looking for timber to cut reported that he almost tripped over a tiger sleeping on a rock.
  6. SWAGMAN.
  1872 G.S. BADEN-POWELL *New Homes for Old Country* 428 The multitudes of 'swagmen', or 'bushmen', wandering about the country will do as little as possible for a living. **1954** *Bulletin* (Sydney) 16 June 12/4 All this talk about 'blueys' and 'Matildas' may be O.K. for you blokes in the 'inside' country, but bushmen in the Territory and Kimberleys always refer to 'swags'.
  7. *pl.* Abbrev. of *Bushman's Contingent;* in *sing.,* a member of this.
  1900 *Truth* (Sydney) 4 Feb. 5/1 Another man failed in horsemanship for both the previous contingents, but managed to pass for the Bushmen. **1901** *Bulletin* (Sydney) 4 May 32/2 The derider of work was now one of a 'mob' .. upon their way to South Africa. He was a full-blown 'Bushman'—a 'Soldier of the Queen'.
  8. In special collocations: **Bushman's Bible,** a name for *The Bulletin* (see BULLY); **bushman's clock,** *settler's clock,* see SETTLER 3 b.; **Bushman's Contingent,** a body of volunteer troops equipped through public

subscription for service in the Boer War; **Bushman's Home** obs., a guest house catering chiefly for country-dwellers (see quot. 1868).

1888 *Bulletin* (Sydney) 15 Dec. 5/4 (heading) The Bulletin is the **Bushman's Bible.** **1846** C.P. HODGSON *Reminisc. Aust.* 165 The Laughing Jackass is a comical creature . . well and truly stiled the **Bushman's clock.** **1900** *Pastoral Times* (Deniliquin) 17 Feb. 2/3 When it was first decided to form a **bushmen's contingent** to go to South Africa Mr Frank V. Weir . . was one of the first to volunteer for service. **1868** W.M. HUGO *Hist. First Bushmen's Club* (1872) 14 Some few months ago we called public attention to the importance of establishing a **Bushmen's Home,** in order to keep poor fellows who come down from the country out of the hands of harpies who prey upon them on their occasional visits to Adelaide.

Hence **bushmanlike** *a*.

1862 H. BROWN *Vic. as I found It* 89, I had crept up to the horses in . . a very scientific, bushman-like manner.

bushmanship. The ability to travel through, or live in, inhospitable country, esp. that which is unfamiliar and unsettled, without getting into difficulty.

1848 H.W. HAYGARTH *Recoll. Bush Life* 134 Notwithstanding all that has been said of the great sagacity of savages in tracking, and of their quickness in catching a distant sound, I strongly suspect that the white man, when he has been accustomed to this kind of 'bushmanship' at an early age, generally proves his superior. **1967** M. SELLARS *Carramar* 46 In recognition of their bushmanship these two young men were made Fellows of the Royal Geographical Society and were given grants of money.

bushrange, *v.* [Back-formation f. BUSHRANGER *n.* 1.] *trans.* To hold up and rob (travellers, dwellings, etc.); to steal. Also *absol.*, and *fig.*

1841 *Omnibus & Sydney Spectator* 4 Dec. 75/1, I, in company with two other men bushranging, was going along the road. **1850** *Bell's Life in Sydney* 15 June 3/1 Then black mugs an' white mugs can run a cleer race, Tal they bushrange the counthry right out uv a face. **1976** C.D. MILLS *Hobble Chains & Greenhide* 123 They were anathema to station managers in the matter of 'bush-ranging' feed for their bullocks. As well to stand between a lioness and her cubs as a bullocky on a bare route with feed through the bordering fence.

bushranger. [f. BUSH *n.* + *ranger* one who ranges over a tract of country. Prob. of U.S. origin: cf. BUSH *n.* and see Mathews *bossloper* and *bushranger*.]

1. One who engages in armed robbery, escaping into, or living in, the bush in the manner of an outlaw; orig. an escaped convict subsisting in the bush, often by resort to robbery (see quot. 1822).

1801 J. ELDER et al. *Jrnl. Rio to Port Jackson* 5 Mar. 25 It is said also, which we are very sorry to observe, that of these Bushrangers, that Williams . . is one. **1822** J.T. BIGGE *Rep. State Colony N.S.W.* 108 The convicts assigned to military officers, according to the custom and necessities of that day, were obliged to furnish to their masters, and to procure for themselves, a certain quantity of kangaroo flesh; and having first gone into the woods for these temporary supplies of food, they gradually acquired a knowledge of the country, and of the means of supporting themselves in it. To this at length they were driven; and the predatory habits of these men, who have since received the common appellation of bush-rangers, have continued from the year 1805, with more or less of violence and rapacity, until the month of October in the year 1818.

2. *Obs.* One skilled in travelling through the bush; BUSHMAN 1.

1805 Banks Papers 19 July XX., If the Bush rangers will always bring plants from the remote parts of their tours, I can form a good idea of what distance they have been. **1843** J. HOOD *Aust. & East* 176, I confess I was again induced to wish that my boys had remained at home in Britain instead of becoming bushrangers in New Holland.

3. *transf.* and *fig.*

1855 F.H. WILSON Overland Expedition No. 2 19 Mar., He abused them terribly and said that we were a regular lot of bushrangers—going from one man's run to another and eating off all the grass—and did not care for anybody. **1977** R. MACKLIN *Paper Castle* 138 Basically, I suppose, everyone has the public interest at heart. But by Christ some of those bushrangers on the other side go the long way round.

bushranging, *vbl. n.*

1. The practice of the bushranger (sense 1); the committing of armed robbery by one who escapes into the bush; orig. living as a fugitive in the bush. Also *attrib.*

1813 *HRA* (1921) 3rd Ser. II. 441 There are no means which can be devised that will so effectually destroy the System of Bush-ranging, as a rigid observance of this order. **1886** R. HENTY *Australiana* 177 He commenced his bushranging tactics under the *rôle* of being the 'swagman's' friend.

2. *Obs.* Travelling cross-country, esp. in an unfamiliar or unsettled region.

1821 Macarthur Papers XII. 57, I reached Home in good time, and in much better health than when I set out bushranging. This sort of Life is to me an efficacious, and at the same time agreeable restorative. Roaming in lonely independence thro' almost trackless wilds, and contemplating without interruption the vast Sublimity of nature, we lose the recollection of those unpleasant circumstances which within the influence of Sydney's Pollutions continually to [*sic*] occur to harrass the Mind. **1839** W.H. LEIGH *Reconnoitering Voyages* 129 Night came on, and we again sought the bush, like all bush ranging, 'The mixture as before'.

3. *fig.* Also as *ppl. a.*

1939 K. TENNANT *Foveaux* 425 The once notorious Bud Pellager . . had taken to a mild and lucrative form of bushranging as owner of a garage on the Main Western Highway. **1951** D. CUSACK *Say no to Death* (1959) 258 You're a bush-ranging, cowardly old bitch! You've black-marketed here all the war, and you're black-marketing still.

bush telegram. BUSH TELEGRAPH *n.* 2.

1894 J.M. MACDONALD *Thunderbolt* 143 These bush telegrams were a source of wonder to the police from the old country. A lighted fire, a burning tree, a slip-rail tied up, a tree allowed to fall across the road, blazed trees, the smoke of a leaf fire rising high in the air—these all had different meanings, cyphers to the bushrangers who could read them. **1980** *Sporting Globe* (Melbourne) 1 July 2/7 Evidently the 'bush telegram' is . . fast as Carlton knew of South's plans to play Teasdale almost as quickly as the Swans.

bush telegraph, *n.*

1. *Hist.* One who alerts a bushranger to the movements of police or to a potential victim. Also *fig.*

1864 *Bell's Life in Sydney* 23 Apr. 2/5 Two or three noted 'bush-telegraphs' were among the crowd who had come in from the country to obtain one more look at the robbers. **1920** B. CRONIN *Timber Wolves* 210 Them [*sc.* white cockies] and the red-bills seem to hold the job of bush telegraph for the rest of the wild things.

2. An informal network by means of which information is conveyed in remote areas; the information or message so conveyed; a rumour; MULGA WIRE 1. Also *attrib.*

1864 *Sydney Punch* 13 Aug. 91/1 The following correspondence has been forwarded to us for publication. It was carried on through the medium of 'Bush Telegraphs'. **1933** S. GRIFFITHS *Rolling Stone on Turf* 200 In 'bush telegraph' fashion the news had spread far and wide. **1965**

D. Martin *Hero of Too* 246 The bush telegraph had it that her lover had struck up a friendship with a rich landholder's son from Balranald.

3. A means of long-distance communication used by Aborigines, usu. employing smoke signals; the message so conveyed; Mulga wire 2.

1930 A.E. Yarra *Vanishing Horsemen* 42 It was a signal that could be seen for miles—the smoke signal of the aboriginals: the bush telegraph. **1952** A.M. Duncan-Kemp *Where Strange Paths go Down* 11 Smoke signals, the bush telegraph which relays in some intricate secret code, tribal news to the outside world.

Hence **bush telegraphist** *n.*, **bush telegraphy** *n.*

1965 D. Martin *Hero of Too* 172 Peter was the greatest **bush telegraphist** of his time. Nothing went on but Quinn knew of it. **1900** *Truth* (Sydney) 17 June 6/3 The nature of the country and the system of **bush telegraphy** prevented arrests.

bush telegraph, *v.* [f. prec.] *trans.* To communicate (information) by means of bush telegraph. Also *intr.* and with a person as obj.

1926 A.A.B. Apsley *Amateur Settlers* 98 A set of blacks could 'bush telegraph'. **1953** *Bulletin* (Sydney) 11 Mar. 13/1 The ranger doing his annual round is bush-telegraphed long before he arrives, and it must be a continual surprise to him to note the rapid decline in the dog population. **1966** 'E. Lindall' *Northward Coast* 160 They were now heading directly into tribal country. Every move they made would be bush-telegraphed ahead.

bushwhack, *v.* [Back-formation f. Bushwhacker.] *intr.* To work, esp. as an unskilled labourer, clearing ground in the country; to fell timber. Freq. as *vbl. n.* and *ppl. a.*

[N.Z. **1907** W.H. Koebel *Return of Joe* 287 Cutting good [plug] terbaccer as if you was bushwacking.] **1927** M.H. Ellis *Long Lead* 187 The resulting regime was, to quote Mrs Aeneas Gunn, a 'friendly, bushwhacking old Government'. **1929** P.R. Stephensen *Bushwhackers* 68 Only a few lived on after the white men came to whack the bush; lived as adjuncts, almost as spectators of the bushwhacking. **1935** H.H. Finlayson *Red Centre* 24 After weeks of bush-whacking in the mulga.

bushwhacker. [U.S. *bushwhacker* backwoodsman.]

1. One who lives in the country (as opposed to the town): cf. Bushy *n.* 1.

1896 M. Hornsby *Old Time Echoes Tas.* 60 Berresford was an old hermit, or bush-whacker. **1981** P. Barton *Bastards I have Known* 19 He hated city-slickers (we had many years to go before Jack accepted us as fellow bushwhackers).

2. *Hist.* A member of the *Bushman's Contingent* (see Bushman 8).

1900 *Tocsin* (Melbourne) 22 Mar. 1/3 Bushwhacker Davey's case disclosed wretched bungling on the part of the Defence authorities. **1901** *Ibid.* 22 Aug. 4/4 You know 'Ginger' wot went away with the 'bushwhackers' to the war?

Hence **bushwhackery** *n.*

1961 *Bulletin* (Sydney) 1 Feb. 32/4 He is nowadays capitalising on his outback years and imposing a self-conscious bushwhackery on his gullible urban admirers.

bushy, *a.* and *n.* Also **bushie.** [f. Bush *n.*3 + -Y.]

A. *adj.* Countrified; lacking the (supposed) refinements of urban life.

1848 *Satirist & Sporting Chron.* (Sydney) 18 Mar. 1/2 We have heard quite enough of *Flash Bill B.*, the horse-dealer... Bill has quite enough to do to look after Mary, and keep her from getting *bushy*. **1975** X. Herbert *Poor Fellow my Country* 1029 'Someone'd sell you the Harbour Bridge within an hour.' 'D'you think I'm that bushy?'

B. *n.*

1. One who lives in the country as opposed to the town; one whose manner or appearance betrays this.

1887 *Tibbs' Pop. Song Bk.* 4 And they poke fun at our clothes. Their own are made to measure, Fitting neatly round the leg, And Bushy's got a tenner Where they've only got a peg. **1986** *Sydney Morning Herald* 15 Feb. 6/3 Tony Adams, an AWU member and lifelong Labor voter, takes his first break... 'Ever since they started treating bushies like dirt, I've stopped being keen on the bastards.'

2. *Hist.* A member of the *Bushman's Contingent* (see Bushman 8).

1900 *Truth* (Sydney) 4 Mar. 5/1 One very drunk Bushie reeled all over the shop, and for a time disorganised the whole outfit. **1903** J. Green *Story Austral. Bushmen* 188 Here a Bushie tipped me a knowing and unbelieving wink.

business. *Aboriginal English.*

1. Traditional lore and ritual; the exercise of this. Also *attrib.*

1943 W.E. Harney *Taboo* 170 'That not proper wind, but blackfellow business.' Blackfellow business! Some native in another tribe had cast some magic and sent this wind to destroy the tribe. **1985** I. White et al. *Fighters & Singers* 13 They might make him a man.. this year at business time up here.

2. In the collocation **Sunday business,** an exclusive ritual (see quots. 1949 and 1962). Also **Sunday business ritual**.

1949 Harney & Elkin *Songs of Songman* 143 The women.. go off to 'dance', that is perform their secret corroboree, their 'Sunday Business'. **1962** D. Lockwood *I, Aboriginal* 32 Henceforth the ceremony was strictly men's Sunday-business.. in which [the women] could not take part. **1964** —— *Up Track* 124, I have seen dozens of corroborees and a few big Sunday Business rituals among today's aborigines.

bust, *n.* [Br. dial. *bust* var. of Burst *n.*^{1}: see OEDS *sb.*^{3} a.] A drinking bout. Freq. in the phr. **on the bust.**

1865 *Sydney Punch* 23 Sept. 554/2, I may here explain that the term 'on the bust' is an expression having reference to a curious religious practice of the inhabitants of these parts, who.. enter into a solemn vow to spend a certain, or uncertain, sum of money, usually all they are possessed of, in the purchase of spirituous liquors. **1891** J. Fenton *Bush Life Tas.* (1965) 164 A man's nothing without a 'bust' now and then.

bust, *v.* [f. prec.] *trans.* To squander (money), usu. on liquor. Formerly also with **up.**

1878 'Ironbark' *Southerly Busters* 24 In Bathurst's busy streets He got upon the spree... He said he'd 'busted up his cheque'. **1980** J. Wright *Big Hearts & Gold Dust* 153 Come on mate, we've got a fiver to bust.

buster, *n.*^{1} *Obs.* [Prob. Br. dial. form of *burster* 'exhausting piece of exercise': see OED 1 b.] A cracking pace, something which 'takes the wind out of one'.

1865 *Austral. Monthly Mag.* (Melbourne) I. 234 He went it a buster for fifteen miles, and then gave in. **1887** A. Nicols *Wild Life & Adventure* 223 The overseer, after bringing them round, gave the mob a 'buster' at a severe pace during the next half-hour, to take the wind out of them.

buster, *n.*^{2} [Abbrev. of Southerly buster.] A strong squally wind, esp. from the south.

1873 W. Thomson-Gregg *Desperate Character* II. 179 We'll have a regular buster in no time; it was just such weather as this last year. **1985** B. Rosser *Dreamtime Nightmares* 120 We used to get a buster out in the bush, too.

buster, *n.*³ [Prob. Br. dial. form of racing slang *burster* (see BURSTER *n.*¹) a fall, a 'cropper' (cf. BUST *n.*).]

1. A heavy fall from a horse.

1878 G. WALCH *Australasia* 28 He wouldn't tell a lie to save his life, but he would put the parson in the way of a 'buster' without compunction. **1980** ANSELL & PERCY *To fight Wild* 103 Go and hop on a rough horse and maybe take a buster.

2. *fig.*

1968 *Sunday Truth* (Brisbane) 30 June 20 The Australian Government has come an incredible double buster on the design for its Vietnam campaign medal.

but, *adv.* [Not in standard use.] At the end of a phrase or sentence: though, however; 'no doubt about it'.

1853 *Austral. Gold Digger's Monthly Mag.* iv. 125 The hero of (not a hundred fights, but) famed Whitechapel, doubtless considered such a feat of valour would greatly exalt him in the eyes of Cockneyism. **1982** P. RADLEY *My Blue-Checker Corker* 3 'Wish we had ashfelt in the school playground, but.' 'Asphalt,' Grandad said. 'I thought Miss Cruikshank had you out of the habit of ending your sentences with 'but'.'

butcher, *n.*¹ *S.A.* [Prob. a. G. *becher* convivial drinking vessel, but see quot. 1956.] A glass or measure of beer; for size, see quots. 1908 and 1984.

1889 W.R. THOMAS *In Early Days* 14/2 Over a good fat 'butcher' of beer, he told me how he was getting on. **1908** M. VIVIENNE *Sunny S.A.* 255 He gives away a good few of what they call 'butchers of beer', which is a long, wide glass, holding more than a pint. **1956** S. HOPE *Digger's Paradise* 232 And what is called a 'lady's waist' in some parts of the country is generally known as a 'butcher'. This originated in bygone days when workers from the abattoirs came unwashed to the pubs after their day's toil. A proportion of drinking mugs was kept separate for them, and a mob of slaughtermen would announce themselves as 'butchers' and be given those mugs. **1984** B. DRISCOLL *Great Aussie Beer Bk.* 99 The South Australian six ounce (170 ml.) has Australia's oddest glass name, a 'butcher'.

butcher, *n.*²

1. As **butcher's (hook)**, rhyming slang for 'crook'.

a. Ill; CROOK 1 c. b. In the phr. **to go butcher's (hook)**, to complain vehemently; to speak angrily; *to go crook*, see CROOK 2 b.

1918 *Kia Ora Coo-ee* Aug. 5/1 A certain New Zealand Regiment, camped on the Jordan flats, recently came under the eagle eye of brother 'Jacko', who immediately went 'butcher's hook' or 'ram's horn' and launched forth much frightfulness. **1967** *Kings Cross Whisper* (Sydney) xxxii. 7/1 *Butchers in the comics*, sick in the guts from the rhyming butchers hook and the comic cuts.

2. In the collocation **butcher's picnic**, an occasion characterized by its lack of decorum; a motley assemblage.

1965 K. SMITH *OGF* 140 Behave yourself, Gadley, and shut your trap—this isn't a butchers' picnic. **1984** S. MACINTYRE *Militant* 137 Terms used to be bandied around like curses at a butchers' picnic.

butcherbird. [Transf. use of *butcher-bird* shrike (fam. Laniidae), referring to the bird's habit of impaling its prey on thorns.] Any of the four birds of the genus *Cracticus* (fam. Cracticidae) having black and white plumage and hooked bills, noted for their predatory habits, and (esp. the *pied butcherbird*, see PIED) as songbirds.

1827 *Trans. Linnean Soc. London* XV. 213 Mr Caley thus observes.. '*Butcher-bird.*—This bird used frequently to come into some *green wattle-trees* near my house, and in wet weather was very noisy; from which circumstance it obtained the name of *Rain-bird*.' **1974** N. CATO *Brown Sugar* 96 As purely as the butcher-birds singing in the dew of a Queensland morning.

butt. [Survival of Br. *butt* bale, pack: see OED *sb.* 10. 1.] A pack, esp. a bale of wool below standard weight.

1913 W.K. HARRIS *Outback in Aust.* 184 Mr Saxons .. 'hitched on' a well-filled 'butt' to the back of the sulky. **1976** DRAGE & PAGE *Riverboats & Rivermen* 75 To plug such holes we carried 'butts' (bags) of flour.

butterbush. [From a fancied resemblance to butter, prob. in the colour of the wood.] Any of several shrubs or trees esp. *Pittosporum phylliraeoides* (fam. Pittosporaceae), which yields seeds used for flour, an edible gum and a hard pale timber; *native apricot* NATIVE *a.* 6 a. See also *native willow* NATIVE *a.* 6 a.

1888 *Proc. Linnean Soc. N.S.W.* III. 538 *Pittosporum Phillyraeoides*... Called variously 'Butter-bush', 'Native Willow', and 'Poison-berry' tree. **1944** *Bulletin* (Sydney) 23 Feb. 13/3 Little whitewood.. or butterbush—they call it Berrigan on the Lachlan—not only provides good fodder but splendid wind-breaks.

butterfish. [From a fancied resemblance to butter, prob. in the flavour of the flesh.] Any of several unrelated fish, esp. (*S.A.*) MULLOWAY.

1849 *Adelaide Miscellany* 28 July 407 A really excellent fish for the table has fallen in my way, as large as a small salmon, and something like it in form; they call it 'butter fish': the flesh is white, but it is much richer than any other I have tasted. **1963** B. CROPP *Handbk. for Skindivers* 116 Butterfish (*Dactylopagrus morwong*).. is the Victorian name for the dusky morwong.

butterfly, *v.* Two-up. *trans.* See quot. 1967. Freq. as *vbl. n.*

1949 G. BERRIE *Morale* 251 *Butterflying*—throwing the coins so that they turn once in the air and then come to the ground without spinning. The coins are always tails upwards and the spinner always backs heads; hence the idea. **1967** F. HARDY *Billy Borker yarns Again* 2 He was butterflying the pennies.—Butterflying?—Butterflying is to throw the pennies sliding off the kip so they flutter like a butterfly but don't really spin.

Also **butterfly** *n.* (*attrib.* in quot.), **butterflied** *ppl. a.*

1946 K.S. PRICHARD *Roaring Nineties* 152 The ring-keeper might object to a spin... A '**butterfly**' fall was in order over a sandy patch, but not if there were any stones about on which she might bounce and start an argument. **1967** F. HARDY *Billy Borker yarns Again* 2 Any experienced swy player can pick a **butterflied** penny from the genuine spinning article.

butterfly cod. *Fire fish*, see FIRE *n.*

1936 N. CALDWELL *Fangs of Sea* 116 Butterfly cod, their long streamers of colour extended, streak about in panic. **1976** E. WORRELL *Things that Sting* 51 Butterfly cod are so beautifully coloured and spectacularly finned that they are easy to see in the water.

button, *n.* [Fig. use of *button.*] Used *attrib.* in Special Comb. **button grass**, **(a)** the large, tufted sedge, *Gymnoschoenus sphaerocephalus* (fam. Cyperaceae) which forms distinctive plains, esp. in w. Tas. (see quot. 1898); **(b)** the short-lived annual grass *Dactyloctenium radulans* of mainland Aust.; **stone**, AUSTRALITE.

1881 *Tas. H. of A. Jrnls.* XLI. lv. 14 A narrow strip of barren **button-grass** land. **1898** E.E. MORRIS *Austral Eng.* 74 Button-grass... So called from the round shaped flower (capitate inflorescence), on a thin stalk four or five feet long, like a button on the end of a foil. **1983** MORLEY & TOELKEN *Flowering Plants Aust.* 391 Among native grasses recorded as being used by Aborigines for food are ..

Dactyloctenium radulans, button grass, which has its seeds adhering to large husks which were methodically removed [etc.]. **1855** *Q. Jrnl. Geol. Soc. London* XI. 403 The smaller very much resembles a button without the shank; and, from this appearance, the diggers call them '**button stones**'. **1934** C. Fenner *Australites* i. 65 Even as far back as 1855, and possibly earlier, australites were well known to the gold diggers, who called them 'button stones'.

button, *v. Obs.* [Back-formation f. BUTTONER.] *intr.* To act as a buttoner. Also as *vbl. n.*

1917 C. Drew *Reminisc. D. Gilbert* 131 His job was to do the 'buttoning'. To be seen in company with the other rogues would have been fatal. **1919** A. Wright *Game of Chance* 116 'It was a slanter,' cried Mason. 'The dice were loaded; I saw that man next the thrower helping to ring the changes. He was buttoning for the other.'

buttoner. *Obs.* [Survival of Br. slang *buttoner* accomplice, decoy: see OED *button sb.* 9 and *buttoner* 3.] The accomplice of a confidence man.

1882 *Sydney Slang Dict.* 2 *Buttoners*, assistants of stage tricksters who mingle with the audience. **1918** J.H.C. Sleeman *Queer Qld.* 51 It is the same honorable tactics as the buttoner practises when assisting his friend, the cardsharper, to defraud the public.

buy, *v.* [Transf. use of the gambling expression *to buy into (a game).*] In the phr. **to buy in(to),** to involve oneself in (an activity).

1929 C.E.W. Bean *Official Hist. Aust. 1914–18* III. 613 While part of the 5th Brigade, ostensibly fresh, had thus subjected itself to considerable strain by 'buying in' (to use an Australianism) to a struggle on its flank. **1943** *Coast to Coast 1942* 188, I haven't got to buy into every fight you pick!

buzzy. *Tas.* [Of unknown origin.] BIDGEE-WIDGEE.

1952 J.R. Skemp *Memories Myrtle Bank* 94 Buzzy is the common Tasmanian name for a creeping native herb which has a very adhesive burr for a seed-head. It is sometimes called 'bidgee-widgee'. **1968** J. Woodberry *Come back Peter* (1974) 87 Treading on buzzies and prickles.

B.Y.O. /ˌbi waɪ ˈoʊ/. Acronym for the phr. *bring your own* (see BRING). Also **B.Y.O.G**(rog).

1968 *Catering* May 12/2 One important alteration in the new Liquor Control Bill is that B.Y.O. permits for unlicensed restaurants have been abolished. **1983** *Canberra Times* 11 July 9/7 The B.Y.O.G. restaurant is something of a rarity in Canberra.

by-yu /ˈbaɪ-ju/. [a. Nyungar *bayu*.] The seed of the cycad of s.w. W.A. *Macrozamia riedlei* (fam. Zamiaceae), formerly an Aboriginal plant food. Also **by-yu nut**.

1841 G. Grey *Jrnls. Two Exped. N.-W. & W.A.* II. 64 The natives had, according to their custom, buried a store of By-yu nuts. **1843** W. Pridden *Aust.* 115 The pulp of the nut of a species of palm is called *by-yu* . . an agreeable and nourishing article of food.

C

cab. [Fig. use of *(taxi) cab.*] In the phr. **first cab off (on) the rank**, the first to seize an opportunity.
   1966 S.J. BAKER *Austral. Lang.* (ed. 2) 421 It must have been in the time of horse-drawn cabs that *the first cab on the rank* came to mean early in the day. **1977** *Austral.* (Sydney) 19 July 10/5 It is unlikely the Ranger partners will agree to new terms without concessions, such as being first cab off the rank if, as expected, the Government agrees to limited mining.

cabbage garden. A nickname for Victoria. Also **cabbage patch, cabbage State**.
   1882 *Bulletin* (Sydney) 8 Apr. 8/1 There is a town in the 'Cabbage Garden', where, after a lot of exertion, two or three were gathered together to petition for rain. **1905** *Bulletin* (Sydney) 7 Dec. 14/1 In Perth .. vegetables .. are cheaper than and equal to those I've met in Victoria the cabbage State. **1967** G. JENKIN *Two Yrs. Bardunyah Station* 71 And I tell you what—I'll never go back to the Cabbage Patch again!
   Hence **cabbage gardener, patcher, Stater** *n.*
   1903 *Sporting News* (Launceston) 14 Feb. 3/6 Subsequently shipped to the other side, he opened the eyes of the '**cabbage gardeners**' by winning an important event. **1955** N. PULLIAM *I traveled Lonely Land* 373 *Cabbage patcher*, a person from Victoria. **1960** *Bulletin* (Sydney) 3 Aug. 19/1 **Cabbage-Staters** and Croweaters reading 'Curio's' dismissal of red-gum for fencing-posts .. must have been undecided whether he was having them on.

cabbage gum. [f. *cabbage* + GUM *n.* 1: see quots. 1889 and 1897, though the diversity of species to which the name applies makes it susceptible of other explanations (see quot. 1956).] Any of several trees of the genera *Eucalyptus* and *Angophora* (fam. Myrtaceae), esp. (*Tas.*) *E. pauciflora*.
   1887 *Proc. Linnean Soc. N.S.W.* II. 279 'White', or 'Cabbage-gum'; useless for timber. **1889** J.H. MAIDEN *Useful Native Plants Aust.* 520 This timber is considered, in the Braidwood and Monaro districts, N.S.W., so soft and perishable for ordinary purposes that it is called 'Cabbage Gum', but it is nevertheless very durable underground. **1897** *Proc. Linnean Soc. N.S.W.* XXII. 706 'White Gum' .. usually goes under some name referring to the softness or brittleness of its timber, *e.g.* 'Cabbage Gum', 'Snappy Gum'. **1956** A.C.C. LOCK *Tropical Tapestry* 171 At last we reached some black soil plains, out of which rose some cabbage gums, so called because the smell they exude resembles that of boiled cabbage.

cabbage palm: see CABBAGE TREE 1 a.

cabbageite, cabbager: see CABBAGITE.

cabbage saltbush. [f. *cabbage* + SALTBUSH: see quots. 1885 and 1887.] *Old man saltbush*, see OLD MAN *n.* 3 a.
   1885 *Trans. & Proc. R. Soc. S.A.* VIII. 25 *Atriplex nummularium*. Often called the 'Cabbage' Saltbush, from the comparatively large size of its leaves. **1887** S. NEWLAND *Far North Country* 15 Cabbage saltbush is extolled as a table vegetable of surpassing excellence.

cabbage tree. [Spec. use of *cabbage tree* a name variously applied in other parts of the world.]
   1. a. Any of several trees, usu. palms (fam. Arecaceae) of the genera *Corypha* and esp. *Livistona*, of n., e., and central Aust. and elsewhere, the young growing shoot of which is edible. See also FAN PALM. Also **cabbage palm, cabbage tree palm**.
   1770 J. COOK *Jrnls.* 8 June (1955) I. 339 The trees we saw were a small kind of Cabbage Palms. **1788** J. HUNTER *Hist. Jrnl. Trans. Port Jackson* (1793) 306 We found a vast number of cabbage-trees... They are a very good substitute for other vegetables, but one tree produces only a single cabbage. **1852** W. HUGHES *Austral. Colonies* 72 In the Illawara district are still left a few specimens of the cabbage-tree palm, the leaves of which are used for making the kind of hat almost universally worn by colonists of all classes.
   b. The plant *Nuytsia floribunda* (see *Christmas bush* (b) CHRISTMAS).
   1832 G.F. MOORE *Diary Ten Yrs. W.A.* 14 Sept. (1884) 136 The cabbage or beef-wood tree, with a splendid orange blossom. **1936** J.E. HAMMOND *Western Pioneers* 126 The bush around contained an interesting variety of timber, including .. cabbage (or Christmas) tree.
   2. Ellipt. for CABBAGE-TREE HAT 1.
   1844 *Dispatch* (Sydney) 20 Apr. 1/2 The very 'cabbage trees' of the squatters seemed to assume a something of defiance in their knowing cock, as their wearers laughed and joked. **1974** *Austral. Folksongs* (Folk Lore Council Aust.) 26 The squatter loves his cabbage-tree With streamers hanging down—He wears it always in the bush, And even when in town!
   3. *Hist.* CABBAGE-TREE MOB (sense 1). Also *attrib.*
   1848 *Austral. Sportsman* (Sydney) 14 Oct. 2/4 The visitors had to run the gauntlet of the 'cabbage-trees', who subjected each carriage to a critical inspection. **1867** J.R. HOULDING *Austral. Capers* 227 Some of the 'cabbage-tree boys' were there too, indulging in their favourite holiday rollick of knocking all the 'black billies' from the heads of the wearers.
   4. *Hist.* See CABBAGE-TREE MOB 2.
   1857 *Bell's Life in Sydney* 17 Oct. 2/1 Our young men, particularly the class familiarly termed the 'cabbage-tree' lads [*sc.* stockmen], are peculiarly fitted for this honorable duty.
   Hence **cabbage-treed** *ppl. a.*
   1857 *Illustr. Jrnl. Australasia* II. 6 A burly-looking carter, blue-shirted and cabbage-treed, according to custom.

cabbage-tree hat. [f. CABBAGE TREE 1 a.]
   1. A wide-brimmed hat woven from cabbage tree leaves. Also **cabbage-palm hat**.
   1841 *Hunter River Gaz.* 11 Dec. 3/3 At present our principal manufactures are cabbage-tree hats and tomb stones. **1853** F. GERSTAECKER *Life in Bush* 13 A squatter from the Adelaide district, with a huge beard, a cabbage-palm hat, .. bush shoes, and a red silk neck handkerchief.
   2. cabbage-tree hat mob: see next.
   Hence **cabbage-tree-hatted** *ppl. a.*
   1876 *Austral. Town & Country Jrnl.* (Sydney) 16 Dec. 982/2 The sabre stroke of a sixteen foot stockwhip dropped fair between the eyes, by a cabbage-tree-hatted black velvet-banded native.

cabbage-tree mob. *Hist.* [f. CABBAGE-TREE 2 + MOB 3.]
   1. A collective term for a class of young urban roughs distinguished by their wearing of cabbage-tree hats; a gang of these. Also **cabbage-tree hat mob**.
   1848 *Atlas* (Sydney) IV. 390/2 The disturbances .. were not begun by the Irish party who were in favour of Captain O'Connell, but originated with a parcel of young blackguards, known by the name of the *Cabbage-tree mob*. **1907**

C. MacAlister *Old Pioneering Days* 54 George Hough .. was a bit inclined to act the bully, perhaps to show his credentials as a leading member of the lower strata of the 'cabbage-tree Hat' mob, which corresponded to some extent to the hooligans and larrikins of to-day.

2. *transf.* and *fig.* Used of other traditional wearers of the cabbage-tree hat, e.g. bushmen, squatters.

1891 *Truth* (Sydney) 5 Apr. 7/3 The fence and the sheep have sent the stockman to Queensland, and the cabbage-tree hat mob to the devil. **1898** *Bulletin* (Sydney) 19 Feb. 6/3 The remnant of the Cabbage-tree Mob has risen to announce that it will do all it knows to prevent any Federation unless N.S. Wales receives a special bribe by the establishment of the Federal capital in its territory.

cabbage tree palm: see CABBAGE TREE 1 a.

cabbagite. *Hist.* Also **cabbageite.** [f. CABBAGE-TREE 2.] A member of the CABBAGE-TREE MOB (sense 1). Also **cabbager.**

1838 *Colonist* (Sydney) 21 July 3/4 The Bench sentenced the young *cabbagers* to a month's industry at the treadmill. **1852** G.C. MUNDY *Our Antipodes* III. 131 Scurrilous and insolent abuse of the constituted authorities had been found to be a dainty dish to set before the Cabbageites. **1976** B. SCOTT *Compl. Bk. Austral. Folk Lore* 52 Unaware of the propensities of the Cabbagites, he was by them furiously assailed—for no better reason apparently than because, like 'noble Percy', 'he wore his *beaver* up'.

cable gum. *Obs.* [f. *cable* (see quots.) + GUM *n.* 1.] GIMLET a.

1833 *Perth Gaz.* 21 Sept. 151 An apparently different species of the Eucalyptus... From its peculiar appearance, some of our party named it the cable gum. **1855** R. AUSTIN *Jrnl. Interior W.A.* 9 Interspersed with patches of gnaleruk, (fluted or cable-gum of Roe) a singular species of eucalyptus, with smooth, glossy bark, and three spiral channels along the trunk, which make it resemble a twisted clustered column growing on the loamy soil.

cabon /ˈkʊbɒn/, *a.* (and *adv.*) Austral. pidgin. *Obs.* [a. Dharuk prob. *gabawan.*] Also **cawbawn, cobborn,** etc.

A. *adj.* Big, great.

1827 P. CUNNINGHAM *Two Yrs. in N.S.W.* II. 28 They could not contain their astonishment .. that '*cobawn* (big) gobernor, had not mout *so* (screwing theirs in the appropriate shape), like the *narang* (little) gobernor'. **1849** S. & J. SIDNEY *Emigrant's Jrnl.* 311 He required a rig out, as a necessary preliminary that he might appear 'a cabon swell'. **1923** J. BOWES *Jackaroos* 137 He elicited the information that three days ago a cobborn (big) mob of white pfeller rode in from the north.

B. *adv.* Extremely.

1881 A.C. GRANT *Bush-Life Aust.* II. 175 'Missis bail bong, only cawbawn prighten' (Missis not dead, only dreadfully frightened).

cacker, var. KAKKA.

cackle tub. [f. *cackle* loquacity + *tub* pulpit.] A pulpit. Also *fig.*

1882 *Sydney Slang Dict.* 2 *Cackle-Tub*, a pulpit. **1905** *Shearer* (Sydney) 26 Aug. 5/2 Miss Locke, like many of her sex, is terribly assertive when mounted on the political 'cackle tub'.

cactus, *n.* and *a.*

A. *n.*

1. In the phr. **in the cactus,** in difficulty.

1943 S.J. BAKER *Pop. Dict. Austral. Slang* (ed. 3) 18 *Cactus, in the*, in trouble. (R.A.A.F. slang.) **1984** A. DELBRIDGE *Aussie Talk* 56 *In the cactus*, in difficulties, in trouble.

2. *fig.* The backblocks.

1945 *Coast to Coast 1944* 174 He got in the car and started the engine. 'Well, it's back to the cactus,' he said. **1980** *Sydney Morning Herald* 31 Dec. 7/9 We are today back to the cactus as our Antipodean friends would say.

B. *adj.* Ruined; finished.

1945 *Atebrin Advocate: Mag.* 2/4 Austral. Armoured Regiment Jan. 1 My Jeep's broken down... The starter's cactus. **1980** ANSELL & PERCY *To fight Wild* 29, I couldn't make up my mind about that dirty-water creek... If I was lucky I might find fresh water in a few hours. If not, if it ran back into salt pans, I'd be cactus. I'd never make up the lost time.

cadet. *Obs.* [N.Z. *cadet* young man learning sheep-farming: see OEDS 4.] JACKEROO *n.* 2.

1879 S.W. SILVER *Austral. Grazier's Guide* 13 The 'colonial experiencer', the 'jackàroo' or 'cadet', as he is variously designated in different colonies, always lodges with the proprietor or the resident manager. **1923** J. BOWES *Jackaroos* 17 They were cadets newly appointed to a cattle station, and from henceforth would be known as 'jackaroos'.

cakker, var. KAKKA.

calabash. *Obs.* [Transf. use of *calabash* vessel made from the shell of a gourd or fruit.]

1. COOLAMON 1.

1835 J. BACKHOUSE *Narr. Visit Austral. Colonies* (1843) 325 They [*sc.* the natives] likewise carry with them .. vessels for water, made of the large, tubercular excrescences of the gum-tree, hollowed out, which are here called Calabashes. **1922** J. LEWIS *Fought & Won* 85 We spied a lubra. The moment she saw us she hid in a bunch of grass, and as we rode up seemed very frightened and ran away, leaving her wooden calabash.

2. *fig. Obs.* A promissory note: see quot. 1882.

1861 *Brisbane Courier* 23 Oct. 2/2 *Calabashes*. Agents or other parties resident in the country are requested to refrain from the practice of forwarding '*calabashes*' to this office by way of payment, since they are not looked upon as cash, and will invariably be returned to the person who transmitted them. **1882** W. COOTE *Hist. Colony Qld.* 82 The absence of a bank and the want of silver, led to the adoption of a system of what were called 'calabashes'—orders drawn upon some agent of the drawer, payable at various dates after presentation, and often for very small amounts.

calico, *attrib.* and *n.* [Spec. use of *calico* cotton cloth.]

A. *attrib.*

1. Applied to temporary or portable structures made of strong cotton or canvas.

1856 G. WILLMER *Draper in Aust.* 140, I was agreeably surprised to receive an invitation to dine with him in his calico-roofed house. **1946** W.E. HARNEY *North of 23°* 16 Camped the sheep at night by erecting a calico yard. **1949** H.E. THONEMANN *Tell White Man* 38 With the party was also the hangman, cooks, and those to care for the large plant of horses... It was the largest calico town most of us had ever seen.

2. Special Comb. **calico muster:** see MUSTER *n.* 5.

B. *n.* A shirt.

1858 *S. Austral. Advertiser* (Adelaide) 13 July 3/2 He .. was fined for the assault .. and damage done to the constable's 'calico'. **1935** P.H. RITCHIE *North of Never Never* 154 Some don't even wear a 'calico'.

calico jimmy. *Obs.* [f. *calico* (see prec.) + the proper name *Jimmy.*] A member of a free-trade lobby advocating the importation of duty-free textiles; a textile merchant.

1889 *Braidwood Dispatch* 14 Sept. 2/4 It had been the habit three years ago when the Parkes Government came into power, for such men as Melville and O'Sullivan to rail at the Government as calico jemmies, but what did they find in Melbourne—why that calico was admitted free. **1917** *Advocate* (Burnie) 3 July 1/5 Why, farmers, you are placing your business in the hands of lawyers and calico jimmies.

Californian, *a. Hist.* In the gold-rush period: applied in collocations to machinery and wearing apparel similar to those used on the Californian goldfields, esp. as **Californian pump** (see quot. 1931). Also **California**.

1851 *Britannia* (Hobart) 26 June 4/5 Others add to it a blue serge shirt and a California hat. **1853** A. MACKAY *Great Gold Field* 30 At the waterhole, they cut a channel for the water of the creek to run off, and then soon emptied the waterhole with a Californian pump. **1931** W. BARAGWANATH et al. *Guide for Prospectors in Vic.* 15 The California pump is an endless belt passing over rollers, and having buckets at intervals attached to it. When the belt is in motion the buckets, as they pass down into the water, fill themselves, and then travel with the belt to the top, where they discharge the water as they turn over into a shoot, by which it passes away.

Hence **Californiate** *v. trans.*

1854 W. SHAW *Land of Promise* 87 The efforts made by the tradespeople to Californiate their city, are rather amusing.

call, *v.* [Spec. use of *call* to announce.] *trans.* To commentate upon (a sporting event).

1906 *Gadfly* (Adelaide) 20 June 14/1 When the sporting writer whose task it is to 'call' an important hockey match focuses his spectacles on the frenzied girls, he talks like a lunatic. **1977** *Sun-Herald* (Sydney) 9 Jan. 67/5 He's calling the dogs for 2UE on Fridays from Richmond and on Saturdays from Wentworth Park.

Hence **caller** *n.*

1949 L. GLASSOP *Lucky Palmer* 247 There's no better race caller in Australia than 'Lucky' Palmer. When he was only fourteen he used to call the races from the verandah of a house.

callistemon /kəˈlɪstəmən/. [The plant genus *Callistemon* was named by British botanist Robert Brown in 1814 (see quot. 1814), f. Gr. καλλι-, comb. stem of κάλλος beauty + στήμων thread, referring to the conspicuous stamens of the individual flowers comprising the 'bottlebrush'.] Any plant of the chiefly Austral. genus *Callistemon* (see BOTTLEBRUSH a.).

1814 R. BROWN *Gen. Remarks Bot. Terra Australis* 15 Callistemon, a genus formed of those species of Metrosideros that have inflorescence similar to that of Melaleuca, and distinct elongated filaments. **1985** *Age* (Melbourne) 3 Dec. 27/1 Prune callistemons after flowering.

callitris /kəˈlɪtrəs/. [The plant genus *Callitris* was named by French botanist E.P. Ventenat (*Decas generum nov.* (1808) 10), f. Gr. καλλι-, comb. stem of Gr. κάλλος beauty and τρεις three, referring to the arrangement of the leaves in whorls of three.] Any plant of the chiefly Austral. coniferous genus *Callitris* (fam. Cupressaceae). See also CYPRESS PINE.

1849 C. STURT *Narr. Exped. Central Aust.* II. 291, I saw no Callitris (Pine of the colonists) in all that country. **1963** A.E. FARRELL *Vengeance* 18 A great belt of Callitris pines. The sturdy, dark blue-green boles, capped with clumps of dark green, needle-like foliage stood out as exquisite etchings against the undulating pink coloured sandhills.

callop /ˈkæləp/. *S.A.* [Prob. f. a S.A. Aboriginal language.] *Golden perch*, see GOLDEN 3.

1921 *Rec. S. Austral. Museum* II. i. 88 *Plectroplites ambiguus* . . (Callop, Tarki). **1986** *Daily Tel.* (Sydney) 24 Apr. 15/4 Callop and Murray Cod, two of Australia's most prized native fish.

camel bush. Any of several shrubs, esp. *Trichodesma zeylanicum* (fam. Boraginaceae), reputedly favoured by camels.

1900 A.A. DAVIDSON *Jrnl. of Explorations Central Aust.* 6 May (1905) 18 From the ridge we passed into a small flat, with a splendid run of camel bush. **1973** C.E. GOODE *Stories Strange Places* 141 That patch of land towards Mount Burgess is rich enough for anything... Plenty .. of camel bush.

camel-neck. [See quot. 1935.] A drought-emaciated rabbit. Also **camel-back.**

1935 D.G. STEAD *Rabbit in Aust.* 87 Rabbits had died out or were dying, and the remnant were all poor, miserable 'camel-necks'—just skin and bone, moving about feebly. **1969** E.C. ROLLS *They All ran Wild* 59 These superior rabbits do not drink... 'Camel backs' and 'camel-necks', they are called when the feed and water dry up.

camel poison. Any of several (poisonous) trees or shrubs, esp. the shrub *Gyrostemon australasicus* (fam. Gyrostemonaceae) and the extremely poisonous tree *Erythrophleum chlorostachys* (fam. Caesalpiniaceae) of n. Aust. See also *black bean* (b) BLACK $a.^2$ 1 a., IRONWOOD.

1926 *Poison Plants W.A.* (W.A. Dept. Agric.) 57 Camel Poison (*Erythrophloeum Labourcherii*) .. is more commonly known as 'Black Bean Tree', 'Ironwood', or 'Steelwood'. **1976** L. BEADELL *Beating about Bush* 145 There could be no doubt that this specimen, with its 'goanna skin' patterned bark and light green foliage, was one of the dreaded camel poison bushes.

camp, *n.* [Spec. use of *camp* temporary quarters.]

1. *Obs.* A name given to Sydney and to any of several other towns which grew out of temporary settlements (see quot. 1792). Usu. with **the.**

1790 *Hist. Rec. N.S.W.* (1893) II. 724 He treats us with more affability, and is all at once so polite as to beg of my only companion, Mr Harris, and self, whenever we come to camp, to let him have our co. **1792** R. ATKINS Jrnl. 4 Apr., I walked by myself to the Brick fields, about a mile from the Camp, for so Sydney is call'd, from its having been on the Spot they pitch'd their tents on their first landing. **1843** *South Briton* (Hobart) May 139 A bark hut, under a great gum tree, in the very middle of *Camp* as they then called the charming port of Hobart Town. **1887** MRS D.D. DALY *Digging, Squatting, & Pioneering Life* 44 The 'camp', to use the name so familiar to every one, and which to this day it [*sc.* Darwin] has retained, consisted of a number of log and iron houses on either side of the gully. **1929** I.A. SCOULER *Dowerin Story* 17 The more scattered mining towns (or 'camps', as they were generally called—Coolgardie is still spoken of by its old timers as the 'Old Camp').

2. An Aboriginal settlement, either temporary or permanent. Also *attrib.*

1840 S. *Austral. Rec.* (London) 18 Apr. 191 We have the chief or king (Wagamy), and his two black queens, or *jins*, always with us, who have their camp just beside us. **1922** 'J. BUSHMAN' *In Musgrave Ranges* 82 These niggers are wild... They're different from the camp blacks who hang round stations.

3. A place where stock choose regularly to congregate; a resting-place for travelling stock; the place where a mustered herd is assembled; travelling stock (see quots. 1868 and 1944). Freq. in the phr. **on camp.** Also **cattle camp, sheep camp.**

1845 *Sydney Morning Herald* 23 Sept. 3/3 Any one who has been upon a cattle camp knows that cattle invariably face about, and stare at the intruder. **1861** H. EARLE *Ups & Downs* 10 Cattle .. become peculiarly attached to a particular camp or locality. **1868** C.W. BROWNE *Overlanding in Aust.* 38 When two sheep-camps meet on the road, there very soon springs up a friendly feeling between them. **1872** 'RESIDENT' *Glimpses Life Vic.* 61 They were driven first on to a large camp, when they were all rounded up together. **1915** *Bulletin* (Sydney) 23 Sept. 22/4 A mob of travelling cows was put on camp. **1944** J.J. HARDIE *Cattle Camp* (ed. 3) 82 Ken led his camp down the Barker on his first muster as head stockman.

4. See quot. 1938 and FLYING FOX CAMP.

1881 A.C. GRANT *Bush-Life Qld.* II. 20 A little distance further on they come to a camp of flying-foxes. **1938** F. RATCLIFFE *Flying Fox & Drifting Sand* 12 A camp of flying foxes was to be found. (The daytime congregations of these beasts are known as 'camps'. A camp is not just a casual meeting place. Many have been inhabited year after year for half a century at least.)

5. A rest.

1899 'S. RUDD' *On our Selection* 127 Sometimes Dan used to forget to talk at all—he would be asleep—and Dad would wonder if he was unwell. Once he advised him to go up to the house and have a *good* camp. **1979** B. SCOTT *Tough in Old Days* 39 He stretched luxuriously on the grass as the sun warmed his bones. 'Think I'll have a camp,' he said.

6. Special Comb. **camp gang**, a convict working party; **horse**, see quot. 1886; **kettle**, a cooking vessel; variously applied to (iron) vessels used over a camp fire; **muster**, see quot. 1933; **oven**, (a) a heavy, iron, three-legged cooking vessel which stands in a fire and has a flat, usu. recessed, lid on top of which hot coals can be placed; **(b)** an Aboriginal cooking place (see quot. 1851); **pie**, a kind of cooked, usu. tinned, meat mixture; **work**, work associated with a camp muster.

1808 *HRA* (1916) 1st Ser. VI. 356 As employed in the **Camp Gang**, which Gang are supposed to be working for the sole advantage of the Crown. **1886** H. FINCH-HATTON *Advance Aust.* 63 A '**camp-horse**' is one used for cutting out cattle on a camp. **1805** J. TURNBULL *Voyage round World* I. 74 Some fish belonging to the sailors .. boiling in a **camp kettle** over the fire on shore. **1933** *Bulletin* (Sydney) 9 Aug. 21/3 The **camp muster** was an annual event in the old days before general fencing, when every station had a general muster on the main cattle camps, and men from all the stations came along to identify and cut out their own cattle. **1832** *Hill's Life N.S.W.* (Sydney) 28 Dec. 1 Iron **camp ovens**, all sizes. **1851** *Australasian* (Melbourne) 303 The 'camp ovens' where in happier times they roasted the kangaroo whole. **1909** *Anthony Hordern Catal.* 1153 Preserved Meat .. **Camp pies**, Maconochie's .. 1s. tin 11s. 6d. doz. **1876** *Austral. Town & Country Jrnl.* (Sydney) 23 Dec. 1022/4 In **camp-work**, there is little or no chance of oppression or hurt. After an hour's 'beating up', and ringing of whips, streams of cattle are seen pouring in from every point of the compass towards, let us say, the main camp. Generally situated at no great distance from the stockyard, this is supposed to be the central and principal trysting place.

camp, *v.* [See prec.]

1. *intr.* Of stock: to settle down to rest, usu. in some number (but see quot. 1872); to use an habitual resting place (see quot. 1849).

1843 A. CASWELL *Hints from Jrnl.* 37 He then lets the cattle camp, or lie down. **1849** S. & J. SIDNEY *Emigrant's Jrnl.* 20 The sheep, for nearly nine months in the year after drinking, *camp*; that is, lie still under the shade, with all their heads turned towards one another. **1872** A. McFARLAND *Illawarra & Manaro* 121 Teams of bullocks—from 6 to 12 in number .. are to be met with 'camped' by creek and stream.

2. *intr.* To take a short rest, usu. for refreshment and not necessarily out of doors (see quots. 1870, 1892 and 1917). Also *fig.*

1848 *Maitland Mercury* 12 July 2/5 Having camped, to breathe the dogs, and partaken of refreshments and 'nobblers' round, the hounds started on a fresh scent. **1870** 'JACKAROO' *Immigration Question* 8 An old gentleman from Bathurst .. camped at our hut in the middle of a broiling day recently. **1892** *Bulletin* (Sydney) 7 May 24/1 We'd camp in some old shanty-bar, And sit a-tellin' lies. **1917** *Ibid.* 29 Mar. 22/2 Six teamsters with their waggons and 30 horses were camped for dinner at 'The Weatherboard'. **1949** *Bulletin* (Sydney) 30 Mar. 15/4 The shearers as they go in for a sheep will naturally select the one they consider the easiest shearing, leaving the culls .. to last. Last one of all is called the 'cobbler'. A shearer just missing that 'choice' would have first pick of the new pen, and the vast difference between the two often leads shearers to 'camp' on their last sheep so that the other fellow would get the rough 'un.

3. *intr.* Of wild animals: to rest; to establish a resting place. Also with **up**.

1861 'OLD BUSHMAN' *Bush Wanderings* 9 It is a pretty sight to watch a mob [of kangaroos] camped up. **1895** *Bulletin* (Sydney) 2 Feb. 3/2 A kangaroo always wears his tail straight out behind. The scrub-wallaby, however, gets his between his legs when camped.

4. *trans.* To keep (stock) together at a particular place, esp. for their rest and refreshment. Also with **out**, and *absol.*

1847 *Maitland Mercury* 28 Aug. 4/4 At stations where I cannot form paddocks, I make the shepherds camp the sheep out. **1897** *Bulletin* (Sydney) 28 Aug. 29/2 Men from outback are camping for grass or water. **1916** *Ibid.* 24 Aug. 22/4 Has any .. orchardist tried camping sheep among his trees to eradicate codlin moth?

camp draft, *n.* [f. CAMP *n.* 3 + *draft* a selection.] A competitive equestrian event in which a rider isolates a steer from its fellows and drives it, against the clock, round a set course. Also *attrib.*

1951 *Bulletin* (Sydney) 23 May 15/2 He now has a horse to handle. It's not really a camp-draft champion. **1963** R.H. CONQUEST *Spurs are Rusty Now* 14 The girls who rode in the rodeos and camp-drafts in those days were hard-boiled customers.

Also **camp-drafter** *n.*, a horse used for campdrafting.

1942 *Bulletin* (Sydney) 27 May 13/4 A sheep on the wheel will leave the best camp-drafter standing.

camp-draft, *v. trans.* Usu. as *vbl. n.*

1. To take part in a camp draft.

1921 *Bulletin* (Sydney) 14 Apr. 24/2 Cracks .. compete annually at one of the best camp-drafting and bull-tossing shows in Australasia. **1981** *Weekend Austral. Mag.* (Sydney) 3 Oct. 9/2 Good shots of the Australian-invented sports of polocrosse (polo-cum-lacrosse) and campdrafting (cattle mustering in a showground).

2. To ride among yarded cattle, with the intention of isolating those required for branding, butchering, etc.

1945 E. MITCHELL *Speak to Earth* 56 Mitchell .. had as great a name for riding after cattle in rough country as he had a bad one for camp-drafting. **1956** T. RONAN *Moleskin Midas* 22 Until midnight they worked erecting a rough but serviceable fork-and-sapling yard. In the morning they mustered their cattle into this, and .. Amos Sides started camp-drafting out the heifers.

camping, *vbl. n.* [f. CAMP *n.* 3, infl. by CAMP *v.* 1.] Used *attrib.* in Special Comb. **camping ground, place, reserve**: see CAMP *n.* 3.

1841 *Omnibus & Sydney Spectator* 27 Nov. 68/4 The whole course of the Mackie is full of dead bullocks, and I have heard that the skeletons of two hundred bullocks are bleaching on one **camping ground**. **1843** *Sydney Morning Herald* 11 May 3/5 Strayed from a **camping place**, about 25 miles north-east of Gloucester. A bay mare. **1903** *Bulletin* (Sydney) 21 Mar. 16/2 **Camping reserves** for travelling stock, which are reserved from sale and lease, are placed at suitable distances along almost every T.S.R. for the convenience of drovers.

canagong /'kænədʒɒŋ/. *Obs.* Also **canajong**. [a. e. Tas. *ganajaŋ*.] PIGFACE.

1834 *Hobart Town Almanack* 133 *Mesembryanthemum equilaterale*, pigfaces, called by the aborigines by the more elegant name of canagong. **1889** J.H. MAIDEN *Useful Native Plants Aust*. 44 The 'canajong', of the Tasmanian aboriginal. The fleshy fruit is eaten raw by the aborigines. The leaves are eaten baked.

canary.
1. a. [See quot. 1829; prob. infl. by Br. slang *canary bird* jailbird (see OED 2).] A convict (from the colour of the clothing); *pl.* (occas.) the clothing. Also **canary bird.**

1827 P. CUNNINGHAM *Two Yrs. in N.S.W.* II. 117 Convicts of but recent migration are facetiously known by the name of *canaries*, by reason of the yellow plumage in which they are fledged at the period of landing. **1829** R. BURFORD *Descr. View Sydney* 11 Convicts .. when first landed .. are termed Canaries, from their yellow clothing; they afterwards attain the more honourable distinction of Government Men. **1849** *Britannia* (Hobart) 26 July 2/6 Pray, are not some men in this colony called canary-birds, from the colour of their clothing? **1871** *Austral. Jrnl.* (Melbourne) June 542/2 We can't bring him off .. in his canaries. He puts on these duds, d'ye see.

b. A punishment of one hundred lashes.

1859 J. LANG *Botany Bay* (1885) 30 There were slang terms applied to these doses of the lash—a hundred was called a 'canary'. **1892** 'P. WARUNG' *Tales Convict System* 9 As he has to go through another little ceremony this morning I'll let him off with a 'canary'—(a hundred lashes).

2. Abbrev. of 'canary bird', a gold coin.

1853 MRS C. CLACY *Lady's Visit to Gold Diggings* 163 In digger's slang, a 'canary' and half-a-sovereign are synonymous. **1928** 'BRENT OF BIN BIN' *Up Country* 203 The 'Sweep Stakes', for which every entrant had to pay a 'canary'.

3. [From the skin colour.] A Chinese immigrant. Also *attrib.*

1898 *Bulletin* (Sydney) 1 Oct. 14/3 A few more W. Q. slang words... Tobacco is 'snout', opium 'twang', a Chinaman a 'canary', and a blackfellow is a 'swatser'. **1912** R.S. TAIT *Scotty Mac* 42 What's the matter, canary face?

candlebark. Any of several trees of the genus *Eucalyptus* (fam. Myrtaceae), esp. *E. rubida* of s.e. Aust. incl. Tas., having a smooth white bark which freq. develops reddish patches in summer and autumn before the bark is shed.

1899 *Proc. Linnean Soc. N.S.W.* XXIV. 456 The name 'Candle-bark' in use in the Queanbeyan district is in reference to its smooth and glaucous trunk... It has usually reddish or plum-coloured patches on the bark. **1974** BUCKLEY & HAMILTON *Festival* 71 'Aren't those pretty trees? Nice white trunks.' 'They're called candlebarks, Delcia.'

cane. [Shortening of *sugar cane*.]
1. Used *attrib.* in various Comb. with reference to the growing or harvesting of sugar cane.

1880 J. BONWICK *Resources Qld*. 73 The cane-growing prospects of Queensland are good. **1895** *Bulletin* (Sydney) 5 Jan. 3/2 Men do *not* fight in Australia so much as 'at 'ome'. But they talk fight. By 'they' I mean .. the shearing, harvesting, racing or cane-cutting lot. **1977** C. McCULLOUGH *Thorn Birds* 260 'This is a cane knife...' It widened into a large triangle instead of tapering to a point, and had a wicked hook like a rooster's spur at one of the two blade ends. **1978** M. PAICE *Shadow of Wings* 5 The cane loco emerged from the field.

2. Special Comb. **cane barracks,** accommodation provided at a cane farm for itinerant workers; **beetle,** a beetle the larva of which attacks cane roots; any of several Austral. species of *Lepidiota* or *Dermolepida*; **cocky,** the proprietor of a cane farm; *sugar cocky*, see SUGAR 2; **-cutter,** an itinerant worker employed in the harvesting of sugar cane; also *transf.* (see quot. 1909); **inspector,** one responsible for regulating the supply of sugar cane to a mill, and for settling industrial disputes; **paddock,** cane field; **season,** the harvesting period (from June to December); **toad,** the large toad *Bufo marinus*, native to Central and S. America and introd. to n.e. Aust.

1967 *Meanjin* 30 His wife had left him in the **cane barracks** fifteen years ago. **1902** *Agric. Gaz. N.S.W.* XXIII. 64 This destructive **cane beetle** .. is .. in general form somewhat like the typical cockchafer. **1899** *Bulletin* (Sydney) 18 Feb. 15/2 Not satisfied with cheap Jap. and kanaka-labor brought to their doors by a piebald Govt. many **cane-cockies** rope in the blacks and make them sink holes and plant and trash cane. **1881** *Bulletin* (Sydney) 30 July 13/4 **Cane-cutters** are scarce on the Clarence. **1909** *Ibid.* 17 Feb. 13/2, I have discovered the longest long beer in the Commonwealth .. is found on some of the Queensland sugar fields and is known as the 'cane cutter'. **1911** *Austral. Sugar Jrnl.* 6 Apr. 45/1 From the official synopsis of **cane inspectors'** reports .. we make the following extracts as to the condition of the cane crops. **1945** *Ibid.* 11 Apr. 13/2 The grasshopper swarm in the hopping stage arrived in the **cane paddocks**. **1955** R. LAWLER *Summer of Seventeenth Doll* (1965) 18 Seven months they spend up there killin' themselves in the **cane season**, and then they come down here to live a little. **1963** HARNEY & LOCKWOOD *Shady Tree* 117 A .. **cane toad**, one of a species that had been introduced to Queensland to destroy beetles that were causing havoc to the crops of sugarcane.

canegrass. Any of several grasses (fam. Poaceae) having cane-like stems, esp. *Eragrostis australasicus* of all mainland States. Also *attrib.*

1861 *Burke & Wills Exploring Exped*. 6 Cane-grass growing in great quantities. **1938** A. UPFIELD *Bone is Pointed* (1966) 50 Trees .. surrounded by what appeared to be a canegrass fence.

Caneite. [Proprietary name.] A soft building board made from the fibres of sugar cane.

1938 *Austral. Official Jrnl. Patents* (Canberra) 1969 *Caneite* 72,201. Structural materials, including fibre board, fibre laths, fibre tiles... The Colonial Sugar Refining Company Limited. **1979** R. DUFFIELD *Rogue Bull* 91 It had developed from sugar-cane a fibre hardboard called Caneite.

cannibal. *Hist.* A term applied undiscriminatingly by the colonists to an Aboriginal. Also *attrib.*

1838 *Sydney Herald* 14 Nov. 21/1 We say, protect the whites as well as the blacks. Protect the white settler, his wife, and children, in remote places, from the filthy, brutal cannibals of New Holland. **1850** *Britannia* (Hobart) 9 May 4/5 The policy of telling a number of cannibal savages that a party of white men is supposed to be approaching.

canoe. *Hist.* A name given by the colonists to any Aboriginal boat. Also *attrib.*

1784 G.W. ANDERSON *New Collection Voyages* 71 The canoes are formed by hollowing the trunk of a tree, and it was conjectured, that this operation must have been performed by fire, as the natives did not appear to have any instruments for the purpose. The canoes are in length about fourteen feet, and so narrow, that they would be frequently overset, but that they are provided with an outrigger... The canoes in the southern parts are formed only of a piece of bark four yards long, fastened together at each end, and the middle kept open by pieces of wood, passing from side to side. **1847** G.F. ANGAS *Savage Life & Scenes* I. 102 The canoe dance of the Rufus is one of the most graceful of these savage amusements.

Canterbury cake. A kind of butter cake containing dried fruit or seeds: see quot. 1909.

1909 MRS H.W. SHAW *Six Hundred Tested Recipes* 65 Canterbury Cake... 1 cup of butter, 2 cups sugar, 1 cup milk, 4 eggs, 3 cups flour, 1 cup fruit or seeds, 2 teaspoons baking powder. Beat butter and sugar to a cream, add milk (a little at a time), well-beaten eggs, then flour with baking powder. Flavour with essence to taste. **1973** A. BURNETT *Wilful Murder in Outback* 42 'Canterbury cake, jubilee Mick and lady drawers.' Meaning tinned cake, jubilee sweets mixture and women's underclothing.

canvas.

1. Used *attrib.* of dwellings, etc., made of canvas.
1855 'RUSTICUS' *How to settle in Vic.* 22 The *canvas-framed house* is merely a tent, brought into the form of a house by means of a timber framing, on which the canvas is stretched. **1945** *Bulletin* (Sydney) 26 Dec. 13/2 Corny had a canvas-and-bark humpy by the lagoon.

2. Special Comb. **canvas muster,** see MUSTER *n.* 5; **town,** a settlement, initially of gold-miners, consisting largely of tents; also **canvas township.**
1851 [**canvas town**] *Empire* (Sydney) 14 Nov. 364/2 About the centre of this canvas village, stand the stores of Mssrs. Fentum and Edmiston and Mr Tucker. **1853** F.J. COCKBURN *Lett.* (1856) 5 'Canvass town', a town or village of tents, made since gold was found. **1900** 'CAS-HAMBA' *Sketchy Characters* 27 Can the reader picture mentally a canvas township, varied in architecture and building material, in the form of bush breakwind and calico roofs, scattered over an area of land as extensive as an estate of an English noble?

cap. [Spec. use of *cap* a part laid horizontally along the top of a structure.] See quot. 1849. Also **cap rail.**
1849 S. & J. SIDNEY *Emigrant's Jrnl.* 43 The stockyard ought to be made very strong; four rails with a cap; that is to say, a long, round rail on the top of all the posts, running from one to the other... The top rail is the cap. **1897** *Bulletin* (Sydney) 11 Dec. 30/1 We heard them lift the post and wire and fling the cap-rails down.

Cape. Used *attrib.* in Special Comb. designating species of flora brought from the Cape of Good Hope: **Cape barley** *obs.*, see quot. 1833; **spinach,** DOUBLE-GEE a.; **weed,** the widespread S. African herb *Arctotheca calendula* (fam. Asteraceae), naturalized in W.A. by 1833 and, although used as fodder, generally regarded as a weed.
1825 *Australasian Pocket Almanack* 84 [January is] the proper season for sowing winter (here commonly called **Cape**) **barley.** **1833** *Launceston Advertiser* 7 Mar. 2 *On sale .. Cape Barley,* (the produce of Seed imported last year from the Cape of Good Hope). **1897** L. LINDLEY-COWEN *W. Austral. Settler's Guide* 541 Mr Wansborough.. sowed a bed with the seed of this '**Cape Spinach**'... The seed was obtained from Mr Tanner... However, the plant did not prove a very palatable spinach. **1878** W.R. GUILFOYLE *Austral. Bot.* 60 **Cape weed** .. which has proved such a pest in many parts of Victoria, was, a few years ago, introduced from the Cape of Good Hope, as a fodder plant.

Cape Barren. [f. the name of *Cape Barren* Island in Bass Strait.] Used *attrib.* in Special Comb. **Cape Barren goose,** the grey waterfowl *Cereopsis novaehollandiae* of s. Aust., breeding mainly on islands off the mainland s. coast; **tea** *obs.*, the shrub of Tas. and s.e. mainland Aust. *Correa alba* (fam. Rutaceae) commonly found on coastal dunes and cliffs; also *attrib.*
1832 J. BACKHOUSE *Narr. Visit Austral. Colonies* (1843) 87 We returned to the Lagoons with.. a man carrying two young **Cape Barren Geese,** one of which died on the way, from the effect of cold and rain. **1827** *HRA* (1923) 3rd Ser. VI. 267 '**Cape Barren Tea** Shrub' .. makes an acrid stimulating drink. **1833** J. BACKHOUSE *Narr. Visit Austral. Colonies* (1843) 179 *Corraea alba,* the Cape Barren tea, becomes a large bush, and covers the sand hills of the western head of the Tamar.

cap rail: see CAP.

captain. A person with money to spend, esp. one who buys drinks for an assembled company.
1961 W.E. HARNEY *Grief, Gaiety & Aborigines* 20 Doleites were calling to other doleite friends... Everywhere I heard the term 'captain' or 'a whale in the bay' and came to realise it meant someone was in town who had money to spend. **1977** K. GILBERT *Living Black* 302 Have you seen 'em bludging up to a captain who's just come onto the mission with money in his pocket? [*Note*] The reserve people's name for a white man who visits them to trade money or grog for sex.

Captain Cook, *n.* and *a.* [The name of James *Cook* (1728–79), navigator and explorer.]

A. *n.* Rhyming slang for 'look'. See also COOK.
1932 L. MANN *Flesh in Armour* 179 Take a captain cook at love's young dream. **1974** D. O'GRADY *Deschooling Kevin Carew* 140 Got a Captain Cook at your dossier—it's thicker than your frickin' head.

B. *adj.* Rhyming slang for CROOK *a.* 1 c.; ill.
1959 E. LAMBERT *Glory thrown In* 46, I never saw anyone who was feeling Captain Cook get any sympathy from Doc.

Captain-General and Governor-in-Chief: see GOVERNOR-IN-CHIEF.

caravan. *Obs.* Box *n.*² 1.
1835 BACKHOUSE & TYLOR *Life & Labours G.W. Walker* (1862) 219 The prisoners lodge in small caravans, capable of containing sixteen at a time, which are moved from one place to another upon small wooden wheels. **1889** *Corresp. on Secondary Punishment* (Great Brit. Parl.) 15 Feb. (1841) 77 The mode of incarceration in boxes or caravans, alluded to by the Committee .. as in existence in New South Wales, was never, so far as I am aware, even thought of in Van Diemen's Land.

carbeen /'kabin/. Also **carbean, karbeen.** [a. Kamilaroi and Yuwaalaraay *gaabiin.*] *Moreton Bay ash,* see MORETON BAY.
1888 *Centennial Mag.* (Sydney) 293 Tall and imposing carbeens and river-gums lined the bank of the Namoi. **1928** B. SPENCER *Wanderings in Wild Aust.* 525 One special gum tree was especially interesting (*Eucalyptus platypoda*)... The tree is popularly called 'Karbeen'. **1956** T. RONAN *Moleskin Midas* 114 The use of knives in this district is restricted to butchering and stockwork, and if you want to carve your name look for a carbean tree.

carby. Also **carbie.** [f. *carb(urettor* + -Y.] A carburettor.
1957 'N. CULOTTA' *They're Weird Mob* 47 'Carburettor, matey,' said Joe. 'We'll start on the carby.' **1963** D. ATTENBOROUGH *Quest under Capricorn* 130 Finally, he looked up, as mystified as we were. 'Well, I dunno,' he said, 'Yer maggie's right and there's mobs of 'ole in the carbie.'

carf. *Timber-getting. Obs.* Also **carve.** [Br. dial. *carf* an incision or notch: see OED 1 and EDD *sb.*¹] The part of the trunk cut out as a tree is felled: see quot. 1885. Also as *v. trans.* (see quots. 1916).
1885 *Illustr. Austral. News* (Melbourne) 25 Nov. 202/2 Having put in the front 'carve', on the side the tree is to fall, the back one, which is usually a little higher than the front, is commenced and the tree is cut across. **1916** *Bulletin* (Sydney) 4 May 22/3 Tassy bushmen of 30 years ago always spoke of 'carfing' a tree, the cut being called front or back carf. The majority of bushmen .. on the mainland .. used the word 'scarf', which I took to be correct and smiled at the Speck splitters' corruption of the term. *Ibid.* 8 June 24/3 Tassy bushmen .. never spoke of 'carfing' a tree when they meant chopping or sawing it down. When referring to

the cut made by axe or saw, they spoke of it as the 'belly-cut' or the 'back-cut'. The opening or angle taken out by the axe was the carf. . . If an axeman marked this angle on his tree before chopping . . he would be said to be carfing his tree.

cark, var. KARK.

cark, v. [Imitative.] *intr.* **a.** Of a crow: to caw. **b.** Of a person: to laugh or speak raucously. Also *trans.,* and redupl. as **cark-cark.** See also KARK.
1936 F. CLUNE *Roaming round Darling* 120 Big mob of crows carking. 1971 F. HARDY *Outcasts of Foolgarah* 6 'Leave my bottles alone,' the Black Crow, who looked after the dump for the Council, cark-carked, poking his head out from under the front-end loader. 1981 —— *Who shot George Kirkland?* 6 Hall carked a laugh.

carn, v. Also **c'arn.** [Altered form of *come on.*] Esp. in supportive barracking at sporting fixtures, 'come on!'; an injunction to greater effort.
1968 B. DAWE *Eye for Tooth* 42 When children are born in Victoria they are wrapped in the club-colours, laid in berib-boned cots, having already begun a lifetime's barracking. Carn, they cry, Carn . . feebly at first. 1969 A. HOPGOOD *And Big Men Fly* 11 'C'arn the Crows' is the battle-cry of the greatest football machine in league history.

carney /'kani/. Also **carni, carnie.** [a. Baagandji *gaani.*] Any of several lizards in the traditional diet of Aborigines, esp. BEARDED DRAGON.
1881 J.C.F. JOHNSON *To Mount Browne & Back* 13 The carnie or Jew Lizard is esteemed a luxury by many of the Central Australian men. 1902 *Bulletin* (Sydney) 8 Nov. 3/2 He cooks Some wood-grubs in a pan, Or carnies roasts in lonely nooks. 1916 *Ibid.* 31 Aug. 24/3 Next in favor is the 'carni' or frill-necked lizard. 1932 M.R. WHITE *No Roads go By* 233 Dick Willow, a full-blooded black, was licking his shiny chops after polishing off a large-sized carney, i.e., a lace lizard.

carpet. [Spec. use of *carpet,* with reference to skin markings.] Used *attrib.* in Special Comb. **carpet shark,** WOBBEGONG; **snake,** the python *Morelia spilotes variegata,* widespread in Aust. and New Guinea.
1896 F.G. AFLALO *Sketch Nat. Hist. Aust.* 221 The Wobbegong or **Carpet-Shark** of Sydney. 1833 *Perth Gaz.* 16 Feb. 27 A young man last week, imprudently laid hold of a **Carpet Snake.**

carrying gang. Chiefly *Tas. Hist.* A party of convicts assigned to hard labour at carrying, esp. the carrying of timber from where it is felled to where it is to be used: see quot. 1842. See also GANG.
1835 *Sydney Herald* 31 Aug. 3/2 He is immediately sent into the 'carrying gang', the severest of all, where he remains for some months. 1842 *Tasmanian Jrnl. Nat. Sci.* I. 287 The carrying gang is deemed the most severe. This body . . transport on their shoulders immense spars (the masts and yards of a 300-ton ship for example) from the forest to the dockyards.

cartwheel. A round damper marked with a cross (resembling the spokes of a wheel). Also **cartwheel damper.** See DAMPER.
1900 *Tocsin* (Melbourne) 13 Sept. 6/1 The march of years and of intellect has flattened the damper into a 'cart-wheel', in which form even the unskilled traveller fresh from the city can very easily produce a tolerably good baking. 1902 R. BRUCE *Reminisc. Old Squatter* 194 On my return to the hut I would put on some more salt junk to boil, or make a cartwheel damper, in order to meet the requirements of our mixed population.

carve, var. CARF.

case moth. Any of several moths of the fam. Psychidae, whose larvae make and inhabit cases: see quot. 1926.
1886 F. COWAN *Aust.* 18 The Case- or Lictor-moths . . marvelous among the marvels of the insect world. 1926 R.J. TILLYARD *Insects Aust. & N.Z.* 435 Psychidae (Case Moths, Bag Moths). . . The larvae construct bags or cases of strong silk into which they weave short twigs or dried leaves.

caser. [Br. slang *caser* a crown, five shillings, orig. f. Yiddish (cf. Heb. *kesef* silver). Recorded earliest in Aust.] (A coin worth) five shillings, a crown; formerly a dollar.
1825 *Austral.* (Sydney) 29 Sept. 3/4 A swell drew out his thimble and handed it to the time keeper, together with a few casers. 1906 H. LAWSON *Lett.* (1970) 153, I want that quid—pound (otherwise four casers) tonight.

casey. [f. the name of *Casey* Jones, hero of an American ballad.] A small mechanical conveyance used by railway workers. In full **Casey Jones.**
1939 T.E. JONES *These Twenty Yrs.* 66 It costs many pounds to use railway engines and . . 'Mary' was only a black lubra. 'Mary' must be taken in a 'casey', a small open trolley. 1964 P. ADAM SMITH *Hear Train Blow* 128 Because of the amount of traffic the fettlers did not use the Caseys or other motorized transport here. . . Instead, they pulled one-man and sometimes four-man hand trolleys. 1969—— *Folklore Austral. Railwaymen* p. x, The most common form of transport is a four-wheeled motor vehicle known to the old-timers as a Casey Jones but nowadays more often referred to as a section car.

cashed up, *ppl. a.* Well supplied with money, 'flush'. See also CHEQUED UP.
1930 L.W. LOWER *Here's Luck* (1955) 115 Straight from the Never-Never by the look of him. Is he cashed up? 1980 S. THORNE *I've met some Bloody Wags* 88 They had just sold a big 'parcel' and were cashed up and ready for some fun among the bright lights.

cask. A plastic or foil-lined container for table wine, fruit juice, etc., enclosed within a cardboard pack, and having a spigot so that wine not drawn off remains under a vacuum. Also *attrib.,* and **wine cask.**
1974 *Wine Buyer* Aug. 429 An agreeable, light cask wine. 1977 *Weekend Austral. Mag.* (Sydney) 22 Oct. 15/4 Already the cardboard cask has found an acceptable place on the table in most homes. 1981 *Canberra Times* 23 July 18/5 Britain has discovered the wine cask. With the curious name of 'bag-in-a-box', the wine container, which for many years was the exclusive domain of Australians, has been launched in London with a big bang.

Casket. Shortened form of *Golden Casket:* see GOLDEN 2. Also *attrib.*
1924 L.M.D. O'NEIL *Dinkum Aussie* 37, I worked an' belonged to me union, an' drew down a sizeable screw; Took tickets in Tatt's an' the Casket; was fairly contented with life. 1977 *Southerly* iii. 303, I found the present she had for me—it was really a whole lot of presents, a shirt, a tie, a pair of socks she'd knitted herself, a couple of paperbacks and a Casket ticket.

cassowary. [Spec. use of *cassowary* flightless bird related to the ostrich; in mod. usage restricted to members of the fam. Casuariidae, as in sense 2.]
1. *Obs.* EMU $n.^1$
1788 J. WHITE *Jrnl. Voyage N.S.W.* (1790) 129 A New Holland Cassowary was brought into camp. This bird stands seven feet high, . . and, in every respect, is much larger than the *common Cassowary.* 1857 *Illustr. Jrnl. Australasia* II. 263 Cassowaries, cranes, swans . . the Botany Bay menagerie.

2. A flightless bird of n.e. Qld., the Austral. cassowary *Casuarius casuarius*, having black plumage, a bare blue neck with red wattles, and standing up to 2 m. in height.

1848 W. CARRON *Narr. Exped. Rockingham Bay & Cape York* 4 Nov. (1849) 64 This morning Jackey .. shot a fine cassowary; it was very dark and heavy, not so long on the leg as the common emu, and had a larger body, shorter neck, with a large red, stiff, horny comb on its head. **1978** R.J. BRITTEN *Around Cassowary Rock* 96 The most dangerous of the lot—the cassowary. That big flightless bird of the Queensland jungle .. can kick with the leg power of any horse, taking a dog or man apart at will with those big toes and hissing, slashing beak.

cast, *n*. [Spec. use of *cast* the spreading out of hounds in search of a lost scent: see OED *sb.* 41.] The sweep that a trained dog makes in mustering sheep: see quot. 1966.

1929 J.L. MOORE *Canine King* 45 Of these, five points are awarded for the 'run out', or as we call it in Australia, the 'cast'. **1966** C. ODELL *Working Dogs* 18 Most dogs are taught to run towards the sheep in a wide arc, so that the sheep are not frightened, and any stragglers near the boundary fence will be rounded up. This is called a 'cast' and many sheep-dogs do it by instinct.

cast, *v*. [See prec. and OED *v.* 60.] *trans*. In mustering, to direct (a sheep-dog) to make a wide sweep; also *intr.*, to make such a sweep. Also with **off**.

[N.Z. **1911** W.H. KOEBEL *In Maoriland Bush* 77 He must acquire the art of 'casting' a sheep-dog.] **1920** J.B. CRAMSIE *Managem. & Diseases Sheep* 28 Have the dog behind you, and by a wave of the hand cast him out wide to the right. **1929** J.L. MOORE *Canine King* 30 The dog is 'cast off' 'on the blind' to use the expression by which a sheep-man admits his own impotence.

cast, *ppl. a*. [Spec. use of *cast* thrown aside, discarded.]
1. Rejected as of inferior quality; esp. in the Comb. **cast fleece**.

1921 L.G. JONES *Flockmaster's Companion* 77 *Cast* relates to wools that are rough or badly bred, found in a clip. **1948** R. RAVEN-HART *Canoe in Aust.* 54 'Cast fleeces', thrown out by the remorseless classer for lack of quality.

2. In the collocation **cast-for-age** *a.*, (of sheep) culled, as too old for good breeding stock.

1930 D. COTTRELL *Earth Battle* 140 He pulled out the particulars of the fifteen thousand 'cast-for-age ewes in lamb by Derford rams'. **1977** A.G. BLACKBURN *Managem. Booms & Busts* 58 Cast-for-age ewes are sold off-shears and 1½ year old wethers are sold at the autumn break.

castor, *a.* [Poss. shortened form of *castor sugar* as (something) sweet.] All right; *apples*, see APPLE 4. Also as *n.* in the phr. **on the castor**.

1945 'MASTER-SARG' *Yank discovers Aust.* 75 'Castor' or 'sweet'—all right. **1953** K. TENNANT *Joyful Condemned* 294 These chaps .. why am I on the castor with them?

casuarina /kæzjəˈriːnə/. [The plant genus *Casuarina* was named by Swedish botanist Carl von Linne (Linnaeus) (*Amoenitates Acad.* IV. (1759) 143), from the fancied resemblance of the tree's drooping branches to the cassowary's plumage.] **a.** Any of many trees or shrubs of the fam. Casuarinaceae, of Aust., s.e. Asia, and the Pacific, the genus *Casuarina* formerly including all species of the fam. The plants have distinctive foliage consisting of whorls of tiny teeth-like leaves on jointed branchlets. **b.** The wood of these trees. See also HE-OAK, OAK 1, SHE-OAK 1.

1799 Banks Papers 28 Nov. XIX. 95 The wood which was so admired just before I left London is what I supposed it to be a Casuarina. **1982** *Austral. Financial Rev.* (Sydney) 5 Feb. 40/3 Due to the limited size of the tree, casuarina was used largely as a veneer. No fine piece of early colonial veneered furniture should now be without it.

cat, *attrib.* and *n*. [From a fancied resemblance to the animal.]

A. Used *attrib*. in Special Comb. **cat bird, (a)** the green cat bird *Ailuroedus melanotis* of rainforests in e. Aust.; **(b)** any of the three Austral. species of *Ailuroedus* (fam. Ptilonorhynchidae); **(c)** any of several other birds (see quots. 1896, 1911, and 1928); **head,** any of several plants having spiny fruits, esp. the annual of all mainland States *Tribulus terrestris* (fam. Zygophyllaceae), often abundant on disturbed ground; also **cat's head; head fern,** any of several ferns, esp. (*Tas.*) *Blechnum nudum* (fam. Blechnaceae), widespread in e. Aust.; also **cat's head fern**.

1827 P.P. KING *Narr. Survey Intertropical & Western Coasts* I. 171 The discordant screams of a bird which had roosted over our fires, and which the people called the **cat-bird**. **1851** J. HENDERSON *Excursions & Adventures N.S.W.* II. 186 The Cat-bird is a pretty green bird .. and at night .. screams like a cat .. but still more, I think, like a child in distress. **1896** B. SPENCER *Rep. Horn Sci. Exped. Central Aust.* I. 120 The 'cat-bird' (*Pomatostomus rubeculus*) attracted attention to itself. **1911** *Bulletin* (Sydney) 26 Jan. 15/2 In the bush .. [babblers] are variously known as .. 'dog birds' or 'cat birds' in tribute to their vocal peculiarities. **1928** B. SPENCER *Wanderings in Wild Aust.* 540 Troops of cat-birds (*Struthidea cinerea*). *c* **1910** W.R. GUILFOYLE *Austral. Plants* 357 'Land Caltrops', 'Indian Caltrops', or '**Cat's-head**'. **1938** F. BLAKELEY *Hard Liberty* 160 Catheads .. of a giant kind .. burned within the flesh like red-hot needles. **1880** L.A. MEREDITH *Tasmanian Friends & Foes* 220 The **cat's head fern** .. is full of beauty. **1900** *Bulletin* (Sydney) 30 June 14/3 The fern-tick .. does not patronise the cat-head fern.

B. *n.*

1. See *native cat* NATIVE *a.* 6 b.

2. *Mining.* See quot. 1977.

1950 K.S. PRICHARD *Winged Seeds* 23 Then a couple a little beauts turned up in the ripples and I got a thirty ouncer with a nest of small slugs in the 'cat'. **1977** J. DOUGHTY *Gold in Blood* 72 This was east of where the bar fell away like a small cliff, and was somewhat deeper than usual, being composed of four to five feet of yellow-striped crumbly clay known as 'cat'.

3. In the phr. **to whip the cat**: see WHIP *v*.

4. [Cf. *cat* 'regular guy' (OEDS *sb.*[1] 2 d.).] A passive homosexual.

1958 F. HARDY *Four-Legged Lottery* 117 The hospital was 'full of cats', as the crims say; a large percentage of its staff were flaunting homosexuals. **1980** B. JEWSON *Stir* 109 'Are you fucken normal or what?' 'Normal?' asked Andrew returning to his bunk. 'Well, t' put it bluntly, are you a cat?' .. 'I don't know what gives you the idea that I might be, er, .. camp.'

catamaran. *Tas. Obs.* A name given by the colonists to an Aboriginal craft.

1804 M. HOOKEY *B. Knopwood & his Times* 21 June (1929) 25 Three of their cattemirans or small boats made of bark that will hold about 6. **1851** H. MELVILLE *Present State Aust.* 361, I tell you dat, him own Wallaby ground—he make 't catamaran, come back so soon as yourself.

catarrh. *Hist.* [Spec. use of *catarrh* inflammation of a mucous membrane.] An infectious and often fatal disease of sheep: see quot. 1848.

1837 *Colonist* (Sydney) 13 June 3/2 The sheep are .. afflicted with the 'Catarrh'. **1848** H.W. HAYGARTH *Recoll. Bush Life* 50 The scourge of the sheepowner is the catarrh; a disease peculiar to Australia... The principal symptoms are a discharge from the nostrils of a dark slimy matter, a drooping of the head, feeble gait, and loss of appetite; the infected animal .. dies, apparently in great pain, often within twenty-four hours from the time of its first seizure.

Also **catarrhed** a.

1846 *Portland Guardian* 22 Sept. 3/2 The bill admitted of the boiling down of catarrhed sheep.

catch. *Shearing.* BELL SHEEP.

[N.Z. **1933** *Press* (Christchurch) 23 Sept. 13/7 Just before stopping time in a wool shed, a shearer tries to finish the sheep he is on and catch another which he can finish at ease after knock-off. This is called *getting a catch.*] **1965** J.S. GUNN *Terminol. Shearing Industry* i. 7 The 'bell sheep', or 'the catch' as it is often called, may be an easy one.

catching pen. [Also used elsewhere.] A pen in a shearing shed from which the shearer takes the sheep to be shorn.

[N.Z. **1857** R.B. PAUL *Lett. from Canterbury* 88 A post and rail catching pen.] **1867** A.K. COLLINS *Waddy Mundoee* 9 Catching pens front the shed. **1980** P. FREEMAN *Woolshed* 18 Before shearing starts, the 'rouseabout', or general hand, drives some sheep into each of the 'catching' pens. The shearer 'catches' the sheep from these pens.

catfish. Any of several marine and fresh-water fish of the fam. Ariidae and Plotisidae, having long barbels near the mouth somewhat resembling a cat's whiskers, and harmful spines. See also *Murray catfish* MURRAY.

1827 P.P. KING *Narr. Survey Intertropical & Western Coasts* I. 31 The river appeared to abound in fish, but the only sort that was caught was what the sailors called cat-fish. **1981** Q. WILD *Honey Wind* 33 The barramundi, the saltwater crocodile and the large catfish were seen on the walls of the rock caves.

Catholic frog. [See quot. 1923.] The yellowish frog *Notaden bennettii* of inland s.e. Aust.; HOLY CROSS TOAD. Also **Catholic toad.**

1891 *Proc. Linnean Soc. N.S.W.* VI. 265 *Notaden bennettii*, the 'Catholic frog' or, as I have heard it called, the Holy Cross toad. **1901** F.J. GILLEN *Diary* 11 June (1968) 113 He also brought us some specimens of frogs one of which Spencer thinks is Notaden Bennetti commonly called Catholic Toad. **1923** *Bulletin* (Sydney) 12 Apr. 24/3 Aestivation .. is practised by .. the 'catholic' frog, which gets its ecclesiastical moniker from the pale cross decorating its back.

cat-shag, *v. intr.* To 'fool around'.

1971 D. IRELAND *Unknown Industr. Prisoner* 143 These men are trained for years, they know more than us, they're bent over books and calculus and things we've never heard of while we're out cat-shagging around and learning to get on the piss. **1977** R. BEILBY *Gunner* 248 Now, lets stop cat-shagging about and get started.

cat's paw. a. PUSSY TAIL. **b.** Any of the smaller perennial herbs of the W.A. genus *Anigozanthos* (fam. Haemodoraceae) having a claw-like flower with a furry appearance (cf. *kangaroo paw* KANGAROO *n.* 5), esp. *A. humilis.*

1901 *Twentieth Century Impressions W.A.* 186 In the order Amarantaceoe [sic], Ptilotus leads with 36 species. . . In the eastern colonies it is known as the cat's paw. **1959** C. & E. CHAUVEL *Walkabout* 33 Patches of 'Cats' paw', which is an edible little bush, enjoyed by the kangaroos.

cattle. Used *attrib.* in Comb. not always excl. Austral. but of local importance.

1. Comb. **cattle bitch, country, dip, draft, -drafting, holder, -holding, property, road, spear, -spearing, walk, work.**

1936 I.L. IDRIESS *Cattle King* 58 The best **cattle-bitch** on the Darling! **1840** *S. Austral. Rec.* (London) 20 June 335, I think the lands nearest the settled districts which are desirable for purchase are .. the **cattle-country**, commencing, say, twelve miles north of Perth. **1909** *Bulletin* (Sydney) 14 Oct. 14/2 A **cattle-dip** stirred up is about the color, consistency and odor of Melbourne's Yarra. **1901** *Advocate* (Burnie) 8 June 4/2 The Duke expressed a desire to see a **cattle draft**, and in 'cutting out' certain animals and clearing them off, very fine stockriding was shown. **1859** H. KINGSLEY *Recoll. Geoffrey Hamlyn* II. 244 Sam, sir, has won a wife by **cattle-drafting**. **1843** *N.S.W. Monthly Mag.* June 270 The **cattle holders** and drivers of New South Wales. **1854** W. SHAW *Land of Promise* 250 **Cattle-holding** differs totally from sheep-farming. **1950** A. GROOM *I saw Strange Land* 209 Henbury is one of the oldest and largest **cattle properties** along the mighty old Finke. **1965** *N. Austral. Monthly* Oct. 17/2 We decided to take the new **cattle road** to the bitumen and on to Katherine. **1879** 'AUSTRALIAN' *Adventures Qld.* 12 Some blacks had got up the trees with their heavy **cattle-spears**, while another party had watched their opportunity till the cattle fed that way, when they rushed from their hiding-places, and hunted them pell-mell down the gully, for the fellows up the trees to spear as they passed under. **1882** A.J. BOYD *Old Colonials* 193 If they are punished, it deters them for a certain time from committing any more overt acts of murder or **cattle-spearing**. **1831** *Acct. Colony Van Diemen's Land* 117 Great part of this fine grazing country has now been located and converted into profitable sheep and **cattle-walks**. **1926** A.A.B. APSLEY *Amateur Settlers* 112 Our '**cattle-work**' was .. amusing.

2. Special Comb. **cattle camp,** see CAMP *n.* 3; **dog,** a dog bred and trained to work with cattle, such as the *blue heeler* (see BLUE *a.*); **driver,** *cattle drover*; **-driving** *vbl. n., obs.,* DROVING; **drover,** DROVER; **grazier,** see GRAZIER, so **-grazing** *vbl. n.*; **hunt** *obs., cattle muster*; **-hunting** *vbl. n., obs.,* MUSTERING; **king** [orig. U.S.] a large-scale cattle farmer; **muster,** see MUSTER *n.* 2; **pad,** a track made by cattle (see PAD 1); **run,** see RUN *n.*² 1 a. and 2; **slut,** a female *cattle dog*; **station,** see STATION 2 a. and 3; **track,** a route followed by cattle drovers (see TRACK *n.* 2 a.).

1868 *Illustr. Sydney News* 7 Aug. 27/4, I remember .. Robardi killed a **cattle dog** belonging to me. **1843** *N.S.W. Monthly Mag.* June 270 **Cattle** holders and **drivers**. **1843** R.D. MURRAY *Summer at Port Phillip* 232 You are now equipped for a steeple-chase of a desperate kind though it be under the modest name of **cattle-driving**. **1844** *Sydney Morning Herald* 15 May 2/7 (*heading*) Caution to **cattle drovers**. **1857** *Queen v. Beaton* 14 A cattle drover brought a mob of cows and calves and put them on my grass. **1845** D. MACKENZIE *Emigrant's Guide* 110 To the emigrant who intends to commence as a **cattle-grazier**, I would recommend to buy a *mixed* herd. **1965** R.H. CONQUEST *Horses in Kitchen* 95 In Queensland's early years the Dawson region and the Burnett country were probably the best **cattle-grazing** areas in the State. **1854** H.B. STONEY *Yr. in Tas.* 91 The settlers in the counties, when in the interior collecting cattle, which they allow to graze at large over the wilds, enjoy above all things a good **cattle-hunt**. **1829** H. WIDOWSON *Present State Van Diemen's Land* 159 From what I have seen of **cattle-hunting**, I must confess there is more fuss and noise made than are necessary. **1901** *Truth* (Sydney) 16 June 5/7 Some of these **cattle kings** rig out their dark inamoratas in all the glory of a loud pink dress. **1845** D. MACKENZIE *Emigrant's Guide* 131 Divers extraordinary and incorrect accounts of Australian **cattle-muster** have been written. **1910** *Emu* X. 22 We .. got through to the west side on a **cattle pad**. **1823** *Hobart Town Gaz.* 4 Oct., Two small Farms, one 100 and the other 50 acres .. affording a good **cattle run**. **1965** R.H. CONQUEST *Horses in Kitchen* 187 Thylungra .. is only a pup of a station compared with some of the huge cattle runs further north, but is nevertheless about 1,600,000 acres. **1915** *Pastoral Rev.* Mar. 239 A valuable **cattle slut** .. developed mange. **1832** *N.S.W. Govt. Gaz.* 14 Mar. 9/1, I arrived .. at

Walamoul . . (a **cattle station** of Mr Brown). **1955** F. LANE *Patrol to Kimberleys* 177 Far below, on the flats, sprawled a cattle station, its homestead, barns, and sheds looking like toy buildings. **1849** *Belfast Gaz.* 14 Sept. 3/3 By following along a well-marked **cattle track** you will arrive at the mouth of the Shaw river.

3. In the names of flora: **cattle bush,** any of several plants, esp. the perennial herb *Trichodesma zeylanicum* (fam. Boraginaceae); **pumpkin,** see quot. 1977.

1886 D. LINDSAY *Exped. across Aust.* 18 Good **cattle bushes** and blue-bush are plentiful. **1925** *Bulletin* (Sydney) 5 Feb. 22/4 He has a mandolin fashioned out of a **cattle-pumpkin** shell. **1977** G.A.W. SMITH *Riding High* 181 Enough grass to fill the beast, using the artificial feed merely as a supplement: this was cattle pumpkin. The pumpkins were huge, twice the size of the table variety.

cattle duff, *v. intr.* To steal cattle; see also DUFF *v.* 1. Freq. as *vbl. n.*

1865 *Tumut & Adelong Times* 23 Mar. 3/1 A very lucrative business in the cattle-duffing at Kiandra. **1886** *Melbourne Punch* 15 July, Cattle duffers on a jury may be honest men enough, But they're bound to visit lightly sins in those who cattle duff.

cattle duffer. A cattle thief; DUFFER *n.* 1.

c **1872** J.C.F. JOHNSON *Over Island* 1 The wild Barrier Rangers, the haunt of the 'cattle duffer'. **1978** R.H. CONQUEST *Dusty Distances* 46 Kangaroo beef . . which we said was cheap beef, bought from the cattle duffers.

caucus. [U.S. *caucus* a private meeting of the leaders or representatives of a political party: see OED 1.] A meeting of the parliamentary members of a political party; collectively, those eligible to attend such a meeting. Also *attrib.*

1887 *Tasmanian News* (Hobart) 25 Feb. 2/3 After the caucus broke up yesterday afternoon, Ministers entertained their supporters at lunch. **1976** K. AMOS *New Guard Movt.* 5 Bitterly disappointed with the result, Hughes stormed from a Labor caucus meeting.

Hence **caucuser** *n.*, **caucusite** *n.*

1898 *Truth* (Sydney) 6 Nov. 4/3 These cursed, cowardly **Caucussers.** **1904** *Ibid.* 27 Aug. 4/2 Albert is a well-known foot-baller, an earnest speaker, and a **Caucusite.**

caustic, *a.* Used in the names of plants from the irritant action of their sap: **caustic bush (plant, vine),** any of several plants, esp. the scrambler or bush *Sarcostemma australe* (fam. Asclepiadaceae) of all mainland States exc. Vic., which is variously regarded as good fodder (*W.A., S.A.*) or as poisonous to stock (*Qld., N.S.W.*); see also *milk-bush* MILK 1; **creeper** (or **weed**), any of several plants usu. of the genus *Euphorbia* (fam. Euphorbiaceae), esp. *E. drummondii* of Aust. and New Guinea which has a milky sap, and is reputed to have either healing or poisonous properties (see quots. 1917 and 1981).

1887 [**caustic bush**] BAILEY & GORDON *Plants reputed Poisonous* 43 *Sarcostemma australe*. . . Known as 'Caustic plant' or 'Caustic vine' in Queensland. **1897** L. LINDLEY-COWEN *W. Austral. Settler's Guide* 591 'Caustic bush' or 'vine'. . . Reported poisonous in Queensland but sometimes found harmless. **1887** BAILEY & GORDON *Plants reputed Poisonous* 79 *Euphorbia drummondii* . . **Caustic creeper**. . . This weed is unquestionably poisonous to sheep. **1917** EWART & DAVIES *Flora N.T.* 170 Caustic Creeper . . is used by the Queensland natives in cases of snake-bite. The fresh milky sap possesses great healing properties, and is in constant use by bushmen. **1981** G.M. CUNNINGHAM et al. *Plants Western N.S.W.* 456 Caustic weed . . when eaten as part of a mixed diet . . has little effect on grazing animals. It has however been blamed for poisoning sheep, and on occasions, horses and cattle.

cawbawn, var. CABON.

Cazaly /kə'zeɪli/. [The name of Roy *Cazaly* (1893–1963), an Australian National Football player who played for South Melbourne (1921–1926).] In the phr. **up there Cazaly,** orig. a supporter's cry (see quot. 1943); now *transf.* as a cry of encouragement or approbation.

1943 S.J. BAKER *Pop. Dict. Austral. Slang* (ed. 3) 86 *Up there Cazaly!* Used as a cry of encouragement. **1981** B. OAKLEY *Marsupials & Politics* 71 I'm telling you the facts about your damn fool, insignificant, down-under, she'll-be-right, fill-'em-up-again, see-yer-later, 'ow-ya-goin', waltzing-matilda, up-there-Cazaly little country.

cedar.

1. Any of several trees resembling the coniferous *Cedrus* in foliage or in the colour, grain, or smell of its timber, esp. the tall rainforest tree *Toona australis* (fam. Meliaceae) of e. N.S.W., e. Qld., and elsewhere, the wood of which is often attractively figured and usu. a deep red colour; the timber of these trees. Also with distinguishing epithet, as **native, pencil, red, Sydney, white** (see under first element). Also **cedar-tree.**

1795 *HRA* (1914) 1st Ser. I. 491, I have permitted the master of the Experiment to take with him a cargo of mahogany and cedar of this country. **1960** E. O'CONNER *Irish Man* 169 He heard the lonely call of a black cockatoo, and knew that this was what he had heard as he stood by the cedar-tree.

2. Comb. (chiefly with reference to *Toona australis*) **cedar brush, cutters, cutting, getter, grounds, party, sawyers, tracks.**

1836 J. BACKHOUSE *Narr. Visit Austral. Colonies* (1843) 397 We took a walk into one of the luxuriant woods, on the side of the Hunter, such as are termed **Cedar Brushes,** on account of the colonial White Cedar . . being one of the trees that compose them. **1827** *Monitor* (Sydney) 10 Feb. 308/1 Before the present **cedar-cutters** could wind up and get out of the trade, their loss of earnings will compel them to live on their capital. **1845** *Star* (Parramatta) 27 Sept. 3/2 *Moreton Bay*. . . **Cedar cutting** had been commenced on an extensive scale. **1876** 'EIGHT YRS.' RESIDENT' *Queen of Colonies* 133 A wandering miner . . presented himself at the camp of a **cedar-getter** on the upper waters of the Mary. **1833** *Monitor* (Sydney) 9 Mar. 3/1 The **cedar-grounds** within 100 miles of Sydney, are now bared of this wood. **1832** *HRA* (1923) 1st Ser. XVI. 713, I collected the prisoner Settlers and these men, as well as many of the **Cedar party. 1845** C. HODGKINSON *Aust., Port Macquarie to Moreton Bay* 10 Ague . . was particularly prevalent among the **cedar sawyers. 1851** J. HENDERSON *Excursions & Adventures N.S.W.* 125 Lost amid the various and endless mazes of **cedar tracks.**

3. Special Comb. **cedar wattle,** the N.S.W. tree *Acacia elata* (fam. Mimosaceae) having large dark-green glossy bipinnate leaves, and freq. planted as an ornamental.

c **1910** W.R. GUILFOYLE *Austral. Plants* 33 *Acacia elata* . . 'Tall Acacia', or 'Cedar Wattle'.

celery-top pine. The rainforest tree *Phyllocladus aspleniifolius* (fam. Phyllocladaceae) which is restricted to (mainly w.) Tas.; the timber of the tree, valued for its durability and resistance to chemicals; ADVENTURE BAY PINE. Also **celery-leafed pine, celery-topped pine,** and *ellipt.* as **celery-top.**

[**1820** *HRA* (1921) 3rd Ser. III. 466 There is another sort of Tree, which grows among the Huon Pine; it is called here the Celery Pine.] **1827** *Ibid.* (1923) 3rd Ser. VI. 265 The 'Celery-leafed Pine' of Van Diemen's Land . . is rather inclined to be knotty in the trunk in small trees. **1832** J. BACKHOUSE *Narr. Visit Austral. Colonies* (1843) 48 Celery-topped Pine—*Thalamia asplenifolia*—so called from the resemblance of a branch clothed with its dilated leaves, to the leaf of Celery, is well calculated for masts. **1842** D. BURN *Narr. Journey Hobart Town to Macquarie Harbour* 11 Apr. (1955) 25 A very fine resinous pine, called the Celery Top, from its resemblance to that production, is a native of these woods. **1905** *Timber Products & Sawmilling* (Tas. Lands & Surveys Dept.) 11 *Celery-top Pine*.. is another valuable tree, which is generally distributed throughout Tasmania, but in limited quantities.

celestial. *Hist.* [Spec. use of *celestial* a Chinese: see OED(S *sb.* 2.] An immigrant from China; an Australian resident of Chinese descent. Chiefly *pl.*

1841 *Port Phillip Patriot* 11 Mar. 2/5, I am glad to find that our disagreements with the *celestials* promise soon to receive a pacific and satisfactory settlement. **1956** A.C.C. LOCK *Tropical Tapestry* 70 The mating of celestial and lubra had produced a woman with unusual features, which were reflected in her children.

cement. *Mining*, esp. *gold-mining*. [Transf. use of U.S. *cement* 'gravel held firmly in a siliceous matrix or the matrix itself': see Mathews.] Any conglomerate. Also *attrib.*

1858 *Colonial Mining Jrnl.* Nov. 46/3 The singular auriferous conglomerate called 'cement', continues abundant and good. **1891** *Hist. Wedderburn Gold Fields* 8 Between the gullies, and surrounding the flats, are innumerable cement hills. These cement hills are mere remnants of ancient river beds.

Centralia. [Blend of *centr(al* and AUSTR)ALIA 1.] A name orig. proposed for the Colony of South Australia (see quots. 1888 and 1896); now applied to the region surrounding Alice Springs. Cf. CENTRE 1. Also *attrib.*

1888 W. BADGER *'Land Transfer' Laws* p. vii, South Australia, geographically speaking, the 'Centralia' of 'The Australias'. **1896** J.S. LAURIE *Story of Australasia* 299 The name 'South' Australia, embracing as it does both the central and the northern territory, is anomalous.. why not *Centralia*; for West Australia, *Westralia*; for New South Wales, *Eastralia*. **1944** M.J. O'REILLY *Bouyangs & Boomerangs* 115 She married a Centralia clay-pan squatter.

Hence **Centralian** *a.* and *n.*

1896 *Bulletin* (Sydney) 24 Oct. 19/3 Your sneer at Percy Hodgkinson's Centralian frogs is unjust. **1897** *Tocsin* (Melbourne) 4 Nov. 9/2 There are men from Northern Croydon, and a crowd of Maorilanders, Westralians and Centralians, round to Murrumbidgee whalers.

central school. A school providing post-primary courses for pupils from primary schools in the surrounding districts: see quots.

1905 *N.S.W. Parl. Papers* 2nd Sess. IV. 1140 The scheme for conveying children to central schools was brought into operation this year under rules specially framed, and the results have been satisfactory. **1927** G.S. BROWNE *Educ. in Aust.* 36 That the bush children should fare as well as town children [*sc.* in N.S.W.], Central Schools were established in 1903 to which children were conveyed free of charge. **1974** J. McLAREN *Dict. Austral. Educ.* 54 Central School. In New South Wales a country school classified as primary but providing both primary and secondary education... In Victoria, a metropolitan primary school with secondary classes for grades 7 to 8.

centre.

1. With **the** and initial capital. Central Australia (see quot. 1965); red centre, see RED *a.* 2.

1899 SPENCER & GILLEN *Native Tribes Central Aust.* 54 In common with all other Australian tribes, those of the Centre have been shut off from contact with other peoples. **1965** *Austral. Encycl.* II. 323 In popular present-day Australian usage 'The Centre' is an area roughly within a radius of 400 to 500 miles from Alice Springs.

2. *Australian National Football.* **a.** *Centre circle* (see sense 4). **b.** The player occupying the position in the centre circle.

1931 J.F. McHALE et al. *Austral. Game of Football* 60 The centre and the half-forward centre are absolutely unguarded. **1936** E.C.H. TAYLOR *Our Austral. Game Football* 34 *Centre*, .. able to kick with either foot, and should be an expert stab kick or a long drop kick, and .. a good mark.

3. *Two-up.* The central part of the ring, where the spinner stands and bets with the spinner are taken. Also *attrib.*

[N.Z. **1917** *Chrons. N.Z. Exped. Force* 16 May 137 The 'ringies' they were bending low And yelled for 'centre hoot!'] **1931** O. WALTERS *Shrapnel Green* 26 The centre was set, the side-bets on, and Mick was ready to toss. **1971** G. MORGAN *We are borne On* 87 In my first two spins I bet three pounds so I decided to give another pound a fly and went into the centre for my last gamble.

4. *Australian National Football.* Special Comb. **centre back,** the player occupying the central back position; **circle,** a circle in the middle of the field in which the ball is bounced by the field umpire to commence play at the start of each quarter and after a goal is scored; **half-back,** the player occupying the centre half back position, between the centre and back positions; **half-forward,** the player occupying the centre half forward position, between the centre and forward positions; **line man,** a player occupying one of the three centre positions; **man,** the player occupying the central position in the centre line; **wing,** a player occupying either of the wing positions in the centre line.

1931 J.F. McHALE et al. *Austral. Game of Football* 59 The **centre back** must kick off to the windward side of the ground. **1964** J. POLLARD *High Mark* 16 The playing surface .. is oval-shaped and apart from the boundary line itself, a **centre circle** and the goal 'square' at each end there are no other markings anywhere on the field. **1942** H.H. PECK *Mem. of Stockman* 103 **Centre half-back** for Essendon. **1963** L. RICHARDS *Boots & All!* 158 Big **centre-half-forward** Ray 'Joe' Poulter was another character. **1964** J. POLLARD *High Mark* 14 The 18 men comprise six defenders or backmen, six forwards or attacking players, three **centre line men,** and three followers who may move to any part of the ground. **1963** L. RICHARDS *Boots & All!* 46 A well-built six-footer, he was tall for a **centreman.** **1931** J.F. McHALE et al. *Austral. Game of Football* 60 The half-backs—or .. the **centre wings.**

centre-board shed. [See BOARD 1.] A shearing shed in which shearing takes place in the middle rather than along each side.

1908 W.H. OGILVIE *My Life in Open* 36 In a 'centre-board' shed the pens containing the sheep are around the outside of this board. **1979** HARMSWORTH & DAY *Wool & Mohair* 141 Sheds may be classified as *side board* or *centre board* sheds.

century. *Shearing.* [Transf. use of *century* (in cricket) a hundred or more runs.] A tally of one hundred sheep.

1905 A.B. PATERSON *Old Bush Songs* 28 For some had got the century who'd ne'er got it before. **1959** H.P. TRITTON *Time means Tucker* 62 Dutchy broke the 'century', and .. the rep... made a speech praising Dutchy, and welcoming him to the ranks of the big-gun shearers.

certificate. *Hist.* A document issued on the expiry of a convict's term of penal servitude, certifying the recipient's status as a freed person: see quot. 1822. Also **certificate of freedom.**

1796 *N.S.W. Instruct. to Watchmen* 11 If they call themselves Free People and off the Store, they are to produce their Certificates. **1810** *Sydney Gaz.* 14 Jan., All Persons whose Term of Transportation to this Colony has expired, and who have not obtained a legal Certificate of Freedom.

1822 J.T. BIGGE *Rep. State Colony N.S.W.* 120 The certificates issued by the secretary attest, that after an examination of the indents, so many years have expired since sentence of that term was passed on the party entitled to it, describing the year and ship in which he arrived, and ending with a declaration, that by reason of the expired service, the said party is restored to all the rights of a free subject.

chain, *n.*[1]
1. *Hist.* Used *attrib.* in Special Comb. **chain gang,** a party of convicts assigned to hard labour in chains, such chains usu. being ankle fetters joined by a chain which, to allow reasonable freedom of movement, was tied up to the belt (convicts wearing irons were also chained together when moving from one place to another); IRONED GANG; see also GANG; so **chain gangsman.**
1822 J.T. BIGGE *Rep. State Colony N.S.W.* 35 The punishment of the chain gang is rightly described . . to be the least efficient, and most prejudicial. **1846** H. EASY *Horrors of Transportation* 11, I now begin to believe what I have often heard old chain gangsmen say.

2. In the phr. **(up)on the chain.**
a. *Hist.* Of a convict: (so as to be) secured with a chain.
1835 J. BACKHOUSE *Extracts from Lett.* (1838) ii. 74 He was committed to jail in irons, with the rest of his fellows, and they were put upon the chain (i.e.) had a chain passed over their irons, and fixed outside of their prison to render them more secure. **1846** *Citizen* (Sydney) 26 Dec. 138/2 He would be put on 'the chain' and sent down to Sydney.

b. *fig.* See sense 3.
1980 *Nat. Times* (Sydney) 2 Nov. 36/2 Shearers are a competitive lot, and watch each other's tallies jealously. There's great prestige in being the ringer; no one wants to shear 'on the chain'.

3. *fig.* In the phr. **to drag the chain,** to lag behind one's fellow workers (orig. in shearing) or companions in an activity.
1912 *Bulletin* (Sydney) 28 Nov. 16/4 One of the fraternity confided to me on the board . . that he 'had peeled 88, and was dragging the chain behind Nugget Smith'. **1961** M. CALTHORPE *Dyehouse* 156 Maybe they could take it easy. Drag the chain just a little.

4. *fig.* In the phr. **off the chain,** free from restraint.
1947 C. FENTON *Flying Doctor* 53 For what followed, little excuse can be offered, except that we were 'off the chain'; we had come from the bush, and our spirits were high with prospect of holiday in the gay town of Darwin.

chain, *n.*[2] [Spec. use of *chain* linear series (of objects).] In the collocation **chain of billabongs (lagoons, lakes, ponds, pools, waterholes),** a series of depressions in the bed of an intermittently flowing watercourse which continue to hold water after the connecting stream has dried up.
1799 D. COLLINS *Acct. Eng. Colony N.S.W.* (1802) II. 185 The creek runs winding between two steep hills, and ends in a chain of ponds that extends into a valley of great beauty. **1845** L. LEICHHARDT *Jrnl. Overland Exped. Aust.* 10 Jan. (1847) 104 The creek . . joined a river. . . It was not, however, running but formed a chain of small lakes, from two to three and even eight miles in length, and frequently from fifty to one hundred yards broad. **1852** G.C. MUNDY *Our Antipodes* II. 40 A fine chain of water-holes, which, after heavy rains, puts on the guise of a continuous stream. **1882** W. SOWDEN *N.T. as it Is* 39 The village is situated near a chain of billabongs. **1887** A. NICOLS *Wild Life & Adventure* 62 Chains of lagoons—some of extraordinary depth—marked the former course of the Maranoa. **1945** *Bulletin* (Sydney) 11 Apr. 12/3 Barramundi and other fish contrive to survive when the river is reduced to a mere chain of pools.

chain *v.*

1. *intr.* Of pools: to form a chain.
1926 *Bulletin* (Sydney) 8 Apr. 22/2 Dawdling down the Diamantina, squandering days where the deep pools chain.
2. *trans.* To clear (land), using a chain stretched between two bulldozers to flatten scrub, etc.
1968 R.M. FADDEN Land Clearing Team Daily Diary 4 Mar. 1 The two operators had no experience on chaining. **1985** *Newsletter* (Soc. for Growing Austral. Plants, Canberra Region) Sept. 10 His wildflower farm is at Coorow, where he purchased 3500 acres of sandplain in 1978. The land had previously been chained and unsuccessfully cropped.

chain-lightning. [U.S. *chain-lightning* inferior whisky: see Mathews.] Any crudely-made spirituous liquor. Also *attrib.*
1876 J.A. EDWARDS *Gilbert Gogger* 96 At three o'clock in the morning, they lighted up, and began to retail 'stone fences', 'shandy gaff', 'chain lightning', 'all my own', etcetera, etcetera, to the assembled diggers. . . Australian fancy drinks. **1892** *Braidwood Dispatch* 31 Dec. 2/3 The sole stock-in-trade consists of an empty beer barrel and some chain-lightning rum, warranted to bite all the way down and scratch all the way back, and to be particularly soothing to the bush-man.

chalkie. Also **chalky.** [f. *chalk* + -Y.] A schoolteacher.
1945 *Bulletin* (Sydney) 2 May 12/1 A country chalkie of my acquaintance. **1953** T.A.G. HUNGERFORD *Riverslake* 29 'I was a chalky before the war—just couldn't settle down to it again, after.' 'Chalky?' 'School-teacher.'

chaney. *Obs.* Also **chanie.** [Of unknown origin.] In the phr. **to play chaneys,** to exert influence; **to play chaneys with,** to bribe (someone).
1892 *Bohemia* (Melbourne) 4 Feb. 3 He hasn't any constitution or manifesto in his breeches-pocket, and only vents a growl at his successor, who really does not appear to have 'played all chanies' in the little game which ends with Berry out and Munro in. **1899** *Truth* (Sydney) 19 Mar. 3/3 She stows whatever morals she has in the south-western corner of her heel, plays chaneys with the police.

change. *Hist.* [Scot. dial. *change* inn: see OED *change, sb.* 11 and *change-house.*] A staging-post at which coach horses were changed. See also *mail change* MAIL *n.*[1] Also **change** (or **changing**) **station,** and *attrib.*
1913 W.K. HARRIS *Outback in Aust.* 110 The pub-keeper drove the coach on to the next 'change'. **1926** C.B. FLETCHER *Murray Valley* p. ii, A small two- or three-house changing-station on the Murray. **1943** H.G. LAMOND *From Tariaro to Ross Roy* 90 Cobb & Co.'s change grooms were always versatile. **1947** W. LAWSON *Paddle-Wheels Away* 145 Might find shanty or a change-station and find out about the coach.
Hence **change** *v. trans.*
1911 *Bulletin* (Sydney) 19 Jan. 14/4 That crib was one of the busiest between Melbourne and Beechworth. Cobb's changed there, while the passengers got their tucker at three bob a time.

chanie, var. CHANEY.

channel-billed cuckoo. [From the channel or groove on each side of the beak.] The large-billed, predom. grey cuckoo *Scythrops novaehollandiae* of n. and e. Aust., a summer visitor from Indonesia and New Guinea, having a loud, harsh call traditionally presaging rain. See also STORM BIRD. Also **channel-bill (cuckoo).**
1801 J. LATHAM *Gen. Synopsis Birds* Suppl. II. 96 N. Holland Channel-Bill . . is not very common, and first appears about *Port Jackson* in *October*. **1914** *Bulletin* (Sydney) 15 Jan. 24/2 The so-called storm-bird—who can't predict storms

worth a cuss—is a cuckoo, the channel-bill cuckoo. **1964** M. SHARLAND *Territory of Birds* 130 The giant Channel-billed Cuckoo . . whose vocal talents are by no means melodious.

channel country. See quot. 1968.

1947 *Proc. R. Soc. Qld.* LIX. 158 Panicum Whitei . . is . . sometimes . . a prominent part of the pasture of the 'channel country'. **1968** A.M. DUNCAN-KEMP *Where Strange Gods Call* p. ix, The term 'channel country' is not necessarily the proper name of a geographical area, but a common expression used by outback residents to designate a definite order of geographical features. These are the wide, twisting rivers and creeks, and the great flood plains that form the inland river system, the natural irrigation channels of the far south-west of Queensland and the north of South Australia.

charcoal tart. A piece of dough baked on embers: see JOHNNY-CAKE.

1909 *Bulletin* (Sydney) 30 Sept. 13/2 The 'Johnny cake' . . is variously known as the 'charcoal tart' or the 'blanker on the coals'. **1976** C.D. MILLS *Hobble Chains & Greenhide* 73, I could hear the plant bells moving in as I flicked the 'charcoal tarts' out of the ashes next morning.

charge, *v*. *Australian National Football*. *trans*. To attack and push (a player) illegally. Also as *vbl. n*.

1929 W.S. SHARLAND *Sporting Globe Football Bk.* (1930) 86 The field umpire shall . . report to the controlling body every player who . . charges an opponent when such opponent is standing still or when he is in the air for a mark. **1959** PARNELL & ANDREW *Austral. Football* 46 Charging takes place when a player bumps or pushes a player when the ball is *more than five yards away, on the ground or in the air*.

charge, *n.*[1] *Australian National Football.* [f. prec.] The act of pushing or bumping illegally.

1931 J.F. MCHALE et al. *Austral. Game of Football* 31 Every charge cannot be effective in upsetting an opponent, and so every player must expect to be charged as well as to charge. **1965** J. DYER *Captain Blood* 190 If you see a charge coming, get out of the way if you can. If you can't, improvise. . . There is no set answer for a charge other than raising as dangerous a front to him as possible.

charge, *n.*[2] [Spec. use of U.S. *charge* a thrill, 'kick'.] A glass of an alcoholic beverage, esp. spirits. Also **charge-on.**

1963 D. ATTENBOROUGH *Quest under Capricorn* 19 Doug took the hint. 'It's my shout,' he said. 'You blokes can ease in another charge I reckon.' **1984** P. READ *Down there with me on Cowra Mission* 115, I went over to where the Aborigine camp is alongside of that, and there's two old fellers having a charge-on.

charity moll. A prostitute who charges less than the usual rate.

1962 'C. ROHAN' *Delinquents* 104 If the cops spring you here, I know nothing and no charity moll capers with my men. **1982** N. KEESING *Lily on Dustbin* 41 A 'charity moll' is the equivalent of a World War II 'EA' or 'enthusiastic amateur': a promiscuous woman whose sexual favours are theoretically not available for sale . . instead, for presents, dinners, theatre and show tickets.

charlie. Also **charley,** and in full **Charlie Wheeler.** [f. the name of *Charles* Wheeler (1881–1977), a painter of the nude.] Rhyming slang for 'sheila'.

1942 *Cheeriodical* (Rathmines) 5 Mar. 12 The Manager knew what they meant by 'Charlie Wheelers'. **1949** L. GLASSOP *Lucky Palmer* 41 'What do you mean by 'Charlie'?' 'Your 'Charlie',' repeated Max. 'Your canary.' 'Canary?' 'Ay, don't you speak English? Your sheila.' **1960** D. MCLEAN *Roaring Days* 1 A female may be my sheila, my bird, my charley, [etc.].

chase, *v*. In the phr. **to chase the dragon**, see quot. 1979; **the (penny) weight,** to prospect for gold; **the sunset,** to tramp the country.

1979 B. DELANEY *Narc* 43 Charlie chased this elusive liquid and inhaled the fumes through the drinking straw! Hence the expression **'chasing the dragon'**. As the heroin burned off, Charlie expertly dropped more granules and sucked the gas into his lungs. **1936** J. KIRWAN *My Life's Adventure* 76 Prospectin' is a rotten life . . . I expect I'll be all my life **chasin' the weight. 1949** I.L. IDRIESS *One Wet Season* 72 And the talk inevitably turned to gold. 'Ah!' sighed Womba. 'I too chased the pennyweight in the days when I had my Ena.' **1915** *Bulletin* (Sydney) 14 Oct. 24/4 Tell me a profession with more *aliases* than the swagman's? Here are a few: 'Waltzin' Matilda', . . 'humpin' the bluey', . . **'chasin' the sunset'**.

chat, *n*. [Br. slang *chat* louse: see OED *sb.*[7]]

1. A louse. Also *attrib*.

1812 J.H. VAUX *Mem.* (1819) 162 *Chats*, lice. **1916** *Battery Herald: Jrnl. 14th Field Artillery* 25 Sept. 2 For sale. Specially selected stud chats. **1918** C.L. HARTT *Diggerettes* 63 Just after we had left the lines a Digger was industriously holding the usual 'chat hunt', when a pal passing by remarked: 'Hello, Bill, picking 'em out?' Bill: 'No, just taking 'em as they come.' **1967** *Kings Cross Whisper* (Sydney) xxxiii. 4/3 *Chat*, a prison bed-bug. A term used to describe an obnoxious person. *Chats' yard*, the section of a prison where grubby people are segregated. **1974** ADAMSON & HANFORD *Zimmer's Essay* 99 George Orwell gives 'chat' as a term for 'louse' . . in usage among Kentish hop-pickers. . . In New South Wales prison argot, it means both 'louse' and a certain type of prisoner. A 'chat' is a social incompetent, though not necessarily a drunk. They are usually gaoled for nuisance offences, such as vagrancy.

2. *Transf.* and *fig.* A debased person. See quots. 1967 and 1974 above.

1967 B.K. BURTON *Teach them no More* 119 He had always felt for the alcoholics in the chat's yard. **1980** M. WILLIAMS *Dingo!* 160 'He's a warb! A chat!' I exclaimed. 'A dirty drunk!'

Hence **chatty** *a.*, afflicted with lice.

1972 W. WATKINS *Don't wait for Me* 45 'I'm so chatty I can bloody near smell myself.' He scratched irritably at his crutch with his free hand as he spoke.

chat, *v*. [f. prec.] *trans.* To remove lice from (one's clothing or person). Also *absol.*

1919 *Waiting Times: Jrnl. 17 Battalion A.I.F.* 1 Mar. 4 A certain officer was one day chatting himself. **1933** E.J. RULE *Jacka's Mob* 16 Like the poor, the 'chats' were with us always, and most of us chatted twice daily.

cheerio. [N.Z., prob. from association with *cheerio* 'cheers'.] A small sausage of the frankfurter type. Also as *cheerio sausage.*

1965 K. SMITH *OGF* 136 Vi looked towards the kitchen where eight pounds of cheerios were bubbling merrily on the stove; they would be splitting their sides already. **1980** S. THORNE *I've met some Bloody Wags* 18 Keith . . tossed cheerio sausages into the fans, played the didgeridoo, and wrestled a stuffed crocodile.

cheer-up. *S.A.* [f. the name of the *Cheer-Up* Our Boys Society, a patriotic organization founded in Adelaide in 1914.] Used *attrib.* in Comb. with reference to the activities of the Cheer-Up Our Boys Society (or of a similar organization). Also *absol.*, a member of the Society.

[**1914** *Register* (Adelaide) 3 Nov. 4/4 Our boys must not be allowed to believe for even one solitary hour that they are forgotten or neglected by the people for whom they have shown their willingness to make the supreme sacrifice or to fancy that nobody cares for them. . . Who will form the first Cheer Up Our Boys Society? *Ibid.* 5 Nov. 4/6 We are pleased to announce that The Register's suggestion of a

'Cheer Up Our Boys Society' has resulted in the formation of such a body.] *Ibid.* 10 Nov. 5/7 Yet, but for this 'Cheer Up' organisation, it is probable that little would have been done to adequately farewell this band. **1920** F.J. MILLS *Cheer Up* 25 The Cheer-Ups—150 strong—arrived with baskets of good things, including oranges and early peaches.

cheque.
1. The total sum received, esp. by a rural worker at the end of a seasonal contract, or from the sale of a crop.
1857 F. DE B. COOPER *Wild Adventures* 66 Drawing my 'cheque' from Wilder, I felt my exchequer sufficiently strong to allow of my embarking in another career, namely, that of an overlander. **1976** B. SCOTT *Complete Bk. Austral. Folk Lore* 167 In a week the spree was over and the cheque was all knocked down, So we shouldered our Matildas and we turned our backs on town.
2. Special Comb. **cheque bu(r)sting** *ppl. a.*, spending freely, engaged in a spree; so **buster; man,** one who has received a cheque and is ready to spend it; **-proud** *a.*, 'flush', elated at being so.
1910 *Bulletin* (Sydney) 5 May 15/1 Shearers were then just about on a par with their present-day confrères in gambling and **cheque-bursting** habits. **1945** *Ibid.* 22 Aug. 12/1 Adelaide was the acme of cities, the vision of all vacationists, the **cheque-busters'** dream. **1881** *Bulletin* (Sydney) 10 Sept. 12/1 Shearing.. is the season when the honest publican gets the 'shearer's bottle' ready under the counter and when he sees a little cloud of dust drawing nearer along the winding track, calls out to the 'stringer'—just brought up from town for the season—'Come into the verandah and smile, Mary Ann; here's another **cheque-man** coming.' **1904** L.M.P. ARCHER *Bush Honeymoon* 276 Any other fellow would have been **cheque-proud** long ago.

chequed-up, *a.* In possession of a CHEQUE (sense 1), and ready to spend it. See also CASHED UP.
1905 *Bulletin* (Sydney) 16 Mar. 3/2, I was chequed-up for a wonder... Course my cheque was not the size of shearing-cheques of long ago. **1977** F.B. VICKERS *Stranger no Longer* 85, I was the lucky bastard who was chequed-up at the end of a run of shearing.

cherry.
1. *Obs.* Any of several plants, esp. those of the genus *Exocarpos* (see BALLART); the wood or 'fruit' of these plants; *wild cherry* WILD 1. See also *native cherry* NATIVE *a.* 6 a. Freq. *attrib.*, as **cherry-tree.**
1793 J. HUNTER *Hist. Jrnl. Trans. Port Jackson* 478 The fruit Captain Cook calls a cherry. **1799** D. COLLINS *Acct. Eng. Colony N.S.W.* (1802) II. 235 The blue gum, she-oak, and cherry tree of Port Jackson were common here. **1884** A. NILSON *Timber Trees N.S.W.* 98 M[*emecylon*] *cerasiformis*—Cherry... a singularly handsome tree, tall and straight.
2. Special Comb. **cherry bob,** a cherry-stone, esp. as used in a game played by children; the name of a game; **pick** *v. trans.* (**a**) to sort or remove (stones, etc.) manually; (**b**) to manipulate (monies in a superannuation fund) for the purpose of tax avoidance; also as *vbl. n.*; so **picker.**
1959 A.D. MICKLE *After Ball* 73, I played '**Cherry-bobs**', 'Kick the Tin', 'Charlie Over', and collected stamps. **1960** K. SMITH *Word from Children* 155 These days cherry stones are cherry stones. When I was a child they were 'cherrybobs', eagerly sought after as currency in a schoolboy's game of skill called 'Bunny-holes'. **1975** L. BEADELL *Still in Bush* 22 Eric drove the workshop Rover, doing a dual job of helping everyone do everything as well as '**cherry picking**' the finished road for odd roots and stones left behind after the last pass of the grader. **1984** *Canberra Times* 5 Apr. 13/8 Legislation to combat the operation of 'cherry-picking' tax-avoidance schemes involving employee superannuation funds was introduced into Parliament yesterday. **1984** *CPD* (Senate) CII. 486 A way in which the employees.. for whose benefit ostensibly the fund was established, are deprived of their entitlements in that fund and the contributions on which exemption from taxable income has already been claimed and on which income earned within the fund has been tax exempt, are ultimately directed or harvested, if you like. I understand that the colloquial term is 'cherry picked'. **1970** B. FULLER *Nullarbor Story* 43 'When everything was set, we cut a track thirty-four feet wide to take a twenty-eight foot surface. And after us came the **cherry pickers**.' 'Cherry pickers?' 'Yeh. The name we had for the old blokes who did smoothing-off work, cleaning up the large stones that we had missed.' **1984** *CPD* (Senate) CII. 497 The cherry picker scheme is a most outrageous and reprehensible tax avoidance mechanism.

chestnut, *n. Obs.* Black bean (a), see BLACK *a.*^{2} 1 a.
1833 W.J. HOOKER *Bot. Miscellany* I. 259 Close to our encampment we observed a number of fires, kindled by the natives, with quantities of *Chestnuts* (*Castanospermum*). **1880** J. BONWICK *Resources Qld.* 82 The Chestnut of the south-east is a *Castanospermum* of magnificent growth and luxuriance of foliage, with dark walnut-like wood.

chestnut, *a.* [Spec. use of *chestnut* the colour.] In the names of birds: **chestnut-breasted shelduck,** *mountain duck*, see MOUNTAIN; **-eared finch,** *zebra finch*, see ZEBRA; **teal,** the small duck *Anas castanea* of s. Aust., the adult male having chestnut underparts.
[**1844 chestnut-breasted shelduck:** J. GOULD *Birds of Aust.* (1848) VII. Pl. 7, *Casarca tadorinodes*... Chestnut-coloured Shieldrake... Mountain Duck, Colonists of Swan River.] **1931** N.W. CAYLEY *What Bird is That?* 246 Chestnut-breasted Shelduck.. is generally shy and wary. **1843** J. GOULD *Birds of Aust.* (1848) III. Pl. 87, The **Chestnut-eared Finch** is one of the smallest of the genus yet discovered in Australia. [**1845 chestnut teal:** J. GOULD *Birds of Aust.* (1848) VII. Pl. 11, *Anas punctata*... Chestnut-breasted Duck... Teal, Colonists of Swan River.] **1945** C. BARRETT *Austral. Bird Life* 50 The chestnut teal.. is absent from northern parts of the mainland and the south-west.

chew, *v. Obs.*
1. In the phr. **to chew** (someone's) **lug** (or **ear**), to cadge. See also BITE *v.*
1896 H. LAWSON *While Billy Boils* 14 Bill said: 'We'll have to sharpen our teeth, that's all, and chew somebody's lug... You know one or two of these mugs. Bite one of their ears.' So I took aside a chap that I knowed and bit his ear for ten bob, and gave it to Bill to mind. **1901** *Truth* (Sydney) 9 June 3/4 The bandsmen, who complained about being half-starved on the Royal yacht, had been indulging freely in the unromantic occupation of what, in polite circles, is called 'chewing a man's ear', or 'biting his lug'. In other words.. the Royal bandsmen.. were *obliged to cadge.*
2. *trans.* To drink (esp. beer). See also BEER CHEWER.
1904 *Shearer* (Sydney) 15 Oct. 8/1 They are well dressed and well behaved, and instead of chewing beer, they were reading good books. **1910** *Bulletin* (Sydney) 14 Apr. 14/3 Twenty years ago the average shearer was a derelict sort of person, whose main ambition in life was to earn a cheque and then chew it up at the nearest shanty. The old-time beer-chewer has been driven out to join the sundowners.
Hence **chewer** *n.*
1922 *Bulletin* (Sydney) 13 July 22/4 A chewer on the promise of a pint of beer swallowed a mixture of tar and kerosene.

chewbac. *Austral. pidgin.* [f. *chew (ing + to)bac(co.*] Tobacco.

1925 M. TERRY *Across Unknown Aust.* 286 There was much chew-bac to be handed to them. 1944 F. BERKERY *East goes West* 26 The black inhabitants .. found the men were not such bad fellows, and inclined to be liberal with the good old 'chewbac'.

chewy. Also **chewie.** [f. chew(ing gum) + -Y.]
1. (A piece of) chewing gum. Also *attrib.*
1924 F.J. MILLS *Happy Days* 115 The boys .. looked round for the chocolate and 'chewy' sellers. 1969 W. DICK *Naked Prodigal* 239 'Have a chewie, Kenny,' he said, passing me one.
2. In the phr. **chewy on your boot,** a barracker's call intended to discourage a player from performing well (at kicking, running, etc.), or to deride one who is performing poorly.
1966 S.J. BAKER *Austral. Lang.* (ed. 2) 370 *Hope you have chewie on your boot!* used to express a wish that a football player kicking for goal misses because there is chewing gum on his boot. 1975 *Sydney Morning Herald* 8 Nov. 4/3 Mr Hawke puzzled the crowd when he described their reaction to the Khemlani disclosure as, 'You were wrong, chewy on your boot'. He did not seem to realise he had used an Australian Rules cat-call.

chiack /'tʃaiæk/, *v.* Also **chyack.** [a. Br. slang *chi-hike,* apparently orig. a costermonger's cry of praise or commendation: see OED(S.] *trans.* To taunt, barrack, or tease (someone). Also *absol.*
1853 [see *chiacking, vbl. n.*]. 1874 G. WALCH *Adamanta* 27 I've learnt to chi-ike peelers. 1885 *Australasian Printers' Keepsake* 139 My mates chyacked me all night. 1948 K.S. PRICHARD *Golden Miles* 180 The groomsmen all red in the face and looking as if they would choke in their stiff white collars, rocked the whole congregation with a desire to chuckle and chiack.
Hence **chiacking** *vbl. n.* and *ppl. a.*
1853 C.R. READ *What I heard, saw, & Did* 148 The 'skyhacking', to which the police were subject .. was brought on principally by their own individual overbearing conduct. [*Note*] Blackguarding. 1964 'E. LINDALL' *Kind of Justice* 30 They were a vociferous crowd, ruggedly vocal in a loud, chiacking anticipation of the heady joys to come.

chiack /'tʃaiæk/, *n.* Also **chyack.** [f. prec.] Banter, barracking.
1869 *Australasian* (Melbourne) 17 July 72/4 The hissing of gallery, or the gods, is called *chy-ike.* 1898 *Bulletin* (Sydney) 17 Dec. (Red Page), *Chyack* is more properly *chyike,* the cockney pronunciation of 'cheek'—impudent badinage. 1971 F. HARDY *Outcasts of Foolgarah* 2 'Hullo, hullo,' Chilla said, always a bit too keen on the old chiack, especially when it came to Tich's unsuccessful carryings on with the female of the species.

chief. *Hist.* KING *n.*[1] 1 a.
1794 G. THOMPSON *Slavery & Famine* II. 11 There are three or four of the Chiefs who attend the Governor's house every day for their dinner and a glass of wine. 1912 A. BERRY *Reminisc.* 178 Two native gentlemen—Lager, the chief of Jervis Bay, and Wagin, the chief of Numba—who were induced to accompany me by the promise of a suit of clothes and an engraved brass plate each, as a badge of their dignity as chiefs or kings!!

child. *Obs.* Usu. in *pl.* In the phr. **child of the bush** and varr., applied to an Aboriginal. Cf. BLACK *a.*[1] 4.
1819 *Sydney Gaz.* 2 Jan., *His Excellency the Governor,* accompanied by the *Lieutenant Governor,* the Members of the Native Institution, and several other Gentlemen entered the circle where these Children of Nature were seated. Chairs were provided for the Chiefs of tribes. 1874 J.J. HALCOMBE *Emigrant & Heathen* 38 Those houseless, homeless children of the bush, the black natives.

child endowment. An untaxed allowance paid by a government (from 1941 by the federal government) to the parents or guardians of a child. Also *attrib.*
1926 *Sydney Morning Herald* 24 Dec. 1/1 The State Cabinet has approved of a child endowment scheme, the rate to be 6s. per child per week. 1978 R.H. CONQUEST *Dusty Distances* 18 Child endowment, for what it's worth, was something for the distant future.

Children's python. [The specific epithet *Childreni* was given by English naturalist J.E. Grey (*Zool. Miscellany* (1842) 44), after J.G. *Children* (1777–1852), a colleague at the British Museum.] The nocturnal python *Liasis childreni* of n. Aust. Also **Children's snake.**
1869 G. KREFFT *Snakes of Aust.* 34 Children's rock snake. 1970 P. SLATER *Eagle for Pidgin* 59 'It's a Children's python, isn't it, Dad?' 'That's right—not called after kids .. but after a Dr Children.'

Chinaman.
1. *Obs.* In the collocation **Chinaman's trot,** a slow but steady jogging pace; a shuffling gait. Cf. CHINKIE (quot. 1930).
1897 J.J. MURIF *From Ocean to Ocean* 22, I frequently caught myself going at a 'Chinaman's trot' where I could not do any riding. 1904 *Sporting News* (Launceston) 10 Sept. 1/3 Why the stewards did not take action is certainly not understandable. It was a Chinaman's trot, in the fullest sense of the term, and should not be countenanced.
2. Used *attrib.* in Special Comb. **Chinaman fish,** any of several fish, esp. the sea perch *Symphorus nematophorus* of n. Qld. Also **Chinaman.**
1906 D.G. STEAD *Fishes of Aust.* 265 Yellow Leatherjacket or 'Chinaman'. *Monacanthus ayraudi.* N.S.W. 1944 J. DEVANNY *By Tropic Sea & Jungle* 81 The Chinaman fish is supposed to be poisonous at certain times of the year.

Chinese. In various collocations: **Chinese burr,** any of several burred plants, esp. *Centaurea melitensis* (see COCKSPUR); the burr itself; **pump** *mining,* a pump consisting of buckets on a continuous belt; **scrub** (or **shrub**), the aromatic shrub *Cassinia arcuata* (fam. Asteraceae) which, from its vigorous growth and seeding, is often regarded as a weed.
1900 *Bulletin* (Sydney) 15 Dec. 15/2 The **Chinese burr** in Cairns district (N.Q.) is densely thick... The Chow always leaves this legacy behind him when he quits leased land. It is supposed to have been brought from China in packing. 1946 'B. JAMES' *Cookabundy Bridge* 20 He wildly explored his feet for Chinese burrs. 1852 A. MACKAY *Great Gold Field* 9 Nov. (1853) 46 The claim .. is situated near the centre of the Bar, and what is called a Californian, but more properly a **Chinese pump,** which lifts a great deal of water, is employed to work it. 1909 A.J. EWART *Weeds Vic.* 1 The following native plants are included under the head of proclaimed weeds: .. the **Chinese Scrub** (*Cassinia arcuata*) [etc.]. 1981 G.M. CUNNINGHAM et al. *Plants Western N.S.W.* 688 As chinese-shrub readily colonizes disturbed and bare soils it has some use in the reclamation of gravel pits or mine dumps. Its name originates from its frequent occurrence around gold diggings and the fact that the Chinese miners used it to thatch roofs of their dwellings.

Chingah, Chingi, varr. JINGY.

Chink. [Altered form of *Chinese,* poss. infl. by *chink* narrow aperture, slit, with reference to the eyes; not excl. Austral. but, like CHINKIE, recorded earliest in Aust.] A Chinese; usu. an immigrant or a descendant of an immigrant.
1887 'WANDERER' *Down on their Luck* 28 The white man must go, because the Chinks can live on the smell of an oil rag. 1965 *Coast to Coast 1963–64* 118, I take a little Chink with the slanty eyes, or a little Black Feller nobody wants.

Chinkie. Also **Chinky.** [See prec.] CHINK. Also *attrib.*
1876 *Queenslander* (Brisbane) 18 Mar. 13/2 Our colonialised 'Chinkie', as he is vulgarly termed (with the single variation 'Chow'). **1930** *Bulletin* (Sydney) 6 Aug. 20/1 An' many a mile across the plains We done the 'chinkie-jog'. **1969** W. DICK *Naked Prodigal* 5 He didn't seem a bad bloke for a chinky-chink.
Hence **Chinkieland** *n.*, China.
1911 *Truth* (Sydney) 29 Oct. 1/5 He sees the Pong start off for dear old Chinkieland.

chip, *v. trans.* To hoe or break up (the surface soil); with **in(to),** to sow (seed) by hoeing it into the ground.
1797 D. COLLINS *Acct. Eng. Colony N.S.W.* (1802) II. 18 Some .. too idle and dissipated to hoe and properly prepare the ground for seed, have carelessly thrown the grain over the old stubble, and afterwards chipped it in, as they termed it, going lightly over the ground with a hoe, and barely covering the seed. **c 1852** A. MANN *Goldfields Aust.* 107 A man with a hoe, and the labour of a few days, may 'chip' into the earth sufficient maize or Indian corn to sustain him for the entire year. **1918** *Bulletin* (Sydney) 18 July 22/3, I have gone to fight the Germans, and I don't know when I'm coming back, somebody chip round my humpy against grass fire.
Hence **chipper** *n.*
1978 D. BALL *Great Austral. Snake Exchange* 97 A work force of 2000 Aboriginal 'chippers', so called because they chip out weeds with five-foot long hoes.

chip heater. A domestic water heater which uses small pieces of wood as fuel.
1946 K. TENNANT *Lost Haven* 101 Grandpa led the way to the bathroom and expected the guest to admire the bath and the chip-heater! **1984** P. READ *Down there with me on Cowra Mission* 26 They didn't have a chip heater, like we got here now.

chiv /tʃɪv/. [Abbrev. of *chiv(v)y* shortened form of *Chevy Chase*, rhyming slang for 'face'.] The face.
1902 *Truth* (Sydney) 20 Apr. 5/1 The class of female under notice has, to use an Australianism, a chiv as tough as the rear end of a native bear, and *a hide like a dugong.* **1916** C.J. DENNIS *Moods of Ginger Mick* 117 'Ow many times 'ave I sat in this chair An' seen is 'ard chiv grinnin' over there.

choc: see CHOCKO.

chock-a-block. See quots. Also abbrev. as **chocka.**
1971 F. HARDY *Outcasts of Foolgarah* 80 They caught me at it once on the sofa in the living room, caught me right in the bloody act with a woman who came to do the cleaning; chocker-block up her, I was, going for me life. **1979** R. DREWE *Cry in Jungle Bar* 146 It was as if he and Gigi had been the couple caught red-handed. On the job. Chocka—as the old schoolboy expression succinctly put it—chockablock.

chock-and-log. A kind of fence or wall built of logs resting on short, transversely-placed blocks of wood. Freq. *attrib.* as **chock-and-log fence.**
1869 E.C. BOOTH *Another England* 132 Tom .. put a 'chock and log' fence round his little property. **1872** G.S. BADEN-POWELL *New Homes for Old Country* 207 Another fence, known as 'chock and log', is composed of long logs resting on piles of chocks, or short blocks of wood.

chocko /tʃɒkoʊ/. Also **choco.** Shortened form of CHOCOLATE SOLDIER. Also **choc.**
1918 R.H. KNYVETT *Over there with Australs.* 154 We carried off the 'championship cup', beating the 'Chocolates' by two or three points. We might not have been so elated had not the 'Chocs.' been such 'nuts' on themselves. **1942** T. KELAHER *Digger Hat* 51 I've a letter here to hand, Saying Chockos, Yanks and Refugees Have overrun the land. **1943** D. FRIEND *Gunner's Diary* 39 Chocos (militia) shouldn't be allowed into the canteen, the conscript rats.

chocolate frog. Rhyming slang for 'dog', an informer (see DOG *n.*²). Also *ellipt.* as **chocolate.**
1971 *Bulletin* (Sydney) 28 Aug. 17/2 He said he preferred any other prisoner to a 'chocolate frog' or an informer. **1973** J. MCNEIL *Chocolate Frog* 18 Trouble is, but, yer never know these days just who is a bloody chocolate, and who ain't!

chocolate lily. Any of the several perennial herbs of the genus *Arthropodium* (fam. Liliaceae), the purplish flowers of which have a sweet scent reminiscent of chocolate or vanilla. Also *ellipt.* as **chocolate.**
1944 A. MARSHALL *These are my People* 201 Say diggers, do you remember picking the ham and eggs, the chocolates, the everlastings, the early nancy? **1965** *Coast to Coast 1963–64* 155 The mullock heaps in their pelts of paspalum and chocolate lilies.

chocolate soldier. [Spec. use of *chocolate (cream) soldier* a soldier who will not fight (see G.B. Shaw *Arms and the Man* (1898) I. 17).]
a. *Hist.* In the war of 1914–18, a soldier in the 8th Infantry Brigade of the Australian Imperial Force, so called because the Brigade arrived in Egypt after the Gallipoli campaign.
1915 T. SKEYHILL *Soldier-Songs from Anzac* 22 But 'e called me a chocolate soldier, A six bob a day tourist, too. 'E says, 'You'll not reach the trenches; Nor even get a view.' **1918** R.H. KNYVETT *Over there with Australs.* 153 There was a good deal of rivalry between us and another brigade known as 'The Chocolate Soldiers'. They received this nickname because they were the most completely equipped unit that ever left Australia.
b. Orig. in the war of 1939–45, a militiaman or conscript, called up for home service and unable, before 1943, to serve outside Australia and its territories.
1943 A. DAWES *Soldier Superb* 83 'Chocko' abbreviates 'chocolate soldier', formerly a term of opprobrium rather than affection applied by men of the A.I.F. to 'Saturday soldiers'—militiamen called up for home defence. **1979** *Southerly* iv. 368 He's in the University Regiment. He's a chocolate soldier.

chokey /tʃoʊki/. [Anglo-Indian *choky* police station lock-up, used also in Br. slang from 1873: see OED 2.] A police station; a gaol. Freq. without article.
1840 A. RUSSELL *Tour through Austral. Colonies* 190 He was politely handed up to the *chokey*, (colonially called) .. more generally known as the police office. **1855** R. CARBONI *Eureka Stockade* 55 Three of the ringleaders of the mob had been pounced upon, and were safe in chokey.

choko /tʃoʊkoʊ/. [a. Brazilian Indian *chuchu*.] The cultivated vine of tropical America *Sechium edule* (fam. Cucurbitaceae), bearing an edible pear-shaped fruit; the fruit itself.
1909 LINDSAY & HOLTZE *Territoria* 58 The choko, to give its Queensland name, likes a loose sandy or loamy substratum. **1979** DOUGLAS & HEATHCOTE *Far Cry* 46, I ate chokos steamed, fried, stewed, in salads, and every other way I could think of.

choof, *v.* Also **chuff.** [Fig use of *chuff* to puff (as a steam engine).] *intr.* To go or move.
1947 *Contact: Jrnl. Air Force Assoc. Victorian Division* Mar. 16 We hope you shall be able to choof along to the next function. **1977** R. BEILBY *Gunner* 139 It's just that the old bloke's sick so it might be better if you chuffed off.

choogar bag, var. SUGAR BAG 1.

chook /tʃʊk/. Also **chookie, chooky, chuckey, chuckie**. [Br. dial. *chuck(y)* chicken, fowl: see OED *sb.*²]

1. A domestic fowl; a chicken. Also *attrib.*

1855 W. Howitt *Land, Labor & Gold* II. 148 They overtook a huge and very fat hen... They tied chuckey up in a handkerchief, and rode on. **1875** R. Thatcher *Something to his Advantage* 149 Gone! gone! are my chuckies, But where are the foes? **1880** *Bulletin* (Sydney) 17 July 4/2 A man was found in the cow-shed of Government House... Was he looking after the housemaid or the 100 little chookies? **1903** *Bulletin* (Sydney) 19 Nov. 36/1 Chuck!—*Chook!*—Cho-ok! Why, there's that white 'un lost another chick today! **1905** *Ibid.* 27 Apr. 16/4 The mallee-hen is not .. any brainier than the barndoor chooky. **1927** *Bulletin* (Sydney) 3 Feb. 24/2 A Digger poultry-farmer .. received a letter from his wife .. announcing a chook hunger-strike.

2. *transf.* and *fig.*

1914 *Bulletin* (Sydney) 22 Oct. 43/2 Over the gaol there is the inscription 'Erected 1836'. There is a rat (or kangaroo) and a common chook (or emu) flanking the inscription. **1984** *Nat. Times* (Sydney) 20 July 2/2 Clancy noted last week that Premier Joh had told his 'chooks' (press gallery members) to cease their practice of gathering outside the Cabinet room for interviews with ministers as they emerged from meetings.

3. Comb. **chook farm, house, raffle, -raiser, run, yard**.

1939 *Bulletin* (Sydney) 17 May 20/4, I called at a **chook-farm** recently when a batch of some thousands of eggs was about to hatch. **1938** *Bulletin* (Sydney) 26 May 20/3 Went into the **chook-house** the other day and found a porcupine. **1979** *Herald* (Melbourne) 18 Aug. 2 The Government is proudly announcing a casino venture .. while the local church footy club secretary can go to jail for running an unregistered **chook raffle**. **1985** *Bulletin* (Sydney) 18 June 72/3 Kevin Parry .. does not have to worry about chook raffles. Parry has personally guaranteed the $10 million budget drawn up. **1931** *Ibid.* 30 Dec. 20/2 A suburban **chook-raiser** added a wallaby to the population of a pen of Leghorn cockerels. **1979** D. Maitland *Breaking Out* 23 'I'll admit I'm more of a hayshed man,' Henry confessed—a skinny fox ogling the surrounding **chook-run**. 'I get nervous in open country.' **1942** G. Casey *It's Harder for Girls* 127, I seen one [*sc.* willy-willy] take the roof off my front veranda an' land it in th' **chookyard** at the back.

choom /tʃʊm/. [Repr. Br. dial. pronunc. of *chum.*] **a.** In the war of 1914–18: an English soldier. **b.** An English person.

1916 Tas. Non-State Rec. 103/11 11 June, The 'Chooms', as our men call the men of Kitchener's new army, pulled the wire rope. **1952** J. Cleary *Sundowners* 157 She's a Choom, like you, Rupe. I married her when I was over in the Old Dart during the war.

chop, *n.*¹ and *a.* [Generalized use of *chop* quality, class, a. Hindi *chhap* seal, mark of quality: see OED(S *sb.*⁵ 4.]

A. *n. Obs.* Something to be valued or prized.

1827 *Monitor* (Sydney) 9 Aug. 575/2 Many native girls, after living in a very decent sort of a way (as they conceive at least) as concubines with several gentlemen, at length will do a Hawkesbury Settler *the honour perhaps to marry* him. And if she be a brisk good-looking active wench, the Settler blesses his stars at his rare luck in getting such *a chop*. **1888** 'R. Boldrewood' *Robbery under Arms* (1937) 461 Life ain't no great chop to a man like me, not when he gets the wrong side o' sixty, anyhow.

B. *adj.* Of quality; good. Freq. in the collocations **no chop, not much chop**, no good, not up to much.

1847 *Moreton Bay Courier* 28 Aug. 3/1 You never hear of masters who, to use a colonial phrase, are no chop, who take very mean advantages of their men. **1950** J. Morrison *Port of Call* 225 Anyway, that verandah's not much chop in bad weather; the south wind blows right in.

chop, *n.*² An event or series of events in which axemen compete under certain rules in a contest of speed.

1899 *North-Western Advocate* (Devonport) 5 Apr. 4/1 'Mugs" chop, 1 ft. blocks. **1988** *Daily Mirror* (Sydney) 19 Jan. 48/3 During the chop the coach stood near the log advising the chopper where to direct his blows.

Also **chopping match** *n. Tas. Obs.*

1896 J.B. Walker Corresp., Chopping match. A favourite contest for bush men in Tasmania.

chop, *n.*³ [Fig. use of *chop* a slice or cut of something.] A share (usu. of winnings); a gain or advantage.

1919 W.H. Downing *Digger Dialects* 16 *Chop*, share. 'To hop in for one's chop'—to enter in, in order to secure a privilege or benefit. **1986** *Good Weekend* (Sydney) 19 Apr. 11/1 A stutter and some early illness made Norm's schooling .. an ordeal with the nuns using the strap liberally. 'They all had their chop,' he says.

chopper.

1. *Obs.* One taking part in a wood-chopping contest.

1901 *Axeman's Jrnl.* (Ulverstone) Sept. 44/2 If the West Coast champion can down the 'Duke's Own' chopper, he will be a strong favourite. **1910** *Huon Times* (Franklin) 26 Feb. 2/3 The choppers had no opportunity, after finishing one event, of getting a 'rub down'.

2. [From the chopping movement of the fish's jaws, most noticeable when a school is feeding in an estuary.] A small Tailor.

1969 J. Pollard *Austral. & N.Z. Fishing* 793 Tailor are silvery white on the belly and pale green to greyish or bluish above... The half-grown fish generally are spoken of by anglers as 'choppers'. **1984** *West Austral.* (Perth) 10 Feb. 40/6 Chopper tailor have been taken from Mosmans downstream and several reports have come in of bigger tailor to 1.5 kg. being caught at Blackwall Reach.

chop picnic. An outdoor meal at which (lamb) chops are cooked and served.

1948 G. Farwell *Down Argent Street* 5 When the stores close, soon after midday, the crowd rapidly ebbs, shifting to sports grounds and dog-races .. chop picnics or an afternoon's drive in the bush. **1980** M. Dugan *Early Dreaming* 42 My mother took me and my friends for chop picnics by a waterfall.

chough. [Transf. use of *chough* a large black bird in fam. Corvidae. The Austral. bird looks similar but is unrelated.] The predom. black bird *Corcorax melanorhamphus* (fam. Corcoracidae) of s.e. Aust., living in groups and building nests of mud. Also **white-winged chough**.

1846 J. Gould *Birds of Aust.* (1848) IV. Pl. 16, The Whitewinged Chough is a very early breeder. **1929** A.H. Chisholm *Birds & Green Places* 130 She [*sc.* a lyre-bird] .. laughed like a kookaburra .. and wailed like a chough.

Chow /tʃaʊ/.

1. [Abbrev. of Chow Chow.] A Chinese, esp. an immigrant or a descendant of an immigrant.

[N.Z. **1872** G.L. Meredith *Adv. in Maoriland* (1935) 22 The solitary Chinaman to take up his abode amongst the hardy Scots at Dunedin... This 'Chow' wanted to study economy.] **1876** *Queenslander* (Brisbane) 18 Mar. 13/2 Our colonialised 'Chinkie', as he is vulgarly termed (with the single variation 'Chow'). **1977** T.A.G. Hungerford *Wong Chu* 25 'The Chows.' She emphasised the word, long discarded I imagine, except among Australians, in a way which whisked me straight to my boyhood in South Perth, and my mother saying: 'Go down the Chows and get me...'

2. The name of a type of playing marble.

1909 J.C.L. Fitzpatrick *When we were Boys Together*, His 'Alley tors' were the choicest, and his 'Chows' the best. **1977** R. McKie *Crushing* (1978) 107 'Glassies or Chows allowed, Doc?' 'Certainly not. I've only got alleys.'

chowchilla /tʃaʊˈtʃilə/. [Dyirbal and Yidiny *jawujalla*.] Log-runner 1, esp. *Orthonyx spaldingii*.

1909 *Emu* VIII. 251 Other names given to different birds by the local aborigines are as follow .. Black-headed Log-runner ('Chow-chilla') [etc.]. **1973** S. & K. Breeden *Wildlife Eastern Aust*. 55 Chowchillas are dark brown birds, round in shape but also with very strong feet and legs. The male Chowchilla has a white throat, that of the female is orange.

Chow Chow /ˈtʃaʊtʃaʊ/. *Obs*. [Transf. use of *chow chow* a mixture or medley of any sort, e.g. mixed pickles: see OED *sb*.] A Chinese.

1864 C.R. Thatcher *Invercargill Minstrel* 72 Chow Chow his hands with glee did rub, 'Cause he'd washed out a half-pennyweight to the tub. **1879** 'Australian' *Adventures Qld*. 38 Then I tell him, 'what for you *momkoll* Chow Chow?'

Chrissie. [f. *Chris(tmas* + -Y.] Christmas. Also *attrib*.

1966 S.J. Baker *Austral. Lang*. (ed. 2) 372 *Chrissie*, Christmas. Whence *Chrissie prezzie*, Christmas present. **1977** E. Mackie *Oh to be Aussie* 42 If the trainee Aussie didn't get a chance to go broke over Chrissie, he can do it now—taking the wife and kids on holidays (they don't say holi*day* here), camping or caravanning.

Christmas. Used *attrib*. in Special Comb. designating flora and fauna, etc. associated with Christmas time: **Christmas beetle,** any of several scarab beetles of the genus *Anoplognathus*, so-called because the adults emerge in summer; **bells,** any of several species of the grass-like plant *Blandfordia* (fam. Liliaceae) of N.S.W., s.e. Qld., and Tas., so called from the abundance of their brightly-coloured red and yellow flowers (see quot. 1896); **billy,** see Billy *n*.[1] 4; **bush** (or **tree**), **(a)** any of several unrelated trees or shrubs known for their decorative qualities, esp. (*N.S.W.*) *Ceratopetalum gummiferum* (fam. Cunoniaceae), the calyx lobes of which enlarge and turn deep pink in summer and (*Tas*. and *Vic*.) the aromatic summer-flowering *Prostanthera lasianthos* (fam. Lamiaceae); **(b)** *W.A*. the semi-parasitic arborescent mistletoe *Nuytsia floribunda* (fam. Loranthaceae) of s.w. W.A., bearing bright orange flowers (see quot. 1937); **eye,** see quot.; **hold** (or **grip**), see quot. 1953.

1932 *Bulletin* (Sydney) 27 Jan. 21/4 The various heavy-bodied flying beetles—the coleopt known in Australia as the **'Christmas beetle'** is notorious for it— .. deliberately butt their heads into every obstruction. **1896** J.H. Maiden *Flowering Plants & Ferns N.S.W*. 51 Large **Christmas bells** .. Vernacular name.—Originally given, of course, because these beautiful flowers were to be seen during the Christmas season. **(a) 1817** A. Cunningham in I. Marriott *Early Explorers Aust*. 8 Mar. (1925) 171 Ceratopetalum gummiferum (**Christmas Bush**). **(b) 1901** M. Vivienne *Travels in W.A*. 65 A handsome painting of the Nutsyia [*sic*] firetree, or **Christmas-bush**. **1937** R. Fairbridge *Pinjarra* 196 The Christmas Tree, a queer parasite of the Mistletoe tribe, growing on roots, but reaching a height of 20 feet or so, which in December bursts forth into a startling blaze of bright orange blossom. **1984** *Canberra Times* 22 Sept. 11/2 The unpleasant habits of larvae of the steel-blue sawfly, or 'spitfires'. . . A sticky secretion from their mouths .. was high in eucalyptus oil and caused severe pain if it got into the eyes. . . The secretions made the eyeball bloodshot—a condition called **Christmas Eye**. **1953** S.J. Baker *Aust. Speaks* 132 **Christmas hold,** a hold applied by grabbing an opponent's testicles (a 'handful of nuts'). **1981** *Weekend Austral. Mag*. (Sydney) 2 May 7/1 A woman in a dental surgery lying on the dentist's couch, put the Christmas grip on the dentist. When the dentist winced with pain, as anyone would wince if a Christmas grip were put upon him, she said, 'We are not going to hurt each other are we, Mr Dentist?'

chromo /ˈkroʊmoʊ/. [Fig. use of *chromo*, abbrev. of *chromolithograph* a picture lithographed in colours, with reference to the painted face of the prostitute.] A prostitute.

1883 *Bulletin* (Sydney) 19 May 11/4 'That fellow is so highly colored that he reminds me of a chromo,' remarked a man of a schnapper-nosed, dissipated-looking creature in a marine suburb. **1977** T. Ronan *Mighty Men on Horseback* 65 He'd butted into some big bloke who had a chromo in tow.

chuck, *v*. [Colloq. substitution for *throw*.]

1. In the phr. **to chuck off,** see *throw off* Throw *v*. 2.

1901 *Bulletin Story Bk*. 147 Aggie 'chucked off' in a particularly nasty way at the porter at Cheltenham. **1959** D. Hewett *Bobbin Up* 150 She waddled away .. grinning at the good-humoured chucking off from the spinners and the reelers.

2. *trans*. To bring (something) up, to vomit. Also *absol*.

1957 D. Niland *Call me when Cross turns Over* 53 Get a feed into you, and then you want to chuck it up again. You chuck it up and your right as pie till you eat again. And so it goes on. **1977** W. Moore *Just to Myself* 53 He nearly chucked everywhere.

chuck, *n*. [See prec.] Vomit; an act of vomiting. Also *attrib*.

1966 *Kings Cross Whisper* (Sydney) Apr. 2/5 He sat down in the gutter to have a bit of a chuck and flaked out. **1976** McDonald & Harding *Norman Gunston's Finest Moments* 12 Were there chuck stains around the toilet?

chuckey, chuckie, varr. Chook 1.

chuck in. [See Chuck *v*. and cf. *to throw in* to put in as a supplement or makeweight.] A bit of luck; a bonus.

[N.Z. **1912** *N.Z. Truth* (Wellington) 11 May 4 Fancy landing thousands of the starving humans from Bull's country. . . What a chuck-in for the local squatters!] **1916** Tas. Non-State Rec. 103/11 Apr., Bound for the Soudan .. and if so their job would be no chuck in. **1961** D. Stuart *Driven* 101 This was a real chuck-in for old Charlie.

chuff, var. Choof.

chum. [Shortened form of New chum *n*. 2.] A recently arrived immigrant. Also **chummy**.

1846 *Britannia* (Hobart) 28 May 3/2 I'm the flashest, fliest chum upon the Derwent River. **1846** C.P. Hodgson *Reminisc. Aust*. 366 'Hand', synonymous with 'Chum'; not elegant appellations, but very significant. **1887** A. Nicols *Wild Life & Adventure* 191 Hi, chummy, didn't quite know where you was jist now, did yer?

chunder /ˈtʃʌndə/, *v*. [Prob. f. rhyming slang *Chunder Loo* for 'spew', after a cartoon figure *Chunder Loo of Akim Foo* orig. drawn by Norman Lindsay (1879–1969), and appearing in advertisements for Cobra boot polish in the Sydney *Bulletin* between 1909 and 1920.] *intr*. To vomit.

1950 'N. Shute' *Town like Alice* 76 The way these bloody Nips go on. Makes you chunda. **1985** *Austral. Short Stories* xi. 42 And lamb chops and fluffy kenebecs drooling melted butter have been known to make me chunder!

2. *transf.* and *fig.* Also *trans.*
1968 B. HUMPHRIES *Wonderful World Barry McKenzie*, Hey Bazza? You chundering off [*sc.* departing] already! **1971** *Bulletin* (Sydney) 17 Apr. 40/1 Ellis with gum-ache, .. Boddy bilious, his candy-striped jeep chundering petrol all over Waverley.

Hence **chunderer** *n.*

1967 F. HARDY *Billy Borker yarns Again* 61, I know a better yarn called 'The Champion Chunderer from Cooper's Creek'.

chunder /'tʃʌndə/, *n.* [f. prec.] Vomit; an act of vomiting. Also *attrib.*
1960 G. TAYLOR *Crop Dusters* 111 Chunder-yellow. You couldn't miss it unless you were colour-blind. **1967** F. HARDY *Billy Borker yarns Again* 37 One of the boys asked him about the chunder and the Gargler says modestly: 'I never chundered in my life; I put it down and keep it down.'

Hence **chunderous, chundersome** *adjs.*, sickening; revolting.

1967 F. HARDY *Billy Borker yarns Again* 66 'Yodeller, me old **chunderous** mate,' he says. **1971** *Bulletin* (Sydney) 4 Dec. 11/2 The Poms are rapacious, mean, cunning. Bazza is beery, **chundersome**, anal.

churinga /tʃə'rɪŋɡə/. Also **tjuringa**. [a. Aranda *tywerrenge*.]
1. A sacred object of Aboriginal ceremonial (but see also quots. 1886 and 1917). Also *attrib.*
1886 *Proc. R. Geogr. Soc. Australasia: S.A.* (1890) 34 Every festival is called 'tjurunga'. They speak, for instance, of an 'emu tjurunga', a 'kangaroo tjurunga'. **1917** M.W. JAMES *'Coo-ee' Call* 21 *'Churinga'* is an Aboriginal expression meaning 'Good Luck'. **1963** I.L. IDRIESS *Our Living Stone Age* 192 Churinga sticks .. are the sacred records of the tribe and the individuals within it, the symbols of their spiritual life, and are looked upon with great reverence.

2. Comb. **churinga stone.**
1933 W. HATFIELD *Desert Saga* 26 He went then to the *ertnalunga* on Gallinanna Creek, the cave wherein lay the *churinga* stones, personal talismans of all the men in the tribe.

chute, var. SHOOT *n.*

chyack, var. CHIACK *n.* and *v.*

cider gum. Any of several trees of the genus *Eucalyptus* (fam. Myrtaceae), esp. the Tas. tree *E. gunnii*, yielding a sweet potable sap. Also **cider tree.**
1826 *Colonial Times* (Hobart) 15 Apr., The tree called the cider tree by the stock keepers .. exudes a rich saccharine juice, capable of making wine or spirits. **1903** *Tasmanian Timbers* (Tas. Lands & Survey Dept.) 20 *Cider gum* .. named from its sweet sap .. is rather a branching tree.

cigarette swag. A small swag, so called because of its size and shape (see SWAG *n.* 1). Also **cigarette-paper swag.**
1938 J.F.W. SCHULZ *Destined to Perish* 33 Jack had brought a somewhat diminutive swag, a cigarette swag, as I was told later. **1953** L. & C. REES *Spinifex Walkabout* 36 Ours was only what was known in these parts as a 'cigarette-paper swag', a light American ground-sheet and a blanket apiece, with an extra blanket and a tiny pillow for the lady.

cigger /'sɪɡə/. [Shortened form.] A cigarette.
1922 A. WRIGHT *Colt from Country* 78 'Wait till I get you a cigger,' said Bucks; 'I knew y'c'd do a smoke.' **1973** R. HALL *Poems from Prison* 40 Last night as we enjoyed a quiet cigger, The stars reflecting open life outback, The knack we had of mateship was much bigger.

citizen. A civilian trained for military service in the event of a national emergency. Chiefly *attrib.*
1903 *Act* (Cwlth. of Aust.) no. 20 Sect. 30, The Defence Force shall consist of the Naval and Military Forces of the Commonwealth, and shall be divided into two branches called the Permanent Forces and the Citizen Forces. **1968** K. DENTON *Walk around my Cluttered Mind* 183 About a year after I arrived in Australia I joined the part-timers, the Citizen Military Forces.

city of churches. Adelaide, the capital city of South Australia.
1873 A. TROLLOPE *Aust. & N.Z.* II. 184, I have said that Adelaide has been called a city of churches. **1983** J. HEPWORTH *Great Austral. Cities, Adelaide.* Supposed to be the 'City of Churches', but actually a city as sinful as they come.

civilize, *v. Hist. trans.* To impose upon (an Aboriginal people) a way of life alien to them. Also *absol.*
1827 P. CUNNINGHAM *Two Yrs. in N.S.W.* I. 134 We trust a strong injunction will be laid on every settler to abstain from all aggression or insult of the natives, who are described as a stately healthy race, easy to be civilized. **1918** C.J. DENNIS *Backblock Ballads* 154 They landed with some rum and Bibles and a gun or two, And started out to 'civilize', as whites are apt to do.

civilized, *ppl. a. Hist.* Of an Aboriginal: having adapted to (some aspects of) the European way of life. See also DOMESTICATED, TAME.
1843 C. ROWCROFT *Tales of Colonies* III. 143 The civilized natives soon catching the colonial predilection for cloth of a superior quality. **1935** R.B. PLOWMAN *Boundary Rider* 224 His assistants were only partly civilized black boys.

claim. [Spec. use of (orig. U.S.) *claim.*]
1. A piece of land formally claimed and taken up for mining purposes. Also with distinguishing epithet, as **amalgamated, bed, creek, extended, reward** (see under first element).
1851 J.H. BURTON *Emigrant's Man.* 121 Numerous claims have already been marked out, and the indications of the plentiful presence of the coveted metal are said to be unmistakable. **1978** B. OAKLEY *Ship's Whistle* (1979) 37 Any more of that, and you'll get a whiff of grapeshot. Back to your claims! Do some work for a change!

2. *transf.* and *fig.*
1918 *Bulletin* (Sydney) 30 May 24/1 One night a red-backed spider pegged out a claim in the corner of my stable.

3. Special Comb. **claim holder,** the holder of a mining claim; **jumper,** JUMPER *n.*[3]; also **jumping** *vbl. n.*
1853 A. MACKAY *Great Gold Field* 49 **Claim holders** who wish to be employed on the work are to have preference over strangers. **1891** 'SMILER' *Wanderings Simple Child* (ed. 3) 167 A band of **claim 'jumpers'** had been at work and had secured all the best shows in that part of the field. **1863** *Bell's Life in Sydney* 3 Oct. 3/1 **Claim jumping** extraordinary. On Thursday afternoon a very extraordinary case of jumping a claim.

clamper. PIN-BULLOCK.
1904 *Bulletin* (Sydney) 15 Dec. 40/1 Eighteen to twenty constitute a team, which includes polers—those nearest the waggon—clampers, body bullocks and leaders. **1980** O. RUHEN *Bullock Teams* 172 On a crest of a road the pull of the bullocks ahead could put an increasing strain on each pair of body-bullocks as they topped it, culminating in that borne by the pin-bullocks; and many animals suffered death or a lesser permanent injury from this factor. Because of this pin-bullocks were often referred to as 'the clampers'.

CLAN

clan. **a.** *Hist.* A name applied by the colonists to an Aboriginal community. **b.** A group of Aboriginal people of common descent. Also *attrib.*

1837 E. Fraser *Narr. of Capture* 14 We reached a cluster of inhabited tents of huts of another and more numerous clan of savages. **1985** I. White et al. *Fighters & Singers* 140 She painstakingly participated in painting clan designs with ochre on the young men—a very unusual and probably new role for a woman.

clap stick. An Aboriginal percussion instrument; Music stick: see quot. 1952. Usu. in *pl.* Also **clapping sticks.**

1952 R.M. Berndt *Djanggawul* 310 Clapping sticks, sometimes called *bilma:* two sticks of resonant wood clapped together by a singing man, while another man blows on the drone pipe. **1979** A. Wells *Forests are their Temples* 45 The old man, seated on the ground, began to clap his music-sticks for quietness. Then verse by verse he told the story while the clap-sticks marked each quiet pause between.

claret ash. The ornamental ash tree *Fraxinus oxycarpa* cv. Raywood (fam. Oleaceae), orig. cultivated in S.A., and having purplish-red autumn leaves.

1934 H. Sargeant *Flowering Trees & Shrubs* 77 Raywoodii is the purple or claret Ash. **1980** R.F. Brissenden *Whale in Darkness* 45 The dripping pinoaks and the claret ash Burn with the first fires of autumn.

class, *n. Hist.* A division of the convict population of a penal colony, graded according to the severity of the punishment to be undergone. Chiefly with distinguishing first element, as **crime, first, second, third,** etc.

1824 Tas. Colonial Secretary's Office Rec. 1/40 164, I was placed in the first Class in the Penitentiary on the Establishment of Classes by His Honor the late Lieut. Governor. **1829** *Ibid.* 1/32 198, It has to supply not only the Washerwomen belonging to the Assignable Class, but also those in the Crime Class with hot water. **1830** *Sydney Monitor* 6 Feb. 2/2 She having lately been condemned to third class . . her auburn locks were shorn or shaven off her fair head. **1833** J. Backhouse *Narr. Visit Austral. Colonies* (1843) 167 Prisoners are divided into a chain-gang, and a first and second class, distinguished by the kind of labour allotted them, by their clothing, and by the second class having an allowance of tea and sugar.

class, *v.*

1. *trans.* To grade (fleeces), esp. in a shearing shed. Also *absol.*, and with 'shed' as obj. Freq. as *vbl. n.*

1845 *Sydney Morning Herald* 8 Aug. 4/3 Large and really substantial Wool Shed . . with every convenience for classing and packing. **1889** H. Egbert *Pretty Cockey* 44 Mr Thompson classed the wool into Long Clothing, Short Clothing [etc.]. **1953** A. Upfield *Venom House* 78 Robin Foster's brother done the wool pressing. Bloke from over Manton way came to do the classing. **1977** D. Whittington *Strive to be Fair* 28, I was paid £5 a week and my keep to class a small shed on Tasmania's east coast.

2. *Hist. trans.* To grade (a convict) according to severity of punishment; see Class *n.*

1851 *Irish Exile* (Hobart) 18 Jan. 3/1 Mr P. O'Donohoe arrived here on Wednesday evening last, and was 'classed' on Thursday morning, for a hard labour party.

classer. One who grades fleeces, esp. in a shearing shed; *wool-classer,* see Wool 2.

1874 *Australasian Sketcher* 31 Oct. 119/3 Some hands then 'skirt' the wool . . and the 'classer' decides on the classification. **1978** J. Dingwall *Sunday too far Away* 48 The *classers, piece pickers, rousies* and *pressers* standing at one end of the shed, looking, waiting.

clay-hole. Claypan 1.

CLEAN

1843 *Sydney Morning Herald* 31 Oct. 4/1 The rain has fallen generally on the interior plains and water may be found in the clay-holes for some months at least to come. **1928** M. Forrest *Reaping Roses* 231 His horse stumbled in a dry clay-hole and pitched the rider right over his head.

claypan. [f. *clay* + *pan* a hollow or depression in the ground, esp. one in which water lies (cf. *saltpan*).]

1. A shallow depression with an impermeable clay base which holds water after rain: see quot. 1889. Also *attrib.*

1858 J.M. Stuart *Explorations in Aust.* 23 June (1865) 9 At fourteen and a half miles we found a clay-pan of water, with beautiful green feed for the horses. **1889** E. Giles *Aust. twice Traversed* I. 39 A clay pan is a small area of ground, whose top soil has been washed or blown away, leaving this hard clay exposed; and upon this surface, one, two, three, or (scarcely) more inches of rain water may remain for some days after rain: the longer it remains the thicker it gets, until at last it dries in cakes which shine like tiles; these at length crumble away, and the clay pan is swept by winds clean and ready for the next shower. **1905** *Emu* V. 19, I did see one after a Native-Hen . . on a claypan flat where there was no shelter.

2. Special Comb. **claypan squatter,** one who occupies land without holding title to it, and grazes illegally acquired stock.

1905 *Observer* (Adelaide) 2 Sept. 47/1 The depredations of what are known as claypan, or waterhole, squatters are a serious menace to pastoralists in the unfenced country of the interior. Taking up a ridiculously small area of pasture, these men raid the outskirts of a run and gather in young unbranded cattle and horses.

Clayton's. [The proprietary name of a soft drink: see quot. 1980.] Something which is largely illusory or exists in name only.

[**1980** *Herald* (Melbourne) 6 Dec. 22/4 Actor Jack Thompson was commissioned for that Clayton's ad by D'Arcy-MacManus & Masius whose national creative director Noel Delbridge wrote the line that, with variations, is now part of the language. . . 'It's the drink I have when I'm not having a drink.'] **1984** *Canberra Times* 20 June 16/7 Academic staff of Commonwealth tertiary-education institutions will now have to pay back their 'Clayton's' pay rise. **1985** *Canberra Times* 13 July B1/1 Australian English is not a Clayton's sort of English, a sort of colonial doggerel you speak when you cannot manage Standard Southern.

clean, *a.* and *adv.*

A. *adj.*

1. a. Of stock: uncontaminated by disease.

1839 *Port Phillip Patriot* 4 July 3/2 An opportunity of at once finding clean flocks. **1960** *N.T. News* (Darwin) 28 Oct. 2/2 Mixing 'clean' cattle with a mob from a pleuro area cost a former transport driver 18 guineas.

b. Of pastoral land: uncontaminated by diseased stock; free from pests.

1840 *Port Phillip Gaz.* 29 Jan. 4 The above Run is . . quite clean. **1943** H.G. Lamond *From Tariaro to Loss Roy* 121 Though the country is clean, the cattle are tied up on account of a fanciful tick line drawn between that station and the markets.

2. In collocations indicating a degree of completeness: **clean burn,** (in clearing land) a controlled fire which leaves little debris; **muster,** (of stock) a complete round-up.

1886 P. Clarke *'New Chum' in Aust.* 268 He has cut them down so that they all lie in the fittest way for a **'clean burn'** when the opportunity comes. **1891** M. Roberts *Land-Travel & Sea-Faring* 72 The sheep hunting began. In this mountainous land they grow very wild; . . so good dogs are essential to anything like a **clean muster.**

B. *adv.* Of mustering: completely.

1925 M. TERRY *Across Unknown Aust.* 121 No country can be mustered 'clean', i.e. entirely.

clean, *v.*
1. *trans. Obs.* To decontaminate (pasture affected by diseased stock).
1845 *Portland Gaz.* 9 Sept. 4/4, I . . have to request your kind permission to vacate my head sheep station, where I have been both dressing and shearing for four months, in order that the run may be cleaned and the grass renewed.
2. *trans.* To clear (a paddock) of stock, to muster (stock from a paddock).
1886 P. CLARKE *'New Chum' in Aust.* 168 This is the paddock we have, in bush phraseology, to 'clean' or 'muster'. **1903** *Bulletin* (Sydney) 17 Jan. 16/2 The men could not have sighted and 'cleaned' every part of the paddock—the true definition of mustering—in time to count 80,000 sheep.

cleanskin.
1. An unbranded animal; CLEARSKIN. Also *attrib.*
1881 A.C. GRANT *Bush-Life Qld.* I. 209 All hands are anxious to try their luck with the clean-skins. **1902** F. RENAR *Bushman & Buccaneer* 9, I have done a bit of brumby running in mountain country, although most of the cleanskin experience has been in mulgoa or brigalow.
2. *transf.* An Aboriginal who has not passed through an initiation rite.
1903 H. BASEDOW *Jrnl. Govt. N.-W. Exped.* 21 May (1914) 111 He is a so-called 'clean-skin', that is, he has not yet been the victim of any personal mutilation ceremonies. **1963** I.L. IDRIESS *Our Living Stone Age* 155 The 'cleanskins' the stockmen referred to were unbranded beasts; as the white man called an unbranded bullock a cleanskin, so he called a blackboy who had not been 'branded' with the initiation knife.
3. *fig.* One who has no criminal record; one new to (a situation or activity) and lacking experience.
1907 A. SEARCY *In Austral. Tropics* 112 The men I met with were good, honest, and hard working, although perhaps it might have been as well for a clean skin to fight shy of some of them. **1979** W.D. JOYNT *Breaking Road for Rest* 80 How would we behave when under fire and in front of tough Anzacs, and what would be their reactions to us cleanskins?

clearing, *ppl. a. Hist.* In collocations referring to the clearing of land: **clearing gang,** orig. a detachment of convicts detailed to clear trees, undergrowth, etc., from a settler's land in order to fit it for cultivation or pasturage; any party so employed; **lease,** an arrangement under which a settler has the use of a tract of land, for little or no rent, in return for clearing it; also *attrib.*; **party,** *clearing gang.*
1824 *HRA* (1921) 3rd Ser. IV. 560 Respecting the appropriation of the **Clearing Gangs.** **1808** *Sydney Gaz.* 4 Sept., Together with several allotments of land on **clearing leases** for 5 to 7 years. **1849** J.P. TOWNSEND *Rambles & Observations N.S.W.* 136 In this district is to be found a numerous class of small settlers called 'clearing-lease men'. They take a small piece of uncleared land (each about thirty acres), on condition of having it rent-free for six years, and form on it a kind of shanty... By the time their original tenancy expires, they have generally got on pretty well in the world, and can afford to pay about ten pounds a-year for their now reclaimed land. **1824** *Hobart Town Gaz.* 16 Apr., In New South Wales . . the settler may have his farm . . entirely cleared, and ploughed fit for the seed... This work is all done by **Clearing Parties,** consisting of several hundred Crown prisoners, employed in that manner by Government.

clearing sale. A sale, esp. of surplus stock, farm machinery, and household goods at a rural property; a retailer's sale of superseded merchandise, usu. at reduced prices.
1884 *Austral. Tit-Bits* (Melbourne) 19 June 2/3 We have also . . clearing sales, land rackets, and bogus auctions. **1983** M. HAYES *Prickle Farm* 47 Clearing sales are big news in the bush. . . Many country people seem to gain satisfaction out of watching someone's property . . go under the hammer.

clearskin. CLEANSKIN 1.
1884 'R. BOLDREWOOD' *Old Melbourne Memories* 109 Calves and clear-skins, are separated at the same time. **1967** E. HUXLEY *Their Shining Eldorado* 247 The rest are 'clearskins' whose males grow up to be scrub bulls.

cleftie, var. CLIFTY.

Cleopatra. [Transf. use of *Cleopatra* the name of a queen of Egypt renowned for her beauty.] A (chiefly Tas.) variety of eating apple. Also **Cleo.**
1936 *Austral. Writers' Ann.* 77 Cleopatras, sweet as Egypt's golden queen. **1961** R. PARKER *Fiddlers' Place* 19 He . . fetched the apple out of his pocket. 'What'd you take a Cleo for?' demanded his brother... 'There were still some red ones.'

clever, *a. Aboriginal English.*
1. Wise; learned in traditional lore. Esp. in the collocation **clever man.** See KORADJI.
1909 *Folklore* (London) XIV. iv. 487 A 'doctor' or clever blackfellow can sometimes go and see a Wahwee. **1935** *Oceania* VI. 33 Several men had the reputation of being 'clever' men.
2. *Transf. and fig.*
1972 *Bulletin* (Sydney) 24 June 59/1 As widely reported, the clever-feller-money-magicians (who are *usually* right) are predicting a further 0.2 percent cut in the long term bond rate. **1986** HERCUS & SUTTON *This is what Happened* 229 There was a white cleverman at Port Augusta—white people call him 'doctor'.

clifty, *v.* Also **cleftie, cliftie.** [f. Gr. κλέφτης a thief; used in Services' speech and prob. not excl. Austral.] *trans.* To steal (something).
1918 *Kia Ora Coo-ee* June 8/1 You discover that the iron rations for your horse have been 'cleftied'. **1956** *Harry Peck's Post* (Sydney) July 18, I cliftie a truck off the lines.
Hence **clifty** *a.,* thieving.
1943 H.E. BEROS *Fuzzy-Wuzzy Angels* 66 We'll remember how we had to watch those sneaking clifty wogs.

climbing, *ppl. a.* Used in the names of fauna: **climbing fish,** MUDSKIPPER; **kangaroo** *obs., tree-kangaroo,* see TREE.
1880 *Proc. Linnean Soc. N.S.W.* V. 614 *Periophthalmus Australis* 'The **Climbing Fish**' of the Northern Queensland Settlers. **1890** *Braidwood Dispatch* 29 Jan. 2/5 Three **climbing kangaroos** . . are said to have been captured safe and sound.

cliner /ˈklaɪnə/. *Obs.* Also formerly **clinah, kleiner.** [a. G. *kleine*: see quot. 1898.] A girl or girl-friend.
1895 *Bulletin* (Sydney) 9 Feb. 15/4 I'm ryebuck and the girl's O.K. Oh, she's good iron, is my little clinah. **1898** *Ibid.* 20 Aug. (Red Page), The 'clinah' of Goodge's 'Australian Slanguage' is simply the German *kleine* (fem. of *klein*, small, little, and meaning 'little', i.e., woman) Australised. I heard the term first in S.A. (where Germans abound) some years ago. **1899** *Truth* (Sydney) 10 Sept. 1/8 He'd wing his kliner with a sock, The toe of which contained some rock. **1902** *Ibid.* 29 June 6/2 He'd a little kleiner stoppin' With him. She went out awl day Workin'. **1915** C.J. DENNIS *Songs of Sentimental Bloke* 22, I carn't describe that cliner's winnin' ways. The way she torks! 'Er lips! 'Er eyes! 'Er hair!

clock. [From the number of hours on a clock-face.] With **the:** a prison sentence of twelve months.
1950 *Austral. Police Jrnl.* Apr. 112 *Clock, The,* 12 months imprisonment. 1968 J. ALARD *He who shoots Last* 2 Anyhow I'd better stall; if I get picked up I'll at least get the clock.

clocker. [Used elsewhere but recorded earliest in Aust.: see Mathews.] One who (surreptitiously) times a racehorse, esp. during a training run.
1895 N. GOULD *On & Off Turf in Aust.* 117 Ruses are resorted to at times to deceive or out-general the 'clocker' on the look-out for a good gallop. 1980 *Daily Mirror* (Sydney) 1 Apr. 111/1 She's an absolute flying machine and today made clockers look twice when she recorded 35 sec. for her 600 m. task.

Cloncurry ringneck. [f. the name of a town in n.e. Qld. + RINGNECK.] The parrot *Barnardius barnardi macgillivrayi* of n.w. Qld. Also **Cloncurry parrot** (or **parakeet**).
1913 G.M. MATHEWS *List Birds Aust.* 134 Cloncurry Parrot . . Range: Interior of Mid-Queensland. 1967 E. HUXLEY *Their Shining Eldorado* 135 Here are colonies of Cloncurry ringnecks. 1977 J. CARTER *All Things Wild* 51 Cloncurry parakeets have a tag of $2500 a pair.

close out, *v.* Surfing. *intr.* Of a wave: to break simultaneously over its whole length, thus preventing a surfer from riding along the breaking crest.
1964 *Surfabout* (Sydney) I. vi. 9 The waves are always right-handers, with the bigger waves 4 ft.–5 ft. closing out. 1967 *Ibid.* III. vii. 8 The other popular surf, the left beach-break, works best at 3–4 feet on high tide. Any bigger and it will close out.

closer settlement. *Hist.* A policy of closely settling land suitable for agricultural purposes, with a view to increasing land utilization and productivity; settlement in this manner. Also *attrib.*
1897 *Act* (S.A.) 60 & 61 Vict. no. 687 Sect. 1, An act relating to the Repurchase of Land. . . 1. This Act may be cited as 'The Closer Settlement Act, 1897'. 1902 *Bulletin* (Sydney) 12 Apr. 14/2 S.A. Govt. is at present very hot on Closer Settlement.
Hence **closer settler** *n.*
1913 *Bulletin* (Sydney) 9 Oct. 22/3 Victoria's closer settlers are not all craven shirkers of the conditions of their agreements.

close up, *adv. Austral. pidgin.* Near; nearly.
1853 H.B. JONES *Adventures in Aust.* 128 It was with some difficulty we could get them to be bearers of the skin, &c. of the bullock to the 'humpy', i.e. station, which was 'close up' (near), for they will not work at all if they are full. 1951 E. HILL *Territory* 320 Rose was 'close up finish'.

clothes hoist. A rotary clothes-drier consisting of a square frame, between the arms of which run lengths of clothes-line, turning about a central pole and adjustable in height.
[1923 *Austral. Home Beautiful* Aug. 66/1 An ingenious circular clothes-line . . revolves on the principle of the merry-go-round on windy days, and helps to dry the clothes quickly.] 1926 *Ibid.* Jan. 9 (Advt.), *Toyne's rotary clothes hoist. The perfect clothes line—props done away with—an ornament to your back yard. . .* Raises as desired up to 7 ft. 6 in. from ground to lines. 1972 *Southerly* iv. 291 The clothes hoist was blown gently round above them, its four aluminium arms spreading thin shadows across them.

clover. Used *attrib.* in the names of plants having a clover-like leaf; **clover burr,** any of several naturalized herbs of the genus *Medicago* (fam. Fabaceae) having a spiny fruit; **fern,** NARDOO.

1878 'R. BOLDREWOOD' *Ups & Downs* 49 We *must* have shearing over by October, or all this **clover-burr** that I see about will be in the wool. 1878 R.B. SMYTH *Aborigines of Vic.* I. 209 The use, as a food, of the **clover-fern,** Nardoo.

clucky, *a.* [From the noise made by a broody hen.] Of a woman: pregnant; broody.
1941 S.J. BAKER *Pop. Dict. Austral. Slang* 18 *Clucky,* pregnant. 1977 H.O. TESHER *Eleven Days* 22, I told you I have been very clucky lately, and I wanted your child.

cluey, *a.* [f. *clue* prob. by analogy with *clueless.*] Knowledgeable; alert (to the possibilities of a situation); 'clued-up'.
1967 *Kings Cross Whisper* (Sydney) xxxiii. 4/3 Cluey, a cluey person is one who has many ideas of ways and means of getting money. 1975 D.G. JENNER *Darlings* 21 Dad wasn't cluey enough to take up the offer.

clumper. A work-horse (see quot. 1980). Also *attrib.*
1916 L. FERRIS *John Heathlyn of Otway* 138 Heathlyn's first equine companion was a brown, hardy clumper. 1980 HOLTH & BARNABY *Cattlemen of High Country* 126 A 'clumper' or heavy type of mare crossed with a blood horse produced a strong horse suitable for a 'remount' or regimental mount.

coach, *v.* [Spec. use of *coach* to teach, train.] *intr.* To use tame cattle as a lure for wild cattle. Also *trans.*, to lure (wild cattle), and as *vbl. n.* and *ppl. a.*
1872 G.S. BADEN-POWELL *New Homes for Old Country* 183 The cattle are often very wild, and the method usually entered upon is that termed 'coaching'. 1880 J.B. STEVENSON *Seven Yrs. Austral. Bush* 128 We often worked all through a long winter's night, coaching round scrub after scrub. 1905 *Bulletin* (Sydney) 13 Apr, 18/1 'Scrub-running' for clean skins . . and then coaching them. 1978 PALMER & MCKENNA *Somewhere between Black & White* 36 He used 'coaching cattle', tame cows that would do exactly as directed and the rougher . . animals tended to follow their lead.

coach, $n.^1$ Abbrev. of COACHER.
1872 G.S. BADEN-POWELL *New Homes for Old Country* 183 The 'coaches' are a mob of quiet cattle. 1962 D. LOCKWOOD *I, Aboriginal* 172 On clear nights we drove quiet decoy cattle we called 'coaches' on to the plains to attract others.

coach, $n.^2$ In the phr. **to rob this** (or **the**) **coach,** to be in charge of an operation.
1945 S.J. BAKER *Austral. Lang.* 251 Disapproval or disagreement is indicated by . . *who's robbing this coach?* [*Note*] Reputed to be associated with bushranging days, this expression is equivalent to 'mind your own business!' 1977 *Austral.* (Sydney) 1 Dec. 8/2 Apart from raising the question as to which of Labor's four Treasurers-elect is robbing the coach, where does this leave Labor policy—except in tatters?

coacher. [f. COACH *v.*] A tame beast used as a lure for others, esp. wild cattle; a tame horse used to attract brumbies.
1876 J.A. EDWARDS *Gilbert Gogger* 137 Now our coachers they start on the track they well know. 1967 E. HUXLEY *Their Shining Eldorado* 247 Coachers are steady-going and reliable cattle, as it were the prefects, who exert a calming influence on the wild scrubs.

coachman. *Obs.* [Fig. use of *coachman.*] COACH-WHIP. Also **coachman bird, coachman's whipbird.**
1822 B. FIELD *Geogr. Mem. N.S.W.* 10 Oct. (1825) 440 Some [notes] are harsh and vulgar, like those of the parrot-

kind, the cockatoo, the coachman's whip-bird. **1827** P. CUNNINGHAM *Two Yrs. in N.S.W.* II. 158 If you should hear a coach-whip crack behind, you may instinctively start aside to let *the mail* pass; but quickly find it is only our native *coachman* with his spread-out fan-tail and perked-up crest, whistling and cracking out his whiplike notes as he hops sprucely from branch to branch. **1836** *Tegg's Monthly Mag.* (Sydney) I. 64 The coachman-bird would almost persuade you that you were listening to the cracking of stage-coach whips on the London City Road.

coach-whip. [Fig. use of *coach-whip*: see quot. 1793.] The bird *Psophodes olivaceus* (see WHIPBIRD). Also **coach-whip bird.**
   1793 W. TENCH *Compl. Acct. Settlement* 175 To one of them, not bigger than a tom-tit, we have given the name of coach-whip, from its note exactly resembling the smack of a whip. **1801** J. LATHAM *Gen. Synopsis Birds* Suppl. II. 222 It has a long single note, not unlike the crack of a coachman's whip, hence called the *Coach-whip Bird*.

coachwood. [From the use of the timber in coach-building.] Any of several trees, esp. the N.S.W. and Qld. *Ceratopetalum apetalum* (fam. Cunoniaceae), having a fragrant bark and serrated leaves, and yielding a versatile light brown to pinkish brown timber; the wood of these trees. Also *attrib*.
   1860 G. BENNETT *Gatherings of Naturalist* 325 Another species is named Coach-wood, Leather-jacket, and also Light-wood by the colonists (*Ceratopetalum apetalum*). **1979** *Sydney Morning Herald* 5 Sept. 6/5 It is impossible to drop trees on these steep slopes without them crashing into the coachwood rainforest below.

coalie. Also **coaley.** [Prob. survival of Br. dial. *coaly* (see quot. 1846).] A wharf labourer who loads coal into ships, a coal-lumper.
   [**1846** 'HON. F.L.G.' *Swell's Night Guide* 78 A most motly [*sic*] group of shicksters, flash-lads, loggers, coalies, watermen, and lightermen.] **1882** *Sydney Slang Dict.* 4 Two quarts of brimming porter, With several goes of gin beside, Drained Bet the Coaley's Daughter. **1907** *Truth* (Sydney) 26 May 1/4 The coalies will be down in the dumps when these machines arrive.

coalopolis. A name given to Newcastle, N.S.W., because of its traditional association with coal-mining.
   1891 *Truth* (Sydney) 8 Feb. 1/3 The honest miners of Coalopolis. **1956** G. MACKANESS *Art of Bk.-Collecting Aust.* 10 Newcastle, the coalopolis and second city of New South Wales.

coast, *n*. Used *attrib*. in Special Comb. **coast disease,** a disease of sheep, formerly prevalent in parts of coastal s. Aust., caused by a deficiency of cobalt and copper; **myall,** the tree *Acacia binervia* (fam. Mimosaceae) of the e. coast, which has silvery foliage and often occurs in rocky soil near creek gullies and rivers; also **coastal myall; she-oak,** any of several coastal trees of the genera *Allocasuarina* and *Casuarina* (fam. Casuarinaceae); see also SHE-OAK 1; **wattle,** BOOBIALLA a.
   1863 W. MILNE *Notes on Journey S. Eastern District* 9 Jan. 28 The frightful **Coast disease** which has always made such havoc all along this part of the Coast of So. Australia amongst Sheep & Cattle. **1895** J.H. MAIDEN *Flowering Plants & Ferns N.S.W.* 13 The wood strongly resembles that of Myall, and as it is purely a coast and coast-range species we propose to designate it '**Coast Myall**'. **1935** E. COLEMAN *Come back in Wattle Time* 25 Only one of our Australian wattles is known to be poisonous. This is the Coastal Myall (*A. glaucescens*), an Eastern species, ranging from South Australia to Queensland. **1880** *Argus* (Melbourne) 2 Feb. 6/7 Casuarina quadrivalvis, the '**coast sheoak**'. **1880** *Argus* (Melbourne) 2 Feb. 6/7 Acacia sophorae.. the '**coast wattle**'.

coast, *v. Obs.* [U.S. *coast* to wander about aimlessly; orig. to travel downhill without exerting effort.] *intr.* With **about:** to travel as a tramp.
   1878 'R. BOLDREWOOD' *Ups & Downs* 295, I ain't like you, Towney, able to coast about without a job of work from shearin' to shearin'. **1945** S.J. BAKER *Austral. Lang.* 104 Expressions to describe being on the tramp.. *to swag it, chase the sun, coast about.*

Hence **coaster** *n*.
   1875 *Austral. Town & Country Jrnl.* (Sydney) 27 Mar. 503/3 A voluble, good-for-nothing loafing imposter, a regular 'coaster'.

coasty, *a*. Also **coastie.** Affected by *coast disease* (see COAST *n*.); associated with the disease.
   1886 J.F. CONIGRAVE *S.A.* 108 Disease is almost unknown.. except occasionally on the swampy land of the coast, where the sheep sometimes become 'coastey'. **1887** *Adelaide Observer* 3 Dec. 27 Some of the coast is coasty in winter. **1911** *Bulletin* (Sydney) 30 Mar. 14/4 'Coastie' stock, when removed to an inland pasture, rapidly recover.

coat. [Of unknown origin; but see quot. 1983.] In the phr. **to be on the coat,** to be ostracized, in disfavour, 'beyond the pale'.
   1940 P. KERRY *Cobbers A.I.F.* 21 Once yer on the coat yeh stay there, an' yer pleadin's go fer nought. **1983** STURGESS & BIRNBAUER *Journalist who Laughed* 28 On the coat... To ostracize someone, particularly a strike-breaker. From the days when seamen or dock-workers would signal by jerking on the right lapel.. that a particular individual was a blackleg.. or that a specific job or ship was blacklisted.

coathanger. [Fig. use of *coathanger*: see quot. 1940.] A name for the Sydney Harbour Bridge.
   [**1940** D. AUCHTERLONIE *Kaleidoscope* 7 Twinkle, twinkle little stars On a million motor-cars, Along the Harbour bridge so high, Like a coat-hanger in the sky.] **1943** *Troppo Tribune* (Mataranka) 12 Apr. 1 A number of New South Welshmen.. anxious for a glimpse of the famous 'coathanger' that means home. **1983** *Sydney Morning Herald* 18 June 31/5, I like it here [*sc.* Melbourne] but I'd give anything for a glimpse of the old coathanger.

Cobar /ˈkoʊbɑ/. [The name of a copper-mining town in w. N.S.W.]
   1. *Obs.* A penny.
   1898 *Bulletin* (Sydney) 1 Oct. 14/3 A few more W.Q. slang words. A penny is a 'Cobar', 3d. a 'traybit', 6d. a 'zack'. **1920** *Bulletin* (Sydney) 15 Jan. 20/2 Western Queensland slang of my day.. 'Cobar', a penny.
   2. Special Comb. **Cobar shower,** a dust storm; also as rhyming slang for 'flower'.
   1952 J. CLEARY *Sundowners* 105 He could feel the dust falling on him like a dry rain. A Cobar shower, they called this. **1959** S.J. BAKER *Drum* 77 Cobar shower, a flower.

cobba-cobba. /ˈkɒbə-kɒbə/. [a. Bardi prob. *goba-goba*.] A corroboree. Also *attrib*.
   1943 *Bulletin* (Sydney) 8 Sept. 12/3 He could take any new scene or experience, from a mass conversion to a hanging, and reproduce.. a cobba-cooba play. **1953** L. & C. REES *Spinifex Walkabout* 100 'They love their cobba-cobba. Why should we interfere?' We realized that probably only one in twenty thousand Australians had ever witnessed a corroboree.

cobber, *n*. [Prob. f. Br. dial. *cob* to take a liking to: see EDD *v*.²]
   1. An intimate; a companion; a friend.
   1893 *Worker* (Sydney) 3 Aug. 2/4 He overloads his 'cobber's' ration bags and gives a strange traveller *nil*. **1982**

Canberra Times 1 Dec. 12/3 'It appears that in Australia it has become popular to clobber your cobber, and we happen to be your cobber,' he said. 'We don't ever publish in New Zealand details of Australian criminals being deported, or how many Australians are on welfare in New Zealand, because that is not the thing you do to your mate.'

2. Special Comb. **cobber dobber,** one who informs on a colleague (see DOBBER).

1966 S.J. BAKER *Austral. Lang.* (ed. 2) 191 *Cobber-dobber,* one who betrays a friend.

Hence **cobberless** *a.,* **cobbership** *n.*

1957 F. CLUNE *Fortune Hunters* 1 His mind was made up, and I was **cobberless**. **1944** S. BROGDEN *Sky Diggers* 107 **Cobbership** and a cool approach to all problems—if there is a more Australian aspect of war it would be difficult to find.

cobber, *v.* [f. prec.] *intr.* To make friends with. Freq. with **up.**

1918 *Kia Ora Coo-ee* June 4/1 I've cobbered up with the bloke on guard here. **1925** E. MCDONNELL *My Homeland* 30, I struck there an old-aged pensioner... We cobbered.

cobbera, var. COBRA *n.*[1] and *n.*[2]

cobbler, *n.*[1] [Of unknown origin.]

a. W.A. The fresh-water catfish *Tandanus bostocki* of w. Aust., having harmful spiny fins. **b.** The marine fish *Gymnapistes marmoratus* of s. Aust. which has similar fins.

1831 G.F. MOORE *Diary Ten Yrs. W.A.* 10 Nov. (1884) 87 Fished for *cobblers* in the evening. **1974** T.D. SCOTT et al. *Marine & Freshwater Fishes S.A.* 174 The name 'Cobbler' as applied to this species, should not be confused with the Catfishes of Western Australia, which are commonly named Cobblers. Our species [*sc. Gymnapistes marmoratus*] is often encountered by net fishermen.. and the pain caused by a sting from the spines.. can be very excruciating.

cobbler, *n.*[2] [Shortened form of *cobbler's last,* as a pun on *last*.] A sheep which is difficult to shear and therefore often the last sheep to be taken from a pen: see quot. 1898, and also SNOB *n.*[2] Also *attrib.*

1871 *Cornhill Mag.* (London) Jan. 87 The 'Cobbler', or last sheep was seized, and stripped of his rather dense and difficult fleece. **1888** *Bulletin* (Sydney) 8 Sept. 9/3 Shearers call the last and always the worst, sheep in the pen 'the cobbler'. **1898** *Ibid.* 17 Dec. 15/1 *Cobbler* need not be the last or any other sheep in a pen. By *cobbler* shearers mean a dirty, sticky or matted and wrinkly sheep—one that is hard to shear. Two men catching out of one pen naturally avoid bad sheep—i.e., *cobblers*—as long as possible; and pens not being refilled until the last sheep has been caught the last sheep is more often a *cobbler* than any other... The term, I think, comes from the old proverb: 'As dirty as a cobbler'. **1974** *Austral. Folksongs* (Folk Lore Council Aust.) 61 The sheep are tall and wiry where they feed on the Mitchell grass, And every second one of them is close to the cobbler class.

cobbler's awl. [Transf. use of *cobbler's awl* the avocet, so called from the shape of the beak.] SPINEBILL.

1843 J. GOULD *Birds of Aust.* (1848) IV. Pl. 61, *Acanthorhynchus tenuirostris*.. Cobbler's Awl, Colonists of Van Diemen's Land. Spine-bill, Colonists of New South Wales. **1919** *Bulletin* (Sydney) 16 Jan. 24/4 'Cobbler's awl' (spinebill).

cobbler's peg. [Fig. use of *cobbler's peg*: see esp. quots. 1882 and 1949.]

1. Usu. in *pl.* Any of several plants, esp. the annual herbs *Bidens pilosa,* having barbed fruits, and *Erigeron linifolius* (both fam. Asteraceae).

1882 *Proc. Linnean Soc. N.S.W.* VII. 78 A species of *Enigeron* [sic] (*canadensis* or *linifolius*). It goes by the name of cobbler's peg, from the ready way in which the erect fragments of old stems penetrate the shoes. **1949** *Bulletin* (Sydney) 27 Apr. 14/2 The sheep were clean and free from 'cobblers' which were small burrs that grew on a plant about 9 in. high and were known as 'cobbler's pegs' because they somewhat resembled the wooden boot-sprig in common use at that time.

2. *pl.* The pneumatophores of certain mangrove species usu. protruding vertically from the submerged roots.

1896 F.G. AFLALO *Sketch Nat. Hist. Aust.* 259 In the Queensland estuaries.. may be seen.. oysters adhering to the horizontal off-shoots (called 'cobbler's pegs') of the White, Red and Orange Mangroves. **1948** R. RAVEN-HART *Canoe in Aust.* 205 The White Mangroves, half-flooded at high tide, with.. the curious stumps which Alan called 'cobbler's pegs', the things that grow up from the roots to get away from the noisome mud into the air.

cobborn, var. CABON.

cobra /'kɒbrə/, *n.*[1] *Obs.* Chiefly *Austral. pidgin.* Also **cobbera.** [a. Dharuk *gabarra.*] The head, skull.

[**1790** J. HUNTER *Hist. Jrnl. Trans. Port Jackson* (1793) 408 *Caberra,* the head.] **1831** *Sydney Herald* 14 Nov. 4/1 After a hard fought battle they parted good friends, some of their *cobberas* having sustained considerable damage. **1833** *Currency Lad* (Sydney) 20 Apr. 3 Defendant.. began to deal some ugly thumps on the *cobra* of complainant.

cobra /'kɒbrə/, *n.*[2] Also **cobbera.** [a. Djangati *gabara.*] A shipworm, a mollusc boring into wood in brackish or sea water and traditionally eaten by Aborigines.

1836 J. BACKHOUSE *Narr. Visit Austral. Colonies* (1843) 366 He was driven by hunger, to eat a species of *Teredo,* or Augur-worm, called by the Blacks, Cobra. **1845** C. HODGKINSON *Aust., Port Macquarie to Moreton Bay* 47 A wooden bowl full of cobberra, a long white worm, eaten by them, which is found in wood that has been immersed for some time in the brackish water.

cockatiel. [a. Du. *kaketielje,* prob. a. Pg. *cacatilha,* dimin. of *cacatua* cockatoo.] The crested, predom. grey parrot *Nymphicus hollandicus,* widespread in mainland Aust. and popular as a cage bird in Aust. as elsewhere; *cockatoo parrot,* see COCKATOO *n.*[1] 4; QUARRION; WEERO.

1877 C.W. GEDNEY *Foreign Cage Birds* 57 Cockatiels are natives of South Australia. **1977** W.A. WINTER-IRVING *Bush Stories* 30 Sometimes grey cockatiels break the silence with their soft intimate call.

cockatoo, *n.*[1] [Spec. use of *cockatoo* crested parrot.]

1. Any of a number of large, noisy, crested parrots, esp. in the genera *Cacatua* and *Calyptorhynchus.* Also with distinguishing epithet, as **black, Major Mitchell's, pink, rose-breasted, sulphur-crested, white** (see under first element).

1770 J. BANKS *Jrnl.* 1 May (1896) 267 The trees overhead abounded very much with loryquets and cockatoos. **1983** J. HEPWORTH *More Birds & Beasties Aust.,* Cockatoo speaks before it thinks, Its voice is rough and raucous.

2. A look-out posted by those engaged in an illegal activity, now esp. the playing of two-up, to give warning of any threat of interruption. Also *attrib.*

1827 P. CUNNINGHAM *Two Yrs. in N.S.W.* (rev. ed.) II. 288 It being a common trick to station a sentinel on a commanding eminence to give the alarm, while all the others divert themselves, or go to sleep. Such are known here by the name of 'cockatoo-gangs', from following the example of that wary bird. **1964** G. JOHNSTON *My Brother Jack* 80 There was a big mob of gamblers playing two-up.. with their 'cockatoos' posted all around to keep watch for the police.

3. *transf.* and *fig.* (With reference to the cockatoo's habit of sitting on a fence: see COCKATOO v.¹ 1.) Freq. *attrib.*

1876 *Austral. Town & Country Jrnl.* (Sydney) 16 Dec. 982/3 Whenever this 'pound' holds cattle of *only one class* you hear the deciding shouts from the cockatoo stockmen, who are doing the 'reviewing' safely on the fence. 1909 R. KALESKI *Austral. Settler's Compl. Guide* 65 A top 'cockatoo' rail is put on top.

4. Special Comb. **cockatoo bush**, the widespread shrub or small tree *Myoporum insulare* (fam. Myoporaceae), bearing edible fruits (see quot. 1888), also known as BOOBIALLA b.; **orchid**, FLYING DUCK ORCHID; **parrot** (or **parakeet**), COCKATIEL.

1888 *Proc. Linnean Soc. N.S.W.* III. 532 'Cockatoo bush'. . . The berries are edible, though somewhat of a saltish and bitter flavour. They are much relished by birds. *c* 1910 W.R. GUILFOYLE *Austral. Plants* 90 'Large Caleana', or 'Cockatoo Orchid' (terrestrial orchid), f[lower] dark purplish. 1836 *Sydney Herald* 21 Mar. 2/4 Among the birds we noticed . . black, red-headed and pink cockatoos, . . **cockatoo parrots**. 1926 K. DAHL *In Savage Aust.* 251 Parrots were plentiful, especially the nymph, the 'cockatoo parakeet'.

cockatoo, *n.*² and *attrib.* [From the name of Cockatoo Island in Sydney Harbour, formerly a prison for intractable convicts.]

1. a. *n.* *Obs.* A convict serving a sentence on Cockatoo Island; one who has served such a sentence. Also **Cockatoo Islander**.

1841 *Sydney Herald* 14 July 2/5 Cockatoo Islanders. . . A report was forwarded to the proper authority in Sydney, from Cockatoo Island, that two of the convicts . . had effected their escape. 1846 *Bell's Life in Sydney* 26 Sept. 3/1 Robert Hunter, an accomplished Cockatoo, was charged with robbing Mr J.R. Torr, of Miller's Point, of two seals.

b. *attrib. Obs.*

1845 *Sydney Morning Herald* 7 Jan. 2/5 *Cockatoo men*. . . The total number of prisoners on Cockatoo Island under sentence yesterday was two hundred and fifty-three. 1911 A.L. HAYDON *Trooper Police Aust.* 71 Jackey Jackey was now sentenced to a life term and became a 'Cockatoo bird'.

2. a. *n.* A small farmer; orig. with reference to tenant farmers, brought from Sydney and settled in the Port Fairy district. Also **cockatoo farmer, selector, settler**.

1845 *Standard* (Melbourne) 13 Aug. 3/2 *The Port Fairy Special Survey*.—Most of the settlers on Mr Atkinson's special survey, either have or are about to flit; it appears that the agreement between 'Cockatoo settlers' and their landlord, was merely verbal. 1849 *Argus* (Melbourne) 6 Feb. 2/4 The harvest has fairly commenced, and the *cockatoo farmers* are in the height of their glory. 1853 F.J. COCKBURN *Lett.* (1856) 32 The Colonial term for a small cultivator is 'Cockatoo', as the Cockatoos scrape the outside of the trees for grub. 1897 J.D. HENNESSEY *New-Chum Farmer* 1 Hire yourself out to a dairyman, take a contract with a rail-splitter, sign articles with a cockatoo selector, but don't touch land without knowing something about it.

b. *attrib.* Of or relating to small farming.

1863 W. MILNE *Notes on Journey S. Eastern District* 9 Jan. 28 Tomorrow we have arranged that he should drive us up to *his Cockatoo* tenants. 1890 'R. BOLDREWOOD' *Colonial Reformer* II. 170 And so you believe in these cockatoo chaps? Now, what's the good of 'em? . . All the crop they'll ever get out of that land you may put in your coat pocket.

3. Special Comb. **cockatoo fence**, a fence improvised from logs and branches; **squatter** *hist.*, see quot. 1862.

1861 *Austral. Settler's Handbk.* 13 A **cockatoo fence** . . consists of forked sticks driven into the ground, and saplings, or young trees laid across them. A second and shorter row is requisite, making it a two railed fence. 1862 C. MUNRO *Fern Vale* I. 47 One or two settlers of minor importance, and dignified with the title of 'stringy bark' or '**cockatoo**' squatters.

cockatoo, *v.*¹ [f. COCKATOO *n.*¹]

1. *intr. Obs.* To perch on a fence: see COCKATOO *n.*¹ 3.

1876 *Austral. Town & Country Jrnl.* (Sydney) 16 Dec. 982/2 The correct thing, on first arriving at a drafting yard, is to 'cockatoo', or sit on the rails, high above the tossing horn-billows, and discuss the never-ending subject of hoof and horn. 1894 E. TURNER *Seven Little Australians* (1912) 209 But everybody else had gone to 'cockatoo'—to sit on the top rail of the inclosure and look down at the maddened creatures: so at length he fastened his bridle to a tree and proceeded gingerly to follow their example.

2. *intr.* To act as a look-out: see COCKATOO *n.*¹ 2.

1954 L. EVERS *Pattern of Conquest* 216 You'd better stay down and cockatoo for us today. 1982 LOWENSTEIN & HILLS *Under Hook* 16, I used to cockatoo for them—watch for the police.

cockatoo, *v.*² *Obs.* [f. COCKATOO *n.*² 2.] *intr.* To farm on a small scale. Freq. as *vbl. n.*

1875 *Austral. Town & Country Jrnl.* (Sydney) 4 Sept. 383/2 A farm! Fancy three hundred acres in Oxfordshire, with a score or two of bullocks, and twice as many black-faced Down sheep. Regular cockatooing. 1876 J.B. STEPHENS *Hundred Pounds* 184 The Government under which I 'cockatooed'.

cockatooer. *Obs.* COCKATOO *n.*² 2 a.

1852 MRS C. MEREDITH *My Home in Tas.* II. 137 'Cockatooers' . . are not . . a species of bird, but human beings; who rent portions of this forest from the proprietors . . and vainly endeavour to exist on what they can earn. 1891 J. FENTON *Bush Life Tas.* (1964) 91 For in those middle days, there were many 'cockatooers', with more money than prudence.

cockeye. Shortened form of COCKEYED BOB. Also *attrib.*

1910 *Bulletin* (Sydney) 18 Aug. 13/1 A strong 'cockeye' struck us from the N.E., making further progress impossible. 1959 *Bulletin* (Sydney) 4 Mar. 16/1 It's cockeye season in Australia's Nor'-west.

cockeye bob. Altered form of COCKEYED BOB. Also *attrib.*

1926 *Bulletin* (Sydney) 25 Feb. 1/1 Cockeye-bob . . seems to have come from the native word 'kikobor'. What the native word means I do not know, but 'cockeye-bob' seems to be the nearest the white man can get to the pronunciation of the native name. *Ibid.* 25 Mar. 24/1 'Kriz' . . attributes the origin of the term 'cockeye-bob' to the native word 'kikobor'. Old North-Westralians relate that it originated on a pearling lugger whose captain and owner was named 'Bob'. His sight was not of the best, and his black-boy diver, on seeing a miniature cyclone on the skyline approaching, used to warn his skipper by singing out 'Cock eye, Bob!' 1960 *N.T. News* (Darwin) 9 Feb. 1/7 A Nightcliff Tornado Distress Fund has been opened . . to help families left homeless by Sunday's 'Cockeye Bob' blow.

cockeyed bob. Chiefly *W.A.* and *N.T.* [Of unknown origin; but see prec. (quots. 1926).] A sudden, violent, but short-lived storm or squall.

1894 *Age* (Melbourne) 20 Jan. 13/4 In some places even on the approach of an ordinary thunderstorm or 'Cock-eyed Bob', they clear off to the highest ground about. 1981 *Weekend Austral.* (Sydney) 15 Aug. 13/2 A cockeyed bob, the West Australian term for an unpredictable wind.

cockie, var. COCKY $n.^1$ and $n.^2$

cockney. [Of unknown origin.] A young SNAPPER: see quot. 1906.
[**1874** N.S.W. Rep. R. Comm. Fisheries (1880) 1288 Juveniles rank the smallest of the fry, not over an inch or two in length, as the 'cock-schnapper'.] **1906** D.G. STEAD Fishes of Aust. 126 Up to about 4 or 5 inches in length, the young fry of the Snapper .. are very often known as 'Cockneys'... Beyond the 'Cockney' stage and up to a weight of about a pound and a half, the Snapper is known as Red Bream. .. Later on in life .. this species is known to the fishermen first as 'Squire' and then as 'School Snapper'; while beyond this stage, we get what is known as the 'Old-Man Snapper'.

cockrag. A loincloth, esp. as worn by an Aboriginal.
1964 T. RONAN Packhorse & Pearling Boat 46 Joe, clad in Malay-style sarong with a grey flannel shirt hanging down outside it .. at night put on the cockrag and joined the blacks in their corroboree. **1981** NGABIDJ & SHAW My Country of Pelican Dreaming 82 Wallambain threw away his woomera and cock rag and jumped in.

cockroach. A hard, dark-coloured lump (of brown sugar).
1903 J. FURPHY Such is Life 229 The prince bounded out through the front door, with a triumphant grin on his brown face, and an enormous cockroach of black sugar in his hand. **1921** G.A. BELL Under Brigalows 41 Stacks of sugar... She and Mamie used to search the bins for hard, brown lumps, called 'cockroaches' by bush children.

cockspur. [Transf. use of cockspur, referring to the spiny flower-head.] Any of several plants, esp. the naturalized annual herb Centaurea melitensis (fam. Asteraceae), having thistle-like flower-heads with short slender spines, and occurring in all States but not N.T.; see also Chinese burr CHINESE.
1891 E.H. HALLACK W.A. & Yilgarn Goldfields 13/2 Raspberry jam-trees, silver-grass, and cockspur, with good soil, are now passed. **1981** G.M. CUNNINGHAM et al. Plants Western N.S.W. 720 Maltese cockspur is a widespread and common plant, invading weak pastures and forming dense stands over wide areas.

cocky, $n.^1$ Also **cockie**. [f. COCKATOO $n.^1$ 1 + -Y.]
1. COCKATOO $n.^1$ 1. Also **cocky-bird**.
1834 G. BENNETT Wanderings N.S.W. I. 244 The reaper's song might be, 'Fly not yet, little cockies.' **1844** Colonial Lit. Jrnl. (Sydney) 18 July 62/2 And I have on the wattle there A speaking Cocky-bird,—And all who pass the Punt declare The like they never heard. **1900** Pastoral Times (Deniliquin) 16 June 2/7 As I was lying on deck I heard the old familiar screech of a 'cockie'. **1958** F. HARDY Four-Legged Lottery 66 I'm practising drawing animals and birds lately. Could I come up tomorrow and draw the cocky?
2. Special Comb. **cocky apple**, the tree Planchonia careya (fam. Lecythidaceae) of W.A., N.T., Qld., and elsewhere in the tropics, bearing an egg-shaped greenish fruit with edible flesh; the fruit.
1936 J. DEVANNY Sugar Heaven 13 Over the range were the swamps full of horny pandanus, the shining red and scarlet leaves and the green of the cocky apple.
3. fig. In the collocation **cocky('s)-cage**, applied attrib. or absol. to the mouth or tongue: unpleasantly furred, usu. as a result of an excessive consumption of alcohol; hence **cocky-caged** a.
1967 Kings Cross Whisper (Sydney) xxxii. 1/2 It will be available in the form of pills which will .. give cocky-cage mouth. **1971** D. IRELAND Unknown Industr. Prisoner 8 His tongue was still cocky-caged from the night before, his huge pink belly tight as a drum. **1974** BUCKLEY & HAMILTON Festival 183 A mouth like the bottom of a cocky's cage.
1975 Bronze Swagman Bk. Bush Verse 53 Head pounding, mouth a cockie's cage.

cocky, $n.^2$ and attrib. Also **cockie**. [f. COCKATOO $n.^2$ 2 a. + -Y.]
A. n. Chiefly used of a small farmer but now often applied to a substantial landowner or to the rural interest generally: see quots. 1969 and 1974. Also **cocky farmer**.
1871 Austral. Town & Country Jrnl. (Sydney) 14 Jan. 58/4 Which prevented good time being made, and led to one horse, ridden by a young cockey, being killed. **1968** F. ROSE Aust. Revisited 30 These small dairy or 'cocky' farmers were and still are the most backward part of the white Australian community. **1969** B. GARLAND Pitt Street Prospector 10 Some of those big Cockies don't know how much land they own, or how many sheep they've got. **1974** New Press (Perth) I. ii. 6/1 The cockies' organisations, the Farmers' Union and the Pastoralists and Graziers' Association.

B. 1. attrib.
1896 Bulletin (Sydney) 25 Apr. 27/4 Your 'road-mending' farmer is all over N.S.W. The members are put in by cockie 'road-menders'. **1977** R. EDWARDS Austral. Yarn 110 The miners and prospectors, mainly from Victoria had to take jobs on cocky farms, and that sort of thing.
2. Special Comb. and collocations: **cocky chaff**, wheat chaff; **country**, a district chiefly devoted to small farming; **cocky's delight**, cocky's joy; **cocky('s) gate**, see quot. 1935; **cocky('s) hours**, dawn to dusk; **cocky's joy**, treacle or golden syrup; **cocky's mile**, an idiosyncratic estimate of distance.
1908 Bulletin (Sydney) 22 Oct. 17/2 Mixed some oats through a bag of '**cocky chaff**', and turned it out in a corner of a small paddock for my hack. **1943** Bulletin (Sydney) 4 Aug. 13/4 Larry, exiled on foot in the **cocky country**, was looking for a job. **1902** Bulletin (Sydney) 5 Apr. 32/2 '**Cockie's Delight**', better known, perhaps, as 'Bullocky's Joy', occupies a prominent position on the table, and may be called the cockie's 'staff of life'. **1926** A.A.B. APSLEY Amateur Settlers 138 Typical Australian '**cocky**' **gates**. **1935** R.B. PLOWMAN Boundary Rider 196 Some of these were what is known as 'cockies' gates... These gates consist of several wires and a piece of wood. At one end the wires are fixed to a gate-post. At the other they are attached to an upright stick at intervals to correspond with those on the gate-post at the opposite end. In between are usually two sticks or droppers to keep the wires apart. **1899** Bulletin (Sydney) 12 Aug. 14/4 '**Cockies' hours**' are supposed to be 'from jackass to jackass'. **1926** Ibid. 14 Jan. 22/3 With a big herd the owner probably has to get down to cocky hours of labor. **1902** Bulletin (Sydney) 4 Oct. 17/1 He has to fetch in cows, .. milk, snatch some damper and **cocky's joy**. **1917** Bulletin (Sydney) 12 Apr. 24/4 Between Belgrave and Emerald a **cocky's mile** is about 10 furlongs; from Croydon to Lilydale it is rarely less than 12 furlongs.

cocky, v. intr. To farm in a small way. Chiefly as vbl. n.
1895 Worker (Sydney) 6 July 3/4 You know Sam Jones .. is going to do a bit of cockying on his own. **1943** G. CASEY Birds of Feather 6 Cockying was tough enough since wheat and wool had gone to glory but it was a proper life.

cockydom. Obs. The community of small farmers.
1904 Bulletin (Sydney) 28 Apr. 16/4 In the very near future cockydom will be down to the primitive aborigine stage. **1923** Ibid. 5 July 22/3 'E.W.' should advise N.S.W. North Coast cockydom to leg-rope every ibis it can catch.

coconut. Aboriginal English. [See quot. 1980 (2).] An Aboriginal who lives in a manner perceived by others as repudiating Aboriginal identity; JACKY JACKY b.

1980 *N.S.W. Parl. Papers* (1981) 3rd Sess. IV. 1798 When the Premier .. sends non-Aboriginal people out into the country, they talk to people that we call coconuts... They are assimilated black people who sit about the towns and all they are proud of is how many white friends they have. *Ibid.* 1799, I was interested in your description of people to whom you referred as coconuts... They are brown on the outside and white underneath.

cod. [Transf. use of *cod* the Atlantic fish *Gadus callarias*.] Any of several fish, some unrelated to the Atlantic cod, incl. the *Murray cod* (see MURRAY 2). Also **codfish.**
1821 T. GODWIN *Descr. Acct. Van Diemen's Island* 9 Fish are caught in abundance .. those most known are skate, mullet, cod. **1825** *Austral.* (Sydney) 8 Dec. 2 Procured a cod-fish from a creek of the river Macquarie.

coffee. Used *attrib.* in Special Comb. **coffee palace** [in Br. use for a coffee house from 1879 (see quot. 1880)], a temperance hotel; **shop, tent,** a place of refreshment, usu. a sly grog shop (see SLY GROG 2).
[**1880** *Argus* (Melbourne) 9 Jan. 6/4 We had no doubt that the **coffee palaces** would have a good influence in promoting temperance and checking drunkenness, and they ought to be encouraged.] **1884** *Sands & McDougall's Melbourne & Suburban Directory* 658 *Melbourne coffee palace*—Coffee Taverns Co. (Limited) .. 89 Bourke-st east. **1852** *Tas. Non-State Rec.* 56/1 6 Oct., Several **Coffee Shops** on the way, Coffee 6d. per pint, meals 2s. 6. Most of them are sly grog sellers. **1853** *Austral. Gold Digger's Monthly Mag.* v. 165 Sighting a **coffee-tent**, we were delighted enough to have a good supper, and soon after, folding our blankets around us, we lay on the floor, and slept in peace.

coffee-room. *Obs.* [Spec. use of *coffee-room* the public dining-room of an hotel: see OED.]
1. The better appointed of two dining-rooms in an hotel. Also as quasi-*adv.*
1947 M. RAYMOND *Smiley gets Gun* 138 Naturally the Quirks must have the best, so they stayed coffee-room—and not dining room, where the residents ate at a long table covered with newspaper instead of a cloth. **1959** H. LAMOND *Sheep Station* 51 The Keystone .. ran two tables: coffee-room for the social aspirants; dining-room for those who were hut men and ate in the kitchen on stations.
2. *fig.*
1936 *Bulletin* (Sydney) 30 Dec. 20/1 In bush changes a noticeable one is the passing of the coffee-room bagmen. These old chaps, gentlemen once, would sooner camp on the creek and go hungry than go to the hut. They were 'inside' men, by gad, sir!

coil, *v. Obs.* [Prob. fig. use of *coil* to roll or curl up.] *intr.* To (lie down to) sleep.
1830 *Launceston Advertiser* 11 Jan. 3 This .. is .. the last aggression these Bandits will be suffered to perpetrate, and we are certain their capture must take place immediately, if the numerous parties detached in pursuit be not too fond of *coiling*. **1905** A.B. PATERSON *Old Bush Songs* 28 A few had taken quarters and were coiling in their bunks.

coil, *n. Obs.* [f. prec.] A sleep.
1849 F.R. GODFREY *Extracts Old Jrnls.* 14 Oct. (1926) 27 We were all very tired and determined to have a good 'coil' this morning; but were awakened at daybreak. **1892** G. PARKER *Round Compass in Aust.* 58 Where is he? Gone to to have a coil.

coiler. [f. COIL *v.*] A loafer or idler; a tramp.
1846 *Hogg's Weekly Instructor* IV. 211/2 Coilers are people in Australia who have been improvident or unfortunate, and who, on retiring, not voluntarily, from town gaieties into the bush, become hangers-on at sheep and cattle stations. **1973** J. MURRAY *Larrikins* 202 *Coiler*, an idler who sleeps on wharves.

coit, var. QUOIT.

colane /kəˈleɪn,ˈkɒleɪn/. [a. Wiradhuri prob. *galayin*. See also GRUIE.] *Emu apple* (a), see EMU *n.*¹ 3.
1903 *Proc. Linnean Soc. N.S.W.* XXVIII. 410 Of *Owenia acidula*, .. the 'Colane', there is a pretty legend told by the aborigines of the Bogan. **1981** J. JESSOP *Flora Central Aust.* 197 *Gruie, colane, gooya, sour apple, emu apple.* .. There are a number of vernacular names but none seems to have achieved very widespread use.

Cold Country. *Obs.* A jocular name for Great Britain. Also *attrib.*
1906 *Bulletin* (Sydney) 24 May 15/3 He could tell on sight whether any man he met came from Queensland, N.S. Wales, Victoria, Tasmania, or the Cold Country. **1911** *Ibid.* 17 Aug. 13/2 Before the rabbit and fox and other Cold Country importations got in their fine work, the cat was the pet curse of the blue-nose settlers.

cold footer. *Obs.* [Prob. orig. U.S., as was *to get (or have) cold feet* (see OEDS *cold, a.* 19).] A cowardly soldier; one who, although eligible for active service, fails to enlist. Also **coldfoot.**
1916 'MEN OF ANZAC' *Anzac Bk.* 102 He was generally considered by all those who knew of him in the squadron to be a 'cold-foot' and his nickname was appropriately 'Icy'. **1916** F.R. CORNEY *Let.* 31 Oct., I would like to get back again for the battalion's sake as soon as I can, as I would not like anyone to think that I was a 'cold-footer'.
Also **cold-footed** *a.*
1916 'MEN OF ANZAC' *Anzac Bk.* 108 If Jessie could see me now, would she turn me down for some cold-footed well-groomed fellow?

coldie. [f. *cold (beer* + -Y.] COLD ONE.
1953 *Tobruk to Borneo* (Perth) Dec. 12, I took a couple of coldies to augment [his] supply. **1981** Q. WILD *Honey Wind* 84 May Father, Son and Holy Ghost keep your oven full of roast help you fill the fridge with coldies bless the young and soothe the oldies.

cold one. A glass, bottle, or can of chilled beer.
1962 MARSHALL & DRYSDALE *Journey among Men* 54 You will find the inevitable bottles and cans discarded along the way, where someone has taken, wrapped in wet paper, a few 'cold ones for the road'. **1979** B. HUMPHRIES *Bazza comes into his Own*, What say youse and me adjourn to the nearest rubbidy and sink a few cold ones.

collar. [Prob. f. *collar* to take possession of, master.] Paid employment; a job.
1896 *Worker* (Sydney) 11 Apr. 1/3 Work was .. easily obtainable here—every day's Kalgoorlie *Miner* had a column or so of ads for miners, and men found no difficulty in getting into 'collar'. **1927** J. MATHIEU *Backblock Ballads* 1 As I've written for a collar To a place called Bundaleer, Where we beat all records holler, In the shearing line one year.

collared sparrowhawk. The bird of prey *Accipiter cirrocephalus*, having a rufous mark round the neck, widespread in Aust. and also occurring in New Guinea; SPARROWHAWK a.
1842 J. GOULD *Birds of Aust.* (1848) I. Pl. 19, *Accipiter torquatus* .. Collared Sparrow Hawk. **1984** M. BLAKERS et al. *Atlas Austral. Birds* 98 The Collared Sparrowhawk lives in New Guinea and Australia.

collar-proud. [Transf. use of *collar-proud*, (of a horse) restive when in harness.] Resentful of constraint.
1919 C. DREW *Doings of Dave* 168, I never seen a man so collar proud. **1930** K.S. PRICHARD *Haxby's Circus* 162 The holiday had lasted long enough, she said. It had run from a

fortnight to a month. Everybody was beginning to get collar-proud.

Collins Street. Also **Collins-street.** [The name of a principal business street in Melbourne.] Used *attrib.* as a Victorian equivalent of PITT STREET.
1938 *Bulletin* (Sydney) 12 Jan. 20/1 They're Collins-street bushies most likely. **1960** *Ibid.* 27 Apr. 18/1 Cooee is translated 'Yoo-hoo', a Collins Street squatter is a drugstore cowboy.

colonial, *a.* and *n.* Now chiefly *hist.*
A. *adj.*
1. Of, belonging to, or characteristic of one of the Australian Colonies, or of these Colonies collectively; Australian, usu. as distinct from British.
1793 D. COLLINS *Acct. Eng. Colony N.S.W.* (1798) I. 298 The *Daedalus* was considered as a colonial ship. **1939** G. DIGBY *Down Wind* 183 What is known in Australia as Colonial Whisky. It is one of those beverages which has to be drunk quickly, or it will corrode the glass.
2. Inferior in some respect, as provincial, lacking polish or cultivation, coarse, vulgar, etc.
1808 *Sydney Gaz.* 25 Sept., The paltry insignificant editor of a paltry insignificant half-sheet colonial news paper. **1979** W.D. JOYNT *Breaking Road for Rest* 3 The word Australian was seldom if ever used and the word Colonial was anathema. 'Don't speak Colonial' was levelled at us if we used slang words or behaved in any other way as 'young gentlemen'.
3. Of, belonging to, or characteristic of Australia before Federation.
1916 *Bulletin* (Sydney) 16 Mar. 22/2 They placed Tom on the 'colonial sofa' in our front room. **1980** *Westerly* i. 10 We stopped at a pub by a crossroads. It had had a plastic facelift recently but its solid old colonial lines were still detectable. There was some fine wrought iron on the balcony and the stonework in the foundation was expert.
4. In collocations: **colonial ale, aristocracy, aristocrat, beer, -born** *a.*, **-bred** *a.*, **-built** *a.*, **cloth, dray, government, language, life, -made** *a.*, **parlance, phrase, phraseology, price, produce, slang, society, tobacco, twang, tweed, vessel, wine, wool.**
1853 *Guardian* (Hobart) 2 July 3/5 **Colonial Ale**.. is a rich pale ale of good flavour. **1832** *Colonist* (Hobart) 7 Sept. 3/3 There exists, both in New South Wales and in Van Diemen's Land, a **colonial aristocracy**, composed of the Government officers and members of the Legislative Councils, *not chosen by the settlers, but 'nominated' by the Government.* **1842** *Colonial Observer* (Sydney) 9 Mar. 177/1 The feeble political orator of five feet high—the would-be **Colonial aristocrat**. **1831** *Sydney Herald* 2 May 3/4 Bones And Kendall.. are supplying Public House and Private Families, with **Colonial Beer.** **1835** *Colonist* (Sydney) 16 Apr. 2/1 Would the **colonial-born** children be warranted to say to those born and still living in England. **1827** P. CUNNINGHAM *Two Yrs. in N.S.W.* I. 333, I had two dogs with me that had acquired the habit of snake-killing—one being a fine pointer newly from England, and the other a **colonial-bred** kangaroo dog. **1808** *Sydney Gaz.* 15 May, The Mercury **colonial built** vessel.. had not arrived when the Venus left. **1811** *Sydney Gaz.* 5 Jan., Constables and Night Watch are to receive **Colonial Cloth** sufficient for a Watch Coat. **1856** 'OLD COLONIST' *How to Farm & Settle in Aust.* 9 The **colonial dray** forms the most complete vehicle for the road carrier. **1808** *To Viscount Castlereagh* 87 On the conduct of Major Johnston, or the other members of the new **Colonial Government**, during their administration, I do not mean to trouble your Lordship with any remarks. **1828** *Tasmanian* (Hobart) 15 Aug. 4 If you know of any person wanting a situation who is a proficient in the **Colonial language**, you will do me a great service by recommending them to me, as I am resolved that my children shall not remain ignorant of the dialect of the land they live in. **1843** J.F. BENNETT *Hist. & Descr. Acct. S.A.* 122 (*heading*) Sketch of Adelaide and surrounding villages—**colonial life** and manners. **1830** Tas. Colonial Secretary's Office Rec. 1/15 141, These latter shoes are part of the 197 Prs. procured from the Commissariat Department at Sydney (**Colonial Made**) in September last year. **1843** J.F. BENNETT *Hist. & Descr. Acct. S.A.* 47 Barracouta... [*Note*] In **Colonial parlance** so called, from a supposed resemblance to that fish. **1832** J. HENDERSON *Observations Colonies N.S.W. & Van Diemen's Land* 38 The settler must.. receive an order to select a grant of land... He must then procure an order to take possession of it, or in **colonial phrase**, to 'Locate'. **1846** C.P. HODGSON *Reminisc. Aust.* 303 Its duration amounted in **colonial phraseology**, to a 'Sundowner'. **1833** J. KING *Information Van Diemen's Land* 15 If they happen not to have any article that is wanted, they procure it, and charge the consumer a profit upon the **colonial price.** **1819** *Sydney Gaz.* 23 Jan. 3/2 British manufactures and **Colonial produce.** **1840** S. *Austral. Miscellany* June 178 The animals were what in **colonial slang** is termed 'planted' (i.e. concealed). **1842** *Tasmanian Jrnl. Nat. Sci.* I. 10 The diffusion of scientific information might be immediately conducive to the advantage of **Colonial society.** **1829** *Sydney Monitor* 12 Jan. 1460/2 There is not only five thousand pounds of colonial *leaf* tobacco in the Colony altogether, but little **Colonial Tobacco** of any kind. **1859** R.H. HORNE *Austral. Facts & Prospects* 67 A different explanation must be given of the vulgarity, illiterateness, public chattering, and **colonial twang** in the speech. **1843** *Sydney Morning Herald* 23 May 3/3 It is generally understood that many gentlemen intend to appear at Government House, at the Levee, in **colonial Tweeds.** **1793** D. COLLINS *Acct. Eng. Colony N.S.W.* (1798) I. 319 Every one was expecting our **colonial vessel**, the Francis. **1831** *Sydney Herald* 7 Nov. 4/2 The *Palambam* is taking home a pipe of **Colonial wine.** **1834** *Hobart Town Mag.* May 122 Perceive the increase and improvement of our **Colonial wool.**
5. In special collocations: **colonial bill,** a promissory note in the name of an individual, circulating as currency; **convict,** one serving a sentence for a crime committed in an Australian Colony; **currency,** any unofficial medium of exchange, esp. that consisting of colonial bills (see also CURRENCY 1); **dollar,** HOLEY DOLLAR; **fever** (chiefly *Vic.*), a typhoid-like disease; also *fig.* (see quot. 1876); **fund(s),** monies assigned to civil administration; **goose,** a boned leg of mutton stuffed with sage and onion; **oath,** a strong oath; in the phr. **my colonial oath,** intensive form of *my oath* (see OATH); **offence,** a crime committed by a transported convict in an Australian Colony; **oven,** see quot. 1941; **pine, (a)** CYPRESS PINE; **(b)** HOOP PINE; **prisoner,** *colonial convict;* **robert,** a shilling; **secretary,** in an Australian Colony, the official responsible for domestic affairs; the chief minister (see PREMIER 1); **sentence,** the punishment inflicted upon a *colonial convict;* **style,** a manner thought of as distinctively Australian; a nineteenth-century Australian style of building, furniture, etc.; **treasurer,** in an Australian Colony, the official responsible for internal finance; **youth,** a young person, born in Australia of immigrant descent; (*collect.*) young persons of this category.
1803 *Sydney Gaz.* 26 June, Several forgeries of **Colonial Bills** have lately made their appearance, some of which are backed with the name of responsible inhabitants, which are also counterfeit. **1843** *Colonial Observer* (Sydney) 18 Mar. 892/4 He was not aware whether they were English or **Colonial convicts** who were detained. **1804** *Sydney Gaz.* 28 Oct., The **Colonial Currency,** as established by the General Order of the 19th November, 1800. **1820** *N.S.W. Pocket Almanack* 72, 1813.. The **colonial dollar** substituted in the place of the local currency, July 1. **1857** *Illustr. Jrnl. Australasia* III. 214 The angel of death.. cut down many victims. The most fatal diseases were fever and dysentery. The former, known as **colonial fever,** was most dangerous. **1876** J.A. EDWARDS *Gilbert Gogger* 189 The

new chum has evidently caught the colonial fever, or in plain English, he is humbugging his maternal relative. **1810** *Sydney Gaz.* 17 Mar., He shall receive an Allowance of Five Shillings per Day out of the **Colonial Fund**. **1849** *Britannia* (Hobart) 19 July 3/2 The Lieutenant-Governor makes payment of the public money from the colonial funds. **1882** J. SCHLEMAN *Life in Melbourne* 6 A haunch of kangaroo, flanked by a '**colonial goose**'. **1859** H KINGSLEY *Recoll. Geoffry Hamlyn* II. 94 'Oh my – (**colonial oath**!)' said the other; 'oh my – cabbage tree!' **1873** W. THOMSON-GREGG *Desperate Character* I. 66 The gaffer wound up his oration with a colonial oath, like the brandy of the same manufacture, uncommonly black and strong. **1838** T.H. JAMES *Six Months S.A.* 43 They have been re-sentenced since their first arrival for **colonial offences**. **1867** 'S. McTAVISH' *Chowla* 9 A. Simpson & Son, patentees and manufacturers of the **colonial ovens**. **1941** *Bulletin* (Sydney) 27 Aug. 17/4 Successor to the camp oven was that one-time pride of the kitchen the colonial oven. It was an oblong box with a full-length door in front. Three-sixteenth—or quarter-inch wrought-iron plate for top and bottom, thinner sheet round back and sides. Open fire on top for boiling or stewing, extra fire underneath when roasting or baking. **1848** H.W. HAYGARTH *Recoll. Bush Life* 147 The dresser, made of **colonial pine**, was as clean and white as snow. **1904** J.H. MAIDEN *Notes on Commercial Timbers N.S.W.* 24 *Cypress pine*. . . In the western districts this timber is often known simply as 'colonial pine'. **1926** *Qld. Agric. Jrnl.* XXV. 437 *Araucaria Cunninghamii* . . Colonial Pine. **1843** *Melbourne Times* 1 Apr. 2/3 On Sunday morning he inspected the **colonial** or second convicted **prisoners**. [N.Z. **1869** R.P. WHITWORTH *Grimshaw, Bagshaw & Bradshaw's Comic Guide to Dunedin* 39 Shall we invest in two **Colonial Roberts** in a seat each in the stalls?] **1885** *Australasian Printers' Keepsake* 71, I paid, as he discovered he hadn't 'the colonial Robert' upon him that he thought he had. **1810** *HRA* (1916) 1st Ser. VII. 259, I . . submit that the Gentleman now holding this Office should henceforth be denominated **Colonial Secretary**, with a Suitable Salary. **1811** *Sydney Gaz.* 16 Feb., Henry Melsom (now under **Colonial Sentence** at Newcastle). **1838** *S. Austral. Rec.* (London) 8 Aug. 83/3 The rest of the party bushed it in true **colonial style**. **1948** R. RAVEN-HART *Canoe in Aust.* 200 One of the Banks had chosen a definitely 'colonial' style of architecture for their new building, with a triangular pediment above two-storey stone pillars. **1826** *Colonial Times* (Hobart) 6 May, **Colonial Treasurer**. This Officer, together with the Receipt and Custody of all Public Money, is charged with the Collection of the Quit rents, and other Sources of internal Revenue. **1834** J.D. LANG *Hist. & Statistical Acct. N.S.W.* I. 176 Contests . . between the **colonial youth** and natives of England, or . . between *currency and sterling*. **1867** J. BONWICK *J. Batman* 4 Mr John Batman, unlike Mr Faulkner, was a colonial youth.

B. *n.*

1. A person born in Australia of immigrant descent.
1827 P. CUNNINGHAM *Two Yrs. in N.S.W.* I. 9 New South Wales (or *Australia* as we colonials say). **1980** *Southerly* ii. 180 You know, Marcel Proust? He giggles. For Christ sake . . I may be a colonial but I'm not a bloody moron.

2. Shortened form of *colonial ale, beer*.
1853 G.B. EARP *What we did in Aust.* 171 No man can open his mouth, and swallow anything, even a glass of 'colonial', in a public-house, under sixpence. **1901** *Truth* (Sydney) 24 Feb. 8/2 A man from the country last week had a pint of the vile stuff called colonial, and it put him dead to sleep.

3. *absol.* In the collocation **my colonial**: shortened form of *my colonial oath* (see COLONIAL *a.* 5).
1873 J.C.F. JOHNSON *Christmas on Carringa* 6 If you was really to say . . will you take a pint of sheaoak . . I'd say, I'd say , . my colonial! **1968** D. O'GRADY *Bottle of Sandwiches* 30 My colonial. . . Sorry I'm a day late, but things kept croppin' up.

colonial experience, *n.* and *attrib. Hist.*

A. *n.*

1. First-hand knowledge of the conditions of life in (outback) Australia; training in self-reliance, esp. in station management and in the skills necessary on a sheep or cattle station.
1838 N.L. KENTISH *Pol. Econ. N.S.W.* 17 These letters could be restricted to the perusal of Gentlemen of Colonial experience. **1975** M. THORNTON *It's Jackaroo's Life* 18 By the late 1840s many young migrants were arriving in Australia with the intention of seeking their fortunes. The first requirement . . was to get what became known as colonial experience.

2. A (British) youth living and working on an (Australian) sheep or cattle station in order to learn the necessary occupational skills: see JACKEROO *n.* 2.
1868 C.W. BROWNE *Overlanding in Aust.* 36 He is usually a man that has been employed on a run as a superintendant, overseer, 'colonial experience', or something of that nature. **1938** F. RATCLIFFE *Flying Fox & Drifting Sand* 122 When I was in Bundaberg forty years ago there was a 'colonial experience' named Thompson.

B. *attrib.* (in sense of *n.* 2).
1886 P. CLARKE *'New Chum' in Aust.* 295 A planter put a new 'colonial experience' man on to 'boss' a gang of black ladies. **1976** B. SCOTT *Complete Bk. Austral. Folk Lore* 130 The Colonial Experience Man, he's there, of course, Shiny boots and leggings, boys, just off his horse.

Hence **colonial experienced** *a.*, **colonial experiencer** *n.*

1873 *Illustr. Sydney News* 16 Apr. 18/4 A large section of land should be most carefully selected by a **colonial-experienced** surveyor. **1879** S.W. SILVER *Austral. Grazier's Guide* 13 The '**colonial experiencer**', the 'jackaroo', or 'cadet', as he is variously designated in different colonies, always lodges with the proprietor or the resident manager.

colonialize, *v. Obs. trans.* COLONIZE. Also as *pa. pple.*, and *fig.*

1852 F. LANCELOTT *Aust. as it Is* II. 162 Too many of the merchants and traders . . delight in what is called 'colonializing the fresh arrivals right off the reel'—that is, taking advantage of their ignorance of colonial matters, and legally cheating them of all they possess. **1854** 'H.J.L.' *Travels & Adventures*, Having colonialised his dress he secures his swag and prepares for a start into the Country. **1882** A.J. BOYD *Old Colonials* 233 A tendency to suicide, when under a cloud, is also amongst the pleasant traits of character in our colonialised 'Chinkie'.

colonially, *adv. Obs.* Locally, i.e. in the Australian Colonies.

1835 H.W. BUNBURY *Early Days W.A.* 16 Aug. (1930) 18 These are all men colonially sentenced, in addition to their former transportation, so are the very *élite* of the English blackguards. **1889** J.H.L. ZILLMANN *Past & Present Austral. Life* 51 'Is it true that you are only a *colonially* ordained clergyman?' Colonially being pronounced *Kah*-lonially with a great and scornful emphasis on the first syllable.

colonist.

1. *Hist.* Prior to Federation: a non-Aboriginal inhabitant of a British Colony in Australia; one taking part in the founding of a Colony (see quots. 1790 and 1833); a settler.

1790 J. HUNTER *Hist. Jrnl. Trans. Port Jackson* 17 July (1793) 455 As the good land could not at present be cultivated by the colonists, it was reserved for the first settlers that should come out. **1833** W.H. BRETON *Excursions* 46 By 'Settlers', I mean the farmers only: and by 'colonists', the whole of the free inhabitants. **1910** *Advocate* (Burnie) 3 Jan. 2/3 The deceased had been a colonist for 85 years.

2. *transf.*
1920 J.H. MAIDEN *Weeds N.S.W.* 70 'Wild Verbena or Vervain', 'Purple-Top or Weed' . . is a very old Australian

colonist, and now it is found practically over the settled parts of Australia.

3. In the collocation **old colonist,** one whose standing in the community derives from the length of the period of residence in Australia. Also *attrib.*

1828 H. DANGAR *Index & Directory River Hunter* 33 This regulation . . was a very proper one in reference to the *old colonists*. **1858** T. MCCOMBIE *Hist. Colony Vic.* 76 He was under the guidance of the old colonist aristocracy of Sydney.

4. In special collocations: **colonists' cement** (see quot.); **colonist's clock,** the bird *Dacelo novaeguineae* (see KOOKABURRA).

1847 *Atlas* (Sydney) III. 62/3 What is the colonists' patent cement? . . The **colonists' cement** is just cow or bullock hide cut into thongs. **1847** *Moreton Bay Courier* 29 May 4/3 They are most absurdly named laughing-jackasses, though some designate them the **colonist's clock**, and the natives, *cucaburra*.

colonize, *v. Obs. trans.* To render (a person) colonial, i.e. Australian, in character or outlook. Freq. as *past pple.*

1849 *Bell's Life in Sydney* 26 May 3/1 'Ma,' said a young lady to her mother the other day, 'What is Emigration?' Mother—'Emigration, dear, is a young lady going to Australia.' Daughter—'What is Colonizing, Ma?' Mother—'Colonizing, dear, is marrying there and having a family.' **1940** J.A. BROOK *Jim of Seven Seas* 67, I did not take kindly to this job, being by now well colonized, and my blood thin and susceptible to keen frost.

Hence **colonization** *n.*, accommodation to life in Australia.

1850 *Monthly Almanac* (Adelaide) 7 He is soon reconciled to this unexpected disbursement by congratulations on the prospect of his rapid 'colonization'.

Colony. Also **colony.**

1. Prior to Federation: one of the British Colonies in Australia or the Australian Colonies collectively; those taking part in the founding of a Colony (see quot. 1788 and cf. COLONIST).

1788 J. HUNTER *Hist. Jrnl. Trans. Port Jackson* (1793) 301 Before the colours were hauled down, I assembled my small colony under them. **1901** *Advocate* (Burnie) 6 Feb. 2/3 The old name of 'colony' has been dropped . . and the word 'State' substituted.

2. After Federation: used loosely of Australia as a former British colony or as one of a number of former British colonies.

1910 *Huon Times* (Franklin) 5 Mar. 4/6 A few words . . to those seeking homes in the colonies. **1978** B. OAKLEY *Ship's Whistle* (1979) 31 All the fools, all the crackpots, they all come out here to the colonies.

colour. *Mining.* Also **color.** [U.S. *color* a trace of gold: see Mathews.]

1. A trace or particle of gold; in opal-mining, esp. in *pl.*, an indication of the presence of opal.

1859 [see sense 2]. **1869** R.B. SMYTH *Gold Fields & Mineral Districts* 607 When only very minute particles of gold are found in a 'prospect' the miner is said to have got the 'color'. **1898** D.W. CARNEGIE *Spinifex & Sand* 89 Wherever we tried a 'dish of dirt', colours were sure to result.

2. In the phr. **to raise the** (or **a**) **colour,** to find a trace of the mineral sought, usu. gold.

1859 W. KELLY *Life in Vic.* I. 222 They had not, to use a current phrase, 'raised the colour'. **1977** J. DOUGHTY *Gold in Blood* 72 After sinking a trench . . and bottoming on green 'country' without raising a colour, we gave it up.

coloured, *ppl. a.* Applied to Aborigines, and others wholly or partly of non-white descent.

1816 *Hobart Town Gaz.* 8 June, The under-mentioned Prisoners having absented themselves . . —Matthew Keegan; Peter Franks (a coloured man); and Wm. Lee, a boy. **1977** T. RONAN *Mighty Men on Horseback* 76 He is no longer a 'blackfellow' or even a 'coloured man' but more formally an 'Aboriginal'.

comb.

1. The lower, fixed, and toothed part of the cutting-piece of a shearing machine.

1887 *Australasian* (Melbourne) 12 Mar. 495/3 Mr Wolseley stated that he had different combs for shearing such sandy sheep. **1984** *Age* (Melbourne) 16 May 3/4 The comb is the leading edge of the shearing handpiece and rakes the wool onto the blade.

2. With distinguishing epithet: **narrow comb,** a comb of the standard breadth of 63.5 mm.; also *attrib.*; **wide comb,** a comb of greater breadth; also *attrib.*

1980 *Austral.* (Sydney) 8 July 9/8 The Sunbeam Corporation has an agreement with the union to sell only **narrow combs** in Australia. **1983** *Sydney Morning Herald* 31 Mar. 3/4 Six of his shearers were attacked by narrow-comb shearers in a hotel last year. **1981** *Austral* (Sydney) 19 Dec. 5/8 If I worked as hard with wide combs as I used to with the narrow combs . . I would shear approximately 40 sheep a day more with the wide combs, and easier. **1984** *Canberra Times* 6 June 1/2 Union to abide by wide-comb decision.

Hence **narrow-comber** *n.*, **narrow-combing** *vbl. n.*, **wide-comber** *n.*, **wide-combing** *vbl. n.*

1984 *People Mag.* (Sydney) 7 May 38 You can hear New Zealand wide-combers accused of nearly every sin bar baby-killing. *Ibid.* 39/1 Standard-gaugers say the bigger combs are too hard to push through dense merino fleece and hurt shearers' wrists—a questionable claim, since I could not find one narrow-comber who'd admit to even trying wide gear. *Ibid.* 39/3 No man labours as hard or lives as rough as the 40-hour-a-week shearer, whether he's wide-combing, narrow-combing or biting the wool off.

combine. A combine seed drill: see quot. 1966. Also **combine drill.**

1966 F. WHEELHOUSE *Digging Stick* 30 When the Australian farmer uses the word 'Combine' he means the grain and fertiliser drill combined with the tyne cultivator in one implement. The term 'Combine' used in Australia is not to be confused with the American Combine, which is a wheat harvesting machine. **1979** J. BIRMINGHAM et al. *Austral. Pioneer Technol.* 24 The 'combine' drill which sowed seed and fertiliser together, and added cultivator tines to prepare the seedbed and bury the seed.

combo. [f. *comb(ination* + -O, earlier than and independent of the U.S. use for a partnership.] A white man who lives with an Aboriginal woman, often within an Aboriginal community; a white man who sexually exploits Aboriginal women. Also as **comboman,** *attrib.*, and as quasi-*adv.*

1896 W.H. WILLSHIRE *Land of Dawning* 72 The *Sydney Bulletin* . . not only reaches the combos and stockmen of Central Australia, but it reaches lepers on isolated islands, [and] lighthouse-keepers. *c* **1934** C. SAYCE *Comboman* 240 You're only a Comboman: That's what yer are. A Comboman. You're only the 'usband of a *lubra.* **1938** X. HERBERT *Capricornia* 36 Once a man went combo he could never again look with pleasure on a white woman unless he blacked her face.

Also **comboing** *vbl. n.*, **comboism** *n.*

1938 X. HERBERT *Capricornia* 194 A lean and faded-looking man, become so through excessive drinking and **comboing. 1907** *Truth* (Sydney) 7 Apr. 10/8 **Comboism** should be wiped out.

come, v.

1. Obs. In the phr. **to come it (on),** to inform (upon someone).

1812 J.H. VAUX *Mem.* (1819) II. 163 *Come it,* to divulge a secret; to tell any thing of one party to another; they say of a thief who has turned evidence against his accomplices, that he is *coming* all he knows, or that he *comes it as strong as a horse.* **1841** B. WAIT *Lett. from Van Dieman's Land* (1843) 266 When the party has a *down* upon either *pal's* (mate) *coming it,* (informing against them,) the *trickster* (a false swearer) makes oath. **1899** J. BRADSHAW *Quirindi Bank Robbery* 16 He was promised a very light sentence if he would come it on his mate.

2. In the phr. **to come at,** to agree to do (something), to accept (a situation, etc.); to 'try (something) on'. Freq. in negative contexts.

1911 A. WRIGHT *Gambler's Gold* (1923) 118 Punters were watching for a move that the stable was backing... It came at last; the word went round that — was 'coming at' Gorki. **1984** *Age* (Melbourne) 18 Sept. 17/6, I was a great advocate of Hawke's... I went to Canberra deliberately to see him. I spent a week there, but watching him at a distance I just couldn't come at it.

comeback.

1. A boomerang which returns to the thrower. Also **comeback boomerang.**

1878 R.B. SMYTH *Aborigines of Vic.* I. 329 The boomerangs.. from the north-east coast in my collection are not 'come-back' or 'play' boomerangs. **1901** *Bulletin* (Sydney) 2 Mar. 15/1, I am a pretty fair boomerang-thrower, except with the 'returner'. Can any reader inform me as to how Westralian 'comebacks' (kylies) are thrown.

2. A sheep three-quarters merino and one-quarter crossbred; the wool of the breed. Also *attrib.*

1891 R. WALLACE *Rural Econ. & Agric.* 360 When a pure Merino ram is put to a cross ewe the produce is termed a 'come-back' or 'quarter-back'. **1896** *Bulletin* (Sydney) 11 Jan. 27/2 His youngsters have a pet sheep, of the comeback denomination. **1905** *Shearer* (Sydney) 2 Dec. 3/2 Wools fine in quality, free, sound, and in good condition were in exceptional request, whilst bright, free, comeback and crossbreds created keen bidding.

comic cuts. Rhyming slang for 'guts'. Also *ellipt.* as **comics.**

1945 *Newsreel* (Launceston) May 4 Patients feel the pills doing them good even before they reach the 'comic cuts'.

commission. [Abbrev. of *Housing Commission* (in some States).] Used *attrib.* of government-owned housing, etc., for people on low incomes.

1926 *Canberra Community News* 11 June 9 Recently I was severely 'ticked off'.. for building a small fireplace in my shanty with Commission bricks. **1981** B. GREEN *Small Town Rising* 12 The families of the two aborigines.. were above suspicion, for they lived in Commission homes in the town.

common. Also in *pl.* [Transf. use of *common* communally owned or shared land.]

1. Unenclosed Crown land available as public pasture; sometimes, as in Br. use, an area specifically reserved, but freq. unallocated land adjacent to settlements.

1808 *Sydney Gaz.* 29 May, Fifty Acres of excellent land... Four acres much elevated immediately contiguous to an extensive Common. **1977** W.A. WINTER-IRVING *Bush Stories* 19 The town common, a huge area of about eight hundred hectares or more, taking in most of the waterhole and contained by a fence.

2. Special Comb. **common ranger:** see quot. 1899.

1899 *Bulletin* (Sydney) 8 Apr. 14/3 Even in the bush exists the desire for titles... The bank-clerks are 'bankers', the herdsman is 'common ranger', the bum is 'sheriff'.

common fringe-myrtle: see FRINGE-MYRTLE.

Commonwealth. [Shortened form of *Commonwealth of Australia.*] The federated States and Territories of Australia; the government of this federation. Also *attrib.*

1891 *Quiz* (Adelaide) 17 Apr. 6/2 Deakin, it is stated, is the real godfather of the term 'Australian Commonwealth'. **1901** F.J. GILLEN *Diary* 9 May (1968) 73 Today the Duke of Cornwall is to open the Commonwealth Parliament.

compo. [f. WORKERS') COMP(ENSATION + -O.]

1. A payment or series of payments made under a workers' compensation scheme. Also *attrib.*

1949 *Coast to Coast 1948* 108 What if I am—dusted? What d'you think I'll do? Get outback, take me compo, and nose around till I strike some of the shiny stuff they call gold. **1966** *Realist* (Sydney) xxii. 20/2 The compo claims on false teeth had reached about their limit.

2. In the phr. **on compo,** in receipt of workers' compensation.

1941 K. TENNANT *Battlers* 291 'If you *do* slice your hand, they put you on compo...' Seeing them puzzled, she explained: 'Compensation money while it heals.' **1978** R.H. CONQUEST *Dusty Distances* 7, I ruined me back workin' as a ganger on the railways so they've super-ed me out on compo.

concertina, *n.* and *attrib.* [Fig. use of *concertina.*]

A. *n.*

1. a. A side of mutton. **b.** A sheep with wrinkles or folds in its skin.

1897 *Bulletin* (Sydney) 7 Aug. (Red Page), Ribs of Mutton—'Concertina'. Ancient, and very common throughout Australia. **1970** J.S. GUNN in W.S. Ramson *Eng. Transported* 65 *A concertina,* a slang term for a wrinkly sheep is now also a side of lamb in some places.

2. See quot. 1981.

1966 S.J. BAKER *Austral. Lang.* (ed. 2) 68 *Concertinas,* a type of leggings with wrinkles in them. **1981** G. MITCHELL *Bush Horseman* 40 Most stockmen.. preferred to make their own and produced soft, short leggings with turned-down tops. They were very comfortable and were adjusted beneath the swell of the calf by two straps at the top which held them in place during hard riding. Because these leggings wrinkled in the centre, they were known as 'concertinas'.

B. *attrib.* (in senses 1b. and 2).

1905 *Shearer* (Sydney) 4 Mar. 6/2 A lot of the shearing done by Harry Livingstone is of 'concertina' merinos, and not plain bodied crossbreds. **1947** E. HILL *Flying Doctor Calling* 19 There are leggings, spring-side or concertina—concertina are the most comfortable, but if you get them wet you can't take them off for six weeks so spring-side are recommended.

conchie, var. CONSHIE.

Condamine /'kɒndəmaɪn/. [The name of a town in Queensland.] A type of animal bell originally made at Condamine. In full **Condamine bell.**

1925 M. GILMORE *Tilted Cart* 103 The Condamine bell in Queensland.. was as famous there as Mennicke's bell in New South Wales. The first Condamine bell was made from a pit saw; in later years it was made from circular and from crosscut saws as well. Horses and cattle alike wore it. Its note was so penetrating that in time it would render horses deaf. As far as I recollect it, it had a hard steely sound something like a hammer-clink on an anvil. **1926** K.S. PRICHARD *Working Bullocks* 295 Dick Hayes tinkled the condamine he was carrying round to start events.

condenser. *Hist.* [Spec. use of *condenser* an apparatus which converts vapour to liquid.] An apparatus by which water is made potable through distillation. Also *attrib.*
1894 F. HART *Miner's Handbk.* 19 The great drawback to the rapid development of the field has, up to the present, been the scarcity of fresh water; but this want has now been, in a great measure, overcome .. by the provision of a public condenser; not to mention that every mine on which machinery has been erected is in a position to supply itself by means of its own condenser, an apparently unlimited supply of salt water having in almost every instance been encountered at no very great depth from the surface. **1981** A.B. FACEY *Fortunate Life* 54 They used to be big condenser contractors on the Goldfields.
Hence **condensing** *vbl. n.* and *ppl. a.*
1939 A. GASTON *Coolgardie Gold* 115 As the number of condensing plants increased the price of water came down. **1940** G. MORPHETT *Simple Story Rural Dev.* 4/1 The neighbors used to say, 'When you start condensing you get the rain.'

conditional, *a. Hist.*
  a. In special collocations: **conditional emancipation, pardon,** a remission of (a convict's) sentence, subject to varying territorial stipulations but always precluding return to the British Isles until the expiration of the term of the original sentence.
1792 D. COLLINS *Acct. Eng. Colony N.S.W.* (1798) I. 228 One of those convicts who left England in the *Guardian*, and who, from their meritorious behaviour before and after the disaster that befel that ship, received **conditional emancipation** by his Majesty's command. **1794** D. COLLINS *Acct. Eng. Colony N.S.W.* (1798) I. 391 James Ruffler, and Richard Partridge (convicts for life), received a **conditional pardon,** or (as was the term among themselves on this occasion) were made free on the ground, to enable them to become settlers.
  b. In the collocation **conditional pardon man.**
1845 *Observer* (Hobart) 26 Sept. 3/4 On the subject of the Conditional pardon men.

condolly /'kɒndəli/. *Obs.* [a. Gaurna *gandali* whale.] Whale blubber.
1893 S. NEWLAND *Paving Way* 31 'Frying-down pots'— huge iron boilers in which the fat, technically called 'condolly', or blubber, of the whales is melting. **1919** S. NEWLAND *Band of Pioneers* 39 There was a strong odour of 'condolly' (blubber), but the aboriginal luxuriates in ointment that makes itself known.

conjuror. *Obs.* KORADJI.
1846 'COLONIAL MAGISTRATE' *Remarks on Probable Origin* 10 Although the word *Priest* does not appear in the vocabulary of the Natives—the words *Doctor* or *Conjuror* is [*sic*] applied to those old men who assume the guidance in *Coroborees.* **1886** E.M. CURR *Austral. Race* I. 45 It is an universal belief of the Blacks that a conjuror, wizard, or doctor (as bushmen commonly call and I shall continue to call that personage) .. can charm.

conkerberry /'kɒŋkəbɛri/. Also **coongaberry, konkleberry, koonkerberry.** [a. Mayi-Yapi and Mayi-Kulan *gaŋgabarri*.] Either of two species of the genus *Carissa* (fam. Apocynaceae), esp. *C. lanceolata*, the spiny shrub or small tree of W.A., N.T., and Qld., having edible fruits.
1888 *Proc. Linnean Soc. N.S.W.* III. 495 *Carissa ovata* .. 'Kunkerberry' of the aboriginals of the Cloncurry River (North Queensland). **1948** H.A. LINDSAY *Bushman's Handbk.* 58 The koonkerberry is a shrub with thin spines and a milky juice carrying a sweet little berry like a sultana grape. **1949** H.G. LAMOND *White Ears* 60 A sandhill ridge thick with coongaberry and gooya apples. **1969** R. LAWRENCE *Aboriginal Habitat* 58 The Konkleberry .. matured quickly after rain, but the harvest lasted for a few weeks only. **1982** ELLIOT & JONES *Encycl. Austral. Plants* II. 464 Conkerberry... A stunted shrub found in stony terrain often in thickets. A useful plant to the Aborigines.

connie, var. COONIE.

connie, $n.^1$ Chiefly in Melbourne. [f. *con(ductor* + -Y.] A bus or tram conductor.
1933 'TRAMWAY WORKERS' *Shock Brigader* 6 A happy young connie from Kew Called some streets, but omitted a few. **1969** P. ADAM SMITH *Folklore Austral. Railwaymen* 207 Passengers often ask the conductor to wake them up on long runs. This passenger said to the old connie, 'Throw me off at Gladstone.'

connie, $n.^2$ [f. *corn(elian* + -Y.] A type of playing marble. Also **connie agate.**
1966 S.J. BAKER *Austral. Lang.* (ed. 2) 284 Marbles of one kind and another are known to Australian children as .. connies, connie agates. **1972** *Bulletin* (Sydney) 6 May 63/3 He managed to win a few 'birdcages', bottle-os, connie agates and other middle-class marbles.

conshie. Also **conchie.** [Abbrev. of *consc(ientious.*] A conscientious person. Also **conch, concho,** and *attrib.*
1969 A. BUZO *Front Room Boys* (1970) 20 'All right, you blokes, let's get on with the work, eh?' .. 'Righto, Thomo, righto, You're a bit of a conch this morning, aren't you?' **1970** R. BEILBY *No Medals for Aphrodite* 14 One lousy stripe, and as soon as you tried to do the right thing you were a 'military maniac' or 'Army-happy' or, worst of all, a 'conshie'. **1972** R. MAGOFFIN *Chops & Gravy* 106 *Concho,* a conscientious person. **1980** G.F. BREWER *On Breadline* 17, I was a 'conchie' worker, but we were still up to our neck in debt as it was, even before the floods came.

consolidated, *ppl. a.* In special collocations: **consolidated miner's right,** see quot. 1869; **run,** *Qld., obs.*, a holding of adjacent tracts of pasture land, the combined area of which does not exceed 200 square miles (see also RUN $n.^2$); **school,** a rural school formed by the amalgamation of two or more small schools.
1869 R.B. SMYTH *Gold Fields & Mineral Districts* 616 A **consolidated miner's right** may be taken out for all the land held by a mining company on payment of a sum equal to that which would be paid for all the miners' rights that the consolidated right represents. **1863** *Act* (Qld.) 27 Vic. no. 17 Sect. 29, Where the licensee or lessee shall have two or more runs adjoining each other not exceeding in the aggregate two hundred square miles he may apply to the commissioner to register the same as a **consolidated run.** **1920** *W. Austral.* (Perth) 15 Nov. 7/7 Toodyay .. is the first district in the State to gain the distinction of having a **consolidated school** opened in its midst. This is a class of school which marks a forward step in the advanced system of education obtaining in Western Australia.

consultation. [Euphem. use of *consultation* the seeking of advice.] A sweepstake (see quot. 1890); a lottery.
1880 *Bulletin* (Sydney) 21 Feb. 7/3 Sydney Cup Consultation, 1880. 2000 Members at One Pound each. **1890** J. HASLAM *Glimpse Austral. Life* 103 In connection with all big races there is carried out by the fraternity what are called consultations. They get fifty thousand subscribers at one pound each, and divide the winnings, less ten per cent., among those individuals who are lucky enough to draw numbers with a horse's name.
Hence **consult** *v. trans.*

1880 *Bulletin* (Sydney) 3 Apr. 2/3 Mr T.F. Whistler .. successfully consulted Mr Ned Jones .. re the Sydney Cup—£950.

contingent vote. *Hist.* A form of preferential voting introduced in Queensland in 1892; a vote cast under this system.
1892 *Act* (Qld.) 56 Vict. no. 7 Sect. 22, Electors may give contingent votes. 1919 C.A. BERNAYS *Qld. Politics during Sixty Yrs.* 296 Frequently a member had during the existence of a Parliament represented a minority of the electors. An attempt was now made to put an end to that by introducing what was known as the 'contingent vote'.

conversation-lolly. [f. *conversation* + LOLLY 1: cf. *conversation lozenge*, OEDS *conversation* 11.] A sweet inscribed with a (sentimental) motto: see quot. 1902. Also *ellipt.* as **conversation.**
1901 *Bulletin* (Sydney) 19 Jan. 32/1 He .. purchased silk handkerchiefs and perfume and conversation-lollies at the store. 1902 *Ibid.* 13 Dec. 21/4 He never did anything much except bring me .. conversation-lollies, with 'What about the ring?' 'Be my loved one', 'Love the giver', 'You are very sweet', etc., on them. 1972 J. JONES *Memories Golden Gate* 6 Southern made sweets included conversations, humbugs and happy moments, containing a lot of hot chilli liquid.

convict, *n.* and *attrib. Hist.* [Spec. use of *convict* a condemned criminal serving a sentence of penal servitude: see OED *sb.*¹ 2.]

A. *n. Hist.*

1. One sentenced in the British Isles to a term of penal servitude in an Australian Colony.
1787 *Hist. Botany Bay New Holland* p. i, Names of the Ships, and Number of Convicts embark'd on board each ship. 1975 J.D. RITCHIE *Aust. as once we Were* 31 The Aborigines who witnessed the convicts' agonies showed disgust at the punishments.

2. *fig.*
1859 'EYE WITNESS' *Voyage to Aust.* 19 The last dinner taken on British soil is the only comfortable one you will take until you return or die; in short, you are the convict of your own choice, and those with a young family leaving home for Australia would be kindly visited if the undertaker had to receive the money paid to the shipping agents.

B. 1. *attrib.*
1793 W. TENCH *Compl. Acct. Settlement* 25 A dozen farthing candles stuck around the mud walls of a convict-hut. 1935 F. CLUNE *Rolling down Lachlan* 7 The convict iron-gang roadmenders wore fetters.

2. Comb. **convict boy, -built** *a.*, **class, clerk, gang, labour, labourer, -made** *a.*, **mechanic, population, shepherd, stock-keeper, woman.**
1833 *N.S.W. Mag.* (Sydney) 248 **Convict Boys** may be procured as apprentices on board ships. 1839 *S. Austral. Rec.* (London) 9 Oct. 246 The new colony will throw their **convict built** importance entirely into the shade. 1837 J. BACKHOUSE *Narr. Visit Austral. Colonies* (1843) 464 Servants of the **convict class**, are amongst the greatest drawbacks upon domestic comfort, in these Colonies. 1827 P. CUNNINGHAM *Two Yrs. in N.S.W.* II. 297 As these lists are at present made out by a **convict-clerk**, the difference of half-a-crown will make a man either saint or fiend. 1832 BACKHOUSE & TYLOR *Life & Labours G.W. Walker* 22 Feb. (1862) 40 J.B. had an interview with the Governor on the subject of gaining access to the prisons and **convict** or chain-**gangs**. 1827 *Third Rep. Select Committee Emigration* 394 The demand for **convict labour** has risen so much that we are not likely to obtain much of it. 1824 E. CURR *Acct. Colony Van Diemen's Land* 105 Government, so far from having a superfluity of **convict labourers**, is unable to supply the number voluntarily required by the settler. 1852 S. MOSSMAN *Voice from Aust.* 3 The gold-digger .. now travels comfortably along the **convict-made** roads. 1837 J. MUDIE *Felony of N.S.W.* 28 The secresy [sic] as well as co-operation of the **convict mechanics** was secured by means of rum. 1834 J.D. LANG *Hist. & Statistical Acct. N.S.W.* II. 1 The whole of the **convict-population** .. were employed on account of the Government. 1834 J.D. LANG *Hist. & Statistical Acct. N.S.W.* II. 111 The **convict-shepherd** or overseer in charge .. brought us a bucket. 1833 W.H. BRETON *Excursions* 108 It would be an interesting point to ascertain the effect on the **convict stock-keepers.** 1827 P. CUNNINGHAM *Two Yrs. in N.S.W.* II. 271 The usual number of **convict-women** proceeding out in one vessel seldom exceeding ninety.

3. Special Comb. **convict barrack(s),** BARRACK *n.*¹ 1 a.; **chaplain,** a clergyman appointed to minister to the spiritual needs of convicts; **colony,** an Australian Colony regarded primarily as a place of penal servitude; **constable,** a convict appointed as an officer of the peace; so **constabulary; days,** the period 1788–1868, during which convicts were transported to Australia; **department,** the government department responsible for the management of the convict population; **establishment,** the buildings and personnel of a convict station; **overseer,** a convict in government or assigned service appointed to supervise convict labourers; **police,** a force of *convict constables*; **servant,** an assigned convict; **settlement,** *convict colony; convict station;* **settler,** one transported as a convict who has subsequently taken up land in Australia; **ship,** a ship in which convicts are transported from Britain to Australia; **slave,** a convict servant; **station,** a place at which convicts are confined; STATION 1 a.; **system,** the transportation of convicts and treatment of them during confinement. See also PENAL, PRISONER.

1819 *HRA* (1917) 1st Ser. X. 96 The New **Convict Barrack** is a Commodious Spacious Building. . It is Surrounded by a very high Stone Wall and is Calculated to Contain between Five and Six hundred Men. 1837 *Rep. Select Committee Transportation* 2 The convicts are kept on board ship until some necessary arrangements are made on shore for their reception and distribution; the place where they are received is called the Convict Barracks. 1844 F.R. NIXON *Pioneer Bishop Van Diemen's Land* 30 Dec. (1953) 41 The Bishop wished particularly to ordain all the **convict chaplains** himself. 1822 J.T. BIGGE *Rep. State Colony N.S.W.* 147 He has thought, and often repeated, that New South Wales was a **convict colony.** 1834 J.D. LANG *Hist. & Statistical Acct. N.S.W.* II. 267 This delicate task was entrusted by the military commandants to **convict-constables.** 1835 *True Colonist* (Hobart) 27 Nov. 4/1 The subject of the **Convict Constabulary.** 1892 'J. MILLER' *Workingman's Paradise* 92 That's .. a little island and in the **convict days** hard cases were put on it. 1842 *Sydney Morning Herald* 2 Aug. 2/6 Three of the convicts attached to this branch of the **convict department.** 1827 *HRA* (1920) 1st Ser. XIII. 471 For the support and maintenance of the **Convict Establishment.** 1829 *Sydney Monitor* 16 Feb. 1500/2 Fulton, a convict servant of our **convict overseer** .. was tied up. 1838 *Rep. Select Committee Transportation* 26 Mar. 127 'There are a great many convicts employed as Constables?'—'Yes, a .. great many...' 'How do you find the **convict police** behave?'—'Very well, I do not think free men would have done the duty that they did.' 1790 R. CLARK Jrnl. 15 Feb. 133 My other **convict servants.** 1831 J.G. POWELL *Narr. Voyage Swan River* p. x, The trade and number of emigrants to the **Convict Settlements** will be reduced. 1851 *Empire* (Sydney) 2 Dec. 423/3 The first convict settlement in this locality was situated at a place called Red Bank. 1792 P.G. KING Jrnl. Norfolk Island Oct. 50 The **Convict Settlers** are all doing very Well, and are at present the most industrious description of Settlers. 1812 E.H. BARKER *Geogr., Comm., & Pol. Essays* 193 The appearance and regulations of a **convict ship** are as singular as the novel punishment of transportation. 1829 D. BURN *Bushrangers* (1971) 23 Kindness! I was your husband's **convict slave**—true, an unruly one.

1834 *Perth Gaz.* 8 Nov. 387 The propriety of petitioning the Home Government that this [*sc.* Albany] should be made a **Convict Station.** **1834** *New Brit. Province S.A.* 134 The great natural advantages of Australia had been counteracted by the moral evils of the **convict system.**

convictism. *Hist.*

1. *Convict system,* see CONVICT *n.* 3; the use of an Australian Colony as a place of penal servitude.

1834 *Colonist* (Hobart) 18 Mar. 2/2 It did not take away, if he might be allowed to use such an expression, 'convictism'. **1965** G. MCINNES *Road to Gundagai* 116 Though convictism had been finally abolished in 1852, the Emigrant Ship still meant Transportation for Life.

2. The convict population (of an Australian Colony).

1847 *Port Phillip Herald* 7 Jan. (Suppl.), A very considerable immigration of exclusively male convictism, undiluted by any admixture of free and untainted persons, has been going on from Van Diemen's Land and from England. **1870** *Austral. Jrnl.* (Melbourne) May 499/1 Convictism had established a tacit right to converse in whispers.

convincing ground. *Obs.* A place at which prize or grudge fights are held.

1830 *Sydney Monitor* 14 Aug. 2/2 The place of punishment '*the convincing ground*'. **1951** I.L. IDRIESS *Across Nullarbor* 19 For this was the Convincing Ground. Those were the bare-knuckle days, 'kinged' over by the grim 'grass fighters'.

cooba /'kubə/. Also **couba**. [a. Wiradhuri *gubaa*.] Any of several plants of the genus *Acacia* (fam. Mimosaceae), esp. *A. salicina* of drier mainland Aust.; WIRRA *n.*^{2} See also *native willow* NATIVE *a.* 6 a., *willow wattle* WILLOW 2.

1878 'R. BOLDREWOOD' *Ups & Downs* 46 A deep reach of the river, shaded by couba trees. **1889** J.H. MAIDEN *Useful Native Plants Aust.* 115 *Acacia salicina* .. called 'Cooba' or 'Koobah' by the aboriginals of Western New South Wales... This is another tree which is rapidly becoming scarce, owing to the partiality of stock to it. **1901** *Proc. Linnean Soc. N.S.W.* XXVI. 209 *Acacia salicina*... Cooba appears to be the aboriginal name for this tree, but there is a growing tendency in the west to pronounce the name Cuba.

cooboo /'kubu/. *W.A.* [Poss. a. Martuthunira *gubuyu* small, child.] An (Aboriginal) baby.

1929 K.S. PRICHARD *Coonardoo* (1961) 10 Their skins darken with exposure to the air and sunshine, so that by the time they are toddling, the cooboos are as bronzed and gleaming as pebbles lying on the red earth. **1931** D.B. O'CONNOR *Black Velvet* 12 In the heat of the sun she exposed her cooboo.

cooee /'kui, ku'i/, *n.* and *int.* [a. Dharuk *guuu-wi*.]

1. Orig. a call used by an Aboriginal to communicate (with someone) at a distance; later adopted by settlers and now widely used as a signal, esp. in the bush (see quots. 1827 and 1845); a name given to the call.

1790 D. SOUTHWELL Corresp. & Papers, *Coo-ee, cō-ee, cō-eé, cō-é*, to come. **1827** P. CUNNINGHAM *Two Yrs. in N.S.W.* (rev. ed.) II. 23 In calling to each other at a distance, the natives make use of the word *Coo-ee*, as we do the word *Hollo*, prolonging the sound of the *coo*, and closing that of the *ee* with a shrill jerk. **1845** C. GRIFFITH *Present State & Prospects Port Phillip* 65 The cooey is a call in universal use amongst the settlers and has been borrowed from the natives. The performer dwells for about half a minute upon one note, and then raises his voice to the octave. It can be heard at a great distance.

2. *fig.*

1894 W. CROMPTON *Convict Jim* 28 An' the river is a banker, an' its current's running strong, An' I don't think I'll be waiting for Death's cooee very long. **1917** M.W. JAMES *'Coo-ee' Call* 9 They bless the day when first he heard His little Wife's 'Coo-ee'.

3. In the phr. **within cooee,** within earshot; within reach, near.

1836 R. PORTER *Hist. Story* 12 He lay there some time, unable to rise, but had eventually managed to crawl within coo-ee of the camp. **1984** *Nat. Times* (Sydney) 6 July 50/2 Holland was our only hope within cooee of winning an Olympic gold medal at Montreal.

4. Special Comb. **cooee bird,** the large cuckoo *Eudynamys orientalis*, the Indian koel, a summer visitor from s.e. Asia to n. and e. Aust.

1912 *Bulletin* (Sydney) 22 Feb. 14/1 The coo-ee bird, a fruit-eating nuisance in Queensland... Even those familiar with this bird will fail to distinguish its call, at a distance, from the human coo-ee.

cooee /'kui/, *v.* [f. prec.] *intr.* To utter a 'cooee'. Also *trans.*

1824 *Austral.* (Sydney) 18 Nov. 3 The little girl told them .. that he intended some mischief, and that he was coo-ing for some of his tribe. **1869** E.C. BOOTH *Another England* 66 Come along into dinner, for I hear the mistress cooeeing me.

Hence **cooeeing** *vbl. n.* and *ppl. a.*

1845 J.O. BALFOUR *Sketch of N.S.W.* 17, I shall never forget the cooing, shouting, roaring, cracking of nulla-nullas. **1881** *Adventures of Strollers Otway Ranges* 8 So one is told off to do the cooee-ing for the lost children. **1885** G. DARRELL *Sunny South* 38 There's no one else within cooeeing distance.

coohoy nut /'kuhɔi nʌt/. *Hist.* [f. *coohoy* (a. Dyirbal *guway*) + *nut*.] The nut of the rainforest tree *Floydia praealta* (fam. Proteaceae) of s.e. Qld. and n.e. N.S.W. Also **coohoy,** the tree itself.

1886 *Trans. & Proc. R. Geogr. Soc. Australasia N.S.W.* (1888) 242 Our dinner consisted of a few coohoy nuts, so named by the aborigines. The nut is perfectly round, and about 6 inches, in circumference, with a thin shell... The nut needs no preparation, only roasting till nicely browned. If eaten raw it resembles the uncooked English potato. *c* **1910** W.R. GUILFOYLE *Austral. Plants* 210 *Helicia praealta* .. 'Tall Queensland Nut Tree'.. or 'Coohoy'.. N.S.W. and Q'land.

Cook. *Obs.* Shortened form of CAPTAIN COOK *n.*

1899 *Truth* (Sydney) 14 May 3/1 The Cap'en, he merely squinted around, cursory-like, and I'm hanged if his name don't stick to that job, too. How do I mean? Why, if a chap just glances at a thing don't we still say he has 'a Cook' at it? **1910** L. ESSON *Woman Tamer* (1976) 70 Soon's we had a cook at the engines, gorblime, we were pinched, five of us.

Cooktown orchid. [f. the name of a coastal town in n. Qld.] The epiphytic orchid *Dendrobium bigibbum* (fam. Orchidaceae) of n. Qld. and Torres Strait islands, the floral emblem of Queensland, having showy, usu. lilac flowers.

1956 A.C.C. LOCK *Tropical Tapestry* 268 One of the most common species, *Dendrobium phalaenopsis*, is so named on account of the resemblance of its flowers to moths. Because they are plentiful in the country west of Cooktown, they have earned the name of Cooktown orchids. **1984** K.A.W. WILLIAMS *Native Plants Qld.* II. 2 The Cooktown Orchid was declared the Floral Emblem of Queensland in November 1959... This beautiful species is rapidly becoming endangered in the natural habitat as poachers continue to gather large numbers of plants for illegal sale.

coola, var. COOLER, KOALA 1.

coolabah, var. COOLIBAH.

coolah grass /'kulə gras/. [f. Wiradhuri prob. *gulu* + (Eng.) *grass*.] Any of several grasses (fam. Poaceae), esp. the introduced *Panicum coloratum*, a summer-growing tufted perennial of N.S.W., Vic., and Qld., and the widespread native *P. prolutum*. See also COOLY.

1847 D. BUNCE *Australasiatic Reminisc.* 20 Apr. (1857) 168 The *Panicum Leavinode* [*sic*] is the plant from which the natives make their bread, and is called by the blacks of Liverpool Plains, *coola grass*. 1981 G.M. CUNNINGHAM et al. *Plants Western N.S.W.* 118 Many forms of coolah grass exist and these differ in habit, size, hairiness and colour.

coolamon /'kuləmən/. Also **coolimon, coolaman, kooliman**. [a. Kamilaroi *gulaman*.]

1. A vessel of wood or bark (but see quot. 1857) used by Aborigines to hold water and other liquids, but also for a variety of other purposes (see quots. 1926 and 1943); PITCHI. See also YANDY *n*.

1845 L. LEICHHARDT *Jrnl. Overland Exped. Aust.* 27 May (1847) 269 Three koolimans (vessels of stringy bark) were full of honey water, from one of which I took a hearty draught, and left a brass button for payment. 1851 J. HENDERSON *Excursions & Adventures N.S.W.* II. 151 The *coolaman* is their jug, or jar, for carrying water. It is a large knot of a tree cut off from it, and hollowed out, a handle of cord being fastened across it. 1857 F. DE B. COOPER *Wild Adventures* 40 Cooliemans (Cameleroi dialect)—vessels for holding water, frequently gourds. 1909 F.E. BIRTLES *Lonely Lands* 203 A favourite dish of theirs is a mixture of iguana and leaves, served in 'coolamons' (native dishes). 1926 A.A.B. APSLEY *Amateur Settlers* 107 The babies are carried in a rude sort of cradle, called a 'coolimon'. 1943 *Bulletin* (Sydney) 11 Aug. 13/3 In the Pilbara district (W.A.) .. abo. gins .. partly fill the coolamons with mullock from the old workings, and by a process known as yandi-ing .. separate from the mullock particles of tin.

2. *fig.*

1891 M. ROBERTS *Land-Travel & Sea-Faring* 197 The water-holes, or as they call them in that part of Australia, cooliman holes, gave out.

cooler /'kulə/, *a*. and *n*. *Austral. pidgin. Obs*. Also **coola, coolie**. [a. Dharuk *gularra*.]

A. *adj*. Angry.

c 1790 W. DAWES Grammatical Forms Lang. N.S.W., *Gulara*, angry. 1830 R. DAWSON *Present State Aust*. 75, I murry cooler (angry). 1839 T.L. MITCHELL *Three Exped. Eastern Aust*. II. 4 The Myalls were coming up ('murry coola' i.e. *very angry*) to meet us. 1845 J.O. BALFOUR *Sketch of N.S.W.* 18, I .. was told that they did not like my interference, and that they would become 'coolie'; in other words, that there would be enmity between them and me.

B. *n*. Anger.

1841 *Port Phillip Patriot* 4 Oct. 4/1 They .. then went away, saying, 'we will return in two or three days, when cooler (white man's wrath) is all gone.'

Coolgardie /kul'gadi/. [The name of a gold-mining town in W.A.]

1. a. Used *attrib*. in Special Comb. **Coolgardie safe,** a safe for keeping foodstuffs cool (see quot. 1925); also **Coolgardie foodsafe.**

c 1924 MAW & JORDAN *Hints Pioneering Homemakers* 5 *Coolgardie safes*—All sizes, both straight and sloping sides, galvanised frames, covered with hessian. 1925 *Makeshifts & Other Home-Made Furniture* (New Settlers League Aust.) 40 To make a Coolgardie safe, build a frame from strong packing cases, and put a shelf about 2 ft. from the ground, and another on top 5 ft. from the ground. Cover the frame with hessian, putting a door on one side. On top, place a kerosene tin cut in half lengthwise. Keep this filled with water, and, hanging from it over the sides of the safe, put strips of hessian, towelling or flannel. Make gutters of pieces of tin to go around the bottom of the safe, making them all slope toward one corner. Here let the water drip into a tin underneath. This water may be used again. Keep in a breezy place. 1959 *Meanjin* 293 Everything spoke of a man of simple tastes and exacting habits: a single bed made up with military efficiency .. a coolgardie foodsafe.

b. In other Special Comb. **Coolgardie cooler,** a refinement of the Coolgardie safe (see quot. 1977); **shampoo,** see quot.; **stretcher** (or **bunk**), a makeshift bed; also **Coolgardie camp stretcher.**

1972 N. KING *Nickel Country* 91 With its tongue flicking in and out, it always headed for the **Coolgardie cooler** where it knew eggs were kept. 1977 B. FULLER *Nullarbor Lifelines* 38 Later, the Coolgardie Cooler came into general use. This had double walls of fine-mesh wire netting, usually placed from two to eight centimetres apart. The space between was filled with charcoal kept wet through percolation. 1908 J.A. BARRY *Luck of Native Born* 48 They did as they saw all others around them doing, stripped mother-naked outside their tent, and gave themselves first a scrubbing with Ned's big clothes-brush, then a rub down with a coarse towel—a process locally known as a '**Coolgardie shampoo**'. 1944 M.J. O'REILLY *Bowyangs & Boomerangs* 39 Sitting on **Coolgardie stretchers** were two old miners. 1949 I.L. IDRIESS *One Wet Season* 85 Scotty insisted on carrying him into the homestead and making him comfortable on a spare Coolgardie bunk. 1981 M. CRITCH *Our Kind of War* 81 The canvas hold-all contained .. four sheets, towels, pillowslips, a folding Coolgardie camp stretcher, a folding canvas chair.

2. A Coolgardie safe.

1936 M. HERRON *Seed & Stubble* 95 There is a cold fowl and trimmings in the 'Coolgardie'. 1978 *Bronze Swagman Bk. Bush Verse* 10 Coolgardies swung and spread their hessian-scented breath.

coolibah /'kuləba/. Also **coolabah**. [a. Yuwaaliyaay (and related languages) *gulabaa*.] Any of several myrtaceous trees, esp. the bluish-leaved *Eucalyptus microtheca* of W.A., N.T., Qld., N.S.W., and S.A., a fibrous-barked tree yielding a heavy durable timber and occurring in seasonally inundated areas. See also *flooded box* FLOODED. Also **coolibah tree**, and *attrib*.

1883 E. PALMER *Plants N. Qld.* (1884) 14 *E. microtheca* .. The Coolibar or flooded box found on all Gulf waters, often in flooded ground, of a crooked growth, about 30 feet high. 1893 'TIMES SPECIAL CORRESPONDENT' *Lett. from Qld*. 60 The timber, of course, when seen close at hand is strange. Boree and gidyah, coolibah .. are the unfamiliar names. 1900 *Proc. Linnean Soc. N.S.W.* XXV. 86 It is mostly a crooked tree; and it is from this feature that the aboriginal name 'Coolabah' is derived. 1956 *Bulletin* (Sydney) 24 Oct. 12/3 The jackeroos were sitting by a coolibah-shaded waterhole, waiting for their quartpots to boil.

coolie, var. COOLER.

coolie, /'kuli/, *n*.[1] *Obs*. [a. Wemba-wemba *guli* person.] A name given by white Australians to the consort of an Aboriginal woman; also applied, usu. in *pl*., to Aboriginal men in general.

1842 *Melbourne Times* 3 Dec. 3/1 About ten days since an aboriginal woman died at the station of Mr Allen of the Pyrenees and was laid by her coolie and others of the tribe upon a piece of bark and burned. 1847 T. MCCOMBIE *Austral. Sketches* 6 He talks of having gone out with his rifle and shot the black coolies by dozens.

coolie /'kuli/, *n*.[2] *Obs*. [Var. of *collie*: see OED 1.] A sheep-dog, a collie. Also **coolie dog.**

1848 H.W. HAYGARTH *Recoll. Bush Life* 44 Here the watchman, after tying up near the folds several of his 'coolie' dogs, who will awaken him on the approach of a 'warragle', or native dog, his only cause of alarm. 1891 M. ROBERTS *Land-Travel & Sea-Faring* 72 Their dogs are always collies—

called by the way in the bush coolies—they come very often from good imported strains.

coolimon, var. COOLAMON.

cool-safe. [Abbrev. of *Coolgardie safe*, with pun on *cool.*] *Coolgardie safe*, see COOLGARDIE 1 a.
1924 *Anthony Hordern Catal.* 421 The 'Cold Cap' Collapsible Cool Safe, made of strong galvanized iron. The perforated zinc sides are covered with White towelling. **1979** W.K. BECKINGHAM *Red Acres* 24 The 'Coolgardie Safe' or 'Cool' Safe kept food a little longer in the heat in the days before country people had refrigerators, which in our case was until 1949.

cooly /'kuli/. *Obs.* [a. Wiradhuri *gulu.*] The edible seed or seeds of *native millet* (see NATIVE *a.* 6 a.), and prob. also COOLAH GRASS.
1848 T.L. MITCHELL *Jrnl. Exped. Tropical Aust.* 90 The *Panicum laevinode* of Dr Lindley seemed to predominate, a grass whereof the seed ('Cooly') is made by the natives into a kind of paste or bread. Dry heaps of this grass, that had been pulled expressly for the purpose of gathering the seed, lay along our path for many miles. **1888** *Proc. Linnean Soc. N.S.W.* III. 536 'Native Millet'... The seed used to be called 'Cooly' by western New South Wales aboriginals.

coon. [Transf. use of *coon* a Black.] An Aboriginal. Freq. as a term of abuse.
1899 *Truth* (Sydney) 9 July 2/2 The mate will never be able to exert his authority over the coon after having been in the same chain-gang with him. **1984** P. READ *Down there with me on Cowra Mission* 22 But they couldn't see that they were hurting me by just using .. 'coon'.

coongaberry, var. CONKERBERRY.

coonie /'kuni/. Also **connie, coondie, cundy.** [Prob. f. a N.S.W. Aboriginal language.] A stone suitable for use as a missile.
1941 S.J. BAKER *Pop. Dict. Austral. Slang* 21 *Cundy*, a small stone. **1968** S. GORE *Holy Smoke* 13 All I needeth is me shanghai here, and a few of these big coonies that's layin' around, and I'll get stuck into it. **1978** W. LOWENSTEIN *Weevils in Flour* 378 One of our blokes threw a great big connie at a policeman who stuck his head out. **1981** D. STUART *I think I'll Live* 316 He hoys me with his right hand, then he heaves this coondie over the fence... I went inside and takes the paper off this rock.

coota. Also **couta.** Shortened form of BARRACOUTA.
[N.Z. **1911** *N.Z. Truth* (Wellington) 1 Apr. 6 Hampton said that the 'couta were rotten and stinking.] **1933** D. MACDONALD *Brooks of Morning* 65 Scattered shoals leaped in terror out of the sea with the 'coota through and after them. **1951** D. COLLINS *Vic.'s my Home Ground* 7 This peculiarly clad but adventurous character was Fisherman Collins, outward bound after the 'coota and crays.

Cootamundra wattle /kutəmʌndrə 'wɒtl/. [f. the name of a town in central N.S.W., referring to the area of the plant's natural occurrence + WATTLE 1.] The N.S.W. shrub or small tree *Acacia baileyana* (fam. Mimosaceae), having pale bluish-grey foliage, now widely planted and naturalized elsewhere (see quot. 1959). Also *ellipt.* as **Cootamundra.**
1902 *Proc. Linnean Soc. N.S.W.* XXVII. 198 *Acacia Baileyana*.. (Cootamundra Wattle) is fairly plentiful. **1959** A.E. BROOKS *Austral. Native Plants* 2 *Cootamundra Wattle*,.. found naturally in only a restricted area near Temora and Cootamundra.. is spreading into the bushland in some areas from garden specimens. **1965** G. McINNES *Road to Gundagai* 84 The .. flower bed between the cootamundra and the peach tree.

cop. Used *attrib.* in Special Comb. **copman, copperman** (both *obs.*), a policeman; **shop** [used elsewhere but recorded earliest in Aust.], a police station.
1898 *Bulletin* (Sydney) 4 June (Red Page), A policeman is a 'johnny' or a 'copman' or a 'trap'. **1916** *Truth* (Sydney) 5 Nov. 12/3 Yet he for the copperman (Flannagan) sent. **1941** S.J. BAKER *Pop. Dict. Austral. Slang* 20 *Copman*, a policeman. *Copperman*, a policeman. **1966**——*Austral. Lang.* (ed. 2) 142 The now-obsolete *copman* and *copperman.* **1941**——*Pop. Dict. Austral. Slang* 20 **Copshop**, a police station.

cop it sweet, to: see SWEET $a.^2$ 2 b.

copper-burr. Any of several spiny-fruited plants, esp. small shrubs of the genus *Sclerolaena*, formerly *Bassia*, (fam. Chenopodiaceae) of all mainland States.
1932 M.R. WHITE *No Roads go By* 45 The flats were sprinkled with .. copper-burr. **1982** G.B. EGGLETON *Last of Lantern Swingers* 46 The copper-burr has vicious little needle-like brown spikes about half-an-inch in length, and sheep dogs need to be fitted with leather foot-guards before they can be worked in this country.

copper-head. [Transf. use of *copperhead* a North American snake.] The venomous snake *Austrelaps superbus* of s.e. Aust. Also **copper-head(ed) snake.**
1878 F. McCOY *Prodromus of Zool. Vic.* (1885) I. i. Pl. 2, The Copper-head Snake... I have adopted the popular name 'copper-head' for this snake from a well-known vendor of a supposed antidote for snake-bites. **1888** *Centennial Mag.* (Sydney) 14 The hill crow-shrike is plentiful; so is the copper-headed snake. **1976** E. WORRELL *Things that Sting* 14 The Copperhead has a thickset body and usually has the scales around its lips edged with cream.

coppertail. *Obs.* [Fig. use of *copper* as contrasting in value with *silver*: see SILVERTAIL.] A person of small social pretension or standing. Also **coppertop.**
1887 *Bulletin* (Sydney) 12 Nov. 4/1 In their thoughts and expressions they betray the demoralisation wrought in the 'copper-top' and 'silver-tail' era. **1901** *Ibid.* 28 Sept. 15/1 'Silvertails' congregate at one end of the room, 'Coppertails' at the other, and the line of demarcation is rarely crossed.

Also **coppertailed** *ppl. a.*
1890 A.J. VOGAN *Black Police* 116 The genus termed in Australian parlance 'silver-tailed', in distinction to the 'copper-tailed' democratic classes.

coral. [Attrib. use of *coral*, with reference either to habitat or to a fancied resemblance.] Special Comb. **coral cod** (or **trout**), the marine blue-spotted fish *Plectropoma maculatum* (fam. Serranidae) of waters off W.A. and Qld., including the Great Barrier Reef; the similar related fish *Cephalopholis miniatus*; **fern,** any of several slender ferns with forked fronds of the genus *Gleichenia* (fam. Gleicheniaceae) of all States and N.Z., New Caledonia, and s.e. Asia; (chiefly *Qld.*) the scrambling tropical fern ally *Lycopodium cernuum* (fam. Lycopodiaceae); **pea, (a)** any of several climbing or trailing plants of the genus *Kennedia* (fam. Fabaceae), with red or purple flowers, esp. *K. rubicunda* (also **dusky coral pea**) of e. Aust. and *K. prostrata* (see RUNNING POSTMAN); **(b)** FALSE SARSAPARILLA; also **purple coral pea; tree,** any of several trees of the genus *Erythrina* (fam. Fabaceae) of n. and central Aust., bearing bright red or yellowish flowers.
1928 S.E. NAPIER *On Barrier Reef* 81 Many **coral cod** .. were caught. **1936** T.C. ROUGHLEY *Wonders Great Barrier Reef* 9 Some fish from the reef .. red emperor and coral trout. **1898** E.E. MORRIS *Austral Eng.* 98 **Coral-Fern**, name given in Victoria to *Gleichenia circinata*. **1985** N. & H. NICHOLSON *Austral. Rainforest Plants* 42 Coral fern makes a

cord pretty ground cover for moist or poorly drained soils in sun or shade. **(a) 1896** *Melburnian* 28 Aug. 53 The trailing scarlet kennedyas, aptly called the 'bleeding-heart' or '**coral pea**'. **1942** C. BARRETT *Austral. Wild Flower Bk.* 44, Dusky coral pea, with its dark-red flowers and long, tough rambling stems. **(b) 1914** E.E. PESCOTT *Native Flowers Vic.* 35 The thick roots of this species, Hardenbergia monophylla, the 'Purple **Coral Pea**', have a certain medicinal value as a blood purifier. **1981** A.B. & J.W. CRIBB *Wild Medicine in Aust.* 76 Quite possibly the imaginary virtues of the coral pea, if trusted strongly enough by those who drank the infusion, were as effective as the more pharmacologically valuable true colonial sarsaparilla. **1848** T.L. MITCHELL *Jrnl. Exped. Tropical Aust.* 218 One thorny tree or shrub.. had a leaf, somewhat like a human hand, and a pod containing two peas of a bright scarlet colour, about the shape and size of a French bean... This proved to be a new species of Erythrina, or **coral tree**.

cord. Abbrev. of *corduroy road* (see CORDUROY B).

1898 *Bulletin* (Sydney) 26 Feb. 14/1 He once started from Waratah to the '13-Mile', the whole distance on 'cords', with a newchum. Godkin left with 75 lb., the towny with about 30 lb.

corduroy, *n.* and *attrib.* [U.S., from the resemblance to the ribbed appearance of *corduroy*: see OED(S *sb.* 3.]

A. *n.*

1. A pathway across swampy ground, made of logs or slabs laid transversely and side by side; the logs or slabs so used: see esp. quot. 1920 (2).

1861 [see *corduroy road*]. **1875** R.P. WHITWORTH *Cobb's Box* 4 Over hill and dale, gully and flat, mudhole and 'corduroy'. **1920** C.C. DUGAN *Old Tasmanian Road* 23 With a jump and a thump and a bump, bump, bump, Over the corduroy. **1920** *Land of Lyre Bird* (S. Gippsland Pioneers' Assoc.) 94 Corduroy was pretty largely used by the settlers in the early days to keep them out of the mud, and the forests of saplings of all kinds through which the roads ran afforded abundance of material for the work. Spars of six or eight inches in diameter were cut into lengths of eight or ten feet and laid close together, transversely to the road, along the worst stretches... A better system of corduroy was adopted by the Shire Councils later on, of splitting slabs of about four inches by nine and ten or twelve feet long out of the big timber, and laying them on longitudinal bed logs.

2. *transf.*

1956 S. GORE *Overlanding with Annabel* 59 The only way to deal with this kind of road hazard is to dig all sand from around the wheels so that it will not grip and bind, then laying spinifex, bushes or matting of some kind under the back wheels, reverse the car out.. and when back on firm ground make another rush at the sand, which will meanwhile have been prepared by laying more 'corduroy' all along in front.

B. *attrib.* Used in various Comb., esp. **corduroy road,** to denote this method of construction or the material used.

1861 L.A. MEREDITH *Over Straits* 160 Corduroy roads of logs were being laid down in some places on the line, because stone for 'road-metal' was scarce. **1880** 'OLD HAND' *Experiences of Colonist* (ed. 2) i. 74 Where the stream was shallow and rapid, an attempt had been made to erect a corduroy bridge over it. **1982** M. WALKER *Making Do* 130 It had a corduroy bottom, that's wood in the bottom of it to stop you from sinking down in the sand. He broke the wagonette's axle.

corduroy, *v.* [f. prec.] *trans.* To surface (a pathway, etc.) with logs or slabs laid transversely and side by side.

[N.Z. **1868** DILKE *Greater Brit.* I. 340 The highway is 'corduroyed' with trunks of tree fern.] **1879** 'AUSTRALIAN' *Adventures Qld.* 94 Bogs and swamps have not been corduroyed, or in any way altered. **1976** J.H. TRAVERS *Bull Dust on Brigalow* 46 He had up to five tethered together by this method and had them corduroying sandy patches on the road close to Borroloola.

Hence **corduroyed** *ppl. a.*, **corduroying** *vbl. n.*

1946 A.J. MARSHALL *Nulli Secundus Log* 89 We found a muddy, **corduroyed** track. **1898 corduroying** [see CORDUROY *v.*]. **1982** R. ELLIS *Bush Safari* 24 After we managed to dig down and jack up the ute, this timber, in lengths of about 60 centimetres, was placed underneath the wheels and along the wheel tracks, giving, in effect, a made 'road' about 12 metres long. This is known as 'corduroying'.

cordy. [Prob. f. *cord*, in allusion to the epaulettes of a dress uniform: see quot. 1945 where the reference is in a military context and to servants.] A member of the Corps of Staff Cadets at the Royal Military College, Duntroon.

[**1945** *Weekend Mag.* 25 Nov. 2 How would you like to be waited on by 1000 people—or should I say Kordies?] **1964** *Woroni* (Canberra) 9 July 8/1 *Blues Undo Cordies.* After indifferent form in our last two matches Uni. played constructive football to defeat R.M.C. at Duntroon. **1981** *Canberra Times* 18 Sept. 2/6 Changing the guard at Yarralumla Palace would become the top tourist attraction in Canberra, says the task force, with the red-coated RMC band marching down Lady Denman Drive with a smartly outfitted detachment of 'cordies' from Duntroon behind them.

corella /kə'rɛlə/. [a. Wiradhuri prob. *garila*.]

1. a. Either of two predom. white, crestless cockatoos of the genus *Cacatua, C. sanguinea* (see *little corella* LITTLE 2) and *C. tenuirostris* (see *long-billed corella* LONG 2). **b.** (Occas.) MAJOR MITCHELL COCKATOO.

1859 H. KINGSLEY *Recoll. Geoffry Hamlyn* II. 77 He had a bird, a white corrella, which could talk and whistle. **1924** L. ST. C. GRONDONA *Kangaroo keeps on Talking* 128 Corellas—pink crested—and galahs.. are all good talkers.

2. Special Comb. **corella pear,** a variety of pear grown in S.A. (see quot. 1975).

1975 *Bulletin* (Sydney) 26 July 50/1 The Corella pear is grown only in South Australia, and is almost manufactured. Cross pollination is done by hand and the beautiful red blush is created by a cold-storage technique. The pear is named after a red-coloured parrot found in South Australia.

cork. [f. the resemblance of a bark or wood to the bark of the cork oak *Quercus suber*.] Used *attrib.* in Special Comb. **cork-bark,** any of several shrubs or trees having a thick, rough, and corky bark, esp. of the genus HAKEA; **tree** (or **wood**), any of several trees or shrubs having light and porous wood or rough corky bark, esp. of the genera *Duboisia* (fam. Solanaceae), *Erythrina* (see *coral tree* CORAL), and HAKEA; also **corkwood tree.**

1890 'LYTH' *Golden South* 196 The timber is good,—the jarrah, pine, cajeput, **cork-bark**. **1788** J. WHITE *Jrnl. Voyage N.S.W.* 23 Jan. (1790) 117 Some few had shields made of the bark of the **cork tree**. **1845** C. HODGKINSON *Aust., Port Macquarie to Moreton Bay* 4 The popular names of the most remarkable brush trees are as follow.. Lightwood, Sassafras, Corkwood. **1935** DAVISON & NICHOLLS *Blue Coast Caravan* 239 The cork-wood-tree, with its large leaves and large yellow flowers with shiny black centres that turn red as they die.

corkscrew.

1. Used *attrib.* in the names of flora: **corkscrew grass,** any of several grasses (fam. Poaceae), esp. the perennial *Stipa nitida* and related species, occurring in all States, bearing sharp pointed fruits with spirally twisted awns; **palm,** SCREW PINE.

1872 [**corkscrew grass**] A. MCFARLAND *Illawarra & Manaro* 118 There are many varieties of grass seed; but the one which causes the most trouble is, from its spiral shape, locally known as the 'corkscrew'. **1897** L. LINDLEY-COWEN *W. Austral. Settler's Guide* 79 The chief pasture plants are corkscrew and silver grass, which are very fattening. **1862** J. McKINLAY *Jrnl. Exploration Interior* 7 June 104 The creeks and the river have lots of **cork-screw palms** in and near them.

2. *Surfing*. See quot. 1963.
1931 *Surf: All about It* 36 *Corkscrew shoot*. Ever tried to do a corkscrew? It's one of the higher flights of surfing. **1963** J. POLLARD *Austral. Surfrider* 46 For the expert body surfer, a number of fancy slides have been worked out over the years. In the *corkscrew*, the surfer's body makes a complete turn as he goes down the slope of a greenback.
Hence **corkscrewing** *vbl. n.*
1956 S. HOPE *Diggers' Paradise* 166 It needs a great deal of practice, and yet more practice if you want to show off by 'corkscrewing' and shooting a 'beacher' on your back.

cormorant. *Obs.* [Spec. use of *cormorant* an insatiably greedy or rapacious person: see OED 2.] A name for a squatter who displays greed in the acquisition of land. Also **cormorant squatter.**
1875 CAMPBELL & WILKS *Early Settlement Qld.* 25 The vicissitudes the early pioneers—or rather cormorant squatters—had to sustain. **1876** J.B. STEPHENS *Hundred Pounds* 186, I *was* a squatter then: not a cormorant, by any means; I am afraid I partook rather of the nature of a cockatoo.

corn.
1. Usu., as in U.S., applied exclusively to maize or Indian corn but formerly also used, as in Br. English, to refer to grain crops generally. Freq. *attrib.*
1804 *Sydney Gaz.* 11 Nov., The Rent of the Premises will be received in the following proportions, viz. One half in Pork; One fourth in Wheat and Corn; and the remaining fourth in Money. **1970** N.A. BEAGLEY *Up & Down Under* 73 The maize crop was ripe and pickers were wanted there. The name for their seasonal occupation was, in Aussie language, 'Corn Snatching'.

2. Special Comb. **corn-bird,** *golden-headed fantail warbler*, see GOLDEN *a.* 3.; *bush lark*, see BUSH C. 3.
1911 J.A. LEACH *Austral. Bird Bk.* 142 Golden-headed Fantail-Warbler,.. Corn (Barley) Bird.

Corner. With **the.** A name for the area in which the borders of N.S.W., Qld., and S.A. meet. Also **Corner Country.**
1891 *Quiz* (Adelaide) 20 Mar. 7/2 The great jaw man of the Corner. **1949** G. FARWELL *Traveller's Tracks* 21 In the extreme north-west corner, where the border fences of three states meet—the 'Corner Country' they call it.
Hence **Cornerman** *n.*, an inhabitant of the Corner.
1949 *Bulletin* (Sydney) 7 Dec. 13/4 As a 'cornerman'—I've spent quite a slice of my life in that conjunction of three States around Tibooburra and parts adjacent—a man is neither Cornstalk, Croweater nor Bananalander.

cornstalk. *Obs.* [Fig. use of *cornstalk*: see quots. 1827 (1) and 1853.]
1. A nickname for a non-Aboriginal native of Australia. Also **cornstalker.**
1827 P. CUNNINGHAM *Two Yrs. in N.S.W.* II. 116 We have .. English and Colonial born, the latter bearing also the name of *corn stalks* (Indian corn), from the way in which they shoot up. **1898** *Truth* (Sydney) 10 July 4/3 The 'cornstalker' from Australia and the smart and sturdy Canadian.

2. A nickname for a non-Aboriginal person, native to or resident in New South Wales. Also *attrib.*
1851 J. HENDERSON *Excursions & Adventures N.S.W.* II. 205 Next day, four young men, natives of the colony and excellent swimmers and divers, as all the *Cornstalks* are, went down to recover the bodies, if possible. **1903** *Bulletin* (Sydney) 16 July 17/2 The old Cornstalk town of Windsor is a weary, sleepy, drowsy place.

coroborey, var. CORROBOREE.

correa /'kɒriə/. Formerly also **corroea.** [The plant genus *Correa* was named by English botanical painter and engraver Henry Andrews (*Botanist's Repository* (1798) I. Pl. 18) after the Portuguese statesman and botanist José Francesco Correia da Serra (1750-1823): see quot. 1984.] Any shrub of the chiefly s.e. Austral. genus *Correa* (fam. Rutaceae), bearing decorative, often bell-shaped, flowers.
1833 H.W. PARKER *Rise, Progress, & Present State Van Dieman's Land* 142 The green corroea (corroea virens) is one of the most remarkable shrubs. **1984** *Canberra Chron.* 1 Feb. 16/1 Correa was named after Jose Francesco Correia de Serra (1750-1823), a Portuguese botanist who published several papers on the family rutaceae.

corroboree /kəˈrɒbəri/, *n.* Formerly with much variety, as **coroborey, corrobbaree, corrobboree, corrobara, corroberee, corrobori, corrobory,** etc. [a. Dharuk *garabari*.]
1. An Aboriginal dance ceremony, of which song and rhythmical musical accompaniment are an integral part, and which may be sacred and ritualized or secular, occasional, and informal. Hence loosely, in extended senses, esp. with reference to a meeting or assembly, or to festivity generally. Also *attrib.*
c **1790** W. DAWES Grammatical Forms Lang. N.S.W., *Car-rib-ber-re*, another mode of dancing. **1811** *Sydney Gaz.* 19 Jan., In the center [*sic*] of the ball-room were the Royal Initials in chrystal .. with a transparent painting .. being the representation of our Native Race .. a striking full-sized figure, drawn in one of the most animated attitudes of the *corrobori* pointed with his *waddy* at the Church of St. Philip. **1825** B. FIELD *Geogr. Mem. N.S.W.* 433 The *corrobory*, or night-dance, still obtains. This festivity is performed in very good time, and not unpleasing tune. The song is sung by a few males and females who take no part in the dance. One of the band beats time by knocking one stick against another. The music begins with a high note, and gradually sinks to the octave, whence it rises again immediately to the top. **1826** S. MACARTHUR ONSLOW *Some Early Rec. Macarthurs* (1914) 455 Let me give you some account of one of our native dances—a 'Corroboree' as they call it, when it is not unusual for two or three hundred to collect, to paint and deck themselves with green boughs, and in sets perform various grotesque figure dances, in most excellent time, which is given by others who sit apart and chant a sort of wild cadence. **1839** W.H. LEIGH *Reconnoitering Voyages* 141 One of the native *Corrobbarees*, or war songs and war dances, which are performed at the full of the moon. **1843** C. ROWCROFT *Tales of Colonies* III. 164 In the meantime a monosyllabic 'corrobara' had taken place between our guide and the chief of the sable community. **1857** J. ASKEW *Voyage Aust. & N.Z.* 83 Thirty or forty .. of both sexes, may be seen occasionally on the banks of the Torrens, near the gaol, throwing the spear, and dancing a coroborey. **1879** 'AUSTRALIAN' *Adventures Qld.* 38 He placed his pipe in his mouth, and threw himself on to his back, relapsing into a merry *corroboree*, into which he introduced some of the principle events of the day, with a considerable amount of self-laudation for his exploit in spearing his uncle... Bony having *corroboreed* himself into a first-rate humour again, sat up and had some more tea and damper, and mutton fat. **1889** J.H.L. ZILLMANN *Past & Present Austral. Life* 132 The story was a grand joke among the blacks for many a day. It became, no doubt, the theme for 'a corroberee'. **1963** R. STOW *Tourmaline* 171 People began to clap, in corroboree fashion, in time to the crash of the bell and the great shattering chords of the guitar.

2. *transf.*
1833 *Perth Gaz.* 24 Aug. 135 Several natives .. expressed some alarm when they perceived the preparations .. for the parade. They were given however to understand, that it was only a corrobora; it seemed to amuse them greatly to find that we had also our corroboras. **1971** *Bulletin* (Sydney) 13 Nov. 13/1 Of all the strange indigenous corroborees that take place in Melbourne, the Melbourne Cup is unquestionably the best.

3. Comb. **corroboree dance, ground, song, stick.**
1839 T.L. MITCHELL *Three Exped. Eastern Aust.* (rev. ed.) I. 114 They .. assumed the attitudes of the **corrobory dance**. **1898** D.W. CARNEGIE *Spinifex & Sand* 421 Near the spring in the scrub was a cleared **corroboree ground**, twenty feet by fifty yards, cleared of all stones and enclosed by a fallen brush-fence. **1845** L. LEICHHARDT *Jrnl. Overland Exped. Aust.* 1 May (1847) 237 Brown tunes up his **corroborri songs**, in which Charley, until their late quarrel, generally joined. **1878** R.B. SMYTH *Aborigines of Vic.* II. 294 The dancers .. commence by beating time simultaneously with their **corrobboree-sticks** (short pieces of green wood which give out a loud ringing sound when struck).

corroboree /kəˈrɒbəri/, v.
1. *intr.* To perform a corroboree.
1790 D. SOUTHWELL Corresp. & Papers, Că-rāb-bă-răi, to dance. **1976** C.D. MILLS *Hobble Chains & Greenhide* 25 A few of us had our 'toes in the ashes', and were smoking and yarning; the boys on watch were quietly corroboreeing to the bullocks who were well settled.
2. *transf.*
1844 *Sydney Morning Herald* 12 Dec. 4/4 The mosquitoes from the swamps corroboreed with unmitigated ardour. **1930** J.S. LITCHFIELD *Far-North Memories* 62 We told him that Dirty corroboreed in Latin hymn tunes.

Hence **corroboreeing** *vbl. n.*; also *transf.* and *attrib.*
1833 BACKHOUSE & TYLOR *Life & Labours G.W. Walker* 5 Dec. (1862) 171 The arrival of a fresh party of blacks has produced a good deal of excitement at Wybalenna, which shews itself in the constant corrobberrying that is kept up. **1860** G. BENNETT *Gatherings of Naturalist* 184 Each bird forms for itself three or four 'Corroboring places', as the sawyers call them.

corroboree frog. [See quot. 1953.] The small frog *Pseudophryne corroboree* of mountainous s.e. N.S.W.
[**1953** *Proc. Linnean Soc. N.S.W.* LXXVIII. 180 *Pseudophryne corroboree*. . . The specific name may be suggested by the resemblance of the dorsal pattern of *P. corroboree* to the body paintings used by some Australian aboriginal tribes in their corroborees.] **1968** V. SERVENTY *Southern Walkabout* 28 Here live the brilliant black and yellow corroboree frogs. **1986** *Sydney Morning Herald* 15 Jan. 13/3 The beautiful black-and-gold corroboree frog lives above the treeline in the Snowy Mountains and the ACT's Brindabella Range. Its breeding spots are snowdrifts in winter.

cossie /ˈkɒzi/. Also **cozzie**. [f. *(bathing) cos(tume* + -Y.] A swimming costume.
1926 'J. DOONE' *Timely Tips New Australs.*, Cossie, a sea-side term applied to a swimming costume. **1959** D. HEWETT *Bobbin Up* 34 A mob of kids, cozzies and towels tucked under their arms.

cotton. Used *attrib.* in Special Comb. **cotton bush**, any of several plants, usu. shrubs of the genus *Maireana* (fam. Chenopodiaceae), having a cotton-like appearance (see quot. 1981), esp. the spiny plant of mainland Aust. *M. aphylla*, often dominant in drier Austral. shrublands; any of several other plants having a similar resemblance to cotton; also *attrib.*; **tree, (a)** any of several plants, esp. the small tree with yellow flowers *Hibiscus tiliaceus* (fam. Malvaceae) of N.S.W., Qld., N.T., and s.e. Asia; **(b)** KAPOK TREE.

1861 *Burke & Wills Exploring Exped.* 6 Saltbush and **cottonbush** plentiful in the hollows. **1898** D.W. CARNEGIE *Spinifex & Sand* 425 It is a stony cotton-bush flat, and on it numerous white clay-holes of water. **1981** G.M. CUNNINGHAM et al. *Plants Western N.S.W.* 265 Cottonbush has become the dominant shrub in many communities it formerly shared with bladder saltbush. . . White cotton-like clusters .. are often seen on the branchlets; these growths (from which the common name of the plant was derived) are galls caused by small grubs. **1815** *Govt. & Gen. Orders* 9 Dec., That noxious Plant called the **Cotton Tree** (though not possessed of any of its valuable Qualities) is suffered to extend itself over large Portions of rich soil. **1845** L. LEICHHARDT *Jrnl. Overland Exped. Aust.* 5 June (1847) 282 We observed a cotton tree (Cochlospermum), covered with large yellow blossoms, though entirely leafless.

couba, var. COOBA.

coucal. Shortened form of *pheasant coucal* (see PHEASANT 2).
1822 J. LATHAM *Gen. Hist. Birds* III. 239 Giant Coucal .. Inhabits New-Holland. **1956** A.C.C. LOCK *Tropical Tapestry* 243 A coucal flew awkwardly and perched on a fence post, giving us a good look at its brown and black plumage.

count, *v.* [Spec. use of *count* to number.] *trans.* With **out**: to count (sheep or cattle as they leave a pen or paddock, esp. sheep after shearing). Freq. *absol.*
1874 *Australasian Sketcher* 31 Oct. 119/3 The fleece is taken off entire, and the shorn sheep is turned by the shearer into the 'count-out pen', whence the sheep are counted out by the overseer three times a day. **1883** *Illustr. Austral. News* (Melbourne) 28 Nov. 194/3 He asks us to see him 'count out', and consequently we return to the shearing floor, watching him from the windows as he lets the sheep out into the big receiving yard.

Hence **counting out** *vbl. n.* and *attrib.*, esp. as **counting-out pen**, a pen, usu. that into which sheep are placed after being shorn, the sheep being counted as they leave it.
[N.Z. **1874** J.A.H. CAIRD *Sheepfarming in N.Z.* 23 A small door for each shearer to put his shorn sheep out of the shed, and into the counting out pens.] *c* **1914** H.B. SMITH *Sheep & Wool Industry* 34 When the shearer has shorn the sheep, he lets it go into another pen, which is known as a counting-out pen, because it is in these pens that the overseer counts the number of sheep each shearer has shorn. **1975** B. FOLEY *Shearers' Poems* 2 The wool appeared much dimmer Than it had ten years before And 'counting out' was difficult With 'shornies' jaw to jaw.

count, *n.* [f. prec.]
1. The number of sheep shorn by a shearer and counted at the end of a day; the number of stock mustered and counted. Also with **out** and *fig.*
1895 J. KIRBY *Old Times in Bush* 147 The shearer did not care how much wool he left on the sheep, all his look out was, 'the count'. . . He would not scruple to leave half an inch long ridges of wool on the sheep, so long as he could get paid for the shearing. **1911** H.G. TURNER *First Decade Austral. Cwlth.* 127 In the Committee stage it was shelved by a 'count out' of the House. **1938** *Bulletin* (Sydney) 26 May 21/2 Biggest count-out I ever saw was 24,000, but over a friendly glass or two I've heard of counts of up to 50,000.

2. Special Comb. **count muster** (*fig.* in quot.), a count; **(out) pen**, *counting-out pen*, see COUNT *v.*
1891 'R. BOLDREWOOD' *Sydney-Side Saxon* (1925) 1 Well, the old man's having a regular **count-muster** of his sons and daughters, and their children and off-side relatives, that is by marriage. **1874 count-out pen** [see COUNT *v.*] **1894** *Western Champion* (Barcaldine) 16 Jan. 12/1 Mates don't like my name put down, And watch the blessed monkeys fill my count pen with a frown.

counter lunch.

1. a. A midday meal served in the bar of an hotel or public house; orig., to attract custom and so at no cost to patrons, now usu. cheap but substantial. Also *attrib.*

1880 *Bulletin* (Sydney) 14 Aug. 10 (Advt.), H. Donaldson's Mercantile Hotel and Luncheon Rooms... Free counter lunch. **1936** *Bulletin* (Sydney) 2 Sept. 21/4 Dad.. had lingered long at the counter lunch bar.

b. Similarly **counter tea**: see quot. 1972.

1971 D. WILLIAMSON *Removalists* (1972) 56 Er.. I.. er.. wasn't expecting you home, so I haven't cooked any tea. Why don't you go and have a counter tea with the boys? **1972** J. O'GRADY *It's your Shout, Mate!* 45, I also discovered evening meals served in bars, called, to my delight, 'counter tea'.

2. *fig.*

1908 *Bulletin* (Sydney) 23 Jan. 15/2 The black cockatoo knows exactly where to bite through the bark to find his breakfast, although there may be no evidence to the eye of man which might lead him to suspect the existence of so much as even a counter lunch.

country.

1. *Obs.* An Australian Colony; after Federation, (rarely) an Australian State.

1833 *Launceston Advertiser* 7 Mar. 2 The Colonists of one country [*sc.* N.S.W.] were trampled upon by a haughty ruler. **1911** *Bulletin* (Sydney) 26 Oct. 13/4 It is Westralia's rotten luck that it is.. one of the lightest stock-carrying countries on earth.

2. The traditional territory of an Aboriginal people; TOWRI. See also quot. 1962. Also *attrib.* as **countryman** (see quot. 1983).

1843 J.F. BENNETT *Hist. & Descr. Acct. S.A.* 59 They are divided into tribes, each tribe having its own district of country or hunting ground. **1962** D. LOCKWOOD *I, Aboriginal* 31 We all belong to the Alawa tribe and the Roper River district, but every man among us owns a particular plot of tribal ground which he calls 'My Country'. **1983** B. SHAW *Banggaiyerri* 235 *Countryman*, person(s) with whom one has an especially close and usually life-long association/camaraderie that is cemented continually through ritual, mutual visiting and responsibilities towards each other.

3. Orig. *S.A. Mining.* [Br. dial. (chiefly Cornish) *country* the rock in which a lode of ore occurs: see OED 11.] The material surrounding a lode of ore. Also **country rock.**

1848 *S. Austral. Register* (Adelaide) 26 Apr. 4/4 The country—that is the ground in which the ore lays. **1898** D.W. CARNEGIE *Spinifex & Sand* 127 The country rock lying immediately above the reef is the 'hanging wall', and that immediately below, the 'foot wall'.

4. A rural land-holding; land suitable for this purpose.

1855 N.L. KENTISH *Question of Questions!* 40 They might locate on any 'country' they chose to 'take up', *i.e.*, to select to any extent. **1923** J. ARMOUR *Spell of Inland* 25 The Wilsons.. are seventy miles away... That is why we have made such a friend of George. His country joins ours, so we see him occasionally.

county. [Transf. use of *county* a territorial division of Great Britain, serving as a divisional unit for administrative, judicial, and political purposes.]

1. One of a number of territorial divisions delineated in each Australian Colony but lacking the administrative functions of the British model. Also *attrib.*

1804 *Sydney Gaz.* 9 Sept., Charged with feloniously Stealing out of the dwelling house.. he was Committed to the County Gaol at Sydney. **1851** H.R. RUSSELL *Short Descr. Austral. Colonies* 3 The settled districts of New South Wales Proper are divided into 21 counties, but a great number of squatters have located themselves beyond these boundaries, occupying above one hundred millions of acres.

2. In local government: a territorial division delineated for a specific purpose; see esp. quots. 1919, 1955 and 1962. Freq. *attrib.*

1892 *NSWPD* 1st Ser. LXI. 2579/2, I should like to see a measure of local self-government brought down which would provide not only that there should be municipalities, shires, and boroughs in New South Wales, but that a large portion of the county of Cumberland, should be incorporated into a Sydney county council, or a county council, to which body should be given large powers of local self-government over the metropolitan area. **1919** *Act* (N.S.W.) no. 41 Sect. 561 (1), The Governor may, by proclamation, constitute as a county district for local government purposes any groups of wholes and parts of municipalities or shires, or of both municipalities and shires, and may, by proclamation, alter the boundaries of county districts. **1955** G.F. ANDERSON *Fifty Yrs. Electricity Supply* 145 The Gas and Electricity Act constituted a county district under the name of 'The Sydney County District'. The Sydney County District consisted of the areas in which the Undertaking supplied electricity direct to customers. **1962** A. & R. BLUETT *Local Govt. Handbk.* 184 One of the many purposes the creation of county councils serve is the destruction of aquatic pests, mainly water hyacinth.

Cousin Jack, *n.* and *attrib.* Orig. *S.A.* [f. the Br. dial. use of *cousin* as a familiar term of address or designation, esp. in Cornwall, hence *Cousin Jan, Jacky* a nickname for a Cornishman.]

A. *n.* A man, usu. a miner, of Cornish descent.

1863 J.B. AUSTIN *Mines S.A.* 103 Things are managed better in Cornwall, and though we are apt sometimes to laugh at 'Cousin Jack' we might occasionally gain some useful lessons from him. **1980** M. MCADOO *If only I'd Listened* ('Michael Llewelyn'), The Cousin Jacks used to wear those stiff-fronted shirts, and down 'ere on the front of them there was a little tab they buttoned to the fly of the pants.

B. *attrib.* passing into *adj.* Cornish.

1896 E. DYSON *Rhymes from Mines* 178 She was killed with a slab from a Cousin Jack cake. **1973** A. BURNETT *Wilful Murder in Outback* 47 He was a fund of Cousin Jack humour.

Hence **Cousin Jinny** (or **Jenny**), the wife of a miner.

1909 W.G. SPENCE *Aust.'s Awakening* 49 Come on, you Cousin Jinnies; bring me the stones and I will fire them. **1962** O. PRYOR *Aust.'s Little Cornwall* 39 We can be damned thankful that women don't usually unite for a common purpose. Those Cousin Jennies up at Moonta showed us what can happen if they do.

couta, var. COOTA.

cove. [Survival of Br. criminal cant *cove* fellow, 'chap': see OED(S *sb.*[2] Used elsewhere but apparently most freq. in Aust.]

1. A man, a 'bloke' or 'chap'.

1828 *Tasmanian* (Hobart) 15 Aug. 41 My friend's eldest son.. replied, 'I have dropped my *thimble.*' His father chid him roundly calling him 'a careless *cove*'. **1978** D. STUART *Wedgetail View* 30 He was a good sort of a cove; quiet.

2. *Obs.* The owner or manager of an establishment, esp. of a sheep station.

1837 *Rep. Select Committee Transportation* 21 Apr. (1838) 32 You must not go on as you have done with the cove; that is the master, the masters are called coves by the convicts. **1916** J. FURPHY *Poems* 42 'Are you the Cove?' He spoke the words As Freeman only can. The squatter freezingly inquir'd, 'What do you mean, my man?'

3. *transf.*

1903 *Bulletin* (Sydney) 11 Apr. 16/4 Dad isn't going to kill that pig he spoke about now. It's gettin' better, an' Mr Mooney, th' hoss doctor, says it didn't have cancer at all. But there's another cove lookin' a bit multy, so I s'pose he'll kill it. **1920** *Ibid.* 24 June 20/2 A brumby (no unbranded cove under seven years old merits the term) is a grown horse and hits the ground much harder than a 'green' thing.

covie. Also **covey.** [Br. slang *covey* (dimin. of COVE): see OED *sb.*[3]] COVE 1; also used as an affectionate mode of address.

1835 *True Colonist* (Hobart) 21 Jan. 2/4 These 'Covies' were very 'jolly', and endeavoured to 'bounce out of it', but it was 'no go'. **1846** L.W. MILLER *Notes of Exile Van Dieman's Land* 265 Tell you what, my covey, if you want these ere .. take 'em. **1914** *Truth* (Sydney) 30 Aug. 5/5 Robert Shannon, a mild-mannered young covie .. looked as if he wouldn't injure the proverbial flea.

cow.

1. Used *attrib.* in Special Comb. with reference to dairy-farming: **cow bail,** BAIL *n.*; **cocky,** a dairy farmer; see also COCKY *n.*[2]; so **cockydom, cockying** *vbl. n.*; **cockyism; farm,** a dairy farm; so **farmer; juice,** milk; **kick,** a violent sideways kick; also as *v. trans.* and *intr.*; so **kicker; paddock,** a paddock in which cows are confined; **spanker,** a dairy farmer; one who works on a dairy farm; so **spanking** *vbl. n.*; **time,** milking time.

[N.Z. **1851** E. WARD *Jrnl.* 12 May (1951) 180 The **cow bails** in the stockyard are fastened up.] **1936** M. FRANKLIN *All that Swagger* 370 He whitewashed the dairy and cowbails. **1902** *Bulletin* (Sydney) 12 July 16/2 The **cowcocky** is the most awful and wonderful of the genus—especially the young rooster. **1911** *Bulletin* (Sydney) 16 Mar. 14/4 When the Big Scrub began to take to dairying he .. took up land, and descended into **cow-cockeydom.** **1936** *Ibid.* 16 Dec. 20/1 The stockman who rides without leggings is usually found in **cow-cockying** country. **1916** *Bulletin* (Sydney) 2 Mar. 48/1 Some time back I wrote that **Cow-Cockyism** and Cow are near the end of Log Paddock. **1910** *Ibid.* 20 Jan. 15/1 She didn't waste time talking to blokes or coves, and any that came to the **cow-farm** were warned off. **1913** *Ibid.* 3 Apr. 15/1 It isn't always the **cow farmer.** Sometimes it is the agriculturist devoted to onions, and on occasion it is the squatter whose speciality is poultry. **1903** *Truth* (Sydney) 25 Jan. 1/5 'Killed by a **cow juice** cart', is the heading used by a country paper, to chronicle the death of a little girl recently killed by a milk cart. **1936** J.C. DOWNIE *Galloping Hoofs* 100 After a few '**cowkicks**' and rearing once or twice, he began trotting round the yard. **1911** 'S. RUDD' *Bk. of Dan* 30 Dan just **cow-kicked** Snowy in the empty stomach and temporarily disabled him. **1927** —— *Romance of Runnibede* 39 The nuggetty grey shook his head violently and cow-kicked under the shaft at his tormentor. **1964** B. WANNAN *Fair Go, Spinner* 138 The boss of the mustering camp scratched his head when it came to finding suitable mounts for Pat and finally decided to try him out on Lasher, whose name was bestowed because of his prowess as a '**cow-kicker**'. **1908** *Bulletin* (Sydney) 24 Dec. 14/3 He had a fairly-large dam in the **cow paddock** .. and on it he ran a cranky boat. [N.Z. **1906** *N.Z. Truth* (Wellington) 11 Aug. 3 The king of Okoia **cow-spankers.**] **1919** *Smith's Weekly* (Sydney) 5 Apr. 9/6 The young cow-spankers of Albion park can now devote all Sunday spare time to the Australian national sport of two-up. **1896** *Bulletin* (Sydney) 14 Nov. 27/3 There is nothing in **cow-spanking** .. My first job was at a place where they milked 120 cows. Talk about slavery! **1906** *Ibid.* 18 Oct. 44/2 Five o'clock! Nearly **cow-time** again.

2. [Cf. Br. slang *cow*, used derogatorily of a woman: see OED(S *sb.*[1] 4.] A term of abuse applied to any person, situation, or thing to which the speaker takes, or pretends to take, exception; often used good-humouredly. Cf. BASTARD *n.*

1864 C.R. THATCHER *Colonial Minstrel* 14 Called each one of them [*sc.* bullocks] an old cow, Whilst blows thick and fast he kept dealing.. **1978** H.C. BAKER *I was Listening* 128 It's a cow not to be able to read.

cowal /'kaʊəl/. [a. Kamilaroi prob. *guwal.*] See quot. 1910.

1882 C. LYNE *Industries of N.S.W.* 213 The homestead .. is situated .. not far from .. the shores of a lake which in this part of the Colony is called, in the language of the aborigines, a 'cowall', or 'cowell'. **1910** C.E.W. BEAN *On Wool Track* 251 If one gets bogged in a creek or a cowal (which is a small tree-grown, swampy depression often met with in the red country), the other will never leave him there.

cowanyoung /'kaʊənjʌŋ/. *N.S.W.* [Prob. f. a N.S.W. Aboriginal language.] The marine fish *Trachurus declivis* of s. Aust. See also JACK MACKEREL.

1897 *Proc. Linnean Soc. N.S.W.* XXII. 761 The true 'Cowanyung' being .. the adult Yellowtail (*Trachurus declivis*) or some closely allied species. **1965** *Austral. Encycl.* IV. 84 Jack mackerel (*Trachurus novaezelandiae*), the cowanyoung of New South Wales and the horse mackerel of South Australia and Tasmania.

cowry pine, var. KAURI PINE.

cowslip orchid. The terrestrial orchid of s.w. W.A. *Caladenia flava* (fam. Orchidaceae), bearing bright yellow flowers.

1926 J. POLLARD *Bushland Man* 207 They plucked .. cowslip orchids. **1967** B.Y. MAIN *Between Wodjil & Tor* 97 Clumps of spider orchids, cowslip orchids and the solitary, yellowish-green Jack-in-the-boxes .. were now in flower.

cozzie, var. COSSIE.

crab. [Shortened form of *crab-shell*: in sense 1 in punning allusion to an artillery shell, in sense 2 a boot.]

1. In the phr. **to draw the crabs.**

a. To attract enemy fire.

1918 *Ca ne fait Rien: 6th Battalion A.I.F.* 8 Mar., J.D. Johnston .. being in command of those horrible people who draw the crabs, the T.M.B. **1978** H.C. BAKER *I was Listening* 169 What were you trying to do—draw the crabs on the camp?

b. *transf.* To attract unwanted attention, esp. from the police.

1959 *Bulletin* (Sydney) 23 Dec. 16/1 Most shearers are .. down on men who 'draw the crabs' through bringing excessive grog to the huts. **1978** D. STUART *Wedgetail View* 90 Just let any bastard talk about underground accidents in a humorous sort of a fashion, an' he's likely to get put back in his place double quick. It's always on, underground, an' I s'pose no one wants to draw the crabs by talking light an' funny about it.

2. In *pl.* A pair of boots.

1896 *Bulletin* (Sydney) 21 Mar. 27/1 If you wear new crabs—I mean boots—out of the shop, instead of having 'em wrapped up, there's several points gained. **1919** V. MARSHALL *World of Living Dead* 85 I'll, moochin' round about it, wear the crabs from off me feet.

crabhole. [Fig. use of *crab-hole* a hole made or inhabited by a crab.] **a.** A hole in the ground of small diameter, made by a terrestrial crustacean (see LAND CRAB); a collapsed hole caused by the burrowing of the animal; any hole resembling this. **b.** Chiefly *s. Aust.* A depression in heavy clay soils, a form of GILGAI. Also *attrib.*

1847 *Maitland Mercury* 28 Aug. 4/4 The Wimera [*sic*] country, especially the low part of it, is at present an immense lake. A great part of it is 'crab-hole' country, or 'dead men's graves', which at present look like so many islands. **1944** C. Fenner *Mostly Austral.* 102 The depressions are mis-called 'crab-holes'... Apparently the aborigines recognised them, for the name 'gilgais' has long been applied thereto... In New South Wales and Queensland such depressions are called 'melon-holes'. **1977** D. Stuart *Drought Foal* 165 The road .. goes across a stretch of crab-hole country .. dark soil littered with shapeless lumps of black rock.

Hence **crab-holed, crab-holey** *adjs.*

1874 'Rev. F.T.P.' *Thirty-Shilling Horse* 36, I had never seen **crab-holed** land before; but now I saw it, and with much fear and trembling passed through it. **1872** 'Resident' *Glimpses Life Vic.* 305 There rises before my mind some waste of dreary plains, **crab-holey** and treeless, on which stands a handsome house.

crack, *v.*[1] [Prob. spec. use of Br. dial. *crack* to boast, brag: see OED *v.* 6 and EDD *sb.*[1] and *v.* 18.]

1. *intr. Obs.* To feign, pretend. Also *trans.*

1900 *Western Champion* (Barcaldine) 10 Apr. 9/2 'He skied his rockets and cracked a deafun. I guyed a whack. Pads it back here.'.. Now, here is the above translated... 'He put his hands in his pocket and would not listen to me. I turned away, walked back.' **1904** L.M.P. Archer *Bush Honeymoon* 45, I cracked it was a mate had tied me up for a lark.

2. In the phr. **to crack hardy,** (in times of difficulty or misfortune) to feign equanimity, to put on a brave front, to 'grin and bear it'.

1904 *Emu* IV. 45 A fair number .. were 'cracking hardy'. **1979** B. Humphries *Bazza comes into his Own,* You don't have to act brave or crack hardy with old Bazza McKenzie. I'll ring youse a doctor or something.

crack, *v.*[2] [Spec. use of *crack* to puzzle out, solve: see OED(S *v.* 9 b.]

1. In the phr. **to crack it,** to succeed (in an enterprise, etc.).

1936 W. Hatfield *Aust. through Windscreen* 199 They had worked alongside men who had 'cracked it' on this field in the early days and kept finds to themselves. **1981** A. Wilkinson *Up Country* 105 Everyone agrees it is splendid to see the 'cocky' (farmer) crack it for a quid for once.

2. *trans. Surfing.* To catch and ride (a wave).

1940 P. Kerry *Cobbers A.I.F.* 10 An' the surf wus runnin' 'owlers—an' the shoots were good 'uns, too When yeh cracked one on the front line, yeh could see right ter the zoo. **1986** *Bulletin* (Sydney) 14 Jan. 30/3 If there were 48 hours in the day I'd be down there cracking a few waves with them.

3. In the phr. **to crack a lay,** (in negative constructions) to 'spill the beans', to 'let on'.

1941 *Air Force News* (Melbourne) 7 June 7 The boys didn't crack a lay—just treated him casual like. **1975** G.A.W. Smith *Once Green Jackeroo* 63 All the time telling me that if I so much as cracked a lay he was gone a bloody million. I never did 'crack a lay', and earned his undying gratitude.

4. In the phr. **to crack on to** (a person), to find (someone) sexually attractive, to pursue with amorous intent.

1955 R. Lawler *Summer of Seventeenth Doll* (1965) 85 'Just cracked on to the very thing. Piece about eighteen. That young enough for yer?' 'What's she like?' 'Only seen her photo, but she looks terrific.' **1979** Carey & Lette *Puberty Blues* 5 'Smile!' 'No. He'll think I'm trying to crack onoo him.'

5. In the phr. **to crack a fat:** see Fat *n.*[3]

crack-a-back, *v. Austral. pidgin. S.A. Obs.* [Poss. a. Jangkudjera dial. of Western Desert *kakapaka.*] *intr.* To die.

1867 'S. McTavish' *Chowla* 53 Caracalinga, one of the native chiefs, came to the door of the saloon, and .. spoke as follows:- 'That Plower, he bery bad man; he want um take um ship, make um plenty people cracabac.' **1893** S. Newland *Paving Way* 68 After getting the fish, he told me the old man had 'crack-a-backed' a little before daylight; and as he was a big man in the tribe, he would be paid all the funeral honours befitting his station.

cracker, *n.*[1] [Br. dial. and U.S. *cracker* small cord at the end of a whip which makes it crack.] A strip of silk, horsehair, etc., attached to the tip of a stockwhip to make a cracking sound.

1852 *Four Colonies Aust.* 52 The stockman .. wears a jacket of colonial tweed... His whip—the handle about a foot and a half long, and the thong 12 or 14 feet, with a 'cracker' at the end generally made of a piece of silk handkerchief twisted, or better still, of a shred of an old infantry sash—is a terrific weapon. **1913** G. Hervey *Australs. Yet* 233 Silk Cracker Days!!—the roaring whips are silent now, and dumb The scarlet, stinging, goading strips.

cracker, *n.*[2] [Fig. use of *cracker* thin hard biscuit.]

1. **a.** A term for the smallest imaginable amount of money; cf. a 'bean', Razoo. Chiefly in negative contexts.

1934 W.S. Howard *You're telling Me!* 300 What about money?... We haven't got a cracker. **1980** *Daily News* (Perth) 22 Dec. 40/1 The pub safe had been knocked off the night before. That left us stranded in Wiluna without a cracker.

b. In the phr. **not worth a cracker,** of no value whatsoever.

1953 T.A.G. Hungerford *Riverslake* 221 Any man without some sort of loyalty to whoever pays his wages isn't worth a cracker. **1978** N. Hasluck *Hat on Letter O* 17 'Tony isn't worth a cracker.' 'He was in the old days. He was pretty tough.'

2. *transf.* A worthless animal.

1946 *Bulletin* (Sydney) 17 July 28/1 Gettin' late in the season for y' t' get sheep now... I got three hundred crackers in me river paddock... Y' c'n have 'em for nothin'. **1982** N. Keesing *Lily on Dustbin* 168 Old cows pretty much beyond their usefulness .. are called 'crackers'.

3. A prostitute; a brothel.

1963 J. Naish *That Men should Fear* 143 My Aunt Helen worked in a cracker in Munro Street. Worked as a madame or a moll. **1967** *Kings Cross Whisper* (Sydney) xxxiii. 4/4 *Cracker,* a prostitute.

cracker night. [Spec. use of *cracker* firework.] An occasion of (public) festivity celebrated by a display of fireworks, orig. a celebration of Empire Day, later of Commonwealth Day, and now of the Queen's official birthday.

1951 *Bulletin* (Sydney) 2 May 14/3 They .. bought bungers out of their shearing cheques .. and 17 of the boys declared to [*sic*] be 'the crackerest cracker night we ever seen!' **1981** Q. Wild *Honey Wind* 95 One cracker night Thommo and his uncle let off a few plugs of dynamite.

crack of the whip: see Fair *a.*[1] 3.

cradle, *n.* Gold-mining. [U.S. *cradle* gold-mining apparatus: see Mathews.]

1. A box-like apparatus, mounted on rockers and agitated by hand, in which gold is separated from its surrounding sand, gravel, etc., and retained: see esp. quot. 1852.

1851 *Empire* (Sydney) 20 May 2/2 Now and then a respectable tradesman who had just left his bench or counter, would heave into sight with a huge something in front of his horse which he called a cradle, 2nd with which he was about to rock himself into fortune. **c 1852** A. Mann *Goldfields Aust.* 33 A cradle .. is six or eight feet long, open at the foot, and its head has a coarse grate .. fixed upon it. The cradle is placed on rockers... The sieve at the head keeps the worse stones from entering the cradle; the current of water .. softens and washes off the earthy matter, which is carried away by the foot of the machine, leaving the gold mixed with sand.

2. Comb. **cradle-man, -rocker.**

1851 *Empire* (Sydney) 13 Sept. 151/7 The tents are struck—the tribes of **cradlemen** .. have dispersed. 1851 *Guardian* (Hobart) 2 July 4/2 The motley group of diggers and **cradle-rockers** in the creek.

cradle, v. [f. prec.] *trans.* To wash (gold-bearing sand, gravel, etc.) in a miner's cradle. Also *absol.*

1851 *Empire* (Sydney) 6 Aug. 19/2 Eaton is to commence cradling on Monday. 1852 J. Shaw *Tramp to Diggings* 254 When gold is mixed with any other rock it is frequently disseminated in such masses as to be recognised at once; but, when mixed with earth, its particles are so small as not to be recognized at all by the naked eye; and, to obtain it, it is necessary to be cradled. 1853 J. Sherer *Gold Finder Aust.* 284 It is good washing dirt, it pays to cradle.

Hence **cradling** *vbl. n.*

1852 G.B. Earp *Gold Colonies Aust.* 167 Much gold is now lost in Australia by the cradling method.

crammer /ˈkræmə/. *Austral. pidgin.* Also **cramma.** [a. Dharuk *garrama.*] *trans.* To steal (something). Also *absol.*

1798 D. Collins *Account Eng. Colony N.S.W.* I. 614 *Carrah-mā,* stealing. 1830 R. Dawson *Present State Aust.* 75 Black pellow crammer (steal). 1912 J. Bradshaw *Highway Robbery under Arms* (ed. 3) 21 Do you want to cramma young gin. Suppose you like it, she very good look out yarra-man.

cranberry: see *native cranberry* Native *a.* 6 a.

cranky fan. [f. *cranky* erratic + *fan(tail* alluding to the bird's rapid changes of direction as it flies after insects.] The predom. grey, fan-tailed, fly-catching bird *Rhipidura fuliginosa,* occurring widely in Aust., and also in N.Z. and some s. Pacific islands; *white-shafted fantail,* see White *a.*² 1 b.

1903 *Emu* III. 27 Dusky Fantail... When flitting from bough to bough it has a rather head-over heels kind of flight; it is from this curious habit it gains the name of 'Cranky Fan'. 1981 M. Sharland *Tracks of Morning* 80 For producing the prettiest nest of any bird, I give full honours to the white-shafted fantail—the 'cranky fan', as it's commonly known.

crash, v. [Abbrev. of Br. naval slang *crash the swede* to get one's head down on the pillow: see Partridge. Used elsewhere but recorded earliest in Aust.] *intr.* To collapse into sleep, esp. following a period of prolonged exertion or alcoholic indulgence.

1943 J.F. Moyes *Scrap-Iron Flotilla* 161 'We crawled into our 'flea bags' and 'crashed'—our first sleep after being on deck continuously for more than thirty-six hours,' a seaman wrote home. 1977 H. Garner *Monkey Grip* 80, I think I'll just go home and crash.

crawfish, var. Crayfish *n.* and *v.*

crawl, *n.* [In joc. allusion to the arm movements of a person swimming the stroke. Used elsewhere but recorded earliest in Aust.] A fast swimming stroke in which the body is prone, the arms reach forward alternately in an overarm action and pull back through the water, and the legs maintain a flutter kick; *Australian crawl,* see Australian *a.* 4. Also *attrib.*

1901 *Arrow* (Sydney) 2 Mar. 4/4 Dick .. will set Hogan and Co. a lively go—especially when he gets fairly moving with that great 'crawl' kick of his. 1972 *Swimmer's Handbk.* (S. Austral. Amateur Swimming Assoc.) (rev. ed.) 25 The stroke outlined here is the 'six beat' crawl, used by almost every world champion.

crawl, v. [Spec. use of *crawl* to move with a slow or dragging motion: see OED v.¹ 2.]

1. *intr.* To move at the pace of grazing sheep: cf. Crawler 1 b.

1846 C.P. Hodgson *Reminisc. Aust.* 34 Sheep, under the charge of no piping shepherd, but a rough bearded and rougher clad 'old hand', crawl down the plain. 1961 M. Kiddle *Men of Yesterday* 60 'Crawling' behind sheep was a job which few except old lags, broken in spirit and diseased in body, accepted kindly.

2. [Used elsewhere but recorded earliest in Aust.] *intr.* To behave (towards someone) in an obsequious manner, to seek to ingratiate oneself.

1880 *Argus* (Melbourne) 9 Feb. 4/6 The Ministers to whom it crawled and truckled have pronounced its condemnation. 1965 *Kings Cross Whisper* (Sydney) Feb. 11/1 Crawl to the boss, dob in your best mate, knock off his wife.

Hence **crawlsomeness** *n.*

1900 H. Lawson *Over Sliprails* 73 If he grafted harder than we did, we'd be sure to feel indignant about that too, and reckon that it was done out of nastiness or crawlsomeness.

crawler. [Fig. use of *crawler,* prob. orig. a term used by convicts: see quots. 1836 and 1838.]

1. **a.** *Obs.* An idle or incompetent person; one who avoids work, a loafer or shirker.

1827 *Monitor* (Sydney) 5 July 496/1 Another 'hated a *crawler* from his heart', and would 'work by himself and get half his time to the good'. 1836 C. Darwin *Jrnl. Researches Geol. & Nat. Hist.* 20 Jan. (1839) III. 527 A 'crawler' is an assigned convict, who runs away, and lives how he can, by labour and petty theft. 1838 *Rep. Select Committee Transportation* 75 The cant name for these among the prisoners themselves was 'the crawlers'. They were scarcely able to work, people whom no settlers wished to employ. 1947 W. Lawson *Paddle-Wheels Away* 102 A dozen river-men, swearing and shouting, erupted into the bar. 'Where are the 'top-end' crawlers? Come and fight, you dingoes.'

b. *Obs.* A shepherd.

1852 S. Mossman *Voice from Aust.* 13 When .. one of your romantic immigrants .. meets one of our Australian shepherds .. he is rather startled... He encounters a bronze-featured, long-bearded 'crawler', as he is termed. 1878 'R. Boldrewood' *Ups & Downs* 67 Do I look like a slouchin', 'possum-eating, billy-carrying crawler of a shepherd?

2. *Obs.* A slow-moving animal, usu. one enfeebled by age or disease.

1838 *Colonist* (Sydney) 22 Aug. 2/5 Fat cattle are now not to be seen anywhere—a few 'crawlers' may now and then be observed nipping the leaves of the stunted bush. 1943 *Austral. New Writing* 43 Taking it like a lamb, a crawler!

3. [Used elsewhere but recorded earliest in Aust.] A sycophant.

1888 R. Thomson *Austral. Nationalism* 122 The cause of these city frauds .. is that you put snobs, title-hunters, society crawlers, and lovers of Tite Barnacles, and of Tite Barnacleism into power. 1973 R. Blair *President Wilson* (1974) 50 *House:* But you like Colonel House. *Edith:* Not necessarily. He's a crawler, or I imagine he is.

4. *Obs.* A snake.

1918 *Bulletin* (Sydney) 12 Dec. 24/2 Dunno if 'H.V.E.' has been sufficiently observant when out snaking. He .. expresses a doubt that the bunda-bunda is a Monaro (N.S.W.) crawler. 1929 P.R. Stephensen *Bushwhackers* 23 Sobbing with a hatred of crawlers; sobbing with the deathlust, they exulted together, thumping the earth-thing.

crawling, *ppl. a.* and *vbl. n.* [f. CRAWL *v.*]

A. *ppl. a.* Slow-moving; indolent.
1852 S. SIDNEY *Three Colonies* 309 Above all, he scorns a 'crawling shepherd'. **1899** *Worker* (Sydney) 21 Jan. 8/1 You hear times out of number about the mean, crawling cockie.

B. *vbl. n.* Obsequiousness.
1891 D. FERGUSON *Vicissitudes Bush Life* 152 He regarded it as a sign of toadyism or 'crawling'. **1965** *Kings Cross Whisper* (Sydney) Dec. 7/2 Some people might think it's crawling to give a present to the turn and toss, but depends on the present.

cray. Abbrev. of CRAYFISH *n.*
1909 *Bulletin* (Sydney) 1 Apr. 43/1 The crays when they're past prayin' fer, takes care to let y' know they're due fer burial. Oysters is different. **1971** D. WILLIAMSON *Removalists* (1972) 27, I can.. grab m'self a cray and half a dozen tubes, .. sit m'self down in front of the box and watch the wrestling.

crayfish, *n.* Formerly also **crawfish.** [Transf. use of *crayfish* any of several fresh-water and marine crustaceans.] Any of several elongated decapod crustaceans, marine or fresh-water, esteemed as food. See also LOBSTER, *painted crayfish* PAINTED.
1770 J. COOK *Jrnls.* 23 Aug. (1955) I. 394 Cockles and Clams of Several sorts, many of these that are found upon the Reefs are of a Prodigious size; Craw-fish, Crabs, Musles [*sic*], and a variety of other sorts. **1784** G.W. ANDERSON *New Collection Voyages* 70 Variety of fish is supplied by the seas in these parts, among which are mullets, cray-fish and crabs.

crayfish, *v.* Also **crawfish.** [f. prec.] *intr.* To move in the manner of a crayfish; to retract or 'back down', to act in a cowardly fashion.
1894 H. LAWSON *Short Stories* 89 All the other chaps crawfished up and flung themselves round the corner and sidled into the bar after Dave. **1936** W. HATFIELD *Big Timber* 242 Dale was his weight, only every ounce of him was bone and sinew... He might have 'crayfished' but for the crowd.

Hence **crayfishing** *vbl. n.*
1931 V. PALMER *Separate Lives* 194 The truth, the whole truth, and no cray-fishing, so help me God.

creamy. [f. *cream(-coloured* + -Y.]
1. A cream-coloured horse; *spec.* a palomino.
1887 *Tibbs' Pop. Song Bk.* 28 He likes all lively hacks, He's very partial to the creamies. **1981** G. MITCHELL *Bush Horseman* 21 Palominos and buckskins were called 'creamies'.

2. A person of part-Aboriginal and part-white descent; freq. *spec.* (see quot. 1941). Also as adj.
1912 *Bulletin* (Sydney) 11 Apr. 14/4 Fully 50 per cent. of the children are half-castes—'creamies', as the blacks call them. **1941** *Argus Weekend Mag.* (Melbourne) 15 Nov. 1/3 Slang applied to the aborigines occurs, of course, only in the Far North, where the natives are commonly seen. They are referred to invariably as 'Boongs'. Half-castes are 'halfies', and quarter-castes 'creamies'. **1960** J. WALKER *No Sunlight Singing* 31 Some o' these creamy bitches.. put on airs as if they was white.

creek. Also (rarely) **crick.** [Br. *creek* a narrow inlet in the coastline, an estuary, but also an inlet or short arm of a river, applied in U.S. and other former British colonies to a tributary river or stream: see OED(S *sb.*[1] 2 b. The earliest Austral. uses retain the Br. meaning (see quot. 1793).]
1. A watercourse, esp. a stream or tributary of a river; in Australian use often varying widely in application: see esp. quots. 1805, 1833, 1848, 1849, 1903, and 1955.

[**1793** J. HUNTER *Hist. Jrnl. Trans. Port Jackson* 489 It will also be necessary.. to make a dam across the creek, in order to prevent the tides making the water brackish at the lower part of it.] **1795** D. COLLINS *Acct. Eng. Colony N.S.W.* (1798) I. 422 The husband.. sold a very good farm.. on a creek of the river. **1804** *HRA* (1921) 3rd Ser. I. 584 There is a small Creek.. that discharges the Water of a beautiful Fall at its head into the main River. **1805** *Ibid.* (1915) 1st Ser. V. 586 A Creek—It's locally applied to all brooks and small Rills that are deeply seated in the Ground and the Sides or Banks very Steep. **1833** W.H. BRETON *Excursions* 98 A creek is commonly the bed of a stream, which being partially exhausted during the dry weather, forms only an occasional pond or water-hole. **1848** H.W. HAYGARTH *Recoll. Bush Life* 127 A creek, which in most other parts of the world signifies a small inlet or arm of the sea, is very differently understood in Australia, where it generally means a valley, or any open space in the forest, with or without water. The use of the word in the colony is in fact very vague, and might well mislead a stranger. 'Which is the way?'—'*Down* the creek.' 'Is Mr so and so at home?'—'No; he's just gone *up* the creek.' 'How shall I find the station?'—'Oh, you can't miss it, it's *in* the creek.' **1849** C. STURT *Narr. Exped. Central Aust.* I. 7 It may be necessary to warn my readers that a creek in the Australian colonies, is not always an arm of the sea. The same term is used to designate a watercourse, whether large or small, in which the winter torrents may or may not have left a chain of ponds. Such a watercourse could hardly be called a river, since it only flows during heavy rains, after which it entirely depends on the character of the soil, through which it runs, whether any water remains in it or not. **1903** *Bulletin* (Sydney) 7 Mar. 16/3 Once watched a creek (a bend of the Lachlan) 'come down', as the bush saying is. It had been dry for months. **1936** F. CLUNE *Roaming round Darling* 54 An old nincompoop, rotting on a horse, called out for our information: 'You're in the crick.' **1955** D. CLARK *Boomer* 38 The mother kangaroo drank at a billabong—a long, clear creek fringed by reeds.

2. Comb. **creek bank, bed, crossing, flat.**
1849 A. HARRIS *Emigrant Family* (1967) 76 The slight sweep of a deep and precipitous **creek-bank.** **1847** A. HARRIS *Settlers & Convicts* (1953) 134 He was down in a deep **creek-bed** in the mountain. **1853** W. WESTGARTH *Vic.* 143 Many.. vexatious gullies, **creek-crossings,** and patches of swamp, might.. have been greatly improved. **1897** J.J. MURIF *From Ocean to Ocean* 96 A wide, fertile and picturesque **creek-flat,** studded with gums.

3. Special Comb. **creek claim,** a mining claim which includes, or is confined to, the bed of a creek; **gum,** any of several trees of the genus *Eucalyptus* (fam. Myrtaceae), esp. *E. camaldulensis* (see RED GUM 1); **oak,** *river oak,* see RIVER 2.
1869 R.B. SMYTH *Gold Fields & Mineral Districts* 608 **Creek claim,** a claim which includes the bed of a creek. **1891** *Proc. Linnean Soc. N.S.W.* VI. 403 *E. rostrata,* var. 'Creek Gum', Tarella, Wilcannia. **1872** C.H. EDEN *My Wife & I in Qld.* 190 The time being chiefly occupied.. in making yokes which are formed from the **creek oaks** (*Casuarina quadrivalvis*).

crescent nail-tailed wallaby: see NAIL-TAILED WALLABY.

crested, *ppl. a.* In special collocations: **crested bellbird,** the bird *Oreoica gutturalis* of arid and semi-arid Aust., the mature male having a black crest; BELLBIRD 2; **bronze-wing,** *crested pigeon* (a); **hawk,** the bird of prey *Aviceda subcristata* of n. and e. Aust.; **pigeon,** a pigeon with a crest, esp. (a) the widespread, predom. grey *Geophaps lophotes;* (b) FLOCK PIGEON b.
1896 B. SPENCER *Rep. Horn Sci. Exped. Central Aust.* II. 74 *Oreoica cristata,* **Crested Bell-bird..** is one of our most widely dispersed birds. [**1854 crested bronze-wing:** J. CAPP *Stanford's Emigrant's Guides* 40 There are about thirty varieties of the pigeon, among which is the crested bronze-

winged.] **1844** J. GOULD *Birds of Aust.* (1848) I. Pl. 25, *Lepidogenys subcristatus* . . **Crested Hawk**. **1823** J. LATHAM *Gen. Hist. Birds* VIII. 106 **Crested Pigeon** . . at the nape of several elongated, narrow, black feathers, some three inches or more in length, giving the appearance of the crest of the Coly. . . Inhabits New-Holland. **1973** V. SERVENTY *Desert Walkabout* 36 Ken had to make do with . . two crested pigeons and damper.

crib. [Br. dial. *crib* food, something to eat between meals: see OED(S 6 b.]

1. A light meal or refreshment, packed to be eaten during a break from work; the break itself. Also *attrib*.

1890 A.S. DAY *Democrat* 17 What say about crib time? Ye're right, Bob. The billy and chuck's on that 'ere log. Crib, ho! below! **1978** M. PAICE *Shadow of Wings* 115 Although I was near enough to go home for lunch I was carrying my crib in a paper bag.

2. Comb. **crib bag, box, can, house, hut, room, time, tin.**

1898 E. DYSON *Below & on Top* 56 He crowded his usual two-pound 'plaster' of cold fried bacon and bread into his **crib-bag**. **1947** *Bulletin* (Sydney) 16 July 29/1 His **crib-box** was perched high in a gum-tree. **1957** *Westerly* i. 33 Miners drinking **Crib cans** clinking. **1948** G. FARWELL *Down Argent Street* 67 The **cribhouse** is habitually a place for relaxation. . . It provides a cleaner lunch-place than the stopes. **1986** *Bulletin* (Sydney) 8 Apr. 36/1 All the men will have access to modern air conditioned **crib huts** close to proper (porcelain) toilet and shower facilities. **1949** *Ibid.* 12 Jan. 29/4 Numerous rats . . overran the **crib-room** on 54 level. **1890 crib time** [see sense 1.] **1894** *Western Champion* (Barcaldine) 6 Feb. 3/3 It was nearly 'crib-time' before they got the four shots ready for firing. **1919** *Smith's Weekly* (Sydney) 8 Mar. 9/5 A pet method is to dump a case of whisky or wine on the wharf so darned hard that a few bottles break. What comes out of the box at the corners belongs to the wharfie, and is caught in a **crib-tin**.

crick, var. CREEK.

crim, *n*. [Abbrev. of *criminal*, prob. orig. U.S.: see OEDS.] One convicted of a crime.

1953 K. TENNANT *Joyful Condemned* 293 When Chigger honoured any crim in the gaol, that was the accolade. **1983** *Open Road* Apr. 7/1 What I hadn't reckoned on is that drink-driving is a criminal offence. I was a crim—not just another blundering motorist.

crim, *v*. [f. prec.] *intr*. To engage in criminal or questionable activities. Also *trans*., to steal.

1968 *Coast to Coast 1968–70* 81 You've been crimming around just this side of the law for years. **1978** H. HAENKE *Bottom of Birdcage* 39, I give a bunch of 'em y' last birthday. . . Yair, but y' crimmed 'em from the cemetery so it don't count.

crimean shirt. *Obs.* [f. the name of the Black Sea peninsula, prob. with reference to the warmth of the material.] A coloured flannel shirt formerly popular amongst workers in the bush.

1864 R. HENNING *Lett.* 25 Dec. (1952) 80 Hatless and bootless and trouserless and arrayed only in a Crimean shirt. **1936** J.E. HAMMOND *Western Pioneers* 42 The 'Crimean' shirts were made of flannel.

crimson, *a*. Used as a distinguishing epithet in the names of flora and fauna: **crimson chat**, the small nomadic bird *Epthianura tricolor* of mainland Aust., the breeding male having crimson, brown, and white plumage; TRICOLOURED CHAT; **finch**, the finch *Neochmia phaeton* of n. Aust., the mature male having predom. crimson plumage; *blood finch*, see BLOOD; **-flowering gum**, see FLOWERING GUM; **rosella (lowry, parakeet, parrot)**, the red and blue parrot *Platycercus elegans* of e. Aust.; *red lory*, see RED *a*. 1 b; **-winged parrot**, *red-winged parrot*, see RED *a*. 1 b.

1943 C. BARRETT *Austral. Animal Bk.* 274 The **crimson chat** (*E* [*pthianura*] *tricolor*) has a wide mainland distribution, but is absent from North Queensland. It is a beautiful little bird, with nomadic habits. **1842** J. GOULD *Birds of Aust.* (1848) III. Pl. 83, *Estrelda phaëton* . . **Crimson Finch**. **1843** [**crimson rosella**] A. MCEVEY *J. Cotton's Birds Port Phillip* 8 June (1974) 36 Shot two crimson lowries or broadtails Platycercus Pennantii. **1907** *Emu* VII. 96 Crimson Parrakeet . . one of those birds that has been pushed back by settlement. **1932** H. PRIEST *Call of Bush* 163 Some, like the beautiful mountain-loving Crimson Parrot, are most conspicuously red. **1945** C. BARRETT *Austral. Bird Life* 79 The crimson rosella . . rivals the common rosella in colour. **1781** J. LATHAM *Gen. Synopsis Birds* I. 299 **Crimson-winged Parrot**. . . All the wing coverts a full crimson.

cripples, *pl.* [f. Br. dial. *cripple* a disease of cattle: see OEDS 1 b.] An affliction of cattle, characterized by staggering due to weakness in the hindlegs or incoordination, and resulting from poisoning by plants of the genera *Xanthorrhoea* or *Macrozamia*, or a phosphorus deficiency.

1901 J.H. MAIDEN *Plants reputed to be Poisonous* 31 The settlers in the vicinity of Jervis Bay inform me that the young shoots of the grass-tree, when in blossom, if eaten by cattle, give them a complaint called 'cripples'. **1929** *Colonial Times* (Hobart) 1 July 15/6 Lack of minerals in pastures causes innumerable diseases, such as . . 'cripples' . . in Australia.

cro, var. CROW *n*.[2]

crockery. [Joc. use of *crockery* earthenware.] False teeth.

1941 *Bulletin* (Sydney) 17 Sept. 14/1 Bill removed his crockery and stood it tenderly on a flat stone while he champed his corned beef sandwiches on his horny gums. **1967** *Kings Cross Whisper* (Sydney) xxxiii. 4/4 Crockery, false teeth.

crocodile. [Prob. joc. formation from *crock* broken-down horse.] A horse.

1897 *Worker* (Sydney) 11 Sept. 1/1 Across a wiry 'cuddy' whom he calls his 'crocodile'. **1966** S.J. BAKER *Austral. Lang.* (ed. 2) 66 The old Scottish use of *crock* for a broken-down horse has probably influenced the evolution of the Australian outback slang *crocodile* for a horse.

cronk, *a*. and *n*. Also **kronk**. [Prob. var. of Br. dial. *crank* crooked, distorted, infirm, weak.]

A. *adj*. Dishonest, illegal, 'crooked'; ill, in poor condition; not genuine.

1890 'R. BOLDREWOOD' *Nevermore* (1892) III. 143 From the look of him . . I shouldn't be surprised if there was something 'cronk' about him, for all his gold-buying. **1981** K. MCARTHUR *Bread & Dripping Days* 11 Every child had to eat 'what was good for you', even parsnips and Swede turnips if fathers liked them. They were 'kronk' in the children's vernacular of the day.

B. *n*. A criminal.

1899 *Bulletin* (Sydney) 22 Apr. 14/3 Spread from the criminal class there to the 'cronks' elsewhere in Australia. **1913** M. CANNON *That Damned Democrat* (1981) 130 All the rooks and crooks and cronks of society assemble at these places.

crook, *a*. [Abbrev. of *crooked* dishonestly come by, made, obtained, or sold in a way that is not straightforward (see OED(S 3 b.); prob. infl. by (orig.) U.S. *crook* swindler, and by CRONK.]

1. **a.** Dishonest; illegal; illicitly obtained.

1898 Bulletin (Sydney) 17 Dec. (Red Page), *Krook* or *kronk* is bad. **1982** R. HALL *Just Relations* 465, I remember some pretty crook things went on there, did some of them meself.

b. Of circumstances, objects, etc.: bad; inferior; unpleasant; unsatisfactory.
1900 *Western Champion* (Barcaldine) 14 Aug. 13/1 At first all the rations were issued to the cooks, and things were very 'crook'. **1986** *Nat. Times* (Sydney) 10 Jan. 4/2 It was pretty crook on the land in the early 1970s.

c. Ill; injured; out of sorts.
1908 *Bulletin* (Sydney) 15 Oct. 14/1 Climb out of bunk, feeling crook—sore head from fever over-night. **1981** *Woman's Day* (Sydney) 9 Sept. 15/1 He did indeed have a crook knee. He'd been riding on a board and a shark had come up and nipped him.

2. In the phr. **to go crook (at, on).**

a. *Obs.* To act dishonestly.
1906 *Bulletin* (Sydney) 20 Sept. 16/1 His integrity was known; Thoughts of snatching pelf he spurned. At suggestions to 'go crook' Righteous wrath within him burned.

b. To become angry (with), to vent one's anger (upon).
1910 L. ESSON *Woman Tamer* (1976) 79 Now, don't go crook, Katie. **1971** *Austral Roadsports & Drag Racing News* 15 Oct. 10/2 Withers went crook at me because I broke the axle.

c. To deteriorate; to cease functioning adequately.
1919 *Smith's Weekly* (Sydney) 21 June 16/5, I neglected to take an overcoat, although it was at that season when the New England weather might at any moment 'go crook'. **1963** S. MUSSEN *Beating about Bush* 36 After four months in Australia I thought I could speak like an Australian. My watch did not *break;* it *went crook on me.*

d. To become ill.
1918 *Kia Ora Coo-ee* June 2/3 What a grafter she is, when she doesn't elect to go 'crook'. **1976** L. OAKES *Crash Through* 237 The last thing we want is to have you start tonight, not turn in a good performance because you're sick, and then in a day or two go crook again.

3. In the phr. **to be crook on,** to be annoyed by (cf. CROOKED).
1955 R. LAWLER *Summer of Seventeenth Doll* (1965) 48 You're crook on me because I stayed up there with Dowdie and didn't walk out with you. **1982** LOWENSTEIN & HILLS *Under Hook* 42, I was there on duty when the police strike was on. I was crook on it because I couldn't get away.

crooked /'krʊkəd/, *a.* [f. CROOK 2 b.] Annoyed; esp. in the phr. **crooked on,** exasperated by, infuriated with.
1942 *Whizz* (Perth) July 1 You're crooked on parasites and profiteers back home. **1978** D. STUART *Wedgetail View* 76 Ah you're just crooked, Col . . 'cos she hasn't got a sister here with her, so's you could have a dash.

crooked maginnis: see MAGINNIS.

croppy. *Hist.* [Transf. use of Br. *croppy* one who has the hair cut short, applied esp. to the Irish rebels of 1798.] Orig. an Irish convict, esp. one transported for participation in the 1798 rebellion; any convict, incl. a convict at large.
1800 *HRA* (1914) 1st Ser. II. 581 Drinking inflammatory and seditious Toasts—'Success to the Croppies' and other improper Expressions. **1888** W.T. PYKE *Bush Tales* 14 From the close governmental crop of their hair, convicts are called croppies by the blacks. Blacks hate croppies . . and croppies hate blacks as heartily, because they so often prove the means of their detection.

Cross, *n.*

1. Abbrev. of SOUTHERN CROSS 1.
1872 MRS E. MILLETT *Austral. Parsonage* 173 Without its 'pointers', however, as the two splendid stars are called that accompany it, the Cross would lose much of its attraction. **1969** D. NILAND *Dead Men Running* 57 You could look out and see the five white stars of the cross.

2. With **the**: abbrev. of 'King's Cross', the name of a district of Sydney, N.S.W. noted for its cosmopolitan character.
1945 H.C. BREWSTER *King's Cross Calling* 5 Just where is King's Cross?—or as it is referred to affectionately by those who live there—The Cross. **1980** M. WILLIAMS *Dingo!* 59 He took me up to the Cross, the city's playground, and introduced me to the molls working in the coffee bars.

Hence **Crossite** *n.*, a frequenter of King's Cross.
1945 H.C. BREWSTER *King's Cross Calling* 112 The Crossite has . . a complacent belief that he may still sit in his beloved cafe.

cross, *a.* [f. *cross* across (as in *cross-country*).] In special collocations: **cross fence,** a fence delineating a part of an externally fenced area; **track,** a cross-country track (see quot. 1849); in *pl.*, an intersection of such tracks, 'cross-roads'.
1840 *S. Austral. Rec.* (London) 29 Aug. 139, I made choice of the E.S.E. corner of section 256, it being the clearest of timber and the most easily inclosed by **cross fences,** the section being previously fenced. **1849** A. HARRIS *Emigrant Family* (1967) 309 The road he had to traverse is a **cross-track,** between districts that have . . little business communication. **1914** *Bulletin* (Sydney) 21 May 24/1 A pub . . we had passed at the cross-tracks.

cross-brand, *v. trans.* To re-brand (an animal): legally, by marking it with the brand of a second or subsequent owner; illegally, by altering the existing brand. Also as *ppl. a.*
1936 W. HATFIELD *Aust. through Windscreen* 59 One suspected cattle-thief . . rode into the police paddock where seventeen head of alleged cross-branded cattle were being held as exhibits. **1978** D. STUART *Wedgetail View* 25 There'd be work . . as soon as they'd cross-branded the young breeders that were to pay for agistment for the mob.

crow, $n.^1$ [Transf. use of *crow* bird of genus *Corvus*.]

1. Any of several large, glossy, black birds of the genus *Corvus*, having a harsh call, esp. *C. orru* of Aust. and New Guinea and *C. bennetti* of mainland Aust. See also RAVEN.
1770 J. BANKS *Endeavour Jrnl.* 19 June (1962) II. 83 There were vast flocks of Pigeons and crows. **1976** *Ecos* viii. 30/2 Most of us would be quite content to label the large black birds of the genus *Corvus* as crows or ravens. . . He has now established that there are in fact five species involved—two crows and three ravens. They all look very much alike.

2. Special Comb. **crow shrike,** (variously) BUTCHERBIRD, CURRAWONG, MAGPIE $n.^1$
1878 R.B. SMYTH *Aborigines of Vic.* II. 38 *Crow shrike,* Wooryung. **1962** B.W. LEAKE *Eastern Wheatbelt Wildlife* 86 The magpie and currawong or squeaker are closely related to the crow and are really crow shrikes.

3. In the phr. **to stone (spare, starve, stiffen) the crows,** an exclamation of surprise, disgust, exasperation, etc. See also LIZARD 2 and STARVE.
1918 H. MATTHEWS *Saints & Soldiers* 116 'Starve the crows,' howled Bluey in that agonised screech of his. **1919** C. DREW *Doings of Dave* 47 Spare the crows! **1927** F.C. BIGGERS *Bat-Eye* 15 Well, stone the floggin' crows! **1932** J. TRURAN *Green Mallee* 75 Stiffen the crows, Fred, a man oughter do it for yer own sake.

4. In the phr. **to draw the crow,** to receive the least desirable share (of anything).
1942 *Wog Jrnl.: Mag. 3rd Austral. Infantry Brigade* 25 Dec. 1 To draw the crow is to be detailed for a job while others [rest]. **1985** N. MEDCALF *Rifleman* 207, I bet I had drawn the crow on some louzy detail.

crow, *n.*² Also **cro**. [Prob. abbrev. of CHROMO.] A prostitute.

1950 *Austral. Police Jrnl.* Apr. 111 *Crow*, prostitute. **1953** K. TENNANT *Joyful Condemned* 47 She's in with all the higher-ups. And what does she do? Slugs a guy like a cro on a beat. **1980** B. HERBERT *No Names* 77 What are you, anyway? A Kings Cross crow. Every Yank in town's been rootin' you.

crowea /ˈkrəʊɪə/. [The plant genus *Crowea* was named by English botanist J.E. Smith (*Trans. Linnean Soc. London* (1798) IV. 222), after the English surgeon and botanist James *Crowe* (1750–1807).] Any shrub of the genus *Crowea* (fam. Rutaceae) of s.w. W.A. and parts of s.e. Aust.

1901 M. VIVIENNE *Travels in W.A.* 61 The delicate pink and white flowers of the crowea hang in loose clusters. **1984** ELLIOT & JONES *Encycl. Austral. Plants* III. 118 Croweas are not prone to any pests or diseases.

croweater. [See quots. 1881 and 1934.] A nickname for a non-Aboriginal person resident in, or native to, South Australia. Also *attrib.*

1881 J.C.F. JOHNSON *To Mount Browne & Back* 13, I was met with the startling information that all Adelaide men were croweaters . . because it was asserted that the early settlers of 'Farinaceous Village', when short of mutton, made a meal of the unwary crow. **1934** M. GILMORE *Old Days* 18 It was said that they ate the crows they caught. With the cruelty of the times people called them 'crow-eaters', and they were despised accordingly by those who lived in the altitudes of 'killed meat'. **1940** *Bulletin* (Sydney) 24 July 16/3 We were humpin' our drums through Croweater country.

Hence **crow-eating** *a.*, **crowland** *n.*

1908 *Truth* (Sydney) 5 July 1/7 In Adelaide . . now it is possible for a man to be tortured to death by **crow-eating** officials. **1908** M. VIVIENNE *Sunny S.A.* 74 The Maoris vied with each other to do honour to their white brother from '**crowland**'. For the South Australians have long been known as 'Croweaters'.

crown, *n.* [Attrib. use of *crown* the authority so symbolized.]

1. *Obs.* In Comb. as a euphemistic term for a convict: **crown labourer, prisoner, servant.**

1824 E. EAGAR *Lett.* 41 A settler possessing £200 capital . . will employ and subsist four **crown labourers**, or convicts. **1819** *Sydney Gaz.* 4 Sept., The trial of several **crown prisoners** charged with robbing His Majesty's store. **1815** M. HOOKEY *B. Knopwood & his Times* 25 Apr. (1929) 111 The whole of the **Crown Servants** are to be mustered every afternoon at sunset.

2. Special Comb., in terms pertaining to land tenure: **crown grant**, a grant of land made to an individual; **land**, unalienated land; **(land) commissioner**, see quots. 1848 and 1852; **lease**, an agreement under which crown land is tenanted; the land so held; **purchase (land)**, crown land which has been sold or is available for sale; **tenant**, one who leases crown land.

1840 S. *Austral. Rec.* (London) 7 Mar. 90 The question of the validity of **crown-grants** of colonial lands has been mooted. [**1789 crown land**: *HRA* (1914) 1st Ser. I. 127 You are also to reserve to Us proper quantities of land in each township.] **1814** *Ibid.* (1916) 1st Ser. VIII. 329 Quit rents to One Shilling per Acre would by no Means answer the Intentions of Government to raise a Revenue from the Crown Lands, intended to be granted. **1846** *Moreton Bay Courier* 5 Sept. 4/3 The days of **Crown Land Commissioners** are numbered. **1848** C. COZENS *Adventures of Guardsman* 123 Each party of border-police was placed under the immediate control of a Crown land commissioner, and generally consisted of four men and horses. One commissioner was appointed to each district beyond the limits of location, i.e. the boundary line laid down as the extent of the police districts. **1852** J.E. ERSKINE *Short Acct. Late Discoveries Gold* 17 Mr Hardy, Police Magistrate at Parramatta, was now nominated in addition 'Crown Land Commissioner' for the Gold Districts, and a force of twelve mounted constabulary was raised, both to enable him to preserve order and to enforce the payment of the license fees. **1862** H. BROWN *Vic. as I found It* 148 The crown Commissioner . . has the responsibility of gathering in the license fee, and of generally superintending the affairs of the gold-fields. **1808** *To Viscount Castlereagh* 10 Tenants under **Crown leases** in the town of Sydney. **1842** *Sydney Morning Herald* 3 Aug. 1/8 Part of a **Crown purchase** of 820 acres. **1920** B. CRONIN *Timber Wolves* 47 Crown purchase land is open for selection. **1855** W. CAMPBELL *Crown Lands Aust.* 21 There could have been no great loss to the Revenue had the **Crown-tenants** got all the lands they applied for.

crown, *v.* [f. *crown fire* a bushfire which moves through the crowns or tops of trees: see OEDS *crown, sb.* 35.] *intr.* Of a bushfire: to move (rapidly) through the tops of trees. Also as *vbl. n.*

1972 B. FULLER *West of Bight* 142 In windy conditions fires travel fast, flames leaping in explosive balls from tree-top to tree-top, a phenomenon known as 'crowning'. **1981** *Bega District News* 27 Nov. 5/6 A tractor and more men were brought in but the fire crowned under the influence of low humidity and strong Westerly winds.

crown of thorns starfish. [f. a fancied resemblance to Christ's *crown of thorns.*] The spiny, coral-eating starfish *Acanthaster planci* of tropical regions, including the Great Barrier Reef.

1964 *Austral. Med. Jrnl.* Apr. I. 592 Usually the 'crown of thorns' starfish is to be found entwined in the branches of living coral, on which it feeds. **1984** *Daily Tel.* (Sydney) 20 Jan. 9/2 Scientists are baffled by the upsurge of activity among the coral-gobbling crown-of-thorns starfish on the Great Barrier Reef.

crow's ash. [See quot. 1981.] The rainforest tree of Qld. and N.S.W. *Flindersia australis* (fam. Rutaceae), having a scaly bark and prickly woody fruits; the timber of the tree, which is yellow and oily. See also TEAK. Also **crow ash.**

1903 *Austral. Handbk.* 279 Other orders . . furnish . . large-sized timber, particularly the following:- . 'Crow's Ash' (*Flindersia australis*). **1949** B. O'REILLY *Green Mountains* 144 Of the vast variety of jungle trees, . . Crow Ash and Lignum Vitae were suitable for fencing, all others used to rot in the ground. **1981** A.B. & J.W. CRIBB *Useful Wild Plants Aust.* 134 The origin of the name crow's ash is obscure. However, it is reported that crows eat the seeds and this may possibly have led to the use of the common name.

crowsfoot. Used *attrib.* in Special Comb. **crowsfoot elm**, BOOYONG; **grass**, the naturalized tussock-forming grass *Eleusine indica* (fam. Poaceae) of all mainland States except Vic.; the related *E. tristachya*; also abbrev. as **crowsfoot.**

1909 *Emu* VIII. 238 The heavy and tall timbers were represented by . . **crow's foot elm**. **1903** G. SUTHERLAND *Australasian Live Stock Man.* (ed. 2) 384 Among the grasses of Riverina . . **crowsfoot**. **1974** S.L. EVERIST *Poisonous Plants Aust.* 227 Crowsfoot grass is a weed of most warm countries.

crudget: see CRUET.

cruel, *v.* [f. *cruel, a.*, perh. infl. by *to queer (the pitch)*.] *trans.* To spoil (an opportunity, etc.); to ruin (the chances of a person or enterprise succeeding).

1899 *Truth* (Sydney) 2 Apr. 4/5 Your brand-new hanky-panky system of drawing in sections 'cruelled' their chances. **1971** D. IRELAND *Unknown Industr. Prisoner* 83 His eagerness for overtime and promotion cruelled him.

cruet. [Prob. altered form of Br. slang *crumpet* the head, as in the phr. *barmy in the crumpet*: see OEDS 4.] Also **crudget.**
1. The (human) head.
1941 S.J. BAKER *Pop. Dict. Austral. Slang* 21 *Crudget*, the head. **1977** R. BEILBY *Gunner* 139 'Where did he get it?' 'Through the cruet.'
2. In the phr. **to do one's cruet,** to lose one's temper.
1976 *Bronze Swagman Bk. Bush Verse* 59 The wife would do her cruet, she would murder me.

cruiser. See quot. 1970.
1966 S.J. BAKER *Austral. Lang.* (ed. 2) 229 Names given to other measures . . *schooner, cruiser*. **1970** N. KEESING *Transition* 202 You Australians call a pint glass a cruiser, a three-quarter-pint a schooner, and a half-pint a middy, all very nautical.

crumpet. [Joc. var. of CRACKER $n.^2$] In the phr. **not worth a crumpet,** worthless.
1944 L. GLASSOP *We were Rats* 153 He won't be worth a crumpet in action, not worth a bloody crumpet. **1968** J. O'GRADY *Gone Troppo* 51 Three trucks and not one of 'em worth a bloody crumpet. Guts driven out of all of 'em.

crush. [Transf. use of *crush* a crowding together.] In a stock yard: a narrow race or passage through which animals can only pass in single file. Also *attrib*.
[N.Z. **1856** W. ROBERTS in J.H. Beattie *Early Runholding in Otago* 18 Dec. (1947) 43 There was no crush pen or drafting race.] **1872** C.H. EDEN *My Wife & I in Qld.* 69 [It] consists of several yards for drafting . . a lane and a crush . . useful for branding or securing a troublesome . . bullock. **1928** B. CRONIN *Dragonfly* 102 I'm going to round-up some cattle. Want to help me with the crush-gate?

crusher. See quots.
1965 F. HARDY *Yarns of Billy Borker* 59 Some blokes beat the game, I hear. Only bookmakers—and crushers. What's a crusher? A crusher's a bloke who backs a horse at, say, five to one; then lays it in a bookmaker's bag, at say three to one. **1985** *Sydney Morning Herald* 25 Jan. 1/1 A crusher really is not a racing man at all. His practice is to back a horse at longer odds, having received some sort of information that its price is likely to shrink during the betting, and then to sell his betting ticket to somebody at odds which are lower than those shown on the ticket, but which are still higher than those currently being offered in the ring. A crusher is not regarded in the betting ring as an admirable figure. He is regarded as something of a hanger-on, a scalper of good odds.

crust. [Fig. use of *crust* a scrap of bread.]
1. A livelihood.
1888 G. ROCK *Colonists* 40, I generally manages to crack a tidy crust. **1980** M. BAIL *Homesickness* (1981) 153 What some people do for a crust.
2. A vagrancy charge; a vagrant.
1910 L. ESSON *Three Short Plays* (1911) 14 You're qualifying for a stiff for the crust . . . You're likely to bring a Sixer, I'm warning you. **1967** *Kings Cross Whisper* (Sydney) xxxiii. 4/4 *Crust*, a vagrant. To be crusted is to be vagged. From the proposal that a person has not enough money to purchase a crust of bread.

crutch, $n.^1$ [Fig. use of *crutch* a support for an infirm person.] See quot. 1965.
1879 S.W. SILVER *Austral. Grazier's Guide* 48 The sheep-washers, armed with a species of crook, called a crutch. **1965** J.S. GUNN *Terminol. Shearing Industry* i. 18 *Crutch*, a mallet-shaped instrument (like a crutch) used to push sheep under in a swimming dip. Improved dips, especially spray dips, have caused this tool to become obsolete.

crutch, $n.^2$ [See CRUTCH *v.*] The hindquarters of a sheep; the removal of wool from this area. Also *attrib*.
1941 *Method Performing Mules Operation* (Austral. Wool Board) 1 Crutch strikes are said to account for over 90 per cent. of the strikes incurred by merino sheep in Australia. **1943** *Bulletin* (Sydney) 27 Oct. 13/2 Ten crutchers doing a full crutch on ewes with a proportion of weaners averaged 597 per man per day for seven days.

crutch, *v*. [f. *crutch* the part of the body.] *trans*. To clip wool from about the tail of (a sheep) to prevent fouling. Also *absol*. and freq. as *vbl. n*.
1913 W.K. HARRIS *Outback in Aust*. 151 'Crutching' is necessary in some districts, when blowflies are prevalent, and consists of cutting away the wool from the hind-quarters of the affected animal. **1977** W.A. WINTER-IRVING *Bush Stories* 76, I crutched sheep stricken with blowfly maggots. **1979** 'BLUE SHEARER' *First Clip* 17 I'd like to be an artist, but I don't quite have the 'touch', And I couldn't be a grazier. I never learned to crutch.

Hence **crutcher** *n*., one who crutches; **crutchings** *n. pl*. (see quot.).
1943 crutcher [see CRUTCH $n.^2$] **1914** H.B. SMITH *Sheep & Wool Industry* 67 Wool which is shorn from the britch of the sheep a few months before shearing is called 'crutchings'.

cuckoo. *Obs*. [Transf. use of *cuckoo*: see quot. 1827.] The owl *Ninox novaeseelandiae* (see BOOBOOK).
[**1827** *Trans. Linnean Soc. London* XV. 188 Boobook Owl . . . The note of the bird is somewhat similar to that of the European *cuckoo*, and the colonists have hence given it that name.] **1852** S. MOSSMAN *Gold Regions Aust*. 64 Hark to the distant Mopauk, with its strange note, which the un-romantic settler translates into 'more pork', while the man who prides himself on having a 'soul above buttons', calls it the cuckoo. **1879** 'AUSTRALIAN' *Adventures Qld*. 129 He heard a hoarse note, resembling that of the cuckoo, or Australian owl, close to his head.

cuckoo-shrike. [See quot. 1945.] Any of several birds of the genus *Coracina* of Aust. and elsewhere. See also *black-faced cuckoo-shrike* BLACK $a.^2$ 1 b.
1898 E.E. MORRIS *Austral Eng*. 109 Cuckoo-shrike . . . This combination of two common English bird-names is assigned in Australia to the following [etc.]. **1945** C. BARRETT *Austral. Bird Life* 196 Cuckoo-shrikes derive their compound name from the fact that their flight is undulating, like that of cuckoos, while they have the bill of a shrike.

cucumber fish. [See quot. 1852.] HERRING 2. Also **cucumber herring, cucumber mullet.**
1843 *South Briton* (Hobart) Apr. 56 Providence has . . not been over-bountiful in peopling our rivers with the finny tribes, the only fresh water fish of note being the mullet, herring, cucumber fish, as it is severally called. **1852** MRS C. MEREDITH *My Home in Tas*. II. 82 A small delicate fish, called 'cucumber fish', from its peculiar odour. **1881** J.F.V. FITZGERALD *Aust*. 35 The Yarra herring . . , called in Tasmania the cucumber mullet, is almost identical with the English grayling. **1986** *Canberra Times* 25 May 5/7 Fisheries inspectors at Eden have identified several small fish, now known to be an endangered species, as Australian Grayling or Cucumber herring.

cuddleseat. [Proprietary name.] A type of baby carrier or sling: see quot. 1949 (2).
1948 *Our Babies* (Victorian Babies Health Centres' Assoc.) (ed. 7) 56 *The comfortable baby is a cuddleseat baby because Cuddleseat is scientifically designed to carry*

babies of from 2 weeks to 2 years with safety and freedom from strain. **1949** *Sydney Morning Herald* 1 May 4/1 The manufacturers of 'Cuddleseat' baby carriers trading as Cuddleseat Manufacturing Co. of Cessnock, New South Wales, hereby notify the trade and the public that they are the registered proprietors under the Trade Marks Act of the Commonwealth of Australia of Trade Mark No. 80931 consisting of the word 'Cuddleseat' registered in respect of 'A carrier device or seat for babies'. **1949** D. WALKER *We went to Aust.* 35 The peculiarly Australian 'cuddleseat' which I believe originated in Sydney but is most popular in Brisbane. This contrivance .. is a form of canvas sling, so that the infant is worn round the shoulders, rather than directly carried.

cuddy. [Transf. use of Br. dial. *cuddy* donkey.] A horse.
1897 *Worker* (Sydney) 11 Sept. 1/1 Across a wiry 'cuddy' whom he calls his 'crocodile' .. in search of shearing work he rides from hut to hut. **1969** W. MOXHAM *Apprentice* 97 This was how he won at Kembla Grange, on a country cuddy.

cudgerie /'kʌdʒəri/. [a. Bandjalang *gajari*.] Any of several rainforest trees, esp. *Flindersia schottiana* (fam. Rutaceae) of N.S.W., Qld., and New Guinea, having large pinnate leaves and prickly woody fruits; the timber of this tree, which is pale and durable. See also BUMPY ASH.
1884 A. NILSON *Timber Trees N.S.W.* 80 F[*lindersia*] *australis*.—Ash; Cugerie... A tree attaining a height of 100 feet, and a diameter of 4 feet, with a dark brown rugged and scaly bark. **1985** P. CAREY *Illywhacker* 117 We would want .. cudgerie for the fuselage.

cue, *n.* Also **kew, q.** [Br. dial. *cue* the shoe of an ox: see EDD *sb.*[1] and *v.*[1].] The shoe of a bullock: see quots. 1935 and 1976.
1902 *Bulletin* (Sydney) 22 Mar. 15/1 Where you can't get the proper cue, old horse-shoes are used, cut in two. **1935** R.B. PLOWMAN *Boundary Rider* 146 Picking up a farrier's toolbox, he .. took from it .. a flat piece of steel—a cue. This was just large enough to cover one half of the horny part of the hoof from the cleft to the heel, and was about an inch and a quarter wide. **1958** *Bulletin* (Sydney) 28 Apr. 18/2 'Kews' .. were carefully nailed to the bullocks' feet. **1976** C.D. MILLS *Hobble Chains & Greenhide* 110 A 'Q' .. is a plate with a flattened, hollowed heel, and a pointed, turned toe. It is the counterpart of a horse-shoe, and serves the same purpose.

cue, *v.* Also **kew.** [f. prec.] *trans.* To shoe (a beast) with a cue.
1902 *Bulletin* (Sydney) 22 Mar. 15/1 Bullocks .. are 'cued' .. but to cue a team you have to build a pen (sort of a crush) and put the comether on 'em. **1958** *Bulletin* (Sydney) 23 Apr. 18/2 'Kewing', or 'cueing' .. was once applied to the shoeing of bullocks in the Kimberley country of W.A.

Hence **cue-er** *n.*, one who cues; **cueing** *vbl. n.*, esp. as **cueing pen.**
1935 R.B. PLOWMAN *Boundary Rider* 147 The bullock recognized the **cue-er** for a stranger and very properly showed his resentment. **1958** *Bulletin* (Sydney) 23 Apr. 18/2 Most stations in the region had their '**kewing**-pens'.

cuff. [With ref. to the *cuffs* and *collars* of a formal shirt.] Used *attrib.* and *absol.* in the collocation **cuff and collar,** white collar (worker).
1896 *Bulletin* (Sydney) 23 May 3/2 You bushmen sneer in the old bush way at the new-chum jackeroo, But 'cuffs-'n'-collers' were out *that day*, and they stuck to their posts like glue. **1936** J. DEVANNY *Sugar Heaven* 211 The 'silver-tails', as the cutters designated the bank clerks and other 'cuff and collar' workers, complained they couldn't get a bath nor a seat at table.

cuffer. *Obs.* [Br. dial. *cuffer* tale, yarn (see EDD *cuff, sb.*[3]); cf. *cuff* to tell a tale (OEDS *v.*[1] 4).] A story or yarn; a 'tall story'.
1887 K. MACKAY *Stirrup Jingles* 40 Alright, boss! If a yarn I must spin, Leastways it won't be a cuffer. **1916** *Truth* (Sydney) 16 Jan. 11/1 They were in no way green, and knew something about the art of leg-pulling... 'Tommy' does so love to spin a 'cuffer'!

cully. [Survival of Br. *cully* fellow, mate: see OED *sb.* 2.] A mate; used esp. as a mode of address.
1905 *Bulletin* (Sydney) 16 Apr. 19/2 You've noticed maybe, cully, that the bush is always callin'. **1976** A. BUZO *Martello Towers* 20 Listen, cully, no man's going to lay a heavy chauve trip on the head of *my* woman.

cultivation. Abbrev. of CULTIVATION PADDOCK. Also *attrib.*
1906 *Bulletin* (Sydney) 18 Oct. 44/1 Dave goes to look after his private enterprise of wallaby trapping, and Dad to the 'cultivation' he has already spent months clearing. **1934** 'S. RUDD' *Green Grey Homestead* 35 The tree with the bees' nest will be cut down and lying across your cultivation fence.

cultivation paddock. An enclosed piece of a rural property, used for the growing of crops.
1841 *Port Phillip Patriot* 25 Feb. 4 There are also considerable improvements on the Estate, having a .. calf paddock, grass paddock, and cultivation paddock. **1973** R. ROBINSON *Drift of Things* 98 Mr Simmonds said that I could exercise him in the soft, ploughed cultivation paddock.

cultural cringe. [Coined by A.A. Phillips (1900–85), literary critic: see quot. 1950.] A phr. alluding to an (Australian) attitude characterized by deference to the cultural achievements of others.
1950 A.A. PHILLIPS in *Meanjin* 299 Above our writers—and other artists—looms the intimidating mass of Anglo-Saxon culture. Such a situation almost inevitably produces the characteristic Australian Cultural Cringe. **1984** *Canberra Times* 26 Apr. 8/5 The expatriate view of a derivative and unimportant people is so much an accepted part of our cultural cringe that we are embarrassed or unbelieving about European enthusiasm for things Australian.

Hence **cultural cringer** *n.*
1977 P. ADAMS *Unspeakable Adams* 24 We're a nation of cultural cringers who tug our forelocks at French cooking while bemoaning our lack of indigenous dishes.

Cumberland disease. [See quot. 1877.] A local name for anthrax. Also *ellipt.* as **Cumberland.**
1863 R. THERRY *Reminisc. Thirty Yrs. N.S.W. & Vic.* 264 We were again visited with a most infectious and fatal disease, known as the Cumberland disease, which killed immense numbers of sheep and cattle. **1877** G. MITCHELL *Cumberland Disease* 19 Cumberland Disease—so called from the circumstance of its having made its first appearance in Australia, in the county Cumberland, New South Wales. **1890** E.T. TOWNER *Selectors' Guide to Barcoo* 3 There is no foot-rot, no scab, no Cumberland and no grass seed, each one of which annoyances and consequent loss has to be borne in many other districts I could mention.

cumbungi /kʌm'bʌŋgi/. [a. Wemba-wemba *gambaŋ*.] BULRUSH.
1878 R.B. SMYTH *Aborigines of Vic.* I. p. xxxiii, The kumpung, a bulrush almost identical with one found in Switzerland—a species of *typha*—is eaten during the summer either raw or roasted, and the fibres are used for making twine. **1942** E. ANDERSON *Squatter's Luck* 14 Cumbungi, sir, 's in ther drain, Skeleton's 'ere again.

cundy, var. COONIE.

cunjevoi /'kʌndʒəvɔɪ/, n.[1] Chiefly *N.S.W.* Also **cungeboy**. [Prob. f. a N.S.W. Aboriginal language.] The ascidian or sea-squirt *Pyura praeputialis*, occurring on intertidal rocks in s. Aust., the flesh of which is used as bait. Also abbrev. as **cunji, cunjy**.

1821 S. LEIGH in Methodist Missionary Soc. Rec. 18 Nov., This Cunguwa is a kind of living fungus, which at certain seasons they detach from the Rocks on the Sea Shore. **1895** C. THACKERAY *Amateur Fisherman's Guide* 32 There is one bait which is par excellence the bait for the rocks. It is called generally 'cungeboy'... The term corresponds with, and is probably a corruption of the word cungevoi or congewoi in the aboriginal vernacular. **1917** —— *Goliath Joe* 29, I .. fell to chuckin' in lumps er cunjy for 'im to eat. **1967** *Surfabout* (Sydney) IV. ii. 22 Another group surf in a decidedly non-functional manner .. which usually results in rather forceful bodily contact with the cunji.

cunjevoi /'kʌndʒəvɔɪ/, n.[2] Also **cunjiboy**. [Prob. f. a N.S.W. Aboriginal language.] The plant *Alocasia macrorrhiza* (fam. Araceae), occurring in moist forests of N.S.W., Qld., and elsewhere.

1845 C. HODGKINSON *Aust., Port Macquarie to Moreton Bay* 225 The root of the Conjeboi, a large-leaved plant, which grows on very moist alluvial land, often flooded, is also eaten. **1888** *Proc. Linnean Soc. N.S.W.* III. 365 *Colocasia macrorrhiza*... I know no aboriginal or colonial name used in New South Wales for this plant, although for Queensland .. 'Cunjevoi' is the one best known. **1926** M. FORREST *Hibiscus Heart* 119 The pale, lily-leafed cunjiboy, which makes an animal's mouth and tongue swell and which the natives use for a mustard plaster and as a cure for rheumatism.

cunji, cunjy, abbrev. of CUNJEVOI n.[1]

cunmerrie /'kʌnməri/. [a. Pitta-pitta *ganmarri*.] In Aboriginal belief: a huge winged spirit which carries off people and animals.

1946 W.E. HARNEY *North of 23°* 79 Fearful cunmerries, bat-like spirits, out to destroy, so powerful that they can lift a horse with its rider into the air. **1959** D. LOCKWOOD *Crocodiles & Other People* 59 They're especially scared of the cunmerrie, a ghastly, ghostly bird with enormous wings, talons, and beak—a bird that can swoop down on a mob and carry away the fattest bullock.

cunning, a. In the phr. **to run cunning,** (of a working dog): see quot. 1914.

1914 R. KALESKI *Austral. Barkers & Biters* 76 He loses his youthful dash and energy, and begins to 'run cunning'— lets the other dog do all the work. **1920** *Bulletin* (Sydney) 6 May 20/2 The alleged tame dingo .. is a heartbreak to the shepherd. He will 'run cunning' when sent round the flock, cutting off a 'wing' of the sheep, which is disastrous to the drover.

Cup. *Horse-racing.*

1. Usu. with **the**: shortened form of *Melbourne Cup*, a handicap race over 3200 m., run annually since 1861, on the first Tuesday in November, in Melbourne. Also *attrib.*

1861 *Argus* (Melbourne) 8 Nov. 5/5 His Excellency visited the saddling paddock during the half-hour preceding the Cup Race. **1981** *Bulletin* (Sydney) 3 Nov. 65/3 For sheer extravagance last year's Cup was hard to beat.

2. Comb. **Cup day, time, week.**

1876 *Illustr. Austral. News* (Melbourne) 29 Nov. 187/3 The **Cup day** of 1876 will be remembered as one of the most successful. **1891** 'ROUSEABOUT' *Jackeroo* 66 Many persons resident in various parts of the colonies, who would never think of visiting Melbourne at any other time, find themselves irresistably drawn thither at **Cup time**. **1882** *Austral. Stories* (ed. 2) 78 Little debts contracted .. in the '**Cup week**', 'bout the Christmas time before.

curl, v. [See quot. 1945.] In the phr. **to curl the mo,** to succeed brilliantly; also as quasi-*adj.*, impressive, outstanding.

1941 S.J. BAKER *Pop. Dict. Austral. Slang* 42 Kurl, good, excellent. Also 'kurl-a-mo'. **1944** *Truth* (Sydney) 13 Feb. 4/3 Breasley saw Kintore donkey-lick a field of youngsters in the Federal Stakes, and had salt rubbed into his wound when the Lewis cuddy Valour curled the mo in the Bond Handicap. **1945** S.J. BAKER *Austral. Lang.* 126 Curl-the-mo was apparently first used to denote the self-satisfaction of a man who twirled the ends of his flowing moustache. **1957** D. WHITTINGTON *Treasure upon Earth* 74 An elbow nudged him on the crowded dance floor later. 'Start getting Josie out,' Mick told him... 'This is going to be a real curl the mo' job.'

curlew. Either of two ground-nesting birds of the genus *Burhinus*, esp. *B. grallarius*, formerly widespread in Aust. but no longer found in closely settled areas; *stone curlew, stone plover*, see STONE n.[1] 3; WEELO.

1834 G. BENNETT *Wanderings N.S.W.* I. 334 At Paramatta [*sic*] I saw two tame specimens of the lesser *Otis*, or Bustard, the 'Curlew' of the colony. **1970** K. WILLEY *Naked Island* 141 Once he killed a curlew, which the Aborigines call the devil bird because of its eerie cry as it circles the camps at night.

curly Mitchell: see MITCHELL GRASS 2.

currajong, var. KURRAJONG.

currant. *Native currant*, see NATIVE a. 6 a. Also **currant bush, tree.**

1817 J. O'HARA *Hist. N.S.W.* 242 A species of currant, green in its state of maturity, afforded an excellent jelly. **1865** R.J. SHOLL *Jrnl. Exped. Camden Harbour to Glenelg River* 205 We bivouacked under what is here called the currant-tree, about 9 or 10 feet high, greyish striated bark, with twisted branches. The leaf is bright-green, smooth on the upper surface, 5 inches long, and 1 to 1½ inch [*sic*] broad. The fruit has a pleasant acid taste—black when ripe. It is of the size of a very small currant, and, like most Australian fruits, has more stone than flesh. **1887** W.H. SUTTOR *Austral. Stories Retold* 117 There grows profusely a sickly -looking greenish-yellow shrub, locally misnamed the currant bush. Its fruit is a pea.

currawong /'kʌrəwɒŋ/. Also **kurrawong**. [a. Yagara (and neighbouring languages) *garrawaŋ*.] Any of the three birds of the Austral. genus *Strepera*, having predom. black or grey plumage and a ringing call; *bell magpie*, see BELL n. Also with distinguishing epithet, as **black, grey, pied** (see under first element).

1905 [see *crow-shrike* CROW n.[1]] **1911** *Bulletin* (Sydney) 26 Jan. 15/2 The pied crow-shrike .. is called by various onomatopoeic renderings of its cry, such as .. corowong. **1916** *Ibid.* 3 Feb. 24/4 The kurrawong, or pied-bell magpie, has a loud, ringing voice. **1918** *Ibid.* 14 Feb. (Red Page), When a bird cheerily shouts *Currawong*, why should a kiddy be asked to pass by that musical word in favor of 'pied bell-magpie'?

currency.

1. *Hist.* A local medium of exchange circulating in the Australian Colonies and discounted against sterling (see also *colonial currency* COLONIAL a. 5). Also *attrib.*

1792 D. COLLINS *Acct. Eng. Colony N.S.W.* (1798) I. 246 They would have suffered great difficulties from the want of public money .. had not the commissary .. given them notes on himself... These notes passed through various hands in traffic among the people... They were intended to serve, and became a species of currency which was found very convenient to them. **1817** *HRA* (1917) 1st Ser. IX. 216 *Currency* Notes, the nature of which was such that the depreciation in the relative Value, when in comparison with Sterling Money, actually became the chief source of profit and advantage . . to the Issuers of those Notes.

2. A non-Aboriginal person native to Australia. Freq. *attrib.* and passing into *adj.*

1824 [see *currency lad, lass*]. **1825** *Austral.* (Sydney) 29 Sept. 3 At peep of day, several persons . . assembled on a spot of ground suitable enough for witnessing a pulley hauley match between two ladies of the fancy; the one a towny, the other of currency worth. **1829** R. MUDIE *Picture of Aust.* 355 Those who are born in the colony are called *Currency*, and those of English or European birth, and who have not found their way there in such a manner as to entitle them to the cant name of *Legitimates*, are called *Sterling*. **1888** 'R. BOLDREWOOD' *Robbery under Arms* (1937) 42 He'd always go to the mischief for the sake of a good horse, and many another 'Currency' chap has gone the same way.

3. *transf.*

1827 *Monitor* (Sydney) 27 Apr. 400/2 Horses started neck and neck—currency-bred. **1848** *Bell's Life in Sydney* 25 Mar. 1/1 The *older* days . . when one or two horses (imported at a vast expense from the *older* country) could enter the colonial arena, triumphantly bearing away the palm of victory from currency cattle.

4. Comb. **currency boy, lad, lass.**

1834 J.D. LANG *Hist. & Statistical Acct. N.S.W.* I. 388 A **currency boy**, or native of the colony. **1824** *Austral.* (Sydney) 18 Nov. 3 Let the **currency lads** and lasses turn Arcadian shepherds and shepherdesses if they choose. **1824 currency lass** [see *currency lad*]. **1825** *Austral.* (Sydney) 28 Apr. 3 The 'Currency Lasses' were 'bumpered, three times three', as we hope they always will be.

curry. [Prob. fig. use of *curry* spiced dish; but see also KURRAJONG 3.] In the phr. **to give** (someone) **curry,** to make life difficult or 'hot' for (a person), esp. to attack (a person) physically or verbally.

1936 *Bulletin* (Sydney) 6 May 21/1 The cocky seems to worry both through drought that gives him curry And through flood that just as ruthlessly destroys. **1986** *Canberra Times* 20 Feb. 1/1 Such actions led the Leader of the Government in the House, Mr Young, to threaten last week to give the opposition a 'bit of curry'.

curse.

1. *Obs.* A jocular name for a swag, esp. in the phr. **curse of God** (or **Cain**).

1921 *Smith's Weekly* (Sydney) 10 Dec. 17/4 A few swag aliases:- Matilda, the drum, bluey, white man's burden, and Curse of Cain. **1926** *Bulletin* (Sydney) 18 Nov. 22/4 An old swaggie with the curse o' God on his shoulders called at our place and asked for a bit of tucker. **1950** *Ibid.* 26 July 12/1 Humping the curse near Bunbury (W.A.), the Count and I found a pick and shovel.

2. Ellipt. for PATERSON'S CURSE.

1932 K.S. PRICHARD *Kiss on Lips* 38 'The curse!' 'Patterson's curse?' 'A noxious weed.' **1984** *Sydney Morning Herald* 6 Apr. 18/1 Beekeepers took out a successful Supreme Court writ in South Australia restraining the CSIRO from destroying the Curse because of its importance to the honey industry.

cushion bush. The rounded, coastal shrub *Calocephalus brownii* (fam. Asteraceae) of N.S.W., Vic., Tas., S.A., and W.A., cultivated as an ornamental.

1911 D.A. MACDONALD *Bush Boy's Bk.* 10 On many of the Victorian sea slopes . . the Cushion Bush forms a natural bed. **1984** E. WALLING *On Trail Austral. Wildflowers* 58 The silvery-grey Cushion-bush, a mass of tangled stems of small dull yellow knob-like flowers.

cut, *n.*

1. A part of a mob of sheep or cattle separated out for a purpose. See CUT OUT *v.* 1.

1874 *Illustr. Sydney News* 28 Mar. 7/4 Small cuts are brought into the woolshed yards and after the lambs are drafted out, the ewes are taken to the woolshed to be shorn. **1963** M. BRITT *Pardon my Boots* 80 My job was to 'hold the cut'—to hold the bullocks or cows which had been cut out of the mob.

2. a. A job as a shearer.

1895 *Worker* (Sydney) 28 Sept. 4/1 Now and then when doing a tramp, Trying to collar a cut. **1962** *Overland* xxiii. 4 The groups tended to merge, shouting indiscriminately for each other, arranging 'cuts' for the coming season.

b. A harvest, esp. of sugar cane; a job cutting (cane).

1934 T. WOOD *Cobbers* 191 To talk about shearing, and wool-presses, and cuts of lucerne. **1962** J. NAISH *Cruel Field* 54 'I've come to cut cane,' said Emery. 'I've got a cut, here in Cook's end with Ruf Craig.'

3. *pl.* A caning or strapping, esp. in the phr. **to get the cuts.**

1915 *Bulletin* (Sydney) 28 Oct. 47/1 'Six cuts yer give him,' roared the whiskers. . . The stick emphasized the last remark by a rapid descent on the meek one's shoulders. **1972** M. GILBERT *Personalities & Stories Early Orbost* 104 Getting 'the cuts' (strap or cane) was preferable to being put in the space under the gallery where the infants sat.

cut, *v.*

1. *trans.* To shear (a fleece, sheep, etc.).

1873 *Illustr. Sydney News* 27 Sept. 7/1 A man, who in one day, can cut eighty fleeces properly is a very good shearer. **1914** *Bulletin* (Sydney) 30 July 24/1 A couple of years back 250,000 fleeces were cut.

2. *trans.* To harvest (sugar cane). Also *absol.*

1936 J. DEVANNY *Sugar Heaven* 9 When a man's a cutter he naturally cuts. **1977** C. MCCULLOUGH *Thorn Birds* 254 How much I earn depends on how much sugar I cut, and if I'm good enough to cut with Arne's gang I'll be pulling in more than twenty quid a week.

Hence **cutting** *vbl. n.*

1957 *Bulletin* (Sydney) 13 Nov. 19/1 The cutting-rate fixed by the cane-inspector . . not being acceptable to the gang, the industrial magistrate was called in to arbitrate.

cut line. [f. *cut* cleared + LINE 1.] A cleared track through scrub country. Also **cut road.**

1927 J. MATHIEU *Backblock Ballads* 19 And the scurried 'possum wonders In his fork all terrified As the flinty cut line thunders Back the rhythm of his stride. [*Note*] Cut line—Cleared track. **1981** A. WILKINSON *Up Country* 7 This was the demanding, gate-strewn track called the 'cut road' from Tibooburra.

cut lunch. [f. *cut* sliced.]

1. A packed lunch, usu. of sandwiches. Also **cut tucker.**

1937 *Bulletin* (Sydney) 30 June 21/1 The 'keep' on my first ten-bob-a-week-and-keep effort was breakfast at five-thirty, followed by milking; three hours' paddock work to develop an appetite for a 'cut' lunch eaten on the job. **1949** H.C. JAMES *Gold is where you find It* 63 All he really expected was to find . . a few tiny nuggets. Enough to give him cut tucker and tools to go on slaving and searching.

2. Special Comb. **cut-lunch commando,** see quot. 1953.

1952 T.A.G. HUNGERFORD *Ridge & River* 123 Think I got nothin' to do but wait around for a bunch of cut-lunch commandos. **1953** S.J. BAKER *Aust. Speaks* 170 *Cut lunch commandos,* soldiers serving with a home base unit.

cut-out, *n.*

cut out

1. The end of a shearing contract or season; a stoppage during shearing (see quot. 1935).

1896 H. Lawson *While Billy Boils* 35 One Saturday morning, about a fortnight before cut-out, The Oracle came late to his stand. **1935** *Red Star* (Perth) 16 Aug. 3/2 On going to their huts the shearers were told that the overseer had declared a cut out, although there were already mustered and in the yards 7,000 to 8,000 sheep.

2. The eradication of a pest, etc., from a piece of land (see quot. 1978).

1908 *Bulletin* (Sydney) 14 Feb. 14/3 A joy in rabbit-infested country is 'cut-out' on a farm. Not 'cut-out' in a shearing sense but the cut-out of each and every cultivation paddock. **1978** A.E. Cosh *Jumping Kangaroos* 4 Wallabies were numerous, and sheltered in the mallee scrub. As the roller went around and around the piece of scrub, the wallabies were herded inwards; and, of course, there would be a day of reckoning when the scrub roller approached the centre. I was very young at the time, but I remember that my father invited neighbours from near and far to join him on the day of the 'cut-out'.

cut out, *v.*

1. *trans.* To separate (an animal or a number of animals) from a mob (usu. of cattle). See also Cutting out.

1844 H. McCrae *Georgiana's Jrnl.* 15 Feb. (1934) 110 Mr Jamieson was able to identify some of his own bullocks.. whereupon, he and Captain Reid, with much shouting and cracking of whips, proceeded to 'cut them out' from the mob. **1976** C.D. Mills *Hobble Chains & Greenhide* 143 A good camp-horse senses the bullock you mean to cut out the moment you sight him.

2. Shearing.

a. *trans.* To reach the end of (a contract, the shearing of the available sheep, etc.); to finish shearing in (a shed, etc.). Also *absol.*

1882 *Sydney Mail* 12 Aug. 246/3 Jim and I stopped at Boree shed till all the sheep were cut out. **1963** D. Niland *Dadda Jumped* 150 I'm a shearer. I come in today from Moombala. We cut-out there first run this morning.

b. *intr.* Of the contract, etc.: to come to an end. Also, of (the shearing at) a shed or station.

1899 *Western Champion* (Barcaldine) 18 July 14/2 During the following week Gobbera Downs 'cut out' and the hotel swarmed with shearers. **1936** *Bulletin* (Sydney) 30 Dec. 20/1 When they got a job they did it well; but when the job cut out they were the dickens of a bother to shift from the station.

3. *intr.* In various extended uses, to come to an end; to become expended or exhausted.

1882 *Sydney Mail* 15 July 86/2 You and George can take a turn at local-preaching when you're cut out. **1962** *Bulletin* (Sydney) 3 Feb. 44/2 The grog cut out. The last bottle emptied. Party over.

4. *trans.* To spend (money); chiefly in the phr. **to cut out a cheque,** to spend one's entire earnings on liquor. See Cheque.

[N.Z. **1906** *N.Z. Truth* (Wellington) 8 Dec. 1 A young man is reputed to have 'cut out' a cheque for £93 at Hastings.] **1913** *Bulletin* (Sydney) 24 Apr. 14/4 Happy.. cut out his cheque on the way to Casterton. **1984** J. Brown *Just for Rec.* 54 After the refund we had a fiver left over so.. we proceeded to cut it out over the bar.

Hence **cut-out** *ppl. a.,* **cutter out** *n.*

1876 *Austral. Town & Country Jrnl.* (Sydney) 30 Dec. 1062/1 The once small drove of '**cut out** cattle' looked important and respectable. **1873** A. Trollope *Aust. & N.Z.* I. 434, I went out one morning at four a.m. to see a lot drafted out of a herd for sale... The owner himself was the '**cutter out**'.

cut-tail. [See quot. 1899.] A tree of the genus *Eucalyptus,* esp. *brown barrel* (see Brown *a.* 1).

1889 *Proc. Linnean Soc. N.S.W.* IV. 612 *E. amygdalina,* var. (near *E. regnans*..) .. 'Cut-tail.' **1899** *Ibid.* XXIV. 548 This fine splitting was carried so far that (given a good tree) they would split a piece into such thin portions that one could bend them like the leaves of a book, which it roughly resembled, with the solid part at one end resembling the back of the book. Those pieces were called 'Cut-tail'... From the piece itself the name was transferred to the tree, and a splitter would point out to you that such and such a tree is a 'Cut-tail'.

cutter, $n.^1$ [f. Cut *v.* 2.]

1. Shortened form of *cane-cutter* (see Cane 2).

1875 *Illustr. Sydney News* 10 Feb. 3/1 The number of labourers is proportioned agreeably to the quantity of cane needed for the day's work. These are divided into three gangs; the first being termed 'Trashers', who with billhooks divest the canes of all their trash, the second is named 'cutters', who afterwards cut them down exactly level with the ground. **1977** C. McCullough *Thorn Birds* 254 The best gang of cutters in Queensland is a gang of Swedes.

2. The blade of a shearing machine.

1891 *Conference Amalgam. Shearers' Union & Pastoralists' Fed. Council* 8 In all sheds where shearing machines are provided, shearers shall pay for cutters and combs a price not exceeding cost. **1968** J. O'Grady *Gone Troppo* 183, I was shearin' outback, by a wayside track; Two sheep the cutter lasted; The Roustabout was a Pommie lout, An' the boss was a hungry bastard.

3. A timber-getter.

1949 J.W.S. Tomlin *Story of Bush Brotherhoods* 43 An encounter with a solitary 'cutter' (timber-getter). **1976** L.R.M. Hunter *Woodline* 1 Unlike the navvies, the cutters on the Woodline were generally a stable lot.

cutter, $n.^2$ *Obs.* [Of unknown origin.] In the phr. **to run the cutter,** to buy beer by the billy to drink elsewhere (see quot. 1904).

1904 *Bulletin* (Sydney) 12 May 17/1 At Mount Morgan they don't breast the bar. The average man 'runs the cutter'. One shilling and a billy are presented to the barmaid with the order for 'a "bob's" worth of beer, and may the Lord strengthen yer arm when yer get "old o' that pump"'. Usually there are seven or eight at the same game and pub., all with billies, and a stranger is cordially invited 'to dip his beak' as he faces them on the footpath. **1911** *Ibid.* 18 May 13/2, I can put 'Jonnel'.. on a fair track to the explanation of the origin of the saying 'running the cutter'. In most parts of Scotland a 'cutter' is the accepted name for a flat flask bottle used by the natives for carrying supplies of lime juice in those savage parts.

cutting grass. [See quot. 1831.] Any of several sedges having sharp-edged and sometimes serrated blades, esp. of the genus *Gahnia* (fam. Cyperaceae).

1831 W. Bland *Journey of Discovery Port Phillip* 61 They had the misfortune to encounter that species of long grass, which is known in the colony by the name of the 'cutting grass', this was betweeen four and five feet high, the blade of it an inch and a half broad, and the edges exquisitely sharp, and fine enough to inflict a severe wound. **1981** J. Jessop *Flora Central Aust.* 513 G[*ahnia*] *trifida*.. Cutting grass.

cutting out, *vbl. n.*

1. The process of separating an animal, or a number of animals, from a mob preparatory to branding, etc. Also *attrib.*

1848 H.W. Haygarth *Recoll. Bush Life* 61 The best exemplification of this faculty is the process of driving, or, as it is called, 'cutting out' a single bullock. **1930** M.M.J. Costello *Life J. Costello* 197 His dam had been a wonderful 'cutting out' mare in her day.

2. *Special Comb.* **cutting-out camp,** a camp established for the purpose of cutting out (animals); see

Camp n. 3; **horse,** a horse trained for this work; see also *camp horse,* Camp n. 6.

1897 *Bulletin* (Sydney) 11 Dec. 22/4 Andy Ferguson, you may go bail, Is yet boss on a **cutting-out camp. 1878** 'R. Boldrewood' *Ups & Downs* 13 No, tell him to get 'Mustang', he's the best **cutting-out horse.**

Cyclone. [The proprietary name of a range of metal and wire products.] Used *attrib.* in Comb. of (fencing) structures made with metal frames or supports and strong interlocking wire: **Cyclone dropper, fence, gate.**

1909 R. Kaleski *Austral. Settler's Compl. Guide* 94 Five No. 8 galvanised wires, posts 40 feet apart, four **cyclonedroppers** in between, rabbit-proof wire netting on the bottom. **1976** R. Prestidge *Cataclysm* 2 Then leaves a bewildered Morris, runs over to a **cyclone fence** and starts talking to a cop. **1912** *Bulletin* (Sydney) 8 Aug. 16/3 The first obstacle was a '**cyclone**' **gate.**

cypress pine. [See quot. 1904.] Any of several trees of the genus Callitris, belonging to the cypress fam. Cupressaceae; the wood of these trees, often termiteresistant; *native pine,* see Native *a.* 6 a., Pine 2; see also *colonial pine* Colonial *a.* 5. Formerly **cypress (tree).**

1820 J. Oxley *Jrnls. Two Exped. N.S.W.* 15 A few cypresses and camarinas [*sic*], scattered here and there. **1825** B. Field *Geogr. Mem. N.S.W.* 14 A little distant from the river, were several brushes or forests of the common Australian cypress-tree (Callitris Australis). **1904** J.H. Maiden *Notes on Commercial Timbers N.S.W.* 24 Under the general name of cypress pine we include a number of Australian trees which, though not true cypresses, more or less resemble those trees in general appearance.

D

daddy. [Used elsewhere but recorded earliest in Aust.] In the phr. **the** (or **a**) **daddy of (them all, the lot,** etc.), the most notable, the biggest.
1898 W.H. OGILVIE *Fair Girls* (1906) 80 Though shaky in the shoulders, he's the daddy of them all; He's the gamest bit of horseflesh from the Snowy to the Bree. **1901** M. FRANKLIN *My Brilliant Career* 194, I never felt such a daddy of a thirst on me before. **1961** I.L. IDRIESS *Tracks of Destiny* 80 Of the Territory pioneer women, perhaps the 'daddy' of the lot is Mrs Phoebe Farrar.

dag, $n.^1$ [Br. dial.: see OED *dag, sb.*^{1} 3 (in Br. usage more commonly *daglock*).]
1. Usu. in *pl.* A lump of matted wool and excreta hanging from about the tail of a sheep; such a lump cut from a sheep.
1891 *Truth* (Sydney) 12 Apr. 73 Smothered in sheep-dung, and pelting one another with 'dags'. **1985** J. HARRISON *Bit of Dag* 65 He got into bed that night and found a pile of dags right at the bottom where the cocky had left them.
2. *fig.*
1956 T. RONAN *Moleskin Midas* 142, I ain't letting one of our prominent local cattlemen, like my friend Mr Yates, be jockeyed out of his lawful due by any sheepman who ever ate fried dags for his supper. **1977** S. LOCKE ELLIOTT *Water under Bridge* 193 Now just frying dags in grim Rockwell Crescent.
3. In the phr. **to rattle (one's) dags,** to bestir oneself, to hurry.
[N.Z. **1968** G. SLATTER *Pagan Game* 161 I'm not over-struck on that new cop.—Told me to rattle my dags out of there.] **1980** S. THORNE *I've met some Bloody Wags* 96 Hurry up! Get down there 'n bleed him! Rattle your dags!
4. Special Comb. **dag-picker,** one employed in a shearing shed to recover wool from dags; hence **-pick** *v. intr.* and **-picking** *ppl. a.*; **-rattler,** a sheep.
1907 *Bulletin* (Sydney) 26 Sept. 13/2 In the woolsheds along the Murrumbidgee there once worked, as bale-brander, an illiterate fellow, who, on the wool-packs, made excellent caricatures of all the shed identities, from squatter to **dag-picker**. **1933** *Bulletin* (Sydney) 8 Feb. 21/1, I work and whistle on my own . . Dag-pickin' all day long. **1934** *Austral. Ring* IX. cvii. 4 When five quid a month was a dag-picker's pay, And the shearers demanded their dues. *Ibid.*, We've camped with the rats on the Warrego side, Fraternised with the drink-sodden wreck, The dag-picking Doctor who swallowed his pride, And the swanker who swallowed his cheque. **1977** A. THOMAS *Bull & Boabs* (1980) 107 Sheep were ground lice . . and **dag-rattlers**.

dag, $n.^2$ [Transf. use of Br. dial. (esp. children's speech) *dag* a 'dare', a challenge: see OEDS *sb.*^{5}]
1. A 'character', someone eccentric but entertainingly so; *hard case,* see HARD.
1875 R. THATCHER *Something to his Advantage* 2 These are 'Charley the Dag', 'Old Daddy', 'the Spring-heeled Immigrant'. **1980** S. THORNE *I've met some Bloody Wags* 44 After a while the novelty of grooming him wore off though, and to Jamie's dismay, they clipped him. Streuth, he looked a dag then!
2. A socially awkward adolescent: see quot. 1985.
1966 S.J. BAKER *Austral. Lang.* (ed. 2) 289 *Dag,* a person who is unenterprising, without courage. (Quite distinct from the old use of *dag* for a 'hard case' or 'character'). **1985** *Canberra Times* 8 June 21/1 The sublime agony of adolescence can be squirmingly funny, especially from the outside. The title 'Dags' sums it up so well: the state most of us feel we are in during those teenage years—awkward social cripples, unattractive and consumed by anxieties about appearance, sex and all the rest.

dag, *v.* [Br. dial.: see DAG $n.^1$ 1.]
1. *trans.* To remove dags from (a sheep).
1867 J.C. JORDAN *Managem. Sheep & Stations* 74 Before sheep-washing, every sheep will have to be 'dagged'. The wool about and below the anus will be covered with dung, dried into hard knobs, caused by the scouring which always follows the fresh green feed in spring. Dagging, therefore, means cutting away these filthy and unsightly encumbrances, as a preparatory step towards a thorough cleansing of the fleece. **1945** E. MITCHELL *Speak to Earth* 149 Many days were now spent with the sheep in the yards or holding-paddocks, dagging them.
2. See quot. 1965.
1965 G. MCINNES *Road to Gundagai* 260 Most of them were not yet 'dagged'. Dagging, which is the castration of baby rams with a dagging knife, was no pastime for the squeamish.
Hence **dagging** *vbl. n.*
1867 [see sense 1]. **1899** *S.A. Parl. Papers* II. no. 77 102 When our sheep require dagging we go down to the Port McLeay Mission Station and get as many blacks as we want. We do not make any agreement with them, but simply pay them so much a hundred for dagging purposes.

daggers, *pl. Shearing. Obs.* Handshears; see also BLADE 1.
1876 J.A. EDWARDS *Gilbert Gogger* 109, I don't think that calling . . a pair of shears, daggers . . [etc.] and a variety of other terms, with which you, my highly educated Australian native, garnish your conversation, is talking pure English. **1966** S.J. BAKER *Austral. Lang.* (ed. 2) There are still many old-timers who can remember such terms for handshears as *daggers*.

daggy, $a.^1$ [f. DAG $n.^1$ 1.] Of (the condition of) a sheep or fleece: fouled with dags.
1895 *Worker* (Sydney) 14 Sept. 4/2 There the sheep are hard and daggy, full of mulga sticks and sand. **1978** HANIGAN & LINDSAY *No Tracks on River* 60 Shearing lambs with daggy tails.

daggy, $a.^2$ [f. DAG $n.^2$, but poss. infl. also by $n.^1$ 1.]
1. Chiefly of clothing and personal appearance: unconventional; unkempt. Also *transf.* (see quot. 1982).
1967 *Kings Cross Whisper* (Sydney) xxxiv. 4/3 *Daggy,* to be dirty. Same as warby and scungy. **1982** *Access* Aug. 23/1 Because tolerance is encouraged throughout the school, unconformity isn't seen as 'daggy'.
2. Unfashionable; graceless.
1983 F. WILLMOTT *Breaking Up* 22 They get fat real young . . and wear daggy dresses and get their hair cut short. **1986** *Nat. Times* (Sydney) 3 Jan. 7/2, I like to write about daggy people who don't get on, mainly because I was a child like that. I never got a look-in.

dago, *n.* and *attrib.* [Orig. U.S., a corruption of *Diego* Sp. proper name, as applied to a Spaniard; now in general use as a derog. term for a foreigner: see OED(S.)]
A. *n.* An immigrant (usu. male) of Latin descent; an immigrant from Europe (exc. the British Isles).
1892 *Bulletin* (Sydney) 19 Nov. 19/1 I've got a down on Dagoes, and a Dutchman I detest; As for Chinkies and Eye-

talians and such like I gives 'em best. **1981** P. CORRIS *White Meat* 104 This dago wants to set it up all his way.

B. *attrib.*

1900 *Truth* (Sydney) 4 Feb. 3/3 A Dago organgrinder fell in with a section of larrikins of the Queen. **1979** J.J. MCROACH *Dozen Dopey Yarns* 101 The Australian farmer developed a deep-seated enmity against these dago-wop bastards who, by working their women, could succeed where a decent Aussie could not.

dairy station. *Obs.* A dairy farm.

1838 T. WALKER *Month in Bush Aust.* 10 We next came to an extensive country .. formerly a dairy station and cattle run. **1878** R.B. SMYTH *Aborigines of Vic.* II. 183 Tea-tree spring (Dairy station).

daisy bush. Any of many shrubs or small trees of the fam. Asteraceae, esp. of the genus *Olearia*, occurring in all States, N.Z., and New Guinea. Also **daisy tree**.

1835 *Hobart Town Almanack* 68 *Aster tomentosus*, daisy tree. A beautiful shrub with oblong toothed leaves, dusky brown underneath. It is highly ornamental and is covered with blossoms for three or four months in summer. **1978** R. ERICKSON et al. *Flowers & Plants W.A.* 195 Among the smaller shrubs Daisybushes, *Olearia*, are often prominent when in flower.

daisy cutter. [Used elsewhere but recorded earliest in Aust.] In Services' speech: see quot. 1947.

1923 F.E. TROTTER *Tales of Billzac* 20 One of those new wide-spreading shells, 'Daisy cutter'. **1947** O. GRIFFITHS *Darwin Drama* 104 The bombs dropped were mostly anti-personnel bombs which do not make a big crater but explode on impact and throw out fanwise, a spray of shrapnel which mows down everything in its way, and for this reason an anti-personnel bomb is known as a 'daisy cutter'.

dalgite /'dælgaɪt/. *W.A.* Also **dalgyte**, etc. [a. Nyungar *dalgaj.*] BILBY a.

1840 T.J. BUCKTON *W.A.* 96 Opossums, dalgerts, and other small animals. **1841** G. GREY *Jrnls. Two Exped. N.-W. & W.A.* II. 291 Some of the smaller animals, such as the *dal-gyte*, an animal about the size of a weasel, burrow in the earth. **1925** *Ibid.* 30 Apr. 24/4 Westralian cockies know the common rabbit-bandicoot by the name 'dalgite'.

dam. [Br. dial. *dam* the body of water confined by a dam or bank, as distinct from the holding barrier: see OED(S *sb.*[1] 2.]

1. An artificial pond or reservoir for the storage of water, usu. run-off rainwater; TANK *n.*[1] 1.

1843 *Sydney Morning Herald* 24 May 3/4 A large waterhole or dam is now being constructed, which will insure a supply of water during the driest seasons. **1986** *Sydney Morning Herald* 12 Apr. 1/4 Bill Morley .. travelled back and forth from his property carting the last water from the last wet dam within cooee.

2. Comb. **dam-digger; -maker; -making; -sinker; -sinking.**

1957 F. CLUNE *Fortune Hunters* 170 The Champion **Dam-digger** raises the dust to finish the job before the rains come. **1878** 'R. BOLDREWOOD' *Ups & Downs* 68 He kept the different parties of teamsters, fencers, splitters, carpenters, sawyers, **dam-makers**, well-sinkers, all in hand. **1897** R. NEWTON *Work & Wealth Qld.* 18 For the rest of the time there is a variety of bush work, fencing, yard-making, **dam-making**. **1893** D. LINDSAY *Jrnl. Elder Sci. Exploring Exped.* 126 Dr Elliot and Mr Wells were over at the **damsinkers'** camp. **1883** C. PROUD *Murray & Darling Trade* 7/2 During the whole of last year the expenditure on tanks, **dam-sinking**, wells, and similar improvements, was not less than £2,000 a month.

dama, damar, vart. TAMMAR.

damper. [Spec. use of Br. *damper* something which takes the edge off the appetite: see OED 1b and OED(S 6.]

1. A simple kind of bread, traditionally unleavened and baked in the ashes of an outdoor fire. Also **damper bread**.

1825 B. FIELD *Geogr. Mem. N.S.W.* 371 We had provided ourselves with but little salt meat; flour for the purpose of making what are termed *dampers* (*i.e.* a flat cake, being merely a mixture of flour and water, baked in wood ashes) forming our chief stock. **1838** T.H. JAMES *Six Months S.A.* 145 There was nothing .. that the blacks could be induced to eat; neither the damper bread nor biscuit.

2. *fig.* Also *attrib.*

1852 J. BONWICK *Notes of Gold Digger* 24 A stray kangaroo .. was soon converted into some exquisite soup for mutton and damper diggers. **1978** TEECE & PIKE *Voice of Wilderness* 42 Asked the time, they would squint at the sun and say, 'She's a damper high', meaning that it was yet forty-five minutes or an hour to sundown. That was the time it took to cook a damper.

3. Comb. **damper-maker, -making.**

1959 *Bulletin* (Sydney) 22 July 18/1 A champion **damper-maker** (ashes-style) along the Dawson River (C.Q.) .. refuses to divulge his recipe. **1862** A. POLEHAMPTON *Kangaroo Land* 76, I became initiated into the mysteries of **damper-making**.

dampiera /dæmpɪ'ɛərə/. [The plant genus *Dampiera* was named by British botanist Robert Brown (*Prodr. Fl. Nov. Holl.* (1810) 587) after the explorer William *Dampier* (1652-1715), who collected the plant in the late 17th century.] Any plant of the Austral. genus of creepers, herbs, and shrubs *Dampiera* (fam. Goodeniaceae) of all States but most numerous in W.A. The flowers of most species are blue.

1844 L. LEICHHARDT *Jrnl. Overland Exped. Aust.* 22 Oct. (1847) 19 On the banks of Hodgson's Creek, grows a species of Dampiera, with many blue flowers, which deserves the name of 'D. floribunda'. **1985** *Age Weekender* (Melbourne) 31 May 7/4 With more than 70 species occurring throughout Australia, numerous Dampieras are becoming .. available for cultivation.

dandy. Chiefly *S.A.* An ice-cream container, now usu. small. See also BUCKET *n.* 1, DIXIE.

1954 *Australasian Confectioner* Sept. 80 Dandies, Dixies or Cartons—Large, 8½d. (Adelaide) 9d. (country); Small, 4½d., 5d. **1955** *S. Austral. Shopkeeper* Apr. 17 *It pays to sell the public's favourite—Amscol Ice-Cream* in Cones, Bricks, Dandies, Dairy-chock, Slice Creams and Fro-Joy Twins.

darg. [Br. dial. (esp. Scot. and northern) *darg* a day's work, a defined quantity or amount of work.] An allotted or fixed amount of work.

1927 F.C. BIGGERS *Bat-Eye* 30 Fillin' our dag we was— wot ain't no play. **1978** *Westerly* iii. 16 It makes me glad I'm a journeyman of literature with my daily darg.

dark, *a.* and *n.*[1]

A. *adj.* As used of Aborigines: a euphemism for BLACK *a.*[1] See DARKSKIN.

1838 T.H. JAMES *Six Months S.A.* 232 Our dark friends were signalizing to their neighbours; shortly afterwards we heard a low 'cooee' from the opposite side of the river; I wished the black boy to answer it. **1984** P. READ *Down there with me on Cowra Mission* 20 He was too strict and too rough with the dark people on the Mission.

B. *n.* An Aboriginal.

1950 *Dark People in Melbourne* (Victorian Council Social Service) 25 Although they would prefer to marry darks, a good number of the dark boys .. cannot provide the amenities which association with whites leads the girls to expect.

dark, *n.*² *Obs.*
  1. See quot. 1873.
  1859 W. KELLY *Life in Vic.* I. 166 Fill us a nobbler—dark; what's yours, mate? **1873** W. THOMSON-GREGG *Desperate Character* I. 39 His companion exclaimed .. 'Two dark, my dear'... The liquor was brandy—colonial brandy—of the darkest hue and most excruciating strength.
  2. In the collocation **fourpenny dark,** cheap wine.
  1955 N. PULLIAM *I traveled Lonely Land* 204 It's too cold for streetcorners and just right for .. a gallon of fourpenny dark with a mate. **1980** HEPWORTH & HINDLE *Boozing out in Melbourne Pubs* 16 The legendary drink of the twenties and thirties was the Fourpenny Dark. This was a stoup of nourishing bombo which, in the great days, was served in a mug with a handle on it.

dark cell. *Hist.* See quot. 1831.
  1831 *Rep. Select Committee Secondary Punishments* (Great Brit. Parl.) 5 There are two modes of solitary confinement; one is in the dark cells, where light is totally excluded, and bread and water is the diet. **1932** W. RADCLIFFE *Port Arthur Guide* 9 Some of the convicts housed in this prison were of the very worst type; many had committed brutal offences, for which they were confined in a special cell called the 'Dark' or 'Dumb' cell. While in there the prisoner could not hear a sound or see any light whatever until he was released.

darkie, *n.*¹ Also **darkey.** [Perh. infl. by U.S. *darky* a Black: see Mathews.] An Aboriginal. Also *attrib.*
  1845 *Parramatta Chron.* 12 Apr. 4/1 Information reaching the settlement, the Military and Police were started in pursuit, but before arriving at the scene of action the Darkies had made themselves scarce. **1854** G.H. HAYDON *Austral. Emigrant* 106 The black protectors had taught the Darkeys to read. **1975** R. HALL *Place among People* 219 If its the darkie woman who comes out first, we grab her.

darkie, *n.*² LUDERICK.
  1895 C. THACKERAY *Amateur Fisherman's Guide* 10 Your noble 'darkie' is a fine fighter, and has more pull to the square inch of his surface than a jewfish or cod has to the square foot. **1978** D. VAWR *Ratbag Mind* 15 Vast breeding grounds for mullet, garfish and luderick ('niggers' or 'darkies' to Sydneysiders).

darkie, *n.*³ See quot. and also DARKUN.
  1982 LOWENSTEIN & HILLS *Under Hook* 17 We was a darkie, a midnight shift.

darkskin. *Obs.* An Aboriginal.
  1845 *Sydney Morning Herald* 8 Apr. 2/7 We have had another affair with the blacks, close to the township... Lieutenant Cooper .. immediately despatched a sergeant and a file of men from his detachment to the scene of the outrage, but before they could reach the spot the darkskins were off. **1911** A. SEARCY *By Flood & Field* 27 Lagoons surrounded by patches devoid of timber, but covered with long grass, which would have made the travelling very trying for anyone but a darkskin.

darkun. [Altered form of *dark one.*] A shift lasting twenty-four hours, worked by a wharf labourer.
  1957 T. NELSON *Hungry Mile* 81 Some 25 years back a gang of us refused an order of the Union Co. to come back after the breakfast break for four hours, after doing a 'darkun' (24 hour shift). **1977** *Sunday Tel.* (Sydney) 6 Mar. 7/2 For 12 years as foreman I worked a weekly 'darkun'—a 24-hour shift. These shifts were inhuman.

darl. Abbrev. of 'darling', chiefly as a mode of address.
  1930 K.S. PRICHARD *Haxby's Circus* 329 'Oh, darl. don't you bother,' he begged. **1984** *Truckin' Life* VII. iv. 91/3 Newcastle to Gosford is only a short run darl.

Darling. [The name of a river in w. N.S.W.] Used *attrib.* in Special Comb. **Darling lily,** the perennial plant of N.S.W., Qld., N.T., S.A., and Vic. *Crinum flaccidum* (fam. Liliaceae), bearing large creamy or white scented flowers; *Murray lily,* see MURRAY 2; **pea, (a)** any of a small number of species of the genus *Swainsona* (fam. Fabaceae), most being perennial herbs of inland Aust., some of which can cause stock-poisoning; see also SWAINSONA; **(b)** such poisoning, usu. affecting sheep, and characterized by stiffness of limbs, incoordination and muscle tremor; also *fig.,* see quot. 1894 (see also PEA *n.*¹); **shower,** a dust storm; **whaler,** see WHALER *n.*¹ b.
  1859 J.D. MEREWEATHER *Diary Working Clergyman* 199 Put into my valise two bulbs of the beautiful **Darling lily. (a)** **1863** W.J. WILLS *Successful Exploration Interior Aust.* 128 A disputed question .. as to the effect of the **Darling pea** on horses, some asserting that they become cranky simply from eating that herb. **(b) 1889** T. QUIN *Well Sinkers* 101 'The man's mad!'.. 'No .. he's got a touch of what we call the **Darling Pea.**' **1894** M. ROBERTS *Red Earth* 246 When you say a man has 'got the Darling pea' you mean that loneliness and desolation—the heat of the sun, and the cursed sameness of the sunburnt plains; the lack of human society; the lack of all the natural outlets of humanity—have made him less than human, that he is mad. **1887** *Observer* (Adelaide) 8 Jan. 43/2 The wind at Birdsville is a caution, quite reminding one of the '**Darling Showers**' of old.

dart. *Obs.* [Fig. use of *dart* repr. U.S. or Br. dial. pron. of *dirt* pay dirt: see quot. 1859 and also *old dart* OLD *a.* 1.] A scheme or dodge; a favoured location, object, or course of action.
  1859 W. KELLY *Life in Vic.* I. 218 The digger will not only work to the boundary of his own claim, but into his neighbour's territory, if word comes down from above that the 'dart' is payable. [*Note*] Dart is the designation of stuff worth washing, as contradistinguished from that considered useless. **1918** L.J. VILLIERS *Changing Yr.* 12 She didn't kid yet long—er bloomin' dart Ud git yer goin' till yer 'ad a rat.

Darwin. [The name of the capital city of the Northern Territory.] Used *attrib.* in Special Comb. **Darwin blonde,** see quot. 1947; **rig,** male attire required by etiquette on semi-formal occasions in Darwin (see quot. 1967); **stubby,** a beer bottle having a capacity of 2.25 litres (see STUBBY 1).
  1947 O. GRIFFITHS *Darwin Drama* 34 At Bagot Compound for Aborigines a big proportion of the inmates were half-caste girls, referred to as '**Darwin blondes**' many of whom were not unattractive. **1964** *N. Austral. Monthly* Sept. 23 Mr Nott will perhaps be best remembered for his insistence on the '**Darwin rig**' for formal affairs here. **1964** K. WILLEY *Eaters of Lotus* 12 Almost his first act as Administrator was to do away with such nonsense as cummerbands and monkey jackets. He decreed 'coats off' at Government House functions. 'Darwin rig' was to be official wear in future. **1967** *Darwin, Way of Life* (N.T. Admin.) 3 For semi-formal wear, including some receptions at Government house, men adopt what has become famous as 'Darwin Rig' .. long-sleeved white shirt, tie, long trousers, and dark shoes, but no coat. **1972** J. O'GRADY *It's your Shout, Mate!* 87 'Try a **Darwin stubby** while you're there. See if you can drink it down in one go.' 'That should not be too difficult,' I said. 'You reckon? They're not the same as our stubbies. A Darwin stubby holds forty ounces.'

Darwinian. An inhabitant of Darwin.
  1928 M.E. FULLERTON *Austral. Bush* 96 At Port Darwin .. the Darwinians. **1968** K. DENTON *Walk around my Cluttered*

Mind 171 Darwinians considered the rest of the country to be full of prissy English.

dash. [Spec. use of *dash* capacity for prompt and vigorous action: see OED *sb.*¹ 9.] In the phr. **to have done (one's) dash,** to have exhausted (one's) energies, to have had (one's) chance.

1910 L. ESSON *Woman Tamer* (1976) 82 'So you want to give me the chuck—me for—Bongo Williams. . .' 'Yes, you've done your dash, Chopsey.' **1973** C. EAGLE *Who could love Nightingale?* 272 'Keep going,' she said. 'Keep going.' 'I've done my dash, Marg, in every sense of the words.'

dasyure /'dæzijʊə/. [a. mod. L. *Dasyurus* f. Gr. δασύς hairy + οὐρά, tail, the name of the genus.] Any of several carnivorous marsupials, now usu. those of the genus *Dasyurus* (see *native cat* NATIVE *a.* 6 b.) of Aust. and New Guinea.

1839 *Proc. Zool. Soc. London* 134 In the Thylacine and Ursine Dasyure . . the condyle of the lower jaw is placed low down. **1935** D.G. STEAD *Rabbit in Aust.* 17 A wall of forest . . containing carnivorous animals like the Dasyures or Native Cats.

date. [Cf. BLOT.] The anus; the vagina.

1961 M. CALTHORPE *Dyehouse* 214 In your bloody date! What do you think we are? **1973** R. EDWARDS *Austral. Bawdy Ballads* 26 His doodle broke off and stayed in her date.

Hence **date** *v. trans.*, to 'goose' (a person).

1972 D. HEWETT *Bon-Bons & Roses* (1976) 52 Remember when I got that plumber in to unblock the sink? I was up on a chair fixing the new curtains and he comes up behind, and dates me. Large as life. Without a word of a lie. He dates me. Cheeky mug. And what did he say? 'Thought you might like *your* plumbing interfered with too, Madam.'

dead, *a.* In special collocations.

1. In the sense of 'without life': **dead heart,** the arid interior of Australia; **house,** see quot. 1855; **marine** [see OED *marine, adj.* 4 b. and *sb.* 4 d.], an empty (beer) bottle; **meat ticket,** an identity disc; **men's graves** *pl.*, mounds in heavy clay soils, often separated by depressions; a form of GILGAI; **wood fence** *Tas.*, see quot. 1852; **wool,** wool taken from a dead sheep.

1906 J.W. GREGORY (title) The **dead heart** of Australia. **1855** P. SAUNDERS *Two Yrs. Vic.* (1863) 126 In the interior and at the diggings . . almost every public house has a room very appropriately called the **dead house.** This room generally has but one window high up in the wall. . . All those who get mad drunk, or insensibly drunk, are deposited in the dead house where they are locked up until the morning. **1864** *Drinkamania* 5 Or sail the ever restless deep, On snow crest wave is seen, Now and again to slyly peep, Its head—a '**Dead Marine**'! [N.Z. **1917** MILLER *Camps, Tracks & Trenches* (1939) 15 **Dead Meat Tickets** (identity discs).] **1920** T. CARLYON *Sons of Southern Cross,* Every second Australian had pawned his 'dead-meat ticket'. **1833** J. BACKHOUSE *Narr. Visit Austral. Colonies* 4 May (1843) 147 The soil is strong, and stands in remarkable ridges, called in this country, '**Dead-mens-graves**'. **1844** *Tas. Non-State Rec.* 103/2, The **dead wood fence** might reach considerably further up the hill. **1852** G.C. MUNDY *Our Antipodes* III. 180 The 'deadwood' fence is one almost peculiar to Van Diemen's land. It is nothing more than the trees of the clearing piled into a sort of wooden wall. **1899** *Bulletin* (Sydney) 16 Sept. 15/2 A sheep, killed lately . . was found with its paunch stuffed with wool. The poor beast had apparently nibbled '**dead**' **wool** in order to ease its hunger.

2. In the sense of 'absolute, complete, unrelieved': **dead beat,** one who is down in luck (not necessarily in the orig. U.S. sense of *loafer*); **bird** *horse-racing,* a certainty; also *fig.*; **frost** *obs.*, a total failure; **knowledge** *obs.* [Br. dial. (see EDD)], deceitfulness, cunning; **nark,** a spoil-sport.

1892 *Truth* (Sydney) 8 May 7/1 Misery and wretchedness were never better exemplified than in the case of those class of unfortunates known as '**dead-beats**'. **1889** A.G. TAYLOR *Marble Man* 18 At night he will be robbing the poorbox to back a '**dead-bird**' at the Carrington. **1906** *Gadfly* (Adelaide) 28 Feb. 17/1 Partridge didn't prove a 'dead bird' . . in the race for Nora Kerin's hand and heart. **1884** *Austral. Tit-Bits* (Melbourne) 3 July 13/1 We have known many Sydney successes a **dead frost** in Melbourne. **1905** *Shearer* (Sydney) 15 July 3/1, I remember once meeting an old swaggie—a genuine '**dead knowledge** man'—on the Darling. **1906** E. DYSON *Fact'ry 'Ands* 27 Up to yeh, too, fer a **dead nark.**

dead finish.

1. The shrub or small tree of the drier parts of W.A., S.A., Qld., N.T., and N.S.W. *Acacia tetragonophylla* (fam. Mimosaceae) which can form tangled prickly thickets; any of several other shrubs or trees of similar habit.

1880 *Proc. Linnean Soc. N.S.W.* V. 10 From the flowers of one, A[*cacia*] *farnesiana* . . called 'Dead-finish' on the Darling Downs, a delicious perfume is distilled. **1981** M. SHARLAND *Tracks of Morning* 71 'Dead-finish' is a native pidgin term for certain plants which have adapted themselves to the blasting heat of summer in Australian deserts where, also, they become skeletonised by hungry cattle and camels. One kind particularly—an ugly, thornarmored acacia—seems always to be hovering between survival and extinction.

2. *transf.* The limit, the end.

1881 A.C. GRANT *Bush-Life Qld.* I. 201 'He's the dead finish—go right through a man,' rejoins Sam, rather sulkily. **1980** ANSELL & PERCY *To fight Wild* 110 If some do-gooder had come along and shoved the poor old buggers in a nice clean home, that would have been the dead finish of them.

dead-set, *a.* and *adv.*

A. *adj.* Genuine; absolute.

1965 F. HARDY *Yarns of Billy Borker* 119 I'm a real crusader against acid stomach, got a dead-set cure for it: Quick-Eze. **1979** CAREY & LETTE *Puberty Blues* 10 'Here comes Darren.' 'What a deadset doll.'

B. *adv.* Truly; really.

1979 CAREY & LETTE *Puberty Blues* 9 Have me lunch. Deadset, I'm not hungry, I just had a curried chop in Home Science. **1984** *Sunday Tel.* (Sydney) 15 Apr. 60/4 Whenever I get the chance to watch Parramatta I'll go and see them just to watch Grothe. Dead set I'm in love with him.

dead-un. A loser, esp. a racehorse which is deliberately restrained from winning.

1896 N. GOULD *Town & Bush* 225 He has a remarkable way of scenting a 'dead un', or of finding out a non-starter. **1982** *Nat. Times* (Sydney) 1 Aug. 14/4 'You hear a lot about dead 'uns *after* the race', said Beirne, 'but 99 per cent of it is sour grapes.'

deaf adder. DEATH ADDER 1.

1827 P. CUNNINGHAM *Two Yrs. in N.S.W.* I. 338 Our *deaf adder* resembles, in its short, puffy, repulsive appearance, the blow-adder of America. **1930** HIVES & LUMLEY *Jrnl. of Jackaroo* 113 The deadly 'deaf' or 'death' adder . . is so venomous that its bite is usually fatal in as short a time as half an hour.

deal, *v. Obs.*

1. In the phr. **to deal it out** (to someone), to attack, esp. verbally.

1901 *Truth* (Sydney) 10 Mar. 4/7 Mr Norton began by dealing it out to E.H. Stobo. **1926** *Illustr. Tasmanian Mail* (Hobart) 17 Nov. 6/3 It is certainly very inconsiderate of the pushes not to give the police fair warning when they are going to 'deal it out'.

2. In the phr. **to deal out stoush,** to assault violently: see STOUSH n. 1.

1900 *Truth* (Sydney) 27 May 5/3 The undesirable denizens of such places as Woolloomooloo or 'the Rocks'.. delight in *dealing out stoush* for their own special delectation. **1973** J. MURRAY *Larrikins* 84 To 'bondi' someone, especially a policeman, became a very transitive verb, with boots, bottles and all, as the push were 'dealing out stoush'.

deaner, var. DEENER.

death. *Shearing. Obs.* In the phr. **to wait for a death,** see quot. 1965.

1898 *Bulletin* (Sydney) 17 Dec. 15/1 Hanging round a shed until someone is sacked—*waiting for a death.* **1965** J.S. GUNN *Terminol. Shearing Industry* ii. 25 The old custom of unemployed shearers waiting round a shed in case someone is sacked was called 'waiting for a death'.

death adder.
1. Any of the three species of venomous snake of the genus *Acanthophis* of Aust., New Guinea, and nearby islands, esp. *A. antarcticus* of s. and e. mainland Aust.; DEAF ADDER.

1833 W.H. BRETON *Excursions* 264 The death, or deaf adder is an ugly creature. **1973** V. SERVENTY *Desert Walkabout* 24 The death adder .. has a thorn-like tail which is twisted and turned in an enticing fashion.

2. *fig.* See quots. 1962 and 1963. Also *attrib.*

1951 E. HILL *Territory* 3 The bagmen of today, the 'old death-adders Major Mitchelling around' were the young men of yesterday. **1962** MARSHALL & DRYSDALE *Journey among Men* 56 These solitary men are usually known as *hatters.* Some of them go under the name of death adder men, for it is reckoned they will bite your head off if spoken to before noon. **1963** X. HERBERT *Larger than Life* 21 Lone prospectors, for all their propensity for living in solitude, are not usually of the retiring type, as witness the lavish good fellowship they invariably show when they make a strike, and that truculent misanthropy of their disappointed age which earns them such names as 'mad-hatter', 'death-adder', 'scrub bull'.

death bone. BONE *n.* 1.

1899 *Proc. Linnean Soc. N.S.W.* XXIV. 330, I discovered the curious bone ornament or implement now to be described. It is made from the fibula of a kangaroo, is 9¾ inches in length, well polished.. Three uses have been suggested for it, viz., netting needle, 'death bone' or 'pointer', and 'nose bone'. **1962** V.C. HALL *Dreamtime Justice* 144 The death-bone might be pointed, and the necessary words sung.

death seat. In a trotting race: the position on the outside of the leader from which overtaking is difficult.

1982 *Weekend Austral.* (Sydney) 7 Aug. 44/8 Prince Jade sat behind a different leader (Rhonda's Al), with Local Honored in the 'death seat'—from where he faded while Prince Jade got a miracle rails run in the final stages to win. **1984** *Sunday Independent* (Perth) 17 June 89/5 He was the first pacer to break 2 min. on a country track in Australia... I sat in the death seat with him and we cruised home.

debil debil. *Austral. pidgin.* Also **debbil debbil, debble debble, dibble dibble.**
1. DEVIL DEVIL 1.

1834 G. BENNETT *Wanderings N.S.W.* I. 210 The following is a definition of a clergyman as once given by one of the aborigines: 'He, white feller, belonging to Sunday, get up top o' waddy, pile long corroberaa all about debbil debbil, and wear shirt over trowsel.' **1838** *Austral. Mag.* (Sydney) 78 The *debil-debil*, they say, will not leap over the bark, and cannot walk under it! **1852** F. LANCELOTT *Aust. as it Is* I. 28 They believe in the existence of an evil spirit, which they call 'Dibble-dibble', and propitiate by offerings. **1883** E.M. CURR *Recoll. Squatting Vic.* 275 This spirit the whites have taught the Blacks to call *debble-debble* (the devil).

2. GILGAI a. Also *attrib.*, esp. as **debil debil country.**

1882 A.J. BOYD *Old Colonies* 189 There only remained six miles more of level country, with a little tract of 'debbil-debbil', and we should stretch our weary limbs in Cardwell. **1913** *Bull. N.T.* vii. 13 Next day we bumped on unceasingly, crossing what is commonly known as 'debill-debill' country, where the earth in dry seasons is hard and seared with cracks .. and covered with a growth of coarse cane-grass.

deciduous beech: see BEECH.

deckie. [f. deck(-hand + -Y.] A deck-hand.

1966 P. PINNEY *Restless Men* 21 There's a few other deckies will be laid off. It'll be harder to find another boat right now. **1984** *Canberra Chron.* 23 May 27/2 His deckie was his son Matthew John, who is only six years old.

deener. *Obs.* Also **deaner, deenar.** [Br. slang *deaner* shilling (prob. ult. identical with L. *denarius*, F. *denier* a coin of low denomination), formerly esp. freq. in Aust. and N.Z.: see OEDS.] A shilling.

1882 *Sydney Slang Dict.* 10 A bludger and his mot 'ticed a cully into the 'Deadhouse', and .. buzzed him for three caser and a deaner. **1949** D. WALKER *We went to Aust.* 194 'Deenar' for a shilling must have come straight from the Yugoslav dinar. **1983** *Canberra Times* 18 Oct. 20/3 The deener went to the NSW Aborigines Protection Board, presumably as a finder's fee; the zac as often as not stayed in the thrifty housewife's purse.

deep, *a.* In special collocations: **deep lead,** an alluvial deposit of gold in the (now subterranean) bed of an ancient river (see quot. 1888 and LEAD *n.*[1]); **leader,** one who mines a deep lead; **noser,** a long glass of beer; **sinker, (a)** *obs., deep leader;* **(b)** a long glass of beer; **sinking** *vbl. n.*, the mining of deep leads.

1858 *Colonial Mining Jrnl.* Sept. 9/1 The **deep leads** on Ballaarat. **1888** *Illustr. Austral. News* (Melbourne) 1 Aug. 16/3 'Alluvial' gold mining includes .. 'deep lead' mining, where the concealed auriferous gravel deposits of ancient river beds are reached by sinking costly shafts. **1898** *Bulletin* (Sydney) 16 July 15/2 Outside Ballarat .. was an old whim-horse, pensioned by some lucky **deep leader**. **1945** A.W. UPFIELD *Death of Swagman* 9 At the only hotel he drank a couple of **deep-nosers** with the licensee. **(a) 1858** *Colonial Mining Jrnl.* Oct. 23/2 There were plenty of men whose faces would be familiar to the **deep-sinkers** at Ballaarat. **(b) 1877** *Pilgrim* (Sydney) 1st Ser. vi. 64 These misguided mortals spend in '**deep sinkers**' .. that money which their landladies are daily sighing for—and sighing for in vain. **1853** *Austral. Gold Digger's Monthly Mag.* iv. 155 There was not much gravel nor **deep sinking**.

Deep North. Applied to Queensland, by analogy with U.S. *Deep South* and with reference to a supposedly similar conservatism.

1972 *Bulletin* (Sydney) 26 Aug. 46/3 Perhaps the author thinks that with our 'Deep North' of Queensland, there is little hope for a crocodilian future. **1985** *Ibid.* 30 July 58/1 In the Deep North it is well-known that a bloodthirsty socialist and, more than likely, a communist tries to hide behind every peanut and pumpkin scone.

de facto. [Spec. use of the L. phr. *de facto* in fact (as opposed to *de jure* by law); in Br. use *adj.* or *adv.*] A common-law spouse.

1952 *Bulletin* (Sydney) 22 Oct. 12/4 The help, plump, 40 and *de facto* to Albert, with whom she had spent 17 far-from-peaceful years after leaving her husband. **1986** *Income Tax Return Form S* (Austral. Taxation Office), Your spouse's or de facto spouse's name? .. Date you were married or started living together as de factos?

delver. [Spec. use of (prob. U.S.) *delver* one who digs.] See quot. 1972.
1919 *Pastoral Rev.* 16 Aug. 759 This delver is being used extensively throughout Queensland and N.S.W. .. for cutting Couchgrass and Bulrushes out of bore drains. **1972** R. MAGOFFIN *Chops & Gravy* 106 A delver is a boat-type apparatus hauled along the boredrain (formerly by horses, now by tractor) to remove weeds, rubbish and slush.
Hence **delving** *ppl. a.*
1972 R. MAGOFFIN *Chops & Gravy* 106 *Delving*, the process of cleaning or dredging a boredrain.

demo. [f. *dem(onstration* + -O. Used elsewhere but recorded earliest in Aust.: see OEDS.] A demonstration; a public display of interest in a cause, usu. a procession or mass-meeting. Also *attrib.*
1904 *Truth* (Sydney) 11 Sept. 7/2 *A dig at demos.* On a charge of distributing certain handbills advertising a 'Monster Democratic Demonstration'. **1986** *Canberra Times* 21 Feb. 3/4 (*heading*) Police condemn policy shift on demo arrests.

democrat. A deep crimson variety of apple, grown chiefly in Tas.
1931 *Tasmanian Jrnl. Agric.* 1 Nov. 173 Amongst all the apples which have ben raised in Tasmania, Tasma, or Democrat, is the most popular throughout Australia. The variety originated as a chance seedling some 25 to 30 years ago at an orchard belonging to Mr J. Duffy, of Glenlusk, in the Glenorchy district. The apple was first known as 'Duffy's Seedling', and later as Democrat but when it was recognised that another variety was in existence under this name, it was subsequently renamed Tasma. **1978** A.F. SIMMONS *Man. Fruit* 30 Democrat .. Discovered about 1900. To avoid confusion with an American variety called Democrat, the name in New Zealand has now been changed to Tasma.

demon. [Spec. use of *demon*, as applied to 'one who seems more than human in the rapidity, destructiveness, etc. of his play or performance, as a *demon bowler*': see OED 3.] A police officer, esp. a detective.
1889 BARRÈRE & LELAND *Dict. Slang* I. 304 *Demons* (Australian), prison slang for police. **1978** H.C. BAKER *I was Listening* 19 You're clear away with the dough before the demons can get near.

depasturing licence. *Hist.* See quot. 1841.
1841 *Rep. Select Committee S.A.* p. xv, It is a practice long established in New South Wales and Van Diemen's Land, and which will, no doubt, be equally followed in South Australia, for the owners of cattle and sheep to occupy large tracts of land under what are called Depasturing Licences, by which they are entitled, in consideration of a very moderate annual payment, to graze their flocks and herds over Land of which the ownership still remains with the Crown. **1851** H. MELVILLE *Present State Aust.* 24 Squatters pay rentals of £10 per annum for depasturing licences, which comprehend a sufficient track of land whereon four thousand sheep may run, or an equivalent number of cattle or horses.

derro. Also **dero.** [f. *der(elict* + -O.] A vagrant, esp. one dependent upon alcohol.
1971 *Southerly* ii. 136 'Just a derro on the meth,' the old men said, the old men on the shop-steps and windows. **1986** H. GARNER *Postcards from Surfers* 67 Bloody Barney, he tells me, Don't you dare bring those hooers of yours back here, you old dero.

derry. [Prob. shortened form of *derry down*, used joc. for DOWN *n.* 2; perh. infl. by Br. dial. *derry* noise, disorder: see EDD and OED *deray*.] In the phr. **to have a derry on**, to have a prejudice against.
1883 *Bulletin* (Sydney) 19 May 7/4 A few years ago some well-to-do young settlers got 17 years each, in West Australia, for shooting, among certain wild cattle, an antiquated working bullock which had strayed amongst the mob. The owner had a 'derry' on them, and the relics of a barbarous law did the rest. **1968** S. GORE *Holy Smoke* 46 The Chaldeans .. had a derry on the Christians anyhow, for mucking up all their forecasts, like Daniel did.

Derwenter. *Hist.* [f. *Derwent* the name of a river in Tas., on the banks of which stood a penal settlement.] An ex-convict from Tasmania.
1827 *Monitor* (Sydney) 16 Mar. 349/2 The Derwent-ers were as scantily provided with Spirituous Liquors as ourselves, previous to the late arrivals. **1918** C. FETHERSTONHAUGH *After Many Days* 384 A chap .. used to come over from the valley to duff Andrew's cattle; he had been an old Derwenter.

Derwent jackass. *Tas.* Grey butcherbird, see GREY *a.* Also **Derwent jack.**
1898 G. DUNDERDALE *Bk. of Bush* 140 Even the Derwent Jackass, the hypocrite with the shining black coat and piercing whistle, joins in the public outcry. **1945** A. RUSSELL *Bush Ways* 120 The Derwent Jack, or grey butcher-bird .. cunning, knavish, joyous and melodious.

desert. Used *attrib.* in Special Comb. **desert gum**, any of several trees of the genus *Eucalyptus* (fam. Myrtaceae), occurring in drier Aust., esp. *E. eudesmioides* of w. W.A., *E. gonglyocarpa* of w. central Aust., and GHOST GUM; **kurrajong**, see KURRAJONG 2; **oak**, any of several trees of drier Aust., esp. *Acacia coriacea* (fam. Mimosaceae) of W.A., N.T., Qld., N.S.W., and S.A., and *Allocasuarina decaisneana* (fam. Casuarinaceae) of W.A., S.A., and N.T.; the timber of these trees; **pea, rose,** *Sturt's desert pea, rose*, see STURT; **sandstone**, see quot. 1872.
1893 D. LINDSAY *Jrnl. Elder Sci. Exploring Exped.* 7 The fine growth of *Eucalyptus eudesmioides* (**desert gum**). **1915** *Bull. N.T.* xiv. 7 A small quartzite ridge was crossed with .. desert gum. **1898** D.W. CARNEGIE *Spinifex & Sand* 254 We saw the first **desert oak**, standing solitary sentinel on the crest of a ridge. **1920** *Smith's Weekly* (Sydney) 28 Aug. 9/4 Desert oak (Casuarina decaisneana) .. has water in both its stem and roots. **1864** *Illustr. Sydney News* Sept. 4/3 The plant is the **desert pea** of Sturt and abounds in the interior of the Australian continent. **1952** A.M. DUNCAN-KEMP *Where Strange Paths go Down* 90 The purple, yellow-eyed blossoms of the **Desert rose**, which grew in scattered masses throughout the plains country. **1872** *Jrnl. & Proc. R. Soc. N.S.W.* (1903) XXXVII. 147 Horizontal beds of coarse grit and conglomerate. .. I have called this upper conglomerate series '**Desert Sandstone**', from the sandy barren character of its disintegrated soil, which makes the term particularly applicable.

detached, *ppl. a. Hist.* Of a convict or party of convicts: separated for a particular purpose from the main body.
1821 *Regulations respecting Assigned Convict Servants* 30 June 15 No Stock-owner should allow his detached stockmen to keep Hunting Dogs. **1849** *Hobart Town Gaz.* 8 May, On route from the Prisoners' Barracks, Hobart, on the 1st instant, to the detached party at Mount Wellington.

deuce, *a.* Of a shearer: capable of shearing two hundred sheep in a day.
1915 *Bulletin* (Sydney) 18 Nov. 24/4 The fastest jumbuck-barber on a board .. is often known as a 'gun', or a 'deuce artist'. **1961** *Ibid.* 3 Feb. 44/2 The young picker-

upper .. boasted, 'I picked for seven 'deuce merchants' on my own last year .. and swept each time they let go.'

Hence as *v. trans.*, to shear two hundred (sheep) in a day.
1939 J. SORENSEN *Lost Shanty* 14 Come tell me is the current rumour true, That recently you 'deuced them' at Murgoo? **1975** B. FOLEY *Shearers' Poems* 9 We're shearing here at Kylie And the frost is on the grain The 'molley dooker' is deucin 'em And the Kiwi's draggin' the chain.

deucer.
1. [See prec.] A shearer capable of shearing two hundred sheep in a day.
1923 *Bulletin* (Sydney) 22 Nov. 22/2 In the blade-shearing days the fastest barber was the 'ringer'; later, he was the 'gun'; nowadays he is a 'deucer'. **1953** *Sydney Morning Herald* 3 Jan. 6/4 'Deucer', a man who can shear 200 or more sheep a day.
2. A double shift (but see also quot. 1979).
1953 D. CUSACK *Southern Steel* 138 'He's doing a deucer,' Landy explained. 'The snipe on the 12 to 4's sick.' **1979** G. STEWART *Leveller* 56 If any of the firemen were sick or injured you were called upon to work a 'Deucer' (two hours of his watch each).

devil.
1. *Tasmanian devil*, see TASMANIAN *a.* 2.
1807 Banks Papers 12 Nov. XX. 177, 2 skulls of an Animal called the Devil. **1981** *Woman's Day* (Sydney) 14 Oct. 65/1 Unique to Tasmania, the devils are marsupial... Tasmanians are proud of their devil—ugly and short-tempered though it is.
2. In the collocation **devil on the coals**, a small damper. See also BEGGAR.
1862 A. POLEHAMPTON *Kangaroo Land* 76 Instead of damper we occasionally made what are colonially known as 'devils on the coals'... Only a minute or so is required to bake them. They are made about the size of a captain's biscuit, and as thin as possible, thrown on the embers and turned quickly with the hand. **1903** H. TAUNTON *Australind* 45 By the time the water had boiled .. the 'devils-on-the-coals' had been cooked, as well as a rasher or two of bacon.
3. In phr.: **devil's grip**, a condition of sheep characterized by a skin fold behind the shoulders that traps moisture and increases the risk of fly-strike; **guts** *obs.*, *devil's twine*; **pool** *obs.*, a game of chance; **twine**, DODDER-LAUREL.
1930 BILLIS & KENYON *Pastures New* 219 They would suffer a *damnosa hereditas*, like the '**devil's grip**', left behind on many an Australian flock by the wrinkly rams from Vermont. **1888** *Proc. Linnean Soc. N.S.W.* III. 496 *Cassytha filiformis*... This and other species of *Cassytha* are called 'Dodder-laurel'. The emphatic name '**Devil's guts**' is largely used. **1892** *Truth* (Sydney) 17 Apr. 2/7 Hon. members can then relieve the monotony of their duties by such innocent recreations as **devil's pool**, dominoes, draughts, penny 'Nap' and 'Three-up'. **1956** T.Y. HARRIS *Naturecraft in Aust.* 183 **Devil's Twine**, another semi-parasite, in which the leaves are reduced to very fine scales, is found forming great twining masses over the branches of trees and shrubs.

devil devil. Orig. *Austral. pidgin.* [Reduplicative form of *devil*, indicating intensity, magnitude.]
1. In Aboriginal belief: an evil spirit; a manifestation of evil; evil itself; DEBIL DEBIL 1. Also *attrib.*
1831 TYERMAN & BENNET *Jrnl. Voyages & Travels* II. 156 A man .. was found lying on the ground .. to drive out the devil-devil—the reduplication of the term signifying the great devil. **1977** T. RONAN *Mighty Men on Horseback* 80 This motor bike bloke reckon white fellers don't know anything about this Devil-Devil business. Only he don't call it Devil-Devil he call it 'Dreamtime'. I never heard that name before.

2. GILGAI a. Freq. *attrib.*, esp. as **devil devil country**.
1844 L. LEICHHARDT *Jrnl. Overland Exped. Aust.* 6 Nov. (1847) 32 Rich black soil, which appeared several times in the form of ploughed land, well known, in other parts of the colony, either under that name, or under that of 'Devil-devil land', as the natives believe it to be the work of an evil spirit. **1864** *Port Denison Times* 17 Sept. 2/4 Ascending out of this swampy gully there extends a swamp composed of what is known to the initiated as 'devil-devil' country. **1870** E.B. KENNEDY *Four Yrs. in Qld.* 20 'Devil devil' .. is simply one formation of holes and hillocks, in some districts of great depth and size.
3. An ant-lion.
1944 J. DEVANNY *By Tropic Sea & Jungle* 178 The ant-lions, or devil-devils, as they are called up there [sc. n. Qld.]. **1945** M. RAYMOND *Smiley* 52 The devil-devil is a fantastic creature that digs ant-traps in the sand.

devon. [f. *Devon(shire* the name of an English county.] A large, bland sausage, usu. sliced and eaten cold; FRITZ.
1962 *Austral. Grocer* Aug. 97/3 Devon .. 2s. 9d. **1984** R.L. REID *Healthy Eating in Aust.* 145 Luncheon meat (devon, pork German, Strasburg, etc.) and salami score 9.

dewfish, var. JEWFISH.

dew lizard, var. JEW LIZARD 1.

dhufish, var. JEWFISH.

diamond, $n.^1$ Used *attrib.* in Special Comb. **diamond bird**, PARDALOTE, esp. the *spotted pardalote*, see SPOTTED; **dove**, the small, predom. grey pigeon *Geopelia cuneata* of n. and central Aust.; **firetail**, the finch *Stagonopleura guttata* of s.e. mainland Aust.; JAVA SPARROW; *spotted-sided finch*, see SPOTTED; see also *diamond sparrow*; **-scaled mullet**, the large-scaled mullet *Liza vaigiensis* of n. Aust. and elsewhere in the tropics; **snake**, any of several snakes incl. *carpet snake* (see CARPET) and (*Tas.*) COPPERHEAD, and esp. *Morelia spilota spilota*, typically black above with pale spots forming more or less diamond-shaped markings; **sparrow**, any of several small finches or finch-like birds, esp. the *spotted pardalote* (see SPOTTED), *zebra finch* (see ZEBRA) and *diamond firetail*.
1827 *Trans. Linnean Soc. London* XV. 238 Pardalotus .. Punctatus... We are informed by Mr Caley, that 'this species is called **Diamond Bird** by the settlers, from the spots on its body'. **1931** N.W. CAYLEY *What Bird is That?* 86 **Diamond dove** *Geopelia cuneata*. **1945** C. BARRETT *Austral. Bird Life* 205 The spotted-sided finch or **diamond firetail** .. popularly known as 'diamond sparrow'. **1906** D.G. STEAD *Fishes of Aust.* 79 The **Diamond-scaled Mullet** .. is notable for its large scales and its broad, flat head. [**1805 diamond snake**: *Sydney Gaz.* 20 Oct., A snake of what is in general termed the *diamond* species was killed at the half-way houses on the Parramatta road and when opened a fine parrot was found within it perfectly entire.] **1825** *Austral.* (Sydney) 8 Dec. 4 On Wednesday se'nnight a man who lives in Pitt-street met with a diamond snake in the bush of the largest dimensions ever seen. **1906** *Bulletin* (Sydney) 12 July 16/1 The diamond snake .. is known as the copper-headed snake in Victoria, and is called the superb snake in N.S.W. Its scientific name is *Denisonia superba*. **1944** J. DEVANNY *By Tropic Sea & Jungle* 137 A true carpet-snake is not a distinct species but a colour variety of the diamond-snake (*Python spilotes*). **1875** P.E. WARBURTON *Journey across Western Interior* 177 Charley's sharp eyes detected some **diamond-sparrows**.

diamond, $n.^2$ *Obs.* [Of unknown origin.] A name given to a soldier by Aborigines.
1846 C.P. HODGSON *Reminisc. Aust.* 234 Having heard

diamond-cracking, *vbl. n. Obs.* Breaking rocks, i.e., undergoing a sentence of hard labour; so **diamond cracker,** one sentenced to this.

some soldiers, or 'diamonds' as they call them, were on the road. **1898** J.J. KNIGHT *In Early Days* 36 The blacks vowed they would kill every 'diamond'—that was the name we gave the soldiers.

1885 *Australasian Printers' Keepsake* 25 He caught a month, and had to 'white it out' At diamond-cracking in Castieau's Hotel. **1916** *Truth* (Sydney) 2 Apr. 7/4 He will be caught knapping (stones) for the next six months, for which period he has gone to join the diamond crackers at Sammacauleytown.

dibble dibble, var. DEBIL DEBIL.

dibbler /'dɪblə/. [a. Nyungar prob. *dibala.*] The rare marsupial mouse *Parantechinus apicalis* of W.A.

1850 A. WHITE *Pop. Hist. Mammalia* 166 The *Antechinus apicalis* of Mr Gray . . is called 'the Dibbler' at King George's Sound. **1970** W.D.L. RIDE *Guide Native Mammals Aust.* 20 Gilbert got several of the little mammals, both at the Moore River and at King George Sound where Aborigines told him that their name for it was 'Dib-bler'.

dice, *v.* [Fig. use of *dice* to lose by dicing.] *trans.* To discard; to reject; to abandon.

1943 S.J. BAKER *Pop. Dict. Austral. Slang* (ed. 2) 25 *Dice*, to upset, reject, throw away. **1984** *N.T. News* (Darwin) 16 Nov. 30/4, I was filleting the jewie on the side of the boat and somehow managed to drop one fillet. . . It must have taken all of 10 seconds to dice the fillet.

dick: see DICKHEAD.

dick. [Familiar form of RICHARD.] In the phr. **to have had the dick,** to be finished, to be irreparably damaged.

1974 D. IRELAND *Burn* 85 Now you've had the dick. . . That's the finish. You're history now. **1976** B. BENNETT *New Country* 34 The cattle trap up there's had the dick.

dicken. Also **dickin, dickon.** [Var. of *dickens* the deuce, the devil.] An interjectional exclamation, usu. expressing disbelief (but see quot. 1966). Also as *n.* and *adj.*, and with **on.**

1894 *Bulletin* (Sydney) 5 May 13/3 'And did yer stouch him back?' 'No.' 'Dicken!' 'Swelp me.' **1898** *Ibid.* 4 June (Red Page), And 'a dickon pitch to kid us' Is a synonym for 'lie'. **1904** L.M.P. ARCHER *Bush Honeymoon* 311 'No dicken (nonsense) now,' said Jim, 'The truth, the whole truth, and nothing but it, old man.' **1966** S.J. BAKER *Austral. Lang.* (ed. 2) 203 Whereas dicken! meaning cut it out! be reasonable! is still known in most parts of Australia, it flourishes quite remarkably in South Australia. Here, depending on the intonation, it can mean 'Yes, of course!' 'Certainly not!' 'Do you really think so?' and 'You don't say!' **1968** S. GORE *Holy Smoke* 52 He rolls his eyes up aloft and starts orf: 'Eh, dickin on it, Lord! How's about givin' a man a fair crack o' the whip. . . Let the dog see the rabbit?'

dickhead. [f. *dick* penis (cf. *prick*). Used elsewhere but recorded earliest in Aust.] A fool. Also **dick.**

1967 R. DONALDSON et al. *Cane!* 150 Nobody made a dick out of Nigger and got away with it. **1976** D. IRELAND *Glass Canoe* 16, I called him a dickhead, but he doesn't know what he's doing when he's real full.

dickin, dickon, varr. DICKEN.

Dickless Tracy. See quot. 1980.

1980 B. HORNADGE *Austral. Slanguage* 197 The only inventive feminine nickname I have come across is *Dickless Tracy* (a woman police officer). **1984** *Sydney Morning Herald* 4 Feb. 37/2 Mangan is one of 18 policewomen at Darlinghurst (out of 136 police) whom one sergeant calls Dickless Tracys.

diddy. Also **didee.** [Prob., in children's speech, altered form of DUNNY.] A lavatory. Also *attrib.*

1958 M. WARREN *No Glamour in Gumboots* 9 The sanitary system was primitive, the 'diddy' being an imposing and conspicuous edifice perched at the back of the house. **1965** F. HARDY *Yarns of Billy Borker* 56 A barbecue in the backyard and a didee in the house. **1971** —— *Outcasts of Foolgarah* 91 Tom has studied the layout of all sorts of houses and can pick the diddy door at a glance.

didgeridoo /dɪdʒəri'du/. Also **didjiridu, didjerry,** etc. [Prob. imit.; not from an Aboriginal language.] An Aboriginal (orig. Arnhem Land) wind instrument, a long, wooden, tubular instrument producing a low-pitched resonant sound with complex rhythmic patterns but little tonal variation; DRONE-PIPE.

1919 *Huon Times* (Franklin) 24 Jan. 4/3 The nigger crew is making merry with the Diridgery doo and the eternal ya-ya-ya ye-ye-ye cry. **1919** *Smith's Weekly* (Sydney) 5 Apr. 15/1 The Northern Territory aborigines have an infernal—allegedly musical—instrument, composed of two feet of hollow bamboo. It produces but one sound—'didjerry, didjerry, didjerry—' and so on ad infinitum. . . When a couple of niggers started grinding their infernal 'didjerry' half the hot night through, the blasphemous manager decided on revenge. **1925** M. TERRY *Across Unknown Aust.* 190 The didjiri-du . . is a long hollow tube, often a tree root about 5 feet long, slightly curved at the lower end. The musician squats on the ground, resting his instrument on the earth. He fits his mouth into the straight or upper end and blows down it in a curious fashion. He produces an intermittent drone. **1960** *N.T. News* (Darwin) 28 Oct. 2/3 Make them a quintet by including the vibrant beat of their own didgeridoo and they would be a sensation.

dig, $n.^1$ Abbrev. of DIGGER 2.

1916 J.F. NUGENT *Lorblimey* 9 'Doc.' sez, 'No 'ope, Dig., y'r've taken th' knock.' **1980** E. BARCS *Backyard of Mars* 209 Frequently, someone in the place wanted to shout us a beer, and inquired whether one of us or both had been at Tobruk or on the Kokoda Trail. They called me 'Dig' and I felt like a fraud.

dig, $n.^2$ [Perh. fig. use of *dig*, with reference to a hole.] See quot. 1962.

1962 'N. CULOTTA' *Gone Fishin'* 48 Shorty talked about 'digs' the name given by fishermen to areas where they can expect to find fish. . . He talked about mullet digs, and bream digs, and 'nigger' digs. **1980** B. SHACKLETON *Karagi* 19 He learned the haunts and the 'digs' and the moods of prawns on the big river.

digger. [Spec. use of *digger* a miner, esp. one working surface or shallow deposits (see OED 2 a.); orig. U.S. in its application to gold-mining.]

1. A miner on the Australian goldfields. Also *attrib.*

1849 *Bell's Life in Sydney* 3 Feb. 3/4 In sheer self-defence I was obliged to turn digger myself. **1944** M.J. O'REILLY *Bouyangs & Boomerangs* 45 The digger swaggies, whom I met in the early days of the Western Australian goldfields, were a fine type.

2. [Transf. use of sense 1: see quot. 1922.] In the wars of 1914–18 and 1939–45, a (private) soldier from Australia or New Zealand; increasingly, an Australian soldier exclusively; also used in civilian as well as military contexts as a term of address, and freq. shortened to DIG $n.^1$ Cf. COBBER, MATE.

1916 C.A. HEMSLEY Diary 12 Aug., The officer in charge of the parade was addressing the men, and at some kindly expressed sentiment one wag interjected with 'Hear, hear, old digger!' **1922** *Bulletin* (Sydney) 8 June (Red Page), 'Digger' is a title coveted and often stolen. It originally meant the infantryman or artilleryman who was always 'digging in' or rebuilding his parapet after enemy fire. . . It did not mean a staff-officer or any of the A.I.F. serving in Palestine or Egypt. It meant the man in the front line in France, and no one else. It is ridiculous to talk of the 'Digger Prince' or to use the word for A.I.F. men indiscriminately; and it is mere swank when claimed by men who did not dig. There were no 'Diggers' at Gallipoli where we dug most—the word had not come then! **1940** 'K. BRUCE' *Digger Tourists* 60, I saw some New Zealand diggers helping along some of our fellows. **1956** S. HOPE *Diggers' Paradise* 13 Very few New Australians whether British, Balts, Italians or Greeks, see Australia through the rose-coloured spectacles worn by the dyed-in-the-wool Diggers. **1968** M. HILLIARD *Excuse me, Mr Sweetenham* 115 Should our suntanned Diggers be fighting in Vietnam? **1980** J. WOLFE *End of Pricklystick* 177 An old man was staring at me. 'How are you, Digger?' he grinned.

3. In the collocation **Little Digger**: a nickname for William Morris Hughes (1864-1952), Prime Minister of Australia during the war of 1914-18 (see quot. 1957).

1919 *Morning Post* (London) 11 Feb. 4/5 'The Little Digger . . is running a great offensive. . . ' From the start it was clear that Mr Hughes was confronted with a formidable task. **1957** W.F. WHYTE *W.M. Hughes* 242 During this visit to France he addressed many units of the Australian Forces, and on several occasions they broke all the rules and mobbed him, carrying him high on their shoulders. They placed a Digger's hat on his head and called him 'the Little Digger'—and by that affectionate name he was to be known to Australian troops for ever after.

4. Special Comb. **digger costume** (or **dress**), see quots.; also **digger's costume; hat,** the felt slouch hat worn as part of the uniform of the Australian soldier; **hunt,** a raid made on a goldfield by police; for the purpose of inspecting miners' licences; also **hunting** *vbl. n.*; **digger-looking** *a.*, having the appearance of a gold miner.

1853 J. SHERER *Gold Finder Aust.* 173 Hundreds of pedestrians in **digger's costume**. **1859** W. BURROWS *Adventures Mounted Trooper* 5 A man dressed in the usual diggercostume, consisting of a black wide-awake hat, blue shirt, and moleskin continuations, came up to the dray. **1865** *Austral. Monthly Mag.* (Melbourne) I. 203, I had the greatest difficulty in persuading him to dismiss his digger's dress. **1940** T. WOOD *Cobbers Campaigning* 159 Distant lands that saw those **digger hats** before; through Victory, and beyond. **1855** *Melbourne Monthly Mag.* May 63 The **digger-hunt** . . was ordered during the excitement against the license-fee. **1855** G.H. WATHEN *Golden Colony* 86 The pursuit and capture of unlicensed diggers, 'man-hunting' or 'digger-hunting' as the miners called it. **1854** W. HOWITT *Boy's Adventures* 272 Six or seven rough **digger-looking** fellows.

Hence **diggerish** *a.*, **diggerism** *n.*

1936 N. CALDWELL *Fangs of Sea* 172 In describing his beloved Barrier he got rather carried away and his language became rather **Diggerish**. **1918** *Aussie: Austral. Soldiers' Mag.* (Sydney) Dec. 20/1 To use a **Diggerism**, 'it's out on its own' as regards its method of work and style of entertainment.

diggerdom. *Obs.* The society established by the gold-miners.

1855 W. HOWITT *Land, Labor & Gold* I. 47 Diggerdom is gloriously in the ascendant here. **1880** G. WALCH *Vic.* 22 The *nouveau riche* of Diggerdom had a lordly taste for playing skittles with bottles of champagne for pins.

digging, *vbl. n.* Usu. in *pl.* [Spec. use of *digging(s* a place where digging is carried out: applied to goldfields in California and then Aust.]

1. A goldfield. Also **diggins**.

1851 *Austral. Gold Digger's Monthly Mag.* (1852) ii. 42 Out of one hundred who flock to the diggings, about three may . . do well. **1851** *Empire* (Sydney) 25 Sept. 191/5 Whilst perambulating the 'diggins' yesterday, Mr Cooper showed me a piece of quartz from about four feet below the surface.

2. Special Comb. **digging mania,** *gold fever,* see GOLD 3; **party,** a group of gold-miners working together; **population,** that part of the population engaged in gold-mining; **price,** the (usu. inflated) cost of retailed goods on a goldfield; **settlement, town, township, village,** the dwellings, etc., on a goldfield; **times,** the gold-rush era.

1857 W. WESTGARTH *Vic. & Austral. Gold Mines* 10 A vision still haunted me of servants ever seized with a **diggings mania**. **1851** *Empire* (Sydney) 6 Aug. 18/5 (*heading*) A **digging party**. **1851** *Empire* (Sydney) 27 Aug. 91/6 A visible thinning of the **digging population** has taken place in some of the richest points of the Turon. **1851** *Empire* (Sydney) 16 Dec. 470/7 Mr Badgery is the most considerable storekeeper, and accommodates the public at a **digging price**. **1861** L.A. MEREDITH *Over Straits* 141 The chief official in a **digging settlement** . . is entitled the Warden. **1862** C. ASPINALL *Three Yrs. Melbourne* 161 There will be a railroad open to Ballarat, one of the most important **'diggings' towns**, containing twenty-five thousand inhabitants. **1881** A.C. GRANT *Bush-Life Qld.* II. 243 John West vowed that his first night passed in the midst of a **digging township** should be the last, if he could help it. **1855** W. HOWITT *Land, Labor & Gold* II. 114 **Digging villages**, with their tents and stores, mark its course for miles, with all their tumbled heaps, tree-stumps and disorderly objects around them. **1853** *Austral. Gold Digger's Monthly Mag.* v. 173 In these **diggings times** the domestic duties of the family fall wholly to the lot of mamma and her daughters.

digging stick. An Aboriginal food-gathering tool made from a piece of wood pointed at each end and used to excavate roots and tubers; KATTA; YAM-STICK.

1841 G. GREY *Jrnls. Two Exped. N.-W. & W.A.* II. 331, I offered to get a spade, but they would not have it; the digging stick was the proper tool. **1979** A. WELLS *Forests are their Temples* 27 You mimic hunting now. Spear and canoe and digging stick will soon mean work to you.

diggins: see DIGGING 1.

dill. [Back-formation from DILLY *a.*] A fool or simpleton.

1941 S.J. BAKER *Pop. Dict. Austral. Slang* 23 *Dil*, a simpleton or fool. **1984** *Canberra Times* 11 Apr. 1/1 God, I'm a dill.

dilli, var. DILLY *n.*

dillon bush /'dɪlən bʊʃ/. [f. Wemba-wemba *dilany + (Eng.) bush.*] The drought-tolerant plant of all mainland States but not N.T., *Nitraria billardierei* (fam. Zygophyllaceae), a rigid spreading shrub bearing edible fruits.

1885 P.R. MEGGY *From Sydney to Silverton* 21 Another succulent shrub known as the 'dillon' bush, the last being the only one of the four which sheep will eat. **1983** *Nat. Farmer* (Perth) 22 Sept. 11/1 When the 84 ha. Kerang property was bought in 1956, it grew mainly barley grass, beadbush and dillon bush, and carried less than two sheep to the hectare.

dillwynia /dɪl'wɪnɪə/. [The plant genus *Dillwynia* was named by English botanist J.E. Smith (in Koenig, K.D.E. and Sims, J. *Ann. Bot.* (1805) I. 510) after English botanist L.W. *Dillwyn* (1778-1855).] Any shrub of the Austral. genus *Dillwynia* (fam. Fabaceae), usu. having yellow or yellow and reddish flowers, and occurring in all States but not N.T.

1850 *Britannia* (Hobart) 7 Nov. 4/5 The narrow valleys of the interior, neither agricultural nor pastoral, and filled with the dylwinnea. **1984** ELLIOT & JONES *Encycl. Austral. Plants* III. 275 Dillwynias usually inhabit sandheath or dry sclerophyll forest communities.

dilly /'dɪli/, *n*. Also **dilli**. [a. Yagara *dili* coarse grass, a bag woven of this.] An Aboriginal bag or basket made from woven grass or fibre.

1830 W.J. HOOKER *Bot. Miscellany* I. 254 On examining the depôt, we found a Kangaroo-Net . . a *Dilly*, or luggage-bag, such as females carry, made of the leaves of a species of *Xanthorrhoea*, and strong enough to bear any weight. **1849** *Tasmanian Jrnl. Nat. Sci.* III. 109 The rock crystal was found in their dillis as far as the gulf.

dilly, *a*. [Br. dial. *dilly* queer, cranky: see EDD.] Foolish, dotty.

1905 L. BECKE *Tom Gerrard* 91 Maybe you've forgotten that when you busted your last cheque at Hooley's pub in Boorala, and had the dilly trimmings, that it was the parson who brought you back here, you boozy little swine. **1970** K. SLESSOR *Bread & Wine* 31 One translation which he has pencilled after the Latin words '*oculos languidum tuens*'—'with a dilly look in her eyes'.

dilly-bag.

1. DILLY *n*.

1867 F.J. BYERLEY *Narr. Overland Exped. Northern Qld.* 68 They . . brought them a villainous compound, in some dilly-bags. **1980** T.A. ROY *Vengeance of Dolphin* 170 She was carrying a woven string dilly-bag to carry the bones of Turrapini.

2. *transf*. A bag of any sort, usu. small (but see quot. 1969).

1906 E. DYSON *Roaring Fifties* 91 There's tea in the pannikin, an' . . grub in the dilly-bag. **1969** W. MOXHAM *Apprentice* 61 He checked the contents of his dilly bag: saddles, and he had some beauties, skull cap, goggles, whip, black boots . . , white breeks and towels, lead bag.

dim-sim /dɪm-'sɪm/. [a. Cantonese *tim-sam* cake or snack.] A small roll of seasoned meat and vegetable encased in a thin dough and steamed or fried.

1961 X. HERBERT *Soldiers' Women* 174 He plied her with *dim-sims* and *sam-sui*, apparently content to rely on the alleged properties of the fare. **1972** *Bulletin* (Sydney) 26 Aug. 6/1 We are also the Dim Sim capital of the world. I wish I could give you conclusive evidence about the origins of the Dim Sim but there is little doubt that it was invented by the Chinese of Little Bourke Street to cater for our very complex palates.

din, var. GIN.

ding, *n*.¹ [Abbrev. of DINGBAT.]

1. An Italian (immigrant to Australia); a European (immigrant). Also *attrib*.

[**1922** *Bulletin* (Sydney) 17 Aug. 22/1, I once saw a couple of 'ding-bats' (Italians) place a packet of gelignite . . on a rock.] **1940** *Ibid*. 17 July 17/1 I've a yearning These city rags to doff And go where 'dings' are burning The northern paddock off. **1976** L.R.M. HUNTER *Woodline* 17 'How do you say 'wood' in Italian?' 'Aw!' said Johnny, 'I don't talk that ding language.' **1979** G. STEWART *Leveller* 24 No matter what race, Slav, Greek, Italian, Maltese, they were all Dings.

2. DINGBAT 2.

1943 S.W. KEOUGH *Around Army* 22 It will be no time at all before he is lending his boss a few 'onks' to tide him over till the ghost wanders, for a 'ding' is never broke.

ding, *n*.² [Shortened form of *ding-dong* or *wing-ding* noisy party.] A party. Also *attrib*.

1956 *Sydney Morning Herald* 15 Oct. 1/10 In New Guinea a party is called a 'ding'. **1963** F. GRANT *Death on my Wing* 28 It was ding night in a few hours with the grog ration together with any black market liquor that could be bought.

ding, *n*.³

1. Abbrev. of DINGER: the backside; the penis.

1957 'N. CULOTTA' *They're Weird Mob* 106 Been sittin' on our dings the last 'alf hour. **1972** G. MORLEY *Jockey rides Honest Race* 209 You can get fined or sent to gaol for kicking a cat in the ding, but it's okay if it's a three-month old baby.

2. *transf*.

1967 V.G.C. NORWOOD *Long Haul* 34 Geoff inspected the gory 'roo meat. 'I'll give you half a quid for a ding (haunch),' he offered.

ding, *v. Obs*. [Br. dial. *ding* to throw, hurl, shake off: see EDD *v*.¹ 2.]

a. *trans*. To throw (something) away; to abandon (a course of action, etc.).

1812 J.H. VAUX *Mem*. (1819) II. 166 *Ding*, to throw, or throw away; particularly any article you have stolen, either because it is worthless, or that there is danger of immediate apprehension. **1903** J. FURPHY *Such is Life* 142 I'm as weak as a sanguinary cat. I must ding it.

b. *spec*. Of a female kangaroo: to discard (a joey) from the pouch (see quot. 1851).

1851 H. MELVILLE *Present State Aust*. 312 When hard pressed in running by the dogs, the mother 'dings her joey', that is, with her forepaws lifts the joey or young one out, and casts it into or alongside a bush or shelter of some kind, here the little thing nestles up and secretes itself; and if the mother escapes, she returns and takes charge of her little beloved. **1891** M. ROBERTS *Land-Travel & Sea-Faring* 159 The flying marsupial . . put its fore-paw into its pouch and threw away its young one, or in Australian parlance 'dinged the joey'.

dingbat. [Perh. f. *ding* (as a bell) + *bat*, joc. formation on *bats in the belfry*.]

1. A simpleton; a halfwit.

1918 *Bulletin* (Sydney) 11 Apr. 47/1 Simon stopped the fight outright by purchasing Bill and presenting him as mascot to the Second Battalion of the Fighting Dingbats. **1980** C. JAMES *Unreliable Mem*. 160 Our office was a transit camp for dingbats. . . It was my first, cruel exposure to the awkward fact that the arts attract the insane.

2. *transf*. An army batman.

1918 *Aussie: Austral. Soldiers' Mag.* Feb. 4/2 He's not a bally Batman he's a Dingbat now, you know, We've changed his blessed monicker for keeps. **1944** *Barging About: Organ 43 Austral. Landing Craft Co*. 1 Sept. 12 He is Scottie's dingbat. To hear him bawl out to the other boongs when they happen to collect some of Scottie's washing, is an education.

3. *pl*.

a. Delusions, esp. those characteristic of *delirium tremens*. Chiefly in the phr. **to have the** (or **to be**) **ding-bats**.

[N.Z. **1911** *N.Z. Truth* (Wellington) 4 Nov. 6 The Taranaki horse led the big field home and paid a big dividend, which gives me dingbats every time I remember it.] **1920** *Aussie* (Sydney) Oct. 16/2 It was a bender—a dinkum jamboree—menageries of dingbats, tiger-headed snakes an' snake-headed tigers. **1925** A. WRIGHT *Boy from Bullarah* 66 It's enough to give a fellow the dingbats. I suppose you've been soaking this damn stuff. **1929** 'F. BLAIR' *Digger Sea-Mates* 128 'You've got 'em, Lockie,' said Tom. 'Got what, you ape?' 'The dinkum dingbats.' 'He'll have 'em worse after that whisky,' observed Kiley.

b. As *adj.* Stupid; eccentric.

1950 *Bulletin* (Sydney) 13 Sept. 13/3 'Dingbats,' nodded Hal. 'Been livin' out with ol' Bill too long, I bet.' **1981** P. BARTON *Bastards I have Known* 97 If you give a mob of sheep something to be frightened of they'll run like mad, but I've walked quietly into a paddock full of them and they just stand there and gawk at you... A mob of ambling shoppers are just as dingbats.

dinger. [Perh. in punning allusion to *ring* anus.] The backside; the anus.

1943 J. BINNING *Target Area* 104 'Dinger', by the way, is a word born in the A.I.F. It describes, neatly, the place on which you sit. **1969** *Kings Cross Whisper* (Sydney) lxxii. 1/3 Their benchmen in supporting roles Would sit upon their dingers.

dingo /ˈdɪŋɡoʊ/, *n.* Pl. **dingoes.** [a. Dharuk *din-gu.*]

1. The native dog, *Canis familiaris dingo* of mainland Aust., typically tawny-yellow, apparently introduced by the Aborigines; *native dingo, dog*, see NATIVE *a.* 6 b.; WARRIGAL *n.* 1; *wild dog*, see WILD 1.

1789 W. TENCH *Narr. Exped. Botany Bay* 83 The only domestic animal they have is the dog, which in their language is called Dingo. **1965** R.H. CONQUEST *Horses in Kitchen* 189 We were like the dingoes in the back paddocks—sleek and contented.

2. *fig.* A term applied to a person who displays characteristics popularly attributed to the dingo, esp. cowardice, treachery. Also *attrib.*

1869 'E. HOWE' *Boy in Bush* 2 He [*sc.* a bushranger] may well call himself Warrigal, the sneaking dingo! **1978** B. ST. A. SMITH *Spirit beyond Psyche* 49 He's not a dinkum RSL man, he's just a yellow, gutless, dingo cur.

3. Comb. **dingo hunter, -hunting, pack, -proof** *a.*, **scalp, scalper, trap, trapper.**

1908 *Emu* VIII. 42 He is a genuine student of the bush, besides being a successful **dingo-hunter.** **1862** G.T. LLOYD *Thirty-Three Yrs. Tas. & Vic.* 384 **Dingo** (native fox) **hunting**.. formed one of the principal sources of amusement. **1892** *Bulletin* (Sydney) 19 Mar. 11/1 We swung with the stride of the **dingo-pack. 1925** M. TERRY *Across Unknown Aust.* 96 Proper wire-fenced paddocks.. with **dingo-proof** netting. **1898** *Western Champion* (Barcaldine) 11 Jan. 2/2 **Dingo scalps** to the number of 2042 have been received and paid for. **1931** *Bulletin* (Sydney) 21 Jan. 21/4 Bourneman was a **dingo scalper**, a taciturn man. **1911** ST. C. GRONDONA *Collar & Cuffs* 51 The poor unfortunate turkey had been caught in a **dingo trap.** **1930** 'BRENT OF BIN BIN' *Ten Creeks Run* (1952) 28, I want to see what the **dingo-trappers** are after.

4. Special Comb. **dingo fence,** a fence erected to exclude dingoes; **-slut,** a female dingo; **stiffener,** one employed to eradicate dingoes.

1914 'B. CABLE' *By Blow & Kiss* 30 The others found Steve waiting for them at the **dingo fence** of the back paddock. **1899** *Bulletin* (Sydney) 4 Feb. 14/1 When a **dingo-slut** produces a litter of pups she leaves them in charge of a mate. **1945** *Ibid.* 31 Jan. 14/1 The rewards hung up for **dingo-stiffeners.** Northern Territory offered a measly seven and sixpence per head.

5. In the collocation **dingo's breakfast:** see quots.

1965 K. MCKENNEY *Hide-Away Man* 101 'Here's yer dinner,' he said, adding with a wink 'I already had me breakfast.' 'What was that?' 'Dingo's breakfast. A piss and a look around.' **1976** B. SCOTT *Compl. Bk. Austral. Folk Lore* 380 A dingo's breakfast is a pee and a good look round.

dingo /ˈdɪŋɡoʊ/, *v.* [f. prec.] *intr.* To behave in a cowardly manner. Also with **it.**

1942 *Sun* (Sydney) 26 Aug. 4/9 A man who avoids an unpleasant job is said to dingo it. **1951** E. LAMBERT *Sleeping House Party* 335 'Where is Allison?' 'He dingoed at the last minute.'

dingy, *a.* Of a fleece: see quots.

1891 *Truth* (Sydney) 19 Apr. 7/3 A lady.. who, if passing through the wool-classer's hands, would have been chucked into the *Dingy* bin. **1970** HARMSWORTH & PAGE-SHARP *Sheep & Wool Classing* 63 Yolk stained, yellowish, dingy, canary stained, green coloured, or fern-stained fleeces should not be blended with white fleeces.

dink, *n.* [Perh. f. Br. dial. *dink* to dandle a baby: see EDD *v.*¹] A lift on a bicycle, or a horse, ridden by another. Also **double dink,** and, as *adv.*, **double dinkie.**

1934 *Bulletin* (Sydney) 5 Sept. 20/1 Victorian philologists are becoming alarmed over an outbreak in the State schools of a new form of slang. Two words in particular have gained great popularity—'dink' and 'pug'. These are, apparently, both used to express a request for a double-bank ride. The fortunate Melbourne schoolkid with a bike, when time comes to go home, is asked by his cobbers for a 'dink'. **1965** L. WALKER *Other Girl* 173 Of course, riding home, double-dinkie on a bronco, was part of it too. **1976** K. BROWN *Knock Ten* 95 'Tell you what, let's get him a bike between us..?' He really felt he was a lucky bloke. He said so to me, giving me a ride double-dink after school.

dink, *v.* [f. prec.] *trans.* To carry (a passenger) on a bicycle or a horse. Also **double-dink.** See also DOUBLE-BANK 3.

1941 S.J. BAKER *Pop. Dict. Austral. Slang* 23 *Double-dink,* to carry a second person on the top bar of a bicycle... Exchangeable terms are 'dink'.. and 'double-bank'. **1942** E. LANGLEY *Pea Pickers* 34 [He] pityingly offered to 'double dink' me. My shame had double damned me, and now, double dinked, I bent over the bar of Kelly's bike and off we went.

dink, *a.* and *adv.* Abbrev. of DINKUM *a.* and *adv.* Also **dinks.**

1906 E. DYSON *Fact'ry 'Ands* 92 'Twasn't fair dink t' go outside the firm. **1974** J. JOST *This is Harry Flynn* 41 The bottle was empty but he sucked at it.. without realising the liquor was gone. 'I have got a secret, true dinks.'

dinki-di, dinkie-di, vart. DINKY-DI.

dinkum /ˈdɪŋkəm/, *n.* [Br. dial. *dinkum* work, a due share of work: see EDD.]

1. *Obs.* Work, exertion.

1888 'R. BOLDREWOOD' *Robbery under Arms* (1937) 35 It took us an hour's hard dinkum to get near the peak.

2. *Hist.* In the war of 1914–18: a member of the 2nd Division of the Australian Imperial Forces (see quots. 1917 and 1919).

1916 *Desert Dust Bin: Official Organ 3rd L.H.F.A.* 3 May 8/1 Anzac Day today. The 'Dinkums' put on blue ribbons. **1917** C.E.W. BEAN *Lett. from France* 224 The sort of Australian who used to talk about our 'tinpot navy' labelled the Australians who rushed at the chance of adventure the moment the recruiting lists were opened 'the six bob a day tourists'. Well—the 'Tourists' made a name for Australia such as no other Australians can ever have the privilege to make. The next shipment were the 'Dinkums'—the men who came over on principle to fight for Australia—the real, fair dinkum Australians. **1919** W.H. DOWNING *Digger Dialects* 19 *Dinkums (the),* the 2nd Division. Also applied to the New Zealanders.

3. *Obs.* Accurate information, the *dinkum* oil (see OIL *n.* 2).

1916 'MEN OF ANZAC' *Anzac Bk.* 56, I was on the beach one day when a friend met me and asked if I had heard the latest dinkum. **1933** *Bulletin* (Sydney) 22 Feb. 34/2 First time I have a cert I'll pass the dinkum to you.

dinkum /ˈdɪŋkəm/, *a.* and *adv.* [f. prec.]

A. *adj.*

DINKY-DI

1. Reliable; genuine; honest; true.

[N.Z. **1905** *N.Z. Truth* (Wellington) 10 Oct. 3 Our sergeant said he would walk from [Palmerston North] to Ashurst to see a 'dinkum go'.] **1908** E.G. MURPHY *Jarrahland Jingles* 168 When up I brings me plumber's kit, An' gives 'em dinkum gabbie. **1984** *Sydney Morning Herald* 9 Feb. 1/8 Jim Kable believes that 'dinkum' may come from the Cantonese expression 'din kum', meaning real gold. It would have come he says, from Chinese workers during the gold rush. Below are the Cantonese characters for 'din kum'.

2. In collocations: **dinkum Aussie, digger.**

1920 A. L'HOTELLIER *Green Fields of Paraguay* 12 And we lead the van, for every man Is a **dinkum Aussie**, see; And we never turn back till we've cut a track On the page of history. **1919** *Ross's Monthly* Sept. 13/1 He's a **dinkum Digger,** Billy (but he doesn't wear a crutch)—and what he'll say and what he'll do, it—doesn't matter much.

3. In the collocation **dinkum oil:** see OIL *n.* 2.

B. *adv.* (also) interrog. and as an asseveration: really; truly; honestly; honourably.

1915 T. SKEYHILL *Soldier-Songs from Anzac* 9, I was sittin' in me dug-out, An' was feelin' dinkum good, Chewin' Queensland bully beef, An' biscuits 'ard as wood. **1960** L.H. EVERS *Make Way for Tomorrow* 43 'You a Park Ranger?' 'A Park Ranger? No I'm not a Park Ranger.' 'Dinkum?' 'Dinkum.' **1975** X. HERBERT *Poor Fellow my Country* 213, I didn't have nothing to do with it... Dinkum. They jes sprung it on me.

C. In the collocation **fair (square, straight) dinkum.**

a. Used with reference to an action, pattern of behaviour, etc., which complies with an accepted code: 'fair play'. Freq. as *exclam.*

1890 A.S. DAY *Democrat* 23 Right ye are partner Dingy, and mind ye, when the job's done, fair dinkum. **1911** 'S. RUDD' *Bk. of Dan* 34 '*Off! Off!* Let go!' Dan cried, assuming the office of referee. 'Square dinkum!'

b. As adj. phr. in emphatic senses of DINKUM *a.*

1890 *Quiz* (Adelaide) 5 Dec. 6/3 In what Literary Society are the terms, 'That's fair dinkum' and 'Oh, yes, whips' to be heard? **1904** *Sporting News* (Launceston) 5 Mar. 1/3 'Oh, it's straight dinkum. You needn't look like that,' he continued.

c. As adv. phr. in emphatic senses of DINKUM *adv.*

1894 A.B. BELL *Austral. Camp Fire Tales* 115 Now Mr Montmorency own up like a man. Wasn't the half of it carried away before they got them ships? Square dinkum, now how about the Goodwin Sands. **1975** D.J. TOWNSHEND *Gland Time* 54 'Ya know old Burt's just told me he's packin' up in a month?' 'Fair dinkum?' Pinhead was astounded. **1986** *Muse Communique* Apr. 21 On the corner a wire-framed Mirror poster swears *Cancer cure—fair dinkum.*

dinky-di /ˈdɪŋki-daɪ/, *a.* and *adv.* Also **dinkie-di, dinky-die.**

A. *adj.* DINKUM *a.*

1918 N. CAMPBELL *Dinky-Di Soldier* 5 An' I lines up nex' day with some more o' th' mob, An' they makes me a dinky-di soldier! **1929** 'F. BLAIR' *Digger Sea-Mates* 36 'You're the dinkie-die legpuller, Blair,' said he.

B. *adv.* DINKUM *adv.*

1915 G.F. MOBERLY *Experiences 'Dinki-Di' R.R.C. Nurse* (1933) 12 Dinki di, boy, how sadly I miss you. **1938** F. BLAKELEY *Hard Liberty* 69 'Yes,' said Dick, 'Dinky-die dead drunk, and buried so.'

dinner.

1. A meal eaten at mid-day, but not the principal meal of the day; lunch.

1911 A. WRIGHT *Gamblers' Gold* (1923) 110 Work started with the rising sun, and ceased when darkness fell... During that time there was a break for dinner and a couple of smoke ohs! At sundown one man would go to the camp to prepare the evening meal. **1977** J. O'GRADY *There was Kid* 57 Our midday meal was called 'dinner', and the more substantial evening one was always known as 'tea'. It still is in many parts of Australia.

2. In the phr. **to do like a dinner,** to defeat; to outwit (usu. in passive).

1847 A. HARRIS *Settlers & Convicts* (1953) 38 If we don't give the rain time to wash out the horse-tracks we shall be done like a dinner. **1978** C. GREEN *Sun is Up* 11 Anyway, within a week I had old Splinters Maloney the fishing inspector knocking on me door wanting to see me licence. Of course I was done like a dinner.

3. Special Comb. **dinner camp,** (in stock droving) the mid-day break; the place where such a break is taken; see also CAMP *n.* 3; so **dinner-camp** *v. intr.*; see also CAMP *v.* 2.

1925 M. TERRY *Across Unknown Aust.* 81 At dinner camp that day (midday). **1937** E. HILL *Great Austral. Loneliness* 90 We dinner-camped at Broken Wagon, a billabong of the Fitzroy. **1960** R.S. PORTEOUS *Cattleman* 88 They were stringing the cattle off the dinner camp when the policeman rode up.

dinnyhayser /dɪniˈheɪzə/. Also **dinnyazer.** [Of unknown origin.]

1. A knockout blow.

1907 N.F. SPIELVOGEL *Cocky Farmer* 14, I gets a dennyaiser in the eye, and sits down suddenly. **1929** *Aussie* (Sydney) Apr. 52/2 One of them, known as Kangaroo Jack, gave him the k.o. with a dinnyazer on the jaw. **1984** W.W. AMMON et al. *Working Lives* 85 Sometimes he let his dinnyhazer go with such viciousness that Stevie shook his head.

2. *fig.*

1949 I.L. IDRIESS *One Wet Season* 141 Here.. the teamsters have their 'last drink'. A dinnyhayser, at times... They had one hundred and twenty-six bottles of whisky and four dozen cases of beer. They drank the lot in eight days! **1966** D.E. CHARLWOOD *Afternoon of Time* 80 'Gunna be a dinnyhazer of a storm,' said Percy.

dip, *n. Obs.* See quot. 1847. See also DOUGHBOY.

1847 D. BUNCE *Australasiatic Reminisc.* 21 Apr. (1857) 171 Dr Leichhardt ordered the cook to mix up a lot of flour, and treated us all to a feed of dips. These were made as follows:- a quantity of flour was mixed up with water, and stirred with a spoon to a certain consistency, and dropped into a pot of boiling water, a spoonful at a time. Five minutes boiling was sufficient, when they were eaten with the water in which they were boiled. **1888** J.F. MANN *Eight Months with Dr Leichhardt* 40 As the last piece of meat had been consumed.. a small additional amount of flour was issued and made into 'dips'—that is, paste dropped from a spoon into boiling water.

dip, *v.*

1. In the phr. **to dip one's lid,** to raise one's hat as a mark of respect. Chiefly *fig.*

1915 C.J. DENNIS *Songs of Sentimental Bloke* 21 'This 'ere's Doreen,' 'e sez. 'This 'ere's the Kid.' I dips me lid. **1984** *Sydney Morning Herald* 9 July (Guide) 16/3 So now three journalists, White, Day and Thomson, own a radio station. Us ordinary journos dips our lids.

2. In the phr. **to dip out (on),** to fail, to miss (an opportunity, etc.)

1952 T.A.G. HUNGERFORD *Ridge & River* 56 There wasn't a man in the section who would dip out on a patrol so long as he could drag one leg after the other. **1984** *N.T. News*

(Darwin) 9 Nov. 26/1 Some of your hopes and wishes hinges on the outcome of this weekend but you have good stars for it so you needn't worry about dipping out.

diprotodon /daɪˈprɒʊtədɒn/. [The fossil animal genus *Diprotodon* was named in 1838 by English palaeontologist Richard Owen (see quot. 1838) f. Gr. δι- two, πρῶτος first + ὀδούς tooth, referring to the two prominent incisors in the animal's lower jaw.] An extinct, very large, herbivorous, quadruped marsupial of the Austral. genus *Diprotodon*.

[**1838** T.L. MITCHELL *Three Exped. Eastern Aust.* II. 362 Genus *Diprotodon*. I apply this name to the genus of Mammalia, represented by the anterior extremity of the right ramus, lower jaw, with a single large procumbent incisor. . . This is the specimen conjectured to have belonged to the Dugong, but the incisor resembles the corresponding tooth of the wombat.] **1848** *Maitland Mercury* 8 Mar. 3/2 *The Diprotodon*. The fossil remains . . found at a branch of the Condamine River. **1986** *Sydney Morning Herald* 18 Sept. 1/6 The diprotodon, a two-tonne precursor to kangaroos, browsed Australia's savannah woodlands during the Ice Age or pleistocene period.

dirt. *Obs.* [Orig. U.S.: see OED *sb*. 3 b. and Mathews.] The alluvial soil or gravel from which gold is separated by washing; wash-dirt. Also *attrib*.

1852 *Murray's Guide to Gold Diggings* 26 The cradleman . . keeps the cradle, when it has been charged with 'dirt', constantly going. **1858** *Colonial Mining Jrnl.* Oct. 29/1 On the whole lead, say a distance of three miles, there are scattered parties sinking and driving for 'blocks' and taking dirt headings.

dirty, *a*. Resentful. Freq. with **on,** resentful of.

1965 *Oz* (Sydney) xxiii. 8 Well Kicker gets a bit dirty on this but I keep him sweet an' we shoot thru an' book in at The Rex. **1972** G. MORLEY *Jockey rides Honest Race* 230 There's Deena talking to her boyfriend. I know he's got a bird out in the car waiting for him. She's gonna get dirty if she finds out.

discoloured, *ppl. a. Obs.* Of a person: neither Aboriginal nor white.

1913 *Bulletin* (Sydney) 6 Nov. 22/1 There were 2054 indented discolored seamen engaged in the pearling industry at Broome. . . Japanese were in the vast majority. **1926** *Illustr. Tasmanian Mail* (Hobart) 27 Jan. 6/1 Alice Springs, with a white population of 30 or more, and a much larger dark and discoloured one.

dish, *n. Gold-mining*.

1. A vessel in which alluvial soil, gravel, etc., is washed to separate out gold; the quantity of alluvial deposit such a vessel contains.

1851 [see *dish man*]. **1852** *Moreton Bay Free Press* 1 Apr. 3/5 He washed two or three dishes full of earth. **1928** M.B. PETERSEN *Jewelled Nights* 65 Sam and Dosey went down to see and they got a 'weight' in two 'dishes'!

2. Special Comb. **dish man,** a gold-miner who uses a dish; **-washing** *vbl. n*., the process of separating gold from the surrounding alluvial deposit by washing it in a dish.

1851 *Empire* (Sydney) 20 Aug. 67/3 Mr Esmonds . . imagines that a cradle in full operation, with a party of four or five miners, might obtain two ounces a day, and that the **dishmen**, when in full practice, might on the average obtain eight or ten shillings. **1852** D. MACKENZIE *Ten Yrs. Aust.* 24 **Dish-washing** consists simply in pouring water into the dish upon the clay, keeping it stirred, and gradually washing off the upper particles.

Hence **dishful** *n*., the quantity of alluvial deposit contained in a dish.

1852 D. MACKENZIE *Gold Digger* 37 A man dug up a tin dishful of slaty-coloured clay, when an individual on the adjoining claim offered £50 for the dishful before it was washed.

dish, *v*. [f. prec.] *trans*. To agitate (a quantity of alluvial deposit) in a dish of water in order to separate out the gold.

1851 *Empire* (Sydney) 27 Nov. 407/3 People are obliged to dish their dirt when they are near enough to the water. **1932** I.L. IDRIESS *Prospecting for Gold* 12 Next day take up the bottom and dish it.

dispersal. [See next.] The clearing of Aborigines from a particular locality; the pursuit and slaughter of Aborigines. Also *attrib*.

1902 W. LEES *Aboriginal Problem Qld.* 11 The issue of distinct orders . . that the aboriginals were to be treated on humanitarian lines, with the result that since then not a single 'dispersal', i.e., by bullet, has taken place. **1926** *Bulletin* (Sydney) 4 Feb. 22/2 Mrs McAuley's husband was killed long ago by the blacks near Cairns. The 'dispersal party' which went out rushed the camp of the suspected tribe.

disperse, *v. Hist.* [Euphemistic use of *disperse* to scatter.] *trans*. Ostensibly, to drive (Aborigines) away from a particular area; commonly, to seek out and kill (an Aboriginal or a party of Aborigines).

1805 *Sydney Gaz.* 19 May, A party composed of the settlers . . went in quest of the natives . . in order to disperse them. **1890** A.J. VOGAN *Black Police* 142 A young 'sub', new in the force . . used the word 'killed' instead of the official '*dispersed*' in speaking of the unfortunate natives left *hors de combat* on the field. The report was returned to him for correction in company with a severe reprimand for his careless wording. . . The 'sub' . . corrected his report so that the faulty portion now read as follows: 'We successfully surrounded the said party of aborigines and *dispersed* fifteen, *the remainder*, some half dozen, succeeded in escaping.'

Hence **dispersing** *vbl. n*. Usu. *attrib*.

1892 *Bulletin* (Sydney) 2 Apr. 6/3 He had crossed the Nicholson to a white's camp, when a 'dispersing party' that had been trailing him came up.

dit. In Services' (chiefly naval) speech: a yarn; a reminiscence. Also *attrib*.

1942 *Rag: H.M.A.S. 'Orara'* 25 Dec. 3 Prowling round the mess-decks listening to the leave dits. **1944** *Dit* (Melbourne) Sept. 3 The two men spinning a dit on the front page of this issue. **1945** *Ibid.* Oct. 152 Ships photographic firms are invited to submit similar photos of dit-spinners.

div. [Abbrev. of *div(idend.*] A sum of money, esp. as won from a bookmaker.

1891 *Bulletin* (Sydney) 28 Mar. 23/1 He borrowed our div. and a lot beside and came out of the fight top dog. **1966** J. WATEN *Season of Youth* 32 We were to meet after each race near the merry-go-round and I would give him my takings and he would give me my div.

dividing mate. *Obs.* A partner, orig. on the goldfields, with whom the rewards of an enterprise are equally shared.

1878 'R. BOLDREWOOD' *Ups & Downs* 11 The great Australian custom of 'dividing mates' by which . . fortunes have been made and shared. **1916** H.L. ROTH *Sketches & Reminisc. Qld.* 10 They had been 'dividing mates' and he insisted on the partnership with the cob continuing.

dividing range. A series of hills or stretch of high country forming a division between adjacent river systems; a watershed.

1834 J.D. LANG *Hist. & Statistical Acct. N.S.W.* II. 105 We were soon obliged to dismount again to climb up the precipitous side of a steep mountain, to gain the summit of what the colonists call 'a dividing range'. These ranges, which are flanked on either side by deep and sometimes impassable ravines, traverse the country in many places for a great distance, either in a northerly and southerly or easterly and westerly direction. **1973** *Official Yr. Bk.* 27 The Great Dividing Range .. extends from the North of Queensland .. and .. terminates in Tasmania.

dixie. Chiefly *Vic.* [Transf. use of *dixie* iron pot.] An ice-cream carton, now usu. small. See also BUCKET *n.* 1, DANDY.

1941 S.J. BAKER *Pop. Dict. Austral. Slang* 23 *Dixie*, an ice-cream carton. **1972** G.W. TURNER *Eng. Lang. in Aust. & N.Z.* (rev. ed.) 124 Why should .. a pot or tub of icecream be a *dandy* in Adelaide, a *dixie* in Melbourne and elsewhere a *bucket*?

dizz, *v.* [Of unknown origin.] *trans.* See quot. 1872.

1872 M.B. BROWNRIGG *Cruise of Freak* 55, I ventured upon tasting a *young* mutton bird 'dizzed', that is, cooked in its own fat. **1968** P. ADAM SMITH *Tiger Country* 173 She .. like most old hands in the mutton-bird islands likes them 'dizzed', very young birds fried in their own fat.

djanga /'dʒæŋə/. *W.A. Obs.* [a. Nyungar *jaŋa* ghost.] A name applied by Aborigines to a white person. Freq. as *pl.*

1838 *Colonist* (Sydney) 31 Jan. 4/1 The name which they invariably apply to the whites, when talking of the latter among themselves, is 'Djanga', or 'the dead'. **1851** *Athenaeum* (London) 24 May 557 The word *Djanga* at Swan River, means the dead; but it is indiscriminately applied to Europeans,—as they are believed to be deceased aborigines.

do, *v.*

1. a. *trans. Obs.* To consume (food or drink), chiefly with reference to alcoholic liquor.

1859 F. FOWLER *Southern Lights & Shadows* 48 A wealthy tavern-keeper who came to England with us used to boast of 'doing' his forty nobblers of brandy a day, a nobbler being in quantity little better than half a wine-glass. **1899** *Western Champion* (Barcaldine) 21 Feb. 3/1 'Can you do a drink,' asked one out-of-work of another in like predicament.

b. To spend (one's available money) completely. Also with **in** and **up.**

1889 *Referee* (Sydney) 19 May 2/1 A young fellow .. rushes to 'do in' every spare fiver or tenner that comes into his possession. **1894** *Bulletin* (Sydney) 20 Jan. 24/1 He could do his cheque up quicker than was ever done before. **1922** A. WRIGHT *Boss o' Yedden* 136 'Done y' dough?' 'Every bean. I'm broke. So long.'

2. With **over:** to assault physically, to 'rough up'. Also as *vbl. n.*

[N.Z. **1866** *Maungatapu Murders*, Since we are going to do these three people over .. I think we had better prevent him from doing us any harm.] **1944** L. GLASSOP *We were Rats* 76 Somebody took my coat. 'Do this galah over,' he whispered in my ear. 'He's a king-hit merchant.' **1977** B. SCOTT *My Uncle Arch* 13 He gave them such a doing over.

dob, *v.* [Fig. use of Br. dial. *dob* to put down, throw down.]

1. a. *trans.* To inform upon; to incriminate. Usu. with **in.**

1955 *Overland* v. 4 He came to me and dobbed in one of the carpenters for talking. **1974** M. GILLESPIE *Into Hollow Mountains* 15 Someone else saw him with the wad of notes and dobbed him to the principal.

b. *trans.* To impose (a responsibility upon).

1968 S. GORE *Holy Smoke* 24 Y' know what happened when I'm in at th' Alice the other day? Some sky-pilot joker tried to dob it on me to go to church! **1981** B. HUMPHRIES *Nice Night's Entertainment* 42 She dropped the broad hint that she'd like to go up to the Elizabethan Theatre at Stratford some time .. and I more or less dobbed myself in.

2. *trans.* [Cf. OEDS *dub, v.*[4]] With **in:** to contribute (money) towards a common cause. Also *absol.*

1956 E. LAMBERT *Watermen* 103 The whole town dobbed in and bought Charlie and Russ a new boat. **1979** S.W. DUTHIE *Fidlers Creek* 2 Anyway, we all dob a bit in to buy the outfit.

3. *Australian National Football.* To kick (a goal).

1965 J. DYER *Captain Blood* 100 He dobbed it through the middle. **1981** L. MONEY *Footy Fan's Handbk.* 37 *Terms for a goal.* It's full points! He's dobbed it! .. Right through the centre!

dobber. [f. DOB *v.* 1.] An informant; a tale-bearer. Also **dobber-in.** See also *cobber dobber* COBBER *n.* 2.

1958 *Coast to Coast 1957–58* 201 How's his flipping form? Dobber-in Number One. **1973** J. POWERS *Last of Knucklemen* (1974) 95 Don't look at me, you bastards! I'm no bloody dobber!

docker. *Obs.* [Br. dial. *docker* struggle; also *fig.* 'of hard work, strenuous living, fatigue' (see SND).] In the phr. **to go (in) a docker,** to embark on an enterprise, activity, etc., with vigour, wholeheartedly.

1866 *Sydney Punch* 21 Apr. 794/1 Somebody else was going in a 'Docker' in reforming the time-honoured abuses of this Gothic Establishment. **1871** *Austral. Town & Country Jrnl.* (Sydney) 22 Apr. 506/1 On Thursday morning when coming home at the finish of a good gallop, and going a docker.

doctor, *n.*[1] KORADJI. Also *attrib.*

1834 G. BENNETT *Wanderings N.S.W.* I. 190 Krardgee Kibba, or Doctor Stone. **1962** D. LOCKWOOD *I, Aboriginal* 9 It was one walkabout time .. in the Never-Never Land south of the Roper River that the Medicine Man, the Doctor Blackfellow, tried to kill me.

doctor, *n.*[2] [Transf. use of *doctor* ship's cook or (U.S.) cook in a logging camp.] One who cooks for shearers, etc., on a station.

1868 C.W. BROWNE *Overlanding in Aust.* 71 Grumbling is contagious in its nature so for this reason alone a good cook, or 'doctor', as he is called, is a necessary individual in camp. **1921** G.A. BELL *Under Brigalows* 147 Next day came another big dish of stew, and another grumbler got up and went outside with the 'Doctor'.

doctor, *n.*[3] [f. the fig. use in the West Indies and S. Africa for a wind with refreshing or cleansing properties.] In the s.w. of W.A., a cool, refreshing sea breeze, with considerable inland penetration, which brings relief at the end of a hot summer day (see quot. 1971). Also **Albany, Esperance, Eucla, Fremantle, Geraldton, Nullarbor, Perth, Southerly doctor.**

1870 W.H. KNIGHT *W.A.* 14 Soon after, the grateful 'doctor', or sea-breeze, sets in. **1908** *Bulletin* (Sydney) 19 Mar. 14/2 Even when the Albany 'doctor' didn't blow, the mornings were quite cool. **1920** BRIGGS & HARRIS *Joysticks & Fiddlesticks* (1938) 108 Every evening .. about five o'clock, a wind springs up from the south. It is called the 'Southerly Doctor'. This wind is remarkably cool, and makes life bearable for the people who live along the east-west railway line from Ooldea to Perth. **1920** *W.A.: Early Vicissitudes* 87 Thanks also to the regularity of the calls of Mr South-West Wind—colloquially termed the 'Fremantle doctor'—the post meridian hours of the warmest days are usually tempered with refreshing zephyrs. **1955** *Austral. Meteorol. Mag.* Dec. 61 Those resident from Norseman southwards were definite in maintaining that the 'Esperance doctor' did reach them. *Ibid.*, Further north, the accounts were rather confused, and diverse, some at least clearly identifying the 'doctor' with cold frontal passages. **1956** S. HOPE *Digger's Paradise* 71 The 'Perth doctor' .. blows toward evening off the Indian Ocean. **1971** J. GENTILLI in *World Survey Climatol.* XIII. 111 In the southwest, sea-breezes have long been recognized as a distinctive feature of the local climate, so much so that they were given local popular names such as (in the likely chronological order of their adoption) *Fremantle Doctor, Albany Doctor, Geraldton Doctor, Esperance Doctor,* and more recently even *Eucla Doctor,* in each case from the name of the coastal locality near which they cross the shore on their welcome way inland. **1977** B. FULLER *Nullarbor Lifelines* 96 The Nullarbor 'doctor' is a desert wind that blows at the equinoxes.

doctor, *n.*[4] [Transf. use of the phr. *to go for the doctor* to seek medical help as a matter of urgency.] In the phr. **to go for the doctor,** to go 'all out', to abandon all restraint.
1949 L. GLASSOP *Lucky Palmer* 74 Go for the doctor. Slap a tenner on it. It's only an even-money shot. **1976** *Sydney Morning Herald* 20 Apr. 13/1, I decided to go for the doctor rather than let Taras Bulba fight for his head.

dodder-laurel. [Transf. use of *dodder* a twining leafless parasitic plant of the genus *Cuscuta* (fam. Cuscutaceae).] Any of several parasitic perennial climbers of the genus *Cassytha* (fam. Lauraceae) of all States; *devil's twine,* see DEVIL 3. Also **dodder, dodder vine.**
1848 T.L. MITCHELL *Jrnl. Exped. Tropical Aust.* 362 One of the Dodder laurels (*Cassytha pubescens*..) a species also found near Port Jackson. **1906** *Emu* V. 134 Matted together in parts with the native dodder vine (Cassytha). **1970** J.V. MARSHALL *Walk to Hills of Dreamtime* 42 A battleground of tree and parasite and vine, with the giant dodders and jikkas choking the life out of all they touched with tourniquet arms.

dodge, *v.* [Br. dial. *dodge* to follow in the track of a person or animal; see EDD.]
1. *trans.* To drive (sheep or cattle). Also *absol.* See also *monkey dodging* MONKEY 5.
1881 A.C. GRANT *Bush-Life Qld.* II. 134 On the road—Aboriginal innocents—a wet night on watch—dodging cows. **1922** 'J. BUSHMAN' *In Musgrave Ranges* 226 'Dodging along' behind cattle, as it is called, is not hard work. **1944** J.J. HARDIE *Cattle Camp* (ed. 3) 85 Armstrong and Phillips cut out the Ardwell cattle to one side, while Ken and Dusty moved through the mob, dodging our cows with unbranded calves, and grown cleanskins to where Scotty and Jerry proudly rode the face of the camp.
2. *trans.* To misappropriate (an animal): see PODDY-DODGE.
1956 T. RONAN *Moleskin Midas* 149 For every poddy that's up in the Coronet breakaways there's a dozen blokes trying to dodge it off.
3. In the phr. **to dodge Pompey**: see POMPEY.

dodger, *n.*[1] [U.S. *dodger* a small handbill or circular.] An advertising leaflet, esp. one carrying political propaganda.
1891 *Truth* (Sydney) 10 May 3/4 Receiving a pink 'dodger' in the street last Saturday week it was found on reference to be a 'startler' from the Centenary Hall. **1973** L. OAKES *Whitlam PM* 54 Margaret Whitlam spent her days folding dodgers, and her husband spent his nights delivering them.

dodger, *n.*[2] [U.S. *(corn) dodger* small cake of cornbread: see Mathews.] Bread.
1897 *Bulletin* (Sydney) 7 Aug. (Red Page), Loaf of bread—'Dodger'. **1980** HEPWORTH & HINDLE *Boozing out in Melbourne Pubs* 141 None of your sliced bread here, but proper hunks of dodger.

dodger, *a.* [Perh. from prec. (but cf. SNODGER).] Good, excellent.
1941 S.J. BAKER *Pop. Dict. Austral. Slang* 24 Dodger, food of any kind. As adj., good, excellent. **1953** D. STIVENS *Gambling Ghost* 3 When we got through the valley mouth everything was dodger. The grass was thick.. and there was plenty of water.

doe. A female kangaroo.
1845 L. LEICHHARDT *Jrnl. Overland Exped. Aust.* 15 Feb. (1847) 155 Brown descried a kangaroo... It proved to be a fine doe, with a young one. **1975** L. WALKER *Runaway Girl* 124 'Would it be 'roo shooters?' Drew nodded. 'A dead doe back there,' he said.

doer. [Transf. use of *doer* an animal that does well, thrives: see OED 3.]
1. a. One who earns respect by coping well with the vicissitudes of life (see quot. 1942); a 'character' (see quot. 1919).
1902 J.H.M. ABBOTT *Tommy Cornstalk* 14 He has unconsciously been taught.. how to be comfortable, how to become a good 'doer' under all adverse circumstances. **1919** W.H. DOWNING *Digger Dialects* 19 Doer, a person unusually humorous, reckless, undisciplined, immoral or eccentric. **1942** H.H. PECK *Mem. of Stockman* 67 Billy.. just on 87, is a wonderful man, and despite several broken limbs in the last few years, still cuts out his own cattle for market.. truly a great old doer.
b. In the collocation **hard doer:** an intensive form of sense 1 a.; a 'hard case' (see HARD *a.*).
1910 *Bulletin* (Sydney) 21 Apr. 14/1 The hard-doer explaining that the names of the Apostles have been written on the slips of paper. **1983** C. BINGHAM *Beckoning Horizon* 22 Many of these men were 'hard-doers', but the majority, whatever their failings, were thoroughly reliable.
c. In the collocation **good doer**: one who thrives; a generous person.
1942 H.H. PECK *Mem. of Stockman* 244 With his happy and kindly nature and general appearance of 'a good doer', he was very popular. **1944** A. TURNER *Royal Mail* 32 He is, in his own words, a 'good doer'. Quick of temper and generous to a fault.
2. *transf.* and *fig.*
1944 K.S. PRICHARD *Potch & Colour* 71 When the mugs were filled.. Bill lifted his old hard-doer of blue-rimmed white enamel, chipped and rusty in every crack. **1976** DRAGE & PAGE *Riverboats & Rivermen* 79 I'd go to the gallery and cook up a batch of what we called 'hard doers', the sweet cakes served up for night time snacks and at change of shifts.

dog, *n.*[1]
1. Used *attrib.* in Comb. with specific reference to the dingo: **dog fence, -net** *v.,* **-netting, -proof** *a.,* **-stiffener.** See also DINGO *n.* 4.
1846 F. DUTTON *S.A. & its Mines* 202 Should the timber not be sufficiently straight for making posts and rails, it will always make a kangaroo or **dog fence**. **1930** D. COTTRELL *Earth Battle* 176 He.. erected.. a six-foot dog-fence.. and men were sorry for him because no one had ever dreamed of **dog-netting** a great station. **1947** E. HILL *Flying Doctor Calling* 108 Crossing the New South Wales border at the Warri Gate in the '**dog-netting**' fence. **1865** *Sydney Punch* 7 Jan. 263/1 Numerous sheep yards, most of them **dog proof. 1898** D.W. CARNEGIE *Spinifex & Sand* 370 The Government is content to pay, not dreaming that '**dog-stiffeners**' (*i.e.,* men who make a living by poisoning dingoes) carry on so base a trade as bartering tobacco for live dog's tails!
2. *transf.* and *fig.*
a. Used *attrib.* in Special Comb. to connote restriction or deprivation: **dog act,** see quot. 1898; **Collar Act,** the Transport Workers' Act (1928), see quot. 1955; **hole** *obs.,* a squalid dwelling, etc.; **licence (certificate, ticket),** a certificate exempting an Aboriginal from legislation pertaining to Aborigines, esp. that prohibit-

ing the sale of alcoholic liquor to Aborigines; **poor** *a.*, in very poor condition; **window,** see quot.
  1898 *Bulletin* (Sydney) 31 Dec. 31/3 There is an Act compelling a publican to refuse drink to an habitual inebriate. This is locally known as the '**Dog Act**', and to be brought under the Dog Act is a glorious distinction, a sort of V.C. of Northern Territory life. **1935** *Workers' Weekly* (Sydney) 16 Aug. 1/2 The Federal Government's threat to apply the **Dog Collar** (Transport Workers') **Act** (work licenses) to break the strike can have no other effect than to make the seamen more determined to struggle for complete victory. **1955** G. HEALEY *A.L.P.* 91 Within one week the Bruce-Page Government had passed a Transport Workers' Act, better known as the 'Dog Collar Act', under which waterside workers were issued licenses which could be withheld or revoked for almost any reason. **1843** *Satirist & Sporting Chron.* (Sydney) 25 Mar. 3/2 Baker, of the *Crown and Anchor,* is about to remove his licence to a **dog-hole** in Market-street. **1955** F.B. VICKERS *Mirage* 257 Monty wants us to get the **dog licence**—that's the paper they give you... If we had this paper, me and you could have walked into that pub and stood at the bar all day and none of 'em could have said a word to us... We'd be as good as the next bloke so long as we could flash the dog licence. **1977** K. GILBERT *Living Black* 297 Before the 1967 referendum, before citizenship, Aborigines could receive these exemption cards—dog certificates—which enabled them to enter a hotel. **1981** *Nat. Times* (Sydney) 15 Nov. 33/2 She carried a Dog Ticket—an exemption card which, despite the evidence of the photograph, stated that she was a white person since she had married a man whose father was white. That ticket allowed her to visit hotels, to vote and to assert her status as an Australian citizen. The catch was that she was no longer allowed to associate with her Aboriginal mother, father and sister or she would be charged with consorting. **1888** 'R. BOLDREWOOD' *Robbery under Arms* (1937) 70 She was **dog-poor** and hardly able to drag herself along. **1981** J. ROBERTS *Massacres to Mining* 70 In most northern pubs the Aborigines are not welcome in the main bar. Instead they are sent to a small side window, or '**dog window**' as it is known, or to a dingy minor bar. In the 330 miles between Alice Springs and Tennant Creek all but one of the pubs has a 'dog window'.
  b. In special collocations: **dog's disease,** any of several ailments (see quots.); **jew's harp,** see quot. 1904; also *fig.*; **show,** a dog's chance, i.e. no chance at all.
  1890 *Braidwood Dispatch* 30 Apr. 2/2 They complain in the first instance of a pain in the head... It is very similar to the epidemic we had some years ago which went by the names of the 'Temora rot' and the '**dog's disease**'. **1953** S.J. BAKER *Aust. Speaks* 166 *Dog's disease,* malaria. **1967** *Kings Cross Whisper* (Sydney) xxxii. 7/1 Brewer's asthma, a very severe hangover. Also brewer's croup. Dog's disease. **1982** N. KEESING *Lily on Dustbin* 77 'Dog's disease' to some people means 'flu, to others gastro-enteritis. **1898** W. DOLLMAN *Bush Fancies* 66 You white-livered son of a gun, you **dog's jew's harp! 1904** *Bulletin* (Sydney) 7 Apr. 16/4 In the heart of the Out-back.. when sugar runs out 'dogs' Jews' harps' are cooked, *i.e.* dumplings punctuated with currants. **1898** E. DYSON *Below & on Top* 179, I don't think you've got a **dog's show.**
  c. As **tinned dog,** canned meat; also **(tin) dog.**
  1895 *Bulletin* (Sydney) 17 Aug. 27/2 We gave him some 'tinned dorg' and a drink. **1913** W.K. HARRIS *Outback in Aust.* 29 In some of the isolated mining camps.. damper, 'dog', and tea is served up meal after meal. **1929** R.D. LANE *Romance Old Coolgardie* 55 Those were the days of tin dog and damper.
  d. As **tin dog,** an improvised rattle used in driving stock: see quot. 1924.
  1924 L. ST. C. GRONDONA *Kangaroo keeps on Talking* 60 If one does not possess a tyke of some description one makes.. a 'tin dog', which.. is evolved by perforating the lids of tobacco tins and threading them on a loop of fencing wire. This makes a horrible din, which,—if efficacious while the novelty lasts,—seems later to amuse, and, finally,

to bore the sheep. The jackeroo who invents a tin dog with a bite as well as a bark should be raised to the peerage. **1979** R. EDWARDS *Skills Austral. Bushman* 157 It has been suggested that the lagerphone, with its cluster of beer-bottle tops, is derived from the tin dog.
  e. In the phr. **a dog tied up,** an unpaid debt, esp. at an hotel.
  1905 *Bulletin* (Sydney) 24 Oct. 14/3 'Scarver'—to flit from town secretly, leaving sorrowing creditors behind... 'Leaving a dog tied up' refers to the debts left by the 'scarverer'. **1977** T. RONAN *Mighty Men on Horseback* 17, I had to live on the cuff till the cheque was made good and by that time I had so many dogs tied up that it took the proceeds to let them go.

dog, *n.*^{2} [U.S. *dog* informer, traitor: see OEDS *sb.* 3 e.]
  a. An informer; one who betrays colleagues or changes allegiance; chiefly in the phr. **to turn dog (on).**
  1848 J. SYME *Nine Yrs. Van Diemen's Land* 273 A man known to give officers information is designated by the epithet 'Dog'. **1863** *Frank Gardiner, or Bushranging in 1863* 14 Some of the lads.. are regular young hands, and might turn dog. **1918** *Truth* (Sydney) 13 Jan. 1/7 Which is the more deplorable—the twistings of Billee Hughes or those of the old cobbers who turn dorg on him?
  b. *fig.*
  1919 *7th Field Artillery Brigade Yandoo* 20 Mar. 136 The weather again 'turned dog on us'. Cold winds and driving rain. **1922** 'TE WHARE' *Bush Cinema* 84 The way-back herbalist.. seldom turns dog on the awful concoction which results from brook-lime (hyssop) boiled down with Epsom salts.

dog, *v.*^{1} [f. DOG *n.*^{2}] *intr.* To change allegiance; with **on,** to betray.
  1896 E. DYSON *Rhymes from Mines* 129 I'm not goin' to dog on a mate. **1953** T.A.G. HUNGERFORD *Riverslake* 228 Perhaps that was why he was pulling out, though he didn't seem to be the type to dog.

dog, *v.*^{2} *intr.* To hunt dingoes: see quot. 1981. Also *trans.*: see quot. 1944. Freq. as *vbl. n.*
  1910 C.E.W. BEAN *On Wool Track* 55 A man is generally kept dogging, and the boundary rider gets a few pounds out of occasional scalps. **1932** M.R. WHITE *No Roads go By* 95 Every man on the station was doing a little 'dogging' as a side-line, scalps were worth twelve and sixpence each, and the game was keen. **1944** *Bulletin* (Sydney) 23 Feb. 12/1, I ran along to see Robbie and found him dogging a paddock near the road. **1981** A. GRANT *Camel Train & Aeroplane* 258 Over the border in Western Australia, dogging. [*Note*] Trapping, shooting or poisoning Dingoes or wild dogs to prevent their inroads into sheep flocks, for which they received a Government bounty paid on each scalp.

dogbox. A compartment in a railway carriage without internal access to other compartments; a substandard carriage.
  1905 N.F. SPIELVOGEL *Gumsucker on Tramp* 44, I found.. railway cars worse than the worst Australia possesses. The one I came down here in was a dog box. **1973** D. FOSTER *North South West* 93 I'm sitting, actually frozen, in the corner of some mail car going west, while outside my second class dogbox (we're stopped) is a platform.

dogger. [See DOG *v.*^{2}] One who hunts dingoes.
  1890 A. WOODHOUSE *Man with Apples* 64 He was up in Mallee Country.. catching dingoes. He was a reg'lar dogger. **1984** *West Austral.* (Perth) 19 Jan. 45/4 'A number of large dingoes apparently evaded the former dogger and are still at large,' Mr Grill said.

dog-leg, *a.* [f. *dog-leg,* of a bent form like a dog's hind leg.] Of a fence: made from logs laid horizontally on

crossed supports (see quots. 1901 and 1980). Also **dog-legged.**
   1836 Tas. Non-State Rec. 103/3 25 Oct., All that portion of Land Bounded on the north by a dog leg and furze fence.   **1901** H. LAWSON *Joe Wilson & his Mates* 99 The clearing was fenced in by a light 'dog-legged' fence (a fence of sapling poles resting on forks and X-shaped uprights).   **1980** HOLTH & BARNABY *Cattlemen of High Country* 83 Another early method of construction was the dog-leg fence. Stumps about half a metre high with a V cut in them were placed in the ground at wide intervals. A log was laid with its ends on the Vs and supported at each stump by two poles—the dog-leg—crossed above the log and dug into the ground beside the stump. A second row of logs was laid through the crossed poles.
   Hence **dogleg** *v. trans.*, to make (timber) into a dog-leg fence.
   1891 E.H. HALLACK *W.A. & Yilgarn Goldfields* 14 One of the wheat paddocks is enclosed by the most valuable fencing material I have ever seen, viz., sandalwood, doglegged and propped to escape the risk of fire.

dogman. [f. *dog* mechanical device for gripping or holding something: see OED *sb.* 7.] A worker who rides on the hook of a crane, or a girder, etc., being lifted by a crane, giving signals to the crane-operator.
   1948 *Act* (N.S.W.) no. 38 Sect. 17A (6), 'Dogman' means a person directly responsible for slinging and controlling the movement of loads by a crane used in building work or excavation work, or other work where the loads are not usually at all times in full view of the crane driver.   **1985** *Canberra Times* 13 Feb. 7/3 BLF dogmen want same 'dirty deal'.

dog watch. *Droving.* [Transf. use of the nautical *dog watch* a short watch of two hours between 4 p.m. and 8 p.m.] A short watch in the early evening.
   1935 G. MCIVER *Drover's Odyssey* 63 Only one man at a time could have supper, for the others were required to keep the sheep on the camp during what was known as 'the dog watch'.   **1979** C. STONE *Riding Brumbies* 8 The first watch, for only one hour, is kept by one of the cattlemen to allow the other men to have their evening meal. This short watch is always called the 'dog watch'.

dogwood. [Transf. use of *dogwood* a shrub of the genus *Cornus.*] Any of several unrelated shrubs or trees, esp. ELLANGOWAN POISON BUSH, and *Jacksonia scoparia* (fam. Fabaceae) of N.S.W. and Qld.; the wood of these plants. See also STINKWOOD. Also *attrib.*
   1828 Tas. Colonial Secretary's Office Rec. 1/14 262, A thick underwood of Dogwood.   **1844** L. LEICHHARDT *Jrnl. Overland Exped. Aust.* 23 Oct. (1847) 20 A . . creek . . which, from the number of Dogwood shrubs (Jacksonia), in the full glory of their golden blossoms, I called 'Dogwood Creek'.

dole.
   1. *Hist.* Used *attrib.*, with reference to unemployment benefits during the Depression of the 1930s.
   1930 *Sydney Morning Herald* 7 June 15/5 Representatives of 15 metropolitan councils yesterday asked the Minister for Labour and Industry (Mr Farrar) to alter the dole system so that men receiving unemployment relief should be allowed to work for it.   **1959** D. HEWETT *Bobbin Up* 90, I remember him draggin' home week after week with those blasted dole tickets.
   2. Special Comb. **dole-bludger,** one who exploits the system of unemployment benefits by avoiding gainful employment; so **dole-bludgery** *n.*, **dole bludging** *vbl. n.* and *ppl. a.*
   1976 *Bulletin* (Sydney) 16 Oct. 20/1 A genuine dole bludger, a particularly literate young man . . explained that he wasn't bothering to look for work any more because he was sick and tired of being treated like a chattel.   **1978** *Westerly* iii. 9, I love the boy: a painty, dole-bludging, sink-full-of-dirty-dishes love, reeking of sentiment, but love.   **1983** *Canberra Times* 26 July 3/3 He said that dole-bludging was a 'socially useful function', as were communes.   **1984** *Austral. Short Stories* viii. 1 He had dole-bludgery down to a fine art: bought the Age every day and memorised the relevant jobs advertised so he could con any Social Services Inspector who came snooping.

doleite. *Hist.* One in receipt of an unemployment benefit, esp. during the Depression of the 1930s.
   1963 HARNEY & LOCKWOOD *Shady Tree* 194 The first wave of people who resembled the present-day tourists, except that they had no money, were the train-jumpers and 'doleites' who spread across the countryside during the great depression.   **1978** G. HALL *River still Flows* 61 The place was quite crowded with Doleites.

doley. Also **dolie.** [f. *dole* + -Y.] One in receipt of an unemployment benefit.
   1953 'CADDIE' *Caddie* 209 You needn't worry about 'im Caddie. 'E's a friend to all us doleys.   **1961** W.E. HARNEY *Grief, Gaiety & Aborigines* 21 'Couldn't make out that old fellow the other day,' concernedly from a newly-arrived dolie.

dollar.
   1. *Hist.* A Spanish dollar circulating in N.S.W.; see also HOLEY DOLLAR.
   1803 *Sydney Gaz.* 21 Aug., The Victorians had however absented themselves carrying off a silver watch, *nine* dollars and several pieces of silver foreign coin.   **1844** C. LYON *Narr. & Recoll. Van Dieman's Land* 27 A kind man, on the road, lent me a dollar to buy food.
   2. *Hist.* [Also in Br. slang.] The sum of five shillings.
   1902 *Sporting News* (Launceston) 13 Dec. 3/4 All the same, were the race run again, my dollar could go on.   **1963** *Meanjin* 387 Give us another dollar. I won't spend more than a bob of it.
   3. Since 1966, and independently of its earlier uses, the standard unit of Australian currency. Also *attrib.*
   1963 *Sun* (Melbourne) 5 June 2/3 You can bet a dollar it's a dollar. . . Federal Cabinet will meet in Canberra today to choose a name for Australia's new basic decimal currency unit. And the strong tip is that the name dollar will be chosen.   **1966** *Age* (Melbourne) 17 Jan. 3/3 The board is now employing 29 Dollar Jills. . . We hope people . . will call the girls for any information they need about decimal currency.

dollar bird. [With ref. to a coin-like white spot on each wing.] A predom. brown and blue-green bird, the roller *Eurystomus orientalis*, a summer visitor to n. and e. Aust. and widespread in s. Asia.
   1827 *Trans. Linnean Soc. London* XV. 202 In Mr Caley's MSS. are the following notices of this bird. . . The settlers call it *Dollar Bird*, from the silver-like spot on the wing.   **1977** W.A. WINTER-IRVING *Bush Stories* 43 That evening the dollar birds called loudly.

dolly, *n. Gold-mining.* [Transf. use of Br. dial. *dolly* wooden instrument used in washing clothes: see OED *sb.*[1] 4.]
   1. An apparatus for crushing auriferous quartz in order to extract the gold.
   1859 W. KELLY *Life in Vic.* II. 67 Numbers of people earning a good livelihood by . . pounding it [*sc.* quartz] in dollies—a simple contrivance, constructed of a rude balance lever, made to act on the stump of a tree, by pulling it down with a rope, and letting it rebound after giving the blow, the blow falling on a common iron grating placed over a hollow in the stump, from which the crushed stuff is taken by means of a hand-hole cut in the side.   **1959** D. STUART *Yandy* 15 The thudding of the iron dolly in the

dolly pot was a familiar sound, and the quartz in the walled ore paddock grew larger day by day.

2. Special Comb. **dolly pot,** the receptacle in which the auriferous quartz is crushed by the dolly.

1931 A.W. UPFIELD *Sands of Windee* 37 It was .. a dollypot used by gold miners to pound up samples of ore to dust, then to flood the dust with water and roughly ascertain the gold content.

dolly, *v.* [f. prec.]
1. *trans.* To crush (auriferous quartz) using a dolly. Also *absol.*

1893 A.F. CALVERT *W.A. & its Gold Fields* 32 The reefs are so rich at the surface that some of the alluvial diggers in slack times have earned fair wages by simply dollying the stone. **1965** L. HAYLEN *Big Red* 64 He had sunk a shaft and dollied along the river, but that was years ago.

2. *fig.*

1890 A.J. VOGAN *Black Police* 56 I'll get dollied if fayther cotched me back at 'ome. **1937** W. & T.I. MOORE *Best Austral. One-Act Plays* 145 No stone un-dollied! I'll swear not.

Hence **dollying** *vbl. n.*

1894 A.F. CALVERT *Coolgardie Goldfield* 21 Only the very rich reefs—those that will give a return for dollying—are being worked.

dolly's wax. In the phr. **to be (full) up to dolly's wax,** to be satiated (with food).

1945 S.J. BAKER *Austral. Lang.* 207 Among nursery expressions which have acquired a fairly stabilized currency .. are .. the catchphrase [*sic*], *up to pussy's bow* and *dolly's wax,* to denote a surfeit, especially of food. **1965** B. HUMPHRIES *Nice Night's Entertainment* (1981) 85 Everyone was full up to dolly's wax and I was absolutely stonkered.

Domain. [Spec. use of *domain* the land immediately attached to a mansion: see OED *demesne* 3 c.] The name given to the land surrounding Government House in Sydney which is now a public park. Used *attrib.* of frequenters of the area in Comb. with various nouns denoting **(a)** a soap-box orator; **(b)** a vagrant, esp. as **Domain dosser.** See also YARRA-BANKER.

(a) **1883** *Bulletin* (Sydney) 17 Nov. 20/4 The question of interference with the 'Domain howlers' is a very much wider one than would be understood by the perusal of the brief discussion in the Assembly the other day. **1979** S. MORAN *Reminisc. of Rebel* p. v, He was a Domain orator and an outstanding one. (b) **1891** *Truth* (Sydney) 25 Jan. 2/4 Then followed all the 'black-legs' of the late strike, most of them bearing the stamp of Domain prowlers and scamps. **1901** *Tocsin* (Melbourne) 3 Jan. 1/2 In Sydney at this boom time were found .. in one day one thousand homeless 'Domain dossers' coming on the same charity for tickets authorising them to obtain one meal a day for a week.

Hence **Domainiac** *n.,* **Domainite** *n.*

1903 *Truth* (Sydney) 15 Feb. 1/5 If cleanliness is next to godliness many **Domainiacs** have wandered far from grace. **1918** *Ross's Monthly* Dec. 5/1 The efforts to convert the Sydney **Domainites** threaten to become popular, like 'slumming' and other forms of patronage and spiritual pride.

domesticated, *ppl. a. Hist.* Of an Aboriginal: trained to live with (and serve) the colonists: see also CIVILIZED.

1835 *True Colonist* (Hobart) 26 Jan. 2/4 The domesticated blacks who have been Mr R's faithful attendants. **1846** *Sydney Morning Herald* 29 Apr. 3/1 Mr Isaacs .. started .. from his station of the Darling Downs, in company with a domesticated aboriginal to act as a guide.

donah /ˈdoʊnə/. Also **dona.** [Br. slang; a. Sp. *dona* a woman.] A woman; a sweetheart (chiefly *c* 1900 in an urban, working-class context).

1874 *Melbourne Punch* 9 July 276/1 'Nobby, 'ere's Nixon with a new dona!' (which, being interpreted meaneth that the young man Nixon is paying his addresses to a fresh sweetheart). **1900** *Truth* (Sydney) 27 May 2/8 Ladies and gentlemen from the swell suburbs and both Society Points, blokes and donahs from the lanes and alleys.

dong, *v.* [Fig. use of *dong* the sound made by a bell or clock, prob. as a play on Br. dial. *ding* to strike, beat.] *trans.* To strike; to hit.

1916 G.I. ADCOCK *Lett.* (1930) 4 (typescript) A Corporal is charged with striking a Sergeant. .. I feel that the Corporal would have failed his manhood had he not 'donged' him. **1982** R. HALL *Just Relations* 113 The publican .. gives young Annie Lang a pat on the bottom as a compliment but she dongs him a beauty.

dong, *n.* [Cf. prec.] A blow; a punch.

1932 L. LOWER *Here's Another* 74 How would they like a dong in the gills with a golf ball? **1959** D. LOCKWOOD *Crocodiles & Other People* 52 'Maybe Darwin, here, wanted a fight, too?' one suggested. .. 'Hey, Darwin,' an athletic giant growled at me, 'is you insulted you wasn't arst into the dinner dong?'

donga. [S. Afr. *donga* a channel or gully formed by the action of water: see OED.]
1. A broad shallow often circular depression most commonly found in dry country.

1902 *Bulletin* (Sydney) 8 Mar. 14/3 The origins of .. 'donga' (a hollow)? **1984** M. BLAKERS et al. *Atlas Austral. Birds* 467 Fire and grazing by rabbits have destroyed the vegetation of many dongas.

2. A makeshift or temporary dwelling: see quot. 1972.

1900 *Truth* (Sydney) 28 Jan. 7/4 And dossed in dongas ev'ry night Daown in the old Dermain! **1972** G.W. TURNER *Eng. Lang. in Aust. & N.Z.* (rev. ed.) 22 *Donga,* a 'gully', expanding its meaning to include any kind of shelter .. seems likely to be traceable to the battlefields of the Boer War.

donk.
1. Abbrev. of *donkey,* an ass; now used elsewhere but perh. orig. Austral.

1907 *Bulletin* (Sydney) 17 Jan. 40/1 The donkey is now much used in the Australian interior. .. The donk.'s constitution is of iron. **1975** X. HERBERT *Poor Fellow my Country* 57 There's an old chap works a donkey-team down inside. .. He's got a lot of donks.

2. Abbrev. of *donkey-engine* a small, usu. subsidiary, engine.

1960 *Meanjin* 10, I thought that if I throttled back the engines a bit, with a few more revs in the starboard donk to keep the wing up, she'd be nose-heavier and wouldn't yaw. **1981** P. BARTON *Bastards I have Known* 61 He lifted the engine cover and peered around the donk.

donkey. *Obs.* [Transf. use of *donkey* a beast of burden.] A swagman's bundle of belongings; SWAG *n.*

1872 C.H. EDEN *My Wife & I in Qld.* 17 They all chaffed us about our swags, or donkeys or drums, as a bundle of things wrapped in a blanket is indifferently called. **1945** S.J. BAKER *Austral. Lang.* 102 A *drum* .. is the equivalent of *swag* .. *donkey.*

donkey-lick, *v.* [f. *donkey* a horse + *lick* to defeat.] *trans.* To defeat (an opponent, etc.) resoundingly. Also **donkey-wallop.**

1890 *Bulletin* (Sydney) 22 Mar. 8/1 He sold for a hundred and thirty, Because of a gallop he had One morning with Bluefish and Bertie, And donkey-licked both of 'em bad. **1975** X. Herbert *Poor Fellow my Country* 897 Pat snarled at him, 'Get donkey-walloped!'

donkey orchid. [See quot. 1942.] Any of several terrestrial orchids of the genus *Diuris* (fam. Orchidaceae) of all States but not N.T., esp. *D. longifolia*.
1926 J. Pollard *Bushland Man* 207 They plucked .. donkey orchids, leek orchids. **1942** C. Barrett *Austral. Wild Flower Bk.* 132 Some of the many kinds of *Diuris* or doubletails are called 'donkey orchids', with reference to the broad, spreading petals which are not unlike a toy donkey's ears.

donkey-vote. In a preferential system of voting: a vote recorded by unthinkingly allocating preferences according to the order in which candidates' names appear on the ballot-paper; such votes viewed collectively.
1962 *Meanjin* 356 Would you care to comment on the fact that your surname begins with the letters 'Ab–'? Yes, I see no reason to believe that the alphabetical system for candidates' names will be abandoned on ballot-papers. That being the case .. it seems that I shall always be at the top of the list. . . If I take you correctly sir, you are subtly stressing the importance of the 'donkey vote'? **1968** G. Mikes *Boomerang* 113 The donkey-votes mostly affect elections for the Senate.

dook /duk, djuk/, *v.* Also **duke**. [f. *dook*, var. *duke* hand.] *trans.* To give.
1954 T. Ronan *Vision Splendid* 119 Did I ever give you that tenner you duked me at the Border Races? **1978** H.C. Baker *I was Listening* 41 You .. just dooks yerself a good hand from the bottom of the pack.

doorknock. An appeal in which agents for a (charitable) cause go from house to house soliciting contributions; a campaign in support of a political party run similarly. Also *attrib.*, esp. as **doorknock appeal**.
1958 *Sun* (Melbourne) 27 May 17/1 All set for 'Campaign Door-knock'. . . With the Lord Mayor .. are some of the girls who helped pack kits for Anti-Cancer Campaign collectors. **1984** *Canberra Times* 26 July 18/4 The doorknock appeal on Sunday will see teams in all suburbs.

doover. /ˈduvə/. [Poss. repr. Yiddish pronunc. of Hebrew *davar* a word or thing.] A thingummyjig; but see quots. 1945, 1959, and 1972.
1940 *Artilleryman: Official Newspaper 2/1 Field Regiment* 6 May 8 Which may be due to the fortnight's 'Douvre' and its attendant change of scenery. **1945** 'Master-Sarg' *Yank discovers Aust.* 17 A doover is anything at all and takes the place of the old 'gadget'. Strictly it seems to mean a slit-trench or other funk hole. **1959** E. Lambert *Glory thrown In* 8 Beneath the camouflage nets and the roofs of dug-outs ('doovers' the Australians called them) the industry of war proceeded. **1972** K. Clift *Saga of Sig* 62 Tubby Allen .. was ensconced in a 'doover'—a rough dugout with a piece of truck canvas and camouflage netting.

dormouse possum. *Pygmy possum*, see Pygmy.
1926 *Bulletin* (Sydney) 25 Feb. 24/1 The dormouse opossum is not as rare as correspondents seem to believe. **1949** B. O'Reilly *Green Mountains* 24 A tiny night rambler in our timber is the dormouse possum, the smallest of our marsupials. . . He sleeps through the winter in a nest deep in a hollow tree.

Dorothy Dix. [f. *Dorothy Dix*, pseud. of E.M. Gilmer (1870–1951), U.S. journalist and writer of a popular question-and-answer column.]
1. A parliamentary question asked of a Minister by a member of the party in government to give the Minister the opportunity to deliver a prepared reply. Also **Dorothy Dix question** and **Dorothy Dixer**.

1963 *Austral. Financial Rev.* (Sydney) 31 Oct. 16/2 Queensland Senator Dame Annabelle Rankin may have been posing a 'Dorothy Dix' (political jargon for a planted question) to Senator Sir William Spooner. **1974** Blazey & Campbell *Political Dice Men* 90 Whitlam, in answer to a Dorothy Dix question, on April 11, roundly attacked Snedden's economic policy. **1983** G.G. Roper *Labor's Titan* 94 Hall was then asked a 'Dorothy-Dixer' as to whether Brookfield had placed the documents in his hand.

2. *Cricket*. Rhyming slang for a 'six'.
1979 *Age* (Melbourne) 2 July 9/5 He still laughs loudly about hitting a 'George Moore' (to the boundary) and a 'Dorothy Dix'—or 'Dorothy' for short—over the fence. **1983** Hibberd & Hutchinson *Barracker's Bible* 131 Cosier had eight Georgie Moores and two Dorothy Dixers in his knock of 65.

Hence **Dorothy Dixish** *a.*, pre-arranged; lacking spontaneity.
1977 D. Jaensch *Govt. S.A.* 87 Each sitting day opens with question time, sometimes prolonged and lively, more often monotonous and increasingly 'Dorothy Dixish'.

dose. *Obs.* [Joc. use of *dose* a quantity of medicine.] With **the:** alcoholic liquor.
1829 *Cornwall Press* (Launceston) 24 Feb. 11/2 This woman has for years been much addicted to the *dose*, in the manner of which too many examples are before us. **1839** *Port Phillip Patriot* 20 Mar. 5/1 He .. came by death, from falling into the river very drunk! *Another* victim to the *dose*!

double, *a.*
1. *Hist.* Used during the convict period in collocations to denote a degree of severity of punishment or sentence: **double cat-o'-nine-tails**, see quot. 1838; **convict**, a transported convict found guilty of a second offence in the colony and sentenced to more severe punishment; so -**convicted** *a.*, **conviction** (see also Second, Secondary *a.*[1]); **irons**, see quot. 1843; also **iron** *v. trans.*, **ironed** *ppl. a.* See also Doubly.
1838 *Rep. Select Committee Transportation* 12 Feb. 38 That which was used at Macquarie Harbour is what is called a thief's cat, or a **double cat-o'-nine-tails**; it did not comprise more than the usual number of tails, but each of those was a double twist of whipcord, and each tail contained nine knots; it was a very formidable instrument indeed. **1827** [**double convict**] P. Cunningham *Two Yrs. in N.S.W.* II. 140 The unpleasant dilemma of rubbing his immaculate shoulders against a man who had been sullied by a double conviction. **1836** J.F. O'Connell *Residence Eleven Yrs. New Holland* 35 The Phoenix was .. made a receiving ship for double convicts, sentenced to penal settlements. **1843** *Sydney Morning Herald* 7 Sept. 2/8 Now, there is another class of double convicted felons—that is, those who, after being in this ironed gang, are again found guilty of robbery. **1802** *N.S.W. Gen. Orders* 19 Oct. (1806) 7 Every Person who may be absent after that Date will, when apprehended, be punished with 500 lashes and kept in **double-irons** in the Gaol Gang during the remainder of their Terms of Transportation. **1827** H. Hellyer Diary 19 July, Threaten to double iron him if they can find him. **1835** *True Colonist* (Hobart) 22 Dec. 3/3 Mr Bryan still continues in prison, double ironed. **1843** B. Wait *Lett. from Van Dieman's Land* 245 On arriving at the place of rendezvous we found eighty or more all invested with double irons... Two rings or bazzles, for the leg, with a chain between them about two feet in length, and weighing about eight pounds.

2. In other miscellaneous collocations: **double board(ed)** *a.*, see quot. 1882; **dipping** *vbl. n.*, see quots. 1981 and 1983; **dissolution** (orig. *Vic.*), the simultaneous dissolution of the upper and lower houses of a parliament preparatory to an election; **drummer**, the black and yellow cicada *Thopha saccata* of s. and e. Aust. (see quot. 1903); see also Union Jack; **dump**, see

quot. 1974; also *attrib.* and as *v. trans.*; see also DUMP *v.* 1; **fleece** *a.*, see quot.

1882 ARMSTRONG & CAMPBELL *Austral. Sheep Husbandry* 174 There are many descriptions of sheds that find favour with our squatters; some consisting of shearing boards on either side, with the sheep in the middle of the shed; others, with the board in the centre and the sheep on each side. These are called single and **double-boarded** sheds.   **1908** W.H. OGILVIE *My Life in Open* 36 In a 'double board' shed the pens [containing the sheep] are in the middle.   **1981** *Bulletin* (Sydney) 6 Oct. 26/1 That phenomenon known as **'double dipping'** whereby the individual taxpayer is given tax concessions aimed at encouraging him to provide for his own retirement only to turn that into a non-income producing asset and put himself on the pension.   **1983** *Ibid.* 22 Mar. 24/1 The practice of taking retirement benefits in the form of near tax-free lump sums has been compounded by the practice of turning such lump sums into assets and then going on the age pension. 'Double dipping', as this practice is known, has played havoc with the pension system since the Fraser Government abolished the asset test on pensions.   **1880** *Argus* (Melbourne) 2 Feb. 4/6 Mr Service's remarks with regard to the proposed **double dissolution** clearly set forth the advantages which are expected to flow from the adoption of that principle.   *Ibid.* 2 July 6/2 The phrase, 'The double dissolution', refers to the provisions by which, when the two houses disagree upon any particular measure... They .. are liable to be dissolved, and to be compelled to appeal to their constituents themselves.   **1895** *Proc. Linnean Soc. N.S.W.* X. 528 From the way in which his musical apparatus projects this Cicada is called the **'Double Drummer'** by the Sydney boys; and the female without this development is called the 'Single Drummer'.   **1903** *Agric. Gaz. N.S.W.* XIV. 340 Though the male is well known as the 'Double Drummer' on account of the large swollen covers over the drums, it is also known as the 'Union Jack' and the 'Washerwoman'.   **1936** [**double dump**] E. SCOTT *Aust. during War* in *Official Hist. Aust. 1914–18* XI. 575 In the process of double-dumping two bales are placed end to end in a machine, subjected to great pressure, and whilst in the compressed state bound together by steel bands or wires.   **1952** *Coast to Coast 1951–52* 170 It's been a long road for most... Bitter struggles 'on the outer' for all the wretched scraps of jobs .. sulphur, superphosphates .. double-dump wool.   **1974** J. GABY *Restless Waterfront* 237 A wool press is sometimes called a dump. When a bale that had been hand-pressed in the shearing shed went into our hydraulic presses, it was subjected to a pressure of four tons per square inch and was pressed or dumped down to half its original size. During the war .. two station-pressed bales were pressed together or double-dumped so that two ships could lift the wool ordinarily carried by three.   **1920** *Bulletin* (Sydney) 29 Jan. 22/2 Every year on big stations there are a few bales of two years' growth, and it is branded **'Double fleece'**.

double, *v. trans.* Abbrev. of DOUBLE-BANK 3.

1950 H.C. WELLS *Earth cries Out* 116 The bicycle ride when Dick 'doubled' her home about midnight.   **1982** P. RADLEY *Blue-Checker Corker* 121 Monte .. spun his bike round madly in the empty waiting room. 'Come on, Kylie! I'll doubleya home if you're game.'

Hence **double** *n.*, **doubler** *n.*, a lift on a bicycle or horse.

1943 *Bully Tin* (Baronta) 3 Oct. 3 The latter offered to give his visitor a 'doubler' on his iron steed.   **1947** M. RAYMOND *Smiley Gets Gun* 173 'I'll give you a double.' Smiley proudly perched himself on the .. horse.

double-bank, *v.* [Transf. use of *double-bank* to double, orig. of rowers either in pairs or two to an oar.]

1. *trans.* Mining. *Obs.* See quot. 1869.

1869 R.B. SMYTH *Gold Fields & Mineral Districts* 609 Double-Bank—To take up a claim parallel with and adjoining another claim in which has been found an auriferous reef or lead; with the object of getting the underlie of the reef, or a bend in the lead or some portion of the washdirt.   **1899** G.R. NICOLL *Fifty Yrs.' Travels* 40 Ten feet was the frontage each man was allowed, and no one could 'double-bank' his claim.

2. *trans.*, becoming *absol.* [In Br. use but apparently more common in Aust.] To yoke on (a second team of bullocks or draught-horses) in circumstances where one is inadequate. Also as *vbl. n.*

1868 R. HENNING *Lett.* (1952) 56 Some of the bad creeks, where they 'double-bank the bullocks', as it is called: that is, put the whole team, thirty yokes perhaps, on to each dray to drag it over.   **1879** 'AUSTRALIAN' *Adventures Qld.* 45 Hooking on two or three teams of bullocks—'double-banking', as it is technically called—to one dray, is commonly resorted to in difficult places, such as steep banks, deep sand, or bog.

3. *trans.*, becoming *absol.* To carry (a second person) on a horse or bicycle. Also with horse as obj.

1876 *Queenslander* (Brisbane) 1 Jan. 12/3 Down goes the mare, dead beat... So we unpacked her, and double-banked my other mail-horse.   **1912** J. BOWES *Comrades* 199 Tony's horse was given to him, while the other two boys 'double-banked' on Sam's.   **1960** M. VIZZERS *She'll do Me!* 83 When Herb wheeled his bicycle through the gates he stopped and said to Mary: 'Hop on Mary, I'll double-bank yer.'

4. *transf.*

1948 G. MEREDITH *Lawsons* 23 With petrol restrictions there was double-banking now, two or even three families to a car.

double dink: see DINK *n.* and *v.*

double-gee. Chiefly *W.A.* [a. Afrikaans *dubbeltjie,* prob. f. *dubbel* double + *-tjie,* dimin. suffix, but poss. alteration of *duiweltjie* little devil.] **a.** The naturalized annual South African herb *Emex australis* (fam. Polygonaceae) of all mainland States, bearing a fruit with three rigid spines; the fruit itself; *Cape spinach,* see CAPE; *prickly jack,* see PRICKLY; *spiny emex,* see SPINY; TANNER'S CURSE; THREE-CORNERED JACK. See also *bull head* BULL *n.*[3], GOATHEAD. **b.** Any of several other plants bearing a similarly spiny fruit; the fruit of these plants.

1872 MRS E. MILLETT *Austral. Parsonage* 102 A poor barefooted child .. refusing to stir another step forward 'because of the double gees'.   **1955** *Bulletin* (Sydney) 28 Sept. 12/4 One theory says 'double-gee' comes from *dubbletge-doorn,* Afrikaans for Devil's thorn; another is that it derives from the same language, but the word is *duiveltje,* meaning 'little devil'.

double-header. A double measure of an alcoholic drink.

1898 *Bulletin* (Sydney) 19 Mar. 3/2 The 'double-header''s out, And it's no one's turn to shout, And 'School's out!'   **1947** *Bulletin* (Sydney) 19 Mar. 28/1 The rather warby-looking man with the sad expression and the faded blue eyes shuffled into Flanagan's shanty pub and ordered 'a double-header o' the strongest whisky y' got'.

doubly, *adv. Hist.* In special collocations: **doubly convicted, ironed,** *double convicted, ironed,* see DOUBLE *a.* 1.

1840 *Sydney Herald* 31 Aug. 6/4 It appears that in 1837, a batch of those **doubly-convicted** from Norfolk Island, and from chain-gangs, were assigned to the trustees of the late Dr Redfern.   **1846** L.W. MILLER *Notes of Exile Van Dieman's Land* 323, I stood before him (**doubly ironed** and handcuffed).

dough-banger. A cook.

1891 *Truth* (Sydney) 3 May 7/4 Poor Joe the dough-banger has still the tea and a heavy day before him.   **1963** *N. Austral. Monthly* Nov. 13/1 Road cooks .. were running under an alias when they classed themselves as dough-bangers.

Hence **dough-banging** vbl. n.
1911 E.S. SORENSON *Life Austral. in Backblocks* 88 Dough-banging does not develop the muscles in the manner that bush-whackers used to imagine.

doughboy. [Also Br. dial., nautical slang, and in other (former) Br. colonies.] A flour dumpling, usu. boiled or fried.
1827 H. HELLYER Diary 19 July, I just ate a little salt pork and a 'doughboy', i.e. a pudding made of flour and water boiled hard. 1983 *West Austral.* (Perth) 31 Dec. 15/2 We hadn't eaten all day and when we asked for a meal, the farmer boiled us up some doughboys in a kerosene tin.

Douglas. [Proprietary name.] An axe. Also *attrib.*
1905 *Shearer* (Sydney) 17 June 6/3 The squatter presents him to 'Douglas' (the axe!). 1937 *Bulletin* (Sydney) 29 Sept. 21/4 A Gippsland Douglas-swinger .. climbed 95 ft. up a fair-sized mountain-ash.

douligah /ˈduləga/. [a. Dhurga prob. *dulaga*.] See quots.
1918 *Bulletin* (Sydney) 4 Apr. 24/1 The existence of 'douligahs' the wild men covered with hair .. was firmly believed in .. on the N.S. Wales South Coast 30-odd years ago. 1922 'TE WHARE' *Bush Cinema* 8 Most of the South Coast, N.S.W., full-blooded aboriginals still believe in the existence of a wild man covered with hair, whom they call 'douligah'. This party is said to inhabit mountain ranges; but he used to come down at night to the camps below.

Dover. *Obs.* Also **dover.** [Proprietary name.]
1. A clasp-knife.
1870 B.L. FARJEON *In Austral. Wilds* 39 He gave me a knife—a first-rate Dover. 1905 A.B. PATERSON *Old Bush Songs* 126 You've only to sport your dover and knock a monkey over—There's cheap mutton for the Wallaby Brigade.
2. In the phr. **to flash one's Dover,** to open one's clasp knife, spec. to begin a meal.
1872 M. CLARKE *His Natural Life* (1970) 616 Hang up your moke, my young Ducrow, sit down, and flash your Dover. 1881 *Bulletin* (Sydney) 26 Mar. 8/3 Who'd think now, to see you a dinin' in state With lords and the devil knows who, You were 'flashin' your dover' six short months ago, In a lambin' camp on the Paroo?
3. *transf.* Food.
1885 *Australasian Printers' Keepsake* 75 Returned with half a loaf of bread, part of a shoulder of mutton, and some cold potatoes. He roared exultingly—'Here's the sanguinary dover for you—now let us have a blooming pint!' 1887 K. MACKAY *Stirrup Jingles* 40 At a pound a week and my dover, Along of a joker named Jack.
4. In the phr. **the run of one's dover,** board and lodging.
1929 G. MEUDELL *Pleasant Career Spendthrift* 247 A salary of £90 a year and the 'run of his dover', meaning his board and lodging. 1942 *Bulletin* (Sydney) 26 Aug. 12/2 In Sydney 80 years ago an employer hiring a man would offer pay at '£30 a year and the run of your Dover', meaning that rations were thrown in.

dowak /ˈdaʊæk/. *W.A.* Also **dowuk.** [a. Nyungar *duwag.*] A wooden club used by Aborigines: see quot. 1962.
1841 G. GREY *Jrnls. Two Exped. N.-W. & W.A.* II. 265 With the dow-uk, a short heavy stick, they knock over the smaller kinds of game. 1962 B.W. LEAKE *Eastern Wheatbelt Wildlife* 55 As a boy I remember how a couple of aborigines, when moving from one place to another .. the male would carry a bundle of spears, dowak, which was a waddy about thirty inches long and one and a quarter inches thick sharpened slightly at one end.

down, n. [Br. criminal cant: see quot. 1812.]
1. *Obs.* A suspicion; a taint of illegality.
1812 J.H. VAUX *Mem.* (1819) II. 168 *A down* is a suspicion, alarm, or discovery. 1849 A. HARRIS *Emigrant Family* (1967) 53 'I know of four or five young cattle now, that never felt the heat of a brand yet.' 'And no down?' rapidly inquired Beck... 'Not a hit of a down,' responded the stockman emphatically.
2. A strong objection (towards a person, etc.); a grudge. Freq. in the phr. **to have a down on** (or **upon**).
1828 *Hobart Town Courier* 2 Feb. 3 When the ill-disposed, the sheep-stealers, runaways and others, know from the public prints that there is what is called a *down* upon them .. their plans of theft and robbery become paralized. 1982 N. KEESING *Lily on Dustbin* 96 Dad says mum's a bit hard on the newcomer. Why 'have a down' on her? .. She's not 'a bad sort'.

down, adv.
1. **a.** In the phr. **to go** (**come,** etc.) **down,** to travel from the country to a capital city.
1806 *Sydney Gaz.* 31 Aug., Who asked him (tho' he, M'Nanimy, was going towards Parramatta), if he had *met* Blundell *going down* to Sydney. 1846 *Moreton Bay Courier* 25 July 2/3 These men coming down from the bush, indulged in vicious habits on the road, and when sickness overtook them came to Brisbane for relief.
b. In the phr. **to come down,** (of a watercourse) to flood, to be in spate.
1868 C.W. BROWNE *Overlanding in Aust.* 7 Whole plains are inundated with water almost instantaneously by the 'coming down' of the Darling. 1983 C. BINGHAM *Beckoning Horizon* 2 There you could hear the river 'come down' in the wet season.
2. *Obs.* In the phr. **down the country,** to or towards a (capital) city.
1827 P. CUNNINGHAM *Two Yrs. in N.S.W.* II. 122, I knew him also to have lately come down the country in a direction which I was about to take on the morrow. 1874 J.J. HALCOMBE *Emigrant & Heathen* 14, I had come down the country to Morpeth.
3. **a.** Of someone or something from the country: in town.
1843 *Sydney Morning Herald* 25 May 3/1 Our wool being all down, we have little else to export, until the salting season commences. 1919 E.S. SORENSON *Chips & Splinters* 67 He was down from Texas Station with a cheque for recreation, And he seemed to own creation by the way he put on side.
b. Of a watercourse: in flood.
1946 L. REES *Austral. Radio Plays* 195 You mightn't get through. The creeks are down, we heard.
4. **a.** In the phr. **down south,** in a more southerly part of the country; freq. with ref. to the urban populace of (esp.) Melbourne and Sydney.
1893 F.W.L. ADAMS *Australs.* 36 Every one over-works, trying to do as much under this devouring sun as they would do 'down south' or in chill and foggy England. 1977 E. MACKIE *Oh to be Aussie* 131 It came from a place out west. Mother gave it to me when I passed the Intermediate down south. That's an exam.
b. *fig.* See quots.
1916 'MEN OF ANZAC' *Anzac Bk.* 47 Along comes the bloomin' officer, so 'Enessy sticks 'is lighted bumper down south into 'is overcoat pocket. 1967 *Kings Cross Whisper* (Sydney) xxxiv. 4/3 *Down south,* the pocket, i.e. in the direction of the pocket.
5. With ellipsis of preposition, so that **down** stands for 'down at' (or 'to').
1911 I.A. ROSENBLUM *Stella Sothern* 32 I'll just see if she is down the bail-yard. 1969 A. BUZO *Front Room Boys* (1970) 48 Been down the pub for lunch?

down country, a., adv., and n.

A. *adj.* Of or pertaining to the more closely settled districts.
1846 *Cumberland Times* (Parramatta) 10 Jan. 4/4 A fire was soon made, a Royal George slung to boil the beef, some flour rubbed up, and leather jackets made, and we made a night of it, having been joined in the course of the evening by two or three down country teams. **1979** B. HARDY *World owes me Nothing* 32 He was a big shot from one of those down-country schools.

B. *adv.* In or towards the more closely settled districts. Cf. *down the country* DOWN *adv.* 2.
1875 CAMPBELL & WILKS *Early Settlement Qld.* 28 Mr Hargrave, to whom I had sold the station on my way down country. **1932** J. TRURAN *Green Mallee* 14 Some day we'll get the better o' the scrub an' 'ave a few good years; then we'll be able to go an' live down country, where there's no sandy-blight or dust-storms.

C. *n. Obs.* A closely settled district, spec. that adjacent to Sydney.
1869 MRS W.M. HOWELL *Diggings & Bush* 253 At last we came to the Blue Mountains. They form the boundary between 'up the country' and the 'down country'.

downer. *Obs.* Shortened form of SUNDOWNER.
1913 W.K. HARRIS *Outback in Aust.* 145 'Garn!' the 'downer snapped viciously, 'Why don't yer mind yer own business?' **1920** *Land of Lyre Bird* (S. Gippsland Pioneers' Assoc.) 26 He had walked along from the head to the butt of an old 'downer'.

down under, *adv.* and *n.*
A. *adv.* In, at, or to the (British) antipodes, freq. with ref. to Australia exclusively.
1886 J.A. FROUDE *Oceana* 92 We were to bid adieu to the 'Australasian'... She had carried us safely *down under*. **1981** *Across Country* xii. 17/1 Back in the States telling his co-entertainers that there's gold 'down-under' waiting to be picked up.

B. *n.* Australia (and New Zealand). Freq. preceded by **from** (or **of**). Also *attrib*.
[N.Z. **1905** *N.Z. Truth* (Wellington) 11 Nov. 3 The men from down under.] **1915** *Honk* x. 5 (*heading*) News from down under. **1933** C.H. HOLMES *We find Aust.* 27 When the peoples of other lands flocked to this continent of 'down under'. **1934** 'E.N. SPEER' *Destiny* 234 He was not handicapped by overbearing English mannerisms and a narrow English outlook, which the 'down-under' people dislike.

dowuk, var. DOWAK.

drack, *a.* and *n.* Also **drac.** [Of unknown origin.]
A. *adj.* Dreary; unprepossessing.
1945 S.J. BAKER *Austral. Lang.* 127 *Sope* is an old larrikin word.. the direct antithesis of *bonzer*... *Drack* and *bodger* are modern equivalents. **1953** T.A.G. HUNGERFORD *Riverslake* 94 The Causeway's all right—a damned sight better than the turns up at the Albert Hall. Anyway, it's a football dance, not just one of those drac turns they slap on for the locals.

B. *n.* An unattractive or unwelcome person, esp. a woman; also, a policeman.
1960 S. WOODFIELD *A for Artemis* 34 It was the police chief. It was as much as I could do to stop yelling, 'Quick Bill, the dracks are in.' **1977** W. MOORE *Just to Myself* 13 She was a bit of a drac, but we put up with her.

draft, *n.* Also **draught**. [Spec. use of *draft* the detachment or selection of a party from the main body (esp. military).]
1. An animal or number of animals separated from the main flock or herd for a particular purpose.
1813 *N.S.W. Govt. & Gen. Orders: Food & Transport*, Riding on any of the Animals in the Drafts or Teams in any of the Towns of Sydney, Parramatta, or Windsor. **1920** *Bulletin* (Sydney) 12 Aug. 20/2 A returned-soldier settler noticed that a couple of his draughts were looking very seedy and were not eating. He sent for a vet.

2. *fig.*
1965 J. WYNNUM *Jiggin' in Riggin'* 37 There's only one other explanation, I reckon. She must have got a draft to another rubbity.

draft, *v.* Also **draught**. [f. prec.] *trans.* To divide (a flock or herd of animals) into smaller lots, according to age, sex, etc.; esp. with **out** (or **off**), to separate (a particular division of animals) from the main body.
1837 *Colonist* (Sydney) 18 May 163/2 We never attempted to draft Coleman's and Grover's cattle, we got no directions. **1848** H.W. HAYGARTH *Recoll. Bush Life* 19 The cattle, numbering perhaps upwards of a thousand, have to be driven into the enclosures, and 'draughted', or subdivided. **1900** *Bulletin* (Sydney) 10 Mar. 31/2 I've seen many a one as would muster a cattle paddock an draft out the strangers before puttin' 'em in the yard. **1980** ANSELL & PERCY *To fight Wild* 49 Then you have to take them all off to a yard somewhere and draft off your bulls.

Hence **drafter** *n.*
1848 H.W. HAYGARTH *Recoll. Bush Life* 68 The chief share of the danger falls upon the draughter, who has to go amongst the cattle.

drafting, *vbl. n.*
1. The process of separating an animal or group of animals from the main body.
1845 D. MACKENZIE *Emigrant's Guide* 130 The cattle being now secured in the yard.. we draft them... Drafting consists in separating those that we want for any particular purpose from those which we do not want, and which, therefore, are turned out into the bush (woods). **1963** M. BRITT *Pardon my Boots* 81 We reached the yard at the same time as the station ringers. The cattle were let out of the yard, and the drafting began.

2. Special Comb. **drafting gate,** a gate at the end of a race designed to close one outlet at the same time as it opens that through which the drafter wishes to direct an animal (see quot. 1882); SWING-GATE; **pen,** a small *drafting yard;* **yard,** an enclosure from which or into which animals are drafted; in *pl.*, the set of pens, yards, races, etc., in which animals are contained and managed, esp. in drafting.
1882 ARMSTRONG & CAMPBELL *Austral. Sheep Husbandry* 177 A second gate hung on the inside of the race will act as a **drafting-gate**, and, when not in use, will, when closed, leave the race secure. **1854** *Illustr. Sydney News* 29 Apr. 33/1 The stockyards are very commodious.. and there are four large yards with **drafting pens** sufficiently extensive to accommodate upwards of 1000 head. **1832** *Sydney Herald* 4 June 1/2 There are erected upon the Estate Men's Huts, Stock, Drafting.. Yards.

drag the chain: see CHAIN *n.*[1] 3.

dragoon bird. [See quot. 1860.] *Noisy pitta,* see NOISY.
1860 G. BENNETT *Gatherings of Naturalist* 210 The beautiful little Dragoon Bird... is seen strutting about... It has received its colonial appellation from its peculiar gait as it hops along the ground, carrying itself quite erect. **1949** C. BENHAM *Diver's Luck* 83 The dragon bird.. loudly calls long before the dawn.

draining, *vbl. n.* Used *attrib.* with **pen, yard,** etc., to designate an enclosure in which animals are held after being dipped, etc., until surplus liquid has drained off into a reservoir.
1879 S.W. SILVER *Austral. Grazier's Guide* 67 The sheep.. emerge saturated and staggering upon the battens of the draining yard. **1886** R. HENTY *Autraliana* 216 The sheep

was .. plunged into cold water and at once held under, a strong flow or jet of cold water being turned completely but slowly round under it, and then permitted to swim out into draining pens.

drake. [Var. of Br. *drawk* a kind of grass growing as a weed among wheat: see OED *sb.*] Any of several native or naturalized grasses (fam. Poaceae) growing as a weed in wheat fields; the seed of the grass among wheat grains.
1796 D. COLLINS *Acct. Eng. Colony N.S.W.* (1798) I. 466 The wheat being almost every where mixed with a weed named by the farmers Drake. **1930** A.J. EWART *Flora Vic.* 200 *L*[*olium*] *temulentum* .. Darnel or Drake... A weed of pastures, cultivation, and waste places found throughout Victoria, native to Europe and Asia, and recorded as naturalized in .. 1878.

draught, var. DRAFT *n.* and *v.*

dray. [Extended use of *dray* a low cart without sides used for carrying heavy loads.]
1. Any two-wheeled cart; see also *bullock dray* BULLOCK *n.* 1.
1827 P. CUNNINGHAM *Two Yrs. in N.S.W.* I. 294, I have seen four bullocks, in yokes, draw a heavy dray with 24 *cwt.* of wool along one of our indifferent roads with the most perfect ease. **1926** 'J. DOONE' *Timely Tips New Australs., Dray,* in Australia this word denotes the springless type of cart generally being equipped with a tipping attachment.
2. Comb. **dray man, road, track.**
1831 *Sydney Herald* 5 Dec. 3/3 Kate O'Hearn .. deeply in love with a **drayman. 1843** *Sydney Morning Herald* 17 May 2/6 The land was sworn to be worth 7s. 6d. per acre, although there were no improvements, and no **dray road** into it. **1843** *Sydney Morning Herald* 4 Nov. 4/4 The poor bullocks and their drivers travelling upon the **dray tracks,** for roads I will not so misname them. **1920** *Land of Lyre Bird* (S. Gippsland Pioneers' Assoc.) 57 At Mr Dunlop's the dray track entered the lordly forest, and after penetrating the scrub country for about nine miles became a mere pack-track.

dreadnought. [Transf. use of *dreadnought* the name of a class of battleship.]
1. *Obs.* A glass of beer.
1909 *Bulletin* (Sydney) 17 Feb. 13/2, I have discovered the longest long beer in the Commonwealth, longer than the 'long sleever', deeper than the 'Dreadnought', and bulkier than the beers of Bourke. **1934** *Ibid.* 21 Feb. 10/2 This is a thin glass holding a quart which is affectionately referred to by its intimates as a 'dreadnought'.
2. *Obs.* A river boat.
1911 C.E.W. BEAN *'Dreadnought' of Darling* 19 He fancied he had been told the name of the boat that ran there was the *Yanda*. Did the Citizen know if she was a comfortable boat? 'Why, she's a **Dreadnought!**' exclaimed the Citizen hopefully. 'You'll be all right in her, I reckon.' **1936** I.L. IDRIESS *Cattle King* 118 Stores came up-river in the 'dreadnoughts' which returned downstream loaded with wool.
3. One who can shear more than three hundred sheep in a day.
1982 P. ADAM SMITH *Shearers* 278 The dreadnought shouts that the Apaches are in and the tomahawks out. Translation: .. a man who can shear up to three hundred a day shouts that he is hacking the animal about. **1982** *Sydney Morning Herald* 23 Oct. 29/4 The mighty men who could knock up a tally of 300 a day are dreadnoughts.

dreaming, *vbl. n.*
1. DREAMTIME 1; esp. as manifested in the natural world and celebrated in Aboriginal ritual; the spiritual identification of an individual with a place, species of plant or animal, etc.; a place, species, or being so regarded; the spiritual significance of a place. Also *attrib.*
1943 W.E. HARNEY *Taboo* 199 Their religion, wherever it came from in the past, is now bound up in those 'dreamings', the traditional sites and memorials of the great deeds of the culture heroes of the past. **1948** C.P. MOUNTFORD *Brown Men & Red Sand* 23 In the beginning, or the 'Dreaming Times' as old Nantawana poetically described the creation period. **1985** I. & T. DONALDSON *Seeing First Australs.* 207 Discussing the history of [Canberra] and being shown archaeological sites and nineteenth century pictures of old Aborigines .. Gurrmanamana said that once, long ago, Aborigines had lived here and that they would have known these attributes of the land which still existed somewhere, but that now, in his own words, 'This country bin lose 'im Dreaming.'
2. Special Comb. **dreaming path, site, track,** a place or route of dreamtime significance.
1978 *Transcript of Proc. Alywarra Land Claim* 2 Oct. 45 It will be the .. transparency showing Dreaming tracks in the claim area. **1983** D. BELL *Daughters of Dreaming* 33 They went on to accuse men of breaches of the Law ranging from the non-maintenance of dreaming sites to misrepresenting .. women's role. **1983** *Canberra Times* 26 Oct. 23/2 Several Dreaming paths go through or close to MMparntwe [*sic*], which is Alice's other name.

dreamtime. [Translation of ALCHERINGA.]
1. In Aboriginal belief: a collection of events beyond living memory which shaped the physical, spiritual, and moral world; the era in which these occurred; an Aboriginal's consciousness of the enduring nature of the era; ALCHERINGA. See also DREAMING. Also *attrib.*
1896 B. SPENCER *Rep. Horn Sci. Exped. Central Aust.* I. 50 They say that in what they call the Alchèringa (or as Mr Gillen appropriately renders it the 'dream times'), a certain noted warrior journeyed to the east. **1938** D. BATES *Passing of Aborigines* 24 A patriarchal or 'dreamtime' father.
2. *fig.* A 'fool's paradise'; a 'period of grace'.
1985 H. GARNER *Postcards from Surfers* 11 Remember that seminar we went to about investment in diamonds?. . . S'posed to be an investment that would double its value in six days. We went along one afternoon. They were obviously con-men. Ooh, setting up a big con, you could tell. .. Anyway, look at this in today's *Age*. 'The Diamond Dreamtime. World diamond market plummets.' Haw haw haw. **1986** *Bulletin* (Sydney) 4 Mar. 30/1 The federal Labor caucus has emerged from the dreamtime it granted Burke's re-election campaign and urged Aboriginal Affairs minister Clyde Holding to bring down his model land rights package.
3. Special Comb. **dreamtime track,** see DREAMING 2.
1934 *Oceania* V. 173 The importance of the 'dream-time' tracks is seen in the custom of approaching sacred totemic and heroic sites by the actual path believed to have been followed by the hero or ancestor.

dredgy, *a. Mining. Obs.* Also **dredgey.** [f. *dredge* ore of mixed quality: see OED *sb.*² 3; cf. EDD *dredgy-ore.*] Of ore: of mixed quality and productivity.
1865 *Wallaroo Times* (Kadina) 28 June 2/4 The western lode .. is looking well, the leader of ore being fully eighteen inches wide in the back of level, the remainder is dredgy as before. **1866** *Ibid.* 17 Nov. 2/4 Lode large but dredgy.

dress, *v. Obs.* [Br. dial. *dress* to apply a lotion to sheep to kill parasites: see EDD 9.] *trans.* To treat (a sheep afflicted with scab). See also *sheep dressing* SHEEP 2.
1831 *Sydney Monitor* 19 Oct. 3/2, I am a shearer, and have at different times had a great many scabby sheep pass through my hands, but have seldom *drest* any for the scab. **1874** C. DE BOOS *Congewoi Correspondence* 50 The sheep there was terribly scabby, and no mistake. Well, he hired us to dress 'em, and the way we set about it was a caution to all sheep never to get scabbed.

dressing shed. At swimming pools, sports grounds, etc.: a changing room.

1917 *St. Kilda Ann.* 25 Dressing sheds are now provided on the beach. 1958 E.O. SCHLUNKE *Village Hampden* 228 'We got a new dressing-shed out of him,' Townshend boasted.

dried out: see DRY *v.*

drift. *Mining.* A deposit of sand, gravel, etc., left by (flood) water: see quot. 1860. Also *attrib.*

1852 *Empire* (Sydney) 20 Feb. 699/3 Whence comes the drift matter which now finds profitable employment for the miners at Sheep Station Point? Is it the wash from the Hills? *c* 1860 'AURIFERA' *Victorian Miners' Man.* 102 *Drift* . . earth and rocks which have been drifted by water, and deposited over a country while submerged. It lies under alluvium and over secondary rocks.

drive, *n.*[1] *Mining.* [f. *drive* to excavate horizontally (see OED *v.* 10); as *n.* apparently chiefly Austral. and N.Z.] A tunnel excavated horizontally.

1857 C.E. GLASS in *Fresh Evidence Early Goldmining Publications* (Austral. Lang. Research Centre, 1966) 11 A main drive shall be carried along the course of such lead or gutter. 1896 H. LAWSON *While Billy Boils* (1975) 5 They lowered the young bride, blindfolded, down a golden hole in a big bucket, and got her to point out the drive from which the gold came that her ring was made out of.

drive, *n.*[2] *Timber-getting.* [Transf. use of (chiefly N. American) *drive* mass of logs driven downstream.] The falling in one mass of a number of trees which have been partially cut through, the impetus or 'drive' being given by the felling of a larger tree (or one uphill of the others) against them.

1904 *Bulletin* (Sydney) 15 Sept. 40/4 We chop all the trees from the back, and only half way through; each cut has to be made so that when the tree goes it will knock the tree below it; in fact to use the scrub term, we are 'choppin' a drive'. 1909 R. KALESKI *Austral. Settler's Compl. Guide* 97 Take the trees in a face, about every half acre or more, as may suit you, knocking them down with a 'driver'. . . When you think you have enough for a 'drive' pick a large tree with a big head above the last one; nick him first in the front, then in the back. He will fall against the one below him and knock him over, that one will knock the next, and so till they are all down.

Hence **driver** *n.*[1], see quot.; **driving** *vbl. n.*

1909 **driver** [see DRIVE *n.*[2]]. 1909 *Bulletin* (Sydney) 26 Aug. 15/2 **Driving** is the making use of falling trees to assist in felling others.

driver, *n.*[2] *Shearing.* A leather strap attached to a set of hand-shears: see quot. 1965.

1905 *Shearer* (Sydney) 23 Dec. 7/5 Half of their time is taken up in fixing fresh 'knockers', 'drivers', and 'dummies' on their shears. 1965 J.S. GUNN *Terminol. Shearing Industry* i. 25 *Driver*, a leather strap on hand shears. This fits firmly round the handle and over the back of the shearer's hand, thus allowing more drive to be given to a blow while preventing the hands from slipping over the blades.

drone-pipe. DIDGERIDOO.

1946 D. BARR *Warrigal Joe* 53 'Didgerydoo,' Dan explained for the benefit of the jackeroo and Bob Greely, who had never before heard the 'music' of the drone-pipe. 1969 A.A. ABBIE *Original Australs.* 173 The *didjeridu*, also known as 'drone pipe', 'bombo pipe' and 'bamboo pipe'.

drongo. [Transf. use of *drongo* the name of a bird. Perh. infl. by its earlier use as the name of a racehorse (running between 1923 and 1925): see quots. 1924 and 1946.] A fool or simpleton, a 'no-hoper' (orig. of a Royal Australian Air Force recruit). Also **drong** and *attrib.*

[1924 *Argus* (Melbourne) 1 Nov. 24/5 Drongo is sure to be a very hard horse to beat. He is improving with every run.] 1941 *Somers Sun* 2 July 2 When you are called Drongo, ignore it. 1946 *Salt* (Melbourne) 8 Apr. 22 Drongo was the name of a horse who failed to win a race. . . The horse retired in 1925 and after that anybody or anything slow or clumsy became a Drongo. 1966 D. NILAND *Pairs & Loners* 135, I didn't waste time like some drongo salesman who can't tell when the customer really means no. 1968 G. MILL *Nobody dies but Me* 14 It's very likely we're the cleanest bunch of drongs in the entire R-bloody-double-A.F.

droob. Also **drube.** [Prob. f. U.S. *droop* a fool, a 'drip'.] An unprepossessing person, usu. male.

1933 H.B. RAINE *Lash End* 33 There's a drube out there wanting to see you. 1949 R. PARK *Poor Man's Orange* 181 A sick feeling entered Dolour's heart when she saw Harry standing there, his hands thrust into his pockets like packages, and a little, saliva-stained fag stuck on his lower lip. Of all the nice boys going to Luna Park . . she had to draw this droob.

Hence **drooby** *a.*

1972 J. SEARLE *Lucky Streak* 50 'These are . . decent!' . . 'You look pretty drooby in them. . .' 'They're just for work.'

drooping, *a. Obs.* In the names of plants having pendulous branches or foliage: **drooping gum,** any of several trees of the genus *Eucalyptus* (fam. Myrtaceae); **tea-tree,** any of several trees of the genus *Melaleuca* (fam. Myrtaceae).

1842 *Geelong Advertiser* 21 Mar. 2/2 A species of Eucalyptus known by the appellation of **drooping gum,** of a dwarf and crooked disposition. 1845 L. LEICHHARDT *Jrnl. Overland Exped. Aust.* 12 Feb. (1847) 144 The **drooping tea-tree** (Melaleuca Leucodendron?) . . was generally the companion of water, and its drooping foliage afforded an agreeable shade.

drop, *n.*[1] [f. *drop* to give birth to.] The number of lambs or calves born on a station in a season.

1838 *S. Austral. Rec.* (London) 11 July 75 His annual drop should be . . 40,000 lambs. 1978 D. STUART *Wedgetail View* 5 A new windmill, tanks and troughs, a good drop of calves, and a steady future.

drop, *n.*[2] *Australian National Football.* Used *attrib.* in Special Comb. **drop punt** (or **pass**), a kick in which a ball held vertically is dropped on to the foot (as in a punt).

1963 *Footy Fan* (Melbourne) I. i. 18 Kick a long drop-kick or stab, a short or long drop-pass. *Ibid.* ii. 18 *Drop punt*, the long seam should be in line with the target and the ball held almost vertically, with the top end slightly away from the body. The fingers should be evenly spread and the top of each middle finger should be near the lacing.

dropper. [Spec. use of *dropper* that which descends or falls away.]

1. *Mining.* [Poss. U.S.: see OED 5 d.] A vein which diverges or drops away from the main lode. Also *attrib.*

c 1860 'AURIFERA' *Victorian Miners' Man.* 102 *Dropper-strings*, small spurs of a vein. 1891 *Hist. Wedderburn Gold Fields* 35 The leaders are barren, except at the intersections with the indicator, or of nearly vertical thin quartz veins, called 'droppers' by the miners.

2. A vertical batten placed at regular intervals between the posts of a wire fence to keep the wires braced.

1897 L. Lindley-Cowen *W. Austral. Settler's Guide* 236 The droppers for six wires can be obtained in the colony from W.D. Moore & Co., Fremantle. **1978** C. Green *Sun is Up* 99 And strong! He could throw a strainer post that would hold the *Queen Mary* up onto a truck as though it was a dropper.

3. A lambing ewe.

1937 D. Gunn *Links with Past* 204 One man .. would be in charge of the lambing ewes, called the 'droppers'.

dropping, *vbl. n.* and *ppl. a.* [f. *drop* to give birth to.]

A. *vbl. n.* A lambing; also with **down,** and *attrib.*

1839 S. *Austral. Miscellany* Oct. 20 The lambs of the first dropping month in the colony will produce in August next. **1872** G.S. Baden-Powell *New Homes for Old Country* 169 Another man .. shepherds out the flock of ewes, and performs all functions connected with 'dropping down'.

B. *ppl. a.* In lamb.

1943 H.G. Lamond *From Tariaro to Ross Roy* 26 The wet flock, as the lambing ewes were known, was a science in itself. Each flock of lambers was sub-divided into three or four smaller flocks: green, dropping, middle and bigger lambs.

Droughtmaster. A breed of cattle having not less than ⅜ or more than ½ Brahman blood and bred to withstand dry conditons. Also **droughtmaster bull.**

1958 *Pastoral Rev. & Graziers' Rec.* 19 Aug. 987/1 Mr De Landelles also awarded the ribbons in the new section provided for Droughtmasters, a name given to cattle that are regarded as a well balanced cross between red British breeds and Brahmans, that carry enough Brahman blood to make them a good beef breed for tropical surroundings. **1977** *Cattleman* (Rockhampton) June 15/2 Droughtmaster bulls have played a valuable role in maintaining production in the large breeding herd.

drove, *n.* [Not excl. Austral. but of local significance.]

1. A herd or flock being driven as a body, esp. over great distances. Also *attrib.*

1829 H. Widowson *Present State Van Diemen's Land* 159 As soon as a drove is brought up, two or three quiet working bullocks lead them into the yard. **1926** A.A.B. Apsley *Amateur Settlers* 118 Drove routes over the roadless, unmapped cattle country.

2. The driving of a herd or flock.

1935 N. Hunt *House of David* 127 Rowel now engaged a reliable drover and outfit and, superintending from time to time himself the 'drove', he brought .. those Queensland shorthorns on to his run. **1973** H. Lewis *Crow on Barbed Wire Fence* 51 They had told me, over the camp fire, of great 'droves' over the route to Adelaide from Central Queensland, with cattle and horses.

drove, *v.* [See prec.] *trans.* To drive (a herd or flock), esp. over a great distance. Also *absol.*

1847 A. Harris *Settlers & Convicts* (1953) 205, I drafted off two-thirds of the herd and drove them out along with the sheep. **1851** *Bell's Life in Sydney* 29 Mar. 6/2, I drove a little, as a boy. **1940** E. Hill *Great Austral. Loneliness* (ed. 2) 124 She droved cattle overland for 2000 miles.

drover. [See Drove *n.*]

1. One who drives a herd or flock, esp. over a great distance.

1841 *Port Phillip Patriot* 4 Oct. 3/3 To be a cattle-jobber or a sheep-drover .. would alike sully the purity of a Barrister's Wig. **1960** *N.T. News* (Darwin) 5 Jan. 1/4 White drover Mick Daly and full-blood aboriginal girl Gladys Namagu were married in St. Mary's.

2. In special collocations: **drover's dog,** one who earns no respect, a drudge; the dog itself, applied in similes; **drover's outfit, plant,** the personnel and equipment employed by a drover; Plant *n.*²

1947 F. Clune *Roaming around Aust.* 30 Taxi-cabs were scarce in Perth. I was told they had been 'Yanked' by the Yanks. In consequence I got as poor as a **drover's dog,** chasing around on foot. **1984** *Canberra Times* 2 Dec. 1/5 Mr Hayden would not comment on whether Labor would have done any better with him as leader. He did, however, make reference to a comment he made early last year when he was replaced as leader by the Prime Minister, Mr Hawke. 'The drover's dog will win again but it looks a bit clapped out this time,' he said. **1912** J. Bowes *Comrade* 91 A **drover's 'outfit'** was expected at the station during the course of a few days to 'overland' the bullocks to Adelaide. This meant driving the cattle right across the continent, a big undertaking, often occupying twelve months. **1935** K.L. Smith *Sky Pilot Arnhem Land* 157 One day we pulled up for dinner not far from a **drover's plant.**

droving, *vbl. n.* [See Drove *n.*]

1. The driving of a herd or flock, esp. over a great distance; the occupation of being a drover. Also *attrib.*

1871 *Austral. Town & Country Jrnl.* (Sydney) 22 Apr. 491/2, I am aware that the necessary steps are intended to be taken by the Survey Department for opening new droving-roads. **1956** A.C.C. Lock *Tropical Tapestry* 142 Droving is a wonderful life for those who enjoy open air; and the pay is high.

2. Special Comb. **droving hand,** one employed by a drover; **plant,** *drover's plant,* see Drover 2.

1930 *Bulletin* (Sydney) 1 Jan. 20/1 To the old **droving-hand** there is some interest in the .. news that the Canadian Government is shifting 300 reindeer. **1902** H. Lawson *Children of Bush* 234 Andy had charge of the '**droving-plant**' (a tilted two-horse waggonette, in which we carried the .. horse-feed).

drube, var. Droob.

drum, *n.*¹ [Perh. with ref. to the usually cylindrical shape of a swag.] A swagman's bundle of possessions; Swag *n.*¹. See Hump *v.* 2 a.

1866 W. Stamer *Recoll. Life of Adventure* I. 304 Our ci-devant millionaire would .. 'humping his drum', start off for the diggings to seek more gold. **1976** B. Scott *Complete Bk. Austral. Folk Lore* 168 Home, it's home I'd like to be, not humping my drum in the sheep country.

drum, *n.*² [Prob. transf. use of *drum* musical instrument used to give a signal, perh. infl. by Drummer *n.*²]

1. A reliable piece of (inside) information. Freq. in the phr. **to give** (or **get**) **the drum.**

1915 Drew & Evans *Grafter* 139 It beats me how the punters get the drum. **1937** K.S. Prichard *Intimate Strangers* 262 If I give my punter the drum from the field, you can't blame me, can you? **1955** D. Niland *Shiralee* 97, I don't want to be quizzy, Mac, but, if it's a fair question, what's the drum?

2. In the phr. **to run a drum,** (of a racehorse) to perform as tipped.

1942 *Truth* (Sydney) 31 May 2/4 Ridden by McMenamin, Vanity Fair was always an unprofitable quotation, more especially when she subsequently failed to 'run a drum'. **1978** J. Hepworth *His Bk.* 113 Warrego Willie went like a hairy goat—never even looked like running a drum.

drum, *n.*³ [Spec. use of *drum* (usu. disreputable) house, lodging-place, etc.: see OEDS *sb.*¹ 9 e.] A brothel.

1879 D. Mayne *Westerly Busters* 27 Farewell to the 'drums' where resided the 'Good Thing'. **1963** 'C. Rohan' *Down by Dockside* 41 Each one of these houses was that dreariest, dullest, loneliest and ugliest institution in the whole history of harlotry—the one-woman drum.

drum, *v.* [f. DRUM *n.*²] *trans.* To give information to (someone); to warn. Also with **up.**
1919 V. MARSHALL *World of Living Dead* 30 He impressed on me the exact location of the maternal abode, and proceeded to 'drum me up' with the message. **1949** L. GLASSOP *Lucky Palmer* 229 Jimmy Daley .. drummed me Herb's on his way here now to get his money or he's going to summons you.

drum country. See quots. See also DRUMMY.
1927 M. TERRY *Through Land of Promise* 82 Some country, like the Georgina River in Queensland, is of very bad repute. Strange cattle do not camp well in that part and only too often make a rush during the night. It is called 'drum country', because a certain hollow ring in the ground enlarges sound. **1970** V. HALL *Outback Policeman* 41 The plain consisted of what is known as 'drum country' having some peculiar property of the soil almost as if it were hollow beneath the surface, so that the stamp of a horse's foot was magnified as enormously as a stroke on a huge drum.

drummer, *n.*¹ Predom. *N.S.W.* [f. U.S. *drum* any of various fish able to make a drumming noise.] Any of several marine fish of the fam. Kyphosidae taken for sport, esp. the rock blackfish *Girella elevata* of N.S.W., Vic., and Tas. and the silver drummer *Kyphosus sydneyanus* of coastal s. Aust. incl. Tas., and N.Z.
1880 *Proc. Linnean Soc. N.S.W.* V. 408 *Girella elevata* .. 'The *Drummer*' .. Port Jackson. **1906** D.G. STEAD *Fishes of Aust.* 91 Such well-known fishes as .. the Drummer (*Kyphosus sydneyanus*).

drummer, *n.*² Obs. [U.S. *drummer* commercial traveller: see OED 2.]
1. a. A commercial traveller.
1886 P. CLARKE *'New Chum' in Aust.* 124 It is possible you may have to share them with a 'drummer'—that is, a commercial traveller—or a 'swagsman'. **1914** *Bulletin* (Sydney) 1 Jan. 24/4 A 'commercial' was busy writing in a room where two old 'merinos' were talking jumbuck, and nothing but jumbuck. The drummer stood it for an hour and a half.
b. One who 'humps his drum'; a swagman.
1898 *Bulletin* (Sydney) 31 Dec. 14/3 The broken-down old drummer, grown cranky from the sun. **1945** S.J. BAKER *Austral. Lang.* 102 *Bender* (1885) and *drummer* (circa 1890) were once popular terms for tramps of slightly better class than the sundowner.
2. Obs. [Prob. joc. use of sense 1.] The slowest shearer in a shed.
1897 *Worker* (Sydney) 11 Sept. 1/1 'The ringer' is the 'cove' who takes the biggest cheque away, And 'drummer' marks the man who gets in silver coin his pay. **1959** H.P. TRITTON *Time means Tucker* 42 It's not every man that is drummer in four sheds running.

drummy, *a.* Of earth or rock: hollow-sounding; apparently unstable. See also DRUM COUNTRY.
1899 *Bulletin* (Sydney) 12 Aug. 14/1 The real terror is the man who's been reefing 10 or 20 years, and who, after sounding a 'drummy' place overhead, casually remarks: 'It'll stand while we get them two shots in.' **1980** O. RUHEN *Bullock Teams* 80 Some site bosses made bullocks uneasy—'drummy ground' for instance, where hollows underneath, perhaps old limestone caves or pressure tunnels .. magnified sounds and could start the bullocks rushing in the night.

dry, *a.* and *n.*
A. *adj.*
1. In special collocations denoting a lack of water:

dry camp [orig. U.S. (see OEDS)], a camp without water; also as *v. intr.*; **country,** country with a very low rainfall; also *attrib.*; **farmer** [orig. U.S. (see OEDS)], one who farms in dry country, also **farming** *vbl. n.*; **feed,** dry grass, etc.; **heart,** central Australia; see also *dead heart* DEAD 1; **season, spell,** a period of low rainfall or drought; **stage,** a part of a journey which is through waterless country; also **dry-staging** *vbl. n.*; **track,** a track through waterless country (see also TRACK *n.* 2 a.).
1897 A.F. CALVERT *My Fourth Tour W.A.* 271 They are fortunate if they do not have to make a '**dry camp**' by sundown. A dry camp means that a teamster must go on with his waggon, or if the horses are too exhausted to drag the load, that they must be unyoked, driven to water, and brought back again to where the freight was left. **1938** F. BLAKELEY *Hard Liberty* 214 We had dry-camped the night before, and there were twenty-two miles to go with very little water in our bags. **1878** 'R. BOLDREWOOD' *Ups & Downs* 161 That capacity for sustaining a high rate of speed for hours together peculiar to '**dry-country** horses'. **1885** P.R. MEGGY *From Sydney to Silverton* 135 He knew many squatters in the dry country who would be only too glad to get rid of their leases at a sacrifice. **1913** *Truth* (Sydney) 23 Feb. 1/7 Niel Nielsen wants the Government to import a number of **dry farmers** from 'Murka. **1925** J.A. COLLUM *New Settlers' Handbk.* 113 It is the intention to allocate a proportionate area of conveniently situated 'dry' land to each holder of irrigated land, thus affording splendid opportunities for mixed irrigated and dry farming. **1934** C. SAYCE *Comboman* 219 Though no rain had fallen for nine months, there was still **dry feed** to be found some miles off the Great North Stock Route, and they came upon a Government bore at long intervals. **1935** T. RAYMENT *Cluster of Bees* 156 His experience, gained in the '**dry heart**' of Australia, has helped me to uncover the secrets of the 'Queen of Diggers', on the beautiful shores of Port Phillip. **1837** J. MUDIE *Felonry of N.S.W.* 51 It was afflicted for three years with the calamitous visitations of 'the **dry seasons**'. **1841** *Omnibus & Sydney Spectator* 27 Nov. 68/4 The river at the present time has much less water in it than it had the last dry season. **1908** *Bulletin* (Sydney) 21 May 14/2 When this **dry spell** passes .. there will be an unholy squaring up of accounts throughout cockiedom. **1908** MRS A. GUNN *We of Never-Never* 150 He faces its seventy-five-mile **dry stage,** sitting loosely in the saddle, with the same cheery, 'So long, chaps.' **1937** M. TERRY *Sand & Sun* 143 Weary with so much dry-staging, they complained of loneliness for their folk. **1941** *Bulletin* (Sydney) 1 Oct. 14/1 'These blokes', said Dusty, 'who skite about the **dry tracks** they've struck mostly talk through their hats. .. They've had to do a bit of a perish, walk perhaps 10 or 15 mile on a hot day without a drink. As the years go by the distance gets longer and the day hotter.'

2. Of sheep during shearing: not sufficiently wet (after rain) to prevent shearing.
1894 *Bulletin* (Sydney) 20 Jan. 9/4, I can recall many instances of *some* shearers voting 'wet sheep' while at the hut, and immediately afterwards, under the boss's eye, voting 'dry sheep'. **1984** P. READ *Down there with me on Cowra Mission* 43 When it's wet, they vote on it. They vote 'em wet or dry, see. The rep comes along and he gives them all a ticket. You shear two sheep then you cast a vote. Say there's ten votes and nine votes 'dry' then they shear 'em.

B. *n.*
1. With **the:** (in northern and central Australia) the dry season, the winter.
1908 MRS A. GUNN *We of Never-Never* 219 It was August, well on in the dry. **1984** *Palmerston Herald* 16 Nov. 6/5 Jackie says they all stuck their necks out and .. took out loans on the 'never-never' to buy tractors... They would farm during the 'Dry' and get casual work during the 'Wet'.

2. A tract of waterless country (of a specified distance).

1908 Mrs A. Gunn *We of Never-Never* 151 Leaving no time for a 'spell' after the 'seventy-five mile dry'. **1950** A. Groom *I saw Strange Land* 7 From the lovely Aghadaghada Waterhole .. an old camel pad led out over the 'eighty miles dry'.

dry, *v.* In the phr. **dried out**, (of land) parched; (of people) driven off drought-stricken land.

1902 *Bulletin* (Sydney) 5 Apr. 14/4 For the first time on record Teryawynia station-homestead, on the lower Darling, is 'dried out'. The country has been held for about 48 years. **1981** G. Pike *Campfire Tales* 51 The Kennedys packed everything on two wagonettes and driving their sheep, they went on the track in search of grass and water, as many pioneers who were 'dried out' were forced to do.

dryandra /draɪˈændrə/. [The plant genus *Dryandra* was named by British botanist Robert Brown (*Trans. Linnean Soc. London* (1810) X. 211 pl. 13), after Swedish botanist Jonas *Dryander* (1748–1810), librarian to Joseph Banks.] Any plant of the genus of shrubs and small trees *Dryandra* (fam. Proteaceae) of s.w. W.A., the flower-heads of which are often large and showy.

1827 *HRA* (1923) 3rd Ser. VI. 579, I observed on these Hills an arborescent species of Dryandra. **1985** *Canberra Times* 16 Oct. 25/4, I go for a contemplative walk in my garden for the next hour or so and talk to my dryandras.

dry bible. [f. *dry* + *bible* the omasum of a ruminant (from the resemblance of the folds to the pages of a book): cf. Br. dial. *bible-tripe* (EDD).] A condition of cattle characterized by dryness of the omasum (third stomach), an affliction which may result from any of several causes, esp. as occasioned by drought.

1917 *Bulletin* (Sydney) 12 July 24/1 The disease called 'dry bible' .. was simply a manifestation of second-hand poison. **1942** E. Anderson *Squatter's Luck* 32 When in a drought the waterholes ran dry, And of 'dry bible' half the herds would die.

dry-blow, *v.*

1. *trans.* To separate (particles of a mineral, esp. gold) from the earth, sand, etc., in which it is found, using a current of air. Also *absol.* and with the area treated as obj.

1894 *Bulletin* (Sydney) 5 May 7/3 On Coolgardie now there are fully 4000 men, most of whom are dry-blowing, and I don't believe there are 20 making much more than full tucker, while most of them are not even getting the colour of gold. **1896** J.M. Price *Land of Gold* 73 Most of the alluvial workings round Coolgardie and its neighbouring 'fields' have been 'dry blown' over and over again. **1946** W.E. Harney *North of 23°* 202 With their wooden dishes, they can dry-blow the precious metal from the earth in which it lies.

2. *fig.*

a. To wash perfunctorily.

1911 A.L. Haydon *Trooper Police Aust.* 333 It was usual for travellers to 'dry blow' each other—that is, knock the dust off each other with a handkerchief and wipe their faces with a hat. **1928** R.M. Macdonald *Opals & Gold* 132 In our camp dry-blowers played for gold for six days in the week and on the seventh washed or 'dry-blowed' their clothes.

b. To recount or tell.

1950 K.S. Prichard *Winged Seeds* 18 Dinny started dryblowing his reminiscences as if Young Bill .. had never heard them before.

Also as *n.*, a perfunctory wash.

1907 *Bulletin* (Sydney) 7 Nov. 14/2 Did a dryblow many a time during the liver-rousing shanghai trips .. water was *terrible* scarce.

dry-blower.

a. One who uses the method of dry-blowing to separate particles of a mineral, esp. gold, from the surrounding earth, sand, etc.

1894 W.H. Barker *Gold Fields W.A.* 101 The distance of the true reef from the blow accounts for the inability of the dry-blowers to find the locality in which the rich slug was hidden. **1975** L. Walker *Runaway Girl* 78 Old dry-blowers like Pete the Prospector never stop looking.

b. An apparatus used for dry-blowing: see quot. 1928. Also *attrib.*

1897 A.F. Calvert *My Fourth Tour W.A.* 146 The gullies and flats below the low hills have been turned over and put through the 'dry-blower'. **1928** R.M. Macdonald *Opals & Gold* 119 'The dry-blower', as generally approved of, consists of a series of sieves mounted on an inclined plane on a frame which allows of their being shaken. A bellows attachment worked by every stroke of the 'shaker' supplies wind, and a hopper is surmounted into which the sand is shovelled. **1941** D. O'Callaghan *Long Life Reminisc.* 134, I decided to put the pack saddles on the camels and my dry blower gold shaker.

dry-blowing, *vbl. n.* The process by which a current of air is used to separate particles of a mineral, esp. gold, from the material in which it is found; see quot. 1881. Also *attrib.* and *fig.*

1881 J.C.F. Johnson *To Mount Browne & Back* 26 'Dry blowing' .. is conducted as follows:- The operator proceeds to sweep the bottom .. of all its superincumbent deposits .. which he places in an ordinary miner's tin dish till that receptacle is about three parts full. He then begins to throw the dirt into the air with a movement somewhat similar to that of a cook tossing pancakes. The wind carries the finest dust away, and the tossing brings the larger fragments of stone to the top, from whence they are swept with the hand... This action is continued till all the dirt but some fine sand and very small particles of stone are left... To finally separate gold from dirt he raises the dish to a level with his mouth and blows the dross over, leaving the prospect of more or less of the much-prized metal exposed on the tin. **1967** K. Tennant *Tell Morning This* 50 Miss Montrose, who realized she had struck pay-dirt at last after much dry blowing at Grandma's conversation, clicked her tongue to express sympathy and interest. **1983** *Canberra Times* 3 Dec. 15/2 Where gold prospectors worked without water supplies, the painstaking dry-blowing process of separating dirt from gold had to be used.

dry digging. Usu. in *pl.* [Orig. U.S.] A place, removed from running water, where gold is found on or near the surface. See Digging.

1851 S. Rutter *Hints to Gold Hunters* 10 Some, bolder than the rest, tried digging deep holes on the plains (called in general, dry diggings, in contradistinction to those mentioned on the banks of rivers). **1980** J. Wright *Big Hearts & Gold Dust* 19 There's a place called th' dry diggin'... Th' years of wind an' rain had eroded away th' old mullock heaps leavin' th' gold slugs lyin' on th' surface.

Hence **dry dig** *v. intr.*; also as *vbl. n.*

1851 *Bell's Life in Sydney* 23 May 2/4 We found located down the creek, from 500 to 700 people, divided into parties from three to eight each, busy dry digging. **1852** W. Hughes *Austral. Colonies* 277 No inconsiderable portion of the Australian gold .. has been procured .. by means of dry-digging .. with no other implement than the pick-axe or the crowbar.

dry fiddle, *v. intr.*, Dry-blow 1. Also as *vbl. n.*

1881 J.C.F. Johnson *To Mount Browne & Back* 26 'Dry blowing' .. is sometimes called 'dry fiddling'. **1976** B. Scott *Complete Bk. Austral. Folk Lore* 79, I then had four weeks 'dry fiddling' on the Gilbert, and made an average 4 ozs. per week.

dry horrors.
1. *Delirium tremens.*
1913 H. LAWSON *Triangles of Life* 1 He had a touch of the 'dry 'orrers', as One-Eyed Bogan said.   1915 N. DUNCAN *Austral. Byways* 86 It was 'a case of the dry horrors' with him (said he); and he was vastly disgruntled with our news that the tavern was closed up.
2. *transf.* Malaria.
1936 K.L. SMITH *Sky Pilot's Last Flight* 193 No-one who has not experienced it can imagine the effect of malaria in its worst form. The bushmen sometimes call it the 'dry horrors'.

dry ration. *Obs.* See quot. 1876.
1846 *Portland Guardian* 15 Sept. 3/4 The cost of shearing is from 2s. 6d. to 2s. 9d. per score with dry rations.   1876 'EIGHT YRS.' RESIDENT' *Queen of Colonies* 290 The squatters.. had no difficulty in obtaining as many as they required by simply finding them.. a 'dry-ration', that is beef and flour and tobacco, without any tea or sugar, and a very small amount of clothing.

dry-shell, *n.* Pearl shell exposed at low tide.
1959 D. STUART *Yandy* 84 S'pose we go for dryshell, what about licence?

dry-shell, *v. intr.* To gather dry-shell; also as *vbl. n.*
1936 N. CALDWELL *Fangs of Sea* 246 There used to be a lot of dry shelling... That is, by those who could not afford a lugger.   1937 E. HILL *Great Austral. Loneliness* 36 Tommy Clark.. dry-shelling on the reefs with an old lubra.. picked up the Southern Cross, jewel of a century.
Also **dry-sheller** *n.*
1912 *Bulletin* (Sydney) 19 Dec. 15/1 Dry-shellers (men who gather pearl-shell at low tides), bêche-de-mer fishers and beachcombers in general are ruled out.

dry-stack, *v. Mining. trans.* See quots. 1931 and 1932. Freq. as *vbl. n.*
1931 C.B. SMITH *Austral. Gold Prospectors' Handbk.* 28 Should your creek be dried up, and you know that the ground is worth working, a good plan is to build a strong dam, dig a series of races along your claim and pile the ground up between the races. This practice is called dry-stacking.   1932 I.L. IDRIESS *Prospecting for Gold* 96 Dry-stacking means loosening ground with the pick, preparing it, throwing away the stones, cutting a race, and when a storm comes and the gully 'runs', rushing the dirt through.

dub. [Shortening of pronunc. of *W.C.*.] A lavatory.
1943 'MRS E.F. BOSWORICK' *Amateur* 9 Privy's a new name to us out here, bein' as we was all brought up to call it the Dub.   1979 E. SMITH *Saddle in Kitchen* 16 The archaic pit-style dub stood some distance from the house on the bank of Ego Creek.

dubbo /ˈdʌbəʊ/. [The name of a country town in N.S.W.] A jocular name for a person who appears something of a country bumpkin. Also *attrib.*
1973 D. FOSTER *North South West* 17 You've only got to look at all the bushwacking, nestfeathering dubbos we get for Education ministers.   1984 *Sydney Morning Herald* 15 Oct. (Guide) 15/4 (*caption*) Sylvester Stallone as Rocky... He's shaken off his dubbo image.

duchess, *v.* [f. *duchess* a woman of high rank.] *trans.* To entertain (esp. a visiting dignitary) lavishly and with ceremony; to give 'red carpet treatment' to. Also as *vbl. n.*
1956 J.T. LANG *I Remember* 64 On arrival in England he was 'duchessed' in a manner that no Australian Prime Minister has ever been 'duchessed' before or since.   1982 *Bulletin* (Sydney) 15 June 25/1 The duchessing by Johnny-come-latelys who are beating their path now to the ALP Federal camp is met with a healthy degree of cynicism.

duck.
a. In the phr. **ducks and drakes,** rhyming slang for 'the shakes'.
1967 *Kings Cross Whisper* (Sydney) xxxiv. 4/4 *Ducks and drakes,* the shakes. From over-indulging.   1978 B. ST. A. SMITH *Spirit beyond Psyche* 209 Don't forget you c'n get the ducks an' drakes from drinkin' too much grog.
b. In the phr. **ducks and geese,** rhyming slang for 'police'.
1950 *Austral. Police Jrnl.* Apr. 112 *Ducks and geese,* police.   1967 *Kings Cross Whisper* (Sydney) xxxiv. 4/4 *Ducks and geese,* police. Shortened to 'ducks and'.

duck-bill. PLATYPUS 1. Also *attrib.*
[1798 Banks Papers 5 Aug. XIX. 49 An Amphibious Animal of the Mole Kind..; it has exactly the Bill of a Duck.]   1802 *Ibid.* 14 Aug. VIII. 106 What I most want to know is the mode of generation of the Duck bill & the Porcupine Ant Eater.   1803 *Ibid.* 8 Apr. VIII. 121 Our greatest want here is to be acquainted with the manner in which the Duck Bill Animal & the Porcupine Ant Eater which I think is the same Genus breed.

duck-billed, *a.* Used as a distinguishing epithet in various Comb. designating the platypus, as **duck-billed animal, mole, platypus, water-mole.**
1799 G. SHAW *Naturalist's Miscellany* X. Pl. 386, The Duck-billed Platypus.   1803 Banks Papers 7 Aug. VIII. 127 The duck billed mole I should have sought.   1837 *Lit. News* (Sydney) 21 Oct. 105, I sought the burrows of those shy animals, the 'water-moles' the ornithorynchus paradoxus of the naturalists, known also as the platypus or duck-billed animal.   1863 F. ALGAR *Handbk. to Colony Vic.* 8 Other remarkable animals are the duck-billed water-mole, or *Platypus Anatinus,* and the *Echidna.*

duckhouse. In the phr. **(one) up against (one's) duckhouse,** used allusively of a person's misfortune or disadvantage: see quots.
1933 N. LINDSAY *Saturdee* 7 You think you hid me cap, so that's one up agen your duckhouse.   1941 S.J. BAKER *Pop. Dict. Austral. Slang* 26 *Duck-house, up against one's,* a phrase used to describe some setback to a person's plans: e.g., 'that's one up against your duckhouse', that baffles you, that makes you think.   1972 *Bulletin* (Sydney) 12 Aug. 7/1 Who, today, ever.. tells you to put something up against your duckhouse?

duck-mole. *Obs.* PLATYPUS 1.
1819 *First Fruits Austral. Poetry* 9 Sooty swans are once more rare, And duck-moles the Museum's care.   1920 *Land of Lyre Bird* (S. Gippsland Pioneers' Assoc.) 49 The platypus, or duck-mole, is found in the creeks.

duck-shove, *v.*
a. *intr. Obs.* In a business: to act unethically. Also as *vbl. n.*
1870 *Notes & Queries* 4th Ser. VI. 111 'Duck-shoving'.. is the term used by our Melbourne cabmen to express the unprofessional trick of breaking the rank, in order to push past the cabman on the stand for the purpose of picking up a stray passenger or so.   1937 L. MANN *Murder in Sydney* 97 He's big enough now not to have to duck-shove or not so openly.
b. *trans.* To evade (responsibilities); to avoid (an issue). Also *absol.* and freq. as *vbl. n.*
1942 *Ack Ack News* (Melbourne) Apr. 3 If it has been the habit to indulge in this form of 'duck shoving' responsibility, the stultifying of initiative will bear fruit at the critical moment.   1949 J. MORRISON *Creeping City* 34 Mishkin had already decided that this was no time for the truth... 'Why should I want to sell out, Bob?' 'Never mind the duck-shoving... Would you?'   1977 *Sun-Herald* (Sydney) 3 Apr. 15/3 All the Public Service duck-shoving will not change the basic arguments.

Hence **duck-shover** n.
1898 E.E. MORRIS *Austral Eng.* 128 A cabman who did not wait his turn on the station rank, but touted for passengers up and down the street in the neighbourhood of the rank, was termed a *Duck-shover*. **1943** *O-Pip: 'P' Battery Austral. Field Artillery* Aug. 1 If there's anything I can't stand its a duck-shover on mess parades.

Duco /ˈdjukoʊ/. Also **duco**. [Proprietary name.] A kind of paint, used esp. on the body of a motor-car; an application of such paint.
1927 *Austral. Official Jrnl. Patents* (Canberra) 106 *Duco* 44,667. Paints, lacquers, varnishes, and enamel paints, and pyroxylin finishes and thinners. E.I. Du Pont De Nemours and Co., Wilmington, New Castle, Delaware, United States of America, manufacturers. **1958** P. COWAN *Unploughed Land* 101 He looked idly at the still serviceable duco, thin over the bonnet.

duff, v. [f. DUFFER n. 1.]
1. *trans.* To steal (stock).
1859 *Gippsland Guardian* 6 May 41 To allow every man who has managed to duff together a mob of cattle. **1978** H.C. BAKER *I was Listening* 77 Complaining to the police that his stock was being duffed.
2. To pasture (stock) illicitly on another's land; to steal (grass).
1900 *Albury Banner* 2 Feb. 16/4 The want of a camping ground with water is sadly felt .. by the wheat carters, causing some of the big teamsters to duff their horses and bullocks into Mr Sloan's for water. **1976** C.D. MILLS *Hobble Chains & Greenhide* 124 If the bullocky did 'duff 'em on the grass' at times .. it was amply repaid by the 'bit of loading at the station, George'.
Hence **duffed** *ppl. a.*
1934 C. SAYCE *Comboman* 141 He's certainly here and so are half a dozen duffed cattle.

duffer, n. [Transf. use of *duffer* one who deals in counterfeit goods; that which is counterfeit or 'no good'.]
1. One who steals stock (and alters brand marks). See also CATTLE DUFFER.
1844 *Sydney Morning Herald* 28 Mar. 2/7 Some line of defence might be adopted which is not known by the 'duffers' (cattle stealers) of other districts. **1984** *Age* (Melbourne) 30 June 17/3 Some time during the night of 7–8 May a group of duffers drove their truck onto Mr Wheelhouse's 50-hectare farm at Mooroopna, near Shepparton, and stole 28 Hereford steers worth about $13,000.
2. a. An unproductive mine or claim. Also *attrib*. See also RANK DUFFER.
1855 *Ovens & Murray Advertiser* (Beechworth) 20 Jan. (Suppl.) 6/2 No one is game to run the risk of sinking two or three 'duffers' in the ridges and gullies. **1915** 'ALPHA' *Reminisc. Goldfields* i. 106 We took some time washing up, during which John Chinaman discovered that he had bought a 'duffer' claim.
b. An unproductive goldfield; the rush to such a goldfield. Also *attrib.*, as **duffer rush**.
[N.Z. **1869** R. WAITE *Narr. Discovery W. Coast Goldfields* 15 Those first arrivals chose to call the expedition a duffer rush.] **1873** R.P. WHITWORTH *Lost & Found* 23 Jim was .. too old a stager to be taken in by these 'storekeepers' rushes', which, nineteen times out of twenty, were the most unmitigated 'duffers'. **1876** 'EIGHT YRS.' RESIDENT *Queen of Colonies* 168 Rockhampton owes its existence to a 'duffer rush'.
3. One who pastures stock illicitly: see DUFF 2.
1911 *Huon Times* (Franklin) 25 Feb. 3/2 Last year an Act was passed which is intended to make an end of the 'grass duffers'. These people run their cattle on the forest areas, and not content with sneaking the grass, start bush fires when it appears necessary to secure a new growth of grass.

duffer, v. [f. DUFFER n. 2.]
1. a. *intr. Mining*. Of a mine, etc.: to prove unproductive; to peter out. Usu. with **out**.
1880 *Austral.: Monthly Mag.* (Sydney) V. 61 The party then .. put down another shaft which 'duffered out'. **1888** *Boomerang* (Brisbane) 7 Apr. 9/4 That hall is going up this year—unless the Eidsvold 'duffers'.
b. *trans.* In passive: to be unsuccessful in the search for gold. Also *intr.*, to fail to find gold.
1890 'R. BOLDREWOOD' *Miner's Right* 58 'So you're 'duffered out' again, Harry,' she said. **1899** *Bulletin* (Sydney) 28 Jan. 3/2 We wish for luck—and duffer out, Or bottom on to payin'' stuff.
2. *transf.* and *fig.*
1895 *Worker* (Sydney) 21 Dec. 6/3 All the stores had stopped our tucker since our luck had duffered out. **1906** *Bulletin* (Sydney) 24 May 14/1 Old Jonas sheared away like fun, Until the shearing duffered out.

duffing, *vbl. n.* [f. DUFF v.]
1. The action or practice of stealing stock (often involving the alteration of brand marks). Also *attrib.*
1865 *Tumut & Adelong Times* 23 Mar. 3/1 A very lucrative business in the cattle-duffing at Kiandra. **1900** C.H. CHOMLEY *True Story Kelly Gang* 22 Until the whole of the professional 'duffing' population was .. safely under lock and key in the gaols .. the police felt it would be futile to hope for a full measure of law and order in the district.
2. The practice of pasturing animals illicitly.
1959 H.P. TRITTON *Time means Tucker* 17 Our horses were in good order, as there was always good feed in the paddocks alongside the route. It was a simple matter to undo the top wire, throw a bag over the next one, and, being old campaigners, they would step over unconcernedly. This was known as 'grass duffing'.

dugite /ˈdjugaɪt/. Also **dukite**. [a. Nyungar *dugaj*.] A predomin. grey, olive, or brown venomous snake, the elapid *Pseudonaja affinis* of s.w. Aust. Also *attrib.*, as **dugite snake**.
1873 J.B. O'REILLY *Songs Southern Seas* 106 If a spirit of evil Ever came to this world its hate to slake On mankind, it came as a Dukite Snake. **1936** *Bulletin* (Sydney) 3 June 21/2 The boss had killed a big dugaight or dukite, South Westralia's tiger-snake. **1950** *Ibid.* 8 Nov. 12/2 The only poisonous snake around Perth that I know of that will attempt to enter a house is the dugite.

dugong grass. Any of several marine flowering plants (seagrasses), esp. of the fam. Potamogetonaceae and Hydrocharitaceae, eaten by the dugong.
1905 T. WELSBY *Schnappering & Fishing Brisbane River* 142 There is no good drift fishing in these coloured banks, for the dugong grass tears your bait away. **1955** V. SERVENTY *Aust.'s Great Barrier Reef* 15 While seaweeds are algae and therefore simple plants, there are true flowering species in the sea. These cling close to land and the most interesting in the Reef area is known as Dugong Grass.

duke, var. DOOK.

dukite, var. DUGITE.

dulachie, var. TOOLACHE.

dummy, *n.*
1. *Hist.* [Spec. use of *dummy* one who is the tool of another.] One commissioned to select a block of Crown land on behalf of another not entitled to do so. Also *attrib.*, esp. as **dummy selector**.
1865 *Australasian* (Melbourne) 24 June 11/5 The differ-

ent grades employed in this profitable occupation [*sc.* dummyism] may be divided into the substantial dummy, the hired dummy, and the speculative dummy. **1920** W. McGuffin *Austral. Tales of Border* 179 Rafferty fell in with a station employee... He was a dummy selector for the squatter there.

2. Chiefly *Vic. Hist.* [Orig. U.S.: see Mathews.] The leading car of a pair of cable tramcars, in which the driver operates the controls: see quots. 1965 and 1967.

1900 *Bulletin* (Sydney) 19 May 19/2 He sat on the dummy of a tram next to an old Irish laborer. **1910** *Truth* (Sydney) Dec. 4 7/1, I was on the 'dummy', as the front outside seat of the car is called. **1965** G. McInnes *Road to Gundagai* 65 The dummy was essentially a hollow square of seats on wheels, in the centre of which stood the driver or 'gripman' with two levers at his disposal. **1967** F.T. Macartney *Proof against Failure* 7 The cable tram, which was in use in Melbourne from 1885 until the 1930s, consisted of 'the dummy' in front and a detachable car behind. The dummy was quite open except for its roof. In a space between the side seats the driver worked levers which passed through a continuous slot midway between the rails to grip or release a cable.

dummy, *v. Hist.* [f. Dummy *n.* 1.] *intr.* To act for another; spec. to select land, ostensibly for oneself but in reality as the agent of another not entitled to do so. Also *trans.* (see quot. 1878).

1878 *Austral.: Monthly Mag.* (Sydney) I. 426 Spoiled with the reckless waste of the 'good times', with their territory dummied, and the dummys' profits spent, they have eaten their cake. **1891** 'Rouseabout' *Jackeroo* 138 'Did you want him to dummy, uncle?' she asked. 'Yes, my dear,' said Old Crusham. 'There's 640 acres must be secured near Brand's.'

Hence **dummied** *ppl. a.*

1878 Mrs H. Jones *Broad Outlines* 266 The dummied land was all forfeited.. and thrown open again for re-selection.

dummying, *vbl. n. Hist.* The practice of employing one entitled to select land as the agent of one not so entitled. Also *transf.* (see quot. 1946).

1873 A. Trollope *Aust. & N.Z.* I. 101 The .. system is generally called dummying,—putting up a non-existent free-selector,—and is illegal. **1946** K.S. Prichard *Roaring Nineties* 394 Tributors suspected of dummying for the company began to move ore from dumps claimed by the alluvial diggers.

dummyism. *Hist.* The practice of dummying.

1865 *Australasian* (Melbourne) 24 June 11/5 Dummyism has made gigantic strides here since the first introduction of this land lottery. **1895** *Worker* (Sydney) 23 Feb. 1/5 They tried to secure the whole with a system of dummyism, persecuting and annoying the selectors.

dump, $n.^1$ *Hist.* [Br. *dump* rough-cast leaden counter used by children in games.]

1. A coin struck from the centre of a Spanish dollar, circulating in N.S.W. from 1813 at a face value equal to one quarter of a dollar.

1816 W.C. Wentworth *Miscellanea* 1816-45 6 Mar., Two Hundred Pounds' a tempting Sum But whence my Heroes must it come Not from your pockets I declare A sum so great was never there... Down with your Dumps and let me see. **1890** J. Joubert *Shavings & Scrapes* 72 During a drunken spree he sold his property for a bottle of rum and a 'dump'.

2. a. *transf.* A small coin; a small amount of money; money in general.

1825 *Austral.* (Sydney) 1 Dec. 3 She had filched from him many a dump. **1828** *Tasmanian* (Hobart) 6 June 2 They will doubtless export large quantities .. in exchange for tobacco, tea and sugar, in lieu of paying away our dumps.

1853 W. Westgarth *Vic.* 175 This occasioned an issue of small fragments of gold or 'dumps', representing a pound in the proportions fixed by the act.

b. *fig.* In negative contexts.

c **1892** J. Cameron *Fire Stick* 175, I don't value the two darkies' lives as worth a dump. **1981** *Sun-Herald* (Sydney) 13 Dec. 97/1 From now on you can have your three pronged Australian pace attack... I wouldn't give you a tuppeny dump for it.

dump, $n.^2$ [f. Dump *v.* 2.]

1. Dumper 1.

1935 *Bulletin* (Sydney) 9 Jan. 11/3 It gave the Duke of Gloucester his first experience of a dump, in the Mooloolaba surf, and he didn't like it. **1959** H. Drake-Brockman *West Coast Stories* 20 There was no slope for the crest to slide down on; it was going to topple in a bone-crushing dump.

2. Dumper 3. Also *attrib.*

1974 J. Gaby *Restless Waterfront* 237 A wool press is sometimes called a dump. **1980** P. Freeman *Woolshed* 155 They installed a giant dump-press to dump or compress the wool bales prior to loading on the wagons.

dump, *v.*

1. *trans.* To compress (a bale of wool). Also as *vbl. n.*

1849 *Portland Gaz.* 9 Mar. 3/5 Wool packed by the spade turns out very badly... It cannot be compressed, or as it is usually termed 'dumped', so well as that packed by the lever or screw. **1980** P. Freeman *Woolshed* 41 The wool bale was often subjected to the final process of 'dumping', which was carried out in the Sydney or Melbourne wool stores.

2. *trans.* Of a wave: to break suddenly and violently into shallow water, throwing (a surfer) down, often against the bottom. Also *absol.*

1932 R.W. Thompson *Down Under* 57 One has to learn to distinguish between the breaker that will carry one in on its crest and the wave that will 'dump'. **1940** P. Kerry *Cobbers A.I.F.* 10 An' 'e rode it like a mermaid, an' wus flyin' on the crest, When it dumped 'im down the mine, an' pounded wildly on 'is chest.

dumper.

1. *Surfing.* A wave which crashes down as it breaks suddenly and violently, driving the surfer towards the bottom.

1920 A.H. Adams *Australs.* 185 A dumper is a badly behaved breaker .. that instead of carrying you on its crest gloriously right up the beach till you ground on the sand, ignominiously breaks as it strikes the shallow water and deposits you, smash! in a flurry of sand and water, any side up. **1979** D. Maitland *Breaking Out* 155 All I could think of was a big fifteen-foot surf, a big dumper, breaking and crashing over at Bondi.

2. *transf.* and *fig.*

1939 *Bulletin* (Sydney) 6 July 21/2 The next capping-rail squatter who tells me 'they don't breed 'em like they useter' when speaking of the young Aussie is inviting a dumper. **1986** *Bulletin* (Sydney) 7 Jan. 78/1 Most of the new-wave floats of the 1970s nickel boom were killed in the dumpers or went industrial.

3. A wool-press.

1948 R. Raven-Hart *Canoe in Aust.* 53 The hydraulic 'dumper', which squashes two bales of wool into the size of one.

dumpling. [See quot. 1888.] *Pl.* Apple berry, see Apple 3; the fruit of this plant.

1888 *Proc. Linnean Soc. N.S.W.* III. 491 'Apple Berry.' The berries are acid and pleasant when fully ripe. From their shape children call them 'dumplings'. **1956** T.Y. Harris *Naturecraft in Aust.* 182 Dumplings, with yellow flowers and

DUMPTY

bright-blue or yellowish-green elongate fruits, is frequently seen in coastal bush in the eastern States.

dumpty. [Prob. joc. formation on DUNNY.] An outside privy. Also **dumpty-doo.**
 1965 N. LINDSAY *Bohemians of Bulletin* 131 There was revealed to us the immense importance Lou attached to an early morning visit to the privy... Mrs Stone had warned us of this ritual by saying, 'Don't go to the dumpty till Father.. has his turn there.' 1965 R.H. CONQUEST *Horses in Kitchen* 85 Find yourself a shady spot behind the dumptydoo, eat the bananas and do some hard thinking.

dungaree settler. *Obs.* A name given to a poor settler: see quot. 1826. Also **dungaree chap.**
 1826 J. ATKINSON *Acct. Agric. & Grazing N.S.W.* 29 The early Settlers, and the lower orders of the present—what are technically termed in the Colony *Dungaree Settlers*, from a coarse cotton manufacture of India which forms their usual clothing. 1880 *Melbourne Christmas Ann.* 2 Byron's 'Address to the Ocean' Would fall rather flat on these 'dungaree' chaps.

dunnart /'dʌnat/. [a. Nyungar *danard*. The name was first applied by John Gilbert to the fat-tailed *Sminthopsis crassicaudata*.] Any of the narrow-footed marsupial mice of the terrestrial genus *Sminthopsis* (fam. Dasyuridae) of all States and New Guinea. See also *marsupial mouse* MARSUPIAL 1, POUCHED MOUSE.
 1928 *Pop. Names for Marsupials* (Public Library, Museum, & Art Gallery W.A., Museum Leaflet no. 1), *Sminthopsis murina*.. Dunnart. 1982 *Bulletin* (Sydney) 13 Apr. 82/1 Dartling from beneath a stone A dunnart caught The quick eye of a hooded bird.

dunny. [f. Br. dial. *dunnekin* privy: see EDD.]
 1. Orig. an unsewered outside privy; now used loosely of any lavatory.
 1933 N. LINDSAY *Saturdee* (1936) 40 Who kidded he wasn't home; only hidin' in the dunny? 1963 B. HESLING *Dinkumization & Depommification* 116 Two cops, according to the inquiry, booked nearly two hundred 'pervs' a year from this one dunny.
 2. Special Comb. **dunny can,** a removable receptacle in a privy; **cart,** a vehicle for the collection and disposal of human excrement, etc.; **man,** one who mans a *dunny cart*. See also SANITARY.
 1962 J. DALTON *Walk back with Me* 102 'I'll say he wasn't cut out for the buildin' trade,' Grist growled. 'The little rat couldn't make a good **dunny can.**' 1963 B. HESLING *Dinkumizatin & Depommification* 52 Tom snorted. 'You're as class-conscious as a bloody squatter! What's it matter whether he built dingo fences, or even worked the **dunny cart**?' 1962 H. PORTER *Bachelor's Children* 280 Early in December, one found a card on the lavatory seat: *Enjoy Christmas as best you can, And don't forget the* **dunny man**.

durry. [Of unknown origin.] A cigarette.
 1941 S.J. BAKER *Pop. Dict. Austral. Slang* 26 *Durry*, a cigarette butt. 1976 S. WELLER *Bastards I have Met* 80 Here's Crot slumped in the saddle, shirt out, feet out of the irons, reins on the horse's neck and a durry stuck to his lip.

dusky, *a.*
 1. As used of Aborigines: a euphemism for BLACK *a.*[1]
 1847 *Moreton Bay Courier* 16 Oct. 3/2 *The blacks in Gippsland* These 'dusky warriors' are 'playing up' pretty lively in Gippsland. 1961 *Bulletin* (Sydney) 8 Feb. 15/1 The dusky handmaidens appeared carrying the marrowbones, the opening course of every 'never never' banquet.
 2. Special Comb. **dusky coral pea,** see *coral pea* CORAL; **flathead,** the dark brownish estuarine fish *Platycephalus fuscus* of e. Aust., valued as food; **robin,** the

DWARF

predom. brown, insectivorous bird *Melanodryas vittata* of Tas.
 1906 D.G. STEAD *Fishes of Aust.* 197 The Common or **Dusky Flathead** .. is very abundant along the coast of New South Wales. 1842 J. GOULD *Birds of Aust.* (1848) III. Pl. 8, *Petroica fusca* .. **Dusky Robin.**

dust.
 1. [U.S., *dust* ellipt. for *gold dust*: see Mathews.] Granular gold; gold dust.
 1851 *Empire* (Sydney) 22 May 3/2 Away, away to the Bathurst ground, Where the 'dust' is brightly shining. *Ibid.* 16 Aug. 55/5 The Bondicar has left since our last report with nearly £30,000 of dust. 1928 M.E. FULLERTON *Austral. Bush* 80 Many a poor miner tramping .. from the field with his 'dust' or nuggets on him.
 2. *fig.*
 a. Flour.
 1878 'IRONBARK' *Southerly Busters* 90 A mildewed crust or a pint o' dust Or a mutton cutlet fried. 1923 *Bulletin* (Sydney) 16 Aug. 24/3, I have used some queer recipes for making the pint of 'dust' rise when jazzing with Matilda around the bush.
 b. Tobacco.
 1903 *Bulletin* (Sydney) 13 Aug. 14/2 'Dust', in the Emperor Edward's free hotel, means the tobacco dust accumulated in the pocket. Remand prisoners .. are, on admittance, often requested to feel their pockets for 'dust'.
 3. A miners' term for silicosis. Also *attrib*. See also DUSTED.
 1937 H.E. GRAVES *Who Rides?* 53 He .. like nearly every other goldminer had contracted the 'Dust'. This meant that having breathed an atmosphere of fine, gritty dust for years, his lungs had become affected and .. he was now suffering from the deadly miners' phthisis. 1959 R. BURNS *My Brain knows Best* 16 We'd want something more than dust money to get others out as well.
 4. Special Comb. **dust-hole (of the (British) Empire),** Tasmania.
 1847 *Melbourne Argus* 9 Nov. 4/3 It will be strange indeed if the outcry against pollution, even in the 'dust-hole of the empire' does not open the eyes of the British Government to the .. necessity of having some consideration for the Colonies. 1851 *Britannia* (Hobart) 17 Feb. 3/2 Freed from its present reproach as emphatically denounced in the House of Lords as the 'Dust-hole of the British Empire'. 1852 *Guardian* (Hobart) 28 Aug. 3/4 Notwithstanding Van Diemen's Land being .. termed the 'dust hole' by our Victorian moralists.

dusted, *ppl. a.* Suffering from silicosis.
 1942 *Mulga* (Alice Springs) 22 Dec. 2 When a miner says he is 'dusted' you realise his lungs are affected. 1948 K.S. PRICHARD *Golden Miles* 119 Dusted miners were cut out of the Workers' Compensation Act. 1978 S. BALL *Muma's Boarding House* 108 I'm dusted. There's nothing to be done about it; I'll die of the dust like all of my mates.

dwarf. Used *attrib.* in Special Comb. **dwarf apple,** the shrub or small tree of N.S.W. *Angophora cordifolia* (fam. Myrtaceae); **grass-tree,** *small grass-tree*, see GRASS-TREE 1 b.; **gum,** any of several small gum trees (see GUM *n.* 1); **honeysuckle** *obs.*, any of several small shrubs of the genus *Banksia* (see BANKSIA).
 1911 A. MACK *Bush Days* 31 Through all the changing seasons, the **dwarf apple** spreads its beauty on that windy hill—an emblem for its lovers of eternal hope and courage. 1832 G.F. MOORE *Diary Ten Yrs. W.A.* 29 Sept. (1884) 141, I have two, or perhaps three acres ready for the plough, that is, cleared from black boys (**dwarf grass trees**), which are grubbed out of it. 1796 D. COLLINS *Acct. Eng. Colony N.S.W.* (1798) I. 557 In the body of the **dwarf gum** tree are several large worms and grubs. 1826 J. ATKINSON *Acct. Agric. & Grazing N.S.W.* 19 At certain seasons of the year, the **dwarf**

honeysuckle .. yields an immense quantity of beautiful transparent honey.

dynamite. Baking powder. Also *attrib*.
1898 *Bulletin* (Sydney) 1 Jan. 14/2 Perhaps the most necessary article on the track is baking-powder. Dampers and johnnie-cakes without 'dynamite' ruin cast-iron livers and galvanised digestions. **1972** F. BLAKELEY *Dream Millions* 59 Damper is made with baking powder that causes much belching—the common term outback is dynamite bread!

E

eagle hawk. A large bird of prey, usu. the *wedge-tailed eagle* (see WEDGE-TAILED).
1805 *Sydney Gaz.* 16 June, An *eagle hawk* rose from the spot with a large *viper* focused within its talons. 1978 L. WHITE *Silent Reach* 122 A pair of hunting eagle hawks, soaring, dipping and wheeling above the expanse of bleached buffel grass.

ear-bash, *v. trans.* To subject (a person) to a torrent of words. Also *absol.*
1944 L. GLASSOP *We were Rats* 205 Are you going to sit there ear bashing all night? 1946 *Strictly Personal* (Ministry Post-War Reconstruction) 4 He was ear-bashing me the other day because he can't get this or that.
Hence **ear-bashed** *ppl. a.,* **ear-bashing** *vbl. n.*
1978 H.C. BAKER *I was Listening* 107 An **earbashed** victim groaned as he worked alongside the garrulous one. 1945 G. POWELL *Two Steps to Tokyo* 190 He had been getting an **ear-bashing** from that worthy gentleman.

earbasher.
1. One who talks incessantly; a bore.
1941 E. LOCKE *From Shore to Shore* (1944) 25 Listen to the champ 'earbasher's' din. 1984 *Sunday Independent* (Perth) 26 Feb. 16/6 Now he's a middle-aged, overweight earbasher who drinks too much and hustles old acquaintances for hours.
2. *fig.*
1967 F. HARDY *Billy Borker yarns Again* p. v, Many new yarns from this most renowned 'ear basher' of modern Australian fiction.

ear-biter. *Obs.* A cadger: see BITE *n.* 1 and *v.*
1899 *Truth* (Sydney) 30 Apr. 5/1 Holiday spirits and careless generosity made them soft marks for the ear-biter. 1934 *Bulletin* (Sydney) 17 Oct. 21/2 No.. earbiters anxious to give you a moral for the lars'.

early, *a.* and *n.*
A. *adj.*
1. Used with reference to the earliest period of white settlement in Australia.
1847 G.F. ANGAS *Savage Life & Scenes* II. 213 With this soil the early settlers were accustomed to manure their gardens. 1981 A.B. FACEY *Fortunate Life* 129 The early settlers and travellers dug a large hole at this spot.
2. In collocations: **early Nancy,** any of several plants of the genus *Wurmbea* (fam. Liliaceae), esp. the small, bulbous-rooted perennial *W. dioica* of all States, but not N.T.; **shed,** a shearing shed which is operative in the early part of the season; **spring grass,** any of several spring and summer grasses of the genus *Eriochloa* (fam. Poaceae), esp. the annual or short-lived perennial forage plant *E. pseudoacrotricha* of all mainland States.
1914 E.E. PESCOTT *Native Flowers Vic.* 91 The small white flower called '**Early Nancy**' is one of the lilies, and is known as Anguillaria dioica. 1901 *Bulletin* (Sydney) 27 June 14/4 Strike-camps have been formed at Cobham and other **early sheds.** 1895 F. TURNER *Austral. Grasses* I. 27 *Eriochloa punctata* . . '**Early Spring Grass**'.
B. *n. pl.* The early years of white settlement in a given area.
1933 C. FENNER *Bunyips & Billabongs* 65 The interesting story of the wild adventurers who lived on this remote island in the 'earlies' is not our subject. 1981 G. PIKE *Campfire Tales* 223 A splendid old pioneer station owner . . came to Queensland in 'the earlies'.

early gluyas: see GLUYAS.

earth tank: see TANK $n.^1$ 1.

Eastern, *a.* Also **eastern.**
1. Of, pertaining to, or situated in, the eastern part of the Australian continent. In special collocations: **Eastern Australia** *hist.,* the Colony of New South Wales; **Colony, State** (usu. in *pl.*) Australia, excluding Western Australia and (occas.) South Australia; also *attrib.;* **Stater,** an inhabitant of an *Eastern State;* **Standard Time,** see quot. 1942.
1829 E.G. WAKEFIELD *Let. from Sydney* 1, I have to give you.. my opinion of **Eastern Australia,** and of the prospects which this penal settlement offers to emigrants. 1865 'SPECIAL CORRESPONDENT' *Transportation* 33 The 'tother side', as they call the **eastern colonies.** 1907 *Truth* (Sydney) 20 Jan. 7/2 The Agriculturalists of W.A. are beginning to feel the pinch of competition with the pioneers of the **Eastern States.** 1937 A.W. UPFIELD *Mr Jelly's Business* 89 Bony's investigations were not progressing as rapidly as the Western Australian Police Chief considered that his eastern States reputation demanded. 1952 *Bulletin* (Sydney) 9 Apr. 13/2 Mention has often been made by **eastern-Staters** in *The Bulletin* of the bloodwood-tree. 1942 C.F. LASERON *Direction Finding* 20 **Eastern Standard Time** as referred to in Australia is that adopted for Tasmania, Victoria, New South Wales and Queensland. It is based on the 150th meridian of east longitude, and is therefore 10 hours ahead of Greenwich time.

2. In the names of animals: **eastern grey kangaroo,** see GREY *a.;* **rosella,** the parrot *Platycercus eximius* of s.e. Aust.; NONPAREIL PARROT; **spinebill,** the small, long-billed honeyeater *Acanthorhynchus tenuirostris* of s.e. and e. Aust.
1931 N.W. CAYLEY *What Bird is That?* 145 **Eastern Rosella** *Platycerus eximius.* 1945 C. BARRETT *Austral. Bird Life* 155 The **eastern spinebill** . . , nicknamed 'cobbler's awl', commonly visits gardens.

Easterner. One from or belonging to an eastern State.
1941 *Bulletin* (Sydney) 24 Sept. 15/2 One tyke.. was paddling in a swamp and had its paw nipped by a gilgie—or yabbie, as you easterners call 'em. 1956 V. COURTNEY *All I may Tell* 14 Native-born Western Australians who profited most by the coming of t'other siders, as the Eastern Staters were referred to, were the most critical... It was almost as if the Easterners belonged to another land.

ebero, var. EBORO.

ebony, *a.* [Cf. U.S. use with reference to a Black (OED(S 4 b.).] Black; Aboriginal. Also *absol.,* as a nickname.
1862 *Bell's Life in Sydney* 1 Feb. 3/2 Old Ebony has kindly been admitted by his captor as a '*sleeping* partner'. 1916 S.A. WHITE *In Far Northwest* 105 My ebony-hued friend.. went to the end of the cleared space and began to dance.

eboro /ˈɛbərəʊ/. *Obs.* Also **ebero, ebroo.** [a. Margu *baaru.*] DIDGERIDOO.
1845 L. LEICHHARDT *Jrnl. Overland Exped. Aust.* 16 Dec. (1847) 534 They tried to cheer us up with their corrobori songs, which they accompanied on the Eboro, a long tube of bamboo, by means of which they variously modulated

their voices. **1846** J.L. STOKES *Discoveries in Aust.* I. 394, I here saw the only musical instrument I ever remarked among the natives of Australia. It is a piece of bamboo thinned from the inside, through which they blow with their noses. It is from two to three feet long, is called *ebroo*, and produces a kind of droning noise. **1890** J. EDGE-PARTINGTON *Album Pacific Islands* i. 363 Musical instrument of bamboo called 'Ebero' Port Essington.

echidna /ə'kɪdnə/. [The genus name *Echidna* was first applied to this animal by French naturalist G. Cuvier (*Tableau Elementaire des Animaux* (1798) 143), a. Gr. ἔχιδνα viper, alluding to the tongue, which resembles that of a snake.] The egg-laying mammal *Tachyglossus aculeatus* of Aust. and New Guinea, which has a long muzzle and spiny back, and eats ants and termites; (occas.) any of several other animals, living or extinct, of the same family, Tachyglossidae; ANTEATER 1; HEDGEHOG; *native hedgehog, porcupine,* see NATIVE *a*. 6 b.; PORCUPINE; *spiny anteater*, see SPINY.

1815 W.E. LEACH *Zool. Miscellany* 90 Porcupine Echidna . . Inhabits New Holland. **1980** J. WOLFE *End of Pricklystick* 79 She looked like an echidna that has just heard of a place where thousands of ants are waiting to be licked up.

economic conscript. *Hist.* A name applied to an unemployed person who enlisted during the war of 1939–45.

1950 J. CLEARY *Just let me Be* 153 There were a lot of other blokes like me. Mr Calwell gave us a name—'economic conscripts'. He'd been angry when the Cabinet Minister came out with that remark, even though he knew it was true: it reduced the sacrifice of Andy Jenkins and Bluey McKenna and all the others who had gone, to something that had been bought for five bob a day. **1975** G.H. FEARN-SIDE *Half to Remember* 11 Others were jobless and found employment with the Army, thereby earning themselves the sobriquet of 'economic conscript'.

Edgar Britt. [The name of Edgar *Britt* (b. 1913), Austral. jockey: see also JIMMY BRITTS.] Rhyming slang for 'shit'.

1969 A. BUZO *Front Room Boys* (1970) 22 He raced out to the john for an Edgar Britt. **1983** B. DAWE *Over here, Harv!* 101 'Jeez,' said Wooffer. 'You give me the Edgar Britts, sometimes.'

educated, *ppl. a. Hist.* Of a convict: fitted by some training or experience prior to transportation for employment in a clerical or professional capacity. See GENTLEMAN CONVICT.

1830 *HRA* (1922) 1st Ser. XV. 832 'Educated Convicts' as they are termed . . includes those transported for *Forgery*. **1851** H. MELVILLE *Present State Aust.* 159 Educated convicts are sometimes transported from the mother country.

egg-and-bacon: see EGGS-AND-BACON.

eggs-a-cook. [From a Cairo street cry: see quot. 1921.] A piece of armed services' badinage: applied *attrib.* to the Third Australian Division and its members (see quot. 1979); see also quot. 1918 (2).

1918 *Aussie: Austral. Soldiers' Mag.* Jan. 8/1 It was the day after the Eggs-a-cook Division's 'stunt' in front of Ypres. *Ibid.* 10/2 *Eggs-a-cook*, an Egyptian dish, also known as '2 for ½', and now used to express that which is expensive and barely worth while. **1921** C.E.W. BEAN *Official Hist. Aust. 1914–18 War* I. 218 Australians and New Zealanders carried with them for years strange tags of 'Arabic' and broken English, such as . . 'Eggs-a-cook', 'oringhes', 'Boots-i-clean'—calls of the Cairo urchins who sold eggs or oranges, or who blacked boots. **1979** W.D. JOYNT *Breaking Road for Rest* 119 Our new 3rd Australian Division, nicknamed the 'Eggs Is Cooked Division', because its colour patch was in the shape of an egg, reminding us of the Arab boys in Egypt trying to sell us cooked eggs and shouting 'Eggs Is Cooked!'

eggs-and-bacon. Any of several leguminous shrubs bearing yellow and reddish-brown flowers, the colours of which suggest those of eggs and bacon. Also **bacon-and-egg(s)**, **egg-and-bacon**, and *attrib*.

1942 E. ANDERSON *Squatter's Luck* 28 Dilwynnia, 'Eggs-and-Bacon'. **1964** E. LANE *Our Uncle Charlie* 47 The yellow-and-brown egg-and-bacon creeper growing beside the track. **1977** D. STUART *Drought Foal* 6 Miles of the brown and gold flowers of bacon-and-egg bushes, cat's paws and kangaroo paws. **1979** WRIGLEY & FAGG *Austral. Native Plants* 182 *Bossiaea* . . are mostly small shrubs with yellow and brown pea-flowers, and provide a significant part of the 'bacon and eggs' element of the Australian bush.

eight. In the phr. **eight, ten, two, and a quarter**, a week's ration of food as issued to a hand by an employer on a rural property: see quot. 1937. See also TEN.

1937 W. HATFIELD *I find Aust.* 84 Rations per man per week were eight pounds of flour, ten pounds of meat, two pounds of sugar and a quarter-pound of tea. Eight-ten-two-and-quarter, it was known. **1978** K. GARVEY *Tales of my Uncle Harry* 72 In those days the squatters had all the money and men like Stevo and me had to exist on 8, 10, 2 and a ¼.

eighteen. A keg of beer which holds eighteen gallons (now seventy-nine litres).

1918 G. DALE *Industr. Hist. Broken Hill* 117 The procession proceeded to the goods stations, loaded some foodstuffs and five 'eighteens' of beer, and started back to the mine. **1971** F. HARDY *Outcasts of Foolgarah* 194 'Two eighteens, twenty dozen hot dogs,' Molly counted to herself, a hostess to the finger tips.

eight hour. Used *attrib.* or in the possessive, usu. in *pl*. [With reference to the slogan 'eight hours' labor, eight hours' recreation, eight hours' rest'.

1. Used in various industrial contexts with reference to the campaign waged during the latter half of the nineteenth century for the mandatory institution of an eight-hour working day. Also *ellipt.* for *eight-hour day*, *eight-hour movement*, etc.

1858 *Illustr. Jrnl. Australasia* IV. 271 Melbourne in 1845, and Melbourne in 1855 . . were two different places. Parks, universities, and 'eight hours labor commemorations' were unknown. **1870** *Eight Hours Hist.* 2 In September, 1858, the ironworkers of Melbourne secured the Eight Hours. **1903** *Truth* (Sydney) 17 May 4/5, I still see you and your thugs . . at Trades' Hall and Eight-Hours' functions. **1917** *Shire & Municipal Rec.* (Sydney) X. Dec. 202, I do hope that my action won't mean that I will be marching in the next Eight-hour procession.

2. Comb. **eight-hour(s') movement, principle, system**,

1856 *Argus* (Melbourne) 13 May 5/1 The inauguration of the **eight hours movement**, now in operation among the various operative trades in this city, was celebrated yesterday by a procession of workmen. **1870** *Eight Hours Hist.* 3 They would perpetuate the honour and dignity of labour, and the **Eight-Hours principle**. **1856** *Argus* (Melbourne) 22 Apr. 5/5 The procession of today may tend to lead the public to believe that a general strike had taken place for the obtainment of the **Eight-Hour system**.

3. Special Comb. **eight-hour(s') day**, a working day of eight hours' duration; the day on which the introduction of this is celebrated; **demonstration**, an assembly in support of the introduction of an eight hour day; a procession commemorating its introduction; **man**, one who supports the principle of, or works, an eight hour day.

[**1887** eight-hour day: *Blackwood's Mag.* (Edinburgh) May 677/1 In Australia .. they thirst for unlimited beer, and uphold the 'eight hours a-day' principle.] **1892** *Bulletin* (Sydney) 18 June 10/1 Eight-hours' Day is not a regular Melbourne holiday. It is only gazetted annually in the hopes of its being abolished. **1909** W.G. SPENCE *Aust.'s Awakening* 510 A clause fixing an eight-hour day. **1869** E.C. BOOTH *Another England* 151 The '**eight-hours' demonstration**' is one of the most interesting gatherings in Victoria. **1896** W.E. MURPHY *Hist. Eight Hours' Movt.* 93 The **Eight Hours' men** early learned that the landed interest retarded settlement and agricultural prosperity in a primary degree.

elastic-side. Usu. in *pl.* Also '**lastic-side.** A boot without laces and having a piece of elastic inset into each side; part of the traditional Australian bush costume.
   1891 *Truth* (Sydney) 1 May 2/4 Every week some eight is spent on 'elastic sides' or blucher. **1896** *Worker* (Sydney) 21 Mar. 1/3 She wore an ill-fitting print frock, and a pair of 'men's 'lastic sides' several sizes too large for her.

elder. A person of recognized authority in an Aboriginal community.
   1879 J. CAMPBELL *Norfolk Island* 29 If the case be of a serious character, and the contending parties are unwilling to submit to the decision of the magistrates, a jury, consisting of 7 Elders is summoned, and the whole case being submitted to them, their decision is final. **1978** 'B. WONGAR' *Track to Bralgu* 35 He reminds me of a tribal elder, serene and calm.

elder colony. *Obs.* A name given to New South Wales.
   1832 *Sydney Herald* 17 May 2/2 The Government of Van Diemen's Land has in several instances, exercised a degree of political wisdom, which the Elder Colony has neglected. **1858** T. MCCOMBIE *Hist. Colony Vic.* 69 The colonists of Australia Felix care little for what has long been considered the great question by the elder colony.

elegant parrot. The small, predom. green parrot *Neophema elegans* of s.w. and central s. Aust., having blue markings on the wings and between the eyes.
   1937 R.H. CROLL *Wide Horizons* 51 Another native of the Inland, commonly called the Elegant Parrot. **1976** *Reader's Digest Compl. Bk. Austral. Birds* 290 The elegant parrot raises four or five young in a nest in a tree hole.

elephant beetle. [From a fancied resemblance.]
   1. Any of several weevils, esp. some species of *Orthorhinus*.
   1890 *Agric. Gaz. N.S.W.* I. 278 Some of the most destructive insects with which the fruitgrower has to contend are the so-called elephant beetles, which pass their early stages in the limbs and branches of the orange, apricot, peach, and vine. **1968** H. FRAUCA *Bk. of Insects* 102 Curculionidae. . . Popularly these beetles are known as Weevils and also as Elephant Beetles on account of the head structure.
   2. The scarab beetle *Xylotrupes gideon* of Qld.
   1891 *Quiz* (Adelaide) 9 Jan. 15/3 Flying foxes and elephant beetles made evening hideous as they disputed possession of stray bits of the anatomy of mine host. **1949** D. WALKER *We went to Aust.* 60 The elephant beetles of northern Queensland are 10 inches long and fight to the death.

elkhorn. [Transf. use of *elk('s)-horn*, the fern *Platycerium alcicorne*.] Any of several epiphytic or lithophytic ferns of the genus *Platycerium* (fam. Polypodiaceae), esp. *P. bifurcatum* of N.S.W. and Qld. Also **elk's-horn.**
   1835 J. BACKHOUSE *Narr. Visit Austral. Colonies* (1843) 240 A fine patch of the Elks-horn Fern, *Acrosticum alcicorne*, retains its native station on a rocky point. **1926** A.S. LE SOUEF et al. *Wild Animals Australasia* 250 One was searching among the elk-horn and orchids.

Ellangowan poison bush /ɛlən'gaʊən pɔɪzən bʊʃ/. [f. the name of Mt. *Ellangowan* in s.e. Qld.] The shrub of drier mainland Aust. *Eremophila deserti* (fam. Myoporaceae), sometimes poisonous to stock; *turkey bush*, see TURKEY *n.*[1] 5. See also DOGWOOD.
   1889 J.H. MAIDEN *Useful Native Plants Aust.* 135 'Ellangowan Poison-bush' of Queensland. . . It is reported from Ellangowan, Darling Downs, Queensland, that out of a flock of 7,000 sheep . . 500 succumbed to eating this plant. **1979** K.A.W. WILLIAMS *Native Plants Qld.* I. 202 Ellangowan Poison Bush . . is a small much branched shrub.

elvan. *Obs.* Also **elvin.** [Br. dial. *elvan* 'the name given in Cornwall to intrusive rocks of igneous origin, so hard as to resist the pick': see OED.] See quot. 1852.
   1845 M. COLLISSON *Miner's Man.* 19 The floors are also found in the granite and elvan. **1852** A. MACKAY *Great Gold Field* 20 Nov. (1853) 62 The rock through which the miners have to tunnel is a dark compact trap of the hardest description called by the miners 'elvan'. **1872** *Yorke's Peninsula Advertiser* (Moonta) 5 Nov. 2/6 The ground consists of a dark elvin containing stains of green carbonates.

emancipate, *v. Hist.* [Spec. use of *emancipate* to release from legal restraint.] *trans.* To discharge as free (a convict who has received a conditional or absolute pardon).
   1787 *Hist. Rec. N.S.W.* 25 Apr. (1892) I. ii. 90 Full power and authority to emancipate and discharge from their servitude any of the convicts . . who shall, from their good conduct and a disposition to industry, be deserving of favour. **1844** *Duncan's Weekly Register* (Sydney) 5 Oct. 175/1 The Queen might choose to emancipate the convicts transported from this colony.

emancipate, *a.* and *n. Obs.* [f. prec.]
   A. *adj.* EMANCIPATED.
   1829 *Sydney Monitor* 12 Jan. 1458/2 A panel of 2000 persons, fit for Jurors could be obtained, and in about the like proportion of Emigrants, Colony born and Emancipate Settlers.
   B. *n.* EMANCIPIST.
   1838 W. BLAND *N.S.W.* 58 The brutal crimes of irresponsible overseers, superintendents, and magistrates, inflicted on defenceless, starved, and wretched convicts, emancipates, or simply paupers. **1848** *Britannia* (Hobart) 20 July 4/1 A diabolical effort was made to antagonise the free population and the emancipates.

emancipated, *ppl. a. Hist.* [f. EMANCIPATE *v.*] Of a former convict: discharged as free having been granted a conditional or absolute pardon, or (loosely) having completed the sentence imposed.
   1803 *Sydney Gaz.* 26 Mar., The quantity of ground allowed to such emancipated convicts as the Governor may think proper to settle is as follows. For every male—30 acres. **1921** J.T. SUTCLIFFE *Hist. Trade Unionism Aust.* 28 The peculiar condition under which convict, indentured and emancipated labour were utilized in production.

emancipation. *Hist.* [f. EMANCIPATE *v.*] The act of discharging as free a convict who has received a conditional or absolute pardon; a document certifying this.
   1793 *Hist. Rec. N.S.W.* (1893) II. 50 Such convicts as become settlers, either on emancipation or upon the expiration of the term for which they have been transported. **1840** *S. Austral. Rec.* (London) 4 July 4 The instrument generally called an Emancipation, a Conditional Pardon, should be given to each.

emancipationist. *Obs.* [f. prec.] EMANCIPIST.
1850 W. GATES *Recoll. Van Dieman's Land* 196 If .. they have succeeded in keeping out of punishment .. they are allowed emancipations, and are then called Emancipationists, having the full privilege of citizenship, and the full freedom of the island.

emancipist. [f. EMANCIPATE *v.*]
1. A convict who has been pardoned or whose sentence has expired.
1822 J. RITCHIE *Evidence to Bigge Reports* 6 Nov. (1971) II. 212 Those persons who came under sentences of Transportation, but have become free by Pardon or Service of the Term, and designated 'Emancipists'. 1972 C. PEARL *Brilliant Dan Deniehy* 4 There was social conflict between the Emancipists, who had been convicts, and the Exclusives .. who had not.
2. Comb. **emancipist class, party**.
1823 *HRA* (1922) 4th Ser. I. 462 This general union and harmony between the Emigrant and **Emancipist Classes** continued unabated and undisturbed until the end of the year 1819. 1835 G. ARTHUR *Defence of Transportation* 93 There is .. no **emancipist party** in Van Diemen's Land.

emigrant, *n.* and *a.*
A. *n.*
1. One who leaves another country to settle in Australia by choice; in early use (like SETTLER 1) freq. contrasted with CONVICT. Cf. IMMIGRANT 1, MIGRANT.
1820 C. JEFFREYS *Van Dieman's Land* p. iv, He has no hesitation in recommending emigrants to the banks of the Derwent and Tamar Rivers. 1881 W. ALLEN *Immigration & Co-op. Settlement* 48 Emigrants from the old country .. might find their way into all parts of the interior.
2. Comb. **emigrant barracks, depot, ship**.
1840 *S. Austral. Rec.* (London) 18 July 34 We left the quarantine ground and went to the **emigrant barracks**, in Sydney. 1848 *Sydney Daily Advertiser* 12 July 2/3 **Emigrant Depot**... Great anxiety .. to provide suitable places in the interior for the reception of newly arrived immigrants. 1837 *Cornwall Chron.* (Launceston) 9 Sept. 2 Two **emigrant ships** and two convict ships have made an addition of 1400 persons to our population.
B. *adj.* In collocations: **emigrant colonist, girl, labour, labourer, settler.**
1821 *Sydney Gaz.* 27 Jan., This state of the law, in its consequences, affects .. a very considerable part of the property of the **Emigrant Colonists**. 1837 *Cornwall Chron.* (Launceston) 19 Aug. 2 Except that little foolery with the **Emigrant girls**—nothing can be said prejudicial to his general official efficiency. 1838 *Southern Austral.* (Adelaide) 30 June 4/2 The Commissioners proceeded with confidence to increase the supply of **emigrant labour**. 1835 R. TORRENS *Colonization of S.A.* 16 If the **emigrant-labourer**, who accepts a free passage to the new colony, will be a slave and a villain, as the Reviewer asserts, then he will not be in a condition to run away from his owner. 1826 *Monitor* (Sydney) 27 Oct. 187/3 Mr Farquharson a respectable **emigrant settler** convicted of sheep stealing.

emigrate, *v. intr.* To leave another country by choice, with the intention of settling in Australia. Cf. IMMIGRATE 1.
1796 'SOCIETY OF GENTLEMEN' *New & Correct Hist. New Holland* 65 Persons induced to emigrate hither, are recommended, before they quit England, to provide all their wearing apparel for themselves, family and servants. 1859 W. KELLY *Life in Vic.* I. 4 They constrained him to emigrate to South Australia.
Hence **emigrating** *ppl. a.*
1852 D. MACKENZIE *Ten Yrs. Aust.* 4 A mania originating in the townland speculations of South Australia .. seized the colonists and the emigrating public.

emigration.
1. The action of leaving another country by choice to settle in Australia. Cf. IMMIGRATION 1.
1820 C. JEFFREYS *Van Dieman's Land* 78 The southern parts of this island .. hold out every possible inducement to emigration. 1852 G.B. EARP *Gold Colonies Aust.* 208 In the Australian colonies there is a land fund, which is annually set apart for the purpose of procuring emigration from the mother country.
2. Special Comb. **emigration agent**, one employed to promote emigration to the Australian Colonies and to assist with settlement; **fund** *S.A.*, a fund accumulating from the proceeds of land sales used to provide financial assistance for emigrants to the Colony (see quot. 1848).
1833 H.W. PARKER *Rise, Progress, & Present State Van Dieman's Land* 221 One of the colonial newspapers, in speaking of parties living in London who advertise themselves as '**Emigration Agents**', says, 'they had much better turn their attention to obtain a livelihood by some more honest and creditable species of industry, than by deceiving, way-laying, entrapping, and kidnapping their fellow-countrymen.' 1835 R. TORRENS *Colonization of S.A.* 83 The minimum price of public land should be fixed sufficiently high, to create an **emigration fund**. 1848 J. BRICE *S.A. as it Is* 5 All the proceeds of the land sales goes into what is called an Emigration Fund, and .. the money is sent over to the English Government, for them to send out as many male and female servants, labourers, tradesmen, &c. of certain trades or callings, as the money sent will pay for.

emperor. [See quot. 1906.] **a.** Any of several tropical or sub-tropical fish, esp. of the fam. Lethrinidae. **b.** *Red emperor*, see RED *a.* 1 b. Also **emperor bream**.
1906 D.G. STEAD *Fishes of Aust.* 130 A closely-allied species [to the Yellow-mouthed Perch] is known in Queensland as 'Emperor', on account of its glorious colouration. 1951 T.C. ROUGHLEY *Fish & Fisheries Aust.* 75 The best-known of the emperor breams is the sweet-lip or red-mouthed emperor, one of the commonest fish caught by both professional fishermen and anglers on the Great Barrier Reef.

empty north: see NORTH 2.

emu /'imju/, *n.*[1] Formerly also **emeu**. [Prob. a. Pg. *ema* applied to any of various ostrich-like birds; now restricted to the Austral. sense.]
1. The flightless bird *Dromaius novaehollandiae*, widespread in mainland Aust., up to 2 m. tall and having exposed blue skin on the neck and long grey-brown feathers on the back; CASSOWARY 1; *New Holland cassowary*, see NEW HOLLAND 2.
[1789 W. TENCH *Narr. Exped. Botany Bay* 123 The bird which principally claims attention is, a species of ostrich, approaching nearer to the emu of South America than any other we know of.] 1803 *Sydney Gaz.* 26 June, Two young Emues, procured at King's Island were sold to a Master of a Vessel for Seven Guineas.] 1865 G.F. ANGAS *Aust.* 97 The largest bird peculiar to Australia is the emeu or New Holland cassowary. 1982 *Weekend Austral. Mag.* (Sydney) 6 Nov. 4/4 Beside a dirt road, a run-down emu like a broken feather duster.
2. *attrib.* Of, obtained from, or relating to the emu.
1794 D. COLLINS *Acct. Eng. Colony N.S.W.* (1798) I. 380 To barter with the natives, and procure emu feathers from them. 1975 R. BEILBY *Brown Land Crying* 50 Emu eggs, skilfully incised like cameos, pale green and pearly white.
3. In the names of flora and fauna: **emu apple, (a)** the small tree of central Aust. *Owenia acidula* (fam. Meliaceae); its edible apple-like fruit with bitter red

flesh; COLANE; GOOYA; GRUIE; MOOLEY APPLE; *sour apple*, see SOUR; see also *sour plum* SOUR; **(b)** any of several other similar plants, esp. *Petalostigma quadriloculare* (fam. Euphorbiaceae); the fruit of these plants; also *attrib.*; **berry,** any of several plants, esp. the small twiggy shrub of tropical and subtropical Aust. *Grewia retusifolia* (fam. Tiliaceae), bearing small edible fruits; the fruit of these plants; **bush, (a)** any of many woody shrubs usu. of the mainland Austral. genus *Eremophila* (fam. Myoporaceae), some species of which bear fruits eaten by the emu; FUCHSIA BUSH; see also *turkey bush* TURKEY n.[1] 5; **(b)** PITURI; **wren,** either of the two small, long-tailed birds of the genus *Stipiturus, S. malachurus* of s.e. and s.w. Aust., and *rufous-crowned emu wren* (see RUFOUS).

1881 *Proc. Linnean Soc. N.S.W.* VI. 740 *Owenia acidula* or '**Emu Apple**' .. mostly confined to the brigalow scrubs in the neighbourhood. **1956** A.C.C. LOCK *Tropical Tapestry* 147 Emu apple trees .. belong to the *Petalostigma* group, the small leaves being ovate and bright green in colour. After its white, clustered flowers have bloomed, it breaks into purple fruit, the size of a large plum. They are bitter, but emus like them, from which the tree derives its common name. **1902** *Emu* II. 31 Emus .. live in very poor country, and seem, from their droppings, to live principally on cranberries, or **Emu berries,** as they are called. **(a) 1885** P.R. MEGGY *From Sydney to Silverton* 57 Jolting over trunks, scrunching along in the scrub, smashing through the **emu bush** .. the party managed to survive without accident. **(b) 1968** W. HILLIARD *People in Between* 118 A branch from the '**emu bush**' (*Duboisia Hopwoodii*). [**1827 emu wren:** *Trans. Linnean Soc. London* XV. 224 Soft-tailed Flycatcher... 'This bird,' Mr Caley observes, 'is called *Emu Bird* by the colonists'.] **1834** J. BACKHOUSE *Narr. Visit Austral. Colonies* (1843) 210 A little bird with open feathers, like those of the Emu, in its tail, whence it has obtained the name of the Emu Wren. **1902** *Emu* II. 71 *Stipiturus malachurus* (Emu Wren). These feathered pygmies were very abundant.

4. Special Comb. **emu dance,** an Aboriginal dance (see quot. 1832); **eye,** *emu stone;* **hunting** *vbl. n.* the pursuit of emus (with dogs) as sport; **parade,** an assembly, esp. of soldiers, for the purpose of picking up litter; **stone,** AUSTRALITE.

1832 J. BACKHOUSE *Narr. Visit Austral. Colonies* (1843) 82 In the **emu dance** they placed one hand behind them, and alternately put the other to the ground and raised it above their heads .. imitating the motion of the head of the emu when feeding. **1937** E. HILL *Great Austral. Loneliness* (1940) 27 Australites, or obsidianites, or meteorites. .. The blacks know them as 'warragetti milki'—**emu-eyes. 1827** P. CUNNINGHAM *Two Yrs. in N.S.W.* I. 308 A very useful breed for **emu-hunting. 1941** T.I. MOORE *Emu Parade* 12 Halters of futility Drag us upon **emu parades,** the Army wasting Prodigal hours while soldiers, eager for the fighting, Billions of butts in hand, bob on to victory! **1902** *Geol. Survey Bull. no. 67* (W.A.) vi. 79 They [*sc.* obsidianites] have been called '**Emu-stones**' in this State [W.A.].

emu /'imju/, *n.*[2] [See EMU-BOB.] See quot. 1966.

1966 S.J. BAKER *Austral. Lang.* (ed. 2) 237 *Emu,* a racecourse lounger who picks up discarded betting and tote tickets in the hope of finding one which has not been cashed. **1984** *Age* (Melbourne) 20 Mar. 50/8 He picks up all the old betting tickets. They call them emus.

emu-bob, *v. intr.* To pick up pieces of timber, roots, etc., after clearing or burning; to collect litter. Also *trans.* (with an area as obj.)

1926 *Bulletin* (Sydney) 25 Feb. 24/1 While in Parilla (S.A.) stump-picking, or 'emu-bobbing' as the old hands termed it, I came across several of the little chaps [*sc.* opossom dormouse]. **1944** *Bulletin* (Sydney) 19 July 12/3 We were emu bobbing on contract and were close to finishing the 200-odd acres. **1949** *Ibid.* 1 June 11/2 As near as we could make it by stepping out the boundaries, we'd emu-bobbed about 400 acres.

Hence **emu-bobber** *n.,* **emu-bobbing** *vbl. n.*

1920 *Bulletin Bk. Humorous Verses* 187 A score of '**emu-bobbers**' came a-tramping from the Bland. **1948** *Bulletin* (Sydney) 19 May 23/1 We had inspected an **emu-bobbing** contract, battled the owner to a price and were set to start.

enamel orchid. Either of the two orchids (fam. Orchidaceae) of s.w. W.A. *Elythranthera brunonis* and *E. emarginata* having glossy flowers of (respectively) purple and pink. Also *ellipt.* as **enamel.**

1951 R. ERICKSON *Orchids of West* 78 Outside the fence grows yet another orchid, a lovely Purple Enamel Orchid. The wax-like flowers would grace a queen's table. **1978** L. WHITE *Memories of Childhood* 1 All the small orchids; spiders, donkeys, yellows, enamels.

endowment. CHILD-ENDOWMENT. Also *attrib.*

1933 J. TRURAN *Where Plain Begins* 140 What wi' the dole an' the endowment money, I'll guarantee there's a lot o' coves gettin' more sittin' on their tails than ever they made when they were workin'. **1978** K. GILBERT *People are Legends* 11, I can't get me welfare cheque no more Nor me 'dowment, the man at the general store Gits me cheque 'n me 'dowment now.

en-suite, *n.* [f. Fr. *en suite, adv.* so as to form a suite; used in Br. English as *a.* and *adv.*] An en-suite bathroom; a bathroom leading off a bedroom.

1970 *Austral. Home Beautiful* Aug. 64 Walk-in robes adjoin a compact en-suite in this house. **1986** *Nat. Times* (Sydney) 21 Feb. 14/4 An *en-suite* (with spa bath) for every bedroom.

entire. [Abbrev. of *entire horse.*] A stallion.

1848 *Observer* (Melbourne) 14 Sept. 205/4 Horses—The show of Entires took place at the Bazaar on Tuesday last. **1961** *Bulletin* (Sydney) 3 May 51/2 It was through this happy association of Rocky with Lame Lass that the fact of his being an 'entire', which is to say a stallion, was discovered.

Enzed. Also **N.Z.** [Repr. pronunciation of the initial letters of *New Zealand.* Used elsewhere but recorded earliest in Aust.] A popular name for a New Zealander, esp. a New Zealand soldier; New Zealand. Also *attrib.*

1915 'LANCE-CORPORAL COBBER' *Anzac Pilgrim's Progress* (1918) 54 An' our Light Horse, the spry N.Z.'s, and the English boys, you bet. **1944** *Sa-eeda Wog* 16/1 In answer to the challenge the Enzed one-pipper in charge yelled 'Waipukurau!' and drew a volley in reply. **1977** C. MCCULLOUGH *Thorn Birds,* I swear that mare has the hardest mouth in En Zed.

Hence **Enzedder** *n.,* a New Zealander.

1933 H.B. RAINE *Whip-Hand* 19 Forty or more of the finest ships afloat sailing out one by one filled with Aussies and Enzedders!

epacris /ə'pækrəs/. [f. Gr. ἐπί upon + ἄκρις dative of ἄκρου summit, from the habitat of some species, orig. given to plants now otherwise classified, by the European naturalists J.R. and G. Forster (*Characteres Generum Plantarum* (1776) 19). The name was first applied to the modern genus *Epacris* by Spanish botanist A.J. Cavanilles (*Icon. et Descr. Plant* IV. (1797) 25).] A shrub (or occas. small tree) of the mainly s.e. Austral. genus *Epacris* (fam. Epacridaceae), some of which bear attractive tube-shaped flowers. See also HEATH.

1805 *Curtis's Bot. Mag.* (London) XXII. 844 (*heading*) Rigid Epacris. **1986** *Canberra Times* 30 Jan. (Suppl.) 11/5 Depending on the time of year, even the less knowledgable gardener will find the 'familiar' growing in the park as nature intended .. kunzea .. and epacris.

eremophila /ɛrə'mɒfələ/. [The name *Eremophila* was given in 1810 by the British botanist Robert Brown (*Prodr. Fl. Nov. Holl.* 518), from the Gr. ἔρημος desert and φιλο- loving, referring to the arid habitat of members of the genus.] Any shrub or small tree of the large genus of mainland Aust. *Eremophila* (fam. Myoporaceae), esp. prevalent in dry inland W.A., and bearing usu. tubular or bell-shaped flowers. See also *emu bush* (a), EMU *n.*[1] 3, POVERTY BUSH.

1935 H. BASEDOW *Knights of Boomerang* 78 The workers carry the honey from the mulga ('acacia') and eremophila blossom to the favoured ants. **1971** J.N. HUTCHINSON *N.W. Austral. Wildflowers* 14 Eremophilas are hardy shrubs which survive under severe conditions.

erky, *a.* [Prob. f. *erk*, orig. a naval rating, later a term of contempt.] Disagreeable, unpleasant.

1959 D. HEWETT *Bobbin Up* 119, I don't like this stew. It's erky. **1960** K. SMITH *Word from Children* 43 It boiled over and ran down the sides of the stove. It looked all erky, too.

escort. *Hist.*

a. *Gold escort*, see GOLD 3. Also *attrib.*

1852 *Murray's Guide to Gold Diggings* 38 The escort came in yesterday from the 'diggings' with £70,000 worth of gold. **1894** *Bulletin* (Sydney) 28 Apr. 9/3 Coolgardie road again blocked for want of water. The escort horses had only two drinks in 130 miles.

b. The consignment carried by a gold escort.

1859 *Colonial Mining Jrnl.* Feb. 93/1 Our last escort is about 2000 OZS.—an increase on the previous one. **1870** *Sydney Morning Herald* 5 July 2/4 We shall soon be able to make up a pretty good escort of gold got in the Valley, as for months past had it not been for Major's Creek, Bell's Creek, and other places round about, we should have shown very poor escorts.

Esky. Also **esky**. [Proprietary name.] A portable insulated container in which food and drink are kept cool.

1953 *Hardware Jrnl.* Nov. 95 The Esky Auto Box is one of the fastest selling lines ever to come out of the Malley's stables... It's a portable ice refrigerator, big enough to take a man-sized family picnic lunch plus six nice cold bottles! **1982** A. JUTE *Festival* 38 Under the table was a styrene cooler, in the vernacular .. an 'esky' and a status symbol judged by the number of 'tinnies' of beer it would hold.

Esperance doctor: see DOCTOR *n.*[3]

establishment. *W.A. Obs.* [Joc. use of *establishment* a public institution.] With **the:** a local name for the Fremantle Gaol.

1857 M.B. HALE *Transportation Question* 8 The men commit some offence against ticket-of-leave discipline, and are committed again to the Establishment. **1897** Z.W. PEASE *Catalpa Exped.* 114 Mr Breslin was invited to inspect the prison, 'The Establishment', as they call it in the colony.

eucalypt. Abbrev. of EUCALYPTUS.

1877 F. VON MUELLER *Introd. Bot. Teachings* 7 The vernacular name of Gum-trees for the Eucalypts. **1984** *Canberra Times* 12 Dec. 25/3, I think that I shall never hum a tune as lovely as a gum. A tune can be a dreadful clamour While every eucalypt has glamour.

eucalyptic, *a.* Of or pertaining to the eucalyptus. Also **eucalypti, eucalyptian,** and *fig.*

1838 *Tegg's N.S.W. Pocket Almanac* 13 The poles should be made from stringy bark or other *Eucalyptic* trees. **1870** A.L. GORDON *Bush Ballads* 8 When the gnarl'd knotted trunks Eucalyptian Seem carved like weird columns Egyptian. **1899** *Truth* (Sydney) 5 Mar. 3/1, I am one of the people—just a simple, plain, blunt, ordinary eucalypti sort.

eucalyptol. A common (and formerly scientific) name for the volatile oil cineole, a principal component of pharmaceutical-grade eucalyptus oil.

1884 *Pall Mall Gaz.* (London) 28 July 12/2 Any preparation from which the slightest odour of eucalyptol is diffused. **1977** R. GENDERS *Scented Flora* 75 Eucalyptol (or cineol) is present in the essential oil of a number of plants.

eucalyptus. Pl. **eucalypti.** [f. Gr. εὖ well (*adv.*) καλυπτός and covered, referring to the bud and the operculum which covers it before the flower opens; the genus was named by the French botanist Charles Louis L'Héritier (*Sertum Anglicum* (1788) 18), from specimens of *Eucalyptus obliqua* collected at Adventure Bay, Tas.]

1. a. Any tree of the genus *Eucalyptus*. See GUM TREE 1. Also *attrib.*

1801 *HRA* (1915) 1st Ser. III. 175 The trees very lofty, mostly blue gum (Eucalyptus). **1927** R.S. BROWNE *Journalist's Memories* 259 Ring-barked eucalypti figured numerously. **1958** C. KOCH *Boys in Island* 16 They wait, the dead-quiet eucalyptus gullies, the damp bracken hollows.

b. Ellipt. for *eucalyptus oil.* Also *attrib.*

1960 B. HARNEY *Cook Bk.* 88 The red young tips of the gum tree, plucked off and eaten, relieve pain in the stomach. The basic ingredient, 'crude eucalyptus', is the medicine. **1982** R. HALL *Just Relations* 84 She placed the cat in the open box of eucalyptus drops... The cat purred from its bed of lollies.

2. Special Comb. **eucalyptus leaf,** GUMLEAF b.; **oil,** any of several volatile oils of trees of the genus *Eucalyptus* valued for medicinal and germicidal properties; EUCY.

1971 *Bulletin* (Sydney) 15 May 25/1 He's also a dab hand at blowing American and Australian tunes on the **eucalyptus leaf** and throwing boomerangs. **1876** E. COOPER *Forest Culture & Eucalyptus Trees* 60 We have in Australia a resource of our own in the **Eucalyptus oil.**

euchre, *v.* [See next.] *trans.* To destroy.

1974 *Austral.* (Sydney) 12 Oct. 19/2 He sits in the mayoral car ('So many dials and buttons! I hope I don't euchre this thing').

euchred, *ppl. a.* [Transf. use of U.S. *euchred* outwitted, orig. in the card game.] Exhausted, finished, 'at the end of one's tether'.

1932 W. HATFIELD *Ginger Murdoch* 194, I always think of you there that time absolutely euchred, cryin' like hell. **1975** D.E. KELSEY *Shackle* 40 'We are euchred,' the poor fellow replied.

Eucla doctor: see DOCTOR *n.*[3]

eucy /'juki/. Also **eucky, euky.** Abbrev. of *eucalyptus oil* (see EUCALYPTUS 2). Also **eucy oil.**

1977 *Overland* lxvi. 7 That eucy is the real McCoy, not that diluted stuff you buy... When she's moppin' the floor .. put just a couple of drops in the water. Makes the house smell good. **1978** W. LOWENSTEIN *Weevils in Flour* 48 The next day I'm back on the eucky with the old man. **1984** *Sun News Pictorial* (Melbourne) 2 Aug. 3/3 Arthur said 'euky oil' could cure anything from a runny nose to tired feet—and, naturally, his brew was the best at the princely sum of $1 a bottle.

eugari, var. UGARI.

Euraustralian. See quot. 1936. Also as *adj.*

1936 *Publicist* (Sydney) i. 15/1 The Aboriginal blends perfectly with the European to make a superior new type of human being, the Euraustralians. **1963** X. HERBERT *Disturbing Element* 82 Handsome Euraustralian people are amongst the most beautiful of the human species.

Eureka. [a. Gr. εὕρηκα used as the name of a lead in the Ballarat goldfield.]

1. A clash between gold-miners and the police and military at Ballarat in 1854, now a symbol of republicanism. Also *attrib*.

1906 *Gadfly* (Adelaide) 20 June 8/1 Dyson's first-hand knowledge of the Eureka days. **1948** F. CLUNE *Wild Colonial Boys* 204 Insurrection is in the air. The word 'Eureka' is frequently heard.

2. *Special Comb*. **Eureka flag**, a blue flag bearing a white cross with a star at the end of each arm, first raised at the *Eureka stockade*; SOUTHERN CROSS 2 a.; **stockade**, the site of the clash; so **stockader**.

1896 *Ballarat Courier* 1 May 4/5 He enclosed to me a fragment of the **Eureka flag**, given to Mrs Clendinning by Dr Alfred Carr who was doing . . general medical duties of the camp at that time. **1854** *Argus* (Melbourne) 11 Dec. 5/4 John Badcock, a constable at Ballarat, was present at the **Eureka Stockade** on Sunday morning when it was charged. **1904** *Bulletin* (Sydney) 25 Feb. 16/2 An old Eureka Stockader . . was sinking a shaft at Ballarat when he broke into a drive where there were six dead Chinamen.

euro /'juroʊ/. Chiefly *S.A.* and *W.A.* Formerly also **uro**. [a. Adnyamadhanha *yuru*.] The reddish, short-haired macropod *Macropus robustus erubescens*, a subspecies of the WALLAROO, of drier Aust. west of the Great Dividing Range.

1855 J. BONWICK *Geogr. Aust. & N.Z.* (ed. 3) 199 The Euro, by Lake Torrens, reaches six feet in height. **1863** J.B. AUSTIN *Mines S.A.* 44 The uro, or huro, is a variety of the kangaroo distinguished chiefly, for its skin being covered with hair, while the common kangaroo has a wooly [*sic*] kind of fur.

European. *Obs.* [Spec. use of *European* one of European extraction who lives elsewhere: see OED(S.] A (British) immigrant to Australia, as distinct from an Australian-born descendant of an immigrant; a non-Aboriginal inhabitant of Australia. Also as *adj*.

1832 *Currency Lad* (Sydney) 1 Dec. 2 We commenced our political career with the expressed determination of publishing the sentiments of the Currency Lads. Whether we do so or not, we leave our countrymen to determine. Many Europeans were surprised at the intemperance, as they termed it, of our last leader. **1855** G.H. WATHEN *Golden Colony* 20 Above the aboriginal scrub, however, appear the towers and public buildings of the European city.

exclusionist. *Hist.* [Spec. use of *exclusionist* one who would exclude another from some privilege: see OED.] One opposed to the integration of ex-convicts into Australian society. Also *attrib*.

1826 *Monitor* (Sydney) 30 June 53/2 We rejoice that the impotent folks, yclept 'The Exclusionists', are not the only persons who can live in the style and adopt the manners of gentlemen. **1827** P. CUNNINGHAM *Two Yrs. in N.S.W.* II. 118 One subdivision of the emigrant class . . is termed the *exclusionist* party, from their strict exclusion of the emancipists from their society.

exclusive. Chiefly in *pl. Hist*. [f. *exclusive, a.* of a class of society disposed to resist the admission of outsiders: see OED 9.] EXCLUSIONIST. Also as *adj*.

1836 *Colonist* (Sydney) 28 Jan. 27/4 Our *Pure Merino*, our *Exclusive* contemporaries, who have been abusing the Governor. **1841** *Port Phillip Patriot* 10 May 2/7 A gentleman, a member of the Melbourne Club, and moreover one of the 'Exclusives'.

Executive Council. The constitutional body, in an Australian Colony (later State) or, since 1901, in the Commonwealth, responsible for the implementation of the laws.

1825 *Sydney Gaz.* 22 Dec., *The Governor* takes this Opportunity to notify, that *His Majesty* has been pleased to constitute an *Executive Council* for this Government. **1986** *Canberra Times* 23 Apr. 2/4 Sir Ninian presided at a meeting of the Federal Executive Council at Government House.

Hence **Executive Councillor** *n.*, a member of the Executive Council.

1825 *AJCP* 851 C.O. 380/140 fo. 88, The persons so appointed by you shall be to all intents and purposes Executive Councillors within our said Territory.

exile. *Hist.* One convicted and imprisoned in Britain, and sent to the Port Phillip District on a conditional pardon which prevented return to Britain until the expiration of sentence. See also PENTONVILLE. Also *attrib*.

1844 *HRA* (1925) 1st Ser. XXIII. 700 The result of our deliberations on the subject is first of all to convince us that there is no sufficient reason why the better class of Prisoners, who have served the prescribed period of secluded punishment at Parkhurst and Pentonville should be transported as Convicts at all. We apprehend that they may with equal advantage to Society at large and with greater benefit to themselves be sent to Australia as Exciles [*sic*]. That is, it appears to us that this class of persons should leave this Country with Free pardons qualified only by the condition of their not returning hither until the expiration of their Sentences. **1848** *Maitland Mercury* 26 July 2/4 Now, if the squatters got exile labour, and paid wages—not in money, but with the stripes and triangles . . what would become of the business of these establishments?

Hence **exile** *v. trans.*; **exileism** *n.*, the practice of sending prisoners to Australia on conditional pardon; the prisoners so treated.

1847 *Port Phillip Herald* 7 Jan. (Suppl.), The experiment of **exiling** the inmates of Pentonville Prison has been attended with perfect success. **1847** *Maitland Mercury* 20 Oct. 2/1 **Exileism**, as at present contemplated by the Whig Ministry, is, in fact, only deferred transportation.

experience. *Obs.* Shortened form of COLONIAL EXPERIENCE *n.* 1. Also *attrib*.

1872 G.S. BADEN-POWELL *New Homes for Old Country* 156 The storekeeper is usually some youth getting his 'experience', and he takes charge of the store and books, and lends a hand generally on the run. *c* **1892** J. CAMERON *Fire Stick* 62 A prostrate Unionist . . was being belaboured by a big lump of a lad, the youngest of the experience men.

expert, *n.*

a. One responsible for the maintenance of machinery, esp. in a shearing-shed. Also *attrib*.

1910 C.E.W. BEAN *On Wool Track* 195 The expert (the man in the engine-room). **1923** J. MOSES *Beyond City Gates* 25 The binder is out of order; I can't get the expert chap to fix it up. **1928** L.A. SIGSWORTH *Various Verse* 2 The experts 'smooge' to the shearers, too, and the pen men stand in awe.

b. *transf.* The manager of a team of shearers.

1967 G. JENKIN *Two Yrs. Bardunyah Station* 66 But for the lowly rouseabout there is no battle—only work and a bit of skylarking when the boss-of-the-board (known usually as the 'Expert' or the 'Super') isn't looking. **1977** J. DOUGHTY *Gold in Blood* 37 They got into trouble with the 'expert' (usual name for the team manager) for arriving late to work.

expert, *v.* [f. prec.] *intr.* To maintain the machinery in a shearing shed. Chiefly as *vbl. n.*

1944 A.E. MINNIS *And All Trees are Green* 97 'I suppose he does the boss of the boarding himself?' 'Yes, and the woolclassing *and* the experting.' **1980** P. FREEMAN *Woolshed* 20 At Kingsvale and most small sheds, the shearer himself did the 'experting'.

expiree. *Hist.* An ex-convict; one whose term of sentence has expired. Also **expiree convict.**

1829 *Sydney Monitor* 15 Aug. (Suppl.), *Expirees*, or those who have served the full period of their sentences, are to all intents and purposes .. restored to all constitutional privileges. **1843** *Sydney Morning Herald* 19 Oct. 2/3 Expiree convicts .. landed in the district of Port Phillip from Van Diemen's Land.

extended claim. See quot. 1869.

1869 R.B. SMYTH *Gold Fields & Mineral Districts* 610 *Extended claim*, a block or frontage claim, the extent of which has been increased by the annexation to the original claim of an additional area of ground or length of lead, or by the amalgamation of one or more claims with the original claim. **1931** C.B. SMITH *Austral. Gold Prospectors' Handbk.* 62 The following claims must be registered within twenty-eight days after possession is taken:- .. Extended alluvial claim. Sluicing claim.

extra-colonial, *a. Obs.* Outside an Australian Colony.

1835 *Van Diemen's Land Monthly Mag.* Sept. 6 We need to apologise to all extra-colonial readers. **1865** 'W.R.L.' *Our Wool Staple* 11 For the benefit of extra-colonial readers, it is deemed advisable to introduce the following pages with a few words of explanation.

-ey, var. **-Y.**

eye. [Transf. use of *eye* mass of ore in a mine, hence 'plum', tit-bit left to the last: see OED(S *sb.*[1] 16 b.]

a. The most desirable piece of land in a holding; esp. in the phr. **to pick (out) the eyes** (see quot. 1889).

1865 *Australasian* (Melbourne) 24 June 11/5 As the day advanced, and sections were taken up, and the 'eye picked from the area', numbers would return and groups form again. **1889** R.W. DALE *Impressions Aust.* 197 Free selectors 'picked out the eyes' of the runs... They selected .. the parts where the sheep or the cattle found water.

b. *transf.*

1981 SANDERCOCK & TURNER *Up where, Cazaly?* 213 There is much interstate resentment against Victoria's ability to 'pick the eyes' out of Australian football.

F

face.

1. The front of a bushfire.
1876 R.P. FALLA *Knocking About* (1976) 65 For some days a large bush fire has been raging . . and on Tuesday night it had a face of fifteen miles. 1925 M. TERRY *Across Unknown Aust.* 206 The wind took the flames to the river. . . When the 'face' got to the river the wind changed slightly, making the fire creep along the banks.

2. In a camp muster: the side of the mob which is being worked. Also *attrib*.
1932 J.J. HARDIE *Cattle Camp* 95 Ken and Dusty moved through the mob, dodging out cows with unbranded calves, and grown cleanskins to where Scotty and Jerry proudly rode the face of the camp. 1975 G.A.W. SMITH *Once Green Jackaroo* 82 Two 'face riders' appeared, and steered the beast into the waiting mob of cut-outs.

3. *Surfing*. The wall of a wave.
1963 B. JOHNSON *Surf Fever* 24 The head dip is usually only done on fast waves with a good high face (a good wall). 1967 *Ibid*. IV. iii. 11 Fred 'Squeaky' Tucker really moves along the face of the wave on his mini.

face plaster. An alcoholic drink.
1941 K. TENNANT *Battlers* 173 It was Uncle who insisted that, as Snow was just out of hospital, they should all stop at the first hotel and get him a 'face plaster'. 1970 J.S. GUNN in W.S. Ramson *Eng. Transported* 50 *Face plaster*, alcoholic drink.

factory, *n.* and *attrib. Hist.*

A. *n.* A prison for the confinement of female convicts, esp. that at Parramatta, N.S.W. In full, **female factory.**
1806 *Sydney Gaz.* 13 July, Catherine Eyres . . ordered to the Factory at Parramatta for the term of six months. 1826 *Austral.* (Sydney) 5 Jan. 4/1 To the care of the lady of that delightful mansion, ycleped the 'female factory'.

B. *attrib.*
1829 *HRA* (1922) 1st Ser. XV. 4 The winter clothing being entirely composed of Factory Cloth. *c* 1891 J. GARDINER *Twenty-Five Yrs. on Stage* 39 This man had been a convict before him, but they got on very well together until a 'factory girl' had been hired by him.

fadge. [Br. dial. *fadge* loosely packed sack of wool, etc.: see OED(S *sb.*[1] and EDD.] An unpressed pack of wool containing less than a bale.
1914 H.B. SMITH *Sheep & Wool Industry* 183 *Fadges*, Australian wool-brokers call any bale or parcel of wool under 200 lb. in weight, and which is too large to be called a sack, a fadge. 1958 S.J. BAKER *Aust. Speaks* 60 *Fadge*, a butt of a bale or two bags sewn together, usual weight 60 lb. to 150 lb.

fair, *a.*[1] [Spec. use of *fair* equitable: see OED(S *a.* 10.] Used to qualify various nouns or collocations which themselves signify an opportunity for displaying or exerting oneself, one's talents, etc., and so indicating that that opportunity is equitable, reasonable, socially just.

1. *Obs.* In the collocation **fair show**, an equitable opportunity; a reasonable choice.
1884 *Austral. Tit-Bits* (Melbourne) 25 Dec. 18/1 We have given you a fair show, and we find that you don't care about working. 1897 *Tocsin* (Melbourne) 25 Nov. 9/1 Give the working man a fair show.

2. In the collocation **fair go**.

a. An equitable opportunity; a reasonable chance.
1904 *Bulletin* (Sydney) 14 Apr. 29/1 A 'fair bonus' is a real trier, a fair go, or a bit of a don. 1986 *Canberra Times* 10 Mar. 3/3, I still believe the average Australian believes in a fair go.

b. *spec.* An equitable contest.
1911 'ROSE BOLDREWOOD' *Complications at Collaroi* 79 We shall have a 'fair go', and the best side will win. 1927 R.S. BROWNE *Journalist's Memories* 285 Chaffed by a 'common bullocky' whom he fought, a really fair 'go'.

c. As *adj*. Equitable, egalitarian.
1935 *Red Star* (Perth) 4 Oct. 2/4 Comrades seem to have a lot of the carefree 'fair go Aussie' left in them, and this is another version of rotten liberalism. 1974 D. IRELAND *Burn* 110 The good old fair-go Aussies.

d. As *exclam*. In the game of two-up: an indication to the spinner that all bets are laid, and an appeal for fairness.
1911 L. STONE *Jonah* 215 The spinner handed his stake of five shillings to the boxer, who cried, 'Fair go!' 1977 R.E. GREGORY *Orig. Austral. Inventions* 117 The coins are tossed by the spinner from a flat piece of wood called a 'kip'. . . When all the bets are laid, the boxer calls, 'Come in, spinner', or 'Fair go, spinner', and the coins are tossed aloft.

e. Hence as *exclam*. in other contexts: 'Steady on!' 'Be reasonable!'.
1938 *Smith's Weekly* (Sydney) 31 Dec. 4/1 When the laugh had gone on long enough, he would silence it by his opening words, 'Fair go, mob.' 1982 R. HALL *Just Relations* 27 Fair go! How can I ask a thing like that?

3. a. [Used elsewhere but recorded earliest in Aust.] In other fanciful collocations: **fair crack of the whip, fair suck (of the sauce bottle),** an equitable opportunity; a reasonable chance.
1924 *Truth* (Sydney) 27 Apr. 6/3 *Fair crack of the whip*, just treatment. 1972 *Bulletin* (Sydney) 21 Oct. 45/2 Humphries . . goes down under a knuckle sandwich, his mouth and detached teeth so reddened you can see he's had more than a fair suck of the sauce bottle.

b. As *exclam*. 'Give (someone) a chance!'.
1966 A. HOPGOOD *Private Yuk Objects* 47 Oh, fair crack of the whip! How corny can ya get! 1976 J. JOHNSON *Low Breed* 198 'Fair suck!' said Gavin, 'If you haven't had a beer for six months you don't walk up to the bar and order half a shandy.'

fair, *a.*[2] [Prob. an amelioration of *fair* expressing moderate commendation, 'pretty good': see OED(S *a.* 11 c.]

1. Thorough-going; absolute.
1903 *Sporting News* (Launceston) 16 May 3/7 Some of his mates in the air were—in the vernacular of the 'talent'—'fair butes'. 1978 J. DINGWALL *Sunday too far Away* 42, I reckon, if he can't cook, he's going to be a *fair bastard* to get rid of.

2. In the collocation **fair cow**: used of a person, situation, etc., to which the speaker takes, or pretends to take, the strongest exception. See also Cow *n.* 2.
1904 *Bulletin* (Sydney) 7 Jan. 16/2 The worst that Australians can call anything, living or dead, is a cow. N.B.—This is a fair cow of a day—with a violent dust-storm, flies, heat. 1978 J. DINGWALL *Sunday too Far Away* 41 He's going to be a fair cow to get rid of.

fair, *adv*. [Br. dial. *fair* completely: see OED(S *adv*. 9 c.] Entirely; absolutely.
1888 G. ROCK *Colonists* 39 Now then, no larks, ye know;

fair horney, my covie. **1966** H. GYE *Father clears Out* 181 A cow . . will come home, and in a most flagrant manner, deposit a pat fair bang in the bail.

fairy, *n.*[1]

1. In the names of birds: **fairy martin,** the predom. black and white insect-eating bird *Hirundo ariel,* widespread in Aust., having a red-brown crown, and building a mud nest shaped more or less like a bottle; *blue martin* (a), see BLUE *a.*; BOTTLE-SWALLOW; see also MARTIN; **penguin,** the small penguin *Eudyptula minor,* which breeds on coasts of s. Aust. and New Zealand; *little penguin,* see LITTLE 2; **wren,** any bird of the genus *Malurus,* all of which are small and long-tailed, the breeding males of most species having brightly coloured plumage.
1842 J. GOULD *Birds of Aust.* (1848) II. Pl. 15, The **Fairy Martin** . . although enjoying a most extensive range, appears to have an antipathy to the country near the sea. **1848** J. GOULD *Birds of Aust.* VII. Pl. 85, *Spheniscus undina* . . **Fairy Penguin. 1983** *Bulletin* (Sydney) 6 Sept. 23/1 Phillip Island, home of the fairy penguins. **1928** *Ibid.* 25 Apr. 23/1 Mrs Daisy Bates . . records that the **fairy** or bluecap **wren** and his mate . . are known to many tribes of natives by the euphonious names of *Miril Yiril Yiri* and *Minning Minning.*

2. Special Comb. **fairy floss,** a confection of spun sugar, usu. pink; candy floss. Also *attrib.*
1945 H. ARTHUR *Flicka Daze* 66, I . . ate another piece of fairy floss. **1956** E. MITCHELL *Black Cockatoos* 40 They threaded their way past stands . . past the Fairy Floss makers, and the canvas snake pit.

fairy, *n.*[2] [Abbrev. of *fairy tale.*] A tall story. Also **fairy twister.**
1892 *Bulletin* (Sydney) 20 Aug. 21/2 Between the acts they treat him While he's swapping 'fairy twisters' with the 'girls behind their bars'. **1897** *Worker* (Sydney) 17 Aug. 4/2 Some bushmen pride themselves upon their storytelling powers, and . . don't stick at a 'fairy' when an impression is to be made around the camp fire.

fake, *v.* [Spec. use of (orig. criminal cant) *fake* to tamper with for the purposes of deception.] *trans.* To change (the brand) on a stolen beast. Also **brand-fake.**
1888 'R. BOLDREWOOD' *Robbery under Arms* (1937) 149 A horse-brand . . had been 'faked' or cleverly altered. **1940** W. HATFIELD *Into (Great?) Unfenced* 211 Taken here in the heart of the property, brand-faking.

Hence **brand faker** *n.*
c **1906** L. BECKE *Settlers Karossa Creek* 150 The sons of the settlers, who were all more or less cattle stealers and horse and cattle 'brand fakers'.

fall, *n.*[1] *Obs.* [Br. dial. *fall* portion of growing underwood ready to fell: see EDD *sb.* 5.] A group of trees.
1847 A. HARRIS *Settlers & Convicts* (1953) 29, I had found a fall of timber (as a group of trees is termed). **1962** B. BEATTY *With Shame Remembered* 199 If one chance to light upon a 'fall' of cedar, none of the others will attempt to cut even a tree out of the group.

fall, *n.*[2]

1. A strip of leather at the end of the plaited lash of a stockwhip: see quot. 1983.
1888 H.S. RUSSELL *Genesis Qld.* 349 A stock-whip with a long green-hide fall. **1983** R. EDWARDS *Whipmaking* 6 The fall is a strip of leather attached to the end of the whip. The end of the whip gets a lot of knocking around so it is better to have a fall that can be replaced rather than let the plaited end take the damage.

2. See quot.
1940 J.A. BROOK *Jim of Seven Seas* 59, I think the most dexterous feat executed by the stock rider is the crack of the whip called 'the fall'. To perform this act he lays out the full length of his whip to the rear on the ground. He then raises the short, eighteen-inch handle over his head, and with one fell swoop will bring the full length of the whip right over to the front, and make the extreme end of the lash strike any pre-selected spot in front of him the full length of the whip away.

fall, *v.* [Br. dial. *fall* to fell (trees): see OED(S *v.* 51 c.] *trans.* To fell (a tree).
1793 P.G. KING Jrnl. Norfolk Island 31 Dec. 110 Falling an Acre of Wood From 10s. to 13s. per day. **1972** B. FULLER *West of Bight* 133 Why, in the south-west, the term should be 'falling' and not 'felling' I cannot say, but so it is.

Hence **fallen** *ppl. a.*; **faller** *n.,* a tree feller.
1808 *Sydney Gaz.* 11 Sept., A capital and extensive farm at George's River, comprising 160 acres, 20 clear, and 6 **fallen** timber. **1793** D. COLLINS *Acct. Eng. Colony N.S.W.* (1798) I. 331 To each [timber] carriage were annexed two **fallers** and one overseer.

fall in, *v. Obs. intr.* To make a mistake.
1894 A.B. PATERSON *Singer of Bush* (1983) 221 If I can't get a copper, by Jingo, I'll stop her, Let the police fall in, it will serve the brutes right. **1922** C. DREW *Rogues & Ruses* 164 I've fell in meself before to-day and I know that it hurts real bad.

Also as *n.*
1902 *Sporting News* (Launceston) 27 Sept. 1/2 With one 'fall in' to their credit, the punters made a mad rush for Benedict . . and again were disappointed.

falling, *vbl. n.* [f. FALL *v.*]

1. The cutting down of timber; felling.
1804 *Sydney Gaz.* 2 Sept., A labouring man who was employed in falling on Livingston's Hill, near Parramatta, was unfortunately killed by a tree which fell in a direction probably contrary to the poor man's expectation. **1960** *Khaki Bush & Bigotry* (1968) 227 Just doin' a bit of scrub fallin'.

2. Comb. **falling axe, gang.**
1792 P.G. KING Jrnl. Norfolk Island 16 Jan. 16 The Settlers . . are totally destitute of many necessaries . . particularly **Falling Axes. 1825** *Austral.* (Sydney) 13 Jan. 2 The numerous road gangs, **falling gangs,** . . are at this moment in the greatest requisition by the settlers.

false sarsaparilla. The twining purple-flowered perennial *Hardenbergia violacea* (fam. Fabaceae) of e. Aust., sometimes confused with *sweet tea* (see SWEET *a.*[1]) which it resembles in leaf and habit; *coral pea* (b), see CORAL; SARSAPARILLA a.
1896 J.H. MAIDEN *Flowering Plants & Ferns N.S.W.* 55 *Hardenbergia monophylla* . . Vernacular name—We know of none except 'False Sarsaparilla'. **1978** B.P. MOORE *Life on Forty Acres* 41 The False Sarsaparilla (*Hardenbergia violacea*), a sprawling and clambering legume that seems to grow best amongst the sandstone flakes.

family reunion. An immigration policy which makes specific provision for immigrants who have relatives already resident in Australia. Also *attrib.*
1972 *Bulletin* (Sydney) 25 Nov. 21/2 Emphasis in immigration changed from government recruitment to 'family reunion' and retaining immigrants already here. **1981** *Austral. Financial Rev.* (Sydney) 3 Nov. 3/4 On the family reunion side the Government made some concessions last week making it easier for brothers and sisters of non-dependent children of resident migrants to settle in Australia.

fancy. *Obs.* In the collocation **the fancy,** the criminal class.

1832 *Sydney Monitor* 22 Aug. 4/2 The offence was of a serious nature, notwithstanding that many gentlemen, termed *the Fancy,* might make light of being transported for seven years. 1903 *Truth* (Sydney) 31 May 3/5 The thieves dealt an unfortunate peeler a blow with an iron bar, and in the expressive language of the 'fancy', laid him out!

fang, $n.^1$
a. A pressing request for a loan or gift, esp. in the phr. **to put the fangs in** and varr.; the loan or gift so secured.

1919 W.H. Downing *Digger Dialects* 22 To put in the fangs, to demand money, etc. 1924 A.W. Bazley et al. *Gloss. Slang A.I.F.* (typescript) 23 *Put the fangs in,* to request a favour or loan. 1932 L. Mann *Flesh in Armour* 250 They were all short of cash... 'I'll stick the fangs in him all right,' Tich averred. 1952 T.A.G. Hungerford *Ridge & River* 218 'Give me a smoke,' Wallace suggested. 'If there's one thing I like, it's to sink the fangs into an officer.' 1967 *Kings Cross Whisper* (Sydney) xxxiv. 4/5 Whereas a snip is only a small loan a fang is a large bite.
b. Special Comb. **fang artist,** one who is skilled at securing loans etc.

1972 A. Chipper *Aussie Swearers Guide* 24 *Fang Artist,* applied to (a) a glutton, (b) a constant borrower, or (c) a lecher.

fang, $n.^2$ [f. the name of Juan *Fangio* (b. 1911), racing driver.] A drive in a motor vehicle at high speed.

1969 A. Buzo *Front Room Boys* (1970) 20 If I were one of the back room boys, you wouldn't see me here before noon. I'd be down by the pool or out for a fang in the Jag.

fang, $v.^1$
1. *trans.* To induce (someone) to give (money or goods) by begging or borrowing, esp. in an exploitative manner.

1967 *Kings Cross Whisper* (Sydney) xxxiv. 4/5 *Fang,* to borrow from a person. 1979 *Herald* (Melbourne) 3 Mar. 41/1 He fanged me for a brick and next thing I know he's shot through all the way to Darwin.

fang, $v.^2$ [f. Fang $n.^2$] *intr.* To drive a vehicle at high speed. Also *trans.* with the vehicle as obj.

1969 A. Buzo *Rooted* (1973) 36 Let's hop in the B and fang up to the beach. 1981 *Bulletin* (Sydney) 10 Nov. 43/3 We pick up sheilas, get drunk, steal cars, fang 'em (drive them fast).. anyfink!

fan palm. a. Any palm of the genus *Livistona* (fam. Arecaceae), occurring in mainland Aust. and elsewhere: see Cabbage tree 1 a.; **b.** The lowland rainforest palm *Licuala ramsayi* (fam. Arecaceae) of n.e. Qld. and elsewhere, having leaf blades divided into many-ribbed segments. Also *attrib.*

1834 J.D. Lang *Hist. & Statistical Acct. N.S.W.* II. 163 The species of palm most frequently met with in the low grounds of Illawarra is the fan-palm or cabbage-tree. 1862 J.M. Stuart *Explorations in Aust.* 10 July (1865) 388 The fan palm .. leaf very much resembles a lady's fan set on a long handle, and, a short time after it is cut, closes in the same manner.

fantail. Any bird of the genus *Rhipidura* of Aust. and the s. Pacific region, insect-eating birds which habitually spread their tail feathers, esp. Willy wagtail and Cranky fan. Also **fantail(ed) fly-catcher.**

1773 W. Wales *Jrnl.* 10 May in J. Cook *Jrnls.* (1969) II. 786 The last I shal mention is the Fan-Tail. Of these there are different sorts, but the body of the most remarkable one is scarce larger than a good Filbert, yet spreads a tail of most beautiful plumage full ¾ of a semi-circle, of, at least, 4 or 5 Inches radius. 1841 *S. Austral. Rec.* (London) 2 Jan. 10 The nest of the fan-tailed fly-catcher, shaped like a wine-glass or egg-cup, with a long stem. 1980 M. Williams *Dingo!* 201 Over me fantail fly-catchers danced.

fantail banger: see Banger.

fan-tailed cuckoo. The predom. blue-grey and rufous cuckoo *Cuculus pyrrhophanus* of e. and s.w. Aust. Also **fantail cuckoo.**

1801 J. Latham *Gen. Synopsis Birds* Suppl. II. 138 Fan-tailed C[uckow]... Inhabits *New Holland.* 1911 A. Mack *Bush Days* 64 The rollicking note of the pallid cuckoo, and the sad wail of his cousin, the fantail cuckoo.

fantail(ed) flycatcher: see Fantail.

fan-tan, *n.* and *attrib.* [a. Chinese *fan .t'an* repeated divisions; used elsewhere but recorded earliest in Aust.]

A. *n.* The name of a Chinese gambling game (see quot. 1937).

1870 *Sydney Morning Herald* 4 July 3/1 The table was crowded with Chinamen eagerly staking their money in a game of 'Fantan'. 1937 E. Flynn *Beam Ends* 164 Fan-Tan is .. a straight out gamble that requires no skill. A handful of beans is taken .. and placed under a metal cover... Bets are laid on four little squares bearing the numbers one, two, three, and four; certain odds being given on certain numbers. The croupier lifts the metal cover and begins to extract the beans four at a time... Those who have bet on the correct number remaining win, while the house collects the rest.

B. *attrib.*

1872 'Demonax' *Mysteries & Miseries of Scripopolis* 42/2 We now made for the fan-tan establishment. 1937 E. Flynn *Beam Ends* 164 There, masquerading as business premises, are to be found large numbers of Fan-Tan joints to satisfy the cravings of those inveterate gamblers, the Chinese.

fantass /ˈfæntæs/. [a. Arabic *finṭās* water tank (pl. *fanāṭīs*).] A water-container, as carried by a camel. Also **fantassy.**

1916 G.M. Berry *Rep. G.O.C. Light Horse Brigade* 14 Nov. 2 A good deal of damage is done to saddlery by leaky fan-tasses. 1976 G.F. Langley *Sand, Sweat & Camels* 146 Let us also be thankful that thro' all the bad desert days we had 'fantassies', as well as water bottles.

f.a.q. /ˌɛf eɪ ˈkju/, *a.* [Acronym f. the initial letters of *fair average quality.*]

1. In the grading of wheat: of fair average quality (see quot. 1956).

1908 *S.A. Parl. Papers* II. no. 20 16 None of this cocky chaff .. is in the f.a.q. sample. 1956 Callaghan & Millington *Wheat Industry Aust.* 349 In those early days a method was evolved that came to be known as the f.a.q. system... The system was adopted in Victoria in 1891, by New South Wales in 1899 and by Western Australia in 1905... The 'quality' in f.a.q. refers not to the baking quality of the flour the wheat will produce but to its milling value. The actual determination of the f.a.q. is organised by the Chamber of Commerce in each State.

2. *transf.* Average.

1930 E. Shann *Econ. Hist. Aust.* 311 It is impossible, however, to 'bear' a land boom by selling f.a.q. land for future delivery. 1986 *Bulletin* (Sydney) 15 Apr. 110/3 On the whole I would say f.a.q. of its type with interesting possibilities as the show moves along.

far, *a.* [Spec. use of *far* remote.]

1. Used as an intensifier with nouns which themselves denote isolation, with reference to places extremely remote from major centres of population: **far bush, interior.**

1843 *Sydney Morning Herald* 27 July 2/7 In the **far bush** the poor settlers are in a miserable condition, should sickness overtake them. **1843** *N.S.W. Monthly Mag.* Apr. 177 South Australians with their corn at the door .. may be able to ship it to this colony at less expense than that at which your farmers convey it to Sydney from the **far interior.**

2. Used with a noun which denotes a place in a particular direction: **far north,** the northern-most part of a particular State (or Colony); **west,** the western regions of New South Wales and Queensland; (less frequently) Western Australia; also *attrib.*; so **far-western** *a.*

1849 *Bell's Life in Sydney* 13 Oct. 3/1 Mr Bilyard (late of North Australia) .. this gentleman having come from the '**far north**'. **1841** *Sydney Herald* 2 Oct. 2/6 It has been observed, by we distant settlers of the '**Far West**' .. that a considerable number of emigrants have lately arrived in the metropolis... Would it not be an act of justice .. were the Government to forward a number of the disengaged emigrants to the principal inland towns say—Yass, Bathurst, Berrima, Goulburn, &c. **1896** *Bulletin* (Sydney) 4 Apr. 22/2 Far western fleeces are light. **1936** W. HATFIELD *Aust. through Windscreen* 132 It would .. prevent the cases of rickets .. which the diligent workers under the Far West Children's Health Scheme come across.

far-back, *a.* and *n.*

A. *adj.* Remote from a major centre of population; OUTBACK *a.*

1851 'SQUATTER' *Let. to Squatters N.S.W.* 9 Did you inform them that they never need hope to hear the innocent prattle of childhood in the far back bush, whither you were leading them? **1964** H.M. BARKER *Camels & Outback* 42 The easy-going ways of those far back places.

B. *n.* A region remote from a major centre of population; OUTBACK *n.*

1898 D.W. CARNEGIE *Spinifex & Sand* 143 Should we find auriferous country in the 'far back', it was not my intention to stop on it. **1926** *Spectator* (London) 11 Sept. 370/1 It [*sc.* Australia] is no longer a pioneering country, except in the far-back.

farewell, *v.* [Spec. use of *farewell* to take leave of, bid or say goodbye to.] *trans.* To take leave of (a person who is departing from a place, job, etc.), usu. in a fairly formal manner (but see quot. 1942).

1897 *Bulletin* (Sydney) 30 Jan. 10/4 Some Kanakas in Bundaberg (Q.) farewelled Parson Eustace, the other day. **1937** F. CLUNE *Dig* 234 He had farewelled Commander Norman at the Albert River. **1942** —— *Last of Austral. Explorers* 125 The manager welcomed and farewelled them with a tot of rum.

Hence **fareweller** *n.*

1942 F. CLUNE *Last of Austral. Explorers* 120 The escorting farewellers were beginning to feel the strain.

farewell, *n.* [f. prec.]

1. An occasion organized to mark a person's departure. Also *attrib.*

1880 *Argus* (Melbourne) 6 Feb. 5/5 Mr George Danell will take his farewell benefit this evening at the People's Theatre, when 'The Forlorn Hope' will be performed for the 37th and last time. **1945** *Queanbeyan Age* 16 Mar. 1/1 A public farewell will be tendered Rev. H.R. Arthur.

2. *fig.*

1974 B. JUDDERY *At Centre* 123 Before 1973 public servants commonly styled them the 'farewell departments'— good for a sinecure, or at worst a routine job that required little serious effort and less serious thought, but offering scant opportunity to the man or woman of ambition or, for that matter, social conscience.

farinaceous, *a. Hist.* [Joc. use of *farinaceous* consisting or made of flour.] Used in various Comb. with reference to Adelaide: see quot. 1873.

1872 W.C. TAYLOR *Jottings on Aust.* 2 Adelaide wheat is very fine, and has led to the city being called by the Melbournites 'the farinaceous village'. **1873** A. TROLLOPE *Aust. & N.Z.* II. 184 Adelaide .. has .. been nicknamed the Farinaceous City... The colony by the sister colonies is regarded as one devoted in a special manner to the production of flour. Men who spend their energies in the pursuit of gold consider the growing of wheat to be a poor employment.

farm.

1. a. Used generally and unspecifically as elsewhere, but esp. of a comparatively small land-holding used primarily for the cultivation of crops.

1803 G. BOND *Brief Acct. Colony Port Jackson* 12 Trotman .. was sent .. to a settler's farm for turnips. **1951** *Bulletin* (Sydney) 13 June 14/4 He worked on the farm after that, eventually taking up a bush-block for himself.

b. Special Comb. **farm constable,** see quot. 1847; **hut,** a farmer's dwelling; **overseer,** a farm manager; **settler,** a farmer; **station,** a holding used primarily for the cultivation of crops.

1834 N.S.W. Magistrates' Deposition Bk. 17 Dec., I then went over to Mr Donald McIntyre's farm and told the **farm constable** there to search the huts. **1847** A. HARRIS *Settlers & Convicts* (1953) 82 The farm-constables .. are prisoners of the crown actually serving their sentence, who have been authorised to act ostensibly for the purposes of convict restraint on the farm. **1823** *First Fruits Austral. Poetry* (ed. 2) 17, I have been musing what our Banks had said And Cook, had they had second sight, that here .. on this south head Should stand an English **farm-hut. 1847** A. HARRIS *Settlers & Convicts* (1953) 9 A gentleman, through misfortunes reduced to the inferior condition of a **farm overseer.** **1847** E.W. LANDOR *Bushman* 108 The **farm-settlers** generally are young men of good birth. **1839** *Southern Austral.* (Adelaide) 10 May 2/2 Every useful requisite for a Dairy and **Farm Station.**

2. A nickname given to Monash University, Melbourne (see quot. 1982).

1963 *Age* (Melbourne) 8 Mar. 18/3 By 1968, it is estimated that 12,000 students .. will be down on 'the farm'. This not-unsuitable nickname has been bestowed by Melbourne University students on the 250-acre campus at Clayton. **1982** *Age* (Melbourne) 22 May (Suppl.) 7/2 It is a far cry from the opening, in 1961, with 363 students, when Monash was called 'The Farm' because cows grazed on campus and rabbits, hares and foxes were a common sight.

3. Australia, or the Australian economy, esp. as supposed to be under the control or influence of foreign investors.

1973 L. OAKES *Whitlam PM* 237 Australia became more jealous about the ownership of its resources, controls on foreign investment were tightened, and plans were laid to expand the Australian Industries Development Corporation to help 'buy back the farm'. **1985** *Canberra Times* 29 Aug. 2/6 Australia will again either incur further net debt abroad or be forced to sell off a bit more of the national 'farm' to foreigners.

farmer.

1. Used generally and unspecifically as elsewhere, but esp. of one whose principal occupation is the cultivation of crops.

1809 *HRA* (1916) 1st Ser. VII. 201 The average crops of the Colony are *generally more* than the consumption and would be considerably increased if the Farmer had any means of disposing of the surplus. **1970** *Bulletin* (Sydney) 18 Apr. 35/2 It is easily the most difficult club in town to join .. and there was a time when neither Catholics nor

FARMING   199   **FAT**

graziers who grew a bit of quiet corn in a far paddock (thus becoming 'farmers', not 'graziers') stood a chance.

2. See COLLINS STREET, PITT STREET, QUEEN STREET.

farming, *vbl. n.*
1. Used generally as elsewhere, as in 'dairy-farming', but esp. of the cultivation of crops. Also *attrib.*
1824 E. CURR *Acct. Colony Van Diemen's Land* 106 The turf hut in which they reside during their labours will serve afterwards to contain the farming men and stock-keepers. 1838 *S. Austral. Rec.* (London) 13 June 66, I think our colony will be more engaged in woolgrowing for the first few years than in farming.
2. Special Comb. **farming overseer** *obs.*, a farm manager; **station,** *farm station* FARM 1 b.
1833 *Launceston Advertiser* 9 May 1 Wanted, a situation, as **Farming Overseer**, by a respectable middle aged man, well versed in Farming. 1838 *S. Austral. Rec.* (London) 11 July 84 There appears no danger to be apprehended from them [*sc.* Aborigines] in establishing sheep or **farming stations** at any point on the great tract through which we passed.

farmstead. [Spec. use of *farmstead* a farm with the buildings upon it.] A farm-house.
1823 *Hobart Town Gaz.* 26 July, The farmstead is a neatly finished residence. 1953 A.W. UPFIELD *Venom House* 4 Here and there were small neat farmsteads.

far-out, *a.* Remote from a major centre of population; OUTBACK *a.*
1879 S.W. SILVER *Austral. Grazier's Guide* 9 It was wonderful upon what indifferent mental pabulum the 'far-out squatter' managed to subsist. 1950 A. GROOM *I saw Strange Land* 1 The transceiver—the two-way radio and telephone transmitter and receiver—has become the speedy messenger . . and far-out homes may talk several times a day with Alice Springs.

farther-back, var. FURTHER-BACK.

farther-out, var. FURTHER-OUT.

farthest-out, var. FURTHEST-OUT.

fat, $a.^1$ [Spec. use of *fat* containing much fat.] In collocations: **fat cake** [orig. Br. dial.], see quots. 1852 and 1888; **jack,** a tallow candle; *fat cake*; **lamp,** an improvised lamp which burns animal fat (see quot. 1886).
1826 *Monitor* (Sydney) 15 Dec. 245/3 He who has fed upon corn for six-months, can eat a '**fat cake**', with a true epicurean relish. 1852 MRS C. MEREDITH *My Home in Tas.* II. 59 That favourite bush dainty, a 'fat cake' . . was hot and brown . . (its composition being that of pie-crust, with abundance of dripping or 'fat' kneaded into it). 1888 J.F. MANN *Eight Months with Dr Leichhardt* 15 Our daily allowance of flour . . was made into a fatcake, that is, it was mixed up solely with fat, no water being used in the composition, and was cooked in the frying pan. 1962 O. PRYOR *Aust.'s Little Cornwall* 166 The Cornish miners of Moonta were singing carols by the light of '**fat jacks**'—tallow candles—stuck on the front of their safety hats. 1883 E.M. CURR *Recoll. Squatting Vic.* 34 The fire, the vapour, the odour of the '**fat lamp**', the scalding hot tea and reeking mutton, were neither pleasant nor inviting. 1886 H. FINCH-HATTON *Advance Aust.* (rev. ed.) 41 The inside of the hut was illuminated by a fat-lamp; a simple contrivance in the form of a jam tin full of fat with a fragment of tweed trousers stuck through a hole in the top for a wick.

fat, $a.^2$ and $n.^1$ [Spec. use of *fat* fattened for slaughter.]
A. *adj.* In collocations: **fat cattle, stock.**
1855 *Illustr. Sydney News* 21 Apr. 187/2 Mrs George Lang's first auction of **fat cattle** was held . . at Camperdown. 1844 *Sydney Morning Herald* 29 July 2/6 Not one moment's delay is occasioned to travellers or teams, or **fat stock**, in passing this hitherto enormous obstacle.

B. *n.*
a. Usu. in *pl.* (but see quot. 1923) or (in *attrib.* use) as a collect. sing. Sheep or cattle ready for slaughter.
1888 A.P. MARTIN *Oak-Bough & Wattle-Blossom* 127 Our 'fats' had been collected from three different stations. 1894 *Bulletin* (Sydney) 27 Oct. 23/2 It only cost a trifle to drive 'fats' to the great Victorian markets. 1923 *Ibid.* 29 Mar. 22/2 The saddler, when assisting the butcher to yard a killer, threw a nigger's null-nulla at the 'fat'. 1946 *Bulletin* (Sydney) 6 Feb. 12/1 The bullock . . was almost ready for the fat market.

b. *transf.*
1912 *Bulletin* (Sydney) 11 Apr. 13/4 Only saw turkey-droving once. That was 26 years ago, when I ran into a mob of prime fats travelling from Tumut to Wagga (N.S.W.).

fat, $a.^3$ and $n.^2$ [Spec. use of *fat* affluent.]
A. *adj.*
1. a. *Obs.* Capitalistic.
1896 *Bulletin* (Sydney) 28 Mar. 10/2 Anti-Sweating League has discovered a woman who earned at the rate of 6s. 9d. for 66 hours' work, and has been cut by the sweater, so that her earnings for the same time would be 4s. 'Let 'em sweat', says the Fat ring in the Leg. Council. 1906 *Gadfly* (Adelaide) 14 Mar. 5/1 According to the Fat Person's fancy picture of him the Australian socialist is a wild-eyed, frantic person, who breathes anarchy.

b. *Obs.* In the collocation **fat man,** a capitalist; also *attrib.*
1893 *Bulletin* (Sydney) 24 June 21/2 And, musing then upon the old-time lags, May doubt, perhaps, if they were more to blame Than modern Fat Man who, unpunished, drags A country's honour through a slough of shame. 1894 *Ibid.* 1 Dec. 16/1 The Fatman party in Vic. Assembly received a nasty pill from Labor-member Cook.

2. In the collocation **fat cat** [spec. use of (orig. U.S.) *fat cat* a wealthy and hence privileged person], a term applied to a person in one of the more highly paid grades of the public service (carrying the assumption that they are overpaid and underproductive); also *transf.*, and *attrib.*
1973 *Bulletin* (Sydney) 25 Aug. 67/3 There are radicals in the government who would really like to reduce the incomes of the various fat-cat groups. 1975 *Ibid.* 7 June 13/1 The number of second division (over $20,600 salary) positions has grown to 31. There are 19 branches, headed by these fat cats as Labor Minister Cameron would call them. 1976 *Ibid.* 11 Sept. 27/3 The ABC has been accused of being a pretty fat cat when it comes to staffing news bulletins or whatever.

Hence **fatmanity** *n.*, capitalism.
1897 *Tocsin* (Melbourne) 28 Oct. 3/3 The present crowd of fawning parasites of Fatmanity.

B. *n. Obs.* A capitalist.
[N.Z. 1905 *N.Z. Truth* (Wellington) 16 Sept. 1 A representative of fat proposed that he and his fellow fats [etc.]. 1906 *Gadfly* (Adelaide) 25 Apr. 5/2 Suggestions have been made to turn the Territory into a black-labour colony for the benefit of the Fat.] 1908 *Truth* (Sydney) 5 Apr. 9/4 And it isn't quite apparent why the Fats love Hingland so, Didn't Mother 'lag' their parents in the days not long ago? 1921 *Industr. News* (Sydney) 1 May 1/1 Quite so, fat, that has always been our lot.

fat, $n.^3$ [f. *fat* distended.] A (sexual) erection; esp. in the phr. **to crack a fat,** to have an erection.
1967 J. HIBBERD *White with Wire Wheels* (1970) 224 By Christ, if he races her off, it'll be the last fat he cracks. 1969 A. BUZO *Front Room Boys* (1970) 21 You'd get a fat as

fattening, *ppl. a.* [Spec. use of *fattening* making fat.] Used with various nouns denoting place, with reference to the suitability of pasture for stock being prepared for slaughter for human consumption: **fattening country, paddock, run, station.**

1875 *Austral. Town & Country Jrnl.* (Sydney) 6 Feb. 223/4 It's first-class **fattening country**; I dare say you saw that if you noticed any mobs as you came along. 1909 M. FRANKLIN *Some Everyday Folk* 17 There was no lack of fodder that season, and even the lanes and byways would have served as **fattening paddocks**. 1848 T.L. MITCHELL *Jrnl. Exped. Tropical Aust.* 15 That country is considered excellent as a **fattening run** for sheep. 1847 *Port Phillip Gaz.* 24 Mar. 3 The improvements are extensive and complete, for either a **fattening**, dairy, or jobbing **station**.

feather foot. *Aboriginal English.* KURDAITCHA 4.

1966 M. BROWN *Jimberi Track* 78 Ralph was thinking: Might be featherfoots watchin' me that side! 1980 *N.S.W. Parl. Papers* (1980–81) 3rd Sess. IV. 1666 At Kinchela we had a feather foot, a Kadachi man, and he came to do the programme... Normally Aborigines are frightened of these people.

fed. [Abbrev. of *federal(ist).*]

1. *Hist.* One who supports federation; FEDERALIST a.

1899 *Progress* (Brisbane) 10 June 1/2 The anti-feds, who were so much distressed by the delusion that in some way the people of Australia were going to pay something towards the maintenance of bounties on Victorian grown beet sugar, will be relieved in their minds when they learn that the factory is to be closed.

2. a. [Transf. use of U.S. *fed* member of the Federal Bureau of Investigation.] A police officer.

1966 P. COWAN *Seed* 2 The car began to gain speed... 'Better take it easy. The feds might pick us up.' 1976 D. IRELAND *Glass Canoe* 76 The Great Lover's got his eyes peeled and a paddy waggon comes round the corner with its lights out. 'The feds!' he yells. And goes for his life.

b. [Transf. use of U.S. *fed* official of the federal government.] A member of the federal parliament; a member of a federal political party.

1978 *Bulletin* (Sydney) 11 Apr. 14/1 At the moment they're leaving it all to Joh, whom they can trust to see that the Feds don't pull any swifties. 1980 *Sun-Herald* (Sydney) 24 Feb. 50/5 My impression is that purges are not on. The Queensland branch is very cocky. It has the cash, and the Feds (according to them) cannot get hold of it.

federal, *a.*

1. *Hist.* Of or pertaining to the association of the Australian Colonies in a federal union.

1835 *True Colonist* (Hobart) 4 Dec. 6/1 A *Federal* Union amongst all the Austral-Asian Colonies, will be most beneficial and desirable. 1944 G. COCKERILL *Scribblers & Statesmen* 105 Lyne was a thorough going Protectionist... Further, he was a 'State rights' man, whose support for the Federal movement was only nominal.

2. Of or pertaining to the Commonwealth of Australia as distinct from the States which constitute it.

1901 *Truth* (Sydney) 23 June 4/2 Fixed firm in the Federal trap, New South Wales is already beginning to feel its iron teeth. 1983 *Open Road* Apr. 2/1 NSW is burdened with an inadequate road system, yet this financial year will receive back for roads only about 22 per cent of total State and Federal fuel tax revenue collected from NSW motorists.

3. In collocations: **federal election, government, parliament.**

1910 *Huon Times* (Franklin) 19 Feb. 2/1 The **Federal elections** are approaching. 1896 C.E. LYNE *Life H. Parkes* 545 The main trunk lines of railway to be at the service of the **Federal Government**. 1898 *Ibid.* 19 Feb. 6/3 It has been decided to leave the fixing of the capital to the **Federal Parliament**.

4. In special collocations: **Federal capital,** Canberra, the capital city of the Commonwealth of Australia; **Capital Territory,** that part of N.S.W. ceded to the Commonwealth of Australia as the site of Canberra and its immediate environs, since 1938 known as the Australian Capital Territory; **House,** either of the two federal Houses of Parliament; **Territory,** the Australian Capital Territory; in *pl.*, the Australian Capital Territory and the Northern Territory.

1898 *Bulletin* (Sydney) 19 Feb. 6/3 The remnant of the Cabbage-tree Mob has risen to announce that it will do all it knows to prevent any Federation unless N.S. Wales receives a special bribe by the establishment of the **Federal capital** in its territory. 1913 *Bulletin* (Sydney) 6 Nov. 22/3 I've been in the **Federal Capital Territory**.. for three months. 1917 *Huon Times* (Franklin) 20 July 2/5 It is proposed to close absolutely the construction work in the Federal Capital territory. 1911 *Ibid.* 30 Sept. 2/4 Seeing that this political machine for the time being dominates both **Federal Houses**. 1961 *Bulletin* (Sydney) 8 Feb. 15/1 The most vocal members of the Federal House are apt to come from pastoral stock. 1917 *Ibid.* 1 Mar. 22/4 This season the **Federal Territory**.. was over-run by the sow thistle... It might be better known to the city folk as 'cocky weed', for it is often gathered for tame cockatoos.

federalist.

a. *Hist.* One who supports the introduction of federation.

1898 *Bulletin* (Sydney) 25 June 20/1 Anti-Federalists in S.A. Assembly.. were sacked by their constituencies. 1907 *Bulletin* (Sydney) 14 Feb. 14/4 There are eighty of us, good Federalists, in a mining camp 100 miles from railway... Our Australia won't give us a mail.

b. One who supports the strengthening and extension of Commonwealth powers; one who seeks to preserve the federal character of the Constitution.

1944 G. COCKERILL *Scribblers & Statesmen* 134 Former 'State-righters' became earnest Federalists. 1978 L. O'CHARLEY *Anatomy of Strike* 44 I'd forgotten you are a federalist.

Hence **federalistic** *a.*, inclined to federalism.

1891 E.H. HALLACK *W.A. & Yilgarn Goldfields* 27 Talk about federation and the small part intercolonially the colony must, from her position, necessarily play, it might with safety be recommended that a more federalistic form of government ought here to exist.

federate, *v. Hist.*

1. *intr.* To enter into a federal association.

1894 *Bulletin* (Sydney) 25 Aug. 6/2 If Australia is going to federate at all it is almost certain that it must start with a machine-made Constitution. 1899 *Austral. Tit-Bits* (Sydney) 25 Feb. 38/2 Oh! do not let us longer wait, Now's the time to federate.

2. *trans.* To bring under the control of the Commonwealth government.

1898 *Bulletin* (Sydney) 9 Apr. 7/1 Many of the residents of Sydney.. are apprehensive lest.. the railways be federated.

Hence **federated** *ppl. a.*, **federating** *ppl. a.*

1899 *North-Western Advocate* (Devonport) 17 May 2/5 Our relationship to **Federated** Australia vastly enhances the question of education. 1900 *Advocate* (Burnie) 8 Dec. 1/8 When the Commonwealth comes into existence the **federating** colonies will drop the name of 'colonies' and be henceforth designated as 'States'.

federation.

1. The association of the Australian Colonies in a federal union; the formation of the Commonwealth of Australia on 1 January 1901. Also *attrib.*

c 1875 *Me an' George* 45 If there's no patriotism, no unselfishness, no natural nobility, no good at all in Australians, why are you appealin' to them to 'make sacrifices' for the sake of federation? **1901** *Truth* (Sydney) 9 June 4/4 Federation, as now consummated and carried on in Melbourne, is a constitutional comedy and a financial farce. **1955** G. HEALEY *A.L.P.* 29 In 1901—Federation year.

2. Abbrev. of *Federation wheat.* Also *attrib.*

1901 *Agric. Gaz. N.S.W.* XII. 429 Federation and Purple Gown were from the same cross. **1984** P. CUFFLEY *Chandeliers & Billy Tea* 194 The 1890s saw superphosphate fertilisers being applied... Seed drills.. when allied to the new Federation strain of wheat, resulted in a new life for the industry.

3. Special Comb. **Federation style,** a name given by Bernard Smith (b. 1916), art historian, to a style of domestic architecture flourishing between 1895 and 1915; **wheat,** an early maturing variety of wheat developed by William Farrer (1845-1906) and released in 1901 (see quot. 1956).

1969 B. SMITH in *Hist. Studies* XIV. 90 The Australian house called Queen Anne has little in common with the English domestic brick architecture of the first decade of the eighteenth century... My own nomination would be **Federation style.** For it was born within the context of a discussion about the nature of an Australian style which parallels the political discussion that led to the foundation of the Commonwealth. **1901 federation wheat** [see sense 2]. **1905** *Agric. Gaz. N.S.W.* XVI. 465 For the country and plains to the west of Warialda, Gunnedah, Narromine, Forbes and Wagga I know of no bread-wheat which is likely to be more suitable than Federation (1 or 2). **1956** CALLAGHAN & MILLINGTON *Wheat Industry Aust.* 275 This new variety was released in 1901 and named Federation to mark the foundation of the Australian Commonwealth, a political event very dear to the heart of Farrer.

Hence **federationist** *n.*

1888 *Plea for Separation* 12 Separationists are essentially Federationists.

feed. [Spec. use of (esp. Br. dial.) *feed* pasture, green crops.] (Natural) vegetation, esp. grasses, suitable as food for stock; PICKING. See also *green feed,* pick GREEN 2, *sheep-feed* SHEEP 2.

1847 *Bell's Life in Sydney* 16 Jan. 3/4 The country however, is looking beautiful just now, the feed being most abundant. **1983** *Canberra Times* 24 May 3/1 At this time of the year there was usually standing dry feed left.

feeding, *vbl. n.* [Br. dial. *feeding, vbl. n.* pasturage.]

1. Used *attrib.* with reference to the pasturing of stock. Cf. GRAZING.

1856 W.W. DOBIE *Recoll. Visit Port-Phillip* 102 The flocks are brought in by the shepherds from their several feeding stations, one by one, to the home-station, to undergo the processes of washing and shearing. **1935** R.B. PLOWMAN *Boundary Rider* 41 Beyond the feeding range of the township stockgrass and saltbush and other feed became plentiful.

2. *transf.* and *fig.*

1869 'Q' *Peripatetic Philosopher* 41 The Wimmera district is noted for the hordes of vagabond 'loafers' that it supports, and has earned for itself the name of 'The Feeding Track'. I remember an old bush ditty, which I have heard sung when I was on the 'Wallaby': Hurrah! hurrah! for the feeding track, I've left the Avoca behind my back, Hurrah! hurrah! for the feeding track, Hurrah! hurrah! for the Wimmera.

feed-shed. An out-building in which fodder is stored.

1941 *Bulletin* (Sydney) 7 May 17/3 In the feed-shed he tackled his son. **1965** H. ATKINSON *Reckoning* 8 Looked.. at the dairy, the feed-shed, the cattle grazing on the flat.

Felician. *Obs.* Shortened form of AUSTRAL FELICIAN.

1848 *Omnibus & Sydney Spectator* 6 Nov. 42/2 It appears he is quite delighted with his trip, and has made the *Felicians* happy by the promise of a visit every year, during his stay in the colony.

fellmonger, *v.* [f. *fellmonger, n.* one whose occupation is the removal of wool from sheepskins.] *trans.* To remove (the wool) from a sheepskin. Also *absol.,* and with 'skin' as obj. Freq. as *vbl. n.* and *ppl. a.*

1847 *Maitland Mercury* 27 Oct. 1/2 *Fellmongering Establishment.* The undersigned.. found it advisable to *open* an *establishment* of the above nature in Maitland. **1871** *Austral. Town & Country Jrnl.* (Sydney) 28 Jan. 106/1 The remaining class was devoted to fellmongered wool, but there were no entries. **1924** E.C. SNOW *Leather, Hides, Skins* 59 The Census of Production of 1907 gave the number of sheep and lambskins fellmongered in England and Wales and Ireland as 8,928,000. **1957** H. PHILLIPS *Survey Fellmongering N.Z. & Aust.* 16 State abattoirs do not fellmonger.

fellmongery. [f. prec.] **a.** An establishment in which wool is removed from sheepskins. **b.** The process involved.

1880 R. ROSE *Austral. Guide: S.A.* 10 There are 60 tanneries and fellmongeries.. and, in addition to these, there are numerous large wool-washing works. **1899** G. JEFFREY *Princ. Australasian Woolclassing* 108 Fellmongery.. here refers to taking the wool off the skin.

fellow. *Austral. pidgin.* Also **fella, feller.** [Transf. use of *fellow* man.]

1. See quots.

1856 W.W. DOBIE *Recoll. Visit Port-Phillip* 91 The flattering compliment meant for my brother and myself, that 'there was no gammon along o' two fellow Dobie'. **1953** L. & C. REES *Spinifex Walkabout* 125 The homestead itself is.. two-storeyed—as the natives say 'him two-fella house'.

2. Chiefly *attrib.* in quasi-adj. (or adv.) phr.: **good fellow,** excellent; **proper fellow,** properly.

1935 K.L. SMITH *Sky Pilot Arnhem Land* 50 To Dan everything that flew, or walked, or creeped, or swam was '**good fellow** tucker'. **1951** I.L. IDRIESS *Across Nullarbor* 145, I can assure Mrs Melang back in Norseman that the meal was '**proper feller**' appreciated.

felon. In occasional use in Australia during the period of transportation as a synonym for CONVICT. Used *attrib.* in Special Comb. **felon colony, constable, constabulary, overseer, police:** see CONVICT B. 3.

1851 *Illustr. Austral. Mag.* (Melbourne) Oct. 210 A narrow jealousy of what we had been pleased, in our virgin purity, to stigmatise as the '**Felon Colony**'. **1835** H. MELVILLE *Hist. Van Diemen's Land* 217 Three witnesses were **felon constables,** John Boswello, a convict attaint, being a prisoner for life. **1835** H. MELVILLE *Hist. Van Diemen's Land* 268 It.. will serve to shew the villainy practised by the **felon constabulary.** **1835** *Ibid.* 14 Nov. 2 All the bolstering of the *Courier,* will never make British free subjects believe, that under any circumstances they are liable to be scourged by **felon overseers,** at the caprice of the Subaltern of a marching regiment. **1834** *True Colonist* (Hobart) 25 Nov. 2/3 Procure a dollar to shut the eyes of any of the **Felon Police,** who may observe an *impropriety.*

felonize, *v. Obs. trans.* To taint (with the human degradation associated with a penal settlement). Also as *ppl. a.*

1827 *Monitor* (Sydney) 20 Apr. 388/2 The sight of human woe and degradation continually before our eyes, will gradually impress upon our imaginations the feelings

FELONRY 202 **FEW**

of gaolers, and *felonise* as it were every conception of our minds. **1841** *Geelong Advertiser* 6 Feb. 2/2 My Lord .. your liberal measures for the division of this colony from the felonized colony of New South Wales.

felonry. *Hist.* [See quot. 1837.] The convict and ex-convict population, conceived of as a class.

1837 J. MUDIE *Felony of N.S.W.* p. vi, The author has ventured to coin the word *felonry*, as the appellative of an *order* or class of persons in New South Wales. **1945** J.A. ALLAN *Men & Manners in Aust.* 164 At Port Arthur the chief use of public worship was the enabling of the felonry to carry on surreptitious conversations.

female factory: see FACTORY.

fence, *n.*[1]

1. a. Used *attrib.* in Special Comb. **fence country,** fenced (hence settled) country, 'civilization'; also as *adj.*; **strainer,** STRAINER.

1940 W. HATFIELD *Into (Great?) Unfenced* 63 'Mister Barton, an' you're sweet. See?' Harry winked. 'What, Sir an' all?' 'Oh, he's not quite **fence-country.** No. Don't lap it round too thick. Might think you're swingin' on his foot. Mister'll do.' **1976** C.D. MILLS *Hobble Chains & Greenhide* 182, I wanted to be in Sydney for Christmas... 'I'm gonna miss you all and I hate to go. Yet I'm glad to be goin' back to see my people again.' I didn't realize as I said it, how much I would miss them and the life I had led once I hit the 'fence country' again. **1944** *Bulletin* (Sydney) 12 Apr. 12/2 Whenever he appeared with a shanty hung on his eye—and that was not seldom. Never did he attribute it to an upflung bit of firewood or a slipped **fence-strainer.**

b. In the phr. **outside the fences,** beyond settled country.

1937 W. HATFIELD *I find Aust.* 101 When the Annandale stock camp rode into town, Jack Gaffney, the manager, gave me a job right away. Over here in the cattle-country, managers were called by their Christian names... I approached him and asked was he Mr Gaffney... 'There's no handles out in this country. You're outside the fences now. Jack Gaffney's my name.'

2. In the phr. **over the fence,** objectionable; unacceptable; 'beyond the pale'.

1918 *Kia Ora Coo-ee* May 4/2 'It's over the blinking fence,' cried one chap, and he voiced the general opinion. **1972** A. CHIPPER *Aussie Swearers Guide* 79 A man who drinks lemonade or milk in a *rubbity* (pub) is *over the fence*.

fence, *n.*[2] Shortened form of *rabbit-proof fence* (see RABBIT-PROOF *a.* 1). Also *attrib.*

1930 E. ANTONY *Hungry Mile* 36 The days I steered the hunchies through the sandhills 'down the fence'. **1937** A.W. UPFIELD *Mr Jelly's Business* 175, I thought Lucy Jelly was sweet on the Fence-rider.

fencer. [Used elsewhere but recorded earliest in Aust.]

1. One whose occupation is the erection of (rural) fences.

1827 P. CUNNINGHAM *Two Yrs. in N.S.W.* II. 167 Carrying up with you three fencers, if you can obtain them, to secure crops by a good four-rail fence. **1981** A. WILKINSON *Up Country* 167 Leonard, a fencer .. had set up camp, with his dogs, just outside a small .. mining settlement.

2. In the collocation **fencer's tea:** see quot.

1942 W. GLASSON *Our Shepherds* 12 The ration supplied to each shepherd was extremely meagre and restricted... ¼ lb. tea, commonly called 'fencer's tea' because of its absence of leaf and preponderance of 'posts and rails'; 1½ lb. dark treacly sugar... 1 lb. of coarse salt; 10 lbs. of flour... 12 lb. of meat.

fencing, *vbl. n.* Used *attrib.* in Special Comb. **fencing camp,** the accommodation, personnel, etc., of a party of fencers; **wire,** heavy-gauge wire used in making fences; also in metaphorical comparisons.

1913 [**fencing camp**] *Bulletin* (Sydney) 6 Nov. 24/2 The most common subject of conversation in any bush camp, whether it's sheep, cattle, scrub cutters', fencing or any other .. is horse: racehorse, stock horse, .. pack horse, .. the take-down horse, the wool-team horse and, of course, the bucking horse. **1917** *Ibid.* 15 Feb. 24/4 A deputation from the fencing camp approached the boss for a change of tucker. **1858** *Royal S. Austral. Almanac* 27 (Advt.), *R.H. Crittenden, iron merchant,* Dealer in Ploughs, **Fencing Wire,** &c. **1922** V. PALMER *Boss of Killara* 145, I thought you had nerves like fencing-wire, Delia.

fern.

1. *spec.* *Obs.* BRACKEN.

1834 *Hobart Town Almanack* 129 *Pteris esculenta* .. is known .. among the European inhabitants of the colony by the name of fern. **1897** L. LINDLEY-COWEN *W. Austral. Settler's Guide* 217 In fern (bracken) country ring-barking appears to be of doubtful benefit.

2. Special Comb. **fern-gully,** a small valley or ravine, esp. in an area of moist forest, characterized by a high incidence of tree ferns; **hook** (or **slasher**), a long-handled arcuate tool used for cutting bracken; **tree,** *tree fern,* see TREE; also *attrib.*, esp. as **fern tree gully.**

1889 A. BRASSEY *Last Voyage India & Aust.* 318 We crossed a large river, the Nepean, passing through some charming **fern-gullies.** **1920** G. SARGANT *Winding Track* 155 Muscles were hardened to the **fern hook** .. cutting off the young bracken. **1952** *Bulletin* (Sydney) 27 Aug. 16/4 'Don't let him see a mattock, either,' the neighbor continued, 'or a fern-slasher.' **1788** J. HUNTER *Hist. Jrnl. Trans. Port Jackson* (1793) 326 The **fern-tree** which is very plentiful is good for hogs. **1880** 'ERRO' *Squattermania* 220 He .. finally deposited him in a gloomy fern-tree gully for the night.

fern root. *Obs.* The edible root of the ferns *Blechnum indicum* (see BUNGWALL) and *B. orientale* (fam. Blechnaceae) of tropical Aust. and elsewhere.

1788 *HRA* (1914) 1st Ser. I. 31, I also found the root of fern, or something like the fern root that had been chewed by one of the natives. **1899** J. MATHEW *Eaglehawk & Crow* 89 Fern roots and the Australian yam .. are perhaps the most common edible vegetables.

fettler. [Spec. use of Br. dial. *fettler* navvy: see EDD *fettle, v.* to repair, maintain, etc., esp. sense 7.] One of a party of workers responsible for the maintenance of a section of railway track.

1887 *V & P* (N.S.W. L.A.) VI. 441 Number and Classification of Persons employed in the Engineer for Existing Railway Branch, year 1886 .. Fettlers .. 1177. **1983** P. ADAM SMITH *When we rode Rails* 154 Permanent-way men .. are known as .. fettlers in Tasmania, New South Wales and Queensland.

Also **fettling gang.**

1937 *Bulletin* (Sydney) 4 Aug. 21/2 Why do swagmen shy clear of fettling gangs?

fever bark. [See quot. 1926.] The tree *Alstonia constricta* (see BITTER BARK). Also **fever tree.**

1888 *Proc. Linnean Soc. N.S.W.* III. 361 *Alstonia constricta* .. 'Fever-bark' or 'Bitter-bark' tree. **1926** *Bulletin* (Sydney) 14 Jan. 22/3 The 'fever'-tree .. is the native quinine .. commonly known on the North Coast of Bananaland as 'bitter bark'.

few. [Used elsewhere but recorded earliest in Aust.] Esp. in the phr. **to have a few (in),** to have (or to have had) a few alcoholic drinks.

1903 *Truth* (Sydney) 12 Apr. 1/6 Senior-sergeant: 'You're charged with being drunk.' Female: 'Guilty on a false oath!' As she had a few in at the time she was sent to the cells. **1912** M. SWEENEY *Melbourne's Armageddon* 22 He was 'havin' a few' with a couple of mates, down in a slum hotel.

fibro. Abbrev. of FIBRO-CEMENT. Freq. *attrib.*
1946 M. TRIST *What else is There* 167 The house was a dishevelled structure of brick, weatherboard and fibro. 1986 *Sydney Morning Herald* 12 Apr. 3/2 The small courthouse has the stateliness of a fibro fishing shack.

fibro-cement. A mixture of asbestos and cement compressed into sheets for use as a building material; asbestos cement. Also *attrib.*
1918 G. WHITE *Thirty Yrs. Tropical Aust.* 202 The church is of fibro-cement. 1964 K. TENNANT *Summer's Tales* 166 She came from the Old Country at the turn of the last century, to a land where there were no fibro-cement cottages, no hospitals, no ballet.

fiddle-back blackwood. [f. *fiddle-back* with reference to the wavy grain of wood traditionally used in the making of violins: see OEDS *fiddle*, *sb.* 8 d.] Figured timber obtained from BLACKWOOD, characterized by a wavy grain and highly prized as a cabinet timber.
1908 J. MANN *Suitability Australasian Timber* 4 Many trees have naturally a very handsome grain... The Fiddle-back, Mottled, and Dark-coloured Blackwood of Victoria and Tasmania.. are examples. 1945 *Bulletin* (Sydney) 6 June 14/2, I had a closer look at the 'curly lightwood'—the best piece of fiddleback blackwood I ever struck.

fiddler. [See quot. 1857.] Any of several fish of the genus *Trygonorrhina*, as *T. fasciata* of N.S.W. and s. Qld.; BANJO 4. Also **fiddler ray**.
1857 J. ASKEW *Voyage Aust. & N.Z.* 229 There is a large flat fish called 'the fiddler', found in shoal water, where there is a muddy bottom... In shape it resembles a fiddle. 1978 N. COLEMAN *Austral. Fisherman's Guide* 34 The fiddler ray inhabits both the sandy sea floor and algae-covered reefs in both shallow and deeper waters, offshore and in estuaries.

fiddley-did. *Obs.* Rhyming slang for 'quid', the sum of one pound; a one-pound note; also *ellipt.* as **fiddley**.
1941 S.J. BAKER *Pop. Dict. Austral. Slang* 28 Fiddley, a £1 note. 1951 E. LAMBERT *Twenty Thousand Thieves* 417 Fiddley-did, rhyming slang for a quid.

field, $n.^1$ Shortened form of GOLDFIELD 1.
1856 H.B. STONEY *Vic.* 10 The Fields are not now worked in the selfish mania that characterized the onset, but rather as an occupation; the digger is not now, as at first, the sole gainer. 1983 *West Austral.* (Perth) 21 Nov. 64/2 Power line a key in Fields growth. The new power line between Muja and Kalgoorlie is expected to be instrumental in bringing many gold prospects in the Goldfields into production.

field, $n.^2$ [Fig. use of *field* the horses, excluding the favourite, in a race: see OED *sb.* 10 a.] The accepted standards of behaviour; esp. in the phr. **to come back to the field,** to relinquish delusions of grandeur; to 'return to the fold'.
1944 L. GLASSOP *We were Rats* 82 'Don't worry,' said Bert... 'The poor bastard's hopeless. He'll come back to the field.' 1954 T.A.G. HUNGERFORD *Sowers of Wind* 4 Young Mark Flannery should come back to the field.

field police. Chiefly *Tas. Hist.* [Spec. use of *field* the country as opposed to a town.] A police force deployed to maintain law and order outside closely settled districts; *border police* see BORDER 3.
1825 *Hobart Town Gaz.* 17 Dec., A Band of Constables shall be forthwith formed, to consist of Thirty Men, to be constantly employed in the Pursuit of Runaway Convicts... The Constables of the Field Police will each receive an ample Allowance of Rations and Slop Clothing. 1862 BACKHOUSE & TYLOR *Life & Labours G.W. Walker* 278 The adult natives were also regarded and made use of as citizens, sixteen of the most active and intelligent having been organized by the police magistrate at Port Phillip into a field police.

field umpire. *Australian National Football.* The umpire or umpires in overall control of a game (see quot. 1965).
1885 D.E. MCCONNELL *Austral. Etiquette* 640 The Goal Umpires shall be the sole judges of goals, and .. in case of doubt may appeal to the Field Umpire. 1965 A. SCOTT *Man. Austral. Football* 66 Before the game, the field umpire should speak with the goal umpires, boundary umpires, and the time-keepers, to make sure that they understand each other's signals.

fifty, $n.^1$ *Obs.* (The punishment of) fifty lashes.
1830 *Sydney Monitor* 14 Aug. 2/3 To have a knife or other weapon in their possession after work-hours is sure to be punished with *fifty*. 1852 J. WEST *Hist. of Tas.* I. 105 The magistrate said 'give him fifty'—an easy compromise with the hangman.

fifty, $n.^2$ *N.S.W.* [Abbrev. of *fifty-fifty*.] See quot. 1978.
1971 F. HARDY *Outcasts of Foolgarah* 76 Five schooners of fifty, thanks, love. 1978 R. MCLELLAND *Outback Touring* 121 In New South Wales some pubs have both old and new beer on tap... A 'fifty' is a 50–50 combination of new and old, i.e. half a glass from one tap and half from the other.

fig. *Obs.* [Spec. use of *fig* a small piece of tobacco.] The unit by which tobacco was customarily sold: see quots. 1846 and 1852.
1834 N.S.W. *Magistrates' Deposition Bk.* 12 Nov., I gave him 7 figs of Tobacco for the Shepherds. 1846 MRS C. MEREDITH *Notes & Sketches N.S.W.* 104 The term 'fig of tobacco', so general here, will not be understood at home... That kept here for general use is 'Negrohead', and comes in large kegs, packed closely in layers of twisted rolls, about eight inches long,and one inch broad; each of these being technically termed a 'fig'. 1852 F. LANCELOTT *Aust. as it Is* II. 87 All the tobacco is uncut, and retailed in square sticks, called figs, each weighing about an ounce.

figbird. The fruit-eating bird *Sphecotheres viridis* of n. and e. Aust., related to the orioles. The male is predom. green and grey, the female brown.
1898 E.E. MORRIS *Austral Eng.* 144 Fig-bird .. *Sphecotheres maxillaris* .. Yellow-bellied, *S. flaviventris.* 1976 *Reader's Digest Compl. Bk. Austral. Birds* 548 Outside the breeding season figbirds move around in flocks, seeking food trees.

fighting-stick. *Obs.* A name given by settlers to an Aboriginal weapon: see quot. 1878.
1878 R.B. SMYTH *Aborigines of Vic.* I. p. xlv, The *Kou-nung* of the Victorian natives .. is not a club, but a fighting-stick. It is sharpened at both ends, and, whether used as a missile or a dagger, is a dangerous weapon. 1883 F. BONNEY *On Some Customs Aborigines* 7 Then throw fighting sticks or boomerangs at the young men, which they ward off with their shields (*oolumburra*).

Fiji. In the phr. **an uncle in** (or **from**) **Fiji** and varr., an imaginary financial backer.
1902 H. FLETCHER *Waybacks Town & Home* 6 'Ain't yer got an uncle in Fiji?' demanded Dads, with scorn. 'Ain't yer got two hundred quid to give to the honest man who will trust you to the same amount?' 1928 A. WRIGHT *Good Recovery* 9 I'm beginning to think that rich uncle is like the one from Fiji, eh, Lance?

financial, *a.* Financially solvent. See also UN-FINANCIAL.

1899 *Bulletin* (Sydney) 30 Dec. 14/3 No outback station refuses to sell rations; very few refuse to *give* when coin is not forthcoming... Stop the rations.. and only 'financial' travellers will venture out, and these.. can refuse work until offered suitable wages. **1973** F. PARSONS *Man called Mo* 4 The Mo character was never financial enough to be a business man. He was the down-trodden employee, but never the employer.

find. [Spec. use of *find* a discovery of archaeological remains, minerals, treasure, etc.]
a. The finding of a deposit of gold or of an area potentially rich in gold; the location of the find.
1851 S. RUTTER *Hints to Gold Hunters* 10 In about a year and a half or two years from the first *find*. **1955** A.C.V. BLIGH *Golden Quest*. 17 There was little mining or fossicking, as everyone was searching for slugs. Barely earning wages, we travelled to many small finds.
b. The gold obtained from the find.
1853 J. SHERER *Gold Finder Aust*. 58 Many instances might be adduced of large 'finds' having been made out of such holes. **1888** A.P. MARTIN *Oak-Bough & Wattle-Blossom* 144 It represented the only result of a strong man's hard toil for many weeks, and, as nuggets go, it was considered by no means a bad 'find'.

fine, *v.* [Br. dial. *fine up* to clear.] *intr*. With **up**. Of the weather: to clear; to become fine.
1926 *Bulletin* (Sydney) 11 Feb. 24/1 What cares the cook if it don't fine up? It's he who'll ring the shed. **1966** S.J. BAKER *Austral. Lang.* (ed. 2) 350 *Bogaduck weather* for heavy rain and *to fine up* (of weather) to become fine, are other Australianisms.

fine-woolled, *a*. Also **fine-wooled**. Of sheep: having wool of fine fibre.
1819 *Sydney Gaz.* 12 June, Some fine woolled Rams of the Spanish Breed. **1843** J.F. BENNETT *Hist. & Descr. Acct. S.A.* 95 Many thousands of fine wooled sheep were driven over by the New South Wales Settlers, and disposed of to the South Australians.

finger. *Obs.* [Prob. joc. use of *finger* policeman: see OEDS *sb.* 10 b.] See quot. 1898.
1897 *Worker* (Sydney) 11 Sept. 1/1 His boss he gives some funny names, when he can't hear the joke, He calls him 'joint' and 'finger', and he sometimes calls him 'bloke'. **1898** *Bulletin* (Sydney) 1 Oct. 14/3 In a shearing-shed: The boss is the 'finger'.

finger cherry. a. The elongated cherry-like fruit of the shrub or tree of Qld. and New Guinea *Rhodomyrtus macrocarpa* (fam. Myrtaceae). **b.** The shrub or tree.
1902 *Truth* (Sydney) 23 Nov. 4/8 Children and animals have become suddenly blind after eating wild berries known as finger cherries. **1982** K. MCARTHUR *Bush in Bloom* 64 The notorious Finger Cherry, Wannaki of the Aborigines. The fruit of this tree, if eaten, can send people blind.

finger-talk. [Spec. use of *finger-talk* sign language using the fingers.] A sign language used by Aborigines. Also *attrib*.
1936 'L. KAYE' *Black Wilderness* 166 Talk to him, Kombi... He might have a word or two of your lingo. Anyway you've both got hands for finger-talk. **1947** V.C. HALL *Bad Medicine* 147 Menikman glanced back and shot up a hand in a 'finger-talk' question.
Hence **finger talk** *v. intr.*
1956 T. RONAN *Moleskin Midas* 48 There's blacks ahead. I was finger talking with one old King and he is bringing two singers.

fire, *n.* [With reference to the colour.] Used *attrib.* in the names of flora and fauna: **fire fish,** any of several reef-dwelling fish of the fam. Scorpaenidae, esp. the red fire fish *Pterois volitans*, having stripes of scarlet and other colours; BUTTERFLY COD; **tail,** any of several finches of the genera *Emblema* and *Stagonopleura*, having red upper tail-coverts; esp. *S. bella* of s.e. Aust. incl. Tas.; also **fire-tailed finch; tree,** any of several trees, usu. so-called from their flame-coloured flowers (but see quot. 1972), incl. the W.A. *Christmas bush* b. (see CHRISTMAS).
1906 D.G. STEAD *Fishes of Aust.* 195 The Red **Fire-Fish** is remarkable for the tremendous elongation of the rays and spines of the fins. **1845** J. GOULD *Birds of Aust.* (1848) III. Pl. 78, *Estrelda bella*. Fire-tailed Finch.. **Fire-tail,** Colonists of Van Diemen's Land. **1872** 'TASMANIAN LADY' *Treasures, Lost & Found* 126 The little firetail. [*Note*] A bird which derives its name from a bright red spot beneath the tail, the rest of the plumage being brown. **1851** *Illustr. Austral. Mag.* (Melbourne) June 357 The *nuytsia floribunda*, whose flame-coloured blossoms have acquired for it the name of the **fire-tree,** exhibits the curious phenomena of a parasitical plant trailing along the ground. **1901** M. VIVIENNE *Travels in W.A.* 65 A handsome painting of the Nutsyia fire-tree, or Christmas-bush, also demanded notice. **1933** C.W. PECK *Austral. Legends* (ed. 2) 116 This fire-tree is a Brachychiton, and it is the same genus as the Queensland bottle-tree. **1972** V. SERVENTY *Singing Land* 81 One of the striking trees of the desert country, with bright green foliage and bell-shaped fruits, is the desert poplar, sometimes called.. fire tree, since it grows vigorously after fire, sending up a long, spindly trunk.

fire, *v. trans.* Esp. of Aborigines: to set fire to (the natural vegetation of an area), for the purpose of trapping animals or maintaining grassland (see quots. 1852 and 1882).
1835 *True Colonist* (Hobart) 14 Feb. 2/4 Caution them against the old system of firing the Bush. **1852** J. MORGAN *Life & Adventures W. Buckley* 100 Natives.. hunt round a kind of circle into which they force every kind of animal and reptile to be found; they then fire the boundary, and so kill them for food. **1882** W. SOWDEN *N.T. as it Is* 33 The natives and the teamsters periodically fire the grass to secure a succulent growth immediately after the late rains.

fire-brand, *v. Obs.* [Prob. independent of the obs. Br. use: see OED *sb.* 3.] *trans*. To mark (an animal) with a branding iron.
1825 *Tas. Non-State Rec.* 61/2 2 Dec., Firebranded the lambs. **1890** 'R. BOLDREWOOD' *Squatter's Dream* 47 'Every sheep of mine will be legibly fire-branded.'.. 'He'll fire-brand too,' said Hawkesbury, 'in the same place.'

fire-plough, *n.* and *attrib*.
A. *n.* An implement which cuts a furrow wide enough to form a fire-break: see quot. 1926.
1907 *Bulletin* (Sydney) 25 Apr. 14/2 The 'fire-plough', devised by C.P. Bell, manager of Westland station, near Longreach (Q.).. will cut a furrow up to 11 ft. wide— enough to keep back a fire except in heavily-grassed country. **1926** A.A.B. APSLEY *Amateur Settlers* 130 A fire-plough is drawn by some fifteen horses, and is a wide metal scoop on a timber frame, after the fashion of a snow-plough. **1954** T. RONAN *Vision Splendid* 156 Old Jack took the lead straight along after the recently passed fire-plough.
B. *attrib*. Made by means of a fire-plough.
1930 D. COTTRELL *Earth Battle* 291 The fire-plough roads were creeping in a mighty cross through the heart of The Block. **1972** R. MAGOFFIN *Chops & Gravy* 59 The car was still racing at ninety miles an hour along the fireplough road.

fire-plough, *v.* [f. prec.] *trans*. To form a fire-break on (land). Also *absol*.

1925 M. Terry *Across Unknown Aust.* 41 One station, which has the homestead in the centre of the run (property), has the ground fire-ploughed like a wheel, with many tracks radiating from the homestead right to the boundary. **1971** W.A. Winter-Irving *Beyond Bitumen* 65, I spent three weeks camped out fire ploughing with a friend.
Hence **fire-ploughed** *ppl. a.*
1935 I.L. Idriess *Man Tracks* 133 Natives showed him Moody's camel pads following a fire-ploughed track leading to a boundary-rider's camp.

fire-stick. A stick used to light a fire; usu. a smouldering stick carried by Aborigines when travelling, but see quot. 1920. Also *attrib.*
1804 *Sydney Gaz.* 11 Nov., These accidents.. are frequently attributed to the.. heedlessness of the natives in transporting fire sticks from place to place. **1920** *Land of Lyre Bird* (S. Gippsland Pioneers' Assoc.) 141 They made fire with their firesticks of 'jealwood'... The method of raising fire with them was very simple—a piece of wood about 1½ inches in diameter was split in half, a countersunk hole made on the flat side, and groove cut from that to the edge of the piece of wood, and then a small round piece of similar wood fitted at the end into the countersunk hole. The small piece of wood was then turned with the hands after the manner of a drill. This caused a friction, and in a very short time this began to smoke. The little black particles were run down the groove on to some very fine bark and then blown into a flame. **1984** B. Dixon *Searching for Aboriginal Lang.* 21 It was nicely printed in Brisbane and had an attractive cover with an Aboriginal firestick design.

firewater. [Spec. use of *firewater* any strong liquor; orig. U.S. and prob. a translation of an Indian word: see Mathews.] Any strong alcoholic liquor, esp. as supplied to Aborigines.
1858 *Austral. Gold Digger's Monthly Mag.* v. 187 Wretches are always found ready to take their cash and give them firewater. **1972** M. Cassidy *Dispossessed* 27 'You like fire water, eh?' and he made a drinking sign with one hand.

fireweed. [Spec. use of *fireweed* any of various weeds that spring up in burnt areas; orig. U.S.: see Mathews.] Any of several shrubs or herbs of the genus *Senecio*, esp. *S. lautus* and *S. linearifolius*, and also *Arrhenechthites mixta* (both genera fam. Asteraceae) which rapidly appear after fire.
1910 *Advocate* (Burnie) 6 Jan. 4/2 'Bullage'—a very bad species of 'fireweed'.. allowed to come up thickly. **1914** H.M. Vaughan *Australasian Wander-Yr.* 111 Most noticeable of all was the fire-weed, a native golden-rod somewhat resembling our own gaudy ragwort... Its local name derives from the circumstances that the fire-weed always springs up in abundance in the clearings made by Bush fires.

fire-wheel tree. [See quot. 1913.] The tree of e. N.S.W. and e. Qld. *Stenocarpus sinuatus* (fam. Proteaceae) which is grown as an ornamental for its striking red flowers. Also **wheel of fire tree.**
1913 F. Sulman *Pop. Guide Wild Flowers N.S.W.* 6 The genus Stenocarpus.. is best known by the Fire Wheel Tree, a handsome species with a very distinctive wheel-like arrangement of scarlet flowers, each resembling those of the Waratah. **1949** B. O'Reilly *Green Mountains* 15 A glorious 'Wheel of Fire' tree in full bloom had smashed into the middle of the road, scattering its blood-red blossoms.

first, *a.*
1. In special collocations referring to the British colonization of Australia: **first fleet,** the eleven British ships under the command of Arthur Phillip which arrived in Australia in January 1788; also *transf.* (see quot. 1945), and *attrib.;* **fleeter,** one who came to Australia aboard one of the ships of the first fleet; a descendant of a first fleeter; **settler,** one of the earliest non-Aboriginal residents of a particular area.
1791 P.G. King Jrnl. Norfolk Island 12 Nov. 6 The far greater part of those Convicts who left England in the **First Fleet** in 1788.. conduct themselves with Honesty. **1896** *Bulletin* (Sydney) 4 July 10/1 'A first fleet family.'—Noah's in the Ark. **1945** *Ibid.* 24 Jan. 13/4 Some of the arrivals by Westralia's First Fleet had to learn the selection of edible fish the hard way. **1826** *Monitor* (Sydney) 1 Sept. 123/2, I am, Sir, Yours, &c. *An Old Hand, but not a* **First Fleeter.** **1952** *Bulletin* (Sydney) 6 Aug. 17/1 Don't know if the hare, like the rabbit, was a 'First Fleeter', but it certainly made better time crossing the Divide than did its cousin. **1961** *Ibid.* 10 May 4/4 How long will it be before 'First Fleeters'—descendants of those who arrived with Governor Phillip—manage to work up the same sort of snobbery about their status as America's Pilgrim Fathers have? **1790** *Extracts Lett. Arthur Phillip* 12 Feb. (1791) 3 The draining.. would be a work of time, and not to be attempted by the **first settlers.**
2. In other collocations: **First Australian,** an Aboriginal; **preference,** see Preference.
1952 R.M. & C.H. Berndt *First Australs.* 11 Let us introduce you to an Australian minority—the Aborigines, the First Australians, who before the coming of the white man occupied the whole of this Continent and its immediate islands.

first-timer. One who is serving a first sentence in prison. Also *attrib.*
1881 *Bulletin* (Sydney) 8 Oct. 9/3 In Darlinghurst.. No. 1 yard contains men convicted three times or more. No. 2, twice-convicted men; No. 3, what is called 'first-timers'. **1903** *Ibid.* 25 Apr. 17/1 In a 'first-timers' prison 12 acres of cabbage garden outside the walls are cultivated by prisoners.

fishbone fern. [Fig. use of *fishbone*, from the resemblance of the shape of the frond of the fern to the skeleton of a fish.] Any of several ferns, esp. the hardy, common *Blechnum nudum* (fam. Blechnaceae) of e. Aust. incl. Tas., and those of the genus *Nephrolepis* (fam. Nephrolepidaceae), esp. *N. cordifolia* of n. Aust. and elsewhere. Also *ellipt.* as **fishbone.**
1923 *Census Plants Vic.* (Field Naturalists' Club Vic.) 2 *Blechnum discolor.*. Fishbone Fern. **1941** C. Barrett *Aust.* 26 Maidenhair grows thickly along the creek.. but tree-ferns have gone and only common 'fishbones' flourish... The young fronds of this poorman's fern.. are tinted rose-pink and salmon-red.

fishing, *vbl. n. Obs.* Used *attrib.* in Special Comb. **fishing station,** Whaling station; a place for catching fish; **weir,** a barrier built across a water-course (by Aborigines) to trap fish.
1836 H. Capper *S.A.* 24 Sept. (1837) 11 The Island [*sc.* Kangaroo Island] commands good harbours which are well adapted for **fishing stations,** refitting whalers, &c. [**1698 fishing weir:** W. Dampier *New Voyage round World* I. (ed. 3) 465 Their only food is a small sort of Fish, which they get by making Wares of stone, across little Coves, or branches of the Sea: every Tide bringing in the small Fish, and then leaving them for a prey to these people, who constantly attend there to search for them at low water.] **1845** L. Leichhardt *Jrnl. Overland Exped. Aust.* 13 July (1847) 330 We crossed two creeks, with good water-holes, in one of which was a fishing weir.

fish spear. A spear used by Aborigines to catch fish.
1845 L. Leichhardt *Jrnl. Overland Exped. Aust.* 27 May (1847) 269 Dillis, fish spears.. and several other small utensils, were in their camp. **1985** F. Birtles *Battle Fronts Outback* 102 He would now and then grab his fish-spear. It

had four eighteen-inch prongs of sharpened wood, fixed to the shaft by means of bloodwood gum.

fit, *v.* [Br. *fit* to visit (a person) with a fit penalty; now apparently obs. outside Aust.: see OED *v.*[1] 12.] *trans.* To fix upon (a person) the responsibility for having committed a criminal offence by securing (or contriving) sufficient evidence to ensure a conviction.

1882 *Sydney Mail* 2 Sept. 374/2 When he gets in with men like his old pals he loses his head, I believe... He'll get 'fitted' quite simple some day if he doesn't keep a better look-out. **1986** *Canberra Times* 2 Apr. 1/1, I feel that they are now determined to fit me on something.

five-corner. Usu. in *pl.* Chiefly *N.S.W.* [See quot. 1834.] The fruit of any of several shrubs of the genus Styphelia (fam. Epacridaceae), esp. *S. triflora* of N.S.W. and Qld.; any of the shrubs themselves. Also *attrib.*

1826 J. ATKINSON *Acct. Agric. & Grazing N.S.W.* 19 The native cherry, five corners, jibbong, and others, are mere tasteless berries. **1834** G. BENNETT *Wanderings N.S.W.* I. 337 Sold in the shops under the popular name of '*five corners*': this name, no doubt, was applied to it on account of the *calyx* projecting in five points above the fruit. **1918** *Bulletin* (Sydney) 1 Aug. (Red Page), Fifty or sixty years ago the ground near Sydney in the vicinity of Centennial Park, Randwick and Botany was covered with five-corner and geebung bushes.

five islands. *Austral. pidgin. Obs.* [Transf. use of a name formerly given to the Illawarra district, N.S.W.: see quot. 1836.] Biscuits.

1836 J. BACKHOUSE *Narr. Visit Austral. Colonies* 16 Apr. (1843) 376 While in Moreton Bay, we were surprised by hearing the Blacks call biscuits, Five Islands. This we learned, arose from some men who, several years ago, were driven from the part of the Illawarra coast called the Five Islands having held up biscuits to the blacks and said, Five Islands, in the hope of learning from them the direction of their lost home. The Blacks, however, mistook this for the name of the biscuits and hence have continued to call them by this name. **1882** W. COOTE *Hist. Colony Qld.* 33 They made him understand they wanted 'bread', 'bacca' and 'five allan'.

five-wire fence. A fence having five horizontal members made of wire.

1909 E. WALTHAM *Life & Labour in Aust.* 40 He would cut through the strands of a 5-wire fence with the palm of his bare hand. **1953** A.W. UPFIELD *Venom House* 157 Old Blaze chuckled and declared he preferred a blacks' wurlie to a house, and in the greatest storm would choose a five-wire fence to the shelter of Venom House.

fizgig. Also **phizgig.** [Prob. transf. use of *fizgig* frivolous woman, one who gads about.] A police informer.

1895 C. CROWE *Austral. Slang Dict.* 29 *Fizgig*, a spy for a detective. **1980** A.S. VEITCH *Run from Morning* 43 You can't get nowhere without good contacts. Phizgigs don't come out of automatic bloody dispensers!

fizz: see FIZZER *n.*[2]

fizz, *v.* [Fig. use of *fizz* to effervesce.] *intr.* Of stock: to behave in a lively or rebellious manner, to be difficult to control. Also as *n.* (see quot. 1968).

· **1966** S.J. BAKER *Austral. Lang.* (ed. 2) 62 *Fizz*, to move rapidly and erratically, originally applied to a lively bull in a yard. **1968** LINKLATER & TAPP *Gather No Moss* 31 A 'rush' was the term used to describe the headlong flight that the westerns of a later day called a stampede. Strings of cattle often break out of a mob and cause trouble. In proper droving language this is only a 'fizz'.

fizzer, *n.*[1] [f. FIZZ *v.*] See quot.

1927 J. MATHIEU *Backblock Ballads* 41 My horse beneath me swerved around, And like a frightened 'fizzer' fled. [*Note*] Fizzer—Untameable brumby.

fizzer, *n.*[2] Also **phizzer.** [f. FIZGIG.] A police informer. Also **fizz.**

1943 S.J. BAKER *Pop. Dict. Austral. Slang* (ed. 3) 32 *Fizgig*, a stool pigeon. *Fizz*, as for 'fiz-gig'. **1950** *Austral. Police Jrnl.* Apr. 112 *Fizz-gig, or Fizzer*, a police informant. **1974** *Bulletin* (Sydney) 15 June 27/1 [The] police commissioner.. told Cairns 'you are wasting your time studying. Your job is to get phizzers.'

fizzer, *n.*[3] [Transf. use of *fizzer* a firework which fails to explode; perh. infl. by *fizzle* a failure or fiasco.] A failure or fiasco.

1957 R.S. PORTEOUS *Brigalow* 101 Good old Carson, I thought. You may be a bit of a fizzer, but you'll do me. **1981** *Austral. Roadsports & Drag Racing News* 27 Feb. 6/1 The Funny Car match.. was something of a fizzer, as both cars were shut down at the first start.

fizzy, *a.* [See FIZZ *v.*] Of stock: rebellious, difficult to control.

1975 D. STUART *Walk, trot, canter & Die* 52 How are you on the real rough horses, or in a yard with fizzy cattle? **1976** C.D. MILLS *Hobble Chains & Greenhide* 175 One old mare was very fizzy, and too old to try and break.

flag.

1. *Australian National Football.*

a. In the phr. **to raise** (or **bring up**) **both flags,** to score a goal (as opposed to a behind), thus causing the goal umpire to signal the event by raising a small flag in each hand.

1908 *Clipper* (Hobart) 27 June 2/2 Ward skyscraped to some tune, and Cook had a try for goal, both flags being raised. **1960** *N.T. News* (Darwin) 12 Jan. 8/3 Bedwell sent it on to P. Marrego who raised both flags. *Ibid.* 5 Jan. 8/5 Cooper snapped a neat handpass to Potts when he got into trouble and Potts brought up both flags.

b. A pennant awarded to the team which wins a competition.

1969 A. HOPGOOD *And Big Men Fly* 3, I promised our supporters that this year I'd get 'em a flag. **1983** HIBBERD & HUTCHINSON *Barracker's Bible* 79 The winners of a premiership receive a special pennant which has emblazoned on it the year of victory. This flag is usually hoisted on the occasion of the first home game for the victors in the following season.

2. *Obs.* The sum of one pound; a one-pound note.

1943 S.J. BAKER *Pop. Dict. Austral. Slang* (ed. 3) 32 *Flag*, a banknote, especially £1. **1955** *Bulletin* (Sydney) 5 Jan. 12/1 Recognised price for a healthy, weaned kid was four-bob, 7s. 6d. for a nanny at the flapper-stage, half-a-flag to twelve-and-a-break for a young milker.

3. In the phr. **to fly the flag:** see quot. 1975.

1975 *Bulletin* (Sydney) 26 Apr. 45/2 Pig.. asks Gulcher why he doesn't fly the flag; that is, appeal the case to a higher court in the hope of having the sentence reduced. **1980** B. HORNADGE *Austral. Slanguage* 81 His cell mate asks him will he appeal against the severity of the sentence to a higher court (*to fly the flag*) and the aggrieved one says that he will.

flag fall. An initial hiring charge incurred as the flag of a taximeter is lowered and the meter engaged.

1931 *N.S.W. Govt. Gaz.* II. 1306 'Flag Fall' means the amount of fare recorded by a taximeter immediately upon the flag being lowered to set the taximeter in motion at the commencement of a hiring. **1978** *Gregory's Sydney Pocket Guide* 6 Charges are.. based on a flat rate flag fall and a metered charge per mile.

flag-flapper. One who, though overtly patriotic, avoids active service.
1918 *Ross's Monthly* July 1/2 *Aghast*—what some war-time flag-flappers (and other flappers) would feel like in the presence of the Real thing. **1954** J. WATEN *Unbending* 249 You bloody cowardly flag-flappers; you stay-at-home fighters.

flagon-wagon. A vehicle used to transport alcoholic liquor to an Aboriginal settlement.
1982 *Bulletin* (Sydney) 7 Dec. 47/1 The 'flagon-waggon' on the grog-run to an isolated settlement, where some people would pay exorbitant prices, has been part of Central Australian culture since the white man introduced alcohol last century. **1985** *Canberra Times* 11 Aug. 5/1 The flagon wagons run less regularly up and down the road.

flame.
1. The brilliant flashes of red found in some opal; an opal gem so characterized. Also **flame opal.**
1932 I.L. IDRIESS *Prospecting for Gold* 245 'Fire' or 'flame', in a stone is the most valuable colour as 'harlequin' is the most prized pattern. **1974** B. MYATT *Dict. Austral. Gemstones* 134 Flame opal describes a precious gem in which the colour occurs as red bands or streaks, similar to flickering flames.
2. Special Comb. **flame robin,** the flycatcher *Petroica phoenicea* of s.e. Aust.; formerly also **flame-breasted robin, flame bird; tree, (a)** the chiefly deciduous tall tree of coastal e. Aust. *Brachychiton acerifolius* (fam. Sterculiaceae) occurring from Illawarra N.S.W. to n. Qld. and cultivated for its conspicuous red flowers; *Illawarra flame tree,* see ILLAWARRA 1; **(b)** coral tree, see CORAL.
1842 [**flame robin**] J. GOULD *Birds of Aust.* (1848) III. Pl. 6, *Petroica phoenicia* . . Flame-breasted Robin. **1891** P.D. LORIMER *Songs & Verses* (1901) 178 Startling the nesting flame-bird, where it lurks. **1942** C. BARRETT *From Bush Hut* 74 The scarlet-breasted species, the flame robin. **1860** G. BENNETT *Gatherings of Naturalist* 355 The **Flame-tree** of Illawarra (*Brachychiton acerifolium*) is of slender growth, lofty, and .. denuded of branches, except at the summit. **1920** *Bulletin* (Sydney) 8 Jan. 20/2 If the flame- or coral-tree .. is any harder to kill than the white ti-tree .. I will hand in the belt.

flaming fury. An outdoor earth-closet, so-called because the contents were periodically doused with an inflammable liquid and ignited.
1960 *N.T. News* (Darwin) 5 Feb. 5/3 Only one dilapidated flaming fury is provided for the present nine people. **1982** *N.T. News* (Darwin) 13 Dec. 7/2 We have heard of a famous Territory dunny that was known far and wide in the post-war years as 'The Blue Room'. . . for a 'flaming fury' it was something out of the ordinary.

flank. *Australian National Football.* An outside position; a player in an outside position.
1931 J.F. MCHALE et al. *Austral. Game of Football* 60 The wings and half-forwards should adopt the same tactics as the halfbacks when the ball is coming down *via* the flanks. **1973** P. MCKENNA *My World of Football* 108 The flank is usually referred to as the 'graveyard' of football, but played by an expert it can become the most dangerous position in a team's attack.

flanker.
1. A beast that travels on the flank of a drove; a stockman who rides on the flank of a drove to prevent straggling. See DROVE *n.* 1.
1843 R.D. MURRAY *Summer at Port Phillip* 233 There is a flanker .. who seems inclined to part company from the 'mob'. **1960** I.L. IDRIESS *Wild North* 204 Often some startled beast would make a wild get-away from the flank, to be rounded back instantly by superb horsemanship on the part of both flanker and horse.

2. *Australian National Football.* See quot. 1968 and FLANK.
1968 EAGLESON & MCKIE *Terminology Austral. Football* ii. 5 *Flanker,* a popular variant recorded by informants in reference to a player occupying outside positions, normally the half-back and half-forward outside positions. **1973** P. MCKENNA *My World of Football* 108 A good flanker relies on his anticipation, elusiveness and cunning.

flannel flower. [From the appearance of the bracts: see quot. 1895.] Any of several annual or perennial plants of the genus *Actinotus* (fam. Apiaceae), esp. the bushy *A. helianthi* bearing conspicuous bracts which are soft, white, and woolly; the flower of these plants.
1888 *Sydney Morning Herald* 24 Jan. (Suppl.) 1/6 The 'flannel flower' (Actimotus [*sic*] helianthi) .. which is found in sandy places, is of the parsley tribe. **1895** J.H. MAIDEN *Flowering Plants & Ferns N.S.W.* 9 The 'Flannel Flower'—a rather unpoetical designation, but a really descriptive one. . . It is .. in allusion to the involucre, which looks as if it were snipped out of white flannel.

flashjack.
1. One whose behaviour or dress is characterized by flamboyance and showiness; a 'swell'.
1898 *Bulletin* (Sydney) 16 Apr. 14/1 Years ago, before the days of paddocks, the 'Flash Jack' was in evidence on every cattle-station, in white moles, cabbage-tree hat, silk neckerchief, and long spurs, and slouching on the back of a raking brumby. **1960** C. YOUNGER *Less than Angel* 124 We don't like flash jacks hanging round our girls. Stick to the tarts, son.
2. *Bridled nail-tailed wallaby,* see NAIL-TAILED WALLABY.
1913 W.K. HARRIS *Outback in Aust.* 130 The 'Flash Jack' is very similar in appearance to the kangaroo known as the 'Blue Flier', but does not grow so large. **1941** E. TROUGHTON *Furred Animals Aust.* 186 Specimens in the Museum collection are from as far south as Wagga, in 1896, where it was locally known as 'Flash Jack' (quite a good name because of its swift actions).

flash jane. A name given to the female equivalent of FLASHJACK 1.
1932 K.S. PRICHARD *Kiss on Lips* 174 Smellin' so as you'd look round to see if a flash Jane from the city was about. **1950** —— *Winged Seeds* 54 You never saw such flash janes: twins with ginger hair.

flat, $n.^1$ [Spec. use of *flat* a piece of level ground.]
a. A stretch of level ground, esp. adjacent to a watercourse (or former watercourse) and of alluvial formation; hence, such a stretch of ground as a source of alluvial gold: see quots. 1855 (1) and 1869. See also *river flat* RIVER 1.
1799 D. COLLINS *Acct. Eng. Colony N.S.W.* (1802) II. 165 In the bottoms of the vallies and upon the damp flats. **1855** *Ovens & Murray Advertiser* (Beechworth) 3 Feb. 5/4 The flats and low grounds, many of which were too wet to be worked last summer, continue to be selected by the miners. **1855** W. HOWITT *Land, Labor & Gold* II. 239 Broad levels, which we should call meadows or plains, are flats. **1869** R.B. SMYTH *Gold Fields & Mineral Districts* 611 *Flat,* a low even tract of land, generally occurring where creeks unite, over which are spread many strata of sand and gravel, with the usual rich auriferous drift immediately overlying the bedrock.
b. With distinguishing epithet, as **apple-tree flat,** such a stretch of ground as characterized by its predominant form of vegetation.
1827 H.S RUSSELL *Genesis Qld.* 19 May (1888) 91 Descending without much difficulty to an apple-tree flat, the valley gradually expanded. **1880** J. BONWICK *Resources Qld.* 36 Such phrases as 'Box forest', 'Iron-bark ranges', 'Apple-tree flats' .. have all had their own respective associations

in the minds of those interested in the pastoral or agricultural capabilities of land.

flat, *n.*² [Spec. use of Br. slang *flat* one who is easily taken in.] A gullible person or dupe, esp. a recent immigrant, a pincher, a picker-up. See also SHARP.
1812 J.H. VAUX *Mem.* (1819) II. 174 *Flat*, in a general sense, any honest man, or *square cove*, in opposition to a *sharp* or *cross-cove*; when used particularly, it means the person whom you have a design to rob or defraud. **1971** H. ANDERSON *Larrikin Crook* 6 He was .. depending for a living on his skill in exploiting the 'flats' who appropriately enough gather on that part of the racecourse known as the flat.

Hence **flatcatcher** *n.*, see quot. 1882; **flat-catching** *vbl. n.*, indulging in sharp practice.
1877 *Vagabond Ann.* 136 You have to be a bit of a magsman, a pincher, a picker-up, a **flatcatcher**, a bester. **1882** *Sydney Slang Dict.* 4 *Flatcatchers*, those who 'work' by false pretences and by fraud. **1849** A. HARRIS *Emigrant Family* (1967) 245 **Flat-catching** is out of season.

flat, *n.*³ *Horse-racing.* [Transf. use of *flat* level piece of ground at the end of some racecourses.] A level and undeveloped enclosure for spectators; the area in the centre of a racecourse.
1846 *Bell's Life in Sydney* 27 June 2/3 After a rapid transit from the flat (not flats) of Campbellfield to .. Bathurst, our Racing Reporter reached .. Wellington. **1920** 'J. NORTH' *Harry Dale's Grand National* 167 The crowds on the lawn and the outer and the flat took up the cheering.

Hence **flatite** *n.*, one who patronizes the flat.
1896 *Bulletin* (Sydney) 19 Dec. 20/3 Flatites don't, as a rule, run to binoculars, so a board, on which starters' numbers and riders' names are legibly exhibited, should be provided by the rich A.J.C. for the multitudinous shilling patrons.

flat, *n.*⁴ See quot. 1950.
1902 *Bulletin* (Sydney) 31 Mar. 31/2 A half plug of 'flat' .. mysteriously disappeared. **1950** *Austral. Police Jrnl.* Apr. 112 *Flat*, fine cut flake tobacco.

flat, *a. Two-up.* Of coins after spinning: landing flat, not rolling on impact. Also *absol.*
1911 A. WRIGHT *Gambler's Gold* (1923) 57 Quickly the coins are up and down. One fell a flat tail. **1934** *Austral. Ring* IX. cviii. 13 He angled for the 'flat'. 'Watch the penny as I spin it—make it vanish in the air.'

flat, *adv.*
1. Usu. in the phr. **flat as a strap** (or **tack**), **flat to the boards**, at the limit of one's powers or resources.
1955 *Bulletin* (Sydney) 14 Dec. 12/4 Mo walked on to the board .. and saw an old pen-mate .. who soon told him he was flat as a strap to get the bare ton. **1963** M. BRITT *Pardon my Boots* 83, I seemed to have been going extra fast just then—'flat to the boards'. **1983** *Sydney Morning Herald* 13 June 25/4 'I rode her in the Brisbane Cup and she went disgracefully,' Quinton said. 'She was as flat as a tack after the hard run.'
2. In the phr. **flat out like** (or **as**) **a lizard (drinking)**, fully extended.
1935 *Bulletin* (Sydney) 23 Oct. 21/4 'Flat out like a lizard drinking' is a well-worn bush phrase. **1938** F. CLUNE *Free & Easy Land* 227 Dirty Dora was as flat out as a drinking lizard. **1952** *Meanjin* 208 I've been flat out like a lizard since eight o'clock this morning.

flatette. A small flat or apartment.
1945 S.J. BAKER *Austral. Lang.* 133 *Flatette*, a small flat, also appears to be indigenous. **1980** *Express* (Brisbane) 28 May 4/1 Granny flats are usually small self-contained flatettes built underneath or attached alongside an existing house.

flathead.
1. [See quot. 1974.] Any of many bottom-dwelling marine and estuarine fish, esp. of the fam. Platycephalidae, having a flattened head and body, and valued as food. Also with distinguishing epithet, as **dusky, long-spined, rock, sand, tiger** (see under first element).
1790 J. HUNTER *Hist. Jrnl. Trans. Port Jackson* (1793), *Paddewah*, a fish called a flat-head. **1974** T.D. SCOTT et al. *Marine & Freshwater Fishes S.A.* 165 The fishes of this family, known as flatheads, are familiar to those with the barest knowledge of our fishes. As the popular name implies, the head is broad and flattened, being much broader than deep.
2. *Qld.* LUNGFISH.
1880 A.C.L.G. GÜNTHER *Introd. Study Fishes* 357 Locally, the settlers call it [*sc. Ceratodus*] 'Flat-head', 'Burnett- or Dawson-Salmon', and the aborigines 'Barramunda'. **1906** D.G. STEAD *Fishes of Aust.* 229 The Australian Lung-Fish (*Neoceratodus forsteri*) .. is a native of the Mary and Burnett Rivers in Queensland... By many Queenslanders this species is known as 'Barramundi'. .. Other names are 'Flathead' and 'Burnett salmon' or 'Mary-River salmon'.

flat-top. An unenclosed, flat-decked railway freight car.
1966 M. BROWN *Jimberi Track* 12 They clambered onto the flat-tops in their bits-and-pieces of cast-off clothing, tugging their blankets and billycans, for they loved nothing so much as travel, and there was nothing in their eyes to match the train. **1973** R. ROBINSON *Drift of Things* 368 Ralph went to the railhead and booked a couple of 'flat-tops' for our six trucks on the next train out of Alice Springs.

flax. *Native flax*, see NATIVE *a.* 6 a.
1824 *Hobart Town Gaz.* 24 Dec., The flax which may be seen growing spontaneously on all the hills, and in nearly all the vales of Tasmania. **1928** J. POLLARD *Bushland Vagabonds* 151 The blue wild flax.

flea. Used allusively in the phr. **to flog** (or **hunt**) **a flea (over)**, apparently with reference to ground being so bare of vegetation that a flea being driven across it would be visible.
1866 *Cornhill Mag.* (London) Dec. 741 The vast natural meadow was, as one of the stockmen feelingly observed, 'as bare of grass as the palm of your hand'; while another gravely professed his belief 'that you could hunt a flea across it with a stock-whip'. **1903** J. FURPHY *Such is Life* 165 The famine was sore in the land. To use the expression of men deeply interested in the matter, you could flog a flea from the Murrumbidgee to the Darling. **1944** *Bulletin* (Sydney) 11 Oct. 13/3 A little concerned over the feed shortage on my own slopes, I entered the new settler's rails to find that one could flog a flea over any of his paddocks.

fleas and itches. Rhyming slang for 'the pictures', the cinema.
1967 *Kings Cross Whisper* (Sydney) xxxiv. 4/5 *Fleas and itches*, movies. Pictures, a hangover from the bughouse days. **1968** D. O'GRADY *Bottle of Sandwiches* 60 When not too tired, a man was able to visit .. the open-air fleas-n' itches.

flick. *Surfing.* With **off** and **out**: see quots.
1963 B. JOHNSON *Surf Fever* 33 *Flick off*, a method of manoeuvring the board whereby the rider is able to pull off the wave before it breaks. **1963** J. POLLARD *Austral. Surfrider* 19 If you bring your board up from the bottom of a wave and over the top you do a 'flick out'

flick pass. [Spec. use of *flick pass* a quick pass.]
1. *Australian National Football.* See quot. 1963 (2).

1936 E.C.H. TAYLOR et al. *Our Austral. Game Football* 23 *The Flick Pass*, this method .. consists of holding the ball in one hand and hitting it with the other hand outstretched. **1963** *Footy Fan* (Melbourne) I. vii. 10 He considers the reaction of the umpires to the flick pass makes it a risky proposition in play. **1963** L. RICHARDS *Boots & All!* 81 Len Smith must also go down in football history for inventing a new style of hand-ball—even though it borders on a throw—he was the first coach to wake up to the fact that the flick pass could be used. His players started using lightning-fast passes in which the ball was hit with the open hand, a more accurate and far quicker method than the ordinary hand pass with the punch or the clenched fist.

2. *fig.* In the phr. **to get the flick pass,** and as **flick-pass** *v. trans.*: see quots.

1983 *Canberra Times* 19 Aug. 8/3 He had recalled the dinner when he heard Mr Ivanov 'got the flick pass'. *Ibid.* 31 Aug. 25/6 (*caption*) The Princess of Wales .. flick-passes her son to a nanny.

flier, var. FLYER.

flimsy. *Obs.* [Survival of Br. slang *flimsy* a bank-note: see OED *sb.* 1.] A bank-note.

1845 *Parramatta Chron.* 19 Apr. 3/2 He .. admitted the finding the *flimsies*, but made the rather *flimsy* excuse that having got the 'kites' he considered he had a right 'to fly them'. **1930** A.E. YARRA *Vanishing Horseman* 220 The white man .. gave him a punch for trying to snatch a bundle of flimsies out of his hand.

Flinders grass. [Prob. from the name of Matthew Flinders (1774–1814), English explorer.] Any of several annual or short-lived perennial fodder grasses, esp. of the genus *Iseilema* (fam. Poaceae) occurring in all mainland States except Vic.; *Barcoo grass,* see BARCOO A. 2.

1886 *N.T. Times Almanac* 5 Mitchell, blue, barley, Flinders, umbrella, and tuft grass are all well represented. **1975** X. HERBERT *Poor Fellow my Country* 429 No more knee-deep Flinder's grass growing on the little flats that wound between the hummocks of raised ground as when only the kangaroo as herbivore roamed the land.

flindosa /flɪnˈdoʊzə, flɪnˈdaʊzə/. [Corruption of *Flindersia* a genus of trees, from the name of Matthew Flinders (1774–1814), English explorer.] CROW'S ASH. Also **Flindosy, Flindozy.**

1861 *Catal. Natural & Industr. Products N.S.W.* 49 *Flindersia australis.* Cedrelaceae. Ash, Beech, and Flindosa... A large sized tree of very general occurrence in the Northern districts... Timber valuable for staves. **1916** *Bulletin* (Sydney) 4 May 22/3 The coastal bullocky's 'Flindozy' (for Flindersia). **1927** *Ibid.* 3 Nov. 27/4 Crow's ash is not known by any other names than 'Flindosy' and teak.

floater, $n.^1$ [f. *float* loose rock or an isolated mass of ore: see OED *sb.* 20 a.; also as *float mineral, ore, quartz.*] A piece of ore detached and removed by water or erosion from the main body. Also *attrib.*

1881 G.C. EVANS *Stories* 300 (Empties the water out of the tub .. and endeavours to find some gold in the gravel.) 'Two specks and a floater. Pshaw.' **1941** D. O'CALLAGHAN *Long Life Reminisc.* 144, I only took that lease up for the floaters. I then took up another 12 acres lease, just south and joining that floater lease.

floater, $n.^2$ *S.A.* [Transf. use of Cockney slang *floater:* see quot. 1864.] A dish consisting of a meat pie floating in pea-soup: see quot. 1976.

[**1864** J.C. HOTTEN *Dict. Mod. Slang* (rev. ed.) 135 *Floater,* a small suet dumpling put into soup.—*Whitechapel.*] **1915** *Pepper Box* Dec. 1 Say, matey, give me two pies and a floater. **1976** M. POWELL *Down Under* 58 You haven't lived if you've never eaten one of Harry's floaters. It's a bowl of pea-soup so thick that the spoon will stand upright in it; floating on the top is a real meat pie, stuffed full of meat, a liberal dousing of tomato ketchup on top.

floater, $n.^3$ *Two-up.* A coin which fails to spin.

1944 E. LOCKE *From Shore to Shore* 27 If they leave the ring we bar 'em; we bar the floaters, too. **1983** HIBBERD & HUTCHINSON *Barracker's Bible* 81 In two-up, a coin which doesn't spin properly is known as a 'floater'.

floating station. *Pearling.* The mother ship of a pearling fleet. Also *attrib.*

1897 *V & P* (Qld. L.A.) II. 1320 Floating stations .. enable between fifty and sixty boats to keep constantly at work on the pearling grounds. **1902** *Cwlth. Parl. Papers* (1901–2) II. 1069 When did the floating-station system commence here [*sc.* Queensland]?—About 1891, the vessels came from West Australia.

flock. *Obs.*
1. Used *attrib.* in Special Comb. **flock-holder, -owner,** a sheep farmer; **station,** a sheep farm.

1825 *HRA* (1921) 3rd Ser. IV. 319 He rapidly becomes a large **Flock-holder. 1829** R. GOUGER *Let. from Sydney* 84 There is no chance of an alteration favourable to the **flock-owner. 1843** D.G. BROCK *Recoll.* 22 Port Gawler is evidently the most desirable port for ships to take in wool, as the bulk of the **flock** stations lie away to the north.

2. Occas. applied to a group of kangaroos.

1835 T.B. WILSON *Narr. Voyage round World* 243 On perceiving a flock of kangaroos .. he walked .. towards them. **1847** G.F. ANGAS *Savage Life & Scenes* I. 203 We observed numerous kangaroos. They frequently appeared in flocks of eight or ten at a time, and gave constant sport to the dogs.

flock pigeon. Either of two species of pigeon that habitually form flocks.

a. The nomadic, predom. brown pigeon *Phaps histrionica* of inland n. Aust.; HARLEQUIN BRONZEWING.

1851 J. HENDERSON *Excursions & Adventures N.S.W.* II. 178 The flock pigeon is of a lead colour, frequents the brushes, and is generally found in large flocks of several hundreds, and sometimes thousands. **1964** M. SHARLAND *Territory of Birds* 15 The Flock Pigeons, a plains bird which .. has derived a new lease of life from the bores that have been drilled in numbers during recent years.

b. The predom. grey pigeon *Lopholaimus antarcticus* of rainforests in e. Aust.; *crested pigeon* (b), see CRESTED; see also TOPKNOT PIGEON.

1845 C. HODGKINSON *Aust., Port Macquarie to Moreton Bay* 33 Large numbers of the crested flock-pigeon were feeding on this fruit. **1982** H.J. FRITH *Pigeons & Doves Aust.* 134 Throughout the range of the Topknot Pigeon, the name Flock Pigeon is used, perhaps more commonly than is Topknot Pigeon. This is undesirable because of the pre-emption of 'Flock Pigeon' by *Phaps histrionica.*

flogger. [In allusion to the whip or cat-o'-nine tails; in sense 1, because the coat is tailed.]
1. A morning-coat. Also *attrib.*

1905 N.F. SPIELVOGEL *Gumsucker on Tramp* 11 A top hat and 'flogger' are signs of a certain amount of—what shall I say—affluence. **1971** F. HARDY *Outcasts of Foolgarah* 10 Little Tich .. unrecognisable in a black flogger-tail coat, grey trousers, pointed toes.

2. *Australian National Football.* A set of streamers in the colours of a team attached to a rod and waved by supporters.

1972 *Bulletin* (Sydney) 5 Aug. 30/2 In Melbourne, most sports-mad of the cities, a VFL Grand Final can draw 100,000 to the Cricket Ground. 'Floggers' have been outlawed this season but the crowds make up for it by

flogging their vocal chords. **1981** *Age* (Melbourne) 28 July 38/8 There you'd be in your decorated coat, a few badges, and a flogger on a stick, and there they'd be.

flood-bird. [See quot. 1894.] CHANNEL-BILLED CUCKOO.
1887 *Illustr. Austral. News* (Melbourne) 20 Aug. 155/1 They were caught on the Diamantina River and only appear in times of great floods... The natives call them flood birds. **1894** E.H. CANNEY *Land of Dawning* 8 Natives .. in the vicinity of Cooper's Creek .. when they heard a bird known in those parts as the 'Flood-bird', whose presence always preceded rain and flood .. would fall flat upon their faces.

flooded, *ppl. a.* Used in collocations to designate species of trees which are characteristically found in a wet habitat, esp. periodically inundated alluvial flats and river banks: **flooded box,** the tree *Eucalyptus microtheca* (see COOLIBAH); **gum,** any of several trees of the genus *Eucalyptus* (fam. Myrtaceae) growing in moist places, esp. the tall tree of e. N.S.W. and e. Qld. *E. grandis,* also known as *rose gum* (see ROSE), the spreading tree of s.w. W.A. *E. rudis,* and (*obs.*) *E. camaldulensis* (see RED GUM 1).
1839 T.L. MITCHELL *Three Exped. Eastern Aust.* (rev. ed.) II. 49 Clumps of trees of the **flooded box. 1819** *Sydney Gaz.* 26 June, To the Productions of the country .. may now be added great Quantities of .. the **Flooded Gum.**

flossy. *Obs.* [Prob. f. U.S. slang *flossy* saucy, showy: see OEDS *flossy* and also *floosie*.] A prostitute.
1899 B. MORANT *Poetry* (1980) 50 Scanty stock of gold— Scanty! yet the whole d–d lot Publicans and Flossies got. **1903** *Truth* (Sydney) 18 Jan. 1/6 An irate Flossie hit a Chow on the head with a large lump of road metal, and drew the 'claret'.

flour-bag, *a. Austral. pidgin.* [With reference to the colour.] Of hair: white.
1857 F. GERSTAECKER *Two Convicts* 35 In the corrupt language used as a means of communication between white and black .. 'flour-bag' means 'white'. **1975** X. HERBERT *Poor Fellow my Country* 1426 They unpacked, with no more conversation than a couple of jests about their age, 'Flour-Bag', as they called themselves, with reference to the white in their hair.

flour gold. [With reference to the fineness of flour.] See quot. 1869.
1869 R.B. SMITH *Gold Fields & Mineral Districts* 611 *Flourgold,* the finest alluvial drift-gold. **1979** B. SCOTT *Tough in Old Days* 31 We heard of 'flour' gold that was so fine it would float out of your dish, of grassroots gold that lay just below the surface of certain kinds of country.

floury baker. [See quot. 1895.] The cicada *Abricta curvicosta* of s.e. Qld. and coastal N.S.W., having a covering of easily detachable hair-like scales resembling flour in appearance; BAKER. Also **floury miller.**
1895 *Proc. Linnean Soc. N.S.W.* X. 530 The whole of the insect is black on the upper surface, but covered with fine silvery white hairs which form little white spots here and there, looking as though it had been dusted with flour. From this circumstance it has received from the Sydney children the rather appropriate name of the 'Floury Miller'. **1982** N. KEESING *Lily on Dustbin* 95 His ambition is to capture a rare 'cherry nose' or an even rarer 'floury baker'.

flowering gum. Any of several species of GUM TREE noted for their beauty while flowering, esp. the widely-cultivated small tree *Eucalyptus ficifolia* (fam. Myrtaceae) of s.w. W.A. See also *scarlet gum* SCARLET. Also **red-** (or **crimson-**)**flowering gum.**
1905 *Emu* V. 79 Where the crimson-flowering gums (*Eucalyptus ficifolia*)—perhaps the most beautiful and ornamental of Australian trees—bloom in varying shades of red. **1935** T. RAYMENT *Cluster of Bees* 54 The rosy blossom of the red-flowering gum, *Eucalyptus calophylla,* is so abundant that it effectively eclipses the green of the foliage. **1981** *Access* Dec. 6/2 Any tree of outstanding aesthetic significance; e.g. *Eucalyptus ficifolia* (Flowering Gum) at the Metropolitan Golf Club, Oakleigh.

Flowery-Lander. *Obs.* [f. *Flowery Land,* a name for China.] A Chinese immigrant.
1851 *Empire* (Sydney) 21 Mar. 3/4 The sulky Mantchoo was consequently sentenced to be imprisoned for one month, which will give him an opportunity of nursing the 'rheumatism' so prevalent among these 'Flowery Landers'. **1888** J. FREEMAN *Lights & Shadows Melbourne Life* 101 The flowery-lander would get the fowls for four shillings.

flow-on. *Industrial Relations.* The wider application of a wage increase, or improvement in working conditions, awarded to one sector of the community (see quot. 1981); the increase or improvement itself. Also *attrib.*
[**1951** *73 CAR* 337 It was contended that it did not follow that whatever was done in regard to margins for tradesmen in the Metal Trades award would flow into other awards.] **1967** *Age* (Melbourne) 12 Dec. 11/1 They appealed to the Arbitration Commission and unions to ensure that the increases did not flow on to other awards.] **1969** *Sydney Morning Herald* 4 Dec. 1/4 All the professional engineers had received was a 'flow-on' of the metal trades decision. **1976** *Ibid.* 27 Nov. 4/2 Workers under N.S.W. awards to get flow-on wage rise. **1981** SHEEHAN & WORLAND *Gloss. Industr. Relations Terms* (ed. 2) 31 *Flow-on.* . . The process by which a wage increase in one section of the wage community is applied to other sectors for the purpose of maintaining a given community wage structure.

flute, *n.* In the phr. **to be** (or **get**) **on the flute,** to monopolize a conversation, to 'hold the floor'. Also **to hold** (or **pass**) **the flute.**
1896 T. HENEY *Girl at Birrell's* 23 'You've got the flute properly to-night, Graham,' returned the other. 'You can gas for all hands.' **1898** *Bulletin* (Sydney) 17 Dec. (Red Page), An incessant talker is a *skiter* or a *fluter,* and a request to him *to pass the flute* or the *kip* is to allow someone else to 'do a pitch'. *c* **1907** C.W. CHANDLER *Darkest Adelaide* 7 The young fellow had the flure, and was, as Mr Bludger informed me, fairly 'on the flute', square an' all. **1920** A. WRIGHT *Rogue's Luck* 59 Cut it out, Chilla; ring orf. Gor blime, oncet you get on th' flute about th' good ole days. **1955** STEWART & KEESING *Austral. Bush Ballads* 278 He never tired while he 'held the flute' of telling what he could do.

flute, *v. Obs.* [f. prec.] *intr.* To hold forth. Also **fluter** *n.*
1898 [see FLUTE *n.*]. **1915** *Truth* (Sydney) 18 Apr. 2/6 It may have suited Premier Holman, when 'fluting' against the totalisator to 'deplore the drinking habits of the working classes'. **1959** D. NILAND *Big Smoke* 178 Where's Phil the Fluter now?

flute-bird. *Obs.* The bird *Gymnorhina tibicen* (see MAGPIE *n.* 1).
1862 H. KENDALL *Poems & Songs* 53 The echu's songs are dying with the flute-bird's mellow tone. **1919** *Bulletin* (Sydney) 16 Jan. 24/4 'Flute-bird' is good for the black-backed magpie.

fluted gum. *Obs.* [See quot. 1833.] GIMLET.
1833 *Jrnls. Several Exped. W.A.* 214 We named them cable or fluted gum, being considerably twisted. **1897** L. LINDLEY-COWEN *W. Austral. Settler's Guide* 215 Fluted gum, or gimlet wood (*E. salubris*).

fly, *n.*[1]

1. Used *attrib.* in Special Comb. **fly blight** *obs.*, an eye infection, supposed to have been transmitted by flies; **bog**, jam; treacle; **cork**, one of a number of pieces of cork dangling from a wide-brimmed hat to keep flies from the wearer's face; **door**, a door fitted with a *fly screen*; **flapper**, a piece of fine material attached to the hat of a person or the harness of an animal to keep flies away; **loo**, see quot. 1910; **net**, **(a)** *fly veil*; **(b)** a piece of fine netting or mesh used to protect the person or a structure from flies; see also quot. 1924; **fly-netted** *ppl. a.*, (of a structure) protected by fly screens; **-proof** *a.*, protected against flies; so **-proofed** *ppl. a.*; **screen**, a frame in or over which fine netting or mesh is stretched, fitted to an aperture to permit ventilation but prevent the entry of flies; also *attrib.*; **veil**, a piece of finely meshed material hanging from a hat brim to protect the wearer's face from flies; **wire**, fine wire mesh used to make fly screens; also *attrib.*, made from or equipped with fly wire; so **-wired** *ppl. a.*; **-wiring** *vbl. n.*

1851 *Empire* (Sydney) 12 Dec. 459/4 **Fly blight** is a curse under which every second person suffers. **1918** *Aussie: Austral. Soldiers' Mag.* Feb. 6/2 Back in the wagon lines we get butter, rooty, rice an' **flybog**. **1943** *Bulletin* (Sydney) 29 Sept. 13/1 Have heard jam called 'fly-bog' as often as treacle. **1939** *Bulletin* (Sydney) 22 Feb. 21/2 We overtook a genuine old-style swaggie, neatly-rolled 'Curse o' Gawd' slung over left shoulder by a towel .. and **fly-corks** dancing from hat-brim. **1900** *Albury Banner* 5 Jan. 16/4 Having then got our **fly doors**, we can set at nought those 'creeping things with horrid wings'. **1853** J.R. GODLEY *Extracts Jrnl. Visit N.S.W.* 16 Flies .. defile everything. Everybody in the interior wears a short veil, or rather **fly-flapper**, made of net, round his hat, to keep them off the face. **1910** *Bulletin* (Sydney) 21 Apr. 15/2 **Fly-loo** is very simple. If there be six thirsts to quench, six pieces of lump sugar are put on the bar, Mr Pub, as referee explaining that he on whose sugar a fly first alights must pay. But five of the pieces have at a former date been damped with whisky, and as a fly is teetotal it alights on the sixth one. **1911** *Bulletin* (Sydney) 16 Feb. 13/2 A .. tin-fossicker ambled in, wearing his big straw hat, decorated with a **fly-net**. **1924** F.J. MILLS *Happy Days* 123 A tall elderly gentleman, with an umbrella and a cork flynet, approached us. **1927** *Bulletin* (Sydney) 7 July 24/3 Fly-nets are not to be had at every small store outback. **1937** A.W. UPFIELD *Mr Jelly's Business* 106 Through open **fly-netted** doors and windows came drifting the soft distinct night-sounds. **1848** T.L. MITCHELL *Jrnl. Exped. Tropical Aust.* 380, I fancied myself .. sun-proof, **fly-proof** and water-proof. **1938** A. UPFIELD *Bone is Pointed* (1966) 50 The fly-proofed veranda along the south side of the house. **1929** A. SMITH *Austral. Home Carpenter* 49 Renewal of **fly-screen** windows and doors. **1932** *Bulletin* (Sydney) 2 Nov. 21/4 The fly-screens outside my laboratory windows have been in places criss-crossed with chalk. **1890** A. WOODHOUSE *Man with Apples* 81 Few of his most intimate associates would have easily recognized Maurice Dalby in the billycock hat, **fly veil**, leggings and general bushman's garb. **1925** *Makeshifts & Other Home-Made Furniture* (New Settlers League Aust.) 19 If **fly-wire** can be bought by the yard and nailed outside the window frame, it serves the purpose better. **1935** K.L. SMITH *Sky Pilot Arnhem Land* 94 In the mustering camps and on the road, it is rarely possible to have fly-wire butchers' shops. **1962** *N.T. News* (Darwin) 13 Jan. 3/4 Immediate fly-wiring of all wards, kitchens, and other areas not yet closed to mosquitoes and flies. **1969** J. PACKER *Leopard in Fold* 57 He pushed open the fly-wired door of the back verandah.

2. a. [With *on* now also used elsewhere.] In the phr. **(there are) no flies on** (or **about**), (there is) no lack of alertness, astuteness, competence or energy in (a person); no fault to be found with.

1845 C. GRIFFITH *Present State & Prospects Port Phillip* 78 The person who excites their greatest respect is the man who is alive to their attempts (or, as they express it themselves, *who drops down to their moves*), and the highest encomium they can pass on such an one is, that *there are no flies about him*. **1859** J. LANG *Botany Bay* (1885) 62 Whether he had faked the swag or not, he was a tip-top nob, and no flies about it. **1904** L.M.P. ARCHER *Bush Honeymoon* 134 Sandy's a *silvertail*. There ain't no flies on Sandy fer grit.

b. In the (exclam.) phr. **no flies (about)**, no possible doubt (about), no fuss.

1858 C.R. THATCHER *Colonial Songster* (rev. ed.) 39 Hurrah, my brave pals, ye may all nobblerize, There's plenty more grog in the camp, and no flies. **1895** *Worker* (Sydney) 26 Jan. 3/2 He was speculator, storekeeper, and gambler, and made no more flies about robbing his own countrymen than he did the 'White Devils'.

3. In the phr. **(to drink) with the flies**, (to drink) alone, usu. in a public drinking place.

1911 *Truth* (Sydney) 10 Dec. 3/4 No person is allowed to 'shout', so each one, 'with the flies', Absorbs his Jimmy Woodser, while the watchful wowser spies. **1963** D. WHITTINGTON *Mile Pegs* 177 'Have a drink?' the larrikin invited. 'Or do you prefer drinking with the flies?'

fly, *n.*² [Fig. use of *fly* act of flying.] In the phr. **to have a fly, to give (it**, etc.) **a fly**, to make an attempt, to take a chance, to 'have a go'.

1915 *Bulletin* (Sydney) 5 Aug. 24/1, I myself have had a fly after a fox in a green-timber paddock on a 6-h.p. cycle. **1982** PAGE & INGPEN *Aussie Battlers* 85, I couldn't see any future but tending someone else's sheep and cows, so me and my brother Ivan decided to give it a fly on our own account.

fly, *v. Australian National Football. intr.* To jump high in an attempt to take a mark. Also as *ppl. a.*

1960 *N.T. News* (Darwin) 23 Feb. 1/1 The high flying tribesmen of Maningrida settlement in Arnhem Land are after your blood .. on the Australian Rules field. **1963** L. RICHARDS *Boots & All!* 68 Dick stood about 5 ft. 11 in. in his socks, and on top of this he had very long arms, which gave him a decided advantage as a rover, because he could fly for marks against bigger men.

fly-blown, *ppl. a.* [Transf. use of *fly-blown* putrid, hence spoilt, 'ruined'.] Ruined financially; penniless. Also **fly-blowed**.

1853 C.R. READ *What I heard, saw, & Did* 51 Being 'flyblown' is a colonial term for being 'done *up*'. **1948** J. FURPHY *Buln-Buln & Brolga* 50 An' on'y thirteen shillin's in my pocket! About as near flyblowed as a man could wish to be.

flyer. Also **flier**. [Spec. use of *flyer* one who or that which moves with exceptional speed.]

1. An exceptionally fast kangaroo, usu. young and esp. female. See also *blue flyer* BLUE *a.*, FLYING DOE.

1826 J. ATKINSON *Acct. Agric. & Grazing N.S.W.* 24 The animals of this kind [*sc.* kangaroos] that are not quite full grown are termed flyers; they are exceedingly swift. **1955** D. CLARK *Boomer* 27 First were the 'fliers', unmated doe kangaroos, fleet, irresponsible creatures.

2. A fast shearer; the fastest shearer in a shed, RINGER *n.*¹ 2 a.

1908 W.H. OGILVIE *My Life in Open* 42 The 'ringer' or flier of the shed. **1949** *Bulletin* (Sydney) 23 Feb. 14/4 The flier rung at Yanco, Eden Plains and Pompadour.

flying, *ppl. a.* Used as a distinguishing epithet in the names of animals: **flying mouse**, the mouse-sized gliding marsupial *Acrobates pygmaeus*, the feathertail glider, of e. and s.e. Aust.; **possum** (or **squirrel**), any of several tree-climbing marsupials, esp. those that glide through the air using flaps of skin between the fore and hind limbs ac 'parachutes'.

1811 D.D. MANN *Present Picture N.S.W.* 50 **Flying Mice** are likewise found, in considerable numbers, in this country, of a very handsome appearance, and .. of the

Opossum species. The tail of this interesting little animal resembles a feather. **1788** [**flying possum**] *HRA* (1914) 1st Ser. I. 31 At the foot of one tree we found the fur of a flying squirrel. **1986** *Sydney Morning Herald* 13 Feb. 6/1 The forests contained great numbers of flying possums, such as the feathertail glider and the greater glider.

flying doctor.

1. A medical practitioner who uses radio communication and travels by aircraft to provide services to patients in places which are remote and without readily accessible medical services; orig. with reference to the service provided by the Australian Inland Mission from Cloncurry, Qld., established in 1928. Also *attrib.*

1920 *Inlander* July 80 A Flying Doctor could be planted down at Winton immediately. **1960** *N.T. News* (Darwin) 22 Jan. 4/6 Mrs Peter Gunning . . immediately sent out an emergency call over the Flying Doctor radio network.

2. Comb. **flying doctor base, service.**

1939 J.W. COLLINGS *8000 Miles by Air* 3, I naturally wasted no time in becoming acquainted with the service on this my first visit to a fully established **Flying Doctor Base**. **1939** J.W. COLLINGS *8000 Miles by Air* 6 At the same time, I imagined what must have been the condition of things before the advent of our **Flying Doctor Service** at Wyndham.

flying doe.
A young female kangaroo, characteristically fleet of foot. See also FLYER 1.

1846 *Tasmanian Jrnl. Nat. Sci.* II. 372 The grey kangaroo... The swiftest runner is the female of the first year before having young, and of the second year with her first young; at this age her speed is so great, that she is termed the 'Flying Doe'. **1952** B. BEATTY *Unique to Aust.* 26 In bush parlance the old male kangaroo is called an old man, the young female a flying doe and the offspring until eight or ten months old, a joey.

flying duck orchid.
[From the fancied resemblance of the appearance of the flower to that of a duck in flight.] Either of the widespread terrestrial orchids *Caleana major* and *Paracaleana minor*; also *P. nigrita* (fam. Orchidaceae) of s.w. W.A. Also **flying duck.**

1914 E.E. PESCOTT *Native Flowers Vic.* 87 A pretty purplish-brown orchid . . known as the 'Cockatoo' or 'flying duck'. **1981** M. CAMERON *Guide Flowers & Plants Tas.* 108 Pollination is effected as the insect struggles out of the body cavity. This interesting mode of pollination occurs also in *Caleana major*, the Flying Duck Orchid.

flying fox.
[Fig. use of *flying fox* fruit bat.] An overhead cable and apparatus for the transport of materials, supplies, etc., esp. over difficult terrain. Also *attrib.*

1901 M. VIVIENNE *Travels in W.A.* 210 What is here called the 'Flying Fox' . . has an iron bucket on a single rope of twisted wire. **1957** D.D. LADDS *We have our Dreams* 3 The flaming flying-fox wire's nearly busted through.

flying fox camp.
[f. *flying fox* fruit bat + CAMP *n.* 4.] A place where flying foxes congregate; a congregation of flying foxes.

1903 *Truth* (Sydney) 8 Mar. 1/7, 50 guns attacked a flying fox camp on the upper Orara, and killed about 2000. **1903** *Bulletin* (Sydney) 1 Oct. 17/1 The fruit bats, popularly known as flying foxes . . do not hibernate. . . There are a number of well known 'flying fox camps' in the County of Cumberland.

flying gang.
A team of railway maintenance workers.

1897 J.J. MURIF *From Ocean to Ocean* 29 The same night Diamond and I reached Lake Eyre cottages where were the husbands and others, a 'flying gang' of navvies. **1969** P. ADAM SMITH *Folklore Austral. Railwaymen* 10 The elite of all maintenance men is the Flying Gang, a group of specialists, experienced fettlers under a ganger who are rushed to wherever their skill is needed.

fly-moth.
Obs. An insect that destroys cereal grain; an infestation of these insects.

1805 *Sydney Gaz.* 13 Oct., The destruction occasioned by the Fly Moth to the Wheat in Stacks. **1838** *S. Austral. Rec.* (London) 12 Dec. 139/3 Finish wheat harvest, and take care that the stacks are of moderate size. . . If housed in barns they should be well ventilated to prevent fly-moth.

Flynn.
[The name of Errol *Flynn* (1909–1959), Australian-born actor with a reputation as a playboy.] In the phr. **to be in like Flynn,** to seize an opportunity; to be actively or impetuously engaged; to be successful.

1959 E. FLYNN *My Wicked, Wicked Ways* 290 A new legend was born, and new terms went into the national idiom. . . A G.I. or Marine or sailor went out at night sparking and the next day he reported to his cronies, who asked him how he made out, and the fellow said, with a sly grin, 'I'm in like Flynn.' **1984** *Nat. Times* (Sydney) 26 Oct. 5/1 All the political heavies covering the campaign . . were in like Flynn.

fly-speck.
[Joc. use of *fly-speck* tiny stain made by the excrement of an insect.]

1. *Obs.* Used *attrib.* in Special Comb. **Fly-speck Isle,** Tasmania; so **Fly-specker** *n.*, a Tasmanian.

1906 *Gadfly* (Adelaide) 25 Apr. 9/3 Tasmania has lost its oldest inhabitant. . . He had inhabited the Flyspeck Isle since 1828. **1912** *Truth* (Sydney) 30 June 1/5 Vandemonians appear to be rather proud of that particularly black page in the history of their little island; but of course the poor 'fly-speckers' haven't much diversion.

2. A minute particle of gold. Also *attrib.*

1932 I.L. IDRIESS *Prospecting for Gold* 105 If you get 'fly specks' in your dish, then try all over the place, higgledy-piggledy. **1939** —— *Cyaniding for Gold* 32 That contained just as much gold, in an exceedingly fine state— all 'fly speck' gold in fact.

fog.
Obs. Used *attrib.* in Special Comb. **Fog Land,** England, the British Isles; **town,** London.

1907 *Bulletin* (Sydney) 7 Feb. 15/2 An English chap and fast shearer . . used to go 'home' to **Fogland** every year. **1906** *Gadfly* (Adelaide) 20 June 17/1 Writes my **Fogtown** correspondent:- '. . . all the South Australians . . who happened to be wandering loose about London just then gathered themselves into a bunch.'

Also **fogwards** *adv.*

1906 *Gadfly* (Adelaide) 13 June 17/1 There departed fogwards on last week's English mail the Misses Clowes.

follow, *v. trans.*
Used in phr. of an itinerant pursuing a specified avocation: (of a gold or opal miner) **to follow the colour, diggings, game**; (of a shearer or swagman) **to follow the sheds**; (of a swagman) **to follow the luck, rivers**.

1890 A.J. VOGAN *Black Police* 35 The true prospecting and working miner, who has 'followed the diggings' since the Canoona rush or the Palmer field excited the mining world, is a veritable Admirable Crichton. **1915** *Bulletin* (Sydney) 14 Oct. 24/4 Tell me a profession with more *aliases* than the swagmans? Here are a few: 'Waltzin' Matilda', . . 'followin' the luck', 'carryin' the swag' . . 'followin' the sheds'. **1922** J. LEWIS *Fought & Won* 105 Some of them were good miners who had been 'following the game' for many years in Queensland. **1940** I.L. IDRIESS *Lightning Ridge* 148 Some of the old sundowners of the old Murrumbidgee Whaler brotherhood, those who 'followed the rivers' all their lives were characters. . . We 'casuals' always felt embarrassed, when in the society of these Knights of the Road. **1948** M. UREN *Glint of Gold* 28 Both had been following the colour most of their life.   **1957** *Overland* ix. 9 They were mates of long standing and had followed the sheds all the way down through Queensland.

follower. *Australian National Football.* Either of two players who, with the rover, do not have fixed positions and so follow play. See RUCK *n.*

1876 T.P. POWER *Footballer* 11 Followers—Be always on the ball and don't hold it too long. Practise the punt and drop-kicks with both feet.   **1971** B. ANDREW *Austral. Football Handbk.* 67 The Rover plays near the Follower to whom the ball is being kicked.

footballer. *Obs.* A prison warder: see quot. 1921.

1919 V. MARSHALL *World of Living Dead* 33 He'd left his mark on a couple of the pet 'footballers' when they come at the kickin' game down in the Parramatta basement.   **1921** D. GRANT *Through Six Gaols* 51 One day while at work in the shop I heard a warder's name mentioned and noticed that the term 'footballer' was applied to him. I discovered that this title had been conferred upon him for his well-known habit of kicking prisoners.

footie, var. FOOTY.

footman. *Obs.* [Spec. use of *footman* one who travels on foot: becoming Obs. *c* 1900 in Br. use.] A swagman.

[**1890** 'R. BOLDREWOOD' *Squatter's Dream* 277 A 'footman' (as a person not in possession of a horse is termed in Australian provincial circles).]   **1900** H. LAWSON *On Track* 76 If it was a footman (swagman), and he was short of tobacco, old Howlett always had half a stick ready for him.   **1938** F. BLAKELEY *Hard Liberty* 18 A sign-writer footman told Taylor that he had a scheme that would stop travellers killing sheep on the back portion of his run.

foot-rot, *v. trans.* To treat (sheep) suffering from footrot. Also **foot-rotting** *vbl. n.*

1870 E.B. KENNEDY *Four Yrs. in Qld.* 7, I asked one man if he had seen or done anything in the Bush, 'Oh yes, I did some 'foot rotting',' was the languid reply.   **1980** G. ROBINSON *Decades of Duntroon Bastard* 189 A holding cradle . . was a most useful invention which made handling sheep generally, and 'foot-rotting' in particular, much easier work.

footwalk, *v. Austral. pidgin. intr.* To travel on foot. Also as *adv.,* on foot.

1946 W.E. HARNEY *North of 23°* 172 Natives went footwalk to Barraloola for assistance through the mud of the rainy season.   **1952** *Bulletin* (Sydney) 17 Dec. 12/1 Rosie, our housegirl, recently received a filial visit from her son. He 'footwalked' direct overland from the Daly River to Darwin.

Hence **footwalker** *n.*

1937 M. TERRY *Sand & Sun* 22 A footwalker appeared over a sandhill... After the footwalker a string of camels.

footy, *n.* and *attrib.* Also **footie.** [f. *foot(ball* + -Y.]

A. *n.* The game of football, esp. Australian National Football; a football.

1906 *Bulletin* (Sydney) 20 Sept. 44/1 They copped 'im on the square, watchin' the 'footy'.   **1934** F.E. BAUME *Burnt Sugar* 58 It all sounds pretty cronk to me, especially the dressing-up and the black shirts and all that. I'd rather go for a swim or play footie.   **1981** C. WALLACE-CRABBE *Splinters* 89 Some brightly besweatered children ran larruping along the footpath, one of them bouncing a footy.

B. *attrib.*

1923 *Aussie* (Sydney) Sept. 28/1 And the old school's gravelled playground, where we often barked our knees, Near the wider 'footie' oval ringed around with hills and trees.   **1981** B. DICKINS *Gift of Gab* 6 Silly Cyril blinks as Old Baldy pins a sprig of wattle to his Fitzroy footyhat.

forcing, *vbl. n.* Used *attrib.* in Comb. of enclosures so designed as to compel the movement of stock confined therein in a particular direction: **forcing pen, yard.**

1935 G. MCIVER *Drover's Odyssey* 7 The men .. were busy constructing **forcing pens** of boughs and logs to cross the sheep to the north side of the river.   **1857** *Moreton Bay Free Press* 5 Jan. 3/2 The animals are generally too wild to be punted, and the only way is to force them into the river and compel them to swim. For this purpose the mobs are driven into a strongly-fenced paddock, covering about half an acre, which is called the '**forcing yard**', and all other means of exit are closed, except a narrow passage called the 'tan' which slopes towards the river, and terminates at a perpendicular bank.

forest. [Spec. use of *forest* tract of land covered with trees and undergrowth, sometimes intermingled with pasture.]

1. *Obs.* A tract of open, well-grassed land, with occasional trees or stands of trees; see OPEN *a.*^{1} 1. In early use usu. *attrib.* as **forest land** (see esp. quot. 1805).

1805 *HRA* (1915) 1st Ser. V. 586 Forest Land—is such as abounds with Grass and is the only Ground which is fit to Graze; according to the local distinction, the Grass is the discriminating Character and not the Trees, for by making use of the Former it is clearly understood as different from a Brush or Scrub.   **1868** J. BAIRD *Emigrant's Guide Australasia* 223 The forest, or bush, is tame, uniform, forever the same endless waste of gum-trees, making all but shepherds and stockmen miserable, and many of *them* too, we should find, were they to favour us with their experience; the scrub only is beautiful; that is, the dense vegetation that grows on the alluvial banks of rivers and creeks.

2. Used *attrib.* in the names of flora and fauna, usu. having the more usual meaning of trees and undergrowth combined: **forest kangaroo** *obs.,* see *grey kangaroo* (a), see GREY *a.*; **mahogany** *obs.,* a tree of the genus *Eucalyptus* (fam. Myrtaceae), esp. *E. resinifera* (see *red mahogany* RED *a.* 1 a.); **oak,** the tree *Allocasuarina torulosa* (fam. Casuarinaceae) of e. N.S.W. and Qld., having slender drooping branchlets and red timber; the wood of the tree; **red gum,** the tall tree *Eucalyptus tereticornis* (fam. Myrtaceae) occurring in e. Aust. from e. Vic. to n. Qld., usu. in open forest, and also in New Guinea; the wood of the tree.

1817 J. MYERS *Life Voyage & Travels Capt. J. Myers* 196 We met several of the **Forest Kangaroos.**   **1830** R. DAWSON *Present State Aust.* 243 The timber .. is generally useless, consisting chiefly of what are called **forest-mahogany** and blood-wood.   **1819** W.C. WENTWORTH *Statistical, Hist., & Pol. Descr. N.S.W.* 46 Full sized gums and ironbarks .. with the beefwood tree, or as it is generally termed, the **forest oak** .. are the usual timber.   **1899** *Proc. Linnean Soc. N.S.W.* XXIV. 468 Ordinary **Forest Red Gum** (*Eucalyptus tereticornis*).

forest devil. A mechanical contrivance used to clear land by pulling out trees and stumps.

1885 F.A. BOYD *Farmer & Settler's Guide* 9 Where .. stumps have to be removed we would recommend a 'Forest Devil'.   **1979** P. PAVY *Bush Surgeon* 4, I was put to felling giant-sized mallee scrub and heaving the roots out with an antique system of levers called a 'forest devil'.

forester. *Obs.* [See quot. 1826.] *Grey kangaroo* (a), see GREY *a.* Also *attrib.*

1804 R. KNOPWOOD in J.J. Shillinglaw *Hist. Rec. Port Phillip* 17 June (1879) 122 Thos. Salmon, my man, killd a very large kangaroo—a forester.   **1826** J. ATKINSON *Acct. Agric. & Grazing N.S.W.* 24 The forester is the largest of the common kinds [of kangaroo], frequently weighing 150 lbs. It is seldom found in an open country, delighting in forests that have occasional thickets of brush.   **1845** R. HOWITT *Impressions Aust. Felix* 273 A boomer, or large forester kangaroo.

form, v. [Spec. use of *form* to make, to bring into existence.]

1. *trans.* To establish (a sheep or cattle station, etc.).

1837 *Colonist* (Sydney) 8 June 188/2 The absolute necessity of forming a Post and that without delay, for the purpose of intercepting runaways and bushrangers. **1946** J.G. EASTWOOD *More about Cairns* 81, I . . received rations for the camp where Cairns now is, but before it was formed.

2. *trans.* To construct (a road). Also as *vbl. n.* and *ppl. a.*

1846 N.L. KENTISH *Work in Bush Van Diemen's Land* 30 The only serious objection to the *forming* of the road . . is a 'bluff', or projecting mass of rock. **1865** 'SPECIAL CORRESPONDENT' *Transportation* 20 The traveller can proceed to Perth . . along a good road, formed by convict labour. **1939** J.W. COLLINSON *Early Days Cairns* 140 A road had been formed, of mangrove mud, which gave a good surface when set. This formed road turned a corner into Abbott Street.

formation road. See quot.

1973 R. ROBINSON *Drift of Things* 55 We are on a dirt 'formation' road. This is a high, mounded road with a ditch on either side and you drive along on one side of the mound. Mr Goldsmith says that the roads are made like this because of the wet weather.

fortescue. [Of uncertain origin, but see quot. 1874.] The fish *Centropogon australis* of e. Austral. coasts, having venomous spines that can inflict painful wounds.

1874 E.S. HILL in J.E. Tenison-Woods *Fish & Fisheries N.S.W.* (1882) 49 The scorpion or Fortescue . . for its number and array of prickles . . enjoys in this country the *alias* 'Forty skewer' or 'Fortescure'. **1915** *Bulletin* (Sydney) 6 May 22/4 The fortescue, found in the rocky shallows and among the oyster-beds of coastal lakes.

forty. *Obs.* Usu. in *pl.* [Of unknown origin.] A sharper, a swindler; orig. a member of a gang in Sydney (see quots. 1876 and 1882). Also **forty thieves**, and *attrib.*

1876 *V & P* (N.S.W. L.A.) VI. 856 What class of men are these 'Forties'—what is their occupation? They are a band of thieves. Some ten years ago, before the Industrial Schools Act came into operation, a number of youngsters were on the streets; they used to sleep about the wharves, lived on thieving, and were ready to snap up anything they came across. I do not know how they came to be christened 'The Forties', but when they grew up to be men the name stuck to them, and they continued their old habits. They prowl about all night, go to one of these places about 4 or 5 o'clock in the morning, and sleep till 1 or 2 in the day. **1882** *Sydney Slang Dict.* 8 *The Forties*, the worst types of 'the talent', who get up rows in a mob, often after midnight and sometimes assault and rob, either in barrooms or the streets. Name originated with a gang in Sydney under 'Dixon the dog hanger', 'King of the Forties'. **1895** J.T. RYAN *Reminisc. Aust.* 219 Mr E. Deas Thompson was the Colonial Secretary who lowered the duty on spirits to 3s. per gallon . . and the 'Forty Thieves' at once found themselves up a tree. **1904** L.M.P. ARCHER *Bush Honeymoon* 144 A small array of bookmakers, with a slight sprinkling of the 'forty' element.

forward pocket: see POCKET.

fossick, v. [Br. dial. *fossick* to obtain by asking, to 'ferret out'; cf. *fursick, fussick* to potter over one's work, *fussock* to bustle about quickly: see EDD.]

1. *intr.* To search or pick about for gold on the surface, usu. in a desultory or unsystematic way and often on an abandoned or unattended claim. Also with **about**.

1852 *Austral. Gold Digger's Monthly Mag.* ii. 49 It is far better to spend time thus rationally and pleasantly, than . . fossick in the holes of absent diggers. **1873** J.C.F. JOHNSON *Christmas on Carringa* 23 Old Dan Rourke, the 'hatter', who was always fossicking about early and late, high day and holiday, in his surface claim at the bottom of the rise . . was just thinking of 'knocking off work' for the night.

2. *intr. transf.* To search or rummage for something.

1853 *Wanderer* (Adelaide) June 75 Usage has extended the term beyond gold matters. If a man were to take a log of fire-wood from a neighbour's heap . . it would be said he had been fossicking. **1978** C. RUHEN *Crocodile* 82 Bob hauled himself up into the boat . . and fossicking in a bag, found a can of beer.

3. *trans.* To search (a place); to find (something) through searching or rummaging about. Also with **out, up**.

1858 C.R. THATCHER *Colonial Songster* 19 Next morning I well fossicked it, And washed the bottom out; The tub turned out a pennyweight, And I began to doubt. **1886** *Bulletin* (Sydney) 26 June 15/2 Who is it fossicks out a pain, So Dr Pills can come again. And with her *tête-à-tête* remain? The lady! **1891** D. FERGUSON *Vicissitudes Bush Life* 160 He fossicked up some white tablecloths.

Hence **fossicking** *vbl. n.* and *ppl. a.*

1852 *Argus* (Melbourne) 14 Jan. 2/6 Let them immediately return, or commence what is called surface-washing, or fossicking. **1859** W. KELLY *Life in Vic.* I. 234, I was highly edified . . at the conduct of three under-sized fossicking coons, who discussed the nature of 'their shout' with the gravity of veteran topers.

fossick, *n.* [f. prec.] The act of fossicking. Also *attrib.*

[N.Z. **1898** H.B. VOGEL *Maori Maid* 332 Ngaia only laughed, and picking up the axe followed her husband, not, however, until she had made a close fossick for any further gold there might be.] **1904** *Bulletin* (Sydney) 17 Nov. 19/1 Brother Coverdale has been doing a 'fossick round'. **1969** B. GARLAND *Pitt Street Prospector* 26 Aw, just having a bit of a fossick; thought I might pick up a stone or two.

fossicker. Also **fossiker**. [f. FOSSICK v.]

1. One who fossicks for gold.

1852 *Argus* (Melbourne) 14 Jan. 2/6 These fossickers are a race of people, resembling drones in a community of bees, collecting their soil from the cells or holes which have been dug and abandoned by more industrious workmen, and occasionally stealing from other holes during the temporary absence of their industrious proprietors. **1852** *Austral. Gold Diggers' Monthly Mag.* ii. 53 *Fossiker*.—We understand that this digger's term has got into town, and is used as a provocative of a most scandalous character. Nothing so excites the ire of our gentle fair ones of Melbourne and of Geelong, as to say that their sweethearts are fossickers.

2. *transf.*

1853 *Wanderer* (Adelaide) June 75 If one in want of a dinner called at his neighbour's tent at mutton time he would be a 'fossicker'. **1874** C. DE BOOS *Congewoi Correspondence* 115 There's no mistake about the Treasurer bein a first-rate fossicker. My word! Why if he was on a tucker diggins I believe he'd fossick good wages in the old drives.

fossicking knife. An implement used to poke out or pry for nuggets of gold.

1853 J. SHERER *Gold Finder Aust.* 284 We came to a pipe-clay which is the bottom, we must now use a 'fossicking knife', and, scraping the pipe-clay, we see a bit of gold stick out. **1893** 'OLD CHUM' *Chips* 21 The man in digger's dress—blue serge blouse, moleskin trousers, and cabbage-tree hat, with his 'fossicking knife'.

fountain. [Spec. use of *fountain* constant source of water.] A cast-iron urn in which water is heated on an

open fire or solid-fuel stove. Also *attrib.*, as **fountain kettle**.
1876 'RESIDENT' *Girl Life in Aust.* 59 A chain and hook holds the fountain, a constant supply of boiling water being required for tea. **1916** J.B. COOPER *Coo-oo-ee!* 11 Over the kitchen fire a fountain kettle hung with boiling water.

four-railer. FOUR-RAIL FENCE.
1851 *Bell's Life in Sydney* 19 Apr. 1/4 Clearing the four-railer like a bird. **1928** M.B. PETERSEN *Jewelled Nights* 161 Nothing she can't do on horse-back .. and she skims a four-railer as if she were merely stepping over a match-box!

four-rail fence. A fence having four wooden rails as its horizontal members. Also **four-railed fence**.
1819 *Sydney Gaz.* 17 Apr., Surrounded with substantial Four-rail Fences, with or without a Range for a limited number of Cattle. **1829** *Sydney Monitor* 16 May 1603/2 Capt Wentworth possesses the beautiful estate at Tongabbee, .. upon which there was in 1822, not less than *thirty miles* of four railed fence.

fourteen years' man. *Hist.* A convict sentenced to fourteen years of penal servitude.
1834 *Perth Gaz.* 14 June 304 Fourteen years' men, four years in the Gangs, four years to be mustered weekly if living in Town; and monthly, if in the Country; and the remainder of their time annually. **1849** J. PATTISON *N.S.W.* 16 Seven-year men received their tickets at the expiry of four years; fourteen-years men after six years' servitude.

foxie. [f. *fox(-terrier* + -Y.] A fox-terrier.
1906 E. DYSON *Fact'ry 'Ands* 246 Like er bally foxie after er rat. **1952** A. MARSHALL *Aust.* (1981) 147 I'll bet you had a half-bred sheepdog... And you would have a foxie, too.

fracture. Also (erron.) **fracteur.** [Transf. use of *fracture* the act of breaking.] (An) explosive. Also *attrib.*
1897 *Bulletin* (Sydney) 21 Aug. 3/2 The 'fracteur smoke hangs thickly and we breathe it till it dies. **1929** W.J. RESIDE *Golden Days* 247 There were sufficient detonators, powder and 'fracture' to blow up all Coolgardie.

frame. [U.S. *frame* emaciated animal: see OEDS *sb.* 9 b.] An emaciated beast.
1903 J. FURPHY *Such is Life* 200 By the way, there's four of your frames left—out near those coolibahs. **1946** A.J. HOLT *Wheat Farms Vic.* 127 You raise and kill a decent beast yourself and divide it with your neighbour. When it comes for his turn to kill he picks out some rangy old frame with only hair on it.

freckle.
1. See quot. 1967. Also *fig.*
1967 *Kings Cross Whisper* (Sydney) xxxiv. 4/5 *Freckle,* anus. **1968** B. HUMPHRIES *Wonderful World Barry McKenzie,* You can put it up your *freckle* if you don't flamin' like it. **1978** —— *Nice Night's Entertainment* (1981) 180, I too believed that the sun shone out of Gough's freckle.
2. Special Comb. **freckle puncher,** a male homosexual.
1968 B. HUMPHRIES *Wonderful World Barry McKenzie,* Kevin huh? Sounds like a flamin' freckle puncher!!

free, *a. Hist.*
1. Of one formerly a convict: released from penal servitude; FREED. Freq. as **free convict**.
1792 D. COLLINS *Acct. Eng. Colony N.S.W.* (1802) I. 238 The people employed about the stores, if not free, should at least have been so situated as to have found it their interest to resist transportation. **1837** *Rep. Select Committee Transportation* 13 The pardoned convict or the free convict enjoys all the political rights of the free emigrants .. from the date of the governor's pardon.

2. **a.** Applied as a distinguishing epithet to a settler in an Australian Colony who had not been transported as a convict: see esp. quots. 1824, 1844, and 1854.
1795, 1804 [see *free settler*]. **1815** *HRA* (1916) 1st Ser. VIII. 489 Persons, *who have been once Convicts,* can never be restored to *a full* participation in the Rights and Privileges of Free British Subjects. **1824** E. CURR *Acct. Colony Van Diemen's Land* 11 In Van Diemen's Land, a line of demarcation has ever existed between convicts and free persons, which the future acquisition of their freedom has never enabled them to overstep. **1844** *Colonial Times* (Hobart) 10 July, The community is composed of three classes, the *free,* the *freed,* and the *bond.* **1854** J. MITCHEL *Jail Jrnl.* 231 She took an early occasion of informing me that she 'came out free'; which in fact is the patent of nobility in Van Diemen's Land.
b. In collocations: **free emigrant, immigrant, native, settler.**
1827 P. CUNNINGHAM *Two Yrs. in N.S.W.* II. 133 A body of proprietors .. the greater portion of whom are **free emigrants**. **1841** *Port Phillip Patriot* 10 June 4/3 The population of New South Wales consists of four classes; the **free immigrants** and their progeny; the convicts; the convicts who have become free through pardon or expiry of their term of service; and the progeny of the convict immigrants—persons who have always been free, but have a 'taint' in their blood. **1819** *Sydney Gaz.* 18 Sept., Hannah Harris, herself, a **free native** of this Territory. **1795** *HRA* (1914) 1st Ser. I. 679 To the Civil, Military, **Free Settlers,** and People serving in the Stores. **1804** *Sydney Gaz.* 10 June, He came to this Colony .. a Free Settler.

3. In collocations which may be used either exclusively as in sense 2, or to include sense 1: **free colonist, female, labour, labourer, man, overseer, people, population, servant, woman.**
1832 *Hill's Life N.S.W.* (Sydney) 9 Nov. 1 The increase of **free Colonists,** by the late numerous discharges within the Colony, of Soldiers of good character. **1837** W.B. ULLATHORNE *Catholic Mission Australasia* 28 The government .. has been sending out ship-loads of **free females**. **1832** J. BACKHOUSE *Narr. Visit Austral. Colonies* (1843) 66 One of them .. has put up about 17 miles of post and rail fence, at the rate of £70 per mile, by **free** and £60 by convict **labour**. **1805** *Sydney Gaz.* 3 Nov., Wanted immediately, several **Free Labourers** to work in the yard of J. Underwood and Company. **1791** P.G. KING *Jrnl.* Norfolk Island 11 Nine **Freemen** .. had served their Terms of Transportation and .. were permitted to become Settlers. **1834** J.D. LANG *Hist. & Statistical Acct. N.S.W.* I. 356 A party of eight or ten convict-labourers, under the charge of a **free overseer**. **1789** J. HUNTER *Hist. Jrnl. Trans. Port Jackson* (1793) 346 A plan had been concerted among the convicts, to surprize me, with the rest of the officers, marines and **free people**. **1827** *Tasmanian* (Hobart) 18 Oct. 2 We wish to learn what the particular grievances are that the **free population** labour under, that could be avoided. **1808** *Sydney Gaz.* 28 Aug., On Tuesday night John Brazil, a **free servant** of Mr Thompson, at Hawkesbury, was found murdered. **1791** D. COLLINS *Acct. Eng. Colony N.S.W.* (1798) I. 181 There were also eight **free women** (wives of convicts) and one died.

4. In special collocations: **free colony** (as distinct from a penal colony), a Colony which was not founded as, and has not been used as, a place of penal servitude; **settlement, (a)** *free colony;* **(b)** part of a penal colony which is not, or is no longer, used as a place of penal servitude. See PENAL.
1828 *Murray's Austral-Asiatic Rev.* i. 33 Government .. aim to make this not only a **free Colony,** but one of the highest order of Colonies under the Crown. **1832** J. HENDERSON *Observations Colonies N.S.W. & Van Diemen's Land* 17 Smaller indulgences should be (within, or near the penal settlement), allowed them after their sentences had been completed, and similar to what they would have been entitled to in the **free settlements**. **1840** *Port Phillip Gaz.* 12 Feb. 2 Two distinct causes may be assigned for these

examples of successful colonization [sc. South Australia and Port Phillip]—The first, originates in the difference between the results of a *penal* and a *free* settlement.

5. In the phr. **free by servitude,** (one who has been) released, having served the full sentence imposed: see quots. 1847 and 1848.

1813 *N.S.W. Pocket Almanack* 63 State the age, description, and country of the deceased; whether free settler, free or conditionally pardoned convict; free by servitude, or then a convict. **1847** A. HARRIS *Settlers & Convicts* (1953) 47 A convict free by servitude (so convicts are designated whose term of sentence has expired). **1848** C. COZENS *Adventures of Guardsman* 163 The 'free by servitude', he who has served his full sentence, is required to show his 'certificate of freedom'.

free, *n. Australian National Football.* Abbrev. of 'free kick'. Also as *v. intr.*

1859 G. ATKINSON *Everything about Austral. Rules Football* (1982) 197 In case of infringements, captain may claim free from where breach occurred. **1908** *Clipper* (Hobart) 19 Sept. 2/2 From the kick-off Abel played grandly; Teddy Russell put in a good bit of graft. Webb freed to Abel, Webb ditto to Molross. Free to Webb.

freebooter. *Obs.* [Spec. use of *freebooter* one who goes about in search of plunder, esp. a pirate.] A runaway convict; BUSHRANGER 1.

1817 *Hobart Town Gaz.* 16 Aug., All who attempt to establish themselves in the Woods as Free-Booters will meet the same Fate as those men who have lately tried it. **1900** C. WHITE *Hist. Austral. Bushranging* 101 The freebooters .. were exceedingly pleased with this prize, which they declared was 'just what they wanted'.

free-born, *a. Obs.* Used as a distinguishing epithet to deny association with convicts and convictism, esp. of one born in an Australian Colony. Also *absol.*

1825 *Austral.* (Sydney) 17 Mar. 1 The Governor has been pleased to approve of the following Appointments: William Eagleton (free born) to be a constable. **1835** *Sydney Herald* 5 Jan. 2/1 It will give much satisfaction to the Emigrants and free-born of Australia, to learn, that the cause of virtual representation was experienced a triumph at Swan River.

freed, *ppl. a. Hist.*

a. Of one formerly a convict: restored to the possession of civil liberties, having served a sentence imposed or obtained a remission thereof.

1829 *Tasmanian Almanack* 97 Governor Macquarie and Lieutenant Governor Sorell promote the objects of the emancipated (or, as the Right Hon. William Huskisson says, *freed*) Colonists. **1852** W. HUGHES *Austral. Colonies* 170 Distinction between the 'free' and the 'freed' is .. becoming weakened.

b. In collocations: **freed convict, man.**

1832 J. BUSBY *Authentic Information N.S.W. & N.Z.* 13 A degree of trust .. cannot be committed to a convict, or a **freed convict. 1847** *HRA* (1925) 1st Ser. XXVI. 1 The desire shown by the Settlers there to receive and employ Exiles and freed Convicts. **1830** *Ibid.* (1922) 1st Ser. XV. 791 Much has been said of the equal Right to protection and legal privileges of the Freemen and **Freedmen.**

freedom. *Obs.* Shortened form of *certificate of freedom* (see CERTIFICATE).

1847 A. HARRIS *Settlers & Convicts* (1953) 153 Free men do not like being continually called upon by prison constables to 'show their freedom'. **1848** J.C. BYRNE *Twelve Yrs.' Wanderings* I. 167 The free immigrant has nothing of the kind to produce, if required by any prying constable to 'show his freedom'.

freedom of contract. *Hist.* The right (of an employer) to hire non-union labour and to set conditions of employment. Also *attrib.*

1891 *Australasian Pastoralists' Rev.* 15 Aug. 217 The following was agreed to:- 'That employers shall be free to employ and shearers shall be free to accept employment whether belonging to Shearers' or other unions or not, without favour, molestation, or intimidation on either side.' This is the definition of 'freedom of contract' by the Pastoralists' Federal Council of Australia. **1900** H. LAWSON *Over Sliprails* 62 We got back, and the crew had to reload the wool without assistance, for it bore the accursed brand of a 'freedom-of-contract' shed.

free grant. *Hist.* The granting of the freehold of a tract of unalienated land; the land so granted. Also *attrib.*

1817 *Hobart Town Gaz.* 24 May, To Be Sold, A Free Grant Farm, situated at Crawfish Point, in the District of Queensborough. **1857** M.B. HALE *Transportation Question* 20 Upon the first formation of the colony, the grants were entirely free; and, when free grants were no longer made, the land was sold at a very low rate indeed.

freeman's key. *Obs.* [f. Br. slang *(to drink, lush at) Freeman's Quay* to drink at another's expense, with ref. to the name of a wharf near London Bridge at which free beer was distributed to porters, etc.: see Hotten, *Dict. Mod. Slang* (1859) and Partridge.] Used allusively with reference to a set of circumstances in which a consumer does not pay for, or is able to defer payment for, alcoholic liquor.

1891 *Truth* (Sydney) 29 Mar. 7/5, I must explain that getting in on the *nod* is the same as on the 'never never', 'Freeman's key', 'the ready'. **1915** 'ALPHA' *Reminisc. Goldfields* i. 51 He .. usually went on the spree every second month, and while in that state lost more than he made, the house being freeman's key for a time, until he again sobered up, after having had what he declared 'a regular soaker'.

free pardon. ABSOLUTE PARDON.

1794 D. COLLINS *Acct. Eng. Colony N.S.W.* (1798) I. 387 Richard Blount, for whom a free pardon had some time since been received. **1875** CAMPBELL & WILKS *Early Settlement Qld.* 56 The Government offered a large reward and a free pardon for .. information.

free-select, *v. Hist. trans.* To acquire (a tract of land) under a free selection scheme. See also SELECT. Also *absol.*

1861 H. PARKES *Speeches* 6 Mar. (1876) 138 Those who free-selected land would enter upon it under conditions enforcing them to its improvement. **1872** A. McFARLAND *Illawarra & Manaro* 133 An application to free-select should preclude all competition for the land.

Hence **free-selected** *ppl. a.,* **free-selecting** *ppl. a.* and *vbl. n.*

1868 *Frank Gardiner, or Bushranging in 1863* 16 Which brought them in a few moments to the door of a partly constructed hut, on the **free selected** block of James Sinclair. **1862** *Bell's Life in Sydney* 27 Sept. 3/2 Easier to get a living by **free selecting** than by working for wages. **1869** *Colonial Soc.* (Sydney) 18 Mar. 2 He tightly pinched his tiny prize—a free-selecting man!

free selection. *Hist.* A scheme under which the freehold of a tract of unalienated rural land, of a size suitable for small farming, could be acquired on terms favourable to the buyer; the land so acquired. See also SELECTION.

1859 *Bell's Life in Sydney* 21 May 1/1 The right of purchase of farms, surveyed or unsurveyed, without competition, and without delay, by persons willing to settle upon and improve them, and generally known as 'Free Selection', I have ever held to be a principle of essential importance. **1956** R.G. EDWARDS *Overlander Songbk.* 81 On my little free selection I have acres by the score Where I unyoke the bullocks from the dray.

free selector. A small farmer who acquires a tract of land under a free selection scheme (but see quot. 1867). See also SELECTOR 2.

1864 J. ROGERS *New Rush* 22 Free selectors we shall be! Deserting mineralogy, Retir'd to farms six foot by three— Free selectors we shall be! 1867 'CLERGYMAN' *Aust. as it Is* 131 The wife of his overseer said to me, that the infant at her breast, and the rest of her children, were 'free selectors'—that is the owner of the station had made use of their names in picking up the best parts of the run, not for the land itself, but to remain in undisturbed possession of the grazing land adjoining.

freezer.
1. An animal bred to be slaughtered for export as frozen meat. Also *attrib.*

[N.Z. 1889 WILLIAMS & REEVES *Colonial Couplets* 21 Be they [sc. sheep], freezers or crawlers or wethers or ewes.] 1897 R. NEWTON *Work & Wealth Qld.* 22 *(caption)* 'Freezers' for the meat works. 1925 *Pastoral Rev.* 16 Dec. 1114 Freezer Lamb Competitions.

2. FREEZING WORKS.

1933 J. TRURAN *Where Plain Begins* 12 Rabbits were worth a shilling a pair that winter: the 'freezer' up at Blayney would take any number of them at that price.

freezing works. An abattoir at which animal carcasses are prepared and frozen for export.

1881 *Queenslander* (Brisbane) 12 Nov. 635/1 Being specially suitable from its position for raising stock for the large Meat Preserving and Freezing Works about to be erected at Townsville. 1942 H.H. PECK *Mem. of Stockman* 94 These were treated at the Deniliquin freezing works.

Fremantle doctor: see DOCTOR n.³

freshy. Also **freshie**. [f. *fresh(water* + -Y.] A fresh-water crocodile.

1964 B. CRUMP *Gulf* 28 Best professional croc-shooter .. would say, '.. me and Andy Meikin shot four hundred and eighty freshies and nine fourteen-foot salties in the Normanby one trip.' 1972 K. WILLEY *Tales Big Country* 174 'What we have got,' Percy said, 'is a bunch of ragged-pants New Australians wiping out the harmless freshwater crocodile with nets. The freshie is protected everywhere else, but not in Queensland.'

friar bird. [See quot. 1841.] Any of the four species of the honeyeater genus *Philemon* of n. and e. Aust., New Guinea, and nearby islands, having bare facial skin, esp. the *noisy friar bird* (see NOISY). Formerly also **friar.**

1790 J. HUNTER *Hist. Jrnl. Trans. Port Jackson* (1793) 410 Wir-gan, A bird called fryar. 1841 J. GOULD *Birds of Aust.* (1848) IV. Pl. 58, Its bare head and neck have .. suggested the names of 'Friar Bird', 'Monk', 'Leather Head', etc.

frib. [Prob. Br. dial.: cf. *fribble* trifling thing (OED *sb.* 2.) ; *frip* anything worthless or trifling (EDD); *frib* small, dirty lock of wool (DAE).] Usu. in *pl.* A small tuft of wool matted with grease, either under a sheep's legs or on the edge of the shorn fleece.

1805 *Sydney Gaz.* 9 Sept., This wool when sorted produced .. Prime Wool .. choice locks .. Fribs. 1961 *Bulletin* (Sydney) 3 Feb. 44/2 The old piece-picker went on: 'I picked for ten guns on me own and not a frib in the broken.'

fribby, *a.* and *n.*

A. *adj.* Characterized by the presence of fribs (see prec.).

1900 A. HAWKESWORTH *Austral. Sheep & Wool* 180 A fleece is said to be fribby when a great number of second cuts or fribs fall out when it is shaken or in the process of rolling. 1929 H.B. SMITH *Sheep & Wool Industry Aust. & N.Z.* (ed. 3) 209 *Fribby*, short locky pieces of wood such as second cuts and small black yolky locks from crutch and under fore-legs of sheep.

B. *n.* See quot.

1951 *Concerning Wool* (Austral. Wool Board) 100 *Fribby*, wool containing an excessive amount of second cuts and sweat points.

frilled lizard. The agamid lizard *Chlamydosaurus kingii* of n. and n.e. Aust., having a layer of loose tissue around the neck that can be erected when the animal is alarmed. Also **frill lizard, frill-neck, frill-necked lizard, frilly.**

1841 G. GREY *Jrnls. Two Exped. N.-W. & W.A.* I. 94 We fell in with a specimen of the remarkable frilled lizard (*Chlamydosaurus Kingii*). 1901 *Bulletin* (Sydney) 23 Nov. 32/1 Yer don't like chuckin' yer swag off all of a sudden to run down a frill-neck. 1904 M. WHITE *Shanty Entertainment* 67 There is nothing so naturally exhilarating as to watch a good big buck goanna making love to a frill-necked lizard on the wing. 1945 M. RAYMOND *Smiley* 36, I thought bees could let go o' their stings like frill lizards let go o' their tails. 1976 C.D. MILLS *Hobble Chains & Greenhide* 162, I saw this dusky imp Pluto approaching Ned with a 'frilly' that he had found.

fringe. An area of sparse settlement bordering the arid inland region of Australia. Also *attrib.*, esp. as **fringe country**.

1902 *Bulletin* (Sydney) 13 Sept. 16/1 Government men stationed on 'The Fringe' are mostly in their right place. . . The 'Fringe' civil servant, being king of his tinpot village, generally has an overweening conceit of his own abilities. 1961 *Meanjin* 264 He had come from the cattle country to the edge of the Desert, and had found the fringe country to his liking.

fringed lily. Any of several perennial herbs of the genus *Thysanotus* (fam. Lilaceae) bearing purple or blue flowers the three broad segments of which are fringed, esp. *T. tuberosus*; also with distinguishing epithet, as **twining fringed lily** (see quot. 1978). Also (esp. formerly) **fringed violet.**

1819 *First Fruits Austral. Poetry* 3 Th' Australian 'fringed Violet' Shall henceforward be my pet! 1901 M. VIVIENNE *Travels in W.A.* 61 The thysanotus, or fringed lily, is a remarkable satiny-looking flower, and has a habit of climbing. 1978 B.P. MOORE *Life on Forty Acres* 43 The less spectacular Twining Fringed Lily (*T. patersonii*), with smaller flowers on twisting stems.

fringe-dweller. An Aboriginal who lives on the outskirts of a town. Also *transf.* and *fig.*

1959 *Fringe Dwellers* (Dept. Territories) 6 Most of these people are 'fringe dwellers'—people living merely on the fringes of Australian towns, of the larger Australian society, of the Australian economy. 1986 *Nat. Times* (Sydney) 21 Feb. 7/1 A gossipy article .. sent .. a number of political fringe-dwellers—staff, journalists, and public servants—into a state of shock.

fringe-myrtle. [Prob. with reference to the long hairs (awns) of the calyx.] Any of several shrubs of the chiefly w. Austral. genus *Calytrix* (fam. Myrtaceae), typically having clusters of attractive, starry flowers, esp. the widely cultivated *C. tetragona*, also known as **common fringe-myrtle.**

1866 J. LINDLEY *Treasury of Bot.* 508 *Fringe-Myrtles*, a name given by Lindley to the Chamaelauciaceae. 1942 C. BARRETT *Austral. Wild Flower Bk.* 173 Common fringe-myrtle .. has long been associated with the Grampians, but it ranges throughout Australia, excepting only the north.

fritz. Chiefly *S.A.* [Transf. use of *Fritz*, nickname for a German, with reference to *German sausage*.] A large, bland sausage; DEVON. Also **pork fritz,** and *fig.*

1914 *Truth* (Sydney) 8 Nov. 7/7 Pork fritz manufacturers have become alarmed, and some are .. advertising that their commodities are really made from pork and veal. **1966** S.J. BAKER *Austral. Lang.* (ed. 2) 347 South Australia .. *yard of fritz,* a tall man. **1981** P. BARTON *Bastards I have Known* 114 With a half-eaten hunk of fritz.

frog. [f. *frog* french (letter).] A condom. Also **froggie.**

1952 T.A.G. HUNGERFORD *Ridge & River* 23 Having a bath and a shave, getting into clean clothes, whacking a froggie into the kick, to lare up at the dance. **1969** A. BUZO *Front Room Boys* (1970) 40 'Jees I forgot the frog,' he said. . . I was disgusted. I put my pants back on and told him to take me home immediately.

frogskin. *Obs.* [From the colour.] A one-pound note; the sum of one pound; TOADSKIN. Also **frog.**

1907 *Clipper* (Hobart) 28 Dec. 4/3 'I'll give yer a quid for yer old red shawl,' and I 'olds out a frogskin. 'The man's mad,' sez she to 'erself, 'but a quid's a quid.' **1919** *Aussie: Austral. Soldiers' Mag.* (Sydney) Jan. 2/1 The Prince pushed his frame in and risked ten 'frogs' and won.

front, *n.* [Deteriorated use of *front* effrontery, impudence (rare in standard English after 1850): see OED *sb.* 4.] Effrontery. Formerly with indefinite article.

1896 H. LAWSON *While Billy Boils* 20 'Well, I'll be blessed!' I says. 'I'll see you further first. You have got a front.' **1981** C. GORMAN *Night in Arms of Raeleen* (1983) 30 That guy's got more front than the National Bank.

front, *v.* [Spec. use of *front* to confront, orig. in Austral. Services' speech.]

1. *trans.* To appear before (a court, etc.); to confront.

1941 *Argus* (Melbourne) 15 Nov. (Suppl.), *Fronting the Bull,* facing a charge. **1968** D. O'GRADY *Bottle of Sandwiches* 28 A man feels a galah fronting a new boss and putting the bite on him for the price of a gallon of juice.

2. *intr.* To make an appearance, to 'turn up'. Also with **up.**

1968 J. ALARD *He who shoots Last* 3 Look like doin a drag wen I front tamorrow. **1982** H. KNORR *Private Viewing* 68 Now she's gone to Canberra to see her parents. So I'm going to Tassie to mine. They get a bit worried if you don't front up now and then.

frontage.

1. Used in the standard sense of land abutting on a river or stretch of water, but acquiring special prominence because of the importance, esp. in rural areas of comparatively low rainfall, of access to water. See also *river frontage,* RIVER 1. Also **water frontage,** and *attrib.*

1832 J. BACKHOUSE *Narr. Visit Austral. Colonies* (1843) 27 He has about a mile of frontage on the Clyde, which at this season of the year is little more than a chain of pools—called here lagoons. **1838** *Tegg's N.S.W. Pocket Almanack* 71 In general, each lot will consist of 640 acres. But if a section, with water frontage does not contain the full quantity, the section behind it will be added to the lot. **1891** 'R. BOLDREWOOD' *Sydney-Side Saxon* (1925) 2 A big block of country that laid back from the frontage runs on the Logan.

2. *Mining.* Used *attrib.* in Special Comb. **frontage claim,** a tract of land of specific measurement in front, but (initially) of otherwise indefinite dimension (see esp. quots. 1869 and 1870); **lead,** an auriferous deposit subject to *frontage claims;* **system,** the division of an area into *frontage claims.*

1869 R.B. SMYTH *Gold Fields & Mineral Districts* 612 **Frontage Claim,** a claim, the lateral boundaries of which are not fixed until the lead has been traced through it. **1870** W.B. WITHERS *Hist. Ballarat* 126 Two kinds of claim have for some years been in existence, one called 'block' and the other 'frontage' claims. The block claim is a fixed area, with bounds ascertained from the first; the frontage is a claim with a given width on a lead or gutter, with boundaries changeable as to direction according to the course of the lead. **1858** *Colonial Mining Jrnl.* Nov. 44/1 The Mining Board have .. under consideration a code of laws applicable to **frontage leads. 1858** *Colonial Mining Jrnl.* Oct. 28/3 The amount of litigation in connection with this lead is great, some of the claims being under the **frontage,** and others the block **system.**

frontier. [U.S. *frontier* that part of a country which forms the border of its settled or inhabited regions: see OED(S 4 b. and Mathews.] An area of newly or sparsely settled country, remote from closely settled districts, esp. as marking either the limit of settlement or habitable country. Also *attrib.*

1840 *S. Austral. Rec.* (London) 19 Sept. 179 We trust that during the ensuing session Sir George and his councillors will look to the evil effects of the rum-selling system on the frontiers, which are inhabited, generally speaking, by the most lawless portion of our lawless population. **1864** *Sydney Punch* 2 July 44/1 Why is the Shoalhaven district like a frontier town? Because it is all Berry, and, of course, that has a resembling sound to Albury.

front verandah: see VERANDAH.

fruit, *n.*[1]

1. Used *attrib.* in Special Comb. pertaining to commercial fruit-growing: **fruit block,** a fruit farm; **cocky,** a fruit farmer; **property,** a fruit farm.

1939 P. MCGUIRE *Austral. Journey* 258 William stayed on at Mildura .. but the population fled and the **fruit-blocks** which had grown along the river front were falling back into the wilderness. **1910** *Bulletin* (Sydney) 13 Jan. 14/2 These fences are prime breeding grounds for sparrows, codlin moths and other tireless foes of the **fruit** and grain **cockies. 1946** A.M. LAPTHORNE *Mildura Calling* 45 'Blockie' .. originally referred to the owner of a block of land comprising ten or more acres, but is now used for smaller land-holders of **fruit properties.**

2. *fig.* In the phr. **fruit for** (or **on**) **the sideboard,** abundant riches, esp. as resulting from gambling; one who is viewed as a source of 'easy' money.

1953 T.A.G. HUNGERFORD *Riverslake* 128 He was not afraid that they would ever wake up to it .. not the poor dopes who came back week after week to buy the fruit for his sideboard. **1982** *Sydney Morning Herald* 6 Mar. 13/7 No political party in Australia, least of all the Liberals, has the courage to stop giving public money to people who do not need it. The political consequences of playing Robin Hood by depriving the most articulate political force in Australia of some fruit on the sideboard would be catastrophic.

fruit, *n.*[2] *Austral. pidgin.* The amount of ore held by a fruit tin: see quots.

1953 J.K. EWERS *Sun on my Back* 81 When a fruit-tin was full it was taken to Dan Thompson's store where it was weighed. .. I asked one blackfellow who was digging for pug how much tin he got a week and he replied, 'Three or four fruits.' Thus, at Moolyella, a new standard of measurement had been evolved—a 'fruit'. **1973** J. GREENWAY *Down among Wild Men* 254 Every man Jack of the community .. had to collect every day one 'fruit' (a thirty-ounce fruit can) of tantalite yandied from surface iron with a magnet. No fruit, no bloody food for you.

fruitologist. [f. *fruit* + -*ologist* one who professes a science.] A fruiterer; a greengrocer.

1958 G. COTTERELL *Tea at Shadow Creek* 26 Mr Tontelli said that he was a fruitologist. He had several fruitariums in the city. 1959 *Times* (London) 30 Oct. 13/4 In my own country I purchased fruit regularly from a 'fruitologist'. Yours faithfully, *Allen Brown*, Australia House, Strand. W.C.2.

fry. [Spec. use of Br. dial. *fry* used of various kinds of offal, usu. eaten fried.] (A) lamb's liver. Freq. as **lamb's fry.**
1847 E.W. LANDOR *Bushman* 158 The tempting savour . . arose from the large dish of sheep's fry. 1925 *Commonsense Cookery Bk.* (N.S.W. Public School Cookery Teachers' Assoc.) 42 *Liver and bacon. Ingredients.*—1 lamb's fry, ¼ lb. fat bacon. . . *Method.*—1. Wash liver and soak in warm salted water. 1973 J. O'GRADY *Survival in Doghouse* 47, I get a leg, and a fry, and a heart, and half-a-dozen chump chops.

frying-pan, *attrib.*
  a. Special Comb. **frying-pan brand,** a crudely applied brand used by a cattle thief to efface the rightful owner's brand; also *ellipt.* as **frying-pan.**
1857 F. DE B. COOPER *Wild Adventures* 104 This person was an 'old hand' and got into some trouble . . by using a 'frying-pan brand'. He was stock-keeping in that quarter, and was rather giving [sic] to 'gulley raking'. . . He ran in three bullocks belonging to a neighbouring squatter, and clapt his brand on the top of the other so as to efface it. 1951 E. HILL *Territory* 310 Those well away from police patrols . . were content with the good old Frying Pan, a blotch.
  b. Of criminals: petty; small-time.
1865 J.F. MORTLOCK *Experiences of Convict* 90 Some, unarmed, prowl about, watch the inmates of a dwelling away [sic], and then pilfer. These are called 'frying-pan' bushrangers, being looked upon with much contempt. 1966 T. RONAN *Strangers on Ophir* (rev. ed.) 46 Oh, just a frying-pan fighting man who blew in from Coronet.

fuchsia bush. [From a fancied resemblance of the flower of the plant to that of the ornamental shrub.] *Emu bush* (a), see EMU *n.*¹ 3; (*spec.*) *Eremophila maculata* (see *native fuchsia* NATIVE *a.* 6 a.). Also **fuchsia tree.**
1883 F. BONNEY *On Some Customs Aborigines* 7 His bed, made of the small branches of a fuchsia bush. 1916 S.A. WHITE *In Far Northwest* 25 It was dotted over with . . bright flowering fuchsia trees (Eremophila).

fuck truck. *Shag-wagon,* see SHAG *n.*² Also *attrib.*
1979 R.D. JONES *Walking Line* 19 The boys wearing blue singlets in their striped fuck trucks yelled & pressed down on the horns but fifi kept going. 1982 *Meanjin* 395 How did you adapt your fuck-truck style of driving to a foreign car?

fuckwit. A nincompoop, a dimwit. Also *attrib.*
1969 A. BUZO *Front Room Boys* (1970) 89 Ooh, temper! Well, ta-ta for now, fuckwit. 1979 *Meanjin* 464 It sounded like a load of fuck-wit shit to me.
  Also **fuckwitted** *a.*
1973 D. WILLIAMSON *Coming of Stork* (1974) 152 That fuckwitted agent of yours is really driving me right off my brain.

full, *a.*¹ [Scot. dial. *fou, fow, full* drunk (cf. *full* replete).]
  a. Inebriated; drunk.
c 1848 'SICK MAN' *Voyage Sydney to S.A.* 7 We stopped, of course, at almost every public-house until we were full. 1980 C. LEE *Bush Week* 19 We were all pretty well full when the van rolled into Mittagong.
  b. [Spec. use of, and elaboration upon, *full as a tick* full to repletion: see OEDS *tick, sb.*¹ 1 c.] In the phr. **full as a tick** and varr., extremely drunk.

1892 *Dialect Notes* I. 210 *Full as a tick,* drunk [Aust.]. Used also of fulness of any kind. 1941 S.J. BAKER *Pop. Dict. Austral. Slang* 30 *Full as an egg (goog, tick),* completely drunk. 1944 F. JOHNSON *F. Johnson's Laugh* 58 One night my husband came home as drunk as Chloe . . as full as a boot, in fact! 1959 J. WYNNUM *Down Hatch* 40 He walked groggily across the restaurant towards the appropriate door and Trunky . . noted that Dusty was making very heavy weather of it. 'Dusty's sloshed to the gills,' he grinned. 'As full as a bull,' confirmed Watts with finality. 1959 *Bulletin* (Sydney) 30 Dec. 45/1 I'm going to get full as a State school, whittled as a penguin, cacko, blind sleeping drunk. 1981 P. RADLEY *Jack Rivers & Me* 156 They're so full of rum if any of the . . genteeler ladies take seconds they'll get full as farts. 1983 *Daily Tel.* (Sydney) 2 Apr. 3/6 The saying 'as full as a Bourke Street tram' is soon to take on a new meaning in Victoria, where alcohol may soon be served to passengers as the rails sing by.
  c. In the phr. **full as a goog,** extremely drunk; replete with food. See GOOG.
1941 [see sense b.]. 1950 'B. JAMES' *Advancement Spencer Button* 95 Well, old Foll was in that bar, as full as a goog. 1982 LOWENSTEIN & HILLS *Under Hook* 27 The seamen'd stagger back to their ships. . . I've seen them like monkeys climbing up this single hawser rope, full as a goog.

full, *a.*² *Obs.* [Survival of Br. *full* sated, weary of; obs. exc. in 'modern colonial slang' as *full up*: see OED *a.* 4 c.]
  a. Usu. with **of**: surfeited (with), disgusted (with), 'fed up'.
1871 *Austral. Town & Country Jrnl.* (Sydney) 21 Jan. 89/2 People are beginning to get 'full' about pony races. 1913 C.J. DENNIS *Backblock Ballads* 88 I'm full Of that crook mob!
  b. With **up**.
1881 J.C.F. JOHNSON *To Mount Browne & Back* 17 Most of the returning diggers will be almost too 'full up on digging' to care about taking much trouble in prospecting on the back track. 1926 E. MCKENZIE-HATTON *Moluscut* 38 Disheartened and weary, they were just about 'full up', but our cheery songs had helped them to 'stick it out'.

full, *a.*³ [Abbrev. of *full-blood.*] Qualifying an ethnic designation: of unmixed race.
1879 G. TAPLIN *Folklore S. Austral. Aborigines* 125 Agnes Bates was a full native of South Australia. 1979 C. GREEN *Burn Butterflies* 18 Settled in the Barossa. Your full kraut cockie. Lutheran; couldn't speak a word of English.

full-blood. [Spec. use of *full-blood* a person of unmixed race.] An Aboriginal. Also *attrib.*
1895 A. MESTON *Qld. Aboriginals* 12 A grand total of 114 full bloods. 1978 D. STUART *Wedgetail View* 18 With a full-blood woman in tow, he'd be greatly handicapped.

full board: see BOARD 2.

full forward. *Australian National Football.* Any of three players who constitute the full, as distinct from the half forward line; *spec.* the centrally positioned player. Also *attrib.*
1928 G. MORIARTY *Teaching Game of Football* iii. 4 The full forward is your goal kicker; shepherd him and play to him. 1967 *Austral.* (Sydney) 24 Apr. 12/5 Peter Hudson, Hawthorn's star full-forward recruit from Tasmania flies in front of his opposing full-back.

full mouth, *a.* and *attrib.* Of an adult sheep: having its full complement of eight incisors.
1855 Tas. Non-State Rec. 103/4 8 June, The Wethers must be from 6 Tooth to full mouth or they will not suit my purpose. 1867 *Ibid.* 103/6 30 Oct., Drop Mr Harrison a line and say that the 1000 full mouth wedders will require to be sold.

full points, *pl. Australian National Football.* The six points awarded for a goal; a goal. Also **full-pointer.**

1960 *N.T. News* (Darwin) 5 Jan. 8/5 Hobson sent the ball right in for Cooper to grab it off hands and run in for a clever full-pointer. **1981** L. MONEY *Footy Fan's Handbk.* 37 *Terms for a goal.* It's full points! He's dobbed it! . . Right through the centre!

full-woolled, *a.* Of sheep: having twelve months (or more) growth of wool.

1916 *Bulletin* (Sydney) 31 Aug. 22/4 O'Shea . . killed and dressed 140 full-woolled ewes. **1975** R.O. MOORE *Sunlit Plains Extended* 31 It was only a small hole . . and the whole of the surface was completely covered with dead full woolled sheep!

fummy. [Prob. f. *foumart* polecat, in standard use but also widespread in Br. dial.] A domestic cat.

1901 *Truth* (Sydney) 27 Oct. 1/7 Charged at the Water with saturating a cat with kerosene and setting poor fummy aflame. **1978** H.C. BAKER *I was Listening* 29 The big 'fummy' would stand up, spit defiance, then take off in undignified flight.

function. [Spec. use of *function* religious or public ceremony, social gathering conducted with form and ceremony.] An organized social gathering, not necessarily characterized by great ceremony: see quots.

1910 *Truth* (Sydney) 28 Aug. 6/1 Frosty female function. (National Council of Women biennial meeting.) *Ibid.* 25 Sept. 5/8 The little *friendly farewell function* extended him by a few of his friends. **1935** K. TENNANT *Tiburon* 61 She . . teaches sewing, runs school functions, makes cakes for school picnics. **1984** *Tourist: Ansett Airlines Mag.* Jan. 12 This two-storey . . restaurant seats 140, caters in fine style for all functions.

funnel web. [Transf. use of the U.S. name for a spider of the fam. Agelenidae.]

1. a. Any of many venomous spiders of the genera *Atrax* and *Hadronyche* (fam. Hexathelidae), some of which make a web with a funnel-shaped entrance. **b.** *spec. Atrax robustus* of N.S.W., having a potentially fatal bite; *Sydney funnel web,* see SYDNEY 2.

1933 *Bulletin* (Sydney) 15 Mar. 21/3 Three people have been killed recently from the bite of a spider, known as the atrax or funnel-web spider. **1976** E. WORRELL *Things that Sting* 24 There are several species of Funnel-webs. The deadliest species is the Sydney Funnel-web.

2. *transf.* and *fig.*

1986 *Sydney Morning Herald* 8 Mar. 1/8 Sydney's Most Feared Q.C. The funnel-web of Phillip Street.

furfy, var. FURPHY.

furnisher. *Mining. Obs.* See quot. 1869.

1859 *Colonial Mining Jrnl.* Feb. 90/3 The old party have a disagreement between themselves and furnisher. . . The furnisher has I believe, taken proceedings. **1869** R.B. SMYTH *Gold Fields & Mineral Districts* 612 *Furnisher,* a capitalist who by erecting machinery for, or otherwise assisting a party of miners working a claim, becomes entitled to a share of the profits.

furphy /ˈfɜfi/. Also **furfy, furphey.** [f. the name of a firm, J. *Furphy* & Sons Pty. Ltd., operating a foundry at Shepparton, Vic., and manufacturing water-carts, etc., the name *Furphy* appearing on such carts.]

1. A rumour or false report; an absurd story: see quot. 1915 (1), but see also quot. 1965.

1915 R. GRAVES *On Gallipoli* 9 To cheer us then a 'furphy' passed around. . . 'They're fighting now on Achi Baba's mound.' [*Note*] *Furphy,* slang for rumour. In Egypt the various rumours were brought into the camps by the drivers of the water carts. As these water carts were branded Furphy, it is easy to see the origin of the slang meaning. **1915** *First Aid Post: Official Organ 2nd Field Ambulance* 30 June 1/1 Furphys are scarce today owing to the Turks capturing . . our wireless. **1916** 'MEN OF ANZAC' *Anzac Bk.* 134 Wanted—man with active imagination to supply furfies to the Beach, where the supply is running short. **1917** *All abaht It* (London) (1919) Feb. 23 He who brings us wild furpheys. **1965** Austral. *Encycl.* IV. 235 Furphy worked for 20 years in Shepparton, and it was there that he turned in a serious way to writing, first as a contributor of paragraphs and articles to the Sydney *Bulletin* under the pen-name 'Tom Collins', which was in those times a synonym for idle rumour; it was an amusing coincidence that during World War I his real name, Furphy, came to mean the same thing.

2. A water-cart. Also **furphy tank.**

1938 *Bulletin* (Sydney) 2 Feb. 20/1 A rotund citizen up our way went to fill his furphy-tank at the creek and, with the first bucketful he tipped in, fluked a fair-sized eel. **1971** W.A. WINTER-IRVING *Beyond Bitumen* 65 An hour to fill the Furphy, an hour home and an hour to pump it into the kitchen tank.

further-back, *adv.* Also **farther-back.** Compar. formed on FAR-BACK *a.* Also *absol.* as *n.*

1887 'OVERLANDER' *Austral. Sketches* 71 Taking up some of that wretched country further back and forming a pastoral company. **1928** M.E. FULLERTON *Austral. Bush* 41 He went into the 'farther back', caught and mastered a 'brumby'.

further-out, *adv.* and *a.* Also **farther-out.** Compar. formed on FAR-OUT *a.*

A. *adv.* Also *absol.* as *n.*

1895 A.B. PATERSON *Man from Snowy River* 117 He came from 'further out', That land of heat and drought. **1905** *Truth* (Sydney) 23 Apr. 7/5 The magsman talks 'em into shout To drink and sorrows drown. There's joy because from 'Farther Out' The Bills have come to town.

B. *adj.*

1908 *Bulletin* (Sydney) 9 Apr. 15/1 It's time *The Bulletin* shut down on those urban outbackers who can't write a Further-Out par without referring to . . 'Jimmie Pannikin'. **1956** T. RONAN *Moleskin Midas* 148 The big movements of cattle to settle the farther-out country were now in their closing stages.

furthest-out, *adv.* and *a.* Also **farthest-out.** Superl. formed on FAR-OUT *a.*

A. *adv.* Most remote from a major centre of population; more so than FURTHER-OUT.

1917 A.B. PATERSON *Saltbush Bill* 26, I own without a doubt That I always see a hero in the 'man from furthest out'. **1964** B. WANNAN *Fair Go, Spinner* 156 A bushman from 'farthest out' was visiting his sister who lived near Melbourne.

B. *adj.*

1917 A.B. PATERSON *Three Elephant Power* 123 He had been for many years pioneering in the Northern Territory, the other side of the sun-down—a regular 'furthest-out' man'.

Fusion. *Hist.* A name given to the alliance of the non-Labor free trade and protectionist groups formed in 1909. Also *attrib.*

1909 *Sydney Morning Herald* 28 May 8/2 The Fusion. How it stands on protection. **1979** J. BARRETT *Falling In* 66 When Protectionists and Free Traders combined in 1909, their 'Fusion' government amended the Defence Act to prescribe compulsory junior cadet training.

Hence **Fusionist** *n.*

1910 *Bulletin* (Sydney) 24 Mar. 8/1 One of the worst disasters that is perpetually striking the Fusionists is the man with the long memory.

fuzzy-wuzzy. *Hist.* [Transf. use of *fuzzy-wuzzy* a soldier's nickname for a Sudanese warrior: see OED *fuzzy* 5.]

1. A name given by Australian soldiers to an indigenous inhabitant of New Guinea during the war of 1939–45. Also *attrib.*

1942 *Wog Jnrl.: Mag. Headquarters 3rd Austral. Infantry Brigade* 25 Dec. 2 The Fuzzy Wuzzies carried them to save their lives. **1944** G. HAMLYN-HARRIS *Through Mud & Blood* 47 We turned under our ground sheets, well satisfied with 'fuzzy-wuzzy postmen'!

2. Special Comb. **fuzzy-wuzzy angel,** one who gave assistance to Australian Service personnel, esp. as a stretcher-bearer.

1942 *Wog Jrnl.: Mag. Headquarters 3rd Austral. Infantry Brigade* 25 Dec. 1 *The fuzzy wuzzy angels* (By an unknown wounded Australian soldier). **1977** M. TUCKER *If everyone Cared* 161 My husband .. was .. sent to Papua-New Guinea, part of the cleaning-up operations to send the Japanese back home. His praise for the 'fuzzy-wuzzy angels' was great.

G

gaff, *v.* [Br. slang *gaff* to gamble with cards, dice, etc.; not attested in Br. use after 1828: see OED *v.*²] *intr.* To gamble, esp. by tossing coins. Freq. as *vbl. n.*

1812 J.H. VAUX *Mem.* (1819) II. 176 *Gaff*, to gamble with cards, dice, etc., or to toss up. 1946 K.S. PRICHARD *Roaring Nineties* 147 The racket of gaffing over the spinning pennies went on into the small hours.

Hence **gaffing school,** a group of gamblers; a place where gamblers meet: see SCHOOL 3.

1899 J. BRADSHAW *Quirindi Bank Robbery* 43 His share came to 11 . . of these new £5 notes. He answered, 'Ribuck I know what to do; I will pass them off at a gaffing school all at once.'

galah /gəˈlɑː/. Formerly also **galar, gillar,** etc. [a. Yuwaalaraay (and related languages) *gilaa*.]

1. The grey-backed, pink-fronted cockatoo *Eolophus roseicapilla*, formerly of n. Aust. and now widespread; *red-breasted cockatoo*, see RED *a.* 1 b.; *rose-breasted cockatoo*, see ROSE. Also *attrib.*

1862 J. MCKINLAY *Jrnl. Exploration Interior* 6 May 88 A vast number of gulahs, curellas, macaws . . here. 1872 MRS J. FOOTT *Sketches Life in Bush* 14 The Galah parrot feeds on its fragrant petals. 1884 A.W. STIRLING *Never Never Land* 169 Flocks of rose-breasted cockatoos, called by the colonists gillars (I spell the name as it is pronounced) are to be met with everywhere. 1886 P. CLARKE *'New Chum' in Aust.* 233 Not far off a large flock of the rose-crested galar—a grey and rose parrot, well known by bird fanciers—is feeding. 1976 N.V. WALLACE *Bush Lawyer* 124 Mobs of corellas and galahs screamed down on the waterholes at evening time.

2. *fig.* A fool, a nincompoop. Also *attrib.*

1938 H. DRAKE-BROCKMAN *Men without Wives* (1955) 103 That Rienzi . . A black-eyed nasty-tempered galah. 1982 *Bulletin* (Sydney) 16 Feb. 35/1 It was once the done thing . . for a galah DJ to put down country music and its performers.

3. *Comb.* **galah pie.**

1932 J.J. HARDIE *Cattle Camp* (1944) 31 Galah pie is not too bad! 1962 MARSHALL & DRYSDALE *Journey among Men* 169 One old country dish, and a very good one too, was galah pie.

4. *Special Comb.* **galah session,** a period allocated for private conversation, esp. between women on isolated stations, over an outback radio network; also *transf.*, a long chat.

1956 H. HUDSON *Flynn's Flying Doctors* 119 At the Cloncurry Base I listened in to the 'Galah Session', as menfolk call it, also known as the Gossip Session, but officially Intercommunication Between Outposts. 1969 A. GARVE *Boomerang* 26 For hours the three men chatted, swapping stories and experiences and attitudes. . . It was Dawes who said at last, '. . I reckon this galah session's gone on long enough.'

galley. [Transf. use of *galley* ship's kitchen.] A crudely-shielded outdoor cooking fire.

1955 H.G. LAMOND *Towser* 21 A few sheets of tin made a wind-break for a fire . . which Jack and all his class termed a 'galley'. 1977 V. PRIDDLE *Larry & Jack* 8 Old Tom always used an outside fire, known by all bushmen as a galley. Just a few bush saplings supporting a few sheets of iron. That was Tom's kitchen.

gallon licence. See quot. 1880. Also *attrib.*

1880 *Act* (W.A.) 44 Vict. no. 9 Sect. 9, A gallon license shall authorise the licensee to sell and dispose of any liquor in any quantities not less than one gallon, not to be drunk on the premises in which such liquor is sold: Provided that such liquor shall consist of but one description of liquor, and be delivered and shall be taken away from the premises at one and the same time, and not by instalments, at the time of sale. 1966 T. RONAN *Once there was Bagman* 8 He . . found me a gallon-licence store where, with the right introduction, beer would be bought a bottle at a time.

gallows. A structure consisting of two uprights and a crosspiece, from which the carcass of a slaughtered animal is hung, esp. to remove the hide. Also *attrib.*

1847 A. HARRIS *Settlers & Convicts* (1953) 159 Another convenience it must contain is what is called 'the gallows' for hauling up a beast that has been slaughtered, to take the hide off. 1898 *Bulletin* (Sydney) 8 Jan. 32/1 They . . took the end of the rope which he passed to them, put it once round the gallows-post.

galvanized, *a.*

1. In the collocation **galvanized iron** [not exclusively Austral. but of special significance because of the extensive use of the material in Aust.], iron coated with zinc to protect it from rust, used esp. in (corrugated) sheets as a building material. Also *attrib.*

1860 *S. Austral. Advertiser* (Adelaide) 2 July 2/4 *Labour market,* Galvanized Iron Workers, 12s. to 14s. 1887 A. NICOLS *Wild Life & Adventure* 65 The store and the woolshed . . were covered in with sheets of galvanized iron. 1972 *Bulletin* (Sydney) 19 Aug. 12/3 Australia was built on meat pies, sausages and galvanised iron.

2. *fig.* In the collocation **galvanized burr,** the low, spreading shrub *Sclerolaena birchii* (fam. Chenopodiaceae) of Qld., N.T., S.A., and N.S.W., bearing a hard spiny fruit.

1934 *Bulletin* (Sydney) 20 June 22/3 Now they [*sc.* graziers] have a new pest—galvanised burr. It resembles roly-poly, but is the colour of galvanised iron. 1983 *Bingara Advocate* 7 Dec., Because it is a native plant, galvanized burr is, unfortunately, not susceptible to biological control by the techniques accepted for introduced weeds.

galvo. [f. *galv(anized iron* + -O.] Galvanized iron, see GALVANIZED 1.

1945 S.J. BAKER *Austral. Lang.* 266 *Galvo*, galvanised iron. 1986 *Nat. Times* (Sydney) 17 Jan. 22/3 It was a small place . . made of vertical galvo with pitched roof of galvo.

gammon, *n.* [Orig. Br. criminal cant: see quot. 1812. Used as elsewhere but of interest because sense 2 is attested chiefly in pidgin: see OED *sb.*⁴ and *v.*⁴]

1. *Obs.* Guile; deceit.

1812 J.H. VAUX *Mem.* (1819) II. 176 *Gammon,* flattery; deceit; pretence; plausible language; any assertion which is not strictly true, or professions believed to be insincere, as, I believe you're *gammoning*, or, that's all *gammon*, meaning, you are no doubt jesting with me, or, that's all a farce. To *gammon* a person, is to amuse him with false assurances, to praise, or flatter him, in order to obtain some particular end; to *gammon* a man *to* any act, is to persuade him to it by artful language, or pretence; to *gammon* a shop-keeper, &c., is to engage his attention to your discourse, while your accomplice is executing some preconcerted plan of depredation upon his property; a thief detected in a house which he has entered, *upon the sneak,* for the purpose of robbing it, will endeavour by some *gammoning* story to account for his intrusion, and to get off with a good grace; a man who is, ready at invention, and has always a flow of plausible language on these occasions, is said to be a *prime gammoner*; to *gammon lushy* or *queer*, is to pretend drunkenness, or sickness, for some private end. **1830** R. DAWSON *Present State Aust.* 179 They never like to be accused of gammon.

2. Chiefly *Austral. pidgin.* Nonsense; pretence; 'humbug'.

1837 *Colonist* (Sydney) 22 June 205/1 He replied, that he thought it was all gammon that master had told him about the Creation, for who was there who saw God create man! **1937** M. TERRY *Sand & Sun* 211 'I'll show them it's all gammon,' Ben sang out.

gammon, *v.* [f. prec.]

1. *trans. Obs.* To deceive, fool, or cheat (a person, etc.).

1812 [see GAMMON *n.* 1]. **1827** P. CUNNINGHAM *Two Yrs. in N.S.W.* II. 232 All these *innocent* rogues .. laugh and vaunt .. how they have gammoned you over. **1831** *Sydney Herald* 25 July 3/2 William Gammon for endeavouring to gammon his master. **1892** *Bulletin* (Sydney) 10 Sept. 19/2 Bob's gammoning the Chow .. he'll wake .. in a minute.

2. *intr.* To pretend; also *trans.* to feign (illness, etc.).

1812 [see GAMMON *n.* 1]. **1826** *Monitor* (Sydney) 2 June 20/1 Nothing but peace and fidelity marked the conduct of these good-natured, easily-pleased Tribes. We have often been delighted at the unreserved *belief of our word* .. taking what we said for truth and gospel until our foolish stockmen with their misplaced love of the ludicrous, related to them such arrant falsehoods, that now they will answer you in an interrogative tone '*gammon you?*' **1916** *Bulletin* (Sydney) 23 Nov. 24/1 They arranged that he .. should gammon sickness. **1947** W.E. HARNEY *Brimming Billabongs* 7 Let's gammon we are old men and talk big.

Hence **gammoner** *n.*, **gammoning** *ppl. a.* and *vbl. n.*

1812 [see GAMMON *n.* 1]. **1916** *Truth* (Sydney) 17 Dec. 5/1 He should be a good 'guffer', or, as it used to be customary to say, a good '**gammoner**'. **1846** C. ROWCROFT *Bushranger Van Diemen's Land* III. 4 We shall have time enough to read that **gammoning** paper afterwards.

gang. *Hist.* [Spec. use of *gang* party of workmen.] A detachment of convicts under the supervision of an overseer detailed to a particular branch of public labour: see e.g. quot. 1842. Also with distinguishing epithet, as **battery, carrying, chain, clearing, gaol, government, invalid, iron, ironed, loan, penal, probation, public, punishment, respite, road, town, working,** etc. (see under first element).

1789 J. HUNTER *Hist. Jrnl. Trans. Port Jackson* (1793) 370 The overseers, or the greatest part of any gang, should have reason to complain of the idleness of any one man belonging to that gang. **1842** *Tasmanian Jrnl. Nat. Sci.* I. 287 The dockyard gang is scarcely less laborious than the carrying, the men being frequently immersed in water to the neck while securing naval timber to the launches.

gang-gang /ˈgæŋ-gæŋ/. [a. Wiradhuri *gang gang* (onomatopoeic).] The predom. grey cockatoo *Callocephalon fimbriatum* of s.e. Aust., the mature male having a red head and crest. Also **gang-gang cockatoo.**

1833 C. STURT *Two Exped. Interior S.A.* I. p. xxxviii, Upon their branches, the satin bird, the gangan, and various kinds of pigeons were feeding. **1950** *Bulletin* (Sydney) 18 Jan. 12/3 The only time gang-gang cockatoos are really quiet is when they are dining.

gaol gang. *Hist.* Also **jail gang.** A punishment gang; one to which a convict is sentenced, esp. for an offence committed in a colony, to be confined in gaol when not engaged in hard labour in irons. See also GANG.

1796 D. COLLINS *Acct. Eng. Colony N.S.W.* (1802) II. 3 The most notorious .. were formed into a gaol gang. **1819** J.H. VAUX *Mem.* 105 My condition in the jail-gang was deplorable enough.

garage sale. [Used elsewhere but recorded earliest in Aust.] A sale of miscellaneous unwanted household goods, usu. for the benefit of a householder but sometimes to raise funds for a charitable cause.

1973 *Canberra Times* 25 Aug. 29/8 *Garage* sale, furniture, odds and ends... Must sell. **1983** *Open Road* Feb. 12/3 Bumper sticker on a car doing a slow crawl down a suburban street: 'Caution. This car stops for garage sales.'

garbage. Used *attrib.* in Special Comb. **garbage man,** one employed to collect and dispose of (domestic) refuse; **tin,** the receptacle in which (domestic) refuse is put for collection, a dustbin.

1944 *Austral. Week-End Bk.* 108 The mule-drawn lorry of the '**garbage man**' was drawn up at the rear of the camp. **1959** *Bulletin* (Sydney) 21 Jan. 18/2, I think the garbage-man has won, by-law or no by-law. **1907** *Ibid.* 5 Dec. 15/3 Saw a number of fat sheep eating out of **garbage-tins**.

garbo. [f. *garb(age* + -O.]

1. *Garbage man*, see GARBAGE.

1953 S.J. BAKER *Aust. Speaks* 105 *Garbo*, a garbage man. **1985** *Canberra Times* 8 Sept. 2/5 Garbos on the job: only a matter of time before one of them becomes a road-accident statistic.

2. Rubbish; garbage. Esp. *attrib.*

1970 *Kings Cross Whisper* (Sydney) lxxxiv. 8/3 He is alleged to have flogged the bottles to highly-placed employees of city and suburban council garbo rounds. **1978** R. WALLACE-CRABBE *Feral Palit* 24 Thought is rubbish, garbo, it has got no purpose.

Garden State. The State of Victoria. See also CABBAGE GARDEN.

1914 *Bulletin* (Sydney) 9 Apr. 22/2, I write from the Garden State. But the garden is a bit wilted just now .. and I start to find the *Argus* disappearing off the verandah in the arms of a northerly gale. **1982** *Bulletin* (Sydney) 21 Sept. 12/2 Victoria may be the Garden State .. but we all know what you put on gardens.

garfish. [Transf. use of Br. *garfish* the long-snouted fish *Belone vulgaris*.] Any fish in the fam. Hemirhamphidae, having a long snout. See also BEAKIE. Formerly also **guard-fish.**

1699 W. DAMPIER *New Voyage round World* (1703) III. 125 Here are also Skates .. and Garfish. **1786** *Hist. Narr. Discovery New Holland & N.S.W.* 10 The sea-fish seen here were .. guard-fish, bonatos, etc. **1984** *Canberra Times* 28 Apr. 13/4 We used to stand and pull in garfish with breadcrumb bait.

gash. [Spec. use of Br. slang *gash* something superfluous, extra.] A second helping of food.

1943 S.J. BAKER *Pop. Dict. Austral. Slang* (ed. 3) 34 *Gash*, a second helping of food; any surplus or residue (R.A.N. slang). **1972** W. WATKINS *Don't wait for Me* 32 He didn't have to beg the cook for left over scran—gash, the crew called it.

gastric brooding frog. Either of two species of aquatic frog of the genus *Rheobatrachus* occurring in e. Qld.: see quot. 1983.

1981 *Animal Behaviour* (London) Feb. 280 (*heading*) Oral birth of the young of the gastric brooding frog *Rheobatrachus silus*. **1983** M.J. TYLER *Gastric Brooding Frog* 1 The Gastric Brooding Frog, *Rheobatrachus silus*, of Queensland, Australia, is one of the most bizarre species of animal in the world. It is not much to look at, but it is unique in the Animal Kingdom in its habit of swallowing its fertilised eggs, converting its stomach to a uterus, and finally giving birth to fully formed young through its mouth.

gather, *v. trans.* To apprehend (a person) legally, to arrest.
1968 J. ALARD *He who shoots Last* 60 Da coppers might arrive any time now and gather us. 1975 *Bulletin* (Sydney) 26 Apr. 45/3 'The Limp was lucky he wasn't gathered because those Goulburn jacks are bad bits of furniture...' To be 'gathered' or 'lumbered' is to be arrested.

gay. *Obs.* Abbrev. of *gay and hearty*, rhyming slang for 'party'.
1965 *Kings Cross Whisper* (Sydney) May 7/1 The mere mention of.. gay, booze-up, turn, rort, do, will have his ears pricked like fish-hooks. 1968 *Swag* (Sydney) ii. 38 The most important point is whether or not the lounge will accommodate a gay. In other words, can 200 people, 200 drinking, singing, fighting.. dancing, chundering people fit into the lounge?

gay house. *Obs.* [f. *gay, a.* living by prostitution: see OED 2 b.] A brothel.
1903 *Truth* (Sydney) 20 Dec. 4/8 Most serious allegations have been made.. such as the bribery of harlots in brothels... £40 worth of champagne having.. found its way into a gay house. 1908 *Truth* (Sydney) 3 May 1/4 It was alleged that he had been taken down in a gay house for $22 worth.

gazob /gəˈzɒb/. *Obs.* [Prob. f. U.S. slang *gazabo* fellow, 'guy', itself prob. a. Sp. *gazapo* sly fellow.] A fool; a bumbler.
1906 E. DYSON *Fact'ry 'Ands* 162, I thought barrer-pushin' was er game fer gazobs? 1966 S.J. BAKER *Austral. Lang.* (ed. 2) 135 Fools of one kind or another.. *gazob, gimp, gup,* [etc.].

g'day, var. GOOD DAY.

geebung /ˈdʒibʌŋ/. Also formerly **geebong, jibbong**. [a. Dharuk *jibuŋ.*]
1. The fruit of any of several shrubs or small trees of the genus *Persoonia* (fam. Proteaceae), predom. of s.w. W.A. and s.e. Aust., having an edible fleshy layer around the stone; the plant itself. Also *attrib.*
c 1790 W. DAWES *Grammatical Forms Lang. N.S.W.,* Mā n mangun tyíung, we will gather tyibungs. 1826 J. ATKINSON *Acct. Agric. & Grazing N.S.W.* 19 There are no indigenous fruits worth mentioning: the native cherry, five corners, jibbong, and others, are mere tasteless berries. 1845 *Colonial Lit. Jrnl.* 13 Feb. 106/2 Just then a gay butterfly, large as his hand! On her beautiful wings sail'd along, Her colours set off by the glistening sand, And she staid on a neighbouring geebong. 1918 *Bulletin* (Sydney) 1 Aug. (Red Page), Fifty or sixty years ago the ground near Sydney in the vicinity of Centennial Park, Randwick and Botany was covered with.. geebung bushes.
2. *transf.* [First used by D.H. Deniehy (1828–1865), writer: see quot. 1859.] A derogatory term, app. applied first to an Australian-born person whose interests are primarily material; then (cf. 'Philistine') to one who is uncultured, unsophisticated. Also *attrib.*
1859 *Southern Cross* (Sydney) 12 Nov. 12/3 Born and bred—(the *geebung* is always a native)—where pecuniary success is with the majority, the only test of worth, intelligence, and respectability—the object of all honour and the aim of life, the Geebung's first business is to make money. 1892 *Truth* (Sydney) 26 June 4/4 The mills owned by the geebung gods of the Pastoralists Union.

geek, *n.* [f. Br. dial. *geek, v.* to peep, peer, spy; to look at intently: see EDD.] A look, usu. in the phr. **to have a geek at**. Also as *v. intr.*
1919 W.H. DOWNING *Digger Dialects* 25 *Geek* (vb. or n.), look. 1954 T.A.G. HUNGERFORD *Sowers of Wind* 190 There's a circus down by the dance-hall, a Jap show... What about having a geek at that?

gee-man. [f. *gee, v.* to encourage (the public) to patronize side-shows at a fair.] One who encourages the public to patronize side-shows at a fair; AMPSTER.
1941 K. TENNANT *Battlers* 141 In the show world a 'geeman'.. is the man who goes out in the crowd and touts for custom with such inspiring cries as: 'Come along now. Come and have your fortune told.' 1966 S.J. BAKER *Austral. Lang.* (ed. 2) 143 A *geeman* or *amster*.. is a decoy who works with a sideshow operator to induce the public to spend its money.

gemfish. [See quot. 1974.] The marine fish *Rexea solandri*, having an elongated body and occurring in coastal waters of s. Aust., and N.Z.; HAKE.
1974 *Bulletin* (Sydney) 12 Oct. 23/2 A N.S.W. fish called 'hake' is felt to suffer by public confusion with 'flake' and is to be renamed 'gemfish'. 1979 GOODE & WILLSON *Orig. Austral. & N.Z. Fish Cookbk.* 74 Bought whole or in fillets, gemfish is medium oily and is best if grilled, baked, fried in batter or poached.

general store. [Used elsewhere but recorded earliest in Aust.: see OED(S *general, a.* 7 b.] A shop stocking a wide range of miscellaneous goods, usu. including clothing, foodstuffs, hardware, etc. See also STORE 2.
1827 *Tasmanian* (Hobart) 4 Oct. 3 G.W. Robson.. has.. opened a General Store, to which he invites the attention of the Public, where all kinds of Groceries will be sold on the most reasonable terms. 1978 K. GILBERT *People are Legends* 11, I can't get me welfare cheque no more Nor me 'dowment, the man at the general store Gits me cheque 'n me 'dowment now.
Hence **general storekeeper** *n.*
1840 *Port Phillip Gaz.* 1 Aug. 1 *M. Cashmore*.. will in a few days, commence business as a General Storekeeper in Elizabeth-street.

general useful, generally useful: see USEFUL.

gentle Annie.
1. [Common in N.Z. from the 1870s.] A jocular name for a steep incline.
1913 W.K. HARRIS *Outback in Aust.* 108 Driving across creeks with 'Gentle Annies' (the coach-drivers and 'bullocky's' term for a stiff pull up a sandy ridge) on the other side is very trying to the nerves of elderly lady passengers. 1930 BILLIS & KENYON *Pastures New* 62 He did not tackle McKillop's Omeo track, with its 'Big Pinches' and 'Gentle Annies', but went round to Yass, where he learnt there were 20,000 cattle ahead of him.
2. See quot.
1965 *Coast to Coast 1963–64* 154 It was.. raining, that soft rain mother used to call Gentle Annie.

gentleman convict. *Hist.* A convict with either a liberal education or some training requiring literacy (acquired prior to transportation), and so fitted for employment in a clerical or professional capacity. See EDUCATED.
1830 T.P. MACQUEEN *Thoughts Present Condition of Country* 33 That most useless class, generally designated as *gentleman convicts*, persons guilty of minor cases of forgery, of breaches of trust as merchant's clerks, etc. 1851 J. HENDERSON *Excursions & Adventures N.S.W.* 111 Port Macquarie, ever since it ceased to be exclusively a penal settlement, has been used as a *depôt* for what are called 'specials'; that is, special, or *gentlemen*-convicts, and for invalids.

George Street. *Obs.* Also **George-street**. [The name of a major street in central Sydney.] Used *attrib.* in various Comb. to indicate an uninformedly urban perception (of rural matters).
1907 *Bulletin* (Sydney) 11 Apr. 14/3 It places us in the same niche as the George-street nomad, to whom a tucker-

bag would be as much a superfluity as a conscience would be to a sweater. **1911** *Ibid.* 19 Jan. 13/4, I . . suggested that the sufferer should disguise himself as a bushman... Reft of his bowler hat, umbrella, boiled shirt, patent leather boots and other accessories, the George-street wattle-hunter looked the part fairly well.

Georgina gidgee: see GIDGEE *n.*[2] 2.

Geraldton doctor: see DOCTOR *n.*[3]

Geraldton wax. [f. the name of a town on the w. coast of W.A.] The shrub of s.w. W.A. *Chamelaucium uncinatum* (fam. Myrtaceae), occurring on coastal land between Geraldton and Perth, and widely cultivated as an ornamental (see quot. 1956). Also *attrib.*, esp. as **Geraldton wax plant**.
1920 *Jrnl. & Proc. R. Soc. W.A.* VI. 42 Geraldton Wax-plant, Ornamental shrub. **1956** F.B. VICKERS *First Place to Stranger* 152 In the centre of it grew a Geraldton wax tree. The Geraldton wax is a native that grows round the Geraldton district some three hundred miles north of Perth; and in its native state is no more than a straggly shrub, and is called wax because of its tiny, flowers—the petals of which seem to be made of wax.

geri /'dʒɛri/. Also **gerri**. [Abbrev. of *geriatric.*] An elderly person.
1977 *Sydney Morning Herald* 5 Apr. 7/1 Geris (short for geriatrics) is applied by the young to anyone over 40, and has replaced 'oldies'. **1984** *Sydney Morning Herald* 3 May 14/3 Enrol now in training schemes for the care of our growing legion of gerris.

German brick. See quots.
1915 *Bulletin* (Sydney) 2 Sept. 26/4 At Niagara (W.A.) there is a township built of 'German bricks', *i.e.* clayey loam which is first puddled then dumped into boxes (18 in. x 9 in. x 9 in.), and left in the sun to dry. **1962** O. PRYOR *Aust.'s Little Cornwall* 66 The best walls were built of 'German bricks' made by placing wet earth lime-stone rubble and straw or long grass in moulds nine inches by fifteen and allowing them to dry.

German wagon. Any of a range of open, all-purpose, (usu. horse-drawn) wagons.
1934 'S. RUDD' *Green Grey Homestead* 67 The Lukins, and Miskins, and Abrahams .. for years have been sending their kids per horse, and per milk-cart and German waggon to school at the township. **1981** P. CUFFLEY *Buggies & Horse-Drawn Vehicles* 102 It seems the name German waggon was applied to a range of designs some bearing little resemblance to the classic style.

gerri, var. GERI.

gerrund, gerun, var. JERRAN.

get, *n.* [f. (orig. U.S.) *to get* to be off, to 'clear out'.] A hasty departure, esp. in the phr. **to do a get**.
1898 *Bulletin* (Sydney) 28 May 31/2 Their inquisitiveness .. compelled Jim to kill his stud-sluts and growing stock, and do a timely 'get'. **1963** A. UPFIELD *Madman's Bend* 55 Musta done a get after bashing up his wife.

get, *v. trans.* With **up**.
1. To prepare (wool) for sale. Also as *vbl. n.*
1835 *True Colonist* (Hobart) 16 Oct. 1/2 He is in possession of *valuable information*, connected with '*getting up the wool*', which he will engage to increase its value. **1866** Tas. Non-State Rec. 103/1, This Season of the year when the getting up of the wool .. is the Principal part of Sheep farming.
2. *intr.* To be successful in an endeavour, orig. of a racehorse. Also *trans.* in the phr. **to get** (someone) **up**, to engineer (someone's) success (see quot. 1986).
1904 H. FLETCHER *Dads Wayback* 100 When ther public fancies yer nag's chance, an' puts ther beans on, ther books gives yer ther office, an' that prad don't quite get up that time; though he runs close. **1986** *Sydney Morning Herald* 14 June 33/3 Virtually the last words Barrie said to me were, 'Well, we've got to get Brereton up.'
3. In the interrogative phr. **(are you) getting any?**, 'is your sex-life satisfactory?'
1941 S.J. BAKER *Pop. Dict. Austral. Slang* 124 The jocular greeting between man and man, *gettin' any?* . . draws such set replies as, *climbing trees to get away from it! got to swim under water to dodge it!* and *so busy I've had to put a man on!* **1984** *Nat. Times* (Sydney) 6 July 5/1 The Prime Minister's informal contact runs to occasional en-route card games lasting for hours with several press favorites—Hawke plays fiercely to win—and social banter of the 'are yer gettin' any' kind.

get up. The preparation and presentation of wool for sale.
1899 G. JEFFREY *Princ. Australasian Woolclassing* 75 The small Farmer who keeps his few hundred sheep, is in no way exempt from the necessity of paying proper attention to the 'get up' of his wool. **1930** BILLIS & KENYON *Pastures New* 191 Asked to advise as to the 'get up' of certain Victorian clips.

'Ghan /gæn/. Also **Ghan**.
1. Shortened form of AFGHAN. Also *attrib.*
1911 *Bulletin* (Sydney) 10 Aug. 14/2 Menzies (W.A.) .. confessed shamefacedly to two Jap laundries and numerous 'Ghan camel-drivers. **1957** *Austral. Lett.* (Adelaide) Nov. 21 Mohammed Hassen was another Ghan that bred good camels.
2. A nickname for a train running on the Central Australian Railway, originally between Port Augusta and Oodnadatta.
1933 F.E. BAUME *Tragedy Track* 21 This train, once known as the Ghan, because it was largely patronised by Afghans going to the then railhead of Oodnadatta, to-day is making history. **1984** *Austral.* (Sydney) 16 Jan. 1/3 The Ghan, which operates between Adelaide and Alice Springs, has been cancelled until further notice.

ghilgai, var. GILGAI.

ghittoe /'gɪtoʊ, 'dʒɪtoʊ/. Also variously, as **jhitu, jidu, jitto.** [a. Dyirbal and Warrgamay *jidu.*] Either of the two rainforest tree species of the genus *Halfordia* (fam. Rutaceae) of N.S.W., Qld., New Guinea, and New Caledonia, yielding a tough and flexible timber easily burnt when green; the wood of these trees. See also *kerosene wood* KEROSENE 2.
1909 F.M. BAILEY *Comprehensive Catal. Qld. Plants* (ed. 2) 81 Halfordia scleroxyla... Kerosene-tree, 'Ghittoe' of Herberton natives. **1927** *Bulletin* (Sydney) 17 Mar. 24/2 Contract scrubfallers usually stipulate that all jhitu may be left standing. **1945** J. DEVANNY *Bird of Paradise* 24 The wood was that remarkable product known variously among bushmen as jitter, jitto and ghito. So saturated with resin is it that when splinters were laid upon the wet mud and a match put to them they flamed up instantly. **1984** B. DIXON *Searching for Aboriginal Lang.* 86 A special long stick called *gugulu* . . was made from the hard Jidu tree (*Halfordia scleroxyla*) carefully shaped and polished smooth.

ghost. See quot. 1967.
1967 *Kings Cross Whisper* (Sydney) xxxv. 6/1 *Ghost*, a creditor. One who haunts for repayment. Usually publicans and bookies. **1968** J. ALARD *He who shoots Last* 87 Ruffy asked: 'Why d'ya calls people wot ya owes money ta ghosts, Ragged?' 'Because I always get such a nasty fright when one appears in view.'

ghost gum. The tree of n. Aust. *Eucalyptus papuana* (fam. Myrtaceae), the bark of which is smooth and white. See also *desert gum* DESERT, WHITEWASH GUM.

1935 H.H. FINLAYSON *Red Centre* 32 The most beautiful picture of the Central vegetation .. is of the dainty ghost gums with chalk-white stems. **1979** J. JOST *Kangaroo Court* 29 An area shaded by the thin, olive-grey leaves of an unusually large white-trunked ghost gum.

giant, *a.* Used as a distinguishing epithet in the names of flora and fauna: **giant earthworm,** any of several long earthworms, esp. *Megascolides australis* of Gippsland, Vic.; **lily,** see GIGANTIC LILY; **perch,** the n. Austral. fish *Lates calcarifer* (see BARRAMUNDI a.); **stinging tree,** the large rainforest tree *Dendrocnide excelsa* (fam. Urticaceae) of N.S.W. and Qld., bearing large, heart-shaped leaves covered with virulent stinging hairs; formerly **nettle (tree).**

1886 F. COWAN *Aust.* 18 The **Giant Earthworm**: six feet long: the Anaconda of the Annelids. **1896** F.G. AFLALO *Sketch Nat. Hist. Aust.* 214 The .. **Giant Perch** (*Oligorus gigas*) of the Fitzroy .. is one of the finest of .. perches. **1836** [**giant stinging tree**] J. BACKHOUSE *Narr. Visit Austral. Colonies* (1843) 363 In the forests, the Giant Nettle, *Urtica gigas,* forms a large tree. **1886** F. COWAN *Aust.* 16 The Giant Nettle-tree: a hive of bees in every leaf. **1909** *Emu* VIII. 252 Got badly stung on the face by the giant or large-leaved stinging-tree. **1938** C.T. WHITE *Princ. Bot. Qld. Farmers* 157 The Giant Stinging Tree (*Laportea gigas*) attains the dimensions of a very large tree.

gibber /'gɪbə/. Formerly also **gibba.** [a. Dharuk *giba.* See also KIPPER *n.*[1]]

1. A stone; a rock or mass of stone; a boulder. In early use applied chiefly to a large outcrop of rock or boulders (see quots. 1833, 1847, 1850 and GIBBER-GUNYAH); now used spec. for *gibber-stone,* and colloq. for a stone of any size. Also *attrib.*

1790 D. SOUTHWELL Corresp. & Papers, *Kee-bah,* a stone. **1833** *Currency Lad* (Sydney) 13 Apr. 2 As the hour appointed for the combat approached, all the 'lads' from the 'gibbers [sc. The Rocks, a district of Sydney] and Cockle-bay' repaired to a spot in the latter place where the mill was to '*come off'*. **1847** A. HARRIS *Settlers & Convicts* (1953) 87 Under the 'gibbers' (overhanging rocks) of the river. **1850** *Australasian Sporting Mag.* 92 The great velocity and ease with which these creatures [*sc.* rock wallabies] ascend or descend the huge gibbas, is truly astonishing. **1973** A. BURNETT *Wilful Murder in Outback* 41 We reached the gibber lands at the dog proof fence.

2. Special Comb. **gibber country, plain,** an arid stony area of low relief in which the stones sometimes form a surface layer; **stone,** a rounded, weather-worn stone, usu. siliceous, of arid, inland Australia.

1894 *Argus* (Melbourne) 1 Sept. 4/2 Our track led across what is called the **gibber country. 1896** B. SPENCER *Rep. Horn Sci. Exped. Central Aust.* I. 12 Nothing could be more desolate than a **gibber plain** when everything is bare and dry, and the outline of the distant horizon is indistinct with the waves of heated air. **1914** *Emu* XIV. 99 The table-land country .. is covered with loose **gibber stones.**

gibber-gunyah /gɪbə-'gʌnjə/. [f. GIBBER + GUNYAH.] A shallow cave used as a dwelling or for shelter; *rock shelter,* see ROCK *n.* 3.

1836 *Tegg's Monthly Mag.* (Sydney) I. 136, I found the shepherd .. safely ensconced from the scorching heat of the sun under the shade of a commodious *gibba gunya.* **1947** *Bulletin* (Sydney) 11 June 28/3, I came on a gibber-gunyah at the foot of Dark Gully.

gidday, var. GOOD DAY.

gidgee /'gɪdʒi/, *n.*[1] Chiefly W.A. Also **gidgie,** etc. [a. Nyungar *giji.*] An Aboriginal spear. Also as *v. trans.* (see quots. 1847 and 1979).

1845 J. BRADY *Descr. Vocab. Native Lang. W.A.* 21 *Gidji,* a spear. **1847** E.W. LANDOR *Bushman* 191 He *gidgied* Womera through the back, because Womera had *gidgied* Domera through the belly. **1960** H.H. WILSON *Where Wind's Feet Shine* 31 Joe knew all about fish, and could throw a gidgie quicker'n you could see! **1979** H. WILSON *Skedule* 192 Mr Brent gidgied a section of bakewell tart which had bounced off his plate. **1983** *West. Austral.* (Perth) 17 Dec. 3/4 A boy was rushed to hospital yesterday afternoon with the head of a three-pronged spear embedded in his stomach. .. He accidentally fell on a 'gidgee'.

gidgee /'gɪdʒi/, *n.*[2] Formerly also **gidgea, gidyea,** etc. [a. Nyungar (and related languages) *giji.*]

1. Any of several trees of the genus *Acacia* (fam. Mimosaceae) of drier inland Aust., esp *A. cambagei,* the foliage of which at times emits an odour often considered disagreeable; the wood of these trees. Also *attrib.*

1862 W. LANDSBOROUGH *Jrnl. Exped. from Carpentaria* 73 Western wood acacia .. is called gidya in some places of Australia. **1892** *Bulletin* (Sydney) 28 May 18/2 The gidya ripped your moleskins, and the mulga rent your shirt. **1898** *Ibid.* 8 Jan. 14/1 Gidgea tea .. gives you the 'barcoo' for a week after. **1979** D.R. STUART *Crank back on Roller* 158 No mulga, no gidgee .. not a bloody thing for a camel.

2. With distinguishing epithet, as **Georgina gidgee,** the small tree *A. georginae* of e. N.T. and the Georgina R. basin in n.w. Qld., sometimes poisonous to stock.

1900 *Proc. Linnean Soc. N.S.W.* XXV. 596 There is an Acacia with a strong smell .. on the Georgina River, and evidently to distinguish it from the original Gidgea (or Gidgee as it is often spelt) of Bourke to Charleville this tree is called Georgina Gidgee (*Acacia georginae*). **1975** *Bulletin* (Sydney) 18 Jan. 48/3 Several thousand cattle die every year in the Northern Territory and north-west Queensland after eating a shrub called Georgina gidyea, or gidgee.

gig, *v.* [Br. dial. *gig* to laugh in a suppressed manner, to laugh at, taunt: see OED *v.*[4]]

a. *trans.* To mock or make fun of (a person); to stare mockingly at (a person). Also *intr.* and as *vbl. n.*

1891 *Truth* (Sydney) 15 Mar. 2/1 His name was written as co-respondent, and the judge rebuked him .. and the people gigged him. **1916** *Ibid.* 5 Mar. 12/7 It was deemed advisable to have her appear in court in woman's dress, so as to avoid having her 'gigged at' by the police and pressmen. **1963** J. POLLARD *Austral. Surfrider* 31 They don't usually try to catch waves as big as the best boy board riders, and sometimes receive a little 'gigging' from the boys.

b. *intr.* To stare.

1967 K. TENNANT *Tell Morning This* 393 'Let's have some light on it,' his host muttered. 'Can't waste our whole bloody life gigging out windows.'

gig, *n.*[1] [f. prec.]

a. An inquisitive look.

1924 C.J. DENNIS *Rose of Spadgers* 65 'Is this 'ere coot,' I arsts, 'well knowed to you?' The parson takes another gig. 'Why yes.' **1978** C. GREEN *Sun is Up* 37 We drove out through the back gate and down the road to 'get a gig at it'.

b. [Cf. FIZGIG.] One who pries; a busybody.

1953 K. TENNANT *Joyful Condemned* 70 She hadn't asked him to bring any women poking about. This was her flat until Julie came out of gaol. 'Just gigs,' Rene commented silently. 'Slumming.' **1975** *Bulletin* (Sydney) 26 Apr. 46/2 There were Mortons nearby (Morton Bay Figs; gigs, meaning busybodies).

gig, $n.^2$ [Br. dial. *gig* a fool, a singular character: see EDD $sb.^4$ and OED $sb.^1$ 5.] A fool, a figure of fun.

1943 J. DEVINE *Rats of Tobruk* 31 We had a saying that any one who did anything so silly as to get caught by a booby trap was a 'gig'. 1984 W.W. AMMON et al. *Working Lives* 83 They'll laugh and talk about it till everybody knows what a hopeless gig I am.

gigantic lily. The plant *Doryanthes excelsa* (fam. Agavaceae) of N.S.W. coastal forests and heathlands, bearing a large red flowerhead on a scape 2 to 4 m. tall; the related *D. palmeri* of n. N.S.W. and s. Qld., bearing red-brown flowers on an elongated panicle. Also **giant lily**.

1818 *N.S.W. Pocket Almanack* 49 The Dorianthus, or Gigantic Lily .. begins to flower about the latter end of September .. and continues .. 120 days from the first bursting of the bud. 1942 C. BARRETT *Austral. Wild Flower Bk.* 64 Giant lilies are related to the aloes, and the big, bright-green leaves, each a mass of fibre, are much like those of some aloes.

giggle.

1. Used *attrib.* in Special Comb. **giggle house**, a psychiatric hospital; **juice**, intoxicating liquor.

1919 W.H. DOWNING *Digger Dialects* 26 **Giggle-house**, lunatic asylum. 1940 *Action Front: Jrnl. 2/2 Field Regiment* Oct. Ode to Beer .. o **giggle juice** divine!

2. Used *attrib.* in Comb. with nouns denoting items of (often ill-fitting) clothing issued as fatigue dress to personnel of the Australian army during the war of 1939–45: **giggle frock, hat, pants, suit**. Cf. GLAMOUR.

1940 *Action Front: Jrnl. 2/2 Field Regiment* 1 Apr. 4 That extra-large Giggle hat. 1940 *Men may Smoke* (Sydney) Dec. 17 Having just struggled into my giggle pants. 1941 *Argus* (Melbourne) 15 Nov. (Suppl.) 1/3 Throughout Australia one of the best Australian slang words of the war has now become 'official'—the 'gigglesuit'. 1943 *Georges Gaz.* (Melbourne) Nov. 6 The giggle frock which our Lieutenant had graciously lent me.

gilgai /'gɪlgaɪ/. Also **ghilgai, gilgie**. [a. Wiradhuri and Kamilaroi *gilgaay*.] **a.** Terrain of low relief on a plain of heavy clay soil, characterized by the presence of hollows, rims, and mounds, as formed by alternating periods of expansion during wet weather and contraction (with deep cracking) during hot dry weather; DEBIL DEBIL 2; DEVIL DEVIL 2. **b.** A hole or hollow in such terrain; *melon hole*, see MELON 1; also **gilgai hole**. See also BAY OF BISCAY, CRABHOLE, *dead men's graves* DEAD 1.

1867 F.J. BYERLEY *Narr. Overland Exped. Northern Qld.* 44 The party camped on a small tea-tree 'Gilgai', or shallow water-pan. 1881 W.E. ABBOTT *Notes Journey on Darling* 12 At the blackfellows' tanks the clay excavated is still seen beside the waterholes, while in the gilgies there is no appearance of any embankment, the ground all round being perfectly level. 1942 F. CLUNE *Last of Austral. Explorers* 101 Gough Senior went for water to some gilgie holes, farther down the creek. 1949 H.G. LAMOND *White Ears* 56 Every ghilgai was full; every creek was running.

gilgaied, *a.* Of soils: characterized by the presence of gilgai holes.

1968 B. WILSON *Pasture Improvement Aust.* 248 The 'brigalow' is a term given to various types of forest .. which are developed mainly on deep gilgaied clay soils. 1976 *Ecos* vii. 24/3 Other soils, like the undulating 'gilgaied' clays, are unattractive to the engineer and agriculturalist alike.

gilgie /'dʒɪlgi/. *W.A.* Also **jilgie**. [a. Nyungar *jilgi*.] Either of the two small fresh-water crayfish of s.w. W.A. *Cherax crassimanus* and *C. quinquecarinatus*.

1937 A.R. GRANT *Memories of Parliament* 29 I'm not sure how to spell 'gilgies', but they are a small fresh water crayfish, caught in the same way as crabs. 1938 D. BATES *Passing of Aborigines* 70 The place where once she had gathered *jilgies* and vegetable food with the women.

gillar, var. GALAH.

gill bird. WATTLE BIRD.

1854 *Illustr. Sydney News* 28 Feb. 162/1 The gill or wattle bird is pleasing in its plumage. .. Under each eye descends a bright red wattle. 1965 *Austral. Encycl.* IV. 294 Gill-birds, a term that used to be freely applied, mainly in New South Wales, to the large honeyeaters known as wattle-birds. .. Both names derive from the birds' possession of fleshy wattles (or gills) at the corners of the beak.

gills, *pl. Obs.* [f. Br. slang *gill* a chap or cove, app. obs. by mid-19th cent.: see OED $sb.^1$] In the collocation **his gills**, a jocular designation for a (self-important) person, 'his nibs'.

1899 J. BRADSHAW *Quirindi Bank Robbery* 37 Riley came round to tell me to go to the closet, as his gills would be going to cover up his horse in a few minutes. 1914 E. DYSON *Spats' Fact'ry* 79 Up comes his gills, the junior partner, Duff.

gimlet. [Fig. use of *gimlet* boring tool: see quot. 1950.]

a. The slender tree of s.w. W.A. *Eucalyptus salubris* (fam. Myrtaceae), the trunk of which is characteristically twisted, shiny, and bronze-coloured. Also *attrib.*

1891 E.H. HALLACK *W.A. & Yilgarn Goldfields* 16 The gimlet gum, the upper branches of which partake of the gimlet twist, with its red, smooth bark throwing off when bent streamers which wave in the wind. 1904 *Emu* III. 218 The .. gimlet gums (E. salubris) .. held sway. 1921 W.H. PHIPPS *Bush Yarns* 87 Flimsy buildings clumsily constructed of hessian cloth and gimlet-wood saplings. 1950 C.E. GOODE *Yarns of Yilgarn* 51 There was a thicket of red gimlets (gum trees which get their name from their twisted trunks).

b. With distinguishing epithet, as **silver-topped gimlet**, the smaller *E. campaspe* of s.w. W.A. which also has a twisted or fluted trunk.

1953 *New Settler in W.A.* (Perth) Jan. 9 There are two distinct trees called gimlets, the common gimlet (Eucalyptus salubris) and the silver-topped gimlet (E. campaspe). 1967 B.Y. MAIN *Between Wodjil & Tor* 1 A mopoke calling .. from its roost on a dead branch in a silver-topped gimlet.

gimme. [Transf. use of *gimme* acquisitiveness, greed: see OEDS.] An acquisitive woman.

1930 L.W. LOWER *Here's Luck* (1955) 61 She kissed me on the ear. She was a gimme, but twenty years of life fell from me. 1966 G. BARRY *Bed & Bored* 122 He doesn't want to leave his knock-kneed, buck-toothed, brass-eyed gimme for a while!

gin /dʒɪn/. Formerly also **din, jin**. [a. Dharuk *diyin*.]

1. An Aboriginal woman or wife. Also *attrib.*

1790 R. CLARK Jrnl. 15 Feb. 133, I heard the crying of children close to me I asked them for to go and bring me there (Dins) which is there [*sic*] woman. 1826 R. DAWSON *Private & Confidential* 11, I observed the women (married women are called 'Jins'). 1975 R. THROSSELL *Wild Weeds & Wind Flowers* 221 Even after a small electric oven was installed, she still liked to do her 'gin cooking' over the open fire in the sitting room.

2. *transf.*

1833 W.H. BRETON *Excursions* 254 The flying gin (gin is the native word for woman or female) is a boomah, and will leave behind every description of dog. 1954 H.G.

LAMOND *Manx Star* 74 'An' he done th' lot on wine, women an' song?' 'On gins, gee-gees and grog,' Wilson corrected.

3. a. Used *attrib.* to designate a white man who sexually exploits an Aboriginal woman, or the activity of so doing.

1902 *Bulletin* (Sydney) 27 Dec. 15/1 Camp-robberies .. were almost always due to nigs. being encouraged around camps by 'gin-mashers'. **1980** P. PEPPER *You are what you make Yourself* 40 Grandfather told us the white men had 'gin-hunts'—come down on their horses to get the women in the camps.

b. gin shepherd, gin shepherder: see main entry.

4. In special collocations: **gin's piss,** beer deemed to be of inferior quality; **gin's sister,** see quot.

1972 J. O'GRADY *It's your Shout, Mate!* 43 Yeah, but you come from England. That's **gin's piss** country. Any kind o' beer'd be better than that English muck. **1878** R.B. SMYTH *Aborigines of Vic.* I. 64 *Djeet-gun* is the superb warbler; the *eering* the emu wren; the former is called the **'gins' sister',** the latter the 'blackfellows' brother'.

gina-gina /'dʒɪnə-dʒɪnə/. *Austral. pidgin.* Chiefly W.A. Also **jinna-jinna.** [a. Mantjiltjara dial. of Western Desert *jina jina.*] A kind of dress worn by an Aboriginal woman: see quot. 1955.

1927 *Bulletin* (Sydney) 7 Dec. 11/4 A gina-gina .. almost black with dust and grease, showed her bony legs and feet. **1955** F.B. VICKERS *Mirage* (1958) 187 The jinna-jinna dress was a shapeless scarlet colored bag with holes in it for neck and arms. It had no trimmings, no finish, except the turned-in hems.

ging. [Prob. onomatopoeic.] A catapult.

1903 *Bulletin* (Sydney) 17 Dec. 35/1 He had in his pocket a 'ging' with a shop-made wire prong, a 'ging' of marvellous power and deadly accuracy. **1980** W.H. O'ROURKE *My Way* 286 In my boyhood days, every boy had a 'shanghai', or 'ging', as it was more generally known, and no bird was safe.

ginger, *n.* [Abbrev. of *ginger ale*, rhyming slang for 'tail'.] In the phr. **on one's ginger,** close behind, 'on one's tail'. Also *fig.*

1967 *Kings Cross Whisper* (Sydney) xxxv. 6/1 *Ginger ale*, bail. Tail. Shortened to ginger when meant tail. 'I got the coppers on my ginger.' **1971** F. HARDY *Outcasts of Foolgarah* 76 The legal-eagles are on our ginger.

ginger, *v.* [Prob. back-formation f. *gingerly* with extreme caution, with stealth.] *trans.* Esp. of a prostitute: to steal from (a man's person or clothing). Also as *n.*

1945 S.J. BAKER *Austral. Lang.* 139 A prostitute who robs a man by taking money from his clothes is known as a *gingerer... To ginger* and *gingering* are associated terms. **1978** H.C. BAKER *I was Listening* 18 The two conspirators 'gingered' his unoccupied trousers for their contents.

Hence **gingered** *ppl. a.*, stolen by gingering.

1978 H.C. BAKER *I was Listening* 18 In Nug's pocket was found the gingered eight pounds.

ginger beer.

1. *Obs.* A euphemism for an alcoholic drink.

1843 *Satirist & Sporting Chron.* (Sydney) 25 Mar. 3/2 If old Smith .. does not leave off visiting Taylor's Public House, and drinking *ginger beer*, we must tip it home to him in character next week. **1898** *Bulletin* (Sydney) 19 Mar. 14/2 An old whaler .. had the usual ('gingerbeer', I suppose), and straightway became a 'corpse'.

2. [Orig. Br. nautical slang.] Rhyming slang for 'engineer', spec. a member of the Royal Australian Engineers.

1941 S.J. BAKER *Pop. Dict. Austral. Slang* 31 *Gingerbeers*, the Aust. Engineer Corps. **1982** J.J. COE *Desperate Praise* 86 This type of job normally fell to the Engineers, but our officer .. volunteered us to give the 'ginger beers' a hand.

gink. [Prob. f. Br. dial. *geek* to peep, spy, stare about: see EDD.] A scrutinizing look.

1945 R.S. CLOSE *Love me Sailor* 227, I kept staring so that he could get a gink at me wide awake. **1962** S. GORE *Down Golden Mile* 205 Come up to my camp on the way home in the morning and have a gink at it then.

gin shepherd.

1. A white man who cohabits with an Aboriginal woman. Also **gin shepherder.**

1929 K.S. PRICHARD *Coonardoo* (1961) 30 Sam Gears had been known as 'a gin shepherder' for some time and a family of half-castes swarmed about his verandahs. **1958** W.E. HARNEY *Content to Lie* 35 'Twas here, on one cold night I witnessed my mate going for his life down a lignum 'pad', with an irate 'gin shepherd' (a white man who lives with a native woman) on his heels.

2. One who seeks to prevent the sexual exploitation of Aboriginal women by white men.

1946 [see GIN 3 a.]. **1954** T. RONAN *Vision Splendid* 111 The reason why most of them left was that 'the Missus was too much of a gin shepherd'.

Hence **gin shepherding** *vbl. n.*

1945 S.J. BAKER *Austral. Lang.* 197 *Gin-shepherding* and *going on a gin spree*, taking to the bush in search of an aboriginal woman.

give, *v.*

1. [See OED *give, v.* 59 f.] In the phr. **to give in,** to give (something) in addition; to 'throw in'.

1849 *Belfast Gaz.* (Port Phillip) 1 June 3/1 Those possessed of runs capable of running more than 100,000 sheep ought to have sold a few head, and 'given in' the remainder of their runs to those who wanted them badly. **1939** J.G. PATTISON *'Battler's' Tales Early Rockhampton* 123, I put in an offer of 17s. 6d. per head for all branded stock, calves to be given in. By this offer I secured a clean run at the clean skin cattle.

2. [Br. dial.: see EDD *best, a.* 3 and OED *give, v.* 39.] In the phr. **to give** (someone, something) **best,** to acknowledge defeat by (a person, set of circumstances, etc.).

1888 'R. BOLDREWOOD' *Robbery under Arms* I. 94, I could hardly stand for laughing, till the calf gave him best and walked. **1978** H.C. BAKER *I was Listening* 139 Suddenly, Kevan threw up his hands. 'I give you best!' .. a schoolboy expression used in an adult fight.

3. [Fig. use of *to give away* to give as a present: see OEDS *give, v.* 54 h.] In the phr. **to give** (something) **away,** to abandon (an activity, etc.); to 'give up'.

1948 *Khaki Bush & Bigotry* (1968) 98 *Andy:* How's the garden going, Ot? *Ot:* Give it away. **1981** P. BARTON *Bastards I have Known* 69 It just wouldn't work... The lunch gong sounded and everyone gave it away.

gladdy. Shortened form of 'Gladiolus', a plant bearing spikes of colourful flowers. Also *attrib.*

1947 M. MORRIS *Township* 193 A proper garden with old-fashioned flowers like stocks and 'snaps' and in the summer 'gladdies' with tall, flowering, scarlet spikes. **1969** *Listener* (London) 24 Apr. 588/1 On a good night she reaches the gallery and when all the absurd phallic blooms have found their place, Edna leads the audience in the Gladdie Song.

glamour. *Obs.* Used *attrib.* in Comb. with reference to dress uniform issued to personnel of the Australian army during the war of 1939-45 (cf. GIGGLE 2).

1941 *Argus* (Melbourne) 15 Nov. (Suppl.) 1/4 *Glamour gowns*, khaki dress uniforms. **1945** *Chocolate & Green*

(Sydney) July 6 The officers, resplendent in what we have learned to call glamour suits.

glass.
1. *Obs.* In the phr. **glasses round,** a drink for everyone present.
1858 A. PENDRAGON *Queen of South* 209 The trooper . . went so far as to offer a bet of 'glasses round' to the foreman of the jury.   1879 'AUSTRALIAN' *Adventures Qld.* 8 I'll bet you 'glasses round' you'll be tight before the yokes is off your bullocks.
2. In the phr. **glass of lunch, steak,** etc., a glass of beer.
1968 J. O'GRADY *Gone Troppo* 112 At the moment, he's having a glass of lunch.   1969 A. BUZO *Front Room Boys* (1970) 48 'Been down the pub for lunch? . . ' 'Yeah, had a glass of steak with Barry Anderson.'

glassy. Also **glassey.** [Fig. use of *glassy* highly-prized marble.] With **the:** someone (or something) prized or admired. Also as *adj.* in the phr. **glassy marble.**
1905 *Steele Rudd's Mag.* (Brisbane) June 553 That girl'll do you bad every time; she's the real glassy, an' no mistake.   1915 C.J. DENNIS *Songs of Sentimental Bloke* 42 'E's jist the glarsey on the soulful sob, 'E'll sigh and spruik, an 'owl a love-sick vow.   1951 CUSACK & JAMES *Come in Spinner* 300 Low profits and quick turnover, and this is the glassy marble.

glory box. A box in which a woman accumulates her trousseau; 'bottom drawer'; the trousseau itself.
1915 L. STONE *Betty Wayside* 244 It was her glory box, containing all her treasures that she had gathered together against such a day as this.   1984 P. CUFFLEY *Chandeliers & Billy Tea* 97 Ladies . . turned out . . beautiful lace, dozens of doilies, and scores of eccentric needleworked knick-knacks. Much of it went into 'glory boxes' and was rarely if ever used.

glue-pot. A wet and muddy section of a road or track in which a vehicle may become bogged. Also *attrib.*
1875 R.P. WHITWORTH *Cobb's Box* 4 The wild gorges, deep swamps, and terrible 'glue pots' of Gipps Land.   1898 G.H. HAYDON *Sporting Reminisc.* 249 Bullock drays would be bogged in some 'glue-pot' hole.

gluyas /ˈgluːjəs, ˈglaɪjəs/. [The name of H.I. *Gluyas,* a wheat-farmer of S.A., who selected and distributed the variety.] A drought-resistant Australian variety of wheat (see quot. 1956). Also **early gluyas.**
1928 R.G. STAPLEDON *Tour in Aust. & N.Z.* 39 'Nabawah,' 'Gluyas' . . are important varieties in Western Australia.   1956 CALLAGHAN & MILLINGTON *Wheat Industry Aust.* 262 Early Gluyas . . was for 30 years, from 1910 onwards, a leading variety in the drier areas of Australia and . . was only displaced by its own progeny.

gnamma hole /ˈnæmə hoʊl/. Also **namma hole.** [f. Nyungar *ŋamar* + (Eng.) *hole.*] A hole (commonly in granite) in which rainwater collects: see esp. quot. 1948; *rock-hole,* see ROCK *n.* 3.
[1842 G.F. MOORE *Descr. Vocab. Aborigines W.A.* 164 *Water,* standing in a rock—Gnamar.]   1893 D. LINDSAY *Jrnl. Elder Sci. Exploring Exped.* 116 Northeast of the station there was a fine 'gnamer' rockhole and well of good water.   1897 A.F. CALVERT *My Fourth Tour W.A.* 141 The hole widened out from its narrow neck like a demijohn, and it appeared to be replenished from a 'soak' or spring. Such reservoirs, more commonly known as 'namma holes', occur here and there all over the back country.   1948 M. UREN *Glint of Gold* 34 Gnamma holes are holes in rock with an impervious bottom and walls, and generally with a narrow neck. Natives enlarge the necks sufficiently to get their arms into the holes and dip out the water. The rock covering prevents the water from evaporating.

gnow /naʊ/. *W.A.* Formerly also **ngowa, ngow-oo.** [a. Nyungar *ŋow.*] *Mallee fowl,* see MALLEE 6.
1840 J. GOULD *Birds of Aust.* (1848) V. Pl. 78, In these close scrubby woods small open glades occasionally occur, and here the Ngōw-oo constructs its nest.   1872 MRS E. MILLETT *Austral. Parsonage* 223 There is, however, amongst edible birds none that can at all compare with the one known to natives as the *Ngowa,* and to naturalists as the *Leipoa.*   1885 M.A. BARKER *Lett. to Guy* 124, I have been given some emeu's eggs for you, and some 'Gnow's' eggs.

go, $n.^1$
1. See *fair go* FAIR $a.^1$ 2.
2. [Used elsewhere but recorded earliest in Aust.]
a. In the phr. **to give** (something) **a go,** to make an attempt to perform (a task, feat, etc.), often incautiously; to 'have a crack (or shot) at'.
1908 *Bulletin* (Sydney) 17 Dec. 14/1, I gave her a 'go' for half-a-mile; And then when her pedigree I'd seen, I bought her, and christened her 'Bidgee Queen.   1977 R. BEILBY *Gunner* 20 'I'll give it a go,' he called back.
b. In the phr. **to give** (someone) **a go,** to give (someone) the opportunity to attempt (a task, feat, etc.); to give (someone) a 'fair go' (see FAIR $a.^1$ 2a.).
1937 J.M. HARCOURT *It never Fails* 45 All right, we'll give you a go. You ought to be all right.   1982 *Weekend Austral. Mag.* (Sydney) 13 Nov. 16/2 He gave that [*sc.* shearing] away, too, 'to give the young blokes a go'.
3. In the collocation **open go,** an unimpeded opportunity, a 'free rein'.
1918 *Twenty-Second's Echo: Mag. 22nd Battalion A.I.F.* 15 May 3 We did not get an open go in the way of food nor medical attention.   1971 P. HASLUCK *Open Go* 2, I found that I could range further afield if my 'open go' took the form of making suggestions, asking questions, or raising doubts rather than asserting what should be done.
4. In the phr. **from go to whoa,** from start to finish.
1971 D. IRELAND *Unknown Industr. Prisoner* 54 Usually he talked from go to whoa.   1983 *Truck & Bus Transportation* Aug. 48/2 The organ-type brake pedal sits several inches off the floor on a metal box which causes an unusually high and awkward lift from 'go' to 'whoa'.

go, $n.^2$ Abbrev. of GOANNA 1.
1904 *Bulletin* (Sydney) 12 May 16/2 The eye can detect no difference in the 'bingy' of the go. when he emerges from his winter quarters . . and the same 'bingy' when it wobbles away from the interior of a dead bullock.   1969 L. HADOW *Full Cycle* 139 If there's any blue this time, I'm heading north like a go up a tree.

go, $v.^1$ With **through.**
1. a. *trans. Obs.* To rob (a person).
1882 *Sydney Slang Dict.* 4 Go through (or run the rule over) a Man—To rob a man in a haunt or the street.   1896 *Worker* (Sydney) 25 Apr. 4/2 He dextrously 'went'through' the three mates and left 'em as closely fleeced as the sheep they had shorn last season.
b. *Obs.* To shear.
1910 *Bulletin* (Sydney) 8 Sept. 13/2 A chap that I knew to be among the best and fastest sheep-shearers in Australia invited me to watch him and some mates 'go through' a shed of Angoras.   1911 *Ibid.* 25 May 13/3, I have seen Wilson day after day go through 140 or 150 rough 'wrinklies'.
2. *intr.* To make a speedy departure, esp. to avoid fulfilling an obligation. Cf. *shoot through* SHOOT *v.* 3.
1943 S.J. BAKER *Pop. Dict. Austral. Slang* (ed. 3) 35 *Go through,* to desert from a northern base to the south. War slang.   1977 B. SCOTT *My Uncle Arch* 113 The first few times she went through on him nearly broke his heart.

go, $v.^2$ [f. *go, n.* a fight or argument: see OED(S *sb.* 4 b.] *trans.* To fight or take to task (a person, etc.).

1938 *Bulletin* (Sydney) 21 Apr. 20/1 Bill developed a cheque, a thirst and a grouch. Riding in to the homestead he decided to 'go' the boss .. collect his cheque and drift. 'Going' the boss would make Bill's name big in the district. **1977** J. O'GRADY *There was Kid* 74 In the words of our father, he would 'go yer'. . . I told myself that that rooster would get an unpleasant surprise if he 'went me'.

go, $v.^3$ In the phr. **to go off.**

a. Of a person or premises: to be raided by the police force.

1941 S.J. BAKER *Pop. Dict. Austral. Slang* 31 *Go off,* when an hotel or club is raided by the police for permitting gambling or after-hours drinking, it is said to 'go off'. **1984** *Bulletin* (Sydney) 10 July 49/2 Mona last went off in December 1983 when she was charged under her real name, Lucy Domingo, and fined $200 for having been the keeper of a brothel.

b. Of a racehorse: see quot. 1941.

1941 S.J. BAKER *Pop. Dict. Austral. Slang* 31 When a horse is expected or 'fixed' to win a race it is said to 'go off'. **1976** S. WELLER *Bastards I have Met* 104 They had a real hotpot ready to go off and they played it very cagey.

c. To be stolen.

1953 T.A.G. HUNGERFORD *Riverslake* 151, I wondered if you'd mind my wireless while I'm in Sydney? If I leave it in my room it'll go off. **1963** F. HARDY *Legends Benson's Valley* 44 There's been a lot of wood goin' orf from yards round the town lately.

goak. [Prob. altered form of *joke,* influenced by Br. dial. *goak* var. *gowk* fool, simpleton: see EDD.] A jest; a practical joke.

1869 *Lictor* (Sydney) 16 Dec. 339 Mr Alderman Andrews made an *impromptu* 'goak', which we cordially endorse. Let us have no 'free selection' among our visitors. If we are to entertain them at all, let us shew that we recognise not only the officer, but the *sailor*. **1931** *N.T. Times* (Darwin) 9 Jan. 8/1 Aussie can best be described in the words of Josh Billings: 'This is a 'goak'!'

goal. *Australian National Football.* Used *attrib.* in Special Comb. **goal sneak,** a player adroit at scoring goals, esp. one who takes the opposition unawares; a full-forward; **square,** a rectangle in front of the goal (see quot. 1968); **umpire,** one of two umpires who judges when a goal or behind is scored.

1881 [**goal sneak**] *Devon Herald* (Latrobe) 14 Sept., Crooks and Henry as goal snicks had their time fully taken up. **1894** J.M. MACDONALD *Thunderbolt* 88 The local goalsneak .. turned round and made a flying drop at the coveted space between the posts. **1959** PARNELL & ANDREW *Austral. Football* 35 It is very poor forward work to crowd the **goal square. 1968** B. HOGAN *Follow Game* 3 Two straight lines are drawn at right angles to the goal line for a distance of 10 yards from each goal post. The outer ends of these lines are joined by another straight line to form a rectangle 10 yards by 7 yards. This rectangle is often referred to as the 'goal square'. **1876** T.P. POWER *Footballer* 1 Umpires are appointed, goal and field, a **goal umpire** standing between the goal-posts at each end, and deciding as to goals, and the field umpire following the ball, throwing it in out of bounds.

goanna /gouˈænə/. Formerly also **gohanna.** [Altered form of *iguana* any of several large lizards.]

1. A monitor, any lizard of the genus *Varanus,* typically large and fast-moving; GUANA; IGUANA, *tree lizard,* see TREE. See also BOBTAIL.

1831 G.A. ROBINSON in N.J.B. Plomley *Friendly Mission* 12 July (1966) 376 The *kie* or rat had torn up the ground in quest of the goanna's eggs. **1980** *Sydney Morning Herald* 13 Oct. 3/4 His Aboriginal employee has told him that though he will keep working, he will go back to goanna hunting for food.

2. Comb. **goanna fat, oil.**

1926 M. FORREST *Hibiscus Heart* 139 A trooper .. was cleaning his boots with **goanna fat. 1895** *Bulletin* (Sydney) 3 Aug. 28/1 Dave had a bottle of **'Goanna' oil** ready to keep his [boots] soft with.

3. Rhyming slang for 'piano': cf. 'joanna'.

1918 *7th Field Artillery Brigade Yandoo* Jan. 97 Did you know the 7th has a Y.M.C.A. now? Rather! We have got a 'gohanna' too. **1965** F. HARDY *Yarns of Billy Borker* 39 Grabbed the grand goanna and lowered it down in a lifeboat, see. They get ashore, load the piano on a truck and hides it.

goat.

1. In the phr. **goat and** (or **or**) **galah,** used *attrib.* of a hotel, town, etc., to indicate a low level of amenity.

1924 V. PALMER *Black Horse* 69 It was a little bit of a township near the Warrego. . . Smaller than this, wasn't it Jack? . . A lot smaller. What they call a goat-and-galah township back there, Mrs Baker. **1945** *Bulletin* (Sydney) 7 Mar. 12/4 We dropped in at a goat-or-galah pub in a little western N.S.W. town. My cobber .. called for boiled eggs. A bowl of about a dozen was set in front of him. "Strewth!' he exclaimed, 'I on'y wanted a couple.' 'That's all right,' the waitress smiled reassuringly, 'you won't get more than two good 'uns out of that lot!'

2. In the collocation **hairy goat,** a horse which performs badly in a race. Also *transf.*

1941 S.J. BAKER *Pop. Dict. Austral. Slang* 34 *Hairy goat, run like a* (used esp. of horses), to perform badly in a race. **1965** J. BEEDE *They hosed them Out* 192 Our skipper, from the time we got near the enemy coast, flew like a hairy goat. **1978** J. HEPWORTH *His Bk.* 113 When the barrier flew up Warrego Willie went like a hairy goat—never even looked like running a drum.

goathead. [Prob. from the fancied resemblance of the spiny fruit of the plant to the horned head of a goat: cf. *bull head,* see BULL *n.*^{3}] The shrub of all mainland States except Vic. *Sclerolaena bicornis* (fam. Chenopodiaceae), the fruits of which have two stout spines; any of several other similar plants, esp. DOUBLE-GEE. Also **goatshead,** and *attrib.*

1945 M. RAYMOND *Smiley* 17 A bindyeye—not the small, common kind, but a goatshead with four ugly barbs. **1952** A.M. DUNCAN-KEMP *Where Strange Paths go Down* 89 The bindi-eye, or useless Goatshead Burr. **1974** S.L. EVERIST *Poisonous Plants Aust.* 410 *Emex australis* . . is known as goathead or bullhead but both these names are also applied to other plants with large spiny fruits.

goburra /ˈgoubərə/. *Obs.* [Prob. f. an Aboriginal language, but poss. an abbrev. form of KOOKABURRA.] KOOKABURRA. Also *attrib.*

1862 H. KENDALL *Poems & Songs* 123 Wild goburras laughed aloud Their merry morning songs. **1891** P.D. LORIMER *Songs & Verses* (1901) 165 'Tis the Goburra choir—they still are filling Their happy lives with joy. **1918** *Barrack: Official Organ Imperial Camel Corps* 1 Feb. 3/2 Laughing goburras perched on the old split rail fence.

God's trousers. See quot. 1900.

1900 *Bulletin* (Sydney) 17 Feb. 14/2 The up-to-date larrikin doesn't really curse now, but has invented curious out-of-the-way expressions. . . The strangest I have heard is 'God's trousers!' . . 'God's trousers!' serves as verb, adjective and noun. It also does duty as curse and interjection. **1954** P. GLADWIN *Long Beat Home* 209 God's trousers, I don't get the chance.

goffer. [f. the name of *Goffe* and Sons Ltd., a Br. manufacturer of mineral waters; orig. Br. naval slang.] A soft drink.

1945 *Dit* (Melbourne) June 29, 1 'goffer' (lemon flavour). **1982** J.J. COE *Desperate Praise* 132 *Goffer*, soft drink. Naval slang adopted by diggers whilst aboard the troopship HMAS Sydney en route to Vietnam.

gohanna, var. GOANNA.

go-in. [Transf. use of *go-in* attack or onslaught upon: see OED *go-in* and *go, v.* 80 f.] A battle; a fight; a row.

1900 *Advocate* (Burnie) 6 July 1/8 We started to march on the morning of the first 'go-in' at 3.30 a.m. . . We had a real good 'go-in'. **1981** A.B. FACEY *Fortunate Life* 61, I heard him say to Mum that her brother was a dirty scoundrel. She didn't like this and they had a real go-in.

going, *pres. pple.* [Used elsewhere but recorded earliest in Aust.] In the phr. **how are you going?** a conventional greeting; cf. 'how's things?'

1958 O. RUHEN *Naked under Capricorn* 118 'Why, hullo, Charlie,' Ben said. 'How are we going?' **1979** D. MAITLAND *Breaking Out* 62 Walking, talking, irreverent identity crises hanging on the fly-screen door with a case of chilled beer, a howyergarnmate—orrite?

gold. *Mining.* In Comb. and Special Comb. chiefly *Hist.*

1. In the phr. **to be (up)on gold**: (of a claim) to contain auriferous material; (of a miner) to be mining auriferous material.

1871 *Austral. Town & Country Jrnl.* (Sydney) 4 Mar. 271/3 Several claims are upon good gold. **1898** J.A. BARRY *Steve Brown's Bunyip* 72 No life can equal that of a digger's if he be 'on gold', even moderately so; if not, none so weary and heartbreaking.

2. Comb. **gold country** [U.S., see Mathews], **find, finder, finding, hunter** [U.S., see Mathews], **hunting** [U.S., see Mathews], **seeker** [U.S., see Mathews], **seeking.**

1851 *Empire* (Sydney) 15 Aug. 51/1 The earliest and most certain information from the **Gold Country**. **1893** *Braidwood Dispatch* 7 June 2/5 Information . . respecting the Tid River **gold-find**, stating that payable gold has been found on the supposed old river bed. **1851** *Empire* (Sydney) 10 July 3/4 Mr Stewart . . and party, amongst whom is the **gold finder** McGreggor, have been successful in finding some beautiful specimens of gold. **1851** *Bell's Life in Sydney* 31 May 1/3 Disgust against **gold-finding**. **1851** *Empire* (Sydney) 18 Aug. 59/1 The very picturesque style of habiliment affected by our **gold-hunters**. **1851** 'OMEGA' *Gold in Aust.* 6 The raging fever for **Gold hunting**, in nine case out of ten, would perhaps invite him to the Diggings. **1852** J. BONWICK *Notes of Gold Digger* 12 The delight of the **gold seeker**, when he first drops upon a good pocket of nuggets. **1852** F. LANCELOTT *Aust. as it Is* I. 302 Numbers were disheartened, and abandoning **gold seeking** in despair, returned to Sydney.

3. Special Comb. **gold broker, buyer,** one who deals in gold; **cart,** a vehicle for the transport of gold; **colony,** an Australian Colony in which gold has been discovered; **commissioner,** an officer responsible for the issue and administration of *gold licences*; **digger** [U.S., see Mathews], a gold-miner, DIGGER 1; **digging** *vbl. n.*, **(a)** [U.S., see Mathews], gold-mining, also *attrib.*; **(b)** [U.S., see Mathews], a place where gold is found or mined; **escort,** an armed party responsible for the protection of gold being transported from the diggings; the vehicle used for this purpose; ESCORT a., *government escort*, GOVERNMENT B. 4; also *attrib.*, and **escorting** *vbl. n.*; **fever** [U.S., see Mathews], an overriding urge to search for gold; the excitement associated with this; so **fevered** *ppl. a.*; **hole,** a hole excavated in the search for gold; **licence,** a permit to dig for gold, later *miner's right*, see MINER *n.*²; **mania** [U.S., see Mathews], *gold fever*; **police,** a force under the command of a *gold commissioner*; **rush,** an influx of people to a newly discovered goldfield; such a goldfield; also **rushing** *vbl. n.*; **show,** a trace of gold; COLOUR 1; **warden,** a judicial officer responsible for the maintenance of law and order on a goldfield; **washer,** one who mines alluvial gold; **washing** *vbl. n.*, **(a)** the process of separating alluvial gold from its surrounding materials; **(b)** [U.S., see Mathews], usu. in *pl.*, the site of an alluvial gold deposit.

1854 W. SHAW *Land of Promise* 94 **Gold-brokers** seem to vie with each other in auriferous exhibition. **1852** *Moreton Bay Free Press* 24 June 3/5 One of the resident . . **gold buyers** on those diggings is Mr Abraham Solomons. **1853** *Moreton Bay Free Press* 1 Mar. 3/4 The driver of the **gold cart** will have enough to do. **1862** C. ASPINALL *Three Yrs. Melbourne* 33 This may naturally be expected in a new **gold colony**. **1852** J. SHAW *Tramp to Diggings* 255 Mr Hardy, a **gold commissioner**, has stated . . that any man might earn his ten shillings a day. **1852** *Moreton Bay Free Press* 1 Jan. 2/2 Bathurst **gold-digger's** first class 'hole'. **(a) 1851** *Empire* (Sydney) 1 Aug. 3/1 **Gold digging** is no child's play. **1926** G. BLACK *Hist. N.S.W. Political Labor Party* i. 11 The gold-digging days. **(b) 1850** *Monthly Almanac* (Adelaide) 60 In the **Gold Diggins** the price of meat is . . high. **1852** *Moreton Bay Free Press* 24 Aug. 3/3 A notice appears in the Government Gazette . . notifying that a **gold escort** will leave Tamworth for Sydney. **1917** W. LEES *Aboriginal Problem Qld.* 26, I was driving the gold escort from Bargo Brush to Campbelltown. **1918** *Bulletin* (Sydney) 30 May 22/3 Gold-escorting nowadays in Westralia has hardly any . . thrill. **1972** ANDERSON & BLAKE *J.S. Neilson* 41 Drive north-east to cut the former gold-escort track. **1851** *Empire* (Sydney) 5 Aug. 15/2 The **Gold fever** has now considerably abated. **1894** *Bulletin* (Sydney) 31 Mar. 9/3 In one week over 1400 gold-fevered passengers left Melbourne for Westralia. **1852** J.E. ERSKINE *Short Acct. Late Discoveries Gold* 22 The weather . . set in cold and wet, which . . retarded the digging by flooding the banks of the creek, and filling the **'gold holes'**. **1851** *Empire* (Sydney) 7 Aug. 22/7 The fund from **gold licenses** alone must, by this time amount to no inconsiderable sum. **1851** J.C. HAWKER *Diary* 19 Dec., Owing to the fearful **gold Mania** both Miners and Smelters are leaving in hundreds for the Melbourne gold diggings. **1853** *Moreton Bay Free Press* 22 Mar. 3/3 The **gold police** have now taken up the pursuit, and it is hoped that the ruffians may soon be in the hands of justices. **1873** [**gold rush**] A. TROLLOPE *Aust. & N.Z.* I. 29 Gold rushing is of all pursuits . . the most alluring and the most precarious. **1893** G. TREGARTHEN *Austral. Cwlth.* 158 The gold-rush had introduced many unruly spirits. **1911** *Bulletin* (Sydney) 19 Jan. 13/4 The Westralian gold rushes of the early '90s never had a lynching. **1923** M.B. PETERSEN *Jewelled Nights* 210 'E's found a **gold show** on Long Plains. **1867** J. BONWICK *J. Batman* 89 Like a rush to a new diggings before the arrival of a **gold** commissioner, or **warden** each new comer to Port Phillip grasped at what he could. **1851** W.B. CLARKE *Researches Southern Goldfields N.S.W.* (1860) 16 The profits of the **gold washers** at present have not been great. **(a) 1850** W.B. BROWN *Narr. Voyage London to S.A.* 16 Gold . . has recently been found in the beds of the Torrens and Onkaparinga Rivers, and **gold-washing** has already commenced. **(b) 1851** *Empire* (Sydney) 20 Aug. 67/3 On Sunday night last, 24 strangers were lodged in Mr Macallum's huts, 5 miles from the **gold washings**.

4. *fig.* Used *attrib.* in Special Comb. as an emblem of privilege or affluence: **gold lace,** uniformed officialdom; also *attrib.*; **pass,** a warrant entitling the bearer (usu. a politician) to free travel on public transport systems; also *transf.*; **top,** champagne; also *fig.* and *attrib.*

1841 *Port Phillip Patriot* 21 Oct. 2/4 We have received from William's Town a communication addressed to 'the **gold lace** fraternity, *alias* the crown and anchor button mob'. **1867** *Essay on Politics in Verse* 4 Our local hero . .

Blackguards 'gold-lace'. **1919** C.A. BERNAYS *Qld. Politics during Sixty Yrs.* 200 He has 'M.L.A.' attached to his name and a **gold** railway **pass** attached to his watch-chain. **1984** *Age* (Melbourne) 22 Mar. 4/3 Building workers on the Arts Centre project remained off the job yesterday in support of their claim for a lifetime gold pass to performances at the centre. **1885** *Australasian Printers' Keepsake* 139, I cracked too much about the '**gold-top**' champagne (speaking candidly, gentlemen, ordinary fizz). **1896** T. HENEY *Girl at Birell's* 245 He stood rather in awe of his son-in-law, who was to him a swell, a squatter, a gold-top. **1901** *Truth* (Sydney) 8 Dec. 5/4 With the uncorking of a dozen or more of full-sized 'gold top', asked them to drink to 'our happy union'.

golden, *a.*

1. Used in special collocations, esp. with reference to an apparent abundance of gold: **golden colony** *hist.*, Victoria; **fever** *hist.*, *gold fever*, see GOLD 3; **hole** *hist.*, a highly productive mining claim; also *attrib.*; **land** *hist.*, Australia, esp. Victoria; **mile,** see quot. 1971; **West,** Western Australia.

1857 W. WESTGARTH *Vic. & Austral. Gold Mines* 11 Streamed over as from an open gaol to the all-attractive shores of the **golden colony**. **1851** *Empire* (Sydney) 18 July 2/3 Bathurst is made again. The delirium of **golden fever** has returned with increased intensity. **1855** J. CHARLESWORTH *Visit to Diggings* 5, I had a **golden hole**, and did not know it until months afterwards. **1892** 'R. BOLDREWOOD' *Nevermore* I. 94 A 'golden-hole man' and the half-owner of one of the richest claims on the field. **1852** *Austral. Gold Digger's Monthly Mag.* ii. 39 The southern mines sustained the honour of the **golden land** when the western fields began to fail. **1901** M. VIVIENNE *Travels in W.A.* 210 From this place one has a glorious view of the other great mines on the **Golden Mile**, so-called on account of the marvellous quantity of gold that has been and is still being extracted from its depths—Lake View, Great Boulder, Ivanhoe, Boulder Perseverance, and Golden Horseshoe. **1971** C. SIMPSON *New Aust.* 557 The Golden Mile lies between Kalgoorlie and Boulder and is an extraordinarily rich auriferous reef area that is actually about two miles long and a third of a mile wide and has been mined to thousands of feet. **1897** *Worker* (Sydney) 13 Feb. 2/2 Men flocking in for another year's 'yacker' in the '**Golden West**'.

2. With reference to privilege or affluence: **Golden Casket,** a State lottery in Queensland (see quot. 1955); **fleece** *hist.*, wool, esp. as perceived as the source of national wealth; **lace** *hist.*, *gold lace*, see GOLD 4; **top** *hist.*, *gold top*, see GOLD 4.

1916 *Telegraph* (Brisbane) 25 Nov. 3/6 Queensland's **Golden Casket** Art Union. Australian Soldiers' Repatriation Fund. (For returned sailors and soldiers.) **1955** N. PULLIAM *I traveled Lonely Land* 75 In Queensland the lottery operates under the unusual name of the 'Golden Casket'. It was started during World War I to raise funds for some sort of patriotic effort and subsequently was taken over by the government, under which it has continued to flourish, producing the money to build and maintain the large and numerous hospitals of Queensland. **1837** *Sydney Herald* 29 June 2/2 Australia's '**golden fleece**'. **1855** R. CARBONI *Eureka Stockade* 24 Who dares to teach the **golden-lace** .. how to shoot? **1908** J. FURPHY *Such is Life* 87 Illicit snake-juice for them, and **golden top** for the other fellow.

3. As a distinguishing epithet in the names of flora and fauna: **golden-headed fantail warbler,** the small warbler *Cisticola exilis* of Aust. and elsewhere; TAILORBIRD; see also *corn-bird* CORN 2; **perch,** the yellowish or white fresh-water fish *Macquaria ambigua* (fam. Percichthyidae, formerly classed in Percidae) of s.e. Aust. and prob. introduced into W.A. and N.T.; CALLOP; YELLOWBELLY; see also *Murray perch* MURRAY 2; **shoulder,** the parrot *Psephotus chrysopterygius* of Cape York Peninsula, Qld., having yellow median wing coverts; see also ANTHILL PARROT; also **golden-shouldered parrot** (or **parakeet**); **wattle,** the heavily flowering small tree *Acacia pycnantha* (fam. Mimosaceae) of N.S.W., Vic., and S.A., popularly regarded as the floral emblem of Australia; PYCNANTHA WATTLE; **(breasted) whistler,** the bird *Pachycephala pectoralis* of s. and e. Aust., the male having yellow on the neck and underparts; *white-throated thickhead*, see WHITE $a.^2$ 1 b.

1911 J.A. LEACH *Austral. Bird Bk.* 142 **Golden-headed Fantail-Warbler**. **1847** G.F. ANGAS *Savage Life & Scenes* I. 92 The **golden perch** are driven out of the rushes. [**1859 golden shoulder:** J. GOULD *Birds of Aust.* Suppl. (1869) Pl. 64, Golden-backed Parrakeet... This bird is in every way a true *Psephotus*... It is allied both to the *P. pulcherrimus* and *P. multicolor*, but differs from them, among other characters, in the rich-yellow mark on the shoulder.] **1865** —— *Handbk. Birds Aust.* II. 65 Golden-shouldered Parrakeet. **1928** G.H. WILKINS *Undiscovered Aust.* 143 The beautiful golden-shouldered parrots, which make their nests in deserted anthills, were disappearing fast. **1946** W.E. HARNEY *North of 23°* 75 Above flashes in the sunlight that marvel of colour and flight, the golden shoulder. **1850** J.B. CLUTTERBUCK *Port Phillip* 32 Few .. of the native Australian flowers emit any perfume except the **golden** and silver **Wattle**. **1917** [**golden whistler**] *Bulletin* (Sydney) 16 Aug. 22/3 Golden-breasted whistler (also called white-throated thick-head). **1942** C. BARRETT *From Bush Hut* 25, I heard the golden whistler's song.

goldfield. [Used elsewhere but recorded earliest in Aust.]

1. A place in which gold is found and mined. Also *attrib.*

1851 J.H. BURTON *Emigrant's Man.* ii. 123 You may suppose a gold-field a most original sight: at a distance it can only be compared to an immense army, encamped in myriads of tents of all shapes, sizes, and colours. **1883** R.E.N. TWOPENY *Town Life Aust.* 245 When speaking of a goldfield a colonist says 'on'. Thus you live 'on Bendigo', but 'in' or 'at' Sandhurst—the latter being the new name for the old goldfield town.

2. In the collocation **goldfields scavenger,** a whirlwind.

1903 J. MARSHALL *Battling for Gold* 85 (*caption*) 'Willy Willy' or Goldfields Scavenger. **1929** W.J. RESIDE *Golden Days* 341 Goldfields residents also knew of the 'Willy-willy', or, as it was sometimes called 'the Goldfields Scavenger'

goldfielder. [Chiefly Aust.: see prec.] One who works or resides on a goldfield.

1903 *Westminster Gaz.* (London) 28 Jan. 9/2 The goldfielders began to clamour for separation, and talked rather wildly of setting up a Government of their own in the interior and using Esperance Bay as a port. **1950** G.S. CASEY *City of Men* 49 The holidaying goldfielder starts off pretty scornful of the seventh-story [*sic*] miners in city office buildings.

goldfish. In Services' speech: tinned fish. Also *attrib.*

1942 T. KELAHER *Digger Hat* 24 You're sick of eating 'goldfish', bully beef and army stew. **1962** MARSHALL & DRYSDALE *Journey among Men* 104 'Tell us about your part in that rather disagreeable goldfish business during the war, Dom.'.. 'It was not goldfish,' said Dom quietly. 'The fish is *Nematalosa erebi*, a so-called bony bream. It is, in fact, a true herring—one of the soft-rayed clupeoid fishes.'

gonce /gɒns/. *Obs.* Also **gons.** [Of unknown origin.] Money.

1899 *Bulletin* (Sydney) 1 July 32/2 Yes, I'm doin' pretty middlin' And I'm layin' up the gonce. **1918** J.A. PHILP *Jingles that Jangle* 52 We hadn't copped the gons yet.

good, *a.*

1. In the collocation **good on you (her, him,** etc.): an expression of approbation, 'well done!'.

1907 *Truth* (Sydney) 11 Aug. 1/7 Good on them! Another ship captain .. has been fined £100 for landing a smelful alien on our shores, to contaminate the country. **1920** A.I. MACLEOD *Hack's Brat* (ed. 2) 14 'MacLure will stay here to start the mine.' 'It ain't moonshine, then?' 'No—it's a jolly good speck.' 'Good on yer!' howled Watty. **1922** A. WRIGHT *Boss o' Yedden* 117 'Miss Goulder warned the train in time, but the bridge went up.' 'Good on her,' cried Tom, admiringly. **1982** R. HALL *Just Relations* 265 'Good on you Uncle', shouted Billy. 'Good on you Uncle', other voices encouraged him.

2. [Perh. f. U.S. *to feel good* to feel in good spirits or health: see OED(S *good, a.* 3 c.] In good health, well.

1934 T. WOOD *Cobbers* 27 He said he was good, which means his health was, and added that it was a bonza day. **1979** *Westerly* i. 7 'Hello... How are you?' 'Good thanks. How about you?'

3. In the phr. **to come good,** to fulfil an expectation or aspiration; (of a situation, etc.) to ameliorate.

1946 A. THURIAN *Bush Tea & Overlanders* 13 There had come good the chance to class some sheep. **1960** M. VIZZERS *She'll do Me!* 83 Australia would 'come good' again. Brighter times were ahead.

good day. Also **g'day, gooday.** [Elliptical form of *(may you) have a good day:* see OED *good, a.* 10 c. and *good day.*] A familiar greeting, used freq. and at any hour.

1857 *Illustr. Jrnl. Australasia* III. 66 Not one of them spoke to me, except to give me an occasional 'Good day, mate'. **1928** *Bulletin* (Sydney) 19 Dec. 20/1 He had little to say—Just a quiet 'G'day'. **1959** D. STUART *Yandy* 53 Ernie said 'Gooday' and pointed to the small fire behind the siding shed where the billy was boiling.

good man. *Obs.* A convict whose behaviour in custody is exemplary: see BAD 1.

1788 D. COLLINS *Acct. Eng. Colony N.S.W.* (1798) I. 43 A convict who had been looked on as a good man (no complaint having been made of him since his landing, either for dishonesty or idleness). **1850** W. GATES *Recoll. Van Dieman's Land* 124 If we continued to be good men till our probation of two years was expired, we should have tickets-of-leave.

good-o, *a., absol.,* and *adv.* Also **good-oh** and without hyphen.

A. *adj.* In a satisfactory or proper state, 'all right'.

[N.Z. **1905** THOMSON *Bush Boys* 34 That was real good-o.] **1914** 'B. CABLE' *By Blow & Kiss* 246 They're good-oh... Chock full of ginger yet. **1946** *Southerly* ii. 75 'Tastes goodoh, eh?'.. 'Tastes absolutely bonzer...' 'I'm out to get stonkered good and proper.' **1970** P. AMOS *Silver Kings* 157 He had always said .. to the union leaders, 'You scratch my back, I'll scratch yours and we'll all feel good-o.'

B. *absol.* Used as an exclamation, expressing assent or approbation.

1918 *Kia Ora Coo-ee* Aug. 5/2 'Fish for dinner to-day, Jack.' 'Good O! What sort?' 'Mafish.' **1970** C. NOLAN *Bride for St. Thomas* 57 'Good-oh,' I said, over-loudly, trying to get closer to the retreating wall, 'Right-oh, bonzer.'

C. *adv.* Satisfactorily, properly, well.

1920 C.H. SAYCE *Golden Buckles* 120 The mills are working good-O.

good oil: see OIL *n.* 2.

goog /gʊg/. [Abbrev. of GOOGIE.]

1. An egg.

1941 S.J. BAKER *Pop. Dict. Austral. Slang* 32 *Goog*, an egg. **1981** P. BARTON *Bastards I have Known* 29 We half filled the tub with water, chucked in a handful of soap powder, and gingerly tipped in about 120 googs.

2. In the phr. **full as a goog:** see FULL *a.*[1] c.

googie /'gʊgi/. [f. Scot. dial. *goggie* child's word for an egg: see SND *googie.*] An egg. Also *transf.* and *fig.,* esp. in the collocation **golden googie,** a coin, a 'golden egg'; in *pl.* riches. Also **googie egg.**

1903 *Truth* (Sydney) 5 Apr. 5/2 At the show he will .. boast of the golden 'googies' he has in his 'kick'. **1958** M.D. BERRINGTON *Stones of Fire* 78, I shall love to teach you Australian... Googies are eggs. **1968** B. HUMPHRIES *Nice Night's Entertainment* (1981) 113 Beryl popped an empty eggshell upside-down in my egg-cup and I pretended I was surprised to find no googie egg inside.

goolie /'guli/, *n.* [Prob. f. a N.S.W. Aboriginal language.] A stone.

1924 *Truth* (Sydney) 27 Apr. 6/3 *Gooley*, a stone. **1960** D. IRELAND *Image in Clay* (1964) 28 Garn, get out of it, before I let fly with a goolie.

goolie /'guli/, *v.* [f. prec.] *trans.* To throw.

1982 *Nat. Times* (Sydney) 3 Jan. 49/1 He catapulted out of doors, shot towards the swimming pool and goolied the box into the chlorinated depths.

goom /gʊm, gum/. [Poss. transf. use of Gabi-gabi (and neighbouring languages) *guŋ* water, alcohol.]

a. Methylated spirits (as drunk by a derelict).

1967 *Kings Cross Whisper* (Sydney) xxxv. 6/1 *Goom*, methylated spirits. **1982** *Meanjin* 453 Goom! What a name for methylated spirits.

b. Abbrev. of GOOMY.

1984 P. CORRIS *Winning Side* 172 You can't inform on your own, Dick. If you do the place'll be finished for sure. No one'll touch it except the *gooms.*

goomy /'gʊmi, 'gumi/. Also **goomee.** [f. prec.] One addicted to drinking methylated spirits.

1973 K. GILBERT *Because White Man'll never do It* 97 Right at the bottom of the pile are the 'goomies'. These are the Aboriginal alcoholics, the metho drinkers. **1984** P. CORRIS *Winning Side* 161 He took a big gulp of wine and remembered, and had a small sip. Lennie had been a *goommee*, a bad one, but he'd reformed with a lot of help.

goon, *n.*[1] *Services' speech.* Abbrev. of GOONSKIN. Also *attrib.*

1941 *Men may Smoke* (Sydney) June 7 Goon trousers. **1946** *They wrote it Themselves* (W.A.A.A.F.) 19 A W.A.A.A.F. refers to her overalls or *jeans* .. as *goons* or goonskins.

goon, *n.*[2] [Prob. f. altered pronunc. of *flagon,* but see also GOOM.] A flagon (of wine).

1982 *Sydney Morning Herald* 13 Nov. 30/2 Tim Stanford started off drinking with 'the goon'. It's a flagon of moselle or riesling. **1983** *Ibid.* 23 Nov. 1/1 Three flagons of port (known as goons) have been consumed noisily by about 8.30.

goondie, var. GUNDY *n.*[1]

goonskin. [f. *goon* simpleton, after a character called Alice the *Goon* in the 'Popeye' series by E.C. Segar (1894–1938), American cartoonist; also used of a flying suit in R.A.F. slang.] In Services' speech: see quot. 1942. Also *attrib.*

1940 *Muzzle Blast* (Sydney) Sept. 7 Stitch in time saves goonskin button. **1942** *Southerly* i. 14 *Giggle Suit* (*Australian.*) Also *Goon Skins,* loose and ill-fitting fatigue dress. The *goon* is a clumsy and shapeless character in the 'Popeye' comic strip.

gooseneck. See quot. 1972. Also *attrib.*
1970 *Matilda* (Winton Tourist Promotion Assoc.) 18 The men who once lived in the saddle, Have put leggings and goosenecks away. 1972 J. BYRNE *Horse Riding Austral. Way* 22 Australia is unique in its styles of saddle .. *The Gooseneck Poley Saddle.* Used by the majority of horse breakers .. a very deep seated saddle, with a short built in surcingle to attach the girth to; also fitted with a ring either side just behind the flap, to use with a cinch girth.

gooya /ˈguja/. [a. Yuwaalaraay *guuya.*] *Emu apple* (a), see EMU *n.*¹ 3. Also *attrib.*
1949 H.G. LAMOND *White Ears* 60 The two dogs came upon the flock of goats feeding on a sandhill ridge thick with coongaberry and gooya apples. 1955 —— *Towser* 82 A clump of gooya, or emu apple, stood out on a small plain.

gordo /ˈgɔdoʊ/. [Abbrev. of Sp. *gordo blanco* lit. 'fat white', a variety of grape known in the industry as 'muscat gordo blanco'.] A popular variety of grape.
1907 *Jrnl. Dept. Agric. Vic.* V. 714 Our raisin growers may have trouble in suiting their Gordos with a stock. 1946 A.M. LAPTHORNE *Mildura Calling* 51 Gordos are generally picked, packed and sent away fresh to the Melbourne markets, or dried in clusters without dipping.

go-slow. [Used elsewhere but recorded earliest in Aust.: see OEDS.]
a. A form of industrial protest in which employees work to rule or at a deliberately slow pace. Also *attrib.*, and formerly **go-slow strike.**
1917 *Sydney Morning Herald* 23 Aug. 6/8 If New South Wales is going to progress in the future .. this 'go-slow' policy which has been preached amongst our people for years past must be put an end to. 1923 C.F. THWING *Human Australasia* 59 Another form, or cause, of the strike is found in what is known as the 'go-slow' or 'lazy' strike. It represents a desire to lessen the output. 1956 J.T. LANG *I Remember* 254 He had made many speeches about 'go-slow' in the railways.
b. One who takes part in such a protest.
1926 G. BLACK *Hist. N.S.W. Political Labor Party* iv. 15 Jobs for go-slows and incompetents.
Hence **go-slowism** *n.*
1917 *Byron Bay Rec.* 18 Aug. 4 The engineers are demanding that in the workshops go-slowism shall be accepted.

gouge, *v. Mining. intr.* To dig in order to secure a mineral deposit, esp. in opal-mining; also *trans.*, to prize (a stone) out of the surrounding material (see also quot. 1971).
1902 [see *gouging, vbl. n.*]. 1906 *Bulletin* (Sydney) 15 Feb. 15/1 We've sunk and we've driven and paddocked and gouged for scarcely a color a week. 1960 D. MCLEAN *Roaring Days* 62 We gouged them from a white clay below the band. 1971 J.S. GUNN *Opal Terminol.* 21 *Gouge*, to cut carefully under the roof searching for a seam of potch so that full scale cutting of the drive can begin.
Hence **gouging** *vbl. n.* and *attrib.*
1902 *Chambers's Jrnl.* (Edinburgh) Mar. 175/1 In the 'back blocks' of New South Wales opal is abundant, and 'gouging'—the term given to opal-mining—is the chief pursuit of every man on the western side of the Darling River. 1932 I.L. IDRIESS *Flynn of Inland* (1965) 233 He sends down a sheath-knife, a 'spider', or a gouging pick.

gouge, *n. Mining.* A hole, freq. off a drive or shaft; a cavity made by a gouger.
1921 K.S. PRICHARD *Black Opal* 253 We'd better get down and clear out some of the mullock... The gouges are fair choked up. 1958 M.D. BERRINGTON *Stones of Fire* 49 The shaft .. had a small gouge in one end.

gouger. *Mining.* An independent miner who works a surface deposit, now usu. an opal miner. See also *opal gouger* OPAL 1.
1898 *Barrier Weekly Post* (Broken Hill) 17 Sept. 13 The reason assigned for the absence of the gouger from this hill is the extreme hardness of the ground not altogether the absence of opal. 1979 D. LOCKWOOD *My Old Mates & I* 144 Several big mines were producing gold, copper, tin and wolfram, and Chinese gougers were active.

Gouldian finch. [f. the name of English natural history artist Elizabeth *Gould* (1804–1841), first applied as the specific epithet *Gouldiae* by her husband, English naturalist John Gould (1844 *Birds of Aust.* (1848) III. Pl. 88): see quot. 1976.] The n. Austral. finch *Erythrura gouldiae,* brilliantly coloured and a popular cage-bird.
1844 J. GOULD *Birds of Aust.* (1848) III. Pl. 88, *Amadina gouldiae* .. Gouldian Finch. 1976 *Reader's Digest Compl. Bk. Austral. Birds* 543 Of all Australian grass finches the Gouldian finch is the most striking. Its beauty inspired the naturalist, John Gould, to name the bird *gouldiae* in honour of his wife, who drew many of the birds illustrating his books.

gouty stem tree. *Obs.* [From the swollen or bulging appearance of the trunk.] BAOBAB. Also **gouty tree.**
1838 J.L. STOKES *Discoveries in Aust.* 21 Mar. (1846) I. 158 We found here [*sc.* Compass Hill] the gouty-stem tree of large size, bearing fruit. 1855 J. BONWICK *Geogr. Aust. & N.Z.* (ed. 3) 205 The Bottle tree, 40 feet high, is a Sterculia, so bulging out as to be called the Gouty tree.

government, *n.* and *attrib.* [Of Austral. significance because of the proliferation of Comb. and Special Comb., perh. reflecting the nature of the role played by colonial governments in the settlement of Australia.]
A. *n.*
1. Freq. without article. The governing power in a (penal) colony, the body of instrumentalities responsible for the administration of a (penal) colony; the administrative arm of (colonial, state, or federal) government.
1793 S. MACARTHUR ONSLOW *Some Early Rec. Macarthurs* (1914) 45 Where Mr Macarthur had been the greater part of his time .. on account of the employment he holds under Government. 1820 C. JEFFREYS *Van Dieman's Land* 97 Government having thought it advisable to form another settlement, or town, called George Town .. Launceston has been suffered to go considerably into decay. 1872 Mrs E. MILLETT *Austral. Parsonage* 331 The frequent reference in West Australia to the word 'Government', and the manner in which it was alluded to, might have led one to suppose it was an imaginary creature whose character varied with that of each person who spoke of it. 1934 J.C. LEE *Boshstralians* 38, I was in the Government in those days, doing relief duty, and necessarily away from home a goodish bit.
2. a. In the phr. **returned to** (or **sent back to**) **government**: (of a convict assigned to private service) returned to official custody.
[1801 *HRA* (1915) 1st Ser. III. 254 If any person cannot support or employ the prisoners they have taken off the stores they are to be returned to Government labour.] 1834 *Austral. Almanack* 140 Convicts returned to Government, without complaint .. may be immediately reassigned. 1848 S. & J. SIDNEY *Emigrant's Jrnl.* 125 If a man wanted twice flogging he was of no use to me; I sent him back to Government.
b. In the phr. **in government,** in official custody (as opposed to private service).
1827 Tas. Colonial Secretary's Office Rec. 1/23 404, I understand this man is now in Government. 1865 S. BENNETT *Hist. Austral. Discovery* 434 Instead of desiring to be assigned to private persons .. it became the almost

universal desire of the convicts to be 'in government', as they termed it.

B. *attrib.*

1. Owned, funded, administered, or in the service of the government (of a Colony, later a State, or the Commonwealth).

1790 R. CLARK Jrnl. 20 May 168 They sowed two bushels of barley at the Government Farm. **1882** J. WOOD *'Neath Southern Skies* 48 The Government railways (and, be it observed, nearly all the railways in the Colony come within this category) run their trains at a rate of speed which for slowness would send a Midland Railway official into the nearest district asylum. **1962** C. GYE *Cockney & Crocodile* 136 In the evening the Government Dogger came to dinner. He wanders here and there, shooting, trapping and poisoning the dingoes that worry the sheep. **1975** L.H. CLARK *Rouseabout Reflections* 98 Should our Queen pen a letter, her armies and navy may bear it, it's true; But the back-o'-Bourke postie, the government rover must still get it through.

2. a. *Hist.* As a euphemism for 'convict'; also *ellipt.* as *adj.* (see quot. 1872); **b.** Of or relating to the apprehension or detention of a criminal.

1803 *Sydney Gaz.* 6 Nov., The Government Workmen are busy in walling in a channel for the run of water which crosses the Row at the lower end in rainy seasons. **1872** M. CLARKE *His Natural Life* 574 The major part of them had been 'government' themselves, and resented the fact that one of their number had been raised up to rule over them. **1894** *Bulletin* (Sydney) 9 June 21/1 Incontinently thrown—yes, *throum*, for I moved slowly and looked round for my cab!—into the Government Coach—Black Maria.

3. Comb. **government cattle, dam, domain, emigrant, emigration, farm, flock, garden, ground, herd, hut, immigrant, immigration, job, land, paddock, reserve, road, run, school, sheep, stock, store, well.**

1794 G. THOMPSON *Slavery & Famine* ii. 5 Here is a large park, called Cumberland Park, where the **government cattle** are put to graze. **1901** *Bulletin* (Sydney) 4 May 32/2 Watson and I were .. pulling some sheep out of a **Government dam** they had got bogged in. **1813** *N.S.W. Pocket Almanack* 72 **Government Domain**—No cattle of any description but those belonging to Government are to be permitted to graze or feed thereon. **1854** W. SHAW *Land of Promise* 40 '**Government emigrants**' have likewise come under the animadversion of the colonist. **1840** *S. Austral. Rec.* (London) 14 Mar. 109 There will in all probability be no funds out of which the expenses of **government emigration** can be defrayed, after the end of 1839. **1791** S. MACARTHUR ONSLOW *Some Early Rec. Macarthurs* (1914) 40 The **Government Farm** did not this year in grain return three times the seed that had been sown. **1802** *Gen. Orders issued by Governor King* 16 Mar. 84 Ewes lately given to Settlers from the **Government flock** to breed from, have been thus purchased, killed and sold. **1806** *N.S.W. Gen. Orders* 15 Mar. 187 A quantity of very fine Acorns being saved from the Oaks in the **Government Gardens**, at Sydney. **1798** D. COLLINS *Acct. Eng. Colony N.S.W.* I. 506 Not more than a third of the **government-ground**, and a fifth of the ground belonging to individuals, was in any state of cultivation. **1803** *HRA* (1915) 1st Ser. IV. 307 Toongabbee will remain some time Fallow and be benefitted by the **Government Herds** manuring it. **1812** *Rep. Select Committee Transportation* 19 Feb. (1838) 31 There were houses which were called **Government-huts**, which by the superintendent of convicts were appropriated to their purpose. **1840** *S. Austral. Rec.* (London) 14 Mar. 110 Receiving and rationing **government immigrants** at the public cost until they obtain situations. **1841** *Port Phillip Patriot* 16 Aug. 2/5 The late Dowager Duchess, Countess of Sutherland, had influence sufficient to procure the sending of a **Government immigration** ship to a neighbouring port. **1905** *Truth* (Sydney) 12 Mar. 3/2 Should he apply for a **Government job**, and be 40 years of age, he is told that he is too old. **1792** R. ATKINS Jrnl. 21 May, The lands here [*sc.* Parramatta] are **Government lands** that is, lands cultivated for the maintenance of the Colony. **1822** *Hobart Town Gaz.* 24 Aug., Strayed or stolen from the **Government Paddock** .. two Working Oxen. **1831** R. ROBISON *Case of Captain Robison* 50 Mr Mackay .. had made use of the **government reserve** (land) at Nelson's Plains, for his private purpose. **1834** J.D. LANG *Hist. & Statistical Acct. N.S.W.* II. 160 The remainder of the route to Illawarra is a mere bush-road, there being no regular **Government road**. **1796** P.G. KING Jrnl. Norfolk Island Apr. 273 Several Swine have been bought from Phillip Island .. and put into the **Government Run** on this Island. **1829** H. WIDOWSON *Present State Van Diemen's Land* 25 The .. gentleman has been lately appointed superintendant of the **government schools**. **1801** *Gen. Orders issued by Governor King* 1 May (1802) 40 A large body of Natives .. have attacked and killed some of **Government sheep**. **1803** *HRA* (1915) 1st Ser. IV. 302 Sent over 18,535 pounds of Salt Pork, part from **Government Stock** and part purchased from Settlers. **1800** *HRA* (1915) 1st Ser. III. 3 Competition will do that which the **Government Store** and arbitary Power of the Government to regulate Price must do now. **1875** P.E. WARBURTON *Journey across Western Interior* 142 The **government well** was quite dry.

4. Special Comb. **government bill** *obs.*, a promissory note issued in payment for commodities purchased by a government instrumentality; **billet**, a position in the public service, esp. one which is well-paid and undemanding; **blanket**, a blanket issued by a government instrumentality, esp. to an Aboriginal; BLANKET 1; **bore**, a bore owned and maintained by a government instrumentality for use by travelling stock; **bounty**, BOUNTY 1; reward, subsidy; **bream**, *red emperor*, see RED *a.* 1 b.; **camp**, a police outpost, esp. on a goldfield; a place for the detention of Aborigines; **cottage** (chiefly *Tas.*), a small residence for the accommodation of a visiting official; **(gold) escort** *obs.*, gold escort, see GOLD 3; **gang** *hist.*, a detachment of convicts assigned to public labour; see GANG; **hours** *pl.*, **(a)** the daily period which a convict was required to work at public labour; **(b)** public service office hours; **labour** *obs.*, (of a convict) forced labour on public works; **labourer** *obs.*, a convict assigned to public labour; the employee of a government instrumentality; **man**, a convict (see quot. 1827); a public servant; **mark** *obs.*, a brand or stamp identifying government property; **ration**, a dole (of foodstuffs); RATION *n.* 1 c.; **resident**, a representative of the Crown in a settlement remote from a centre of government; (chiefly *N.T.*) the principal resident representative of a government in a territory administered by that government; **servant**, a convict; a public servant; **settlement, station**, an outpost, esp. as established for agricultural purposes or to promote Aboriginal welfare; a community of Aborigines established and maintained by a government instrumentality; **stroke** (orig. of a convict; now freq. of a public servant), a deliberately slow pace of working; also **stroker**, one who works in this way; **tank**, a dam owned and maintained by a government instrumentality to provide water for travelling stock; **town, township** *obs.*, a settlement established and laid out by a government instrumentality; **woman** *obs.*, a female convict; **work**, public labour, esp. as performed by convicts; **works** *pl.*, constructions as roads, etc., for public use.

1808 *Sydney Gaz.* 18 Dec. Payment to be made in Paymasters' or **Government Bills**. **1870** E.B. KENNEDY *Four Yrs. in Qld.* 7 A certain class of men .. come back to Brisbane, and either get a **Government 'billet'**, or go home. **1839** T.L. MITCHELL *Three Exped. Eastern Aust.* (rev. ed.) II. 335 Having a superfluity of **government blankets**, I have taken the liberty of giving her one. **1899** *Bulletin* (Sydney) 9 Sept. 17/1 The Richmond .. **Govt. bore** gives splendid water. **1836** *Tegg's Monthly Mag.* I. 6 The **Government bounty** might not be sufficient to pay the passage money to Australia. **1896** F.G. AFLALO *Sketch Nat. Hist. Aust.* 225

The so-called arrow-marked '**Government Bream**'
1841 *Geelong Advertiser* 7 Aug. 1/4 The **Government camp**,
Corio. **1855** R. CARBONI *Eureka Stockade* 66 They had been
sticking up some three or four tents, called the Eureka
government Camp. **1920** C.H. SAYCE *Golden Buckles* 54 If
one of them does for a white man, he only gets about a year
in a Government camp, down country, petted by the ladies
and missionaries, and fed on the best of tucker. **1829**
Hobart Town Almanack 44 At the township . . is erected a
Government cottage, the residence of a military officer,
stationed here with a detachment of troops. **1852** *Murray's
Guide to Gold Diggings* 38 We have a '**government escort**' or
conveyance, bringing every week into town from the gold-
field, a *ton* of gold. **1872** 'TASMANIAN LADY' *Treasures, Lost &
Found* 46 The Government escort for conveying the gold to
Melbourne consisted of about a dozen mounted and well-
armed troopers, with officer and sergeant. **1913** J. SAD-
LEIR *Recoll.* 46 The Government Gold Escorts were insti-
tuted in the very earliest digging days. **1808** *Sydney Gaz.* 22
May, A search to be made to discover whether any of the
Government gangs were absent. **1809** *N.S.W. Pocket
Almanack* 8 Persons secreting or employing such servants
during **Government hours** will be punished for a breach
of public orders. **1887** MRS D.D. DALY *Digging, Squatting, &
Pioneering Life* 55 The office hours were from ten to four, the
ordinary Government hours. **1802** *HRA* (1915) 1st Ser.
IV. 325 Settlers have been in the habit of employing those
who have left **Government Labour.** **1807** *Sydney Gaz.* 5
Apr., A charge of employing *John Campbell*, a **Government
labourer**, without demanding his certificate or pass.
1846 'SQUATTER' *Visit to Antipodes* 97 Government labourers
were . . getting 17s. 6d. a day, while the South Australian
Company were only paying 12s. **1797** D. COLLINS *Acct.
Eng. Colony N.S.W.* (1802) II. 25 A **government man**
allowed to officers or settlers in their own time. **1827**
P. CUNNINGHAM *Two Yrs. in N.S.W.* II. 117 Convicts . . when
fairly domiciliated . . are . . spoken of under the loyal
designation of *government-men*, the term *convict* being erased
by a sort of general tacit compact from our Botany dictionary. **1902** *Bulletin* (Sydney) 13 Sept. 16/1 Government men stationed on 'The Fringe' are mostly in their
right place. . . The 'Fringe' civil servant, being king of his
tinpot village, generally has an overweening conceit of his
own abilities. **1813** *N.S.W. Pocket Almanack* 58 The Superintendant of the Government Herds is enjoined to continue . . to renew the **Government Mark** on all cattle, if
by time or accident obliterated. **1801** *HRA* (1916) 1st Ser.
VI. 202 The Expense of supporting them by **Government
Rations**. **1842** *Austral. & N.Z. Monthly Mag.* 28 The church
service is . . read at Freemantle and Albany by the **government residents**. **1918** G. WHITE *Thirty Yrs. Tropical Aust.*
98 The first step was to abolish the Government Resident,
who had hitherto sufficed to conduct affairs, and administer justice, and appoint an Administrator with the title of
His Excellency and absolute and autocratic powers. **1802**
HRA (1915) 1st Ser. III. 644 A proportion of **Government
servants** are employed. **1946** F. CLUNE *Try Nothing Twice*
63 My career as a government servant had ended. I didn't
get the sack. I just left. **1837** *S. Austral. Rec.* (London) 8
Nov. 3 We then went forward on the sand for about three
miles, to the **government settlement**, where there still
remain many capital huts, made of brush wood, by the first
people who came here, before the site of the city of Adelaide was determined on. **1977** V. PRIDDLE *Larry & Jack* 132
Old Wambo, his faithful old aboriginal stockman was taken
away to a Government Settlement to spend the evening of
his life with his own people. **1825** *Austral.* (Sydney) 12
May 4 Sarah Brown . . saw the prisoners at the bar at a
government station at . . the Cowpastures. **1886** E.M.
CURR *Austral. Race* I. 40 It is noticeable on the Government
stations, on which the Blacks have been collected and well
fed for over twenty years, that the females who have grown
up on them have entirely ceased to show this disparity of
stature. **1842** *Geelong Advertiser* 7 Mar. 2/3 The men are
employed on the public works; but we are sorry to say that
they do not appear to be of much use, apparently from the
want of an active overseer. The '**government stroke**' is
soon learned; and the proficiency of the new hands appears
to exceed that of the oldest gang in the colony. **1943**
E. MERCIER *Giggles* 13 There appear to be two occasions
when the Government stroke is not noticeable in a Government department—when it is hounding a private citizen
for money, and when it is trying to pass a liability on to
another department. **1892** *Truth* (Sydney) 7 Feb. 4/4
Mr Dibbs . . bluntly declared that if the '**Government
Strokers**' didn't like the present arrangements they could
clear out at once, for thousands of others were ready to fill
their billets and submit to the terrible inconvenience of
being paid *a fine fat 'screw'*. **1894** A.F. CALVERT *Coolgardie
Goldfield* 40 **Government tanks** here quite dry. **1827** W.J.
DUMARESQ in G. Mackaness *Fourteen Journeys Blue Mountains*
(1950) ii. 93 As the *town* of Bathurst is exclusively a
government town, every tenement in it is occupied by
government officers. **1848** J.C. BYRNE *Twelve Yrs.' Wanderings* I. 148 Parramatta, Maitland East and West, Windsor,
Newcastle . . are all **government townships**, established
and laid out by the executive. **1834** J. MUDIE *Vindication* 8
She was Mr Larnach's **Government woman**. **1803** *Sydney Gaz.* 17 July, Thomas Higgins . . for neglect of his
Government work was sentenced to receive twenty-five
lashes. **1822** J.T. BIGGE *Rep. State Colony N.S.W.* 39 The first
of these individuals acts as superintendent of the **government works** at Windsor.

government house.

1. a. The official residence of the principal represen-
tative of the Crown in each Colony (now State); since
Federation, also the official residence of the Governor-
General of Australia. Also *attrib.*

1788 *HRA* (1914) 1st Ser. I. 48 The ground marked for
Government House is intended to include the main guard.
1899 *Austral. Tit-Bits* (Sydney) 25 Feb. 34/2 Francisco
Miranda . . was hospitably entertained by the Government
House party both in Melbourne and Sydney. **1978**
B. OAKLEY *Ship's Whistle* (1979) 42 It is not Government
House, Mr Horne, but it is roomy enough for the single
person.

b. *transf.* The principal residence on a sheep or cattle
station.

1884 J. BAKER *Diary & Sketches Journey S.A.* 23 Were well
recd. by acting Manager (Napier) & had 'Government
House' to ourselves. **1982** M. WALKER *Making Do* 105, I
would be cooking in the manager's house on a station,
which was always called Government House.

2. A dwelling built and maintained at public expense,
esp. in a newly established town or to provide low-cost
accommodation.

1827 P. CUNNINGHAM *Two Yrs. in N.S.W.* I. 147 Few
except the government houses are worthy of much notice,
being chiefly small detached cottages of brick or wood,
presenting no very imposing appearance. **1969** *Bulletin*
(Sydney) 22 Feb. 32/3 Paul Hasluck now moves from
a small Government house in the Canberra suburb of
Deakin . . to Yarralumla.

Governor.

1. The principal representative of the sovereign in an
Australian Colony (later State); formerly an abbreviation of GOVERNOR-GENERAL 1, GOVERNOR-IN-CHIEF,
LIEUTENANT GOVERNOR 1. See also *State Governor* STATE
2 b.

1793 J. HUNTER *Hist. Jrnl. Trans. Port Jackson* 244, I called
them Phillip Islands, after Arthur Phillip, the governor of
New South Wales. **1972** *Bulletin* (Sydney) 21 Oct. 34/3
The roles of Queen Elizabeth's Australian representatives,
the six governors and the governor-general, are three-
fold—constitutional, ceremonial and what has come to be
described as charismatic.

k. *Hist.* In the collocation **Governor's Court**: see
quot. 1819.

1812 *HRA* (1916) 1st Ser. VII. 673 There should be
established two Courts in the Settlement, one the Supreme
Court, the other the Governor's Court. **1819** W.C.
WENTWORTH *Statistical, Hist., & Pol. Descr. N.S.W.* 30 The

Governor's Court consists of the Judge Advocate and two inhabitants of the colony, appointed by precept from the governor, and takes cognizance of all pleas where the amount sued for does not exceed £50 sterling, (except such pleas as may arise between party and party at Van Dieman's Land) and from its decisions there is no appeal.

Governor-General.

1. *Hist.* A title bestowed on a Governor of the Colony of New South Wales whose jurisdiction extended also to other Colonies.

1827 P. CUNNINGHAM *Two Yrs. in N.S.W.* II. 312 New South Wales and Van Dieman's Land are under the jurisdiction of a governor-general, who resides in the former, with a lieutenant-governor under him for each colony. **1873** A. TROLLOPE *Aust. & N.Z.* I. 205 In 1856 . . responsible government was established in New South Wales. . . This happened during the reign of Sir William Denison. . . He, however, still kept the title of Governor-General of Australasia, which was not borne by his successor.

2. The principal representative of the sovereign in the Commonwealth of Australia.

1898 *Austral. Handbk.* 122 The Queen may from time to time appoint a Governor-General, who shall be Her Majesty's Representative in the Commonwealth. **1972** *Bulletin* (Sydney) 21 Oct. 34/3 Constitutionally . . the governor-general is the commander in chief of the Australian armed forces; he opens and closes Federal Parliament; he may grant pardons to criminals; and must give his assent to acts of parliament.

Governor-in-Chief. *Hist.* A title formerly bestowed on the Governor of an Australian Colony; in full **Captain-General and Governor-in-Chief.**

1787 *HRA* (1914) 1st Ser. I. 2 We . . do constitute and appoint you the said Phillip to be our Captain-General and Governor-in-Chief in and over our territory called New South Wales. **1881** J.F.V. FITZGERALD *Aust.* 76 Sir William Dennison . . and Sir Charles Fitzroy were styled 'Governors-General'; they were supposed to have some sort of pre-eminence over the other Governor. Sir John Young (Lord Lisgar) succeeded . . in May, 1861, with the title of 'Governor-in-Chief': this has continued to be the style.

govie, var. GUVVIE.

Goyder's line. *S.A.* [From the name of G.W. *Goyder* (1826-1898), Surveyor-General of South Australia.] A line north of which the annual rainfall is less than 355 mm., and the land in consequence unsuitable for wheat-farming. Also **Goyder's line of rainfall.**

1873 A. TROLLOPE *Aust. & N.Z.* II. 195 The surveyor-general, Mr Goyder, has drawn an arbitrary line across the map of South Australia, which is now known as Goyder's line of rainfall. **1967** R. HAWKER *Emu in Fowl Pen* 162 The country slowly growing drier all the way, to well beyond Goyder's line, which indicated a settled and predictable rainfall.

Grabben Gullen pie /ˈɡræbən ɡʌlən ˈpaɪ/. [f. the name of a town in N.S.W.] See quot. 1899.

1899 *Bulletin* (Sydney) 2 Sept. 14/2 'Grabben Gullen pie' . . is properly . . a pumpkin scooped out and stuffed with 'possum. **1980** B. HORNADGE *Austral. Slanguage* 207 Another old timers' dish was the Grabben Gullen Pie, also known as Possum Pumpkin Pie.

graft, *n.* [Br. dial. *graft* work of any description: see EDD.] Work of any sort, esp. demanding work. Also *attrib.*

[N.Z. **1853** J. ROCHFORT *Adventures of Surveyor* 47, I could make more money by 'hard graft', as they call labour in the colonies.] **1873** J.C.F. JOHNSON *Christmas on Carringa* 15 My name is Jim, the Cadger, I'm a downy cove you see, 'Hard graft', it ain't my fancy. **1981** H. LINDSAY *Echoes H. Lawson* 19 Home is a suddenly-strange and old-fashioned farmhouse away to hell in a lousy hard-graft valley nobody ever heard of.

graft, *v.* [Br. dial. *to graft* to do work of any description.] *intr.* To work; to labour strenuously.

[**1859** J.C. HOTTEN *Dict. Mod. Slang* 47 *Graft*, to go to work.] **1890** *Argus* (Melbourne) 9 Aug. 4/2 You graftin' with him? **1946** M. FRANKLIN *My Career goes Bung* 214 At home grafting away like fury.

Hence **grafting** *ppl. a.*

1980 *Sydney Morning Herald* 24 Apr. 32/3 The mountain men—Penrith Rugby League team—knuckled to a grafting 26-14 win against Cronulla-Sutherland in the Tooth Cup match at Leichhardt Oval last night.

grafter. [f. prec.] One who works hard.

1891 *Truth* (Sydney) 11 Jan. 1/7 Is your husband a good hard 'grafter', or is he lazy and slack? **1981** *Austral.* (Sydney) 3 June 14/1 *A grafter* in Trevor Chappell or a dasher in Martin Kent?

gramma. [Of unknown origin.] A variety of pumpkin having a sweet, fibrous flesh. Also *attrib.*

1964 P. WHITE *Burnt Ones* 183 'But why pick on a poor pumpkin? If it had been a gramma,' she said. **1982** N. KEESING *Lily on Dustbin* 116 Although the Americans invented pumpkin pie, we adapted it, and gramma pie is its close cousin.

Granny, *n.*[1]

1. A nickname for *The Sydney Morning Herald.* Also **Granny Herald.**

1851 *Press* (Sydney) 189/2 'My Grannie O,' (which we beg to submit as a very good cognomen for the *Herald* and its antiquated and obsolete notions on the subject of Government). **1950** J. CLEARY *Just let me Be* 241 'You're beginning to talk like some old spinster,' Harry said. 'You'll be writing letters to Granny Herald next.'

2. *transf. Obs.* A nickname given to other daily newspapers.

1884 *Adelaide Punch* 25 Apr. 2/2 Every day the old dame of Grenfell Street is becoming more feeble and ridiculous. Last Wednesday Mr H. Gawler wrote complaining of some aspersions Granny had cast upon his father. **1905** *Tocsin* (Melbourne) 3 Nov. 6/1 According to the 'Argus', 'an old man died in London at the age of eighty one'. When a young man dies at the age of 81, we wish Granny would ring up the 'Tocsin' and let us know about it.

granny, *n.*[2]

a. Abbrev. of GRANNY SMITH.

1944 C.S. WATTS *Selected Verse* 13 Cast-off clothes and greasy bacon, and . . 'Grannies! Ten a bob!' **1979** *Mercury* (Hobart) 3 Sept. 11/1 The Yugoslav freighter . . unloaded 42,000 cases of Grannies.

b. In the phr. **she'll be Grannies,** all will be well: see APPLE 4.

1963 B. BEAVER *Hot Summer* 115 'She'll be Grannies,' cackled the ragged informant. 'And I know the girls will be in it because they tipped me off to tell you.'

Granny Smith. [f. the name of Maria Ann *Smith* (c 1801-1870), cultivator of the apple.] A variety of apple, green-skinned and especially suitable for cooking.

1895 *Agric. Gaz. N.S.W.* VI. 900, I think that the Sturmer Pippin, Stewarts, Granny Smith's Seedling . . would be worth a trial. **1985** *Sydney Morning Herald* 23 Feb. 109/4 Granny Smith, of Granny Smith Apple fame, grew her apples on a farm near North Road and Threlfall Street, Eastwood, in the 1860s.

grant. *Hist.* Between 1788 and 1831 (when the practice ceased): the granting to an individual (emancipated

convict, settler, marine officer, etc.) of a tract of Crown land; the tract of land so granted; the document or deed in which the conditions of the grant are stated.

1793 J. Hunter *Hist. Jrnl. Trans. Port Jackson* 531 To Philip Schaffer, .. one hundred and forty acres; called in the grant, the *Vineyard*. **1804** *HRA* (1921) 3rd Ser. I. 246 The Parties will become entitled to Grants at the New Settlement of Port Dalrymple. **1827** P. Cunningham *Two Yrs. in N.S.W.* II. 157 In searching for a suitable grant, it is a great point to fix upon a place where the land *round* it is all so indifferent that no new settler is likely to place himself near you .. enabling you thus to have a free run for your stock for miles without being encroached on.

grantee. *Hist.* The recipient of a grant of land.

1800 *HRA* (1914) 1st Ser. II. 514 You assign to each grantee, the service of any number of them [*sc.* convicts] that you may judge necessary. **1853** S. Sidney *Three Colonies* (ed. 2) 87 Persons desirous of becoming grantees without purchase might obtain land in satisfying the governor that they had the power and intention of expending in the cultivation of the land a capital equal to half the estimated value of it.

grape. [Prob. infl. by the expression *sour grapes*.] In the phr. **a grape on the business**: see quot. 1941.

1941 S.J. Baker *Pop. Dict. Austral. Slang* 32 Grape on the business, A (of a person), one who is a blue stocking, a wallflower or a drag on cheery company. **1946** A. Marshall *Tell us about Turkey, Jo* 62 She hasn't got a bloke. She is a grape on the business.

grape-cocky. [See Cocky *n.*²] One who grows grapes, esp. for the dried-fruits industry.

1941 *Bulletin* (Sydney) 28 May 16/2, I lands a job helpin' one of them grape-cockies stack lucerne. **1968** S. Gore *Holy Smoke* 62 These grape cockies think to themselves, Strewth, it's us that's doin' all the hard yakka round the joint.

grape-snatching, *vbl. n.* Grape-picking. Also *attrib.*

1952 *Bulletin* (Sydney) 9 Jan. 16/2 A gang of us congregated in a Mildura boarding-house waiting for the grape-snatching to start. *Ibid.* 2 Apr. 17/1 A temperance advocate joined our grape-snatching gang in Mildura.

grass. In the phr. **on the grass**: see quot. 1941.

1885 *Australasian Printers' Keepsake* 93 I'm *on the Grass* (worse luck!) for now I find I dare not shift. I'm tethered to this state. **1941** S.J. Baker *Pop. Dict. Austral. Slang* 51 On the grass, free, at large. A criminal is 'on the grass again' after being released from gaol.

grass-fed, *a.* and *n.*

A. *adj.* Of a horse: inexperienced; not trained as a racehorse. Of a race(-meeting): organized for such horses. Also *transf.*

1878 G. Walch *Australasia* 28 In the heyday of his grass-fed youth while being ridden just beyond the Sapling Camp he had inadvertently grazed with his hoof an unwary snake. **1891** *Truth* (Sydney) 5 Apr. 2/4 There are plenty of intelligent, honest, educated men in the ranks of Labor who are well enough 'grass fed', but can't stand corn. **1973** R. Robinson *Drift of Things* 92 There was a grass-fed race meeting coming up and Mr Simmonds wanted to try out his horses.

B. *n.* A horse which has not been trained as a racehorse: see quot. 1945.

1940 E. Hill *Great Austral. Loneliness* (ed. 2) 125 Horses are hacks and grass-feds from the drovers' plants and the stations. **1945** F. Cork *Tales from Cattle Country* 51 Among racing enthusiasts in the Outback you will hear much talk about 'corn-feds' and 'grass-feds' that is confusing to the uninitiated. 'Corn-feds' are horses prepared for the regular meetings—training solidly and being fed on such hardening foods as chaff, oats, and corn. The picnic gallopers must be 'grass-feds' unless drought conditions preclude 'grass-fed' meetings, in which case picnic races are held under 'corn-fed' conditions.

grass-fighter. One who fights 'with no holds barred'.

1951 I.L. Idriess *Across Nullarbor* 19 Those were the bareknuckle days, 'kinged' over by the grim 'grass fighters'. **1965** R.H. Conquest *Horses in Kitchen* 123 He reckoned any good Australian grass-fighter, fast on his feet, could skittle a shillelagh man in no time.

Also **grass-fighting** *vbl. n.*

1978 D. Stuart *Wedgetail View* 99 Professional pug, yes, he makes money .. though it's a pretty crook way of making a quid. But grass fighting; hell .. it's crazy.

grasshopper. *fig.* A nickname for a tourist, esp. one visiting Canberra.

1955 S. Rudd *Far & Near* 67 Pioneer tourists are nicknamed the 'Grasshoppers', by the country folk, who state that they fly into a town, devour all there is to eat, drink and see and then fly out again. **1976** C. Forsyth *Governor-General* 117 He picked his way past a group of tourists de-bussing... Grassies, short for grasshoppers, they were called in Canberra because of their habit of descending on the national capital in plague proportions.

grass parrot. Any of various parrots that habitually frequent grassy country, esp. species of *Psephotus* and *Neophema*. Also **grass parakeet**.

1840 J. Gould *Birds of Aust.* (1848) V. Pl. 47, Swift Lorikeet .. in its style of colouring and in its more lengthened and slender tail .. is beautifully intermediate between the Grass Parakeets and the *Trichoglossi*. **1972** J. Hibberd *Stretch of Imagination* (1973) 19, I can see her now .. on a wicker chair .. under a pergola of everlastings .. enjoying the sunsets over Lake Hindmarsh .. feeding a grass parrot or two.

grass roots, *pl. Mining.* [Prob. f. *grass* earth's surface: see OED *sb.*¹ 9 b.] The surface of a mine. Also *attrib.*

1932 I.L. Idriess *Prospecting for Gold* 264 'Grass roots', a term used where a working is started from, or worked up to, the surface. **1979** B. Scott *Tough in Old Days* 31 We heard of .. grassroots gold that lay just below the surface of certain kinds of country.

grass-tree.

1. a. Any of many small trees of the fam. Xanthorrhoeaceae, usu. of the genus *Xanthorrhoea*, having a crown of grass-like leaves; Blackboy 2 a.; Yacca 1. See also Xanthorrhoea.

1794 G. Thompson *Slavery & Famine* ii. 12 Their spears are made of the stem of the grass tree. **1981** A.B. Facey *Fortunate Life* 20 The blackboy is a native grass-tree that grows in the Western Australian bush.

b. With distinguishing epithet: **small grass-tree,** any of several smaller species of grass-tree, esp. (in e. Aust.) *Xanthorrhoea minor,* having a tuft of leaves less than 1 m. tall topped by a slender scape of similar height; *dwarf grass-tree,* see Dwarf.

1844 L. Leichhardt *Jrnl. Overland Exped. Aust.* 23 Oct. (1847) 21 The first appearance of the small grass-tree (Xanthorrhaea). **1972** *Lal Lal Blast Furnace* (Forests Comm. Vic.) 3 An unusual flora feature of the Reserve is the density of *Xanthorrhoea minor,* or small grass tree.

c. Special Comb. **grass-tree gum,** the resin exuded by any of several species of grass-tree, rich in picric acid, usu. red, and formerly much used as an adhesive; Blackboy 2 b.; *yacca gum*, see Yacca 2. See also Yellow gum 1 a.

1835 J. Backhouse *Narr. Visit Austral. Colonies* (1843) 288 He used a spear in fishing, made of a long stick, with four, long, wooden prongs attached to it, by means of string and

Grass-tree Gum. **1973** V. SERVENTY *Desert Walkabout* 27 Near the coast blackboy or grass tree gum was used as an adhesive.

2. Any of several species of the chiefly Tasmanian genus *Richea* (fam. Epacridaceae), having prickly grasslike leaves, esp. *R. dracophylla* and *R. pandanifolia*.

1833 J. BACKHOUSE *Narr. Visit Austral. Colonies* (1843) 159 The Broad-leaved Grass-tree, *Richea Dracophylla*, forms a striking object; it is very abundant, and on an average, from ten to fifteen feet high; it is much branched, and has broad, grassy foliage. **1968** V. SERVENTY *Southern Walkabout* 54 The giant grass tree or 'pandanni'.

grazier. [In Br. use apparently uncommon and applied chiefly to one who raises cattle for market.] One who raises sheep or cattle; in early use distinguishing one who raises stock from a crop-farmer, in later use denoting a land-holder whose interests are substantial. See also *cattle grazier* CATTLE 2, PASTORALIST, *sheep grazier* SHEEP 2.

1804 *HRA* (1915) 1st Ser. IV. 462 Forms the most inviting and extensive country for the comfort and benefit of the cultivator and grazier. **1981** Q. WILD *Honey Wind* 69 Too much rain this year, Harry, all the graziers have got to get webbed feet fitted to their Mercedes.

grazing, *vbl. n.* [Not necessarily excl. Austral. but of local significance because of the importance of the grazing industry.] Used *attrib.* in Special Comb. **grazing country,** land suited to or used for the raising of sheep or cattle; **district,** an area in which sheep or cattle raising is the principal industry; **establishment, farm,** a rural property on which sheep or cattle raising is the principal activity; also **farmer,** one who owns such a property; **paddock,** an enclosure in which sheep or cattle pasture; **property,** *grazing farm*; **run, station,** *grazing farm*; an area of pasture detached from the principal landholding; see also RUN $n.^2$ 1 a., STATION 2 a.

1831 *Acct. Colony Van Diemen's Land* 117 Part of this fine **grazing country** has now been located and converted into profitable sheep and cattle walks. **1831** *Acct. Colony Van Diemen's Land* 84 The road continues through a fine **grazing district**. **1835** *Colonist* (Sydney) 30 July 243/3 Widely-scattered **grazing establishments** in the interior. **1810** *Sydney Gaz*. 23 June, Wanted .. a careful man to take the charge of a **Grazing Farm** with about 100 Head of Horned Cattle. **1855** 'RUSTICUS' *How to settle in Vic*. 104 The undisputed occupation of the **grazing farmer** or squatter, as he has hitherto been termed. **1827** P. CUNNINGHAM *Two Yrs. in N.S.W*. II. 167 A good stock-yard and **grazing-paddock** for your working bullocks, should follow as speedily as possible. **1876** 'CAPRICORNUS' *Colonisation* 12 **Grazing properties** had been formed on which for over thirty years the labours and earnings of thousands of people were sunk. **1826** J. ATKINSON *Acct. Agric. & Grazing N.S.W*. 136 These roads .. have generally been formed by people who have .. taken possession of a **grazing run** beyond the occupied part of the country. **1834** J.D. LANG *Hist. & Statistical Acct. N.S.W*. II. 121 The sheep and young horses were sent, under charge of a hired overseer and two convict-servants, to form a **grazing station** at the distance of thirty miles.

greasy.

1. One who cooks for an assemblage of employees, esp. on a sheep or cattle station; an army cook.

1873 J.C.F. JOHNSON *Christmas on Carringa* 1 Bill .. was our *chef d'cuisine* .. in the vernacular, cook or 'greasy'. **1918** *Twenty-Second's Echo: Mag. 22nd Battalion A.I.F*. 15 Oct. 2 Someone suggested that the German had been a 'greasy' who was being boiled to extract the grease.

2. A shearer.

1939 *Bulletin* (Sydney) 14 June 20/1 When the mob lined up at Drill Park the greasies found that one of the two learners was a cocksure little beggar. **1956** F.B. VICKERS *First Place to Stranger* 134 When those five greasies get moving they'll shear a lot of sheep.

great Australian adjective: see *Australian adjective* AUSTRALIAN *a*. 4.

great brown kingfisher. *Obs*. The kookaburra *Dacelo novaeguineae*. Also **great brown kingsfisher, great kingfisher.**

1782 J. LATHAM *Gen. Synopsis Birds* I. 609 Great Brown Kingfisher. This is the largest species [of kingfisher] yet known, and is in length eighteen inches. **1822** J. LATHAM *Gen. Hist. Birds* IV. 10 Great Brown Kingsfisher .. the note compared to human laughter, which should give the idea of cheerfulness; hence called the Laughing Bird, or Laughing Jack-Ass. **1893** *Western Champion* (Barcaldine) 24 Jan. 1/2 A period of protection shall be in certain districts .. for the whole year, in respect of .. great kingfisher (laughing jack-ass).

greater glider. The large gliding possum *Petauroides volans* of e. mainland Aust. See also SQUIRREL 1. Also **great glider,** and formerly **greater flying phalanger.**

1943 C. BARRETT *Austral. Animal Bk*. 66 Largest of all the 'flying squirrels' is the greater or taguan flying phalanger (*Petauroides volans*); a beautiful creature with dusky black or dark-grey, soft, silky fur, and a long, pendulous tail, cylindrical and bushy. **1956** T.Y. HARRIS *Naturecraft in Aust*. 75 The Great Glider Possum of the coastal highlands of eastern Australia is noted for the jewel-like glow of its eyes when the light from a torch is focussed on them. **1983** R. STRAHAN *Compl. Bk. Austral. Mammals* 134 The abundance of the Greater Glider in undisturbed forests is in strong contrast to its absence from pine plantations and its paucity in regenerated forest.

great grey kangaroo. *Grey kangaroo* (a), see GREY *a*. Also **great kangaroo.**

1836 *Proc. Zool. Soc. London* 188 When sitting in a state of repose the *great Kangaroo* throws the tail behind him. **1980** C. ALLISON *Hunter's Man. Aust. & N.Z*. 34 The great-grey or 'forester' kangaroos (there are two sub-species) prefer the more timbered coastal slopes and the open western forests.

great kingfisher: see GREAT BROWN KINGFISHER.

Great South Land: see SOUTH LAND.

Greek. In the collocation **the Greek's**: a small café.

1946 M. TRIST *What else is There* 144 She caught up with Mamie and Teddy outside the Greek's. 'How about an ice-cream?' asked Teddy. **1977** A. SYKES *Five Plays* 234 Should be out celebrating. What about a feed at the Greeks?

green.

1. Used as a distinguishing epithet in the names of flora and fauna: **green ant,** *green tree-ant*; **head,** the predom. metallic bluish-green ant *Rhytidoponera metallica*; **leek,** any of several predom. green parrots; **mallee, (a)** the small tree *Eucalyptus viridis* (fam. Myrtaceae) of inland e. mainland Aust., having narrow green leaves; **(b)** (occas.) a similar tree, as *E. oleosa*; **monday,** GREENGROCER; **parrot** (or **parakeet**), any of several predom. green parrots (cf. *green leek*); **snake,** any of several snakes sometimes having a greenish hue, as the *green tree-snake*; **tree-ant,** the ant *Oecophylla smaragdina* of n. Aust. and elsewhere, having a green body and living in trees, where it makes nests from leaves; *green ant*; **tree-snake,** the tree-snake *Dendrelaphis punctulata* (fam. Colubridae) of n. and e. Aust. and New Guinea, some specimens of which have green upperparts; **wattle,** any of several trees of the genus *Acacia* (fam. Mimosaceae), esp. *A. decurrens* of e. N.S.W. and naturalized elsewhere; also *attrib*.

1843 J.L. Stokes *Discoveries in Aust.* (1846) I. 429 Found ourselves under a tree covered with large **green ants.** 1879 *Queenslander* (Brisbane) 20 Sept. 365/2 You .. find you have pitched your bed on or near a nest of '**green-heads**' or soldier ants. 1845 *Bell's Life in Sydney* 18 Jan. 3/4 A most extraordinary bird of the parrot species, commonly called the **green leek**, a native of New South Wales. 1900 *Proc. Linnean Soc. N.S.W.* XXV. 301 *Eucalyptus viridis*... A Mallee of dense growth, the stems usually 2–3 inches in diameter, though occasionally measuring 20 feet in height. . The name '**Green Mallee**' refers to the vivid lustreless green of the leaves. 1926 J.M. Black *Flora S.A.* iii. 418 A form [of *Eucalyptus oleosa*] .. growing in the scrub near Pinnaroo .. is only 1–2 m. high and is locally called 'Green Mallee'. 1895 *Proc. Linnean Soc. N.S.W.* X. 528 *Cyclochila Australasiae* .. **Green Monday** .. is our commonest Sydney Cicada. 1798 J. Hunter *Hist. Jrnl. Trans. Port Jackson* 69 There are a great variety of birds in this country; all those of the parrot tribe, such as the macaw, cockatoo .. **green parrot.** 1861 'Old Bushman' *Bush Wanderings* 165 The commonest of all the paroqueets is the *Green Paroqueet*, which in shape and habits rather resembles the blue mountaineer. 1806 *Sydney Gaz.* 16 Mar., A beautiful **green snake** made its appearance on a summer house. 1845 L. Leichhardt *Jrnl. Overland Exped. Aust.* 16 June (1847) 291 It was at the lower part of the Lynd that we first saw the **green-tree ant;** which seemed to live in small societies in rude nests between the green leaves of shady trees. 1869 G. Krefft *Snakes of Aust.* 24 The **Green Tree Snake**, in a state of excitement, is strongly suggestive of one of the popular toys of childhood, by the peculiar white marks which become visible when its skin is distended. 1814 *HRA* (1916) 1st Ser. VIII. 223, I beg to turn my Ideas to the **Green Wattle** Bark. 1982 Elliot & Jones *Encycl. Austral. Plants* II. 40 *Acacia decurrens* .. Green Wattle. . . Leaves suitable as a dyeing material. Cultivated as a glasshouse plant in Europe. Has also been called *A. normalis.*

2. Used to designate a class (or area) of vegetation: **green drought,** the phenomenon of new but insubstantial growth (of forage), promoted by rain during or after a drought and unsupported by standing dry feed; **feed,** forage (grown to be) fed fresh to livestock; **pick,** new growth (of forage) promoted by rain; **shoot,** new growth (of vegetation) immediately after a fire.

1980 *Sydney Morning Herald* 5 Sept. 1/7 The rain has to be heavy, to sink into the earth, to push up grass with guts—not the water-filled junk around some areas now, after last week's sprinkling. That's a '**green drought**'. 1876 'Eight Yrs.' Resident' *Queen of Colonies* 202 The sorghum, or Chinese sugar-cane, is a small species of sugar-cane which is propagated from seed. It is a most excellent **green feed,** for which purpose it is alone grown. . . Market-gardeners .. cut it when four to five feet high and sell it in bundles as 'green-stuff'. 1966 J. Carter *People of Inland* 13 Kidman usually managed to get his sheep or cattle under some rain, so they could have a decent feed of young '**green pick**' before moving on again. 1953 H.G. Lamond *Big Red* 197 As the shooters knew, a **green shoot** always followed a burn of spinifex.

3. Used with various nouns to denote youth or immaturity: **green hand,** one who lacks experience; **lamb,** a very young lamb; **skin,** the hide of a freshly slaughtered sheep.

1872 *Illustr. Sydney News* 13 Apr. 55/1 Should any infatuated **green hand** decline the 'spell' and continue to work while the others rest, he becomes a marked man. 1888 *Bulletin* (Sydney) 10 Mar. 14/2, I went a lambing down to fetch home the **green lambs**; But I couldn't find 'em green—for lambs are mostly white. 1845 *Portland Gaz.* 3 June 2/5 **Green skins** are not to be purchased from the butchers, owing to all being contracted for.

greenback.

1. *Obs.* [Transf. use of U.S. *greenback* a legal tender note.] A one-pound note.

1919 C.A. Bernays *Qld. Politics during Sixty Yrs.* 16 He did not understand the futility of flooding Queensland with 'greenbacks' without a gold backing. 1967 J. Wynnum *I'm Jack, all Right* 11, I also happen to have a roll of greenbacks big enough to choke a horse.

2. See Greenie 2.

1963 *Bulletin* (Sydney) 23 Nov. 13/2 The roaring greenbacks can make the blood sing, but they can also break a limb or gulp the swimmer in a rip. 1963 J. Pollard *Austral. Surfrider* 20 Just out a little further are the 'greenbacks', the unbroken waves.

green ban. [Used elsewhere but recorded earliest in Aust.] A prohibition (esp. as imposed by a trade union) which prevents construction work from proceeding on a site within a green belt; a similar prohibition made to protect a building, site, etc., of natural or cultural significance. See also *black ban* Black *a.*[4] 2. Also *attrib.*

1973 P. Thomas *Taming Concrete Jungle* 43 A unionist coined a happy phrase for such bans to save natural bush and park. 'They're not black bans,' he said; 'they're green bans.' 1976 *Bulletin* (Sydney) 27 Nov. 18/3 Unions will provide the industrial muscle but the left will also try to reconvene the coalition of workers, middle-class conservationists and intellectuals which proved so effective for the 'green ban' movement.

green cart. See quot. 1982.

1935 D.G. Stead *Rabbit in Aust.* 14 We were suitable for cargo for the 'green cart', or for whatever other vehicle is used to take us to the mental hospital. 1982 L. Keesing *Lily on Dustbin* 164 *Green cart*, vehicle allegedly sent to convey mad people to the asylum. 'He wants to look out, they'll be sending the green cart for him next.'

greengrocer. The cicada *Cyclochila australasiae*, when green. See also *yellow monday* Yellow 1.

1905 *Bulletin* (Sydney) 28 Dec. (Red Page), There's heaps of different kinds of locusts, heaps! .. Greengrocers, and floury bakers, and yellow Mondays. 1985 *Northern Herald* (Sydney) 10 Jan. 1/2 There are several species of noisy cicada about Sydney but the prime culprit, the Greengrocer, may be undergoing a natural cycle.

greenhide, *n.* and *attrib.* [In Br. use from 1577 (see OED *green, a.* 9 c.) but of special significance in Aust.: see quot. 1980.]

A. *n.*

1. The untanned hide of a beast; untanned hide, rawhide.

1809 *Sydney Gaz.* 18 June, For Sale .. Leather both English and colonial. . . No expence is spared to manufacture it from the Green Hide to the Shoe or Boot. 1980 P. Freeman *Woolshed* 28 For stringybark and greenhide will never, never fail yer, Stringybark and greenhide is the mainstay of Australia.

2. *transf.* See quot.

1918 *Huon Times* (Franklin) 24 Dec. 3/3 Away in the misty past the Greenhides were a society of young bucks who dwelt on the neighboring stations, where they maintained English traditions and always dressed for dinner, but when they came to town they put off all restraint.

B. *attrib.*

1. Of or pertaining to greenhide.

1847 A. Harris *Settlers & Convicts* (1953) 125 The beast's hide was cut through in all directions with the green-hide lash of the heavy bullock whip. 1978 D. Stuart *Wedgetail View* 24 They were seated .. on rough bush-timber chairs strung with greenhide thongs.

2. *fig.* Strong, sinewy.

1918 C.J. Dennis *Backblock Ballads* 29 He was tall and tough and stringy, with the shoulders of an axeman, Broad and loose, with greenhide muscles; and a hand shaped to the reins.

3. Comb. **greenhide bucket, rope.**
1888 'R. Boldrewood' *Robbery under Arms* (1937) 227 Winding up **greenhide buckets** filled with gravel from shafts. **1843** *Sydney Morning Herald* 8 Sept. 2/7 He took a **green hide rope** with him to tie up the horse in the bush.

4. Special Comb. **greenhide station,** a primitively appointed station; one at which rough-and-ready methods are employed.
1942 *Bulletin* (Sydney) 16 Dec. 12/1 On our greenhide station, when abo. camps were numerous, we ran out of shot.

greenhood. Any of many species of the genus of terrestrial orchids *Pterostylis* (fam. Orchidaceae) of Australasia and the s.w. Pacific, having a hooded greenish flower.
1914 E.E. Pescott *Native Flowers Vic.* 86 The 'greenhoods' belong to the genus Pterostylis; they are usually greenish in colour, and the upper portion of the flower is shaped like a hood, covering the rest of the flower. **1985** *Age* (Melbourne) 20 Sept. (Suppl.) 7/1 Many varieties of greenhoods are like scattered, tiny gems in a sea of muted green.

greenie. Also **greeny.** [f. green + -Y.]
1. Any of several predom. green birds or animals.
1890 *Quiz* (Adelaide) 19 Sept. 6/2 Two Hindmarsh young gentlemen went out with a gun..shot a little 'greenie'. **1933** *Bulletin* (Sydney) 4 Jan. 21/4 As to the frog's persistency, I can vouch for that. I once saw a big 'greeny', who used to come up on the table at nights.

2. *Surfing.* A large unbroken wave; Greenback 2.
1940 P. Kerry *Cobbers A.I.F.* 12 About 'alf a mile from shore, Where 'e was loafin' on the greenies, an' lookin' out fer more. **1964** B. Humphries *Nice Night's Entertainment* (1981) 77 The surf was *fantastic.* You should have seen those greenies.

3. One who supports a Green ban; a conservationist.
1973 *Nation Rev.* (Melbourne) 28 Sept. 1572/1 The local greenies have despaired of stopping the dreaded post office tower by indirect means. **1985** J. Miller *Koori* 218 Since I believe in Koori land rights and no dams on the Franklin River, that makes me a black, greenie, pinko.

green slip. *S.A. Obs.* A portion of Crown land remaining unalienated as a result of a discrepancy between the size of section into which the land was surveyed, and that into which it was divided.
1888 *Southern Austral.* (Adelaide) 3 Nov. 3/1 The Treasurer, could he have known these tenders were for the green slips, would not have received the deposit, because the regulations were not complied with. **1839** *S. Austral. Gaz.* (Adelaide) 7 Nov. 2 In reference to those portions of land usually called 'Green Slips'.. the Resident Commissioner is of opinion that they never have been thrown open to general selection and tender, and that therefore no valid claims upon them exist.

grevillea /grəˈvɪliə/. [The plant genus *Grevillea* was named by the British botanist R. Brown (in Knight, J. (1809) *Proteeae* 120) after the botanist C.F. Greville (1749–1809), Vice-President of the Royal Society.] Any shrub or tree of the large, chiefly Austral. genus *Grevillea* (fam. Proteaceae) many of which are cultivated as ornamentals. See also Spider flower. Also *attrib.*
1825 B. Field *Geogr. Mem. N.S.W.* 422 All the other indigenous trees and shrubs, that I have seen, are evergreens.. the curious grevillea. **1958** *Coast to Coast 1957–58* 138 The grevillea bushes bore a fleece of snowy blossom.

grey, *n.* [Orig. Br. slang; of unknown origin but see OED *grey, sb.* 10.] A coin having two heads or two tails; in the game of two-up, esp. a coin with two tails. Cf. Nob.
1812 J.H. Vaux *Mem.* (1819) II. 179 *Gray,* a half-penny, or other coin, having two heads or two tails, and fabricated for the use of gamblers. **1975** L. Ryan *Shearers* 153 *Greys,* double tail pennies.

grey, *a.* Used as a distinguishing epithet in the names of flora and fauna: **grey box,** any of several trees of the genus *Eucalyptus* (fam. Myrtaceae), usu. having a rough, grey bark, esp. *E. moluccana* of e. N.S.W. and e. Qld.; the wood of these trees; also *attrib.*; **butcherbird,** the woodland bird *Cracticus torquatus,* widespread in Aust., having black, grey, and white plumage; Derwent jackass; Jackass 2; **-crowned babbler,** the bird *Pomatostomus temporalis* of n. and e. Aust. and s. New Guinea, having a grey stripe on the crown; Yahoo *n.*^{2}; see also Happy Jack; **currawong** (or **magpie**), the predom. grey or black bird *Strepera versicolor* of s. Aust. incl. Tas.; **gum,** any of several trees of the genus *Eucalyptus* having a predom. grey bark, esp. *E. punctata* of e. N.S.W. and s.e. Qld.; the wood of these trees; **handlewood,** any of several trees esp. *Aphananthe philippinensis* (see *axe-handle wood* Axe-handle 1); **ironbark,** any of several ironbark trees having a greyish bark, esp. *Eucalyptus paniculata* of near-coastal N.S.W.; **kangaroo, (a)** the eastern grey kangaroo *Macropus giganteus* of e. Aust., having silvery-grey fur; Forester; *forest kangaroo,* see Forest 2; Great grey kangaroo; **(b)** *western grey kangaroo,* see Western; **mangrove,** *white mangrove,* see White *a.*^{2} 1 a.; **nurse,** the shark *Odontaspis arenarius* of e. and s. Aust. coasts, usu. having a grey back; also **grey-nurse shark; teal,** the small, nomadic, predom. grey duck *Anas gibberifrons* of Aust. and s.w. Pacific; **thrush,** the predom. grey woodland bird *Colluricincla harmonica* (fam. Muscicapidae) of Aust. and e. New Guinea; *whistling dick,* see Whistling; also **grey shrike-thrush.**
1878 R.B. Smyth *Aborigines of Vic.* II. 160 Grey box—Boo-loitch. **1935** *Honey Flora Vic.* (Vic. Dept. Agric.) (rev. ed.) 8 When heating Grey Box honey to reliquefy it.. care should be taken that the temperature does not rise beyond 150° Fahr. **1902** *Emu* I. 82 **Grey Butcher Bird**.. *Cracticus cinereus* is a true 'Butcher Bird' in its habits, and he has apparently the same propensity for 'spitting' its prey on thorns as its English namesake. **1928** G.H. Wilkins *Undiscovered Aust.* 31 Soon after we established our camp two groups, the one of **grey-crowned babblers,** and the other of Apostle-birds, came and made their home with us. **1889** [**grey currawong**] *Proc. Linnean Soc. N.S.W.* IV. 404 *Strepera cuneicaudata*... Local names, 'Rain-bird' and 'Grey Magpie'. **1945** C. Barrett *Austral. Bird Life* 217 The grey currawong is at home in humid ranges and hills of the eastern states. **1887** *Colonist* (Sydney) 350/2 The trees used in the colony for domestic purposes are.. **grey gum,** fencing, building, etc. **1926** *Qld. Agric. Jrnl.* XXV. 438 *Aphananthe Philippinensis*.. **Grey Handlewood. 1900** *Proc. Linnean Soc. N.S.W.* XX. *E. paniculata*.. the **Grey** or White **Ironbark** of the coast. **1793** W. Tench *Compl. Acct. Settlement* 171 The large, or **grey kanguroo,** to which the natives give the name of Pa-ta-ga-ràn. **1953** H.G. Lamond *Big Red* 11 A grey kangaroo sat in a huddled position at the foot of a gidyea tree. **1926** *Qld. Agric. Jrnl.* XXV. 440 *Avicennia officinalis*.. **Grey** or white **Mangrove. 1852** G.C. Mundy *Our Antipodes* I. 390 If the **'grey nurse'** or old solitary shark be hooked, the cable is cut. **1934** T. Wood *Cobbers* 223 Even I got a fish: a grey-nurse shark... He had seven rows of teeth. **1900** A.J. Campbell *Nests & Eggs Austral. Birds* 1039 The **Grey Teal**.. has a more extensive habitat than the chestnut-breasted. **1861** 'Old Bushman' *Bush Wanderings* 138 The common **Gray Thrush** is a dull-looking bird, of a uniform ash-gray colour. **1976** *Reader's Digest Compl. Bk. Austral. Birds* 379 The grey shrike-thrush is well named *harmonica,* for it is among the world's most pleasing songbirds... In eastern Australia the bird is often

called simply the grey thrush—a misleading name because it is not a member of the thrush family.

grey billy. [Prob. f. Br. dial. *bully* a rounded stone: see EDD *sb.*[3]] A hard, strongly cemented silcrete of a greyish or cream colour; BILLY *n.*[3]

1942 M.L. MACPHERSON *I heard Anzacs Singing* 54 'Gray Billy?' 'Uh-huh. You have to dig right through that before you come to the opal.' **1973** V. SERVENTY *Desert Walkabout* 62 The hard silica capping of the breakaways... Called 'grey billy' this breaks to a sharp cutting edge and is suitable for a variety of purposes from cutting flakes to stone axes.

greycoat. *Obs.* A prisoner.

1902 *Bulletin* (Sydney) 31 May 31/2 The Spider, Rajah Riley, Pincher Wilson, and three other greycoats comprised the representatives of the bond, and compared very favorably with the six freemen, amongst whom was the gaol wood-carter. **1907** *Ibid.* 17 Jan. 40/1 Corpse-watchers guard the doom-cell in 'B' wing all the night; The sleepless 'grey-coats' mumble and start in sudden fright.

grey death. See quot. 1967.

1967 *Kings Cross Whisper* (Sydney) xxxv. 6/1 *Grey death,* weak prison stew. The cause of many prison 'rally ups'. **1979** L. NEWCOMBE *Inside Out* 27 The food was atrocious. In particular the evening meal... In 1957 they called it the Grey Death. *Ibid.* 32 The riot over the 'Grey Death' involved everybody in the boys' wing.

grid, *n.*[1] [Br. slang *grid* bicycle: see OED(S *sb.* 7.] A bicycle.

1927 A. WRIGHT *Squatter's Secret* 118 Sorry about your grid... It's a good bike. **1965** G. MCINNES *Road to Gundagai* 122 'Where's the grid?' 'My bike!' 'Yeah, the old mangle; isn't this where we left it?'

grid, *n.*[2] In an opening in a fence: a set of rails above a shallow trench, so spaced as to prevent the passage of stock.

1930 *Bulletin* (Sydney) 16 July 20/2 The grids.. are fast outnumbering the licensed public gates. **1964** *Mount Isa Mail* 19 May 7/5 All the Grids on the Gregory to Almora section of the.. Road would be completed.

grill. A person of southern European descent: see quot. 1967 and GREEK.

1957 J.M. HOSKING *Aust. first & Last* 123 We call them New Australians now; once we called some Dagoes, Others Balts and Squareheads, Pongoes, Grills and Rice and Sagoes. **1967** *Kings Cross Whisper* (Sydney) xxxv. 6/1 *Grills,* Greeks. From the ability of industrious Greeks to control country town cafes.

grip. *Obs.* A job; employment.

1903 *Bulletin* (Sydney) 24 Sept. 16/2 For myself, I must be goin'—yes I must be movin' quick; For I've got a 'grip' with sheep that are a-comin' up from Vic. **1915** C.J. DENNIS *Songs of Sentimental Bloke* (1936) 63 Ferever yappin' like a tork-machine About 'The Hoffis' where 'e 'ad a grip.

gripman. [U.S. *gripman* operator of a cablecar: see Mathews.] The driver and operator of a cable-drawn tram.

1894 *Bulletin* (Sydney) 10 Feb. 9/4 Any tram-man having a shop in his family is ignominiously 'fired'. The gripman or conductor whose industrious wife runs a greengrocery or lolly-stall is a comparatively independent individual. **1967** F.T. MACARTNEY *Proof against Failure* 7 He was then no longer a bus-driver but a 'gripman', as the driver of a cable tram was called.

grog, *n.* [Generalized use of Br. *grog* drink of spirits (usu. rum) and water.]

1. Alcoholic liquor of any kind; a drink of an alcoholic beverage. See also SLY GROG 1 a. Also *attrib.*

1832 *Currency Lad* (Sydney) 22 Sept. 2 A parcel of young 'bloods', generally termed 'cocks of the first water', with more grog aboard than brains, appeared to have assembled for the express purpose of creating a disturbance. **1986** *Centralian Advocate* (Alice Springs) 5 Feb. 1/1 Mr Forrester agreed that the main 'grog problem' on the town camps was caused by the licensed stores.

2. In the phr. **on the grog,** engaged in a drinking bout or session.

1959 *Never kill Dolphin* (Writers' Guild Qld.) 185 It's Christmas Eve and they're all on the grog. **1979** K. GARVEY *Absolutely Austral.* 19 On the grog till they do every deener, Stony broke and regretful next day.

3. Special Comb. **grog artist,** a heavy drinker (see also ARTIST); **seller,** an (unlicensed) retailer of alcoholic beverages; also **selling** *vbl. n.,* the (unlicensed) retailing of alcoholic beverages; **shanty,** a roughly constructed (unlicensed) public house, esp. on a goldfield; also *attrib.*; **tent,** a tent on a goldfield for the unlicensed retailing of alcoholic beverages.

1965 *Kings Cross Whisper* (Sydney) Oct. 6/2 Your correspondent, being a **grog-artist** of merit and renown, is also the World Champion Hangover Sufferer. **1827** *Colonial Times* (Hobart) 21 July, Last week, Mrs Jillett, a notorious **grog seller** at the Green Ponds, was convicted. **1829** *Launceston Advertiser* 14 Sept. 3 On Saturday last, Mrs Townsend was indicted for selling liquor without a license... Mr William Duncan was next on the list for the offence of **grog-selling.** **1858** *Colonial Mining Jrnl.* Dec. 59/3 **Grog-shanties** are superabundant. **1982** P. JAMES *Stories Central Qld.* 7 Grog shanty towns sprouted and decayed like mushrooms in those days of alluvial gold. **1852** *Guardian* (Hobart) 10 Jan. 3/6 The Commissioner received intelligence of a **grog-tent.**

grog, *v.*

1. *intr.* To drink an alcoholic beverage. Also *trans.* (see quot. 1978).

1959 R. BURNS *Mr Brain knows Best* 79 You'd be enlisting with the no-hopers, the types you see getting into crutch kicking fights when they've been grogging at the football. **1978** K. GILBERT *People are Legends* 42 A real man don't grog away money.

Hence **grogging** *vbl. n.* and *attrib.*

1965 D. ELLIS *Screw Loose* 122 What 'appens on New Year's Day, besides grogging and what-not? **1980** B. SANSOM *Camp at Wallaby Cross* 50 The point is that grogging restrictions have become very sensitive indicators of the political state of Territory communities.

2. With **on**: to engage in a protracted drinking session. Also as *vbl. n.* and *attrib.*

1951 E. LAMBERT *Sleeping House Party* 31 We were over with Helen and John and Paul, grogging on regardless. **1978** B. ST. A. SMITH *Spirit beyond Psyche* 20 You an' me, like, when we retire, we can go down t' the RSL of an arvo an' grog on regardless.

3. With **up**: to drink, usu. to excess. Also as *ppl. a.*

1956 J.E. MACDONNELL *Commander Brady* 249 Now don't forget. Nobody grogged-up. Nobody rortin' it up with them Yanks. Behave yerselves. **1977** K. GILBERT *Living Black* 303 When a man grogs up his kids' food money you straighten him out.

grog-up. A drinking party or session. Also **grog-on.**

1959 D. HEWETT *Bobbin Up* 31 The noise and abuse at one of Hazel's regular grog-ups was worse than usual. **1978** WARD & SMITH *Vanishing Village* 123 Apex-wise, the service work that we do is probably not as enjoyable as it used to be, but a lot of them used to be grog-ons, there wasn't much service done.

groper /'groʊpə/, *n.*[1] [Var. of *grouper* any of several fish of the fam. Serranidae.] Any of several fish, esp. *Promicrops lanceolatus* (fam. Serranidae), a large marine species of n. Aust. and elsewhere in the Pacific and Indian Oceans; *Queensland groper* QUEENSLAND 2. See also *blue groper* BLUE *a*.

1833 W.H. BRETON *Excursions* 160 Fish are plentiful, and the most abundant are snappers .. gropers, etc. **1979** A.J. BURKE *Bite Pineapple* 5 An old groper took a man holus bolus near the Victoria Bridge.

Groper, *n*.² and *attrib*. [Abbrev. of SAND-GROPER.]
A. *n*. A nickname for a non-Aboriginal person native to or resident in Western Australia, esp. an early settler or a descendant of an early settler.

1899 *Bulletin* (Sydney) 1 July 7/2 Apparently the Old Gropers who govern Westralia have decided to throw in their lot with the Provincialists. **1979** W.D. JOYNT *Breaking Road for Rest* 47 A local 'groper' (the name given to the West Australian born at the time) assured me that it took many years of grazing and cultivation before land could grow crops, or even grass.

B. *attrib*.
1900 *Truth* (Sydney) 20 May 6/2 The settlers in the North-West are almost entirely composed of the old groper group, and many of them are wealthy. **1963** X. HERBERT *Disturbing Element* 37 The *jilgie* in Groper lingo is the yabbie of the T'othersiders.

Hence **Groperdom** *n*., **Groperism** *n*.

1900 *Bulletin* (Sydney) 13 Jan. 7/2 (*heading*) The moan of old **groperdom**. **1907** A. BUCHANAN *Real Aust.* 54 The *West Australian* occupies a unique position. It is the accented mouthpiece of '**groperism**'; that is to say, of those privileged few who came to the State in early days, and monopolised as much of the earth as seemed worthy of their attention.

Groperland. A nickname for the State of Western Australia.

1900 *Bulletin* (Sydney) 14 July 6/1 The Parochialists of Groper Land have girded up their intelligence for the fray. **1963** X. HERBERT *Disturbing Element* 40 Wild flowers of loveliness, variety and profusion to be found nowhere else on earth but in poor arid Groperland.

Hence **Groperlander** *n*., a Western Australian.

1906 *Bulletin* (Sydney) 13 Sept. 17/1 A Groperlander .. has been gathering facts about big Australian grape vines.

ground, *n*.¹ Used *attrib*. in Special Comb. **groundberry**, the edible fruit of any of several small, often prostrate, shrubs of the genera *Acrotriche* and *Astroloma* (both fam. Epacridaceae); any of the plants themselves; **parrot** (or **parakeet**), any of several parrots typically seen on the ground (cf. GRASS PARROT), now usu. spec. *Pezoporus wallicus* of heaths and grassland in s. Aust.; see also *swamp parrot* SWAMP *n*.; also *fig*.; **thrush**, any of several birds typically seen on the ground, esp. *Zoothera dauma* (fam. Muscicapidae) of e. Aust., in size, shape, and plumage resembling the song thrush of Britain, and the species of *Cinclosoma* (fam. Orthonychidae) of s. and central Aust.; see also *mountain thrush* MOUNTAIN, QUAIL-THRUSH.

1849 *Bell's Life in Sydney* 13 Oct. 1/1 The most luxuriant crops of **ground-berries**. **1888** *Proc. Linnean Soc. N.S.W.* III. 489 *Astroloma humifusum* .. Commonly called 'Groundberry'. In Tasmania the fruits are often called 'Native Cranberries'. **1794** G. SHAW *Zool. New Holland* 10 The **Ground Parrot** .. differs from all the rest of its tribe in never perching on trees, but constantly frequenting low and sedgy places, running along the ground in the manner of a rail. **1841** J. GOULD *Birds of Aust.* (1848) V. Pl. 38, *Euphema elegans* .. Elegant Grass-Parrakeet. .. Ground Parrakeet of the Colonists. **1980** H.W. CUMMINGS *Confessions of 'Mud Skipper'* 74 There had been an Air Force camp during war time .. and some of the 'Ground Parrots' .. had relieved their boredom by shooting .303 bullets through the ship's side. **1840** J. GOULD *Birds of Aust.* (1848) IV. Pl. 4, Spotted **Ground-Thrush** .. *Cinclosoma Punctatum* .. gives a decided preference to the summits of low stony hills and rocky gullies. **1978** B.P. MOORE *Life on Forty Acres* 95 The Ground Thrush (*Zoothera dauma*) is .. a true thrush that occurs widely in eastern Australia and New Guinea.

ground, *n*.² *Obs*. [Br. dial. *ground* a piece or parcel of land; OED records this as obs. in the singular from *c* 1733 (see *sb*. 10 b.) but see also EDD *sb*. 4, 'a field; a piece of land enclosed for agricultural purposes'.]

1. A piece of land suitable for cultivation or for grazing stock; see also BACK GROUND 1.

1792 D. COLLINS *Acct. Eng. Colony N.S.W.* (1798) I. 234 The settlers late belonging to the Sirius, whose grounds had, on a careful survey by Mr Grimes, been found to intersect each other. **1835** 'IMPARTIAL OBSERVER' *Illustr. Present State N.S.W.* 46 She and her husband were *Squatters*, the name given in the Colony to persons who cultivate unoccupied Ground, belonging therefore, as they say to Government.

2. *Gold-mining*. A goldfield, a piece of land being worked for gold; a claim. Esp. in the phr. **on the ground**.

1851 *Empire* (Sydney) 4 Aug. 11/2 There were a great many purchasers of gold on the ground. **1852** *Austral. Gold Digger's Monthly Mag*. iii. 79 Persons desirous of changing their ground, were required to notify the same to the Commissioner. **1853** *Ibid*. v. 192 Mr Selwyn, our Government Geologist, is on the ground.

ground, *n*.³ [Spec. use of *ground* the soil of the earth, obs. elsewhere exc. in *Mining*: see OED *sb*. 16.] Used *attrib*. in Special Comb. **ground floor**, an earthen floor; **tank**, an excavation sited to retain rain-water, a dam.

1894 H. LAWSON *Short Stories* 28 The kitchen has 'no floor', or rather an earthen one called a '**ground floor**'. **1973** R. ROBINSON *Drift of Things* 127, I asked at an isolated homestead if I could put my horses in the paddock and camp by the **ground tank**.

Group. *W.A. Hist*. Abbrev. of GROUP SETTLEMENT. Also *attrib*.

1922 [see GROUP SETTLEMENT]. **1927** T.S. GROSER *Lure of Golden West* 29 The conditions attached to 'Groups' are as follows:– A settlement under the 'Group' system is arranged... A 'Group' consists of twenty settlers. **1965** *Tracks we Travel* 148 You don't have to worry about interest and paying off a mortgage, like those poor devils on the Groups.

grouper.
1. *W.A. Hist*. Shortened form of GROUP SETTLER.
1926 A.A.B. APSLEY *Amateur Settlers* 164 Each Grouper as a rule working. **1927** T.S. GROSER *Lure of Golden West* 33 The 'Groupers' come out without any capital at all.

2. A member of one of the 'Industrial Groups', factions formed within trade unions by the Australian Labor Party to support Labor policies and oppose Communist influence; (loosely) a member of a right-wing faction of the Australian Labor Party; a member of the Democratic Labor Party.

1955 *Sydney Morning Herald* 27 Apr. 1/1 Last year the groupers altered the rules to give two delegates for every 250 members from a State electorate council. **1985** *Sydney Morning Herald* 24 Apr. 5/5 He said that activities of the 'groupers' meant that he and his mates spent the best years of their political lives in the wilderness.

groupie. *W.A. Hist*. [f. GROUP (SETTLER + -Y.] GROUP SETTLER.

1926 A.A.B. APSLEY *Amateur Settlers* 195 Some of the Groupies .. were clever carpenters. **1983** J.K. EWERS *Long* *enough for Joke* 111 The Collie miners were earning good money; the groupies were earning only sustenance.

Group Settlement. *W.A. Hist.* A scheme developed in the 1920s for establishing settlements of British immigrants in the underdeveloped s.w. of Western Australia; such a settlement. Also *attrib.*

1922 *West Austral.* (Perth) 4 Aug. 8/2 Dealing with Group Settlement the Premier said there were 26 groups and the work was past the experimental stage. 1927 T.S. GROSER *Lure of Golden West* p. x, The 'Group Settlement' scheme in the south-west, inaugurated only five years ago by Sir James Mitchell.

Group Settler. *W.A. Hist.* A member of a Group Settlement.

1926 A.A.B. APSLEY *Amateur Settlers* 198 Other Group Settlers spent with considerably less sense. 1965 *Tracks we Travel* 139 Several of the Group Settlers had abandoned their farms after the first two or three years.

grouse, *a.* [Of unknown origin.] Very good of (its) kind; highly desirable. Freq. with the intensive **extra**.

1944 L. GLASSOP *We were Rats* 5 You know them two grouse sheilas we've got the meet on with tomorrer night? 1967 *Kings Cross Whisper* (Sydney) xxxvii. 9/2 'Whisper's' super colossal, humdinger, extra grouse, beaut competition for all the family.

grouse, *n.* [Prob. f. prec.] In prison speech: a cigarette, superior in quality to prison issue; also *pl.* and as *adj.*

1968 J. ALARD *He who shoots Last* 125 Da stuff's like gold in here... Gees, it's da grouse weed too—we gits a coupla ounces a week, but boob weed is like smokin' horse dung. 1971 J. McNEIL *Chocolate Frog* (1973) 17 'I was kind of hopin' somebody might lob from court with a grouse cigga...' 'Hey? Oh, yeah.. a grouse'd go well, all right... ' 'Like, a tailor-made, I mean.' 1974 ADAMSON & HANFORD *Zimmer's Essay* 53 'You got any grouse?'.. 'You bring any smokes in with you?'

grouter. [Of unknown origin.] A fortuitous circumstance; an unfair advantage; in the game of two-up, an opportune bet, esp. one made as a run of heads or tails ends. Esp. in the phr. **to come in on the grouter, to run a grouter**. Also *attrib.*, as **grouter bet, grouter bettor**.

1902 *Truth* (Sydney) 6 Apr. 7/2 For Chamberlain with cast-iron cheek Has come in on 'the grouter' And told us that our statesmen are Of the grimy outer outer. 1918 *Port Hacking Cough* (Sydney) 14 Dec. 11 The orderly sergeant, grouter seeking, chanced upon a meek looking person shaving. 1946 K.S. PRICHARD *Roaring Nineties* 152 Sometimes a successful bettor twisted, after backing heads, and backed tails. 'Catching the grouter', that was called. But a grouter bettor could only have one or two bets a night. 1949 L. GLASSOP *Lucky Palmer* 174 A real grouter bet, gents... Any tailie who missed out on that run of heads can come in on the grouter now. 1968 S. GORE *Holy Smoke* 51 He decides he'll run a grouter on the Lord, and took his bait.

grouter, *v.* [f. prec.] *trans.* To acquire (something) fortuitously; to take advantage of (a situation, etc.); see quot. 1967.

1918 G.C. COOPER *Diary* 24 Feb., Drew rations, also two lots of Canteen; 'groutered' some NZ Canteen Stores. 1967 *Kings Cross Whisper* (Sydney) xxxv. 6/1 *Grouter*, to come in on the tail end of a game of chance and clean up.

grow, *v. Aboriginal English.* In the phr. **to grow** (someone) **up**, to bring up; to rear.

1938 V.E. TURNER *Good Fella Missus* 91 You won't .. leave me?... You growed me up. 1977 J. & P. READ *View of Past* 5 Apr. (1978) 249 (typescript) That's all, my old boss. He grow me up. Poor feller, my old boss.

Hence **grower-up** *n.*

1943 W.E. HARNEY *Taboo* 155 Accordingly he claimed Sarah... Claimed her by the right of a feeder, or as the natives say, a 'grower up'.

grub. WITCHETTY 2.

1793 J. HUNTER *Hist. Jrnl. Trans. Port Jackson* 516 The natives were known to eat a grub which is found in the small gum-tree. 1955 F. LANE *Patrol to Kimberleys* 214 The blacks prefer bush tucker—lizards, snakes, etc. Grubs are eaten raw; other foods are merely scorched in hot ashes. For the most part, the aborigines like their meat underdone.

grudge match. [Cf. Br. *grudge fight* (see OEDS *grudge, sb.* 6.).] A game or contest in which there is bitterness or personal antipathy between the opponents. Also in shortened form, as **grudgie**.

1973 P. McKENNA *My World of Football* 173 Imagine the interest that would be injected into Sydney football if Collingwood and Richmond played one of their annual 'grudge matches'—as part of the normal season on the Trumper Oval. 1973 *Kings Cross Whisper* (Sydney) clii. 4/2 To see the stoush which this day is between Easts an' Saints and the beats have been tellin' everybody .. that the game's a 'grudgie' because one a Easts' lot was found in bed with one of the Saints' wives.

gruie /'gruɪ/. [a. Kamilaroi *garuy*.] *Emu apple* (a), see EMU *n.*[1] 3. Formerly also as **gruie-colaine**, a compound formed from the Kamilaroi and Wiradhuri names (see COLANE).

1888 *Proc. Linnean Soc. N.S.W.* III. 534 *Owenia acidula* .. Aboriginal names are .. 'Gruie-Colaine', [etc.]. 1938 C.T. WHITE *Princ. Bot. Qld. Farmers* 217 Associated with the various species of Wattles and beelah are other trees such as .. Emu Apple or Gruie.

grunter. [Spec. use of *grunter* any fish that makes a grunting noise.] Any of many fish of the fam. Teraponidae, usu. fresh-water species, incl. *Bidyanus bidyanus* (see *silver perch* SILVER 1) and the spangled grunter *Leiopotherapon unicolor*, widespread in Aust.

1906 D.G. STEAD *Fishes of Aust.* 123 The Silver Perch .. in many parts of western New South Wales .. is familiarly-known as 'Grunter'. 1982 R. ELLIS *Bush Safari* 85 The spangled grunter, an edible fish that grows up to 15 centimetres long.

guana *Obs.* Also **guaner, guano.** [Aphetic form of *iguana.*] GOANNA 1.

1699 W. DAMPIER *New Voyage round World* (1703) III. 124, I think my Stomach would scarce have serv'd to venture upon these *N. Holland* Guano's, both the Looks and the Smell of them being so offensive. 1786 *Hist. Narr. Discovery New Holland & N.S.W.* 10 The guana of New Holland. 1859 H. KINGSLEY *Recoll. Geoffry Hamlyn* II. 45 Well, I've eaten guaners myself.

guard-fish: see GARFISH.

gub. Also **gubb.** Abbrev. of GUBBA.

1971 K. GILBERT *End of Dreamtime* 9 They called me, Kalari, a 'Pommy' and 'Gub', laughed at my speaking, laughed when I tried to join in their song and dance. 1984 P. READ *Down there with me on Cowra Mission* 135 Now even can't get down to the place because the gubbs have moved in with them white goats and .. they've got twelve foot high fences.

gubba. [Of unknown origin.] Also **gubbah, gubbar, gubber.** A name given by Aborigines to a white person.

1963 *Bulletin* (Sydney) 13 Apr. 8/1 Any aborigine living

in New South Wales who is over the age of 18 can go into a hotel and have a drink like any 'gubbar' (white man). **1971** K. GILBERT *End of Dreamtime* 7 Now we wander crying and the gubbahs go on lying:- O Land of hope and glory! Southern stronghold of the free! **1975** *Bulletin* (Sydney) 18 Jan. 44/3 He makes him repulsive, frightening, and human, putting one of our stereotypes live on stage for probably the first time—our own white trash, the black man's gubba. **1983** *Sydney Morning Herald* 14 Feb. 7/8 There are two Aboriginal words for the races in Moree. One is 'murri', an Aboriginal word for themselves, which is quite acceptable. The other, for whites, is 'gubber', which is derogatory.

gudgeon. [Transf. use of *gudgeon* a fish of the genus *Gobius*.] A small fish of any of several genera of marine, estuarine, or fresh-water fish of the fam. Eleotridae.
1793 W. TENCH *Compl. Acct. Settlement* 176, I shall not pretend to enumerate the variety of fish which are found; they are seen from a whale to a gudgeon. **1974** L. WEDLICK *Sporting Fish* 19 The river gudgeon found in the Murray River is often confused by anglers with the young Murray cod.

guernsey. [Spec. use of *guernsey* 'thick, knitted, closely fitting vest or shirt, generally made of blue wool, worn by seamen': see OED(S 2 a.]
1. *Obs.* A kind of shirt, esp. as worn by a gold-miner.
1850 *Monthly Almanac* (Adelaide) 9 In their place appear the sober Guernsey—the humble moleskin—the strong fossil shaped colonial Blucher. **1892** 'MRS A. MACLEOD' *Silent Sea* I. 288 Well, and he left all that behind him, and ran away for what? To scrape dirt underground till his guernsey pours over wid sweat.
2. A football jersey, esp. the (usu.) sleeveless shirt worn by an Australian National Football player. Also **football guernsey**.
1925 *Bulletin* (Sydney) 30 Apr. 22/4 The majority was with an urchin who 'wasn't takin' any chance with a snake in a football guernsey'. **1978** *Overland* lxxii. 16, I left it in the tram... Had me guernsey, boots and jockstrap in it. Sheila clippie found it.
3. In the phr. **to get** (or **to be given**) **a** (or **the**) **guernsey**, to win selection (for a team); *fig.* to win selection, recognition, or approbation.
1918 E.J. RULE *Jacka's Mob* 26 Sept. (1933) 319, I was told I'd be given a 'guernsey' this time in the line, which was welcome news; I'd missed the 8 August show, and did not want to miss this one. *c* **1920** 'HAMER' *Search for Bonzer Tart* 72 The infamous conduct of the referee awarding a penalty against the Eastern Glebes roused him once more. 'Yah! Get a guernsey!' he yelled disgustedly. **1975** *Bulletin* (Sydney) 22 Feb. 12/1 Doug was the next man on the NSW Liberal Country Party ticket.. and if everything goes according to the rules.. then he should be the one to get the guernsey for Canberra.

Guildford grass. [f. the name of a town in W.A. (see quot. 1948).] The S. African perennial herb *Romulea rosea* (fam. Iridaceae) naturalized in s. Aust. See also **onion grass** ONION 1.
1909 A.J. EWART *Weeds* 58 *Romulea*.. *cruciata*.. The Guildford or Onion Grass. **1948** *Bulletin* (Sydney) 26 May 22/1 Early in Westralia's history a well-meaning pastoralist introduced.. Guilford grass—the pest takes its name from the district in which it first appeared.

guinea-flower. [See quot. 1968.] Any of many plants of the large, chiefly Austral. genus *Hibbertia* (fam. Dilleniaceae) of all States, bearing showy, usu. gold or yellow, flowers. Also *attrib*.
1923 *Census Plants Vic.* (Field Naturalists' Club Vic.) 45 *Hibbertia densiflora*.. Silky Guinea-flower. **1933** C.W. PECK *Austral. Legends* (ed. 2) 200 A tangle of Hibbertia, or Guinea-flower vine. **1968** G.R. COCHRANE et al. *Flowers & Plants Vic.* 28 There is no brighter display on Australian heathlands than that provided by the various guinea-flowers, popularly so called from their flat, regular, golden blooms.

guiver, var. GUYVER *n*.

Gulf.
a. Used *attrib.* with reference to the hinterland of the Gulf of Carpentaria, esp. in the Comb. **Gulf Country**.
1867 *Australasian* (Melbourne) 3 Aug. 134/5 It is the unanimous opinion of the squatters that this year's lambing is the best they have had since the Gulf country was first opened. **1893** E. FAVENC *Last of Six Tales* 50 The new super. was a young man from the South, and Tranter was an old Gulf hand.
b. Gulf fever, malaria.
1901 P.D. LORIMER *Songs & Verses* 13 The Gulf fever, as it is called, is of a very malignant character. **1911** E.J. BRADY *King's Caravan* 269 He was not the only man I met coming down from the North to shake off Gulf fever.
Hence **Gulfer** *n.*, see quot. 1977; **Gulfite** *n.*, one who lives in the Gulf Country.
1977 B. SCOTT *My Uncle Arch* 55 It seems that once every eight years this cloud comes down from Arnhem Land and rains on them from a very great height. They call this cloud the **Gulfer** out there, because it isn't so much a cloud as part of the Gulf of Carpentaria, and it brings all its contents with it. You've heard of those fishes that rain out of the sky in Western Queensland haven't you? Well, these are normally only the fringe of the Gulfer. The real middle of it has dugongs, turtles, and all kinds of other wildlife. **1963** *N. Austral. Monthly* Dec. 31/1 When I came to the Gulf Country to take up work.. I was to become a permanent '**Gulfite**'.

gully. [Extended use of *gully* ravine, small gorge: see OED(S *sb.*^{1} 2.]
1. a. A ravine; an eroded watercourse; an elongated water-worn depression; a (small) valley. See also *fern-gully*, FERN 2. Also *attrib*.
1793 J. HUNTER *Hist. Jrnl. Trans. Port Jackson* 525 They came to a hollow, in which they found some very good water; here they stopped near an hour: after passing this gully, and a rocky piece of ground, the soil grew better. **1981** K.M. OLD et al. *Eucalypt Dieback* 11 Hopkins.. singled out several diebacks which were insufficiently studied. These included high altitude dieback, gully dieback and regrowth dieback, all located in Tasmania.
b. *fig.*
1975 *Nat. Times* (Sydney) 30 June 26/1 Wheeler has crossed a few dry gullies in his career. **1982** *Bulletin* (Sydney) 6 Apr. 80/3 'Life is interesting,' he muses. 'I've crossed a few dry gullies in my time.'
2. a. *spec.* A gully in which alluvial gold is sought.
1852 *Austral. Gold Digger's Monthly Mag.* ii. 38 The gold of the Californian gulches and Australian gullies is not found in veins. **1975** *Southerly* ii. 195 The sides of the gully had a mined-over look, resembling fresh mullock heaps.
b. *fig.*
1872 'DEMONAX' *Mysteries & Miseries* 17 He is rich. Unlike the run of typos, his 'case' is full, and he's got in a good 'gully'

gully-rake, *v*.
1. *intr.* To muster unbranded cattle from country not readily accessible (see quot. 1900); to appropriate illegally cattle so mustered. Chiefly as *vbl. n.*
1847 A. HARRIS *Settlers & Convicts* (1953) 144 Gully-raking.. derives its name from the circumstance of cattle straying away.. and forming wild herds which chiefly congregate down in the wild grassy gullies of the mountains... The gully-rakers eventually driving them out and branding

all the young ones, and any others they can manage, with their own brands. **1900** T. MAJOR *Leaves from Squatter's Note Bk.* 11 A large number of wild cattle were to be found in the scrubby ranges, and could only be yarded by gully-raking.

2. *Gold-mining. intr.* To search for surface gold. Also as *vbl. n.*

1881 J.C.F. JOHNSON *To Mount Browne & Back* 21 The principal work done on it .. has been mere gully-raking or surfacing in the bed of the creek. **1932** I.L. IDRIESS *Prospecting for Gold* 3 Where men are 'gully raking' in the ranges.

gully-raker. *Obs.* [f. prec.]

1. A cattle-thief; one who engages in gully-raking.

1840 *Colonist* (Sydney) 17 Oct. 3/1 The slanderous expressions used .. were the epithets of 'gulley-raker' and 'cattle-stealer'. **1950** G.M. FARWELL *Land of Mirage* 171 Many a man who stuck up a gold escort or a Cobb & Co. coach had started out as a mere gully-raker, putting his brand on scrubbers, or cross-branding in another man's yard.

2. A stockwhip.

1873 *Illustr. Sydney News* 5 July 11/1 At first crack of the stockman's 'gully-raker', as his long-thonged whip is termed, the cattle fly in all directions. **1945** E. MITCHELL *Speak to Earth* 71 The scrub in the gullies was impenetrable and they used a great heavy stockwhip called a 'gully-raker'.

gum, *n.* and *attrib.*

A. *n.*

1. Abbrev. of GUM TREE 1.

1805 *Sydney Gaz.* 16 June, With my dog and my gun to the forest I fly, Where in stately confusion rich gums sweep the sky. **1974** A. BUZO *Coralie Lansdowne says No* 61, I .. sat on the beach and looked at the outline, the rocks and gums.

2. With distinguishing epithet, as **apple, blue, brittle, cabbage, cider, creek, desert, flooded, flowering, fluted, forest red, ghost, grey, lemon-scented, manna, mountain, Murray red, poplar, red, ribbon, river, rose, salmon, scarlet, scribbly, shining, snappy, snow, spotted, Tingaringy, water, white, whitewash, yellow, York,** etc.: see under first element.

B. 1. *attrib.*

1827 *Tasmanian* (Hobart) 1 Nov. 3 Manifest of the cargo on board the ship Harvey .. 86 pieces cedar, 256 gum planks. **1969** D. CUSACK *Half-Burnt Tree* 46 Hungry for the meat that they would grill over a fire of gumwood that smelt like incense.

2. Comb. **gum flat, forest.**

1846 *Moreton Bay Courier* 28 Nov. 3/2 There are also numerous apple-tree and **gum flats**. **1843** J. GOULD *Birds of Aust.* (1848) III. Pl. 12, The thickly-wooded **gum-forests** of the mountain districts.

3. Special Comb. **gum creek,** a creek bed of drier Aust. (see quot. 1896); **grub** *obs.*, WITCHETTY 2; **nut,** the inedible, woody, seed-bearing capsule of the gum tree; also *attrib.*; **tips** *pl.*, the young, often red, growing shoots of the gum tree.

1860 J.M. STUART *Exploration of Interior* 4 Crossed the bed of a large **gum creek**, but no water. **1896** B. SPENCER *Rep. Horn Sci. Exped. Central Aust.* I. 74 They gave rise to what have always been termed by the early explorers 'Gum creeks', that is sandy beds which only contain water, if at all, at rare intervals, but along the sides of which grow a line of gum trees (*Eucalyptus rostrata*). **1840** T.J. BUCKTON *W.A.* 83 The **gum-grub,** or *grungru,* is by some gastronomists considered a great dainty. **1916** M. GIBBS *Gumnut Babies* 4 On all the big Gumtrees there are **Gum-Nut** Babies. **1928** J. POLLARD *Bushland Vagabonds* 48 Other sounds were few— a leaf fluttering down; a gum-nut thudding on the gravel soil. **1942** *Troppo Topics* 21 Dec. 5 With two bottles of beer apiece and plenty of **gumtips**.

gumleaf.

a. The leaf of a gum tree.

1803 *Sydney Gaz.* 21 Aug., An Animal whose species was never before found in the colony .. has a false belly like the opposim [*sic*] and its food consists solely of *gum leaves* in the choice of which it is excessively nice. **1941** *Bulletin* (Sydney) 9 Apr. 16/2 Bushmen working in bull-ant country always light a few gumleaves and twigs on any nearby nests so that they can work undisturbed.

b. A gumleaf used to make musical sounds, serving as a resonator when cupped in the hands and blown upon.

1939 *Bulletin* (Sydney) 11 Jan. 19/3 The gumleaf can be added to the jew's-harp as a bush musical instrument that's outdated. **1977** D. WHITTINGTON *Strive to be Fair* 32 They .. played haunting tunes on gum leaves.

Also **gumleaf band** *n.*

1951 D. COLLINS *Vic.'s my Home Ground* 107 They played for us on their gumleaves, lovingly, with a kind of tenderness. Odd though it may seem, I'd never heard a gumleaf band before.

gummy. [f. *gum* + -Y.]

1. A sheep that has lost or is losing its teeth, esp. a six-year-old sheep.

1871 *Austral. Town & Country Jrnl.* (Sydney) 22 Apr. 487/2 Fat sheep are sent to the butcher; gummies and thin-woolled sheep are culled, and sold to beginners. **1961** J.W. JORDAN *Practical Sheep Farming* 21 At six years they may have lost all their teeth. They are then known as 'gummies', and become a liability to the sheep farmer.

2. Any of several sharks of the genus *Mustelus,* esp. the widespread *M. antarcticus* (see quot. 1898). See also SWEET WILLIAM. Also **gummy shark.**

1898 *Funk's Stand. Dict.,* Gummy, a galeoid shark. **1898** E.E. MORRIS *Austral Eng.* 185 The word *Gummy* is said to come from the small numerous teeth, arranged like a pavement, so different from the sharp erect teeth of most other sharks. **1922** F.C. GREEN *Fortieth* 19 One man puts forward the claims of a dog he once had that would catch 'gummy' sharks.

3. A toothless person; an old person.

1907 *Truth* (Sydney) 30 June 9/5 In the train—upon the dummy, And across the billiard baize, From the 'kiddie' to the 'gummy', We discuss the toeball craze. **1939** *Bulletin* (Sydney) 19 July 20/2 Located these past 40 years anywhere other than the Cabbage Garden, it makes me wonder to hear present-day Gummies raving about the iniquitous blackberry. **1941** *Ibid.* 17 Sept. 14/1 Old Bill had been a 'gummie' for over eighteen months, and when he collected his uppers-and-lowers from the travelling dentist there was no prouder man in Saltbush.

gumsucker. A nickname for a native-born, non-Aboriginal Australian; a Victorian. Also *attrib.*

1840 G.T.W.B. BOYES *Diary* 2 June, These colonial chaps, Gumsuckers as they are not inappropriately called are my aversion—puffed up with success of his father .. without education or manners. **1905** N.F. SPIELVOGEL *Gumsucker on Tramp* 40, I trink two glass Gomsucker beer, I get head top. I trink twenty glass Deutscher beer, not so bad.

gum tree. [Spec. use of *gum tree* gum-exuding tree.]

1. **a.** Any tree of the large, chiefly Austral. genus *Eucalyptus* (fam. Myrtaceae), the dominant tree genus of Austral. forests and woodlands. **b.** *spec.* Any of many species of *Eucalyptus* distinguished by having a smooth bark (see quot. 1860). **c.** Any of several other usu. myrtaceous trees, as *Angophora.* **d.** The wood of any of these trees. See GUM *n.* 1. Also *attrib.*

1789 A. Phillip *Voyage to Botany Bay* 107 The gum-tree is highly combustible. **1860** G. Bennett *Gatherings of Naturalist* 358 The *Eucalypti*, commonly called Gum-trees by the colonists, have smooth bark, which is shed annually in long strips; among these, the Peppermint .. and others are classed. The species with rough, fixed bark, as the .. Stringy-Bark, Box, and others, are not named gum-trees, but are designated by the above appellations. The *Eucalypti* are thus popularly divided into two distinct classes. **1972** *Bulletin* (Sydney) 30 Dec. 41/2 A clinker brick house in the North Shore gum tree belt.

2. [f. U.S. *up a tree* entrapped, in a 'fix' (see OED *tree, sb.* 7), *'possum up a gum tree* in great difficulties (see OED(S *gum-tree* 2).] In the phr. **up a gum tree,** in another place, another state of mind; 'treed', cornered; in a state of confusion; in a predicament.

1851 J. Henderson *Excursions & Adventures N.S.W.* I. 64 My convicts were always drinking rum, I often wished they were up a gum-tree. **1882** J.I. Watts *Memories Early Days S.A.* 10 A tame opossum .. was in the habit of indulging in frequent nightly excursions amongst the furniture on the rafters, doubtless fondly imagining itself to be 'up a gum tree'. **1982** *Nat. Times* (Sydney) 15 Aug. 12/2 It was not until the analyst sent back his magnificent document .. that we realised we were up the original gum tree.

3. *transf.* Used *attrib.* and derogatorily in various contexts: see quots.

1845 R. Howitt *Impressions Aust. Felix* 298 If a poor fellow .. is caught trespassing .. on Crown land, he is summoned before the monarch of the Gum-tree-court. **1983** *Weekend Austral.* (Sydney) 10 Sept. 5/4 Fifty traditional Australian paintings of a group sometimes irreverently called the Gum Tree School.

gum-wattle. *Obs.* Any of several species of *Acacia* (fam. Mimosaceae) yielding quantities of gum (see quot. 1839).

c **1810** *Trans. Linnean Soc. London* (1827) XV. 261, I have known large flocks of these birds come occasionally into the small trees (*Gum-wattle*) about Government House. **1839** *S. Austral. Rec.* (London) 11 Sept. 232 The gum wattle .. seldom exceeds 12 or 14 feet in height; it yields an immense quantity of gum, and the bark is used for tanning and various medicinal purposes.

gun, $n.^1$ and *attrib.* [Spec. use of *(big, great) gun* one eminent in anything: see OED(S *sb.* 7 b.]

A. *n.*

1. A shearer who has a consistently high daily tally (of sheep shorn); an expert shearer. Also **gun shearer**.

1897 *Worker* (Sydney) 11 Sept. 1/1 To shear a thou. or more a week, which is but seldom done, Will gain a shearer high respect and the title of a 'gun'. **1940** I.L. Idriess *Lightning Ridge* 152 The 'gun shearer' there was a two hundred-a-day man.

2. *transf.*

1913 *Bulletin* (Sydney) 13 Mar. 13/2 'Ginger's' tally .. of 600 to 900 chaff bags sewn per day .. is worthy of the most enthusiastic disbelief... The highest tally for one day (10 hours) was 480, and my mate taking turns with me was considered to be one of the 'guns' of the West. **1955** Stewart & Keesing *Austral. Bush Ballads* 282 To those chopping guns you mention Lachlan Jack can give you a mile!

B. *attrib.*

1. Pre-eminent (in an occupation or activity); exceptionally talented or skilled.

1916 *Bulletin* (Sydney) 27 Jan. 22/3 Young .. had the reputation amongst 'gun' sheep men of being the fastest lamb-marker in Australia... He could keep eight catchers busy. **1979** K. Dunstan *Ratbags* 17 So maybe the Yabba was for the gun rabbit skinner.

2. Comb. **gun** (cane) **cutter, drover**.

1922 *Bulletin* (Sydney) 19 Oct. 22/2 We've settled all the shearing and post-hole tallies; now what about the **gun** cane-**cutter**? **1977** B. Scott *My Uncle Arch* 62 When my Uncle Arch was cutting cane in North Queensland .. he was the gun cutter in the area. **1923** *Six Austral. One-Act Plays* (1944) 18 The old bloke'll pull them through. He's the big **gun drover** of the North.

gun, $n.^2$ [Prob. transf. use of Br. slang phr. *in the gun* drunk.] In the phr. **in the gun,** in bad favour; likely to attract criticism or punishment.

1924 R. Daly *Outpost* 36 They've got you in the gun, all right. There have been half-a-dozen Residents there in the last few years, and every man-jack of them has gone out to it. **1982** Lowenstein & Hills *Under Hook* 105 Everybody seemed to have the wharfies in the gun, we were no good, people didn't want to know us.

Gundaroo /gʌndəˈruː/. *Obs.* [The name of a town in s.e. N.S.W.] Used *attrib.* in Special Comb. **Gundaroo bullock, mutton,** see quots.

1899 *Bulletin* (Sydney) 6 May 14/3 A native bear is not .. a 'Grabben-Gullen bullock'; it is mostly known in the South as a 'Gundaroo bullock'. *Ibid.* 3 June 14/3, I was myself in Yass court-house when some members of a Gundaroo family were tried for having supposed stolen mutton in their possession, but they produced testimony that the salted meat .. was native bear. Ever since native bear has in that locality been 'Gundaroo mutton'.

gundy /ˈgʌndi, ˈgʌndi/, $n.^1$ Also **goondie**. [a. Wiradhuri and Kamilaroi *gunday* stringybark, a hut made therefrom.] Gunyah 1.

1876 *Austral. Town & Country Jrnl.* (Sydney) 2 Dec. 902/1 There were a dozen 'goondies' to be visited, and the inmates started to their work. Each blackfellow at the reveillé caught up a few waddies. **1980** S. Thorne *I've met some Bloody Wags* 82 My mate Tom and I went there after a busy afternoon bending the elbow around at his gundy.

gundy /ˈgʌndi, ˈgʌndi/, $n.^1$ Also **goondie**. [a. Wiradhuri and Kamilaroi *gundhi* stringybark, a hut made therefrom.] Gunyah 1.

1906 *Bulletin* (Sydney) 19 Dec. 14/1 Re .. origin and meaning of .. 'No good to gundy'. 'Gundy' is a corruption of a Welsh word meaning to steal, shake, pinch, or hook, and the expression simply means that a thing is not worth stealing. **1907** *Ibid.* 19 Dec. 14/2 The origin of the expression 'No good to Gundy'. Gundy is an abbreviation of Gundagai and the phrase originated way back in 1852— the year of the big flood... A bullocky .. disentangling a few codfish from his whiskers .. looked towards the blank that had been Gundagai, and remarked sadly, that "Tweren't much good to Gundy." **1908** *Ibid.* 2 Jan. 14/4 'No good to Gundy'... This is the only explanation of its origin I could discover: A mounted constable was bringing a darky named Gundy down to Bathurst for trial. .. In the same carriage were some young men who procured much whisky at Wellington .. and when one of the boys playfully held the bottle about a foot in front of the aboriginal's nose and begged of him to [*sic*] 'Do have a drop', Gundy threw one black foot in the air, and deftly kicking the bottle of whisky through the carriage window, yelled 'No plurry good to Gundy.' **1908** *Truth* (Sydney) 30 Aug. 1/7 A temperance fanatic many years ago lectured at Gundy. .. The cold tea advocate was going to shut up every hotel in the land. 'What!' yelled the audience in united voice, 'shut up our pub.' 'Precisely,' replied the ranter. 'Be hanged,' chorused the crowd, 'that's no good to Gundy.'

b. In the phr. **good enough for Gundy**: see quot.

1949 C. Benham *Diver's Luck* 151 When yer got a job ter do yer wants ter do it prop'ly, none o' yer, 'That's near enough', or 'That's good enough for Gundey'.

guneah, var. Gunyah.

gungurru /gʌngəˈruː/. Also **gungunnu**. [Prob. a. Kalaaku *gaŋurru*.] A small tree of s.w. W.A., of the genus *Eucalyptus* (fam. Myrtaceae), usu. *E. caesia*, cultivated as an ornamental.
1949 S. KELLY *Forty Austral. Eucalypts* 20 The vernacular name 'Gungurru' is of Aboriginal origin, and therefore wholly Australian. It applies to one of the loveliest of our ornamental trees. **1954** *Jrnl. Agric. W.A.* 105 Gungunnu (*Eucalyptus caesia* . .). For the want of a good descriptive common name for this handsome mallee I have used the name which Richard Helms stated was used by the aborigines of the Fraser Range district.

gunna. [Not excl. Austral.: cf. OEDS *gonna*.] Repr. colloq. pronunc. of 'going to'.
1950 J. CLEARY *Just let me Be* 11 They could feel the sun hot on their backs. . . 'It's gunna be a beaut again today,' Harry said. **1988** *Truck & Bus* July 126/3, I want answers outa you, Crackers. More than answers—I want them spuds replaced! What are yer gunna do about it?

gunyah /ˈgʌnjə/. Also **gunya** and formerly with much variety as **guneah, gunneah, gunnie, gunyer,** etc. [a. Dharuk *ganyi*.]
1. A temporary shelter of the Aborigines, usually made of sheets of bark and/or branches; any makeshift shelter or dwelling. Cf. HUMPY, MIA-MIA, WILTJA, WURLEY.
1803 J. GRANT *Narr. Voyage N.S.W.* 96 The native . . led us . . very near a *gunnie*, or house, which he made us understand was the place of his birth. **1817** J. OXLEY *Jrnls. Two Exped. N.S.W.* (1820) 117 He threw down with apparent fierceness the little bark guneah which had sheltered him and his family during the night. **1827** *Monitor* (Sydney) 5 July 496/1 A sheet of bark was stripped, and a *gunyah* rigged while others were looking about them. **1830** R. DAWSON *Present State Aust.* 70 The poor natives . . soon made me one of their gunyers, (bark huts). **1833** *Austral. Almanack* p. xv, Nor cease their revels till the morning gun Booms o'er the waves to greet the rising sun; Then to their *gunneahs*, sullenly repair, Like wolves retreating to their caverned lair.
2. *transf.* and *fig.*
1827 *Austral.* (Sydney) 27 Mar. 2/3 At my friend L–'s *gunha*, the native name for house, our breakfast table was never without beefsteaks, roast wild duck, fried bream and potatoes, besides the more usual accompaniments of pancakes, eggs, cream, and bread superior to any out of Sydney. **1911** *Truth* (Sydney) 18 June 5/6 (*heading*) The Guv's gunyah. Deserted Government House.

gunyang /ˈgʌnjæŋ/. [a. Ganay *gunyaŋ*.] Any of several plants, esp. the shrub *Solanum vescum* (fam. Solanaceae) of s.e. Aust. and Tas., bearing a green to ivory-coloured globular berry. See also *kangaroo apple* KANGAROO *n.* 5.
1855 J. BONWICK *Geogr. Aust. & N.Z.* (ed. 3) 204 The Gunyang fruit of the Gipps Land sand ridges is of the taste and size of a Cape gooseberry, on a sort of night-shade shrub 6 feet high. **1981** G.M. CUNNINGHAM et al. *Plants Western N.S.W.* 589 Gunyang [*sc.* fruit] globular, to 3 cm diameter, green to ivory.

gurnet. *Obs.* [Var. of *gurnard* a fish of the fam. Triglidae: see quot. 1898.] Any of several marine fish of fam. Triglidae and Scorpaenidae.
1828 *Hobart Town Courier* 9 Feb. 3 No fish were caught except a few gurnet. **1898** E.E. MORRIS *Austral Eng.* 187 The word *Gurnet* is an obsolete or provincial form of Gurnard, revived in Australia.

gurry. *Tas.* [Transf. use of *gurry* fish offal, of unknown origin and chiefly U.S.: see OED 4 and Mathews.] The stomach contents of the mutton-bird *Puffinus tenuirostris*, after removal of oil for commercial use.
1975 *Linguistic Communications* xiii. 88 The gurry go to the bottom. **1982** *Victorian Naturalist* XCIX. 52 Patches of oil and gurry were seen in much of the rookery. [*Note*] Gurry is a birding term for the partly-digested stomach contents, exclusive of the oil, of muttonbird nestlings. The killed nestlings are squeezed to empty their stomach contents through their bills.

gutless, *a.* [Used elsewhere but recorded earliest in Aust.] In the collocation **gutless wonder,** one who lacks courage or determination.
1955 D. NILAND *Shiralee* 64 'You're a gutless wonder, Christy,' he gibed. 'What's holding you back?' **1982** H. KNORR *Private Viewing* 29 'Try!' it mimicked. 'Why, you gutless wonder, your generation doesn't know what trying is!'

guts.
1. [Used elsewhere but recorded earliest in Aust.] Information, the facts (of a matter); freq. in the collocation **good guts.**
1919 W.H. DOWNING *Digger Dialects* 27 Guts, the substance or essential part of a matter; information. **1975** 'N. CULOTTA' *Gone Gougin'* 72 'We'll go to the cop shop an' see if that mob . . were havin' us on about that Miner's Right lurk. . . ' 'Righto, matey. We'll organise the grog. You front the wallopers an' get the good guts.'
2. In the phr. **to come** (or **give**) (**someone's**) **guts,** to divulge incriminating information, to inform.
1953 K. TENNANT *Joyful Condemned* 295 The sullen, big oaf, baited and jeered at by everyone, a man who had 'come his guts to the coppers', was almost driven desperate. **1959** D. HEWETT *Bobbin Up* 135 She's in the manager's office half the day, with her legs crossed so you can see everythin' she's got, givin' him all our guts.
3. *Two-up*. The ring in which the spinner operates; CENTRE 3 (bets being placed either in the centre or as side-bets).
1941 *Wagflagger: Mag. Signals 6th Austral. Division Abroad* Sept. 7 Toss up pennies bright and clean. . . 'Some money in the guts.' **1974** *Warrumbungle Bk. of Verse* (1978) 20 Another swy in the guts boys For two-up is the game.
4. In the phr. **rough as guts**: (of a person) lacking in refinement or sophistication.
1966 B. BEAVER *You can't come Back* 118 I'm shy all right, but I'm not smooth. . . I'm rough as guts. **1978** *Southerly* iii. 260 The rough-as-guts but dinkum workers in bars he would have to tape in order to support his—and her—style of living.

gutser, var. GUTZER.

gutta-percha tree. [Transf. use of *gutta-percha* a tree yielding a rubbery juice: see OED.] The small tree of Qld. and N.T. *Excoecaria parvifolia* (fam. Euphorbiaceae), having an irritant milky sap. Also **gutta-percha.**
1883 E. PALMER *Plants N. Qld.* (1884) 15 Excoecaria parviola [*sic*] . . The gutta-percha tree; grows all over the Gulf waters and also on the Mitchell River. **1962** T. RONAN *Deep of Sky* 163 Avenues of gutta-percha . . form an archway of branches.

gutter.
1. *Mining*. The lowest part or deepest channel in a former watercourse, where auriferous matter is likely to be most concentrated: see quot. 1856.
1853 W.H. ARCHER *Papers NLA MS 266/5* 28 Aug., We are forced to sink a new shaft on the hillside of our claim to follow up the gutter if we can get at it again without being smothered with water. **1856** 'OLD COLONIST' *How to Farm & Settle in Aust.* 58 The idea generally pervading the mind of the miner is to this effect, that there is a lead, or particular direction of the main charge or accumulation of gold

formed by the in-pourings in former times from the surrounding country. This lead takes a very irregular and wholly uncertain direction. It is not found in directions at all conformable to the lines of the lowest level of the present valleys. 'The gutter' is a term applied to a supposed central line of this lead, into which, as into a groove or ditch, the main mass of the gold had been brought together.

2. A nickname for the Darling River. Also **Gutter of Australia.**

1937 A.W. UPFIELD *Winds of Evil* 179 'You're a stranger to this district.' 'Yes. I've come over from The Gutter for a change.' **1963** A. UPFIELD *Madman's Bend* 73 This Darling River, sometimes called the Gutter of Australia.

gutzer, *n.* Also **gutser.**

a. A (heavy) fall; a collision; *fig.*, a 'let down' or disappointment; a failure.

1918 *Aussie: Austral. Soldiers' Mag.* Oct. 7/1 'What do you boys mean, exactly, when you refer to a gutzer?'.. 'It means a "thud".'.. 'A fall-in.'.. 'A bad sort of failure.' **1937** L. MANN *Murder in Sydney* 71 'I'm going to make a splash, too.' 'Mind it isn't a gutser.' 'Oh, no. I'm doing quite well for myself.' **1979** B. SCOTT *Tough in Old Days* 135 Smashes were known colloquially as 'gutzers', and it was a lucky and skilful driver who did not have at least one a week.

b. In the phr. **to come a gutzer,** to fail as a result of miscalculation, to 'come a cropper'.

1918 N.P.H. NEAL *Back to Bush* 10 The man who came to the war to get away from a nagging wife came a horrible—gutzer, didn't he? **1983** *Canberra Times* 23 Oct. 2/3 'The Opposition,' raged Mr Dawkins during Wednesday's Question Time in the House of Representatives, 'has come an absolute gutser on this one!'

c. In the phr. **to bring** (someone) **a gutzer,** to engineer (someone's) downfall.

1939 FRANKLIN & CUSACK *Pioneers on Parade* 218 You didn't tell him! Of all the poor soft mugs you're the softest. You let slip the chance to bring him a gutser. **1964** E. LANE *Our Uncle Charlie* 35 Skitchem became entangled in his legs and—as Uncle himself would say—'brought him a gutzer', flinging him to the floor like a bag of potatoes.

gutzer, *v. intr.* To fail miserably.

1924 *Aussie* (Sydney) Feb. 42/2 Most of our time was spent in trying to invent some excuse to get us a few days' leave in London, but no matter what excuse we put up, we always 'gutzered'. **1976** S. WELLER *Bastards I have Met* 3 He bought a pub in Charters Towers and gutzered.

guvvie. Also **govie.** [f. GOV(ERNMENT HOUSE 2 + -Y.] GOVERNMENT HOUSE 2. Also as **guvvie flat.**

1984 *Canberra Times* 8 Apr. 9/3 House: Brick veneer guvvie, South Gowrie. **1985** *Ibid.* 15 Apr. 20/2 Probably the most attractive govie in this suburb. **1986** *Ibid.* 9 Apr. 3/1 (*heading*) Pets get the push in guvvie flats blitz.

guy a whack, *v. phr. Obs.* [Prob. joc. formation on Br. dial. and slang *guy* act of decamping: see OED *sb.*[2] 3 b.] *intr.* To decamp, to take (oneself) off, to abscond.

1882 *Sydney Slang Dict.* 5 Hoop (or Hook) it, or Guy Avack—To run. **1915** *Truth* (Sydney) 10 June 1/7 Madam Melba is on the eve of returning to the old country... There are many who would (like Melba) guyawhack if they had the wherewithal (like Melba).

guy-a-whack, *n.* [f. prec.] The act of decamping or absconding; one who does this.

1899 *Truth* (Sydney) 17 Sept. 4/5 At the slightest scent of troubles, Why, it does a 'duck' and doubles, By a process pusillanimous that's known as guy-a-whack! **1922** A. WRIGHT *Colt from Country* 131 'Lookin' fer th' guy what had y' in tow all day?' he asked. 'Yes,' moaned Yalty. 'Where is he?'.. 'Done er guy whack, I expect,' he grunted.

guyver, *n.* Also **guiver, gyver.** [Used elsewhere but recorded earliest in Aust.] An affectation of speech or behaviour, esp. empty or ingratiating talk, persiflage.

1864 C.R. THATCHER *Colonial Minstrel* 13 I'll give you the sack pretty quick, If my wife you offend with your guiver. **1896** *Truth* (Sydney) 7 June 1/3, I knew it was merely gyver, so my answer was straight an' blunt. **1919** E. DYSON *Hello, Soldier* 15 But the parsons and the poets couldn't teach him to discourse When it come to pokin' guyver at a pore, deluded horse.

guyver, *v. Obs.* [f. prec.] *trans.* To abuse (a person) verbally.

1882 *Bulletin* (Sydney) 17 June 10/2 Larrikin mob guyvored a Sydney Chinese storekeeper.

gympie: see GYMPIE HAMMER.

gympie /'gɪmpi/. [a. Gabi-gabi (and other s.e. Qld. languages) *gimbi.*] Any of several trees of the genus *Dendrocnide* (fam. Urticaceae), esp. the shrub or small tree *D. moroides* of n. N.S.W. and Qld., the hairs of which inflict an extremely painful recurring sting. See also STINGING TREE. Also *attrib.*

1895 A. MESTON *Geogr. Hist. Qld.* 55 *Gympie*, the Mary River blacks' name for the stinging tree. **1949** B. O'REILLY *Green Mountains* 103 The Gympie stinging tree, or Gympie Gympie, as it is called by the blacks, is readily identified by its huge dinner plate leaves a foot across. The leaves and young stems are hairy with transparent, stinging spines and contact with them is as painful as a scald.

Gympie hammer. *Mining.* [Also U.S.; of unknown origin.] A lightweight hammer used in hand-drilling; a single-jack. Also *ellipt.* as **gympie.**

1945 S.J. BAKER *Austral. Lang.* 94 *Gympie work*, single-handed hammer and drill work (a Queensland use). **1946** K.S. PRICHARD *Roaring Nineties* 248 A bit of gym, which was what they called the gold they got out of a mine with the Gympie hammer.

gyver, var. GUYVER *n.*

H

ha-ha. [Cf. LAUGHING JACKASS 1.] Used *attrib.* in Special Comb. **ha-ha pigeon (bird, duck),** the kookaburra *Dacelo novaeguineae*.

1938 F. CLUNE *Free & Easy Land* 257 The Ha Ha pigeons (Kookaburras) of Woothakata can Ha Ha without fear and trembling. **1969** P. ADAM SMITH *Folklore Austral. Railwaymen* 128 They .. even shot 'Ha-Ha birds' and magpies until I stopped them. **1970** J.S. GUNN in W.S. Ramson *Eng. Transported* 50 In certain areas along the Murray River the kookaburra is also called a *ha-ha duck* because some migrants eat them.

hair-trigger. *Obs.* TRIGGER PLANT.
1852 MRS C. MEREDITH *My Home in Tas.* II. 71 The *Stylidium*, or as we named it, the 'Hair-trigger', is common all over the colony. **1898** E.E. MORRIS *Austral Eng.* 189 Hair-trigger .. a Tasmanian name for any plant of genus *Stylidium*. Called also Trigger-plant.

hairy goat: see GOAT 2.

hairy Mary. See quots. 1936 and 1979.
1936 J. DEVANNY *Sugar Heaven* 41 The 'hairy Mary', fine prickles which clothed leaves and cane, penetrated every pore of the cutters' arms and hands. **1979** B. SCOTT *Tough in Old Days* 110 There is a substance, called by cutters 'Hairy Mary', which coats the underside of the young leaves and the top of the stalk with what looks for all the world like velvet.

hairy-nosed wombat. Either of two wombats of the genus *Lasiorhinus* of s. and e. Aust., having fine hairs on the snout.
1867 *Illustr. Sydney News* 18 July 205/1 The broadfaced or hairynosed wombat .. of South Australia. **1983** *Sydney Morning Herald* 15 Oct. 32/5 Identifying S.A.'s State pet as the hairy-nosed wombat.

hake. [Transf. use of *hake* a gadoid fish.] GEMFISH.
1951 T.C. ROUGHLEY *Fish & Fisheries Aust.* 128 In the Sydney fish market it [*sc.* the king barracouta] is known as 'hake'. **1974** *Bulletin* (Sydney) 12 Oct. 23/2 A N.S.W. fish called 'hake' is felt to suffer by public confusion with 'flake' and is to be renamed 'gemfish'.

hakea /'heɪkɪə/. [The plant genus *Hakea* was named by H.A. Schrader (1797) (*Sert. Hannov.* 27 Pl. 17) after the Hanoverian patron of botany Baron C.L. von *Hake* (1745–1818).] Any shrub or small tree of the large Austral. genus *Hakea* (fam. Proteaceae) of all States, characterized by spidery inflorescences and woody fruits with winged seeds. See also *cork-bark, cork tree* CORK, NEEDLEWOOD.
1827 *HRA* (1923) 3rd Ser. VI. 579, I observed on these Hills .. several Species of Hakea. **1985** *Age* (Melbourne) 20 Sept. (Suppl.) 7/1 Shrubs, such as the beautifully adorned grevilleas and spiky hakeas, sometimes form dense patches of bush.

half.
1. *pl. Obs.* [Cf. Br. dial. and U.S. *to (the) halves* so as to have a half-share in the profits: see OED *half, sb.* 7.]
a. In the phr. **on (the) halves, for halves:** see quot. 1845.
1829 *Launceston Advertiser* 4 May 5 From One to Two Hundred Head of *cattle*, will be taken on the halves, on one of the best runs on the Island. **1845** D. MACKENZIE *Emigrant's Guide* 106 A sheepowner .. will have no difficulty in meeting a respectable stockholder, who will receive and graze his sheep on what is called *halves*; that is the grazier receives yearly one-half of all the wool, and one half of the increase from the flock. *c* **1852** A. MANN *Goldfields Aust.* 61 It is usual to buy sheep and stock, and entrust them to a respectable stockholder, who pastures and tends them for *halves*—that is .. he takes half the wool and increase, the owner receiving the other half.

b. Used *attrib.* in Special Comb. **halves man,** one who farms 'on halves'.
1900 *Albury Banner* 5 Jan. 16/3 Farmers, selectors, and halves-men seem to care very little about comfort in their small shantys, as long as they get plenty of black billy, tough burnt chops, and half-baked bread.

2. *Australian National Football.* Used *attrib.* in Special Comb. **half-back,** any of the three positions on the line between the centre-line and the full-back line; a player occupying one of these positions; **-back flank** (or **flanker**), a player occupying either outside position on the half-back line; **-forward,** any of the three positions on the *half-forward line*; **-forward flank** (or **flanker**), a player occupying either outside position on this line; **-forward line,** the line between the centre-line and the full-forward line.
1931 J.F. MCHALE et al. *Austral. Game of Football* 60 The backs should kick wide in order to allow the **half-backs**— or very often the centre wings, because the back men may kick right over the half-back lines—to receive the ball on the run. **1936** E.C.H. TAYLOR et al. *Our Austral. Game Football* 34 Half-Back, Centre .. should be a very good high mark and excellent kick, and able to move off the mark. **1963** L. RICHARDS *Boots & All!* 217 **Half-Back Flank,** an ideal back flank should be around about the six-foot mark, vigorous, dashing and a strong mark and kick. **1978** J. DUNN *How to play Football* 78 Obviously, a half-back flanker has to defend. He is pitted against a half-forward flanker and basically his job is to stop his opponent from slicing open the defence for a goal feast. **1876** T.P. POWER *Footballer* 11 Centres and **half-forwards**—Keep your places and kick at once. Never run unless the coast be very clear. **1963** L. RICHARDS *Boots & All!* 36 At South one day Jack Hamilton wasn't getting a kick at full-back... He was being murdered, so Jock decided to shift him to a **half-forward flank.** **1964** *Footy Fan* (Melbourne) II. ii. 19 After making a name for himself as an elusive half forward flanker, Hassa got his chance to play pivot in 1961. **1963** L. RICHARDS *Boots & All!* 105 He knew how to make position on the **half-forward line.**

3. In the phr. **half your luck:** exclam. form of 'I wish I had a half of your luck'.
1933 H.B. RAINE *Lash End* 60 'From now on, Marie and I will be seen together very frequently. Get me?' 'Half your luck, son.' **1963** X. HERBERT *Disturbing Element* 159 Cyril delighted me with his frank comment on her: 'Half your luck, old chap!'

half-axe. [Fig. use of *half-axe* a small axe.] A youth.
1938 *Bulletin* (Sydney) 12 Jan. 21/2 When I was a half-axe .. me ole man had given me a boyproof watch. **1978** G. HALL *River still Flows* 110 In Dad's young days, to call any young half-axe a 'sissy' was the worst possible insult... Now the young feller was wearing much the same as his girlfriend.

half-blood. HALF-CASTE (but see quot. 1959). Also *attrib.*
1952 *Bulletin* (Sydney) 19 Mar. 15/4, I remarked to

HALF-BRED 251 HAND

Townie, a half-blood aboriginal yardman, that he, no doubt, didn't feel the heat. **1959** E. WEBB *Mark of Sun* 112 Anyone with twenty-five per cent of aboriginal blood in him is legally classified as a half-blood under Queensland law.

half-bred, *a.*
a. Of sheep: see quots.
1819 *Sydney Gaz.* 12 June, Three Half-bred Merino Rams. **1959** S.J. BAKER *Drum* 116 *Half-bred sheep,* orig. a sheep by a longwool ram from a merino ewe; now loosely applied to the type.
b. HALF-CASTE *attrib.*
1891 'R. BOLDREWOOD' *Sydney-Side Saxon* (1925) 118 All those half-bred brats of his are sure to give him the slip as they get older. **1901** *Bulletin* (Sydney) 28 Dec. 31/2 Only the last of six persons met proves to be a 'clean white', and the other five are half-bred and drunk—*i.e.,* it was in Western Queensland.

half-caser. *Obs.* A half-crown. See also CASER. Freq. **half-a-caser.**
1882 *Sydney Slang Dict.* 2 *Half a-caser,* half-a-crown. **1891** *Truth* (Sydney) 10 May 3/4 The solicitude he showed over the little half-crowns of the youths who plunge to that extent on the horse of their fancy, made very evident the sorrow he felt that their two-and-a-tanner was not devoted to the Centenary Hall collection plate. The way he hung and lingered over these half-casers was most interesting.

half-caste. Formerly also **half-cast.** [Spec. use of *half-caste* one of a mixed race.] One of mixed Aboriginal and non-Aboriginal parentage or descent. Freq. *attrib.*
1836 *Colonist* (Sydney) 7 July 211/4 They often kill their half-cast offspring. **1986** *Centralian Advocate* (Alice Springs) 15 Jan. 10/3 What I want to know is where the half-caste kids are going to drink now.

half-civilized, *a. Obs.* Of an Aboriginal: living outside colonial society, or incompletely assimilated into it. See also CIVILIZED.
1819 *Sydney Gaz.* 17 Apr., The poor half civilized native. **1900** T. MAJOR *Leaves from Squatter's Note Bk.* 155 This rough, honest old sea-dog .. with the assistance of two half-civilized black boys, managed to work his station.

halfie. [f. HALFCASTE + -Y.] HALF-CASTE.
1941 *Argus* (Melbourne) 15 Nov. (Suppl.) 1/3 Slang applied to the aborigines occurs, of course, only in the Far North... Half-castes are 'halfies', and quarter-castes 'creamies'. **1960** J. WALKER *No Sunlight Singing* 175 Say, Les, what's the drill with these halfies? .. That dance I went to th' other night. There was all colours there – black, white, brown and brindle.

half-masters. A pair of trousers too short for the wearer.
1924 F.J. MILLS *Happy Days* 112 Those trousers .. were what was known as half-masters. There was a space of three inches between the bottom of each leg and top of each boot. **1943** A. STEWART *Let's get Cracking* 55 My Malayan-issue trousers – weird garments which looked like bell-bottomed 'half-masters' when turned down.

half-time school. *Hist.* See quot. 1912.
1873 H. PARKES *Speeches* 5 Aug. (1876) 379 The half-time school means that the teacher goes to one place where there are 8 or 10 children and teaches them for three days, and then rides on to another place 30 miles distant and teaches another group there for three days. **1912** *Cwlth. of Aust. for Farmers* (Dept. External Affairs) 92 In still more thinly-peopled areas, half-time schools are to be found, *i.e.,* schools which are visited alternately by the one teacher, while itinerant teachers visit the scattered settlers in the 'back blocks'.

halves, on (the): see HALF 1.

ham and beef shop. A shop that specializes in the sale of cooked meats. Also *attrib.,* and *ellipt.* as **ham and beef**.
1905 *Truth* (Sydney) 23 Apr. 1/7 The small goods in a Leichhardt ham and beef shop have a row every morning while settling the question as to who is the oldest inhabitant. The German sausage that has sat in a window for about three weeks .. should be dipped in Condy's fluid and buried. **1907** *Ibid.* 18 Aug. 1/7 The ham and beef shopman will persist in doctoring his goods with boric acid preservatives. **1959** D. NILAND *Big Smoke* 114 That old hen would be either going to church or to the ham-and-beef for a headache powder.

ham and egg. a. In the collocation **ham and egg daisy,** *poached egg daisy,* see POACHED. **b.** *pl.* Any of several yellow-flowering plants.
1932 M.R. WHITE *No Roads go By* 230 Patches of ham-and-egg daisies, or Soldier's Buttons as bush folk call them. .. These flowers are really more like poached eggs than anything else, with their yellow lopsided centre and setting of white. **1948** G. FARWELL *Down Argent Street* 87 Thick with wild flowers; paper-petalled white everlastings, yellow ham-and-eggs.

hambone. [Prob. transf. use of *ham-bone* inferior actor: see OEDS 2.] A striptease performed by a male.
1966 C. MCGREGOR *Profile Aust.* 64 In March 1964 the citizens of Sydney were shocked when a medical student did a 'hambone'—a male striptease which continues until the man is stark naked—in front of a packed audience of freshers during a Sydney University orientation week; what they did not know was that the 'hambone' had been a popular entertainment at parties in the exclusive suburbs of the North Shore for many months beforehand! **1972** *Bulletin* (Sydney) 21 Oct. 45/3 It is not repeated—during the hambone nor the mass Percy-pointing event that follows.

hammer. [Abbrev. of *hammer and tack,* rhyming slang for 'back'.] In the phr. **to be on** (someone's) **hammer,** to be in hot pursuit of (a person, etc.); to hound or pester.
1942 *Truth* (Sydney) 31 May 12/2 Someone 'drums' me there's two 'Jacks' on me 'hammer'. **1986** *Canberra Times* 20 June 2/3 Things have really gone bad .. when a peaceful demonstrator can't even break a few windows on a foreign embassy without someone getting on her hammer.

hammer-and-tap. A method of drilling rock by hand. Also *attrib.*
1977 J. DOUGHTY *Gold in Blood* 243 We went to work with gympie and drill, 'hammer-and-tap', and bored and fired our first cut. **1982** M. WALKER *Making Do* 68 There were miners doing 'hammer and tap' demonstrations, with two men on top of a waggon, with a great piece of stone, belting it with a double-header hammer and drill.

hand, *n.*[1] *Hist.* [Cf. *for one's own hand* for one's own interest: see OED *hand, sb.* 27.]
1. In the phr. **on** (or **upon**) **one's own hands**: (of a convict) permitted to work for one's own interest or benefit, as distinct from being assigned to public labour or into private service.
1801 *HRA* (1915) 1st Ser. III. 254 Several settlers and others who have been allowed to take prisoners off the stores have abused that indulgence by receiving payment from the prisoners to allow them to be on their own hands. **1803** *Sydney Gaz.* 7 Aug., Patrick Shannon exhibited a complaint against John Hunter, his Government servant, for intending to defraud him of nine days pay, at the rate of Ten shillings per week, for allowing him the indulgence of

being on his own hands. **1810** *Ibid.* 17 Feb., Those who take prisoners off the Stores shall not permit them to go upon their own hands, under penalty of 2s. 6d. per diem for every day the prisoner shall be absent from their service.

2. In the phr. **on the hands of the government**: (of a convict) in official custody; also *transf.*: see quot. 1874.

1829 *HRA* (1922) 1st Ser. XV. 309 The Number of female Convicts who remained on the hands of the Government. **1874** J. FORREST *Explorations in Aust.* (1875) 339 A source of employment for paupers on the hands of the Government.

hand, *n.*² *Shearing.* Used *attrib.* in Special Comb. **hand-piece,** the part of a shearing machine that is held in the hand, the shearing attachment; **(-blade) shearer,** one who uses manually operated shears; **(-shearing) shed,** a shed in which the shearers use manually operated shears.

1912 R.S. TAIT *Scotty Mac* 9 The **hand pieces** are adding their chatter to the din. **1904** *Shearer* (Sydney) 30 July 1/3 **Hand** and machine **shearers**. **1949** G. FARWELL *Traveller's Tracks* 100 Eighty-four years old Jim Huxley, one of the original hand-blade shearers. **1904** *Shearer* (Sydney) 15 Oct. 8/5 Until this year this place was a **hand shed**, but Mr Chomley, wishing to be up to date, installed the latest pattern of the Wolseley sheep-shearing machine. **1910** *Bulletin* (Sydney) 22 Dec. 44/2 Men follow machine sheds or hand sheds. **1919** *Ibid.* 23 Jan. 24/2 In some hand-shearing sheds a couple of stands are set apart for learners.

handball. *Australian National Football.* HANDPASS *n.*

1859 C.C. MULLEN *Hist. Austral. Rules Football* (1959) 11 Handball will only be allowed if the ball is held clearly in one hand and punched or hit out with the other. **1982** *Bulletin* (Sydney) 28 Sept. 36/3 Standard handball.. punching an oval ball with the clenched fist.

Also as *v. intr.*

1963 *Footy Fan* (Melbourne) I. vii. 10 He is able to hand-ball with both hands.

handle. Chiefly *S.A.* and *N.T.* A measure of beer; the glass (having a handle) in which it is contained.

[N.Z. **1909** *N.Z. Truth* (Wellington) 29 May 7/3 Did he have 'a handle' of beer every time, or just a drop o' Scotch?] **1948** *Bulletin* (Sydney) 14 Apr. 27/4 As no bottles can be bought for love or money Mum and the girls and the little wife go to the hotels. And do they drink it from nice dainty little glasses? Not on your life—from handles and schooners, and some will order pints if they can get them. **1982** *Bulletin* (Sydney) 28 Sept. 28/2 They troop in at the end of the day for a 'handle' (pot or middy) costing $1—living in Darwin is not expensive.

handpass, *n. Australian National Football.* A pass in which the ball is held in one hand and struck with (usu. the clenched fist of) the other hand.

1931 J.F. MCHALE et al. *Austral. Game of Football* 56 Hand-pass, the ball may be held in one hand and hit with the open palm of the other hand, not necessarily with the clenched fist. **1973** J. DUNN *How to play Football* 41 The handpass, therefore, is tremendously important in football, and almost as important as the kick itself.

handpass, *v. Australian National Football. intr.* To deliver a handpass. Also as *vbl. n.*

1960 *N.T. News* (Darwin) 5 Jan. 8/6 Sparks marked well within kicking distance but foolishly handpassed to Lew Fatt. **1968** *Footy Fan* (Melbourne) I. xiii. 13 Hand passing is now divided into two categories—the conventional and the modern.

hand-throw, *v. trans.* To cast (a beast) to the ground preparatory to branding.

1921 *Bulletin* (Sydney) 15 Sept. 22/4, 107 fat calves .. were hand-thrown ('scruffed'). **1931** *Ibid.* 29 July 21/3 To hand-throw 300 nuggety calves before breakfast might be considered a good morning's work.

hang, *v.*

1. a. *trans.* Usu. with **up**: to tether (a horse). Also *intr.*

1859 W. KELLY *Life in Vic.* I. 49 In Melbourne there are posts sunk in the ground almost opposite every door, with rings and latches for affixing the bridles to them... Fastening your horse to one of these posts is termed 'hanging him up'. **1962** J. MARSHALL *This is Grass* 60 Why didn't you hang up your horse outside?

b. *intr.* With **up**: to stop work, esp. in shearing. Also as *vbl. n.*

1891 H.W. HARRIS *Shearers or Shorn* 5 In decreeing this present 'hanging up' of the mine of unionist labour, the unionist leaders seem to have acted as though they were frightened that calm deliberation would too glaringly expose their present errors in the past. **1975** L. RYAN *Shearers* 123 The greasies have hung up. Why can't we?

2. In the phr. **to hang (it) out,** to endure (hardship, etc.), to hold out.

1890 'R. BOLDREWOOD' *Colonial Reformer* II. 130 As long as they have their grub and their wages they'll hang it out. **1946** K. TENNANT *Lost Haven* 132 The old punt had broken down at last. He had been hoping against hope that it would hang out until the war ended, but the luck was against him.

hanging, *vbl. n. Obs.* A perquisite. Usu in *pl.*

1847 *Guardian* (Hobart) 8 Sept. 3/5 A friend at our elbow, acquainted with Colonial *slang*, tells us, that the *hangings* have been monstrous heavy!!! **1899** L. BECKE *Old Convict Days* 63 While the flogger was fixing me up [to the triangles] he said to me quietly, 'Is there any hangings to it?' meaning had I anything to give him to lay it on lightly.

happy family. [From the bird's gregarious habit.] APOSTLE. Occas. as collective.

1901 *Emu* I. 113 Variously known as 'The Happy Family', 'The Twelve Apostles' and 'Seven Sisters'.. my particular flock numbers twelve usually. **1938** F. BLAKELEY *Hard Liberty* 179 The cock-a-whizzle is found in all mulga country; it belongs to the group of 'Happy Family' and 'Twelve Apostles'—always good camp birds.

Happy Jack. Either of two babblers, the *grey-crowned babbler* (see GREY *a.*) and the *white-browed babbler* (see WHITE *a.*² 1 b.), both of which live in groups; APOSTLE b.

1921 'J. O'BRIEN' *Around Boree Log* 31 Happy Jacks (alias Gray-crowned Babblers) are brown with white markings. **1953** A. RUSSELL *Murray Walkabout* 103 Hardly had we settled down in camp when we had a visit from a company of gambolling white-browed babblers, or 'happy jacks'.

harbour. In the collocation **our harbour** (freq. **'arbour**), Sydney Harbour.

1880 *Bulletin* (Sydney) 20 Mar. 1/3 Gentle Reader,— What do you think of our Harbour? And having mastered this time-honoured question, tell me what do you think of our Circular Quay? **1965** G. MCINNES *Road to Gundagai* 71 So the battle raged. 'Our 'Arbour, Our Bridge and Our Bradman' was the Melbourne jibe at Sydney.

hard, *a.* In miscellaneous collocations: **hard case** [transf. use of U.S. *hard case* hardened criminal (OED(S *a.* 7)], a character; one who does not conform; an incorrigible (drinker, liar, eccentric, etc.); **hitter,** a bowler hat; **labour** [used elsewhere but recorded earliest in Aust.], physically hard labour imposed on a convict; also *attrib.*; **stuff** [used elsewhere but recorded earliest in Aust.], spirituous liquor; **timer,** one who has experienced hard or difficult times; **tucker,** lean rations; **word** [Br. dial. in various senses (see OEDS 6 b.)], an importunate request, esp. in the phr. **to put the hard word on.**

1892 *Truth* (Sydney) 8 May 3/7 What a study were those faces! Many of them real '**hard cases**'. **1892** 'J. MILLER' *Workingman's Paradise* 156 He turned and looked at her as he passed; he had a short beard and wore a '**hard hitter**'. **1803** *Sydney Gaz.* 10 July, They will on conviction be put to **Hard Labour** for six months. **1851** *Irish Exile* (Hobart) 18 Jan. 3/1 Mr P. O'Donohoe arrived here on Wednesday evening last, and was 'classed' on Thursday morning, for a hard labour party. **1832** *Hill's Life N.S.W.* (Sydney) 6 July 4 Lots of swizzle, **hard stuff,** two waters, heavy wet, 'weed', and long steamers, were the *last act.* **1892** 'J. MILLER' *Workingman's Paradise* 114 On a seat in the rain, near a lamp, was a poor devil of a woman, a regular **hard-timer** .. sleeping with her head hung over the back of the seat like a fowl's. **1932** M. TERRY *Out Back* 2 Good honest work, **hard tucker**—with plenty of it. **1918** J.A. PHILP *Jingles that Jangle* 23 An Irish friend to whom I was reading the proof of this preface gave me 'the **hard word**'. **1985** H. GARNER *Postcards from Surfers* 68, I can go into any one of them and get myself a fuck, without having to *fight* for it. I never put the hard word on you, did I Watto, in all those years?

hardenbergia /ˈhɑːdənˈbɜːɡiə/. [The Austral. plant genus *Hardenbergia* was named by English botanist G. Bentham (*Enu. Pl. Huegel* (1837) 40) after Countess Franziska von *Hardenberg,* an Austrian patron of botany.] Any species of the genus of trailing or climbing plants *Hardenbergia* (fam. Fabaceae). See also FALSE SARSAPARILLA.

1879 'OLD HAND' *Journey Port Phillip to S.A.* 19 The scarlet Kennedia and the purple hardenbergia climbed over the verandah. **1984** E. WALLING *On Trail Austral. Wildflowers* 11 The purple Sarsaparilla or *Hardenbergia* (one of the plants with a botanical name as familiar as the common one).

hard-gut mullet. [With reference to a large, hard lump in the gut of the fish.] A young *sea mullet* (see SEA). Also abbrev. as **hard-gut.**

1874 *N.S.W. Rep. R. Comm. Fisheries* (1880) 12 The smaller Australian varieties [of mullet] consist of—*Mugil argentens,* or hard-gut [etc.]. **1896** F.G. AFLALO *Sketch Nat. Hist. Aust.* 232 The Sydney Sea Mullet keep well out in the offing, wherein they differ from the younger generation known as Hard Gut mullet, which frequent the estuaries and generally keep inshore.

hardwood. The relatively hard wood of any of many genera of Australian trees, esp. of the genus *Eucalyptus* (see EUCALYPTUS); a tree having such wood; *spec.* the wood of an angiosperm (see quots. 1957 and 1984). Also *attrib.*

1842 *Sydney Herald* 12 Apr. 3/3 The forests .. abound with rosewood, cedar, and hardwood, of a very fine description. **1853** J. SHERER *Gold Finder Aust.* 61 The earnings of hard-wood sawyers can scarcely be estimated. **1957** *Forest Trees Aust.* (Cwlth. Forestry & Timber Bureau) 16 The forest trees of Australia may be arranged conveniently into two broad categories, 'hardwoods' and 'softwoods'. Hardwoods, also known as 'broad-leaved' plants, include all the woody plants except the conifers. **1984** D.J. BOLAND et al. *Forest Trees Aust.* (rev. ed.) 650 Hardwood. Wood from trees classified botanically as angiosperms. The term does not denote the relative hardness of the wood, though it is sometimes used in this sense.

hardyhead. Any of several small marine and freshwater fish of the fam. Atherinidae, often occurring in schools.

1881 *Proc. Linnean Soc. N.S.W.* VI. 38 *Atherina pinguis* .. 'Hardyhead' of Sydney Fishermen. **1977** J.M. THOMSON *Field Guide Common Sea & Estuary Fishes* 107 Not unlike small mullet, the hardyheads are often called silversides from the broad silver stripe which many of the species carry along the sides.

hare-wallaby. [From the resemblance of the wallaby to the European hare: see quot. 1841.] Any of several small wallabies of the genera *Lagorchestes* and *Lagostrophus* of mainland Aust. Also with distinguishing epithet (see *spectacled hare-wallaby* SPECTACLED).

[**1841**] J. GOULD *Birds of Aust.* (1848) I. Pl. 12, The name of Hare Kangaroo has been given to this species [*sc. Lagorchestes leporoïdes*], as much from the similarity of its form, its size, and the colour and texture of its fur, as from its habits assimilating in many particulars to those of that animal.] **1896** B. SPENCER *Rep. Horn Sci. Exped. Central Aust.* I. 109 At Mount Sonder we had obtained specimens of the hare-wallaby (*Lagorchestes conspicillatus var. leichardtii*). **1983** R. STRAHAN *Compl. Bk. Austral. Mammals* 195 The distribution of all hare-wallabies has declined severely since European settlement.

harlequin. A highly prized form of opal (see quot. 1974); a stone of this type. Also *attrib.*

1873 C. ROBINSON *N.S.W.* 62 Opals... Amongst polished stones are some of the harlequin class. **1960** D. McLEAN *Roaring Days* 62 The opal is the most beautiful of all gems, and the most beautiful opal is the harlequin. .. It's a round stone covered with little angular surfaces as if it has been cut by a master hand; these surfaces flash every colour known to nature in a constantly changing, shimmering mosaic. **1974** B. MYATT *P. Hamlyn Dict. of Austral. Gemstones* 134 Harlequin opal shows a mosaic-like pattern of colour in angular, roughly rectangular or rounded patches of about equal size.

harlequin bronzewing. FLOCK PIGEON a. Also **harlequin pigeon.**

1841 J. GOULD *Birds of Aust.* (1848) II. Pl. 66, *Peristera histrionica* .. Harlequin Bronzewing. **1845** L. LEICHHARDT *Jrnl. Overland Exped. Aust.* 20 June (1847) 296 Large flocks of *Peristera histrionica* (the Harlequin pigeon) were lying on the patches of burnt grass on the plains.

harness-cask. [Transf. use of *harness-cask* shipboard container in which salt meat is kept.] A container in which salt meat is stored prior to use.

1848 T.L. MITCHELL *Jrnl. Exped. Tropical Aust.* 39 The dray—already there with the harness casks. **1921** G.A. BELL *Under Brigalow* 211 The 'duffers' were suspected of replenishing their own 'harness' casks from their neighbours' herds.

hash. Used *attrib.* to designate a cheap eating house, boarding house, etc., or one who works in such an establishment.

1892 *Truth* (Sydney) 15 May 1/5 'D'ye love me Bill?' the hash girl said, While out with her Waterloo mash. **1945** *Atebrin Advocate: Mag. 2/4 Austral. Armoured Regiment* Jan. 2 They want a drum of Range fuel at the hash foundry or there'll be no tea.

hashmagandy. Also **hash-me-gandy.** [f. prec., perh. infl. by *salmagundi* mixture of meats, etc.]

1. A stew.

1919 W.H. DOWNING *Digger Dialects* 28 *Hashmagandy,* an insipid and monotonous army dish. **1945** S.J. BAKER *Austral. Lang.* 81 For stews our only original contributions appear to be *hash-me-gandy* and *mulliga stew.*

2. Special Comb. **hashmagandy bag,** see quot.

1944 *Bulletin* (Sydney) 23 Feb. 12/3, I wonder if any Murray fisherman these days ever uses a 'hashmagandy' bag. First you got hold of one of those old-fashioned open-wove potato sacks. Then from any handy boiling-down works a couple of bucketfuls of cooked-to-rags mutton; or, failing that you cooked a similar quantity and quality of rabbit. Hung over the stern of the moored flattie such a bag, given an occasional shake, discharged a stream of tasty meat particles... The modern angler would probably call it 'burley', but present-day mixtures of bran and pollard and soaked bread can never come near the old 'hashmagandy' as a fish-enticer.

hat, *n.* In the phr. **to throw** (one's) **hat in (first),** to declare an intention with a view to ascertaining the response, to 'test the water'.

1953 'CADDIE' *Caddie* 248 As he walked in through the back door I said: 'Hadn't you better throw your hat in first?' **1960** R. TULLIPAN *Follow Sun* 53 There is, I suppose, a need to throw my hat in where you're concerned, Julie.

hat, *v.* [Back-formation f. HATTER.] *intr.* To live a solitary life, esp. as a gold-miner; *transf.,* to fossick.

1868 *Wallaroo Times* (Kadina) 4 Mar. 6/3 A German named Jacob.. had been 'hatting' in Splitters Gully, Whipstick. **1900** H. LAWSON *On Track* 88 He 'hatted' and brooded over it till he went ratty. **1980** *Canberra Times* 18 Aug. 7/1 On the Victorian gold fields he averages 85 gms. a day by 'hatting', searching through the tailing heaps left by the original gold diggers.

hatter. [Prob. f. the phr. *(one's) hat covers (one's) family,* used of one who is alone in the world (see OED *hat, sb.* 5 c.); later infl. by the phr. *mad as a hatter.*]

a. *Mining.* A miner who works independently (rather than in partnership).

1853 J. ROCHFORT *Adventures Surveyor* 66 The Bendigo diggings are suitable for persons working singly... Such persons are called 'hatters'. They live alone, in a tent often not more than six feet long, three feet high, and three feet wide. **1978** M. WALKER *Pioneer Crafts Early Aust.* 104 Some of the solitary prospectors became known as 'hatters'—their isolation had severed their connection with mankind.

b. A rural worker pursuing a solitary occupation; a single man; a misanthrope; an eccentric.

c **1872** J.C.F. JOHNSON *Over Island* 2 'Hatter', in bush phraseology, is a man who shepherds or lives by himself. **1977** G.W. LILLEY *Lengthening Shadows* 22 Boundary-riders on the big Queensland sheep runs.. were a varied lot. The married men were more or less normal but the single tended to be hatters, that is, somewhat queer, the monotonous and solitary life they led tended to make them so.

c. *transf.*

1893 D. LINDSAY *Jrnl. Elder Sci. Exploring Exped.* 23 No sign of the lost brute [*sc.* a camel], which is, I find, a regular 'hatter', always poking away by himself. **1945** E. MITCHELL *Speak to Earth* 113 Fences meant nothing to two of those eighteen-month steers. A white one—'a bit of a hatter, always on his own', Mr Herbert described him—was the first to jump back into the Kurrajong.

have, *v.* In the phr. **to have** (someone) **on,** to engage (someone) in a fight, contest, etc.

1941 S.J. BAKER *Pop. Dict. Austral. Slang* 34 *Have (someone) on,* to be prepared to fight a person; to accept a challenge to a contest or fight. **1962** S. GORE *Down Golden Mile* 137 What! I'm as good as some o' you young jokers. I'll have any one of yer on—old and all as I am.

Hawkesbury Rivers, *pl.* [f. the name of a river in N.S.W.] Rhyming slang for 'shivers'.

1941 S.J. BAKER *Pop. Dict. Austral. Slang* 35 *Hawkesbury Rivers,* the shivers. **1962** D. MCLEAN *World turned upside Down* 12 Danny would have been the first to admit that he was as game as Ned Kelly in most things, but girls gave him the Hawkesbury Rivers.

hay, *v. trans.* With **off**: to dry (standing grass, etc.). Chiefly as **hayed-off,** *ppl. a.,* dried while standing.

1948 *Bulletin* (Sydney) 24 Nov. 29/2 Sudden heat and a dry westerly hayed-off Mac's oats and he put the binder in. **1983** *Canberra Times* 24 May 3/1 At this time of the year there was usually standing dry feed left.. to bolster the green pick that came through with autumn rain. Because of the extended drought, there was no such hayed-off feed.

hay burner. [Also U.S.: see Mathews.] A jocular term for a horse. Formerly **hay motor.** Also *attrib.*

1900 E.L. HOLMES *Pioneer Motor Car Trip* 8 We had matched against us a pair of iron grey 'hay motors', but we.. beat them badly into Cootamundra. **1920** *Character Glimpses: Australs. on Somme* 28 What's the idea of socking our hard earned jack in that hay burner? **1969** P. ADAM SMITH *Rails go Westward* 14 Within a few months agitation began for horse-drawn railways.. what has been called 'the hay burner railway'.

hazel. [Transf. use of *hazel*: see quot. 1827.] Either of the two shrubs or trees *Pomaderris aspera* and *P. apetala* (fam. Rhamnaceae) of e. Aust., having rough, wrinkled leaves.

1827 G.W. BARNARD in *HRA* (1923) 3rd Ser. VI. 267, A Shrub.. I shall call the 'Hazel' to which it has a similitude, is found commonly in the Creeks of V.D. Land; it has an appearance between the 'Curryjong' and the 'Hazel'. **1973** D. WOLFE *Brass Kangaroo* 195 A dense under-forest of blackwoods, hazel, musk and other mountain species.

head, $n.^1$ *Two-up.*

1. In *pl.* A fall of the coins in which the heads face upwards; a bet that the coins will fall this way; a call declaring this.

1897 *Worker* (Sydney) 18 Dec. 3/4 Hey, bar that toss! Heads it is! **1944** G.H. FEARNSIDE *Sojourn in Tobruk* 24 It is just like a game of two-up... A man can have a run of heads and get out while he's still winning.

2. Comb. **head backer, bettor.**

1925 A. WRIGHT *Boy from Bullarah* 18 From all around the ring **head backers** rose to gather in their winnings, and stake again on the next spin. **1946** *Austral. New Writing* 36 Taily wanted for a dollar.. there y' are, mate, **head bettor** over here.

head, $n.^2$ A rogue, a sharper.

1918 *Euripidean: Troopship Souvenir* 6 Cold foot was a gentlemanly epigraph; 'ead.. those.. Johns addressed me as. **1964** P. ADAM SMITH *Hear Train Blow* 125 When the 'head' gave up and went back to the van, the guard motioned me to put the window up.

head, $v.^1$ [Spec. use of *head* to get ahead of so as to turn back: see OED(S *v.* 13 b. and c.] *trans.* To get ahead of (a travelling, often stampeding, mob of sheep, cattle, etc.) so as to arrest its progress.

1846 *Bell's Life in Sydney* 17 Jan. 3/3 The defendant driving a mob of cattle, and Jones being apprehensive of receiving an injury from them—not being able to reach a fence, from the position of that part of the road—'headed them', as it is termed, which so irritated Kennedy that he struck at him with his whip. **1938** D. BATES *Passing of Aborigines* 53 At last the galloping drovers 'headed' them again.

head, $v.^2$ *Two-up.*

1. a. In the phr. **to head them** (also **'em**), to play the game of two-up; to toss the coins so that they fall with the head side upwards.

1902 *Truth* (Sydney) 14 Sept. 1/6 The life of the Domain dosser is indeed hard. He is not allowed to even 'head 'em'. **1981** *N.S.W. Parl. Papers* (1980–81) 3rd Sess. IV. 1970/2, I was playing two-up... I got barred because I headed them twice.

b. *transf.*
1945 'MASTER-SARG' *Yank discovers Aust.* 75 '*Headed 'em*', got a homer or pulled off some other good thing.

2. As ppl. (and n.) phr. in the collocation **heading them**: the playing of two-up; the spinning of two coins so that they fall head side upwards. Also *ellipt.* as **heading**.
1871 *Austral. Town & Country Jrnl.* (Sydney) 10 June 730/2 The course was soon deserted, save by a select circle of the 'heading-em' brotherhood. **1887** K. MACKAY *Stirrup Jingles* 58 Then an hour was devoted to blowing And drinking and handling the 'kip', For at 'heading' these shearers were knowing, And at talk creation could whip. **1959** A. VON BERTOUCH *February Dark* 69 'I see that we might just as well take up heading 'em for a living,' said Peter. 'Heading 'em?' said Helen. 'Two-up,' said Max. 'Tossing coins.'

headings, *vbl. n. pl. Gold-mining*. [Spec. use of *heading* top layer: see OED 12.] See quot. 1869.
1859 *Colonial Mining Jrnl.* May 145/2 Their wash-dirt principally consists of the pipeclay found in the old drives, together with 2 feet of headings. **1869** R.B. SMYTH *Gold Fields & Mineral Districts* 613 *Headings*, coarse gravel or drift overlying the washdirt.

head serang: see SERANG.

head-station. *Home-station*, see HOME *attrib.*[2] b.
1835 J. LHOTSKY *Journey from Sydney to Austral. Alps* 97 This time of year is the conclusion of sheep-shearing, where the persons employed in it (free and bond), were returning home, or to the head-stations. **1978** R.H. CONQUEST *Dusty Distances* 55 They established an outstation, naming it after their home town... Over the range into the Dawson and Callide Valleys, and from there to Gracemere, where they established their head-station.

heady. *Two-up.* [f. HEAD *n.*[1] + -Y.] A person reputedly skilled in spinning the coins so that they fall head side upwards; one who bets on the coins so falling.
1950 F.J. HARDY *Power without Glory* 323 Big Bill spun first. He was considered to be one of the best 'headies' in Queensland. **1946** *Austral. New Writing* 37 Tail bettor here.. heady over there, mate.

heaps. In the phr. **to give** (someone) **heaps**, to oppose (an adversary, team, etc.) with vigour.
1978 *Sydney Morning Herald* 26 Sept. 2/1 *Good luck Kangaroos (and give 'em heaps)* Tooths KB is proud to sponsor the 1978/79 Kangaroo tour of Great Britain and France. And wish players and officials good luck in their quest to keep the Ashes. **1982** *Sunday Mail* (Brisbane) 5 Sept. 80/5 Punters give Malcolm heaps... Malcolm Johnston was booed after champion galloper Kingston Town was beaten into fourth place.. at Randwick yesterday.

heart-leaf poison. [See quot. 1853.] Any of several shrubs of the genus *Gastrolobium* (fam. Fabaceae) poisonous to stock, esp. (*W.A.*) *G. bilobum* of s.w. W.A. and (*Qld.*) *G. grandiflorum* of central and n. Aust. Also **heart-leaf poison bush** (or **plant**).
[**1853** E. SAUNDERS *Our Austral. Colonies* 4 There are very few horses, cattle, or sheep in the settlement, in consequence of there being a plant called 'heart-poison' (so-called because the leaf is in shape like a heart) which is very destructive to them.] **1865** 'SPECIAL CORRESPONDENT' *Transportation* 14 Whole districts are overrun with strong quick-growing bushes.. These are the York-road, the heart-leaf, the rock, and the box-scrub. **1897** L. LINDLEY-COWEN *W. Austral Settler's Guide* 42 Heartleaf poison is found in patches. **1916** *Bulletin* (Sydney) 16 Mar. 22/4 The sudden and deadly effect of the 'heart leaf' poison plant. **1944** *Ibid.* 5 July 13/2 Queensland seems to lead Australia in the number of poison plants; perhaps the deadliest of all is the heartleaf poison bush (*Gastrolobium grandiflorum*).

heath. [Transf. use of *heath*, from the similarity of habitat.] Any of several plants occurring in heathland, usu. of the fam. Epacridaceae, and esp. of the genus *Epacris* including the shrub of s.e. mainland Aust. *E. impressa*, the floral emblem of Vic.; *native heath*, see NATIVE *a.* 6 a. See also EPACRIS.
1849 J.P. TOWNSEND *Rambles & Observations N.S.W.* 28 This open ground produced many specimens of 'the beautiful genus *Epacris*, which may be called the Heaths of Australia, being nearly allied to them, and perhaps superior in beauty' (Sir William Hooker). **1984** E. WALLING *On Trail Austral. Wildflowers* 11 It is still winter when the.. heath comes into flower. Tall slender stems with tiny bells clustering closely to them wave gently beneath a thin canopy of gum trees.

heavy, *a. Obs.* In the collocation **heavy gold**: see quot. 1869.
1855 R. CARBONI *Eureka Stockade* 10 A party of Britishers had two claims; the one, on the slope of the hill, was bottomed on heavy gold. **1869** R.B. SMYTH *Gold Field & Minerals Districts* 613 *Heavy gold*, gold in large particles. Sometimes called 'shotty gold', when it has the appearance of gun-shot.

heavy, *n.* Usu. in *pl.*
1. *Surfing.* A large wave.
1962 *Austral. Women's Weekly* (Sydney) 24 Oct. (Suppl.) 3/2 *Heavy*, a big wave. **1964** *Surfabout* (Sydney) I. vi. 20 Cyclonic weather.. had an enormous effect and influence on the North Narrabeen surf... The cyclonic pattern produced big-day heavies.

2. A person of influence or importance.
1973 A. BROINOWSKI *Take One Ambassador* 85 'Wow,' said Andy. 'This Fujita must be a real heavy.' '.. I beg your pardon?' 'Fujita is a very important man?' **1976** J. HOLMES *Govt. Vic.* 23 Cabinet 'heavies' have multiple portfolios which keep them constantly in the parliamentary eye.

heavy, *v. trans.* To harass (a person), to put pressure on. Chiefly in *pass.*, and also as *vbl. n.*
1974 M. GILLESPIE *Into Hollow Mountains* 31 The Free Store harbored a few criminals from time to time.. and we got heavied by the police a few times. **1986** *Sydney Morning Herald* 14 June 33/5 Heavying doesn't mean you ask someone to do something and tell them they're a mug if they don't. Heavying is 'I want you to do this but if you don't do it, there's a penalty.'

hedgehog. *Obs.* ECHIDNA.
1827 P. CUNNINGHAM *Two Yrs. in N.S.W.* I. 317 Our *porcupine*, or Australian hedgehog, serves for another native dish. **1906** *Bulletin* (Sydney) 13 Sept. 17/2 My landlady was liberal with native 'game', from kangaroo-rat to the hedgehog.

hedgewood. [Transf. use of *hedge-wood* trees or timber grown in hedgerows.] A plant of arid Aust. forming dense thickets; perh. BULWADDY (see quot. 1951). Also *attrib.*, and formerly **hedge-tree**.
1861 J.M. STUART *Explorations in Aust.* 29 May (1865) 299 We have again met with the mulga... Amongst it is the hedge-tree. **1883** E. FAVENC *Rep. Country N.T.* 3 After crossing this branch we got into thick mulga and hedgewood scrub. **1897** J.J. MURIF *From Ocean to Ocean* 147, I led Diamond to a hedgewood tree. **1951** E. HILL *Territory* 299 Hedgewood, allumbo, the 'bulwaddi'... These gnarled dark woods are the hardest timber on earth—when very old it will break and burn, but it never bends.

heeler. Abbrev. of *blue heeler* BLUE *a.* Also *attrib.*
1914 R. KALESKI *Austral. Barkers & Biters* 36 These

speckled heelers are like a small thick-set dingo. **1980** HOLTH & BARNABY *Cattlemen of High Country* 103 Mountain cattlemen also need a heeler dog to push lagging cattle along a highway.

heifer. Used *attrib.* in Special Comb. **heifer paddock,** an enclosure in which calves are isolated from their mothers until weaned; also *fig.* a girls' school; **station** *obs.*, see quot. 1849.

1845 D. MACKENZIE *Emigrant's Guide* 120 Without a weaning or **heifer paddock,** you will be obliged to allow your calves to continue sucking their mothers for a whole year. **1885** MRS C. PRAED *Austral. Life* 50 Next year I shall look over a heifer-paddock in Sydney and take my pick. NB.—Heifer-paddock in Australian slang means a ladies' school. **1839** D. MACKELLAR *Austral. Emigrant's Guide* 10 When the increase of the cattle are ready for weaning, a **heifer station** is established at a considerable distance from the home station, at which a stock-yard is erected. **1849** J.P. TOWNSEND *Rambles & Observations N.S.W.* 182 The squatter has need of many stations distinct from each other. He has first his 'sheep station', then his 'breeding station' for cattle, then his 'heifer station', where young heifers are kept until they are old enough to be transferred into the breeding herd.

hell. In the phr. **hell, west and crooked,** all over the place; in disarray.

1951 E. HILL *Territory* 295 One big stampede to unnerve them, and the cattle are off every night, 'hell, west and crooked'. **1970** V. HALL *Outback Policeman* 43 Everything went 'hell, west and crooked' as the mob divided at the tree.

helmet orchid. [See quot. 1984; cf. *helmet-flower* (OED *helmet, sb.* 9).] Any of several dwarf ground orchids of the genus *Corybas* (fam. Orchidaceae), occurring in all States but not N.T., and from s.e. Asia to N.Z.

1923 *Census Plants Vic.* (Field Naturalists' Club Vic.) 19 *Corysanthes unguiculata.* Small Helmet-orchid. **1984** D.T. & C.E. WOOLCOCK *Austral. Terrestrial Orchids* 56 Helmet orchids... The helmet is formed by an erect dorsal sepal, usually enlarged, concave, and bending forward as a hood, and a large labellum.

helmeted honeyeater. The rare honeyeater *Lichenostomus melanops cassidix,* occurring in a small area e. of Melbourne (Vic.), and a faunal emblem of Vic.

1867 J. GOULD *Birds of Aust.* Suppl. (1869) Pl. 39, Helmeted Honey-eater... The *P[tilotis] cassidix* differs from *P. auricomis* in its much larger size, in the dark olive-black colouring of its upper surface, wings, and tail. **1983** *Sun* (Sydney) 17 Aug. 17 At similar peril are the regent and helmeted honeyeaters.

Henare /'hɛnəri/. [Maori form of 'Henry'.] A Maori; the typical Maori. Cf. HORI.

1921 *Smith's Weekly* (Sydney) 1 Jan. 9/3 Henare made his first aeroplane flight at Palmerston North (N.Z.) the other day. **1933** *Bulletin* (Sydney) 12 July 21/1 Binghi could probably lick Henare at tree-climbing any day in the week, but the old-time Maori had a technique which was safe if slow.

he-oak. *Obs.* [f. the pronoun *he* (see quots. 1855 and 1857) + OAK 1. Cf. SHE-OAK.] Any of several trees of the fam. Casuarinaceae.

1792 *Hist. Rec. N.S.W.* (1893) II. 799 There are two kinds of oak, called the he and the she oak, but not to be compared with English oak. **1855** J. BONWICK *Geogr. Aust. & N.Z.* (ed. 3) 202 The Casuarinae, or He and She Oak, have no leaves, but long knotted twigs at the end of branches. The He oak is Cas. stricta, or upright; the She oak is C. tortulosa [*sic*], or bending. **1857** D. BUNCE *Australasiatic Reminisc.* 33 The trees forming the most interesting groups were the *Casuarina torulosa* she-oak; and *C. stricta,* he-oak... *C. stricta,* or he-oak, has been named in contradistinction of the sexes, as if they constituted one dioecious plant, the one male and the other female, whereas they are two perfectly distinct species.

herbs. The horsepower of an engine, esp. of a motor vehicle; also *fig.*

1957 R. STOW *Bystander* 116 'I think you're beaut... You're the nicest boy in this car,' she said. Derek said sardonically, 'Go on, give him the herbs. Bet he doesn't even notice you're there.' **1975** D.J. TOWNSHEND *Gland Time* 140 Them glands have given him more herbs than a tractor. **1977** W. MOORE *Just to Myself* 80 Got plenty of herbs. Get in and I'll take ya for a drag.

herd. *Obs.* [Spec. use of *herd* a company of animals of any kind: see OED *sb.*^{1} 2.] Used formerly of a number of kangaroos, etc., feeding or travelling together; now replaced by MOB *n.* 2 or 'flock'.

1831 *Acct. Colony Van Diemen's Land* 62 Herds of kangaroos were seen in the plains, but they quickly bounded away. **1926** A.S. LE SOUEF et al. *Wild Animals Australasia* 19 A herd of kangaroos.

herring. [Transf. use of *herring* an edible sea fish.]

1. *W.A.* **a.** *Obs.* BONY BREAM. **b.** TOMMY ROUGH.

1832 G.F. MOORE *Diary Ten Yrs. W.A.* 14 Sept. (1884) 136 Fish, which are very numerous in the river about and below Perth.. of the kind *called* herrings, but do not look very like them; they make a noise when out of the water, and on that account are also called trumpeters. **1980** N. COLEMAN *Austral. Sea Fishes* 152 When the 'herring' (an inaccurate term) are 'on', people turn out in their hundreds.

2. The Australian grayling *Prototroctes maraena,* a fresh-water fish of s.e. Aust.; CUCUMBER FISH; *native herring* (b), see NATIVE *a.* 6 b.

1841 *Port Phillip Patriot* 1 Apr. 4/1 A stream.. abounding in black-fish, herring and lobsters. **1921** *Bulletin* (Sydney) 16 June 26/3 In many rivers of Tasmania there is a lively little fish, usually called 'herring'.

Hewie, var. HUGHIE.

Hexham grey. [f. the name of a town on the Hunter River near Newcastle, N.S.W.] The widespread, dappled grey mosquito *Aedes alternans,* the largest biting mosquito in Australia; SCOTCH GREY.

1889 'SALTBUSH' *Sydney to Croydon* 4 The famous swamps, rendered memorable as the breeding-grounds of the well-known and duly appreciated 'Hexham Greys', those noted mosquitos. **1981** L. MCLEAN *Pumpkin Pie* 15 He was almost eaten alive by mosquitoes at a place called Hexham, where he said the mossies were the biggest, and blood thirstiest he had ever met. They were called 'Hexham Greys'.

hickory. [Transf. use of *hickory* a North American tree of the genus *Carya,* yielding a tough timber.] Any of several trees, usu. of the genus *Acacia* (fam. Mimosaceae), yielding a tough, close-grained timber; the wood of these trees. Also **hickory wattle.**

1840 *S. Austral. Rec.* (London) 27 June 356 Various shrubs—as the tea-tree, hickory (which may be called a tree).. were abundant. **1889** J.H. MAIDEN *Useful Native Plants Aust.* 350 *Acacia aulacocarpa.*. 'Hickory Wattle'. Wood hard, heavy, tough, and dark-red; useful for cabinet-work.

hide. [Ellipt. use of *thick hide*: see OEDS *sb.*^{1} 2 c. Used elsewhere but recorded earliest in Aust.] Impertinence; effrontery.

1902 *Truth* (Sydney) 9 Feb. 4/2 Last week I had a caligraphic cut at what I called, for want of a better name, your 'hide', a word which, in Australian 'slanguage', signifies a

HIDEY 257 **HOBBLE**

tough moral, or rather immoral, article. **1979** K. Dunstan *Ratbags* p. xx, If they've got the hide to do this, then I've got the hide to photograph it.

hidey. [f. *hide(-and-seek* + -Y.] The game of hide-and-seek.

1957 A. Marshall *Aust.* (1981) 73 'Kick the Tin' was a version of 'Hidey' with a race back to the tin when the person who was 'he' found anyone. **1978** M. Walker *Pioneer Crafts Early Aust.* 85 The girls played less vigorously—tiggy touchwood, hidey, domestic games, mothers, fathers and naughty children.

hieleman /'hiləmən/. Also with much variety, esp. formerly as **yeelaman, yelaman**. [a. Dharuk *yilimaŋ*.] An Aboriginal shield made from bark or wood; Shield.

1793 W. Tench *Compl. Acct. Settlement* 191 Their shields are of two sorts: that called *Il-ee-mon*, is nothing but a piece of bark, with a handle fixed in the inside of it. **1839** T.L. Mitchell *Three Exped. Eastern Aust.* (rev. ed.) II. 349 There is.. much originality in the shield or *hieleman* of these people. **1861** *Bell's Life in Sydney* 30 Nov. 4/3 Lo! yeelamans splinter and boomerangs clash. **1889** E.B. Kennedy *Blacks & Bushrangers* 60 He was able to point out and name to Tim spears, woomeras, yelamans, boomerangs, stone tomahawks, and nullah-nullahs.

High Court. The federal supreme court established by the Constitution as the final arbiter of constitutional questions and final court of appeal from State and federal courts. In full **High Court of Australia.**

1900 J.H. Symon *Austral. Cwlth. Bill* 4 From the High Court appeals lie to the Privy Council. **1911** H.G. Turner *First Decade Austral. Cwlth.* 112 A test action by the Government of New South Wales against a trades union connected with the brewing industry was brought before the High Court of Australia.

hill. With **the.**

1. An uncovered area of rising ground for spectators at a sporting event:

a. At Flemington Racecourse, Melbourne.

1872 'Resident' *Glimpses Life Vic.* 399 A crowd numbering some thirty thousand persons is seen moving to and fro on the hill. **1900** *Advocate* (Burnie) 8 Nov. 4/2 People who go to the hill do not make nearly so much litter or give us half so much trouble as.. the grandstand.

b. In front of the scoreboard at the Sydney Cricket Ground.

1925 S. Hicks *Hullo Australs.* 246 The Hill is occupied by thousands of barrackers.. who are sure they understand cricket better than the umpires. **1986** *Canberra Times* 20 Jan. 1/1 (*heading*) The Hill disappearing under sea of alcohol.

2. Broken Hill, a mining town in N.S.W.

1948 G. Farwell *Down Argent Street* 1 The place which had been named.. by the station people on Mount Gipps the 'broken hill', because of its hog-back silhouette against the sky, and by cynics and baffled prospectors the 'hill of mullock'.. came at last to be called, casually and with spare affection, just The Hill. **1979** D.G. Postlethwaite *Home to Hill* 14 A rock hound who visited the hill, Picked up a round black stone.

Hence **hillite** *n.*

1902 *Sporting News* (Launceston) 11 Oct. 1/5 Withdraw Grand Flaneur at the very last moment, much to the disgust of the hillites and others, who were not slow in significantly showing their disapproval.

hill crow-shrike. *Obs.* The Tasmanian race of the grey currawong (see Grey *a.*).

1888 *Centennial Mag.* (Sydney) 14 Up on the sand-hills a few wallaby are seen, and the hill crow-shrike is plentiful. **1902** *Emu* II. 98 Large companies of Hill Crow-Shrikes.

hill kangaroo. Wallaroo.

1902 F.S. Brockman *Rep. Exploration N.-W. Kimberley* 4 Between the Chamberlain and the Charnley Rivers we saw no game, except a few hill kangaroos in the sandstone ridges. **1962** V.C. Hall *Dreamtime Justice* 121 The guide was still moving with the ease and grace of a hill-kangaroo.

hipper. A pad of soft material arranged so as to protect the hip of a person sleeping on hard ground; a hollow made in the ground to serve this purpose. Also **hipper-hole.**

1875 R. Bruce *Dingoes* 134 Feather beds as aids to sleep By none are here possessed; And he is lucky who obtains One sheepskin for a hipper. **1938** F. Blakeley *Hard Liberty* 223 In this old camp the ground was dry and nice and soft, and just the place in which to scoop out a hipper-hole.

hit-out. *Australian National Football.* In a ball-up, or after a throw-in from the boundary: the striking of the ball towards a team-mate.

1931 J.F. McHale et al. *Austral. Game of Football* 69 The importance of the 'hit-out' at the centre has been stressed. **1969** A. Hopgood *And Big Men Fly* 43 It's gone forty yards. At least forty yards! What a hit-out!

Hence **hitter-out** *n.*

1931 J.F. McHale et al. *Austral. Game of Football* 72 Stalwart 'hitters out'.

hoary-headed grebe. The bird *Poliocephalus poliocephalus* of Aust. incl. Tas., having a black or grey head, with narrow white plumes in the breeding season.

1843 J. Gould *Birds of Aust.* (1848) VII. Pl. 82, *Podiceps poliocephalus* .. Hoary-headed Grebe. **1976** *Reader's Digest Compl. Bk. Austral. Birds* 29 (*caption*) The head of the hoary-headed grebe looks hoary only in the breeding season.

Hobart trumpeter. *Obs.* The fish *Latris lineata* (see Trumpeter *n.*[1] 1).

1892 *Bohemia* (Melbourne) 7 Jan. 19 From Tasmania they get the famed Hobart trumpeter, as well as other finny denizens.

hobble, *n.* [Fig. use of *hobble* a rope, strap, etc.] In the phr. **to snap one's hobbles,** to die.

1911 *Bulletin* (Sydney) 5 Oct. 16/1 His mates in the tunnel variously informed me that Uncle Dick had.. 'snapped his hobbles', 'run a bye', 'heaved the sponge', [etc.]. **1980** Ansell & Percy *To fight Wild* 30 The only real consciousness was riveted on the one thing: water.. and staying alive long enough to reach it. I wasn't going to snap my hobbles while there was still the faintest chance.

hobble, *v.*

1. *trans.* With **out**: to put (a horse, etc.) out to rest, fettered so as to prevent straying. Also *absol.*

1849 S. & J. Sidney *Emigrant's Jrnl.* 162 Young bullocks are almost always broken in at plough... When they have done working, they are hobbled out; that is their fore feet are confined in a kind of handcuff, colonial [*sic*], called hobbles. **1909** A.R. Richardson *Early Memories Great Nor-West* 38 Take a good brisk canter for a couple of miles in the dark and then off-saddle and hobble out in a quiet place.

2. *fig.* See quots. Also as *vbl. n.*

1958 W.E. Harney *Content to Lie* 48 Here we all camped and waited in a time that was known to all as 'Hobbling out'—waited till the next mustering season—then off we would go once more. **1963** Harney & Lockwood *Shady Tree* 79 Camooweal was the 'hobbling-out' place for the drovers and the stockmen for hundreds of miles around. To 'hobble-out', in the patois of the stock-routes, simply meant that the horses were being rested while their human owners caught up on a bit of back drinking.

hobble chain. Also **hopple chain.** [Chiefly Austral.: see OEDS *hobble, sb.* 3.] A length of chain or other material used to fetter an animal.
1901 M. FRANKLIN *My Brilliant Career* (1966) 52 The sound of camp-bells and jingle of hobble chains.. had come to these men. **1946** W.E. HARNEY *North of 23°* 75 Out of the distance comes the jingle of hopple chains and the tinkle of bells.

hod. [Prob. a. Arabic *hod* a pool.] An oasis.
1918 G.C. COOPER *Diary* 10 Aug., Left Oghratina and went out looking for a Hod—after riding all the morning, we found it—we waited up at Hod-el-Bakieh; others went on to Hod-el-Oghra, and waited there all day, had a good night's sleep. **1931** 'D. BLACK' *Red Dust* 12 The only shelter, an occasional *hod.*

hoddie. [f. *hod(man* + -Y.] A bricklayer's labourer, a hodman.
1952 *Bulletin* (Sydney) 23 Apr. 17/4 Our hoddie recognised the new bloke the moment he stepped on the scaffold. **1978** H.C. BAKER *I was Listening* 60 He had been a hodcarrier, and hoddies either died young or lived forever.

hoe, *v.* In the phr. **to hoe in(to),** to begin (a task, activity, etc.) with energy and enthusiasm; to 'dig in'.
1935 R.B. PLOWMAN *Boundary Rider* 119 'Us blokes'.. not averse to using the backs of our hands to wipe our mouths, 'hoe into the scran'. **1939** I.L. IDRIESS *Cyaniding for Gold* 86 The local cow.. took a lick; fancied the salty taste and hoed in for breakfast.

Hogan's Ghost. [An unexplained euphemism for *Holy Ghost.*] An expletive; also, rhyming slang for 'toast'.
1930 *Listening Post* (Perth) Aug. 22 And a sleepy voice would answer From the dug-out 'Hogan's Ghost!' **1968** D. O'GRADY *Bottle of Sandwiches* 101 All of us well-fortified with a before-sunrise Saturday morning breakfast of bacon, cackleberries, Hogan's ghost, and two quarts of tea.

hoist, *v.* In the phr. **to hoist one's bluey (drum, Matilda,** etc.), to (set off on a) journey as a swagman.
1897 *Worker* (Sydney) 18 Sept. 3/3 That highly intelligent shearer had to hoist 'Matilda' a sadder, and let us hope a wiser, man. **1912** *Bulletin* (Sydney) 15 Feb. (Red Page), Next day a mulga coaxes him to pack; He hoists his drum, and ambles down the track. **1947** *Ibid.* 16 Apr. 28/2 After hoisting our blueys over most of the State we felt ready to take it easy.

holding, *pres. pple.* Possessing money, in funds. Esp. in the phr. **(how) are you holding?**
1924 *Truth* (Sydney) 27 Apr. 6/3 *Holdin'*, possessing money. **1944** *Gabber: Qld. Lines of Communication Army Trade Training Depot* Oct. 4 Are you holding?.. Let me have ten bob then. **1980** J. ANDERSON *Impersonators* 93 His message was: *how are you holding?*.. 'Oh,' she said.. 'how am I holding for money? I'm quite all right.'

holding, *vbl. n.* Used *attrib.* in Special Comb. relating to the confinement of stock, as: **holding paddock, pen, yard,** an enclosure in which stock is kept for some particular purpose.
[N.Z. **1933** *Press* (Christchurch) 28 Oct. 17/7 **Holding paddock,** a small paddock, close to yards, woolshed, or mustering hut, for holding (not feeding) sheep.] **1934** *Bulletin* (Sydney) 16 May 38/4 At midday the cattle, mad with thirst, broke out of the holding paddock. [N.Z. **1923** *N.Z. Jrnl. Agric.* 20 Mar. 144 The **holding-pens** in the shed.. should never be too large.] **1965** J.S. GUNN *Terminol. Shearing Industry* i. 32 *Holding pen,* one of the small pens or yards in which sheep are held, usually within the shed, under shelter, while awaiting shearing. **1929** *Bulletin* (Sydney) 22 May 23/1 No vestige remains of the **holding-yards** close by, Where the must'rers and dogs yelped a tune.

hole.
1. Shortened form of WATERHOLE 1 a. and c.
1843 *Sydney Morning Herald* 26 Aug. 3/3 The River Page has been constantly running several weeks; a rather unusual state of things, as previous to these late soakings, it was totally destitute of water (except here and there a hole) for nearly four years. **1950** G.M. FARWELL *Land of Mirage* 212 It was on one of these very holes, forty feet deep and permanent, that Burke and Wills both met their deaths.
2. *Gold-mining.* An excavation made in the ground by a miner.
1851 *Empire* (Sydney) 5 Aug. 15/1 If our hole keeps as good as it seems, we will make £3 per day each, for some time. **1960** D. MCLEAN *Roaring Days* 124 There's many a record of placer gold being above the reef, so I took over and sank that hole another twenty feet.

holey dollar. Also **holy dollar.** A coin, circulating as official currency between 1814 and 1828, which was that part of a Spanish dollar remaining after a circular piece (see DUMP *n.*[1] 1) had been struck from its centre; *colonial dollar,* see COLONIAL *a.* 5; RING DOLLAR. Also *attrib.*
1840 *S. Austral. Miscellany* June 175 The *holey* dollar was the rim, the *dump* the centre struck out of the Spanish dollar, the former passing for 3s. 9d., the latter for 1s. 3d. currency. **1857** D. BUNCE *Australasiatic Reminisc.* 59 Our first change for a pound consisted of two dumps, two holy dollars, one Spanish dollar, one French coin, one half-crown, one shilling, and one sixpence. **1982** *Austral. Financial Rev.* (Sydney) 5 Feb. 40/4 The holey dollar market appeared to ease in one sale last year when a big buyer who spent over $100,000 on holey dollars at the sale appeared to exhaust himself.

hollow, *a.* In the collocation **hollow log:** used allusively with reference to a statutory authority's ability to retain its funds instead of having to pay them into consolidated revenue.
1982 *Nat. Times* (Sydney) 31 Oct. 15/1 Was he planning to do a Wran, keeping all charges steady while he emptied the hollow log? 'We left the Treasury in a hollow log situation but that has eroded considerably since.' **1985** *Canberra Times* 11 Sept. 2/4 Canberra's cash-rich hollow logs, to adopt the phrase used for such bodies in Victoria and N.S.W., are the sort of trading enterprises run by all State Governments.

holts. [Var. of Br. dial. *in holds* at grips: see OED(S *hold, sb.*[1] 2 b. and *holt, sb.*[2] 1.] In the phr. **in(to) holts,** in conflict, at grips.
1902 *Truth* (Sydney) 17 Aug. 1/7 A few Cooma parsons nearly got into 'holts' on Sunday night. **1922** A. WRIGHT *Boss o' Yedden* 37 Men were in holts, wrestling and punching.

Holy City. A nickname for Adelaide, the capital city of South Australia. Cf. CITY OF CHURCHES.
1908 M. VIVIENNE *Sunny S.A.* 36 Adelaide is frequently described as the 'Holy City'. **1909** *Truth* (Sydney) 2 May 9/2 There is not another city in the whole of the Commonwealth that can boast such a large and variegated collection of canines than can Adelaide... It is time someone took a hand in ridding the Holy City of one of its chief pests.

Holy Cross toad. [See quot. 1956.] CATHOLIC FROG.
1891 *Proc. Linnean Soc. N.S.W.* VI. 265 '*Notaden bennettii*',

the 'Catholic frog' or, as I have heard it called, the 'Holy Cross toad'.   **1956** T.Y. HARRIS *Naturecraft in Aust.* 55 The Holy Cross Toad is readily identified by the crude warty cross of black with orange and whitish spots on its green back.

holy dollar, var. HOLEY DOLLAR.

Holy Land. *Obs.* A nickname for Tasmania.
1888 C.D. FERGUSON *Experiences of Forty-Niner* 373 The well understood slang of the 'Holy Land', as Van Diemen's Land or Tasmania is called.   **1889** *Bulletin* (Sydney) 5 Oct. 8/2 In the rouse-abouts' hut .. they always spoke of the Cabbage Garden as 'Port Phillip', of the Holy Land as 'tother side.

home, $n.^1$ and *attrib.*^{1} [Spec. use of *home* native land: see OED(S $sb.^1$ 6 and 11 b.]
  A. *n.* Applied to the United Kingdom, esp. England, orig. by colonists and later by their descendants.
1808 *To Viscount Castlereagh* 24 The Government at home, and their instructions to the Governor.   **1975** X. HERBERT *Poor Fellow my Country* 1063 'A condition that's giving us a bad name throughout the world, and particularly at Home.' 'You mean Britain?' 'Of course.' 'But you're Australian born.' 'To me Britain is spiritual home.'
  B. *attrib.*
  a. English; British.
1858 T. MCCOMBIE *Hist. Colony Vic.* 334 The first number was issued on the 1st October, 1850, and was about the size of a home magazine.   **1943** *Bulletin* (Sydney) 29 Sept. 13/4 Till 1840 jarrah was called mahogany. But the Swan Riverites found that the Home folk were accepting the name all too literally.
  b. Special Comb. **home authorities, government,** the British government; the Colonial Office; **sentence** *hist.*, a term of transportation from the United Kingdom to an Australian Colony.
1851 H. MELVILLE *Present State Aust.* 135 The **home authorities** determined to interfere with local arrangements respecting convicts.   **1830** H. SAVERY *Quintus Servinton* III. 172 Representation, after representation had continued to be made in allusion to him, to the **Home Government**.   **1848** C. COZENS *Adventures of Guardsman* 165 Whenever any convict incurs a sentence to an ironed gang, the treadmill, or cell, the term of punishment .. is added to his original or **home sentence**.

home, *attrib.*^{2} and $n.^2$ [Spec. use of *home* dwelling-place. For the *attrib.* use see OED(S $sb.^1$ B. 2, for the *n.* OEDS $sb.^1$ 2.]
  A. *attrib.*
  a. Used to denote relative proximity to the *home station* (see sense b. below).
1823 *Hobart Town Gaz.* 26 July, The farmstead is a neatly finished residence, having .. home-yards fenced in for cattle-stock.   **1849** A. HARRIS *Emigrant Family* (1967) 140 Cattle having been drafted off from the home herd, had been sent to Manaroo.
  b. Special Comb. **home paddock, (a)** a paddock adjacent to a homestead or *home station;* **(b)** *fig.*, familiar territory; **station,** the principal residence on a large stock-raising property, together with the associated buildings and establishment (yards, accommodation for employees, etc.); HEAD-STATION; also *attrib.*
  (a) [N.Z. **1866** M.A. BARKER *Station Life N.Z.* (1874) 66 The country outside the **home paddock** is too rough.] **1872** Mrs E. MILLETT *Austral. Parsonage* 125 She was asked, she said, to look after the sheep in a home paddock for part of a day.   **(b) 1920** *Emu* XIX. 292 They had been liberated from their '**home paddock**'.   **1827** *Monitor* (Sydney) 12 June 433/3 This Farm is situate near the Cowpastures, and is well qualified for a **Home Station**.   **1845** *Portland Gaz.* 7 Oct. 4/1 Defendant ordered Rutherford to move Payne's sheep, which were unyarded round the home station hut.
  B. *n.*
  1. A house; a house and its material embellishments. Also *attrib.*
1848 *HRA* (1925) 1st Ser. XXVI. 691 The ill advised method, by which tenure of our homes is to be obtained. **1961** *Bulletin* (Sydney) 14 Oct. 29/1 Don't let's sell houses, let's sell 'dream' homes.   **1971** *Ibid.* 1 May 66/2 Most people still prefer to live in homes rather than home units, but the number of units is rising.
  2. Special Comb. **home-unit,** a flat or apartment, usu. one owned by the occupant.
1949 *Sydney Morning Herald* 4 May 13/2 Commands *glorious views* of Elizabeth Bay and is *ideal for the erection* of a block of *modern home units.*   **1984** *Sydney Morning Herald* 10 Nov. 10/5 (Advt.), Live in the lap of luxury with one of Hordern Place's top of the range 2 bedroom home units that provide panoramic and spectacular City and Harbour views.

home, *adv.*
  1. [See HOME $n.^1$] To England (from Australia).
1791 *Hist. Rec. N.S.W.* (1893) II. 784 There are in the bay with us two ships .. which afford us an excellent opportunity of writing home. But, why should I say *home?* What is England, or Ireland, or Scotland to me now?   **1969** G. JOHNSTON *Clean Straw for Nothing* (1971) 74 The only really happy person on the deck .. is a middle-aged Australian... He has been saving for years for his trip Home... He wept when we raised the Lizard and saw the green Cornish folds beyond, and wept again for the Isle of Wight and the Dover cliffs.
  2. [In Br. usu. *home and dry:* see OED(S *home, adv.* 2 and 3 b.] In the phr. **home and dried,** having safely and successfully completed (a task, journey, sporting contest, etc.); apparently certain to do so. Also **home and hosed, home on the pig's back** (or **ear**), and varr.
1918 *Kia Ora Coo-ee* Oct. 14/1 All being home and dried, 'Shorty' went over to the 'Q. Emma's' to borrow a bit of 'buckshee' sugar.   **1945** C. MANN *River* 52 He's a monty! We always were lucky. He's home on the pig's ear.   **1948** H. DRAKE-BROCKMAN *Sydney or Bush* 207 The chap advised no one to sell. Hang on, he said. It's going to rise. Home on the pig's back we are—talk about a merry Christmas! **1959** E. LAMBERT *Glory thrown In* 219 'Look!' he yelled to Christy. 'A and C Companies home and hosed!'

homeland. Used *attrib.* in Special Comb. **homeland centre,** OUT-STATION 3 (see quot. 1978); **movement,** the practice of Aboriginal people forming out-stations on their traditional lands. Also **homelands.**
1978 H.C. COOMBS *Kulinma* 150 The descriptive term 'outstation' is increasingly used for such settlements, reflecting probably the use of this term for settlements around Elcho Island which for many years had been serviced by Harold Sheppardson. However, the term somewhat misrepresents the Aboriginal conception of them, for each clan appears to consider its settlement as existing in its own right and not as an off-shoot from a larger unit, although some sense of affiliation with the central unit continues. The Yirrkala community now refers to these settlements in English language contexts as '**homeland centres**'. This phrase probably reflects more accurately the Aboriginal conception.   **1979** *Identity* Nov. 35/3 The outstation or **homeland movement** .. is alive and well across the north and centre of Australia.   **1980** *Aboriginal News* ix. 28//1 This movement to outstations, also frequently called the 'decentralisation' or 'homelands' movement, has been gaining momentum since 1972.

homer. In the war of 1939–45: a wound of sufficient severity to ensure the recipient's repatriation.

[N.Z. **1942** *2nd N.Z. Exped. Force Times* 5 Oct. 5 He wagged his stumps at me. 'Look at me... I've got a homer.'] **1945** 'MASTER-SARG' *Yank discovers Aust.* 17 *A homer,* a wound which sends a man home. **1977** —— *Gunner* 87 She's apples. Now you just lie back an' take it easy. Ya got a homer, mate, you arsey bastard.

homestead, *n.*[1] [Spec. use of *homestead* house with its dependent buildings, esp. a farmstead: see OED(S 2.] A house, usu. the principal residence on a rural property (but see quot. 1878).

1822 J. DIXON *Narr. Voyage N.S.W. & Van Dieman's Land* 73 When he has received his grant and pitched on the spot for his homestead, he ought to take as many necessaries as will serve him for a long time into the country. **1878** *Squatter's Plum* 36 For a distance of 14 miles the visitor will see deserted claims and abandoned homesteads of miners, who once resided there. **1986** *Sunday Examiner* (Launceston) 30 Mar. 49/3 The homestead, which was built in 1898, had been converted into flats.

homestead, *n.*[2] *Hist.* [U.S. *homestead* lot of (rural) land adequate for the maintenance of a family: see OED 3 and Mathews.]

1. A small rural land-holding, esp. as (variously) designated in land acts of the Australian Colonies (but see also quot. 1954). Also *attrib.*

1832 *Hill's Life N.S.W.* (Sydney) 17 Aug. 1 *The quid-pro-quo estate*; consisting of 1,000 acres .. will be divided into four homesteads, for the convenience of purchasers. **1871** *Austral. Handbk.* 40 Heads of families and persons of 21 years of age are allowed to select as 'homesteads' lots not exceeding 80 acres of agricultural or 160 acres of pastoral land... No person is allowed to acquire more than one 'homestead' allotment. **1954** A. UPFIELD *Death of Lake* (1956) 5 The great homestead .. which comprised eight hundred thousand acres .. was populated by sixty thousand sheep.

2. Comb. **homestead block, farm, selection, selector, settlement, settler.**

1890 *Quiz* (Adelaide) 9 May 2/1 *Quiz* has never lost his mental balance in gushing on the subject of **homestead blocks.** **1897** L. LINDLEY-COWEN *W. Austral. Settler's Guide* 261 The **homestead farm** settler .. will be content with a single furrow plough and a couple of good horses. **1880** J. BONWICK *Resources Qld.* 75 The **homestead selection** cannot be more than 80 acres within the homestead area. **1880** R. ROSE *Austral. Guide: Qld.* 13 The Government always favours the **homestead selector**, as it desires the settlement of the land in moderate sized farms by responsible parties. **1877** 'CAPRICORNUS' *Land Law of Future* 7 The leaders of thought elsewhere have by no means overlooked the advantages of '**homestead settlement**'. **1859** R.H. HORNE *Austral. Facts & Prospects* 105 The great majority will be respectable small farmers and **homestead settlers.**

3. Special Comb. **homestead area,** a district reserved for small land-holdings; the land-holding itself; **clause** *Qld.*, see quot. 1870; **lease,** an agreement setting out the terms of tenure of a homestead; the land so held.

1879 *Queenslander* (Brisbane) 26 Apr. 539/1 Certain areas are proclaimed as '**Homestead areas**'; you can select by 'conditional purchase' even in a homestead area. **1910** *Huon Times* (Franklin) 21 May 6/4 A 'homestead area' upon which he would have to reside for five years continuously and make improvements to the value of £1 per acre annually. **1870** C.H. ALLEN *Visit to Qld.* 72 The '**Homestead Clause**' .. allows any one who is head of a family, or is of the age of twenty-one years to enter upon 80 acres of agricultural land, or 160 acres of pastoral land, open to selection, on payment annually, for five years, at the rate of ninepence an acre for the former, and sixpence for the latter, description of land. **1889** *Braidwood Dispatch* 25 Sept. 2/3 The amendments made by the Legislative Council in the Crown Lands Bill .. which relate to the extension of **homestead** and pastoral **leases** by way of compensation for improvements were first considered. **1897** L. LINDLEY-

COWEN *W. Austral. Settler's Guide* 6 The area of a homestead lease shall not be less than 1,000 acres, or more than 3,000 acres in second class land, nor less than 1,000 acres nor more than 5,000 acres in third class land.

homesteader. [Orig. U.S.: see OED(S.] A small farmer (see HOMESTEAD *n.*[2] 1).

1897 *Bulletin* (Sydney) 19 June 9/4 Great game in 'goldfields homesteads' at Gympie. Some of the homesteaders pay 1s. an acre rent to Govt. and sub-let to Chinese lettuce .. man for 10s. an acre. **1983** K.W. MANNING *In their Own Hands* 142 They were 'gentlemen farmers' .. but in an era when planters did not do much manual work, they worked as hard as many a homesteader.

hominy. Also **ominny, ominy.** [U.S. *hominy* maize meal boiled with milk or water: see Mathews.] A gruel or thin porridge made from maize meal, esp. as part of a prison diet. Also *attrib.*

1827 P. CUNNINGHAM *Two Yrs. in N.S.W.* II. 72 If a sentimental shoplifter, fresh run from the trade, is heard pathetically descanting upon the sorrows of sour *smiggins* (cold-meat hash), and the horrors of *homony* (maize pudding), the old voyageur will facetiously remind him of the 'hundred hungry days' of yore. **1830** *Monitor* (Sydney) 14 Aug. 2/4 The cook brings in a kind of *ominy* (made of maize meal and water boiled together). **1836** J.F. O'CONNELL *Residence Eleven Yrs. New Holland* 47 Indian corn meal stirred in boiling water, called in American hashy pudding, or mush, in Australian hominy, makes the breakfast. **1847** *Gleaner* (Sydney) 4 Dec. 252 Convert the meal into ominny, Hawkesbury cakes, and bread. **1921** D. GRANT *Through Six Gaols* 35 They develop what is known among prisoners as 'a hominy stomach'. That is, they suffer from a gastric trouble that is most unpleasant.

honey. Used *attrib.* in the names of flora and fauna: **honey(-pot) ant,** an ant of any of several genera, including *Melophorus* and *Camponotus,* able to store a honey-like liquid in its distended crop; *honey-bag ant* HONEY-BAG 2; **flower,** the shrub *Lambertia formosa* (fam. Proteaceae) of e. N.S.W., having nectar-rich flowers; *mountain devil* (b), see MOUNTAIN; **-parrot,** LORIKEET; **possum** (formerly **mouse**), the small nectar-eating possum of s.w. W.A. *Tarsipes rostratus.*

1896 B. SPENCER *Rep. Horn Sci. Exped. Central Aust.* I. 87 We went out into the Mulga scrub in search of **honey ants.** **1973** V. SERVENTY *Desert Walkabout* 88 Honeypot ants .. those extraordinary insects. **1861** *Sydney Mail* 6 July 3/3 The *Lambertia formosa*, by some called **Honeyflower**, is only found in sandy soil. **1914** H.M. VAUGHAN *Australasian Wander-Yr.* 72 Another very striking plant was the Honey Flower. **1888** *Centennial Mag.* (Sydney) 129 Thousands of **honey parrots**, the light of the spring sun glancing from their lustrous wings. **1923** [**honey possum**] *Austral. Zoologist* III. 148 The *Tarsipes* are known throughout the district as 'Honey Mice'. **1976** *Bulletin* (Sydney) 2 Oct. 42/3 The tiny honey possums which suck nectar from the banksias.

honey-bag.

1. The honeycomb or hive of the wild bee: see SUGAR BAG 1.

1928 B. SPENCER *Wanderings in Wild Aust.* 499 To secure what the natives call a 'honey-bag'. This is the honeycomb of the native bee that makes its rough hive in a hollow tree or bough. **1983** C. BINGHAM *Beckoning Horizon* 11 A young Aborigine climbing high on a river gum for a wild bee hive ('the honey bag', which we harvested in kerosene tins).

2. Special Comb. **honey-bag ant,** *honey ant,* see HONEY.

1896 B. SPENCER *Rep. Horn Sci. Exped. Central Aust.* II. 386 The honey-bag ants were found hanging in clusters to the roof of the chambers by the feet, their large globular bodies looking like bunches of grapes.

honey cart. [Cf. U.S. *honey-bucket*; OEDS *honey, sb.* 7.] *Sanitary cart*, see SANITARY.
   1970 J.S. GUNN in W.S. Ramson *Eng. Transported* 50 *Honey cart*, or *17- door sedan*, sanitary cart. 1971 *Bulletin* (Sydney) 3 July 13/1 A honey cart is the dear little vehicle that the airlines use to empty the aircraft lavatories.

honeycomb. *Obs.* Used *attrib.* in Special Comb. **honeycomb ground,** land having an uneven surface. See CRABHOLE. Also **honey-combed,** *ppl. a.*
   1849 W. CARRON *Narr. Exped. Rockingham Bay & Cape York* 54 During the day's journey, we passed over some flats of rotten honeycomb ground, on which nothing was growing but a few stunted shrubs. 1861 T. M'COMBIE *Austral. Sketches* 79 The land [was] what is termed 'honey-combed' and covered by dwarfed ungainly trees.

honeyeater. [Transf. use of *honey-eater* an African bird, the honey-guide.] Any bird of the fam. Meliphagidae of Aust. and nearby, having a brush-tipped tongue for feeding on nectar and other foods. Also with distinguishing epithet, as **black-headed, helmeted, Keartland, Lewin, New Holland, painted, pied, red-headed, regent, scarlet, singing, spiny-cheeked, warty-faced, white-bearded, white-cheeked, white-eared, white-fronted, white-gaped, white-naped, white-plumed, white-throated, yellow, yellow-faced, yellow-plumed, yellow-spotted, yellow-tufted** (see under first element). Also *attrib.*, and formerly also **honey-bird, honey-sucker.**
   1790 J. COOK *Collection Voyages round World* VI. 2034 There are four species that seem to belong to the trochili, or honey-suckers of Linnaeus. 1822 J. LATHAM *Gen. Hist. Birds* IV. 208 None of them, although the tongue be cloven into two filaments, are at all fringed on the edges, as is the case with very many of the Honey-eaters. 1854 W. HOWITT *Boy's Adventures* 36 The honey birds.. suck the flowers like humming birds. 1986 *Canberra Times* 16 Apr. 19/2 The annual honeyeater migration is one of the highlights of the bird-watchers year.

honeysuckle. [See quot. 1895.] Any of several trees or shrubs bearing nectar-rich flowers, esp. of the genus *Banksia* (see BANKSIA); the wood of these trees; *native honeysuckle*, see NATIVE *a.* 6 a. Also with distinguishing epithet, as **dwarf, red, white** (see under first element), and *attrib.*
   1803 *Sydney Gaz.* 26 June, Timber in this Colony includes Box, Honeysuckle, Cedar. 1861 'OLD BUSHMAN' *Bush Wanderings* 32 A fire of honeysuckle cones and other rubbish. 1895 J.H. MAIDEN *Flowering Plants & Ferns N.S.W.* 31 'Honeysuckle' is so called because the spikes of flowers are often full of honey, which the aborigines used to consume either by passing them over their tongues, or by soaking in water, when a sweetish liquid would be obtained, which was drunk either before or after fermentation.

hooded, *ppl. a.* Used in the names of birds distinguished by the dark colour of the head or crown, esp. of the mature male: **hooded dotterel,** the wading bird *Charadrius rubricollis* of coastal s. Aust. incl. Tas., and inland salt lakes of s.w. Aust; **parrot,** the parrot *Psephotus dissimilis* of the N.T.; see also ANTHILL PARROT; **robin,** the widespread black and white bird *Melanodryas cucullata*; *pied robin*, see PIED.
   1848 J. GOULD *Birds of Aust.* VI. Pl. 18, *Hiaticula monacha*. **Hooded Dottrel.** 1929 A.H. CHISHOLM *Birds & Green Places* 98 The golden-shouldered and **hooded parrots,** of northern Australia, bore into the earthern homes of termites (white ants). 1896 B. SPENCER *Rep. Horn Sci. Exped. Central Aust.* II. 77 *Melanodryas bicolor*.. **Hooded Robin**.. were very tame and easily approached.

hooer. [Prob. repr. dial. pronunc. of *whore*.] A term of abuse; used with varying degrees of strength and applied to a person of either sex. Cf. BASTARD.
   1937 E. PARTRIDGE *Dict. Slang & Unconventional Eng.* 403 *Hoor, hooer, hooa or hua*, a sol. pronunciation of *whore*. 1952 T.A.G. HUNGERFORD *Ridge & River* 31 Cranky old hooer! White thought... Always on the bloody job. 1985 N. MEDCALF *Rifleman* 121 Anyone would think you were professional pox-doctors, checking the hooers in Palmer Street!

hook. A riding spur.
   1920 B. CRONIN *Timber Wolves* 41, I touches my horse with the hooks and away we goes, helter-skelter across the button-grass. 1968 W. GILL *Petermann Journey* 23 Horses being what they are, there comes the time when, mounted on a strange animal, a touch of the 'hook' becomes a necessity.

hoon. [Of unknown origin.] A lout; an exhibitionist; a man who manages a prostitute.
   1938 X. HERBERT *Capricornia* 338 'You flash hoon,' he went on. 'Kiddin' you're white, eh?' 1982 *Canberra Times* 27 Jan. 17/5 Sydney .. the city which had invented the word bludger .. was just starting to use the word hoon, successive terms for the same occupation.

hoop. [Transf. use of *hoop* coloured band on a jockey's blouse.] A jockey.
   1941 S.J. BAKER *Pop. Dict. Austral. Slang* 36 *Hoop*, a jockey. 1984 *Bulletin* (Sydney) 18 Dec. 66/1 Now Moore and Higgins two of the best hoops in the history of racing.

hoop pine. [From the bark hoops (see quot. 1969) which remain conspicuously on the forest floor after the wood has decayed.] The tall conifer *Araucaria cunninghamii* (fam. Araucariaceae), of near-coastal N.S.W. and Qld., and New Guinea; the pale-coloured softwood timber of the tree; *colonial pine* (b), see COLONIAL *a.* 5; *Moreton Bay pine*, see MORETON BAY.
   1861 J.D. LANG *Qld., Aust.* 118 Timber exists; cedar, cowrie, and hoop pine. 1969 T.H. EVERETT *Living Trees of World* 25 The Richmond-river-pine or hoop-pine .. the latter name deriving from its bark, which has horizontal cracks in encircling bands.

hooray /ˈhureɪ/, *exclam.* [Var. *hurrah* a shout.] A conventional form of farewell, 'good-bye'.
   1898 *Bulletin* (Sydney) 4 June (Red Page), In many places the salutation 'good-day' or 'good-night' is simply 'Hooray!' 1977 V. PRIDDLE *Larry & Jack* 10 As George moved to go, Tom said: 'Hooray George, promise now, you will come back and see me before you leave.'

hooroo /ˈhuru/. Also **hurroo, ooroo.** HOORAY.
   1906 *Bulletin* (Sydney) 22 Nov. 44/4 Hurroo. See yer termorrer. 1916 *Truth* (Sydney) 23 Jan. 10/5 Page said, 'Well, too-ra-loo; I'm getting off here.' 'Hoo-roo,' he replied. 1967 D. HEWETT *This Old Man* (1976) 21 Ooroo, Laurie. You there, love?

hooshter /ˈhʊʃtə/. *Hist.* [Transf. use of *hooshter* a command or shout (of encouragement) to a camel.] One who rides a camel, esp. a member of the Imperial Camel Corps.
   1917 *Barrack: Offical Organ Imperial Camel Corps* 1 Sept. 2/2 *The camelier's lament.* Out east with the 'Hooshters'. 1978 P. ADAM SMITH *Anzacs* 235 He remained with the 'hooshters' until April 1918 when the camel corps was disbanded, its members forming the 5th Light Horse.

hoot. [N.Z. slang *hoot* money, a. Maori *utu* payment, recompense.] Money.
   [N.Z. 1864 *Saturday Rev.* iii. 12 We shall soon have no 'hoot' to pay the piper.] 1881 G.C. EVANS *Stories* 265 Why

the very stuff you are now drinking has been bought with 'hoot', obtained from stolen goods. **1977** *Sun-Herald* (Sydney) 24 July 111/1 It's about a QC and his wife, who live in Point Piper and obviously have lots of hoot.

hop, *n.*[1] [Used elsewhere, but chiefly Austral. and N.Z.]

1. Usu. in *pl.* Beer; esp. in the phr. **on the hops,** engaged in a drinking session.
1930 *Bulletin* (Sydney) 1 Jan. 11/4 The proprietor provided a beer party, and the riot that arose out of the hop-drinking led to the school's first raid. **1966** D. NILAND *Pairs & Loners* 102 I'm on the hops and yakking away and neither is any trouble to me.

2. Special Comb. **hophead,** a heavy drinker.
[N.Z. **1942** *2nd N.Z. Exped. Force Times* 17 Aug. 16 Private Harry Hophead.] **1957** D. NILAND *Call me when Cross turns Over* 31 A terror for the grog, my old woman, a real hophead.

Hop, *n.*[2] Abbrev. of JOHN HOP. Also *attrib.*
1916 *Truth* (Sydney) 19 Nov. 1/7 The shooting of our Bluebottles in Sydney is wretched, that is, more honored in the 'breech' than the Hopp-servants. **1933** *Bulletin* (Sydney) 8 Feb. 12/3 The Hops were taking the shattered body out of the water.

hop, *v.*

a. *intr.* With **in(to)**: to begin on (a meal, activity, etc.) with alacrity. Also in the phr. **to hop in for one's chop** etc., to seize an opportunity.
1939 J. CAMPBELL *Babe is Wise* 307 An' hop in, 'cause if you don't you'll just have to see how fast we c'n run. **1968** S. GORE *Holy Smoke* 21 Come on, you Adam, hop in for your chop. Good peller tucker orright! **1971** B. HUMPHRIES *Bazza pulls it Off*, 'You're not tryin' to kid me youse invited me all the way up here for a chin wag!' 'Course she didn't ya stupid drongo cut the cackle and hop into the horsecollar!'

b. *trans.* To attack (a person, meal, etc.).
1945 R.S. CLOSE *Love me Sailor* 160 Did you see young Ernie hopping into Christenson? **1958** G. CASEY *Snowball* 207 'All right, kid, hop into your tucker,' Plugger ordered briskly.

hop-bush. [Transf. use of *hop*, from the bitter leaf or hop-like winged fruit of the plant.] Any shrub or small tree of the widespread genus *Dodonaea* (fam. Sapindaceae), the bitter fruits of which have been used as a substitute for hops; any of several other plants, esp. the shrub *Daviesia latifolia* (fam. Fabaceae), with leaves used similarly. See also *native hop* NATIVE *a.* 6 a., *wild hop* WILD 1. Also **hop scrub**.
1853 W. HOWITT *Land, Labor & Gold* 15 Jan. (1855) I. 201 The country was covered with hop-scrub up to their very heads. **1984** E. WALLING *On Trail Austral. Wildflowers* 24 Hop bushes with clear green leaves and rusty-red papery fruits.

hop-over. *Obs.* The action of 'going over the top', of leaving a trench (to attack an enemy). Also *transf.*
1918 *Aussie: Austral. Soldiers' Mag.* Jan. 10/2 Hopover, a departure from a fixed point into the Unknown, also the first step in a serious undertaking. **1932** *Whiz-Bang* (Brisbane) 1 July 15 We are warning our readers that should they wish .. to start a 'hop-over' with Harry, all they will need to do is to ridicule Australians.

hopper. [Spec. use of *hopper* an animal characterized by hopping.] A kangaroo.
1879 *Queenslander* (Brisbane) 5 July 27/3 The late invasion by the marsupials of the settled districts induced the settlers to wage a war of extermination against the 'hoppers and jumpers'. **1942** T. KELAHER *Digger Hat* 22 The flat Is now dotted with the 'hoppers' who have lately .. come in from the scrub to flog the frontage of its feed.

hopping mouse. Any of several mice of the genus *Notomys* (fam. Muridae) of drier Aust., having long hind legs and a rapid hopping gait; JERBOA; *kangaroo mouse*, see KANGAROO *n.* 5.
1941 E. TROUGHTON *Furred Animals Aust.* 319 This beautiful little hopping-mouse is at once recognized by the distinct pouch-like skin-pocket on the throat. **1977** *Ecos* xiv. 11/1 Two species of hopping mouse of Australia's arid zone can survive without water on a diet of dry seed.

hopple chain, var. HOBBLE CHAIN.

Hori /'hɒri/. [Maori form of 'George'.] A nickname for a Maori. Cf. HENARE.
1922 *Smith's Weekly* (Sydney) 19 Aug. 17/5 As Hori was notoriously lazy, it was a mystery how he managed to get the birds. **1944** *Bulletin* (Sydney) 8 Nov. 13/3, I struck Hori along the bush road, cranking vigorously at his ancient T model... I continued on into town, returning two hours later. The Maori was still cranking away, but with noticeably less vigor.

horizontal scrub. [See quot. 1888.] The small tree or shrub *Anodopetalum biglandulosum* (fam. Cunoniaceae), of central, w., and s. Tas., the interlocking trunks and branches of which may form an almost impenetrable thicket. Freq. *ellipt.* as **horizontal**.
1875 *Papers & Proc. R. Soc. Tas.* (1876) 96 A tall and tangled growth of wireweed (*Bauera*) and cutting-grass, with horizontal scrub (*Anodopetalum*). **1888** R.M. JOHNSTON *Systematic Acct. Geol. Tas.* 6 The Horizontal is a tall shrub or tree... Its peculiar habit—to which it owes its name and fame—is for the main stem to assume a horizontal and drooping position after attaining a considerable height, from which ascend secondary branches which in turn assume the horizontal habit. From these spring tertiary branchlets, all of which interlock, and form .. an almost impenetrable mass of vegetation.

horned dragon. *Mountain devil* (a), see MOUNTAIN.
1930 *Bulletin* (Sydney) 26 Mar. 21/3 The most formidable looking thing in the bush is the thorny devil (*Moloch horridus*), which is also called the horned dragon. **1968** G. MIKES *Boomerang* 160 The horned dragon .. grows to seven inches in length and its appearance is really fearsome; but it is a gentle and harmless creature often kept as a pet.

horny. [Scot. dial.: see OEDS B. 3.]
1. A bullock.
1901 *Bulletin* (Sydney) 30 Nov. 32/1, I am getting tired of roving Round those hornies in the lead, And I'm tired, sick tired of droving On the stock-routes bare of feed. **1976** C.D. MILLS *Hobble Chains & Greenhide* 43 Nugget gave me a spell after smoke-oh, and I went to the crush to deal with the 'hornies'.

2. Special Comb. **horny-steerer,** a bullock-driver.
1905 *Bulletin* (Sydney) 27 July 16/4 A bullock-driver is called a bullocky, a bovine-puncher, an ox-persuader, a horny-steerer. **1943** S.J. BAKER *Pop. Dict. Austral. Slang* (ed. 3) 40 *Horney-steerer*, a bullock driver.

horse.
1. Used *attrib.* in Special Comb. which have a local significance but may not be excl. Austral.: **horseduffer,** a horse thief; **-duffing** *vbl. n.*, horse-stealing; see DUFFING 1; **-hunt** *v. intr.*, to attempt to round up strayed or wild horses; so **-hunt** *n.*, **-hunting** *vbl. n.*; **paddock, (a)** an enclosure for horses, usu. small and for horses in regular use; **(b)** a large paddock on a horse-raising property; **plant,** a team of working

horses; **planter** obs., a horse-thief; **-police** hist., a force of mounted police; so **- policeman; station,** a property used primarily for raising horses; **-sweating** vbl. n., obs., see quot. 1922; **-tailer,** one responsible for the care of working horses; so **-tailing** vbl. n.; **yard,** a yard for the temporary detention of horses.

1892 'R. BOLDREWOOD' *Nevermore* II. 39 So you've dropped down to it at last, my flash **horse-duffer,** have you? **1882** *Sydney Mail* 1 July 6/3 Poaching must be something like cattle and **horse duffing**—not the worst thing in the world itself, but mighty likely to lead to it. **1848** H.W. HAYGARTH *Recoll. Bush Life* 61 Cattle-hunting in Australia is excellent sport .. with less speed than in **horse-hunting**. **1926** J. POLLARD *Bushland Man* 48 The few words at the Stroner home with regard to the horse-hunt had placed him in a false position. **1911** *Huon Times* (Franklin) 7 June 4/3 He had told him that he was going horse-hunting at Corella. **1839** *Port Phillip Gaz.* 4 Dec. 3 This allotment is admirably adapted for a **Horse** or Cattle **Paddock,** and on an eligible order being made, it will be immediately enclosed with a substantial three-rail fence. **1987** W. HATFIELD *I find Aust.* 59 The 'horse-paddock' near the homestead was eight miles by eight, and that wasn't a big 'paddock'. **1930** D. COTTRELL *Earth Battle* 103 In addition to Big Harry's teams, six other **'horse plants'** dragged plough and scoop in the slow piling of dam and tank. **1841** *Port Phillip Patriot* 28 Oct. 2/6 George Kilpatrick, the notorious horse **'planter'** .. was .. committed to take his trial for stealing a grey mare. **1838** L.E. THRELKELD *Ann. Rep. Mission to Aborigines, Lake Macquarie* 2 The engagement .. took place betwixt the **Horse police,** commanded by Major Nunn, and the Aborigines in the interior. **1854** C.A. CORBYN *Sydney Revels* 126 Andreas Brown, a horse-policeman. **1842** R.G. JAMESON *N.Z., S.A., & N.S.W.* 113 Gentlemen from the interior, who have left their inland **horse,** sheep, or cattle **stations,** for the purpose of transacting business. **1887** S. NEWLAND *Far North Country* 33 When horse-stealing, horse-swindling and **horse-sweating** are put down .. then the 'spieler' must reform or seek pastures new. **1922** *Bulletin* (Sydney) 23 Feb. 22/1 In the old days in N.S. Wales the law—in practice if not by Act of Parliament—made a distinction between horse-stealing and horse-sweating... Borrowing a horse without the owner's knowledge or consent, and turning it adrift at the end of the ride, was called 'sweating'; and though it was punishable by law, the penalty was usually light. **1913** W.K. HARRIS *Outback in Aust.* 100 I've had some experience as **'horse-tailer'** for drovers. **1925** M. TERRY *Across Unknown Aust.* 195 One usually takes a black boy to help with the saddles and horse-tailing. **1931** A.W. UPFIELD *Sands of Windee* 26 In the **horse-yards** is a light-draft gelding with white forefeet.

2. [Transf. use of *dead horse* the type of that which is no longer of use: see OED *horse, sb.* 18.] In the collocation **dead horse.**

a. An undischarged debt.

1847 A. HARRIS *Settlers & Convicts* 327 From the constant practice among settlers of ill-using free men in point of rations, it often happens that men run away leaving jobs half finished; in other cases it is the consequence of a dishonest endeavour on the part of the labourer, after having largely overdrawn his account, to get rid of the debt; they call working out such a debt, *riding the dead horse*. **1978** L. HORSPHOL *Turn down Empty Glass* 42 Until we finish up findin' ourselves having to work for naught. Now if there's one thing I don't fancy, it's workin' out dead horses.

b. Rhyming slang for 'sauce'.

1940 *Puckapunyal: Official Jrnl. 17th Austral. Infantry Brigade* Oct. 2 How would the Q.M. go if he was faced with an order like this .. a couple of pounds of stammer and stutter with a bottle of dead horse. **1968** *Swag* (Sydney) i. 24/3 A pie is called a dog's eye... 'Two dogs, one with dead 'orse,' was a favorite catchcry.

3. In the phr. **to sell a horse,** to organise or participate in a simple game of chance or lottery: see quots. 1899 and 1964.

1899 *Austral. Tit-Bits* (Sydney) 8 Apr. 130/1 Selling Horses. (An Australian Game.) No, this title does not refer to the selling of that noble animal 'the friend of man', but merely to a curious game that is played in some Australian pubs., when a few meet to pass a convivial hour or two, to settle the question as to who will bear the expense of the drinks... The 'modus operandi' of the game is as follows:- Assuming the 'crowd' to be six, and the amount to be pooled to be sixpence each man, a half-dozen matches will be procured, and one of the party will be the seller and the rest the purchasers. The seller will take the matches and, concealing them behind his back, will produce a certain number in his closed hand. Then he will go round the purchasers asking them how many 'horses' they will buy. If, for example, the seller offers for sale three 'horses' and buyer No. 1 states three, then No. 1 will be 'stuck' for sixpence, will receive the six matches, and in his turn become seller. If buyer No. 1 states a number not agreeing with the 'horses' offered for sale, then he escapes, and the rest of the purchasers will be invited to buy in a similar fashion... The 'art of the game' is always to dodge stating the correct number of horses for sale, and if you are a smart hand at this you can score many a free drink at the game of 'selling horses'. **1964** T. RONAN *Packhorse & Pearling Boat* 234 'Selling a horse' is a very simple substitute for the cards and dice and, when there are fourteen in the party, much quicker. The barman collects the two bobs and, on a scrap of paper, writes down a number between fifty and a hundred. Then the party forms up in a group, someone starts counting at any number between one and ten, and whoever calls the figure the barman has written down scoops the pool.

horse-collar swag. A long, thin swag, carried around the neck. Also **horseman's swag, horse-shoe swag.**

[N.Z. **1873** PYKE *Wild Will Enderby* 3 He proceeded forthwith to arrange his blankets in the form known to the initiated as 'horse-collar swag'.] **1880** 'ERRO' *Squattermania* 215 Giving a hitch to his horse-shoe swag, he strode off. **1898** *Bulletin* (Sydney) 19 Mar. 14/2, I saw an old whaler—must have been nearing 60—not an ounce of flesh on him .. with a horse-collar swag 85 lb. weight. **1956** *Ibid.* 15 Feb. 12/2, I watched him weaving carefully across the roadway to pay his debt, half-empty bottle in one hand and his thin horseman's-swag in the other.

horse mackerel. [Spec. use of *horse-mackerel* any of several fish allied to the mackerel.] Any of several marine fish, esp. JACK MACKEREL and the Austral. bonito *Sarda australis,* abundant along the e. coast of Aust.

1793 W. TENCH *Compl. Acct. Settlement* 176 Grey-mullet, bream, horse-mackarel [sic]. **1965** *Austral. Encycl.* IV. 84 Jack mackerel (*Trachurus novaezelandiae*), the cowanyoung of New South Wales and the horse mackerel of South Australia and Tasmania.

horseman's swag: see HORSE-COLLAR SWAG.

horseradish tree. [See quot. 1889.] The shrub or tree *Codonocarpus cotinifolius* (fam. Gyrostemonaceae) of drier Aust., the bark and leaves of which have a pungent taste. See also *mustard tree* MUSTARD, *native poplar* NATIVE *a.* 6 a.

1886 F.A. HAGENAUER *Rep. Aboriginal Mission Ramahyuck, Vic.* 47 You can see .. the horseradish tree. **1889** J.H. MAIDEN *Useful Native Plants Aust.* 164 *Codonocarpus cotinifolius* .. called .. 'Horse-radish Tree', owing to the taste of the leaves.

horse-shoe swag: see HORSE-COLLAR SWAG.

hospital. Used *attrib.* of sheep: diseased. Also, of a paddock, etc.: reserved for such sheep.

1855 W. HOWITT *Land, Labor & Gold* I. 192 The squatters are killing off first what they call their hospital flocks—the scabbiest sheep, and those worn to skeletons with foot-rot. **1934** *Bulletin* (Sydney) 14 Nov. 22/3 Some owners run a

hostie /ˈhoʊsti/. [f. *(air) host(ess* + -Y.] A female flight attendant.

1960 'N. CULOTTA' *Cop This Lot* 27 'That hostie's a slashin' line,' Dennis said. 1981 *Sydney Morning Herald* 28 Apr. 1/2, I have been talking to the hosties since last Thursday and they are not concerned about Qantas picking up passengers here and there.

hostile, *a.* Angry. Also with **on** and in the phr. **to go hostile (at).**

1937 E. PARTRIDGE *Dict. Slang & Unconventional Eng.* 408 *Hostile,* .. angry, annoyed; esp. *go hostile,* to get angry: Australian and New Zealand military. 1941 S.J. BAKER *Pop. Dict. Austral. Slang* 36 *Hostile,* angry, annoyed. Also 'go hostile at', express annoyance (towards someone). 1957 *Overland* ix. 5 She's hostile about the money she's getting. 1960 *Ibid.* xviii. 5 A bloke comes to steal my chooks. He knows I'm hostile on it, and I'll do something about it.

hot box. An insulated container for keeping food hot (see also quot. 1982).

1925 *Makeshifts & Other Home-Made Furniture* (New Settlers League Aust.) 32 The principle of the Hot Box is .. to surround the central vessel (with food in it) with a nonconductor of heat, so that the heat is retained for a long time. 1982 J.J. COE *Desperate Praise* 133 *Hot box,* hot meal contained in insulated 'esky'.

hot coffee. *Obs.* (A show of) antagonism; a display of anger.

1885 *Australasian Printers' Keepsake* 121 He was an Englishman—one of the worst sort—overbearing, ignorant, and impudent, and between him and me there usually was hot coffee. 1915 *Truth* (Sydney) 26 Sept. 3/1 Like all such 'trimmers' and 'twicers', however, he is beginning to get 'hot coffee' from both sides.

hot pot. *Horse-racing.* [f. *hot* heavily backed + *pot* favourite: see OED *hot, a.* 8 e. and *pot, sb.*[1] 9 c.] A heavily-backed favourite. Also *transf.*

1904 *Sporting News* (Launceston) 16 Apr. 3/1 Baden Powell was made a hot pot for the Flying Stakes .. but he failed to come on. 1969 *Sporting Globe* (Melbourne) 9 July 22/5 A southern 'hot-pot'—Lord Setay—dismally let his supporters down at Albion Park last Saturday night.

hottie. Also **hotty.** *Obs.* [f. *hot (shot* + -Y.] A 'hot shot'; someone of importance.

1910 L. ESSON *Woman Tamer* (1976) 78 How is it, Katie? What's up? Blime, you've cleaned the knives. Cake? 'Struth, we are hotties. Boronia? Are you expecting the gawd Mayor for tea? 1911 *Bulletin* (Sydney) 23 Nov. 13/4 Micko, from Collingwood, may be a 'tug' or a 'crook' or a 'rough-up' or a 'hotty', but if you called him a larrikin he'd look at you and wonder.

hot wind.

1. An extremely hot, dry wind, blowing periodically from the interior during summer.

1791 Macarthur Papers 18 Mar. XII., We have need of cooling fruit in the warm season—particularly when the hot scorching winds set in—but which however are followed by what is termed the Sea Breeze, and this keeps down the temperature of the air, but when they are overpowered by the hot wind the heat is excessive. 1937 L.R. MENZIES *Gold Seeker's Odyssey* 138 The heat was terrific with the hot wind blowing sand in gusts across our faces.

2. Comb. **hot-wind day.**

1862 C. ASPINALL *Three Yrs. Melbourne* 6, I .. found it to be rather refreshing to the eye .. on a 'hot wind' day.

house.

1. The principal residence on a rural property (as distinct from accommodation provided for employees); prob. perpetuating a distinction made in penal settlements (see HUT *n.* 2 and 3, and also quots. 1788 and 1812). Also *attrib.*

[1788 J. HUNTER *Hist. Jrnl. Trans. Port Jackson* (1793) 310 Two sawyers were sawing timber to build me a house; two men were employed in building huts. 1812 *HRA* (1916) 1st Ser. VII. 583 A few Houses for the Civil and Military Officers .. and a few Huts for Convicts.] 1832 *Colonial Times* (Hobart) 25 Apr., There is a new House .. a good Hut for the men, and other Out-houses, on the Grant. 1903 *Bulletin* (Sydney) 21 Feb. 17/1 At Merungle I saw house-tea vilified; we got a box by mistake in the hut.

2. Special Comb. **house gin (girl, lubra),** a female Aboriginal employed as a domestic servant; **man,** one whose social status secures him accommodation in the house (rather than in the huts); **paddock,** an enclosure, usu. for horses, adjacent to the house; **people,** see *house man.*

1890 A.J. VOGAN *Black Police* 144 We can see the darkskinned, brightly dressed aboriginal '**house gins**'. 1913 *Bulletin* (Sydney) 6 Mar. 16/2 Scraggy was the house gin on an outstation. 1934 *Ibid.* 7 Mar. 21/4 Nellie, the house lubra, hitched up her Mother Hubbard and showed us women the scar. *c* 1947 *Home Building Inland* (Flying Doctor Service Aust.) 13 Aboriginal house girls can only do simple jobs. 1936 W. HATFIELD *Aust. through Windscreen* 64 Find out where he stayed at Whereisit Downs. If he's a **house man** ask him in. If he isn't, tell him he can go down to the kitchen for tea and take his swag over to the hut. 1894 *Bulletin* (Sydney) 20 Oct. 23/2 The **house-paddock** slip-rail edges a side-slope leading down to 'the crossing'. 1891 *Truth* (Sydney) 15 Mar. 7/3 In a general way, the hybrid between **house-people** and the hut is, *ex officio,* a Jackeroo.

house of accommodation. *Obs.* ACCOMMODATION HOUSE.

1804 *Sydney Gaz.* 12 Aug., Halted at a distant house of accommodation. 1928 'BRENT OF BIN BIN' *Up Country* 146 They started a house of accommodation in the most unlikely place for patrons, and their neighbours had a sage intuition that it was a sly grog-shanty and fly-trap for the unwary.

House of Assembly. The lower legislative house in the States of South Australia and Tasmania.

1853 *S. Austral. Register* (Adelaide) 9 Aug. 3/4 With reference, then, to the three provinces remote from Sydney, at present the nominal capital of Australia, my belief that the existence of a general Senate, independent of and possessing higher powers than the local Houses of Assembly sitting in Adelaide, Melbourne, and Hobart Town, would prove beneficial. 1956 F.C. GREEN *Century Responsible Govt.* 18 The House of Assembly or Lower House is also known as the 'People's House'.

House of Representatives. The lower legislative house of the Federal Parliament.

1898 *Austral. Handbk.* 122 The Legislative powers of the Commonwealth shall be vested in a Federal Parliament, which shall consist of the Queen, a Senate, and a House of Representatives. 1986 *Canberra Times* 15 Mar. 3/2 The Departments of the House of Representatives and the Senate were logically separate.

hovea /ˈhoʊviə/. [The Austral. plant genus *Hovea* was named by the British botanist Robert Brown (in Aiton (1812) *Hort. Kew.* ed. 2, VI. 275) after the Polish botanist A.P. Hove (*fl.* 1785–1798).] Any shrub of the genus *Hovea* (fam. Fabaceae), having pea-flowers which are usu. purple or blue, some species being cultivated as ornamentals.

1926 A.A.B. APSLEY *Amateur Settlers* 207 Decorated with a jar full of Hovea—a bright blue kind of pea flower. **1981** *Bulletin* (Sydney) 21 Apr. (Suppl.) 25/2 Purple hovea beside our feet.

how, *adv.* In the phr. **how are you going?** and varr., 'how are you?', a conventional greeting.
1930 V. PALMER *Passage* (1957) 182 Well, how's it going, Peter? Getting the wind up? **1977** E. MACKIE *Oh to be Aussie* 7 The most the Aussie will do, if well disposed towards you is to ask you 'howyergoin?' In answer to this *never* say more than 'Good thanks!' and hang the grammar! **1978** P. ADAM SMITH *Anzacs* 94 Private W.S. Percival of the 15th Battalion told of 7 August, after the futile but desperate attack on Hill 971... Clumsily turning the man over, he shouted, 'How's she going, mate?' There was no answer. He yelled, 'Strike me pink the poor bugger's just about outed.'

hoy. A game of chance, resembling bingo, in which playing cards are used. Also *attrib.*
1965 *Courier-Mail* (Brisbane) 2 Mar. 15/2 A hoy evening which the Royal Society of St. George planned to hold at St. George House. **1978** H. HAENKE *Bottom of Birdcage* 49, I go to the Hoy 'n Euchre, up the Catholic Hall.

Hoyt's. [f. the name of *Hoyt's* Theatre in Melbourne.] In the phr. **the man outside Hoyt's,** the commissionaire outside Hoyt's Theatre in Melbourne in the 1930s; also *fig.* (see quot. 1953).
1953 S.J. BAKER *Aust. Speaks* 133 Hoyt's, the man outside, a mythical person who starts all false rumours; the source of stolen property which an innocent (!) receiver is found to have in his possession. **1975** *Sydney Morning Herald* 5 July 9/4 We might be better off to abandon pre-selections and elections, and choose our politicians by having the Governor (or the man outside Hoyts) stick pins into the telephone book.

Hughie. Also **Hewie.** [Of unknown origin.] The 'rain god', esp. as invoked in the phr. **send it** (or **her**) **down Hughie.** Also *transf.* as **send 'em up Hughie** (see quot. 1981).
1912 *Bulletin* (Sydney) 5 Dec. 15/2 *Re* the shearer's 'Send it down, Hughie!'.. when needed rain is threatening. I first heard the expression in Narrandera (N.S.W.)... I believe that it originated in that district, by reason of a Mr Huie.. an amateur meteorologist, who had luck in prophesying rain... Hence, 'Send it down, Huie'. **1946** K.S. PRICHARD *Roaring Nineties* 43 Miners and prospectors would turn out and yell to a dull, dirty sky clouded with red dust: 'Send her down! Send her down, Hughie!' **1981** *Nat. Times* (Sydney) 20 Dec. 26/4 Incoming waves may be assessed, and sometimes the ancient cry will rise during a lull: 'Send 'em up Huey!' Meaning: push some waves in. Some surf scholars believe Huey to be a corruption of Jupiter Pluvius. **1985** *N.T. News* (Darwin) 19 Apr. 37/1 Who would have expected such a flushing so late in the year? Hewie pulled the chain over the whole of the Top End and every river.. responded with massive flooding.

hum, *n.* [f. the *v.*]
1. An habitual borrower; a cadger. Also *attrib.*
1915 J.P. BOURKE *Off Bluebush* 190 If you cannot be a spendthrift, be a hum. **1921** *Aussie* (Sydney) July 40/2 In one of the Aussie re-inforcement camps in England were two tough Diggers... They were 'hum' experts, their speciality being smokes and drinks.
2. In the phr. **on the hum,** engaged in cadging.
1932 C. HADE *Ebeneezer* 8 At 'run-the-rule' or a two-up school he took the bun—Half his time hungry—always on the hum.

hum, *v.* [Prob. spec. use of *hum*, abbrev. of *humbug* to impose upon, take in: see OED *hum, v.*²]

1. *trans.* To cadge (a cigarette, etc.). Also *intr.*
1913 *Bulletin* (Sydney) 30 Jan. 15/2 He has promised to 'hum' a stamp to post this at the first town we strike. **1915** J.P. BOURKE *Off Bluebush* 77 Got no coin to treat a pal! Got no face to hum!
2. *trans.* To work one's way through (a town) begging.
1918 A. WRIGHT *Breed holds Good* 148 The travellers have 'hummed' the towns with varying success. **1935** *Bulletin* (Sydney) 30 Jan. 21/4 Where other 'Bidgee whalers 'hummed' a town for booze, Mick 'hummed' it for tea, going from house to house with his plea: 'Missus, could y' spring a cup o' tea?'
Hence **humming** *vbl. n.*
1913 W.K. HARRIS *Outback in Aust.* 47 What'll happen to *us* if you town-ies start on the 'humming' game?

hummer, *n.*¹ *Obs.* A name given to an Aboriginal ceremonial object; BULLROARER.
1887 *Proc. R. Geogr. Soc. Australasia, S.A. Branch* 29 Occasionally the 'hummer' is used, but not frequently; probably because it is considered too sacred to be seen by women or young men. **1903** *Bulletin* (Sydney) 3 Sept. 16/2 The 'bull-roarer', or 'gooanduckyer'.. is merely what was known in my boyhood days as a 'hummer'.

hummer, *n.*² [f. *hum, v.*] One who makes a practice of cadging.
1916 *Battery Herald: Jrnl. 14th Field Artillery* 9 Oct. 9 Hummers. During the week our old friend 'Duke Mullins' was caught napping. As usual.. he put the.. sting for a fag. **1945** S.J. BAKER *Austral. Lang.* 108 *Hummer, poler* and *bot-fly* are additional synonyms for a cadger.

hump, *n.*¹ [f. the *v.*]
a. *Obs.* An arduous walk, carrying a load on one's back.
[N.Z. **1863** J.G. WALKER Jrnl. 27 Jan. 4 It was a precious hump [over the hill].] **1890** 'R. BOLDREWOOD' *Miner's Right* 46 We get a fair share of exercise without a twenty mile hump on Sundays.
b. A swagman.
1955 D. NILAND *Shiralee* 51 'I tell you, them humps out there, they want shootin'.' 'Oh, well some like to have fun.' Macauley hoisted the swag. 'So long.'

hump, *n.*² A camel.
1935 H. FINLAYSON *Red Centre* 120 We were heading for a camp in the Everard forty miles away, with a string of twenty-two 'humps'. **1978** D. STUART *Wedgetail View* 65, I see old Dotty Stanley once.. with a pair o' camels; it was the first time he'd ever had humps, an' he wasn't too sure of 'em.

hump, *v.* [Transf. use of *hump, v.* to make humped.]
1. a. *trans.* To carry (a load, etc.), esp. on one's back. Also *fig.*
1851 *Empire* (Sydney) 4 July 4/1 No sooner is the Commissioner seen on the creek than.. those who have not paid may be seen 'humping' their cradles to some secluded spot. **1908** *Bulletin* (Sydney) 16 Apr. 43/1 Take up your cross and hump it—what tho' the way be long.
b. *trans.* Freq. with **it:** to travel on foot, carrying one's bundle of possessions.
1891 M. ROBERTS *Land-Travel & Sea-Faring* 84, I packed my clothes in a rough kind of 'swag', or bundle, and 'humped' it down to Albury. **1908** *Bulletin* (Sydney) 29 Oct. 13/2 We humped the lonely road to Sydney city 'on our pad'.
2. a. In the phr. **to hump one's swag (bluey, drum, knot, Matilda),** to travel on foot carrying, esp. on one's back, a bundle of possessions.
1851 *Empire* (Sydney) 17 Oct. 266/4 The Messrs

Owen .. are 'humping the swag' to the washing hole, and doing fairly; but the labour is immense. **1870** E.B. KENNEDY *Four Yrs. in Qld.* 14 They might hear of a station where shearers were wanted .. and after 'humping their drum' for many hot dusty miles, find there was no room for them. **1891** *Truth* (Sydney) 1 Feb. 5/3 Some time in September 1890, they packed their traps, and humping 'bluey', set out with cheerful faces. **1902** *Ibid.* 17 Aug. 1/8 It isn't all beer and skittles humping 'Matilda' at the best of times. **1937** *Bulletin* (Sydney) 10 Mar. 20/2 Humping their knots west of Condoblin (N.S.W.), Bluey and Dutch discovered a mob of wethers.

b. *fig.* To strive (towards the achievement of a goal).

1891 *Extracts from 'Worker'* (Qld. Patriotic League) 14/3 Australia's a big country, An' Freedom's humping bluey, An' Freedom's on the wallaby—Oh, don't you hear 'er cooey. **1952** H.E. BOOTE *Sidelights Two Referendums* 25 England has declared war on Germany. Progress is humping bluey now, for many a long day, perhaps.

humper.

a. *Obs.* One who carries a heavy load.

1851 *Empire* (Sydney) 12 Dec. 459/4 This is profitable digging certainly, yet the work is exceedingly laborious, the humpers having to walk twenty-three and a-half miles each day, and to carry on the average one and a-half cwt. of clay for upwards of eleven miles of that distance.

b. A swagman.

1944 C. SHAW *Sheaf of Shorts* 96 Who was I, a lonely humper of a bluey. **1945** *Bulletin* (Sydney) 12 Dec. 13/1 A fairly well set-up humper of bluey.

humpty-doo, var. UMPTY-DOO.

humpy /'hʌmpi/. Formerly chiefly *Qld.* [a. Jagara (and neighbouring languages) *yumbi.*] A temporary shelter of the Aborigines (see quot. 1853); *transf.,* any makeshift or temporary dwelling, esp. one made with primitive materials. See also GUNYAH.

1846 C.P. HODGSON *Reminisc. Aust.* 238 A 'Gunyia' or 'Umpee'. **1853** *Moreton Bay Free Press* 13 Dec. 4/6 These *humpeys* or *gunyahs*, as they are called, are constructed by placing a few young boughs or saplings tightly in the ground, in a semi-circular form, the upper parts are then woven or fastened together, and the framework of the structure is thus completed. **1862** C. MUNRO *Fern Vale* I. 2 If we succeed in forming a station, as soon as we can get up a decent sort of a 'humpie', and comfortably settled, I will come and fetch you.

hunchy. A camel. Also *attrib.*

1919 R.J. CASSIDY *Gipsy Road* 58 Some of the best 'hunchy' persuaders in Never-Never Land are Australians. **1930** E. ANTONY *Hungry Mile* 7 I've steered the 'hunchies' the desert thro'.

hungry, *a.*

1. Niggardly; grasping; mean.

1855 W. HOWITT *Land, Labor & Gold* II. 314, I asked two men who were resting with their cart by the road-side whose station that was?—'Hungry Scott's', was the reply. **1980** B. HORNADGE *Austral. Slanguage* 157 In the last century the derogatory term *hungry* was universally applied to anyone who was mean, or grasping. It was a particular term of abuse for station owners who refused to give food to swagmen.

2. Special collocations: **hungry mile,** a stretch of Sussex Street, Sydney, frequented by unemployed wharf-labourers in search of work; **quartz** [see OED *hungry* 6 c.], quartz with a very low yield (see quot. 1853); **track,** a stretch of country in which an itinerant has difficulty in obtaining work and sustenance.

1930 E. ANTONY *Hungry Mile* 5 They toil and sweat in slavery, 'twould make the devil smile, To see the Sydney wharfies tramping down the **hungry mile**. **1853** A. MACKAY *Great Gold Field* 19 Samples, selected on account of their unpromising appearance, called '**hungry quartz**', yielded 13 dwts. per ton, while samples selected as favourable gave 35 ounces to the ton. **1895** *Bulletin* (Sydney) 26 Oct. 7/4 Eight weeks on a **hungry track**. Got a week's work at last for a blacksmith cocky—*such* a nice man. . . Have just got my wages—a pair of good pusher boots (second-hand) and a 2d. stamp.

hunting, *vbl. n. Obs.* Used *attrib.* in Special Comb. **hunting ground,** a stretch of country which is the hereditary possession of an Aboriginal community; **smoke,** a cloud or column of smoke rising from a fire lit by Aborigines to drive game towards hunters.

1830 *Van Diemen's Land Correspondence* 15 Mar. (1831) 55 The Natives are as tenacious of their **hunting-grounds** as settlers are of their farms. **1875** P.E. WARBURTON *Journey across Western Interior* 207 Nothing was to be seen .. except several '**hunting smokes**' in different directions.

huntsman spider. [Spec. use of *huntsman*, from the hunting habits of the spider, which stalks and pounces on its prey.] Any of many spiders of the fam. Heteropodidae (Sparassidae) (esp. of the genus *Isopoda*), members of which are typically large, flat-bodied spiders which dwell under the bark of trees; TARANTULA; TRIANTELOPE. Also *ellipt.* as **huntsman**.

1936 K.C. MCKEOWN *Spider Wonders Aust.* 68 This .. power of the eyes of spiders to reflect light is strongly present in the large Huntsman Spiders. **1978** N. COLEMAN *Look at Wildlife Great Barrier Reef* 35 The huntsman is a ground-dwelling spider which may grow to almost 70 mm across the leg span.

Huon pine. [From the name of a river in s. Tas.] The conifer *Lagerostrobus franklinii* (fam. Podocarpaceae) of s. and w. Tas., having weeping foliage and occurring in damp forests; the durable softwood timber of the tree; *Macquarie Harbour pine*, see MACQUARIE HARBOUR. Also *attrib.*

1810 *Derwent Star* (Hobart) 3 Apr. 2 The Body was placed in a Shell of Huon pine wood. **1983** *Sydney Morning Herald* 3 Feb. 13/1 Huon pines can live for more than 2,000 years.

hurl, *v. intr.* To vomit. Also as *n.*, the act of vomiting; vomit.

1964 B. HUMPHRIES *Nice Night's Entertainment* (1981) 78 I've had liquid laughs in bars And I've hurled from moving cars. **1967** F. HARDY *Billy Borker yarns Again* 63 Calling for Herb, see, that's one of the many euphemisms for vomit, others include spue, burp, hurl, the big spit, the long spit, throw.

hurroo, var. HOOROO.

hurry-scurry. At a country race-meeting: a final event for horses unplaced in previous races.

1878 G. WALCH *Australasia* 33 He asked Harry if he could let him have Tearaway to ride in the Hurry-Skurry. **1969** A. FADDEN *They called me Artie* 12 The final race of the day was a consolation event for beaten horses, known as the 'Hurry-Scurry'.

hurry-up. [f. the vbl. phr. *to hurry up.*] A spur to action, esp. in the phr. **to give** (someone) **a bit of hurry-up.**

1916 O. HOGUE *Trooper Bluegum at Dardanelles* 171 We were giving Abdul a 'bit of hurry-up' . . at Quinn's. **1986** *Canberra Times* 26 May 3/1 (*heading*) A hurry up for late ratepayers.

hut, *n.*

1. *Obs.* An Aboriginal dwelling.

1770 J. COOK *Jrnls.* 29 Apr. (1955) I. 305 We found here a few Small Hutts made of the bark of trees in one of which were four or five small children. **1901** G. WHITE *Across Aust.* 16, I found two well-made blacks' huts shaped like a Kaffir kraal, well thatched and waterproof.

2. *Obs.* A building for the accommodation of a convict (or convicts).

1793 J. HUNTER *Hist. Jrnl. Trans. Port Jackson* 303 The huts were building at the distance of one hundred feet from each other, and each hut was to contain ten convicts. **1834** *HRA* (1923) 1st Ser. XVII. 338 A Tub of Water and a drinking vessel, together with one or more Tubs for Wine, is however to be placed in each Hut previous to the Evening Muster.

3. A dwelling, esp. in the country, not necessarily either temporary or mean (see e.g. quots. 1841 and 1864); such a dwelling as provided for the accommodation of assigned convicts and, later, of employees; also **men's hut**. Also *attrib*.

1803 *Sydney Gaz.* 19 Mar., She saw two men approach a hut in which one of Mr Declamb's men-servants then was. **1841** *Port Phillip Gaz.* 20 Mar. 6 [On] the Cattle Station .. is a comfortable Hut, containing five rooms .. also two huts for stockmen and servants. **1856** W.W. DOBIE *Recoll. Visit Port-Phillip* 70 One large hut, called 'the men's hut', is usually set apart for the working-men engaged in various jobs on the station, and who are without the encumbrances of wives or families. **1864** H. JONES *New Valuations* 28 Nearly all the huts are of stone, and well built by competent masons. **1956** F.B. VICKERS *First Place to Stranger* 233 The accommodation he provided for the shearing team to live in was up to the standard laid down by the Hut Accommodation Act.

4. Comb. **hut-mate**.

1827 *Monitor* (Sydney) 5 July 496/1 Five matched themselves together, as hut-mates, for each of the four huts.

5. Special Comb. **hut-man**, a person, esp. a shepherd, who is accommodated in a hut; a HUT-KEEPER; also *transf*. (see quot. 1936).

1826 *Monitor* (Sydney) 19 May 2/2 The distant Woods of the Colony, where neither the Clergyman nor the Missionary penetrates to remind the poor Hutmen and lonely Settlers, either of the difference between the Sabbath and the week-day, or, that they have Souls which may be lost for want of consideration. **1936** W. HATFIELD *Aust. through Windscreen* 64 It was policy to have a policeman in the house, as an ally against the cattle-thieves. 'But,' said a manager once to me, 'they're really hut men, below the rank of sub-inspector. Yet what can you do?'

hut, *v. Obs.* [Prob. back-formation f. HUTTER, but cf. HAT.] *intr.* To live alone.

1888 *Centennial Mag.* (Sydney) 499 Sauerkraut had worked his claim with varying success, always hutting, or in other words living alone.

hut-keep, *v.* [Back-formation f. HUT-KEEPER.] *intr.* To perform the duties of a hut-keeper.

1840 J. GUNTHER *Jrnl.* 14 Dec. 44 On my road I called at a Shepherd's hut where a Scotchwoman was hutkeeping as they call it. **1891** D. FERGUSON *Vicissitudes Bush Life* 148 The shepherd for whom he was hutkeeping was tending a flock of ewes.

Hence **hutkeeping** *vbl. n.*

1841 *Geelong Advertiser* 13 Dec. 2/5 Reardon returned, but Captain Webster refused to let him have any other work than hut-keeping.

hut-keeper. One who takes care of a hut, esp. as occupied by convicts or employees (e.g., shepherds, shearers, etc.), providing for the occupants and attending to certain menial tasks.

1794 G. THOMPSON *Slavery & Famine* ii. 8 Those who are not fortunate enough to be selected for wives .. are made hut-keepers. **1982** PAGE & INGPEN *Aussie Battlers* 22 A hut-keeper is different from what he was when I was young. I just look after the shearer's quarters, cook their grub and so on.

hutter. [f. HUT *n.* 3, poss. infl. by HATTER.] One who prefers to live alone.

1878 F.W. FENTON *This Side Up* 8 The few 'hutters' who vegetated on Boggy Creek, earning a few shillings a week in working ground that had been turned over and over again. **1937** D. GUNN *Links with Past* 207 After a time .. shepherds' huts were made larger and better. ... If the country was very good, two flocks were camped at the same locality, which meant two single men could live together, but still there were many old hutters who preferred to be alone.

hyena. Prob. *obs.* [Transf. use of *hyena*, from a fancied resemblance to a carnivore of the fam. Hyaenidae.] *Tasmanian tiger*, see TASMANIAN *a.* 2; *opossum hyena*, see OPOSSUM *n.* 3. Also **hyena opossum**.

1810 *HRA* (1921) 3rd Ser. I. 771 The only animal unknown on the Continent is the Hyaena Opossum. **1919** *Huon Times* (Franklin) 14 Mar. 2/7 Plaintiff used to assert that a wild hyena was killing his sheep.

I

ibis. [Transf. use of *Ibis* a genus of large grallatorial birds.] Any of three species of long-legged wading birds of the genera *Plegadis* and *Threskiornis*, occurring in Aust. and elsewhere. Also with distinguishing epithet, as **straw-necked, white** (see under first element), and *attrib.*

1836 *Sydney Herald* 21 Mar. 2/4 Among the aquatic birds we recognised the .. white crane, and Ibis. **1986** *Sydney Morning Herald* 26 Apr. 6/4 Grain farmers recognise the value of ibis birds which are native to the area and which are important in controlling locust plagues.

iceberg. One who makes a practice of swimming regularly during the winter in unheated water.

1932 L. LOWER *Here's Another* 12 One of the toughest surfs I've experienced this winter. All the Icebergs agreed. **1986** *Good Weekend* (Sydney) 26 Apr. 60/2 The Bondi Icebergs .. begin their season on Sunday, May 4, at their freshwater pool in South Bondi. Hardy male swimmers are welcome.

ice-block. A confection of flavoured and frozen water, a water-ice.

1948 C.B. MAXWELL *Cold Nose of Law* 45 Her father .. had given her a paper-wrapped ice-block, a brilliant green water-ice. **1970** J.S. GUNN in W.S. Ramson *Eng. Transported* 64 We should investigate the areas of use of such duplications as *lolly/iceblock*.

Icy-pole. Also **icy-pole.** [Proprietary name.] An ice-block.

1932 *Austral. Official Jrnl. Patents* (Canberra) 1067 *Icy-pole* 59,348. Ice cream, ice cream sherbert, water ice and frozen fruit juices. *Peters American Delicacy Company (Vic.) Ltd.* **1986** *Austral. Short Stories* xiii. 12 The worst they can do is not make up their minds whether to have a lemonade icypole or a raspberry one.

identity. [Spec. use of *identity*; prob. orig. N.Z. (see quot. 1874).] One who is a well-known and long standing resident of a place; a local 'character'. Esp. in the collocation **old identity.**

[N.Z. **1862** C. THATCHER *Dunedin Songster No. 1* 18 (*title*) The old identity.] **1874** A. BATHGATE *Colonial Experiences* 26 The term 'old identities' took its origin from an expression in a speech made by one of the members of the Provincial Council, Mr E.B. Cargill, who, in speaking of the new arrivals, said that the early settlers should endeavour to preserve their old identity... [An Austral.] comic singer [C.R. Thatcher] helped to perpetuate the name by writing a song. **1980** F. MOORHOUSE *Days Wine & Rage* 302, I remember a local identity was picked up for driving under the influence after the picnic races.

-ie: see -Y.

ignore. In the phr. **to treat with ignore,** to disregard the presence or advice of someone or something. Also *transf.* and *fig.*

1936 *Bulletin* (Sydney) 6 July 26/1 The habit of 'treating with ignore' our own industrial experience is quite wrong. **1975** *Sydney Morning Herald* 1 July 7/4 With gathering speed downhill, the train treated Wollstonecraft with ignore.

iguana. *Obs.* [Transf. use of *iguana* any of several large lizards.] GOANNA 1.

1801 M. FLINDERS *Observations Coasts Van Diemen's Land* 21 Amongst other reptiles, are poisonous snakes, and some brown iguanas. **1914** H.M. VAUGHAN *Australasian Wander-Yr.* 240 The iguana, or lace monitor .. is, at least to the 'new chum', most alarming in his attitude and aspect.

ijjecka, var. ADJIGO.

Illawarra /ɪləˈwɒrə/. [The name of a coastal district south of Sydney, N.S.W.]

1. Used *attrib.* in Special Comb. **Illawarra flame tree,** *flame tree* (a), see FLAME 2.

1902 *Proc. Linnean Soc. N.S.W.* XXVII. 578 During the year of heaviest flowering the Illawarra Flame-tree, *Sterculia acerifolia* .. is almost leafless. **1980** L. FULLER *Wollongong's Native Trees* 90 Illawarra flame tree can be found in most rainforest communities on the escarpment.

2. A popular breed of dairy cattle developed in the Illawarra district. Also **Illawarra (milking) Shorthorn.**

1911 *N.Z. Jrnl. Agric.* May 274 The breed .. known as the Illawarra Milking Shorthorn, a dairy type of Shorthorn evolved on the south coast districts of the State from a Shorthorn-Ayrshire foundation, but now bred for about thirty years to a Shorthorn dairy type. **1981** A. WILKINSON *Up Country* 155 The red heifers actually belonged to one of Australia's own breeds, the Illawarra shorthorn. These mature into monumental milkers.

illywhacker /ˈɪliwækə/. Also **illywacker.** [Of unknown origin.] A small-time confidence trickster.

1941 K. TENNANT *Battlers* 145 An illy-wacker is someone who is putting a confidence trick over, selling imitation diamond pins, new-style patent razors or infallible 'tonics'. . 'living on the cookies' by such devices... A man who 'wacks the illy' can be almost anything, but two of these particular illy-wackers were equipped with a dart game. **1985** P. CAREY *Illywhacker* 245 'What's an illywhacker?'.. 'A spieler .. a trickster. A quandong. A ripperty man. A con-man.'

Hence **illywhack** *n.*, the patter of an illywhacker.

1955 *Overland* iv. 10 Within the ring a horse cavorts. Buck on, you beaut! I'd give a fiver To see you smash snake-headed through Palings, poons, illywhack and guyver.

imbo /ˈɪmboʊ/. [f. *imb(ecile* + -O.] A gullible person, esp. the victim of a criminal.

1953 S.J. BAKER *Aust. Speaks* 125 Australia's underworldsters have commemorated the services of their victims by calling them any of these assorted terms: .. *imbo* [etc.]. **1981** P. RADLEY *Jack Rivers & Me* 50 'What *is* an imbo, Connie? Please?' 'If you don't know what imbeciles are far be it from me to tell you.'

immigrant.

1. One who has come to Australia from another country by choice and with the intention of settling. Cf. EMIGRANT *n.* 1, MIGRANT 1. Also *attrib.*

1838 *HRA* (1923) 1st Ser. XIX. 290 This has been a great disappointment to many immigrants. **1939** J.T. MCMAHON *Bushies' Scheme in W.A.* 37 The 'Big Brother' assumes a paternal interest in some immigrant boy, promising to care for him when out of employment, and to guard him while in it.

2. One who moves from one Australian Colony or State to settle in another.

1845 *Portland Gaz.* 1 July 2/2 About 70 immigrants are expected to arrive at Geelong per the schooner David from Hobart Town. **1902** *Bulletin* (Sydney) 28 Oct. 36/2 The culprit is frequently a new-chum or an immigrant from the Paroo country, where bush fires are unknown.

3. *transf.* A species of bird, etc., introduced into Australia.

1925 *Bulletin* (Sydney) 1 Oct. 24/2 Quarrians, rosellas, green-leeks and red-backs, all very numerous on the N.S.W. tablelands, are now eagerly searching for nesting-places which they have carelessly let fall into the hands of immigrants. **1936** *Ibid.* 15 Apr. 20/2 The house-sparrow, aptly termed 'the rat of the air', is certainly Australia's most successful bird immigrant.

4. Comb. immigrant barracks, depot, ship.

1842 *Sydney Morning Herald* 2 Aug. 2/3 The admission into the **Immigrant Barracks,** and the temporary maintenance there of . . labourers with families. **1848** *Sydney Daily Advertiser* 12 July 2/3 A better place could not be selected to form an **immigrant depot.** **1841** *Port Phillip Patriot* 21 Oct. 2/2 The *Agricola*, an **immigrant ship** from London and Cork.

5. In the collocation **immigrants' home,** an establishment in which newly-arrived immigrants are given temporary accommodation.

1852 J. Morgan *Life & Adventures W. Buckley* 150, I was soon afterwards appointed assistant to the storekeeper at the Immigrants' Home, Hobart Town.

immigrate, *v.*

1. *intr.* To come to Australia from another country with the intention of settling. Cf. Emigrate.

1837 *Lit. News* (Sydney) 9 Dec. 180 Those Gentlemen who immigrated on the faith of the Home Government Regulations of 1827. **1982** *Sydney Morning Herald* 13 Dec. 2/1 Prospective immigrants . . must get 60 points under the department's point system before they are allowed to immigrate.

2. *Obs.* To move from one Australian Colony to live in another.

1889 J.H.L. Zillmann *Past & Present Austral. Life* 92 Moonlight and his gang . . were for the most part a band of 'larrikins' that immigrated from the Melbourne side and started as bush-rangers in the neighbouring colony of New South Wales.

Hence **immigrating** *ppl. a.*

1896 *Bulletin* (Sydney) 17 Oct. 10/4 As the immigrating Chows did not report themselves to the police, the Government and its officials took no cognisance of this increase in the pig-tailed population.

immigration.

1. The action of coming to Australia from another country with the intention of settling; [also U.S.: see Mathews] the body of immigrants. Cf. Emigration 1.

1824 *HRA* (1921) 3rd Ser. IV. 567 The chief of the Immigration being directed to Van Diemen's Land. **1912** *Register* (Adelaide) 28 Mar. 4/3 By various means the facilities to immigration will be increased or made easier.

2. Special Comb. **immigration agent,** one employed to promote immigration and to assist with the settlement of immigrants; **department,** the (government) department responsible for the implementation and administration of an immigration policy; **lecturer,** one employed to promote the advantages of immigration to Australia; **society,** an organization established to encourage immigration and to provide assistance to immigrants.

1841 *Morning Advertiser* (Hobart) 5 Aug. 1/3 The regulations of the Bounty system are laid down in the Government Notice of the 14th May, 1840, and by these the **Immigration Agent** will be governed. **1842** *Aust. & N.Z. Monthly Mag.* 47 This excess arises from an increase of . . £1,200 for the **immigration department.** **1868** *Coalition between Squatters & Free Selectors* 7 In 1861 . . the two well known gentlemen (Mr Dalley and Mr Parkes) were immediately instructed to start for England, as '**Immigration Lecturers**'. **1847** *Maitland Mercury* 24 Nov. 3/2 In consequence of . . the organization of several **immigration societies**, chiefly in Port Phillip, who pay emigrants' passages, the stream of emigration from Van Diemen's Land . . is diverted to that district.

imperial convict. *W.A. Hist.* A convict the cost of whose penal servitude was met by the British as distinct from the Colonial government.

1873 A. Trollope *Aust. & N.Z.* II. 112, 240 are imperial convicts,—convicts who have been sent out from England, and who are now serving under British sentences, or sentences inflicted in the colony within twelve months of the date of their freedom. **1885** *V & P* (W.A. L.C.) no. 25 5 It would be liberal to offer to the Colony the same sum per head for the Imperial Convicts as the Colony has paid for Colonial Convicts, viz; £42.

imported, *ppl. a.* Immigrant. Also *absol.*

1849 A. Harris *Emigrant Family* (1967) 198 The inferior portion of the imported free population sympathises. **1910** *Bulletin* (Sydney) 10 Nov. 13/2, I had to fall back on an assisted immigrant, who was journeying to nowhere in particular. Now, I've found most 'importeds' have a failing, and mine had his.

improve, *n.* In the phr. **on the improve,** showing signs of betterment.

1959 S.J. Baker *Drum* 119 *Improve, on the,* improving in health or proficiency. **1984** *West Austral.* (Perth) 4 Jan. 92/5 Regal Martin on the improve. . . Three-year-old Regal Martin showed improvement with a smart trial over 800 m. on the wood fibre track at Ascot yesterday morning.

improve, *v.* [U.S. *improve* to bring land under cultivation: see Mathews *v.* 1., and also OED(S *v.*² 2 b. for the older and more general meaning of which this is a spec. use.]

1. *trans.* To bring (land) into agricultural or pastoral use; to clear, fence, provide with buildings, etc., so making more productive and more valuable.

1834 H. Melville *Two Lett. Van Diemen's Land* 4 Mr Auley . . may dispose of his grant—without ever having seen it, without ever having improved it. **1905** *Bulletin* (Sydney) 19 Oct. 40/2 The land is half-cleared (improved they call it; Nature forgive them).

2. *trans. Obs.* To increase (the quality or yield of stock or of animal produce).

1820 *Hobart Town Gaz.* 2 Dec., Settlers, improving Wool on an extensive Scale, are requested to take this Opportunity of pointing out any Facilities which they consider might be afforded them. **1833** *Trumpeter* (Hobart) 19 Nov. 242 The Proprietors of Cows wishing to improve their breed, may do so, by sending them to Mr Rawling's highly-improved Bull.

Hence **improver** *n.*, **improving** *vbl. n.*

1824 *Hobart Town Gaz.* 9 July, The very best shipments of the oldest **improvers** in New South Wales fetch from 1s. 3d. to 2s. **1956** K. Tennant *Honey Flow* 113 The **improving** and clearing and ring-barking went on until the foothills of the enclosing ranges were almost bare of trees save ring-barked, dead skeletons.

improved, *ppl. a.* [U.S.: see Mathews.] Of land: brought into agricultural or pastoral use; made more productive.

1839 *Sydney Standard* 1 Apr. 3/3 Did not include . . the sale of improved lands. **1986** *Canberra Times* 5 Mar. 18/4 The growth of the wheat industry and the spread of improved pasture in inland Australia provided ideal conditions for the great 20th-century galah boom, but the factors that contributed to the success of the galah around Canberra since the 1940s remain obscure.

improvement. [U.S.: see OED(S 2 a. and b.]
1. The bringing of land into agricultural or pastoral use; the provision of fences, buildings, etc., associated with this process; the increasing of productivity. Also *attrib.*
1834 H. MELVILLE *Two Lett. Van Diemen's Land* 4 No improvements were being made on Mr Auley's grant. **1956** *Westerly* i. 13 Schemes for the reduction or abolition of income taxation have often been proposed . . to compel owners to carry out the improvement clauses in their pastoral leases.
2. *transf. Obs.* An increase in the value or quality (of sheep or cattle).
1835 *Cornwall Chron.* (Launceston) 21 Feb. 3 The proprietor . . paid the greatest attention towards the improvement of his cattle. **1837** *Perth Gaz.* 30 Sept. 981 The improvement effected by the system of crossing, generally adopted of late years by the flock-holders.
3. Special Comb. **improvement lease** [U.S.; see Mathews], IMPROVING LEASE; the land so held.
1895 *Act* (N.S.W.) 58 Vict. no. 18 Sect. 26 (*heading*) Improvement leases. **1910** *Bulletin* (Sydney) 7 Apr. 14/3 The Hay (N.S.W.) Land Board recently wrestled with some Improvement Leases totalling 31,000 acres.

improving lease. *Obs.* An agreement by which the occupation of land is subject to the carrying out by the lessee of specified improvements.
1823 *Hobart Town Gaz.* 4 Oct., To be Let, upon an improving Lease, a small Farm. **1857** *Tas. Non-State Rec.* 103/4 9 Oct., I intend to let it on an improving lease.

imshi /'ɪmʃi/, *v. imp.* Also **imshee.** [Services' speech of the war of 1914–18, f. the colloq. (Egyptian) Arabic. Chiefly Austral.] 'Be off'; 'go away'. Also as *v. intr.*
1916 'MEN OF ANZAC' *Anzac Bk.* 135 It is enough. *Imshee!* [*Note*] Imshee is the Arabic for 'go away'. The Australasian Corps, which had so far employed it only to street hawkers in Cairo, used this war cry on April 25. **1918** R.H. KNYVETT *Over there with Australs.* 83 The first Egyptian word we learned was '*Imshi!*' literally, 'Get!'—but it generally required the backing of a military boot to make it effective.

in, *adv.* Following a verb of motion either expressed or implied, esp. **come**: within the bounds of the settled districts; at a (sheep or cattle) station; in town.
1798 D. COLLINS *Acct. Eng. Colony N.S.W.* (1802) II. 80 Wilson . . lately came in from the woods. **1960** *N.T. News* (Darwin) 22 Jan. 6/4 Visitors to Borroloola recently were old-timer Jack Shadforth and Arthur Alpin, both of whom were in for rations.

in, *prep.* [Spec. use of *in it* partaking, sharing: see OED(S *prep.* 27.] In the phr. **to be in it,** to take part (in an activity, etc.), usu. with some enthusiasm.
1928 A. WRIGHT *Good Recovery* 37 'It's a queer business,' ventured Trilet, 'and if I am to be in it, I want to know the strength of it.' **1982** R. HALL *Just Relations* 129 Naturally they'd all be in it. They'd hitch a ride down the Yalgoona road with the cheese delivery.

inclusions, *pl.* Soft furnishings as included in the purchase price of a residence.
1970 *Canberra Times* 7 Nov. 31/1 Built on concrete slab. Double carports, quality inclusions. **1981** *Ibid.* 4 Nov. 38/7 This is a *solid brick* builders own home with quality inclusions. **1985** *Ibid.* 13 July 5/3 An upgraded kitchen, good quality inclusions and tasteful decor.

incorrigible. *Obs.* A recalcitrant convict.
1827 P. CUNNINGHAM *Two Yrs. in N.S.W.* I. 149 From . . the lazy habits of the *incorrigibles* who are sentenced to this labour, the produce does not at all correspond with what may be expected. **1912** A. BERRY *Reminisc.* 180 We managed our convicts chiefly by moral influence as we had no police. Occasionally we had troubles with incorrigibles.

indent. *Hist.* [Spec. use of *indent* official list.] A document recording the names of a party of convicts transported to Australia and transferring a property in these convicts to the relevant governor, usu. detailing name, date of trial, sentence, etc.
1802 *HRA* (1915) 1st Ser. III. 564 Frauds . . have been practised . . by making an alteration in the indents sent out with the convicts, and thereby shortening the periods by which certain of them were sentenced to transportation. **1965** L.L. ROBSON *Convict Settlers Aust.* 241 The convict records consolidated as 'Convict Indents' . . vary from little more than lists of convicts' names in the early years to much fuller descriptions after 1825.

indented, *ppl. a. Hist.* [Spec. use of *indented* bound by a formal agreement.] Of a convict: assigned into private service.
1804 *HRA* (1915) 1st Ser. IV. 480 There is now a great demand for indented convicts. **1816** *Hobart Town Gaz.* 30 Nov., All Persons are hereby Cautioned against Employing Robert Manders, Carpenter, as he is my indented Servant, from the 6th of August last, for twelve months.

Indian. *Hist.* A name formerly applied to an Aboriginal. Also *attrib.*
1770 J. BANKS *Jrnl.* 28 Apr. (1896) 263 Our boat proceeded along shore, and the Indians followed her at a distance. **1823** *First Fruits Austral. Poetry* (ed. 2) 16 This must be the place Where our Columbus of the South did land; He saw the Indian village on that sand, And on this rock first met the simple race Of Australasia.

indications, *pl. S.A. Mining. Obs.* [Also U.S.: see OEDS *indication* 2 b.] Evidence of the presence of ore in sufficient quantity to make mining profitable.
1846 F. DUTTON *S.A. & its Mines* 281 Several sections with mineral indications have . . been surveyed by Government. **1865** *Wallaroo Times* (Kadina) 15 Feb. 2/4 New Cornwall Mine—Present indications are encouraging.

indicator. *Mining.* [Used elsewhere but recorded earliest in Aust.: see OEDS 2 c.] A geological pointer to the presence of gold: see quot. 1932.
1894 *Miner's Handbk.* (Vic. Dept. Mines) 5 Where the gold ceases is usually near and above the line of reef or vein whence it was derived... 'Indicators' or small veins of pyrites, ironstone, and often thin bands of peculiar slate, intersected by small quartz veins, should . . be carefully looked for. **1932** I.L. IDRIESS *Prospecting for Gold* 189 Some reefs have 'indicators'. A trail of a particular kind of stone which only occurs with the gold in that reef, will lead right up to the gold.

indigo. [Spec. use of *indigo* plant of the genus *Indigofera* yielding a blue dye.] **a.** Any of several plants of the genus *Indigofera* (fam. Fabaceae), esp. the widespread *I. australis* of all States, having pinnate leaves and (usu. purple) flowers; *native indigo*, see NATIVE *a.* 6 a.; *wild indigo,* see WILD 1. **b.** (Rarely) any of several species of *Swainsona* (fam. Fabaceae), esp. *S. galegifolia*.
1825 B. FIELD *Geogr. Mem. N.S.W.* 181 We penetrated through a barren forest of box, abounding in brushes of the native indigo (indigofera australis). **1861** J.D. LANG *Qld., Aust.* 189 Indigo is indigenous in Australia, and could be cultivated.

Indon /'ɪndɒn/. Abbrev. of 'Indonesian'. Also as *adj.*
1972 J. HIBBERD *Stretch of Imagination* (1973) 37 The Indon and Kanaka we will civilize. **1982** *Age* (Melbourne) 30 June 10/6 (*heading*) End Indon arms aid, inquiry told.

indulge, *v. Hist. trans.* To grant (a convict) some mitigation of the conditions under which a sentence is being served. Chiefly in *pass.*

1805 *Sydney Gaz.* 14 July, Several of the Prisoners under Sentence of the Law .. have been indulged with Permission to be off the Stores on Tickets of Leave. 1849 J.P. TOWNSEND *Rambles & Observations N.S.W.* 221 When a 'lifer' had held a ticket-of-leave for six years, and could produce good testimonials to character, he was further indulged with a conditional pardon.

indulgence. *Hist.* A mitigation of the conditions under which a convict's sentence is served.

1794 D. COLLINS *Acct. Eng. Colony N.S.W.* (1798) I. 391 Some warrants of emancipation passed the seal of the territory and received the lieutenant-governor's signature. The objects of this indulgence were, Robert Lidaway .. and William Leach. 1858 N.L. KENTISH *Treatise on Penal Discipline* 24 The runaway's indulgence shall be cancelled, and he returned to the Government to work in a Roadgang.

informal, *a.* Of a vote or ballot paper: invalid. Also as quasi-*adv.* in the phr. **to vote informal.**

1948 R. RAVEN-HART *Canoe in Aust.* 66 The official (not slang) uses of 'to be financial' for to have paid one's dues, and of 'informal vote' for our invalid vote were .. novelties. 1984 *Courier-Mail* (Brisbane) 5 Dec. 4/7 Saturday's large informal vote was, I hope, the start of a strong and healthy reaction against trivialised TV democracy. *Ibid.*, I voted informal for the first time in my life, and did it with a clear conscience.

inked, *ppl. a.* [Obscurely f. *ink.*] Intoxicated.

1898 *Bulletin* (Sydney) 1 Oct. 14/3 To have a whisky is to 'oil up'; .. to get drunk is to get 'inked'. 1969 P. ADAM SMITH *Folklore Austral. Railwaymen* 85 Driver found well and truly inked and lying down to it.

inkweed. The tropical American perennial herb *Phytolacca octandra* (fam. Phytolaccaceae) of all mainland States but not N.T., having a fruit which is purplish-black when ripe and yields a red juice.

[N.Z. 1906 T.F. CHEESEMAN *N.Z. Flora* 1085 *Phytolacca octandra* .. Ink-plant; Poke-weed.] 1909 *Emu* VIII. 278 Red-winged Lories .. feeding .. on the introduced inkweed. 1981 A.B. & J.W. CRIBB *Useful Wild Plants Aust.* 222 Inkweed is closely related to the American pokeweed, well-known in herbal medicine; the pokeweed has been introduced to Australia but is uncommon.

inky, *a.* [f. INKED.] Intoxicated. Also **inky-poo.**

1907 *Truth* (Sydney) 28 Apr. 9/7 He was 'inky', but was happy, for he roared with mad refrain, 'Salley Stiggins, show your pegs and drink your beer!' 1955 A. UPFIELD *Cake in Hat Box* 5 'Doc in town?' asked Silas of the licensee. 'Yes, but he's inky-poo. Be out to it till morning.'

Inland. [Spec. use of *inland* interior part of a country.] With **the:** the sparsely populated interior of Australia; the outback; the inhabitants of this region collectively. Also *attrib.*

1912 *Messenger Presbyterian Church N.S.W.* 29 Nov. 764/3 The '*Australian Inland Mission*'. . . The Presbyterian Church is launching an enterprise which it is fondly hoped .. will be of the utmost importance to the national well-being of the continent. 1972 C. DUGUID *Doctor & Aborigines* 134 It was the coldest trip that I have ever made through the Inland.

inlander. Freq. with initial capital. [Spec. use of *inlander* one who dwells in the interior of a country.] One who lives in the sparsely populated interior of Australia.

1911 E.S. SORENSON *Life in Austral. Backblocks* 282 There is one thing about the inlander that favourably impresses itself upon those who have to look after a city's water supply, and that is his careful use of the liquid. 1962 *N. Austral. Monthly* Feb. 29/2 A Mission which would concentrate on making the Christian Gospel a reality to inlanders.

inside, *a.* and *adv.*

A. *adj.*

1. a. Of or pertaining to a (comparatively) closely settled part of Australia.

1864 R. HENNING *Lett.* (1952) 73 When Biddulph first took up Exmoor it was the very outside run northwards. . . Now it is quite an inside station, every bit of country is taken up for several hundred miles round it. 1922 *Bulletin* (Sydney) 23 Mar. 22/4 She had never seen a train. One expects to find such cases in the back country, but with 'inside' people it is hard to understand.

b. In the collocation **inside country.**

1902 *Blackwood's Mag.* (Edinburgh) May 639 We can always make tucker shootin' kangaroos and emus .. an' if any man wants a cheque bad, for a spell or anything, he can always go shearing inside country.

2. Having some expectation of accommodation in the house (as distinct from the huts) of a sheep or cattle station.

1936 *Bulletin* (Sydney) 30 Dec. 20/1 These old chaps, gentlemen once, would sooner camp on the creek and go hungry than go to the hut. They were 'inside men, by gad, sir!' and if they couldn't put their legs under the manager's table they spread them under the coolibah.

B. *adv.*

1. Within a more closely settled part of Australia. Also as quasi-*n.*

1909 *Bulletin* (Sydney) 28 Oct. 13/3, 1000 head of fat bullocks .. from the Northern Territory .. going 'inside' for sale. 1965 G.W. BROUGHTON *Turn again Home* 50 'Inside', as men in the North called all the southern part of Australia.

2. In the house of the owner or manager of a sheep or cattle station.

1930 *Bulletin* (Sydney) 5 Mar. 25/1 Among the allegedly 'silvertail' jobs of Outback is that of station book-keeper. Its lucky possessor lives 'inside'.

intercolonial, *a. Hist.* Existing, conducted, etc., between two or more Australian Colonies.

1841 H.S. CHAPMAN *New Settlement Australind* 40 Steam .. in a very few years will be established, at all events for intercolonial, if not for European intercourse. 1892 *Truth* (Sydney) 22 May 3/2 'Victoria, New South Wales, and South Australia are provoked by one another's border taxation.' . . Intercolonial taxation will be abandoned.

Hence **intercolonially** *adv.*

1891 E.H. HALLACK *W.A. & Yilgarn Goldfields* 27 Talk about federation and the small part intercolonially the colony must, from her position, necessarily play.

intermediate, *a. Hist.*

a. Of a tract of land: lying between a part of the country which is settled and one which is not yet settled.

1847 *Britannia* (Hobart) 26 Aug. 4/3 The lands of New South Wales are to be divided into the settled, the intermediate, and the unsettled districts. 1882 W. COOTE *Hist. Colony Qld.* 74 The colony of New South Wales was divided into 'settled' 'intermediate' and 'unsettled' districts.

b. Of a person: living in such a part of the country.

1902 *Bulletin* (Sydney) 8 Feb. 32/4 The intermediate man, neither out-backer nor 'inside man' .. is met with about Winton, Cloncurry, the Birdsville district .. [etc.].

interstate, *a.* and *adv.*

A. *adj.*

1. Chiefly since Federation: existing, conducted, etc., between two or more Australian States.

1900 *Advocate* (Burnie) 24 Apr. 2/5 It is provided by the Bill that all inter-state duties must be repealed by the end of two years. **1986** *Canberra Times* 15 Mar. 16/5 For details of interstate buses in and out of Canberra, telephone Ansett Pioneer.

2. Of a person, etc.: in or belonging to an Australian State other than that in which one is normally resident; 'out-of-state'.

1903 *Emu* II. 138 Mr J.W. Mellor, on behalf of the two inter-State visitors. **1977** D. WILLIAMSON *Club* (1978) 23 Some interstate club might offer you money.

B. *adv.* In, into, or from an Australian State other than that in which one is (normally) resident. Also as quasi-*n.*

1957 J. WATEN *Shares in Murder* 110 Stan's away interstate. **1985** *Canberra Times* 2 Sept. 3/3 Police said .. the man they are seeking had only recently arrived in Adelaide from interstate.

invalid gang. *Hist.* A detachment of convicts unfit for hard work.

1832 BACKHOUSE & TYLOR *Life & Labours G.W. Walker* (1862) 47 We arrived at Deep Gully, where the huts of an Invalid Gang are situated... Many of them are labouring under debility or indisposition, the result of intemperance, others are cripples or superannuated. **1846** L.W. MILLER *Notes of Exile Van Dieman's Land* 342 Miller, you look very ill. You cannot be able to perform such heavy work, and I shall shift you to the invalid gang.

Irish-Australian. A person of Irish descent normally resident in Australia. Also as *adj.*

1907 *Westminster Gaz.* (London) 17 Sept. 1/3 The .. Irish-Australian baronet. **1966** *Bulletin* (Sydney) 22 Jan. 13/3 It is not easy for an Irish-Australian to pay tribute to a Pom.

iron, *n.*

1. *Hist.* Used *attrib.* in Special Comb. to denote a fetter: **iron collar,** a band of iron worn round the neck; **iron gang,** IRONED GANG; see also *single iron* SINGLE *a.*, *double irons* DOUBLE *a.* 1; also *attrib.*

1791 D. COLLINS *Acct. Eng. Colony N.S.W.* (1798) I. 165 To make it a chearful day to every one, all offenders who had for stealing Indian corn been ordered to wear **iron collars** were pardoned. **1829** *Sydney Monitor* 3 Jan. 1453/4 A large party of prisoners destined for **iron gangs** at remote parts of the interior, left the Sydney Gaol. **1851** *Empire* (Sydney) 30 Dec. 519/3 Upon examining them he found they were branded with an iron gang mark.

2. Used *attrib.* in Comb. to distinguish a structure made wholly or partly of sheets of (corrugated) iron.

1859 W. BURROWS *Adventures Mounted Trooper* 45 The men no longer live in tents, but have also a good row of iron houses. **1983** *Sydney Morning Herald* 30 Apr. 32/7 His modest fibro and iron home in the township was bought on an eight-year term loan with repayments of $245 a month.

3. *fig. Obs.* [See quot. 1899.] In the collocation **good iron,** deserving of approbation. Freq. as *exclam.*

1894 E. TURNER *Seven Little Australians* (1912) 54 'Good iron,' Pip whistled softly, while he revolved the thing in his mind. **1895** *Bulletin* (Sydney) 9 Feb. 15/4 Oh, she's good iron, is my little clinah; She's my cobber an' I'm 'er bloke. **1899** *Ibid.* 22 Apr. 14/3 'Ringer' and 'good iron' are both derived from the game of quoits... 'Good iron' corresponds to 'good ball' at cricket.

iron, *v. trans.* To knock (someone) down. Usu. with **out.**

1953 S.J. BAKER *Aust. Speaks* 104 *To iron,* to attack or fight (a person) i.e. *to flatten* him. **1984** *Sunday Independent* (Perth) 9 Sept. 86/3 He was absolutely ironed out .. with a shirt-front bump that you could feel in the press box.

ironbark.

1. Any of several trees of the genus *Eucalyptus* (fam. Myrtaceae) having a characteristic thick, hard, deeply furrowed, usu. black bark and occurring in e. Aust.; the wood of these trees. Also with distinguishing epithet, as **broad-leaved, grey, narrow-leaved, red, silver-leaved, white** (see under first element), and *attrib.*

1799 D. COLLINS *Acct. Eng. Colony N.S.W.* (1802) II. 145 A sort of gum tree, the bark of which along the trunk is that of the iron bark of Port Jackson. **1935** F. CLUNE *Rolling down Lachlan* 11 The main shaft was an ironbark log.

2. *fig.* (Something) hard, unyielding; of notable quality. Freq. *attrib.* passing into *adj.*

1833 *Currency Lad* (Sydney) 30 Mar. 2 We would advise all such iron bark politicians .. to resume the strains of Orpheus of old and 'fiddle to the trees!' **1845** *Star* (Sydney) 25 Oct. 1/2 Braveo Billy! You're a right good, proper mark; There's no stringy stuff about you, You're the real iron-bark. **1907** *Truth* (Sydney) 14 July 1/8 'Girls are not like they were in my young days,' said an elderly ironbark lady seated in an Abbotsford tram.

3. Special Comb. **ironbark pumpkin,** a variety of pumpkin having an exceptionally tough skin. Also *ellipt.* as **ironbark.**

1849 A. HARRIS *Guide Port Stephens* 96 Pumpkin .. especially the iron-bark species, as large as a bucket, and, literally in favourable seasons and soils, covering the ground. **1966** J. WATEN *Season of Youth* 29 He was an enthusiast for pumpkins .. the grey-blue ironbarks, Queensland blues. **1974** B. KIDMAN *On Wallaby* 96 Ironbark pumpkins .. made a welcome addition to our ration food.

ironed gang. *Hist.* A detachment of convicts assigned to hard labour in fetters; *iron gang,* see IRON *n.* 1. See *chain gang* CHAIN *n.*[1] 1. Also *attrib.*

1832 *Currency Lad* (Sydney) 6 Oct. 1 Superintendents of ironed gangs. **1841** *Sydney Herald* 4 Jan. 2/5 He was appointed constable to the ironed-gang stockade, but allowed to reside at home.

ironshot. BUCK-SHOT (*attrib.* in quots.).

1902 *Blackwood's Mag.* (Edinburgh) May 643 We plunged into a clump of gidgyas, and in a few minutes burst out on the ironshot plain. **1916** A.I. MACLEOD *Hack's Brat* (1920) 3 The whole sandy, iron-shot slopes near him dotted with spasmodic groups of dry salt-bush.

ironstone.

1. A hard, sedimentary rock rich in iron oxides (see quot. 1967). Freq. *attrib.*

1843 *Sydney Morning Herald* 12 July 2/6 Large masses of iron ore, or iron-stone, as the colonists call it. **1912** T.E. SPENCER *Bindawalla* 98 Crossed the ironstone ridge at a gallop. **1967** R.O. CHALMERS *Austral. Rocks* 30 *Ironstone,* as the term is used in England, Europe and America, strictly applies to shales heavily impregnated with siderite... There are beds of this rock .. in the Sydney district. However more generally in Australia, this name popularly applies to sandstones, siltstones, and shales that are coloured various shades of brown, red and purple, and are hard, due to the amount of iron oxide present.

2. *Tas. Obs.* An igneous rock, prob. dolerite, used in the construction of buildings and roads.

1852 MRS C. MEREDITH *My Home in Tas.* I. 161 The walls of our cottage were to be built of the common 'iron-stone' of the country. **1863** F. ALGAR *Handbk. to Colony Tas.* 9 A

iron tree. IRONWOOD. Also *attrib*.
1830 W.J. HOOKER *Bot. Miscellany* I. 241 They [*sc.* fig-trees] had immediately vegetated, and thrown out their parasitical and rapacious roots, which adhering close to the bark of the *Iron Tree*, had followed the course of its stem downwards to the earth. 1853 W. WESTGARTH *Vic.* 253 The punch of an iron tree waddy upon the skull of an aboriginal lubra.

ironwood. [Spec. use of *ironwood* the hard wood of any of various trees: see OED.] Any of several trees yielding a particularly hard, heavy timber, esp. *Acacia estrophiolata* and *A. excelsa* (fam. Mimosaceae), and *Erythrophleum chlorostachys* (fam. Caesalpiniaceae) of n. Aust.; the wood of these trees. Also *attrib*.
1802 G. BARRINGTON *Hist. N.S.W.* 479 They .. made fast a club of iron wood, which the cannibals had left in the boat. 1891 'OLD TIME' *Convict Hulk 'Success'* 25 One of the convicts was badly hurt through having had his head dashed by the other repeatedly on the iron-wood floor. 1984 *Advertiser* (Adelaide) 27 June 1/3 The ironwood tree .. forlorn on the perimeter of farming land.

irrigation. Used *attrib*. in Comb. to denote that the productivity of the land is dependent upon an artificially engineered water supply, as **irrigation block, colony, farm, settlement.**
1891 *Bohemia* (Melbourne) 24 Dec. 10 Let him be content with a three hundred and twenty-acre selection, and if that is too much, let him settle down on a ten-acre **irrigation block**. 1890 *Braidwood Dispatch* 1 Feb. 5/1 We understand that overtures have been made to the government of this colony for the establishment of an extensive **irrigation colony** by Messrs Chaffey Bros. 1927 *Bulletin* (Sydney) 21 Apr. 24/4 The ibis is the yabbie's greatest enemy, and should be a welcome guest on every **irrigation farm**. 1920 H.S. TAYLOR *Pioneer Irrigationists' Man.* lxx. 3 The Australian **irrigation settlements** are still in their infancy.

island. Used *attrib*. in Special Comb. **island continent,** mainland Australia; **State,** Tasmania.
1835 *Sydney Herald* 19 Mar. 2/1 The establishment of a New Colony in Southern Australia, is so much connected with the interest of the settlements now existing on the same **Island-Continent**, that it would at any time excite great sensation in the inhabitants of those Colonies. 1910 *Huon Times* (Franklin) 12 Nov. 6/4 He left Tasmania to take part in the rushes of the fifties, and was ready to do fight for the **Island State**.

Israelite. A member of the Christian Israelite sect: see BEARDIE.
1852 *Murray's Guide to Gold Diggings* 17 Amongst the miners now at work is a party of Israelites. 1967 F.T. MACARTNEY *Proof against Failure* 13 Music was provided by a brass band, consisting of the male members of a sect who .. were known as the Israelites, but we boys called them the Beardy-bucks.

itchy grub. Any of many caterpillars capable of causing skin irritation, esp. the PROCESSIONAL CATERPILLAR.
1940 *Bulletin* (Sydney) 4 Dec. 16/2 Of all the miscellaneous assortment of wogs that bountiful Nature inflicts on her sons, the 'itchy grub' is the most insidious. A harmless-looking hairy caterpillar, about two inches long, it leaves an invisible irritant behind that lingers long after it has gone. 1973 C. AUSTIN *I left my Hat in Andamooka* 100 One gum tree in the caravan park was infested and campers were warned not to camp under it because this 'itchy grub' as it is called, on coming into contact with the skin, can cause intense irritation or even a serious infection.

itinerant teacher. A peripatetic teacher employed to visit, and supervise the schooling of, children living in areas remote from a school; orig. (*N.S.W.*) a teacher serving in two small half-time schools.
1866 *Act* (N.S.W.) 30 *Vict.* no. 22 Sect. 12, In districts where from the scattered state of the population or other causes it is not practicable to establish a public school the Council of Education may appoint itinerant teachers under such regulations as may be framed by them for that purpose. 1963 *Cwlth. Office Educ. Bull.* xxviii. 4 There are now several itinerant teachers who make brief annual visits to the homes of all correspondence children in the North-West and West Kimberley districts.

ivorywood. [See quot. 1965.] The tree *Siphonodon australis* (fam. Celastraceae), of near-coastal and seasonally dry vine forests of e. Qld. and n.e. N.S.W.; the wood of the tree.
1887 *Colonial & Indian Exhib. Rep. Col. Sect.* 429 Ivorywood. 1965 *Austral. Encycl.* II. 310 The ivorywood .. possesses a fine-textured, hard, ivory-coloured wood excellent for carving.

J

jabiru /dʒæbə'ru/. [Transf. use of *jabiru* a large wading bird *Jabiru mycteria*, of the stork family.] The large wading bird *Ephippiorhynchus asiaticus*, having glossy greenish-black and white plumage and red legs and occurring along the n. and e. coasts of Aust., in New Guinea, and in s. Asia; *policeman bird*, see POLICEMAN.

1847 L. LEICHHARDT *Jrnl. Overland Exped. Aust.* 194 We saw a Tabiroo [*sic*] (Myceteria) and a rifle bird. **1979** D. LOCKWOOD *My Old Mates & I* 11 A solitary jabiru .. stalking its prey, occasionally jumping ludicrously and jabbing at fish with its monstrous bill.

jacana. [Spec. use of *jacana* any bird of the fam. Jacanidae, having long claws enabling it to walk on floating aquatic plants.] LOTUS BIRD.

1921 S.A. WHITE *Bunya* 8 That strange bird, the jacana, was espied running over the waterlily leaves, being able to do this owing to its remarkably long toes. **1970** J.V. MARSHALL *Walk to Hills of Dreamtime* 38 A family of long-legged jacaras [*sic*] were walking single file across the billabong.

Jack, *n.*[1] Also **jack.** [Shortened form of LAUGHING JACKASS 1, assimilating with the proper name *Jack*.] A nickname for a kookaburra; JACKO *n.*[1]; JACKY *n.*[1]

1898 E.E. MORRIS *Austral Eng.* 216 The bird is generally called only a *Jackass*, and this is becoming contracted into the simple abbreviation of *Jack*. **1922** A.D. MICKLE *Wee Dog* 11 Never was a madder jollification than that of the 'jacks' in the great gums.

Jack, *n.*[2] [Cf. prec.] Abbrev. of JACKEROO *n.* 2.

1904 L.M.P. ARCHER *Bush Honeymoon* 211 Dad had two *Jacks*, who did the out-station work with the help of men about the place. **1967** G. JENKIN *Two Yrs. Bardunyah Station* 29 'How does that soliloquy of Macbeth's go in Act I Scene 7, Jack?' .. (Jack stood for Jackaroo).

Jack, *n.*[3] *Two-up.* [Of unknown origin.] A counterfeit penny having a head on both sides.

1936 'SWEENEY, EX-CROOK' *I Confess* 100 The 'double-headed' penny or 'Jack' as it is generally known. **1967** *Kings Cross Whisper* (Sydney) xxxv. 6/3 *Jack*, a double-headed penny in two-up.

Jack, *n.*[4] [Abbrev. of *Jack (McNab*, rhyming slang for 'scab'.] A member of the Permanent and Casual Waterside Workers' Union.

1947 J. MORRISON *Sailors belong Ships* 29 An air of strained expectancy pervades the great bleak shed. In the outer divisions—'Jacks', 'Seconds', 'Unattached', 'Blanks'—the bell is hardly heard over the babel of four thousand voices. **1982** LOWENSTEIN & HILLS *Under Hook* 88 The Permanent and Casual Waterside Workers' Union (popularly known as Jacks or scabs).

jack, *n.*[5] [Abbrev. of *jack in a box*, rhyming slang for 'pox'.] Venereal disease; an attack of venereal disease.

1954 T.A.G. HUNGERFORD *Sowers of Wind* 3 Penicillin'll take care of that! They reckon they just pump you full of it, and bingo! No more jack! **1960** J. IGGULDEN *Storms of Summer* 297 Some rotten poxy bitch of a chromo dobbed them in... They reckon she was rotten with the jack so they never paid her.

jack, *v.* [Spec. use of *jack up* to give up suddenly: see OED *v.*[1] 3 b.] *intr.* With **up:** to refuse to participate or co-operate; to show disapproval. Freq. with **on.**

1898 'R. BOLDREWOOD' *Romance of Canvas Town* 253 The half-used plates and dishes were to me as things loathsome... So, as a man, a gentleman, and a squatter, I 'jacked up' at the cookery. **1978** H.C. BAKER *I was Listening* 177 Now you're on the point of jacking up on me.

Hence **jacked up** *ppl. a.*, disenchanted, 'fed up'.

1981 D. STUART *I think I'll Live* 5 The local sheilahs .. they're jacked up to the eyebrows.

jack, *a.* [f. *jack up* to give up: see prec.] Disenchanted; tired of (a person, activity, etc.), 'fed up with'. Esp. in the phr. **to be jack of.**

1889 J.L. HUNT *Bk. of Bonanzas* 79 We've hed two ov them trips already, an' we'er getting Jack about the business. **1986** *Austral. Geographic* Apr. 68/1 'The missus might get jack of it and clear out for the city,' observed one miner, 'but most of them come back.'

jackaburra /'dʒækəbʌrə/. [Blend of LAUGHING JACKASS 1 + KOOKABURRA.] A kookaburra.

1917 *Bulletin* (Sydney) 22 Feb. 24/4 There is a flock of Jackaburras near my place. **1944** *Ibid.* 4 Oct. 15/4 The jackaburra has not varied the landing technique inherited from his laughing ancestors.

jackaroo, var. JACKEROO *n.* and *v.*

jackass.

1. Abbrev. of LAUGHING JACKASS. See also JACKO *n.*[1], JACKY *n.*[1]

1805 J. GRANT *Jrnl.* 17 May 76 Will send you where they flog Jack-asses. **1979** B. MARTYN *First Footers S. Gippsland* 138 Jackasses had awakened and were breakfasting at the roots of fallen trees.

2. *Tas.* Grey butcherbird, see GREY *a.*

1880 L.A. MEREDITH *Tasmanian Friends & Foes* 110 We, too, have a 'jackass', a smaller bird, and not in any way remarkable, except for its merry gabbling sort of song. **1931** *Bulletin* (Sydney) 6 May 21/3 The 'jackass' of Tassie is the grey butcher-bird.

3. *fig.* In the phr. **(from) jackass to jackass** and varr., (from) dawn to dusk.

1899 *Bulletin* (Sydney) 12 Aug. 14/4 'Cockies' hours' are supposed to be 'from jackass to jackass'. **1912** *Ibid.* 11 Jan. 44/4, 15 bob a week and tucker—jackass to jackass and Sundays off. **1930** *Ibid.* 29 Jan. 25/3 The kookaburra used to be known in N.S.W. as the settlers' clock, and the working day was from 'jackass to mopoke', which was generally interpreted as 'from dawn to dark'.

jackass-fish. The marine fish *Nemadactylus macropterus*, widely distributed in Austral. waters and having a distinctive elongated ray of the pectoral fin. See also MORWONG. Also **jackass morwong.**

1886 *Proc. Linnean Soc. N.S.W.* I. 880 *Chilodactylus macropterus* .. is known as the 'Jackass-fish'. **1983** *Canberra Chron.* 23 Nov. 19/1 Dave Gill .. fished out of Bermagui .. 15 jackass morwong.

jackeroo /dʒækə'ru/, *n.* Also **jackaroo.** [Orig. unkn.; there is no evidence for the statement made in quot. 1896.]

1. Orig. *Qld. Obs.* A white man living beyond the bounds of close settlement.

1845 *Bell's Life in Sydney* 4 Jan. 4/1 The Jackeroos all smoke their pipes and sit still. **1896** *Bulletin* (Sydney) 18 Apr. 27/3 The word 'jackeroo', a station new-chum, comes also from the old Brisbane blacks, who called the pied crow shrike (*Stripera* [sic] *graculina*) 'tchaceroo', a gabbling and garrulous bird. They called the German missionaries of 1838 'jackeroo', a gabbler, because they were always talking. Afterwards they applied it to all white men.

2. A young man (usu. English and of independent means) seeking to gain experience by working in a supernumerary capacity on a sheep or cattle station (see COLONIAL EXPERIENCE *n.* 1); a person working on a sheep or cattle station with a view to acquiring the practical experience and management skills desirable in a station owner or manager; COLONIAL EXPERIENCE *n.* 2.

1870 'JACKAROO' *Immigration Question* 5 A species of Pariah, or Anglo-Bedouin, or whatever category the Jackaroo proper may be presumed to come under, ought perhaps to be the last to offer any remarks upon a political question affecting a country in which he can have little interest... A philanthropic friend got me upon an inland station as a 'jackaroo', and a jackaroo I shall remain to the end. **1984** B. DIXON *Searching for Aboriginal Lang.* 123 We were in full swing when the jackeroo—white lad training to be a manager somewhere, someday—came and said we'd better break it up.

jackeroo /dʒækə'ru/, *v*. Also **jackaroo**. [f. prec.] *intr.* To work as a jackeroo. Freq. as *pres. pple.*

1875 *Austral. Town & Country Jrnl.* (Sydney) 28 Aug. 343/3 A year or two more Jackerooing would only mean the consumption of so many more figs of negrohead, in my case. **1981** *Bulletin* (Sydney) 29 Sept. 64/3 Alas there is no time what with horses and young Old Etonians learning to jackaroo.

Hence **jackerooing** *vbl. n.*

1900 T. MAJOR *Leaves from Squatter's Note Bk.* 22 A young friend.. was learning colonial experience—afterwards termed 'Jackarooing'.

jacket, *v. Obs.* [Transf. use of *jacket* to swindle, betray: see quot. 1812.] *trans.* To inform on (someone).

[**1812** J.H. VAUX *Mem.* 181 *Jacket,* to jacket a person .. is more properly applied to removing a man by underhand and vile means from any birth or situation he enjoys.] **1825** *Austral.* (Sydney) 10 Feb. 3 Maurice Welsh .. knew that Griffiths had a spite against the prisoners; heard Griffiths say frequently, he would *jacket* him. **1888** J.C.F. JOHNSON *Austral Christmas* 48 I'm blessed well sure it was him as blowed the gaff an' jacketted me to the 'cove' about them three bottles of grog I brought out from the township.

jackie, var. JACKY *n.*[1] and *n.*[4]

jack-jumper. [f. the name *Jack,* in names of animals sometimes signifying *small* (OED *sb.*[1] 37) + JUMPER *n.*[1]] JUMPER *n.*[1] Also *attrib.*

1921 *Bulletin* (Sydney) 7 Apr. 20/3 The publican directed my attention to some small, dark-green ants, known, I believe, as jack-jumpers. **1980** J. WOLFE *End of Pricklystick* 64 There's jack-jumper ants live in the flowers [*sc.* ragwort] .. and sometimes you get stung on the hand.

jack mackerel. [Transf. use of *jack* as used in the names of fish: see OED *jack, sb.*[1] 30.] Either of the fish *Trachurus novaezelandiae* (see YELLOWTAIL) and *T. declivis* (see COWANYOUNG).

1950 *Rep.* (Dept. Commerce & Agric., Fisheries Division) 7 At the conference of Commonwealth and State Fisheries Officers in 1947, steps were taken to introduce uniform names for certain species of fish common to more than one State. One of the new names was Scad, previously known as horse mackerel or cowanyoung. From the marketing point of view the name Scad was not satisfactory and in addition had to compete with a closely related species known as jack mackerel in the United States. To help the Australian pack compete with the American pack on the same markets, the Division after consultation with the canners, State Fisheries Departments, C.S.I.R.O. Fisheries Division and others, was instrumental in having the species renamed jack mackerel. **1980** *Ecos* xxiv. 28/2 Jack mackerel is not considered a good table fish in Australia.

Jacko, *n.*[1] [f. JACK *n.*[1] + -O.] A kookaburra.

1907 *Bulletin* (Sydney) 31 Oct. 15/3 The goburra has been called the 'settler's clock', but he should be altogether an unreliable one. Jacko is apt to go off at any time. **1955** N. PULLIAM *I traveled Lonely Land* 381 *Laughing jackass,* one nick-name for the kookaburra... Other names are: jacky, jacko [etc.].

Jacko, *n.*[2] *Hist.* [Joc. use of the proper name *Jack* + -O.] In the war of 1914–18: a nickname for a Turkish soldier; the Turkish army. Cf. ABDUL 1. Also as *adj.*

1916 'MEN OF ANZAC' *Anzac Bk.* 126 By jingo! how your bloomin' grit Must make old Jacko dance. **1918** *Kia Ora Coo-ee* Apr. 18/2 We spotted a Jacko, with a big bulge on his left side, sneaking away. **1949** G. BERRIE *Morale* 43 There's a Jacko general out there trying to tell them something, and they think he's talking French.

Jack Rice. [The name of a racehorse which ran successfully in hurdling and steeplechasing events between 1915 and 1919.] In the phr. **a roll** (**pile,** etc.) **Jack Rice couldn't jump over**: see quot. 1945.

1945 S.J. BAKER *Austral. Lang.* 107 A man well supplied with cash .. may even be fortunate enough to have *a roll Jack Rice couldn't jump over.* Jack Rice was a racehorse noted for his performances over hurdles. **1970** J. CLEARY *Helga's Web* 297 'I never seen twenty thousand in cash before. Somehow you'd think it'd amount to a pile Jack Rice couldn't jump over.' Helidon wondered who Jack Rice was; then remembered it was a famous hurdle horse with a prodigious leap.

Jack Shay. *Obs.* Also **Jack Shea,** without initial capital(s), and as one word. [Perh. f. *jack* black (leather) drinking vessel or container (see OED *sb.*[2] 2) + *O')Shea* Irish surname, as rhyming slang on /teɪ/, obs. and Irish pronunc. of *tea.*] A tin vessel holding a quart (cf. QUARTPOT 1) used for brewing tea and incorporating a smaller vessel for drinking. Also *attrib.*

1879 'AUSTRALIAN' *Adventures Qld.* 17 He .. never, by any chance, irritated her, unless he had previously swallowed at least five inches of strong rum out of a 'Jack Shea'. Not that that small quantity (a good quart) of alcohol affected his brain. **1926** M. FORREST *Hibiscus Heart* 133 A magpie, head on one side, perched on the jack shay. **1948** H.G. LAMOND *From Tariaro to Ross Roy* 42 That was just about the time the Jack Shea quart-and-pint was being introduced.

Jack Shepherd. *Obs.* Also **Jack Sheppard.** [Prob. quasi-proper name indicating familiarity or contempt: see OED *jack, sb.*[1] 35.] A rogue. Also *attrib.*

1841 *Morning Advertiser* (Hobart) 1 Oct. 2/1 This town has been invested with a new denomination of juvenile Jack Shepherds, commonly called *Bricks,* who to the reproach of the police and their parents, have been permitted to commit acts. **1846** *Britannia* (Hobart) 1 Oct. 4/3 The convict Comptroller-General must have felt it, no doubt, together with all the probation Jack Sheppard Nix my Dolly lockers-up, to be an abominable nuisance. **1847** *Ibid.* 8 Apr. 2/3 A certain Jack Sheppard audacity suited only to a convict police.

Jack the painter. *Obs.* A coarse green tea, so named because of its staining properties.

1852 G.C. MUNDY *Our Antipodes* I. 329 Another notorious ration tea of the bush is called 'Jack the painter'. This is a *very* green tea indeed, its viridity evidently produced by a discreet use of the copper drying pans in its manufacture.

1937 D. GLASS *Austral. Fantasy* 89 'Jack the Painter', which extra potent version was apt to leave its mark around the drinker's mouth.

jack up. [f. the vbl. phr. *to jack up*: see JACK *v.*] A dispute; a refusal to co-operate (esp. with an employer or superior).

1948 *Khaki Bush & Bigotry* (1968) 94 By gee, if I'm not on the next draft I'm telling you there's going to be the biggest jack-up you ever saw. **1983** *Canberra Times* 22 Apr. 2/7 Those miners who took arms against authority and staged the first Australian 'jack-up'.

Jacky: see *Jacky Winter* JACKY *n.*²

Jacky, *n.*¹ Also **jackie.** [f. JACK *n.*¹ + -Y.] A kookaburra.

1898 *Bulletin* (Sydney) 10 Sept. 14/4, I have four tame 'jackies' which roam about a large garden. **1931** *Bulletin* (Sydney) 20 May 21/4, I happened on only one kookaburra... This jackie had adopted a small flock of sheep as his companions. **1964** *N. Austral. Monthly* Sept. 12 A small brown snake.. with a jackass (kookaburra) in pursuit... Jacky juggled it around for a while until he got its head in his beak.

Jacky, *n.*² [Attrib. use of *Jacky*, dimin. form of *Jack*, in names of animals signifying *small*: see OED *sb.*¹ 37.] Special Comb. **Jacky lizard,** the small, grey, mainly arboreal dragon lizard *Amphibolurus muricatus* of e. Aust.; **Winter,** the small, predom. grey-brown and white flycatcher *Microeca leucophaea*, widespread in mainland Aust. and also found in n.e. New Guinea; *brown flycatcher*, see BROWN *a.* 1; PETER PETER; POST-BOY; also abbrev. as **Jacky.**

1967 H. COGGER *Austral. Reptiles* 38 The lining of the mouth is brightly coloured in some species. In.. the **Jacky Lizard** (*Amphibolurus muricatus*) it is bright yellow. **1889** *Proc. Linnean Soc. N.S.W.* IV. 407 *Micraeca fascinans*.. locally known as '**Jacky Winter**'. **1925** E. MCDONNELL *My Homeland* 68, I have often noticed Jacky in the Sydney Parks.

Jacky, *n.*³

1. Abbrev. of JACKY JACKY. Also *attrib.*

1890 *Adelaide Observer* 15 Feb. 15/3 We have very few friends as it is, but those we have will feel inclined to shun us after reading the Jackey correspondence. **1985** J. MILLER *Koori* 156 The popular Press of Australia makes a joke of us by presenting silly and out-of-date drawings and jokes of 'Jacky' or 'Binghi', which have educated city-dwellers and young Australians to look upon us as sub-human.

2. In the phr. **to sit up (settle in,** etc.) **like Jacky,** to sit up straight; to display an ingenuousness (supposedly characteristic of an Aboriginal).

1941 S.J. BAKER *Pop. Dict. Austral. Slang* 42 *Jacky, sit up like*, to behave, sit up straight. **1950** E.M. ENGLAND *Where Turtles Dance* 102 She's settled in like Jacky and might take some shifting now.

jacky, *n.*⁴ Also **jackie.** [f. JACK *n.*² + -Y.] JACKEROO *n.* 2.

1945 *Bulletin* (Sydney) 24 Oct. 12/1 The new jackie was an all-wool, double-weft know-all. **1957** *Ibid.* 24 July 16/2 It took an effort to break myself in to the idea of jilleroos replacing jackies on stations.

Jacky Howe. [f. the name of *John Robert Howe* (?1861–1920), a champion Queensland shearer of the 1890s.] A (navy or black) sleeveless singlet worn esp. by shearers, rural workers, etc. Also as *adj.* and **Jacky Howe'd.**

1930 *Bulletin* (Sydney) 9 Apr. 19/2 It took nine bars of soap to wash his 'Jacky Howe' flannel. **1949** R. PARK *Poor Man's Orange* 122 He had finished his tea and was sitting in his Jackie Howe, which is a singlet with the sleeves out of it, and called after a famous shearer of the blade days. **1954** *Bulletin* (Sydney) 24 Feb. 13/3 He was able to stride bow-yanged and 'Jackie Howe'd' to his place on the board.

Jacky Jacky.

a. A nickname for an Aboriginal; the typical Aboriginal.

1845 *Portland Gaz.* 1 July 3/2 Jacky Jacky suddenly turned round and slipped a large jagged spear in his wamera. **1960** *Realist* (Sydney) ii. 10 White men that call us all 'Jacky-Jacky' are no good white men.

b. COCONUT.

1974 C. BUCHANAN *We have bugger All*, Bullymen do not like Aboriginals to be strong and stand together fighting for land rights. But they do like Jacky Jackys.

Jacky Raw. Altered form of *Johnny Raw* (see JOHNNY 2).

1906 *Bulletin* (Sydney) 28 June 14/2 New chums were originally called Johnny Raws. From that it got to Jacky Raw. And from Jacky Raw to Jackeroo is but a slip of the tongue. **1962** D. MCLEAN *World turned upside Down* 79 What th' ell's th' matter with you today? Y' moonin' about like a jacky raw.

jaffle /'dʒæfəl/. [Transf. use of a proprietary name: see quot. 1965.] A sandwich, with a savoury or sweet filling, sealed and toasted (freq. over an open fire) in a jaffle-iron, a long-handled device consisting of two (usu.) saucer-shaped moulds, hinged and locking together.

1950 *Hardware Jrnl.* May 50 A 'Jaffle' is actually a sealed, toasted sandwich. **1965** *Austral. Official Jrnl. Patents* (Canberra) 1542 *Jaffle* A180,630. 28th May, 1963. Toasters. Hi-Craft Manufacturing Co. Pty. Ltd.

jail gang, var. GAOL GANG.

jakeloo, *a.* Also **jakealoo, jakerloo.** [Joc. formation on (orig. U.S.) *jake*: see quot. 1924.] All right, in good order; 'fine'.

1919 W.H. DOWNING *Digger Dialects* 29 Jake-aloo. **1924** A.W. BAZLEY et al. Gloss. Slang A.I.F. (typescript), 17 *Jakerloo* or *jake*, 'jake' was in use before the war, in Australia by drivers & others to indicate that the load and harness were secure and everything ready for a start. It was also used to indicate that all was well with the speaker. The addition of the last two syllables appear to have been made in the A.I.F. abroad; perhaps.. to [rhyme] with 'Bakerloo' the name of the underground railway that connected Waterloo station with Baker Street, both in London. **1927** F.C. BIGGERS *Bat-Eye* 10 These dancin' stunts was jakeloo—a bloke Jist prats 'is frame in, an' selects a girl.

jam, *n.*¹ Shortened form of RASPBERRY JAM. Also **jam-tree, jam-wood,** and *attrib.*

1837 *Perth Gaz.* 977 Jam-wood.. grows in such abundance over the mountain range. **1844** J. GOULD *Birds of Aust.* (1848) IV. Pl. 22, In Western Australia the nest.. is usually constructed in a dead jam-tree. **1855** R. AUSTIN *Jrnl. Interior W.A.* 15 Grassy land.. timbered with jam, sandal-wood, and tuart-trees. **1973** *Meanjin* 251 The jam scrub he disliked because it looked regimented, like so many open umbrellas standing in rows or ordered clumps.

jam, *n.*² Affectation; pretentious display; 'side'. Freq. in the phr. **to put on jam.** Also *attrib.*

1882 *Sydney Slang Dict.* 5 *Jam (Putting on)*, assuming fast airs of importance. **1884** *Austral. Tit-Bits* (Melbourne) 19 June 14/3 Jam is a drug in the English market. So it is here—if you go down Collins street in the afternoon you can get tons of it for nothing. **1936** F. CLUNE *Roaming round*

jamberoo /dʒæmbəˈruː/. [Altered form of U.S. *jamboree*, perh. infl. by the place-name in N.S.W.] A spree: see quot. 1909.

1889 J.L. HUNT *Bk. of Bonanzas* 83 Jones was on the 'Jamberoo' the other night, and .. he was zig-zagging along the pathway home. 1909 F.E. BIRTLES *Lonely Lands* 115 It was here I met a party of station hands out on what is termed locally a 'shivoo'. In other parts this function is called a jamberoo, a beano, a bender.

jammy, a. [f. JAM n.²] Affected.

1911 A. SEARCY *By Flood & Field* 291 A new chum fellow with notions of city decorum, and not a little 'jammy'. 1966 H. PORTER *Paper Chase* 67 The landlady's 18 year old daughter, a head-tosser with a jammy accent.

japanning, vbl. n. Obs. [Perh. with reference to the *japanned* or glossy black finish of a cash-box.] The act of stealing a cash-box.

1902 *Bulletin* (Sydney) 31 May 31/1 Pincher Wilson .. undergoing a sentence of two years for 'japanning', known to the initiated as cash-box or till-snatching, was a gambler. 1904 *Truth* (Sydney) 16 Oct. 7/1 Paddy Toole, serving two years' for 'japanning' (thieving a cash-box).

jarrah /ˈdʒærə/. [a. Nyungar *jarrily*.]

1. The (usu. tall) tree of s.w. W.A. *Eucalyptus marginata* (fam. Myrtaceae), valued for its hard, durable, reddish-brown wood; the wood itself; *native mahogany*, see NATIVE a. 6 a.; SWAN RIVER MAHOGANY. See also MAHOGANY 1. Also *attrib.*, esp. as **jarrah wood**.

1846 *Portland Guardian* 18 Sept. 3/3 As a ship-building timber the Jarrah is not only firm-grained, remarkably free from defect, and naturally durable, but seems to be proof against the salt-water worm which is so destructive even to well-seasoned English oak. 1915 N. DUNCAN *Austral. Byways* 39 A devil-may-care little locomotive, which ate jarrah-wood for breakfast.

2. Special Comb. **jarrah-jerker**, see quot. 1980; **Jarrahland**, the State of Western Australia.

1965 H. PORTER *Cats of Venice* 110 An unmistakable Australian—Joe Blow the Sandgroper; the **jarrah-jerker** doing his dough. 1980 E. & J. TRAUTMAN *Jinkers & Jarrah Jerkers* 1 The descriptive term 'jarrah-jerker' was one term coined to cover all men who 'worked the bush'. 1911 A.S. STEPHENS *Pearl & Octopus* 136 **Jarrahland** jingles.

Java sparrow. [f. the resemblance of the finch to the Java sparrow *Padda oryzivora*.] *Diamond firetail*, see DIAMOND n.¹

1855 R. AUSTIN *Jrnl. Interior W.A.* 49 We shot .. four small finches, resembling, but smaller than Java sparrows. 1978 D. STUART *Wedgetail View* 41 Empty waterbag, and the start of thirst but the Java sparrows had shown where the water was.

javelin fish. [See quot. 1965.] Any of several marine fish of n. Aust. of the genera *Pomadasys* and *Hapalogenys* (fam. Haemulidae), incl. *Pomadasys hasta*.

1896 F.G. AFLALO *Sketch Nat. Hist. Aust.* 225 Of perches, there are .. the Javelin-fish (*Pristi poma hasta*), Hussar (*Genyoroge amabilis*). 1965 *Austral. Encycl.* V. 123 Javelin-fish .. is regarded as a good food-fish. One of the spines of the anal fin is enlarged to form a stout spike, from which the fish takes its popular name.

jay. [Transf. use of *jay* a noisy bird with striking plumage.] Any of several birds, usu. having a loud call, including the *grey currawong* (see GREY a.), and CHOUGH. Also **jay bird**.

1836 J. BACKHOUSE *Narr. Visit Austral. Colonies* 438 Some of the birds of V.D. Land abound; such as the Piping Crow .. the Jay or Black Magpie, *Coronica fuliginosa*. 1981 A.B. FACEY *Fortunate Life* 90 The rosella .. was .. destructive on cereal crops and fruit, as was the jay bird.

jeerun, var. JERRAN.

jelly blubber. A jelly-fish.

1980 C. JAMES *Unreliable Mem.* 171 At Sans Souci baths I dive-bombed a jelly blubber for a dare. 1981 G. CROSS *George & Widda-Woman* 9 We could not swim there, because of the sharks and the jelly blubbers.

jelly leaf. [See quot. 1897.] *Paddy's lucerne*, see PADDY.

1888 *Proc. Linnean Soc. N.S.W.* III. 391 'Paddy Lucerne'... In some parts of this colony the plant bears the name of 'Jelly leaf'. 1897 L. LINDLEY-COWEN *W. Austral. Settler's Guide* 537 *Sida rhombifolia* (.. jelly leaf in Queensland. Synonym—*Sida retusa*) .. when old, hard and dry, but when young mucilaginous, which characteristic accounts for Queensland vernacular.

jemmy. Obs. [Altered form of EMIGRANT n. 1, by analogy with JIMMY 1.] An emigrant.

1850 W.B. BROWN *Narr. Voyage London to S.A.* 9 They call all government emigrants New Jemmies, and all passengers New Chums, both of which names are now used by the colonists to all new comers. 1897 H. HUSSEY *Colonial Life & Christian Experience* 61 The word 'emigrant' was considered too long for ordinary use, and, as a substitute, the term 'Jemmies' was usually applied: thus, 'There's another batch (or lot) of 'Jemmies'.'

Jemmy Low: see JIMMY LOW.

jerboa. Obs. [Transf. use of *jerboa* a small rodent of arid regions.] HOPPING MOUSE.

1845 J.H. BROWNE *Jrnl. Sturt Exped.* 11 Oct. in *S. Australiana* (1962) Mar. 51 The Jerboa is [a] beautiful little animal about as big [as] a large mouse but formed like a Kangaroo with a very long tail with a brush at the end. 1896 B. SPENCER *Rep. Horn Sci. Exped. Central Aust.* I. 75 In the jerboa burrows (*Hapalotis mitchelli*) there was never more than one adult.

jerran /ˈdʒɛrən/, a. Chiefly *Austral*. pidgin. Obs. Also **gerrund, gerun, jeerun, jerrund, jirrand**. [a. Dharuk *jirran*.] Afraid. Also as n., a coward.

[c 1790 W. DAWES *Grammatical Forms Lang. N.S.W.*, *Tyérun kamarigál*, the kamarigals are afraid.] 1798 D. COLLINS *Acct. Eng. Colony N.S.W.* I. 549 A man who would not stand to have a spear thrown at him, but ran away, was a coward, jee-run. 1827 P. CUNNINGHAM *Two Yrs. in N.S.W.* II. 38 'Come on, white fellow—black fellow no *jirrand*' (afraid). 1829 *Sydney Monitor* 12 Dec. 4/2 The Black .. endeavoured to turn the whole into a joke and called out, 'what for you so *gerrund* (frightened)?' 1839 T.L. MITCHELL *Three Exped. Eastern Aust.* (rev. ed.) I. 64 'What for you jerran budgerry whitefellow?' .. Meaning; why are you afraid of a good white man? 1841 'LADY LONG RESIDENT N.S.W.' *Mother's Offering to Children* 213 Too much *gerun* me: (meaning frightened). 1867 A.K. COLLINS *Waddy Mundoee* 12 I'm a bit jerrund to stay out at Crowther's with nobody but my mate. Them darkies are knockin' about, I know.

jerry, v. [f. U.S. slang *jerry*, a., in the phr. *to be jerry* to be 'wise' to: see OEDS a.²] *intr*. To understand; to realize. Also *trans*. and with **to**, and as n. in the phr. **to take a jerry to**.

1894 J.W. LONGFORD *Under Lock & Key* 12 The bearer of this stiff has been a good kobber of mine in stir, and as he jerrys to the lingo in this stiff, he will be able to explain everything. 1917 *Bulletin* (Sydney) 15 Feb. 22/3 An old Riverina squatter .. lost a thousand pounds' worth of rams before he jerried that musty ensilage was the murderer.

1924 *Ibid.* Feb. 6/1 ' 'Ave sense!' snorted Jimmy. 'Don't yer jerry w'y I reneged?' **1938** X. HERBERT *Capricornia* 232 'Use y' bit o' brains,' he says, 'an take a jerry to y'self.'

jerryang /ˈdʒɛriæŋ/. [a. Dharuk *jirraŋ*.] Little lorikeet, see LITTLE 2.
1843 J. GOULD *Birds of Aust.* (1848) V. Pl. 54, *Trichoglossus pusillus* . . Jerryang, Aborigines of New South Wales. **1925** *Bulletin* (Sydney) 23 Apr. 23/2 The blacks usually named a bird from its call. . . Jerryang (green lorikeet), gang-gang (cockatoo) . . are a few of the survivals.

Jerusalem screw. [f. *screw* a prison warder.] See quot. 1978.
1972 J. MCNEIL *Old Familiar Juice* (1973) 82 Our favourite provo, a bastard named Hunter, a bloody Jerusalem screw if there ever was one. **1978** E. HARDING *A. Marshall Talking* 57 The most brutal warders were always called Jerusalem Screws—and this was from the first war where the British in Palestine trained some Australians in the way to break really tough prisoners; the name had stuck.

jew. Abbrev. of JEWFISH.
1902 *Bulletin* (Sydney) 7 June 16/2 Have frequently caught 'jews' by throwing a jag-hook on to the nest. **1978** K. GARVEY *Tales of my Uncle Harry* 19 Little jews are tastier than all the big cod and yellow-belly.

jewel beetle. Any of many brightly-coloured beetles of the fam. Buprestidae. Also *attrib.*
1933 H.J. CARTER *Gulliver in Bush* 18 Here with delight came the capture of our first jewel-beetles. [*Note*] *Stigmodera grandis, S. goryi, S. affinis.* **1970** P. SLATER *Eagle for Pidgin* 1 Jewel beetle grubs bored into trees and wrecked them for timber companies.

jeweller's shop. *Mining.* A rich deposit of gold (or opal).
1853 *Guardian* (Hobart) 3 Dec. 3/2 The greatest activity is now displayed in opening new spots, not only in the vicinity of the 'jeweller's shops', but also, higher up the Buninyong Gully. **1960** D. MCLEAN *Roaring Days* 62 When you strike what you call the 'steel band' of hard sandstone you know you're on the last layer before the opal dirt. A jeweller's shop might be under your feet.

jewfish. Also **dewfish, dhufish.** [Transf. use of *jewfish* any of various fish, chiefly of the fam. Serranidae.] Any of several large, edible, marine fish, esp. *Glaucosoma hebraicum*, found only in the coastal waters of W.A., *Johnius diacanthus*, and MULLOWAY; any of several eel-tail catfishes; JEW; JEWIE.
1803 J. GRANT *Narr. Voyage N.S.W.* 159 We caught . . a species of jew fish. **1877** *Proc. Linnean Soc. N.S.W.* II. 233, I was astonished to find that a *Sciaena* was amongst the most common fishes of Moreton Bay. . . It is called *Dew-fish*, on account of its beautiful silvery grey colour. . . At Sydney this fish is common, and . . it is generally called *Jew-fish*. **1977** J. O'GRADY *There was Kid* 52 Sandgropers are not like us 'from the East'. . . They spell jewfish 'dhufish'.

jewie. Also **jewy.** [f. JEW(FISH + -Y.] JEWFISH.
1917 C. THACKERAY *Goliath Joe* 25 But about ther jewy. Yes! We got some more fish I needn't bother about. **1984** *N.T. News* (Darwin) 16 Nov. 30/4, I was filleting the jewie on the side of the boat.

jew lizard. Formerly also **dew lizard.** [Fig. use of *Jew*, in allusion to the lizard's bearded appearance.]
1. BEARDED DRAGON.
1845 C. HODGKINSON *Aust., Port Macquarie to Moreton Bay* 43 My black companions . . killed an opossum and a large dew-lizard. **1849** *Tasmanian Jrnl. Nat. Sci.* III. 105 Chlamydophorus (the Jew-lizard of the Hunter). **1978** K. GARVEY *Tales of my Uncle Harry* 84 You don't see many Jew lizards about the bush these days.
2. *fig.* Also *attrib.*
1895 *Worker* (Sydney) 14 Sept. 4/2 A jewlizzard-looking angel is the manager. **1930** 'BRENT OF BIN BIN' *Ten Creeks Run* (1952) 91 You don't mean to say the ould jew lizard is quoite as mean as that!

jewy, var. JEWIE.

jhitu, var. GHITTOE.

jibbong, var. GEEBUNG.

jidu, var. GHITTOE.

jig, *v. trans.* To play truant from (school).
1977 J. RAMSAY *Cop it Sweet* 50 Jig, run away, play truant. **1983** *Sydney Morning Herald* 26 July 1/3 'I used to jig school almost every day because I just hated the place, and did not like the teachers very much either,' Sarah said.

jigger, $n.^1$ [Spec. use of *jigger* any of numerous contrivances: see OED(S $sb.^1$ 5.]
1. In prison speech: an improvised radio receiver.
1953 K. TENNANT *Joyful Condemned* 293 He was offered . . a wireless concealed in the false bottom of a treacle tin, a beautiful job, the coil wire being part of an old scrubbing-brush, and most of the rest stolen from the fuse-box outside the cell. A complete jigger such as this was worth at least five pounds money, or forty-eight ounces of tobacco. **1967** B.K. BURTON *Teach them no More* 155 We could make jiggers right under the noses of the screws.
2. A device for administering an electric shock, usu. illegally during a horse race.
1958 *Bulletin* (Sydney) 7 Oct. 13/1 The stewards put me in the sweat-box, fanned me and me gear to see if I've got a 'jigger', and after a long inquiry paid out. **1982** J. ANDERSEN *Winners can Laugh* 99 Hand held devices were designed just to make a sound similar to that made by the painful jigger used only in track gallops. When the horse heard the sound during a race it anticipated a coming shock and accelerated in order to avoid it.
3. See quot. 1981. Also **jigger root**.
1954 *Bulletin* (Sydney) 29 Sept. 12/2 Why . . should dry, fibrous roots that could be smoked with no injury but much pretence of pleasure be universally known as 'jigger'? **1981** L. MCLEAN *Pumpkin Pie* 99 One of them produced a box of matches, broke off a piece of root from an old apple tree gum, and set alight to it. These roots have holes running through them. . . You would draw the smoke through just like a cigarette. This was called smoking 'Jigger Root'.

jigger, $n.^2$ [f. JIG.] A truant.
1983 *Sydney Morning Herald* 26 July 1/3 Sarah was sent to Ormond where she and the 39 other school children there have one thing in common: they are chronic 'jiggers', or truants.

jilgie, var. GILGIE.

jill. Abbrev. of JILLEROO.
1974 J. DINGWELL *Cattleman* 87 Noel came in with a pacific: 'She's a first-class jill on a station.'

jilleroo. /dʒɪləˈru/. Also **jillaroo.** [Joc. formation on JACKEROO *n.* 2.] A female station-hand. Also as *v. intr.*, to work as a jilleroo.
1943 S.J. BAKER *Pop. Dict. Austral. Slang* (ed. 3) 42 *Jillaroo*, a land girl (War slang). **1973** H. LEWIS *Crow on Barbed Wire Fence* 214 Our eldest daughter at twenty-two went alone to Australia to check up on some of my tales and worked as a jilleroo on an up-country sheep station in South Australia.

1984 *Age* (Melbourne) 2 June 2/6 She reckoned she learnt it while jillarooing in the outback.

jim. *Obs.* Also as *pl.* [Abbrev. of *Jimmy O'Goblin*, rhyming slang for 'sovereign'.] The sum of one pound; a sovereign.

1889 *Bulletin* (Sydney) 6 July 5/4 Won fifty 'jim' it all got 'blown', In 'arf a week I spent it. **1921** W.H. PHIPPS *Bush Yarns* 80 Dropped half-a-sovereign in the plate. . . I thort th' good old priest wud drop dead. . . He first picked up that half er jim as ef it were dirt.

Jim Gerald. Rhyming slang for 'Herald', applied to newspapers bearing that name.

1956 *Overland* vi. 17, I see there's a bloke who claims to be thirty-third cousin of the Tsar, and says he's an authority on Russia, writing his memoirs for the Jim Gerald. **1974** *Bulletin* (Sydney) 2 Nov. 57/2 Melbourne's evening newspaper was, and sometimes still is, called the Jim Gerald (Herald) which would simply confuse the Cockneys.

Jimmy.

1. *Obs.* Abbrev. of JIMMYGRANT.

[N.Z. **1850** D. McLEAN *Papers* VIII. 177 The 'Jimmies' usurpers of the soil.] **1859** H. KINGSLEY *Recoll. Geoffry Hamlyn* II. 154 'Why, one,' said Lee, 'is a young Jimmy (I beg your pardon, sir, an emigrant).' **1918** *Truth* (Sydney) 22 June 7/7 *Weedy Jimmygrants.* The class of English chawbacon at present being imported into the Commonwealth to 'go on the land' belong to the 'weedy order'. . . Certainly many of the Jimmies look a bit on the 'weedy' side, but appearances are sometimes deceptive.

Also **jimmygration** *n.* [f. IMMIGRATION].

1908 *Truth* (Sydney) 27 Dec. 1/4 One of those Jimmygration Leagues wants to get the reservists from India out here.

2. *pl.* Abbrev. of JIMMY BRITTS.

1945 *Certo Insana: 5th Austral. Division Signals* 3 All the staff have got the Jimmys. **1955** D. NILAND *Shiralee* 50 Men was growlin' crook tucker, gettin' the jimmies, an' all that, they said.

Jimmy Britts, *pl.* Also **Jimmy Brits.** [f. the name of Jimmy Britt (1879–1940), an American-born boxer.] With **the**: rhyming slang for 'shits'. Cf. EDGAR BRITT. Also *fig.*

1954 J. CLEARY *Climate of Courage* 292 Malaria and the jimmy britz have sucked him dry. **1959** D. NILAND *Gold in Streets* 169 Strike a light Danno, you gimme the jimmy britts at times. **1960** J. WYNNUM *Sailor Blushed* (1962) 10 'You gimme the Jimmy Brits,' grunted Lofty, darting a left fist into Tony's eye.

jimmygrant. Also **Jimmy Grant.** Rhyming slang for IMMIGRANT 1.

[N.Z. **1845** E.J. WAKEFIELD *Adventure in N.Z.* I. 337 The profound contempt which the whaler expresses for the 'lubber of a *jimmy-grant*', as he calls the emigrant.] **1859** J.D. MEREWEATHER *Diary Working Clergyman* 4 Speaking contemptuously of some newly-arrived immigrants ('Jimmy Grants', I think, was the slang term she applied to them). **1887** W.H. SUTTOR *Austral. Stories Retold* 144 Looked upon the 'Jimmygrants' (with an expletive)—as newcomers were called—as intruders, and to be treated with hatred and contempt.

Jimmy Low. *Qld. Obs.* [See quot. 1904.] The tree *Eucalyptus resinifera*, also known as *red mahogany* (see RED *a.* 1 a.). Also **Jemmy Low.**

1882 *Austral. Handbk.* 391 'Jemmy Low'. . is a very large tree, and much in demand for fencing. **1904** J.H. MAIDEN *Forest Flora N.S.W.* I. 67 In Queensland it [*sc. Eucalyptus resinifera*] is often called 'Jimmy Low', after the late Mr James Low, of Maroochie River, a locality for some of the finest specimens in that State.

Jimmy Woodser. [f. *Jimmy Wood*, the name of a character in the poem of that name (see quot. 1892, 1) by Barcroft Boake, and perh. the name of an actual person.] One who drinks alone in a public bar; a drink taken on one's own. Also **Jimmy Wood,** and as *v. intr.*

1892 B.H. BOAKE in *Bulletin* (Sydney) 7 May 17/3 Who drinks alone, drinks toast to Jimmy Wood, sir. [*Note*] A man who drinks by himself is said to take a 'Jimmy Woodser'. *Ibid.* 2 July 7/3 Dear Bulletin—A 'Jimmy Woodser' may mean a solitary drink (or a solitary drinker) in some places. . but in the Western district of Victoria, if a man takes a drink by himself, he is said to 'go Ballarat'. **1967** *Kings Cross Whisper* (Sydney) xxxv. 6/3 *Jimmy Woodser,* to drink by oneself.

jim-rags, *pl. Obs.* [Var. of Br. dial. *jamrags* rags, tatters, shreds: see EDD.] Small pieces, 'smithereens'. Esp. in the phr. **to kick** (one) **to jim-rags** and varr.

1894 H. LAWSON *Short Stories* 65 If yer starts playin' any of yer jumpt-up pranktical jokes on me. . I'll kick yer to jim-rags, so I will! **1899** *Austral. Mag.* (Sydney) Apr. 77 Me and you ain't goin' to fight, Andy. . . If you try it on I'll knock you into jim-rags!

jims, *pl. Obs.* Abbrev. of 'jim-jams' delirium tremens.

1894 G.H. GIBSON *Ironbark Chips* 55 Cure him of D.T.s and 'jims'. **1906** E. DYSON *In Roaring Fifties* 168 Only a touch o' the jims.

jin, var. GIN.

Jindyworobak /dʒɪndi'wɒrəbæk/. [Wuywurung.] A member of a literary group formed in 1938 by the poet R.C. Ingamells (1913–1955), to promote Australianism in art and literature. Also *attrib.*

1938 R. INGAMELLS *Conditional Culture* 4 'Jindyworobak' is an aboriginal word meaning 'to annex, to join', and I propose to coin it for a particular use. The jindyworobaks, I say, are those individuals who are endeavouring to free Australian Art from whatever alien influences trammel it, that is, to bring it into proper contact with its material. **1979** B. ELLIOT (*title*) The Jindyworobaks.

Jinga, var. JINGY.

jingera /'dʒɪndərə/. [The name of a town in s. N.S.W.] Remote and mountainous bush-covered country. Also *attrib.*

1870 *Illustr. Sydney News* 13 Apr. 379/3 Here and there set among the thickly wooded ridges. . pieces of pasture land of small extent upon which the 'Jingera squatter' or 'gully-raker' locates himself. . . The real occupation of the Jingera squatter is to 'spot' the cattle-drove wandering about outlying stations, or straying among the gullies, to 'tail off' the cows heavy with calf, and run them home to lonely mountain gulches, where feed is plentiful. **1977** G.C. JOYNER *Hairy Man of S. Eastern Aust.* 20 It was supposed to be in the Tinderry mountains, and what is known as the 'jingera' behind—the wild, rough country.

Jingie, var. JINGY.

jingle.

1. *Hist.* A covered two-wheeled carriage.

1862 C. ASPINALL *Three Yrs. Melbourne* 122 Gentlemen who have lived in India will persist in calling this vehicle a jingle. . . It is a kind of dos-a-dos conveyance, holding three in front, and three behind, it has a waterproof top to it . . and oilskin curtains to draw all round. **1981** A.S. VEITCH

Roses & Boronia 51 There was a line of cabs waiting, what the townsmen called 'jingles'.

 2. Money in small coins, change.

 1906 E. Dyson *Fact'ry 'Ands* 99 Ther Elder dug in 'n' brought up er 'andful iv jingle. **1958** *Bulletin* (Sydney) 11 June 19/1 If he is a youngish man, his pockets are lined with coin, oof, dough, sugar or hay. If he is getting on in years his pockets will hold jingle.

jingling johnny.

 1. *Sheep-shearing.* **a.** One who uses hand shears. **b.** *pl.* A set of hand shears.

 1941 S.J. Baker *Pop. Dict. Austral. Slang* 39 *Jingling johnnies,* hand shears. **1965** J.S. Gunn *Terminol. Shearing Industry* i. 33 *Jingling Johnny,* originally a swagman or bagman but in many districts this was also another name for a hand-shearer.

 2. Lagerphone.

 1963 *Gumsuckers' Gaz.* (Melbourne) Aug. 10 Interesting to those who play the lager-phone, or jingling johnnie, is the information that hand shears were also called *jingling johnnies.*

Jingy /'dʒɪndʒi/. W.A. Obs. Also Chingah, Chingi, Jinga, Jingie. [a. Nyungar *janga*.] A devil or evil spirit. Also *attrib.*

 1837 G.F. Moore *Evidences Inland Sea* 48 One .. was considered by our guide to be the peculiar residence of a 'Chingah', (a spirit) which he described as having large head and horns. **1847** E.W. Landor *Bushman* 208 They have some indistinct ideas about Chingi, the Evil Spirit. **1851** Mrs R. Lee *Adventures in Aust.* 243 Everybody believed in an evil spirit, which haunts dark caverns, wells, and gloomy plains; that its name is Jinga, and that they are afraid of him at night. **1872** Mrs E. Millett *Austral. Parsonage* 58, I heard a native speak of them as 'Jingy birds', that is, Satan's birds, Jingy being the name of the evil spirit. **1901** M. Vivienne *Travels in W.A.* 337 They greatly fear an evil spirit, Jingie.

jinker, *n.* [Var. of Scot. dial. *janker* long pole on wheels used esp. for carrying logs.]

 1. A wheeled conveyance used for moving heavy logs, etc.: see quot. 1889. Also **timber jinker,** and *attrib.*

 1889 A. Brassey *Last Voyage India & Aust.* 238 We followed a double team of sixteen horses drawing a timber-cart composed of one long thick pole between two enormous wheels some seven or eight feet in diameter. Above these wheels a very strong iron arch is fastened, provided with heavy chains, by means of which and with the aid of an iron crowbar used as a lever, almost any weight of timber can be raised from the ground. The apparatus is called a 'jinka'. **1935** Davison & Nicholls *Blue Coast Caravan* 54 Earth was ploughed deep by the wheels of the timber jinkers. **1980** M. Williams *Dingo!,* Watch the crouching jinker driver bring his haul across the bridge.

 2. A light, two-wheeled, horse-drawn cart. Also *attrib.*

 1916 *Bulletin* (Sydney) 28 Dec. 24/3 A small boy was sitting in a jinker drawn up at the roadside. **1976** C.D. Mills *Hobble Chains & Greenhide* 140 Clarabelle .. jogged a jinker load of mates with you on exciting bird-nesting forays.

jinker, *v.* [f. prec.] *trans.* To convey (a log, etc.) using a jinker.

 1903 R. Bedford *True Eyes & Whirlwind* 240 Waiting for a fine day to jinker those trees out of the bush. **1938** F. Clune *Free & Easy Land* 267 Walnut logs jinkered down the hills.

jinna-jinna, var. Gina-gina.

jirrand, var. Jerran.

jitto, var. Ghittoe.

jockey.

 1. *pl.* Horizontal wooden poles used to hold a bark roof in place: see quot. 1905.

 1905 *Bulletin* (Sydney) 2 Mar. 17/1 The logs which 'anchor' the roof—known as 'riders' and 'jockeys'. The first-named are perpendicular, in pairs; and the ends overlapping the ridge are loosely held together with wooden pins, to allow their spread to conform to the roof-angle and lie close to the bark when the weight of the jockey comes on their loose ends—those nearest the eaves. The jockeys are laid horizontally across these lower ends, and are held in position by wooden pegs driven into the underlying rider. **1911** E.S. Sorenson *Life in Austral. Backblocks* 26 It was roofed with stringybark, the latter being hung with greenhide and held down with poles ('riders' and 'jockeys') pegged together.

 2. One who acts as an assistant to a carrier, taxi-driver, etc. Also as *v. intr.*

 1910 Stephens & O'Brien *Materials Austrazealand Slang Dict.* 26 *Brewer's jockey,* (Melbourne) a man who rides about with the driver of a brewer's waggon helping him load and unload on the chance of a share of the drinks which fall to the lot of a brewer's man. **1945** S.J. Baker *Austral. Lang.* 140 A jockey is a taxi-driver's accomplice who pretends to be a passenger in order to encourage legitimate travellers to pay extortionate fares to secure the taxi. **1973** J. Powers *Last of Knucklemen* (1974) 58 One of the cattle stations used a helicopter for spottin' stray cattle. I jockeyed for the pilot.

jockey spider. [From the resemblance of the striking colours of the female to those of a jockey's blouse.] Red-back. Also *ellipt.* as **jockey.**

 1922 *Bulletin* (Sydney) 16 Mar. 20/4 The red-back or jockey spider (*Latrodectus hasselti*) is being discussed by the country medicoes of N.S.W. **1942** C. Barrett *On Wallaby* 30 An infant bitten by a 'jockey', to give the little horror one of its nicknames, died six hours later.

Joe, *n. Hist.* [Prob. from the name of Charles *Joseph* La Trobe (1801–1875), Lieutenant-Governor of Victoria, but see quot. 1859.]

 1. A policeman, trooper, etc., esp. one charged with the implementation of licensing regulations of the Victorian goldfields; a cry warning of the approach of such a person.

 1854 *Illustr. Sydney News* 28 Oct. 234/3 Some of the police .. were now ordered to fall back on the hotel for its protection if necessary. The Joe!, Joe! soon began and some boys threw stones at the windows. **1859** W. Kelly *Life in Vic.* I. 191 Joe is a term of opprobrium hurled after the police ever since the diggings commenced, but the derivation is still a mystery. Some commentators trace it to the Christian name of Mr Latrobe; but this is an error; the ex-governor was never personally unpopular, except with the editor of the *Argus.* **1868** *Wallaroo Times* (Kadina) 4 Nov. 3/4 The stupid and formerly incessant cry of 'Joe' is seldom heard.

 2. *transf.* A term of derision or abuse, esp. as applied to one whose appearance, dress, etc., is not that of a miner.

 1857 *Illustr. Jrnl. Australasia* III. 65 'Did you go down dressed as you are now?' 'I did.' .. 'Then I'll be bound .. that you are annoyed because they called 'Joe' after you.' **1921** *Bulletin* (Sydney) 17 Nov. 20/2 My dad who 'followed the diggings' tells me that to call a man 'Joe' on the Vic. rushes was the surest way of buying a fight.

joe, *v. Hist.* [f. prec.] *trans.* To taunt (a person) by calling out 'Joe'; to jeer. Also *absol.* and as *vbl. n.*

 1854 R. Carboni *Eureka Stockade* 26 Aug. (1855) 16 A mob soon collected round the hole; we were respectful, and there was no 'joeing'. **1855** *Ibid.* 103 The Ballaarat diggers.. considered themselves luckily cunning to have got off safe, and therefore could afford to 'joe' again. **1955** H. ANDERSON *Colonial Ballads* 47 If they were out for licences we'd stand and joe the traps.

Joe Blake.
1. Rhyming slang for 'snake'.
1905 J. MEREDITH *Learn to talk Old Jack Lang* (1984) 12, I saw a lot of *Joe Blakes*, but don't know if they were dinkum or just the after effects of the grog. **1981** P. BARTON *Bastards I have Known* 21 I'd never heard of anyone actually being bitten by a 'joe blake' in the hills.

2. *pl.* Rhyming slang for 'the shakes'; delirium tremens.
[N.Z. **1942** *2nd N.Z. Exped. Force Times* (Johnny Enzed) 41/6 The Joe Blakes.] **1944** A. MARSHALL *These are my People* 155 You feel nothin' when you're on a bender... You get the Joe Blakes bad after a few weeks. **1971** W.G. HOWCROFT *This Side Rabbit Proof Fence* 85 As Phil arrived, a shooter suffering from a bad attack of the morning after 'Joe Blakes' was trying to take aim.

joes, *pl.* [Of unknown origin.] An attack of revulsion or depression.
1910 L. ESSON *Three Short Plays* (1911) 8 Yer giv 'er man ther joes. **1947** M. RAYMOND *Smiley gets Gun* 207 'You look as if you've got the joes reel bad,' she commented. Smiley blurted out the whole story. 'Oh, well don't drop yore bundle,' advised his mother cheerfully.

joey, *n.*[1] [Of unknown origin.]
1. A young possum. Also **joey possum.**
1828 *Trumpeter* (Hobart) 3 Oct. 3 A young opossum (perhaps two or three days old) was put to a cat which had two kittens... It is really amusing to see the kittens crawling about with Joey clinging to one of their backs. **1928** W. ROBERTSON *Coo-ee Talks* 19 Give her wattle blossom, and a joey 'possum, She's a good Australian piccaninny.

2. A young kangaroo or wallaby. Also **joey kangaroo.**
1839 W.H. LEIGH *Reconnoitering Voyages* 94 The wallaba.. are of the kangaroo species... The young of this animal is called by the islanders a joè. **1862** G.T. LLOYD *Thirty-Three Yrs. Tas. & Vic.* 73 The little shapeless pimple.. is in reality no other than the Joey kangaroo in its truly wonderful and peculiar embryo state.

3. **a.** Any young creature.
1874 R.W. MAYNE *Two Visions* 39 And parrots numerous, trainable to talk—the best for this, the Parrot-Cockatoo, familiarly called 'Joey' from his cry. **1913** C.G. LANE *Creature-Life* 36 It is strange that the term 'joey' is usually applied by bush-folk to any young creature, whether beast or bird, common to Australia; a young opossum, parrot, 'native bears', cockatoo—all may be called 'joey'. The juvenile kangaroo also rejoices in the same title.

b. A baby or young child.
1887 *All Yr. Round* (London) 30 July 67 'Joey' is a familiar name for anything young and small, and is applied indifferently to a puppy, or a kitten, or a child. **1959** D. NILAND *Gold in Streets* 46 Got the wife down with another joey.

c. In the phr. **to get a joey in the pouch,** to become pregnant; also **with a joey in the pouch,** pregnant.
1957 D. NILAND *Call me when Cross turns Over* 227 Dorry's boy-friend had blown through. She's in a spot. Nobody wants to take her on with a joey in the pouch. **1968** W. GILL *Petermann Journey* 14 An' you can stuff that bloody muck I bought off you. Ma's got another joey in th' pouch, that's how good it is.

joey, *n.*[2] [f. JOE *n.* 1 + -Y.]
1. JOE *n.* 1.
1869 'E. HOWE' *Boy in Bush* 219 Policemen lounged about, striving to look unconscious of the 'Joey!' which the miners found time to shout after them in scorn. **1976** B. SCOTT *Complete Bk. Austral. Folk Lore* 64 If you do join the Joeys, I hope you'll be shot. I'd shoot the hull blessed lot of 'em if I had my way.

2. *Obs.* A recent arrival on a goldfield; an inexperienced miner. See JOE *n.* 2.
1864 E. WARDLEY *Confessions Wavering Worthy* 171 As we threaded our way, with peering and new-chummish curiosity, through the mammon-worried labyrinth.. we were hailed as Joeys, and asked if we wanted a feather-bed, or a 'sophy'. **1895** *Worker* (Sydney) 9 Feb. 3/2 He had had but three weeks' experience of colonial life. In digging parlance he was a 'joey'.

joey, *n.*[3] Shortened form of WOOD-AND-WATER JOEY.
1949 *Bulletin* (Sydney) 14 Dec. 42/4 The old Joey seemed to think that now Marks might just as well go and cut his throat.

John.
1. [Abbrev. of *johndarm*, a. F. *gendarme*; used elsewhere but recorded earliest in Aust.: see OED(S *John* 1 c.] A police officer.
1898 *Worker* (Sydney) 8 Jan. 8/2 There was not a sign when the 'Johns', as the police are called in that neighbourhood, passed along. **1982** R. HALL *Just Relations* 144 He took possession of the book... The johns'll get it if we leave it here.

2. In Special Comb. with a second element forming a quasi-name: **John Bull,** rhyming slang for 'full', intoxicated; **Dunn** *obs.,* **(a)** rhyming slang for 'one' (pound, etc.); **(b)** [perh. infl. by *johndarm*, see JOHN 1] a police officer; **Hop** [prob. formed on JOHN 1] rhyming slang for 'cop', a police officer.
1967 *Kings Cross Whisper* (Sydney) xxxv. 6/3 **John Bull,** full, inebriated. **1895** *Western Champion* (Barcaldine) 31 Dec. 9/5 A profitable profession it seemed, too, judging from the cool way they talked of '**John Dunns**' (£1), 'thick 'uns' (sovs.), 'canarys' (half-sovs.), 'finn' (£5), &c. **1908** *Truth* (Sydney) 25 Oct. 1/4 Wowsers who are interesting themselves in trying to get policemen Sunday off, assume that the John Dunns want to go to church to put a thrum in the plate. [N.Z. **1905** *N.Z. Truth* (Wellington) 12 Aug. 4 An incident occurred which.. robbed **John Hop** of his glory.] *c* **1907** C.W. CHANDLER *Darkest Adelaide* 7 Mr Bludger told me that the Adelaide demons had a quick and ready eye for strange faces. So to prevent any prying inquisitiveness on the part of the John Hops we decided to meet in Whitemore-square.

Johnny.
1. **a.** Abbrev. of JOHNNY-CAKE *n.* Also **johnny on the coals.**
1893 *Western Champion* (Barcaldine) 7 Nov. 12/1 Now I'm mixing up a 'Johnny' on a Barcoo billybong. **1895** *Worker* (Sydney) 14 Dec. 4/1 My tucker-bags were full of dainties, such as cake—And nothing like the johnnies on the coals that shearers make.

b. *Obs.* [Shortened form of *John Chinaman.*] A Chinese immigrant; a generic name for the Chinese.
1886 D.M. GANE *N.S.W. & Vic.* 69 A spare and weazen-looking Johnny was standing by, ready to recharge the pipes, when called upon, with a fresh supply of the inspissated juice of the white poppy. **1891** H. NISBET *Colonial Tramp* I. 101 'Johnny' in Victoria is a model of cleanliness and industry, and as the times go, honest also.

c. *Obs.* Abbrev. of *Johnny Raw* (see sense 2).
1895 A.B. PATERSON *Man from Snowy River* 10 But maybe you're only a Johnnie And don't know a horse from a hoe? **1946** G.E.L. WATSON *But to what Purpose* 98, I was still conspicuous of being such a mere 'Johnnie', as Englishmen were then called.

d. *Obs.* Abbrev. of *Johnny Government* (see sense 2).

1900 *Bulletin* (Sydney) 6 Jan. 15/1 The disheartened villager says 'It's all for Johnny'—meaning a benevolent Govt., to whom they owe over £80,000.

Hence **Johnniedom** n., England.

1904 M. WHITE *Shanty Entertainment* 26 Fancy Fred was English and A 'Simon Pure' of Johnniedom. **1906** *Truth* (Sydney) 28 Oct. 5/6 He had a very haw-haw voice and the high-pitched intonation peculiar to well-to-do Johnniedom.

2. In Comb. with a second element, freq. forming a quasi-name: **Johnny all sorts** *obs.*, a dealer in (secondhand) goods; such a shop; **Government** *obs.*, an agency responsible for the administration of public affairs; such agencies collectively; **jumper,** MUDSKIPPER: **Raw** [spec. use of *Johnny Raw* novice], a newly-arrived immigrant; **Russell** *obs.*, rhyming slang for 'bustle', esp. in the phr. **on the Johnny Russell** (see quot. 1897); **Turk,** a Turkish soldier; the Turkish army; **Warder** *obs.*, a vagrant, esp. one habitually intoxicated (see quot. 1880); **Woodser,** JIMMY WOODSER.

1887 S. ELLIOTT *Fifty Yrs. Colonial Life* 49, I .. displayed my goods in the open air. They consisted of tents, cradles, blankets, shovels, hobbles, tin dishes; in fact, I kept one of those popular shops, a '**Johnny all sorts**'. **1901** *Tocsin* (Melbourne) 19 Sept. 7/3 Usually, he would succeed somewhere in obtaining a gift, which he would forthwith sell to a Johnny-All-Sorts. **1914** *Truth* (Sydney) 1 Mar. 2/5 The ways of '**Johnny Government**' are really very funny at times. **1937** E. HILL *Water into Gold* 156 'Johnny Government' was an enemy, to be side-tracked and duped. **1915** *Bulletin* (Sydney) 24 June 26/1 That little lung-breathing fish called the **Johnnie-jumper,** or mud-skipper .. can climb a vertical mangrove tree with ease. **1840** *Temperance Advocate* (Sydney) 11 Nov. 4/2 Why man you are a regular **Johnny-raw** to be in Sydney two months, and not know how to do business yet. **1897** *Bulletin* (Sydney) 7 Aug. (Red Page), *Battling* .. struggling—On the **Johnnie Russel.** **1916** E.F. HANMAN *Twelve Months with Anzacs* 90 'Hullo!' say the men, '**Johnny Turk** is not expecting us, we shall get ashore unnoticed.' **1918** R.H. KNYVETT *Over There with Australs.* 126 Evidently Johnny Turk could not understand the Australian disregard for conventionality. **1872** *Punch Staff Papers* 218 On the kerbstone sat one of those amiable old ladies who are popularly known as '**Johnny Warders**'. She was very drunk. **1880** *Bulletin* (Sydney) 4 Dec. 4/2 The title 'Johnny Warder' applied to vagrants of a certain description, had its origin from the fact that a man named John Ward, who kept a public house in Sussex-street many years ago, used to allow persons of that class to congregate and sleep in a large room adjoining his hotel. **1895** C. CROWE *Austral. Slang Dict.* 40 **Johnnie Woodser,** taking a solitary drink at the bar.

johnny-cake, *n.* and *attrib.* [Transf. use of U.S. *johnny-cake* a flat cake of corn bread.]

A. *n.* A small, usu. thin, damper.

1827 *Monitor* (Sydney) 12 July 507/1 The carcase divided, gave each a good share, and 'a screech in the pan', 'a pot of soup', 'a fat cake', 'a johnny-cake', or 'fritters', alias 'pancakes', were the delicacies which such a God-send would plentifully afford. **1978** K. WILLEY *Joe Brown's Dog* 8 She could .. cook damper and johnny-cakes, and make a decent meal out of very little.

B. *attrib. Obs. fig.* Of an illicit activity: petty, small-time.

1908 *Bulletin* (Sydney) 2 May 17/2 The bush spieler .. often owns a 10th-rate racehorse or a 'johnnycake' book, with which he takes down the public. **1930** A.E. YARRA *Vanishing Horsemen* 58 Somerville who seemed to have become sober with remarkable suddenness, booked several bets with those who had seen 'johnny-cake' spielers at work before.

Johnstone River hardwood. [f. the name of a river in n.e. Qld. + HARDWOOD.] The tall, rainforest tree *Backhousia bancroftii* (fam. Myrtaceae), occurring along the lower Johnstone and Russell Rivers, and yielding a very hard, close-grained timber. Also **Queensland Johnstone River hardwood,** and *attrib.*

1905 P. MACMAHON *Merchantable Timbers of Qld.* 54 Queensland Johnstone River hardwood. *Backhousia Bancroftii*. . . Found in the neighbourhood of Johnstone River, in Northern Queensland, and it is coming into favour for carriage-finishing. **1909** *Emu* VIII. 269 Numbers of dead, ring-barked scrub trees, known locally as Johnstone River hardwood. **1978** R.J. BRITTEN *Around Cassowary Rock* 94 A couple of wild scrub hens .. far up in the topmost branches of a big Johnstone River hardwood tree.

Johnstone's crocodile. [f. the name of explorer and police officer R.A. *Johnstone* (1843–1905), after whom the Johnstone River (Qld.) was also named.] The narrow-snouted fresh-water crocodile *Crocodylus johnstoni,* occurring only in coastal and near-coastal n. Aust. Also **Johnston crocodile, Johnstone crocodile, Johnstone River crocodile.**

1925 M. TERRY *Across Unknown Aust.* 230 The other, commonly misnamed alligator, is the . . Johnstone's crocodile. **1935** F. BIRTLES *Battle Fronts Outback* 75 These 'Johnstone' crocodiles are comparatively harmless. They grow up to a length of about twelve feet. **1948** *Bulletin* (Sydney) 7 July 12/3 In an anabranch of the Copperfield (N.Q.) my mate and I stumbled on about a score of Johnston crocodiles. **1986** *Woman's Day* (Sydney) 24 Feb. 6/3 Val had been told by old crocodile shooters that some Johnson [sic] River crocodiles grew to nearly four metres long and should be regarded with caution.

joint. *Obs.* [Recorded by Partridge as chiefly Cockney.] A chap.

1897 *Worker* (Sydney) 11 Sept. 1/1 His boss he gives some funny names, when he can't hear the joke, He calls him 'joint' and 'finger', and he sometimes calls him 'bloke'. **1922** A. WRIGHT *Colt from Country* 131 He's one of the hottest joints at the game.

joker. [Br. slang use of *joker* jester, merry fellow, now chiefly Austral. and N.Z.]

1. A fellow, a chap.

1810 *Sydney Gaz.* 20 Oct., Six jokers on horseback were standing stock still, Like as many dragoons that were learning to drill. **1978** D. HUTLEY *Swan* 54 There's nothing as stupid as an older joker with long hair.

2. *transf.*

1914 R. KALESKI *Austral. Barkers & Biters* 37 Try the black sheep-dog called the barb. This joker shoos frightened cattle along nicely. **1918** *Bulletin* (Sydney) 12 Sept. 22/2 It is the green turtle that is chiefly used for food. The shell variety .. is the joker that provides the ladies with combs and other fal-lals.

jollo. [f. *joll(ity* + -O.] A spree; a party.

1907 *Truth* (Sydney) 6 Jan. 11/8 On the day of the jollo there was a trifling dispute about the nightman omitting to empty the pans at the hall, of which witness was the caretaker. **1952** C. SIMPSON *Come away, Pearler* 112 Laughs and banter came from the hold. . . Gympie was pleased at the mood created by what he called a 'bit of a jollo'.

jollytail. Chiefly *Tas.* Any of several small fresh-water fish of the genus *Galaxias*, esp. *G. attenuatus* common in coastal streams of s. and s.e. Aust. incl. Tas.

1892 P.L. SIMMONDS *Commercial Dict. Trade Products* (rev. ed.) Suppl. 463/2 *Jolly-tail*, a small fresh-water fish of Australia .. highly esteemed as a delicacy for the table. There are several species. **1985** *Mercury* (Hobart) 30 May 4/7 The jollytail .. lives in fresh water then migrates to spawn in estuaries.

jonick /'dʒɒnɪk/, *a.* Also **jonic, jonnic, jonnik**. [Var. of Br. dial. *jannock* fair, straightforward: see OED *a.*] Fair; genuine; honest; true. Also as *adv.* See also DINKUM *a.* and *adv.*

1874 C. DE BOOS *Congewoi Correspondence* 173, I don't harf like the way as Brown sarved us... I don't think as he acted jonick. 1897 J. FARRELL *How he Died* 61, I know what's Jonnik, coves, and no mistake. 1945 S.D. RAILTON *Southern Cross* 28 Marty gimme th' oil you wanted to see me... That jonnic? 1953 T.A.G. HUNGERFORD *Riverslake* 166 'Got the knife right into him.' 'Jonic?' 'Jonic!'

joss. [Br. dial. *joss* foreman, employer, 'boss': see OEDS.]

a. A person of influence or importance; a boss.

1919 *Ross's Monthly* Jan. 19/1 Despite all the smirks of your josses .. you're snug as a bug in a rug, with your One Big Union of Bosses. 1956 *Coast to Coast 1955–56* 36 A big joss among the young bucks and gins.

b. *fig.*

1922 F.C. GREEN *Fortieth* 71 The Australian is unconventional, and surrounded by others, whose 'josses' are tradition and convention, he is proud of it.

josser. [f. *joss* Chinese idol, esp. as in *joss-house* temple.] A clergyman.

1887 J. FARRELL *How he Died* 22 The Reverend josser .. hammering the pulpit. 1973 G. ROSE *Clear Road to Archangel* 35 The old josser, all black robe and beard and upsidedown hat and silver cross, addressed himself to me. In German.

journo /'dʒɜːnoʊ/. [f. *journ(alist* + -O.] A journalist.

1967 *Kings Cross Whisper* (Sydney) xxxv. 6/3 *Journo*, journalist. 1986 *Bulletin* (Sydney) 15 Apr. 90/3 They accepted a view, vigorously put by the journo who was to interview him, that Irving deserved obscurity.

jug-handle. See quot. 1958.

1958 J.R. SPICER *Cry of Storm-Bird* 115 To aid mounting, the rider often twisted a short strap on the right side of the pommel, a fixture that came in very useful when dealing with a lively horse... The strap in question was known as a 'monkey' or 'jug-handle'. 1976 C.D. MILLS *Hobble Chains & Greenhide* 31, I was unashamedly swinging on the jug-handle, and showing a foot of daylight every buck.

juju tree. [Alteration of *jujube* tree of the genus *Ziziphus*.] A tropical tree of the genus *Ziziphus* (fam. Rhamnaceae), bearing an edible fruit.

1960 E. O'CONNER *Irish Man* 136 Saw a patch of burnt country, a ju-ju tree, gnarled and bent by the wind. 1962 *N. Austral. Monthly* Jan. 21, I was asked for the 'Sunday name' of the China apple or Juju tree. I couldn't think of the name but Mr Dan Corney tells me it is Zixphus jujuba.

July fog. *Obs.* See quot. 1893.

1893 F.W.L. ADAMS *Australs.* 167 The 'July fog' (the dead season when no shearing is done). 1927 J. MATHIEU *Backblocks Ballads* 1, I don't succumb to swagging, July fogs, or charcoal tarts.

jumbuck /'dʒʌmbʌk/. [Of unknown origin: orig. in *Austral. pidgin* and poss. an alteration of an English word (see e.g. JUMP UP *v.*).]

1. A sheep.

1824 Methodist Missionary Soc. Rec. 26 Jan., To two Brothers of mine, these monsters exposed several pieces of human flesh, exclaiming as they smacked their lips and stroked their breasts, 'boodjerry patta! murry boodjerry!— fat as jimbuck!!' i.e. good food, very good, fat as mutton. There is no doubt of their cannibalism. Pray for me, and for them. 1981 P. BARTON *Bastards I have Known* 57 My favourite was a little grey mare that .. knew more about handling sheep than most sheep dogs. She sensed the first day I was on her that I was a novice with the jumbucks.

2. Special Comb. **jumbuck barber,** BARBER *n.,* so, **jumbuck barbering** *vbl. n.* and *attrib.*

1913 *Bulletin* (Sydney) 24 Apr. 14/3 You have no earthly of securing a partner if you are not a jumbuck barber. 1915 *Ibid.* 1 July 22/2, I was quite young at the time, earning a few bob picking-up at a shed. Jumbuck-barbering looked easy enough. 1926 *Bulletin* (Sydney) 14 Jan. 24/3 With a board of 16 shearers a jumbuck-barbering firm this season cut out 105,000 sheep.

jummy. [f. JUM(BUCK + -Y.] JUMBUCK. Also *attrib.*

1943 *Bulletin* (Sydney) 3 Nov. 12/1 My Queensland paper has it that a bunch of greasies downed handpieces in a Longreach shed because they thought they'd catch something from a few jummies with scabby mouths. 1946 *Ibid.* 20 Nov. 29/2 More than one casual stroller was upset in a flying tangle as Ned made a dive for the next woolly, though the jummie barber was usually the last to become aware of it.

jump, *v.*[1] [U.S. *jump* to take possession of without legal procedure: see Mathews *v.* 2.]

1. *trans. Mining.* To occupy or take summary possession of (a claim), in the absence of the former occupant or by resort to legal technicalities.

1852 *Empire* (Sydney) 16 Jan. 578/5 In some instances, parties have 'jumped' claims .. that is, taken possession of claims not registered, and worked in them for two days without being disturbed by the owners, and hence acquiring a right of ownership to them. If the owners of the claims order them out before they have been two clear days at work, they must decamp; but if not their two days' working and possession entitles them to keep the claim. 1977 V. PRIDDLE *Larry & Jack* 21 The mining business is very flat at the moment and all the fossickers are down and out more or less. We hear of them fighting between themselves, jumping claims and doing anything to get a quid.

2. *transf.* To occupy or take possession of (a tract of land) in this manner.

1880 *Argus* (Melbourne) 20 Jan. 6/3 He resolved to jump the selection, and took advantage of the temporary absence of my son. 1907 *Truth* (Sydney) 24 Feb. 2/4 We denounced the audacious attempt on the part of Manager W. Anderson to 'jump' a valuable section of 'the people's heritage', the land known as Tamarama Bay.

3. *fig.*

1868 *Sydney Punch* 29 Aug. 117/2 It has been reserved to an individual of Sydney to arrive at similar 'blushing honors' without either process being employed. In other words, he has 'jumped another's claim'. 1956 R.G. EDWARDS *Overlander Songbk.* 61, I *shepherded* that girl, sir, And soon got in such a flame, That I fancied every fellow there Was going to *jump my claim.*

Hence **jumpable** *a.,* **jumped** *ppl. a.,* **jumping** *vbl. n.* and *attrib.*

1884 'R. BOLDREWOOD' *Old Melbourne Memories* 114 The Heifer station was what would be called in mining parlance 'an abandoned claim', and possibly '**jumpable**', to use another effective expression with which the goldfields have enriched the Australian vernacular. 1858 *Colonial Mining Jrnl.* Nov. 45/2 Some quartz crushed from some **jumped** ground between the Welshman's and New Chum Claim. 1855 R. CARBONI *Eureka Stockade* 11 For the commissioners, this **jumping** business was by no means an agreeable job. 1875 *Australasian Sketcher* (Melbourne) 17 May 19/1 'Jumping' of claims .. is, taking possession of them on the plea that they are illegally held by the parties working them.

jump, *v.*[2] In the phr. **to jump** (a horse, etc.) **over the bar,** to trade one's horse for liquor.

1895 *Bulletin* (Sydney) 27 Apr. 24/1 Oh! when a landlord has your cheque, Think what a hopeless fool you are, You poor, degraded spineless wreck, To jump your crock across the bar. **1923** *Aussie* (Sydney) Dec. 11/1 We had 'jumped our horses over the bar', in other words, handed over our nags to the publican so as to wipe off the slate.

jumper, *n.*[1] Any of several smaller species of ant of the genus *Myrmecia*, many of which are capable of jumping and of inflicting a painful sting; JACK-JUMPER. Also **jumper ant.**

1845 C. HODGKINSON *Aust., Port Macquarie to Moreton Bay* 51, I was severely bitten by the stinging-ants, called Jumpers, which leap like grasshoppers, and inflict a sharp pain. **1972** K. WILLEY *Tales Big Country* 151 Then there's jumper ants. Those blokes will leap six feet in the air to get at you and they've got teeth like a crocodile's.

jumper, *n.*[2] *Hist.* [Spec. use of *jumper* loose outer jacket or shirt worn by seamen, labourers, etc.: see OED(S *sb.*[2]] A smock-like outer garment, distinctive in Australia as part of the conventional attire of a goldminer.

1852 R. CECIL *Gold Fields Diary* (1935) 15 We saw a digger in his jumper and working dress walking arm in arm with a woman dressed in the most exaggerated finery. **1921** M.E. FULLERTON *Bark House Days* 117 He wore a grey 'jumper' reaching to the knees.

jumper, *n.*[3] *Mining.* [f. JUMP *v.*[1] 1.] One who jumps another's claim; *claim jumper,* see CLAIM 3.

1854 *Guardian* (Hobart) 25 Mar. 3/4 Some Scotchmen jumped a hole... The Commissioner.. decided in favour of the jumpers. **1969** E. WALLER *And There's Opal* 25 If I get a couple of roo carcases and dump them down the shaft, it should keep the 'jumpers' out.

jumping snake. Any of several lizards of the fam. Pygopodidae of mainland Aust.

1919 *Bulletin* (Sydney) 6 Nov. 22/1 Tom Ward.. describes a reptile known to Westralians.. as the 'jumping snake'. **1954** C. BARRETT *Wild Life Aust. & New Guinea* 180 'Jumping snake' and 'saltbush snake' are popular names for scaly-foot, which timid people who have met with it declare is so aggressive that it jumps at anyone who disturbs it.

jump up, *v. Austral. pidgin.*

1. *intr.* To come back to life; esp. in the phr. **to jump up whitefellow,** to be reincarnated as a white person.

1826 *Monitor* (Sydney) 29 Dec. 259/3 One of them saw the eye of the deceased glisten, and imagining he might still 'jump up' (to use their own expression, for they are horribly afraid of the resurrection of a dead corpse) he beat the skull till it parted. **1843** *Sydney Morning Herald* 2 Nov. 4/3 He was perfectly aware of the fate which awaited him; but appeared to have the notion that he would soon 'jump up, white fellow'!

2. *intr.* To come; to appear.

1845 D. MACKENZIE *Emigrant's Guide* 241 The black fellow returned.. to complain that the young potatoes did 'not yet jump up'. **1853** *Visit to Aust. & Gold Regions* (S.P.C.K.) 162 The black fellow.. went to his instructor, and told him with much chagrin that the potatoes had not yet 'jumped up', and inquired if they would 'jump up' in two days more.

jump-up, *n.* [Prob. infl. by prec.]

1. An elevated, step-like obstacle on an ascending road or track; a sudden, steep rise; an escarpment. Also *attrib.*

[**1844** MRS C. MEREDITH *Notes & Sketches N.S.W.* 70 The main portion of the road is *bad* beyond an English comprehension; sometimes it consists of natural step-like rocks protruding from the dust or sand, one, two, or three feet above each other, in huge slabs the width of the track, and over these *'jumpers'*, as they are pleasantly termed, we had to jolt and bump along as we best might.] **1847** *Maitland Mercury* 27 Oct. 2/4 Here and there are also to be found, by way of variety, a few of what are expressively termed 'jumps up', and other numerous obstacles. **1981** *Austral. Women's Weekly* (Sydney) 26 Aug. 43 Rolling grasslands give way to 'jump-up country', isolated flat-topped mountains, stark against the sky. Red sandhills undulate away to the north.

2. a. See quot.

1859 W. BURROWS *Adventures Mounted Trooper* 101 A young colonist.. was in the habit of giving the black near him a feed of 'jump up' as they call it; this stuff consists of flour and water boiled into a paste, and sugar put into it, and from the bubbles rising to the surface when boiling, they call it 'jump up'.

b. A raising agent.

1915 *Bulletin* (Sydney) 20 May 22/3 How to make a damper... One large bag of flour, plenty of 'jump up' and water to mix with.

junga. /ˈdʒʊŋə, ˈdʒʌŋə/. [a. Panyjima *jaŋa.*] PARAKEELIA.

1932 I.L. IDRIESS *Flynn of Inland* (1965) 141 It held.. the parakelia, the 'chunga' (milk) and 'junga' (water) plant of the natives. **1984** W.W. AMMON et al. *Working Lives* 151 There was a plant there called junga or parakeelya. It is very sappy and keeps the sheep from needing water till late in the summer.

jungle-fowl. [Transf. use of *jungle-fowl* an East Indian bird of the genus *Gallus.*] *Scrub fowl,* see SCRUB *n.* 5. Also **jungle-hen.**

1842 J. GOULD *Birds of Aust.* (1848) V. Pl. 79, I came to a mound of sand and shells, with a slight mixture of black soil... On pointing it out to the native and asking him what it was, he replied, 'Oooregoora Rambal', Jungle-fowls' house or nest. **1889** R.B. ANDERSON tr. Lumholtz's *Among Cannibals* 96 The melancholy note of the jungle-hen.

jungle juice. [Used elsewhere but recorded earliest in Aust.] Orig. in Services' speech in New Guinea: any crude alcoholic drink.

1942 H.E. BEROS *Fuzzy Wuzzy Angels* (1943) 18 An epidemic hit the camp, it travelled fast and loose, It was started by a liquid with the name of Jungle Juice. **1968** G. DUTTON *Andy* 268 The Americans had two bottles of bourbon and one of jungle juice made from fermented coconut milk and surgical alcohol.

K

kadaitcha, kaditcha, varr. KURDAITCHA.

kadoova /kə'duvə/. *Obs.* [Of unknown origin.] In the phr. **to be off one's kadoova,** to be mentally unbalanced.
1889 BARRÈRE & LELAND *Dict. Slang* 94 A man had tried to prove a man wrong who said he was *off his kadoova.* **1946** D. STIVENS *Courtship of Uncle Henry* 72, I reckoned then Thompson was a bit off his kadoova.

kai /kaɪ/. [a. *kai, v.* to eat, and *n.* food, widespread in Polynesian languages and adopted in its reduplicated form *kai-kai* in Pacific pidgins.] Food.
[N.Z. **1845** E.J. WAKEFIELD *Adventure in N.Z.* I. 265 The determination of the natives not to move until all the *kai* was exhausted.] **1872** 'RESIDENT' *Glimpses Life Vic.* 253 'Kai! me get that fellow [*sc.* an iguana] out quick,' said the native. **1946** *Austral. New Writing* 50 A long-snouted pig grunting always for 'kai'.
So, in reduplicated form, **kai-kai,** food, a meal. Also **ki-ki.**
[N.Z. **1807** J. SAVAGE *Some Acct. N.Z.* 75 *Kiki*, food.] **1893** *Antipodean* (Melbourne) 82 An hour for 'ki-ki' and 'Smoke, oh!' in the middle of the day. **1970** *Coast to Coast 1967–68* 48 No, she didn't say tucker. The kanakas said kai-kai. And I guess the word spread.

kai-yai /'kaɪ-jaɪ/, *a.* Also **ki-eye.** [Prob. transf. use of U.S. slang *ki-yi* dog.] Used *attrib.* as **kai-yai bones:** see quots.
1953 J.K. EWERS *With Sun on my Back* 177 That night, back at the homestead, we had rib-bones grilled over an open fire... 'Ki-eye' bones they call them up there. **1976** C.D. MILLS *Hobble Chains & Greenhide* 95 We grilled the 'kai-yai' bones for lunch. These are the short ribs, and a really epicurean delicacy.

kakka /'kækə/. *W.A.* Also **cacker, cakker.** [Of unknown origin.] An undersized crustacean, esp. a marine crayfish. Also *attrib.*
1965 *R.A.N. News* (Sydney) 30 Apr. 2 'Any kakkas?' .. (A kakka is an undersize crayfish). **1969** *W. Coast Fisherman* May 1 A rise in numbers of lobsters following the clampdown on 'cakkers'. **1983** *Sunday Independent* (Perth) 21 Aug. 47/1 Cacker-catchers .. are generally recognisable by the size of their buckets, and their habit of indiscriminately slaughtering as many undersized fish and crustaceans as they can.

Kanaka /kə'nækə/, *n.* and *attrib. Hist.* [a. Hawaiian *kanaka* man.]
A. *n.* A Pacific islander, esp. one brought to Australia to work as an indentured labourer in the sugar and cotton industries of Queensland.
1836 J.F. O'CONNELL *Residence Eleven Yrs. New Holland* 75 The Kanakas (South Sea Islanders) discharged from American and English whalers, at Sydney, supply the Sydney whalers with half their crews. **1980** *Westerly* i. 6 'You're a Solomon Islander eh?' I said. 'That's right, both sides. Course I was born here, and so was me mum, but me dad was a kanaka.'
B. *attrib.*
1. Of or pertaining to a Pacific islander employed as a labourer in Australia, or to this as a practice.
1881 W. FEILDING *Austral. Trans-Continental Railway* 51 The native constable and our Kanaka lad (Walter) .. got drunk. **1959** *Meanjin* 143 About the time the kanaka-workers appeared my grandmother left us.
2. Comb. **Kanaka labour, labourer.**
1882 J. ALLEN *Hist. Aust.* 213 'Kanaka' labour was a mild form of slave labour. **1887** MRS D.D. DALY *Digging, Squatting, & Pioneering Life* 24 Planters left their estates in the care of their **Kanyaka** [*sic*] **labourers** for a time.
3. Special Comb. **Kanaka question,** the subject of the use of Kanaka labour in Queensland as a matter of debate, controversy, etc.
1901 *Brisbane Courier* 1 July 7/1 He confessed he did not hold any very strong opinions on the Kanaka question until he visited the Bundaberg district.
4. Prefixed by **anti-**: opposed to the employment of Kanakas in Queensland.
1883 T. ARCHER *Alleged Slavery in Qld.* 10 The journal you quote (one of the most rabid of the Anti-Kanaka papers).

Kanakaland. *Obs.* A nickname for Queensland. Also *attrib.*
1892 *Bulletin* (Sydney) 31 Dec. 9/1 The wholesale perfidy and corruption of the present Kanakaland Parliament. **1942** F. CLUNE *Last of Austral. Explorers* 124 Donald .. reached Port Mackay, the metropolis of Kanakaland.
Hence **Kanakalander,** a resident of Queensland.
1903 *Bulletin* (Sydney) 17 Sept. 35/1 The limp Kanakalander gloomily looks up from his lounge.

kanga.
1. Abbrev. of KANGAROO *n.* 1.
1917 *Bulletin* (Sydney) 15 Feb. 24/4, I have had many opportunities of measuring the jump or stride of the kanga. **1981** A.J. BURKE *Pommies & Patriots* 66 The machine gun is being used to kill as many as a thousand kangaroos at a time and approximately five million kangas are being destroyed annually in the 1980s.
2. [Abbrev. of *kangaroo* rhyming slang for 'screw'.] **a.** Money. **b.** A prison warder.
1953 S.J. BAKER *Aust. Speaks* 133 *Kangaroo*, a warder, by rhyme on 'screw'; also used in the abbreviated form, *kanga.* **1978** E. HANGER *2D & Other Plays* 44 Your daughter's got a bit of kanga, but, hasn't she? .. Kanga? .. Cash. That's what they say in the bush.
3. See quot.
1975 *Sun-Herald* (Sydney) 20 July 13/2 Her friend .. prefers a bone-shaking ride on a 'kanga'—a jackhammer, to the uninitiated.
4. Special Comb. **Kanga Cricket,** see quot.
1986 *Canberra Chron.* 2 Apr. 1 (*caption*) Nine-year-old Matthew Pampling .. has a mighty swing during a match of Kanga Cricket... Kanga is a fast-developing form of cricket with rules and equipment especially designed for youngsters.

kangaroo /kæŋgə'ru/, *n.* Pl. **kangaroos** but formerly also **kangaroo.** [Extended use of Guugu Yimidhirr *gaŋurru* a large black or grey kangaroo, prob. *spec.* the male *Macropus robustus.*]
1. a. Any of the larger marsupials of the chiefly Austral. fam. Macropodidae (see quot. 1956), having short forelimbs, a tail developed for support and balance, long feet and powerful hind limbs, enabling a swift, bounding motion. **b.** Occas. loosely, referring to any or all of the members of the fam. Macropodidae and Potoroidae: see quots. 1839, 1870, and 1970. **c.** The

flesh or hide of the animal. See also WALLABY n. 1. Also attrib.

1770 J. BANKS *Endeavour Jrnl.* 14 July (1962) II. 94 Kill Kanguru. 1839 H. CAPPER *S.A.* (rev. ed.) 52 Kangaroos are of five different species, viz., the forest, the brush, the wallaby, the kangaroo rat, and the kangaroo mouse. 1870 *Illustr. Austral. News* (Melbourne) 28 Feb. 52/4 Of the kangaroo, which is too well known to need description, there are between twenty and thirty species in Australia. 1956 T.Y. HARRIS *Naturecraft in Aust.* 76 There is no clear anatomical distinction between a kangaroo, a wallaroo, and a wallaby. In general, 'wallaby' is used for the smaller forms, 'wallaroo' for the stockily-built types of mountain and open forest type of habitat, and 'kangaroo' for the larger forms. 1970 W.D.L. RIDE *Guide Native Mammals Aust.* 44 In some parts of Australia, and in particular where great kangaroos are rare, such as in Tasmania, or in the Kimberley, the local people may refer to large wallabies as kangaroos.

2. With distinguishing epithet, as **brush, bush, eastern grey, great grey, grey, hill, Kangaroo Island, red, western grey:** see under first element.

3. *fig.*

a. An Australian, esp. a member of the armed services or one representing Australia in a sport; Australia as so represented.

1883 BEESTON & MASSIE *St Ivo & Ashes* 8 The battle for the 'ashes' was over, and once more the Englishmen had regained their lost supremacy in the cricket field. Neither Lion nor Kangaroo, however, was satisfied, apparently. 1906 *Truth* (Sydney) 22 July 6/1 The muddied oafs from Auckland also gave the kangaroo a father of a beating. 1949 G. BERRIE *Morale* 197 Well, if you bloody Kangaroos aren't sick of the war, I *am*.

b. *pl.* The name of the Australian international Rugby League team; in *sing.*, a member of such a team. Cf. SOCCEROO and WALLABY *n.* 4.

1933 *Sydney Morning Herald* 27 Oct. 11/2 Widnes attacked early, bustling into the 'Kangaroos' territory. 1985 *Sydney Morning Herald* 4 Apr. 32/4 When the 1982 Kangaroos left for England Steve Mortimer was considered to be Australia's first-string Rugby League half-back.

c. In the phr. **(to have) kangaroos in the (your,** etc.) **top paddock,** to be crazy or eccentric.

1908 *Austral. Mag.* (Sydney) Nov. 1250/1 If you show signs of mental weakness you are either balmy, dotty, ratty, or cracked, or you may even have .. kangaroos in your top paddock. 1968 S. GORE *Holy Smoke* 59 'Strewth what's wrong with this nut?' says one of 'em. 'Kangaroos in the top paddock, by the seem of it.'

4. Comb. **kangaroo flesh, fur, hide, hunt, hunter, -hunting, leather, meat, scalp, shoot, shooter, -shooting, skin, stew.**

1806 *HRA* (1915) 1st Ser. V. 643, I have directed that **Kangaroo Flesh** be received into the Stores. 1842 *Colonial Observer* (Sydney) 23 Mar. 198/4 The officer .. obtained from them a belt composed of small **kangaroo fur,** commonly worn by the natives of this coast. 1828 *Tasmanian* (Hobart) 29 Aug. 3 Cash Price allowed for **Kangaroo** Skins and **Hides.** 1827 *Monitor* (Sydney) 15 Nov. 767/1 Which is the least demoralising .. the Theatre or the **Kangaroo hunt?** 1841 *Port Phillip Patriot* 5 Aug. 2/4 The **kangaroo hunters** of his department. 1828 *Tasmanian* (Hobart) 11 July 3 **Kangaroo hunting** and fowling, although innocent in themselves, are *real crimes* when practised on a Sunday. 1833 *Trumpeter* (Hobart) 31 Dec. 287 **Kangaroo leather,** for shoe-making purposes. 1851 H. MELVILLE *Present State Aust.* 308 In the event of **kangaroo meat** being wanted, he skins the forepart and cuts it off. 1885 *Bulletin* (Sydney) 5 Dec. 10/4 **Kangaroo-scalps** are paid for at the rate of 9d. each. 1936 F. CLUNE *Roaming round Darling* 119 A young grazier .. made up a party for a **kangaroo shoot.** 1886 P. CLARKE *'New Chum' in Aust.* 215, I knew a **kangarooshooter** who employed himself occasionally in killing and salting hams from wild pigs. 1886 J.A. FROUDE *Oceana* 122 Two young English lords on their travels .. who had been up the country **kangaroo-shooting.** 1809 *Sydney Gaz.* 16 Apr. 2/1 On Sunday last arrived the colonial vessel Eliza from the South West coast of this Territory with .. about 1000 **Kangaroo skins.** 1834 M. DOYLE *Extracts Lett. & Jrnls. G.F. Moore* 100 Dined on **kangaroo stew.**

5. In the names of flora and fauna: **kangaroo acacia,** see *kangaroo thorn;* **apple,** any of several shrubs of the genus *Solanum* (fam. Solanaceae), chiefly of s. and e. Aust., esp. *S. aviculare, S. laciniatum* and *S. vescum* (see GUNYANG), bearing an egg-shaped fruit edible when completely ripe; the fruit of these plants; **bush, (a)** PUNTY; **(b)** SANDHILL WATTLE; **fish, (a)** BURNETT SALMON; **(b)** MUDSKIPPER; **fly,** a small and intensely irritating fly, prob. any of several species, poss. incl. *Ortholfersia macleayi* and *Austrosimulium pestilens;* **grass, (a)** the tall, tussocky, perennial grass *Themeda triandra* (fam. Poaceae), widely distributed throughout Aust. and occurring elsewhere; **(b)** (occas.) any of several other similar grasses; **mouse,** HOPPING MOUSE; **paw,** see main entry; **prickly acacia,** see *kangaroo thorn;* **rabbit** *obs., kangaroo rat* (a); **rat, (a)** any of the small macropodoids of the fam. Potoroidae, incl. the BETTONG and POTOROO, most species of which have a fast hopping gait and construct a nest with material carried in the tail; RAT-KANGAROO; **(b)** *transf.* WEET-WEET; **thorn,** the prickly shrub *Acacia paradoxa* (fam. Mimosaceae), of all mainland States but not N.T., naturalized in Tas. and often planted as a hedge; formerly also **kangaroo (prickly) acacia; tick,** either of two ticks having the kangaroo or wallaby as chief host, the argasid tick *Ornithodoros gurneyi* of arid inland Aust., the bite of which can severely affect a human, and the ixodid tick *Amblyomma triguttatum.*

1828 *Hobart Town Courier* 2 Feb. 3 We have had occasion .. to remark the great luxuriance of what is called the **Kangaroo apple,** or New Zealand potato, a species of Solanum common to this country and New Zealand. 1834 J.D. LANG *Hist. & Statistical Acct. N.S.W.* I. 133 *Solanum laciniatum,* the kangaroo-apple, resembling the apple of a potato. 1888 *Proc. Linnean Soc. N.S.W.* III. 544 *Solanum aviculare* .. 'Kangaroo apple', 'Gunyang' .. of the Gippsland and other aboriginals. 1901 *Proc. Linnean Soc. N.S.W.* XXVI. 318 The Acacias noticed were .. *A. Burkittii* (**Kangaroo Bush**). 1956 T.Y. HARRIS *Naturecraft in Aust.* 194 A light sandy soil in the 10-inch rainfall belt carries fairly large shrubs, such as .. Kangaroo Bush. 1931 *Bulletin* (Sydney) 14 Jan. 21/4 The **kangaroo fish** or mudskipper, found in the mangroves of N.Q., does not always use its gills for breathing. 1971 P. BODEKER *Sandgropers' Trail* 191 Wyndham's waterfront at low tide was literally jumping with mudhoppers... Northerners call them .. kangaroo fish .. because they like to elbow themselves up on mangrove roots to enjoy the sunshine. 1833 C. STURT *Two Exped. Interior S.A.* I. 72 We had left the immediate spot at which the **kangaroo flies** (cabarus) seemed to be collected. 1826 J. ATKINSON *Acct. Agric. & Grazing N.S.W.* 20 The principal grasses are, the oak grass, **kangaroo grass,** two sorts of rye grass. 1984 B. DIXON *Searching for Aboriginal Lang.* 22 A flock of brolgas dancing over the long green kangaroo grass. 1833 W.H. BRETON *Excursions* 410 The **kangaroo,** or opossum **mouse,** is a mouse formed like a kangaroo. 1839 J.C. HAWKER *Diary* 33 The Wallaby and **Kangaroo** rat or **rabbit** are a small species of the kangaroo and abound in the scrubs. **(a)** 1788 J. WHITE *Jrnl. Voyage N.S.W.* (1790) 182 Every animal in this country partakes, in a great measure, of the nature of the Kangaroo. We have the Kangaroo Opossum, the **Kangaroo Rat,** &c. *Ibid.* 286 The Poto Roo, or Kangaroo Rat... The forelegs are short in comparison to the hind. **(b)** 1870 J.G. WOOD *Nat. Hist. Man* II. 42, I have seen an Australian stand at one side of Kennington Oval, and throw the '**kangaroo-rat**' completely across it. *c* 1856 F. GERSTAECKER *Life in Bush* 9 'And your men?' 'Are looking for you on the beach, or among the **kangaroo thorns.**' 1854 *Hobarton Guardian* 1 Feb. 3/2 The very dangerous character of the kangaroo prickly acacia as a fence in case of fire. 1874 'SPECIAL

KANGAROO

REPORTER' *Agric. in S.A.* 21 The only hedges seen are of patchy untended kangaroo acacia, which in this condition are neither ornamental nor useful. **1938** *Austral. Vet. Jrnl.* Apr. 69 The **kangaroo tick**, as a parasite of kangaroos and other native fauna, dogs and occasionally man, is to be found in parts of the north-western division of this State [*sc.* N.S.W.]. **1975** *Bulletin* (Sydney) 1 Nov. 25/1 In N.S.W. and Queensland another kangaroo tick (*Ornithodorus* [*sic*] *Gurneyi*) has caused a few cases of sickness; and there is one recorded instance of temporary blindness.

6. Special Comb. **kangaroo bar**, BULLBAR; **bone**, a bone from a kangaroo, used by Aborigines as a tool or as an item of personal adornment; **camp**, a place where kangaroos habitually congregate (cf. CAMP *n.* 3 and 4); **cloak**, a cloak made of kangaroo skin; **closure** [orig. Br. (see OEDS *sb.* 4 b.], see quot. 1936; **corroboree**, *kangaroo dance*; **court** [orig. U.S. (see OEDS *sb.* 4 b.)], an improperly constituted court having no legal standing; **dance**, an Aboriginal ceremonial dance in which the dancers' movements represent those of a kangaroo; **dog (bitch, hound)**, a dog used for hunting the kangaroo; (*spec.*) a breed of dog evolved in Aust. from the Scottish deerhound and the greyhound for this purpose; a dog of this breed; **drive**, an operation in which kangaroos are herded, trapped, and slaughtered, or otherwise hunted; **feather**, (in the war of 1914–18), a jocular name for an emu plume worn on the hat of a member of the Australian Light Horse; **fence**, a fence made to exclude kangaroos (see quots. 1852 and 1978); **ground** *obs.*, a place habitually frequented by kangaroos; **hedge** *obs.*, a hedge of *kangaroo thorn* (see sense 5); **jack**, a heavy-duty, lever-action jack, used esp. to lift logs, stumps, etc.; **joey**, a young kangaroo; **knapsack**, a knapsack made from kangaroo skin; so **-knapsacked** *a.*; **land**, Australia; **leap**, a sudden or jolting bound; also *fig.*; **mat**, a floor rug made from kangaroo skin; **net**, a net used by Aborigines to snare kangaroos; **route**, a name for the Sydney-Singapore-London air route, orig. as flown by Qantas Airways Ltd.; **rug**, a rug made from kangaroo skin; **sinew**, a kangaroo tendon used for binding, tying, etc., or for personal adornment; also *attrib.*; **soup**, soup made from kangaroo meat; **spear** *obs.*, a spear used by Aborigines to kill kangaroos; **start**, (of a motor vehicle) a jerking start (see KANGAROO *v.* 2 a.); **steak**, a piece of kangaroo meat cut and cooked in the manner of beef-steak; **steamer**, a stew made from kangaroo meat (see quot. 1864); STEAMER; **tail**, the tail of a kangaroo as an article of food, esp. *attrib.* as **kangaroo-tail soup; tooth**, the tooth of a kangaroo, as used for personal adornment; **Valley**, a name given to Earls Court, a district of London (see quot. 1965).

1969 L. HADOW *Full Cycle* 207 He took a folded handkerchief from the glove box, wet it from the water-bag on the **kangaroo bar**. **1842** *Colonial Observer* (Sydney) 23 Mar. 198/4 The officer . . obtained from them a . . nosepiece of **kangaroo bone**. **1846** C.W. SCHÜRMANN *Aboriginal Tribes Port Lincoln* 3 A small hole is bored by means of a sharp kangaroo bone. **1878** R.B. SMYTH *Aborigines of Vic.* II. 63 *Burrai gurrai* . . a **kangaroo camp**. **1830** S.H. COLLINS *Geogr. Descr. Australasia* 17 Most of them wore **kangaroo cloaks**, which were their only clothing. **1936** H.D. INGRAM *Australasian Secretarial Principles* 75 **Kangaroo Closure**. A method adopted in Parliamentary committees by which the chairman is permitted to select what amendments he considers are relevant to the question and 'jump over' those he thinks are not worth considering. **1883** A.W. HOWITT *On Some Austral. Beliefs* 11 He . . dreamed for several consecutive nights that he was present at a **Kangaroo Corroboree**. **1967** *Kings Cross Whisper* (Sydney) xlii. 9/3 Mr Justice Collusion interrupted to point out that he was not running a **kangaroo court** . . and adjourned for lunch. **1833** *Currency Lad* (Sydney) 27 Apr. 3 The **kangaroo-dances** . . of the aborigines. **1805** *Sydney Gaz.* 21 July, Capital **kangaroo dog**—To be sold. **1827** *Monitor* (Sydney) 17 Sept. 642/2 Stolen, a black brindled kangaroo bitch, with a white spot on the breast. **1839** W.H. LEIGH *Reconnoitering Voyages* 96 We untied the kangaroo hounds, and they gave it a splendid chace. **1870** C.H. ALLEN *Visit to Qld.* 169 In some places there are what are called '**kangaroo drives**', and then immense numbers are killed. **1916** *Kangaroosilite: On Board 'Wandilla'* Jan. 4 Stolen. Brown felt hat as worn by young children, decorated with several '**Kangaroo feathers**'. **1846** F. DUTTON *S.A. & its Mines* 203 The '**kangaroo**' fence is composed of pieces of timber large and small. **1852** F. LANCELOTT *Aust. as it Is* I. 138 Where timber is plentiful, the 'Kangaroo' fence is preferred before all others, as it keeps out sheep, pigs, and such like quadrupeds; it is formed of pieces of timber, large and small, all cut into equal lengths, either of 7 or 8 feet, and placed close and upright in a trench 2 feet deep and tightly rammed; a rough batten being nailed along the top as a band. **1978** M. WALKER *Pioneer Crafts Early Aust.* 28 An early form of hemming in the paddock was the palisade fence, also known as the kangaroo fence, being made up with split trunks, straighter branches and saplings, all being cut to a consistent length, which varied from seven to ten feet (2.1–3 m.). A continuous two to three feet (0.6–0.9 m.) trench was dug and the timbers stood upright; the earth was backfilled and tightly rammed about the uprights. **1833** W.H. BRETON *Excursions* 76 The grounds that enclose the ravines are level . . the **kangaroo ground** being one of the most remarkable. **1875** R. & F. HILL *What we saw in Aust.* 236 *Acacia armata* . . as a hedge and well pruned . . forms an impervious fence. . . Coming originally from Kangaroo Island, the fences thus made are called **Kangaroo hedges**. **1911** *Settlers' Handy Pamphlet* (W.A. Lands Dept.) 7 The cost of clearing is greatly reduced by the use of 'jacks', gelignite, and fire. . . When the roots are burned through and the tree falls the roots are run and lifted with a '**Kangaroo**' or 'Wallaby' **jack**. **1941** W.J. DENNY *Digger at Home & Abroad* 150 The familiar picture . . of units preceded by a **kangaroo joey** . . is not of recent origin. **1888** *Cornwall Chron.* (Launceston) 22 Sept. 2 On Saturday night last, four men, well armed, and with **kangaroo knapsacks**, entered a sawyer's hut. **1850** *Irish Exile* (Hobart) 5 Oct. 2/2 A shifting population of blue-shirted, kangaroo-knapsacked labourers. **1827** *Monitor* (Sydney) 20 Apr. 386/3 Easter Monday . . was signalized among us of **Kangaroo Land**, in the *usual mode* adopted at seasons of joy. **1852** *Austral. Gold Digger's Monthly Mag.* III. 98 We have some amazing **kangaroo leaps** in our mineralogical conformations. **1972** D. MARTIN *Frank & Francesca* 5 Francie gave a kangaroo leap and half fell over the bike. **1861** E.P. RAMSAY-LAYE *Social Life & Manners* 123 My drawing-room was made quite gay with some handsome **kangaroo mats**. **1830** W.J. HOOKER *Bot. Miscellany* I. 253 It is customary for the tribes, when leaving a district, to deposit in such a situation their **Kangaroo-Nets**, *Dillies, Bass-mats*, chissels, and superfluous implements, until their return. [**1946** kangaroo route: *Sydney Morning Herald* 8 Nov. 6/4 Because of the European winter and the wet season in North Australia the 'Kangaroo' flying boat service between Sydney and the United Kingdom has been modified. **1948** *Ibid.* 7 Aug. 2/7 The Qantas Kangaroo land plane service between Australia and the United Kingdom is to be increased from three to four trips a fortnight.] **1961** *Nation* (Sydney) 12 Aug. 11/2 On the Kangaroo route, the flight to Britain, strange things have been happening. **1828** *Hobart Town Courier* 5 July 4, I . . wrapped myself in my **kangaroo rug**, and reposed like a king until day. **1832** J. BACKHOUSE *Narr. Visit Austral. Colonies* (1843) 84 They also wear necklaces formed of **Kangaroo-sinews** rolled in red ochre. **1846** *Tasmanian Jrnl. Nat. Sci.* II. 414 The women generally wear a kangaroo skin, likewise the kangaroo sinew belt. **1829** *Cornwall Press* (Launceston) 17 Feb. 8/2 The additional luxuries of **kangaroo soup** and *opossum gravy*!!! **1875** CAMPBELL & WILKS *Early Settlement Qld.* 44 One of the gins with a **kangaroo spear**, Had sadly annoy'd Billy Ure in the rear. **1971** D. IRELAND *Unknown Industr. Prisoner* 308 The Mercedes made a few **kangaroo starts** then lurched off up the road. **1826** *Monitor* (Sydney) 15 Dec. 243/3 The common dinner at Hunter's River is salt pork, or a **Kangaroo steak**, without vegetables, and with dumpling-like bread unleavened.   **1833** C.O. BOOTH *Jrnl.* 24 Aug. (1981) 160 Had a capital **Kangaroo Steamer** for B-fast.   **1849** J. PATTISON *N.S.W.* 73 There is another very good colonial dish, called kangaroo steamer; which .. is the best parts of animal stewed in its own gravy without water.   **1864** *Colonial Cook Bk.* (1970) 70 Kangaroo Steamer... Take the most tender part of the kangaroo .. chop it very fine, about the same quantity of smoked bacon (fat); season with finely-powdered marjoram, pepper, and a very little salt. Let it 'steam', or 'stew', for two hours; then pack or press tight in open-mouthed glass bottles.   **1830** R. DAWSON *Present State Aust.* 207 Dinner consisted of a dish of fine perch, and some excellent **kangaroo tail** soup.   **1862** G.T. LLOYD *Thirty-Three Yrs. Tas. & Vic.* 129 Kangaroo-tails baked in wood ashes.   **1833** W.H. BRETON *Excursions* 210 The only ornament that I procured was a string of **kangaroo teeth**.   **1965** H. PORTER *Cats of Venice* 108 Londoners call Earl's Court—you can readily imagine the tone of voice—**Kangaroo Valley**. That's because it's the address of the Australians, the invaders, the temporary, the hit-and-run, cut-and-come-again yahoos, the colonial vagabonds, the loud-mouthed and light-fingered rowdies, the uncouth, irreverent, cock-sure, yankee-ized and so on and so forth so-and-sos.

kangaroo /kæŋgə'ru/, *v.* [f. prec.]

1. *intr.* To hunt the kangaroo. Chiefly as *pres. ppl.* and *vbl. n.*

1803 J. GRANT *Narr. Voyage N.S.W.* 91 He had been Kangarooing, had lost his way, and was almost starved.   **1949** G. FARWELL *Traveller's Tracks* 168 If you're a good hand with a gun, there's all the kangarooing you want.

2. a. *intr. transf.* To leap in a manner resembling that of a kangaroo; (of a motor vehicle) to move forward in jerks. See also KANGAROO-HOP. Also as *vbl. n.*

1867 *Sydney Punch* 30 Mar. 142/1 A daring spirit then initiated a peculiar description of jumping which he called 'Kangarooing'.   **1915** *Bulletin* (Sydney) 9 Sept. 26/2 That'll stop any kangarooing, because a horse when about to spring places his front paws together, and he can't do it when the piece of timber is in the way.   **1971** C. MCGREGOR *Don't talk to me about Love* 187 The car jerked and kangarooed off into the night.

b. *trans. fig.* To squat over (a lavatory) with one's feet on the seat. Also as *vbl. n.*

1955 D. NILAND *Shiralee* 129 There was a notice on the wall .. 'Craphouse Duties'... It ended up with the injunction in snaggled capitals: 'Kangarooing is not allowed.' And in smaller letters: 'Remember others have to sit where you shat.'   **1981** P. RADLEY *Jack Rivers & Me* 6 An accumulation of advice. 'Yeah! Like: 'No use to kangaroo this seat; the crabs here jump fifteen feet'.'

kangarooer. One who hunts kangaroos.

1836 'W. R–s' *Fell Tyrant* 40 This man was a constant visitor at Government House, and was chiefly kept by the commandant as kangarooer, and when his services were required, as flogger.   **1970** P.J. BAILLIE *Bush Ballads* 73 Three kangarooers up the Coast Once shot a tidy pile.

kangaroo-hop, *v. intr.* **a.** To move in a manner resembling that of a kangaroo; to move with an awkward gait; to leap or move in bounds (also *fig.*).   **b.** (Of a motor vehicle) to move forward in jerks. See also KANGAROO *v.* 2 a.

1943 *Double Gee* (Kalgoorlie) Christmas 5 Recently when on leave he found himself in an unenviable situation kangaroo-hopping.   **1960** H.H. WILSON *Where Wind's Feet Shine* 43 There was Cousin Millie coming down the track from the sandhills, her tight shoes making her look as though she were kangaroo-hopping over burning hot ground.   **1979** J.J. MCROACH *Dozen Dopey Yarns* 75 She .. rushes past us .. and into a volkswagen. She starts it, jumps it forward about eight feet, stalls, starts again and kangaroo hops.

Kangaroo Island kangaroo. [See quot. 1941.] The kangaroo *Macropus fuliginosus fuliginosus*.

1926 A.S. LE SOUEF et al. *Wild Animals Australasia* 177 Gould never actually saw a specimen of the Kangaroo Island kangaroo.   **1941** E. TROUGHTON *Furred Animals Aust.* 219 Kangaroo Island Kangaroo *Macropus fuliginosus* .. restricted to Kangaroo Island, off Yorke Peninsula, South Australia, where it inhabits the dense scrub and bushland.

kangaroo paw.

1. [See quot. 1926.] Any plant of the genera *Anigozanthos* and *Macropidia* (fam. Haemodoraceae), perennials of s.w. W.A. having distinctive elongated, paw-like flowers, esp. the red-and-green flowering *A. manglesii*, floral emblem of W.A.

1901 M. VIVIENNE *Travels in W.A.* 61 The anygoxanthus (kangaroo paw), a most wonderful flower, was to be seen in many different hues.   **1926** A.A.B. APSLEY *Amateur Settlers* 207 A curious tufted sedge-like plant called a Kangaroo Paw .. so called from its quaintly shaped flowers so like the paws of a kangaroo.

2. [See KANGAROO *n.* sense 3 a.] A name given to tenosynovitis, in the belief that it occurs more commonly in Aust. than elsewhere.

1985 *Med. Jrnl. Aust.* Feb. CXLII. 237 So what are we left with? Obviously a unique Aussie 'disease' which one day no doubt will find its place into [*sic*] the small print of an occupational health medical tome—possibly under the eponym of 'Kangaroo paw'. Perhaps 'Kangaroo poor' would be more appropriate, as that's the likely result of the burgeoning spiral of costs associated with an epidemic which, however it started, could only be perpetuated with the approbation of the medical profession, either through ignorance or avarice or both.

kangarooster. *Obs.* An Australian.

1909 *Truth* (Sydney) 2 May 1/4 The Kangaroosters have arrived back. Their tails aren't even half-mast high.   **1922** 'J. NORTH' *Black Opal* 164 The Kangaroosters .. were privileged to view that contest.

kanooka /kə'nukə/. Also **kanuka**. [Poss. transf. use of Maori *kanuka* the tea-tree *Kunzea ericoides*.] The tree *Tristaniopsis laurina* (see *water gum* WATER); the wood of the tree. Also *attrib.*

1914 E.E. PESCOTT *Native Flowers Vic.* 62 Tristania laurina, the 'Kanuka', is a compact growing shrub.   **1979** DOUGLAS & HEATHCOTE *Far Cry* 78 At Nambour we were camped on the side of a hill near a kanooka forest (a cousin of the eucalypt).

kapok tree. [Transf. use of *kapok tree* the fibre-producing *Ceiba casearia*: see OED(S *kapok*.] Any of several small deciduous trees of the genus *Cochlospermum* (fam. Bixaceae), bearing a fruit containing seeds embedded in soft cottony fibres; *cotton tree* (b), see COTTON. Also **kapok**.

1933 *Bulletin* (Sydney) 6 Sept. 21/1 The kapok-tree has its habitat among the rocky escarpments of Queensland and certain parts of Centralia.   **1976** C.D. MILLS *Hobble Chains & Greenhide* 41 The flowering kapok.

karara /kə'rarə/. Also **karrara, kurara.** [Panyjima *kurarra.*] The plant *Acacia tetragonophylla* (see DEAD FINISH 1). Also *attrib.*

1929 K.S. PRICHARD *Coonardoo* (1961) 117 Hugh and the boys threw themselves in any shred of shade beside a clump of karrara bush, or thicket of mulga.   **1942** *Bulletin* (Sydney) 22 July 13/1 Every blackfellow in my mustering team carried on his saddle a koondy—a heavy stick, usually of karara wood, sharpened at each end by charring and scraping.   **1966** M. BROWN *Jimberi Track* 32 Everything was different here—no gidgie tree, karara, no quondong of the little round nuts.   **1984** W.W. AMMON et al. *Working Lives* 150 The kurara grows mostly in watercourses and, like the `spinifex further north, give it a few millimetres of rain and it throws out thousands of new green leaves.

karbeen, var. CARBEEN.

karbi /ˈkabi/. [Prob. a. Yagara *gabay*.] The small, dark-coloured, stingless bee *Trigona carbonaria*.
1884 *Trans. Entomol. Soc. London* 149 (OEDS) Of these stingless bees of Australia two varieties only have come under my immediate observation... 'Karbi' or 'Keelar' and 'Kootchar' are the names given to them by the natives... 'Karbi' gather but little honey. 1948 *Bull. Amer. Museum Nat. Hist.* XC. 22/1 (OEDS) The spiral staircase type of nest was recorded by Hockings.. in the case of an Australian *Trigona* known as 'karbi' or 'keelar' that he believed to be *carbonaria*.

kark, v. Also **cark**. [Prob. fig. use of CARK to caw, from the assoc. of the crow with carrion.] *intr.* To die.
1977 R. BEILBY *Gunner* 302 'That wog ya roughed up—well, he karked.' Sa'ad dead! 1982 N. KEESING *Lily on Dustbin* 50 A 'stiff dunny' is dead or, in other words 'has carked it', and a patient who has 'sloughed off' has disappeared.

karkalla /kaˈkælə/. [a. Gaurna *garrgala*.] Any of several species of PIGFACE, incl. *Carpobrotus rossii* of coastal Tas., Vic., S.A., and W.A.
1846 C.W. SCHÜRMANN *Aboriginal Tribes Port Lincoln* 6 The fruit of a species of cactus, very elegantly styled pig-faces, by the white people, but by the natives, called karkalla. 1984 *Flora Aust.* IV. 27 *Carpobrotus rossii*.. Karkalla. A native species found primarily in coastal areas in S.A., Vic. and Tas.

karri /ˈkæri/. [Prob. a. Nyungar *karri*.] The tall timber tree of s.w. W.A. *Eucalyptus diversicolor* (fam. Myrtaceae), having a straight, smooth-barked trunk and reaching a height of 70 m.; the hard, heavy, red wood of the tree. Also *attrib*.
1866 *S. Austral. Register* (Adelaide) 17 May 3/7 The Karri gum-tree (*Eucalyptus diversicolor*) attains.. stupendous dimensions. 1983 P. ADAM SMITH *When we rode Rails* 66 The many little milling lines in the area called the 'Kingdom of the Karri'.

Kathleen Mavourneen, *a.* and *n.* [In allusion to the song 'Kathleen Mavourneen', the refrain of which is: 'it may be for years, it may be forever.']
A. *adj.* Of indeterminate duration.
1903 J. FURPHY *Such is Life* 161 Heaven grant that that parting may be a Kathleen Mavourneen one; and let me have some other class of difficulty to deal with next time. 1983 *Sydney Morning Herald* 20 May 16/2 Two on a lengthening list of the Bowen Basin's 'Kathleen Mavourneen' mines whose development could be for years or could be forever.
B. *n.*
a. A gaol sentence of indeterminate duration.
1910 L. ESSON *Three Short Plays* (1911) 16 It's a Kathleen Mavourneen, you know. It may be for years, or it may be for ever. 1978 H.C. BAKER *I was Listening* 41 The judge declared him an 'habitual criminal' and gave him a 'Kathleen Mavourneen' ('It may be for years and it may be forever', as the old song went).
b. *transf.* An habitual criminal.
1917 *Bulletin* (Sydney) 1 Nov. 24/1 The hawk.. spells danger and death to many.. sweet bush singers.. and so he should get a place with the Kathleen Mavourneens. 1950 *Austral. Police Jrnl.* Apr. 116 *Kathleen Mavourneen*, declared an habitual criminal.
c. *fig.* A swag.
1922 *Smith's Weekly* (Sydney) 28 Jan. 17/4 Swag aliases are.. 'Kathleen Mavourneen' [etc.].

katta /ˈkætə/. *Obs.* Also **kiatta**. [a. Gaurna *gada*.] DIGGING STICK.
1839 *Tasmanian* (Hobart) 5 Apr. 110/3 The only instruments he used were a *katta* (cudgel) and a *joko* (wooden scoop). 1879 *Native Tribes S.A.* 214 The kiatta or grubbing stick is a gum or sheoak sappling.

kauri pine /ˈkaʊri paɪn/. Also **cowry pine**. [Transf. use of Maori *kauri* the N.Z. tree *Agathis australis*.] Any of three tall, coniferous, rainforest trees of the genus *Agathis* (fam. Araucariaceae), *A. microstachya* and *A. atropurpurea* of n. Qld. and *A. robusta* of n. and s. Qld.; the pale, light, easily worked wood of the tree. Also **kauri**, and *attrib*.
1861 J.D. LANG *Qld., Aust.* 122 The principal timber is Kauri, of large growth and it stands thicker on the ground than in any scrubs I have seen on the Mary. 1879 *Illustr. Austral. News* (Melbourne) 2 Aug. 122/1 She is composite built, with.. Kauri decks and teak fittings. 1901 C. MOYNIHAN *Feast of Bunya* 32 From woody-crowned Maroochie, Where grow the kauri pines. 1930 HIVES & LUMLEY *Jrnl. of Jackaroo* 212 Huge cotton, cedar and cowry pine-trees grew in great numbers.

Keartland honeyeater /kətlənd ˈhʌniitə/. [f. the name of G.A. *Keartland* (1848–1926), an ornithologist who accompanied the Horn expedition to central Aust. and collected the type specimen.] The grey-headed honeyeater *Lichenostomus keartlandi* of inland n. Aust., a predom. yellowish-green bird. Also **Keartland's honeyeater**.
1896 B. SPENCER *Rep. Horn Sci. Exped. Central Aust.* II. 65 Keartland's Honey-eater is here burdened with the trouble of rearing young cuckoos. 1903 *Emu* II. 147 Keartland Honey-eater... A nest of this Honey-eater was found.

kebarra, kebarrah, varr. KIPPER $n.^1$

keenly, *a.* S.A. *Obs.* [Cornish dial. *keenly* (of a mine) promising: see EDD.]
a. *Mining.* Of ore, a lode, etc.: promising; likely to yield the mineral sought.
1849 *S. Austral. Register* (Adelaide) 25 July 3/2 We venture to express an opinion experimentally in favour of a mining log-book.. that 'she's looking keenly'. 1872 *Yorke's Peninsula Advertiser* (Moonta) 8 Nov. 2/7 Some very 'keenly stone' has already been found on the surface.
b. *transf.*
1872 *S. Austral. Register* (Adelaide) 9 Oct. 3/6 The crops look 'keenly', being refreshed by late rains.

keepara, keeparra, varr. KIPPER $n.^1$

keet. [Shortened form of LORIKEET.] Any of several small parrots, incl. the *little lorikeet* (see LITTLE 2). Often with distinguishing epithet.
1874 C. DE BOOS *Congewoi Correspondence* 148 The keets and the blue mountainers seems to be the only birds as don't mind it. 1948 J. FAIRFAX *Run o' Waters* 58 A little colony of green 'keets would dive between the forest trees with shrill screams.

keg. [Spec. use of *keg* small barrel or cask.]
1. A barrel of beer.
1896 *Bulletin* (Sydney) 5 Sept. 3/2 We wore our knuckle-dusters, and we took a keg on tap For our friendly game of football with the fellows at the Gap. 1965 J. O'GRADY *Aussie Eng.* 16 Containers run from five-ounce glasses to eighteen-gallon kegs.
2. Special Comb. **keg party,** a party at which a keg of beer (the cost of which is met by subscriptions from the participants) is the principal refreshment.

1950 K.S. Prichard *Winged Seeds* 60 They were in demand at all the dances and keg parties of the smart set.

kellick. [Var. of Br. *killick* (of unfixed spelling, *killick, killock* being preferred elsewhere): see OED(S *killick*.] A stone; an anchor. Also *attrib.*

1867 J.R. Houlding *Austral. Capers* 215 Vainly did he implore his jovial companions to up kellick, and land him on the nearest point. **1873** R.P. Whitworth *Lost & Found* 44 Left the boat afloat with the German in her, and moored by a kellick rope and a large stone.

Kelly, *n.*[1] [f. the name of Ned *Kelly* (1857–1880), bushranger.]

1. Used *attrib.* in Special Comb. **Kelly country,** a district in n.e. Victoria in which Ned Kelly and his brothers were active as bushrangers; **gang** *transf.*, see quots. See also Ned Kelly *n.* and *v.*

1880 *Argus* (Melbourne) 2 Feb. 5/4 A gentleman . . had come through from Sydney, and stayed for a time to have a look at 'the **Kelly country**'. **1902** *Truth* (Sydney) 28 Sept. 8/3 English papers have been referring to *our Boer-baiting braves* as **Kelly gangs** owing to their pleasant little ways. **1941** S.J. Baker *Pop. Dict. Austral. Slang* 41 *Kelly gang*, a term applied to any business firm whose practices are not above suspicion, and esp. to a ruling Government, with reference to tax-grabbing propensities.

2. [Prob. *transf.*] A crow. Also **kelly crow.**

1924 *Smith's Weekly* (Sydney) 23 Feb. 23/5 'Kelly' was found guilty and sentenced to six months in chains on hard food. A chain was attached to the crow's leg and thence to a stake in the ground. **1981** A.J. Burke *Pommies & Patriots* 44 In times of frequent drought the Kelly Crows descend on millions of dead cattle like vultures.

3. One whose behaviour is supposed in some way to resemble that of Ned Kelly.

1947 *Bulletin* (Sydney) 11 June 28/1 When he was camped by Naracan Creek a couple of louts bailed him up. . . The amateur Kellies rushed. **1980** C. James *Unreliable Mem.* 155 The inspectors were called Kellies, after Ned Kelly, and were likely to swoop at any time. A conductor with twenty years' service could be dismissed if a Kelly caught him accepting money without pulling a ticket.

Kelly, *n.*[2] Also **kelly.** [Proprietary name.] A type of axe; (loosely) an axe. Also **Kelly axe,** and *attrib.*

1909 R. Kaleski *Austral. Settler's Compl. Guide* ii. 11, I try every axe on the market, but the only two I care to use are either Plumb's or the black Kelly, the Kelly for choice as the best all-round axe. **1945** D. Robinson *Pop's Blonde* 84 'Up the Alley,' roared a big Australian, an ex-kelly swinger from Queensland. **1983** R. Beckett *Axemen* 12 Most axemen . . use a standard axe. . . It used to be referred to as a 'Kelly' because it was just that . . the 'Kelly' axe.

kelp fish. [Attrib. use of *kelp*, from the fish's habit of lying among algae and seagrasses.] Any of several marine fish, esp. of the fam. Chironemidae, incl. *Chironemus georgianus* and *C. marmoratus* of s. Aust., and (*Tas.*) *Neoodax balteatus* (fam. Odacidae).

1842 *Tasmanian Jrnl. Nat. Sci.* I. 102 *Odax*, known at Port Arthur by the name of Kelp Fish. **1974** T.D. Scott et al. *Marine & Freshwater Fishes S.A.* 232 Kelp Fish. . . This species is quite good eating.

kelpie /'kɛlpi/. [f. the name of an individual bitch *Kelpie* a progenitor of the breed. An Australian breed of short-haired, prick-eared dog, noted for its hardiness and ability to tend and work sheep; a dog of this breed. See also Barb.

1895 *Australasian* (Melbourne) 12 Jan. 60/2 There is a little smooth-coated sheep dog with prick ears . . in several parts of Australia called Kelpies. I have seen them at Wagga and other shows. **1983** *Bulletin* (Sydney) 28 June 44/2 Exporting kelpies to Scotland is particularly interesting since they are descendants of dogs brought from that country to Australia in the 1860s.

kennedia /kə'nɛdiə/. [The plant genus *Kennedia* was named by the French botanist E.P. Ventenat (*Jard. Malm.* II. (1805) 104, Pl. 104) after the London nurseryman John *Kennedy* (1759–1842).] Any plant of the genus of climbing or trailing perennials *Kennedia* (fam. Fabaceae), occurring in s.w. W.A. and all other States but not N.T., some species being cultivated for their colourful pea flowers and trifoliolate leaves.

1845 *Florist's Jrnl.* 75 (OED) An early vinery is exactly the place in which to grow Kennedyas. **1976** *Ecos* vii. 11/1 In the jarrah forest . . the mild fires of prescribed burning produce very little regeneration of nitrogen-fixing plants, particularly wattles and ground-hugging kennedias.

kero /'kɛroʊ/. Abbrev. of 'kerosene'. Freq. *attrib.*

1930 *Bulletin* (Sydney) 10 Sept. 22/3 With little stalls and cut-down kero.-tins . . calves can be fed quickly enough. **1968** S. Gore *Holy Smoke* 94 You'll be like them Foolish Virgins, who never had a skerrick of kero left in their lamps to greet the second coming of the Lord!

kerosene.

1. Used *attrib.* with a second element designating a container for the storage or transport of kerosene subsequently used to improvise a utensil or article of furniture: **kerosene box,** (**-tin**) **bucket, case, tin.**

1901 *Advocate* (Burnie) 8 June 4/2 The Duchess sat down on a **kerosene box**, covered with a rug. **1901** H. Lawson *Joe Wilson & his Mates* (1902) 64, I ran down to the creek with the big **kerosene-tin bucket**. **1927** K.S. Prichard *Brumby Innes* (1974) 59 Two smoke-blackened kerosene buckets for water on the hearth. **1903** J. Furphy *Such is Life* 157 Bendigo Bill, sitting on the same **kerosene-case**, long afterward narrated the episode fully. **1896** M. Clarke *Austral. Tales* 61 A band of merry boys would have exploded in his back yard, and have banged **kerosene tins** beneath his wedding window.

2. In the names of highly flammable plants: **kerosene bush,** the small, aromatic shrub *Helichrysum hookeri* (fam. Asteraceae), occurring in mountainous Tas., Vic., and s.e. N.S.W., esp. in swamps and near watercourses; the related *H. ledifolium*; **wood** (or **tree**), Ghittoe.

1965 *Austral. Encycl.* V. 181 The highly resinous *Helichrysum hookeri*, which flares up when ignited, has been called **kerosene-bush** in Tasmania, where it is a common mountain shrub. **1919** [**kerosene wood**] R.T. Baker *Hardwoods of Aust.* 63 *Halfordia scleroxyla* . . 'Kerosene Tree.' **1944** J. Devanny *By Tropic Sea & Jungle* 18 Take kerosene wood, or jitter, as some people call it.

kestrel. [Spec. use of *kestrel* a hovering bird of prey.] Nankeen kestrel, see Nankeen.

1893 *Argus* (Melbourne) 25 Mar. 4/5 The kestrel's nest we always found in the fluted gums that overhung the creek, the red eggs resting on the red mould of the decaying trunk being almost invisible. **1984** M. Blakers et al. *Atlas Austral. Birds* 111 The Kestrel inhabits any country where it can hunt over open space, often urban areas, even town centres.

kew, var. Cue *n.* and *v.*

kiatta, var. Katta.

kick, *v.*[1] In the phr. **to kick the tin,** to contribute money to a cause.

1965 J. O'Grady *Aussie Eng.* 53 'Kick the tin' . . when it's your turn to buy a round of drinks. **1982** *Austral.* (Sydney) 11 Aug. 9/1 The Tasmanian Premier would do all (except, presumably, kick the tin) that the Victorian Premier would not do.

kick, *v.*² *intr.* With **on**: to maintain momentum; to gain momentum. Also *trans.*
1949 L. GLASSOP *Lucky Palmer* 153 'I knew him when I used to slip ten bob out of the till . . so he could kick on with it.' 'You can often kick on with ten bob,' said 'Lucky' judicially. 1955 R. LAWLER *Summer of Seventeenth Doll* (1965) 48 What about all those times you've carried me—every year when I've run dry down here you've kicked me on.

kick-off. *Australian National Football. Obs.* In the collocation **kick-off post,** *behind post* (see BEHIND 2).
1859 C.C. MULLEN *Hist. Austral. Rules Football* (1959) 10 Two posts to be called the 'kick off' posts shall be erected at a distance of 20 yards on each side of the goal posts.

Kidman. [The name of Sidney *Kidman* (1857–1935), grazier.]
1. Used *attrib.* with ref. to large-scale stock-raising.
1946 C.T. MADIGAN *Crossing Dead Heart* 88 Annandale was a typical example of what is often called the Kidman blight on the country. 1949 G. FARWELL *Traveller's Tracks* 88 The country can only be held in large holdings, preferably in the Kidman manner, so that stock can be shifted from one property to another, instead of droving them straight down.
2. In the collocation **Kidman's blood mixture (delight, joy),** golden syrup or treacle.
1935 R.B. PLOWMAN *Boundary Rider* 187 The better class employer added a tin of jam per week, or its equivalent in 'Bullocky's Joy' (treacle) or what was later known as 'Kidman's Delight' (golden syrup). 1945 S.J. BAKER *Austral. Lang.* 200 *Kidman's joy or Kidman's blood mixture,* treacle or golden syrup. Commemorating the late Sir Sidney Kidman, noted squatter.

kidstakes, *pl.* [Prob. joc. formation on Br. slang *kid humbug.*] Nonsense; pretence. Also *attrib.* and *v. intr.*
1912 *Huon Times* (Franklin) 9 Mar. 6/3, I thought whirlwinds were kid stakes, just bits of games, but I don't want to see another. 1927 F.C. BIGGERS *Bat-Eye* 7 This 'ere ain't now no kidstakes yarn ter touch yer 'earts. 1950 F.J. HARDY *Power without Glory* 525 Sent him to manage those milk-bars in Brisbane. . . Kidstaked to him a bit at the finish to sugar-coat the pill.

ki-eye, var. KAI-YAI.

ki-ki: see KAI.

kiley, var. KYLIE.

killer. An animal, esp. a bullock or sheep, selected and killed for immediate consumption.
1897 I. SCOTT *How I stole over 10,000 Sheep in Aust. & N.Z.* 9 'You know the killers, don't you?' . . i.e., the sheep the boss used for his own mutton at the house. 1980 ANSELL & PERCY *To fight Wild* 133 Christopher cooked the rib bones from our killer that night.

killing, *vbl. n.*
1. Used *attrib.* in Comb. with reference to the butchering of animals, as: **killing day, gallows, paddock, pen, season, yard.**
c 1877 W. ARCHER in R. Stanley *Tourist to Antipodes* (1977) 33 As **killing day** comes round generally not oftener than once a week, fresh meat is regarded as quite a delicacy. 1893 E. FAVENC *Last of Six Tales* 97 On the **'killing-gallows'** hung a freshly-slaughtered beast. [N.Z. 1907 W.H. KOEBEL *Return of Joe* 281, I see'd [the dog] after some sheep in the **killing paddock**.] 1922 V. PALMER *Boss of Killara* 77 The fattest bullocks had been brought into the killing-paddock. 1925 M. TERRY *Across Unknown Aust.* 143 There is also the **'killing pen'**, paved with slabs, where the butcher kills his beast. 1939 J.G. PATTISON *'Battler's' Tales Early Rockhampton* 61 My mission was to ride to Laurel Bank in the **killing season** on every Saturday morning to collect a cheque for my father who had the contract to supply the works with cattle. 1870 C.H. ALLEN *Visit to Qld.* 139 The **killing-yards** and boiling down houses are on a very extensive scale.
2. Special Comb. **killing sheep,** a sheep selected to be killed for food (esp. for the employees on a station).
1901 *Bulletin* (Sydney) 22 June 32/3 I've seen a native sent on the road with a mob of killing sheep (native name cookinjerry).

Kimberley /'kɪmbəli/. [f. the name of the *Kimberley Range* in n.w. W.A.] Used *attrib.* in Special Comb. **Kimberley (horse) disease** *n. Aust.*, a usu. fatal illness of horses in which liver damage, the cause of which is believed to be the consumption of certain species of *Crotalaria* (fam. Fabaceae), occurs; see also WALKABOUT DISEASE a.; also **Kimberley walkabout (disease); knot,** see quot.; **mutton,** goat meat; **oyster,** *Burdekin duck* (b), see BURDEKIN.
1915 *Bulletin* (Sydney) 18 Feb. 13/3 The 'walkabout' disease of the Northern Territory, the **Kimberley disease** of Westralia and the Birdsville disease of Queensland have been identified as one and the same. 1954 *Bulletin* (Sydney) 25 Aug. 12/2 Gardiner has established that the Kimberley (walkabout) horse disease is caused by the animals eating the wedge-leaved rattlepod. 1971 K. WILLEY *Boss Drover* 72 Horses . . would die in hundreds from what we called the Kimberley walkabout. This was a disease which set a horse walking, round and round and up and down, knocking into trees and rocks and never stopping to eat, until in a few hours or days he would literally have walked himself to death. 1975 R. EDWARDS *Austral. Traditional Bush Crafts* 93 The Gulf knot is used for attaching reins to the bit without the use of a buckle. In north-west Australia it is known as a **Kimberley knot.** 1953 L. & C. REES *Spinifex Walkabout* 119 You've tasted goat, of course—they call it **Kimberley mutton** up here. 1945 T. RONAN *Strangers on Ophir* 39 A meat fritter known in the Kimberleys as a 'Burdekin Duck', and on the Burdekin as a **'Kimberley Oyster'**.

kinchela /kɪn'tʃelə/. *Shearing. Obs.* Also **kinshela.** [Poss. f. the name of John *Kinsella* (d. 1902), labourer.] An adjustment made to shears to increase the width of the blow: see quots. 1911 and 1937.
1897 *Bulletin* (Sydney) 25 Sept. (Red Page), 'Putting Kinchela on 'em' is evidently inspired by the fact that one Kinchela, some years ago, wrote and published a pamphlet on the art of sharpening and 'keeping' shears. The expression was at first confined exclusively to shear-sharpening but in time came to have a wider application. 1911 E.S. SORENSON *Life in Austral. Backblocks* 233 The blades are pulled back and the knockers filed down, so the shears will take a bigger blow. This is called 'putting Kinchler on them', from the fact that it was first adopted by John Kinsella. 1937 *Bulletin* (Sydney) 14 July 20/1 Bar 'kinshela', no bladesmen sought for artificial aids to pace. . . 'Kinshela' consisted of putting the bottom blade back so as to obtain a wider cut.

kinder. Abbrev. of 'kindergarten'. Also *attrib.*
1955 *Meanjin* 308 Like Billy in the Kinder. 1959 D. HEWETT *Bobbin Up* 130 It was his version of a particularly sissy 'kinder' song, that offended his rugged masculinity.

kindy. Also **kindie.** [f. *kind(ergarten* + -Y.] A kindergarten. Also *attrib.*
[N.Z. 1959 G. SLATTER *A Gun in my Hand* 146 Two kids at school now and the little joker's at a kindy.] 1973 *Courier-Mail* (Brisbane) 4 June 15/6 The State Education Department will provide children in isolated areas with a pre-school education. . . A scheme for 'kindy by correspondence' would be available by the start of 1974. 1981

P. RADLEY *Jack Rivers & Me* 66 They sound like Kindie-kids. Run, fish, run, here comes the sun, fish.

king, *n.*[1] *Hist.*

1. a. A title given by colonists to the male leader of an Aboriginal community; CHIEF; *native chief*, see NATIVE *a.* 5.

1830 G.C. INGLETON *True Patriots All* 27 Nov. (1952) 122 We have to announce the death of his Aboriginal Majesty King *Boongarie*, Supreme Chief of the Sydney tribe. **1978** E. SIMON *Through my Eyes* 78 'King' Billy Ridgeway .. used to wear a brass plate around his neck; it had been given to him when Parliament had made it fashionable to call the elders 'kings'.

b. *Special Comb.* **King Billy** [prob. in joc. allusion to King William IV (1830- 37)], a generic term for an Aboriginal leader; an Aboriginal; **plate,** see quot. 1817.

1847 *Maitland Mercury* 24 July 3/1 We were in conversation with 'King Billy Boomee'. **1883** *Bulletin* (Sydney) 10 Nov. 6/4 Boomerang, spear, and bow Laid by for ever—lo, Dead is King Billy! [**1817 king plate:** *Sydney Gaz.* 4 Jan., His *Excellency*.. assembled the chiefs .. confirmed them in the ranks of chieftains to which their own tribes had exalted them, and conferred on them badges of distinction, whereon were engraved their names as chiefs and those of their tribes. **1849** A. HARRIS *Emigrant Family* (1967) 233 He picked up from the ground a brass-plate, of a half-moon shape, such as the settlers give to favourite leading blacks as a distinguishing badge, to be worn slung from the neck by a chain. On it was engraved 'Bondi, King of the Snowy Mountains'. **1894** *Bulletin* (Sydney) 13 Jan. 4/3 The honour of being King Billy fell into contempt when every male member of the Australian aboriginal race began to lay claim to an elaborately engraven brass half-moon of his own.] **1980** *Catal. Fine & Rare Bks.* (James R. Lawson Pty. Ltd.) 14 Dec. 58 An exceptionally fine solid brass king plate or breastplate weighing 14 oz., bearing engraved crown to centre and engraved with figures of an emu and a kangaroo.

2. *Special Comb.* In the names of flora and fauna: **king brown (snake),** the large, venomous snake *Pseudechis australis*, occurring throughout n. and drier s. mainland Aust.; *mulga snake*, see MULGA *n.*[1] B. 3; **fern,** either of the two large ferns, *Todea barbara* (fam. Osmundaceae) of shady forests in e. Aust., N.Z., and S. Africa, and the tropical *Angiopteris evecta* (fam. Marattiaceae), chiefly of Qld., Malaysia, and Polynesia; **honeysucker** *obs., regent bird*, see REGENT 1; **parrot,** any of several parrots, esp. the predom. scarlet and green *Alisterus scapularis* of coastal and near-coastal mountain regions of e. mainland Aust., and (*W.A.*) the *red-capped parrot* (see RED *a.* 1 b.); **pigeon** *obs.*, WOMPOO PIGEON; **prawn,** a large prawn of the genus *Penaeus* valued as food, *P. plebejus* occurring in the waters of e. Aust., and *P. latisulcatus* in w. and n. Aust. and throughout the Indo-Pacific region; **quail,** the small, wide-ranging bird *Coturnix chinensis*, occurring in near-coastal e. and n. Aust. and through s.e. Asia to China; **snapper,** any of several fish incl. *red emperor* (see RED *a.* 1 b.).

1935 D. THOMSON *In Arnhem Land* (1983) 35 *Pseudechis australis,* the **King Brown Snake** .. a fine showy snake, rich copper-brown .. and about seven feet long and very thick. **1980** ANSELL & PERCY *To fight Wild* 48 If I was bitten by a king brown out in the bush and didn't get antivenene for six hours I'd be dead anyway. *c* **1910** W.R. GUILFOYLE *Austral. Plants* 354 *Todea barbara.* '**King Fern**' or 'Swamp Sponge Fern'. **1981** G. ELLIS *Hey Doc, let's go Fishing!* 72 Even the huge King ferns, *Angiopteris evecta*, with huge fronds five metres in length, have vanished. **1813** J.W. LEWIN *Birds N.S.W.* 16 **King Honeysucker.** Inhabits Banks of Patterson's River. Frequents thick brushy Woods. **1803** J. GRANT *Narr. Voyage N.S.W.* 111 Mr Cayley shot a **king parrot. 1857** W.S. BRADSHAW *Voyages* 87 There are a great variety of parrots, namely .. the king parrot, the walkinger .. and the red-crested. **1889** R.B. ANDERSON tr. Lumholtz's *Among Cannibals* 214 Up here I saw several nests of the beautiful **king-pigeon** (*Megaloprepia magnifica*). **1950** *Fisheries Newsletter* IX. vii. 5 The **King prawns** were going out into deeper water. **1889** *Proc. Linnean Soc. N.S.W.* IV. 419 *Excalfatoria australis* .. known as '**King-quail**'. **1951** T.C. ROUGHLEY *Fish & Fisheries Aust.* 98 A species closely related to the nannygai and caught in the Great Australian Bight is known commonly as '**king snapper**'.

3. *Special Comb.* **king post** [transf. use of *king-post* upright post in the centre of a roof-truss], one of the main uprights in a fence, etc.; **tide,** a spring tide; an unusually high tide.

1892 *Bulletin* (Sydney) 30 July 7/3 Nigh a shattered drum and a **king-post** rotting, Are the bleaching bones of the old grey horse. **1926** M. FORREST *Hibiscus Heart* 261 There was a **king tide** coming in: to-night the full moon would see itself in a vast assemblage of waters, thundering on the trunks of the pandanus, flooding the milk-white beaches.

king, *n.*[2] Abbrev. of KINGFISH.

1939 *Bulletin* (Sydney) 1 Mar. 21/2 He talks about night-angling for kingfish. Our kingies, or the things we call kings, observe early closing hours and don't bite after dark. **1983** *Canberra Chron.* 15 June 18/3 Tracy, 13, took another big king.

king, *n.*[3] Abbrev. of KING-HIT *n.*

1952 *Argus Mag.* (Melbourne) 18 Jan. 4/3, I brought him back to the subject of the king-hit again, and he said, 'You've always got to connect with a king. It's no good swinging one and missing.'

king, *v.* Abbrev. of KING-HIT *v.*

1940 W. HATFIELD *Into (Great?) Unfenced* 124 He would slip in now and 'king' him. **1975** *Bulletin* (Sydney) 26 Apr. 45/3 He kinged a floorwalker just to let the bagman off the hook.

King Billy pine: see KING WILLIAM PINE.

kingfish. [Transf. use of *kingfish* a fish remarkable for its size or value as food, etc.] Any of several fish, esp. the large, common *Seriola lalandi*, having edible flesh and a yellow caudal fin, and MULLOWAY. See also YELLOWTAIL.

1825 B. FIELD *Geogr. Mem. N.S.W.* 22 The bay abounds with what are called in the colony .. king-fish. **1983** *Canberra Chron.* 15 June 18/3 They finally managed to salvage a saurie that a hooked kingfish spat our near their boat, caught a kingfish with it, then gutted him to obtain even more sauries.

King George whiting. [See quot. 1974.] *Spotted whiting,* see SPOTTED.

1968 D. O'GRADY *Bottle of Sandwiches* 15 The bay was alive with .. King George whiting, and many other mouth-watering finny pan-fillers. **1974** J.M. THOMSON *Fish Ocean & Shore* 126 The King George or spotted whiting (*Sillaginodes punctatus*) ranges from south-western Australia, where the name King George is derived from King George Sound, to the southern coast of New South Wales.

king-hit, *n.* A sudden, damaging blow; a knock-out punch; an unfair punch. Also *fig.*, and *attrib.*

1917 A.C. PANTON *Dinkum Oils,* K is the King-hit we'll give to the guy, Who started this war, or we'll want to know why. **1923** *Communist* (Sydney) 16 Mar. 4/1 No doubt Ted will take warning from James and get in on the Queensland Central Executive with his king-hit. **1985** *N.T. News* (Darwin) 16 Apr. 35/4 The final chapter of the ugly 'king-hit' incident from last month's NTFL grand final will unfold tonight.

king hit, *v.* [f. prec.] *trans.* To punch (a person) suddenly and hard, often unfairly; to knock out.
   1959 E. LAMBERT *Glory thrown In* 150 They stopped us and tried to arrest us. I king-hit the sergeant and we up and off.   **1985** *N.T. News* (Darwin) 17 Apr. 40/1 Nikoletos was reported by goal umpire Peter Hardy after 'king-hitting' McPhee in the first term of the grand final.
   Hence **king hitter** *n.*, **king hitting** *vbl. n.* and *ppl. a.*
   1952 *Argus Mag.* (Melbourne) 18 Jan. 4/3 King-hit Delaney of Bourke, a man who earned his nickname over the fallen bodies of a score of victims, once gave me the low-down on **king-hitters**.   **1979** G. STEWART *Leveller* 35 'You **king-hitting** bastard, out the back and fight like a man,' Paddy screamed.   **1981** A.B. FACEY *Fortunate Life* 224 If you won't withdraw what you said I'm prepared to test you with your king-hitting business.

kingie. [f. *king* (as first element indicating size) + -Y.]
   1. KINGFISH.
   1936 N. CALDWELL *Fangs of Sea* 90 The immense schools of striped tuna, locally called 'kingies' (kingfish) work into the warmer waters.   **1970** I. GALL *Fishing for Fun of It* 16 The kingie probably headed for New Zealand or at least Norfolk Island, for we never, at any stage, saw that rod and reel again.
   2. *King prawn*, see KING *n.*¹ 2.
   1966 P. PINNEY *Restless Men* 20 We export our Australian prawns to .. Japan, so that .. the Japs can cut up our Kingies and sell 'em back to us as prawn-flake.   **1980** B. SHACKLETON *Karagi* 23 The school and ground prawners of the estuaries battled to compete with the big 'Kingie' running at about ten to the pound.

King Street. [The name of a street in central Sydney, used in allusion to the hearing of bankruptcy cases in the Supreme Court located there.] In the phr. **up** (or **in**) **King Street**, in financial difficulty.
   1864 *Bell's Life in Sydney* 11 June 3/1 Always avoid the society of obstinate 'jolly good fellows' who 'won't go home till morning', for late hours are very expensive, and generally lead to an *early* 'walk up King-street'.   **1887** *Bungendore Mirror* 8 Oct. 2 The speculation would not pay at present and could but land us in King-street.

King William pine. [Prob. f. the name of the *King William* Range in w. Tas.] The coniferous tree *Athrotaxis selaginoides* (fam. Taxodiaceae) of w. and s.w. Tas.; the softwood timber of the tree, being straight-grained, light, and very durable. Also **King Billy pine.**
   1903 *Tasmanian Timbers* (Tas. Lands & Survey Dept.) 25 King William pine .. *Athrotaxis selaginoides* .. is so named from the leaf resembling the selaginela, an ornamental tree-moss.   **1916** *Bulletin* (Sydney) 10 Aug. 24/2, I move that a D.S.O. be awarded to King Billy pine, which grows on the wet side of Tassy, as the best timber for huts.

kinshela, var. KINCHELA.

kip. *Two-up.* [Perh. f. Br. dial. *kep, v.* to catch; to throw up in the air: see EDD.] A small, flat piece of wood with which the coins are tossed.
   1887 K. MACKAY *Stirrup Jingles* 58 Then an hour was devoted to blowing And drinking and handling the 'kip' For at 'heading' these shearers were knowing, And at talk creation could whip.   **1977** R. BEILBY *Gunner* 297 Gunner waited with the kip at the ready: it was a small rectangle of sweat-darkened wood, smoothed by handling and scored with cross-hatching which gave it a rudimentary but professional look.

kipper /'kɪpə/, *n.*¹ *Hist.* Formerly also with much variety, as **kebarra, kebarrah, keepara, keeparra,**

kippa. [a. Dharuk *gibara* an initiated boy; poss. related to *giba* stone (see quot. 1798).]
   1. a. An Aboriginal male who has been initiated into manhood. Also as quasi-*adj.*
   1798 D. COLLINS *Acct. Eng. Colony N.S.W.* I. 580 They were also termed Ke-bar-ra, a name which has reference in its construction to the singular instrument used on this occasion, ke-bah in their language signifying rock or stone.   **1841** *Colonial Observer* (Sydney) 14 Oct. 10/4 We went with some of the natives to see the spot where the solemnity of making *kippers* is to take place.   **1869** 'E. HOWE' *Boy in Bush* 204 One of them asked, 'Was not the son of Kaludie a kipper?' and then pointed to Harry's mouth, out of which, of course, no tooth had been knocked, black-fellow fashion, at the 'kipper' age.   **1923** T. HALL *Short Hist. Downs Blacks* 6 Each pole or post bore the distinct mark belonging to each 'Kippa' (or youth), and the Councillors knew which Kippa belonged to the different posts.
   b. The ceremony in which such an initiation takes place. Also **kipper ceremony, kipper making.**
   1833 *N.S.W. Mag.* (Sydney) I. 11 'Bappo' .. the deity supposed to preside at the celebration of the 'Kebarrah'.   **1876** 'EIGHT YRS.' RESIDENT' *Queen of Colonies* 327 Among the customs of our blacks, perhaps the most curious and mysterious is that of kipper making.   **1899** R.H. MATHEWS *Folklore Austral. Aborigines* 23 The rocks .. enclosed a large oval or circular space, like the *kackaroo* ring at the keeparra ceremony.
   2. *Special Comb.* **kipper ground, ring,** the place reserved for the holding of an initiation ceremony.
   1851 *Empire* (Sydney) 22 Oct. 284/3 Nor are they treated in any manner as men, nor allowed to take to themselves a wife or wives (for Polygamy is allowed among them) until they have their allotted probation at the **Kipper ground.**   **1876** 'EIGHT YRS.' RESIDENT' *Queen of Colonies* 328 '**Kipper rings**' may be seen, where these mysteries are performed and the initiations take place.

kipper, *n.*² [f. the popular assoc. of *kipper* a cured herring with the English.] A sailor in the Royal Navy; an English person.
   1943 J.F. MOYES *Scrap-Iron Flotilla* 105 The soldiers were mostly Australians, the nurses were 'Wallabies', 'Kiwis' and 'Kippers'.   **1948** H.W. CRITTENDEN *Rogues' Paradise* 172 It is this ignorance that inspires a Royal Australian Navy rating in uniform to publicly describe the British Navy men as 'kippers', and proudly proclaim that he is 'Anti-British'.

kipper /'kɪpə/, *v.* [f. KIPPER *n.*¹] *trans.* To initiate (an Aboriginal male) into manhood.
   1873 J.B. STEPHENS *Black Gin* 39 Where of old with awful mysteries and diabolic din, They 'kippered' adolescents in the presence of their kin.   **1972** M. CASSIDY *Dispossessed* 174 Murac .. had broken the tribe's law by marrying a girl before he was kippa-ed.

kippy. *Two-up.* [f. KIP + -Y.] SPINNER *a.*
   1946 K.S. PRICHARD *Roaring Nineties* 152 The ring-keeper might object to a spin, on the grounds that the kippy had put a 'gig' on it, or touched the kip with his fingers.

kipsy. Also **kipsie.** [Elaboration of *kip* lodging-house.] A house; a shelter.
   1905 J. BUFTON *Tasmanians in Transvaal War* 95 Rigged a kipsie up on truck to keep the wet off.   **1909** *Bulletin* (Sydney) 16 Sept. 14/2 Cocky's first rain-water reservoir is usually a barrel, stuck at one corner of the kipsy with a sheet of stringy-bark connecting it with the roof.

kiss-and-ride, *attrib.* See quot 1975.
   1974 *Sydney Area Transportation Study* III. vi. 8 The statistics include both 'park-and-ride' and 'kiss and ride' passengers.   **1975** *Sydney Morning Herald* 16 Jan. 6/7 The alternative is the kiss-and-ride system—the wife drops her

husband off at the station or terminal, keeps the car for her own use during the day, and picks him up at night.

kit, *v. S.A. Mining. Obs.* [Prob. f. Br. dial. *kit* to pack in a kit or wooden vessel: see OED *v.*¹] *trans.* To steal (ore). Chiefly as *vbl. n.*

1865 *Wallaroo Times* (Kadina) 9 Dec. 5/2 Three men . . were discharged from the mine minus a good character for stealing or, to use the mining term 'kitting' ores from the company's piles. **1962** O. PRYOR *Aust.'s Little Cornwall* 56 There were dire penalties for 'kitting' as the stealing of ore was known.

kitchen.

1. In the phr. **the rounds of the kitchen,** a severe reproof; a scolding.

1873 J.C.F. JOHNSON *Christmas on Carringa* 4 He had been getting from Mrs M. . . what he termed 'the rounds of the kitchen', for being such a fool. **1939** J. CAMPBELL *Babe is Wise* 211 An does she gimme the rounds of the kitchen! Pitches into me like I dunno w'at.

2. Special Comb. **kitchen tea,** a party given for a bride-to-be to which the (usu. female) guests bring gifts of kitchen equipment.

1934 T. CLARKE *Marriage* 17 Tom Rawlings led me off to see the bride at a 'kitchen tea'. . . In the centre of affairs was the young bride in whose honour the 'kitchen tea' had been arranged; and it was so called because each guest brought a kitchen utensil as a wedding-gift.

kitehawk. The predom. brown, carrion-eating bird *Milvus migrans,* common in n. Aust. and widespread to Europe and Africa.

1909 LINDSAY & HOLTZE *Territoria* 24 There are the . . hawks (eagle, brown, and kite hawks). **1979** D. LOCKWOOD *My Old Mates & I* 58 Kitehawks (fire hawks) feeding on the perimeter of a grass fire, swooping on insects, rodents, lizards.

Kiwi, *n. Obs.* [f. KIWI *v.*] A soldier, esp. one with highly-polished accoutrements.

1916 *Astra* (Melbourne) Sept. 1/2 Demands . . are made on them as Kiwi Kids. **1917** *Southern Cross Gaz.: Jrnl. H.M.A.T. 'Thermistocles'* 28 May 3 This army . . consists of soldiers and 'Kiwis'. . . 'Kiwis'. . Australia's bad bargains are much more easily distinguished by the high polish of their boots.

kiwi, *v. Obs.* [f. the proprietary name of a brand of shoe polish.] *trans.* To polish (shoes); to spruce up (one's appearance). Usu. with **up.** Also *absol.*

1917 *All abaht It* (London) Feb. (1919) 51 Hair sleekly brushed and kiwi-ed up as much as possible. **1929** 'F. BLAIR' *Digger Sea-Mates* 112 Whose boots were not bright as a mirror 'Kiwied' to the highest perfection? **1949** G. BERRIE *Morale* 210 Men will shave and wear bandoliers. They don't need to kiwi up specially.

kleiner, var. CLINER.

knap, *v. Gold-mining.* Also **nap.** [Spec. use of Br. (chiefly dial.) *knap* to strike sharply, to tap (esp. stone): see OED *v.*² and EDD *v.*²] *trans.* To break off (pieces of an outcropping reef) in order to ascertain if gold is present.

1898 W. DOLLMAN *Bush Fancies* 22 We'd been prospecting and hunting for miles, We'd 'napped' full many a reef. **1946** K.S. PRICHARD *Roaring Nineties* 59 Dinny went loaming along the ridge for several days before he knapped a rock that showed fine shotty gold.

knight. Used ironically in fig. collocations, as: **knight of the blades, of the bright** (or **shining**) **sword,** a shearer who uses hand shears; **of the road, (a)** a bushranger; **(b)** a swagman.

1896 *Worker* (Sydney) 5 Sept. 3/4 If the '**knights of the blades**' and their comrades will resolve to sink all minor issues . . Unionism must soon flourish and become all powerful throughout Australia. **1949** *Bulletin* (Sydney) 23 Feb. 14/4 Another common way to describe the ringer is to say that he 'swung the gate'. . . Can any old '**knights of the bright swords**' say how that term originated? **1978** M. WALKER *Pioneer Crafts Early Aust.* 151 The 'Knights of the Shining Swords'—the blade shearers. **(a) 1864** *Bell's Life in Sydney* 9 Jan. 2/6 A member of the Fighting Blues . . while out on horseback last week with the ostensible purpose of bushranger-hunting, accidentally stumbled over one of the **Knights of the Road.** **(b) 1936** I.L. IDRIESS *Cattle King* 351 Gone . . were the picturesque characters of the bush. . . Numerous similar **Knights of the Road** who had brought countless laughs to the tracks.

knock, *n. Australian National Football.* The striking of the ball towards a team-mate after a ball-up or throw-in.

1960 *N.T. News* (Darwin) 2 Feb. 8/8 Shields won the knock and Buffs brought the ball down for Frankie Ah Mat to goal. **1964** J. POLLARD *High Mark* 37 Shepherding . . is illegal when . . players are going for the knock in the ruck as the ball is bounced.

knock, *v.*

1. **a.** *trans.* With **down**: to spend (one's available resources) in a spree or drinking bout; esp. in the phr. **to knock down a (one's,** etc.) **cheque.** See also CHEQUE.

1845 *Sentinel* (Sydney) 15 Jan. 1/6 Inns . . where the profligate or improvident resorts when released from the engagement with his master, and in three or four days 'knock down' [*sic*] the hard earned gains of perhaps six months. **1912** *Bulletin* (Sydney) 29 Feb. 44/2 The ebony ones get *carte blanche*. . . To get the true sense of the words 'knocked down', you must go to one of these outposts. There is no doctoring of liquor and no dead house. **1923** *Ibid.* 11 Jan. 22/3 Among a crowd of us busy knocking down our cheques at a bush shanty was one who had just bought a new pair of boots. **1946** *Ibid.* 16 Aug. 28/3 Nowadays a bushman knocking down a cheque . . is a rarity.

Hence **knocking down** *vbl. n.* and *attrib.*

1873 A. TROLLOPE *Aust. & N.Z.* I. 172 The knocking down of an imaginary cheque would be dreadful to the publican. **1895** *Worker* (Sydney) 9 Feb. 4/2 The knocking-down-cheque trick is fast becoming a matter of the past.

b. [Spec. use of *knock up* to accumulate.] In the phr. **to knock up a cheque,** to get or accumulate (a total sum) by one's labour.

1890 A.J. VOGAN *Black Police* 258 Here he is, working hard to 'knock up' another cheque. **1949** G. BERRIE *Morale* 102 They had knocked up a cheque on a seven-months job, and they were going to knock it down before they signed on for another.

2. *trans.* With **out: (a)** to extract (payable dirt); **(b)** to earn (a living).

1853 S. SIDNEY *Three Colonies* (ed. 2) 375, I tried surface washing, and knocked out an ounce a day. **1949** I.L. IDRIESS *One Wet Season* 103 There's old-timers still knocking out a crust in the Kimberleys could tell you of those days.

3. [f. *knock out* to stun or kill.] *trans.* To kill (esp. in *pass.*). Also (formerly) *intr.*, to die.

1911 *Bulletin* (Sydney) 5 Oct. 16/1 His mates in the tunnel variously informed me that Uncle Dick had 'kicked the bucket' . . 'knocked' [etc.]. **1920** W.H. DOWNING *To Last Ridge* 177 'Eat, drink and be merry as possible, for tomorrow we may get knocked,' was the prevailing faith.

4. [f. KNOCKBACK *n.*] *trans.* With **back**: to reject; to rebuff.

1918 *Kia Ora Coo-ee* July 12/1 Have you ever got arrangements completed for your holidays to commence on a Monday at home, and then about six of your fellow workers got sick on the Saturday, and you have been knocked back? **1979** B. HUMPHRIES *Bazza comes into his Own,* If you try makin' me a lord I'll more than likely knock it back!

knockabout.
1. An unskilled labourer on a rural property; ROUSEABOUT *n.* a. Also *attrib.,* esp. as **knockabout man (hand, joey).**
1867 *S.A. Parl. Papers* no. 14 28 What were they principally?—Shepherds, and knock-about hands. The usual bush hands. **1869** *Bushmen, Publicans, & Politics* 5 They have .. to serve an often hard apprenticeship, as what is locally known as knock-about men, doing small jobs by weekly labour, shovelling up along fences, sheep-washing, yard work. **1893** R. BRUCE *Echoes from Coondambo* 195 So then a job to make a bob I takes as 'knockabout'. **1909** E. WALTHAM *Life & Labour in Aust.* 44 We were very dubious as to whether he was the 'Boss' or the Knockabout Joey.
2. A loafer; a tramp. Also *attrib.*
1888 *Centennial Mag.* (Sydney) 234 Here he was, a ragged, hard-up tramp, a 'knock-about' as Talgai called him. **1958** F. HARDY *Four-Legged Lottery* 117 The prisoners can be divided roughly into three categories. First offenders and 'knock-about men' (semi-criminals who come here at infrequent intervals); hardened criminals; and, thirdly, 'poofters' (homosexuals).

knockback. [Br. dial. *knock-back*: see OEDS.] A repulse; a rebuff. See also KNOCK *v.* 4.
1915 B. GAMMAGE *Broken Yrs.* (1974) 13 Things are now looking so serious, and the Russians and Allies are getting so many knock backs, that .. I have decided to [enlist]. **1975** *Bulletin* (Sydney) 1 Feb. 17/2, I called 15 and got 15 knockbacks, with reasons ranging from the old favourite 'Me truck's broken down' to 'Only got one bloke on the job'.

knock-down. [Orig. U.S.: see OEDS.] An introduction (to a person).
1915 C.J. DENNIS *Songs of Sentimental Bloke* 125 Knockdown, a formal introduction. **1981** *Sun-Herald* (Sydney) 1 Mar. 97/1 That's a grouse-looking little sheila over there, Sal. Any chance of a knockdown to her later on?

knock 'em down, *a.* Chiefly *N.T.* of rain: torrential. Chiefly in the collocation **knock 'em down rain.**
1946 W.E. HARNEY *North of 23°* 99 With the final storms—'knock 'em down' they call them—it bends to the ground. **1960** J. GLENNON *Heart in Centre* 240 Another spring had gathered up her remnants of green and departed, followed by a sweltering summer and the 'knock 'em down' rains which flattened the spear grass that had lately flourished.

knocker, *n.*[1] *Obs.* [Of unknown origin.] Common sense; gumption.
1891 *Truth* (Sydney) 15 Mar. 7/3 This kit consisted of a tin can, a tin mug, a blanket, and a good deal of assurance. These, in bush parlance, are *billy, pannikin, bluey, and knocker.* **1900** H. LAWSON *On Track* 120 The old woman might have had the knocker to keep away from the bush while I was in quod.

knocker, *n.*[2] [Spec. use of *knocker* that which knocks.]
1. *Shearing.* See quots. 1941 and 1959.
1895 *Worker* (Sydney) 28 Sept. 4/1 And set to work with my file—Levelled my knockers quickly, and then I rigged them up in style. **1941** S.J. BAKER *Pop. Dict. Austral. Slang* 42 *Knocker,* a leather pad fixed near the heel of a pair of hand shears to prevent the blade closing too deeply. **1959** H.P. TRITTON *Time means Tucker* 31 Shears do not click. The gullets of the blade are filled with soft wood, or sometimes with cork. These are called 'knockers' and they stop the heels of the blade from meeting.
2. [Cf. Br. slang *on the knocker* on credit (see OEDS 2 e.).] In the phr. **on the knocker,** (payment made) immediately, on demand, 'on the nail'.
1962 J. CLEARY *Country of Marriage* 297 Sid was a man who wanted cash on the knocker. **1975** *Austral.* (Sydney) 12 Aug. 9/4 He has to pay cash on the knocker for everything he buys, but he has to wait two or three months for payment from the big firms.

knock-off. [Used elsewhere but recorded earliest in Aust.: see OED(S *sb.* 2.] The time set for the day's work to finish. In full **knock-off time.**
1867 J.S. BORLASE *Night Fossickers* 97 By knock-off time I had taken out five pounds' weight of gold. [*Note*] Hour of leaving work. **1960** *Bulletin* (Sydney) 10 Aug. 19/2 Walking around the job after knock-off, he found a piece of timber almost cut through.

knot. [See quot. 1898; later infl. by *knot* a mass as formed by a knot in string.]
1. In the phr. **to push the knot,** to travel carrying a swag.
1896 *Bulletin* (Sydney) 3 June 14/1 'Push the knot to 'Ungry'—walk to Hungerford. **1898** *Ibid.* 8 Oct. 15/1 *Re* derivation of 'pushing the knot'. When I wore the Order of the Wallaby .. swag was fastened near the ends with the binders, through which was passed the sling, so arranged that the knot came just below the breast and gave a rest for the hand, which thus acquired a habit of pushing the sling outwards from the body as the man neared the end of his tramp.
2. A swag. Also *attrib.*
1911 *Bulletin* (Sydney) 20 July 13/2, I remember the time when a man could arrive per boot, with his 'knot' up, and obtain a contract for (say) grubbing or fencing. **1949** *Ibid.* 6 Apr. 15/4 The knot-humper had been given a feed at the farmhouse.

knuckle. In the phr. **to go the knuckle** (or **knuckles**), to fight; to punch.
1944 J. DEVANNY *By Tropic Sea & Jungle* 160, I always got on well with the blacks, because I never went the knuckle on them. **1968** S. GORE *Holy Smoke* 46 The biggest jokers among his mob .. able to go the knuckles a bit themselves.

koala /koʊ'alə/. Formerly also **coola, koolah.** [a. Dharuk *gula, gulaway.*]
1. The arboreal, mainly nocturnal marsupial of e. Aust. *Phascolarctos cinereus,* having a stout body, thick grey-brown fur with a pale underside, large rounded furry ears, a leathery nose, strong claws and a vestigial tail. It feeds largely on the leaves of certain eucalypts, and is the faunal emblem of Qld.; BEAR; MONKEY BEAR; *native bear, sloth,* see NATIVE *a.* 6 b.; SLOTH; *tree-bear,* see TREE. Also *attrib.,* esp. as **koala bear.**
1798 *Hist. Rec. N.S.W.* (1895) III. 821 There is another animal which the natives call a cullawine, which much resembles the stoths [*sic*] in America. **1803** *Sydney Gaz.* 9 Oct., Serjeant Packer of Pitt's Row, has in his possession a native animal .. called by the natives, a Koolah. **1808** *Philos. Trans. R. Soc. London* XCVIII. 305 The koala is another species of the wombat... The natives call it the koala wombat; it .. was first brought to Port Jackson in August, 1803. **1827** P. CUNNINGHAM *Two Yrs. in N.S.W.* I. 317 Our *coola* (sloth or native bear) is about the size of an ordinary poodle dog, with shaggy, dirty coloured fur, no tail, and claws and feet like a bear, of which it forms a tolerable miniature. **1937** C. KEARTON *I visit Antipodes* 132 The Koala Bear was first seen by a young explorer who journeyed to the Blue Mountains in 1798.
2. *transf.* and *fig.* A person, etc., treated as a protected species.

1942 *CPD* (H. of R.) VII. 1418 Does the Minister for the Army intend to deal with the naughty, nasty people who insist on referring to members of his beloved Militia as Koalas, because, under Australian law you must not shoot at them, and you must not export them. **1953** *Sydney Morning Herald* 3 Jan. 6/2 'Koalas', police or diplomatic cars, immune from being booked for parking offences, and therefore 'protected creatures'.

kobong /'koʊbɒŋ/. *Obs.* [a. Nyungar *gubuŋ*.] A totem.
1841 G. GREY *Jrnls. Two Exped. N.-W. & W.A.* II. 228 Each family adopts some animal or vegetable, as their crest or sign, or *kobong*, as they call it. **1901** M. VIVIENNE *Travels in W.A.* 337 Each family has its kobong, or cognisance, some animal or vegetable for which they have a reverence.

koel /'koʊəl/. [Transf. use of *kóēl* a cuckoo of India.] *Cooee bird*, see COOEE *n.* 4. Also *attrib.*
1908 *Emu* II. 211, I have only come across the Koel about Homestead. **1929** A.H. CHISHOLM *Birds & Green Places* 157 A koel cuckoo . . was rendered almost frantic by imitations of its curious notes.

koepanger /'kupæŋə/. [f. Du. *Koepang* (Kupang), the name of a town in w. Timor.] A diver, crew-hand, etc., recruited from or through Kupang to work in the pearling industry; a Timorese. Also *attrib.*
[**1902** *Cwlth. Parl. Papers* II. 1079 The Asiatics are got from three sources: . . (2) Koepang (in Timor). These men sign a 'musterrol' in Koepang before the Dutch authorities for a term of 20 months, at the end of which they have to be returned at employers' expense. **1933** L. KORNITZER *Trade Winds* 18 But these others, Corporal, Japs, Filipinos, Koepang men—they aren't whites?] **1936** T.E.A. HEALY *And far from Home* 57 The Malays, Koepangers and other coloured races conducted their religious services privately. **1937** I.L. IDRIESS *Forty Fathoms Deep* 168 The Japanese . . had almost displaced the Manilamen and Koepanger divers.

koie-yan /'kɔɪ-jæn/. *Obs.* [Prob. a. Warrgamay *guri-yan*.] The vigorous climbing plant *Faradaya splendida* (fam. Verbenaceae) of rainforest in n.e. Qld., having large leaves and clusters of fragrant white flowers.
1908 E.J. BANFIELD *Confessions of Beachcomber* 270 Another method by which the blacks secure fish in pools left by the receding tide is to scrape off the inner bark of the 'Koie-yan' (*Faradaya splendida*) with a shell. **1914** *Bulletin* (Sydney) 26 Feb. 22/4 Of these [fish poisons] the best is 'koie-yan', a Queensland vine, from which the outer bark is scraped, while the inside is macerated and thrown into the water.

kombo, var. COMBO.

konkleberry, var. CONKERBERRY.

kooditcha, var. KURDAITCHA.

kooka. Abbrev. of KOOKABURRA.
1906 *Bulletin* (Sydney) 22 Mar. 14/2 Our kookas fairly cackled with delight at the sight of raw beef. **1984** *Age Weekender* (Melbourne) 7 Dec. 4/5 As the sun went down the kookas gave us a grand finale as we toasted the first of the season's great catches—and the first of the memorable outdoor feasts.

kookaburra /'kʊkəbʌrə/. Formerly also with much variety, esp. **kukuburra**. [a. Wiradhuri *gugubarra*.] Either of two Austral. kingfishers, the large, predom. brown and white laughing kookaburra, *Dacelo novae-guineae*, of s. and e. Aust. (introduced into Tas. and s.w. W.A.), having a distinctive loud, laughing call, and the *blue-winged kookaburra* (see BLUE *a.*); GOBURRA. See also LAUGHING JACKASS 1.
1834 G. BENNETT *Wanderings N.S.W.* I. 222 The natives at Yass call the bird 'Gogera', or 'Gogobera', probably from its peculiar note, which has some resemblance to the sound of the word. **1926** A.A.B. APSLEY *Amateur Settlers* 41 Kukuburras echoed their evening chorus. **1975** *Bronze Swagman Bk. Bush Verse* 24 O carol, carol, magpies gay, While shy koala peeps; Laugh, kookaburra, laugh with glee While little Jesus sleeps.

kooky. [f. KOOK(ABURRA + -Y.] KOOKABURRA. Also **kooky jack** (see JACK *n.*[1]).
1918 L.J. VILLIERS *Changing Yr.* 24 Too flamin' soon we're roused be Kooky Jack. **1930** *Bulletin* (Sydney) 14 May 20/2, I found two kookies—full-grown birds—under a small bush.

koolah, var. KOALA.

kooliman, var. COOLAMON.

koonkerberry, var. CONKERBERRY.

koori /'kʊri/, *n.*[1] Also **koorie, kuri, kurri**. [a. Awabakal (and other n. N.S.W. languages) *gurri* man or person.] An Aboriginal (now used chiefly by Aborigines). Also *attrib.*
1834 L.E. THRELKELD *Austral. Grammar* 87 *Ko-re*, man, mankind. **1892** J. FRASER *Aborigines N.S.W.* 2 The kuri, or 'blackman' is usually kind and affectionate to his jin, 'wife'. **1966** M. BROWN *Jimberi Track* 40 At any moment the dogs were liable to be sent racing through the camp, or some koorie or other set screaming. **1970** R. ROBINSON *Altjeringa* 30 These wild Kurris were runnin' out of the scrub. **1985** J. MILLER *Koori* 218 Since I believe in Koori land rights and no dams on the Franklin River, that makes me a black, greenie, pinko.

koori, /'kʊri/, *n.*[2] [a. Panyjima *kurri* marriageable teenage girl.] A young Aboriginal woman.
1908 *West Austral.* (Perth) 22 Feb. 12/3 Do you remember . . there was a coorie and two piccaninnies. . . What was her age? About ten or eleven. **1985** MARIS & BORG *Women of Sun* 94 If you were a koori, what chance did you have of finding a job?—except . . cleaning up whitefeller's dirt?

kopi /'koʊpi/. Also **kopai**. [Prob. a. Bagandji *gabi*.] A fine powdery gypsum occurring near salt lakes in arid areas, and used in ritual Aboriginal mourning; a more cohesive, gypsum-rich mass, sometimes a rock, found where opal is mined. Also *attrib.*
1889 *Rec. Geol. Survey N.S.W.* I. 3 There is abundance of earthy gypsum, locally called 'Copi', present in patches over this country. **1897** J.J. KNIGHT *Brisbane* 42 We came on a small tract of 'kopi country' (powdered gypsum). **1978** D. STUART *Wedgetail View* 92 Lake beds dry and salt-crusted with islands of dirty white kopai country where stunted mallees struggled to survive.

koradji /kə'rædʒi/. Also formerly in a wide variety of unfixed spellings. [a. Dharuk *garraaji*.] An Aboriginal having recognised skills in traditional medicine and (freq.) a role in ceremonial life. For words taken from other Aboriginal languages, see BOYLYA and WARRA-WARRA; for those applied by colonists to denote a perceived function or power of such a person, see *clever man* CLEVER 1, CONJUROR, DOCTOR *n.*[1], MEDICINE MAN, *native doctor* NATIVE *a.* 5, PRIEST, SORCERER, WISE MAN, and WIZARD.
1793 W. TENCH *Compl. Acct. Settlement* 232 Yellomundee was a Cár-ad-yee, or Doctor of renown. **1899** J. MATHEW *Eaglehawk & Crow* 142 The titles of these magicians varied with the community. . . *Koradji* was the name applied in the neighbourhood of Sydney, and it still holds the ground among Europeans.

Kosciusko minnow /kɒziɒskoʊ 'mɪnoʊ/. [See quot.

1906.] The small fresh-water fish *Galaxias olidus*, widespread in e. mainland Aust.
1906 D.G. STEAD *Fishes of Aust.* 50 The Kosciusko Minnow .. is found on the highlands of the Monaro and Snowy River Districts, particularly in the neighbourhood of Mount Kosciusko, the 'roof' of Australia, from which it takes its name. **1933** D. MACDONALD *Brooks of Morning* 115 The clear, cold pinnacle stream, of which the spotted Kosciusko minnow is still the sole occupant.

kukuburra, var. KOOKABURRA.

kunzea /'kʌnziə/. [The plant genus *Kunzea* was named by German botanist H.G.L. Reichenbach (*Conspect. Reg. Veg.* (1828) 175) after the botanist and physician G. *Kunze* (1793–1851), Professor of Botany at Leipzig.] Any shrub or small tree of the genus *Kunzea* (fam. Myrtaceae) of s. Aust., having attractive, fluffy flowers for which some species are cultivated.
1942 C. BARRETT *Austral. Wild Flower Bk.* 149 Some of the Kunzeas are small trees up to about twenty feet high; others never grow out of shrubhood and one lives close to the ground. **1981** *Bulletin* (Sydney) 21 Apr. (Lit. Suppl.) 25/2 Purple hovea beside our feet, Snow daisies and kunzea's foam.

kurara, var. KARARA.

kurdaitcha /kə'daɪtʃə/. Also **kadaitcha, kaditcha, kooditcha**. [Poss. a. Aranda *gwerdaje*.]
1. A malignant spirit. Also **kurdaitcha spirit**.
1886 E.M. CURR *Austral. Race* I. 148 It was discovered in 1882, or thereabouts, that the Blacks to the westward of Lake Eyre .. wear a sort of shoe when they attack their enemies by stealth at night. Some of the tribes call these shoes *Kooditcha*, their name for an invisible spirit .. The soles were made of the feathers of the emu, stuck together with a little human blood. .. The uppers were nets made of human hair. The object of these shoes is to prevent those who wear them from being tracked. .. It is only on the softest ground that they leave any mark, and even then it is impossible to distinguish the heel from the toe. **1901** G. WHITE *Across Aust.* 28 During the night the blackboy rushed up to the fire crying out that the Kadaitcha was out after him with a spear and a firestick. The Kadaitcha is an evil spirit or ghost. **1936** 'L. KAYE' *Black Wilderness* 108 'Thos' fellers like catch 'm me or Kombi. Fright of this country, me. All same *kaditcha*.' .. '*Kaditcha*' he said in fear, as he trekked not through darkness filled with spearmen merely, but with things supernatural and terrible. The witch doctors and witch-craft of an alien tribe were out there in the night. **1952** A.W. UPFIELD *New Shoe* 13 A mopoke 'Ma-parked' at him .. and later still a curlew screamed like a kurdaitcha spirit is alleged to do when after an aborigine away from his camp at night.

2. A shoe, worn esp. on a mission of vengeance, so made as to leave no trace of the wearer's movements: see quot. 1886. Also **kurdaitcha boot (shoe, slipper)**.
1886 [see sense 1]. **1901** G. WHITE *Across Aust.* 28 When a black is about some nefarious purpose he puts on Kadaitcha shoes, made of emu's feathers, and leaving no track. **1933** F.E. BAUME *Tragedy Track* 84 The dogs fail to hear the approach of the warriors who have been chosen to wear the trackless kaditcha boot of emu feathers stuck together with human blood and woven into a shoe without toe or heel, so that no one can tell from the tracks how a native is moving. **1952** *Bulletin* (Sydney) 23 Apr. 17/3 They are Kadaitcha slippers, not 'boots'. **1970** K. WILLEY *Naked Island* 138 Whenever they found a patch of stony ground the party would put on the kadaitchas, spirit shoes of emu and turkey feathers which made the wearers' tracks invisible.

3. a. A mission of vengeance; the ritual accompanying this. Also *attrib.*
1895 *Proc. R. Soc. Vic.* (1896) 66 The shoes themselves in this district are known by the name of 'Urtathurta', and the occasion on which they were used is spoken of as 'Kūrdaitcha lūma ' (Kūrdaitcha—a bad or evil spirit, and luma, to walk). The wearing of the Urtathurta and going Kūrdaitcha lūma appears to have been the medium for a form of vendetta. **1940** E. HILL *Great Austral. Loneliness* (ed. 2) 175 Kurdaitcha, the blood vengeance .. extends throughout the whole of unoccupied Central Australia. **1962** V.C. HALL *Dreamtime Justice* 138 This water country would hold no tracks for the eyes of any men who walked the Kadaitja trail—the mission of revenge.

b. In the phr. **to go kurdaitcha**, to embark on such a mission.
1901 F.J. GILLEN *Diary* 23 May (1968) 88 The members of a group fully realise that they cannot go Kurdaitja, that they cannot in fact impart to the feather shoes the magic properties which make them leave no track. **1927** SPENCER & GILLEN *Arunta* 458 Many will .. confess that they do go Kurdaitcha.

4. One who undertakes a mission of vengeance. Also **kurdaitcha man**.
1927 SPENCER & GILLEN *Arunta* 458 We have met several Kurdaitcha men who claim to have killed their victim. **1953** A.W. UPFIELD *Murder must Wait* 121 Those prints would be followed back to the tree, where the kurdaitcha put on his great boots and mounted a bike to go back to Mitford.

kuri, var. KOORI.

kurrajong /'kʌrədʒɒŋ/. Also **currajong**. [a. Dharuk *garrajuŋ*.]
1. A name given to any of several plants yielding a useful fibre; spec., any of several such trees of the genera *Brachychiton* (see also BOTTLE TREE) and *Sterculia*, esp. the fodder tree *B. populneus* of N.S.W., Qld., Vic., and N.T.; ORDNANCE TREE. Also *attrib.*
1801 *HRA* (1915) 1st Ser. III. 179 Many parts are covered with a new hibiscus, which the natives use as flax for making their nets and for other purposes. This plant is much superior to the carradgan, which is of the same species. **1889** E. GILES *Aust. twice Traversed* I. 73 We passed the night under the umbrage of a colossal Currajong-tree. **1986** *Sun-Herald* (Sydney) 26 Jan. 7/3 Kurrajongs are highly prized as feed for livestock during drought. Large trees can take 100 years to grow. At this time of the year they are usually so leafy a cockatoo could fly into them and not be seen.

2. With distinguishing epithet: **desert kurrajong**, the tree of W.A., N.T., and S.A. *Brachychiton gregorii*, occurring in sandy country in drier Aust.
1948 C.P. MOUNTFORD *Brown Men & Red Sand* 129 The desert kurrajong (*Brachychiton gregorii*) with its smooth, light-green trunks, and symmetrical heads of lush-green foliage, is one of the most beautiful of the desert trees. **1969** A.A. ABBIE *Original Australs.* 74 Ground into flour, as are the seeds of the Desert Kurrajong tree.

3. Austral. pidgin. Obs. In the phr. **to give** (someone) **kurrajong**, to hang (someone) with a rope made from kurrajong fibre.
1848 *Maitland Mercury* 8 Nov. 2/1 When the white men tried to prevent these outrages the blacks told them plainly that the magistrate would give them curryjong (i.e. hang them). **1851** J. HENDERSON *Excursions & Adventures N.S.W.* II. 284 Up to the last moment, he thought the threat to 'give him curryjung', that is, to hang him, was 'all gammon'.

kurrawong, var. CURRAWONG.

kurri, var. KOORI.

kwee-ai, var. QUEEAI.

kylie /'kaɪli/. Also **kiley**. [a. Nyungar (and other w. Austral. languages) *garli*.]

1. Chiefly *W.A.* BOOMERANG *n.* 1.

1835 G.F. MOORE *Diary Ten Yrs. W.A.* (1884) 358, I am sorry that nasty word 'boomerang' has been suffered to supercede [*sic*] the proper name. Boomerang is a corruption used at Sydney by the white people, but not the native word, which is tur-ra-ma; but 'kiley' is the name here. **1971** K. GILBERT *End of Dreamtime* 24 Whirling high to beating kylies and the thump of stamping feet while didjeridoos are dreeing to the weird outlandish beat.

2. *transf.* See quot. 1945.

1945 S.J. BAKER *Austral. Lang.* 176 The small piece of board upon which the two pennies are rested for spinning is called the *kip, stick, bat* or *kiley*. **1955** N. PULLIAM *I traveled Lonely Land* 76 The game is played with two pennies, a mattress, a thin piece of wood called a 'kip' (sometimes a stick or a kiley), and amazing dexterity and ardor.

L

laap, var. LERP.

labour. Also **labor.**

1. As **labor**. **a.** The wage-earning sector of the population, viewed with regard to its political interests. **b.** With initial capital: short for 'Labor Party', from 1918 for 'Australian Labor Party'. Freq. *attrib.*

1870 *Age* (Melbourne) 5 Nov. 2/5 In August last a labor convention was held at Cincinatti to consider the desirability of forming a political party that should be consecrated to 'labor reform'. **1983** *Sydney Morning Herald* 7 Sept. 9/2 N.S.W. provides an excellent example of how Labor can get on with the bush.

2. Usu. as **labour.** *Hist.*

a. Used *attrib.* as a euphemism for KANAKA B. 1.

1872 *Australasian* (Melbourne) 5 Oct. 434/1 Dr Murray, of 'labour-collecting' fame, gets off very well indeed. **1898** *Bulletin* (Sydney) 12 Mar. 14/3 T'other day at Bundaberg (Q.) the cook of a labor-vessel took up his headquarters.

b. With reference to communities established to provide rural work for the unemployed.

1893 *Act* (N.S.W.) 56 Vict. no. 34, An Act to establish and regulate Labour Settlements on Crown Lands. **1924** S.H. ROBERTS *Hist. Austral. Land Settlement* 330 At the same time 'labour colonies' were set up for a totally different class of persons, the 'absolutely destitute'.

lace monitor. [See quot. 1962.] The large, tree-climbing monitor *Varanus varius*, widespread in e. mainland Aust.; any lizard of the genus *Varanus* (see GOANNA 1). Also **lace lizard, laced lizard.**

1789 A. PHILLIP *Voyage to Botany Bay* 279 Laced Lizard. . . This beautiful Lizard is not uncommon at *Port Jackson*, where it is reputed a harmless species. **1962** B.W. LEAKE *Eastern Wheatbelt Wildlife* 101 The lace lizard is so called because of the yellow spots all over the body, which is dark green in colour, though less so than that of the bungare. **1968** R. HILL *Bush Quest* 56 The lace monitor is the common goanna of our eastern States. It can be found almost anywhere in lightly timbered country, being largely arboreal in its habits.

Lady Blamey. [f. the name of the wife of *Sir* Thomas Blamey (1884–1951), soldier.] See quot. 1972.

1945 *Action Front: Jrnl.* 2/2 Field Regiment May 11 Ernie Stagg wanted to know where his large supply of 'Lady Blameys' would go in the kit layout. [**1972** *Sydney Morning Herald* 28 Oct. 8/8 Lady Blamey stayed put and continued her welfare work. During this time she gave her name to the 'bottle' drinking glass used by thousands of Diggers. She taught them to slice an empty bottle cleanly in half with the aid of kerosene-soaked string. The string was wound round the bottle, and set alight. When the bottle was hot it was plunged into water and would break cleanly. The men used the lower part for drinking.]

lady's finger. Also **lady finger.**

1. A tall-growing variety of banana of commercial importance in Aust.; the short, sweet fruit of the plant. Also **lady('s) finger banana.**

1893 MRS C. PRAED *Outlaw & Lawmaker* II. 91 They were sitting . . in the banana grove, whither Elsie had gone on pretext of finding some still ungathered 'Lady's fingers'. **1959** N.W. SIMMONDS *Bananas* 145 The cultivation of the tall 'Lady's finger' banana on the Queensland flats. **1965** *Austral. Encycl.* I. 406 Another variety of some importance is the Lady Finger or Manilla banana. **1981** P. BAXTER *Growing Fruit in Aust.* 164 The main types of banana grown commercially in Australia are the smaller 'Cavendish' . . and the taller sugar banana ('Lady Finger').

2. A variety of grape; the fruit of this, a large, elongated dessert grape. Also **lady('s) finger grape.**

1892 E. REEVES *Homeward Bound* 90 The very finest ladies'-fingers, sweet-waters, and muscatels. **1924** L.H. BRUNNING *Austral. Gardener* 198 The following sorts are all suitable for growing for table use in the Home Garden . . Black Hambro, Lady Finger. **1966** H. PORTER *Paper Chase* 17 Bunches of Lady Finger and Black Hambro grapes.

lady's waist. A small, slender, waisted beer glass; the drink contained in this.

1934 *Bulletin* (Sydney) 4 Apr. 20/1 A daintier goblet I never fingered than the hourglass shape of a lady's waist. **1985** *Bulletin* (Sydney) 24 Dec. 62/2 The shearers and drovers I met at Coonabarabran drank from the smallest, known as a lady's waist (five ounces)—probably because it was so hot the beer in a schooner would get flat and warm.

lag, *v.* [Spec. use of *lag* to transport to penal servitude: see OED *v.*^{3} 2.]

1. *trans.* To transport (a convict) from Britain to a penal settlement in Australia; to sentence (a criminal) to a term of imprisonment.

1812 J.H. VAUX *Mem.* (1819) II. 185 *Lag*, to transport for seven years or upwards. **1948** J. DEVINE *Rats of Tobruk* 95 Though it had not been his fault he was blamed and 'lagged'. When he got out he managed to get two years for pinching three hundred fowls.

2. **a.** *trans.* To inform against (a person) with the object of securing arrest and imprisonment.

1832 *Currency Lad* (Sydney) 10 Nov. 3 Morrison had uttered threats that 'if his master turned him in, he would turn *him* in, and lag him'; if he could not *lag* him right, he would do it wrong. **1970** K. MACKEY *Cure* 63 Maybe I should split. This flip might just lag me to the jacks.

b. To inform against (a fellow-prisoner).

1968 L.H. EVERS *Fall among Thieves* 177 The rights and wrongs of 'lagging' (reporting fellow prisoners to the authorities) formed the sole topic of debate. **1971** J. MCNEIL *Chocolate Frog* (1973) 32 It ain't just any sort of maggot gets to be a dog . . only those that lag other people . . who co-operate with bastards in uniform . . see?

lag, *n.* [f. prec.]

1. A convict who has been transported to a penal settlement in Australia; any convict. Also *attrib.*

1812 J.H. VAUX *Mem.* (1819) II. 185 *Lag*, a convict under sentence of transportation. **1903** *Truth* (Sydney) 5 Apr. 5/3 Botany Bay law, while hampering an outraged husband 'under the ban', aided and abetted the adulterous wife. The old lag law is still law.

2. In the collocation **old lag**, an ex-convict; a former prisoner.

1812 J.H. VAUX *Mem.* (1819) II. 193 *Old lag*, a man or woman who has been transported, is so called on returning home, by those who are acquainted with the secret. **1977** B. SCOTT *My Uncle Arch* 48 Another old lag . . used to make dud two-bobs for a sideline.

Hence **(old) lagdom,** the convict period; **lag(s')land,** Australia.

1900 *Bulletin* (Sydney) 29 Dec. 15/2 Darlinghurst . . is the pet prison of **Old Lagdom,** which some of the 'Botany Bay Aristocracy', or their convict progenitors, helped to build. **1858** A. PENDRAGON *Queen of South* 76 What right have such as you to come here, to this island—to our country—to the **lags' land** .. to rob us of our gold?

lagerphone. [Prob. f. *lager* (with reference to the beer-bottle tops employed) + *xylo*)*phone*.] See quot. 1979.

1956 *People Mag.* (Sydney) 11 Jan. 26/3 The lagerphone, a broomstick and crosspiece studded with beer bottle tops, produces a jingling sound, something like that of a big tamborine, when shaken. **1979** R. EDWARDS *Skills Austral. Bushman* 157 The lagerphone .. a percussion instrument .. made by loosely tacking rows of bottle tops to a stick, usually a worn-out broom or a stick of similar length with a crossbar at the top. The tops are vibrated by banging the instrument on the floor, and also by 'bowing' it with a serrated stick.

lagger. [f. LAG *v.*]
1. *Obs.* A sailor.
1812 J.H. VAUX *Mem.* (1819) II. 185 *Lagger*, a sailor. **1847** A. HARRIS *Settlers & Convicts* (1953) 50 Old George was always hocussing some poor lagger (sailor).
2. A police informer, esp. a prisoner who informs against a fellow prisoner.
1967 B.K. BURTON *Teach them no More* 17, I knew an old lagger once. He was quite famous. He made little statues out of his mush. Didn't eat breakfast for years. **1974** *Gayzette* (Sydney) 14 Nov. 13/3 Maitland also houses the cretins, and the laggers.

lagging, *vbl. n.* [f. LAG *v.*] A term of penal servitude; a sentence or term of imprisonment.
1832 *Hill's Life N.S.W.* (Sydney) 16 Nov. 4 All the risques I ran Of *lagging, scragging*, and so forth, To be a *swell-mob-man*. **1979** L. NEWCOMBE *Inside Out* 106 About six more prisoners made up the van load, some with brand-new 'laggings' (prison slang for sentences) and others remanded to a later date.

lagoon. [In Br. use applied only to an area of salt or brackish water; in U.S., infl. by Sp. *laguna*, applied also to an area of fresh water: see DAE.] An expanse of fresh water, usu. shallow but of indeterminate extent: see quots. 1805 and 1878.
1797 *Hist. Rec. N.S.W.* (1895) III. 765 Walked 8 miles and came to a river, where we met fourteen natives, who conducted us to their miserable abodes in the wood adjoining to a large lagoon. **1805** *HRA* (1915) 1st Ser. V. 586 Some local Expressions that have obtained in this Colony .. *A Lagoon*—Is a large Pond of Stagnant water; Although in many places the water does not Stagnate being supplied with Springs. **1878** J.H. NICHOLSON *Opal Fever* 32 In some parts of this vast colony [of Queensland] two buckets of water and a frog would be called a 'lagoon'.

lair, *n.* and *a.* Also **lare.** [Back-formation from LAIRY.]
A. *n.*
a. One who displays vulgarity, esp. in dress or behaviour; a show-off; a larrikin.
1923 C.E. SAYERS *Jumping Double* 60 A hit behind the ear from one of those back street lairs. **1956** K. TENNANT *Honey Flow* 188 When Blaze and Big Mike were working around in boiler suits, they were men. When they dressed best, they looked cheap lares, the type you see leaning against the hotel or the general store.
b. In the collocation **mug lair**, a term of abuse applied to a person supposed to be both stupid and vulgar. Also *attrib*.
1965 *Oz* (Sydney) xxiii. 8 Now I reckon any bloke that goes for your technical apparatus is a mug lair mongrel! **1974** J. GOODWOOD *Last Gamble* 98 There was real venom in his parting words. 'You're just a mug lair poofter.'

B. *adj.* Vulgarly flamboyant.
1971 *Bulletin* (Sydney) 10 Apr. 37/3 There are four broad styles of Australian automobile decor—Domestic, Functional, Speed and Lair.

lair, *v.* [f. prec.] *intr.* To behave in the manner of a lair. Usu. with **up.**
1928 L.A. SIGSWORTH *Various Verse* 2 The 'babbling brook' will let the guns lare up in the shearers' mess. **1983** A.F. HOWELLS *Against Stream* 1 Earning something in the vicinity of three pounds ten shillings a week .. I could still afford to lair up a bit, get on the scoot occasionally with my mates.

lairize, *v.* [f. LAIR *n.*] *intr.* LAIR *v.* Also (rarely) as *n.*
1953 K. TENNANT *Joyful Condemned* 22 You came lairizing round at our place like you owned it. **1967** *Kings Cross Whisper* (Sydney) xxx. 4/3 'The boys in the local brigades are getting very toey, indeed,' a Country Fire Authority official said. 'They haven't had a chance for a good lairise.'

lairy, *a.* Also **leary, leery.** [Transf. use of Cockney slang *lairy* knowing, 'fly': see OED(S *lairy*, $a.^2$ and *leery*, $a.^2$] Flashily dressed; showy; socially unacceptable.
1898 *Tocsin* (Melbourne) 15 Sept. 3 Height, about 5 ft. 6½ in.; style 'lairy'. Shop made suit, tight fit and cheap. Flower in slouched hat, well over eyes. 'Silk' rag around neck. **1899** *Bulletin* (Sydney) 1 Apr. 26/2 The dressy larrikin .. is the 'leary one'. *c* **1907** C.W. CHANDLER *Darkest Adelaide* 7/2 Sitting on the seat with him was a nice specimen of the Australian larrikin. Not so leery, perhaps, as his prototypes of Melbourne and Sydney, but a choice specimen of his class nevertheless. **1979** B. MARTYN *First Footers S. Gippsland* 106 He was a stout fleshy chap wearing a dazzling fat and fancy waistcoat. He was popularly described as a 'bit lairy'.
Hence **lairiness** *n.*
1965 D. MARTIN *Hero of Too* 318 By no means all Queenslanders are lairs, nor is every politician, but all Queensland politicians are, or endeavour to be, lairs. .. Their lairiness is of the type that captures the national imagination.

la-la. A euphemism for 'lavatory'.
1963 B. HESLING *Dinkumization & Depommification* 116 Couldn't you last out to the Wentworth? Even Judge Willis said on the bench that he wouldn't be game to risk a visit to the Lang Park la-la. **1984** *Canberra Times* 28 Apr. 13/4 Once we were caught in a hurricane that caused a small amount of damage, including knocking over someone's outside dunny. The lady in whose house we were sheltering was laughing fit to burst. 'Ho! Ho! There goes old Fitz's la-la!'

lamb. Used *attrib.* in Special Comb. **lamb-catcher,** one who assists a *lamb-marker*; **-marker,** see *-marking*; **-marking** *vbl. n.* the marking of an ear of a lamb with the owner's brand; the completing of other processes, as castrating male lambs, docking, etc., at the same time (see quot. 1975).
1882 ARMSTRONG & CAMPBELL *Austral. Sheep Husbandry* 139 The required number of **lamb-catchers** have been employed and despatched, under the overseer, with from 50 to 60 hurdles, for the purpose of arranging the yards in the paddock. **1891** *Truth* (Sydney) 22 Mar. 7/1 His brother, a union shearer, was slushing for the **lamb-markers. 1882** ARMSTRONG & CAMPBELL *Austral. Sheep Husbandry* 136 Successful **lamb-marking** is one of the most important items in the management of a station. **1975** M. THORNTON *It's Jackaroo's Life* 90 *Lamb-marking*, castration; however, the term is used to cover a series of operations undertaken in conjunction with castration, including ear-marking, tailing, mulesing, drenching, inoculating, ear-tagging, jowlsing.

lamb down, *v.* [Br. *lamb (down)* to tend (ewes) at

lambing time; app. rare as OED records only 1850 and 1851: see OED *v.* 3 and, for sense 2, OED *v.* 4.]

1. a. *trans.* To tend (ewes) at lambing time. Also *absol.*

1848 S. & J. SIDNEY *Emigrant's Jrnl.* 31, I have known two little fellows, under ten years of age, sons of a settler, lamb down a flock of 1,000 ewes. **1888** *Bulletin* (Sydney) 10 Mar. 14/2 And next I went a lambing down to fetch home the green lambs; But I couldn't find 'em green—for lambs are mostly white.

b. *trans. Obs.* To accommodate (ewes) at lambing time; to provide accommodation for (a client). Also *absol.*

1863 R. HENNING *Lett.* (1952) 53 Biddulph bought the station in question .. and Palmer asked him to let him 'lamb-down', as it is called, on some part of his country as he (Palmer) had no place of his own. Biddulph gave him leave to go on this new station for a few months, and then the fellow claimed it on the ground of prior occupation. **1873** M. CLARKE *Holiday Peak* 21 As the Three Posts was to Trowbridge's, so was Trowbridge's to the Royal Cobb... True, that Trowbridge's did not 'lamb down' so well as the Three Posts, but then the Three Posts put fig tobacco in the brandy casks, and Trowbridge's did not do that.

2. *fig.*

a. *trans.* To inveigle (a client, esp. a shearer or shepherd) into spending accumulated earnings on liquor. Esp. in *pass.* Also *transf.* (see quot. 1879).

1850 *Bell's Life in Sydney* 12 Jan. 2/6 There are such things as roadside public houses .. and shepherds and shearers, in about three days are quietly *lambed down.* **c 1879** *Ye Prodigal* (Sydney) 54 He proved that he had very considerably more money than brains; and the [gambling] Ring, not taking long to discover the fact, he was 'lambed down' to a very respectable tune.

b. *trans.* To squander (one's accumulated earnings) on liquor. Also *absol.*

1899 F. CRAWFORD *Native Companion Songster* 11 'I'll cash your cheque and send you on.' He stopped, and now his money's gone—Lambed down. **1890** *Argus* (Melbourne) 9 Aug. 4/5 The old woman, of course, thought that we were on gold, and would lamb down at the finish in her shanty.

Hence **lambed-down** *ppl. a.*, **lamber-down** *n.*

1889 F. CRAWFORD *Native Companion Songster* 11 A man whom you could plainly see Had just come off a drunken spree, **Lambed down.** **1880** 'ERRO' *Squattermania* 168 What thrown over the pick and sluice-box, and gone among the '**lambers-down**' [*sc.* sheep-farmers]?

Lambert's wren. [Applied as the specific epithet *Lamberti* in 1825 by ornithologists N.A. Vigors and T. Horsfield (*Trans. Linnean Soc. London* (1827) XV. 221) after English naturalist A.B. Lambert (1761–1842), Vice-President of the Linnean Soc. London.] VARIEGATED WREN. Also **Lambert's (superb) warbler.**

1841 J. GOULD *Birds of Aust.* (1848) III. Pl. 24, *Malurus lamberti* .. Lambert's Wren... Lambert's Superb Warbler is a species with which we have been long acquainted. **1928** B. SEMMENS *Wanderings in Wild Aust.* 96 Lambert's Warbler .. is also striking on account of the presence of a patch of cinnamon-brown, edged with deep cobalt-blue, on the top of its head.

lambing. Used *attrib.* in Comb. with reference to the provision made for the accommodation of ewes at lambing time, as **lambing camp, paddock, station, yard.**

1851 *Illustr. Austral. Mag.* (Melbourne) Sept. 171, I have to go to a lambing station the first thing in the morning. **1881** *Bulletin* (Sydney) 26 Mar. 8/3 You were 'flashin' your dover' six short months ago, In a lambin' camp on the Paroo? **1888** 'R. BOLDREWOOD' *Robbery under Arms* (1937) 78 We were out at the back making some lambing yards. **1907** *Bulletin* (Sydney) 12 Sept. 14/4 With paddocked sheep, if tucker-bags Runs low .. You 'aven't Buckley's show to strike A (lurid) lambin' camp. **1948** J.K. EWERS *For Heroes to Live In* 17 He walked with her one evening out to the lambing paddock. The air was loud with the bleating of the young lambs.

lambing down, *vbl. n.* [f. LAMB DOWN *v.*]

1. The tending of ewes about to lamb. Also as *ppl. a.*

1864 'E.S.H.' *Narr. Trip Sydney to Peak Downs* 20 The grass was all eaten by the lambing-down flocks. **1874** *Illustr. Sydney News* 28 Mar. 7/4 The very great mistake of early lambing down is often committed from an erroneous opinion that the flocks can be shorn earlier.

2. a. The process of spending one's earnings on liquor.

1870 W.H. KNIGHT *W.A.* 76 The man comes into the town for the confessed purpose of 'lambing down', as it is called. He places his money in the hands of a publican, and instructs him to let him know when the amount is reduced to what he reckons will be sufficient to carry him back to his district or home. **1890** *Argus* (Melbourne) 7 June 4/2 The paying off of drovers, the selling off of horses, the 'lambing down' of cheques.

b. The process of inveigling a shearer, shepherd, etc., into spending his entire resources on liquor. Also as *ppl. a.*

1882 *Bulletin* (Sydney) 10 June 1/1 The business of 'lambing down' has of late exhibited a singular briskness... One of the most singular circumstances which successive inquests have brought to light, is the inherent capacity of the 'lambing down' publican to tell when a man has had more drink than is good for him. **1886** *Once a Month* (Melbourne) June 489 The periodical spree, when they submitted themselves to the 'lambing-down' process at the hands of the tender publicans.

3. Comb. **lambing down shanty, shop.**

1894 *Bulletin* (Sydney) 13 Jan. 74 Close the swagger's port of departure—the **lambing-down shanty.** **1889** F. CRAWFORD *Native Companion Songster* 9 A filthier place you'd not find in a week—A regular **'lambing down' shop.**

lamb poison. [See quot. 1981.] Any of several shrubs or herbs of the genus *Isotropis* (fam. Fabaceae), apparently sometimes toxic to stock.

1897 L. LINDLEY-COWEN *W. Austral. Settler's Guide* 591 *Isotropis juncea* .. 'Lamb poison.' Suspected. **1981** G.M. CUNNINGHAM et al. *Plants Western N.S.W.* 398 Wheeler's lamb-poison has a scattered distribution... As its name suggests, it has been suspected of poisoning stock, although no definite evidence is available.

lamb's fry: see FRY.

lambswool. The shrub of s.w. W.A. *Lachnostachys eriobotrya* (fam. Verbenaceae), having a white, woolly flowering panicle and felt-like leaves.

1926 J. POLLARD *Bushland Man* 127 This .. is the wild violet; this is 'lamb's wool'. **1973** R. ERICKSON et al. *Flowers & Plants W.A.* 187 Lambswool .. is a grey shrub with linear leaves and open panicles of white flowers.

Laminex. Also **laminex.** The proprietary name of a hard, durable, plastic laminate used esp. as a surfacing material; any similar surface. Also *attrib.*

1945 *Austral. Official Jrnl. Patents* (Canberra) 2226 *Laminex.* 83,123. Articles (included in this class) moulded, cast or otherwise formed from or incorporating synthetic resin or similar moulding material and including laminated sheets, blocks, tubes, rods, gear wheels and other goods comprising superposed sheets of fabric, paper or other material impregnated with synthetic moulding material. **1969** F. MOORHOUSE *Futility & Other Animals* 62 Into the bright, laminex and detergent kitchen.

lamington. [Prob. f. the name of Charles Wallace Baillie, Baron *Lamington* (1860–1940), Governor of Queensland (1895–1901).]

1. A square of sponge cake coated in chocolate icing and desiccated coconut. Also *attrib.*

1909 *Guild Cookery Bk.* (Holy Trinity Church Ladies Working Guild) 66 Quarter lb. butter, 1 cup icing sugar; beat to cream; 2 tablespoons of cocoa, mixed with 2 tablespoons boiling water. Mix all well together, and put over the Lamington. **1985** *Canberra Chron.* 31 July 4/3 Students set sight on lamington record.

2. Special Comb. **lamington drive,** an organized effort (by a community group) to raise money from the sale of lamingtons.

1979 C. KLEIN *Women of Certain Age* 37 'It's lamington day,' she informed Elissa, full of virtue. 'I made four dozen lamingtons for the lamington drive.'

lamplighter. [See quot. 1860.] The cicada *Cyclochila australasiae* (see *yellow monday* YELLOW 1).

1860 G. BENNETT *Gatherings of Naturalist* 271 From the circumstances of these having three ruby-coloured spots in the front of the head, they are called *Lamplighters* by the boys. **1966** S.J. BAKER *Austral. Lang.* (ed. 2) 283 When cicadas are shouting in the summer trees, who but an expert or a child could identify them? There are many types .. *lamplighter* [etc.].

lancewood. [Transf. use of *lancewood* the tough, elastic wood of a W. Indian tree.] Any of several trees, usu. yielding a tough, durable timber, incl. *Acacia shirleyi* of Qld. and N.T., often forming dense stands; such a stand; the wood itself. Also *attrib.*

1861 J.M. STUART *Explorations in Aust.* 3 May (1865) 278 A thick scrub of dwarf lancewood, as tough as whalebone. **1881** W. FEILDING *Austral. Trans-Continental Railway* 38 The Lancewood Range .. is covered with lancewood bushes about 12 feet high, which grow on the bare rock.

land. Chiefly *hist.*

1. Used *attrib.* in Comb., not always excl. Australian, with reference to the occupation and tenure of land: **land agent, board, boom, boomer, commissioner, court, jobber, -jobbing, mania, order.**

1839 *Southern Austral.* (Adelaide) 2 Oct. 2/5 Messrs O'Halloran, Nixon & Co. The above firm have now commenced business as **Land Agents.** **1828** *Sydney Gaz.* 12 Jan., The *Governor* has been pleased, under the Authority of the Secretary of State, to form a Board, to be termed the **Land Board,** for the Purpose of assisting Him in investigating such Particulars as may appear necessary to an impartial Decision, on the Applications which may be made for Grants, or to purchase Land. **1890** J. HASLAM *Glimpse Austral. Life* 11 Soon after I got fairly settled to work, what is called a **Land Boom** set it [*sic*]. **1890** *Truth* (Sydney) 3 Aug. 2/6 As a natural result, that enterprising philanthropist, the **land boomer,** will be found on the war-path over again. **1828** H. DANGAR *Index & Directory River Hunter* 41 The assigning of boundaries to parishes, as well as counties, belongs to the **land commissioners.** **1877** 'CAPRICORNUS' *Land Law of Future* 7 At the first sitting of the **Land Court** .. the land agent shall read aloud a report. **1835** *True Colonist* (Hobart) 27 Nov. 2/4 A celebrated and very successful **Land Jobber.** **1809** *Hist. Rec. N.S.W.* (1901) VII. 33 They had for years commenced **land-jobbing.** This went so far as the selling of land before the grant for land was obtained. **1844** *HRA* (1925) 1st Ser. XXIII. 343 **Land Mania** was an evil. **1838** *Southern Austral.* (Adelaide) 23 June 1/4 The Owners and Representatives of Owners of Preliminary or other **Land Orders** .. are requested to meet at My Office .. J.H. Fisher, Colonial Commissioner.

2. Special Comb. **land council,** a body appointed to represent the interests of Aborigines in Aboriginal land (see quot. 1976); **fund,** the revenue realized from the sale of Crown land; **-grant railway,** a railway built in return for a grant of land; **rights,** the entitlement of Aborigines to possess their traditionally occupied territory (see COUNTRY 4); the acknowledgement of this entitlement; **-shark,** one who speculates in land transactions; also **-sharking** *vbl. n.*

1973 *Cwlth. Parl. Papers* no. 138 41 It is recommended that two Aboriginal **land councils** be set up in the Northern Territory: one for the central region, based on Alice Springs, and the other for the northern region, based on Darwin. **1976** *Act* (Cwlth. of Aust.) no. 191 Sect. 23, The functions of a Land Council are .. to ascertain and express the wishes and the opinion of Aboriginals living in the area of the Land Councils as to the management of Aboriginal land in that area and as to appropriate legislation concerning that land. **1835** *Colonist* (Sydney) 28 May 170/2 The whole of the **land-fund** appropriated in bringing out virtuous and industrious families from the mother-country, to occupy our waste lands, and to cultivate those that are already located. **1883** *Victorian Rev.* Aug. 460 If the example be once set on a large scale in Queensland, **land-grant railways** are almost sure to be constructed, whether for good or for evil, in other parts of Australasia. **1964** *Anthropol. Forum* Nov. 294 What is at issue here is the actual acknowledgment of Aboriginal **land rights** as having any contemporary relevance at all. **1984** *Age* (Melbourne) 16 Aug. 11/2 Nearly 24 per cent of the Northern Territory population is Aboriginal (or 29,088 people) and they have been granted about 32 per cent of the Territory in land rights. **1836** *Sydney Herald* 4 July 2/7 When these allotments are put up for sale, those persons on the spot, who would become purchasers, cannot contend against the **land-sharks.** **1840** D. BURN *Vindication Van Diemen's Land* 45 All the **land-sharking** put together will make land very cheap.

3. a. In the phr. **(up)on the land,** in(to) a rural occupation, esp. owning or managing a rural property.

1902 *Advocate* (Burnie) 20 Feb. 4/1 Go on the Land! **1911** *Huon Times* (Franklin) 14 Jan. 3/4 Are there no men upon the land who are still struggling to try and get an existence?

b. In the phr. **the man on the land,** one who owns or manages a rural property, esp. as representative of those engaged in rural occupations.

1911 *Huon Times* (Franklin) 8 Feb. 3/4 We could not possibly oppose it as advocates for assistance for the man on the land. **1979** *Cattleman* (Rockhampton) Feb. 11/2 The Australian man on the land places unique demands on all his machinery, particularly his multi-purpose workhorse—the farm car.

land crab. Any of several small, fresh-water crayfish, esp. of the genus *Engaeus.* Also **land crayfish.**

1844 L. LEICHHARDT *Jrnl. Overland Exped. Aust.* 16 Dec. (1847) 78 Mr Gilbert found a land crab in the moist ground under a log of wood. **1965** *Austral. Encycl.* III. 92 A number of smaller aberrant members of the same crayfish family (Parastacidae) are the so-called land crayfish. These have a limited distribution in the temperate areas of eastern Australia, being mainly concentrated in Victoria and northern Tasmania.

land mullet. [See quots.] The large skink *Egernia major* of e. Aust.

1945 S.J. BAKER *Austral. Lang.* 214 Various Australian lizards are known in popular speech as the .. *land mullet,* mallee trout, railway lizard and stump-tail. **1979** D.R. MCPHEE *Observer's Bk. Snakes & Lizards Aust.* 136 This species [*sc. Egernia major*] .. receives its vernacular name from the large scales which almost cover the ear openings, adding to the superficial likeness of its head to that of the mullet fish. .. The Land Mullet is endowed with considerable lung capacity and if antagonized exhales a loud hissing blast.

Landsborough grass. *Obs.* [f. the name of William *Landsborough* (1826–1886), explorer.] FLINDERS GRASS.

1881 T. Archer *Some Remarks on Proposed Qld. Trans-Continental Railway* 18 Over all these plains [near Burketown] we rarely lost sight of the Mitchell, blue, and Landsborough grasses. **1923** E. Breakwell *Grasses & Fodder Plants N.S.W.* 18 *Iseliema* [sic] *membranacea* (Flinders or Landsborough grass). Common in the north-west; less abundant elsewhere in interior.

land train. *Road train,* see Road 3.
1968 D. Attenborough *Quest under Capricorn* 130 Once or twice we passed a land-train, a line of gigantic trailers, each the size of a large furniture van, stretching for fifty yards and drawn by an immense diesel lorry, the size of a military tank transporter, with twenty-two gears and the speed of a saloon car. **1969** A. Garve *Boomerang* 61 An enormous land train of three linked trailers drawn by a gigantic diesel truck.

lane. An enclosure in a stock yard from which animals may be fed in small numbers into the appropriate pen (see esp. quots. 1880 and 1890).
1880 J.B. Stevenson *Seven Yrs. Austral. Bush* 115 First of all the cattle are driven into what is called the 'receiving yard', which is the largest subdivision. From this they are drafted in small numbers into the 'lane', which is an oblong enclosure, and serves as a feeder for the 'drafting pen', where the work of separating the different ages, etc., is performed. **1886** H. Finch-Hatton *Advance Aust.* (rev. ed.) 70 Five or six men .. go into the receiving yard and jam the cattle up into the corner against the gate of 'the lane'. **1890** 'R. Boldrewood' *Colonial Reformer* II. 113 About fifty head have been run into the drafting lane and are ready for separating. The 'lane' is a long narrow yard about three panels wide and eight in length—a panel of fencing is not quite nine foot in length—immediately connected with the pound or final yard, and leading into it by a gate opening into the latter.

langeel, var. Leangle.

lapunyah /ləˈpʌnjə/. [a. Gunya *yapan*ʸ.] **a.** The tall, smooth-barked tree *Eucalyptus argophloia* (fam. Myrtaceae) of s.e. Qld. **b.** Yapunyah. Also *attrib.*
1940 W. Hatfield *Into (Great?) Unfenced* 41 A strong growth of eucalypts, the common river-gum, and .. lapunyah. **1955** Stewart & Keesing *Austral. Bush Ballads* 108 And still the yellow wattles rose through the thin lapunyahtrees.

lare, var. Lair.

larrikin. [Br. dial. *larrikin* 'a mischievous or frolicsome youth': see OED(S).]
1. *Hist.*
a. A young, urban rough, esp. a member of a street gang; a hooligan.
1868 W. Cooper *Colonial Experience* 58 Allow me to introduce you to .. one of the most accomplished swindlers ever imported into the colonies... Why, you infernal old larrikin! **1975** *Bulletin* (Sydney) 22 Nov. 30/1 Whitlam, under the shock of his dismissal, revealed some of those characteristics which seem to lie so close beneath his urbane exterior. The larrikin came out in the unseemly attack on the Governor General.
b. Comb. **larrikin class, element.**
1879 *Kelly Gang* 108 Sympathy and admiration for the Kellys .. by the **larrikin class**, are not only barely disguised in some cases, but openly vaunted in others. **1877** J. Vicars *Tariff, Immigration, & Labour Question* 22 The hourly and daily surroundings, and the circumstances in which this **'larrikin' element** is placed, exert a very great deal of influence in moulding their habits and modes of life.
c. Special Comb. **larrikin push,** a street gang; Push b.
1890 *Braidwood Dispatch* 5 Nov. 2/6 The larrikin 'pushes' are about again. On Friday night a gang of them assaulted a young lad.
2. a. One who acts with apparently careless disregard for social or political conventions. Also *attrib.,* and as *adj.*.
1891 *Truth* (Sydney) 15 Mar. 7/3 Jackeroos .. are such fun, and vary, from the sensible one, in a fair way for promotion, to the larrikin, who will either sling station life or hump the swag. **1891** *Bohemia* (Melbourne) 3 Sept. 21 Roseate hopes are entertained that the experiment may yet produce male and female voters far less larrikin than many of those who—but that has been said often before. **1984** *Sydney Morning Herald* 9 Feb. 1/7 She .. grins and accepts cheerfully enough the description of being an Australian intellectual larrikin.
b. *transf.*
1881 G. Walch *Little Tin Plate* 28 While larrikin spiders aloft, like youths trammelled in sin, Exhausted their vital resources to keep 'on the spin'. **1912** *Bulletin* (Sydney) 15 Aug. 15/2 When the inkweed .. is seeding, this harshvoiced air larrikin darts round with the push, devouring the ripe berries.
3. In the collocation **bush larrikin,** a rural larrikin.
1889 J.H.L. Zillmann *Past & Present Austral. Life* 159 There is now the bush 'larrikin' as well as the town 'larrikin', and it would be difficult sometimes to say which is the worse. Bush 'larrikins' have gone on to be bush-rangers.

larrikiness. *Hist.* A female associate of a Larrikin 1 a.
1871 *Collingwood Advertiser & Observer* 22 June 3/5 Evidence was tendered as to the manner of life led by these larikinesses. **1956** J.E. Webb *So much for Sydney* 10 These children of the new slums are natural recruits for the strange legion of 1955-56 larrikins and larrikinesses called 'bodgies' and 'widgies', and they know enough to realise that they have little to fear from a 'Labor' régime which has abolished the hangman.

larrikinism. Behaviour such as characterizes a larrikin.
1870 *Austral.* (Richmond) 10 Sept. 3/3 A slight attempt at 'larrikinism' was manifested. **1983** *Austral.* (Sydney) 29 Oct. 3/3 (*heading*) One of its two artistic directors .. believes it should not lose its essential 'larrikinism'.

larry, var. Lary.

Larry.
1. [Used elsewhere but recorded earliest in Aust.: see OEDS *sb.*³] In the phr. **as happy as Larry,** extremely happy.
1905 *Barrier Truth* (Broken Hill) 29 Dec. 1 Now that the adventure was drawing to an end, I found a peace of mind that all the old fogies on the river couldn't disturb. I was as happy as Larry. **1984** B. Dickins *Crookes of Epping* 13 There are such nights and days of joy, the Crookes are happy as Larry.
2. [Perh. f. Br. dial. *larry* a disturbance, a scolding (see OED *sb.*¹ and EDD *sb.*¹ 2.), infl. by the name of *Larry* Foley (1849-1917), pugilist.] In the collocation **Larry Dooley,** a beating; a disturbance or fracas. Chiefly in the phr. **to give** (someone) **Larry Dooley.**
1943 *Coast to Coast 1942* 12, I had driven him back a week before, and that morning I gave him Larry Dooley. **1973** J. Murray *Larrikins* 169 The country towns at race time saw the wild boys rampage about, throwing stones on corrugated iron roofs, smashing windows, and creating Larry Dooley, in honour of the boxer named Foley.

larry-doo. Abbrev. of *Larry Dooley,* see Larry 2.
1978 Saw & Milbank *Back to Back Tango* 21 The sport and

games and, hum, gaming and larry-doo that could, just *could* be lined up.

lary. Also **larry.** Abbrev. of LARRIKIN.
1891 *Bohemia* (Melbourne) 3 Sept. 20 The 'lary' who has come to the years of indiscretion. 1970 P. WHITE *Vivisector* 109 Once a mob of larries happened to pass underneath, and he spat.

lash. [Spec. use of *lash* a sudden blow, esp. as infl. by the *v. to lash out*.] An attempt, a 'go'; a fight; fighting. Chiefly in the phr. **to have a lash at** (a person, an object, etc.).
1894 A.A. MACINNES *Straight as Line* 222 The fighting blood was roused within him, and he longed to have a 'lash', as he put it, at the gang. 1976 K. BROWN *Knock Ten* 135, I reckon meself that carting'd be the lash... There's always no end of stuff getting shipped out for construction.

'lastic-side, var. ELASTIC-SIDE.

latchet. [Transf. use of *latchet(t)* the gurnard.] The edible marine fish *Pterygotrigla polyommata*, having large pectoral fins and a reddish-coloured skin.
1951 T.C. ROUGHLEY *Fish & Fisheries Aust.* 130 Originally the sharp-beaked gurnard was known as 'latchet', but this name has come to refer to the more slender species. 1980 N. COLEMAN *Austral. Sea Fishes* 103 The latchet is often caught around reefs by line and is also taken in large numbers by trawling.

lathered, *ppl. a.* [Prob. joc. formation on BLITHERED. Used elsewhere but recorded earliest in Aust.] Drunk.
1910 L. ESSON *Three Short Plays* (1911) 17, I don git lathered on ther takin's, do I? 1945 J.A. ALLAN *Men & Manners* 167 When you have over-indulged in intoxicants.. you may be.. 'lathered'.. but you are never 'drunk'.

latrine wireless. [Formed by analogy with *latrine rumour*: see OEDS *latrine* 2.] In Services' speech: the latrine block (of a barracks, camp, etc.) as a source of rumour; a rumour. Also *attrib*.
1918 *Two Blues: Mag. 13th Battalion A.I.F.* Dec. 3 In our Australian camps all we now call 'Furphies' were called 'Latrine Wireless Messages'. 1944 G. MANT *You'll be Sorry* 67 The Latrine Wireless indeed kept us on considerable tenterhooks.

laughing jackass.
1. The kookaburra *Dacelo novaeguineae*. Also **laughing jack** and formerly **laughing bird**.
1798 D. COLLINS *Acct. Eng. Colony N.S.W.* I. 615 Go-gan-ne-gine, Bird named by us the Laughing Jack-Ass. 1849 W.S. CHAUNCY *Guide to S.A.* 28 The laughing bird.. may also be noticed.. for the peculiar strains in which it indulges. 1885 J. HOOD *Land of Fern* 14 Day woke, on the stream I saw its first beam glide, And heard the first notes of the laughing jack's song.

2. *fig*.
1874 C. DE BOOS *Congewoi Correspondence* 2, I couldn't believe that Australians would ever send into Parliament such a lot of chattering, laughing jackasses. 1899 *Progress* (Brisbane) 4 Feb. 1/2 Laughing-jackasses of the Press took up the cry with becoming fidelity.

laughing owl. Either of two nightjars, the *spotted nightjar*, see SPOTTED *a*., and the *white-throated nightjar*, see WHITE *a*.² 1 b.
1929 A.H. CHISHOLM *Birds & Green Places* 157 A 'laughing owl', the white-throated nightjar of ornithology. 1964 M. SHARLAND *Territory of Birds* 199 The curtain of night came down.. slow enough to persuade a 'Laughing Owl' to utter its curiously eerie herald to the night.

laughing-side. Usu. *pl.* A jocular name for an ELASTIC-SIDE. Also **laughing side(d) boot.**
1937 *Bulletin* (Sydney) 6 Jan. 20/3 'Laughing-sides' wouldn't last long in a boggy cowyard. 1960 J. WALKER *No Sunlight Singing* 51 The dirty bare ankles.. disappeared into a broken-down pair of 'laughing-side' riding boots. 1968 F. HARDY *Unlucky Australs.* 8 High-heeled elastic-sided boots (which the Aborigines, with their genius for turning their limited vocabulary and pronunciation into poetry, call laughing-sided boots).

lavender bug. [See quot. 1976.] A bug, prob. a burrowing bug of the fam. Cydnidae.
1944 *Troppo Tribune* (Mataranka) 15 Apr. 2 At the closing of each day Lavender bugs come out to play. 1976 B. SCOTT *Complete Bk. Austral. Folk Lore* 379 Re '*stinking, stinking wogs*' mentioned in the poem; these are undoubtedly the little beetles known in Innisfail as the '*lavender*' bug, or '*stink*' bug. When distressed these squirt out a corrosive fluid or gas which stings severely, especially if it gets you in the eye. The smell is unmistakable, like bitter almonds raised to the power of ten.

lawn sale. N.T. (chiefly in Alice Springs). GARAGE SALE. Also *attrib*.
1974 *Centralian Advocate* (Alice Springs) 21 Mar. 19/5 Lawn sale.. Clothing, toys, baby gear, records, typewriter, bicycle and more. Good buys. 1980 *Ibid.* 9 Oct. 46/7 Bring your leftover lawn sale stuff down to the Sunday Market and sell it there.

lawyer vine. [Spec. use of Br. dial. *lawyer* a long bramble: see OED 3.] Any of several plants, chiefly of tropical and subtropical e. coastal Aust., esp. climbing plants of the genus *Calamus* (fam. Arecaceae), having long, whip-like leaf appendages armed with strong, pointed, recurved hooks; BUSH LAWYER 3. See also WAIT-A-WHILE. Also **lawyer**.
1871 *Austral. Town & Country Jrnl.* (Sydney) 18 Mar. 330/4 Lawyers make excellent clothes-lines, lasting for as many years as the hemp lines do months, and being always clean. 1876 'EIGHT YRS.' RESIDENT' *Queen of Colonies* 117 One [Chinaman] was engaged in making baskets from the split canes of the 'lawyer' vine.

lay-by, *n.* A system of payment whereby a purchaser puts a deposit on an article which is then reserved by the retailer until the full price is paid. Freq. in the phr. **on (the) lay-by.** Also *attrib*.
1926 *Smith's Weekly* (Sydney) 9 Oct. 18/2 Farming on the Lay-by. 1927 *Memo* (Governing Director's Office, Grace Bros. Ltd. Sydney) 29 July, Please arrange for Mr Roach to exchange Lay By 7691 & to credit the full amount. 1959 D. HEWETT *Bobbin Up* 10 Lovingly she'd pressed the blue silk dress for her wedding... She'd had it on lay-by ever since that night on Bondi Beach. 1967 D. HORNE *Educ. Young Donald* 95 Mum paid off, at two shillings a time, the collection of Shakespeare's plays she had put on the 'lay-by' for me. 1969 *Bulletin* (Sydney) 15 Feb. 4/3 Castlereagh Street swarms with girls assessing the lay-by situation in gear.

lay-by, *v. trans.* To purchase (an article), using the lay-by system. Freq. *absol*.
1969 *Bulletin* (Sydney) 15 Feb. 10/2 The girls from the Rural are lay-bying like crazy. 1985 P. READ *Down there with me on Cowra Mission* 29 My mother used to lay-by about six or seven months before Christmas.

lazy strike. *Obs.* GO-SLOW *a*.: see quot. 1920.
1920 *Argus* (Melbourne) 24 Feb. 6/9 The tramway employees put into force what was described as a 'lazy' strike... The men observed the regulations to the letter, limiting the number of passengers standing on the platform and paying strict attention to the speed at turns

and crossings. The result was a slowing down of the service, with inconvenience to the passengers. **1923** C.F. THWING *Human Australasia* 59 The 'go-slow' or 'lazy' strike . . represents a desire to lessen the output.

Leach's kingfisher. [The specific epithet *Leachii* was applied by ornithologists N.A. Vigors and T. Horsfield, after English naturalist William *Leach* (1790–1836), founder of the genus *Dacelo*: see quot. 1825.] *Blue-winged kookaburra*, see BLUE a. Also **Leach kingfisher**.

[**1825** *Trans. Linnean Soc. London* (1827) XV. 205 [*Dacelo*] *Leachii* . . In honorem Gulielmi Elford Leach, Medicinae Doctoris, Sócietatum Regiae et Linneanae Socii . . ornithologi eximii, qui primùm hoc genus detexit characteribusque illustravit, haec species perpulchra nominatur.] **1848** J. GOULD *Birds of Aust.* II. Pl. 19, *Dacelo leachii* . . Leach's Kingsfisher. **1903** *Emu* II. 151 Dacelo leachii (Leach Kingfisher). . . The various nests I have personally found of these birds have all been holes drilled in the earthen nests of termites. **1917** *Bulletin* (Sydney) 5 July 22/2 Leach's kingfisher is aboriginally known as kitticarrara.

lead /lid/, *n.*[1] [Used elsewhere but recorded earliest in Aust.: see OED *sb.*[2] 6 b.] See quot. 1869 and also *deep lead* DEEP.

1852 *Empire* (Sydney) 16 Jan. 578/5 Experience . . proves that the *chief* deposit of gold is to be found at the turns of the stream on the inner side, in a line or *lead*, as it is termed. **1869** R.B. SMYTH *Goldfields & Mineral Districts* 614 Lead, a deep alluvial auriferous deposit or gutter. A lead, correctly defined, is an auriferous gully or creek, or river, the course of which cannot be determined by the trend of the surface, in consequence of the drainage having been altered either by the eruption of basalt or lava, or the deposition of newer layers of sand and gravel.

lead /lid/, *n.*[2] [Spec. use of *lead* the front or leading place.]

1. a. The front part of a travelling mob (of sheep, cattle, etc.).

1904 *Bulletin* (Sydney) 8 Dec. 19/3 When cattle have 'rushed' . . the rider has seldom need to urge the good nag beneath him to 'get to the lead of 'em'. **1972** *Bronze Swagman Bk. Bush Verse* (1973) 9 'Twixt the river bank and the myall scrub Where Gold Star wheeled the lead.

b. In the phr. **on the lead,** at the head of a travelling mob.

1919 *Bulletin* (Sydney) 17 July 22/3 A dog on the lead of bolting jumbucks should turn out. By so doing he meets sheep that are breaking behind him. A stockman on the lead of rushing cattle or horses always turns his mount's tail to the herd for the same reason. **1981** A.B. FACEY *Fortunate Life* 168 The cow on the lead had to go back and come over in front of each lot to show them the way.

2. *transf.* A route followed by travelling stock.

1962 MARSHALL & DRYSDALE *Journey among Men* 54 In an odd way they have even affected the landscape, for on the long leads you will find the inevitable bottles and cans, discarded along the way, where someone has taken . . a few 'cold ones for the road'. **1978** D. STUART *Wedgetail View* 5 On a hard track with a mob of cattle that wasted away week after week, crawling down the long leads.

Leadbeater's cockatoo /lɛdbitəz kɒkəˈtu, lɛdbɛtəz kɒkəˈtu/. [f. the name of the nineteenth-century English natural history agent Benjamin *Leadbeater* (see quot. 1831).] MAJOR MITCHELL COCKATOO.

[**1831** *Proc. Zool. Soc. London* 61 Mr Vigors exhibited, from the collection of Mr Leadbeater, an undescribed species of Cockatoo from New Holland . . *Plyctolophus leadbeateri*.] **1843** J. GOULD *Birds of Aust.* (1848) V. Pl. 2, *Cacatua leadbeateri* . . Leadbeater's Cockatoo. **1943** C. BARRETT *Austral. Animal Bk.* 225 Known to all Australians as the 'Major Mitchell', the pink or Leadbeater's cockatoo . . is the handsomest of all the species, and the least plentiful.

Leadbeater's possum /lɛdbitəz ˈpɒsəm, lɛdbɛtəz ˈpɒsəm/. [f. the name of the naturalist John *Leadbeater* (c 1832–1888), taxidermist at the National Museum, Melbourne, Vic. (see quot. 1968).] The rare possum *Gymnobelideus leadbeateri*, having a grey to greyish-brown back with a dark stripe and a pale underside, restricted to the mountain ash forests of the central highlands of Victoria, and a faunal emblem of that State.

1926 A.S. LE SOUEF et al. *Wild Animals Australasia* 249 Leadbeater's opossum *Genus Gymnobelideus*. . . The one species of this family was restricted to a very small district, that of the Bass River valley, in South-eastern Victoria. **1968** V. SERVENTY *Wildlife of Aust.* 30 In 1867 a new possum was found in the forests of south-eastern Victoria. It was named Leadbeater's possum in honour of the taxidermist then at the Melbourne Museum.

leaden flycatcher. [See quot. 1929.] The flycatcher *Myiagra rubecula* of n. and e. Aust. incl. Tas., and New Guinea, having a swift, darting flight.

1908 E.J. BANFIELD *Confessions of Beachcomber* 95 Leaden Fly-catcher, *Myiagra rubecula*. **1929** A.H. CHISHOLM *Birds & Green Places* 77 The leaden flycatcher is a shapely and pretty bird. Light-lead colour on the coat, head and chest is set off by pure white on the abdomen in the case of the male, and in the female the leaden hue is relieved by rich rust-red on throat and chest.

leader. [Transf. use of *leader* front horse.] One of the leading bullocks in a team: see quot. 1959.

1843 H. CASWELL *Hints from Jrnl.* 33 A two-wheeled dray with a pole, is certainly better than with shafts. . . The shafter should be a large heavy animal. . . Two good leaders are also indispensable. **1959** H.P. TRITTON *Time means Tucker* 36 A bullock-team is made up in four parts: polers, pin, body and leaders. The leaders are the most important, being the mainstay of the team.

leaf-cutting bee. [See quot. 1960.] Any of several bees of the fam. *Megachilidae*, using pieces of leaf to construct or line cells for their eggs. Also **leaf-cutter (bee)**.

1935 T. RAYMENT *Cluster of Bees* 213 There were wildflowers to yield nectar for the innumerable wild bees, including . . black leaf-cutters. **1955** *Bulletin* (Sydney) 5 Oct. 12/4 There are more than one species of leaf-cutter bee. **1960** J. CHILD *Austral. Insects* 67 Leaf-cutting bees, Megachilidae. Many bees in this family cut circular pieces of leaf with which they construct a case in which the food supply and egg are deposited.

leangle /liˈæŋgəl/. Formerly with much variety, as **langeel, leangil, liangel, liangle, liangra.** [a. Wemba-wemba and Wuywurung *liengel*.] An Aboriginal fighting club with a hooked striking head: see quot. 1845. See also LEONILE.

1841 *Geelong Advertiser* 26 June 2/4 The Aborigines got drunk . . and gave vent to their blood-thirsty passions by quarrelling and fighting with each other. Some of them are frightfully wounded. The liangra, a hatchet-shaped club, is the weapon generally used in such brawls. **1845** C. GRIFFITH *Present State & Prospects Port Phillip* 155 The liangle is . . of the shape of a pickaxe, with only one pick. Its name is derived from another native word, *liang*, signifying tooth. **1861** 'OLD BUSHMAN' *Bush Wanderings* 225 The root of the shey-oak is much used by the Blacks in making their weapons, such as boomerangs, liangels, etc. **1867** G.G. MCCRAE *Mamba* 9 The long leangle's nascent form Forespoke the distant battle-storm. **1910** J. MATHEW *Two Representative Tribes Qld.* 122 A weapon called *bokkan*, from *bokka*, a horn or projection, corresponded to the leangil of the Victorians. **1936** *Amer. Anthrop.* (Menasha, Wisconsin)

83 In slightly varying forms, the marpungy is often met with under such names as burrong, langeel, leonile, and bendi, according to district.

learner. *Shearing.* One not yet fully trained as a shearer.

1917 *11 C.A.R.* 433 'Learner' means a shearer or intending shearer who has not yet shorn under engagement through three sheds. **1979** M. RUTHERFORD *Departmental* 42 Shearing was okay. Dad took me everywhere to get me learner's pen but I could never get a run of me own.

leary, var. LAIRY.

lease. [Spec. use of *lease* a piece of land leased.]
  a. An area of land used for mining.
  1883 *Northern Daily Leader* (Tamworth) (1983) 2 Dec. 6/3 There is no progress being made with the mines owing to the want of machinery, and several leases have been taken up with a view to floating them to Sydney, mostly abandoned leases. **1962** O. PRYOR *Aust.'s Little Cornwall* 65 The mining company.. realized that it would be better to have most of their employees living on the leases than in the towns.
  b. An area leased for farming.
  1897 *Tocsin* (Melbourne) 9 Dec. 4/1 Those gifts by the State.. are euphoniously termed 'selections', 'leases', and even 'purchases'! **1960** *N.T. News* (Darwin) 12 Feb. 7/5 Rain extended to Katherine and relieved near-drought conditions on a number of leases there.

leatherhead. [See quot. 1854.] Any of several friar birds, esp. the *noisy friar bird* (see NOISY).

1841 J. GOULD *Birds of Aust.* (1848) IV. Pl. 58, Its bare head and neck have also suggested the names of 'Friar Bird', 'Monk', 'Leather Head', etc. **1854** W. HOWITT *Boy's Adventures* 27 The leatherhead is a very odd bird. It is as large as a fieldfare, with ash-coloured back and whitish stomach, but the singularity of it lies in the head, which is destitute of feathers, and covered with a brown skin resembling leather—whence its name.

leatherjacket.
  1. [See quots. 1770 and 1974.] Any of many marine fish of the fam. Monacanthidae, widely distributed in Austral. waters and elsewhere in the Pacific and Indian oceans, having a tough skin.
  1770 J. COOK *Jrnls.* 5 May (1955) I. 310 They had caught a great number of small fish which the sailors call leather Jackets on account of their having a very thick skin. **1974** J.M. THOMSON *Fish Ocean & Shore* 140 Leatherjackets have small fine spines which are modified scales scattered over their bodies giving the body a velvety feeling and providing the name for the group.
  2. [See quot. 1853.] A thin cake made of a (sometimes leavened) flour and water dough, cooked (usu. with fat) in a pan over a fire.
  1843 *Melbourne Times* 11 Mar. 4/6 A damson tart of goodly dimensions, was sent to a baker, to receive the benefit of his oven, upon its return, lo! it had become a gooseberry tart, a veritable leather jacket, unsightly to the eye, tough and sour to the palate. **1853** MOSSMAN & BANISTER *Aust. Visited & Revisited* 126 'Leatherjackets', an Australian bush term for a thin cake made of dough, and put into a pan to bake with some fat. The term is a very appropriate one, for tougher things cannot well be eaten.
  3. Usu. as **leather-jacket.** Any of several trees, sometimes so-called from the toughness of their bark.
  1860 G. BENNETT *Gatherings of Naturalist* 325 Another species is named Coach-wood, Leather-jacket, and also Lightwood by the colonists (*Ceratopetalum apetalum*). **1937** D. GLASS *Austral. Fantasy* 12 The leaves point long fingers to the ground, and hesitate to fall throughout the seasons. So the bark peels off instead: not only the stringy 'messmate' variety, but iron-bark, leather-jackets, black-butts and all.

leatherneck. *Obs.* A rouseabout.
  1897 *Worker* (Sydney) 11 Sept. 1/1 The 'rouseabout'.. he sneeringly terms 'loppy' and a 'leatherneck'. **1905** *Shearer* (Sydney) 4 Feb. 4/2 What do you know of.. 'loppies', 'leather-necks' and 'blue-tongues'.

leatherwood. [See quot. 1969.] The rainforest tree or (occas.) tall shrub *Eucryphia lucida* (fam. Eucryphiaceae) of Tas., yielding a tough timber, and bearing showy, scented flowers from which a pale, distinctively scented honey is made; any of several other trees or shrubs, esp. the related shrubby *E. milliganii* of Tas.; the wood of these trees. See also *pink wood* PINK *a.* Also *attrib.*

1903 *Tasmanian Timbers* (Tas. Lands & Survey Dept.) 27 Leatherwood (*Eucryphia billardieri*).. is very useful in the manufacture of implements being somewhat akin in nature to the English ash, but stronger. **1923** M.B. PETERSEN *Jewelled Nights* 298 She had decorated both camps with big jars of leatherwood blossom. **1969** KING & BURNS *Wildflowers Tas.* 36 The name 'leatherwood' was originally given to *Acradenia franklinii*, possibly on account of the toughness of its wood, but by 1903 was being transferred by common usage to the *Eucryphias*, which produce honey.

leave.
  1. *Obs.* Of a convict: in the phr. **on leave,** in possession of a ticket of leave.
  1811 *Sydney Gaz.* 19 Jan., Those who have received Emancipations or Pardons will be required to produce them, as will also those who are off the Store on leave, be required to produce their Tickets of Leave. **1840** A. RUSSELL *Tour through Austral. Colonies* 184 The runaway telling him he was travelling on a message, the native.. demanded a sight of.. the passport, which every convict on leave carries.
  2. Special Comb. **leave pass** [transf. use of *(leave) pass* written authority for Services' personnel to be on leave], 'permission' to be away from home.
  1973 J. O'GRADY *Survival in Doghouse* 11 We had a bit of trouble getting leave passes from our wives, and had to make all sorts of impossible promises. **1979** A.J. BURKE *Bite Pineapple* 86 A husband could get a much sought leave pass from kerosene lamps and Home, Sweet Home which lacked colour T.V. and other modern amenities. His excuse was that he was going to the lodge.

lechenaultia, var. LESCHENAULTIA.

leek. Shortened form of *green leek* (see GREEN *a.* 1).
  1854 W. HOWITT *Boy's Adventures* 34 We have seen thousands of small green parroquets, which they call leeks. **1902** *Bulletin* (Sydney) 6 Sept. 16/3 A great pest to N.S.W. orchardists is the common 'green-leek' parrot. Just as the fruit is ripening these 'leeks' swoop down upon it.

leek orchid. Any of many terrestrial orchids of the chiefly Austral. genus *Prasophyllum* (fam. Orchidaceae), having a single onion-like leaf and spike of very small flowers.

1914 F. SULMAN *Pop. Guide Wild Flowers N.S.W.* II. 190 *Prasophyllum elatum*. 'Tall Leek Orchid'.. the tallest terrestrial orchid in Australia. **1984** D.T. & C.E. WOOLCOCK *Austral. Terrestrial Orchids* 82 Leek orchids.. are well represented in Australia... Their distinguishing.. features are the smooth, long leaf, like that of the onion plant [etc.].

leery, var. LAIRY.

leg. Used *attrib.* in Special Comb. **leg-iron** *hist.* [used elsewhere but recorded earliest in Aust.], a shackle or fetter for the leg; also *fig.*; so **-ironed** *a.*; **-rope,** a noosed rope used to secure an animal by one hind leg; also *fig.*, and as *v. trans.*

[**1827** *leg iron*: P. CUNNINGHAM *Two Yrs. in N.S.W.* I. 46 The jail-gang straddling sulkily by in their jingling leg-chains.] **1849** A. HARRIS *Emigrant Family* (1967) 310 The clank of the leg-iron .. sounded in his ears. **1892** 'R. BOLDREWOOD' *Nevermore* II. 91 Lance found himself early next morning driven off to Ballarat, leg-ironed and hand-cuffed. **1903** *Truth* (Sydney) 5 Apr. 5/3 What was good enough for a leg-ironed community seems now to be good enough for the 'new nation' sprung from its lecherous loins. **1849** A. HARRIS *Emigrant Family* (1967) 129 The **leg-rope** is now passed round his hind legs. **1898** *Bulletin* (Sydney) 14 Nov. 27/3 Bailing up cows is nice, too... When you have got them bailed, its ten to one that the first you go to leg-rope plants her foot in your stomach. **1911** *Truth* (Sydney) 7 May 7/6 (*heading*) Lee leg-roped for lurid language.

Legacy.
   1. An organization dedicated to the care of dependants of deceased Services' or ex-Services' personnel. Also **Legacy Club.**
   1923 *Argus* (Melbourne) 31 Oct. 20/3 Mr C.V. Watson .. at the Legacy Club luncheon yesterday, addressed members on the subject of 'The Protection of Industrial Property'. **1932** C. BLATCHFORD *Legacy* 5 'The Spirit of Legacy is Service.' Legacy has been aptly defined as 'A Practical Expression of the Comradeship of the War'.
   2. Used *attrib.* to designate a recipient of support from Legacy.
   1958 *Meanjin* 136 James is a Legacy boy. No one is more pleased at the boy's success than Ned Williams, who has been acting in loco parentis since the lad's father died in action at Gallipoli. **1965** *Legacy* (Legacy Club Adelaide) 6 The Gellibrand Scholarship .. provides Legacy children with post-graduate education overseas.

leger /'lɛdʒə/. [f. St. *Leger* the name of a classic horse-race held annually at Doncaster in England since 1776.] A stand or section of a racecourse, usu. at some distance from the finishing-post. Also *attrib.*
   1907 *Truth* (Sydney) 20 Jan. 7/8 The iron fence which divides the leger stand from the grandstand on the Mudgee racecourse was the means of cutting off the poor man's beer on the occasion of the Spring Flat races. **1949** L. GLASSOP *Lucky Palmer* 66 'I'm going round to the Leger.' .. Forcing his way through the crowd in the Leger, the cheaper section of the course, 'Lucky' noticed that Norm Carston .. had Glittering Gold at seven to one.

legislative, *a.* In special collocations: **Legislative Assembly,** the title of a Colonial (later State) legislature, now esp. the lower house of a State parliament; **Council,** the title of a Colonial (later State) legislature, now the upper house of a State parliament.
   1823 *Act* (G.B.) 4 Geo. IV. no. 96 Sect. 24, It is not at present expedient to call a **Legislative Assembly** in the said Colony. **1918** C.H. NORTHCOTT *Austral. Social Dev.* 27 In every Australian State and in the Commonwealth, there are two legislative houses. One of these, known in the States by the term Legislative Assembly, and in the Commonwealth as the House of Representatives. **1823** *Act* (G.B.) 4 Geo. IV. no. 96 Sect. 33, In the case of the Death, Absence, or permanent Incapacity of any Member or Members of the said **Legislative Council,** the Governor, or Acting Governor .. shall and may appoint some fit and proper person to act in the Place and Stead of such Person. **1986** *Canberra Times* 3 Mar. 2/4 The legislation was defeated by the then Liberal-dominated Legislative Council.

legitimacy. *Obs.* See quot. 1827.
   1827 P. CUNNINGHAM *Two Yrs. in N.S.W.* I. 16 *Legitimacy,* a colonial term for designating the *cause* of the emigration of a certain portion of our population; i.e. having legal reasons for making the voyage. **1836** J.F. O'CONNELL *Residence Eleven Yrs. New Holland* 34 Legitimacy, in all other parts of the world a coveted qualification, is in New Holland a term of reproach.

legitimate. *Obs.* One who came to Australia as a convict. Also *attrib.*
   1827 P. CUNNINGHAM *Two Yrs. in N.S.W.* II. 116 We have the *legitimates,* or *cross-breds,*—namely, such as have *legal* reasons for visiting this colony; and the *illegitimates,* or such as are free from that stigma. **1836** J.F. O'CONNELL *Residence Eleven Yrs. New Holland* 34 The veracity of this narrative is not so questionable as it might be, were he left to the presumption that the narrator was a *legitimate, legal,* or *sentenced* visiter [*sic*] of Botany Bay.

Leichhardt pine. [f. the name of the Prussian naturalist and explorer F.W.L. *Leichhardt* (1813–?1848).] The tree *Nauclea orientalis* (fam. Rubiaceae) of coastal n. Aust. and elsewhere in the tropical Indo-Pacific region, having large leaves and yielding an edible fruit and a close-grained, yellowish, soft wood. Also **Leichhardt tree,** and *ellipt.* as **Leichhardt.**
   1860 F. VON MUELLER *Essay* 12 The opportunity is an apt one for offering here some remarks on the 'Leichhardt-tree' of the settlers of Rockhampton. **1882** W. SOWDEN *N.T. as it Is* 55 Leichhardt pine .. is not really a pine at all, but its timber is useful. **1886** H. FINCH-HATTON *Advance Aust.* (rev. ed.) 231 Both fig-trees and Leichardt are very handsome.

leipoa /laɪ'poʊə/. *Obs.* [The bird genus *Leipoa* was named in 1840 by English naturalist John Gould (*Birds of Aust.* (1848) V. Pl. 78), f. Gr. λειπ- stem of λείπειν to leave + ὠά eggs, referring to the bird 'leaving' its eggs in a mound.] Mallee fowl, see MALLEE 6.
   1840 *Proc. Zool. Soc. London* 126 This new species .. Mr Gould proceeded to characterize .. as a new genus, under the name of *Leipoa,* signifying 'a deserter of its eggs'. **1872** MRS E. MILLETT *Austral. Parsonage* 223 There is, however, amongst edible birds none that can at all compare with the one known .. to naturalists as the *Leipoa.*

lemon.
   1. Used *attrib.* in the names of flora and fauna: **lemon-breasted flycatcher,** the flycatcher *Microeca flavigaster,* a predom. olive-brown bird with a lemon-yellow belly, occurring in n. Aust. and New Guinea; **-crested cockatoo** *obs., white cockatoo* (a), see WHITE *a.*[2] 1 b.; **gum,** any of several trees, usu. of the genus *Eucalyptus* (fam. Myrtaceae), esp. *lemon-scented gum*; **-scented gum-tree,** the tree *Eucalyptus citriodora* (fam. Myrtaceae) of e. Qld., having a smooth, sometimes spotted bark and leaves which are strongly lemon-scented when crushed.
   1901 *Emu* I. 59 The little **Lemon-breasted Flycatcher** (Microeca flavigaster) has a habit of covering its tiny nest with pieces of bark. **1832** J. BACKHOUSE *Narr. Visit Austral. Colonies* (1843) 30 **Lemon-crested Cockatoos** .. are .. a great annoyance to the farmer. **1899** *Proc. Linnean Soc. N.S.W.* XXIV. 467 E[*ucalyptus*] *tereticornis* .. var. *brevifolia* .. is the 'Orange Gum' or '**Lemon Gum**' of the Port Macquarie district. **1980** B. SCOTT *Darkness under Hills* 45 Downstream was a tall stand of black bean trees, red cedar and lemon gums. **1860** G. BENNETT *Gatherings of Naturalist* 265 The **Lemon-scented Gum-tree** (*Eucalyptus citriodora*) is peculiar to the Wide Bay district [of N.S.W.]... The leaves .. on being bruised, yield a delightful citron-like odour.
   2. In the phr. **to go (in) lemons,** to act with enthusiasm and vigour; to make a fuss.
   1872 G.S. BADEN-POWELL *New Homes for Old Country* 186 A boy, as soon as he gets old enough and strong enough to manage a horse, delights in mustering. He will then, in his Australian, 'go in big lemons' whenever he gets the chance. **1905** J. FURPHY *Rigby's Romance* (1946) 78, I drops like a cock, jumps up agen, an' goes for him lemons.

3. *pl. Australian National Football.* A break in the game at three-quarter time for refreshment taken on the field.

1960 *N.T. News* (Darwin) 12 Jan. 8/3 At lemons, Wanderers led by 8.11 to 8.6. **1968** EAGLESON & MCKIE *Terminol. Austral. Nat. Football* ii. 21 *Lemons*, three-quarter time.

lemony, *a.* Irritable; aggressive.

1941 S.J. BAKER *Pop. Dict. Austral. Slang* 31 *Go lemony at*, to become angry, express anger towards someone. **1968** S. GORE *Holy Smoke* 35 Oh, blimey, they went real lemony on 'im!

lend, *v. Obs. trans.* To give to another the temporary use of the labour of (a convict in one's charge). See also LOAN GANG.

1827 *Tasmanian* (Hobart) 18 Oct. 2 The Government can either lend or assign the prisoner to a master. **1849** A. HARRIS *Emigrant Family* (1967) 30 If he's a prisoner, the master can lend him, if he likes: it's not allowed I suppose; but nobody cares about that.

leonile /'liənil/. *Obs.* Prob. var. LEANGLE, but poss. from a related language.

1894 *Jrnl. Anthrop. Inst.* (London) XXIII. 317 The Australian Aboriginal *weapon*, termed the *leonile, langeel, bendi* or *buccan*... The *leonile* consists, speaking generally, of a more or less long straight handle, or shaft, and a sharp pointed head, of greater or less length, either at right angles to the former, or opposed to the shaft at an angle somewhat greater than a right angle. **1921** *Mid-Pacific Mag.* June 541/1 The boomerang.. appears to possess the greatest affinity to the bent hand clubs, which were very often thrown, and it is certain that the first boomerangs were modifications of the leonile, for intermediate forms of this weapon have been met with.

leopard orchid. Either of two terrestrial orchids (fam. Orchidaceae) bearing a yellow flower with brown markings: in s.e. Aust. applied to *Diuris maculata* of s.e. Aust. incl. Tas., and in W.A. to *Thelymitra fuscolutea* of s.w. W.A., S.A., and Vic.

1923 *Census Plants Vic.* (Field Naturalists' Club Vic.) 21 *Diuris maculata*.. Leopard Orchid. **1978** B.P. MOORE *Life on Forty Acres* 41 The taller and attractively spotted Leopard and Tiger orchids (*Diuris maculata* and *D. sulphurea*) in butter yellow and chocolate brown.

leopard-wood. [See quot. 1863.] Either of two trees of the genus *Flindersia* (fam. Rutaceae) having a distinctive spotted trunk and occurring in N.S.W. and Qld., *F. maculata* of drier country and *F. collina* of rainforest and drier scrub; the wood of these trees. Also *attrib.*, and **leopard tree.**

1863 W.J. WILLS *Successful Explorations Interior Aust.* 130, I have never seen in any other part of the country—the leopard tree (called so from its spotted bark). **1924** J.A. REID *Pioneer Grazier Aust.* 7 The.. homestead was a six-roomed structure, built of locally pit sawn 'leopard wood' weatherboards. **1966** J. CARTER *People of Inland* 57 On the horizon, a ragged line of mulga and leopard trees, vividly green.

Leperland. *Obs.* A nickname for Queensland.

1896 *Bulletin* (Sydney) 17 Oct. 25/2 Barcoo rot.. extends all over Western Leperland. **1898** *Worker* (Sydney) 20 Aug. 3/3 He had to cross a creek up Leperland way, which is infested with alligators.

leper-line. *W.A. Hist.* See quot. 1977.

1966 S.J. BAKER *Austral. Lang.* (ed. 2) 354 What is known as the *leper line* in Western Australia. **1977** F. B. VICKERS *Stranger no Longer* 167 The Western Australian Native Welfare Act was approved for reprint on 22nd August 1955.. and section 10 in its preamble *says: In order that the spread of leprosy within the State may be limited the following provisions shall operate.. no person shall cause a native to travel from a place north of the boundary line to a place south of the boundary line*... The 20th parallel of south latitude was the boundary line, more usually referred to as the Leper line.

lerp /lɜp/. Also (esp. formerly) **laap, loap.** [a. Wemba-wemba lerab.] **a.** The whitish, sweet, waxy secretion produced by insect larvae of the fam. Psyllidae, often in the form of a conical covering of scales; the insect secreting this. Also *attrib.*, esp. as **lerp scale.**
b. MANNA 1 a.

1845 *Papers & Proc. R. Soc. Tas.* 25 Mar. (1851) 242, I had no dinner, but I got plenty of lerp. Lerp is very sweet, and is formed by an insect on the leaves of gum-trees; in size and appearance like a flake of snow, it feels like matted wool, and tastes like the ice on a wedding-cake. **1848** W. WESTGARTH *Aust. Felix* 73 The natives of the Wimmera prepare a luscious drink from the laap, a sweet exudation from the leaf of the mallee (Eucalypt dumosa). **1856** J. BONWICK *W. Buckley* 50 The Loap, or Manna, causes quite a festival in its season. **1907** W.W. FROGGATT *Austral. Insects* 363 Their popular name of 'Lerp Insects' [comes] from the habit of the larvae of many species of forming 'lerp scales', shell-like protective coverings formed from exudations from the insects.

leschenaultia /lɛʃə'nɒltiə/. Also **lechenaultia.** [The plant genus *Lechenaultia* was named by British botanist Robert Brown (*Prodr. Fl. Nov. Holl.* (1810) 581) after the French botanist J.L.C.T. *Leschenault* de la Tour (1773–1826).] Any plant of the genus of perennial herbs and shrubs *Lechenaultia* (fam. Goodeniaceae), occurring chiefly in s.w. W.A., some of which are widely cultivated for their colourful flowers.

1825 *Curtis's Bot. Mag.* (London) LII. 2600 (OEDS) Handsome Lechenaultia. **1916** L.H. BAILEY *Standard Cyclop. Hort.* IV. 1844 The leschenaultias require special care in watering.

leso /'lɛzoʊ/. Also **lezo, lezzo.** [f. *les(bian* + -O.] A lesbian. Also as *adj.*

1945 S.J. BAKER *Austral. Lang.* 123 A lesbian is known mainly as a *lezo* and *a lover under the lap*. **1972** *Bulletin* (Sydney) 21 Oct. 45/1 The Tories, trendies, lesos, poofters, four-be-twos and just plain Pommy bastards. **1974** D. HEWETT *Tatty Hollow Story* (1976) 118 What's up with you? Are you leso or something? **1983** *Nat. Times* (Sydney) 22 July 37/3 And *Gay*! What an insult to the poofs and lezzos who made this country what it is today!

Lesueur's rat-kangaroo /ləsɜː ræt-kæŋgə'ru/. [f. the name of the French illustrator and naturalist C.A. *Lesueur* (1778–1846), who sailed on an expedition to the Pacific led by T.N. Baudin.] BOODIE.

1926 A.S. LE SOUEF et al. *Wild Animals Australasia* 235 Lesueur's rat-kangaroo... Islands of Sharks Bay, Western Australia. **1981** *Ecos* xxix. 21/2 Smaller macropods.. such as.. Lesueur's rat-kangaroo, fared less well, becoming scarce or extinct with the disappearance of the long grass in which they had sheltered.

let go, *v. phr. Shearing.* Of a shearer: to release a shorn sheep.

1879 *Austral. Grazier's Guide* 54 Previously to letting go the sheep.. the shearer marks it with a piece of chalk, putting on his own hieroglyph. **1961** *Bulletin* (Sydney) 3 Feb. 44/2 The young picker-upper.. boasted, 'I picked for seven 'deuce merchants' on my own last year.. and swept each time they let go.'

Hence **letting-go** *ppl. a.*

1925 *Pastoral Rev.* 16 Jan. 31 C, in the plan, denotes the pens where the sheep are caught for shearing; B the shearing board; and L the letting-go pens.

letter-stick. MESSAGE-STICK.
   1887 *Proc. Linnean Soc. N.S.W.* II. 621 Mr Palmer exhibited two 'letter-sticks' obtained from the Aborigines of the Gascoigne River district where, as in other parts of Australia, they are used for inter-tribal communication. **1977** X. HERBERT *Dream Road* 13 George told Prindy he had made up a Letter Stick for sending to the Wise One to say that they two would be going on to the Alice Country.

letter-winged kite. [See quot. 1976.] The bird of prey *Elanus scriptus* of mainland Aust., predom. light to dark grey with white underparts, feeding chiefly on rodents.
   1842 J. GOULD *Birds of Aust.* (1848) I. Pl. 24, *Elanus scriptus* .. Letter-winged Kite. **1976** *Reader's Digest Compl. Bk. Austral. Birds* 117 The letter-winged kite .. in flight .. is clearly distinguished by its underwing pattern—a black line in the shape of a W or an M.

leubra, var. LUBRA.

Lewin /'luən/. [f. the name of the naturalist and artist J.W. *Lewin* (1770–1819), author of a work on Austral. birds.] In the names of birds: **Lewin('s) honeyeater,** the bird of forested e. mainland Aust. *Meliphaga lewinii,* having olive-green plumage with yellow neck markings; **Lewin's rail** (or **water rail**), the mottled grey and white bird *Rallus pectoralis,* inhabiting areas of dense vegetation in Aust., New Guinea, and Indonesia.
   [**1808 Lewin honeyeater:** J.W. LEWIN *Birds New Holland* 9 Yellow-Eared Honeysucker... These birds inhabit the banks of the Hawkesbury and Patterson rivers, frequenting thick bushes.] **1931** N.W. CAYLEY *What Bird is That?* 9 Lewin Honey-eater *Meliphaga lewini* .. also called Yellow-eared Honey-eater and Banana-bird. **1980** L. FULLER *Wollongong's Native Trees* 46 Lewin's Honeyeater .. the only rainforest honeyeater may also [be] found in wet sclerophyll forests and nearby gardens. **1848 [Lewin's rail]** J. GOULD *Birds of Aust.* VI. Pl. 77, *Rallus lewinii* .. Lewin's Water Rail. **1984** *Age* (Melbourne) 7 July 2/3 Hands up all those who knew that Lewin's Rail had disappeared from Western Australia.

lezo, lezzo, varr. LESO.

liangel, liangle, liangra, varr. LEANGLE.

licence. *Hist.* Also **license.**
   1. A formal, annually renewable, permission to occupy Crown land for grazing purposes; a certificate of this. See also TICKET OF OCCUPATION. Also *attrib.*
   1820 *Hobart Town Gaz.* 2 Dec., The Licenses for Occupation of Grazing Grounds for the Year commencing September 29, 1820, will be delivered at this Office on Saturday, December 9th. **1853** *Visit to Aust. & Gold Regions* (S.P.C.K.) 83 The squatter pays his licence-fee of ten pounds for liberty to occupy his land for a year.
   2. a. Prior to the introduction of the *miner's right* (see MINER $n.^2$): a permit, renewable monthly, to remove gold. Also *attrib.*
   1851 *Illustr. Austral. Mag.* (Melbourne) Nov. 262 The Commissioner has a busy post, issuing licenses, (thirty shillings for the month is charged) receiving gold, and arranging matters brought for adjudication. **1870** W.B. WITHERS *Hist. Ballarat* 94 Provoked hostilities by the peculiarly despotic action taken in the last license-collecting raid.
   b. Special Comb. **licence fee,** the fee for a mining permit; **hunt,** an inspection, carried out by police and troopers, to ensure that anyone engaged in gold-mining has a permit; also **-hunting** *vbl. n.*
   1851 *Britannia* (Hobart) 26 June 4/5 The diggers who were without means, for the immediate payment of the **license fee. 1855** R. CARBONI *Eureka Stockade* 13, I was often compelled to produce my licence twice at each and the same **licence hunt.** *Ibid.* 17 Up to the middle of September, 1854, the search for licences happened once a month; at most twice: perhaps once a week on the Gravel Pits, owing to the near-neighbourhood of the Camp. Now, licence-hunting became the order of the day.

licensed, *ppl. a. Hist.*
   1. To whom or for which a permit to occupy Crown land for grazing purposes has been granted.
   1839 *Port Phillip Patriot* 27 May 3 No such licensed person, nor his or her Overseer or Manager, shall keep any stock whatever, belonging to any other person. **1858** T. McCOMBIE *Hist. Colony Vic.* 185 The licensed occupiers of Crown lands, and the tenant farmers.
   2. To whom or for which a permit to remove gold has been granted.
   1851 *Empire* (Sydney) 3 Sept. 115/3 A party of three men were dispossessed of their licensed diggings by a number of impudent fellows walking coolly into the hole and commencing operations. **1856** H.B. STONEY *Vic.* 103 The licensed digger was granted a power to change his locality as often as he pleased during the month.

lick. [Spec. use of *lick* a spurt at racing, speed: see OED(S *sb.* 6.] In the phr. **for the lick of one's life,** at a cracking pace.
   1915 *Honk* x. 7 Straight for his own lines he goes for the lick of his life. **1966** *Sunday Mail Mag.* (Brisbane) 3 Apr. 6/3 A section of the miners agreed that the happiest solution to the sorry affair would be to lynch Mr Chapple. The little Cornishman got wind of this thinking and .. went for the lick of his life.

lick hole. [f. U.S. *lick* place at which animals lick salt or salt earth: see OED(S *sb.* 2.]
   a. A shallow depression in which stock lick for salt which occurs naturally or is supplied. Also **licking hole,** and *attrib.*
   1848 T.L. MITCHELL *Jrnl. Exped. Tropical Aust.* 53 Salt wort plants .. were .. efficacious .. as wholly preventing cattle and sheep from licking clay, a vicious habit to which they are so prone that grassy runs in the higher country near Sydney are sometimes abandoned only on account of the 'licking holes' they contain. **1871** *Austral. Town & Country Jrnl.* (Sydney) 22 Apr. 490/4 Cattle depasturing .. in the up-lying 'lickhole' country are more subject to the ailment. **1928** 'BRENT OF BIN BIN' *Up Country* 143 No horse .. was safe .. in the lick-hole country of its myriad spring-heads. Pool found a way with rock-salt to make the lick-holes a trap.
   b. *fig.* A public house.
   1911 *Bulletin* (Sydney) 16 Feb. 13/2 Some of us .. were anxious to get back to the pub to collect .. so when .. he acknowledged defeat .. we got back to the 'lick-hole'.

Lieutenant-Governor /lɛftɛnənt-'gʌvənə/.
   1. One who deputizes for the Governor of an Australian Colony (later State), or for the Governor-General; formerly also, in Tasmania, Victoria, and Western Australia before their independence from New South Wales, the principal resident representative of the sovereign.
   1787 *HRA* (1914) 1st Ser. I. 3 Our Judge-Advocate in our said territory is hereby required to tender and administer unto you and in your absence to our Lieutenant Governor. **1973** W.G. WALKER *Gloss. Educ. Terms* 74 *Lieutenant-Governor,* (A) official representative of the Sovereign when a temporary vacancy in the office of either Governor-General *q.v.* or Governor *q.v.* occurs; *syns.* Administrator; Deputy Governor.
   2. The title given to a deputy State Governor (in some States).
   1902 *N.S.W. Govt. Gaz.* I. 374 His Excellency the Lieutenant-Governor .. directs the publication .. of the

substance and prayer of a Petition. **1963** *Austral. Encycl.* IV. 351 The vice-regal representative in each State is .. called the Governor of that State, and he generally has a Lieutenant-Governor as his deputy.

life.

1. [Used elsewhere but recorded earliest in Aust.: see OEDS *sb.* 8 d.] A sentence of transportation to Australia and penal servitude for life; imprisonment for life. Freq. *attrib.*

1833 T. BANNISTER *Let. on Colonial Labour* 12 The number of years, for a .. life Convict to serve in the Gangs, before he can get his ticket-of-leave, to be mentioned. **1857** *Vic. Parl. Papers* (1856–57) III. no. 48 46, That is the time I am satisfied he got life.

2. In the phr. **to go for one's life,** to engage (in an activity, etc.) with vigour and enthusiasm. Now chiefly as an exhortation.

1920 H.F. MOLLARD *Humour of Road* 14 You'll have to go for your life now, Jim, if you want your firm's boots to keep walking. You have a keen competitor up against you. **1985** *Canberra Times* 15 Aug. 3/8 If you have a Prime Minister like Bob Menzies who, when asked by the British for anything, was accustomed to drop his strides and say 'Go for your life', you must expect the worst.

lifer. [Used elsewhere but recorded earliest in Aust.] One sentenced to transportation to Australia and penal servitude for life; one sentenced to life imprisonment. Also *attrib.*

1827 *Monitor* (Sydney) 29 Oct. 728/1 As the law, affecting male Prisoners of the Crown now stands, 'lifers' have either a very remote, or as it regards 999 out of every thousand of them, no chance whatever of being permitted to marry. **1892** *Bulletin* (Sydney) 9 Jan. 10/1 The gaol at 'the Pivot' is a sort of Benevolent Asylum for used-up assassins, and in the 'lifer' yard of that drowsy institution you can see groups of mild-looking ancients.

lift, *v.* [Br. *lift* to drive (cattle) away or to market; now chiefly Austral.: see OED(S *v.* 11.] *trans.* To move (stock) from one place to another. Also as *vbl. n.*

1875 *Austral. Town & Country Jrnl.* (Sydney) 27 Feb. 343/2, I haven't lifted a finer mob [of cattle] this season. **1935** N. HUNT *House of David* 126 The 'lifting' of starving stock on the 'drove' so far 'out' .. was a business too risky to anyone who knew his business.

light, *n.*

1. *Austral. pidgin. Obs.* In the phr. **to make a light,** to see; to understand.

1834 G. BENNETT *Wanderings N.S.W.* I. 325 My fadder no see white feller trowsers—*if make a light* (see) make get; but no white feller sit down this place when my fadder here. **1893** S. NEWLAND *Paving Way* 325 First time make-a-light (see) white fellow, then come back yabber (tell).

2. As a mild oath, in the imp. phr. **strike a light.**

1936 A. RUSSELL *Gone Nomad* 44 'Strike a light!' he broke in suddenly. 'See them?' **1979** K. DUNSTAN *Ratbags* 9 Gawd strike a light.

light, *a.* With **on**: in short supply; under-weight.

1944 L. GLASSOP *We were Rats* 122 'You're a bit light on too, aren't you?' 'Purely a temporary state of poverty, Reynolds old boy.' **1960** N. CATO *Green grows Vine* 17 Mike .. never goes crook at yer if your tins is a bit light-on. Only thing he hates to see good fruit left behind on the vine.

lightning fence. A wire fence strung from widely spaced posts and therefore quickly constructed; fencing of this kind.

1913 *Bulletin* (Sydney) 13 Mar. 14/3 New settlers in the Vic. and South Aus. mallee run up 'lightning' fences (posts a chain apart and one barb). **1981** A.B. FACEY *Fortunate Life* 194 The fence consisted of two barbed wires strung from tree to tree. Where the distance between trees was more than five yards, we put a post in. The barbed wire was nailed to the trees and posts. This kind of fence was called a 'lightning fence'.

lightwood. Any of several trees yielding a timber which is light in weight or pale in colour, esp. the shrub or small to medium tree *Acacia implexa* (fam. Mimosaceae) of e. mainland Aust., having a rough, greyish bark and pale yellow flower-heads; the wood of these trees.

1803 *Sydney Gaz.* 26 June, Timber in this Colony includes .. Light-wood. **1981** L. COSTERMANS *Native Trees & Shrubs S.-E. Aust.* 327 Lightwood .. common and widespread in Vic.–N.S.W. hill country.

lignum.

1. [See quot. 1981.] Any of several plants, usu. of the genus *Muehlenbeckia* (fam. Polygonaceae) and esp. *M. cunninghamii* of all mainland States, a twiggy shrub with slender, tangled stems, often forming dense, almost impenetrable thickets; POLYGONUM 1. Also *attrib.*, esp. as **lignum swamp.**

1872 Mrs J. FOOTT *Sketches Life in Bush* 15 The poor animals were glad to munch the roots of salt-bush or lignum. **1933** *Bulletin* (Sydney) 7 June 21/1 Lignum swamps on the dry Paroo Take the place of the ledger page. **1981** J.A. BAINES *Austral. Plant Genera* 246 *Muehlenbeckia cunninghamii*, Tangled Lignum, all States (named after Allan Cunningham, who placed the Aust. spp. in the genus *Polygonum*, of which Lignum is a corruption).

2. Abbrev. of LIGNUM VITAE.

1893 D.J. FROST *Crown Lands N.S.W.* 19 Among the timbers which these northern river forests contain are .. lignum .. and hickory.

lignum vitae. [Transf. use of *lignum vitae* a timber tree of the genus *Guaiacum.*] Any of several trees, esp. the tall, rainforest tree *Premna lignum-vitae* (fam. Verbenaceae) of Qld. and n.e. N.S.W., yielding a durable timber; the wood of these trees; LIGNUM 2.

1803 *Sydney Gaz.* 26 Mar., Lignum Vitae, used in sheaves and pins for blocks. **1986** STANLEY & ROSS *Flora S.-E. Qld.* II. 374 *Premna lignum-vitae* .. Lignum-vitae... Flowers found throughout the year.

likely, *a. Mining.* [Spec. use of *likely* apparently suitable (for a purpose): see OED *a.* 3.] Of rock, country, etc.: promising, likely to yield ore.

1873 W. THOMSON-GREGG *Desperate Character* I. 160 We'll go up the gully a bit; and if I don't think the ground up there looks likely; why, we must just take up an outsider. **1946** K.S. PRICHARD *Roaring Nineties* 49 He had come on likely country about twenty-five miles north-east of the camp.

lilac. *Obs.* [See quot. 1834.] *White cedar*, see WHITE *a.*[2] 1 a.

1834 G. BENNETT *Wanderings N.S.W.* I. 205 *Melia azedarach* .. the fragrance of the flowers so closely resembles those produced by the tree known in England as the 'lilac', that the same appellation is given to it in this colony. **1886** F. COWAN *Aust.* 17 The Lilac or White Cedar-tree: deciduous: its purple bloom, night-scented, beautiful.

lil-lil /'lil-lil/. [Prob. related to LEANGLE.] An Aboriginal weapon used both as a missile and in close combat (see quot. 1974).

1878 R.B. SMYTH *Aborigines of Vic.* I. p. xlv, The *Lil-lil* is not so often used as a missile as to strike at and cut the enemy, and may indeed be properly called a wooden sword. **1974** M. TERRY *War of Warramullas* 121 Boomerang-shaped clubs were used in eastern and central Australia. The lil-lil, a short, bladed weapon with a curved

LILLY-PILLY   311   **LIPPY**

handle was much used in New South Wales and Victoria for hand-fighting or throwing.

lilly-pilly /'lɪli-pɪli/. Also **lilli-pilli**. [Of unknown origin.] The tree *Acmena* (syn. *Eugenia*) *smithii* (fam. Myrtaceae), having glossy, dark green foliage, occurring in rainforest and sheltered gullies of e. Vic., N.S.W., and Qld., and widely cultivated esp. as a street tree; the purplish to white, edible fruit of the tree. Also *attrib*.
    1854 F. ELDERSHAW *Aust. as it really Is* 43 Five-Corners, Lillypillies . . are . . well-recognized delicacies among the rising Anglo-Australian generation. **1947** *Bulletin* (Sydney) 26 Mar. 44/1 Ripe lillipillies dropped on the dry forest bed. **1972** M. GILBERT *Personalities & Stories Early Orbost* 41 Flying foxes could be found hanging in the lilly-pilly jungles.

lily. In the phr. **like a lily on a dust bin** (**dirt tin**, etc.), used as an emblem of incongruity.
    1943 *Signals* (Melbourne) Christmas 41 Girl sitting on Piano like lily on dirt tin. **1982** N. KEESING *Lily on Dustbin* 14 One woman says to look like a lily on a dustbin (or garbage or dirt bin) is to dress inappropriately for an occasion and/or to wear over-fussy, frilly clothes. Another uses it for a variety of incongruous matters: an informal or poor family meal table might have newspaper instead of a cloth and cracked and battered utensils and one pretty milk jug stands in the centre of it like a lily on a dustbin.

lily-trotter. [See quot. 1934.] LOTUS BIRD. Also **lily-walker**.
    1934 *Bulletin* (Sydney) 7 Feb. 21/3 Lotus birds . . are essentially swamp dwellers and get their colloquial name of 'lilly trotters' from their ability to scamper over the wide leaves of the lotus and other water plants. **1945** J. DEVANNY *Bird of Paradise* 114 A lotus-bird, or lily-walker, pattered across the surface of the pond.

lime-juice. *Obs.* [Fig. use of *lime-juice* the juice of the lime used as an antiscorbutic on a long sea voyage.] Used allusively of a recently arrived British immigrant.
    1855 G.H. WATHEN *Golden Colony* 39 He is quite green; he has only been here eighteen months; he hasn't got the lime-juice off. **1897** *Jrnl. Pioneers & Old Residents Assoc. Castlemaine* 12 I'll never forget how I was stared at. The diggers cried, 'Look at him; you can smell the lime-juice.'

lime-juicer. *Obs.* [f. prec.] A recently arrived British immigrant. See also LIMEY.
    1857 J. ASKEW *Voyage Aust. & N.Z.* 55 The black gins kept calling out as I passed each 'whurlie'—'Ah! white fellow, limejuicer' (which is a term used in all the colonies to newly arrived emigrants). **1906** E. DYSON *In Roaring Fifties* 68 They've been hazing you properly, mate. Pea-soupers and lime-juicers are strangers off shipboard.

limewood. [See quot. 1981.] Either of the two trees *Eucalyptus papuana* (GHOST GUM) and *E. aspera* (fam. Myrtaceae) of n. Aust., having a white bark yielding a chalky powder.
    1931 M. TERRY *Hidden Wealth* 326 Limewood is a very handsome tree, shapely, with a white trunk and light green foliage; it is very plentiful in the Tanami district. **1981** A.B. & J.W. CRIBB *Useful Wild Plants Aust.* 214 The very white bark of the ghost gum is covered with a fine white powdery layer which comes off on the hand; this is responsible for the less common name of limewood.

limey. [f. LIME(JUICER + -Y. In later use prob. infl. by U.S. *limey* English sailor or ship (see OEDS).] A British immigrant. Also *attrib.*
    1888 D.B.W. SLADEN *Austral. Ballads & Rhymes* 31 They'd seen old stagers and limey new chums. **1937** WISBERG & WATERS *Bushman at Large* 92 All you limeys are nutty. **1953** J.E. MACDONNELL *Wings off Sea* 125 Them Limeys sure fan the breeze.

limits, *pl. Hist.* Abbrev. of *limits of location* (see LOCATION 4).
    1821 J. WALLIS *Hist. Acct. Colony N.S.W.* 17 The strictest orders were . . given to prevent the convicts from straggling beyond the limits which were marked and known. **1980** P. FREEMAN *Woolshed* 48 The 1836 Squatting Act . . allowed squatting beyond the Limits, providing a license fee of £10 per annum was made for each 'run'.

line.
    1. In the collocation **line of road,** a course marked out for a road; the completed road.
    1828 *Tasmanian* (Hobart) 9 May 3 Three prisoners in the chain gang at Oatlands, succeeded in slipping off their fetters, while at work in the new line of road at a distance from the huts. **1949** *Main Roads* Sept. 15 The building of the main railway to the west during the sixties and seventies of the last century altered the line of road in some places.
    2. [Also Canadian and N.Z. from 1828: see OEDS *sb.*² 26 e.] Abbrev. of *line of road*. Also *attrib*.
    1837 *Perth Gaz.* 25 Mar. 872 In an E.N.E. course from the same point (York), we have now the satisfaction of knowing that . . about eight or ten farmsteads and sheep runs could be formed on that *line*. **1890** 'R. BOLDREWOOD' *Miner's Right* 76 The impatient holders of claims on 'the line' frontage.
    3. In the collocation **back line** *obs.*, a rear boundary.
    1847 *Britannia* (Hobart) 8 July 2/3 His back line may be Macquarie Harbour. **1899** *North-Western Advocate* (Devonport) 10 Feb. 4/1 The part of Forest tapped by the Back Line road west has gone ahead wonderfully.
    4. *Hist.* Abbrev. of *black line* (see BLACK *a.* 7).
    1831 G.A. ROBINSON in N.J.B. Plomley *Friendly Mission* 5 Nov. (1966) 503 Miles Opening was where the natives got through at the time of the Line. **1886** *Austral. Handbk.* 554 In 1830 an attempt on a gigantic scale called The Line was made to drive the aborigines into a corner of the island.
    5. [Poss. transf. use of *line* a department of activity, branch of business: see OED(S *sb.*² 28 but also 13 d.] In the phr. **to do a line with,** to behave amorously towards (another).
    1933 N. LINDSAY *Saturdee* 242 'I suppose you're going with Elsie Coote, aren't you?' 'Oh, yes, I'm doin' a line with her,' said Peter. **1961** N. GARE *Fringe Dwellers* 286 I'm gunna do a line with the little gel that wants to go to Perth with me.

line-ball. [Fig. use of *line-ball* a ball striking the line and therefore almost out of play.] An indecisive event; a borderline case.
    1915 DREW & EVANS *Grafter* 54, I don't know how he'd sling if he had a good winning day. Last day was a line ball. **1951** S. HICKEY *Travelled Roads* 4 Con was clearly a line-ball so decorous conviviality marked his wake.

ling. [Transf. use of *ling* a long, slender fish.] Any of several marine fish, usu. of the fam. Ophidiidae, esp. *Genypterus blacodes*, having a long, tapering pinkish-white body, and the reddish-brown *Lotella callarias*, both of s. Aust.
    1895 C. THACKERAY *Amateur Fisherman's Guide* 57 Tumbledown is the . . habitat of . . ling. **1906** D.G. STEAD *Fishes of Aust.* 86 The Cod family . . is comparatively unimportant so far as our Australian waters are concerned . . the most important being the Beardie or Ling (*Lotella callarias*).

lippy. Also **lippie.** [f. *lip(stick* + -Y.] Lipstick.
    1955 *Meanjin* 310 Jest . . for fun I put some of Mums [*sic*] lippy on. **1983** *Sydney Morning Herald* 19 Dec. (Guide) 1/2

On radio, Miss Buttrose sounds as though she is wearing a sunfrock, bit of lippie and a pair of orthopaedic sandals.

liquid, *a.* In special collocations: **liquid laugh,** a vomit; **lunch,** a mid-day meal consisting mainly of an alcoholic beverage, esp. beer.

1964 B. HUMPHRIES *Nice Night's Entertainment* (1981) 78 I've had **liquid laughs** in bars. **1969** A. BUZO *Front Room Boys* (1970) 21 We used to go down to Jim Buckley's . . for a **liquid lunch.**

little, *a.*

1. In special collocations: **Little Brother,** a British youth who emigrates to Australia under the auspices of the *Big Brother Movement* (see BIG BROTHER); **-go** *obs.*, a nickname for the Court of Requests; also **little-go court,** and *attrib.*; **house** [Br. dial. (see EDD *little, a.* 30)], a euphemism for an outside privy; **lunch,** light refreshment eaten during a mid-morning break at school.

1927 J.A.R. MARRIOTT *Empire Settlement* 81 The idea is that a band of well-established Australian citizens, clergymen, government officials, bankers, farmers, etc., should individually undertake to act the part of a Big Brother to an individual **Little Brother** from the homeland. **1837** *Cornwall Chron.* (Launceston) 5 Aug. 3 First, an Under Sherriff of the Supreme Court . . now a **Little-go** Sherriff! *Ibid.* 12 Aug. 3 But for the strictest exactness in matters of accounts carried into the 'Little Go' Court, a system of roguery would take place. **1843** *Melbourne Times* 10 June 3/2 Your carriage hire you must pay or they will put you in the 'Little-go'. **1886** N. ROBINSON *Stagg of Tarcowie* 9 Aug. (1977) 84 Building at the **little house.** **1982** N. KEESING *Lily on Dustbin* 120 In Queensland 'eleveners' have disappeared in favour of the universal '**little lunch**' to eat during the morning; 'big lunch' is eaten at lunch time.

2. As a distinguishing epithet in the names of birds: **little corella,** the predom. white, crestless cockatoo *C. sanguinea* of Aust., esp. arid regions, and New Guinea; see also CORELLA; **eagle,** the bird of prey *Hieraaetus morphnoides* of mainland Aust. and New Guinea; **falcon,** the bird of prey *Falco longipennis* of Aust. and islands to the north; *white-fronted falcon*, see WHITE *a.*² 1 b.; **kingfisher,** the smallest Austral. kingfisher *Ceyx pusillus*, a blue and white bird of coastal N.T. and n. Qld.; **lorikeet,** the small lorikeet *Glossopsitta pusilla* of e. and s.e. Aust., a predom. green bird with a red face; JERRYANG; see also KEET; **penguin,** *fairy penguin*, see FAIRY *n.*¹ 1; **quail,** the small, nomadic bird *Turnix velox* of mainland Aust.; **wattle bird,** either of the two smaller wattle birds, *Anthochaera lunulata* of s.w. Aust., and *A. chrysoptera* (see *brush wattle bird* BRUSH *n.*¹ B. 2); **wood swallow,** the predom. grey-brown bird *Artamus minor* of n. and central Aust.

1948 A. MARSHALL *Ourselves writ Strange* 247 **Little corellas,** those cockatoos with naked blue skin around their eyes, were feeding in the long grass. **1902** *Emu* II. 10 The **Little Eagle** . . are constant visitors during summer, autumn and winter. **1841** J. GOULD *Birds of Aust.* (1848) I. Pl. 10, *Falco frontatus* . . **Little Falcon,** Colonists of Western Australia. **1843** J. GOULD *Birds of Aust.* (1848) II. Pl. 26, *Alcyone pusilla* . . **Little Kingfisher.** [**1843 little lorikeet:** J. GOULD *Birds of Aust.* (1948) V. 54 *Trichoglossus pusillus* . . Little Parrakeet.] **1929** A.H. CHISHOLM *Birds & Green Places* 209 The tiny red-faced species, known as the 'gizzie' or little lorikeet. [**1785** J. LATHAM *Gen. Synopsis Birds* III. 572 **Little Pinguin** [*sic*] . . This species is found among the rocks on the southern parts of *New Zealand*. . . The inhabitants of *Queen Charlotte's Sound* kill the birds with sticks, and, after skinning them, esteem the flesh as good food.] **1844** J. GOULD *Birds of Aust.* (1848) VII. Pl. 84, *Spheniscus minor* . . Little Penguin. **1841** J. GOULD *Birds of Aust.* (1848) V. Pl. 87, *Hemipodius velox* . . **Little Quail,** of the Colonists. **1846** J. GOULD *Birds of Aust.* (1848) IV. Pl. 57, *Anthochaera lunulata* . . **Little Wattle-Bird,** Colonists of Swan River. **1945** C. BARRETT *Austral. Bird Life* 162 The red wattle-bird . . and the little wattle-bird (*A*[*nthochaera*] *chrysoptera*) range from southern Queensland to Victoria. **1842** J. GOULD *Birds of Aust.* (1848) II. Pl. 28, *Artamus minor* . . **Little Wood Swallow.**

littley. [f. *little* + -Y; prob. independent of Br. dial. *littly* small person: see OEDS.] A child.

1965 *Coast to Coast 1963–64* 84, I take a bunch of littlies for Bible lessons, hymns, you know. **1968** D. O'GRADY *Bottle of Sandwiches* 62 The amount of grog consumed there really separated the boys from the littleys.

liver. In the phr. **shit on the liver**: see SHIT 2.

lizard.

1. One employed: **(a)** to muster sheep; **(b)** to maintain boundary fences. Also *attrib.*

1897 *Worker* (Sydney) 11 Sept. 1/1 By 'lizards' he means musterers, sometimes he calls them 'snails'. **1905** *Shearer* (Sydney) 4 Feb. 4/2 What do you know of . . 'tick-jammers', or of 'lizards' and 'wire inspectors'? **1912** *Bulletin* (Sydney) 30 May 16/3 He does the lizard act along a fence, and pulls up at water by noon.

2. In the exclam. **starve** (or **stiffen**) **the lizards,** an expression of surprise or exasperation. See also CROW *n.*¹ 3.

1927 *Bulletin* (Sydney) 27 Jan. 22/2 'Starve the lizards,' he said, 'there ain't no kangaroos in the West now.' **1959** M. RAYMOND *Smiley roams Road* 17 Stone the crows and stiffen the lizards.

3. In the phr. **flat out like a lizard**: see FLAT *adv.* 2. Hence **lizarding** *vbl. n.*, mustering; also *transf.*, lazing.

1908 'G. SEAGRAM' *Bushmen All* 240 This blessed lizarding is bad enough, but wood and water joey is worse. **1975** *Sun* (Sydney) 16 May 13/2 He likes his golf and just lizarding in the sun.

loading, *vbl. n.*¹ [Br. *loading* a load, cargo, but app. now rare: see OED *vbl. n.* 4.] Freight carried by a vehicle; a load.

1862 C. MUNRO *Fern Vale* I. 127 By this time the drays were seen making their approach; and great was instantly the bustle in preparation for the reception of the 'loading'. **1976** K. BROWN *Knock Ten* 59 A teamster . . took loading out from the railhead at The Mount to any point . . in the Gulf.

loading, *vbl. n.*² A payment in addition to an award wage or salary, in acknowledgement of conditions of employment, degree of skill, a prosperous economy, etc.

1941 *44 CAR* 456 In addition to amounts otherwise payable a special loading at the rate of 3s. per week shall be payable to occupants of any of the callings specified. **1983** J. CARROLL *Austral. Industr. Relations Handbk.* (rev. ed.) 86 Whether or not an employee is entitled to payment of the loading on pro rata annual leave on termination of his employment depends primarily on the terms of the relevant award.

loam, *n.*

1. *pl.* Particles of gold found by loaming (see LOAM *v.*) and indicating the presence and location of a deposit. Also **loam gold.**

1934 S.J. CASH *Prospecting for Gold* 8 Quartz of a sugary nature would . . throw loam gold or 'loams' as it is called, more freely than harder quartz. **1977** J. DOUGHTY *Gold in Blood* 196 Near The Castlemaine outcrop, I had discovered a shed of loam gold.

2. Special Comb. **loam bag,** the bag in which a sample of soil which is to be tested for gold particles is placed.

1896 J. HOLT *Virgin Gold* 42 The prospector, pure and simple . . sets out with his pick and shovel, his dish and his loam-bag.

loam, *v.* Also **loom.** [f. *loam* clay, soil.] *intr.* To search (an area) for a mineral, usu. gold, by washing loam: see quot. 1932. Also *trans.* and as *vbl. n.*
1896 J. HOLT *Virgin Gold* 19 That important branch known as '*loaming*'. **1932** I.L. IDRIESS *Prospecting for Gold* 264 *Loaming*, a method of prospecting for a metal-bearing vein or mineralized area in which dirt is washed from places chosen systematically around and up the slope of a hill. Presence, absence, and the number of colours in the dish eventually indicate the mineral source. **1946** K.S. PRICHARD *Roaring Nineties* 59 Dinny went loaming along the ridge for several days before he knapped a rock that showed fine shotty gold. **1950** —— *Winged Seeds* 21 'Ye've loomed her north, a bit, Mick?'. . 'Got colours in every dish,' Mick told him.

loamer. Also **loomer.** One who searches for gold by loaming: see LOAM *v.*
1931 W. BARAGWANATH et al. *Guide for Prospectors in Vic.* 6. The 'loamer' digs a small hole to bedrock. **1980** M. MCADOO *If only I'd Listened* ('Pop Doherty'), Now those fellows . . could find the source of the gold; they called it 'looming', and oh it was an art because there wasn't much water about. The Cash brothers . . they were famous loomers.

loan. [Var. of Br. dial. *to take the lend of a person* to take advantage of, to cajole: see EDD *lend, v.* and *sb.*[1] 4.] In the phr. **to get (or have) the loan of** (someone), to trick (a person); to treat (a person) as a fool.
1903 J. FURPHY *Such is Life* 143 'Jist what I told you!' she replied, with a sunny laugh. 'Think I was tryin' to git the loan o' you?' **1955** R. LAWLER *Summer of Seventeenth Doll* (1965) 95 It's all fellers—Barney wouldn't take a girl to the races with a crowd of fellers. He's havin' a loan of yer.

loan gang. *Hist.* A detachment of artisan convicts employed on public works but made available to settlers: see quot. 1840. See also LEND.
1833 *Colonist* (Hobart) 4 Jan. 2/4 Much as has been said about the Loan-Gang, we are firmly persuaded, that had it not been for this gang, the price of labour would have risen. **1840** D. BURN *Vindication Van Diemen's Land* 14 The loan-gang . . is formed of artisans employed in government works, who . . are lent . . to assist settlers in building, or other needful improvements.

loap, var. LERP.

lob, *n.* [Spec. use of Br. dial. *lob* lump (of money): see EDD *sb.*[1] and OED *sb.*[2] 4.] A rich deposit of gold: see quot. 1869. Also **lob of gold.**
1861 H. EARLE *Ups & Downs* 287 The gold perhaps may tempt us the diggings to try, In a hole or fine 'lob' we may see. **1869** R.B. SMYTH *Gold Field & Minerals Districts* 164 *Lob of gold*, a very large quantity or rich deposit of gold contained within a small area.

lob, *v.* [Transf. use of *lob* to move heavily or clumsily: see OED(S *v.* 3.] *intr.* To arrive, esp. without ceremony; to turn up. Freq. with **in, on to, up,** etc.
1911 *Bulletin* (Sydney) 17 Aug. 14/3 I first lobbed on to the 'far Barcoo' . . years ago. **1918** A. WRIGHT *Over Odds* 121, I beat it to the West on my share of Skimmy's roll; only lobbed back two days ago. **1925** *Aussie* (Sydney) Aug. 57/2 The next day we all lobbed up to the local hall. **1965** R.H. CONQUEST *Horses in Kitchen* 47 Any man who lobbed in with an empty tucker-bag was promptly fed.

lobby. Chiefly *Qld.* [f. LOB(STER + -Y.] YABBY 1.
1952 W.J. DAKIN *Austral. Seashores* 183 In Queensland they are known as lobbies (the derivation of this can be guessed)—in that State yabbies are something quite different. **1984** H.W. DAVIS *Bachelors in Bush* 51 Harry and me was fishing for them little freshwater lobsters what they call 'lobbies'.
Hence **lobbying,** *vbl. n.*
1977 K. MCARTHUR *Bread & Dripping Days* 10 For a day's lobbying, first a kind mother had to supply meat bones which were well and truly picked over on the way to the creek.

lobster. [Transf. use of *lobster* a large marine decapod crustacean of the genus *Homarus*.] Any of several crayfish, esp. those having claws the flesh of which is esteemed as food. See also CRAYFISH *n.*
1826 J. ATKINSON *Acct. Agric. & Grazing N.S.W.* 25 Lobsters, crayfish, and prawns, are also found in many places. **1985** *Age* (Melbourne) 19 Mar. 29/2 The light sauce with the dish . . and the freshness and perfect cooking of the crayfish (please let us break the 'lobster' habit; lobsters have claws) were laudable.

local government. *Hist.* Any one of the Colonial administrations as distinct from the *home government* (see HOME *n.*[1] B b.).
1835 *Cornwall Chron.* (Launceston) 14 Nov. 1 The Local Government is guilty at the least of an injudicious arrangement of the means placed at its disposal for the benefit of the whole Colony. **1845** *Portland Gaz.* 1 Apr. 4/4 The state of the Great Southern Road is positively a disgrace to the local government.

locatable, *a. Obs.* [f. LOCATE *v.* 3.] Of land: available for occupation by a settler.
1833 *Launceston Advertiser* 13 June 2 *For sale. A maximum grant*, free from Quit Rent, to be taken where the purchaser may choose from Land yet locatable.

locate, *v. Hist.* [Spec. use of *locate*, not always excl. Austral. but of local significance: see OED *v.* 3, 4, and 5, and Mathews.]
1. [See esp. OED *v.* 5.] *trans.* To allocate (a specified block of land or an entitlement to a specified area of unidentified land), esp. to a settler or for the purpose of grazing stock; to grant.
1811 *HRA* (1921) 3rd Ser. I. 458 No New Town Allotment is to be located to any person whatever in 'George Square' or in 'Macquarie Street'. **1851** H. MELVILLE *Present State Aust.* 226 Sir William Denison trusted that his locating the allotment to the captain, would be sanctioned by the home authorities.

2. [See esp. OED *v.* 3 and 4.] **a.** *trans.* To establish (a settler, etc.) in a place suitable for permanent occupation; to settle. Freq. *refl.*
1823 *HRA* (1914) 1st Ser. II. 122 On obtaining the promise of a grant, the settler formerly went and located himself. **1837** *S. Austral. Rec.* (London) 8 Nov. 3 Colonel Light will send to Sydney for assistance, to prevent disappointment to those who come out and expect to be located immediately.

b. *trans.* To establish (a person) in a place for a period of limited or uncertain duration. Freq. *refl.*
1839 *Southern Austral.* (Adelaide) 10 May 4/1 The recent murders were committed by a tribe of natives whom I can assert to have been two months absent from Adelaide. . . I am the owner of the property on which they located themselves during that period. **1847** *Port Phillip Herald* 11 Mar. 2/6 Prisoners in future to be located at Maria Island.

3. *trans.* To select (a piece of land as specified in the terms of a grant).
1823 *Hobart Town Gaz.* 4 Oct., New Settlers, or those who have not yet located their Grants. **1839** *Tegg's Handbk. for Emigrants* 11 You intend to locate a maiden tract.

4. [See esp. OED v. 4.] **a.** *intr.* To establish oneself (as a settler) in a place.

1827 *Tasmanian* (Hobart) 7 Dec. 2 On coming here, they get land in proportion to their property, on which they can locate with as little expense as at Canada. **1855** N.L. KENTISH *Question of Questions!* 40 They might locate on any 'country' they chose to 'take up', *i.e.*, to select to any extent.

b. *transf.*

1842 *Portland Mercury* 14 Sept. 3/2 Mr James Allison .. had .. started from Portland on horseback, armed to the teeth, with the dire intention of proclaiming war against the ducks located at Bridgwater. **1843** *Ibid.* 24 May 3/4 It is reasonable to suppose that these insects will locate where they can obtain water.

Hence **locating** *vbl. n.*

1827 *Monitor* (Sydney) 3 Mar. 362/3 His resignation was tendered upon the condition usually granted to public servants, namely a grant of land. For the present 'granting' and 'locating' are at a stand still.

located, *ppl. a. Hist.*

1. Of land: allocated, granted; occupied by settlers. See also UNLOCATED.

1825 *Hobart Town Gaz.* 8 June, Even those whose sheep and cattle are not numerous, find a difficulty in depasturing on their located grounds. **1848** J.C. BYRNE *Emigrant's Guide* 12 Secure a good master and a comfortable home within the located parts of the colonies.

2. In the collocation **located district,** a district occupied by settlers.

1825 M. HINDMARSH *Lett.* (1945) 20 Government is now about selling all the Crown Lands in the Located Districts which is mostly choice land.

locatee. *Hist.* One to whom an allocation of land has been made.

1834 H. MELVILLE *Two Lett. Van Diemen's Land* 6 Numerous instances of the resumption of land .. have taken place, in order to bestow them gratuitously upon other locatees. **1855** N.L. KENTISH *Question of Questions!* 11 Subjecting it, by the conveyance deed, to *certain conditions* binding on each locatee.

locater, var. LOCATOR.

location. *Hist.* [Spec. use of *location*, as infl. by prec.]

1. An allocation or grant of land; the piece of land so allocated.

1813 *HRA* (1921) 3rd Ser. I. 35, I cannot sanction nor confirm some of the Locations you directed Mr Meehan to make. **1865** 'W.R.L.' *Our Wool Staple* 9 They were to be accredited cultivators of wool fixed down to particular locations, and subjected to rentals proportioned to the area of their runs.

2. The act of establishing a settler in a place; settlement.

1819 *HRA* (1921) 3rd Ser. II. 411 Preclude my authorizing any extensive location thereon. **1865** G.S. LANG *Aborigines of Aust.* 39 The grand foundation of all the evil is the absence of any systematic provision .. for the location of the blacks, when their country is occupied by the whites.

3. Special Comb. **location duty,** an obligation imposed on the occupier of a location by the terms under which the land was allocated; **order,** a warrant authorizing the holder to select and occupy a piece of land on certain stipulated terms.

1832 G.F. MOORE *Diary Ten Yrs. W.A.* 1 July (1884) 122 Here I have as much as I can manage, perhaps more, as the **location duties** are heavy. **1832** *Colonist* (Hobart) 28 Sept. 3/5 It will require .. more than all the casuistry of all the lawyers to prove that **location order** can be substituted for the term *grant*.

4. In the phr. **the limits (boundaries, bounds) of location,** the frontier of settlement; *spec.* boundaries delimiting those parts of an Australian Colony within which land is available for alienation. See also BORDER 1 and BOUNDARY *n.*

1837 *Rep. Select Committee Transportation* 23 May (1838) 190 They take their sheep establishments not beyond the limits of the colony, but beyond the limits of location. **1837** *Colonist* (Sydney) 25 May 169/4 The following gentlemen have been appointed Commissioners of Crown Lands in the .. districts .. beyond the boundaries of location. **1840** *Port Phillip Gaz.* 25 Jan. 4 The Brickmakers .. are always close upon the town, and cannot therefore be said to live beyond the bounds of location, a position which can alone demand the protection of a Border Police.

locator. *Obs.* Also **locater.** One who takes up an allocation of land.

1829 H. WIDOWSON *Present State Van Diemen's Land* 46 February 26, 1827—Orders all locaters of town grants to build their houses in such a way as to leave 60 feet for carriage and foot roads. **1847** *HRA* (1925) 1st Ser. XXV. 563 The Establishments of the licensed Locators of the Crown Lands.

lock, *v.* [Spec. use of *lock* to shut off from: see OED *v.*[1] 4, esp. quot. 1785.] *trans.* With **up:** to shut (land) off from small settlers; to prevent the release of (land). Also as *vbl. n.* See also UNLOCK.

1855 P. SAUNDERS *Two Yrs. Vic.* (1863) 6 The immediate effect of this locking up of the land was the enormous prices paid. **1947** F. CLUNE *Roaming around Aust.* 146 The best land is all 'locked up' in these big leaseholds. They have the river frontage and all the good land, so there's no chance for small-farming to develop.

locust. [Extended and transf. use of *locust* an insect of the fam. Acrididae.]

1. A winged insect of the fam. Acrididae or Tettigoniidae; applied esp. to those species able to form a destructive, migratory swarm, incl. the plague locust *Chortoicetes terminifera*.

1822 J. DIXON *Narr. Voyage N.S.W. & Van Dieman's Land* 67 A kind of grasshopper, or locust .. spread over the land, and ate up the herbage of the colony. **1969** *Victorian Yr. Bk.* LXXXIII. 6 The Australian plague locust (*Chortoicetes terminifera*) breeds in plague numbers in inland Australia under certain conditions.

2. A cicada.

1834 J. BACKHOUSE *Extracts from Lett.* (1838) II. 54 The cicadae (here called locusts), of which there are several species, keep up a constant rattle. **1956** S. HOPE *Diggers' Paradise* 206 Juveniles rapturously hail a lush cicada season .. 'locusts', as they erroneously call them.

3. *transf.* A tourist.

1972 A. CHIPPER *Aussie Swearers Guide* 41 *Locust*, a popular Australian term for a tourist pest.

log, *n.*[1]

1. Used *attrib.* in (orig. U.S.) Comb. **log fence, fencing, hut.**

1846 F. DUTTON *S.A. & its Mines* 203 There are the 'ditch and bank', 'American or **log-fence**' and the 'dog-leg fence'. **1851** H. MELVILLE *Present State Aust.* 109 Yards are commenced; if for sheep, brush fence serves very well for a time,—but for cattle more substantial work, such as **log fencing,** is required. **1825** T. KENT *Lett. to B. Field* 45 Another Englishman living in a **log hut** on his farm in Van Diemen's Land.

2. In *pl.* with **the.** A gaol, orig. (see quots. 1796 and 1873) one constructed of logs.

[**1796** D. COLLINS *Acct. Eng. Colony N.S.W.* (1802) II. 2 A strong and capacious Log Prison at each of the towns of Sydney and Paramatta.] **1872** *Austral. Jrnl.* Jan. 327

To-morrow morning, Mac, we'll have all these fellows comfortably in the logs. **1873** *Austral. Town & Country Jrnl.* (Sydney) 2 Aug. 147/1 The aforesaid lockup, popularly known as 'the Logs', from the preponderating quantity of these massive timbers displayed in the floor, the wall, and indeed the ceiling of the edifice. **1928** N.F. SPIELVOGEL *Affair at Eureka* 15 Lalor drew himself up to his full height of 6 ft. 6 in. . . 'Remember your thirty-five friends lying in 'the logs' to-night.'

3. Special Comb. **log-chop,** a wood-chopping competition.
1905 *Bulletin* (Sydney) 31 Aug. 36/1 'I bet on the log-chop,' the one bookmaker reminds the public.

4. *fig.* A block-head. Also **log of wood.**
1959 S.J. BAKER *Drum* 124 *Log,* any person regarded contemptuously for his lack of ability, brains and energy. **1961** F. HARDY *Hard Way* 12 On the way to the lift, I remembered with a start that I had forgotten to empty my pockets. What a log of wood I am!

log, $n.^2$ *Industrial Relations.* [Spec. use of *log* a record.]

1. A set of claims for an increase in wages, improvement in working conditions, etc., esp. as lodged by a trade union with an industrial tribunal. See also AMBIT. Also **log of claims.**
1911 5 *CAR* 181 The claims of the employees have been framed into a log of wages and conditions. **1948** G. FARWELL *Down Argent Street* 102 When the unions submitted their log of claims for the 1925 Agreement, they asked for increased wages and yet shorter hours. **1983** D.J. BAILEY *Holes in Ground* 15 In 1920 Queensland miners endorsed a Federal claim. The log included: six hours, bank to bank; a five-day working week.

2. With qualifying element, as **Lygon Street log**: see quot. 1976.
1976 *10 ALR* 473 The log of claims for improved wages and conditions is in the standard form currently used by many trade unions and is described as a Lygon Street log (referring to the Trades Hall, Lygon Street, Melbourne).

log, *v.*

1. *Mining. intr.* With *up*: to construct a log frame to support a windlass. Also *trans.*
1871 *Austral. Town & Country Jrnl.* (Sydney) 8 Apr. 431/3 They have . . logged up and covered their shaft. **1888** *Tasmanian* (Hobart) 1 Sept. 21/2 Have logged up shaft and made paddock for quartz.

2. *intr.* Of an animal: to take refuge inside a hollow log.
1920 *Bulletin* (Sydney) 8 Jan. 20/2 Big Murray cod when closely pursued scoot into hollow logs... The 'yellow belly' (golden perch), like the hare, 'logs' only in the last extremity. **1943** *Ibid.* 27 Oct. 12/3 When I was a nipper I hunted kangaroo-rats and bandicoots with a cattle-dog and I never knew one to escape him except by 'logging'.

Hence **logged-up** *ppl. a.*
1905 *Horlick's Mag.* (London) Feb. 108/1 Reaching a logged-up hole on the flat, I returned for a moment to hide behind it and reconnoitre.

Logie /'lougi/. [f. the name of John *Logie* Baird (1888–1946), British inventor of television.] One of the statuettes awarded annually since 1958 by the magazine *TV Week* for excellence in acting, etc., in a television production. Also **Logie award,** and *attrib.*
1968 *TV Week* (Melbourne) 5 Jan. 3 *Logie votes* are flowing in to the *TV Week* office in their thousands this month. **1968** *Austral.* (Sydney) 30 Mar. 11/4 One of the rites involved in this apotheosis of the mediocre is the annual presentation of the Logies, those squat statuettes named after John Logie Baird. **1985** *Sydney Morning Herald* 27 Apr. 3/8 *A Country Practice* dominated the 27th annual Logie Awards in Melbourne last night.

log-runner.

1. Either of two ground-dwelling, rainforest birds of the genus *Orthonyx*, the dark-plumaged *O. spaldingii* of the Atherton region in Qld., and the *spine-tailed log-runner*; CHOWCHILLA.
1898 E.E. MORRIS *Austral Eng.* 272 *Log-runner* . . an Australian bird, called also a *spinetail.* **1954** C. BARRETT *Wild Life Aust. & New Guinea* 145 Log-runners, or 'chowillas' [*sic*] as they are called by naturalists, are birds of the rain-forest floor.

2. With distinguishing epithet: **spine-tailed log-runner,** the mottled brown bird *Orthonyx temminckii* of e. coastal Qld. and N.S.W., having tail feathers in which the central shaft projects in a spine-like tip.
1909 *Emu* VIII. 242 The southern species, known as the Spine-tailed Log-runner (*O. spinicauda*). As their name implies, their habit is running more than flying. **1945** C. BARRETT *Austral. Bird Life* 135 Jules Verreaux nearly a century ago published field notes on the southern spine-tailed log-runner.

Lola Montez /ˌloʊlə ˈmɒntɛz/. [The name of *Lola Montez* (1818–1861), an Irish dancer and courtesan, who toured Australia in 1855.] A drink with a rum base: see quot. 1859.
1859 F. FOWLER *Southern Lights & Shadows* 52 The following are a few of the names of favourite beverages:- . . A Lola Montez . . Old Tom, ginger, lemon, and hot water. **1981** *Bulletin* (Sydney) 1 Aug. (Red Page), If you murmured 'a Lola Montez', the barman of the fifties handed you over a concoction of Old Tom, ginger, lemon and hot water.

lolly. [Br. dial. *lolly* a sweetmeat, abbrev. of *lollipop.*]

1. A sweet of any kind, esp. boiled. Also *attrib.*
1854 C.H. SPENCE *Clara Morison* II. 102 Fanny ran away to the nearest lolly shop, and all her brothers and sisters followed her. **1986** *Canberra Times* 24 Feb. (Suppl.) 2/1 It is one of those programs which is bad for the brain in the same way that lollies are bad for the teeth.

2. Comb. **lolly paper, shop, tin.**
1968 D. IRELAND *Chantic Bird* 13 Plenty of litter with milk cartoons, soft drink cans, **lolly papers,** sandwich crusts. **1854 lolly shop** [see sense 1]. **1883** J.E. PARTINGTON *Random Rot* 95, I noticed one enterprising man had over his shop, 'The largest lollie shop on earth'. **1901** F. GILLEN *Diary* 3 Aug. (1968) 193 Two Warramunga kiddies . . frequently raid our **lolly tin.**

3. Special Comb. **lolly boy,** one who sells refreshments from a tray at a cinema, sports ground, etc.; also *fig.*; **money,** cash given to a child to buy sweets; **-pink** *a.*, shocking pink; **stick,** a boiled sweet on a stick or shaped like a stick; **water,** a soft drink.
1950 F. HARDY *Power without Glory* 460 Above the mumble of five thousand voices could be heard the calls of the drink and **lolly boys** with their trays. **1980** *Sydney Morning Herald* 4 Nov. 2/8 The former Finance Minister, Mr Eric Robinson . . was prepared to speak his mind and . . was not one of the Prime Minister's lolly boys. **1917** *Truth* (Sydney) 12 Aug. 7/8 The tramways have taken **lolly-money** from the kiddies. **1958** M. WARREN *No Glamour in Gumboots* 214 Joe came, and the post-girl, who produced, as a parting gift, a particularly repulsive boutonnière of **lolly pink** duck feather flowers. **1911** 'S. RUDD' *Bk. of Dan* 26 'Look,' Dan said, extending his big toe to the infant as though offering it a **lollie stick.** **1905** J. MEREDITH *Learn to talk Old Jack Lang* (1984) 14, I can . . have a lemonade . . and no one ever laughs at me or calls me sissy because I am drinking **lolly water.**

4. *transf.* and *fig.* The head; esp. in the phr. **to do one's (or the) lolly,** to lose one's temper; to lose one's head; to 'do one's nut'.

1951 *New Settler in W.A.* (Perth) Feb. 77 That joint has a clothes line in the front yard so go slow or get your lolly lopped off. **1956** *Truth* (Sydney) 15 Jan. 21/2 Punters were inclined to do their 'lolly' at Alan Burton. **1965** F. HARDY *Yarns of Billy Borker* 77 'She cursed and swore at the moon. And the moon did the lolly'—I slipped into the Australian language again there for a minute.

London fog. A nickname for a person who loafs on the job: see quots.

1967 *Kings Cross Whisper* (Sydney) xxxvi. 4/1 *London fog*, any person who will not lift. **1981** *Nat. Times* (Sydney) 25 Jan. 24/2 A lazy wharfie would be known as 'the Judge' because he was always sitting on a case, and another 'the London Fog' because he would never lift.

long, *a*.
1. Used in special collocations to indicate greater than usual length: **long blow** *shearing*, a stroke of the shears which extends from the tail to the neck; **paddock**, a *stock route* (see STOCK 2); a public road the sides of which are used for grazing; **-sentence(d) man** *obs.*, a convict serving a long sentence; **-sleever**, a tall beer glass; the drink so contained; **'un**, a long beer.

1904 *Shearer* (Sydney) 10 Dec. 4/4 In a shed can be seen all the latest styles—**long blow**, three-quarter blow, and the blow which is a mixture of both. **1929** *Bulletin* (Sydney) 16 Oct. 25/2 The **'long paddock'** is not the only place in which sheep-owners have had .. cheap feed. **1840** *Tasmanian Weekly Dispatch* 5 June 4/2 This **'long sentenced man'** .. had .. the power of mustering. **1875** J. FORREST *Explorations in Aust.* 334 The residue of convicts are, many of them, men of the doubly reconvicted class and long-sentence men. **1877** *Pilgrim* (Sydney) Ser. I. viii. (Suppl. no. 2) 18, I should blow the froth from off the festive '**long sleever'**. **1902** *Bulletin* (Sydney) 1 Mar. 16/3 A blacktracker .. used to boast that, although he was only as high as 12 'long-sleevers', he could drink 13 inside the hour. **1895** *Bulletin* (Sydney) 5 Jan. 3/2 He can't fight; he always gets beaten; he has no science, no constitution, and won't train as long as '**long 'uns'** are plentiful.

2. As a distinguishing epithet in the names of flora and fauna: **long-billed corella** (or **cockatoo**), the predom. white bird *Cacatua tenuirostris* of s.e. Aust., having orange-red markings on the head and throat, and a long, curved upper bill; see also CORELLA 1 a.; **-leaved acacia** (or **wattle**) *obs.*, *Acacia longifolia*, see *sally wattle* SALLY 2; **-necked tortoise**, the tortoise of s.e. and e. mainland Aust. *Chelodina longicollis*, occurring in various fresh-water habitats, esp. swamps; also **long-neck(ed) turtle**; **-spined flathead**, the marine fish *Platycephalus longispinis* of s.e. and w. Aust.; see also SPIKEY; **yam**, the twining plant *Dioscorea transversa* (fam. Dioscoreaceae) of n. Aust.; the long, edible tuber of the plant.

[**1822 long-billed corella:** J. LATHAM *Gen. Hist. Birds* II. 205 *Long-nosed cockatoo*. Psittacus nasicus... The general colour of the plumage is pure white, but the whole face or front of the head is rose-colour.] **1847** J. GOULD *Birds of Aust.* (1848) V. Pl. 5, *Licmetis nasicus*. Long-billed Cockatoo. **1945** C. BARRETT *Austral. Bird Life* 72 The long-billed corella .. is a favourite, ranking first as a talking bird. **1820** J. OXLEY *Jrnls. Two Exped. N.S.W.* 103 There were only four different kinds of plants at this terminating point of our journey, viz. the small eucalyptus, the **long-leaved acacia** [etc.]. **1856** *Jrnl. Australasia* I. 37 You may now plant .. acacia longifolia, long-leaved wattle. **1794** G. SHAW *Zool. New Holland* 19 Testudo Longicollis. The **long-necked tortoise** .. is a species never before figured or described... The neck extremely long, and (as it should seem) always exserted. **1886** F. COWAN *Aust.* 19 The Long-necked Turtle of the inland creeks: reptilian crane. **1960** B. HARNEY *Cook Bk.* 65 Freshwater turtles (known as 'Long Neck' turtles) are caught in the swamps where they lie during the dry months of the year. **1906** D.G. STEAD *Fishes of Aust.* 198 The **Long-spined Flathead** is a small, large-bellied species, occurring on the coast of New South Wales. It is not uncommon on sandy patches in deep water off a number of the beaches in the vicinity of Sydney. **1878** R.B. SMYTH *Aborigines of Vic.* I. 229 *Dioscorea punctata* .. **long yam**. **1981** D. LEVITT *Plants & People* 41 Long Yam grows in jungles... The long, thin root .. can be eaten raw but was usually cooked in hot sand and ashes.

longa, *prep. Austral. pidgin.* Belonging to; near; about; with.

1879 'AUSTRALIAN' *Adventures Qld.* 21 Then mine ask him look out sugar-bag long a me—mine kill him behind *cobra*. **1951** E. HILL *Territory* 108 'Debil-debil piccaninny walk-about longa sit-down,' he informed the astonished tribe. **1955** F. LANE *Patrol to Kimberleys* 215 *Longa*, aborigine pidgin for 'at' or 'with'. Instead of saying the boss is down at the billabong, an aborigine will say: 'Boss longa billabong.' **1968** S. GORE *Holy Smoke* 104 *Longa*, to do with; pertaining to. (Pidgin.)

long service leave. A period of paid leave granted to an employee who has served a specified period of continuous employment: see e.g. quots. 1918 and 1927. Also *attrib*.

1900 *Act* (W.A.) 64 Vict. no. 21 Sect. 29, Public servants shall be entitled to long service leave. **1918** *Act* (Tas.) 9 Geo. no. 69 Sect. 90 (1), Every officer under the age of Sixty-five years, of or over Twenty years' continuous service in the Public Service shall, for the *bonâ fide* purpose of furlough only, be entitled to .. long-service leave of absence for Six months on full pay, or, at the option of the officer, Twelve months on half-pay. **1927** *N.S.W. Industr. Gaz.* 30 June 1202 Long Service Leave. Four weeks' leave of absence on full pay shall be granted to each employee on the completion of twenty years' service with the Company. **1984** *Austral. Financial Rev.* (Sydney) 16 May 1/1, 60 of Australia's largest companies have among them, provisions for annual leave and long service leave payments totalling $1.5 billion.

long tom.
1. *Gold-mining*. [U.S.: see OED(S 2.] A trough used for washing auriferous material: see quot. 1865. Also **long-tom sluice**.

1852 *Empire* (Sydney) 23 Jan. 602/4 Long-toms are coming into use on the river—they do more work than an ordinary cradle. **1865** J.F. MORTLOCK *Experiences of Convict* 149 They had first dammed the river, a mere brook; they then constructed a 'long Tom' sluice; merely a wooden trough some ten feet in length having at its lower end a compartment lined with tin, perforated in many places, so as to permit the mud and water freely to escape, but to retain in a shallow tray underneath the minutest particles of weightier ore.

2. ALLIGATOR PIKE.

1881 *Proc. Linnean Soc. N.S.W.* VI. 241 *Belone ferox* .. 'Long Tom' of the Fishermen .. Port Jackson. **1983** HUTCHINS & THOMPSON *Marine & Estuarine Fishes S.-W. Aust.* 22 Like most longtoms it can 'run' across the sea's surface using the tail for propulsion.

Hence **long-tomming** *vbl. n.*, the act of using a long tom.

1856 G. WILLMER *Draper in Aust.* 78, I resolved to try the experiment of 'long-tomming'; and accordingly, without delay, I procured one of the long troughs known in digging parlance as a 'tom'.

lookout. [Transf. use of *lookout* view, prospect, infl. by *lookout* place for keeping watch: see OED(S.] An elevated place from which a particular scenic attraction can be viewed.

1930 M.B. PETERSEN *Monsoon Music* 51 After driving some miles, the party reached the turning to the well-known 'Jimmie's Look Out'. **1981** *Meanjin* 153 'This is called Mitchell Lookout,' he said, 'but as you see it is not a Lookout in the Rotary sense.' It was just a shelf of rock.

loom, var. LOAM v.

loomer, var. LOAMER.

loppy. [Prob. f. Br. (dial.) *lop* to hang about, to idle: see EDD v.² and OED v.² 2; but see also OEDS *loppy, sb.*, which suggests a derivation f. *loppy, a.* flea-ridden.] A rouseabout.
   1897 *Worker* (Sydney) 11 Sept. 1/1 The 'rouseabout' .. he sneeringly terms 'loppy' and a 'leatherneck'. 1981 K. GARVEY *Rhymes of Ratbag* 76 The loppies all complain a lot Because it didn't rain a spot.

loranthus /ləˈrænθəs/. *Obs.* [The plant genus *Loranthus* was named by French botanist N.J. Jacquin (*Enum. Stirp. Vindob.* (1762) 55,230): all Austral. plants once included in this genus are now classified in different genera.] Any of several mistletoes.
   1827 A. CUNNINGHAM *Gen. Remarks Vegetation* 18 The genus Loranthus .. is .. sparingly scattered on all the Coasts of Australia, where about eleven species have been recently observed, parasitical upon certain trees. 1844 L. LEICHHARDT *Jrnl. Overland Exped. Aust.* 3 Oct. (1847) 6 The Loranthus and Myal in immense bushes.

Lord Howe Island woodhen. [f. the name of *Lord Howe Island*, n.e. of Sydney, N.S.W.] The small brown bird *Tricholimnas sylvestris* of Lord Howe Island.
   1977 *Ecos* xi. 18 Lord Howe Island lies about 600 km. off the coast of northern New South Wales. .. It provides refuge for one of the world's rarest birds—the Lord Howe Island woodhen. The entire breeding population of this flightless fowl numbers about 25. 1985 *Parks & Wildlife News* Winter 20 Apart from being small and having a less than spectacular plumage that can only be described as dag brown, its other notable non-attribute is that it can't fly. .. A Lord Howe Island Woodhen.

lorikeet. Any of several small, and usu. predom. green, nectar-feeding parrots most common in n. and e. Aust.; *honey parrot,* see HONEY. Also with distinguishing epithet, as **little, musk, purple-crowned, rainbow, red-collared, scaly-breasted, varied** (see under first element).
   1770 J. BANKS *Jrnl.* 1 May (1896) 267 The trees overhead abounded very much with loryquets and cockatoos. 1979 C. KLEIN *Women of Certain Age* 43 She saw her mother holding a tray of bread and honey for the lorikeets.

lotus bird. The wading bird *Irediparra gallinacea novaehollandiae* of e. and n. Aust. and southernmost New Guinea, having exceptionally long toes which enable it to walk on aquatic plants; JACANA; LILY-TROTTER.
   1870 E.B. KENNEDY *Four Yrs. in Qld.* 114 The lotus bird .. runs along the leaves of the water-lily. 1982 R. ELLIS *Bush Safari* 55 Quite close to camp Jacanas or Lotus-birds ran across waterlilies on their long spider-like feet.

loubra, var. LUBRA.

lounge room. [In Br. use usu. *lounge.*] The sitting-room of a private house.
   1917 *Huon Times* (Franklin) 26 Oct. 5/2 A lounge room presents a very cosy and attractive appearance. 1979 P. ADAMS *More Unspeakable Adams* 92 Paul .. lumbered out to the loungeroom where he switched on the telly.

louse, v. [Fig. use of *louse* to search for lice.]
   a. *Mining. trans.* To pick over (waste material) looking for pieces of the mineral sought; esp. in the phr. **to louse the dump.** See also NOODLE. Freq. as *vbl. n.*
   1934 *Geol. Survey: Mineral Resources* 36 (N.S.W. Dept. Mines) 117 Small parcels have been obtained by the method known locally as 'lousing', which is simply picking the material over. 1950 *Coast to Coast 1949–50* 137 She loused the dumps, sifting the dirt that came up, and she found chips which she bottled and a few nobbies that the buyers bought for a quid or two.
   b. *trans.* To pilfer (food, etc.).
   1957 W.E. HARNEY *Life among Aborigines* 66 Not that the natives wished to 'louse' much—a bush term for minor pilfering of small quantities of food to feed their kin, and as such considered wages.
   Hence **louser** n.
   1948 K.S. PRICHARD *Golden Miles* 27 A louser's always suspected of pimping for the boss.

lousy jack. APOSTLE a.
   1933 J. MCCARTER *Love's Lunatic* 220 To-day they did not .. hear the chattering lousy-jacks. 1980 S. THORNE *I've met some Bloody Wags* 69 Lousyjacks are small, grey, ugly, nasty-looking birds, which are found in the west grouped together, continually screeching in an irritating manner.

love-bird. [Transf. use of *love-bird* a small African parrot: see quot. 1842.] BUDGERIGAR.
   1837 *S. Austral. Rec.* (London) (1838) 13 Jan. 30 Strictly speaking, there are no real parrots, except the small love birds, the rest are parroquets, cockatoos, and macaws. 1842 R.G. JAMESON *N.Z., S.A., & N.S.W.* 71 There is another species, called the love-bird, which usually associate in pairs, perching so close together, that it is generally impossible to shoot them singly.

love creeper. The Austral. twining plant *Comesperma volubile* (fam. Polygalaceae) bearing racemes of (usu. bluish) flowers. Also *ellipt.* as **love.**
   1894 J.K. ARTHUR *Kangaroo & Kauri* 26 Among Australian flowering plants, 'Love' is the pet name bestowed on a most beautiful little creeper bearing flowers of a lovely blue. 1973 J. MORRISON *Austral. by Choice* 74 The whole hillside was speckled with colour: blue love-creeper, yellow leopard orchids [etc.].

lowan /ˈloʊən/. [a. Wemba-wemba (and neighbouring languages) *lawan.*] Mallee fowl, see MALLEE 6.
   1847 *Port Phillip Herald* 16 Mar. 2/5 The eggs of the Lowan, a bird frequenting the barren plains on and about the Lower Murray. 1972 ANDERSON & BLAKE *J.S. Neilson* 41 More than once as a youth he watched the lowans building.

lowey, var. LOWIE.

low-heel. [Perh. infl. by orig. U.S. *round heels,* used transf. of a sexually compliant woman: see OEDS *round, a.* 15 a.] A prostitute; a sexually promiscuous woman.
   1939 K. TENNANT *Foveaux* 311 In this crowd of low heels, quandongs and rippery men, she looked at her ease and yet not one of them. 1965 J. BEEDE *They hosed them Out* 193 My well-bred low-heel declared it was the first time she'd been done on the floor and voted it an exceedingly diverting experience.

lowie /ˈloʊi/. Also **lowey.** [f. LOW(-HEEL + -Y.] LOW-HEEL.
   1953 K. TENNANT *Joyful Condemned* 21 There's many a man thought he was going to stand over some little lowie and now he's either looking through the bars, or else he's mowing the lawn for her. 1967 *Kings Cross Whisper* (Sydney) xxxvi. 4/1 *Lowey,* an immoral young hussy very popular among young knockabouts.

lubra /ˈlubrə/. Formerly also with some variety, as **leubra, loubra.** [orig. uncert.]
   1. An Aboriginal woman. Also *attrib.*
   [1829 G.A. ROBINSON in N.J.B. Plomley *Friendly Mission*

18 May (1966) 59 The husband soon followed me, his cheeks wet with tears. Said *leuberer lowgerner unnee* (his wife asleep by the fire).] **1830** *Ibid.* 19 Mar. (1966) 133 Dray told me that the natives had gone away last night and that Woorrady and *lubra* or *lore* went after them. **1841** *Geelong Advertiser* 8 May 2/5 Within the last few days, we have been informed, two leubras were killed and eaten, at the Protector's station, near Killembeet. **1843** *Port Phillip Gaz.* 10 June 3 The reward offered for the apprehension of the murderers of the Loubras. **1856** J. BONWICK *W. Buckley* 76 A female friend of ours was once talking with a lubra pensioner.

2. *transf.* and *fig.*

1950 *Southerly* iii. 142 So we grew gamblers, tough, hardbitten, taking The lubra of luck for a mistress. **1971** D. WILLIAMSON *Don's Party* (1973) 49 Any man who isn't married with four kids is a lecher in your book, you flopbellied, breast-sucked old lubra.

Lucky Country, the. [The title of a book by Donald Horne (b. 1921), published in 1964.] A (chiefly ironic) name for Australia; the popular assumption that Australia is 'a land of opportunity'.

1968 K. DENTON *Walk around my Cluttered Mind* 168 We take it for granted that this *is* the Lucky Country, ignoring the fact that when Donald Horne titled his book he was writing in acid. **1986** *Bulletin* (Sydney) 28 Jan. 24/1 As a rapidly falling relative standard of living focuses their minds, Australia's educators are wondering how to cope with the loss of the 'lucky country'.

lucky digger. *Obs.* A successful gold-miner.

1852 *Austral. Gold Digger's Monthly Mag.* i. 13 Tom, the lucky digger, is to be bridegroom. **1903** N. CRAIG *My Adventures* 228 He is a lucky digger, and considers himself quite good enough to mate with a scion of Royalty.

lucky shop. *Vic.* See quot. 1982.

1979 *Age* (Melbourne) 19 Dec. 24/4 He was intrigued by the number of people at the so-called 'Lucky Shop' frittering away all kinds of money on undisciplined quadrella betting. **1982** *Sun-Herald* (Sydney) 7 Mar. 144/5 Victoria's TAB (quaintly called lucky shops) now seems to be the place to spend a pleasant Saturday afternoon.

luderick /'ludərɪk/. Formerly also **ludrick**. [a. Ganay *ludarag*.] The largely herbivorous *Girella tricuspidata*, a brown or silvery-grey marine and estuarine fish with dark vertical bands, of commercial importance in e. Aust.; DARKIE *n.*[2]; NIGGER 3. See also BLACKFISH.

1886 *Argus* (Melbourne) 13 Mar. 4/2 The ludrick is a rare and fine fish, something like a bream, but striped with dark bands. **1985** *Canberra Chron.* 10 July 19/5 The big winter luderick are turning up in the estuaries.

lug-bite, *v. trans. Obs.* To cadge (money, food, etc.): see BITE *n.* and *v.* Also as *n.*

1891 *Truth* (Sydney) 29 Mar. 7/5 Getting in on the *nod* is the same as . . 'the bustle', 'the whisper', 'the lug-bite', 'on the have'. **1902** *Ibid.* 25 May 1/1 'Lugbiting' meaning in the Australian vernacular, cadging—impudent, outrageous begging.

Hence **lug-biter** *n.*

[N.Z. **1905** *N.Z. Truth* (Wellington) 5 He looked so much more like a low-down lug biter than a wool king.] **1911** L. STONE *Jonah* 223 Joe Grant, a loafer by trade and a lugbiter by circumstance, shifted from one foot to another.

lumber, *v.* [Transf. use of Br. slang *lumber* to place (property) in pawn: see quot 1812 and OED(S *v.*[3] Used elsewhere but chiefly Austral.] *trans.* To arrest; to imprison; to punish judicially (see quot. 1827). Chiefly *pass.*

1812 J.H. VAUX *Mem.* (1819) 188 *Lumber, to lumber* any property, is to deposit it at a pawnbroker's or elsewhere for present security; to retire to any house or private place, for a short time, is called *lumbering yourself.* A man apprehended, and sent to gaol, is said to be *lumbered,* to be *in lumber,* or to be in *Lombard-street.* **1827** *Monitor* (Sydney) 2 Aug. 559 He was sentenced to be *lumbered* for six months; i.e. to go on the tread-mill every Saturday. **1984** P. READ *Down there with me on Cowra Mission* 57, I got lumbered. Copper pulled up and asked me my name, where I was going.

lumber yard. *Obs.* [f. *lumber* 'disused articles of furniture and the like, which take up room inconveniently': see OED(S *sb.*[1] 1. Cf. U.S. *lumber house* building in which various things may be stored: see DAE.] See quot. 1837.

1793 D. COLLINS *Acct. Eng. Colony N.S.W.* (1798) I. 324 The lumber yard near Sydney being completed, the convict millwright Wilkinson was preparing his new mill. **1837** J. MUDIE *Felonry of N.S.W.* 28 The lumber-yard, as it was called, was an establishment containing workshops for convict mechanics of various descriptions, in the employ of government, and was also a depot for materials and stores used in the carrying on of the government works.

lumpy, *a.* Of an animal: afflicted with lumpy jaw (actinomycosis). Also as *n.*

1907 *Bulletin* (Sydney) 6 June 4/4 An old 'lumpy' bullock was missed . . when the herd was removed to fresher fields. **1974** B. KIDMAN *On Wallaby* 16 He found some of the beasts were infected with pleuro pneumonia; they were easily recognised by a swelling on the cheek or the neck. These 'lumpies' were shot at once.

lunar. *Obs.* Esp. in the phr. **to take a lunar.** [Shortening of 'to take a lunar observation', Br. slang *to take a sight* to make an observation with an instrument, *transf.* to make a gesture with the fingers in front of the nose similar to the action of doing this: see OED *sight, sb.*[1] 7 b. and c. and OED(S *lunar, sb.* 2. Sense 2 is now used elsewhere but is recorded earliest in Aust.]

1. An offensive gesture (see quot. 1847, 1). Also *transf.* (see quot. 1866).

1847 *Bell's Life in Sydney* 8 May 3/5 This worthy, upon meeting me in the streets lately, saluted me with a *lunar,* by placing his thumb on his nose and extending his fingers. **1847** *Maitland Mercury* 28 July 2/4 Davis's much enduring spirit was driven beyond all bounds by Mrs Tennant and a friend of hers 'taking a lunar' at him as he was returning towards his house. **1866** *Sydney Punch* 7 Apr. 791/2 Is it not just possible that the writer may be 'taking a lunar' at human credulity.

2. A look.

1849 A. HARRIS *Emigrant Family* (1967) 16 You go towards 'the Rocky Springs' and 'take a lunar' at them. **1880** *Bulletin* (Sydney) 28 Aug. 12/1 Young ladies . . used to believe there was a man in the moon. . . What are the fair ones to do now, having no object in view 'when taking a lunar'?

lunatic soup. Alcoholic liquor of poor quality.

1933 *Bulletin* (Sydney) 6 Sept. 42/1 Lunatic soup, as the few fellows who knew him as Darkie called the brandy he drank. **1986** *Transair* Mar. 9/1 They went about destroying themselves with the lunatic soup crippling their larynx as surely as if they'd downed an economy size tin of paint stripper.

lunette. [Transf. use of *lunette* the figure of a crescent moon.] A usu. curved or crescent-shaped dune, largely of wind-borne material, formed on the lee side of a lake basin in parts of arid s. Aust. and elsewhere, having smooth contours and with the concave edge along the shore.

1940 E.S. HILLS in *Austral. Geographer* Mar. 15 Along the eastern shores of almost every lake and swamp in the plains of northern Victoria there occurs a crescentic ridge of silty clay or clay 'loam', whose smooth and regular outlines, rising above the plains, at once catch the eye in an otherwise monotonous landscape... The present writer can find no record of the occurrence of such land forms in any other part of the world. It is therefore proposed to designate them by a new term—*lunette*. **1977** J.A. MABBUTT *Desert Landforms* 208 Sand lunettes are less stable than clay lunettes.

lungfish. [Spec. use of *lung-fish* a dipnoan fish.] The lungfish *Neoceratodus forsteri* of Qld. rivers; BURNETT SALMON. See also *mud fish* MUD 1.
1896 F.G. AFLALO *Sketch Nat. Hist. Aust.* 211 'Barramunda', a name that more properly belongs to the *Ceratodus*, or Lung Fish. **1982** *Bulletin* (Sydney) 26 Jan. 18/2 Dead lungfish, believed to have been killed by water pollution, were discovered in Brisbane's Breakfast Creek.

lurk. [Generalized use of Br. slang *lurk* a method of fraud: see OED(S *sb.*¹] A profitable stratagem; a dodge or scheme (not necessarily implying fraud); a job (see quots. 1915 and 1958).
1891 *Truth* (Sydney) 15 Mar. 2/1 The young man took thought within his bosom, and he said within his own heart, 'Now, what's his lurk?' **1915** C.J. DENNIS *Songs of Sentimental Bloke* 20, I found 'er lurk wus pastin' labels in a pickle joint. *Ibid.* 125 *Lurk*, a regular occupation. **1958** R. STOW *To Islands* 126 'What's your lurk, mate?' 'Me? Stockman on a mission.'

lurkman. One who lives by sharp practice.
1945 S.J. BAKER *Austral. Lang.* 138 We are .. originators of the following terms for various sharpers, tricksters and others who live by their wits: *spieler* .. *lurk man* .. and *amsterdam*. **1978** W. LOWENSTEIN *Weevils in Flour* 139 You couldn't get a deener where there was no deener to be got. You had to be there where it was, so we became lurkmen. Not bad people but sharp!

lyre-bird. [See quot. 1886.]
1. Either of the two species of ground-dwelling bird of the genus *Menura*, the ALBERT LYRE-BIRD or the more widespread and common *superb lyre-bird* (see SUPERB), *M. novaehollandiae* of forest in s.e. mainland Aust. and introduced into Tas. The bird is noted for its resounding call and remarkable power of mimicry, and for the long, lyre-shaped tail displayed by the male; MENURA; *mountain pheasant*, see MOUNTAIN; *native pheasant* (a), see NATIVE *a.* 6 b.; PHEASANT 1 a. Formerly also **lyre(-tailed) pheasant, lyre-tail bird.**
1834 G. BENNETT *Wanderings N.S.W.* I. 277 The 'Lyre bird' of Australia... The lyre-pheasant is a bird of heavy flight, but swift of foot. **1851** MRS R. LEE *Adventures in Aust.* 356 What is the reason I have never met with the Lyre-tail Birds? **1886** J.A. FROUDE *Oceana* 146 We saw a lyre-bird .. the body being like a coot's and about the same size, the tail long as the tail of a bird of paradise, beautifully marked in bright brown, with the two chief feathers curved into the shape of a Greek lyre, from which it takes its name. **1896** C.E. LYNE *Life H. Parkes* 398 And have we no visions pleasant Of the playful lyre-tailed pheasant.
2. *transf.* (Punningly) a liar; a mimic.
1895 G. RANKEN *Windabyne* 234 Boggs and Nipper were certainly unbusiness-like .. and Short blurted out that they were 'lyre birds' of the most pronounced type. **1969** A. GARVE *Boomerang* 86 'You're like a ruddy lyre bird.' 'Oh, lord—not *more* ornithology! What does that one do?' 'Imitates everything.'

M

Ma: see MA STATE.

macadamia /mækə'deɪmɪə/. [The plant genus *Macadamia* was named by the botanist F. von Mueller (*Trans. Philos. Inst. Vic.* (1858) II. 72) after the chemist John *Macadam* (1827–1865), Secretary of the Philos. Inst. Vic.] Any rainforest tree of the genus *Macadamia* (fam. Proteaceae) of e. Qld., n.e. N.S.W., and the Celebes, esp. *M. integrifolia* and *M. tetraphylla* which are cultivated for their edible nuts; the nut of these trees; BOPPLE NUT; *Queensland nut*, see QUEENSLAND 2. Also **macadamia (nut) tree**, and *attrib*.
    1927 H.J. RUMSEY *Austral. Nuts* 8 A rather strange feature of the Macadamia is that the nut adheres to the bottom of the exocarp or husk, instead of hanging from the stem like other nuts and the seeds of stone fruit. **1970** *Coast to Coast 1967–68* 4 The butcher-birds and magpies in the macadamia-trees. **1978** S. GOULDSTONE *Austral. & N.Z. Guide Food Bearing Plants* 48 The macadamia nut tree is a beautiful evergreen tree which is indigenous to northern New South Wales and Queensland.

macaroni. Rhyming slang for 'baloney'; nonsense.
    1924 LAWRENCE & SKINNER *Boy in Bush* 46 Yes. Jam, macaroni, cockadoodle. We're plain people out here-aways. Not mantle ornaments. **1984** A. DELBRIDGE *Aussie Talk* 201 *Macaroni*, nonsense.

macaw. *Obs.* [Transf. use of *macaw* any of several birds of tropical America of the genus *Ara*.] A black cockatoo, prob. PALM COCKATOO.
    1793 J. HUNTER *Hist. Jrnl. Trans. Port Jackson* 69 There are a great variety of birds in this country; all those of the parrot tribe, such as the macaw. **1862** J. MCKINLAY *Jrnl. Exploration Interior* 6 May 88 A vast number of gulahs, curellas, macaws .. here.

macca, var. MACKER.

machine.
    1. *Obs.* A totalizator.
    [N.Z. **1889** A.E. WOODHOUSE *N.Z. Farm & Station Verse* (1950) 26 What a lot [of money] you left behind in the 'machine'.] **1893** *Bird o' Freedom* (Sydney) 7 Jan. 7/3 Shortly after the machine opened it was seen that the party behind St. Nipps were backing him. **1903** *Sporting News* (Launceston) 11 July 1/5 His or her investment on the machine, either straight-out or for a place.
    2. Abbrev. of *shearing machine* (see SHEARING B. 3). Freq. *attrib*.
    1891 *Conference Amalgam. Shearers' Union & Pastoralists' Fed. Council* 20 The strong desire shown by men who have never shorn by machine to get into machine sheds. **1940** *Bulletin* (Sydney) 10 Jan. 16/1 Anyone .. could put up tallies with machines.

Mackenzie bean. [f. the name of the *Mackenzie* River: see quot. 1982.] The trailing creeper *Canavalia rosea* (syn. *C. maritima*) (fam. Fabaceae) of tropical n. Aust. and elsewhere, the immature pod of which may be cooked and eaten.
    1845 L. LEICHHARDT *Jrnl. Overland Exped.* 15 Mar. (1847) 180 The scrub is generally an open Vitex... The Mackenzie-bean and several other papilionaceous plants .. grow in it. **1982** K. MCARTHUR *Bush in Bloom* 25 We call it simply the Beach Bean because that describes it sufficiently for people living near the coast, as here it is a plant of the sand dunes... Leichhardt called it the Mackenzie Bean because he found it on the Mackenzie River in Central Queensland.

macker. Also **macca.** [Of unknown origin.] A recruit in the armed forces; a newcomer.
    1944 *H.M.A.S. 'Westralia'* Dec. 5 All the tried and noted 'mackers' from the messes near and far. **1965** J. WYNNUM *Jiggin' in Riggin'* 112 Only a macca in the outfit, too. Only been in half as long as us.

mackerel. [Transf. use of *mackerel* the marine fish *Scomber scombrus*.] Any of several marine fish, usu. of the fam. Scombridae, esp. *Scomber australasicus*, a silvery-greenish fish of s. Aust. and elsewhere.
    1770 J. COOK *Jrnls.* 23 Aug. (1955) I. 394 The sea is indifferently well stock'd with Fish of various sorts, such as .. Mackarel [*sic*]. **1974** T.D. SCOTT et al. *Marine & Freshwater Fishes S.A.* 289 The Mackerel is a migratory fish and occurs in large numbers in the open ocean off the coasts of southern Australia.

macnoon, var. MAGNOON.

Macquarie Harbour. [f. the name of an inlet on the w. coast of Tas.] Used *attrib*. in the names of flora and fauna: **Macquarie Harbour pine** *obs.*, HUON PINE; **vine**, (chiefly *Tas.*) the twining plant *Muehlenbeckia gunnii* (fam. Polygonaceae) of Tas. and S.A., bearing edible fruit in loose, grape-like clusters; also **Macquarie harbour grape (vine), Macquarie vine.**
    1851 *Hobarton Guardian* 8 Jan. 4/2 On Sale .. 150,000 feet of **Macquarie Harbour pine**. **1831** [**Macquarie Harbour vine**] *Hobart-Town Almanack* 265 The Macquarie harbour grape .. produces its fruit in large bunches, resembling grapes. **1843** J. BACKHOUSE *Narr. Visit Austral. Colonies* p. xxxvi, Macquarie Harbour Vine or Grape. This large climber was introduced into Hobart Town from Macquarie Harbour about 1831 or 1832; but it also abounds in almost every other humid forest in the Colony. **1857** D. BUNCE *Australasiatic Reminisc.* 39 *Polygonum adpressum*, or Macquarie harbor grape vine... Its quick growth, dense foliage, and white blossoms, succeeded with clusters of waxy transparent fruit, slightly acid, renders it a desirable ornament. **1975** A.B. & J.W. CRIBB *Wild Food in Aust.* 66 Macquarie Vine is a woody, twining plant, sometimes prostrate but often climbing over other plants in moist forests.

Macquarie Island parrot. [f. the name of an island s.e. of Tas.] See quot. 1965. Also **Macquarie Island parakeet, Macquarie parrot.**
    1827 P. CUNNINGHAM *Two Yrs. in N.S.W.* I. 326 The Macquarie parrot is the inmate of an island even more bleak and cold than the Orkneys. **1831** *Hobart-Town Almanack* 260 Macquarie island parrot—Pacificus. **1965** *Austral. Encycl.* VII. 28 Unfortunately, the Macquarie Island parakeet (*Cyanoramphus novaezelandiae erythrotis*) is extinct; it was exterminated by sealers seeking food.

Macquarie perch. Also **Macquarie's perch.** [f. the name of a river in central N.S.W.] The fresh-water fish *Macquaria australasica* of rivers and lakes in Vic. and N.S.W., valued for its fine flesh.
    1906 D.G. STEAD *Fishes of Aust.* 99 Macquarie's Perch attains a length of from 12 to 15 inches. **1984** *Age* (Melbourne) 30 Jan. 1/5 The survival of the Murray cod and Macquarie perch is threatened by silt, filling the deep holes

in river beds they inhabit and killing the bottom-dwelling insects they feed on.

Macquarie vine: see *Macquarie Harbour vine*, MACQUARIE HARBOUR.

macrozamia /mækroʊˈzeɪmɪə/. [f. Gk. μακρο-, comb. form of μακρός large and *Zamia* a plant genus, a name given by the Dutch botanist F.A.W. Miquel (*Monogr. Cycad.* (1842) 35).] Any plant of the genus *Macrozamia* (fam. Zamiaceae) of e., s.w., and central Aust., typically having stiff, palm-like leaves and cone-bearing seeds edible after treatment (see quot. 1951). See also *wild pineapple* WILD 1, ZAMIA. Also *attrib*.
1871 *Illustr. Sydney News* 30 Sept. 158/4 On the Manning River there grows a noble arborescent Macrozamia .. which attains a height of eight or ten feet, with a splendid canopy of leaves at the top, bearing resemblance to the arborescent fern. 1951 C. SIMPSON *Adam in Ochre* 138 Between the trees there were often macrozamia palms. These are a good food-palm to the natives, who know that the nuts must be crushed, washed, and baked before they are eaten.

mad, *a*.
1. In the phr. **(as) mad as a (cut) snake,** (or **as a meat axe**), angry; crazy; eccentric.
1917 A.L. BREWER *'Gators' Euchre* 29 When a new-chum gets lost, why in thunder does he lose his head? .. White or colored, they run as mad as snakes. 1932 W. HATFIELD *Ginger Murdoch* 30 'But you're mad,' said Mick, 'mad as a cut snake!' 1946 *Coast to Coast 1945* 252 The cow's mad—mad as a meat-axe!
2. In the collocation **mad mick,** rhyming slang for 'pick'.
1919 *Aussie: Austral. Soldiers' Mag.* Jan. 8/1 We were issued with .. 'Mad Micks', as the Diggers call .. picks. 1975 F. HUELIN *Keep Moving* 78 Well! I won't buy drinks f'r any bloody ganger, just f'r a chance to swing a mad mick.

made, *ppl. a*. [Spec. use of *made* artificially (as opposed to naturally) constructed: see OED *ppl. a.* 1.]
1. In the collocation **made road** [in Br. use an artificially constructed road], a formed but freq. unsealed road; see also UNMADE.
1827 P. CUNNINGHAM *Two Yrs. in N.S.W.* I. 123 A *made* bush-road is one where the brushes have been cleared, banks of rivers and gullies levelled, and trees notched, on the route, and cuts made on the faces or tops of hills when necessary, the remainder being all left in a natural state. 1981 A.B. FACEY *Fortunate Life* 44 The road was just a winding track—there were no made roads in those days.
2. *Obs*. In the collocation **made ground,** ground composed in part of drifts of sand, soil, etc., washed from elsewhere; also *fig*.
1871 *Austral. Town & Country Jrnl.* (Sydney) 25 June 778/4 Here springs and the rainfall are carrying away the soil which supports the timber on the flanks of the ranges and spurs, and depositing it, as what miners call 'made ground', in the small hollows which are tributary to the larger plains, and which they gradually assist to form. 1890 'R. BOLDREWOOD' *Miner's Right* 277, I had been actuated by the best and purest motives, if such there be within this strangely concocted entity, this jumble of 'made ground' (to use the miner's phrase) that we call humanity.

mado /ˈmeɪdoʊ/. [Prob. f. a N.S.W. Aboriginal language.] Either of two small marine fish *Atypichthys mado* and *A. strigatus*, commonly found near wharves and inlets of e. Aust.
1906 D.G. STEAD *Fishes of Aust.* 134 The Mado [*sc. Atypichthys strigatus*] is a handsome little fish. 1978 N. COLEMAN *Austral. Fisherman's Fish Guide* 139 The mado seems to prefer a somewhat sheltered habitat and is more likely to be found in bays, inlets and estuaries than open water.

mag, *v.* [Br. dial. *mag* to chatter (as in *magpie*): see EDD.] *intr.* To prattle; to talk incessantly. Also *trans*.
1895 [see *magging, vbl. n.*]. 1918 'LANCE-CORPORAL COBBER' *Anzac Pilgrim's Progress* 82 He's no bully, doesn't mag, Doesn't swank around an' sprag, You will never hear him brag. 1981 D. STUART *I think I'll Live* 170 Get him talking, an' he'd mag the leg off a campoven.
Hence **magger** *n.*, **magging** *vbl. n.*
1973 *Bronze Swagman Bk. Bush Verse* (1974) 6 One could out-talk all the rest Of **maggers** that I know. 1895 *Worker* (Sydney) 14 Sept. 4/2 You never get a rest From his growling and his **magging**.

mag, *n.* [See prec.] Talk; a gossip or chat; a 'tale'.
1895 *Worker* (Sydney) 28 Sept. 4/1 When a couple of fast men draw a pen There is always a lot of mag. 1980 D. HEWETT *Susannah's Dreaming* (1981) 8 She wants ter stay and 'ave a bit of a mag with Freddy.

maga, var. MOGO.

maggie. Also **maggy.** [Br. dial.: see OED(S 2 b.] A hypocoristic name for MAGPIE *n.* 1 a.
1901 *Bulletin* (Sydney) 5 Oct. 17/1 *Re* the black-backed Monaro magpies... Has 'Gumleaf' .. ever seen two 'maggies' marked alike? 1917 C. THACKERAY *Goliath Joe* 46, I was jest skinnin' a black maggy fer bait fer my 'and-line wen I seen my springer bend. 1975 T. SCHURMANN *Shop!* 71 'Just where did you get this pipe?' .. 'I found it in a maggie's nest.'

maggotty, *a*. Also **maggoty.** [Br. dial. *maggoty* queer-tempered, fractious, etc.: see EDD.] Angry; bad-tempered. In the phr. **to go maggotty,** to become irritable.
1919 W.H. DOWNING *Digger Dialects* 33 Maggotty, angry. 1959 'D. FORREST' *Last Blue Sea* 74 He's down there .. going maggotty about doctors and Japs and boongs. 1977 B. SCOTT *My Uncle Arch* 63 Scotty got a bit maggoty about this.

maggy, var. MAGGIE.

maginnis /məˈgɪnəs/. [Of unknown origin.] *Obs*. Also **McGinness, McGinnis, McGuiness.** A (wrestling) hold from which escape is difficult. Freq. *fig.*, and esp. in the phr. **to put** (or **clap**) **(the) maginnis on.** Also **crooked maginnis.**
1901 *Truth* (Sydney) 6 Oct. 6/4 And if I see a drunken man I soon gets on his trail; I claps McGinness on to him And hugs him off to jail. 1904 *Ibid*. 13 Nov. 3/3 He was followed by the two accused, one of whom (the colored man) 'put the McGuiness on' witness. 1905 J. FURPHY *Rigby's Romance* (1946) 67, I could see my way to Agnes in a more manly, off-hand way than depending on the sort of crooked maginnis I had on her. 1941 S.J. BAKER *Pop. Dict. Austral. Slang* 46 *McGinnis on, put the,* to render an opponent hors-de-combat, to put on the pressure.

magnetic, *a*. [See quot. 1909.] In the name of a termite, and its nest: **magnetic ant hill (bed, nest),** the wall-like nest constructed by the *magnetic termite,* with the long axis pointing roughly north-south; **termite,** the termite *Amitermes meridionalis* of n. Qld. and N.T.; MERIDIAN ANT.
[1897 **magnetic ant hill:** *Proc. Linnean Soc. N.S.W.* XXII. 727 This is the species which constructs the remarkable 'meridional' or 'magnetic nests' found from near the Bloomfield River, North Queensland, to Palmerston, Port Darwin.] 1909 F.E. BIRTLES *Lonely Lands* 198 They are sometimes called 'magnetic' ant hills, owing to the fact of

their pointing due north and south. **1934** WARBURTON & ROBERTSON *Buffaloes* 12 The magnetic ant beds .. were fashioned like huge tombstones. **1935** K.C. MCKEOWN *Insect Wonders Aust.* 140 The **Magnetic Termite**.. with a world-wide reputation, builds an amazing nest like a brick wall.

magnificent, *a.* In the names of fauna having a striking appearance: **magnificent (fruit) pigeon,** WOMPOO PIGEON; **spider,** the spider *Dicrostichus magnificus* of e. Aust.

1846 J. GOULD *Birds of Aust.* (1848) V. Pl. 58, *Carpophaga magnifica.* **Magnificent Fruit Pigeon. 1916** *Bulletin* (Sydney) 23 Nov. 24/2 The 'Big Scrub', towards the Tweed (N.S.W.) and the jungles further north, once teemed with pigeons, among them the .. 'magnificent'.. and 'topknot'. **1936** K.C. MCKEOWN *Spider Wonders Aust.* 107 Fully justifying the name of **Magnificent Spider** .. about the size of a large Barcelona nut; it is cream-coloured above... Along the front edge of the abdomen is an intricate mosaic of fine lines and small salmon-pink dots.

magnoon /mæg'nun/, *a.* Also **macnoon, magnune, mangoon.** [f. the colloq. (Egyptian) Arabic.] Mad; eccentric.

1917 P. AUSTEN *Bill-Jim* 8 I'll be orl rite nex' wick!—Why kid I ain't magnoon. **1918** *Kia Ora Coo-ee* Apr. 18/2 Poor old Bob Gordon's gone magnune. **1919** O. HOGUE *Cameliers* 5 Admittedly their language, when a camel went mangoon, was simply shocking. **1932** I.L. IDRIESS *Lasseter's Last Ride* 116 A bolting camel travels at an amazing speed. These beasts, gone 'macnoon', covered the ground in giant strides.

mago, var. MOGO.

magpie, *n.* and *a.* [Transf. use of *magpie* a black and white bird of the crow family.]

A. *n.*

1. a. The black and white bird *Gymnorhina tibicen,* widespread in Aust., occurring also in New Guinea and introduced to New Zealand, having a melodious, carolling call; BREAK O' DAY BIRD; MAGGIE; *native magpie,* see NATIVE *a.* 6 b.; PIPING CROW. **b.** (Occas.) Any of several other birds having black and white plumage. See also ORGAN BIRD.

1792 R. ATKINS Jrnl. 13 Nov., We .. made some excellent Soup of 1 Duck 1 Pidgeon 1 Crow & 3 Magpies. **1931** M.M. BANKS *Memories Pioneer Days Qld.* 74 The magpie, a shrike thrush by classification, is, like the butcher bird, also pied black and white.

2. *transf.* Used *attrib.* in the names of birds having black and white plumage: **magpie goose,** the large bird *Anseranas semipalmata,* occurring near fresh water in n. Aust. and New Guinea, having a resonant honking call and the male a conspicuous knob on the head; *pied goose,* see PIED; SEMIPALMATED GOOSE; **lark,** the common, widespread bird *Grallina cyanoleuca* of Aust. and New Guinea having a loud, piping call and building a mud nest; *mud lark,* see MUD 1; *Murray magpie,* see MURRAY 2; PEEWEE 1; *pied grallina,* see PIED.

1861 'OLD BUSHMAN' *Bush Wanderings* 70 As the name denotes, the colour of the **magpie-goose** is pied, dull black and white. **1848** J. GOULD *Birds of Aust.* (1848) II. Pl. 54, *Grallina australis* .. **Magpie Lark,** Colonists of New South Wales.

3. A nickname for a South Australian. Also *attrib.*

1915 *Truth* (Sydney) 10 Oct. 6/16 *Magpie magsters.*— South Australian Wowserdom worked itself into a fine frenzy. **1955** N. PULLIAM *I traveled Lonely Land* 381 *Magpie,* a person from South Australia.

4. HALF-CASTE.

1982 *Austral.* (Sydney) 30 Aug. 9/7 'It's difficult if you're a 'magpie'. You cop it from both sides,' he says.

B. *adj. Obs.*

1. Of cattle: two-coloured (one colour usu. being white).

1824 *Hobart Town Gaz.* 12 Nov., Impounded, at Iverdon, a magpie Cow, branded S R on the off hip. **1884** 'R. BOLDREWOOD' *Old Melbourne Memories* 45, I missed a magpie steer to-day, and I didn't see that fat yellow cow with the white flank.

2. Of convict clothing: black and yellow (see quot. 1850). Also as quasi-*n.*

1841 B. WAIT *Lett. from Van Dieman's Land* (1843) 350 Near the dock, you cannot but observe a mass of beings, dressed in magpie (black and yellow) clothes, with chains coupling the legs together. **1850** W. GATES *Recoll. Van Dieman's Land* 112 The day after the capture of our friends, we were ordered to be dressed in 'magpie' and changed to another station... This 'magpie' suit is intended for chain gangs and doubly convicted prisoners, and is ordered by government as a badge of the deeper disgrace. It is composed of black and yellow cloth, of the same quality as the grey. The left side of the front part of the body, with the front of the left arm and leg, together with the right side of the back part of the body were yellow, whilst the remainder was black. **1865** J.F. MORTLOCK *Experiences of Convict* 105, I .. having made for Hobart Town, knocked at the barrack gate and reported myself a 'bolter'... They immediately ordered me to put on a vile, dirty, coarse threadbare cloth suit (no lining, no drawers) of yellow and black, called 'magpie'.

magsman. [Survival of Br. slang *magsman* swindler: see OED.]

1. A confidence trickster.

1877 *Vagabond Ann.* 136 You have to be a bit of a magsman, a pincher, a picker-up, a flatcatcher, a bester. **1975** *Bulletin* (Sydney) 31 May 26/1 My mate was a top-shelf magsman on the phone and could mimic the tone of gruff arrogance .. so characteristic of the cop in my day.

2. A talker; a raconteur.

1935 K. TENNANT *Tiburon* 182 He became very antistrikers when he discovered that the Magsman was the same Dennis Kelly. **1974** F. MOORHOUSE *Electrical Experience* 121 Now he would dearly love to be a Bachelor of Arts or a Bachelor of Science. He had been a real magsman in his day. Nothing more than a magsman.

mahleesh /ma'liʃ/, *int.* Also **mahlish, maleesh, malish.** [f. the colloq. (Egyptian) Arabic.] See quot. 1962.

1918 H. DINNING *Byways on Service* 124 If you missed, a consolatory *Malish*! (never mind). **1919** O. HOGUE *Cameliers* 116 The word cannot be translated into English. The nearest approach is 'What matter'. So in days to come Australian settlers, viewing the devastation brought by fires and floods and drought, will grin and exclaim, 'Maleesch.' **1944** L. GLASSOP *We were Rats* 138 Oh well, *mahlish!* We'll get no promotion this side of the Ocean, so cheer up, my lads, bless 'em all. **1962** A. SEYMOUR *One Day of Yr.* 18 Mahleesh. Expression Dad brought back from the Middle East. 'Never mind.' 'Forget it.'

mahogany. [Transf. use of *mahogany* the tree *Swietenia.*]

1. Any of several tree species, esp. of the genus *Eucalyptus* (fam. Myrtaceae), incl. JARRAH, yielding a hard, usu. reddish-brown, timber; the wood of these trees. Also *attrib.,* and with distinguishing epithet, as **red, swamp, white** (see under first element).

1792 *Hist. Rec. N.S.W.* (1893) II. 799 A kind of pine and mahogany, so heavy that scarce either of them will swim. **1986** *Parkwatch* (Vic. Nat. Parks Assoc.) Mar. 13 Cape Conran is a popular destination where people enjoy camping amongst banksias and mahogany gums 100 metres from an excellent beach.

2. Special Comb. **mahogany beef** (or **shavings**), jerked beef.
1846 *Cumberland Times* (Parramatta) 10 Jan. 4/4 As he had some old mahogany beef, and the other flour, a fire was soon made, a Royal George slung to boil the beef; some flour rubbed up, and leather jackets made.   **1922** B. THREADGILL *S. Austral. Land Exploration* 70 The party were without flour, depending on native vegetables, 'mahogany shavings' (jerked beef), and the small amount of euro they could kill.

maidenhair. [Transf. use of *maidenhair* a fern having fine hair-like stalks and delicate fronds.] Any of several ferns of the genus *Adiantum* (fam. Adiantaceae), incl. the European maidenhair *A. capillus-veneris* of scattered parts of mainland Aust., but referring more commonly to other species, esp. *A. aethiopicum*. Also *attrib.*, esp. as **maidenhair fern.**
1867 *Lang. Native Flowers Tas.* 5 Maiden Hair Fern .. concealed love.   **1893** R. RICHARDSON *Willow & Wattle* 11 Knee-deep lies the maiden hair Which no garden craft hath planted there.

maiden's blush. [Transf. use of *maiden's blush* a delicate pink colour.]
1. The small rainforest tree *Sloanea australis* (fam. Elaeocarpaceae), occurring from n.e. Qld. to s.e. N.S.W., often along creeks and in gullies; the wood of the tree.
1884 A. NILSON *Timber Trees N.S.W.* 54 E[*chinocarpus*] *australis*—Maiden's Blush—A beautiful tree, sometimes attaining a height of 150 feet... *Timber* of a delicate rosy tint, close-grained, but soft and easily wrought.   **1985** N. & H. NICHOLSON *Austral. Rainforest Plants.* 59 Maiden's Blush .. was named by timber-workers for the colour of its heartwood... The young toothed leaves are a beautiful pink, another possible reason for the name.
2. See quots.
1941 S.J. BAKER *Pop. Dict. Austral. Slang* 45 Maiden's blush, ginger beer and raspberry.   **1966** G.W. TURNER *Eng. Lang. in Aust. & N.Z.* 116 *Maiden's blush*, a drink, either of port and lemonade or rum and raspberry.   **1970** W. FEARN-WANNAN *Austral. Folklore* 32 Usually in old-time bushmen's meaning, a drink of rum and raspberry is a Barmaid's Blush. This drink is also known as a 'Maiden's Blush'.

mail, *n.*¹ Used *attrib.* in Special Comb. **mail car,** a motor vehicle used primarily for the conveyance of the mail; **change,** a staging-post on a mail route; also *attrib.*; **driver,** the driver of a horse-drawn vehicle in which the mail is conveyed; **man** [also Br. and U.S. but recorded earliest in Aust.], one who conveys the mail (see quot. 1977); **track,** the route by which the mail is delivered.
[N.Z. **1942** *N.Z. New Writing* I. 55 Martin heard the **mail-car** go past.]   **1945** C. MANN *River* 4 Fish .. sent by the mail-car up to town.   **1905** *Bulletin* (Sydney) 31 Aug. 16/2 'Crooked Mick', the **mail-change** groom at the Seventeen Mile, had an old 'oss.   **1944** *Bulletin* (Sydney) 30 Aug. 13/4 This superb drover worked his epic way till he reached a mail-change on the Ayrshire Downs road, whence he collected a few monkey conductors suffering a holiday.   **1891** E.H. HALLACK *W.A. & Yilgarn Goldfields* 15 The part of the track most dreaded by teamsters and **maildrivers.**   **1849** J.P. TOWNSEND *Rambles & Observations N.S.W.* 161 The road .. crosses a height, where it is usual for the '**mailman**' to pull up his vehicle.   **1977** W.A. WINTER-IRVING *Bush Stories* 98 Our only reliable contact with the outside world was the mailman. He was paid by the government to carry the letters; but he also carried a hell of a lot of other things, for which he was subsidised by us and the other people on his round. He would bring flour, potatoes, onions, bags of loose salt to rub into the meat to keep it fresh, pumpkins, sugar, loaves of bread, and barbed wire. He even carried a block of ice a metre long, wrapped in newspaper and stuffed into a sack... He also brought a private supply of illegal goods such as rum, gin, beer [etc.].   **1924** H.E. RIEMANN *Nor'-West o' West* 96 He could .. follow the creek until he came to the Nanunabberra River **mail-track.**

mail, *n.*² [See BUSH TELEGRAPH and MULGA WIRE.] Information; rumour.
1966 S.J. BAKER *Austral. Lang.* (ed. 2) 77 Along with the variations *mulga mail* (or *wire*), it [*sc.* mulga] can mean a source of rumour.   **1984** *Age* (Melbourne) 19 Sept. 38/2, I had never heard of the horse before. I didn't receive any special 'mail' on it, but I've gone to races all my life—money speaks all languages.

mai-mai, var. MIA-MIA.

mainland. The continent of Australia, as opposed to any of the offshore islands and esp. Tasmania. Also *attrib.*
1829 Macquarie Harbour Commandant's Letter-Bk. 20 Aug., One of the gangs sent to the mainland opposite the Settlᵗ to cut Timber.   **1978** L. HORSPHOL *Turn down Empty Glass* 32 He suggested that I pay a visit to the Cadbury-Fry chocolate factory, posing as a mainland tourist.
Hence **mainlander** *n.*, one who dwells on the Australian mainland.
1910 *Advocate* (Burnie) 8 Jan. 3/2 A number of mainlanders.

maisonette. [Transf. use of *maisonette* a small house.] A semi-detached house. Also **maisonette house,** and *attrib.*
1949 *Argus* (Melbourne) 4 June 17/6 Brick Maisonette, mod. 6 rms. in each.   **1971** *Bulletin* (Sydney) 8 May 25/3 Joined or semi-detached houses are called 'maisonette houses' in Queensland and South Australia and 'duplexes' in Western Australia and the Northern Territory.   **1982** *Advertiser* (Adelaide) 8 Aug. 33/5 Lockleys $46,500 Maisonette style strata unit. Ent. hall/sunroom. Spacious lounge, 2 b.r., large kitchen, laundry.

major. *Australian National Football.* A goal, scored when the ball is kicked between the goal-posts and earning six points.
1951 *Football Rec.* (Melbourne) 8 Sept. 18 They opened with four behinds, and then rattled on sixteen majors.   **1960** *N.T. News* (Darwin) 8 Mar. 10/1 Saints .. kicked only two majors and four behinds.

Major Mitchell, *n.*: see MAJOR MITCHELL COCKATOO.

Major-Mitchell, *v. Obs.* [f. the name of T.L. *Mitchell* (1792–1855), Surveyor-General of N.S.W. and explorer.] *intr.* To pursue a zig-zag course, orig. as a method of exploration; to meander; to become lost. Also **Major-Mitchelled** *ppl.a.*, lost.
1900 *Bulletin* (Sydney) 28 July 14/4, I don't mean 'bushman' in its ordinary acceptation; that term is applied to timber-getters in general, except when tracking, mustering, overlanding, or Major-Mitchelling is the subject.   **1934** *Bulletin* (Sydney) 2 May 21/2, I don't know what originated the expression, and I don't know if Mitchell himself warranted it; but to Major-Mitchell meant to work in zig-zags, to poke about a lot, avoid a straight line, and, in some cases, a man who was lost was referred to as being 'Major-Mitchelled'.

Major Mitchell cockatoo. [As prec.] The predom. pink and white cockatoo *Cacatua leadbeateri*, having a scarlet crest with a central yellow band, and occurring in arid and semi-arid Aust.; LEADBEATER'S COCKATOO;

pink cockatoo, see PINK *a*.; WEE JUGGLER. Also **Major Mitchell cocky, Major Mitchell's cockatoo**, and *ellipt*, as **Major Mitchell.**

1898 E.E. MORRIS *Austral Eng.* 280 *Major Mitchell, n.* vernacular name of a species of Cockatoo. **1927** *Bulletin* (Sydney) 3 Mar. 24/2, I brought a Major Mitchell cockie from the bush and put him in an enclosure. **1945** A.W. UPFIELD *Death of Swagman* 30 A Major Mitchell cockatoo spread its multicoloured crest. **1982** *Ecos* xxxiii. 13/1 Major Sir Thomas Livingstone Mitchell, the explorer whose enthusiasm for the pink cockatoo led to its being popularly known as Major Mitchell's cockatoo.

Major's line. *Hist.* The route followed by the explorer T.L. Mitchell on his return to Sydney from Portland Bay in 1836.

1853 T.F. BRIDE *Lett. Victorian Pioneers* (1898) 52 We followed the track of those before us .. and in a short distance came on to the Major's line, which was easily recognised at that time. **1886** *Once a Month* (Melbourne) Mar. 233 Settlers began to arrive along the 'Major's line' from the 'Sydney side'—the Major's line being the track by which Major Mitchell returned to Sydney from Portland Bay.

makarrata /mækə'ratə/. Also **makharata, makkarata**. [a. Yolŋu sub-group *makarrata*.] An Aboriginal ceremonial ritual symbolizing the restoration of peace after a dispute; an agreement.

1946 D. BARR *Warrigal Joe* 105 Dan went on to describe the 'makkarata' of Arnhem Land tribes... 'It's a sort of ceremonial ordeal, this makkarata business, and there are rules which all must obey.' **1979** A. WELLS *Forests are their Temples* 50 The ancient ceremony of makharata began with calm deliberation. **1980** *Canberra Times* 5 July 2/2 Makarrata, described by the National Aboriginal Conference subcommittee on the subject as 'a coming together after a struggle'. The subcommittee is likely to be right about this meaning because one of its members, Mr Peter Minyipirrwuy, comes from Elcho island [*sic*] in north-east Arnhem Land, where the word is used.

make, *v.*[1] *Mining.* [Spec. use of *make* to extend: see OED *v.*[1] 73 b.]

a. *intr.* Of a mineral deposit: to occur.

1850 *S. Austral. Register* (Adelaide) 14 Nov. 2/5 The ore makes in small bunches or lumps and then disappears. **1932** I.L. IDRIESS *Prospecting for Gold* 189 A patch of golden stone may 'make' anywhere at all in a reef. Often you known nothing about it until your pick 'breaks' gold.

b. *trans.* To yield (a mineral). Also *intr*. See also *to make values* VALUES.

1932 I.L. IDRIESS *Prospecting for Gold* 190 A reef may 'make' gold when it strikes a change of country. *Ibid.* 236 Be very careful when on potch and colour—at any moment they may 'make' into a 'stone'. **1939** [see VALUES].

Hence **making** *vbl. n.*, an occurrence of ore.

1862 J.A. PATTERSON *Gold Fields Vic.* 17 At Poverty Reef and Nuggetty Reef (Maldon), the stone has been found, not in one unbroken mass, but in separate 'makings'.

make, *v.*[2] *trans.* To initiate (an Aboriginal male) ceremonially into manhood. Esp. in the phr. **to make a (young) man.** Also as **man-making** *vbl. n.*

1856 J. BONWICK *W. Buckley* 77 Man making is attended with several mysterious and often torturing ceremonies. **1930** J.S. LITCHFIELD *Far-North Memories* 126, I told Marion how keen I felt to see the 'making-young-man' ceremonial. **1979** *Aboriginal Hist.* III. 65 The first of my examples was compared by the late Jack King, father of Archie King, the lone survivor of those who were 'made men' in 1914.

make, *n. Mining*. [f. prec.] A deposit or pocket of ore.

1887 H.Y.L. BROWN *Rec.of Mines S.A.* 36 The fourth lode is similar in character to the third lode. Its features .. indicate that it and the foregoing ones are 'makes' of the same great lode. **1919** *Guide Bk. Prospectors N.S.W.* (ed. 2) 14 Attention is chiefly directed to the mining for Wolfram, which occurs in 'bunches' or 'makes'.

makharata, var. MAKARRATA.

makings, *pl.* [U.S.: see OEDS *making, vbl. sb.*[1] 8 b.] Paper and tobacco as materials for rolling a cigarette; a hand-made cigarette.

1924 *Aust.* (Sydney) Apr. 8 Drawing the 'makings' from my pocket, I proceeded .. to roll a cigarette. **1944** *Aust. Week-End Bk.* 108 Winters was seen smoking a Wog 'makings', which is the lowest form in which tobacco can be introduced to the human lungs.

makkarata, var. MAKARRATA.

maleesch, var. MAHLEESH.

malga, var. MALKA, MULGA *n.*[1]

malgun /mæl'gun, mæl'gʌn/. *Obs.* [a. Dharuk *malgun.*] The ceremonial amputation of the first two joints from the fourth finger of the left hand of a female Aboriginal infant: see quot. 1878.

1798 D. COLLINS *Acct. Eng. Colony N.S.W.* I. 553 Mutilation of the two first joints of the little finger of the left hand... They name it Mal-gun. **1878** R.B. SMYTH *Aborigines of Vic.* I. p. xxiii, The practice of mutilating the body prevails in all parts of Australia. In New South Wales, at an early age, the women are subjected to an uncommon mutilation of the first two joints of the little finger of the left hand. This operation is performed when they are very young, and is done under an idea that these little joints of the left hand are in the way when they wind their fishing lines over the hand. This amputation is termed *Mal-gun*.

malish, var. MAHLEESH.

malka /'mælkə, 'mʌlkə/. Also **malga** and now usu. **mulga.** [a. Wuywurung *malga.*] An Aboriginal shield: see quot. 1856.

1839 T.L. MITCHELL *Three Exped. Eastern Aust.* (rev. ed.) II. 269 The malga is a weapon .. but that with which these natives were provided somewhat resembled a pick-axe with one half broken off. **1856** J. BONWICK *W. Buckley* 71 Buckley tells us that the Yarra Blacks called .. the two shields, Malka and Seaugwell... The Malka, to ward off blows, is two or three feet long, and is provided with a handle. **1944** C. FENNER *Mostly Austral.* 81 From the mulga the blacks made a special implement of war, the mulga, from which the plant got its name.

mallee /'mæli/. [a. Wemba-wemba *mali*.]

1. a. Any of many trees of the genus *Eucalyptus* (fam. Myrtaceae), characteristically small and having several stems usu. arising from a lignotuber, as *E. dumosa, E. socialis* and *E. oleosa*; the wood of these trees. **b.** A vegetation community in drier Aust., characterized by the presence of mallee eucalypts. Also *attrib.*, esp. as **mallee scrub.**

1845 *Standard* (Melbourne) 7 June 2/6 The stock .. are with all possible expedition driven into an almost impenetrable scrub, termed by the natives 'Malley'. **1944** C. FENNER *Mostly Austral.* 90 Jack has gone to the mallee, And Mary, she's gone too. They're going to cut down mallee scrub, And live on kangaroo.

2. Any of the semi-arid areas of N.S.W., S.A., W.A., and esp. Vic., the principal natural vegetation of which is mallee scrub. Also *attrib.*, esp. as **mallee country, desert, district, land.**

1851 *Empire* (Sydney) 13 Feb. 3/3 The flock masters in the Mallee country . . are compelled to move their flocks. **1890** *Illustr. Austral. News* (Melbourne) 1 Feb. 6/2 The Mallee districts in particular, which are among the earliest in the colony, have come out well with respect to the average yield and the quality of the grain. **1902** *Bulletin* (Sydney) 28 Jan. 14/3 Nobody knows who made the mallee, but the Devil is strongly suspected. **1962** H.J. FRITH *Mallee-Fowl* 63 The spinifex and mallee desert near Mossgiel, New South Wales. **1983** *Bogong* (Canberra) IV. v. 4 The mallee lands are found in the southern parts of Australia, in a broad band stretching from south-western Western Australia to central New South Wales with a break at the Nullarbor plain. In New South Wales the mallee occurs across the central slopes and western plains.

3. Used, with reference to eucalypts of mallee regions and elsewhere, to designate the many-stemmed form typical of the mallee eucalypt. Also *attrib.*

1938 C.T. WHITE *Princ. Bot. Qld. Farmers* 65 In some plants such as certain Eucalypts in Western Australia there is a tree form and shrub (mallee) form of the same species. **1956** T.Y. HARRIS *Naturecraft in Aust.* 192 These many-stemmed Eucalypts characteristic of so much of our inland, are known as Mallees; a general term applied to any species of Eucalypt which grows after this fashion.

4. *fig.* Also *attrib.*

1853 MOSSMAN & BANISTER *Aust. Visited & Revisited* 191 The promontory of his nose being only visible through the scrubs which, from his lips downwards to his chin, were impervious. No Leichardt razor had penetrated there; it was all 'Mallee'. **1867** *Pasquin* (London) 16 Nov. 267 Black people disguised and made ridiculous as mallee Christians—half thieves half methodists.

5. In the phr. **fit as a mallee bull,** 'fighting fit'.

1960 *Overland* xvii. 7 'How's Bubby?' 'Fit as a Mallee bull! Got another tooth.' **1981** *Sun-Herald* (Sydney) 14 June 151/4 He looked as fit as a Mallee bull.

6. In the names of birds: **mallee fowl** (**hen** and formerly **bird**), the mound-building *Leipoa ocellata*, a mottled grey, brown, and white bird of dry, inland, southern mainland Aust.; GNOW; LEIPOA; LOWAN; *native hen* (b), *native pheasant* (b), see NATIVE *a.* 6 b.; **ringneck (parakeet, parrot),** the parrot *Barnardius barnardi* of e. Aust., a predom. green bird with a green head, blue back, and yellow collar.

1849 [**mallee fowl**] *Belfast Gaz.* (Port Phillip) 30 Nov. 3/4 Mr White . . has sent to Portland the drawing of 'the Mallee bird', which is peculiar to the Mallee scrub. **1862** J.A. PATTERSON *Gold Fields Vic.* 15 All between and around is a mass of mallee and whipstick, in the shelter of which that strange bird, the mallee hen, builds her nest from year to year. **1953** A. RUSSELL *Murray Walkabout* 79 The Australian mallee fowl, that archaic mound-building bird . . is among the bird wonders of the world. **1898** [**mallee ringneck**] E.E. MORRIS *Austral Eng.* 341 Mallee Parrakeet—*Platycercus barnardi*. **1932** H. PRIEST *Call of Bush* 162 Less commonly seen, but no less beautiful, is the Mallee Parrot. . . The scheme of its colouring is green, melting into blue-grey and blue on the wings. **1943** C. BARRETT *Austral. Animal Bk.* 232 The Mallee ringneck . . frequents trees growing along the banks of rivers and creeks.

7. Comb. in the sense of MALLEE 2: **mallee cocky, farmer, town.**

1902 *Bulletin* (Sydney) 22 Nov. 16/1 You can meet the starved-out **mallee cocky** anywhere in Vic. **1899** *Bulletin* (Sydney) 11 Mar. 14/1 The editor of a way-back Vic. paper was misinformed of the death of a far-out **mallee farmer,** an old identity. **1913** *Bulletin* (Sydney) 9 Oct. 24/3 My brother is a doctor in a **Mallee town.**

8. Special Comb. **mallee gate,** a makeshift gate (see quot.); **roller,** a heavy roller used to crush and flatten mallee scrub (see quots. 1926 and 1977); **root,** the large, woody rootstock of any of several species of mallee eucalypt, valued as firewood; **soil,** a brownish, alkaline soil commonly having calcareous concretions in the subsoil; **stump** (usu. *pl.*) *mallee root.*

1964 *Overland* xxx. 21 'D' you know what a **Mallee gate** is, Bob?' 'Yes, it's a short loose panel, just droppers and wires.' **1910** *Jrnl. Dept. Agric. Vic.* 780 **Mallee roller.** . . The accompanying drawings show the usual type of roller in the Mallee districts. The roller itself varies in length from 8 feet to 12 feet, and in diameter from 1 ft. 6 in. to 3 ft. 6 in., and may be either a log, an old boiler, or a specially constructed iron cylinder. **1926** A.A.B. APSLEY *Why & how I went to Aust.* 14 The invention of the mallee roller. . . It was found that by hitching a large iron roller, generally an old boiler with a heavy timber framework, to a team of from ten to twelve horses, the mallee could be crushed and rolled flat on the ground. **1977** R.E. GREGORY *Orig. Austral. Inventions* 78 In the case of the mallee and brigalow scrub, it was the Mallee Roller. This was an invention which in its simplest form consisted of a hollow tree trunk with a strong branch through it for an axle. . . These Mallee Rollers were pulled by horses or bullocks and either dragged the trees out . . or smashed them down. **1892** *Bulletin* (Sydney) 27 Aug. 19/1 The two old cronies sat together over a fire of **mallee-root.** **1920** H.S. TAYLOR *Pioneer Irrigationists' Man.* lxx. 2 The **mallee soils** of Berri may be conveniently grouped into two classes, deep and shallow. **1926** A.A.B. APSLEY *Why & how I went to Aust.* 17 **Mallee stumps** which were split with a blunt axe . . make a most excellent fuel.

mallet /'mælət/. [a. Nyungar *malard.*] Any of several trees of the genus *Eucalyptus* (fam. Myrtaceae) of s.w. W.A., typically having a bark rich in tannin. Also *attrib.*

1837 G.F. MOORE *Evidences Inland Sea* 49 Here we saw another variety of the *Eucalyptus*, called 'Mallat'. **1984** *West Austral.* (Perth) 24 Mar. (Country ed.) 58/2 Mallet wood is one of the strongest and most flexible woods in the country.

Maltese cross. [Transf. use of *Maltese cross* a form of cross.] The right-angled form of the cross-shaped twinned crystals of the mineral staurolite.

1963 N. *Austral. Monthly* Nov. 10 The Staurolites—commonly called 'Maltese Crosses'—are geologically known as 'twin crystals'. **1978** C. AUSTIN *I left my Hat in Andamooka* 142 Were we interested in going out after some 'Maltese crosses'? . . A well-formed ninety degree twin makes a perfect cross and they can be used as attractive charms to hang on a necklace or the tiny ones as earrings.

Maluka /mæ'lukə/. Also **Maluga.** [a. Djingulu *marluga.*] The person in charge; the boss.

1905 MRS A. GUNN *Little Black Princess* 3, I was 'the Missus' from the homestead, and with the Boss, or 'Maluka' (as the blacks always called him), was 'out bush', camping near the river. **1937** *Oceania* VII. 311 The widespread North Australian term *maluka* or *maluga* implies both status and age.

man. [Spec. use of *man* as the correlative of *master*: see OED $sb.^1$ 10 c.]

1. Used in the possessive pl. in collocations designating accommodation, etc., provided on a rural property for workers (as distinct from that for the owner, manager, etc.).

1826 *Colonial Times* (Hobart) 14 Oct., An Eighty acre Farm, with Cottage, Men's Skilling, a stock-yard and Pigstye. **1937** *Bulletin* (Sydney) 28 July 21/4 My mate and I took a job with a cocky in the Bendigo district, and after showing us the 'men's quarters' (a disused calf pen) he took us in to tea consisting of bread, rancid butter and stewed pears.

2. In the collocation **men's hut:** see HUT *n.* 3.

manatee. *Obs.* [Transf. use of *manatee* a large aquatic mammal of the genus *Trichechus*, incl. the West Indian *T.*

manatus.] The large, herbivorous marine mammal *Dugong dugon*, the dugong, occurring in coastal waters of n. Aust. and elsewhere.

1698 W. DAMPIER *New Voyage round World* (ed. 3) I. 33 The Manatee .. on the Coast of *New Holland*. This creature is about the bigness of a Horse, and 10 or 12 foot long. **1933** C. FENNER *Bunyips & Billabongs* 2 As long ago as 1821 the explorer Hamilton Hume reported the existence in Lake Bathurst of a large animal, supposed .. 'to be a manatee (dugong) or a hippopotamus'.

manchester. [Ellipt. and transf. use of *Manchester wares* cotton goods manufactured at Manchester.] Household linen; the department of a shop in which such goods are sold. Also *attrib*.

1907 *Anthony Hordern Catal.* 60 *Manchester Department.* So called from the majority of the goods included within its scope being of what is popularly known as Manchester manufacture. But the department, as arranged at our store, goes far beyond, for in it will be found, not only fabrics which owe their substance to Cotton, but Linen, Holland, Damask, Flannel, and scores of other materials of domestic and general utility. **1977** E. MACKIE *Oh to be Aussie* 42 When *he's* finished spending, 'Mum' carries on buying Manchester at the January sales.

maned goose. [f. the mature male bird's 'mane' of elongated, black, hair-like feathers.] *Wood duck*, see WOOD *n.*[1] 3 b. Also **maned duck.**

1845 J. GOULD *Birds of Aust.* (1848) VII. Pl. 3, *Bernicla jubata*. Maned Goose .. Wood Duck, Colonists of New South Wales and Swan River. **1984** *A.N.U. Reporter* (Canberra) 26 Oct. 4 (*caption*) Two Maned Ducks out for a stroll on the banks of Sullivans Creek.

man fern. *Tas.* [Perh. with ref. to a supposedly male characteristic, as size: see *male fern*, OED *male, a.* 2 b.] *Tree fern*, see TREE.

1900 *Bulletin* (Sydney) 30 June 14/3 The fern-tick .. smoodges in the dry seeds of the todia and man-ferns. **1985** *Tasmanian Travelways* Aug. 32 Manferns have taken over a long abandoned carriage from the old Kelly Basin railway line.

mangle. [Fig. use of *mangle* device for pressing water from washed clothes, etc.] A bicycle.

1941 S.J. BAKER *Pop. Dict. Austral. Slang* 45 *Mangle*, a bicycle. **1965** G. McINNES *Road to Gundagai* 226 It's clear you weren't a bicycle fan in Australia in the Twenties. Oppie was the idol of all, boy and man, who could 'push a mangle'.

mango. Used *attrib.* as an emblem of 'midsummer madness'.

1978 H. LUNN *Joh* 203 Queenslanders call it the Mango Season. . . It is the season of destruction—of cyclones and floods and whirly-whirlys. **1984** *N.T. News* (Darwin) 22 Sept. 6/2 The season of mango madness is one of many dangers. Who knows what crazy idea a Commissar might come up with while under the influence of the dreaded mango fruit. *Ibid.* 21 Dec. 35/2 It seems 'mango madness', that mystery affliction which hits Darwin during November and December, struck Top End footballers last weekend.

mangoon, var. MAGNOON.

mangrove. Used *attrib.* in the names of fauna: **mangrove (swimming) crab,** *mud crab,* see MUD 1; **heron** (or **bittern**), the predom. grey or brown bird *Butorides striatus* of warmer coastal Aust., and elsewhere in the tropics and sub-tropics; **jack,** the chiefly marine and estuarine fish *Lutjanus argentimaculatus* of n. Aust. and elsewhere; **kingfisher,** the predom. white and blue-green kingfisher *Halcyon chloris sordida* of coastal n. Aust.; **mullet** (chiefly *Qld.*) any of several fish, usu. of the genus *Mugil*, esp. *M. cephalus* (see *sea mullet* SEA); **pigeon,** the bar-shouldered dove *Geopelia humeralis*, occurring near water in n. and e. Aust., and in s. New Guinea.

1930 [**mangrove crab**] C.M. YONGE *Yr. on Great Barrier Reef* 217 The mangrove swimming crab (*Scylla serrata*) and the blue mudcrab (*Portunus pelagicus*) .. are excellent eating. **1935** DAVISON & NICHOLLS *Blue Coast Caravan* 193 He asked if we had ever eaten mangrove crabs. **1948** [**mangrove heron**] R. RAVEN-HART *Canoe in Aust.* 202 Another 'permanently-folded' heron stumped him, like the Nankeen but bluish .. the Mangrove Bittern. **1955** V. SERVENTY *Aust.'s Great Barrier Reef* 55 The Mangrove Heron looks a little like a dark Reef Heron, but has a much more skulking habit and creeps stealthily over the reef. **1951** T.C. ROUGHLEY *Fish & Fisheries Aust.* 69 The **mangrove jack** .. is an inhabitant of the rivers, which it penetrates right into fresh water, its favourite haunt being amongst the mangrove roots. **1945** C. BARRETT *Austral. Bird Life* 144 There are several other northern species: the **mangrove kingfisher** (*Halcyon chloris*) [etc.]. **1884** *Proc. Linnean Soc. N.S.W.* IX. 870 The '**Mangrove Mullets**' of the Brisbane fishermen are M[ugil] *tade* .. and *M. longimanus.* **1844** J. GOULD *Birds of Aust.* (1848) V. Pl. 72, It may often be seen among the mangroves in flocks of several hundreds, and hence its colonial name of **Mangrove Pigeon.**

man-hunting, *vbl. n. Gold-mining. Obs.* See *digger-hunt* DIGGER 4.

1855 G.H. WATHEN *Golden Colony* 86 The pursuit and capture of unlicensed diggers, 'man-hunting' or 'digger-hunting' as the miners called it. **1888** G. ROCK *Colonists* 51 'Man-hunting' has become a recognized pastime of the gentlemen in blue.

Hence **man-hunter** *n.*, see quot. 1855.

1855 W. HOWITT *Land, Labor & Gold* II. 15 The foot police .. generally are the man-hunters, or bloodhounds.

manna. [Spec. use of *manna* a sweet exudation from a plant.]

1. a. The white, sugary, soluble exudation of a tree, usu. of the genus *Eucalyptus* (fam. Myrtaceae), esp. *E. viminalis* and *E. rubida.* **b.** LERP.

1808 *HRA* (1921) 3rd Ser. I. 692 An insect which produces very fine Manna. **1827** P. CUNNINGHAM *Two Yrs. in N.S.W.* I. 203 A species of our eucalyptus produces also the finest manna, and that in very considerable abundance. It is named by Mr Allan Cunningham, the able botanist from Kew, the *eucalyptus mannifera*.

2. *Special Comb.* **manna gum.**

a. Any of several trees yielding manna, esp. *Eucalyptus viminalis* of s.e. Aust. incl. Tas. Also *ellipt.*

1837 *Lit. News* (Sydney) 21 Oct. 108 The lofty and majestic gum-trees, the graceful manna. **1904** *Bulletin* (Sydney) 4 Feb. 17/1 Manna gums .. supply various birds and insects with snow-white sugar.

b. *Obs.* MANNA 1.

1868 J. BAIRD *Emigrant's Guide Australasia* 71 The 'bush' of Western Australia yields a 'manna gum', which is coming into much request.

many-coloured parakeet. *Mulga parrot*, see MULGA *n.*[1] B. 3. Also **many-coloured parrot.**

1847 J. GOULD *Birds of Aust.* (1848) V. Pl. 35, *Psephotus multicolor*. Many-coloured Parrakeet. **1916** S.A. WHITE *In Far Northwest* 51 They belong to those known as the many-coloured parrot.

Maori /'mauri/. [See quot. 1974.] The brightly coloured marine fish *Ophthalmolepis lineolatus* of s. Aust. See also *rainbow fish* RAINBOW 2. Also **Maori wrasse.**

1882 J.E. TENISON-WOODS *Fish & Fisheries N.S.W.* 74 Those [Labridae] that are most familiar to the Sydney public are .. the 'Maori' (*Coris lineolatus*) [etc.]. **1974** T.D. SCOTT et al. *Marine & Freshwater Fishes S.A.* 302 Maori... Head green, with narrow blue lines below the eye, and on the throat, rather resembling the tatto marks of the Maoris, from which the common name is no doubt derived. **1984** *Austral. Gourmet* June-July 59 The choicest of local seafood, such as coral trout, red emperor, maori wrasse.

Maoriland /'maʊrılænd/. [Used elsewhere but recorded earliest in Aust.: see OEDS.] A name for New Zealand.
1859 *Bell's Life in Sydney* 30 Apr. 2/2 To gallop in Maoriland. **1979** J. DAVIES *Souvenir Kangaroo Island*, Of all the walls I've painted, and some in Maori land Corrugated iron walls, are tough to understand.
Hence **Maorilander** *n.*
1892 *Truth* (Sydney) 19 June 4/7 A colonist of the 'three islands' is proud to be a Maorilander.

mapi /'mapi/. [a. Dyirbal and Yidiny *mabi*.] BOONGARRY. Also **mappy-mappy**.
1895 *Proc. Linnean Soc. N.S.W.* IX. 573 When engaged in obtaining *D. lumholtzi* .. he seldom saw them at rest... The native name is Mapi (Marpee, according to English pronunciation). **1919** *Bulletin* (Sydney) 30 Jan. 22/4 In the southern States the tree-kangaroo of North Q., known locally as 'mappy-mappy', is ignorantly regarded as a myth.

maple. [Transf. use of *maple* a tree of the genus *Acer*.] Any of several trees yielding an attractive, usu. pinkish, cabinet timber, esp. *Queensland maple* (see QUEENSLAND 2); the wood of these trees.
1889 J.H. MAIDEN *Useful Native Plants Aust.* 611 *Villaresia Moorei* .. 'Maple'.. a most extellent wood, white in colour, and durable. **1985** *Age* (Melbourne) 31 Oct. 11/3 We came to a giant maple, about 200 centimetres in diameter.

mappy-mappy: see MAPI.

maramie /'mærəmi/. [a. Wiradhuri prob. *marramin*.] A fresh-water crayfish.
1844 MRS C. MEREDITH *Notes & Sketches N.S.W.* 108 The moramies, or crayfish, live in holes in the muddy banks of these pools. **1951** J. DEVANNY *Travels N. Qld.* 195 A real delicacy .. was a small crayfish: maramie to the Aborigines.

marara /mə'rarə/. [Prob. f. a Qld. Aboriginal language.] Either of two large rainforest trees of the fam. Cunoniaceae, *Pseudoweinmannia lachnocarpa* and the rose-leaf marara *Caldcluvia paniculosa* (*Ackama paniculata*), both of e. Qld. and N.S.W.; the wood of these trees.
1884 A. NILSON *Timber Trees N.S.W.* 124 *W*[*einmannia*] *rubifolia*—Marara .. *timber* close-grained and tough, but easily wrought. **1981** H. HANNAH *Together in Jungle Scrub* 19 To start with they lived in a big marara tree. They've got big spurs on the hips. They felled that and they used it until they got a hut built.

marble.
1. *Obs.* In the phr. **to pass** (**chuck**, etc.) **in one's marble**, to die; to give up. See ALLEY 1.
1908 *Austral. Mag.* (Sydney) Nov. 1250/1 Instead of dying you can .. 'pass in your marble'. **1911** *Bulletin* (Sydney) 5 Oct. 15/1 On one was a man who had just handed in his marble; on the other was his drunk and morbid friend, bemoaning the loss of his pal. **1918** *Passed by Censor: Souvenir Austral. Naval & Military Exped. Force New Guinea* Christmas 7 Verily hath the Hun chucked in his marble.
2. a. In the phr. **to make** (or **keep**) **one's marble good**, to ingratiate oneself; to improve one's position. See ALLEY 2.

[N.Z. **1909** *N.Z. Truth* (Wellington) 15 May 7 He 'made his marble good', he alleged, by paying up a score he owed.] **1928** L.A. SIGSWORTH *Various Verse* 2 And the classers keep their marbles good with 'guns', for they have pull. **1950** B. JAMES *Advancement Spencer Button* 162 You can't get that class any time—that bloody Button's got them all the time. He's trying to make his marble good, all right.
b. In the phr. **one's marble is good,** one is in a favourable position.
1966 D. NILAND *Pairs & Loners* 80 My marble's good there for a cushy job and a few quid picking apples and pears.
3. *Horse-racing.* The number drawn by a jockey which determines the horse's position on the starting line.
1924 'S. RUDD' *Me an' Son* 90 To see who were th' rider ov Sardinia, an' what was his marble. **1964** *Sydney Morning Herald* 10 Aug. 2/5 A good marble in the racing game can be a lower number giving the inside running, and a good marble in Sydney today can mean a hundred thousand quid.

marbled frogmouth. The bird *Podargus ocellatus* of e. Qld. and N.S.W., having red, brown, and white marbled plumage. Formerly also **marbled frogsmouth**.
1898 E.E. MORRIS *Austral Eng.* 155 The mouth and expression of the face resemble the appearance of a frog. The species are .. Marbled F[rogsmouth].—*P*[*odargus*] *marmoratus* [etc.]. **1913** *Emu* XII. Suppl. 56 *Podargus marmoratus* .. Marbled Frogmouth.

marblewood. Any of several trees yielding timber with an attractive mottled grain, esp. the tall rainforest tree *Acacia bakeri* (fam. Mimosaceae) of Qld. and N.S.W.; the wood of these trees.
1889 J.H. MAIDEN *Useful Native Plants Aust.* 580 *Olea paniculata* .. 'marble-wood'... The heart-wood is nicely mottled. It is of a whitish colour, darkening towards the centre, and prettily figured. **1981** PUGH & RITCHIE *Guide to Rainforests N.S.W.* 12 Brunswick Heads Nature Reserve... Rare tree species occurring here include .. Marblewood.

March fly. [f. the name of the month (see quot. 1948), although the fly is usu. most noticeable in the spring or wet season.] A blood-sucking fly of any of several genera of the widely-distributed fam. Tabanidae.
1852 J. BONWICK *Notes of Gold Digger* 22 The nuisance is the flies, the little fly and the stinging monster March fly. **1948** W.W. FROGGATT *Insect Bk.* 96 These thickset active flies are known as March Flies because they usually appear about the end of summer. In England they are better known as Horse or Gad Flies.

marching, *vbl. n.* Used *attrib.* in Special Comb. **marching chain** *hist.*, a connecting chain to which the fetters of each member of a party of travelling convicts are attached to prevent escape.
1837 *Rep. Select Committee Transportation* 14 July (1838) 82 He will apply to the officer of the guard for an adequate escort and will, in all cases, attach the hand cuffs of the prisoners to a marching chain before they quit the stockade. **1899** G.E. BOXALL *Story Austral. Bushrangers* 278 The prisoners were seated in the body of the coach, and were connected together by 'a marching chain', to which their handcuffs and leg irons were attached.

marching, *ppl. a.* In the collocation **marching girl,** a girl trained to march in formation.
[N.Z. **1952** *Here & Now* 9 July, Not for a long time have I observed such a symptom of our *malaise* as the business of 'marching girls'.] **1953** *About Turn* Dec. 3 The badge features a Marching Girl in the centre. **1974** *Herald* (Melbourne) 28 Feb. 21/6, I wanted to become a marching girl but my father said no.

margoo /'magu/. [a. Western Desert language *magu*.] WITCHETTY 2.

1916 S.A. WHITE *In Far Northwest* 78 These grubs are much sought after by the natives who call them 'margoo'. 1973 V. SERVENTY *Desert Walkabout* 13 He had dragged out a four-inch long white grub and swallowed it with much satisfaction. 'Margo,' he exclaimed, eyes gleaming with epicurean delight.

marine settler. *Hist.* One who, having served as a marine, remains in an Australian Colony as a settler.

1792 P.G. KING Jrnl. Norfolk Island 24 Those Marine Settlers, who brought their Wives & Families from England, were supplied. 1804 *HRA* (1915) 1st Ser. V. 28 In your Return I observe Nine old Marine Settlers.

mark, n.[1] [Spec. use of *mark* target, that which may be aimed at: see OED(S *sb.*[1] 7 d. (but see also OED(S *sb.*[1] 21 and 22).] A person who is an object of attention: freq. with qualifying *adj.*, as **good** (**bad**, etc.) **mark**, having reference esp. to the person's financial probity.

1835 *Cornwall Chron.* (Launceston) 14 Mar. 3, It is currently reported that several *gentlemen*—known amongst the trades-people of Sydney as 'bad marks'—intend embracing the present opportunities of leaving the Colony with a 'flying topsail'. 1845 R. HOWITT *Impressions Aust. Felix* 233, I wondered often what was the meaning of this, amongst many other peculiar colonial phrases, 'Is the man a good mark?' Our bullock-driver had it familiarly in his mouth. I heard it casually from the lips of apparently respectable settlers as they rode on the highway. 'Such and such a one is a good mark!'—simply a person who pays his men their wages, without delays or drawbacks; a man to whom you may sell anything safely. 1854 C.A. CORBYN *Sydney Revels* 132 They knows I'm the wrong mark to peach on 'em.

mark, n.[2] *Hist.* [Spec. use of *mark* symbol in respect of conduct: see OED *sb.*[1] 11 g.] A point or unit of credit (or penalty) counting towards a total which may earn the remission or measure the passage of a convict's sentence.

1839 J. WARD Diary of Convict Nov. 118 Marks of approval were kept by the Doctor; and when you got three of these good marks, your irons was taken off. 1845 A. MACONOCHIE *On Managem. Transported Criminals* 2, I propose that a form of *Wages* (marks) be introduced into all our penal Establishments.

Hence **mark system** *n.*

1862 BACKHOUSE & TYLOR *Life & Labour G.W. Walker* 272 The experiments which were made on Norfolk Island and elsewhere, of the Mark System . . were considered by some to be unsuccessful.

mark, n.[3] *Australian National Football.* [Transf. use of *mark* heel-mark made by a Rugby Union player who has made a 'fair catch': see OED(S *sb.*[1] 12 d.]

1. a. (The taking of) a fair catch (see quot. 1931); the catch itself.

1859 C.C. MULLEN *Hist. Austral. Rules Football* 11 A mark is made when a player catches the ball before it hits the ground and after it has been clearly kicked by another player. 1931 J.F. MCHALE et al. *Austral. Game of Football* 48 A mark may be obtained either from a place, drop, or punt kick, and consists of catching a ball directly from a kick or bounce from below the knee, not less than ten yards distant, the ball being held a reasonable time and not having been touched while in transit from kick to catch. 1964 B. WANNAN *Fair Go, Spinner* 138 Cynical barracker to showy player who goes through flash actions after a mark: 'Orlright, mate, we've got yer photo!'

b. See quot. 1968.

1894 J.M. MACDONALD *Thunderbolt* 87 A burly Bendigonian kicked it into the hands of the Melbourne skipper. He could have had a mark—*i.e.* a free kick behind a mark on the ground. 1968 EAGLESON & MCKIE *Terminol. Austral. Nat. Football* ii. 23 *Mark*, . . the spot at which a player caught the ball ('took a mark') and behind or over which he must make his kick.

c. The kick awarded to a player who has taken a fair catch.

1894 J.M. MACDONALD *Thunderbolt* 89 Harrison kicked off along the right lower side to Greaves . . marked the ball, and chose to take his mark. . . He coolly went back ten yards, and then kicked a drop-kick on along the lower centre. 1960 *N.T. News* (Darwin) 5 Jan. 8/4 Saints won the knock and . . a soaring mark was followed by a sixer.

d. A player skilled at taking a fair catch and gaining advantage with the subsequent kick.

1936 E.C.H. TAYLOR et al. *Our Austral. Game Football* 34 *Centre back* . . a good kick and safe mark, cool and intelligent. 1963 L. RICHARDS *Boots & All!* 105 A terrific mark, he knew how to make position on the half-forward line with perfection.

2. In the collocation **high mark,** a fair catch taken in the course of a high leap; a player who does this.

1936 E.C.H. TAYLOR et al. *Our Austral. Game Football* 20 It is not necessary to be very tall to become a good high mark. 1963 *Footy Fan* (Melbourne) I. iii. 22 What better satisfaction can a player have than taking a well judged high mark over the top of the pack?

mark, v.[1] *trans.* To mark the ear of (a lamb), completing at the same time other processes, as the castration of male lambs, docking, etc. Also as *vbl. n.* See also *lamb-marking* LAMB *n.*

1883 E.M. CURR *Recoll. Squatting Vic.* 153 Shortly after taking charge I marked two thousand lambs. 1907 C. MACALISTER *Old Pioneering Days* 17 One morning just before the marking—or 'docking' as it was then called—Brentnall and his mate found they were six or seven lambs short of their tally.

mark, v.[2] *Australian National Football.* [f. MARK n.[3]] *trans.* To take (the ball) in a fair catch; to kick (the ball) after taking a fair catch. Freq. *absol.*

1894 J.M. MACDONALD *Thunderbolt* 94 The ball sailed long and low . . about four feet above the forest of hands raised to mark it. 1900 B. KERR *Silliad* 31 He passed it neatly to Adonis Vane Who, driving forward, marked to Green again.

Hence **(high) marking** *vbl. n.* and *ppl. a.*

1936 E.C.H. TAYLOR et al. *Our Austral. Game Football* 20 Marking is perhaps the most spectacular feature of our game, especially high marking. 1939 P. MCGUIRE *Austral. Journey* 285 The most spectacular feature of the game is its 'high-marking'. If a man catches the ball cleanly from a kick, he is entitled to an unimpeded kick himself, and when one sees three or four young giants soaring into the air together to battle for a ball ten feet above the ground, it is enough to set any crowd roaring. 1960 *N.T. News* (Darwin) 8 Jan. 6/3 Pott, a high-marking rover for the aboriginal team, Wanderers, pleaded not guilty.

marked, *ppl. a. Obs.* [f. U.S. *mark, v.* to blaze (a tree): see DAE *v.* 1 and OED *marked, ppl. a.* 1.] Of a series of trees: marked with blazes to indicate the line of a track or road. Freq. in the collocation **marked tree line (road, track).**

1831 *Acct. Colony Van Diemen's Land* 40 The traveller has now only marked trees to guide him along a thick, scrubby road, which is as yet impassable for carriages. 1832 J. BACKHOUSE *Narr. Visit Austral. Colonies* (1843) 25 There was 'a marked tree road', or a way through 'the bush' . . marked by pieces of bark being chopped off the sides of trees. 1840 H.S. RUSSELL *Genesis Qld.* 2 July (1888) 167 We encamped the drays . . and making my way by our own marked tree line, I met Dalrymple. 1854 H.B. STONEY *Yr. in Tas.* 192 Offering his services to set us on the marked-tree track the next morning.

market. In the phr. **to go to market,** to lose one's temper, to behave angrily; to behave excitably.
1870 *Austral. Town & Country Jrnl.* (Sydney) 12 Nov. 13/4 He slackens the rein, and saying, 'Go to market now old fellow', sits the wild plunge of the colt like a Mexican vaquero. **1950** F.J. HARDY *Power without Glory* 35, I have me instructions, so it's no use going to market on me.

marl /mal/. [a. Nyungar *maarl.*] The small bandicoot *Perameles bougainville,* light grey-brown above and white below, with a striped rump, now occurring only on Bernier and Dorre Islands, Shark Bay, W.A.
1941 E. TROUGHTON *Furred Animals Aust.* 67 Marl or Western Barred-Bandicoot .. *Perameles myosura.* .. The native's name of 'Marl' has been advocated as the popular name for the western race. **1983** R. STRAHAN *Compl. Bk. Austral. Mammals* 101 Marl appears to be derived from *Mala,* quoted by Gould as the Aboriginal name for the Barred Bandicoot from the Toodyay district of Western Australia. This is actually an Aboriginal name of the Rufous Hare-wallaby in Western Australia and its application to a bandicoot is confusing.

marlock /'mɒlɒk/. [a. Nyungar *malag.*] Any of several small, mallee-like trees of the genus *Eucalyptus* (fam. Myrtaceae) occurring in s.w. W.A.: see quot. 1971. Also *attrib.*
1894 A.F. CALVERT *Coolgardie Goldfield* 46 The first 14 miles consists of broken sand-plain and marlock country. **1971** C. DEBENHAM *Lang. Bot.* (ed. 2) 131 The marlock is noted for its mallee-like form but poor development of a ligno-tuber.

marloo /ma'lu/. *W.A.* Also **merloo.** Pl. **marloo.** [a. Western Desert language *marlu.*] The kangaroo *Macropus rufus* (see **red kangaroo** (a), RED *a.* 1 b.).
1935 H.H. FINLAYSON *Red Centre* 57 The kangaroo, or merloo as the Luritjas call him, is the familiar red kangaroo (*Macropus rufus*) of the saltbush tablelands farther south. **1984** W.W. AMMON et al. *Working Lives* 149 The big red roos, the marloo, keep to the plain country.

marmalade. Also **marmelade.** [See quot. 1919.] In Services' speech: a new recruit.
1918 R.H. KNYVETT *Over there with Australs.* 53 New arrivals in camp were always called 'Marmalades', because they were distinguished by their relish for marmalade jam. **1919** *7th Field Artillery Brigade Yandoo* Sept. 160 'Marmelade!' .. The term arose through the frequency of marmelade in the jam ration and was an appellation which would be applied to the new troop until he became familiar with the ways and methods of a soldier.

marri /'mæri/. [a. Nyungar *marri.*] The tree *Eucalyptus calophylla* (fam. Myrtaceae) of s.w. W.A., having rough grey-brown bark and ornamental flowers; the hard, durable wood of the tree.
1833 *Jrnls. Several Exped. W.A.* 133 The mahogany and red gum, of Perth, (the tyarreil and marré of the natives here) are predominant. **1985** *West Austral.* (Perth) 6 Nov. 54/4 Very hot fires .. severely reduced the occurrence of fungus in the marri forest.

marron /'mærən/. In the pl. freq. **marron.** [a. Nyungar *marran.*] The large fresh-water crayfish of s.w. W.A. *Cherax tenuimanus.*
1943 *Land Girls Gaz.* (Perth) Apr. 7 Last night we caught twelve marrons in a fishing bag. **1983** *Austral. Fisheries* Jan. 31/2 The Minister for Fisheries and Wildlife .. said the bag limit was not more than 20 marron in any one day... The only means by which marron could be legally taken were by drop net, pole snares or hand scoop nets.

marsh. Chiefly *Tas. Obs.* [Br. dial. *marsh(-land)* rich alluvial soil: see EDD *marsh, sb.*[1] 1. (5 b) and 4.] A tract of rich alluvial land, suitable for agricultural use after draining. Also **marsh land.**
1833 *Trumpeter* (Hobart) 24 Sept. 178 The convenient distance from town, and the great advantage of water carriage, so essential to convey to market the superabundant crops, which the marsh land affords, are indeed objects of some importance. **1836** *Cornwall Chron.* (Launceston) 1 Oct. 3 *The Forton Estate* .. about one third of which is of the richest possible description of Marsh, and at a very small expense if desirable, may be made secure from floods, about 75 acres is under cultivation.

marshmallow. [Transf. use of *marshmallow, Althaea officinalis,* of marshy country.] Any of several plants of the fam. Malvaceae esp. the naturalized European *Malva parviflora,* widespread in Aust. and generally regarded as a weed, and the tall *Lavatera plebeia* of all mainland States.
1835 J. BATMAN *Settlement Port Phillip* 4 June (1856) 18 We travelled over the richest land I had ever seen in my life; marsh mallows, with leaves as large as those of the cabbage tribe, and as high as my head. **1974** S.L. EVERIST *Poisonous Plants Aust.* 364 *Malva parviflora* .. commonly known in Australia as *marshmallow* .. is now widespread as a weed in many parts of the world.

marsh tern. The black-crowned, predom. grey and white bird *Chlidonias hybrida,* of inland swamps, lagoons, and lakes.
1848 J. GOULD *Birds of Aust.* VII. Pl. 31, *Hydrochelidon fluviatilis* .. Marsh Tern. **1964** M. SHARLAND *Territory of Birds* 42 Marsh Terns were dipping into the water for insect food.

marsupial.
1. Used *attrib.* in the names of animals: **marsupial lion,** the extinct, carnivorous marsupial *Thylacoleo carnifex* of Aust. incl. Tas.; **mole,** the small, blind, burrowing marsupial *Notoryctes typhops,* widely distributed in sandy country in arid Aust.; **mouse,** any of many small carnivorous marsupials of the fam. Dasyuridae, esp. of the genera *Sminthopsis* (see DUNNART) and *Antechinus,* some of which are also known as bush mice (see *bush mouse* BUSH C. 3), and pouched mice (see POUCHED MOUSE); **rat,** the small carnivorous marsupial of arid central Aust. *Dasyuroides byrnei* (fam. Dasyuridae); **wolf,** *Tasmanian tiger,* see TASMANIAN *a.* 2.
1867 *Illustr. Sydney News* 16 July 204/2 The fossil remains picked out, yielding a rich harvest of many bones and teeth, among them the left incisor of the much talked about **marsupial lion** (*Thylacoleo carnifex*). **1901** C. WRIGHT *Historic Melbourne* 46 In real life the **Marsupial Mole** is unlike any other animal, and very like nothing else... It was first discovered by whites in the neighbourhood of the Finke River. **1872** 'RESIDENT' *Glimpses Life Vic.* 18 A tiny **marsupial mouse. 1906** J.W. GREGORY *Dead Heart Aust.* 150 On its shores lived .. wallabies, bandicoots, and **marsupial rats. 1885** *Illustr. Austral. News* (Melbourne) 19 Dec. 218/3 The group of the **marsupial wolf** .. represents the largest, most formidable and, in many respects, the most remarkable of the carnivorous marsupial animals. It is now entirely confined to Tasmania.

2. Special Comb. **Marsupial Board,** a body established in a rural district to control kangaroos, wallabies, etc., and other animals regarded as pests.
1881 *Act* (Qld.) 45 Vict. no. 4 Sect. 2, The following items in inverted commas shall bear the meanings set against them... 'Board.'—The Marsupial Board to be elected or appointed for any district hereinafter defined... 'Marsupial.'—Any kangaroo, wallaroo, wallaby, or paddamelon.

martin. [Transf. use of *martin* the bird of the swallow fam. *Chelidon urbica.*] Any of several swallow-like migratory birds, some of which build a mud nest, usu. nesting in colonies, incl. the *fairy martin* (see FAIRY n.[1] 1), *tree martin* (see TREE), and *masked wood swallow* (see MASKED). Also *attrib.*

1838 *S. Austral. Rec.* (London) 14 Mar. 45 Two beautiful little martins are building their nests over the porch of the door-way. **1981** A.B. FACEY *Fortunate Life* 89 The martin sparrow went in packs of hundreds; it lived on small insects and made its nest in hollow limbs of large trees... It was.. about the size of a canary, and had a black head, brown feathers along the sides and back, light grey underneath.. and around the neck, and bright brown under its wings.

Martin Place. [The name of a street, now a pedestrian plaza, in central Sydney.] Used allusively to connote urban decadence.

1938 *Bulletin* (Sydney) 28 Dec. 19/3 Martin-place outbackers. **1979** S. MORAN *Reminisc. of Rebel* 59 More unusual ones [*sc.* nicknames] were .. Martin Place (full every lunch time) [etc.].

Marvellous Melbourne. See quot. 1966.

1885 *Argus* (Melbourne) 8 Aug. 5/1 *The land of the golden fleece by George Augustus Sala*... *Marvellous Melbourne*... It was on the 17th of March in the present year of grace, 1885, that I made my first entrance, shortly before high noon, into Marvellous Melbourne. **1966** M. CANNON *Land Boomers* 3 Visitors to the colony of Victoria in the 1880s were awed and dazzled by the astonishing progress of the city. They began to call it 'Marvellous Melbourne'.

Mary. *Austral. pidgin.* [Also in other Pacific pidgins.]

a. An Aboriginal woman.

1830 R. DAWSON *Present State Aust.* 65 Mary come me. Dat husband murry bad man: he waddy (beat) Mary. Mary no like it, so it leabe it. Dat pellow no goot, massa. **1980** L.G. FOGARTY *Kargun* 28 Are they told that Jacky Jackys and Marys are going to be killed Tell the abo child the true history.

b. Any non-white woman.

1886 P. CLARKE *'New Chum' in Aust.* 294 If you set a kanaka 'Mary' or woman to clean a floor you must expect it to be somewhat dirtier after than before... The women .. were all 'Mary' if you didn't know their proper name. **1952** T.A.G. HUNGERFORD *Ridge & River* 172 The kanaka shrugged and walked out of the hut... 'What did he say, Alec?'... 'The coons reckon he's been having a lash at the maries.'

c. A white woman. Freq. as **white Mary**.

1853 H.B. JONES *Adventures in Aust.* 147 He wished to know, pointing to a hut, whether my wife and children lived there. 'You white fellow—Mary—piccaninie—sit down humpy,' pointing to the building. We gave him to understand we were blessed with neither a Mary nor piccaninie. **1974** N. CATO *Brown Sugar* 139 They made their usual inquiries, saying they were investigating the death of a 'white Mary' at the coast.

masked, *ppl. a.* Used as a distinguishing epithet in the names of birds: **masked gannet,** the large seabird *Sula dactylatra*, of islands of n.w. and n.e. Aust. and elsewhere in the tropics and subtropics, having white and black plumage with black face-markings; **plover,** the wading bird *Vanellus miles miles* of n. Aust. and nearby parts of the s.w. Pacific, having predom. olive-brown and white plumage, with a black crown and yellow wattles on the face; **wood swallow,** the nomadic, predom. grey bird *Artamus personatus* of mainland Aust. (see quot. 1849); see also *blue martin* b., BLUE *a.*, MARTIN.

1846 J. GOULD *Birds of Aust.* (1848) VII. Pl. 77, *Sula personata*.. **Masked Gannet. 1890** G.J. BROINOWSKI *Birds of Aust.* II. Pl. 42, This **Masked Plover** .. frequently utters a cry not unlike the name bestowed on it by the natives (Al-ga-ra-ra). **1842** J. GOULD *Birds of Aust.* (1848) II. Pl. 31, *Artamus personatus*.. **Masked Wood Swallow. 1849**
C. STURT *Narr. Exped. Central Aust.* II. 20 App. *Masked wood swallow.* So called because of a black mark on the throat and cheek resembling a mask in some measure.

mason wasp. [Transf. use of *mason-wasp* a solitary wasp *Odynerus murarius.*] Any of many stout-bodied, solitary wasps, esp. of the fam. Eumenidae and Sphecidae, building mud cells in which to store food for the larvae; *mud wasp*, see MUD 1. Formerly also **mason fly** (or **hornet**).

1872 MRS E. MILLETT *Austral. Parsonage* 56 Hanging nests of puddled clay, looking somewhat as if they belonged to a colony of swallows. The proprietors, however, were not birds, but of the race of mason-hornet, properly called a sphex. **1894** *Proc. Linnean Soc. N.S.W.* IX. 27 *Alastor eriurgus* .. a very common 'mason wasp' in the neighbourhood of Sydney. **1896** B. SPENCER *Rep. Horn Sci. Exped. Central Aust.* I. 98 A black and white mason fly was making persistent efforts to drag a heavy spider up the smooth trunk of a red gum to its nest.

Ma State. A name for New South Wales, the earliest Australian Colony (see quot. 1914). Also abbrev. as **Ma.**

1906 *Bulletin* (Sydney) 18 Jan. 14/4 Strange how the importing mania clings to the Ma State. **1914** H.M. VAUGHAN *Australasian Wander-Yr.* 61 The mother colony of New South Wales is often referred to as 'Ma State'. **1927** *Bulletin* (Sydney) 12 May 24/2 Within certain shires of the Ma State .. the cape-tulip has spread apace. **1934** *Ibid.* 24 Jan. 25/1 The Cabbage Gardeners will have to be licked outright if Ma is to have a hope.

Hence **Ma Stater** *n.*

1933 *Bulletin* (Sydney) 2 Aug. 10/3 In 1923 a warrant was issued for a Ma Stater charged with disobeying a magisterial order.

master. *Hist.* One to whom a convict is assigned: see ASSIGN *v.*

1796 *N.S.W. Instruct. to Watchmen* 11 Gentlemen's Servants will have Passes from their respective Masters. **1900** W. DELAFORCE *Life & Experiences Ex-Convict Port Macquarie* 6 If a man had a seven years' sentence, he had to serve four years with a master before he got a 'ticket-of-leave'.

matchbox bean. [See quot. 1933.] The large, shiny, dark brown seed of the vigorous climber *Entada phaseoloides* (fam. Caesalpiniaceae); the long flattened pod of the plant; the plant itself, occurring in Qld., N.T., and elsewhere; *Queensland bean*, see QUEENSLAND 2.

1917 *Bulletin* (Sydney) 7 June 22/4 The bucks went into the surrounding scrubs and gathered matchbox beans .. and clothes-line props. **1933** *Ibid.* 27 Dec. 21/4 A matchbox bean (*Entada scandens*) was washed up on a beach near Eden... Bushmen scoop out the kernel and make very fine waterproof matchboxes from these beans.

mate. [Spec. use of Br. *mate* 'habitual companion, an associate, fellow, comrade; a fellow-worker or partner. Now only in working-class use': see OED(S *sb.*[2] 1.]

1. a. An equal partner in an enterprise: see quots. 1838, 1845, and 1921. Also **working mate.**

1834 N.S.W. Magistrates' Deposition Bk. 19 Nov., Just before I got to my own hut I heard the dogs making a great noise and I asked my mate John Rolfe whose dogs they were. **1838** A. MACONOCHIE *Thoughts on Convict Managem.* 220 These men when they contract to do heavy work, as clearing, fencing, etc. almost always do it in parties of two, or more, being prompted to this in the first place by the hardness of the work, which a man cannot face alone, requiring always the assistance of 'neighbours', or 'mates', or 'partners', as they are severally called, even in the minute details. **1845** C. GRIFFITH *Present State & Prospects Port Phillip* 79 Two generally travel together, who are called mates; they are partners, and divide all their earnings.

1921 W.H. CORFIELD *Reminisc. Qld.* 46, I have alluded several times to 'partners', or 'mates', which was the more popular term. These partnerships were quite common amongst carriers and diggers in bygone days. It was simply chums, owning and sharing everything in common, and without any agreement, written or otherwise. **1952** *Bulletin* (Sydney) 20 Aug. 16/1 I've been working 'mates' with a very New Australian.

  b. In the phr. **to go mates,** to work as an equal partner (with someone, etc.).

1876 'EIGHT YRS.' RESIDENT' *Queen of Colonies* 119 They [sc. the Chinese] appear to have no quarrels among themselves when working in partnerships, or as the digging phrase is, 'going mates'. **1940** I.L. IDRIESS *Lightning Ridge* 188 None of us liked going mates with a man unless we could pay our own way.

  2. An acquaintance; a person engaged in the same activity.

1841 *Port Phillip Patriot* 23 Dec. 4/3 We told him our mates were gone, and that we had heard two shots fired. **1985** *Canberra Times* 21 June 1/1 High Court judge Mr Justice Murphy denied yesterday that he had ever said to N.S.W. Chief Magistrate Mr Briese anything like, 'And now, what about my little mate?'

  3. One with whom the bonds of close friendship are acknowledged, a 'sworn friend'.

1891 'SMILER' *Wanderings Simple Child* (ed. 3) p. iv, Where his mate was his sworn friend through good and evil report, in sickness and health, in poverty and plenty, where his horse was his comrade, and his dog his companion, the bushman lived the life he loved. **1986** *Bulletin* (Sydney) 21 Jan. 36/1 Silence was the essence of traditional mateship. . . The gaunt man stands at his wife's funeral; his mate comes up, says nothing but rests a gentle hand briefly on his shoulder.

  4. A mode of address implying equality and goodwill; freq. used to a casual acquaintance and, esp. in recent use (but see quot. 1855), ironic.

1843 *Trifler* (Launceston) 12 July 2/2 Before Comray fired, he said, 'Where are you, mate?' **1855** R. CARBONI *Eureka Stockade* 4 'Your licence, mate', was the peremptory question from a six-foot fellow in blue shirt, thick boots, the face of a ruffian, armed with a carabine and fixed bayonet. **1983** *Bulletin* (Sydney) 13 Sept. 60/1 When they call you 'mate' in the N.S.W. Labor Party it is like getting a kiss from the Mafia.

mateless, *a.* Companionless; lone.

1896 H. LAWSON *While Billy Boils* 170 The everlasting stars . . keep the mateless traveller from going mad as he lies in his lonely camp on the plains. **1926** L.C.E. GEE *Bush Tracks & Gold Fields* 72 'Possum Bill was a 'hatter', that is, a mateless river man, who roamed about by himself.

mateship. [Spec. use of *mateship* the condition of being a mate, companionship: see OED(S.] The bond between equal partners or close friends; comradeship; comradeship as an ideal. Also *attrib.*

1864 J. ROGERS *New Rush* 54 As typical of mate-ship ever true, Accept this melody—my last. Adieu. **1954** J. WATEN *Unbending* 95 You've always told me . . that the boss class works the mateship business in this country.

matey. [f. MATE 4 + -Y.] A mode of address implying friendliness and goodwill.

1854 C.A. CORBYN *Sydney Revels* 93, I say matey . . go and lie down in my bunk. **1981** C. WALLACE-CRABBE *Splinters* 30 'Listen, matey, I don't want any fancy academic analyses of the situation.

Matilda. [Transf. but unexplained use of the female name.]

  1. A swag. Also *fig.*

1892 *Bulletin* (Sydney) 9 Apr. 18/2 An old stager of a sundowner . . slung 'Matilda' off his back, and leant across the rail. **1905** *Truth* (Sydney) 26 Feb. 1/8 A man dressed in clerical garb passed through recently carrying a 'matilda'. **1916** *Ibid.* 21 May 7/4 The full private in Napoleon's army carried a Marshall's baton *in his matilda*.

  2. In the phr. **to waltz Matilda,** to carry one's swag; to travel the road. Also *fig.*

1893 *Bulletin* (Sydney) 18 Nov. 20/3 No bushman thinks of 'going on the wallaby' or 'walking Matilda', or 'padding the hoof'; he goes on the track—when forced to 't. **1925** *Smith's Weekly* (Sydney) 14 Mar. 21/3 The turtle is a pretty considerable land-traveller on occasions. When the billabongs dry up in drought time he waltzes Matilda to the river as straight as the crow flies.

  3. In the phr. **(with) Matilda up,** carrying a swag.

1895 K. MACKAY *Yellow Wave* 58 D' ye mind that day on the Flinders when you met me with Matilda up. **1912** M.C. DONALD *Real Austral.* 48, I wonder whether Miss Desmond ever . . fell into step with the lean, brown, dusty, travelling worker, 'Matilda up'.

  4. Special Comb. **Matilda-bearer (-carrier, -hawker, -lumper, -man, -waltzer),** a swagman.

1910 *Bulletin* (Sydney) 26 May 15/2 The average Matilda-hawker, if he happens on a 'stiff' mate, rushes into the nearest town with the news. **1911** *Ibid.* 19 Jan. 14/4 We were joined by a veteran Matilda-carrier. **1927** *Smith's Weekly* (Sydney) 30 Apr. 19/7 Hence the hearty welcome to any Matilda bearer who . . succeeds in passing the deep crossing. **1933** *Bulletin* (Sydney) 3 May 20/2 Matildawaltzers with one black (or brown) shoe or boot are an everyday sight. **1936** *Ibid.* 30 Sept. 21/2, I struck a veteran Matilda-man preparing his bed. **1939** *Ibid.* 28 June 20/3 Your modern Matilda-lumper doesn't fool around on a wet day with damp chips.

McGinness, McGinnis, McGuiness, varr. MAGINNIS.

meara, var. MEERA.

meat. Used *attrib.* in Special Comb. **meat ant, (a)** any of a small group of related species of ant of the large genus *Iridomyrmex*, esp. the mound-building *I. purpureus* (= *detectus*), having a reddish head and purple body, and capable of inflicting a painful bite; *road ant*, see ROAD 3; **(b)** *fig.*, in the phr. **game as a meat ant,** courageous; **-bag,** a hessian safe used to protect meat from flies; **-billy,** a billy in which meat is cooked; **pie, (a)** *attrib.* in **meat-pie bookie** (or **bookmaker**), a smalltime bookmaker; see also PIE; **(b)** in the phr. **as Australian as (a) meat pie,** quintessentially Australian; **-works,** an abattoir; an establishment where meat is processed.

  (a) 1900 *Bulletin* (Sydney) 7 Apr. (Red Page), On the nest of a colony of these **meat ants** I placed a large green caterpillar. **(b) 1932** J.J. HARDIE *Cattle Camp* (1944) 9 She's like a well-bred filly—**game as a meat-ant**. **1904** *Bulletin* (Sydney) 4 Feb. 36/2 Flies have got into the **meat-bag** and the meat is only fit to throw to the dogs. **1902** *Bulletin* (Sydney) 11 Jan. 32/1 Every traveller has . . one or two billies. Some have three—of varying sizes to fit one in the other. The tea-billy and **meat-billy** are the most common. **1915** A. WRIGHT *Sport from Hollowlog Flat* 24 Don't bet with these **meat-pie bookies**. Dave Doem'll offer a fair price directly. **1919** C. DREW *Doings of Dave* 89 I've done with all these meatpie bookmakers for good. **1972** *Sunday Austral.* (Sydney) 16 Apr. 4/6 Apart from his name and his forebears, Barassi with his wide grin and fierce desire to win is **as Australian as a meat pie**. **1979** K. DUNSTAN *Ratbags* p. xiv, As Australian as meatpie. [**1895 meat-works**: T.A. COGHLAN *Wealth & Progress N.S.W. 1894* 367 All the cattle killed, except 27,891 treated in the meat-processing works, were required for local consumption.] **1936** *Bulletin* (Sydney) 23 Sept. 20/4 The Koolinda called at Wyndham recently to convey 200 returning meatworks employees to Fremantle.

medicine man. [Spec. use of orig. U.S. *medicine man.*] KORADJI.
1865 G.S. LANG *Aborigines of Aust.* 8 The second class is that of the sorcerers or medicine men. 1962 D. LOCKWOOD *I, Aboriginal* 9 The Medicine Man, the Doctor Blackfellow.

medifraud. [f. *medi(cal insurance + fraud.*] The practice of making fraudulent claims against a medical insurance scheme; an instance of this. Also *attrib.*
1982 *Age* (Melbourne) 6 Aug. 3/7 PS staff rapped on attitude to medifraud... Senior officials of the Commonwealth Health Department.. were severely criticised at a Federal inquiry into medifraud yesterday. 1986 *Canberra Times* 4 Mar. 7/1 A former Department of Health medifraud investigator has failed in his attempt to force the Australian Federal Police to hand over documents concerning a joint medifraud case involving a medical practitioner.

Mediterranean. Used allusively to refer to behaviour supposedly characteristic of an Australian of Italian or Greek descent: (of an injury, illness, etc.) feigned.
1973 *Bulletin* (Sydney) 24 Feb. 12/1 There was.. the case of the laborer suffering a severe case of 'Mediterranean Back' after an accident at work. 1983 *Austral.* (Sydney) 9 Dec. 9/1 A report by the Human Rights Commission published yesterday dwells on complaints which can be an incitement to racial hatred. 'Mediterranean back', 'ethnic jokes' (especially Irish ones) and the use of the word 'Pom' receive special mention.

meera /ˈmirə/. Also **meara, merro, meru.** [a. Nyungar *mirra.*] An Aboriginal throwing stick used to launch a spear.
1828 *Austral. Q. Jrnl. Theol., Lit. & Sci.* Jan. 29 The hammers and knives were of singular formation, and the *mearas* ingeniously constructed. 1841 G. GREY *Jrnls. Two Exped. N.-W. & W.A.* I. 304 The old lady.. went up to him.. seizing his merro, or throwing stick. 1878 R.B. SMYTH *Aborigines of Vic.* I. p. xlvi, The lever used to propel the spear— the *Kur-ruk, Gur-reek, Murn-wun, Meera,* or *Womerah,* of the east, west, and south, the *Logorouk* or *Wondouk* of the north—is the same in principle in all parts of Australia. 1935 H.H. FINLAYSON *Red Centre* 80 The *meru* or spearthrower.

meet. [Spec. use of *meet* a meeting, an appointment.] An assignation with a person of the opposite sex; a 'date'.
1915 C.J. DENNIS *Songs of Sentimental Bloke* 23, I dunno 'ow I 'ad the nerve ter speak, An' make that meet wiv 'er fer Sundee week! 1974 N. PHILLIPSON *As Other Men* 118 This guy had a meet on with the girl.

melaleuca /mɛləˈlukə/. [The plant genus *Melaleuca* was named by Swedish botanist Carl von Linné (Linnaeus) (in *Syst. Nat.* ed. 12 509; *Mantissa Plant.* I. 14, 105 (1767).) f. Gr. μέλας black + λευκός white, referring to the fire-blackened white bark of some Asian species.] Any plant of the large, chiefly Austral. genus *Melaleuca* (fam. Myrtaceae) many of which are cultivated as ornamentals; the wood of these plants. See also TEA-TREE. Also *attrib.*
1814 R. BROWN *Gen. Remarks Bot. Terra Australis* 15 The maximum of Melaleuca exists in the principal parallel, but it declines less towards the south than within the tropic. 1982 R. HALL *Just Relations* 111 Granny Collins buys a dark brocade curtain.. and hangs it on a melaleuca rod hammered to the slab-timber wall of her shack.

Melba /ˈmɛlbə/. [f. *Melbourne* and adopted by Helen Mitchell (1861–1931), an operatic soprano.] Used allusively of a person who retires but makes repeated 'farewell' performances or come-backs. Esp. in the phr. **to do a Melba.** See also quot. 1972.
1971 *Austral.* (Sydney) 20 Feb. 22/4 The later years were marked by a seemingly endless round of farewell performances. 'Doing a Melba', they call it. 1972 *Bulletin* (Sydney) 22 Jan. 33/3 *Germaine Greer's* visit to Australia to promote the paperback edition of her book, 'The Female Eunuch', is in the classic, Melba tradition: the expatriate returning to her homeland at the close of her public career.

Melbourne, Marvellous: see MARVELLOUS MELBOURNE.

melon. [Spec. use of *melon* a gourd: see PADDYMELON $n.^2$]
1. Used *attrib.* in Special Comb. **melon blindness,** an illness of horses, characterized by blindness and believed to result from feeding on the paddymelon; also **melon-blind** *a.*; **hole,** GILGAI b.; *paddymelon hole,* see PADDYMELON $n.^2$ 2; freq. *attrib.*; **vine,** PADDYMELON $n.^2$ 1.
1932 M.R. WHITE *No Roads go By* 108 Paddy-melons grew in a green riot along the base of this hill, and many horses were afflicted with **melon blindness** that year—a disease caused through eating the vines. 1976 C.D. MILLS *Hobble Chains & Greenhide* 146 Some bullocks are melon-blind like horses. They're menaces. They'll rush your mob every night if you're not careful. 1844 L. LEICHHARDT *Jrnl. Overland Exped. Aust.* 8 Oct. (1847) 9 The soil of the Bricklow scrub is a stiff clay, washed out by the rains into shallow holes, well known by the squatter under the name of **melon-holes.** 1984 H.W. DAVIS *Bachelors in Bush* 12 The area to be fallen for the season.. would embrace a few acres of 'melon hole' country. I have never learned how the name 'melon-holes' originated. They appeared to be natural depressions or holes in certain parts of the standing scrub, several yards in circumference. 1911 *Bulletin* (Sydney) 6 Apr. 15/3 Pretty well every noxious weed.. finds a barracker.. **melon-vine,** sweet briar and the rest.. turn up as 'capital fodder for stock in drought time'.

2. *fig.*
a. A head.
1907 *Truth* (Sydney) 12 May 8/5 (*heading*) Woodford wields a waddy *and mangles Monaghan's melon.* 1971 D. IRELAND *Unknown Industr. Prisoner* 98 One of the engineers.. bravely approached the hole, lowering his head to look inside. 'Why don't you shove your melon right in?' roared the Humdinger.
b. A fool. Also **melonhead.**
1937 E. PARTRIDGE *Dict. Slang & Unconventional Eng.* 516 *Melon..* the Australian and New Zealand sense.. a simpleton, a fool. 1941 S.J. BAKER *Pop. Dict. Austral. Slang* 46 *Melon,* a simpleton or fool. Whence 'melonhead'.

melt, $v.^1$ *Obs.* [Spec. use of *melt* to reduce to a liquid condition by heat.] *trans.* Freq. with **down.** In the preparation of tallow: to render animal fats. Also *absol.*
1840 *Port Phillip Gaz.* 30 Nov. 3 The Proprietors are purchasers of fat Stock or will melt down for the settlers upon reduced terms. 1847 *Port Phillip Herald* 16 Nov. 1/1 The undersigned is prepared to melt stock on the usual terms. 1848 *Ibid.* 16 Mar. 2/4 Tens of thousands of sheep and thousands of cattle *melted down* that their mere tallow may be sent to Europe, their flesh being cast away in the fields.
Hence **melter** *n.*
1844 *Port Phillip Gaz.* 30 Nov. 3 *Important Sale of 150 Head of Cattle without reserve.* To butchers, melters, dairymen, and stockholders.

melt, $v.^2$ *Obs.* [Spec. use of Br. (slang) *melt* to spend, squander (money): see OED $v.^1$ 13 *a.* Perh. also infl. by MELT $v.^1$] *trans.* To squander (one's accumulated earnings) on alcoholic drink, esp. in the phr. **to melt**

(down) a cheque. Also with the publican as subject (see quot. 1914).

1869 *Bushmen, Publicans, & Politics* 8 Whatever he may want at the bush township he may choose to visit, he has to cash his cheque to obtain it. Its amount is immediately known, and it is no less sad than true that every snare is thereafter employed to induce him to 'melt it down'. **1882** *Bulletin* (Sydney) 17 June 9/2 A played-out shearer was ordered off the premises of a shanty-keeper out west after he had melted his cheque. **1914** *Ibid.* 15 Jan. 22/1 He said he'd made enough money to do without melting down drunks' cheques, so when they got to a certain stage he limited them to a beer an hour.

melting, *vbl. n. Obs.* [f. MELT *v.*¹]

1. In the preparation of tallow: the rendering of animal fats. Also *attrib.*

1843 *Port Phillip Patriot* 10 Aug. 4/2 No process, whether of boiling, roasting, or melting, will ever be found to answer when the *fat* and *lean* portions, or the whole carcass of the sheep is put down together. The juices of the *flesh* will *soften* and *discolour* the tallow, and render it much less valuable in the home market. **1847** *Port Phillip Herald* 16 Nov. 2/2 The market continues much overstocked with fat cattle, and good quality are selling a shade over melting prices.

2. Comb. **melting(-down) establishment.**

1840 *Port Phillip Gaz.* 30 Nov. 3 Melbourne. Melting Establishment, the first steam establishment formed in the colonies. **1843** *Colonial Observer* (Sydney) 23 Aug. 1257/1 Messrs. Watson and Wright .. made application for a squatting license, to enable them to form a melting-down establishment in the neighbourhood of Melbourne.

menura /mɛnˈjurə/. *Obs.* [mod. L. *menura* f. Gr. μήνη moon + οὐρά tail: see quot. 1800.] LYRE-BIRD 1.

[1800 *Trans. Linnean Soc. London* (1802) 207 *Menura superba*... The general colour of the under sides of these two [tail] feathers is of a pearly hue, elegantly marked on the inner web with bright rufous colured crescent-shaped spots, which, from the extraordinary construction of the parts, appear wonderfully transparent.] **1823** J. LATHAM *Gen. Hist. Birds* VIII. 161 The Menura inhabits New-Holland. **1874** J.G. WOOD *Nat. Hist.* (1885) 337 (OED) The Menura seldom, if ever, attempts to escape by flight.

merejig, var. MERRYJIG.

meridian ant. *Magnetic termite*, see MAGNETIC.

1896 B. SPENCER *Rep. Horn Sci. Exped. Central Aust.* I. 129 We came across a small patch of the mound nests of what are called the meridian or compass ants. **1927** M. DORNEY *Adventurous Honeymoon* 79 They were flat slab-like structures .. built by a particular kind of termite called the meridian ant.

merino. *Hist.* [Fig. use of *merino* a breed of fine-woolled sheep introduced early in small numbers and valued more highly than coarse-woolled sheep.] One who has chosen to settle in Australia (as opposed to a convict or ex-convict); one who finds in this a basis for social pretension. Esp. as **pure merino.** Also *attrib.*

1826 *Monitor* (Sydney) 24 Nov. 221/2 One of the late petit-jury has this week been committed for compounding felony, and another is expected shortly to be put in the House of Correction, as he is constantly amusing himself with beating his wife and his father. Remember, reader, these are all *pure Merinos*! **1837** *Cornwall Chron.* (Launceston) 5 Aug. 3 Proceedings .. commenced against this Merino paper, whose Editor considers his own writing to be the very quintessence of everything that is good and virtuous.

merloo, var. MARLOO.

mernong, var. MURNONG.

merro, var. MEERO.

merryjig /ˈmɛrɪdʒɪg/, *a. Austral. pidgin. Obs.* Also **merejig, merrijig, merrygig.** [a. Wathawurung *mirijig.*] Very good.

1839 *Port Phillip Gaz.* 13 Nov. 3 *Constable*: My name Harry Stokes. *Native*: Ah ha! merrygig you. **1843** *Colonial Observer* (Sydney) 1 Feb. 790/3 'Merri jig' means in English 'very good'. **1862** G.T. LLOYD *Thirty-Three Yrs. Tas. & Vic.* 427 The natives .. discovered that the 'piccaniny boulganas merejig cogalla'—the little sheep were very good eating. **1872** 'RESIDENT' *Glimpses Life Vic.* 25 'Merryjig' that fellow!

meru, var. MEERA.

mesembryanthemum. Also **mesembrianthemum.** [Transf. use of *mesembryanthemum* the name of a plant genus.] PIGFACE.

1840 J. FRANKLIN Diary Visit S.A. 31 Dec. 52 (typescript) Covered with mesembrianthemum. **1935** T. RAYMENT *Cluster of Bees* 131, I had searched .. the blossoms of the coast tea-tree .. the Mesembryanthemum, and dozens of other plants .. and there were no plumed bees.

message-stick. A piece of wood carved with symbolic patterns which convey a message from one Aboriginal community to another and which may also indicate the bearer's standing or totem; LETTER-STICK.

1878 R.B. SMYTH *Aborigines of Vic.* I. p. xliv, It is by no means certain that message-sticks were in common use amongst the people of the southern parts of Australia. **1980** T.A. ROY *Vengeance of Dolphin* 135 Clutched in her right hand was the paperbark cover belonging to the message-stick.

messmate. [See quots. 1889 and 1902.] Any of several rough-barked trees of the genus *Eucalyptus* (fam. Myrtaceae), esp. the tall *E. obliqua* of s.e. Aust. incl. Tas., and the Gympie messmate, *E. cloeziana*, of e. Qld.; the wood of these trees. Also *attrib.*

1861 'OLD BUSHMAN' *Bush Wanderings* 223 The 'messmet' as we called it—a species of bastard gum. **1880** J. BONWICK *Resources Qld.* 80 The Messmate, of Moreton Bay corner, may reach 300 feet... It is the *E. obliqua*. **1889** J.H. MAIDEN *Useful Native Plants Aust.* 429 *Eucalyptus amygdalina*.. has even more vernacular names than botanical synonyms... Because it is allied to, or associated with, 'Stringybark', it is also known by the name of 'Messmate'. **1902** *Proc. Linnean Soc. N.S.W.* XXVII. 573 The appellation of Messmate infers that these trees 'messmate' with or partake of the characters of other trees. **1943** *Bulletin* (Sydney) 11 Aug. 13/2 Out hunting on the messmate flat my foxies disturbed a kangaroo-rat.

metallic starling. The bird *Aplonis metallica* of rainforests of n.e. Qld. and nearby s.w. Pacific, having glossy black plumage with a metallic green and purple sheen; *shining starling*, see SHINING.

1912 *Emu* XII. 25 We do not refer to them as the Metallic Starling .. or *Calornis metallica*, but as 'Tealgon', the accent on the first syllable. **1982** R. ELLIS *Bush Safari* 63 We stopped .. to observe a nesting colony of Metallic Starlings, a native species.

metho, *n.*¹ [f. *meth(ylated spirits* + -O.]

1. Methylated spirits. Also *attrib.*

1933 *Bulletin* (Sydney) 18 Oct. 10/2 A metho. drinker—a regular visitor—came into the pharmacy the other day. **1938** F. CLUNE *Free & Easy Land* 138 'Metho' drinkers of the Domain.

2. One who is addicted to drinking methylated spirits.
1933 *Bulletin* (Sydney) 1 Nov. 11/1 A John Hop who has helped to deal with many 'methos.' tells me not a few prefer petrol. 1973 *Brisbane City Mission* Sept. 17/2 The methos... When a man takes to drinking methylated spirits you know .. that he has no thought for betterment of his lot.

Metho, n.² Abbrev. of 'Methodist'. Also as adj.
1940 *Rutherford Rumblings* (Tamworth) 17 May 1 Why did the 41st pinch our Metho. Padre? 1965 J. O'GRADY *Aussie Eng.* 60 Members of the Methodist Church are also known as 'Methos', or 'Metho drinkers', although they don't drink metho.

mial, var. MYALL n.¹

miall, var. MYALL n.¹ and n.²

mia-mia /'maɪə-maɪə/. Formerly with much variety, as **mai-mai, miam, miami, miam-miam, mi-mi, myam-myam, mya-mya**. [a. Nyungar *maya*, or *maya-maya*.]
1. A temporary shelter of the Aborigines: see quot. 1851. See also GUNYAH 1. (Quot. 1839 may be *transf.*: see sense 2.)
1839 *Port Phillip Gaz.* 2 Nov. 3 Where stood .. two years past the 'myam myam', or hut of the first settler, will tower five years hence the ceiled and painted roof of some gaudy theatre. 1840 P.L. BROWN *Clyde Co. Papers* 9 Dec. (1952) II. 400 They walked in regular order, each carrying his spear, & a cockatoo's feather in his head; the women and children followed, & made thier [*sic*] miam miams close to the house. 1841 *Geelong Advertiser* 27 Dec. 3/1 At their mi-mis we found two double-barrelled guns and one single-barrelled, and a brace of pistols. 1843 *Melbourne Times* 25 Mar. 4/2 Should the arrangements entered into be of a friendly nature they retire and fix up their miams, and a grand corrobery is given in honour of the strange tribes. 1845 *Observer* (Hobart) 18 July 4/5 Three blacks came to Mr Cameron's and made a 'mia-mia' by the garden fence. 1851 H.R. RUSSELL *Short Descr. Austral. Colonies* 11 They are still the same wanderers as at first .. living in the same 'mai mais', consisting of a sheet of bark stripped from a tree, and laid to windward against a forked stick, opposite which they light a fire, and under the shelter of which they rarely sleep two nights in succession. 1857 *Illustr. Jrnl. Australasia* II. 60 That liquid evening star no more Shall gleam his fragile mya-mya o'er. 1872 'RESIDENT' *Glimpses Life Vic.* 21 The murderer slunk with cat-like steps round the mia-mi, where his victim was sleeping.
2. *transf.* A temporary shelter erected by a traveller.
1855 G.H. WATHEN *Golden Colony* 153 We received a volley of shots from a sort of mia-mia on the side of the road. 1984 P. READ *Down there with me on Cowra Mission* 48 The first time I came to this place [sc. Erambie, near Cowra] there was only four houses, and there used to be mia mias .. built all around. That'd be about 1918.

mick, n.¹ Abbrev. of MICKEY 1.
1894 A.B. BELL *Oscar* 67 Some few of the wildest mickeys broke away through the cordon of stockmen and scoured round the yard, only to be tackled by the cattle dogs. One fierce mick, about eighteen months old, became enraged. 1976 C.D. MILLS *Hobble Chains & Greenhide* 145 This bloke's a 'thick-horn'. Evidently been a mick. He is almost a stag—coarse as hell too.

mick, n.² [Transf. use of U.S. *Mick* an Irishman. Used elsewhere but recorded earliest in Aust.] A Roman Catholic.
1902 *Truth* (Sydney) 20 July 6/4 He's a tyke. He's a Mick. Chuck him out. 1985 *Canberra Times* 1 Sept. 8/4 No wonder we 'Micks' used to have slanging matches .. with the State-school kids.

mick, n.³ *Two-up.* [Of unknown origin.] The reverse side of a coin; the tail.
1918 *Aussie: Austral. Soldiers' Mag.* (Sydney) Dec. 3/1 They were playing the good old game and a big dope they called Snow was spinner. Presently, up went two browns in the air. They came down showing two micks. 1953 T.A.G. HUNGERFORD *Riverslake* 126 'Ten bob he tails 'em!' he intoned... 'I got ten bob to say he tails 'em—ten bob the micks!'

mick, v. *Two-up.* [f. MICK n.³] *trans.* To spin (the coins) so that they land tail uppermost.
1918 *Home Trail: Souvenir Issue Voyage H.M.T. 'A. 30'* Dec. 12, I bet a quid he Micks 'em. 1977 T.A.G. HUNGERFORD *Wong Chu* 56 Ten bob the mick! I got ten bob says he micks 'em.

mickery /'mɪkəri/. Also **mickeri, mickerie, mickri**. [a. Wangganguru *migiri*.] SOAK; *spec.*, an excavated and formed soak, esp. in a dry river bed (see quots. 1947 and 1971). Also *attrib.*
1899 *Western Champion* (Barcaldine) 25 July 3/2 Then to a sandal wood break .. and he stuck himself, into the mickerie just where the niggers' brush gunyahs were. 1915 F.R.B. LOVE *Aborigines* 12 At times one finds a 'mickri' or native well, containing water. 1947 A.W. NOAKES *Water for Inland* 6 Stock was watered from mickeries in the Flinders River, that is a chock and log structure about four feet wide, twenty feet long and eight to ten feet high, according to the depth of water from the surface, which was lowered down through the sand to the water. 1956 T. RONAN *Moleskin Midas* 76 The elder lubras dug the postholes squatting on their haunches, breaking the soil with mickeri sticks and scooping it out with their fingers. 1971 W.A. WINTER-IRVING *Beyond Bitumen* 118 The mickery was two long logs four feet apart sunk in the sand for about thirty feet or more. Between the logs we dug out the dry sand to water level where it stayed to water the cattle.

mickey. Also **micky**. [Spec. use of *Mick(e)y* familiar form of *Michael*, prob. infl. by (orig. U.S.) *Mick* an Irishman.]
1. A bull calf, usu. unbranded and freq. wild.
1876 *Austral. Town & Country Jrnl.* (Sydney) 9 Dec. 942/2 The wary and still more dangerously sudden 'Michie', a two-year-old-bull (so called after an eminent Australian barrister famous for bringing his 'charges' to a successful issue). 1881 A.C. GRANT *Bush-Life Qld.* I. 227 The branding-pen is getting .. lively now. There are three or four Mickies and wild heifers who are determined to have their owner's hearts-blood. 1984 *N.T. News* (Darwin) 22 Dec. 13/1 Mike told us a mickey was a bull that had escaped castration, gone wild and gathered a harem of wild cows.
2. *fig.* In the phr. **to throw** (or **chuck**) **a mickey,** to have a tantrum.
1952 T.A.G. HUNGERFORD *Ridge & River* 22 And he don't chuck a micky every time something goes off behind him! 1960 M. HENRY *Unlucky Dip* 90 Not that it was such a terrible thing really—but the Boss threw a mickey.
3. *Noisy miner*, see NOISY.
1911 J.A. LEACH *Austral. Bird Bk.* 173 Noisy Miner, Garrulous Honeyeater, Snake-Bird, Cherry-eater, Soldier, Micky, Squeaker, *Myzantha garrula*. 1981 M. SHARLAND *Tracks of Morning* 74 A brown goshawk preening itself on a dry branch not far from its nest, with half a dozen 'mickeys' (noisy miners) to whom it is normally Public Enemy No. 1, preening on a branch a few feet below.
4. The vulva.
1969 A. BUZO *Front Room Boys* (1970) 49 Barry Anderson reckons he got her in the locker room the other day. Mucked around, played with mickey, she didn't mind.

1975 D.J. TOWNSHEND *Gland Time* 238 Can't blame her for it, 'cause her mickey was probably throbbin' for it.

mickri, var. MICKERY.

micky, var. MICKEY.

middla, var. MIDLA.

middy. A medium-sized measure of beer; the glass containing this.
1945 S.J. BAKER *Austral. Lang.* 169 The *middy*, a beer glass containing nine ounces, is a measure used only in N.S.W. hotels. **1986** *Age* (Melbourne) 13 Mar. (Green Guide) 8/3 'How much do you drink a day? Six middies?'—'Look, son, I'd spill more than that.'

midla /'mɪdlə/. *Obs.* Also **middla, midlah**. [a. Gaurna *midla*.] An Aboriginal throwing stick: see quot. 1863.
1842 *S. Austral. News* (London) 15 Oct. 46/2 The weapon is thrown by the midla (propelling stick) a distance of sixty or eighty yards with considerable precision. **1847** G.F. ANGAS *Savage Life & Scenes* I. 111 Their weapons are the throwing-stick (*midlah*), which is made of the she-oak wood, [etc.]. **1860** *Trans. & Proc. R. Soc. Vic.* (1861) 169 This kind of spear . . is always thrown with the so-called 'middla'. **1863** J. BONWICK *Wild White Man* 50 The *Wommera, Midla* or *Throwing Stick* is an ingenious contrivance for accelerating and directing the motion of the spear.

migrant. [Spec. use of *migrant* one who leaves a country to settle in another.]
1. An immigrant to Australia. Now more usual than IMMIGRANT 1. Also *attrib.* See also EMIGRANT *n.* 1.
1922 *Daily Mail* (Sydney) 17 Jan. 1/2 Please don't speak of those arriving in Australia from Britain as immigrants. . . Call them rather migrants, because to go from Britain to Australia is only to pass from one part of Great Britain to another. **1980** S. ORR *Roll On* 3 A great deal of nonsense has been written in recent years about the changes in Australian eating habits brought about by the Great Migrant Invasion.
2. Special Comb. **migrant camp, hostel,** a place in which temporary accommodation is provided for newly-arrived immigrants; **ship,** a vessel carrying (assisted) immigrants to Australia.
1953 T.A.G. HUNGERFORD *Riverslake* 68 It had been worked for him by a Lithuanian girl in the **migrant camp** at Bathurst. **1964** *Bulletin* (Sydney) 18 Jan. 12/1 This is Villawood, biggest of Australia's **migrant hostels** (population around 1,425 at last count, capacity 2,750) and temporary home for a steady flow of assisted newcomers, English, Dutch, Italian and other nationalities. **1948** *Listening Post* (Perth) July 15 Films depicting various phases of life and conditions in Australia . . shown on **migrant ships.**

Mike. Shortened form of 'Michael': see quot. 1967 and see also OEDS *angel, sb.* 8.
1954 *Sporting Life* Jan. 31/1 It was suggested that he become a bookmaker's 'Mike' (a man who finances a bookie's bag). **1967** *Kings Cross Whisper* (Sydney) xxxvi. 4/2 *Mike,* a backer. Usually for a promoter. From Michael the Archangel, guardian angel.

Mile. Abbrev. of *golden mile* (see GOLDEN 1).
1938 W. HATFIELD *Buffalo Jim* 34 'That'll see you pretty well to the Mile.' 'The Mile?' 'Kalgoorlie. They call it the Golden Mile.' **1978** D. STUART *Wedgetail View* 238 She's a town and a half, that Kal[goorlie]. . . Booze enough to flood every stope on the Mile.

military settler. *Hist.* One who, having served as a military officer in an Australian Colony, elects to remain as a settler.

1837 *Perth Gaz.* 11 Feb. 847 It has become necessary to make a . . change in the arrangements which have hitherto been in force with respect to Military Settlers. **1838** *Tegg's N.S.W. Pocket Almanac* 73 Officers on Half-pay, residing in the Colony where they propose to settle, may be admitted to the privileges of Military and Naval Settlers.

milk.
1. Used *attrib.* in the names of plants: **milk-bush,** any of several plants having a milky sap, esp. *Sarcostemma australe* (see *caustic bush* CAUSTIC); **-wood,** *milky pine,* see MILKY; also *attrib.*
1886 *N.T. Times Almanac* 6 The country abounds in edible bushes; those which stock are most partial to are the orangebush and whitewood or **milkbush. 1880** R. ROSE *Austral. Guide: Qld.* 17 The tulip wood is one greatly admired in cabinet work, so also is the **milk-wood. 1908** E.J. BANFIELD *Confessions of Beachcomber* 214 The edge of the precipice looks over a tangle of jungle down upon the top of a giant milkwood tree (*Alstonia scholaris*).
2. Special Comb. **milk billy,** a billy used as a container for milk; **opal,** white opal, a variety of precious opal (see quot. 1974); **run,** *transf.* [cf. Br. *milk round,* OEDS *milk, sb.* 10], a regular trip with stops at a number of places.
[N.Z. **1912** K. MANSFIELD *Stories* (1984) 113 She trailed over to us with a basket in her hand, the **milk billy** in the other.] **1935** DAVISON & NICHOLLS *Blue Coast Caravan* 154 We were invited across to the farm to have our milk billy filled. **1961** F. LEECHMAN *Opal Bk.* 129 **Milk Opal** . . probably owes its colour to white clay in the solutions from which it was made. **1974** B. MYATT *Dict. Austral. Gemstones* 134 Milk opal is the name given to a translucent to opaque milk white, pale bluish-white or greenish-white variety of opal. **1942** *Bulletin* (Sydney) 25 Nov. 13/2 A Winton (Q.) boundary rider . . established his '**milk run**' during the great rat plague.

milkie. An opaque playing marble.
1908 *Bulletin* (Sydney) 10 Dec. 16/4 Peter signified his willingness to adventure two alleys. 'Commonies or milkies?' demanded Sam. **1936** N. LINDSAY *Saturdee* 50 After consultation with his alley-bag, he selected two peewees, a chalkey and a slatey, which he placed in the ring. Enraged at this proposal to fob off such stuff on honourable milkies, Waldo snatched them up and threw them out of the ring.

milkmaids, *pl.* Any of several plants, usu. of the genus *Burchardia* (fam. Liliaceae), esp. *B. umbellata* of temperate Aust. incl. Tas., bearing an umbel of scented white flowers.
1930 A.J. EWART *Flora of Vic.* 287 *B*[*urchardia*] *umbellata* . . Milkmaids . . Flowers white, often tinged with red on the outside, very fragrant. **1965** *Austral. Encycl.* II. 186 The name 'milkmaids' is popularly applied in allusion to the cluster of white flowers.

milko. Also **milk-oh.** [f. the call 'Milk-O!' (see quot. 1865). Used elsewhere but recorded earliest in Aust.: see -O.]
1. A milkman.
[**1865** J.F. MORTLOCK *Experiences of Convict* 115 He proposed that I should carry his pails round the town and shout out 'Milk O!' at the customers' doors.] **1907** *Truth* (Sydney) 20 Jan. 1/7 A milk-oh . . has been convicted of selling adulterated milk more than once. **1985** *Canberra Chron.* 10 July 19/3 He has spent a fair bit of time in banking and an oil company business, but also doubled as a pretty good milko.
2. A cow-hand.
1946 F. CLUNE *Try Nothing Twice* 111 What with watering the milk and letting calves strip the cows, I was candidly a failure as milk-oh.

milky, *a.* Used as a distinguishing epithet in the names of plants: **milky mangrove,** the mangrove tree of tropical and subtropical Aust. and elsewhere *Excoecaria agallocha* having an irritant milky sap, and known also as BLIND-YOUR-EYE; **pine,** any of several trees or shrubs of the fam. Apocynaceae having a milky sap, esp. the tall rainforest tree *Alstonia scholaris* of n.e. Qld., and its soft whitish wood; *milkwood,* see MILK 1.

1888 *Proc. Linnean Soc. N.S.W.* III. 380 Excaecaria agallocha..'**Milky Mangrove**', 'Blind-your-eyes'. **1934** C. MACKNESS *Young Beachcombers* 128, I thought I never would get up that **milky-pine** you made me tackle. **1980** H.W. CUMMINGS *Confessions of 'Mud Skipper'* 268, I have noticed in several placed along the inland road to Cooktown, the Milky Pine (Alstonia Scholaris) growing alongside the road.

milli-milli /'mɪli-mɪli/. [Prob. reduplication f. (Eng.) *mail.*] A written message. Also **milli.**

1929 K.S. PRICHARD *Coonardoo* (1961) 16 The milli-millis passed from Wytaliba to Nunniewarra. **1976** C.D. MILLS *Hobble Chains & Greenhide* 24 Long Jack turned up with a 'milli'—'Start bullock-muster as soon as you can' the letter read.

million. In the phr. **gone a million,** done for, finished; beyond redemption.

1913 *Bulletin* (Sydney) 25 Sept. 22/2 Inebriated.. loaded.. gone a million [etc.]. **1976** *Austral.* (Sydney) 1 Mar. 1/2 'Gough's gone. Gone a million. He's had it. I'd give him inside two weeks before we get his resignation..' a Federal executive member said.

mi-mi, var. MIA-MIA.

mimi /'mimi/. [a. Gunwinygu *mimi.*] A category of spirit people depicted in rock and bark paintings of western Arnhem Land: see quots. 1956 (2) and 1981. Freq. *attrib.*

1949 *Nat. Geographic Mag.* (Washington) Dec. 780 The art of the Mimi consists largely of single-line drawings, almost exclusively of human beings... One design of a man throwing a spear shows remarkable resemblance to figures painted by primitive bushmen of Africa and Stone Age men of Europe. **1956** C.P. MOUNTFORD *Rec. American-Austral. Sci. Exped. Arnhem Land* I. 112 The *Mimi* artists had a feeling for composition and movement which the X-ray artists lacked. Their main subject was man in action, running, fighting and throwing spears. All *Mimi* paintings were executed in red which, according to the myth, was made up of blood and red ochre. *Ibid.* 181 The general term of *Mimi* covers a large group of spirit people. Some.. live under similar conditions to the aborigines; that is, they have the same hunting implements, eat the same foods, and know the way to make fire... The cave-painting *Mimi,* whose specific name I did not find out, are supposed, by the aborigines, to have been responsible for the single-line rock paintings in the caves of the Arnhem Land plateau, adjacent to Oenpelli, particularly those of human beings. **1981** J. MULVANEY et al. *Aboriginal Aust.* 163 Mimi spirits are characterised by their elongated and slender form. They are trickster spirits, sometimes cannibalistic, which inhabit rocky places. Where they disappear into the rock walls of caves and shelters, they sometimes leave their shadows behind, which appear as paintings on the rock surfaces.

mimosa. Used *attrib.* in Special Comb. **mimosa bush,** the tangled spiny shrub or small tree *Acacia farnesiana* (fam. Mimosaceae) of n. Aust. and elsewhere in the tropics, having foliage and pods palatable to stock.

1959 H. LAMOND *Sheep Station* 87 A pair of top-knot pigeons had nested in the thorny tangle of a mimosa bush. **1981** J.A. BAINES *Austral. Plant Genera* 15 A[*cacia*] *farnesiana,* Mimosa Bush, unique in that it is native in five continents.

mina, minah, vart. MINER *n.*[1]

mindi /'mɪndaɪ/. *Obs.* Also **mindai.** [f. Wemba-wemba *mirnday.*] A fabulous serpent: see quots.

1844 H. MCCRAE *Georgiana's Jrnl.* 21 Aug. (1934) 129 The natives north of the Grampians talk about a species of Boa called *Mindi,* which lies in wait by waterholes, and, if an emu comes to drink, makes a meal of the complete bird! **1896** F.G. AFLALO *Sketch Nat. Hist. Aust.* 83 Nor did I give any account in the foregoing of the black-maned 'Bunyip' and 'Mindai' of Lake George and elsewhere. These fabulous creatures rank with the sea-serpent.

mindic /'mɪndɪk/, *a. Austral. pidgin.* [a. Nyungar *mindik.*] Ill; sick.

1845 E.J. EYRE *Jrnls. Exped. Central Aust.* II. 35 He would lie down, and roll and groan, and say he was 'mendyt' (ill). **1984** W.W. AMMON et al. *Working Lives* 180, I began to think he must be 'mindic', 'sick fella', or 'gone walkabout' even as far as Lake Way or Wiluna.

miner, *n.*[1] Also **mina, minah, mynah,** the latter two being increasingly reserved for *Acridotheras tristis.* [Spec. use of *miner,* var. of *mina* any of various birds of India and elsewhere.] **a.** Any of the several yellow-billed, Austral. honeyeaters of the genus *Manorina.* **b.** The introduced, starling-like *Acridotheras tristis,* native to India and s. China, an omnivorous, ground-feeding, predom. brown bird with yellow bill, eye patches, and legs, often confused with the *noisy miner* (see NOISY). Also *attrib.*

1832 J. BACKHOUSE *Narr. Visit Austral. Colonies* (1843) 30 Birds of various kinds.. abound.. the Wattle-bird, the Miner. **1832** J. HENDERSON *Observations Colonies N.S.W. & Van Diemen's Land* 41 The restless and noisy minas are disputing. **1914** *Bulletin* (Sydney) 13 Aug. 26/1 Here in Tassy, where it never droughts to any extent, a spell of dry weather will bring the.. minahs hustling to the troughs. **1973** V. SERVENTY *Desert Walkabout* 52 Miner is a name given to several rather similar honeyeaters. All have the brush tongue of the group and use this for sopping up pollen and nectar in flowers... The name miner is interesting and not to be confused with mynah, an introduced bird from Asia and related to the starlings. It too has the yellow beak and legs and I feel that this coloration led to the name for the Australian birds. **1975** D. MALOUF *Johno* 83 The glossy black mynah birds, picking about between the roots of the Moreton Bay figs.

miner, *n.*[2] In special collocations: **miner's complaint (disease, lung),** a name given to a pulmonary disease, such as silicosis, to which a miner is especially susceptible; **licence,** LICENCE 2 a.; *miner's right;* **right,** a document entitling the holder to search for and remove a mineral (orig. gold); land occupied under such an entitlement.

1896 J. HOLT *Virgin Gold* 48 *Phthisis,* or what is popularly termed The **Miner's Complaint.** **1909** W.G. SPENCE *Aust.'s Awakening* 27 A form of phthisis called 'miner's lung' overtook men after a few years, and led to a more or less lingering death. **1977** STIRLING & RICHARDSON *Memories of Aberfeldy* 8 Men died young with the dust from mining on their chests that they called Miners' Disease. **1862** H. BROWN *Vic. as I found It* 148 Every person carrying goods into the gold fields ought to have a **miners' license.** **1855** *Illustr. Sydney News* 14 Apr. 181/3 To exact a registration fee of £1 per annum per head, on miners, the production of which constitutes a '**Miner's Right**', without which, in case of dispute, no claim can lie. **1936** *Bulletin* (Sydney) 17 June 21/4 Near Laurel Hill, southern N.S.W. tablelands, I was occupying a miner's right.

mingil /'mɪŋɡəl/. Also **mingle, mingul.** [a. Western Desert language *miŋgurl* native tobacco (synonym of *ugiri,* see OKIRI).] PITURI.

MIN-MIN   **MISTLETOE**

1935 H. BASEDOW *Knights of Boomerang* 67 To 'dope' the emus .. they had employed only the leaves of a plant they called 'mingul' ('Duboisia hopwoodii'), the same as they themselves use for chewing. **1935** H.H. FINLAYSON *Red Centre* 85 The narcotic known variously as mingil or okiri .. a true tobacco .. which grows luxuriantly at the foot of the ranges. **1959** C. & E. CHAUVEL *Walkabout* 62 Bushes called Quondong and Yarran and Mingle.

min-min /ˈmɪn-mɪn/. [orig. unkn.; no evidence of an Aboriginal etymology.] A will-o'-the-wisp: see quot. 1956. Also **min-min light.**

1956 H. HUDSON *Flynn's Flying Doctors* 115 'We're catching up with the Min-Min.' 'What's that?' I asked. My mates explained that it is an Aboriginal name for a mysterious dancing light or will-o'-the-wisp that moves about on the plains. Some say it is caused by luminous gases or luminous insects, but the Aborigines believe it is an apparition of evil spirits, anyway nobody has ever caught up with a Min-Min. **1964** *N. Austral. Monthly* Aug. 11 That was where the mysterious debbil-debbil glow, known as 'The Min Min Light', used to do its tricks.

minnerichi /mɪnəˈrɪtʃi/. Also with much variety, as **minnaritchi, minni ritchi.** [Prob. f. an Aboriginal language.] The shrub or small tree *Acacia cyperophylla* (fam. Mimosaceae) of arid inland Aust., having typically thin, peeling curls of reddish bark; the wood of the tree; *red mulga,* see RED *a.* 1 *a.* Also *attrib.*

1929 K.S. PRICHARD *Coonardoo* (1961) 102 If the room got too hot and stuffy with the smoke of mulga, minnerichi, and tobacco, she opened a door. **1970** *Matilda* (Winton Tourist Promotion Assoc.) 40 Trunks of Minnaritchis smouldering Ruby-red upon the screes. **1983** *Austral. Plants* June 131 It .. resembles the rich red-brown crisped bark of some species of *Acacia* for which the term 'Minni Ritchi' bark is now widely used.

minor. *Australian National Football.* BEHIND 1. See also MAJOR.

1903 *Sporting News* (Launceston) 16 May 4/4 Brown from a mark on the magazine wing put up the first minor. **1981** L. MONEY *Footy Fan's Handbk.* 39 'Only a minor', a behind.

mint. Used *attrib.* in the names of plants: **mint bush** (formerly **mint tree**), any shrub of the large genus *Prostanthera* (fam. Lamiaceae) of Aust. incl. Tas., many of which are cultivated as ornamentals for their aromatic leaves and profusion of flowers in spring, incl. *P. lasianthos* (see *Christmas bush* (a) CHRISTMAS); **weed,** the naturalized annual plant *Salvia reflexa* (fam. Lamiaceae) of North America, having aromatic, greyish-green leaves, and being sometimes poisonous to stock.

1887 [**mint bush**] *Proc. Linnean Soc. N.S.W.* II. 9 *Prostanthera lasiantha* .. from the scent of its foliage is sometimes called the 'Mint Tree'. **1942** C. BARRETT *Austral. Wild Flower Bk.* 39 There are more than forty kinds of *Prostanthera,* all popularly known as mint bushes. **1933** *Bulletin* (Sydney) 5 Apr. 21/3 A plant that is rapidly spreading in Queensland is the wild mint weed (*Salvia lanceifolia*), the eating of which has resulted in the death by poisoning of hundreds of cattle on the Darling Downs.

Mintie. Also **mintie.** [The proprietary name of a peppermint flavoured sweet. The advertising slogan 'It's moments like these you need Minties' is now widely current as a catch-phrase (see quot. 1963).] Used allusively as an emblem of solace.

1926 *Austral. Official Jrnl. Patents* (Canberra) 879 *Minties* 42,344. Confectionery. James Stedman-Henderson's Sweets Ltd. **1932** *Listening Post* (Perth) May 16 Weak moments, when even minties will not put things to rights. **1963** F. HARDY *Legends Benson's Valley* 192 It's moments like these you need Minties!

mirr'n-yong, var. MURNONG.

mirrnyong /ˈmɜnjɒŋ/. Also **mirnyong.** [Prob. f. a Vic. Aboriginal language.] A mound of ashes, shells, and other debris, accumulated in a place used by Aborigines for cooking; a kitchen midden; *native oven,* see NATIVE *a.* 5. Also **mirrnyong heap.**

1878 R.B. SMYTH *Aborigines of Vic.* II. 232 As we travel through the country, we find but few indications of a previous race having occupied it. Two of these are, the marks cut on trees, which will soon disappear; and the 'native ovens', or mirnyongs. **1890** *Proc. Linnean Soc. N.S.W.* V. 259 Fragments of tomahawks and bone needles have been dug out of *Mirrn-yong* heaps on the sea-coast, covered wholly or partially by blown-sand.

mirror dory. [See quot. 1965.] The marine fish *Zenopsis nebulosus* of s. Aust. incl. Tas., and elsewhere.

1951 T.C. ROUGHLEY *Fish & Fisheries Aust.* 28 The mirror dory .. grows to a length of 14 inches. **1965** *Austral. Encycl.* III. 272 Another rarer but equally palatable species is the mirror dory .. of deep water, whose smooth, scaleless, and circular body is brilliantly silvered like a looking-glass.

miserable, *a.* [Br. dial. *miserable* miserly: see OED *a.* 6.] Parsimonious; stingy.

1903 J. FURPHY *Such is Life* 14 The more swellisher a man is, the more miserabler he is about a bite o' grass for a team, or a feed for a traveller. **1976** *Austral.* (Sydney) 20 May 6/5 A 'lousy dollar a day!' Could any government be more miserable?

mission. [Spec. use of *mission* missionary post.]

1. Used *attrib.* and in Comb. to denote an establishment administered by a religious community for the spiritual and material welfare of Aborigines, as **mission black, boy, native, station.**

1841 *Geelong Advertiser* 27 Dec. 2/4 Mr Hurst .. I believe, is now at the mission station. **1910** *Huon Times* (Franklin) 14 Sept. 4/3 Bowman was speared in the head by mission blacks. **1935** K.L. SMITH *Sky Pilot Arnhem Land* 38 There is a mission boy here .. waiting for the mail. **1937** *Bulletin* (Sydney) 8 Sept. 21/1 The mission natives excitedly prepared for David's wedding.

2. *transf.* Such an establishment or community administered by a government agency or by Aborigines themselves. Also *attrib.*

1948 A. MARSHALL *Ourselves writ Strange* 219 Milingimbi mission did not interfere in 'native trouble', the term used to distinguish disagreements and quarrels of a tribal nature, or those misdemeanours for which the native laws provided a punishment. It concerned itself with 'mission trouble', which covered thieving from the mission .. or the breaking of certain rules and regulations governing the permanent residents. **1984** *Aboriginal Hist.* VIII. 34 Three successive governmental moves institutionalised the Ngiyampa on 'Aboriginal stations', or, as the people themselves called them, 'missions'.

mistletoe. [Transf. use of *mistletoe* the parasitic plant *Viscum album.*]

1. Any of many partly-parasitic plants, usu. dependent from the branches of a tree, and chiefly of the fam. Loranthaceae and Viscaceae of mainland Aust. Also *attrib.*

1862 R. HENNING *Lett.* (1952) 52 We hung over the pictures some Australian mistletoe, a pretty parasite, with bright-yellow drooping branches—like willow in the autumn—which grows in the gum trees here. **1981** D. LEVITT *Plants & People* 21 The hardwood pegs came from .. the Mistletoe Tree (*Exocarpos latifolius*).

2. Special Comb. **mistletoe bird,** the small bird *Dicaeum hirundinaceum,* widespread in mainland Aust.

and also occurring on islands to the north, feeding chiefly on mistletoe berries.
1878 R.B. SMYTH *Aborigines of Vic.* II. 38 Mistletoe-bird, *Chirtgang.*

mistress. *Hist.* A woman to whom a convict is assigned; the wife of a man to whom a convict is assigned: see ASSIGN *v.*
1813 *Regulations respecting Assigned Convict Servants* 24 July (1821) 17 If any Female Convict Servant be ill-treated by her Master or Mistress, she is . . to prefer her Complaint to a Magistrate. 1856 J. BONWICK *Bushrangers* 9 No female convict was allowed to be in the streets after dusk without her master or mistress.

Mitchell. Abbrev. of MITCHELL GRASS.
1906 G.M. SMITH *Days of Cobb & Co.* 37 On the country there's a blight, There's not a blade of blue, or mitchell on the plain. 1976 C.D. MILLS *Hobble Chains & Greenhide* 136 That's Mitchell, good feed, 'specially when its hayed-off like it is now.

Mitchell grass. [f. the name of the explorer T.L. Mitchell (1792–1855): see MAJOR MITCHELL *v.*]
1. a. Any species of the genus *Astrebla* (fam. Poaceae), hardy, tussock-forming perennial grasses of arid and semi-arid Aust. providing valuable fodder; MITCHELL.
1880 J. BONWICK *Resources Qld.* 44 As to native grasses, one has forty varieties growing . . the perennial, fattening, drought-resisting *Mitchell.* 1983 *Ecos* xxxvi. 30/2 Even during drought, hardy Mitchell grass tussocks usually can be relied upon to provide some fodder for sheep and cattle.
b. Comb. **Mitchell grass(ed) country, plains.**
1890 W.F. BUCHANAN *Aust. to Rescue* 59 We emerged from the timber into an open Mitchell grassed plain. 1927 M.H. ELLIS *Long Lead* 76 It is a series of long, golden, Mitchell grass plains, more coarsely pastured than the Mitchell country of the South. 1969 A. GARVE *Boomerang* 56 It's not like the Mitchell grass country up on the Tableland. That's real bonza.
2. With distinguishing epithet, as **bull Mitchell (grass),** *Astrebla squarrosa;* **curly Mitchell grass,** *A. lappacea;* **wheat-eared Mitchell grass,** a Mitchell grass, esp. *curly Mitchell.*
[1937 **bull Mitchell**: *Publicist* (Sydney) xvii. 15/1 Mitchell grass has three species, Hoop (Astrebla elymoides), Curly (A. pectinata) and Bull (A. triticoides) of which the two latter are perhaps better than the first.] 1938 C.T. WHITE *Princ. Bot. Qld. Farmers* 200 *Astrebla squarrosa* is the Bull Mitchell. . . It yields a very large seed-head and correspondingly large grain. 1903 E. PALMER *Early Days N. Qld.* 236 **Curly Mitchell grass**; plant forming erect tufts one or two feet high, the leaves narrow and much curved. 1903 E. PALMER *Early Days N. Qld.* 236 'A. triticoides', **wheat-eared Mitchell grass** . . is taller and coarser than [common Mitchell grass], attaining a height of four or five feet.

mixed, *n.* [Abbrev. of *mixed train.*] A train which carries both passengers and freight.
1934 T. WOOD *Cobbers* 192 Goods trains and sheep trains and cattle trains run . . but they do not concern the passenger. He has to rely on the Mail and the Mixed. 1969 P. ADAM SMITH *Folklore Austral. Railwaymen* 39 My longest trip with the 'mixed' from Alice Springs took me two weeks. It was January 1938. This 'mixed' ran alternate weeks to the Ghan.

mixed, *ppl. a.* In special collocations: **mixed allotment** *W.A., hist.,* see quots.; **business,** see quots. 1904 and 1962; **farmer,** one engaged in more than one kind of farming; **herd** *obs.,* a herd of heterogeneous cattle; **lounge,** a public room in which both men and women may drink.

1841 H.S. CHAPMAN *New Settlement Australind* 126 To each of the lots of 100 rural acres are attached . . four town sections of one quarter of an acre each, which rural acres and town selections (called **mixed allotments**) are offered at £101 each. 1843 *Sketch W.A.* 36 A 'mixed allotment' . . consists of 100 rural acres and four quarter-acre sections in the town. 1903 *Sydney Morning Herald* 6 Nov. 8/6 **Mixed businesses.** I have a Special Selection of Genuine Concerns Suitable for 1 or 2 ladies. 1904 *Ibid.* 16 Jan. 11/8 Mixed bus., Groc., Conf., Haberd., Tob., Cigar., Drinks, chp. rent, gd. liv. 1962 HUNT & TOAL *Princ. Profitable Retailing* 29 Many hundreds of Australian retailers conduct what is called a 'mixed' business . . centred around a milk bar and/or delicatessen and/or sub-newsagency, with a bit of stationery and confectionery thrown in. 1909 R. KALESKI *Austral. Settler's Compl. Guide* 12 The . . **mixed farmer** selects too much. 1843 A. CASWALL *Hints from Jrnl.* 46 A person beginning should buy (besides cows and heifers) three and two-year-old steers and yearlings (called a **mixed herd**). 1969 *On Guard* (Broken Hill) Mar. 1 The work entails extending the **mixed lounge.**

mo. Abbrev. of 'moustache'.
1894 *Bulletin* (Sydney) 4 Aug. 2/2 He used to sport a ragged 'mo', my face was then quite bare. 1981 K. GARVEY *Rhymes of Ratbag* 54 His mo he paused to wipe.

mob, *n.* [Transf. use of *mob* a rabble, a riotous crowd: see OED(S *mob, sb.*[1]]
1. a. *Hist.* A (potentially hostile) party of Aborigines.
b. An Aboriginal community.
1828 *Hobart Town Courier* 13 Sept. 3 The tribe of natives who murdered the unfortunate man named Samuel Clarke, at the Lakes last week, consisted of what is generally known as the Big river mob and another united. 1984 *Aboriginal Hist.* VIII. 37 The old people . . when talking about the past, do not . . retain these names in their Ngiyampa form. Instead, they use names which link people with parts of the country by reference to pastoral stations. Thus the Nhiiyikiyalu are referred to as the 'Marfield mob'.
2. An assembled body of animals (orig. with some sense of the body being threatening); a flock or herd; a group.
1828 *Hobart Town Courier* 12 July 2 The wild mob [of cattle] . . not content with devouring our grass, walk off with every horn and hoof belonging to us. 1978 D. STUART *Wedgetail View* 56 Four or five thousand wethers in one mob.
3. A number, or class, of people sharing a distinctive characteristic, identity, etc.
1848 *Atlas* (Sydney) IV. 379/1 The Electors of Geelong and Portland have been disfranchised by a Melbourne mob. 1985 *Bulletin* (Sydney) 18 June 72/2 His crew was 'certainly not a mob of high rollers'.
4. A (large) quantity; a (considerable) number: see quot. 1934 (1). Now esp. in *pl.* and also as quasi-*adv.*: see quot. 1934 (2). See also **big mob** BIG 3 d.
1852 *Wanderer* (Adelaide) (1853) June 53, I took down a mob of quarts and pints, so strung together that for a time I could not disentangle them. 1853 H.B. JONES *Adventures in Aust.* 114 Wool from the interior is brought down, to be placed on board these steamers, and then shipped for Sydney, by schooners from Brisbane. 'There will be a great mob of things going down to-day,' said one to another, which meant, that there would be a heavy cargo in number. 1934 T. WOOD *Cobbers* 175 The supplanting of all collectives by one single upstart—mob. When two or three are gathered together, then you have a mob. Men, birds, animals, fish—all mobs. Mountains and mosquitoes—all mobs. 1934 A. RUSSELL *Tramp-Royal* 91 There'll be mobs of water on the track, we'll get mobs of beef at the runs, the stages'll be mobs shorter, an' there'll be mobs better camping grounds . . and of course we'll be able to take it mobs easier.

mob, v. [f. MOB n. 2.] trans. To muster (stock). Also as vbl. n.

1856 J. BONWICK *Bushrangers* 45 A long continued course of success in the art of mobbing, branding and slaughtering had made him less cautious. 1913 W.K. HARRIS *Outback in Aust.* 137 Many of my Missionary friends have shorn sheep with them, mobbed and drafted cattle and sheep.

mock. [Transf. use of *mock* a mocking: see OEDS *mock*, sb.[1] 1 b. and *mocker*, sb.[1] 1 d.] A jinx; a stop (to an activity, etc.). Also **mocker**. Esp. in the phr. **to put a mock** (or **mocker**) **on** or **the mock** (or **mockers**) **on**.

1911 E. DYSON *Benno & Push* 33 'All toms is 'erlike t' me,' he said .. 'but, all the same, it's up t' me t' put a mock on that tripester.' 1922 C. DREW *Rogues & Ruses* 115 I've got a mocker hung on me. 1938 X. HERBERT *Capricornia* 523 'He put the mocks on me,' roared Norman... 'What's he saying, dear?' 'He—he reckons I told the police on him.' 1983 *Bulletin* (Sydney) 2 Aug. 34/2 The double loss put the mockers on everything. Lake Macquarie is not the place to live without wheels.

mocker. Also **mokker**. [Of unknown origin.] Attire; dress.

[N.Z. 1947 P. NEWTON *Wayleggo* 147 Climbing out of bed and donning clammy, greasy shearing mocker.] 1953 S.J. BAKER *Aust. Speaks* 106 *Mocker*, clothes in general. 1984 *Austral. Short Stories* viii. 54 Just wear ordinary mokker.

Also **mockered up** *ppl. a.*, dressed up.

[1938 E. PARTRIDGE *Dict. Slang & Unconventional Eng.* (rev. ed.) 1014 *Mockered up*, dressed in one's best: low: late C. 19-20.] 1943 S.J. BAKER *Pop. Dict. Austral. Slang* (ed. 3) 5 *All laired up*, flashily dressed, dressed up to the nines, also 'All Mockered Up'.

model. *Obs.* Abbrev. of MODEL PRISON. Also *attrib*.

1845 *Cumberland Times* (Parramatta) 27 Dec. 4/3 Forgery is become of common occurrence in Melbourne—the last offender was one of the recently arrived 'model' pets. 1845 *Standard* (Melbourne) 8 Jan. 2/4 *The Pentonvillains*. Some idea may be formed of the worst of the model men, by the sample we have just seen.

model prison. *Hist.* A prison in which the inmates are kept in separate confinement and considerable emphasis is placed upon their reformation.

1846 *Moreton Bay Courier* 24 Oct. 3/1 These convicts are mostly from the model prison, where they have been taught useful trades, and will have the opportunity of making themselves useful men in the new convict colony. 1975 I. BRAND *'Separate Prison' Port Arthur* 7 Of all the buildings at Port Arthur, the one which raises most interest is the 'Model Prison', or, as it was officially known, the 'Separate Prison'.

mogo /ˈmoʊɡoʊ/. *Obs.* Also **maga, mago, mogin, moko**. [a. Dharuk *mugu*.] An Aboriginal stone hatchet.

[1793 W. TENCH *Compl. Acct. Settlement* 68 *Bùlla Mògo Parrabiùgò* (two hatchets tomorrow) I repeatedly cried.] 1798 D. COLLINS *Acct. Eng. Colony N.S.W.* I. 586 This is the Mogo, or stone hatchet. 1801 *HRA* (1915) 1st Ser. III. 178 From what I observed of trees cut down by the natives, which must have been with a much sharper edged tool than what their stone maga is. 1840 T.J. BUCKTON *W.A.* 99 The *mago* is a stone-hatchet, the handle of which is so light and elastic as greatly to aid the effect of the blow. 1848 *Bell's Life in Sydney* 5 Feb. 1/1 The silence of the woods is startling—you do not hear even the 'moko' of the aborigines, all of whom have been exterminated in the march of civilization, and in accordance with our national system of ethics. 1895 G. RANKEN *Windabyne* 275 He had not a weapon, not even the little stone 'Mogin' that stands for axe, and carpenter's chest in general, with the blacks.

moiety. *Anthropology.* [Spec. use of *moiety* one of two parts into which something is divided. Used earliest in reference to Aborigines: see OED(S 4.] One of two units into which an Aboriginal people is divided, esp. on the basis of lineal descent.

1882 *Jrnl. Anthrop. Inst.* (London) (1883) XII. 510 If we now .. separate the whole into its two constituent moieties, we shall have exactly a representation in each of the assumed forms of the divided commune, in which the two divisions are in fact totems. 1946 W.E. HARNEY *North of 23°* 46 Divisions, perhaps based on the mother's local group, and moieties are again divided into totems.

moit. Usu. in *pl.* [Br. dial. *moit* particle of wood, stick, etc., caught in the wool of a sheep: see OEDS.] See quot. 1899.

1899 A. SINCLAIR *Clip of Wool* 66 *Moits*, short pieces of stick and scrub, principally found in the neck wool. 1953 R.F. COOPER *Practical Woolclassing* 31 Moits (such as sticks, straw and vegetable matter).

moity, *a.* [Br. dial. *moity*: see prec.] Of wool: containing particles of wood or other foreign substances.

1878 'R. BOLDREWOOD' *Ups & Downs* 83 The 'heavy and moity' parcels were not touched by the cautious operators at any price. 1928 C.E. COWLEY *Classing Clip* 36 The wool grown on the scragg .. is .. often 'moity', that is, containing pieces of vegetable matter, sticks, pieces of thistles, etc.

mokani /məˈkani/. *Obs.* [a. Yaralde *mogani*.] See quot. 1846.

1846 H.E.A. MEYER *Manners & Customs Aborigines Encounter Bay* 8 The mokani is a black stone, shaped something like the head of an axe, fixed between two sticks bound together, which serve for a handle. The sharp side of the stone is used to enchant males, the other side females. 1879 *Native Tribes S.A.* 195 They fancy that they can charm or enchant by means of two instruments, one called plongge, the other mokani.

moke. [Transf. use of *moke* a donkey.] A horse; sometimes an inferior horse.

1863 *Frank Gardiner, or Bushranging in 1863* 9, I didn't know what had become of the moke. 1976 C.D. MILLS *Hobble Chains & Greenhide* 29 'How's my horse?' .. 'Your old moke's alright,' laughed the Boss.

mokker, var. MOCKER.

moko, var. MOGO.

molared, var. MOLO.

mole, n.[1] *Obs.* [Transf. use of *mole* a small, burrowing mammal.] PLATYPUS.

1825 B. FIELD *Geogr. Mem. N.S.W.* 462 This is New Holland .. where the mole (ornithorhynchus paradoxus) lays eggs, and has a duck's bill. 1837 *Lit. News* (Sydney) 21 Oct. 106 The young moles .. were 'cobbong fat',and in plump condition, whilst the old one was miserably thin.

mole, n.[2] [Abbrev. of MOLESKIN.]

a. Used *attrib.* in Comb. **mole pants, trousers.**

1860 *Northern Star* (Kapunka) 26 May 1/3 Men's Mole Trousers at 4s. 6d. 1896 W.H. WILLSHIRE *Land of Dawning* 101 Here you get a rough book, by a rough author, written in the garb of a real bushman, viz., mole pants and a cotton shirt.

b. *pl.* Moleskin trousers, see MOLESKIN.

1879 *Kelly Gang* 125 His dress .. consisted of .. an ordinary flannel singlet, covered by an olive-green Crimean shirt; trousers of a kind known in the slop-shops as 'coloured moles'. **1953** A. MARSHALL *Aust.* (1981) 2 Those pants were white moles but they're covered with mud.

mole, *n.*[3] [Prob. var. of *moll* girl or woman.] A girl or woman: see esp. quot. 1983.

1965 W. DICK *Bunch of Ratbags* 270 Just because you've got yourself some rich bloke's mole of a bloody daughter, don't come telling me and the boys what to bloody do. **1983** *Sun-Herald* (Sydney) 15 May 51/2 'If a girl does it all the time then she's a mate. Moles are scum, worse than dirt.'.. 'I know one girl who goes out with someone for one night and hops into bed with them—I'd call her a mole.'

moleskin. [Spec. use of *moleskin* a strong, cotton cloth: see OED(S 2 and 4. As *moleskin trousers* recorded earliest in Aust.]

1. Used *attrib.* in Special Comb. **moleskin trousers,** trousers made of moleskin, esp. as regarded as part of the customary dress of a rural worker or gold-miner.

1839 *Tasmanian* (Hobart) 15 Feb. 51/1 Moleskin and cord trowsers. **1894** J.K. ARTHUR *Kangaroo & Kauri* 12 Moleskin trousers are much patronized by the colonists who have manual labour or much riding to do.

2. Usu. in *pl.* Abbrev. of *moleskin trousers.* Also *attrib.* and *fig.*

1850 *Monthly Almanac* (Adelaide) 10 The body of the moleskins is napless—the soles of the Bluchers become attenuated—the cabbage-tree hat has acquired a suitable greasiness in the region of the ribbon. **1978** F. HOWARD *Moleskin Gentry* 2 In a country that still thought in English terms and judged by English values, they were the gentry— the moleskin gentry.

Hence **moleskinned** *ppl. a.,* clad in moleskin trousers.

1885 N.W. SWAN *Couple of Cups Ago* 122 The public, moleskinned and pipeclayed, looked on.

molled, var. MOLO.

molly. In the phr. **molly the monk,** rhyming slang for 'drunk'.

1966 *Kings Cross Whisper* (Sydney) xxvi. 6/1 Now the basic type of booze.. and that which induces the most popular result (gets you molly the monk) is—wait for it— beer. **1973** *Ibid.* cliv. 2/4 Ophelia was more than a little bit Molly the Monk after Parkinson had been loosening her up a bit with three bottles of Quelltaler hock.

molly-dook. Also **molly-dooker, molly-duke.** [Prob. f. *molly* an effeminate man, a milksop (see OED *sb.*[1] 2) + *dook,* var. *duke* hand.] A left-handed person. Also *attrib.,* and **molly-hander.**

[**1926** 'J. DOONE' *Timely Tips New Australs.,* Mauldy, left handed.] **1934** *Bulletin* (Sydney) 21 Mar. 11/3 Hence the trade is taboo to the molly-hander. **1941** S.J. BAKER *Pop. Dict. Austral. Slang* 47 Mollydooker, a left-handed person. Whence, *mollydook* (adj.), left-handed. **1943** *Signals* (Melbourne) Christmas 7 Who is the molly duke Lieut. who forgot to endorse her cheque?

Hence **molly-dooked.** *a.,* left-handed.

1969 *Southerly* xxix. 8 It could be being written by someone else with the same absurdly decorous aim, someone molly-duked, atheist, over-educated.

molo /'moʊloʊ/, *a.* Also **molared, molled, mowlow.** [Of unknown origin, but see OED *molly, sb.*[2] 2., a meeting of ship-captains: the quots. (1874 and 1885) suggest this might also be a drinking party.] Inebriated.

1906 *Truth* (Sydney) 28 Oct. 9/4 She herself told me she was half-molled. What did you understand her to mean by that? That she was half-drunk. **1916** *Rising Sun: On Board 'Themistocles'* 26 Aug. (Suppl.), When you're 'molo' in a crowd. **1926** M. FORREST *Hibiscus Heart* 146 Most people in the township considered him not much more than a fool, who was always 'half molared'. **1978** H.C. BAKER *I was Listening* 56 He got mowlow at a dance one night.

moloch. [See quot. 1898.] *Mountain devil* (a), see MOUNTAIN. Also **moloch lizard.**

1845 J.E. GRAY *Catal. Specimens Lizards Brit. Museum* 263 The Moloch, *Moloch horridus,* Gray. **1855** J. BONWICK *Geogr. Aust. & N.Z.* (ed. 3) 200 The Moloch lizard has horns on its head and spines on its back. **1898** E.E. MORRIS *Austral Eng.* 300 Moloch.. an Australian lizard.. the adjective (Lat. *horridus,* bristling) seems to have suggested the noun, the name probably recalling Milton's line ('Paradise Lost', I. 392)—'First Moloch, horrid king, besmeared with blood'.

monaych /'mɒnaɪtʃ/. Also **monarch.** [a. Nyungar *manaj* white cockatoo; *transf.* a police officer.] A police officer; the police.

1961 N. GARE *Fringe Dwellers* 35 Skippy gets off. An ya know the first thing e says ta them monarch? E turns round on em an yelps, 'An now ya can just gimme back that bottle.' **1981** A. WELLER *Day of Dog* 2 'Nuh, gotta go. See Mum.' 'Yeah, well, look out for the monaych, budda.' '.. 'Ard luck if 'e goes back, first day out.'

mong /mʌŋ/. [Abbrev. of *mongrel* a dog of mixed breed.]

1. A dog (not necessarily of mixed breed).

1903 *Sporting News* (Launceston) 2 May 1/3 Trotting like 'mongs' in the two mile events. **1980** J. WRIGHT *Big Hearts & Gold Dust* 127 Gor'on, ya bloody mong. Git ta buggery. Ya probably lousy with fleas.

2. *transf.* Applied to a person: see MONGREL. Also *attrib.*

1926 *Aussie* (Sydney) Jan. 36/3 'E never gave anybody er chance.. the dirty mong. **1968** W.N. SCOTT *Some People* 120 The little bloke said, 'Mong jew!!'

Mongolian. *Obs.* [Transf. use of *Mongolian* a native of Mongolia.] A Chinese immigrant to Australia; Chinese immigrants to Australia in general.

1859 *Colonial Mining Jrnl.* Feb. 94/1 The mongolian.. follows the caucasian as the scavenger succeeds civilization. **1913** J.B. CASTIEAU *Reminisc. Detective-Inspector Christie* 19 He saw a Chinaman, the first he had ever seen. Curiosity caused him to regard the Mongolian attentively.

mongrel. [Survival of Br. use: see OED *sb.* 1 b.] Applied to a person: a term of contempt or abuse (cf. 'cur'). Also *attrib.,* and *transf.*

1919 A. WRIGHT *Game of Chance* 20 A mongrel she'd known before me.. put a tale over on her. **1956** J.E. MACDONNELL *Commander Brady* 248 The ladies of this here mongrel joint are puttin' on a gut-rub for Navy gents ternight.

monkey. [Transf. and fig. use of *monkey.*]

1. See MONKEY BEAR.

2. A sheep. Also *attrib.*

1876 J.A. EDWARDS *Gilbert Gogger* 109, I don't think that calling a sheep, a jumbuck or a monkey.. is talking pure English. **1905** A.B. PATERSON *Old Bush Songs* 126 You've only to sport your dover and knock a monkey over— There's cheap mutton for the Wallaby Brigade. **1921** *Bulletin* (Sydney) 3 Feb. 22/2 To corn mutton.. soak a couple of thick cornsacks in water and lay them out... Then kill and dress.. 'monkey' and divide it longitudinally. **1944** *Ibid.* 30 Aug. 13/4 This superb drover worked his epic way till he reached a mail-change on the Ayrshire Downs road, whence he collected a few monkey conductors suffering a holiday.

3. *Mining.* A vertical shaft: see quots. 1869 and 1968. Also **monkey shaft.**

1869 R.B. Smyth *Gold Field & Minerals Districts* 616 *Monkey-shaft* is a shaft rising from a lower to a higher level (as a rule perpendicularly) and differs from a blind-shaft only in that the latter is sunk from a higher to a lower level. **1968** M.T. Clark *Spark of Opal* (1973) 133 Sometimes a miner put down an exploratory hole, known as a 'monkey', to the next level through the floor of the drive instead of working back from the main shaft, and sometimes it rewarded him.

4. A looped strap attached to a saddle pommel and used by a (novice) rider as an aid to mounting and when riding a spirited horse. Also **monkey strap**.

1911 E.S. Sorenson *Life in Austral. Backblocks* 207 Novices and others who lack proficiency use .. a monkey (a strap looped between the D's for the right hand to grip). **1915** V. Palmer *World of Men* (1962) 35 He always was a grip rider... No broncho-straps, or monkey-straps or top rails for him.

5. Special Comb. **monkey dodger,** one who musters sheep; **dodging** *vbl. n.*, the mustering of sheep.

1912 R.S. Tait *Scotty Mac* 138 Head **monkey dodger** to .. Hungry Harris. **1900** *Western Champion* (Barcaldine) 27 Nov. 9/1 By jove, this game beats **monkey dodging** all to pieces.

monkey bear. Koala 1. Also **monkey**.

1836 *Saturday Mag.* (London) 31 Dec. 249 They are called by some monkeys, by others bears, but they by no means answer to either species. **1980** P. Pepper *You are what you make Yourself* 23 They made the toe-holds to go up after possums and monkey bears (koala).

monotreme. [f. Gr. μονο-, comb. form of μόνος sole + τρῆμη, var. of τρῆμα hole, referring to the single opening for reproductive and excretory organs.] Any of the egg-laying mammals of the order Monotremata, occurring only in Aust., incl. Tas., and New Guinea. See also Echidna, Platypus. Also *attrib.*

1835 W. Kirby *On Power Wisdom & Goodness of God* II. 483 This Sub-class is divided into two Orders, *Monotremes*, and *Marsupians*. **1943** C. Barrett *Austral. Animal Bk.* 25 A motherless monotreme bairn, discovered in the scrub near Cranbourne, Victoria, was brought .. by the finder, who was puzzled by the little naked creature not unlike an animated rubber toy of nondescript shape.

monster, *v. trans.* To attack (a person, policy, etc.); to put pressure on.

1967 *Kings Cross Whisper* (Sydney) xxxvi. 4/2 *Monster*, make unwelcome passes at a female. **1983** *Sydney Morning Herald* 5 Mar. 13/6 Ian Macphee was in trouble for saying something good about the prices and incomes policy while the Prime Minister was monstering it, although at times Fraser seemed to have trouble deciding whether it was a monster or a mouse.

monte. Also **monty**. [Transf. use of U.S. *monte* a game of chance played with cards.]

1. *Obs.* A racecourse tipster. Also **monte man**.

1887 K. Mackay *Stirrup Jingles* 6 In the Leger the 'Monties' are shouting. **1909** A. Wright *Rogue's Luck* 2 The monte man (with his following of buttoners) still works hard to make an honest crust, but the breed of 'mugs' on whom he lives .. has lessened.

2. A certainty.

1894 *Worker* (Sydney) 18 Aug. 2/5 Chaps, I've got a vote for Hughie—but it ain't no monte yet. **1976** Lloyd & Clark *Kerr's King Hit* 7 Kerr was regarded as a 'monte' for school captain but he was pipped at the post.

monterry, montry, vart. Muntry.

mook-mook owl /'mʊk-mʊk aʊl/. [a. many N.T. Aboriginal languages *mug mug*.] **a.** An owl, perh. *barking owl* (see Barking). **b.** *transf.* See quot. 1978 (1). Also **mook-mook, muk-muk**.

1946 W.E. Harney *North of 23°* 266 The mook mook owl gives its cry. **1961** —— *Grief, Gaiety & Aborigines* 21 We were lulled to sleep by the glass-blower's tunes that blended with a muk-muk's call in the still night's air. **1978** R.D. Eagleson *Urban Aboriginal Eng.* 61 *Muk-muk*, spirit, ghost. **1978** J. & P. Read *View of Past* (typescript) 254 Why they rush, those bullocks .. ? Yeah, they gettem fright. Mook-mook (owl) dingo.

mooley apple. /'muli æpəl/. [a. Malyangaba *muli* + *apple*.] *Emu apple* (a), see Emu *n.*[1] 3. Also **mooley plum**.

1888 *Proc. Linnean Soc. N.S.W.* III. 534 'Emu apple.' 'Mooley apple' is a western New South Wales name. **1933** C.W. Peck *Austral. Legends* (ed. 2) 48 The Owenia acidula or 'mooley plums' quickly grew.

Moomba. /'mumbə/. [See quot. 1981.] A carnival, held annually in Melbourne from 1955. Also *attrib.*

1955 *Herald* (Melbourne) 12 Mar. 1/1 All was set for the Governor, Sir Dallas Brooks, to open the Moomba officially. **1981** B.J. Blake *Austral. Aboriginal Lang.* 84 Undoubtedly the most unfortunate choice of a proper name from Aboriginal sources was made in Melbourne when the city fathers chose to name the city's annual festival 'Moomba'. The name is supposed to mean 'Let's get together and have fun', though one wonders how anyone could be naive enough to believe that all this can be expressed in two syllables. In fact 'moom' (*mum*) means 'buttocks' or 'anus' in various Victorian languages and '-ba' is a suffix that can mean 'at', 'in' or 'on'. Presumably someone has tried to render the phrase 'up your bum' in the vernacular. **1985** *Age* (Melbourne) 4 Mar. 1/2 Moomba antics. Melbourne's annual festival has begun.

moon, *v. trans.* To hunt (a possum) on a moonlit night: see quot. 1893. Freq. as *vbl. n.*

1886 D.M. Gane *N.S.W. & Vic.* 177 It is necessary to 'moon them', as the bushmen say, that is, to get them in a line with the moon. **1893** E.D. Cleland *White Kangaroos* 66 A 'possum was amongst the branches somewhere but though all three peered into them nothing could be seen. Then they had to go through the process known as 'mooning'. Walking backwards from the tree, each one tried to get the various limbs and branches between him and the moon, and then follow them out to the uttermost bunch of leaves where the 'possum might be feeding.

moonlight, *v. trans.* To muster (wild cattle) by night: see quot. 1887. Chiefly as *vbl. n.*

1880 J.B. Stevenson *Seven Yrs. Austral. Bush* 128 Moonlighting on frosty nights is severe work, particularly when there are not many cattle about. We often worked all through a long winter's night, coaching round scrub after scrub, without coming across a single mob. **1887** W.S.S. Tyrwhitt *New Chum in Qld. Bush* 151 Wild cattle .. are commonly called 'scrubbers' because they live in the larger scrubs... There is a way of catching them .. called 'moonlighting'... A party of men go out at night, or more often in the small hours of the morning, with a mob of quiet cattle, and take their places on the edge of a scrub so as to intercept the scrubbers as they return from watering and feeding outside. They are then driven in amongst the quiet ones, and if possible the whole mob is taken down to a yard or put in a paddock.

moonlighter.

1. [f. prec.] One who musters wild cattle by night.

1886 F. Cowan *Aust.* 32 The manor-born Moonlighter: austral Guacho [sic]: fearless, skillful, breakneck rider: in the bush and in the open: over stones and through marshes. **1892** 'R. Boldrewood' *Nevermore* 46 Have you had a ride with the moonlighters lately?

2. [Infl. by U.S. *moonshiner* one who makes 'moonshine' or illicitly distilled liquor.] One who distils liquor illicitly.

1913 J.B. CASTIEAU *Reminisc. Detective-Inspector Christie* 113 Public-housekeepers of a certain class were always ready customers of the 'moonlighters', as they could purchase spirit for about 5s. per gallon. **1926** *Bulletin* (Sydney) 7 Jan. 24/2 The bush has made a good many powerful beverages, but the most powerful of the lot was potato spirit. The moonlighter cut up the spuds, skins and all.

3. [See quot. 1974.] The marine fish *Vinculum sexfasciatum*, having a silver head and body with six vertical black bands, occurring near rocky reefs of s. Aust. incl. Tas.

1948 W. HATFIELD *Barrier Reef Days* 20 Bream and 'moonlighters' and 'fingermarks' that took your bait. **1974** T.D. SCOTT et al. *Marine & Freshwater Fishes S.A.* 221 It is said that it takes the hook . . better at night, and the species is often called the Moonlighter by fishermen. The flesh is of a fine texture and well flavoured.

moorhen. [Transf. use of *moorhen* the bird *Gallinula chloropus*.] Any of several waterbirds of the genus *Gallinula*, incl. *G. ventralis* (see *native hen* (a), NATIVE *a.* 6 b.), and the predom. black *G. tenebrosa* of e. and s.w. Aust., New Guinea, and Indonesia.

1820 C. JEFFREYS *Van Dieman's Land* 35 This lake abounds with . . moor-hens. **1860** G. BENNETT *Gatherings of Naturalist* 169 The Black-tailed Tribonyx, or Moor Hen of the colonists . . when strutting along the bank of a river, has a grotesque appearance, with the tail quite erect like that of a domestic fowl.

moosh, var. MUSH.

mopoke /ˈmoʊpoʊk/, *n.* [Imitative of the bird's call, the forms *mope-hawk* and *morepork* being interpretative.]

1. a. BOOBOOK. **b.** TAWNY FROGMOUTH (to which the call has often been erroneously attributed). **c.** Any of several other nocturnal birds. Also **mope-hawk, morepork.**

1825 J.H. WEDGE *Diaries* 31 Aug. (1962) 19 They killed one [possum]—and a More Pork. **1852** W.H. HALL *Practical Experience* (ed. 2) 22 The low, melancholy but pleasing cry of the Mope-hawk, broke the unearthly silence. **1896** B. SPENCER *Rep. Horn Sci. Exped. Central Aust.* I. 124 In the gum trees the 'mopokes' (*Ninox boobook*) were calling to one another. **1900** *Bulletin* (Sydney) 28 July 14/2 Recently saw two magpies trying to drive a mopoke (genuine caprimulgus—not the Boobook owl) out of the fork of a tree near their nest.

2. The call of the mopoke.

1827 J. BISCHOFF *Sketch Hist. Van Diemen's Land* 13 Mar. (1832) 177 The owl's doleful cry of 'more pork', and the screaming of the opossum, were the only disturbances we experienced during the night. **1968** D. FLEAY *Nightwatchmen* 4 The sound itself was reminiscent of the 'mopoke' of the Boobook Owl.

3. *fig.* A tedious or stupid person. Also *attrib.*

1845 R. HOWITT *Impressions Aust. Felix* 233 'A more-pork kind of fellow', is a man of cut-and-dry phrases; a person remarkable for nothing new in common conversation. This, by some, is thought very expressive; the more-pork being a kind of Australian owl, notorious for its wearying nightly iteration, 'More pork, more pork'. **1930** 'BRENT OF BIN BIN' *Ten Creeks Run* (1952) 182 He must know it now or else he's a bigger mopoke than ole Teddy O'Mara.

mopoke /ˈmoʊpoʊk/, *v.* [f. prec.] *intr.* **a.** Of a mopoke: to call. **b.** To imitate the call of a mopoke.

1915 *Bulletin* (Sydney) 4 Mar. 14/4 The ardent Billjim . . imitates the call of the mopoke to announce that he has arrived. . . I mopoked under a big peach tree. **1968** D. FLEAY *Nightwatchmen* 87 Trees from which the Boobook Owl has 'mopoked' the prior night.

moral. [Survival of Br slang *moral*, abbrev. of *moral certainty*. Now chiefly Austral.: see OED(S *sb.* 9.] A certainty.

1878 *Austral. Town & Country Jrnl.* (Sydney) 30 Mar. 602/2 It was understood that he was entered on the chance of the two cracks destroying each others chances, in one of the numerous accidents to which such races are liable, in which case Bargo would be a 'moral'. **1986** *Canberra Times* 7 May 25/5 The senior puisne judge (who is an absolute moral for the Chief Justiceship come February next year) . . is almost certainly among the ranks of the deeply concerned.

morepork: see MOPOKE *n.*

Moreton Bay. [The name of the bay at the mouth of the Brisbane River, Qld., given by James Cook as *Morton*, after James Douglas (1702–1768), 14th Earl of Morton and member of the Royal Society, and subsequently spelt *Moreton*. The name was applied to the penal settlement on the bay (1824–1839) and until 1859, when separation from N.S.W. was effected, to the whole of Queensland.] Used *attrib.* in the names of flora and fauna: **Moreton Bay ash,** the tree of Qld., n. N.S.W., and New Guinea *Eucalyptus tesselaris* (fam. Myrtaceae); the wood of the tree; CARBEEN; also *attrib.*; **bug,** any of several marine crustaceans valued for their edible tail flesh, esp. *Thenus orientalis* of n. Aust.; see also SHOVEL-NOSED LOBSTER; **chestnut,** *black bean* (a), see BLACK *a.*² 1 a.; **fig, (a)** any of several large trees of the genus *Ficus* (fam. Moraceae), esp. the massive, spreading *F. macrophylla* of near-coastal n. N.S.W. and s. Qld., widely planted as an ornamental and shade tree; also **Moreton Bay fig-tree** and *ellipt.* as **Moreton Bay; (b)** rhyming slang for FIZGIG, an informer; also *ellipt.*; **oyster,** *Sydney rock*, see SYDNEY 2; **pine,** HOOP PINE; **rosella,** the parrot of Qld., and n. N.S.W. *Platycercus adscitus*, having a blue body, and mottled black and yellow back.

1844 L. LEICHHARDT *Jrnl. Overland Exped. Aust.* 15 Dec. (1847) 75 The **Moreton Bay ash** (a species of Eucalyptus)—which I had met with, throughout the Moreton Bay district, from the sea coast of the Nynga Nynga to Darling Downs—was here also very plentiful. **1978** R.J. BRITTEN *Around Cassowary Rock* 10 The few uprights were made of skinny little Moreton Bay ash saplings that *were* all sap. **1970** HEALY & YALDWYN *Austral. Crustaceans* 58 The 'Balmain bug' of New South Wales and the similar-looking '**Moreton Bay bug**', *Thenus orientalis*, of Queensland and northern Australia, are both taken with prawn trawls. **1836** J. BACKHOUSE *Extracts from Lett.* (1838) iii. 57 Some of the pods of the **Moreton Bay chesnut** [sic], which is a fine tree, with leaves like those of the European walnuts, are ten inches long and eight round. **(a) 1849** J. PATTISON *N.S.W.* 95 The oak, the elm, and those of the mother country, are seen growing along side the **Moreton Bay fig**. **1953** C. WILLS *Austral. Passport* 15 Moreton Bay fig trees, extraordinary trees, vast and spreading as old oaks, with grey bark like elephant-hide, dark, glossy leaves, and round fruit of the size of chestnuts that ripened to a purplish red and dropped in sticky masses . . with a sweet, lazy smell. **1967** D. HEWETT *This Old Man* (1976) 23 Kisses in Moore Park under the Moreton Bays after the pitchers on Saturdee nights. **(b) 1953** S.J. BAKER *Aust. Speaks* 134 **Moreton Bay (fig)**, any witness who lays an information, anyone who unwarrantably attends to or meddles in the affairs of others; by rhyme of *gig* . . which may be a contraction of *fiz-gig*, an informer. **1975** *Bulletin* (Sydney) 26 Apr. 46/2 There were Moretons nearby (Moreton Bay Figs; gigs, meaning busybodies). **1984** *Ibid.* 19 June 69/1 Fifty percent of the Drug Squad's arrests are based on information received and woebetide a user, supplier or anyone else who becomes a dog, a gig or, as the police term it, a Moreton Bay. **1870** *Sydney Morning Herald* 6 July 3/3 **Moreton Bay oyster** . . could be made to yield an annual local and export value second to none. **1826** J. ATKINSON *Acct. Agric.*

& *Grazing N.S.W.* 13 **Moreton Bay Pine**—Found in great abundance at Moreton Bay. [**1841 Moreton Bay rosella:** J. GOULD *Birds of Aust.* (1848) V. Pl. 26, *Platycercus palliceps* . . Moreton Bay Rose-hill, Colonists of New South Wales.] **1845** L. LEICHHARDT *Jrnl. Overland Exped. Aust.* 30 Oct. (1847) 460, I observed a Platycercus, of the size of the Moreton Bay Rosella.

morning glory. See quots. Also **morning glory cloud.**

1934 *Bulletin* (Sydney) 12 Sept. 20/4 A 'morning glory' is a frequent occurrence in the Gulf Country . . . A low bank of clouds lined the horizon early in the morning, and gathered speed at an alarming rate. . . Soon the sky was completely overcast. A few drops of rain fell; then we had a delightful breeze which lasted for a couple of minutes. Away went the dark cloud as quickly as it had come, and the sun continued to blaze as mercilessly as ever. **1984** *Bulletin* (Sydney) 13 Nov. 75/2 Another phenomenon, the solitary wave, is much more common and is beginning to worry meteorologists and pilots. The waves are induced by the flow of air over the Australian land mass. They can be up to 500 km. long . . . Sometimes the wave is visible because it generates cloud. The classical instance is the 'morning glory' cloud of the Queensland and Northern Territory Gulf Country . . a daily occurrence at this time of year.

morning tea. A mid-morning break; the refreshment taken during that break. See also SMOKO 1 a. Also *attrib.*

1916 V.G. DWYER *Conquering Hal* 139 She had stayed to pull Sandra's hatpins out, and drink morning tea with her. **1942** *Bulletin* (Sydney) 19 Aug. 12/3 At the morning-tea roll up of the Works and Parks gang, tea was scarce and coffee not plentiful. **1963** A. LUBBOCK *Austral. Roundabout* 6 One of the first things to get straight on arrival in Australia is the meals called 'tea'. There are three; and they are all as indispensable as breakfast or dinner. First you have 'morning tea', which consists of cups of tea and biscuits, or savouries, at eleven o'clock.

morrel /'mɒrəl, məˈrɛl/. Also **morrell.** [a. Nyungar *murril.*] Any of several trees of the genus *Eucalyptus* (fam. Myrtaceae) of s.w. Aust., esp. the rough-barked trees *E. longicornis*, yielding a strong, durable, reddish wood, and *E. melanoxylon*, yielding a very hard, strong, blackish wood; the wood of these trees. Also *attrib.*

1837 G.F. MOORE *Evidences Inland Sea* 48 We passed another variety of *Eucalyptus*—a tall, straight stem and scaly bark, called 'Morrail'. **1897** L. LINDLEY-COWEN *W. Austral. Settler's Guide* 47 The morrell gum is . . commonly met with on the eastern agricultural lands, and is indicative of rich country. **1973** G.M. CHIPPENDALE *Eucalypts W. Austral. Goldfields* 99 The name 'morrel' is an aboriginal name applied to several species.

morrison. [See quot. 1981.] Any of several shrubs bearing decorative flowers of the genus *Verticordia* (fam. Myrtaceae), chiefly of W.A. Also *attrib.*

1929 I.A. SCOULER *Dowerin Story* 7 The numerous varieties of morrison, and the many shades of leschenaultia are perhaps the more conspicuous. **1935** T. RAYMENT *Cluster of Bees* 191 The larvae . . feast on the sweet blossoms of the tea-tree . . and, in Western Australia, on the Morrison flower, *Verticordia nitens.* **1981** J.A. BAINES *Austral. Plant Genera* 390 *V* [*erticordia*] *nitens*, Morrison Feather-flower, Yellow Morrison (after Alexander Morrison, 1849–1913, Govt. botanist W.A. 1897–1906; few botanists have been commemorated in this way as a vernacular name).

morwong /'mɔːwɒŋ, 'məʊwɒŋ/. [Prob. f. a N.S.W. Aboriginal language.] Any of several edible marine fish of the fam. Cheilodactylidae, esp. *Nemadactylus douglasii* of s. Aust. and N.Z., having a distinctive elongated ray of the pectoral fin, and the JACKASS-FISH; MOWIE.

1871 *Industr. Progress N.S.W.* 791 The . . morwong . . may be taken by the line in almost unlimited quantities. **1978** J. ROWE *Warlords* 206 The red bream, snapper and morwong . . were being hauled up from the reef twenty metres below.

moscow, *v.* [Altered form of Br. slang *moskeneer* to pawn an article for more than it is worth.] *trans.* To pawn (an article).

1910 STEPHENS & O'BRIEN *Materials Austrazealand Slang Dict.* 100 *Moscow*, the pawnshop: to moscow anything is to pawn it. **1917** C. DREW *Reminisc. D. Gilbert* 50 Do you know where a man can 'moscow' a couple of snakes?

moscow, *n.* [f. prec.] A pawnshop. Also **gone to Moscow, in Moscow,** in pawn.

1941 S.J. BAKER *Pop. Dict. Austral. Slang* 47 *Moscow*, a pawnshop. **1953** 'CADDIE' *Caddie* 217 Me clobber's already in Moscow, an' so is me tan shoes. . . There don't seem nuthin' a man can raise a deaner on. **1955** N. PULLIAM *I traveled Lonely Land* 377 *Gone to Moscow*, pawned.

mosh. [Of unknown origin.] An illegal gambling game. Also **mosh game** and *attrib.*

1925 A. WRIGHT *Boy from Bullarah* 14 Sporting clubs, gambling 'schools', mosh, faro, two-up. **1934** F.E. BAUME *Burnt Sugar* 176 All nationalities met at Parks' mosh shop and two-up school. *Ibid.* 194 Throwing the dice became boring to everyone. The mosh game at Speranthos' place was without a minyon.

mosquito fleet. *Australian National Football.* [Transf. use of *mosquito fleet* a fleet of small light vessels adapted for rapid manoeuvring.]

1. *Hist.* See quot. 1931.

1931 J.F. MCHALE et al. *Austral. Game of Football* 66 The Essendon team of 1922–1926 contained a number of very fast, skilful little players, known as the 'mosquito fleet', and by their tactics they worked havoc among the opposing back players. **1963** *Footy Fan* (Melbourne) I. xii. 18 They developed what has come to be known as the famous 'mosquito' fleet—a naval term of First War origin. And I firmly believe that Essendon's 'mosquito' fleet was the means of whipping up the tempo of our game.

2. *transf.* See quot. 1968.

1968 EAGLESON & MCKIE *Terminol. Austral. Nat. Football* ii. 24 *Mosquito fleet*, small players in a team, especially if the team exploits the fleetness of its small men in attack. **1983** HIBBERD & HUTCHINSON *Barracker's Bible* 132 *Mosquito fleet*, . . a batch of shortish players, sawn-offs, usually rovers, who dominate or distinguish a team.

mosquito peg. One of two or more stakes used to support a mosquito net over a person sleeping in the open.

1908 MRS A. GUNN *We of Never-Never* 27 Our camp was very simple; just camp sleeping mosquito nets . . hanging by cords between stout stakes driven into the ground. 'Mosquito pegs', the bushmen call these stakes. **1935** K.L. SMITH *Sky Pilot Arnhem Land* 28 Each one has his own camping necessities, and as a rule requires little save a couple of 'mosquito pegs' for his net.

mossie /'mɒzi/. Also **mozzie.** [f. *mos(quito* + *-Y*; now used elsewhere but recorded earliest in Aust.: see OEDS *sb.*²] A mosquito. Also *attrib.*

1936 C.P. CONIGRAVE *N. Aust.* 146 The net has not yet been made that will prevent some of the North Australian 'mossies' from finding a way into their human prey. **1972** *Kings Cross Whisper* (Sydney) cxxxiv. 2/2 Down the pub Clarry has fixed up one of the rooms real nice for the Premier with a mossie net and a clean bedspread. **1985** *Age* (Melbourne) 20 Feb. 1/3 Scientist develops a soap that offends no one but the mozzie.

mote, v. [Prob. abbrev. of *motor* to travel (in a motor car).] *intr.* Of a car, person running, etc.: to move fast.
1937 *Bull. Australasian Eng. Assoc., Sydney Branch* July 3 To mote is defined by Mr Partridge as 'to drive or ride in a motor car', but for many years now Australian schoolboys have been using it in the more general sense of 'move quickly', so that often they say in praise of an athlete 'There is no doubt he can mote.' **1938** H. HODGE *Death in Morning* 31 Yes, he'd seen the Packard. Yes, two men in the front seat... Yes, they were certainly 'moting'.

mother. Used *attrib.* in Special Comb. **(a) mother country** (or **-land**) [spec. use of *mother country* (or *mother-land*) a country in relation to its colonies], the British Isles; **(b) mother colony (province, state),** New South Wales. See also PARENT.
(a) 1832 J. HENDERSON *Observations Colonies N.S.W. & Van Diemen's Land* 27 Bathurst is to Sydney, as Sydney is to the **Mother Country. 1907** F.T. BULLEN *Advance Australasia* 114 What strikes one as being quite touching is the way the Motherland is continually being spoken of affectionately, regretfully as 'Home'. **(b) 1824** J. LYCETT *Views in Aust.* 12 The native dog of the **mother colony** is, however, unknown here. **1892** *Bulletin* (Sydney) 9 July 7/2 To uplift the honour, glory, and credit of the mother-province, the N.S.W. Government is now actively engaged in carrying on the patriotic work of holding up the mirror to convict nature. **1907** *Truth* (Sydney) 17 Feb. 1/2 See what blessings of peculiar promise Barton's Victoria Policy has in store for this unhappy Mother State.

motherless, a. and quasi-*adv.* Used as an intensive, esp. in the phr. **motherless broke,** destitute of money; also *ellipt.* for *motherless broke*.
1898 *Bulletin* (Sydney) 17 Dec. (Red Page), To these are prefixed the adjectives *motherless* and *dead*, thus *dead motherless broke.* **1920** *Smith's Weekly* (Sydney) 18 Sept. 10/6 He was motherless broke. **1958** *Bulletin* (Sydney) 11 June 19/2 The worrying starts when he is flat, skinned, motherless, stony hearts-of-oak, or has 'gone bad'. **1976** B. BENNETT *New Country* 34 He let half-a-dozen others out at the same time. The motherless hooer.

motser /'mɒtsə/. Also **motsa, motza, motzer.** [Prob. a. Yiddish *matse* bread.] A large sum of money, esp. as won in gambling; a great amount. Also *transf.*, a certainty.
1936 A.B. PATERSON *Shearer's Colt* 180 It's a motzer. It's a schnitzel. We'll have to pack 'em in on the roof of the grandstand. **1943** S.J. BAKER *Pop. Dict. Austral. Slang* (ed. 3) 51 *Motser, motza,* a large sum of money. **1970** R. BEILBY *No Medals for Aphrodite* 214 You better let that bugger get well ahead... The Stuka'll be a motsa to have a go at him.

mound-bird. *Obs. Mound-building bird:* see MOUND-BUILDING.
1886 F. COWAN *Aust.* 19 *The Mound-birds,* Megapods: as yet which have not learned to build a nest and hatch their young themselves, but still, remembering their reptile origin, when they have scratched and scraped together a great mound of sand and herbage mold, depositing their eggs therein, and leaving them to be brought forth by the engendered heat and moisture of the heap fermenting in the sun. **1896** B. SPENCER *Rep. Horn Sci. Exped. Central Aust.* I. 83 Riding through the scrub.. we passed a mound-bird's nest (*Leipoa ocellata*).

mound-building, *ppl. a.* [Used elsewhere but recorded earliest in Aust.] Used to describe the habit of a ground-dwelling bird of the fam. Megapodiidae, having strong legs, feet, and claws, and incubating its eggs in a large mound. Esp. as **mound-building bird.** See also *brush turkey* BRUSH n.[1] B. 2, *mallee fowl* MALLEE 6, MOUND-BIRD, *scrub fowl* SCRUB n. 5.
1846 J.L. STOKES *Discoveries in Aust.* I. 417 This.. must have been the *Leipoa ocellata* of Gould, one of the mound or tumuli-building birds, first seen in Western Australia. **1962** H.J. FRITH *Mallee-Fowl* 23 Throughout the whole mound-building process, the rainfall has a great influence on the rate at which the birds work.

mound spring. *Mud spring,* see MUD 2.
1891 *Jrnl. & Proc. R. Soc. N.S.W.* XXV. 290 Natural artesian water rises to the surface in many parts of the east-central portions of Australia from mud or mound springs. **1985** *Austral. Nat. Hist.* Spring 432 Some of the mound springs are within the Lake Eyre National Estate Area.

mountain. Used *attrib.* in the names of flora and fauna: **mountain ash,** any of many trees, usu. of the genus *Eucalyptus* (fam. Myrtaceae), and esp. (*Vic.*) *E. regnans* of Vic. and Tas., favouring cool, moist mountain gullies; the wood of these trees; **devil, (a)** the small, spiny lizard *Moloch horridus* of arid and semi-arid central, s., and w. Aust.; HORNED DRAGON; MOLOCH; THORNY DEVIL; **(b)** *honey flower,* see HONEY; **duck** [see quot. 1976], the large duck *Tadorna tadornoides* of w. and s.e. Aust. incl. Tas., having predom. black and brown plumage with a white ring around the neck; *chestnut-breasted shelduck,* see CHESTNUT *a.*; **eagle** *obs., wedge-tailed eagle,* see WEDGE-TAILED; **gum,** any of several trees of the genus *Eucalyptus* (fam. Myrtaceae), esp. the tall *E. dalrympleana* subsp. *dalrympleana* of Vic., N.S.W., and Tas., having a smooth white and grey bark, and *E. cypellocarpa* of Vic. and e. N.S.W., having smooth greyish bark; the wood of these trees; **hickory,** the shrub or small tree *Acacia penninervis,* occurring on rocky hills in N.S.W., Qld., and e. Vic.; the tough, durable, and flexible wood of the tree; **oak,** any of several trees incl. *Allocasuarina verticillata* (fam. Casuarinaceae) of s.e. Aust., having slender drooping branchlets and occurring on stony ridges and rocky soils; **pheasant** *obs.,* LYRE-BIRD 1; **pygmy possum,** the small terrestrial marsupial *Burramys parvus* of alpine and subalpine n.e. Vic. and s.e. N.S.W.; see also *pygmy possum* PYGMY; **shrimp,** the small fresh-water crustacean *Anaspides tasmaniae,* occurring in mountain waters of Tas.; **thrush,** the bird *Zoothera dauma* (see *ground thrush* GROUND n.[1]); **trout,** any of several small fresh-water fish of the fam. Galaxiidae, found at higher altitudes in s. Aust.
1837 *Colonist* (Sydney) 350/3 **Mountain ash,** for carriage work. **1934** W.A. OSBORNE *Visitor to Aust.* 65 The great Mountain Ash (*Eucalyptus regnans*) soars to heights that challenge the Californian sequoias. **(a) 1872** MRS E. MILLETT *Austral. Parsonage* 183 The '**Mountain Devil**' is about five or six inches long. **(b) 1949** B. O'REILLY *Green Mountains* 91 **Mountain devils** are the joy of Blue Mountain children; following a tulip-shaped flower of flame-red comes the seed pod—a perfect little devil's head with two sharp horns and a sinister-looking pointed beard. **1820** C. JEFFREYS *Van Dieman's Land* 35 This lake abounds with.. teal, **mountain ducks,** coots. **1976** *Reader's Digest Compl. Bk. Austral. Birds* 100 Contrary to its popular name, most mountain ducks do not live or breed in high places. The main populations live in the lowland areas. **1800** D. COLLINS *Acct. Eng. Colony N.S.W.* (1802) II. 288 (Pl.) **Mountain Eagle** of New South Wales will kill a large sized Kangaroo. **1831** W. BLAND *Journey of Discovery Port Phillip* 16 They are at present among a species of **mountain gum,** of the finest description. **1891** *Braidwood Dispatch* 14 Jan. 2/1 On our coast ranges are to be found the mountain gum, blackwood [etc.]. **1882** *Illustr. Austral. News* (Melbourne) 24 Jan. 10/3 Here also were found many other woods, equally if not more valuable, myrtle, dogwood, **mountain hickory,** and blackwood. **1900** *Proc. Linnean Soc. N.S.W.* XXV. 713 Another tree now appearing for the first time is *Casuarina quadrivalvis* (She Oak and **Mountain Oak**). **1911** *Bulletin* (Sydney) 20 July 14/2, I do not know the Dago names for the two oaks... Locally they are distinguished by the

names 'mountain-oak' and 'meadow-oak'. **1800** Banks Papers 20 Feb. XIX. 124 The **Mountain Pheasant** (as it is called) which I sent by Captain Raven for Lady Banks. **1971** J. CALABY et al. *Mountain Pigmy Possum* (CSIRO Division Wildlife Research Techn. Paper no. 23) 3 The **mountain pigmy possum** . . was unknown as a living animal until August 1966 when a specimen was caught in the kitchen of a ski-lodge at Mt. Hotham in the Victorian alps. **1909** G. SMITH *Naturalist in Tas.* 80 The remarkable **Mountain Shrimp** of Tasmania (*Anaspides tasmaniae*) . . is found at a high elevation on Mount Wellington and in the clear tarns upon Mount Field, the Harz [sic] Mountains, and on some of the mountains on the west coast. **1848** J. GOULD *Birds of Aust.* IV. Pl. 7, *Oreocincla lunulata* . . **Mountain Thrush**, Colonists of Van Diemen's Land. **1882** J.E. TENISON-WOODS *Fish & Fisheries N.S.W.* 108 In the upper and shallower parts of the creeks and rivers rising in the Blue Mountains one or two species of *Galaxias* are found. . . They are known to some as the '**Mountain trout**'.

mountaineer. *Obs.* A (wild) beast which has strayed from the main herd into high country which is difficult of access.
1849 A. HARRIS *Emigrant Family* (1967) 125 They'd better go into that mob of mountaineers that always runs separate from your quiet cattle in the ranges. **1857** F. DE B. COOPER *Wild Adventures* 58, I went with a party of four to beat up the ranges, and bring in any stray mob of mountaineers.

mounted police. *Hist.* A cavalry force responsible for the maintenance of law and order in (remote) rural districts; orig. (see quot. 1825) such a force engaging in the pursuit and capture of bushrangers.
1825 *HRA* (1919) 1st Ser. XII. 85, I had some time since carefully selected and equipped as light cavalry, 2 Officers, 2 Serjeants, and 22 Rank and File from the Regiment under my Command to act as a Mounted Police, for the express Purpose of pursuing and capturing Bushrangers. **1884** J.T. HINKINS *Life amongst Native Race* 34 The mounted black police . . had been camping at our station for several days.
Hence **mounted policeman** *n.*
1834 'EMIGRANT' *Party Politics Exposed* 36, I saw the mounted policeman . . fire. **1914** C.H.S. MATTHEWS *Bill* 27 You can guess that in those days the mounted policeman's lot was an exciting, if not always a happy, one.

mounter. *Obs.* [f. Br. slang *mount* to give false evidence for money: see OED *v.* 7.] One who gives false evidence in return for payment.
1812 J.H. VAUX *Mem.* (1819) II. 189 *Mounter*, a man who lives by *mounting*, or perjury, who is always ready for a guinea or two to swear whatever is proposed to him. **1896** M. HORNSBY *Old Time Echoes Tas.* 38 For ten bob I could find mounters (false swearers) enough to hang a county.

Mount Pitt bird. *Obs.* Also **Mount Pit bird.** [f. the name of *Mount Pitt*, Norfolk Island.] The brown and grey bird *Pterodroma solandri*, now breeding only on Lord Howe Island, but formerly abundant on Norfolk Island; BIRD OF PROVIDENCE.
1790 R. CLARK Jrnl. 18 Apr. 159 The haversack contained 68 of the Mount Pit Birds. **1805** *HRA* (1921) 3rd Ser. I. 327 Kangaroos and Emus affording us as providential a Supply as the Mount Pitt Birds once did.

mouser. *Shearing.* See quot. 1965.
1895 *Bulletin* (Sydney) 13 July 23/2 And there isn't any hurry, as it takes you all the day To get the 'sweet-lips' going, and the boss severely damns The mercenary 'mouser' who opens out on rams. **1965** J.S. GUNN *Terminol. Shearing Industry* ii. 5 *Mouser*, a slang name given to the man who is out to make all the money he can and never 'misses a trick'. Such a person could disturb the peace and good fellowship in a shed, and thus upsets the boss as well as the other shearers.

mouse spider. [See quot. 1976.] Any of several large, black, burrowing spiders of the genus *Missulena*, widespread in mainland Aust., esp. *M. occatoria*.
1965 *Austral. Encycl.* VIII. 233 Two of the species [of *Missulena*] are widely distributed over Australia; they are *M. occatoria*, sometimes termed the 'mouse' spider, and *M. insigne*. **1976** B.Y. MAIN *Spiders* 65 Many years ago *Missulena* was designated the mouse spider apparently as a result of someone finding a spider, probably a male specimen, in a deep sinuous burrow. Presumably the spider had crawled down an old hole of a beetle or perhaps even a mouse.

mouth, *v. trans.* To examine the mouth of (a sheep), in order to estimate its age. Also as *vbl. n.*, and *attrib.*
1870 J.R. GRAHAM *Treatise Austral. Merino* 32 When they were 'mouthed', at the time of delivery, fully 25 per cent. of them were found with teeth worn down to the gums. . . None of these sheep could by any possibility be over six, and many no more than four or five years old. **1896** G. SUTHERLAND *Australasian Live Stock Man.* 174 On large stations where sheep are frequently boxed up for various reasons, it enables the overseer to draft, by the swing gate, all the separate ages without resort to 'mouthing'. **1961** J.W. JORDAN *Practical Sheep Farming* 214 In the days when 'bullocking' was in favour, owners had mouthing races. They used to 'up-end' every sheep, and open its mouth, to find out its age from its teeth.

Movement. *Hist.* Shortened form of 'Catholic Social Studies Movement', a body formed in 1945 to counter the influence and activity of communists in trade unions. See GROUPER 2.
1945 *Catholic Action at Work* 4 Because of this necessity to hide its religious affiliation, the report points out, it was decided to call the organisation '*The Movement*'. **1982** *Bulletin* (Sydney) 7 Sept. 63/2 Although the Movement rarely had more than 5000 members at any one time, it was a formative influence on the early years of some 100,000 Australian Catholics.

mowie /ˈmoʊi/. [f. MOR(WONG + -Y.] MORWONG.
1973 *Kings Cross Whisper* (Sydney) clv. 16/4 A nice haul of snapper, mowies and even a dozen or so trag. **1984** *Canberra Chron.* 25 July 19/1 At Montague Island . . there have been a few good mowies around the north-western corner.

mowlow, var. MOLO.

mozz, *n.* Also **moz.** [Abbrev. of MOZZLE.] In the phr. **to put the moz on**, to exert a malign influence upon (a person), to jinx.
1924 C.J. DENNIS *Rose of Spadgers* 75 Too much soul-ferritin' might put the moz On this 'ere expedition. **1985** *Canberra Times* 6 Sept. 1/1 He has put the mozz on runners before. He backed Mr Peacock against Mr Fraser and lost.

mozz, *v.* Also **moz.** *trans.* To jinx; to deter. Also as *vbl. n.*
1941 S.J. BAKER *Pop. Dict. Austral. Slang* 47 *Moz*, to interrupt, to hinder. **1983** HIBBERD & HUTCHINSON *Barracker's Bible* 132 *Mozz* . . to attempt to distract a player kicking for a goal, or a batsman waiting for the bowler to deliver. . . 'No mozzing' is a schoolkids' rule often adopted in the interest of fair play.

mozzie, var. MOSSIE.

mozzle. [a. Heb. *mazzāl* luck.] Luck; fortune.
1898 *Bulletin* (Sydney) 17 Dec. (Red Page), *Mozzle* is luck . . *Good mozzle* = good luck; *Kronk mozzle* = bad luck.

1919 E. Dyson *Hello, Soldier* 32 'Twas rotten mozzle, Neddo. We had blown every clip.

Mrs Potts. *Hist.* [Of unknown origin.] The name of a type of smoothing-iron: see quot. 1913.

1907 *Anthony Hordern Catal.* 542 Mrs Potts' Chinese Polishing Irons . . 2s. 6d. each. Extra Handles . . 8d. **1913** *Lassetters' Compl. Gen. Catal.* 333 'Mrs Potts" Irons. Nickel-Plated. The great merits of these irons are universally known. They are better made and fine finished, and hold the heat longer than any other iron, and being double pointed will iron either way. The handle is made of walnut, and detachable by a spring, and being circular shape fits the hand naturally, so all straining is avoided. The sets comprise three irons and one handle.

mud.

1. Used *attrib.* in the names of fauna: **mud crab,** the large swimming crab *Scylla serrata,* valued as food, occurring along muddy shores in estuaries of n. Aust., and widespread in the Indo-Pacific region; *mangrove crab,* see Mangrove; Muddie; **-eye,** the larva of a dragonfly, used by anglers as bait; **fish,** any of several marine, estuarine, or fresh-water fish living amongst or over mud beds, incl. Lungfish and Mudskipper; **lark,** *magpie lark,* see Magpie n. 2; **oyster,** the oyster of s.e. Aust. *Ostrea angasi;* **wasp,** Mason wasp.

1966 T.C. Roughley *Fish & Fisheries Aust.* (ed. 7) 127 **Mud** or Mangrove **Crab**. . . This large crab has a powerful pair of nippers which can easily crush a finger carelessly placed. **1911** D.A. Macdonald *Bush Boy's Bk.* 95 They live on the yabbie, the shrimp, and the **mud eye**—which is the water form of the dragon-fly. **1829** R. Mudie *Picture of Aust.* 196 A **mud-fish**, found on the north-west coast . . is about nine inches in length, and buries itself under the mud with more rapidity than any other fish that is known. **1906** J.W. Gregory *Dead Heart Aust.* 151 Crocodiles swarmed in the lake and its estuaries, and preyed on the primitive Queensland mudfish (*Ceratodus*). *Ibid.* 49 Our sportsmen did good practice on the birds—teal . . and **mud-larks**—that swarmed around the pond. **1770** J. Cook *Jrnls.* 23 Aug. (1955) I. 394 The Shell-fish are Oysters of 3 or 4 sorts, viz. Rock oysters and Mangrove Oysters which are small, Pearl Oysters, and **Mud Oysters,** these last are the best and largest. **1894** *Proc. Linnean Soc. N.S.W.* IX. 29 *Abispa splendida*. . . Among our 'mason or **mud wasps**' this takes the palm for being one of the largest and handsomest.

2. Special Comb. **mud-fat** *a.* [Br. dial.] in prime condition; **map,** a diagram of a district, route, etc., drawn with a stick in earth or dust; so **mud-map** *v. trans.;* **rain,** see quot. 1872; **spring,** see quot. 1901; Mound spring; **tank,** an earth dam.

1880 *Argus* (Melbourne) 17 Feb. 9/3 Bullocks are '**mud-fat**' almost all the year round. **1919** E.S. Sorenson *Chips & Splinters* 14 Phineas Jones was a native of Wattle Gully, an obscure little place that isn't marked on any map excepting always the **mud maps** that Phineas draws, when directing some unfortunate wanderer to the awful place. **1930** A.E. Yarra *Vanishing Horsemen* 116 While waiting for the trial the two men spent many an hour 'mud-mapping' the scene of their arrest and advancing theories to account for the startling event. **1872** 'Resident' *Glimpses Life Vic.* 109 Rain has fallen which was impregnated with dust, and the drops of which left deep stains of reddish brown. . . This phenomenon is familiarly known as **mud-rain**. **1881** *Proc. Linnean Soc. N.S.W.* VI. 155 In putting down some tube-bores at the so-called '**Mud Springs**' of Wee Wattah and Mulyeo, at Killarah, Mr David Brown . . struck a strong flow of water. **1901** E.F. Pittman *Mineral Resources N.S.W.* 466 An account of the Artesian basin would be incomplete without a reference to the peculiar occurrences known as Mud Springs. They are the visible evidence of the efforts of the water, stored underground in a state of pressure, to force its way through the Cretaceous shales to the surface; in other words, they are natural Artesian wells. They consist of mounds of yellow clay mixed with water-worn pebbles, and in outward appearance they are not unlike large ant-hills; in the centre of each is a vertical pipe through which water, or rather liquid mud comes to the surface. The mounds have been formed by the very slow overflowing of the liquid mud, and, as some of them are of very large dimensions, they must have been forming for a very long period. **1898** *Bulletin* (Sydney) 1 Jan. 3/2 The weak are falling back; Closely guarded by the **mud-tank** just abreast the western wing.

3. In the phr. **up to mud,** unsatisfactory.

1931 G.C. Bolton *Fine Country to starve In* (1972) 157 We meet by chance in the street. 'Hullo! How's things?' 'Up to mud!' **1965** J. O'Grady *Aussie Eng.* 60 Anything 'up to mud' is 'not up to much'. It's no good. It's buggered.

4. *fig.* In the sugar industry: see quot. 1966.

1938 F. Clune *Free & Easy Land* 236 The juice from the mills now runs into juice tanks, where it is steam-heated and treated with lime, which precipitates the impurities to the bottom. The precipitate is known as 'mud'. **1966** B. Beatty *Around Aust.* 224 Nothing goes to waste in the North Queensland sugar industry. 'Mud', the residue left after the juices have been filtered from the crushings, makes a rich fertilizer.

muddie. Also **muddy.** [f. *mud(crab* + -Y.] *Mud-crab,* see Mud 1.

1953 S.J. Baker *Aust. Speaks* 104 *Muddy,* a mud crab. **1981** *Weekend Austral. Mag.* (Sydney) 26 Dec. 4/3 They don't even know what a mangrove is in America, let alone muddies.

muddlo, var. Mudlo.

Mudgee stone. /mʌdʒi 'stoʊn/. [f. the name of *Mudgee* a town in N.S.W.] A slate found in the Mudgee district and particularly suitable for use as a whetstone; a whetstone of this material. Also **Mudgee.**

1909 R. Kaleski *Austral Settler's Compl. Guide* 24 The oil-stones I prefer are the Lily white Washita or the best Mudgee stone. **1964** H.P. Tritton *Time means Tucker* (rev. ed.) 47 A good whetstone was a prized possession and 'Mudgee Stones' (a slate found only in that district) were always admired and envied. . . Few shearers would allow anyone to use their 'Mudgee'.

mudhopper: see Mudskipper.

mudlo /'mʌdloʊ/. *Obs.* Also **muddlo.** [a. Yagara *mulu.*] See quot. 1876.

1876 'Eight Yrs.' Resident' *Queen of Colonies* 333 When one of the tribe is sick he is said to have a 'mudlo'. Mudlo is a stone, and their belief is that death is caused by some hostile black placing a stone in that portion of the body which is affected. We have seen blacks with mudlos in their heads, some in their stomachs or breasts, and some in the legs. They will tell you with the greatest composure whether the mudlo will be got out, or whether the patient will 'go bong'. **1923** T. Hall *Short Hist. Downs Blacks* 26 Unless a medicine man sucked the Muddlo out they would die with fear.

mudskipper. [Transf. use of *mudskipper* any fish of the genus *Periophthalmus:* see OED(S *mud, sb.*[1] 4 b.] Any of several small, amphibious marine fish of the fam. Gobiidae of tropical n. Aust. and elsewhere, esp. of the genera *Periophthalmus* and *Periophthalmodon,* having modified pectoral and ventral fins which enable it to move about on mudflats; *climbing fish,* see Climbing; *Johnny jumper,* see Johnny 2; *kangaroo fish* (b), see Kangaroo *n.* 5. See also *mud fish* Mud 1. Also **mudhopper.**

1896 F.G. Aflalo *Sketch Nat. Hist. Aust.* 248 The curious little Mudhoppers (*Periopthalmus*) of Queensland . . springs [*sic*] in advance of the rising tide and leaps and skips over the wet mud. **1906** D.G. STEAD *Fishes of Aust.* 187 The Mud-Skipper 'is an essentially-tropical species'.

mug, *v*. [Used elsewhere but recorded earliest in Aust.: see OEDS *v*.³ 4 and *vbl. n.* 3.] *intr.* To kiss; to 'neck'. Freq. as *vbl. n..* Also with **up**.
1890 *Bull-Ant* (Melbourne) 28 Aug. 17/3 B.M. was specially favoured with the mugging and kissing which M.E. (a new arrival) bestowed so freely on certain young ladies. **1977** T.A.G. HUNGERFORD *Wong Chu* 82 You been mugging up with the postie.

mugga /ˈmʌgə/. [a. Wiradhuri *magar*.] The tree *Eucalyptus sideroxylon* (see *red ironbark* RED *a.* 1 a.).
1834 G. BENNETT *Wanderings N.S.W.* I. 253 Different species of *Eucalypti*.. among them.. 'iron bark' ('Mucker' of the natives). **1956** K. TENNANT *Honey Flow* 5 Good bee country.. ironbark mainly, narrow-leaf, a bit of mugga.

mug lair: see LAIR *n.* b.

muk-muk: see MOOK-MOOK OWL.

Mules /mjulz/, *n.* [The name of J.H.W. *Mules* (1876–1946), sheep-raiser.] Used *attrib.* in Special Comb.
Mules operation, a surgical procedure designed to reduce the incidence of blowfly strike in sheep: see quots. 1945 and 1950. Also **Mules' operation**.
1932 *Jrnl. Dept. Agric. S.A.* Aug. 115 *Blowfly strike in sheep and the 'Mules' operation for reducing the incidence...* 'Mr J.H.W. Mules.. carried out some observations which led him to believe that the irritation of the skin by urine in the breech of the Merino ewe, was the chief predisposing factor to blowfly strike... Mr Mules' treatments date back from 1929.' **1933** *Council Sci. & Industr. Research Pamphlet* no. 37 9 The surgical removal of the side folds (e.g., Mules' operation). **1945** E.H. PEARSE *Sheep, Farm & Station Managem.* 388 The Mules operation is designed, by cutting away the wrinkles that are causative of this susceptibility, and by stretching the bare skin area below the tail, to deprive the ewe of her attraction for the fly. **1950** H.G. BELSCHNER *Sheep Managem. & Diseases* 157 The modified Mules operation reduces the tendency to crutch strike, partly by removing the wrinkles beside the vulva, but chiefly, it would appear, by stretching and enlarging the area of wool-less skin around the vulva, that is, the so called 'bare area'.

mules /mjulz/, *v.* [f. prec.] *trans.* To perform a Mules operation. Freq. as *ppl. a.* and *vbl. n.*
1946 *Qld. Country Life* 18 Apr. 3 Mulesed sheep are much easier to crutch. *Ibid.*, We don't say that mulesing will stop the fly altogether. **1984** *Sydney Morning Herald* 11 June 8/4 Mulesing.. is a severe surgical procedure which.. involves literally skinning the animal alive (in the crutch area) without any anaesthetic.

mulga, var. MALKA.

mulga /ˈmʌlgə/, *n.*¹ and *attrib.* Formerly also **malga, mulgah, mulgar.** [a. Yuwaalaraay *malga*.]
A. *n.*
1. Any of several plants of the genus *Acacia* (fam. Mimosaceae) of dry inland Aust., esp. the widespread shrub or tree *A. aneura*, having grey-green foliage regarded as useful fodder, and yielding a distinctive brown and yellowish timber; the wood of these trees. Also *attrib.*, esp. as **mulga bush, tree, wood.**
1848 T.L. MITCHELL *Jrnl. Exped. Tropical Aust.* 176 On the summit, grew the Malga tree; which is an acacia of such very hard wood. **1858** J.M. STUART *Explorations in Aust.* 18 June (1865) 6 The hills are very stony with a little salt bush, and destitute of timber, except.. the mulga bushes in the sand hills. **1861** *Ibid.* 11 Apr. (1865) 267 The first four miles was over a beautiful grassy plain with mulga wood.
1862 W. LANDSBOROUGH *Jrnl. Exped. from Carpentaria* 106 The scrub consisted of mulgah with a few other trees. **1875** R. BRUCE *Dingoes* 164 Perch'd on some mulgar bare and dead.
2. a. With **the:** remote, sparsely populated country, as opposed to that which is more closely settled; the outback. Also **Mulgaland.**
1898 *Worker* (Sydney) 28 May 6/3 'That's right,' says the man from the Mulga, 'I think I'll do the rest myself.' **1905** *Steele Rudd's Mag.* (Brisbane) June 568 Mulgaland, with its vast open spaces, impressed them in a way that would be utterly impossible in crowded Surrey.
b. An inhabitant of such country.
1904 *Bulletin* (Sydney) 15 Sept. 18/2 The back-'o-beyond Jay Pee is often a tricky bit of mulga. **1908** *Ibid.* 16 Jan. 15/1 The bushy-detection question arouses much difference of opinion. Know how we pick them in Brisbane? If in a mixed party, the mulgas invariably clasp hands before venturing to cross the street—girls inside, older boys at each wing.

B. *attrib.*
1. Characterized by the presence of mulga, as **mulga country, flats, paddocks, scrub.**
1858 J.M. STUART *Explorations in Aust.* 25 July (1865) 27 Our journey has been through a very thick mulga scrub and sand hills. **1889** W.H. TIETKENS *Jrnl. Central Austral. Exploring Exped.* 21 Apr. (1891) 15 These mulga flats are intersected by small gum creeks. **1896** *Bulletin* (Sydney) 15 Feb. 3/2 Where the mulga paddocks are wild and wide, That's where the pick of the stockmen ride. **1898** *Ibid.* 19 Feb. 14/2 Scrub-cutting will soon be a thing of the past in mulga country

2. Rustic; countrified.
1895 *Worker* (Sydney) 23 Feb. 4/1 He forgets his Mulga-verses aren't very high in rank. **1942** F. CLUNE *Last of Austral. Explorers* 104 A mob of mulga miners were ready at Clune's pub.

3. In the names of flora and fauna: **mulga ant,** the ant *Polyrachis macropus* of inland Aust. which builds a mud nest to which mulga leaves are applied; **apple,** a large, edible gall produced by the mulga tree; **grass,** any of several grasses (fam. Poaceae) of mulga country and elsewhere, esp. the common *Thyridolepis mitchelliana*, a tufted perennial regarded as good fodder, and *Aristida contorta*, having tufts which whiten on drying; see also WIND-GRASS; **parrot** (or **parakeet**), the parrot of drier mainland Aust. *Psephotus varius*, a predom. green bird with yellow, blue, and red markings; MANY-COLOURED PARAKEET; **snake,** *king brown*, see KING *n.*¹ 2.

1948 C.P. MOUNTFORD *Brown Men & Red Sand* 58, I saw many homes of the curious **mulga ant,** an insect which builds a mud wall, up to fourteen inches in diameter and five inches in height, round the mouth of its nest, and then thatches the wall with dead mulga leaves. **1888** *Proc. Linnean Soc. N.S.W.* III. 483 *Acacia aneura*... In western New South Wales two kinds of galls are commonly found on these trees; one kind is very plentiful.. but the other is less abundant, larger, succulent and edible. These latter galls are called '**Mulga apples**', and are said to be very welcome to the thirsty traveller. **1882** *Austral. Handbk.* 392 The '**Mulga Grass**'.. is valuable as thriving under shade in poor soil. **1966** A. MORRIS *Plantlife W. Darling* 7 Grasses which favour hilly situations are.. Neurachne Mitchelliana.. (Mulga Grass) [etc.]. **1951** [**mulga parrot**] *Bulletin* (Sydney) 3 Jan. 12/1 We rise as mulga-parakeets go whirring through the dawn. **1952** A.M. DUNCAN-KEMP *Where Strange Paths go Down* 95 The Mulga parrot, one of the most beautiful of the outback species. Because of its rich and varied colouring.. [bushmen] have named it 'Joseph's coat'. Its general colour scheme is green, but the chest and thighs are a bright scarlet. **1941** *Bulletin* (Sydney) 16 Apr. 16/4 For sheer pugnacity I'll put the blue ribbon on the **mulga snake** of the Lower Thompson (W.Q.) as champ. of the ophidian world.

4. Special Comb. Mulga Bill, see quot. 1972; **black,** an Aboriginal from a remote place; **-bred** *a.*, reared in the country; **madness,** eccentricity attributed to living in the outback; also *attrib.*; **mafia,** a name for the National Country Party; **message,** a message conveyed by MULGA WIRE; also *fig.*; **rum,** crude or illicitly made alcoholic liquor; **scrubber,** see quot. 1945; **wireless (radio, telegram, telegraph),** MULGA WIRE.

1905 *Truth* (Sydney) 23 Apr. 7/5 The spieler notes his vacant gaze And quickly he swoops down, The magsman understands the ways Of **Mulga Bills** in town. **1972** A. CHIPPER *Aussie Swearers Guide* 66 *Mulga Bill*, a simpleton, specifically from the Bush. **1900** J. BRADSHAW *20 Yrs.' Experience Prison Life* (c 1927) 105 The disgraceful stupidity of a doctor who knew as little about the game as a **Mulga black. 1899** *Bulletin* (Sydney) 21 Jan. 3/2 I'd forgotten for a moment you are not all **mulga-bred. 1905** *Bulletin* (Sydney) 13 Apr. 18/2 He said he had had several rums but the **mulga madness** brands never upset his digestion. **1980** S. THORNE *I've met some Bloody Wags* 115 He was a prime example of 'mulga madness'. Given a good drench and put on a small lush block in the 'inside country' he would be a new man. **1978** *Sydney Morning Herald* 24 Feb. 7/2 The National Country Party is .. a rustic clan of tough, like-minded politicians who know what they want and how to get it. Its critics might see the party as a kind of **mulga mafia. 1985** *Bulletin* (Sydney) 29 Oct. 30/1 In Malcolm Fraser's government he was one of the mulga mafia, with Anthony and Peter Nixon. **1926** *Ibid.* 8 Apr. 22/1 Watching the red coals fashion a picture filming a bar-girl's business smile—Only a sordid **mulga message,** blacking out in a little while! **1943** L. McLENNAN *Spirit of West* 24 They sent a mulga message through all of cattle-land For Dingo Joe, the trapper, to come and try his hand. **1910** *Bulletin* (Sydney) 21 Apr. 39/2 You .. poured gallons of **Mulga rum** down your throat! **1897** *Bulletin* (Sydney) 20 Mar. 28/1 And he loves the merry rattle of the stockwhip and the tramp Of the cockhorned **mulga scrubbers** when they're breaking in the bush. **1945** S.J. BAKER *Austral. Lang.* 67 *Mulga scrubbers*.., stock that have run wild and deteriorated in condition. **1932** I.L. IDRIESS *Flynn of Inland* (1965) 138 '**Mulga wireless**' had advertised the coming of those dresses far and wide. **1984** W. HATFIELD *River Crossing* 102 You've heard about 'mulga-telegrams'—say something away in the mulga scrub, an' the trees theirselves seems to pass it along. **1948** F. CLUNE *Wild Colonial Boys* 171 The 'mulga telegraph' was the word-of-mouth link of communication. **1950** G.M. FARWELL *Land of Mirage* 98 'We heard the Inspector was on his way up.' For once the mulga radio had proved unreliable.

mulga /ˈmʌlgə/, *n.*² Abbrev. of MULGA WIRE 1; a (false) rumour; a tall story.

1899 *Bulletin* (Sydney) 4 Mar. 15/2 A lie or false report is, in N.S.W., a 'Mulga' or 'Mulga-wire', while in Centralia it's 'gidyea'. **1950** K.S. PRICHARD *Winged Seeds* 297 The troops've had it all by mulga.

mulgara /ˈmʌlgərə/. [Prob. Wangganguru *mardagura*.] The small carnivorous marsupial *Dasycercus cristicauda* (fam. Dasyuridae) which inhabits burrows in sandy regions of drier Aust.

1941 E. TROUGHTON *Furred Animals Aust.* 33 A rat which provided a meal for three hungry Mulgaras was skinned as by a skilled taxidermist, no bones being left attached to the skin which was inside-out and almost perfect. **1984** *Daily Tel.* (Sydney) 22 Aug. 15/7 The Mulgara has an unusual ability to conserve precious water by producing extremely concentrated urine and surviving only on the moisture gained from its prey.

mulga wire /ˈmʌlgə ˈwaɪə/.

1. BUSH TELEGRAPH *n.* 2.

1899 *Bulletin* (Sydney) 15 July 31/1 Swaggie .. pulled up .. and hailed the boss. 'Any show of a job, *sir*?' (The 'mulga wires' had posted him as to civilities.) **1983** M. DURACK *Sons in Saddle* 123 Local gossip flourished through a word-of-mouth medium referred to as 'the bushman's mulga wire'.

2. An Aboriginal smoke signal; the message so conveyed; BUSH TELEGRAPH *n.* 3.

1927 M. DORNEY *Adventurous Honeymoon* 134 The blacks have a wonderful code for signalling by smoke. Messages sent in this way are said by the whites to have been sent by 'mulga wire'. **1944** A.W. UPFIELD *No Footprints in Bush* 65 This morning I found Itcheroo squatted before a little fire and sending or receiving a mulga wire.

mulla mulla /ˈmʌlə mʌlə/. [a. Panyjima *mulu-mulu*.] PUSSY TAIL.

1967 V. SERVENTY *Nature Walkabout* 31 Mulla mullas were in flower and tall speargrass rose seven feet into the air. **1984** *Age Weekender* (Melbourne) 7 Dec. 7/3 Pussy Tails or Mulla Mulla (*Ptilotus exaltatus*) carpet the rocky slopes with pink and grey hairy flowers.

mullenize, *v. Hist.* [Prob. f. the name of Charles Mullen, farmer: see quot. 1962.] *trans.* To clear and prepare for cultivation (scrub-covered land): see quots. 1962 and 1979. Chiefly as *vbl. n.*

1892 *Trans. & Proc. R. Soc. S.A.* XV. 196 Wherever that mode of cultivation known as 'mullenizing' has been sufficiently prolonged to ensure the death of the primitive growth by uprooting the underground stem—popularly known as the 'mallee root'—regeneration is almost wholly unknown. **1962** O. PRYOR *Aust.'s Little Cornwall* 180 Many farms were cleared in this way before the job was rendered easier by the introduction, by Charles Mullen, of Wasleys, of the process known as mullenizing. In mullenizing, the larger mallees were cut off at ground level with an axe, and the smaller stuff was left standing, ready to be broken down by a four-horse team, dragging a heavy roller made from the shell of an old Cornish boiler. **1979** J. BIRMINGHAM et al. *Austral. Pioneer Technol.* 21 'Mullenising' involved smashing down the mallee using a heavy roller (often an old boiler) drawn by twelve oxen; burning the felled mass of timber; and scratching over the soil with a spiked log to prepare for the first sowing. *Ibid.*, Many variants of this plough were made as the innovation caught on and as more and more mallee was mullenised.

Hence **mullenizer** *n.*, a heavy roller for crushing scrub.

1910 C.H. SPENCE *Autobiogr.* 44 The stump-jumping plough and the mullenicer, which beats down the scrub or low bush so that it can be burnt, were South Australian inventions, copied elsewhere, which have turned land accounted worthless into prolific wheat fields.

mullet. In the phr. **like a stunned mullet,** dazed; uncomprehending; unconscious.

1953 S.J. BAKER *Aust. Speaks* 267 Dullness: (looking) *like a stunned mullet.* **1980** R. DAVIDSON *Tracks* 62 They turned to me like stunned mullets, Frankie's eyes popping out, Clive's downcast with guilt.

mullock /ˈmʌlək/, *n.* [Spec. use of Br. dial. *mullock* rubbish, refuse matter.]

1. a. Mining refuse.

1855 R. CARBONI *Eureka Stockade* 13 Crossing the holes, up to the knees in mullock, and loaded like a dromedary. **1979** *Ecos* xxii. 22/3 Have you ever heard of mullock? It's waste rock from mining operations.

b. Comb. **mullock dump, heap.**

1925 *Smith's Weekly* (Sydney) 10 Jan. 23/7 Not all the **mullock** and gravel **dumps** marking the deserted mines in Victoria .. have been put to practical use. **1859** *Colonial Mining Jrnl.* Feb. 88/3 It would be well always to prospect its value before it is thrown away in the **mullock heap.**

2. *fig.*

a. Rubbish; nonsense; 'muck'.

[N.Z. **1866** R. BURGESS *Autobiogr.* 127 (typescript) No

b-y fear. I should know it was a lot of mullock they were telling for you are not like this Jew.] **1878** 'HUMANITY' *Sketches Chinese Character* 7 'A lot of *mullock*' .. is a gold fields phrase, and means, according to my views, anything of no use. **1981** P. RADLEY *Jack Rivers & Me* 172 Most of the men went to the Rugby union field to watch the Chadla Chickens make mullock of the still-pissed Boomeroo Bulls.

b. In the phr. **to poke mullock,** to mock; to deride.

1916 *Bostall Boshter* (Bostall Heath, England) 3 Apr. 1 After photographing .. and poking mullock at it. **1981** D. STUART *I think I'll Live* 163 You're no Mister bloody Australia y'self .. so don't poke mullock at anyone for being a bit skinny.

mullock /'mʌlək/, *v.* [f. prec.]

1. *trans.* With **over:** to shear (sheep) in a rough and careless fashion; to perform (a task, etc.) in a slovenly manner.

1893 *Age* (Melbourne) 23 Sept. 14/4 No man could shear 321 sheep in eight hours, although .. he might do what we shearers call 'mullock over' that number. **1965** J.S. GUNN *Terminol. Shearing Industry* ii. 5 *Mullock over*, to rush the work quickly and carelessly, thus turning out badly shorn sheep.

2. With **up:** to excavate mullock; to litter or block with mullock.

1940 I.L. IDRIESS *Lightning Ridge* 96 The owners had found their drives mullocked up, broken opal everywhere. **1977** J. DOUGHTY *Gold in Blood* 243 In stoping to the surface on both ends we had mullocked up the shaft.

mullocker /'mʌləkə/. One who clears away the refuse in a mine.

1905 *Steele Rudd's Mag.* (Brisbane) Dec. 1073 A young clerk .. had an argument with a mullocker from the Lady Shenton. **1982** M. WALKER *Making Do* 84 What was taken out from underground and processed, the residue, had to be put back to fill it up again, and I was one of those that helped in that department, pushing the trucks. I was a mullocker.

mullocky /'mʌləki/, *a.*

1. Rubbishy: see quot. 1886.

1862 'W.T.G.' *Quite Colonial* (c 1948) 18 It is bottom, and a preciously mullocky looking one it is, too. **1886** H. FINCH-HATTON *Advance Aust.* (rev. ed.) 168 Having hit on the reef, if it is what is known as 'mullocky'—that is soft and rotten—the next thing is to take out a prospect from between the walls.

2. In the collocation **mullocky leader,** see quot. 1944.

1882 W. SOWDEN *N.T. as it Is* 59 Those mullocky leaders are curious. **1944** M.J. O'REILLY *Bowyangs & Boomerangs* 37 Working what was known as a 'Mullocky leader'. That is a quartz leader running through soft, barren country.

mulloway /'mʌləwei/. Formerly also **mullaway.** [a. Yaralde *malowe.*] The large, edible fish *Argyrosomus hololepidotus*, occurring in marine and estuarine waters of Aust. See also BUTTERFISH, JEWFISH, KINGFISH.

1846 H.E.A. MEYER *Manners & Customs Aborigines Encounter Bay* 6 They use the spear at the Murray in catching the large fish, *Mallowe.* **1871** *Austral. Town & Country Jrnl.* (Sydney) 22 Apr. 486/4 As much as three tons at a haul, consisting principally of mullaway, bream [etc.]. **1933** D. MACDONALD *Brooks of Morning* 180 Adelaide has called a particular fish of the Murray mouth, quite large enough for angling romance, a mulloway. If the mulloway .. ranges as far east as Port Phillip it becomes a kingfish.

mullygrub. [Prob. transf. use of Br. dial. *mullygrub* meal grub: see EDD *mullygrub-gurgin.*] A grub, esp. WITCHETTY 2.

1924 F.J. MILLS *Happy Days* 61 If fruit-trees are not sprayed at the correct time .. leaves will curl up (caused by a mullygrub shaped like a corkscrew). **1966** *Courier-Mail* (Brisbane) 26 Nov. 8/8 The woman .. had told him frequently to 'go and eat his mully grubs', and to 'go back to the bush where you came from'.

multy /'mʌlti/, *a. Obs.* [Shortened form of Parlyaree *multicattivo*, a. It. *molto cattivo* very bad: see Partridge *multee kertever.*] Bad; in poor condition; unpleasant; low.

1880 *Bulletin* (Sydney) 11 Sept. 8/1 The Franzini Variety Company, at St. George's Hall, Melbourne, did not fizzle; the houses were 'multy', and the shutters are up. **1908** *Truth* (Sydney) 19 Apr. 10/5 The only fairies as she seen Were a multy kind of set.

mundic /'mʌndɪk/. Also **mundick.** [A Cornish miners' term: see OED.] Iron pyrites.

1834 C.O. BOOTH *Jrnl.* (1981) 179 Descended the new Shaft—crawled into the 'level'—the Mundick just above the second stratum of Coal lying in a bed of grey or dark Stone bind. **1858** *Colonial Mining Jrnl.* Nov. 40/3 The Old Man vein .. contains a quantity of mundic where cut in the levels, but little gold.

mundie /'mʌndi/. *Obs.* Also **mundy.** [Prob. a. Kattang *mundi.*] See quot. 1847. Also **mundie-stone.**

1847 G.F. ANGAS *Savage Life & Scenes* II. 224 Mundie is a crystal, believed by the natives to be an excrement issuing from the Deity, and held sacred. **1851** J. HENDERSON *Excursions & Adventures N.S.W.* II. 157 The natives have charms which they carry about with them. .. These are bits of rock crystal, which they find on the mountains, and are called *mundy-stones*.

mundowie /mʌn'dovi/. Chiefly *Austral. pidgin.* Also **mundoey, mundoie.** [Perh. a. Dharuk *manuwi* or Awabakal *manduwaŋ.*] A foot; a footstep.

1822 A. CUNNINGHAM Table of Lang., *Foot*, mundoe. **1896** *Bulletin* (Sydney) 18 Apr. 27/1 The Botany dialect .. gave us 'mundowie', the word for leg, though widely used for the foot by the whites. **1909** *Ibid.* 16 Dec. 13/3 Chocking one of the wheels of bullock-dray with his big mundoeys. **1976** C.D. MILLS *Hobble Chains & Greenhide* 11 We saw tracks about a mile from the hole, and though the big, splayed 'mundoies' meant nothing to me, Pebble could read them like a printed page.

munga /'mʌŋɡə/. Also **mungar, munger, mungey.** [Abbrev. of Br. slang *mungaree* food, f. It. *mangiare* to eat: see OEDS *mungaree* and also *munga, n.²*] In Services' speech: food.

1918 *Kia Ora Coo-ee* Oct. 14/3 I've enjoyed munger in a 'special' more than six course dinners in Cairo. **1920** *Aussie* (Sydney) Apr. 18/3 'What'll you have, Maisie?' .. 'A meat pie, please, Bob.' It was a little bit of heaven to see her put the mungar away. **1933** E.J. RULE *Jacka's Mob* 206 They had made a present of our 'mungey' to some Digger whom they'd never seen before. **1945** *Chocolate & Green* (Sydney) July 16 Seven say their record attendance is due to the 'Hungry Nine' hogging the 'Munga' and leaving them weak from malnutrition.

mungite /'mʌŋɡaɪt/. *W.A.* [a. Nyungar *maŋɡayit* a sweet substance, esp. the flower of the banksia.] The nectar-rich flowering spike, becoming a woody cone, of the BANKSIA; the plant itself.

1886 H.W. BUNBURY *Early Days W.A.* (1930) 80 At this season food was plentiful—both fish .. and 'Munghites' as they call the flower of the Banksia, from which they extract by suction a delicious juice resembling a mixture of honey and dew. **1979** E. SMITH *Saddle in Kitchen* 26 Grandpa had strange names for some things too—native names many of them. Banksias he called what sounded like 'mungites', though I've never heard the term used by anyone else.

mungo /'mʌŋgoʊ/. [Prob. a. Ngiyambaa *maŋgar* bark (canoe).] An Aboriginal bark canoe.

1847 G.F. ANGAS *Savage Life & Scenes* I. 219 The natives, in their canoes of bark (*mungo*). **1853** A. KINLOCH *Murray River* 13 We managed to upset a native canoe or 'mungo', propelled by a black and his 'lubra', or spouse.

munjon /'mʌndʒən/. *W.A.* Also **mungus, munjong, murndong**. [a. Yinjibarndi *manyjaɲu* stranger.] An Aboriginal who has had little contact with white society. Also *transf.*, an Aboriginal brought up in white society and unfamiliar with the traditional way of life.

1948 M. UREN *Glint of Gold* 250 The Munjons, the wild bush aboriginals. **1975** R. BEILBY *Brown Land Crying* 107 Ya a bit of a newchum ain'tcha? What we call a murndong. **1975** X. HERBERT *Poor Fellow my Country* 628 Anyone of them who could not ride a horse or was scared of a train or motor vehicle was considered a 'mungus' or a 'myall'. **1984** W.W. AMMON et al. *Working Lives* 42 There was nearly always work at the dead-end job of fencing .. waiting for the mugs, the munjongs and the new chums.

muntry /'mʌntri/. Now usu. in the pl. form **muntries**, constr. as sing. Formerly also **monterry, montry, muntree** and **muntri**. [a. Yaralde *mandharri*.] The edible fruit of the prostrate shrub *Kunzea pomifera* (fam. Myrtaceae) of dry sandy soils and near-coastal w. Vic. and e. S.A.; the plant itself; *native apple* (a), see NATIVE *a.* 6 a. Also *attrib.*.

1847 G.F. ANGAS *Savage Life & Scenes* I. 65 Monterries, or native apples. This fruit is a little berry, the production of a running plant that grows in profusion upon the sand-hills. These berries are precisely like miniature apples, and have an aromatic flavour, which is not unpleasant. When the monterry is ripe, the natives disperse themselves over the sand-hills in search of them. **1893** S. NEWLAND *Paving Way* 137 Before leaving the beach .. he gathered a handful of *montries*, a small indigenous berry with the flavour of a sour apple. **1926** J.M. BLACK *Flora S.A.* iii. 405 The berries, called 'muntries' in Victoria, are used for making tarts. **1937** *Bulletin* (Sydney) 7 July 20/1 On swampy areas inland from the S.A. coast between Robe and Beachport grows a small creeping plant which bears heavy crops of a berry. . . The abos. knew it as 'muntry' berry. **1948** H.A. LINDSAY *Bushman's Handbk.* 54 Muntrey or muntree, small creeping ground plant, bearing a fruit exactly like a tiny apple in appearance, smell and flavour. Can be eaten raw but is better stewed. **1955** M. BUNDEY *My Land* 34 There is a berry called the muntri and with this you can make a lovely pie and tasty jam.

munyeroo /mʌnjə'ru/. Also **munyeru**. [a. Diyari (and related languages) *manyurra*.] Either of two succulent plants of the fam. Portulacaceae having seeds and leaves used as food, orig. *Calandrinia balonensis* (see PARAKEELIA), and now usu. *pig weed* (see PIG *n.*[1]).

1885 *Trans. & Proc. R. Soc. S.A.* (1886) VIII. 27 *Claytonia Balonnensis*—This showy plant, called 'Munyeroo' by the aboriginals .. has a cluster of thick fleshy leaves, with a flower stem some six or more inches high, crowned with bright deep pink flowers as large as a shilling. **1896** B. SPENCER *Rep. Horn Sci. Exped. Central Aust.* IV. 56 *Claytonia balonnensis*... By the blacks of Alice Springs (Arunta) this seed is called 'Ing-witchika', which appears to be the real native name, though the term 'Munyeru', by which it is known to Europeans, is invariably understood.

murawirrie, var. MURRAWIRRIE.

murlonga /mɜ'lɒŋgə/. Also **murlonger, myrnonga**. [Perh. f. an Aboriginal language.] A white man who sexually exploits Aboriginal women.

1912 *Bulletin* (Sydney) 15 Feb. 13/2 There is the much less widely known aboriginal term 'myrnonga'. The myrnonga is a person of more promiscuous habits [than the combo] who .. prowls with furtiveness when the moon is young. **1949** H.G. LAMOND *White Ears* 9 'Don' you talk 'bout my mother thataway!' Emma screamed. 'You combo-you! You murlonga!'. **1971** K. WILLEY *Boss Drover* 45 Combos, murlongers, or gin burglars.

murndong, var. MUNJON.

murnong /'mɜnɒŋ/. Also with much variety, as **mernong, mirr'n-yong, murnung, murrnong, myrnong**. [a. Wathawurung and Wuywurung *mirnaŋ*.] The edible tuber of the perennial herb *Microseris scapigera* (fam. Asteraceae) of temperate Aust.; the plant itself, bearing a yellow, dandelion-like flowerhead. See also YAM.

1836 *Bent's News* (Hobart) 3 Sept. 3 Pigs .. feed well on the 'murnung', a root on which the natives here often subsist. **1837** P.L. BROWN *Clyde Co. Papers* 16 Aug. (1952) II. 91 Saw a woman digging murnong, a native root, about five miles from the scrub. **1851** H. MELVILLE *Present State Aust.* 68 Mr Gellibrand .. almost lived upon the nutritious root, 'Mernong', or native parsnip. **1859** D. BUNCE *Lang. Aborigines Vic.* p. xi, The whole of the tribes to form one great family, where they may adopt their primitive habits of .. digging for myrnong, burrowing for wombats and porcupines. **1965** *Austral. Encycl.* IX. 524 *Microseris scapigera* .. is called yam throughout Victoria. Its tuberous roots furnished one of the chief vegetable foods of many native tribes, those near Melbourne calling it *murrnong* (literally, 'the fingers of a hand', from the clusters of small finger-like tubers). **1983** J. FLOOD *Archeol. of Dreamtime* 202 The men could have existed on .. the region's one abundant plant food, the daisy yam or mirr'n-yong (*Microseris scapigera*).

murrawirrie /mʌrə'wɪri/. Also **murawirrie**. [a. Diyari *mara* hand + *wirri* throwing club.] A heavy boomerang used for striking at an opponent: see quot. 1879.

1879 *Native Tribes S.A.* 288 Murawirrie .. two-handed boomerang, from 6 to 14 ft. long, and 4 in. broad. **1931** A.W. UPFIELD *Sands of Windee* 108 Moongalliti, attired only in a loincloth, clutched a heavy murrawirrie in his left hand, and three or four wooden spears.

Murray. [The name of a river in s.e. Aust.]

1. Used *attrib.* in Comb. **Murray scrub.**

1843 *S. Austral. Mag.* Jan. 129 The Murray scrub is well known.

2. In the names of flora and fauna: **Murray catfish**, the fresh-water catfish *Tandanus tandanus*, a thickset, robust fish brown to olive-green above and paler below, formerly widespread in the Murray River; **cod**, the large, groper-like *Maccullochella peeli*, a mottled, greenish, fresh-water fish of the Murray-Darling river system and elsewhere in Aust.; **crayfish**, the large fresh-water crayfish *Euastacus armatus*; also **Murray River crayfish; grey**, a breed of grey, beef cattle (see quot. 1964); **lily** obs., Darling lily, see DARLING; **magpie**, *magpie lark*, see MAGPIE *n.* 2; **perch**, any of several fresh-water fish of the Murray-Darling river system, incl. *golden perch* (see GOLDEN 3), and MACQUARIE PERCH; **pine**, any of several trees of the genus *Callitris* (fam. Cupressaceae), esp. *C. preissii* subsp. *murrayensis* of N.S.W., Vic., and S.A. and *white pine* (see WHITE *a.*[2] 1 a.); the close-grained, resinous wood of these trees; **red gum**, the tree *Eucalyptus camaldulensis* (see RED GUM 1); **smoker**, *yellow rosella*, see YELLOW 1.

1873 F. DE CASTELNAU *Edible Fishes Vic.* 15 The **Murray catfish** (*Copidoglanis Tandanus*) from the Murray river. It is a hideous-looking fish, but fit for the table. **1843** *S. Austral. News* (London) 15 Dec. 166/2 So plentiful are the **Murray cod** that the men at the station merely throw out their lines in the evening and the next morning they find them full. **1878** [**Murray crayfish**] R.B. SMYTH *Aborigines of Vic.* I. 205 The cray-fish commonly found in creeks and ponds—the large Murray one (*Astacoides serratus*), and the smaller (*A. quinquecarinatus*) afford excellent food. **1880** 'OLD HAND' *Experiences of Colonist* (ed. 2) i. 79 The antennae of a number of Murray crayfish. **1944** A. MARSHALL *These are my People* 28 He brought us a bag of Murray River crayfish. **1963** *Pastoral Rev. & Graziers' Rec.* 18 Oct. 1135 The unusual feature of this year's beef cattle section was the inclusion for the first time of two breeds, Galloways and **Murray Greys**. **1964** *Ibid.* 19 Oct. 1146 Murray Greys. 'Crossley', writing in *The Pastoral Review* of November 1955 . . is acknowledged to be the first to have placed on record a detailed chronicling of the origins of this interesting breed. On his way to the Melbourne Royal of that year he visited Thologolong, the upper-Murray River property of Mr Keith Sutherland. He also wrote at length about the intriguing new breed of 'Scottish Greys', as they were then known. Having been first recognized by Mr Keith Sutherland's father in 1914, the Murray grey is fast becoming a force to be reckoned with in the rough country in the southern half of Australia. **1847** G.F. ANGAS *Savage Life & Scenes* I. 62 We frequently met with that large and beautiful straw-coloured amaryllis, the **Murray lily**; the perfume of its blossoms frequently betraying its locality, at a considerable distance. **1940** L.E. SHEARD *Austral. Youth among Desert Aborigines* (1964) 5 Remarking on the number of '**Murray Magpies**' about, the hotel proprietor told us that these birds have been proved by tagging to migrate to the north of Japan. **1880** G. WALCH *Vic.* 124 Our noble old 1,400-mile river, the Murray, well christened the Nile of Australia . . produces 'snags' and that finny monster, the Murray cod, together with his less bulky, equally flavourless congener, the **Murray perch**. **1853** J. SHERER *Gold Finder Aust.* 188 A new tree, a species of pine, with foliage like a Scotch fir, but tapering like a larch or silver fir. Its cones are about the size of marbles. I believe it is the **Murray pine**. **1880** R. ROSE *Vic. Guide* 11 The Murray pine is a handsomely marked useful wood. **1916** S.A. WHITE *In Far Northwest* 44 Among the rocks grew the shapely trees of the Murray pine (Callitris robusta). **1904** J.H. MAIDEN *Notes on Commercial Timbers N.S.W.* 17 **Murray red gum** (*Eucalyptus rostrata*) . . is the red gum *par excellence* of the States of New South Wales, Victoria and South Australia. **1917** *Bulletin* (Sydney) 7 June 24/4 A very rare bird, the yellow parrot, or '**Murray smoker**' (*Platycercus flaveolus*), appears occasionally on the Monaro (N.S.W.) plains.

3. Special Comb. **Murray whaler**: see WHALER *n.*¹ b.

4. In the phr. **on the Murray (cod)**, rhyming slang for 'on the nod', on credit.

1967 *Kings Cross Whisper* (Sydney) xxxvi. 4/2 *Murray cod*, on the nod, to bet on credit, on the Murray. **1977** *Weekend Austral. Mag.* (Sydney) 23 July 1/6 A punter, well known in Sydney, who bets on 'the murray cod' (the nod) walked into City Tattersalls on Monday settling day carrying $240,000 cash in two suitcases.

Murray Valley. [The name of the valley of the *Murray* River (see MURRAY).] Used *attrib.* to designate (**a**) a severe form of encephalitis; (**b**) the mosquito-borne virus that causes it.

1951 *Med. Jrnl. Aust.* I. 526 A severe human encephalitis of virus origin spread diffusely along the Murray Valley during the early months of 1951. This has been provisionally referred to as Murray Valley encephalitis. **1985** *A.N.U. Reporter* (Canberra) 22 Nov. 1 In the last year attention has been focussed on Murray Valley encephalitis virus. Under certain climatic and ecological conditions the virus can break out in epidemics around Australia.

murri /'mʌri/. Also **murrey**. [a. Kamilaroi (and many Qld. languages) *mari* Aboriginal man, Aboriginal person.] An Aboriginal person; the Aboriginal people.

1884 J.B. GRIBBLE *Black but Comely* 125 It has been the misfortune of the Murri . . to be found in the way of European colonisation. **1930** K.G. TAYLOR *Pick & Duffers* 49 'I bet it's someone dressed up to frighten the blacks.' 'No fear; murreys never come to Yeller Cap in the moon.'

murrillo /məˈriloʊ/. *Obs.* Also **murilla**. [a. Yuwaalaraay *murrila*.] See quot. 1881. Also *attrib.*

1881 *Jrnl. & Proc. R. Soc. N.S.W.* XV. 43 A conglomerate composed chiefly of waterworn quartz pebbles, called on the Barwon and Narran murrillo, but not known by this name in other parts of the country where the conglomerate is found. On making inquiries among the blacks I found that in their language murrillo means ant-hill. . . These anthills are nearly always built on the highest ground in that part of the Colony, to avoid floods, and as the highest ground is generally that which is composed of the quartz conglomerate it is easy to understand how the word which first meant ant-hill came also to mean the ridges on which the ant-hills are found. **1915** T. SKEYHILL *Soldier-Songs from Anzac* 13 By yarran clumps and coolabah, and up murilla ridges.

murrnong, var. MURNONG.

Murrumbidgee /mʌrəmˈbɪdʒi/, *attrib.* and *n.* [The name of a river in s. N.S.W.]

A. Used *attrib.* in Special Comb. **Murrumbidgee blanket**, see quot. 1926 and WAGGA; **camper,** *Murrumbidgee whaler*, see WHALER *n.*¹ b.; **jam**, see quot. 1901; **pine**, the tree *Callitris glaucophylla* (see *white pine* WHITE *a.*² 1 a.), and poss. other trees of the genus *Callitris*; **rug**, see quot. 1924; **whaler, whaling** *vbl. n.*, see WHALER *n.*¹ b.

1906 *Bulletin* (Sydney) 26 July 16/2 *Re* Wagga rugs and **Murrumbidgee blankets** . . the latter is a bare bag, split open. **1926** *Aussie* (Sydney) Aug. 50/1 The 'Murrumbidgee blanket' . . was a wheat bag split down the seams, and used as a quilt. **1936** *Bulletin* (Sydney) 19 Aug. 21/1 You rarely see . . a Murrumbidgee blanket in a swag these days. **1906** *Ibid.* 5 July 17/1 Swears they'll join some push o' rampers or some **Murrumbidgee campers**. **1901** *Ibid.* 14 Sept. 16/4 '**Murrumbidgee jam**' consists of brown sugar muddled up with cold tea. **1834** G. BENNETT *Wanderings N.S.W.* I. 263 Large quantities of a species of Callitrys, called the '**Murrumbidgee pine**' by the colonists, from having been seen first on the hills in the vicinity of that river. **1924** *Smith's Weekly* (Sydney) 24 May 23/6 The . . **Murrumbidgee rug** . . is . . a split bag . . with an old woollen blanket that has become too thin to keep out the cold, sewn on for lining.

B. *n.* A game of chance played with dice, resembling craps. Also *attrib.*

1917 *Bk. of Ballarat* 41 Producing a dice-box, he invites all and sundry to 'have a go at the good old game of Murrumbidgee'. **1941** D. O'CALLAGHAN *Long Life Reminisc.* 5 He experienced . . the sly-grog shops and the two-up and Murrumbidgee rings.

murry /'mʌri/, *adv. Austral. pidgin. Obs.* [a. Dharuk *mari*.] Very. Also as *adj.*, great.

[**1793** W. TENCH *Compl. Acct. Settlement* 65 They called him Mùr-ree Mùl-la (a large strong man).] **1803** J. GRANT *Narr. Voyage N.S.W.* 90 You know me *murrey jarrin*, that is much afraid. **1818** J. HOLT *Mem.* (1838) II. 150 They say . . that there is a *murry* devil, of whom they are very much afraid.

mush. Also **moosh**. [Spec. use of U.S. *mush* a kind of porridge: see OED *sb.* 1.] Gaol food, esp. porridge.

1945 S.J. BAKER *Austral. Lang.* 141 Jail food is *moosh*. **1967** B.K. BURTON *Teach them no More* 17, I knew an old lagger once. . . He made little statues out of his mush. Didn't eat breakfast for years.

mushy, *a.* [Spec. use of *mushy* soft, pulpy.] Of wool: yielding a high percentage of waste (see quot. 1951).
  1901 *Bulletin* (Sydney) 12 Oct. 16/3 'Strong' wool is fashionable now because .. in a hot climate it is not nearly so liable to become 'mushy' or 'wasty' as 'fine'. 1951 *Concerning Wool* (Austral. Wool Board) 102 *Mushy,* wool which is lacking character, open, badly weathered, and very wasty or noily.

music stick. CLAP STICK.
  1944 *Coast to Coast 1943* 1 From his left hung a long bag of banyan-cord containing his big painted dijeridoo and music-sticks. 1981 D. LEVITT *Plants & People* 21 Boomerangs were clapped together as 'music-sticks' during corroborees.

musk. [Transf. use of *musk* odoriferous glandular secretion of the male musk-deer.]
  1. The small tree or tall shrub *Olearia argophylla* (fam. Asteraceae) of Tas., Vic., and s.e. N.S.W., the leaves of which are silvery underneath and have a musky aroma; the wood of the tree. Also **musk tree, muskwood.**
  1827 H. HELLYER Diary 5 July, Thickly wooded with .. musk and Dogwood. 1880 R. ROWE *Roughing It* 11 He had to cross a lonely ridge, covered with evergreen beeches and musk-trees. 1904 J.H. MAIDEN *Notes on Commercial Timbers N.S.W.* 28 Muskwood (*Olearia argophylla*) .. requires the most careful seasoning, otherwise it warps and twists very much.
  2. Special Comb. **musk duck,** the brown and black duck *Biziura lobata* of s. Aust. incl. Tas., the male of which has a large, pendulous lobe under the bill and a musky odour; **lorikeet** (formerly **parakeet),** the lorikeet *Glossopsitta concinna* of s.e. Aust. incl. Tas., having bright green plumage with a red face stripe.
  1805 Banks Papers 7 Jan. XX. 13 Wild Ducks several kinds, a large Bird which I think is new from the very strong smell it has of Musk they have here named it the **Musk Duck.** 1843 [**musk lorikeet**] J. GOULD *Birds of Aust.* (1848) V. Pl. 52, In the more southern country of Van Diemen's Land .. it is known by the name of the Musk Parrakeet, from the peculiar odour of the bird. 1969 J.M. FORSHAW *Austral. Parrots* 35 The Musk Lorikeet derives its name from a musky odour that is said to be associated with it.

muskwood.
  1. The rainforest tree *Alangium villosum* (fam. Alangiaceae) of e. Qld. and N.S.W.; the wood of the tree. Also **musk tree.**
  1880 J. BONWICK *Resources Qld.* 82 The Musk-tree, *Marlea,* though of bright yellow wood, is black at the centre. 1906 *Proc. Linnean Soc. N.S.W.* XXXI. 374 There is only one genus and species (*Marlea vitiensis* ..) of *Cornaceae* known in Australia, and this .. yields a very good timber, which is known locally as 'Muskwood'.
  2. See MUSK 1.

muso /'mjuzoʊ/. [f. *mus(ician* + -O.] A musician.
  1967 *Kings Cross Whisper* (Sydney) xxxix. 9/1 *Musos blow cold.* Members of the Sydney symphony orchestra will work to rule. 1977 K. GILBERT *Living Black* 162, I used to be a muso and a hustler from the city but I'm a tribal man too.

mustard. Used *attrib.* in Special Comb. **mustard gold,** gold in extremely fine particles; **tree** (or **bush),** any of several plants, esp. the almost-leafless shrub or small tree *Apophyllum anomalum* (fam. Capparaceae) of N.S.W. and Qld., and the HORSERADISH TREE.
  [N.Z. 1912 N.Z. Geol. Survey Bull. No. 15 New Ser. 110 Some of these small sulphide patches showed **'mustard gold'**.] 1932 I.L. IDRIESS *Prospecting for Gold* 57 Black sands on the sea beach have been very rich with 'mustard gold'.

1898 [**mustard tree**] D.W. CARNEGIE *Spinifex & Sand* 179 Little clumps of what is locally termed 'mustard bush', so named from the strong flavour of the leaf. 1956 GARDNER & BENNETTS *Toxic Plants W.A.* 26 The native poplar .. also known as the mustard tree .. contains a mustard oil.

muster, *n.* [Spec. use of *muster* an assembly of soldiers, etc., for inspection: see OED(S *sb.*[1] 3 and *v.*[1] 2.]
  1. *Hist.* **a.** A routine assembling of convicts in order to ascertain that all are present. **b.** An assembly of the population of a district, Colony, etc., or a specified sector thereof, for the purpose of taking a census; a census.
  1788 J. WHITE *Jrnl. Voyage N.S.W.* 5 Feb. (1790) 124 On a muster of the convicts this morning, some were found to be missing, and supposed to have gone to Botany Bay. 1804 *HRA* (1915) 1st Ser. V. 9, I have the honour to transmit the result of the free people and convicts' muster. 1831 *HRA* (1923) 1st Ser. XVI. 418 No Muster of them having been received in this Country since the year 1825.
  2. *transf.* The gathering together of (freq. widely dispersed) livestock in one place for the purpose of branding, counting, etc.
  [N.Z. 1841 S. REVANS Lett. I. 90 (OEDS), I am not yet confident of the mode in which flock and stock musters will be dealt with by the natives.] 1844 Macarthur Papers LXII. 106, I hope this year we shall have a great increase to this muster, as the Ewes will lamb in September next. 1956 T. RONAN *Moleskin Midas* 74 Yates volunteered to tail right through the muster with Wilmot Lake for offsider.
  3. In the collocation **general muster.**
  a. *Hist.* MUSTER *n.* 1 b.
  c 1795 G. BARRINGTON *Voyage to Botany Bay* 51 In the morning a general muster took place. 1850 *Irish Exile* (Hobart) 29 June 6/4 The woman was discharged to the service of Government, her ticket-of-leave being revoked, because she did not attend the last general muster.
  b. A muster of all stock on a property.
  [N.Z. 1892 W.E. SWANTON *Notes on N.Z.* 97 There is the general muster, which means the rounding up and bringing in of all the sheep, good or bad, on the 'run'.] 1927 A. CROMBIE *After Sixty Yrs.* 41 Arranged for a general muster of their herd. 1931 *Bulletin* (Sydney) 29 July 20/4 On the big cattle stations of western Queensland .. a general muster on such occasions as the sale of the run is necessary.
  4. Special Comb. *Hist.* **muster bell,** a bell which is rung to summon convicts (later prisoners) to an assembly; **book,** a register of the population of a Colony; a register of the names, etc., of convicts; **clerk,** a clerk employed in keeping the record of a census; **day,** a day appointed for a census; a day on which livestock are mustered; **ground,** a place at which a muster is held; **master,** an official responsible for keeping a *muster roll;* **roll,** a register of convicts (see quot. 1822); **station,** the office in which a *muster roll* is kept; **yard,** *muster ground;* an enclosure into which livestock are mustered.
  1846 L.W. MILLER *Notes of Exile Van Dieman's Land* 263 At six o'clock the **muster bell** rang, and about twelve hundred men answered their names, took their place in their respective gangs, and under the charge of overseers marched out of the barracks to their daily labour. 1973 R. HALL *Poems from Prison* 33 A muster bell hangs from a wrought iron frame where a warder parades on the square. 1826 *Colonial Times* (Hobart) 6 May, To this Officer also the General Muster of the Colony will be entrusted. He will have charge .. of the **Muster Books.** 1849 T. ROGERS *Corresp. relating to Dismissal* 100 He had the muster-book in his hand calling the names. 1830 *Sydney Monitor* 10 Mar. 3/2 Alexander Still, Esq. late principal **muster-clerk.** 1844 *Colonial Times* (Hobart) 9 Nov., A number of ticket-of-leave men have been variously dealt with for their accustomed jollification on **muster day.** 1849 A. HARRIS *Emigrant Family* (1967) 91 To keep an eye on the gathering in the stockyard when the next muster-day came. 1848 J. SYME

Nine Yrs. Van Diemen's Land 277 The whole gang .. hear prayers read on the **muster-ground** morning and evening. **1827** *HRA* (1922) 3rd Ser. V. 766, I have .. appointed Mr Josiah Spode to be **Muster Master**. **1802** *N.S.W. Gen. Orders* 22 Oct. (1806) 8 The **Muster Rolls** are to continue the same as when delivered to the *Governor* by Captain Balmain. **1822** J.T. BIGGE *Rep. State Colony N.S.W.* 15 The lieutenant-governor's secretary proceeds on board the convict ships, attended by the lieutenant-governor's clerk, and makes a list or muster roll of the convicts, describing the number, name, time and place of trial, their sentences, age, native place, trade, description of person and character. **1820** *Sydney Gaz.* 19 Sept., It is further ordered and directed that the Clerk of the General Muster do furnish to the Principal or Senior Magistrate at each **Muster Station**, a suitable Book and Forms for the taking the said Musters. **1845** *Port Phillip Gaz.* 23 July 3 A good .. cottage, with .. stock and **muster yards** for 1500 head of cattle. **1892** *Bulletin* (Sydney) 7 May 21/4 The System sent a masked man into the muster-yard of the ironed men.

5. *fig.* With distinguishing first element: **tarpaulin muster** [spec. use of nautical slang *tarpaulin muster* a collection of money (see OEDS *tarpaulin, sb.* 4)], **(a)** the collecting of a pool of money, to be used either to buy drinks for the contributors or to provide assistance to some other person or cause (see quot. 1960); **(b)** *transf.*, see quot. 1945. Also **blanket, calico, canvas, tambaroora muster.**

1897 *Bulletin* (Sydney) 18 Dec. (Red Page), The essence of a present-day tambaroora is a sweep for the purchase of drinks—frequently on the principle that more liquor can be purchased wholesale for 1s. 6d. than six thirsty people can buy for 3d. each. Hence 'tambaroora muster', when the droughty party musters all the coin it's possessed of, and one individual goes and bargains for the beer. **1904** *Sporting News* (Launceston) 27 Aug. 2/8 Then raked through all our pockets, 'mongst tobacco, string, and grease; Till by tarpaulin muster, we raised just a drink a piece. **1945** E. GEORGE *Two at Daly Waters* 102 As she had not brought a town outfit Daly Waters had what we call in the bush a tarpaulin muster (the loan of everybody's best clothes). **1960** *Bulletin* (Sydney) 30 Nov. 18/2 A calicomuster .. dates from the time when shearers and other casual bush-workers all had swags usually with calico or tarpaulin covers. At night a swag-cover would be spread on the ground for a table, and the shearers would sit around .. and gamble against their earnings. When cut-out came, a calico-muster or, more commonly, tarpaulin-muster, might be held for the benefit of the hospital .. or any other suitable object of charity; that is, the swag-cover was spread as usual, and contributions were thrown into it. **1964** K. WILLEY *Eaters of Lotus* 45 He leapt off the bunk and broke both his toes. Everyone thought that was very humorous, so they held a blanket muster and sent him off to hospital in an aeroplane. **1965** *Mount Isa Mail* 16 Nov. 2/1 Claimed his department colleagues were to take up a canvas muster to provide him with sufficient money to survive.

muster, *v.* [As prec.]

1. *Hist.*

a. *trans.* To assemble (convicts) for counting, inspecting, etc.; to take a census of (the population, or a sector thereof).

1789 J. HUNTER *Hist. Jrnl. Trans. Port Jackson* (1793) 361, I gave orders for the convicts to be mustered in their huts three times every night. **1816** *Hobart Town Gaz.* 16 Nov., The Lieutenant Governor will Muster the Settlers, Prisoners, and other Persons resident in the District of Pitt Water.

b. *refl.*

1811 *Sydney Gaz.* 2 Mar., Many Persons have omitted to come forward and muster themselves.

c. *intr.* for *refl.* To assemble (for inspection, a census, etc.). With **for**: to declare at a muster.

1810 *Sydney Gaz.* 7 Jan., Some ill-disposed Person or Persons, with an Intent to injure me most maliciously have falsely propagated a Report, that I had not the Number of Acres of Wheat, Barely, and Corn in Cultivation that I mustered for at the last General Muster. **1814** L. MACQUARIE *Let.* 10 Sept. (1821) 88 Ticket of Leave Men are to muster on the right of Assigned Government Men.

2. *transf.*

a. *trans.* To gather (livestock) together in one place for the purpose of branding, counting, drafting, etc. Also *absol.*

1813 *HRA* (1916) 1st Ser. VII. 747 You must in Person Muster the whole of the Horned Cattle, Sheep and Horses belonging to the Crown. **1886** H. FINCH-HATTON *Advance Aust.* (rev. ed.) 55 Neighbouring stations always .. send up a spare hand or two to help muster and brand.

b. *trans.* To clear (an area specified) of livestock in order to gather them together in one place.

1886 P. CLARKE *'New Chum' in Aust.* 168 This is the paddock we have, in bush phraseology, to 'clean' or 'muster'. **1962** D. LOCKWOOD *I, Aboriginal* 172 We mustered the open country around the billabongs on the river flats.

musterer. One who musters livestock.

[N.Z. **1863** E.R. CHUDLEIGH *Diary* 19 Dec. (1950) 114 All the musterers dogs have come home.] **1889** *Illustr. Austral. News* (Melbourne) 1 May 74/2 The distribution of the musterers under the leadership of one of the stockmen that knows the most likely places to find cattle suitable for the southern market. **1980** ANSELL & PERCY *To fight Wild* 76 Any faint possibility that might have crossed my mind about some musterers turning up, from anywhere .. was dispelled.

mustering, *vbl. n.*

a. The action of gathering together in one place (freq. widely dispersed) livestock. Also *attrib.*

1847 T. WOORE *Diary* May (1935) 68 Should 'Pomeroy Run' be leased separately from the Homestead then its stock yards, mustering paddock of 300 acres, [etc.]. **1872** C.H. EDEN *My Wife & I in Qld.* 69 Here take place the annual musterings.

b. *Comb.* **mustering camp, dog.**

1911 E.S. SORENSON *Life in Austral. Backblocks* 82 This class of cook is frequently met with in **mustering-camps** on the big cattle stations of Western Queensland. **1937** *Bulletin* (Sydney) 16 June 20/2 Jack was the finest **mustering dog** I ever saw.

c. Special Comb. **mustering plant**, see PLANT *n.*^{2}

1934 C. SAYCE *Comboman* 217 A mustering plant! It was Jim Hindley's plant. He had been out for a fortnight, mustering horses and was taking a mob back to Kendal station for drafting.

mutting /'mʌtɪŋ/. *Obs.* Also **mutach, muton**. [a. Dharuk *mudiŋ*.] An Aboriginal fish spear.

1790 D. SOUTHWELL *Correspondence & Papers*, *Mūding*, fish-gig. **1803** J. GRANT *Narr. Voyage N.S.W.* 163 He threw down his *muton*, so they name the fish-gig, and came readily to us. **1851** J. HENDERSON *Excursions & Adventures N.S.W.* II. 137 They spear fish from a canoe, or from the bank, in which case they use commonly a *mutach*, or smaller spear, having four or five points, and discharged from the hand. **1892** HILL & THORNTON *Notes on Aborigines N.S.W.* 2 A blackfellow in his way, as a rule, is very clever .. and with the mutting (four-pronged spear) .. not easily surpassed.

mutton. [Transf. use of *mutton* the flesh of sheep, used as food.]

1. The flesh of goat, used as food. Also **goat mutton.**

1897 J.J. MURIF *From Ocean to Ocean* 57 No sheep beyond Oodnadatta either. .. The goat's flesh is called 'mutton'. **1930** D. COTTRELL *Earth Battle* 125 She put .. the damper and cold goat mutton on a newspaper.

2. In the collocation **underground mutton**, the flesh of rabbit, used as food.
1919 *Bulletin* (Sydney) 1 May 22/2 Here where I am (4th A.G.H.) the Diggers call rabbit 'underground mutton'.

mutton-bird, *n.* [See quot. 1839 (2).]
1. The brownish-black, migratory bird *Puffinus tenuirostris*, breeding in s.e. Aust., esp. on Bass Strait islands, and harvested for its fat, feathers, and edible flesh; any of several other birds of similar appearance or usefulness. See also *short-tailed shearwater* SHORT-TAILED.
1790 R. CLARK Jrnl. 28 Aug. 202 A Box for my beloved woman, Containing.. a Mount Pit Bird, a Mutton Bird. **1839** W.H. LEIGH *Reconnoitering Voyages* 109 There is .. a bird called the 'Mutton Bird', which is salted and dried, but it requires a desperate stomach to attack such an oily mess. **1839** W. MANN *Six Yrs.' Residence* 51 They are web-footed, of the puffin species, and are commonly called *mutton birds*, from their flavour and fatness; they are migratory, and arrive in Bass's Straits about the commencement of spring, in such numbers that they darken the air.
2. *fig.* A non-Aboriginal resident of northern Tasmania.
1892 *Truth* (Sydney) 19 June 4/7 North Tasmanians resent being nicknamed Mutton birds. **1941** S.J. BAKER *Pop. Dict. Austral. Slang* 48 *Mutton-bird*, a resident of Northern Tasmania. Also, 'mutton-bird eater'.
3. *attrib.* esp. as **mutton-bird feather, oil, pillow, rookery.**
1830 G.A. ROBINSON in N.J.B. Plomley *Friendly Mission* 18 June (1966) 176 The Stack Island is a small rocky island with herbage, and there is a mutton bird rookery. **1846** *Britannia* (Hobart) 10 Sept. 3/2 A protest against 'the abomination of mutton bird feather beds'. **1852** MRS C. MEREDITH *My Home in Tas.* II. 122 The odour of the abominable 'mutton-bird' pillow on which he had lain was most sickening. **1872** *Illustr. Sydney News* 20 Jan. 12/4 At present it [*sc.* Phillip Island, Vic.] is inhabited by a few Chinamen, whose chief avocation is the procuring of mutton bird oil and fishing.
4. Special Comb. **mutton-bird eater**, MUTTON-BIRD 2; **gales** *pl.* (but see quot. 1980), seasonal gales coinciding with the annual arrival of flocks of mutton-birds to nest on islands in Bass Strait and on the coast of Tasmania; *transf.* the flocks of mutton-birds themselves.
1914 *Bulletin* (Sydney) 28 May 22/3 'Moana'.. has never been in Tassy, or he would include the inhabitants of the Fly Speck in his category as **muttonbird-eaters**. **1910** F.M. LITTLER *Handbk. Birds Tas.* 167 The birds commence to come in for laying purposes just a few minutes after sunset. Just at this time of the year heavy gales usually blow, which are known as '**Mutton-bird gales**'. **1958** *Papers & Proc. R. Soc. Tas.* 169 This association of boisterous weather with the egg-laying season of the mutton-birds has led to the use of the term 'mutton-bird gales' in Bass Strait. **1980** H.W. CUMMINGS *Confessions of 'Mud Skipper'* 42 As we ran for Bass Strait it turned into a full 'mutton bird gale'.

mutton-bird, *v.* [f. prec.] *intr.* To catch mutton-birds as food; to catch mutton-birds and prepare their flesh and by-products for the market. Chiefly as *vbl. n.*
1872 M.B. BROWNRIGG *Cruise of Freak* 55 To this place Mr Baudinet and his family annually resort for about two months, for mutton-birding operations. **1881** G. WALCH *Vic.* 49 One of the sports of the neighbourhood is 'mutton-birding'. **1896** *Papers & Proc. R. Soc. Tas.* (1897) p. vi, Mutton-birding, a unique industry, and only carried on in the Furneaux Islands as a regular one... The 'birding' begins on March 20.
Hence **mutton-birder** *n.*
1881 G. WALCH *Vic.* 49 Armed with a piece of stout curved wire, fastened at the end of a long stick, the mutton-birder fishes in the holes for his prize, and is generally rewarded.. by either the egg or the young bird.

mutton-fish. Any of several marine gastropods with an edible flesh, esp. *Haliotis ruber*, having a flat, oval shell with a nacreous lining. See quot. 1974.
1830 G.A. ROBINSON in N.J.B. Plomley *Friendly Mission* 16 Feb. (1966) 120 The natives procured some mutton-fish, which the natives of the south call *par.rar*. **1974** J.M. THOMSON *Fish Ocean & Shore* 89 Abalone .. were known as mutton fish in Australia before the American term abalone took over.

muzzlewood. [See quot. 1982.] *Black sallee*, see BLACK *a.*^{2} 1 a.
1895 *Proc. Linnean Soc. N.S.W.* X. 597 *Eucalyptus stellulata*... It is called 'Muzzle-wood' in Gippsland, but the meaning of the name is unknown to us. **1982** K. HUENEKE *Huts of High Country* 189, I passed several stands of black sallies (*Eucalyptus stellulata*) and he told me the origin of their common name—the muzzlewood. It was in the days of shepherds and unfenced holdings that cattle owners hit on the idea of a wooden muzzle to help wean young calves. Without fences they could not be kept away from their mothers so they fashioned a wooden flap suspended from the nostrils. The calves could still eat grass and drink from a dam or a creek but as soon as they lifted their heads to suckle the muzzle flopped down and prevented access... It was discovered that black sally was the most durable and naturally enough it became the muzzlewood tree.

myall /'maɪəl/, *n.*^{1} and *attrib.* Formerly also **mial, miall, myal.** [a. Dharuk *mayal* a stranger.]
A. *n.*
1. *Obs.* In Aboriginal use: a stranger.
1798 D. COLLINS *Acct. Eng. Colony N.S.W.* I. 610 *Mi-yal*, a stranger... This word has reference to sight; *Mi*, the eye. **1826** Macarthur Papers XII. 4 Feb., This festivity is .. always given to do honor to and entertain strangers, whom they call 'Myall'.
2. An Aboriginal living in a traditional manner (esp. as distinct from one accustomed to, or living amongst, whites). See also WARRIGAL *n.* 2.
1837 *Colonist* (Sydney) 2 Feb. 40/2 'They are only *myalls*' i.e. *wild* natives. **1848** *Sidney's Austral. Hand-Bk.* 7, I have encountered hundreds of wild blacks, fierce myals, who had never before eaten bread, smoked tobacco, or beheld a white face. **1976** S. WELLER *Bastards I have Met* 98 Charlie's people were Myalls and never saw a white man.
3. *transf.* One who is placed in an unfamiliar environment.
1982 *Yulngu* Aug. 23 Chips lost the *Mimi* Toyota out bush one weekend!!... He is a bit of a myall in the bush.
B. *attrib.* passing into *adj.*
1. *Obs.* In Aboriginal use: strange.
1827 W.J. DUMARESQ in G. Mackaness *Fourteen Journeys Blue Mountains* (1950) ii. 96 These *mial* or strange blacks have related .. to us, that there exists in the western country, many days off, a vast interior sea. **1845** *Sydney Morning Herald* 10 June 2/5 On my return .. I found that some myall blacks, belonging to the north-west .. had been in.
2. *transf.* Of an Aboriginal. **a.** *Obs.* Hostile. **b.** Living in a traditional manner; unaccustomed to white society. See also WARRIGAL *a.* 1.
1839 T.L. MITCHELL *Three Exped. Eastern Aust.* (rev. ed.) I. 50 He had been unwilling to acknowledge to me, his dread of the 'myall' tribes. **1870** E.B. KENNEDY *Four Yrs. in Qld.* 34 The term Miall denotes Blacks who are perfectly wild. **1984** B. DIXON *Searching for Aboriginal Lang.* 49 Willie was the most myall of all, and if anyone knew any language it would be him.
3. *fig.* Of an animal or plant: wild.
1851 J. HENDERSON *Excursions & Adventures N.S.W.* I. 271 We were unable to feed our dogs, and they had assumed somewhat the appearance of the *Myall Dingo* or wild dog.

1963 D. ROBERT *Look at me Now* 92, I found a bush of wild lemons or 'myall lemons' as they are called.

myall /ˈmaɪəl/, $n.^2$ Formerly also **miall, myal**. [Perh. related—in some way that is not understood—to prec.] Any of several trees of the genus *Acacia* (fam. Mimosaceae), esp. *A. pendula* of inland N.S.W., Qld., and Vic., having silvery foliage sometimes used as fodder, and the similar *A. melvillei*; the wood of these trees. See also BOREE, *weeping myall* WEEPING. Also *attrib*.

1840 J. GOULD *Birds of Aust.* (1848) II. Pl. 22, The only parts where I observed it [sc. the Red-backed Halcyon] was the myall-brushes (*Acacia pendula*) of the Lower Namoi. **1851** *Empire* (Sydney) 30 Jan. 2/2 The sable Australian .. never contrived a defter thing than .. his boomerang of plain-cut miall. **1896** A. MACKAY *Austral. Agriculturist* (rev. ed.) 301 The wattles and myals of the Australian bush.

myall country. An area inhabited by Aborigines living in a traditional manner; an area in which myall (see $n.^2$) is predominant.

[**1857** F. DE B. COOPER *Wild Adventures* 68, I was well-known to be acquainted with the topography of the 'myal' districts... Myal—(Comeleroi dialect)—Wild; unreclaimed.] *Ibid.* 123 A similar question in the myal country would have been taken as an insult. **1867** 'CLERGYMAN' *Aust. as it Is* 20 Cattle are very fond of eating the leaves, and, as a consequence, 'Myall country' is usually considered first-class.

myam-myam, mya-mya, var. MIA-MIA.

myna(h), var. MINER $n.^1$

myrnong, var. MURNONG.

myrnonga, var. MURLONGA.

myrtle. [Transf. use of *myrtle, Myrtus.*]

1. The tall tree of Vic. and Tas. *Nothofagus cunninghamii* (fam. Fagaceae) which has small, shiny, dark-green leaves; the wood of the tree; *Tasmanian myrtle*, see TASMANIAN *a.* 2. Also *attrib.*, esp. as **myrtle beech.**

1816 *Hobart Town Gaz.* 15 June, The Mountains on the Northern Shore where the Coal is, are barren, but the rest are generally covered with Myrtle. **1957** *Forest Trees Aust.* (Cwlth. Forestry & Timber Bur.) 220 Celery top pine occurs in cool temperate rain forest .. with myrtle beech.

2. Any of several other trees or shrubs, sometimes of the myrtle fam. (Myrtaceae); also with distinguishing epithet, as *native myrtle* (see NATIVE *a.* 6 a.).

1825 B. FIELD *Geogr. Mem. N.S.W.* 461 Myrtle trees (myrtaceae) are burnt for fire-wood. **1958** *Coast to Coast 1957–58* 138 Leschenaultia made patches as blue as the sky everywhere, with the peach-blossom pink of wild myrtle.

3. Special Comb. **myrtle acacia,** the shrub *Acacia myrtifolia* (fam. Mimosaceae): see quot. 1942; also **myrtle-leaved acacia, mimosa, wattle.**

1793 J.E. SMITH *Specimen Bot. New Holland* 51 Mimosa myrtifolia. Myrtle-leaved Mimosa .. is now not uncommon in our greenhouses, having been raised in plenty from seeds brought from Port Jackson. **1828** R. SWEET *Flora Australasica* Pl. 49, *Myrtle-leaved Acacia* .. a handsome evergreen bushy Shrub, with slender smooth branches. **1856** *Jrnl. Australasia* I. 37 You may now plant .. myrtle-leaved wattle. **1935** E. COLEMAN *Come back in Wattle Time* 37 Myrtle Acacia (*A. myrtifolia*). Broad green phyllodes (myrtle-like). **1942** C. BARRETT *Austral. Wild Flower Bk.* 35 Myrtle Acacia, a small shrub with pale yellow flower-heads and myrtle-like leaves, which ranges throughout Australia, excepting only the Northern Territory.

myxo /ˈmɪksoʊ/. [Abbrev. of *myxo(matosis* a disease introduced (into several countries) to exterminate rabbits. Now used elsewhere but recorded earliest in Aust.: see OEDS.] Myxomatosis.

1953 *Sydney Morning Herald* 3 Jan. 6/2 'Myxo', an abbreviation of myxomatosis, the rabbit-killing disease. **1982** J. MORRISON *North Wind* 101 The myxo'll look after the rabbits... You could walk right across this property and never see a rabbit.

N

Nabawa /'næbəwɔ/. [The name of the town in W.A.] A variety of wheat: see quots.

1917 *V & P* (W.A.) (1918) II. no. 7 541 At Chapman we have a variety we call Nabawah. I always endeavour to give names taken from the district in which the wheat is grown. This has been grown now for two seasons, and has given us more satisfaction than any other variety. Next year it will be out amongst the farmers in large enough quantities for them to work on. 1956 CALLAGHAN & MILLINGTON *Wheat Industry Aust.* 277 Amongst the material was the progeny of a cross between Early Gluyas and Bunyip made at Wagga Experiment Farm in 1908, and from it was developed the variety Nabawa. Although it was selected initially because of its resistance to stem rust, Nabawa is also very resistant to flag smut.

naga. /'nagə/. Also **naga-naga, narga, nargar, narger.** [a. Wuna *naga* dress, covering.] A loin-cloth (as worn by an Aboriginal).

1907 A. SEARCY *In Austral. Tropics* 81, I employed about thirty niggers . . and paid them with tobacco and rice, and Turkey-red for the women for nargers (waist cloths). 1911 —— *By Flood & Field* 55 The hunter, naked save for a nargar (waist-cloth), speeding on the outskirts of the mob. 1959 D. LOCKWOOD *Crocodiles & Other People* 82 A dozen natives, men and women, in brief nargas or no clothes at all. 1962 C. GYE *Cockney & Crocodile* 50 There a bush native, tall and thin and proud and black in a tiny red naga-naga (loincloth). 1981 A. MARSHALL *Aust.* 52 He had a loose naga (loin cloth) around his loins.

nagoora burr, var. NOOGOORA BURR.

nailcan. [Prob. alteration of *nail-keg (-kag)* a small barrel containing nails; also (U.S.) a hat of similar shape.]

1. A container for nails. Also *attrib.*

1904 L.M.P. ARCHER *Bush Honeymoon* 39 Cold, soaking rain falling outside, and three scrub-cutters drawn up close to a *nailcan* filled with hot coals. 1956 T. RONAN *Moleskin Midas* 77 With his beefhouse completed, he got himself a killer from the Twin Hills side and picked up a nailcan beef-bucket from Sam Slack's deserted homestead.

2. See quot. 1955. Also **nailcan hat.**

1941 S.J. BAKER *Pop. Dict. Austral. Slang* 48 *Nail-can*, a tall (top) hat. 1955 N. PULLIAM *I traveled Lonely Land* 382 *Nail can*, a top hat. 1971 H. ANDERSON *Larrikin Crook* 2 The clerks sneered at in *Truth* and called suburban snobs 'going to the city every day on a first class ticket in a nail can hat and bum-banger coat'.

nailrod. [Transf. use of *nailrod* a strip or rod of iron from which nails are cut.] Coarse dark tobacco in the form of a thin roll.

[N.Z. 1886 *N.Z. Herald* (Auckland) 8 Nov. 7/3 Nailrod and 1 lb. bars . . with Havana . . Cigars.] 1890 A.J. VOGAN *Black Police* 200 He hands out his black friend a piece of 'nail-rod' with which to charge his evening pipe. 1967 J. STUART *Part of Glory* 157, I could smoke or leave it alone, and as the jail weed was 'nail rod' or 'sheep dip' I left it severely alone.

nail-tailed wallaby. a. Any of the three species of wallaby of the genus *Onychogalea*, members of which have a horny nail at the tip of the tail. **b.** With distinguishing epithet: **bridled nail-tailed wallaby,** the wallaby *O. fraenata*, now known only from e. central Qld., with bridle-like white markings on the head and shoulder; also **bridled wallaby; crescent nail-tailed wallaby,** WURRUNG; also **crescent nail-tail wallaby.** Also **nail-tail, nail-tailed kangaroo.**

1859 J. GOULD *Mammals of Aust.* (1863) II. 52 *Onychogalea unguifer*, Nail-tailed Kangaroo. 1894 R. LYDEKKER *Handbk. Marsupialia & Monotremata* 48 The three species of Nail-tailed Wallabies, which are confined to Australia . . form a well-marked group. *Ibid.* 50 Bridled Wallaby. *Onychogale frenata.* 1926 A.S. LE SOUEF et al. *Wild Animals Australasia* 211 Mr G.S. Shortridge found the crescent nail-tailed wallaby very local, living in low scrubby thickets. 1975 *Ecos* v. 28/1 A few bridled nail-tailed wallabies turned up last year at Dingo, between Emerald and Rockhampton. 1978 M. DOUGLAS *Follow Sun* 199 'It's a nail-tail.' The little macropod lay still, limp and exhausted. 1984 *Age* (Melbourne) 9 Aug. 1/7 Species already extinct in Australia . . crescent nailtail wallaby.

namma hole, var. GNAMMA HOLE.

nana /'nanə/. Prob. f. *banana.*]

1. In the phr. **off one's nana,** mentally deranged; **to do** (or **lose**) **one's nana,** to lose one's temper.

1966 S.J. BAKER *Austral. Lang.* (ed. 2) 293 *Lose one's nana,* . . an equivalent of *lose* (or *do*) *one's block.* 1968 *Coast to Coast 1967–68* 9 Arright, Mister Mighty Boss. Don't do your nana. 1975 *Austral.* (Sydney) 8 Feb. 13/6 'We've all learned to laugh at ourselves and at our predicament,' Trevor England said. 'If we hadn't we'd all be off our nanas.'

2. [Used elsewhere but recorded earliest in Aust.] A foolish person; a fool. Also *attrib.* as **nana-cut,** a style of hair-cut.

1941 S.J. BAKER *Pop. Dict. Austral. Slang* 48 *Nana (hair) cut*, a utilitarian haircut in which the back of the head is closely shaved. 1965 G. MCINNES *Road to Gundagai* 148 Although he was obviously a gent, he was not a 'tonk' or a 'nana'.

nangry /'næŋgri/, *v. Austral.* pidgin. *Obs.* Also **nangerie.** [a. Dharuk *nan-ga(ra).*] *intr.* To sleep; to rest; to reside. Also as *n.*, a sleep.

1790 D. SOUTHWELL Corresp. & Papers, *Nan-gă-ră*, to sleep. 1830 R. DAWSON *Present State Aust.* 73 It was much too far without nangry (sleep, rest, or night). 1839 T.L. MITCHELL *Three Exped. Eastern Aust.* (rev. ed.) I. 269 They violently shook their boughs at me, and having set them on fire, dashed them to the ground, calling out 'Nangry' (sit down). 1853 H.B. JONES *Adventures in Aust.* 147 'Where you 'nangerie',' i.e., where do you live? was his next interrogatory.

nankeen. [Transf. use of *nankeen* the colour.] Used *attrib.* in the names of birds having a red-brown back: **nankeen kestrel** (formerly **hawk**), the small falcon *Falco cenchroides* of Aust. and New Guinea, having a characteristic hovering flight; KESTREL; SPARROWHAWK b.; **night heron,** the nocturnal heron *Nycticorax caledonicus*, occurring near water throughout Aust. and widespread in the s.w. Pacific; also **nankeen crane, heron,** and (formerly) **bird.**

1827 [nankeen kestrel] *Trans. Linnean Soc. London* XV. 184 This bird . . is called Nankeen Hawk by the settlers. . . On the 3rd of August 1804, I made the following note:- I saw no *Nankeen Hawks* this autumn.—I never observed it attacking the fowls. 1849 C. STURT *Narr. Exped. Central Aust.* II. 14 App. *Tinnunculus* Cenchroïdes. *Nankeen Kestrel.* . . This bird is generally distributed over the conti-

NAN-NAN

nent and is known by the nankeen colour of his back. **1837** [**nankeen night heron**] J. BACKHOUSE *Narr. Visit Austral. Colonies* 13 Nov. (1843) 500 We also noticed the Nankin-bird, a species of Heron, which is cinnamon-coloured on the back, sulphur-coloured on the breast, and has a long, white feather, pendant from the back of the head. **1846** J. GOULD *Birds of Aust.* (1848) VI. Pl. 63, *Nycticorax caledonicus*. Nankeen Night Heron. **1849** C. STURT *Narr. Exped. Central Aust.* II. 52 App. Nycticorax Caledonicus. *Nankeen Bird.* A Night Heron with nankeen-coloured back and wings. **1886** D.M. GANE *N.S.W. & Vic.* 200 The nankeen crane . . is seldom within gunshot.

nan-nan. *Obs.* [Perh. f. *nancy* effeminate man.] A straw hat (in quot. 1899 used *attrib.*); also *transf.*, a dandy.

1899 *Bulletin* (Sydney) 8 Apr. (Red Page), A boarding-house keeper with two or three grown-up, white-shirted . . straw-hatted, cigarette-smoking sons. . . I'd like to paint her and the children—and the 'nan-nan' sons. **1907** *Truth* (Sydney) 24 Feb. 1/7 Colonel Bell has given politics best while he explains to the University nan-nans the theory of earthquakes. **1910** STEPHENS & O'BRIEN *Materials Austrazealand Slang Dict.* 104 *Nan-nan*, a straw hat for men's wear: by transference, to the gangs of youths who affect these hats, either for cheapness or for showiness. They are well known in Sydney as the 'Nan-nan or Straw-hat' push. A straw hat a few years ago was known as a donkey's breakfast. The cry to the wearer was 'Ba, ba, who shook/stole the donkey's breakfast?' The genesis, no doubt, of 'Nan-nan'.

nannygai /'nænɪgaɪ/. [Prob. f. a N.S.W. Aboriginal language.] The marine fish of s. Aust. *Centroberyx affinis*, a short-bodied, reddish fish valued as food. See also *red fish* (b), RED *a.* 1 b.

1871 *Industr. Progress N.S.W.* 791 The . . king-fish, 'moorra nennigai' . . and a variety of other less familiar forms, may be taken by the line in almost unlimited quantities. **1968** G. DUTTON *Andy* 176 Some good fish in Tasmania. Nannygai, now there's an incomparable fish!

nanto /'næntoʊ/. *Obs.* Also **nanta, nantah, nantu.** [a. Gaurna (and neighbouring languages) *nhandu* kangaroo, (*transf.*) horse.] A horse.

1839 W. WILLIAMS *Vocab. Aborigines S.A.* 16 *Nan-tah*, horse. **1893** H.J. WHITE *Round Camp Fire* 61 Well the 'nantos' were ready and the tucker-box stowed away snug. **1929** 'A. RUSSELL' *Bungoona* 7 Bungoona . . means 'good', or, rather, the superlative of good. That is to say, if I were to remark that old Blossom was a *bungoona nanta*, I'd really mean to convey to you, in the lingo of the blacks, that Bloss was a jolly good old horse. **1957** W.E. HARNEY *Life among Aborigines* 12 They saw many 'kutebas' come to Mudba with their strange 'nantus' (a word in reference to the distended nose of a horse after it has been ridden hard).

nap, var. KNAP.

nap, *n.*¹ [Prob. f. *knapsack*.] A bed-roll; a swag.

1892 *Bulletin* (Sydney) 2 Apr. 13/1 Drip, drip, drip! and one's 'nap' is far from dry Tis hard to keep the water out—however one may try. **1968** W. GILL *Petermann Journey* 24, I knew where to put my 'nap', the Territory word for a 'swag'.

nap, *n.*² [Neg. use of *to go nap* to stake all one can: see OED(S *sb.*⁵ 2 b.] In the phr. **not to go nap on,** to have no enthusiasm for (someone or something).

1918 *Kia Ora Coo-ee* Dec. 3/3 Talking of souvenirs, I don't go nap on any of the ordinary kind which lose their interest after they have been looked at once or twice. **1966** D. NILAND *Pairs & Loners* 143, I got a marquee. Don't go nap on this tent-living, but what can a man do?

NARGA

napunyah /nə'pʌnjə/. YAPUNYAH. Also *attrib.*

1949 H.G. LAMOND *White Ears* 21 A giant napunia-tree had fallen across two rocks. **1968** LINKLATER & TAPP *Gather No Moss* 6 The manager of a sheep station . . set me taking out napunya roots near the homestead to fill in time till the shearing began.

narang /nə'ræŋ/, *a.* Chiefly *Austral. pidgin.* *Obs.* Also **narrangy, nerangy.** [a. Dharuk *ŋarraŋ.*] Little.

1790 J. HUNTER *Hist. Jrnl. Trans. Port Jackson* (1793) 409 *Narrong*, any thing small. **1827** P. CUNNINGHAM *Two Yrs. in N.S.W.* II. 28 They could not contain their astonishment . . that the '*cobawn* (big) gobernor, had not mout *so* (screwing theirs into the appropriate shape), like the *narang* (little) gobernor'. **1861** *Burke & Wills Exploring Exped.* 8 Sandy said he could only understand 'narrangy word' they said; but I believe that he could not understand them at all. **1879** 'AUSTRALIAN' *Adventures Qld.* 31 That fellow been sit down here *nerangy* while (a little while).

narangy /nə'ræŋgi/. [See NARANG.] See quot. 1967. Formerly also **rangie.**

1891 *Truth* (Sydney) 8 Mar. 7/3 Remember that the jackeroo without perfolio (alias the *rangie* pur et simple) has a chance of promotion to drover, shed-boss, overseer, and manager. **1967** G. JENKIN *Two Yrs. Bardunyah Station* 73 *Narangies*, salaried people on the staff of a station, as distinct from the stockmen and others on a weekly wage.

nardoo /na'du/. Formerly also **nardu.** [a. Diyari *ŋardu* or Kamilaroi *nhaaduu.*]

1. The perennial, rhizomatous fern *Marsilea drummondii* (fam. Marsileaceae) of mainland Aust., having clover-like fronds and occurring chiefly in arid areas along stream-beds and near lakes; any of several other ferns of the genus *Marsilea*; the sporocarp of these plants, which is ground into flour and used by Aborigines as a food; *clover fern*, see CLOVER. Also *attrib.*

1860 *Trans. & Proc. R. Soc. Vic.* 203 While the foregoing sheets were going through the press, intelligence having reached Melbourne of the value, as an edible seed, of the *Marsileae hirsuta* (or Nardo), as found so useful in the Victorian Expedition . . it has occurred to me that it would be well to mention that I found the same plant growing in Dumby Bay, Port Lincoln. **1861** *Bell's Life in Sydney* 9 Nov. 2/6 For some time we were employed gathering nardoo, and laying up a supply. **1892** J. FRASER *Aborigines N.S.W.* 77 From many kinds of seeds, such as the 'nardu' . . the natives make a rough kind of meal which is baked into 'damper'. **1977** J. O'GRADY *There was Kid* 39 Although often short of food on the farm, our father said that he hoped we would never have to 'come at nardoo bread', or porridge.

2. Comb. **nardoo cake, flour, stone.**

1861 *Burke & Wills Exploring Exped.* 30 Next came a supply of **nardoo cake** and water. **1861** *Burke & Wills Exploring Exped.* 30 Fetched a large bowl of the raw **nardoo flour.** **1912** SPENCER & GILLEN *Across Aust.* 16 The natives make a kind of flour out of them by grinding them to powder between their so-called **nardoo stones.**

Naretha parrot /nərɪθə 'pærət/. [f. the name of a railway station in s.e. W.A.] See quot. 1976.

1922 *Bulletin* (Sydney) 12 Jan. 20/3 From so accessible a place as Naretha, on the East-West line, F. Whitlock lately secured a new species of parrot, the Naretha. **1976** *Reader's Digest Compl. Bk. Austral. Birds* 287 There are four rather distinct forms of the blue bonnet. One, the Naretha parrot *Northiella haematogaster narethae*, lives along the south-western fringe of the Nullarbor Plain, and differs mainly from others in its pure yellow belly, red undertail-coverts, turquoise brow and small size.

narga, nargar, narger, varr. NAGA.

nark, *v. Obs.* [Spec. use of *nark* to exasperate.] *trans.* To thwart (a scheme, etc.).

1891 *Truth* (Sydney) 15 Mar. 2/1 They would surely know that I lied to them, and would crab my pitch, or to speak more plainly.. they would nark my lurk. **1975** R. BEILBY *Brown Land Crying* 200 Ya'd do anything to nark me, anything to put me down, wouldn't ya?

Nar Nar Goon /na na 'gun/. [The name of a small town s.e. of Melbourne.] Used allusively to denote a small and insignificant place.

1918 *Kia Ora Coo-ee* Sept. 18/2 Jimmy was thinking of home, how his mother would be feeling, what his father would say about him, and how things in general were at Nar Nar Goon. Yes, dear, old, sleepy Nar Nar Goon. **1981** *Age* (Melbourne) 8 June 2/2 Television football commentaries tend to be about as rewarding as a night game at Nar Nar Goon football ground in a power strike.

narrangy, var. NARANG.

Narrawa burr /nærəwə 'bɜ/. [Perh. f. the name of the small town *Narrawah*, N.S.W.] The small, prickly shrub *Solanum cinereum* (fam. Solanaceae) of s.e. Qld., N.S.W., Vic., and naturalized in the Flinders Ranges, S.A.

1917 *Bulletin* (Sydney) 27 Sept. 22/4 There is but one 'native' in that bunch—the Narrawa burr. **1958** J.N. WHITTET *Weeds* 358 Narrawa burr is considered to be responsible for causing mortalities in sheep and horses in New South Wales.

narriwadgee /nærə'wædʒi/. [Prob. f. an Aboriginal language.] *Night well*, see NIGHT.

1923 *Bulletin* (Sydney) 25 Jan. 22/3 The mysterious waterhole.. is no doubt a 'narriwadgee', or night well. **1930** *Ibid.* 16 July 21/2 The night well, known to abos. as narriwadgee.

narrow-billed bronze cuckoo. The cuckoo *Chrysococcyx basalis*, widely distributed in Aust. and occurring elsewhere, having a copper-green back, black bill, and barred underparts.

1903 *Emu* II. 165 Narrow-billed Bronze Cuckoo (*Chalcoccyx basalis*).. very common on the plains. **1945** C. BARRETT *Austral. Bird Life* 149 [The egg colour] of.. the narrow-billed bronze cuckoo.. is pinkish, with a uniform sprinkling of tiny reddish spots.

narrow comb: see COMB 2.

narrow-leaved, *a.* Used as a distinguishing epithet in the names of plants: **narrow-leaved ironbark,** a tree of the genus *Eucalyptus* (fam. Myrtaceae), esp. *E. crebra* of N.S.W. and Qld.; also **narrow-leafed ironbark**; **peppermint,** the tree *Eucalyptus radiata* (fam. Myrtaceae) of s.e. mainland Aust., having narrow green to grey-green leaves with a peppermint smell when crushed; **poison,** any of several shrubs of the genus *Gastrolobium* (fam. Fabaceae), esp. *G. stenophyllum* of s.w. W.A., having narrow leaves, and yellow and red flowers; also **narrow-leaf poison.**

1845 L. LEICHHARDT *Jrnl. Overland Exped. Aust.* 18 Jan. (1847) 112 We came across an open forest of **narrow-leaved Ironbark** (E. resinifera). **1976** *Ecos* ix. 29/3 The woodlands include.. narrow-leafed ironbark, and grey box communities. **1896** *Proc. Linnean Soc. N.S.W.* X. 603 *E. amygdalina*.. var. *radiata*... We have a fairly distinct tree which goes under the names of 'White Gum', 'River Gum', 'River White Gum', 'Ribbon Gum', and even '**Narrow-leaved Peppermint**'. **1897** [**narrow-leaved poison**] L. LINDLEY-COWEN *W. Austral. Settler's Guide* 582 Narrow-leaf and marlock poison bushes. **1926** *Poison Plants W.A.* (W.A. Dept. Agric.) 33 The name 'Narrow-leaved Poison' as here adopted for *Gastrolobium crassifolium*.. in some districts.. is also applied to Champion Bay Poison.. Pituri.. White Gum Poison.. and Rock Poison.

nasho. [Abbrev. of *nat(ional* + -O.] Compulsory military training, as introduced under the National Service Act of 1951; one who undergoes this. Also **nasho training.**

1966 B. BEAVER *You can't come Back* 5 Sam, the new one, was just eighteen and due for his Nasho training. **1973** *Bulletin* (Sydney) 27 Jan. 27/1 Some 'nashos' have shown outstanding zeal by signing on with the Regular Army. **1981** Q. WILD *Honey Wind* 85 One of the worst things.. was something that happened in nasho.. before there was any fighting or anything.

national game.

1. Two-up.

1930 L.W. LOWER *Here's Luck* 50 He had a small piece of flat wood in his hand, on which were balanced two pennies. The national game was in progress. **1983** *Sun-Herald* (Sydney) 23 Jan. 35/3 You can't wipe out two-up; it's our national game.

2. Australian National Football.

1936 E.C.H. TAYLOR et al. *Our Austral. Game Football* 9 'The University of Hard Knocks' as Sir Isaac Isaacs so aptly termed our National Game. **1985** *Canberra Times* 11 Aug. 9/4 Failing attendances this year should be sharp enough to jolt the VFL out of the smug complacency and token concern for the future of the national game.

native, *n.*

1. An Aboriginal; AUSTRALIAN *n.* 1.

1770 J. COOK *Jrnls.* 29 Apr. (1955) I. 305 Saw as we came in on both points of the bay Several of the natives and a few hutts. **1963** *Bulletin* (Sydney) 23 Nov. 10/3 Most of West Australia's 20,000 'natives', within the meaning of the Act, should be able to have a legal drink soon.

2. A non-Aboriginal person born in Australia; AUSTRALIAN *n.* 2.

1806 *Sydney Gaz.* 20 July, Thomas Ford and William Evans, Boys; the latter a native of this Colony. **1964** J.S. MANIFOLD *Who wrote Ballads?* 43 They were a bit of a problem to thoughtful Governors, these local-born among the currency men. Even to give them a collective name was a problem. Some called them 'natives'—unsatisfactorily because it confused them with aboriginals.

3. An animal or plant indigenous to Australia.

1793 J.E. SMITH *Specimen Bot. New Holland* 31 *Flax-leaved Pimelea*.. is a native of the coast of New South Wales, among rocks. **1985** *Canberra Times* 23 Aug. 34/6 Old style home nestled among natives and orchard trees.

4. *Obs.* In phr.

a. **native of New Holland,** an Aboriginal.

1805 J. TURNBULL *Voyage round World* I. 43 The natives of New Holland.. have gained nothing in civilization since their first discovery. **1852** J. SHAW *Tramp to Diggings* 21 Generally, the natives of New Holland have dark brown skins, large eyes, massive foreheads, broad noses, wide mouths, short lower jaws, large white teeth, and long sinewy limbs.

b. **native of the colony,** a non-Aboriginal person born in an Australian Colony.

1834 *Sydney Herald* 17 Nov. (Suppl.) 1/6 Samuel Leverton, a Native of the Colony, who had shipped himself a few weeks back, as Steward of the *Australia*. **1880** 'ERRO' *Squattermania* 36 They were natives of the colony, bred in the Bush.

c. **native of Australia, native of New South Wales: (i)** an Aboriginal; **(ii)** a non-Aboriginal person born in Australia.

1830 R. DAWSON *Present State Aust.* 132 It is not customary with the **natives of Australia** to shake hands. **1883** R.E.N. TWOPENY *Town Life Aust.* 245 An aboriginal is always a 'black fellow'. A native of Australia would mean a white man born in the colony. **1805** J. TURNBULL *Voyage round World* I. 73 It is one thing to catch, and another to civilize, a **native of New South Wales. 1867** J. BONWICK *J. Batman* 12 Mr Batman .. is a native of New South Wales.

native, *a.*

1. a. Of or pertaining to the Aborigines; Aboriginal.
1807 Banks Papers 18 Dec. XX. 177, 3 Kangaroo Skins, Two of which are native mantles. **1986** *Sydney Morning Herald* 8 Mar. 41/6 The Pope has expressed a desire to visit 'the native people of Australia'. A committee of 15 people—all Aborigines—is being formed to plan the encounter.

b. In collocations: **native black, camp, canoe, children, constable, encampment, grave, guide, hut, inhabitant, man, name, path, savage, shepherd, tongue, track.**

1816 *HRA* (1917) 1st Ser. IX. 53 The **Native Blacks** of this Country, Inhabiting the distant Interior parts. **1842** *Portland Mercury* 31 Aug. 2/5 A double-barrelled gun, which had belonged to the man, was found at the **native camp. 1853** A. KINLOCH *Murray River* 13 We managed to upset a **native canoe** or 'mungo', propelled by a black and his 'lubra'. **1819** W.C. WENTWORTH *Statistical, Hist., & Pol. Descr. N.S.W.* 18 A school for the education and civilization of the aborigines of the country .. was founded by the present governor three years since, and by the last accounts from the colony, it contained eighteen **native children,** who had been voluntarily placed there by their parents, and were making equal progress in their studies with European children of the same age. **1839** W. MANN *Six Yrs.' Residence* 287 Onkaparinga Jack, Captain Jack, both **native constables. 1841** G. GREY *Jrnls. Two Exped. N.-W. & W.A.* II. 329 When I went to the **native encampment,** I found that the first forms of the marriage ceremony had taken place. **1856** G. WILLMER *Draper in Aust.* 68 Encamped for the night very near a **native grave.** I particularly noticed the care which the relatives had taken to fence it all around with sticks. **1808** *Sydney Gaz.* 18 Sept., I have frequently occasion to traverse the interior .. and finding the utility of a **native guide,** always made election of such as I found most tractable and obliging. **1803** C.M.H. CLARK *Select Documents* (1950) 90 Saw a canoe and two **native huts. 1808** *Sydney Gaz.* 21 Aug. The little attention which we pay to the customs of the **native inhabitants** of this country. **1793** J. HUNTER *Hist. Jrnl. Trans. Port Jackson* 132, I observed a **native man** of this country, who was decently cloathed, and seemed to be as much at his ease at the tea-table as any person there. **1834** G. BENNETT *Wanderings N.S.W.* I. 70 As well as the scientific (or hard names, as the ladies call them), let also the popular, colonial and **native names,** be attached. **1791** S. MACARTHUR ONSLOW *Some Early Rec. Macarthurs* (1914) 33 Nor do I think there is any probability of my seeing much of the inland country until it is cleared, as beyond a certain distance round the Colony there is nothing but **native paths,** very narrow and very incommodious. **1831** *Independent* (Launceston) 24 Sept. 2/3 The dogs in the possession of the hordes of **native savages. 1845** E.J. EYRE *Jrnls. Exped. Central Aust.* II. 447 On the Murray River **native shepherds** and stock-keepers have hitherto been employed almost exclusively. **1840** S. *Austral. Rec.* (London) 15 Jan. 11 This proclamation is .. the first that has ever appeared in Australia in the **native tongues. 1837** J. BONWICK *Wild White Man* 6 Feb. (1863) 5 We .. crossed the Yallack by a **native track.**

2. a. Of a non-Aboriginal person: born in Australia.
1821 *Austral. Mag.* 217 The Society employs 32 Clergymen .. and Settlers, European and Native. **1887** W.S.S. TYRWHITT *New Chum in Qld. Bush* 201 England is spoken of as home, even by native colonials, who are never likely to see it.

b. In collocations: **native colonist, lad, settler, white.**

1824 E. CURR *Acct. Colony Van Diemen's Land* 150 The **native colonist** has no recollections to raise discontent; what he never knew, he can never miss. **1828** *Hobart Town Courier* 16 Aug. 2 The leader of the band is a **native lad** called Biffin or Bevin, who made his escape from gaol here sometime ago. **1822** J. DIXON *Narr. Voyage N.S.W. & Van Dieman's Land* 67 The **native settlers,** born in this colony .. have been long inured to it. **1837** *Rep. Select Committee Transportation* 18 Apr. (1838) 28 Is juvenile prostitution among the **native whites** of the lower order common?— I believe it to be so.

3. a. Of flora and fauna: indigenous.
1804 S. MACARTHUR ONSLOW *Some Early Rec. Macarthurs* (1914) 81 The Native Woods instead of making the Grass sour are generally so open as not to deteriorate its quality. **1986** *Canberra Times* 16 Feb. 5/5 After nearly two centuries of believing that Australia's rainforests were invading outliers of South-East Asia's rainforests, botanists had finally arrived at the view Australia's rainforests were not 'secondhand' but truly native.

b. In collocations: **native animal, bird, flower, forest, pasturage, pasture, plant, shrub, timber, tree.**

1856 J. BONWICK *Bushrangers* 2 The commissariat was obliged to rely upon **native animals** furnished by hunters. **1860** 'LADY' *My Experiences in Aust.* 53 The few *native* animals among the collection were the only ones that possessed much interest for me. *Ibid.* 54 Of the **native birds,** there was the Emu, with its long legs and curious *fibry* feathers. **1843** *Teetotal Advocate* (Launceston) 2 Oct. 3/5 Bouquets of **Native Flowers. 1831** TYERMANN & BENNET *Jrnl. Voyages & Travels* II. 149 In travelling through the **native forests** .. we found many ants' nests. **1833** *Colonist* (Hobart) 13 Aug. 3/3 The benefit of occasionally burning off the **native pasturage. 1835** *Hobart Town Almanack* 10 The **native pasture** on the hills now puts on a verdant appearance. **1803** *N.S.W. Gen. Orders* 4 Oct. (1806) 69 The Trees and other **Native Plants** had been suffered to remain. **1828** *Tasmanian* (Hobart) 2 May 3 Gentlemen's grounds most tastefully laid out, and ornamented with **Native,** and other Plants and **Shrubs. 1837** *Perth Gaz.* 4 Feb. 845 No tenders having been received for the supply of **native timber** for the use of His Majesty's Dock-yard at Portsmouth. **1828** *Tasmanian* (Hobart) 22 Aug. 3 The ground is cleared and laid out with English grasses, and ornamented with **Native Trees.**

4. In collocations occurring in both sense 1 and sense 2: **native Australian, boy, girl, population, race, son, woman, youth.**

1832 *Colonist* (Hobart) 28 Sept. 2/4 The new Sydney journal, called 'The Currency Lad' produced .. entirely by **native Australians. 1852** W. HUGHES *Austral. Colonies* 2 Even amidst the crowded streets of the populous and busy city, is seen the scarcely half-clothed form of the native Australian—the 'black fellow'. **1800** *HRA* (1914) 1st Ser. II. 404 Enquiring of them if they knew anything about the two **Native Boys** being murdered. **1827** *Monitor* (Sydney) 22 Nov. 783/1 All our six-feet high native boys and girls, have sprung from these 'reprobates'. **1826** M. HINDMARSH *Lett.* (1945) 27 The **Native girls** of the Country or Currency Girls are so very pert that I do not think I will ever have one of them for a wife. **1856** J. BONWICK *Bushrangers* 49 He was attended by a faithful native girl called Black Mary. **1829** E.G. WAKEFIELD *Let. from Sydney* 129 That low-lived Englishman who .. distinguishing the Emigrant and **Native population** of New South Wales, by nicknaming the one Sterling, and the other Currency, was, no doubt, a man of taste. **1843** J.F. BENNETT *Hist. & Descr. Acct. S.A.* 59 The native population of Australia is by no means numerous. Within the settled districts of South Australia, the whole number of aborigines does not exceed 700. **1811** *Sydney Gaz.* 19 Jan., In the center [*sic*] of the ball-room .. the representation of our **Native Race. 1848** S. & J. SIDNEY *Emigrant's Jrnl.* 73 It is a fashion .. of many British colonists to abuse and despise the native race; that is to say, Australians born in the country, of European parents. **1968** G. BAKER *Montgomery & I* 62 Montgomery sternly replied: Surely the **native sons** should have my autograph before migrants and dagos. **1973** *Bulletin* (Sydney) 20 Jan.

40/1 New South Wales was still guilty about the way it had treated its brilliant native son. **1827** *Monitor* (Sydney) 3 Feb. 299/2 A humane Correspondent describes an outrage upon the person of a **native woman** on Tuesday night near the new Court House. **1857** J. ASKEW *Voyage Aust. & N.Z.* 223 Much has been said and written touching the loveliness of the 'currency lasses', or native women of New South Wales. **1804** *Sydney Gaz.* 2 Dec., On Wednesday a **native youth** died at Sydney of a dysentery, who was the first of the savage inhabitants of this colony introduced to civil society. **1826** *Austral.* (Sydney) 19 Jan. 3/1 The name which the Native Youth have acquired for loyalty, steadiness, and sobriety.

5. In special collocations (freq. *obs.*): **native affairs**, Aboriginal welfare; a name given to a government department responsible for this; also *attrib.*; **chief**, KING *n.*¹ 1 a.; **doctor**, DOCTOR *n.*¹; **evidence**, evidence given by an Aboriginal as admitted in a court of law; **fire**, a fire lit by an Aboriginal (see quots. and also FIRE *v.*); **honey** *obs., bush honey*, see BUSH C. 2; **industry**, Australian, as distinct from foreign, industry; **Institution**, a publicly-funded establishment for the care and education of Aboriginal children; **interpreter**, one who translates from or into an Aboriginal language; **king**, KING *n.*¹ 1 a.; **language**, an Aboriginal language; **location**, land allocated to an Aboriginal community; **oven (a)**, an Aboriginal cooking-place (see quot. 1845); **(b)** MIRRNYONG; **pock**, see quot. 1892; **(mounted) police**, a police force of male Aborigines recruited to serve (esp. in rural districts) under white officers; also *attrib.*; **policeman**, a member of the *native police*; **protector**, PROTECTOR; **reserve**, an area of land set aside for the exclusive use of Aborigines; **school**, a school for the instruction of Aboriginal children; **smoke**, a column of smoke rising from a fire, as indicating the presence of Aborigines; **soak**, a SOAK frequented by Aborigines; **tracker**, Tracker; **tribe**, TRIBE; **trooper**, a member of the *native police*; **village**, a (temporary) Aboriginal settlement; **weir**, *fishing weir*, see FISHING; **well**, a natural source of water used by Aborigines; see also *native soak*, GNAMMA HOLE.

1938 J.F.W. SCHULZ *Destined to Perish* 10 There could be .. a permanent commission for **native affairs** with a national policy and a continuous programme of development. **1947** V.C. HALL *Bad Medicine* 277 He was a policeman, acting as a Native Affairs Officer. .. He had police powers and he had Native Affairs powers. **1818** *Hobart Town Gaz.* 31 Jan., His Excellency the Governor held his usual annual Meeting of the **Native Chiefs** and their Tribes at Parramatta. **1841** G. GREY *Jrnls. Two Exped. N.-W. & W.A.* I. 215 The cave was frequented by some wise man or **native doctor**, who was resorted to by the inhabitants in cases of disease or witchcraft. **1845** E.J. EYRE *Jrnls. Exped. Central Aust.* II. 497 For the purpose of obtaining redress for a wrong, or of punishing cruelty, or the atrocity of the European, no amount of **native evidence** would be of the least avail. **1805** *Sydney Gaz.* 31 Mar., The plaintiff's property was in danger of being destroyed by **native fires** the night before the unfortunate event took place. **1851** H. MELVILLE *Present State Aust.* 346 Native fires were .. easily distinguished from those of bushrangers or settlers. **1861** J. DAVIS *Tracks of McKinlay* 22 Nov. (1863) 119 Many native watch fires on the other side of the lake. **1841** *Sydney Herald* 26 Apr. 2/2 **Native honey** is delicious, from the flavour of the wild flowers. **1861** W. WESTGARTH *Aust.* p. vii, The miners .. petitioned the authorities for the expulsion of the Chinese, 'protection to **native industry**'. **1818** *Hobart Town Gaz.* 31 Jan., The Children of the **Native Institution** were conducted by their Tutor to the Meeting, where their interview with their parents became a most interesting spectacle. **1856** J. BONWICK *W. Buckley* 46 My **native interpreter** told them who I was. **1857** W. WESTGARTH *Vic. & Austral. Gold Mines* 51 These '**native kings**', as the ready colonial nomenclature might have styled them. **1831** *HRA* (1923) 1st Ser. XVI. 14 Form an acquaintance with the **Native Languages** of the country. **1839** *Southern Austral.* (Adelaide) 9 Oct. 3/2 The Public Officers of the Colony are invited to attend his funeral, and to meet for this purpose at the Old **Native Location**. **1834** G. BENNETT *Wanderings N.S.W.* I. 170 A **native oven** is made in the ground, similar to those in use among the New Zealanders, and throughout the Polynesian Archipelago. **1845** E.J. EYRE *Jrnls. Exped. Central Aust.* II. 289 The native oven is made by digging a circular hole in the ground, of a size corresponding to the quantity of food to be cooked. It is then lined with stones in the bottom, and a strong fire made over them. **1855** W. HOWITT *Land, Labor & Gold* II. 95 We saw here what we have seen nowhere else in this colony—heaps of wood ashes, partly overgrown with grass, and resembling the barrows of the ancient Britons. They are called native ovens. **1832** *Sydney Monitor* 4 Jan. 3/1 The **native pock** is prevalent in many parts of Sydney, and the effects of the malady are as conspicuous as those of the small pox. **1892** HILL & THORNTON *Notes on Aborigines N.S.W.* 4 The natives all over the continent, at the time the first white people arrived for the purposes of settlement, were subject to a disease resembling small-pox; the native name of this disease was 'Galgala', and it was known to the early settlers as 'Native Pock'. **1839** *Southern Austral.* (Adelaide) 27 Feb. 4/4 The **native police** .. left this place under Mr De Villiers, in quest of the murderers. **1846** *Melbourne Argus* 7 July 3/1 The Native Police Force do not seem to have been of any great use, and this is said to be caused by the difficulty of keeping the natives to their duty. **1852** W. HUGHES *Austral. Colonies* 101 The experiment which has met with most success .. has been that of enrolling a native mounted police .. to act as a border force against bushrangers and other depredators. **1848** *Arden's Sydney Mag.* Oct. 78 Under this system, the **Native Policemen** have become, in a few months, civilized beings. **1842** *Austral. & N.Z. Monthly Mag.* 26 Habits of decorum, order, and regularity, have gradually been introduced amongst them .. owing principally to the continued watchfulness .. of the two gentlemen who have been appointed **native protectors** for the colony. **1842** *Austral. & N.Z. Monthly Mag.* 171 **Native reserves** .. the whole of the sections reserved for the use of the aborigines are to be let on lease for a term not exceeding seven years. **1838** *Aboriginal Claims Discussed* 14 In the formation of **native** and colonial **schools**, it should be a matter for serious consideration, whether there is not a fundamental error in all *general* schools. **1831** G.A. ROBINSON in N.J.B. Plomley *Friendly Mission* 23 Nov. (1966) 528 Ascended to the top of a hill, when the chief descried the **native smoke**. **1898** D.W. CARNEGIE *Spinifex & Sand* 200 Between us and the hills one or two native smokes were rising. *Ibid.* 80 **Native soaks** dug out with sticks and wooden 'coolimans' .. are by no means uncommon. **1878** R.B. SMYTH *Aborigines of Vic.* I. 7 The **native trackers** have on many occasions rendered important services to the Government, and when any one is lost in the bush the whites rely with the utmost confidence on the sagacity and skill of the 'black-tracker'. **1805** *Sydney Gaz.* 7 July, She had never been observed to intermingle with the Native **Tribes**. **1847** *Port Phillip Herald* 20 Apr. 2/7 The **native troopers** are now on the Murray, endeavouring to capture .. the two undetected murderers of Mr Beveridge. **1835** T.B. WILSON *Narr. Voyage round World* 210 We suddenly came to a **native village**. **1841** G. GREY *Jrnls. Two Exped. N.-W. & W.A.* II. 85 Across the bed, where we passed it, was a **native weir**. **1836** H.W. BUNBURY *Early Days W.A.* (1930) 75 We found some at a low promontory in a small **native well** amongst the Tea trees, but it was exceedingly bad, brackish, and stinking.

6. a. Used as a distinguishing epithet in the names of plants: **native apple (a)** *obs.*, MUNTRY; **(b)** any of several trees of the genus *Angophora* (fam. Myrtaceae); see also *apple tree* APPLE 3; **apple tree** *obs., apple tree*, see APPLE 3; **apricot**, the tree *Pittosporum phylliraeoides* (see BUTTERBUSH); **artichoke** *Tas.*, the tufted perennial herb *Astelia alpina* (fam. Liliaceae) of alpine N.S.W., Vic., and Tas., having rosettes of stiff, silvery, pointed leaves; **banana**, any of several species of banana of the genus *Musa* (fam. Musaceae) of n.e. Qld.; *wild banana*, see

WILD 1; **bluebell,** BLUEBELL; **box (thorn),** *sweet bursaria,* see BURSARIA b.; **bramble,** *native raspberry;* **bread,** the large, heavy, tuber-like sclerotium of the fungus *Polyporus mylittae* of s. Aust. incl. Tas.; *blackfellow's bread,* see BLACKFELLOW n. 2; *black's bread,* see BLACK n. 2; **cabbage,** any of several plants used as a vegetable, esp. the succulent shrub *Scaevola frutescens* (fam. Goodeniaceae) of n. Aust. and elsewhere; **carrot,** any of several plants, esp. the annual herb *Daucus glochidiatus* (fam. Apiaceae) of temperate Aust., having carrot-like leaves eaten by stock; the root of these plants; *wild carrot,* see WILD 1; **cedar** CEDAR 1; **cherry, (a)** the small cypress-like tree *Exocarpos cupressiformis* (fam. Santalaceae); **(b)** CHERRY; also **cherry-tree;** **cotton,** *cotton tree* (a) and (b), see COTTON; also **cotton bush, cotton tree; cranberry,** any of several plants of the fam. Epacridaceae and Ericaceae with edible fruits, esp. the prostrate shrub *Astroloma humifusum* (fam. Epacridaceae) of N.S.W., Vic., Tas., S.A., and W.A., bearing an edible greenish drupe with a sweet viscid pulp; the fruit of these plants; also *ellipt.* as **cranberry; cucumber,** any of several plants bearing a melon-like fruit, esp. the trailing vine *Cucumis melo* (fam. Cucurbitaceae) of n. Aust.; the fruit itself; *native melon;* **cumquat** (or **kumquat**), the tangled, often spiny, shrub or small tree *Eremocitrus glauca* (fam. Rutaceae) having greyish-green foliage and an edible, globular fruit yellow when ripe; *native lime* (a); *wild lime,* see WILD 1; **currant,** any of many plants bearing fruit resembling the currant in appearance or flavour, esp. *Leptomeria aphylla* (fam. Santalaceae) and *Coprosma quadrifida* (fam. Rubiaceae) of s.e. Aust. incl. Tas.; the fruit of these plants; CURRANT; *wild currant,* see WILD 1; **fig,** any of several plants of the genus *Ficus* (fam. Moraceae), esp. the small tree or shrub *F. platypoda* of drier Aust., often growing among rocks, and bearing a globular reddish fig; the fruit of these plants; **flax,** the perennial plant *Linum marginale* (fam. Linaceae) of temperate Aust. which, like the related European flax, yields a strong fibre; FLAX; **fuchsia,** any of several plants bearing flowers reminiscent of those of the *Fuchsia,* esp. the species of the genus *Correa* (see CORREA), *Epacris longiflora* (fam. Epacridaceae) of Vic. and N.S.W., and *Eremophila maculata* (fam. Myoporaceae) of drier mainland Aust.; **grape,** any of several perennial woody climbers of the fam. Vitaceae, esp. *Cissus hypoglauca* (see *water vine* WATER); **grass,** any of many grasses of the fam. Poaceae; **heath,** HEATH; **hibiscus,** any of several Austral. species of *Hibiscus* (fam. Malvaceae), incl. ROSELLA n.²; also *attrib.*; **honeysuckle,** HONEYSUCKLE 1; **hop** (or **hops**), any of several plants resembling the hop *Humulus* (often in the winged fruit or bitter leaves), incl. HOP-BUSH; *wild hop,* see WILD 1; also *attrib.*; **indigo,** INDIGO a.; **jasmine,** any of several plants bearing fragrant, often pale-coloured, flowers, incl. the desert jasmine *Jasminum didymum* ssp. *lineare* (fam. Oleaceae) of inland Aust.; **laurel** *Tas.,* the tall shrub or small tree *Anopterus glandulosus* (fam. Cunoniaceae) of Tas., having glossy, serrated, dark green leaves and showy, usu. white, flowers; **leek,** any of several plants of the genus *Bulbine* (fam. Liliaceae) of temperate Aust. incl. Tas., and elsewhere, having narrow, succulent, hollow leaves; *native onion;* see also *onion weed* ONION 1; **lilac,** any of several plants incl. FALSE SARSAPARILLA; **lime, (a)** *native cumquat;* **(b)** the thorny shrub or small tree *Microcitrus australis* (fam. Rutaceae) of Qld., bearing a green, rough-skinned, edible fruit; **mahogany** *obs.,* JARRAH 1; **melon,** *native cucumber;* **millet,** any of several grasses (fam. Poaceae), usu. of the genus *Panicum,* esp. the tussock-forming perennial *P. decompositum* of all mainland States; see also COOLY; **mulberry,** the small, soft-wooded tree *Pipturus argenteus* (fam. Urticaceae) of e. Qld., n.e. N.S.W., and elsewhere, bearing a white, mulberry-like fruit; **myrtle,** any of several plants incl. the shrub *Myoporum acuminatum* (fam. Myoporaceae) of all mainland States, having bright green leaves; **oak,** SHE-OAK 1; **onion,** *native leek;* **orange,** any of several shrubs or trees, usu. bearing a rounded, edible fruit, esp. of the genera *Capparis* (see *wild orange* WILD 1) and *Citriobatus* (fam. Pittosporaceae) of n. Aust.; the fruit itself; also **orange-tree; parsley** *obs.,* the herbaceous plant *Apium prostratum* (fam. Apiaceae) of all States and elsewhere, occurring on coastal land and swampy areas inland; **peach,** any of several plants esp. QUANDONG 1 a.; the fruit of the plant; **pear,** the fruit of any of several plants, often of the genus *Xylomelum* (fam. Proteaceae), esp. the shrub or small tree *X. pyriforme* of N.S.W. and Qld., and ALUNQUA; the plant itself; see also WOODEN PEAR; also *attrib.*; **pepper,** any of several plants bearing a pungent fruit, incl. species of the genus *Piper* (fam. Piperaceae), and PEPPER TREE 1; the fruit itself; **pine,** CYPRESS PINE; **plum,** any of several trees or shrubs bearing a plumlike fruit, incl. *Santalum lanceolatum* (fam. Santalaceae) of drier mainland Aust., having greyish foliage and an edible bluish fruit, *Planchonella australis* (see *black apple* BLACK a.² 1 a.) and (Tas.) *Cenarrhenes nitida* (fam. Proteaceae) of Tas.; the fruit itself; PLUM; *wild plum,* see WILD 1; **pomegranate, (a)** *wild orange,* see WILD 1; **(b)** W.A. the low shrub *Balaustion pulcherrimum* (fam. Myrtaceae) of s.w. W.A.; **poplar,** any of several trees, esp. HORSERADISH TREE; **potato, (a)** POTATO ORCHID; **(b)** either of the two twining plants *Marsdenia viridiflora* and *M. flavescens* (fam. Asclepiadaceae), having tuberous roots; **raspberry,** any of several prickly shrubs of e. Aust. of the worldwide genus *Rubus* (fam. Rosaceae), bearing an edible, red fruit, as *R. parvifolius* of s.e. Aust. incl. Tas., and elsewhere; the fruit itself; *native bramble; wild raspberry,* see WILD 1; **rose,** any of several plants, esp. the shrub *Boronia serrulata* (fam. Rutaceae) of sandstone heaths of e. N.S.W., bearing fragrant bright-pink (or occas. white) flowers; **sarsaparilla,** any of several plants esp. *sweet tea* (see SWEET a.¹); **spinach,** any of several plants used as a green vegetable; **tamarind,** the large tree *Diploglottis australis* (fam. Sapindaceae) of s.e. Qld. and n.e. N.S.W., the fruit of which has an edible, acid pulp; the fruit itself; TAMARIND; **tobacco,** any of several plants resembling, or used as, tobacco, incl. soft-leaved species of the genus *Nicotiana* (fam. Solanaceae) and PITURI; **tulip** *obs.,* the plant *Telopea speciosissima* (see WARATAH 1); **willow,** any of several trees of pendulous habit incl. *Pittosporum phillyraeoides* (see BUTTERBUSH), and esp. *Acacia salicina* (fam. Mimosaceae), usu. occurring near watercourses in drier mainland Aust.; see also COOBA; **yam,** YAM.

1843 J.F. BENNETT *Hist. & Descr. Acct. S.A.* 44 There are some kinds of small berries which have been dignified with the names of the '**native apple**', 'cherry', &c., but most of them are no larger than peas. **1965** *Austral. Encycl.* I. 218 The names native apple and apple-myrtle are used for indigenous trees of the genus *Angophora* .. so conspicuous on Hawkesbury sandstone formations, N.S.W. **1805** *Sydney Gaz.* 3 Feb., The fine foliage of the iron bark and **native apple tree**. **1967** B.Y. MAIN *Between Wodjil & Tor* 27 On the pendulous boughs of the *Pittosporum phillyraeoides* or **native apricots** a faint yellow was beginning to tinge the green bivalved fruits. **1909** G. SMITH *Naturalist in Tas.* 60 Wherever the ground is at all marshy the **native Artichoke**, which is really a Lily (*Astelia alpina*), forms profuse, dense tufts. **1878** R.B. SMYTH *Aborigines of Vic.* I. 231 *Musa Brownii* .. **Native banana**. **1911** A.J. BOYD *Banana in Qld.* 31 In the dense scrubs of North Queensland the Banana is indigenous, and may be seen growing everywhere in great luxuriance, but the fruit .. is quite inedible... The three best known of these native bananas are—*Musa Banksii* .. *Musa Fitzalani* .. *Musa Hillii*. **1900** H. LAWSON *Verses Pop. & Humorous* 28 Where groves of wattle flourish And **native bluebells** grow. **1835** *Hobart Town Almanack* 73 *Bursaria* spinosa. **Native Box** . . is easily propagated from the seeds, which are produced very abundantly, and when planted in rows and clipped makes excellent hedges. It has already been introduced into the conservatories in England, to which its elegant odoriferous flowers are a great ornament. **1916** *Emu* XV. 177 The islet . . is covered in parts with a prickly shrub locally known as 'native box thorn'. **1848** T.L. MITCHELL *Jrnl. Exped. Tropical Aust.* 351 On the river bank, we observed this day the **native bramble**, or Australian form of *Rubus parvifolius*. **1831** G.A. ROBINSON in N.J.B. Plomley *Friendly Mission* 23 Oct. (1966) 490 One of the native women, Sall, found a bulbous plant called by the white people '**native bread**'. **1863** *Adelaide Observer* 5 Dec. 6/6 They fish, shoot, hunt up **native** potatoes, carrots, **cabbage**, and a multiplicity of other strange edibles which require a considerable deal of looking after before the seekers can eat. **1842** *Tasmanian Jrnl. Nat. Sci.* I. 36 *Geranium parviflorum*. Small-flowered Geranium . . . The Aborigines were in the habit of digging up its roots . . and roasting them. It was called about Launceston '**native carrot**'. **1966** A. MORRIS *Plantlife W. Darling* 74 *Daucus glochidiatus* . . 'Native carrot'. Common annual. Spring. **1854** G.E. SARGENT *Frank Layton* (1865) 139 Its furniture was . . manufactured of **native cedar** principally. **1817** A. CUNNINGHAM in I. Marriott *Early Explorers Aust.* 21 May (1925) 217 The **Native Cherry**, our common eastern coast plant, Exocarpus cupressiformis. **1844** *S. Austral. Odd Fellows' Mag.* Oct. 191 The thick foliage of the native cherry-tree . . studded with small fruit just blushing into ripeness. **1908** W.H. OGILVIE *My Life in Open* 5 A quandong or a native cherry stands like a trim bush in the grounds of some country houses. **1838** *Sydney Herald* 30 July 2/5 A **native cotton** tree, and a small kangaroo, with a nail or hook at the end of its tail, comprise the whole of the curiosities discovered. **1878** R.B. SMYTH *Aborigines of Vic.* I. 226 *Mootcha*, native cotton-bush. When the leaves sprout and become quite green, the natives gather and cook them, and at same-time they pluck and eat the pods. **1903** F. TURNER *Bot. Darling, N.S.W.* 409 One of the most beautiful flowering plants of this family is the 'native cotton', *Gossypium sturtii* . . which I have seen successfully cultivated in a garden at Bourke. **1829** R. MUDIE *Picture of Aust.* 151 The Australian **cranberry** (*lissanthe sapida*) is a beautiful fruited shrub. **1834** *Hobart Almanack* 133 *Astroloma humifusa*. The native cranberry has a fruit of green, reddish, or whitish colour. **1840** *Aust., Van Dieman's Land, & N.Z.* 5 The only species of *native* eatable fruit produced by New Holland is the cranberry. **1859** J.M. STUART *Explorations in Aust.* 13 Apr. (1865) 49 The **native cucumber** grows about here. **1880** J. BONWICK *Resources Qld.* 81 The **Native Cumquat**, an *Atalantia*, is a Darling Downs shrub with a close grain, and taking a good polish. **1888** *Proc. Linnean Soc. N.S.W.* III. 489 *Atalantia glauca* . . 'Native Kumquat', 'Desert Lemon.' The fruit is globular, and about half-an-inch in diameter. **1826** J. ATKINSON *Acct. Agric. & Grazing N.S.W.* 19 The **native currant** . . resembling the cranberry. **1829** G.A. ROBINSON in N.J.B. Plomley *Friendly Mission* 19 Sept. (1966) 74 Learnt that the Kangaroo eat the prickly mimosa and likewise the **native fig**. **1799** Banks Papers 28 Nov. XIX. 95 There is also some of the **Native Flax** which grows all over the Country but near the [Hawkesbury] River it is much stronger. **1860** G. BENNETT *Gatherings of Naturalist* 372 The *Correa virens*, with its pretty pendulous blossoms (from which it has been named the '**Native Fuchsia**'). **1890** 'LYTH' *Golden South* 209 Pillars wreathed with . . epacris longiflora or native fuchsia. **1901** J.H. MAIDEN *Plants reputed to be Poisonous* 27 *Eremophila maculata*—called 'Native Fuchsia' in parts of Queensland. It is often sent to Sydney as a suspected plant. **1838** *Sydney Herald* 30 July 2/5 A **native grape** of good flavour, was found near the banks of the Fitzroy River. **1804** *HRA* (1915) 1st Ser. VI. 491 Dry weather . . has dried up all the **native grasses**. **1860** 'LADY' *My Experiences in Aust.* 45 There is the **native heath**, or *Epacris*, of which there are many varieties. **1935** H. BASEDOW *Knights of Boomerang* 60 Under the cover of a **native hibiscus**-bush. **1980** L. FULLER *Wollongong's Native Trees* 51 Native hibiscus (*Hibiscus heterophyllus*) with its 100 mm. wide white and red throated flowers is an attractive and easily grown plant. **1831** W. BLAND *Journey of Discovery*

Port Phillip 6 The plains . . were interspersed with occasional clumps of the **Native Honeysuckle**. **1841** *S. Austral. Mag.* (Adelaide) Dec. 198 The native honeysuckle, which, with many other sweet smelling plants sends its delicate perfume on the air. **1855** W. HOWITT *Land, Labor & Gold* I. 109 The **native hop** . . only so called because it is intensely bitter—is a shrub with oval leaves, growing in the bush. . . Instead of a humulus, it is a Daviesia, the latifolia. **1967** B.Y. MAIN *Between Wodjil & Tor* 25 In the undergrowth . . native hop bushes (*Dodonaea attenuata*) with covered with withered papery fruits, pinkish-green in colour. **1981** J. JESSOP *Flora Central Aust.* 32 Much photographed by tourists as 'Native Hops'. This vernacular name is unsuitable because it [*sc. Rumex vesicarius*] is neither native nor a hop. **1826** *Hobart Town Gaz.* 15 Apr., Of all our indigenous plants, none equals in value the **native indigo**. **1860** 'LADY' *My Experiences in Aust.* 45 There is also a **native Jasmine**, its flower precisely resembling the white Jasmine we are all familiar with at home, but the plant itself bearing more likeness to the broom. **1842** D. BURN *Narr. Journey Hobart Town to Macquarie Harbour* 11 Apr. (1955) 25 A singularly beautiful shrub, styled in unlearned phrase, the '**Native Laurel**'. **1866** *Australasian* (Melbourne) 25 Aug. 665/2 There are a variety of herbs on which stock are found to thrive exceedingly; amongst which may be enumerated 'salt-bush', '**native leeks**' [etc.]. **1847** G.F. ANGAS *Savage Life & Scenes* I. 225 The brilliant clusters of the **native lilac**. **1880** J. BONWICK *Resources Qld.* 81 The Native Orange, a *Citrus* of the scrubs, has a hard close-grained wood, like the **Native Lime**. **1912** *Emu* XII. 73 Noticed a flock of several of the little white-browed Babblers . . moving amongst the native lime trees (*Atalantia glauca*). **1975** A.B. & J.W. CRIBB *Wild Food in Aust.* 42 *Microcitrus australis* Native Lime, Native Orange. . . Found in rainforests, *M. australis* is a taller tree than the finger-lime. **1837** *Perth Gaz.* 7 Jan. 825 His Excellency the Governor . . received authority for the supply of 200 loads . . of **Native Mahogany** for the use of His Majesty's Dock-yard, Portsmouth. **1844** L. LEICHHARDT *Jrnl. Overland Exped. Aust.* 29 Dec. (1847) 87 The **native melon** of the Darling Downs and of the Gwyder. **1888** *Proc. Linnean Soc. N.S.W.* III. 536 '**Native Millet**'. . . The seed used to be called 'Cooly' by western New South Wales aboriginals. . . The grains pounded yield excellent food. . . This plant is not endemic in Australia. **1846** *Portland Guardian* 18 Sept. 4/3 A **native mulberry**, with small white fruit of a sweet taste, grew on the fields of lava, at the Burdekin. **1835** *Hobart Town Almanack* 84 *Dodonaea truncata*. **Native Myrtle**. . . Their beauty consists only in the foliage, the flowers being green and inconspicuous. **1831** G.A. ROBINSON in N.J.B. Plomley *Friendly Mission* (1966) 386 The **native oak** (sheoak). **1891** *Proc. Linnean Soc. N.S.W.* VI. 135 *Bulbine bulbosa* . . '**Native Onion**' . . is recorded as poisonous to stock in Queensland and South Australia. **1860** J.M. STUART *Explorations in Aust.* 24 Apr. (1865) 166 The **native orange**-tree abounds here. **1863** J. DAVIS *Tracks of McKinlay* 300 We found abundance of the native oranges. Why it should be called 'orange' I don't know, as it is as much like that fruit as a gooseberry is like a pine-apple. **1835** *Hobart Town Almanack* 67 *Apium prostratum*. **Native Parsley**. **1839** H. WARD *Diary* 6 Farther in land I soon discovered several sorts of Bryanthemuns in flower and one the purple I found to be of Grate use in plucking of the pericarp or seed vessel and peelling of the outer skin and sucking it there are called heer by some **native peaches** and I have had some trouble to pursuade some to the contrary. **1853** J. ALLEN *Jrnl. River Murray* 55 The native peach-tree (not dissimilar to the English peach) grows along the bank in profusion, giving the land quite a cultivated appearance. **1805** S. MARSDEN *Some Private Corresp.* 15 Jan. (1942) 36 Mr — . . promised to call on you and deliver a letter and small box containing some **native pears**. **1853** MOSSMAN & BANISTER *Aust. Visited & Revisited* 270 A few specimens of what is called the native pear-tree of New Holland, from the exact shape its seed-vessel bears to that fruit. **1826** *Colonial Times* (Hobart) 2 Dec., Most interesting of all is the **native pepper**, which grows on a small prickly bush, and is red until ripe, when it has generally attained a black colour. The pepper corns are then stronger than any from the spice islands. **1838** *Southern*

Austral. (Adelaide) 29 Sept. 2/4 On sale .. half-inch and inch **native pine. 1818** A. CUNNINGHAM in I. Marriott *Early Explorers Aust.* 6 Oct. (1925) 404 *Podocarpus sp.* (**native Plum**), a low, humifuse, spreading plant, of the habit of Taxus, with a large purple fleshy receptacle. **1880** J. BONWICK *Resources Qld.* 82 The **Native Pomegranate**, a *Capparis*, has a hard, close-grained scrubwood. **1965** *Austral. Encycl.* I. 394 *B[alaustion] pulcherrimum* is known as the native pomegranate, from the shape of its small, brilliantly scarlet bell-flowers. **1889** E. GILES *Aust. twice Traversed* II. 195 There was nothing but the **native poplar** for the camels to eat, and they devoured the leaves with great apparent relish, though to my human taste it is about the most disgusting of vegetables. (**a**) **1833** J. Backhouse *Narr. Visit Austral. Colonies* 2 Jan. (1843) 119, I dug up a *Gastrodium sesamoides*. . . It grows among decaying vegetable matter, and has a root like a series of kidney potatoes . . and is sometimes called **Native Potato.** (**b**) **1890** *Ibid.* V. 275 *Marsdenia flavescens* . . and *M. viridiflora* . . the tuberous roots of these species are edible. They are called '**Native Potatoes**', and the blacks were accustomed to eat them after some preparation. **1844** L. LEICHHARDT *Jrnl. Overland Exped. Aust.* 9 Dec. (1847) 67 The **native raspberry**, and *Ficus muntia*, were in fruit. **1827** R. SWEET *Flora Australasica* Pl. 19, Boronia serrulata. . . Its beauty and the delightful fragrance of its flowers . . has [sic] obtained for it the name of the **native Rose** in New South Wales. **1856** *Jrnl. Australasia* I. 38 Glycine monophylla; one-leaved glycine, the rich blue flowering trailer, erroneously known as the **native sarsaparilla. 1846** *Portland Guardian* 18 Sept. 4/2 We boiled the young shoots of **native spinach** (mesembrianthemum) . . as vegetables. **1854** F. ELDERSHAW *Aust. as it really Is* 43 The **native** Plum, **Tamarind**, Chestnut . . are . . well-recognized delicacies among the rising Anglo-Australian generation. **1844** L. LEICHHARDT *Jrnl. Overland Exped. Aust.* 2 Oct. (1847) 5 **Native tobacco** in blossom. **1826** J. ATKINSON *Acct. Agric. & Grazing N.S.W.* 19 The wood of the warrataw or **native tulip**, the most magnificent flower of New Holland. **1861** *Sydney Mail* 6 July 3/3 The graceful *Acacia floribunda*, the sallee, or '**native willow**', is golden with bloom . . a slender tree, with long lance-shaped leaves. **1827** P. CUNNINGHAM *Two Yrs. in N.S.W.* I. 300 They [*sc.* the pigs] feed on the grasses, herbs, wild roots, and **native yams**, on the margins of our rivers or marshy grounds.

b. In the names of animals: **native bear,** KOALA 1; **bee**, any of several small, stingless bees of the genus *Trigona*, producing honey which is stored in a comb, often in the hollow of a tree trunk; **canary**, any of several birds having an attractive song or yellowish colour, esp. *white-throated warbler* (see WHITE *a.*[2] 1 b.); **cat**, any of the several carnivorous, long-tailed, spotted marsupials of the genus *Dasyurus* of Aust. incl. Tas., and New Guinea, incl. the *tiger cat* (see TIGER *n.* 6); QUOLL; *spotted native cat*, see SPOTTED; WILD CAT *n.*[1]; see also DASYURE; also *ellipt.* as **cat; companion,** BROLGA; **devil** *obs.*, *Tasmanian devil*, see TASMANIAN *a.* 2; **dingo** *obs.*, **dog**, DINGO *n.* 1; **hedgehog,** ECHIDNA; **hen**, (**a**) either of two species of moorhen, the *Tasmanian native hen* (see TASMANIAN *a.* 2), and the black-tailed native hen *Gallinula ventralis*, a nomadic bird occurring near water in inland mainland Aust.; (**b**) *mallee fowl*, see MALLEE 6; **herring** *obs.*, (**a**) TOMMY ROUGH; (**b**) HERRING 2; **hyena** *obs.*, (**a**) *Tasmanian tiger*, see TASMANIAN *a.* 2; (**b**) *Tasmanian devil*, see TASMANIAN *a.* 2; **magpie** *obs.*, MAGPIE *n.* 1 a.; **pheasant,** (**a**) LYRE-BIRD 1; (**b**) *mallee fowl*, see MALLEE 6; **porcupine,** ECHIDNA; **salmon**, the fish *Arripis trutta* (see SALMON); **sloth** *obs.*, KOALA 1; **tiger** *obs.*, *Tasmanian tiger*, see TASMANIAN *a.* 2; **turkey** *obs.*, TURKEY *n.*[1] 1.

1827 P. CUNNINGHAM *Two Yrs. in N.S.W.* I. 317 Our *coola* (sloth or **native bear**) is about the size of an ordinary poodle dog, with shaggy, dirty coloured fur, no tail, and claws and feet like a bear, of which it forms a tolerable miniature. **1845** L. LEICHHARDT *Jrnl. Overland Exped. Aust.* 12 Feb. (1847) 148 In the scrub Fusanus was observed in fruit . . and the white Vitex in blossom; from the latter the **native bee** extracts a most delicious honey. **1889** *Proc. Linnean Soc. N.S.W.* IV. 407 *Gerygone albigularis* . . local name '**Native Canary**'. **1804** *Sydney Gaz.* 11 Mar. 3/3 From the prodigious increase of the brood of wild or **native cats** great quantities of poultry have been destroyed. **1825** *London Mag.* May II. 61 There is the native cat, a very pretty animal, mostly dark brown with white spots all over them as thick as they can well be, they are the sise [sic] of our cats. **1817** J. OXLEY *Jrnls. Two Exped. N.S.W.* 12 May (1820) 33 That large species of bittern, known on the east-coast by the local name of **Native Companions**, I believe from the circumstance of their being always seen in pairs, was observed. **1833** W.H. BRETON *Excursions* 408 Of the **native devil** (dasyurus ursinus) I saw only one specimen. **1842** *S.A. News* (London) 15 Jan. 69/1 The **native dingoes**, now spread thinly over the country, skulking in holes and caves, seek to avoid the light of day. **1788** *HRA* (1914) 1st Ser. I. 32 Five ewes and a lamb had been killed in the middle of the day, and very near the camp, I apprehend by some of the **native dogs. 1848** *Portland Gaz.* 27 Oct. 3/5 **Native hedge-hog.** . . In shape and size it resembles the Hedgehog of the Mother Country, but is covered with strong, short, and sharp quills or bristles, somewhat different from that well-known animal. **1804** M. HOOKEY *B. Knopwood & his Times* 24 Mar. (1929) 20 Killed a **Native Hen**, which first took the sea. **1861** 'OLD BUSHMAN' *Bush Wanderings* 63 The *Lowan* or native hen, is peculiar to the country in the vicinity of the 'Mallee Scrub'. **1864** *Colonial Cook Bk.* (1970) 52 **Native herring**, or ruff. A small but delicate fish. **1889** 'MOOSAFIR' *N.-W. Coast Tas.* 30 The River Mersey . . abounds with . . the native herring or cucumber fish as it is called—really the grayling. **1831** *Acct. Colony Van Diemen's Land* 53 Considerable numbers of the **native hyena** prowl the mountains near this in quest of prey among the flocks at night. **1857** D. BUNCE *Australasiatic Reminisc.* 25 Mr Davidson submitted to our notice the *Dasyurus*, or native hyena, or devil. **1842** *S. Austral. Mag.* (Adelaide) Aug. 469 **Native magpies**—properly, a very beautiful species of the jack-daw tribe—colours, black, white, and grey; their notes about daylight are exceedingly melodious. **1826** J. ATKINSON *Acct. Agric. & Grazing N.S.W.* 26 The **native pheasant** is remarkable for its beautiful tail, but is not fit to eat. **1889** E. GILES *Aust. twice Traversed* I. 153 We saw a native pheasant's nest. . . This bird is known by different names in different parts of Australia. On the eastern half of the continent it is usually called the Lowan, while in Western Australia it is known as the Gnow. **1834** G. BENNETT *Wanderings N.S.W.* I. 299 The *Echidna*, or '**native porcupine**'. **1889** 'MOOSAFIR' *N.-W. Coast Tas.* 22 The river contains plenty of . . mullet, **native salmon**, etc. **1852** W. HUGHES *Austral. Colonies* 79 There is a **native sloth**—a kind of bear, about the size of a poodle dog, with shaggy, dirty-coloured fur. It climbs trees with facility, getting very fat and unwieldy: the flesh is esteemed by the natives. **1832** *Hobart-Town Almanack* 85 During our stay, a **native tiger** or hyena bounded from its beautiful lair beneath the rocks. **1822** B. FIELD *Geogr. Mem. N.S.W.* 12 Oct. (1825) 443 At Bathurst, saw what is called the **native turkey**. It is the New Holland vulture of Dr Latham, and is one of the most remarkable birds found in Australia, appearing to form a connecting link between the rapacious and gallinaceous orders.

native-born, *a.* [Spec. use of *native-born* belonging to a place by birth, applied esp. to persons of immigrant race in a colony.]

1. Of a non-Aboriginal person: born in Australia (as opposed to 'immigrant' or 'naturalized'). Also as quasi-*n.*

1820 *HRA* (1921) 3rd Ser. III. 442 Four out of the Five marriages performed, since I have been here, are between native born people. **1827** *Monitor* (Sydney) 21 June 460/3 It is alleged, that the Colonists who were British-born, are loyal; but the adult native-born in this respect, are but so so.

2. In collocations: **native-born Australian, colonist, population, white, youth.**

1842 *Colonial Observer* (Sydney) 16 Nov. 612/3 One half of the whole number of the City Councillors, are not **native-born Australians** at all, but free immigrants from the mother-country. **1831** *Independent* (Launceston) 22 Oct. 2/2 Recommend it to the attention of a **native born colonist. 1848** H.W. HAYGARTH *Recoll. Bush Life* 123 The **native-born population** (I allude, of course, only to the whites).. are not, upon the whole, equal in form to the parent stock. **1835** BACKHOUSE & TYLOR *Life & Labours G.W. Walker* (1862) 233 The bulk of the population are **native born whites. 1827** *Hobart Town Courier* 1 Dec. 1 One of them is Edward Hannigan, a **native born youth.**

nature strip. A name applied in some Australian towns to a piece of publicly-owned land between the front boundary of a dwelling or other building and the street, usu. planted with grass; a median strip.
1948 *Architecture in Aust.* Jan. 34, I did not see one allotment where the whole of the ground was cared for and the street nature strip in front attended to. **1973** *Bulletin* (Sydney) 3 Feb. 62/1 If you drive through many country towns these days you see the nature strips in the centres of roads and parks neat and tidy and lots of new kerbing and guttering.

naughty. (An act of) sexual intercourse.
1959 E. LAMBERT *Glory thrown In* 106 Until I met Thelma, I always thought sheilas had to be talked into a bit of a naughty. **1985** *Sydney Morning Herald* 20 June 11/6 The Poms are often accused of spending all their time at a party chatting up girls—an offence against Mateship. Not for nothing do Australians call sexual intercourse 'having a naughty'.
Hence **naughty** *v. trans.*, to have sexual intercourse with.
1977 C. KLEIN *Pomegranate Tree* 61 He didn't want to dob the hard word on her, last thing he had on his mind was to try and naughty her.

near enough, *phr.* See quot. 1962.
1939 H.M. MORAN *Viewless Winds* 12 This has begotten the slipshod character of all we make and the spirit of 'near enough will do'. **1962** *Texas Q.* 62 'Near enough' is the national philosophy: a deliberate cult of antifinesse, of outbackmanship.

Nebuchadnezzar. [So called in allusion to Daniel's interpretation of the dream of *Nebuchadnezzar* King of Babylon (d. 562 B.C.): see Daniel iv. 25.] A salad.
1859 F. FOWLER *Southern Lights & Shadows* 53 At some of the taverns they serve bread-and-cheese, salads, and sandwiches for luncheon. The vernacular for these stands thus: .. Salad .. Nebuchadnezzar [etc.]. **1941** S.J. BAKER *Pop. Dict. Austral. Slang* 48 Nebuchadnezzar, salad.

neck, *n.*
1. *pl.* The wool shorn from the neck of a sheep.
1928 C.E. COWLEY *Classing Clip* 36 In large sheds it may be advisable to remove the 'necks', that is, the wool grown on the scragg.
2. a. In the phr. **under** (someone's) **neck,** see quot. 1966.
1953 T.A.G. HUNGERFORD *Riverslake* 220 Why jack up?.. You just race in the mob from the office and go under our necks. **1966** S.J. BAKER *Austral. Lang.* (ed. 2) 239 Worthy of record is the expression *get under someone's neck*, which is in general use and apparently has horsey antecedents. A person who beats, outwits or anticipates the moves of another is said to *get under his neck*; it means to get in front of him.
b. In the *attrib. phr.* **neck-to-knee,** see quot. 1902.
[**1902** *N.S.W. Govt. Gaz.* VI. 8690 All persons bathing in any waters exposed to view from any wharf, street, public place, or dwelling-house in the Municipal District of Manly, before the hour of 7.30 in the morning and after the hour of 8 o'clock in the evening, shall be attired in proper bathing costume covering the body from the neck to the knee. Any person committing a breach of this By-law shall be liable to a penalty not exceeding one pound.] **1910** *Daily Tel.* (Sydney) 20 June 17/8 Neck-to-knee costumes have been for some time past insisted on at all the popular resorts. **1965** G. McINNES *Road to Gundagai* 261 Refusing to wear the regulation 'neck-to-knee' bathing togs.
3. Special Comb. **neck-bag,** a water-bag; **rope,** a rope used to tether an animal by the neck; so, **rope** *v. trans.*
1936 *Bulletin* (Sydney) 12 Aug. 20/2 Another test is with a **neck-bag.** The city cove will put his mouth to the nozzle of the bag; the mulga-trained one will pour the water from the bag to his pint. **1849** A. HARRIS *Emigrant Family* (1967) 129 The leg-rope is first cautiously unloosed; next the **neck-rope** is slackened. **1938** A. UPFIELD *Bone is Pointed* (1966) 49 Both animals .. appeared to be neck-roped to their respective trees.

neck, *v. trans.* To carry (a burden) across the shoulders.
1976 R. THIELE *Ketch Hand* 43 Sometimes even the skipper did an hour 'necking a few bags' to speed up the loading. **1982** LOWENSTEIN & HILLS *Under Hook* 50 With bags you arsed 'em or necked 'em. .. Necking 'em means that you carried them across your shoulders, on your neck.

necking, *vbl. n.* See quot. 1967.
1967 *Kings Cross Whisper* (Sydney) xxxvi. 4/2 *Necking*, the practice of putting one arm around a victim's neck and a free hand into his pocket. **1968** J. ALARD *He who shoots Last* 173 All his boob dreams of performing future neckings (his favourite method of earning a living) were fading.

neddy. [Transf. use of *neddy* a donkey.]
1. A horse.
1887 *Tibbs' Pop. Song Bk.* 9 So they saddled up their Neddys And like loafers sneaked away. **1981** *Bulletin* (Sydney) 8 Sept. 47/2 Needing extra money for the neddies, he'd let it be known that guests were expected to cough up.
2. *transf.* A swagman's tucker-bag.
1898 *Bulletin* (Sydney) 30 July 32/2 'Neddy' the tucker-bag is of more importance than the 'blue one', and by way of precedence dangles in front, mostly hanging to Matilda's apron-strings.

Ned Kelly, *n.* [f. the name of *Ned Kelly* (1857-1880), bushranger.]
1. Used allusively to designate one who is unscrupulous in seeking personal gain or resistant of authority. See also *Kelly gang* KELLY *n.*[1] 1. Also *attrib.*
1893 F.W.L. ADAMS *Australs.* 66 This Ned Kelly of colonial politics .. may yet jockey himself into a local immortality, as the father of Australian Federation. **1982** *Bulletin* (Sydney) 20 July 41/1 Unfortunately the old Ned Kelly syndrome rears its head. People look up at all the big insurance buildings and reckon they can afford it.
2. In the phr. **(as) game as Ned Kelly,** fearless in the face of odds; foolhardy.
1938 *Point* (Melbourne) I. i. 8 Sleet-smarted face and snow-filled eye, Vigilant in the dark before the dawn Game as Ned Kelly. **1956** S. HOPE *Diggers' Paradise* 89 A common expression on the lips of Aussies of both sexes to describe someone engaged in a risky enterprise is 'he's as game as Ned Kelly'.
3. Rhyming slang for 'belly'.
1945 S.J. BAKER *Austral. Lang.* 271 *Ned Kelly*, the belly. **1951** D. STIVENS *Jimmy Brockett* 86, I got his arm and rammed a right into his Ned Kelly. **1971** B. HUMPHRIES *Bazza pulls it Off*, If I don't get a drop of hard stuff up me old Ned Kelly there's a chance I might chunder in the channel.

4. *Fishing.* An unsporting fishing rig: see quots.
1948 F.D. MARSHALL *Let's go Fishing* 45 The 'Ned Kelly' is the answer. It consists of a bamboo pole (Indian Cane) approximately 12 feet long. At the end, whip on a loop of greenhide to which is attached the line .. from 12 to 15 feet of steel wire. 1951 S.H. EDWARDS *Shooting & Bushcraft* 48 A 'Ned Kelly' rig to a fisherman is a rod without a reel and a short line to skull-drag a fish.

Ned Kelly, *v.* [f. prec.] *intr.* To bushrange; also *trans.*, to kill (a bird, etc.) unsportingly.
1906 *Gadfly* (Adelaide) 2 May 9/3 Gipsy Smith was a second-rate bushranger, who Ned-Kellied on a small scale about Bendigo in the days of the Forest Range goldfield. 1951 S.H. EDWARDS *Shooting & Bushcraft* 48 When raising yourself above .. the bank of a dam, go up very, very slowly .. and you will have ample time to plan your shot, whether you intend to 'Ned Kelly' them or take them on the wing.

needlebush: see NEEDLEWOOD.

needle-tail. [See quot. 1968.] *Rainbow bird*, see RAINBOW 2.
1941 *Bulletin* (Sydney) 20 Aug. 16/2 A needle-tail .. is more like Willie Wagtail than a kingfisher, and his favorite insect is the good old working bee. A few of them will clean up a dozen hives in no time. 1968 F. HARDY *Unlucky Australs.* 48 She waged a constant war with her shotgun against the needletails. These are beautiful birds, with red eyes, long savage beaks and two long tail feathers sharp as needles.

needlewood. Any of several shrubs or small trees, chiefly of the genus *Hakea* (see HAKEA), having rigid needle-like leaves, esp. *H. leucoptera* and *H. tephrosperma* of drier inland Aust.; PIN BUSH. See also *water tree* WATER. Also **needlebush,** and *attrib.*
1884 *Once a Month* (Melbourne) Dec. 453 The *hakea stricta*, or needlebush of the colonists, with its roots just under the surface, had them full of water. 1898 W. REDMOND *Shooting Trip* 35 This timber is called needlewood, because the foliage resembles fine needles. 1936 C.T. MADIGAN *Central Aust.* 76 The twisty needlewood sticks of the desert.

neelia, var. NELIA.

neg, *a.* [Abbrev. of *negligent.*] In the collocation **neg driving:** see quot. 1984.
1969 A. BUZO *Rooted* (1973) 44 Hammo had a prang in his B and got dobbed in for neg driving. 1984 A. DELBRIDGE *Aussie Talk* 217 *Neg driving, n.,* the offence of negligent driving.

negro. *Obs.* A name applied by colonists to an Aboriginal.
1834 G. BENNETT *Wanderings N.S.W.* I. 171 It is probable that the negroes of New Holland have extended into the Australian continent, by New Guinea and the eastern islands, and that the migration has been made from the coast of Africa. 1878 R.B. SMYTH *Aborigines of Vic.* I. 245 The Jardines, on their overland expedition from Rockhampton to Cape York, found 'at a native fire the fresh remains of a negro roasted'.

negrohead. [Used elsewhere but recorded earliest in Aust.: see quot. 1802.] NIGGERHEAD 1.
1802 M. FLINDERS *Voyage Terra Australis* 5 Oct. (1814) II. 83 The reefs were not dry in any part, with the exception of some small black lumps, which at a distance resembled the round heads of negroes. 1931 J.S GARDINER *Coral Reefs & Atolls* 7 Corals are broken off to be swept perchance on to an island shore behind, and fractured rock masses may be cast on to the reef as giant sentinels or 'negroheads'.

negrohead beech: see BEECH.

nelia /'niliǝ/. Formerly also **neelia, nilyah.** [Ngiyambaa *nhiilyi* the tree *Acacia loderi.*] Any of several small trees or shrubs of inland Aust. of the genus *Acacia* (fam. Mimosaceae), esp. *A. rigens*, having needle-like foliage, and *A. loderi.*
1867 *Illustr. Sydney News* 16 Jan. 104/2 The banks of the Murray .. abound in fancy woods. .. The sweetly scented myall is known, but there is another description, known by the blacks as Nelia 1910 *Emu* X. 89 The neelia (*Acacia rigens*) just coming into bloom. 1984 *Aboriginal Hist.* VIII. 24 'Nilyah' spelt 'nelia' in many reference books is the local English name for *Acacia loderi*.

Nelly. Also **nelly.** [Transf. use of *Nelly* a female name.]
1. A cheap wine. Also **Nelly's death.**
1935 K. TENNANT *Tiburon* 128 Staines .. tenaciously kept a bottle of Nellie's Death out of circulation. 1973 *Kings Cross Whisper* (Sydney) cliii. 16/2 You've got to get up very early in the morning to catch them sober and then you can't always be sure on account of their habit of keeping a flagon of nellie by the bed.
2. In the collocation **nervous Nelly,** a timid or cautious person.
1974 *Bulletin* (Sydney) 30 Nov. 15/1 The Nervous Nellies—those people in the Federal Government who take fright at some of the devil-may-care attitudes of Prime Minister Whitlam. 1984 *N.T. News* (Darwin) 10 Dec. 7/1 Another architectural masterpiece in the same mould is not required. I am neither a 'flat earther' nor a 'nervous nellie', just a concerned Territorian.
3. As **Nelly Bligh,** rhyming slang for 'pie'; also *ellipt.* as **Nelly.**
1967 *Kings Cross Whisper* (Sydney) xxxvi. 4/2 *Nelly Blighs*, eyes, meat pies. *Ibid.* xxxiv. 5/4 *Nellie at Expo* 67. An Australian meat pie is to be sent to Expo '67. 1968 *Swag* (Sydney) i. 24/3 A pie is called a dog's eye, or perhaps, a Nelly Bligh.

nerangy, var. NARANG.

net, *v. trans.* To surround (an area) with wire-netting in order to protect it from vermin. Also with **in, round.**
1896 *Bulletin* (Sydney) 4 Apr. 22/2 Rabbit-net the country, of course, answers the man who knows all about Eastern and Central squattages. .. This 'net the paddocks' solution of the problem will be seen to have weak features about it. 1900 *Ibid.* 28 Apr. 14/3 A 'remittance' farming drunk .. wired in alarm to his wealthy English father that the rabbits were approaching, and please wire £140 for netting round selection. 1938 J.F.W. SCHULZ *Destined to Perish* 22 Though the station was netted in, the rabbits gradually broke through from the South.

net fence. NETTING FENCE.
1905 *Bulletin* (Sydney) 16 Mar. 16/1 The net fences are banked up by roly-poly and sand.

netted, *ppl. a.* Protected with a wire-netting fence; made of wire-netting.
1936 *Bulletin* (Sydney) 5 Feb. 21/1 In a netted paddock beside the Wollondilly .. we had paused to watch a platypus in the stream. 1949 *Walkabout* May 18/2 It rushed men and materials by rail to Burracoppin .. and constructed the fence which is known as the longest netted fence in the world.

netting fence. [Abbrev. of *wire-netting fence.*] A fence of wire-netting erected as a barrier against vermin.
1900 *Bulletin* (Sydney) 1 Sept. 14/2 Have never *seen* a rabbit climb a netting-fence. 1936 W. HATFIELD *Aust.*

through Windscreen 244 Netting fences defeated the rabbits, and everything was lovely.

nettle tree. STINGING TREE. Also **nettle**.

1827 P. CUNNINGHAM *Two Yrs. in N.S.W.* I. 201 The nettle-tree will tell you at once by the touch whence comes its designation. **1837** *Colonist* (Sydney) 350/1 The nettle is a lofty tree, and the poplar a dwarfish shrub.

neutral. *Obs.* A recruit not yet on active service (see quot. 1917); a deserter.

1917 C.E.W. BEAN *Lett. from France* 224 Then the 'Neutrals', 'We know they are not against the Allies', the others said when news came of the latest drafts still training under peace conditions, 'we know they are not against us—we suppose they are just neutral.' **1919** C.H. THORP *Handful of Ausseys* 202 A neutral .. is a bloke who's fed up with soldierin', an' hops it, so's the Jacks can't trace 'im.

never.

1. Abbrev. of NEVER-NEVER 1 a. Also *attrib.*

1892 *Bulletin* (Sydney) 29 Oct. 24/1 Harry .. back to old Vic, man, Down from the Never Land? Now, what's yer game? **1903** *Ibid.* 18 Apr. 16/1 They stood beside a 'Never' pub. **1978** G. HALL *River still Flows* 16 We rode in the 'Never' by twos and by threes.

2. [Used elsewhere as *never never, a.* denoting a system of periodic payments (see OEDS *never* 9 c.) but recorded earliest in Aust.] In the phr. **on the never,** at no cost to oneself; in a (financially) exploitative manner. Also **on the never-never.**

1882 *Sydney Slang Dict.* 6 *On the Never*, to take advantage of, to best. **1893** F.W.L. ADAMS *Australs.* 95 We don't let our theatrical critics go into the theatres on the never-never. .. We pay for their places.

3. In special collocations: **never-sweat** [Br. dial.: see EDD *never, adv.* 12], one who works without exertion, a loafer; **-touch-it,** a teetotaller.

1939 *Menace of Speed Coursing* (Plympton Park Citizen's Committee) 4 Dog racing produces nothing. It simply keeps a number of bookmakers and '**never-sweats**' in their jobs. **1895** *Worker* (Sydney) 26 Jan. 4/3, I am a **never-touch-it** of some years' standing.

never-fail. Any of several plants, usu. of the genus *Eragrostis* (fam. Poaceae), regarded as useful, drought-resistant fodder, esp. the tussocky perennials *E. setifolia* and *E. xerophila* of inland Aust. Also **never-fail grass.**

1923 E. BREAKWELL *Grasses & Fodder Plants N.S.W.* 19 In the dry periods only drought-resistant grasses like *Eragrostis* (Never-fail) .. grow to any extent. **1930** D. COTTRELL *Earth Battle* 204 He was riding over a low open hill shoulder covered with short grey never-fail grass.

nevergreen. [Punning alteration of *evergreen.*] See quot. 1945.

c **1840** ST. HUBERT Foreign & Colonial Stations Brit. Army Van Diemen's Land, Those persons who remain at home in the old country have been led to suppose that the beauty of the scenery must be much enhanced, by the trees described as 'evergreens', with far .. greater propriety would they have been called 'nevergreens'. **1945** S.J. BAKER *Austral. Lang.* 215 *Never greens*, a semi-humorous description for our eucalypts.

Never-Never.

1. a. The far interior of Australia; the remote outback. Also *attrib.*

1833 W.H. BRETON *Excursions* 213 The Never-never blacks .. are so called because they have hitherto kept aloof from the whites. **1986** *Canberra Times* 19 May 19/2 The Never Never .. is pock-marked with places of interest.

b. Comb. **never-never country, land.**

1877 'CAPRICORNUS' *Land Law of Future* 47 The outside districts have next to be dealt with—the dry, waste, '**never-never country**'. **1884** A.W. STIRLING *Never Never Land* p. vi, Queensland some day, and above all the '**Never Never Land**'—as the colonists call all that portion of it which lies north or west of Cape Capricorn—will be among the greatest of England's dependencies.

2. *fig.* The abode of the dead.

1891 *Truth* (Sydney) 3 May 4/5 Most of these subjects are .. shattered old derelicts who would have a short lease of life anyhow, but the departure of some of them for the Never Never is .. hastened by harsh treatment. **1911** *Bulletin* (Sydney) 5 Oct. 16/1 His mates .. informed me that Uncle Dick had 'kicked the bucket', .. 'gone to the Never Never' [etc.].

3. In the phr. **on the never-never:** see *on the never* NEVER 2.

new, *n. N.S.W.* [Abbrev. of *new beer.*] A light beer, made by the bottom fermentation method and so-called because it was regarded as a 'new' style when introduced. See OLD *n.*

1935 *First Hundred Yrs.* (Tooth & Co. Ltd.) 71 We make our way across a wide platform on which barrels full of 'Old' and 'New' are being assembled in readiness for despatch. **1984** B. DRISCOLL *Great Aussie Beer Bk.* 22 When bottom-fermented lagers were introduced into New South Wales they became the 'new' style of brewed beers. Therefore, the dark top-fermented ale as brewed by, say, Toohey's, was called Tooheys' Old, while the lighter, bottom-fermented lager became Tooheys' New.

new, *a.*

1. Used with nouns denoting land or an area, region, etc., to mean 'not previously occupied or worked by white people', as **new colony, country** [also U.S. (see OED *a.* 6 e.)], **district, field, ground, land** [also U.S. (see Mathews 2 b.)], **settlement.**

1835 *True Colonist* (Hobart) 21 Feb. 2/2 We continue this day the extracts from the Westminster Review relating to the **New Colony. 1821** Macarthur Papers XII. 56 Our son James has lately made a Tour into the **new Country,** as it is called in 'Westmoreland', where we have an Establishment of Cattle. **1811** *Sydney Gaz.* 23 Feb., All those Persons to whom he has promised to give small Grants of Land in the **New District** of Airds, shall attend at Mr Meehan's Farm. **1890** A.J. VOGAN *Black Police* 35 The Warden of the **new field** has only just arrived .. besides being Police Magistrate, Warden, Senior-constable Surveyor, Clerk of Petty Sessions, etc., etc. **1857** F. DE B. COOPER *Wild Adventures* 140 Working in the old gullies is always a safe speculation, while sinking in **new ground** is never certain. .. In the latter it is mere chance whether gold lies there or not. **1849** A. HARRIS *Emigrant Family* (1967) 12 A farm .. would suit you, in the first instance, rather better than **new land. 1792** R. ATKINS Jrnl. 2 June, Walked to the **New Settlement** and shot some beautiful Parraquets.

2. Used with nouns denoting people to mean 'recently arrived (in Australia)', as **new arrival, -comer, settler.**

1842 *Sydney Morning Herald* 1 Aug. 1/7 The great advantage to a **new arrival** especially, of having a station and herd broke in to it all ready formed to hand. **1843** *Sydney Morning Herald* 21 Aug. 4/1 To give **new-comers** an idea of the financial state and requirements of the colony. **1840** *S. Austral. Rec.* (London) 11 July 18 In consequence of such large and frequent arrival of '**new settlers**', there is always a great demand for all kinds of live stock.

3. In miscellaneous collocations: **new-come-up** *n. phr.,* see quots.; **New Guard,** a right-wing, paramilitary organization formed in Sydney in 1931; a member of this organization; **hand,** NEW CHUM *n.* 1, 2, and 3; also *attrib.*; **New Protection,** an approach to the protection of Australian industries which was conditional on employers paying reasonable wages (see quot. 1899); **rush,** a fresh movement of people to a newly discovered goldfield; such a goldfield; see also RUSH *n.* 2 a. and c.; **New State,** an additional (proposed) State, to be formed by the division of an existing State; freq. *attrib.*; so **New Stater** *n.*, a proponent of such a proposal.

1913 W.K. HARRIS *Outback in Aust.* 42 The new chum (or the '**New-come-up**' as the new chum is termed Outback) cannot tell the difference. **1968** W. GILL *Petermann Journey* 6 When he spoke, it was in the Territory idiom. For example, I heard him call a recent arrival in the country, 'a new-come-up'. **1932** C. HADE *Ebenezer* 12 The leader of all was a big white card, Said, 'I'm a member of the **New Guard.**' **1977** L. Fox *Depression Down Under* 54 Mr Steve Purdy.. was being attacked by three New Guards, one holding his arms while the others rained 'rabbit-killers' on the back of his neck. **1817** *HRA* (1921) 3rd Ser. II. 643, I Have not the least Doubt But you are glad that these **New Hands** joaning [*sic*] Us. **1902** *Bulletin* (Sydney) 8 Feb. 14/3 A couple of new-hand tank-sinkers—Australians, too—on the Rock Station (N.S.W.), once conceived the brilliant idea of undermining the 'face' of the tank. **1899** *Age* (Melbourne) 8 Nov. 6/4 What is called the '**New Protection**' extends beyond the manufacturer's industry to his workers. Protectionists are now claiming that just as the manufacturer shall be adequately protected by tariff duties against the competition of sweater-made goods from abroad, so the domestic worker shall be adequately protected by Factory legislation against any possible sweating of the laborer at home. **1855** *Ovens & Murray Advertiser* (Beechworth) 20 Jan. 6/1 We received intelligence of a **new rush** having taken place on Spring Creek. **1858** *Colonial Mining Jrnl.* Dec. 62/2 The Indigo has progressed.. from the position of a 'New Rush' to that of a large and established gold-field. **1891** *Draft Bill to constitute Cwlth. Aust.* (Nat. Australasian Convention) 66 The Parliament of the Commonwealth may from time to time establish and admit to the Commonwealth **new States.** **1960** *N.T. News* (Darwin) 2 Feb. 2/3 The New State movement had another important victory. **1923** *Austral.* (Sydney) Mar. 34 So many misleading criticisms of the **New Staters'** proposals.

New Aussie: see NEW AUSTRALIAN *n.* 2.

New Australia. *Hist.* The name of a socialist utopian settlement formed in Paraguay in 1893 by members of the New Australia Co-operative Settlement Association under the leadership of William Lane (1861–1917).

1893 *Braidwood Dispatch* 26 Apr. 2/2 The Jesuits taught the world how to manage a 'model colony' in Paraguay long before 'old Australia' was discovered or 'New Australia' thought of. **1978** P. WOOLLEY *Art of living Together* 98 In 1893 Lane established the socialist community of New Australia in Paraguay.

New Australian, *n., attrib.* and *a.*
A. *n.*

1. *Hist.* A colonist of NEW AUSTRALIA.

1893 *Braidwood Dispatch* 26 Apr. 2/2 It is said that 500 'New Australians' will leave Sydney early in May. **1931** *Century of Journalism* 339 The people of this Colony will follow the story of this movement to Paraguay... It is unnecessary to recount the disappointments, and the struggles which the 'New Australians' were forced to encounter.

2. An immigrant to Australia, esp. one (from continental Europe) whose first language is not English. Also **New Aussie.**

1905 *Bulletin* (Sydney) 21 Sept. 39/1 For what the new Australian knows as 'shikker' is just another word for good old 'fou'. **1961** *Realist* (Sydney) v. 10 It was twenty minutes later when Tess led a flushed and excited Pepita and all the new Aussies out into the rain again.

3. *fig.*

1955 *Bulletin* (Sydney) 8 June 13/1 Some once-'new' Australians, who don't figure in the statistics of heavy drinkers, are being exported—some wild camels that are wanted by American zoos and circuses. **1980** S. THORNE *I've met some Bloody Wags* 33 Yarding and drafting Brahman cattle always meant plenty of action. Those lop-eared 'New Australians' could really give you a lift!

B. *attrib.* becoming *adj.* Immigrant; foreign.

1955 N. PULLIAM *I traveled Lonely Land* 313 Almost the entire mining colony there is New Australian. **1985** *Canberra Times* 18 Aug. 17/6 A sprinkling of Englishmen and Scotsmen play and watch the game, but it is overwhelmingly and accurately regarded as a 'New Australian' code—to use another archaism.

new chum, *n.* and *a.*
A. *n.*

1. *Hist.* A prisoner newly admitted to a gaol or hulk; a newly arrived convict.

1812 J.H. VAUX *Mem.* (1819) II. 163 *Chum*, a fellow prisoner in a jail, hulk, &c.; so there are *new chums* and *old chums*, as they happen to have been a short or a long time in confinement. **1865** J.F. MORTLOCK *Experiences of Convict* 110 Rather a clever 'new chum'. Had the attempt failed, he, as a ticket-of-leave 'bolter', would have been sentenced to three years at Port Arthur.

2. *transf.* A newly arrived immigrant. Also *attrib.*

1828 *Tasmanian* (Hobart) 15 Aug. 4, I understood.. that I was called a *new chum*, my English name being Stranger. **1912** *Truth* (Sydney) 25 Feb. 12/4 At a large works recently erected.. a new-chum Scotchman will get preference to a colonial.

3. A novice; one inexperienced in a particular activity, occupation, etc. Also *attrib.*

1851 J. HENDERSON *Excursions & Adventures N.S.W.* I. 182 He seemed to think that his being a beginner, or (as it is termed) 'new chum', had been taken advantage of. **1973** F. PARSONS *Man called Mo* 128 A sketch in which he played a new-chum dairy farmer who picked up a cow-pad under the impression that it was Field-Marshal Montgomery's beret.

4. *Obs.* Abbrev. of *new-chum hole* (see sense 5).

1869 Mrs W.M. HOWELL *Diggings & Bush* 5 'My word, Tom, come up quick,' exclaimed a dirt-begrimed digger, who was looking over a hole resembling a well, 'this must be a new chum'.

5. Special Comb. **new chum gold,** a name given to any of several mineral substances commonly mistaken for gold by an inexperienced miner; also **new chum's gold; hole,** see quot. 1944.

1873 'DEMONAX' *Mysteries & Miseries* 16 He was shown some stone which was streaked with '**new chum' gold**—a sort of coppery, cobwebby, affair, like Dutch metal. **1948** M. UREN *Glint of Gold* 102 He spat on the shiny mineral. 'That,' he said slowly, 'is pyrites; new chum's gold.' **1881** J.C.F. JOHNSON *To Mount Browne & Back* 14 Some of them.. were amusing themselves by putting down small '**new chum holes**' in the neighbouring gullies. **1944** M.J. O'REILLY *Bowyangs & Boomerangs* 41 He started a real 'new chum hole', that is a hole in the loose ground without any means of holding the sides or ends.

B. *adj.* Inexpert; raw.

1903 *Bulletin* (Sydney) 28 Feb. 16/2 One is struck by the new-chum methods of conserving water. **1956** B. BEATTY *Beyond Aust.'s Cities* 14 He was so tolerant of my new-chum ignorance that I pursued my questions.

Hence **new chumism** *n.*, behaviour which is characteristic of a newly arrived, and therefore inexperienced, immigrant; an instance of this; **new chumship** *n.*, the condition of being a new chum.

1850 *Australasian Sporting Mag.* 124 The other, needs but the addition of local experience to his preformed habits of life, to exempt him from those retributive pains and penalties, which follow from the ridiculous follies, vices, and conceits, of genuine and unmitigated **new chumism**. **1898** *Bulletin* (Sydney) 8 Jan. 29/2 It is a stupid error to call the Australian tea-tree a 'ti-tree'. More than this, it is a new-chumism, a relic of Gov. Phillip. **1848** *Sydney Morning Herald* 9 Sept. 4/3 Those who, on their first arrival among us .. looked upon the traffic as wicked and discreditable, gradually become familiarised with the aspect of the monster, and yet ere out of their **new chumship** begin to consider the profession of usurer as not only righteous but even honourable.

new chummy. NEW CHUM *n.* 2 and 3. Also *attrib.*
1869 'PERAMBULATOR VON VELOCIPEDESTRIAN' *Anecdotes Vic.* 11 The largest of dreaded blackfellows came up, and he and the young farmer exchanged a few guttural sounds which were gibberish to new chummie. **1926** *Aussie* (Sydney) Jan. 12.1 Near Emudilla I was joined by a young man of fresh and new-chummy appearance.

New Holland. [An anglicization of L. *Nova Hollandia* a name given by Dutch navigators in the seventeenth century to that part of the Australian continent lying west of the meridian which passes through Torres Strait.]
1. *Hist.* A name formerly given to the Australian continent or part thereof, sometimes including Tasmania.
1770 J. HAWKESWORTH *Acct. of Voyages* (1773) III. 237 New Holland, or, as I have now called the eastern coast, New South Wales, is of a larger extent than any other country in the known world that does not bear the name of a continent. **1870** *Illustr. Sydney News* 17 Feb. 343/2 At best New Holland was regarded as a convenient spot to which the overflowings of vice might be exported.
2. In the names of birds: **New Holland cassowary** obs., EMU *n.*[1] 1; **honeyeater,** the honeyeater *Phylidonyris novaehollandiae* of s.w. and s.e. Aust. incl. Tas., having black and white plumage with yellow on the wings and tail; *white-bearded honeyeater,* see WHITE *a.*[2] 1 b.; *yellow-wing,* see YELLOW 1; **vulture** *obs., brush turkey,* see BRUSH B. 2.
1789 A. PHILLIP *Voyage to Botany Bay* 271 **New-Holland Cassowary**... This is a species differing in many particulars from that generally known, and is a much larger bird, standing higher on its legs, and having the neck longer than in the common one. **1822** J. LATHAM *Gen. Hist. Birds* IV. 171 **New-Holland Honey-eater**.. inhabits New South Wales, chiefly seen in January. **1822** B. FIELD in G. Mackaness *Fourteen Journeys Blue Mountains* 12 Oct. (1950) 44 At Bathurst, saw what is called the native turkey. It is the **New Holland vulture** of Dr Latham, and is one of the most remarkable birds found in Australia, appearing to form a connecting link between the rapacious and gallinaceous orders.

New Hollander. *Obs.* An Aboriginal.
1699 W. DAMPIER *New Voyage round World* (1703) III. 147 Among the N[ew] Hollanders.. there was one who.. seem'd to be the Chief of them. **1888** R.J. FLANAGAN *Aborigines Aust.* 50 The corroboree appears to be the great festival among the New Hollanders.

newie. [Abbrev. of NEW (CHUM *n.* 2 and 3 + -Y: see also the perh. independently formed *newie* something new (OEDS 1947).]
1. One who has recently arrived in Australia; one who is new to a place or situation.
1917 *Truth* (Sydney) 1 Apr. 6/7 Two newies had a rough-up at Rozelle. **1951** *Bulletin* (Sydney) 21 July 13/4 Bloke that carries his swag through town is either a newy, a galoot or a sympathy chaser.
2. *transf.*
1924 H.E. RIEMANN *Nor'-West o' West* 60 I've got a few newies since you were here last. **1976** D. IRELAND *Glass Canoe* 55 Someone in the government got rid of it [*sc.* a car] and bought a newie.

New South. Abbrev. of 'New South Wales'.
1892 *Bulletin* (Sydney) 17 Dec. 19/1, I took a turn in New South, and tried Tassy and New Zealand. **1981** B. GREEN *Small Town Rising* 149 He .. set out into New South on his bicycle.

New South Waler. *Obs.* A non-Aboriginal inhabitant of the Colony of New South Wales.
1844 *Sydney Morning Herald* 12 Apr. 3/1 The New South Walers could obtain immigrants at half the Coolie cost. **1864** *Sydney Punch* 27 May 4/1, I feel rather doggedly dyspeptic myself among these South Sea whalers—New South Walers I mean—beg pardon.

New South Wales Corps. *Hist.* A military force raised in Great Britain for service in the penal colony of New South Wales.
1789 *Hist. Rec. N.S.W.* II. 422 Warrant for Raising New South Wales Corps—George R... we have thought proper to direct that a corps of foot shall be forthwith raised, which is intended to be stationed in New South Wales. **1945** J.A. ALLAN *Men & Manners in Aust.* 33 The Rum Corps—officially the 'New South Wales Corps'.. garrisoned the settlement.

New South Welshman. A non-Aboriginal inhabitant of the Colony of New South Wales; one who is native to or resident in the State of New South Wales. Also **New South Welsher.**
1860 *Bell's Life in Sydney* 26 May 3/2 A batch of New South Welshmen. **1891** *Bohemia* (Melbourne) 26 Nov. 6 He is a New South Welsher.

Newstralian. *Obs.* Shortened form of NEW AUSTRALIAN *n.* 2.
1951 *Bulletin* (Sydney) 12 Dec. 13/4 Some Newstralians are nothing if not thorough. **1952** *Ibid.* 27 Feb. 17/3 His housekeeper is a Newstralian still a bit shaky on our language.

New Zealand flax. [The name perh. became established because of the importance of the flax from N.Z. as a source of fibre in the Austral. colonies.] The perennial, tufted plant *Phormium tenax* (fam. Agavaceae) of New Zealand and Norfolk Is., having long, stiff, pointed leaves yielding a useful fibre, and cultivated as an ornamental.
1789 W. TENCH *Narr. Exped. Botany Bay* 147 The New Zealand flax, plants of which are found growing in every part of the island. **1978** V.H. HEYWOOD *Flowering Plants World* 316 The Agavaceae is a family of considerable economic importance. A number of species are the source of strong, durable fibres... Examples include .. *Phormium tenax* (New Zealand flax).

ngoora burr, var. NOOGOORA BURR.

ngowa, ngowoo, vart. GNOW.

nick, *v.*[1] [Prob. fig. use of Br. dial. or slang *nick* to steal: cf. *steal* to depart, withdraw surreptitiously (OED *v.*[1] 9); but see also OED(S *nick, v.*[2] 13 b.]
1. *intr.* To go on the spur of the moment; to slip (away, out, etc.).
1896 E. TURNER *Little Larrikin* 274 Trying to induce the driver of the motor, for whom he had a friendship, to promise at the end of the journey to 'nick away and come too'. **1981** *Sydney Morning Herald* 11 Apr. 13/2 There is no lavatory so the Labor candidate .. and his helpers nick across the road to use Ansett's.
2. With **off**: to depart (often without ceremony or surreptitiously). As an imperative, 'Clear out!'
1901 M. FRANKLIN *My Brilliant Career* 258 If you go to a picnic, just when the fun commences you have to nick off

home and milk. **1981** P. Barton *Bastards I have Known* 96, I was in this spot first . . so nick off.

nick, *v.*² [Spec. use of *nick* to make a nick or notch in.] *trans.* In clearing scrub: to cut a 'scarf' or notch in (the trunk of a small tree), esp. to facilitate the progress of a *mallee roller* (see Mallee 8).

1920 *Land of Lyre Bird* (S. Gippsland Pioneers' Assoc.) 72 As the scrub-cutting progressed, the process known as 'nicking' became popular. This was done by cutting a small notch front and back in each tree; in hazels and small growths, just a few blows front and back would be sufficient, and in gum saplings, blackwoods, or wattles, a 'scarf' say, a third through front and back, and so on . . as it required both skill and judgment to successfully negotiate a good 'fall'. **1983** A. Cannon *Bullocks, Bullockies & Other Blokes* 20 If there were any heavy trees—in that country one of four inches diameter was considered heavy—they had to be 'nicked' at the base with an axe, before the scrub could be rolled.

nicked, *past pple.* In the imprecation **get nicked,** 'get lost'; esp. euphemistically.

1968 D. O'Grady *Bottle of Sandwiches* 179, I yelled, 'Last one in can get nicked' and took off after Boof. **1982** J. Hibberd *Country Quinella* (1984) 75 Hello, Marmalade. I'm your great aunty Val. . . Get nicked.

nicki-nicki /'nɪki-nɪki/. *Austral. pidgin.* Also **nikki-nikki,** etc. [Austral. pidgin; formed on *niggerhead.*] Black twist tobacco; *nigger tobacco, twist,* see Nigger 4.

1938 X. Herbert *Capricornia* 137 It was a parcel from a Chinese store, containing . . one pound of niki-niki. **1964** K. Willey *Eaters of Lotus* 87 We smoked nikki-nikki (native twist tobacco). **1985** B. Rosser *Dreamtime Nightmares* 21 They used to get this tobacco sent out to the outstations, but you couldn't really call it tobacco. We called it *nicki-nicki.* You couldn't smoke it, it was too hard.

nig. Abbrev. of Nigger 1.

1880 H. Kendall *Songs from Mountains* 107 I'll give him education; A 'nig' is better when he's tamed, Perhaps, than a Caucasian. **1981** A. Weller *Day of Dog* 48 Ya want to look out for those wackers. They hate us nigs.

nigger. [Transf. use of *nigger* a Black.]

1. An Aboriginal. Also *attrib.*

1845 G. de C. Lefroy in C.T. Stannage *New Hist. W.A.* (1981) 95 It is shocking . . to see a fine young fellow cut off by the odious detestable niggers. **1969** F.B. Vickers *No Man is Himself* 58 He came back to my bloody nigger camp that same night.

2. *Obs.* A Kanaka.

1869 P.A. Taylor *Colony of Qld.* 11 One planter . . said, 'What can you supply me a hundred niggers for?' **1903** *Truth* (Sydney) 6 Dec. 1/7 There is no possibility of plutocratic slave-owners in the sugar districts getting supplies of fresh niggers to replace the 'returns'.

3. *transf.* Luderick.

1927 A. Wright *Squatter's Secret* 38 The big catch of lively 'niggers' splashing in a rock-bound pool behind him. **1983** *Sun* (Sydney) 30 Sept. 28/4 Brisbane Water has been best of the estuaries, with bream, niggers and mullet.

4. Special Comb. **nigger country,** an area inhabited by Aborigines living traditionally; also **nigger's country; farming** *vbl. n.,* the exploitation by a non-Aboriginal of a government subsidy paid to an employer of Aboriginal labour or to fund an Aboriginal welfare project; **hunt,** the organized pursuit of Aborigines (see Disperse); so **hunting** *vbl. n.;* **tobacco, twist,** strong, coarse tobacco of the type issued to an Aboriginal worker on a rural property; Nicki nicki.

1915 N. Duncan *Austral. Byways* 86 Traveling the edge of the '**nigger country**' to the north, he had fallen in with a roving band of gins. **1942** G. Casey *It's Harder for Girls* (1944) 57 "Strewth!' said a bloke who was leaning through the window. 'It's nigger's country, ain't it?' **1968** F. Hardy *Unlucky Australs.* 17 A person is said to engage in '**nigger farming**' in the Northern Territory when he relies on income from aboriginal subsidies to keep his station solvent. **1882** P. O'Farrell *Lett. from Irish Aust.* (1984) 68 Crawford apologised to Lillie for the monotony of his letters: 'the only incidents that occur are '**nigger hunts**'.' **1917** *Life & Experiences Successful W. Austral.* 76 We started out on our nigger hunting enterprise, and making a wide circle, closed in behind the native camp. **1910** *Bulletin* (Sydney) 22 Dec. 13/4 Each nig. received his wages mostly in '**nigger tobacco**'. **1937** Wisberg & Waters *Bushman at Large* 21, I filled a pipe with **niggertwist,** a cheap tobacco the very smell of which would knock a white man into a coma.

niggerhead.

1. [Spec. use of *niggerhead* a rock, stone, etc.: see OED(S 2 and Negrohead.] A large block of coral deposited high on a reef by a storm, frequently blackened and rounded; a submerged isolated coral spire, pinnacle, or head, usu. reaching close to the surface; Negrohead.

1876 J. Moressy *Discovery New Guinea* 3 A crowd of 'nigger heads', black points of coral rock, peep up in places. **1979** R. Miller *Sugarbird Lady* 64 After drifting for three days it was wrecked on a coral 'niggerhead' about a mile from Bernier Island.

2. The small, tufted perennial grass *Enneapogon nigricans* (fam. Poaceae) of all mainland States but not N.T., having dark seed-heads; (occas.) any of several other grasses of the genus *Enneapogon.* Freq. in *pl.*

1923 *Census Plants Vic.* (Field Naturalists' Club Vic.) 9 *Pappophorum nigricans* . . Niggerheads. **1975** E.R. Rotherham et al. *Flowers & Plants N.S.W. & Southern Qld.* 180 In the winter . . the flexible silky heads of the Spear Grass bend to the inland wind whilst in summer they are replaced by the stiffer black-green Nigger-Heads (*Enneapogon nigricans*).

niggerhead beech: see Beech.

night. Used *attrib.* in Special Comb. **night-camp,** the overnight, outdoor rest taken by a traveller, esp. a drover; the resting-place; also as *v. intr.;* **-cart,** *sanitary cart,* see Sanitary a.; so **-cartman; fossicker** *obs.,* one who raids a gold-miner's claim by night; **-horse** [also U.S. (see OEDS *night, sb.* 14)], a horse used at night, esp. one used to round up the animals required for the coming day (see quots. 1923 and 1977); **-horse paddock,** an enclosure in which such horses (or other animals required during the coming day) are kept; also **night paddock; -man,** *sanitary man,* see Sanitary a.; **watch,** a watch kept over (unenclosed) stock at night; the time this occupies; *night watchman;* **watchman,** one who keeps watch over (unenclosed) stock at night; **-well,** see quots. 1906 and 1908.

1882 Mrs J.C. Stanger *Journey from Sydney* 12 A smell of burning, which proved to be the drivers' **night-camp**. **1953** *Bulletin* (Sydney) 28 Oct. 13/2 Bringing a mob through Pooncarie . . we night-camped on the Gampang-No Man's Land boundary. **1957** F. Clune *Fortune Hunters* 34 In the cool of the evening we pushed on a few miles . . looking for a spot for a night-camp. **1840** *Tasmanian Weekly Dispatch* (Hobart) 1 May 8/1 **Night Cart!!!** The above is kept in constant readiness. Any orders for the emptying of Cesspools, etc. . . immediately attended to. **1965** D. Martin *Hero of Too* 9 A nightcartman's professional view of local inhabitants is as valid as anyone else's. **1853** C.R. Read *What I heard, saw, & Did* 149 The man was what they called a **night fossicker,** who slept or did nothing during the day, and then went around at night to where he knew claims to be rich, and stole the stuff by candle light. **1904** *Bulletin* (Sydney) 8 Dec. 19/3 When cattle have 'rushed'.. Wheelbarrow, like every other **night horse**, takes simultaneous action. **1923** *Ibid.* 1 Nov. 24/4 A practice which hasn't much to recommend it is that of keeping a 'night horse' yarded all night on the far-out stations, so that it can be used to run up the mob in the morning. **1977** *Pastoral Rev. & Graziers' Rec.* Sept. 303 The nighthorse is of no particular breeding and is kept on his own. His singular duty is to run in (muster) the working horses every morning. As his job is generally completed before daylight, it is desirable that he be sure-footed and possess good eyesight. **1922** [**night-horse paddock**] V. PALMER *Boss of Killara* 124 He stole softly over the dewy grass of the night-paddock. **1977** *Pastoral Rev. & Graziers' Rec.* Sept. 303 Some three hundred yards from the homestead there was .. the night-horse paddock. **1898** *Truth* (Sydney) 27 Nov. 1/3 *Molong*, a sweet town of the west, is in the throes of a municipal crisis—and all about a **night man**. **1907** *Bulletin* (Sydney) 10 Oct. 14/1 They were for years most valuable to drovers saving **night watches**, dogs, calico fences, etc. **1954** T. RONAN *Vision Splendid* 163 There's enough of us for the night watches. **1836** J. BACKHOUSE *Extracts from Lett.* (1838) iii. 73 The different flocks are counted into the folds at night, and committed to the charge of a **night-watchman**, and are re-counted to the respective shepherds in the morning. **1906** *Bulletin* (Sydney) 17 May 15/3 Ever hear of a **night-well**? Thirty or forty miles east of Wagin .. W.A., there is a hill, on top of which is a small cavern. Part of the floor of the cavern is water-worn into a basin holding about 50 gallons. A little after sundown a tiny thread of water starts trickling from an inlet in the wall of the cave, and continues till shortly before sunrise. During the day not a drop flows. **1908** *Ibid.* 6 Aug. 14/3 As to 'night-wells', I know one on the Ravensthorpe road, sixty miles east of Broome Hill. It is in the bed of a salt-water river. You can get fresh water from it at any time... The strange thing about these 'night wells' is that the water rises every night to the surface and sinks about a foot during the day.

night parrot. The rare, nocturnal parrot *Geopsittacus occidentalis*, a ground-dwelling, predom. green, yellow, and black bird of arid and semi-arid inland Aust. See also *spinifex parrot* SPINIFEX 4.

1913 *Emu* XIII. 16 The Night-Parrot (*Geopsittacus occidentalis*). **1985** *Sydney Morning Herald* 11 Apr. 10/4 The quite fabulous night parrot, said to be near extinction.

nikki-nikki, var. NICKI-NICKI.

nilla-nilla, var. NULLA-NULLA.

nine. A keg containing nine gallons of beer. Also **niner**.

1943 *Bully Tin* (Baronta) 17 Apr. 3 Now, there is *the nine*. This must be of course the nine gallon keg. **1980** H. STEPHENSON *Cattlemen & Huts High Plains* 336 W'jer 'appen to 'ave a niner?

ning nong. [f. Br. dial. *ning-nang* a fool: see EDD and OEDS.] A fool.

1957 'N. CULOTTA' *They're Weird Mob* 15, I 'ave ter get landed with a bloody ning nong who doesn't know where he's bloody goin'. **1977** E. MACKIE *Oh to be Aussie* 43 The trainee Aussie must not go to King's Cross—it's only for the tourists, ningnongs and geezers all the way from Woop Woop.

nip, *n.* [See BITE *n.*]

1. a. In the phr. **to put the nips in** (or **into**) (someone), to cadge (from).

[N.Z. **1917** *Chrons. N.Z. Exped. Force* 19 Sept. 63, I put the nips in the other night.] **1919** [see NIP *v.*]. **1937** W. & T.I. MOORE *Best Austral. One-Act Plays* 398 He came along to put the nips in, so I gave him a couple of bob. **1949** L. GLASSOP *Lucky Palmer* 230 You can't put the nips into old Alf. He's got death adders in his pockets.

b. In the phr. **to get the nips into** (someone), to attempt to gain an advantage, etc., from (a person).

1959 D. NILAND *Gold in Streets* 60 That sheila's got the nips into me. She must have, or she wouldn't have been so easy.

2. One who responds sympathetically to a cadger; a 'soft touch'.

1987 *Bulletin* (Sydney) 4 Aug. 21/2 Most 'bucks' would be good nips for .. a handout from their always loaded tucker-boxes.

nip, *v. trans.* To cadge (something); to cadge from (someone). See BITE *n.* and *v.*

1919 W.H. DOWNING *Digger Dialects* 35 *Nip*, to cadge (or 'Put in the Nips'). **1978** H.C. BAKER *I was Listening* 7 No chance of nippin' the bricky for a smoke—he don't smoke.

nipper, *n.*[1] [Spec. use of *nipper* one who nips.] Any of several small burrowing shrimp-like marine crustaceans, commonly used for bait.

1882 J.E. TENISON-WOODS *Fish & Fisheries N.S.W.* 126 *Alphaeus socialis* .. locally named the 'Nipper', is abundant in Port Jackson, and is a good deal sought for, but not so much for food as for bait for black bream fishing. **1983** *Fishing Information & Services Handbk.* 76 The top baits .. would naturally include .. nippers, harbour prawns.

nipper, *n.*[2] [Spec. use of *nipper* the smallest or youngest of a family.] A youth employed to do odd jobs in a labouring gang, esp. to make tea.

1915 *Bulletin* (Sydney) 9 Dec. 22/1 When the slips were all written out the jobless ganger sent the nipper after the 'head'. **1953** 'CADDIE' *Caddie* 29 A nipper was the name given to a young boy whose job it was to boil the billies and carry the various tools .. to the men when required.

Hence **nippering** *pr. pple.*

1938 F. BLAKELEY *Hard Liberty* 22 My job was nippering in a navvy gang for the contractors.

nit. [Prob. var. of *nix* 'a word used as a signal that someone in authority is approaching', also used in the phr. *to keep nix*: see OED(S *nix, sb.*[1] 3 and *nit, sb.*[2]]

1. *Obs.* A word used as a signal to warn an accomplice of the approach of a third party. Also as *v. intr.*, to escape, to flee.

1882 *Sydney Slang Dict.* 10 *Nit*, get away (usually from a foe), make tracks. **1895** *Worker* (Sydney) 15 June 4/2 'Nit, you chaps,' said Bill, 'and wait for me.'

2. In the phr. **to keep nit**, to keep watch while an accomplice engages in an (illegal) activity.

1903 *Truth* (Sydney) 19 July 3/5 She was aided in securing patrons by a bludger, who .. stood near the Railway Bridge and *kept 'nit' for the traps* so that Amy could walk freely when she got on her beat. **1977** B. SCOTT *My Uncle Arch* 3 They'd pick a couple of the mob to keep nit then they'd hoe into the corn.

nit-keeper. One who keeps watch while an accomplice engages in an (illegal) activity.

1935 *Bulletin* (Sydney) 22 May 21/1 That outlaw the sulphur-crested cockatoo is not the only bird to post a 'nit-keeper' when transgressing against society. **1981** M. GRANT *Inherit Sun* 183 Red knew there would be a nit-keeper, a man keeping watch who could slip out for the police if there was trouble.

Hence **nit-keeping** *vbl. n.*

1978 W. LOWENSTEIN *Weevils in Flour* 139 In Kandos I'd get a day nit-keeping for the SP bookmaker bloke now and again.

no, *a.*

1. *Obs.* Of a cheque: in the phr. **no mercy**, 'the full value is to be spent (on alcoholic drink)'.

1916 *Bulletin* (Sydney) 10 Feb. 22/2 When a drover, fencer or tank-sinker handed a cheque over the bar Pat would ask, 'Is it 'No mercy'?' 'Yes.' Then 'No mercy' would be written across the back, and Pat would take down a bugle . . and blow . . and a general rush would be made for the pub. *Ibid.* 30 Mar. 24/3 He passes his cheque which is seized in a crack, And the landlord takes pen and writes 'No Mercy' on the back.

2. Used in various conventional tags, as **no risk**, without doubt; **worries**, no bother, no trouble; also *attrib.*

1969 G. JOHNSTON *Clean Straw for Nothing* (1971) 285 Everything duty free, you know. You know, you could spend a bloody fortune. **No risk**. **1967** J. HIBBERD *White with Wire Wheels* (1970) 159 'Well. How was she?' . . 'Who, Sue? **No worries**.' **1986** *Mercury* (Hobart) 25 Mar. 10/1 'No worries' reaction to Bell pullout.

Noah's Ark.

1. Rhyming slang for 'nark'.

1898 *Bulletin* (Sydney) 17 Dec. (Red Page), An informer or mar-plot is a nark or a Jonah or a Noah's Ark. **1968** J. ALARD *He who shoots Last* 97 Ya knows Bill, yer gettin' to be a real Noah's Ark.

2. Rhyming slang for 'shark'. Also **Noah**.

1945 *Dit* (Melbourne) Sept. 129 'Poor blighter, what about the 'Noah's Arks'?' voices exclaimed. **1982** *Bulletin* (Sydney) 13 July 65/1 'I'll tell you what's worse than the Noahs,' said Edgar. 'What about those bloody dragon-flies?'

nob. [Spec. use of Br. slang *nob* head.] A coin having two heads, esp. in the game of two-up. Cf. GREY *n*. Also *attrib.*

1903 *Bulletin* (Sydney) 2 May 17/2 Amongst the peculiar animals evolving in Australia the bush spieler is one of the most interesting. . . His methods are still of the old order . . 'nob-ringing', and double-banking lone-hand simpletons in play. **1918** *Aussie: Austral. Soldiers' Mag.* Dec. 3/1 Snow had spun the pennies himself and that was just his way of getting out of paying up when he found that he had failed to ring in the nob.

nobbler. Also **nobler.** [f. *nobble, v.*, either in the sense 'to drug or lame (a horse)' or 'to strike (esp. on the head or 'nob')': see OED(S *v*. 1 and 3.] A measure of spirits; the glass in which this is served.

1842 *Sydney Herald* 19 May 2/7 A wag enquired whether Mr Tegg . . was endeavouring to escape the licensing act by an admixture of a little salt and at the same time selling 'nobblers' instead of glasses. **1849** *Argus* (Melbourne) 12 Nov. 4/1, I always take things in their due moderation, I never exceed thirty *noblers* a day. **1926** M. FORREST *Hibiscus Heart* 145 The tall nobbler of whisky neat.

nobblerize, *v*. [f. prec.] *intr*. To drink nobblers; to drink spirits generally, esp. in company with others. Freq. as *vbl. n.*

1847 *Port Phillip Gaz.* 30 June 2 He was comfortably nobblerizing in the William Tell. **1899** MRS A. HAY *Footprints* 107 It is said that in the early years of the colony there was a terrible habit of 'nobblerizing'.

Hence **nobblerizer** *n*., one who drinks nobblers.

1858 R. ROWE *Peter 'Possum's Portfolio* 92 She is flirting with an early nobbleriser.

nobby, *n*. Opal-mining. See quot. 1976.

1919 *Huon Times* (Franklin) 21 Nov. 3/3 A little seam-opal is found on the field, but most of the gem occurs in 'nobbies', a species of flat, pebble-shaped stone. To test these (for colour) a small pair of pincers (termed 'snips') is used. **1976** STONE & BUTT *Guide Austral. Precious Opal* 108 *Nobby*, a nodule of opal coated with sandstone or opal dirt—commonly found at Lightning Ridge, N.S.W.

nobby, *a*. [Alteration of Br. dial. *knobby* lumpy, as applied to a beast: see EDD.] Of a beast: lean, and therefore having protuberant bones, joints, etc.

1860 *S. Austral. Advertiser* 2 July 4/5 One white nobby steer. **1977** T. RONAN *Mighty Men on Horseback* 94 He'd eaten all the nobby cattle.

nod, *v*. In the phr. **to nod the nut** (or **head**), to plead guilty.

1950 *Austral. Police Jrnl.* Apr. 116 *Nod the nut*, plead guilty. **1968** J. ALARD *He who shoots Last* 140, I sez I ain't gonna nod me head ta dat. Den dey sez 'suit yerself, but we'll make it stick'.

nodding blue lily. The tufted perennial plant *Stypandra glauca* (fam. Liliaceae) of s. and e. Aust. incl. Tas., having starry, usu. bright blue flowers on slender nodding stalks.

1914 E.E. PESCOTT *Native Flowers Vic.* 91 A fine blue lily, with bright green grassy foliage, is Stypandra glauca, or the 'nodding blue lily'. **1985** J. GALBRAITH *Garden in Valley* 9 In the silver-lichened granite outcrops, crevices overflowed with heath-myrtle, nodding Blue-lily and small orchids.

nog. [Transf. use of *(nig-)nog* f. *nigger.*] A Vietnamese (soldier).

1969 J.J. COE *Desperate Praise* (1982) 49 During the night the 41 ambush killed 6 nogs. **1975** W. NAGLE *Odd Angry Shot* 15 'We suspect that there are about twenty or thirty nogs dug in. . .' 'VC or NVA?' asks Harry.

noggy. [f. *(nig-)nog* + -Y. See also NOG.] An Asian, esp. an Asian immigrant to Australia. Also *attrib.*

1954 N. BARTLETT *With Australs. in Korea* 217 This old bloke says there are about a hundred noggies [*sc.* Chinese soldiers] in the village. **1981** C. WALLACE-CRABBE *Splinters* 56 They had led him on a fair treat with questions about Noggy women.

no-hoper.

a. A racehorse with no chance of winning; a rank outsider.

1943 S.J. BAKER *Pop. Dict. Austral. Slang* (ed. 3) 54 *No-hoper*, an outsider (Racing slang). **1957** J. WATEN *Shares in Murder* 30 I've given the mare away. She's a no-hoper . . I wouldn't put a penny on her again.

b. [Used elsewhere but recorded earliest in Aust.] An incompetent or ineffectual person; a failure. Also *attrib.*

1944 *Atebrin Advocate: Mag.* 2/4 *Austral. Armoured Regiment* 9 Dec. 1 Probably the greatest little bunch of No-hopers. **1955** *Khaki Bush & Bigotry* (1968) 185 *None* of my children's going to marry a no-hoper rouseabout.

Hence **no-hoping** *ppl. a.*

1957 *Westerly* i. 6 Save me from a no-hoping whinger.

noisy, *a*. Used as a distinguishing epithet in the names of birds: **noisy friar bird**, the honeyeater *Philemon corniculatus* of e. mainland Aust. and New Guinea; see also FRIAR BIRD; **miner**, the honeyeater of e. Aust. *Manorina melanocephala*, a predom. grey and white bird with black face-markings; MICKEY 3; **pitta**, the bird *Pitta versicolor* of rainforest in n.e. Qld., having a loud, whistling call; ANVIL-BIRD; DRAGOON BIRD; **scrub-bird**, the ground-dwelling, predom. brown bird *Atrichornis clamosus* of s.w. W.A., having a loud, penetrating whistle and inhabiting areas of dense heathy vegetation.

1943 C. BARRETT *Austral. Animal Bk.* 292 The **noisy friar-bird** is nomadic in its habits. An amusing and pugnacious bird . . its head is ink-black and naked, and the friar-bird's long, curved bill bears a knob. **1901** *Emu* I. 137 **Noisy Miner** (*Manorhina garrula*). Two of these were shot at Malkuni. **1942** J. GOULD *Birds of Aust.* (1948) IV. Pl. 1, *Pitta strepitans* . . **Noisy Pitta**. [**1844 noisy scrub-bird**: J. GOULD *Birds of Aust.* (1848) III. Pl. 34, *Atrichia clamosa*. . .

Noisy Brush-bird. Few of the novelties received from Australia are more interesting than the species to which I have given the generic name of *Atrichia*.] **1891** G.J. BROINOWSKI *Birds of Aust.* V. Pl. 17, *Atrichia clamosa* . . Noisy scrub-bird. From . . the little that is known of its habits, this species will no doubt prove to be one of the most interesting of all the Australian birds.

nolla-nolla, var. NULLA-NULLA.

nominated, *ppl. a.* In the collocation **nominated emigrant (immigrant, migrant),** one proposed as an assisted immigrant by an Australian resident (who normally meets some part of the cost and takes some responsibility for the person on arrival).

1873 A. TROLLOPE *Aust. & N.Z.* II. 138 Nominated emigrants would remain—emigrants nominated by friends in the colony. **1896** J.M. PRICE *Land of Gold* 180 The Government grant assisted passages to Western Australia to nominated immigrants, upon the payment of £7 10s. per adult by sailing vessel. **1949** A.A. CALWELL *Immigration* 21 The categories approved by the Premiers' Conference in order of priority were: 1. Nominated migrants who can be accommodated by their nominators and are classed as essential workers for Australian industry.

nonda /'nɒndə/. [Prob. f. a Qld. Aboriginal language.] The tree *Parinari nonda* (fam. Chrysobalanaceae) of Qld. and N.T., bearing an astringent, edible, yellow fruit; the fruit itself. Also *attrib.*

1845 L. LEICHHARDT *Jrnl. Overland Exped. Aust.* 3 July (1847) 315 A middle sized shady wide spreading tree, resembling the elm in the colour and form of its leaves, attracted our attention, and excited much interest. Its younger branches were rather drooping, its fruit was an oblong yellow plum, an inch long and half an inch in diameter, with a rather rough kernel. When ripe, the pericarp is very mealy and agreeable to eat, and would be wholesome, if it were not so extraordinarily astringent. We called this tree the 'Nonda', from its resemblance to a tree so called by the natives in the Moreton Bay district. **1965** *Austral. Encycl.* VI. 483 Nonda timber is yellowish, close-grained and strong, but soft enough to be worked easily.

nong. [Prob. shortened form of NING NONG.] A fool; also as quasi-*adj.* Also **nong-nong.**

1944 *RAF RAAF: Souvenir Crenferry Cruise No. 3* Feb. 9 That we were just collossal [*sic*] nong Was the theme of his daily song. **1962** *Overland* XXVI. 12 I'm not gunna stand around exchanging words with any long-haired nong. **1967** D. HEWETT *This Old Man* (1976) 17 'Ere comes the Bride, fair, fat and wide, Who's that poor nong-nong she's got by 'er side.

nonpareil parrot. *Eastern rosella,* see EASTERN 2.

1794 G. SHAW *Zool. New Holland* 1 *Psittacus Eximius.* The Nonpareil Parrot. . . It may indeed be doubted whether any bird can exhibit a plumage more elegant, or colours of a nobler hue. **1931** N.W. CAYLEY *What Bird is That?* 145 Eastern Rosella *Platycerus eximius.* . . Also called Rosella, Rosehill Parakeet, and Nonpareil Parrot. . . It spends much of its time on the ground in search of seeds of grasses, which, with wild fruits and berries, constitute its normal food.

noodle, *v.* [Of uncertain origin: perh. transf. use of Br. dial. *noodle, v.* to saunter about aimlessly, to waste time (see EDD); but see also quot. 1948.]

1. *trans.* To search (an opal-mining dump or mullock heap) for opals. Also *intr.* and as *vbl. n.* See also LOUSE a.

1902 *Geol. Survey No. 177* (Qld. Dept. Mines) 20 (OEDS) Some splendid opal is found . . by turning over and searching the old heaps and mullock—'noodling'. **1948** E.F. MURPHY *They struck Opal* 129 Small egg-shaped opals in an open cut in a gully. A visiting geologist tabbed these 'nodules', and explained that they had originally formed inside a soft stone (like yowah nuts), which had later decomposed. The miners soon altered the name to 'noodles'—and hence the 'noodling' game. **1963** A. LUBBOCK *Austral. Roundabout* 79 Anyone can . . 'puddle' or 'noodle' in the gravelly tailings of the mine. **1965** K.J. BUCHESTER *Austral. Gemhunter's Guide* 80 Most of the old heaps have been noodled for opal of all grades, even down to a low grade of 'potch with a bit of colour'. **1975** 'N. CULOTTA' *Gone Gougin'* 22 Noodlin' means pickin' over the old mullock. Abos are the best at it. They've got sharp eyes. Palefaces need a bit of rain.

2. a. *trans.* To remove surrounding matter from (an opal). Also *transf.*

1921 K.S. PRICHARD *Black Opal* 68 The brushwood shelters near the mines in which the men sit at midday to eat their lunches and noodle—go over, snip, and examine—the opal they have taken out of the mines. **1976** *Bulletin* (Sydney) 20 Mar. 40/3 It takes two months for a novel to germinate with me. One fiddles with it, noodles it and then the day comes when I'm ready to go.

b. To obtain (an opal) by searching through mining refuse.

1931 M.S. BUCHANAN *Prospecting for Opal* 10 Dick Huggard's famous claim on Bald Hill must have produced ten thousand pounds, with what was 'noodled' or picked up from the dumps.

noodler. One who 'noodles'.

1919 *Smith's Weekly* (Sydney) 21 June 17/6 Should he see nothing, nor feel anything with his pick, he is apt to bring the dirt down in lumps—which accounts for the number of stones found on his dump by 'noodlers'. **1982** *Sun-Herald* (Sydney) 31 Jan. 100/7 Thousands of noodlers will have been there before you, but the chances of digging a cuttable opal from the dumps are good provided you work at it.

nooer /'nuə/. [Repr. pronunc. of abbrev. of *manure.*] In the phr. **in the nooer,** in a difficult situation.

1970 R. BEILBY *No Medals for Aphrodite* 88 How come you blokes blew the bridge so soon? . . You really dropped us in the nooer, you did. **1975** B. FOLEY *Shearers' Poems* 9 Two Kiwis left, their mother sick And took off for Rotorua Two Aussies occupied their pen Now the cockie was in the 'nooer'.

Noogoora burr /'nəgurə 'bɜ/. Also **nagoora, ngoora, nugura burr.** [See quot. 1973.] The naturalized annual *Xanthium occidentale* (fam. Asteraceae), a proclaimed noxious weed having rough, lobed leaves and a spiny, woody burr; the burr itself, a nuisance, esp. in the wool of sheep.

1883 F.M. BAILEY *Synopsis Qld. Flora* 259 *X*[*anthium*] *strumarium* . . known as 'Noogoora Burr', and supposed injurious to stock. **1957** *Westerly* ii. 26 The grey Gulf country stretched away into the hot afternoon. . . I chopped viciously at an obstreperous bush of ngoora burr. **1973** W.T. PARSONS *Noxious Weeds Vic.* 117 Noogoora burr . . was first discovered in Australia in the 1860s at Noogoora Station near Ipswich in Queensland, from where it has now spread to all mainland states. **1976** S. WELLER *Bastards I have Met* 8 Jock was the big dark Scotchman . . and he had a burr thicker than the nagoora after a good wet season. **1978** HANIGAN & LINDSAY *No Tracks on River* 48, I had them nugura burrs all over me. In my hair, in my jeans, in my t-shirt.

noongah, noongar, varr. NYOONGAH.

Norfolk Island. [The name of an island some 1500 kilometres n.e. of Sydney.]

1. *Hist.* Used *attrib.* in allusion to the penal settlement

established on the island (1788-1814 and 1825-1856), and esp. for the detention of recalcitrant convicts.
1843 *Sydney Morning Herald* 16 May 2/5 Terry M'Guigan, a Norfolk Island expiree, for neglecting to register his place of abode, to be confined in Sydney Gaol for fourteen days. **1876** H. PARKES *Speeches* p. ix, Their fixed idea of the only political institutions suitable for the mass of their fellow-colonists was what, in one of the speeches, is caustically but truthfully described as a 'Norfolk Island Government'.

2. Special Comb. **Norfolk Island grant** *hist.*, a grant of land made to a settler removed from Norfolk Island, chiefly in Tasmania and without conditions as to use or disposal; **pine**, the tall coniferous tree *Araucaria heterophylla* (fam. Araucariaceae) of Norfolk Island, having a symmetrical, conical shape and widely planted elsewhere; also **Norfolk pine**.
1820 Tas. Colonial Secretary's Office Rec. 1/44 40, The Estate at Pitt Water consists of three separate Grants (unconditional, or what are termed **Norfolk Island Grants**). [**1788 Norfolk Island pine**: J. WHITE *Jrnl. Voyage N.S.W.* (1790) 212 It [*sc*. Norfolk Island] promised some advantages; particularly in furnishing us with pine trees, which grow here to a size nearly equal to those of Norway.] **1803** *HRA* (1915) 1st Ser. III. 743 An island upon which grows the Norfolk Island pine. **1804** *Ibid.* (1921) 3rd Ser. I. 620 The Mimosa .. grows here .. not unlike the Norfolk Pine in miniature.

Hence **Norfolk-Islandized** *a.*
1840 D. BURN *Vindication Van Diemen's Land* 34 *Norfolk-islandised*—that is, utterly degraded and hardened in depravity.

Norfolk Islander. *Hist.* One who is, or who has been, a convict sentenced to penal servitude on Norfolk Island.
1842 *Sydney Herald* 21 Apr. 3/2 *Norfolk Islanders*. The Superintendent of Police some time since issued an order that expirees from Norfolk Island shall be visited at their residences once a week at least, by the inspectors of the parishes in which they reside. **1855** W. HOWITT *Land, Labor & Gold* II. 23 A striking example of the character and doings of escaped Norfolk Islanders in this colony.

nork. [Of uncertain origin: see quot. 1966.] A woman's breast. Freq. in *pl.*
1962 'C. ROHAN' *Delinquents* 157 Hello, honey, that sweater—one deep breath and your norks will be in my soup. **1966** S.J. BAKER *Austral. Lang.* (ed. 2) 215 *Nork*, a female breast, usually in plural. (Ex Norco Co-operative Ltd., a butter manufacturer in N.S.W.).

north. Freq. with **the**.
1. The northernmost part of Australia: the northern parts of Queensland, the Northern Territory, and Western Australia. See also DEEP NORTH. Also **northland**.
1891 *Truth* (Sydney) 5 Apr. 6/1 His tour—or 'tower', as it is usually called up North—has been a prodigious 'burst'. **1927** A. WRIGHT *Squatter's Secret* 41 Get back to the great Northland, where he could bury himself in the bush, and forget. **1979** R. DUFFIELD *Rogue Bull* 124 The Great North would be so invaluable to the rest of the world that it would be permanently protected from predators.

2. In the collocation **Empty North**, the northernmost part of Australia as an especially sparsely populated region.
1918 G. WHITE *Thirty Yrs. Tropical Aust.* 261 The empty North and the White Australia ideal. **1947** F. CLUNE *Roaming around Aust.* 182 The trouble is, that taxpayers 'Down South' are not interested in developing our 'Empty North'.

northern, *a*. Used as a distinguishing epithet in the names of birds: **northern fantail**, the grey and white bird *Rhipidura rufiventris* of open forest in n. Aust. and elsewhere; **rosella**, the rosella *Platycercus venustus* of n.w. Aust.
1847 J. GOULD *Birds of Aust.* (1848) II. Pl. 85, *Rhipidura isura* .. **Northern Fantail**. **1945** C. BARRETT *Austral. Bird Life* 80 The **northern rosella** (P[*latycercus*] *venustus*) is found in the north-west of the state [*sc.* W.A.] and the Northern Territory.

northerner. A non-Aboriginal inhabitant of any of the northernmost parts of Australia.
1889 F. CRAWFORD *Native Companion Songster* 16 'Neath a ragged banana a Northerner sat, A'twisting the leaf of his cabbage-tree hat. **1964** *N. Austral. Monthly* Feb. 6 Hardened Northerners go prepared for anything.

northland: see NORTH 1.

nor'-west. Also **north-west**. The northern part of Western Australia. Also *attrib.*
1899 *Bulletin* (Sydney) 19 Aug. 32/1 Battled from the Diamantina to the 'North West Corner' without having so much as got their hands into wool during the whole dreary ten weeks. **1929** K.S. PRICHARD *Coonardoo* (1961) 158 His spurs, the ends of his narrow pull-on stockman boots and his big Nor'-West hat were struck against the light behind him. **1962** C. GYE *Cockney & Crocodile* 142 South and West of that is the other large area of stations, mostly sheep and not usually quite a million acres, called the North-West.

Hence **nor'westy** *a.*, characteristic of n. Western Australia.
1977 J. DOUGHTY *Gold in Blood* 158 Here .. the country began to turn definitely Nor-westy. The dirty looking greyness of the south was gone.

nor'-wester. A non-Aboriginal inhabitant of n.w. Australia. Also *attrib.*
1900 *Truth* (Sydney) 28 Jan. 3/5 The beauty of these names is singularly indicative of the poetic temperament of the Nor'Wester. **1965** L. WALKER *Other Girl* 10 Four men's faces stared out from under dusty nor'-wester ten-bale hats.

nose. In the phr. **on the nose**, distasteful, offensive; smelly.
1941 S.J. BAKER *Pop. Dict. Austral. Slang* 49 *Nose, on the*, (said of things) disliked, offensive. **1982** *Bulletin* (Sydney) 5 Jan. 25/1 The swing against us in Bass was about 17 percent. .. We were on the nose, electorally speaking.

nose-bag. [Transf. use of *nose-bag* a horse's feeding-bag.]
1. A bag in which a swagman carries provisions.
1894 *Bulletin* (Sydney) 12 May 2/1 The 'nose-bags' heavy on each chest (God bless one kindly squatter!). **1927** A. WRIGHT *Squatter's Secret* 123 He was attired in the orthodox swagman outfit, with swag, billy and nosebag complete.

2. *fig.* A meal; in the phr. **to put on the nose bag**, to have a meal.
1919 C. DREW *Doings of Dave* 28 What's wrong with us putting on our nose-bags? I ain't had a feed all day. **1968** D. O'GRADY *Bottle of Sandwiches* 66 After the third beer .. Bill's shout .. the first carpenter said, 'Better put the nose-bag on.'

nosey bob. [The nickname of R.R. Howard (c 1836-1906), public executioner in N.S.W. (c 1874-1904), so-called because of a facial disfigurement.] A hangman; an inquisitive person, a 'nosey parker'.
1892 *Truth* (Sydney) 1 May 4/7 He would not risk his own carcase, or do anything likely to put his neck in Nosey Bob's noose. **1930** *Listening Post* (Perth) 24 Jan. 23, I suggest that space be devoted to the 'nosey bobs'.

note. [Spec. use of *note* a bank-note.] A one-pound note; the sum of one pound.

1863 *Frank Gardiner, or Bushranging in 1863* 10 If I had known that the boot was only fifteen notes and a ticker, I wouldn't have started on such a wet night. 1978 K. GILBERT *People are Legends* 11 I'll sell me moot for half a note And a bottle of wine.

Novocastrian. [Transf. use of *Novocastrian* a native or inhabitant of Newcastle upon Tyne.] A non-Aboriginal native or resident of Newcastle, N.S.W.

1902 *Newcastle Morning Herald* 8 Nov. 7/7 (*heading*) Novocastrians on tour. 1986 *Sydney Morning Herald* 12 Apr. 11/4, 30,000 Novocastrians crowded on to the main beach.

nuddy /'nʌdi/. Also **nudee**. [f. *nud(e* + *d* + -Y. Used elsewhere but recorded earliest in Aust.] In the phr. **in the nuddy**, in the nude, naked.

1953 *Bulletin* (Sydney) 11 Nov. 12/2 The young matron of the 'blacksoil country' whom the artist depicted in the nuddie killing a snake . . did a good job. 1959 D. HEWETT *Bobbin Up* 139 The sheet slipped down and bared her little pendulous breasts. 'What are you lyin' there in the nuddy for?' 1966 H. PORTER *Paper Chase* 127 That we euphemistically say 'swimming in the nud-ee' indicates our respectability, our tender consciences.

nudge. [Fig. use of *nudge* a slight push.] Esp. in the phr. **to give it (a bit of) a nudge,** to drink (alcoholic liquor) to excess; to over-indulge. Also *transf.*, and as *v. trans.* and *intr.*

1966 S.J. BAKER *Austral. Lang.* (ed. 2) 178 *Nudge*, used in reference to drinking, e.g. *give it a nudge, nudge it*, to drink alcoholic liquor. 1977 H. GARNER *Monkey Grip* 15 Today I gave the junk a nudge. 1978 R. MACKLIN *Newsfront* 51 Gave it a bit of a nudge last night, did you?

nugget, *n.* [Br. dial. *nugget* a lump of anything; a short, thickset person or animal: see EDD. Used elsewhere in senses 1 a. and b. but recorded earliest in Aust.]

1. a. A lump of native gold. Also *attrib.*

1851 J.H. BURTON *Emigrant's Man.* ii. 116 Small lumps, called 'nuggets', are . . discovered in a remarkably pure state. 1941 D. O'CALLAGHAN *Long Life Reminisc.* 5 The prospector's 'nugget-kickers' led out into the shimmering and pitiless Never Never.

b. *transf.* Someone or something precious.

1853 MOSSMAN & BANISTER *Aust. Visited & Revisited* 191 She was delirious with joy, as she clasped Browne in her arms, and called him her 'nugget'. 1897 *Bulletin* (Sydney) 19 June 28/1 He's mastered a method of 'turning' That never was taught in a school. His manners are rugged and vulgar, But he's nuggets of gold in our need.

2. A small stocky animal or person; also, a runt. Hence freq. as a nickname for a small person.

1852 G.C. MUNDY *Our Antipodes* III. 322 The word nugget among farmers signifies a small compact beast—a runt; among gold miners a lump, in contradistinction to the scale or dust gold. 1971 *Sydney Morning Herald* 28 Oct. 7/1 Widely known as 'Nugget' because of his short, stocky build . . he [*sc.* H.G. Coombs] was one of a number of young intellectuals recruited during World War II to work in Canberra.

3. An unbranded calf.

1872 G.S. BADEN-POWELL *New Homes for Old Country* 182 Fresh-born calves as yet unbranded . . go by the name of 'nuggets'. 1976 J.H. TRAVERS *Bull Dust on Brigalow* 23 We saw quite a few cattle and plenty of nuggets (unbranded cattle).

nugget, *v. Obs.* [f. prec.]

1. *trans.* To search for and prise out from surrounding material (gold in nuggets); also *intr.*, to search for and obtain nuggets of gold. Also as *vbl. n.*

1851 *Empire* (Sydney) 22 Aug. 75/5 One old man, while nuggetting on the hills was fortunate enough to turn out a piece of gold weighing thirteen ounces. 1874 S.W. SILVER *Handbk. Aust. & N.Z.* 148 Nuggeting is a pleasant and profitable occupation. 1881 G.C. EVANS *Stories* 129 My mate and I sunk a hole about 10 feet deep, and nuggeted two ounces off the bottom.

2. *trans.* To steal (unbranded calves). Also *intr.* and freq. as *vbl. n.*

1881 MRS C. PRAED *Policy & Passion* I. 52 My lady breaks in the horses and takes care that the calves are branded. It is said that she has an eye to business, and does not disdain nuggeting. [*Note*] To *nugget*: in Australian slang, to appropriate your neighbours' unbranded calves. 1885 —— *Head Station* III. 100 Nobody would go there except after calves to nugget.

nuggetty, *a.* Also **nuggety**. [f. NUGGET *n.* + -Y.]

1. a. Of gold: occurring as nuggets.

1852 F. LANCELOTT *Aust. as it Is* II. 2 The gold is nuggetty, and often found in the schist rocks. 1935 *Vic.: Gold & Minerals* (Vic. Dept. Mines) 26 Nuggety patches of gold were obtained from the quartz veins cutting the Indicators.

b. Rich in nuggets.

1853 *Austral. Gold Digger's Monthly Mag.* v. 192 Nuggetty Gully has turned out fine golden boulders. 1980 R. SHEARS *Gold* 17, I went out at weekends to areas in Gippsland because my research had shown me there were nuggety gullies there.

2. a. Of a person: compactly built; stocky; tough.

1856 W.W. DOBIE *Recoll. Visit Port-Phillip* 40, I was nuggety-looking, not enough of the digger, bushman, or old leg [*sic*] about me to command the respect of the public. 1974 *Southerly* ii. 170 He was the type . . who became more and more unwholesomely noticeable; too nuggety, his hair too grizzled.

b. Of an animal: stocky; small but sturdy.

1893 *Pall Mall Gaz.* (London) 28 Jan. 3/1 The light spring waggon drawn by a pair of sleek, nuggetty cobs. 1940 I.L. IDRIESS *Lightning Ridge* 126 All the horses were nuggety little grey ponies.

nugura burr, var. NOOGOORA BURR.

nulla /'nʌlə/. Also **nullah**. Shortened form of NULLA-NULLA.

1878 R.B. SMYTH *Aborigines of Vic.* I. 85 He saw the gins carrying spears and shields on the march, the men carrying only a nulla or two. 1912 J.H.L. ZILLMAN *Austral. Poetry* 12 The crash on shield by nullah thrust.

nulla-nulla /'nʌlə-nʌlə/. Formerly also with much variety, as **nilla-nilla, nolla-nolla, nullah-nullah**. [a. Dharuk ŋala ŋala.] An Aboriginal war club: see quot. 1808.

c 1790 W. DAWES Grammatical Forms Lang. N.S.W., *Gnallangulla* . . a particular club. 1808 *Sydney Gaz.* 6 Nov., A perhaps deadly stroke with a *nulla-nulla*. . . [*Note*] This weapon is formed by affixing to the end of a club a circular piece of a very hard wood, 8 or 10 inches in diameter, with a sharp edge, and of a mushroom form. It is frequently carried as a weapon of defence, but the natives seldom exercise it against each other. 1833 W.H. BRETON *Excursions* 239 The waddies . . and nullah-nullahs, are clubs. 1895 A.C. BICKNELL *Travel & Adventure Northern Qld.* 44 A weapon the native usually carries is the 'nolla-nolla', or club. 1903 J. FURPHY *Such is Life* 241 A sharp jerk, and the whipstick would snap, supplying a nilla-nulla which would make him an over-match for a dozen Folkestones in rotation.

Hence as *v. trans.*, to strike (a person) with a nulla-nulla.

1849 A. HARRIS *Emigrant Family* (1967) 239 Three fellows I nullah-nullahed on their way home.

Nullarbor doctor: see DOCTOR *n.*³

numbat /'nʌmbæt/. [a. Nyungar *numbad.*] The small, termite-eating marsupial *Myrmecobius fasciatus*, now occurring only in s.w. W.A., having red to grey-brown fur with light stripes across the back and rump; ANTEATER 2.

1923 F.W. JONES *Mammals S.A.* i. 123 Banded Ant-eater. Marsupial Ant-eater. White-banded Bandicoot. *Myrmecobius fasciatus.*.. These names are all merely book designations, for the animal appears never to have been sufficiently common or conspicuous to have earned a popular or familiar name. To the aboriginals, however, it is known as the Numbat, and this name will be adopted here. **1984** *Age* (Melbourne) 10 Apr. 28/7 The numbat—an attractive marsupial anteater the size of a large rat.

number. [From the practice of declaring the result of a horse-race by posting the numbers of the winners.] In the phr. **the numbers are** (or **go**) **up**, and varr., the result is known.

1890 'TASMA' *In her Earliest Youth* III. 228 'And then your children, a growing family, you know, you have *two* already,' suggested the agent blandly. 'Yes, we've got two,' said George meditatively; 'and as for the family, it's the same as with everything else—you never can tell till the numbers are up.' **1920** F.A. RUSSELL *Ashes of Achievement* 199 He thinks the chances are in favour... And my guess is as good as his, before the numbers go up.

nun. [Spec. use of *nun* a name applied to any of various birds.] *White-fronted chat*, see WHITE *a.*² 1 b.

1918 *Bulletin* (Sydney) 14 Feb. (Red Page), *White-fronted Bush-Chat* (Tang, Nun, Tintac) and other members of the genus *Epthianura*. **1942** E. ANDERSON *Squatter's Luck* 28 'Nun', the white-throated chat.

nunga, var. NYOONGAH.

nunger. Usu. in *pl.* [Of unknown origin.] A woman's breast.

1966 G. WYATT *Strip Jack Naked* 54 'I see she's got the raffle books stuck down the front of her dress.' 'That's not raffle books,' Evan said. 'That's her. She was born with paper nungers.' **1967** J. HIBBERD *White with Wire Wheels* (1970) 161 I'll never forget those nungers, and their red jelly-bean nipples.

nut-brown. *Obs.* A name applied to a convict. Also **nut-brown face.**

1834 *Sydney Herald* 20 Oct. 2/4 It is a common saying 'spare the rod and you spoil the child'; this nursery proverb is fully verified in the spoiled *innocents* of the Government gangs, y'clept by Humanitas the 'Nut-brown faces'. **1840** *Sydney Herald* 17 Feb. 2/2 Captain Maconochie has applied to the Government to be allowed a band of musicians to accompany him to Norfolk Island to entertain the gentlemen 'nutbrowns' there.

nutmeg. [Transf. use of *nutmeg* the tree *Myristica fragrans.*]

1. Either of two trees, *Myristica muelleri* and *M. insipida* (fam. Myristicaceae), occurring in n.e. Qld. and n. N.T.; the fruit of these trees; *wild nutmeg*, see WILD 1.

1814 M. FLINDERS *Voyage Terra Australis* II. 188 We found upon Chasm Island .. many large bushes covered with nutmegs... It is the *Myristica insipida* of Brown's *Prodrom. Nov. Holl.* p. 400. **1825** B. FIELD *Geogr. Mem. N.S.W.* 291 Two species of nutmeg were found, but they are not fit for use.

2. Special Comb. **nutmeg pigeon,** TORRES STRAIT PIGEON.

1901 *Emu* I. 130 The Nutmeg Pigeon (*Myristicivora spilorrhoa*).. build substantial nests. *c* **1960** C. MACKNESS *Clump Point & District* 4 Nutmeg pigeons were then very numerous... They could be pulled off their nests with the bare hands at dusk.

nut tree. [Spec. use of *nut-tree* a tree that bears nuts, esp. the hazel.] A nut-bearing tree, any of several species, perh. incl. NUTWOOD and QUANDONG 1 a.

1834 *Perth Gaz.* 10 May 283/2 In the neighbourhood of York we found the nut tree in flower: it belongs to the same class and order, and agrees in the form of the seed with the sandal wood of India; but the seeds of our plant are about four times as large: they contain a large portion of pure, tasteless oil, and burn with a clear light. **1986** K. BRENNAN *Wildflowers of Kakadu* 57 Nut Tree *Terminalia grandiflora*... This tall, slender, narrow-leafed tree is partly deciduous in the Dry Season.

nutwood. The tree *Terminalia arostrata* (fam. Combretaceae), of N.T. and the n.e. Kimberley region (W.A.), the fruit of which has an edible kernel.

1915 *Bull. N.T.* xiv. 7 Then more volcanic downs with bauhinia and nutwood for about six miles. **1983** R.J. PETHERAM *Plants Kimberley Region W.A.* 517 *Terminalia arostrata* Nutwood, Crocodile Tree... A small tree, 4 to 10 m. high, with willow-like drooping branches.

nyoongah /'njʊŋə/. Also **noongah, noongar, nunga.** [a. Nyungar *nyungar* an Aboriginal person.] A person of Aboriginal, or part-Aboriginal, descent. Also *attrib.*

1845 E.J. EYRE *Jrnls. Exped. Central Aust.* II. 396 Men or people... Yoon-gar. **1954** *Coast to Coast 1953–54* 105 N-Yoongars not black. Most all us N-Yoongars brown. **1961** *Polynesian Soc. Jrnl.* (Wellington, N.Z.) June 202 Adelaide people .. use .. different native words to refer to aborigines... Point Pearce people say *Nunga*. **1975** R. BEILBY *Brown Land Crying* 3 You're as much coloured as white, as much Noong-ah as wadjullah. **1977** K. GILBERT *Living Black* 88 The most effective means of communication .. we call .. the 'noongar grapevine'... It used a sort of communication that can only be understood by Aborigines and it's highly functional.

N.Z., var. ENZED.

O

o-, *suffix*. [Prob. infl. by the use of the *-o* suffix as a final syllable in street cries such as 'milk-o' (see MILKO 1) and in other calls such as RUSH-OH, 'smoke-o' (see SMOKO 1 a., quot. 1872), SPELL-OH; similarly attached to personal names, as 'John-o', and so widespread as elsewhere in informal English, esp. as a mark of familiarity.] Added as a final syllable to **(a)** shortened forms, as **carpo** [f. *car(pet snake)*], **cemo** [f. *cem(etery)*], **delo** [f. *del(egate)*], **euco** [f. *euc(alyptus)*], **evo** [f. *ev(ening)*], **fiftho** [f. *fifth (columnist)*], **houso** [f. *hous(ekeeping)*], **Jappo** [f. *Jap(anese)*]; **(b)** monosyllabic forms, as **Greeko, juggo, kicko, maddo**. See separate entries for the following settled forms: ARVO, BIZZO, BOMBO, BOTTLE-OH, BRONZO, BULLO, COMBO, COMPO, DEMO, DERRO, GALVO, GARBO, IMBO, JACKO (*n.*[1] and *n.*[2]), JOLLO, JOURNO, LESO, METHO *n.*[1], MILKO, MUSO, NASHO, PANNO, PLONKO, PRESBO, PROVO, RABBIT-OH, RABBO, REFFO, REGGO, REO, ROBBO, SALVO, SAMBO, SANO, SARVO, SECKO, SMOKO, SPEARO, SPELL-OH, SUSSO, TOADO, etc.

1907 *Truth* (Sydney) 30 June 9/5 If a forward miss his 'kicko' He's not 'worth his blanky oats'. **1911** *Ibid.* 14 May 11/4 Mary Neary was fined £3, in default a month's juggo. **1914** E. DYSON *Spats' Fact'ry* 90 Here's a maddo offerin' marriage to all ours. **1934** *Bulletin* (Sydney) 14 Nov. 41/3 A carpet-snake was thrown into the car by a wheel, landing across the driver's shoulder... In the end carpo called it a day; he was probably as frightened as we were. **1942** *Plane Speaking from R.A.A.F. Amberley* 15 Oct. 8 We'd rather be in Tokio drinking Jappo beer. **1943** H.E. BEROS *Fuzzy Wuzzy Angels* 73 A dirty thieving rotter came, a proper fiftho pest. **1944** L.J. LIND *Escape from Crete* 64, I was awakened by.. two black-bearded Greekos. **1955** N. PULLIAM *I traveled Lonely Land* 114 Tot it all up and then communicate with the headwaiter at the place where the mob's going that evo. **1964** *Bulletin* (Sydney) 22 Aug. 32/1 Merely ran a little way in among the graves and hid... The birds and lizards in the cemo taught us. *Play dead*, they said. **1974** J. GABY *Restless Waterfront* 204 According to the delegate, a dello wasn't only as good as the master.. but he was better. **1975** *Bulletin* (Sydney) 1 Nov. 19/1 My wife's increasing demands for more housekeeping money.. 'Could you give me the houso?' she said. **1982** K. HUENEKE *Huts of High Country* 182 Harry and Plonkey were both avid 'euco cutters' in the 1930s and 1940s. The new term had me stumped... They were humble old gum tree cutters.

oak. [See quot. 1965.]

1. Any of many trees thought to resemble the English oak, generally in the appearance of the timber, esp. those of the fam. Casuarinaceae (see CASUARINA); the wood of these trees. Also *attrib.*

1789 J. HUNTER *Hist. Jrnl. Trans. Port Jackson* (1793) 357 Pines, and oak-trees of the largest size, were blown down every instant. **1965** *Austral. Encycl.* VI. 381 The word 'oak' is usually applied in Australia to various members of the genus *Casuarina* .. because the grain of their timbers resembles that of the English oak, having large conspicuous medullary rays.

2. With distinguishing epithet, as **desert, forest, he, river, she, silky, swamp, Tasmanian,** etc.: see under first element.

3. Special Comb. **oak grub,** the large larva of a variety of insects, usu. beetles or moths, sometimes used as bait.

1900 H. LAWSON *Over Sliprails* 111 We got a rusty pan without a handle, and cooked about a pint of fat yellow oak-grubs... We had broken a new pair of shears digging out those grubs from under the bark of the she-oaks. **1933** *Canberra Chron.* 26 Oct. 19/5 Bob Reid.. has begun his famous summer-bait service again and has good stocks of large oak grubs.

oat grass. Any of several usu. tufted grasses used as fodder, esp. TALL OAT GRASS. Formerly also **oaten grass.**

1825 *Austral.* (Sydney) 21 July 4 A late *danthonia*, or gigantic oatgrass was most remarkable. **1846** *Sydney Morning Herald* 26 Mar. 2/5 The oaten grass of the Isaacks, which grew to a considerable height, and the stem of which is very juicy and sweet.

oath. In the phr. **my oath,** an emphatic exclamation of agreement or endorsement; an expletive. See also BLOODY *a.* 2, COLONIAL *a.* 5.

1869 *Lictor* (Sydney) 16 Dec. 347 My oath! I'm as right as a first-rate quondong. **1981** H. MILLIGAN *Sprig of Light* 28 'You're not going to ring up now are you?' 'My oath I am, you can't let the grass grow under your feet.'

obsidianite. AUSTRALITE.

1898 *Proc. R. Soc. Vic.* 23 As long as this uncertainty exists, some other name would be more appropriate, and I suggest and will refer to them in this paper as 'obsidianites', a term which will at least not be open to this objection, and will be more convenient for use. **1933** C. FENNER *Bunyips & Billabongs* 40 Most of us have seen an Australite, either in our own or in a friend's collection, or in a museum. They are also known as 'blackfellows' buttons', obsidianites, emu-stones, and 'trans-line' meteorites.

occupation licence. *Hist.* A permit to graze stock on a specified tract of Crown land for a stipulated period.

1843 *Colonial Observer* (Sydney) 25 Mar. 909/2 Occupation Licenses... The sale of Licenses for the occupation of Crown Lands, within the boundaries of location. **1932** B.U. BYLES *Rep. on Reconnaissance Mountainous Part River Murray Catchment N.S.W.* 42 Occupation licences cover very large areas of country of very low grazing value, rentals vary from 6d. to 12d. per acre per annum and the size of the blocks from 14,000 to 20,000 acres.

Ocean Hell. *Hist.* A name given to the penal establishment on Norfolk Island.

1850 *Britannia* (Hobart) 4 Apr. 2/2 We designated it [*sc.* Norfolk Island] for the first time '*the Ocean Hell*'. **1939** J.G. PATTISON *'Battler's' Tales Early Rockhampton* 42 Haynes left the Albion on her return to Sydney and joined the 'Morayshire', which ship had been hired by Sir William Denison to remove any of the Pitcairn Islanders who wished to go to Norfolk Island, known as 'The Ocean Hell' and 'Earthly Paradise'.

ock. Abbrev. of OCKER *n.* 2.

1976 *Bulletin* (Sydney) 21 Aug. 21/3 Get the average Ock to take a holiday in his own country. **1982** *Ibid.* 6 July 65/1 He had tins of beer zipped into the front of his parka jacket, resting on his fat stomach... 'That's the historical ock.'

ocker /ˈɒkə/, *n.* and *attrib.* Also **okker.** [A nickname, esp. for a person named *Oscar*, used as a nickname for a character devised and played by Ron Frazer (1924–1983) in a television series, 'The Mavis Bramston Show' (1965–1968), and hence applied generically.]

A. *n.*

1. a. Used as a masculine nickname.

1916 R.H. ADAMS *Diary* 26 Feb., Considerable helio work done on the station owing to fault on line to Bde. called up by Ocker's Co. Heard a voice, could swear it was Jim's. **1972** *Bulletin* (Sydney) 26 Feb. 11/1, I only realised afterwards that I was suspected of being 'Ocker' Campbell, the notorious Australian smash-and-grab man.

b. Used as a derisive nickname for a person who exploits an exaggerated Australian nationalism.

1968 *Kings Cross Whisper* (Sydney) li. 3/3 This was the theme in the winter showing of fashion designer Fred 'Ocker' Smith. **1978** *Ibid.* lxxx. 1/2 'It is in keeping with our image as a fair dinkum all-Australian company,' the general manager, Mr W. (Ocker) Leadhead, said today.

2. *transf.* A rough and uncultivated Australian male, often aggressively Australian in speech and manner.

1971 G. JOHNSTON *Cartload Clay* 71 The big man would be a good player, a vigorous clubman, a hearty participant in the companionship of the club bar. He was .. what the boy called an 'Ocker'. **1981** B. DICKINS *Gift of Gab* 28 Huge mobs of Orange-Fanta ockers queueing up for beach tickets.

3. Australian English.

1979 DOUGLAS & HEATHCOTE *Far Cry* 29 Talking okker. Mother used to whip us if we pronounced anything incorrectly. This meant I grew up with a New Zealand accent and I have always felt sorry that I could never sound like a true Aussie.

B. *attrib.* passing into *adj.* Characterized by a discernibly Australian vulgarity.

1972 *Australasian Post* (Melbourne) 30 Nov. 4/1 'I've got a Charger parked out the front and some classy clob-ber on me back,' he said, in an accent only a shade less Strine than his Ocker alter ego. **1979** *Overland* 78/37 Make it ocker, sing a song, show muscles and boobs.

Hence **ocker** *v. intr.*, to behave as an ocker; **ockerization** *n.*, vulgarization; **ockerized** *a.*, vulgarized.

1976 B. BENNETT *New Country* 42 Winter liked to **ocker** it up occasionally. **1975** *Bulletin* (Sydney) 6 Sept. 21/1 The annual general meeting of the Australian Society of Authors threw up its hands in horror at the idea, many a silver-haired lady and tweedy gentleman getting up to protest at the **ockerisation** of modern society, the well known crassness of marketing people, et cetera. **1978** K. GARVEY *Tales of my Uncle Harry* 8 Both would writhe in their graves if they could see some of the modernized, deodorized, glamorized, Americanized, televisionized, **Ockerized**, socialserviceized, Aussies of the present permissive decadent era.

ockerdom. Ockers collectively; their social impact.

1974 *Gayzette* (Sydney) 19 Sept. 19/3 We are going through an artificial revival, not of the Lawson male ethic, but of a curious and pugnacious Ockerdom. **1979** K. DUNSTAN *Ratbags* p. xv, Ockerdom and the whole cult of the Ocker is so engaging.

ockerina. A female ocker.

1975 *Sunday Tel.* (Sydney) 27 July 96/6 Ockerina of the week was surely the woman on the Eastern Suburbs bus, studying a race guide while slurping down a meat pie. **1980** B. HORNADGE *Austral. Slanguage* 136 The use of bad language was entirely a male prerogative, but it seems the Ockerinas of the nation are fast catching up.

ockerism.

1. Behaviour characteristic of an ocker: see quot. 1974.

1974 *Austral.* (Sydney) 5 Oct. 13/4 The new Australian boorishness is known as Ockerism, from a slob-like character called Ocker in a television series, the embodiment of oafish, blinkered self-satisfaction. **1984** *Canberra Times* 14 Apr. 2/1, I would find it easier to read *The Canberra Times* .. if some members of your team of sports writers were to rein in the ethnocentric machismo, also commonly known as ockerism.

2. AUSTRALIANISM 1; Australian English.

1975 *Daily Mirror* (Sydney) 9 May 5/4 'A few of 'em are adoptin' a few ockerisms that don't come natural to 'em,' says Hogan. **1981** *Bulletin* (Sydney) 15 Dec. 6/2 If on the other hand we choose to invent a new language .. teach our children 'ockerism' instead of English and end confusion.

ocky. [f. *oc(topus* + -Y.] An octopus; octopus flesh.

1968 R. HILL *Bush Quest* 101 There were two buckets of octopus pieces for bait. The 'ocky', as they call it, was bluish white and rather slimy looking. **1984** *Canberra Chron.* 29 Feb. 19/3 Watch out for the ockies that roam all over the sand flats.

octo. Abbrev. of 'octopus'.

1912 *Bulletin* (Sydney) 24 Oct. 16/2 The octo. let go and sunk [*sic*] hurriedly, and the girl shrieked. **1936** N. CALDWELL *Fangs of Sea* 202, I never went looking for that octo again.

octoroon. [Transf. use of *octoroon* a person of oneeighth Negro descent.] A person of one-eighth Aboriginal descent.

1933 R.S. SAMPSON *Through Central Aust.* 28 The child of a white person and a mulatto is a quadroon; of a white person and a quadroon, an octoroon. **1984** *A.N.U. Reporter* (Canberra) 27 Apr. 3 Archie describes himself as an 'octoroon', being one-eighth Aborigine.

offside, *a.*[1] [Spec. use of *offside* the right side of an animal, vehicle, etc.] Of a bullock team: of or pertaining to the right-hand side (as opposed to the near or left-hand side).

1847 *Bell's Life in Sydney* 25 Dec. 3/2 I'd sooner .. be an off-side bullock driver. **1981** E. ROLLS *Million Wild Acres* 28 (caption) The offside leader and the offside pinner both shook their heads during the long exposure necessary to the slow film.

offside, *a.*[2] [Transf. use of *offside* away from one's own side (in football, hockey, etc.).]

a. *transf.* Unacceptable; in bad taste.

1910 H. LAWSON *Rising of Court* 90 It seems that Brutus objected to Cassius's or one of his off-side friends' methods of raising the wind. **1939** K. TENNANT *Foveaux* 142 You only had to say something a bit offside to Bramley and he would blush like a girl.

b. In the phr. **offside with,** on the wrong side of; in bad odour with.

[N.Z. **1947** COMBS *Half-Lengths* 8 Harris began to put himself off-side with some of the leading citizens.] **1979** *Southerly* i. 54 It was about this time, by the way, that I got offside with some of the sports writers.

offside, *v.* [Back-formation from OFFSIDER 1 a.] *intr.* To act as an offsider. Also as *vbl. n.*

1883 M. DURACK *Kings in Grass Castles* (1959) 256, I have put up a yard on Galway since Uncle Jerry left—Pumpkin and Kangaroo offsiding. **1946** *Bulletin* (Sydney) 21 Aug. 28/3, I went off-siding to a professional bird-catcher. **1980** M. MCADOO *If only I'd Listened* ('Tom Parker'), My father broke me in with some of the bullocks. I used to 'ave to offside for 'im.

offsider. [f. OFFSIDE *a.*[1]: see quot. 1910.]

1. a. A bullock-driver's assistant; an assistant in an occupation or enterprise.

1879 'AUSTRALIAN' *Adventures Qld.* 108 Mr Brown, George Martin, and the Malcolms, lent him two hands each, who, with his off-sider and himself, made a good strong clearing party. **1910** C.E.W. BEAN *On Wool Track* 168 An 'offsider', by the by, is a gentleman who is learning bullock-driving, and who is allowed to try his apprenticetongue on the offside of the bullock team. **1983** *Canberra Times* 18 Sept. 7/1 Her common-law husband .. was a bricklayer, and she had often worked as his offsider and gained the reputation of being able to do the work of two men.

b. With occupation specified: **cook's offsider.**
1910 *Bulletin* (Sydney) 28 Apr. 13/1, I can .. smell the buns the cook's offsider is bringing. 1979 W.D. JOYNT *Breaking Road for Rest* 42, I took over as men dropped out, and handled in turn nearly every one of the vacant jobs, even cook's offsider and butcher.

2. *transf.* and *fig.*
1924 F.J. MILLS *Happy Days* 8 A chap lookin' as if 'e 'ad crawled out of a rabbit's burrow, came up, leadin' a 'orse, what looked like as if 'e was offsider to the missin' link. 1944 *Bulletin* (Sydney) 1 Mar. 12/1 The yarn about the bullant and its offsiders raiding the honey .. isn't as far-fetched as it reads.

oil, *n.* [Fig. use of *oil* as the substance essential to the running of a machine.]

1. Information; news.
1915 DREW & EVANS *Grafter* 56, I can guarantee that he's trying, because I got the right oil about it. 1977 F.B. VICKERS *Stranger no Longer* 73 'That's if all goes well, mate,' said the man who was giving me the oil.

2. With qualifying epithet: **dinkum** (or **straight**) **oil,** reliable information; an accurate report; also *fig.* (see quot. 1918); **good oil,** reliable (and therefore welcome) information.
1915 (*title*) The **Dinkum Oil** War News. 1916 R.H. ADAMS *Diary* 8 Mar., We hear dinkum oil re Turks having thrown in the sponge. 1918 N. CAMPBELL *Passing Cheer* (1919) 8 You'll give the Hun the 'dinkum oil' The Anzacs gave of old. 1923 *Bulletin* (Sydney) 21 June 24/4 Here's the straight oil for keeping ants out of safes. 1916 *Astra* (Melbourne) Sept. 2/1 The **Good Oil.** 1933 H.B. RAINE *Whip-Hand* 140 This was the good oil, too. The nice little haul of 'white stuff' proves that.

oil, *v.*[1] [Fig. use of *oil* to lubricate.] *trans.* To gratify (one's taste for alcoholic liquor). Also with **up** and freq. in *pass.*
1898 *Bulletin* (Sydney) 1 Oct. 14/3 To have a whisky is to 'oil up'. 1936 *Bulletin* (Sydney) 22 Apr. 21/1 An' you can gamble that the cove 'oo, when 'e's oiled, looks round fer fight Will, if 'e's challenged when 'e's on the wagon, damn near die of fright.

oil, *v.*[2] [f. OIL *n.* 1.] *trans.* With **up**: to provide (a person) with information.
1968 S. GORE *Holy Smoke* 106 *Oil up,* to explain; or to warn someone about something. 1968 D. O'GRADY *Bottle of Sandwiches* 30, I gotta go to Perth tomorrow for a couple o' weeks, so I'll oil you blokes up on what's what.

okiri /'ɒkəri/. [a. Yankunytjatjara dial. of Western Desert *ugiri.*] A plant of the genus *Nicotiana* (fam. Solanaceae): see *native tobacco* NATIVE *a.* 6 *a.*
1891 *Trans. & Proc. R. Soc. S.A.* (1896) XVI. 293 The blacks had gathered some native tobacco plants which they call 'okiri'. 1935 H.H. FINLAYSON *Red Centre* 85 The narcotic known variously as mingil or okiri .. a true tobacco .. which grow[s] luxuriantly at the foot of the ranges.

okker, var. OCKER.

old, *n. N.S.W.* [Abbrev. of *old beer.*] An ale, so-called because made by top fermentation in the traditional manner. See NEW *n.*
1935 *First Hundred Yrs.* (Tooth & Co. Ltd.) 71 We make our way across a wide platform on which barrels full of 'Old' and 'New' are being assembled in readiness for despatch. 1976 B. HOWARD-SMITH *Adult Gift Bk. Poetry* 20 I'll have a middie of new An old and a squash.

old, *a.*

1. Used in collocations denoting the British Isles, esp. England: **old country** [also U.S.: see OED(S *a.* 12 b.]; **Dart** [dial. pronunc. of *dirt;* see also DART and cf. *(old) sod* (OED(S *sb.*[1] 4 b.)]; **land.**
1834 G. BENNETT *Wanderings N.S.W.* I. 142 The barndoors about the farms (in imitation of a similar custom in the '**old country**') were decorated by the brushes and tails of that shepherds' pest, the Dingo. 1892 *Quiz* (Adelaide) 18 Nov. 7/2 He was from England. . . He is one of the sort who return to the **old dart** and say that fruit-growing here is a failure. 1891 E. HULME *Settler's 35 Yrs. Experience Vic.* 1 When living in the '**Old Land**' . . I belonged to a class of which there are many thousands.

2. *Obs.* In miscellaneous collocations: **old chum,** OLD HAND; also *attrib.;* **colonist,** see COLONIST 3; **colony,** New South Wales; **settler,** see SETTLER 3; **squatter,** a long-established, substantial land owner (see SQUATTER 2 and 3); **thing,** see quots.
1832 *Sydney Monitor* 25 July 2/5 A gold mine, which a fellow-servant, an **old chum,** had gulled him with the belief was in existence. 1859 W. KELLY *Life in Vic.* I. 34, I should be afraid to repeat the valuation put upon these properties .. by my old chum friend. 1853 S. SIDNEY *Three Colonies* (ed. 2) 91 The remoteness of Swan River from the **old colony** rendered importations of any kind difficult, expensive, and uncertain. 1849 S. & J. SIDNEY *Emigrant's Jrnl.* 4 Let him buy no land, but go up the country two or three hundred miles, and settle on one of the rivers with some **old squatter.** 1848 H.W. HAYGARTH *Recoll. Bush Life* 6 The traveller's entertainment is confined to the '**old thing**' as it is contemptuously called, that is to say, beef and 'damper'. 1945 S.J. BAKER *Austral. Lang.* 80 It was what W.W. Dobie called the *muttonous* diet of the outback that produced the expression *the Old Thing* for a meal of mutton and damper.

old fellow. The penis. Also **old boy.**
1968 B. HUMPHRIES *Wonderful World Barry McKenzie,* All that ice cold Fosters has gone straight to the old feller. Am I bustin' for a nice long snakes! 1982 *Bulletin* (Sydney) 9 Mar. 96/1 I'll never forget the look on guests' faces in a Manchester hotel one night, when they arrived back to find a well-known Australian player draped on a chaise-longue in the public lounge, having what is commonly referred to as his 'old boy' autographed by a member of the opposite sex.

old hand.

1. *Hist.* A convict with long experience of life in a penal colony (as opposed to one newly arrived); an ex-convict.
1826 *Colonial Times* (Hobart) 14 Jan., We want a Governor-in-Chief, No dummies to afford relief, No subjects for a Lawyer's brief, And 'old hands' in the Council! 1897 *Bulletin* (Sydney) 28 Aug. 21/1 Yet another of the 'old hands' who connect the convict-days with the present, has gone. Solomon Blay, ex-convict and ex-public executioner, died last week at Hobart.

2. *Hist.* An immigrant with some experience of life in Australia (as opposed to one newly arrived).
1839 W. MANN *Six Yrs.' Residence* 163 Combinations are .. entered into by what are termed the old hands who are long established in the colony. 1870 *Sydney Morning Herald* 1 July 5/2 Those gentlemen of extensive colonial experience, who are popularly known as 'old hands'.

3. One who has had long experience of an activity, occupation, or place.
1846 N.L. KENTISH *Work in Bush Van Diemen's Land* 12 The 'old hands' on the north and western side of the island. 1945 E. GEORGE *Two at Daly Waters* 32 Mrs Cranston .. was an old hand at Territory housekeeping. 1964 *Bulletin* (Sydney) 8 Feb. 13/1 The real 'old hands', the early originals, will tell you that Palm Beach has been spoilt.

Hence **old-handish** *a.*, **old-handism** *n.*

OLD MAN

1873 W. Thomson-Gregg *Desperate Character* II. 57, I never saw a more **old-handish** looking customer since I've been in the colony. **1859** F. Fowler *Southern Lights & Shadows* 15 The battle of '**old-handism**' against 'new-chumism' is not everlasting waging in Victoria as it is New South Wales, where the natives are more intolerant and intolerable than the Bowery boys of America.

old man, *n.* and *attrib.*

A. *n.*

1. A fully grown male kangaroo, esp. the *grey kangaroo* (a) (see Grey *a.*). Also **old man kangaroo, 'roo.**

1827 P. Cunningham *Two Yrs. in N.S.W.* II. 160 One of our backwoodsmen .. relates .. that he has been fortunate enough to kill *an old man*.. The 'old man' turns out to possess the appendage of *a tail*, and is in fact no other than one of our acquaintances, the kangaroos! **1843** *Portland Mercury* 23 Aug. 4/2 Betts replied that he wanted to kill some old men kangaroo. **1935** F. Birtles *Battle Fronts Outback* 159 A big old man 'roo rose from his noon-day camp.

2. An Aboriginal elder (see also quot. 1854).

1848 T.L. Mitchell *Jrnl. Exped. Tropical Aust.* 269 Each of them carried .. three or four missile clubs. . . They said, by signs, that the whole country belonged to the old man. **1854** W. Howitt *Boy's Adventures* 306 The Old Man, as they call Pungil their god, not unlike the Hebrew term, Ancient of Days, now held out his hand to 'Gerer', the sun, and made him warm.

3. In the collocation **old man's beard,** any of several climbing plants of the genus *Clematis* (fam. Ranunculaceae), esp. *C. aristata*.

1914 E.E. Pescott *Native Flowers Vic.* 101 We are familiar with the Clematis or 'old man's beard', with white starry flowers.

B. 1. *attrib.* passing into *adj.* Of exceptional size, duration, intensity, etc.

1845 R. Howitt *Impressions Aust. Felix* 233, I stared at a man one day for saying that a certain allotment of land was 'an old-man allotment': he meant a large allotment—the old-man kangaroo being the largest kangaroo. **1968** D. O'Grady *Bottle of Sandwiches* 201 Between a large submerged log and an old-man willow.

2. Comb. **old man cod, crocodile, drought, fern, flood, goanna, possum, wombat.**

1902 *Bulletin* (Sydney) 22 Mar. 14/2 *Re* cod fish. . . In '95 one was caught in the Burdekin .. the *head and shoulders* thereof weighing 87 lbs. This **'old man' cod** smelt as rank as a W.A. boom prospectus. **1929** H. MacQuarrie *We & Baby* 26 A great **'old man' crocodile** emerged. **1904** *Truth* (Sydney) 25 Sept. 1/6 In many parts of the interior the **'old man' drought** never broke. **1879** 'Recent Settler' *Emigration to Tas.* 51 One of the most remarkable features of Myrtle Bank is the immense number of tree ferns, commonly called **'old men ferns'**, the stems of which are often from ten to twenty feet high. **1916** T. Warlow *By Mirage & Mulga* 51 At last it rained, and the blacks predicted an **old-man flood**. **1947** *Bulletin* (Sydney) 23 July 28/1 There was an old-man flood on the river. **1900** *Ibid.* 7 July 15/2 Found an **old-man-goanna** with nearly half the arm down his throat. **1847** A. Harris *Settlers & Convicts* (1953) 17 In one place we saw a very large opossum (in the language of the country an **old man 'possum**). **1909** *Bulletin* (Sydney) 21 Jan. 14/1, I was hailed by an **old-man wombat** who was much the worse for wear. . . His wombatess was not at home at the time.

3. Special Comb. **old man saltbush,** either of two shrubs of the fam. Chenopodiaceae, *Atriplex nummularia* (also Cabbage saltbush) of arid and semi-arid Aust., having grey-green foliage used as fodder, and (occas.) *Rhagodia parabolica* of central and e. Aust.; formerly also **old man's saltbush; snapper,** a large Snapper (see quots. 1965 and 1974); also **old man schnapper; spinifex** *obs.*, Buck spinifex.

1885 P.R. Meggy *From Sydney to Silverton* 13 The plains on either side are fairly covered with this not very pleasant-tasting bush—common salt bush, **old man's salt-bush** [etc.]. **1984** *West Austral.* (Perth) 10 Dec. 58/2 Plants such as 'old man' saltbush are preferred hosts for the young [sandalwood] plants. **1882** J.E. Tenison-Woods *Fish & Fisheries N.S.W.* (*caption*), An **'old man schnapper'**. **1965** *Austral. Encycl.* VIII. 169 Full-grown specimens develop a large bony protuberance on the nape, and a peculiar flabby and fleshy nose, which produces a somewhat human appearance and has earned for them the name of old-man snapper. **1974** J.M. Thomson *Fish Ocean & Shore* 126 A squire becomes a snapper at about one and a half kilos and thereafter matures to the old man snapper stage which may reach eighteen kilos. **1882** *Illustr. Austral. News* (Melbourne) 25 Jan. 10/3 After travelling some miles through **'old man' spinifex**, it is almost impossible to force horses along.

old people. Aborigines who live in the traditional manner; Aborigines of an earlier generation, regarded by their descendants as repositories of traditional knowledge.

1938 X. Herbert *Capricornia* (ed. 6) 324 Let's consider the Old People for a jiffy. . . They're starved and sickened and kicked and stupefied and generally jiggered out of all recognition. **1983** *Bulletin* (Sydney) 1 Nov. 80/2 The 'Old People' (as the part-Aborigines called their full-blood progenitors).

old wife. [Spec. use of *old wife* any of various fish of several families.] Formerly any of several marine fish, now usu. *Enoplosus armatus* of s. Aust., a silvery fish with black vertical stripes. See also *zebra fish* Zebra.

1699 W. Dampier *New Voyage round World* (1703) III. 140 In the night while Calm we fish'd with Hook and Line, and caught good store of Fish, *viz* Snappers, Breams, Old Wives, and Dog-Fish. **1983** Hutchins & Thompson *Marine & Estuarine Fishes S.-W. Aust.* 44 Old Wife .. named after its habit of 'grunting like an old wife' when caught. Dorsal fin spines reputed to be venomous.

olive, *a.* Used as a distinguishing epithet in the names of birds: **olive-backed oriole,** the bird *Oriolus sagittatus* of n., e., and s.e. mainland Aust., and s.e. New Guinea, having olive to grey upper parts; **whistler,** the bird *Pachycephala olivacea* of s.e. Aust. incl. Tas., having olive-brown upper parts; formerly also **olive thickhead.**

1945 [**olive-backed oriole**] C. Barrett *Austral. Bird Life* 137 The yellow oriole .. is restricted to tropical Northern Australia. The olive-backed species (*O. sagittatus*) has a much wider range—Northern, Eastern, and Southern Australia. **1956** A.C.C. Lock *Tropical Tapestry* 281 The olive-backed orioles were named cedar birds. **1903** [**olive whistler**] *Emu* II. 207 *Pachycephala olivacea* (olive thickhead)—this large Thickhead with beautiful aesthetic markings. **1911** J.A. Leach *Austral. Bird Bk.* 152 Olive Whistler, Olivaceous Thickhead .. olive brown; head dark-gray .. liquid, whistling note.

ominny, ominy, varr. Hominy.

on, *prep.*

1. [Chiefly Austral.: see OED(S *prep.* 26 b. and quot. 1883.] Denoting 'place where': at; in.

1853 *Bendigo Advertiser* 9 Dec. 1/1 We have .. endeavoured to procure suitable materials for publishing a Newspaper on Bendigo, to be devoted Exclusively to the Mining Interests. **1883** R.E.N. Twopeny *Town Life Aust.* 245 When speaking of a goldfield a colonists says 'on'. Thus you live 'on Bendigo', but 'in' or 'at' Sandhurst—the latter being the name for the old goldfield town. **1976** C.D. Mills *Hobble Chains & Greenhide* 162 On dinner camp I saw this dusky imp Pluto approaching Ned with a 'frilly'.

2. In phr.: **on gold,** see Gold 1; **on opal,** see Opal 2.

3. [See OED(S *prep.* 1 l.] In the phr. **on it,** drinking (alcoholic liquor) heavily.

1908 *Truth* (Sydney) 19 July 1/7 People who have in the dim religious light of the previous evening, been 'on it', next morning are fined 'five shillings'. **1978** D. STUART *Wedgetail View* 69 Y' know he got on it once in a while.

4. [See OED(S *prep.* 6 b. and 26 b.] In the phr. **on (the) weekend(s),** at or during (the) weekend(s).

1958 R. ROBINSON *Black-Feller White-Feller* 3 Jack, as usual on week-ends, was drunk. **1985** *Good Weekend* (Sydney) 25 Aug. 19/2 More urgent .. is a review of the food retailing outlets that appear on the weekends.

on, *adv.* [Br. slang *on* on the way to intoxication: see OED *adv.* 10 c.]

1. Under the influence of alcohol.

1871 *Austral. Town & Country Jrnl.* (Sydney) 18 Feb. 20/1 Perks, poor fellow, was well—yes, a trifle 'on'. **1970** K.E.C. GRAVES *Third Chance* 27, I won't serve anyone who's getting a bit on.

2. **a.** In the phr. **on with,** amorously involved with.

1903 *Truth* (Sydney) 8 Mar. 3/5 Thousands of grande dames will be only too anxious to be 'on with' the man who could win the .. love of a Crown Princess. **1972** *Southerly* iv. 281 Soon after she was on with David Murray, Nina arranged a dinner party.

b. In the phr. **on for,** amorously interested in.

1907 *Truth* (Sydney) 6 Jan. 9/2 You're on for the donah up there. **1936** N. LINDSAY *Saturdee* (ed. 2) 181 'Conkey Mender! Is he on for Trix?' 'He's on any day.'

3. In the phr. **it is (was,** etc.) **on (for young and old):** a description of a battle, party, argument, etc., characterized by the participants' lack of inhibition or restraint.

1945 'MASTER-SARG' *Yank discovers Aust.* 17 'Its on' means that a battle or something else has started. **1951** E. LAMBERT *Twenty Thousand Thieves* (1952) 258 Peter Dimmock bounded between the tents leaping into the air at every few paces and whooping: 'It's on! It's on for young and old!' **1971** D. MARTIN *Hughie* (1972) 106 He almost forgot about it until the evening of Sunday when the party was due and when, in Harry's words, it was on for young and old.

oncer. [Spec. use of *oncer* one who does a particular thing only once.] A person elected as a member of parliament (esp. in a marginal seat), who is considered unlikely to hold the seat for more than one term.

1974 BLAZEY & CAMPBELL *Political Dice Men* 47 When he got to Canberra, with all the other new Liberal members, he found he was treated with sympathy because everyone regarded him as a 'oncer'. **1983** *Austral.* (Sydney) 4 Feb. 11/4 However, it soon became apparent that Mr Hayden was something more than one of those political irrelevancies, the 'oncer'—the bolter who wins a seat for one term, which he spends gazing wide-eyed at the activities around him before returning to obscurity.

one, *a.*

1. [Cf. *one too many, etc.* OED(S 1 d.] With ellipsis of *glass* or *drink,* not always with the implication 'sole'. Also in the phr. **one for the bitumen,** 'one for the road'.

1945 *Aust. Week-end Bk.* 164 'What the hell are you two doing here, eh? Have one with me!' Presently Bill says, 'You'd better have one with me now. . . ' and a little while later Jack says, 'This one's mine.' **1977** B. SCOTT *My Uncle Arch* 108 Two hours later it's have one for the bitumen.

2. In the phr. **one day of the year,** ANZAC DAY. Also *transf.*

1962 A. SEYMOUR (*title*) The One Day of the Year. **1971** F. HARDY *Outcasts of Foolgarah* 211 A retired officer of high rank .. out late celebrating the One Day of the Year. **1985** *Centralian Advocate* (Alice Springs) 6 Sept. 2/2 Aborigines throughout Australia are gearing up to celebrate their 'one day of the year' next week. National Aborigines' Week .. will culminate in a march and speeches on National Aborigines' Day on Friday.

3. In collocations: **one flag (only),** the signal for a BEHIND 1 b.; **-pub** *a.* (of a settlement), small, uninteresting, 'one-horse'; **-teacher school,** see quot. 1973.

1968 EAGLESON & MCKIE *Terminol. Austral. Football* ii. 26 *One flag* [*only*], a behind (a goal is signalled by two flags, a behind by one). **1901** H. LAWSON *Joe Wilson & his Mates* 54 Along the bush roads and tracks that branch out fanlike through the scrubs to the **one-pub** towns and sheep and cattle stations out there in the haunting wilderness. **1931** B. CRONIN *Bracken* 90 Guruwa's only a **one-teacher school** as they call it. **1973** W.G. WALKER *Gloss. Educ. Terms* 84 *One-teacher-school,* a school usually in an isolated area, in which one teacher teaches all grades.

ones, *pl. Two-up.* A call indicating that one coin has landed with the head facing upwards and one with the tail facing upwards. In full, **two ones.**

1911 L. STONE *Jonah* 217 He set two pounds of his winnings, and tossed the coins. 'Two ones!' cried the gamblers, with a roar. **1979** *Bulletin* (Sydney) 14 Aug. 36/3 If one head and one tail showed, then it was 'ones', meaning that the spinner must continue spinning until two sides showed together.

Hence **one** *v. trans.,* to throw (the coins) so that they land showing a head and a tail.

1949 L. GLASSOP *Lucky Palmer* 168 The pennies hit the canvas. One jumped in the air, landed and lay flat. It was a tail. 'And he's—' began the fat man. The other penny ran a few feet and stopped. It was a head. '—one'd 'em!' finished the fat man.

onion.

1. Used *attrib.* in the names of plants: **onion-grass,** any of several species of the introduced genus *Romulea* (fam. Liliaceae), incl. GUILDFORD GRASS; **orchid,** any species of the chiefly Austral. genus of terrestrial orchids *Microtis* (fam. Orchidaceae), having a single, onion-like leaf and flower-spike of small, usu. green flowers; **weed, (a)** the naturalized perennial herb *Asphodelus fistulosus* (fam. Liliaceae), common on disturbed land and along roadsides; **(b)** the S. American perennial *Nothoscordum inodorum* (fam. Liliaceae), having leaves which smell of onions when crushed; **(c)** any of several other similar herbs, esp. of the widespread genus *Bulbine* (fam. Liliaceae); *wild onion,* see WILD 1.

1909 J.M. BLACK *Naturalised Flora S.A.* 147 [*R. Bulbocodium*] .. **Onion-grass** in Victoria. **1961** *Meanjin* 6 Cucumber, potato and even **onion orchids.** **1909** A.J. EWART *Weeds Vic.* 60 *Asphodelus fistulosus.* . . This plant, known locally as the **Onion Weed,** is a native of Southern Europe. **1935** T. RAYMENT *Cluster of Bees* 264 The tiny pink funnel-flowers of the onion weed. **1977** J. GALBRAITH *Wild Flowers S.-E. Aust.* 37 Onion Weed .. with greyish onion-like leaves and small bell-flowers that turn miles of the drier sandy country into a lilac-brown sea.

2. *fig.* An occasion upon which a number of males have intercourse one after another with the same female; the female.

1969 *Sydney Morning Herald* 16 July 13/4 When he had passed the circle of men, he knew an 'onion was going on'. . . The court was told on Monday that the expression 'onion' meant a girl was available for sexual intercourse with two or more men. **1976** *Southerly* ii. 136, I would like to win his confidence so that he would admit me to their brotherhood and to rites that I could write about, the inside story of onions, gang-bangs, pack rapes. **1978** *Weekend Austral.* (Sydney) 1 July 3/8 Woodhouse told the man the girl was to be the 'onion' for the night. . . He understood that an 'onion' in bikie jargon meant a girl having repeated intercourse.

onka: see ONKAPARINGA 2.

onkaparinga /ɒŋkəpə'rɪŋgə/. Also **onkaparinka**.
1. With initial capital. The proprietary name of a blanket; such a blanket.
1926 *Austral. Official Jrnl. Patents* (Canberra) 336 *Onkaparinga* 41,194. Cloths and stuffs of wool, worsted and hair. *South Australian Woollen Co. Ltd.* **1968** *Coast to Coast 1967-68* 121 Bodies were carried out of the crumpled cars, and she remembered a past occasion when she had run with blankets, and Hazel's Onkaparinka, and a pillow from their own beds.
2. Rhyming slang for 'finger'. Also abbrev. as **onka**.
1967 *Truth* (Sydney) xxxviii. 10/1 *Onkaparingas*, fingers. **1974** *Bulletin* (Sydney) 2 Nov. 57/3 When one gets around to plighting one's troth to a charlie, one claps a frank on her onka .. a Frank Thring on her Onkaparinga .. a ring on her .. aaar, work it out for yourself.

onkus, *a.* [Of unknown origin.] Disagreeable; distasteful; disordered.
1918 G.C. COOPER *Diary* 17 Nov., Felt pretty 'onkus' in consequence of fall I had on deck the previous night. **1962** D. McLEAN *World turned upside Down* 121 All this yabber about Danny is onkus.

oooah, var. YOHI.

Oodnagalahbi /udnəgə'labi/. Also **Oodnagalabie**. [f. *Oodna(datta* the name of a town in n. S.A. + GALAH + -*bi*.] An imaginary place, remote and supposedly backward. See also BULLAMAKANKA, WOOP WOOP 1.
1968 *Kings Cross Whisper* (Sydney) xlviii. 9/3 Secretary of the Oodnagalabie branch of the United Pastoralists Union .. said yesterday politicians had reached plague proportions in many areas of Australia. **1969** *Sydney Morning Herald* 1 Dec. 6/4 Last night the show was firmly bogged down in Oodnagalahbi (may it be eaten by grasshoppers) and Dad and Dave and Mabel wore felt hats pulled down on their foreheads and cracked jokes about carpet snakes in the dunny.

oont /ʊnt/. [a. Hindi (and Urdu) ūṇṭ camel; also in Indian English: see OEDS.] A camel. Also *attrib*.
1918 *Barrack: Official Organ Imperial Camel Corps* 1 Feb. 9/2 *The laws of the oont*. Now these are the Laws of the Camel. **1957** *Bulletin* (Sydney) 16 Oct. 19/1 Any Moslem oont-driver knows that the bull-camel is frustrated and resentful of humans.

ooroo, var. HOOROO.

oowa, var. YOHI.

opal.
1. Used *attrib.* in Special Comb. **opal dirt,** the type of earth in which opal occurs; **-gouger,** an opal-miner (see also GOUGER); so, **-gouging** *vbl. n.*
1925 *Ann. Rep.* (N.S.W. Dept. Mines) 85 The **'Opal Dirt'** is picking ground, being simply a layer of clay or sandy clay overlain by sandstone. **1904** *Bulletin* (Sydney) 17 Mar. 16/3 Came the way of a White Cliffs (N.S.W.) **opal-gouger** lately. **1965** A.W. UPFIELD *Lure of Bush* 9 He spent twenty years in the bush, working at many kinds of jobs: .. opal gouging [etc.].
2. In the phr. **to be on opal,** to have found or to be mining an opal deposit.
1878 J.H. NICHOLSON *Opal Fever* 4 I'm on opal sure as beans. **1932** I.L. IDRIESS *Prospecting for Gold* 235 A patch means, generally, hundreds of stones. You may be weeks, months, 'on opal'.

open, *a.*[1] [Spec. use of *open* unobstructed, clear: see OED *a.* 8 and, for U.S. examples, Mathews.]
1. a. Of land bearing scattered trees or stands of trees: without undergrowth or similar obstruction to movement or to use as pasture. See FOREST 1.
1829 [see *open forest land*]. **1840** *S. Austral. Rec.* (London) 27 June 351 North of the Great Bend, the brush almost wholly disappears, and the open brush spreads out into enormous plains. **1960** R.S. PORTEOUS *Cattleman* 20 The coolibah gave way to brigalow, in places open brigalow that made excellent grazing country.

b. Also **open forest country, land.**
1834 G. BENNETT *Wanderings N.S.W.* I. 163 We passed an interesting **open forest country**, possessing some good land for cultivation, and abundance of fine herbage. **1829** *Hints Emigration New Settlement Swan & Canning Rivers* 41 Mr Frazer did not rate the trees upon an average of more than two to an acre, but *probably* he referred only to large trees or what is termed **open forest land.**

2. a. Of land: without any obstruction to movement or use; *spec.,* without (or with very few) trees.
1849 J.S. ROE *Rep. Exped. S.-Eastward Perth* 5 They soon joined a continuous river of brackish water .. flowing E. and S.W. through open scrubby plains. **1934** 'S. RUDD' *Green Grey Homestead* 131 Ahead a clump of grass trees and patches of wallaby bush obscured an open valley coated with feathery grass from view.

b. In collocations: **open downs, paddock, plain** (chiefly in *pl.*).
1848 T.L. MITCHELL *Jrnl. Exped. Tropical Aust.* 158, I travelled steadily .. over the **open downs,** but with scrubs on either side. **1929** *Bulletin* (Sydney) 31 July 19/2 A gum-tree .. grew in solitary state in an **open paddock.** **1841** G. ARDEN *Recent Information Port Phillip* 32 The spur-winged plover, with its plaintive cry, the native companion a gigantic species of crane, and the stately emu, dwell in the **open plains.**

c. In the collocation **open forest**: a tract of such land. See also FOREST 1.
1832 J. BACKHOUSE *Narr. Visit Austral. Colonies* (1843) 26 Much of the country was settled: it consisted of hills, generally covered with open grassy forest, and interspersed with little patches of cultivated ground.

open, *a.*[2] [f. OPEN *v.*[1]] Of land: available for settlement. Also in the phr. **to throw open,** to make (land) available.
1830 [see OPEN *v.*[1] 1]. **1855** *Ovens & Murray Advertiser* (Beechworth) 24 Feb. (Suppl.) 5/3 The Government has at length seen the necessity for throwing open the lands in the vicinity of the gold fields for farming and agricultural purposes. **1886** P. FLETCHER 'Hints to Immigrants' in P. Fletcher *Qld.* 8 All Queensland is not open for anyone to go and pick out a piece of land, but from time to time large districts are proclaimed open, and you can take up your block anywhere in those districts.

open, *v.*[1] *Hist.* [Spec. use of *open* to render accessible or available for settlement: see OED *v.* 12.]
1. a. *trans.* To release (Crown land) for settlement. Also with **up.**
1793 D. COLLINS *Acct. Eng. Colony N.S.W.* (1798) I. 266 The lieutenant-governor proposing to open and cultivate the ground commonly known by the name of the Kangaroo Ground. **1900** *Bulletin* (Sydney) 1 Dec. 15/1 Newly 'opened-up' farming district, consequently great preponderance of men.

b. *trans.* To occupy (such land) as a settler.
1794 D. COLLINS *Acct. Eng. Colony N.S.W.* (1798) I. 340 Williams and Ruse .. were permitted .. to open ground on the banks of the Hawkesbury... They chose for themselves allotments of grounds conveniently situated for fresh water. **1940** G. MORPHETT *Simple Story Rural Dev.* 4

Great-hearted folk, the people who opened up our country lands!

2. *intr.* To become settled.

1794 D. COLLINS *Acct. Eng. Colony N.S.W.* (1798) I. 375 A country gradually opening, and improving every where upon us as it opened.

open, $v.^2$ [Spec. use of *open* to cut or break into.]

1. *Mining. trans.* To break (the surface of the earth) preparatory to a mining operation. Also with **up**.

1845 *S. Austral. Register* (Adelaide) 11 Oct. 2/2 The face of the hill . . had been opened in three separate places. **1869** *Wallaroo Times* (Kadina) 4 Sept. 5/2 Levels driven and the ground opened up.

2. *Shearing. trans.* To begin the removal of (the fleece) from a sheep. Usu. with **up**.

1882 ARMSTRONG & CAMPBELL *Austral. Sheep Husbandry* 167 The fleece should be opened up the neck, commencing at the brisket. **1914** H.B. SMITH *Sheep & Wool Industry* 37 The machine is then driven up the front of the neck several times till the neck wool is well opened.

open call. An informal Stock Exchange: see quot. 1898. Also **open call Stock Exchange**.

1896 J.M. PRICE *Land of Gold* 74 One of the principal features of Coolgardie, and one which struck me as being quite unique, was the evening 'open call' Stock Exchange. **1898** R. RADCLYFFE *Wealth & Wild Cats* 39 'Open calls' . . are curious. At night, about eight o'clock, all the miners and gamblers stroll into one of the tin-roofed halls. . . Presently a Jewish gentleman comes in and takes the chair. 'We will call the list,' says he, and with stentorian voice shouts, 'Adelaide Queens—who sells?' . . It is a rough-and-ready Stock Exchange, and thousands of shares change hands.

open go: see Go $n.^1$ 3.

open slather: see SLATHER.

opossum, *n.* [Transf. use of *opossum* an arboreal marsupial; now largely superseded by POSSUM.]

1. POSSUM 1.

1770 J. BANKS *Jrnl.* 26 July (1896) 291 While botanising to-day I had the good fortune to take an animal of the opossum (*Didelphis*) tribe. **1973** R.J. DOOLIN *Boy from Bush* 15 The dogs had an o'possum up a tree.

2. Comb.

a. **opossum belt, cloak, fur, hair, rug, skin, yarn**.

1830 R. DAWSON *Present State Aust.* 226 He stuck one end of it in his **opossum belt**. **1832** J. HENDERSON *Observations Colonies N.S.W. & Van Diemen's Land* p. xiii, We had carried . . our **oppossum cloaks**. **1833** *Perth Gaz.* 7 Sept. 143 Mr Armstrong has shown us some **oposum** [*sic*] **fur**, worked up into a ball, similar to a ball of worsted, and equally fine. A stocking of this fur is nearly finished. **1844** *Swan River News* 1 June 40/1 Their sole clothing is a kangaroo skin . . and a girdle round the loins, woven from **opossum hair**. **1841** *Port Phillip Patriot* 11 Nov. 2/1 Thomas Arbuthnot, ship, for Calcutta . . 1 parcel (**oppossum rug**). **1820** J. OXLEY *Jrnls. Two Exped. N.S.W.* 19 They were covered with cloaks made of **opossum skins**. **1830** R. DAWSON *Present State Aust.* 115 His long hair was turned up and bound about the head with **opossum yarn**.

b. **opossum hunt, hunter, -hunting, -shooting**.

1837 *Perth Gaz.* 18 Mar. 869 We enjoyed a capital **opossum hunt**. **1855** W. HOWITT *Land, Labor & Gold* I. 214 Prim . . is a famous **opossum hunter**, following them often, where a tree slants, right up it. **1840** *S. Austral. Rec.* (London) 24 Oct. 269 At **opossum-hunting**, they observe the marks of the animal's claws on the trunks of trees before they get close up to them. **1845** *Star* (Parramatta) 18 Jan. 2/1 He was . . staying away all night **opossum shooting**.

3. Special Comb. **opossum hyena,** HYENA; **mouse,** *pygmy possum,* see PYGMY.

1824 J. LYCETT *Views in Aust.* 12 The kangaroo, the emu . . and the **opossum-hyena**, are all natives of Van Diemen's Land. **1832** H. MARTINEAU *Homes Abroad* 112 Susan is taming an **opossum mouse**.

opossum, *v. intr.* To hunt possums. Also as *vbl. n.*

1847 *Atlas* (Sydney) III. 93/2 The Worrigals went out 'oppossuming'. **1917** 'H.H. RICHARDSON' *Fortunes of Richard Mahony* 211 There is to be opossuming and a moon-light picnic to-night.

opportunity shop. A shop run by a charitable organization in which donated second-hand goods, esp. clothes, are sold.

1961 B. HUMPHRIES *Nice Night's Entertainment* (1981) 52 It ruined the lining of a lovely raffia bag that Beryl had bought at the opportunity shop. **1978** J. COLBERT *Ranch* 35 Keep it up and people will think I get my clothes from the opportunity shop.

op shop. Also **opp shop.** Shortening of OPPORTUNITY SHOP. Also *ellipt.* for 'op shop clothes'.

1978 P. WOOLLEY *Art of living Together* 91 Be sure to donate your old clothes and old furniture to the opp shop in your neighbourhood. **1979** H. WELLER *Lip Service* 86 Likes toffee apples, live theatre and people who wear Op Shop when Fiurucci [*sic*] would do. **1985** *Austral. Women's Weekly* (Sydney) Jan. 160 Why do I have to have new clothes, there are a lot of much nicer things in the Op shop.

orange, *a.* Used as a distinguishing epithet in the names of animals and birds: **orange-bellied parrot,** the rare, chiefly coastal parrot *Neophema chrysogaster* of w. Tas., s. Vic., and s.e. S.A.; also **orange-breasted parrot,** and formerly **orange-bellied grass-parakeet; chat,** the nomadic bird *Epthianura aurifrons* of arid inland Aust., the mature male having an orange-yellow head and underparts; also **orange-fronted chat; horseshoe bat,** the bat of tropical n. Aust. *Rhinonicteris aurantius;* -**speckled hawk** *obs.,* brown hawk, see BROWN *a.* 1; -**winged sittella,** the s.e. Austral. form of the bird *Daphoenositta chrysoptera,* having striped plumage and an orange patch on the wing; formerly also **orange-winged nuthatch, tree-runner**.

1841 [**orange-bellied parrot**] J. GOULD *Birds of Aust.* (1848) V. Pl. 39, *Euphema aurantia* . . Orange-bellied Grass-Parrakeet. **1943** C. BARRETT *Austral. Animal Bk.* 235 Distinguished by a rich orange colour-patch on the undersurface, the orange-breasted parrot (*N* [*eophema*] *chrysogaster*) has grass-green plumage above, and is a brilliant little bird. **1969** J.M. FORSHAW *Austral. Parrots* 261 Orange-bellied Parrots are generally seen singly, in pairs, or in small flocks. . . When alarmed they emit a '*chitter-chitter*', repeated so rapidly as to produce an overall 'buzzing' effect. This strange call is a valuable aid to identification. [**1842 orange chat:** J. GOULD *Birds of Aust.* (1848) III. Pl. 65, *Epthianura aurifrons* . . Orange-fronted Epthianura.] **1916** S.A. WHITE *In Far Northwest* 124 The pretty little orange-fronted chats . . were also plentiful. **1984** M. BLAKERS et al. *Atlas Austral. Birds* 570 The Orange Chat lives in acacia scrub, spinifex, tussock grassland and salt-bush, specially round salt lakes. **1926** A.S. LE SOUEF et al. *Wild Animals Australasia* 53 **Orange horseshoe bat.** *Rhinonycteris aurantia* . . North and North-west Australia, especially abundant in the Coburg Peninsula. **1827** *Trans. Linnean Soc. London* XV. 185 It is called by the settlers **Orange-speckled Hawk. 1801** [**orange-winged sittella**] J. LATHAM *Gen. Synopsis Birds* Suppl. II. 146 Orange-winged N[uthatch] . . inhabits New Holland. **1844** J. GOULD *Birds of Aust.* (1848) IV. Pl. 101, *Sittella chrysoptera* . . Orange-winged Sittella. **1903** *Emu* II. 165 Orange-winged Tree-Runner . . in the Otway.

orchardist. [App. in more freq. use in Aust. and N.Z. than elsewhere.] A commercial fruit-grower.
1887 *Illustr. Austral. News* (Melbourne) 23 July 126/2 Orchardists also have reason to rejoice, as their trees have been watered to the very lowest roots. **1986** *Canberra Times* 15 Mar. 7/3 Jeff Ashmann, part-time teacher and orchardist, Moruya.

order. *Hist.* [Spec. use of *order* an instruction.]
1. Abbrev. of *land order* (see LAND 1).
1836 A. BARCLAY *Life* (1854) 7 Governor Macquarie gave me an order for a grant of 500 acres there, and also for a [*sic*] allotment of building-ground in the town of Launceston. **1855** H. HUME *Brief Statement* 13 An order to select 1,200 acres of land was given me; that order, however, I was under the necessity of selling.
2. A written direction to a third party to discharge a financial obligation: see quots. 1848 and 1977. Also *attrib.*
1848 H.W. HAYGARTH *Recoll. Bush Life* 86 The 'order' system, which has long been adopted in the interior of the colony, being found desirable as a substitute for payment in cash. It is usual for proprietors of stations 'up the country' to keep an account current with a Sydney merchant or agent, from whom they also purchase their annual supplies, and, when discharging any debt in the interior, they simply draw an 'order' upon him for the amount. **1977** T. RONAN *Mighty Men on Horseback* 83 The 'order on Monger & Co.'. I would say that this would have been an order, engraved, or perhaps printed, on heavy parchment much thicker and less durable than what is used for banknotes; it would have been an order on Monger & Co.'s bankers and it would have been signed in ink by the head of the establishment.

ordnance tree. *Obs.* [See quot. 1855.] KURRAJONG 1.
1855 R. AUSTIN *Jrnl. Interior W.A.* 27 The tree resembling the fig tree .. and which we called the Ordnance Tree, as the leaf was formed like a broad arrow. **1893** D. LINDSAY *Jrnl. Elder Sci. Exploring Exped.* 38 Numerous kurrajong or ordnance trees.

organ bird. [See quot. 1847.] Either of two birds of the fam. Cracticidae having a melodious song, the *pied butcherbird* (see PIED), and *Gymnorhina tibicen* (see MAGPIE *n.* 1 a.). Also **organ magpie.**
1847 J. GOULD *Birds of Aust.* (1848) II. Pl. 48, When perched on the dead branches of the trees soon after daybreak, it pours forth a succession of notes of the strongest description that can be imagined, much resembling the sounds of a hand-organ out of tune, which has obtained for it the colonial name of the Organ-Bird. **1852** G.C. MUNDY *Our Antipodes* II. 287 The organ-magpie, pied crow, or barita, is somewhat larger than the English magpie, with a tail as much shorter as his voice is sweeter.

organ-grinder. [See quot. 1930.] Any of many lizards of the fam. Agamidae having a characteristic waving movement of a forelimb, as members of the genera *Diporiphora* and *Lophognathus*. Also **organ-grinder lizard.**
1930 J.S. LITCHFIELD *Far-North Memories* 172 Organ-grinder—Small lizard, with a long, whip-like tail. Has a habit of sitting erect, and 'grinding the organ' with a paw. **1980** N. WATKINS *Kangaroo Connection* 103 An organ-grinder lizard .. paused, stood up on its hind legs, waving its forelegs in a circular motion, as if turning a handle of an old fashioned organ.

oriental pratincole. [f. *oriental*, first applied by English naturalist William Leach in 1820 (*Trans. Linnean Soc. London* (1822) XIII. 132) as the specific epithet *orientalis* eastern or Asian.] The bird *Glareola maldivarum*, breeding in Asia and migrating to n. Aust. in summer, having brownish-grey to olive plumage with a black throat band.
1824 J. LATHAM *Gen. Hist. Birds* IX. 365 *Oriental pratincole*... In this the bill is black; gape yellow; plumage above brownish ash-colour, beneath white... Inhabits Java, and called Tre; brought by M. Leschenault. **1984** M. BLAKERS et al. *Atlas Austral. Birds* 189 The Oriental Pratincole feeds on insects, many taken on the wing.

original, *a. Hist.*
1. ABORIGINAL *a.* 1.
1840 S. Austral. *Miscellany* Mar. 117 This poor fellow, who was the last of the original lords of the soil known to be left at liberty in his native land, died at Pitwater. **1883** *Bulletin* (Sydney) 7 July 6/3 Near Braidwood are five of the original proprietors of the soil of N.S.W. They have their ancient jins with them.
2. Of a colonist: first, earliest.
1839 *Sydney Standard* 7 Jan. 2/4 The increasing wealth of the original settlers. **1891** 'ROUSEABOUT' *Jackeroo* 43 Mr Sharp, the owner of Bulletta Station .. was the original holder, or, to speak more plainly .. he was the first and only man who had ever leased the station from the Crown.
3. Of a soldier: belonging to the first Australian contingent to serve in the war of 1914–18. Also as *n.*
1919 C.H. THORP *Handful of Ausseys* 161 Whether he is of an 'original' battalion or a reinforcement company. **1941** *Bulletin* (Sydney) 15 Jan. 16/3 My mate, Kelly, never previously out of Melbourne, got away with the originals in 1914.

ornithorhynchus /ɔnəθəˈrɪŋkəs/. Formerly also with unsettled variety. [The animal genus *Ornithorhynchus* (orig. *Platypus*) was named in 1800 by German anatomist J.F. Blumenbach (*Götting. gel. Anz.* 1 609) f. Gr. ὀρνιθο- comb. form of ὄρνις bird + ῥύγκος bill, referring to the duck-like bill of the animal.] PLATYPUS.
1800 *Philos. Trans. R. Soc. London* XC. 432 My opportunities of examining the *Ornithorhynchus* were procured through Sir Joseph Banks. **1944** C. BARRETT *Platypus* 11 The Platypus was the greatest zoological puzzle that the learned men of Europe had ever tried to solve. Solve it they did at last—almost a century after the first specimen of Ornithorhynchus reached England.

Orstralia /ɔˈstreɪljə, ɔˈstraɪljə/. Also **Orstralier.** A representation for comic effect of an exaggerated pronunciation of 'Australia'.
1918 N. CAMPBELL *Dinky-Di Soldier* 29 All the bush in wide Orstralia can't compare with Shepherd's Bush! **1955** STEWART & KEESING *Austral. Bush Ballads* 252 Lord, I don't know wot Orstralier is comin' to.
Hence **Orstrylian, Ostrylian,** etc., *n.* and *a.*
1948 J. FAIRFAX *Run o' Waters* 44 That famous cabbage-tree hat .. led to the old cockney jibe 'That's an Orsetrillian,' 'e's got on a cabbage-tree 'at'. **1956** S. HOPE *Diggers' Paradise* 121 Why don't you get someone to learn you how to speak Ostrylian? **1965** G. MCINNES *Road to Gundagai* 30 Corcoran lacked the more outrageous diphthongs of what, at that early time, she still called the Orsetrylian Accent. **1981** A.J. BURKE *Pommies & Patriots* 62, I conducted an accountancy practice which did Taxation Returns for emigrant pommies, ethnics or orstraleens.

ort. [Of unknown origin.] The backside; the anus.
1952 P. PINNEY *Road in Wilderness* 62 You're a big bronzed Anzac sitting on your ort drinking free tea. **1962** J. WYNNUM *Tar Dust* 116 Take it from me, there's more ways of killin' a cat than fillin' its ort with sand.

oscar. Abbrev. of OSCAR ASCHE.
1917 *Ca ne fait Rien: 6th Battalion A.I.F.* Oct. 1 So readers may rest assured they will get value for their oscar. **1959** D. NILAND *Big Smoke* 21 If you'd been fighting all those

blokes in the ring you'd have more oscar in your kick now than the Prime Minister.

Oscar Asche. [The name of *Oscar Asche* (1871–1936), an actor.] Rhyming slang for 'cash'.

1905 J. MEREDITH *Learning to talk Old Jack Lang* (1984) 15 Two years ago I was .. spending all my *Oscar Asche* on .. two-up, fighting and brawling, stoushing *John Hops*, hetting run in. **1929** *Rising Sun* (Melbourne) Oct. 7 Billee Hughes will pay zee Oscar Asche.

Oss, var. OZ.

Ossie, var. AUSSIE.

ossie. [f. *os(miridum* + -Y.] Osmiridum, a natural alloy. Also *attrib*.

1936 M.J. O'REILLY *Pinnacle Road* 19 When old Adamsfield is finished and the pioneers are gone, And we ossie diggers all have passed away. **1968** P. ADAM SMITH *Tiger Country* 76 Saviour Simmonds ran a billiard-saloon-cum-slygrog-shop and he'd buy your 'ossie' when you were hard up.

ostrylian: see ORSTRALIA.

O.T. Abbrev. of OVERLAND TELEGRAPH. Also **O.T. line,** and *attrib*.

1898 *Bulletin* (Sydney) 31 Dec. 31/2 The Overland telegraph ends at Palmerston and employs a large staff, known as the O.T. men. **1915** E.R. MASSON *Untamed Territory* 19 The value of the Overland Telegraph has never diminished. .. A man from out back will tell you that he lives 'three weeks from the O.T.'. **1927** M.H. ELLIS *Long Lead* 201 Illegal for travellers to pass down the 'O.T.' line unless they carried firearms.

other side.

1. Used variously to designate a part of Australia which is removed from the speaker by a natural barrier or border. See also SIDE *n.*[1] 1, TOTHER SIDE *n.*[1] 1.

1827 *Tasmanian* (Hobart) 24 May 2 The districts, at the other Side, require a Pastor like Mr Robinson. **1952** J.R. SKEMP *Memories Myrtle Bank* 221 Quite a number went 'over the other side', as the Australian mainland is rather ambiguously described by Tasmanians.

2. a. A place in the northern hemisphere; *spec.* England.

1892 *Quiz* (Adelaide) 29 Apr. 6/2 When a politician visits England he generally has a job on hand. Dibbs .. is going to float a bank. Most banks on the other side hequire floating. **1937** A.R. GRANT *Memories of Parliament* 1 Five years on the 'other side' had given me a love for Australia.

b. *W.A.* The eastern States; TOTHER SIDE 2.

1893 *Quiz* (Adelaide) 7 Apr. 6/1 The West Australian cricketers underwent a terrible collapse on the other side. Perhaps it was the Melbourne stinks that overcame them. **1950** G.M. FARWELL *Land of Mirage* 167 The plain fact about rustling—as they call cattle-lifting, poddy-dodging, or gully-raking over the other side—is that after all it is only droving, with an extra note of gambling and suspense.

other-sider. *W.A.* TOTHERSIDER 1.

1883 *Bulletin* (Sydney) 17 Nov. 20/4 To 'other-siders' as they are called some Western Australian experiences have been of a decidedly phenomenal character. **1891** E.H. HALLACK *W.A. & Yilgarn Goldfields* 5 'Othersiders', as they in the west call Adelaidens.

out, *adv.*[1]

1. At a distance from one's place of origin: in or to Australia.

1790 *Extracts Lett. Arthur Phillip* 12 Feb. (1791) 5 If settlers are sent out, and the convicts divided amongst them, this Settlement will very shortly maintain itself. **1978** J. ANDERSON *Tirra Lirra* 88, I got out of hospital, weakened and considerably poorer, but there were no more passenger ships out.

2. Absent from a place of confinement; at large.

1792 P.G. KING Jrnl. Norfolk Island 50 A convict who has been some time past, a vagabond in the woods, was seen plundering some maize but could not be taken, this man has been out since the 25th September. **1946** L. PIRANI *Old Man River* 27, I remember the trembling and hushed voices that spread around the news: 'The Kelly's are out'.

3. In the phr. **to go out (to),** to die (from).

1929 C.E.W. BEAN *Official Hist. Aust. 1914–18* III. 598 He had found it more than he could bear, put his rifle to his head, and 'went out' uncomplaining. **1948** K.S. PRICHARD *Golden Miles* 118, I reckon there's more accidents on the mines and more men going out to miner's complaint, now, than there was in the old days.

out, *adv.*[2] Abbrev. of OUTBACK *adv.* Also **out there.**

1897 *Bulletin* (Sydney) 19 June 3/2 And I thought of piny sand-ridges!—and somehow I could swear That this tailor-made young johnnie had at one time been 'out there'! **1917** A.L. BREWER *'Gators' Euchre* 44 On the way out I met many fences, mostly with sheep-wires, while now and then one was rabbit-proof.

out, *a.* (or as an adv. combinative element) [Not necessarily excl. Austral. but of historical interest.]

1. *Obs.* Used in collocations in the sense of 'distant from a central establishment or main settlement', as **out-district, -farm, -gang, -settlement, -settler, -squatter.**

1835 *Hobart Town Almanack* 191 The carelessness of persons engaged in the **out-districts**, the remote stock-keepers. **1805** *Sydney Gaz.* 28 Apr., The impropriety of encouraging any of these people about the **out-farms**. **1805** J. TURNBULL *Voyage round World* I. 113 One of the prisoners belonging to the **out-gangs**, being sent into camp on Saturday .. fell unfortunately into the company of a party of convicts. **1803** *HRA* (1915) 1st Ser. IV. 330 When any person is sent to an **Out-Settlement** as a punishment, the Magistrate or Magistrates before whom they were convicted will inform the Magistrate of the place they are sent to of their crime and term of punishment. **1802** *HRA* (1915) 1st. Ser. III. 582 Prevent the **out-settlers** from being robbed and plundered. **1847** G.F. ANGAS *Savage Life & Scenes* II. 192 The settler and the **out-squatter**, who, perhaps, have lived like hermits in the bush.

2. Used in collocations in the sense of 'situated at some distance from the principal establishment on a rural property', as **out-camp, -hut, -paddock.**

1905 *Bulletin* (Sydney) 7 Dec. 15/2 Every year resolutions are made in **out-camps** and huts to .. go down and see the Melbourne Cup. **1873** *Tas. Non-State Rec.* 103/11 19 July, The two boys and myself left our bedding at the **out hut** three miles from the yards. **1886** *Bulletin* (Sydney) 12 June 20/1 And the **out-paddocks**—holy frost! .. They really are immense.

out, *v.* [Spec. use of *out* to dismiss.] *trans.* To suspend (a football player) from a team.

1962 *N.T. News* (Darwin) 1 Feb. 1/5 Noted footballer Brien Durrington was 'outed' by the Australian Rules Tribunal for five years last night .. charged with knocking down a goal umpire. **1984** *N.T. News* (Darwin) 17 Oct. 47/3 This suspension is the first he has received since 1976 when he was outed for two matches for striking.

outback, *adv., a.,* and *n.* Now usu. as one word, but formerly often as two or hyphened. [Ellipt. *out* in(to) the *back* country.]

A. *adv.* Out in or to country which is remote from a major centre of population.

1869 *Wagga Wagga Advertiser* 17 Apr. 3/3 Grass will be

abundant out back, and those pleasant and welcome visitors the travelling sheep will have comfortable quarters all the way down the river. **1981** A. MARSHALL *Aust.* 24 He talked of his experience outback.

B. *adj.* Of, pertaining to, or characteristic of remote parts of the country.
1893 *Bulletin* (Sydney) 18 Nov. 20/4 We wish to Heaven that Australian writers would leave off trying to make a paradise out of the Out Back Hell. **1984** *N.T. News* (Darwin) 26 Sept. 18/4 An outback road could become a new tourist corridor linking two of Australia's greatest attractions, the Great Barrier Reef and Ayers Rock.

C. *n.*
a. Sparsely inhabited country which is remote from a major centre of population.
1893 J.A. BARRY *Steve Brown's Bunyip* 51 'Yes, I'm from out back,' said a dark, wiry little man, as he dismounted from his horse at a Queensland frontier-township hotel. **1984** *Bulletin* (Sydney) 7 Feb. 6/2 People of the outback still do not have an efficient telephone service.
b. In the collocation **great (Australian) outback,** the outback, esp. as perceived in a romanticized literary depiction of life there.
1936 C.P. CONIGRAVE *N. Aust.* 54 Only one of the many, many lonely graves in the great Australian Outback. **1972** *Bulletin* (Sydney) 30 Sept. 40/3 He describes the Great Outback or Heart as a place where 'the drover is driven and the shearer is shorn'.
Hence **outbackmanship** *n.*
1962 *Texas Q.* 62 'Near enough' is the national philosophy: a deliberate cult of antifinesse, of outbackmanship.

outbacker, *n.*[1] A non-Aboriginal person native to or resident in the outback.
1900 *Bulletin* (Sydney) 1 Sept. 15/1 Surat (Q.), from a travelled 'out-backer's' view, may be considered an elysium. **1981** *Austral. Women's Weekly* (Sydney) 18 Nov. 21/1 Part of the route was along a 'highway'—the Connie-Sue, cleared by legendary outbacker Len Biddell.

out-backer, *n.*[2] *Two-up.* See quot. 1941.
1919 C. DREW *Doings of Dave* 34 The 'out' backers were winning. **1941** E. BAUME *I lived These Yrs.* 122 If they both come down heads the man who is tossing wins; if tails the 'out' backer, or man betting against the tosser, collects the bet.

outbackery. [f. OUTBACKER *n.*[1]] The cultivation of attitudes and values supposedly characteristic of those who live in the outback. Also *attrib.*
1961 *Bulletin* (Sydney) 1 Feb. 32/3 People .. are suspicious of the current outbackery cult. **1986** *Bulletin* (Sydney) 14 Jan. 44/1 On the whole issue of outbackery, the author finds curious contradictions in the Australian psyche.

out beyond. OUTBACK *n.*
1906 *Bulletin* (Sydney) 25 Jan. 14/4 What is this strange fascination to the sundowner, the Out Beyond? **1907** A. SEARCY *In Austral. Tropics* p. v, It is only the man who has lived in the far-removed 'out-beyond' .. who can understand the charm and poetry of the Australian bush.

out bush, *adv.* and *a.*
A. *adv.* Into or in an area of back country.
1908 Mrs A. GUNN *We of Never-Never* 220 Out-bush we take the good with the bad as we find it. *Ibid.* 256 Our life was .. peaceful and regular, with an occasional single day 'out-bush'. **1963** X. HERBERT *Disturbing Element* 94 They called him Bushy .. because he was lately from somewhere out bush.
B. *adj.* Situated in the back country.
1911 A. SEARCY *By Flood & Field* 274 We chanced on a little fellow camped on the track, who some time before had left one of the outbush stations with a mate. **1927** M. TERRY *Through Land of Promise* 230 The man who does the 'bronco-ing' (the local term for this roping of cattle, only found in the most bushy out-Bush stations) rides amongst the mob.

outer.
1. An uncovered area for non-members at a racecourse or sports ground and, as such (at a racecourse), a place where bets can be laid; (*two-up*) the periphery of the ring in which the game is played.
1915 DREW & EVANS *Grafter* 54 'Hello, Grafter!' .. 'What's the strong of this? I thought you were fielding on the Outer?' **1944** F. BRUNO *Sa-eeda Wog!* 10 You and I, brother, can pierce the cloak of harmless amusement which hovers about the 'outer' of the two-up school.
2. *fig.* In the phr. **on** (or **of**) **the outer,** disadvantaged; ill-favoured; excluded.
1902 *Truth* (Sydney) 6 Apr. 7/2 Our statesmen are Of the grimy outer outer. **1975** 'N. CULOTTA' *Gone Gougin'* 41, I was feeling depressed because I did not understand. .. 'Well,' he said, 'that's a relief. I thought I was on the outer.'

outlaw. [Spec. use of *outlaw* a wild, untamed beast.] An intractable horse. Also **outlaw horse.**
1900 *Truth* (Sydney) 28 June 5/6 Several .. of the horses presented to the Bushman are 'outlaws'—that is, horses with whom it has been found impossible to do anything. **1960** R.S. PORTEOUS *Cattleman* 18 One old hand tried to outdo the other in tales of wild cattle or outlaw horses!

outside, *a., n.,* and *adv.*
A. *adj.*
1. a. Situated at or pertaining to the outer limit of settlement; situated in an area remote from a major centre of population.
1847 E.B. KENNEDY *Extracts Jrnl. Exped. Central Aust.* 233 After travelling 14 miles reached Roach's, the outside station of the settlers. **1951** E. HILL *Territory* 310 In the early days these 'outside' men .. worked their cattle with lubras, quicker to learn and more to be trusted.
b. In collocations: **outside country, district, track.**
1879 *Queenslander* (Brisbane) 31 May 684/1 A man knows what he has to expect in the **outside country.** **1876** 'CAPRICORNUS' *Colonisation* 21 In the **outside districts** there is always hanging about a sprinkling of population which partakes in some degree of the character of the original squatters. **1888** 'R. BOLDREWOOD' *Robbery under Arms* (1937) 95 We kept working by all sorts of **outside tracks** on the main line of road.
2. *Fishing.* Off-shore.
1896 F.G. AFLALO *Sketch Nat. Hist. Aust.* 201 The skill employed by the 'outside men', 'groper-men', 'black-brimmers', and others in catching their favorite fish, is such as to astonish .. fishermen all the world over. **1982** R. HUNGERFORD *Compl. Bk. Austral. Fishing* (ed. 3) 95 We have no banks or extended shallow continental shelf. Thus, most of our outside fishing is in deep water.

B. *n.* An area remote from a major centre of population.
1869 'E. HOWE' *Boy in Bush* 171 The Kakadua was then 'outside'—as the colonists used to call unsettled districts. **1979** D. LOCKWOOD *My Old Mates & I* 157 The Territory was once back-of-Bourke, back-of-beyond, the Outside.

C. *adv.*
1. In a remote area.
1911 C.E.W. BEAN *'Dreadnought' of Darling* 317 Be the 'inside' country never so tame and densely populated, there will always be a huge stretch of country 'outside' which cannot by any known means be closely settled. **1930** J.S. LITCHFIELD *Far-North Memories* 207 Perhaps a

young man brings up a bride from the south, and takes up work 'outside', i.e., in the bush.

2. *Fishing.* Out to sea.

1902 *Bulletin* (Sydney) 11 Oct. 33/1 We were 'outside' schnappering. **1982** R. HUNGERFORD *Compl. Bk. Austral. Fishing* (ed. 3) 95, I avoided the wide, blue water—until two friends invited me to 'have a day outside'.

outsider. *Obs.* One who lives in a remote place.

1867 *S.A. Parl. Papers* II. no. 14 40, I believe you have been engaged on runs all your life?—Ever since I was ten years old. Since 1840 I have been an outsider. **1879** *Queenslander* (Brisbane) 19 Apr. 492/4 Ye gentlemen of Brisbane, who sit at home at ease, How little do ye know of—the sort of life we poor unfortunate 'outsiders' have to pass.

out-station.

1. a. *Obs.* An outpost, esp. a military garrison or convict settlement.

1817 *Hobart Town Gaz.* 9 Aug., At this Muster are to attend all Free Men and Women resident at .. Stony Hut Plains, and all Out-stations and Stock Yards in that Quarter. **1880** J. BONWICK *Resources Qld.* 10 The so-called *Moreton Bay District* was an out-station of New South Wales.

b. *Obs.* An outpost of settlement; a run or station established at a distance from a settled district. Also *attrib.*

1834 J.D. LANG *Hist. & Statistical Acct. N.S.W.* II. 64 Ticket-of-leave holders, of reputable character, might be advantageously settled in the out-stations of the colony. **1856** D.J. GOLDING *Emigrant's Guide Aust.* (1973) 103 The out-station settlers furnish their dwellings with few articles of domestic convenience.

2. a. On a grazing property: a subordinate station at some distance from the main establishment (see quot. 1853). See *home station* HOME *attrib.*[2] **b.**

1829 R. DAWSON *Statement* 50 They visited the principal out-stations, and nearly all the sheep folds. **1853** MOSSMAN & BANISTER *Aust. Visited & Revisited* 65 An out-station is simply a hut at a convenient distance from the homestead, or from any other out-station on the 'run' or sheep-walk, so as to allow ample feeding-ground for two flocks of sheep.

b. Comb. **out-station hut.**

1844 *Port Phillip Gaz.* 18 May 3 On the night of the 23rd March, Peter Stratton came to the out station hut.

3. An autonomous Aboriginal community located at some distance from a centre on which it is dependent for services and supplies: see quot. 1981 (1). See also HOMELAND. Also *attrib.*, esp. as **outstation movement.**

1972 DOUGLAS & OLDMEADOW *Across Top* 29 One of Sheppy's deepest interests is in his 'out-stations'; small groups of Aborigines still clinging to their traditional ways in their tribal territories. **1976** *West Austral.* (Perth) 10 July 9/4 The 'outstation movement'—under which family groups moved away from settlements and used them only as service centres—appeared to have achieved some success by returning to tribal patterns of authority. **1981** Q. WILD *Honey Wind* 148 On the way back to Darwin, they visited Aboriginal out-stations on several locations, and saw how Aborigines were experimenting in developing their own cattle runs.

out west, *adv., n.,* and *a. Eastern States.*

A. *adv.* In or to the sparsely populated western districts; OUTBACK *adv.*

1895 *Worker* (Sydney) 21 Dec. 1/3 We were tank-sinking out West when the news came that one of our crowd had struck the first in Tattersall's big sweep. **1977** R. MCKIE *Crushing* (1978) 131 It came from a place out west. Mother gave it to me when I passed the Intermediate down south.

B. *n.* The sparsely populated western districts; OUTBACK *n.*

1902 *Blackwood's Mag.* (Edinburgh) May 638/1 On the streets of Sydney or Melbourne the appearance of a copper-skinned back-blocker excites as much comment as might a being from another planet. The man from 'out west' cares little for the opinion of the townsman. **1969** A. GARVE *Boomerang* 39, I was thinking rather of the interior—'out west' I believe you call it—where my Corporation could expect to get in on the ground floor.

C. *adj.* Of or pertaining to, or situated in, the sparsely populated western districts; OUTBACK *a.*

1917 *Bulletin* (Sydney) 22 Nov. 22/3 The most wicked parrot of my acquaintance was the property of Janet O'Brown an Out West licensee. **1923** *Ibid.* 1 Nov. 24/3 At many Out-West peeling establishments goats—always more manageable than the woollies—are regularly used as leaders, and poddied calves are also often pressed into the service.

oval. [Transf. use of the name of Kennington *Oval*, the Surrey County cricket ground in s. London.] A sports ground (not necessarily elliptical in shape).

1822 T. REID *Two Voyages N.S.W. & Van Diemen's Land* 113 The greater part of the fence enclosing the Cricketing Association's oval was levelled to the ground. **1977** D. WILLIAMSON *Club* (1978) 33 We're going to graze 'em on the oval and save on lawn mowing costs.

oven. Abbrev. of *native oven* (see NATIVE *a.* 5).

1878 R.B. SMYTH *Aborigines of Vic.* II. 232 When a company of natives returns after a day's hunting and foraging, the women take a fresh supply of firewood and stones. These last are sometimes found in the 'ovens' in localities remote from where any stones are known to exist. **1951** A. MARSHALL *Aust.* (1981) 157 In a wind-scooped patch of red sand, lie the remains of a blackfellow's midden— 'ovens' the bushmen call them. Mussel shells lie scattered around. There are lumps of baked clay and quite a number of artifacts.

over, *adv.* In the phr. **over there,** on the other side of the world, in Europe (esp. during the war of 1914–18).

1918 R.H. KNYVETT *Over there with Australs.* 5 Only earth that has been blown on by the wind is fresh 'over there'. Don't, if you have a weak stomach, ever turn up any earth; though there may not be rotting flesh, other gases are imprisoned in the soil. **1978** G. HALL *River still Flows* 69 Something happening 'over there' while we went on living lives that were almost normal.

overcoat. *transf.* The fleece of a sheep.

1919 *Bulletin* (Sydney) 11 Dec. 20/2 It was widely circulated that a Westralian shearer barbered 321 jumbucks in one day. True, he was paid for 321, but he took the overcoats off only 180. **1941** *Ibid.* 22 Jan. 16/3 The shearing contractor .. had been urging his team on, resulting in their 'skimming the wrinkles' and leaving the sheep with a fair overcoat.

overdrive, *v.* [Spec. use of *overdrive* to drive or work to exhaustion.] *trans.* To drive (cattle) too hard. Freq. as *vbl. n.* and *ppl. a.*

1851 *Empire* (Sydney) 15 Mar. 7/2 Cattle are known to die .. from overdriving. **1923** *Bulletin* (Sydney) 4 Jan. 22/2 If you want cattle to camp you must feed and water them well and not overdrive them. **1936** 'L. KAYE' *Black Wilderness* 59 He was in sight again, driving on his mob of over-driven cattle.

overland, *a.* and *n.* [Spec. use of *overland* proceeding across land.]

A. *adj.*

1. a. *Hist.* Of or pertaining to a journey by land from

OVERLAND   387   **OVERLAND TELEGRAPH**

New South Wales to South Australia. **b.** *transf.* Of or pertaining to a long journey by land, esp. the driving of stock over a long distance.
1838 *S. Austral. Rec.* (London) 11 July 76 An *overland* importation on a great scale, which we hail as the introduction of a system of internal communication and supply between the Colonies. Nearly 2,000 head of cattle, and from 4,000 to 6,000 sheep, were on the route overland from New South Wales to the Province. **1954** T. RONAN *Vision Splendid* 165 Marty, pack-bags bursting with all available varieties of rations, was excelling himself as an overland chef.

2. In collocations: **overland herd, party.**
1839 *S. Austral. Rec.* (London) (1840) 27 June 358 Three **overland herds** of cattle have just arrived, consisting in all of about 1,800 head. **1840** *S. Austral. Register* (Adelaide) 30 Apr. 4 The peace .. has been sometimes interrupted between the **overland parties** and the aborigines.

3. In the collocation **overland fish** (or **trout**), a lizard or snake, esp. when used as food.
1881 J.C.F. JOHNSON *To Mount Browne & Back* 13 The Jew lizard is known as 'overland fish'. **1940** *Bulletin* (Sydney) 6 Mar. 17/4 Jack's oft-expressed desire for a feed of 'overland trout' induced a couple of us to take a bush walk. The tally was half a dozen... Jack .. managed to .. build a fire and cook his lizard abo. style.

B. *n.*
1. Ellipt. for 'overland stock route'.
1894 *Bulletin* (Sydney) 10 Feb. 20/3 From South and East the shearers come across the Overland. **1927** M.H. ELLIS *Long Lead* 74 'Where might you be bound?' he asked 'Darwin,' we said, 'and back to Sydney down the Overland.'

2. Ellipt. for 'overland journey (driving stock)'.
1936 J.C. DOWNIE *Galloping Hoofs* 111 The 'fats' are culled out for the overland to the freezing works. **1974** *Austral. Folksongs* (Folk Lore Council Aust.) 36 We rolled our swags and packed our bags, and, taking our lives in hand, We started away with a thousand goats on a Billygoat Overland.

overland, *v.*
1. **a.** *trans.* To drive (stock) overland, esp. for a great distance.
1882 A.J. BOYD *Old Colonials* 9 As to droving, I have overlanded sheep and cattle. **1979** D. LOCKWOOD *My Old Mates & I* 81 The annual droving schedule of cattle being overlanded from Halls Creek to Thargomindah.

b. To convey (a cargo) by land.
1948 B. CRONIN *How runs Road* 39 Joseph Hawdon .. agreed to overland the mails for £1,200 a year.

2. *intr.* To travel by land. Also *trans.*
1885 *Australasian Printers' Keepsake* 126 Jerry proposed to 'overland' the distance. **1948** M. UREN *Glint of Gold* 154 They left the ship and overlanded to Coolgardie.

overland, *adv. Hist.* [Spec. use of *overland* over or across land.] From New South Wales to South Australia by land.
1837 *S. Austral. Gaz.* (Adelaide) 8 July 4 During the period that .. Messrs Barnard and Fisher were at Sydney as Commissioners from this Government to purchase supplies for the use of the Colony, they made some enquiries on the important subject of transporting cattle, horses, and sheep, *over land*. **1871** M. CLARKE *Old Tales of Young Country* 163 Young men .. purchased cattle and sheep in New South Wales and drove them 'overland'.

overlander.
1. Orig. one who drove stock from New South Wales to the new Colony of South Australia; one who drives stock over a long distance.
1841 G. GREY *Jrnls. Two Exped. N.-W. & W.A.* II. 195 The first step taken by the Overlanders was the connexion of Port Phillip with Sydney... At this period they did not, however, bear the name of Overlanders, which was only given to them after Adelaide had been reached in 1838.
1979 D. LOCKWOOD *My Old Mates & I* 81 When I was an overlander I hated bull trains. I could see they were going to take my living from me.

2. One who travels overland: see quots.
1847 T. McCOMBIE *Austral. Sketches* 68 The term Overland is not .. confined to such alone as brought over stock; as, whoever arrives at a new settlement overland, is designated an Overlander. **1941** S.J. BAKER *Pop. Dict. Austral. Slang* 52 *Overlander*, a traveller... (3) A settler from another State. (4) A drover. (5) A sundowner.

3. *transf.*
a. A motor vehicle equipped for rugged conditions.
1957 F. CLUNE *Fortune Hunters* 35 We pushed on another few miles and found an overlander with a trailer sandbogged in another creek. **1965** L. WALKER *Other Girl* 10 The car, a great fawn-coloured overlander thickly red with the desert dust, thundered round the curve.

b. See quots.
c **1887** K.G. GALLOP In Never Never Land, Huge mosquitoes known here as 'Scotch Greys' or 'Overlanders' added their quota of misery. **1934** *Bulletin* (Sydney) 14 Nov. 24/1 Take a sugar-bag, sew together the sides of the open end, and leave about the centre of the bag as one does with a split bag—the old time drover's 'overlander'... The stuffed split bag will keep the saddle well off the sore.

overlanding, *vbl. n.*
1. The driving of stock over a long distance. Also *attrib.*
1847 *Port Phillip Herald* 5 Jan. 3/2 Wanted.—the situation of Overseer upon a Sheep and Cattle Station, by a party who can give the most unexceptionable references. N.B.— The above would be glad to engage in the overlanding of stock, &c. *c* **1891** Mrs P. MARTIN *Coo-ee* 272 When you are sitting over a camp fire brewing quart-pot tea and smoking store tobacco .. ask one of the overlanding hands to tell you what he knows about the Bunyip.

2. *transf.*
1937 *Bulletin* (Sydney) 25 Aug. 20/3 In other countries besides Australia overlanding crocodiles .. are a commonplace.

3. Special Comb. **overlanding camp,** a drover's overnight camp; a resting place for stock being overlanded.
1868 C.W. BROWNE *Overlanding in Aust.* 61 These opinions are all very well when kept in his own bosom, but they will not do in any overlanding camp.

overland mail. [Also U.S.: see Mathews.]
a. An inter-colonial postal service operating by land (as opposed to 'by sea'); the mail so conveyed.
1838 *Melbourne Advertiser* 15 Jan. 4 The overland mail for Sydney closes this day at 6 oclock. **1931** *N.T. Times* (Darwin) 13 Jan. 2/2 An overland mail will be sent away by the train on Wednesday 28th. inst.

b. A vehicle used for the conveyance of mail.
1954 T. RONAN *Vision Splendid* 119 He just missed the connection to the Port by sea and his shortest road home was to go to Big Knob by the overland mail.

Overland Telegraph. The telegraph line between Port Augusta in South Australia and Darwin in the Northern Territory, completed in 1872 and linking by submarine cable to Java with the telegraphic networks of Asia and Europe. Also **Overland Telegraph line.**
1870 *Illustr. Austral. News* (Melbourne) 5 Dec. 208/1 (*heading*) Planting first post of the Overland Telegraph at Port Darwin. **1942** H.H. PECK *Mem. of Stockman* 85 The country beyond, until they struck the overland telegraph line about Newcastle Waters, was unknown.

overseer. [Spec. use of *overseer* one who superintends.]

1. *Hist.* One appointed, freq. from the convict body, to superintend the work of a party of convicts; *convict overseer* CONVICT B. 3.

1788 D. COLLINS *Acct. Eng. Colony N.S.W.* (1798) I. 33 Had a few persons been sent out who were not of the description of convicts, to have acted as overseers, or superintendents [etc.]. 1848 C. COZENS *Adventures of Guardsman* 118 An overseer (generally speaking, one of themselves) is appointed to each gang, who marches his men by twos to their respective scenes of operation.

2. One who manages a rural property or who supervises a part of the work on such a property.

1806 *Sydney Gaz.* 15 June, *Wanted*—A Free man as an Overseer on a large Farm. 1955 F. LANE *Patrol to Kimberleys* 145 Both station owners and their overseers are out mustering.

3. In the collocation **overseer's hut**, a (temporary) dwelling occupied by the overseer of a convict gang or an employee on a rural property: see also HUT *n.* 2 and 3.

1835 *Colonist* (Sydney) 23 July 237/2 A road party stationed near, called after the name of their overseer, Thorpe's gang, and the escort .. proceeded to the overseer's hut. 1856 W.W. DOBIE *Recoll. Visit Port-Phillip* 94 His lubra was generally about the overseer's hut during the day.

Hence **overseer** *v. trans.*

1841 *Morning Advertiser* (Hobart) 15 Oct. 4/2 We .. abhorred his system of keeping the prisoner gangs overseered by prisoners.

overstock, *v.* [Spec. use of *overstock* to stock to excess; also U.S. (see DAE).] *trans.* To stock (an area of land) with more animals than can be supported. Also *absol.*

1825 J.H. WEDGE *Diaries* (1962) 12 It is only adapted for a cattle and sheep run and it may easily be over-stocked. 1945 *Bulletin* (Sydney) 26 Sept. 13/2 Joe had overstocked and was one of the first to be hit by the drought. Soon he was looking for agistment country.

Hence **overstocked** *ppl. a.*

1848 J.S. ROE *Rep. Exped. S.-Eastward Perth* 20 Nov. (1849) 59 Render available a tract of pasturage sufficiently extensive to relieve the present overstocked districts.

overstocking, *vbl. n.* The stocking of an area of land with more animals than it can support.

1867 'CLERGYMAN' *Aust. as it Is* 204 Experience comes so much to the aid of the Australian settler, in the making of 'dams', and guarding against the great danger of 'overstocking'. 1936 E.W. COX *Evol. Austral. Merino* 135 Rabbits, overstocking, and wanton destruction of timber, bringing about soil erosion, have sadly depleted the land of many of its most valuable grasses.

over there: see OVER.

Owen. [From the name of E.E. *Owen* (1915–1949), the Australian inventor of a sub-machine-gun.] A type of sub-machine-gun. Also **Owen gun.**

1941 *Sydney Morning Herald* 30 Sept. 5/6 When all three guns were subjected to the test of being buried in a heap of sand the Owen gun was the only one to continue firing automatically. 1948 *Listening Post* (Perth) Oct. 27 Facing them, with owens at the ready, stood four big men.

owlet nightjar. The small nocturnal bird *Aegotheles cristatus*, predom. grey or brown with barred wing and tail feathers, widespread in Aust. incl. Tas., and also occurring in s. New Guinea.

1840 J. GOULD *Birds of Aust.* (1848) II. Pl. 1, *Aegetholes novae-hollandiae* .. Owlet Nightjar. 1982 *Ecos* xxxiii. 15/2 Specimens of stone curlews and owlet nightjars have also been found.

ox. Used *attrib.* in facetious Special Comb. as: **ox conductor**, a bullock driver; **persuader**, a bullock driver; a bullock whip (see PERSUADER); see also BULLOCK *n.* 1.

1902 *Truth* (Sydney) 3 Aug. 7/3 The **ox-conductor**, we're often told, Can make the air turn blue. 1899 W.T. GOODGE *Hits! Skits! & Jingles* 170 Jack McCamley, Lank and long, **Ox-persuader**, Billabong. 1980 O. RUHEN *Bullock Teams* 164 The terms 'ox' and 'oxen' haven't had much currency in Australia, except perhaps as persiflage: 'ox-persuader' for the bullock whip and 'oxen-conductor' for the teamster.

oxy-weld, *v.* [Abbrev. of *oxy(-acetylene* + *weld.*] *trans.* To weld (metal), using a mixture of oxygen and acetylene. Also as *vbl. n.*

1945 J. DEVANNY *Bird of Paradise* 31, I went into Atherton to get some oxy-welding done. 1956 K. TENNANT *Honey Flow* 54 What looked like the spine of a dinosaur was a set of caterpillar tractor-treads waiting to be oxy-welded.

oyster, *a.* [Abbrev. of *oyster-like* uncommunicative.] Unforthcoming; secret.

1910 L. ESSON *Woman Tamer* (1976) 63 You might tell us, Chopsey. Don't be oyster. I won't word nobody, not me. 1971 H. ANDERSON *Larrikin Crook* 3 The boy was dragged off to the police station where he remained 'oyster'.

Oyster Bay pine. *Tas.* [f. the name of *Oyster Bay*, on the e. coast of Tas.] The pyramidal tree or tall shrub *Callitris rhomboidea* (fam. Cupressaceae) of s.e. Aust. incl. Tas.

1832 J. BACKHOUSE *Narr. Visit Austral. Colonies* (1843) 73 On the hills, are the Blue Gum, the Oyster Bay Pine. 1956 W.M. CURTIS *Student's Flora Tas.* 5 *C[allitris] tasmanica* .. Oyster Bay Pine. .. Locally abundant on the east coast from Prosser River to Elephant Pass.

oyster blenny. [See quot. 1974] The small marine fish *Cyneichthys anolius* of e. Aust.

1906 D.G. STEAD *Fishes of Aust.* 211 The Oyster Blenny .. is very often to be found amongst dead and empty oyster-shells, along the coast of New South Wales. 1974 T.D. SCOTT et al. *Marine & Freshwater Fishes S.A.* 277 Oyster Blenny. *Cyneichthys anolius.* .. This unusual little fish shelters in the empty shells of oysters, and deposits its eggs therein, guarding them till they hatch.

Oz /ɒz/, *n.* and *a.* Also **Aus, Oss.** [Repr. pronunc. of abbrev. of 'Australia' or 'Australian'.]

A. *n.* Abbrev. of 'Australia'.

1908 *Bulletin* (Sydney) 2 July 15/3 My home is near Kingston, which is in the S.E. of South Oss. 1944 *Barging About: Organ of 43rd Austral. Landing Craft Co.* 1 Sept. 6 All the tribes of Oz did gather together. 1981 C. WALLACE-CRABBE *Splinters* 162 Foreign countries sound so horrid nowadays. Dad was right to always stay home in the old Aus.

B. *adj.* Abbrev. of 'Australian'. Also as **Ozman.**

1971 *Bulletin* (Sydney) 18 Dec. 30/2 Then I got back to England and found myself facing the 'Oz' educational attitudes. 1985 *Bulletin* (Sydney) 15 Oct. 10/3 Modern Ozman is the direct descendant of the first white boat people.

Ozzie, var. AUSSIE.

P

Pacific, *a.* Used as a distinguishing epithet in the names of birds occurring on the Pacific coast: **Pacific gull,** the large gull *Larus pacificus* of coastal s. Aust. incl. Tas., having white and black plumage and a heavy yellow beak; **heron,** the predom. grey-black waterbird *Ardea pacifica,* chiefly of mainland Aust., having a white head and neck; *white-necked heron,* see WHITE *a.*^{2} 1 b.

1801 J. LATHAM *Gen. Synopsis Birds* Suppl. II. 332 **Pacific G**[**ull**] inhabits *New South Wales.* **1801** J. LATHAM *Gen. Synopsis Birds* Suppl. II. 305 **Pacific H**[**eron**] .. inhabits the sea-shores in various parts of *New Holland*.. but is not a common species.

pack, *a.*

1. Used *attrib.* in Special Comb. not necessarily peculiar to Aust. but of local historical significance: **pack bullock, camel,** a bullock or camel used for carrying a pack; **(horse)bike,** a second bicycle, attached alongside the one being ridden and used to carry a pack.

1832 *Sydney Monitor* 19 Dec. 3/6 Pack-saddles constructed on this tree will .. save the back of many a poor **pack-bullock** from writhing sores. **1919** G.W. HANDSLEY *Two-&-Half Yrs. P.O.W. in Turkey* 16 Not the ordinary camel, but old scraggy, bony beasts, who had been used formerly for **pack camels**. **1903** *Bulletin* (Sydney) 6 Aug. 16/2, I saw a **pack-horse bike**... The biker had a huge swag strapped on, over, under, and round his second jigger, which was attached to the riding bike by a curious outrigger contrivance. **1912** *Ibid.* 10 Oct. 15/2, I have often met a party of shearers, camped for tucker-time, with their bikes all set up in a mulga garage... Even in the time of my sunset sojourn, the pack-bike was not uncommon.

2. a. In the phr. **to send** (someone or something) **to the pack,** to discard; to dismiss.

1915 C.J. DENNIS *Songs of Sentimental Bloke* 94 I've sent the leery bloke that bore me name Clean to the pack wivout one pearly tear. **1926** *Bulletin* (Sydney) 18 Feb. 22/2 The local vet. says I may as well send her to the pack any time, as a horse with founder never completely recovers.

b. In the phr. **to go to the pack,** to decline or deteriorate to a lower state; to 'go to pieces'; to 'go to the dogs'.

1919 W.H. DOWNING *Digger Dialects* 26 *Go to the pack,* deteriorate. **1980** F. MOORHOUSE *Days of Wine & Rage* 357 All the places overseas where the British have pulled out are going to the pack.

pack, *v.* In the phr. **to pack them,** to be frightened, to have lost one's nerve (see quot. 1970). Also with explicit objs.

1945 *Atebrin Advocate: Mag.* 2/4 Austral. Armoured Regiment 31 Mar. 1, I don't mind admitting I was packing them. **1970** J.S. GUNN in W.S. Ramson *Eng. Transported* 52 It is some time since I heard anyone talk of *packing the tweeds* for being scared. **1979** CAREY & LETTE *Puberty Blues* 10 I'm so nervous. I didn't do *any* study. I'm packin' shit.

pack-rape. The rape of a woman by a number of men in turn. Also *attrib.* and as *v. trans.,* and *fig.*

1965 *Bulletin* (Sydney) 17 Apr. 27/2 I've had letters from girls who have been pack-raped. **1970** *Ibid.* 16 May 22/2 Organisers of the Moratorium are political bikies pack-raping democracy. **1976** *Southerly* ii. 136 The bikie has just been acquitted on a pack rape charge. **1986** *Canberra Times* 26 May 2/3 It does not take a war to engender rape—pack or otherwise.

pad. [Spec. use of *pad* a path.]

1. A track made by animals: see also *cattle pad* CATTLE 2.

1893 D. LINDSAY *Jrnl. Elder Sci. Exploring Exped.* 23 He must have been on one of the pads close to the camp instead of on the main track. **1981** *Overland* lxxxvi. 58 The 'pads' (camel- and man-made) were so important to the travel of local cyclists that 'the Goldfields Bicycle Pad Protection League' was formed in mid-1897.

2. *transf.* A journey on foot, esp. as made by a swagman.

1897 A.F. CALVERT *My Fourth Tour W.A.* 84 A camel that has done a dry 'pad' for the last few days will scream with impatience while his drink is being run out of the tap for him. **1913** *Bulletin* (Sydney) 30 Jan. 15/2 From Wagga they tramped .. to Yanco, 70-odd miles, doing the pad in three days.

3. Special Comb. **pad-flogger,** a swagman.

1938 *Bulletin* (Sydney) 29 June 20/1 Various pad-floggers .. nominated their entries for the worst walking in the outback.

paddock, *n.* [Spec. use of *paddock* small field or enclosure.]

1. a. A piece of land, fenced, defined by natural boundaries, or otherwise considered distinct; usu. a section of a rural property and, on a sheep or cattle station, often of considerable size. Also *attrib.*

1808 *HRA* (1916) 1st Ser. VI. 370 A six railed Fence forming different Paddocks or enclosures for stock. **1849** N.L. KENTISH *Proposals* 90 In one instance I have surveyed a bend of the Murray, (or series of bends) of six miles, enclosing for my fortunate employer, a paddock of many thousand acres, (for no enclosed tract of land is too large to be designated 'a paddock' in these colonies) by a fence of a few rods. **1906** *Bulletin* (Sydney) 15 Feb. 39/3 'Rouse up. The Paddock weaners—they're amongst us.' The paddock sheep must have come up during my watch.

b. *transf.* A playing field.

1839 *Tasmanian* (Hobart) 8 Feb. 43/1 The Match .. will take place, in the Paddock. **1984** *Daily Mirror* (Sydney) 6 Apr. 85/3 Young set the example for the team where it mattered most in the centre of the paddock.

c. *transf.* and *fig.* [In some cases prob. influenced by ACCOMMODATION PADDOCK.]

1876 *Argus* (Melbourne) 1 July 4/5 We have as yet only seen the doings of the *demi-monde* in the stalls, vestibules and paddock of the Theatre Royal. **1960** *N.T. News* (Darwin) 5 Feb. 18/3 Merv Hunt must have been in a very good paddock. He put on three stone while on holidays in the City of Churches.

2. *Mining.*

a. In shallow alluvial mining, an area marked out and systematically excavated for wash-dirt.

1855 W. HOWITT *Land, Labor & Gold* II. 161 We have since tried to reach the bottom of the river, and see what gold there was there, by making what they call a paddock; that is, enclosing a square piece of the river with a strong bank of earth between two walls of stones. **1980** R. SHEARS *Gold* 58 If you do want to find .. areas of gold you will have to do a bit of farming—digging portions of the river bed in designated sections. These divisions .. are known as 'paddocks'.

b. A storage place for wash-dirt or uncrushed quartz.

1858 *Colonial Mining Jrnl.* Sept. 3/2 The new shaft is being sunk .. and a close and substantially constructed paddock has been erected. **1974** B. MYATT *Dict. Austral. Gemstones* 32 Old alluvial workings in which all the unwanted material ended on the 'paddock'.

3. On a racecourse: an enclosure for spectators adjacent to the saddling paddock.

1892 *Truth* (Sydney) 27 May 1/6, I was punting in the paddock at Swindle Park one day When the gaffer of some ponies comes up and says 'I say'. **1981** *Austral.* (Sydney) 3 Nov. (Cup Suppl.) B/7 Television coverage in more recent years, when we have had more than 100,000 congregated in the paddock area.

4. Comb. **paddock fence**.

1808 *HRA* (1916) 1st Ser. VI. 363 A Paddock Fence with Posts and Railing.

paddock, *v.*

1. *trans.*

a. To confine (livestock) within a paddock; to provide pasture for (livestock), as in agistment.

1847 *Bell's Life in Sydney* 11 Dec. 3/1 The horses were paddocked for the night. **1892** *Western Champion* (Barcaldine) 7 June 12/1 After a week's spell, a move was made towards Muswellbrook, where the 'Boss' intended paddocking the sheep for a week or so before trucking them to further south.

b. *fig.*

1849 *Bell's Life in Sydney* 10 Mar. 3/4 These suspicions were subsequently made certainties, which rendered it necessary for the Ministers of Justice to *paddock* Thomas instead of allowing him free *run* of the country without paying the *licence-fee*. **1937** *Bulletin* (Sydney) 17 Feb. 21/1 Net-fishers yarded up about five tons of Westralian kingfish... They gathered about half for the Perth market, leaving the rest paddocked. **1967** E. HUXLEY *Their Shining Eldorado* 247 Less than half the property is paddocked, and beyond the fences cattle live and breed free.

c. To fence or enclose (an area) in a paddock.

1873 A. TROLLOPE *Aust. & N.Z.* I. 302 When a run is 'paddocked', shepherds are not required;—but boundary-riders are employed, each of whom is supplied with two horses, and these men are responsible not only for the sheep but for the fences. **1967** E. HUXLEY *Their Shining Eldorado* 247 Less than half the property is paddocked, and beyond the fences cattle live and breed free.

d. *intr.* Of livestock: to enter into, and accept the confinement of a paddock.

1959 E. WEBB *Mark of Sun* 49 The cattle were tired and paddocked easily for the night.

2. *Mining.* **a.** *trans.* To excavate (a PADDOCK *n.* 2 a.); also *absol.* or *intr.* **b.** To store in a PADDOCK *n.* 2 b.

1855 G.H. WATHEN *Golden Colony* 56 In Eagle-Hawke Gully parties were 'paddocking' the old workings... That is, marking out and working large areas of ground already once wrought. **1880** 'ERRO' *Squattermania* 28, I looked over the heap they've got paddocked, and couldn't find a speck.

Hence **paddocked** *ppl. a.*, **paddocker** *n.*, **paddocking** *vbl. n.*

1871 *Austral. Town & Country Jrnl.* (Sydney) 4 Feb. 138/3 Ours are shepherded sheep running on black soil, and are therefore not so easily washed as **paddocked** sheep. **1862** J.A. PATTERSON *Gold Fields Vic.* 319 The **'paddocker'** is another class of the alluvial diggers. **1871** *Austral. Town & Country Jrnl.* (Sydney) 8 July 42/4 The splendid herds .. are the result of a gradual but sure process of improvement by selection, special importation, and **paddocking**.

Paddy. In collocations: **Paddy's lucerne**, the perennial shrub *Sida rhombifolia* (fam. Malvaceae) of n. Aust. and widespread in the tropics, having mucilaginous leaves and fibrous stems; JELLY LEAF; *Queensland hemp*, see QUEENSLAND 2; also **Paddy lucerne; Paddy's Market**, a name applied to any of various markets; also **Paddy market**, and *fig.*

1888 *Proc. Linnean Soc. N.S.W.* III. 391 *Sida rhombifolia* .. called **'Paddy Lucerne'** on the Richmond and Clarence Rivers, New South Wales, and 'Lucerne' in other parts of the colony (cows being very fond of it). **1896** A. MACKAY *Austral. Agriculturalist* (rev. ed.) 120 The 'paddy's lucerne' of colonial farming populations, is one of the best known fibre-yielders. **1875** R. THATCHER *Something to his Advantage* 120 **Paddy's market**, as it is popularly called, is a kind of bazaar, or poor man's fair, which is held every Saturday in the three, long narrow, stable-like buildings in the Haymarket Square. **1915** E. BELLAMY *Diary* 18 Dec., Got leave in the afternoon and went into Cairo and wandered around the bazaars. They are weird and strange and you can buy all sorts of things, produce, curios and a regular paddy markets sort of a place. **1950** J. MORRISON *Port of Call* 20 Ships have been scarce for days, and every division is packed with work-hungry men... It's impossible to be shy in this Paddy's Market of human flesh and blood, because everybody else is pushing.

paddymelon /'pædimɛlən/, *n.*[1] [Poss. a. Dharuk *badi-maliyan*.] Also **pademelon** (esp. in modern scientific literature) and formerly with much variety, as **padememella, paddymalla, paddymellon**.

1. Any of several small, compact-bodied wallabies of the genus *Thylogale*, inhabiting dense vegetation in moist forests of e. Aust. incl. Tas., and New Guinea; (occas.) any of several other, usu. small, macropods; the flesh of the animal. Also *attrib.*

1802 Banks Papers 1 June VIII. 103 Patty mellon. It is of reddish colour and much inferior in size to the forest one. **1827** P. CUNNINGHAM *Two Yrs. in N.S.W.* I. 310 The *wallabee* and *paddymalla* grow to about sixty pounds each, and inhabit the brushes and broken hilly country. **1830** R. DAWSON *Present State Aust.* 212 The natives however had shot several guanas, and had hunted down a paddymelon (a very small species of kangaroo, which is found in the long grass and thick brushes). **1844** *Sydney Morning Herald* 20 Apr. 2/5 Mr Strange found in its stomach a paddymellon, a species of wallaby. **1845** C. HODGKINSON *Aust., Port Macquarie to Moreton Bay* 33 This tribe left us to go on a pademella hunt. **1983** R. STRAHAN *Compl. Bk. Austral. Mammals* 224 Pademelons .. are grazers upon rather succulent grasses and also browse on shrubs.

2. Special Comb. **paddymelon stick** *obs.*, an Aboriginal weapon used as a missile in hunting small game.

1851 J. HENDERSON *Excursions & Adventures N.S.W.* II. 129 These are hunted in the brushes, and killed with paddy mellon sticks, with which they are knocked down. These sticks are about two feet long, and an inch or less in diameter.

paddymelon /'pædimɛlən/, *n.*[2] Also **pademelon**. [Prob. from an erroneous assoc. with PADDYMELON *n.*[1] 1.]

1. Any of several plants of the fam. Cucurbitaceae, esp. the trailing or climbing annual plant *Cucumis myriocarpus* of Africa, naturalized in inland Aust., bearing a small, bristly, melon-like fruit, and widely regarded as a weed; the fruit itself; *melon vine*, see MELON 1. Also *attrib.*

1891 *Bulletin* (Sydney) 19 Dec. 19/4 They stole my pears—my native pears—Those thrice convicted felons, And ravished from me unawares My crop of paddymelons. **1907** *Ibid.* 19 Sept. 14/2 The pademelon vine .. is a prolific plant, which bears spiky little melons about the size of gooseberries. There are hundreds of acres of them Outback, and countless patches of them Inback.

2. Special Comb. **paddymelon hole**, GILGAI b; *melon hole*, see MELON 1; also ellipt., as **paddymelon country**, and *attrib.*

1910 C.E.W. BEAN *On Wool Track* 79 Up in the north, whirling along a hilltop amongst paddymelon holes—which, whether the paddymelon really makes them or not, are uncomfortable little pitfalls, nearly a yard deep. **1948** *Bulletin* (Sydney) 8 Dec. 12/4 Viewed from surrounding hills or the sand dunes which separate it from the sea, southern Queensland's 'paddymelon-hole country' appears as a fine series of flats level enough for a landing ground.   **1957** V. PALMER *Seedtime* 159 She had gone out early in search of wild-flowers in the paddymelon country behind the settlement losing herself in the tall grass, falling into swampy gutters.

pademella, var. PADDYMELON *n.*[1]

pademelon, var. PADDYMELON *n.*[1] and *n.*[2]

pai-alla, var. PIALLA.

paint, *v.* [Ironic use of *paint* to colour.] *trans.* To bruise (a person or part of the body).
1841 *Port Phillip Gaz.* 29 Oct. 3/2 Connell said he was certainly drunk, but the constables had 'walloped' him sober; to which Constable Waller, who appeared to be suffering under the effects of a severe thrashing, replied that if he had 'painted' Connell's face, the defendants had returned the compliment by 'painting' his ribs. **1896** M. HORNSBY *Old Time Echoes Tas.* 145 Even after the handcuffs were on him he painted Sam a trifle.

painted, *ppl. a.* Used as a distinguishing epithet in the names of animals: **painted burrowing frog,** the frog *Neobatrachus pictus* of s.e. mainland Aust., grey, light brown, or green above with dark brown to olive patches; **crayfish,** any of several colourful tropical rock lobsters, esp. *Panulirus ornatus* and *P. versicolor*; also **painted cray, (spiny) lobster; dragon,** the lizard *Amphibolurus pictus* of drier s. and central Aust., bluegrey to reddish-brown above, usu. with black markings; **finch,** the bird *Emblema pictum* of arid Aust., esp. in the n.w., inhabiting rocky hills and gorges near permanent water; (occas.) any of several other colourful finches; **honeyeater,** the honeyeater *Grantiella picta* of e. mainland Aust., having black, white, and yellow plumage; **pigeon,** WOMPOO PIGEON; **quail,** the mottled chestnut-coloured bird *Turnix varia* of s.w., s., and e. Aust. incl. Tas.; see also PARTRIDGE.
1969 D. CLYNE *Austral. Frogs* 104 **Painted Burrowing Frog**.. is found near temporary pools and marshes after rain.   **1928** [**painted crayfish**] S.E. NAPIER *On Barrier Reef* 129 Deserves his name of Painted Spiny Lobster.   **1955** V. SERVENTY *Aust.'s Great Barrier Reef* 37 Similar to the less colourful crayfish of southern waters, at least where structure is concerned, the painted crayfish is a thing of beauty. **1962** N. MONKMAN *Quest Curly-Tailed Horses* 185 Out came a gorgeous crayfish, the painted lobster, as it is called by the fishermen of the reef. What a pity that they are such a delicacy! It is as if one cooked and ate a Picasso. **1978** N. COLEMAN *Look at Wildlife Great Barrier Reef* 90 Painted crays do not readily enter traps or pots and in the past this has led fisherman [*sic*] to believe they are vegetarian. **1948** *Bulletin* (Sydney) 17 Nov. 29/2 A minute or two of digging will disclose half a dozen inches of lizard—the little '**painted dragon**' (*Amphibolurus pictus*) of the sandhills. **1842** J. GOULD *Birds of Aust.* (1848) III. Pl. 97, *Emblema picta* .. **Painted Finch. 1843** J. GOULD *Birds of Aust.* (1848) IV. Pl. 50, I had been led to suspect that the actions and economy of the **Painted Honey-eater** would be found to differ materially from those of the other members of its family, and such proved to be the case. **1870** E.B. KENNEDY *Four Yrs. in Qld.* 111 One may find a large one with green back and purple and yellow breast, called the Whompoa, or **painted pigeon. 1845** J. GOULD *Birds of Aust.* (1848) V. Pl. 82, *Hemipodius varius* .. **Painted Quail,** Colonists of Van Diemen's Land and Swan River.

paint-gold. See quot. 1869.
1869 R.B. SMYTH *Gold Fields & Mineral Districts* 616 *Paint-gold,* gold found in cement, of such remarkable fineness as to resemble paint or gilding. **1896** B.S. JAMES *Westralian Goldfields* 37 Paint gold is often produced on the surfaces of quartz along its cleavage planes.

pair. *Hist.* Also **pare.** [Br. dial. *pair*, used chiefly in Cornwall: see OED *sb.*[1] 7.] A party of miners working together.
1848 *S. Austral. Register* (Adelaide) 22 Nov. 3/5 The vast heaps .. are now being let to 'pairs' or parties of workmen (a 'pair' of miners generally consisting of some half dozen). **1962** O. PRYOR *Aust.'s Little Cornwall* 15 It was usual for a party—known as a *pare*—of tributers to form themselves together to work a *pitch*, or portion of a lode, sharing equally between them the money they earned.

pakapoo. Also **pakapu** and with some variety. [a. Chinese *pai ko p'iao* white pigeon ticket; used elsewhere but recorded earliest in Aust.: see OEDS.]
1. A Chinese gambling game played with slips of paper marked with columns of characters. Freq. *attrib.*
1886 F.J. STEEL *Miscarriage of Justice* 13 There is no pretence to any sort of trade except in pak-ah-pu tickets. These are sold by a blank little Pagan. .. His customers plank a 'lokolooey' (sixpence, or any multiple of it) and mark off 10 characters out of the 80 printed upon the rice-paper voucher handed them by the blank heathen, who, thereupon, proceeds to take a duplicate for the use of the 'bank'. **1903** *Truth* (Sydney) 22 Feb. 6/2 A gambling den at 48 Campbell-street, Haymarket .. one of the most important pak-a-pu banks of the celestial sub-city.   **1974** J. GABY *Restless Waterfront* 235 They wanted multiple marks on the bales, 'more marks than on a pak-a-poo ticket', as the wool foreman said, and he was pretty right.
2. *fig.*, and in fig. contexts, as **pakapoo ticket,** something which is difficult to decipher.
1951 E. LAMBERT *Twenty Thousand Thieves* (1952) 89 Henry opened Dooley's pay-book, the pages of which showed liberal sprinklings of the red ink with which fines and convictions were entered. 'What a pay-book!' he sighed. Dooley grinned. 'Like a pak-a-poo ticket,' he agreed.

paling, *vbl. n.*
1. Used *attrib.* in Special Comb. **paling knife,** a cutting tool used to split palings, shingles, etc., from the block; a froe; **splitter,** one whose occupation is the cutting of palings, etc.; also **splitting** *vbl. n.*
1881 *Australasian Sketcher* (Melbourne) 8 Oct. 327 The **paling knife** is made to work by leverage, but in this beautiful free-splitting timber, little leverage is required, and the knife almost divides the clean, smooth shingles by merely driving it with the mallet into one end.   **1837** *S. Austral. Rec.* (London) 27 Nov. 24 We have .. men come .. as labourers .. that is to say, stock keepers, shepherds, and **paling** and shingle **splitters. 1902** *Axemen's Jrnl.* (Ulverstone) Mar. 168/2 Thirty years ago paling splitting was probably the leading industry of the North-West Coast of Tasmania.
2. Used *attrib.* with nouns designating a construction in the sense 'made from palings'.
1849 A. HARRIS *Emigrant Family* (1967) 89 The construction of paling-yards, or hurdle enclosures, being a job of some time.   **1910** *Emu* X. 128 Wherever a settler .. erects his slab or paling hut.

pallid cuckoo. [f. *pallid*, first applied as the specific name *pallida* by the English ornithologist J. Latham (*Index Ornithol.* (1801) lx.).] The cuckoo *Cuculus pallidus* occurring throughout Aust., incl. Tas.; BRAIN-FEVER BIRD.
1883 A.J. CAMPBELL *Nests & Eggs Austral. Birds* p. iii, The egg of the Pallid Cuckoo, being about half the size of the foster-bird's eggs and of a uniform pinkish tint—a beautiful specimen.   **1984** E. ROLLS *Celebration of Senses* 76 The Pallid Cuckoo arrives in the spring with a lovely rising five-note song.

palm cockatoo. [See quot. 1943.] The large, slaty black cockatoo *Probosciger aterrimus* of Cape York Peninsula (n. Qld.) and northwards to New Guinea. See also MACAW.

1898 E.E. MORRIS *Austral Eng.* 92 Palm C[ockatoo]— *Microglossus aterrimus.* **1943** C. BARRETT *Austral. Animal Bk.* 220 Few naturalists have observed the palm cockatoo in a wild state... A shy bird in its native haunts, it usually associates in pairs, frequenting the palm scrubs.

palmer. [Of unknown origin.] The fish *Lates calcarifer*: see BARRAMUNDI a. Also **palmer perch.**

1896 F.G. AFLALO *Sketch Nat. Hist. Aust.* 211 The Fitzroy perch, allied to the 'palmer' of the Mackay. **1971** P. BODEKER *Sandgropers' Trail* 231 *Lates calcarifer* (palmer perch, giant perch). Biggest freshwater fish of the North.

pandanny /pæn'dæni/. Also **pandani, pandanni.** [See quot. 1965.] The palm-like tree or shrub *Richea pandanifolia* (fam. Epacridaceae) of Tas. See also GRASS-TREE 2. Also *attrib.*, and **pandanus palm.**

1944 C. BARRETT *Isle of Mountains* 33 There were tall 'pandanny' Richeas—a whole colony of them in a swampy glade. **1963** W.M. CURTIS *Student's Flora Tas.* ii. 460 *R[ichea] pandanifolia* .. Giant Grass Tree, Pandani. **1965** *Austral. Encycl.* VI. 443 Pandanus, the generic name (often used as a vernacular) for palm-like tropical plants better known as screw pines .. in the family Pandanaceae. A corruption of this name is 'pandanny', by which the tall mountain heath *Richea pandanifolia* .. is commonly known in Tasmania. **1968** V. SERVENTY *Southern Walkabout* 54 There is the giant grass tree or 'pandanni'... Richea is the scientific name, and it is called pandanni because of the resemblance of the leaves to the pandanus of the mainland. **1979** B. ROBERTS *Stones in Cephissus* 19 You could be lost forever in this dank forest of King Billy Pine and Richea (the tall pandanus palm). **1984** *Austral. Plants* Sept. 372 *Richea pandanifolia*... Known locally as .. 'Pandani', it can be a large shrub or even a tree to 15 m.

panel van. [Cf. U.S. *panel truck.*] A motor vehicle similar in size and shape to a station wagon, having a single row of seats and a flat tray in the rear.

1955 *Wheels* July 10 Station wagons .. aren't yet as popular for private owners as cars, or as favored as panel vans for light commercial work. **1986** *Mercury* (Hobart) 27 Mar. 1/4 A girl gets pregnant .. from smoking a cigarette injected with hashish oil and then climbing into the back of a panel van to have nookie-nookie.

pan jam. *Obs.* See quot. 1864.

1864 *Colonial Cook Bk.* 72 Pan Jam. This dish used to be made from kangaroo tails. Roast them in the ashes with the skin on. When nearly done, scrape them well, and divide at the joints. Then put them into a pan, with a few slices of fat bacon, to which add a few mushrooms, pepper, etc. Fry gently, and serve. **1970** J.S. GUNN in W.S. Ramson *Eng. Transported* 63 Such food references as *saddle pouch tucker, salt junk, slippery bob* and *pan jam* are well left to history.

pannikin. Formerly also **pannican, pannakin, panniken.** [Br. dial. *pannikin* small (earthenware) pan or jar: see EDD and OED(S.)]

1. a. A metal drinking vessel; the contents of such a vessel.

1830 R. DAWSON *Present State Aust.* 101 Several tin pannicans .. served us for tea and drinking-cups. **1835** BACKHOUSE & TYLOR *Life & Labours G.W. Walker* 17 Sept. (1862) 223 A pannakin of tea however restored me. **1837** *S. Austral. Gaz.* (Adelaide) 8 July 3 We picked up several pints of periwinkles, filled our bottles with salt water, returned to some sand-hills at the side of the creek, lighted a fire, cooked them in a panniken we fortunately had with us, and made a hearty supper. **1857** J. BONWICK *Early Days Melbourne* 24 Shepherds and bullock-drivers were seen drinking champagne out of buckets with pannikins. **1945** S.J. BAKER *Austral. Lang.* 169 *A friendly pannikin*, a drink with a companion.

b. With distinguishing epithet, as **pint pannikin,** a pannikin holding one pint.

1842 *Legends of Aust.* Mar. 48 A three-legged stool, formed the table, on which were placed two pint pannikins, and half a 10 lb. damper.

c. *fig.*

1866 *Austral. Monthly Mag.* (Melbourne) II. 14 Jack .. swore .. 'a pannikin full' at Mr Graham.

2. Abbrev. of *pannikin boss.*

[N.Z. *c* **1926** 'MIXER' *Transport Workers' Songbk.* 7 My power is such to make or break—I'm a Pannikin, get me?] **1951** *Bulletin* (Sydney) 21 Feb. 12/2 By 'smoke-oh' he'd thawed out enough to say that his hand was crook... When, at blow-up, the 'pannikin' succeeded in bringing him back to life he crawled back to work like a blue-tongued lizard.

3. *Obs.* The head; in the phr. **off one's pannikin,** 'off one's head'.

1894 'H. GOLDSMITH' *Our Alma* 128 He's a bit off his pannikin to-night and I can't do nothin' with him. **1934** B. PENTON *Landtakers* 383 He's gone off his pannikin in Sydney.

4. Special Comb. **pannikin boss, overseer,** one who has only a small degree of authority; **snob,** a small-time snob; **squatter,** a small-time landholder; **wash,** see quot.

1898 E.E. MORRIS *Austral Eng.* 339 **Pannikin-boss..** applied colloquially to a man on a station, whose position is above that of the ordinary station-hand, but who is only a 'boss' .. in a small way. **1891** *Truth* (Sydney) 15 Mar. 7/3 So we bushmen changed the names Colonial experience, **pannikin-overseer,** rangie-boss, and all that 'push' into Jackeroo. **1953** 'CADDIE' *Caddie* 41 My mother-in-law was a **pannikin snob** as my father would have said. **1919** *Smith's Weekly* (Sydney) 10 May 14/2 A certain N.S.W. **pannikin squatter** once stuck up notices all over his shed. **1974** B. KIDMAN *On Wallaby* 29, I had to be content with a '**pannikin wash**'. This consisted of putting some water from the bag into the mug which formed the lid of my quartpot, holding the handle between the teeth and tipping a little into my cupped hands. A lather was then rubbed up .. another trickle .. washed it off and the remainder .. rubbed over my face and neck.

panno. [f. *pann(ikin boss* + -O.] *Pannikin boss*, see PANNIKIN 4.

1957 T. NELSON *Hungry Mile* 50 So we decided to follow the 'panno' and tracked her to the Australian Stevedoring Industry Board. **1961** *Realist* (Sydney) vii. 4/1 The worst pannos (pannikin bosses, otherwise foremen) on the waterfront.

pants man. A womanizer.

1968 *Swag* (Sydney) i. 19 You remember he was Sydney's greatest pants man. He's doing even better now, knocking off daughters of barons and earls, etc. **1979** B. HUMPHRIES *Bazza comes into his Own,* Dad was always a bit of a pants man before he dropped off the twig. They dunno what killed him: booze or stalk-fever.

paper. *Austral. pidgin.* Used *attrib.* in Special Comb. **paper talk, yabber,** a written message; a letter; also *transf.*

[**1849** C. STURT *Narr. Exped. Central Aust.* I. 139 'Papung,' he exclaimed, meaning paper or letters.] **1857** W.S. BRADSHAW *Voyages* 106 The natives have a superstitious belief respecting letters, or as they term them **paper talk.** **1887** 'OVERLANDER' *Austral. Sketches* 24, I determined to send him off first with a **paper yabber** to the other stockman telling him where we had gone. **1958** *Coast to Coast 1957–58* 34 Even the songmakers of the white people had made a 'paper-yabba' of the story.

paper-bark. [See quot. 1955.]
1. Any of several trees of the genus *Melaleuca* (fam. Myrtaceae) having a papery, often peeling, bark, as *M. leucadendra* of n. Aust. and elsewhere. Also **paperbark(ed) tree** (**tea-tree**, etc.), **paper-tree**, and *attrib.*
1827 *HRA* (1923) 3rd Ser. VI. 267 'Tea Tree' of which there are two or three varieties, the 'paper Barked' with white wood affecting moist situations. **1837** G.F. MOORE *Evidences Inland Sea* 9 Each family had its separate hut soon completed from the ready materials of blackboy spears and paper-tree bark. **1841** G. GREY *Jrnls. Two Exped. N.-W. & W.A.* I. 93 Lofty paper-bark trees grew here and there. **1863** J. DAVIS *Tracks of McKinlay* 352 This river .. is the 'Flinders'. It has lots of paper-barked trees on it. **1926** *Bulletin* (Sydney) 21 Oct. 22/3, I personally conducted experiments on timber ranging from saplings to the giant paperbarked 'ti-tree'. **1955** F. LANE *Patrol to Kimberleys* 216 Paperbarks belong to the Melaleuca family, trees of the lowlands, following the water courses... The bark resembles several sheets of thin, pale-brown papers laid together, and appears as thin and flimsy as tissue. Yet it provides a finer water-proof, grease-proof wrapping than any manufactured product which can be bought.
2. The bark of these trees.
1836 H.W. BUNBURY *Early Days W.A.* (1930) 75 Many deserted huts, some of them made with some care of the paper bark, i.e. the bark of the tea tree. **1978** B. SCOTT *Boori* 6 He gently straightened the wasted body, and rolled it in great sheets of paper-bark brought from the level country at the foot of the mountain.
3. Comb. **paper-bark** (or -**tree**) **swamp**, **torch**.
1869 *Illustr. Sydney News* 23 Dec. 310/3 Large **paperbark swamps** existing between the west bank of the river and the highest lands flanking the plain. **1918** B. CRONIN *Coastlanders* 9 Over yonder, in the paper-tree swamp. **1935** K.L. SMITH *Sky Pilot Arnhem Land* 45 We lit great **paper-bark torches**, and waved them to an fro during the crossing, in order to keep any venturesome crocodiles at bay.

paper daisy. Any of many plants of the genera *Helipterum* and *Helichrysum* (fam. Asteraceae) bearing a daisy flower-head with stiff, papery, petal-like bracts.
1921 K.S. PRICHARD *Black Opal* 5 The faint, dry fragrance of paper daisies was in the air. **1981** G.M. CUNNINGHAM et al. *Plants Western N.S.W.* 692 Common white sunray is the most widespread and common of the paper-daisies in the region.

paper man. *Hist.* A convict holding a ticket-of-leave.
1848 *Guardian* (Hobart) 25 Mar. 6/4 As to punishment (being a 'paper man') he was ordered 3 months road-making. **1851** *Guardian* (Hobart) 26 Apr. 2/3 Recommended the unlucky wight of a 'paper' man, to have his indulgence revoked.

paper-tree: see PAPER-BARK 1.

Papua. *Hist.* A name formerly applied to an Aboriginal. Also **Papuan**, *n.* and *a.*
1833 *N.S.W. Mag.* (Sydney) 181 Our *Papuas* (the aborigines) generally know nothing but to starve and to die. **1841** *Port Phillip Patriot* 9 Aug. 4/1 Mr Gould took the opportunity of visiting Flinders Island, where the scanty remnants of the Papuan Indigines of Van Diemen's Land still exist. **1853** *Visit to Aust. & Gold Regions* (S.P.C.K.) 156 The aboriginal inhabitants of Australia belong to the class of Papuans, or oriental negroes.

paradise honeysucker: see PARADISE RIFLE-BIRD.

paradise parrot. [See quot. 1976.] The parrot *Psephotus pulcherrimus*, a predom. brown, red, and turquoise bird now poss. extinct, formerly known from central e. Aust. See also ANTHILL PARROT.
1929 A.H. CHISHOLM *Birds & Green Places* 98 The paradise-parrot, of central and southern Queensland and the north of New South Wales. **1976** *Reader's Digest Compl. Bk. Austral. Birds* 286 The name paradise parrot was conceived by bird-keepers in England when live specimens began to arrive there.

paradise rifle-bird. [*Paradise*, first applied as the specific name *paradiseus* by English naturalist William Swainson: see quot. 1825.] The rainforest bird *Ptiloris paradiseus* of e. Qld. and e. N.S.W., the mature male having velvety black plumage with iridescent blue-green markings. Formerly also **paradise honeysucker**.
[**1825** *Zool. Jrnl.* (London) I. 481 *Ptiloris paradiseus*... It is impossible for any written description, or coloured representation, to convey an adequate idea of the rich and varied tints of this superb creature. Its *size* is about that of the six shafted Paradise bird.] **1860** G. BENNETT *Gatherings of Naturalist* 215 The Paradise Honeysucker, the Rifleman or Rifle-bird of the colonists (*Ptiloris paradiseus*). **1941** C. BARRETT *Aust.* 85 Paradise rifle-birds frequent the palm brush.

paradox. *Obs.* [f. the specific epithet *paradoxus* of paradoxical character, applied by the German anatomist J.F. Blumenbach (*Voigt's Mag. Naturk.* (1800) II. 205, *Götting. gel. Anz.* (1800) I. 609).] PLATYPUS.
1815 *HRA* (1916) 1st Ser. VIII. 573 In the reaches or pools of the Campbell River, the very curious animal called the Paradox, or Watermole is seen.

parakeelia /pærə'kiljə/. Also with much variety, as **parakeelya, parakelia, parakylia, parrakeelya**. [a. Guyani *barrgilya*.] Any of several herbs of the fam. Portulacaceae, having thick succulent leaves and occurring in arid inland Aust., usu. of the genus *Calandrinia*, esp. *C. balonensis* and *C. polyandra*; JUNGA. See also MUNYEROO. Also *attrib.*
1885 *Adelaide Observer* 22 Aug. 10 Pigface and parakylia abound. **1898** D.W. CARNEGIE *Spinifex & Sand* 215 'Parakeelia' .. is a local, presumably native, name in Central Australia for a most wonderful and useful plant. A specimen brought back by me from this locality was identified at Kew as *Calandrinia balonensis*. **1920** C.H. SAYCE *Golden Buckles* 114 There were plenty of cattle tracks about, but it was parakelia country, and .. the beggars can go for weeks without a drink if that stuff is at all green. **1967** M. & M. LEYLAND *Where Dead Men Lie* 122 He came upon the green jelly-like Parakeelya plant with its juicy water-filled leaves. **1978** K. WILLEY *Joe Brown's Dog* 6 A drink of water at considerable intervals and a feed of parrakeelya or some of the other desert herbages, and a camel would go anywhere.

paralytic, *a.* [Used elsewhere but recorded earliest in Aust.] Extremely intoxicated, 'dead drunk'. Also **paralytic drunk.**
1891 *Truth* (Sydney) 10 May 3/3 This friend was paralytic drunk. **1962** A. SEYMOUR *One Day of Yr.* 10 You'd stick up for him if he was paralytic.

Paramatta, var. PARRAMATTA.

parcel. [Spec. use of *parcel* a quantity or amount. Used elsewhere but recorded earliest in Aust. and prob. of Br. dial. origin: see OED(S 4 b.] A quantity of a mineral, esp. as prepared for sale.
1848 *S. Austral. Register* (Adelaide) 25 Oct. 3/5 A parcel of Burra Burra ore. **1980** S. THORNE *I've met some Bloody Wags* 74, I was told he had just sold a 'parcel' (meaning a quantity of opal) to the opal dealer sitting behind us.

parcel post. [Joc. use of *parcel post* branch of a postal service.] **a.** Used *attrib.* to designate the inexperience or recent arrival of a station hand. **b.** Used allusively with reference to such a person's acquisition of a job.

1931 W. HATFIELD *Sheepmates* 118 Hallett took charge of the three 'parcel post' men and showed them a bunk where they could deposit their belongings. **1951** E. HILL *Territory* 431 'Parcel post' was influence—a station manager, or a jackeroo from the cities, who might be the boss's nephew, or going to marry his daughter... 'He come up by parcel post,' they still say. 'He don't know nothin'.'

Hence **parcel poster** *n.*

1935 R.B. PLOWMAN *Boundary Rider* 151 'He's a parcel-poster, that bloke,' the padre heard a bushman say, referring to the English-man... 'Up one mail an' down the next... A few sticks it out; but most of 'em don't.'

parchment. *Hist.* [Spec. use of *parchment* a document on parchment.] A certificate issued to a pardoned convict.

1848 R. MARSH *Seven Yrs. of my Life* 175 We are now in Hobart Town and at the office receiving our parchments or pardon. **1853** *Guardian* (Hobart) 8 June 3/1 On presenting his 'parchment', to the Captain, it was found illegible, and the Captain, refused to take him.

pardalote /'pɑːdəloʊt/. [The bird genus *Pardalotus* was named by the French ornithologist L.J.P. Vieillot (*Analyse d'une nouvelle Ornithologie* (1816) 31), a. Gr. παρδαλωτός spotted like a pard.] Any bird of the genus *Pardalotus*, of all States. See also *diamond bird* DIAMOND *n.*[1] Often with distinguishing epithet, as **red-browed, red-tipped, spotted, striated** (see under first element).

1841 *S. Austral. Rec.* (London) 2 Jan. 10 The pardalotes, beautiful little birds, of which .. two species are figured. **1984** SIMPSON & DAY *Birds of Aust.* 332 Pardalotes are distinctive in appearance—small and colourful with short tails and short blunt beaks.

pardon. *Hist.* [Spec. use of *pardon* remission of the legal consequences of a crime.] A remission of (a convict's) sentence; a document certifying this. See also ABSOLUTE PARDON, *conditional pardon*, CONDITIONAL.

1793 J. HUNTER *Hist. Jrnl. Trans. Port Jackson* 563 A general pardon was therefore promised to all those who came back within a certain time. **1850** W. GATES *Recoll. Van Dieman's Land* 191, I saw my name gazetted for a free pardon... We called at the police office for our 'Pardons'.

Also **pardoned** *ppl. a.*

1818 T.E. WELLS *M. Howe* (1945) 31 Howe .. being in fact considered a *pardoned offender* .. was afforded a last chance of atoning in some degree for his past crimes by an amended life.

pare, var. PAIR.

parent. Used *attrib.* in Special Comb. **(a) parent country, land, state,** the British Isles; **(b) colony,** New South Wales. See also MOTHER.

(a) 1789 W. TENCH *Narr. Exped. Botany Bay* 5 Some have been sanguine enough to fore-see the most beneficial effects to the Parent State, from the Colony we are endeavouring to establish. **1808** *To Viscount Castlereagh* 3 Indebted originally to the parent country. **1853** J. CAPPER *Emigrant's Guide to Aust.* (ed. 2) 15 There will no longer be a convicted criminal from the parent land within its [*sc.* New South Wales] limits. **(b) 1821** J. WALLIS *Hist. Acct. Colony N.S.W.* 10 The population of Norfolk Island would be very considerably increased by this detachment from the parent Colony.

parentie, parinti, varr. PERENTIE.

Parkhurst. *Hist.* [f. the name of *Parkhurst* Prison on the Isle of Wight.] Used *attrib.* of a juvenile who, having served part of a sentence in Parkhurst Prison, was sent to Australia or New Zealand between 1842 and 1852.

1844 *Parramatta Chron.* 22 June 3/2 *Swan River.*—John Gavin, one of the Parkhurst boys, has been tried and found guilty at the Supreme Court of this colony for the murder of a youth named George Pollard. **1852** G.C. MUNDY *Our Antipodes* III. 226 The worst class of men .. were separated from a more juvenile class, the Parkhurst lads.

parkinsonia tree. [The plant genus *Parkinsonia* was named by Swedish botanist Carl von Linné (Linnaeus) (*Species Plantarum* (1753) 375), after English apothecary John *Parkinson* (1569-1629).] The introduced tree or shrub *Parkinsonia aculeata* (fam. Caesalpiniaceae), naturalized and cultivated in n. Aust., having fragrant yellow flowers.

1953 J.K. EWERS *With Sun on my Back* 90 Clusters of date palms, and Parkinsonia-trees bright with yellow blossom. **1963** O. RUHEN *Flockmaster* 177 There was an aborigine camp .. and dotted all about were planted stands of parkinsonia trees, white cedars, athel pines and pepperinas.

park lands, *pl. S.A.* A green belt along the Torrens River, and surrounding the centres of Adelaide and North Adelaide, as planned by Colonel William Light (1786-1839) in 1837.

1838 T.H. JAMES *Six Months S.A.* 32 Most of the new comers settle down on what is called the Park Lands, where they are handy to the little rivulet. **1979** K. BONYTHON *Ladies' Legs & Lemonade* 224 We lived with his oft-repeated catchcry of 'Hands off the parklands! Restore Adelaide to Colonel Light's Vision!'

Hence **Park Lander** *n.*

1838 *Southern Austral.* (Adelaide) 17 Nov. 3/3 In December next all Park Landers would be compelled to quit.

parma wallaby /ˌpɑːmə ˈwɒləbi/. [The specific name *Parma,* a. Dharawal *bama,* was applied by the English naturalist G.R. Waterhouse (*Nat. Hist. Mamm.* I. (1845) 149).] The greyish-brown wallaby *Macropus parma* of N.S.W., and introduced to Kawau Is., New Zealand, having a white throat and white cheek stripe. Formerly also **parma (kangaroo).**

1845 J.E. GRAY *List of Specimens Mammalia Brit. Museum* 91 The Parma. *Halmaturus Parma,* Gould, P.Z.S. *a.* Male. New South Wales.—From Mr Gould's Collection. *b.* Female. **1845** G.R. WATERHOUSE *Nat. Hist. Mammalia* I. 149 *Macropus* (Halmaturus) Parma. Parma Kangaroo. *Halmaturus Parma.* .. Fur moderate; general colour rich rufous brown, pencilled with whitish. **1894** R. LYDEKKER *Handbk. Marsupialia & Monotremata* 40 Parma Wallaby... This species seems to be very rare and locally distributed.

parrakeelya, var. PARAKEELIA.

Parramatta. /ˌpærəˈmætə/. *Hist.* Also **Paramatta.** [f. the name of the second settlement in New South Wales, now a city in the Sydney metropolitan area.]

a. Used *attrib.* in Special Comb. **Parramatta cloth,** a coarse woollen cloth, orig. manufactured by the inmates of the Female Factory at Parramatta: see quot. 1946.

1826 J. ATKINSON *Acct. Agric. & Grazing N.S.W.* 131 The coarse woollens are known in the Colony by the appellation of Parramatta cloth, having been first made there. **1946** *Concerning Wool* (Austral. Wool Board) 91 Simeon Lord who had established a mill on the swamps at Botany in 1816 entered into an agreement with Governor Macquarie to burl, mill, dye and dress the cloth from the Parramatta factory. Known as 'Parramatta cloth', this was well spoken of in the wool trade for many years. Other

mills followed and in 1852 the output had reached 235,000 yards a year, and Parramatta tweed exported to England gained such a favourable reputation that Bradford manufacturers began production of a tweed which they called Parramatta cloth.
b. Abbrev. of *Parramatta cloth.* Freq. *attrib.*
1827 P. CUNNINGHAM *Two Yrs. in N.S.W.* I. 46 The government gangs of convicts .. with their white woollen Parramatta frocks and trowsers .. tell a tale too plain to be misunderstood. **1884** J.B. MARTIN *Reminisc.* 41 The great tailor artist, Hayes, used to boast that he served the swell and the bullock driver from the same roll of 'Parramatta', but that the refinements of his art preserved their identities.
c. A blanket made from *Parramatta cloth.*
1883 'ONE WHO WAS THERE' *Prison Sketches* 11 Touching the bedding, I may remark that it consists of a sort of a flock and a kind of flax bed, two single blankets and a rug in summer, and in winter an extra rug, called a 'parramatta'.

Parramatta grass. The naturalized African grass *Sporobolus africanus* (fam. Poaceae), an erect, tussocky perennial; the similar, closely-related native grass *S. elongatus.*
1895 F. TURNER *Austral. Grasses* I. 52 *Sporobolus indicus* .. 'Parramatta' or 'Tussock Grass'... An erect-growing, tussocky grass, sometimes attaining a height of 2½ feet, and found in all the Australian Colonies. **1983** G.G. ROBINSON *Native Grasses Northern Tablelands* 10 Parramatta grass [*sc. Sporobolus elongatus*] is generally more frequent on the lighter soil types where it is very persistent even under intense grazing... It is one of the poorer of the common native grasses.

parrot. The flesh of a parrot, used as food. Freq. *attrib.*, esp. as **parrot pie.**
1837 *S. Austral. Rec.* (London) 11 Nov. 14 Strange as it may appear to you, a stewed cockatoo, a parrot pudding, a steak off the leg of an emu, or a tureen of kangaroo soup, is a dish that you would relish even in London. **1977** *Westerly* iv. 16 Geoff promised you parrot pie for dinner and slunk off behind the bulkhead.

parrot fish. [Transf. use of *parrot-fish* a fish having a brilliant colour or beak-like mouth.] **a.** Any fish, usu. brightly coloured, of the fam. Scaridae, having fused teeth resembling a parrot's beak. **b.** Any of many brightly coloured marine fish of the fam. Labridae.
1827 *HRA* (1923) 3rd Ser. VI. 271 The Fish we caught were 'Parrot Fish'. **1889** *Lord Howe Island* 66 *Labrichthys inscripta.*.. This 'Parrot Fish' (all the members of the family go by the same name) is abundant.

Parry's wallaby. [First applied as the specific name *Parryi* by E.T. Bennett, secretary of the Zool. Soc. London (*Proc. Zool. Soc. London* (1834) 151) after the English naval officer and Arctic explorer Sir William Edward Parry (1790–1855), who took the type specimen to England.] WHIPTAIL WALLABY.
1894 R. LYDEKKER *Hand-Bk. Marsupialia & Monotremata* 30 Parry's Wallaby. *Macropus parryi.* .. Size medium; form slender and graceful... General colour of upper-parts clear grey, with a bluish tinge. **1954** C. BARRETT *Wild Life Aust. & New Guinea* 6 Parry's wallaby, with a slender body and very long tail, and white and grey markings.

parson's bands, *pl.* [See quot. 1911.] The terrestrial orchid *Eriochilus cucullatus* (fam. Orchidaceae), of all States exc. W.A. and N.T.
1911 R.S. ROGERS *Introd. S. Austral. Orchids* (rev. ed.) 11 The 'parson's bands', so called from the two little white sepals which stick out in front. **1978** B.P. MOORE *Life on Forty Acres* 51 Parson's Bands .. a pale pink and very delicate orchid that blooms in late summer.

part, *adv.* [Spec. use of *part* in part, partly.] Of an Aboriginal: partly descended from another race.
1959 E. WEBB *Mark of Sun* 133 It's going to look good, him having a part-aborigine boy working for him. **1981** A.B. FACEY *Fortunate Life* 39 He was a part-blood Aboriginal. *Ibid.* 140 Six part-blooded Aboriginals and two full-bloods.

partridge. *Obs.* [See quot. 1847.] Either of two birds, the *painted quail* (see PAINTED) and the *brown quail* (see BROWN *a.* 1). Also **partridge quail.**
1803 J. GRANT *Narr. Voyage N.S.W.* 110 We sprung some coveys of quails, or more properly the partridges of New Holland. **1847** J. GOULD *Birds of Aust.* (1848) V. Pl. 90, They are distinguished as the greater and lesser Brown Quail, and sometimes the name of Partridge was given to the bird here figured [*sc.* the 'Van Diemen's Land Partridge']; doubtless from its going in coveys and resembling the Common Partridge of Europe in many of its actions. **1878** R.B. SMYTH *Aborigines of Vic.* II. 159 Partridge quail—Chooirrp.

partridge pigeon. [See quot. 1976.] The bird of tropical woodlands of the Kimberley Ranges (W.A.) and Arnhem Land (N.T.) *Geophaps smithii;* occas. *G. scripta* (see *squatter pigeon* SQUATTER 5).
1842 J. GOULD *Birds of Aust.* (1848) V. Pl. 68, *Geophaps smithii* .. Partridge Pigeon, Residents at Port Essington. **1976** *Reader's Digest Compl. Bk. Austral. Birds* 246 Partridge pigeons fly like partridges, in short, swift bursts close to the ground.

part up, *v.* [f. *part* to give or pay money, prob. infl. by *to pay up.*] *intr.* To pay money. Also *trans.*
1889 *Bulletin* (Sydney) 21 Sept. 20/1 An' then they reckoned I'd been usin' 'em all the time, and they made me part up. *c* **1907** W.C. CHANDLER *Darkest Adelaide* 84 If Christ came down again He would have to part up the full traybit, or sleep out in the park, no matter how cold and frosty the night might be.

pass. *Hist.* [Spec. use of *pass* a written permission.]
1. A document authorizing and regulating the movement of a convict.
1796 *Instruct. for Constables Country Districts* 13 They are to apprehend all Persons passing to and from the different Settlements who are not furnished with proper Passes signed by any of the Acting Magistrates, the Governor's Aid de Camp or the Commanding Officer at the Hawkesbury. **1865** J.F. MORTLOCK *Experiences of Convict* 87 Foot-travellers must exhibit their 'pass' and satisfy enquiries on pain of apprehension.
2. Special Comb. **pass-holder,** a convict to whom a pass has been issued.
1845 *Sydney Morning Herald* 13 Mar. 2/6 The remainder, ticket-of-leave men and pass-holders, remain in this colony.
Also **passed** *ppl. a.,* issued with a pass.
1827 *Monitor* (Sydney) 20 Sept. 655/2 Some of the vigilant Constables were not to be deprived of their prey .. and Buler Hewson .. seized upon the '*passed*' fugitives, and lodged them in custody.

passport. *Hist.* [Transf. use of *passport.*] PASS 1. Also **passport of leave.**
1796 *N.S.W. Instruct. to Watchmen* 11 If they are People travelling from Parramatta, the Hawkesbury or any other distant place to Sydney, they are to produce their Passports of Leave from the persons authorised to give them. **1843** *Sydney Morning Herald* 23 Aug. 3/5 All passports or passes for more than fourteen days, enabling ticket of leave holders or assigned servants to visit Sydney shall cease to be in force.

pastoral, *a.* [Spec. use of *pastoral* 'relating to, or occupied in, the care of flocks or herds'; (of land) used for pasture: see OED(S *a*. In Austral. use there is a firm distinction between AGRICULTURAL (q.v.) and PASTORAL and the latter is substantially without literary connotations.]

1. Of, pertaining to, or engaged in, stock-raising as distinct from crop-raising.

1839 S. *Austral. Rec.* (London) 15 Nov. 271 Does not every quality and inclination they have shown prove their fitness for *pastoral* occupations? **1965** G.H. FEARNSIDE *Golden Ram* 160 It has been estimated that present agricultural and pastoral production in Australia is being achieved with 250,000 fewer rural workers than was required under pre-war methods.

2. Of a tract of land: used for, or suitable to be used for, stock-raising.

1839 S. BUTLER *Hand-Bk. Austral. Emigrants* 115 Both colonies must necessarily be pastoral settlements for a long time to come. **1973** *Agriscene Aust.* Jan. 44/1 For the better part of three years now the crisis in the wool industry, especially in the Pastoral Zone, has been widely heralded.

3. Special Comb. **pastoral company,** a commercial enterprise engaged in large-scale stock-raising; **country,** a territory, or tract of land within a territory, devoted principally to stock-raising; **district,** an area in which the principal industry is stock-raising; an area officially designated for this purpose; **lease,** an agreement under which an area of land is held on condition that it is used for stock-raising; the land so held; **lessee,** one who holds a *pastoral lease*; **property, run,** a stock-raising establishment (see also PROPERTY, RUN *n.*² 2); **settlement,** the occupation of land for stock-raising; **settler,** one who takes up land for the purpose of stock-raising; **station,** a stock-raising establishment (see also STATION 3); **town,** a town which depends for its existence upon the stock-raising industry in the surrounding district.

1852 J. WEST *Hist. of Tas.* I. 110 Captain Dixon .. came to Van Diemen's Land in 1820. .. He suggested the formation of a **pastoral company,** with a capital divided into £100 shares, as a profitable scheme. **1840** S. *Austral. Rec.* (London) 15 Jan. 11 Concentration can never exist in a **pastoral country** like Australia. **1831** *Acct. Colony Van Diemen's Land* 27 The road .. passes through a **pastoral district** of fine thinly wooded downs, principally adapted for sheep grazing. **1876** *Austral. Handbk.* 104 The colony of New South Wales is divided into thirteen Pastoral Districts. **1850** *Illustr. Austral. Mag.* (Melbourne) July 78 There appears to be no power over the Crown lands except for **pastoral leases,** and these confined to one year. **1869** *Bushmen, Publicans, & Politics* 18 The remaining quarter million of acres held under pastoral lease. **1880** *Argus* (Melbourne) 6 Jan. 5/5 It would be a great help .. if every **pastoral lessee** were to report to the Government all particulars relating to every well sunk. **1883** *Illustr. Austral. News* (Melbourne) 28 Nov. 194/3 Shearing time on **pastoral properties** and stations is the busiest and most important time of the whole year. **1868** J.K. TUCKER *Aborigines & Chinese Question* 6 A **pastoral run** was leased from the Government with a view of establishing an industrial farm and self-sustaining mission. **1841** S. *Austral. Almanack* 3 The quantity of stock stated as in the possession of those colonists only *commencing* their **pastoral settlement,** gives no fair criterion to judge of the extent of their intended operations. **1839** *Port Phillip Patriot* 24 Apr. 3 A clause in the **Pastoral Settlers** Act. **1848** W. WESTGARTH *Aust. Felix* 109 It is common practice to have an aboriginal boy at the **pastoral stations** for assisting in tracking stray cattle. **1901** H. LAWSON *Joe Wilson & his Mates* 47 The place was only a dusty little **pastoral town** in the scrubs.

pastoral, *n. Obs.* PASTORALIST.

1890 'R. BOLDREWOOD' *Colonial Reformer* 20 One of the pastorals looked at the other in astonishment.

pastoralist. [Spec. use of *pastoralist* 'one who lives by keeping flocks of sheep and cattle': see OED(S.)] The owner of a substantial stock-raising establishment or of a number of such establishments. See also GRAZIER.

1880 *Gentleman's Mag.* (London) CCXLVI. 62 The outside districts, occupied only by pastoralists. **1985** *Bulletin* (Sydney) 28 May 66/3 An outback pastoralist who fitted in a war between incredibly varied and tough days on the land in Queensland.

pat. Abbrev. of PAT MALONE.

1908 *Austral. Mag.* (Sydney) 1 Nov. 1251 'On my own' (by myself) became 'on my Pat Malone', and subsequently the tendency to abbreviation .. soon had the effect of rendering this 'on my Pat' a very general expression nowadays. **1978** R.H. CONQUEST *Dusty Distances* 10 He rode, on his pat, close on 800 miles.

patch. [Spec. use of *patch* an area, body of material, etc., different from its surrounds.] A (profitable) mining claim; an isolated body of mineral.

1857 A. FAUCHERY *Lettres d'un Mineur en Australie* 197 Une simple plaque souterraine,—ce qu'un nomme, en langage de mines, une *tache* (patch) ou une *poche* (pocket). **1940** I.L. IDRIESS *Lightning Ridge* 77 The 'Big Four' had 'struck it', had 'bottomed on large nobbies' (black opal) and looked like developing into a big patch!

Paterson's curse. Also **Patterson's curse.** [Prob. f. the name of Richard Eyre *Patterson* (1844–1918), a grazier occupying various stations near Albury from *c* 1874.] Any of several naturalized European herbs of the genus *Echium* (fam. Boraginaceae), esp. the common *E. plantagineum*, having usu. bluish-purple flowers, variously regarded as a noxious weed, useful drought fodder, or valuable honey plant; *the curse*, see CURSE 2; RIVERINA BLUEBELL; SALVATION JANE.

1904 J.H. MAIDEN *Weeds N.S.W.* (1920) 67 Mr P. Hore, of Mugwee Estate, kept a number of sheep in a small paddock last spring that was covered with 'Paterson's Curse', and the sheep completely ate it out, and appeared to do well on it. **1982** K. HUENEKE *Huts of High Country* 181 Dilapidated dairies and weatherboard homesteads contrasted against less sympathetic modern brick veneer farm houses, many hectares of Patterson's curse and big fat black cattle. Here and there are miniature clusters of beehive villages, no doubt moved elsewhere when the rich deep blue carpet has wilted.

Pat Malone. Rhyming slang for 'own'; esp. in the phr. **on one's Pat Malone,** on one's own; alone. Also **Pat Maloney.**

1908 MRS A. GUNN *We of Never-Never* 146 A thousand miles on horseback, 'on me Pat Malone', into the Australian interior and out again. **1950** J. MORRISON *Port of Call* 174 'All on your Pat Maloney?' .. 'I guess.'

patter /'pætə/, *v. Austral.* pidgin. *Obs.* Also **patta.** [a. Dharuk *bada* to eat.] *trans.* To eat (food). Also *absol.*

1790 D. SOUTHWELL Corresp. & Papers, *Pat-ta*, to eat. **1803** J. GRANT *Narr. Voyage N.S.W.* 109 These natives would kill and *patter*, that is, *eat him*. **1847** *Maitland Mercury* 27 Oct. 4/4 White fellow too much sick, patter too much jumbuck.

patter /'pætə/, *n. Austral.* pidgin. *Obs.* Also **pattor.** [f. prec.] Food.

1824 Methodist Missionary Soc. Rec. 26 Jan., 'Boodjerry patta! murry boodjerry!—fat as jimbuck!!' i.e. good food, very good, fat as mutton. **1880** J.B. STEVENSON *Seven Yrs. Austral. Bush* 147 Billy .. made his appearance, holding a large carpet-snake aloft in triumph, 'Buddgery Pattor this fellow'. **1904** *Shearer* (Sydney) 17 Dec. 2/2 Almost anyone from a 'slushy' to a spieler .. can become a parrot and

Patterson's curse, var. PATERSON'S CURSE.

pav. Abbrev. of PAVLOVA.
1966 G.W. TURNER *Eng. Lang. Aust. & N.Z.* 173 *Pavlova cake*.. sometimes shortened to *pav*. **1981** *Bulletin* (Sydney) 13 Jan. 74/1 The Pav, a kind of meringue the size and shape of a truck wheel, is the country's national dish.

pavlova. [f. the name of Anna *Pavlova* (1885–1931), Russian ballerina: see quot. 1971.]
1. A dessert; a large, soft-centred meringue topped with whipped cream and fruit.
[N.Z. **1927** *Davis Dainty Dishes* (Davis Gelatine N.Z., Ltd.) (ed. 6) 11 Pavlova... Dissolve all but a teaspoonful of Gelatine in the hot water, and all the sugar [etc.].] **1929** K. MCKAY *Practical Home Cookery* 155/1 *Pavlova cakes*... Cook like meringues... They are delightful and simple to make besides being a novelty.] **1940** WESTACOTT & LOWENSTERN 275 *Choice Recipes* 40 Pavlova Cake. Four eggs, 8 ozs. castor sugar, 1 dessertspoon vinegar, 1 dessertspoon cornflour, 1 pinch cream of tartar. Beat whites stiff, fold in sugar, beat till dissolved, add other ingredients, lastly vinegar. Line a 9-inch tin with grease-proof paper slightly moistened; allow sides to stand up 4 inches as it rises very much, bake 1½ hours in slow oven. Turn out and leave upside down to cool. Turn over and put whipped cream and passion fruit on top. **1971** *Bulletin* (Sydney) 11 Dec. 13/1 Harrods is still London's most classy department store.. so I felt a touch of satisfaction when I saw in their cake department a sign saying 'Pavlova Cake—20 p. a slice' (that is, A43 cents). The Pavlova, a distinctive Australian contribution to cuisine, had been officially recognised as posh. But I was shocked to read the rest of the notice. It said: 'Pavlova Cake was created in New Zealand as a tribute to the dancer Anna Pavlova'. Furthermore, the specimen on display was not authentic. Instead of the traditional passionfruit on top of the cream it had strawberries. And the base did not seem to be the proper meringue; it was some brown crusty stuff.
2. Used allusively as an emblem of insubstantiality. Also *attrib*.
1972 BERMAN & CHILDS *Why isn't she Dead!* 63 As a graduate of the pavlova belt he was too inhibited to try anything novel or unfamiliar. **1972** *Bulletin* (Sydney) 30 Dec. 15/1 What it most sadly didn't seem to merit was the recent final softening of TDT into television's equivalent of the pavlova, a nightly pudding of feeble comedy and stingless comment.

pay, *v. Mining.* [Spec. use of *pay* to yield an adequate return; to be profitable.] *intr.* Of a mine, mineral-bearing deposit, etc.: to be profitable to work. Also *trans.*, to yield (a return).
1852 *Murray's Guide to Gold Diggings* 24 The rock was too deep for them to reach, or to pay well even if there was gold when they did. **1902** *Bulletin* (Sydney) 22 Mar. 3/2 Two ounces to the dish she pays.

payable, *a.* [Spec. use of *payable* capable of yielding an adequate return: see OED *a.* 3.]
a. In collocations: **payable gold, goldfield, ground, ore.**
1859 *Colonial Mining Jrnl.* May 145/1 A claim at the end of Wilson's lead has struck **payable gold**. **1863** F. ALGAR *Handbk. to Colony Tas.* 10 By a **payable gold-field** is meant one capable of yielding five thousand ounces a week for a period of twelve months. **1859** *Colonial Mining Jrnl.* May 145/2 The company found a small patch of **payable ground** of some 50 feet square. **1868** *Wallaroo Times* (Kadina) 1 Apr. 5/3 The lode.. is yielding good **payable ore.**
b. In the collocation **payable dirt,** pay-dirt.
1859 *Colonial Mining Jrnl.* June 162/2 The party has driven across two or three wide runs of payable dirt.

pay-back. *Austral. pidgin.* An act of revenge, as sanctioned by traditional Aboriginal practice; the code governing this. Also *attrib.*, and *transf.*
1935 D. THOMSON *In Arnhem Land* (1983) 67 Many remembered feuds of long standing—for blood feuds among these people are carried on for many generations. The 'pay back' as they call it, may be delayed for years in order to catch a man, or a group, off guard. **1962** D. LOCKWOOD *I, Aboriginal* 22 Aborigines never forget. All wrongs must be set right by a system known as *Pay-Back*. **1970** M. KELLY *Spinifex* 63 'I can remember him taking part in a big pay-back raid a few years later.' 'Pay-back?' 'Pidgen [*sic*] for vendetta.' **1984** *Age* (Melbourne) 19 Sept. 11/3 It is simply asking too much of human nature for people not to see Mr Wran's advertising switch as pay-back to Fairfax.

Paymaster. *Hist.* Used with reference to a paymaster of the New South Wales Corps in the collocations **Paymaster's bill, note,** a note recording payment due to a member of the Corps, which was consolidated into a bill on a regimental agent in London.
1803 *Sydney Gaz.* 24 Apr., Paymaster's Bills and Copper Coin received in payment of any of the above Articles. **1811** *Ibid.* 9 Feb., Payment to be made on delivery, in Government or Paymaster's Notes.

pay note. *Obs.* Shortened form of *Paymaster's note* (see PAYMASTER).
1804 *Sydney Gaz.* 25 Nov., New South Wales Corps.. the Committee of Paymastership of the said Corps will consolidate their Pay Notes for this and the preceding months. **1809** *Ibid.* 26 Mar., The Pay Notes issued for the subsistence of the Corps.. will be consolidated in Cash or Bills on the 30th instant, at the Paymaster's Office.

pea, *n.*[1] [Shortened form of *Darling pea* (a) (see DARLING).] Used *attrib.* in Special Comb. **pea-eater,** an animal which has been poisoned as a result of eating Darling pea; **-struck** *ppl. a.*, afflicted by this poisoning; also **-stricken.**
1901 J.H. MAIDEN *Plants reputed to be Poisonous* 16 'Darling Pea'... It's effect on sheep is well-known; they separate from the flock, wander about listlessly, and are known to the shepherds as '**pea-eaters**', or 'indigo eaters'. **1916** *Bulletin* (Sydney) 5 Oct. 24/2 Can any.. scientist put a name to the toxic principle in the Darling pea..? When a cow develops a wild glare.. and doesn't appear to have any real desire for tucker.. it is safe to assume in pea country that she has become a 'pea-eater'. **1902** [**pea-struck**] *Ibid.* 17 May 14/3 Concerning a certain pea-stricken horse: 'D.H.R.'.. recommends hand-feeding as a possible remedy for the effects of Darling pea. **1934** A. MELROSE *Song & Slapstick* 96 A pea-struck steer.

pea, *n.*[2] [Fig. use of *pea*, as in the (swindler's) game of *thimblerig*, in which one of three inverted thimbles allegedly conceals a pea; *obs.* except in Aust.: see OEDS *n.*[1] 1 e.]
1. In horse-racing: a favourite; a likely winner (see quot. 1953). Also *transf.*, one in a favoured or favourable position.
1911 E. DYSON *Benno & Push* 206 Mr Dickson.. ran his eye down the card and chanced it. 'Dandy's the P,' he said. 'Put yer whole week's wash on Dandy, 'n hold me responsible if the goods ain't delivered.' **1953** S.J. BAKER *Aust. Speaks* 118 Other expressions used by racing fans include: *pea*, a horse that is being ridden to win, especially when there is doubt about the genuineness of other runners. **1969** A. BUZO *Rooted* (1973) 92 He's had his eye on her for some time, you know, but I'm the pea, she said.
2. In the *attrib.* phr. **pea and thimble,** engaged in swindling.

1918 *Euripidean: Troopship Souvenir* 6 An me arunnin' messages for th' barmaid at th'. 'Spreading Sun' and workin' in conjunction with a pea an' thimble joint. **1966** J. WATEN *Season of Youth* 32, I started to walk, hardly taking any notice of the horses pounding round the course... There were pea and thimble men displaying their skill and fleecing the half-shrewd mugs.

pea-bush. Any of several shrubs of the genus *Sesbania* (fam. Fabaceae) occurring in n. Aust., as *S. benthamiana* of N.S.W., Qld., and N.T.
1881 T. ARCHER *Some Remarks on Proposed Qld. Trans-Continental Railway* 18 The pea-bush, a species of *sesbania*, also found abundantly on the flooded flats of the Gilbert, growing in patches, or more open scrubs, to a height of from ten to fifteen feet, is eagerly devoured by stock when green. **1981** A.B. & J.W. CRIBB *Useful Wild Plants Aust.* 207 *Sesbania benthamiana* (*S. aculeata*) Sesbania Pea, Pea-bush... The dried stems were used by the Aborigines as drills for making fire.

peaceful dove. The dove *Geopelia placida* of e. and n. mainland Aust. and elsewhere, a predom. grey to brown bird with black bars.
1845 J. GOULD *Birds of Aust.* (1848) V. Pl. 73, *Geopelia tranquilla*.. Peaceful Dove. **1984** SIMPSON & DAY *Birds of Aust.* 310 Many pigeons, including this Peaceful Dove, drink by sucking.

peacock, *v. Hist.* [In punning allusion to the eye-like markings on the tail feathers of a peacock: see EYE.] *trans.* To obtain (the choicest parts of a tract of land, esp. those controlling access to water), in order to render the surrounding land of little or no value to others. Also *intr.*
1892 *Truth* (Sydney) 17 Apr. 2/1 'Peacocked' in the most scientific manner all over the vast holding, literally 'picking the eyes out' of this fine country. **1945** H.S. ROBERTON *Now blame Farmer* 16 They 'peacocked' the land and held the squatter up for ransom. They selected where it would do the squatter the greatest harm, and then they offered to sell. They were our first land-jobbers.
Hence **peacocker** *n.*
1892 *Truth* (Sydney) 17 Apr. 4/3 These princes among 'peacockers'.

peacocking, *vbl. n.* [f. prec.] See quot. 1945.
1892 *Truth* (Sydney) 17 Apr. 2/1 This 'peacocking' was commenced.. under Sir John Robertson's new Land Act of 1861. **1945** H.S. ROBERTON *Now blame Farmer* 15 The squatters had exercised their right of pre-emption. When their licences had been converted to leases they were given the right to buy at the unimproved capital value, and they bought. But they did not buy the whole of their runs. They bought small and strategically situated areas all over their runs, in the pious hope that it would discourage intrusion. The device came to be known as 'peacocking'.

peacock sole. [See quot. 1969.] The marine fish *Pardachirus pavoninus* of n. Qld., having the typically flattened body of a sole, and the similar *P. hedleyi* of N.S.W. and Qld.
1906 D.G. STEAD *Fishes of Aust.* 183 Amongst other species of our Flat-Fishes might be mentioned.. the Peacock Sole (*Achirus pavoninus*). **1969** J. POLLARD *Austral. & N.Z. Fishing* 200 Peacock Sole... This is a prettily-marked sole, with an array of dots or spots that are paler than the rest of the fish scattered across a reddish-brown background.

pea-dodger. *Obs.* A bowler hat.
1933 *Bulletin* (Sydney) 5 Apr. 12/3 'Elizabeth Owen':.. the different terms applied to 'bowler' hats—I have also heard them called 'egg-boiler' and 'pea-dodgers'. **1945** S.J. BAKER *Austral. Lang.* 181 Among.. the Australia equivalents of what the Englishman calls a *bowler*.. peadodger.

pear.
1. *Obs.* Any of several plants, esp those of the genus *Xylomelum* (see WOODEN PEAR); the fruit of the plant. Also **pear-tree.**
1804 *Sydney Gaz.* 7 Oct., The timber consisted chiefly of cedar, pear and tea tree. **1805** J.H. TUCKEY *Acct. Voyage to establish Colony Port Phillip* 228 The pear-tree is so called from its bearing a fruit resembling a pear in shape, but of the hardness of wood.

2. a. Shortened form of 'prickly pear'.
1908 *Bulletin* (Sydney) 9 July 15/3 Runs have been given up as hopeless for stock owing to the prickly anathema. Right down the line from Roma to Dalby pear is seen all the way. **1973** H. LEWIS *Crow on Barbed Wire Fence* 29 You seen pear? It's cactus. Put a piece on that barbed wire fence and it'll grow.

b. *attrib.*, esp. as **pear country.**
1914 H.M. VAUGHAN *Australasian Wander-Yr.* 231 The sole method of destruction that has so far proved serviceable is the injection of some poisonous fluid.. which is squirted into each leaf of the plant by means of a 'peargun'. **1977** *Pastoral Rev. & Graziers' Rec.* Sept. 302 The pear country was alive with the dreaded death adder.

pearl. Used *attrib.* in Special Comb. **pearl-cleaner, -doctor, -faker,** one who prepares pearls for sale (see quots.).
1937 J.M. HARCOURT *It never Fails* 130 The **pearl-cleaner** sat at a table working on a blister with a file. **1937** I.L. IDRIESS *Forty Fathoms Deep* 158 Layers of nacre are the coats or skins of the pearl. Some skins may be slightly discoloured, dinted, or spotted. To find this perfect skin is the job of the **'pearl doctor'**. **1903** H. TAUNTON *Australind* 226 Defective and blotchy pearls are often rendered valuable by the art of the **'pearl-faker'**

pearler, var. PURLER.

pearl perch. [See quot. 1974.] The greenish to silvery-grey marine fish *Glaucosoma scapulare* of offshore reefs in n. N.S.W. and s. Qld.
1884 *Proc. Linnean Soc. N.S.W.* IX. (1885) 7 *Glaucosoma scapulare*.. is known to some of the fishermen as the 'Pearl Perch', and is said to be a most excellent food fish. **1974** J.M. THOMSON *Fish Ocean & Shore* 135 The name pearl perch is derived from a bony protuberance behind the head which in life is covered by a thin black skin. But this is often ruptured during handling so that the pearly white bone beneath is revealed.

peasouper. *Obs.* [In allusion to the 'pea-soup fog', long associated with London.] A recently arrived British immigrant.
1862 C. STRETTON *Mem.* II. 40 Twig that new chum; he's a real pea-souper. **1906** E. DYSON *In Roaring Fifties* 66 'Peasouper!' trumpeted a horseman through his hands. There were sarcastic references to 'lime-juice', and Jim was asked by several strangers.. if his mother knew he was out.

peb. *Obs.* [Abbrev. of PEBBLE 1.] A larrikin.
1908 R. BEDFORD *True Eyes & Whirlwind* 129 The session broke up—pebs and donahs wandered off in couples. **1916** C.J. DENNIS *Moods Ginger Mick* 102 They wus pebs, they wus narks, they wus reel naughty boys.

pebble. [Br. slang, but chiefly Austral.: see OED(S *sb.* 1 c.]
1. A person, esp. a convict or (later) a prisoner in a gaol, whose behaviour is incorrigible; a reprobate.
1848 *Port Phillip Herald* 29 June 2/4 A few days ago, a carpenter showed a note in one of the public houses in

PEDAL   399   **PENAL**

town which circumstance having been observed by three 'pebbles', who were watching him outside, they followed him till he got opposite the Church, when they attacked and attempted to rob him, but having a hand-saw with him he resisted and eventually put them to flight... The Pentonvillains are becoming a complete pest to Corio. **1962** D. McLean *World turned upside Down* 10 You're new round here and I think I ought to warn you that those two pebbles you was talkin' to would oozle the eyes out of y'r head.

2. *transf.* and *fig.* A stayer, esp. in the phr. **(as) game as a pebble.**

c **1863** T. Taylor *Ticket-of-Leave Man* 11 Doctor? Nay; I'm as game as a pebble and as stell as a tree! **1888** 'R. Boldrewood' *Robbery under Arms* III. 123 The Turon favourite—a real game pebble of a little horse—began to show up. **1918** C. Fetherstonhaugh *After Many Days* 277 Traveller was game as a pebble, and he just passed Quadrant on the post and no more.

pedal. *Hist.*

1. Used *attrib.* with various nouns, as **pedal radio, set, transceiver, wireless,** etc., to designate a small radio transceiver with a generator powered by a foot-pedal, invented by A.H. Traeger (1895–1980) to provide a means of communication in remote inland areas.

1930 *A.I.M. Frontier News* Aug. 3 (*caption*) A 'Woman of the West', busy at her work of shattering isolation with the aid of an A.I.M. 'Pedal' Radio Transmitter. **1932** *Ibid.* Mar. 35 The installation of a pedal wireless set at the Wimmera Home at Victoria River Downs is recommended for consideration by the Executive. **1939** J.W. Collings *8000 Miles by Air* 1 Mr A.H. Traeger, well-known to all in the Outback as the manufacturer of the Pedal Transceiver (wireless receiving and transmitting set). *Ibid.* 3 That evening, Dr Vickers had arranged for me to address the pedal set outposts.

2. In the phr. **on the pedal,** through the medium of the *pedal transceiver.*

1962 C. Gye *Cockney & Crocodile* 71 Mr and Mrs Arnold welcomed us with tea and scones at Ivanhoe, having heard us 'on the pedal' (the radio telephone, or Traeger transceiver, so called as it used to be worked by pedalling on a thing like a bicycle while speaking).

Hence **pedal** *v. trans.*, to transmit (a message) in this way.

1940 *Frontier News* Apr. 2/3 He called us periodically and we pedalled back news to him.

peel, *v.* [Joc. use of *peel* to strip.] *trans.* To shear (a sheep). Also as *ppl. a.*

1912 *Bulletin* (Sydney) 28 Nov. 16/4 One of the fraternity confided to me on the board.. that he 'had peeled 88, and was dragging the chain behind Nugget Smith', but had bet him a bottle of sheep dip 'that he'd 'wheel him next day'. **1923** *Ibid.* 1 Nov. 24/3 At many Out-West peeling establishments goats—always more manageable than the woollies—are regularly used as leaders.

peewee /'piwi/. [Transf. use of *peewee*, var. of imitative *pe(e)wit* lapwing.]

1. *Magpie lark*, see Magpie *n.* 2. Also **peeweet, peewit.**

1904 *Emu* IV. 72 Peewees (*Grallina*) with young in the nest. **1922** M. Gilmore *Hound of Road* 141 A peeweet clashed his wings as he called with plangent cries to his mate. **1981** A.B. Facey *Fortunate Life* 90 The peewit was a light brown bird with some black streakings on its back and wings, and a white breast marked with a U-shaped black half circle.

2. A bowler hat. Also **peewee hat.**

1910 *Truth* (Sydney) 13 Mar. 11/6, I bought some bran' noo clobber, an' a little peewee hat. **1926** G. Black *Hist. N.S.W. Political Labor Party* ii. 10 In Sydney, most city men wore either tall hats, or straw boaters (stiff and hard), or 'pee-wees' (now known as 'bowlers') [etc.].

peg, *n.*[1] *Obs.* [Scot. dial. *peg* a shilling.] One shilling (but see quot. 1950).

1882 *Sydney Slang Dict.* 3 *Deaner*, a shilling. Also, Peg, Twelver, &c. **1904** L.M.P. Archer *Bush Honeymoon* 213 I'm old an' lonely an' poor—ten peg per week, an' lucky to get it. **1950** *Austral. Police Jrnl.* Apr. 117 *Peg*, 2s.

peg, *n.*[2] *Obs.* [Of unknown origin.] In the phr. **to put in the peg,** to desist from an activity, esp. the consumption of alcoholic liquor.

1896 *Bulletin* (Sydney) 22 Feb. 27/2 Mr Murphy.. had been 'on a fair bend' for a week. The grog had got on to his nerves, and there was a hand of iron gripping the back of his neck. The doctor said that it was 'cerebral congestion', and that if Mr Murphy didn't put the peg in there would be trouble. **1929** W.J. Reside *Golden Days* 334 For several weeks he had 'put in the peg'.

peggy. [Transf. use of *peggy* a ship's mess-steward.] An unskilled worker responsible for tea-making, etc.

1971 J.P. Gilders *Man Alone* 44 'Who'd work on the railways for a lousy $36 a week. Only a poor bastard like me.' 'You've got it easy,' Paul laughed. 'You're only the 'peggy' aren't you?' **1986** *Bulletin* (Sydney) 8 Apr. 36/1 There are refrigerated water fountains.. a subsidised canteen and a 'peggy', a man paid by the contractors to make the tea and organise the lunches in each of the crib huts.

peg-leg. Chiefly *N.T.* [See quot. 1985.] A disease of cattle attributed to phosphorus deficiency. Also *attrib.*

1953 T.G. Hungerford *Diseases of Livestock* (ed. 3) 469 *Phosphorus deficiency disease in cattle*. Other names.. peg-leg disease (Northern Territory). **1985** P.J. Schmidt *Beef Cattle Production* (ed. 2) 48 *Hypophosphorosis* or phosphorus deficiency is very widespread in Australia... The classical symptoms are increasing porosity and fragility of the bones, painful stiff-legged gait (hence the alternative name of 'peg-leg'), depraved appetite and bone chewing.

pen. [Spec. use of *pen* a small enclosure for domestic animals.]

1. A division in a shearing shed.

1879 'Australian' *Adventures Qld.* 113 There was a pen in front of the shearing-floor, holding from thirty to sixty sheep, according to the number of shearers. **1912** J. Bradshaw *Highway Robbery under Arms* (ed. 3) 37 You could not leave the shed without the permission of the man over the board, or you would be fined the ensuing pen of sheep.

2. *transf.* A job as a shearer.

1897 *Worker* (Sydney) 11 Sept. 1/1 Now when by chance he gets a 'pen' he buys a pair of 'tongs'. **1984** P. Read *Down there with me on Cowra Mission* 43 'Yes, I want to ring up about a pen.' That's what they call the shearing, see, a pen.

3. Special Comb. **pen-mate,** a shearer who takes sheep from the same pen as another shearer.

1895 *Worker* (Sydney) 28 Sept. 4/1 And when I asked my pen-mate's name Off one of the chaps I know, 'Why old son,' says he 'that's Billy McGee, 'Big dog' of the old Barcoo.' **1980** J. Wright *Big Hearts & Gold Dust* 83 Just tell him ya was pen-mates with Barney Walsh.

penal, *a. Hist.* [Spec. use of *penal* of, pertaining to, or relating to punishment. Used elsewhere but esp. with reference to Aust.] In special collocations: **penal colony, establishment, settlement, station,** *convict colony, establishment, settlement, station,* see Convict B. 3; **gang,** Gang; **servitude,** see Servitude.

1827 P. Cunningham *Two Yrs. in N.S.W.* I. 212 A **penal colony,** however, to prove fully beneficial to the mother country, must be regulated so as efficiently to *punish* the crime committed, before the *reform* of the criminal is thought of; and in this particular has hitherto consisted the great defect of our New South Wales system. **1837** W.B. ULLATHORNE *Catholic Mission Australasia* 8 From 1803 .. to 1821, it continued to be a mere **penal establishment.** **1827** P. CUNNINGHAM *Two Yrs. in N.S.W.* II. 297 The police magistrate .. should .. sentence him to work a certain period, in single or double irons, in a **penal gang** employed in the distant interior of the colony upon road and bridge making. **1820** H.G. BENNET *Let. to Earl Bathurst* 20 It has now risen from the degraded state of a **penal settlement,** to the station of a colony, peopled by many thousand free Englishmen. **1824** *HRA* (1921) 3rd Ser. IV. 143 A penal Settlement like Macquarie Harbour .. can only be effectual with those whose habits of life require very strong measures to change them. **1825** Tas. Colonial Secretary's Office Rec. 1/2 154, The privations he must necessarily be subject to at that **Penal Station.**

penalty rate. A 'penalty' imposed on an employer: an additional payment prescribed in an award for work required of employees outside normal hours or under abnormal conditions: see quots. 1950 and 1981.
1948 *Industr. Information Bull.* Feb. 89 The Commissioner made orders increasing the penalty rate applicable to work performed on a holiday. **1950** *Ibid.* July 599 The insulation board concerned .. was not loose insulation material, for which the award prescribed a penalty rate. **1981** SHEEHAN & WORLAND *Gloss. Industr. Relations Terms* (ed. 2) 56 Penalty rates are special payments prescribed in awards for work outside the normal spread of hours, e.g. overtime, work on weekends, and public holidays.

pen and ink. Rhyming slang for 'drink'.
[N.Z. **1963** *N.Z. Truth* (Wellington) 21 May 19 We wander over to the bar for a pen and ink.] **1967** *Kings Cross Whisper* (Sydney) xxxviii. 10/1 *Pen and ink,* drink. **1968** J. ALARD *He who shoots Last* 106 Are ya gonna have a pen an' ink?

pencil, *n.* Used *attrib.* in the names of plants: **pencil cedar,** any of several trees of various fam., yielding a useful timber, as *Glochidion ferdinandi* (fam. Euphorbiaceae) of n. and n.e. Aust.; the wood of these trees; **orchid,** either of two epiphytic orchids (fam. Orchidaceae) of Qld. and N.S.W., *Dendrobium teretifolium,* having long pendulous leaves, and *D. beckleri,* having thick, erect leaves; **pine** *Tas.,* a coniferous tree, usu. *Athrotaxis cupressoides* (fam. Taxodiaceae) of wet sites in Tas.
1820 *HRA* (1921) 3rd Ser. III. 18 An inferior kind called **pencil Cedar** is abundant and useful as a Common Wood. **1909** F.M. BAILEY *Comprehensive Catal. Qld. Plants* (ed. 2) 526 *Dendrobium teretifolium* .. **Pencil Orchid. 1935** DAVISON & NICHOLLS *Blue Coast Caravan* 239 The green-leafed and delicate-hued blooms of the pencil orchid and golden orchid. **1846** N.L. KENTISH *Work in Bush Van Diemen's Land* 22 The Celery-topped Pine is met with in the ranges of the upper part of the River Forth. [*Note*] This wood, also called the '**Pencil Pine**', is a handsome specimen of the Fir species.

pencil, *v.* Horse-racing. [Extended use of *pencil* to enter (a horse's name) in a betting book (apparently rare in Br.): see OED *v.* 2 b.] *intr.* To act as a bookmaker's clerk. Also as *vbl. n.*
1919 C. DREW *Doings of Dave* 84 The first thing to be done was to find a clerk, as Thimble could not pencil. **1978** N. EVERS *Tas. Paradise & Beyond* 40 She recalled doing some 'pencilling' for Gunboat Smith who was S.P. Bookie.

penciller. [Survival of Br. slang *penciller* bookmaker's clerk: see OED 2 a.] A bookmaker or bookmaker's clerk.
1891 *Truth* (Sydney) 11 Jan. 55 The recognised professional 'pencillers'. **1978** H.C. BAKER *I was Listening* 187 This fellow should make a fair bricklayer, but his real vocation would be as a bookmaker's penciller.

penda /'pɛndə/. [Prob. f. a Qld. Aboriginal language.] Any of several trees of the genera *Xanthostemon* and *Ristantia* (both fam. Myrtaceae), esp. (and orig.) the large *X. oppositifolius* of s.e. Qld., having very hard, brown wood; the wood of the tree. Also **penda tree.**
1890 F.M. BAILEY *Catal. Indigenous & Naturalized Plants Qld.* (ed. 2) 101 Penda-tree—Xanthostemon oppositifolius. **1944** J. DEVANNY *By Tropic Sea & Jungle* 130 The penda, startlingly heavy, weighing like iron in the hand, has the rosy glow of the sky after sunset.

Penguin award. [From the supposed resemblance between the award, a stylized sculpture of the human ear surrounded by a television screen, and a penguin.] One of the annual awards for excellence in the industry made by the Television Society of Australia.
1966 *Age* (Melbourne) 7 Nov. 11/4 Two Penguin awards were given for documentary films after 13 entries had been considered. **1985** *Age* (Melbourne) 26 Jan. 13/4 The society held its annual Penguin Award presentation last night.

penner-up. In a shearing shed: one who pens sheep preparatory to their being shorn. Also **penner.**
1887 K. MACKAY *Stirrup Jingles* 46 It was during last shearing that the boss gave a penner the go. **1963** D. NILAND *Dadda Jumped* 58 Maybe I had a yarn with the presser, or the penner-up, or one of the shearers.

pensioner. *Hist.* [Spec. use of *pensioner.*]
1. A person in receipt of a pension for military service, as a Chelsea pensioner, who has commuted the pension for a passage and emigrated to Australia. Also *attrib.*
1832 *Colonist* (Hobart) 28 Sept. 3/2 Useless free people, such as the poor pensioners, who have in fact been defrauded by the British Government. **1933** J.L. GLASCOCK *Jarrah Leaves* 32 Her own father had been one of the pensioner guards.
2. See quot. 1812.
1812 J.H. VAUX *Mem.* (1819) II. 195 *Pensioner,* a meanspirited fellow who lives with a woman of the town, and suffers her to maintain him in idleness in the character of her *fancy-man.* **1903** *Truth* (Sydney) 20 Dec. 5/3 Pragmatical police .. permit pensioners on prostitutes to pollute the pavements.

Penton. *Obs.* Abbrev. of PENTONVILLE. Also *attrib.*
1847 *Port Phillip Herald* 29 July 2/5 At the trial of Dr Barker's 'Penton' pets, at the Supreme Court on Tuesday, it oozed out that the five stolen books specified in the indictment were of a rather heterogeneous nature. **1848** *Ibid.* 6 Jan. (Suppl.), The other fellow that escaped is a noted robber, and turns out to be a Van Diemonian; the present prisoner is a Penton.

Pentonvillain. *Obs.* Also **Pentonvillian.** [Blend of PENTONVILLE and *villain.*] An opprobrious term for a PENTONVILLE. Also *attrib.*
1844 *Melbourne Weekly Courier* 21 Dec. 2/3 The degrading of our free and untainted immigrants to a level with the crime-stained Pentonvillains, of whom the first sample came by the *Royal George.* **1847** *Port Phillip Herald* 16 Mar. 2/5 A Pentonvillain named George Rolfe, was fully committed for uttering a forged order. **1848** *Ibid.* 25 May 2/7 If our Downing-street rulers will insist upon our receiving their Pentonvillain and other prison 'pets', they, or the Colonial Government must very soon be prepared to defray the expense of another gaol. **1855** W. HOWITT *Land, Labor & Gold* I. 22 Several of these escaped Van Demonians, or Pentonvillians.

Hence **Pentonvillainy** n., the Pentonvilles collectively; the scheme under which they were sent to the Port Phillip District.
  1847 *Port Phillip Herald* 12 Oct. 2/3 With respect to the question of *Pentonvillainy*, it would appear .. that Port Phillip is to be converted into a vast *reportiorum* [sic] of sublimated felony.

Pentonville. [f. the name of *Pentonville* Prison, London.] One sentenced in Britain to transportation, but required first to serve eighteen months in Pentonville (or another reformatory prison) receiving moral and religious instruction and learning a trade, before being sent to Australia, esp. to the Port Phillip District, on a conditional pardon. Also **Pentonville exile** (see EXILE), **man, prisoner,** etc.
  1845 *Portland Gaz.* 22 Jan. 3/1 Pentonville Exiles .. are not so dangerous as colonial convicts. 1845 BACKHOUSE & TYLOR *Life & Labours G.W. Walker* 10 Apr. (1862) 521 The Pentonville men are decidedly the most hopeful set I have seen land here. 1846 W. WESTGARTH *Commercial, Statistical & Gen. Rep. Port Phillip* 21 Some opposition was displayed as to the meeting being committed to an entire approval of an influx of criminal population, even under the mitigated aspect of the Pentonville prisoners. 1847 *Port Phillip Herald* 16 Sept. (Suppl.), The Colonial Government has determined upon defraying one-half the expense of conveying to this colony the families of all Pentonvilles who may have arrived at Port Phillip.
  Hence **Pentonville system** n.
  1847 *Hobart Town Herald* 6 Mar. 2/1 Either by the Probation or Pentonville system.

pepper, v. Obs. [Spec. use of *pepper* to sprinkle like pepper, to scatter in small particles.] *trans.* To make (a mine) appear to be profitable by fraudulently introducing samples of the mineral sought. Also as *vbl. n.*
  1851 *Empire* (Sydney) 1 Dec. 418/7 The fraudulent practice of 'peppering', as it is termed—disposing of a barren hole, in which grains of gold are judiciously interspersed to deceive the unwary purchaser. 1858 C.R. THATCHER *Colonial Songster* (rev. ed.) 19 Of course you know they'd peppered it, The gold was all a hum; They'd sold it me because they saw I was a green new chum.

peppercorn tree. PEPPER TREE 2. Also **peppercorn.**
  1954 *Coast to Coast 1953–54* 76 Who do you think we see sittin' under a pepper-corn tree but this old sundowner. 1984 *Sun* (Sydney) 2 Oct. 18/2 If the meat has a scented taste, most probably the lambs were eating peppercorns, which are grown as shade trees on many western properties.

pepper grass. [Perh. transf. use of *pepper-grass* a plant of the genus *Lepidium* having a pungent taste.] The leafy annual or short-lived perennial grass *Panicum whitei* (fam. Poaceae), of drier parts of all mainland States exc. Vic.
  1927 M. TERRY *Through Land of Promise* 265 Spinifex, nardoo, box or pepper grass. 1981 G.M. CUNNINGHAM et al. *Plants Western N.S.W.* 122 Pepper grass should be grazed early to retard maturity and encourage new growth.

pepperina. PEPPER TREE 2. Also **pepperina tree.**
  1930 V. PALMER *Men are Human* 166 Nothing grew save the drooping pepperina that trailed its sheeny leaves over the kitchen roof. 1978 D. STUART *Wedgetail View* 102 Two buildings, roofless, with window spaces gaping, walls leaning, and a few pepperina trees.

peppermint. [Transf. use of *peppermint*: see quot. 1790.]
  1. Any of many small to large trees of s.e. Aust. incl.

Tas., of the genus *Eucalyptus* (fam. Myrtaceae), the leaves of which yield aromatic, peppermint-like essential oils, the trunk often having a fine, fibrous bark; the wood of these trees. Also *attrib.*
  1790 J. WHITE *Jrnl. Voyage N.S.W.* 227 App. The name of Peppermint Tree has been given to this plant by Mr White on account of the very great resemblance between the essential oil drawn from its leaves and that obtained from the Peppermint (*Mentha piperita*) which grows in England. 1984 D.J. BOLAND et al. *Forest Trees Aust.* (rev. ed.) 332 Most peppermint species are notable for their 'peppermint' bark which is persistent, rather short-fibred .. at first brownish weathering to grey.
  2. Any of several other plants, esp. (*W.A.*) the tree or shrub *Agonis flexuosa* (fam. Myrtaceae) of s.w. W.A., having pendulous, peppermint-scented foliage and widely cultivated as an ornamental. See also *willow myrtle* WILLOW 2. Also **peppermint tree.**
  1838 *Swan River Guardian* (Perth) 15 Feb. 4 Our peppermint tree is a fine species of *Metrosideros*. 1977 H. BUTLER *In Wild* 79 Peppermint's not a eucalypt—it's a plant called *Agonis*.

pepper-pot, v. intr. See quot.
  1980 *N.S.W. Parl. Papers* (1981) 3rd Sess. IV. 1749 What is the policy of the Housing Commission—does it pepperpot? A. We are pepperpotting, which is one of the recommendations of the previous select committee, that we should put them [sc. Aborigines] into towns and spread them round various streets. What we are doing in non-black towns .. is trying to keep it at two or three to a street... Our policy is one of scatteration.

pepper tree. [Transf. use of *pepper-tree* a name given to various trees.]
  1. Any of several small trees or shrubs of the genus *Tasmannia* (fam. Winteraceae) having a pungent fruit (but see also quots. 1839 and 1979), esp. *T. lanceolata* of e. N.S.W., e. Vic., and Tas., having reddish stems and a purplish-black fruit. See also *native pepper* NATIVE a. 6 a. Also **pepper bush, pepper shrub.**
  1827 *HRA* (1926) 3rd Ser. VI. 267 'Pepper Shrub' .. found in Land [sic], good soil. 1839 T.L. MITCHELL *Three Exped. Eastern Aust.* (rev. ed.) II. 280 We also found the aromatic tea, *Tasmania aromatica*... The leaves and bark of this tree have a hot biting cinnamon-like taste, on which account it is vulgarly called the pepper-tree. 1979 WRIGLEY & FAGG *Austral. Native Plants* 292 *Tasmannia* spp. vary from medium-sized shrubs to trees and most bear the common name of pepper or pepper bush, because of the hot flavour of fruit, seeds or sometimes foliage.
  2. [U.S. *pepper tree* the tree *Schinus molle.*] The introduced S. American tree *Schinus molle* var. *areira* (fam. Anacardiaceae), bearing a small, red, aromatic fruit, widely planted as an ornamental and shade tree, esp. near homesteads in inland Aust.; PEPPERCORN TREE; PEPPERINA.
  1892 'Mrs A. MACLEOD' *Silent Sea* I. 241 There was also an avenue of blue gums and pepper-trees round the house. 1981 *Woman's Day* (Sydney) 16 Sept. 6/1 Pink and grey galahs wheeled over the shining tin roof of the infants' school and fluttered through the pepper trees and the blue gums.

per boot, adv. phr. [f. *per* by means of + *boot.*] On foot.
  1895 K. MACKAY *Yellow Wave* 58 'When you were on the wallaby, you mean?' said Dick, with a laugh. 'Yes, per boot.' 1941 *Bulletin* (Sydney) 3 Dec. 14/1 Touring Gippsland per boot, Mat was hailed .. by a dog-tired cocky.

perch. [Transf. use of *perch* the fresh-water fish *Perca fluviatilis* and other fish of the fam. Percidae.]
  1. Any of many fresh-water or marine fish of various

fam., usu. of the order Perciformes and esp. those of the fam. Teraponidae.
1825 B. FIELD *Geogr. Mem. N.S.W.* 48 We were fortunate enough to .. catch a good dish of perch. **1978** D. VAWR *Ratbag Mind* 21 The 'perch' (bass) .. would never take anything except, rarely a live prawn in the darker creeks.
2. With distinguishing epithet, as **giant, golden, Macquarie, Murray, pearl, sea, silver,** etc.: see under first element.

perentie /pə'rɛnti/. Also with much variety, as **parentie, parinti, perenty, prenti, printhy, printy**. [Prob. a. Diyari *pirrinthi*.] The large monitor lizard *Varanus giganteus* of rocky country in arid central and w. Aust. Also *attrib*.
1905 *Observer* (Adelaide) 30 Sept. 48/2 But this is not the Territory you read of—might as well call a printhee an alligator. **1925** H. BASEDOW *Austral. Aboriginal* 127 Of the Lizards, the most favoured are the species of *Varanus*, popularly known as the printhy and the goanna. **1929** E.R. WAITE *Reptiles & Amphibians S.A.* 125 The Perentie is .. the largest Australian species. **1944** M.J. O'REILLY *Bouyangs & Boomerangs* 120 Circling around and around as far as the sapling would allow was a six-foot prenti caught across the loins with the steel-wire snare. **1946** W.E. HARNEY *North of 23°* 30, I listened wide-eyed to his tales of 'parintis', giant monitor lizards, that would attack a man. **1957** F. CLUNE *Fortune Hunters* 56 A man could .. live happily .. on a diet of parentie lizards, grubs, berries, roots, honey-ants and grilled euro. **1958** M.D. BERRINGTON *Stones of Fire* 56 'Sounds to me like a printy,' he said. .. He told us about printies as we went. The creature he described .. was a very good word-picture of a dragon. It looked, he said, like a cross between a lizard and an alligator. **1978** O. WHITE *Silent Reach* 203 Carrying her riding boots in one hand and dragging a dead perenty lizard with the other.

perform. [Transf. use of *perform* to act in a play.] *intr.* To display anger or bad-temper; to make a fuss.
1891 *Truth* (Sydney) 3 May 4/5 The 'doing' they get in the padded cells, and often in the associated cells, is explained to the doctor by the allegation that they 'performed'. **1911** L. STONE *Jonah* 45 Ow'l Chook perform, if 'e ain't at Ada's?

perish, *n.* [f. *perish, v.* to come to a violent, sudden, or untimely end.]
1. **a.** A period of extreme privation, esp. as caused by lack of water.
1884 A.V. PURVIS *Heroes Unsung,* I am nearly perished I have left two mates behind both nearly perished. .. I found the three men none the worse for their bit of a perish. **1964** D. LOCKWOOD *Up Track* 52 Not that they ever stopped laughing, even at the height of the 'perish'.
b. PERISHER 3.
1968 LINKLATER & TAPP *Gather No Moss* 95 According to bush ethics the dying 'perish' must free his animals to give them a chance of survival.
2. In the phr. **to do a perish. a.** To suffer a period of extreme privation; to be without sustenance (esp. water). See also PERISHER 2.
1897 P. O'FARRELL *Lett. from Irish Aust.* (1984) 94 We were lucky enough to get water and only did a perish twice and then only for the horses. **1984** *Overlander* Apr. 29 It must have been mighty reassuring for him to know he had that water to fall back on .. even though he might have to do a 'perish' while covering the intervening distance.
b. To die, esp. of thirst.
1897 A.F. CALVERT *My Fourth Tour W.A.* 141 The party had, indeed, very narrowly escaped 'doing a perish', as the expressive phrase goes out West to describe the fate of a gold-seeker, whose skeleton, picked clean by carrion birds, is found by those who chance upon his tracks. **1980** ANSELL & PERCY *To fight Wild* 31 Something was saying 'maybe you've made a boo-boo, that you'll die, do a perish, which is a pity, a bit of a shame really'.
c. *transf.* To suffer hardship or privation of any kind, not always of an extreme nature (see quot. 1907).
1899 H. LAWSON *Lett.* (1970) 91 Did a three-months' unemployed 'perish', and then went with a mate to a sawmill. **1907** *Bulletin* (Sydney) 11 July 14/2 At Milparinka did a 'perish' several times at one pub—no whisky, no nothing, except flies and goat.

perish, *v.* [f. prec.]
1. *intr.* To suffer (extreme) thirst. Also *fig.*
1909 *Truth* (Sydney) 25 July 1/6 Many a big skulking fellow in this city reports himself as perishing if he be only two hours without beer and counter lunch! **1944** K.S. PRICHARD *Potch & Colour* 56 'There we were,' said Bill, 'the three of us, perishin' for water, eighty miles from anywhere.'
2. [Apparently independent of the obs. Br. use: see OED *v.* 3 a.] *trans.* To kill (a person, etc.).
1934 T. WOOD *Cobbers* 202 'Longreach, the Glory of the West.' Masts & Yards [*sc.* travelling salesmen] .. said it would perish the crows. **1975** B. FULLER *Ghan* 75 'I'll perish you,' he threatened. 'I'll put a half-moon in your belly.'
Hence **perished** *ppl. a.,* **perishing** *vbl. n.* and *ppl. a.*
1876 *Queenslander* (Brisbane) 22 Apr. 11/4 It's a fools' errand we're on, and it would be better to give in and turn back before we get **perished** for want of water. **1879** *Ibid.* 12 Apr. 461/2 The greatest **perishings** I have ever had were in country which I knew, and occurred because I didn't take the simplest precaution. **1957** F. CLUNE *Fortune Hunters* 49 I've had to put up with a lot of tough going to bring in perishing blokes who got off the beaten track, and a few who were on the beaten track!

perisher.
1. In the phr. **to go in a perisher,** to pursue (a course of action) with dedication or vigour.
1864 *Sydney Punch* 23 June 40/1 Like a second Quintus Curtius, 'go in a perisher' against that quagmire of slush and corruption known as the Circular Quay. **1888** 'R. BOLDREWOOD' *Robbery under Arms* III. 87 He .. went in an awful perisher—took a month to it, and was never sober day or night the whole time.
2. PERISH *n.* 2 a. and c. Esp. in the phr. **to do** (or **perform**) **a perisher.**
1892 *Bohemia* (Melbourne) 3 Mar. 15 Many thirsty travellers arrived and were languishing for a 'reviver'. Doing, in bush parlance, a 'perisher' for a 'nip'. **1905** J. FURPHY *Rigby's Romance* (1946) 43 'Have it so, then,' says the Lord, 'but they got to go back into the Wilderness of Sin an' do another perisher.' **1911** *Bulletin* (Sydney) 19 Oct. 43/2 The stinging tree and the lawyer vine are unpleasant .. but they keep out of the way in dark scrubs, and, when your business takes you there, and they get hold of you, though you perform a perisher for a minute, you see the 'joke' immediately afterwards.
3. One who suffers a period of privation; PERISH *n.* 1 b.
1956 H. HUDSON *Flynn's Flying Doctors* 187 Before the days of Flying Doctors, he rescued many a perisher lost in the lonely regions, going out on the track with his camels and blackboys. **1957** F. CLUNE *Fortune Hunters* 49 Australia's Number One Salvager of Desert Perishers squatted on his haunches, tilted his hat, scratched his ear, and grinned.

perk, *n.*[1] *Obs.* [Abbrev. of Br. slang *perkin* beer, 'dandy or affected shortening of the widely-known firm, Barclay and Perkins' (Hotten 1864). Partridge also records *purko.*] Beer.
1913 *Truth* (Sydney) 6 July 3/1 *A battalion of bobbies* put in an appearance, and proceeded to search the house for

perk. Their search revealed two demijohns, one of which was about half-full.

perk, n.² [f. PERK, v.] A vomit.

1965 J. O'GRADY *Aussie Eng.* 67 'Perks' are the little extras... There is, however, another kind of 'perk'... You'll know when you're going to do it.

perk, v. [Poss. f. PERK n.¹] intr. To vomit, esp. after excessive drinking.

1941 S.J. BAKER *Pop. Dict. Austral. Slang* 53 *Perk, to,* to vomit. 1965 J. O'GRADY *Aussie Eng.* 67 Never, never, never, perk into the wind.

permanent, a.

1. Used as a qualifying element with nouns designating a watercourse or other natural source of water, to signify the security of the source in all seasons: **permanent creek, water, waterhole.**

1890 'R. BOLDREWOOD' *Colonial Reformer* III. 117 By degrees it began to be asserted that 'back country'.. paid the speculative pastoral occupier better than the 'frontage', or land in the neighbourhood of **permanent creeks.** 1843 *Sydney Morning Herald* 31 Oct. 4/1 When once known.. the **permanent waters** could be followed, and journeys made accordingly. 1845 L. LEICHHARDT *Jrnl. Overland Exped. Aust.* 13 June (1847) 289 It.. was the almost constant companion of the **permanent waterholes.**

2. In the collocation **permanent head,** the senior executive officer of a department in the public service; the Secretary of such a department.

1915 *Sydney Morning Herald* 14 July 9/3 He said Mr Edwards was recalled on the recommendation of the permanent head of the department.

permit. In the collocation **permit to travel,** see quot. 1878.

1878 *Act* (N.S.W.) 41 Vict. no. 19 Sect. 14, Every owner intending to travel three hundred or more sheep from any run shall before leaving the Sheep district in which such run is situated forward to the Inspector of the district a statement in writing of the number description brands and marks of the said sheep and of their intended route and destination and shall obtain from the Inspector a permit containing the particulars set forth in the Second Schedule hereto to travel the said sheep. And every owner introducing sheep from any of the adjoining Colonies shall in like manner obtain a permit to travel as aforesaid from the Inspector for the district into which such sheep shall first pass on crossing the Border. 1957 *Law Bk. Company's N.S.W. Land Laws Service* Mar. 307 The defendant made an application.. for a permit to travel one hundred and twenty sheep from Dalrye Station to Wagga Wagga.

persuader. [Spec. use of *persuader* something used to compel obedience.] A whip, esp. that used by a bullock driver.

1890 *Observer* (Adelaide) 15 Mar. 41/5, I soon dismounted and from a bush cut a nice pliant 'persuader' for my camel. 1984 A. DELBRIDGE *Aussie Talk* 235 *Persuader,*.. a jockey's whip.

Perth doctor: see DOCTOR n.³

perv, n. and a. Also **perve.** [Abbrev. of (sexual) *perversion, pervert.*]

A. n.

1. *Obs.* Pornographic literature (*attrib.* in quot.).

1942 'Havildar' Havalook: Mag. H.M.A.T. 'Havildar' 14 Mar. 1 'Logical Love'.. by that well-known perv-merchant, John.. Hunt.

2. A sexual pervert.

1949 R. PARK *Poor Man's Orange* 38 That dirty old cow, always making up to kids... Merv, Merv, the rotten old perv. 1978 L. HORSPHOL *Turn down Empty Glass* 125, I don't want your dirty old perv, you lying slut! Why, I wouldn't touch the bastard with a fifty foot pole!

3. One who observes another (or others) with erotic or sexual interest; the act of so observing.

1963 J. CANTWELL *No Stranger to Flame* 15 'Never even saw him. Might have been a spook.' She did up the top button on the green blouse. 'Even spooks like a bit of a perv.' 1968 B. HUMPHRIES *Wonderful World Barry McKenzie,* I feel a bit of a *perve* standing here like this, but I can't help getting an earful of them two lovebirds.

B. adj. *Obs.* Pornographic.

1944 L. GLASSOP *We were Rats* 177 Bluey brought a perv book back from Cairo with him.

perve, v. [As prec.] intr.

a. To act in a sexually perverted manner. Now usu. in weakened sense: to observe with erotic or sexual interest. Freq. with **on,** and as *vbl. n.*

1941 S.J. BAKER *Pop. Dict. Austral. Slang* 53 *Perve, to,* to act as a sexual pervert. 1944 L. GLASSOP *We were Rats* 183 'Doing a bit of perving again?' I asked, looking at the gallery of nudes he had gathered from all sorts of magazines. 1960 *Westerly* iii. 30 He saw our naked bodies and we couldn't tell if he 'perved' on us or was just dreary of watching the same scenery.

b. *transf.* To observe with interest.

1984 *Sydney Morning Herald* 12 July (Life & Home Suppl.) 4/3 More than a million people a year set out on sea trips from the east and west coasts of the United States with the sole purpose of perving on whales.

per.-way. Shortened form of 'permanent way', a railway track. Freq. *attrib.*

1919 *Smith's Weekly* (Sydney) 19 Apr. 10/6 Several gangs of per.-way workers belonging to the Railway Workers' Branch of the A.W.U. are.. denouncing the Commissioners, who refuse to pay award rates. 1953 *Bulletin* (Sydney) 7 Oct. 13/4 One of the per.-way men got hold of an ancient recipe for honeymead.

peter. [Transf. use of Br. slang *peter* a box or safe.]

1. A prison cell; a prison. See also *black peter* BLACK a.² 2.

1890 BARRÈRE & LELAND *Dict. Slang* II. 125 *Peter*.. (Australian prison), punishment cell. 1979 L. NEWCOMBE *Inside Out* 26 Gotta see the doc this morning. Probably get a couple of days in the 'peter'.

2. A witness box.

1895 C. CROWE *Austral. Slang Dict.* 56 *Peater,* the witness box. 1958 V. KELLY *Greedy Ones* 14 Mounting the peter. Going into the witness box.

3. *Obs.* A pack-saddle.

1897 *Worker* (Sydney) 11 Sept. 1/2 Now when the shed at last 'cuts out' he gets his 'little bit' And straps his 'peter' on his 'croc' and quickly does a get. 1898 *Bulletin* (Sydney) 17 Dec. 15/2 The pack-saddle is called the *peter.*

Peter Peter. [Imitative.] *Jacky Winter,* see JACKY n.²

1917 *Bulletin* (Sydney) 23 Aug. 22/2 Some appropriate names bestowed by the white pfella are.. four-o'clock (the friar-bird or leatherhead) and Peter Peter (the brown flycatcher). 1954 C. BARRETT *Wild Life Aust. & New Guinea* 157 'Post-boy' and 'Peter Peter' (the call note) are other names for 'Jacky Winter', who ranges throughout Australia.

petrol bowser.

1. See BOWSER 1.

2. *pl.* Rhyming slang for 'trousers'. Also **petrols.**

1971 B. HUMPHRIES *Bazza pulls it Off,* This *randy* Australian bastard passed out cold even before I could get him out of his petrols. 1974 *Bulletin* (Sydney) 2 Nov. 57/2 Trousers are petrols—petrol bowsers.

phascogale /ˈfæskəgeɪl, fæskəˈgali/. [The animal genus *Phascogale* was named by Dutch naturalist C.J. Temminck (*Monographies de Mammalogie* (1824) I. 56), f. Gr. φάσκωλος pouch + γαλῆ weasel, with reference to the long-bodied appearance of the marsupial. The genus formerly included many of the smaller carnivorous Austral. marsupials.]

1. a. Either of the two species of largely arboreal, carnivorous marsupials of the genus *Phascogale* (fam. Dasyuridae); TUAN a.; WAMBENGER. **b.** (Formerly) any of several other marsupials of the fam. Dasyuridae. Formerly also **phascologale**.

1852 J. WEST *Hist. of Tas.* I. 324 The Phascogales are small insectivorous animals, found on the mountains and in the dense forest parts of the island. 1896 B. SPENCER *Rep. Horn Sci. Exped. Central Aust.* II. 19 *Phascologale cristicauda* . . the crest-tailed Phascologale. 1926 A.S. LE SOUEF et al. *Wild Animals Australasia* 332 *Genus Dasycercus* . . and *Phascogale*. . . Small rat-like carnivorous animals.

2. With distinguishing epithet, as **brush-tailed, Swainson's**: see under first element.

pheasant. [Transf. use of *pheasant*.]
1. a. LYRE-BIRD 1. **b.** *Pheasant coucal*.

1798 D. COLLINS *Acct. Eng. Colony N.S.W.* (1802) II. 88 A few birds which, from the length of the tail feathers, they denominated pheasants. 1970 W.S. RAMSON *Eng. Transported* 42 In the case of the *lyrebird*, described also as a *pheasant* or *bird of paradise*, it was the bird's arresting appearance that gave rise to the name.

2. Used *attrib.* in the names of birds: **pheasant coucal**, the long-tailed nest-building cuckoo *Centropus phasianinus* of n. and e. Aust., New Guinea, and nearby islands; COUCAL: *swamp pheasant*, see SWAMP *n*.; also ellipt. as PHEASANT 1 B., and formerly **pheasant cuckoo**; **parrot**, ADELAIDE ROSELLA; **-tailed pigeon**, *brown pigeon*, see BROWN *a.* 1; also **pheasant pigeon**.

[1801 **pheasant coucal**: J. LATHAM *Gen. Synopsis Birds* Suppl. II. 137 Pheasant C. This is a beautiful species . . the whole of the back and wings varied with rufous, yellow, brown, and black, somewhat similar to a *Pheasant* or *Woodcock*. . . Inhabits *New South Wales*, known there by the name of *Pheasant*.] 1827 P.P. KING *Narr. Survey Intertropical & Western Coasts* II. 8 Several black cockatoos and the pheasant cuckoo were seen. 1908 E.J. BANFIELD *Confessions of Beachcomber* 103 The swamp pheasant, or pheasant coucal (*Centropus phasianus*) is also an early bird. 1841 J. GOULD *Birds of Aust.* (1848) V. Pl. 22, *Platycercus adelaidiae* . . Adelaide Parrot . . **Pheasant Parrot**, Colonists of South Australia. 1844 J. GOULD *Birds of Aust.* (1848) V. Pl. 75, From what I could personally observe during my residence in New South Wales, the **Pheasant-tailed Pigeon** resorts entirely to the brushes, as in no instance did I meet with it in the open parts of the country. 1929 A.H. CHISHOLM *Birds & Green Places* 156 The 'Whoop-a-whoop' of the brownie or pheasant-pigeon.

Phillip Island parrot. *Hist.* [f. the name of an island s. of Norfolk Island.] The extinct parrot *Nestor productus* formerly found on Norfolk and Phillip Islands.

1841 J. GOULD *Birds of Aust.* (1848) V. Pl. 6, *Nestor productus* . . Phillip Island Parrot. 1886 F. COWAN *Aust.* 20 The extinct Phillip Island Parrot: cousin-german to the honeysucking, sheep-destroying and -devouring kea of Zealandia.

phizgig, var. FIZGIG.

phizzer, var. FIZZER *n.*²

pialla /paɪˈælə/ *v. Austral. pidgin. Obs.* Also with much variety, as **pai-alla, pialler, pile, piola**. [a. Dharuk *bayala*.] *trans.* To tell (news, etc.). Also *intr.*, to talk.

1790 D. SOUTHWELL Corresp. & Papers, *Pī-ă-la*, to speak or talk. 1828 *Sydney Gaz.* 2 Jan., 'All gammon white fellow pai-alla cabon gunyah, me tumble down white fellow.' It was all false that the white fellows said in the Court house, that I killed the white fellow. 1830 R. DAWSON *Present State Aust.* 162 What for piola (talk to) me dat. 1834 G. BENNETT *Wanderings N.S.W.* I. 210 The following is a definition of a clergyman, as once given by one of the aborigines: 'He, white feller, belonging to Sunday, get up top o' waddy, pile long corrobera all about debbil debbil, and wear shirt over trowsel.' 1845 C. HODGKINSON *Aust., Port Macquarie to Moreton Bay* 52, I . . sent Wongarini Paddy, and Billy, to pialla (tell the news) to them. 1846 *Cumberland Times* (Parramatta) 25 Apr. 4/1 Hearing some alarm was felt in Sydney respecting them, they at once dispatched one of the tribe to Sydney, as a special Courier, to *pialler* news, as to their whereabouts.

pic. Abbrev. of PICCANINNY *n.* 1.

1906 *Bulletin* (Sydney) 25 Jan. 14/2 A black gin died . . leaving . . a 'pic' of eight months. 1976 C.D. MILLS *Hobble Chains & Greenhide* 12, I waited behind an anthill, and the 'pics' worked them up close.

picaninna, picaninny, varr. PICCANINNY.

piccabeen /ˈpɪkəbin/. Chiefly *Qld.* [a. Jagara (and neighbouring languages) *bigi* or *bigibin*.] The palm *Archontophoenix cunninghamiana* (see BANGALOW). Also **piccabeen palm**.

1926 M. FORREST *Hibiscus Heart* 118 All along the banks were piccabeen and full-skirted tree fern. 1935 DAVISON & NICHOLLS *Blue Coast Caravan* 165 They ate also the green heart of the piccabeen palm.

piccaninny, *n.* and *a.* Chiefly *Austral. pidgin.* Also with much variety, as **picaninna, picaninny, piccanin, pickaninny,** etc. [Transf. use of West Indian *piccaninny* a little one, a child: see OED(S for use elsewhere.]

A. 1. *n.* An Aboriginal child; any child.

1817 *Sydney Gaz.* 4 Jan., Governor, that will make good Settler—that's my Pickaninny! 1826 *Monitor* (Sydney) 18 Aug. 106/3 He had seen the white woman often with her daughter and younger '*picaninna*'. 1832 *Hill's Life N.S.W.* 27 July 2 *Margaret Shannon*, a very *dacent* sort of a body from the Isle of Isles, with a *picaninny* slung gracefully across her shoulders, was accused by her spouse Michael of being too *obstropolus*. 1845 *Port Phillip Gaz.* 13 Sept. 4 A most important looking fellow, with an unusual number of lubras and piccaninnies at his heels.

2. *transf.* A young animal.

1824 Methodist Missionary Soc. Rec. 14 Sept., Young—shot her down: and he thought she had something in her belly, so he took his knife and cut her open, and a little *pickerninny* tumbled out. 1965 R. OTTLEY *By Sandhills* 132, I show you kangaroo. Big fella one, an' mary gottim piccanin. Piccanin along belly.

B. *adj.*

a. Little; tiny.

1842 J. HAYTER *Landsman's Log-Bk.* 126 They are afraid of . . pistols, which they call '*pickaninny muckett*'. 1951 E. HILL *Territory* 322 Somewhere there he had heard of a native well or soak—picaninny water, he showed them with his hand.

b. Special Comb. **piccaninny dawn, daylight, light, sun,** the approach of dawn, first light; **twilight,** the last glow of the setting sun.

1936 M. FRANKLIN *All that Swagger* 125 At **piccaninny dawn**, the billy with the lid off was found rolling on the floor. 1866 *Adventures ashore & Afloat* (1887) 172 He . . refused, on the plea that it was '**picaninny daylight**'—*i.e.*, that the day was short, and we had no time to lose. 1962 J. MARSHALL *Journey among Men* 107 We were up at **piccaninny light**. After breakfast we loaded the dinghy with guns and cameras and sailed up the gorge. 1846 *Port Phillip Patriot* 23 Nov. 2/5 You no sleep to-night—plenty thousand Murray black fellow come **piccannini sun** (daylight) take him other one black fellow all same quamby hut and plenty Gilbert (kill) white fellow. **1965** L. HAYLEN *Big Red* 180 The **piccaninny twilight** shimmered and died.

Hence **piccaninnyhood** *n.*, childhood.

1920 *Smith's Weekly* (Sydney) 22 May 17/5 The late John Nevell . . reared a blackfellow from piccanninyhood.

pick, *n.* Abbrev. of PICKING *vbl. n.*

1960 *N.T. News* (Darwin) 11 Mar. 7/4 On the Goyder there is a good feed from No. 7 to Mallee Bore with a fair pick from there to Finke. **1977** V. PRIDDLE *Larry & Jack* 102 'It's surprising the way the country has changed colour in such a short time,' said George. 'Why in another few days the cattle will be able to get hold of that pick.'

pick, *v.*¹ *Shearing. trans.* With **up**: to gather up (a shorn fleece), preparatory to placing it on a table for skirting, classing, etc. Freq. *absol.*, and as *vbl. n.*

[N.Z. **1862** J.G. WALKER Jrnl. 10 Nov. 24 (typescript) My job at first was picking up fleeces.] **1897** *Bulletin* (Sydney) 30 Oct. 14/1 During the late shearing, black gins were employed 'picking-up'. **1928** C.E. COWLEY *Classing Clip* 32 'Picking-up' is sometimes looked upon as a very simple task, and, consequently, does not always receive the consideration it is entitled to. **1974** J. HORNER *Vote Ferguson* 4 In July 1896, when he was legally entitled to leave school at fourteen, young Ferguson went to the shearing sheds, 'picking up' the shorn wool.

pick, *v.*² *intr.* To pick fruit. Freq. as *vbl. n.*

1913 W.K. HARRIS *Outback in Aust.* 70 Even overlanders from Queensland, have been in evidence during the picking season. **1941** K. TENNANT *Battlers* 211 Anyway, we might get a married couple's job in Orion, if we don't get on picking. **1955** J. MORRISON *Black Cargo* 155 We've been picking here for four weeks, and the A.W.U. is the wealthiest trade union in Australia.

pick, *v.*³ [Shortening of *to pick on.*] *trans.* To pick on (a person), to victimize.

1953 T.A.G. HUNGERFORD *Riverslake* 212 'If you're picking me,' he said at length, 'don't go off half-cocked.' **1981** *Bulletin* (Sydney) 10 Nov. 46/3 'Chicks fight heaps round here,' said Cheryl, 14, 'Ya get picked if ya look at someone too long, if there's somethin' about cha someone doesn't like, if ya dob, or wear the wrong clothes.'

pickaninny, var. PICCANINNY.

picker.

1. Abbrev. of PICKER-UP.

1895 *Bulletin* (Sydney) 13 July 23/3 There's the flying hurry-scurry up and down the greasy floors Of the pickers and the broomies; there's the banging of the doors, And the rattle of the wool-press.

2. Shortened form of 'fruit picker'.

1913 W.K. HARRIS *Outback in Aust.* 70 The pickers earn from 6s. to 8s. a day of eight hours. **1980** *Southerly* iii. 335 The return rail voucher that employment officers issued to pickers, had to be endorsed by the employer before a free return rail pass was issued. But as long as a picker stuck out the season, the blockie couldn't refuse to sign.

picker-up. *Shearing.* A shed-hand who gathers up the shorn fleeces: see quot. 1899. Also **picker-upper.**

1870 *Austral. Town & Country Jrnl.* (Sydney) 12 Nov. 13/4 The woolpress-men—the fleece-rollers—the pickers-up—the yarders—the washers' cooks—the hut cooks—the spare shepherds . . all . . paid off. **1899** G. JEFFREY *Princ. Australasian Woolclassing* 39 As soon as the fleece is off the sheep's back, the pickers-up take it by the breeches and place it on the rollers' tables, then sweep the floor clean of trimmings or locks as they are called. **1962** *Bulletin* (Sydney) 3 Feb. 43/3 The young picker-uppers got frisky after a couple of ponies.

picking, *vbl. n.* [Spec. use of *picking* that which may be picked up; *pl.* gleanings.] Sparse pasture; FEED; PICK *n.* See also *green pick* GREEN 2.

1901 F.J. GILLEN *Diary* 16 Oct. (1968) 290 There is good green picking here for the horses. **1938** J. MATHESON *Day Dreams*, There's picking upon those flats below and shade.

picking-up, *vbl. n.*

1. The process of clearing land of fallen timber, branches, etc., after burning off: see quot. 1952.

1879 'RECENT SETTLER' *Emigration to Tas.* 73 The picking up should be done as soon as possible after the fire, and consists in collecting in piles, and burning whatever timber and rubbish the fire may have spared, hoeing up and adding to the heaps, fern heads, roots, etc., so as to leave the land ready for chipping in the first grain crop. **1952** J.R. SKEMP *Memories Myrtle Bank* 67 The next job of the settler was 'picking up', the pieces not consumed by the fire being carried into heaps or piled against a fallen tree, and there burnt.

2. See PICK *v.*¹

pickle and pork. Rhyming slang for 'walk'. Also **pickled pork.**

1940 *Sixer* (Mornington) 22 May 9 Pickle and pork . . a walk. **1957** D. WHITTINGTON *Treasure upon Earth* 87 What about coming bush with me? . . We'll go for a pickled pork into Queensland, pick up some work harvesting.

pick up. The act of engaging casual employees; the time and place at which this is done.

1940 E.A. McCOMBE *Whales & Whalers* 30 Of the thirty-five signed on at Hobart . . seventy-five per cent . . were . . Tasmanians, while the remainder had travelled from the mainland to be present at the 'pick up'. **1946** F. CLUNE *Try Nothing Twice* 85 There was an army . . of shearers and rouseabouts waiting for the 'pick-up' at Yanco shed.

picnic.

1. [Ironic use of *picnic* a pleasurable excursion.] An awkward or disordered occasion or experience; an unpleasant situation. Also *attrib.*

1896 E.E. MORRIS *Austral Eng.* (1898) 351 If a man's horse is awkward and gives him trouble, he will say, 'I had a picnic with that horse', and so of any misadventure or disagreeable experience when travelling. **1903** *Sporting News* (Launceston) 12 Sept. 3/4 As heavy showers of rain fall during the engagement, enthusiasts in the pastime can easily realise the 'picnic' time the teams had.

2. a. Special Comb. **picnic (race) meeting, races** (*pl.*), a race meeting which is primarily an informal social occasion, usu. in a rural district. Also **picnic race** *attrib.*, see quot. 1985.

1896 N. GOULD *Town & Bush* 224 Picnic race-meetings are got up in various parts of the country. These meetings are for amateur riders only, and as a rule they are well managed. **1911** *Bulletin* (Sydney) 23 Mar. 40/2 It was the first meeting of the Sandy Creek Amateur Turf Club Picnic Races. **1936** I.L. IDRIESS *Cattle King* 350 Gone were nearly all the station and bush 'picnic meetings'. **1985** *Bulletin* (Sydney) 2 July 12/2 His view of the country is obviously obtained by mixing with the picnic race set. These people who grace the social pages do rural Australia a great disservice by perpetuating the myth of the wealthy farmer.

b. A *picnic meeting*; also *attrib.* as **picnic horse.**

1904 *Sporting News* (Launceston) 30 Apr. 1/2 Recently one of those New South Wales 'picnic' horses took up quarters in J.H. Davis's stables at Caulfield. **1942** T. KELAHER *Digger Hat* 36, I miss the chestnut filly, I thought she'd have some pace, And when the 'Picnics' came again be fit to win a race.

Hence **picnicker** *n.*, a horse which runs at a picnic race meeting.

1921 G.A. BELL *Under Brigalow* 89 None of them were really trained racehorses, only what bushmen call 'good picnickers'.

picture-show. *Obs.* [Transf. use of *picture-show* a film showing.] A cinema. Also **picture theatre.**

1915 *St. Kilda Ann.* 137 Seven years ago there was but one important picture theatre in Melbourne. **1918** A. WRIGHT *Over Odds* 51 It was hard indeed to have to daily play the clown outside a picture-show to amuse a frivolous crowd.

pie. [Shortened form of *meat pie*.]

1. Used *attrib.* in Comb., as **pie-biter, -eater, -eating** *ppl. a.*, to connote 'second rate', 'small-time'. See also *meat pie bookmaker* MEAT.

1911 E. DYSON *Benno & Push* 144 He was that angry with the South pie-biters, he didn't care what happened to them. **1949** L. GLASSOP *Lucky Palmer* 96 The trouble is, Mr Hughes, you're too good for the pie-eating bookmakers round these parts. You bet too well for them Mr Hughes. **1953** K. TENNANT *Joyful Condemned* 166 He's one of those big he-men that go sneaking round the park waiting to snitch some chromo's handbag. Just a pie-eater.

2. *transf.* and *fig.* An informal grouping of wool buyers who do not bid against one another at a wool sale, and divide the wool purchased amongst their number. Also *attrib.*

1959 *N.S.W. Parl. Papers* 2nd Sess. IV. 1310 The facts that pies are formed, generally speaking, between buyers interested in the same types of wool, and that their admitted purpose is to avoid the competition of members *inter se* show clearly the distinct advantages to pie members. **1966** S.J. BAKER *Austral. Lang.* (ed. 2) 58 The Australian public became aware in 1958 that wool-buying was not always a straightforward operation... Some buyers were combining into pies (also called rings) to bid and then share purchases, so that competition was reduced.

piebald, *a.* and *n.*

A. *adj.*

1. Half-caste; of part white and part non-white descent.

1899 *Progress* (Brisbane) 13 May 7/3 Even in Mount Morgan we see the piebald population increasing—mixing in our public schools with our children. **1911** R.J. CASSIDY *Land of Starry Cross* 200 This is the song of a piebald love—of a love that is White and Brown.

2. Applied as a derogatory epithet to: **(a)** one who favours admitting non-whites, esp. Kanakas, to Australia, and **(b)** the resultant society.

1901 *Tocsin* (Melbourne) 3 Oct. 1/2 Victoria has 23 members in the Federal House of Representatives, 19 of whom are 'Piebald Austr-Aliens'. **1903** *Truth* (Sydney) 15 Mar. 1/8 Here's something for the advocates of a piebald Australia to chew before they encourage the immigration of smellful and cruel aliens.

B. *n.* One who is of mixed race.

1903 'BOONDI' *Boondi's Bk.* 35 So few full-blooded blacks and so many 'piebalds'. **1908** *Truth* (Sydney) 5 Apr. 7/3 Are you an Englishman?—No, *I am an Australian*. 'No,' retorted Mr Levien, 'by God you are not! (Laughter) You are a piebald!'

Hence **piebaldism** *n.*

1901 *Bulletin* (Sydney) 20 July 15/2 Piebaldism in North Queensland. A sugar-planter has a half-caste illegitimate son, whose mother is an aboriginal gin. This young man recently married his half-caste *cousin*, whose mother is a Kanaka woman who is now 'kept' indiscriminately by Chows and other aliens.

piece. [Spec. use of *piece* (small) portion.]

1. *pl. Shearing.* Oddments of wool detached from the skirtings of a fleece; the skirtings.

[N.Z. **1881** A. BATHGATE *Waitaruna* 173 The 'pickers up' were.. carrying [the fleeces] to the sorting table, where they were stripped of the 'pieces', which were thrown aside.] **1891** R. WALLACE *Rural Econ. & Agric.* 384 The washing of wool, either before or after shearing, is, with the exception of locks and pieces, which are generally scoured, almost entirely given up. **1979** E. SMITH *Saddle in Kitchen* 80 There'd be catching pens to fill and wool to be pressed, with us jumping and tramping on 'pieces' and 'bellies' in two bales held upright from the shed rafters by wire.

2. Special Comb. **piece picker,** one who gathers up and sorts the pieces; so **piece picking** *vbl. n.*

1899 G. JEFFREY *Princ. Australasian Woolclassing* 51 The skirtings are thrown on the floor until the 'Piece Pickers' gather them up and sort them. **1928** C.E. COWLEY *Classing Clip* 41 To carry out the duties of 'piece-picking' with the fullest measure of success, a certain degree of skill and dexterity is required.

3. In the phr. **to have** (or **take**) **a piece (out) of** (someone), to rebuke, to take to task.

1958 *Coast to Coast 1957* 125 I'd made up my mind to 'have a piece of him', as the good Australian phrase goes, and had, therefore, confined my activities to a few minor jobs which could be cleared up at a minute's notice. **1984** A. DELBRIDGE *Aussie Talk* 237 *Take a piece out of*, to reprimand severely.

pied, *a.* Used as a distinguishing epithet in the names of black and white birds: **pied butcherbird,** the bird *Cracticus nigrogularis* of mainland Aust., except parts of the south; see also ORGAN BIRD; **cormorant,** the large bird *Phalacrocorax varius* occurring near coastal and inland waters of Aust. and N.Z., having a black back, white front, and orange-yellow face patch; **currawong** (or **crow-shrike**), the bird *Strepera graculina* of e. Aust. exc. Tas.; *black magpie* (b), see BLACK *a.*^{2} 1 b.; **goose,** *magpie goose*, see MAGPIE *n.* 2; **grallina** *obs., magpie lark,* see MAGPIE *n.* 2; **heron** (or **egret**), the predom. blueblack and white bird *Ardea picata* of coastal and near-coastal n. Aust. and elsewhere; **honeyeater,** the bird *Certhionyx variegatus* of arid mainland Aust., the male of which has black and white plumage; **oystercatcher,** the bird *Haematopus longirostris* of coastal Aust. and elsewhere; see also *red bill* RED *a.* 1 b.; **robin,** *hooded robin*, see HOODED.

1902 *Emu* II. 90 **Pied Butcher Bird.**.. These birds generally go in pairs. **1843** J. GOULD *Birds of Aust.* (1848) VII. Pl. 68, The **Pied Cormorant** may be regarded as a gregarious species. **1844** [**pied currawong**] J. GOULD *Birds of Aust.* (1848) II. Pl. 42, *Strepera graculina*. Pied Crow-Shrike. **1945** C. BARRETT *Austral. Bird Life* 216 Currawongs.. feed chiefly upon native fruits and berries, and insects. Perhaps the best known species are the pied currawong and the grey bird. **1884** 'R. BOLDREWOOD' *Old Melbourne Memories* 22 The **pied goose**, here in large flocks, with.. an occasional wild turkey, were our chief support and sustenance. **1843** J. GOULD *Birds of Aust.* (1848) II. Pl. 54, *Grallina australis*.. **Pied Grallina. 1846** [**pied heron**] J. GOULD *Birds of Aust.* (1848) VI. Pl. 62, *Herodias picata*.. Pied Egret. **1981** C. THIELE *Little Tom Little* 23 The pied heron put on his mating plumage and danced and nodded to his love. **1844** J. GOULD *Birds of Aust.* (1848) IV. Pl. 49, *Melicophila picata*.. **Pied Honey-eater. 1901** *Emu* I. 102 *Entomophila leucomelas*.. Pied Honey-eater.. will rise to a great height in the air, and then fall suddenly into another tree. **1785** J. LATHAM III. 219 **pied Oister-catcher.**.. The *Oister-catcher* is pretty common in England. **1842** J. GOULD *Birds of Aust.* (1848) III. Pl. 7, *Petroica bicolor*.. **Pied Robin.**

pie-dish beetle. [See quot. 1935.] Any of many beetles, usu. of the genus *Helaeus* of drier Aust.

1896 F.G. AFLALO *Sketch Nat. Hist. Aust.* 271 The nocturnal *Tenebrionidae*.. include the grotesque Pie Dish Beetle

(*Helaeus princeps*). **1935** K.C. McKeown *Insect Wonders Aust.* 5 The so-called 'Pie-Dish' Beetles are typical of the drier areas. They are queer creatures, flattened in shape, and with a wide flange running round the outer edge of the elytra or wing-covers, a feature which gives them their popular name.

pie-melon. [Poss. transf. use of U.S. *pie-melon* a melon used for pies.] Any of several plants bearing a melon-like fruit, esp. a cultivated variety of the watermelon *Citrullus lanatus* (fam. Cucurbitaceae). See also *wild melon* WILD 1.

1907 *Truth* (Sydney) 24 Feb. 12/5 The scallywags who would rob a chinkie's pie melon patch deserve nothing better than a seat on an ounce of shot. **1975** L. BEADELL *Still in Bush* 140, I had founda wild pie-melon . . so for tea I had my first sample of a melon boiled in claypan water. . . It could easily have resembled stewed apples.

pig, *n.*[1] In the names of flora and fauna: **pig fish,** any of several marine fish, esp. those of the fam. Congiopodidae, and some of the fam. Labridae, as *Bodianus oxycephalus* of n. and e. Aust. and elsewhere; -**footed bandicoot,** the bandicoot *Chaeropus ecaudatus* of drier southern and central Aust., having only two well-developed toes on the forefoot, prob. now extinct; **melon,** see quot. 1872; **weed** [transf. use of *pigweed* a plant used as animal fodder or as a pot-herb], the spreading, prostrate plant *Portulaca oleracea* (fam. Portulacaceae) of Aust. and elsewhere, having thick, succulent stems and leaves, and often regarded as a weed of cultivation; PORTULAC; see also MUNYEROO.

1842 *Tasmanian Jrnl. Nat. Sci.* I. 104 Ostracion . . known at Port Arthur by the name of Pig-fish. [**1836 pig-footed bandicoot**: T.L. MITCHELL *Three Exped. Eastern Aust.* II. 131 This animal was of the size of a young wild rabbit, and of nearly the same colour. . . The feet, and especially the fore-legs were singularly formed, the latter resembling those of a hog.] **1838** *Proc. Zool. Soc. London* 26 Mr Ogilby exhibited a drawing, made by Major Mitchell, of a Marsupial animal found by that officer on the banks of the river Murray. . . It would appear that there were only two toes on the fore-feet, which were described as having been so perfectly similar to those of a pig, as to have procured for the animal the name of the pig-footed bandicoot, among the persons of the expedition. **1872** MRS E. MILLETT *Austral. Parsonage* 103 A large field-melon, called the **pig** or cattle **melon**, which, in spite of its insipidity, produced, when largely helped out with vinegar and sugar and baked under a crust, an imitation by no means despicable of apple-pie. **1862** G. BOURNE *Jrnl. Landsborough's Exped. from Carpentaria* 30 Pigweed, or portulac, is plentiful here.

pig, *n.*[2]

1. [f. U.S. *in a pig's eye, ear, arse*: see OEDS *sb.*[1] 10 g.]

a. In the possessive, as an abbrev. of 'pig's eye', etc.: used as a derisive retort. Also with **to**.

1906 E. DYSON *Fact'ry 'Ands* 5 'Pigs to you!' said Benno, with incredible scorn. **1953** T.A.G. HUNGERFORD *Riverslake* 102 'Kerry's all right.' 'Pigs, is he! He's tailing round with Mister bloody Randolph an' that flamin' Balt!'

b. As a possessive with various anatomical nouns: used as a derisive retort; freq. as a strong negative.

1919 W.H. DOWNING *Digger Dialects* 38 Pig's ear, a contemptuous ejaculation. **1966** D. NILAND *Pairs & Loners* 13 'You know my reputation then,' I said. He snapped his fingers. 'Pig's bum to your reputation!' **1974** D. WAUGH *Master White Grass* 23 'The pidgin for bully beef is bullamacow.' 'Pig's tit!' **1978** HANIGAN & LINDSAY *No Tracks on River* 60 'Pigs foot,' said Mike. 'They just put up signs like that to scare you.' **1981** J. SAXTON *Something will Come* 163 'Pig's arse' could mean almost anything. . . 'I won ten thousand pounds. . . ' P.A.—disbelief. 'Me crop caught fire. . . ' P.A.—sympathy. 'Western Australia should secede. . . ' P.A.—one hundred per cent agreement. 'Me wife ran off. . . ' P.A.—half your luck.

2. Abbrev. of PIG-ROOT *n.*

1911 A. SEARCY *By Flood & Field* 251 He contented himself with a couple of 'pigs', and then walked quietly away.

pig-dog. A dog bred to hunt the wild pig.

[N.Z. **1845** E.J. WAKEFIELD *Adventure in N.Z.* II. 6 It soon became a fashion for travelling settlers like myself to have a pack of pig-dogs, known for their strength, skill, and courage.] **1925** *Bulletin* (Sydney) 19 Nov. 24/4 To bail up a pig in its jungle without trained dogs is almost impossible and certainly unsafe. This explains why . . a good 'pig-dog' is prized. **1978** D. LAVERS *Vet in Clouds* 55 Most hunters breed pig-hunting dogs (colloquially known as 'pig-dogs') by mating a bull terrier with another breed like a staghound or boxer.

pigeon-berry ash. [Prob. transf. use of U.S. *pigeonberry* any of several plants having fruit attractive to birds.] Any of several, usu. large, rainforest trees of e. Aust., esp. *Cryptocarya erythroxylon* (fam. Lauraceae), having a fragrant, pinkish-brown wood and *Elaeocarpus obovatus* (fam. Elaeocarpaceae), having a pale, tough wood; the wood of these trees. Also **pigeon-berry tree.**

1884 A. NILSON *Timber Trees N.S.W.* 55 *E*[*laeocarpus*] *obovatus*—Ash; Pigeon-berry Tree. A noble tree, attaining sometimes a height of 130 feet and a diameter of 5 feet. **1965** *Austral. Encycl.* III. 137 The rose maple or rose walnut (*C*[*ryptocarya*] *erythroxylon*), found in the hill rain-forests of south-east Queensland and northern New South Wales, where it is most generally known to timber-getters as pigeon-berry ash.

pigface. [See quot. 1965.] Any of several succulent, prostrate, perennial plants of the genera *Disphyma* and *Carpobrotus* (fam. Aizoaceae) of coastal and dry inland Aust., esp *D. crassifolium* which also occurs in N.Z. and S. Africa; CANAGONG; MESEMBRYANTHEMUM. See also KARKALLA. Also **pig's face,** and *attrib.*

1830 G.A. ROBINSON in N.J.B. Plomley *Friendly Mission* 1 Feb. (1966) 113 The natives gathered a marine plant called pigface which they eat and of which they appear very fond. **1926** *Bulletin* (Sydney) 15 July 24/3 Abos. have more uses for pigface-weed than curing jellyfish sting. **1947** F. CLUNE *Roaming around Aust.* 16 'Pig's Face'—that's an ugly name for a pretty little flower. **1965** *Austral. Encycl.* VII. 112 Pigface, a name widely applied in Australia to fleshy-fruited succulent plants of the genus *Carpobrotus* . . because the ripe, reddish fruiting structure is subtended by two ear-like floral leaves and the whole bears a fanciful resemblance to a pig's head.

pig-iron polisher: see quot. 1982.

1968 J. O'GRADY *Gone Troppo* 85 'Pig-iron polishers go last.' he said. The Engineer put money on the bar. **1982** LOWENSTEIN & HILLS *Under Hook* 175, I remember the only time I was sorry for a ship's engineer—pig iron polishers you'd call them if you wanted to annoy them.

pig-jump, *v. intr.* Of a horse: to jump as a pig does, from all four legs but without bringing them together (as in a buckjump). Freq. as *vbl. n.*

1884 A.W. STIRLING *Never Never Land* 190 She habitually rode a skittish pony of about fourteen hands, who used to buck, or, as she called it, pig jump for about five minutes after its mistress got seated. **1916** J.M. CREED *Recoll. Aust.* 88 The prairie horses rarely do more than buck straight ahead, which in Australia is looked on with contempt and called 'pig-jumping'.

Hence **pig-jumper** *n.*

1920 *Bulletin* (Sydney) 24 June 20/2 In far-western Queensland, where you *do* get brumbies and rough horses, they are considered soft snaps unless they can 'spin' and 'buck back'. The straight-ahead prad, no matter with how great a jar he hits the ground, is a mere 'rooter' or 'pig-jumper'.

pig-jump, *n.* [f. prec.] The act of pig-jumping.

1924 FUNK & WAGNALLS *New Standard Dict.* 1873 *Pig-jump, vi.* [Austral.] To buck, as a horse.—*pig-jump, n.—pig-jumper, n.* 1946 *Bulletin* (Sydney) 28 Aug. 29/2 'C'n y' ride?' asked the boss. 'Aw,' mumbled Skinny, 'I c'n ride a quiet hack.' 'S'pose you're good for a few pigjumps?'

pigmeater. *Obs.* A beast which is unfit for human consumption: see quot. 1890.

1879 S.W. SILVER *Austral. Grazier's Guide* 14 He has learned to comprehend what .. 'scrubbers', 'pigmeaters', and 'stags' mean as disparaging terms when applied to live stock. 1884 'R. BOLDREWOOD' *Old Melbourne Memories* 105 The original cattle had been neglected... Among them was a large proportion of bullocks, which declined to fatten... They were what are known by the stock-riders as 'ragers' or 'pig-meaters'. 1890 — *Colonial Reformer* II. 100 'Pigmeaters!' exclaimed Ernest; 'what kind of cattle do you call those? Do bullocks eat pigs in this country?' 'No, but pigs eat them, and horses, too,' affirmed Jack Windsor; 'and a very good way of getting rid of rubbish.'

pig-root, *v.*

1. *intr.* Of a horse or other animal: to kick upwards with the hind legs, head down and forelegs firmly planted. Also as *vbl. n.*

1900 *Bulletin* (Sydney) 14 July 15/1, I saw a colt after much buck jumping and pig-rooting, get rid of rider, saddle and girth. 1980 A. HOPGOOD *And here comes Bucknuckle* 48 He fell out of the stall, pig-rooted and the jockey went sailing into the air.

2. a. *Joc. intr.* To ride.

1919 E. DYSON *Hello, Soldier* 17 'N' Privit Artie Rowe along with others in the force Goes pig-rootin' inter battle, holdin' converse with his horse.

b. *trans.* (in *pass.*). To be thrown by a pig-rooting horse.

1965 *Coast to Coast 1963–64* 158, I was pig-rooted off a horse, and broke my wrist.

c. *intr. fig.*

1925 M. TERRY *Across Unknown Aust.* 48 He announced laconically that his car was pig-rooting!

Hence **pig-rooting** *ppl. a.*

1913 *Bulletin* (Sydney) 20 Mar. 16/4 I've seen a monkey in a circus remain on a pig-rooting Australian outlaw, but was it a horseman?

pig-root, *n.* [f. prec.] The act of pig-rooting.

1917 A.L. BREWER *'Gator's Euchre* 30 Starlight snorted frequently, and delivered a few violent pig-roots; though these did not perturb Walsh, who had sat the horse on more than one occasion when it was fresh after a long spell. 1960 R.S. PORTEOUS *Cattleman* 194 Ken was moderately fond of riding. He had his own pony and could even stick its playful winter-morning pigroot, but he showed none of Dan's reckless horsemanship.

pig-rooter. An animal that 'pig-roots'.

1933 J. MCCARTER *Love's Lunatic* 123 I've fallen as heavy as a mug rider from a pig-rooter. 1977 H. TOWSON *Black & White* 69 This is Old Charlie's pig-rooter. He's never been ridden for years.

pigsty. [Transf. use of *pigsty* a pen for pigs.] A (temporary) structure of logs built as a support on a mine, for a section of railway track, etc.

1911 E.D. CLELAND *W. Austral. Mining Practice* 145 In wide stopes it is sometimes found necessary to support the ore at points where it threatens to come away... The support given usually takes the form of 'pig-stys'. These are constructed of round logs, built up in the form of a hollow square, and forming a support of great strength. 1969 P. ADAM SMITH *Folklore Austral. Railwaymen* 15 In 1929 we put in pig-sties at the washaways for nearly a hundred miles down as far as Bundoomah.

pigtail. *Obs.* [Transf. use of *pigtail*: used elsewhere but recorded earliest in Aust.] A Chinese immigrant to Australia.

1858 A. PENDRAGON *Queen of South* 169 There's no good to be done by a whitefellow where those thundering pigtails are. 1907 C. MACALISTER *Old Pioneering Days* 207 The fall broke the poor 'pigtail's' neck.

Hence **pigtailed** *a.*, Chinese.

1871 *Austral. Town & Country Jrnl.* (Sydney) 10 June 720/2 A solid stare and 'No savee' being the extent of news to be elicited from the pig-tailed geologists.

pike. [Transf. use of *pike* a large, voracious, fresh-water fish of the fam. Esocidae.] Any of several voracious marine fish, esp. of the fam. Sphyraenidae, having an elongated head and sharp teeth, as *Sphyraena novaehollandiae* and *S. obtusata.*

1847 *Port Phillip Herald* 25 Mar. 2/4 The banks of the Yarra may be daily seen lined with anglers... The bream is the principal sport, although occasionally a pike of large size rewards the angler's perseverance and tact. 1983 *Age* (Melbourne) 19 Sept. 11 Fifteen years ago 38 per cent of Westernport Bay was covered with seagrass. Rock flathead and pike grazed in the grass.

piker. [Transf. use of *piker* a vagrant: see OED(S *piker, n.*^{3} 2.] A bullock living in the wild.

1887 K. MACKAY *Stirrup Jingles* 16 Gone is the rush and rattle Of pikers on the rails, When wings were full of cattle, And thongs came down like flails. 1980 S. THORNE *I've met some Bloody Wags* 9 Back to Queensland—back to where the scrubs are deep and dense, to God's own land where the pikers roam, across the border fence.

pile, var. PIALLA.

pile. *Mining. Obs.* [Transf. use of *pile* a heap of money.] A very rich claim. Also **pile claim, pile hole.**

1854 *Illustr. Sydney News* 28 Oct. 324/2 The writer states (with all the enthusiasm of a fortunate digger who has at length discovered his pile) that himself and his party had been successful in striking the gutter. 1871 *Austral. Town & Country Jrnl.* (Sydney) 4 Feb. 143/3 There is little fear but their labours will be soon rewarded with what they deserve—a pile hole. *Ibid.* 17 June 751/3 There is doubtless a large area of payable ground in it; but we think no 'pile' claims.

pilot bird. [Transf. use of *pilot bird* a name applied to a number of birds.] The reddish-brown, chiefly terrestrial bird *Pycnoptilus floccosus* of s.e. mainland Aust., having a penetrating whistle.

1893 *Argus* (Melbourne) 25 Mar. 4/6 Here, close together, are eggs of the lyre bird and the pilot bird—the last very rare, and only found quite lately in the Dandenong Ranges, where the lyre bird, too, has its home. 1984 M. BLAKERS et al. *Atlas Austral. Birds* 456 The range of the Pilotbird is completely within that of the Superb Lyrebird but they are rarely seen together.

pimelea /pɪˈmiljə, paɪˈmiljə/. [The plant genus *Pimelea* was named by naturalists Daniel Solander and Joseph Banks (in Gaertner, J. (1788) *De Fructibus et Seminibus Plantarum* I. 186) from Gr. πιμελή fat, perh. referring to the oily seeds of the plant.] Any plant of the genus *Pimelea* (fam. Thymelaeaceae), shrubs and herbs of the

Australasian region, many of which are cultivated as ornamentals. See also *rice-flower* RICE.
1793 J.E. SMITH *Specimen Bot. New Holland* 32 The name of *Pimelea*.. is derived from πιμελή, fat, but is rather a pleasantly sounding than a very apt denomination, unless there may be any thing oily in the recent fruit. 1986 *Canberra Times* 30 Jan. (Suppl.) 11/5 Depending on the time of year, even the less knowledgeable gardener will find the 'familiar' growing in the park as nature intended—grevilleas in many forms, mint bushes, pimelea, kunzea.

pimlico. *Obs.* [Imitative, prob. assimilating to the name of a London suburb.] FRIAR BIRD.
1841 J. GOULD *Birds of Aust.* (1848) IV. Pl. 58, The Friar Bird.. has obtained from the Colonists the various names of 'Poor Soldier', 'Pimlico', 'Four O'Clock', etc. 1944 L. WELSH *Kookaburra* 12 Noisy friar birds.. have many names—Leatherhead, Monk, Four O'Clock, Pimlico, and Poor Soldier.

pimp, *n.* [Transf. use of *pimp* a pander.] An informer; a tell-tale.
1899 J. BRADSHAW *Highway Robbery under Arms* (1912) 8 Yes, savagely they murdered him, The cowardly Blue Coat imps, Who were led on to where he slept By informing Peeler's pimps. 1974 *Age* (Melbourne) 12 Oct. 12/1 You fat pimp! The standard response to 'I'm going to tell on you'.

pimp, *v.* [f. prec.] *intr.* To tell tales; to inform. Usu. with **on.**
1938 X. HERBERT *Capricornia* 524 He reckons I pimped on him—and that's how the johns went out and grabbed 'em both. 1957 J. WATEN *Shares in Murder* 155 You made up to me so you could get me to pimp on Charlie for you.

pin-bullock. [Transf. use of *pin* the middle place in a tandem team of three horses + BULLOCK.] One of the two (or four) bullocks in a team harnessed to the end of the pole: see quot. 1959; CLAMPER; POINTER $n.^3$ 1.
1898 *Bulletin* (Sydney) 13 Aug. 3/2 From pin-bullocks to the leaders, every beast was wearied out. 1959 H.P. TRITTON *Time means Tucker* 36 A bullock-team is made up in four parts: polers, pin, body and leaders... The pin-bullocks take the pull.

pin bush. [See quot. 1902.] NEEDLEWOOD.
1888 *Proc. Linnean Soc. N.S.W.* III. 518 *Hakea leucoptera*.. 'Needle bush', 'Pin bush'. Good drinking water is got from the fleshy-roots of this bush in the arid districts in which it grows. 1902 *Ibid.* XXVII. 580 Various shrubs and trees passed between Cowra and Grenfell were:.. *Acacia diffusa* (sometimes called Pin Bush from the shape of the rigid pointed leaves) [etc.].

pinch. [Br. dial. *pinch* short, steep hill; recorded earliest in U.S.: see OED(S.] A steep or difficult part of a road; a steep hill. Also *fig.*
1846 *Bell's Life in Sydney* 25 July 3/3 The passage through the gap is not very difficult until you begin to descend on the eastern side, when the pinches are real bursters. 1923 J. MOSES *Beyond City Gates* 37 I'm trottin' along the road of life.. and I feel the uphill pinches.

pindan /ˈpɪndæn/. [a. Bardi *bindan*.]
1. A tract of arid, sandy country characteristic of the s.w. Kimberley region, in n. W.A.; the low, scrubby vegetation occurring on the sandy soils of such country; any of several plants typifying such vegetation, as *Acacia tumida* (fam. Mimosaceae). Also *attrib.*
1888 *Proc. Linnean Soc. N.S.W.* II. 1018 The coast on the east side of King's sound is low and swampy, bounded eastwards by 'Pindan' sands and gravels, a pliocene formation which extends inwards for upwards of 60 miles. 1962 C. GYE *Cockney & Crocodile* 111 We drove the eighty four miles along the straight red road through the pindan, that low scrub of spindly fire-blackened trees and tall grass which looks hopeless but with a bore or two will support sheep and cattle well. 1983 R.J. PETHERAM *Plants Kimberley Region W.A.* 363 In the North Kimberley region periodic burning is considered necessary to prevent Pindan Wattle invasion of improved pastures.

2. Comb. **pindan country, scrub.**
1910 *Emu* IX. 148 The country immediately around Broome is covered with fairly dense scrub, and is known locally as **Pindan country.** 1952 I.L. IDRIESS *Outlaws of Leopolds* 18 A darkness before them darker than the night was the dense edge of the **pindan scrub**—small trees densely growing together, interlaced by creeper and vine.

pindaner. Chiefly *W.A.* Also **pindana.** [f. prec.] An Aboriginal from the inland. Also *attrib.*
1938 D. BATES *Passing of Aborigines* 20 Big pindana (inland) mob blackfellows come up. 1954 I.L. IDRIESS *Nor'-Westers* 220 At Lulugui station a skinny pindaner came in from the bush... Dick the stockman christened him Spider.

pine. [Transf. use of *pine* a tree of the genus *Pinus* or various allied coniferous species.]
1. Any of several, usu. large, coniferous trees generally yielding a useful timber, now usu. with distinguishing epithet, as **celery-top, Huon, Norfolk Island** (see under first element); the wood of the tree. Also *attrib.*
1788 *HRA* (1914) 1st Ser. I. 21 The pine-trees [on Norfolk Island] rise fifty and sixty feet before they shoot out any branches. 1965 *Austral. Encycl.* VII. 119 The name 'pine' is popularly given to a number of different indigenous conifers.

2. CYPRESS PINE. Also *attrib.*
1805 J.H. TUCKEY *Acct. Voyage to establish Colony Port Philip* 161 Timber trees are very thinly scattered... They are.. box, and a kind of pine. 1938 C.T. WHITE *Princ. Bot. Qld. Farmers* 142 The inner bark.. contains an oleo-resin which, when the bark is injured, exudes in tears, the resin being variously known as 'Pine Resin', 'Cypress Pine Resin', [etc.].

3. Used *attrib.* in both senses in Comb. **pine brush, scrub.**
1839 *S. Austral. Register* (Adelaide) 11 July 4 Belts of scrub and **pine brush.** 1827 *Monitor* (Sydney) 20 Aug. 599/2 Towards evening my route eastward was completely terminated, by mountains covered with **pine scrubs**, to the summit.

pineapple.
1. Used *attrib.* in Special Comb. **pineapple grass-tree** *obs.* [see quot. 1842], the plant *Richea pandanifolia* (see GRASS-TREE 2); also **pine-apple tree.**
1842 D. BURN *Narr. Journey Hobart Town to Macquarie Harbour* (1955) 25 The pathway is everywhere skirted by.. a very remarkable and exceedingly graceful plant, which, from its striking similitude to the lordly fruit, is styled the 'Pine-Apple Tree'. 1877 *Illustr. Austral. News* (Melbourne) 3 Sept. 138/1 The pine-apple tree (richea pandanifolia) may also be frequently met with.

2. [See quot. 1974.] An opal cluster, formed where glauberite crystals are replaced by opal.
1928 M.E. FULLERTON *Austral. Bush* 212 Bunches of crystal, belonging to a remote geological period, and called by the miners 'pineapples'. 1974 *Austral. Gem & Minerals Fossicker* I. 74/3 The types of opal to be found in the rock at White Cliffs are fascinating in themselves. The favorite, and most valuable form is a 'pineapple'. Although it may look nothing like a pineapple, it gets its name from the way it is formed from many small pieces apparently glued together by nature.

piner.

3. In the phr. **the rough** (or **wrong**) **end of the pineapple,** a raw deal; inequitable treatment.

1961 R. LAWLER *Piccadilly Bushman* 37 He'll know what I mean when I talk of getting the wrong end of the pineapple. 1976 *Sydney Morning Herald* 23 Oct. 9/1 Waffling witnesses, even those of lofty social standing, were given short shrift, if not the rough end of the pineapple.

piner.

a. *Tas.* One employed in felling Huon pine trees and getting the logs to market.

1871 *Mercury* (Hobart) 5 Apr. 2 The piners have to go some 15 or 20 miles up the Davey River to the timber beds. 1983 P. DOMBROVSKIS *Wild Rivers* 26 He often passed beneath the Angel and grew to believe that anyone who destroyed it would meet with ill-fortune. For the piners it was a unique, sacred presence in the heart of the rivers region.

b. *transf.* An artefact made of pine.

1895 *Bulletin* (Sydney) 26 Jan. 15/1 A Melbourne undertaker complains that the local cadaver is now almost invariably content with a stained 'piner'.

pining, *vbl. n. Tas.* The occupation of a piner.

1919 *Huon Times* (Franklin) 28 Sept. 3/3 This gentleman has for many years engaged in pining at the Craycroft, Picton, and Huon rivers. 1984 J. & K. HEPPER *Gordon River Cruise Bk.* 11 Pining was .. taking place to the south at Port Davey.

pink, a.
Used as a distinguishing epithet in the names of flora and fauna: **pink bells** *pl.,* see PINK-EYE $n.^1$ 2; **-breasted robin,** the small bird *Petroica rodinogaster* of Vic. and Tas., the mature male having predom. grey-brown plumage with a deep pink breast and belly; also **pink robin,** and formerly **pink-breasted woodrobin; cockatoo,** MAJOR MITCHELL COCKATOO; **-eared duck,** the nomadic duck *Malacorhynchus membranaceus,* having a pink patch behind the eye, white underparts with brown bars, and a shovel-shaped bill; PINK-EYE $n.^1$ 1; *whistling duck,* (b) see WHISTLING; *zebra duck,* see ZEBRA; see also WIDGEON; also **pink-ear; wood,** any of several trees or tall shrubs, esp. of the genus *Eucryphia* (fam. Eucryphiaceae), as *E. moorei* (see PLUMWOOD) of s.e. N.S.W. and e. Vic., having dark-green, pinnate leaves and large, white, showy flowers, *E. lucida* (see LEATHERWOOD), and (*Tas.*) *Beyeria viscosa* (fam. Euphorbiaceae) of s. Aust.; the wood of these trees.

1842 J. GOULD *Birds of Aust.* (1848) III. Pl. 1, *Erythrodryas rhodinogaster.* **Pink-breasted** Wood-**Robin.** . . The food of the Pink-breasted Wood-Robin consists solely of insects. 1903 *Emu* II. 163 Pink-breasted robin (*Petroeca rhodinogastra*) abundant in parts of the Otways, as on the Upper Erskine. On the plains it is not to be seen except in the scrub near the coast, where it is plentiful. 1976 *Reader's Digest Compl. Bk. Austral. Birds* 357 The nest of the pink robin .. is a beautiful compact cup of soft green moss, deftly bound with spiderweb and camouflaged outside with pale green or grey lichen. 1843 J. GOULD *Birds of Aust.* (1848) V. Pl. 2, *Cacatua leadbeateri* .. **Pink Cockatoo,** Colonists of Swan River. 1898 E.E. MORRIS *Austral Eng.* 127 **Pink-eared D[uck],** or Widgeon .. *Malacorhynchus membranaceus.* 1964 M. SHARLAND *Territory of Birds* 106 The delightful little Pink-ear, with broad bill, zebra stripes, and white-rimmed eye, is well distributed. 1824 *Hobart Town Gaz.* 1 Oct., Colonial Timber may at any time be purchased of an inhabitant of this town... Cherry Tree and **Pink Wood,** for furniture and gun stocks. 1877 *Illustr. Austral. News* (Melbourne) 3 Sept. 138/1 The bases of the mountains are clad with the most luxuriant growth of forest vegetation, such as .. the beautiful pinkwood (eucryphia billardieri). 1967 N.A. WAKEFIELD *Naturalist's Diary* 20 The Pinkwood (*Eucryphia moorei*), a large jungle tree resembling a beech but with foliage like that of an ash.

pink, v. trans.
To shear (a sheep) so closely that the colour of the skin is visible. Also *absol.*

1897 *Worker* (Sydney) 11 Sept. 1/1 He 'shaves' his sheep, or 'pinks 'em', when he shears them nice and clean. 1911 A.G. STEPHENS *Pearl & Octopus* 105 He had finished that big wether in five minutes .. and had pinked as if the boss was at his hip.

Hence **pinker** *n.,* one who shears carefully (and therefore slowly).

1939 J. SORENSEN *Lost Shanty* 22 Now 'Billy the Pinker' and 'Quality Jack', With 'Jimmy the Moulder', were shearing out back.

pink-eye, $n.^1$

1. *Pink-eared duck,* see PINK a. Also **pink-eyed duck.**

1845 J. GOULD *Birds of Aust.* (1848) VI. Pl. 13, *Malacorhynchus membranaceus* .. Pink-eyed Duck, Colonists of Swan River. 1941 C. BARRETT *Aust.* 53 A few pairs of pink-eyes rose from the creek.

2. *pl.* Any of many small shrubs of the genus *Tetratheca* (fam. Tremandraceae) of s.w. and s.e. Aust. incl. Tas., having often pendant, usu. purplish-pink to red flowers with a dark centre. Also **pink-bells.**

1914 E.E. PESCOTT *Native Flowers Vic.* 31 Tetratheca ciliata and Tetratheca ericfolia [sic] .. are low-growing plants, known as 'pink-eyes', sending out long sprays of magenta bells in spring and early summer. 1984 E. WALLING *On Trail Austral. Wildflowers* 24 Heathy Tetratheca or Pink-bells, a low slender plant with open mauve flowers at the tips of the wiry stems.

pink-eye /ˈpɪŋkaɪ, ˈpɪŋki/, $n.^2$
Chiefly *W.A. Austral. pidgin.* Also **pinki.** [Perh. a. Yinjibarndi *biŋgayi* f. *biŋga* to hunt.] WALKABOUT 3 a. and 4 a.

1899 [see PINK-EYE *v.*]. 1901 *Bulletin* (Sydney) 22 June 32/3 A common practice at these stations is .. 'Pinki' (native holiday)—a picnic where the tucker is flying in the air, or crawling the earth, the natives having first to catch before they can satisfy their hunger. This 'pinki' takes place when the kind 'master' has no immediate work for his 'indentured' black goods. 1902 *Ibid.* 29 Mar. 14/2 A squatter .. sends the blacks (signed-on) whom he does not want, out on what is termed pinki (or holiday)—that is to say, he stops their rations and turns them out where there is no food till he wants them again. 1984 W.W. AMMON et al. *Working Lives* 21 Dido and me are in for a bit of pink-eye and to do some business as well.

pink-eye, $n.^3$
[Of unknown origin.] A labourer who is given preferential treatment when work is allocated. See BULL $n.^4$

1915 *Bulletin* (Sydney) 9 Dec. 22/1, I was wielding the pick and banjo in a gang on a big channel job once when the ganger got his 'slip' for giving his 'pink-eye' (pet) an easy job. 1982 LOWENSTEIN & HILLS *Under Hook* 81 As soon as the deck cargo was off, you'd be finished. Now you might get that once a week, but the regular gangs, the bloody pink-eyes, they'd be kept on till the ship was finished.

pink-eye, $n.^4$ [Prob. altered form of PINKY $n.^2$]

a. Cheap alcoholic liquor; alcoholic liquor in general. See also quot. 1945. Also *attrib.*

1922 *Bulletin* (Sydney) 6 July 22/2 The Speck's early settlers learned from the blacks how pink-eye can be got from the cider-tree. 1945 S.J. BAKER *Austral. Lang.* 166 Recipes as published by an outback newspaper in 1936. . . Methylated spirits and Condy's crystals (*Pinky*). . . Addicts of these noxious drinks are known as *meths* .. and *pinkeyes.* 1956 A. UPFIELD *Battling Prophet* 84 I'm game to bet there was fifty empty Pink-Eye brandy bottles. He hadn't been dead long. . . Lying on the floor, and the place stinking of Pink Eye.

b. A drinking bout.

PINK-EYE 411 **PIPE**

1958 F.B. VICKERS *Mirage* (ed. 2) 247 He reckoned we'd been havin' a pink-eye—layin' up on the grog. **1982** M. WATTONE *Winning Gold in W.A.* 51 Jim Clarke was often having a go at these three men and named them the roadside prospectors because he believed they just went out having a pink eye (boozing).

pink-eye, *v.* [See PINK-EYE *n.*^{2} 1.] *intr.* To go on a walkabout; to holiday. Also as *vbl. n.* and *ppl. a.*, and **pink-eyer** *n.*, a holiday-maker.

1899 *Truth* (Sydney) 9 Apr. 5/4 The diabolical and dastardly doing of the 'Pinkeyeing' Squattocracy of the norwest. **1919** *Smith's Weekly* (Sydney) 10 May 11/2 Pearlers crowd away for a holiday—known as a 'pink-eye' in norwest slang—in the off-season, when the boats cannot operate. One such party happened to 'pink-eye' on a small island off the N.W. coast... The island soon disappeared, all but a rock or two, from which derisive crabs watched the shivering 'pink-eyers' steer for the mainland. **1929** K.S. PRICHARD *Coonardoo* (1961) 24 I'll be glad when all this pink-eyeing is over.

pinko, see PINKY *n.*^{1}

pinky /'pɪŋki/, *n.*^{1} *S.A.* Also **pinkie**. [a. Gaurna *biŋgu.*] BILBY. Formerly also **pinko**.

1840 TEICHELMANN & SCHÜRMANN *Outlines of Grammar* 39 Pingko, *s.* a small animal with a white tail that burrows in the earth. **1898** *Bulletin* (Sydney) 23 July 15/3 Something apparently new in zoology has been taken into Kalgoorlie from way-out—something between the 'bilbee' (of N.S.W. and Q.) and the 'pinkie' (of S.A.). **1969** E.C. ROLLS *They All ran Wild* 49 'Pinky' referred to the bare skin on the nose and 'pinto' probably to the black and white tail.

pinky, *n.*^{2} Also **pinkie**. [Orig. Br. slang but chiefly Austral.: see OEDS *sb.*^{3}]

1. Cheap or home-made (fortified) wine. Also *attrib.*

1904 *Worker* (Sydney) 10 Sept. 2/2 One vile decoction, known locally as 'Pinky', is so full of ether and raw spirit that it sends drinkers stark, staring mad. **1970** N.A. BEAGLEY *Up & Down Under* 80 Port was called 'Pinkie', and those who preferred port were Pinkie drinkers.

2. Comb. **pinky joint, shop.**

1958 M.D. BERRINGTON *Stones of Fire* 7 'That's the store and the wine saloon,' Roger told me. 'The bush name for them is **'pinky joint'**—don't ask me why.' **1920** *Bulletin* (Sydney) 5 Aug. 24/2 Jacky had just recovered from the horrors which he had contracted at the local **pinky shop.**

Hence **pinkyite** *n.*

1904 *Worker* (Sydney) 10 Sept. 2/2 The following day the wine .. was sold to the pinkyites.

pinnaroo /pɪnə'ru/. [a. Diyari *pinarru* an elder.] An Aboriginal elder (in quot. 1938 *attrib.*, and *fig.*).

1938 R. INGAMELLS *Sun-Freedom* 17 Dark pinnaroo gums go straggling over the plain. **1966** K. WALKER *Dawn at Hand* 42, I look at you and am back in the long ago, Old pinnaroo lonely and lost here, Last of your clan.

pint pannikin: see PANNIKIN 1 b.

piola, var. PIALLA.

pioneer. [U.S. *pioneer* one who goes into new country to settle: see Mathews.]

1. One of the first or early settlers in a district. Also *attrib.*, esp. as **pioneer settler.**

1842 *Austral. & N.Z. Monthly Mag.* 23 Considerable augmentation .. has been received by the arrival .. of the pioneers of the new settlement of Austral-Ind. **1956** *Bulletin* (Sydney) 23 May 12/4 The farm on which I was born carried the whole range of fences marking the progress of the pioneer-settlers, with wire unknown.

2. Comb. **pioneer colonist, squatter.**

1871 *Great Northern Run Case* 111 An enterprising **pioneer colonist** embarked capital, and risked both life and health in occupying the runs Ludwig, Dura, and Kilmore, situated in the pastoral district of Leichhardt. **1841** G. ARDEN *Recent Information Port Phillip* 75 The first faint bush track of the **pioneer squatter.**

pioneering, *vbl. n.* [f. U.S. *pioneer* to go into new country as a settler.]

1. The opening up of new country by settlers.

1867 'CLERGYMAN' *Aust. as it Is* 49 The work of pioneering, and 'taking up country', still continue to be prosecuted with as great vigour as ever. **1940** G. MORPHETT *Simple Story Rural Dev.* 1 Pioneering on the West Coast was a grim affair.

2. Comb. **pioneering days.**

1902 *Bulletin* (Sydney) 21 June 17/1 J.D. Moore, who writes as an old-chum .. I take to belong to a class which is over-fond of blowing about its 'pioneering days'.

Hence **pioneerage** *n.*

1939 FRANKLIN & CUSACK *Pioneers on Parade* 12 Felonry, of whatever virtue, was taboo in the pioneerage, but descendants of free settlers, however humble or undesirable, were recognized.

piosphere /'paɪəsfɪə/. [f. the stem πι- of Gr. πίνειν to drink + combining -o- + *sphere.*] An ecological system defined as the area around a watering point, in an arid zone, in which grazing animals interact: see quot. 1969. Also *attrib.*

1969 R.T. LANGE in *Jrnl. Range Managem.* (Baltimore) vi. 396 In an arid zone, the animals forage outwards from a watering-point, to which they are obliged to return frequently for drink... This leads to the development of a distinct ecological system... For convenience, the system is called in this paper the *piosphere* (from the Greek word 'pios' = to drink). It may be envisaged as a zone, but it is defined by the interactions, not by any spatial limits of area. **1979** GRAETZ & HOWES *Chenopod Shrublands* 83 The more or less radial vegetation pattern generated by the dependence of stock on a particular water point in a paddock (Lange's 'piosphere' effect).

pipe.

1. *Hist.* A lampoon against a prominent person, written on a piece of paper rolled into a tube and left in a public place; a pasquinade. Also *attrib.*

1816 W.C. WENTWORTH *Miscellanea* 1816-45 6 Mar., By the Pipe Maker on seeing the advertisement in the Gazette offering on the part of the Officers of the 46th a reward of two Hundred Pounds for the detection of him. **1816** *Sydney Gaz.* 9 Mar. 1/1 Copies of a *paper,* usually called a *pipe,* were circulated in the Town of Sydney .. containing a false, malicious, and scurrilous Attack upon the Character of His Honour the Lieutenant Governor.

2. A long, tubular cavity in the centre of a tree trunk or log of wood.

1882 A.J. BOYD *Old Colonials* 20 Logs with a bit of a pipe in suits me best. They ain't so hard to burst. **1908** *Bulletin* (Sydney) 27 Feb. 15/1 From a perfectly-solid log a few more sleepers could certainly be sawn than may be chopped; but where there is a pipe in the log, the difference isn't worth arguing about.

Hence **piped** *ppl. a.,* **pipy** *a.*

1898 R. RADCLYFFE *Wealth & Wild Cats* 20 Poor Coolgardie has only its bush—and what bush! Wretched, miserable gum trees, half-grown, most of them '**piped**'. **1879** *Queenslander* (Brisbane) 12 July 58/3 The bigger the tree the better for shingle-splitting... If it is '**pipey**', that is, hollow all up the centre, it does not matter.

pipe-clay. [Spec. use of *pipe-clay* fine white clay used for making tobacco-pipes.]
1. A fine white clay which forms a paste when mixed with water and is used as body paint by Aborigines. Also *attrib.*

1832 *Sydney Monitor* 21 Mar. 3/3 The widow went into the usual mourning for her gallant husband, by streaking her face, breast, and arms with pipe clay. **1854** W. SHAW *Land of Promise* 73 Pipe-clay hieroglyphics adorn her countenance; her main article of covering is an opossum-skin cloak.

2. *transf. Gold-mining.* A layer of soft clay lying immediately below an auriferous stratum: see quot. 1869.

1852 J. BONWICK *Notes of Gold Digger* 9 Some greasy substance with streaks of yellow sand, is at once concluded by you to be the pipe clay bottom. **1869** R.B. SMYTH *Gold Fields & Mineral Districts* 617 *Pipe-clay*, a soft white clay, which is often found lying between the bed-rock and the wash-dirt. Its thickness varies from a mere trace to many feet.

Hence **pipe-clay** *v. trans.*, to paint (part of the body) with a paste made from pipe-clay.

1852 J. MORGAN *Life & Adventures W. Buckley* 43 They all pipe-clayed themselves, and had another corrobberree.

pipi /ˈpɪpi/. Also **pippie**. [Transf. use of N.Z. *pipi*, usu. referring to the edible bivalve *Amphidesma australe*.] The edible marine bivalve *Plebidonax deltoides* of coasts from s. Qld. to s. W.A., incl. Tas., often used as bait; UGARI.

1895 C. THACKERAY *Amateur Fisherman's Guide* 70 The absolutely best baits are the lug or sea worm, and the pippie, a species of mussel. **1985** I. & T. DONALDSON *Seeing First Australs.* 150 (*caption*) Gathering pipis (*Plebidonax deltoides*), ocean beach shellfish species, on Tacking Point Beach.

piping crow. MAGPIE *n.* 1 a. Also **piping crowshrike, piping shrike.**

1832 J. BACKHOUSE *Narr. Visit Austral. Colonies* 31 Numbers of Piping Crows called also White Magpies, were hopping about. **1933** C. FENNER *Bunyips & Billabongs* 188 A beautiful songster, the Australian magpie or piping crowshrike. **1981** *Bulletin* (Sydney) 13 Jan. 93/3 Now South Australia has its State emblem—the piping shrike... The symbol depicts a piping shrike with wings spreading in the shape of a Union Jack.

pippie, var. PIPI.

pippy. [Prob. independently f. *pip* ill-humour, poor health, but see OEDS 2 b. for an 1886 instance.] Depressed; irritable.

1941 S.J. BAKER *Pop. Dict. Austral. Slang* 54 *Pipped, pippy*, irritated, angry, out of sorts. **1978** MULLALLY & SEXTON *Libra & Leprechaun* 115 I'll admit I get a bit pippy at times.

pirate, *n.*
1. One who seeks a casual acquaintance with the intention of having a sexual relationship.

1916 *Truth* (Sydney) 23 Jan. 9/3, I have not for many years past been a 'Pirate', one of those men who molests young women in the streets.

2. The act of seeking such an acquaintance; esp. in the phr. **on the pirate.**

1948 *Gabber: Qld. Lines of Communication Army Trade Training Depot* Oct. 4 She sees them and laughs when a pirate is attempted. **1964** G. GELBIN *Australs. have Word for It* 99 They are on the pirate. We goes round St. Kilda and tries a few but we want three together.

pirate, *v.* [f. prec.] *trans.* To seek a casual acquaintance with (a person) with the intention of having a sexual relationship. Also as *vbl. n.*

1927 F.C. BIGGERS *Bat-Eye* 26 An' me an' Skin—we pirates two young tarts. **1981** L. MCLEAN *Pumpkin Pie* 53 They were supposed to be shopping, but most of the time was spent in 'Pirating', or looking for suitable members of the opposite sex.

pirri /ˈpɪri/. Also **pirrie.** [a. Arabana (and neighbouring languages) *birri*.] An Aboriginal engraving tool made of stone: see quot. 1961.

1924 HORNE & AISTON *Savage Life Central Aust.* 90 The last stone of the ideal type to be described is the *pirrie*; this is a small pear-shaped tool running to a fine point. It is used as a graving tool to make decorative marks on wooden weapons, and occasionally it is used as a drill for light boring work, such as making the hole to take the string of an *inchitcha* (bull-roarer). **1961** *Proc. Prehist. Soc.* (Cambridge) XXVII. 75 A pirri is a symmetrical, leaf-shaped, uniface point, retouched over all or part of its upper surface, apparently by pressure flaking... Specimens vary in length from about 1 to 7 centimetres, and even the smallest are made sometimes from intractable quartz. This combination of superb craftsmanship with the production of aesthetically pleasing artefacts.. makes the pirri one of the most distinctive items of prehistoric culture.

pisonia /pɪˈzoʊniə/. [The plant genus *Pisonia* was named by Swedish botanist Carl von Linné (*Species Plantarum* (1753) II. 1026, *Genera Plantarum* (1754) ed. 5 451) in honour of the Dutch physician Willem Piso (*fl.* 1648), author of a work on medicinal plants of Brazil.] Either of two trees or shrubs of the widespread tropical and subtropical genus *Pisonia* (fam. Nyctaginaceae), occurring in n. and e. Aust., and elsewhere, *P. grandis* and *P. umbellifera*.

1928 S.E. NAPIER *On Barrier Reef* 86 The trunks and limbs of the pisonia are gnarled and twisted. **1978** N. COLEMAN *Look at Wildlife Great Barrier Reef* 25 Pisonias are large, easily recognised trees which dominate inner forest areas of most vegetated coral cays.

piss, *v.* In the phr. **to piss in** (someone's) **pocket,** to ingratiate oneself with (someone).

1967 K. TENNANT *Tell Morning This* 283 Soon's they knew you was in with Numismata, they all want to piss in your pocket. **1980** E. BARCS *Backyard of Mars* 52 'It's just that we Australians don't piss in one another's pockets.' The colloquialism mystified me with my struggling English.

pissant, *n.* In the phr. **game as a pissant,** brave; foolhardy.

1944 J. HETHERINGTON *Austral. Soldier* 13 'The Trump'll do us,' his men said. 'He's as game as piss-ant!' **1962** R. TULLIPAN *March into Morning* 59 The old white lady makes you as game as a pissant.

pissant, *v. intr.* With **around:** see quot. 1945.

1945 S.J. BAKER *Austral. Lang.* 87 Someone is pissanting around when he is messing about. **1959** G. HAMILTON *Summer Glare* 138 Struth, you pissant around like a rooster that's too old.

piss pot. [Fig. use of *piss-pot* a chamber-pot.] A heavy drinker.

1974 *Bulletin* (Sydney) 2 Nov. 65/3 Eventually every house in the area will have a bottle collection crate and we'll be collecting more than Mosman. As the Mayor told me, they're much bigger pisspots over here. **1981** C. WALLACE-CRABBE *Splinters* 53 Me poor dad used to say that God never speaks to a drunk man. Dear old dad was never a pisspot.

pitch. *Mining. Obs.* [Cornish dial.: see OED *sb.*^{2} 12.] A specific portion of a mine allotted to a particular workman, esp. a tributer (one who receives a proportion of the ore raised). Also *transf.*, a productive claim.

1846 S. *Austral. Register* (Adelaide) 9 Dec. 2/5 The present pitch at the Burra Burra Mines ends on the 23rd inst., and the next will not be made till the 11th January, that the men may have time, if they wish it, to enjoy the Christmas holidays. **1855** G.H. WATHEN *Golden Colony* 65 Thus a likely 'pitch' we seek, Such is life on the Forest Creek!

pitcheri, pitcherie, varr. PITURI.

pitcher plant. [Spec. use of *pitcher-plant* any of several plants having leaves modified as pitchers.] The insectivorous, perennial herb *Cephalotus follicularis* (fam. Cephalotaceae) of s.w. W.A. Also **Albany pitcher plant.**

1818 A. CUNNINGHAM in I. Marriott *Early Explorers Aust.* 31 Jan. (1925) 323, I made a diligent search for the curious Pitcher Plant, *Cephalotus follicularis.* **1985** *Age* (Melbourne) 29 July 15/3 One Australian insect-eating species that has been declared endangered from collection is the Albany pitcher plant *Cephalotus follicularis.* The W.A. Government has banned all commercial exploitation of the plant in the wild but according to Mr Cheers 'backyarders are still digging up the plants'.

pitchery, var. PITURI.

pitchi /ˈpɪtʃi/. Also **pitchie, pittji.** [a. Western Desert language *bidi.*] COOLAMON 1.

1896 B. SPENCER *Rep. Horn Sci. Exped. Central Aust.* IV. 56 'Munyeru'.. is collected in large quantities by the females on their 'Pitchis' or wooden boat-shaped receptacles. **1934** C. SAYCE *Comboman* 107 It was Koomilya with a pitchie of food. **1936** C. CHEWINGS *Back in Stone Age* 1 All the women and most of the young girls carried wooden trays, or *pittjis*, mostly.. shallow.. and twice as long as they were broad.

Pitt Street. Also **Pitt-street.** [The name of a principal business street in Sydney.] Used allusively with reference to urban incomprehension of rural matters; freq. *attrib.* in Comb. with nouns designating a rural occupation, as *bushman, farmer*, etc., in (usu.) derogatory reference to a person whose principal interests are in the city but who invests in rural property: see quot. 1972. See also COLLINS STREET, QUEEN STREET.

1842 *Colonial Observer* (Sydney) 23 Feb. 161/1 The Pitt-Street Corrobbory! We were in no way disappointed at the result of the late meeting in the Victoria Theatre, to petition the Queen and Parliament for a Representative Government for this Colony. **1962** V.C. HALL *Dreamtime Justice* 82 'You got bushed,' I pointed out. 'Came down the wrong river. That's the worst of you Pitt Street bushmen.' **1972** K. WILLEY *Tales Big Country* 28 Communities where the same families had cultivated their land for 150 years are having their own quiet revolutions as 'Pitt Street farmers'—doctors, lawyers, businessmen, and so on—buy up the properties for a combined weekend retreat and tax dodge. **1985** *Bulletin* (Sydney) 2 July 41/2 Pitt and Collins Street farmers are people with incomes earned in cities by stockbrokers—doctors, dentists, businessmen and lawyers—who buy farms. They operate these enterprises at losses, ensuring that the funds expended on the land and written off against taxable non-farm income go to enhance its capital value.

pituri /ˈpɪtʃəri/. Also with much variety, esp. as **pitcheri, pitcherie, pitchery.** [a. Pitta Pitta *bijirri.*] The shrub *Duboisia hopwoodii* (fam. Solanaceae), widespread in arid, sandy, central Aust., the leaves being traditionally used as an animal poison and a narcotic; any of several other plants of the fam. Solanaceae, used as a drug. See also *emu bush* (b), EMU *n.*[1] 3, *native tobacco* NATIVE *a.* 6 a. Also *attrib.*

1861 *Burke & Wills Exploring Exped.* 13, I distributed the few remaining presents, and they gave in return some chewed pitchery and nardoo balls. **1872** *Austral. Med. Jrnl.* (1876) Nov. XXI. 368, I obtained.. a quantity of dried leaves.. of a plant used by the natives as a stimulating narcotic. These leaves, called 'pituri', were obtained in the neighbourhood of the water-hole Kulloo, eight miles beyond Eyre's Creek. **1878** *Queenslander* (Brisbane) 1 June 262/1, I have seen pitcherie growing only five miles to the west. **1928** B. SPENCER *Wanderings in Wild Aust.* 158 The Pitcheri, or Pituri, plant, which is presumably its native name in some part of Australia. The natives use it both as a narcotic and as a means of catching emus.

piturine. An alkaloid derived from PITURI: see quot. 1979.

1880 *Jrnl. & Proc. R. Soc. N.S.W.* (1881) XIV. 127 Piturine mixes with every proportion of water, alcohol, and ether... The yield was about 1 per cent. of alkaloid from the dried plant. **1979** J.G. HAWKES et al. *Biol. & Taxon. Solanaceae* 42 The active alkaloid in D[*uboisia*] *hopwoodii* was variously identified as pituria, piturine, duboisine and nicotine... Eventually in 1934, Hicks and Le Messurier established that it was not nicotine, but d-nor-nicotine... However.. chemical properties of the plant vary not only with seasons and state of maturity, but apparently by region.

Pivot City. *Obs.* A name given to the city of Geelong, Victoria: see quot.

1859 W. KELLY *Life in Vic.* I. 160 The Pivot City is a sobriquet invented by the citizens of Geelong to symbolise it as the point on which the fortunes of the colony would culminate and revolve.

Hence **Pivotite** *n.*

1884 *Austral. Tit-Bits* (Sydney) 26 June 14/2 The Pivotites won a very easy victory from the Melbournites on Saturday.

pizzle. [Br. dial., now apparently more freq. in Aust. than elsewhere: see OED(S and quot. 1965.]

1. The penis of an animal, esp. of a bull or ram. Also *attrib.*

1891 *Conference Amalgam. Shearers' Union & Pastoralists' Fed. Council* 8 The shearer shall not.. cut the teat of any ewe or pizzle of any wether or ram. **1965** J.S. GUNN *Terminol. Shearing Industry* ii. 8 *Pizzle*, a sheep's penis. This word has no taboo and is the formal word in written articles. **1973** H. LEWIS *Crow on Barbed Wire Fence* 172 The machine clipper was steered through the yellow pizzle wool.

2. *transf.*

1969 F.B. VICKERS *No Man is Himself* 153 'He cut me pizzle off with a bit o' broke bottle.' He felt at his penis through the cloth of his trousers. 'He never made much of a job of it. It's got a head on it now like a bloody frilly lizard.'

placer. See quot. 1945.

[N.Z. **1921** H. GUTHRIE-SMITH *Tutira* 383 'Placer' is a term used to denote a gold digger who remains year after year on the one spot, on the one place.] **1940** *Bulletin* (Sydney) 31 Jan. 41/2 (*title*) The placer sheep. **1945** S.J. BAKER *Austral. Lang.* 66 *Placer*, a sheep which becomes attached to a spot and refuses to budge.

plain. [Spec. use of *plain* a tract of country of which the general surface is comparatively flat.]

1. a. An extensive tract of land which is open and generally suitable for pasture, freq. undulating and lightly treed.

1814 M. FLINDERS *Voyage Terra Australis* II. 66 Towards Double Mount and Shoal-water Bay, the country consisted of gently-rising hills and extensive plains, well covered with wood and apparently fertile. **1948** F. CLUNE *Wild Colonial Boys* 21 Ben wondered why timbered land should be called 'plains', but realized that the trees were more sparse here than on the lower regions of the stream, and that the country was level—in parts swampy.

b. A flat expanse of arid, or semi-arid, land, freq. covered with low scrub.

1847 E.W. LANDOR *Bushman* 291 The cracked, baked, clay-plains in the interior. **1962** J. MACKENZIE *Austral. Paradox* 42 The dry plains of the dead heart.

2. Used *attrib*. in the names of animals: **plain turkey, (a)** *wild turkey*, see WILD 1; also **plains turkey; (b)** *transf.*, see quot. 1978; **wanderer,** the terrestrial bird *Pedionomus torquatus* of s.e. mainland Aust., having mottled brown plumage with a black and white spotted collar in the female; also **plains wanderer.**

(a) 1872 C.H. EDEN *My Wife & I in Qld.* 122 The bird that repaid the sportsman best was the **plain turkey. 1914** H.M. VAUGHAN *Australasian Wander-Yr.* 241 Now and again a 'Plains turkey', or great grey bustard.. would be seen.
(b) 1955 D. NILAND *Shiralee* 27 An old bundle of a man came down the road from the west. Macauley watched him approaching and recognized him at once for what he was, a flat-country bagman, a type on his own... In his time he had met plenty of these **plain-turkeys,** as they were known. **1978** T. DAVIES *More Austral. Nicknames* 80 *Plain Turkey*, a generic nickname for any swaggie who plodded the Central Queensland plains. Such men were usually loners, like the game bird from which they took their name. **1849** C. STURT *Narr. Exped. Central Aust.* II. 45 App. Pedionomus Torquatus.. the **plain Wanderer**.. was first discovered on the plains of Adelaide by Mr Gould. **1984** *Age* (Melbourne) 27 Mar. 26/8 Declining are the thick-billed grass-wren and that odd quail, the Plains Wanderer (of which the latest reports are that new populations have been discovered).

plant, $n.^1$ [Extended use of Br. slang *plant* hidden stolen goods, their hiding-place: see OED(S $sb.^1$ 7.]

1. a. Something hidden, esp. a quantity of stolen goods; the hiding-place.

1812 J.H. VAUX *Mem.* (1819) II. 196 Any thing hid is called, *the plant*, when alluded to in conversation; such article is said to be *in plant*; the place of concealment is sometimes called *the plant*, as, I know of a fine *plant*; that is, a secure hiding-place. To *spring a plant*, is to find any thing that has been concealed by another. **1967** S. LLOYD *Lightning Ridge Bk.* 8 Gibson never located this plant of opal again.

b. In the phr. **to spring a** (or **the**) **plant,** to discover that which has been hidden. See also SPRING.

1812 [see sense 1 a.]. **1828** *Tasmanian* (Hobart) 4 Jan. 3 After some search .. a *plant* of two casks were *sprung* one containing rum and the other wine. **1918** C. FETHERSTONHAUGH *After Many Days* 250 The Scotchmen had by some means 'sprung' the bushrangers' plant, and got away to Scotland with it.

c. In the phr. **in** (or **out of**) **plant,** in (or out of) a hiding-place.

1841 *Sydney Gaz.* 4 Sept., Mr Dogherty .. while riding over the run in the vicinity of Mookia, discovered 'in plant', a large number of calves .. variously branded, which he laid down at once as having been stolen. **1854** G.H. HAYDON *Austral. Emigrant* 100 Happening to have a half bottle of rum in store, I took it out of plant.

2. *Obs.* A salted claim; a quantity of the mineral sought placed in a claim: see PLANT *v.* 3.

1859 W. KELLY *Life in Vic.* I. 189 It was a regular plant—a salted hole... Salting a hole is sprinkling it artificially, with the view of perpetrating a cheat. **1871** 'IOTA' *Kooroona* 139 The surface copper was what, among miners, is called a plant, which, translated into modern English, means that it was not deposited in the place where it was found.

plant, $n.^2$ [Spec. use of *plant* equipment, implements, etc., used in an (industrial) operation: see OED(S $sb.^1$ 6.] The working animals, equipment, vehicles, and sometimes personnel employed by a drover, stockman, etc., on the move.

1867 S.A. *Parl. Papers* no. 14 86 One pound per head for the sheep, with plant and all included. **1982** D. HARRIS *Drovers of Outback* 13 In my day most of the big back country plants were about forty to fifty horses and an open wagonette (often an old Cobb & Co. coach cut down) pulled by four or five horses.

plant, *v.* [Br. slang *plant* to hide (stolen goods): see OED *v.* 8.]

1. *trans.* To hide (articles, animals, etc.); freq. (esp. formerly) used of stolen goods.

1793 J. HUNTER *Hist. Jrnl. Trans. Port Jackson* 373 Some villains dug up every one of the potatoes .. a very strict search was made, in order to find out the offender, but to no purpose, as the potatoes were (in the cant phrase) *all planted*; viz. buried in the ground, so as to be taken out as they were wanted. **1978** H.C. BAKER *I was Listening* 69 He'd lift anything. Tom's yarn went that Jack had whizzed off an electric drill and planted it.

2. *trans.* Of an animal: to settle (another animal, esp. its offspring) in a safe place.

1849 *Argus* (Melbourne) 13 Nov. 4/1 When the calf is too young to follow the cow, she conceals it, colonially, *plants* it, when she goes to feed. **1936** J.C. DOWNIE *Galloping Hoofs* 148 Bush-bred or wild cattle always 'plant' their calves for safety when they have to go a distance to water, the young animals being too weak to undertake the long journey.

3. *trans. Obs.* To salt (a claim); to place (a quantity of the mineral sought) in a mining claim in order to give a false impression of its productivity. Also as *vbl. n.*

1853 C. READE *Gold* 17 *Levi*: This dust is from Birmingham, and neither Australian or natural. *Rob*: The man planted it for you. **1853** H.B. JONES *Adventures in Aust.* 287 The Bishop of Sydney, in laying the foundation stone of a church at Sofala, at each turn of the trowel brought to light a nugget of some value, which however it appeared had been placed there with a view of enhancing the value of the neighbouring land. This in technical gold-digging phraseology, is called 'planting'.

4. *intr.* and *refl.*

a. To conceal oneself.

1846 C.P. HODGSON *Reminisc. Aust.* 347 The ladies however more provident of their offspring, 'planted' in the rushes or creeks, till we had passed. **1983** G. SAVAGE *Tournament* 9, I nicked around the house and planted myself behind the mile-high pile of fruit cases standing there.

b. *transf.* Of an animal: to conceal itself.

1890 Mrs H.P. MARTIN *Under Gum Tree* 173 A dense scrub, in the edges of which horses would often 'plant', and remain concealed for hours. **1951** S.H. EDWARDS *Shooting & Bushcraft* 49 If only wounded he may 'plant', so, look round a bit. . . He is probably quite handy.

planter. [f. PLANT *v.*] One who steals and hides stock.

1890 'R. BOLDREWOOD' *Colonial Reformer* III. 54 What's a little money .. if .. your children grow up duffers and planters. **1955** N. PULLIAM *I traveled Lonely Land* 384 *Plant,* to hide sheep or cattle which have been stolen. *Planter,* one who does so.

planter's friend. A plant of the genus *Sorghum* (fam. Poaceae), cultivated as a crop.

1870 'JACKAROO' *Immigration Question* 10 The 'Planter's Friend' bids fair to be tested this year, and I shall look forward with interest to the result. **1902** *Bulletin* (Sydney) 7 June 16/2 The frequent poisoning of cows by young sorghum and 'planters friend' begins to alarm South Coast (N.S.W.) dairymen.

planting, *vbl. n.* The hiding of stolen goods; esp. the

practice of hiding stolen horses and 'discovering' them when a reward is offered.
1799 *HRA* (1914) 1st. II. 288 The witness discovered the tobacco, but did not remove it in order that from the *planting* of a constable over ye same some discovery might be made by someone coming for it. **1895** G. RANKEN *Windabyne* 92 They opened a business for the 'planting' of horses and the sale of adulterated rum at the solitary waterhole.

plate. [Also N.Z.: see OEDS *sb.* 18 h.] A plate of food contributed by a participant towards the catering at a social gathering; BASKET *n.*
1961 *Gumsuckers' Gaz.* (Melbourne) Aug. 2 Visitors will be welcome. Ladies bring a 'plate', and gentlemen make a donation. **1986** *Sydney Morning Herald* 14 June 41/7 At the Australian Opera.. Veitch announces a new Australian production of Patrick White's Kerr, to be performed on alternate Tuesdays by the Police Choir and Pipe Band: BYO; ladies, a plate please.

platibus, var. PLATYPUS.

platman. *Mining.* One who works on a plat; the person responsible for loading a cage for despatch to the surface.
1934 *Red Star* (Perth) 14 Dec. 1/3 One skipman went on, and a platman was transferred to be his mate and another platman was sent for. **1978** D. STUART *Wedgetail View* 19 Machine miners, boggers, platmen, timbermen, and the men on the surface jobs, all known to him.

platypus /'plætəpʊs/. Pl. **platypuses.** Formerly with much variety, as **platibus, platybus,** etc. [mod. L. *platypus,* a. Gr. πλατύπους, given as the name of the genus by English naturalist G. Shaw (see quot. 1799) but changed in 1800 to *Ornithorynchus.*]
1. The amphibious, burrowing, egg-laying mammal *Ornithorhynchus anatinus* of fresh-water lakes and watercourses of e. Aust. incl. Tas., having thick brown fur, a bill with leathery skin, webbed feet, and a broad, flattened tail; DUCK-BILL; DUCK-MOLE; MOLE *n.*[1]; ORNITHORHYNCHUS; PARADOX, *water mole,* see WATER. See also DUCK-BILLED. Also *attrib.*
1799 G. SHAW *Naturalist's Miscellany* X. Pl. 386, The Platypus is a native of Australia or New Holland, and is at present in the possession of Mr Dobson, so much distinguished by his exquisite manner of preparing specimens of vegetable anatomy. **1833** A. PRINSEP *Jrnl. Voyage Van Diemen's Land* 100 An extraordinary animal is common on the banks of rivers and in lagoons, of which you may have heard, combining the species of quadrupeds and birds; it is called the Platibas, or Platibus. **1854** G.H. HAYDON *Austral. Emigrant* 87 A pouch made from the skin of a platybus. **1915** W.J. WYE *Souvenirs Sunny South* 34 Her velvety coat, that had never known brands, shone soft as the platypus fur. **1952** B. BEATTY *Unique to Aust.* 38 Platypuses inhabit fresh water rivers and lagoons from Tasmania to North Queensland.
2. Special Comb. **platypus frog,** GASTRIC BROODING FROG (esp. *Rheobatrachus silus*).
1983 *Courier Mail* (Brisbane) 21 Nov. 13/2 A search for the rare platypus frog in the Sunshine Coast's Conondale and Blackall ranges at the weekend was unsuccessful.

platypusary. Also **platypusery, platypussery.** [f. prec.] An enclosure in which the natural conditions preferred by the platypus are simulated.
1942 A.L. HASKELL *Waltzing Matilda* 95 It was necessary to create an artificial burrow on the banks of an artificial river, which in itself created a new word—platypusery. **1958** *Bulletin* (Sydney) 16 Apr. 18/3 'A platypussery is to be made in a plane to take platypusses to New York'... The late Harry Burrell.. built (and christened) a platypusary—not 'platypussery'—at his home in the Sydney suburb of Kensington. **1968** V. SERVENTY *Southern Walkabout* 37 The platypusary was in full swing... It was an excellent idea to have a tape recording which concisely explained all the average visitor would want to know about the platypus, then a polite request to keep moving so that the people waiting could come and see the show.

play, *v. Australian National Football. intr.* With **on:** to keep the ball in play without stopping to take a mark or penalty. Freq. as *imp.*
1885 D.E. MCCONNELL *Austral. Etiquette* 641 The Field Umpire, on being appealed to, may either award a 'free kick', call 'play on', or stop the play and throw the ball in the air. **1969** A. HOPGOOD *And Big Men Fly* 36 A beautiful stabpass, right down the throat of team-mate Morris.. and Morris is playing on.

play-about, *n.* and *a. Austral. pidgin.*
A. *n.* A corroboree the main purpose of which is to provide entertainment.
1914 *Bulletin* (Sydney) 11 June 24/2 Charlie found himself 'disqualified' from ever again taking part in a 'play-about'. **1959** E. WEBB *Mark of Sun* 116 The stock-boys and their lubras.. were preparing to stage a small-fella corroboree or 'playabout' for the visitors on Christmas night.
B. *adj.* Of an artefact, activity, etc.: for entertainment or recreation.
1914 *Bulletin* (Sydney) 11 June 24/1 Port Darwin residents used to enjoy going out at sundown towards the Junction to see the 'play-about' spear fights between different Northern Territory Tribes. **1955** M. DURACK *Keep him my Country* 36 'Was she fighting?' 'Playabout,' Liddy said shortly.

play-boomerang. A boomerang designed for entertainment or recreation. See also PLAY-ABOUT *a.*
1851 J. HENDERSON *Excursions & Adventures N.S.W.* II. 147 Some are made and used for amusement, and are called play-boomerangs. With these, the boys practice a great deal. **1878** R.B. SMYTH *Aborigines of Vic.* I. 329 The boomerangs.. from the north-east coast in my collection are not 'come-back' or 'play' boomerangs.

play-lunch. A snack taken by children to school to eat during the mid-morning break; the break itself.
1963 E. SPENCE *Green Laurel* 109 She was not hungry enough to go back for her play-lunch, and to stay close to the classroom appeared to be the safest thing to do. **1982** N. KEESING *Lily on Dustbin* 120 The Queensland coal mining town of Blair Athol gave the world 'eleveners'—the morning break, or recess in a school day or 'playlunch' as it might be called further south.

plenty, *a. Austral. pidgin.* Many; much. Also as quasi-*adv.*
1834 *Perth Gaz.* 10 May 283, I told *Weeip* to put down their spears, when they all threw them down, and ran towards us, calling out *'babbin babbin* (friend) plenty'. **1951** I.L. IDRIESS *Across Nullarbor* 53 We were 'plenty feller' hungry.

pleuro /'plʊroʊ/. Also **pleura, ploorer.** [Chiefly Austral.: see OED(S).]
1. Abbrev. of 'contagious bovine pleuro-pneumonia'.
[N.Z. **1863** E.R. CHUDLEIGH *Diary* 13 Aug. (1950) 98 A horse that was showing signs of pleura. **1864** C.R. THATCHER *Songs of War* 13 We are by this Pleuro haunted.] **1871** *Austral. Town & Country Jrnl.* (Sydney) 25 Feb. 230/3 There were some indications of pleuro in several herds during the very wet season. **1881** A.C. GRANT *Bush-Life Qld.* I. 190 It is a two-year-old steer... As we ride past he shows the white of his eye, and gathering up his strength, he gives a deep hollow cough... 'Pleura,' said Fitzgerald, reading West's enquiring glance. 'We always have it more

or less on the run.' **1896** H. LAWSON *While Billy Boils* 10 The cows contracted a disease which was known in those parts as 'plooro permoanyer', but generally referred to as 'th' ploorer'.

2. Special Comb. **pleuro line**, see quot. 1978.

1960 *N.T. News* (Darwin) 26 Feb. 3/2 The Central Australian area is now officially recognised as a 'pleuro free zone' because of the A.I.B. pleuro line separating the south from the north. **1978** D. STUART *Wedgetail View* 5 The Government drew a line on the map. . and declared the country north of the line an area infected with bovine pleuro-pneumonia. Pleuro. Contagious. . . It meant the end of all their plans, that pleuro line.

plink. [Joc. var. of PLONK.] Wine of very poor quality: see quot. 1943.

1943 S.J. BAKER *Pop. Dict. Austral. Slang* (ed. 3) 60 *Plink*, described as 'a cheap form of plonk'. **1950** *Southerly* iii. 145 A Gargantuan zest for that common horror of the dipsodes: plink.

plod. [Cornish dial. *plod* 'a short or dull story; a lying tale': see OEDS *sb.*^{2}]

1. A tale; a 'line'; a piece of information.

1928 *Bulletin* (Sydney) 5 Sept. 27/1, I 'ad to grin When 'e starts pitchin' that plod to me. **1975** X. HERBERT *Poor Fellow my Country* 1126 Put in a plod for me, mate.

2. *transf.* Chiefly *W.A.* A work-sheet recording details of an employee's day's work; the day's work. Also **plod card.**

1935 *Red Star* (Perth) 20 Sept. 2/1 As the day's plods had not been signed the men decided to get them at the timekeeper's office. **1974** N. PHILLIPSON *As Other Men* 103 He . . showed them how they were supposed to fill out their plod cards, listing the number of holes drilled [etc.]

plongge /ˈplɒŋgi/. *Obs.* [a. Yaralde *bloŋge*.] A club used in Aboriginal ritual: see quot. 1846.

1846 H.E.A. MEYER *Manners & Customs Aborigines Encounter Bay* 8 The plongge is a stick about two feet long, with a large knob at the end. They believe that if a person is tapped gently upon the breast with this instrument he will become ill and die, or if he should shortly afterwards receive a wound that it will be mortal. **1879** *Native Tribes S.A.* 195 They fancy that they can charm or enchant by means of two instruments, one called plongge, the other mokani.

plonk. [Prob. altered form of Fr. *blanc* in *vin blanc* white wine: see early quots. and cf. PLINK. Now also used elsewhere.]

1. Wine, or fortified wine, of poor quality. Also *attrib.*

[**1919** W.H. DOWNING *Digger Dialects* 52 *Vin blank*, white wine. **1924** A.W. BAZLEY et al. Gloss. Slang A.I.F. 22 (typescript) *Point blank*, the white wine commonly used in France.] **1933** *Bulletin* (Sydney) 11 Jan. 12/3 The man who drinks illicit brews or 'plonk' (otherwise known as 'madman soup') by the quart does it in quiet spots or at home. **1955** D. NILAND *Shiralee* 76 Getting blown about like an old moll at a plonk party.

2. Comb. **plonk bar, shop.**

1965 E. LAMBERT *Long White Night* 187 Prim . . rented a room above the **plonk bar**. **1965** D. MARTIN *Hero of Too* 58 'We will give them wine to make it special.' 'They'll call it a **plonk shop**.'

Hence **plonk-up** *n.*, a party; **plonked-up** *ppl. a.*, intoxicated.

1966 *Kings Cross Whisper* (Sydney) xxv. 5/2 Entertained the four and a half Persians to a **plonk-up** on the shores of Lake Hurley-Burley. **1972** J. DE HOOG *Skid Row Dossier* 6 You get **plonked up** and the bouncer chucks you out.

plonker. *Obs.* In the war of 1914–18: a shell.

1918 *Aussie: Austral. Soldiers' Mag.* Jan. 3 Fritz was putting over some big stuff. Every time a plonker landed near them, one of the officers energetically fired his revolver into the air. **1920** *Aussie* (Sydney) Dec. 36/3, I had helped him out when he had got chucked into a shell-hole by a plonker.

plonko. [f. PLONK + -O.] One who is addicted to 'plonk'. Also **plonky.**

1963 A. MARSHALL *In mine Own Heart* 187 You end up a plonko with bells ringing in your head. **1978** K. GILBERT *People are Legends* 21 I'm Joe. Tired Joe. The 'plonky' the wino you see on the street I piss at the public corner, I'm a drunk, I'm never discreet.

ploorer, var. PLEURO.

ploughed, *ppl. a.* In special collocations: **ploughed field** *Tas.*, see quot. 1896; **land** *obs.*, terrain characterized by ridges resembling the furrows made by a plough.

1885 *Once a Month* (Melbourne) June 457 On the summit there is a singular assemblage of boulders, which have not been inappropriately designated the '**Ploughed Field**'. **1896** J.B. WALKER Corresp., Ploughed field. In Southern Tasmania applied to extensive fields of large stones, usually basaltic, which occur on mountain sides. The name had its origin in a noticeable area of this kind near the summit of Mount Wellington, which seen from Hobart has the colour and appearance of a ploughed field. **1831** [**ploughed land**] T.L. MITCHELL *Three Exped. Eastern Aust.* 28 Nov. (1838) I. 14 Portions of the surface . . bore that peculiar, undulating character which appears in the southern districts, where it closely resembles furrows, and is termed 'ploughed ground'. **1833** W.H. BRETON *Excursions* 97 The land rises in ridges exactly as though it had once been in a state of cultivation. . . This 'ploughed land', as it has been termed, was observed only where the soil was a rich black mould.

pluck, *v.* In the phr. **to pluck a brand:** see quot. 1945.

1911 A.L. HAYDON *Trooper Police Aust.* 352 One popular form of 'faking' that has been introduced with success is that of 'plucking a brand'. This is done by pulling out hairs from a colt. . . Such a mark only lasts a comparatively short time. **1945** S.J. BAKER *Austral. Lang.* 50 *To pluck a brand*, to fake a new brand on stolen cattle or horses by pulling out the hairs round the existing brand.

plugger. [f. *plug* to keep on persistently.] One who runs, rides, etc., doggedly.

1896 *Bulletin* (Sydney) 14 Mar. 17/3 Wallace, after all, is only a great 'plugger'. The chestnut can't come with a rush at the finish. **1900** *Western Champion* (Barcaldine) 24 Apr. 13/1 The two bicycle races fell to Hoskins, who is a genuine 'plugger'.

plug hat. *Obs.* [U.S. *plug hat* hat with a tall cylindrical crown: see Mathews.] A top hat (quot. 1941 appears erroneous).

1883 G.E. LOYAU *Personal Adventures* 78 Frank . . disguises himself in a 'plug hat' and great coat, and carries a banjo. **1941** S.J. BAKER *Pop. Dict. Austral. Slang* 55 *Plug hat*, a bowler hat.

Hence **plug-hatted** *ppl. a.*

1903 *Truth* (Sydney) 4 Jan. 7/3 Alexander is . . entitled to as much protection . . as is the most bloated, plug-hatted plutocrat in the State.

plum. [Transf. use of *plum* the fruit of *Prunus domestica*; the tree itself.] *Native plum*, see NATIVE *a.* 6 a.; the wood of a native plum. Also *attrib.*

1770 J. BANKS *Jrnl.* 26 Aug. (1896) 299 A fruit we called plums—like them in colour, but flat like a little cheese.

1935 H.H. FINLAYSON *Red Centre* 31 On the fringes of the mulga colonies .. a score or more of large shrubs or small trees .. quondong, plum-bush [etc.].

plumed, *a.* Used as a distinguishing epithet in the names of birds: **plumed egret** [see quot. 1976], the waterbird *Egretta intermedia* of n. and e. Aust. incl. Tas., and elsewhere; **pigeon,** *spinifex pigeon,* see SPINIFEX 4; **tree duck,** the duck *Dendrocygna eytoni* (see *whistling duck* (a), WHISTLING).
1848 J. GOULD *Birds of Aust.* VI. Pl. 57, *Herodias plumiferus* .. **Plumed Egret.** **1976** *Reader's Digest Compl. Bk. Austral. Birds* 80 Long, lacy, filamentous nuptial plumes have given the plumed egret its name. As with its relatives .. only breeding birds have these plumes. **1945** C. BARRETT *Austral. Bird Life* 66 The **plumed pigeon** (*Lophophaps plumifera*) frequents stony areas in the interior of Southern Australia. [**1945 plumed tree duck**: C. BARRETT *Austral. Bird Life* 48 Those curious birds called tree-ducks are better known in Northern Australia than in the south. However, the plumed species (*Dendrocygna eytoni*) ranges into South Australia, and is an occasional visitor to Victoria.] **1955** S. OSBORNE *Duck Shooting Aust.* 16 Plumed tree duck... These have the same general appearance as the Whistling Tree Duck, but they are a paler greyish colour and have no chestnut on the shoulders.

plume grass. [Transf. use of *plume-grass* a grass of the genus *Erianthus* having a plume-like inflorescence.] Any of several perennial grasses (fam. Poaceae) having a plume-like flower-head, esp. those of the genus *Dichelachne* of all States.
1847 G.F. ANGAS *Savage Life & Scenes* I. 152 Tufts of a gigantic species of plume grass, with sharp-edged leaves, grew in vast quantities upon several of the flats. **1966** N.T. BURBIDGE *Austral. Grasses* I. 78 Plume Grass is very common in dry forest and woodland areas and is also found in the mountains.

plum pine. [See quot. 1985.] *She pine,* see SHE 2.
1904 J.H. MAIDEN *Notes on Commercial Timbers N.S.W.* 24 We have another timber allied to 'colonial pine', but much harder and more durable, namely, that one which is variously known as .. 'plum pine', and 'berry pine'. **1985** N. & H. NICHOLSON *Austral. Rainforest Plants* 55 *Podocarpus elatus* Plum Pine. Although the swollen stalks of the fruit are sweetish and quite edible, they are hardly as delectable as a plum.

plumpton. [The name of a village in Sussex, England, where the first enclosed greyhound racing took place in 1877.] A kind of enclosed racecourse for greyhounds; a race held on such a course (as opposed to one held in the open). Also *attrib.*
1884 *Australasian Coursing Calendar* 30/1 We much question whether any enclosed ground in the old country can hold a candle to the colonial Plumpton. *Ibid.* 35/1 The opening day of the important produce meeting at the Oval was anything but favourable or inviting to coursers who affect the Plumpton system.

plumwood. The tree *Eucryphia moorei* (see *pinkwood* PINK *a.*). Also **plum.**
1889 J.H. MAIDEN *Useful Native Plants Aust.* 530 *Eucryphia moorei* .. 'Plum' of the Southern districts of New South Wales .. is a beautifully clear, moderately hard wood, of a warm, light brown colour. **1965** *Austral. Encycl.* III. 411 *E*[*ucryphia*] *moorei* .. is sometimes called plumwood or stinkwood—an unfortunate name for such a handsome tree.

plurry, *a.* [Joc. representation of a Maori pronunc. of BLOODY.] An intensive: BLOODY. Also as *adv.*
1900 H. LAWSON *Verses Pop. & Humorous* 227 Their language that day, I am sorry to say, Mostly consisted of 'plurry'. **1927** W. BLACKET *May it please your Honour* 238 Knowing but two words of the Kamilaroi dialect, I could only advise them to 'make plenty of plurry yabber longa plurry big fella plurry jury'.

plute. *Obs.* [Used elsewhere but recorded earliest in Aust.: see OEDS.] Abbrev. of *plutocrat.* Also *attrib.*
1894 *Vagabonds* 2 It is by this monopolisation of currency as well as of the land and other means of production that the Plutes are enabled to levy their weighty taxes on human industry. **1903** *Truth* (Sydney) 27 Dec. 1/3 No wonder the defeated and dismayed 'plute' push cry aloud in real alarm, 'Where the devil is Labor driving us?'
Hence **plutish** *a.*, plutocratic.
1907 *Truth* (Sydney) 25 Aug. 4/7 They 'sool' their plutish prints on to proclaim him a cocktail, a renegade, a coward.

poached, *ppl. a.*
1. In special collocations: **poached egg,** see quot. 1941; **egg daisy,** the annual herbaceous plant *Myriocephalus stuartii* (fam. Asteraceae); also **poached eggs daisy.**
1941 S.J. BAKER *Pop. Dict. Austral. Slang* 55 **Poached egg,** a yellow-coloured 'silent cop' placed in the centre of intersections as a guide to traffic. **1965** *Austral. Encycl.* II. 494 The so-called 'ham-and-eggs' or '**poached-egg daisy**' (*Myriocephalus stuartii*) grows prolifically on mallee sandhills across Australia; its hairy viscid stems are up to 2 feet high, with rather large yellow compound heads surrounded by a common involucre of white bracts, the whole reminiscent of a poached egg. **1986** *Trees & Natural Resources* Mar. 2 Wild Turnip .. and Poached Eggs Daisy (*Myriocephalus stuartii*), became the dominant plants in the dune grasslands.

pobblebonk. [Prob. f. Br. dial. *pobble* the noise made by water bubbling as it starts to boil (see EDD *sb.*^{2}) + imitative *bonk.*] Either of two frogs of the genus *Limnodynastes* having a loud, single note call, *L. dorsalis* of s.w. W.A. and *L. dumerilii* of s.e. Aust. incl. Tas.
1967 B.Y. MAIN *Between Wodjil & Tor* 84 The resonant twangs of the 'banjo' or pobble-bonk frogs. **1978** B.P. MOORE *Life on Forty Acres* 113 The most distinctive call .. is that of the local Pobblebonk (*Limnodynastes dumerili*). Each male utters but a single 'bonk' at a time but others immediately follow.

pocket. *Australian National Football.* A side position, esp. in the forward and back rows; a player occupying such a position. Freq. as **back pocket, forward pocket.** Also *attrib.*
1931 J.F. MCHALE et al. *Austral. Game of Football* 66 The back pocket players always kept slightly in front of their opponents. **1936** E.C.H. TAYLOR et al. *Our Austral. Game Football* 56 The extra man will most probably be taken from one of the full forward 'pockets'. **1978** P. MCKENNA *My World of Football* 90 The pocket specialists are a new idea in League football.

podargus /pə'dagəs/. [The bird genus *Podargus* was named by the French ornithologist L.J.P. Vieillot (*Nouveau Dict. Hist. Nat.* (ed. 2, 1818) XXVII. 151) f. Gr. πόδαργος swift-footed.] A nocturnal, grey to brown frogmouth of the genus *Podargus* of all States, New Guinea, and adjacent islands, esp. the TAWNY FROGMOUTH.
1841 *S. Austral. Rec.* (London) 2 Jan. 10 Besides the owlet night-jar .. there is the podargus, another night-bird, that sleeps so soundly during the day as only to be disturbed by being knocked off its perch, when it flies lazily to another tree, and resumes its slumbers. **1961** *Coast to Coast 1959–60* 66 'You know the podargus?' 'It's a bird. The tawny-shouldered frogmouth.'

poddied, *ppl. a.* [f. PODDY *v.*]
1. Of an animal: hand-fed.
1921 *Bulletin* (Sydney) 17 Feb. 20/2 The reason the poddied sheep-pups.. turned out duffers was more likely psychological than physiological. **1952** *Meanjin* 19 There were three poddied calves frisking in the overgrown grass.

2. *Obs.* Intoxicated.
1905 *Shearer* (Sydney) 4 Mar. 4/2 Personal effort, self-abnegation, libertarian ideas, and ethical standards are, however, very distressing and distasteful to the 'poddied' State socialist or befooled A.W.U. member. **1909** J.S. RYAN *Splinters on Wall* 8, I long to be 'poddied' with beer; Have brandy on every shelf.

poddy: see PODDY MULLET.

poddy, *n.* and *a.* [Spec. use of Br. dial. *poddy* corpulent, f. *pod* large protuberant stomach: see OED *pod, sb.*^{2} 3 and OED(S *poddy*.]
A. *n.*
1. **a.** A calf; orig. one old enough to wean and fatten, later (esp.) one as yet unbranded. Also *attrib.*
1872 A. MCFARLAND *Illawarra & Manaro* 76 Three or four 'selections', good for wheat, 'poddies', and snipe. **1963** HARNEY & LOCKWOOD *Shady Tree* 84 A poddy is a calf, and a poddy-dodger is a man who spirits them away from their owners before they've been branded, and quickly gets his own brand on them.
b. A calf (less freq. a lamb or foal) which is hand-fed.
1898 *Bulletin* (Sydney) 8 Jan. (Red Page), Prof. Morris defines 'Poddy' as 'a Vic. name for sand-mullet', but leaves out its meaning of motherless calf or foal (common in the bush). A poddy calf or a poddy foal is heard all over Australia. **1983** M. HAYES *Prickle Farm* 80 A little one-eyed ewe, who'd obviously been someone's poddy and considered herself a little above the common throng of paddock sheep.
c. *transf.* See quots.
1958 J. BECKETT *Study Mixed Blood Aboriginal Minority* (M.A. thesis) 145 In fact, young men, or 'poddies' as they are called, find single life very pleasurable. **1982** G.B. EGGLETON *Last of Lantern Swingers* 13 Occasionally, a pair of rabbits may be overlooked in the 'gutting' operation, and on reaching the freezing room would be found to be bloated and unfit for use. These were known as 'poddies'.

2. A bottle containing an alcoholic beverage.
1891 *Truth* (Sydney) 5 Apr. 7/3 Formerly the riding men did not drink much, but as there is now a pub. on every run they frequently come home rolling from side to side and with a poddy in their kick. **1953** H.M. EASTMAN *Mem. of Sheepman* 58 For anaesthetic he would use a couple of 'poddies' (lemonade bottle of whisky) obtained from Coree pub.

B. *adj.* Hand-fed; most freq. in the collocation **poddy calf.**
1899 *Bulletin* (Sydney) 18 Mar. 14/2 She .. talked a lot about pigs and 'poddy' calves. **1983** M. HAYES *Prickle Farm* 11 Six poddy calves some enterprising cattle baron has grazing on the reserve behind the War Memorial.

poddy, *v.* [f. prec.] *trans.*
a. To feed (a young animal) by hand. Also **poddy-feed.**
1896 *Worker* (Sydney) 21 Mar. 1/3 He carried the slop-buckets to the pig sty for her, and helped to 'poddy' (hand-feed) a young calf. **1902** *Bulletin* (Sydney) 29 Mar. 14/4 When calves are being reared, he has to poddy-feed his share daily.
b. *transf.*
1924 *Bulletin* (Sydney) 17 Jan. 24/2 Mrs Cocky came in carrying an infant about a month old. I offered my congratulations. 'Oh, it's not ours,' exclaimed Cocky; 'it belongs to the missus's sister. But she's too crook to rear it, so the missus is poddying it for her.'

Hence **poddying** *vbl. n.*
1913 *Bulletin* (Sydney) 29 May 48/3 The cows had been milked, buckets washed and 'poddying' completed, all in record time.

poddy-dodge, *v.* [f. PODDY *n.* 1 + DODGE *v.* 2.] *trans.* To steal (unbranded cattle). Also *absol.*, and freq. as *vbl. n.*
1919 *Bulletin* (Sydney) 25 Sept. 22/3 Owing to the rise in price of cattle and the difficulty stations have in branding-up, 'poddy-dodging' has become an established trade about Cloncurry (Q.). **1925** M. TERRY *Across Unknown Aust.* 125 Whites may be poddy-dodging. **1977** W.A. WINTER-IRVING *Bush Stories* 96, I don't think anybody will .. poddy-dodge our calves.

poddy-dodger. [See prec.] One who steals unbranded cattle.
1919 *Smith's Weekly* (Sydney) 26 Apr. 19/4 The luck of the poddy-dodgers in these parts is right out just now. They expend time and cunning in mustering cleanskins, and .. a station manager or policeman comes nosing around. **1972** D. SHEAHAN *Songs from Canefields* 37 They took him to court but old Bill had them tricked—A wise poddy dodger is hard to convict.

poddy-feed: see PODDY *v.* a.

poddy mullet. [f. *poddy*, poss. alteration of Jagara *punba* (see PUDDING-BALL) + (Eng.) *mullet.*] Any of several fish, esp. the young of *Mugil cephalus* (see *sea mullet* SEA). Also **poddy.**
1890 *Act* (Vic.) 54 Vict. no. 1093 2nd Sched., Sand-mullet or poddies. **1941** *Bulletin* (Sydney) 29 Oct. 14/1 We caught two pickle-jar full o' poddy mullet, shoved 'em in the fire an' ate them. **1977** *Commercial Fish Aust.* (Dept. Primary Industry) 50 Sea mullet, also known as poddy or grey mullet, are distributed worldwide.

poddy-rear, *v.* [f. PODDY *n.* 1 b.] *trans.* To hand-feed (a young animal). Also as *vbl. n.* and *ppl. a.*
1901 M. FRANKLIN *My Brilliant Career* 17 They do all the milkin', and pig-feedin' and poddy-rarin'. **1934** *Bulletin* (Sydney) 28 Mar. 20/3 This year a merino wether, poddy-reared, is to be broken in. **1976** C.D. MILLS *Hobble Chains & Greenhide* 82 A pet camel that has been 'poddy-reared' is a menace about a homestead. It will reach out and eat anything available.

pogie /'pouɡi/. *Hist.* Also **pogey, poggy, poogie.** [Of unknown origin.] Used *attrib.* in the Special Comb. **pogie pot** (or **tub**), a vat in which oysters are left to decompose before being boiled down, pearls being removed from the residue: see quot. 1979.
1903 H. TAUNTON *Australind* 145 He cheerfully replied, 'Oh! it's only some one stirring his poogie tub', and then went on to explain the process of obtaining pearls from the oysters. **1940** E. HILL *Great Austral. Loneliness* (ed. 2) 26 To obtain the pearls, the oysters are placed in 'pogey-pots', boilers and barrels that line the seashore. **1955** A.C.V. BLIGH *Golden Quest* 31 The waters of the bay are leased .. to .. pearlers and .. they gather the shell by dredging... After gathering the shell it is filled into large iron pots called 'poggy pots'. **1979** *Pearling Industry W.A.* 8 Recovery of the pearl was by an extremely primitive and offensive method. The shucked oysters were put into large drums called 'pogie pots', allowed to rot, and the pearls then recovered from the residue in the bottom.

pogo. Rhyming slang for *pogo stick*, 'prick', as a term of abuse.
1972 R. POLLARD *Cream Machine* 2 Be men, not mouths .. men, not Pogos and 'support' turd-burglars who spin war

point

yarns and bullshit in the bars and R.S.L.s. **1982** J.J. COE *Desperate Praise* 24 'We're on road clearing again. . .' 'What about bloody 7 section doing it . .?' 'Yeah, bloody pogos.'

point, $n.^1$ Shearing. Usu. in *pl*. See quot. 1899.

1871 *Austral. Town & Country Jrnl.* (Sydney) 18 Mar. 331/2 Sheep that strip at the points, and lose the belly-wool, having a clean head without topknot. **1899** A. SINCLAIR *Clip of Wool* 66 *Points*, the points or extremities of the fleece, i.e., the flanks, shanks, neck and head pieces.

point, $n.^2$ *Hist*. A unit in measuring rainfall, the hundredth part (.01) of an inch.

1889 *Australasian* (Melbourne) 20 Apr. 816/2, 92 points were registered at Wilcannia, and more rain has already fallen this year than during the whole of 1888. **1968** R. MAGOFFIN *We Bushies* 75 It was the wettest year we've had, Our score was sixty points!

point, $v.^1$ *Obs*. [f. the phr. *to get points* to gain an advantage.] *intr*. To take unfair advantage of a person, situation, etc. Freq. as *vbl. n.*

1853 H.B. JONES *Adventures in Aust*. 216 Doubtless, as the colony advances, this spirit of 'pointing' will disappear, and a fair legitimate system of trading and commerce will be introduced. **1886** J.F. STEEL *Miscarriage of Justice* 14 There is the glaring swindling of the tan-dealer and the frequent 'pointing' of the cashier.

point, $v.^2$ *Point the bone*, see BONE *n*. 1. Also as *vbl. n.*

1927 SPENCER & GILLEN *Arunta* 402 Take part in the 'pointing'. **1977** J. CARTER *All Things Wild* 58 My informants claimed another Aranda artist had been 'pointed', about the time of Joshua Ebatarinja's death. (Since then I've heard on the mulga wire that this man was repeatedly 'sick', and died in 1975.)

pointer, $n.^1$ *pl*. [Transf. use of *pointers, pl*. the two bright stars in the Great Bear.] The two stars Alpha and Beta *Centauri* in the Southern Cross, a line drawn through which passes almost through the head of the Cross.

1864 J. BONWICK *Astronomy for Young Australs*. 63 Look at the two bright ones pointing toward the Cross. . . They are the Pointers to the Cross. **1950** W.A. MCNAIR *Starland of South* 13 They are sometimes called the Pointers, because they point to the Southern Cross. But their usual names are Alpha Centauri and Beta Centauri.

pointer, $n.^2$ *Obs*. [f. POINT $v.^1$] A sharper; an idler.

1853 H.B. JONES *Adventures in Aust*. 301 For safety the well disposed camp together, for the 'pointers' go in gangs and large bodies. **1954** T. RONAN *Vision Splendid* 164 There was no nark or pointer in the camp, they rode good horses by day and champions at night.

pointer, $n.^3$ [Spec. use of *pointer* that which points out.]

1. PIN-BULLOCK.

1872 C.H. EDEN *My Wife & I in Qld*. 36 Twelve bullocks is the usual number in a team, the two polers and the leaders being steady old stagers; the pair next to the pole are called the 'pointers'. **1941** S.J. BAKER *Pop. Dict. Austral. Slang* 55 *Pointers*, two of the bullocks in a team, placed next to the 'polers'.

2. *Pointing-bone*, see POINTING.

1899 *Proc. Linnean Soc. N.S.W*. XXIV. 330, I discovered the curious bone ornament or implement now to be described. It is made from the fibular of a kangaroo, is 9¾ inches in length, well polished. . . Three uses have been suggested for it, viz., netting needle, 'death bone' or 'pointer', and 'nose bone'.

POKER MACHINE

pointing, *ppl. a*. In special collocations: **pointing bone, stick**, BONE $n.^1$

1904 SPENCER & GILLEN *Northern Tribes Central Aust*. 459 The pointing apparatus . . consists of a long strand of human hair-string, to one end of which five small **pointing-bones** are affixed. **1901** F.J. GILLEN *Diary* 21 Aug. (1968) 235 The Puntudia crept up and 'boned' him with their **pointing sticks**. . . He became very ill and finally died.

poison. Any of several plants poisonous to stock, esp. shrubs of the genus *Gastrolobium* (fam. Fabaceae) occurring mainly in s.w. W.A. Also *attrib*., esp. as **poison bush, plant,** and with distinguishing epithet, as **heart-leaf, York road** (see under first element).

1843 *Port Phillip Gaz*. 18 Apr. 4 A tolerable sheep country badly watered, but a fair average feed and plenty of poison. **1948** C.P. MOUNTFORD *Brown Men & Red Sand* 71 Camels . . which have lived in 'poison bush' country for any length of time seem to learn that the plant is dangerous. **1985** *W. Austral*. (Perth) 6 Nov. 54/2 The regrowth of marri and the poison plant Gastrolobium biloba.

poison-cart. A vehicle designed to lay poison for the destruction of vermin, esp. the rabbit: see quots. 1910 and 1931.

1898 'R. BOLDREWOOD' *Romance Canvas Town* 61 All this time the poison-cart was kept going. **1910** C.E.W. BEAN *On Wool Track* 113 A poison-cart is a cart which lays poison for rabbits. It has a knife underneath it which scratches a furrow in the surface of the ground, into which the poison falls and is covered up. Rabbits will grub for poison but sheep do not. **1931** A.W. UPFIELD *Sands of Windee* 26 The poison-carts . . were light two-wheeled affairs, carrying an iron cylinder in which was placed the poisoned pollard when it was churned up into small pills and carried by a pipe down to a position behind a disk-wheel and dropped into the furrow the wheel made.

poisoner. A cook, esp. one catering for a party of shearers, etc.

1905 E.C. BULEY *Austral. Life* 23 The shearer's cook is always a competent man, and supplies his clients with the best fare obtainable, utterly 'belying' the name of 'poisoner', usually bestowed upon him. **1969** L. HADOW *Full Cycle* 208 'I'm not much good at cooking but I'll try.' 'Never you mind about that. Up north we've got the best poisoners in the country.'

Hence **poison** *v. intr*., to serve as cook.

1934 C. SAYCE *Comboman* 138 He engaged Mick as station cook, a grizzled old man who boasted that he had 'poisoned'—as he described his occupation—on every station in Queensland.

poke, *v*. [Shortened form of *to poke borak* (see BORAK *n*. 2).] In the phr. **to poke it at** (a person), to ridicule or deride. Also **to poke crap, to poke mud**.

1890 *Bull-Ant* (Melbourne) 28 Aug. 15/1 There was a big crowd drawd up about th' worfs watchin' th' toffs, an' pokin' mud at them. **1902** *Truth* (Sydney) 2 Nov.4/7 He had imbibed more 'inspiration' than he was licensed to carry, and got 'poking it' at the 'boys', who 'dealt out stoush'. **1960** D. IRELAND *Image in Clay* (1964) 61, I don't hear her slinging off at you; why poke crap at her?

poker machine. A coin-operated gaming machine which pays out according to the combination of symbols (often representations of playing-cards) appearing on the edges of the wheels spun by the operation of a lever.

1903 *Advocate* (Burnie) 6 Jan. 2/6 It was considered that the use of the poker machine was too much in the publican's favor; it was a one-sided game of chance. **1977** E. JONES *Barlow Down Under* 22 Spent time developing their muscles at one-arm bandits of which the club had only some four dozen. To call them poker machines is an insult to a great game of skill.

pokie. Also **pokey.** [f. POK(ER MACHINE + -Y.] POKER MACHINE. Also *attrib.* and freq. in *pl.*

1965 I. HAMILTON *Persecutor* 87, I always know how much I lose on the pokies. **1970** *Kings Cross Whisper* (Sydney) lxxxii. 2/3 Jackpots on pokey bandits.

pole, *n.* [Spec. use of *pole* a shaft fitted to the forecarriage of a vehicle and attached to the yokes or collars of the draught-animals.] Used *attrib.* in Special Comb. **pole bullock,** POLER 1; **cart, dray,** a vehicle fitted with a central pole rather than a pair of shafts.

1844 *Sydney Morning Herald* 29 July 2/7 He was kicked by one of the **pole bullocks**, and the wheel passed over his chest. **1824** E. CURR *Acct. Colony Van Diemen's Land* 97 It may also be advisable to take with him a pair or two of strong broad wheels and iron axles for a **pole cart**. **1843** A. CASWALL *Hints from Jrnl.* 33 A two-wheeled dray with a pole, is certainly better than with shafts, as if it upsets it turns in the ring-bolt of the pole yoke, and the bullocks sustain no injury; whereas when one with shafts is capsized, the shafter is frequently killed; besides, the shafter should be a large heavy animal, and therefore more valuable, but two indifferent ones suffice for a **pole dray**.

pole, *v.*

1. *intr.* [See quot. 1924.] To take advantage of someone; to contribute less than one's share to a group enterprise. Freq. with **on**.

1906 E. DYSON *Fact'ry 'Ands* 66 'What rot, girls; why don't yer get er shift on?' cried Feathers virtuously... 'Taint ther mealy pertater, polin' on the firm like this.' **1924** A.W. BAZLEY et al. Gloss. Slang A.I.F. 22 (typescript) Poling, to do less than one's share thereby rendering the other fellows more difficult. This term was also borrowed from Australian Bullock driving parlance. The 'Polers' the pair of bullocks nearest to the pole of the wagon, are generally regarded as being not only the strongest, but next to the leaders the cutest pair in the team, and therefore more inclined to take things easy and let the other bullocks do the pulling, if the driver is not observant.

2. *trans.* POLE-FISH. Also *intr.*

1965 *Canberra Times* 9 Jan. 9/1 The Australians take only the smaller bluefin, poling nearer the shoreline. **1983** *Canberra Chron.* 7 Dec. 19/1 Ken Stevenson, on the Carmela T, is reported to have spotted a massive school of bluefin tuna offshore... He poled seven to have a look at them.

pole-fish, *v. intr.* To fish (esp. for tuna), using a pole, a short line, and a barbless lure. Chiefly as *vbl. n.*

1951 *Daily Tel.* (Sydney) 4 Jan. 7/1 Australian tuna can be caught by live bait pole fishing. **1981** *Encycl. Austral. Fishing* XII. 1856 Four-fifths of the Australian catch.. are taken chiefly by means of pole fishing with feather jigs or live baits.

poler.

1. One of the pair of bullocks harnessed to the pole of a vehicle; *pole bullock*, see POLE *n.*

1860 'LITTLE JACOB' *Colonial Pen-Scratchings* 85 There was a bullock dray going lazily down the road—one of the bullocks, a poler (see colonial dictionary), fell from sheer exhaustion. **1959** H.P. TRITTON *Time means Tucker* 3 A bullock-team is made up in four parts: polers, pin, body and leaders: The polers have to be good.. for they have the job of steadying the dray or wagon while the pin-bullocks take the pull.

2. [f. POLE *v.* 1.] A loafer; a shirker.

1938 X. HERBERT *Capricornia* 528 'You long-jawed poler,' Norman roared. 'Living on the fat of the land, while your poor damn flock feeds on soup and coconuts and what they root out of the bush.' **1953** C. WILLS *Austral. Passport* 43 When an' 'orse.. when he's loafin', he leans agin the pole, an' let's the other one carry 'im. So we call 'im a poler... And when a man loafs.. we call him a poler, too.

3. [See POLE-FISH.] One who hoists tuna fish on board with the aid of a pole.

1969 C. THIELE *Blue Fin* 2 With four polers they would really tumble the fish aboard if each man could work by himself; but when they had to team into pairs or even threes it slowed everything down. **1975** *West Austral.* (Perth) 10 Feb. 16/6 The boats were manned by some of the most experienced tuna polers in Australia.

poley, *a.* and *n.* Also **poly.** [Br. dial. *poley*, etc. f. *poll* a hornless cow or ox: see EDD *poll, sb.²*]

A. *adj.*

1. Hornless.

1843 *Port Phillip Patriot* 9 Jan. 3/4 One yellow-sided poly cow. **1933** J.L. GLASCOCK *Jarrah Leaves* 15 Red, white, spotted, and roan; long horn, short horn, and poley; baby 'fats' of three short summers.

2. *transf.* and *fig.*

a. *Obs.* Of a domestic utensil: having a broken handle.

1848 *Bell's Life in Sydney* 4 Mar. 1/1 A poley-quart-pot is simmering at the fire. **1901** M. FRANKLIN *My Brilliant Career* 233 A couple of dirty knives and forks, a pair of cracked plates, two poley cups and chipped saucers.

b. *Obs.* [Perh. in punning allusion to CROPPY.] Of a person: at large; wanted by the police. Also as *n.*

1854 C.A. CORBYN *Sydney Revels* 43 A wild looking man.. who responded to the name of Henry Bull, and who only lacked the horns of his patronymic (being a poley), was summoned. **1884** J.B. MARTIN *Reminisc.* 14 These men [*sc.* police].. zigzagged about.. in search of what they called their 'poley cattle' [*sc.* bushrangers].

c. Of a rifle: see quot. 1918.

1918 *Bulletin* (Sydney) 25 July 22/2 The breech-loader was then a rarity on Monaro, and the 'poly'—hammerless—gun had hardly been evolved, much less perfected. **1954** *Coast to Coast 1953–54* 14 Home made cartridges? There they go again! No. Poley chokes on their guns. That American idea for greater range.

B. *n.*

1. Abbrev. of 'poley bullock', 'poley cow,' etc.

1843 *Sydney Morning Herald* 16 Aug. 3/4, I think another motion is imperatively called for, namely, a return of all the sheep, horned cattle (not forgetting the *poleys*) horses, and pigs in the colony. **1976** C.D. MILLS *Hobble Chains & Greenhide* 138 'That slab-sided poly,' indicating a poor-quality beast moving almost under Laddies' nose, 'Spoil the look of any mob.'

2. *transf.* A type of saddle which does not have kneepads. Also **poley saddle.**

1930 A.E. YARRA *Vanishing Horsemen* 16 Maggie gets the blue-roan, and I'll throw in the old poley saddle for her—and a bridle! **1975** *Sunday Mail Mag.* (Brisbane) 26 Jan. 15/1 My own poley had had its day... Good second-hand saddles were not easy to come by.

police. Used *attrib.* in Special Comb. **police boy,** an adult Aboriginal male employed in the police force, esp. as a *police tracker*; **paddock,** an enclosure for the confinement of impounded animals or animals used by the police; **tracker,** TRACKER; **trooper,** TROOPER.

1937 M. TERRY *Sand & Sun* 269 'Then there's all the sorts of 'em,' Stan added. 'Stock boy,.. camp boy, mission boy, **police boy,** camel boy.' **1840** *Port Phillip Gaz.* 21 Mar. 4 The Public are hereby cautioned against putting Cattle, or any other description of Stock, in the Paddock.. which is situated immediately beyond the **Police Paddock**, and enclosed by a four railed fence. **1910** *Huon Times* (Franklin) 18 May 4/2 Normanton.. had been a **police tracker**, and was running away because he wanted to go to the Baranibah mission. **1839** *Tasmanian* (Hobart) 17 May 159/4 Two mounted **police troopers**.

policeman. Used *attrib.* in the names of animals: **policeman bird,** JABIRU; **fly,** any of many small wasps, esp. of the subfamily Nyssonidae, hunting flies as food for the larvae.

1928 C.G. LANE *Adventures in Big Bush* 131 Wallabies were numerous, also .. Australian storks (commonly called 'Policeman-birds'). 1963 *N. Austral. Monthly* Nov. 34 For two seasons now we have watched this 'Policeman Bird' nest in the same tall scrub-tree at the edge of the swamp. 1905 *Bulletin* (Sydney) 23 Mar. 16/2 The '**policeman fly**' .. is a black fly... When 'the force' arrives at a camp, the common fly has to clear out. I have seen a camp swarming with common flies, and a few days after the 'policemen' appeared it was hard to find one... Consequently the 'policeman fly' is very popular in a camp.

pollutionist. *Hist.* One who advocates the continuation of transportation.

1847 *Abolitionists & Transportationists* 32 From you Pollutionist I sickening turn, To feel my soul's indignant feelings burn. 1847 *Guardian* (Hobart) 26 June 2/5 The emigrant will allow himself to be lured from his home, and remain amongst us, for the convenience of anti-pollutionists.

polly. [Orig. U.S.: see OEDS.] Abbrev. of 'politician'.

1967 *Kings Cross Whisper* (Sydney) xxxviii. 10/2 *Polly*, politician. 1986 *Sydney Morning Herald* 1 May 13/1 Pollies don't matter much any more.

Polwarth /'pɒlwəθ/. [The name of a county in s.w. Vic.] A breed of sheep (see quot. 1965); a sheep of this breed. Also as **Polwarth sheep.**

1919 *Pastoral Rev.* 16 Oct. 965 The standard type of Polwarth sheep is a sheep of fairly level top, with well-sprung ribs and generally robust frame. 1965 *Austral. Encycl.* VII. 184 The name comes from the district in which the sheep were evolved and was officially given to the breed in 1919. The Polwarth was evolved by Richard and Alexander Dennis by mating first-cross Lincoln x Merino ewes with Carr's Plains Merino rams (Ercildoune blood). 1975 L.A. POCKLEY *Handbk. for Jackeroos* 55 *Polwarth*, developed in Australia to suit light cold country and agricultural areas... The Lincoln Merino cross matched back to the Merino is the basis.

poly, var. POLEY.

polygonum /pə'lɪgənəm/. *Obs.* [Spec. use of *polygonum* a herb of the genus *Polygonum*, formerly incl. members of the genus *Muehlenbeckia*.]

1. LIGNUM 1.

1819 *HRA* (1917) 1st Ser. X. 28 A barren marsh, overrun with a species of polygonum. 1901 K.L. PARKER in M. Muir *My Bush Bk.* (1982) 62 The next day seemed more monotonous; all coolabah and polygonum—the 'leafless bramble' of Sturt.

2. Used *attrib.* in Comb. **polygonum bush, scrub, swamp.**

1849 *Adelaide Miscellany* 11 Oct. 50 It was not long before two pretty little crested pigeons fluttered out of a **polygonum-bush.** 1851 *Bell's Life in Sydney* 15 Mar. 7/2 A high condition is so easily sustained by the abundance of salt Bush (Rhagodia) and **Polygonum scrub.** 1879 *Queenslander* (Brisbane) 26 Apr. 531/3 We came to a coolibah forest .. from this into a vile **polygonum swamp,** the worst I was ever in. [*Note*] That is, a swamp after a wet season—the driest of dry country during a dry season.

pom. Abbrev. of POMEGRANATE, and subsequently of POMMY. Also *attrib.*, and as *adj.*

1912 *Truth* (Sydney) 10 Nov. 1/8 The immigrant ('desirable') Will p'r'aps amuse you most—The comic British citizen, That leans against a post; They used to say colonials did, But I'm very much afraid, Upon the 'Poms' I'd put my quid, At the gay 'Chateau de Wade'. 1970 C. NOLAN *Bride for St. Thomas* 45 You'll never fit into the Pom way of life. 1971 B. HUMPHRIES *Bazza pulls it Off*, I've never been overseas before—youse wouldn't count Pom-land.

pomegranate. *Obs.* Also **pommygranate, pommygrant.** [Formed by word-play: see quot. 1920.] An immigrant from the British Isles (now superseded by POM and POMMY *n.*).

1912 *Bulletin* (Sydney) 14 Nov. 16/4 The other day a Pummy Grant (assisted immigrant) was handed a bridle and told to catch a horse. 1912 *Truth* (Sydney) 22 Dec. 1/3 Now they call 'em 'Pomegranates' and the Jimmygrants don't like it. 1916 W.C. WATSON *Mem. Ship's Fireman* 61 As I hailed from the Old Dart, I of course, in their estimation, was an immigrant, hence the curl up of the lip. But 'pommygrant' or 'jimmygrant', they always had a helping hand for me. 1920 H.J. RUMSEY *Pommies* Introd., The colonial boys and girls .. ready to find a nickname were fond of rhyming 'Immigrant', 'Jimmygrant', 'Pommegrant', and called it out after the new-chum children. 1963 X. HERBERT *Disturbing Element* 91 He still wore the heavy clumsy British type of clothing of the day. When we kids saw people on the street dressed like that we would yell at them: 'Jimmygrants, Pommygranates, Pommies!'

pommy, *n.* and *attrib.* Also **pommie.** [f. POM(EGRANATE + -Y.]

A. *n.* An equivocal term for an immigrant from the British Isles; applied also, more recently, to an inhabitant of the British Isles (esp. of England). Also *transf.* (see quots. 1922 and 1953). See also POM, WHINGEING POM.

1912 *Bulletin* (Sydney) 14 Nov. 16/4 The other day a Pummy Grant (assisted immigrant) was handed a bridle and told to catch a horse... Pummy sneaked up behind the quadruped. 1922 *Bulletin* 23 Feb. 20/2 One pommy who is rapidly becoming a good Aussie is that wonderful songster, the blackbird. 1944 J. HETHERINGTON *Austral. Soldier* 32 Their discussion drifted round to the British units who were fighting with the Australians in the desert. 'You know, Bill,' said Australian Number One, 'these 'Pommies' a man meets here are good blokes.' 'My oath!' said Australian Number Two. 'As a matter of fact, Bill, after what I've seen of 'Pommies' out here, I'm never going to sling off at a 'Pommy' again.' 'No, Harry, neither will I.' 'In fact, Bill,' said Australian Number One, warming to his subject, 'I'll go so far as to say this. They're as good as us.' 'Cripes, Harry,' said Australian Number Two, 'you can't say that. But they're bloody wonderful fellers just the same.' 1953 D. STIVENS *Gambling Ghost* 28 You and I are Australians but the rabbits ain't—they're pommies. 1984 B. DIXON *Searching for Aboriginal Lang.* 53 The weatherbeaten, red faces of the cattlemen sitting on stools around the bar all slowly swivelled and surveyed me. 'Pommy!' ejaculated one of them. I was made to feel that no one had ever asked for a gin and tonic in that pub before.

B. *attrib.* or as *adj.*

1. Of or pertaining to a 'pommy'; British, English. Esp. (often as a term of affectionate abuse) as **pommy bastard.**

1915 *Bulletin* (Sydney) 18 Mar. 14/4 The river was 'a swim', and the pommy rouseabout who had been cut off couldn't cross. 1922 *Bulletin* (Sydney) 9 Mar. 20/2 And help with sunwarmed Pommie blood to keep Australia white. 1958 J.R. SPICER *Cry of Storm-Bird* 8 Why Rob Saunders, you old pommy bastard. Jeez, it's good to see you, mate!

2. Special Comb. **pommy jackeroo,** an English jackeroo (see JACKEROO *n.* 2); *transf.* an inept or inexperienced person; **land,** the British Isles; England.

1915 B. GAMMAGE *Broken Yrs.* (1974) 240 They're only a b– lot of **Pommie Jackeroos** and just as hopeless. 1964 J.S. MANIFOLD *Who wrote Ballads?* 86 The jackaroos .. were usually educated young men studying the art and mystery of station management; sometimes they included a 'colonial-experiencer' or 'pommy jackaroo'. **1916** *Truth* (Sydney) 1 Oct. 12/1 It amuses me to hear the way the Pommies run the Australian girls down. They are forgetting that they come out here for their bread and butter, and also good money in hand, more than they got in **Pommyland**.

Hence **pommified** *a.*, affecting an English manner; influenced by an English model.

1936 *Publicist* (Sydney) iv. 10/1 The West is not yet yankified and pommified to the same extent as is Sydney.

pommygranate, pommygrant, VART. POMEGRANATE.

Pompey. *Obs.* [Poss. f. Br. dial. *pompey*, a name for a house of correction or reformatory: see EDD *sb.* 3.] In the phr. **to dodge Pompey**, to evade detection (while engaged in an illegal activity); to avoid carrying out one's responsibilities, esp. to malinger, out of the sight of one's supervisor.

1868 C.W. BROWNE *Overlanding in Aust.* 53 He is necessitated to do a little trespassing on the quiet, which he calls 'dodging Pompey', thereby getting his sheep better feed. **1920** C.W. BRYDE *Chart House to Bush Hut* 67 Didn't like to palm myself off as an expert mill hand. I thought even the 'rat-gangers' had to be skilled men. Afterwards I was one of a rat-gang myself for awhile, and found one only had to be expert at 'dodging Pompey'.

Hence **Pompey dodger** *n.*

1905 *Shearer* (Sydney) 2 Dec. 3/5 State payment to 'Pompey dodgers', when taken advantage of for a lifetime, only benefits the few at the cost of the many.

pond. [In Br. use applied mainly to an artificially-formed body of water, in U.S. to a small naturally-formed lake: see OED(S *sb.* 1 a. and b.] A pool in a watercourse; such a body of water remaining after the watercourse has ceased flowing, esp. in the collocation **chain of ponds** (see CHAIN *n.*²). Freq. in place-names.

1835 *Trans. Zool. Soc. London* I. 234 A tranquil part of the river, such as the colonists call a 'pond'. **1886** D.M. GANE *N.S.W. & Vic.* 197 It abounds, as do most Australian rivers, in 'ponds' or occasional basins, which are distinguishable by their dark and placid surfaces.

Pong. [Joc. formation in resemblance to a Chinese name.] A Chinese. Also as *adj.* and *transf.* (quot. 1985 refers to a Japanese).

1906 *Truth* (Sydney) 28 Oct. 11/1 To-day there are 20 whites to 150 *Ah Pongs*. **1951** *Southerly* iv. 208 It didn't sound like English to us but more like Pong yabber or Eyetoe or Dago gibberish. **1985** N. MEDCALF *Rifleman* 18 Me and that Pong... I got him.

pongello /pɒŋ'gɛloʊ/. *Obs.* [Transf. use of *pongelo* beer: see OEDS.] A game in which the throw of a die determines which of the participants pays for a round of drinks.

1898 *Bulletin* (Sydney) 1 Oct. 14/3 To shake for drinks is a 'pongello'. **1920** *Ibid.* 15 Jan. 20/2 Some Western Queensland slang of my day:... to get drunk was to get 'inked'. To shake for drinks 'pongello'.

Pongo /'pɒŋɡoʊ/. [Transf. use of *pongo* a soldier, a marine.] An Englishman. Also as *adj.*

[N.Z. **1942** *2nd N.Z. Exped. Force Times* 7 Sept. 5 A big bronzed Pongo came in.] **1944** *RAAF Saga* 65 Amazing blokes, the Pongos. **1982** *Weekend Austral. Mag.* (Sydney) 30 Jan. 6/5 It came from somebody in the British Legion (the pongo equivalent of the RSL).

pony. *Shearing.* [Transf. use of *pony* small (working-) horse.] See quot. 1915.

1911 *Bulletin* (Sydney) 2 Mar. 14/2 At one of the biggest sheds in the land of the Prickly Pear..a..meeting was held, and it was decided to approach a shearer who was known to be a 'rousies' man'. The result of the vote.. was a majority of one for 'wet sheep'... But on the Monday our man deserted us, and the verdict was 'dry sheep'... Result: 'Classers' pony' instructed to become ill. I happened to be the 'pony', and by first smoko I had a very bad cough. **1915** *Ibid.* 28 Oct. 22/4 A 'pony' is a rouseabout who carries the fleeces from the classer to the wool-bins.

poofter /'pʊftə/. Also **poofta, poufter.** [Formed on *poof* homosexual: see OEDS *sb.*¹]

1. A male homosexual; a man whose manner or behaviour does not conform with that conventionally regarded as masculine. Also used (of a man) as a general term of abuse. Also *attrib.*

1903 *Truth* (Sydney) 5 Apr. 5/6 It was the sort of talk that put the political 'poofter's' nose out of joint. **1910** O'BRIEN & STEPHENS *Materials Dict. Austral. Slang* (typescript), *Pouf* or *poufter*, a sodomite or effeminate man. **1967** J. HIBBERD *White with Wire Wheels* (1970) 154, I wish I'd puked all over his poofta pants.

2. Special Comb. **poofter basher,** a male who engages in physical violence against, or verbal denigration of, homosexuals; so **bashing** *vbl. n.*; **rorter,** see quots.

1974 N. PHILLIPSON *As Other Men* 143 The sergeant had that sort of look about him. The look of a confirmed **poofter-basher. 1978** *Weekend Austral. Mag.* (Sydney) 4 Mar. 5/6 Poofter-bashing in Australia is an ancient and honourable sport, and quite a few men have died of it. **1945** S.J. BAKER *Austral. Lang.* 123 A procurer for homosexuals is known as a **poofter rorter. 1967** *Kings Cross Whisper* (Sydney) xxxviii. 10/2 *Poofter rorter*, one who preys on homosexuals.

Hence **poofterish** *a.*, **poofterism** *n.*

1969 W. DICK *Naked Prodigal* 89 'Oh, yes,' he said in a **poofterish** voice. **1978** L. HORSPHOL *Turn down Empty Glass* 29 The only rules that we're strict about are the ones governing rowdiness, drunkenness and **poofterism**.

poogie, var. POGIE.

pooh. In the phr. **in the pooh,** a euphemism for 'in the shit', in trouble.

1961 'J. DANVERS' *Living come First* 177 You're rather in the pooh with the Adelaide police. **1975** X. HERBERT *Poor Fellow my Country* 873 She'll put you in the poo if she writes anything 'bout you.

pool, *v.* [Spec. use of *pool* to share.] *trans.* To implicate (a person); to inform on. Also as *ppl. a.*

1907 M. CANNON *That Damned Democrat* (1981) 92 The Poor, Pooled Public. Buncoed, Boomed and Busted. **1981** K. GARVEY *Rhymes of Ratbag* 141 It doesn't do to shake some beef. The police narks always pool yer.

pool, *n.* [See prec.] In the phr. **in** (or **out of**) **the pool,** in (or out of) trouble.

1923 C.E. SAYERS *Jumping Double* 97 You're not the only one who has a cover at headquarters. You don't think I've kept out of the pool so long without feeding the D's, do you? **1928** A. WRIGHT *Good Recovery* 145 'They're gone to the pack now,' put in Ric. 'Punting put them in the pool properly.'

poon, *n.* [Of unknown origin.] A simpleton or fool. See also quot. 1941. Also *attrib.*

1941 S.J. BAKER *Pop. Dict. Austral. Slang* 56 *Poon*, a lonely, somewhat crazy dweller in the Outer Beyond... A simpleton or fool. **1982** T. WINTER *Mountain Verse* 51 'Golden

Triangle is a euphemism for 'poon-patch' also known as antigravity land' i.e. the area between Perisher Range and Perisher Creek.

poon, *v.* [Of unknown origin.] *intr.* With **up**: to dress in order to impress. Also as *ppl. a.*

1943 S.J. BAKER *Pop. Dict. Austral. Slang* (ed. 3) 61 *Poon up*, to dress up, especially in flashy fashion. **1972** A. CHIPPER *Aussie Swearers Guide* 48 *Pooned up*, dressed to impress, often with sexual success in view.

poonce /pŭns/. Formerly also **punce**. [Var. of *ponce* one who lives off the earnings of a prostitute, perh. infl. by POON *v.*] An ineffectual male; a homosexual; a general term of abuse for a man.

1941 S.J. BAKER *Pop. Dict. Austral. Slang* 57 Punce (pronounced with a short vowel as in 'book'), an effeminate man, a homosexual. **1982** T. WINTON *Open Swimmer* 28 'Bit of fight for a small fish,' said Jerra... 'That's 'cause they swim sideways coming up.' 'Smart fish, skippy.' 'Trevally.' 'Not this side of the border.' Jerra cast again. He spread some pollard onto the water. 'What are you, a Sydney poonce?'

Hence **poonc**y *a.*, affectedly refined; 'precious'.

1982 T. WINTON *Open Swimmer* 76 Sean's pissed off to his poonc**y** townhouse in South Perth.

poor black. *Hist.* Used with intense irony of an Aboriginal miscreant.

1837 *Colonist* (Sydney) 20 Apr. 130/4 An assigned servant of Lieutenant Wood's, at West Maitland was speared and killed a few days since by a *poor black*. **1845** *Sydney Morning Herald* 19 Aug. 2/7 Speaking to you some time since about the doings of our 'poor' dark brethren in this quarter. I send you a list of unfortunate white beings murdered by these 'poor blacks'.

poor man. *Gold-mining.* [Also U.S.] Used in the collocation **poor man's digging(s), (gold)field, rush,** etc., (alluvial) terrain from which gold may be mined without substantial capital investment.

1855 W. HOWITT *Land, Labor & Gold* II. 226 You now hear Bendigo called the Poor Man's Digging. **1870** E.B. KENNEDY *Four Yrs. in Qld.* 215 What are known as 'a poor man's diggings' are *alluvial*, while *reefs* require capital to work them. **1901** H. LAWSON *Joe Wilson & his Mates* 158 She went with the rush to Gulgong (about the last of the great alluvial or 'poor-man's' goldfields). **1907** M. CANNON *That Damned Democrat* (1981) 93 The ground was ridiculously easy to work. It was eminently a poor man's field. **1980** D. STONE et al. *Metal Detecting for Gold* 154 There were still some of the so called 'poor man's rushes' (where little skill or capital was needed) occurring in the 1860s and 70s in Victoria, Queensland and New South Wales.

Hence **poor man's gold** *n.*, gold obtained from such terrain.

1946 K.S. PRICHARD *Roaring Nineties* 360 You know as well as I do alluvial's been recognized as poor man's gold on every field in the colonies.

poor soldier. *Obs.* [See quot. 1841.] FRIAR BIRD; (occas.) any bird having a similar call.

1841 J. GOULD *Birds of Aust.* (1848) IV. Pl. 56, The Friar Bird.. from the fancied resemblance of its notes to those words.. has obtained from the Colonists the various names of 'Poor Soldier', 'Pimlico', 'Four O'Clock', etc. **1896** F.G. AFLALO *Sketch Nat. Hist. Aust.* 119 There are five Friar Birds... Of these, the Poor Soldier (*Tropidorhynchus corniculatus*) occurs only in New South Wales and Queensland.

pop, *v. Obs.* In the phr. **how are you popping (up)?**, 'how are you getting on?'

1894 H. LAWSON *Short Stories* 89 'How are yer?' 'Oh! I'm alright!' he says. 'How are ye poppin' up!' **1942** 'S. CAMPION' *Bonanza* 207 Howya poppin', cobber?

pop, *adv.* In the phr. **to go off pop,** to explode into angry speech.

1904 *Shearer* (Sydney) 17 Sept. 4/5 McManus is having a hot time at sheds in the Cobar district; and how he does go off, pop! when the boys corner him. **1972** F. BLAKELEY *Dream Millions* 101 When he made this statement I went off pop at him, and told him that it was very unlikely that the West Australian Government was paying for dingo scalps in those days.

poplar gum. [See quot. 1846.] The partly deciduous tree *Eucalyptus alba* (fam. Myrtaceae) of n. Aust., New Guinea, Timor, and nearby islands, having a pale, smooth bark and broad juvenile foliage.

1846 *Sydney Morning Herald* 26 Mar. 2/5 A new species of gum, which we called poplar gum, as its leaf and its foliage resembles very much in form and verdure the trembling poplar of Europe. **1963** *N. Austral. Monthly* Dec. 11 The white-trunked poplar gums are always beautiful especially in the spring with their new pale-green leaves. The leaves are broad and vary in shape; the creamy flowers and gum-nuts are small.

poppy. [See OED *poppy* 1 b. and *poppy-head* 1 for 17th century examples of a similarly allusive use.] In the collocation **tall poppy,** a person who is conspicuously successful; freq. one whose distinction, rank, or wealth attracts envious notice or hostility.

1902 H.L. NIELSEN *Voice of People* 8 The 'tall poppies' were the ones it was desired to retrench, but fear was expressed that, as usual, retrenchment might begin at the bottom of the ladder, and hardly touch those at the top at all. **1986** *Canberra Times* 26 Jan. 1/5 Our national immaturity led us to cut down tall poppies and denigrate achievements.

populate or perish. A slogan coined by W.M. Hughes (1864–1952) when, as Minister for Repatriation and Health, he drew attention to Australia's falling birth-rate: see quot. 1937.

1937 *Sydney Morning Herald* 2 Feb. 10/4 'Australia must advance and populate, or perish,' said the Federal Minister for Health (Mr Hughes) to-day. **1986** *Sydney Morning Herald* 1 May 13/7 Calwell would no doubt be pleased to hear his call 'populate or perish' resurrected decades later.

porcupine. [Transf. use of *porcupine* a rodent of the fam. Hystricidae.] ECHIDNA. Also **porcupine anteater.**

1799 D. COLLINS *Acct. Eng. Colony N.S.W.* (1802) II. 145 The dogs found a porcupine ant-eater but could make no impression on him; he escaped from them by burrowing in the loose sand, not head foremost, but sinking himself directly downwards, and presenting his prickly back opposed to his adversaries. **1981** K. GARVEY *Rhymes of Ratbag* 170 The spiny echidna, or porcupine Is considered by murries a meal divine.

porcupine grass.

1. SPINIFEX 1 a. Also **porcupine bush** and (*ellipt.*) **porcupine.**

1842 G.C. HAWKER *Diary Station Life Bungaree* 15 June, Passed through a few patches of scrub & some very bad country covered with porcupine grass. **1950** A. GROOM *I saw Strange Land* 58 It was hard going.. with the stabbing needles of the spinifex 'porcupine'-bush. **1984** E. WALLING *On Trail Austral. Wildflowers* 76 Grasses, poa and porcupine that mulch and hold the dry inland.

2. Special Comb. **porcupine grass resin** (or **gum**), *spinifex gum*, see SPINIFEX 3.

1927 SPENCER & GILLEN *Arunta* 24 Small lump of porcupine-grass resin. **1938** A. UPFIELD *Bone is Pointed* (1966) 145 Nero from his dilly-bag took a ball of porcupine-grass gum and proceeded to knead it into the form of a plate.

pork and bean. Rhyming slang for 'queen', a male homosexual.

1967 *Kings Cross Whisper* (Sydney) xxxviii. 10/2 *Pork and bean*, queen. Also a feminine homosexual. 1972 L. IRISH *Time of Dolphins* 114 If a pork-and-bean as much as comes near me I want to vomit. Can't help it.

pork fritz: see FRITZ.

port. [Abbrev. of *portmanteau*.] A suitcase; any (travelling) bag; hence (in *pl*.) baggage. Also locally with distinguishing epithet, as quots. 1968 and 1982.

1898 *Western Champion* (Barcaldine) 3 May 7/1 Various styles of traps laden with swags, ports, and refreshments. 1968 P. ADAM SMITH *Tiger Country* 10 He brought his 'Gordon River port' (a chaff bag carried on the back and supported by hessian strips across the chest) to the camp. 1982 N. KEESING *Lily on Dustbin* 107 In Queensland a Millaquin port was a sugar bag, the term deriving from the Millaquin Sugar Mill.

portable soup. *Hist*. Dehydrated meat which may be reconstituted in liquid form: see quot. 1846.

1843 *Colonial Observer* (Sydney) 16 Aug. 1235/4 Gelatine, or German Portable Soup . . from its extreme convenience as a provision for travelling in the bush we feel little doubt that it will soon become an article of considerable consumption. One ounce of the cake will make a quart and two thirds of a pint of excellent soup. 1844 *Sydney Morning Herald* 26 July 4/1, With reference to the exertions now being made to manufacture a portable soup, erroneously called gelatine, at the boiling down establishments, Mr Hogg . . assures us that he is confident large quantities of it would be purchased by the Indian Government for hospital use. 1846 *Ibid*. 27 May 2/7 We are glad to perceive that the portable soup made at the boiling-down establishments, is beginning to attract notice in England. . . In a London paper of December, the following paragraph appeared:— Recent arrivals of ships from Australia have introduced a new article of food into the London market. It is a kind of concentrated gravy, the result of the boiling down of sheep and cattle for the supply of the English tallow market, and which has hitherto been of little or no value. It is imported in a good state of preservation, and, on the addition of a few condiments, makes a very palatable soup.

port cart. *Hist*. A light cart used to convey passengers between Adelaide and Port Adelaide: see quot. 1848.

1848 *Adelaide Miscellany* 9 Sept. 90 Looking about for some conveyance to take me to the City of Adelaide, I discovered that a man . . was the driver of what is here called a *Port cart*, which is a Colonial imitation of our English short stages. 1915 *Lone Hand* June 52 The journey from Port Adelaide to the capital was accomplished in a 'Port cart'.

Hence **port-cart** *v. intr*., to travel by port cart.

1850 *Monthly Almanac* (Adelaide) 43 We went ashore, and an hour or two afterwards, port-carted it to Adelaide.

porter-gaff. [f. *porter* a dark beer + *shandy*)*gaff*.] A drink made by mixing stout with lemonade.

1891 *Truth* (Sydney) 8 Mar. 5/1 He brought her a porter-gaff, but she refused to drink it. 1979 P. PAVY *Bush Surgeon* 8, I was afraid to drink too many beers, so I spent several hours consuming glasses of 'Portergaff', a mixture of stout and lemonade.

port-hole. In the wall of a shearing-shed: a small doorway, adjacent to a shearer's stand, through which a shorn sheep is pushed into a counting-out pen.

1882 ARMSTRONG & CAMPBELL *Austral. Sheep Husbandry* 175 'Port-holes', or small doorways are made (one for each shearer), through which the sheep are turned when shorn. 1965 J.S. GUNN *Terminol. Shearing Industry* i. 14 The 'port-hole' . . is a low opening and ramp through which the shorn sheep are passed down to the counting-out pen.

Port Jackson. [The name of the port of Sydney, N.S.W.] Used *attrib*. in the names of flora and fauna: **Port Jackson fig,** the shrub to large tree *Ficus rubiginosa* (fam. Moraceae) of e. N.S.W.; **shark,** any shark of the fam. Heterodontidae, esp. *Heterodontus portusjacksoni* of s. Aust.

1889 J.H. MAIDEN *Useful Native Plants Aust*. 225 *Ficus rubiginosa* . . 'Port Jackson Fig' . . like other figs, exudes a juice when the bark is wounded. 1789 A. PHILLIP *Voyage to Botany Bay* 283 **Port Jackson Shark**. . . At first sight the above might be taken for the *Prickly Hound-fish*, or *Squalus Spinax* of Linnaeus.

Port Lincoln parrot. [f. the name of a town in S.A.] The parrot of central and w. Aust. *Barnardius zonarius*, a predom. green bird with a black head, and yellow collar and belly. See also TWENTY-EIGHT. Formerly also **Port Lincoln parakeet.**

1896 B. SPENCER *Rep. Horn Sci. Exped. Central Aust*. II. 63 Port Lincoln Parrakeet . . were afterwards found throughout the trip wherever water existed. 1976 *Reader's Digest Compl. Bk. Austral. Birds* 282 The Port Lincoln parrot is much more widely distributed than its name suggests.

Port Phillip. *Hist*. [Named after *Port Phillip* Bay, a large inlet on the south coast of Victoria, near which the city of Melbourne now stands.] The name given to that part of the Colony of New South Wales which in 1851 became the Colony of Victoria. Also *attrib*., esp. as **Port Phillip District.**

1836 G. MERCER *Copy Lett*. 2 If Port Phillip be constituted a subordinate colony . . the proximity . . to Van Dieman's Land might be taken to render Hobart Town a more eligible station for controls than Sidney. 1858 T. MCCOMBIE *Hist. Colony Vic*. 62 This formed what was afterwards known as the southern or Port Phillip district of the colony of New South Wales until separation.

Port Phillipian. A resident of the Port Phillip District. Also as *adj*.

1836 *Cornwall Chron*. (Launceston) 17 Dec. 2 We have statements before us of the extreme dissatisfaction caused to the Port Phillipians generally, by the troublesome interference of Captain Lonsdale in matters, in which, as Commandant, he supposes himself justified—but in which the Phillipians think that he is not. 1930 BILLIS & KENYON *Pastures New* 179 If the broad Australian rather than the Port Phillipian view be taken.

portulac. *Obs*. [Var. of *portulack* the common purslane, *Portulaca oleracea*.] Pigweed, see PIG *n*.¹

1861 *Burke & Wills Exploring Exped*. 18 There had been a considerable fall of rain in some places, which had raised a fine crop of grass and portulac. 1911 C.E.W. BEAN *'Dreadnought' of Darling* 234 They helped their provisions by eating a good deal of a shrub known as portulac.

possie /'pɒzi/. Also **possy** and less freq. **pozzy**. [f. *pos(ition* + -Y.] A position of supposed advantage to the occupant; a place; a job. Orig., in trench warfare, an individual soldier's place of shelter or firing position.

1915 I.L. IDRIESS *Diary* 29 Aug. i. 25 His possy is in a good position and he had already got 105 Turks, which is the record for a single man on the Peninsula. 1915 T. SKEYHILL *Soldier-Songs from Anzac* 16 'E climbs up stunted pine-trees, An' snipes away at us. But 'e never shows 'is pozzy. 1969 L. HADOW *Full Cycle* 250 Only the odd, dead-end jobs until they were eighteen . . all dead-end possies that led, inevitably, to the mines. 1984 *Palmerston & Northern*

Suburbs Herald (Darwin) 16 Nov. 5/1 The bridge will not only link south western areas with Palmerston, locals say it could provide a good fishing possie.

Hence **possie** *v. trans.*, to position (*refl.* in quot.).

1963 *Sunday Mirror* (Sydney) 20 Jan. 43/2 Gilli, with Mulley apparently 'curling the mo' was possied behind them for his challenge.

possum, *n.* [Transf. use of *possum*, aphetic form of *opossum*; now the preferred form in Aust.]

1. Any of many chiefly herbivorous, long-tailed, arboreal marsupials of the fam. Phalangeridae, Petauridae and Burramyidae, some of which are gliding animals; OPOSSUM *n.* 1. Often with distinguishing epithet, as **brush-tailed, dormouse, flying, honey, mountain pygmy, pygmy, ringtail** (see under first element). See also LEADBEATER'S POSSUM.

1770 J. COOK *Jrnls.* 4 Aug. (1955) I. 367 Here are .. Possums. **1979** K. GARVEY *Absolutely Austral.* 72 We used to find a possum once in every hollow spout On all the river-gums before the myxo thinned them out.

2. *transf.*

a. Used as a mildly derogatory term for a person: a 'creature'. Also as an (affectionate) mode of address.

1894 A.B. BELL *Austral. Camp Fire Tales* 104 Bob Fogarty, as I'm a living sinner, delighted to meet you, old possum. **1982** R. HALL *Just Relations* 88 Goodness what an ugly little possum you've turned into.

b. A fraudulent substitution, RING-IN *n.* 1; the practice of this.

1903 *Sporting News* (Launceston) 17 Jan. 1/2 Although the field was a painfully weak one, the game of ' 'possum' appeared in more than one instance to have been well rehearsed. **1955** *Bulletin* (Sydney) 27 July 12/3 Whence do we get the colloquialisms 'playing possum' and 'a possum' (meaning a racetrack ring-in)?

3. [Prob. as the obverse of *to play possum.*] In the phr. **to stir** (or **rouse**) **the possum,** to excite interest or controversy; to liven things up.

1900 *Truth* (Sydney) 29 Apr. 5/7 Why, old George Reid would be comparatively forgotten if he didn't keep stirring the possum. **1981** *Age* (Melbourne) 18 July 15/2 Treasury secretary John Stone has a grand way of stirring the possum.

4. In the phr. **possum up a gum tree,** used allusively as an expression of approbation.

1885 R. CANNON *Savage Scenes Aust.* 16 The Australian delights in 'possum up a gum tree'. **1928** B. SPENCER *Wanderings in Wild Aust.* 151 The expression ' 'possum up a gum tree' was really brought over to Australia in early days by miners of the celebrated 'forty-niner' period, who left California to try their luck on the gold-fields.

5. Comb. **possum cloak, hunt, hunting, rug, shooting, skin, snarer, snaring trapper.**

1848 H.W. HAYGARTH *Recoll. Bush Life* 21 He rolls himself for the night in the blanket or **'possum cloak'**, which by day is strapped on before him. **1857** W. DENISON *Varieties Vice-Regal Life* 20 July (1870) I. 249 On coming down the hill we had a **'possum' hunt**: a shepherd had set fire to a hollow tree, and smoked the opossum out of his hole; he was sitting disconsolately at the end of a branch, watching a dog that was barking below, and bobbing his head occasionally to get out of the way of the sticks and stones which flew about his ears; he was often hit, but kept his post to the last, and in fact tired us out. **1849** A. HARRIS *Emigrant Family* (1967) 258 There is actually good **'possum hunting** now, within a day's stage of Sydney. **1840** S. *Austral. Rec.* (London) 26 Dec. 410 The natives are a harmless race of people .. a blanket, or **possem rug**, completes their dress. **1860** 'LITTLE JACOB' *Colonial Pen-Scratchings* 94 The two young men were very thick, and cattle-hunted and went **possum-shooting** together. **1854** *Illustr. Sydney News* 7 Jan. 108/3 The invaluable qualities of the cloak made from the rich grey and buff fur of the animal and which is vulgarly called a **'possum skin'**. **1864** J. MORRILL *Sketch of Residence* 219, I was .. making a possum skin rug. **1908** *Bulletin* (Sydney) 16 Jan. 14/2 The **'possum-snarer** is no longer known in the land; his place has been taken by the rabbit-snapper. **1922** *Ibid.* 31 Aug. 20/3 How's this for a 'possum-snarer's cheque? *Ibid.*, He thought he'd try his hand at **'possum-snaring. 1899** *Bulletin* (Sydney) 7 Oct. 14/3, I know a **'possum-trapper's** horse that will eat raw 'possum.

6. Special Comb. **possum eater,** a parsimonious person; a country bumpkin; **-eating** *ppl. a.*, countrified; **guts,** a coward; **-gutted** *ppl. a.*, cowardly; **(pumpkin) pie,** see quot. 1960.

1942 H.H. PECK *Mem. of Stockman* 72 That .. was characteristic of James Tyson as a young man, when he denied himself many a necessity in order to save money, and no doubt was the origin of his reputation as a ' **'possum eater'**, of which he was not ashamed. **1878** 'R. BOLDREWOOD' *Ups & Downs* 67 Do I look like a slouchin' **'possum-eating,** billy-carrying crawler of a shepherd? **1962** D. MCLEAN *World turned upside Down* 10 The big bloke's Danny Fenton, one of the Rocks push, and his mate's Skinny Harford, a proper **possum-guts. 1959** D. NILAND *Gold in Streets* 194, I ought to push your bloody teeth down your throat, you **possum-gutted** halfwit. **1871** 'OLD BOOMER' *Story of Mathinna* 10 Her full and restless coal-black eye Turned sometimes to the passer-by And sometimes to the **'possum pie. 1960** B. HARNEY *Cook Bk.* 35 *Possum pumpkin pie.* In the early days, possums were caught, cleaned and cut up, put into a hollowed-out pumpkin which was then roasted until the meat was cooked.

possum, *v.* [Also U.S.] *intr.* To hunt possums. Freq. as *pres. pple.* and *vbl. n.*

1852 J. BONWICK *Notes of Gold Digger* 22 Some amuse themselves with going out 'possuming. **1957** R.S. PORTEOUS *Brigalow* 88 Mick and Wonga .. knew, from their possuming experiences, every gully, every water-hole, and every patch of open plain.

possumer. One who hunts possums.

1905 J. FURPHY *Rigby's Romance* (1946) 47 'Allowed to be the best (adj.) possumer on the track,' he resumed. **1979** J. LINDEMAN *Red Rumps & White Faces* 42 By that time the semi-professional 'possumers had just about finished the cream. New chums arriving on the opening day of the season .. reported that the 'possums were almost extinct.

possy, var. POSSIE.

post, *v. trans.* To leave (someone) in the lurch. Freq. as *ppl. a.*

1967 *Kings Cross Whisper* (Sydney) xxxviii. 10/2 *Posted*, to be left waiting. **1975** *Bulletin* (Sydney) 26 Apr. 45/3 The guy's willin' and there's no way he'll post you on the job.

postal note. An order issued by a post office for any required sum of money, payable at any other post office.

1885 *Victorian Yr.-Bk. 1884–85* 481 Postal notes were first issued on the 1st January, 1885. **1978** *Bulletin* (Sydney) 25 Aug. 3 Enclosed please find my cheque/postal note.

post and rail. [Used elsewhere (esp. U.S.) but of considerable local significance: see OEDS.]

1. a. *pl.* The component parts of a *post and rail fence* (see sense 1 b.).

1802 D. COLLINS *Acct. Eng. Colony N.S.W.* II. 313 A stockyard, consisting of about 30 acres, was inclosed [*sic*] with posts and rails. **1948** F. CLUNE *Wild Colonial Boys* 171 The stockyards were built of heavy posts and rails, seven feet high.

b. In the phr. **post and rail fence,** a strongly constructed wooden fence, consisting of two or more horizontal rails morticed into upright posts. Also **post and rail fencing**.

1820 *Sydney Gaz.* 20 May, Supposed to have a cross-cut saw, and other implements for putting up post and rail fence. **1978** M. WALKER *Pioneer Crafts Early Aust.* 32 Station owners found the costs of maintaining shepherds and the outposts with their temporary fencing too large a cost to bear and enclosed and subdivided their large holdings with post and rail fencing.

c. Used *attrib.* and *ellipt.* for *post and rail fence*.

1829 R. DAWSON *Statement* 127 Above *fifteen miles* of permanent Post And Rail inclosures had been finished. **1947** J.W. GORDON *Under Wide Skies* 20 And my thoughts drift back to childhood with a sentimental yearning For the oldtime dog-leg fences and the sturdy post-and-rail.

2. a. In the phr. **post and rail tea**, a coarse tea of inferior quality, so-called because particles of stalk, etc., float on its surface (but see also quot. 1907, sense 2 b.).

1843 *Sydney Morning Herald* 5 Oct. 4/3 Awful accounts related of cruel masters, boney meat, post-and-rail tea, black flour, etc. **1975** R.O. MOORE *Sunlit Plains Extended* 17 The 'post and rail' tea cost about 1s. 6d. per lb.

b. *Ellipt.* for *post and rail tea*. Also **posts and rails**.

1858 'A. PENDRAGON' *Queen of South* 19 'Good tea this,' asserted Jack... 'Rather full of stems,' ventured Frank, dubiously. 'Stems be hanged,' replied Jack; 'you should have tried the 'posts and rails' at Currumbumbula.' **1907** C. MACALISTER *Old Pioneering Days* 12 The tea for which we paid 6s. per lb. was known as 'posts and rails', because it was generally retailed mixed with small chips or shavings to add to the grocer's weight. **1976** C.D. MILLS *Hobble Chains & Greenhide* 105 Give us another mug of that 'post and rail' and don't be so damn curious.

post and wire. *Obs.* In the phr. **post and wire fence**, a fence of vertical uprights and wire horizontals. Also *ellipt.*

1891 'ROUSEABOUT' *Jackeroo* 50 Brand's next move was to let a contract to grub and burn off one hundred acres of land for cultivation. This he enclosed with a post-and-wire fence, known as a cattle fence. **1897** *Bulletin* (Sydney) 11 Dec. 30/1 We heard them lift the post and wire and fling the cap-rails down.

post-boy. *Jacky Winter*, see JACKY *n.*² Also **post-sitter**.

1911 J.A. LEACH *Austral. Bird Bk.* 121 Australian Brown Flycatcher.. Post-Boy. **1954** C. BARRETT *Wild Life Aust. & New Guinea* 157 'Post sitter', 'post-boy'.. are other names for 'Jacky Winter'.

pot, *n.* [Spec. use of *pot* vessel for cooking, boiling or (sense 2) for holding liquor.]

1. *Obs.* Boiling establishment, see BOILING 3.

1847 J.D. LANG *Cooksland* 135 They are 'sent to pot', as it is termed, or boiled down for their tallow. **1888** A.P. MARTIN *Oak-Bough & Wattle-Blossom* 126 A good time had arrived for the squatters of the Heaton district, an actual buyer having suddenly come amongst them, and for the time, at any rate, they were independent of 'the Pots', as the boiling-down establishments were called.

2. A medium-sized measure of beer.

1915 A.T.M. JOHNSON *Austral. Life* 55 'Oh! Colonial Beer. Well give me a glass.'.. 'Ain't got no glasses; sell it by the pot.' **1984** *Canberra Times* 6 July 1/6 'In my youth I used to drink up to 30 pots a day,' he said. 'My body doesn't need it any more. I still have a few grogs, but now I like to get to bed at about half past seven.'

3. *fig.* In the phr. **to put the** (or someone's) **pot on**, to inform on, to thwart the prospects of.

1864 *Bell's Life in Sydney* 4 June 2/6 The police are, of course, severely censured by everybody for 'neglect of duty', and they, in turn, 'put the pot on' magistrates for the mischievous leniency they show. **1957** V. PALMER *Seedtime* 119 There's an election coming on, and there's a chance I'll be dumped... This afternoon's work has probably put my pot on.

pot, *v.* [f. prec., perh. infl. by *pot* to outdo, outwit.] *trans.* To inform on (a person); to secure the conviction of.

1911 A. WRIGHT *Gamblers' Gold* (1923) 100 You can't come that tale. Why should I pot th' bloke?

potato.

1. [Prob. Br. dial.: see OED(S 5 c. and EDD 2. Used elsewhere but chiefly Austral.] In the collocation **clean potato**, a person whose character is beyond reproach; a plan, activity, etc., which is 'above board'. Freq. in the negative.

1853 H.B. JONES *Adventures in Aust.* 119 You do not know whether the man who addresses you is or has been a convict; and it is not very complimentary to ask one who speaks to you, 'Are you', in the idiomatic phraseology of the bush, 'a clean potato?' **1962** T. RONAN *Deep of Sky* 42 Some of the grand old pioneers and land-takers of history were not quite the clean potato.

2. Used *attrib.* in Special Comb. **potato field** *Tas. obs.*, *ploughed field*, see PLOUGHED; **land**, fertile land; land esp. suitable for growing potatoes.

1909 G. SMITH *Naturalist in Tas.* 61 Another feature is the presence upon the plateau of Wellington and Ben Lomond of extensive level fields of large rounded boulders of diabase, known locally as 'potato' or 'ploughed' **fields**, which do not support any soil or vegetation owing to the gaps between the rocks, through which the rain washes all the detritus away. **1886** J.A. FROUDE *Oceana* 92 Behind the crags the land was green and undulating, and extremely rich. They call it the **Potato Land**; all the Australian sea-towns are supplied from it.

3. Shortening of 'potato peeler', rhyming slang for SHEILA.

1959 D. NILAND *Gold in Streets* 54 'He got hold of a potater. He'll see us later.' 'Any good?' Danno whispered. 'Who?' 'The sheila.' **1971** B. HUMPHRIES *Bazza pulls it Off*, If I don't make it with a nice broadminded potato tonight I'll give that quack a knuckle sandwich!!!

potato orchid. The saprophytic terrestrial orchid *Gastrodia sesamoides* (fam. Orchidaceae) of s. and e. Aust., incl. Tas., and N.Z., having large, thick rhizomes; *native potato* (a), see NATIVE *a.* 6 a.

1914 F. SULMAN *Pop. Guide Wild Flowers N.S.W.* II. 179 *Gastrodia sesamoides*. 'Potato Orchid'... The potato-like tubers of this species were roasted and eaten by the natives of Tasmania. **1984** D.T. & C.E. WOOLCOCK *Austral. Terrestrial Orchids* 74 The cinnamon-brown colouring of the flower has given it one common name of Potato Orchid.

potch. Also **potsh.** [Of unknown origin; now used elsewhere but recorded earliest in Aust.] Opal that has little or no play of colour and is of no value; opaliferous material found in association with precious opal. Also in the phr. **potch and** (or **with**) **colour** and as **potch opal**.

1896 *Jrnl. & Proc. R. Soc. N.S.W.* XXX. 256 The dull, milky, and opaque stones are called 'potsh' by the miners. **1900** J.S. GUNN *Opal Terminol.* (1971) 35 Demand for potch with color.. active. **1912** *Empire Mag.* (London) Nov. 282/1 A pocketful of 'potch-and-colour'—that is 'potch' with a slight 'colour' of opal. **1956** B.J. RAYMENT *My Touri* 36 Opals were almost always dotted through the band, but a great number were valueless, being what is usually called 'potch' opal.

pot-hole. *Mining.* [Transf. use of *pot-hole* a naturally-worn hole.] A shallow excavation made in prospecting for gold or opal.

1890 'R. Boldrewood' *Miner's Right* 55 All the gold in the locality appeared to have been shovelled by malignant gnomes into one crevice, in the familiar phrase of the miners, 'a pot hole'. **1940** I.L. Idriess *Lightning Ridge* 90 For a time I sank pot-holes alone then went mates with little Archie Campbell.

Hence **pothole** *v. trans.*, to search (an area) for gold or opal by digging such holes. Also as *vbl. n.*

1885 H. Finch-Hatton *Advance Aust.* 185 In Queensland the run of gold is very irregular, and never of any great extent. Seldom at any depth, it is generally confined to 'pot-holing' and 'crevicing' in the banks and bed of the creeks. **1896** J.W. Roberts *Mining Industry N.S.W.* 64 These gullies . . were potholed by jackaroos, paddocked by Chinese, and afterwards ground-sluiced by Europeans!

potoroo /pɒtəˈruː/. [Prob. a. Dharuk *badaru*.] A small, long-nosed, nocturnal macropodoid of the genus *Potorous* inhabiting areas of dense ground vegetation of s.e. (and formerly s.w.) Aust. See also *kangaroo rat* Kangaroo *n.* 5.

1789 J. White *Jrnl. Voyage N.S.W.* (1790) 286 (*caption*) A Poto Roo. **1981** *Bulletin* (Sydney) 17 Mar. 35/1 Scientists in Tasmania have been given nearly $150,000 to study baby potoroos.

potsh, var. Potch.

potstick. [Transf. use of *potstick* a stick for stirring food or washing in a pot.] A pole used to agitate a fleece immersed in a cleansing liquid. Also *attrib.*, and as *v. trans.*

1899 G. Jeffrey *Princ. Australasian Woolclassing* 89 When wool is scoured by the pot-stick system it is first soaked in one or two tanks of scouring liquid, and then lifted out and drained before being finally washed off. **1977** G.W. Lilley *Lengthening Shadows* 73 They did not overload the boxes with wool but what they did put in was pot-sticked from one end to the other until it was clean.

pouched mouse. [f. *pouched* marsupial + *mouse*, from the mouse-like appearance and size of the animal.] Any of several small carnivorous marsupials, esp. Dunnart and Phascogale 1. See also *marsupial mouse* Marsupial 1.

1888 O. Thomas *Catal. Marsupialia & Monotremata* 287 Little Pouched Mouse. Size rather small, general form murine. **1974** *Bulletin* (Sydney) 30 Nov. 27/3 The pouched mouse has caused quite a stir of excitement in the Wildlife Service.

poufter, var. Poofter.

poultice, *n.* [Fig. use of *poultice* a medicament.]

a. *Obs.* A large wager.

1902 *Sporting News* (Launceston) 22 Nov. 3/1 The connections of the stable which shelters the son of Tostig followed the nag, and put a good 'poultice' on him. **1915** A. Wright *Sport from Hollowlog Flat* 3 We're going to put a poultice on a cert.

b. *transf.* A (large) sum of money.

1904 *Truth* (Sydney) 28 Aug. 1/8 Well, it would take a pretty big 'poultice' to enable a girl to stand being cuddled by coal-black Merzouk! **1979** *Sun-Herald* (Sydney) 24 June 143 A bloke . . made a poultice in recent weeks when he sold Rupert a quarter of a million Channel Ten shares.

c. *spec.* A mortgage.

1932 K.S. Prichard *Kiss on Lips* 184 Mick Mallane . . sayin' if the bank wanted his farm, poultice or no poultice, it'd have to go out and take it from him. **1934** T. Wood *Cobbers* 134 Men talked about their blister, or their poultice, which means a mortgage, with complacency.

poultice, *v. Obs.* [f. prec.] *trans.* To back (a horse) heavily; to exact money from.

1904 *Sporting News* (Launceston) 2 Jan. 3/1 The figures would have been larger had there been no other channel available for punters to 'poultice' their fancies. **1907** *Truth* (Sydney) 26 May 10/7 (*heading*) *A common cabby* has the haw-don't-cher-know-dacity to *poultice patrician Egan, of Parramatta*, for a 'arf jim cab fare.

pound. [Prob. transf. use of *pound* enclosure.]

1. See quot. 1953.

1937 M. Terry *Sand & Sun* 247 Issuing from a low gap, where it drained a 'pound', a sandy creek linked up with an attenuated arm of Lake White. **1953** C.F. Laseron *Face of Aust.* 93 In the Flinders Range [S.A.] . . pressure came from north and south also, resulting in the formation of large domes and basins. In the final erosion the hills retained their dome-shaped forms; the harder layers stand out in series of concentric steps, the outward slopes gradual but the inward slopes steep. The basins remain as huge natural amphitheatres encircled by tier above tier of rocky ledges. These basins are known locally as pounds.

2. A punishment cell in a prison; solitary confinement.

1967 *Kings Cross Whisper* (Sydney) xxxviii. 10/2 *Pound*, punishment cells in boob. **1974** J. McNeil *How does your Garden Grow* 54 Yer know it's a *pinch*, I suppose? Get sprung with it and yer off tap, yer know that? . . Three days pound its likely to get yer.

poverty bush. [Spec. use of *poverty*, as in the names of plants growing in poor soil: see OED 8.] Any of many shrubs of drier Aust., usu. of the genera *Eremophila* (see *emu bush* (a), Emu *n.*^{1} 3) and *Sclerolaena* (fam. Chenopodiaceae).

1931 M. Terry *Hidden Wealth* 41 Poverty bush, fresh young spinifex . . scrub of a hundred kinds and shapes hide the red sand of this land. **1977** D. Stuart *Drought Foal* 182 Poverty bush stretching from the grey green salt grass coastal flats to the pitiless sands and pindan scrub.

poverty pot. A (small) container in which an alluvial miner accumulates particles of gold.

1948 M. Uren *Glint of Gold* 40 Dryblowing is a term used for the process of obtaining gold from the surface material without the use of water. . . The gold won is put in a receptacle called by the miners the 'poverty pot'. **1980** N. King *Colourful Tales* 75 Father taught us how to pan off correctly and to save the specks of gold in 'poverty pots', which in our case were glass jars.

powerful owl. The large owl *Ninox strenua* of e. and s.e. mainland Aust., having predom. brown and cream plumage and a deep, resonant, two-note hoot.

1844 J. Gould *Birds of Aust.* (1848) I. Pl. 35, *Athene strenua* . . Powerful Owl. **1984** M. Blakers et al. *Atlas Austral. Birds* 306 The Powerful Owl . . lives alone or in pairs and occupies a permanent territory containing a number of roost sites.

pozzy, var. Possie.

P-plate. One of a pair of plates bearing the letter P which must be displayed on the front and rear of a vehicle being driven by the holder of a provisional licence. Also *attrib.*

1969 *Statutory Rules* (Vic.) 94 These Regulations may be cited as the Motor Car ('P' Plates) Regulations 1969. **1971** J. O'Grady *Aussie Etiket* 55 With four surf boards on top, and a P-plate on the stern, they will overtake you.

prad. [Br. slang *prad* a horse, by metathesis from Du. *paard*. Not attested in Br. use after *c* 1900: see OED(S.)] A horse.

1812 J.H. VAUX *Mem.* (1819) II. 198 *Prad*, a horse. **1977** *Courier-Mail* (Brisbane) 31 Mar. 4/5 It would surely be more appropriate for the riding [for democracy] to be done on some business man rather than on a prad.

prat, *v.* [Perh. f. *prat* the backside: see OED(S *sb.*² Prob. not excl. Austral.: see Partridge.] In the phr. **to prat** (oneself, one's frame) **in,** to butt in, to push oneself forward. Also *intr.*

1903 *Truth* (Sydney) 1 Feb. 5/4 When speaking about the safe at Auburn Woolford said, 'You ought to 'prat' yourself in with the two men,' and witness replied, 'No, I am too weak.' **1927** F.C. BIGGERS *Bat-Eye* 10 These dancin' stunts was jakeloo—a bloke Jist prats 'is frame in, an' selects a girl.

prawn.

1. *fig.* [In sense 1 a. used elsewhere but chiefly Austral.]

a. A fool; also as a generalized term of contempt.

1893 D. HEALEY *Cornstalk* 50 Well, boys, the 'Worker' is a prawn—A fool for all his pains; He has the muscle and the brawn, The 'Fat Man' has the brains. **1977** C. MCCULLOUGH *Thorn Birds* 385 'Jussy, this is Cardinal de Bricassart!.. Kiss his ring, quickly.' The blind-looking eyes flashed scorn. 'You're a real prawn about religion... Kissing a ring is unhygienic.'

b. (i) In the collocation **raw prawn,** an act of deception; a 'swiftie'; an unfair action or circumstance, a 'raw deal'; something which is 'difficult to swallow'. Also *attrib.*

1940 *Any Complaints* (Newcastle) 4 Apr. 2 Voice.. is invariably heard muttering something about a raw prawn. **1972** *Bulletin* (Sydney) 21 Oct. 45/3 It's that kind of inventive grossness that's going to sell the film to those who've got the taste for raw prawn culture.

(ii) In the phr. **to come the raw prawn (on, over, with,** etc.), to attempt to deceive (a person); to misrepresent a situation.

1942 A.J. MCINTYRE *Putting over Burst* 9 They argue there for hours—They start at early morn; Till a loud disgusted voice drawls out, 'Don't come the old raw prawn'. **1951** CUSACK & JAMES *Come in Spinner* 306 Coupla bastards come the raw prawn over me on the last lap up from Melbourne and I done me last bob at Swy. **1963** J. WYNNUM *No Boats to Burn* 38 'Don't come the raw prawn stunt with me,' the girl cried. 'That feller wouldn't shout his old woman a glass of water if she was dying of thirst out in the middle of the Nullabor!' **1948** *Khaki Bush & Bigotry* (1968) 36 The filthy rotten Crab, he'd better not come the raw prawn on us.

2. Special Comb. **prawn (and beer) night,** a social function, chiefly for the male members of a club, at which prawns and beer are served and entertainment offered.

1976 *Bulletin* (Sydney) 19 June 17/1 The RSL was in the ambivalent position of seeming to foster, through its various clubs .. a State network of 'prawn nights' complete with seedy strippers and 'blue movies'. **1980** S. ORR *Roll On* 84, I wouldn't have invited the wives to an RSL prawn and beer night.

preference.

1. [Used elsewhere but important in Aust. where a preferential voting system is commonly employed.] In a system of preferential voting:

a. The numerical ranking given to a candidate on a ballot paper.

1900 E.J. NANSON *Real Value of Vote* 7 All the elector has to do is to number the names on his voting paper in accordance with the order of his preferences for the candidates so far as he has any preferences. **1984** *Sydney Morning Herald* 16 Mar. 4/7 The Liberals admit that even a 10 per cent leakage of preferences would be disastrous.

b. In the collocation **first preference (vote),** the first choice, as expressed by a voter on a ballot paper.

1911 E.E. STENBERG *Principal Electoral Systems* 24 If, for argument's sake, the candidate whom a certain elector has marked on his Ballot Paper as his No. 1 choice, is found to have the *lowest number of 'First Preference' votes*, such candidate is declared 'defeated', and the Returning Officer then proceeds to re-examine and transfer such candidate's Ballot Papers, according to the preferences shown thereon. **1972** M. MACKERRAS *Austral. Gen. Elections* 245 Even when the final first preferences are counted, there remains a most important element to consider—the distribution of preferences.

2. With reference to the employment of waterside workers. In the collocation **first** (or **second) preference:** see quot. 1934. Freq. *attrib.* as **first** (or **second) preference man.** See also BLANK.

1934 *Statutory Rules* (Cwlth. of Aust.) 335 After the expiry of a period of one month from the date of the appointment of a [Waterside Employment] Committee in respect of a port to which Part III. of the Act applies, engagement of waterside workers at that port shall be made in the following order of priority: (a) Waterside workers who are available for employment and are holders of current licences bearing the endorsement 'First Preference'; and (b) Waterside workers who are available for employment and are holders of current licences bearing the endorsement 'Second Preference'; and (c) Waterside workers to whom neither of the last two preceding paragraphs applies who are holders of current licences. **1955** J. MORRISON *Black Cargo* 24 It is divided into four parts; one for members of the Permanent and Casual Waterside Workers' Union .. one for Second Preference men, and one for Blank Licence men.

preggo, *a.* [f. *preg(nant* + -O.] Pregnant. Also as *n.*, a pregnant woman.

1951 CUSACK & JAMES *Come in Spinner* 226 Guinea's face lighted with unholy glee. 'A Parker prego? Did I hear right?' **1984** P. ADAM SMITH *Austral. Women at War* 288 We were very down to earth in the WAAF... To us, preggos were preggos. Contraceptives were available to the RAAF.

preliminary, *a. S.A. Hist.* Used with reference to the sale of lots of land prior to settlement: see quot. 1859. Freq. as **preliminary land order, section.**

1837 *S. Austral. Rec.* (London) 11 Nov. 13 The situation being one of the best next to the 437 selected by the preliminary holders, there was great competition. **1839** *Southern Austral.* (Adelaide) 15 Dec. 3/2 The Commissioner has waived all idea of granting any leases which may have a tendency to defer the right of prior choice, to which the holders of Preliminary Land Orders are undoubtedly entitled. **1843** J.F. BENNETT *Hist. & Descr. Acct. S.A.* 14 The price was reduced from *one pound* to *twelve shillings* per acre—one hundred and thirty-four acres of Country, and one acre of Town Land, being given for £81. Hence the 'Preliminary Sections', as those originally purchased were termed, consisted of 134 acres instead of 80 acres as at present. **1859** W. FAIRFAX *Handbk. to Australasia* 145 The first purchasers of land, to whom the colony was indebted for its very existence .. were called 'preliminary' land holders. And, as they had purchased in London, of course, before the first settlers had landed, or surveys had commenced, it became necessary to hit upon some expedient for determining the priority of choice of the land, or 'preliminary section', as it was termed.

premier.

1. With initial capital. The chief minister of the government of an Australian Colony or State. Also used as a title prefixed to the surname of a premier.

1858 N.L. KENTISH *Valedictory ('P.P.C.') Let.* 5 John O'Shanassy, Esq... presented my petition to the Legislature .. being himself ex-Premier. **1892** *Bulletin* (Sydney) 7

May 8/1 For the farewell dinner to Premier Dibbs .. tickets were sold.
2. *pl.* A team which wins a PREMIERSHIP.
1891 *Bohemia* (Melbourne) 18 June 20 'I know I'm an awful barracker', admitted the elder frankly, 'but I do so hope the South Melbourne Club will be premiers this year.' **1973** *Sunday Tel.* (Sydney) 24 June 54/2 Walgett must start favorites to beat last year's premiers Cobar on their home ground.

premiership. [Spec. use of *premiership* the state of being first.] Any organized sporting competition, esp. for team games; the winning of this. Also *attrib.*
1891 *Bohemia* (Melbourne) 11 June 10 Don't go off your heads and back Geelong for premiership. They won't be higher than third, if so high. **1930** *Australasian* (Melbourne) 20 Sept. 28/2 A B grade challenge match in connection with the premiership contests of the Victorian Women's Hockey Association was played on September 13.

prenti, var. PERENTIE.

Presbo. [f. *Presb(yterian* + -O.] A Presbyterian.
1965 L. HAYLEN *Big Red* 78 Catholics were Catholics, Methos were Methodist, Presbos were Presbyterian and the other Protestants were Protestant. **1978** *Bulletin* (Sydney) 28 Nov. 35/3 My sympathies are with the 'continuing' Presbos, who decided they weren't going to have any truck with the Methos, and the Congros and so on.

preselection. [Spec. use of *preselection* selection in advance. Used elsewhere but recorded earliest in Aust.] The process by which a political party selects a candidate to stand in an election; the ballot which decides this. Freq. *attrib.*
1930 W.K. HANCOCK *Aust.* 207 Members of branches join with the unionists who live in the same area to choose by a preselection ballot the local party candidate and to elect delegates to attend the State conference of the party. **1988** *N.T. News* (Darwin) 27 Sept. 2/4 The blame for bad blood over preselection must go to Pam O'Neil.

press, *n. Shearing.* Shortened form of *wool press* (see WOOL 2).
1848 H.W. HAYGARTH *Recoll. Bush Life* 48 The fleece is .. set aside to be ready for the press, which is in full operation throughout the day. **1926** *Bulletin* (Sydney) 11 Feb. 24/1 The pressmen swear that the cross-eyed bum who fed at the shearers' mess Stalked through the shed to dodge the boss and looked at the blasted press.

press, *v. Shearing.* [Spec. use of *press* to compress.] *trans.* To compress (wool) into bales; also with shed as obj.
1840 *Port Phillip Gaz.* 15 Jan. 5 Having engaged a very experienced sorter .. it is their intention to Store, Sort, and Press Wool. **1965** *Tracks we Travel* 97, I had a shed to press at Stagmount, for ten shearers.
Hence **pressed** *ppl. a.*
1889 H. EGBERT *Pretty Cockey* 45 Some of the rouseabouts did duty as .. sewer-ups of the pressed bales.

presser. *Shearing.* Shortened form of *wool presser* (see WOOL 2).
1872 G.S. BADEN-POWELL *New Homes for Old Country* 176 'Pressers' fill bales out of one of these bins, sew them up, and brand them. **1965** L. WALKER *Other Girl* 44 Neither of the girls could be shed-hand, presser or shearer, that was clear.

pretty face. [See quot. 1943.] WHIPTAIL WALLABY. Also **pretty-face wallaby.**

1887 W.S.S. TYRWHITT *New Chum in Qld. Bush* 145 The smaller kind, known as pretty faces or whip tails .. are rather smaller and of a grey colour, with black and white on the face. **1943** C. BARRETT *Austral. Animal Bk.* 93 'Pretty face' (*Wallabia elegans*) is among the most beautiful of all marsupials, with its slender, graceful body, its very long and slender tail, and white-and-grey face markings. **1956** T.Y. HARRIS *Naturecraft in Aust.* 77 The Pretty-face Wallaby .. grazes quietly in open country, usually in the cooler parts of the day, and is not easily disturbed.

prezzie. [f. *pres(ent* + -Y.] A present.
1961 J. ROSE *At Cross* 141 Bella said, 'I brought you quite a lot of prezzies.' **1986** *Nat. Times* (Sydney) 14 Feb. 2/2 Last year's his-and-hers prezzies, matching yellow diamonds.

pricker.
1. A device studded with sharp points, attached to the side of the snaffle against which a horse with a one-sided mouth leans.
1871 *Austral. Town & Country Jrnl.* (Sydney) 13 May 601/3 The followers of The Pearl accounted satisfactorily for his Saturday performance, by his having been ridden in 'prickers', which cut him so much about the mouth as to completely cow him. **1898** *Western Champion* (Barcaldine) 15 Feb. 12/1 The charge arose out of the use of a 'pricker', which was affixed to Passion Fruit's bridle to prevent his habit of 'hanging out'.
2. In the phr. **to have** (or **get**) **the pricker,** to be angry.
1945 S.J. BAKER *Austral. Lang.* 121 A man in a temper is said .. *to have the dingbats, the pricker* or *the stirks.* **1965** K. McKENNEY *Hide-Away Man* 103 Trevor said, easily, hiding his interest in a cloak of colloquialism, 'What you got the pricker about?'

prickly, *a.* Used as a distinguishing epithet in the names of plants: **prickly acacia (mimosa, wattle),** any of several prickly shrubs of the genus *Acacia* (fam. Mimosaceae), esp. *A. paradoxa* (see *kangaroo thorn* KANGAROO *n.* 5), and *A. verticillata* of e. Aust., which is also known as *prickly Moses;* **box,** *sweet bursaria,* see BURSARIA; **jack,** DOUBLE-GEE; **Moses** [see quot. 1953], any of several prickly shrubs of the genus *Acacia* (fam. Mimosaceae), esp. *A. verticillata* and *A. ulicifolia* of e. Aust., and *A. pulchella* of w. Aust.; **poison,** the spiny shrub *Gastrolobium spinosum* (fam. Fabaceae) of W.A.
1827 P. CUNNINGHAM *Two Yrs. in N.S.W.* II. 176 The attention of the colony is beginning to be directed toward the **prickly acacia** for hedges. **1829** G.A. ROBINSON in N.J.B. Plomley *Friendly Mission* 19 Sept. (1966) 74 Learnt .. that the kangaroo eat the prickly mimosa. **1856** *Jrnl. Australasia* I. 37 You may now plant .. acacia virticulata [*sic*] .. commonly known as the prickly wattle. **1904** *Emu* III. 216 Found a Fire-tailed Finch's .. nest just begun in a **prickly box.** **1903** H. BASEDOW *Jrnl. Govt. N.-W. Exped.* 23 June (1914) 150 The **prickly Jacks** and burrs are more than a tax on a fox terrier's patience. **1887** *Austral.* (Melbourne) Apr. 9/3 (OEDS) An expedition was now made into the scrub for fishing rods. .. I cannot recommend .. that awful thing which our philosopher called '**prickly moses**'. **1953** T.Y. HARRIS *Austral. Plants* 212 *Acacia juniperina.* .. This species has been known in many localities as 'Prickly Moses', a modification no doubt, both of the now obsolete older generic name 'Mimosa', and of the descriptive title for the foliage. **1897** L. LINDLEY-COWEN *W. Austral. Settler's Guide* 580 **Prickly Poison.** *Gastrolobium spinosum.* A shrub of two to four feet.

priest. *Obs.* KORADJI.
1845 *Sentinel* (Sydney) 29 Jan. 2/6 About half an hour after the body has lain, the Doctor or Priest provides each of the inner class of mourners with a short stick about 6 inches long. **1878** R.B. SMYTH *Aborigines of Vic.* I. 28 With

them was an old man of an odd and striking appearance, supposed to be a coradje or priest.

prill. *S.A. Mining. Hist.* [Br. dial. (Cornwall) *prill*: see OED sb.[4] 1.] Rich copper ore. Freq. as **prill ore**.
1871 *Austral. Town & Country Jrnl.* (Sydney) 4 Mar. 270/3, I was informed that, although only 'prill ore', it would yield from 25 to 35 per cent. pure copper. **1962** O. PRYOR *Aust.'s Little Cornwall* 85 The pickey-boys .. picked out the prill or high-grade ore and dropped it into boxes.

primary. *First preference*, see PREFERENCE 1 b. In full **primary vote**.
1902 G.A. WOOD *Electoral Reform* 4 He knew he had a chance of just getting through on his primaries only. **1985** *Sydney Morning Herald* 29 Apr. 6/2 An academic has branded coming changes to Queensland electoral system as 'the world's worst zonal gerrymander'. The 'Bjelkemander', as it is known locally, is partly responsible for allowing the National Party to rule Queensland with 38.9 per cent of the primary vote.

Prince Alberts, *pl. Hist.* [Ironic use of the name of *Prince Albert* (1819–1861), Consort of Queen Victoria: see quot. 1945.] Strips of cloth wound round the toes or feet and worn, esp. by a swagman, in place of socks (see esp. quot. 1974); TOE-RAG 1. Also **Royal Alberts**.
1893 K. MACKAY *Out Back* 191 They 'mouched' along .. showing glimpses of brown, unwashed skin above the frayed edges of their 'Prince Alberts', the toes of their bluchers gaping wide. **1900** *Truth* (Sydney) 29 Jan. 7/4 It was a dreary, dirty man, With furtive, foxy leer, And royal-alberts round his toes. **1945** S.J. BAKER *Austral. Lang.* 105 Prince Alfreds or Prince Alberts ... These terms developed from the malign suggestion that the Prince Consort was so poor when he came to England to marry Queen Victoria that he wore toe-rags instead of socks. **1974** B. KIDMAN *On Wallaby* 58, I was introduced to 'Prince Alberts' as a substitute for socks .. long strips of calico, rubbed with a little suet to minimise chafing and wrapped around the foot after the style of puttees.

Prince Alfreds, *pl. Hist.* [The name of *Prince Alfred* (1844–1900), second son of Queen Victoria.] PRINCE ALBERTS.
1896 H. LAWSON *While Billy Boils* (1975) 53 Occasionally someone gets some water in an old kerosene-tin and washes a shirt or pair of trousers, and a pair or two of socks—or foot-rags—(Prince Alfreds they call them). **1945** [see prec.].

Prince of Wales feather. [Amplified and transf. use of *prince's feather* a garden plant of the genus *Amaranthus*.] Any of several plants of the genera *Amaranthus* and *Ptilotis* (both fam. Amaranthaceae). Also **Prince of Wales's feather**, and in *pl.*
1945 J. DEVANNY *Bird of Paradise* 36 The leaves of the Prince of Wales Feather weed which abounded among the grass in the grazing paddocks was used by the farmers as a substitute for cabbage. **1948** H.A. LINDSAY *Bushman's Handbk.* 59 There are many patches of Prince-of-Wales's Feather plant (Amaranthus) whose young leaves make good greens. **1973** H. HOLTHOUSE *S'pose I Die* 37 There was a weed they called Prince of Wales Feathers growing down by the fence along the river. It was a sort of wild spinach.

Princess parrot. [f. the title of Alexandra (1844–1925), Princess of Wales and later Queen-Consort of King Edward VII: see quot. 1863.] The delicately-coloured parrot *Polytelis alexandrae* of arid inland central and w. Aust.; ALEXANDRA PARAKEET. See also *spinifex parrot* SPINIFEX 4. Also **Princess Alexandra('s) parakeet (or parrot), Princess of Wales('s) parakeet**.

[**1863** *Proc. Zool. Soc. London* 232 It will enable me to make known .. a new and very beautiful species of Parrakeet pertaining to the genus *Polyteles*... The specific appellation I would propose for this novelty is *alexandrae*, in honour of that Princess who .. is destined at some future time to be the queen of these realms and their dependencies.] **1867** J. GOULD *Birds of Aust.* Suppl. (1869) Pl. 62, *Polytelis Alexandrae*, Gould. The Princess of Wales's Parrakeet. **1896** B. SPENCER *Rep. Horn Sci. Exped. Central Aust.* I. 100 It was during this part of the journey that the only specimens seen of the rare Princess Alexandra Parrakeet (*Spathopterus (Polytelis) alexandrae*) were secured. **1903** H. BASEDOW *Jrnl. Govt. N.-W. Exped.* 20 Sept. (1914) 236 Several Princess of Wales parrakeet (*Spathopterus alexandrae*) were found breeding in the hollows of the gums. **1937** M. TERRY *Sand & Sun* 171 On the Finke River .. at least one hundred Princess Alexandra parrots made life worth while. **1945** C. BARRETT *Austral. Bird Life* 78 Long-tailed birds are the regent parrot or 'smoker' (*Polytelis anthopeplus*) .. the 'green leek' or superb parrot (*P. swainsonii*) .. and the exquisitely coloured Princess parrot (*P. alexandrae*). **1982** R. ELLIS *Bush Safari* 79 He thought he had seen a pair of rare Princess Alexandra's Parrots... I had seen them in the Gibson Desert some years before... One of our party .. recorded them as a possible sighting on her Australian bird-atlassing sheets.

printhy, printy, vart. PERENTIE.

prisoner. *Hist.*
1. CONVICT *n.* 1. Also *attrib.*, and **prisoner of the Crown**.
1800 *Gen. Orders issued by Governor King* 6 Sept. (1802) 11 No Prisoner or Free-man (who is not a Settler) is to leave the place where he is stationed or resides, without a Pass from the nearest Magistrate. **1822** *Hobart Town Gaz.* 10 Aug., All Prisoners of the Crown (except those employed on Government Duty), are forbidden to enter the Domain at any Time. **1847** *Port Phillip Herald* 28 Sept. 2/3 Instead of having now, as formerly, prisoner shepherds and stockkeepers for nothing, they are compelled to employ men as uncontaminated as themselves at .. more than remunerative wages.

2. Comb. **prisoner labour, labourer, population**. See also CONVICT B. 2.
1828 *Tasmanian* (Hobart) 18 July 2 **Prisoner Labour** cannot be obtained without considerable difficulty. **1828** *Tasmanian* (Hobart) 15 Aug. 3 We cannot help congratulating the Colony on the arrival of so many **prisoner labourers**. **1827** *Ibid.* 18 Oct. 2 His uneasy mind seems not to be at rest, till he shall see the **prisoner population** bound down as slaves to their several masters.

3. Special Comb. **prisoner constable, overseer, police, servant, settler**: see *convict constable*, etc. CONVICT B. 3.
1834 J. BACKHOUSE *Narr. Visit Austral. Colonies* (1843) 227 Attended by a **prisoner constable**, we returned to Norfolk Bay. **1829** *Sydney Monitor* 16 Feb. 1500/3 On what ground of propriety did Capt. Crotty employ **prisoner-overseer** Chrawn .. to shoot him birds. **1839** *Extracts Papers & Proc. Aborigines Protection Soc.* Aug. 110 Field Police .. would also be more steadily well-behaved than a **Prisoner Police**, otherwise so common in the Australian colonies. **1807** *HRA* (1916) 1st Ser. VI. 147 **Prisoner Servants** of the Crown are allotted to Settlers. **1832** *HRA* (1923) 1st Ser. XVI. 713, I collected the **prisoner Settlers** and these men .. and performed Divine Service to them.

prison population. *Hist.* [See also *prisoner population* PRISONER 2.] The convict population (of an Australian Colony).
1827 *Monitor* (Sydney) 1 Oct. 679/2 Malicious and libellous comments were dangerous in a colony like this, where the prison population was so great as compared with the free population. **1845** J. DREDGE *Brief Notices* 20 In the older portion of the colony .. the native tribes had long been in pernicious contact with the prison population.

probation, *n.* and *attrib. Hist.* [Transf. use of *probation* 'testing or trial of a person's conduct' (see OED 2); this precedes the U.S. and Br. use of the term in criminal jurisdiction (see OED 3).]

A. *n.*

1. A system for the management of convicts, introduced in Tasmania after the abolition of assignment in 1839: under the system a convict whose conduct continued satisfactory progressed through stages, as confinement, supervised public labour, paid employment, etc., to a pardon. Usu. as **probation system.**

1840 *True Colonist* (Hobart) 24 Jan. 4/1 The Colony is already beginning to feel the effects of the new 'probation system'. **1852** J. BONWICK *Notes of Gold Digger* 162 The old Assignment system of convictism was changed for that of Probation in 1840.

2. The condition of one serving a sentence under the probation system; the period of probation; a stage in this.

1840 *True Colonist* (Hobart) 24 Jan. 4/2 Under the new system .. they must work out their advanced probation in the Government gangs, and when they become free, they will be turned loose upon society. **1846** C. ROWCROFT *Bushranger Van Diemen's Land* I. 35 Nearly a hundred and fifty government servants working on their probation.

B. 1. *attrib.*

1841 *Van Diemen's Land Papers Legis. Council* no. 26 46 The present ticket-of-leave man has served an apprenticeship; the Probation man has learned nothing but to work with pick and shovel. **1848** *Britannia* (Hobart) 2 Nov. 2/3 Four magistrates in favour of the probation police.

2. Special Comb. **probation department,** the government department responsible for the administration of *probation gangs*; **gang, party,** a detachment of prisoners required to complete a term of supervised labour on public works; also *attrib.*; **pass,** a document issued to a prisoner who has served a term of probation, authorizing the holder to obtain private employment; also **pass-holder**; **station,** an establishment for the accommodation of prisoners serving in probation gangs.

1844 *Colonial Times* (Hobart) 6 Feb., Salaries for the superintendents and overseers in the **Probation Department,** two thousand pounds, and contingent expenses eight hundred and three pounds eight shillings. **1841** *Van Diemen's Land Papers Legis. Council* no. 26 39 Would you think a large Immigration so desirable, if you knew that any considerable number of men from the **Probation gangs** would soon be available, when holding tickets-of-leave? **1841** *Morning Advertiser* (Hobart) 1 Oct. 4/2 We hear so much said against the **probation party** system. **1843** *Colonial Observer* (Sydney) 17 June 1103/1 An officer, entitled Comptroller of Convicts, to be appointed to the charge of the probation parties. **1843** *HRA* (1924) 1st Ser. XXII. 519 After a Convict shall have passed through the Probation Gang, he will next proceed to the third stage of punishment and become the Holder of a **Probation Pass.** **1844** *Colonial Times* (Hobart) 9 Jan., In order to afford every facility to the hiring of probation pass-holders, two principal hiring depôts will be formed. **1842** *Tasmanian Jrnl. Nat. Sci.* I. 283 Complete **probation station** is governed by a superintendent, three assistant-superintendents, a competent number of overseers (all free men) a surgeon, a catechist, and a military detachment.

probationary, *a. Hist.* [f. PROBATION *n.* 2.] (That consists of) undergoing probation.

1840 *Tasmanian Weekly Dispatch* (Hobart) 21 Aug. 4/3 The immediate effects of the establishment of Probationary Gangs, and the consequent non-assignment of the Convicts on arrival, are already seriously felt. **1851** *Illustr. Austral. Mag.* (Melbourne) Mar. 159 Among the convict gangs of Tasmania, there prevails an extent of vice and infamy, not exceeded, perhaps never equalled, in the worst ages of pagan darkness. And these gangs too, after their 'probationary' ordeal, are finally scattered over Australasia.

probationer. *Hist.* [f. PROBATION *n.* 1.] One who is serving a sentence under the probation system.

1840 *S. Austral. Rec.* (London) 29 Aug. 133 By the introduction of the probationers, after a sojourn at Norfolk Island .. more vice will be introduced than by the present system. **1858** T. MCCOMBIE *Hist. Colony Vic.* 227 Two thousand probationers, and the like number of free emigrants.

probationism. *Hist.* [f. PROBATION *n.* 1.] The probation system.

1844 *Colonial Times* (Hobart) 27 Feb., He offered them wages at £9 a year, with rations, etc., for a further period: but the men, feeling the high importance of Probationism, declined so paltry an offer. **1856** J. BONWICK *Bushrangers* 7 Convictism, according to most old settlers, was attended with fewer evils when in the early days, and before the hated period of Probationism.

processional caterpillar. [See quot. 1926.] The caterpillar *Ochrogaster lunifer*, having slender hairs which can cause severe skin irritation. See also ITCHY GRUB. Also **processionary caterpillar, procession caterpillar.**

1918 *Emu* XVIII. 75 The heads waved in exactly the threatening manner of the tails of processional caterpillars. **1926** J. POLLARD *Bushland Man* 231 When they migrate, or when seeking a place to pupate, they trek along the ground in single line... 'Processional caterpillars' they are called. **1935** K.C. MCKEOWN *Insect Wonders Aust.* 110 This is the Bag-Shelter Moth, the parent of the well-known Processionary Caterpillar... When the caterpillars are full fed, they emerge from their shelter, and wander about the countryside in long chains or processions. **1980** F.D. HOCKINGS *Friends & Foes Austral. Gardens* 42 (caption) Procession Caterpillar. These destructive, hairy caterpillars appear in large numbers... Unless removed, they will soon defoliate plants.

Progress Association. An association of residents, usu. in a suburb or small town, concerned primarily with the improvement of local amenities.

1907 *Truth* (Sydney) 9 June 1/7 The Sefton Park Progress Association take themselves seriously... The principal result of their efforts last year was the establishment of a telephone bureau at the local post-office. **1985** *Bombala Times* 18 July 20/2 The Delegate Progress Association has once again achieved a successful public service for our community.

prop, *v.* [Prob. f. Br. dial. or slang *prop* 'the leg; also, the arm extended in boxing; hence, a straight hit': see OED *sb.*[1] 1 e.]

1. a. *intr.* Of a horse: to stop abruptly when moving at speed. Also *transf.*

1844 H. MCCRAE *Georgiana's Jrnl.* 15 Feb. (1934) 110 Suddenly my pony propped, and I had just time to disengage my limb from the pommel before he started to roll himself on the beach. **1984** *Courier-Mail* (Brisbane) 30 June 26/2 A joey wallaby .. hopped and propped not three metres away.

b. *trans.* Of a horse: to throw (a rider) as a consequence of stopping abruptly.

1887 A. NICOLS *Wild Life & Adventure* 83 If he should happen to prop you off when turning a beast, he'll stand by till you get on again.

2. *intr.* Of a person: to stop (often with the intention of establishing a presence). Also *trans.*, to accost.

1950 *Austral. Police Jrnl.* Apr. 117 *Prop,* stop; stop and question. **1976** B. BENNETT *New Country* 34 He leapt out of the driver's seat .. and propped in the doorway.

prop, *n.* [f. Prop *v.* 1.] A sudden stop made by a horse moving at speed.
1881 A.C. Grant *Bush-Life Qld.* I. 201 A sudden fierce prop, and Roaney has shot behind Sam's horse. 1895 G. Ranken *Windabyne* 47 Once or twice, when Stumpy tried to double on us, an electric-like 'prop' by the grey mare showed me the quickness and mettle of the true stock-horse.

property. [Spec. use of *property* 'a piece of land owned, a landed estate': see OED *sb.* 2 b.] A rural landholding which is used for stock-raising or crop-growing.
1825 *Hobart Town Gaz.* 18 Mar., Every Property on which the Proprietor is not actually resident, as well absolute Grants, as Reserves, distant Farms, Stock runs or Grazing Grounds. 1985 A. Hill *Bunburyists* 77 Suburban householders may own property. Graziers, however, have Properties. And they do not farm. Small people do that.

proppy, *a.* [See Prop *v.* 1.]
1. Of a horse: disposed to be restive when being ridden.
1866 *Australasian* (Melbourne) 10 Nov. 1002/4 We listened in wrapt attention to the horsey crowd as they severally gave their opinion of the quadrupeds. No. 1 says she is every inch a racer. No. 2 is of the opinion that she is 'proppy'. 1969 *Austral.* (Sydney) 24 May 35/5 King's Delight had a bruised sole on the near fore, and Clare said the horse was proppy in its action.
2. *transf.* Unsteady.
1904 L.M.P. Archer *Bush Honeymoon* 134 Old cove's gettin' a bit *proppy*, too, since last shearin'.
Hence **proppily** *adv.*
1951 Murdoch & Drake-Brockman *Austral. Short Stories* 213 Both [dogs] walked proppily on tiptoes.

proprietary company. A private company.
1890 *Act* (Vic.) 54 Vict. no. 1074 Sect. 354, Every proprietary company shall provide a book to be called the 'Shareholder's Address Book'. 1986 P. Latimer *Austral. Business Law* 570 A proprietary company need have only two members, whereas a public company must have five.

protection area. *Gold-mining. Obs.* See quot. 1895.
1871 *Austral. Town & Country Jrnl.* (Sydney) 18 Feb. 207/4 We hear of several protection areas being taken up, some of which look well. 1895 G.C. Addison *Miners' Man.* 7 Any miner shall be entitled to mark off a protection area double the length by four times the width of the prospecting claim . . and shall be protected in holding and occupying such area until payable gold shall have been discovered therein, or until it shall have been abandoned.

Protector. *Hist.* [Spec. use of *protector* one who protects from injury or harm.] An official responsible for the welfare of the Aboriginal population of a particular district: see quot. 1845 (where the reference is to South Australia); *black protector*, see Black *a.*[1] 7; *native protector*, see Native *a.* 5. In full **Protector of (the) Aborigines.**
1835 *Colonist* (Sydney) 25 June 201/3 It is the intention . . to recommend the appointment of a Protector of the Aborigines of this territory. 1839 *Tasmanian* (Hobart) 26 Apr. 132/3 On Thursday last, the chief Protector, aided by the four assistant Protectors, gave a feast. 1845 M. Collisson *S.A.* 46 An officer entitled the 'Protector of Aborigines' . . whose duty it is to secure to the natives 'the due observance of justice and the preservation of their rights, and in particular to protect them from personal violence; to secure for them permanent subsistence, shelter, and lodging, and to afford them moral and religious instruction'. 1947 V.C. Hall *Bad Medicine* 277 He made a special report to the Chief Protector of Aborigines.

Protectorate. *Hist.* [Spec. use of *protectorate*: see prec.]
1. The office or function of a Protector of (the) Aborigines; the body of Protectors collectively. Also **protectorate of (the) Aborigines.**
1841 *Herald* (Melbourne) 5 Jan. 2/1 It was devised by somebody strongly imbued with the prevailing Whig ideas . . that what is called a Protectorate of the Aborigines should be established in Australia. 1847 A. Harris *Settlers & Convicts* (1953) 213 The final mischief, and indeed infinitely the worst was done by the 'Protectorate of Aborigines', as it was called. 1856 J. Bonwick *W. Buckley* 91 The Squatters in their meetings condemned the Protectorate, and recommended the establishment of Land Reserves and Provision Depots for the Blacks.
2. Special Comb. **Protectorate station,** an area of land reserved for Aborigines under a *protectorate system*; **system,** the practice of delegating responsibility for Aboriginal welfare to Protectors of (the) Aborigines.
1840 *Port Phillip Herald* in *S. Austral. Rec.* (London) (1841) 2 Jan. 4 In future each protector shall have under his superintendence a reserve of ten square miles, one square mile of which will be kept in cultivation for the purpose of affording subsistence for such blacks as may rendezvous at the **Protectorate station.** 1842 *Geelong Advertiser* 29 Aug. 2/2 This absurd conduct of the Government is harmless, compared to the evils which they intend again to inflict upon both *settlers and blacks* by the re-institution of the **Protectorate system.**

pro-transportationist: see Transportationist.

province. *Hist.* Before Federation: used as an alternative to 'colony'; also used of the Port Phillip District to designate its relationship to New South Wales.
1829 D. Burn *Bushrangers* (1971) 15 Let official Proclamations forthwith be circulated throughout the Province, offering—let me see—yes—one hundred sovereigns for each of those miscreants, dead or alive. 1898 A.P. Martin *Beginnings Austral. Lit.* 23 'Rolf Boldrewood' here describes the 'up-country' social life among the delightful sheep and cattle stations of the Western District of what is now the colony of Victoria, but which was then the Port Phillip province of the mother-colony—New South Wales.

provisional school. *Obs.* A private school established in a district too sparsely populated to support a public school, receiving government support and subject to inspection.
1873 H. Parkes *Speeches* 7 Aug. (1876) 379 The provisional school is a school established where there are not 25 children, the number legally required to found a public school. 1916 E. & M.S. Grew *Rambles in Aust.* 178 'Bush' children have 'Provisional' . . schools, provided for them.

provo /ˈproʊvoʊ/. [f. *prov(ost-marshal*, an army officer acting as head of the military police in a camp, etc. + -O.] A military policeman.
1948 *Gabber: Qld. Lines of Communication Army Trade Training Depot* May 6 Those provos seek him everywhere! 1972 J. McNeil *Old Familiar Juice* (1973) 82 Our favourite provo, a bastard named Hunter.

prunella. *Obs.* [Transf. use of *prunella* material used for the uppers of women's shoes.] A shoe; a boot. Usu. in *pl.*
1908 E.G. Murphy *Jarrahland Jingles* 151 From her downat-heel prunellas peeped her corn-encrusted toes. 1912 *Truth* (Sydney) 28 Jan. 1/5 Fined three quid for shaking a pair of workmen's prunellas from a Salvation Army building.

pubbery. [f. *pub* + *-ery* suffix designating place or establishment.] A public house.
1910 *Bulletin* (Sydney) 2 June 15/3 Five miles from Fred Daylight's wayside pubbery you meet your old friend

Bill... After a chat you say: 'I'll leave a drink for you at Fred's.' **1939** *Bulletin* (Sydney) 11 Jan. 18/1 Bung and myself were the only occupants of the bar of his pubbery in a one-dog s.w. Q. township.

public, *a. Hist.* [Spec. use of *public* provided at public expense, under public control: see OED(S 4.]

1. Provided, maintained, or employed by the government (of a penal colony) for the benefit of the community.

1788 J. HUNTER *Hist. Jrnl. Trans. Port Jackson* (1793) 340 If they wish to remain as settlers .. you may give them such part of the public stock to breed from as you may judge proper. **1843** *HRA* (1924) 1st Ser. XXII. 509 A large portion of the produce of the public Farm in Norfolk Island.

2. In special collocations: **public gang,** a party of convicts detailed to perform *public labour*; **labour,** forced labour on a project or construction which benefits the community; **store,** the stock of provisions, clothing, etc., maintained by the government; the building which houses this; STORE 1 a.; **work** (usu. in *pl.*), *public labour*; a project or construction so undertaken.

1796 D. COLLINS *Acct. Eng. Colony N.S.W.* (1798) I. 485 Two men from each officer were ordered to join the **public gangs. 1813** *HRA* (1916) 1st Ser. VIII. 45 Several Convicts having absconded and deserted from the Public Govt. Gangs. **1792** *Ibid.* (1914) 1st Ser. I. 372 The colony, having been almost constantly on a reduced ration, is a great check on the **public labour. 1790** *Extracts Lett. Arthur Phillip* 12 Feb. (1791) 5 He has returned the quantity of corn .. into the **public store. 1789** J. HUNTER *Hist. Jrnl. Trans. Port Jackson* (1793) 345 The convicts would have an opportunity of saving time to themselves; and, as that time was to be employed in clearing gardens and ground to cultivate for their own use, what was thus saved from the **public work** would not be lost to society. **1801** G. BARRINGTON *Sequel to Voyage N.S.W.* 27 Will be found to amount to an enormous sum when the expences of the public works erected in this colony come to be calculated.

public, *n.* Abbrev. of PUBLIC SCHOOL 1; a pupil of such a school.

1956 'B. JAMES' *Bunyip of Barney's Elbow* 140 People spoke of keeping their children at home, or .. 'putting them to the convent', or 'the public', as the case might be. **1984** *Nat. Times* (Sydney) 20 Apr. 13/1 These were known as the Publics. They went to public school, they ran about in the streets, they didn't believe in the Pope, and they went to something called Sunday school instead of Mass. The Publics never seemed to have to go to boarding school.

public school. [Used elsewhere in both senses: see OED(S 1 and 3.]

1. A school established and maintained at public expense as part of a system of public (and usually free) education. Also *attrib.*

1813 *N.S.W. Pocket Almanack* 30 Masters of the Public Day Schools throughout the Territory. **1895** *Bulletin* (Sydney) 28 Dec. 16/3 A Bill to abolish public-school fees and make education absolutely free in N.S.W. was pushed halfway through the Assembly by Griffith.

2. A private, fee-paying school on the English model. Also *attrib.*, and **great public school.**

1848 J. FOWLES *Sydney* 7 Those considered as *public,* are—the Sydney and Australian Colleges (each a School under the control of a Committee), the Anglican College at Lyndhurst, the St. James' Grammar School, the Archiepiscopal Seminary at St. Mary's, and the Normal Institution. **1919** *Argus* (Melbourne) 24 May 21/1 That public school rowing has an extraordinary hold on the public was demonstrated yesterday, when the heats of the Head of the River boat race attracted a crowd of 20,000 people to the River Yarra. **1961** *Bulletin* (Sydney) 7 Oct. 51/3 The *Armidale School N.S.W.* The only *great public school* situated in the Country.

public servant.

a. Obs. A convict assigned to public labour.

1797 *HRA* (1914) 1st Ser. II. 18 Thus you will discover, my Lord, how impossible it was for me to do anything on Government account for want of public servants. **1820** *HRA* (1917) 1st. Ser. X. 221 Whose Conduct, as a Public Servant of the Crown, Since his Arrival .. has been irreproachable.

b. A member of the PUBLIC SERVICE, a civil servant.

1812 *HRA* (1916) 1st Ser. VII. 477 Institute Judicial Proceedings against one of the Public Servants who is accused of the grossest acts of Fraud and Peculation. **1986** *Sydney Morning Herald* 8 Mar. 11/2 The time had come to make it pretty clear that public servants had a clear professional responsibility to act professionally.

public service. Service to the community as provided under the direction of the government; now the preferred term (cf. Br. and U.S. 'civil service') for the administrative departments of each State and Territory Government, and the non-military administrative departments of the Commonwealth of Australia; the body of people so employed. Also *attrib.*

1793 W. TENCH *Compl. Acct. Settlement* 176 Many a night have I toiled .. on the public service .. hauling the seine in every part of the harbour of Port Jackson. **1979** R. BATH *Jamaica* 7, I start in February, so I'm getting in early—check the lie of the land, dirty up my trendy little Public Service flat.

puddenba, puddinba, varr. PUDDING-BALL.

pudding. The fruit of any of several plants, popular with children for chewing.

1903 *Bulletin* (Sydney) 31 Jan. 36/2 We knew all about five-corners, ground berries, 'puddings'. **1978** E. SIMON *Through my Eyes* 126 The apple berries which we called 'puddings' and which we chewed because they were supposed to be good for general health.

pudding-ball /ˈpʊdɪŋ-bɔl/. Also **puddenba, puddinba.** [a. Yagara *bunba.*] An edible marine fish resembling a mullet, perh. *Mugil cephalus* (see *sea mullet* SEA).

1847 J.D. LANG *Cooksland* 96 The species of fish that are commonest in the Bay are mullet, bream, puddinba (a native name, corrupted by the colonists into puddingball)... The puddinba is like a mullet in shape, but larger, and very fat; it is esteemed a great delicacy. **1896** *Australasian* (Melbourne) 29 Aug. 407/4 'Pudding-ball' is the name of a fish. It has nothing to do with pudding, nothing with any of the various meanings of ball. The fish is not specially round. The aboriginal name was 'pudden-ba'.

puddle, *v.* [Spec. use of *puddle* to stir (wet clay, etc.) into a puddle; used elsewhere but recorded earliest and used chiefly in Aust.] *trans.* To work (clayey auriferous or opal-bearing material) with water in a tub so as to separate out the mineral sought. Also *intr.*

1852 J. BONWICK *Notes of Gold Digger* 13 The dirtied water is gently poured off every now and then, and, with a fresh supply from the stream, you puddle away. **1967** S. LLOYD *Lightning Ridge Bk.* (1968) 1 Opal-dirt can be brought to the surface and examined or puddled.

puddler. [f. PUDDLE.]

1. One engaged in puddling for gold or opal.

1855 *Ovens & Murray Advertiser* (Beechworth) 14 Apr. 5/1 The rejected tailings of the ordinary miner are eagerly sought after by the puddlers. **1967** S. LLOYD *Lightning*

Ridge Bk. (1968) 99 Puddlers have ruined the whole Lightning Ridge Field.

2. A puddling machine.

1888 F. HUME *Madame Midas* 44 The wash was carried along in the trucks from the top of the shaft to the puddlers, which were large circular vats into which water was constantly gushing. **1971** J.S. GUNN *Opal Terminol.* 37 There are two dams .. at which miners rent sites .. where they operate power-driven wet puddlers capable of handling several tons of dirt in one operation.

puddling, *vbl. n.* [f. PUDDLE.]

1. The working (of clayey auriferous or opal-bearing material) with water so as to separate out the mineral sought. Also *attrib.*

1852 J. BONWICK *Notes of Gold Digger* 13 Good puddling makes easy and profitable cradling. **1971** J.S. GUNN *Opal. Terminol.* 37 *Puddling tank*, large dam at which wet puddling takes place.

2. Special Comb. **puddling claim,** see quot. 1890; **machine,** an apparatus in which puddling is done mechanically; **tub,** a container in which puddling is done by hand.

1862 J.A. PATTERSON *Gold Fields Vic.* 59 A **puddling-claim** .. had given an average of three pounds per week after paying expenses. **1890** *N.T. Times Almanac* 123 A puddling claim may be taken up on alluvial ground which has been previously worked and abandoned, or on ground which has been tested, and found to be too poor to pay for the ordinary method of working, such ground to be worked in connection with a puddling machine, and must be registered. **1855** *Illustr. Sydney News* 13 Jan. 19/2 They intend to construct a large drain sufficient to contain water for three or four months and also to erect a **puddling machine** on the Bendigo principle. **1851** R. TESTER *Wombat Wallaby* 61 (OEDS), I spurred my little mare off, and in doing so she made a plunge, and very nearly bundled me and my mutton into the **puddling tub.**

puffs, *pl.* With **the:** a disease of stock, esp. horses, in hot climates, characterized by absence of sweating.

1898 D.W. CARNEGIE *Spinifex & Sand* 366 Another horse-sickness common in the North is called the 'Puffs'. **1911** *Cwlth. Parl. Papers* III. 519 There are three diseases, however, that seem to constitute drawbacks to horse breeding in this part of the country. These are commonly known as (1) the 'Walk-about' disease, which is generally fatal; (2) the 'Puffs', and (3) the so-called 'Swamp-cancer'.

puftaloon /pʌftə'luːn/. Also with some variety, as **puff de loon, puff de looney, pufftaloona, puffta-looner,** etc. [Of unknown origin; perh. f. *puff* light pastry, light porous cake.] A small fried cake, usu. spread with jam, sugar, or honey.

1871 *Austral. Jrnl.* July 602/2 'Have a puffterlooner, Master Dick,' suggests Derwent Jack, 'or a bit o' sweetcake.' **1887** W.H. SUTTOR *Austral. Stories Retold* 121 Mrs Maybud prepares some pufftalooners and eggs and tea. **1908** MRS A. GUNN *We of Never-Never* 189 The cooking lessons proceeded until the fine art of making 'puff de looneys', sinkers, and doughboys had been mastered. **1921** G.A. BELL *Under Brigalows* 121 Golden brown crisp 'puff-de-loons', very good if somewhat greasy. **1933** W.L. OWEN *Cossack Gold* 124 The puftaloon .. is a member of the immense fritter family, a sort of unsweetened doughnut. **1959** H. LAMOND *Sheep Station* 34 He fried some pufftaloonas. Those fried scones did not rise in the frying-pan and offer the delicacy of taste they had done when other and more expert hands had cooked them.

pug, $n.^1$ [Transf. use of *pug* clay used as a building material.] An auriferous clay. Also *attrib.*

1896 E. DYSON *Rhymes from Mines* 66 To puddle off the pug and clay And pan the gleaming prospect bare. **1941** D. O'CALLAGHAN *Long Life Reminisc.* 107 The valley was more like a Kaline pug lead. The gold was mostly in the pug and was very fine.

Hence **puggy** *a.*

[N.Z. **1907** *N.Z. Geol. Survey Bull. No. 3* New Ser. 98 Quartz and puggy material.] **1932** I.L. IDRIESS *Prospecting for Gold* 41 Puggy clay is unusual. 'Puggy' ground often breaks up under the pick to form into sticky clay balls exceptionally awkward to disintegrate.

pug, $n.^2$ *Obs.* [Of unknown origin.] A lift on a horse ridden by another. Also as *v. trans.*

1934 *Bulletin* (Sydney) 5 Sept. 20/1 Victorian philologists are becoming alarmed over an outbreak in the State schools of a new form of slang. Two words in particular have gained great popularity—'dink' and 'pug'. These are, apparently, both used to express a request for a double-bank ride. The fortunate Melbourne schoolkid with a bike, when time comes to go home, is asked by his cobbers for a 'dink'. In the country the other word seems more popular, horses being largely used there. When a cobber wants a lift home behind the kid in the saddle he asks for a 'pug'. *Ibid.* 26 Sept. 20/2 In 1915 I was riding to my first job in Mildura when another boy asked me to 'pug' him to Fourteenth-street.

pull, *v.*

1. *trans. Timber-getting.* To pull out (a tree) by the roots; to haul (felled timber).

1920 *Bull.* (W.A. Dept. Forests) xii. 4 All persons pulling, cleaning and carting sandalwood must be registered at the Forests Department, Perth, in accordance with forest regulations, and may only operate on Crown lands after obtaining an order from one of the firms who hold a license to pull and remove a stipulated quantity of sandalwood per month from Crown lands. **1923** *W.A. Govt. Gaz.* 30 Oct. 2096/1 All sandalwood trees removed under this license shall be pulled up by the roots. The main trunk of the tree shall not be severed until the tree is pulled. **1975** G.A.W. SMITH *Once Green Jackaroo* 115, I had me own team pullin' timber outa them bloody gorges and mountains in the Northern Rivers.

2. *Opal-mining.* In the phr. **to pull dirt,** to haul the material excavated by a miner to the surface.

1931 M.S. BUCHANAN *Prospecting for Opal* 12 You can use your motor car instead of pulling the dirt by hand. **1973** C. AUSTIN *I left my Hat in Andamooka* 19 Maybe I should meet a lone miner who would be glad to have, even for a short period, an extra pair of hands to 'pull dirt' or scratch at the promising clay and sandstone.

3. In the imperative phr. **pull your head** (or **skull**) **in,** 'shut up', 'mind your own business'.

1942 *Whizz* (Perth) Aug. 1 Pull your skull in, sport. **1953** T.A.G. HUNGERFORD *Riverslake* 199 'Pull your flaming heads in!' he cried in answer to their unspoken criticism.

4. To play (a didgeridoo).

1949 W.E. HARNEY *Songs of Songmen* 7, I heard .. the didjeridoo player 'pulling' (blowing) his instrument.

pull-away hand. *Obs.* On a whaling-boat: an oarsman.

1845 *Inquirer* (Perth) 7 May 2/1 Wanted, For the Fremantle Whaling Company, a few stout pull-away hands. **1878** R.B. SMYTH *Aborigines of Vic.* II. 244 Wherever whaling stations have been established, the natives have proved themselves to be very valuable assistants... They enter heartily into the sport, and make excellent 'pull-away hands' in the whale-boats.

puller.

1. *Timber-getting.* One who pulls sandalwood from the ground.

1920 *Bull.* (W.A. Dept. Forests) xii. 4 In order that the sandalwood getter may be protected, payment to the puller for sandalwood of fair average quality is fixed. **1933**

P. ADAM SMITH *When we rode Rails* 68 The line opened on 1 June 1889 and it was claimed..that it followed.. the tracks of sandalwood pullers. These gatherers of the fragrant scrubby timber that was pulled out, rather than cut, for sale to the Chinese for use in the manufacture of incense had driven their horse and camel teams into uninhabited areas.

2. One who plays the didgeridoo.
1943 W.E. HARNEY *Taboo* 80 From the river bank came the droning of the didgeredoo. The player—or puller as he is called—was playing a walika. **1953** J.K. EWERS *With Sun on my Back* 25 Each group had its own 'puller', as they call the didjerdoo player.

pumpkin beetle. A beetle of the genus *Aulacophora*, esp. *A. hilaris*, commonly feeding on pumpkins and other plants of the fam. Cucurbitaceae.
1915 *Bull. N.T.* xiii. 3 Pumpkin beetles. *Aulacophora hilaris..Aulacophora palmerstoni..*are common pests of cucurbitaceous plants in the northern part of the Territory. **1982** F. HUTCHINSON *What Pest is That?* 42 *Pumpkin beetle*, Australian native insect that is a serious pest of pumpkins.

pumpkin-squatter. *Obs.* A small farmer.
1898 *Bulletin* (Sydney) 15 Jan. 14/2 *Pumpkin-squatter*, a little cocky with a swelled head. **1903** *Truth* (Sydney) 18 Jan. 1/6 'I believe you had a pretty tough time in Sydney,' said the pumpkin squatter to his friend who had just returned from a trip to the big smoke.

punce, var. POONCE.

punch, *n. Obs.* [Fig. use of *punch* a blow.] In the phr. **to make a punch,** to make a killing.
1902 *Bulletin* (Sydney) 8 Feb. 32/3 If the mounted man does make a 'punch' in the tucker line he can carry it, whilst the swaggie has either to sit down and eat it or else leave it behind. **1914** M. CANNON *That Damned Democrat* (1981) 98 The only chance a punter in shares has of making a punch is an unforeseen heavy rise.

punch, *v.* [Spec. use of *punch* to poke or prod; also U.S. but recorded earliest in Aust.: see OED(S *v.*^{1} 2 a.]

1. *trans.* To drive (a beast) forward by poking or prodding (see quot. 1859); to drive (cattle). Also *intr.*, and as *vbl. n.* See also BULLOCK PUNCHING.
1859 W. KELLY *Life in Vic.* I. 172 The teamster, whose whip-shaft is always armed with a spike to punch an overobdurate animal. **1911** E.S. SORENSON *Life in Austral. Backblocks* 58 Punching is the mainspring of Bullocky Bill's existence, and he could hardly be happy if released from the thraldom of the yoke. **1918** *Kia Ora Coo-ee* Mar. 15/1 Once I was punching with a team of bullocks up in North Queensland.

2. *transf.*
1933 R.B. PLOWMAN *Camel Pads* 67 Loading half a ton of gear on to his camels nearly every morning required plenty of brute strength, and 'punching' them over an almost roadless area..was no weakling's job. **1984** W.W. AMMON et al. *Working Lives* 157 We covered twenty-seven kilometres that day—a bit different to punching the sheep on the stock routes at thirteen kilometres a day.

punch pass. *Australian National Football.* HANDPASS *n.* Also as *v. intr.*
1936 E.C.H. TAYLOR et al. *Our Austral. Game Football* 23 *Punch pass*, stand still, and hold the ball in one hand, and punch it with the other with the fist clenched. Then try it on the run. **1963** *Footy Fan* (Melbourne) I. v. 12 If you can only do a flick pass as a youngster it would be very hard to learn to punch pass properly with speed and accuracy if you were to play senior football later. **1964** *Ibid.* II. viii. 27 Players must practise, and master, the two methods of hand passing. The 'punch pass'—hitting the ball with the clenched fist—and the 'open hand pass'—hitting the ball with the front of the four fingers of the hand.

puncture, *v.* [Fig. use of *puncture*: see quot. 1980.] *intr.* To tire. Also as *ppl. a.*
1903 *Sporting News* (Launceston) 13 June 2/4 Both men were 'punctured' but finally, amid cheers, the Forth veteran got his block down. **1911** C.E.W. BEAN *'Dreadnought' of Darling* 16 The tank may have dried up, and indeed the hut may be in the next paddock, or you may walk along the fences and give out ('puncture' as they say out there) before you reach it. **1980** J. FITZPATRICK *Bicycle & Bush* 231 The pneumatic tyre made its own contribution to Australian English. The word 'puncture', with the meaning extended through the concept of deflation to mean giving out, or tiring, was in use by early this century at least.

punishment gang. *Hist.* A detachment of convicts subject to severe disciplinary measures as a punishment.
1832 *Sydney Monitor* 12 Dec. 2/5 If it be a punishment gang, we think that it would form a very proper part of their punishment to withhold their tobacco. **1846** *Observer* (Hobart) 6 Mar. 3/3 Acting as overseer over a punishment gang at Swan Port.

punk. [Spec. use of *punk* rotten wood or a fungus growing on wood, used when dry as tinder: see OED(S *sb.*^{3}] The fruiting body of any of many fungi, sometimes used as tinder when dry, esp. *white punk* (see WHITE *a.*^{2} 1 a.).
1798 D. COLLINS *Acct. Eng. Colony N.S.W.* I. 561 She made use of the small bone of the leg of the kangooroo, round the point of which Bennilong had rolled some punk, so that it looked not unlike the button of a foie. **1977** M. TUCKER *If everyone Cared* 38 There was a fungus that grew on the gum trees, sometimes weighing six pounds, all shapes and sizes. We called it *punk*. When it was dry, we would soak it with white man's kerosene and light it at night.

punkari /ˈpʌŋkəri/. Also **punkary**. [a. Yaralde *baŋgari*.] *White-eyed duck*, see WHITE *a.*^{2} 1 b.
1879 *Native Tribes S.A.* 42 Dense flocks of widgeon (native, punkeri)..abound on the lakes. **1955** S. OSBORNE *Duck Shooting Aust.* 11 Punkary are generally fat and well rounded in the body. **1974** J. BYRNE *Duck Hunting Aust. & N.Z.* 189 White-eyed Duck or Punkari.

punt. [f. *punt, v.* to bet upon a horse, etc.] A gamble, usu. in the phr. **to take a punt.**
1965 J. O'GRADY *Aussie Eng.* 71 To 'take a punt at' anything is the equivalent of to 'have a go'. **1969** *Sydney Morning Herald* 7 June 25/9 Melbourne..selectors have 'taken a punt' in naming 20-year-old Russell Collingwood as centre half-forward.

punty /ˈpʌnti/. [a. Western Desert *bundi*.] Any of several shrubs of the genus *Cassia* (fam. Caesalpiniaceae), incl. *C. nemophila* var. *nemophila* of all mainland States; *kangaroo bush* (a), see KANGAROO *n.* 5. Also **punty bush.**
1892 G. PARKER *Round Compass in Aust.* 43 The sheep have gone from grass to salt-bush..and from salt-bush to the puntie..for their food. **1981** G.M. CUNNINGHAM et al. *Plants Western N.S.W.* 379 Numerous paddocks adjacent to homesteads and once cleared and ploughed for the growing of oats..now support dense pure stands of punty bush.

pup. In the phr. **the night's (only) a pup,** 'the night is young'. Also **the day's (only) a pup,** and in other contexts.
1915 *Bulletin* (Sydney) 11 Dec. 32/2 The night was not even a pup yet; it was broad daylight, being Northern

summer. **1928** 'BRENT OF BIN BIN' *Up Country* 167 The night is only a pup yet. **1934** T. WOOD *Cobbers* 138 'What's the worry?' they say; 'the day's a pup.' **1949** L. GLASSOP *Lucky Palmer* 73 We'll get him in. The day's only a pup yet. **1968** G. DUTTON *Andy* 198 'Are you thinking of driving out to Hangingstone to-night?' 'It's only forty miles and the night is a pup.' **1983** *Newcastle Herald* 26 Apr. 2/7 So far the national shearers' strike is only a pup. Four weeks may be a long time without work in most industries, but in shearers' terms it is nothing.

pure merino: see MERINO.

purge. *Obs.* [Joc. use of *purge* an aperient medicine.] Alcoholic liquor.
1891 *Truth* (Sydney) 17 May 3/4 We had no credit for purge at the nearest shop. **1929** *Bulletin* (Sydney) 13 Mar. 23/3 That's larrikin jargon of a 50-year-old vintage... We used to call food 'scran' and beer 'purge'.

purler. Also, and now more commonly, **pearler**. [Transf. use of *purler* 'a throw or blow that hurls anyone head-foremost; a knock-down blow': see OED(S.] Something surpassingly good, or otherwise remarkable (of its kind).
1935 R.B. PLOWMAN *Boundary Rider* 149 My face was covered in blood and I had a pearla of a headache. **1948** R. RAVEN-HART *Canoe in Aust.* 66 'A purler' meant something super-excellent and not a bad fall, usually from a horse. **1984** *Age* (Melbourne) 12 June 40/8 Michael Egan played a pearler in the back pocket for Footscray.

purple, *a.* Used as a distinguishing epithet in the names of flora and fauna: **purple apple berry**, the twining shrub *Billardiera longiflora* (fam. Pittosporaceae) of N.S.W., Vic., and Tas., bearing a shiny, usu. purple, berry; **-backed wren**, the bird *Malurus lamberti assimilis* of arid Aust., the male having a purplish mantle; **coral pea**, see *coral pea* (b), CORAL; **-crowned lorikeet**, the brightly-coloured lorikeet *Glossopsitta porphyrocephala* of s.w. and s.e. mainland Aust.; **-crowned wren**, the predom. brown and white, blue-tailed bird *Malurus coronatus*, occurring near water in parts of n. Aust., the breeding male having a purple and black crown; **-top**, any of several plants bearing purple flowers, esp. the naturalized S. American perennial *Verbena bonariensis* (fam. Verbenaceae).
1835 *Hobart Town Almanack* 71 **Purple** fruited **Apple berry**... The purple berries, full of seed, hang in elegant festoons for several months in the latter part of the season. **1903** *Emu* III. 36 *Malurus assimilis* (**Purple-backed Wren**).. not uncommon on coast and inland. **1945** C. BARRETT *Austral. Bird Life* 193 The purple-backed wren.. is a northern and western species. **1902** *Emu* I. 124 *Glossopsittacus porphyrocephalus*, **Purple-crowned Lorikeet**... The distinctive porphyry-coloured patch on the crown of the head showed itself. **1898** E.E. MORRIS *Austral Eng.* 519 **Purple-crowned W[ren]**—*M[alurus] coronatus*. **1890** A. MACKAY *Austral. Agriculturist* (ed. 2) 148 Malignant weeds.. are taking the place of so many valuable grasses.. cobblers' pegs.. **purple top** (*Vitadenia Australis*), and several other pests.

push. [Spec. use of *push* a 'press' of people, a crowd: see OED(S *sb.*[1] 8 and 9.]
a. A group of people having a common interest or background; a coterie.
1884 *Bulletin* (Sydney) 30 Aug. 10/1 We wished we were in the 'push' to go with them overland to Sydney. **1986** *Sydney Morning Herald* 8 Mar. 3/6 The piece was produced by a New York push which appears so far to be dominating the festival.
b. *Hist.* A gang of larrikins; *larrikin push*, see LARRIKIN 1 c. Also *attrib.*
1890 *Truth* (Sydney) 19 Oct. 3/6 Suppose a live policeman is on the ground while the gay and festive members of a 'push' are 'giving him Bondi'. **1932** K.S. PRICHARD *Kiss on Lips* 45 Deceased, who was an associate of thieves and criminals, has probably paid the penalty of a push vendetta.
c. *Hist.* A libertarian group in Sydney: see quot. 1963.
1963 *Sunday Tel.* (Sydney) 20 Jan. 2/2 The Royal George Hotel, at the corner of King and Sussex Streets.. has for some years been the headquarters of members and ex-members of the Sydney University Libertarian Society—known simply as 'The Push'. **1971** *Bulletin* (Sydney) 28 Aug. 6/3 The Push to my knowledge consists of a strange pack of academic bores, bar-room intellectuals of various persuasions, homo-sexuals, crooks and alcoholics, with some reasonable, human and charming people in all sections.
d. *transf.*
1903 H. TAUNTON *Australind* 92 We suddenly darted from our hiding-places with loud yells and cracking of stock-whips to gallop round between the wild mob and the edge of the thicket to force them to take refuge in the midst of our tame 'Push'. **1913** *Bulletin* (Sydney) 25 Sept. 22/2 It was a common, barnyard fowl that squared the deal between me and the scorpion push.

Hence **pushism** *n.*, the practice of forming street gangs; **pushite** *n.*, a member of a push, esp. in sense b; **pushy** *a.*, having the characteristics of a *pushite*.
1892 *Truth* (Sydney) 15 May 3/7 'Larrikinism' and '**pushism**' are growing, and it is time to take steps. **1899** *Worker* (Sydney) 11 Feb. 2/2 Strike the fear of the law deep down into the hearts of the '**pushites**'. **1902** *Bulletin* (Sydney) 12 July 16/3 Hard faces, shaven upper lips, straw and Mount Rennie hats, shoddy suits and bludger's neckerchiefs—all of the 'Push', **Pushy**!

pusher. Alteration of 'push-chair'.
1953 A.W. UPFIELD *Murder must Wait* 60 Several prams and pushers parked in an alcove. **1965** D. MARTIN *Hero of Too* 311 Lacy was standing there, too, looking proud, with Charlie in his pusher.

push the knot, to: see KNOT 1.

pussy, *v. intr.* To move (in) quietly or unobtrusively.
1919 E. DYSON *Hello, Soldier* 31 We held that stinkin' cellar, though, 'n' when the day was done Son pussied on his bingie where a Maxie trim 'n' neat Had spit out loaded lightnin'. **1975** *Bulletin* (Sydney) 26 Apr. 45/3 Ratty Jack was stallin' for me to pussy in as soon as Limp slews the tart.

pussy tail. Any of many herbs or shrubs of the large genus *Ptilotus* (fam. Amaranthaceae), chiefly of arid Aust., bearing a soft, fluffy flower-head; MULLA MULLA. Also **pussy tails**.
1916 *Emu* XV. 154 Many acres were covered in the fluffy purple plumes of *Trichinium exaltum*, commonly called 'pussy tails'. **1937** M. TERRY *Sand & Sun* 67 Salvation Jane, buck-bush, and pussy-tail predominated.

put, *v.*
1. [See OED(S *v.*[1] 44 l. *put in.*] In the phr. **to put in**, to inform on; to 'frame'; to secure the conviction of (a person); to send to prison.
1911 A. WRIGHT *Gambler's Ghost* (1923) 82, I ain't wantin' anythin' ter do with th' police... They put me in fer six weeks after your affair. **1975** *Sydney Morning Herald* 3 July 11/1 A lagger is someone who puts people in to the police.
2. [See OED(S *v.*[1] 53 *put up.*] In the phr. **to put up a drink**, etc., to buy (an alcoholic drink) on credit.
1896 H. LAWSON *While Billy Boils* (1975) 13 We walked right into the bar, handed over our swags, put up four drinks, and tried to look as if we'd just drawn our cheques

and didn't care a curse for any man. **1986** *Bulletin* (Sydney) 4 Mar. 21/1 Murlonga . . can 'put up' a beer in my name anywhere.

3. [See OED(S v.^{1} 50 b. *put through*.] In the phr. **to put through,** to shear (sheep).

1908 C.H.S. MATTHEWS *Parson in Austral. Bush* 137 At one station last shearing season 110,000 sheep were 'put through', as the shearers say, in about 7 weeks. **1987** E. HILL *Great Austral. Loneliness* 266 Mrs Giles was woolclassing. . . She has a little flock that she 'puts through' herself for pin money.

4. [See OED(S v.^{1} 46 *put on*.] In the phr. **to put it on** (a person), to exert strong pressure (upon someone), esp. to secure a favour. See also *to put the acid* ACID and *to put the hard word on* HARD.

1943 *Austral. New Writing* 44 Put it on the boys yet, Sid? . . Pull 'em all out, eh, Sid? **1977** B. SCOTT *My Uncle Arch* 135 He came good, when we put it on him for a job without any argument.

put the acid: see ACID.

Putt's pine. [f. the name of the settler Edward A. *Putt* (1865-1951) of Barron River, n. Qld.: see quot. 1945.] The rainforest tree *Flindersia acuminata* (fam. Rutaceae) of the Atherton Tablelands, n. Qld.; the soft, silvery wood of the tree, having an unpleasant smell when green.

1926 *Qld. Agric. Jrnl.* XXV. 435 Flindersia acuminata. Putts Pine (Atherton). **1945** J. DEVANNY *Bird of Paradise* 37 A chap named Putt came to my father in the mill and offered to sell him some pine. . . When it reached the yard he found it was timber he had never seen before. . . A timber man . . asked him what sort of wood it was. . . Dad answered: 'That's Putt's pine.'

putty. [Perh. fig. use of *putty* a powder, in contradistinction to *snuff* in the phr. *up to snuff* 'up to scratch' (see OED(S *snuff, sb.*^{3} 3 a.).] In the phr. **up to putty,** worthless; ineffectual; 'in a mess'.

1916 'MEN OF ANZAC' *Anzac Bk.* 32 A man's got a chance to hit back there, but down 'ere it's up to putty. **1973** *Bronze Swagman Bk. Bush Verse* (1974) 14 Can't ya see her tail was broken. . . And her breeding's up to putty.

pycnantha wattle /pɪknænθə 'wɒtl/. [The specific epithet *pycnantha* was applied by the English botanist George Bentham (Hooker in *Lond. J. Bot.* (1842) I. 351); a. Gr. πυκνός dense + ἄνθος a flower, referring to the dense flowering of the plant.] *Golden wattle*, see GOLDEN 3.

1938 C.T. WHITE *Princ. Bot. Qld. Farmers* 181 The wattle yielding bark richest in tannin is the Golden Wattle of South Australia (*Acacia pycnantha*), commonly known in commerce as 'pycnantha wattle'. **1979** C. KLEIN *Women of Certain Age* 60 The gold of the last pycnantha wattles shone strident.

pygmy. Used *attrib.* in the names of birds and animals: **pygmy goose,** either of the two short-billed waterbirds of the genus *Nettapus* occurring on deep lagoons in Aust. and elsewhere, *N. pulchellus* of n. and n.e. Aust. and *N. coromandelianus* of e. Aust.; see also *white-quilled goose* WHITE *a.*^{2} 1 b.; **possum** (formerly **opossum, phalanger**), any of the small, mainly nocturnal, marsupials of the fam. Burramyidae of n.e., e., and s. Aust. incl. Tas., and New Guinea; DORMOUSE POSSUM; see also *mountain pygmy possum* MOUNTAIN.

1842 J. GOULD *Birds of Aust.* (1848) VII. Pl. 5, *Nettapus coromandelianus.* **Pygmy Goose. 1980** C. ALLISON *Hunter's Man. Aust. & N.Z.* 115 A number of other birds are rare enough to be fully protected, including the Green pygmy goose, the White pygmy goose and the Burdekin Duck. **1794** [**pygmy possum**] G. SHAW *Zool. New Holland* 5 *Didelphis Pygmaea.* The Pygmy Opossum . . (exclusive of its diminutive size, not exceeding that of a common domestic mouse) forms as it were a kind of connecting link between the genera of Didelphis and Sciurus, or Opossum and Squirrel. **1855** *Illustr. Sydney News* 7 Apr. 156/1 The Pigmy Phalanger . . much resembles the common dormouse of Europe. It inhabits the southern portions of Australia especially the Swan River district. Its habits are strictly nocturnal, it secretes itself during the day in the hollows of trees, and at night leaves its retreat for the flowering branches of low shrubs. **1985** *New Idea* (Melbourne) 20 Aug. 3 Rob rears all varieties of possums, from pygmy possums . . to the big fellows cursed by orchardists and householders.

pyjama cricket. Cricket as played under the rules governing one-day international matches: see quot. 1983.

1982 *Sun-Herald* (Sydney) 31 Jan. 35/3 He feels indulgent towards 'pyjama' cricket, the name he gives to the one-day variety, but prefers the challenge that Test cricket poses. **1983** *Ibid.* 9 Jan. 4/2 The very mention of 'pyjama' cricket—a name born of the players' multi-coloured uniforms—makes veteran observers like former Test bowler, Bill O'Reilly, cringe.

python. [Fig. use of *python* a snake.] In the phr. **to syphon the python**: (of a male) to urinate.

1968 B. HUMPHRIES *Wonderful World Barry McKenzie*, I'm flamin' urgently desirous to syphon the python! **1978** D. BALL *Great Austral. Snake Exchange* 16 Brooks was struck with an overpowering urge to piss. Syphon the python, he thought.

Q

q, var. CUE *n.* and *v.*

Q fever. [See quot. 1964.] An acute infectious disease caused by the rickettsial organism *Coxiella burneti*.

1937 *Med. Jrnl. Aust.* II. Aug. 282 The suspicion arose and gradually grew into a conviction that we were here dealing with a type of fever which had not been previously described. It became necessary to give it a name, and 'Q' fever was chosen to denote it until fuller knowledge should allow a better name. 1964 *Qld.'s Health* Dec. 11/2 'X' is a recognised term for an unknown quantity. But Australia already had an 'X disease', now known as Murray valley encephalitis. However, the rest of the alphabet was open. Query also signified the unknown. 'Q (for query) fever' it became... Many have wrongly assumed that the 'Q' stands for Queensland.

quack. [Joc. use of *quack* (medical) charlatan; used elsewhere but recorded earliest in Aust.] A medical practitioner; an army medical officer.

1919 W.H. DOWNING *Digger Dialects* 40 *Quack*, a medical officer. 1976 D. IRELAND *Glass Canoe* 136, I go along to this quack and he says Get back to the surf and get some green vegetables into you.

quadroon. [Transf. use of *quadroon* one who has a quarter of Negro blood.] A person of one quarter Aboriginal descent; also (loosely) one of part Aboriginal descent. Also as *adj*.

1901 *Truth* (Sydney) 17 Mar. 4/6 The common method of procuring a wife (gin, quadroon, or white) is to buy her. 1965 C. JOHNSON *Wild Cat Falling* 70 He has a right to challenge me to produce my exemption ticket. As a quadroon I would be eligible for this.

quagga, var. QUOKKA.

quail. [Transf. use of *quail* a migratory bird allied to the partridge, esp. *Coturnix coturnix*.]

1. a. Any of several small, ground-dwelling birds of the fam. Phasianidae, as STUBBLE QUAIL. **b.** Any of several similar birds of the genus *Turnix* (fam. Turnicidae). **c.** *Plain wanderer*, see PLAIN 2.

1770 J. BANKS *Endeavour Jrnl.* (1962) II. 59, I made a small excursion in order to shoot anything I could meet with and found a large quantity of Quails, much resembling our English ones. 1945 C. BARRETT *Austral. Bird Life* 67 While all the quails are engaging birds, some are useful too, since they eat the seeds of noxious plants. 1976 *Reader's Digest Compl. Bk. Austral. Birds* 141 Quails are small, plump birds with rounded wings and tails so short as to seem absent. They are separated as a group from the button quails as they have a small hind toe.

2. With distinguishing epithet, as **brown, king, little, painted, stubble, swamp**: see under first element.

quail-thrush. Any bird of the genus *Cinclosoma*: see *ground thrush* GROUND *n.*1

1926 *Official Checklist Birds Aust.* (R. Australasian Ornith. Union) p. iv, Vernacular names have also been closely examined. Some indefinite names like Ground-bird have been replaced by more appropriate names, such as Quail-thrush. 1984 SIMPSON & DAY *Birds of Aust.* 324 Genus *Cinclosoma*, the quail-thrushes, includes four endemics. Shy, elusive, ground-dwellers, they usually flush away with a quail-like 'whirr'.

Qualup bell /'kweɪləp bɛl/. Also **Quailup**. [f. the name of *Qualup* in s.w. W.A.: see quot. 1933 and 1977.] The shrub *Pimelea physodes* (fam. Thymelaeaceae) of s.w. W.A.: see quot. 1981.

1916 *Bulletin* (Sydney) 9 Mar. 22/2 Almost every bush and tree has its blossom. The two most beautiful are the hibiscus.. and the Quailup bell. 1933 *W. Austral. Hist. Soc. Jrnl. & Proc.* II. xiii. 25 Riding along Wellstead's bullock dray track, which rises from the Qualup Valley.. the writer, in the spring of 1878 suddenly found himself surrounded by a galaxy of beautiful blooms... The 'Qualup Bell', as it is now called, has great bell-shaped flowers of a delicate greenish-yellow colour, splashed and flushed with crimson. 1977 M. BIGNELL *Fruit of Country* 4 Among the unending variety of plants.. is to be found the exquisite Qualup bell (*Pimelea physodes*)... Originally the area of the West Mount Barren was known as 'Queelup' and a derivation of this word was given to a small outpost that was eventually made in the locality by an early settler. 1981 J.A. BAINES *Austral. Plant Genera* 286 The magnificent.. Qualup Bell, the only sp. in this genus with a large bell-like inflorescence, which consists of reddish-green bracts enclosing greenish-yellow flowers, extending from Gairdner River to Ravensthorpe but named from Quallup [*sic*].. near the mouth of that river.

quamby /'kwɒmbi/, *n.* [f. next.] A camp; a temporary shelter.

1841 *Geelong Advertiser* 9 Jan. 3/5 The name of the town was originally the same as that of the district in Geelong... We defy the English gazetteer to produce a prettier name for a prettier township, than the one given by the ignorant aboriginal blacks, to this white man's *quamby*. 1846 G.H. HAYDON *Five Yrs. Experience Aust. Felix* 128 We.. erected our shelters or quambys as they are generally called after the native name.

quamby /'kwɒmbi/, *v.* Also **quambi, quambie, quomby**. [a. Wuywurung and Wathawurung *guwambi* to sleep; a sleeping place.] *intr*. To lie down; to camp. Also, as an imp., 'stop' (see quot. 1830).

1830 *Hobart Town Almanack* 53 This native.. is said to have fallen on his knees, calling out Quamby! quamby! that is, in the native language, mercy, mercy, spare me, spare me. 1839 *Port Phillip Gaz.* 3 Native—Where that white fellows 'quambi' (lie down)? 1845 T. MCCOMBIE *Adventures of Colonist* 75 Even the aborigines say the 'Dible, Dible quambies there,' and avoid it. 1859 W. BURROWS *Adventures Mounted Trooper* 112 'Black fellow quomby dead, by and by jump up white fellow...,' meaning, that if a black should 'quomby' i.e. lie down, and die, they would rise again white.

quandong /'kwɒndɒŋ/. Also **quondong**, and formerly **quandang, quantong**. [a. Wiradhuri *guwandhaaŋ*.]

1. a. The shrub or small tree *Santalum acuminatum* (fam. Santalaceae) of dry country in s. Aust., bearing a globular, usu. bright red fruit with a deeply wrinkled stone containing an edible kernel; the edible fruit of the plant; see also *native peach* NATIVE *a.* 6 a. **b.** With distinguishing epithet, as **bitter quandong**, *S. murrayanum* (see quot. 1975, 2). **c.** The large rainforest tree *Elaeocarpus grandis* (fam. Elaeocarpaceae) of e. Qld. and e. N.S.W., bearing a globular blue edible fruit with a deeply wrinkled stone, and yielding a useful timber (see quot. 1937); *blue fig*, see BLUE *a.* **d.** Any of several other plants, usu. of the genera *Santalum* and *Elaeocarpus*. Also *attrib.*

1836 T.L. MITCHELL *Three Exped. Eastern Aust.* 9 May (1838) II. 69 The plain we traversed this day exactly resembled the best of the ground on the Darling, and in some places I observed the Quandang bushes having their branches covered with a parasitical plant, whose bright crimson flowers were very ornamental. **1859** H. KINGSLEY *Recoll. Geoffry Hamlyn* II. 249 There's plenty of quantongs over there, eh, mother, and raspberries? **1937** *Bulletin* (Sydney) 15 Sept. 20/1 The quandong, known in some parts as the 'blue-fig', mills into a light, strong, hard timber. **1975** X. HERBERT *Poor Fellow my Country* 467 He .. made up a little fire .. nibbling the thin rosy flesh of quondongs and spitting out their great pitted seeds. **1975** A.B. & J.W. CRIBB *Wild Food in Aust.* 140 Bitter quandong, as the name suggests, has bitter and inedible fruit.

2. *transf.*

a. In the phr. **to have (the) quandongs,** to be stupid.

1899 *Bulletin* (Sydney) 4 Mar. 15/2 F'rinstance .. the man with wheels in his head .. in the Cobar and Lachlan country .. has 'quandongs' or 'rabbits' ('Rabbits' means very severe quandongness). **1945** S.J. BAKER *Austral. Lang.* 130 The state of being stupid is described variously as .. having any one or more of .. *the quandongs* [etc.].

b. One who exploits or imposes upon another.

1939 K. TENNANT *Foveaux* 311 In this crowd of low heels, quandongs and ripperty men, she looked at her ease and yet not one of them. **1985** P. CAREY *Illywhacker* 246 'What's an illywhacker?' .. 'A spieler .. a trickster. A quandong. A ripperty man. A con-man.'

c. A country bumpkin.

1978 T. DAVIES *More Austral. Nicknames* 84 *Quandong*, was born and bred in the bush.

quanger /'kwæŋə/. [Prob. f. Fr. *coing* quince.] A quince. Also *attrib.*

1966 S.J. BAKER *Austral. Lang.* (ed. 2) 344 *Quanger*, a quince (reported from Gippsland). **1977** *Sydney Morning Herald* 5 Mar. 11/4 We had an abandoned quince orchard where we used to wage the most fantastic quanger wars.

quantong, var. QUANDONG.

quarrion /'kwɒriən/. Also **quarien, quarrian, quarrien.** [a. Wiradhuri *guwarrayiŋ.*] COCKATIEL.

1900 A.J. CAMPBELL *Nests & Eggs Austral. Birds* 622 The Grey and Yellow Top-knotted Parrot ('Quarrion', native name among bushmen) flies round about waterholes. **1925** *Bulletin* (Sydney) 1 Oct. 24/2 Quarriens .. are now eagerly searching for nesting-places. **1944** *Bulletin* (Sydney) 23 Aug. 12/3 Galahs, budgerigars and quarriens were plentiful in the early days on the eastern Darling Downs (Q.). **1958** O. RUHEN *Naked under Capricorn* 20 All the noisy parrot world was momentarily silent—the budgerigars, the galahs .. and the quariens.

quart. Abbrev. of QUART-POT.

1857 W. HOWITT *Tallangetta* I. 146 Cooling it by pouring it repeatedly from the quart to the pannikin and back. **1980** S. THORNE *I've met some Bloody Wags* 31 We'd chuck our sandwiches to the dogs, and put our mudcrabs on the hot coals after we had boiled our quarts.

quart-pot. [Spec. use of *quart-pot* vessel capable of containing a quart: see OED(S.]

1. A tin vessel, orig. of a quart capacity, used for boiling water, etc.

1806 *Sydney Gaz.* 11 May, Iron Kettles, quart pots, frying pans. **1977** W.A. WINTER-IRVING *Bush Stories* 85 In preparation for our trip we packed corned beef, blankets, and quart pots.

2. *fig.* Used *attrib.* in various contexts: see quots.

1880 *Bulletin* (Sydney) 13 Mar. 6/2 New Chum 'Quart Pot Overseer' (*who has missed his way*): 'Haw, my abowiginal fwiend. Pway infawm me the diwection to the homestead.' **1973** D. STUART *Morning Star, Evening Star* 9 Tom went off horsedealing, or droving, or working at anything .. to get money for his run. 'A pair of quart pot squatters' they called themselves.

3. Special Comb. **quart-pot tea,** tea made in a quart-pot.

1854 W. HOWITT *Boy's Adventures* 112 Made our quart-pot tea.

queeai /'kwiaɪ/. Also **kwee-ai, quee-eye, qui-ai.** [a. Aranda *gweye.*] An Aboriginal girl; but see also quot. 1965.

1886 D. LINDSAY *Exped. across Aust.* (1889) 11 While I was after the Quus (girls) a native crossed the creek in sight of the camp. **1933** R.B. PLOWMAN *Man from Oodnadatta* 168 Ordered the blackfellow to return Maggie's qui-ai (little girl). **1945** S.J. BAKER *Austral. Lang.* 197 *Kwee-ai*, a young lubra. **1957** F. CLUNE *Fortune Hunters* 55 Mick told me how Lasseter was found by the tribe, south of Lake Amadeus. .. Then he continued: 'There was a *nungoo* (big mob) of *waddies* (men), *koonga* (married women), *quee-eyes* (girls), *nuringa* (boys) and *chidgee* (babies). **1965** F.G.G. ROSE *Wind of Change* 137 He had a wife in the Petermann Ranges .. and as he expressed it, [she] .. is a 'proper Queeai' and not a young girl. **1976** C.D. MILLS *Hobble Chains & Greenhide* 12, I would look at one of the 'queeais', who, like little girls the world over, would turn her head away, suddenly overcome with the giggles.

queen. *Hist.* A title occas. given by colonists to the consort of an Aboriginal leader: see KING *n.*[1] 1.

1830 G.C. INGLETON *True Patriots All* 27 Nov. (1952) 112 His Aboriginal Majesty .. will be interred at Rose Bay, beside the remains of his late Queen Gooseberry. **1840** *S. Austral. Rec.* (London) 18 Apr. 191 We have the chief or king (Wagamy), and his two black queens, or *jins*, always with us, who have their camp just beside us.

queenfish. [See quot. 1965.] Any of several marine fish, esp. of the genera *Scomberoides* and *Chorinemus* (fam. Carangidae), valued as game in n. Aust., and *Nemadactylus valenciennesi* (fam. Cheilodactylidae) of s. Aust.

1906 D.G. STEAD *Fishes of Aust.* 264 Queen-Fish. *Scomberoides sancti-petri.* Found principally in Q[ueensland]. **1965** *Austral. Encycl.* VII. 317 *Queenfish*, a name applied in southern and western Australia to *Nemadactylus valenciennesi* .. is also loosely applied by fishermen to a number of other fishes, the implication being that they are the consorts of 'kingfish' of various species.

Queensland. [The name of the British Colony established in n.e. Aust. in 1859 and previously part of New South Wales (see MORETON BAY); one of the federated States of the Commonwealth of Australia.]

1. Used *attrib.* in Special Comb. **Queensland billy,** a semi-circular billy; **cattle,** goat meat; **gate,** an improvised gate (see quot. 1928); **hitch,** see quot. 1979; **lamb,** goat meat; **rum,** (illicitly distilled) rum; also *attrib.;* **salute,** see quot.; **sore,** *Barcoo sore*, see BARCOO A. 2; **stock saddle,** see quot. 1972.

1902 *Bulletin* (Sydney) 11 Jan. 32/2 The **Queensland billy** is the handiest for mounted men. It is flat on one side, and has a D in the centre of the round side for a strap. **1915** *Truth* (Sydney) 19 Sept. 12/6 Although Western Queensland is largely sheep country, quite a quantity of **Queensland cattle** (goats) are consumed, instead of the orthodox beef and mutton. **1928** *Bulletin* (Sydney) 25 July 25/2 The stick-and-wire gate .. is merely a number of wires, spaced apart by stakes or droppers, and attached at each end to a stake, over which the catch, usually a piece of fencing-wire is slipped... Victorian settlers refer to these as '**Queensland gates**', while the Bananalanders blame the Victorians for introducing them. **1979** R. EDWARDS *Skills Austral. Bushman* 23 A **Queensland hitch**.. requires no skill to tie; a length of fencing wire is doubled and then put around whatever is to be tied. A piece of metal.. is put into the loop and turned around until the hitch is tight. **1936** N. CALDWELL *Fangs of Sea* 39, I had my first helping of **Queensland lamb**! Tender and sweet, I would never have known it was goat flesh. **1892** 'E. KINGLAKE' *Austral. at Home* 132 These men.. get gloriously drunk on spirits or wine with a little cognac flavouring in it, or a fearful decoction called **Queensland rum**. **1908** *Bulletin* (Sydney) 6 Aug. 15/1 Queensland rum.. isn't altogether a myth even now. The sugar mills up north sent 520,000 gallons of molasses to the distilleries last year, and 223,573 gallons of rum resulted. Not, of course, that bush rum necessarily has any connection with molasses. **1913** *Ibid.* 13 Mar. 14/3 In the N. Queensland forest and scrub country you can see more snakes when you're sober than you can in most places after you've started a bad attack of Queensland rum-fever. **1958** J.R. SPICER *Cry of Storm-Bird* 76 As they ate, the men kept their hands waving continuously before their faces and over their food. It had become an almost unconscious gesture, born of habit, and was generally known as 'the **Queensland salute**'. **1892** G.L. JAMES *Shall I try Aust.?* 242 '**Queensland Sores**'.. are, I believe, generally attributed to excessive thinness and poverty of the blood, caused by the great heat and an absence of vegetable diet. **1901** *Australasian Saddler* Dec. 77/2 No. 2 shows the main features of a popular **Queensland stock saddle**. **1972** J. BYRNE *Horse Riding Austral. Way* 21 Australia is unique in its styles of saddle... (1) Queensland Stock Saddle with its 6 inch kneepad set high on the pommel, so the front of the rider's thigh lies comfortably on it, with a small 3 inch back thigh pad and a 4½ inch to 5 inch dip in the centre to give our boundary rider.. the comfort necessary for arduous work.

2. In the names of flora and fauna: **Queensland bean**, MATCHBOX BEAN; **blue (heeler)**, *Queensland heeler*; **blue (pumpkin)**, a variety of pumpkin having a deep blue-grey skin, cultivated in Qld. and elsewhere; **blue grass**, the tufted perennial grass *Dichanthium sericeum* (fam. Poaceae), widespread in e. and central mainland Aust.; **bottle tree**, the tree *Brachychiton rupestris* (fam. Sterculiaceae) of Qld., having a swollen, bottle-like trunk; see also BOTTLE TREE; **cane toad**, *cane toad*, see CANE 2; **fruit fly**, a small fly of the genus *Dacus*, esp. *D. tryoni* of Qld. and elsewhere, a pest of cultivated fruits; **groper**, GROPER n.[1]; **heeler**, *blue heeler*, see BLUE a.; **hemp**, *Paddy's lucerne*, see PADDY; **Johnstone River hardwood**, see JOHNSTONE RIVER HARDWOOD; **maple**, the wood of either of two rainforest trees of the genus *Flindersia* (fam. Rutaceae), *F. brayleyana* of n.e. Qld. and New Guinea, and (occas.) *F. pimenteliana* (see SILKWOOD); the trees themselves; see also MAPLE; **nut**, MACADAMIA; **stinging tree**, STINGING TREE; **tick**, the introduced cattle tick *Boophilus microplus* of n. Aust. and elsewhere; also **Queensland cattle-tick**; **walnut**, the tall, rainforest tree *Endiandra palmerstonii* (fam. Lauraceae) of n.e. Qld.; the wood of the tree.

1882 *Proc. Linnean Soc. N.S.W.* VII. 139 *Entada scandens*.. is the well known '**Queensland Bean**', the large seeds of which are made into match boxes. **1956** *Coast to Coast 1955–56* 80 It was a noble animal, a true **Queensland-blue**, with jaws like an alligator, sagacity in its eye, and limbs like a well-muscled leopard. **1980** M. GRANT *Barrier Reef* 210 There was a Queensland Blue Heeler dog on the verandah. **1966** H. COX *Are Pigs People* 20 'How are your pumpkins?'.. 'Not coming away,' said Sam. 'How much have you got in?' 'Three acres. All **Queensland Blues**.' **1986** *Canberra Times* 22 Apr. 5/2 Hot soup of Queensland blue pumpkin. **1901** *Advocate* (Burnie) 6 June 2/7 Supply seed of the **Queensland blue grass**. **1902** *Proc. Linnean Soc. N.S.W.* XXVII. 579 The soft wood of the **Queensland Bottle Tree**, *Sterculia rupestris*.. after being sawn and put through a chaff cutter, is useful as a fodder. **1966** *Kings Cross Whisper* (Sydney) xxvii. 2/4 The frogs will be the large, **Queensland cane-toads** which will be guaranteed to frighten hell out of anyone. **1899** *North-Western Advocate* (Devonport) 13 Feb. 3/1 The discovery of the dreaded **Queensland fruit fly** in Hobart. **1906** D.G. STEAD *Fishes of Aust.* 103 The **Queensland Groper**.. frequents the coast of Queensland and the northern portions of that of New South Wales. **1948** *Bulletin* (Sydney) 8 Dec. 13/3 Boozer, the **Queensland heeler**, came idly along, stopped, nipped in with his inimitable, silent, sidelong rush and chopped her heels. **1888** *Proc. Linnean Soc. N.S.W.* III. 391 *Sida rhombifolia*.. '**Queensland hemp**.' **1919** R.T. BAKER *Hardwoods of Aust.* 33 The soft woods.. such as Red Cedar, Red Bean, **Queensland Maple** [etc.]. **1981** A.B. & J.W. CRIBB *Useful Wild Plants Aust.* 135 Queensland maple is one of the most highly regarded and widely used cabinet timbers in Australia. **1870** *Illustr. Sydney News* 6 June 3/1 The Government have proclaimed that the cutting and removal of certain timber, named the 'Bunya Bunya' and the '**Queensland nut**' is now absolutely prohibited. **1930** HIVES & LUMLEY *Jrnl. of Jackaroo* 212 **Queensland 'stinging' trees**, with their large heart-shaped leaves and fruit resembling mulberries, were seen and given a wide berth; for a touch of the leaves meant days of agony, swollen glands and disablement. **1897** L. LINDLEY-COWEN *W. Austral. Settler's Guide* 56 The introduction into the herds of the colony of the destructive **Queensland tick**. **1935** DAVISON & NICHOLLS *Blue Coast Caravan* 103 One of us suggested that the purpose of the fence and gate was to keep Queensland cattle-ticks out of New South Wales. **1919** R.T. BAKER *Hardwoods of Aust.* 339 *Cryptocarya Palmerstoni*.. '**Queensland Walnut**'.. is fairly heavy, of a chocolate colour, approaching English and American Walnut.. takes a good polish, and possesses a fine figure.

Queenslander. One who is native to or resident in Queensland. Also *transf*.

1860 *Moreton Bay Courier* 6 Mar. 2/5 In your issue of Thursday last appeared a letter signed a 'Queenslander'. **1911** I.A. ROSENBLUM *Stella Sothern* 9 Your business was the sale of some Queenslanders—cattle, you know.

Queen Street. [The name of a principal business street in Brisbane.] Used *attrib*. in Comb. as a Queensland equivalent of PITT STREET.

1898 'OLD COLONIST' *How Constitutional Govt. was Won* 30 The planting of a race of sturdy yeomen on the soil by the Queen Street (Brisbane) politicians of the period, as well as in later times, was regarded as an infringement of the rights of the class who have controlled the destinies of Australia so long. **1983** P. KILVINGTON *P. Kilvington* 88 The Queen Street cockie who publicly said my friend was a 'lucky dog' is probably still wondering why he got a thump.

Queen Victoria rifle-bird: see VICTORIA RIFLE-BIRD.

Queen Victoria's lyre-bird. *Obs.* [f. the name and title of *Queen Victoria* (1837–1901), first applied as the specific name *victoriae* by English naturalist John Gould (see quots. 1862 and 1865) + LYRE-BIRD 1.] The southern form of *Menura novaehollandiae* (see LYRE-BIRD 1), formerly regarded as a distinct species.

[**1862** *Proc. Zool. Soc. London* 23 Mr Gould exhibited a specimen of a Lyre-bird (*Menura*) from Port Philip [*sic*], and pointed out the characters in which it differed from the closely allied *Menura superba* of New South Wales. Mr Gould proposed the name *Menura victoriae* for this new species.] **1865** J. GOULD *Handbk. Birds Aust.* I. 302 Queen Victoria's Lyre-bird. *Menura victoriae*. **1956** A. CHISHOLM *Bird Wonders of Aust.* 22 About forty years after the initial discovery, John Gould, the English birdman, examined a Lyrebird from Victoria which appeared to differ slightly from the Sydney form, and he called this Queen Victoria's Lyre-bird.

qui-ai, var. QUEEAI.

quick smart, *adv. phr.* Very quickly.
  1966 S.J. BAKER *Austral. Lang.* (ed. 2) 215 *Quick smart*, rapidly. 1973 C. EAGLE *Who could love Nightingale?* 162 He hunted us off quicksmart.

quid. [Fig. use of *quid* the sum of one pound.] In the phr. **the full quid,** (in) full possession of one's faculties.
  1944 *Austral. New Writing* 36 He'll back down; I said he wasn't the full quid, just a skite. 1984 J. HIBBERD *Country Quinella* 101 Though not the full quid, a bit sawn-off, impossible to live with.

quietly, *adv.* [Also N.Z.: see OEDS *quietly, adv.* b.] In the phr. **just quietly,** confidentially, between ourselves.
  1938 X. HERBERT *Capricornia* 145 He'd love to see you 'fore you goes. Thinks a lot of you, you know, just quietly. 1979 *N.T. News* (Darwin) 17 Oct. 6/6 Apparently the team has nothing to do with houses and just quietly, doesn't agree with the present policy.

quilt, *v.* [Br. dial. *quilt* 'to beat, thrash, flog': see OED(S *v.*^{3}] *trans*. To punch (a person), to beat soundly. Also as *vbl. n.*
  1895 *Bulletin* (Sydney) 23 Nov. 19/2, I quilted Jim. Jim, senr., quilted me; nine stone seven cannot argue against 13 odd. 1980 G. BEER *Dust, Sweat & Tears* 28, I was promptly set upon by the school's bully and given a proper workover. I sure got a quilting.

quince. [Fig. use of *quince*, the fruit.] In the phr. **to get on** (one's) **quince,** to irritate or exasperate.
  1941 S.J. BAKER *Pop. Dict. Austral. Slang* 58 *Get on one's quince*, to annoy or aggravate deeply. 1974 D. O'GRADY *Deschooling Kevin Carew* 95 In an unguarded moment, he told Bill Moynihan 'This joint is getting on my quince.'

quinine tree. [Spec. use of *quinine*, referring to the bitterness of part or parts of the plant, formerly attributed to the presence of quinine.] **a.** Any of several bushes or small trees esp. of the genus *Petalostigma* (fam. Euphorbiaceae), bearing bitter orange fruits. **b.** BITTER BARK. Also **quinine bush** and, as **quinine berry,** the fruit of the tree.
  1886 F.A. HAGENAUER *Rep. Aboriginal Mission Ramahyuck, Vic.* 47 You can see the .. quinine tree. 1973 H. HOLT-HOUSE *S'pose I Die* 67, I knew it was going to be a dry trip and as a precaution I brought with me a supply of 'quinine berries', a native berry about the size of a cherry. 1986 K. BRENNAN *Wildflowers of Kakadu* 46 Common, widespread shrubs are the Quinine Bush *Petalostigma quadriloculare*, the Turkey Bush [etc.].

quinkan /'kwɪŋkən/. Also **quinkin.** [a. Kuku-Yalanji *guwin-gan* ghost, spirit.] A category of spirit people depicted in rock paintings of n. Qld.: see quots. Also *attrib.*
  1969 BAGLIN & MULLINS *Aborigines Aust.* 22 Aborigines will make a Quinkan trap by placing dry leaves—or nowadays a sheet of newspaper—between two twigs .. so they will hear his movements. *Ibid.*, Many of these galleries feature Quinkans, a phenomenon of northern Queensland. According to the Aborigines, these strange creatures live in rock crevices and emerge at night, waiting just outside the light of the campfire to grab the unwary. 1982 R.M. BERNDT et al. *Aboriginal Austral. Art* 149 Galleries of rock abound near Laura, north-west of Cairns... In the one noted here, the paintings belong to what has been called the 'Quinkin' tradition because many concern spirits known by this general term.

quoit. Also **coit.** [Fig. use of *quoit* rope ring.]
  1. The backside.
  1941 S.J. BAKER *Pop. Dict. Austral. Slang* 58 *Quoit*, the buttocks. 1972 J. BAILEY *Wire Classroom* 82 'I think he needs a good kick up the coit,' says Cromwell.
  2. In the phr. **to go for one's quoit,** to hurry.
  1941 S.J. BAKER *Pop. Dict. Austral. Slang* 58 *Go for one's quoits*, to travel quickly, go for one's life. 1952 J. CLEARY *Sundowners* 42 Going for the lick of his coit up the street.

quokka /'kwɒkə/. Also **quagga.** [a. Nyungar *gwaga*.] The small, short-tailed wallaby *Setonix brachyurus* of s.w. W.A., incl. Rottnest and Bald Islands, having long, greyish-brown fur; *short-tailed wallaby*, see SHORT-TAILED. Also *attrib.*
  1855 J. GOULD *Mammals of Aust.* (1863) II. Pl. 38, At Augusta .. its [*sc.* the short-tailed wallaby's] native name, Quăk-a, is the same as at King George's Sound. 1928 J. POLLARD *Bushland Vagabonds* 225 A shadow skippin' among them rocks looked to me like a quagga or some other wallaby. 1970 W.D.L. RIDE *Guide Native Mammals Aust.* 50 Until the mid-1930s the Quokka was a very common animal in the South West where it occurred in swampy thickets; Quokka-shooting was even a familiar sport.

quoll /kwɒl/. [a. Guugu Yimidhirr *dhigul*.] *Native cat*, see NATIVE *a.* 6 b.
  1770 J. BANKS *Endeavour Jrnl.* (1962) II. 117 Another [quadruped] was calld [*sic*] by the natives *Je-Quoll*. 1983 R. STRAHAN *Compl. Bk. Austral. Mammals* 16 The similarity of quolls to European carnivores was noted by early settlers.

quomby, var. QUAMBY *v.*

quondong, var. QUANDONG.

R

rabbit, *attrib.* and *n.*

A. Used *attrib.* in Special Comb.

1. In the names of animals having a supposed resemblance to the rabbit: **rabbit bandicoot**, BILBY; also **rabbit-eared bandicoot; rat**, (a) any of the rodents of the chiefly n. Austral. genera *Mesembriomys* and *Conilurus*, having long ears and a long, somewhat brushy tail, incl. the prob. now extinct *C. albipes* of inland s.e. mainland Aust.; (b) any of several other animals, incl. BILBY and STICK-NEST RAT.

1832 J. BISCHOFF *Sketch Hist. Van Diemen's Land* 28 The bandicoot is as large as a rabbit. There are two kinds, the rat and the **rabbit bandicoot**. 1982 M. WATTONE *Winning Gold in W.A.* 29 Nullagine is 110 km. from Marble Bar... While staying there a photograph .. of a rabbit-eared bandicoot was given me. 1837 G. BENNETT *Catal. Specimens Nat. Hist. Austral. Museum* 6 (OEDS) The **Rabbit Rat** of the Colonists. Habitat, Interior of Australia. 1970 W.D.L. RIDE *Guide Native Mammals Aust.* 142 Little is known of the habits of the White-footed Tree-rat of eastern Australia; early settlers called this the Rabbit Rat because of its rounded form and long ears. It has not been seen alive this century.

2. With reference to the control and extermination of rabbits, esp. on rural properties: **rabbit board**, a (local) body responsible for the control of rabbits; **fence**, *rabbit-proof fence*, see RABBIT-PROOF *a.* 1; also *attrib.*; **inspector**, an officer appointed to enforce rabbit-control regulations; **netting**, rabbit-proof netting; **poisoner**, one employed to poison rabbits; **scalper**, one who kills rabbits, retaining the scalps in order to obtain a bounty.

1898 C.L. MORGAN *Rabbit Question Qld.* 5 Netting fencing in use by the **Rabbit Boards** and others. 1896 *Bulletin* (Sydney) 19 Sept. 10/3 Queensland boasts altogether 4719 miles of **rabbit fence**, inside which the rabbits are gaily breeding in millions. 1980 J. FITZPATRICK *Bicycle & Bush* 204 Harry Jordan, a 'lengthrunner' along the Kalgoorlie pipeline, met a rabbit fence rider still using a bicycle sometime between 1912 and 1916. 1896 *Western Champion* (Barcaldine) 22 Sept. 3/2 The **rabbit inspector** at Broken Hill recently reported that very few of the land owners are taking any steps to destroy the rabbits, which are increasing at an alarming rate. 1925 *Makeshifts & Other Home-Made Furniture* (New Settlers League Aust.) 29 Make a strainer .. of fencing wire and **rabbit netting** of small mesh. 1913 W.K. HARRIS *Outback in Aust.* 90 Sometimes the 'dogger' is independent, but in most cases he is the **rabbit-poisoner** employed by the station. 1906 *Bulletin* (Sydney) 22 Mar. 15/2 The Victorian and Grampian Ranges (Vic.) .. are well stocked with emus, wallaby, and a few 'great reds' in spite of the exertions of the **rabbit scalper** and station hand to exterminate them.

3. *fig.* As **rabbit-killer:** a 'rabbit punch', a sharp, chopping blow to the back of the neck delivered with the side of the hand. Also *attrib.*

1942 G. CASEY *It's Harder for Girls* 23, I took a rush and gave him a rabbit-killer that must have nearly broken his neck. 1951 D. STIVENS *Jimmy Brockett* 99 'He told me he was going to use a rabbit-killer punch on Hill.' 'If he does, I'll disqualify him,' Bob said.

B. *n.*

a. *fig.* Alcoholic liquor, usu. beer. In the phr. **to run the rabbit**, to procure this, sometimes illegally.

1895 E. GIBB *Thrilling Incidents Convict System* 46 'Ikeing the rabbit for a fake for his Bingy' .. convict slang... It may be freely translated as having surreptitiously concealed some liquor under the excuse that one was ill and it was required for medicine. 1914 *St. Kilda Ann.* 143 He .. rose to the level of respectability of 'running the rabbit'.

b. *transf.* See quot.

1956 *Bulletin* (Sydney) 15 Feb. 13/4 My apprenticeship started in the railway-workshops... First you had to 'run the rabbit'; pulling a hand-cart loaded with rivets and coke to the lines of butty gangs, and returning with clinker and scrap as back-loading.

rabbit, *v.*

1. *intr. Australian National Football.* To duck down in the path of an opposing player, so causing the player to trip or fall. Also *trans.*, to trip (a player) in this way, and as *vbl. n.*

1885 D.E. MCCONNELL *Austral. Etiquette* 641 Tripping, hacking, rabbiting, slinging, or catching hold of a player below the knee are prohibited. 1918 J.A. PHILP *Jingles that Jangle* 28 In the game Ginger Mick was a tricky galoot, He might 'trip', he might 'rabbit'—or 'put in the boot'. 1983 HIBBERD & HUTCHINSON *Barracker's Bible* 165 A player 'rabbits' another when he ducks down as the other is about to use his back to take a mark... Regarded as poor form.

2. *trans.* To borrow; to steal.

1943 S.J. BAKER *Pop. Dict. Austral. Slang* (ed. 3) 63 *To rabbit*, to borrow, 'scrounge'. (R.A.N. slang.) 1953 K. TENNANT *Joyful Condemned* 198 Why were Australian Navy men better at 'rabbiting' little valuable articles than Americans?

rabbit-eared bandicoot: see *rabbit bandicoot* RABBIT A. 1.

rabbit-ears, *pl.* The terrestrial orchid *Thelymitra antennifera* (fam. Orchidaceae) of s. Aust. incl. Tas., occurring on coastal heaths and inland.

1923 *Census Plants Vic.* (Field Naturalists' Club Vic.) 19 *Thelymitra antennifera* .. Rabbit-ears. 1985 *Austral. Plants* Dec. 223 *Thelymitra antennifera* (Rabbit Ears). Bears 1–3 large scented yellow flowers which open freely on warm days in spring. It has brown 'ears' on top of the column.

rabbit-oh. Also **rabbit-o.** [f. *rabbit* + -O.]

a. One who sells rabbits as food (usu. an itinerant but see quot. 1946). Also *attrib.*

1902 *Truth* (Sydney) 11 May 5/7 The poor animal finishes its slavery in the shafts of the 'bottle-oh' van, or amidst the floggings of the 'rabbit-oh' push. 1946 F. CLUNE *Try Nothing Twice* 21, I made for the haven of Paddy's Markets, seeking a refuge among the rabbit-ohs. 1977 D. STUART *Drought Foal* 68 There is the rabbit-o, with a horse pulling a two-wheeler flat-top, with boxes of rabbits.

b. *transf.* A rabbit sold as food; also a rabbiter.

1920 J.N. MACINTYRE *White Aust.* 196 Gathering old bottles and rags or selling 'rabbitohs' in the cities. 1937 A.W. UPFIELD *Mr Jelly's Business* 16 'The men employed along the pipe-line are called Water Rats because often they have to work deep in water when a pipe bursts.' 'Thank you. And what are the Snake Charmers?' 'They are the permanent-way men. Now that you are a Rabbit Department employee you are a Rabbitoh.'

rabbit-proof, *a.* and *n.* [Not necessarily excl. Austral. but of local significance.]

A. *adj.* Secure against rabbits.

1. In the collocation **rabbit-proof fence**.

a. A fence erected to exclude rabbits, esp. on the border of a State.

1883 J.E. Partington *Random Rot* 270 The rabbits here [*sc.* S.A.] are so numerous that they have had to adopt rabbit-proof fences. **1962** *N. Austral. Monthly* Feb. 26 The rabbit scare was at its top then; the government offered extension of leases to owners erecting rabbit-proof fences.

b. Such a fence as marking the border of a State.

1927 T.S. Groser *Lure of Golden West* 221 Beyond the Rabbit-Proof Fence. **1971** J. O'Grady *Aussie Etiket* 30 You would be the greatest bloody galah this side of the rabbit-proof fence.

2. In collocations: **rabbit-proof fencing, gate, netting, wire (netting).**

1886 *Bulletin* (Sydney) 4 Sept. 13/1 **Rabbit-proof fencing** . . is nothing to the intruder-proof phalanx which surrounds Lady Carrington. **1898** C.L. Morgan *Rabbit Question in Qld.* 123 **Rabbit-proof gates** can be left [in the fence] for the purpose of enabling stock to water during the day. **1900** *Bulletin* (Sydney) 28 Apr. 14/3 **Rabbit-proof netting** is *not* any good. If the rabbits don't climb over, crawl under, or break through, the swaggie who wants work heaves them over. **1909** R. Kaleski *Austral. Settler's Compl. Guide* 94 Five No. 8 galvanised wires, posts 40 feet apart, four cyclone-droppers in between, **rabbit-proof wire netting** on the bottom. **1980** S. Orr *Roll On* 88 We have managed to rescue about 80 metres of tolerable rabbit-proof wire.

B. *n. ellipt. Rabbit-proof fence.*

1894 *Bulletin* (Sydney) (1895) 20 July 27/3 Beyond the furthest rabbit-proof, barbed wire and common wire. **1972** D. Hewett *Bon-Bons & Roses* (1976) 28 Best little ticket this side of the rabbit-proof.

Hence **rabbit-proof** *v. trans.*, to make secure against rabbits. Also *absol.*

1949 J. Morrison *Creeping City* 141 Clavering came upon Smith while the latter was rabbit-proofing his fence on the frontage. **1981** A.B. Facey *Fortunate Life* 200 The Western Australian Water Supply wanted men to go into the country fencing-in Government dams, rabbit-proofing, and fixing dam pumps.

rabbo. [f. *rabb(it* + -O, a street-cry.] A rabbit, or rabbit meat, sold as food.

1911 I.A. Rosenblum *Stella Sothern* 121 The bawling of hawkers with vegetables and 'Wild rabbo,' and 'Fish, O!' almost distracted her. **1911** *Bulletin* (Sydney) 19 Jan. 14/4 'Pick' may be an authority on the keeping qualities of 'rabbo' on a hand-cart in a disembowelled and negotiable condition.

race, *n.*[1] [Transf. use of *race* artificial channel (of water): see OED(S *sb.*[1] 8 c. and f.] A narrow passageway in a stock yard; esp. one through which animals pass singly, for branding, loading, washing, etc.

1862 A. Polehampton *Kangaroo Land* 216 When the sheep had undergone a preparatory cleansing in the first pen, they were passed . . under the dividing beam, into the next pen, and so on from one pen to another; till . . they were passed into the last division, called the 'Race'. **1978** M. Walker *Pioneer Crafts Early Aust.* 153 In the morning the sheep are driven into a 'race' running along the middle of the shed, and from that find their way into the 'shearer's pens', on each side of the race.

race, *n.*[2] [Fig. use of *race* contest of speed.] In the phr. **to be in the race,** to have an opportunity of succeeding (used in negative contexts).

1904 *Worker* (Sydney) 6 Aug. 3/3 'What snout!' said Din; 'it's emu dung, and not too bad in place Of 'bacca when you're stony broke And graft's not in the race.' **1984** *Sydney Morning Herald* 10 May 18/5 'How could three men fight so? They were not in the race,' he said.

race, *v.* In the phr. **to race** (a person) **off,** to seduce; to hurry (a person) off with the intention of seduction.

1965 W. Dick *Bunch of Ratbags* 185 Three of Knuckles's boys had raced Sharon off to the park to see if they could do any good for themselves. **1977** H. Garner *Monkey Grip* 137 What do you reckon my chances are of—you know— racing him off?

racehorse. [Spec. use of *racehorse* anything sleek or racy: see OEDS 3.]

1. Used *attrib.* in the names of swift, usu. sleek, lizards: **racehorse goanna,** any of several goannas, esp. the large *Varanus tristis* of central and n. Aust.; **lizard,** any of several lizards, esp. the small *Amphibolurus caudicinctus* of central and n. Aust.; also *ellipt.* **racehorse.**

1962 B.W. Leake *Eastern Wheatbelt Wildlife* 100 The lace goanna . . generally called **racehorse goanna** is well distributed through the Eastern Wheatbelt . . growing up to four feet long. **1923** A.G. Bolam *Trans-Austral. Wonderland* 36 The **racehorse** or bicycle **lizard** . . runs at an incredible speed (hence it receives the name of 'the Racehorse'). **1924** *Smith's Weekly* (Sydney) 17 May 17/7 One of the fastest things in the Australian reptile world is the racehorse lizard. . . They are found on the Nullabor Plains.

2. A thinly-rolled cigarette, swag, etc. Also *attrib.*

1953 K. Tennant *Joyful Condemned* 164 He sat rolling a very thin cigarette, known as a 'racehorse'. **1965** R.H. Conquest *Horses in Kitchen* 46 A hobo's swag was known as a 'racehorse' swag—long and lean. **1967** *Kings Cross Whisper* (Sydney) xxxviii. 10/3 Racehorse, a very thin cigarette. More the rule than the exception in nick.

rack, *v.* [Of uncertain origin; perh. transf. use of *rack* (of a horse) to move with the gait called a rack: see OED(S *rack, v.*[4]] In the imp. phr. **rack off,** 'clear out', 'get lost'.

1975 *Sun-Herald* (Sydney) 29 June 83/2 (*title of record*) Rak off Normie. **1984** R. & P. Thyer *Streetlight* 21 'Rack off mate, or you are going to cop it,' he bellowed.

raddle, *v. Shearing.* [Spec. use of *raddle* to mark with raddle.]

1. *trans.* To mark (an imperfectly shorn sheep) with raddle: see quots. 1891 and 1980. Also as *vbl. n.*

1879 S.W. Silver *Austral. Grazier's Guide* 57 He . . 'raddles', or marks, for non-payment any specially discreditable sheep. **1891** *Braidwood Dispatch* 6 May 2/4 Freedom of contract . . proposed by pastoralists . . said that 'any sheep not shorn to the satisfaction of the employers or their managers would be raddled or not paid for'. **1909** W.G. Spence *Aust.'s Awakening* 63 Another scheme was known as 'raddling'. This means that a whole penful of sheep would be marked and not paid for because the last one or any other one was not done to please the boss. **1980** P. Freeman *Woolshed* 124 The raddle stick was the pencil used for putting a mark on the sheep's wool to indicate that the sheep was improperly shorn and should not be counted. In some cases, the board manager might even condemn a whole penful of sheep when only a few had been actually 'raddled'.

2. *Obs.*

a. *transf.* To swindle (a person).

1897 *Worker* (Sydney) 11 Sept. 1/2 But when he puts the 'stopper' on, because he finds he's broke, He swears that he was 'raddled' by that shanty-keeper 'bloke'.

b. *fig.* In the phr. **to raddle** (someone's) **toe,** to call on (a person) to buy a round of drinks.

1899 *Truth* (Sydney) 3 Apr. 8/3 According to custom, her Ladyship's toe was 'raddled'. I suppose everybody ought to know what that means, but for those who don't, I will explain. To 'raddle' the toe of a visitor to a shearing shed, means that the visitor shouts for the crowd.

radjah shieldrake, var. Rajah shieldrake.

Rafferty. [Joc. use of the Irish surname *Rafferty*, in punning allusion to Br. dial. *raffety* irregular, f. *raff* confused heap, medley: see EDD but also OEDS for the suggestion that the word is a var. of *raffatory* or *reffatory*, a Br. dial. form of *refractory*.]

a. Used *attrib.* or in the possessive, as **Rafferty('s) rules,** no rules at all. Also **the rules of Rafferty.**

1918 *Port Hacking Cough* (Sydney) 14 Dec. 8 *Rafferty's rules*... A dog is kept to do all the barking on the premises. **1930** E. ANTONY *Hungry Mile* 38 There's two thousand scrapping with you 'neath the rules of 'Rafferty'. **1935** *Sydney Morning Herald* 28 Dec. 11/7 Rafferty rules may suit.. the Communist party, but they are repugnant to the trade union movement.

b. *ellipt.* for **Rafferty's rules.**

1948 H.W. CRITTENDEN *Rogues' Paradise* 8 Who could imagine any Rafferty Labor Prime Minister repeating.. 'We are with you to the last man and the last shilling'?

rager. *Obs.* An (old) untamed and aggressive bullock or cow: see quot. 1876.

1876 *Austral. Town & Country Jrnl.* (Sydney) 16 Dec. 982/1 The resources in attack or defence, developed in the confirmed 'rager', are only to be learned by experience. He is the grizzly bear of Australia. **1894** A.B. BELL *Oscar* 66 The cows were real old ragers, rag-eaters.

Rag Fair. *Obs.* [Transf. use of *rag-fair* a market in London for the sale of used clothing.] A market in Melbourne at which newly arrived immigrants sold clothing, etc.: see quot. 1856.

1853 J. ROCHFORT *Adventures Surveyor* 62 Emigrants who arrive with a large outfit and little money stand in a spot called 'Rag Fair', in the midst of their pile of clothes, etc., selling them to passers-by at an *awful sacrifice*. **1856** W.H.G. KINGSTON *Emigrant's Home* 169 At Melbourne, the beach is called Rag Fair, because there the poor creatures who have just landed turn out the contents of their boxes and sell them at ruinous prices, to enable them to go to the diggings.

rahzoo, var. RAZOO.

rail-splitter: see SPLITTER.

rain. Used *attrib.* in Special Comb. with reference to Aboriginal rain-making ritual: **rain-maker** (or **-doctor**), one competent to perform such a ritual; so **-making** *ppl. a.*; **(-making) stone,** a stone used in such a ritual (see quot. 1883).

1847 G.F. ANGAS *Savage Life & Scenes* I. 59 The green bough being symbolical of his situation, according to the '**rain-makers**' or wise old men. **1898** *Bulletin* (Sydney) 26 Mar. 14/4 These rev. gentlemen led a rain-making corroboree which lasted five nights. **1898** D.W. CARNEGIE *Spinifex & Sand* 348 The implement.. is used by the 'Mopongullera', or Rain-doctor, at their ceremony which they hold annually when they are making the rain. **1883** *Proc. Linnean Soc. N.S.W.* VIII. 436 Gypsum occurs abundantly in the soil, but the fibrous variety known as Satin Spar.. is highly prized by the natives, and is called by them '**rain-stone**', for they believe that the Great Spirit uses it in making rain. **1964** *N. Austral. Monthly* Nov. 4 Spider, our pathfinder, had mentioned earlier that the stone was his tribe's 'rainmaking' stone... He had better bring some back and throw it in the river to break the drought.

rain bird. [Transf. use of *rain-bird*, orig. the green woodpecker *Picus viridis*.] Any of several birds, esp. cuckoos, whose call is believed to presage rain, as the CHANNEL-BILLED CUCKOO, *grey currawong* (see GREY *a.*), and PALLID CUCKOO.

1827 *Trans. Linnean Soc. London* XV. 213 Vanga.. Destructor.. Mr Caley thus observes on this species. '*Butcherbird*.—This bird used frequently to come into some *green wattle-trees* near my house, and in wet weather was very noisy; from which circumstance it obtained the name of *Rain-bird*.' **1965** *Austral. Encycl.* VII. 381 Rain-bird, a name casually applied to various birds whose calls in special circumstances are supposed to presage rain. Australia's chief 'rain-birds' are cuckoos and black cockatoos.

rainbow.

1. In Services' speech: a late reinforcement (see quots.). Also *attrib.*, as **rainbow soldier,** and *transf.*

1919 W.H. DOWNING *Digger Dialects* 40 *Rainbow*, a reinforcement, or member of non-combatant corps, who joined a fighting unit after the Armistice. **1944** T.R. ST. GEORGE *C/O Postmaster* 104 Even we Selective Service men could more or less look down on the A.M.F. and refer to them as 'Rainbow Soldiers'. **1947** V. PALMER *Cyclone* 181 Rainbow, eh? Mighty good, Clive always was, at showing up after the storm was over!

2. Used *attrib.* in the names of flora and fauna: **rainbow bird,** the bee-eater *Merops ornatus*, a largely migratory, insectivorous bird of mainland Aust. and islands to the north; NEEDLE-TAIL; **fish,** any of several fish, esp. the marine *Odax acroptilus* of s. Aust., the MAORI, and fresh-water fish of the fam. Melanotaeniidae, esp. *Melanotaenia splendida*; **lorikeet,** the very brightly-coloured lorikeet *Trichoglossus haematodus* of e. Aust., and introduced to the Perth (W.A.) area; *blue mountain parrot*, see BLUE *a.*; **pitta,** the predom. black and green bird *Pitta iris* of Arnhem Land (N.T.) and the Kimberley region (W.A.); **plant** (chiefly *W.A.*), any of several insectivorous plants, esp. those of the genus *Drosera* (fam. Droseraceae), and *Byblis gigantea* (fam. Byblidaceae) of s.w. W.A.; also *ellipt.* as **rainbow.**

1911 J.A. LEACH *Austral. Bird Bk.* 107 **Rainbow-bird,** Aust. bee-eater.. *Merops ornatus*. **1895** C. THACKERAY *Amateur Fisherman's Guide* 57 *Tumble-down* is the.. habitat of the beautiful **rainbow** and parrot **fish.** [**1911 rainbow lorikeet:** J.A. LEACH *Austral. Bird Bk.* 88 Blue Mountain Lorikeet.. Rainbow Lory.. *Trichoglossus novae-hollandiae*.] **1929** A.H. CHISHOLM *Birds & Green Places* 209 Just a sprinkling of the larger 'blueys' (rainbow lorikeets). **1842** J. GOULD *Birds of Aust.* (1848) IV. Pl. 3, *Pitta iris*.. **Rainbow Pitta. 1901** [**rainbow plant**] M. VIVIENNE *Travels in W.A.* 322 The desert octopus or tiger-plant is most remarkable.. and is also known as 'Rainbow' or 'Fly-trap'. **1917** *Bulletin* (Sydney) 15 Feb. 22/2 The Darling Ranges of Westralia produce a great number and variety of carnivorous plants. Commonest among these is one called by children rainbow-plant. It is a creeper which grows to a length of about 18 inches and has tiny sundew cups on short stems at irregular intervals.

3. Special Comb. **rainbow serpent,** a widely venerated spirit of Aboriginal mythology: see e.g. quot. 1970. Also **rainbow snake, spirit.**

1926 *Jrnl. R. Anthrop. Inst. London* LXI. 24 The rainbow-serpent is not confined in Australia to any particular ethnological province. **1928** W. ROBERTSON *Coo-ee Talks* 38 There was a time when stinging-nettles grew so thickly round the lake that the aborigines regarded them as having been placed there by the rainbow-spirit to keep away intruders. **1970** J.V. MARSHALL *Walk to Hills of Dreamtime* 156 *Rainbow serpent*.. (*Yurlunggur* to the Bindubi) moves through the myths of all the tribes of Australia.. nearer to godhead than any other creature. The great snake is said to have appeared in Dreamtime, the time of creation, to have fashioned the earth and then gone to ground east of the Kimberleys at a place where the rainbow plunges from earth to sky. Rain, according to some tribes, is the serpent spitting; and when the rainbow appears they say *Kaio Kuriaio* (no more rain). **1986** *Canberra Times* 22 Apr. 15/1 The spring was where the Rainbow Snake, or Wagyl, had come out of the river and gone underground. It had laid an egg.. and is now near the start of Perth's Narrow Bridge.

rajah shieldrake. Also **radjah shieldrake.** [Spec. use of *rajah* Indian title, first applied as the specific epithet *radjah* by French physician and naturalist Prosper Garnot (in L.I. Duperry *Voy. la Coquille* (1828) I. 303 Pl. 49).] Burdekin duck (a), see BURDEKIN. Also **radjah shelduck.**

1844 J. GOULD *Birds of Aust.* (1848) VII. Pl. 8, *Tadorna radjah* . . Radjah Shieldrake. **1845** C. HODGKINSON *Aust., Port Macquarie to Moreton Bay* 204 There are several varieties of ducks in New South Wales, such as . . the white-headed or Rajah shieldrake, the Australian shoveller, etc. **1976** *Reader's Digest Compl. Bk. Austral. Birds* 101 Burdekin duck *Tadorna radjah*. Other names Radjah shelduck, whiteheaded shelduck. . . Nowadays seldom found on east coast except in small numbers in some places in northern Queensland.

ram, *n.*

1. Used *attrib.* in Special Comb. **ram paddock,** an enclosure in which rams are kept segregated from ewes; **stag,** a ram castrated after reaching maturity; also *attrib.*

1882 ARMSTRONG & CAMPBELL *Austral. Sheep Husbandry* 147 By having the **ram paddock** enclosed by a good chock and log fence the evil effects of constant lambing will be avoided. **1897** L. LINDLEY-COWEN *W. Austral. Settler's Guide* 642 *Stags* (or **ram stags**). Rams that are no longer wanted for use in the flock . . are a trouble if kept as rams, and it seems a waste to destroy them. The usual plan is to castrate them, and use them for food next season. . . Ram stags when fattened make excellent mutton, though some people have a prejudice against it. **1956** R.G. EDWARDS *Overlander Songbk.* 96 You'll forget the ram-stag mutton on the Banks of the Condamine.

2. *fig.* See quot. 1941 and RAM *v.*

1941 S.J. BAKER *Pop. Dict. Austral. Slang* 59 *Ram*, a trickster's confederate. **1966** —— *Austral. Lang.* (ed. 2) 246 The ram would say, 'Give the old boy a fair go; he's nearly too old to spin them!'

ram, *v.* [f. prec.] *intr.* To act as a swindler's accomplice.

1952 *Coast to Coast 1951–52* 199 Siddy might have been ramming for you, but what you didn't know, my lad, was that he was helping me to hook you. You were a goner from the start. **1964** H.P. TRITTON *Time means Tucker* (rev. ed.) 33 A gentleman with an umbrella, three thimbles and a pea was demonstrating how 'the quickness of the hand deceives the eye' and was raking in the money at a great rate. When business slackened, another gentleman would pick the pea with surprising regularity. This would bring the crowd back to try their luck again. No one seemed to wake up to the fact that the second gentleman was 'ramming' for the first gentleman.

rammies, *pl.* Altered form of 'round me (or the) houses', rhyming slang for 'trousers'.

1906 *Bulletin* (Sydney) 20 Dec. 15/3 Philological research has . . enabled me to discover how a pair of pants was transmogrified into rammies. Rhyming slang transmuted trousers . . into 'round my houses'—cockney pronunciation, 'rahand me 'ouses'. **1982** *Bulletin* (Sydney) 25 May 50/2, I well remember my father describing trousers as *rammies*.

ramp, *n.*[1] [Spec. use of *ramp* swindle: see OED(S *sb.*[5]] A search made in a gaol of a prisoner's person or cell.

1919 V. MARSHALL *World of Living Dead* 85 Toe the arrer for the ev'nin' ramp. **1980** B. JEWSON *Stir* 34 China stood looking at the door. . . He must have missed Tony telling him there would be a ramp—a search.

ramp, *n.*[2] GRID *n.*[2]

1948 R. RAVEN-HART *Canoe in Aust.* 82 The road had grating across it at every gate. . . (The gratings are locally 'ramps', a curious misnomer). **1955** 'M. HILL' *Land nearest Stars* 107 We were coming at last to the great sheep stations and the instructions in the Itinerary now consisted of several pages of monotonous repetition of a single word: *ramp*. This was sometimes expanded to *ramp and gate*, or *ramp and shed*.

ramp, *v.* [f. RAMP *n.*[1]] *trans.* To search (a prisoner or cell) in gaol.

1919 V. MARSHALL *World of Living Dead* 12 It would take minutes to make him secure, for he must deliver up his braces, his boots, his books, and be ramped to the skin. **1982** R. DENNING *Diary* 177 The screws ramped every cell in the jail this morning looking for Xmas brews.

ranch. Chiefly *n. Qld.* [Joc. use of *ranch(-house)*.] A canteen (or boarding-house) for employees.

1937 W. HATFIELD *I find Aust.* 198 There were eighty-four men eating at the 'ranch' as they called it. **1944** J. DEVANNY *By Tropic Sea & Jungle* 21 We hiked a few miles to a sawmill, where we ate at the mill ranch—'ranch' in North Queensland means cookhouse.

Hence **rancher** *n.*

1967 F. HARDY *Billy Borker yarns Again* 70 Ah, not real ranchers. In North Queensland a rancher is a bloke who runs a sort of boarding house out in the bush, near some big job.

range, *n.* [Spec. use of *range* line or series of mountains: see OED(S *sb.*[1] 2 c.]

1. Chiefly in *pl.* Hilly or mountainous country, not necessarily forming a single divide. Also *attrib.* in sing.

1805 *HRA* (1915) 1st Ser. V. 580 Those Cow tracks sometimes branch off to the most inaccessible parts of the Hills. The Range and Summits of which appear to be the general Resort of the Cattle. **1890** 'MRS A. MACLEOD' *Austral. Girl* 108 One day . . she discovered a whole range-side of early epacris.

2. a. In the phr. **over the range(s),** on the other side of a tract of mountainous country.

1864 'E.S.H.' *Narr. Trip Sydney to Peak Downs* 8 We proceeded to what is called 'over the ranges', on a good sound road. **1940** E. HILL *Great Austral. Loneliness* (ed. 2) 88 Kimberley is a country of wanderers, stockmen and 'ringers', swaggies . . men 'out dogging' in the wilderness. 'Over the ranges', the rugged King Leopolds to the north, lies a magnificent coast.

b. [U.S.: see Mathews *n.* 4 b.] In the phr. **to go over the range,** to die.

1936 J.C. DOWNIE *Galloping Hoofs* 72 Of course a lot of them do go 'over the range', and are laid to rest in the great outback. **1942** *Frontier News* (Sydney) Sept. 4/2 The only set item is the reading of the list of those Old-timers who, since we last met, have gone on 'Over the Range'.

range, *v. Obs.* [Spec. use of *range* to rove.]

a. *intr.* To live in the bush in the manner of an outlaw: see BUSHRANGER 1.

1805 *Sydney Gaz.* 24 Nov., *Desmond* . . is again a fugitive from the settlement of King's Town and ranges about the skirts of these settlements. **1829** *Sydney Monitor* 1 Aug., Several bushrangers are reported as ranging about Botany Bay.

b. *trans.* In the phr. **to range the bush**.

1834 J. MUDIE *Vindication* p. vii, He was, for absconding and ranging the bush several weeks without means of subsistence (except by pilfering or robbing on the road to Sydney . .) sent twelve months to an ironed-gang. **1846** *Bell's Life in Sydney* 12 Sept. 1/3 Some miscreants by way of raising the wind without pawning, have been deriving a profit by ranging the bush.

ranger. BUSHRANGER 1.

1817 *HRA* (1921) 3rd Ser. II. 194 The party under Ensign

Mahon of the 46 had just before killed two and wounded a third of the Rangers. **1980** O. RUHEN *Bullock Teams* 86 A few experiences with bushrangers had taught him to be careful of the way he carried money... Usually, however, the 'rangers did not rib the teamsters.

rangie: see NARANGY.

rangy, *a*. [f. RANGE *n*. 1 + *-y*.] Hilly, mountainous.
1861 *Burke & Wills Exploring Exped.* 2 Between the tropics and Carpentaria a considerable portion is rangy. **1909** E. WALTHAM *Life & Labour in Aust.* 64 We were now rapidly approaching the 'Rangy' or hilly district.

rank duffer. *Obs.* A complete failure (orig. of a gold mine): see DUFFER *n*. 2.
1873 W. THOMSON-GREGG *Desperate Character* II. 177 Their neighbours, outside, bottomed a rank 'duffer' at sixty-four feet. **1913** W.K. HARRIS *Outback in Aust.* 167 The wild rush to Port Curtis, in Queensland, took place in 1857, and proved a rank duffer.

rap, *n*. Also **wrap**. [See next.] A boost; a commendation. Also **rap up**.
1939 K. TENNANT *Foveaux* 176 Everyone wants to be seen with a high-up feller. When I pass the time of day to a cove he feels that's a rap for him, see? **1978** H.C. BAKER *I was Listening* 170 One verse gave the nursing sisters from Baggot a good rap-up. **1980** A. HOPGOOD *And here comes Bucknuckle* 58 You had to put your money where your mouth was. I've never heard anybody give a horse a wrap like the one you gave Bucknuckle after that first race at Manangatang.

rap, *v*. Also **wrap**. [Prob. transf. use of Br. dial. *rap* to boast: see EDD *v.*[1] 11.] *trans*. To praise (exaggeratedly). Freq. with **up**.
1957 D. NILAND *Call me when Cross turns Over* 138 'You dream and feel hopeless, I don't.' 'Rapping yourself up a bit, aren't you?' **1967** *Kings Cross Whisper* (Sydney) xliii. 11/3 To praise a person is to give him a wrap. If you can't wrap a bloke don't roast him.

rapt: see WRAPPED.

raspberry jam. [See quot. 1872.] The shrub or small tree of s.w. W.A. *Acacia acuminata* (fam. Mimosaceae), yielding a fragrant, durable timber; the wood of the plant; JAM *n.*[1] Also **raspberry jam tree** (or **wood**).
1833 *Perth Gaz.* 10 May 283 The acacia, called from the smell of the wood, raspberry-jam tree. **1837** *Ibid.* 11 Nov. 1004, 4 logs (5 cwt.) raspberry-jam wood. **1872** MRS E. MILLETT *Austral. Parsonage* 49 An acacia of that kind familiarly named the 'raspberry jam', because the perfume of the wood when freshly cut resembles that of the preserve.

rat, *n*.
1. a. In the phr. **to get** (or **have**) **a rat** (or **rats**), to be eccentric, disturbed, or deranged; also **to give** (someone) **a rat**, to cause derangement.
1898 G.T. BELL *Coolgardie* 51 They get fat fees for their reports, but oft times they get rats, When the ten-ounce reef a duffer proves and the mines are called 'wild cats'. **1899** *Truth* (Sydney) 23 July 3/5 The solitude of the bush is giving him rats. **1911** V. DESMOND *Awful Austral.* 75 The Australian bushman has, what is generally known as a 'rat'; in fact, the lunacy of Australia is most alarming.
b. In the phr. **in the rats,** in a state of derangement, esp. as a result of excessive consumption of alcoholic liquor.
[N.Z. **1921** LORD 'Stunology' in *Ballads of Bung* (1976), We say a man is.. A 'ribald reveller', 'on the rag', or mayhap 'in the rats'.] **1937** W. HATFIELD *I find Aust.* 138 A brumby-runner .. was 'in the rats' after a prolonged boozing spell. **1957** D. NILAND *Call me when Cross turns Over* 116 Your own brother is half in the rats with worry and anxiety. Unless something's done he'll end up in the giggle-house.
2. RATTER.
1921 K.S. PRICHARD *Black Opal* 34 Rats, the men who sneaked into other men's mines when they were on good stuff, and took out their opal during the night, were never Ridge men.
3. In the phr. **like a rat up a drainpipe**, very quickly, 'quick as a flash'.
1962 C. ROHAN *Delinquents* 76 He'd be up you like a rat up a drainpipe, given the chance. **1981** P. BARTON *Bastards I have Known* 4 Old Bert lived just up the road and I took to him like a 'rat up a drainpipe'.
4. Special Comb. **rat-house,** a psychiatric hospital.
1900 J. BRADSHAW *Highway Robbery under Arms* (*c* 1927) 120 The doctor certified him to be a madman. Bertrand then got packed off to the rat-house.

rat, *v. trans*. To loot; to rob (a person, claim, etc.); to steal (money, etc.). Also as *vbl. n.* and *ppl. a.*
1898 *Bulletin* (Sydney) 17 Dec. 15/2 Ratted or robbed is meant by *raddled*. **1921** K.S. PRICHARD *Black Opal* 47 There had been ratting epidemics on the Ridge before; but robbery of a mate by a mate had never occurred before. **1980** S. THORNE *I've met some Bloody Wags* 73 Occasionally a specker is lucky, but a lot of stones sold as 'specked' opal are in reality 'ratted' opal.

ratbag. A trouble-maker, a rogue; an eccentric; a person to whom some opprobrium attaches. Also *attrib.*
1890 *Quiz* (Adelaide) 1 Aug. 2/2 The Imperial ratbag amongst us brings these insults upon us. **1986** *Canberra Times* 15 Feb. 2/4 A self-opinionated mediocrity .. this guru of the ratbag right.
Hence **ratbaggery** *n.*
1943 S.J. BAKER *Pop. Dict. Austral. Slang* (ed. 3) 64 *Ratbag*, an unpleasantly disposed or vicious person: a term of contempt, though not always offensive. Whence, 'ratbaggery'

ration, *n*. Freq. in *pl.* [Transf. use of *ration* the daily amount of certain articles of food allotted to military personnel: see OED(S 3 a.]
1. a. An allowance of provisions made to a hand on a rural property as a condition of employment. Also *attrib.*
1843 *Sydney Morning Herald* 6 Oct. 3/7 Wanted some shepherds. Wages, £15, and a good ration. **1959** *Bulletin* (Sydney) 1 July 18/2 Station ration-scales, as authorised by the Central Queensland Pastoral Employers' Association in 1893 .. included: Flour 8 lb.; tea, 6 oz.; sugar, 3lb.; meat, 20 lb.; salt, ½ lb.; soda, 2 oz. **1960** *N.T. News* (Darwin) 22 Jan. 6/4 Visitors to Borroloola recently were old-timer Jack Shadforth and Arthur Alpin, both of whom were in for rations.
b. A gift of food made to an itinerant.
1879 S.W. SILVER *Austral. Graziers' Guide* 41 The labourer generally arrives at the station store about sundown, with a request for 'a little ration' (always supplied gratis) and a rather languid inquiry as to whether 'there's any work goin''. **1974** W.G. HOWCROFT *Sand in Stew* 2 Some sundowners acquired a sinister reputation for allegedly using veiled threats of 'letting the red steer loose' to station owners who refused them rations.
c. An allowance of provisions (but see also quot. 1913) made to a member of an Aboriginal community or group by a government or religious body.
1884 *V & P* (N.S.W. L.A.) XI. 943 Gresford—Clothing and rations supplied to old and infirm aborigines. **1913** W.K. HARRIS *Outback in Aust.* 115 A patronising Government doles out rations and blankets to those who have been in the settlement the longest.
d. With distinguishing epithet, as **dry, govern-**

ment, station, track, travelling, etc.: see under first element.

2. Special Comb. **ration bag,** a bag used by the recipient of a ration; **carrier,** one employed on a rural property to deliver rations to out-stations; **cart,** a cart used for the conveyance of rations; **day,** the day appointed for the issue of rations to employees on a rural property; **dray,** *ration cart;* **hut,** the provision-store on a rural property; **man,** *ration carrier;* **sheep,** a sheep killed for immediate consumption, esp. as part of an allowance; **sugar,** an inferior grade of sugar issued as rations; **tea,** an inferior grade of tea issued as rations.

1849 A. HARRIS *Emigrant Family* (1967) 198 Carrying up their **ration bags** to the farm-store. 1868 C.W. BROWNE *Overlanding in Aust.* 59 Such is his daily routine varied by the visit of the **ration-carrier** once a week. 1849 A. HARRIS *Emigrant Family* (1967) 41 Willoughby .. was seen conveying three ladies in the little green **ration-cart** towards the Rocky Springs. 1849 A. HARRIS *Emigrant Family* (1967) 198 The hands found **ration-day** again come round, and no supply. 1859 H. KINGSLEY *Recoll. Geoffrey Hamlyn* II. 163 Send him down on the **ration dray.** 1896 *Bulletin* (Sydney) 11 Jan. 18/1 Mrs Mitchins and the kids amid the general fray Got access to the **ration-hut** and took the 'junk' away. 1900 *Ibid.* 29 Dec. 14/1 Old Andy, a boundary-rider, was much-valued by the boss, who, whenever the drink-crave attacked the old chap, would send him by the **ration-man** a couple of bottles of brandy. 1872 G.S. BADEN-POWELL *New Homes for Old Country* 156 Meat has to go out twice a week, unless the system of '**ration sheep**' be in vogue. Then each shepherd will have in his flock, sheep which he is allowed to kill. 1873 J.C.F. JOHNSON *Christmas on Carringa* 1 Jam ingeniously concocted of brown **ration sugar** and water. 1878 E. BRADDON *Lett. to India from Tas.* (1980) 88, I quite wonder why anybody goes through the farce of buying **ration tea** for these sons of toil. It would answer just as well to go into the bush and pick a teapotful from the bushes there.

ration, *v.* [Used elsewhere but recorded earliest in Aust.: see OED *v.* 1.] *trans.* To supply (a person) with an allowance of provisions. Also as *ppl. a.*

1834 BURNS & SKEMP *Van Dieman's Land Correspondents* 10 May (1961) 33 Assist me by the loan of three labourers for about two months rationed by the Government. 1950 V.F. TURNER *Ooldea* 8 The Aborigines' Board received the proposal to open the Station with sympathy, and eventually removed the ration depot from Tarcoola to Ooldea, Miss Lock becoming the rationing officer.

rat-kangaroo. *Kangaroo-rat* (a), see KANGAROO *n.* 5.

1896 B. SPENCER *Rep. Horn Sci. Exped. Central Aust.* I. 28 On the Porcupine sandhills the Rat-kangaroos (*Bettongia lesueuri*) are constantly dodging in and out amongst the tussocks. 1983 R. STRAHAN *Compl. Bk. Austral. Mammals* 177 Referred to in the past simply as 'rat-kangaroos', the Potoroidae is now seen to comprise three subgroups; potoroos, bettongs and the Musky Rat-kangaroo.

ratshit. Used allusively to denote insignificance, the lowest point or level; also as *adj.*, 'rock-bottom', and as a general term of opprobrium.

1970 *Kings Cross Whisper* (Sydney) lxxxiv. 5/4 Look at Ample's plan to drill the Barrier Reef to rat-shit in our greed to get our grubby hands on more oil. 1980 F. MOOR-HOUSE *Days of Wine & Rage* 421 In 1970 I thought that various things would happen, that, spectacularly, didn't, but now I have a much better idea of why they should and a much improved estimation of their chances (ratshit).

ratter. [f. RAT *v.*] One who steals, esp. opal from another's mine.

1932 I.L. IDRIESS *Prospecting for Gold* 239 Ratters are men, a gang as a rule, who work your opal out for you while you sleep. 1980 S. THORNE *I've met some Bloody Wags* 73 The miners usually deal with ratters (people who steal opals from someone else's claim) themselves.

rattlepod. [U.S.: see Mathews *rattle, n.* 5.] Any of many herbs or shrubs of the genus *Crotalaria* (fam. Fabaceae) of central and n. Aust. and elsewhere.

1935 DAVISON & NICHOLLS *Blue Coast Caravan* 268 Rattle-pod, a shrub that lived up to its name .. when its branches were shaken. 1981 J.A. BAINES *Austral. Plant Genera* 108 *Crotalaria* .. Gk. krotalon, a rattle or clapper; because the seeds rattle in the inflated pods, hence the common name rattlepods.

ratty, *a.* [f. RAT *n.* 1 + *-y.*]

a. Mad, deranged.

1895 *Worker* (Sydney) 5 Jan. 1/5, I suppose its the heat that makes all of us a bit ratty at times. *Ibid.* 14 Dec. 3/3 Further, that persons like myself are 'ratty' who think otherwise. 1973 C.E. GOODE *Stories Strange Places* 80 The bush life may have been making him a bit 'ratty' like several others in the neighbourhood. The incendiarist patiently waited for the next harvest.

b. In the phr. **to be ratty over (on, about),** to be infatuated with.

1900 *Western Champion* (Barcaldine) 24 Apr. 11/1 The girls are real 'ratty' on anyone in dungarees. You cannot shake them off. 1923 *Aussie* (Sydney) July 20/3 He can't sleep for lovin' you... It's the truth. He's fair ratty over you. 1932 *Listening Post* (Perth) Aug. 4 But you needn't have kept on praising [the girl] you are ratty about.

raven. [Transf. use of *raven* the large black bird *Corvus corax.*] Any of three large, glossy black birds of the genus *Corvus, C. coronoides* of e. and s.w. mainland Aust., *C. mellori* of s.e. mainland Aust., and *C. tasmanicus* of Tas., southernmost Aust., and n.e. N.S.W. See also CROW $n.^1$ 1.

1805 J.H. TUCKEY *Acct. Voyage to establish Colony Port Phillip* 163 The land birds are eagles, crows, ravens. 1903 *Emu* II. 205 *Corone australis* (Raven)—Parties of these birds frequently cross the Strait to and from Tasmania. 1978 B.P. MOORE *Life on Forty Acres* 98 'Crows' to the layman, or more correctly ravens, are .. ready to accept any titbit.

raw prawn: see PRAWN 1 b.

razoo /ra'zu/. Also **rahzoo.** [Of unknown origin.] A (non-existent) coin of trivial value, a 'jot' or 'tittle'. Also in the phr. **brass razoo.** Used in negative contexts only.

1919 C. DREW *Doings of Dave* 28 'Did you have any bank to kick off with?' 'Not a razoo.' 1932 W. HATFIELD *Ginger Murdoch* 35 Ginger had not a rahzoo. 1982 R. HALL *Just Relations* 487 For all their pestering they never got a brass razoo.

razor-back. [The name of a steep ridge south of Sydney; now also used elsewhere.] A narrow, steep-sided ridge of land. Also as *adj.*

1901 F.J. GILLEN *Diary* 19 Apr. (1968) 41 Had a pleasant drive for 14 miles over undulating country with razor back hills of desert sandstone scattered here and there. 1979 J. WILLIAMS *White River* 40 You didn't know the half of it till you were cornered in these barren razor-backs, working for nothing till you paid off your air-fare.

razor gang. [Transf. use of Br. Railway slang *razor gang* 'economy men from Headquarters': see OEDS *razor* 3 c.] A parliamentary committee established to examine ways of reducing public expenditure: see quot. 1981. Also *attrib.*

1981 *Bulletin* (Sydney) 5 May 20/1 Canberra reports said that Sir Phillip Lynch's 'Razor Gang' had recommended an overall staff cut in the Federal public service of 2 percent. **1985** *Good Weekend* (Sydney) 5 Oct. 5/3 The Government, in the midst of the infamous razor-gang cost cuts, agreed to fund and complete the building's shell.

Hence **razor ganging** *vbl. n.*

1986 *Canberra Times* 9 Feb. 2/4 A long season of razor-ganging has made the problem much worse. The Canberra bus fleet is getting old and .. has not been replaced at anything like the rate it needs.

razor-grinder. [Transf. use of *razor-grinder* one who grinds or sharpens razors.] RESTLESS FLYCATCHER.

1822 B. FIELD in G. Mackaness *Fourteen Journeys Blue Mountains* 9 Oct. (1950) ii. 42 The notes of the birds of New Holland are rather cries than songs. . . Some are harsh and vulgar, like those of the .. razor grinder. **1911** A. MACK *Bush Days* 13 A razor-grinder stopped a few minutes on the fence, and, instead of his usual harsh scold, uttered a few, soft tender notes.

read, *v.* In the phr. **you wouldn't read about it (in Pix):** an exclamation used to express incredulity and chagrin.

1950 J. CLEARY *Just let me Be* 135 Everything I backed ran like a no-hoper. Four certs I had, and the bludgers were so far back the ambulance had to bring 'em home. You wouldn't read about it. **1981** P. BARTON *Bastards I have Known* 127 Mathematical genii, or is it genius's? I dunno; you wouldn't read about this language of ours.

reap-hook. *Obs.* (except in place-names). Used *attrib.* to describe a hill resembling a reap-hook in shape: see quot. 1863.

1860 J.M. STUART *Explorations in Aust.* 17 Apr. (1865) 160 There are three reap-hook hills about three miles west. **1863** J.B. AUSTIN *Mines S.A.* 43, I must not omit to mention the remarkable form assumed by many of the hills in the North, and hence called 'reap-hook ranges'; one side rises abruptly and culminates, generally, in a knob of rocks, while the other side slopes away gradually in a graceful concave form, very much the shape of a sickle.

receiving yard. The enclosure in a stock yard into which mustered sheep or cattle are first driven.

1848 H.W. HAYGARTH *Recoll. Bush Life* 68 A cattle enclosure is usually subdivided into five yards: two of them facing the entrance are large, the three others are smaller; the former are known as 'receiving', and the latter as 'draughting' yards, all of which communicate with one another. **1960** M. HENRY *Unlucky Dip* 25 They all looked across the receiving-yard to the iron side, roof and supports of the dip.

recovery. In the phr. **to suffer a recovery,** to be afflicted with a hangover.

1885 *Australasian Printers' Keepsake* 72 He had indeed the appearance of one 'suffering a recovery'. **1941** S.J. BAKER *Pop. Dict. Austral. Slang* 74 *Suffer a recovery*, to recover from a drinking bout.

recruiting, *vbl. n. Obs.* [Transf. use of *recruiting* the raising of an army.] BLACKBIRDING. Also *attrib.*

1892 *Truth* (Sydney) 5 June 4/4 There is every reason to believe the 'recruiting' for Queensland plantations will develop into simple slave-trading. **1911** E.J. BRADY *King's Caravan* 275 He had been in the recruiting trade. As he whisked me from one place of refreshment to another, he poured out stories of blackbirding in the South Seas.

red, *n.* Red kangaroo (a), see RED *a.* 1 b.

1896 *Western Champion* (Barcaldine) 25 Aug. 3/4 Starting now to cross the long-furred reds with the blue flyers. You should see the joeys—big and strong as young lions. **1973** V. SERVENTY *Desert Walkabout* 60 The 'red' is the kangaroo of the inland plains, being found everywhere in Australia or in every Australian mainland State.

red, *a.*

1. a. Used as a distinguishing epithet in the names of plants: **red almond,** either of the trees *Alphitonia excelsa* and *A. petriei* (see *red ash*); **ash,** any of several trees, esp. *Alphitonia excelsa* (fam. Rhamnaceae) of N.S.W., Qld., W.A., and N.T., and the related *A. petriei* of N.S.W. and Qld.; the wood of the tree; see also *red almond,* SOAP TREE; **bean,** any of several trees, esp. the large *Dysoxylum muelleri* (fam. Meliaceae) of n.e. N.S.W. and e. Qld., yielding a deep red timber; the wood of the tree; see also TURNIPWOOD; **bloodwood,** the tree *Eucalyptus gummifera* (fam. Myrtaceae) of s.e. mainland Aust., yielding a durable red timber; the similar *E. intermedia* of n.e. mainland Aust.; the wood of the tree; **box,** any of several trees yielding a reddish timber, esp. *Eucalyptus polyanthemos* (fam. Myrtaceae) of s.e. mainland Aust.; the wood of the tree; also *attrib.*; **cedar,** the tree *Toona australis* (see CEDAR 1); the wood of the tree; *native cedar,* see NATIVE *a.* 6 a.; **-flowering gum,** see FLOWERING GUM; **grass,** any of several grasses, esp. *red leg grass*; **heart,** either of two trees, the rainforest tree *Dissiliaria baloghioides* (fam. Euphorbiaceae) of Qld., having a hard, durable timber, and *Eucalyptus decipiens* (fam. Myrtaceae) of s.w. W.A.; the wood of the tree; **honeysuckle,** the tree or shrub *Banksia serrata* (fam. Proteaceae) of near-coastal s. Qld., N.S.W., Vic., and n.w. Tas.; the wood of the tree; **ironbark,** any of several IRONBARK trees, esp. *Eucalyptus sideroxylon* (also known as MUGGA) of Vic., N.S.W., and s. Qld., having a deeply furrowed dark bark which is red under the surface, and yielding a tough, durable, red timber; **leg grass,** any of several grasses of the genus *Bothriochloa* (fam. Poaceae) esp. *B. macra* of e. mainland Aust., usu. having red to purple stems; *red grass;* **mahogany,** any of several trees of the genus *Eucalyptus* (fam. Myrtaceae) yielding a red timber, esp. the rough-barked *E. resinifera* and *E. pellita* occurring on sandy near-coastal soils in N.S.W. and Qld.; the durable wood of the tree; see also JIMMY LOW; **mallee,** any of several mallee eucalypts of drier s. Aust. having red branchlets or other parts, as *Eucalyptus oleosa* and *E. calycogona* (fam. Myrtaceae); **mangrove,** any of several trees, chiefly of the fam. Rhizophoraceae, as *Rhizophora stylosa* of n. Aust. and elsewhere in the tropics; **mulga,** MINNERICHI; **myrtle,** any of several trees, esp. *Syzygium australe* (see *brush cherry* BRUSH n.[1] B. 2); the wood of the tree; **pine,** a tree having a reddish wood, esp. *Callitris endlicheri* (fam. Cupressaceae) of e. mainland Aust.; the wood of this tree; **river gum,** the tree *Eucalyptus camaldulensis* (see RED GUM 1); the wood of this tree; **stringybark,** any of several rough-barked trees of the genus *Eucalyptus* (fam. Myrtaceae), esp. *E. macrorhyncha* of s.e. mainland Aust.; the wood of the tree; also **red stringy.**

1948 P.J. Hurley *Red Cedar* 158 In the Forestry Offices some of our treasures in timber are displayed. . . Polished **red almond** (*Alphitonia*) adorned the walls. **1889** J.H. MAIDEN *Useful Native Plants Aust.* 373 *Alphitonia excelsa* .. variously called 'Mountain Ash', '**Red Ash**', [etc.] . . . Wood near the outside somewhat pinkish, the inner wood dark-brown, or parti-coloured. **1981** A.B. & J.W. CRIBB *Useful Wild Plants Aust.* 106 Red ash is a common tree in both rainforests and eucalypt forests. **1895** *Agric. Gaz. N.S.W.* V. 1 Because of the dark colour of the wood, and partly by way of distinction from the **red bean,** it is usually known by timber merchants as black bean. **1907** J.H. MAIDEN *Forest Flora N.S.W.* II. 28 The wood loses considerably more weight than the **Red Bloodwood** as it seasons. **1878** R.B. SMYTH *Aborigines of Vic.* II. 160 **Red-box**—Teering. **1928** M.E. FULLERTON *Austral. Bush* 108 Red-box and yellow-box honey are among the best. **1818** J. OXLEY *Jrnls. Two Exped. N.S.W.* 29 Sept. (1820) 317 In this brush was a quantity of fine **red cedar** trees. **1980** B. SCOTT *Darkness under Hills* 45 Downstream was a tall stand of black bean trees, red cedar and lemon gums. **1886** *N.T. Times Almanac*

6 Flinders or **red grass**. **1911** *Bulletin* (Sydney) 28 Sept. 13/4 Nobody has nominated **red-heart**, a timber which frequents the coastal scrubs of Queensland, for the hardest wood championship. **1973** G.M. CHIPPENDALE *Eucalypts W. Austral. Goldfields* 93 Redheart is a spreading, twisted, gnarled tree up to 30 ft. (9 m.), or a mallee up to 15 ft. (4.5 m.) high. **1824** *Austral.* (Sydney) 21 Oct. 2 Red and white **honey-suckle** for boat timbers. **1880** *Proc. Linnean Soc.N.S.W.* V. 505 *E. crebra*, which is commonly known as the narrow-leaved or **Red Ironbark**, is a tree of considerable size, rising to 100 or 120 feet in height. **1923** E. BREAKWELL *Grasses & Fodder Plants N.S.W.* 202 **Red Leg grass** is fairly easily eradicated by cultivation. It is very sensitive to frosts, and is therefore best ploughed in the winter months. **1817** A. CUNNINGHAM in I. Marriott *Early Explorers Aust.* (1925) 176 *E. resinifera*; (**red mahogany**). **1882** *Proc. Linnean Soc. N.S.W.* VII. 625 The Red or Forest Mahogany **1855** J. BONWICK *Geogr. Aust. & N.Z.* (ed. 3) 202 The **red** or water **mallee**, from the cut rootlets of which water may be procured. **1880** J. BONWICK *Resources Qld.* 81 The **Red Mangrove** is proof against ant attack. **1896** B. SPENCER *Rep. Horn Sci. Exped. Central Aust.* I. 13 The lines of the watercourses are marked by belts of gum trees and acacias.. *Acacia cyperophylla*, the **red mulga**, a very local tree. **1889** J.H. MAIDEN *Useful Native Plants Aust.* 531 *Eugenia myrtifolia*.. called '**Red Myrtle**' in Southern New South Wales. **1803** *Sydney Gaz.* 9 Oct., And 72 **red pine** spars, from 28 to 33 feet in length. **1899** *Proc. Linnean Soc. N.S.W.* XXIV. 469 'Forest Red Gum' (*E[ucalyptus] tereticornis*) as compared with '**Red River Gum**' (*E. rostrata*). **1896** *Proc. Linnean Soc. N.S.W.* XXI. 447 *E. macrorrhyncha*.. '**Red Stringybark**'. This is considered the best stringybark in regard to durability of timber, and is highly prized. **1911** *Bulletin* (Sydney) 27 July 14/2 Ordinary 'stringy' takes fire easily enough, while red 'stringy'.. does not.

b. In the names of animals: **red ant**, see *red meat ant*; **-bellied black (snake)**, the snake *Pseudechis porphyriacus* (see *black snake* BLACK *a.*² 1 b.); **bill**, any of several birds having a red bill, esp. *swamp hen* (see SWAMP *n.*), *pied oystercatcher* (see PIED), and formerly *red-browed finch*; **bream**, a young SNAPPER (see quot. 1906); **breast** *obs.*, ROBIN REDBREAST 1; also **red-breast(ed) robin** (or *warbler*); **-breasted babbler**, the bird *Pomatostomus temporalis rubeculus* of central and w. mainland Aust., the reddish-breasted form of the *grey-crowned babbler* (see GREY *a.*); formerly also **red-breasted pomatorhinus** (or **pomatostomus**); **-breasted cockatoo** *obs.*, GALAH 1; **-browed finch** (or **firetail**), the small bird *Neochmia temporalis* of e. Aust. and naturalized elsewhere, having predom. olive-green and grey plumage with scarlet rump, eyebrow, and sides of the bill; see also *red-head*; **-browed pardalote**, the small bird *Pardalotus rubricatus* of n. and central Aust., nesting in a tunnel which it excavates in sandy banks; formerly also *red-lored pardalote*; **-capped dotterel** (or **dottrel**), the wading bird *Charadrius ruficapillus* of all States and elsewhere, having predom. grey-brown and white plumage with a rufous crown; *sand lark*, see SAND; also **red-capped plover**; **-capped parrot** (or **parakeet**), the red-crowned parrot of s.w. W.A. *Purpureicephalus spurius*, having green, blue, yellow, and red plumage, and occurring in eucalypt forests, where it feeds on marri; **-capped robin**, the small bird *Petroica goodenovii* of s. and central mainland Aust., esp. the drier inland; **-collared lorikeet** (or **parrot**), the brightly-coloured lorikeet *Trichoglossus rubritorquis* of forested country in n. W.A. and N.T., having a yellowish-orange collar on the nape; *blue bonnet* (b), see BLUE *a.*; **-crowned pigeon** (or **fruit-pigeon**), the predom. green and grey bird *Ptilinopus regina* of n. and n.e. Aust., and elsewhere, having a reddish crown; **-eared finch** (or **firetail**), a red-eared bird, usu. the small bird *Stagonopleura oculata* of s.w. W.A., having a scarlet bill and earpatch; **emperor**, the red and white marine fish *Lutjanus sebae* of n. Aust.; *government bream*, see GOVERNMENT B. 4; see also EMPEROR; **fish**, **(a)** any of several holothurians, esp. *Actinopyga echinitis* and *A. mauritiana* of n. Aust. and elsewhere; **(b)** (usu. as **redfish**) any of several fish, esp. NANNYGAI; **-footed booby** (or **gannet**), the brown or black and white,oceanic bird *Sula sula* of islands in n. Aust., and elsewhere in the tropics; formerly also **red-legged gannet**; **fruit bat**, the reddish, nomadic bat *Pteropus scapulatus* of e., n., and n.w. Aust.; **gurnard** (or **gurnet**), any of several fish, esp. the usu. reddish, marine *Chelidonichthys kumu* of all States and elsewhere; **-head**, a bird having red head markings, esp. *red-browed finch*; **-headed honeyeater**, the honeyeater *Myzomela erythrocephala* of n. Aust. and elsewhere, the mature male having a glossy red head; see also *blood-bird* BLOOD; also *ellipt.* as **red head**; **kangaroo, (a)** the large kangaroo *Macropus rufus*, widely distributed in drier inland Aust., having red to blue-grey fur above and white below; MARLOO; RED *n.*; also **red plain kangaroo** (or **'roo**), **red 'roo**; **(b)** any of several other rufous macropods, esp. (*N.T.*) the wallaroo *Macropus antilopinus*; **-kneed dotterel** (or **dottrel**), the widespread *Erythrogonys cinctus* of Aust. and s. New Guinea, a black, brown, and white bird having greyish legs with red around the knees; **-lored pardalote** *obs.*, *red-browed pardalote*; **lory (lowrie, lowry)**, *crimson rosella*, see CRIMSON; **meat ant**, *meat ant* (a) (see MEAT), esp. the red *Iridomyrmex sanguineus* of n. Aust.; **morwong**, the marine fish *Cheilodactylus fuscus* of N.S.W. and s. Qld.; **-necked avocet**, the bird *Recurvirostra novaehollandiae* of mainland Aust., having a bright chestnut head and neck, and black and white body; **-necked stint**, the migratory wading bird *Calidris ruficollis*, occurring in all States from spring to autumn; **-necked wallaby**, the wallaby *Macropus rufogriseus* of e. and s.e. Aust. incl. Tas.; see also BENNETT'S WALLABY; **rock cod, (a)** the reddish marine fish *Scorpaena ergastulorum* (fam. Scorpaenidae) of e. Aust. incl. Tas.; **(b)** any of several other, usu. related, fish; **-rump(ed) parrot (parakeet, paroquet)**, the predom. green parrot *Psephotus haematonotus* of s.e. mainland Aust.; *red-backed parrot*, see RED-BACKED; **-shouldered parakeet** (or **paroquet**) *obs.*, SWIFT PARROT; **soldier (ant)** *obs.*, *soldier ant*, see SOLDIER *n.* 1; **-tailed black cockatoo**, the predom. black cockatoo *Calyptorhynchus banksii* of mainland Aust., the mature male having a bright red band on the tail; *western black cockatoo*, see WESTERN; see also BANKSIAN COCKATOO; also **red-tailed cockatoo**; **throat**, the small, predom. greyish-brown bird *Sericornis brunneus* of drier s. and central mainland Aust., the mature male having a rufous throat patch; **-tipped pardalote**, the small bird *Pardalotus striatus ornatus*, a form of the STRIATED PARDALOTE; **wattle bird**, the large, common honeyeater *Anthochaera carunculata* of s. mainland Aust., a brown and white streaked bird having reddish facial wattles; **-winged parrot (or lory)**, the predom. green parrot *Aprosmictus erythropterus* of n. and n.e. Aust., the mature male having a crimson patch on the wing; *crimson-winged parrot*, see CRIMSON; **-winged wren**, the small bird *Malurus elegans* of s.w. W.A.

1936 *Bulletin* (Sydney) 1 Apr. 20/2 While snake yarns grow taller and fewer laborers use the wrigglers as bowyangs, there *are* a few genuine close shaves. A **redbellied black** went up with the last sheaf of hay aboard the dray. **1985** P. CAREY *Illywhacker* 301 A jut-jawed child in short pants, playing with a red-bellied black snake, cooing to it on the floor. **1799** D. COLLINS *Acct. Eng. Colony N.S.W.* (1802) II. 146 There were a few ducks, teal.. and a bird named from its bill the **Red-bill**, upon the lagoons. **1982** N. KEESING *Lily on Dustbin* 99 It was commonly said of him that 'he fed his family on cracked corn and redbill soup', the redbill being a native swamp hen, common in that region but regarded as virtually useless tucker. **1857** J. ASKEW *Voyage Aust. & N.Z.* 228 The harbour abounds with fish, of which the.. black and **red bream** and the yellowtail, are used for food. **1906** D.G. STEAD *Fishes of Aust.* 126 Beyond the 'Cockney' stage and up to a weight of about a pound and a half, the Snapper is known as Red Bream. **1804** G. CALEY in A.E.J. Andrews *Devil's Wilderness* (1984) 66 Saw .. 2 small **red breasts**, with black and white heads. **1813** J.W. LEWIN *Birds N.S.W.* 5 Red Breast Warbler .. inhabits Forests Frequents low trees. **1878** R.B. SMYTH *Aborigines of Vic.* I. 225 The animal and vegetable food of the people of the Dieyerie tribe (Cooper's Creek) is, according to Mr Samuel Gason, as follows .. *Choonda*—Red-breasted robin. **1844** [**red-breasted babbler**] J. GOULD *Birds of Aust.* (1848) IV. Pl. 21, *Pomatorhinus rubeculus* .. Redbreasted Pomatorhinus. **1896** B. SPENCER *Rep. Horn Sci. Exped. Central Aust.* II. 91 Red-breasted pomatostomus .. are extremely sociable... Their habit of mewing like a cat has gained for them the local cognomen of 'cat-birds'. **1900** A.J. CAMPBELL *Nests & Eggs Austral. Birds* 274 Red-Breasted Babbler... This bird is numerously dispersed over the northern parts of Australia. **1845** L. LEICHHARDT *Jrnl. Overland Exped. Aust.* 29 Aug. (1847) 380 We .. came to a plentiful supply of water, which was indicated .. by the call of the **red-breasted cockatoos**, noticed a few days since; but which was probably only a variety of the common species. **1898** E.E. MORRIS *Austral Eng.* 145 **Red-browed F[inch]**—*Aegintha temporalis*. **1903** *Emu* II. 164 Red-browed Finch . . in immense numbers on all the creeks in the Otway. **1945** C. BARRETT *Austral. Bird Life* 206 While the beautiful firetail is a rare bird around Sydney and Melbourne, the red-browed firetail .. is fairly common in the neighbourhood of those cities. **1898** E.E. MORRIS *Austral Eng.* 340 **Red-browed P[ardalote]**—*P[ardalotus] rubricatus*. **1846** J. GOULD *Birds of Aust.* (1848) VI. Pl. 17, The **Red-capped Dottrel** is universally dispersed over every part of the sea-shores of Australia that I have visited. **1976** *Reader's Digest Compl. Bk. Austral. Birds* 176 A friendly and attractive small wader, the red-capped dotterel is common over much of its range. **1984** M. BLAKERS et al. *Atlas Austral. Birds* 159 The Red-capped Plover lives on sand or shingle beaches along the coast or inland waters. **1845** [**red-capped parrot**] J. GOULD *Birds of Aust.* (1848) V. Pl. 32, *Platycercus pileatus*... The Red-capped parrakeet is an inhabitant of Western Australia. **1972** B. FULLER *West of Bight* 5 'What about birds? Any unique to the southwest?'.. 'Yeah. We've got some. Like the Red-capped Parrot.' **1842** J. GOULD *Birds of Aust.* (1848) III. Pl. 5, *Petroica goodenovii* .. **Red-capped Robin** of the Colonists. **1842** J. GOULD *Birds of Aust.* (1848) V. Pl. 49, *Trichoglossus rubritorquis* .. **Red-collared lorikeet**. **1984** M. BLAKERS et al. *Atlas Austral. Birds* 253 The Red-collared is one of the commonest parrots in the Top End. **1898** [**red-crowned pigeon**] E.E. MORRIS *Austral Eng.* 156 Red-crowned F[ruit]-P[igeon]—*P[tilinopus] swainsonii*. **1981** PUGH & RITCHIE *Guide to Rainforests N.S.W.* 15 A good area for fruit pigeons with many Red-crowned Pigeons coming here to feed. **1845** J. GOULD *Birds of Aust.* (1848) III. Pl. 79, *Estrelda oculea*. **Red-eared Finch**. **1976** *Reader's Digest Compl. Bk. Austral. Birds* 530 The shy and beautiful red-eared firetail is the most solitary of all Australian grass finches. **1936** T.C. ROUGHLEY *Wonders Great Barrier Reef* 9 Some fish from the reef .. **red emperor** and coral trout. We like the name 'red emperor' and .. find ourselves repeating our order for its white, flaky flesh is delicious. (a) **1880** *Proc. Linnean Soc. N.S.W.* V. 128 He enumerates four, viz. *Trepang edulis, T. ananas, T. impatiens*, and *T. peruviana*. The first of these is certainly found on the reefs, and is called by the fishermen '**red fish**'. It is an elongated oval, somewhat shapeless mass of dull, reddish-brown color. (b) **1944** J. DEVANNY *By Tropic Sea & Jungle* 5 The weedfish—other names for him are **redfish** .. and pigfish—likes deep water and bites mostly at night. **1846** [**red-footed booby**] J. GOULD *Birds of Aust.* (1848) VII. Pl. 79, The Red-legged Gannet is very abundant along the northern shores of the Australian continent. **1945** C. BARRETT *Austral. Bird Life* 96 The red footed species (*S[ula] sula*), and the masked gannet .. are tropical birds which nest on islands off the coast. **1965** *Austral. Encycl.* IV. 239 The smallest species [of gannet] is the red-footed booby, which is the only gannet that nests off the ground. **1965** *Austral. Encycl.* I. 458 Another much smaller species, which also migrates south to the Victorian border, is the little **red fruit-bat** (*P[teropus] scapulatus*). It is more exclusively a blossom feeder. **1873** [**red gurnard**] F. DE CASTELNAU *Edible Fishes Vic.* 9 The red gurnet (*Upeneichthys porosus*) .. is highly considered as a table fish, and is also remarkable for its beautiful carmine hues, and the pretty blue stripes of its head. **1978** N. COLEMAN *Austral. Fisherman's Fish Guide* 20 A brilliantly coloured fish when landed on the deck, the red gurnard is, like many other sea floor dwellers, able to change its colours to suit its surroundings. **1889** *Proc. Linnean Soc. N.S.W.* IV. 411 *Estrilda temporalis* .. called '**Red-head**'. **1965** *Austral. Encycl.* VI. 64 The spotted-sided finch .. and the red-browed finch or 'red-head' (*Aegintha temporalis*) are confined to eastern Australia. **1843** J. GOULD *Birds of Aust.* (1848) IV. Pl. 64, The **Red-headed Honey-eater** is so distinctly marked as almost to preclude the possibility of its being confounded with any known species of the genus. **1973** R. ROBINSON *Drift of Things* 32 In spite of belonging to the school's 'Gould League of Bird Lovers', many of the boys had shanghais with which they were expert in knocking 'Red 'eads' out of the branches as they fed on the flowers. **1793** W. TENCH *Compl. Acct. Settlement* 269 One of them we called the **red kangaroo**, from the colour of its fur, which is like that of a hare, and sometimes is mingled with a large portion of black; the natives call it Bàg-a-ray. **1952** R. ROBINSON *Legend & Dreaming* 38 When Koopoo, the red plainkangaroo, was travelling from Arnhem Land. **1962** MARSHALL & DRYSDALE *Journey among Men* 30 We saw the big red 'roos pause and prop. In turn they watched us curiously and with caution as we passed. **1974** D. STUART *Prince of my Country* 44 There are the red plain 'roos, bigger than the dark brown hill 'roos. **1903** *Emu* II. 212 **Red-kneed Dottrel** (*Erythrogonys cinctus*)—This smart-looking Dottrel is fairly common from December to May. **1945** C. BARRETT *Austral. Bird Life* 102 The red-kneed dotterel .. really is a wattled plover without the wattle. **1846** J. GOULD *Birds of Aust.* (1848) II. Pl. 36, *Pardalotus rubricatus* .. **Red-lored Pardalote**. **1861** [**red lory**] 'OLD BUSHMAN' *Bush Wanderings* 161 In certain places they are as common as the red lowry. **1902** *Emu* II. 17 The Red Lory (*Platycercus elegans*) are only found visiting the hills to the south. **1952** A.C.C. LOCK *Travels across Aust.* 174 A gorgeous red lowrie, or a crimson rosella, flashed its geranium-like plumage. **1834** [**red meat ant**] G. BENNETT *Wanderings N.S.W.* I. 114 Avoid making their dormitory upon the nest of the red ant, which cannot endure intrusion. **1981** *Ecos* xxviii. 26/1 The nest of a colony of red meat ants looks a careless affair, resembling a spill of gravel from a passing truck. **1882** J.E. TENISON-WOODS *Fish & Fisheries N.S.W.* 46 The **red Morwong** or Carp, *C[hilodactylus] fuscus* .. is of a uniform reddish colour. **1824** J. LATHAM *Gen. Hist. Birds* X. 40 **Red-necked avoset** [sic] .. inhabits the shores of the south of Asia, and is to be met with in various ornithological collections. **1934** H.G. LAMOND *Aviary on Plains* 141 They are sandpipers (**Red-necked stint**). **1894** R. LYDEKKER *Hand-Bk. Marsupialia & Monotremata* 26 **Red-necked Wallaby**. *Macropus ruficollis* .. general colour of upper parts greyish-fawn, with the back of the neck and rump bright rufous. **1880** *Proc. Linnean Soc. N.S.W.* V. 430 *Scorpaena cruenta* .. the '**Red Rock Cod**' .. Tasmania, Port Phillip, Port Jackson. **1975** *Bulletin* (Sydney) 9 Aug. 17/2 The *ling* (long, pinkish) and the *sea perch* (bright red, plump, sometimes called red rock cod) were magnificent in both taste and texture. [**1837 red-rumped parrot:** *Proc. Zool. Soc. London* V. 88 Mr Gould exhibited from his Australian collection of Birds two species of the genus *Platycercus* .. for one of these he proposed the specific name of *haematonotus*, from the red spot upon its rump.] **1849** C. STURT *Narr. Exped. Central Aust.* II. 39 App. *Red-rumped Parroquet* .. is a bird of the interior, and was found on the most distant creeks, amongst the gum-trees. **1896** B. SPENCER *Rep. Horn Sci. Exped. Central Aust.* II. 64 They were always in pairs, and were never seen in flocks like the Red-rumped Parrakeet (*P. haematonotus*). **1984** M. BLAKERS et al. *Atlas Austral. Birds* 280 The Red-Rumped Parrot has expanded its range towards the coast in the South-East Region. **1789** A. PHILLIP *Voyage to Botany Bay* 269 **Red-Shouldered Parrakeet**... This species inhabits New South Wales; and we believe it to be hitherto non-descript. **1790** J. WHITE *Jrnl. Voyage N.S.W.* 263 Red shouldered paroquet. *Psittacus discolor.* Long tailed Green Parrot, with the tail feathers ferruginous towards the base, the shoulders blood-red beneath. **1872** G.S. BADEN-POWELL *New Homes for Old Country* 272 In Australia, there are vast numbers of ants: one, a large red variety, nearly an inch in length .. goes by the name of the '**red soldier**'. **1889** G.T. BLAKERS *Useless Young Man?* (1986) 62 There are in Australia a great variety of ants... Another kind.. reach fully three-quarters of an inch in length; and .. from their colour and viciousness, are popularly called red soldier ants... They make a hill only a few inches high. **1836** J. BACKHOUSE *Narr. Visit Austral. Colonies* (1843) 434 **Red-tailed Black Cockatoos**, numerous Aborigines, and many plants of truly Australian features, prove we are still at the antipodes. **1969** J.M. FORSHAW *Austral. Parrots* 64 Red-tailed Cockatoos are impressive in captivity and will thrive if housed in spacious flight aviaries. **1896** B. SPENCER *Rep. Horn Sci. Exped. Central Aust.* II. 84 *Pyrrholaemus brunnea* .. **Red-throat** .. was first found amongst the scrub at Hermannburg [*sic*]. **1898** E.E. MORRIS *Austral Eng.* 340 **Red-tipped P[ardalote]**—*P[ardalotus] ornatus*. **1913** *Emu* XII. Suppl. 92 *Anthochaera carunculata* .. **Red Wattle-Bird** .. Range: S. Queensland, New South Wales, Victoria, S. and W. Australia. **1842** [**red-winged parrot**] J. GOULD *Birds of Aust.* (1848) V. Pl. 18, *Aprosmictus erythropterus*. Red-winged Lory .. Crimson-winged Parrot. **1984** M. BLAKERS et al. *Atlas Austral. Birds* 261 In northern Australia the Red-winged Parrot lives in eucalypt woodland and mangroves. **1898** E.E. MORRIS *Austral Eng.* 519 **Red-winged W[ren]**—*Malurus elegans*.

2. In special collocations: **red blanket**, see quot. 1926; **centre**, CENTRE 1 (so called because of the reddish colour of iron oxide in the soil and rocks); **country**, country with reddish soil; **hand**, an impression of a human hand made with red ochre, a freq. motif in Aboriginal rock-painting; **heart**, *red centre*; **ned**, red wine of inferior quality; **steer**, a destructive fire, esp. a bushfire; **terrors**, a dust storm.

1926 A. GILES *Exploring in 'Seventies* 127 Tinned meat in six-pound tins ('**red blanket**' we called it). The tins were painted red, without labels or description of contents. **1935** H.H. FINLAYSON *Red Centre* 22 The Luritja Country—the south-west portion of Central Australia and contiguous tracts in the adjoining States .. might well be known as the **Red Centre**. Sand, soil, and most of the rocks are a fiery cinnabar. **1910** C.E.W. BEAN *On Wool Track* 117 Almost every possible plant—grows when irrigated in the **red country** along the Darling. [**1803 red hand**: M. FLINDERS *Voyage to Terra Australis* 14 Jan. (1814) II. 188 In the steep sides of the chasms were deep holes or caverns, undermining the cliffs; upon the walls of which I found rude drawings, made with charcoal and something like red paint upon the white ground of the rock. These drawings represented porpoises, turtle, kanguroos, and a human hand.] **1852** W. HUGHES *Austral. Colonies* 100 Some strange and mysterious belief is associated with this figure of the 'red hand', and the natives are reluctant to communicate any information regarding it, except that it was made 'before white fellow came'. **1931** 'BRENT OF BIN BIN' *Back to Bool Bool* 45 The dawn was murky. Particles of the **red heart** of Australia had reached the pampered city, staining the arum lilies and irritating the housewives. **1941** S.J. BAKER *Pop. Dict. Austral. Slang* 59 **Red Ned**, cheap red wine. [**1930 red steer**: *Bulletin* (Sydney) 21 May 20/3 There had been a number of grass fires in the district, and suspicion falling on 'Monkey' Brown .. he was accused of loosing the 'red bull' on the community.] **1936** J. DEVANNY *Sugar Heaven* 100, I put 'red steer' in cane. That'll fix the bloody bosses. **1956** H. HUDSON *Flynn's Flying Doctor* 211 Broken Hill is a fine modern city, but until recently was subject to violent dust storms, known as **Red Terrors**, due to soil erosion caused by denuding the surrounding country.

red-back. [From the distinctive red to orange-red stripe on the upper abdomen of the female spider.] The small, venomous, black and red spider *Latrodectus hasselti* of Aust., the female having a pea-sized body and toxic bite; JOCKEY SPIDER. Also **red-back(ed) spider**, and *attrib*.

1898 *Bulletin* (Sydney) 8 Jan. 13/4 Are insects—red-back spiders and the like—more venomous some seasons than others? **1947** E. HILL *Flying Doctor Calling* 77 A woman bitten by a red-backed spider. **1984** *Canberra Times* 9 Apr. 10/4 Before the discovery of an anti-venene in 1956, the health of bite victims would fail gradually over several days. There had been no fatalities from red-back bites since the treatment was introduced.

red-backed, *a*. Used as a distinguishing epithet in the names of birds: **red-backed kingfisher** (formerly **halcyon**), the predom. blue-green and white kingfisher *Halcyon pyrrhopygia*, widespread in mainland Aust.; **parrot** (formerly **parakeet**), *red-rumped parrot*, see RED *a*. 1 b.; **sea eagle**, the white and chestnut-brown bird of prey *Haliastur indus*, the Brahminy kite, of coastal n. Aust. and elsewhere; *white-headed sea eagle*, see WHITE *a*.^{2} 1 b.; see also *white-headed fishing-eagle* WHITE *a*.^{2} 1 b.; **wren** (or **fairy wren**), the small bird *Malurus melanocephalus* of n. and n.e. Aust.

1840 [**red-backed kingfisher**] J. GOULD *Birds of Aust.* (1848) II. Pl. 22, *Halcyon pyrrhopygia* .. Red-backed Halcyon. **1984** M. BLAKERS et al. *Atlas Austral. Birds* 328 Inland, the Red-backed Kingfisher is often present far from water but always where there are trees. **1845** [**red-backed parrot**] J. GOULD *Birds of Aust.* (1848) V. Pl. 36, *Psephotus haematonotus* .. Red-backed Parrakeet. **1968** R. HILL *Bush Quest* 29 Red-backed parrots tore down wind, shrilling as they came, to land in the tossing branches of the wattles and red gum. **1945** C. BARRETT *Austral. Bird Life* 33 The Brahminy kite of India and Ceylon is identical with the **red-backed sea eagle** (*Haliastur indus*). **1901** *Emu* I. 89 *Malurus dorsalis* .. **Red-backed wren**... Fifteen skins have been received. **1984** SIMPSON & DAY *Birds of Aust.* 325 The fairy-wrens are well-known for the beauty of the male's plumage, usually consisting of blues (red and black in Red-backed Fairywren).

Redfern. [The name of a suburban railway station in Sydney which immediately precedes the terminus of the line.] In the phr. **to get off** (or **out**) **at Redfern**, to employ the practice of *coitus interruptus*.

1970 *Times Lit. Suppl.* (London) 4 Dec. 1422/5 *To get off at Redfern* .. is dull and unoriginal. Since the nineteenth century, natives of Newcastle upon Tyne have described the procedure alliteratively as *getting out at Gateshead*. **1984** P. JARRATT *Aussie* 179 Cheryl and Troy .. concluded their lovemaking in the fashion Troy knew as 'getting out at Redfern'—one stop short of the final destination.

redfin. The European fresh-water fish *Perca fluviatilis*, naturalized in streams of s. Aust. incl. Tas., having a deep, banded body and orange to bright red pectoral, ventral, and anal fins. Also **redfin perch**.

1946 A.D. BUTCHER *Freshwater Fish Vic.* 9 Non-indigenous or introduced species .. English perch or redfin. **1985** *Benalla Ensign* 5 Dec. 1/1 Juvenile redfin perch are extremely susceptible to the virus.

red gum. [Orig. referring to trees yielding a reddish gum-like kino, and later applied also to trees having a smooth bark and yielding a hard red wood.]

1. Any of many trees, often considered a group, of the genus *Eucalyptus* (fam. Myrtaceae), esp. the widespread *E. camaldulensis* (formerly *E. rostrata*), typically a large spreading tree with smooth mottled bark, and (*W.A.*) MARRI; the wood of the tree. See also *creek gum* CREEK 3, *flooded gum* FLOODED, *Murray red gum* MURRAY 2, *red river gum* RED *a*. 1 a., *river gum, river red gum* RIVER 2. Also *attrib*.

1788 J. WHITE *Jrnl. Voyage N.S.W.* (1790) 201 We picked up .. plants and shrubs of different genera and species, specimens of which I have transmitted to Mr *Wilson*, particularly the Red Gum Tree. **1984** *Canberra Times* 10 Sept. 12/5 Red gum, a hard, close-grained timber with a dark ruby-red colouring, is water-resistant and virtually immune from attack by termites, which makes it ideal for use in bridge and wharf constructions and for fencing and stumps.

2. The astringent kino of any of several trees of the genera *Eucalyptus* and *Angophora*, used for medicinal purposes and tanning.

1788 J. WHITE *Jrnl. Voyage N.S.W.* (1790) 178 The trees of this country are immensely large... At the heart they are full of veins, through which an amazing quantity of an astringent red gum issues. This gum I have found very serviceable in the obstinate dysentery that raged at our first landing. **1946** *Bulletin* (Sydney) 25 Sept. 28/1 In Westralia there is nothing better than redgum or kino for the tanning of fishing nets or lines.

red hot, *a.* and *n.*

A. *adj.* As **red-hot,** unfair; unreasonable.

1896 H. LAWSON *While Billy Boils* 281 When .. she paused for breath, he drew a long one, gave a short whistle, and said: 'Well, it's red-hot!' **1980** *Sun* (Sydney) 22 Feb. 21/4 *(heading)* Tomato prices are red hot.

B. *n. pl.* Rhyming slang for 'trots'. Also *attrib.*

1979 *Herald* (Melbourne) 24 Feb. 35/6 It's not often I'd consider giving the red hots a miss on Saturday night—especially when I've got a couple of certainties. **1983** *Sydney Morning Herald* 22 Apr.27/6 The reason for the press conference, was to defend trotting and lay to rest the 'red hots' stigma. It is an unjustified tag which has remained with the industry since the late 1920s and early 1930s when, Judge Goran pointed out, someone with a penchant for rhyming slang coined the term.

Red Indian fish. [See quot. 1965.] The scarlet marine fish *Pataecus fronto* of Qld., N.S.W., S.A., and W.A. Also **Red Indian.**

1906 D.G. STEAD *Fishes of Aust.* 212 The Red-Indian Fish .. lives in weedy, rocky localities, along parts of the coast of New South Wales. **1934** *Bulletin* (Sydney) 16 May 20/3 Someone identified the thing as *Pataecus fronto*, better known as the 'Red Indian' in N.S.W., where it is sometimes caught on the reefs. **1965** *Austral. Encycl.* VII. 395 Red Indian fish .. of the southern Australian rocky shore-lines. Its high dorsal fin forms a crest like the feathers of a Red Indian's head-dress.

red light. *Obs.* [Fig. use of *red light* a sign of danger.] A supervisor; a manager.

1915 *Bulletin* (Sydney) 9 Dec. 22/1, I was wielding the pick and banjo in a gang on a big channel job once when the ganger got his 'slip' for giving his 'pink eye' (pet) an easy job. The riding 'redlight' then unknowingly picked out another 'spur' in the horde, gave him the book and rode away. **1933** L.A. SIGSWORTH *Verse* 7 'The redlight' strolls with an easy gait, but his lamps are everywhere; His time book peeps from 'is side coat 'kick', like a signboard says 'beware!'

red-ragger. [In allusion to the *red flag* as a symbol of revolution, socialism, or communism.] A communist; a socialist.

1916 *Ross's Monthly* June 13/2 Dear Editor .. I can honestly say I have read a lot of Labor papers, also socialist literature, but I never saw any that would come within coo-ee of 'Ross's' for straightforwardness and sincerity. 'A red ragger.' **1985** N. MEDCALF *Rifleman* 78 Bluey was considered a bit of a red-ragger.

reed-bird: see REED-WARBLER.

reed spear. *Obs.* An Aboriginal spear: see quots. 1859 and 1884.

1847 G.F. ANGAS *Savage Life & Scenes* I. 93 The reed spear .. is like an arrow, and pointed with wood hardened by fire. **1859** W. BURROWS *Adventures Mounted Trooper* 97 The reed spear is made, as its name implies, of reeds, joined together by the fibres of the bark of trees, and kangaroo sinews, terminating in a point of hard, heavy wood. They can throw this spear a distance of eighty or a hundred yards with surprising accuracy. It is used for killing small game. **1884** E. PALMER *Notes Austral. Tribes* 12 All the northern tribes of blacks use the reed-spear, generally barbed, which is thrown by the aid of the *wommera*.

reed-warbler. [Transf. use of *reed-warbler* the British bird *Acrocephalus streperus*.] The predom. brown bird *Acrocephalus stentoreus australis* of reedy wetlands. Also **reed-bird.**

1808 J.W. LEWIN *Birds New Holland* 22 *(caption)* Reed Warbler... These birds frequent the banks of rivers, and the sides of ponds in the Summer months; they harbour among the reeds, where they also breed and sing both night and day. **1889** *Proc. Linnean Soc. N.S.W.* IV. 410 *Calamoherpe australis* .. known as 'Reed-bird'.

reef, *n. Gold-mining.* [Transf. use of *reef* a narrow ridge or chain of rocks. Used elsewhere but recorded earliest in Aust.] A lode or vein of auriferous quartz (but see also quots. 1869 and 1895). Also *attrib.*

1854 *Illustr. Sydney News* 28 Oct. 324/3 A new reeff has been lately opened in Lang Gulley .. and several new claims have been taken up .. in the quartz reeff. **1869** R.B. SMYTH *Gold Fields & Mineral Districts* 619 *Reef*, the term is applied to the up-turned edges of the palaeozoic rocks. The reef is composed of slate, sandstone, or mudstone. The bed-rock anywhere is usually called the reef. **1895** G.C. ADDISON *Miners' Man.* 31 The terms 'vein' and 'reef' shall mean any substance, other than alluvial, containing gold. **1935** F. CLUNE *Rolling down Lachlan* 122 An old-timer told me that reef-mining started on the Mount in 1891.

reef, *v. Gold-mining.* [f. prec.] *intr.* To mine auriferous quartz. Freq. as *vbl. n.*

1859 *Colonial Mining Jrnl.* May 143/1 Reefing bids fair to be the main feature, but alluvial workings are also likely to turn out satisfactorily. **1890** *Truth* (Sydney) 3 Aug. 7/1 He started 'reefing', and for a time he did pretty well.

reefer. *Gold-mining.*

a. *Obs.* A mining claim in a reef.

1854 *Illustr. Sydney News* 28 Oct. 234/3 Few claims have been bottomed on the gravel pits for some considerable time and such as have been lately bottomed are reefers, by which however we do not mean blanks as many of these same reefers are paying as much as eight ounces to the tub.

b. One who mines such a claim.

1859 *Colonial Mining Jrnl.* Mar. 108/3 The Reefers have objected to mining leases, and I do not think they are far wrong as far as the reefs are concerned. **1964** H.P. TRITTON *Time means Tucker* (rev. ed.) 58 We found we were 'diggers', not miners, mining being the work of the 'reefers', or hard rock men.

reef heron. The bird *Egretta sacra* of coastal mainland Aust. and elsewhere, having either white or bluish-grey plumage.

1848 J. GOULD *Birds of Aust.* VI. Pl. 60, *Herodias jugularis* .. the Blue Reef Heron is universally distributed over the whole of the coasts of the great continent of Australia. **1976** *Reader's Digest Compl. Bk. Austral. Birds* 81 Reef herons occur in two forms—white, which is the more common in tropical areas, and dark or slate-blue, which is the more numerous in temperate regions.

reffo. Also **refo.** [f. *ref(ugee* + -O.] Orig. a refugee from Europe; any migrant other than from the British Isles. Also *attrib.*

1941 S.J. Baker *Pop. Dict. Austral. Slang* 59 *Reffo*, a refugee from Europe. **1970** J. Cleary *Helga's Web* 37 Bloody reffo women... You get 'em all da time. **1984** *Canberra Times* 10 May 9/7 Bloody refos, I hate them.

regent. Used *attrib.* in the names of birds.

1. regent bird. [Named in compliment to the Prince Regent, later King George IV.] The bower bird *Sericulus chrysocephalus* of dense forests in near-coastal Qld. and N.S.W., the adult male having brilliant golden-yellow and black plumage. Also **regent bower bird,** and *ellipt.* as **regent.**

1813 T. Skottowe *Select Specimens Birds & Animals N.S.W., Regent.* This charming Bird is given as large as Life... I am I believe the first possessor of any of its Kind, and having procured the specimen from which the Drawing here given is taken on the same day that I receiv'd in this distant part of the World the news of the Regency Restrictions on His Royal Highness, the Prince Regent, having been taken off, as a small tribute from the Esteem I bear that exalted Character, I have named it as above. **1929** A.H. Chisholm *Birds & Green Places* 168 Regent bowerbird... Distribution: throughout approximately a thousand miles of coastal jungle from central Queensland to central New South Wales. **1959** *Meanjin* 135 He .. follows the flight of a black-and-orange regent-bird.

2. *transf.* [Prob. from the similarity in colouration.] **regent honeyeater,** the predom. black and yellow honeyeater *Xanthomyza phrygia* of s.e mainland Aust.; Warty-faced honeyeater; **parrot,** Smoker.

1913 G.M. Mathews *List Birds Aust.* 270 *Zanthomiza phrygia phrygia.* **Regent Honey-eater.** **1945** C. Barrett *Austral. Bird Life* 77 Long-tailed birds are the **regent parrot** or 'smoker' (*Polytelis anthopeplus*) [etc.].

reggo /'rɛdʒoʊ/. Also **rego.** [f. *reg(istration* + -O.] (Motor vehicle) registration. Also *attrib.*

1967 J. Wynnum *I'm Jack, all Right* 39 Everything is sweet except for the bloody silly reggo sticker. **1984** *N.T. News* (Darwin) 15 Sept. 42/3 Nissan MQ 4X4 S/Wagon Diesel Air-con tow/bar Air shocks, Bullbar, Driving lights, F.W.H. long rego.

Hence **reggo** *v. trans.*

1967 J. Wynnum *I'm Jack, all Right* 35 A car doesn't have to be reggoed in Queensland to have an accident up there.

rehab /'rihæb/. Abbrev. of 'rehabilitation': see quot. 1966.

1945 *Weekend: 15th Austral. Infantry Brigade* 14 Nov. 1 The stands were packed to hear Mr Mash .. on demob and rehab respectively. **1966** G.W. Turner *Eng. Lang. Aust. & N.Z.* 172 *Rehab,* pronounced with stress on the first syllable, was a common word in the years following the Second World War for 'rehabilitation', referring to loans, bursaries and other help given to returned soldiers.

reinstoushment. *Obs.* [Insertion of Stoush *n.* 2 in *rein(force)ment.*] One of a number of soldiers, etc., sent as reinforcements.

1918 *Aussie: Austral. Soldiers' Mag.* Aug. 11/2 A dopy reinstoushment recently lobbed into our wagon lines. **1943** S.W. Keough *Around Army* 17 It is a common sight to see one of the hard-heads, tough in the ways of war, taking one of the 'green' reinstoushments under his wing.

relief country. An area having pasture available for stock from drought-affected areas.

1905 *Shearer* (Sydney) 18 Mar. 8/5 Probably 40,000 sheep will leave this station for relief country. **1942** W. Glasson *Our Shepherds* 11 It was decided to send on agistment nineteen thousand sheep to Hall's property .. where relief country was available.

remittance man. [Spec. use of *remittance man* an emigrant supported by remittances from home. Used elsewhere but recorded earliest in Aust.: see OED(S *remittance* 2.] A male immigrant to Australia financially supported by his family: see quot. 1984. Formerly also **remittance immigrant.**

1873 *Austral. Handbk.* 51 The Commissioner for Railways is authorized to grant a free railway ticket to any assisted, free, or remittance immigrant, being a steerage passenger, who may be desirous of proceeding into the country within fourteen days after arrival in the colony. **1984** *Midweek Territorian* (Darwin) 24 Oct. 5/2 A remittance man, for the benefit of those who don't know of them .. was generally an Englishman unwanted by his family for one or another reason. He was paid to live as far away as possible .. definitely in another country. They were generally unwanted because they drank too much, or had been caught in compromising circumstances with the maid .. or worse still with the butler, or had committed some other dreadful social sin.

rendezvous. *Obs.* [Transf. use of *rendezvous* a meeting place.] The habitual resting place of a mob of cattle.

1848 H.W. Haygarth *Recoll. Bush Life* 59 A spot on which cattle are thus in the habit of assembling and basking during the day is called a 'rendezvous', and is easily known, for, from the constant pressure of innumerable vast bodies, the surface of the ground becomes smooth and hard, resembling a blighted ring in the midst of verdure. **1865** G.F. Angas *Aust.* 282 From the main body of the herd, dimly seen through a dense cloud of dust, a succession of furious animals break off on all sides, some making back to their 'rendezvous' (as the spot where the herd is in the habit of resting is called).

reo. [f. *re(inforcement* + -O.] In Services' speech: one of a party of reinforcements. Usu. in *pl.*

1931 O. Walters *Shrapnel Green* 19 For the 'reos' were talking of Passchendaele. **1958** R. Graves *On Gallipoli* 12 The re-o looked at us—we saw a child.

rep. [Spec. use of *rep.*, abbrev. of *representative.*] The elected representative of a party of employees, esp. shearers (see quot. 1919); *shearer's rep* Shearer b. Also **rep shearer.**

1899 *Bulletin* (Sydney) 19 Aug. 32/1 Sheedy asked to see the 'Rep.' The latter .. was ringer as well as union representative. **1919** A.B. Paterson *Song of Pen* (1983) 411 The shearers then drew apart and held a ballot for a 'rep', i.e. shearers' representative, whose duty it would be to bring forward any grievances, see that union rules were observed, and union dues collected from all hands in the shed. **1973** J. Morrison *Austral. by Choice* 127 It lasted six weeks, and when it cut out the rep shearer, with whom I'd palled up took me with him as a fully blown presser to Mingowallah Station.

Repat /'ripæt/. [Abbrev. of *repatriation.*] The Repatriation Commission. Also used *attrib.* of benefits made available to former Service personnel through the agency of the Commission.

1920 *Smith's Weekly* (Sydney) 24 Apr. 23/2 The Repat. will give him £10 worth of instruments as tools of trade. **1960** *Bulletin* (Sydney) 14 Sept. 18/3 Five a.m. in the Repat. Hospital.

reporter. *Obs.* A member of a droving team who goes ahead of a mob to give notice of its approach.

1890 'R. Boldrewood' *Colonial Reformer* II. 267 The usual 'reporter' of travelling sheep. **1914** C.H.S. Matthews *Bill* 97 With a mob of 1000 bullocks there will be about ten drovers, a cook, and a man, who is known as a Reporter... The reporter has charge.of the spare saddle-horses.

Also **reporting** *vbl. n.*

1904 L.M.P. Archer *Bush Honeymoon* 281 What game are you at—*reportin'?*

rep shearer: see REP.

reserve. [Spec. use of *reserve* a district or place set apart for some particular use, or assigned to certain persons: see OED(S *sb.* 5 b.]

1. a. [Also U.S.: see Mathews n. 6.] A piece of land set aside for a specific public use. See also *government reserve* GOVERNMENT B. 3, *town reserve*, TOWN 3, *township reserve* TOWNSHIP 1, *village reserve* VILLAGE 3.
1815 *HRA* (1916) 1st Ser. VIII. 638, I have no information upon the Nature of the large Reserves above alluded to, which are marked E on the Charts of the Colony. **1978** B. KENNEDY *Silver, Sin, & Sixpenny Ale* 8 The town's planners optimistically set apart reserves for a school, hospital, several public buildings, and parklands.
b. A public park.
1851 H. MELVILLE *Present State Aust.* 60 On either side of the Torrens is a reserve or Government domain of two hundred acres. **1960** *N.T. News* (Darwin) 12 Jan. 7/3 The need to declare the Katherine River low-level bridge camping area a reserve is becoming more urgent. Judging by the number of 'dead marines' it is the site of regular drinking orgies.
2. *Obs.* [Also U.S.: see Mathews n. 2.] A piece of land reserved for the future use or occupancy of an individual.
1822 *HRA* (1822) 3rd Ser. IV. 55 Mr Meredith .. proposed then to waive his Claim to the reserve adjoining his Grant. **1843** *HRA* (1925) 1st Ser. XXIII. 267 Let him receive authority to select four square miles as a Reserve, on condition of its being Stocked and improved.
3. A piece of land set aside for the exclusive use of Aborigines; *Aboriginal reserve*, see ABORIGINAL a. 2; *native reserve*, see NATIVE a. 5. Also *attrib.*
1839 *Extracts Papers & Proc. Aborigines Protection Soc.* Oct. 133 The reserves for the Aborigines .. will be enclosed and cultivated. **1984** P. CORRIS *Winning Side* 14, I was going to wipe the fact that I was a reserve Aborigine off the slate, that was essential, especially for the union ticket.

Reserve Bank. A central bank; that bank which is responsible for the administration of the monetary policy of a government.
1959 *CPD* (H. of R.) XXII. 377 The Reserve Bank will be a worthy successor to the Commonwealth Bank as Australia's central bank. **1985** *Nat. Times* (Sydney) 22 Nov. 17/1 The Reserve Bank no longer collects exchange control data.

reserved, *ppl. a.* [Also U.S.: see Mathews b.] Of land: retained unsold for some public use.
1823 *Hobart Town Gaz.* 26 July, As a sporting farm, or farm for profit, is perhaps equal to any on the island... A reserved road to this estate, from the brook .. gives it the advantage of communication by land with Hobart Town. **1934** 'S. RUDD' *Green Grey Homestead* 151 'The Mount' consisted of waste country reserved by a Government of squatters for 'closer settlement' and bordering this reserved area were mighty stations .. lying there within their cheap, pointed sheep fences, like living land sharks.

respite gang. *Hist.* A detachment of convicts whose capital sentences have been commuted to sentences of penal servitude for life.
1834 *N.S.W. Mag.* (Sydney) 220 Proceeded towards the goal [*sic*], headed by the man in the apparel of the doctor's mate, and were taken by the guard as the respite gang. *c* **1844** T. COOK *Exile's Lamentations* (1978) 47 Another Wild and desperate undertaking was put into execution at the Boat Harbour by Eight of the Respite Gang, who had been respited from Death in Sydney to be worked here for Life in chains.

rest. Imprisonment for one year.
1882 *Sydney Slang Dict.* 9 He's gone in the country for a rest... He's gone to jail for one year. **1945** S.J. BAKER *Austral. Lang.* 141 Here is a brief glossary of jail sentences: *lag*, three months .. *rest*, twelve months [etc.].

restless flycatcher. The black and white bird *Myiagra inquieta* of mainland Aust. and s. New Guinea; RAZOR-GRINDER; SCISSORS-GRINDER. Formerly also **restless thrush**.
1801 J. LATHAM *Gen. Synopsis Birds* Suppl. II. 181 Restless Thr[ush] .. inhabits *New Holland*, said to be a restless species. **1984** E. ROLLS *Celebration of Senses* 76 Another busy black and white bird, the Restless Flycatcher, stops grating out his daytime scissors-grinder notes and instead calls musically 'Jury. Jury. Jury.'

retention money. *Cane-cutting.* A sum withheld from earnings: see quots.
1936 J. DEVANNY *Sugar Heaven* 20 The cockies keep sixpence a ton out of our cheque as a guarantee that we'll stay the season... The cockies are supposed to pay this retention money into the bank and we are supposed to draw interest on it but normally they don't pay it in. **1965** J. BECKETT *New-Chum looks at Qld.* 39 Sixpence per ton is retained by the farmer. This is called retention money. It is part of the contract to induce the men to stay on until all the crop is cut... At the finish of 'crushing' the retention money is paid and the men are often engaged on day labour chipping the young cane to keep it free of weeds.

retransport, *v. Hist. trans.* To commit (a convict guilty of a further offence) to a penal settlement, esp. one at which a more severe form of punishment is imposed. Usu. *pass.*
1799 *HRA* (1914) 1st Ser. II. 352 They are well aware of the consequences of detection in their robberys [*sic*], many having been retransported, a sentence they dread more than death. **1862** BACKHOUSE & TYLOR *Life & Labours G.W. Walker* 53 They were punished .. lastly, by being retransported, as it were, to a penal settlement.
Hence **retransportation** *n.*
1845 *HRA* (1925) 1st Ser. XXIV. 603 The position of these men essentially differs from that of Expirees from a Settlement for re-transportation, such as Norfolk Island.

retread. [Used elsewhere but recorded earliest in Aust.] A retired person (orig. a discharged soldier) who is re-engaged.
1941 *Salt* (Melbourne) 22 Dec. 36 Characteristically the Australians call .. a 1914–1918 soldier enlisted a second time a 'retread'. **1984** *Sydney Morning Herald* 9 July 3/5 During his long service Mr Culgin did work with some retired teachers for brief periods and they were referred to as 'retreads'.

return boomerang: see RETURNING BOOMERANG.

returned, *ppl. a.*
a. *Obs.* Designating a miner who has returned from the goldfields, as **returned digger**.
1852 *Guardian* (Hobart) 24 July 2/2 A Returned Digger. **1904** *Rec. Castlemaine Pioneers* (1972) 193 The soldiers were carousing with returned diggers, who 'shouted' freely.
b. [Used elsewhere but recorded earliest in Aust.: see OEDS 2 b.] Designating a person discharged from the armed services who has returned home from a war.
1902 *Truth* (Sydney) 6 July 5/8 In the present state of Australia, with a dearth of employment owing to the drought, these returned soldiers, who were offered good opportunities in South Africa, are no welcome addition to the country's population. **1981** A.B. FACEY *Fortunate Life* 289 He said that if I wasn't a returned soldier he would

have had to fail me but they could not reject a returned man on war injuries.

returning boomerang. See BOOMERANG *n.* 1. Also **return boomerang, returner.**

1901 *Bulletin* (Sydney) 2 Mar. 15/1, I am a pretty fair boomerang-thrower, except with the 'returner'. **1905** *Ibid.* 8 June 16/2 The 'return' boomerang... According to authentic records, the earliest European visitors to Australia found the coastal aborigines provided with this weapon. **1928** W. ROBERTSON *Coo-ee Talks* 8 Another toy was the 'returning boomerang'. It was a rather weighty toy-weapon, one arm of which was a little longer and heavier than the other.

reward claim. *Mining.* A mining claim granted to a miner who discovers payable gold in a new district: see quot. 1944. Also *ellipt.* as **reward.**

1894 W.H. BARKER *Gold Fields W.A.* 32 The White Feather Claim.. is a 'reward' claim, and is about forty miles from Coolgardie. **1944** M.J. O'REILLY *Bowyangs & Boomerangs* 11 A Reward Claim is granted to a prospector for finding new ground carrying payable gold, outside a specified distance from an existent goldfield. **1946** K.S. PRICHARD *Roaring Nineties* 136 We never seen colours on that trek, got wind of Paddy Hannan's reward on our way back, and Gord, did we whip the cat!

ribbed-up, *ppl. a.* Having ample money (for a purpose), 'flush'.

1918 *Home Trail: Souvenir Issue Voyage H.M.T. 'A. 30'* Dec. 5 The others were well 'ribbed-up' too. **1933** *Bulletin* (Sydney) 6 Sept. 40/3 And we would have run out of tucker, too, if I hadn't been well ribbed up with coin.

ribbon gum. [See quot. 1902.] Any of several trees of the genus *Eucalyptus* (fam. Myrtaceae) having bark which tends to hang in ribbons as it is shed, esp. *E. viminalis* (see **manna gum** a., MANNA 2). Also **ribbony gum.**

1889 *Proc. Linnean Soc. N.S.W.* IV. 609 *E[ucalyptus] amygdalina* var. *radiata.* 'Ribbon Gum.' Nelligen, Clyde River, N.S.W. **1902** *Ibid.* XXVII. 574 *E[ucalyptus] radiata..* is known sometimes as Peppermint but often as Ribbony Gum from the appearance of the streamers of decorticating bark as they hang from the upper parts of the trees.

ribuck, var. RYEBUCK.

Rice: see JACK RICE.

rice. Used *attrib.* in the names of plants having some resemblance to cultivated rice (*Oryza sativa*): **rice flower,** any of many species of the genus *Pimelea* (see PIMELEA); **grass,** any of several plants, esp. *Leersia hexandra* (fam. Poaceae), occurring in or near water in N.S.W. and Qld.

1898 E.E. MORRIS *Austral Eng.* 355 A gardener's name for some of the species [of Pimelea] is **Rice-flower.** **1849** C. STURT *Narr. Exped. Central Aust.* I. 274 At that time they [*sc.* pigeons] were feeding upon the seed of the **rice grass,** and were scattered about.

richard. [Ellipt. form of *Richard the Third,* rhyming slang for 'bird'; f. theatrical slang *to get the bird* (or *goose*), to be hissed, to be given a bad reception.] In the phr. **to have had the Richard,** to be finished, to be irreparably damaged. See also DICK.

1967 *Kings Cross Whisper* (Sydney) xxxv. 6/1 Had the Richard, tired, weary, same as frigged. **1980** HEPWORTH & HINDLE *Boozing out in Melbourne Pubs* 44 What he didn't know.. was that actually she had shot through to London with another feller... He was going to discover at the end of the three months that he'd had the richard.

richea /'rɪtʃɪə/. [The plant genus *Richea* was named by British botanist Robert Brown (*Prodr. Fl. Nov. Holl.* (1810) 555) after French naturalist Claude *Riche* (1762–1797) of the Bruny D'Entrecasteaux expedition.] A shrub or tree of the chiefly Tas. genus *Richea* (fam. Epacridaceae).

1850 *Papers & Proc. R. Soc. Van Diemen's Land* (1851) 278 The graceful palm-like Richea (*Richea pandanifolia*), found in the dense forests between Lake St. Clair and Macquarie Harbour, where it attains the height of 40 to 50 feet in sheltered positions. **1980** G.R. COCHRANE *Flowers & Plants Vic. & Tas.* (rev. ed.) 160 A number of the smaller Richeas.. favour a damp windy site.

ride, *v. trans.* To traverse (the line of a boundary, an area occupied by stock, etc.) on horseback in order to make an inspection or carry out maintenance.

1914 'B. CABLE' *By Blow & Kiss* 173 Up to the Ridge from the back paddocks, where now there were no sheep to ride boundary on. **1967** R. HAWKER *Emu in Fowl Pen* 52 'You'll have to do your bit of work... We don't keep horses to play with here.' 'She can fetch the mail.'.. 'And ride paddocks.'

riders, *pl.* [Transf. use of *riders* additional set of timbers used to strengthen the frame of a ship.] Wooden poles used to hold a bark roof in place: see quot. 1945.

1872 G.S. BADEN-POWELL *New Homes for Old Country* 162 The hut is of oblong shape, slab walls, and bark roof, with heavy wooden framework of 'riders', to keep the bark from being blown away. **1945** S.J. BAKER *Austral. Lang.* 78 Riders are slabs or logs running from the ridge of the roof to the eaves.

ridge, *a.* [Fig. use of *ridge* gold, gold coin: see OED(S *sb.*²] All right; genuine; 'dinkum' (see DINKUM *a.* 1.).

1938 E. PARTRIDGE *Dict. Slang & Unconventional Eng.* (ed. 2) 1026 *Ridge*, adj., good; valuable: Australian. **1978** H.C. BAKER *I was Listening* 166 Within seventy miles we heard (and that was supposed to be 'ridge'—direct from the ship's officers).

ridgey-dite. [After RIDGY-DIDGE.] Rhyming slang for 'all right'.

1953 K. TENNANT *Joyful Condemned* 295 He'd tell you himself I'm ridgey-dite. I worked for him.

ridgy-didge, *a.* Also **ridgey-(the-)didge, ridgie-didge, ridgy-dig.** [Elaboration of 'ridgy', f. RIDGE + -*y.*] RIDGE.

1953 S.J. BAKER *Aust. Speaks* 102 *Ridgy-didge* or *ridgy-dig*.., honest, genuine, okay. **1963** L. GLASSOP *Rats in New Guinea* 153 'It's ridgie-didge,' said Eddie. 'Spit me death.' **1967** *Kings Cross Whisper* (Sydney) xxxii. 6/3 The ridgey didge Australian dictionary. **1968** S. GORE *Holy Smoke* 65 'Yes. Ridgey-the-didge, mate,' says Jesus.

rifle-bird. [See quot. 1898.] Any of three species of bird of the genus *Ptiloris* of e. Aust., the mature male having velvety black plumage with metallic patches. Also with distinguishing epithet, as **paradise, Victoria** (see under first element). Formerly also **rifleman.**

1827 P. CUNNINGHAM *Two Yrs. in N.S.W.* I. 325 The regent and *rifle-bird* outvie all I have seen from any part of the world, in the chaste splendour of their plumage. **1833** *N.S.W. Mag.* (Sydney) 12 In the long recesses of their thick and trackless scrubs.. the call of the 'khagghak', or rifleman, would be most likely heard. **1898** E.E. MORRIS *Austral Eng.* 387 Rifle-bird... The male is of a general velvety black, something like the uniform of the Rifle Brigade. This peculiarity, no doubt, gave the bird its name, but, on the other hand, settlers and local naturalists sometimes ascribe the name to the resemblance they hear in the bird's cry to the noise of a rifle being fired and its bullet striking the target.

rifle-fish. [See quot. 1926.] A fish of the fam. Toxotidae, occurring in fresh water and estuaries of n. Aust. and elsewhere in the tropics.
1906 D.G. STEAD *Fishes of Aust.* 95 One species of this family is found on the coast of Queensland, where it is known by the name of Rifle-Fish (*Toxotes jaculator*). 1926 J. MCLAREN *My Crowded Solitude* 45 On the shore-reef he showed me a rifle-fish—so called because of its habit of shooting with a drop of water insects which flew close to the water.

right, *n.* Abbrev. of *miner's right,* see MINER *n.*²
1870 J.O. TUCKER *Mute* 42 But who are these to whom the digger yields Obedience prompt, when questioned for his 'right'?

right, *a.*
1. In the phr. **all right.** [Spec. use of *all right* satisfactory, acceptable: see OED(S *right, a.* 15 c. and 8 e.]
a. *Obs.* In morally dubious contexts: (of a person) trustworthy, safe, 'on side'; (of a situation) 'all clear'.
1841 *Register of Flash Men* 11 This man was apprehended .. by Inspector Ryan. . . A person known to Ryan came up at the time saying, This man is all right, he has two horses at stables. 1875 A. PYNE *Reminisc. Colonial Life* 287 Seeing (to use a colonial phrase) I was 'all right', he cried out.
b. In neutral contexts, often with deliberate understatement: up to standard.
1898 *Bulletin* (Sydney) 4 June (Red Page), On the N.S.W. plains, say from Liverpool to Bourke, the word 'alright' is used by bushmen as an adjective; and it means a lot, too. 1918 *Kia Ora Coo-ee* Oct. 5/2 Later I was informed that I had missed a bit of 'all right duff'.
2. [Spec. use of *right* in good health and spirits: see OED(S 13 b. Now chiefly Austral. and N.Z.] Of a person: in good shape, 'all right'.
1864 *Bell's Life in Sydney* 28 May 3/2 So people imagined, and well they might, That, like Croesus of old, our hero was 'right' In the matter of 'tin'; for money still sends, To those who possess it, a number of friends. 1974 *Bulletin* (Sydney) 14 Dec. 27/2 'You right?' It is—for the benefit of new settlers—an abbreviation of 'Are you all right?' which, in turn, is a shorter way of asking: 'Are you, in the matter of looking for, selecting and purchasing something .. or could I do something to help you .. ? Could I .. even sell you something?'
3. [Used elsewhere but recorded earliest in Aust.: see OEDS *right, a.* 14 c. and *too, adv.* 5 h.] In the phr. **too right,** an expression of agreement or approval.
1919 W.H. DOWNING *Digger Dialects* 51 *Two eyes right* or *too right,* certainly. 1980 *Westerly* i. 8 'Jacky is it?' 'Too right, and a mate,' said Jacky.
4. **a.** In the phr. **she'll be right,** 'all will be well': see quots. 1962 and 1967. Also as *adj. phr.*, designating an attitude of unreasoning optimism (see quot. 1971).
1947 G. CASEY *Wits are Out* 154 'I only hope Kitty'll be willing to forget it, too.' 'She'll be right,' Jerry promised. 'I'll square her off, don't you worry.' 1962 J. MACKENZIE *Austral. Paradox* 154 So long as individuals are not obviously adversely affected, Australians show little concern about matters of principle. 'She'll be right' is a well used and familiar phrase revealing an attitude which implies: 'Why bother, why fuss; it will all turn out right in the end.' 1967 D. HORNE *Southern Exposure* 22 '*She'll be right.*' Their combination of high hope and deep doubt can make Australians devastatingly cool-headed and wry-witted. 1971 *Bulletin* (Sydney) 10 July 21/1 With social consciences progressively insulated by more and more creature comforts and with a sense of 'she'll be right' isolationism, the yarn and the shrug were seeming to become national characteristics.

b. In the phr. **she's right,** 'all is in order'.
1958 F.B. VICKERS *Though Poppies Grow* 76 'You're free until we take a firm order. But bring the permit with you.' 'She's right mate. Thanks a lot.' 1978 D. STUART *Wedgetail View* 21 'What d' y' reckon, should I drop back a bit an' put up a smoke, let them know where we are?' 'No, she's right, Col. Davey's got one going.'

righteous, *a.* Jocular alteration of 'riotous (behaviour)'.
1891 *Truth* (Sydney) 8 Feb. 6/5 Abe Willis was lumbered and fined 10s. and costs for being 'righteous' in Auckland Street. 1919 V. MARSHALL *World of Living Dead* 71 The grisly 'toe-ragger', who is doing a 'sleep' of three months for 'righteous' .. will tell him of the best road to take if it comes to 'hoofin' it'.

ring, *n.*¹ [Abbrev. of (orig.) U.S. *ringer* an exact counterpart: see OEDS *ringer, sb.*² 5 and *ring, sb.*² 3 d.] In the phr. **the dead ring for** (or **of**), the exact likeness of, the 'spitting image' of.
1899 J. BRADSHAW *Quirindi Bank Robbery* 37 You are the dead ring for the veiled prophet himself. 1951 E. HILL *Territory* 318 Now you're the dead ring o' that girl, and you speak the same.

ring, *n.*² *Two-up.* [Spec. use of *ring* (enclosed) circular space within which a sport or performance takes place.]
1. The site of a two-up game; the area within which the coins are tossed and must fall; the assembly of players; the game itself. Also **two-up ring.**
1896 [see *ring-keeper*]. 1913 *Bulletin* (Sydney) 30 Jan. 15/2 Two spins in the two-up ring. 1920 *Huon Times* (Franklin) 21 May 5/2 Near the 'ring' the constable found a lunch bag. 1941 D. O'CALLAGHAN *Long Life Reminisc.* 5 He experiences .. the two-up and Murrumbidgee rings.
2. Special Comb. **ring-keeper,** (formerly **-master**), the person in charge of a two-up game.
1896 *Worker* (Sydney) 4 July 4/1 Well, Charlie is 'ringmaster' (I believe that's the correct title, the 'two-up' ain't a pet vice of mine) of the Boulder 'school'. 1977 R. BEILBY *Gunner* 180 A two-up game proceeded intermittently, the ring-keeper's calls pealing faintly. . . 'Set in the centre! Up 'n' do 'm, spinner!'

ring, *n.*³ [f. RING *v.*²] A milling mob of restless cattle.
1890 'R. BOLDREWOOD' *Colonial Reformer* II. 111 If the 'ring' crowds too near the fence, the men on that side would walk along the middle rail. 1934 J. KIRWAN *Empty Land* 202 Others will follow, forming a ring of cattle swimming round and round. . . In 1904 no fewer than 300 cattle were drowned in crossing the Georgina, the result of their 'ringing' in midstream whilst crossing.

ring, *v.*¹ [Spec. use of *ring* to deprive (a tree) of a ring of bark: see OED *v.*¹ 9 b.] *trans.* RING-BARK *v.* 1. Also *absol.*
1846 J.L. STOKES *Discoveries in Aust.* I. 315 Ringing the trees; that is to say, they cut off a large circular band of bark, which destroying the trees, renders them easier to be felled. 1905 *Steele Rudd's Mag.* (Brisbane) July 695 Gangs of Chinamen ring for sixpence in parts of West Queensland.

ring, *v.*²
a. *intr.* Of livestock, esp. cattle: to keep moving restlessly round and round in a mass, to mill. Also *fig.*
1868 [see RINGING 2]. 1876 *Austral. Town & Country Jrnl.* (Sydney) 16 Dec. 982/2 A desultory entry into the receiving yard then takes place. . . The 'ragers' observing this moment keep wildly and excitedly 'ringing', like a first-class Maëlstrom. 1938 F. BLAKELEY *Hard Liberty* 65 Although we were getting opal we soon found ourselves 'ringing', as miners term it when restlessness begins.

b. *trans.* To turn (a mob, esp. of cattle) back on itself; to cause (a mob) to mill.

1907 *Bulletin* (Sydney) 11 Apr. 15/3, I collared the spare night-horse and lit out to the old man's assistance. He had the lead blocked on the edge of the scrub when I came up, and was ringing 'em finely. **1957** R.S. PORTEOUS *Brigalow* 38 Albert . . quite often turning the entire mob about-face. At other times he achieved the highly undesirable effect of ringing them and we would find ourselves with a milling, bewildered herd.

c. *intr.* To work with cattle as a drover, musterer, etc. Also *trans.*, to drive (a mob), and as *vbl. n.*

1949 *Bulletin* (Sydney) 26 Jan. 15/3 Now, especially in North Queensland and the Territory . . 'How do you like 'ringing' for a job?' 'I was yarning with a mob of 'ringers' from the Gulf', are common expressions. **1961** *Ibid.* 7 Oct. 29/1 Our ringer had come up from Pandy Pandy, over the South Australian border, after breaking down a cheque. But for a tube of tooth paste, he'd be ringing the ghost herds in the sky.

ring, $v.^3$ [Back-formation f. RINGER $n.^1$ 2 a.] *trans.* To beat (one's fellow shearers) by shearing the most sheep in a given period. Also *transf.* (see quots. 1926 and 1967). Usu. with 'shed' as obj.

1894 *Bulletin* (Sydney) 13 Jan. 7/3 Legge got the run, Fogg cleared, Bell 'rung' the shed, and Warte turned out to be a 'scab'. **1899** *Western Champion* (Barcaldine) 15 Aug. 5/1 George Eyre 'rung' the shed, with an average tally of 175 sheep. **1926** *Bulletin* (Sydney) 11 Feb. 24/1 What cares the cook if it don't fine up? It's he who'll ring the shed. **1967** *Telegraph* (Brisbane) 25 Mar. 2/5 To 'ring the shed' a shearer's cook has to earn more money than the top shearer.

ring, $v.^4$ In the phr. **to ring the tin (on),** to summon a meeting (of workers) to consider a specific (industrial) matter; to refuse to communicate with a foreman, etc. Also as **ring the tin ruling**.

1958 M.D. BERRINGTON *Stones of Fire* 93, I had often heard the expression used jokingly, 'we ought to ring the tin on him', and, on inquiry, had heard all about this outback custom so seldom practised nowadays—a custom that was common in remote places when transport was slow and it took days to contact the police. Except in major offences, the residents administered their own law and order. The entire population was called together to decide what course of action must be taken. They were summoned by 'ringing the tin'. **1972** *Sydney Morning Herald* 24 Feb. 12/1 A recent meeting of about 70 men who work under the foreman, decided to 'ring the tin' because they had no confidence in him. According to union officials 'ring the tin' ruling means that the foreman will not be spoken to by WIU men who work under him. **1977** B. FULLER *Nullarbor Lifelines* 73 It was no soothing bell, but a kerosene tin. . . If any officer or ganger had fallen from grace in Union eyes he knew that that evening the tin would be 'rung on him'.

ring-bark, *v.* [f. RING $v.^1$]

1. *trans.* To kill (a tree) by cutting a ring of bark from around the trunk; to prepare (land, scrub, etc.) for clearing in this way. Also *absol.*, and as *vbl. n.* and *ppl. a.*

1866 *Australasian* (Melbourne) 30 June 409/5 Will you, or some of your practical readers, kindly inform me if what is called 'ring-barking', or the cutting and removal of a piece of bark from the indigenous trees, can be carried on successfully throughout the year, with a view to kill the trees? **1965** R.H. CONQUEST *Horses in Kitchen* 87 The local doctor had to go ringbarking in the brigalow belts to make ends meet. **1982** R. HALL *Just Relations* 111 The hillsides of forest trees are ringbarked to clear the land for pasture, tree by tree the ringbarking work goes forward.

2. *transf.* and *fig.*

1899 *Western Champion* (Barcaldine) 1 Mar. 3/3 'Oh no, dash it all, don't go and spoil a cove for riding,' protested the lively young man from outback; 'just you ringbark it.' **1981** Q. WILD *Honey Wind* 107 All that pioneering has been cordoned off in suburbia, ringbarked with picket fences.

Hence **ring-bark** *n.*, a tree which has been ringbarked.

1951 G. FARWELL *Outside Track* 52 Reckless early settlement, particularly in western New South Wales, bequeathed us a landscape whose ghostly ringbarks symbolize not only erosion and declining land values but poverty of the imagination.

ring-barker. One engaged in ring-barking trees.

1886 D.M. GANE *N.S.W. & Vic.* 191 The country has been devastated far and wide by the ring-barker, a person who cuts off a circle of bark round the tree, the consequence being that in a very short time the leaves fall, and the tree, lacking sustenance, rots and tumbles to the ground. **1972** *Bulletin* (Sydney) 11 Nov. 61/2 One job that gave me great pride, if only from an etymological point of view, was that of ring-barker, sucker-basher.

ring-coachman. THUNDER-BIRD.

1931 J. DEVANEY *Earth Kindred* 14 The little ring-coachman crackt his whip. **1944** L. WELSH *Kookaburra* 10 One of the earliest of dawn-singers is the Rufous-breasted Whistler, alias the Ring Coachman.

ring dollar. Chiefly *Tas. Hist.* HOLEY DOLLAR.

1828 *Tasmanian* (Hobart) 29 Aug. 3 George Jones, charged with fraudulently obtaining a ring dollar from J. Hardy, was found *Guilty.* **1855** J. BONWICK *Geogr. Aust. & N.Z.* (ed. 3) 161 One fourth part punched out of the centre was a substitute for a shilling, and was called a Dump; the other part was known as the Ring dollar.

ringed snake: see RING SNAKE.

ringer, $n.^1$ [Spec. use of Br. dial. *ringer* anything superlatively good: see EDD $sb.^2$]

1. a. One who excels (at an activity, etc.).

1848 *Port Phillip Herald* 20 June 2/7 Another Melbourne 'Ringer' named Edwards has proceeded to Sydney, resolved to defeat his man there as well as Sinclair. **1921** *Bulletin* (Sydney) 25 Aug. 20/2 The top scorer at a hare- or wallaby-drive still earns his three cheers for being the 'ringer' when the day's slaughtering is done; the best dog in a rabbiter's pack is always his 'ringer', and there is a 'ringer' in every bullock-team.

b. Something surpassingly good of its kind.

1891 *Truth* (Sydney) 1 Feb. 6/5 I'd like to see the mill, for it will be a ringer if the officials let them fight to a fair decision. **1904** *Ibid.* 2 Oct. 1/7 The sugar season is a ringer; 11,000 or 12,000 tons of sugar are being shipped weekly.

2. a. The shearer with the highest tally of sheep shorn in a given period.

1871 *Cornhill Mag.* (London) Jan. 85 Billy May stood for the fashion and 'talent', being the 'Ringer', or fastest shearer of the whole assembly, and as such truly admirable and distinguished. **1984** *People Mag.* (Sydney) 7 May 40/2 (*caption*) Des Bourke . . the ringer with a small comb, is out of work, out of hope and 3300 km. from home.

b. *transf.*

1890 *Braidwood Dispatch* 26 Nov. 2/2 *Wallaby drive.* . . The country . . was thoroughly scoured with the result that no less than 250 of the marsupial pests were destroyed. Mr John Gumel was 'ringer' with 26, Mr McWilliams being close up with 23. **1949** B. O'REILLY *Green Mountains* 245 The guns fell silent; the wallabies which had not fallen had escaped through the line. A count was made and the man with the biggest bag was proclaimed 'ringer'.

ringer, *n.*² [Prob. f. RING *v.*² b and c.] A stockman, esp. as employed in droving: see quot. 1977.

1909 J. CAMERON *Spell of Bush* (1910) 48 Dam-sinkers, fencers, scrub-cutters, ringers, and other men doing contract work in the vicinity. **1977** T.L. McKNIGHT *Long Paddock* 12 The ordinary members of the droving team are usually referred to simply as *ringers*. Their job is primarily to ride along with the stock, keeping the mob out of trouble, mustering strays etc. In cattle droving night riding around the perimeter of the resting stock is normally also required.

ringer, *n.*³ *Two-up.* [f. RING *n.*² 1.] *Ring-keeper*, see RING *n.*² 2.

1943 H.M. MURPHY *Strictly for Soldiers* 17 And you throw the caser yonder to the boxer's waiting hand; Then the ringer loudly bellows: 'Spread the ring—now fair go, fellows!'

ringie. *Two-up.* [f. RING *n.*² 2 + -Y.] *Ring-keeper*, see RING *n.*² 2.

[N.Z. **1917** *Chrons. N.Z. Exped. Force* 16 May 137 The 'ringies' they were bending low And yelled for 'centre hoot!'] **1941** S.J. BAKER *Pop. Dict. Austral. Slang* 54 *Ringie*, the keeper of a two-up school. **1977** R. BEILBY *Gunner* 298 'Right! Up 'n do 'em, spinner,' the ringie sang.

ring-in, *v.* [Spec. use of *ring in* to substitute fraudulently: see OED *ring*, *v.*² 13 b.]

a. *trans. Horse-racing.* To substitute fraudulently (a horse) for another entered in a race. Also as *vbl. n.*

1898 *Western Champion* (Barcaldine) 18 Jan. 10/1 The disgraceful practices now going on, such as 'ringing-in' horses, pulling, foul riding. **1984** *Austral.* (Sydney) 23 Aug. 7/5 Endeavour to frustrate those who would attempt to ring in horses.

b. *Two-up.* To substitute (a double-headed or double-tailed coin) for a genuine coin.

1898 *Western Champion* (Barcaldine) 11 Jan. 4/5 He had been playing 'two-up' on the racecourse, and took a man down for 23s. by 'ringing-in a grey' (a two-tailed penny) on him. **1964** E. LANE *Our Uncle Charlie* 87 Even with his double-headed penny being occasionally 'rung into' the game of two-up he usually came home from a shearing trip not much better off.

ring-in, *n.* [f. prec.]

1. A fraudulent substitution, esp. of one horse for another in a race; the act of making such a substitution.

1918 A. WRIGHT *Breed holds Good* 79 Wiseacres would declare that it was another of Maff's 'hot 'uns', a 'ring-in' probably. **1971** G. MORGAN *We are borne On* 354 It was not often a horse that had been racing as a ring-in got away with it.

2. One who, or that which, is not of a kind with others in a set: see quots. 1967 and 1975.

1945 *Mud & Blood* 18 Every starter has four legs, even those few 'ring-ins' that were picked up for a song after being boarded out of the Labor Corps because of flat feet. **1967** E. HUXLEY *Their Shining Eldorado* 82 'I'm a ring-tail, or ring-in.' That means an outsider, one not born in Broken Hill. **1975** *Bulletin* (Sydney) 3 May 42/1 The entrance to his establishment is a 20-foot high glass tower made entirely of stubbies... He has used only standard South Australian stubbies, no ring-ins.

ringing, *vbl. n.*

1. [f. RING *v.*¹] The removal of a ring of bark (from around the trunk of a tree) in order to kill it.

1860 *T.H.A.J.* no. 84 3 The system of 'scrubbing' by which the underwood alone is removed, and of 'ringing' whereby the larger trees are simply killed (by cutting through the bark and sapwood all round). **1934** 'S. RUDD' *Green Grey Homestead* 56 You'll have a notion of 'doing a bit of ringing in one of the gorges where the grass always seems to be sour'.

2. [f. RING *v.*² a.] Of livestock: the action of milling (see quot. 1868).

1868 C.W. BROWNE *Overlanding in Aust.* 77 Sometimes two or three commence butting each other, and then start running round the mob; this is taken up by all the rest, and away they go round and round like a whirlpool, kicking up their legs and buckjumping like horses. They then suddenly turn and go the other way, blowing and puffing the whole time, and kicking up an awful dust... After an hour's amusement of this sort, they stop of their own accord. This evolution is termed 'ringing'. It is a good sign rather than otherwise, and proves the sheep are in good pluck. **1934** C. SAYCE *Comboman* 73 There's one thing that'll make a mess of the mob more than anything else and that's ringing.

ringneck. Any of several predom. green parrots of the genus *Barnardius*, having a narrow yellow collar on the darker plumage of the neck. Also **ringneck** (or **ring-necked**) **parrot**.

1888 W.H. WILLSHIRE *Aborigines of Central Aust.* 6 Parrots of many kinds—ring-necks, blue bonnets, and goolahs, furnish the natives with many a meal. **1897** J.J. MURIF *From Ocean to Ocean* 60 Now and again . . one catches sight of the gaudier galah or the gay ring-necked parrot. **1945** C. BARRETT *Austral. Bird Life* 80 The ringneck parrot (*Barnardius barnardi*) inhabits the interior of southern Queensland, New South Wales, Victoria (north-western areas), and South Australia.

ring snake. Any of several banded snakes, esp. BANDY-BANDY. Also **ringed snake**.

1844 *Duncan's Weekly Register* 16 Nov. 246/1 The Water or Ring snake is usually found in wells, water holes, or stagnant pools. **1956** T.Y. HARRIS *Naturecraft in Aust.* 51 The Bandy Bandy or Ringed Snake, which is also venomous but not dangerous, grows from 1 foot 8 inches to 2 feet 6 inches long.

ringtail.

1. [See quots. 1854 and 1941.] Any of several possums of the genera *Pseudocheirus* and *Hemibelideus* of e. Aust. incl. Tas., s.w. W.A., and New Guinea, esp. the common *P. peregrinus*. In full **ring-tail** (or **ring-tailed**) **possum**. Also *attrib.*

1820 J. OXLEY *Jrnls. Two Exped. N.S.W.* 171 He went down to us the game he had procured (a ring-tailed opossum). **1854** W. HOWITT *Boy's Adventures* 185 There is a smaller kind, called the ring-tailed opossum, because the tail curls itself up into the shape of a ring, not upwards, but downwards. **1886** A.W. HOWITT *On Austral. Medicine Men* 52, I used to keep it in a bag of ringtail 'possum skin. **1909** E. ASH *Austral. Oracle* 15 The dogs had scented a ringtail to a gum tree. **1941** E. TROUGHTON *Furred Animals Aust.* 104 In its broadest scope, this genus [*Pseudocheirus*] embraces all the familiar little ring-tailed possums which derive their popular name from the long and tapered tail, the prehensile end of which is usually curled into a ring owing to its constant use in gripping branches when climbing.

2. RING-IN *n.* 1; also *transf.*, RING-IN *n.* 2.

1908 *Truth* (Sydney) 19 Jan. 9/5 Then you'll follow our example, and you'll never run a bye—When you've got a good old 'ringtail' on the job. **1919** *Smith's Weekly* (Sydney) 5 July 5/1 Ringing-in has become a lost art. Racing officials, and followers of the sport are too keen to permit of its success nowadays; the ringtail is quickly recognised, and the plans of the schemers fall through. **1967** [see RING-IN *n.* 2].

3. A coward. Also as *v. intr.*, to act in a cowardly manner; to desert.

1941 S.J. BAKER *Pop. Dict. Austral. Slang* 60 *Ringtail*, a coward. **1959** E. LAMBERT *Glory thrown In* 212 'Private

Watford back?' asked Christy. 'Yair. Why?'.. 'Reckon he might ringtail?' 'Anyone of us might.'

Hence **ringtailer** *n.*, one who hunts possums.

1919 *Bulletin* (Sydney) 18 Sept. 20/2 Up in the north-east of Tasmania there has been a dreadful slaughter of 'possums. Some 'ringtailers' have raked in as much as £200 for skins this winter.

ring the tin ruling: see RING *v.*[4]

ringy, *a.* Of cattle: inclined to mill.

1976 C.D. MILLS *Hobble Chains & Greenhide* 40 'I was coming down from the top end one time', he related, 'with eighteen hundred ringy six and seven year olds.'

rip, *v.*

1. In the phr. **to rip (it) into** (someone), 'to tear a strip off' (someone).

1940 *Cobbers* (Brisbane) 20 Dec. 1 Many.. watched Sgt. Gordon Owens.. drilling the two culprits and ripping it into them. **1970** D. WILLIAMSON *Coming of Stork* (1974) 5 They've been ripping into me about punctuality. I can't afford to be late.

2. [Prob. as a euphemism for ROOT *v.*[2] 2.]

a. In the phr. **wouldn't it rip you**: see WOULD. **b.** In the imp. phr. **get ripped,** 'shut up!' 'get lost!'

1948 *Khaki Bush & Bigotry* (1968) 96 'Aw, get ripped.'.. 'You big galah.. get a great big woolly pup.' **1966** D. NILAND *Pairs & Loners* 16 'So I pity you.' 'Get ripped,' he said. 'What's more', I said, 'you're unintelligent.'

ripper. [Br. slang and dial. *ripper* something especially good; now chiefly Austral. (see OED(S *sb.* 3 a.).] Something (or someone) which excites admiration. Also *attrib.* and as *exclam.*

1858 C.R. THATCHER *Colonial Songster* (rev. ed.) 87 One of them had a frying-pan, And 'twas a regular ripper; And another laid about him With an old tin dipper. **1977** W. MOORE *Just to Myself* 82 'Hang on!' yells Tip, trying to get back to the steering wheel. 'Watch this for a skid!' and next thing you know we go into this almighty skid, do a beaut figure eight, and finish up the way we came. 'Bloody ripper, eh?' bawls out Tip. **1977** E. MACKIE *Oh to be Aussie* 58 Everyone had a ripper time on rum at the Rocks.

rise. [f. U.S. *to make a rise* to win or make money: see Mathews *rise, n.* 2 b.] A substantial profit or gain, esp. from gold-mining. Freq. in the phr. **to make a rise.**

1876 'EIGHT YRS.' RESIDENT' *Queen of Colonies* 165 Hundreds who had before been in great poverty, 'made a rise' on Jimna. **1898** *Bulletin* (Sydney) 2 July 15/1 A Gippslander tells of the origin of his 'rise'... I picked up a stone to throw at my dog.. but saw gold glistening... It was a half ounce specimen, an' set me hunting for the reef.

rising. Short for 'the rising of the court' (see quot. 1908).

1907 *Truth* (Sydney) 9 June 9/6 Some people after 'doing' their sentence find themselves in a queer position. At the Water Police Court.. a woman.. was fined 5s. or 'the rising'. Not having the 5s., she did the latter, and then, when discharged, found herself without even the fare back to Manly. **1908** *Ibid.* 19 July 1/7 People who have in the dim religious light of the previous evening, been 'on it', next morning are fined 'five shillings, or the rising'... Those that choose the alternative are escorted back to the cells, and again placed under lock and key, where they are kept until 'checked'. It is quite a common occurrence, however, for those so incarcerated to be liberated long after the rising of the court.

rising sun. A badge, originally a half-circle of swords and bayonets radiating from a crown, esp. as worn by a member of the Australian Imperial Force in the war of 1914–18. Also *transf.* (see quot. 1919).

c **1919** J.A. GAULT *Padre Gault's Stunt Bk.* 125 A surprise for this Hun was the 'Old Rising Sun', That smashed up his Hindenberg Line. **1929** 'F. BLAIR' *Digger Sea-Mates* 112 Whose boots were not bright as a mirror, 'Kiwied' to the highest perfection? Whose 'rising suns' were not as resplendent as their shining prototype above?

rissole, *v. trans.* Euphem. var. of ARSEHOLE.

1971 *Bulletin* (Sydney) 3 July 40/3 When today's footie heroes look like yesterday's poofters there's not much spice in rissoling short-hairs. **1979** *Age* (Melbourne) 2 July 9/1 He was West Australian, he reminded his team-mates. Over there pitches played truly, and if you picked the right ball you could '*safely tug four bits off the deck at the WACA without fear of getting rissoled for a gozzer by a guzunder'*.

river.

1. Used *attrib.* in Special Comb. **river claim** [also U.S., see Mathews 2], a mining claim that extends into a watercourse; **flat,** FLAT *n.*[1]; **frontage,** FRONTAGE 1.

1859 *Colonial Mining Jrnl.* June 79/1 Claims are divided into three sorts—alluvial claims, **river claims,** and quartz claims. **1888** *Southern Austral.* (Adelaide) 8 Sept. 3/1 Lagoons and creeks intersected the **river flats.** **1839** R. TORRENS *Emigration Ireland to S.A.* 28 The Surveyor-General, sold some rural land having **river frontage,** and containing brick earth, for £90 per acre.

2. In the names of flora and fauna: **river blackfish,** the fish *Gadopsis marmoratus* (see BLACKFISH); **garfish,** any of several fish of the fam. Hemirhamphidae, esp. *Hyporhamphus ardelio* of all mainland States but not N.T.; see also BEAKIE, GARFISH; **gum,** any of several trees of the genus *Eucalyptus* (fam. Myrtaceae) occurring near watercourses, esp. *E. camaldulensis* (see RED GUM 1); **oak,** any of several trees of the fam. Casuarinaceae, esp. the usu. large *Casuarina cunninghamiana,* occurring along rivers and fresh-water streams in N.S.W., Qld., and N.T.; **creek oak,** see CREEK 3; **red gum,** the tree *Eucalyptus camaldulensis* (see RED GUM 1).

1906 D.G. STEAD *Fishes of Aust.* 210 The so-called 'Slippery' or **River Blackfish** (*Gadopsis marmoratus*), also known occasionally as the 'Marbled River-Cod'. **1881** *Proc. Linnean Soc. N.S.W.* VI. 245 *Hemirhamphus regularis*.. '**River Gar Fish**' of Sydney Fishermen. **1974** J.M. THOMSON *Fish Ocean & Shore* 131 In contrast to.. primarily marine garfish, the river garfish (*Hemirhamphus ardelio*) is very common in estuaries and the young penetrate even into fresh water. **1881** W.E. ABBOTT *Notes Journey on Darling* 42 After crossing the Darling on the western side, except along the edge, I saw nothing deserving the name of a tree. The coolabar.. and the **river gums,** which grow only within about 100 yards of the water, are the only trees to be found. **1817** A. CUNNINGHAM in I. Marriott *Early Explorers Aust.* 9 Apr. (1925) 176 *Casuarina torulosa* (**River Oak**).. with another species of Eucalyptus called by the colonists 'Stringy Bark'. **1900** *Proc. Linnean Soc. N.S.W.* XXV. 712 Forest Red Gum, in some situations, is scarcely distinguishable from *E[ucalyptus] rostrata* (**River Red Gum**) except by the fruits.

Riverina bluebell. [f. the name of a district in s. N.S.W.] PATERSON'S CURSE.

1976 W.A. BAYLEY *Border City* (rev. ed.) 84 Patterson's curse.. has been sold as Riverina Bluebell on the flower stalls in Martin Place, Sydney and as Riverina Heath in Melbourne. Its beauty blooming in paddocks remains undisputed. **1980** *Canberra Times* 23 July 1/2 Paterson's curse, sometimes known as Salvation Jane or Riverina bluebells, is a purple-flowered plant which grows extensively throughout southern Australia.

road.

1. *pl. Obs.*

a. [Orig. Br. but not attested after 1771: see OED *sb.* 5 b.] In the phr. **to take to the roads**: see quot 1835.

1835 *Colonist* (Sydney) 330 July 243/2 Punishments of runaways have not been sufficiently felt to discourage a repetition of the crime of absconding. 'Taking to the bush', or roads, as usually termed, must in general be considered as taking to robbery. **1889** J.H.L. ZILLMANN *Past & Present Austral. Life* 77 Scoundrels from every part of the world . . infested the gold-fields to 'take to the roads', as it was called, and make themselves the possessors of immense wealth by one daring onslaught upon the gold escort.

b. Of a convict (later a convicted person): in the phr. **(up)on** (or **to**) **the roads,** *ellipt.* for 'forced labour on the roads'.

1837 *Rep. Select Committee Transportation* 283 The principal superintendent holds in his hand the assignment list . . stating to what service he is assigned, whether he is to go to any individual, or whether to be sent upon the roads. **1840** *Tasmanian Weekly Dispatch* (Hobart) 7 Feb. 7 Indulgence suspended, and three months to the roads. **1843** *Sydney Morning Herald* 10 July 2/5 The Court sentenced the prisoner to be kept at hard labour on the roads for twelve calendar months. **1871** *Austral. Town & Country Jrnl.* (Sydney) 29 Apr. 516/1 At the circuit court today, Jacob Donovan was convicted of cattle stealing, and sentenced to five years on the roads.

2. Used allusively with reference to droving, esp. in the phr. **on the road.** See also TRACK *n.* 2 a. Also *attrib.*

1901 *Bulletin* (Sydney) 7 Dec. 30/2 Cattle 'on the road' are unaccountable animals. **1929** *Bulletin* (Sydney) 14 Aug. 23/3, I wanted a cook on a road camp. . . A dapper chap blew along with Matilda and said: 'You want a cook?'

3. Special Comb. **road ant,** *meat ant* (a), see MEAT; **board** [used elsewhere but recorded earliest in Aust. (see OEDS *road, sb.* 10 a.)], a local body having responsibility for the maintenance of roads (but see also quot. 1927); also **roads board; gang** *hist.*, a detachment of convicts (later prisoners) detailed to work at road construction; **hut** *obs.*, a dwelling provided for the accommodation of convicts working on the roads; **paddock,** a paddock adjacent to a road; **party** *obs.*, *road gang*; also *transf.* and *attrib.*, as **road party boots; station** *obs.*, an outpost at which a road gang is based; **train,** see quot. 1968; LAND TRAIN.

1925 *Bulletin* (Sydney) 25 June 24/4 If they are '**road**' or 'meat' **ants,** let him run a circle of coal tar around the nests. **1856** W.H.G. KINGSTON *Emigrant's Home* 170 A letter to the **Road Board,** offering to construct the bridges at £60 each. **1927** J. POLLARD *Rose of Bushlands* 174 'The Culgoa Roads Board', he explained, 'allows us three months in which to fumigate and poison. . . It means that a farmer is frequently done with it before his neighbour begins, and naturally rabbits come from his neighbour's farm to his.' **1819** *Sydney Gaz.* 23 Jan., Four Men who had eloped from the Sydney **Road Gang. 1825** *Hobart Town Gaz.* 8 Oct., If it is thought requisite to inspect all cattle and sheep brought into Hobart Town, it is surely no less necessary to have those intended for the road parties examined before slaughtering them; yet those supplying are allowed to kill, either at their own houses, or at the **road huts. 1902** *Bulletin* (Sydney) 8 Nov. 16/4 My mate and I were stripping wattle in the **road-paddock. 1822** J.T. BIGGE *Rep. State Colony N.S.W.* 38 The labour of the **road parties,** and the shell gangs, exposes the convicts to the evil effects of slight control and great temptation. **1945** S.J. BAKER *Austral. Lang.* 182 Leggings worn by outback travellers and workers are known as *dog stiffeners*. . . Heavy boots were called road party boots. **1831** *Sydney Herald* 8 Aug. 3/1 Masters are to pay twenty shillings for every assigned servant they may receive from the ship or **road stations,** as a remuneration to Government for slops. **1940** *Aust.: Nat. Jrnl.* Sept. 17 Recent developments in the use of **road trains** carrying over 20 tons of goods. **1968** D. O'GRADY *Bottle of Sandwiches* 159 In case you don't know what a road-train is, it's a prime-mover pulling anything up to half a dozen big trailers loaded up with live cattle, or all sorts of everything.

roany. [f. *roan* + -Y.] A roan-coloured animal.

1891 *Truth* (Sydney) 17 May 1/5 He was cremating the dead 'Roany' or 'Strawberry'. **1929** W.J. RESIDE *Golden Days* 381 Castieau's raking roanies Could show their dust to most.

roar, *v.* [Chiefly Austral.: see OEDS *roar, v.* 4 C.] *trans.* With **up:** to reprimand; to berate. Also as *vbl. n.*

1917 *Advocate* (Burnie) 13 July 3/6 Mag will roar me up if I get back without a settlement. **1933** 'TRAMWAY WORKERS' *Shock Brigader* 5 'You were tryin' to scale me, you young varmint,' said Mick with an angry scowl, and didn't he give that young varmint a 'roaring up'?

roarer. Abbrev. of BULLROARER.

1928 B. SPENCER *Wanderings in Wild Aust.* 274 When whirled round the little slab rotates in the air, tightening the string, which then vibrates and gives out a sound, the quality of which depends upon the size of the 'roarer'. **1963** I.L. IDRIESS *Our Living Stone Age* 113 Hidden somewhere where the formation of rock and earth would cause sound to reverberate with increasing volume, there would be forty or more practised men whirling those roarers round their heads.

roaring, *ppl. a.* [Spec. use of *roaring,* characterized by riotous or noisy behaviour.] In special collocations: **roaring days,** the time of the gold rushes; **fifties,** the 1850s, the time of the gold rushes in Victoria.

1896 H. LAWSON *In Days when World was Wide* 33 And you and I were faithful mates All through the **roaring days**! **1896** *Worker* (Sydney) 26 Dec. 1/1 One . . has been privileged to listen to the yarns of the 'old timers', the diggers of the '**roaring fifties**'.

roart, var. RORT *n.*

robbery under arms. BUSHRANGING 1.

1864 *Illustr. Sydney News* 16 Nov. 2/3 Three troopers . . have arrested a man . . suspected of . . several charges of robbery under arms. **1912** J. BRADSHAW *Highway Robbery under Arms* (ed. 3) 41 Bushranging, for instance—or robbery under arms.

robbo. *Obs.* [f. *Rob(inson* (see quots. 1897) + -O.] Orig. in the derisive call **four-bob robbo:** see quot. 1897 (2). Used *transf.* of something in a deteriorated or unsatisfactory condition, esp. a (horse and) light conveyance. Also *attrib.*

1897 *Bulletin* (Sydney) 2 Jan. 13/4 Sydney's wild-rabbit and bottle-merchants now take their 'donahs' out driving on Sundays in a 'four-bob robbo', *i.e.,* sulky. Now what is the derivation of 'robbo'? **1897** *Ibid.* 23 Jan. 11/3 'Four Bob Robbo'—four shillings Robinson, who lived in the classic suburb of Waterloo, Sydney . . came into a bit of money and bought a horse and trap. The money was spent, and Robinson tired of the horse, which got poor; so he then sometimes let out the horse and trap (both somewhat worse for wear) for 4s. per half-day. There was a run on the cheap hire, and Rob. bought two other horses and traps, which he let out at the same price. A neighbouring livery-stable keeper and his employés resented Rob's cutting-down prices; and, when any of the rival's equipages passed, used to cry out, in derision, 'Four Bob Robbo!' The cry was taken up by the kids, and has now become a Waterloo classic. **1909** R. KALESKI *Austral. Settler's Compl. Guide* 20 Carefully avoid delivery vans, 'robbo' fruit carts and such like, they are too wide and heavy.

robin. [Transf. use of *robin* the robin redbreast: see next.] Any of many small, active birds, some having a brightly coloured breast, of the fam. Pachycephalidae. Also with distinguishing epithet, as **dusky, flame, pink-breasted, red-capped, rose, scarlet, scrub, white-breasted, yellow** (see under first element).

1825 J. LATHAM *Gen. Hist. Birds* VI. 211 [Scarlet-bellied Flycatcher] .. called the Robin of New South Wales, and Norfolk Island, where it is most numerous. **1985** *Age* (Melbourne) 9 Sept. 15/5 The Australian wrens, warblers and robins are quite unrelated to their namesakes in the Northern Hemisphere.

robin redbreast. [Transf. use of *robin redbreast* the European bird *Erithacus rubecula*.]
1. A red-breasted robin, esp. *scarlet robin* (see SCARLET); *red breast*, see RED *a*. 1 b.
1845 C. GRIFFITH *Present State & Prospects Port Phillip* 127 The robin-redbreast is worthy of particular mention. It is a beautiful little bird, with black and grey body, and bright scarlet breast. **1948** P.J. HURLEY *Red Cedar* 160 They are robin red breast, rose and hooded robins. Few birds are more loved.
2. *fig. Obs.*
1886 *Once a Month* (Melbourne) IV. 33 My attention was attracted by a bullock-driver taking his team along the bank... He was one of the old stamp known as 'Robin Redbreasts'. His open serge shirt exposing his chest to the sun and weather had made it as red as an Aberdeen moon.

rock, *n.*
1. *Gold-mining. Obs.* Bedrock: see quot. 1856.
1856 S.C. BREES *How to farm & settle in Aust.* 57 This lowest bottom, 'the rock', as it is emphatically termed, in reference to its character as a bar to further digging for gold, is often the depository upon its irregular surface of considerable gold deposits. **1857** W. WESTGARTH *Vic. & Austral. Gold Mines* 248 They reached 'the rock' without finding any auriferous drifts.
2. In the names of flora and fauna: **rock cod,** any of several marine fish inhabiting reefs and rocky waters, incl. *Pseudophycis barbata* of s. Aust.; also with distinguishing epithet, as **black, red** (see under first element); **fern,** any of several ferns of the genus *Cheilanthes* (fam. Adiantaceae), esp. *C. austrotenuifolia* of all States and elsewhere; **flathead,** any of several marine fish of the fam. Platycephalidae, living among weed-covered rocks or reefs, esp. *Platycephalus laevigatus* of s. Aust. and *Thysanophrys cirronasus* of W.A., S.A., and N.S.W.; **kangaroo,** any of several macropods, esp. WALLAROO; **lily** (or **orchid**), an epiphytic or lithophytic orchid of the genus *Dendrobium* (fam. Orchidaceae), esp. *D. speciosum* of e. mainland Aust., cultivated as an ornamental; **lobster,** any of several marine crayfish, some of which are fished commercially for the tail-meat, the most important being the western rock lobster *Panulirus cygnus*; **melon** [also U.S.], the fragrant edible fruit of the cultivated melon *Cucumis melo* ssp. *agrestis* (fam. Cucurbitaceae); the plant itself; any of several other similar plants; **oyster,** any of several oysters occurring on the rocky substrate of estuaries and bays, esp. *Saccostrea commercialis* (see *Sydney rock* SYDNEY 2); **parrot** (or **parakeet**), the predom. olive to yellow-olive parrot *Neophema petrophila* of rocky islands and coastal s. and s.w. Aust.; **pebbler (pebblar, peplar),** SMOKER; also *attrib.*; **pigeon,** either of two brown pigeons of the genus *Petrophassa* inhabiting rocky parts of n. Aust., the *white-quilled rock pigeon* (see WHITE *a.*[2] 1 b.) and the chestnut-quilled rock pigeon *P. rufipennis*; any of several other pigeons of similar habitat; **poison,** the poisonous shrub *Gastrolobium callistachys* (fam. Fabaceae) of s.w. W.A.; **python,** any of several snakes of the fam. Boidae, esp. *Morelia amethistina* of n.e. Qld. and elsewhere, the largest Austral. python, and the olive python, *Bothrochilus olivaceus* (syn. *Liasis olivaceus*) of n. Aust.; **ringtail,** the possum *Pseudocheirus dahli* of n.e. W.A. and n. N.T.; WOGOIT; also **rock possum, rock-haunting ringtail; wallaby,** any small wallaby of the genera *Petrogale* and *Peradorcas,* inhabiting rocky ranges and rock-strewn outcrops of mainland Aust.; WIRRANG; also with distinguishing epithet, as **brush-tailed, yellow-footed** (see under first element); **warbler,** the predom. dark brown and rufous bird *Origma solitaria* of rocky sandstone gullies and caves in e. N.S.W.; **whiting,** any of several marine fish of the fam. Odacidae, esp. *Haletta semifasciata* of s. Aust.; STRANGER 2.

1790 R. CLARK Jrnl. 19 Apr. 159, 16 fishes consisting of Snappers Blue fish and one **Rock Cod. 1923** *Census Plants Vic.* (Field Naturalists' Club Vic.) 3 *Cheilanthes tenuifolia*.. **Rock Fern. 1873** F. DE CASTELNAU *Edible Fishes Vic.* 11 They [*sc.* the flat-heads, or *Platycephalus*] form several sorts, of which the two most common are the *Bassensis* and the *Laevigatus*; the latter is called **rock flat-head. 1826** J. ATKINSON *Acct. Agric. & Grazing N.S.W.* 23 The wayrang or **rock kangaroo. 1833** W.H. BRETON *Excursions* 89 **Rock lillies**.. are uncommonly beautiful. **1923** *Census Plants Vic.* (Field Naturalists' Club Vic.) 18 *Dendrobium speciosum*.. Rock Orchid. **1909** G. SMITH *Naturalist in Tas.* 108 In Tasmania the term crayfish is applied to the marine **Rock Lobster** (*Panulirus*). **1841** *Sydney Herald* 6 Mar. 2/6 The **rock** and water **melons** are even superior to what you see in Sydney. **1858** A.C. & F.T. GREGORY *Jrnls. Austral. Explorations* 29 Apr. (1884) 39 A small species of rock-melon was.. found in great abundance. **1770** J. COOK *Jrnls.* 23 Aug. (1955) I. 394 The Shell-fish are Oysters of 3 or 4 sorts, viz **Rock oysters** and Mangrove Oysters which are small, Pearl Oysters, and Mud Oysters, these last are the best and largest. **1844** [**rock parrot**] J. GOULD *Birds of Aust.* (1848) V. Pl. 40, *Euphema petrophila*.. Rock Parrakeet, Colonists of Swan River. **1867** 'COLONIST' *Life's Work* 118 Many of the parrots are most gorgeous in plumage.. blue mountain parrots, rock parrots, ground parrots. **1890** 'MRS A. MACLEOD' *Austral. Girl* (1894) 231 'And parrots scream rather loudly, too; don't they?' 'Yes; but there are times when they warble most musically; not only the smaller kinds.. but also larger ones, like the **rock-pebblers. 1952** A.C.C. LOCK *Travels across Aust.* 173 At Wood Wood the river was close, and among the gums here we caught glimpses of rock pebblar parrakeets. **1965** *Austral. Encycl.* VII. 474 Rock pebbler.. rock-peplar... It may be that 'pebbler', or 'peplar', was corrupted by dealers through the specific name, *anthopeplus*, meaning 'robed in flowers'. **1845** L. LEICHHARDT *Jrnl. Overland Exped. Aust.* (1847) 11 Nov. 476 A new species of **rock pigeon** (Petrophassa..) with a dark brown body, primaries light brown without any white. [**1865 rock poison:** 'SPECIAL CORRESPONDENT' *Transportation* 14 Whole districts are overrun with strong quick-growing bushes, the juices of which are fatal to animal life. There are no less than fourteen known varieties of these plants, but only four are commonly pointed out. These are the York-road, the heart-leaf, the rock, and the box-scrub.] **1875** J. FORREST *Explorations in Aust.* 61 Country studded here and there with granite rocks, with good feed around them—in some places rock poison. **1934** A. RUSSELL *Tramp-Royal* 251 We rode almost on top of a **rock python** one day... He was ten feet long. [**1895 rock ringtail:** *Zoologischer Anzeiger* (Leipzig) XVIII. 464 *Pseudochirus dahlii* n. sp. The Rock Phalanger... 7 Specimens (1 male, 6 females) collected by a Norwegian traveller, Dr Knut Dahl, May 1895.] **1941** E. TROUGHTON *Furred Animals Aust.* 115 It seems therefore that the rock ring-tail has somewhat lowered the arboreal standard of its near relatives in adapting its habits to the unusual surroundings, at the north-west extremity of its mainland range. **1942** C. BARRETT *From Bush Hut* 37 'Got it from a lubra for half a stick o' 'bacca,' he informed me, holding up the spitted *wogoit* (that's a blackfellow name for the rock-possum). **1943** —— *Austral. Animal Bk.* 71 The rock-haunting ringtail (*Petropseudo dahli*).. lives among granite formations in the Northern Territory, and was discovered by Dr Knut Dahl, after whom it was named, in the Mary River country. **1844** L. LEICHHARDT *Jrnl. Overland Exped. Aust.* 25 Nov. (1847) 49 According to Mr Gilbert, **rock wallabies** were very numerous. **1813** J.W. LEWIN *Birds N.S.W.* 3 **Rock Warbler**.. frequents caverns inaccessible to Mankind, and deep rocky Gullies, creeping in the Cavities and Chasms. **1878** *Proc. Linnean Soc. N.S.W.* III. 390

Odax semifasciatus.. is called '**rock whiting**' at Sydney, and is fourteen inches long; obtained in May. **1974** T.D. SCOTT et al. *Marine & Freshwater Fishes S.A.* 313 This species [*sc. Haletta semifasciata*] is our most abundant Rock Whiting in South Australia. It is usually found in weedy and rock areas in shallow to moderately deep-water.

3. Special Comb. **rock ape,** a derogatory term for a (black) person; **-chopper,** a navvy; also *transf.*, a Roman Catholic; so **-chopping** *vbl. n.*; **-hole,** GNAMMA HOLE; also **rock water-hole; -hopper,** one who fishes from coastal rocks; **shelter,** an Aboriginal cave-dwelling (see also GIBBER-GUNYAH); also *attrib.*

1972 *Bulletin* (Sydney) 17 June 4/3 The good relationships which these expatriates develop is too often counteracted by the Territorian who refers to his workers as '**rock apes**'.. or 'kanakas' and treats them as 'idle, useless blacks'. **1984** M. ELDRIDGE *Walking Dog* 217 Who's walking you home, not those rockapes, I trust? **1908** *Truth* (Sydney) 22 Mar. 4/7 Ninety per cent. of the **rock-choppers** do not follow the vocation more than about three or four years before they are in an advanced stage of consumption, victims to what is known among them as the 'sewer disease'. This is caused by the stone-dust continually inhaled by the men. **1918** *Huon Times* (Franklin) 20 Dec. 3/2 Mrs Bill Smith, whose old man has got a job rock-chopping at Cremorne. **1982** E. CAMPION *Rockchoppers* 2 A symbol of such unfriendliness was the nickname 'rock-choppers'. Unknown to most Catholics, the word was used privately by ascendant Protestants to express their dislike of the Irish-Australians whose proletarian roots went back to the convict rockchoppers. 'Rockchoppers' remained an underground word, outside the reference books, until last year, when the *Macquarie Dictionary* gave it an entry, guessing (wrongly, in my view) that its origins lay in the initials RC. **1875** J. FORREST *Explorations in Aust.* 111 Camped on a grassy rise, close to a small **rock** water-**hole**. **1973** V. SERVENTY *Desert Walkabout* 24 Bunjil rockhole was unusual in that a vertical tunnel went down about twenty-four feet into the rock. **1917** C. THACKERAY *Goliath Joe* 74 Several **rock-hoppers**—users of long rods and landing nets—were clustered round the corner. **1892** *N.S.W. Geol. Survey Rec.* 34 The aboriginal name for these **Rock-shelters** appears to have been that of 'Gibber-gunyas', literally, 'houses of rock', at any rate, in the Port Jackson and Hawkesbury Districts. **1954** A.P. ELKIN *Austral. Aborigines* 191 The ritual means of increasing man and natural species.. is associated with cave and rock-shelter paintings.

rock, *v. Gold-mining.* [Orig. U.S.: see OED $v.^1$ 4 b.] *trans.* To wash auriferous material (in a CRADLE *n.* 1). Also *absol.*

1851 *Empire* (Sydney) 20 May 2/2 Many a hand which had been trained to kid gloves.. became nervous to clutch the pick and crow-bar or 'rock the cradle' at our infant mines. **1884** 'R. BOLDREWOOD' *Old Melbourne Memories* 168 Each man dug, or rocked, or bore, As if salvation with the ore Of the mine monarch lay.

rocker. *Gold-mining. Obs.* [Orig. U.S.: see OED(S $n.^1$ 4 c.]

a. CRADLE *n.* 1.

1851 *Bell's Life in Sydney* 31 May 1/4 The rocker or cradle may be made of half inch soft stuff—and consists essentially of first, a trough say 10 inches deep, 18 inches broad, and 4 feet long... This trough, placed on rockers like a cradle.. forms the rocker. **1855** G.H. WATHEN *Golden Colony* 71 The method of washing the earth has been also much modified by time and experience. At first, all was done by the *cradle* or *rocker*, and the tin dish.

b. Abbrev. of *cradle-rocker* (see CRADLE *n.* 2).

1853 J. SHERER *Gold Finder Aust.* 60 When all the earth is washed away, the rocker and washer cast their longing eyes into the sieve to see if there be a 'nugget' too large to get through the holes.

rocking horse. Used allusively of something not readily obtainable, esp. in the phr. **as rare as rocking-horse manure.**

1944 G.H. FEARNSIDE *Sojourn in Tobruk* 33 Australian cigarettes were as rare as rocking-horse manure hereabouts. **1981** *Bulletin* (Sydney) 16 June 81/2 The price in Australia, allowing freight and costs, is nearly par with the sterling price. And that, these days, is as rare as rocking horse manure.

rogaine /ˈroʊgeɪn/. [See quot. 1986.] A rogaining event.

1982 N. & R. PHILLIPS *Rogaining* 1 Although rogaines are defined as being 12 hours or longer, the classic rogaine is the 24 hour event. **1986** *ACT Orienteering News* Mar. 7 According to the book 'Rogaining—cross-country navigation' by Neil and Rod Phillips, the term was introduced in 1976 to coordinate and promote a rapidly developing sport which had originated as the Melbourne Uni. Mountaineering Club 24 hour walk (a line event).. and, later, the Surrey Thomas Rover Crew annual hike. The contribution of Neil, Rod and also Gail Phillips in promotion of the sport initially in Victoria and later in W.A. and Tas. is understated in the book, and no explanation is offered for the term which *they* introduced. However, it is altogether too much of a coincidence that '*rogaine*' is a compound word of the first letters of each of their names: Rod, Gail and Neil.

rogaining /ˈroʊgeɪnɪŋ/, *vbl. n.* [f. prec.] A sport similar to 'orienteering', in which teams compete over a course which requires at least twelve hours to complete: see quot. 1982.

1982 N. & R. PHILLIPS *Rogaining* 1 Rogaining is the sport of long distance cross-country navigation in which teams of two to five members visit as many checkpoints as possible in an allocated period. Teams travel entirely on foot, navigating by map and compass in terrain that varies from open farmland to thick, hilly forest. A central base camp provides hot meals throughout the event and teams may return there at any time to eat, rest or sleep. **1984** *5th Austral. Rogaining Championships* (Advt.), Rogaining is a relatively new sport which may be described as competitive bushwalking or marathon orienteering.

Hence **rogainer** *n.*, one who engages in rogaining.

1982 N. & R. PHILLIPS *Rogaining* 8 The easy terrain of Kimbolton Forest suited the many beginners and was a new experience for the seasoned rogainers.

roley-poley, var. ROLY-POLY.

roll, $v.^1$ *Hist.* [Spec. use of *roll* to travel or move about (see OED(S $v.^2$ 12 a. and b.); the sense 'to arrive, to appear on the scene' is later and used elsewhere.] *intr.* With **up**: to assemble for a meeting (see ROLL UP 1). Freq. *imp.*

1861 *Miner & General Advertiser* (Lambing Flat) 20 Feb. 3/2 '*Roll up! Roll up!*' is the general watchword of the miners on the diggings. **1892** 'R. BOLDREWOOD' *Nevermore* III. 16 We heard as the Ballarat men was talking of 'rolling up' if the licenses wasn't lowered.

roll, $v.^2$ [Spec. use of *roll* to form into a roll or ball: see OED(S $v.^2$ 8.]

1. *trans.* To pack (one's belongings, swag, etc.) prior to departure. Freq. *absol.* with **up**.

1872 G.S. BADEN-POWELL *New Homes for Old Country* 124 In the morning one of them starts the flock, leaving his mates to 'roll up' and follow. **1978** R.H. CONQUEST *Dusty Distances* 37 We rolled our swags, the two New South Welshmen giving me hints about balance, tightness of binding straps, and so on.

2. *Shearing. trans.* To roll (a newly-shorn fleece): see quot. 1979.

[N.Z. **1863** E.R. CHUDLEIGH *Diary* (1950) 75, I was picking up and rowling [*sic*] the fleeces.] **1874** *Illustr. Sydney News* 19 Dec. 15/1 Mr Fisher had a shed erected at his own expense, floored with deal, fitted up with pens for sheep, bench for rolling fleece and press for packing. **1979** HARMSWORTH & DAY *Wool & Mohair* 159 The reason for rolling the fleece is to keep each fleece separate so that it can be handled readily for classing and pressing, to command the attention of the buyer by presenting it in an attractive manner, and so that it can be readily opened when being sorted for the manufacturer.

Hence **rolling-table** *n.*, a bench upon which a fleece is rolled.

1899 G. JEFFREY *Princ. Australasian Woolclassing* 39 Second cuts .. fall beneath the spokes of the rolling tables and are called locks, and do not bring one-third of the price of fleece wool.

roll, $v.^3$ [Spec. use of *roll* to flatten with a roller: see OED $v.^2$ 10.] *trans.* To crush and flatten (mallee scrub). Also with **down**.

1910 'YARRAN' *Mallee* 5 In some districts the Government, by means of a traction engine, rolls down the scrub, charging the settler 3s. per acre. **1983** A. CANNON *Bullocks, Bullockies & Other Blokes* 19 Rolling scrub, which was necessary to clear the land before farming could commence, was too rough and risky for horses, and, as few settlers owned bullock teams, they let out these jobs to contractors.

roll-call. *Shearing. Obs.* The reading out of names of shearers who have booked a stand in a shed in advance.

1899 *Bulletin* (Sydney) 19 Aug. 32/1 They never seemed to strike a union shed until at least a week after roll-call. **1909** W.G. SPENCE *Aust.'s Awakening* 82 Organisers were kept very busy, often knocking up several horses during the season in rapid riding to get from one shed to another in time to be at roll-call.

roller. *Shearing.* [f. ROLL $v.^2$ 2.] One who rolls a newly-shorn fleece. Also **roller-man**.

[N.Z. **1892** W.E. SWANTON *Notes on N.Z.* 96 The woolclasser with his assistant rollers.] **1899** G. JEFFREY *Princ. Australasian Woolclassing* 39 As soon as the fleece is off the sheep's back, the pickers-up take it by the breeches and place it on the rollers' tables. **1927** J. MATHIEU *Backblock Ballads* 7 And the pickers-up are streaking To the tables all a-grin, But the roller-men ain't peaking Though they've nearly built them in.

roll up. [f. ROLL $v.^1$]

1. *Hist.* A mass meeting of gold-miners called to consider an individual grievance or an issue of common concern; a summons to attend such a meeting: see quots. 1861 (2) and 1896. Also *attrib.*

1861 *Sydney Morning Herald* 28 Jan. 8/1 On the 18th instant there was a small roll up against the unfortunate Chinese. **1861** *Miner & General Advertiser* (Lambing Flat) 3 July 2/2 *Monster roll up.* The words which head our article have a peculiar meaning and significance; they remind us at once of those movements which had for their object the removal from amongst us of the Chinese, and which a few months ago caused the most profound sensation from the remotest interior to the metropolis. **1896** J.M. PRICE *Land of Gold* 103 Immediately a man is caught stealing, the 'roll up' is sounded, that is to say, a tin pannikin is beaten vigorously drumwise, and, on hearing this ominous sound, all the miners in the camp hurry up to the place. The case is roughly explained to them, an impromptu court is immediately formed, a president elected, and there and then the culprit is tried. If he is found guilty, and when he has been caught *in flagrante delicto*, there is of course no doubt about it, he is ordered to leave the camp .. and never return to it again under the risk of being tarred and feathered. **1929** R.D. LANE *Romance Old Coolgardie* 59 He had been reading in his tent (not playing at the two-up school) when, in response to the roll-up call he ventured forth.

2. *transf.* An assembly.

1889 *Bulletin* (Sydney) 2 Mar. 12/4 And of such men there'll many be, and of such leaders some, In the roll-up of Australians on some dark day yet to come. **1965** K. SMITH *OGF* 186 'We should get a big roll-up, Darce.' 'Yeah. It should be a great show. We'll keep the poker machines locked up and turn on the sherry.'

rolly-poley, rolly-polly, varr. ROLY-POLY.

roly. Abbrev. of ROLY-POLY.

1911 *Bulletin* (Sydney) 30 Mar. 44/2 A hundred rolies racing across a plain in the moonlight is a weird sight. **1973** R. ROBINSON *Drift of Things* 129 On a property near the Pilliga Scrub I landed a job cutting galvanized roly.

roly-poly. Also **roley-poley, rolly-poley** (or **-polly**). [See quot. 1907.] Any of several plants, usu. of arid and semi-arid Aust., which break off at ground level and roll along in the wind, esp. the rounded shrubs *Salsola kali* (fam. Chenopodiaceae), also known as BUCKBUSH, and *Sclerolaena muricata*. Also *attrib.*

1857 D. BUNCE *Australiasiatic Reminisc.* 168 Very common to these plains, was a large-growing *salsolaceous* plant, belonging to the *Chenopodeaceae.*.. These weeds grow in the form of a large ball. .. No sooner were a few of these balls (or, as we were in the habit of calling them, 'rolly-poleys') taken up with the current of air, than the mules began to kick and buck. **1862** G. BOURNE *Jrnl. Landsborough's Exped. from Carpentaria* 33 Far as the eye can reach these Downs extend, seldom relieved by timber, and covered with the eternal 'roley poley'. **1881** *Proc. Linnean Soc. N.S.W.* VI. 742 We saw .. *Salsola Kali* 'Salt-wort' or 'Rolly polly'. **1898** *Bulletin* (Sydney) 12 Mar. 14/3 Around a station near Breeza, the plains for miles were covered with what are known as 'rolly-poleys', and the crows were in swarms. **1907** *Ibid.* 13 June 15/1 The strange 'roly-poly'... This plant is one of Nature's marvels. Growing to a height of about 20 in., it looks like the back of a porcupine. It overturns sideways when a strong wind arrives, and rolls along and so scatters its seeds over the soil. **1946** W.E. HARNEY *North of 23°* 61 The rolypoly grass bounding past, jumping and leaping in the wind.

Rome Beauty. [Of unknown origin.] A variety of eating apple; the tree bearing such apples.

1893 D.A. CRICHTON *Australasian Fruit Culturist* I. 179 *Rome Beauty (Gillett's Seedling)*—An excellent American variety .. a first-class dessert Apple, and an excellent variety for a local market and export. **1972** *Mercury* (Hobart) 18 Nov. 1/2 Rome Beauty is probably the only variety which escaped serious damage, being much later to bloom.

roo, $n.^1$ Also **'roo.** Shortened form of JACKEROO $n.$ 2.

1891 *Truth* (Sydney) 19 Apr. 73 They .. will allow the dealers to feed in the hut, or even alongside of the *Roos*. **1976** *Bulletin* (Sydney) 3 Apr. 20/2 There soon became a certain fascination about jackarooing for the Minister for War, as one 'roo put it.

roo, $n.^2$ Also **'roo.**

a. Shortened form of KANGAROO $n.$ 1. Also *attrib.*

1898 *Bulletin* (Sydney) 12 Nov. 14/4 There is a brisk demand for 'roos tails among London epicures. **1946** *Bulletin* (Sydney) 24 July 29/1, I was runnin' the herd in the paddick with the 'roo-proof fence at night. **1983** *Daily News* (Perth) 11 Aug. 10/7, I used to shoot roos.

b. Used *attrib.* in Comb., as **roo dog, hunter, -hunting, -killing, meat, scalper, shooter, -shooting, skin, tail soup.**

1900 *Bulletin* (Sydney) 7 July 32/1 'I've seen the same thing ..,' said the 'roo-hunter. **1900** *Ibid.* 28 July 14/4 The dingo and 'roo-scalper can shoot.   **1917** T.J. BRIGGS *Life & Experiences Successful W. Austral.* 120, I was there for a certain purpose . . namely to obtain 'roo skins. *Ibid.* 122, I put in another winter at 'roo hunting.   **1932** I.L. IDRIESS *Lasseter's Last Ride* 17 'Roo-tail soup was a welcome addition to the bill of fare.   **1932** K.S. PRICHARD *Kiss on Lips* 83 She was as good a 'roo dog as I've seen and no mistake.   **1946** J.J. FAHEY *Slim Sullivan hits Wallaby* 14 His decision to become a roo shooter.   **1968** D. O'GRADY *Bottle of Sandwiches* 142 A hunk of roo meat skewered onto the biggest fork we had.   **1979** D. MAITLAND *Breaking Out* 127 We fell in with this bloke from out West who'd done a lot of roo-shooting for the dog-food factories.   **1986** *Canberra Times* 30 Aug. 6/2 (*heading*) Qld. 'threatening' mass roo-killing.

c. Special Comb. **roo bar, guard,** BULLBAR.

1973 J. GREENWAY *Down among Wild Men* 135 Unbendable **'roo bar'** to shunt kangaroos as the cowcatchers on our old locomotives.   **1972** *Southerly* iii. 216, I rinsed my mouth and drank sparingly from the waterbag on the **'roo guard**.

roo, *v. intr.* Shortened form of KANGAROO *v.* 1.

1907 *Bulletin* (Sydney) 17 Oct. 14/1 Meeting the boss 'rooing . . Midnight was invited to join the hunt.   **1964** E. LANE *Our Uncle Charlie* 134 It always amazed anyone going rooing with Uncle how he could ride into the scrub.

roof. *Opal-mining.* [Transf. use of *roof* the stratum lying immediately over a bed of coal.] The stratum lying immediately above opal-bearing material.

1931 M.S. BUCHANAN *Prospecting for Opal* 8 Almost all the sheet of potch containing opal lies within two ft. from the roof.   **1960** *People Mag.* (Sydney) 27 Apr. 51 Pipe opal . . is mostly found in soft white clay between one and six inches below the over-lying sandstone 'roof'.

Rooshan, Rooshian, varr. RUSSIAN.

root, *n.*[1] Shortened form of PIGROOT *n.*

1930 'BRENT OF BIN BIN' *Ten Creeks Run* (1952) 7 'He can't ride! The colt's only pig-rootin'!' 'Pooh! He's hangin' on by his spurs!' 'The next root will bring him a buster.'

root, *n.*[2] [See ROOT *v.*[2]]

a. An act of sexual intercourse.

1959 R. CHAMBERLAIN *Stuart Affair* (1973) 111 Did you have a root?   **1985** *Canberra Times* 6 Dec. 12/2 Which one of you girls is going to take your clothes off and give me a root?

b. A (female) sexual partner.

1961 F. HARDY *Hard Way* 77 The conversation led inevitably to women. Our shabby criminal struck a match revealing . . a sign scrawled on the wall: 'Best American root—ring such and such a number.'   **1982** *Bulletin* (Sydney) 9 Nov. 34/1 Globe trotting Australians certainly have become noted for their high sex drive. . . At their mother's knee, little Australians learn that 'good root' is the highest term of approval.

root, *v.*[1] *intr.* Shortened form of PIGROOT *v.* 1.

1929 K.S. PRICHARD *Coonardoo* (1961) 49 He'd begin with a flying root and a couple of high bucks . . and go on buckin' and rootin' in a circle.   **1955** H.G. LAMOND *Towser* 269 A horse 'roots' when not bucking hard.

root, *v.*[2] [Of unknown origin: it is likely that sense 2 is older and sense 1 a fig. use of sense 2.]

1. *trans.* To ruin; to exhaust; to frustrate. Freq. in pass. and as *ppl. a.*

1944 J. HETHERINGTON *Austral. Soldier* 28 'Listen', the dying man said, 'I'm rooted.'   **1976** K. CLIFT *Soldier who never grew Up* 145 'God, Ken, where have you been?' . . I was too rooted to explain. I ate some iron rations . . then I fell asleep.

2. *trans.* To have sexual intercourse with (a person); also *intr.*, to engage in sexual intercourse.

1958 R. CHAMBERLAIN *Stuart Affair* (1973) 12, I took her bathers off. Then I raped her. She was hard to root.   **1974** *Southerly* 271 'She's obviously a convent girl,' Singleton said, with the aplomb of a connoisseur. 'They root like rabbits.'

3. In phrases.

a. wouldn't it root you: see WOULD **b.**

b. root (someone's) **boot,** an expression of exasperation.

1967 J. HIBBERD *White with Wire Wheels* (1970) 153 Root my boot. What a night.   **1981** B. DICKINS *Gift of Gab* 5 'Gawd, it's flamin' rainin'?' says Old Baldy. . . 'Wouldn't it root your boot?'

c. get rooted, 'get lost', 'get fucked'.

1961 M. CALTHORPE *Dyehouse* 186 'He can get rooted, for all I care,' Collins said bitterly.   **1979** J. SUMMONS *Lamb of God* 30 Get rooted. I can't write in the bus. I'll lend you mine to copy—you'll get it right for a change.

rootable, *adj.* Sexually attractive.

1973 D. WILLIAMSON *What if you died Tomorrow* (1974) 156, I had a gorgeous young dancer lined up. Quite stupid—apologies to you two feminists—but very rootable.

rooter, *n.*[1] Shortened form of PIG-ROOTER.

1920 *Bulletin* (Sydney) 24 June 20/2 In far-western Queensland, where you *do* get brumbies and rough horses, they are considered soft snaps unless they can 'spin' and 'buck back'. The straight-ahead prad, no matter with how great a jar he hits the ground, is a mere 'rooter'.   **1933** *Ibid.* 13 Dec. 25/2 The only rooter that got the better of Jack was a sullen brute that threw himself down and rolled.

rooter, *n.*[2] One who is sexually promiscuous.

1965 J. BEEDE *They hosed them Out* 149 It was at one of these unscheduled bludging periods that the Rooters' Club was born. Its function was for a closer and more intimate relationship with all females.   **1984** B. REED *Crooks* 159 Club Finese is still for the higher class naughty little rooter.

ropable, var. ROPEABLE.

rope, *v.* [Also U.S.] *trans.* To catch (an animal) with a noosed rope; to lasso.

1827 P. CUNNINGHAM *Two Yrs. in N.S.W.* I. 291 The young heifers in their first calf, too, ought to be broken in to milk, as, if that period is passed over, they are afterwards most untractable milkers:—by *roping* two or three times, they are soon taught to walk quietly up to the milking pail.   **1960** E. O'CONNER *Irish Man* 210 He and Paula and Dalgliesh mustered near the homestead, and worked cattle in the yards close to the house. He learned to rope a calf, and to have the hot brand ready to be placed quickly in Dalgliesh's outstretched hand.

Hence **roper** *n.*

1849 A. HARRIS *Emigrant Family* (1967) 129 The pole drops clear, leaving the rope only in the roper's hands.

ropeable, *a. fig.* Also **ropable.** Requiring to be restrained; angry; bad-tempered.

1874 C. DE BOOS *Congewoi Correspondence* 195, I don't know a nastier smell than the smeller new togs just fresh from the tailor's goose, and the thoughter that amost made me ropable.   **1947** N. LINDSAY *Halfway to Anywhere* 167 Cripes, the idea of a bloke going with rough tarts gets my old man absolutely ropeable.

roping, *vbl. n.* [f. ROPE.]

1. The action of catching (an animal) with a rope.

1890 'R. BOLDREWOOD' *Colonial Reformer* (1891) 119 The drafting, the roping, the branding . . were novelties of a very high order.

2. Special Comb. **roping pole, stick,** a long pole used to drop a noosed rope over the head of an animal.

1890 'R. BOLDREWOOD' *Colonial Reformer* I. 192 Jack Windsor being a first-class stockman, and handy with the **roping-pole**, was always invited to join the party. **1846** C.P. HODGSON *Reminisc. Aust.* 115 A **roping-stick** about ten feet long, to which is attached a noose for throwing round the calf's neck.

rort, *n.* Also **roart, wrought.** [f. *rorty* boisterous, rowdy; of dubious propriety.]

1. An act of fraud or sharp practice; a 'lurk'.

1926 'DRYBLOWER' *Verses* 50 A bank-roll unto him is 'Oscar Asche', A swindle is to him a 'joke', a 'wrought'. **1945** *Atebrin Advocate: Mag. 2/4 Austral. Armoured Regiment* 10 Feb. 4 Insurance was his civil 'roart'. **1985** *Canberra Times* 28 May 1 (*heading*) Tax rorts hit collections.

2. A wild party; an escapade.

1952 T.A.G. HUNGERFORD *Ridge & River* 81 Out we go on another bloody rort, so what's the use of saving a day? **1985** *Canberra Times* 6 Mar. 23/1 (*heading*) Big annual rort a blunt peace push.

rort, *v.* [As prec.]

1. **a.** *intr.* To engage in sharp practice. Freq. as *vbl. n.*

1919 C. DREW *Doings of Dave* 142 'Melbourne . . I've been down there doin' a bit of rortin'.'. . 'What line are you on?' 'Clocks', answered Tiger, 'They're the best line of clocks you ever slung your eyes on.' **1980** *Sunday Mail* (Brisbane) 15 June 6 (*heading*) Overseas tax havens and 'rorting' claimed. $3,000 m. a year in tax dodges.

b. *trans.* To manipulate (a ballot, records, etc.) fraudulently, to rig: see quot. 1981. Freq. as *vbl. n.*

1980 *Sydney Morning Herald* 21 July 1/2 He felt the ALP should urgently close several inner city branches, including one whose real membership was only a tenth of its fraudulently manipulated membership records. 'This rorting is all about control over public office preselections and particularly in local government and the avenues for graft which it provides.' **1981** *Sydney Morning Herald* 10 June 6/1 Both sides blamed the other for massive 'rorting' in party branches. Rorting, in Labor jargon, is a charmingly flexible term to cover such practices as stacking branch membership, rigging elections, cooking branch records and as a last resort, losing all branch records to frustrate a head office inquiry. Rorting, in short, means working hot in the Labor Party.

2. *intr.* To go 'on the town'. Also with **up**, and as *vbl. n.*

1956 J.E. MACDONNELL *Commander Brady* 249 Now don't forget. Nobody grogged-up. Nobody rortin' it up with them Yanks. Behave yerselves. **1981** D. STUART *I think I'll Live* 179, I got to be mates with him, out dancing, shielah rortin' together.

Hence **rorted** *ppl. a.,* rigged.

1981 *Austral.* (Sydney) 1 Apr. 8/6 Mr Wright said the fund involved a 'rorted system' of adjusting rates in the party's newspaper.

rorter. Also **wroughter.** [f. RORT *n.* 1.]

1. One who engages in sharp practice: see quot. 1941.

1926 'DRYBLOWER' *Verses* 93 He'd been a race course wroughter In the years that yester dwell. **1941** S.J. BAKER *Pop. Dict. Austral. Slang* 61 *Rorter*, a professional sharper: a hawker of worthless goods: one who practises sly dodges to obtain money.

2. One who engages in rorting (see RORT *v.* 1 b.).

1981 *Nat. Times* (Sydney) 6 Dec. 18/3 On balance the Right—because they have much more experience and also happen to run the party's head office—are more accomplished rorters.

3. With distinguishing element, as **poofter rorter**: see POOFTER 2.

rose, *a.* Used as a distinguishing epithet in the names of flora and fauna: **rose apple,** any of several plants, incl. *Burdekin plum* (see BURDEKIN), trees of the genus *Owenia* (fam. Meliaceae), and esp. the rainforest tree *Syzygium moorei* (fam. Myrtaceae) of n.e. N.S.W. and s.e. Qld.; **-breasted cockatoo,** GALAH 1; formerly also **rose (-coloured) cockatoo; -crowned (fruit) pigeon,** the bird *Ptilinopus regina ewingii* of Arnhem Land (N.T.) and the Kimberley region (W.A.); **gum,** the tree *Eucalyptus grandis* (see *flooded gum* FLOODED); **robin,** the small, predom. grey bird *Petroica rosea* of s.e. mainland Aust., the mature male having a rose-coloured breast; also **rose-breasted robin.**

1846 *Portland Guardian* 18 Sept. 4/3 We collected three species of **rose-apple** (eugenia), one was a large scarlet fruit, with longitudinal ribs of a coarse and strong aromatic taste; another was of a delicate rose colour, and extremely pleasant. **1888** *Proc. Linnean Soc. N.S.W.* III. 534 *Owenia cerasifera* . . 'Sweet plum', 'Rose apple'. . . This plant bears a fine juicy red fruit with a large stone. **1965** *Austral. Encycl.* III. 412 *S*[*yzygium*] *moorei* . . has dense masses of large rosy-red flowers springing from the older branchwood, and is sometimes called 'rose apple'. **1838** [**rose-breasted cockatoo**] *S. Austral. Gaz.* (Adelaide) 21 July 4/1 Those very beautiful birds the rose cockatoo and the crested pigeon of the marshes. **1841** *Port Phillip Patriot* 9 Aug. 4/2 Flocks of . . rose-breasted cockatoos, were seen in every direction, restless and busy. **1845** J. GOULD *Birds of Aust.* (1848) V. Pl. 4, *Cacatua eos* . . Rose-coloured Cockatoo. **1903** *Emu* II. 153 *Ptilopus ewingi* (**Rose-crowned Fruit-Pigeon**). . . This bird was found breeding in the mangroves. **1982** H.J. FRITH *Pigeons & Doves Aust.* 107 For the north-western form [of the Red-crowned Pigeon], 'Rose-crowned Pigeon' is a common name. **1945** J. DEVANNY *Bird of Paradise* 20 The tractor had deposited two scrub gum—or **rose-gum**-logs. **1968** D. FLEAY *Nightwatchmen* 62 The tall flooded or rose gum (*E. grandis*). **1887** [**rose robin**] *Illustr. Austral. News* (Melbourne) 21 Dec. 218/1 Three kinds of robins were found—the dusky, the flame-breasted and the rose-breasted, all fairly numerous. **1984** SIMPSON & DAY *Birds of Aust.* 321 Rose Robin, the most arboreal and acrobatic [of *Petroica* spp.], catches flies in outer canopies of trees.

Rose Hill parrot. *Obs.* [f. *Rose Hill*, the original name for Parramatta, w. of Sydney.] ROSELLA *n.*[1] 1. Also **Rose Hill (parakeet).**

1810 E. BENT Lett. 27 July 187, I have now . . two Rose Hill Parrots. **1845** J. GOULD *Birds of Aust.* (1848) V. Pl. 29, *Platycercus icterotis.* . . *Moy-a-duk*, Aborigines of the mountain districts of Western Australia. *Rose-hill* of the Colonists. **1846** *Ibid.* Pl. 27, *Platycercus eximius* . . Rose-hill Parrakeet, Colonists of New South Wales.

rosella /rou'zelə/, *n.*[1] Formerly also **roselle.** [Altered form of the place-name *Rose Hill*: see ROSE HILL PARROT.]

1. Any of the brightly-coloured parrots of the genus *Platycercus* of all States, originally and still esp. the *eastern rosella* (see EASTERN 2). Also with distinguishing epithet, as **Adelaide, crimson, eastern, Moreton Bay, northern, red-headed, western, yellow** (see under first element), and *attrib.,* esp. as **rosella parrot.**

1829 *Sydney Gaz.* 21 July, The doleful dying quails, And roselles golden. **1836** J. BACKHOUSE *Narr. Visit Austral. Colonies* (1843) 438 Some of the birds of V.D. Land abound. . . The Rosella, Rosehill, or Nonpareil Parrot, *Platycercus eximius.* **1981** A.B. FACEY *Fortunate Life* 90 The ring-neck parrot . . was most destructive on cereal crops and fruit. Another parrot, smaller and of different markings, was the rosella. This bird was also destructive on cereal crops and fruit.

2. *transf.* A sheep which is losing its wool, and is therefore easy to shear.

1849 *Stephen's Adelaide Miscellany* 8 Nov. 81 If at shearing he chooses to pick all the 'Rosellas' (clean-bellied sheep), no one grumbles. **1963** O. RUHEN *Flockmaster* 47 Oh, we lost a ewe yesterday. The eagles got it... It was that little Roman-nosed one, the rosella, the one that's always going.

3. *Military.* A staff officer.

1919 *Aussie: Austral. Soldiers' Mag.* Jan. 11/1 A certain Rosella in the Aussie Army is known as Old Bloodlust. **1943** *Troppo Tribune* (Mataranka) 5 July 1 This accounts for the success he has attained with the big birds of the Army in later years; rosellas also hold a prominent position.

rosella /rou'zelə/, *n.*² Also **rozella**. [Transf. use of *rosella, roselle* the red sorrel *Hibiscus sabdariffa*.] The shrub or small tree of n. Aust. *Hibiscus heterophyllus* (fam. Malvaceae), used as a food plant and an ornamental; the flower bud of the plant. See also *native hibiscus* NATIVE *a.* 6 a. Also *attrib.* as **rosella jam**.

1854 *Moreton Bay Free Press* 10 Jan. 3/5 This is the plant from the fruit of which Rosella jam is made. **1928** W. ROBERTSON *Coo-ee Talks* 7 Central Queensland is the home of the rozella-bush, and the women of that day made large quantities of rozella jam. **1953** *Bulletin* (Sydney) 22 July 13/4 'It's rosella jam—it's made out of rosellas,' insisted Stan. 'Gaw starve the crows,' breathed his best mate. 'I always knew you were a bit weak in the skull. Now I suppose you'll tell me them Bananalanders make pickles out of peewees and tomato-sauce out of galahs?' 'You blasted idiot', yelled Stan, 'a rosella is a *flower* in Queensland; it's a big red blossom that grows on a bush and people make jam out of it.'

rosener, var. ROSINER.

rosewood. Any of several trees or shrubs having a fragrant or reddish timber, esp. the tall rainforest tree *Dysoxylum fraserianum* of n.e. N.S.W. and s.e. Qld., *Synoum glandulosum* of e. N.S.W. and e. Qld. (both fam. Meliaceae), and the small tree *Heterodendrum oleifolium* (fam. Sapindaceae) of drier mainland Aust.; the wood of these trees, esp. that of *D. fraserianum*. See also BOON-AREE, *bullock bush* BULLOCK *n.* 2. Also *attrib.*

1819 *Sydney Gaz.* 26 June, To the Productions of the Country as then reported, may now be added great Quantities of Rose Wood, the Flooded Gum and Coal. **1844** *Sydney Morning Herald* 12 Dec. 4/4 We were stopped by an impenetrable rosewood scrub, running north and south. **1984** E. ROLLS *Celebration of Senses* 153, I sit to write on a chair of leather and Australian rosewood made by a craftsman... One sits among a soft perfume, a suggestion of distant roses.

rosiner /'rɒzənə/. Also **rosener, rozener, roziner**. [f. *rosin* (var. of *resin*), alcoholic drink. Also Irish slang: see OEDS.] A (generous) measure of spirits.

1933 *Bulletin* (Sydney) 10 May 20/1 Fill up the cup, a rozener, a hummer! **1947** H. DRAKE-BROCKMAN *Fatal Days* 114 I've not had a solitary spot since four. I need a rosiner. **1976** S. WELLER *Bastards I have Met* 25 Dad had a regular who came in twice a day for a scotch and if you gave him a bloody bucket he'd fill it. He was a dead loss. One day he poured himself a rosener. Dad took his shilling and gave him three-pence change. He said, 'Mr Weller—haven't you made a mistake?' Dad said, 'No—that's right. It's cheaper when you buy it in bulk.' **1978** D. STUART *Wedgetail View* 33 He got him to get outside a bit o' breakfast, an' a good roziner of whisky.

Ross River virus. [f. the name of a river near Townsville, Qld.] A mosquito-borne virus causing a non-fatal disease characterized by a rash, and joint and muscle pain; the disease itself, also known as **Ross River fever.** Also *attrib.*

1966 *Austral. Jrnl. Exper. Biol. & Med. Sci.* 365 Infections of man with Ross River virus or a closely related agent were shown to have occurred on at least 4 occasions between 1957 and 1964 at Mitchell River Mission near the Gulf of Carpentaria. **1984** *Area News* (Griffith) 21 Nov. 3/2 If the Ross River Fever mosquito is to be beaten the CSIRO will need to become involved in research to destroy its larvae.

rotate, *v.* In the phr. **wouldn't it rotate you**: see WOULD **b.**

rotten, *a.*

1. In the phr. **to knock rotten,** to kill or stun. Also *fig.*

1919 W.H. DOWNING *Digger Dialects* 31 *Knocked rotten*, killed or stunned. **1968** S. GORE *Holy Smoke* 47 I'd say he was knocked rotten.

2. Drunk. Also in the phr. **to get rotten**.

1864 *Drinkamania* 8 In 'lush' we are not merely ripe, But only—nearly rotten. **1966** R. MORLEY *Cool Change* 13 Something the late Ezra Norton designed himself when he got rotten after a clean-up at the races.

3. In the collocation **rotten egg**, a children's game: see quot. 1957.

1957 A. MARSHALL *Aust. (1981)* 73 Do you remember 'Rotten Egg' in which a row of our caps lay against the school wall and turns were taken to throw a ball into one of them? I forget exactly how the game developed but there came a stage when, at the shout of Rotten Egg there was a scatter and the ball was thrown at those fleeing. **1979** B. MARTYN *First Footers S. Gippsland* 125 He held a little girl by each hand. He had been out by the barn playing 'rotten egg' with them.

rough, *a.*

1. In the names of plants: **rough-bark(ed) apple,** a rough-barked tree of the genus *Angophora* (fam. Myrtaceae), esp. *A. floribunda* of e. mainland Aust.; **(-leaved) fig,** SANDPAPER FIG.

1919 R.T. BAKER *Hardwoods of Aust.* 7 Pale [timber colour].—*Angophora intermedia* **Rough-barked,** or Narrow-leaved **Apple. 1956** T.Y. HARRIS *Naturecraft in Aust.* 131 Common Angophoras of the bush are:.. Rough-bark Apple—*Angophora intermedia* [etc.]. **1845** L. LEICHHARDT *Jrnl. Overland Exped. Aust.* 4 Aug. (1847) 359 The **rough-leaved fig** tree.. grew on its sandy banks. **1917** EWART & DAVIES *Flora N.T.* 80 F[*icus*] *scabra*.. (*F. aspera*)—Roper River, Gilruth and Spencer, July-August, 1911. Rough or Purple Fig.

2. In special collocations: **rough cut** *obs.*, a careless style of shearing; **sheep,** a sheep which is difficult to shear; also *ellipt.* as **rough; shop** *obs.*, a place which presents difficulties of some kind (cf. ROUGH-UP c); **spin,** see SPIN *n.*¹ 2; **trot,** a period of misfortune.

1898 *Bulletin* (Sydney) 17 Dec. 15/1 Cut stands for shedjob. There are *fine cuts* and **rough cuts**. In the former the boss is particular. In a *rough-cut* he is lenient, and shearers can shear anyhow. **1904** *Shearer* (Sydney) 10 Sept. 4/4 Amongst the noted **rough sheep** at Nowranie, a board of 25 has shorn 2,600 in a day of seven hours. **1915** *Bulletin* (Sydney) 28 Oct. 22/3 As the pen cuts out there is keen rivalry among.. pen-mates, each trying to force the other to take the roughs. **1892** 'R. BOLDREWOOD' *Nevermore* 199 Well you know Growlers' always was a **rough shop**. **1944** H.M.A.S. *Westralia* Dec. 8 Hell, wouldn't that be a **rough trot.**

3. *Obs.* [See quot. 1885.] In the phr. **rough on rats,** bad luck.

[**1885** *Australasian* (Melbourne) 11 July 91/2 (Advt.) 'Rough on rats' clears out rats, mice, roaches, flies, ants, bed-bugs, beetles, insects, skunks, jack-rabbits, gophers. At druggists.] **1888** J. POTTS *One Yr. Anti-Chinese Work Qld.* 16 The foregoing may appear 'rough on rats'; but Northerners speak their minds and do not take shelter behind flowery terms. **1889** *Bulletin* (Sydney) 15 June 13/4 Tho' his last and he have parted (Meaning 'rough on rats' for some): Still more game than chicken hearted Is the 'broke' new chum.

rough, *v.*

1. *trans.* To shear (a sheep) carelessly and unevenly.

1878 'IRONBARK' *Southerly Busters* 180, I allus roughs 'em when the boss Ain't on the shearin' floor. **1896** *Bulletin* (Sydney) 14 Nov. 11/2 A Darling-shed shearer was roughing his sheep. Next morning he found a note over his pen: 'Sheep rough; please improve.' He sheared cleaner next day and the following morning found this note: 'Improved. Thanks.'

2. See quot.

1945 F. CORK *Tales from Cattle Country* 37 Some riders prefer to 'rough' a horse. This consists in blindfolding, saddling, and 'riding the buck'.

rough and tumble. [Spec. use of *rough and tumble* roughly improvised: see OED(S 4.] A fence made from untreated saplings and branches: see quot. 1956. Also **rough and tumble fence.**

1956 *Bulletin* (Sydney) 23 May 12/4 The bush-paddock was still enclosed by the original 'rough-and-tumble'; just saplings and heavier branches piled in line to resist big stock. **1980** HOLTH & BARNABY *Cattlemen of High Country* 37 We'd cut the snow-gums off so high up and built what they call a brush fence, a 'rough and tumble' fence.

roughie. Also **roughey, roughy** [f. *rough* + -Y.]

1. A cheat; a deception; a 'swiftie'; esp. in the phr. **to put a roughie over.**

1914 *Kan-Karoo Kronikle: Mag. H.M.T.S. 'Karroo'* 24 Oct. 20 Ginger springs a roughy: 'Though we are not aboard a P & O we have a PI-AN-O aboard. **1924** A.W. BAZLEY et al. Gloss. Slang A.I.F. 24 (typescript) *Roughey,* a statement difficult to believe. **1970** R. BEILBY *No Medals for Aphrodite* 269, I bluffed him, put a roughie over him.

2. In dog- and horse-racing: an outsider.

1922 C. DREW *Rogues & Ruses* 11 Dig into them roughies. **1985** *Bulletin* (Sydney) 29 Oct. 48/1 Picking a winner is difficult... Alan Jones must be considered a roughie.

3. An unbroken horse.

1929 K.S. PRICHARD *Coonardoo* (1961) 124 Hugh was there to see that the roughie, as they called him, got more riding and handling before he went out of the yards again. **1978** R.H. CONQUEST *Dusty Distances* 16 Ready to ride a real roughie?

rough-up. [Spec. use of *rough-up* an informal encounter: see OED(S.]

a. A fight; a brawl. Also *fig.*

1891 *Truth* (Sydney) 1 Feb. 6/5 Mr Sydney Broomfield is one of the hardest sort of men in a rough-up of his inches in the city, and he absolutely loves a turn up now and then. **1933** *Bulletin* (Sydney) 6 Dec. 24/4 The council.. wants to make it clear that in future all inter-State rough-ups will be *its* pigeon.

b. A thug.

1911 *Bulletin* (Sydney) 23 Nov. 13/4 Micko, from Collingwood, may be a 'tug' or a 'crook' or a 'rough-up' or a 'hotty', but if you called him a larrikin he'd look at you and wonder. **1920** G. SARGANT *Winding Track* 43 He had no time for me, anyway; he thought me too much of a rough-up.

c. *transf.* A difficult stretch of terrain: cf. *rough shop* ROUGH *a.* 2. Also *attrib.*

1938 C.P. CONIGRAVE *Walk-About* 79 We took the risk of descending a 'rough-up', in the hope of getting water at the bottom of it. *Ibid.* 120 Looking behind we saw range after range that we had crossed on our 'rough-up' journey from Mount Casuarina.

roughy, var. ROUGHIE.

roughy. [f. TOMMY) ROUGH + -Y.] **a.** TOMMY ROUGH. **b.** *transf.* The small, reef-dwelling fish *Trachichthys australis.*

1864 *Colonial Cook Bk.* (1970) 49 Ruffy—Small. Exquisitely delicate. **1906** D.G. STEAD *Fishes of Aust.* 89 The curious little fish known as the Roughy (*Trachichthys australis*).. inhabits very similar situations to those in which the Nannygai is found.

round, *v.* [The Austral. use precedes and is apparently independent of U.S. *round up, v.*: see OED(S *round, v.*^{1} 5 e. and Mathews *round up, v.* 1.] *trans.* To gather (scattered livestock) together by riding round a paddock, etc., to muster. Freq. with **up**. Also *transf.*

1847 C. STURT *Narr. Exped. Central Aust.* (1849) I. 228 We rounded up cattle till the moon should rise. **1929** C.E.W. BEAN *Official Hist. Aust. 1914–18* III. 73 Several hundreds from one ship streamed into the town, and were partly 'rounded up' the same night by an armed party from the nearest Australian camp.

rouse, *n. Obs.* Abbrev. of ROUSEABOUT *n.* a.

1898 *Worker* (Sydney) 26 Feb. 7/2 As rouses we may not be of electric breed, but for all that we are quick and lively, especially on 'Duff Days'.

rouse /raʊs/, *v.*^{1} [f. Scot. dial. *roust* to roar, to bellow: see EDD *roust, v.*^{2} and OED(S *roust, v.*^{1} and *v.*^{3}] *intr.* To scold. Freq. with **at, on**: to berate (someone).

1896 *Worker* (Sydney) 29 Aug. 3/3 Some very thin-skinned individuals have been 'rousing' on me for what they term my 'strong language'. **1922** *Aussie* (Sydney) Sept. 10, 7.30 oklok: Mum rouses and bangs me hed becos the blarsted wood won't burn. **1984** H.W. DAVIS *Bachelors in Bush* 82, I called out loudly. Tommy heard me and he had to stop the team and take me back home. Naturally I was roused at for that.

Hence **rousing** *vbl. n.*

1923 M.J. PETERSEN *Jewelled Nights* 164 He told me to give you a good rousing for not looking him up.

rouse /raʊs/, *v.*^{2} *Obs. intr.* Abbrev. of ROUSEABOUT *v.*

1919 *Bulletin* (Sydney) 9 Oct. 20/2, I was coming in for a spell after 'rousin'' at a run of sheds in the West.

rouseabout, *n.* [Spec. use of Br. dial. *rouseabout* a rough, bustling person: see EDD and OED(S.]

a. A general hand on a rural property, esp. in a shearing shed.

[N.Z. **1861** *Lett. from N.Z.* 20 July (1914) 54 Shearing, it happens, is in full swing, so there are a number of extra men, besides the shepherds of the station, shearers, fleece-pickers, wool-sorters, and 'rouse-abouts'.] **1881** *Austral.: Monthly Mag.* (Sydney) V. 147 At Warrena my billet was that of 'rouseabout', or in more civilized terms generally useful. **1984** *People Mag.* (Sydney) 7 May 40/2 My father was a woolpresser and I was a rouseabout at 15... If my son wanted to be a shearer now I'd steer him away from it.

b. *transf.*

1906 E. DYSON *Fact'ry 'Ands* 15 Billy the Boy, the juvenile rouseabout from the printer's flat. **1978** R.H. CONQUEST *Dusty Distances* 154 A rouseabout looking after the caravan horses, helping to put up the big tent and pull it down and so on.

c. *attrib.* Also *fig.*

1884 *Bulletin* (Sydney) 28 June 18/3 What Granny would call an 'embarrassing predicament', happened recently in the gay rouseabout city of Paris. **1974** D. IRELAND *Burn* 49, I stayed with him for a bit and did some rouseabout stuff and got my tucker and a sleep in the feed shed.

rouseabout, *v.* [f. prec.] *intr.* To work as a rouseabout. Freq. as *vbl. n.*

1897 *Tocsin* (Melbourne) 23 Dec. 6/1 It was grand fun most of the time—rabbit trapping, emu hunting, rouseabouting first and then to the mastership of shearing. **1979** B. HARDY *World owes me Nothing* 167 He'd left school to go rouseabouting in the sheds.

rouser. Shortened form of ROUSEABOUT *n.* a.

1896 H. LAWSON *While Billy Boils* (1975) 52 They are all shearers, or at least they say they are. Some might be only 'rousers'. **1967** G. JENKIN *Two Yrs. Bardunyah Station* 66 The aim of the rouser is eventually to become a shearer.

rousie. Also **rousy.** [f. ROUSE(ABOUT *n.* + -Y.] ROUSEABOUT *n.*

1906 *Bulletin* (Sydney) 22 Feb. 14/3 The local 'rousies' are gluttons .. after living for a month or two in a shearers' hut. **1972** W. WATKINS *Suddenly of Age* 7 'Are you a shearer?' 'No, just a rousy.'

Hence **rousy** *v. intr.*, to work as a rouseabout.

1979 J. DAVIES *Souvenir Kangaroo Island,* As a neighbour, and rousying for a change of tucker Good days, good country.

roust, *v. intr.* ROUSE *v.*[1] Also with quasi-obj. in the phr. **to roust hell out of** and as *vbl. n.*

1904 L.M.P. ARCHER *Bush Honeymoon* 113, I was to *go lightly* on it, and bring it back in good repair, if I didn't wanted to be *rousted* on about it. **1938** X. HERBERT *Capricornia* 314 He rousted hell out of the surveyor fellers for keepin' lubras in their camp. **1950** N. LINDSAY *Dust or Polish* 116 If you don't stop rousting on me I'll do for meself with a chisel.

rousy, var. ROUSIE.

rover. *Australian National Football.* One of three players making up the ruck, usually small, fast, and adept at securing possession of the ball. See RUCK *n.* 1 a.

1894 M. SHEARMAN *Athletics & Football* (ed. 4) II. 422 The rover is an individual chosen for his quickness and readiness to go wherever he is wanted. **1973** J. DUNN *How to play Football* 6 No matter how many rabbits a rover can pull out of his top hat he is no good unless he can kick accurately, and even more importantly, with both feet.

Hence **rove** *v. intr.*, and as *vbl. n.*

1936 E.C.H. TAYLOR et al. *Our Austral. Game Football* 75 The full forward centre has a roving commission within kicking distance and must always be trying to make position. **1963** L. RICHARDS *Boots & All!* 78 He went to Fitzroy as a rover, but had to be content with a place on the wing because Bunton was roving.

roving party. *Tas. Hist.* A detachment of men engaged in the pursuit and detention of Aborigines.

1831 *Van Diemen's Land Corresp. Military Operations* 23 Feb. 82 The Council advised the Lieutenant-Governor to discontinue the roving parties, as the measure appeared to have a bad effect upon the Natives. **1870** J. BONWICK *Last Tasmanians* 132 After much discussion, it was determined to depend no longer upon the feeble operations of the Roving Parties—the *Five Pounds' Catchers* as they were called.

rowdy, *a.* [Transf. use of *rowdy* rough and disorderly.] Of animals: resistant of control.

1872 C.H. EDEN *My Wife & I in Qld.* 69 [It] consists of several yards for drafting... A lane and a crush .. useful for branding or securing a troublesome or colonially a 'rowdy' bullock. **1897** R. NEWTON *Work & Wealth Qld.* 39 Gardens cover the ridges that in his day were dense with ironbark, bloodwood, and sweet-smelling wattle, and in place of the 'rowdy mob' who grazed in these ravines are troups of children returning from school.

Hence **rowdiness** *n.*

1887 A. NICOLS *Wild Life & Adventure* 203 The cattle .. showed frequent signs of rowdiness.

Roy. *Obs.* [Transf. use of the proper name *Roy.*] A derogatory name for the type of the consciously fashionable Australian. See also ALF.

1960 *Encounter* (London) May 29 A Roy .. would patronise *Art Nouveau* every pay-day .. for arty knick-knacks for his lovely Wahroongah home. **1971** C. McGREGOR *Don't talk to me about Love* 130 It's like those signs hung out by London landladies: *Sorry, no Roys.*

royal, *n. Hist.* [Also Br.: see OEDS *sb.* 2 e.] A name proposed, but not adopted, for a unit of decimal currency.

1963 *Daily Tel.* (Sydney) 6 June 1/1 Federal Cabinet decided tonight to call the major new decimal currency unit a royal. **1963** *Daily Mirror* (Sydney) 6 Aug. 29/1 The Federal Government will decide next week whether to change the name royal as the major unit of decimal currency... Dollar is the most favoured name for the unit.

royal, *a.* In the names of flora and fauna: **royal bluebell,** the small perennial herb *Wahlenbergia gloriosa* (fam. Campanulaceae) of higher altitudes in s.e. mainland Aust., the floral emblem of the Australian Capital Territory; **spoonbill,** the large wading bird *Platalea regia,* having white plumage and black face, bill, and legs.

[**1914 royal bluebell:** F. SULMAN *Pop. Guide Wild Flowers N.S.W.* II. 124 *Wahlenbergia gracilis.* 'Australian Blue Bell.'] **1950** J. GALBRAITH *Wildflowers Vic.* 143 *W*[*ahlenbergia*] *gloriosa,* Royal Bluebell... Flowers large, rich dark blue or blue purple. **1842** J. GOULD *Birds of Aust.* (1848) VI. Pl. 50, The **Royal Spoonbill** is tolerably common on the eastern and northern coast of Australia.

royal alberts: see PRINCE ALBERTS.

Royal Alfred. *Obs.* [f. the name of Prince *Alfred* (1844–1900), second son of Queen Victoria, who visited Australia in 1867–68.] A heavy swag: see quot. 1902.

1896 H. LAWSON *While Billy Boils* (1975) 62 A little farther on we saw the first sundowner. He carried a Royal Alfred, and had a billy in one hand and a stick in the other. **1902** —— *Children of Bush* 139 The weight of the swag varies from the light rouseabout's swag, containing one blanket and a clean shirt, to the 'royal Alfred', with tent and all complete, and weighing part of a ton.

Royal George. *Obs.* [f. the name of King *George* IV (1762–1830).] See quot. 1827.

1827 *Monitor* (Sydney) 12 July 507/2 The 'Royal George', (an iron pot holding four gallons of water) was then placed on the fire; tea and sugar were thrown in it by the handful. **1846** *Cumberland Times* (Parramatta) 10 Jan. 4/4 A fire was soon made, a Royal George slung to boil the beef, some flour rubbed up, and leather jackets made, and we made a night of it, having been joined in the course of the evening by two or three down country teams.

rozella, var. ROSELLA *n.*[2]

rozener, roziner, varr. ROSINER.

rub, *v.* [Transf. use of *rub out* to wipe out, to kill.] In the phr. **to rub out,** to disqualify (a competitor).

1902 *Advocate* (Burnie) 29 Jan. 2/5 When men are

proved to be non-tryers they will be 'rubbed out'. **1983** HIBBERD & HUTCHINSON *Barracker's Bible* 173 Players, jockeys and reinsman get 'rubbed out' when they are disqualified from participation by a tribunal or stewards. 'The Derwent Dobber's been rubbed out for a fortnight.'

rub-a-dub-dub. Altered form of RUBBITY-DUB.

[N.Z. *c* **1926** 'MIXER' *Transport Workers' Song Bk.* 81, I gazed upon the motley crowd Within this 'rub-a-dub'.] **1941** S.J. BAKER *Pop. Dict. Austral. Slang* 62 *Rubberdy* .., a public house. Rhyming slang on 'rub-a-dub-dub' for 'pub'. **1971** *Nat. Times* (Sydney) 13 Dec. 20 Let's grab some Kate and Sidney and a pint of apple fritter at the rub-a-dub-dub.

rubbedy, rubberdy, varr. RUBBITY.

rubbie, var. RUBBY.

rubbish, *v.*

1. [Used elsewhere but recorded earliest in Aust.] *trans.* To denigrate (a person); to disparage. Also as *vbl. n.*

1953 T.A.G. HUNGERFORD *Riverslake* 20 'If Verity was going to tramp you for burning the tucker, Slim', one of the cooks.. observed.. 'he would have rubbished you long before this.' **1971** B. HUMPHRIES *Bazza pulls it Off*, Am I to take it you want to know the secret of my romantic prowess? Look, I can't ask any of me mates or they'd give me a flamin' rubbishing.

2. *Surfing.* (Chiefly in *pass.*) To tip (a surfer) off a wave.

1962 *Austral. Women's Weekly* (Sydney) 24 Oct. (Suppl.) 3/3 *Rubbished*, to be thrown off wave and dumped on shore. **1966** *Surfabout* (Sydney) III. v. 11 Bob McTavish gets rubbished.

Hence **rubbisher** *n.*

1969 D.S. WILKINS *Diary* 1 June 44 The entertainers expose themselves to the roughest audience of rubbishers in existence.

rubbish, *a. Austral.* pidgin. Inferior in quality.

1959 W.E. HARNEY *Tales from Aborigines* p. xvi, In the early days the native girls travelled around with their white companions, and being excellent cattle and horse-women they became the ones who helped the early settlers to open up the land. They were classed as 'Rubbish-one-whites', 'Comboes', 'clay-pan squatters'. **1969** J. DINGWELL *One String* 46 Don't be offended if all they can address you by is 'Missus', and don't be offended, either, if they reject what you offer as 'rubbish tucker'.

rubbity. Also with much variety, as **rubbedy, rubberdy, rupperty.** Abbrev. of RUBBITY-DUB.

1898 *Bulletin* (Sydney) 17 Dec. (Red Page), *Drum*, derived from the kettle-drums (evening parties) of the days of the Georges—was a high-class word, but it fell. The cockney turned it into *rub-a-dum-dum*; the Australian now calls the same thing a *rubadey*. **1944** *Action Front: Jrnl 2/2 Field Regiment* May 15 Overheard in a Melbourne rupperty. **1957** D. NILAND *Call me when Cross turns Over* 101 Gord, I can hardly talk, I'm that dry. How about a gargle? Down to the rubberdy, come on. **1974** W. HOWCROFT *Sand in Stew* 68 They would usually blow their wages on a three or four day spree at the nearest bush rubbedy. **1977** *Southerly* ii. 202 I'll take it up to the rubbity after breakfast and show it to the mates.

rubbity-dub. Also with much variety, as **rubbitty-dub, rubby dub.** Rhyming slang for 'pub'.

1898 *Bulletin* (Sydney) 29 Oct. 15/1 His home is 'the rubby dub', his occupation 'the joint'. **1905** J. MEREDITH *Learn to talk Old Jack Lang* (1984) 12, I rambled over to the *rubbity dub* and had a pint of *oh my dear*. In fact I had several and finished up in the dead house, broke to the wide. **1969** B. GARLAND *Pitt Street Prospector* 32 'Ow about we ducks into the rubbitty-dub fer a quick 'un?

rubby. *Obs.* Also **rubbie.** Abbrev. of RUBBITY-DUB.

1897 *Worker* (Sydney) 11 Sept. 1/2 And I will lay an oil-rag to a pound of 'Darling Pea' He gallops straight away towards a 'rubbie' for a 'spree'. **1926** 'DRYBLOWER' *Verses* 34 So down at a rubby along the road, We lunched on steak and eggs.

ruck, *n. Australian National Football.* [Transf. use of *ruck* scrimmage.]

1. **a.** A group of three players (two FOLLOWERS and a ROVER) who do not have fixed positions but follow the play.

1900 B. KERR *Silliad* 21 No peer had he for keeping on the ball And in the ruck he marked above them all. **1983** HIBBERD & HUTCHINSON *Barracker's Bible* 173 Players without fixed positions, who follow the ball, are in the ruck.

b. Abbrev. of *ruckman.*

1931 J.F. MCHALE et al. *Austral. Game of Football* 64 The position of the ruck and rover when the umpire bounces the ball in the centre should not be a stereotyped one. **1963** *Footy Fan* (Melbourne) I. i. 18 It is no coincidence that a majority of players who can perform most football tasks (all-round players) finish either in the centre as a ruck or a rover because it is here that they have to be able to perform almost any football feat.

2. Special Comb. **ruckman,** FOLLOWER; **play,** play following no set pattern; **rover,** a tall ruckman selected for an ability in loose play; so, **roving** *vbl. n.*

1900 B. KERR *Silliad* 25 The sweeping **ruck-men** on the ball descend. **1936** E.C.H. TAYLOR et al. *Our Austral. Game Football* 62 The Australian Football Council has.. eliminated a great deal of **ruck play**. **1963** L. RICHARDS *Boots & All!* 73 His ruck-play improved year after year. *Ibid.* 90 By far the greater part of his success has been at centre half-back or centre half-forward and in later years as a **ruck-rover** changing in the forward pocket. **1963** *Footy Fan* (Melbourne) I. ii. 24 Kevin Rose turned in a terrific ruck-roving performance against Richmond on opening day.

ruck, *v.* [f. prec.] *intr.* To play as one of the ruck. Also as *ppl. a.*

1963 *Footy Fan* (Melbourne) I. vii. 21 When he rucked with Bill Morris, he always feared he might spoil Morris' leaps for the ball and more or less played the role of understudy. **1963** L. RICHARDS *Boots & All!* 79 A cagey left-footer, he used big Bert Clay's rucking ability to full advantage.

rufous, *a.* In the names of birds and animals: **rufous bristlebird,** the brown bird *Dasyornis broadbenti* of coastal scrub in w. Vic. and s.e. S.A., and formerly s.w. W.A.; formerly also **rufous-headed bristlebird; -crowned emu wren,** the small brown and blue bird *Stipiturus ruficeps* of parts of drier mainland Aust.; **fantail,** the bird *Rhipidura rufifrons* of n. and e. mainland Aust. and the s.w. Pacific; formerly also **rufous-fronted fantail; owl,** the owl *Ninox rufa* of n. Aust. and New Guinea, having barred rufous plumage; **rat-kangaroo (kangaroo-rat, bettong),** the small marsupial *Aepyprymnus rufescens* of e. mainland Aust.; **scrub-bird,** the predom. rufous-brown ground-dwelling bird *Atrichornis rufescens*, inhabiting areas of dense ground cover in s.e. Qld. and n.e. N.S.W.; **song-lark,** the migratory bird *Cinclorhamphus mathewsi* of mainland Aust., having brown and whitish plumage with a rufous rump; see also SONG-LARK; **treecreeper,** the bird *Climacteris rufa* of s. W.A. and S.A.; **whistler,** the bird *Pachycephala rufiventris*, widespread in mainland Aust. and occurring elsewhere, the mature male having a rufous breast and belly; WIREE; see also THUNDER-BIRD, WHISTLER; also **rufous-breasted whistler** (and formerly **thickhead**).

1897 [**rufous bristlebird**] *Proc. Linnean Soc. N.S.W.*

XXII. 58 *Sphenura broadbenti* . . Rufous-headed Bristle-bird. **1903** *Emu* II. 163 Rufous Bristle-Bird . . very common throughout the Otways. **1901** *Emu* I. 56, I saw a family party of **Rufous-crowned Emu Wrens** (*Stipiturus ruficeps*). One of the young birds . . had no trace of the bright rufous crown of the adult bird. **1846** [**rufous fantail**] J. GOULD *Birds of Aust.* (1848) II. Pl. 84, The Rufous-fronted Fantail is one of the most beautiful and one of the oldest known members of the group to which it belongs. **1903** *Emu* II. 163 Rufous Fantail (*Rhipidura rufifrons*)—common in the Otways. **1846** J. GOULD *Birds of Aust.* (1848) I. Pl. 36, *Athene rufa* . . **Rufous Owl.** **1894** R. LYDEKKER *Hand-Bk. Marsupialia & Monotremata* 71 **Rufous Rat-Kangaroo.** *Aepyprymnus rufescens* . . the largest of the Rat-Kangaroos. **1898** E.E. MORRIS *Austral Eng.* 239 A fourth genus (*Aepyprymnus* . .) includes the Rufous Kangaroo-Rat. . . It is . . distinguished by its ruddy colour, black-backed ears, and hairy nose. **1983** R. STRAHAN *Compl. Bk. Austral. Mammals* 190 At night the Rufous Bettong feeds on grasses and herbs and forages for roots and tubers, dug from the ground with its strongly clawed forelegs. [**1869 rufous scrub-bird:** J. GOULD *Birds of Aust.* Suppl. Pl. 26, *Atrichia rufescens.* Rufescent Scrub-bird.] **1898** E.E. MORRIS *Austral Eng.* 406 The Noisy Scrub-bird . . and the Rufous S[crub]-b[ird]. **1900** A.J. CAMPBELL *Nests & Eggs Austral. Birds* 276 *Cinclorhamphus rufescens* . . **rufous song lark.** . . While the Black-breasted or Brown Song Lark appears partial to grassy plains, the Rufous loves the grassy glades of the forest or lightly timbered country. **1841** J. GOULD *Birds of Aust.* (1848) IV. Pl. 94, *Climacteris rufa* . . **Rufous Tree Creeper. 1896** [**rufous whistler**] B. SPENCER *Rep. Horn Sci. Exped. Central Aust.* II. 72 *Pachycephala rufiventris* . . Rufous-breasted Thickhead . . were always found near water and in the scrub along the Finke River. **1918** *Bulletin* (Sydney) 14 Feb. (Red Page), *Rufous-breasted Whistler* . . and other members of the musical genus *Pachycephala*. **1984** E. ROLLS *Celebration of Senses* 77 The Rufous Whistler makes a few musical calls, then cracks like a whip, a good alarm.

rugged billy: see BILLY *n.*[1] 4.

Rules. Shortened form of AUSTRALIAN RULES. Also *attrib*.

1946 D. STIVENS *Courtship of Uncle Henry* 18 In those days in the Mallee before they got the latest city ideas, they played Rules in long pants. **1960** *N.T. News* (Darwin) 11 Mar. 16/6 (*heading*) Big rules game could be close.

rum. *Hist.* Used *attrib.* in Special Comb. reflecting the importance of spirits as a medium of exchange during the early days of the Colony of New South Wales: **Rum (Puncheon) Corps,** NEW SOUTH WALES CORPS; **currency,** see quot. 1870; **Hospital,** a hospital in Sydney the building of which was undertaken in return for the granting of a monopoly on the import of spirits from 1810 to 1814; **rebellion,** the rebellion against William Bligh, Governor of New South Wales, by officers of the New South Wales Corps in 1808.

1897 M. CLARKE *Stories Aust.* 31 The New South Wales Veteran Corps (a regiment of pensioners tempted by promise of privilege to emigrate) was called the '**Rum-Puncheon Corps**'. **1944** R. BEDFORD *Naught to Thirty-Three* 37 Our 'history' became a laudation of the ruffians of the Rum Corps, and their successors, the pure Merinos. **1870** J. BONWICK *Curious Facts* 124 In the primitive period the **rum currency** prevailed. In purchase, the worth was estimated in quarts or gallons of rum. One Serjeant-major Whittle sold a house to Governor Macquarie for two hundred gallons of rum. **1834** J.D. LANG *Hist. & Statistical Acct. N.S.W.* II. 138 Governor Macquarie . . made an agreement on the part of the Colonial Government with Messrs D'Arcy Wentworth, Blaxcell, and Riley, by which these gentlemen stipulated to erect a building agreeably to the plan proposed, on condition of receiving a certain quantity of rum from the King's Store and having the sole right to purchase, or to land free of duty, all the ardent spirits that should be imported into the colony for a term of years. The **Rum Hospital,** as it was called at the time, was accordingly erected on these conditions. **1855** W. HOWITT *Land, Labor & Gold* II. 125 From the date of this '**rum-rebellion**', and the forcible deposition of poor Bligh, in 1809 up to 1823, the system of political grants went on swimmingly.

rumper. [Prob. transf. use of Br. dial. *rumper* a large sheep.]

1. SCRUBBER 1 a.

1899 *Worker* (Sydney) 14 Jan. 3/4 Sometimes I thought it hard When I struck a stranger's yard, And a 'rumper' worked with malice in his eye. **1936** I.L. IDRIESS *Cattle King* 190 A mob of rumpers like these.

2. See quot.

1970 J.S. GUNN in W.S. Ramson *Eng. Transported* 65 A *rumper* in the poultry trade is now a domestic fowl with a peculiar feather growth from lack of a tail-bone, but it was earlier a possum or koala whose backside fur had been worn away, thus damaging the pelt.

run, *n.*[1] *Obs.* [Chiefly Br. dial. and U.S.: see OED *run, sb.*[1] 9 a.] A small watercourse.

1793 J. HUNTER *Hist. Jrnl. Trans. Port Jackson* 458 They came to a run of water, which they supposed to be the head of the Nepean river. **1878** R.B. SMYTH *Aborigines of Vic.* II. 303 Other food includes fish of three or four kinds, which are caught in nets, or in grass weirs placed across runs of water when the floods subside.

run, *n.*[2] [Prob. Br. dial. in origin, superseding *walk* both in the sense of an enclosure for poultry, etc., and a tract of land used for pasture. There is an isolated North American example (1658) but the earliest sustained evidence of use is Austral.: see OED(S *run, sb.*[1] 21 b. and 22, and *walk, sb.*[1] 11 a. and 12.]

1. a. A tract of land used as pasture; *spec.* a tract of Crown land situated adjacent to a holding and leased or occupied as pasture (see quot. 1849); such a tract situated at some distance from the user's dwelling or holding (see quot. 1828). See also STATION 2 a.

1804 *Sydney Gaz.* 12 Feb., A commodious dwelling-house [with] an extensive Run for Stock. *Ibid.* 24 June, The premises are pleasantly situate in Sydney, being a corner house, and an excellent run for stock. **1828** *Blossom* (Sydney) i. 82 Numerous herds of cattle are moving for pasture to Bathurst and Argyle has the benefit of more extensive 'runs'. **1849** S. & J. SIDNEY *Emigrant's Jrnl.* 11 A *run* is a tract of wild land on which cattle or sheep are depastured on a poll-tax, and license or lease from the Crown. **1973** D. STUART *Morning Star, Evening Star* 18 There's nothing quite so dismal as a station with every one out on the run.

b. *Obs.* Pasturage.

1820 *Sydney Gaz.* 23 Sept. (Suppl.), A Farm . . well adapted for a Person'having Stock, being adjacent to one of the greatest Outlets in the Colony for the Run of Cattle. **1835** *Cornwall Chron.* (Launceston) 30 May 4 The unlimited run for stock upon unlocated lands, must necessarily produce plenty.

c. *Hist.* In the phr. **right of run,** legal entitlement to the use of a tract of grazing land; such a tract of land. See also STATION 2 b.

1840 *Port Phillip Gaz.* 1 Jan. 2 If desired, the whole or portion of the herd will be sold with the Right of one of the finest Runs in Port Phillip. **1961** M. KIDDLE *Men of Yesterday* 48 He intended to buy the 'right of run' rather than take up a station.

2. A tract of land used for the raising of stock, together with the requisite improvements such as dwellings, yards, etc. Also with distinguishing epithet, as **cattle, grazing, sheep, squatting, stock** (see under first element). See also STATION 3.

1810 *Sydney Gaz.* 24 Feb., A capital Forty Acre Farm, at the Nepean, well watered, and one of the best runs for Stock in the Country. **1982** R. ELLIS *Bush Safari* 96 The ruins of Annandale Station, one of Sir Sidney Kidman's early runs, and the most remote station he ever owned.

3. *transf.* The territory traditionally occupied by an Aboriginal community.

1838 *Port Phillip Gaz.* 22 Dec. 4/3 These poor creatures [*sc.* Aborigines], aware of the penalty that await [*sic*] them when trespassing on the ground of another tribe .. dare not leave their own runs. **1909** W.G. SPENCE *Aust.'s Awakening* 11 When the white man came to Australia he found in possession the aboriginal squatter, whose runs were tribal and whose stock were kangaroos and opossums.

4. Special Comb. **run-holder,** the owner of a stock-raising establishment; one who has a legal entitlement to the use of a tract of grazing land; so, **-holding** *vbl. n.*; **hunter** *obs.*, one who seeks unoccupied grazing land; so, **-hunting** *vbl. n.*; **-jobbing** *vbl. n., obs.*, see quot. 1861.

1863 B.A. HEYWOOD *Vacation Tour Antipodes* 112 Several **run-holders** have jointly subscribed towards the support of a clergyman. **1872** *Causes Ruinous Condition Coal Trade N.S.W.* 15 He may .. invest one portion of his means in a coal-mine, another portion, say £30,000, in a copper-mine, whilst these two may be supplemented by run-holding and stock and station agency. **1881** W. FEILDING *Austral. Trans-Continental Railway* 23 Mr Turnbull says that the opinion generally held before my arrival here was that the Railway Company would turn out the present run-holders, and cutting up their runs, offer them for sale or lease to small sheep or cattle farmers. **1848** *Maitland Mercury* 8 Jan. (Suppl.) 1/2 A gentleman recently arrived in town from .. the interior .. met several **runhunters**, who were resorting to the most extraordinary and even fraudulent means to secure right of possession by pre-occupation. **1916** H.L. ROTH *Sketches & Reminisc. Qld.* 9 He found himself stock-driving and run hunting (i.e., looking for new country) in the Central and Northern lands of the then young Colony of Queensland. **1861** F. ALGAR *Handbk. to Colony Qld.* 10 The 'Tenders for Crown Lands Act' was passed with the view of putting an end to the system of **'run-jobbing'**... Parties were fitted out for the object of travelling into the unsettled country, observing what portions of it were fit for occupation, and then tendering for it .. for the purpose of selling the untenanted blocks at enormous prices, to those about to engage in squatting.

run, *n.*³ [Spec. use of *run* regular track made by an animal.] The bower made by a bower bird.

1840 *Proc. Zool. Soc. London* (1841) 94 Mr Gould then called the attention of the Members to an extraordinary piece of Bird-architecture, which he had ascertained to be constructed by the Satin Bird, *Ptilonorhynchus holosericeus*, and another of similar structure, but still larger, by the *Chlamydera maculata*. These constructions, Mr Gould states, are perfectly anomalous in the architecture of birds, and consist in a collection of pieces of stick and grass, formed into a bower... They are used by the birds as a playing-house, or 'run', as it is termed, and are used by the males to attract the females. **1913** *Emu* XII. 173 The birds like a dry run, not too stony, and within call of several of the different berries which they eat. I know of about ten different runs now.

run, *n.*⁴ [Spec. use of *run* a period of allowing a liquid, machinery, etc. to run: see OED(S *sb.*¹ 19.]

a. *Shearing.* An uninterrupted period worked during a day; a period of employment as a shearer.

1904 *Shearer* (Sydney) 6 Aug. 3/5 To Shearers... Can give Runs of Three and Four Sheds. **1963** D. NILAND *Dadda Jumped* 150 I'm a shearer. I come in today from Moombala. We cut-out there first run this morning.

b. *transf.* A period of employment.

1979 B. SCOTT *Tough in Old Days* 112 We entered the hall to face the Cane Inspectors from the mill to sign on for our 'run'. **1984** *N.T. News* (Darwin) 22 Sept. 40/2 Bricklayer wanted, good money, long run... Solid plasterers required, long run of work.

run, *n.*⁵ [Spec. use of *run* the act of running.] In the phr. **to get the run,** to be dismissed from one's employment.

1889 BARRÈRE & LELAND *Dict. Slang* I. 403 *Get the run, to,* (English and Australian), to be discharged. **1894** *Bulletin* (Sydney) 13 Jan. 7/3 Legge got the run, Fogg cleared, Bell 'rung' the shed, and Warte turned out to be a 'scab'

run, *v.*¹ [Used elsewhere but recorded earliest in Aust. and apparently chiefly Austral.: see OED(S *v.* 43 c.]

1. *trans.* To provide pasture for (sheep, cattle, etc.); to raise (livestock). Also *absol.*

1795 R. ATKINS Jrnl. 15 Feb., By the sale of the late farms it appears many people run upon the Hawkesbury. The land is certainly very fine. **1867** J. BONWICK *J. Batman* 38 One of the so-called party of anti-squatters, Mr Evans, assured me that he went with the avowed intention to run sheep. **1963** X. HERBERT *Disturbing Element* 8 We ran horses. Dad's sideline, hobby, and delight was horses. He broke them, trained them, traded them.

2. *intr.* Of livestock: to graze.

1810 *Sydney Gaz.* 21 Apr., All Persons having Horses or Stock .. running at Castle Hill are requested to take them away. **1927** 'S. RUDD' *Romance of Runnibede* 78 Did you see the mob that those roan poley cows run with, in that wattle gorge?

3. a. *trans. Obs.* Of land: to provide sustenance for (animals).

1840 *Port Phillip Gaz.* 24 Oct. 1 *For sale*, about one hundred head of Cattle, with a splendid Cattle Station, watered by three rivers, and capable of running at least six hundred head of cattle and two thousand sheep. **1849** *Belfast Gaz.* (Port Phillip) 3/1 Those possessed of runs capable of running more than 100,000 sheep, ought to have sold a few head and 'given in' the remainder of their runs to those who wanted them badly and would have paid for them liberally.

b. *transf.* To cover the expense of; to 'run to'.

1905 *Bulletin* (Sydney) 20 July 3/2 He was rabbiting, he told me, and the job would 'run a mate'. **1946** A.J. HOLT *Wheat Farms Vic.* 112 This Mallee country won't run holidays.

run, *v.*² [Transf. use of *run* to pursue, follow up (a scent): see OED *v.* 34 b.] *trans.* To follow (the trail of a person, animal, etc.). Esp. in the phr. **to run the track.**

1841 *Sydney Herald* 21 Jan. 2/6 Lieutenant Christie and his party, who had been running his track with an aboriginal native for three days, came up the next morning and escorted him to Queanbeyan. **1904** L.M.P. ARCHER *Bush Honeymoon* 350 First we'll set the nigger to track 'bout the place; then *runnin' the track's* simple.

run, *v.*³ *Obs.* [U.S. *run* to tease, nag: see OED(S *v.* 52 c.] *trans.* To harass (a person).

1846 L.W. MILLER *Notes of Exile Van Dieman's Land* 330 Every new load of prisoners from town [for Port Arthur] always brought some money with them. This was strictly prohibited, and many ingenious plans were devised to smuggle it, one of which was, swallowing pieces of gold. Every person in the gang was of course liable to be suspected of possessing these hidden treasures, and in order to discover the real *Simon pures*, and compel them to '*fork over*', the whole were continually '*run*', as it was termed, for months. Loads which it was impossible to carry were heaped upon them, until some excuse was found to take them to the office. **1892** 'R. BOLDREWOOD' *Nevermore* II. 132 'Well, I knocked over the head warder at Ballarat.' 'Good boy! What for?' 'He had been 'running' me—wanted to make me break out, I suppose.'

run, $v.^4$ [Transf. use of *run* to chase or hunt: see OED(S 42 a.]

1. To round up (wild cattle, horses, etc.). Also as *vbl. n.* and *ppl. a.*

1871 *Austral. Town & Country Jrnl.* (Sydney) 22 Apr. 490/2 In fact the running of wild horses is the initiation of many of our youths into the vile habit of duffing, which next to drinking is the most demoralizing evil in the country districts. **1889** *Illustr. Austral. News* (Melbourne) 1 May 74/2 On stations where there are any scrub cattle, running coachers, or quiet cattle, are used as decoy for the purpose of running the wild cattle into the yards. **1979** C. STONE *Running Brumbies* 46 Running brumbies like branding is an exciting experience.

2. In phrases.

a. To run in, to pursue and confine (cattle). Also *transf.* (see quots. 1900 and 1907).

1885 MRS CAMPBELL-PRAED *Head Station* I. 124 No end of sport . . in shooting wild horses and running in scrubbers. **1900** *Bulletin* (Sydney) 21 Apr. 14/1, I heard a man from the backblocks say the other day that he intended to run in a mob of 30 black lepers, and see what the Govt. would do then. **1907** *Truth* (Sydney) 7 Apr. 9/7 'But they use them on the stations?' 'Oh, yes, they use them, gins and bucks. Soon as they get tame enough, both squatters and missionaries run 'em in, and the one lot can use the stockwhip just as well as another.'

Hence **run-in** *ppl. a.*

1934 J.C. LEE *Boshstralians* 226 Owen, astride a 'run-in' brumby, cantered briskly up to his own slip-rails.

b. To run into, to drive (an animal) into (a yard, etc.).

1849 A. HARRIS *Emigrant Family* (1967) 138 The mingled flocks must be run into the stockyard. **1946** F. CLUNE *Try Nothing Twice* 100 Run that creamy heifer into the bail . . then leg-rope her and milk her—it's easy.

c. To run off, to separate (animals) from a mob.

1861 H. EARLE *Ups & Downs* 43 When you can run off any stock from the station, leave two stones on the table in the hut, and one of the party will carry them off into the mountains. **1965** J.S. GUNN *Terminol. Shearing Industry* 15 *Run-off*, to take a group of sheep from the flock without necessarily 'cutting-out' all of this group or 'drafting' them into special lots, for example 'I'll run off some fats'.

d. To run up, to bring (a horse, etc.) in from pasture.

1876 J.A. EDWARDS *Gilbert Gogger* 163 After breakfast, the several guests retired to their rooms to don riding apparel; the stockmen ran up the horses, side-saddles were fastened to the backs of the steeds destined to carry the fair equestrians. . . Dear reader, this phrase is colonial, and not *ours*; we certainly never saw a stockman running *up* a horse. **1923** *Bulletin* (Sydney) 1 Nov. 24/4 A practice which hasn't much to recommend it is that of keeping a 'night horse' yarded all night on the far-out stations, so that it can be used to run up the mob in the morning.

run, $v.^5$ [Spec. use of *run* to cause to move.] *trans.* With **out**: to split (a plank, post, slab, etc.) from a log of wood. Also *absol.*

1873 C.H. EDEN *Fortunes of Fletchers* 72 Posts and rails are 'run out', as it is technically expressed, from an iron bark, or some other hardwood tree. **1874** C. DE BOOS *Congewoi Correspondence* 119 He 'ud take a big chip outer the sap wood, and he 'ud split it up runnin out ways and grain ways, and he 'ud say, lookin at me, 'Why, it 'ud run out like matches, Johnny!'

runaway. *Hist.* A convict who has escaped from official custody or from assigned service. Also **runaway convict, prisoner, transport.**

1790 R. CLARK Jrnl. 4 Sept. 204 Thos. Streets one of the convicts . . has . . gone into the wood to live with Gray and Jones the other Runaway convicts. **1791** D. COLLINS *Acct. Eng. Colony N.S.W.* (1798) I. 190 A boat . . had been taken off by some runaways to get on board one of the ships then about to sail. **1828** *Tasmanian* (Hobart) 18 July 3 A Mr McKevett was fined this week by the Police Magistrate, in the sum of 50 dollars, for harbouring Mary Ann Heagan, a runaway prisoner. **1850** J. PLATT *Horrors of Transportation* 6, I was described as a run-away transport from my master.

runaway hole. A hole in the soil through which surface water drains away.

1878 MRS H. JONES *Broad Outlines* 177 There is water, but I am inclined to think it comes from those curious runaway holes we have on most of the runs. . . They partially drain the country, and are supposed to empty themselves into the Blue Lake at Mount Gambier. **1906** *Bulletin* (Sydney) 23 Aug. 16/3 The creek . . is fed from the Wimmera, and empties into swamps and 'runaway' holes. . . Curious things are these same 'runaway' holes—the smaller, when dry, are like rabbit burrows leading down to some great subterranean river; when water is running the vortex may be plainly seen.

rung, *ppl. a.* [f. RING $v.^1$] Of a tree: ring-barked. Of an area: having ring-barked trees still standing. See RINGBARK *v.* 1.

1885 MRS C. PRAED *Austral. Life* 35 They were only pressed into service when shepherds were scarce, or 'rung' trees (that is, gums which had been barked and allowed to wither) required felling. **1952** J.R. SKEMP *Memories Myrtle Bank* 67 The first act in clearing was to go through the bush and ringbark the larger trees—anything over a foot in diameter; trees so treated were said to be 'rung'.

runner.

1. One who rounds up (wild cattle, horses, etc.). See RUN $v.^4$

1917 C. DREW *Reminisc. D. Gilbert* 34 The manager of Calendoon Station gave the runners permission to clear the brumbies from off the Calendoon run. **1968** W. GILL *Petermann Journey* 46 Cattle duffers; cattle killing natives, and their cum'-uppance; horse thieves who became station owners; the iniquities of brumby 'runners'. Once he was convinced of my interest, he talked on and on.

2. A proprietor of a stock-raising establishment. See RUN $v.^1$ 1.

1963 X. HERBERT *Disturbing Element* 57 As runners of stock ourselves . . we had to share grazing and water with them.

running postman. [See quot. 1981.] The widespread, prostrate, perennial plant *Kennedia prostrata* (fam. Fabaceae), having trifoliolate leaves and scarlet pea flowers. See also *coral pea* (a), CORAL.

1898 E.E. MORRIS *Austral Eng.* 247 *K[ennedya] prostrata* is called the *Coral Pea* . . or *Running Postman*. **1981** J.A. BAINES *Austral. Plant Genera* 203 Running Postman (so named from red flowers and prostrate habit of growth, in allusion to the scarlet uniforms of postmen in former times).

run-through.

1. See quot. 1956.

1956 S. GORE *Overlanding with Annabel* 74 Sometimes, to the great joy of the traveller, there is no gate at all! In its place is a 'run-through', which is a deep pit roofed over with equally-spaced iron bars. Animals cannot walk over these but a car can be driven. **1978** D. STUART *Wedgetail View* 101 Hard rough road. . . Rattling grids or twisting run-throughs where fences crossed the road every five or six miles.

2. *Australian National Football.* A screen made of crepe paper or some similar material and in the colours of a team, through which the players run on to the field.

1973 P. MCKENNA *My World of Football* 90 The carnival atmosphere, the tier after tier of packed stands encircling the MCG, the cheer squads with their long club banners and until recently the highly colourful floggers and run-throughs. **1979** *Age* (Melbourne) 1 Oct. 1/5 The giant run-throughs were raised and the Carlton and Collingwood teams battered their way through them on to the ground.

rupee. *Hist.* An Indian coin which circulated in New South Wales during the earlier part of the nineteenth century: see esp. quot. 1835.

1825 *Austral.* (Sydney) 22 Dec. 3/2 Rupees .. might properly pass as half-dollars. **1835** *True Colonist* (Hobart) 4 Sept. 2/3 The *Rupee* Bill has passed, fixing the value of that coin at two shillings, as a legal tender between the Inhabitants. . . Let [the People] resolve not to buy a Treasury Bill, until the Commissary will receive the '*Rupee*' at the legalized Colonial value.

rupperty, var. RUBBITY.

rural school. A name given to any of several kinds of educational institution: see quots. 1926, 1927, and 1974.

1875 *Act* (Qld.) 39 Vict. no. 11 Sect. 14, It shall be lawful for the Minister from time to time to make provision for the establishment of training schools rural schools night schools and such other State schools as may be authorised by the regulations and deemed expedient. **1926** J.W. ELIJAH *Rural School* 1 The Victorian Education Department defines a rural school as one 'the allotment of which does not exceed 150 pupils'. **1927** G.S. BROWNE *Educ. in Aust.* 41 In New South Wales it has a technical significance, a Rural School being a special type of Superior School which has recently been discriminated from the others. *Ibid.* 274 One of the most important developments in Queensland education was the inauguration of a system of rural schools in 1917. . . The Rural School is part of a carefully organized scheme of agricultural education for all grades of students from those in the primary school to University students in the proposed University Faculty of Agriculture. **1974** J. MCLAREN *Dict. Austral. Educ.* 167 *Rural School*, a school with only one teacher and with all the students combined in a single class. Each grade of students is given its own program, but the whole school will combine for excursions, singing or school broadcasts. . . More than half the schools in Australia are still of this kind.

rush, *n.*

1. *Hist.* The sudden escape of a number of prisoners.

[**1812** J.H. VAUX *Mem.* (1819) II. 202 A sudden and violent effort to get into any place, or *vice versa* to effect your exit, as from a place of confinement, &c., is called *rushing them*, or *giving it to 'em upon the rush*.] **1816** *Hobart Town Gaz.* 13 Sept., On Thursday morning . . a most daring Rush was committed by some of the Prisoners in the Prison Room at Hobart Town, by taking out of the window an Iron Bar. **1964** J.V. BARRY *Life & Death J. Price* 79 When a body of prisoners banded together to effect an escape it was called a 'rush'.

2. a. [Used elsewhere but recorded earliest in Aust.: see OED(S *sb.*^{2} 4 a.] A sudden movement of numbers of people to a particular place, esp. to a newly discovered goldfield; the people who take part in such a movement. See also *new rush* NEW *a.* 3.

1841 *Omnibus & Sydney Spectator* 27 Nov. 68/4 Parties who now want runs go over the range to the Moreton Bay side. . . I understand there is a fine river about one hundred miles to the northward of Moreton Bay called White Bay River which is navigable for a considerable way upwards for large vessels, so that this will no doubt be the next rush. **1893** 'OLD CHUM' *Chips* 65 We came upon a 'rush' of diggers marking out new claims. **1962** O. PRYOR *Aust.'s Little Cornwall* 91 At Wallaroo, as in all cases where a deposit of a valuable mineral is discovered, there was a rush to peg claims on all the surrounding ground.

b. In the phr. **a rush set in,** 'a sudden movement of people began'.

1866 *Colony of Qld. as Field for Emigration* 17 Rockhampton . . was precipitated into importance some seven years since by a 'rush' which set in from the southern colonies to the Canoona diggings, about forty miles from the town. **1901** *Brisbane Courier* 5 July 4/8 Shortly after Westcott's prospecting party had met with success, what is known as a 'rush' set in. Within a few weeks from 2000 to 3000 Europeans arrived with horses, stores, mining batteries, &c.

c. *transf.* A goldfield to which a sudden movement of numbers of people has taken place. Also of opal-mining. See also *new rush* NEW *a.* 3.

1855 W. HOWITT *Land, Labor & Gold* II. 249 They are bound for . . distant rushes. **1966** H. GYE *Father clears Out* 52 Why is he so poor now, after finding all the rich reefs and rushes.

d. A newly-discovered deposit of gold on a goldfield.

1871 *Austral. Town & Country Jrnl.* (Sydney) 3 June 687/4 This rush is an important addition to the workings of the gold-field. **1887** 'OLD GOLD DIGGER' *Gold Digger's Guide* 3, I . . know of two quartz reefs containing gold, a few miles from the present rush at Teetulpa.

3. A stampede, esp. of cattle.

1881 A.C. GRANT *Bush-Life Qld.* II. 132 A sudden rush—a whirr—a tearing, crashing, roaring, thundering noise was heard; a confused whirl of dark forms swept before him, and the camp, so full of life a minute ago, is desolate. It was 'a rush', stampede. **1981** G. PIKE *Campfire Tales* 4 Robbie often spoke of a long droving trip he made in 1894. . . He told of many 'rushes' and wild rides in the darkness.

rush, *v.*

1. *trans.* To cause (cattle, etc.) to stampede.

1834 N.S.W. Magistrates' Deposition Bk. 6 Nov., He [*sc.* the shepherd] came home and reported to Mr Wightman that his Sheep had been rushed by a native dog. **1920** L. ESSON *Dead Timber* 34 Fancy the Jackeroo firing his revolver and rushing the mob like that—it's the dead finish.

2. [Transf. use of *rush* to attack (in a military context): used elsewhere but recorded earliest in Aust. (see OED(S *v.*^{2} 5 b.] *trans.* To assail (a person, etc.) by means of a sudden rush.

1840 *S. Austral. Miscellany* June 181 They would then, in the emphatic phrase of colonial description, *rush him*—the issue of such a conflict being all but certain. **1981** *Bulletin* (Sydney) 15 Dec. 82/1 The long war of attrition between the races, when 'rushing the gins' was a euphemism for rape and 'dispersing the natives' or 'snipe-shooting' meant murder.

3. a. [Used elsewhere but recorded earliest in Aust.: see OED(S *v.*^{2} 5 d.] *trans.* To occupy by a rush (esp. of gold-miners).

1852 *Bell's Life in Sydney* 19 June 2/3 Campbell's Hill, has been 'rushed' after the fashion of Rose Hill. **1973** *Nation Rev.* (Melbourne) 31 Aug. (Suppl.) 1/1 It was first explored by Hume and Hovell, then opened up by cattlemen, rushed by gold seekers, and finally developed as a prosperous agricultural area.

b. *trans.* To exhibit enthusiasm for (something or someone).

1858 L. PEARSON *Emigrants' Guide Port Curtis* 25 The shipping passenger trade has been—to speak colonially—tolerably well *rushed* in the prevailing excitement. **1930** M.B. PETERSEN *Monsoon Music* 17 'In Australia we are more sensible, our people don't rush stars as a rule.' 'They'll rush him all right,' the big fair man asserted.

4. *intr.* Of animals: to stampede.

1838 G.C. INGLETON *True Patriots All* 19 Nov. (1952) 198 With respect to 'rushing' of cattle, our readers lately arrived in the Colony will please to understand, that Cattle when much left to themselves, 'rush', that is, make off at full gallop to a great distance and into the glens. **1977** R. EDWARDS *Austral. Yarn* 32 The cattle rushed every night and Snuffler used to be out risking his life while the boss and the jackeroos and all the silvertails were back in camp.

Hence **rushing** *vbl. n.* and *ppl. a.*

1919 *Bulletin* (Sydney) 17 July 22/3 A stockman on the lead of rushing cattle or horses always turns his mount's tail to the herd. **1978** TEECE & PIKE *Voice of Wilderness* 36 The cattle were wild and known for 'rushing', the bushman's term for stampede.

rusher.

1. [Used elsewhere but recorded earliest in Aust.: see OED 2.] One who takes part in a rush to a new goldfield.

1853 *Austral. Gold Diggers Monthly Mag.* iv. 141 The dishes of the first rushers up refused to show the golden sediment. **1946** K.S. PRICHARD *Roaring Nineties* 388 There must 've been six or seven thousand rushers, most of 'em foot-sore and shaggy.

2. One who escapes from confinement in a rush (see RUSH *n.* 1).

1891 'OLD TIME' *Convict Hulk 'Success'* 39 The year 1856 was a very important one in the penal records of Victoria. There had been a rush of prisoners in the month of March of that year, and one of the 'rushers'.. had been shot.

3. A stampeding animal.

[N.Z. **1889** HAY *Brighter Britain* I. 158 Occasionally we find it necessary to slaughter some unmanageable rusher, a cow, or bullock.] **1892** *Truth* (Sydney) 31 July 1/2 Could you hang to a buckjumper with your knees, Or rattle a rusher through the trees.

rush-oh. *Obs.* An exclamatory call, announcing the discovery of a new goldfield.

1864 J. ROGERS *New Rush* 29 The cry 'Rush oh!' reverberating wide, Attracts the claimless to the rushing tide. **1887** *Rec. Castlemaine Pioneers* 30 Sept. (1972) 3 Early in 1854 there were constant rumors of fresh discoveries. The cry of 'Rush, Oh!' to Bryant's Ranges was raised.

Russian. *Obs.* Also **Rooshan, Rooshian.** [Prob. a pun on RUSH *n.* 3 and *v.* 4.] Esp. of cattle: a beast which is wild or difficult to handle.

1838 J.C. CRAWFORD *Diary* 15 Dec. in *S. Australiana* (1964) Mar. 56 The bullocks.. were not so easily managed as we expected, perhaps from being imperfectly broke at first, or else from having been long turned out to grass they proved to be as wild as Rooshians (to use an Australian phrase). **1847** A. HARRIS *Settlers & Convicts* (1953) 197 When a real 'Russian' happens to be among the mob, circumspection must positively be practised as well as bravery. **1849** —— *Emigrant Family* (1967) 53 Are there any 'Rooshans' in the mountains?

rustbucket. [Transf. use of (orig. U.S.) *rustbucket* an old and rusty ship. Used elsewhere but recorded earliest in Aust.] A rusty and dilapidated motor vehicle.

1965 *Daily Tel.* (Sydney) 23 Apr. 20/1 A motor mechanic yesterday described a car which broke in two as a 'rust bucket'. **1984** *Truck & Bus Transportation* Jan 12/1 The oldest Volvos.. are far from being rust buckets.

rusty gum. [See quot. 1963.] Any of several trees, esp. *Angophora costata* (fam. Myrtaceae) of N.S.W. and Qld., having a smooth bark and twisted branches.

1845 L. LEICHHARDT *Jrnl. Overland Exped. Aust.* 6 Feb. (1847) 139 A rather stunted rusty gum grew plentifully on the sandstone ridges. **1963** C. BURGESS *Blue Mountain Gums* 60 'Rusty Gum'... The smooth *bark* is rich, rusty orange-red in mid-summer, changing to salmon-pink and sometimes leaden-grey in autumn and winter.

Rutherglen bug. [f. the name of a town in n.e. Vic.: see quot. 1948.] The small bug *Nysius vinitor*, large aggregations of which cause damage to cultivated food plants.

1900 *Proc. Linnean Soc. N.S.W.* XXV. 760 Mr Froggatt exhibited specimens of cherries from the Armidale district showing the effect of the depredations of the Rutherglen Bug (*Nysius venator*). **1948** W.W. FROGGATT *Insect Bk.* 106 The Rutherglen bug, 1/6th of an inch long, gets its name from a town in Victoria, where it was first discovered as a pest among the vines.

ryebuck /ˈraɪbʌk/, *int., a.,* and *n.* Also **ribuck, rybuck.** [Br. slang *ryebuck,* perh. a. G. *reibach,* var. of *rebbach* profit, and orig. Yiddish: see OED *rybek* and OEDS *ryebuck.*]

A. *int.* An expression of agreement or assent, 'all right'.

1890 *Truth* (Sydney) 7 Dec. 4/7 But the boy by his gods he swore, 'Ri-buck, old man, true dinkum,' he said. 'The betting was ten to four.' **1900** *Tocsin* (Melbourne) 4 Jan. 3/1 The general hesitancy was soon dispelled, however, by a hoary-headed old tramp exclaiming: 'Rye buck, matey, wire in.'

B. *adj.* Good; excellent.

1892 *Truth* (Sydney) 31 July 4/2 He is, as he gracefully would express it, 'rybuck', quite at home. **1967** MEREDITH & ANDERSON *Folk Songs Aust.* 23 The first song Luscombe recorded for John Meredith concerned a man's ambition to become a ryebuck shearer. (Ryebuck means expert; the term 'gun shearer' is used in the same sense).

C. *n.* The 'genuine article'.

1896 H. LAWSON *While Billy Boils* 329 There were cakes of tobacco, and books, and papers, and several flasks of 'ryebuck'. **1942** *Action Front: Jrnl. 2/2 Field Regiment* July 9 A Ryebuck is not a wheat cake.

S

sable, *a. Obs.* [Spec. use of *sable* as applied to a black-skinned person.]

a. A literary epithet for an Aboriginal, with a rhetorical range extending from romantic elevation to ironic denigration. Cf. BLACK *a.*[1] 4 and 5.

1823 W.C. WENTWORTH *Australasia* 5 To you, ye sable hunters, sweeter too To spy the track of bounding kangaroo. **1880** *Bulletin* (Sydney) 15 May 1/1 The Executive in its wisdom decided to execute the blackfellow who a little while ago shot one of his sable countrymen at Dubbo.

b. In collocations: **sable brethren, companion, friend, gentleman, majesty, tribe, warrior.**

1839 *S. Austral. Rec.* (London) 1 Nov. 254 Many a right-hearted colonist will join me in ascribing equal forbearance to our **sable brethren**. **1845** L. LEICHHARDT *Jrnl. Overland Exped. Aust.* (1847) 11 Oct. 430 To shew my **sable companions** that their secret manoeuvres only tended to increase their own labour, I ordered the bullocks to be loaded immediately. **1833** BACKHOUSE & TYLOR *Life & Labours G.W. Walker* 3 Dec. (1862) 170 W.J. Darling appeared much pleased to see us, and hardly less so, our **sable friends**. **1843** *Sydney Morning Herald* 6 July 2/7 It is to be hoped the lately appointed Commissioner of Crown Lands for the Upper District here will, with his border police force, teach these **sable gentlemen** that their recent outrages will not escape unpunished. **1831** *Sydney Herald* 14 Nov. 4/1 Before the party broke up, his **sable Majesty** became done up with *bull*; and .. was floored by a waddie. **1819** *Sydney Gaz.* 24 July, Nothing of this kind is done for the **sable tribes** of New Holland. **1843** *Sydney Morning Herald* 24 May 4/6 We have had the pleasure of seeing some of these **sable warriors**.

sac, var. ZAC.

sacred kingfisher. The predom. blue, green, and buff kingfisher *Halcyon sancta* of Aust. and elsewhere. Formerly also **sacred kingsfisher**.

1782 J. LATHAM *Gen. Synopsis Birds* I. 621 Sacred K[ingsfisher]... This species is common to many parts of the South Seas. **1984** SIMPSON & DAY *Birds of Aust.* 317 Sacred Kingfishers nest in Australia, including the south, then migrate to northern Australia, New Guinea, Timor and the Solomon Islands in winter.

sacred site. A place venerated by Aborigines because of its spiritual significance to them: see quot. 1979. See also DREAMING 1. Also *attrib.*

1933 *Oceania* III. 266 Their sons will preserve the myths, ceremonies and sacred sites, if there be such. **1979** *N.S.W. Parl. Papers* (1980–81) IV. 735 A sacred site should be understood to mean any object or location whether a natural phenomenon or man-made .. that is sacred to Aborigines or is otherwise of significance according to Aboriginal tradition. **1983** D. BELL *Daughters of Dreaming* 38 The opportunity of returning .. to work alongside Aboriginal women in the *realpolitik* of land claims, law reform and sacred site registration.

saddle, *v. fig.* In the phr. **to saddle up,** to prepare oneself (for something).

1922 C. DREW *Rogues & Ruses* 38 That night .. Finger's saddlin' up for bed. **1967** *Kings Cross Whisper* (Sydney) xxxix. 4/4 *Saddle up,* prepare for work, get into harness.

saddle-my-nag. A game resembling leap-frog. Also **saddle-my-nagger,** one who plays this game.

1953 G.H. FEARNSIDE *Bayonets Abroad* 311 Later events went how to prove how badly built were these mess-hut structures... The end fell out of one building, followed by some half-a-score of eager 'saddle-me-naggers' who had been leaning a little too heavily on its delicate structure. **1966** A.R. CHISHOLM *Familiar Presence* 78, I don't think the name 'Saddle-my-nag' was ever applied to the complicated, difficult and sometimes painful form of leap-frog that we played in Sydney... I believe that in Victoria 'Saddle-my-nag' was the stock term, afterwards transformed by popular etymology into 'Solomon Egg'.

saddling, *vbl. n. Horse-racing.* Used *attrib.* in Special Comb. **saddling enclosure,** *saddling paddock* a.; **paddock, (a)** an enclosure in which the horses are saddled before a race; **(b)** a nickname for a bar in the Theatre Royal, Melbourne, frequented by prostitutes in the late nineteenth century; a similar bar elsewhere; hence, a known place of assignation.

1969 *Sun-Herald* (Sydney) 13 July 33/1 Mr Swales told us he could not get through to the stewards on the phone and gave us permission to return to the **saddling enclosure** to put our case to the stewards. **(a) 1861** *Argus* (Melbourne) 8 Nov. 5/5 His Excellency visited the **saddling paddock** during the half-hour preceding the Cup Race. **(b) 1876** *Argus* (Melbourne) 1 July 4/4 The stranger sees that the women, possibly picking up a male companion, all enter the apartment which was previously closed, and which is now guarded by swing doors. Curiosity will doubtless prompt him to enter, and he will find himself in the far-famed '**saddling paddock**' of the Royal. **1958** G. CASEY *Snowball* 28 The Government Dam was the inland town's beach and playground, its courting-place and secret rendezvous... The ribald, popular name of the enclosure round the Government Dam was 'the saddling paddock'.

saffron thistle. [Transf. use of *saffron-thistle* the dye-yielding plant *Carthamus tinctorius.*] The introduced Mediterranean annual *Carthamus lanatus* (fam. Asteraceae), naturalized, and proclaimed a noxious weed, in all States.

1909 A.J. EWART *Weeds Vic.* 37 The Saffron Thistle is widely spread over the whole State, and in many districts is reported to be the worst of all the thistles. **1986** *West Austral.* (Perth) 25 Jan. (Country ed.) 60/1 Saffron thistle is a widespread and troublesome weed in W.A. About 200,000 ha. of land in the Geraldton region is infested by the weed.

sagg. *Tas.* [Br. dial. *sag* a sedge: see OED *sb.*[1]] A tufted perennial, esp. *Lomandra longifolia* (fam. Xanthorrhoeaceae) of e. Aust.

1898 E.E. MORRIS *Austral Eng.* 399 Sagg .. the name given in Tasmania to the plant *Xerotes longifolia* .. and also to the White Iris, *Diplarhena moraea*. **1908** *Emu* VII. 150 This little frequenter of rushes, saggs (*Xerotes longifolia*) and patchy undergrowth in the open.

Hence **saggy** *a.*

1908 *Emu* VII. 151 In some soils saggy growth is still provokingly persistent.

Saint Andrew's Cross spider. The orb-weaving spider *Argiope aetherea,* which aligns its legs in pairs along the arms of the cross in the centre of its web.

1936 K.C. MCKEOWN *Spider Wonders Aust.* 44 The St. Andrew's Cross Spider .. is of fair size, and is arrayed in remarkably gaily coloured attire. Its general colour is brown .. while the abdomen is striped crossways with alternate bands of brown, silver, and yellow. **1952** B. BEATTY *Unique to Aust.* 63 The St. Andrew's Cross spider superimposes upon the web proper after it has been completed, a broad St. Andrew's Cross.

saleyard. An enclosure in which livestock is sold; a set of such enclosures.
1839 *Tasmanian Weekly Dispatch* (Hobart) 29 Nov. 2/3 Mr Davis' newly erected and well constructed Sale Yards. 1910 *Emu* X. 30 Two large mobs of Queensland horses were approaching on their way to a southern sale-yard.

sally. Also **sallee**. [Transf. use of Br. dial. *sally*, var. of *sallow* a willow.]
1. Any of several trees of the genera *Eucalyptus* (fam. Myrtaceae) and *Acacia* (fam. Mimosaceae), resembling the willow in habitat, habit, or foliage. Formerly also **sallow**.
1826 J. ATKINSON *Acct. Agric. & Grazing N.S.W.* 19 A species of sallow, growing about the sides of rivers, furnishes good materials for basket-making. 1897 *Worker* (Sydney) 18 Sept. 1/1 The hand that trimmed its greenhide fall Is hidden underground—There, in the patch of sallee shade Beneath that grassy mound. 1955 STEWART & KEESING *Austral. Bush Ballads* 189 They reached the low sally before he could wheel the warrigal mob.
2. Special Comb. **sally wattle**, any of several plants of the genus *Acacia* (fam. Mimosaceae), esp. the shrub or small tree *A. longifolia* of s.e. Aust. incl. Tas., having narrow, elongated phyllodes; also **sallow wattle**.
1943 *Bulletin* (Sydney) 20 Oct. 13/2 For .. Australian trees, graceful and able to weather the worst winds, I'll nominate the shapely 'Sally Wattles' that dot the rolling hilly landscapes near Robertson (N.S.W.). 1965 *Austral. Encycl.* VII. 539 *A*[*cacia*] *longifolia, A. mucronata* and several related species with long flower-spikes are known as sallow wattles in Victoria.

salmon. [See quot. 1974.] Any of several marine and fresh-water fish, esp. the marine *Arripis trutta* and *A. esper*, abundant in s. and e. Aust. See also *native salmon* NATIVE *a.* 6 b., SALMON TROUT.
1790 D. COLLINS *Acct. Eng. Colony N.S.W.* (1798) I. 136 Near four thousand of a fish, named by us, from its shape only, the salmon. 1974 T.D. SCOTT et al. *Marine & Fresh-water Fishes S.A.* 239 It is thought that the name 'Salmon' was first used in the early days .. possibly from a confusion of the young Australian Salmon with its trout-like spots, with the Salmon-trout of Europe.

salmon gum. The tree *Eucalyptus salmonophloia* (fam. Myrtaceae) of the drier parts of s.w. W.A., having smooth salmon-red bark when freshly exposed; the durable red to red-brown wood of the tree. Also *attrib.*, and *ellipt.* as **salmon**.
1894 A.F. CALVERT *Coolgardie Goldfield* 49 This was another high rock, surrounded by salmon gum. 1908 E.G. MURPHY *Jarrahland Jingles* 114 Or underneath the salmons, where on sultry nights we sit. 1934 *Bulletin* (Sydney) 24 Oct. 20/3 At Ismailia (Egypt) a Digger mate and myself saw three salmon gums, trees of the Westralian wheatbelt and eastern goldfields—and you don't see them anywhere else in Australia. 1952 *Ibid.* 9 Jan. 17/2 Salmon-gum country, hard enough itself to kill any but the experienced bush-man, is Garden of Eden stuff compared with the Great Victoria Desert.

salmon trout. [Transf. use of *salmon-trout* a fish of the rivers of n. Europe, *Salmo trutta*.] The young of either of two fish, *Arripis trutta* and *A. esper* (see SALMON), having brown trout-like markings on the upper surface.
1848 J. SYME *Nine Yrs. Van Diemen's Land* 14 Fish are plentiful and reasonable. You have .. gurnett, a description of salmon trout .. and a variety of others. 1940 *Bulletin* (Sydney) 3 Jan. 16/2 Down on the Hopkins .. a shoal of what we Cabbage Gardeners call salmon trout had come in.

salt, *a. Obs.* Used in collocations as an abbrev. of SALT WATER 1, as **salt creek** [also U.S. (see Mathews *n.* 1)], **lagoon**.
1770 J. COOK *Jrnls.* 23 Aug. (1955) I. 395 In the Rivers and **salt Creeks** are some Aligators. 1835 *True Colonist* (Hobart) 23 Feb. 2/4 Another [river] .. disappointed expectation by ending in a **salt lagoon**, within a few miles of the sea.

saltbush. [See quot. 1965.]
1. Any of many shrubs or herbs of the fam. Chenopodiaceae, esp. those of the large genus *Atriplex* and the smaller genus *Rhagodia*, typically dominating tracts of saline and alkaline land in drier Aust.
1846 *Sydney Morning Herald* 8 Dec. 3/2 The myall tree and salt bush (*Acacia pendula*, and *salsoloe*), so essential to a good run are also there. 1965 *Austral. Encycl.* VII. 541 Saltbush .. alludes both to the salty character and habitat of these plants, which often grow naturally within the influence of salt water—near the seashore, in saline marshes or associated with salt-pans in the arid interior.
2. Comb. **saltbush country, flat, plain**.
1859 J.M. STUART *Explorations in Aust.* 14 Apr. (1865) 49 The country travelled over was fine **salt-bush country**. 1855 R. AUSTIN *Jrnl. Interior W.A.* 24 We struck a small samphire and **salt bush flat** about half a mile from the base of the hills we were steering for. 1848 T.L. MITCHELL *Jrnl. Exped. Tropical Aust.* 66 We encamped on the edge of a **salt-bush plain**.
3. Special Comb. **saltbush snake** [see quot. 1943], the lizard of s. mainland Aust. *Pygopus lepidopodus*, having rudimentary, scaly hind limbs.
1932 M.R. WHITE *No Roads go By* 32 A saltbush snake (whose bite it was said meant death in twenty minutes) ran across the back of her hand. 1943 C. BARRETT *Austral. Animal Bk.* 319 The scaly-foot (*Pygopus lepidopodus*), whose tail is more than twice the length of head and body combined, frequents salt-bush country. Rapid in its movements, often it is called the 'salt-bush snake'.
4. With distinguishing epithet: **creeping saltbush**, any of several plants, esp. the spreading *Atriplex semibaccata* (fam. Chenopodiaceae) of all mainland States; **old man saltbush**, see OLD MAN B. 3.
1903 G. SUTHERLAND *Australasian Live Stock Man.* (ed. 2) 384 Saltbush proper is the principal feed in the back country, and good feed it is. Then there is Mallee Salt Bush, and also Creeping Salt Bush—both good. 1984 *Flora Aust.* IV. 110 *Atriplex semibaccata* .. prostrate or decumbent perennial herb with slender spreading branches .. Creeping Saltbush.

saltie. [f. SALT (WATER 3 + -Y.] *Salt-water crocodile*, see SALT WATER 3.
1951 J. DEVANNY *Travels N. Qld.* 203 Mr Walker had shot a medium-sized 'saltie' as the man-eating crocodile of the coastal plains was called. 1985 *Age* (Melbourne) 3 Aug. (Saturday Extra) 15/1 It's the 'salties', the saltwater crocs that are really dangerous.

salt water.
1. Used *attrib.* in Comb. to distinguish an expanse of water which is salt, as **salt-water creek, lagoon**.
1837 *S. Austral. Gaz.* (Adelaide) 8 July 3 A **salt water creek**, running into Vivonne Bay. 1843 *S. Austral. Odd Fellows' Mag.* Oct. 44 There are numerous **salt-water lagoons**, around which may be traced several ancient reaches, far above the present water level, indicating different elevations of the land.
2. Used *attrib.* of an Aboriginal who lives near the sea, as distinct from one who lives inland.
1900 R. BRUCE *Benbonuna* (1904) 347 He also knew perfectly well that the old lubra would attribute their disappearance to the visit of a 'salt-water black'. 1981 NGABIDJ

& Shaw *My Country of Pelican Dreaming* 1 The Gadjerong were not solely 'saltwater people' like those further north.
 3. Special Comb. **salt-water crocodile,** the large crocodile *Crocodylus porosus* of coastal and near-coastal n. and n.e. Aust. and elsewhere, inhabiting estuarine, sea, and fresh water; Saltie.
 1943 C. Barrett *Austral. Animal Bk.* 314 The saltwater crocodile (*Crocodilus porosus*) also frequents estuaries and coastal waters. **1986** *Courier-Mail* (Brisbane) 6 Jan. 4, Male saltwater crocodiles take 16 years to become sexually mature and by that time they are 3 m. to 4 m. long. Females are 2 m. to 3 m. long when they mature at about 10 years of age.

salute: see *Australian salute* Australian *a.* 4; *Queensland salute* Queensland 1.

salvage, *v. Obs.* [Also U.S.: see OEDS *v.* 2.] *trans.* To steal; Salve; Souvenir.
 1918 *Aussie: Austral. Soldiers' Mag.* Jan. 11/1 *Salvage,* to rescue unused property and make use of it. The word is also used of the property rescued. Property salvaged in the presence of the owner leads to trouble and is not done by an expert. **1941** S.J. Baker *Pop. Dict. Austral. Slang* 63 *Salvage, to,* to steal, purloin.

Salvarmy. Shortened form of 'Salvation Army'. Freq. *attrib.*
 1899 *Bulletin* (Sydney) 10 June 14/1 A Brisbane Salvarmy captain lately held an audience .. entranced. **1915** *Bulletin* (Sydney) 18 Mar. 44/3 The Salv. Army band blew the palate out of its trombone in welcome.

Salvation Jane. Chiefly *S.A.* [See quot. 1973.] Paterson's Curse.
 1910 *Jrnl. Dept. Agric. S.A.* Dec. 524 It was also decided to ask other Branches to co-operate with the object of preventing the blue weed (Salvation Jane, Paterson's Curse, &c.) from being declared a noxious weed north of Petersburg. It was good fodder for sheep, especially in times of drought, and if it was desired to eradicate it the sheep would quickly do it. **1973** W.T. Parsons *Noxious Weeds Vic.* 32 In South Australia the plant is known as 'salvation jane', presumably because it can provide valuable fodder especially in the drier northern areas. It has been suggested, however, that the flower resembles the shape of the bonnets worn by Salvation Army lasses and that the plant was named accordingly.

salve, *v. Obs. trans.* Abbrev. of Salvage. Also as *ppl. a.*
 1918 M. Abson Diary 1 Feb. 29 (typescript) My batman 'salved' a couple of bags of cake. **1918** *Aussie: Austral. Soldiers' Mag.* Dec. 9/1 The brazier .. did .. duty .. for a jumped-up dish of Maconochie, bully beef, and salved spuds.

Salvo. [Abbrev. of *Salv(ation Army* + *-O.*] A member of the Salvation Army; the Salvation Army. Also *attrib.*
 1891 *Truth* (Sydney) 12 Apr. 7/3 Some of them ran behind the huts, some under the wood heap, and one poor devil got stuck in a hollow log, and had to be chopped out. But Salvo prayed. **1985** *Nat. Times* (Sydney) 2 Aug. 12/1 Some are too embarrassed to use the Salvo food vouchers they are given and welfare workers have to do the shopping for them.

sambo. [f. alteration of *sand(wich* + *-O.*] A sandwich. Also **sambie.**
 1976 B. Humphries *Dame Edna's Coffee Table Bk.* 71 Some exciting sambies .. an increasingly popular diminutive for 'sandwiches'. **1984** *Sydney Morning Herald* 2 Nov. 35/5 The last sprig of parsley disappeared from the final platter of sambos.

Sammy. [See quot. 1976 (1).] An award presented for excellence in the television industry by the Variety Club of Australia. Also **Sammy award.**
 1976 *TV Times* (Sydney) 25 Sept. 13/1 The new awards have been christened the Sammys, following a Variety Club custom of nearly 50 years of giving circus names to club officials, such as Chief Barker for Paul Hogan. The Sammys are designed like a circus seal. **1976** *Ibid.* 2 Oct. 10/1 Here come the Sammys .. the presentation of the first Australian TV and Film Awards. **1980** *Sydney Morning Herald* 18 Oct. 5/1 Last night in Sydney the fifth annual Sammy Awards were handed out... Bert Newton, Australia's best known second banana, was awarded the male Golden Sammy Award for consistent excellence.

samson fish. [See quot. 1882.] Any of several marine fish, esp. the large *Seriola hippos* of s. Aust., valued as a game fish.
 1871 *Industr. Progress N.S.W.* 791 Flat-head, samson-fish, and a variety of other less familiar forms, may be taken by the line in almost unlimited quantities. **1882** J.E. Tenison-Woods *Fish & Fisheries N.S.W.* 60 The great strength of these fishes is remarkable, and which probably is the cause that gave it the name of Samson-fish, as sailors or shipwrights give to the name of a strong post resting on the keelson of a ship, and supporting the upper beam, and bearing all the weight of the deck cargo near the hold, Samson post.

sand. Used *attrib.* in Special Comb. **sand flathead,** any of several fish of the fam. Platycephalidae inhabiting sandy seabeds, esp. *Platycephalus bassensis* of s. Aust. and *P. arenarius* of e. and n. Aust.; **goanna,** Bungarra; **lark,** red-capped dotterel, see Red *a.* 1 b.; **monkey,** see quot. 1981; **mullet,** the small marine and estuarine fish *Myxus elongatus* of s. Aust. exc. Tas.; Tallegalane; (occas.) any of several other similar fish; **palm,** the small, fan-leaved palm *Livistona humilis* (fam. Arecaceae) of n. N.T., usu. occurring on sandy soils; also *attrib.;* **soak,** a sandy Soak from which water can be obtained by digging; **whiting,** the marine fish *Sillago ciliata* of e. Aust., valued as food; (occas.) a similar, related fish.
 1885 *Proc. Linnean Soc. N.S.W.* X. 578 *Platycephalus arenarius* .. **Sand Flathead** of Sydney. **1978** N. Coleman *Austral. Fisherman's Fish Guide* 132 The sand flathead has spots on the top of the tail and the lower half is dark in colour. The body also has brown or red spots along the side. **1907** W.R.O. Hill *Forty Five Yrs. Experience N. Qld.* 75 The bites had come from small **sand 'goannas'**! **1802** M. Flinders *Voyage Terra Australis* (1814) II. 145 On the shores were pelicans .. and **sand-larks. 1958** H.D. Williamson *Sunlit Plain* 59, I was over on a bit of a **sand-monkey** about a mile off, setting a string of traps, so I didn't see you come in. It's marvellous how you can miss a man in this flat country. **1981** E. Rolls *Million Wild Acres* 260 The belts of white sand where the best pine grew were raised about half a metre above the rest of the country and were known as sand monkeys. **1844** *Sydney Morning Herald* 3 May 3/2 The **sand** or sea-**mullet** are just coming in. **1906** D.G. Stead *Fishes of Aust.* 75 The Sea Mullet is the largest .. of all our Mullets... In Victoria it is known as 'Sand Mullet', a name which we, in New South Wales, more judiciously apply to the Mullet which is also known as Tallegallane or Lano (*Myxus elongatus*). **1935** F. Birtles *Battle Fronts Outback* 157, I lived on young **sand palm** tops and black bream from the creek. **1984** D. Jones *Palms in Aust.* 134 *Livistona humilis* .. Sand Palm... This species is very common in open forest frequently growing in scattered colonies and sometimes in pure stands. **1936** C. Chewings *Back in Stone Age* 36 The water .. is ordinary ground water, from .. **sand-soaks.** **1882** J.E. Tenison-Woods *Fish & Fisheries N.S.W.* 65 The 'whitings' are not like those of Europe. There are in all four Australian species—the common **sand whiting** (*Sillago maculata*) [etc.].

SANDALWOOD

sandalwood, n.[1] [Spec. use of *sandalwood* the scented wood of several species of *Santalum*.]

1. Used *attrib.* with reference to the sandalwood industry.

1849 J.S. ROE *Rep. Exped. S.-Eastward Perth* 53 Mr Maxwell had a sandal-wood cutting station, at a good spring. **1981** *Austral. Women's Weekly* (Sydney) 18 Nov. 21/1 Most sandalwood camps are deep in remote country, hundreds of kilometres north and east of the gold-mining town of Kalgoorlie, Western Australia.

2. Comb. **sandalwood carter, getter.**

1865 'SPECIAL CORRESPONDENT' *Transportation* 22 It is the great rendezvous .. of the **sandal-wood carters**. **1913** *Bulletin* (Sydney) 17 Apr. 16/3 A hardy group of men are the **sandalwood-getters**.

3. Special Comb. **sandalwood track,** a track made by sandalwood cutters.

1849 J.S. ROE *Rep. Exped. S.-Eastward Perth* 53 We proceeded along the beaten sandal-wood track on the eastern side of the Stirling Range.

sandalwood, n.[2] [Transf. use of SANDALWOOD n.[1]] Any of several trees or shrubs of drier Aust. yielding wood with a fragrant aroma (esp. when burnt), esp. *Eremophila mitchellii* (see BUDDA), and *Myoporum platycarpum* (both fam. Myoporaceae); the wood of these plants.

1852 J. MACGILLIVRAY *Narr. Voyage H.M.S. Rattlesnake* I. 98 An inferior kind of sandal wood, the produce of *Exocarpos latifolia* (but which afterwards turned out to be useless) was met with. **1954** H.G. LAMOND *Manx Star* 260 *Sandal wood*, shrub with brittle leaves (*Eremophila Mitchelii*).

sandalwood, v. In the phr. **to go sandalwooding,** to seek out and cut sandalwood. See SANDALWOOD n.[1]

1894 J.K. ARTHUR *Kangaroo & Kauri* 23 The high price it once attained induced many of the colonists to go 'sandalwooding', travelling with their teams in search of this odorous wood. **1973** W.G. WALKER *Gloss. Educ. Terms* 9 Pioneer farmers after putting in their crop might go sandalwooding, to return in time for the harvest.

sandalwooder. One engaged in the cutting of sandalwood. See SANDALWOOD n.[1]

1932 C.E. GOODE *Grower of Golden Grain* 18, I saw a sandal-wooder with his camel team arrive. **1974** N. CATO *Brown Sugar* 9 Of course they were not the first white men the villagers had seen. Before that there had been the sandalwooders.

sand-grope, v. *Obs.* [See SAND-GROPER.]

a. *intr.* To walk in soft sand.

1924 LAWRENCE & SKINNER *Boy in Bush* 21 They walked off the timber platform into the sand, and Jack had his first experience of 'sand-groping'. The sand was thick and fine and soft, so he was glad to reach the oyster-shell path running up Wellington Street.

b. *fig.* To bungle. (In quot. as *ppl. a.*)

1898 *Bulletin* (Sydney) 15 Jan. 20/1 The W.A. sand-groping Forrest Govt. has a great penchant for importing second-hand English clerks.

Sand-groper. A non-Aboriginal person, native to or resident in Western Australia. (The statement made in quot. 1899 is erroneous). Also *attrib.*

1896 H. LAWSON *Lett.* 3 Sept. (1970) 62 The old Sandgropers are the best to work for... The Totherslders are cutting each others' throats. **1899** *Austral. Tit-Bits* (Sydney) 2 Dec. 6/1 'Sand-groper' is the name given to the aboriginals of West Australia. **1963** X. HERBERT *Disturbing Element* 2, I doubt if born West Australians have got over the Sand Groper Complex even yet.

SANITARY

Sandgroperland. A nickname for Western Australia.

1908 *Truth* (Sydney) 12 July 1/3 They do things differently over in Sandgroperland. **1920** *Referee* (Sydney) 11 Feb. 13/5 How the swimmers of Sandgroperland attained the standard they reached under such conditions surpasses my understanding.

sandhill wattle. The tall shrub or small tree *Acacia burkittii* (fam. Mimosaceae), usu. of sandy plains in N.S.W., S.A., and W.A., having long, needle-like phyllodes; *kangaroo bush* (b), see KANGAROO n. 5.

1946 C.T. MADIGAN *Crossing Dead Heart* 68 There was green sandhill wattle. **1975** E.R. ROTHERHAM et al. *Flowers & Plants N.S.W. & Southern Qld.* 150 *Acacia burkittii* sandhill wattle .. is scattered throughout the Plains of N.S.W. and in northern S.A.

sand map. A makeshift diagram of an area, route, etc., drawn in sand.

1932 I.L. IDRIESS *Lasseter's Last Ride* 58 'Sand maps' were drawn .. eloquent with .. fingernail in making depressions along the proposed route where soakages were found. **1959** A. UPFIELD *Bony & Mouse* 221 Bony smoothed the ground, and with a finger rapidly drew a map of the mulga forest... About this sand map, white men and black elders squatted on heels.

sandpaper fig. [See quot. 1965.] Any of several trees of the genus *Ficus* (fam. Moraceae) having rough leaves, as *F. coronata, F. opposita,* and *F. fraseri; rough fig,* see ROUGH a. 1. Also *attrib.*

c **1910** W.R. GUILFOYLE *Austral. Plants* 177 *Ficus aspera* .. 'Sand- paper Fig Tree' .. (evergreen tree, 80 to 100 ft.) .. Vic., N.S.W., and Q'land. **1965** *Austral. Encycl.* IV. 59 A number of figs are noted for the roughness of the leaves to the touch and are popularly known as sandpaper figs.

sandy blight. [See quot. 1892.] An acute conjunctivitis, usu. infectious and trachomatous, characterized by granular follicles and common in arid areas; BLIGHT. Also **sand blight.**

1846 H. McCRAE *Georgiana's Jrnl.* 19 July (1934) 197 Cuts, splinter-wounds, boils, and sand-blight, have been successfully treated. **1892** G.L. JAMES *Shall I try Aust.?* 242 One pest of the bush and plains is 'Sandy Blight', or inflammation of the eyes—it is, I believe, called 'sandy' owing to the pain being exactly similar to that which grains of sand upon the eyeball would cause.

sanger. Alteration of 'sandwich'. Also **sango.**

1943 *O-Pip:* 'P' *Battery Austral. Field Artillery* Aug. 3 We beheld an outsize in double-decker sangos clamped in Irvine's jaw. **1980** *Sunday Mail* (Brisbane) 24 Aug. 3/8 A colleague went to order a chicken 'sanger' and decided to ask the serving lady why they seemed 'a little thin of late'.

sanguineous honeyeater: see *scarlet honeyeater* SCARLET.

sanitary, a.

a. Used in collocations with reference to the collection of excrement from unsewered areas, as **sanitary cart (truck, van),** a vehicle used for this purpose; *dunny cart,* see DUNNY 2; *night-cart,* see NIGHT; also *ellipt.*; **man,** one who operates such a vehicle; *dunny man,* see DUNNY 2; *night-cart man, night-man,* see NIGHT.

1894 [**sanitary cart**] A.B. BELL *Austral. Camp Fire Tales* 95 The cabby .. set that horse going full sail, and no mistake: as we dashed through the city, everyone stared aghast, while the Jehu remarked as he coughed and spit: 'Oh! Lor, Oh! Lor, they'll take us for a sanitary van.' **1958** F.B. VICKERS *Though Poppies Grow* 202, I was the half-caste bastard working on the sanitary-cart. **1968** *Kings Cross Whisper* (Sydney) li. 2/1 The speed limit for sanitary trucks—better known as night carts and dunny carts—is to be raised. **1984** P. READ *Down there with me on Cowra Mission* 26 They never had the sewerage... We had the sanitary coming once a week. **1903** *Truth* (Sydney) 31 May 1/4 Crapp is the euphonious name of the **sanitary man** in a New South Wales town.

b. In the phr. **on the sanitary,** working on a sanitary cart.

1963 P. WHITE *Four Plays* (1965) 113 I've got me run, Digger. I told you I was on the sanitary. I've gotta make meself scarce. Late already. We're short of personnel. The night-soil's not everybody's cuppa tea.

sano. Also **sanno.** [f. *san(itary* + -O.] A sanitary inspector; *sanitary man,* see SANITARY a. Freq. *attrib.* as **sano man.**

1959 S.J. BAKER *Drum* 142 *Sanno,* a sanitary inspector. **1969** *Kings Cross Whisper* (Sydney) lxvi. 5/5 Fifty Sydney dunny carts, manned by sano men carrying dozens of cut lunches, will leave Sydney next week on a survey of the marathon route. **1971** F. HARDY *Outcasts of Foolgarah* 49 Sanitary carters .. known not too favourably locally as Sanos, or more precisely, shitties.

sap, *v. trans.* To cut a ring round (the trunk of a tree) of sufficient depth to penetrate the sap wood. Also **sap-ring (bark)** *v.,* and as *vbl. n.*

1826 J. ATKINSON *Acct. Agric. & Grazing N.S.W.* 85 Another plan is to stump-fall the trees, and then to open out the stump all round, so as to expose as many of the roots to the air as possible, at the same time *sapping* the stump, as it is termed, that is, cutting off about a hand's breadth of the bark all round, as low down as possible. **1827** *Monitor* (Sydney) 5 July 495/1 There were many of these worthies, who had never handled an axe or a hand-spike, and to whom, 'felling' and 'lopping', 'sapping', and 'cutting-out', would be almost as strange and irksome, as it would be for a ship's carpenter to attempt the making of a chronometer. **1967** W. *Austral. Selector's Guide* (W.A. Lands Dept.) 6 York Gum is apt to throw out suckers, particularly if sap-ringed. **1947** *Bulletin* (Sydney) 24 Sept. 29/3, I have found that trees 'sap'- ringbarked decay much more rapidly than trees 'collar'-ringbarked.

saratoga. [Of unknown origin.] The fish *Scleropages leichardti* (see BARRAMUNDI c.).

1969 J. POLLARD *Austral. & N.Z. Fishing* 661 *Scleropages leichardti...* The species is known as saratoga or saratota in all North Australia, with local exceptions on the Jardine and Dawson River. **1984** MERRICK & SCHMIDA *Austral. Freshwater Fishes* 71 This immature saratoga (*Scleropages leichardti*) is 300 mm. long.

sardine. [Used elsewhere but recorded earliest in Aust.] Used *attrib.* in Special Comb. **sardine box, tin,** an extremely small dwelling or other building.

1899 G.E. BOXALL *Story Austral. Bushrangers* 136 Later some boxes, made of corrugated iron, were put up as cells and these were known as 'the Dutch ovens' or 'the **sardine boxes**' and prisoners confined to them on hot summer nights suffered tortures and begged to be put 'on the chain' as a relief. **1888** 'SPECIAL CORRESPONDENT' *Barrier Silver & Tin Fields* 6 The '**sardine-tin**', 'rag houses', and 'bandbox' buildings were in ill contrast.

sarsaparilla. [Transf. use of *sarsaparilla,* orig. applied to *Smilax.*]

a. FALSE SARSAPARILLA. **b.** *Sweet tea,* see SWEET *a.*[1] Also *attrib.*

1830 R. DAWSON *Present State Aust.* 199 Sarsaparilla .. grew wild on the banks. **1887** *Proc. Linnean Soc. N.S.W.* II. 274 *Kennedya .. monophylla ..* everywhere .. usually called 'Sarsaparilla' and used in the same way as a bitter, *Smilax* the true Sarsapilla not extending to this district. **1981** E. POTTER *Scone I Remember* 24 Over the years we watched a small sarsaparilla vine slowly climb to the top of the fence, grow into a luxuriant purple mass and spill over the far side.

sarvo. [f. *thi)s* + ARVO.] 'This afternoon'.

1942 *Welcome to Aust.* 7 Sarvo, this afternoon. **1978** D. STUART *Wedgetail View* 244 An' after the Company parade, 'sarvo, what'll it be, Eddie?

sassafras. [Transf. use of *sassafras* an American tree of the genus *Sassafras.*] Any of several trees, usu. of the fam. Monimiaceae, having an aromatic bark, esp. the rainforest trees *Atherosperma moschatum* of s.e. Aust. incl. Tas. and *Doryphora sassafras* of e. N.S.W. and s.e. Qld.; the bark, leaves, or wood of these trees. Also *attrib.*

1802 *HRA* (1915) 1st Ser. III. 571 The Sassafras wood grows in great abundance. **1981** A.B. & J.W. CRIBB *Wild Medicine in Aust.* 58 *Atherosperma moschatum* is given the common name of sassafras because of the spicy scent, rather like nutmeg, in the leaves and bark.

satin, *a.* Used as a distinguishing epithet in the names of flora and fauna: **satin bird,** *satin bower-bird*; (occas.) *shining flycatcher,* see SHINING; **bower-bird,** the bird *Ptilonorhynchus violaceus* of e. mainland Aust., the mature male having glossy black plumage with a blue sheen; **flycatcher,** the bird *Myiagra cyanoleuca* of e. Aust. incl. Tas., and elsewhere, the mature male having glossy bluish-black upperparts and chest, and white belly; **oak,** a tall rainforest tree of the genus *Oreocallis* (fam. Proteaceae), esp. *O. wickhamii* of n.e. Qld.; also **satin silky oak; top,** any of several grasses (fam. Poaceae), esp. the tufted perennial *Bothriochloa erianthoides* of N.S.W. and Qld., valued as fodder; also **satin top (ped) grass.**

1827 *Trans. Linnean Soc. London* XV. 264 Mr Caley says that 'the male of this species is reckoned a very scarce bird, and is highly valued. The natives call it *Cowry,* the colonists **Satin Bird**'. **1860** *Sydney Mail* 21 July 6/2 The satin birds seek in the gardens and shrubberies for seeds. **1841** J. GOULD *Birds of Aust.* (1848) IV. Pl. 10, *Ptilonorhynchus holosericeus..* **Satin Bower-bird** .. Satin Bird, of the Colonists of New South Wales. **1898** E.E. MORRIS *Austral Eng.* 404 Satin-Robin .. a Tasmanian name for the **Satin Flycatcher,** *Myiagra nitida.* **1919** [**satin oak**] R.Γ. BAKER *Hardwoods of Aust.* 5 Timber Colours .. Pink ... *Embothrium Wickhami ..* Satin Silky Oak. **1982** K. MCARTHUR *Bush in Bloom* 140 The brilliant North Queensland *Oreocallis wickhamii*—the Satin Oak. **1882** [**satin top**] *Austral. Handbk.* 392 There are nearly 200 indigenous grasses, amongst which are .. the 'Satin-topped grass' (*Andropogon erianthoides*) [etc.]. **1923** E. BREAKWELL *Grasses & Fodder Plants N.S.W.* 17 *Andropogon bombycinus* (Satin Top grass) .. very rare everywhere; found in protected areas in the northwest. **1965** *Austral. Encycl.* VI. 366 *Bothriochloa erianthoides* (satin-top) is a valuable fodder grass usually found in bluegrass country.

satinwood. [Transf. use of *satin-wood* the satiny, yellowish wood of various trees.] Any of several trees of e. Aust. yielding a glossy, usu. yellowish timber, esp. *Zanthoxylum brachyacanthum* and *Phebalium squameum* subsp. *squameum* (both fam. Rutaceae), and *Daphnandra micrantha* (fam. Monimiaceae); the wood of these trees.

1853 J. CAPPER *Emigrant's Guide to Aust.* (ed. 2) 9 Cedar and satin-wood are also found in the western and southern sides of the island. **1981** J.A. BAINES *Austral. Plant Genera* 403 Satinwood, so-called from the glossy yellow timber.

saucy, *a. Austral. pidgin.* See quot. 1860.

1860 G. BENNETT *Gatherings of Naturalist* 108 The aborigines saying (alluding to the spur), 'It is very saucy', such

sausage.

being their English expression when they wish to imply that anything is hurtful or poisonous.   **1914** J. MATHEW *Ballads Bush Life* 9 Their saucy-fellow dillies And sugarbag and billies, Their shells and reeds and rugs and other store.

sausage.
1. *fig.* The penis. Also *attrib.*
1944 *Action* (Toowoomba) July 11 'Sausage Brigade'.. to live up to this term, then, a soldier must have his wife in the area.   **1971** B. HUMPHRIES *Bazza pulls it Off,* Yeah, you old sausage grappler!!!
2. Special Comb. **sausage wrapper,** a newspaper.
1891 'SMILER' *Wanderings Simple Child* (ed. 3) 6 I'd write a better leader than your old one-horse show has ever had in its columns since it first started on its wild career as a sausage wrapper.

savage. *Obs.* Used freq. during the nineteenth century, not necessarily pejoratively, of an Aboriginal.
1792 R. JOHNSON *Address to Colonies N.S.W. & Norfolk Island* 67, I would farther plead with you for the sake of the poor unenlightened savages, who daily visit us, or who reside amongst us.   **1830** *Launceston Advertiser* 15 Feb. 3 Much has been said about the Savages, whom by the mere right of *power* we have bereaved of their dominion, and against whose defenceless wretchedness we have waged a war directly tending to extermination.

saver. *Horse-racing.* [Used elsewhere but recorded earliest in Aust.: see OED(S 5.] A hedging bet, a bet laid to insure against loss on another bet.
1891 N. GOULD *Double Event* 123 Wells says Perfection will win .. but I've put a saver on Caloola.   **1983** *Sydney Morning Herald* 12 Mar. 13/8 The electorate clearly has had 'a saver' on the Democrats and the Senate. While giving the Labor Party a clear mandate to govern in the House of Representatives, voters have left 'the minders' in control in the Senate, just in case the Government should get out of line.

sawn. Abbrev. of 'sawney' a simpleton.
1953 K. TENNANT *Joyful Condemned* 145 Get back, or I'll bung a rock at you. I'm always getting into trouble through sawns.   **1961** *Bulletin* (Sydney) 15 Mar. 6/1 During the war, when overcrowding at Parramatta became a scandal .. younger, meeker girls who were there as a result of wretched home and living conditions were contemptuously termed 'sawns'.

saw shark. [See quot. 1974.] A shark of the fam. Pristiophoridae of s. Aust. and elsewhere.
1882 J.E. TENISON-WOODS *Fish & Fisheries N.S.W.* 98 The saw-shark must not be confounded with saw-fish, as their gill-openings are lateral not underneath.   **1974** T.D. SCOTT et al. *Marine & Freshwater Fishes S.A.* 42 The Saw Sharks form an unusual group of fishes which are not uncommon in southern Australian waters... They are recognized readily by the long produced and flattened snout, armed with a row of teeth on each side. This formidable weapon is used in defence, or when in search of prey.

scabbery. The betrayal of one's fellow workers; scab workers collectively.
1918 B. KENNEDY *Silver, Sin, & Sixpenny Ale* 160 One militant denounced the local Trades and Labor Council as .. 'born in Scabbery'.   **1939** E.H. LANE *Dawn to Dusk* 25 Scabbery was exalted by the blatant capitalist press as the sacred duty of every freedom-loving Australian worker.

scabby, *a.* Non-union.
1892 *Bulletin* (Sydney) 24 Dec. 22/1 There were eight or ten dashed Chinamen a-shearin' in a row... And I left his scabby station at the old jig-jog.   **1985** J. SCHULTZ *Steel City Blues* 25 In the Combined Mining Unions, the Burragorang Valley is also known as 'scabby valley', the miners not being noted for their industrial militancy.

scalded, *ppl. a.* Of land: bare of vegetation, often because of soil erosion or salination.
1920 J.N. MACINTYRE *White Aust.* 74 It meant that when I opened it up and had the stumps grubbed out, that it would have been a remarkably fast motor track, as miles and miles of it ran over scalded country.   **1977** *Weekly Times* (Melbourne) 19 Jan. 17/2 Deep gullies and scalded country are evidence of the worst abuses of valuable farming country.

scale, *n.* Gold-mining. *Obs.* [U.S.: see Mathews *n.*^{2} 2.] A flake of gold. Chiefly as **scale gold,** gold found in flakes.
1851 *Empire* (Sydney) 18 Aug. 59/4 The other specimen consisted of scale gold of a deep yellow colour, nearly orange.   **1852** *Moreton Bay Free Press* 24 June 3/5 The greater part of the gold was of a nuggety character, but there was also a great number of scales; there were no large nuggets amongst the lot; the colour principally dark, and the gold evidently water-worn.

scale, *v.* [Perh. transf. use of *scale* to weigh (a jockey): see OED(S *v.*^{1} 3 b. but also *v.*^{2} 2 c.]
1. *intr.* To avoid paying what is due; *spec.* to avoid paying one's fare. Also *trans.*, to defraud (a person); to ride (a tram, truck, etc.) without paying; to take (a ride) in this way.
1904 *Truth* (Sydney) 7 Aug. 9/5 'Scaling' consists in the bilking of the woman that has agreed to behave unchastely in return for a pecuniary consideration.   **1917** C. THACKERAY *Goliath Joe* 87 Wen 'e tried to scale on the tram for a section he bumped a rough guard who knew 'im by name an' repitation an' 'ad 'im prosecuted.   **1933** 'TRAMWAY WORKERS' *Shock Brigader* 5 'Phwere's your ticket?' Mick's suspicions were confirmed. The boy opened his hand and exposed sixpence. 'So you were tryin' to scale me, you young varmint.'   **1984** *Sydney Morning Herald* 7 Jan. 31/4 The tram guards .. were generally much admired by little boys, even though we did our best to outwit them by 'scaling' a ride, crouching unseen on the footboard on the other side of the tram.
2. To depart stealthily or speedily; also with advs. and *trans.*, to absent oneself from.
1917 G.C. COOPER *Diary* 30 Sept., Scaled Church Parade—got hand dressed. *Ibid.* 30 July, Went to a concert at night (scaled out and nearly got caught) by the Magpies.   **1929** *Aussie* (Sydney) Aug. 52/3 When the dressing gong woke me a couple of hours later, Dad had scaled—carpetbag and all.

scaler. [f. SCALE *v.* 1.] One who 'scales', a cheat.
1915 *Honk* ix. 5 If you wear a sling, people put their arms around you and weep, but if you have a couple of bullets in your liver and nothing to show them you must be a scaler.   **1981** G. CROSS *George & Widda-Woman* 50 The Tramway is very down on scalers, and brings a court action whenever possible .. against people who try to swindle His Majesty's government.

scalie. Also **scaly.** [f. *scale* a weighing machine + -Y.] An official who checks the weight of the load carried by a road transport vehicle. Also **scalie man.**
1976 *Truckin' Life* I. iii. 47 His parting words to Harry left no doubt that the scalies would be waiting for him at the end of the tough road.   **1977** *Lights on Hill* 13 Dodge the weights and measure boys, yeah, dodge those scaly men.

scalp. [U.S.: see OEDS *sb.*^{1} 2 c.] Used *attrib.* to designate the scalp of an animal retained as evidence of its death, usu. in order to obtain a bounty.
1891 H.W. HARRIS *Shearers or Shorn* 26 One young

Queenslander who has lived the greater portion of his life in the bush, has worked as a shearer, drover, brumby hunter, and scalp collector. **1950** G.M. FARWELL *Land of Mirage* 43 No one has ever reckoned the cost of rabbit fencing, nor of bounties, bonuses, scalp money paid to rabbit trappers.

Hence **scalper** n.
1897 *Western Champion* (Barcaldine) 12 Oct. 3/3 There is a great commotion amongst the scalpers owing to the reduction in price for kangaroo scalps. **1919** *Smith's Weekly* (Sydney) 26 July 4/3, I was a fortnight in a Maranoa scalper's camp.

scaly, var. SCALIE.

scaly-breasted lorikeet. The lorikeet of e. Aust. *Trichoglossus chlorolepidotus*, having green plumage (see quot. 1976) with bright orange-red underwings, and often occurring in flocks with the *rainbow lorikeet* (see RAINBOW 2). Also **scaly-breasted parrot**, and *abbrev*. as **scaly-breast**.
1843 J. GOULD *Birds of Aust*. (1848) V. Pl. 50, The Scaly-breasted Lorikeet breeds in all the large *Eucalypti* near Maitland on the Hunter. **1929** A.H. CHISHOLM *Birds & Green Places* 209 Just a sprinkling of the larger 'blueys' (rainbow lorikeets) and 'greenies' (scaly-breasts). **1945** C. BARRETT *Austral. Bird Life* 76 The scaly-breasted parrot (T[*richoglossus*] *chlorolepidotus*) bears a bad name among orchardists. **1976** *Reader's Digest Compl. Bk. Austral. Birds* 261 'Scaly-breasted' aptly describes this bird, which has yellow breast feathers broadly edged with green that look like scales... Scaly-breasted lorikeets can be identified in flight by their conspicuous orange-red underwing-coverts and green head.

scarf, v. [Prob. var. of CARF, infl. by *scarf* to cut a scarf-joint, but see OED(S *scarf*, sb.^{5} and v.^{3}] *trans*. To cut a scarf in (a tree trunk). Also as *vbl. n*.
[N.Z. **1899** J. BELL *Shadow of Bush* 83 The smaller trees.. had been 'scarfed', or cut partly through in readiness, and skilfully, so that each, when struck, might again in its turn strike and bring down another.] **1909** *Bulletin* (Sydney) 26 Aug. 15/2 The judgment is required, in the first place to sufficiently kerf (why do bushmen use the carpenter's term 'scarf'?) the front tree or trees. **1938** F. RATCLIFFE *Flying Fox & Drifting Sand* 102 The two fallers then took up their positions.. and the process of 'scarfing' began... The 'scarf' penetrated about half-way to the centre.

scarlet, a. Used as a distinguishing epithet in the names of flora and fauna: **scarlet-chested** (or -**breasted**) **parrot**, the parrot *Neophema splendida* of drier s. Aust.; formerly also **scarlet-chested grass parakeet** (or **grass parrot**); **gum**, either of two small to medium trees of the genus *Eucalyptus* (fam. Myrtaceae), *E. phoenicea* of n. Aust. and *E. ficifolia* (see FLOWERING GUM), cultivated for their showy clusters of red to orange flowers; also **scarlet flowering gum**; **honeyeater**, the honeyeater *Myzomela sanguinolenta* of e. Aust. and elsewhere, the mature male having predom. scarlet plumage; see also *blood-bird* BLOOD; formerly also **sanguineous honeyeater**; **robin**, the small bird *Petroica multicolor* of s. Aust. incl. Tas., the mature male having black and white plumage with a scarlet breast; see also ROBIN, ROBIN REDBREAST 1; also, esp. formerly, **scarlet-breasted robin**.
1822 [scarlet-chested parrot] J. LATHAM *Gen. Hist. Birds* II. 121 *Scarlet-breasted parrot*. Length fifteen inches. Bill red.. chin and throat yellow, the latter bounded on the breast by a broad scarlet band... Inhabits New-Holland. **1900** A.J. CAMPBELL *Nests & Eggs Austral. Birds* 654 (heading) Scarlet-chested Grass Parrakeet. **1913** *Emu* XII. Suppl. 54 *Euphema splendida*.. Scarlet-chested Grass-Parrot... *Range*: New South Wales, Victoria, S. and W. Australia. **1931** N.W. CAYLEY *What Bird is That?* 152 Scarlet-chested Parrot... Rarely recorded, then only as isolated pairs. **1880** [scarlet gum] *Argus* (Melbourne) 21 Jan. 7/1 The flame tree of Illawarra and northern New South Wales—Brachychiton acerifolium—is very beautiful when in flower; but it is not equal to the splendour of the scarlet flowering gum. **1947** W.A.W. DE BEUZEVILLE *Austral. Trees for Austral. Planting* 166 Scarlet Gum (*Euc. ficifolia*). This is an extremely ornamental plant when in bloom, producing freely bunches of very striking scarlet to flame coloured blossoms, very attractive in appearance. [**1801 scarlet honeyeater:** J. LATHAM *Gen. Synopsis Birds* Suppl. II. 167 *Sanguineous creeper*... All the upper parts of the bird crimson.. with a few irregular large black spots.] **1822** —— *Gen. Hist. Birds* IV. 201 *Sanguineous honey-eater*.. inhabits New South Wales; common in the neighbourhood of the River Nepean, among bushes and thick woods. **1984** M. BLAKERS et al. *Atlas Austral. Birds* 568 The Scarlet Honeyeater lives in Sulawesi, New Caledonia and in Australia. **1842** [scarlet robin] J. GOULD *Birds of Aust*. (1848) III. Pl. 3, *Petroica multicolor*.. Scarlet-breasted Robin. **1978** B.P. MOORE *Life on Forty Acres* 95 Scarlet Robins.. with bright red breasts in true robin fashion, are at best locally in early spring.

scarp, v. *intr*. Abbrev. of 'scarper', to depart hastily.
1910 L. ESSON *Woman Tamer* (1976) 82 *Katie*:.. Get! *Chopsey*: Gaud struth Katie... *Katie*:.. Scarp off! **1941** *Ack Ack News* (Melbourne) Nov. 4 A semi-nude figure, draped only in a towel.. was seen scarping in the direction of the predictor pit at terrific speed.

scarver, v. *Obs*. [Alteration of *scarper* to depart hastily.] *intr*. See quot.
1905 *Bulletin* (Sydney) 24 Oct. 14/3 Scarver, to flit from town secretly, leaving sorrowing creditors behind... 'Leaving a dog tied up' refers to the debts left by the 'scarverer'.

scatter. [Spec. use of *scatter* a dispersion.] In the phr. **to get a scatter on,** to lose touch with someone.
1949 I.L. IDRIESS *One Wet Season* 269 We'd got a scatter on and.. didn't hear of the wedding until too late to send a present. **1978** D. STUART *Wedgetail View* 29 Never seen ole John again. Heard of him once in a while, but y' know how it is; a bloke gets an awful scatter on across the face o' the country over the years.

scheme. W.A. Used *attrib*. to designate water supplied to arid inland areas by pipeline from Mundaring Weir, on the Helena River near Perth. Also *absol*.
1915 J.P. BOURKE *Off Bluebush* 81 And thoughts tramp back where I lost the track Of a 'leader' of five-ounce dirt, Before I knelt with a 'Scheme'-cleansed pelt At the shrine of a laundried [*sic*] shirt! **1950** G.S. CASEY *City of Men* 151 She interrupted Joseph and dragged her children off to the bathroom, but they were no longer enthusiastic about it. After all, she thought unhappily, it was only a Scheme-water shower she had to offer.

scheisser, var. SHICER.

schleinter, schlenter, vart. SLANTER.

schnapper, var. SNAPPER.

school.
1. In the phr. **School of Arts,** an institution founded in many centres during the nineteenth century which provided a library and arranged lectures, etc., for the local public.
1834 J.D. LANG *Hist. & Statistical Acct. N.S.W.* I. 178 We may hail the present establishment of a 'Mechanics' School of Arts' in Sydney as opening altogether a new era in the history of the colony. **1948** R. RAVEN-HART *Canoe in Aust*. 13 The oddly-named 'Mechanics Institute' or 'School of

Arts', used mainly for dances and meetings though perhaps containing also a library.

2. School of the Air, a government-funded educational program which uses a two-way radio communication system to enable children in remote areas to participate in 'classroom' activities for part of each day.

1950 *Centralian Advocate* (Alice Springs) 8 Sept. 1/1 It has been learned that the scheme envisages a broadcast direct from Alice Springs in the form of a 'School of the Air' catering for a normal curriculum. 1983 *Bicentenary '88* (Austral. Bicentennial Authority) Nov. 11/1 With the help of the Katherine School of the Air, the radio signal 'Calling all Penguins' broke the air-waves on 17 May this year.

3. *transf.* A group of people assembled for the purpose of playing a gambling game, esp. TWO-UP *n.*; the place where such an assembly takes place; *gaffing school,* see GAFF *v.*

1812 J.H. VAUX *Mem.* (1819) II. 203 School, a party of persons met together for the purpose of gambling. 1950 H.C. WELLS *Earth cries Out* 80 'Had a good win at the 'school' last Sunday.' . . 'I've never played two-up in my life.'

schoolie, *n.*[1] Also **schooley.** [f. *school(teacher* + -Y.] A schoolteacher.

1889 H. EGBERT *Pretty Cockey* 57 The rest addressed him sometimes as 'Schoolmaster', sometimes as 'Schooley'. 1982 R. HALL *Just Relations* 86 She was the last schoolie of Whitey's Fall.

schoolie, *n.*[2] [f. *school* a flock, company (of animals) + -Y.] **a.** SCHOOL SHARK. **b.** A school prawn.

1980 S. SALISBURY et al. *Fishermen's Views* E71 All the sharks and catfish all get into this lukewarm water. Because its [*sic*] only a shark about that long, a schoolie. They won't bite you. 1980 B. SHACKLETON *Karagi* 26 Daylight prawns are light shelled 'schoolies' that run spasmodically soon after sunup.

school shark. [See quot. 1980.] The medium-sized shark *Galeorhinus australis,* abundant in s. Aust., and occurring in New Zealand, an important commercial species.

1852 G.C. MUNDY *Our Antipodes* I. 390 The 'school shark' is dealt with as above. But if the 'grey nurse' or old solitary shark be hooked, the cable is cut. 1980 ANSELL & PERCY *To fight Wild* 57 The school sharks are genuine sharks, and go around in packs.

schooner. [U.S. *schooner* a tall beer glass: see OED(S *sb.*[2]] A large beer-glass of locally variable capacity; the (measure of) beer contained in such a glass.

1892 *Truth* (Sydney) 8 May 3/6 Maybe you'd like a good schooner, now, wouldn't you? A nice long sleever, hay? 1985 *Bulletin* (Sydney) 24 Dec. 62/2 We thought that heroic drinkers drank from the largest glasses—schooners (15 ounces) or pints.

Hence **schoonerful** *n.*

1981 K. GARVEY *Rhymes of Ratbag* 76 We start makin' tracks To the village and a schoonerful of two-mile ale.

scissors-grinder. [See quot. 1985.] RESTLESS FLY-CATCHER.

1917 [see RESTLESS FLYCATCHER]. 1934 S. KING *Molly's Yr. in Camp* 34 Scissors-grinders seemed to be trying over their parts. 1985 *Austral. Nat. Hist.* Spring 429 The Restless Flycatcher with its whirring, rasping call, which sounds like scissors being sharpened on a grind stone, is often referred to as the Scissors-grinder.

scone /skɒn/, *n.* [Fig. use of *scone cake:* see OEDS *sb.* 3 a. and b.]

1. The head.

[N.Z. 1942 *2nd N.Z. Exped. Force Times* 19 Oct. 5 Don't do your plurry scone, Dig!] 1945 *Atebrin Advocate: Mag.* 2/4 Austral. Armoured Regiment 12 May 3 Pull yer scone in. 1975 'N. CULOTTA' *Gone Gougin'* 62 He's not right in the skull. Musta got concussion in that blue he started last night. He's gone in the scone.

2. In the phr. **to go** (someone) **scone-hot,** to attack (someone) with vigour, esp. verbally; to become angry with.

1927 F.C. BIGGERS *Bat-Eye* 15 Ter see a dinkum parson go a bloke scone 'ot, An' chuck 'im out . . Gawd spare me days! 1981 H. HANNAH *Together in Jungle Scrub* 20 One time old Jones sold the last tin of strawberry—his wife went him scone hot!

scone, *v.* [f. Br. dial. *scon* to beat with the flat of the hand: see EDD.] *trans.* To hit.

1948 *Coast to Coast 1947* 187 The bottle broke. Damn! he hadn't meant to scone the bottle first go-off. 1957 D. WHITINGTON *Treasure upon Earth* 79 'I'd like to see the mug that could scone me,' Mick said belligerently.

scoot. Also **skoot.** [Transf. use of *scoot* to go suddenly.] In the phr. **(up)on the scoot,** engaged in a drinking bout or spree.

1916 *Truth* (Sydney) 29 Oct. 12/2 Elsie Long, a puffeck Lydie, Got upon the scoot one Friday. 1927 K.S. PRICHARD *Brumby Innes* (1974) 73, I can be a bit of use here, John. . . Look after things when Brum's out musterin' . . or on the skoot.

score, *v.* [Used elsewhere but recorded earliest in Aust.: see OEDS *v.* 16 f.] *intr.* To achieve sexual intercourse with another.

c 1907 C.W. CHANDLER *Darkest Adelaide* 5 In Flinders street the other night several [prostitutes] were congregated together when one of them was called on one side. . . The following dialogue ensued: He—'Come on. Sling!' She (to her mates)—'Gor' blime have I scored?' Chorus of Shes—'She's never scored to-night, and won't while you keep hanging round.' 1978 *Southerly* iii. 268 'You can't seduce that young man. He doesn't know anything about life,' he said. 'You're just jealous because I'm scoring better than you are,' she goaded.

Scotch, *a.* [Spec. use of *Scotch* (supposedly) characteristic of Scotland or its people.] In special collocations: **Scotch coffee,** ersatz coffee (see quots.); **navigation,** see quot. 1907; so, **navigator.**

1836 J.F. O'CONNELL *Residence Eleven Yrs. New Holland* 47 At dinner they have animal food and vegetables, and at supper '**Scotch coffee**', i.e. burned corn. 1904 *Bulletin* (Sydney) 7 Apr. 16/4 In the heart of the Out-back, when the tucker-bag gets low . . tea is replaced by 'Scotch coffee', *i.e.,* flour roasted in an oven. 1907 C. MACALISTER *Old Pioneering Days* 32 Mr Siggs, also bound to Sydney with a cargo of wool, showed us a better way of running our team than by '**Scotch navigation**' (i.e. brute strength and stupidity). 1903 J. FURPHY *Such is Life* 215 Some carriers never learn the great lesson, that to everything there is a time and a season. . . Moreover, the same rule holds fairly well throughout the whole region of industry. But the **Scotch-navigator** can't see it. He is too furiously busy. *Ibid.* 236 Straight into the lion's mouth! Heaven help—but does heaven help the Scotch-navigator?

scotch grey. [Fig. use of the sing. of *Scotch* (for *Scots*) Greys, a cavalry regiment. Cf. the obs. Br. slang use for *louse.*] HEXHAM GREY. Also **Scots grey.**

c 1887 R.G. GALLOP In Never Never Land, Huge mosquitoes known here as 'Scotch Greys' or 'Overlanders' added their quota of misery. 1934 WARBURTON & ROBERTSON *Buffaloes* 29 The mosquitoes acquainted us of their presence. They were mostly the famous Scots Greys; they literally stood on their heads and bored in.

scotty, *a*. [Fig. use of *scotty* having the temperament of a Scot; used elsewhere but recorded earliest and chiefly in Aust.: see OED(S *a*. b.] Irritable; bad-tempered.
1872 'DEMONAX' *Mysteries & Miseries* 10 My 'scotty' friend tore his hair and threw his belltopper at the pier-glass. 1981 P. RADLEY *Jack Rivers & Me* 169 'I got a pretty scottie teacher, Dad.' 'You're lucky.' 'He means his teacher is a grumpy old bat.'

scour. A shed in which wool is scoured. Also *attrib*.
1896 *Worker* (Sydney) 5 Sept. 3/2 The men's only offence was that they welcomed the scour hands, who are standing out against the day wage sought to be introduced by their board. 1959 H. LAMOND *Sheep Station* 43 Shearing was no trouble; there were scours with shearing sheds at Longreach, Ilfracombe, Barcaldine, Winton, almost any western town which aspired to be a Queen City.

scoured. [Used elsewhere but recorded earliest in Aust.: see OED *scoured, ppl. a.* 2 b.] Abbrev. of 'scoured wool'.
1851 *Empire* (Sydney) 21 Aug. 72/1 *Wool*. A few lots of scoured have been offered during the week. 1977 *Pastoral Rev.* July 212 The market indicator recovered from the end of May low of 297 to 300 cents per kg. clean scoured.

scrammy, *a*. Also **skrammy**. [f. *scram* withered: see OED.] Being or afflicted with a defective hand or arm. Also *absol.* as *n*.
1841 *Port Phillip Patriot* 28 Oct. 2/5 Should the bantling have a 'scrammy' hand, he is the property of the contracted gentleman. 1895 G. RANKEN *Windabyne* 8 One was 'Skrammy', or one-armed; another was 'Bothered' or deaf. 1898 *Bulletin* (Sydney) 21 May 14/1 At a woolshed, near Condoblin .. a traveller who 'chucked a scrammy' (pretended to have paralysed arms) .. 'had' the sympathising shearers to the extent of £8.

scrape, *v. intr*. To engage in sexual intercourse. Also *trans*., to have intercourse with (someone), and as *n*.
1955 *Meanjin* 169 Larrian was ready to scrape with the whitefellers. 1969 O. WHITE *Under Iron Rainbow* 64 She said she didn't mind lying down for white men at three dollars a time... All the girls got scraped by someone... She'd give the old sergeant a scrape for free and he'd make things easy for her while she was in the lock-up.

scratch, *v*.
1. *Obs*. In the phr. **to scratch** (someone's) **back**, to flog (someone).
1858 A. HARRIS *Secrets* (1961) 109 None of the other magistrates dared say no when D'arcy Wentworth said yes. 'Ha!' says the old doctor .. 'not a word out of your head sir. I'll have your back scratched sir, three times a week... Two hundred lashes!' 1882 *Austral. Stories* 88 If a cove does get his back scratched now and then, it's easier to stand it with a full belly not an empty one.
2. *trans*. To mine (an area) for gold. Also *intr*. See also *tin-scratching* TIN *n.*[1] 2 a.
1881 W. FEILDING *Austral. Trans-Continental Railway* 45 This mine is about 10 miles from the township, and there are two other reefs which have been 'scratched' close by. 1971 *Island Authors* 76 He was always rootin' around the other blokes' gear while they were out scratching, trying to find out where they hid their bottles of gold.
3. [Also Br. dial. and U.S.: see EDD *v*. 3 and OEDS *v*. 5 c.] To move; to travel, esp. in the phr. **to scratch (the) gravel**.
1888 'R. BOLDREWOOD' *Robbery under Arms* (1937) 192, I runs his horses up into a yard nigh the angle of his outside paddock and collars this little 'oss, and lets old Johnny go in hobbles. My word, this cove can scratch! 1912 'IRONBARK' *Ironbark Splinters* 18 And assisted in the chase When they had to 'scratch the gravel' for their grub. 1940 W. HATFIELD *Into (Great?) Unfenced* 67 Gawd, but she can scratch gravel! I thought *I* could move a bit!
4. To accept (someone's) resignation. Usu. with **off**.
1915 *Bulletin* (Sydney) 9 Dec. 22/1 Hopping out of the 'gutter' the coot snapped out at him, 'Write it out'... The coot's mate .. drawled, 'Scratch me off, too.' 1982 LOWENSTEIN & HILLS *Under Hook* 130 So the Federation bloke says, 'Who's me mate?' I said, 'Him.' The Federation bloke said, 'No, scratch me,' and the other bloke said, 'Scratch me too,' so they both went. They just wouldn't work with each other.

scratcher. One who cultivates the land or engages in surface mining. See also *tin scratcher* TIN *n.*[1] 2 a.
1905 *Truth* (Sydney) 19 Mar. 1/8 The outback ground scratcher is a sadly irreligious person. 1978 D. LAVERS *Vet in Clouds* 244 Bill, an agate and topas 'scratcher', had spent years picking over the arid, but mineral-rich wastes of the outback.

screamer. In the collocation **two pot (middy, pint, schooner) screamer**, one who has a very low tolerance of alcohol.
1959 D. HEWETT *Bobbin Up* 21 Look at Lou. She's a two-pot screamer, always 'as been. 1967 *Kings Cross Whisper* (Sydney) xli. 4/5 *Two schooner screamer*, a pest who cannot hold liquor. 1967 J. WYNNUM *I'm Jack, all Right* 25 Our Cocky is a two pint screamer. 1972 *Bulletin* (Sydney) 3 June 67/1 Sefton said she'd become a two middy screamer. He said when she had a few drinks she began to shout and tried to dominate the conversation.

screaming-woman bird. [See quot. 1958.] *Barking owl*, see BARKING; (occas.) any of several other nocturnal birds to which a screaming call has been attributed.
1958 N.W. CAYLEY *What Bird is That?* (rev. ed.) 40 Barking Owl... It is believed to utter appalling nocturnal screams—calls that have caused their author to be termed Screaming-woman Bird and Murder-bird; these cries were formerly ascribed to the Powerful Owl. 1961 *Bulletin* (Sydney) 19 Apr. 28/3 Hearing what I swore was the call of the Screaming-woman Bird (tawny frogmouth), I went out into the orchard to investigate. For frogmouths never scream in the daytime.

screen door. A door fitted with a *fly screen* (see FLY *n.*[1] 1).
1969 *Meanjin* 234, I had raised the venetians, and left the screen door open. 1984 O. MASTERS *Loving Daughters* 96 The kitchen had a screen door to keep out the flies.

screw, *n*.
1. *Obs*. Abbrev. of SCREW-PRESS.
1893 *Bulletin* (Sydney) 29 July 17/1 An' they never ask you whether There is room enough to stand in, or a blessed breath o' air When your layin' on the screw When your haulin' on the screw.
2. [Used elsewhere but recorded earliest in Aust.: see OEDS *sb.*[1] 16.] A look; esp. in the phr. **to have a screw**.
c 1907 W.C. CHANDLER *Darkest Adelaide* 20 My heart did not pit-a-pat extra much after I got a screw of her phizog. If the back view was attractive, the face was absolutely repulsive, for the whilom charmer turned out to be one of the ugliest old battlers I ever struck. 1951 R.H. WHITECROSS *Slaves* 232 You're the smallest bird around here. Come over to me and I'll hoist you up to the ventilator to have a screw around.

screw, *v*.
1. *Obs. trans. Shearing*. To compress (bales of wool) in a SCREW-PRESS.
1851 *Guardian* (Hobart) 15 Oct. 3/2 The Captain of the

Marmion had to come from Launceston to Hobart Town to employ men to screw his wool. **1892** *Bulletin* (Sydney) 19 Nov. 19/1 Fact, there ain't no mortal man can beat a stevedore to swear, But its screwing wool in summer or its stowing frozen meat An' the stevedore must yacker for the bit he gets to eat.

2. [As for SCREW *n.* 2: see OEDS *v.* 13.] *intr.* To look. Also *trans.*

1917 A.L. BREWER *'Gators' Euchre* 42 'E stood in me blanky cowyard, Surrounded be cows untold. 'E screwed at me blanky milker—Poor cow!—an' 'is feet froze cold. **1922** 'J. NORTH' *Black Opal* 132 From the way he was screwin' her phiz.

screwed, *ppl. a.* [Prob. spec. use of *screwed* awry, contorted: see OED *ppl. a.* 4 but also *screw* a nag (OED *sb.*[1] 17).] Of a horse: irrevocably worn out.

1872 G.S. BADEN-POWELL *New Homes for Old Country* 202 The greater proportion of .. wild horses are worthless; a large number of them being more or less 'screwed'. **1891** *Bulletin* (Sydney) 20 June 24/1, I cast one look at the poor old gray; Weary and battered and screwed, of course.

screw pine. Any of several trees of the genus *Pandanus* (fam. Pandanaceae), of W.A., N.T., Qld., N.S.W., and the Old World tropics, yielding edible pulp and nuts. Also **screw palm.**

1829 R. MUDIE *Picture of Aust.* 128 The farinaceous seeds of the screw-pine (*pandanus spiralis, Br.*) and of several cone-bearing trees, are occasionally bruised and eaten by the natives. **1967** V.G.C. NORWOOD *Long Haul* 77 Bushy pandanus palms, sometimes called 'screw' palms because of the spiral arrangement of the leaves.

screw-press. *Shearing. Obs.* A machine in which pressure is applied (to a bale of wool) by means of a screw.

1848 *Colonial Observer* (Sydney) 3 May 993/1 The mortgages it held should be foreclosed and the Directors subjected, like their own woolpacks, to the screw-press. **1980** P. FREEMAN *Woolshed* 40 The screw press required two men to push a lever around the wool box 150 times, taking 30 minutes.

scribbly gum. [f. *scribbly* (see quot. 1963) + GUM *n.* 1.] Any of several smooth-barked trees of the genus *Eucalyptus* (fam. Myrtaceae) having characteristic scribbles on the bark, formed by the burrowing larvae of the scribbly gum moth, *Ogmograptus scribula*, incl. *E. haemastoma, E. racemosa, E. rossii, E. sclerophylla,* and *E. signata,* some of which are also known as SNAPPY GUM; the wood of the tree.

1902 *Proc. Linnean Soc. N.S.W.* XXVII. 568 *E. coriacea* .. shares with some other trees the names of White Gum, Cabbage Gum, and Scribbly Gum. **1963** C. BURGESS *Blue Mountain Gums* 54 *'Scribbly gum'*. . . The trunk is invariably marked with the 'scribbles' of an insect which burrows between the layers of bark, the scribbles appearing on the new bark as the old flakes off.

scroucher /'skraʊtʃə/. Also **scrousher, scrowcher.** [Perh. altered form of Br. dial. *scringer* 'a person who pries about, looking out for trifles', *skreenger* 'a person of energetic character; esp. used in a bad sense': see EDD *scringe, v.*[1] and cf. *scrounger* (see OEDS *scrounge, v.*[1]).] A derogatory term for a person. Cf. BLUDGER 2 a. Also *attrib.*

1901 *Truth* (Sydney) 22 Sept. 1/3 Some of the scroucher toffs of Sydney, both male and female, treat decent tramguards in a dirty, snobbish manner. **1966** D. NILAND *Pairs & Loners* 111 Ah, I could puke. That scrousher, that roughhouse annie, what's she got to get uppety about? **1982** N. KEESING *Lily on Dustbin* 89 Where is she off to? To a disco. . . Chorus: Don't mix with scrowchers; Remember what the girl did.

scrub, *n.* [Used elsewhere but chiefly Austral. and N.Z.: see OED(S *sb.*[1]]

1. A name given to any of a wide range of generally low and apparently stunted forms of vegetation, often thick, impenetrable, and freq. growing in poor soil; a constituent of such vegetation; its wood.

1805 *HRA* (1915) 1st Ser. V. 586 In general rocky Scrub and Brush may with propriety be called the Underwood of the Forest. **1860** J.M. STUART *Explorations in Aust.* 16 Apr. (1865) 160 For five miles the plain was open and well grassed: afterwards it became thick, with mulga bushes and other scrubs. **1882** ARMSTRONG & CAMPBELL *Austral. Sheep Husbandry* 196 Bush Drop Fence .. is commenced .. by placing posts, of any description, about 1 foot apart, with panels suitable to the length of the scrub to be used. **1911** ST. C. GRONDONA *Collar & Cuffs* 69 Bendi, as a very thick scrub is called, is almost impenetrable, certainly so for a horseman. I have never seen any of it alive... I have encountered a good deal of dead stuff, however, and it is most awkward if the stock you are after take it into their heads to investigate the interior of a patch of bendi.

2. a. A tract of land covered in such vegetation: see esp. quots 1805 and 1882.

1805 *HRA* (1915) 1st Ser. V. 586 A Scrub—Consists of Shrubs of low growth, Soil of a bad quality with small Iron gravelly Stones. . . It is not infrequent on the Sea Coast for Scrubs to be void of Trees. **1882** *Proc. Linnean Soc. N.S.W.* VII. 565 The vast plains of the interior are .. covered with trees, and when these grow in thickets they go by the colonial name of 'scrubs'. The term is of very varied application. Just as the trees in different localities are of different kinds and different heights, so are the scrubs. There is the greatest possible diversity between what is called a 'scrub' in New South Wales, in Victoria, and in Queensland. The trees are different and the whole aspect is different. To describe the distinctive features of each would be a kind of descriptive botany for each colony. A scrub is usually a dense thicket of the trees which happen to be most common in the locality. **1980** S. THORNE *I've met some Bloody Wags* 9 At the ripe old age of nineteen I decided that I was sick of Australia, and would go back to Queensland—back to where the scrubs are deep and dense, to God's own land where the pikers roam, across the border fence.

b. As **underscrub,** undergrowth.

1861 L.A. MEREDITH *Over Straits* 35 The underscrub is rich in lovely plants. **1933** C.W. PECK *Austral. Legends* (ed. 2) 71 There was no underscrub.

3. Usu. with **the.** Country which remains in its natural and generally inhospitable state; the country as opposed to the town. Cf. BUSH *n.* 2 and 3. Also *attrib.,* and as quasi-*adv.*

1827 *Monitor* (Sydney) 13 Jan. 274/1 A district of 20,000 acres, where nine-tenths are *scrub* (to use a colonial term for land perfectly barren). **1900** H. LAWSON *Over Sliprails* 39 The banker, the storekeeper, one of the publicans, the butcher .. the postmaster, and his toady, the lightning squirter, were the scrub-aristocracy. The rest were crawlers, mostly pub-spielers and bush larrikins. **1955** J. MORRISON *Black Cargo* 93 'We had a bloke in the last gang told his wife he had to work a year's probation before he got full money.' 'He must have lived out in the scrub.' **1985** J. SCHULTZ *Steel City Blues* 108 We won't be able to afford to stay there. I'll just have to go over the mountain, go scrub and look for work.

4. Comb. in senses of 1 and 2: **scrub country, land, plain, timber, wood.**

1847 G.F. ANGAS *Savage Life & Scenes* I. 99 The vast **scrub country** to the north west of this part of the Murray. **1833** W.H. BRETON *Excursions* 130 Maize .. grows very luxuriantly on what is termed '**Scrub Land**'. **1844** L. LEICHHARDT *Jrnl. Overland Exped. Aust.* (1847) 10 Nov. 35 The **scrub plains** were thickly covered with grasses and vervain. **1876** 'EIGHT YRS.' RESIDENT' *Queen of Colonies* 41 Many beautiful scrub woods known by the generic name of '**scrub timber**' are capable of receiving a high polish and are very beautiful. **1841** J.D. LANG *Austral. Emigrant's Man.*

5 Dec. (1852) 53 The timber consists chiefly of oak .. with a great many species of **scrub wood.**

5. In the names of flora and fauna: **scrub bloodwood,** the tree *Baloghia lucida* (fam. Euphorbiaceae) of coastal N.S.W. and Qld.; **box,** any of several trees incl. *Lophostemon confertus* (see brush box BRUSH n.[1] B. 2); **fowl,** the mound-building *Megapodius reinwardt,* a uniformly grey-brown bird of forested coastal n. and n.e. Aust., s.e. New Guinea, and nearby islands; JUNGLE-FOWL; *scrub hen;* **gum,** any of several trees of the genus *Eucalyptus* (fam. Myrtaceae); also *attrib.;* **hen,** *scrub-fowl;* also *attrib.;* **ironwood,** any of several plants, esp. the large rainforest tree *Choricarpia subargentea* of Qld., and some species of the genus *Austromyrtus* (both fam. Myrtaceae) of e. Qld. and e. N.S.W.; **itch,** a skin irritation caused by the parasitic larvae of mites of the fam. Trombiculidae, affecting humans in tropical n. Aust., New Guinea, Asia, and the Pacific; the (larval) mites themselves; also *attrib.;* **kangaroo,** any of several kangaroos incl. *Macropus giganteus* (see grey kangaroo (a), GREY a.) and *M. rufus* (see *red kangaroo* (a), RED a. 1 b.); **leech,** a terrestrial leech, perh. esp. the common *Chtonobdella limbata* of forested coastal and near-coastal e. Aust.; **oak,** any of several trees, esp. some species of the fam. Casuarinaceae; **robin,** either of two small, long-tailed birds of the genus *Drymodes, D. superciliaris* of Cape York Peninsula (n. Qld.) and New Guinea, and the more widespread *D. brunneopygia* of s. Aust.; **tick,** any of several ticks that attack humans, esp. *Ixodes holocyclus* or the introduced *Haemaphysalis longicornis;* BOTTLE TICK; *bush tick,* see BUSH C. 3; **tit,** the small bird *Sericornis magnus* of temperate rainforest in Tas.; **turkey, (a)** *brush turkey,* see BRUSH n.[1] B. 2; also *attrib.;* **(b)** *transf.,* a swagman (see quots.); **wallaby,** any of several macropodids of various sizes inhabiting rainforest, brigalow or other densely vegetated country, esp. *Macropus dorsalis* of e. Qld. and e. N.S.W., having a brown back with a dark mid-dorsal stripe; **wattle,** a shrub or tree of the genus *Acacia* occurring in scrub country, as *A. leprosa* of e. Vic. and N.S.W.; **wren,** any of several small, ground-feeding birds of the genus *Sericornis,* usu. inhabiting dense undergrowth and rainforest; also with distinguishing epithet, as **white-browed, yellow-throated** (see under first element).

1889 J.H. MAIDEN *Forest Flora N.S.W.* 382 *Baloghia lucida* .. 'Scrub', or 'Brush **Bloodwood'**... Wood fine and close-grained. It is impregnated with a resinous substance, and burns readily in a green state. **1840** J. FRANKLIN Diary Visit S.A. 31 Dec. 52 (typescript) **Scrub box** & salsolaceous plants. **1965** *Austral. Encycl.* VII. 142 *Tristania conferta* (scrub box, brush box..) is a giant tree in the wet sclerophyll forests. **1903** *Emu* II. 155 *Megapodius duperreyi* (**Scrub Fowl**) .. is found right across Northern Australia. **1889** J.H. MAIDEN *Useful Native Plants Aust.* 640 *Eucalyptus cosmophylla* .. a '**Scrub Gum**'... Baron Mueller has suggested this gum as being highly suitable for decorative purposes. **1945** J. DEVANNY *Bird of Paradise* 20 The tractor had deposited two scrub gum—or rose-gum—logs. **1890** A.J. VOGAN *Black Police* 210 The **scrub hen** (Megapodius tumulus), saves herself from the monotonous duty of sitting on her eggs by depositing them in a capital natural incubator, formed of rotting and heated leaves. **1984** B. DIXON *Searching for Aboriginal Lang.* 35 Paddy also described some of the traditional foodstuffs, like black bean nuts, and scrub-hen eggs. **1880** J. BONWICK *Resources Qld.* 82 The Lily Pillies .. of close wood, like the **Scrub Ironwood,** a myrtle. **1965** *Austral. Encycl.* VI. 238 *A[ustromyrtus] hillii* .. a small glabrous tree up to 60 feet in height, is called 'scrub-ironwood', but its timber is prone to warp and is not much used. **1984** K.A.W. WILLIAMS *Native Plants Qld.* II. 82 *Choricarpia subargentea* .. Scrub Ironwood... This tree .. is now an uncommon species as most of its habitat has been cleared. **1890** A.J. VOGAN *Black Police* 210 The two travellers .. pick the bush-ticks and **scrub-itch** insects from their flesh with the point of the long scrub-knife the old digger carries. **1945** J. DEVANNY *Bird of Paradise* 20 The scrub itch is bad... A small tick is the cause. **1984** B. DIXON *Searching for Aboriginal Lang.* 15 This turned out to be scrub-itch, a parasitic red mite a bit like ring-worm. **1903** H. BASEDOW *Jrnl. Govt. N.-W. Exped.* 25 Apr. (1914) 79 Large **scrub-kangaroo** (*Macropus rufus*) plentiful. **1983** R. STRAHAN *Compl. Bk. Austral. Mammals* 244 Eastern Grey Kangaroo *Macropus giganteus*... Other common names .. Scrub Kangaroo [etc.]. **1880** J.B. STEVENSON *Seven Yrs. Austral. Bush* 87 We were greatly tormented by **scrub leeches.** **1881** *Proc. Linnean Soc. N.S.W.* VI. 742 *Casuarina glauca* or '**Scrub oak**'. **1959** L. ROSE *Country of Dead* 154 The mulga and the scrub-oak gave them shade and food. **1842** J. GOULD *Birds of Aust.* (1848) III. Pl. 10, *Drymodes brunneopygia* .. **Scrub Robin.** **1933** *Bulletin* (Sydney) 6 Dec. 34/3 Of scrub-robins (*Drymodes*) there are three species, two occurring in Australia and the third in New Guinea and the Aru Islands. **1886** P. CLARKE '*New Chum*' *in Aust.* 272 In the scrub of Queensland it is well to guard by reasonable caution and occasional attention to the state of one's garments from the unpleasant adherence of the **scrub-tick.** **1983** *Gold Coast Bull.* 15 July 5/1 The CSIRO said it is trying to develop a vaccine that will protect dogs and livestock against paralysis and death caused by the scrub tick ixodes holocyclus. **1898** E.E. MORRIS *Austral Eng.* 470 **Scrub T**[**it**]—*Sericornis magna.* **(a)** *1846* C.P. HODGSON *Reminisc. Aust.* 166 The **Scrub Turkey** is very plentiful, and a magnificent dish. **1980** B. SCOTT *Darkness under Hills* 43 He built his fire .. and roasted a swamp-pheasant and some scrub turkey eggs. **(b) 1955** A. MARSHALL *I can jump Puddles* 152 Father .. was familiar with the ways of swagmen... The bearded men who kept to the bush he called 'Scrub **Turkeys**'. **1973** F. HUELIN *Keep Moving* 178 *Scrub Turkey,* bagman who has gone Bush. Usually slightly mental or eccentric. **1845** L. LEICHHARDT *Jrnl. Overland Exped. Aust.* 14 Feb. (1847) 151 All hands were now employed in shooting crows; which, with .. a small **scrub wallabi,** gave us several good messes. **1921** A.J. CAMPBELL *Golden Wattle* 40 In the east, notably in Gippsland, there is the **Scrub Wattle** (*Acacia leprosa* of the botanist), of pendulous habit, which illuminates the forested hills with its bunches of blossom of rich lemon chrome. **1898** E.E. MORRIS *Austral Eng.* 407 **Scrub-Wren**... Any little bird of the Australian genus *Sericornis.* The species are—Brown Scrub-Wren—*Sericornis humilis* [etc.].

6. Special Comb. **scrub block,** a rural landholding which in its natural state is scrub-covered; **bull,** a bull which was bred in, or has escaped into, the wild; also *transf.,* and **scrub bullock, cattle; -chopper,** *scrub-cutter;* **-clearing** *vbl. n.,* the action of clearing land of scrub; **-cutter,** one employed to cut scrub, either to clear land or to provide fodder; so **-cutting** *vbl. n.;* **-faller,** one employed in *scrub-felling;* **-falling** *vbl. n.; scrub-felling;* **farm,** a small farm on poor, originally scrub-covered, land; so **farmer; -felling** *vbl. n.,* the felling of some types of scrub, esp. those marketable as timber; **fire,** a bushfire which burns mainly scrub and undergrowth (see quot. 1956); **-hook,** an implement with a hooked blade used for cutting small scrub; **horse,** BRUMBY 1; **-knife** *obs.,* see quot. 1882; **lease,** an agreement under which Crown land classified as scrub land may be held (see quots. 1885 and 1906); **mob** *obs.,* a mob of wild cattle; **native,** an Aboriginal living in an area remote from white settlement; **paddock,** an uncleared paddock; **rider,** one who rounds up strayed or wild livestock; so **-riding** *vbl. n.;* **roller,** *mallee roller,* see MALLEE 8; so **scrub-roll** *v.;* **run,** a tract of inferior grazing land; **-running** *vbl. n.* and *pr. pple.,* the rounding up of wild livestock; **selection** *Qld., scrub lease;* a tract of land so held; **soil,** fertile soil in an area of cultivable land cleared of scrub; **(trap) yard,** a makeshift stock yard constructed of pieces of scrub.

1927 *Murray Pioneer* (Renmark) 27 May 3/3 They purchased a square red iron tank from Chaffeys for £2 10s., which tank the Chaffeys were good enough to cart out to their **scrub block** for them. **1881** A.C. GRANT *Bush-Life*

Qld. 226 Dexterously lassoes a yearling **scrub bull. 1977** X. HERBERT *Dream Road* p. x, A man like Jeremy Delacy, the 'scrub bull'. **1890** W.F. BUCHANAN *Aust. to Rescue* p. xvi, The principal topics were the various adventures in the bush of celebrated **scrub bullocks** .. and the turf. **1880** J.B. STEVENSON *Seven Yrs. Austral. Bush* 109 A small mob of quiet cattle .. indispensable in working for **scrub cattle. 1909** R. KALESKI *Austral. Settler's Compl. Guide* 97 Employ two good **scrub choppers. 1916** *Truth* (Sydney) 16 Jan. 8/5 There are plenty of men in this country who earn their bread by **scrub-clearing. 1845** *Standard* (Melbourne) 28 May 3/3 *Mr Hoddle at the public expense.* With an equipment of six **scrub cutters**, a groom and butler, drays, bullocks and horses, a spacious tent, containing an elegant brass bedstead and *requisite accompaniments.* **1905** *Bulletin* (Sydney) 14 Sept. 40/1 We are mainly scrub-cutters .. called sheep-caterers, because the scrub is to keep alive the flocks and herds. **1980** *Sydney Morning Herald* 13 Oct. 3/2 Mr Keith Cochrane, of Calgary station between Walgett and Collarenebri, sold 1,800 sheep in March, and has kept between 1,500 and 2,000 others alive by scrub-cutting. **1927** *Bulletin* (Sydney) 17 Mar. 24/2 Contract **scrubfallers** usually stipulate that all jhitu may be left standing. **1905** *Ibid.* 15 June 35/2 He would escort me home from **scrubfalling** every night .. on the off-chance of my getting bushed. **1876** 'EIGHT YRS.' RESIDENT' *Queen of Colonies* 188 In Canada and the States farmers .. can to a large extent rely on a harvest at a certain time and to a certain amount. This the Queenslander can hardly do; there may be a drought and nothing grows, or, if he is on a **scrub-farm**, a flood may come just as his crop is ripe, and destroy the whole. **1893** *Adelaide Observer* 26 Aug. 43/3 'Concert Camp', as the place was duly named after a jolly evening round the camp fire with songs, recitations, and tall yarns, wherein the 'squatter' vied with the 'scrub farmer'. **1903** *Sporting News* (Launceston) 20 June 2/4 The annual **scrub felling** period has arrived. **1939** M. MORRIS *Dark Tumult* 185 A blaze that, beginning as a mere **scrub fire**, easy to handle and curb, could develop into that implacable horror, a crown-fire, which leaping along the tops of trees, sending its sparks and flying embers a mile in advance, was impossible to check. **1956** A. MARSHALL *How's Andy Going?* 164 There's three kinds of bushfires. One just creeps along in a calm. It burns leaves and that on the floor of the bush. It's easy to belt out. This one behind Barret's is a scrub fire. It can travel at a fair bat, but it stops below the heads of the trees. But say it comes out hellishun hot and a north wind comes up. The scrub fire gets going then. It climbs up the messmate bark and sets off on its own. It travels in the tops of the trees. **1909** *Bulletin* (Sydney) 26 Aug. 15/2 You cut all the small undergrowth, vines, etc., with a slasher (or **scrub-hook**); this is 'vining' in N.S.W., 'brushing' in Queensland. **1897** J.D. HENNESSY *New-Chum Farmer* 38 A **scrub horse** does not know much for a horse; neither can he learn. **1882** *Proc. Linnean Soc. N.S.W.* VII. 568 Without a **scrub-knife**, an instrument which is a combination of a thin sword-blade and a bill-hook, such forests are absolutely impenetrable. **1885** *Australasian Farmer* 322 **Scrub leases** for areas not exceeding 10,240 or less than 640 acres, for terms not exceeding 15 years, and at rentals not less than 2s. 6d. per section for the first five years, 5s. for the second five years, and 20s. for the last five years, may be granted on prescribed conditions as to the clearing of scrub. **1906** *N.S.W. Yearbk. 1904–5* 66 The holder of a scrub lease must take such steps as the Land Board may direct for the purpose of destroying such scrub as may be specified in his lease, and must commence to destroy the same within three months from the beginning of the lease, and when destroyed to keep the land free from the same. **1847** *Bell's Life in Sydney* 20 Mar. 3/1 Have you tried near the water-holes t' other end of the flats .. for the **scrub mob. 1847** G.F. ANGAS *Savage Life & Scenes* I. 99 The **scrub natives** who are called Wirramayo .. occupy the vast scrub country to the north-west of this part of the Murray. **1955** E.O. SCHLUNKE *Man in Silo* 212 The teamster's guess was that he was 'in the dead centre of your father's big **scrub paddock**'. **1881** A.C. GRANT *Bush-Life Qld.* I. 207 It is .. a favourite plan amongst the bold **scrub-riders** to take advantage of the bright moonlight nights, when, shrouded in the misty light, and undistinguishable from the surrounding shadows, they burst on the unsuspecting mob. **1883** E.M. CURR *Recoll. Squatting Vic.* 291 Come to the front in scrub-riding. **1914** *Pastoral Rev.* 16 Dec. 1143 In the first place we roll the Mallee with a **scrub roller. 1950** C.E. GOODE *Yarns of Yilgarn* 11 Harry .. was getting all the contracting he could—seeding, fallowing, and then scrub-rolling. **1880** C. PROUD *S.E. District S.A.* 17 On entering the Bangham property we found it to be a **scrub run**, consisting of 114 square miles of inferior land, and carrying only about 10,000 sheep and lambs. **1905** *Bulletin* (Sydney) 13 Apr. 18/1 Throwing and tying is the ordinary daily occupation of scores of stockmen on part of the Dawson River country (Q.), especially in winter, when they go .. **'scrub-running'** for clean-skins. **1980** ANSELL & PERCY *To fight Wild* 81 They'd have twenty or thirty dogs on the place, even when they're not doing much scrub running. **1900** *Austral. Handbk.* 97 The applicant .. becomes entitled to receive a license to occupy the land in the case of an Agricultural Selection or a Grazing Selection, or a lease in the case of a **Scrub Selection** or Unconditional Selection. **1919** C.A. BERNAYS *Qld. Politics during Sixty Yrs.* 331 The tenure was known as 'scrub selection', and was divided into four classes according to the proportion of land overgrown with 'scrub'. **1880** J. BONWICK *Resources Qld.* 65 The best **scrub soil** of Albert River gives 10.623 of organic matters. **1897** *Bulletin* (Sydney) 11 Dec. 7/2 **Scrub-yards** and new bark shanties. **1946** *Ibid.* 13 Mar. 15/4 They sighted the ringers racing to hold and head them into the wings of a scrub trap-yard.

scrub, *v.* [f. prec.]

1. *intr. Obs.* To travel through scrub.

1847 *Sydney Morning Herald* 11 Oct. 2/3 We entered into bricklow scrub, which became so dense, that after five miles scrubbing we were glad to follow a very winding watercourse to the S.E.

2. *trans.* To clear (land) of scrub; to clear (scrub) from land. Freq. as *vbl. n.*

1860 *T.H.A.J.* no. 84 3 The system of 'scrubbing' by which the underwood alone is removed, and of 'ringing' whereby the larger trees are simply killed. **1945** J. DEVANNY *Bird of Paradise* 28 Mrs Brown alternated these activities with 'scrubbing' timber and driving a bullock team.

3. *Obs. trans.* To feed (cattle, etc.) on scrub. Also as *ppl. a.*

1880 *Blackwood's Mag.* (Edinburgh) Jan. 62/1 They .. maintain a precarious existence by .. breeding a few scrubbing horses and cattle. **1902** *Bulletin* (Sydney) 20 Dec. 17/1 Experience in 'scrubbing' cattle and sheep has taught me that mulga and kurrajong are the only scrubs that cattle will thrive on.

scrub-bash, *v.*

1. *intr.* SCRUB-DASH.

1963 *Gumsucker's Gaz.* Nov. 14 Scrub-bash (chase strays through the bush, throw them by the tail and knife-brand them). **1977** W.A. WINTER-IRVING *Bush Stories* 112 When Big John was seventy-three and galloping the hell out of his horse, scrub-bashing to round up a cow or a wild bull, his horse hit a tree and came down.

2. *intr.* To make a track through the scrub; to travel cross-country. Also as *vbl. n.*

1964 D. LOCKWOOD *Up Track* 13 More often than not we will be off the Track, hundreds of miles from it, scrub-bashing in out-of-the-way spots where it's a good idea to have either double-reduction gears or stout walking shoes. **1981** P.B. CRESWELL *Granite Peak* 1 Herbert's vehicle was a 4 cylinder Dodge, with everything except the bare essentials removed, mostly forcibly as a result of scrub-bashing.

3. *intr.* To clear land of scrub. Also as *vbl. n.*

1966 S.J. BAKER *Austral. Lang.* (ed. 2) 77 *Scrub bashing,* the clearing of scrub-covered land. **1970** N.A. BEAGLEY *Up &*

Down Under 58 Well, I got a job scrub-bashing, which means that one contracts to knock off the suckers on the trees that had previously been ring-barked.

scrubbed, *a. Obs.* Scrub-covered.
[N.Z. **1870** R.P. WHITWORTH *Martin's Bay Settlement* 13 The land was densely scrubbed with undergrowth.] **1899** *North-Western Advocate* (Devonport) 10 Mar. 3/2 The country.. was a succession of undulating, heavily-scrubbed land. **1910** *Huon Times* (Franklin) 5 Nov. 2/5 It was necessary for a gate to be erected owing to the property being densely scrubbed and heavily timbered.

scrubber. [f. SCRUB *n.*]
1. a. As applied to cattle: a beast which has been bred in, or has strayed and established itself in, the wild; RUMPER 1.
1848 *Adelaide Miscellany* 2 Dec. 280 My bucolical knowledge.. left me in total ignorance of the nice distinction between yearlings, steers, heifers, stags, poleys, workers, rooshians, and scrubbers. **1982** G.B. EGGLETON *Last of Lantern Swingers* 67 The scrubbers remained far out west.. managing to obtain sufficient moisture for their needs from native shrubs and grasses.
b. *transf.* and *fig.* A 'wild' person, one only partially assimilated into a society; a person of rough and unkempt appearance.
1858 R. ROWE *Peter 'Possum's Portfolio* 99 A third juridicial grandee.. who walketh up and down, driving his thumb into the ribs, and his toe against the shin of any acquaintance less wealthy than himself, exclaiming therewithall, 'Scrubber, Sir, scrubber—show us your bank-book.' **1868** *Colonial Monthly* Apr. 140 'And do you mean.. that those poor children are heathens?' 'I can answer for it, that they are scrubbers—to use a bush phrase—have never been brought within the pale of any church.'.. 'Scrubbers, sir—never been branded.'
c. An inferior horse..
1874 *Illustr. Sydney News* 28 Mar. 4/1 Horses sell very well, any sort of scrubber will bring from £25 to £30. **1914** J.H.L. ZILLMAN *Career of Cornstalk* 28 When I had purchased one of these animals, I felt like proposing to go back on my bargain, for, as I said at the time, 'he looks a regular scrubber'.
2. One who dwells in the bush: see SCRUB *n.* 3.
1867 *Pasquin* (London) 31 Aug. 194 Taken altogether, the Scrub Lands Act is a very amusing piece of business. What with District Councils, rights of commonage, and migratory mallees, the 'scrubbers' seem destined to come to grief. **1927** *Murray Pioneer* (Renmark) 11 Nov. 8/3 *Bushed on Lake Victoria.* Mr Watson went rabbitting, and while crossing Lake Victoria station nearly perished from thirst. His story is a bush epic of rare determination and grip... Let the old scrubber speak.
3. *Special Comb.* **scrubber runner,** one who rounds up scrubbers (sense 1 a.); so, **-running** *vbl. n.*
1917 C. DREW *Reminisc. D. Gilbert* 33 Gilbert threw in his lot with some scrubber runners. **1943** *Bulletin* (Sydney) 4 Aug. 13/4, I was one of three who did a spot of scrubber-running on a neighbor's place.

scrubby, *a.* [Spec. use of *scrubby* covered with scrub: see OED(S *a.*¹ 2 and SCRUB *n.*] Covered with scrub; consisting of or in the form of scrub; barren, infertile.
1802 J. FLEMMING in J.J. Shillinglaw *Hist. Rec. Port Phillip* 18 Dec. (1879) 17 The land appeared barren, a scrubby brush. **1952** *New Settler in W.A.* (Perth) July 55 Third class land included the sandy and gravelly scrub plain areas with a variety of scrubby vegetation and small mallees.

scrub-dash, *v. intr.* To ride at speed through thick scrub, esp. in pursuit of wild or straying livestock. Also as *vbl. n.*
1904 L.M.P. ARCHER *Bush Honeymoon* 144, I pick out some assorted timber which I have acquired in my back hair during our *scrub-dashing.* **1977** G.W. LILLEY *Lengthening Shadows* 7 It was in this paddock that I ran my second dingo... It was possible to scrub-dash up to a point, after that it was too risky for man and horse.
Hence **scrub dasher** *n.*
1911 ST. C. GRONDONA *Collar & Cuffs* 33 The professional scrub dasher, on a horse that knows his business, just drops the reins and trusts to Providence to bring him through with a whole carcase.

scruff, *v.* [f. *scruff* the nape of the neck.]
1. *trans. Obs.* To seize (a person) by the nape of the neck; to manhandle. Also *fig.*
1837 *Sydney Herald* 16 Oct. 2/7 The luckless wight was, what is technically called 'scruffed' to the watchhouse, and the next morning was fined five shillings for being drunk. **1890** *Truth* (Sydney) 16 Nov. 4/5 The 'gentlemen' M.'s P. must do the fighting in Parliament now that Crick's 'scruffed' and kept out for more than a month.
2. *transf.* To seize and hold (a calf) for branding, castrating, etc., without the use of a rope: see quot. 1887. Also *absol.*, and as *vbl. n.*
1881 A.C. GRANT *Bush-Life Qld.* I. 228 The smaller calves are scruffed, and soon finished. **1887** W.S.S. TYRWHITT *New Chum in Qld. Bush* 137 Jim and the Boss run after them, and 'scruff' them, seizing them by the hind leg and the scruff of the neck, and in another ten minutes they are all branded and let out with the cows. **1905** *Bulletin* (Sydney) 28 May 17/3 Now for 'scruffing'—throwing a calf by twisting the head. **1976** C.D. MILLS *Hobble Chains & Greenhide* 17 We do 'scruff' in the yards on light stuff, but I'm sure most ringers will agree that in good hands ropes are the better in the long run.
Hence **scruffer** *n.*, one who so seizes and holds a calf.
1905 *Bulletin* (Sydney) 25 May 17/3 The scruffer's mate—we work in pairs—meanwhile puts a swing-over on to the tail.

scrum. *Obs.* [Rhyming slang for 'thrum', three pence: see OEDS *thrums.*] A threepenny piece; THRUMMER.
1891 *Truth* (Sydney) 10 May 3/5 The slim audience were mighty slow with their money, and it was fun to watch the plates seized by the end man of the seat, sent careening along and returned to the collector without the addition of a solitary 'scrum'. **1902** *Truth* (Sydney) 16 Mar. 4/4 The popular 'tray-bit', 'thrum', 'scrum', or 'boozer's life-saver'.

scrummy. *Obs.* [f. SCRUM + -Y.] SCRUM.
1894 A.B. BELL *Austral. Camp Fire Tales* 108 Well that's mean, dirt mean, only a scrummy and the valuable information I gave him was worth a quid. **1915** *Byron Bay Rec.* 25 Dec. 8 Notify the public that they must bring along their scrummies (the fee for using the dressing-sheds is reported 3d. for adults, 1d. children).

scuff, *v.* SCRUFF 2. Hence **scuffer** *n.* (see quot. 1945).
1945 F. CORK *Tales from Cattle Country* 29 Scuffing.. calls for expert rope work and perfect co-ordination between the scuffers. A stockman selects a calf and skilfully casts a rope over its head, the strain being taken by passing the rope around a rail of the fence. While the calf bucks and plunges in an effort to free itself, smaller ropes are cleverly thrown over a front and a hind leg, and a quick jerk brings the calf to the ground where it lies, practically helpless, while the iron is applied. **1977** W.A. WINTER-IRVING *Bush Stories* 7 Scuffed by the men at the branding panel.

scungy /'skʌndʒi/, *a.* and *n.* Also **scungie, skungy.** [f. Ir. and Scot. dial. *scunge,* n. a sly or vicious person, a sponger, a vague term of abuse; also as *v.* to sponge: see OEDS.]
A. *adj.* Disagreeable; sordid.

SCURVY GRASS

[N.Z. **1964** *Salient* (Vic. Univ. Wellington) 1 *Pitch-hacking* has been in the news... Scungy anonymous louts tore up the sacred turf for the first cricket test.] **1965** *Kings Cross Whisper* (Sydney) Dec. 11/2 This is a week for good relations. Unfortunately you don't have any, because they are all a bunch of scungie cruds. **1966** J. SPENCER *Cross Section* 18, I always dislike the scungy feel when you don't show. **1983** R. WILLIAMS *Best of Science Show* 72 This skungy sediment which accumulates in the settling tanks of the carwash.

B. *n. pl.* Sporting briefs.

1979 CAREY & LETTE *Puberty Blues* 3 Changing in and out of boardshorts at the beach was always done behind a towel or when your girlfriend was at the shop. The ultimate disgrace for a surfie was to be seen in his scungies. They were too much like underpants.

scurvy grass. [Transf. use of *scurvy-grass* a cruciferous plant believed to be an antiscorbutic: see quot. 1951.] Any of several species of the genus *Commelina* (fam. Commelinaceae), erect or spreading annual or perennial herbs commonly with blue flowers, esp. *C. cyanea* of n.e. Aust., often regarded as a garden weed. See also BOGGABRI.

1805 J.H. TUCKEY *Acct. Voyage to establish Colony Port Phillip* 162 Of potable vegetables, wild celery, wild parsnip, scurvy-grass.. were found in great abundance. **1951** J. DEVANNY *Travels N. Qld.* 13 Comelina.. commonly called scurvy grass, because formerly mariners threatened with scurvy came ashore and gathered it for food.

sea. Used *attrib.* in the names of fish: **sea garfish,** any of several fish of the fam. Hemirhamphidae, esp. *Hyporhamphus melanochir* of s. Aust. and *H. australis* of coastal Qld. and N.S.W.; see also BEAKIE, GARFISH; **mullet,** the marine, estuarine, and fresh-water fish *Mugil cephalus* of s. Aust., and widely distributed elsewhere; (occas.) any of several other similar fish; see also HARD-GUT MULLET, *mangrove mullet* MANGROVE, PODDY MULLET; **perch,** any of several marine fish incl. those of the chiefly tropical fam. Lutjanidae, and *Helicolenus papillosus* of s. Aust. and New Zealand.

1906 D.G. STEAD *Fishes of Aust.* 66 The **Sea Garfish** is found in abundance along the greater part of the Australian coastline (including Tasmania); as well as in New Zealand, the Seas of China, Japan, the Malay Archipelago and other waters. **1974** J.M. THOMSON *Fish Ocean & Shore* 131 The single biggest garfishery is that for the sea garfish (*Hemirhamphus melanochir*) in South Australia. The sea garfish of the eastern States is another species (*Hemirhamphus australis*) which enters only the lower estuaries, preferring the gutters along sea beaches. **1844** *Sydney Morning Herald* 3 May 3/2 The sand or **sea-mullet** are just coming in. **1906** D.G. STEAD *Fishes of Aust.* 80 The Yellow-eye Mullet.. is distributed right round the southern half of Australia... In Victoria, this Mullet is known as 'Sea Mullet'. **1873** F. DE CASTELNAU *Edible Fishes Vic.* 8 Some [members of the Perch family] inhabit the sea, such as the **sea perch** (*Lates Antarcticus*). **1898** E.E. MORRIS *Austral Eng.* 409 Sea-Perch.. a name applied to different fishes—in Sydney, to the *Morwong*.. and *Bull's-eye*.. in Melbourne, to *Red-Gurnard*.

sea-gull. [See quot. 1983.]

1. A casual, non-union, waterside worker.

[N.Z. *c* **1926** 'MIXER' *Transport Workers' Songbk.* 46 What a study! Let us paint it As the sea-gulls fly about, While the stringer birds are anxious for the meeting to come out.] **1965** F. HARDY *Yarns of Billy Borker* 115 He was a casual wharfie at the time I'm telling you about, during the Second World War it was, and they call casuals 'seagulls'. **1983** H.M. MILLER *My Story* 45, I would become a 'seagull'; a casual labourer loading and unloading ships... A 'seagull' was a scavenger who hung around the pick-up points,

SECOND

waiting for whatever jobs were going after union members had snapped up the plums.

2. *transf.* A tourist.

1977 A. THOMAS *Bulls & Boabs* (1980) 92 Tourists, known by the wonderfully descriptive word, seagulls... 'They fly in, do what they have to do, and fly off again.'

sealed, *ppl. a.* [Spec. use of *sealed,* f. *seal, v.* to render (a surface) impervious: see OEDS *seal, v.*^{1} 8 c. and *sealed, ppl. a.* 2 h.] Of a road: surfaced with tar macadam, etc.

[N.Z. **1928** R.G. STAPLEDON *Tour in Aust. & N.Z.* i. 12 Practically every mile of the road so traversed is 'tar sealed'.] **1938** *Ann. Rep. 1937* (N.S.W. Dept. Main Roads) 4 (OEDS) Generally for country roads in New South Wales the sealed gravelled pavement has proved to be quite adequate. **1983** *Open Road* Aug. 19/2 From Warren you can make a 220 km. round trip by taking a sealed road north to Willan.

sealing, *vbl. n. Hist.* [Used elsewhere but of local significance: see OED(S *vbl. sb.*^{2}]

1. The action or occupation of hunting the seal.

1804 *Sydney Gaz.* 28 Oct., *Wanted,* Four or Five Seamen, or other able Men who are accustomed to the work of a boat; if acquainted with the business of sealing they will find a preference. **1834** *Perth Gaz.* 8 Nov. 386 Their capital [*sc.* that of settlers at Albany] can be applied to much greater advantage to themselves and the community, in the Fisheries or Sealing.

2. Comb. **sealing gang, ground, party.**

1804 *Sydney Gaz.* 29 July, A charge was brought by the master of a vessel trading to the straits against a person going to join a **sealing-gang,** of having embezzled the vessel's provisions. **1808** *Ibid.* 14 Aug., On Monday last sailed the Albion whaler for the fishery, and the colonial vessel Perseverence for the **sealing grounds.** **1828** *Tasmanian* (Hobart) 12 Dec. 2 On Thursday, Dec. 4, the *Henry* sailed from Launceston for the Sealing Grounds. *Ibid.* 26 Dec. 3 *Seal Fishery*—We regret to learn that the **sealing party** on the White Rock, and another party somewhat farther down the river, have as yet not been successful.

secko. Also **secco, sekko.** [Shortened form of *sex* + -O.] A sexual pervert; a sex offender.

1949 R. PARK *Poor Man's Orange* 38 'Just look at that dirty ole secko, will you?' he said disgustedly. **1961** F. HARDY *Hard Way* 75 'The woman copper picked me up—having a piss, I was. The bitch charged me with indecent exposure.' 'A secco,' the bush lawyer whispered, 'Been flashing it.' **1984** *Bulletin* (Sydney) 20 Mar. 47/1 It was a risk to talk with a bloke who was 'suss'—a risk of being identified with a 'sekko' (sex offender).

second, *a.* In special collocations: **second bottom,** a second stratum of gold-bearing material: see BOTTOM *n.*^{1}; so **-bottoming** *vbl. n.*; **-convicted** *ppl. a. hist., double-convicted,* see DOUBLE *a.* 1; **cut,** (the mark of) a blow made to remove poorly-cut fleece; a piece of short or inferior wool resulting from this; so **-cutter** *n.*; **fleet,** see quot. 1851; **-fleeter** *n.*, one who came to Australia aboard one of the ships of the second fleet; **preference,** see PREFERENCE 2; **-sentence(d)** *a. hist., double-convicted,* see DOUBLE *a.* 1; **shed,** the second shearing shed in which a shearer is employed during a particular season.

1855 G.H. WATHEN *Golden Colony* 230 The diggers have sunk shafts through the pipeclay to a great depth in search of 'a **second bottom**', but without success. **1856** S.C. BREES *How to farm & settle in Aust.* 56 Hence arose the terms first and second bottoms: the first, relating to drift resting upon a soft shaly bed of various light hues, called the pipeclay; the second to another drift-mass, arrived at in boring through the pipe clay, and beyond which it is supposed there are no further auriferous drifts. *Ibid.* 57 The deep-sinking and second-bottoming have been chiefly exemplified at Ballaarat, where gold digging has .. become even more precarious than elsewhere. **1840** *Corresp. on Secondary Punishment* (Great Brit. Parl.) 26 Dec. (1841) 65, I observe that no more **second-convicted** men are to be sent here; but are those now with me to be removed? **1882** ARMSTRONG & CAMPBELL *Austral. Sheep Husbandry* 168 In shearing the first side of the sheep, each blow should be continued round until the back-bone is passed; this avoids the **second cut** caused by the blow up the back which should not be allowed, as the cutting through which results considerably depreciates the value of the wool. **1899** G. JEFFREY *Princ. Australasian Woolclassing* 39 Second cuts .. fall beneath the spokes of the rolling tables and are called locks, and do not bring one-third of the price of fleece wool. **1975** G.A.W. SMITH *Once Green Jackaroo* 151 A man shearing a sheep for the second time .. trying to get rid of the ridges he had left .. was what is known as a first-class 'second-cutter'. **1791** D. COLLINS *Acct. Eng. Colony N.S.W.* (1798) I. 156 Came in the **second fleet**. **1851** H. MELVILLE *Present State Aust.* 19 In September 1791 His Majesty's ship Gorgon, with ten transports .. reached Sydney, and this convoy is designated in the colony the *second fleet*. **1831** *Sydney Herald* 18 Apr. 3/1 His Excellency .. gave permission to the **second-fleeter** to occupy his land. **1827** P. CUNNINGHAM *Two Yrs. in N.S.W.* II. 3 The Newcastle mine has been hitherto worked by the **second-sentence** men, sent down for punishment. **1848** J. SYME *Nine Yrs. Van Diemen's Land* 189 The second or local sentenced men .. are all sent to such labour stations with the view first of undergoing 'hard labour'. **1904** *Shearer* (Sydney) 17 Sept. 4/3 Bringagee should be out about last week of month. **Second sheds** now being allotted.

secondary, *a.*[1] *Hist.* [Spec. use of *secondary*, pertaining to a second period or condition.] Pertaining to a criminal offence committed by a convict after arrival in Australia and to the punishment inflicted for such an offence, esp. in the collocation **secondary punishment**. See also *double convict*, etc., DOUBLE *a.* 1, *second-convicted, second-sentence* SECOND.
1824 E. CURR *Acct. Colony Van Diemen's Land* 47 George's Town .. is a place of secondary banishment, and possesses a factory for women, the people are for the most part of the worst description of convicts. **1835** *Colonist* (Sydney) 30 July 243/2 No. 111 should be designated the Black Gang, to wear the heavy criminal irons now in use for secondary punishments in the gangs.

secondary, *a.*[2] *S.A. Hist.* [Spec. use of *secondary* of minor importance, subsidiary.] Used in special collocations **secondary town, township,** to designate a settlement, or proposed settlement, other than Adelaide.
1838 *Southern Austral.* (Adelaide) 23 June 1/4 The lands .. except such parts as shall be reserved for **Secondary Towns** .. will from and after the 7th day of July next be open to purchase. **1839** *S. Austral. Rec.* (London) 13 Feb. 149/1, It is fair, therefore, to expect that land in **secondary townships**, if well selected, will command the attention of the capitalist, and may even prove more valuable than that in Adelaide.

section. *Hist.* [Spec. use of *section* one of the portions into which a thing is divided. Orig. U.S. and in Aust. generally superseded by BLOCK *n.*[1]]
a. Orig. a tract of Crown land, one square mile in area, made available for development; a tract of such land of variable size; such a tract of land after development.
1830 *Sydney Monitor* 16 June 2/1 A respectable settler having an order for two sections of land (1,240 acres). **1846** S. DAVENPORT *Lett.* 29 Apr. in *S. Australiana* (1977) Sept. 131, I have let about eight acres of the thirty-two acre section claimed by you of Mr Luck's. **1861** *Number One* (Adelaide) Apr. 12 A few yards brought us to the slip-panel,

and we struck off for the homestead, situate about half way up the section.
b. A plot of Crown land made available for urban development; such a plot of land after development.
1836 *S. Austral. Gaz.* (London) 18 June 4/2 Surveyed land shall be divided, as nearly as may be, into sections of eighty acres each, with the exception of the site of the first town, which shall be divided into acre sections. **1838** *Southern Austral.* (Adelaide) 23 June 1/2 To Let, Acre Section No. 800, delightfully situate in North Adelaide, with a House thereon, consisting of three apartments, as now occupied by Mr Hibernia Smyth.

sekko, var. SECKO.

select, *v.* [Spec. use of *select* to choose or pick out in preference to another or others.]
1. a. *trans.* To choose (a tract of Crown land), esp. with a view to farming it. **b.** *spec.* FREE-SELECT.
1826 *Monitor* (Sydney) 29 Dec. 258/2 The authority given to *select* land shall not be considered sufficient to possess it. **1865** 'SPECIAL CORRESPONDENT' *Transportation* 12 A man selects an allotment of not less than forty acres of land, anywhere, pays for it at the rate of 10s. per acre, and obtains large grazing rights. **1982** J. MORRISON *North Wind* 103 'This used to be one of the best farms in this district.' 'Did you select it?' 'Yes, I did. I suppose I'm what you'd call a pioneer. I broke it in myself.'
2. *absol.* To obtain land under a free-selection scheme; to occupy such land.
1880 J. BONWICK *Resources Qld.* 75 No minor or unmarried woman can select. **1974** *Austral. Folksongs* (Folk Lore Council Aust.) 85 So you rode from the range where your brothers 'select', Through the ghostly grey bush in the dawn.

selection.
1. a. The formal choosing of a tract of Crown land by one who has an entitlement to a specified area of unidentified land or by one who intends to purchase. **b.** FREE SELECTION.
1826 *Monitor* (Sydney) 29 Dec. 258/2 The Public Notice that the authority given to *select* land shall not be considered sufficient to possess it, ought to have been made *at the time*, for it requires settlers to be lexicographers, to understand the difference between selection and possession. **1957** J. HAWKE *Follow my Dust* 52 My, that used to be a great station at one time. Three shearing sheds, and one year they broke all records by shearing a million sheep. The Gov'ment took bits and pieces off it for selection and now there's only a million acres left.
2. a. Land acquired by selection; a small to medium sized rural property however acquired. Also *attrib.*
1830 *Austral. Almanack* 145 If the selection do not adjoin land already granted, it will be necessary for the applicant to state the exact bearing and distance from some surveyed boundaries. **1927** T.S. GROSER *Lure of Golden West* 154 A mere pocket-handkerchief block of 25,000 or 50,000 acres would be a 'small man's' block, and be called a grazing farm or selection. **1930** D. COTTRELL *Earth Battle* 123 The actual man-handling of her sheep was the one form of selection work that she dreaded.
b. *transf.* A mining claim.
1878 J.H. NICHOLSON *Opal Fever* 26 If you convince me that you have opal in payable quantities, I advance you money to take up the selection jointly between us, and I also find money to set the whole thing going.

selector.
1. *Hist.* One who selects a tract of Crown land: see SELECTION 1.
1840 *S. Austral. Rec.* (London) 29 Feb. 83 This person is a 'land shark', who has acquired large means by regularly attending sales and buying up land which he knows to be

coveted by another; his object in opposing the original selector being, either to commute his threatened opposition by a high bribe, or to buy with the intention of compelling him to repurchase at an exorbitant profit. *Ibid.* 20 June 334 Whilst the present good feeling exists (it probably arises from no great want of land being experienced) restraining settlers from bidding against the selector, he can almost always calculate on purchasing the number of square miles equal to the 5,000 acres.

2. *spec.* Shortened form of FREE SELECTOR; also *transf.*, a small farmer (see SELECTION 2).

1866 'J.W.T.' *Land Question in Qld.* 23 The Minister for Land and Works shall appoint some duly qualified person or persons to point out to immigrants or intending selectors .. the several farms on the Agricultural Reserves in each district. 1964 J.S. MANIFOLD *Who wrote Ballads* 100 No squatter is mentioned so contemptuously in bush songs as the selector, the 'cockatoo' or 'cocky' as he became.

semaphore crab. [See quot. 1969.] The burrowing estuarine crab *Heloecius cordiformis* of e. Aust. incl. Tas.

1952 W.J. DAKIN *Austral. Seashores* 194 *Heloecius cordiformis*, the semaphore-crab... When the tide recedes even a little on the mud-flats .. myriads of crabs appear... One of the most common is *Heloecius*. 1969 *Crabs Sydney Foreshores* (Austral. Museum Leaflet no. 62) 7 The Semaphore Crab .. has received its popular name from the quaint habit of holding the claw-bearing limbs outstretched while the body is being raised and lowered in a manner simulating signalling.

semi, *n.* [U.S.: see OEDS *semi, prefix*^{2} 5.]

1. Abbrev. of 'semi-trailer'. Also *attrib.*

1956 H. FRAUCA *In New Country* 46 The driver and co-driver .. told us that they had been travelling from Meekatharra to Port Hedland together with another 'semi' when one of the axles of their vehicle had broken. 1965 R. FIELD *All over Down Under* 45 You know some of those 'semi' drivers are a bit rough.

2. A semi-detached house.

1959 D. HEWETT *Bobbin Up* 5 Always fighting a losing battle with life in the grey, warped weatherboard semi in Maddox Lane. 1980 N. SCOTT *Wherever we step Land is Mined* 22 Semi, comprising two-and-a-half bedrooms, kitchen, bath, inside W.C., rear access, very handy position.

semi-, *prefix. Obs.*

1. As **semi-civilized, -myall, -wild** *adjs.*, used to designate an Aboriginal still living in part in a traditional manner.

1853 *Austral. Gold Digger's Monthly Mag.* v. 163 A semi-civilized native .. was tending sheep. *c* 1879 A. MACPHERSON *Mount Abundance* 27 Charley and I started by ourselves, taking with us a semi-wild Balonne black (mounted). *c* 1947 *Home Building Inland* (Flying Doctor Service Aust.) 17 Patient was a semi-myall native with two broken legs.

2. With nouns designating a non-white person, as **semi-native,** (one) of part-Aboriginal and part-white descent.

1901 *Bulletin* (Sydney) 15 June 7/2 What about the rising population of semi-Kanakas that pass as Europeans? 1914 *Ibid.* 2 Apr. 24/3 Decided by the legal advisers of S.A. Government, that 'aboriginal' does not include half-caste, for the purposes of the Birds' Protection Act. Binghi is allowed, if hunting for food, to murder the nesting swan when other people are forbidden to, but semi-Binghi will in future have to rank as one of the other people. 1926 L.C.E. GEE *Bush Tracks & Gold Fields* 69 There was some sort of semi-native names applied by those early, bold navigators.

semipalmated goose. [See quot. 1964.] *Magpie goose,* see MAGPIE *n.* 2.

1824 J. LATHAM *Gen. Hist. Birds* X. 295 *Semipalmated goose...* Inhabits New-Holland: found in flocks near Hawkesbury River, and called New South Wales Goose; its note said to be tuneful, and melodious. 1964 M. SHARLAND *Territory of Birds* 56 Although the Territory has other geese .. the Pied Goose is the chief one... Alternative names for it are 'magpie' and 'semipalmated' goose. The 'semipalmate' refers to the feet being only partly webbed.

senate. [Transf. use of *senate* the upper branch of the U.S. legislature.] The upper house of the Federal Parliament. Also *attrib.*

1898 *Austral. Handbk.* 122 The Legislative powers of the Commonwealth shall be vested in a Federal Parliament, which shall consist of the Queen, a Senate, and a House of Representatives. 1931 *Century of Journalism* 386 As we have seen, practically all the problems that had worried the *Herald* in 1891 had been those represented by 'States' rights' and 'Senate representation'.

senator. A member of the SENATE.

1898 A.B. PIDDINGTON *Pop. Govt. & Federation* 16 To a Senator 'public opinion' will mean .. the opinion of the public of his own particular province. 1984 *Canberra Times* 5 Jan. 1/2 Bob Menzies tried to pull a swifty in the 1953 half-Senate election that would have resulted in the Liberals obtaining two more senators.

send, *v.*

1. In the imp. phr. **send it** (or **her**) **down Hughie**: see HUGHIE.

2. In the phr. **to send** (something) **off,** to steal.

1951 *Barbed Wire & Bamboo* (Sydney) June 13 Everyone chose his own method of 'sending off' (that being the transitive form of the intransitive verb 'to go off') petrol. 1968 G. MILL *Nobody dies but Me* 21 So much stuff is sent off that I wouldn't be surprised if someone tries to send home a complete hut through the post, and no one seems to worry about getting caught. Except the pigs, of course, but amongst the men it's mostly always spoken of as simply *sending something off.* It's very common to hear someone say, 'So and so's sent off an Aldis lamp', or 'I wouldn't mind sending off that hammer.'

sensitive plant. [Transf. use of *sensitive-plant* the shrub *Mimosa pudica,* having sensitive leaflets which fold when touched.] Any of several plants of the fam. Mimosaceae, the leaflets of which fold when touched, esp. *Neptunia gracilis* of mainland Aust. (and the naturalized *Mimosa pudica*).

1822 G.W. EVANS *Geogr., Hist., & Topogr. Descr. Van Diemen's Land* 54 Our naturalist observed .. the *sensitive plant.* 1965 *Austral. Encycl.* VI. 90 No *Mimosa* is indigenous to Australia, but the common sensitive plant (*M. pudica*) from the American tropics has been a widespread prickly weed in North Queensland for many years.

separate, *a.* and *n.* [Used elsewhere but apparently chiefly Austral.: see OED *separate, a.* 1 b. and *sb.* 5.]

A. *adj.* Used with reference to the prison system to designate solitary (confinement), esp. in the collocation **separate treatment.**

1839 A. MACONOCHIE *Gen. Views Convict Managem.* 32 With the philosophy of the Separate system .. social management concurs, *so far as it goes.* 1881 *Bulletin* (Sydney) 8 Oct. 9/3, I will first deal with what are termed long-sentenced prisoners. Anyone who gets a sentence of three years and upwards is sent to Berrima for nine months' 'separate treatment'. This .. consists in being absolutely secluded for that period—or nearly so.

B. *n.* Solitary confinement; a solitary confinement cell.

1866 *Cornhill Mag.* (London) Apr. 512 It is absurd to talk about reforming criminals when you ruthlessly corrupt those with whom lies your only chance. For charity's sake these men, at least, should be kept 'in separates', or only associate with each other. **1891** *Truth* (Sydney) 1 Feb. 3/3, I knew one fellow who 'come it very strong' though. He was doing three years .. and used to try all sort of cringing dodges with the doctor to get taken out of 'separate', all to no purpose. **1891** *Ibid.* 17 May 2/1 He had got 'put away' for forgery; and he escaped separate (which, for the benefit of the innocent, I may say, once for all, means nine months solitary confinement on starvation regimen) on the plea that he was subject to epilepsy.

separation. [Spec. use of *separation* the action of separating or parting.]

1. a. *Hist.* The division from the Colony of New South Wales, and subsequent establishment in 1851, of the Colony of Victoria. Also *attrib.*

1839 *Port Phillip Patriot* 29 Apr. 3 The 'Sydney Herald' falsely states, that we deprecate the idea of becoming a separate or independent Colony... One short statement will show that we have nothing to lose, but every thing to gain by *separation.* **1852** G.C. MUNDY *Our Antipodes* III. 283 One of the *five* newspapers of this little town contains an advertisement for the sale, at a music-shop, of a new air, 'the Separation Polka'—inapplicable title for a dance of which personal proximity in the dancers is a leading feature.

b. Special Comb. **Separation Day,** 1 July, the anniversary of the proclamation of the independent Colony of Victoria; **tree,** see quot. 1977.

1855 *Vic. Govt. Gaz.* (Index) 10 **Separation day** falling on Sunday, holiday to be kept on Monday. **1939** *Bulletin* (Sydney) 2 Aug. 20/1 The **Separation Tree** in Melbourne was an old-man red-gum more than 100 years ago. **1977** *Austral. Encycl.* VI. 148 The Separation Tree. A eucalypt in the Botanic Gardens, Melbourne, bears an inscription commemorating the separation of the colony of Victoria from New South Wales on 1 July 1851.

2. *transf.* Used of similar movements in other parts of Australia: see quots. Also *attrib.*

1860 *S. Austral. Advertiser* 2 July 3/1 In New South Wales I went up to the north as far as Brisbane and Ipswich. The people were then (June, 1858) full of the idea of becoming independent. The question of 'separation' was constantly coming up. **1980** P. FREEMAN *Woolshed* 10 The call for the creation of a 'Riverine' state continued well into this century, and was perhaps strongest in the depression of the early 1930s when Charles Hardy junior of Wagga Wagga, gained a seat in the New South Wales Parliament on a 'Separation' ticket.

separationist. *Hist.* One who advocates the political independence of a part of an existing Colony, esp. that of the Port Phillip District from New South Wales.

1843 *Colonial Observer* (Sydney) 22 Mar. 898/2 Curr expounded his political views. He is a thorough separationist, and is sure to be triumphantly returned. **1897** J.J. KNIGHT *Brisbane* 25 Petitions to the Queen were got up by the advocates of Separation. The mother colony had to be fought... The Separationists desired to include in the new colony the Clarence, Richmond and Tweed River districts.

septic.

1. a. Abbrev. of 'septic tank'.

1939 M.I. Ross *Dawn Hill Brand* 14 'It says here 'septics'. Have we got any?' Sidge asked. 'It means septic tanks,' Gene explained. **1977** *Weekly Times* (Melbourne) 19 Jan. 65/2 (Advt.), Lovely new home .. 2 bathrooms, 2 septics and large living area.

b. A 'Yank': see sense 2.

1976 *Cleo* Aug. 33 Even before R and R, Americans were septics (septic tanks—yanks). Septic is now general usage. **1981** D. STUART *I think I'll Live* 31 Jesus, lover of my soul, if it isn't the Goddams, the Septics themselves! .. Stick around long enough, I told myself, and .. you'll see some real live Yanks.

2. In the collocation **septic tank,** rhyming slang for 'Yank', an American.

1967 *Kings Cross Whisper* (Sydney) xxxix. 4/4 *Septic tank*, yank or bank.

serang. Also **sherang.** [Transf. use of Anglo-Indian *serang* a native boatswain, or captain of a Lascar crew: see OED.] A person in authority. Freq. as **head serang.**

1911 *Bulletin* (Sydney) 19 Jan. 14/4, I hereby threaten to produce affidavits from several boundary-riders and one serang that my facts are right. **1968** *Kings Cross Whisper* (Sydney) lv. 10/3 It's a real happy farm. The head sherang and the boys are still calling me Wally.

sergeant baker. [Of unknown origin: see quot. 1965.] The crimson, purple, and white marine fish *Aulopus purpurissatus* of all States.

1871 *Official Rec. Intercolonial Exhib. Australasia* 791 The beautiful 'aulopus' (serjeant baker) .. and a variety of other less familiar forms, may be taken by the line in almost unlimited quantities. **1965** *Austral. Encycl.* VIII. 74 Sergeant baker (*Latropiscus purpurissatus*), a red, variegated marine fish named after an early colonial sergeant who was probably florid of complexion; possibly it was William P. Baker, one-time sergeant of marines at Norfolk Island, where this fish is common.

serrated tussock. [See quot. 1973.] The introduced South American grass *Nassella trichotoma* (fam. Poaceae), naturalized as a weed of pasture in much of s.e. Aust.; TUSSOCK GRASS b.

1958 J.N. WHITTET *Weeds* 294 In New South Wales serrated tussock mainly infests the central and southern tablelands. Its general growth, excepting seed heads, is somewhat similar to the native tussocky poa grasses (*Poa caespitosa*). **1973** W.T. PARSONS *Noxious Weeds Vic.* 151 'Serrated tussock' is an obvious name describing the serrated leaves and the tussock type of growth.

servant. *Hist.* [Shortened form of *assigned servant* (see ASSIGNED 2).]

1. A convict assigned to be the servant of a private person.

1802 *Gen. Orders issued by Governor King* 6 Feb. 81 If any person should beat or use their servants ill, they will be taken from them to Government labour, and the offenders dealt with according to their situations in the Colony. **1835** *Tegg's N.S.W. Pocket Almanac* (1838) 95 Should the master of any servant applying for a ticket, consider the applicant undeserving the indulgence, he is required to state his opinion in writing to the Bench, stating the grounds of it.

2. In the phr. **servant of the crown,** a euphemism for CONVICT *n.* 1, whether in private or official custody.

1788 *HRA* (1914) 1st Ser. I. 34 The convicts being the servants of the Crown till the time for which they are sentenced is expired, their labour is to be for the public. **1843** C. ROWCROFT *Tales of Colonies* (1858) 266, I am a servant of the Crown. I am assigned to Mr Kale.

serve. In the phr. **to give** (someone) **a serve,** to criticize adversely, to reprimand sharply. See also quot. 1967.

1967 *Kings Cross Whisper* (Sydney) xxxix. 4/5 *Serve*, to give a person a thrashing. 'Give the mug a serve.' **1983** *Woman's Day* (Sydney) 27 June 18/1 'Yeah', he said, 'Oges is set to give the Poms a serve.'

service. *Hist.*

1. Shortened form of *assigned service* (see ASSIGNED 2).

1832 *Hill's Life N.S.W.* 21 Dec. 3, I am assigned to Colonel Damaresq. Two years ago, I was in Mr John M'Intyre's service, lent to him by Mr Potter M'Queen. **1833** *Launceston Advertiser* 31 Oct. 2 The Convicts by the Stakesby who have not been taken off according to their assignments published in the Gazette, September 13, 1833, have been this day ordered to the service of other applicants.

2. In the phr. **service of government,** official custody (of a convict) as opposed to private assignment.

1848 C. COZENS *Adventures of Guardsman* 113 Two young men, prisoners .. happened to be returned from their master's private assignment to the service of Government. **1850** *Irish Exile* (Hobart) 29 June 6/4 The woman was discharged to the service of Government, her ticket-of-leave being revoked, because she did not attend the last general muster.

servitude. *Hist.* [Spec. use of *servitude* absence of personal freedom; for *penal servitude* see OED *penal, a.*[1] 1 c.] The compulsory labour to which a convict (later, a prisoner) is sentenced. Also as **penal servitude** (occas. *attrib.*).

1787 *Hist. Rec. N.S.W.* 25 Apr. (1892) I. ii. 90 Full power and authority to emancipate and discharge from their servitude any of the convicts .. who shall, from their good conduct and a disposition to industry be deserving of favour. **1857** P.J. MURRAY *Not so Bad* 17 The principle of giving a Ticket-of-Leave to the Transport and refusing it to the Penal Servitude man. **1890** *Braidwood Dispatch* 23 Aug. 2/5 Samuel Charles who was in Sydney on Tuesday sentenced to 10 years' penal servitude for breaking and entering a dwelling-house, had, since 1865, served no less than 15½ years in gaol.

session. A period spent drinking; GROG-UP.

1949 L. GLASSOP *Lucky Palmer* 215 I'll join you in a beer later, but I don't want to get into a session. **1981** C. WILLIAMS *Open Cut* 148 She has to go longer hours. .. Bloke'll shoot off for a session. She has to make up her own entertainment.

set, var. SETT.

set, $n.^1$ [Spec. use of *set* 'dead set': see OED(S $sb.^1$ 7.] A hostile attitude; esp. in the phr. **to get (make, take) a set on** (a person), to exhibit a hostile attitude towards.

1866 *Austral. Monthly Mag.* (Melbourne) II. 144 Rather angrily; for he considered we were all making a set on him. **1885** *Australasian Printers' Keepsake* 24 The Boss had 'got a set on him' to *set* The mullock of the whole establishment. 'You'd better far believe it!' So he said. **1946** K. TENNANT *Lost Haven* (1947) 228 If the Old Man hadn't tried to give Mark Thorne such particular hell when he was starting his shop, perhaps Thorne wouldn't have taken a set on all the Sudermans. **1956** *Tennant Creek Times* 15 June 7/3, I did notice .. a set against Territorian officialdom.

set, $n.^2$

1. *Surfing.* [Spec. use of *set* a number or group: see OED $sb.^2$] A series of waves followed by a lull.

1963 J. POLLARD *Austral. Surfrider* 20 A group of waves is called a 'set'. **1979** CAREY & LETTE *Puberty Blues* 47 Yet that's all the boys *did* talk about, way out on the flat sea, sitting on their boards, in between sets.

2. *transf.* A pair of female breasts.

1967 J. HIBBERD *White with Wire Wheels* (1970) 155 Jesus. Get on to these for a set. .. This bird. Just have a look at those knockers. **1979** B. HUMPHRIES *Bazza comes into his Own,* Cripes! I wish they only gave seven days for rape! This sheilah's got a set on her like a pair of Mudgee mailbags! I bet she goes off like a tin of bad fish!

set, $v.^1$ [Spec. use of *set* to fix on as a victim: see OED(S $v.$ 125.] In the phr. **to have** (or **get**) (a person) **set,** to be ill-disposed towards, to 'have it in for' (a person).

1899 *Truth* (Sydney) 5 Nov. 1/3 In bush parlance Speaker Abbott evidently has John Norton set. What's in Reid's mouth but a playful word, is in Norton's rank disorder. **1929** 'A. RUSSELL' *Bungoona* 7 It ain't too bad, but when the Jacks get er man set, like they did me over in Melbourne, its got ter slump.

set, $v.^2$ [Spec. use of *set* to wager: see OED $v.$ 14.]

a. *trans.* To wager (a sum).

1911 A. WRIGHT *Gamblers' Gold* 56 Taking the 'kip' and pennies. .. Yer set 'arf-a-dollar. **1946** K.S. PRICHARD *Roaring Nineties* 152 The spinner backed himself to head 'em. The ring-keeper started the betting; got his bet set.

b. *trans.* (in *pass.*) and *intr.* To arrange (a wager), esp. in the game of two-up. Freq. in the phr. **to get set.**

1915 DREW & EVANS *Grafter* 62, I had forty pounds to put on it. Twenty of my mate's, and twenty of my own, and I wanted to get it 'set' all in one lump. I didn't want to draw attention to myself by dribbling it on a fiver at a time. **1986** *Canberra Times* 9 Mar. 1/1 Whether you want a $1 flutter on your fancy or whether you are a big punter, you will have no trouble getting set with a bookmaker.

c. *trans.* To arrange a wager with (a person).

1915 DREW & EVANS *Grafter* 126 'How much do you want?' 'Six pounds to four. .. ' Brummy 'set' him.

d. *Two-up.* In the phr. **to set the centre,** to ensure that the sum waged by the spinner is covered by the players.

1930 L.W. LOWER *Here's Luck* (1955) 50 He had a small piece of flat wood in his hand, on which were balanced two pennies. The national game was in progress. .. 'I spin for the lot,' he called. 'Seven and eightpence. Set the centre! Set the centre!' **1970** R. BEILBY *No Medals for Aphrodite* 278 Turk .. heard the ring-keeper's wheedling chant: 'Right-oh, who'll set the centre?'

sett. *S.A. Obs.* Also **set.** [Used chiefly in Cornwall: see OED *set, sb.*[1] 3 b.] A mining lease.

1846 F. DUTTON *S.A. & its Mines* 300 Two brothers .. obtained the first set, for the space of twelve months, at Kapunda .. whose tribute for that period amounted to above £500. **1890** H.Y.L. BROWN *Rec. of Mines S.A.* (ed. 2) 6 The operations of the company were confined to leasing setts of its land for mining purposes.

settle, *v.* [Used as elsewhere but of local significance: see OED *v.* 4 and 11 b.]

1. **a.** *trans. Hist.* To settle (a place) with non-Aboriginal inhabitants.

1788 J. HUNTER *Hist. Jrnl. Trans. Port Jackson* (1793) 293 Governor Phillip signified his intention of sending me to Norfolk-Island, with a few people, and stock to settle it. **1924** *Smith's Weekly* (Sydney) 11 Oct. 22/3 The big cattle runs in the north-east corner of N.S.W. are gradually disappearing. Much of that country was close-settled many years ago.

b. *trans.* To establish (a person or body of persons) in a place. Also with **down.**

1812 *HRA* (1916) 1st Ser. VII. 595 The Tract of Country now Occupied by the Wild Cattle will be required in a few Years more for the purpose of Agriculture and Settling People on. **1857** M.B. HALE *Transportation Question* 29 Reasons .. may be put forward .. for settling down the convict population in Western Australia.

2. *intr.* To establish oneself, esp. as a farmer, on land not previously occupied by non-Aboriginal inhabitants.

1788 J. HUNTER *Hist. Jrnl. Trans. Port Jackson* (1793) 341 You will make the report to me .. of such who are not convicts, and who are desirous of settling on the island.

1981 A.B. FACEY *Fortunate Life* 49 A settler could take up land and settle on it without much or any money.

settled, *ppl. a.* [Used as elsewhere: see OED 10 and Mathews.]

1. a. Of land (*spec.* that available for alienation): peopled with settlers. See also UNSETTLED.

1816 *Hobart Town Gaz.* 15 June, Lime can be obtained for erecting buildings on the newly settled Farms. **1960** *N.T. News* (Darwin) 19 Feb. 9/2 Darwin .. is the closest settled community in Australia to the East.

b. In collocations: **settled country, district, land.**

1861 W. LANDSBOROUGH *Jrnl. Exped. from Carpentaria* (1862) 7 We saw large quantities of the small white cockatoos, and the rose-coloured ones, which are to be found only in the inland **settled country** of New South Wales and Queensland. **1822** J.T. BIGGE *Rep. State Colony N.S.W.* 165 The retirement of the useless or unemployed convicts from the **settled districts** to those that are more remote. **1820** *HRA* (1921) 3rd Ser. II. 252 The Mountainous Districts adjoining the **Settled Lands.**

2. Of a non-Aboriginal: established in Australia.

1839 *Port Phillip Patriot* 10 June 3 This vile hankering after the filthy lucre, is it not picking the pockets of the newly settled Emigrant. **1964** *Bulletin* (Sydney) 18 Jan. 13/3 A British woman who was a settled migrant .. gave regular talks on board.

settlement. [Spec. use of *settlement*: see esp. OED 6, 14, and 15.]

1. a. *Hist.* The British community established in Australia in 1788 and as subsequently enlarged; the land so occupied.

1788 J. HUNTER *Hist. Jrnl. Trans. Port Jackson* (1793) 301 Drank the healths of his Majesty, the Queen, the Prince of Wales and success to the settlement. **1865** 'SPECIAL CORRESPONDENT' *Transportation* 7 The settlement was hapless from the first. Old colonists give lively descriptions of how ladies, blood horses, pianos, and carriages, were landed on a desolate coast .. and no one knew where his particular allotment lay.

b. A place where non-Aboriginal inhabitants of Australia have established themselves, esp. a small town. See also BACK SETTLEMENT.

1792 *Hist. Rec. N.S.W.* (1893) II. 794 Sydney is the spot where the first settlement was formed. **1972** ANDERSON & BLAKE *J.S. Neilson* 2 The children watched bullock teams moving slowly out of the settlement, hauling lumbering drays, loaded with supplies, to up-country stations in the hinter-land.

2. The act of settling in Australia: see SETTLE 2.

1828 J.D. LANG *Narr. Settlement Scots Church* 5 A very great number of free Scottish emigrants have arrived in the Colony .. and effected settlements in all parts of the territory. **1899** *Progress* (Brisbane) 1 Apr. 1/2 The rental obtained is a secondary matter so long as settlement is secured, the prime consideration of land legislation being the settlement on the land of a white population which will open up the land and create traffic.

3. a. *Obs.* A tract of rural land held by a settler.

1834 H. CARMICHAEL *Hints relating to Emigrants* 6 The substantial advantages of obtaining a settlement in New South Wales are .. questionless.

b. Special Comb. **settlement lease,** a form of agreement governing the tenure of some rural landholdings; the landholding itself (see quot 1912); **scheme,** a plan to bring about rural development by encouraging the establishment of farmers in underdeveloped areas.

1896 *Austral. Handbk.* 99 Small settlement is provided for by conditional purchase, homestead, **settlement** and improvement **leases.** **1912** *Cwlth. of Aust. for Farmers* (Dept. External Affairs) 99 *Settlement Lease*—Areas up to 1,280 acres for agricultural purposes, and 10,240 acres for grazing, may be obtained as settlement leases. Such leases have a term of forty years, and provision is made for the reappraisement of the rent every ten years. **1965** *N. Austral. Monthly* Feb. 21 The Daly flows through good agricultural land .. and it would seem that a **settlement scheme** there could be a wonderful thing for the Territory.

4. An Aboriginal community administered by a public authority. Also *attrib.*

1911 A. SEARCY *By Flood & Field* 285 A strange Myall native reported (through the Settlement blacks) .. a big mob of cattle. **1961** *Bulletin* (Sydney) 15 Feb. 32/1 The aborigines at the Settlement said that if you were an aboriginal you did not have to do anything.

settler. [Spec. use of *settler* one who settles in a new country: see OED(S 2.]

1. One who settles in Australia: see SETTLE 2; a (small) farmer; an immigrant. See also BACK SETTLER. Also *attrib.*

1788 J. HUNTER *Hist. Jrnl. Trans. Port Jackson* (1793) 340 After the time for which they are sentenced may expire, lands will be granted them, if they wish to remain as settlers. **1917** *Huon Times* (Franklin) 18 May 5/3 We can take it for granted that the settler class will nominate someone for the position and we may look forward to having to pay for an election.

2. *Hist.* In the phr. **settler of the first class**: see quot. 1815.

1811 *Sydney Gaz.* 27 Apr., To Gentlemen Settlers, or Settlers of the first Class and the Wives of absent Civil and Military Officers. **1815** *HRA* (1916) 1st Ser. VIII. 559 Settlers of the first Class (that is Gentlemen who are Supposed to be possessed of Sufficient Property to maintain themselves).

3. a. [Also U.S.] In the collocation **old settler,** one of the earliest settlers in Australia or in a particular district. Also *attrib.*

1827 P. CUNNINGHAM *Two Yrs. in N.S.W.* I. 195 An old settler can always readily tell whether it is to be a dewy night or not, by the appearance of the sky and state of the air. **1979** S.W. DUTHIE *Fiddlers Creek* 129, I suppose that there's lots of old settler families around the place besides the Kinnears but I bet not many of them like to look too far back in their family history

b. In special collocations: **settler's cake** *obs.*, see quot.; **clock,** the kookaburra *Dacelo novaeguineae*; *bushman's clock,* see BUSHMAN 8; SHEPHERD'S CLOCK; **friend** *obs., settler's matches* (and see quot.); **man** *obs.*, a convict assigned to a settler; **matches,** strips of bark useful as kindling.

1843 C. ROWCROFT *Tales of Colonies* (1858) 325 There's a real **settler's cake** for you, gentlemen, made nice and light, like a pancake, only it wants eggs and milk. **1827** P. CUNNINGHAM *Two Yrs. in N.S.W.* I. 232 The loud and discordant noise of the *laughing jackass* (or **settler's clock,** as he is called), as he takes up his roost on the withered bough of one of our tallest trees acquaints us that the sun has just dipped behind the hills. **1856** G. WILLMER *Draper in Aust.* 217 It is no uncommon thing still to hear men in the bush speak of this bark and the green hide (the latter is used for halters) as the **settler's friend.** **1804** *Sydney Gaz.* 11 Mar., The Prisoners at Public Labour at Castle Hill, and the **Settlers** [sic] **men,** were in a state of Insurrection. **1891** *Bulletin* (Sydney) 19 Dec. 21/2 And we walked so very silent—being lost in reverie—That we heard the '**settler's matches**' gently rustle on the tree.

settling, *vbl. n. Hist.*

1. The action of SETTLE 1.

1789 *HRA* (1914) 1st Ser. I. 127 It has been found by experience that the settling plantees in townships hath very much redounded to their advantage. **1839** *S. Austral. Rec.* (London) (1840) 22 Feb. 63 An hour and a quarter's drive of nine miles brought us to the station of Mr Henty, distant from Portland bay about forty miles. . . The Messrs Henty have the merit of discovery and first settling this fine

seven.

1. *Hist.* In the *attrib. phr.* **seven year(s')**, used to designate a convict sentenced to seven years of penal servitude. See also SEVENER.

1827 P. CUNNINGHAM *Two Yrs. in N.S.W.* II. 269 The youngster I speak of was therefore the second son induced to entitle himself to a seven years' trip to Botany. **1948** F. CLUNE *Wild Colonial Boys* 7 Only three classes of convicts were transported to New South Wales... Lifers and fourteeners were destined for hard labour on the roads and public buildings of the colony, while the seven-year men.. were.. assigned as unpaid servants to private employers and landowners in the colony.

2. In the phr. **to chuck (do, throw) a** (or **the**) **seven**, to die; to faint, vomit, or otherwise lose one's composure.

1894 *Worker* (Sydney) 18 Aug. 2/5, I am pretty cronk and shaky—too far gone for hell or heaven, An' the chances are I'm goin'—that I'm goin' to 'do the seven'. **1908** *Truth* (Sydney) 3 May 1/7 We miss him in the morn, We miss him in the noon, We did not think our darling brother Would chuck a seven so soon. **1958** V. KELLY *Greedy Ones* 73 'The padre had gone out to it—thrown a seven.' 'Mr Mathieson had fainted,' said Murrill. **1978** HANIGAN & LINDSAY *No Tracks on River* 96 Of course, his Mum straight away chucked a seven and squealed, 'Careful, Deryck, careful. Oh, do be careful!' **1982** *Bulletin* (Sydney) 25 May 50/3 If you drink enough you'll get *shickered*.. or even *chuck a seven* (which means succumb, in whole or in part).

3. A measure of beer. Also **seven-ounce**.

1962 *Meanjin* 323 He stood erect in the far corner and drank a seven-ounce. **1984** P. CORRIS *Winning Side* 69 'Get you a seven,' he said. It came, along with his fresh schooner, and he emptied it into my half-full glass.

4. *pl.* See quot. 1982.

1965 K. SMITH *OGF* 106 Bernard Borker.. condemned all lotteries, games of chance.. cards (including fish, sevens and grab) and the T.A.B. **1982** P. ADAM SMITH *Shearers* 280 These men remember the big tin shed on the banks of the Thompson River where they broke down their cut-out cheque playing local variants of Crap called Yankee Grab, Murrumbidgee and Sevens.

sevener. *Hist.* A convict sentenced to seven years of penal servitude: see also SEVEN 1.

1847 *Port Phillip Herald* 3 Aug. 3/1 The Pentonville convict.. exclaimed to a fellow 'exile', 'halloo! there's an old bloke of a 'seven'ner' for you!' **1948** F. CLUNE *Wild Colonial Boys* 7 The lifers and long-sentence men lorded it over the seveners.. for the lifers and long-termers had abandoned hope.

shade. Used *attrib.* and *absol.* to designate a shelter made to afford protection from the sun, esp. for plants.

1886 J.F. CONIGRAVE *S.A.* 87 It is hardly possible to grow camellias, ericas, and similar plants that can be affected by hot drying winds, except under what are termed 'shade houses', which are structures made with lath roofs, having a space of about an inch between each lath. **1952** *Meanjin* 197 Mary packed her three children and belongings into the mailman's truck at Kakarra, and went out to live with Jim in his tent and the brushwood shade he had made for her.

shaft. *Obs.* [Spec. use of *shaft* one of the long bars between a pair of which a draught animal is harnessed to a vehicle.] Used *attrib.* in Special Comb. **shaft bullock**, a bullock harnessed between the shafts of a vehicle; **dray**, a two-wheeled cart having a pair of shafts rather than a central pole.

1827 P. CUNNINGHAM *Two Yrs. in N.S.W.* I. 294 Harness, however, is absolutely necessary for the **shaft-bullock**, when setting your carts to work. **1848** H.W. HAYGARTH *Recoll. Bush Life* 49 In some districts, chiefly in the vicinity of Bathurst, **shaft-drays** are used; but pole-drays are found to be more suitable to the nature of the country.

shafter. [Transf. use of *shafter* a shaft-horse.] *Shaft bullock*, see SHAFT; also (loosely) POLER 1.

1843 A. CASWALL *Hints from Jrnl.* 33 A two-wheeled dray with a pole, is certainly better than with shafts, as if it upsets it turns in the ring-bolt of the pole yoke, and the bullocks sustain no injury; whereas when one with shafts is capsized, the shafter is frequently killed. **1939** J. SORENSEN *Lost Shanty* 16 The shafters prop, the leaders pull, The wheels creak dismally.

shag, $n.^1$ Used esp. in the phr. **a shag on a rock** (or **stick**) as an emblem of isolation, deprivation, or exposure.

1845 R. HOWITT *Impressions Aust. Felix* 233 The common people are not destitute of what Wordsworth calls 'the poetry of common speech'... 'Poor as a bandicoot', 'Miserable as a shag on a rock', &c.; these and others I very frequently heard. **1951** I.L. IDRIESS *Across Nullarbor* 7 Left us sitting there like shags on a stick!

shag, $n.^2$ [Spec. use of *shag* an act of sexual intercourse.] Used *attrib.* in Special Comb. **shag-bag**, a derogatory term for a woman; **-wagon**, a panel van (or station wagon), appointed as a convenient place in which to engage in sexual intercourse; also **shaggin' wagon**.

1944 *Troppo Tribune* (Mataranka) 21 Feb. 2 Old '**Shag-bag**' is very fond of snakes. **1975** S. FRENCH *Hey Phantom Singlet* 56 'Didja see Hustler posing off in his **shag wagon** this morning?'.. 'It's not so old—69 Holden.' **1978** L. O'CHARLEY *Anatomy of Strike* 25 The spectre of surfing bums and shaggin' waggons had faded from the scene.

shake, $v.^1$ [Survival of Br. slang *shake* to steal: see OED *v.* 16 b.] *trans.* To steal (something); to rob (someone). Also as *vbl. n.*

1812 J.H. VAUX *Mem.* (1819) II. 204 *Shake*, to steal, to rob; as, I *shook* a chest of *slop*, I stole a chest of tea. **1847** *Melbourne Argus* 10 Sept. 2/4 He heard the prisoner boast of having given the flour bag a 'shaking', and it was then discovered that a considerable quantity of flour had also been stolen. **1903** W. CRAIG *My Adventures* 191 They had been sitting on the side of their bed for some time, smoking and conversing, when the man lowered his voice to a whisper, and wondered if 'he' was worth 'shaking' (*i.e.* robbing).

shake, $v.^2$ [Spec. use of *shake* to cause to quiver: see OED(S 11 d.] In the phr. **to be shook on** (or **after**), to be enamoured of; to be well-disposed towards.

1868 *Sydney Punch* 11 July 58/1 And thither I'll quickly repair With the maiden on whom I am shook. **1901** H. LAWSON *Joe Wilson & his Mates* 26 He was supposed to be shook after Mary too.

shaker. *Gold-mining.*

a. A machine in which auriferous gravel, sand, etc., is agitated to separate out alluvial gold without the use of water.

1901 *Twentieth Century Impressions W.A.* 202 The gold is being found, not on the surface of the earth, but a thousand feet beneath it, and the rattle of the 'shaker' has long been changed to the 'growl of the sluicing stamphead'. **1972**

N. King *Nickel Country* 3 This is the most primitive form of extracting alluvial gold. The men who owned 'shakers', or dry-blowers, shovelled the earth in and began shaking the dirt away.

b. Special Comb. **shaker dryblower** (or **blower**), a machine which combines the properties of a shaker and a DRYBLOWER b.

1939 A. GASTON *Coolgardie Gold* 76 Several different kinds of dryblowing machines were at work, but the shaker and Steve Lordern's patent dryblower were the most popular. The shaker dryblower came in some time later. It is the most perfect dryblowing goldsaver ever invented. **1977** J. DOUGHTY *Gold in Blood* 91 Only it wasn't a shaker now. It was a shaker-blower that I had built myself in Coolgardie under the guidance of Tom Collings. My first dryblower.

Shaky Isles. Also **Shakey Isles.** New Zealand (from the frequency there of earthquakes). Cf. SHIVERY ISLES.

1933 *Bulletin* (Sydney) 2 Aug. 20/2 The widespread notion that they're peculiar to the Shaky Isles. **1943** *Bully Tin* (Baronta) 21 Aug. 1 A team of husky Aussies..sailed to the Shakey Isles.

shaler, var. SHEILA.

shallow, *a. Gold-mining. Obs.* Used in collocations with reference to the mining of gold occurring close to the surface, as **shallow (-ground) rush**, (the working of) a goldfield having deposits of gold close to the surface (see RUSH *n.* 2 c.); **sinker,** a miner who works deposits of gold close to the surface; **sinking** *vbl. n.*, see quot. 1871.

1859 *Colonial Mining Jrnl.* Feb. 90/2 One or two **shallow rushes** have taken place on the ground between the Norfolk head and the Catholic Chapel. **1870** B. WITHERS *Hist. Ballarat* 138 To an old goldfields man .. the sight of a little shallow-ground 'rush' now, is like a sweet vision of childhood. **1868** J. BAIRD *Emigrant's Guide* 171 The diggers were of diverse kinds—surfacers, **shallow-sinkers**, deepsinkers, and quartz crushers—some being all these in turn. **1854** *Bell's Life in Sydney* 2 Sept. 1/1 It took its rise at the base of the Black Hill in **shallow sinking**, and has all along been remarkable for the depth and richness of its washing-stuff and the steadiness of its yield. **1871** J. BALLANTYNE *Homes & Homesteads* 40 *Shallow sinking*—digging holes in the creeks and low grounds, and getting the gold-impregnated soil from the surface of clay stones, sandstones, and slates.

shammy. *Gold-mining.* A bag of chamois leather in which a miner keeps the gold he finds. Also **shammy bag.**

1874 G. WALCH *Head over Heels* 83 Here it is—in this old Shammy bag. **1960** I.L. IDRIESS *Wild North* 179 On the grass outside, spilt carelessly on chaff-bags, were shammies of 'shotty' gold.

shandygaff. *Obs.* [Fig. use of *shandygaff* a drink composed of a mixture of beer and ginger-beer.] A compromise which pleases neither side. Also **shandygaffer.** Freq. *attrib.*

1897 *Worker* (Sydney) 11 Sept. 1/1 But when its only second-class (it often makes me laugh) He calls the blessed document a blanky 'shandy-gaff'. **1908** *Official Rep. Austral. Labour Conference* 27 If alliances and immunity were allowed, it would have a serious disintegrating effect on the Movement in Victoria—and he believed in Australia—and they would get in return nothing but political 'shandygaffers'. **1937** *Publicist* (Sydney) xv. 6/1 These are the half-and-halfs, the shandy-gaff Australians, who don't know yet what they are.

Hence **shandygaffy** *a.*, prone to compromise.

1895 *Worker* (Sydney) 10 Aug. 1/4, I want to growl. Your Newcastle contributor 'Shandy Gaff' is true to name—he's very *shandy-gaffy* in politics, judging from his 'Notes' in your issue of August 3.

shanghai /ˈʃæŋhaɪ, *n.*¹ [Prob. altered form of *shangie*, var. of Scot. dial. *shangan* a stick cleft at one end: see OED.] A catapult.

1863 *Leader* (Melbourne) 24 Oct. 17/1 Turn, turn thy shanghay dread aside, Nor touch that little bird. **1982** *Yulngu* Dec. 36 When we got up Gary and Simon were making some shanghais.

shanghai /ˈʃæŋhaɪ/, *n.*² *Obs.* [Prob. altered form of *shandrydan* a rickety old-fashioned vehicle.] A ramshackle old vehicle.

1906 *Bulletin* (Sydney) 3 May 14/2 Waiting .. once for the ramshackle shanghai at Port Pooncarie, I noticed a local blackfellow .. walloping his gin. **1914** T.C. WOLLASTON *Spirit of Child* 30 A station shanghai with two mules in it.

shanghai /ˈʃæŋhaɪ, ʃæŋˈhaɪ/, *v.* [f. SHANGHAI *n.*¹] *trans.* To catapult. Also *fig.*

1938 C.P. CONIGRAVE *Walk-About* 97 An animal would get irritated at being baulked, would rush ahead, and then the springy, resilient saplings would 'shanghai' him backwards. **1938** F. CLUNE *Free & Easy Land* 41 Shanghai the sugar down this way, Danny Boy.

shanty, *n.*¹ [Spec. use of *shanty* small, mean dwelling: see OED(S *sb.*¹]

a. A small public house, usu. in a rural area and freq. unlicensed. See also *grog shanty* GROG *n.* 3, *sly-grog shanty* SLY GROG 2.

[N.Z. **1848** W.T. POWER *Sketches N.Z.* 168 A 'pakeha' had built a shanty on the opposite side of the river for the purpose of entertaining travellers.] **1863** *Bell's Life in Sydney* 7 Feb. 2/4, I told him there was a shanty at the crossing-place. **1982** R. HALL *Just Relations* 104 Such is Main Ridge settlement with its shanties selling rum.

b. Comb. **shanty-keeper, -keeping.**

1862 *Bell's Life in Sydney* 22 Mar. 3/1 Burly **shanty keepers** from the gold fields. **1894** *Western Champion* (Barcaldine) 12 June 12/2 Nell had followed her father, an old reprobate, from diggings to diggings, where he usually followed the occupation of **shanty-keeping**, otherwise sly grog selling.

shanty, *n.*² [U.S. *shanty* a bruised eye.] In the phr. **to hang a shanty on** (someone's) **eye,** to give (someone) a black eye.

1943 S.W. KEOUGH *Around Army* 31 When, not unjustifiably narked, she wrote and told him off, and why the sapper thought that to hang a decent shanty on the censor's eye worth ninety days' No. 2 f.p. **1944** *Bulletin* (Sydney) 12 Apr. 12/2 Whenever he appeared with a shanty hung on his eye—and that was not seldom. Never did he attribute it to an upflung bit of firewood or a slipped fence-strainer.

shanty, *v. Obs.* [f. SHANTY *n.*¹] *intr.* To frequent a shanty; to drink habitually.

1888 'R. BOLDREWOOD' *Robbery under Arms* I. 34, I was put out at his laying it down so about the Dalys and us shantying and gaffing. **1980** B. HORNADGE *Austral. Slanguage* 223 In the outback the illegal seller of spirits was the bush shanty, and this did give rise to the verb *to shanty* (to drink habitually) and *shanty-keeper*. These terms were short-lived.

share. Used *attrib.* in Special Comb. to designate an arrangement under which two or more persons participate in the risks and profits of an undertaking, as **share-cocky,** *share-farmer*; so **-cockying** *pr. pple.*; **-farm** [also U.S.], a rural property the profits from which are shared in an agreed proportion between the owner and

the person who farms it; -**farmer,** one who farms such a property; -**farming** vbl. n., the activity of so doing.
1929 Bulletin (Sydney) 28 Aug. 25/4 Working for a **share-cocky** on the lower Murray I noticed .. that .. the meat was always slightly 'high'. **1961** Ibid. 19 Apr. 28/1 They drive the dour and casual Australian alike mad with their wants, share-cockyin' the land, shame him with their industry and return to Italy rich men before they've time to learn the language. **1909** N.S.W. for Settler (N.S.W. Immigration & Tourist Bureau) 40 Throughout the whole of New South Wales .. the owners of large estates, which have been hitherto given over solely to sheep-raising, are recognising that greater profits are to be made from agriculture, and are cutting up their properties and making blocks available as '**share farms**'. **1928** R.G. STAPLEDON Tour in Aust. & N.Z. 28 Many successful men have started as **share-farmers**. **1924** New Settlers' Handbk. Vic. 129 Four model **share-farming** agreements.

shark. Used attrib. in Special Comb. **shark bait** (or **baiter**), one who swims alone or well out from the shore; so -**baiting** vbl. n.; **bell,** see quot. 1945; -**meshing** vbl. n., the netting of sharks; **patrol,** a patrol of surfing beaches, by boat or aircraft, to give warning of the presence of sharks; -**proof** a., secure against sharks; **spotter,** one who watches for sharks; so -**spotting** vbl. n.
1912 [shark bait] A. WRIGHT Rung In (1921) 29 It might be only some foolhardy 'shark baiter', as he heard the more venturesome of the bathers termed. **1920** A.H. ADAMS Australs. 177 Farther out in the deep water swam the venturous line of experts, technically known as 'shark-bait'. **1967** K.S. PRICHARD Subtle Flame 99 I'm no good at shark baiting! **1940** P. KERRY Cobbers A.I.F. 14 An' 'e didn't pause fer breath till 'e wus ringin' the **shark bell**. **1945** J.A. ALLAN Men & Manners 138 All beaches of note have their watch-towers and 'shark-bells'—the latter rung in warning whenever a black fin appears inshore. **1936** Sydney Morning Herald 24 Nov. 12/5 The State Government has accepted a tender .. for **shark meshing** off the metropolitan beaches from Broken Bay to Port Jackson. **1951** Ann. Rep. (Surf Life Saving Assoc. Aust., Qld. State Centre) 8 Once again the Courier-Mail provided an aerial **shark patrol** over the waters of the South Coast during the Xmas holidays. **1968** Herald (Melbourne) 20 Jan. 10/8 Told of the surf boats which surf life saving clubs use for shark patrols off Australian beaches, he said: 'There is no reason why they couldn't be equipped with electrodes to drive off sharks.' **1857** J. ASKEW Voyage Aust. & N.Z. 259 A neat little bathinghouse, with .. a space in front entirely surrounded with a **sharkproof** netting of wattles. **1958** V.M. COPPLESTON Shark Attack 207 For some time great faith was placed in the air shark patrol which comprised a Dragon DH4 carrying a **shark spotter.** **1978** Herald (Melbourne) 14 Jan. 6/10 Shark spotting is only one of our functions,' Mr Stewart said.

shark, v. Australian National Football. trans. See quot. 1969. Also absol.
1960 N.T. News (Darwin) 5 Jan. 8/4 Then Bruno Wilson sharked cleverly and brought up Wanderers' second major. **1964** Footy Fan (Melbourne) II. xv. 3 If he did not get the hit-outs from his own followers, he certainly 'sharked' plenty from the opposition. **1969** EAGLESON & MCKIE Terminol. Austral. Nat. Football iii. 15 Sharking, in bounces, throw-ins and knock-outs, intercepting the ball as it passes between an opposing ruckman, who won the knock, and his rover.

sharp. Obs. [Spec. use of sharp a cheat, a swindler, a rogue.] One who exploits the simple or inexperienced, orig. an ex-convict as opposed to a newly arrived immigrant. See also FLAT n.²
1812 J.H. VAUX Mem. (1819) II. 205 Sharp, a gambler, or person, professed in all the arts of play; a cheat, or swindler; any cross-cove, in general, is called a sharp, in opposition to a flat, or square-cove; but this is only in a comparative sense in the course of conversation. **1909** A. WRIGHT Rogue's Luck 196 As the breed of 'flats' grows less in the cities, the 'sharps' who prey on them are forced to travel far afield in search of plunder.

sharpie. [f. sharp, stylish, fashionable, smart + -Y.] A young person who affects certain extreme or provocative styles of hair, dress, etc.: see quot. 1975. Also attrib.
1965 Kings Cross Whisper (Sydney) Feb. 11/2 Although you might think you're a bit of a sharpie, everyone else reckons you're a cockroach. **1974** M. GILLESPIE Into Hollow Mountains 15 We didn't recognise each other until we'd almost passed, because he'd had a sharpie haircut. **1975** Sun-Herald (Sydney) 13 Apr. 7 A sharpie is usually aged between 14 and 19 years. The boys wear their hair cropped short on the top and sides and longer at the back. The girls often wear 'dolly' makeup and have their ears pierced. Tattoos are often worn by both sexes. The sharpies wear blue jeans or high-waisted slacks supported by old-fashioned braces, matched with a tee shirt and sometimes a woollen cardigan.

shave, v. Shearing. trans. To shear (a sheep), esp. closely.
1895 Worker (Sydney) 14 Sept. 4/2 Fleecing, scraping, shaving, skinning, fit for show or exhibition. **1910** Bulletin (Sydney) 22 Dec. 13/4 An extra stick of tobacco was awarded each barber who shaved over 50 jumbucks a day.

she, pers. pron.
1. [Chiefly Austral. and N.Z.: see OEDS 2 e.] Applied to things (both material and immaterial) to which the female sex is not conventionally attributed: see quots. See also APPLE 4, RIGHT a. 4, SWEET a.² 2 a.
1863 J.B. AUSTIN Mines S.A. 96 The miners say the Moonta will be a mine when the Burra is forgotten—because she has lodes and the Burra has none. **1935** N. HUNT House of David 156 The men .. sprinkled along the fences, which were likely to take fire... 'She's euchred, boss! She's hemmed in on all sides! She can't pass them there breaks, nohow.' **1980** J. WRIGHT Big Hearts & Gold Dust 2 Goodnight, mate. Come on over and warm your toes, she's startin' to get a bit chilly.

2. [As used attrib. in the names of plants: see OED 10 e. and also SHE-OAK.] **she beech,** any of several rainforest trees of e. Qld. and e. N.S.W., of the genera Cryptocarya and Litsea (both fam. Lauraceae), esp. L. reticulata; the wood of the tree; **pine,** any of several plants of the genus Podocarpus (fam. Podocarpaceae), esp. the rainforest tree P. elatus of e. N.S.W. and e. Qld., having a small seed at the head of a short, egg-shaped, edible receptacle similar in appearance to a bluish-black plum; the wood of the tree; PLUM PINE.
1894 Proc. Linnean Soc. N.S.W. IX. 583 Mr Maiden exhibited specimens of Litsaea (Tetranthera) reticulata .. a plant new for the Colony, from Lismore, Richmond River, where it is known as '**She Beech**'. **1926** Qld. Agric. Jrnl. XXV. 437 Cryptocarya obovata .. She Beech (N.S.W.). **1880** J. BONWICK Resources Qld. 81 The **She Pine** of the colonists is a Podocarpus, living in the sea-side scrubs, and much admired by the cabinet-makers.

sheaf tossing, vbl. n. The sport of throwing a sheaf: see quot. 1986.
1961 Advertiser (Adelaide) 9 Sept. 1/2 The Governor was cheered by the crowd at the sheaf tossing arena when he tried his hand. **1986** Canberra Times 27 Jan. 3/4 The aim of sheaf tossing is to toss, with a pitchfork, a 3.6 kg. bag of straw as high as possible, simulating the old country skill of tossing sheaves of hay on to a hay cart.

Also **sheaf-tosser** n.
1947 Hoofs & Horns May 25 We cannot close without

shea oak, var. SHE-OAK.

shear, v. [Spec. use of *shear* to cut the fleece from (a sheep).]
1. intr. To be employed as a shearer.
1892 *Bulletin* (Sydney) 5 Nov. 20/1 At the last station where he shore he gave the super a sheol of a hiding. **c 1918** R. McJANNETT *Saltbush Jim V.C.* 3 He'd shorn way back to the far Paroo Then he trekked to the Condamine.
2. In the phr. **to shear (non-)union,** to employ shearers in accordance (or not) with conditions laid down by their trade union.
1891 *Conference Amalgam. Shearers' Union & Pastoralists' Fed. Council* 22, I don't think they ever sheared Union in that shed. **1892** *Bulletin* (Sydney) 24 Dec. 22/1 'We shear non-union, here,' says he. 'I call it scab,' says I.

shearer. [Spec. use of *shearer* one who removes the fleece from a sheep.]
a. An itinerant worker hired seasonally to shear sheep.
1826 J. ATKINSON *Acct. Agric. & Grazing N.S.W.* 77 Considerable difficulty is sometimes experienced in obtaining good shearers. **1984** *People Mag.* (Sydney) 7 May 39/2 No man labours as hard or lives as rough as the 40-hour-a-week shearer, whether he's wide-combing, narrow-combing or biting the wool off.
b. In special collocations: **shearers' ball,** an annual dance marking the end of shearing at a particular place; **cook,** one seasonally employed on a rural property to cook for the shearers; **hut, quarters,** accommodation provided for shearers during their period of employment on a rural property; **rep,** REP.
1899 J. BRADSHAW *Quirindi Bank Robbery* 23 Murphy and I went up to Louth, where at Matthew's pub we thoroughly enjoyed ourselves at the **shearers' ball.** **1872** W.M. HUGO *Hist. First Bushmen's Club* 216 Mr Peter Campbell, **shearer's cook,** seconded the motion. **1873** A. TROLLOPE *Aust. & N.Z.* I. 301 About a quarter of a mile from the wool-shed was the **shearer's hut,** in which the men slept, and ate, and smoked their pipes. **c 1892** J. CAMERON *Fire Stick* 46 While these simple arrangements were making in the **shearers' quarters,** they were not idle up at . . Wycomb's residence. **1903** *Bulletin* (Sydney) 31 Jan. 17/1 A **shearers' rep.,** in sending an order to a local store, asked the storekeeper to send out 5s. worth of newspapers.

shearing, vbl. n. and attrib. [Spec. use of *shearing* the action of cutting the fleece from a sheep; not necessarily excl. Austral.]
A. vbl. n.
1. The period during which sheep are shorn at a particular establishment.
1834 N.S.W. *Magistrates' Deposition Bk.* 24 Dec., Daniel Hogan and Thomas Miller came to me on the 25th Nov[r] with their shears and refused to shear any longer for me being under an engagement to remain during the shearing. **1933** J. TRURAN *Where Plain Begins* 150 Old Bill . . noted, for the hundredth time that shearing, the inroads made by his little friends the blow-flies.
2. The occupation or activity of the shearer.
1852 G.B. EARP *Gold Colonies Aust.* 112 Shearing is a separate occupation, men travelling from station to station for the purpose. **1978** N. EVERS *Tas. Paradise & Beyond* 34 A few more old wethers, the last to be brought down from the bush run, and the shearing was finished.
B. attrib.
1. Of or pertaining to the occupation of shearing.
1829 R. DAWSON *Statement* 86, I visited the shearing Station no less than *ten* times during the period alluded to.
1977 F.B. VICKERS *Stranger no Longer* 113 We were . . to develop the poultry farm so that I might unroll my swag and say goodbye to the shearing tracks forever.
2. Comb. **shearing season, team, time.**
1833 *Van Diemen's Land Almanack* 53 When the **shearing season** arrives, a place should be assigned wherein the sheep may be driven. **1926** *Bulletin* (Sydney) 11 Feb. 24/1 None of the swanky **shearing team** have cut their exes. yet. **1842** *Sketch of Shepherd's Duties N.S.W.* 49 At **shearing time,** the flocks are brought in rotation to the home station.
3. Special Comb. **shearing board,** see BOARD; **cheque,** the gross earnings of a shearer at the end of a period of employment at a particular place; **contractor,** one who employs a gang of shearers, etc., and who enters into a contract with an owner to shear sheep; **floor,** the part of the floor in a shearing shed on which the sheep are actually shorn; BOARD 1; **machine,** a mechanized device for shearing sheep; **shed,** a building in which sheep are shorn and fleeces processed and packed; *wool shed,* see WOOL 2; also attrib., and transf. a job as a shearer.
1882 ARMSTRONG & CAMPBELL *Austral. Sheep Husbandry* 174 There are many descriptions of sheds that find favour with our squatters; some consisting of **shearing boards** on either side, with the sheep in the middle of the shed; others, with the board in the centre and the sheep on each side. **1905** *Bulletin* (Sydney) 16 Mar. 3/2 My cheque was not the size of **shearing-cheques** of long ago. **1936** *Bulletin* (Sydney) 8 Jan. 19/1 The best picker-up I ever saw was Barefooted Joe. Any **shearing contractor** would find a job for him. **1850** W. GATES *Recoll. Van Dieman's Land* 162 The sheep to be sheared are driven at night under a long shed . . . From this shed a door opens to the **shearing floor,** which is sufficiently large for ten or fifteen men to work upon. **1852** *Guardian* (Hobart) 20 Oct. 3/4 **Shearing Machine.** A gentleman has invented a machine for shearing sheep, which can be employed by hand or steam. **1829** R. DAWSON *Statement* 83 He complains . . that the **shearing-shed** was not erected until the season was *close at hand.* **1976** B. SCOTT *Complete Bk. Austral. Folk Lore* 398 An account of life on the McConnells' station in Queensland in the 1860s in *Tales of Australian Pioneer Women,* by F.M. Johnson, says 'Shearing was followed by the Shearing Shed Dance, opened with a quadrille, followed by sets of lancers, polkas and country dances, with a caller to instruct us when to set partners and swing.' **1977** V. PRIDDLE *Larry & Jack* 6 He'd hump his swag further west to the big sheep stations and follow the shearing sheds.

shears, n. pl. In the phr. **off (the) shears:** (of sheep) newly shorn. Also as quasi-n. and attrib.
[N.Z. **1888** J. BRADSHAW *N.Z. of Today* 110 The hoggett . . in 1882 could be readily sold 'off the shears' at twelve shillings.] **1896** T. HENEY *Girl at Birrell's* 69 Now and again a buyer visited the stations to get cheap sheep 'off shears'. **1905** *Shearer* (Sydney) 18 Mar. 8/5 Drover Wood goes out to-morrow to lift 12,000 off the shears, bound for the Darling Downs. **1965** L. HAYLEN *Big Red* 199 We credit the proceeds from the 'off shears' sheep disposed of to No. 2 account.

shed, n. Shearing. [Abbrev. of *shearing shed* (see SHEARING B. 3) or *wool shed* (see WOOL 2).]
1. a. *Shearing shed,* see SHEARING B. 3.
1853 J. SHERER *Gold Finder Aust.* 233 Thousands of bales of wool were lying in the settlers' sheds. **1978** J. DINGWALL *Sunday too far Away* 6 I'm on my way to a shed.
b. The gang of shearers working in a particular shed. Also attrib.
1891 *Truth* (Sydney) 15 Feb. 7/2 He makes his sons . . manager of out-station, boss drover, over the shed, chief of burr-cutters—anything, in fact that draws pay *chargeable to the company.* **1982** *Sydney Morning Herald* 23 Oct. 29/4 The man who tops the shed tally is the ringer.

c. A job in a shearing gang; a contract to shear (an owner's) sheep.
1893 *Southerly* (1964) iii. 204 Men tramping in search of a 'shed' are not called 'sundowners' or 'swaggies'; they are 'trav'lers'. **1963** C.H. SMITH *How y' going Mate?* 7 Sproggins my name—shearing contractor. Eight in the team. Starting a shed near Hobart tomorrow.

2. *Comb.* **shed boss, manager, overseer.**
1887 *Bungendore Mirror* 12 Nov. 2 The highest tally we have heard of this season comes from the Narrowmine Shed... The work was not scamped either, but executed to the full satisfaction of the **shed 'boss'**. **1879** S.W. SILVER *Austral. Grazier's Guide* 50 The object of the overseer or **shed manager**.. is.. to get his sheep into the shed the moment they are dry. **1896** T. HENEY *Girl at Birrell's* 109 The **shed overseer**, the 'man over the board', was present to see that the shearing was properly done.

3. *Special Comb.* **shed hand,** a labourer employed to do the unskilled work in a shearing shed; **representative,** REP; **work,** unskilled work in a shearing shed; **worker,** *shed hand.*
1898 *Bulletin* (Sydney) 21 May 14/1 At a woolshed, near Condoblin.. a traveller.. 'had' the sympathising shearers to the extent of £8... After thanking the **shed-hands**.. he set out for the nearest township. **1909** W.G. SPENCE *Aust.'s Awakening* 181 The Union agent, Mr Arthur Rae, at Hay. As agent, he gave a letter to the **shed representative** at Mungadel. **1902** *Bulletin* (Sydney) 12 July 16/3 Looking for **shedwork**.. I one evening struck a shed that was to start shearing. **1899** *Western Champion* (Barcaldine) 18 July 7/4 On the night of Wednesday, the 12th.. the shed was visited by Mr P. Langston, who addressed a somewhat meagre meeting of the **shed workers** under the verandah of the rouseabouts hut.

sheelah, var. SHEILA.

sheep.
1. Used *attrib.* in *Comb.* **sheep bridge, country, downs** *obs.,* **establishment** *obs.,* **fence, -grazing,** *obs.,* **-grower, -growing, -herder, hill** *obs.,* **-holder** *obs.,* **-holding, land** *obs.,* **master, -net, -netting, overseer, owner, paddock, -proof** *a.,* **property, proprietor** *obs.,* **watchman** *obs.,* **-work, -yard.**
1940 G.W. LOVEJOY *In Journeyings Often* 101, I had perforce to travel twenty miles up the creek to cross by the Narrawin **sheep bridge**. **1822** W. BEARD *Old Ironbark* (1967) 11 Delightful country.. best **sheep country** in the world. **1831** *Acct. Colony Van Diemen's Land* 79 About 6 miles above New Norfolk the country becomes more open, consisting of fine **sheep downs**. **1833** *Sydney Morning Herald* 19 Sept. 2/3 Mr C.F. Koelz.. has been for some years employed at the extensive **Sheep Establishments,** at Camden, pointing out to the flock masters in this colony the advantages to be derived from a judicious classification of their sheep. **1909** R. KALESKI *Austral. Settler's Compl. Guide* 94 Ran a **sheep-fence** around it (six wires). **1926** *Illustr. Tas. Mail* (Hobart) 14 Apr. 1/2 Sheep Farming v. **Sheep Grazing**.. the advantages of intensive sheep farming as compared with ordinary grazing. **1840** *Port Phillip Gaz.* 8 Jan. 4 Portland Bay at present forms a great scene of attraction to all **sheep growers** in Van Diemen's Land. **1923** 'J. NORTH' *Son of Bush* 26 The most picturesque part of the great Wooroodil run was.. utterly unlike the portion of the estate used for **sheep-growing**. **1937** H.E. GRAVES *Who Rides?* 160 It was a rough single-room structure of boards, used by stockmen and **sheep-herders** when on duty. **1834** J. BACKHOUSE *Narr. Visit Austral. Colonies* (1843) 188 We proceeded over some fine **sheep-hills**. **1819** W.C. WENTWORTH *Statistical, Hist., & Pol. Descr. N.S.W.* 112 The majority of the **sheep-holders** are actively employed in crossing their flocks with tups of the best Merino breed. **1928** C.E. COWLEY *Classing Clip* 157 On any **sheep-holding** serviceable drafting-yards are necessary. **1832** *Colonial Times* (Hobart) 3 July, For Sale, a Fine Sheep Farm.. 2,560 acres of fine **Sheep Land,** well watered at all seasons.

1835 *Sydney Herald* 2 Feb. 2/2 Our **sheep-masters** should therefore prepare for a change. **1849** C. STURT *Narr. Exped. Central Aust.* I. 318 He mistook the **sheep net** for a fishing net, and gave them to understand that there were fish in those waters so large that they would not get through the meshes. **1837** H. CAPPER *S.A.* 70 The materials for large cattle and sheep enclosures, which will require little time to erect, have been obtained; and the **sheep-netting** and chains, to render them more complete for the purposes designated, have been sent out with them. **1834** N.S.W. Magistrates' Deposition Bk. 6 Nov., I am **Sheep Overseer** to Mr McIntyre and the prisoner himself is employed as a Shepherd and Taylor as Watchman at the same Station. **1839** *Southern Austral.* (Adelaide) 16 Oct. 4/2 Our **sheepowners** should be constantly on the watch to prevent the disorder [*sc.* foot rot] from gaining ground. **1883** W.A. BRODRIBB *Recoll. Austral. Squatter* 123 This timely assistance enabled me to.. fence a portion of the station into **sheep paddocks**. **1872** G.S. BADEN-POWELL *New Homes for Old Country* 169 A run is cut up into several portions, or 'paddocks', by **sheep-proof** fences. **1957** *Bulletin* (Sydney) 30 Jan. 13/1 They'd been on that particular **sheep-property** doing contract post-cutting. **1835** F.C. IRWIN *State & Position W.A.* 65 He.. has, for some time, been a **sheep proprietor**. **1822** B. FIELD in G. Mackaness *Fourteen Journeys Blue Mountains* 15 Oct. (1950) ii. 45 The settlers' convict-servants (stockmen and **sheep watchmen**) do little but drone. **1931** A.W. UPFIELD *Sands of Windee* 85 The men are late to meals having been delayed by **sheep-work** in a paddock. **1809** *Sydney Gaz.* 22 Jan., Farm.. with capital cow houses, **sheep yards**, and all other conveniences.

2. *Special Comb.* **sheep barber,** BARBER *n.;* **boiler** *obs.,* one who engages in *sheep-boiling;* **-boiling** *vbl. n., hist.,* BOILING 1; also *attrib.;* **camp,** see CAMP *n.* 3; **cocky,** a sheep-farmer on a small scale (see COCKY *n.*^{2}); **district, (a)** a district suitable for grazing sheep; **(b)** see quot. 1878; **dressing** *obs.,* see DRESS; **-drove** *v. intr.,* see DROVE *v.;* also as *vbl. n.;* so **-drover,** see DROVER 1; **-feed,** vegetation suitable for sheep to graze (see FEED); **feeder** *obs.,* a sheep-farmer; **-feeding** *vbl. n.,* the pasturing of sheep; **grazier** *obs.,* see GRAZIER; **king,** a large-scale sheep-farmer; **-man,** a sheep-farmer; one employed to tend sheep; **race,** see RACE *n.*^{1}; **run,** see RUN *n.*^{2} 1 a. and 2; **selection,** see SELECTION 2 a.; **shed,** *shearing shed,* see SHEARING B. 3; **-sick** *a.,* see quot. 1979; **slut,** a female sheep-dog; **squatter** *obs.,* see SQUATTER 2 and 3; **station,** see STATION 2 a. and 3; **tank,** see TANK *n.*^{1} 1; **tobacco** *obs., sheepwash tobacco;* **town,** a town which serves a sheep-farming district; **-wash** *obs.,* adulterated or inferior alcoholic liquor; **-wash tobacco,** inferior tobacco.

1912 *Bulletin* (Sydney) 14 Nov. 15/2 The shearers.. the **sheep barbers**. **1843** *Sydney Morning Herald* 18 July 3/3 Surely such a line of procedure is as necessary to be observed by the editor of a paper as by a **sheep-boiler**. **1843** *Colonial Observer* (Sydney) 26 July 1199/1 Mr Wentworth has commenced **sheep boiling** on his estate... Such settlers as may choose to take advantage of the opportunity, may have their surplus stock rendered down. **1844** *Sydney Morning Herald* 8 Jan. 2/3 The flockowners of the southern district.. are about to call a meeting for the purpose of forming a sheep boiling establishment. **1897** *Worker* (Sydney) 7 Aug. 3/3 Now, Mr Editor, I wish all our lads to be warned against those **sheep cockeys** who are going to cut down the price. **1843** *Arden's Sydney Mag.* Oct. 119 His surveyors are at work opening up a direct line of communication with the Maneroo **sheep district**. **1878** *Act* (N.S.W.) 41 Vict. no. 19 Sect. 14, Every owner intending to travel three hundred or more sheep from any run shall before leaving the Sheep district in which such run is situated forward to the Inspector of the district a statement in writing of the number description brands and marks of the said sheep and of their intended route and destination and shall obtain from the Inspector a permit containing the particulars set forth in the Second

Schedule hereto to travel the said sheep. And every owner introducing sheep from any of the adjoining Colonies shall in like manner obtain a permit to travel as aforesaid from the Inspector for the district into which such sheep shall first pass on crossing the Border. **1841** G. ARDEN *Recent Information Port Phillip* 27 Tobacco .. has been cultivated by squatters .. in quantities sufficient to supply their ordinary demands for **sheep dressing**. **1888** *Bulletin* (Sydney) 10 Mar. 14/1 A young fellow .. was **sheep-droving** with the writer away in the 'New Country' north of the alligator line, during the early sixties. **1925** M. TERRY *Across Unknown Aust.* 24, I went sheep-droving and he went south, far away to a distant cattle station. **1841** *Port Phillip Patriot* 4 Oct. 3/3 A cattle-jobber or a **sheep-drover**. **1903** *Bulletin* (Sydney) 25 Feb. 16/2 Though splendid rains have fallen .. the prospect for **sheep-feed** even is very remote. **1840** *Port Lincoln Herald* 7 Mar. 4 A small water hole is valued by an Australian **Sheep feeder** as much as one of Niobe's tears preserved in spirits would be by an English Antiquarian. **1838** *S. Austral. Rec.* (London) 11 July 76/2 **Sheep-feeding** has made the fortune of Australia. **1833** *Colonist* (Hobart) 18 June 1/4 This Estate is admirably adapted for an extensive **Sheep Grazier**. **1899** *Bulletin* (Sydney) 14 Oct. 14/3 The chum .. was bidden to drive to the station for the expected **sheep-king**. **1901** *Bulletin* (Sydney) 7 Dec. 30/2 The **sheepman** and his satellites came out; all riding stable-fed horses. **1980** J. WOLFE *End of Pricklystick* 39 An old man was driving a mob of sheep through the Strzelecki Ranges .. then slowly he collapsed on the hot road. .. Luckily for the sheepman, his progress was being watched. **1956** *Bulletin* (Sydney) 4 Jan. 13/1 The boss says for you to pick-up in No. 2 road, kick two down the **sheep-race** and clear the shed-road. **1823** *Hobart Town Gaz.* 4 Oct., A Farm of 200 acres .. with a good but small **sheep run**. **1965** G. MCINNES *Road to Gundagai* 147 Bourchier had a sheep run—it was too modest to be called a station—of about three hundred acres. **1943** *Bulletin* (Sydney) 22 Sept. 13/2 There is near Adavale (s.w. Q.) a **sheep selection** without a horse on the place. **1829** R. DAWSON *Statement* 83 Mr J. McArthur is compelled to admit .. that the **sheep-shed** .. was a 'well-adapted building'. **1895** *Leader* (Melbourne) 3 Aug. 6/1 Certain country in which severe losses have occurred in recent years has been too long carrying sheep, and .. the land has become what is termed '**sheep sick**'. **1979** J. LINDEMAN *Red Rumps & White Faces* 111 Due to poor seasons and heavy stocking, the country became 'sheep sick'. The majority of the good grasses .. gradually died out and were replaced by natural causes with both black and white spear grasses, both lethal to sheep. **1925** *Bulletin* (Sydney) 9 Apr. 24/4 A well-bred **sheep-slut** of ours in Western Queensland has developed the atrocious habit of devouring her litter. **1844** *Parramatta Chron.* 9 Nov. 3/1 The lordly **sheep squatter** and over-grown stock holder that comes in and out. **1886** D.E. BANDMANN *Actor's Tour* 88 The Cup of last year (1883) was won by a Mr White, a sheep squatter. **1825** *HRA* (1919) 1st Ser. XII. 69 Their Shepherds' Huts and **Sheep Stations** are established on different parts of it. **1982** R. HALL *Just Relations* 56 Could have made a fortune and bought hisself a sheep station by now. **1890** G.J. BROINOWSKI *Birds of Aust.* II. Pl. 35, The present specimens were found among the herbage usually growing about the **sheep tanks**. **1912** *Emu* XII. 66 This tree stood close to a sheep-tank or dam. **1843** *Portland Mercury* 4 Jan. 1/4 **Sheep tobacco**. **1948** F. CLUNE *Wild Colonial Boys* p. xix, My peregrinations .. brought me as a commercial traveller to .. Binalong, near the old **sheep-town** of Yass. **1891** M. ROBERTS *Land-Travel & Sea-Faring* 177 In the hotel we did not flourish, for both of us had something there described as brandy, but known to colonials as '**sheepwash**'. It is said that in order to make the vile concoction take quicker effect on the unwary tobacco is put in the cask. **1860** *S. Austral. Advertiser* (Adelaide) 2 July 2/5 *Proposed Amended South Australian Tariff.* Cigars, per lb., 4s. Snuff, per lb., 2s. **Sheepwash Tobacco**, per lb., 3d.

3. In the phr. **on** (or **off**) **the sheep's back**, used in allusion to wool as the source of national prosperity.

1932 R.W. THOMPSON *Down Under* 65 The phrase 'riding on the sheeps' [*sic*] back' was heard in a small and quickly hushed voice from certain wiser quarters. **1970** *Bulletin* (Sydney) 14 Feb. 17/1 Off the sheep's back, into the iron age.

sheep bush. [See quot. 1885.] WILGA. Also *attrib.*

1885 *Trans. & Proc. R. Soc. S.A.* (1886) 20 *Geijera parvifolia*—The Sheep Bush. Sheep only are particularly fond of this bush, which grows on hard limestone soils, and seems quite unaffected by droughts. **1903** G. SUTHERLAND *Australasian Live Stock Man.* (ed. 2) 385 The 'Sheep-bush willow' is the *Geijera parvifolia* belonging to a peculiarly Australian genus of trees.

sheep-ho, *int.* and *n.* Also **sheep-o**, **sheep-oh**.

A. *int.* A shearer's call for a sheep to shear.

1900 *Bulletin* (Sydney) 13 Jan. 32/2 'Go it, you—tigers!' yells a tar-boy. 'Wool away!' 'Tar!' 'Sheep Ho!' **1963** C.H. SMITH *How y' going Mate?* 53 Sometimes, when the shearers called 'Sheep-oh!' Sam would be at the back. **1982** *Sydney Morning Herald* 23 Oct. 29/4 There are cries of Sheep-O! when more sheep are needed in the pen.

B. *n. Obs.* PENNER-UP.

1900 *On Track* 131 Others, the sheep-ho's or the engine drivers at the shed or wool-wash, call him.

sheep-wash, *v. Hist.* [Used elsewhere but recorded earliest in Aust.] *intr.* To wash sheep before shearing. Chiefly as *vbl. n.*

1834 'EMIGRANT' *Party Politics Exposed* 41, I was sheep-washing at Castle Forbes. **1980** P. FREEMAN *Woolshed* 18 Sheep washing has long since been discontinued and the brush pens of Henry King's time have given way in modern woolsheds to well-designed drafting-yards that allow the proper storage, movement and handling of the sheep destined to be shorn.

sheep-washer. *Hist.* [See prec.] One who is employed to wash sheep before they are shorn.

1841 *Geelong Advertiser* 11 Oct. 2/3 The Governor himself dare not offer a glass of wine to a friend, nor a settler give a pannikin of grog to his sheep-washers, without subjecting himself to a penalty of £30. **1943** H.G. LAMOND *From Tariaro to Ross Roy* 27 The boss of the board would appeal for sheep washers from among the shearers.

sheepy. *Austral. pidgin. Obs.* Mutton; sheep.

1839 *S. Austral. Rec.* (London) (1840) 1 Feb. 22 They [*sc.* aborigines] call mutton *sheepy*, and pork *piggy*, and bread *bready*. **1842** *Tasmanian Jrnl. Nat. Sci.* I. 118 *Sheepi-kangallangalla* (sheep-mother) is the name of a shepherd.

sheevo, var. SHIVOO.

sheila. Formerly also **shaler**, **sheelah**, **sheilah**, **shelah**. [Prob. from the generic use of the (orig. Irish) proper name *Sheila*: see quot. 1828. Now Austral. and N.Z. but previously also Br. slang: see OEDS.] A girl or (young) woman.

[**1828** *Monitor* (Sydney) 22 Mar. 1053/2 Many a piteous Shela stood wiping the gory locks of her Paddy, until released from that duty by the officious interference of the knight of the baton.] **1832** *Hill's Life N.S.W.* (Sydney) 17 Aug. 2 *Daniel Delaney*, from Donoghadee, was charged with making love to a Shelah in the Domain, at the unseasonable hour of eleven p.m. **1895** C. CROWE *Austral. Slang Dict.* 72 *Shaler*, a girl. **1919** C.H. THORP *Handful of Ausseys* 130 Fellows would ride in from anywhere up to twenty miles around to have a hop and see all the sheilas. **1920** *Aussie* (Sydney) Apr. 21/1 For the sheelahs know the Aussie hat, from France to Scapa Flow. **1943** *Bulletin* (Sydney) 27 Oct. 12/1 'I wouldn't have cared if he'd been a good-lookin' feller', lamented Bill, 'but an ugly-looking cow like that beatin' a man to a sheilah.'

shelf, *n*. [Prob. in allusion to the phr. *on the shelf* out of the way.] An informer. Also **shelfer**.

1916 *Bulletin* (Sydney) 6 July 24/1 Here are a few of the pet names given by the wielder of the pick and banjo to the ganger: 'The red light', 'the big bloke', 'the gun', 'the nark', 'the spur', 'the shelfer', and 'the nit'. **1969** W. MOXHAM *Apprentice* 18 'Who's going to split? His word wouldn't carry much weight.' 'I'm no shelf.' Rufe took a notch in the collar.

shelf, *v*. [f. prec.] *trans*. To inform upon. Also as *vbl. n*.

1936 'SWEENEY, EX-CROOK' *I Confess* 123 No crime is so heinous as that called 'shelfing'—betrayal. **1984** *Sun-Herald* (Sydney) 9 Sept. 63/3 For all the pre-planning and agreements not to 'shelf' one another by being seen to start a rush to back Fine Cotton, several of those in the know could not contain their greed.

shell. Shortened form of 'pearl-shell'. Also *attrib*.

1913 *Cwlth. Parl. Papers* III. 747 They have not yet proved themselves as shell-getters. There is no doubt about their being divers. But, at the same time, getting the shell is called the scavenging of the bottom of the sea. **1936** N. CALDWELL *Fangs of Sea* 250 'There it is, lad, that's shell.' He pointed to the dirty looking disks.

Also **sheller** *n*., one who fishes for pearl-shell; **shelling** *ppl. a*., of or pertaining to this.

1902 *Cwlth. Parl. Papers* II. 1009 From this outward the '**shellers**' became divided into two parties. **1900** *Qld. Geogr. Jrnl*. XV. 32 The population of the island is about 1,500, and the population working in the **shelling** boats a little over 2,000.

shell-open *v. intr*. To open pearl-shells. Also as *vbl. n*.

1933 J.M. HARCOURT *Pearlers* 111, I know shell-opening isn't a pleasant occupation. **1937** —— *It never Fails* 132, I wouldn't shell-open for another week for another pearl like that one.

Also **shell-opener** *n*.

1925 *Bulletin* (Sydney) 14 May 22/4 In the bad old days of Broome there was one shell-opener who realised that there is luck even in dishonesty.

shell parrot. [Perh. in allusion to the colour patterns of the plumage.] BUDGERIGAR. Also **shell parakeet**.

1845 J.H. BROWNE *Jrnl. Sturt Exped*. 12 Mar. in *S. Australiana* (1962) Mar. 43 The Crested Parrot and Shell Parrakeet .. came to this part of the country in November in flights, they immediately paired off and commenced breeding. **1852** F. LANCELOTT *Aust. as it Is* I. 40 The little shell parrot, may be mentioned as exquisitely beautiful both in shape and plumage.

shelter-shed. A roofed structure, usu. partly enclosed, affording protection from inclement weather.

1856 *Plea on Behalf Aboriginal Inhabitants Vic*. 6 When 'Shelter Sheds' were talked of, no one ever thought of suggesting an extra one or two .. for them. **1977** K. GILBERT *Living Black* 47 When I went to school, I remember that the teachers used to make the black kids go out and clean up the shelter shed because they felt we wouldn't learn anything anyway.

she-oak /ʃiˑoʊk/. Also **sheoke** and formerly **shea oak, shiac**. [f. SHE 2 + OAK, the pronoun prob. being indicative of the perceived inferiority of the timber. See also HE-OAK.]

1. Any of many trees or shrubs of the fam. Casuarinaceae, incl. *Casuarina cunninghamiana* (see *river oak* RIVER 2), the rough-barked small tree *Allocasuarina verticillata* of s.e. Aust. incl. Tas., and (*W.A.*) *A. fraseriana* of s.w. W.A.; any plant of this fam. (see CASUARINA); the wood of the tree, the grain of which resembles that of the English oak; *native oak*, see NATIVE *a*. 6 a. Also with distinguishing epithet, as *coast she-oak* (see COAST), and *attrib*.

1792 *Hist. Rec. N.S.W*. (1893) II. 799 There are two kinds of oak, called the he and the she oak, but not to be compared with English oak. **1833** *Perth Gaz*. 27 July 119 The Shea Oak, or Casuarina of this Colony, admitted to be of a superior description to that of either our Eastern or Southern neighbours, is likely to become an article of more extensive export to the Cape than our Mahoganies. **1845** R. HOWITT *Impressions Aust. Felix* 231 Shiac-trees are waving their tresses in the wind. [*Note*] Shiac is the native name—vulgarised to she-oak. **1931** *Bulletin* (Sydney) 4 Feb. 20/3 'Sheoke' and 'buloke' are the names that have been adopted for two kinds of casuarinas. It was considered that 'she-oak' and 'bull-oak', the previous names would suggest a relationship with the oak of Europe which the casuarinas cannot claim.

2. *transf*. Beer brewed in Australia.

1848 *Guardian* (Hobart) 5 Apr. 5/1 She had only taken two glasses of 'she-oak', and for so doing was sentenced. **1948** R. RAVEN-HART *Canoe in Aust*. 21 What Jack called 'she-oak' (or you may spell it shea-oak, or she-oke or shea-oke—it is also slang for beer in Australia).

3. Special Comb. **she-oak net**, a safety net slung under the gangway of a ship (see quots).

1886 D.M. GANE *N.S.W. & Vic*. 51 It is called by sailors 'she-oak', whence the term 'she-oak nets' is given to the life-preservers which the Victorian authorities have thought it wise to have slung under the gangways of every ship which is moored to the Melbourne wharves. **1934** T. WOOD *Cobbers* 163 The 'She-oak Net' .. is to catch a man if he slips when going aboard; and the name .. is in memory of She-oak beer, which used to be, and may be still, a powerful agent in making him slip.

shepherd, *v*. [Transf. use of *shepherd* to tend.]

1. *trans. Obs*. To effect token occupation of (a gold-mining claim) in order to comply with the regulations governing possession: see quot. 1869. Freq. as *vbl. n*.

1852 *V & P* (Vic. L.C.) (1852–53) II. 327 There is now a practice of 'shepherding claims'... The way in which this is done is as follows: whenever a new gully is opened, one of the party goes there and marks out a claim, taking out two spits of earth to shew that he has 'taken it up and worked at it'. He repeats this daily until some other party has gone down the full depth, and has discovered whether the locality is worth working or not, and acts accordingly. This being done by the same party in perhaps eight or ten different places at once, men who would really 'set in' to work steadily are driven about from place to place. **1869** R.B. SMYTH *Gold Fields & Mineral Districts* 621 *Shepherding*, the holding possession of claims by doing the minimum amount of labour enforced by the mining by-laws. A system whereby auriferous lands are monopolized by speculators and idlers, often to the injury of the industrious miner.

2. *transf*. [Used elsewhere but recorded earliest in Aust.: see OED *v*. 4.] To keep under close surveillance.

1853 H.B. JONES *Adventures in Aust*. 299 A digger who was known to have about forty pounds weight of gold, was 'shepherded' for a considerable time, i.e. watched till a favourable opportunity presented itself to attack him. **1948** K.S. PRICHARD *Golden Miles* 98 He .. gave his instructions for the bags to be counted and shepherded to the treatment plant.

shepherd, *n. Obs*. [f. SHEPHERD *v*. 1.] One who effects token occupation of a gold-mining claim (see esp. quots. 1862 and 1909); one employed to do this.

1855 R. CARBONI *Eureka Stockade* 71 The shepherds' holes inside the lower part of the stockade had been turned into rifle-pits. **1862** J.A. PATTERSON *Gold Fields Vic*. 318 The 'shepherd' is one who marks off a claim on the supposed site of a lead or reef, and watches it while another party are 'bottoming', doing only the minimum of work requisite to secure his right to the ground .. abandoning his claim without trial if those near him should prove 'duffers'—that is to say, unfurnished with gold. **1909** W.G. SPENCE *Aust.'s Awakening* 47 They opposed the 'shepherd'—the man or company who took up a lease and did nothing but merely await a chance to sell.

shepherd's clock. *Settler's clock,* see SETTLER 3 b.

1879 'OLD HAND' *Experiences of Colonist* 24 The first sound heard in the wood was the peculiar note of the laughing jackass (dacelo gigantea), a bird so celebrated in New South Wales for his particular virtue of punctuality, that the colonists gave it the name of the 'shepherd's clock'. **1955** N. PULLIAM *I traveled Lonely Land* 381 *Laughing jackass*—one nickname for the kookaburra, the lovable mischievous and favorite bird of Australia. Other names are .. alarm bird, bushman's clock, clock-bird, settler's clock or shepherd's clock [etc.].

shepherd's companion. WILLY WAGTAIL. Also **shepherd's friend.**

1844 L. LEICHHARDT *Jrnl. Overland Exped. Aust.* 20 Dec. (1847) 80 We also observed .. the shepherd's companion, or fan-tailed fly-catcher (Rhipidura). **1903** *Bulletin* (Sydney) 2 May 16/3 Just before the western Q. heavy rains arrived a 'willie-wagtail', 'shepherds' friend' .. or whatever other alias the vivacious little black and white bird is known by.

sherang, var. SERANG.

sherbet. Also **sherbert.** [Joc. use of *sherbet* a cooling drink.] Alcoholic liquor, esp. beer.

1904 *Truth* (Sydney) 14 Feb. 1/4 The fellow that frequents a pub draws corks—the chap that drinks sherbert draws cheques. **1965** J. WYNNUM *Jiggin' in Riggin'* 36 How about .. organising after dinner entertainment before we get stuck into the sherbet.

sherrocker. *Obs.* [Of unknown origin: perh. f. Br. dial. *sherry* to scurry, run away.] In the phr. **to take sherrocker:** see quot. 1912.

1908 *Truth* (Sydney) 6 Sept. 1/5 After the Fleet had taken sherrocker, some of the Sydney business establishments which now belatedly being properly decorated. **1912** *Ibid.* 17 Mar. 7/7 Why, in a remarkably short space of time they (small blame to them) took 'sherrocker', i.e. French leave.

shiac, var. SHE-OAK.

shicer /'ʃaɪsə/. Also **scheisser, shiser, shycer.** [Transf. use of Br. slang *shicer* a worthless person: see OED(S).] An unproductive claim, mine, or goldfield.

1853 F.J. COCKBURN *Lett.* (1856) 23 When a hole is found to be contain [*sic*] no gold it is called a 'shicer'. **1855** R. CARBONI *Eureka Stockade* 10 One fine morning, a hole was bottomed down the gully, and proved a scheisser. **1861** H. EARLE *Ups & Downs* 330 How great the disappointment, when .. they discovered their hole to be a 'shycer', or a goldless one. **1880** 'ERRO' *Squattermania* 53 'That reef they were blowing about so much only went five pennyweights to the ton when they crushed ... ' 'I always said it would turn out a shiser.'

Hence as quasi-*adv.,* unproductively.

1887 *Illustr. Austral. News* (Melbourne) 25 June (Suppl.) 7/2 God pity the poor solitary wretch .. who had bottomed hole after hole a 'schicer', i.e., without finding gold in it.

shick, *a.* and *n.* [Abbrev. of SHICKER *a.* and *n.*]

A. *adj.* Drunk.

1907 *Bulletin* (Sydney) 21 Feb. (Red Page), Ah, Joy don't *all* consist in Getting Shick! **1966** J. WATEN *Season of Youth* 3 'I'm sick,' was his everlasting plea. 'Shick you mean,' she screamed.

B. *n.*

1. Alcoholic liquor.

1907 *Bulletin* (Sydney) 7 Mar. 14/2 Went on the shick and stoushed a trap wot tried to snare 'im. **1925** A. WRIGHT *Boy from Bullarah* 44 A nice job I'll have with you soon. What with th' shick, and now goin' crazy over a woman.

2. A drunkard.

1907 *Bulletin* (Sydney) 5 May 1/5 Not a soul behind the barrier at the Water on Wednesday, only one woman in the cowpen (a wretched beggar), and only a few shicks in the men's stockyard.

shicker, *a., n.* and *exclam.* Also **shiker, shikker.** [a. Yiddish *shiker* drunk: see OEDS *shicker* and also *shickery* (EDD *shiggry*). See also SHICKERED, quot. 1843.]

A. *adj.* Drunk.

1898 *Bulletin* (Sydney) 17 Dec. (Red Page), *Shiker*, drunk. **1908** *Truth* (Sydney) 27 Sept. 1/8 And Caldecott doth now relate That he and every bowling mate, Were never in that beastly state Termed 'shikker'. **1977** D. STUART *Drought Foal* 57 She goes crook when he lands home shicker.

B. *n.*

1. Alcoholic liquor; a drink of this. Esp. in the phr. **on the shicker.**

1901 *Truth* (Sydney) 31 Mar. 2/5 Toby was taking on the gold-top 'shikker' and the chicken. **1966** *Kings Cross Whisper* (Sydney) Mar. 7 Surfers Paradise beer garden, where everyone got on the shicker.

2. A drunkard.

1906 E. DYSON *Fact'ry 'Ands* 180 It's these cheap 'n' easy shickers rollin' round on their ear what brings discredit on beer. **1938** X. HERBERT *Capricornia* 257 He's the biggest shikker in Town. Now nick off, you old sponge.

C. *exclam.* As a mild oath.

1914 E. DYSON *Spats' Fact'ry* 16 S'elp me shicker, Twenty, you was the on'y pebble. **1943** *Austral. New Writing* 18 See that pup? Shicker me grandmother, she's a great bitch!

shicker, *v.* Also **shikker.** [f. prec.] *intr.* To take alcoholic liquor (to excess).

1908 *Truth* (Sydney) 19 July 9/3 But here in Australia! Well, this is a sell, We thought they all shickered, The parsons as well. **1937** WISBERG & WATERS *Bushman at Large* 279 'You haven't been shikkering have you, Nugget?' 'Shikkering and business don't mix,' declared Nugget.

Hence **shikkering** *ppl. a.*

1919 *Bulletin* (Sydney) 18 Sept. 22/4 As a God-fearing, non-shikkering Abo. let me discourse freely.

shickered, *ppl. a.* Also **shikkered.** Drunk.

[**1843** *Satirist & Sporting Chron.* (Sydney) 11 Mar. 3/3 A certain Teetotal Gent, accompanied by a companion *Just-it,* entered a public-house the other night, quite 'shuck'.]
1898 *Bulletin* (Sydney) 29 Oct. 15/1 A glass of beer is 'a pot of wollop', and the previous night he was 'on his pink', 'juiced', 'wined', or 'shikkered'. **1979** D. STIVENS *Demon Bowler* 77 By five o'clock Metho Bill wasn't the only one shickered.

shield. *Obs.* HIELEMAN.

1787 *Descr. Botany Bay, on East Side New Holland* 7 They use a shield or target of an oblong form, of about three feet long and about half that width, made of the bark of a tree. **1923** T. HALL *Short Hist. Downs Blacks* 17 *Helimon or shield* .. was used for precisely the same purpose as that of our ancient European warriors. It was made out of stinging tree wood, which was very light and soft, but tough.

shiker, shikker, varr. SHICKER a. (etc.) and v.

shikkered, var. SHICKERED.

shilling.
1. *Hist.* In the phr. **shilling-a-month-man**, see quot. 1898.

1898 G. DUNDERDALE *Bk. of Bush* 3 On the ships conveying women there were no soldiers, but an extra half-crew was engaged. These men were called 'Shilling-a-month' men, because they had agreed to work for one shilling a month for the privilege of being allowed to remain in Sydney. **1933** A.J. COTTON *With Big Herds in Aust.* 52 Most of the crew were 'shilling a month' men; that is, men who used to ship out to Australia for a shilling a month and their passage.

2. A game in which each participant contributes a shilling, the winner buying a round of drinks; a collection, esp. for the purpose of buying a round of drinks; BOB-IN.

[N.Z. **1880** *Evening Post* (Wellington) 7 Jan. 17 A man had paid his shilling in a game of 'shilling in and the winner shout'.] **1900** *Advocate* (Burnie) 29 May 4/1 They were having 'a shilling in and the winner shouts' when he arrived. **1942** G. CASEY *It's Harder for Girls* 83 We had another shilling in, and bought some bottles to take to the restaurant.

shin cracker. *Opal-mining.* Very hard, brittle, splintery rock. See also ANGEL STONE.

1919 *Huon Times* (Franklin) 21 Nov. 3/3 In a hole of that depth you would first sink through about 10 or 12 feet of 'shincracker', a hard, white substance, very brittle and somewhat resembling limestone. **1962** WHITING & RELPH *Occurrence of Opal* 7 A fine-grained white to cream claystone is associated with sandstone throughout the area. Where it is exposed at the surface it has been hardened by the concentration of secondary chalcedony and opaline silica and is known locally as 'shin-cracker'.

shindykit. *Obs.* [Alteration of *syndicate*.] A derogatory name for a business consortium.

1890 *Truth* (Sydney) 16 Nov. 1/7 When shindykits get on a job That makes their hearts with rapture throb, And I have helped them hook their fish, Do I refuse a small commish? **1916** *Ibid.* 3 Dec. 4/4 (*heading*) The tricky tote. What's Holman giving us? Will the state or a shindykit snavel the siller?

shingle. [Spec. use of *shingle* a thin piece of wood used as a house-tile.]

1. *Hist.* Used in Comb. with reference to the occupation of preparing shingles for use as a building material, as **shingle cutter, getter, splitter**.

1828 *Tasmanian* (Hobart) 3 Oct. 2 A Coroner's Inquest was lately held at Bothwell, on the body of Samuel Cok *alias* Clarke, a shingle splitter in the employ of Mr Kemp. **1842** R.G. JAMESON *N.Z., S.A., & N.S.W.* 46 Mr Cock carried his operations into the Stringy Bark Forest, where he employed a number of sawyers, splitters, and shingle cutters. **1882** A.J. BOYD *Old Colonials* 20 If I am working close alongside a shingle-getter . . we swops [*sic*] logs.

2. *fig.* A mental faculty, esp. in the phr. **to be a shingle short** and varr.

1844 D.G. BROCK *To Desert with Sturt* (1975) 64 Strolled among the hills with Kirby; poor fellow is certainly 'wanting a shingle'. **1968** *Southerly* i. 3, I reckon we're a shingle short to 'uv ended up on the Parramatta Road.

shingleback. [See quot. 1978.] BOBTAIL. Also *attrib.*

1898 *Bulletin* (Sydney) 24 Dec. 15/1 Nack's legged-snake was probably a 'shingleback'. Oily-looking reptile, either jet-black or yellow-and-brown, and never much more than 18 in. long; body thick, comparatively. **1962** H.J. FRITH *Mallee-Fowl* 53 The scrub is silent and breathless; nothing moves: the only signs of life are a few shingle-back lizards lying in the sun. **1978** B.P. MOORE *Life on Forty Acres* 107 The skink family includes an amazing variety of lizards. . . The slowest, roughest and perhaps, most interesting is the Shingleback (*Trachydosaurus rugosus*), a thick-set species with coarse, overlapping scales so large as to give it the appearance of an animated pine-cone.

shining, *a.* Used as a distinguishing epithet in the names of flora and fauna: **shining flycatcher**, the bird *Myiagra alecto* of n. Aust., New Guinea, and adjacent islands, the mature male having glossy black plumage with a blue sheen; see also *satin bird* SATIN; **gum**, the tall tree *Eucalyptus nitens* (fam. Myrtaceae) of e. Vic. and e. N.S.W.; also *attrib.*; **starling**, METALLIC STARLING.

1844 J. GOULD *Birds of Aust.* (1848) II. Pl. 88, *Piezorhynchus nitidus* . . **Shining Flycatcher** . . *Uñg-bur-ka*, Aborigines of Port Essington. **1923** *Census Plants Vic.* (Field Naturalists' Club Vic.) 47 *Eucalyptus nitens* . . **Shining Gum**. **1986** *Parkwatch* (Vic. Nat. Parks Assoc.) Mar. 17 An understorey to a long-undisturbed shining gum forest. **1909** *Emu* VIII. 256 (*caption*) Native climbing Kauri Pine in quest of nests of Shining Starling (*Calornis metallica*).

shin-plaster. *Hist.* [U.S. *shin-plaster* a piece of privately issued paper money, esp. one of a low denomination, depreciated in value, or not sufficiently secured.] A promissory note: see quot. 1920.

1900 *Truth* (Sydney) 24 June 2/6 Buchanan used to pay his men in orders on his Sydney agents, and the Coonamble storekeeper or publican could never cash these orders except by giving 'shin-plasters', as they were termed, or orders of his own. **1920** *Smith's Weekly* (Sydney) 28 Feb. 9/1 Shinplasters, issued by local business men, were simply promises to pay—flimsy notes of the face value of 10s. and 20s., not drawn on any bank, and with no real guarantee behind them.

shiny, *n.* Abbrev. of *shiny arse* (see SHINY *a.* 2).

1971 D. IRELAND *Unknown Industr. Prisoner* 287 Five days later, a shiny in the pay office was rushing about trying to find out why . . number 1208 had not clocked off. **1980** H. LUNN *Behind Banana Curtain* 191 'Don't worry, I will take you fellas,' the driver said. 'All the other cabs are taking the calls for the shiny arses but I won't be in it for the shinies.'

shiny, *a.*

1. In the phr. **just the shiny** (**shilling** or **bob**), an expression of approbation.

1901 *Western Champion* (Barcaldine) 26 Feb. 9/2 'Just the shiny bob', remarked the loquacious Bardy. . . 'We'll get the horses in alright.' **1904** *Worker* (Sydney) 6 Aug. 3/3 An it's just the shiny shilling when you larn to cure it right. **1920** *Aussie* (Sydney) Nov. 23/2 The real and compleat Cobber is very rare, like most good things, but he is 'just the shiny' when you've got him.

2. *fig.* In the collocation **shiny arse (bum, seat)**, an office worker. Also **shiny-arsed** *a.*

1945 *Atebrin Advocate: Mag. 2/4 Austral. Armoured Regiment* 28 Apr. 3 He liked being a sailor. He didn't like being a 'shiny-bum'. **1945** *Fore & Aft: 42 Austral. Landing Craft Co. A.I.F.* 26 Feb. 3 The North must . . give the 'shiny-seats' . . an idea of the work that is really being done. **1971** D. IRELAND *Unknown Industr. Prisoner* 36 The little bosses protested as reasonably as they could to the office staff—the shiny arses. **1978** B. ROSSER *This is Palm Island* 51 Some shiny arsed chair jockey down in the city . . is administering and enforcing the Queensland Aboriginal Act.

shipoo, var. SHYPOO.

shiralee /ʃɪrə'li/. Also **shirallee**. [Of unknown origin.] A swag.

1892 G. PARKER *Round Compass in Aust.* 49 Let him down easy and slow... Drop in his shirallee and water-bag by him... That's right. 1974 *Sunday Sun* (Brisbane) 5 May 4/2 The fences, the barns, the houses—they're all gone and I'm out on the road with my shiralee.

shire, *n.*
1. A rural administrative district in some Australian States. Also *attrib.*
1863 *Act* (Vic.) 27 Vict. no. 176 Sect. 279, If at any time in any district whether single or united which shall contain an area of not less than one hundred square miles the total amount actually paid in respect of the general rate then last made shall have amounted to one thousand pounds it shall be lawful for the Governor in Council to proclaim if it seem fit such district by such name as in and by such Order in Council may be assigned thereto to be a shire within the meaning of this Act. 1985 *Bombala Times* 18 July 6/3 The Shire engineer .. said that instructions had been issued to gas and destroy the rabbit burrows at the cemetery.
2. Comb. **shire council, councillor.**
1880 *Argus* (Melbourne) 7 Jan. 6/7 The council expressed itself in favour of tolls, as advocated by the South Barwon **Shire Council.** 1935 F. CLUNE *Rolling down Lachlan* 105 We admired the forethought of **shire-councillors**, who had set aside this beautiful spot for the travelling public.

shirker. *Obs.* [Spec. use of *shirker* one who evades responsibility.] SLACKER.
1918 A. WRIGHT *Breed holds Good* 33 They are not all stay-at-homes, or shirkers if you will, like me. 1936 E. SCOTT *Aust. during War* in *Official Hist. Aust. 1914–18* XI. 317 The indiscriminate labelling of apparently eligible but unenlisted men as 'shirkers'.

shirt. Used *attrib.* in Special Comb. **shirt-front** *Australian National Football.*, see quot. 1983; also *attrib.* and as *v. trans.*; **-lifter,** a male homosexual.
1964 J. POLLARD *High Mark* 75 There is a vast difference between a deliberate charge and a **shirtfront**. 1983 HIBBERD & HUTCHINSON *Barracker's Bible* 182 *Shirtfront*, a rib rattling tackle; a fiercely delivered shoulder to the chest of an opponent who is 'open', i.e. not ready. 1984 *Sunday Independent* (Perth) 9 Sept. 86/1 The Sharks overwhelmed hot favourites Swan Districts using non-stop, tear-through, shirt-front tactics in the first quarter. *Ibid.*, They were not going to tolerate being shirt-fronted all day. 1966 S.J. BAKER *Austral. Lang.* (ed. 2) 216 **Shirt lifter,** a sodomite.

shiser, var. SHICER.

shit.
1. Used *attrib.* in Special Comb. **shit catchers** *pl.*, knickerbockers (see also quot. 1981); **kicker,** an unskilled worker; a person of little consequence; **ringer,** a stockman.
1967 D. HORNE *Educ. Young Donald* 96 Knickerbockers, known among boys as 'poop catchers' or '**shit catchers**'. 1981 P. RADLEY *Jack Rivers & Me* 90 We're wearin' bowyangs... That's like when you tie a rope round the legs of your pants to stop snakes from crawling up. The boys call them shit-catchers. 1969 C. BRAY *Blossom* 35 'What's yer job?' asked Brody, grinning. 'What's yer line of country?'.. '**Shitkicker**,' he said. 'What's yours?' 1973 J. POWERS *Last of Knucklemen* (1974) 23 Thing is, you see, Pansy's not just an ordinary shitkicker like the rest of us. Pansy's had money. 1940 W. HATFIELD *Into (Great?) Unfenced* 61 How d' you mean—a job?—Here? I'm not a **shit ringer**. Don't know which end of a bull 'd bite me! No, I'm a shearer.
2. In the phr. **shit on the** (or **one's**) **liver** and varr., used in allusion to a supposed cause of ill-temper; S.O.L.
1935 H.R. WILLIAMS *Comrades of Great Adventure* 147 What's up with you, you big stiff. Got hobnails on your liver? 1951 'S. MACKENZIE' *Dead Men Rising* 14 And how is Captain Hyacinth? I trust the Captain has no more 'n 'is usual amount of s–t on the liver this morning?

shitters, *pl.* Cattle.
1940 W. HATFIELD *Into (Great?) Unfenced* 75, I don't have to frowst out here in these sand-hills chasin' shitters for a livin'.

shitty, *a.* and *n.*
A. *adj.* Bad-tempered.
1971 D. IRELAND *Unknown Industr. Prisoner* 188 'Why doesn't someone tell me?' 'Why don't you keep your ear to the ground?' 'What are you shitty about?' 'I'm not shitty.' 1971 D. WILLIAMSON *Removalists* (1972) 52 She won't be as shitty if she knows I'm getting paid.
B. *n.* A fit of bad temper.
1982 LOWENSTEIN & HILLS *Under Hook* 76 They'd say: 'Go up and tell him that it's too dirty to work today. How about letting us go home?' We wouldn't work, we'd be sitting there for two hours and if he had a shitty, old McKinnon, he wouldn't let us go home.

shiveau, var. SHIVOO *n.*

shivery grass. [Altered form of *shivering grass* a name for the quaking-grass *Briza media.*] The naturalized annual Mediterranean grass *Briza minor* (fam. Poaceae), common throughout s. Aust. incl. Tas.; the similar *B. maxima.*
1935 F. CLUNE *Rolling down Lachlan* 18 Plenty of shivery grass, shivering in the shade of stunted she-oaks. 1978 L. WHITE *Memories of Childhood* 1 Prickly bacon-and-egg bushes, shivery grass, blackboys.

Shivery Isles. New Zealand. Cf. SHAKY ISLES.
1933 *Bulletin* (Sydney) 30 Aug. 14/1 He .. lived in the Shivery Isles only a few years. 1951 *Ibid.* 18 July 14/1 Maorilanders inform me that the shellfish is regarded as a luxury in the Shivery Isles; and .. the pippi lives and feeds in a much cleaner environment than many oysters.

shivoo, *n.* Also **sheevo, shiveau.** [a. Fr. *chez vous* 'at your place', used erroneously to mean 'a party or celebration' and variously Anglicized: see OEDS *chez* (quot. 1804), *shiveau* (where Br. dial. forms are cited), and *shivoo.*] A party or celebration; a revel; a 'shindig'.
1844 J. TUCKER *Ralph Rashleigh* (1952) 165 The notes of a fiddle and tambourine, the staple music of a colonial *sheevo*, or merrymaking. 1849 A. HARRIS *Emigrant Family* (1967) 62 A 'Shiveau' at the Hut. 1985 *Bulletin* (Sydney) 15 Oct. 68/3 Tell your wife to stop scaling the mullet and .. buy a nice hat for a shivoo at Government House.

shivoo, *v.* *Obs.* [f. prec.] *intr.* To celebrate. Also *trans.*, to entertain, and as *vbl. n.*
1906 *Gadfly* (Adelaide) 18 Apr. 18/2 Last night the Semaphore shivoo'd at the Ward Street Hall to farewell popular Canon Swan. 1908 *Truth* (Sydney) 28 June 1/6 The shivooing now going on in the Big Smoke. 1908 *Ibid.* 11 Oct. 1/4 Australia, judging by the manner in which it pelted its good splosh away, shivooing the Yankee Fleet .. will shortly be known as 'The Golden Calf'.

shlanter, shlinter, varr. SLANTER.

shoddy dropper. [f. *shoddy* woollen yarn + *dropper* one who delivers goods: see OEDS *shoddy, n.* 5 and *dropper* 1 d.] One who peddles cheap or falsely-described clothing; a hawker.
[1937 E. PARTRIDGE *Dict. Slang & Unconventional Eng.* 759 *Shoddy-dropper*, a seller of cheap serge: New Zealand c. (-1932).] 1950 *Austral. Police Jrnl.* Apr. 118 *Shoddy droppers*,

a hawker [sic] of inferior or shoddy clothing which is not true to label. **1973** A. BURNETT *Wilful Murder in Outback* 42 Cotadabeen was a shoddy dropper—a travelling draper.

shoe. *Timber-getting*. See quot. 1983.
1901 *Bulletin* (Sydney) 12 Jan. 15/2 Scaffolding of big timber by means of the 'shoe'.. is an every-day occurrence with the splitters in Tasmanian gum forests. The 'shoe' is a piece of timber roughly shaped with the axe, unshod, and driven into a narrow hole previously cut into the tree about 7 in. **1983** R. BECKETT *Axemen* 53 A jigger board was a relatively simple thing... It narrowed at one end and at this end it had an iron tip or shoe. In Australia, because the boards were made of hardwood, the iron shoe was not often seen in the early days... The axemen would cut a small wedge-shaped hole for the tip of the board, insert it, iron tip first, and then balancing on the first board cut his next stand, until he had levered himself up to the required height.

shonky, *a.* and *n.* Also **shonkie.** [Prob. f. *shonk* an offensive name for a Jew: see OEDS.]
A. *adj.* Unreliable; unsound; dishonest; out of sorts.
1970 R. BEILBY *No Medals for Aphrodite* 98 'You shonkie sod!' Harry drove his fist into that vulnerable belly. **1985** *Canberra Times* 29 Sept. 2/5 (*heading*) Rajneeshees, like Liberals, a 'shonky sect'.
B. *n..* One who engages in sharp practice.
1979 *Austral. Financial Rev.* (Sydney) 25 July 11/6 Mr Groom is right when he refers to the building industry as being characterized by initiative and drive, but unless something is done to eliminate these shonkies quickly, then such qualities will be characteristic of the past.

shoofty /ˈʃʊfti/, *n.* Also **shoofti.** [Var. of Br. slang *shufti* a look, orig. Arabic: see OEDS *shufti, shufty, n.* and *shufty, v.*] A look.
1959 *R.A.N. News* (Sydney) 9 Jan. 2 No, you may *not* have a shoofty through me look-stick. **1977** R. BEILBY *Gunner* 14 'What have they got? Fuck all! No planes, buggerall transport...' 'I'll take a shoofti,' he muttered tautly.

shoofty, *a.* Also **shooftey.** [Alteration of *shifty* not straightforward.] Dishonest; deceitful; 'slippery'.
1962 J. WYNNUM *Tar Dust* 15 Trouble with you is you've been working too many shoofty moves during your long period of shore time. **1963** F. HARDY *Legends Benson's Valley* 207 Years of unemployment had given them the ability to work more shooftey points than any share jobber on the stock exchange.

shook, on (or **after**): see SHAKE *v.*²

shoot, *n.* Also **chute.**
1. *Shearing.* An inclined passage down which shorn sheep pass into a counting-out pen.
1900 H. LAWSON *On Track* 134 A great-horned ram, in poor condition, but shorn of a heavy fleece, picks himself up at the foot of the 'shoot', and hesitates, as if ashamed to go down to the other end where the ewes are. **1965** J.S. GUNN *Terminol. Shearing Industry* i. 14 Chute, also called the 'porthole', this is a low opening and ramp through which the shorn sheep are passed down to the counting-out pen.
2. *Surfing.* A breaking wave which carries a surfer towards the beach; the act of riding such a wave.
1914 M. GROVER *Minus Quantity* 14 Try a shoot... The great thing is to catch them at the right time. **1978** B. ST. A. SMITH *Spirit beyond Psyche* 99 Days of sun, laughter and vigour in the Surf Life-saving Club; long, tough swims across the pull of the sweep, the cross-currents; coming in *on the body* on a *shoot* in the company of whooping friends.

shoot, *v.*
1. *Obs. trans.* [f. *shoot* dismissal, sack: see OEDS *sb.*¹ 3 f.] To dismiss (someone) from employment.
1892 G. PARKER *Round Compass in Aust.* 447 Shot me dead, discharged me. **1899** *Bulletin* (Sydney) 19 Aug. 32/2 The boss hinted that he could make room for Sheedy and his mate by 'shooting' two less competent hands.
2. *trans. Surfing.* To ride (a wave); also *absol.*
1912 *Truth* (Sydney) 18 Feb. 8/3, I think respectable people may go surf-bathing and, still remain respectable, but people who aren't moral and respectable do not become so by shooting the breakers and airing their figures on the beaches. **1953** *Sydney Morning Herald* 3 Jan. 6/3 'Body shooting', a surfing term for catching a wave without the use of a surf board or surf ski, hence, 'shooting on the body'.
3. In the phr. **to shoot through,** to escape; to disappear; to leave. See also BONDI *n.*²
1947 *Pix* (Sydney) 20 Sept. 15 Shoot through, escape, abscond. **1960** D. IRELAND *Image in Clay* (1964) 95 Well, we were only coming back for a day or two, then we were going to shoot through. **1985** *Bulletin* (Sydney) 26 Nov. 80/1 Me wife's shot through... Can't get a bird... Can't pay the rent.
4. In the phr. **to be shot in,** to be thrown in (to gaol).
[N.Z. **1947** P. NEWTON *Wayleggo* 38 How we saw that day out without getting 'shot in' is a mystery to me yet.] **1968** S. GORE *Holy Smoke* 108 Shot in, to be, thrown in. **1972** J. BOOTH *Only Tracks Remain* 31 Your mate has been 'shot in'; I saw the police take him.

shooter. *Surfing.* [f. SHOOT *v.* 2.] One who shoots a wave.
1949 C.B. MAXWELL *Surf* 8 Bathers hitherto content to find unadventurous pleasure in the swirl round their knees became unhappily aware of the new-style human torpedoes powered by the sea. Early on there came to be a sharp .. cleavage between 'shooters' and 'non-shooters' in the South Steyne surf.

Shop. [Spec. use of Br. slang *shop* a place of business: see OED(S *sb.* 4.] With **the:** a nickname for the University of Melbourne.
1889 *Centennial Mag.* 218 It related how 'a medical student came up to the Shop' as a freshman, and 'thought through exams. he would speedily pop'. **1968** G. BAKER *Montgomery & I* 53 *Melbourne University*. The first University in the province of Victoria. Sometimes referred to in ancient documents as 'The Shop'.

shore station. *Pearling.* See quot. 1913. Also *attrib.*
1902 *Cwlth. Parl. Papers* II. 1009 The 'shellers' became divided into two parties, one called the 'shore station party', from their working from the shore, the other called the 'floating station party', from their working from their schooners. **1913** *Ibid.* III. 747 What do you mean by a shore station? In Thursday Island they send the luggers out, and have the schooner coming in periodically. They get all their supplies on shore, instead of on the boats. That is what is known as a shore station?

shornie. *Shearing.* [f. *shorn* + -Y.] A newly-shorn sheep.
1965 R.H. CONQUEST *Horses in Kitchen* 187 The shearer, be he a 'gun' or just an average man, could not maintain a steady output of shornies unless he enjoyed the loyal co-operation of the rouseabouts, to wit, the shedhands. **1982** *Bulletin* (Sydney) 13 Apr. 97/2 Instead of a penful of hard-won shornies, there was only one sheep left in the pen.

short-nosed bandicoot. [See quot. 1941.] Any of several marsupials of the genus *Isoodon* of all States, esp. *I. obesulus* of s.w., n.e., and s.e. Aust. incl. Tas.
1894 R. LYDEKKER *Hand-Bk. Marsupialia & Monotremata* 144 Short-nosed Bandicoot. *Perameles obesula.* **1941**

short-sentenced, *ppl. a. Obs.* Of a convict: sentenced to seven years of penal servitude.

1835 *Sydney Herald* 27 July 2/3 The Wollombi, comprising its own thickly-settled valley, the small farms on Ettalong, the cattle stations in the mountain ranges, and the retreats of squatters.. themselves short-sentenced expirees.. forms a district of itself. **1851** H. MELVILLE *Present State Aust.* 51 Only a sufficient number of short sentenced men should be sent there.

short-tailed, *a.* Used as a distinguishing epithet in the names of animals: **shearwater,** the bird *Puffinus tenuirostris* (see MUTTON BIRD *n.* 1); formerly also **short-tailed petrel; wallaby,** QUOKKA; also **short-tailed pademelon.**

1847 [short-tailed shearwater] J. GOULD *Birds of Aust.* (1848) VII. Pl. 56, *Puffinus brevicaudus..* Short-tailed Petrel. **1977** *Ecos* xi. 19/1 Bands were first used in 1912, when members of the Melbourne Bird Observers' Club.. placed them on Tasmanian mutton-birds (short-tailed shearwater). **1898** E.E. MORRIS *Austral Eng.* 494 **Short-tailed W[allaby]**—*M[acropus] brachyurus*. **1941** E. TROUGHTON *Furred Animals Aust.* 197 The reference occurs in a brief account published in 1658 by.. Samuel Volckersen, concerning Rottnest Island and the presence of 'two seals and a wild cat... ' The 'wild cat' was actually the short-tailed pademelon.

shot, *n.*

1. *Obs.* Dismissal from employment: see SHOOT *v.* 1.

1897 *Worker* (Sydney) 11 Sept. 1/1 'Percentage' is the thing he says the shearer-man has got Who shears his sheep just as he likes but doesn't get the 'shot'. **1898** *Bulletin* (Sydney) 17 Dec. 15/1 *Discharge,* sack, shot, or spear.

2. An attempt to provoke or 'get at' a person, esp. in the phr. **to have a shot at.**

1903 J. FURPHY *Such is Life* 125 'By heaven! I'd like to have a shot at you for a thousand!' I continued, eyeing him greedily. **1982** R. HALL *Just Relations* 52 The two branches of Swans having a shot at one another, somebody forever getting stoushed.

3. *Obs.* See quot.

1913 W.K. HARRIS *Outback in Aust.* 146 All the greatest.. celebrities of the day, were 'on the wallaby', 'humping bluey', and had called at his particular station for the proverbial free pannikin of 'dust' (flour), pinch of 'shot' (baking powder).

4. An expedient course of action; esp. as an expression of approbation in the phr. **that's the shot.**

1953 T.A.G. HUNGERFORD *Riverslake* 30 Ready to go, eh? That's the shot. **1981** C. WALLACE-CRABBE *Splinters* 56 'Beer, Bob?' Sandstone asked... 'Just the shot, thanks.' Bob was thirsty now.

shot, *ppl. a.* [U.S.: see OEDS *ppl. a.* 4 b.] Drunk.

1913 *Bulletin* (Sydney) 25 Sept. 22/2 *Inebriated..* shot. **1979** D.R. STUART *Crank back on Roller* 218 Ah well, I got shot, real staggery.. but that arrack, hell, it's great stuff.

shotty, *a. Gold-mining.* [Spec. use of *shotty* resembling shot or pellets of lead. Chiefly Austral.: see OED(S.] Of a particle of gold: small and round, resembling gun-shot. Freq. in the collocation **shotty gold.**

1860 *Rep. Mining Surveyors* (Vic. Dept. Mines) Aug. 236 There were also some very good patches of shotty gold and small nuggets found in the vicinity of this nugget. **1893** *Braidwood Dispatch* 27 May 6/2 The gold being coarse, shotty and showing no trace whatever of water action.

shoulder, *v.* In the phr. **to shoulder** (one's) **drum (knot, Matilda, swag,** etc.), to take to the road.

1894 *Bulletin* (Sydney) 14 Apr. 24/3 With a strong right arm and a willing hand, He shouldered his 'drum' to the Thirsty Land. **1896** H. LAWSON *While Billy Boils* (1975) 41 Macquarie afterwards shouldered his swag and staggered and struggled along the track ten miles to the Union Town hospital. **1914** *Bulletin* (Sydney) 21 May 24/1 We took the rattler to Echuca, but.. shouldered our knots from there. **1940** I.L. IDRIESS *Lightning Ridge* 125 Nearly broke, it was a case of again shouldering Matilda and looking for a job.

shouse. Also **shoush, sh'touse.** [Syncopated form of *shit-house.*] A lavatory. Also *fig.* and *attrib.*

1941 S.J. BAKER *Pop. Dict. Austral. Slang* 66 *Shouse,* a privy. **1978** B. ROSSER *This is Palm Island* 39 Instantly a black head.. appeared above the door of the next cubicle... He bounded out of that shoush like a rocket. **1981** B. GREEN *Small Town Rising* 119 That's a pretty sh'touse deal and you know it.

shout, *n.* [f. SHOUT *v.* Used elsewhere but recorded earliest in Aust.]

1. a. The purchase of a round of drinks for an assembled company; the round of drinks itself.

1854 T.F. BRIDE *Lett. Victorian Pioneers* (1898) 127 Do you forget the shout you stood—the shout for all hands? **1979** K. GARVEY *Absolutely Austral.* 73 So I'll put down my ignorant pen, and stand you all a shout.

b. *transf.* and *fig.* Also **shout-out,** a helping hand.

1916 H. LAWSON *Lett.* (1970) 238 The receipt for boots represents one 'shout' for the children, two pairs each. **1980** O. RUHEN *Bullock Teams* 232, I offered to give him a 'shout-out' and he accepted gladly. I remarked what big sturdy stock he had in the pole and pin. 'No good trying to stir those bastards,' he said... 'When I start your load moving call the bullocks in front.'

2. One's turn to buy a round of drinks for an assembled company.

1882 *Sydney Slang Dict.* 8 *Shout,* to pay for drinks. 'It's my 'shout'!' **1982** R. HALL *Just Relations* 56 My shout, he said, slapping the money down beside the hand.

shout, *v.* [Transf. use of *shout* to call (for drinks).]

1. a. *intr.* To pay for a round of drinks, esp. one given freely to an assembled company.

1850 *Monthly Almanac* (Adelaide) 7 Well, he gets out, and is immediately enjoined to 'shout' on the spot... A moderate request which he, in his innocence, is about complying with literally.. but being naturally apt, ultimately discovers that 'shouting' signifies paying for nine nobblers, four spiders, various glasses, and an indefinite quantity of blunted stunted things, called by courtesy cigars. **1986** *Bulletin* (Sydney) 28 Jan. 46/3 Anyone shooting a hole in one must shout for all players present on the course at that time.

b. *transf.* and *fig.*

1861 H. EARLE *Ups & Downs* 223 The governor shouted heavy, and gave us all a excellent feed. **1925** *Bulletin* (Sydney) 26 Mar. 24/3, I flatly deny the statement.. that when swifts circle high up in a desultory fashion the clouds are about to 'shout' for the thirsty earth.

2. a. *trans.* To buy (a drink or round of drinks); to buy a drink for (a person); also with indirect obj.

1854 *Illustr. Sydney News* 14 Oct. 292/3 The fortunate owners when they bottom on the gutter generally 'shout' champagne for all hands in the immediate neighbourhood. **1916** J.M. CREED *Recoll. Aust.* 73, I did not think it necessary to insult any elector by supposing it was necessary to shout grog for him in order to secure his vote. **1977** W. MOORE *Just to Myself* 102 All Merv's mates shouted him at the pub for a week.

b. *transf.* To make (a present), to give (a treat), etc.;

to make a present to (someone); also with indirect obj.

1896 *Bulletin* (Sydney) 9 May 3/2 In a Melb. restaurant, the other night, a certain flash young jock condescended to chaff his two middle-aged companions, one of whom had 'shouted' the dinner. **1912** *Ibid.* 26 Dec. 15/4 I'll shout a trip (first-class) for him from Sydney to Narrandera. **1981** P. RADLEY *Jack Rivers & Me* 137 'I pay my way!' 'You wouldn't shout a moll a packet of Condy's Crystals.'

shouter. One who 'shouts': see SHOUT *v.* 1 a.

1862 C. MUNRO *Fern Vale* I. 50 'A shout', in the parlance of the Australian bush, is an authority or request to the party in waiting in a public-house to supply the bibulous wants of the companions of the shouter, who of course bears the expense. **1919** A. WRIGHT *Game of Chance* 113 Expressing admiration for the 'shouter'.

shouting, *vbl. n.* The practice of 'shouting': see SHOUT *v.* 1 a. Also *attrib.*

1850 [SEE SHOUT *v.* 1 a.]. **1855** R. CARBONI *Eureka Stockade* 67 Their glory is to stand oceans of grog, joined to their benevolence of 'shouting', for all hands. **1919** A. WRIGHT *Game of Chance* 69 Showed no inclination to lose sight of him while he held some shouting silver.

shoveller. Also **shoveler.** [Transf. use of *shoveller* the Northern Hemisphere duck *Anas clypeata*, having a broad shovel-like beak, and recorded as a rare visitor to Aust.] The duck *Anas rhynchotis rhynchotis* of s.w. and e. Aust. incl. Tas.

1845 J. GOULD *Birds of Aust.* (1848) VII. Pl. 13 [The 'Membranaceous Duck'] passes through the air with great quickness, like the Green-necked Duck and Shoveller, with both of which species it is frequently found in company. **1984** M. BLAKERS et al. *Atlas Austral. Birds* 80 The Shoveler feeds by filtering surface water through its bill, sometimes upending and dredging on the bottom.

shovel-nosed lobster. Any of several marine crustaceans having a flattened appearance and characteristic shovel-shaped ends of the main feelers, incl. the *Moreton Bay bug* (see MORETON BAY) and BALMAIN BUG.

1966 T.C. ROUGHLEY *Fish & Fisheries Aust.* 315 Lobster, shovel-nosed [minimal legal length in inches] 3. **1983** J. JONES *Macquarie Dict. Cookery* 200 Balmain bug. An edible crustacean, *Ibacus incisus*, known also as shovel-nosed lobster, and related to the Moreton Bay Bugs of Queensland.

shovel-spear. An Aboriginal weapon: see quot. 1962. Also **shovel-head(ed spear), shovel-nose(d) spear.**

1930 J.S. LITCHFIELD *Far-North Memories* 122 Another kind of blade was made of one flat piece of iron about an inch and a half broad, with its sides and point as sharp as a blackfellow could make them. These were known as 'shovel' spears, and were mostly used for slaying enemies. **1946** W.E. HARNEY *North of 23°* 84 He promptly ordered a ton of shovels to build dams to hold water. These the blackmen used to make shovel-nosed spears to kill the cattle. I believe that is where the name of these things came from. **1962** D. LOCKWOOD *I, Aboriginal* 96 The shovel-nose spear, as its name implies, has a killing-head made of iron. This may be an old horseshoe, a piece of galvanized pipe, or a flat section cut from an abandoned water-tank. In my grandfather's day iron was scarce on the Roper and was highly prized. In his grandfather's day it was unknown. Spears were than made entirely of wood, or with a stone killing-head. **1976** C.D. MILLS *Hobble Chains & Greenhide* 20 I'd got to about fifty yards and I reckoned I would draw a bead on him when a big buck raced up the ant-bed from the back and downed him with a shovel-head (shovel-headed spear).

show, *n.*[1] [U.S.: see OED(S *sb.*[1] 3 c.]

a. An opportunity for doing something; a chance.

1876 *Austral. Town & Country Jrnl.* (Sydney) Nov. 11 782/2 As he's a gentleman, he's bound to give you a show. **1959** D. NILAND *Gold in Streets* 181 Goo' fight, Johnny. I didn't have a show.

b. In the collocation **fair show:** see FAIR *a.*[1] 1.

show, *n.*[2] [Transf. use of *show* an indication of the presence of the mineral sought: see OED(S *sb.*[1] 5 c.] A mine.

1898 E. DYSON *Below & on Top* 130 Jump this show, Humpy! Why there is not gold enough in a mile of it to buy a peanut. **1978** D. STUART *Wedgetail View* 42 'Yes, you'll get a job in the Bar, no trouble now that a company's taken over the Comet.' 'She's a good show, is she? A goer?'

shower. [Used elsewhere but recorded earliest in Aust.] In the phr. **I (he, they,** etc.**) didn't come down in the last shower,** an indication that one is not without experience.

[**1906** J. FURPHY *Rigby's Romance* (1946) 256 He didn't come down with the las' rain. Pity that sort o' bloke ever dies.] **1944** L. GLASSOP *We were Rats* 51 'Listen, Mr Wilkerson', I says, 'I'm awake-up, I am. Ya doan need ter come that stuff with me. I didden come down in the last shower.' **1984** *Weekend Austral. Mag.* (Sydney) 30 June 12/6 An irate theatregoer says its about time they stopped treating patrons as though they had come down in the last shower, especially when they are being charged $25 for the privilege. This week he went to hear Shirley Bassey and had to spend the first hour listening to a ventriloquist.

show pony. One who gives more attention to appearances than to performance.

1964 J. POLLARD *High Mark* 19 Don't become one of those football 'show ponies' who wear more bandages than some of those race horses we see. **1985** *Bulletin* (Sydney) 10 Dec. 25/3 He may be an extrovert but he's not a show pony.

shrewdie. Also **shrewdy.** [f. *shrewd* + -Y; used elsewhere but recorded earliest in Aust.]

1. A shrewd or cunning person.

1904 *Truth* (Sydney) 17 July 10/7 He was regarded as what the Sydney boys of the present would call a 'shrewdie'. **1929** 'F. BLAIR' *Digger Sea-Mates* 254 'You're one of the 'shrewdies', Lockie, ain't you?' 'You'll need to know a lot', spoke up Robertson, 'before you'll be a 'shrewdy' in old London yonder.'

2. A crafty scheme.

1960 J. WYNNUM *Sailor Blushed* (1962) 120 I'll have a gander at that as soon as I'm free, and if I think you're trying to pull a shrewdie, you'll finish up doing jankers.

shrike. [Transf. use of *shrike* a bird of the fam. Laniidae.] Used *attrib.* in the names of birds: **shrike-robin,** any of several greyish or grey and yellow robins of the genera *Eopsaltria* and *Tregellasia* of mainland Aust. (see *white-breasted robin* WHITE *a.*[2] 1 b., *yellow robin* YELLOW 1); **-thrush,** any of the several birds of the genus *Colluricincla* of all States and the New Guinea region, having a melodious song, esp. the widespread *grey thrush* (see GREY *a.*); see also THRUSH; **- tit,** the bird *Falcunculus frontatus* of e., s.w., and n. mainland Aust., having a black and white striped head and a heavy, hooked bill; *yellow-bellied shrike-tit*, see YELLOW 1.

1895 *Rep. Sixth Meeting Australasian Assoc. Advancement of Science, Brisbane* 447 By retaining the term 'Robin' for the best known member of the group (*Petroica*), and applying a qualifying noun to the allied genera, such titles as . . **Shrike-robin** were easily evolved. **1942** C. BARRETT *From Bush Hut* 74 Three kinds of robins frequent the garden: the scarlet-breasted species, the flame robin, and 'Yellow Bob', the shrike-robin. **1896** *Melburnian* 28 Aug. 54 The spotted thrush of England gives forth .. his full and varied notes; notes which no Australian bird can challenge, not even the **shrike-thrush** on the hill side, piping hard to rival his song every bright spring morning. **1965** *Austral. Encycl.* VIII. 494 Other Australian birds known as thrushes, but more correctly shrike-thrushes, are members of the genus *Colluricincla*. These comprise seven species of thrush-like insectivorous birds which are in general grey or brown. **1890** *Act* (Vic.) 54 Vict. no. 1095 3rd Sched., **Shrike-tit** .. from the first day of August to the twentieth day of December next following in each year.

sh'touse, var. SHOUSE.

shycer, var. SHICER.

shypoo /ʃaɪˈpuː/, *n.* and *a.* Chiefly *W.A.* Also **shipoo**. [Of unknown origin; but see sense 2, quot. 1962.]

A. *n.*

1. Inferior alcoholic liquor, esp. beer.
1897 *Bulletin* (Sydney) 25 Sept. 3/2 And he paid for the shypoo With the crispy notes and new. **1962** MARSHALL & DRYSDALE *Journey among Men* 160 Men in cotton shirts and corduroys met there to buy provisions and to 'blue' their cheques on fiery spirits or *shypoo*, as Colonial beer was called.

2. An (unlicensed) establishment which sells such liquor. Usu. in Comb. as **shypoo joint, shop,** etc.
1903 MARSHALL & DRYSDALE *Battling for Gold* 25 Despite the fact that all drinks were 1s. each, all the hotels, as well as the 'shypoo' shops (unlicensed groggeries) were doing splendid business. **1914** *Truth* (Sydney) 8 Nov. 1/3 Some of Sydney's flash shypoo pubs. **1936** H. DRAKE-BROCKMAN *Sheba Lane* 237 How about managing that shipoo for me? **1947** F. CLUNE *Roaming around Aust.* 115 Along the beach were sly-grog shops—which are called 'shypoo joints' in the West. **1962** T. RONAN *Deep of Sky* 218 It ran to two pubs and a hostelry named the Bull and Bush Inn, the licensee of which was restricted to the sale of beer and wine. Locally this was known as the 'Shypoo Shop'. I'm not sure of the derivation of 'Shypoo'. I think it is bastard Chinese for soft drink. To the sturdy second wave of pioneers of West Kimberley, beer and wine were soft drinks.

B. *adj.* Inferior.
1902 *Truth* (Sydney) 3 Aug. 7/1 He was a solicitor of the 'shypoo' sort—that is, a lawyer who had few, if any, clients, and who lived 'on his wits'. **1952** C. SIMPSON *Come away, Pearler* 230 There's half a dozen .. decided the beer at the Dampo wasn't such shypoo stuff after all, the week after she arrived.

shyster. Alteration of SHICER. Also **shyster mine.**
1910 L. ESSON *Woman Tamer* (1976) 71 We're all thieves. .. One bloke, he says, does the trick with a silk hat on the Stock Exchange, and a shyster mine. We do it with a jemmy. **1941** S.J. BAKER *Pop. Dict. Austral. Slang* 66 *Shyster*, a worthless mine.

sickie. [f. *sick(-leave* + -Y.]

1. A day's sick leave; esp. as taken without sufficient medical reason. Also *attrib.*
1953 T.A.G. HUNGERFORD *Riverslake* 197 Why don't you go back to bed and have a sickie? **1961** *Bulletin* (Sydney) 7 Oct. 20/2 They allow new restrictive practices to grow up and curry favor .. by extending meal-hours or smoko-breaks, by tolerating absenteeism and actively encouraging 'sickies' and overtime rackets. **1966** *Kings Cross Whisper* (Sydney) May 2/3 Will prescribe 'sickie' certificates at the usual rates of reward.

2. *transf.* A sick person or animal.
1968 G. MILL *Nobody dies but Me* 138 There were two sickies in the waiting room when I barged in. **1977** C. McCULLOUGH *Thorn Birds* 400 The bunnies have died in millions. .. You'll sometimes see a few sickies around with huge lumps all over their faces.

side, *n.*^{1}

1. Used as an abbrev. for (a specified) side of a natural barrier or border; orig. of New South Wales from a South Australian perspective. See also OTHER SIDE, *Sydney-side* SYDNEY 1, TOTHER SIDE.
1846 [see *Sydney-side* SYDNEY 1]. **1847** G.F. ANGAS *Savage Life & Scenes* I. 167 This was one of the sheep stations of Messrs. Arthur, who had penetrated into this charming country from the New South Wales side, and had brought several of their flocks for the purpose of squatting upon these new pastures. **1977** D. WHITTINGTON *Strive to be Fair* 28 He'd rung some sheds of larger size out on the Queensland side.

2. *transf.* [Prob. an independent development from sense 1, but see OED *sb.*^{1} 15 b.] A (specified) district or region.
1892 N. BARTLEY *Opals & Agates* 105, I soon met Matthew Goggs (also well heard of on the Murrumbidgee side). **1956** T. RONAN *Moleskin Midas* 77 With his beefhouse completed, he got himself a killer from the Twin Hills side.

Hence **sider** *n.*, an inhabitant of a (specified) district.
1865 [see *Sydney sider* SYDNEY 1]. **1904** *Bulletin* (Sydney) 15 Dec. 18/2 The Murray-siders are then giving up the ghost.

side, *n.*^{2} *Two-up.*

1. The body of players as distinct from the SPINNER and *ring-keeper* (see RING *n.*^{2} 2). Esp. in the phr. **on the side:** see *side bet* below.
1918 C.E.W. BEAN *Diary* 8 May 45 Franc wanted .. Heads one Any on the side Heads ten. Heads forty, forty on the nut. **1953** T.A.G. HUNGERFORD *Riverslake* 129 'All right, gents', he called out, 'there's one hundred and forty quid in the guts—get it set before you bet on the side.'

2. Special Comb. **side bet,** a wager laid by a player with another player rather than with the spinner; so **side bettor.**
1931 O. WALTERS *Shrapnel Green* 26 The centre was set, the side-bets on, and Mick was ready to toss. **1946** *Austral. New Writing* 36 Tail bettors toss in their money and soon the pound is covered. Again the side bettors 'get set'.

side board. A shearing shed in which the shearing is done along the two long sides rather than in the centre. Also **side board shed.** See BOARD 1.
1893 'TIMES SPECIAL CORRESPONDENT' *Lett. from Qld.* 81 A shearing shed in full swing is a striking sight. There are two kinds, known respectively as 'central boards' and 'side boards'. In the one the shearing is done in the middle and the sheep penned all round. In the other the sheep are penned in the middle and the shearing is done upon the sides. **1979** HARMSWORTH & DAY *Wool & Mohair* 141 Side board sheds are unsatisfactory because, when sheep are shorn, they must either be dragged cross the board or allowed to walk across at a time when the fleece may still be on the board.

side verandah: see VERANDAH.

siding. Alteration of 'sideling', a slope or declivity.
1852 *Hobarton Guardian* 26 May 4/1 No *culverts* on the 'sidings' of the hills along which the roads passed. **1931** F.D. DAVISON *Man-Shy* (1962) 126 On a certain morning .. the scrubbers were grazing along an ironbark siding.

sight. *Mining.* In the phr. **in sight:** (of a mineral) potentially able to be mined.
1845 *S. Austral. Register* (Adelaide) 19 Nov. 2/5 A gentleman who paid a visit to the Burra Burra Mines found 300 tons lying at the mine ready for sending away—and large masses of ore 'in sight' equal to the production of 3000 tons

more. **1911** E.D. CLELAND *W. Austral. Mining Practice* 15 Lessen the apparent amount of ore 'in sight' between any two levels.

silent cop. See quot. 1934.
1934 T. WOOD *Cobbers* 122 A circle in the middle of crossroads .. round which all traffic changing direction must swing; a round yellow blob, known here as the Silent Cop, or the Poached Egg. **1969** E. WALLER *And there's Opal* 41 Look, if you find a hill higher than a 'silent cop', you'll have the Shire people out and naming it Mount Everest.

silkwood. Any of several trees, esp. the rainforest tree *Flindersia pimenteliana* (fam. Rutaceae) of n.e. Qld. and New Guinea; the wood of these trees.
1909 F.M. BAILEY *Comprehensive Catal. Qld. Plants* (ed. 2) 91 Flindersia Chatawaiana .. has .. been called 'Silkwood'. **1986** *Herald* (Melbourne) 2 May (Suppl.) 5/1 Despite the use of timbers such as silkwood .. the cost of each dinghy is around $350 in materials.

silky heads. A tussocky perennial grass of the genus *Cymbopogon* (fam. Poaceae), esp. the aromatic *C. obtectus* of inland mainland Aust.
1895 F. TURNER *Austral. Grasses* I. 4 *Andropogon bombycinus* .. (Referring to the inflorescence resembling masses of silk.) 'Silky Heads'. **1981** J.A. BAINES *Austral. Plant Genera* 113 *C[ymbopogon] obtectus*, silky-heads, all mainland States, but extremely rare in V[ictoria].

silky oak. Any of many trees of the fam. Proteaceae, usu. rainforest species of n. and e. Aust. yielding an oak-like timber of silky texture; esp. the tall, commonly cultivated *Grevillea robusta* of n.e. N.S.W. and s.e. Qld., having feathery foliage and golden orange flowers, and *Cardwellia sublimis* of n.e. Qld., having pinnate leaves and a large, woody fruit; the wood of these trees. Formerly also **silk oak**.
1836 J. BACKHOUSE *Narr. Visit Austral. Colonies* (1843) 365 The Silk Oak, *Grevillea robusta*, also forms a large tree. **1938** C.T. WHITE *Princ. Bot. Qld. Farmers* 158 To the Queenslander, the main interest in *Proteaceae* arises in the beauty and value of the timbers, several of which are cut and sold indiscriminately under the name of Silky Oak. In previous years the familiar *Grevillea robusta* provided all the Silky Oak of the trade, but now practically all comes from various North Queensland trees—mostly *Cardwellia sublimis*.

silver, *a.*
1. Used as a distinguishing epithet in the names of flora and fauna: **silver ash**, any of several rainforest trees of the genus *Flindersia* (fam. Rutaceae) yielding a silvery, ash-like wood, incl. *F. bourjotiana* of n.e. Qld.; the wood of the tree; **banksia,** the shrub or tree *Banksia marginata* (fam. Proteaceae) of s.e. Aust. incl. Tas., having leaves which are silvery-white underneath; **belly,** any of many small marine fish, esp. those of the fam. Gerreidae (also *silver biddy*), incl. the common *Gerres ovatus*; **biddy,** a small fish of the fam. Gerreidae (see *silver belly*); **bream,** any of several fish, esp. *Acanthopagrus butcheri* (see *black bream* BLACK *a.*[2] 1 b.); **dory,** the marine fish *Cyttus australis* of s. Aust.; **eel,** any of several silvery eels incl. *Muraenesox cinereus* and *Anguilla australis*; **-eye,** a small bird of the genus *Zosterops* of Aust. and elsewhere, having a conspicuous white eye-ring, esp. the common widespread *Z. lateralis*; *white-eye*, see WHITE *a.*[2] 1 b.; **fish,** any of several silvery fish, esp. of the fam. Atherinidae, having a silvery band along the sides; **grass,** any of several annual or perennial grasses (fam. Poaceae) incl. the native *Aristida contorta* (see *mulga grass* MULGA *n.*[1] 3), and the introduced European *Vulpia bromoides*; **gull,** the predom. white and grey gull *Larus novaehollandiae* of coastal and inland waters of all States, and elsewhere; **-leaf** (or **-leaved**) **box,** the small tree *Eucalyptus pruinosa* (fam. Myrtaceae) of n. Aust.; **-leaved** (**-leaf, -leafed**) **ironbark,** the small to medium tree *Eucalyptus melanophloia* (fam. Myrtaceae) of Qld. and n. N.S.W., having bluish-grey foliage; **perch,** any of several fish, esp. the fresh-water *Bidyanus bidyanus*; see also GRUNTER; **wattle,** any of several shrubs or trees of the genus *Acacia* (fam. Mimosaceae), esp. *A. dealbata* of N.S.W., Vic., and Tas., and naturalized in S.A., usu. having silvery foliage; the wood of the tree.

1927 *Bulletin* (Sydney) 3 Nov. 27/4 Bumpy ash is .. known also as cudgerie, mountain ash and **silver ash**. **1970** W.D. FRANCIS *Austral. Rain-Forest Trees* (ed. 3) 429 *Flindersia pubescens* .. Northern Silver Ash. .. Swain includes this species with *F. schottiana* and *F. bourjotiana* under the common name of Silver Ash on account of the similar qualities and applications of the timbers of the three species. The timbers are described by him as firm, tough, strong and usually lustrous white, straight and open grained. **1923** *Census Plants Vic.* (Field Naturalists' Club Vic.) 24 *Banksia marginata* .. **Silver Banksia**. **1882** J.E. TENISON-WOODS *Fish & Fisheries N.S.W.* 44 It is necessary to cook the **silver-belly**, as it is often called, perfectly fresh .. otherwise .. it is flavourless, flabby, and soft. **1906** D.G. STEAD *Fishes of Aust.* 118 Other names by which it [*sc.* the common Silverbelly] is sometimes known are: 'Silver Bream' and '**Silver-Biddy**'. **1870** E.B. KENNEDY *Four Yrs. in Qld.* 123 There are plenty of fish in all the lagoons and rivers; black bream, **silver bream**. **1906** D.G. STEAD *Fishes of Aust.* 176 The **Silver Dory** (*Cyttus australis*) .. is of a beautiful uniform silvery appearance (though more roseate when first captured). **1871** *Austral. Town & Country Jrnl.* (Sydney) 21 June 88/3 A small yellow-backed variety with a shining white belly forming what are denominated '**silver-eels**' abound in waterholes. **1862** E. WARD *Vineyards & Orchards S.A.* 40 A border of trees of various kinds which had been planted on the east of one vineyard were grubbed up two years ago, because they afforded a shelter to the '**Silver-eye**', a bird very destructive to vines. **1832** F. MOORE *Diary Ten Yrs. W.A.* 14 Sept. (1884) 136 The **silver fish** (perch), and the guard fish, sometimes come up the river. **1848** W. ARCHER *Diary* 18 Feb., Preparing for burning off the **silver grass** &c. on lower Stony Pt. **1897** L. LINDLEY-COWEN *W. Austral. Settler's Guide* 79 The chief pasture plants are corkscrew and silver grass, which are very fattening. **1848** J. GOULD *Birds of Aust.* VII. Pl. 20, *Xema jamesonii* .. **Silver Gull**. **1884** [**silver-leaf box**] E. PALMER *Notes Austral. Tribes* 47 *Eucalyptus pruinosa*... Native name on Cloncurry *Kullingal*. Silver-leaved box, 20 feet high, stunted and crooked growth. **1983** R.J. PETHERAM *Plants Kimberley Region W.A.* 445 *Eucalyptus pruinosa* Silver Box, Silver-leaf Box. .. A small straggly tree with blue-grey foliage. **1844** L. LEICHHARDT *Jrnl. Overland Exped. Aust.* 5 Nov. (1847) 30 Extensive flooded gum-flats and ridges, clothed with a forest of **silver-leaved Ironbark**. **1849** *N.S.W. Sporting Mag.* (Sydney) 1 Jan. 162 It consisted of alternate downs and open forest, the latter silver-leafed iron bark. **1934** 'S. RUDD' *Green Grey Homestead* 82 You'll turn your thoughts to the bee's nest in the gully near your cultivation paddock. It's been there in that silver-leaf ironbark for three years. **1861** *Burke & Wills Exploring Exped.* 9 Caught five **silver perch**, weighing from 1½ lb. to 3 lb. **1824** *Austral.* (Sydney) 21 Oct. 2 Black and **silver wattle** .. for house work and furniture. **1878** R.B. SMYTH *Aborigines of Vic.* I. 378 The wood of the silver wattle (*Acacia dealbata*) was used for making the handles of tomahawks.

2. In miscellaneous special collocations: **silver cheque,** a (shearer's) wage-cheque for less than £2; **city,** the silver-mining town of Broken Hill, N.S.W.

1897 *Worker* (Sydney) 13 Nov. 3/4 They not only go in for 'freedom of contract', but likewise, endeavour to apply that principle to 'free drinks' and, when they receive their '**silver cheques**' at the cut-out, *Fold their tents like the Arabs And as silently steal away*. **1891** *Quiz* (Adelaide) 1 May 7/1 The **Silver City** is the scene of the following story.

silvertail, *a.* and *n.* [Prob. orig. with reference to the wearing of dress uniforms.]

A. *adj.* Socially prominent; having social aspirations; privileged.

1887 *Bulletin* (Sydney) 12 Nov. 4/1 In their thoughts and expressions they betray the . . 'silver-tail' era. **1986** *Canberra Times* 31 Mar. 19 (*heading*) Rundown Roos first hurdle for silvertail Swans.

B. *n.* One who is socially prominent or who displays social aspirations; a privileged person.

1891 *Truth* (Sydney) 12 Apr. 1/3 Sir Henry always was a 'silvertail', and his love for a lord is as great to-day as ever. **1985** *Canberra Times* 18 Dec. 28/5 Mr Justice Barry Maddern, who has been described as a silvertail and lives in Toorak, Melbourne, once tried to gain Liberal preselection for the Federal seat of Gellibrand.

silvertail, *v.* [f. prec.] *trans.* See quot.

1922 H. LAWSON *Lett.* (1970) 266 When they pointedly gave him the cold shoulder, he wanted to know what they were 'silver-tailin" *him* for?

silvertailed, *ppl. a.* SILVERTAIL *a.*

1890 A.J. VOGAN *Black Police* 116 A select circle of long-limbed members of those upper circles who belong to the genus termed in Australian parlance 'silver-tailed', in distinction to the 'copper-tailed' democratic classes. **1984** *Nat. Times* (Sydney) 9 Mar. 18/1 Last month in Parliament he spat out a string of acidic references to her as 'this whited sepulchre', 'this scion of society' and as a member of the 'silvertailed aristocracy'.

silvertop.

1. Any of several trees of the genus *Eucalyptus* (fam. Myrtaceae) having smooth-barked, silvery-white upper branches, esp. *E. sieberi* of N.S.W., Vic., and Tas., the trunk of which has a dark, deeply-furrowed bark. Also *attrib.*, and (esp. outside Vic.) **silvertop ash**.

1896 *Proc. Linnean Soc. N.S.W.* XXI. 800 The most westerly locality . . is Mudgee, where it [*sc. Eucalyptus capitellata*] is called 'Silvertop'. **1969** S. KELLY *Eucalypts* 51 Silvertop ash . . grows on sandy soils. **1985** J. GALBRAITH *Garden in Valley* 9 On the drier slopes . . Silvertop forests were more open.

2. [Also U.S.: see Mathews *silver* 1.] An expensive drink: cf. *gold top* GOLD 4.

1855 *Ovens & Murray Advertiser* (Beechworth) 17 Feb. 5/2 This is the first time that we have witnessed a storm of 'sherry cobblers' and 'silver tops'. **1940** *Sentry Go* (Keswick) July 29 Hardly expect a Silver Top for a tray a mile.

silver-topped gimlet: see GIMLET b.

silvery, *a.* Ostentatiously expensive: see SILVERTAIL.

1979 M. RUTHERFORD *Departmental* 37 Big executive houses just out of town but near the beach. Pool, couple of garages, a few big trees—private you know. . . Yeah. You don't live in one yourself, I hope? . . No, that would look a bit silvery.

sin-bin, *n. Rugby League*. [Transf. use of N. Amer. *sin-bin* penalty box (in ice hockey): see OEDS *sin*, *sb.* 6.]

1. A penalty box; the place where a player sent off the field for an infringement of the rules spends a specified period of time.

1981 T. RAUDONIKIS *Rugby League Stories* 11 As we start the 1981 season, we have more changes to get used to, such as differential penalties and the 'sin bin'. **1985** *Sydney Morning Herald* 22 June 2/6 They started to head-butt each other like a couple of randy Rocky Mountain goats while on their respective ways to the sin bin.

2. *transf. Shag-wagon*, see SHAG *n.*²

1980 *Age* (Melbourne) 5 Sept. 1/2 One group of locales that escaped the name of brothel . . was cars, panel vans, and other sin-bins.

sin-bin, *v.* [f. SIN-BIN *n.* 1.] *trans.* To send (a player) from the field as a penalty. Also *fig.* and as *vbl. n.*

1983 *Nat. Times* (Sydney) 1 July 14/3 While Wran is 'sin-binned' the party should be loyal to acting Premier Ferguson. **1984** *Austral.* (Sydney) 21 June 17/2 McInerney was sin-binned for 10 minutes in the second half along with Counties' lock and captain Alan Dawson after a dust-up between the pair. **1986** *Canberra Times* 1 May 30/1 Sin-binning will be introduced in ACT rugby from Saturday.

sing, *v.*

1. *trans.* Of an Aboriginal: to impart supernatural powers to (an object) by incantation; to bring a (freq. malign) supernatural influence to bear on (a person or thing) by incantation.

1896 B. SPENCER *Rep. Horn Sci. Exped. Central Aust.* IV. 130 The man, on being told that the spear which had caused the injury had been 'sung', that is, had undergone an incantation which bewitched it, proceeded to pine away, and he eventually died without the supervention of any surgical complications which could be detected. **1984** *N.T. News* (Darwin) 20 Sept. 6/5 'I like to think the black man sang them,' he says. 'They did a lot of singing the white man. They're sort of having their revenge.'

2. *transf.* In the phr. **to sing the cattle**, to soothe resting cattle: see quot. 1971.

1969 J. DINGWELL *One String* 47 Brother Seb rode her once again up the hill to listen to the stockmen 'singing the cattle'. **1971** P. ADAM SMITH *No Tribesman* 9 And then it began. Gently, softly at first, the stockmen began to 'sing' the cattle, make them aware and content in the presence of men. . . So, they sing the cattle.

Singapore ant. [See quot. 1930.] The small ant *Monomorium destructor*, introduced into tropical Aust. Also *attrib.*

1930 *Northern Standard* (Darwin) 7 Oct. 3/4 Singapore Ants. It is said that these ants came from Singapore secreted in cargo landed at Darwin from India. . . Anything smellful will draw them to concentrate upon it in straight lines from their nookeries. . . Townships and bushlands are in a state of Singapore ant saturation. **1965** *Austral. Encycl.* I. 212 The few species [of *Monomorium*, etc.] that have been introduced are collectively known (according to locality) as house ants, ship ants and Singapore ants. These pests cause most trouble in Western Australia and Queensland, but are bad enough elsewhere at times.

singing, *ppl. a.* Used as a distinguishing epithet in the names of birds: **singing honeyeater**, the predom. grey-brown honeyeater *Lichenostomus virescens* of mainland Aust.; **lark**, SONG-LARK.

1845 J. GOULD *Birds of Aust.* (1848) IV. Pl. 33, *Ptilotis sonorus* . . **Singing Honey-eater**. **1847** J. GOULD *Birds of Aust.* (1848) III. Pl. 76, *Cincloramphus rufescens* . . **Singing Lark** of the Colonists.

singing string. OVERLAND TELEGRAPH.

1957 F. CLUNE *Fortune Hunters* 41 The Aborigines called the O.T. line the 'Singing String'. **1962** D. LOCKWOOD *I, Aboriginal* 44 The Singing String—the Overland Telegraph Line—was thrown across the country in my grandfather's day.

single, *n. Australian National Football*. BEHIND 1.

1960 *N.T. News* (Darwin) 5 Jan. 7/5 Three successive kicks . . got singles that should have been goals. **1969** EAGLESON & MCKIE *Terminol. Austral. Nat. Football* iii. 16 *Single*, a behind. . . It is difficult to determine whether this variant for *behind* has been derived from the fact that only one flag is raised by the goal umpire when a behind is scored, or from the fact that a behind is worth only one point.

single, *a. Hist.* In special collocations: **single cat,** a whip of nine knotted cords; a cat-o'-nine-tails; cf. *double cat-o'-nine-tails* DOUBLE *a.* 1; **iron,** one fetter, also **single-ironed** *ppl. a.*
1838 *Rep. Select Committee Transportation* 12 Feb. 38 Was the cat with which the floggings were inflicted at Macquarie Harbour of the same description as the ordinary cat-o'-nine-tails?—No, it was a much heavier instrument, and larger; the cat which is generally used in the colony for the punishment of convicts is what is called a **single cat,** such as is generally employed for the punishment of soldiers and sailors. **1802** [**single iron**] *HRA* (1915) 1st Ser. III. 546 Q.2.—Was he in Irons? A.—He was single-Ironed. **1804** *Sydney Gaz.* 23 Dec. 3/2 To labour in a single iron every evening until dusk.

singlet. A woven or knitted undergarment covering the body from the shoulders to the hips; also worn as an outer garment. See also JACKY HOWE.
1882 W. SOWDEN *N.T. as it Is* 27 The Minister in a slashed slouch-hat with a veil—a *la* bushranger—light tweed trousers, with singlet, black umbrella, and long white oil leggings. **1969** *On Guard* (Broken Hill) Feb. 10 Persons wearing a singlet only will be asked to leave.

sink, $v.^1$ [Spec. use of *sink* to excavate (a shaft, etc.) by digging downwards: see OED *v.* 18.]
1. *intr.* To dig downwards in search of gold.
1851 *Empire* (Sydney) 30 Sept. 207/3 The kind of gold the men of Tarshish are obtaining, is similar to the very fine dust found on the surface of the soil at the Turon. In no case that I saw, have the men sunk deeper than four feet, and the greater number are rooting on the very top; not deeper than a foot or two. **1932** I.L. IDRIESS *Prospecting for Gold* 51 Remember to apply your 'water knowledge' whenever possible, if you happen to work at other forms of alluvial—sinking or tunnelling for an old river-bed.
2. *trans.* To dig (a hole, etc.) in the ground in search of gold. Also *fig.*
1852 A. ADAMSON *Lett.* 9 May (1901) 25 On Tuesday Adam and Joseph bottomed the hole they were sinking last week, and again found nothing. **1896** *Bulletin* (Sydney) 18 Jan. 3/2 Allus sinkin' duffers, allus bottomin' on 'tish'. **1908** *Ibid.* 23 Jan. 15/2 The black cockatoo knows exactly where to bite through the bark to find his breakfast. . . I have never known him to sink a duffer hole in the bark.

sink, $v.^2$ [Spec. use of *sink* to cause (a thing) to descend: see OED(S *v.* 17 e. Used elsewhere but recorded earliest in Aust.] *trans.* To consume (an alcoholic drink); to quaff.
1911 *Bulletin* (Sydney) 31 Aug. 14/2 Poison-Cart Bill had been 'sinking' the proceeds of months of driving the rabbit 'bus, and he was loaded to the nines by the time he . . subsided gloriously on a garbage heap. **1986** *Canberra Times* 27 Jan. 1/2 The typically Australian activity of sinking a cold can on a hot day.

sinking, *vbl. n.* Gold-mining. The process of digging downwards in search of gold; the cavity so formed.
1851 J.H. BURTON *Emigrant's Man.* ii. 121 Several parties have commenced sinking about a mile from Sofala. **1896** M. CLARKE *Austral. Tales* 51 The place is underlined with 'sinkings', and the inhabitants burrow like moles beneath the surface of the earth.

sirocco. *Obs.* [Transf. use of *sirocco* a hot wind blowing from the north coast of Africa over the Mediterranean.] HOT WIND 1.
1842 *S. Austral. News* (London) 15 May 99/2 We are occasionally afflicted with irregular, or extraordinary visitations of heat, in the shape of hot winds, or siroccos, blowing from the centre of the continent. **1903** *Ibid.* 16 May 16/3 A sirocco could bury a good slice of B.H. beneath thousands of tons of tailings.

sis. Also **siss.** Abbrev. of 'sissy', an effeminate person.
1944 A. MARSHALL *These are my People* 59 Jim . . I understood, was regarded as a siss. **1977** W. MOORE *Just to Myself* 10 We all reckoned he was a sis because his mother wouldn't let him get his clothes dirty.

sister. [Spec. use of *sister* in the sense of 'fellow': see OED *sb.* 10.] Used *attrib.* to designate an equality of status between Colonies (occas. States), esp. in the Comb. **sister colony.** Cf. BROTHER COLONIST.
1820 C. JEFFREYS *Van Dieman's Land* 118 They are certainly a superior race to those of the sister colony of Port Jackson. **1903** *Truth* (Sydney) 18 Jan. 1/6 Ben . . has celebrated his 64th year of residence in Victoria. When Ben arrived in the sister State he could have bought half Port Phillip for a bottle of rum.

sit, *v.* With **down.** [Spec. use of *sit down* 'to establish oneself in some position or place; to settle, take up one's abode': see OED *v.* 21 c.]
1. [Survival of the Br. and U.S. sense, strengthened by the development of sense 2.] *intr.* Of non-Aborigines: to settle, take up residence, esp. to SQUAT 1. See also quot. 1871.
1798 D. COLLINS *Acct. Eng. Colony N.S.W.* I. 489 There was indeed a woman, one Ann Smith, who ran away a few days after our sitting down in this place, and whose fate was not exactly ascertained. **1871** *Great Northern Run Case* 3 Their agent had requested permission to 'sit down' for a time with his sheep, owing to the scarcity of water elsewhere.
2. *intr.* Freq. in Austral. pidgin. Of Aborigines: to be (in a place); to settle (somewhere) permanently. Also *transf.* (see quots. 1880 and 1944).
1805 *Sydney Gaz.* 7 May, A Number of Natives . . are *sit down* at the Brush between Prospect and George's River, they are not to be molested in that situation. **1880** J.B. STEVENSON *Seven Yrs. Austral. Bush* 144 Plenty Possum sit down up there. **1944** M.J. O'REILLY *Bouyangs & Boomerangs* 88, I told one of the old men, who could jabber fairly good English, about the incident. This is what he told me: 'That fellow bean tree is one place where big fellow 'Kaditcha' all the time sit down; no whitefellow, no blackfellow allowed camp alonga that place.' **1978** H.C. COOMBS *Kulinma* 228 In some communities work on the projects continued while materials were available but increasingly Aborigines became content to 'sit-down'.

Hence **sitting-down** *vbl. n.* (used *attrib.* in the examples).
1959 *Bulletin* (Sydney) 6 May 16/2 The latest for N.T. abos. is three weeks walkabout on full pay, as they are now holding their jobs long enough to get paid annual holidays at native resorts such as Snake Bay, Shoal Bay, and various islands. . . For the less energetic, the most attractive resort is a shady banyan-tree for three weeks 'sitting-down walkabout' at the boss's expense. **1978** H.C. COOMBS *Kulinma* 228 Aborigines found that they would receive in unemployment benefit ('sitting-down money' it was called in some communities) more than it had been possible for them previously to earn for work on their community projects.

sit down, *n.* Austral. pidgin. [f. prec.]
1. A rest; a stay. Also *attrib.*
1931 I.L. IDRIESS *Lasseter's Last Ride* 137 Warts said it was only a little way—'one sit down'. **1981** *Central Austral. Land Rights News* Dec. 13 They say they're very worried that cattle stations won't be used as cattle stations and become sitdown places.
2. Special Comb. **sit-down money,** unemployment or welfare benefits. Also *transf.*
1978 H.C. COOMBS *Kulinma* 202 Community advisers

became active in some communities in assisting Aborigines to apply for unemployment benefit... Generally Aborigines have been content to accept the 'sit-down' money without working. **1981** *Weekend Austral. Mag.* (Sydney) 31 Oct. 19/1 Mr Tuxworth said these companies should pay the out-of-work miners sit-down money to keep them in the territory for when the uranium boom begins.

sittella /sɪˈtɛlə/. Also **sitella**. [The bird genus *Sittella* was named by English naturalist William Swainson (*On Nat. Hist. Classif. Birds* (1837) II. 317), f. mod. L. *sitta*, a. Gr. σίττη nuthatch + dimin. suffix *-ella*.] The small, arboreal bird *Daphoenositta chrysoptera* of mainland Aust., usu. grey or brown and white streaked, and having several distinctive forms sometimes regarded as separate species, as **black-capped sittella, orange-winged sittella** (see under first element). See also WOODPECKER 1.

1844 J. GOULD *Birds of Aust.* (1848) IV. Pl. 103, *Sittella leucoptera*.. White-winged Sittella. **1982** J. MORRISON *North Wind* 212 Some pardalotes and sitellas were fluttering about the drooping branch of [a] pepper tree.

six, *a*.

1. In *attrib.* collocations designating the number of horizontal barriers in a fence, as **six-rail (-strand, -wire) fence.**

1897 *Bulletin* (Sydney) 11 Dec. 30 Great curly horned Brewarras bred among the back belars To a scorn of six-wire fences and a dread of twelve-foot bars. **1908** *Ibid.* 22 Oct. 14/3 Was once accelerated over a six-rail fence by a masculine cow, and landed fair in the middle of a clump of the Queensland curse. **1960** E. O'CONNER *Irish Man* 209 They came to a six-strand fence and after following it for a mile or so saw a few freshly branded calves.

2. In the collocation **six-by-eight,** a tent measuring 6 feet by 8 feet.

1898 *Worker* (Sydney) 21 May 1/2 He'd pitched his little 6 x 8; and when he saw me there He promptly bade me enter, with a spirit cheering swear. **1929** W.J. RESIDE *Golden Days* 364 Where are they who with me camped Within the six by eights.

3. In the phr. **six bob a day,** used with reference to the daily rate of pay to designate an Australian soldier serving in the war of 1914–18, esp. *attrib.* as **six bob a day tourist.**

1915 T. SKEYHILL *Soldier-Songs from Anzac* 22 But 'e called me a chocolate soldier, A six bob a day tourist, too. 'E says, 'You'll not reach the trenches; Nor even get a view.' **1948** H.W. CRITTENDEN *Rogues' Paradise* 36 It will appease his Irish sectarian soul.. to learn that.. the 'saviors' marched as part of the valiant mob who called the Diggers, among even less complimentary epithets, 'six-bob-a-day-murderers'.

sixer. *Australian National Football.* A scoring kick worth six points; a goal.

1908 *Clipper* (Hobart) 19 Sept. 2/2 Molross took a bonza mark on the wing, and from a pass Rait scored a sixer against great applause. **1960** *N.T. News* (Darwin) 5 Jan. 8/5 The pass found its mark and Lew Falt got the sixer.

sixes, *n. pl.* [Spec. use of *six* the number used to grade the uniform.] In naval use: white (summer) dress uniform.

1944 *Quickmatch: Souvenir Mag. H.M.A.S. 'Quickmatch'* 87 Admirably dressed in spanking sixes. **1983** *Canberra Times* 22 May 10/1 The top brass, dressed in 'sixes' (which were very smart uniforms indeed).

six o'clock swill: see SWILL b.

sixpence. *Austral. pidgin. Obs.* Money; TICKPENS.

1851 *Athenaeum* (London) 24 May 557 Never mind, I jump up white fellow—plenty of sixpence. **1859** W. BURROWS *Adventures Mounted Trooper* 112 'Black fellow quomby dead, by and by jump up white fellow, plenty tixpence', meaning, that if a black should 'quomby' *i.e.* lie down, and die, they would rise again white, and have plenty of money, sixpence being their name for money.

sked. [Orig. U.S. abbrev. of *schedule*] An appointed time for a radio call: see quots.

1946 E.A. FELDT *Coast Watchers* 10 Previously the small stations in the area had communicated with key points at fixed times, 'skeds' as they were called. **1983** *Yulngu* Mar. 6 The radio 'skeds' are so easy to do these days as all communities.. shut up when Katherine Base is talking.

skee. Shortened form of 'whisky'.

[N.Z. **1959** G. SLATTER *Gun in my Hand* 145 In this country a bulged pocket would not mean a gun. More likely a flask of skee or mother's ruin.] **1962** P.A. KNUDSEN *Bloodwood Tree* 122 'Any skee?' Happy squeaked hopefully. 'Yair, git a coupla bottles. Not Scotch—Australian stuff 'll do us peasants.' **1967** G. JENKIN *Two Yrs. Bardunyah Station* 16 And for this here quid and a bottle of skee I'm betting at ten to one.

skeleton weed. [Also U.S.] The naturalized perennial herb *Chondrilla juncea* (fam. Asteraceae), orig. of central Asia, generally regarded as a weed, esp. of wheat and other cereals.

1935 *Agric. Gaz. N.S.W.* XLVI. 16 Skeleton weed is well liked by sheep, especially when it is in the young stages. **1981** *Bulletin* (Sydney) 9 June 36/3 Take the case of skeleton weed. Wheat farmers regard it as a pest, but some sheep men call it the 'poor man's lucerne' because in a drought it can provide sheep with much needed high-protein feed.

skelly. *Obs.* Alteration of 'skilly', a thin, watery porridge or gruel. Also *attrib.*

1846 *Britannia* (Hobart) 8 Oct. 2/5 He had not been poking his nose into flour bags, and skelly-tubs as part of his duty. **1853** I. CHAMBERLAYNE *Austral. Captive* 82 A pint of *skelly*—a very thin gruel, without salt.

skerrick. [Br. dial. *skerrick* a small amount: see OEDS.] The smallest amount, a 'scrap'. Usu. in negative contexts.

1854 S. SIDNEY *Gallops & Gossips* 88, I have plenty of tobacco, but not a skerrick of tea or sugar. **1985** J. CLANCHY *Lie of Land* 201 'Eighty-seven? For that skerrick of —?' Couldn't be more than ten squares.

skilling. Also **skillen.** [Spec. use of *skilling* a shed or outhouse: see EDD *skeeling* and OED(S *skilling, sb.*¹]

1. A lean-to attached to a dwelling and providing additional accommodation (freq. a kitchen); a small dwelling built in the style of a lean-to (see quot. 1840).

1799 *Lett. to London Missionary Soc. Murder S. Clode* 300 Jones went into the skilling, and coming out a second time took up a large knife. **1840** *Port Phillip Gaz.* 5 Sept. 6 *A weather-boarded skilling*, with a piece of Garden ground attached; well adapted for a Mechanic.. situated in the suburbs. Price £100. **1874** J.J. HALCOMBE *Emigrant & Heathen* 34 Sometimes there is a skillen at the back of the hut.

2. *Skillion roof,* see SKILLION B. 2. Also as **skilling roof.**

1861 L.A. MEREDITH *Over Straits* 94 Stray little bits of dwellings, with perhaps one window and a door to the street, and a slant roof or 'shilling' [*sic*] behind. **1891** J. FENTON *Bush Life Tas.* (1964) 42 With tea-tree rafters nailed on the plate for a skilling roof.

skillion, *n.* and *attrib.* [Alteration of SKILLING.]

A. *n.*

SKIMPS   512   **SKIRTY**

1. SKILLING 1.
1808 *Sydney Gaz.* 13 Nov., A house in Pitt's Row, a skillion of which was tenanted by a person with whom the prisoner was in habits of intimacy. **1949** *Coast to Coast 1948* 48 Nim .. put skillions on the northern, the eastern, and the southern sides of the original building he had constructed for his wife and the children, so that there was no longer any overcrowding, even if the house appeared to ramble somewhat.
2. Such a structure attached to a shearing shed and accommodating the sheep.
1846 C.P. HODGSON *Reminisc. Aust.* 39 Skillions formed by a sloping verandah to receive the sheep in from the fold as required. **1951** *Bulletin* (Sydney) 18 July 14/4 Our shed was simply a very long building with skillion on one side and the other open. The shearers were placed at the posts.
3. *Skillion roof.*
1879 S.W. SILVER *Austral. Grazier's Guide* 53 Sloping roofs, after the fashion of a 'lean-to', are called in the colonies 'skillions'. **1953** *Bulletin* (Sydney) 3 June 12/4, I recall one silver-grey who went too far—too far down the skillion of the sleep-out veranda.
B. *attrib.*
1. Lean-to.
1857 *Vic. Parl. Papers* (1856–57) III. no. 48 21 At Pentridge .. a den in the shape of a skillion-building was used as an exempt-ward. **1963** X. HERBERT *Disturbing Element* 7 It was only a three-room shack, for all the bits and pieces added in the way of verandahs and skillion kitchen.
2. Special Comb. **skillion roof,** the sloping roof characteristic of a lean-to building; also **skillion-roofed** *ppl. a.*; SKILLING 2.
1901 *Bulletin* (Sydney) 7 Dec. 28/1 In a four-roomed, skillion-roofed, red-brick dwelling, upon a 'donkey' sofa, sat a woman. **1965** G.H. FEARNSIDE *Golden Ram* 105 He led Sam to the room adjoining the printery. It sheltered beneath a skillion roof appended to the main building—an architectural afterthought that was realised at minimum expense.

skimps, *pl.* [Abbrev. of *skimpings* mining waste (chiefly in Cornwall): see OED.] Mining refuse. Also **skimpy** *n.* (see quot. 1982).
1978 B. KENNEDY *Silver, Sin, & Sixpenny Ale* 35 Slag Street, aptly named since it ran parallel to the slag tailings or skimps and mullock at the foot of the hill. **1982** M. WALKER *Making Do* 84 What was taken out from underground and processed, the residue, had to be put back to fill it up again, and I was one of those that helped in that department, pushing the trucks. I was a mullocker or a skimpy, because the mullock was nick-named 'skimps'.

skin, *n.*[1] MOIETY. Also *attrib.*
1927 *V & P* (W.A.) I. no. 3 83 The hurt, or the injury that I might do to one A, a native, is a hurt not done primarily to him, but done to the — group or skin, as they call it, of which he is a member. **1986** *Canberra Times* 2 Apr. 7/2 The 'skin' name was the way of identifying an Aboriginal as part of a group.

skin, *n.*[2] In the phr. (one's) **skin is cracking** and varr., used allusively of a craving for alcoholic liquor.
1955 H.G. LAMOND *Towser* 48 In the language of the bush, 'Jack's skin was crackin''. He craved a drunken spree. **1963** S. MUSSEN *Beating about Bush* 63 'His skin's fair cracking.' 'Fair cracking?' I asked. 'He can't wait to start a drinking spree,' translated Tim.

skinless barley. *Obs.* A variety of barley (see quots.).
1828 *Tasmanian* (Hobart) 12 Dec. 2 On Wednesday last a field of what is called *skinless barley*, was cut on the farm of Mr Mather, at Muddy Plains. **1849** W.S. CHAUNCY *Guide to S.A.* 38 There is another kind which is in much esteem, it is termed by the colonists, *skinless barley*, from its resemblance to wheat; it is highly valuable, yielding a large crop and weighing as much as 70 lbs. to the bushel.

skinner. [Spec. use of Br. slang *skinner* one who strips another of money: see OED(S 4 b.] A horse that wins a race at very long odds; a betting coup.
1891 *Truth* (Sydney) 1 Feb. 6/2 Then came a complete skinner, in the doubles, straight out and post betting. **1980** A. HOPGOOD *And here comes Bucknuckle* 20 The bookies are cheering of course. That was a fair dinkum skinner. Not one punter left standing after that.

skinny. Any of several fish of the fam. Carangidae, incl. *Scomberoides lysan* of n. Aust. and elsewhere, having a notably compressed body: see quot. 1971. Also **skinnyfish.**
1962 *N.T. News* (Darwin) 10 Apr. 1/1 The trawling was good. Skinnies averaging 10 lbs. were coming in fast. **1971** P. BODEKER *Sandgropers' Trail* 25, I had never heard of queenies coming so far south... Side-on, it looked as if it had been run through a mangle—the reason they call them shinnies [sic] up around Darwin. **1980** G.P. WHITLEY *Handbk. Austral. Fishes* 134 Leatherskin .. also called .. skinnyfish .. are mainly tropical with strongly compressed bodies covered with a shiny, leathery skin.

skippy. Chiefly *W.A.* and *Tas.* The silvery marine fish *Pseudocaranx dentex* of s. Aust.
1982 T. WINTON *Open Swimmer* 27 'Smart fish, skippy.' 'Trevally.' 'Not this side of the border.' Jerra cast again. He spread some pollard onto the water. 'What are you, a Sydney poonce?' **1984** *Overlander* Oct. 61 His one great ambition was to get among the big skippy for which Esperance is famed. 'Skippy' are silver trevally.

skirt, *v. Shearing.* [Br. dial.: see EDD *skirt, sb.* 8 and *skirting* 5.] *trans.* To trim the skirtings from (a fleece).
1833 H.W. PARKER *Rise, Progress, & Present State Van Dieman's Land* 167 The fleeces should next be *skirted*, that is, unfolded .. and the coarser extremities taken off. **1981** A.B. FACEY *Fortunate Life* 299 He gave my wife a lesson in wool-classing... He went to a lot of trouble making my wife understand how to class wool and how to skirt a fleece.

skirter. *Shearing.* One who trims the skirtings from a fleece.
1883 *Leisure Hour* (London) 244 A barefooted boy .. gathers up the fleece and carries it to the skirters' table. **1946** *Bulletin* (Sydney) 28 Aug. 28/4 'Black,' called the classer, as the picker-up flicked out a fleece with a black patch on the rump... 'Aw, cripes, it's only got a tinge or one shoulder,' pointed out an emergency skirter.

skirting, *vbl. n. Shearing.* [f. SKIRT.]
1. *pl.* The trimmings or inferior parts of a fleece.
1881 A.C. GRANT *Bush-Life Qld.* I. 85 The roller-up, with a rapidity which is the result of long practice, separates the skirtings. **1980** P. FREEMAN *Woolshed* 20 The 'fleece' itself .. is immediately removed from the board by the 'pickers-up', and cleverly thrown over a 'wool' table where the 'skirtings' or rough flanks are removed.
2. Special Comb. **skirting table,** the table at which the skirtings are removed.
1890 *Argus* (Melbourne) 20 Sept. 13/7 At the 'skirting table' we will .. watch while the fleece .. is opened out by the 'roller' and the inferior portions removed.

skirty, *a. Shearing.* Of a fleece: roughly trimmed.
1928 C.E. COWLEY *Classing Clip* 35 If the fleeces are not properly trimmed, or, in other words, are 'skirty', the value of the fleece-wool is lessened.

skite, *n.* [Spec. use of Br. dial. *skite* 'an opprobrious epithet for an unpleasant or conceited person': see EDD *sb.*[1] 3 and OED(S.]

1. A boast; boasting; ostentation.
1860 C.R. THATCHER *Vic. Songster* v. 160 You don't often see a chap given to 'skite, Can do very much when it comes to a fight. **1968** S. GORE *Holy Smoke* 12 'Y' could give anyone a shade of odds on the skite,' says the King.

2. A braggart, a boaster; a conceited person. Also *transf.*
1897 *Bulletin* (Sydney) 11 Dec. 14/1, I banged a pewter pot And cried, 'Who is this drunken skite That talks this tommy rot?' **1906** *Bulletin* (Sydney) 1 Nov. 16/2 Mr Mag is .. the skite of the feathered tribe.

skite, *v.* [See prec.] *intr.* To boast; to brag. Also as *vbl. n.*
1857 C.R. THATCHER *Colonial Songster* 18 If you ever get into a fight, Of course you'll not forget to skite. **1982** R. HALL *Just Relations* 130 That's skiting if you want to hear me skite. We'd beat the lot of youse, him and me.

skiter. One who boasts; SKITE *n.* 2.
1898 *Bulletin* (Sydney) 17 Dec. (Red Page), An incessant talker is a skiter. **1976** M. POWELL *Down Under* 130 What an independent lot they were, not like the skiters in New South Wales and Victoria.

skol, *v.* [Transf. use of *skoal* to drink a health.] *trans.* To drink (a glass, etc. of alcoholic liquor) in a single draught.
1976 J. JOHNSON *Low Breed* 244 Octavia picked up a loose glass of claret and skolled it. **1982** *Ozbike* (Sydney) July 44/3 She picked up her drink, skolled it and said, 'How about another?'

skoot, var. SCOOT.

skrammy, var. SCRAMMY.

skull-drag, *v. trans.* To haul (someone or something) along by force. Also *fig.*
1872 'DEMONAX' *Mysteries & Miseries* 11/2 A barrister of note .. was gloriously tight. The barrister had a wife. In the morning that lady drove up in a stylish affair, and 'skull-dragged' her better half from the scene of his excesses. **1978** B. KENNEDY *Silver, Sin, & Sixpenny Ale* 53 George Dale .. remembered how certain recalcitrant individuals were 'skull-dragged' into the union.

skull-driving, *vbl. n.* School-teaching.
1899 *Bulletin* (Sydney) 7 Oct. 14/1 The champion cool hand was a man with whom I boarded when skulldriving 'out-back'. **1925** *Ibid.* 9 Apr. 22/3 The best damper ever I had was made by a woman in whose house I lodged when skulldriving handy to Gundagai (N.S.W.).

skungy, var. SCUNGY.

slab, *n.* and *attrib.* [Spec. use of *slab* flat, broad, thick piece of wood, etc.: see OED(S *sb.*[1] 2 b. and 4 a.]

A. *n.* A thick, rough-hewn plank of wood used for building purposes.
1829 H. WIDOWSON *Present State Van Diemen's Land* 86 Logs, or as they are more commonly called, slabs, for erecting barns or small buildings. **1934** *Red Star* (Perth) 22 June 4/1 We were offered two hours to cut slabs of green jarrah bark for ourselves but no green is standing for at least two miles around, all the country having been ringbarked.

B. *attrib.*

1. Constructed from slabs.
1847 *Port Phillip Herald* 16 Nov. 3/6 Slab verandah cottage and garden, wool-shed, men's and out-station huts and hurdles, will be given in. **1979** J. WILLIAMS *White River* 11 My charges, Sheila, Curly and Baldy, were the meekest and stood for me calmly by the slab fence.

2. Comb. **slab building, -built** *ppl. a.*, **cottage, house, humpy, hut, road, shanty, table, wall.**
1836 J. BACKHOUSE *Narr. Visit Austral. Colonies* (1843) 395 We walked about two miles, to the school-house, which we found a miserable **slab-building**, in a ruinous condition. **1854** G.H. HAYDON *Austral. Emigrant* 147 The largest was a long **slab built** and bark roofed hut. **1856** W.H.G. KINGSTON *Emigrant's Home* 125 We found the family living in a comfortable **slab cottage**. **1839** D. MACKELLAR *Austral. Emigrant's Guide* 9 One **slab-house** for overseer. **1865** *Colony of Qld. as Field for Emigration* 14 The **slab 'umpie'** or hut of the small farmer or gardener .. situated here and there along the wide sweeping banks of verdure. **1836** J. BACKHOUSE *Narr. Visit Austral. Colonies* (1843) 418 The married soldiers have built themselves very small, **slab-huts**, covered with sheets of bark, and white-washed. **1877** 'ANGLO-INDIAN' *Visit Tas.* 22 The **slab road** is 9 miles long from the coast. **1897** *Bulletin* (Sydney) 6 Mar. 3/2 It crowds some forty youngsters (sometimes less and sometimes more) In an iron-roofed **slab shanty** fifteen feet by twenty-four. **1880** 'ERRO' *Squattermania* 108 On the **slab table** beside them stood a half-emptied bottle. **1853** *Austral. Gold Digger's Monthly Mag.* vii. 251 Two rude bush bedsteads were rigged against the **slab-wall**.

slab, *v. Mining.* [f. prec.] *trans.* To support (the sides of a shaft) with slabs. Also as *vbl. n.*, and *absol.*
1854 *Guardian* (Hobart) 25 Mar. 3/4 The Commissioner .. considering the depth, water, slabbing etc., decided in favour of the jumpers. **1857** W. WESTGARTH *Vic. & Austral. Gold Mines* 205 These long shafts became very expensive, as it was necessary also to 'slab' them, or build up their sides with split slabs so as to prevent water and material from pouring down the pit. **1859** W. KELLY *Life in Vic.* I. 216 As they could not be well or securely slabbed downwards from the surface, the digger first sinks nine feet and slabs upwards, and so continues proceeding in spells of nine feet all the way down.

slabbed, *ppl. a. Obs.*

a. Constructed from slabs; faced with slabs.
1835 *Commercial Jrnl. & Advertiser* (Sydney) 17 Aug. 3/4 There are twenty acres cleared and stumped, with a good Well of Water, and two slabbed and shingled Huts. **1883** G.E. LOYAU *Personal Adventures* 23 When you go to a bush inn out North .. the landlord usually takes you into a large-sized slabbed room.

b. *Mining.* Supported by slabs.
1859 W. KELLY *Life in Vic.* I. 216 Slabbed holes are generally four feet by two feet ten inches.

slacker. *Hist.* [Spec. use of *slacker* one who shirks work.] One who has failed to volunteer for military service, esp. during the war of 1914–18; SHIRKER.
1917 *Huon Times* (Franklin) 19 Jan. 5/1 This should make the slackers feel their position and go and help those poor wounded heroes who are war-worn and weary. **1963** X. HERBERT *Disturbing Element* 141 She had been sending white feathers round to what she now called Slackers ever since Phil's enlistment.

slag, *v.* [Br. dial. *slag* to besmear: see EDD *sb.*[2] and *v.*[2]] *intr.* To spit.
1965 W. DICK *Bunch of Ratbags* 238 He cleared his throat and spat on the car grille, 'Hell', muttered Ritchie, 'he's slaggin' on me car!' **1985** *Bulletin* (Sydney) 8 Oct. 148/4 'Where do I stick it in?' asked the former minister for the Yartz, wielding the knife. 'Jesus', he laughed, 'I've slagged all over it!'

slanguage. Also **slangwidge**. [Spec. use of *slanguage* a slang expression.] A distinctively Australian expression, esp. of the more colourful variety; colloquial Australian speech. Freq. **Australian slanguage.**

1899 W.T. GOODGE *Hits! Skits! & Jingles* 151 And our undiluted English Is a fad to which we cling, But the great Australian slanguage Is a truly awful thing! 1929 'F. BLAIR' *Digger Sea-Mates* 149 'They're round in the barracks now .. the pair of blasted hobos.' 'Hush-h-h,' said Kiley, inclining his head in the direction of a lady not far away. 'No slanguage here.' 1967 M. SELLARS *Carramar* 69 'The Orstralian slangwidge as it is spoke,' he drily commented.

slant. *Obs.* [Spec. use of Br. slang *slant* a chance: see OED(S *sb.*[1] 6 and 7.] An opportunity to go somewhere procured as the result of a stratagem.

1835 *Cornwall Chron.* (Launceston) 2 May 3 This was a prosecution at the instance of Constable Thomas Perkins, who is stationed at Birch's Bay and Long Bay, and has detained him in town from his situation as constable for a week. No prosecutor appeared, and there was not the slightest evidence adduced of a felony. This charge appeared to have been trumped up for no other purpose than but for him to get a *slant* to Hobart Town. 1897 'P. WARUNG' *Tales Old Regime* 217 Pedder had got tired of things in general, and had organized that movement which was popularly known in Norfolk Island and Port Arthur as a 'slant', that is, he had planned a murder or a mutiny on purpose to obtain a trial in Hobart or Sydney.

slanter /'slantə/, *n.* and *a.* Also **schleinter, schlenter, shlanter, shlinter, slinter.** [a. Du. *slenter* knavery, trick, perh. through S. African English: see OEDS *schlenter*.]

A. *n.* A trick; a fraudulent stratagem.

1864 C.R. THATCHER *Invercargill Minstrel* 15 'Twas a 'shlinter' for the tenant one morning departed Without paying his rent. 1919 A. WRIGHT *Game of Chance* 116 'It was a slanter,' cried Mason. 'The dice were loaded; I saw that man next the thrower helping to ring the changes.' 1925 —— *Boy from Bullarah* 133 'A shlanter!' he bellowed, 'Acted for the pictures, an' me layin' two hundred.. Robbery.' 1966 D. NILAND *Pairs & Loners* 118 'Mistaken, nothing!' roared Tiny. 'You're crazy, Sergeant—can't you see it's a slinter? They've cooked this up between them.'

B. *adj.* Dishonest; crooked.

[N.Z. 1889 WILLIAMS & REEVES *Colonial Couplets* 51 Broke! Broke! Broke! At the will of the C.J.C. For the slenter race with the favourite dead Will never come back to me.] 1895 *Bulletin* (Sydney) 5 Jan. 3/2 The long-beerians, rabbiters, spielers, fat-heads, slanter-bookies, etc., were all there. 1901 *Truth* (Sydney) 20 Oct. 4/8 They are usually about Bourke-street, near the 'schleinter' betting clubs. *c* 1919 W. LAWLESS *Darcy Story* 26 If he was attempting any schlenter work would it not have been detected.

slather /'slæðə/. [f. Br. dial. and U.S. *slather* to use in large quantities, to squander: see OED(S *v.* and *sb.*).] In the collocation **open slather:** freedom to operate without impediment, a 'free rein'; a free-for-all.

1919 V. MARSHALL *World of Living Dead* 71 Try the races up Dingo Creek way... They say she's an open slather up there. Not a demon in the burg. 1983 *Canberra Standard* 9 Feb. 1/4 Introduction of draw poker machines and similar machines for gambling purposes was a step towards 'open slather' gambling in the A.C.T.

slaty gum. [See quots. 1889 and 1969.] Any of several trees of the genus *Eucalyptus* (fam. Myrtaceae) having a smooth, greyish bark, esp. *E. dawsonii* of N.S.W.; the wood of these trees.

1889 J.H. MAIDEN *Useful Native Plants Aust.* 470 *Eucalyptus largiflorens* .. is also called 'Slaty Gum', from the grey and white patches on the bark. 1969 S. KELLY *Eucalypts* 66 Slaty gum is a eucalypt of relatively restricted natural distribution... The common name refers to the branchlets, leaves and buds which are covered with a waxy bloom and give a greyish appearance to the tree from a distance.

sledge, *v. Cricket.* [See quot. 1982 (2).] *trans.* Of a fielder: to attempt to break the concentration of (a person batting) by the offering of abuse, needling, etc. Freq. as *vbl. n.*

1975 *Sun-Herald* (Sydney) 21 Dec. 49/4 'Sledging' .. or the gentle art of talking a player out .. has no place in women's cricket. 1982 *Canberra Times* 2 Nov. 8/7 N.S.W.'s fast-bowling hero Len Pascoe, involved in one of Sheffield Shield's ugliest days at the SCG yesterday, was fired up by a barrage of racist 'sledging'. 1982 *Sydney Morning Herald* 4 Nov. 10/2 The court has been told by Ian Chappell that the expression 'sledging' first came into vogue among cricketers in 1963–64. It came from the expression 'subtle as a sledgehammer' at a time when a man called Percy Sledge had a song on the English hit parade. It meant using words to exploit an opponent's weaknesses and put him off his game.

sleeper. Used *attrib.* in Comb. designating the activity of procuring and preparing timber for use as railway sleepers, as **sleeper chopper, cutter, getter, -getting** *vbl. n.*, **hewer, -hewing** *vbl. n.*, **squarer, -squaring** *vbl. n.*

1903 *Bulletin* (Sydney) 24 Dec. 36/3 Gum rings in the trees are a frequent and especial trouble. No good **sleeper-chopper** will work a 'ringy' tree, for the sleepers will split along the gum rings. 1899 *Worker* (Sydney) 14 Jan. 4/4 The **sleeper-cutters** on the Moree-Inverell railway complain of the rate of wages received. 1900 *Bulletin* (Sydney) 18 Aug. 15/1, I .. was always sure of having at least four yarns in the week—two to the mailman and two to a couple of **sleeper-getters.** 1903 *Bulletin* (Sydney) 17 Jan. 16/4, I was camped out last Dec. **sleeper-getting** for Narrabri-Walgett railway. 1927 T.S. GROSER *Lure of Golden West* 104 See the **sleeper-hewer** at work. 1927 T.S. GROSER *Lure of Golden West* 104 **Sleeper-hewing**, in itself, is an important branch of the timber industry. 1885 *Evening News* (Sydney) 3 Mar. 1/5 Goulburn and Cooma railway... **Sleeper squarers** .. wanted... Apply Fishburn and Co., Young. 1903 *Sporting News* (Launceston) 5 Sept. 2/5 With sundry sawing contests, **sleeper-squaring** matches, and other events.

sleeping lizard. [See quot. 1899.] Any of several lizards, incl. BOBTAIL and some species of the genus *Tiliqua* (see *blue-tongue lizard* BLUE *a.*); BOGGI 1. Also **sleepy lizard.**

1844 L. LEICHHARDT *Jrnl. Overland Exped. Aust.* 27 Dec. (1847) 85 Mr Gilbert found a new species of sleeping lizard, with four lighter stripes on the dark brown ground along the back, and with dark spots on the sides. 1899 R. SEMON *In Austral. Bush* 183 The lazy torpid 'sleeping lizards' (*Tiliqua scincoides*). 1970 R. BUSTARD *Austral. Lizards* 116 The sleepy lizard (*Trachydosaurus rugosus*), more commonly known outside Australia as the stump-tailed skink, is widely distributed on the mainland occurring in inland areas of all States.

sleep-out.

1. A place to sleep outdoors.

1919 *Bulletin* (Sydney) 4 Dec. 20/2 While enjoying a casual after-tea walk in search of a suitable 'sleep-out' an unsympathetic policeman put an end to the great adventure.

2. A verandah, porch, or outbuilding providing sleeping accommodation. Also *attrib.*

1927 *Link* (Melbourne) 1 Oct. 8 The jobs that can be done .. building sleep-outs. 1929 A. SMITH *Austral. Home Carpenter* 126 A sleep-out room for the children. An open-air bedroom that is easily and cheaply constructed.

sleepy lizard: see SLEEPING LIZARD.

sleever. *Obs.* Abbrev. of *long-sleever* (see LONG 1).

1901 *Bulletin* (Sydney) 28 Dec. 32/4 Striking a pub .. I unyoked, thinking that a 'sleever' would be welcome.

slew, *v.* Also **sleu.** [Prob. f. *slewed* drunk: see OED.]

1. In the phr. **to get** (or **be**) **slewed,** to be(come) lost, esp. in the bush.

1879 *Truth* (Sydney) 30 Oct. 3/1, I guess you thought that I was high up the river with the Inspector and his black trackers close on my heels, but it is not the first time they have been slewed. 1978 TEECE & PIKE *Voice of Wilderness* 179 That is where I must have got 'slewed' for .. the sun came out and I could see we were heading into the sun instead of having sundown at our backs.

2. *trans.* To defeat (a person), to 'settle'.

1890 H.A. WHITE *Crime & Criminals* 152 The fellow, placing his thumb to his nose, said in a jeering manner, 'That slues you mate.' 1975 *Bulletin* (Sydney) 26 Apr. 45/3 Ratty Jack was stallin' for me to pussy in as soon as Limp slews the tart.

slice. A one-pound note.

1946 A. GREEN *We were (Riff) R.A.A.F.* 54 He played the national game until he had lifted a few 'slices' (N.T. slang for pound notes). 1966 S.J. BAKER *Austral. Lang.* (ed. 2) 115 £1, .. slice.

sling, *n.* [f. SLING *v.* 2.] A gift; a bribe. Also **slingback.**

1948 K.S. PRICHARD *Golden Miles* 74 'There's some hungry bastards', the men said, 'makin' big money on their ore, and never give the poor bugger boggin' for 'em a sling back.' The sling back might be ten bob on pay-day, or no more than a few pots of beer, but was always appreciated. 1982 *Canberra Times* 29 Apr. 1/4 To have a house, in effect, given to you is, to put it colloquially, a sling of major proportions.

sling, *v.*

1. In the phr. **to sling the billy (kettle, pot):** see BILLY *n.*[1] 6.

2. *intr.* To make a gift; to pay a bribe. Also *trans.*

c 1907 W.C. CHANDLER *Darkest Adelaide* 5 'Come on. Sling... If you don't dub up I'll punch you on the blanky jaw.' This seemed to have the desired effect, for she freely parted with two bob out of the four she had. 1959 *Bulletin* (Sydney) 16/3 Annual sports-meeting at a Victorian town, and Bung slung a bottle of whisky for the married ladies' race.

3. In the phr. **to sling off,** *throw off,* see THROW *v.* 2.

1900 *Tocsin* (Melbourne) 18 Jan. 8/1 If the Tocsin had for a moment supposed that Brassey's bike and boat idea was inspired by a desire to be unostentatious, it would not have 'slung off' at it. 1977 R. BEILBY *Gunner* 90, I wasn't slinging off at your religion.

slinging, *vbl. n.* Australian National Football. See quot. 1973.

1885 D.E. MCCONNELL *Austral. Etiquette* 641 Tripping, hacking, rabbiting, slinging, or catching hold of a player below the knee are prohibited. 1973 B. HOGAN *Follow Game* (rev. ed.) 73 Slinging is the act of catching a player by or around the neck and throwing or attempting to throw him on to the ground.

Hence **slinger** *n.*

1931 J.F. MCHALE et al. *Austral. Game of Football* 58 A sling round the neck .. is always penalised by a free kick given against the 'slinger'.

slinter, var. SLANTER.

slip, *n. S.A. Hist.* Abbrev. of GREEN SLIP.

1838 *Southern Austral.* (Adelaide) 6 Oct. 3/2 These slips, or residues of preliminary sections, have been tendered for by parties claiming a legal right. 1839 *S. Austral. Rec.* (London) 10 Apr. 176 After the holders of preliminary sections had chosen their land in that district, the purchasers of 80 acre sections were allowed to select their land out of the remaining unselected 134 acre sections, thus leaving unappropriated about 54 acres on each preliminary section. These portions or *slips* were regularly marked on the Surveyor-General's maps and coloured green; some of these *slips* have been tendered for in the usual manner.

slip, *v.*

1. *trans.* With **up**: to defraud or swindle (a person); to disappoint.

1874 'SPECIAL REPORTER' *Agric. in S.A.* 35 Mr Hughes has obtained notoriety as a gentleman who has been 'slipped up' by his dummies. This phrase is the one commonly used to describe the breaking of faith with the squatter by the dummy, and the conversion of the land by appropriation or commercial transfer to his own benefit. 1904 L.M.P. ARCHER *Bush Honeymoon* 117 When he came back, he found the girl had slipped him up and married a boundary rider.

2. *intr.* [Survival of Br. slang: see OED *v.*[1] 2 c.] With **into**: to give a beating to (a person). Also *fig.*

1972 J. MCNEIL *Old Familiar Juice* (1973) 66 Yer forgot ter bring 'em up... Yer must be slipping... I'll slip inter you inner minute! 1974 STACKPOLE & TRENGOVE *Not just for Openers* 83 When the crowd reacted by giving Bill a bit of hurry-up, he turned to the grandstand and expressed his feelings. The Press slipped into him over that.

slip-panel. SLIP-RAIL a.

1844 *Parramatta Chron.* 21 Sept. 2/2 John Star, the plaintiff's servant, was in his master's paddock when the defendants and another man pulled down the slip pannel, and insisted on riding through the paddock. 1934 J.C. LEE *Boshstralians* 187 Spikey .. was in the act of swinging himself on to the top rail of the slip-panel.

slippery. [f. the heavy coating of slime on the skin of the fish.] The fish *Gadopsis marmoratus* (see BLACKFISH).

1906 D.G. STEAD *Fishes of Aust.* 210 Amongst the Australian Blennies, there is one of considerable economic importance. This is the so-called 'Slippery' or River Blackfish. 1984 MERRICK & SCHMIDA *Austral. Freshwater Fishes* 269 River Blackfish or Slippery... This furtive species .. is usually less than 300 mm. long and 220 to 450 g.

slippery bob. *Obs.* See quot. 1864.

1864 *Colonial Cook Bk.* (1970) 72 Slippery Bob. Take kangaroo brains, and mix with flour and water, and make into batter; well season with pepper, salt, etc.; then pour a table-spoonful at a time into an iron pot containing emeu fat, and take them out when done. 1970 J.S. GUNN in W.S. Ramson *Eng. Transported* 63 Such food references as .. slippery bob and pan jam are well left to history.

slip-rail.

a. A fence-rail, forming one of a set which can be slipped out so as to leave an opening; the opening so formed: see quot. 1844. Also *attrib.*

1827 P. CUNNINGHAM *Two Yrs. in N.S.W.* I. 206 Some of the young saplings do contract most amazingly, and most quickly. Twice were the slip-rails of a gate reported to me as too short, and tumbling out. 1844 Mrs C. MEREDITH *Notes & Sketches N.S.W.* 130 You never see a *gate*... 'Slip-rails' are the substitute; five or six heavy long poles loosely inserted in sockets made in two upright posts. 1900 *Bulletin* (Sydney) 21 Apr. 3/2 The lovers standing at the sliprail gate.

b. *fig.*

1892 *Bulletin* (Sydney) 7 May 24/1 He soon must mount his bluey for The last long tramp of all; I trust that when in bush an' town, He's lived and learnt his fill, They'll let the golden slip-rails down For poor old Corny Bill. **1894** W. CROMPTON *Convict Jim* 36 Till I enter through ther slip-rails of ther never never gate.

slop, *n.*[1] *Obs.* [Transf. use of *slops* ready-made clothing and other furnishings supplied to seamen from a ship's stores: see OED(S *sb.*[1] 5. The word is used elsewhere during the 19th century but has a strong local significance.]

A. *n. pl.* Clothing issued by a colonial administration; clothing in general, usu. ready-made, but see quot. 1892.

1791 *HRA* (1914) 1st Ser. I. 239 A supply of provisions we have had, but cloathing not a rag, notwithstanding a great part of the slops sent in the Sirius for the use of the convicts were never put into store. **1892** 'MRS A. MACLEOD' *Silent Sea* III. 293 'Mother, the greatest happiness of your life is having slops made for people,' Rachel says to me sometimes, laughing, and perhaps it is true in a way.

B. *attrib.*

1. a. Of or pertaining to clothing issued by a colonial administration or to ready-made clothing in general.

1789 [see *slop clothing* below]. **1800** *HRA* 1st Ser. II. 634 A clothing and slop-expence book, for those supported by the Crown. **1978** M. WALKER *Pioneer Crafts Early Aust.* 74 People could buy apparel 'off the hook' from the town retailer but this cheap, standardised costume was anathema to many country women, who referred to it as 'slop clothes'.

b. *transf.* Supported by the government.

1832 *Hill's Life N.S.W.* (Sydney) 27 Aug. 2 The beaks .. sent the two victorines among others to the slop shop. *Seven days imprisonment.* **1836** *Bent's News* (Hobart) 3 Sept. 3 *The Courier.* We were much amused this morning with the leading article in the Slop Journal. *Ibid.* 22 Oct. 2 Poor Bent had worked hard, and he also had a large family, when the bread was taken out of their mouths, to pay for the silly drivellings of the Slop Editor.

2. Comb. **slop clothing, made** *a.*, **seller, shop.**

1789 J. HUNTER *Hist. Jrnl. Trans. Port Jackson* (1793) 371 Every free person or convict is strictly forbid buying or selling any article of **slop cloathing**. **1856** G. WILLMER *Draper in Aust.* 232 There is abundance of **slop-made** goods at present in Australia. **1843** *Dispatch* (Sydney) 11 Nov. 3/4 Draper, hosier, haberdasher, and **slopseller**. **1841** *Bell's Life in Sydney* 6 Sept. 1/1 Nearly every tailor in Sydney charges such high prices that it has driven a great portion of the middle and lower classes of society to obtain their clothes from Drapers and **Slop Shops**.

slop, *n.*[2] *pl.* [Orig. U.S.: see OEDS *sb.*[2] 3 c.] Beer; alcoholic liquor generally.

1944 L. GLASSOP *We were Rats* 120 If I ever get ter Germany I'll have a go at their slops. In one er them big beer gardens. **1982** R. HALL *Just Relations* 31 You and my grandson here on the slops, is that it?

sloper. [Spec. use of Br. dial. *sloper* trickster, defrauder: see EDD *slope, v.*[1]] One who leaves a place without discharging a debt.

1896 *Bulletin* (Sydney) 18 Jan. 3/2 You strike the stores for credit. They've all 'heard that yarn before'—They've 'had enough of slopers', an' they 'don't take any more!' **1981** H.C. MILLS *No Regrets* 78 The 'sloper'—the man who decamped without paying his debts, the worst of criminals.

slot. A prison cell; also, a prison.

1947 *Pix* (Sydney) 20 Sept. 15 *Peter* or *slot*, cell. **1976** *Cleo* Aug. 33 Some of the old heads are in the slot, he says. The slot is jail.

sloth. *Obs.* [Transf. use of *sloth* an arboreal mammal.] KOALA 1.

1811 G. PATERSON *Hist. N.S.W.* 417 The Koolah, or Sloth, a singular animal of the Opossum species, having a false belly, was found by the natives. **1886** F. COWAN *Aust.* 21 A makeshift Monkey, Bear, and Sloth.

slouch hat. [Fig. use of *slouch hat* the hat worn by an Australian soldier.] Used allusively as an emblem of patriotism and courage.

1927 K. BURKE *With Horse & Morse* 67 The 'butterfly' badges on their slouch hats had faded to a leaden grey. **1985** M. WALSH *May Gibbs* 126 Calendars featuring all the bush creatures, the favourite being a kookaburra depicted as a world war veteran wearing the Australian slouch hat.

Slowbart. *Obs.* Alteration of 'Hobart', the name of the capital city of Tasmania.

1895 *Bulletin* (Sydney) 10 Aug. 15/3 At Slowbart recently, a defending solicitor was questioning a publican, witness for the prosecution. **1905** *Truth* (Sydney) 24 Sept. 1/7 Parramatta has always been regarded as a Sleepy Hollow—sleepier than Slowbart, Tasmania.

slow strike. *Obs.* GO-SLOW *a.*

1917 *Award for Shearing, Crutching, & Wool-Scouring* (Cwlth. Court Conciliation & Arbitration) 42 A 'slow strike' has been held to be a breach of Clause 1 in that men deliberately shearing slowly are not shearing 'with all reasonable despatch'. **1918** J.H.C. SLEEMAN *Queer Qld.* 32 At the Ross River meatworks, the employees on contract hit upon a 'slow strike' as a means to harass the employers.

slow-worm. [Transf. use of *slow-worm* a small, harmless lizard.] Any of the small, worm-like, burrowing snakes of the genus *Ramphotyphlops* of mainland Aust. and elsewhere; any of many lizards of the fam. Pygopodidae of mainland Aust.

1824 J. LYCETT *Views in Aust.* 4 Of poisonous reptiles, the .. slow-worm and snake, are the most hurtful. **1970** R. BUSTARD *Austral. Lizards* 81 In Australia they [*sc.* the Pygopodidae] are sometimes called 'slow-worms' perhaps because the early European settlers were familiar with the slow-worm (*Anguis fragilis*) of their original homeland.

slug. [U.S. *slug* a piece of crude metal; a nugget (of gold): see OED(S *sb.*[2] 3 a.]

a. A large piece of crude metal found on or just below the surface; a nugget of gold. Also **slug gold,** and *attrib.*

1888 [see sense b. below]. **1891** 'SMILER' *Wanderings Simple Child* (ed. 3) 34 Silver was found lying round on the surface in lumps, or, as they were called, 'slugs'. **1903** *Bulletin* (Sydney) 7 Feb. 16/3 Lake Way was a great 'specking patch', and the gins .. were great speckers, and brought in a lot of slug gold. **1977** J. DOUGHTY *Gold in Blood* 49 For weeks they failed to raise a 'colour'. It was slug-or-nothing ground they were told. 'If you get a colour you'll get a slug.'

b. In the phr. **to travel on the slug:** see quot. 1888.

1888 'SPECIAL CORRESPONDENT' *Barrier Silver & Tin Fields* 11 It was a common thing for miners to travel 'on the slug'. A man would walk into a mining township, produce to the storekeeper a slug of very rich silver, and on the strength of having discovered a good claim get anything he wanted in the way of stores for himself and camp for weeks. Travelling 'on the slug' does not obtain now. **1891** 'SMILER' *Wanderings Simple Child* (ed. 3) 35 It would be worse than useless for an enterprising loafer to try to travel on the slug in the present day.

Hence **sluggy** *a.*, (of gold) in the form of a slug.

1881 J.C.F. JOHNSON *To Mount Browne & Back* 25 The gold, which for the most part is heavy and, to use of digger's term, 'sluggy' rather than nuggety, is found in these gullies.

sluicer, *v*. *Gold-mining*. An alluvial miner who uses a sluice to separate the particles of gold from the auriferous earth.
1855 W. HOWITT *Land, Labor & Gold* II. 193 It will not pay the cradler or the tommer to put through much rough earth. But the sluicer will come after him, and even out of the earth that he has cast aside as containing little, or nothing, will obtain in the aggregate large quantities. 1932 I.L. IDRIESS *Prospecting for Gold* 30 The sluicers mainly rely on lining the bottom of the box with a blanket, 'paving' the last two feet of the box with stones, and on the bottom ripple, to save their gold.

slum, *v*. [Prob. spec. use of Br. slang *slum* to cheat: see OED(S.)]
a. *trans.* To perform (a task) carelessly, lazily, or incompetently. Also *intr.*, to work carelessly, etc., and as *vbl. n*.
1847 *Hobart Town Courier* 7 Apr. 2/2 The 'Government step' and 'slumming' are fundamental articles of the convict creed, in which willing belief, established by constant habit, is maintained with marvellous tenacity. 1886 P. FLETCHER 'Hints to Immigrants' in P. Fletcher *Qld.* 29 If *well* put up it will last you for many years, but if 'slummed' it will soon get shaky and lean askew. 1891 *Truth* (Sydney) 8 Mar. 7/3 Of course he slums a lot, and makes the work as easy as possible.
b. *spec. Shearing.* To shear (a sheep or a number of sheep) carelessly, lazily, or incompetently.
1878 *Squatters' Plum* 42 At one time, shearers might 'slum' their work, and cut the sheep about, so long as the wool came off somehow, but, now, it requires a practised hand to shear 85 sheep a day, so as to please the overseer. 1966 J. CARTER *People of Inland* (1967) 165 At shearing time, these same 'guns' can slum pen after pen of fine, clean sheep, because the opportunity to set a new record has presented itself.

slush, *v*. *Obs.* [f. SLUSHY *n.*¹] *intr.* To work as a cook's assistant.
1891 *Truth* (Sydney) 22 Mar. 7/1 His brother, a union shearer, was slushing for the lamb-markers.

slush lamp. [Spec. use of *slush* waste fat, etc., aboard a ship: see OED *sb.*¹ 2.] An improvised light made from a container holding fat and fitted with a wick (see quot. 1893); SLUSHY *n.*². Also **slush light**, and *ellipt.* as **slush**.
1862 E.R. CHUDLEIGH *Diary* (1950) 40 Turned into our blankets and read by the light of some slush lamps which is a pot full of fat with a bit of lighted rag in the middle and soon fell asleep, the dogs at our feet, the cats at our head ... and rats everywhere. 1904 M. WHITE *Shanty Entertainment* 14 When the other fellows had dowsed their slushes or blown out their candle-lights. 1964 K. WILLEY *Eaters of Lotus* 54 Out in the camps he used to read by 'slush-light'—a piece of moleskin trousers shoved into a tin of fat like a wick, which used to give off 'a horrible light'.

slushy, *n.*¹ [Transf. use of *slushy* a ship's cook: see OED(S.)]
1. An assistant to a cook, esp. for a shearing gang.
1880 'OLD HAND' *Experiences of Colonist* (ed. 2) ii. 7 He was cook for the men, and bore the usual title of 'Slushey'. 1974 C. THIELE *Albatross Two* 67 'He's been offered a job on the oil rig.'... 'A kitchen rouseabout,' Aunt Jessica said scornfully. 'A pot-walloper; a slushy.'
2. *transf.* An unskilled assistant.
1900 *Truth* (Sydney) 11 Mar. 1/7 Tommy Atkins in Boerland does the real graft, the contingenters are genteel slushies or offsiders. 1953 'CADDIE' *Caddie* 25 Slushie was the name given to anyone who worked at a camp boarding-house. No one minded being called that.
Hence **slushy** *v. intr.*, to work as a cook's assistant.
1942 'Havildar' *Havalook: Mag. H.M.A.T. 'Havildar'* 16 Mar. 1 It must be rather hard to have to slushie one's way to Australia.

slushy, *n.*² [f. SLUSH (LAMP + -Y.] SLUSH LAMP.
1928 *Bulletin* (Sydney) 16 May 21/1 The venerable fat lamp, alias 'slushy' and 'greasy', is still used in hundreds of N.S.W. farmers' barns. 1931 J.R. FIDDIAN *R. Mitchell of Inland* 20 They made acquaintance with the primitive bush illuminant, the 'slushie', a piece of rag acting as wick for the melted fat which in burning gave light and smoke, more or less, to all that were in the house.

slutzkin /'slʊtskən/. See quot.
1982 *Age* (Melbourne) 14 Oct. 9/5 Slutzkins go back to February 1977 and a majority judgment by Sir Garfield Barwick, Sir Keith Aickin and Sir Ninian Stephen. In this case, litigants by the name of Slutzkin won court approval for the taxpayer to convert company income, on which tax has been paid, into a capital gain. Thus the shareholder's income is in the form of a capital gain, which is tax free.

sly, *a*. and *n*.
A. *adj.* [Spec. use of *sly* secretive: see OED(S *a.* 5 b. Chiefly Austral.]
1. Illicit, illegal; esp. of the retailing of alcoholic liquor. See SLY GROG.
1828 *Tasmanian* (Hobart) 15 Feb. 3 An application is sent in for a grant of land, and .. there is little difficulty in obtaining it. A house is immediately built, and a license applied for; but—if that cannot be obtained—it then becomes a '*sly house*', and grog is sold without it. 1973 *Bulletin* (Sydney) 27 Jan. 33/2 The Board of Works has actually asked people to dob in their neighbours for sly watering.
2. *Obs.* In the collocation **sly digging** *vbl. n.*, unlicensed gold-mining; the site of this.
1851 *Empire* (Sydney) 8 Aug. 27/4 One of the uninitiated, who had been doing a little sly digging, came to town a few days ago with a sample of something which he believed to be gold. 1852 G.C. MUNDY *Our Antipodes* III. 338 They are watched and followed by others who have been less successful, and the 'sly' diggings .. become known to the Commissioner.
B. *n.* [Spec. use of *on the sly* in a secret manner: OED(S *sb.* 2.] In the phr. **(up)on the sly**: (of the retailing of alcoholic liquor) without a licence.
1830 T. BETTS *Acct. Colony Van Diemen's Land* 49 These small settlements would become the resort of run-a-ways; and .. many of them would turn vendors of grog, on what is called 'the sly'. 1835 BACKHOUSE & TYLOR *Life & Labours G.W. Walker* 13 Dec. (1862) 231 There is hardly a single house or hut belonging to the lower description of settlers from the Nepean River to Bathurst, where grog may not be obtained 'upon the sly'.

sly grog.
1. **a.** Alcoholic liquor as sold by an unlicensed vendor. Freq. *attrib*.
1825 *Hobart Town Gaz.* 18 Mar., We therefore felt convinced that in the sequel they would altogether decline applying for licenses, whilst many of them would become sly grog-men to the manifest injury of Government. 1898 D.W. CARNEGIE *Spinifex & Sand* 351 She came overland from Queensland, accompanying her husband who, in the early days of the rush, sought to turn an honest penny by the sale of 'sly grog'.
b. Abbrev. of *sly-grog shop* (see sense 2 below).
1955 R. LAWLER *Summer of Seventeenth Doll* (1965) 42

Keepin' nit for the S.P. bookies, eh—drummin' up trade for the sly grogs. **1975** LATCH & HITCHINGS *Mr X* 224 I'll tell you where the brothels are and who's running them, the sly grogs, the bookies.

2. Comb. **sly-grog seller, selling** *vbl. n.*, **shanty, shop, tent.**

1826 *Hobart Town Gaz.* 11 Nov., **Sly Grog Sellers.** These avaricious panders to the vices of the worst part of this population have adopted a new method to evade the penalties of the late Act. **1827** *Tasmanian* (Hobart) 6 Sept. 4 The abominable system of **sly-grog selling**. **1882** A.J. BOYD *Old Colonials* 104 As soon as farmers are settled the *bona fide* publican settles amongst them, and the **sly grog shanty**, as it is familiarly called, cannot stand. **1826** *Monitor* (Sydney) 4 Aug. 90/3 We see our sister Colony is cursed .. with heavy licences on public-houses and its consequence, '**sly grog shops**', i.e. back places where grog is drank [*sic*] in stealth, and coupled with gambling and lewdness. **1855** G.H. WATHEN *Golden Colony* 184 At the Diggings every gully and flat was infested with '**sly grog-tents**'.

sly-grogger. One who sells alcoholic liquor without a licence. Also **sly-grogster.**

1897 *Bulletin* (Sydney) 10 Apr. 10/2 A couple of shanty-keepers were trapped by an excise-officer who gained the confidence of the sly-grogsters by making himself known to them as a brother Mason. **1980** W.H. O'ROURKE *My Way* 67 Although there was no hotel nearer than Manjimup, a 'sly grogger' attended the local dances and provided the thirst quenchers.

sly-groggery. An establishment at which alcoholic liquor is sold illegally.

1907 *Truth* (Sydney) 9 June 7/8 *Sly groggery*. A 'rum' case at the Central. **1957** J. WATEN *Shares in Murder* 76 What if you were running a sly groggery? It's nothing to us. We're not the licensing squad.

sly-grogging, *vbl. n.* Illegal dealing in alcoholic liquor.

1952 *Bulletin* (Sydney) 3 Dec. 13/1 The local publican went in for a bit of sly-grogging—at a price. **1981** P. CORRIS *White Meat* 89 Ted's instincts, bred in the SP game and sly grogging, were to avoid the police.

sly-grogster: see SLY GROGGER.

smallgoods, *pl.* Cooked meats and meat products. Freq. *attrib.* as **smallgoods shop.**

[N.Z. **1879** W.J. BARRY *Up & Down* 181, I had also tradesmen at work making up 'small goods' which I sold to retail butchers.] **1905** *Truth* (Sydney) 25 Apr. 1/7 The small goods in a Leichhardt ham and beef shop. **1955** *Bulletin* (Sydney) 7 Dec. 12/1 A kitten .. was abandoned in a suburban smallgoods shop.

small grass-tree: see GRASS-TREE 1 b.

smalls, *pl.* Mining. [Spec. use of Br. dial. *smalls* 'thinly powdered tin-stuff': see EDD *small, sb.* 7.] Pieces of ore graded as small: see quot. 1914.

1847 *S. Austral. Register* (Adelaide) 21 Apr. 2/5 The ores .. sent from Glen Osmond mine we beg to inform them that the intended shipment was pretended to be what the miners call 'smalls' and consequently bags were necessary. **1914** *Wallaroo & Moonta Mines* 26 The ores received from the Company's mines comprise, 'roughs' (2½ in.), 'toppings' (¾ in.), 'smalls' (½ in.) [etc.].

small-scaled snake. The highly venomous large snake *Parademansia microlepidota* of e. central Aust., formerly confused with the related TAIPAN.

1980 *Ecos* xxiv. 32/1 The small-scaled snake, *Parademansia microlepidota*, was first found in 1879 by a naturalist named Frederick McCoy. **1983** *Age* (Melbourne) 22 Nov. 3/2 The small-scaled snake which, fortunately, occupies only a small part of central Australia, has the most powerful snake venom in the world, with enough in each bite to kill 250,000 mice.

Smellbourne. Also **Smellbun, Smellburn.** Alteration of 'Melbourne', the name of the capital city of Victoria: see quot. 1898.

1890 A.J. VOGAN *Black Police* 380 My trip to Melbourne—Smellbourne the *Bulletin* calls it, and rightly. **1898** H. MATTHEWS *Chat about Aust.* 44 Melbourne, situated as it is on the banks of the Yarra, which, coupled with a very faulty system of drainage, has often caused that wonderful city to be called 'Smellbourne'. **1907** *Truth* (Sydney) 27 Oct. 1/4 There has been a rumpus lately in the good old Sydney town, All the 'Holy Joes' of Smellbourne wear the mourning garb and gown. **1911** *Ibid.* 14 May 1/8 Oh, the dear old Smellbun matron Is a model in her house. **1955** N. PULLIAM *I traveled Lonely Land* 225 Beaches? Beaches? In Smellburn?

smelt. [Transf. use of *smelt* the small European fish *Osmerus eperlanus* and other species of the fam. Osmeridae.] Any of several small fish, esp. those of the fam. Retropinnidae, as *Retropinna semoni* of s.e. Aust. and *R. tasmanica* of Tas.

1821 T. GODWIN *Descr. Acct. Van Diemen's Island* 9 Fish are caught in abundance... Those most known are .. smelt, John Dory, oysters. **1984** MERRICK & SCHMIDA *Austral. Freshwater Fishes* 109 This smelt .. is most frequently found in lakes and slowly flowing water.

smoke, *n.*

1. [Also U.S.] A column of smoke serving as a signal or as a sign of an encampment, etc.

1770 J. HAWKESWORTH *Acct. of Voyages* (1773) III. 490 Seeing a smoke on the shore, we directed our glasses to the spot, and soon discovered ten people, who, upon our nearer approach left their fire. **1968** W. GILL *Petermann Journey* 91 When the wind dropped at sunset, the natives sent up a 'smoke' from a fire they made in the bed of the creek.

2. Abbrev. of *big smoke* (see BIG 2).

1892 *Bulletin* (Sydney) 20 Aug. 21/2 He left 'the smoke' to wander where the wattle-blossoms wave. **1966** B. BEAVER *You can't come Back* 12, I wasn't struck on working for the railways up in the bush or down in the smoke but so far it was the only job I'd held down.

3. *Obs.* Abbrev. of *smoke concert* (see sense 5 below). Also *attrib.*

1904 *Truth* (Sydney) 28 Aug. 7/2 The National Sporting Club has decided to entertain the English Football Team at a farewell smoke concert... Something extra special in the way of a programme for the smoke. **1906** *Gadfly* (Adelaide) 16 May 8/2 At a farewell 'smoke' to an Adelaide man recently a genial Scot took the chair, and .. declared pathetically that the departing guest left the firm 'respected by all'.

4. In the phr. **in(to) smoke,** in(to) hiding.

1908 *Lone Hand* Dec. 166 When not 'in smoke' (i.e. in hiding), the cheerful Smithy sometimes 'fights in the 'alls'. **1938** W. HATFIELD *Buffalo Jim* 35 You'd better go into smoke now till old Jerry routs you out and says you're Oke.

5. Special Comb. **smoke concert, night, social,** an informal social occasion at which guests smoke and chat, and at which light entertainment is freq. provided. Also *attrib.*

[N.Z. **1888** J.D. WICKHAM *Casual Ramblings* 42 They had a **smoke concert** with a Salvation Army accompaniment.] **1891** *Bird o' Freedom* (Sydney) 25 Apr. 8/3 The Pyrmont Rangers Football Club open their season by a smoke concert, to be held in Pyrmont on May 8. **1906** *Gadfly* (Adelaide) 18 July 20/1 The Sydney Pressman's **smoke-night.** **1965** K. TENNANT *Summer's Tales* 226 I'm coming, wind, I'm nearing the door with the C.W.A. and Smoke Night notices drawing-pinned on. **1901** *Advocate* (Burnie) 31 Aug. 2/7 A well-attended **'smoke social'** was tendered.

smoke, *v.*

1. a. *intr.* To make a hasty departure. Also with **off**.
1893 *Sydney Morning Herald* 26 June 8/8 'Let us 'smoke'.' Smoke, it may be explained, is the slang for the 'push' to get away as fast as possible. **1961** P. WHITE *Riders in Chariot* 415 Dubbo had gone all right. Had taken his tin box, it seemed, and smoked off.

b. *trans.* To effect the departure of (a person). Also *reflex*.
1917 C. DREW *Reminisc. D. Gilbert* 51 They always smoke themselves away like that. They're under them leaves. *c* **1930** 'N. GHURKA' *Graft* 5, I got the 'whisper' (information) that Lillian Philby had been 'smoked', and that a police officer had stage-managed her departure for a substantial consideration from Clark.

2. To signal (a message, etc.) by means of smoke from a fire. Also **smoke-talk** *intr.*
1931 I.L. IDRIESS *Lasseter's Last Ride* 140 He bargained with them to .. 'smoke-talk' to distant myalls. **1976** C.D. MILLS *Hobble Chains & Greenhide* 5 Next morning Pebble and Mollampi rode off to 'smoke' the news that we were on to him and would be ready for the run first thing on Thursday morning.

smoke bush. [See quot. 1933.] Any of several shrubs or trees of the genus *Conospermum* (fam. Protaceae), chiefly of s.w. W.A., having white woolly flowers.
1888 *Centennial Mag.* (Sydney) 15 The whitey-blue green of the smoke bush. **1933** H.J. CARTER *Gulliver in Bush* 232 We journeyed over plains dotted with smoke bush (of which the popular name comes from the woolly white flower showing like smoke in the distance).

smoke-ho, smoke-o, smoke-oh, varr. SMOKO.

smoker. The long-tailed parrot *Polytelis anthopeplus* of s.w. and s.e. Aust., the adult male of which has mustard-yellow plumage and a dark tail; *regent parrot*, see REGENT 2; *rock pebbler*, see ROCK n. 2.
1933 D. MACDONALD *Brooks of Morning* 49 The Black-tailed Parrakeet—the 'smoker' of the Mallee—is heard, and seen often in gleams of golden green, amongst the gums. **1984** E. WALLING *On Trail Austral. Wildflowers* 48 We had seen .. Smoker Parrots, smoke black and sulphur yellow.

smoke talk: see SMOKE *v.* 2.

smoko. Also **smoke-ho, smoke-o, smoke-oh.** [f. *smoke* a spell of smoking tobacco + -O.]

1. a. A tea-break; a rest from work; the food and drink provided for this period (see also quot. 1969). Also *attrib*.
1865 *Austral. Monthly Mag.* (Melbourne) I. 234 They in a 'smoke oh!' time, commenced to recount feats that they had seen done. **1872** G.S. BADEN-POWELL *New Homes for Old Country* 175 At stated times throughout the day there comes a general spell, commenced as soon as the phrase 'smoke-oh!' is heard. **1914** *Bulletin* (Sydney) 30 July 24/1 Fifty-two shearers were employed, exclusive of rouseabouts, pickers, classers, cooks, slushies and whalers .. and to save time the cook's off-sider took the 'smoke-ho' around on roller skates. **1936** F. CLUNE *Roaming round Darling* 115 At smoke-o a visitor 'got the bird' for taking out his teeth, in order to drink more comfortably. **1969** J. PACKER *Leopard in Fold* 55 Their smokos—the packed lunches prepared by Mrs Wale—were beside their plates. **1986** *Sydney Morning Herald* 29 Aug. 17/1 Restrictive work practices—from heavily subsidised housing to the provision of pink salmon and oysters for workers' 'smoko' breaks.

b. *transf.*
1915 *Bulletin* (Sydney) 28 Jan. 22/3 A gentle breeze zephyred from Monday to Friday, not even knocking off for smoko, and taking no notice of Wages Boards' awards respecting holidays. **1946** F. CLUNE *Try Nothing Twice* 108 My heart went out to the calves, so I let them do the stripping, by opening up the calf pen, so they could have ten minutes smoke-oh with their mothers in the cow-yard.

2. *Smoke concert*, see SMOKE *n.* 5. Also *attrib*.
1918 G.A. TAYLOR *Those were Days* 30 It was a rare incident for that distinguished party to grace an Art Society 'Smoko'. **1940** *Any Complaints* (Newcastle) 4 Apr. 8 No. 12 Platoon .. held a smoko evening last week.

smoodge, *v.* Also **smooge**. [Br. dial. *smudge* to kiss, to sidle up to: see EDD *v.*¹ 2. Cf. OED *smouch*, *v.*¹ and OEDS *smooch*, *v.*³]

1. *intr.* To behave in an ingratiating manner; to 'make up to' a person.
1898 *Worker* (Sydney) 6 Aug. 4/3 The principal industries and businesses are owned by Japs, Kanakas, Chows and other colored citizens to whom the 'white trash' must smoodge if they are not to be starved out. **1959** E. WEBB *Mark of Sun* 173 Barney here used to hang around, smooging to mum for the kind of favours she wasn't the kind for giving, see?

2. *transf. trans.* To smooth; to smooth the passage (of something).
1910 W. MOORE *Tea-Room Girl* 18 Watching the wavelets smoodge the glistening sand. **1934** C. STEAD *Seven Poor Men* 66 Marion had little difficulty when she went down to smoodge Fulke's interdicted books in French and German through the customs.

Hence **smoodging** *vbl. n.* and *ppl. a.*
1904 *Shearer* (Sydney) 17 Sept. 3/3 All his .. 'smooging' failed to score him any wins. **1949** J. MORRISON *Creeping City* 8 You pay sixpence to go in and have a gig at his .. fishponds and smoodging nooks.

smoodge, *n.* Also **smooge**. [f. SMOODGE *v.*] Flattery; an act of ingratiation; a display of amorous affection. In the phr. **to do a smoodge, to come the smoodge,** to behave in such a way.
1909 *Truth* (Sydney) 2 May 1/8 It is certainly better to speak In support of your honest beliefs Than in attitude humble and meek Do a smooge for a few paltry briefs. **1955** D. NILAND *Shiralee* 136 If there was no blokes about, he'd come the smoodge to the women for a bit of a love-up. **1980** D. HEWETT *Susannah's Dreaming* (1981) 21 What's wrong with a bit of a smooge between friends? You didn't useta be so choosy. What is it? Got annuver lover or somethin'?

smoodger. Also **smooger**. A flatterer; a sycophant. Also *transf*.
1897 *Worker* (Sydney) 11 Sept. 1/1 While he who 'crawls' and 'runs the cut' and lacks a bushman's pluck, Is known by men as 'smoodger', while the tarboys call him 'suck'. **1928** *Bulletin* (Sydney) 12 Dec. 25/2 A wily old smooger was Jimmy Harrin, who kept a tanglefoot house in Mulgatown. **1976** C.D. MILLS *Hobble Chains & Greenhide* 116 Gentle, affectionate and a real 'smoodger', with plenty of life though very quiet to ride.

smooge, var. SMOODGE *v.* and *n.*

smooger, var. SMOODGER.

smoogy /'smudʒi/, *a.* Also **smoogey**. Ingratiating; affectionate. Also as quasi-*adv.*
1900 *Truth* (Sydney) 4 Feb. 1/4 You have brass enough for a whole park of artillery, with all your nice, smoogy ways. **1959** A. UPFIELD *Bony & Mouse* 208 Harmon called me into the office, all smoogey-like.

smooy /'smui/. Also **smooie**. [Abbrev. of SMOO(DGE *n.* + -Y.] See quot. 1967.

1967 *Kings Cross Whisper* (Sydney) xl. 4/4 Smooy, 'a bit of smooy' to make love. 1970 R. BEILBY *No Medals for Aphrodite* 279 'We should be able to take it easy, have a swim, bit of grog, perhaps a few sheilas. . . ' 'You tell me what's better than grog and smooie, sarn,' he challenged.

smother.

1. *Obs.* An undercover enterprise; a strategem.

1902 *Truth* (Sydney) 3 Aug. 8/4 We could name several other 'smothers' where the proprietor combines the business of prostitution with that of criminal coddling. 1903 *Sporting News* (Launceston) 23 May 2/6 He has a 'smother' which has saved him from many a well-directed blow, using this in preference to his feet.

2. In the phr. **to put the smother on,** to suppress.

1963 B. SUTTON *Snow & Me* (1966) 18 They are to put the smother on how much dough the toilers are getting done for.

smoush /smuʃ/. [Var. of *smooch*: see OEDS *sb.*^{2}] A kiss.

1963 D. NILAND *Dadda Jumped* 182 He clutched the girl and gave her a smoush like the smack of a rubber glove. 1971 D. IRELAND *Unknown Industr. Prisoner* 173 Reminds me of a widow I knew at Richmond. Whenever I visited her and a plane went over she'd drop whatever she was doing and rush over for a smoush.

snack. Something easy to accomplish, a 'pushover'.

1941 S.J. BAKER *Pop. Dict. Austral. Slang* 68 Snack, a certainty. 1970 R. BEILBY *No Medals for Aphrodite* 274 'How could I do that, Harry?' 'Easy. It'll be a snack.'

snag, *n.*^{1} [Fig. use of *snag* an obstacle.] An adversary to be reckoned with.

1905 J. FURPHY *Rigby's Romance* (1946) 78 Grand thing to be a (adj.) snag like him. 1978 D. STUART *Wedgetail View* 50 I'm not too bloody sure Sandy wouldn't be a snag himself. . . He's rangy, he's strong, an' he's certainly not awkward. I think he'd be a surprise packet if anyone put him out too much. An' he's not a bloody flyweight, y'know.

snag, *n.*^{2} [Prob. spec. use of Br. dial. *snag* a morsel, a light repast: see EDD *v.*^{2} and *sb.*^{3} and cf. *snack* (see OED *sb.*^{2} 4 b.).] A sausage.

1941 S.J. BAKER *Pop. Dict. Austral. Slang* 68 Snags, sausages. 1972 *Bulletin* (Sydney) 12 Aug. 7/3 As an experiment our committee bunged on a rort for some of them, with plenty of snags and red Ned.

snag, *v.*^{1} *Obs.* [f. *snag* short stump.] *intr.* To clear away stumps, etc., before cultivation. Also *trans.*

1904 *Bulletin* (Sydney) 22 Dec. 16/4 After rolling, the right thing is to 'snag' level with the ground. Feverish haste of cocky to 'get crop in', however, leaves him no time for this. 1910 'YARRAN' *Mallee* 7 As early as possible after the first year, the beginner should 'snag' a portion of his original clearing, so as to render it fit for a binder to work.

snag, *v.*^{2} *intr.* To shear: see SNAGGER.

1927 J. MATHIEU *Backblock Ballards* 1 And I reckon I'll be snagging Too, this season, when it starts.

snagger. *Shearing.* [Transf. use of *snagger* a bill-hook.] A slow, inexpert, or inept shearer.

1887 *Tibbs' Pop. Song Bk.* 11, I found a lot of snaggers Not a shearer in the mob. 1985 J. HARRISON *Bit of Dag* 7 One old snagger now retired, having shorn for forty years . . is living on $15,000 a year.

snail. *Obs.* See quot. 1898.

1897 *Worker* (Sydney) 11 Sept. 1/1 Musterers, sometimes he calls . . 'snails'. 1898 *Bulletin* (Sydney) 17 Dec. 15/1 Musterers are snails (originally applied to slow musterers who couldn't keep up with the sheep and stopped the shearing. Now a general term).

snaily, *a.* and *n.* Also **snailey**. [Cf. Br. dial. *snailhorn(ed* (see OED).]

A. *adj.* Of an animal's horn: curled like a snail-shell. Of cattle: having horns of this description.

1884 'R. BOLDREWOOD' *Old Melbourne Memories* 123 That black bullock . . him with the snaily horn. 1891 —— *Sydney-Side Saxon* 133 There's a snailey Wallanbah bullock I haven't seen this two years.

B. *n.* A beast having snaily horns.

1884 'R. BOLDREWOOD' *Old Melbourne Memories* 68 Snaileys and poleys, old and young, coarse and fine, they were a mixed herd in every sense. 1894 A.B. BELL *Oscar* 9 The big, red baldy's in the lead as usual, so is the magpie, the fat roan, the old razorback, and the white snailey.

snake.

1. Used *attrib.* in Special Comb. **snake charmer** W.A., a railway maintenance worker; **Gully,** an imaginary place, perceived as remote and backward; **-headed** *a.*, angry; vituperative; **juice,** alcoholic liquor, esp. of an inferior sort; a drink of this; also *attrib.*; **yarn,** a tall story.

1937 A.W. UPFIELD *Mr Jelly's Business* 16 'What are the **Snake Charmers?**' 'They are the permanent-way men.' 1945 *Tropic Spread: Mag. 18th Austral. Advanced Ordnance Depot* July 7 Report from our **Snake-Gully** correspondent. 1900 *Bulletin* (Sydney) 28 Apr. 32/2 He owed Milligan a big score in bar and store and Pat was turning '**snake-headed**'. 1890 *Pall Mall Gaz.* (London) 3 Sept. 3/2 This whisky, or **snake-juice,** as bushmen often call the hell-broth prepared for them. 1914 *Bulletin* (Sydney) 27 Aug. 24/4, I would like to know the ingredients of a particular brand of snake-juice that the Japs have popularised in the pearling industry at Broome (W.A.) . . known as 'corpse reviver'. 1920 *Ibid.* 24 June 22/4 The boss was afraid we would break away to the nearest snake-juice factory before the job was done. 1930 A.E. YARRA *Vanishing Horsemen* 55 'Two snakejuices,' he said to the man behind the bar. 1903 *Advocate* (Burnie) 27 May 2/6, I believe the crop is near 30 tons per acre. . . This is no '**snake yarn**'.

2. In Services' speech: a sergeant. Freq. *attrib.* as **snake pit,** the sergeants' mess.

1941 *Action Front: Jrnl. 2/2 Field Regiment* Aug. 3 Have increased our contribution to the Snake Pit. 1951 E. LAMBERT *Twenty Thousand Thieves* 314 Baxter reckons the officers and snakes are pinching our beer.

snake flower. See quot. 1916.

1916 *Bulletin* (Sydney) 11 May 24/1 Any flower of a certain unattractive shade of purple is 'snake-flower'. 1981 G. CROSS *George & Widda-Woman* 9 We gathered small bunches of flowers for Mum . . snake flowers, flannel flowers, Christmas bush.

snakewood. A tree having twisted branches, as *Acacia grasbyi* (fam. Mimosaceae) of W.A.

1817 A. CUNNINGHAM in I. Marriott *Early Explorers Aust.* 23 May (1925) 218 We saw some fine specimens of a tree which our people termed Snakewood. 1982 *Bulletin* (Sydney) 23 Nov. 45/1 A kilometre-long belt of bowgada bean and snakewood—wattles known to botanists as *Acacia linophylla* and *Acacia grasbyi.*

snaky, *a.* Also **snakey.** Savage; angry. Also *fig.*

1894 *Bulletin* (Sydney) 28 Apr. 23/1 That night I started drinking at the shanty on the Flat Where the o.p. grog is snaky. **1935** P. LAWLOR *Confessions of a Journalist* 29 'Crikey,' whispered the 'Truth' man sitting next to me. 'Look at the Beak. He looks so snakey. I think he's going to put on the black cap.'

snap, *n. Australian National Football.* A quickly taken and opportune kick at goal. Also *attrib.* as **snap drop**.
   1894 J.M. MACDONALD *Thunderbolt* 93 Hanks took a snap-drop at the goal, and through it went, score No. 2 for Bendigo. **1960** *N.T. News* (Darwin) 19 Jan. 10/2 Joe Bonson grabbed the ball from a throw-in and shot a major with a neat snap. *Ibid.* 9 Feb. 11/4 Cooper sent to Peter Marrego who raised both flags with a good snap.

snap, *v. Australian National Football.* trans. See quot. 1969.
   1960 *N.T. News* (Darwin) 12 Jan. 8/3 Vierk snapped a goal which was disallowed for a free to Wanderers. **1969** EAGLESON & MCKIE *Terminol. Austral. Nat. Football* iii. 17 *Snap a goal (or behind)*, score a goal (or behind) with a sudden opportune kick.

snap and rattle. Also **snappin' rattle**. [See quot. 1935.] Any of several trees, incl. *Eucalyptus gracilis* (fam. Myrtaceae) of s. mainland Aust.
   1935 L.J. GOMM *Blazing Western Trails* 171 A tree they call 'snap and rattle' was quite new to me. It grows big like other trees, but just at this time of the year the bark peels off in great long strips... The wind blows these streamers about... They snap and rattle in the wind, hence the name. **1950** C.E. GOODE *Yarns of Yilgarn* 85 Shingly rises begrudgingly supporting snappin' rattle or thorny-oak or mulga.

snap drop: see SNAP.

snapper. Also **schnapper**. [Spec. use of *snapper* used widely as a name for a fish.] Any of several marine fish of the fam. Sparidae, esp. the pinkish-silver *Chrysophrys unicolor* of w. Aust., *C. auratus* of s. Aust. and elsewhere, and *C. guttulatus* of e. Aust., valued as food. See also COCKNEY, *old man snapper* OLD MAN B. 3, *red bream* RED *a.* 1 b., SQUIRE. Also *attrib.*
   1699 W. DAMPIER *New Voyage round World* (1703) III. 140 In the night while Calm we fish'd with Hook and Line and caught good store of Fish, *viz* Snappers, Breams, Old Wives, and Dog-Fish. **1897** 'OLD HOUSEKEEPER' *Austral. Plain Cooking* 46 Trevalla and schnapper.. must be cut across, in pieces about half an inch in thickness, or may be filleted. **1969** J. POLLARD *Austral. & N.Z. Fishing* 707 Various other fish may be called snapper. Those most commonly confused are the various members of the emperor or sweetlips family, *Lutjanidae*, and the quite unrelated fish of the red snapper family *Berycidae*.

snappin' rattle, var. SNAP AND RATTLE.

snappy gum. [See quot. 1897.] Any of several tree species of the genus *Eucalyptus* (fam. Myrtaceae) yielding a brittle timber, incl. *E. brevifolia*, *E. haemastoma*, and *E. rossii*. See also BRITTLE GUM, SCRIBBLY GUM.
   1897 *Proc. Linnean Soc. N.S.W.* XXII. 706 *E[ucalyptus] haemastoma* var. *micrantha*.. in one or other of the many districts in which it occurs, usually goes under some name referring to the softness or brittleness of its timber, *e.g.*, 'Cabbage Gum', 'Snappy Gum', 'Brittle Gum'. **1978** K. WILLEY *Joe Brown's Dog* 99 Bluey found the next man, Wunduk, in a clump of little snappy gums where he must have tried to hide.

snarler. [Quasi-acronym, f. the initial letters of 'services *no longer* required'.] In Services' speech: see quot. 1943.
   1943 S.J. BAKER *Pop. Dict. Austral. Slang* (ed. 3) 74 *Snarler*, a soldier or flier sent back home from overseas service because of some misdemeanour. **1983** *Sun-Herald* (Sydney) 17 July 57/3 In the Navy's Weekly Postings he receives an official 'snarler' which is nautical for a 'services no longer required' notification.

snatch, *v.* In the phr. **to snatch it**, or (one's, the, etc.,) **bit, rent, time,** to resign; to take the wages due and leave a job.
   1911 *Bulletin* (Sydney) 13 July 14/3 Will someone on the mainland tell me whether the slang phrase, 'Snatch it', is used there by miners when they announce their intention of 'drawing their time'? It is common on the mining fields of Tassy. **1915** *Ibid.* 28 Oct. 22/4 A shearer.. never gets 'sacked'. He always 'pelts it in' or 'snatches his bit'. **1953** L. & C. REES *Spinifex Walkabout* 76 The cook had a bit of a row with the overseer and had 'snatched his rent'—given notice. **1979** J. WILLIAMS *White River* 40 Once they got you here, you felt the power of the company... To hell with the civil liberties you once thought you possessed. Snatching your time didn't pay.

snavel, *v.* Also **snavvel**. [Br. dial. but now chiefly Austral.: see EDD *v.*² and OEDS.] *trans.* To steal; to appropriate; to grab. Also *absol.*
   1892 *Truth* (Sydney) 15 May 1/6 He has only managed to 'snavel' £4000 this year. **1902** *Ibid.* 13 July 4/3 Finding that he can neither finger nor filch, snavel nor sneak. **1934** *Austral. Ring* VIII. xcv. 6 Lurich snavvled first fall in the third round.

sneezeweed. [See quot. 1965.] Any of the several aromatic herbs of the genus *Centipeda* (fam. Asteraceae) of Aust. and elsewhere.
   1877 F. VON MUELLER *Introd. Bot. Teachings* 58 The Sneeze-weed (*Cotula* or *Centipeda Cunninghamii*). A dwarf, erect.. odorous herb... Can be converted into snuff. **1965** *Austral. Encycl.* VIII. 169 Sneezeweed, the vernacular name for low aromatic herbs in the genus *Centipeda*.. which, when crushed, are strongly irritant to the mucous membranes; the vapour causes sneezing.

snide. *Pearling.* [Transf. use of *snide* counterfeit.] A stolen pearl. Also *attrib.*, and as **snide pearl**.
   1933 J.M. HARCOURT *Pearlers* 116 As if every mother's son of them wouldn't buy snides from his own brother's boat! **1937** J.M. HARCOURT *It never Fails* 110 Snides, Julius gathered, were stolen pearls, and snide-buying an industry that yielded precedence in importance only to pearling itself. **1941** K.S. PRICHARD *Moon of Desire* 120 He had been buying snide pearl, as well as the best stuff in the town, for years.

snig, *v. Timber-getting.* Past tense **snigged, snug, snugged.** [Br. dial.: see EDD *v.*¹ and OEDS *v.*²]
   1. *trans.* To haul (a log) by means of ropes and chains. Also with **out** and **up**.
   [N.Z. **1866** B. HARPER *Kettle on Fuchsia* (1967) 69 Snigging firewood out.] **1897** L. LINDLEY-COWEN *W. Austral. Settler's Guide* 229 There is a fourth method [of clearing forests], which is certainly the most expeditious, but it requires a large amount of capital and would only pay where a large area of country had to be cleared. I refer to the use of traction engines fitted with long wire ropes by means of which the trees can be pulled down as they stand, without any preliminary preparation, and then 'snigged' up into rows eight or ten chains apart. **1917** *Bk. of Ballarat* 32 When he had the job of cleaning up the Green Swamp.. it was David who fastened the chains and snugged them in on the slippery boulders. **1920** *Land of Lyre Bird* (S. Gippsland Pioneers' Assoc.) 83 The construction of the hundreds of miles of chock and log fencing, the materials for which had to be 'snigged' up hill and down dale through a veritable labyrinth of stumps and logs and holes. **1945** J. DEVANNY *Bird of Paradise* 19 After a log is snug the heart

pops out still further and finishes up about a quarter of an inch beyond the rest of the log. **1983** *Overlander* Jan. 84 Diesels .. no more stalling when you stop halfway up a steep hill to .. snig out a log.

2. *transf.*

[N.Z. **1966** P. Newton *Boss's Story* 97 Saw one of the chaps snigging a dog away by its tail.] **1976** J.H. TRAVERS *Bull Dust on Brigalow* 54 Sometimes a brumby horse would be shot and snigged near the house by a couple of draught horses. **1981** H. HANNAH *Together in Jungle Scrub* 42 There were big fireplaces, where you'd open a door and snig a big log in.

Hence **snigging** *vbl. n.* and *attrib.*, esp. as **snigging track**, a track along which timber is hauled.

1910 *Emu* X. 209 Some 'snigging' track, cut for the purpose of timber hauling. **1944** J. DEVANNY *By Tropic Sea & Jungle* 118 The grappling and snigging of the logs.

snig-track. *Timber-getting. Snigging track*, see SNIG.

[N.Z. **1953** N.Z. Forest Gloss. (N.Z. Forest Service) (typescript), *Snig track*, a path constructed for snigging.] **1979** *Sydney Morning Herald* 5 Sept. 6 In order to extract logs from the buffer zone, roads and 'snig' tracks will have to be cut through the virgin rainforest. **1985** *Age* (Melbourne) 31 Oct. 11/3 The two foresters were proud that guidelines for logging are now being enforced, including .. routes that roads and snig tracks must follow.

snipe, *n.* [Spec. use of U.S. *snipe* an outdoor advertising poster.] See quot. 1966.

1966 S.J. BAKER *Austral. Lang.* (ed. 2) 355 *Snipe*, a political election poster, the size of which is limited to 10 in. by 6 in. **1977** F. DALY *From Curtin to Kerr* 75 He went to the same printer as me, got the same kind of snipes printed in blue and white with his photograph and pasted them up all over the electorate on every post: *Vote No. 1* Clark... He pasted snipes on nearly every post and on the day had his booths well manned.

sniper. See quot. 1945. Also **sniping** *vbl. n.*

1945 S.J. BAKER *Austral. Lang.* 248 A waterfront term of fairly recent origin is *sniper*, a non-union labourer. **1950** J. MORRISON *Port of Call* 222 Don't you know what sniping is? Taking work outside the 'Pound or outside pick-up hours.

snob, *n.*[1] S.A. Obs. In *pl.*: see quot. 1863.

1852 *Four Colonies Aust.* 39 The retailers, and all not within a certain indescribable line, were dubbed the 'snobs'; the officials and self-elected aristocracy, the 'nobs'. **1863** J.B. AUSTIN *Mines S.A.* 19 The Princess Royal Mining, and .. the South Australian Mining Association .. were called the 'nobs' and the 'snobs', the former representing the 'aristocracy' of the colony, and the latter the merchants and tradespeople.

snob, *n.*[2] [Punning use of *snob* a shoemaker or cobbler.] COBBLER *n.*[2]

1915 *Bulletin* (Sydney) 28 Oct. 22/3 The last sheep left in the pen is always a very rough one, and is termed the 'cobbler' or the 'snob'. **1975** L. RYAN *Shearers* 49 'Get on to this wrinkled bludger!' he said. It was the last sheep in the pen... 'Real snob ain't it?'

snodger, *a.* [Of unknown origin. Cf. Br. dial. *snod* sleek, neat, in good order: see OED *a.* and EDD *a.*] Excellent, very good, first-class. Also as *n.* and *adv.*

1917 *O.P.: Lit. Chron. 10th Battery A.F.A.* 35 An' at that he hits me a snodger in the neck. **1921** F. GROSE *Rough Y.M. Bloke* 26 We went through a lot of gardens right up to a 'snodger' 'ouse. **1946** *Sun* (Sydney) 11 Aug. (Suppl.) 15 There they find the con-ships fitted up snodger with bulkheads studded with nails.

snodgollion: see SNOTTYGOBBLE.

snooker, *n.* [f. SNOOKER *v.*] A hiding-place.

1967 *Kings Cross Whisper* (Sydney) xxxv. 6/2 *In smoke*, to hide out. Similar to being in snooker. **1979** L. NEWCOMBE *Inside Out* 84 'It's O.K. they won't find us here.' 'We've still gotta find a better snooker than this.'

snooker, *v.* [Transf. use of *snooker* to prevent (someone) from reaching an object.] *trans.* To hide.

1968 J. ALARD *He who shoots Last* 224 We'll have to snooker da dough some place. **1979** L. NEWCOMBE *Inside Out* 80, I suggested to Kevin that .. we could 'snooker' ourselves for a while in the boot of one of the cars parked outside.

snoot. [f. *snooty, a.* supercilious, snobbish.] A supercilious person.

1955 N. PULLIAM *I traveled Lonely Land* 388 *Snoot*, a very disagreeable person. **1977** S. LOCKE ELLIOTT *Water under Bridge* 15 Those Melbourne snoots .. look down their noses at us Sydneyites.

Hence **snoot** *v. trans.*, to snub.

1977 S. LOCKE ELLIOTT *Water under Bridge* 19 Better than being snooted by those plutos.

snore, *n.*

1. As **snore-off**: a sleep or nap, esp. after drinking.

[N.Z. **1950** *Landfall* (Christchurch) 127, I notice Little Spike's legs sticking out from .. where he is having a snore-off.] **1952** C. SIMPSON *Come away, Pearler* 185, I go into me room for a bit of a snore-orf, only it turns out to be 'er room... She's only 'alf-'arnessed. **1968** D. O'GRADY *Bottle of Sandwiches* 49 He surfaced from his plonk-induced snore-off.

2. A sleeping place, esp. as provided for transients.

1967 *Kings Cross Whisper* (Sydney) xl. 4/4 *Snore*, a place to rest the bod. **1975** *Bulletin* (Sydney) 24 May 26/3 The alternative is a night shelter—one of the eight round Surry Hills and Woolloomooloo run by the Salvation Army, St Vincent de Paul and the Methodists. For skid row derelicts they have about 700 beds. The deros don't choose much between what they call 'snores'—many have lice, they say, except the Catholics—and everyone involved with them is a 'bastard', tough and unfriendly.

snore, *v. intr.* In the phr. **to snore off**, to fall asleep.

1925 S. HICKS *Hullo Australs.* 145 'Good-night, I hope you'll snore off.' 'Snore what,' said Green. 'Snore off, sir—It's Australian. Means go to sleep.' **1962** P.A. KNUDSEN *Bloodwood Tree* 150 'Well,' Art said, 'you fellas can do what y' like—I'm goin' to snore-off.' .. Presently all the men in the camp were stretched out dozing.

snork. [Transf. use of *snork* a young pig.]

1. A baby.

1941 S.J. BAKER *Pop. Dict. Austral. Slang* 68 *Snork*, a baby. **1944** L. GLASSOP *We were Rats* 273 Got a scar on his hand, but probably he's had it since he was a little snork.

2. A sausage.

1941 S.J. BAKER *Pop. Dict. Austral. Slang* 68 *Snork*, .. a sausage. **1948** R. RAVEN-HART *Canoe in Aust.* 14 Sausages are also 'snags' in Australia, or 'snorks'.

snottygobble. [Transf. use of Br. dial. *snotty-gobble*, var. of *snotergob* the fruit of the yew-tree: see EDD.] Any of several plants incl. (chiefly W.A.) trees or shrubs of the genus *Persoonia* (fam. Proteaceae); the fruit of these plants. Also **snodgollion, snot-goblin.**

1854 F. ELDERSHAW *Aust. as it really Is* 43 Snodgollions, etc., are .. well-recognized delicacies among the rising Anglo-Australian generation. **1906** *Bulletin* (Sydney) 4 Oct. 17/2 The toothsome 'snot-goblin', a pink delicacy growing in the ti-tree mistletoe, whose slimy pulp taxed the powers of the toughest stomach among us. **1981**

J.P. GABBEDY *Forgotten Pioneers* 73 The 'snotty-gobble' (*Persoonia longifolia*..) had another.. application... The Muir ladies.. used to steep the red-coloured inner bark of the tree and dye their straw hats a vivid and lasting red.

snout, *n.* [Fig. use of *snout* nose.] In the phr. **to have a snout on** or **against** (someone or something), to be ill-disposed towards (someone); to have an aversion to (something).

[N.Z. **1905** *N.Z. Truth* (Wellington) 12 Aug. 1 The Grey candidate has a snout on the law courts. 'I got fourteen days,' he said.] **1919** V. MARSHALL *World of Living Dead* 33 It was all part of the 'snout' they had ag'in him. **1977** V. PRIDDLE *Larry & Jack* 13 He.. would often say the police had a snout on him and had him before the bench many times.

snout, *v.* [See prec.] *trans.* To harass; to rebuff; to bear ill-will towards. Freq. as *pa. pple.* and *ppl. a.*

1913 *Bulletin* (Sydney) 25 Sept. 24/1 I'll.. work the other sheds down to Yanco... That's where some blokes settle themselves... They hang around the town, an' the Johns and pubs get 'em snouted. **1944** A. MARSHALL *These are my People* 155, I was sore as a snouted sheila for weeks.

snow.

1. Used *attrib.* in the names of plants: **snow daisy,** any of several perennial herbs, usu. of the genus *Celmisia* (fam. Asteraceae) and esp. *C. asteliifolia* of high country in s.e. Aust. incl. Tas., and New Zealand; **grass,** any of many grasses (fam. Poaceae) of high country in s.e. Aust. incl. Tas., esp. some densely tufted perennials of the genus *Poa*; also *attrib.*; **gum,** any of several trees of the genus *Eucalyptus* (fam. Myrtaceae), esp. *E. pauciflora* (fam. Myrtaceae), of s.e. Aust. incl. Tas., occurring both above and below the snow-line, and having a smooth, usu. whitish bark and thick leathery leaves, and (*Tas.*) *E. coccifera*; the wood of the tree; see also CABBAGE GUM, *weeping gum* WEEPING, *white sally* WHITE *a.*[2] 1 a.

1941 C. BARRETT *Aust.* 90 Millions of **snow-daisies** were out below the drifts. **1898** E.E. MORRIS *Austral Eng.* 425 **Snow-Grass**.. *Poa caespitosa*. **1945** E. MITCHELL *Speak to Earth* 55 Sleek young Herefords come in from Groggin with older steers that have ranged the snow-grass tops. **1905** *Emu* V. 66, I saw between 20 and 30 male and female Lyrebirds on the stunted **snow gums** (*E. pauciflora*) on the high ridge running from Feathertop. **1985** *Mt. Field Nat. Park* (Tas. Nat. Parks & Wildlife Service), Here the dominant trees are yellow gums (*E*[*ucalyptus*] *subcrenulata*), with the snow gums (*E. coccifera*) higher up among the lakes.

2. Special Comb. **snow country,** those areas of s.e. New South Wales and n.e. Victoria which are snow-covered for all or part of the winter; **lease,** a contract governing the tenure of an area of Crown land in the snow country; the land so held; also *attrib.*

1906 *Bulletin* (Sydney) 19 July 16/1 Got into the **snow country** of Vic. recently to bring cattle to a warmer situation. **1905** *Austral. Handbk.* 95 **Snow Leases**—Vacant Crown lands or lands held under Annual Lease or Occupation License, which for a part of each year are usually covered with snow, and in consequence unfit for continuous use or occupation, are offered by lease for auction. **1953** E. MITCHELL *Flow River, blow Wind* 7 Two mobs were starting on their way to the mountain snowlease country.

snuffle-buster. *Obs.* A puritanical person.

1890 *Bull-Ant* (Melbourne) 28 Aug. 4/3 This is a fearful blow to the cause of the snuffle-busters and the Pharisees, whose horror of a free and genial Sunday is only equalled by their sycophantic adulation towards their gracious Queen. **c 1907** W.C. CHANDLER *Darkest Adelaide* 57 The matter was passed over by the sanctimonious snuffle-busters, whose pharisaical plea was that the evil could not be a very alarming one, otherwise the Advertiser and Register would have written it up.

snuffle-busting, *ppl. a. Obs.* Puritanical.

1895 *Worker* (Sydney) 9 Feb. 4/2 Painted by him I am a narrow, bigoted, snuffle-busting son of a gun whose grog blossomed 'conk' gives the lie to his watery protestations. **1905** M. CANNON *That Damned Democrat* (1981) 153 The eminently respectable firm of Beath, Schiess and Co... have done more to make a hell upon earth in Melbourne than any other gang of snufflebusting sweaters we wot of.

snug, snugged: see SNIG.

soak. [Br. dial. *soak* a percolation of water; water which has oozed through or out of the ground: see OED *sb.*[2]] A hollow in (often sandy) soil where water collects, on or below the surface of the ground; a water-hole. Also *attrib.*

1838 T.W. WALKER *Month in Bush Aust.* 44 It appeared.. well watered, for we frequently met with springs or land-soaks. **1932** I.L. IDRIESS *Lasseter's Last Ride* 16 Numbers of dry creeks contain 'soak' water just a few feet below the surface.

soakage. SOAK. Also *attrib.*

1892 A.F. CALVERT *Narr. Exped. N.-W. Aust.* 14 To detect the basins or natural rock bed, catchments, or using the local term 'soakages' fell to my lot. **1927** *Smith's Weekly* (Sydney) 7 May 22/4 Binghi makes soakage tapping a quick and simple operation.

soap. In the phr. **not to know** (someone) **from a bar of soap,** not to have the remotest acquaintance with.

1918 C. PEARL *Morrison of Peking* (1967) 367 No respect except among very restricted class for Gov.-General or Lieut. Gov. 'Don't know 'im from a bar of soap' would be the comment. **1970** J. CLEARY *Helga's Web* 145 I've never met any of his—interests. Certainly not this girl. I dunno her from a bar of soap.

soapie. [See quot. 1983.] A young fish, esp. a jewfish. Also *attrib.*

1978 *Sydney Morning Herald* 27 Oct. 23/8 Small 'soapie' jewfish are plentiful but most anglers are not rigging heavily enough to land big jewfish. **1983** *Sun-Herald* (Sydney) 20 Nov. 74/1 Mulloway grow to a weight of more than 50 kg., but.. fishermen are happy when their scales register 5 kg. or 10 kg., while the smaller 'soapie' of 2 kg. or 3 kg. is the norm. The term 'soapie' is used to describe the flavour of the smaller mulloway's flesh. It's unwarranted because such a fish is quite good eating if properly prepared.

soap tree. [Spec. use of *soap-tree* any of several plants the leaves (etc.) of which yield a substitute for soap.] The tree *Alphitonia excelsa* (see *red ash* RED *a.* 1 a.).

1923 *Bulletin* (Sydney) 8 Feb. 22/2 Queensland possesses what we called 'the soap-tree'. It is not unlike the silver-gum, having long tapering leaves and rough bark. **1979** K.A.W. WILLIAMS *Native Plants Qld.* I. 14 *Alphitonia excelsa*.. Soap Tree... The underside of the leaf is silvery and when rubbed in the hand in the presence of water they form a 'soapy' froth.

Socceroo /sɒkəˈruː/. [f. *soccer* + KANGAR]OO *n.* 3.] In the *pl.*: the name of the Australian international soccer team; in *sing.*, a member of such a team. Cf. KANGAROO *n.* 3 b. and WALLABY *n.* 4.

1978 *Sydney Morning Herald* 15 Nov. 1/10 Now that the Australian Soccer team is basking in honour and glory after its World Cup victory over South Korea it can surely do without the name 'Socceroos' which is being increasingly applied to it. **1985** *Border Morning Mail* (Albury-Wodonga) 30 Nov. 75/1 Scotland's soccer team manager had high praise for the Socceroos' secret weapon, Jim Patikas.

social system. *Hist.* A method of convict management formulated by Alexander Maconochie (1787-1860), penal reformer: see quot. 1839.

1839 A. MACONOCHIE *Gen. Views Convict Managem.* 23 Prisoners under the Social System would be exactly as free men labouring for wages, and be just as easily managed—or rather, they would be more so, for both their dependance and stake would be greater. **1841** *Morning Advertiser* (Hobart) 19 Aug. 2/2 The Hulks, the Penitentiary . . the Silent, and as it termed, the Social or Maconochie systems.

sock, *v.* [Fig use of *sock* to drive or strike into something.] *trans.* To drink (alcoholic liquor) quickly. Also with **away, down.**

1915 *Euripides Ensign: on Board 'Euripides'* 2 June 1 Is a soldier less a soldier 'Cause he socks a pint of beer? **1967** J. HIBBERD *White with Wire Wheels* (1970) 217 Think I'll dash down to the milk bar and sock away a pint or so before I head off to the office. **1969** —— *Dimboola* (1974) 23 Cheer up Reen, it'll seem beaut tomorrow. Sock another one down.

sod. [f. *sod, ppl. a.* (of bread) sodden, poorly risen: see OED *pa. pple., ppl. a.,* and *sb.*^{2} 2 a.]

a. A damper which has failed to rise: see also quot. 1980. Also **sod damper** and **soddy damper.**

1852 *Austral. Gold Digger's Monthly Mag.* iii. 86 Beware of bad water and sod damper. **1887** 'OVERLANDER' *Austral. Sketches* 15 Showing us . . how to make a damper—which, I am sorry to say, was a regular sod. **1980** R. BROPHO *Fringedweller* 19 You'd have . . soddy damper and tea. Soddy damper is plain flour with no self-raising flour or baking powder in it.

b. Hence, loosely, any damper.

1918 *Jackass: First Austral. Gen. Hospital* Christmas 20 He is consolingly informed that everyone buries his first 'Sod', as a Damper is called. **1939** *Bulletin* (Sydney) 7 June 20/2, I agree . . *re* the general awfulness of damper. Still some sod-punchers are worse than others. . . Most sodmakers get . . the dough too wet. . . Show me the padflogger who wouldn't swap a sod as big as a cartwheel for just one loaf of baker's bread.

Hence **sod** *v. trans.*, to spoil (a damper) by failing to make it rise.

1946 F. CLUNE *Try Nothing Twice* 86, I had my first lesson in damper-making, and I've been an expert in charring them and sodding them ever since.

soda. [Prob. transf. use of *soda* deal card in Faro: see OEDS 4.] Any easy victim; a simple task; a 'pushover'

1917 *All abaht It* (London) Feb. (1919) 10 He is a 'Soda' for anyone who has had any service. **1966** H. PORTER *Paper Chase* 74 The job, for which I have no really specialized training, is nevertheless a soda.

sod hut. *Obs.* [Used elsewhere but recorded earliest in Aust.] A dwelling built with sods of turf.

1827 Tas. Colonial Secretary's Office Rec. 1/47 238, I would also propose to construct forthwith a *Sod Hut* for the Detachment of 1 Serjent and G of the 40th Reg^t. **1884** 'R. BOLDREWOOD' *Old Melbourne Memories* 37 The walls of a sod hut were indeed already up.

S.O.L. /ɛs oʊ 'ɛl/. *Shit on the liver,* see SHIT 2.

1951 D. STIVENS *Jimmy Brockett* 137 'I don't care what you write about my wrestling matches, brother,' I told him. 'I had a bit of S.O.L. the other day, but I hope you'll lay off my wife.' **1978** R. MCKIE *Bitter Bread* 119 This was the first human sign for hours. Blue must be improving, getting rid of his s.o.l.

soldier, *n.* **1.** Used *attrib.* (and *ellipt.*) in the names of animals: **soldier ant,** a BULLDOG ANT, esp. one which is red, and perh. esp. *Myrmecia gulosa*; **bird,** any of several birds, esp. the *noisy miner* (see NOISY); **crab,** a small crab of the genus *Mictyris* occurring in large numbers on sandy tidal flats, esp. the bluish *M. longicarpus.*

1844 L. LEICHHARDT *Jrnl. Overland Exped. Aust.* 20 Nov. (1847) 47 The **soldier ant,** and the whole host of the others, were everywhere. **1845** R. HOWITT *Impressions Aust. Felix* 142 The **soldier-bird** . . is the very sentinel of the woods. **1948** R. RAVEN-HART *Canoe in Aust.* 207 Soldier-birds (Noisy Miners) chasing a kookaburra, speckly grey birds with yellow facings, keeping up a stream of insulting 'Nyah-nyahs'. **1861** 'OLD BUSHMAN' *Bush Wanderings* 254 One, which we called the **soldier-crab,** was handsome and curious. **1969** *Crabs Sydney Foreshores* (Austral. Museum Leaflet n. 62) 6 Low tide is feeding time for perhaps the most spectacular of Sydney's foreshore crabs—the Soldier Crab (*Mictyris longicarpus*).

2. *Obs.* An animal used without its owner's knowledge.

1918 [see SOLDIER *v.*]

3. *Hist.* As a shortening of SOLDIER-SETTLEMENT and SOLDIER-SETTLER. Freq. *attrib.*

1919 C.A. BERNAYS *Qld. Politics during Sixty Yrs.* 349 The aggregate area of the soldier leases already taken up (they are all leaseholds). **1939** *Bulletin* (Sydney) 27 Sept. 16/2 When Mac, one of the hard-doers of the old A.I.F., took over his soldier's block in the mallee . . only two things clouded his horizon.

soldier, *v. Obs. trans.* To use (another's animal) without the owner's knowledge.

1879 'AUSTRALIAN' *Adventures Qld.* 93 If a 'nobby' bullock . . makes off . . so artfully as to evade all attempts to find him within a reasonable time . . when the runaway is caught, it may be he is in someone else's team, and the poor brute is worked down as poor as a crow. . . Of course, the poor man who 'soldiered' him was quite innocent! **1918** C. FETHERSTONHAUGH *After many Days* 211 These I recovered next day, and let my two 'soldiers' go. . . It was the first time I had ever 'soldiered' a horse. Soldiering means using a horse without the owner's leave or knowledge. Two of our lost horses were never found. Probably someone was soldiering them!

soldier-settlement. *Hist.* A scheme under which ex-service personnel are allocated grants of land, usu. land not previously cultivated; the land so acquired. Also **soldier's settlement** and *attrib.*

1919 C.A. BERNAYS *Qld. Politics during Sixty Yrs.* 347 We have a different class of soldier settlement in the fruit-growing Stanthorpe district. **1920** *Huon Times* (Franklin) 24 Aug. 3/2 Last week Mr C.T. Hassie, the Secretary of the South Australian branch of the O.B.U. visited the soldiers' settlement at Glossop. **1948** *Bulletin* (Sydney) 1 Sept. 22/4 A fellow . . came up to the Tweed to grow bananas on a soldier-settlement. **1972** *Kings Cross Whisper* (Sydney) cxl. 2/3 It was back in 1921 when they was having all that fuss about the soldier settlement blocks.

soldier-settler. *Hist.*

1. An ex-serviceman who acquires land under the soldier-settlement scheme.

1917 *Huon Times* (Franklin) 2 Nov. 5/1 The services of such advisory committee to be available in connection with the valuation of stock, implements, etc., which returned soldier settlers wish to obtain. **1979** C. THIELE *Chadwick's Chimney* 28 When he had been discharged from the Navy he had applied for a Government loan to become what was called 'a soldier settler'.

2. Comb. **soldier-settler block**.
1933 *Bulletin* (Sydney) 13 Dec. 24/1 A young Englishmen took up one of the soldier-settler blocks on Kongbool, Balmoral (Vic.), in 1920.

sole. [Transf. use of *sole* the European fish *Solea solea* and other fish of the fam. Soleidae esteemed as food.] Any of many flatfish, incl. those of the fam. Soleidae and Cynoglossidae.
1786 *Hist. Narr. Discovery New Holland & N.S.W.* 50 Among a variety of fish, we caught some .. bream, soles, flounders. **1969** J. POLLARD *Austral. & N.Z. Fishing* 213 *Ammotretis rostratus*... One of the commonest of the flatfishes, sometimes incorrectly labelled sole in both Tasmania and Victoria.

solid, *a.* [See OED(S *a.* 18.] Severe; difficult; unsparing.
1916 C.J. DENNIS *Moods Ginger Mick* 155 *Solid*, severe, severely. **1948** R. PARK *Harp in South* 62 After all, Auntie Josie's got all them kids to look after. It must be pretty well solid for her with Grandma as well. **1966** P. COWAN *Seed* 53 'Beer's run out,' he said. Walter laughed. 'You were too solid on it.'

sollicker. Also **soliker.** [Prob. of Br. dial. origin: see EDD *sollock* impetus, force.] Something very big, a 'whopper'.
1898 R. GRAEME *From England to Back Blocks* 82 Who was it I heard that in cutting-out some cattle on one of the Methvin plains, did come down a soliker and broke his horse's knees? **1955** P. WHITE *Tree of Man* 91 'You can jump down, can't you? You're quite big, you know.' 'Of course he can', said the man .. 'he's a sollicker.'
Hence **sollicking** *a.*
1917 C. DREW *Reminisc. D. Gilbert* 54 He gives a bit of a lecture about snakes, first; then he let's a sollickin' cove, as big as a new-chum's swag, bite him.

song-lark. Either of the two birds of the genus *Cinclorhamphus*, *C. cruralis* (see *brown song-lark* BROWN *a.* 1) and *C. mathewsi* (see *rufous song-lark* RUFOUS); *singing lark*, see SINGING.
1898 [see *brown song-lark* BROWN *a.* 1]. **1932** A.H. CHISHOLM *Nature Fantasy in Aust.* 62 The fire had returned and completely destroyed the song-lark's home. **1965** *Austral. Encycl.* V. 242 The two song-larks, which belong to the genus *Cinclorhamphus*, are peculiar to Australia and are widely distributed throughout the continent.

songman. An Aboriginal who memorizes and performs the traditional songs of a community.
1943 W.E. HARNEY *Taboo* 19 He is considered a great 'song man' in the tribe. **1980** M. DUGAN *Early Dreaming* 34 There was the night in Arnhem Land by the banks of the Koolatong river when I talked to a songman who told me how he explained to his people why rivers ran.

sonk. [Back-formation f. SONKY.] A figure of fun; a foolish or ungainly person.
1959 D. NILAND *Gold in Streets* 144 Silly looking sonk. Head like a melon, big feet, shovel hands. King of the cowbails, possum eater, the pride of Woop-Woop. **1966** H. PORTER *Paper Chase* 131 Her husband .. upsets the good-clean-fun pattern of an open-air drinking bout at Eagle Point Park by accusing his wife and a sonk of a bank clerk of unchaste designs on each other.

sonky, *a.* [f. Br. dial. *sonkie* 'a man like a sack of straw': see EDD *sonk, sb.* 2.] Foolish; gawky. Also as *n.*
1917 C.J. DENNIS *Doreen* 5 Aw, I ain't no silk-sock sonkie 'oo ab'ors the rood an' rough. **1958** F. HARDY *Four-Legged Lottery* 93 Jim and his father began to tease Meg about her handsome lover. 'That sonky thing,' she replied with all the scornful pride of a beautiful young woman. 'When I'm courted it will be by a real man with real prospects in life.'

soogee /'sudʒi/. Also **soojee, souge, sougee, sugee, sujee.** [Transf. use of *soojee* a flour obtained by grinding Indian wheat.] Used *attrib.* of a bag in which Indian flour was sold, esp. with reference to the inferiority of the material. Hence used allusively as an emblem of poverty or deprivation.
1836 'W.R.–s' *Fell Tyrant* 46 There are four sorts of settlers, the Swell settler, that is the rich, the Dungaree, the Souge, and the last and poorest of all is the Stringybark settler. **1847** *Launceston Examiner* 12 May 301/4 The old prisoners they called 'corn stalks', the present were know [*sic*] as 'sougee bags'; every farmer knew the difference between a good striped Dundee corn sack and a sougee bag, and there was just that difference in the comparison of the two classes of labour. **1862** G.T. LLOYD *Thirty-Three Yrs. Tas. & Vic.* 262 A host of ticket-of-leave men, who flourished under the significant cognomen of 'sugee settlers' .. were evidently guided by the doctrine, that a ticket-of-leave awarded the positive right of appropriating other men's goods and chattels. **1891** D. FERGUSON *Vicissitudes Bush Life* 48 You will let the traveller see, be he common swagger, or 'sujee swell', that you are glad to make him welcome. **1905** J. FURPHY *Rigby's Romance* (1946) 43 I'll jist wipe out these (adj.) soojee (cravens), an' make a great nation out o' you an' yer own piccaninnies. **1942** *Bulletin* (Sydney) 11 Nov. 13/4 The man with the soogee swag and makeshift sandals was discoursing on hardship.

sook /sʊk/. [Transf. use of Br. dial. *suck* a 'duffer', stupid fellow: see OEDS *sb.*[1]]
1. A coward, a sissy.
[N.Z. **1933** N. SCANLAN *Tides of Youth* 155 He looked a big sookie and wouldn't say a word.] **1941** S.J. BAKER *Pop. Dict. Austral. Slang* 69 *Sook*, a coward, a timid person. **1983** *Bulletin* (Sydney) 5 July 86/3 The girl applied a hefty hip .. and flattened him. Sprawled on the bitumen, he began to howl. 'Bloody sook!' said the girl, disgustedly.
2. A timid (race)horse.
1980 *Sydney Morning Herald* 2 Aug. 59/7 White, answering charges that Panamint is unsound, described the horse as a 'big sook'... Invariably when he is taken in and out of the box he is timid. **1984** *Age* (Melbourne) 16 Apr. 28/1 According to Smith, the horse lost his confidence and became a dreadful 'sook'.

sooky /'sʊki/, *a.* [See prec.] Babyish; stupid.
1901 *Bulletin* (Sydney) 2 Nov. (Red Page), Big, sooky-looking fellow he was, with ears like little turn-over tarts. **1985** *Austral. Short Stories* xii. 89 Rosa never failed her sums... Annie felt sick with fear. 'Sookie sook, I'm going to tell on you,' chanted Rosa.

sool /sul/, *v.* Formerly also **sowl.** [Transf. use of Br. dial. *sowl* (of a dog), to seize (a pig) by the ears: see OED *sowl, v.*[3] 1 and OEDS *sool, v.*]
1. *trans.* Of a dog: to worry; freq. *transf.* to harass. Freq. as imperative.
1849 A. HARRIS *Emigrant Family* (1967) 135 'Hey! hey! sowl her, boys!' roared Morgan: and on went the whole pack, seizing the poor beast by the ears, nose, and even eyelids. **1903** *Truth* (Sydney) 15 Nov. 1/6 Dave Wiley, the Newtown State School dominie, has been teaching his pupils to model from Nature. Sool him, ye gimlet brigaders. **1981** K. GARVEY *Rhymes of Ratbag* 141 The ringers all are drunk and mad With savage dogs they sool yer.
2. *trans.* To urge or goad; to importune. Freq. with adv., esp. **on**.
1889 *Bulletin* (Sydney) 10 Aug. 8/1 He wakens with a shock, And 'sools' his dog around a score Of 'crawlers' from his flock. **1944** 'S. CAMPION' *Pommy Cow* 256 'You're always tryin' to put thoughts into me head an' sool me into thinkin' this or that.' 'Anyone can sool *you* without much

trying.' **1971** K. WILLEY *Boss Drover* 11 Each time she broke away I would sool her into the mob again. **1985** *Sun-Herald* (Sydney) 28 July 19/2 He had sooled their pet doberman on to her, saying 'Kill, Blitzen, kill'.

Hence **sooling** *ppl. a.*, insistently importunate; also with **on**.

1916 *Truth* (Sydney) 29 Oct. 4/7 God help Australia if it had to depend for soldiers on the shrieking, sooling, 'race suicide' shemales of snobbish suburbia. **1936** N. LINDSAY *Saturdee* (ed. 2) 249 When willing hands thrust him again to action, he hung back, and Ponkey employed the sooling-on tactics without effect.

3. *intr.* To run; to travel.

1945 M. RAYMOND *Smiley* 77 The man pulled two half-crowns and handed them to the boy. 'There y' are. Now sool.' Smiley sooled off at top speed. **1951** J. DEVANNY *Travels N. Qld.* 137 He 'sools' along quietly for a time, as though he does not mean business.

sooler /'sulə/. One who exerts pressure upon another, esp. one who supported the campaign to introduce conscription during the war of 1914–18. Also **sooler-on**.

1916 *Truth* (Sydney) 6 Aug. 6/3 Never before was there so much delight among the sweaters, extortioners, forestallers, 'soolers', sycophants, proxy 'patriots', and bawlers for blood as there is now at the return of 'Billee'. **1933** G.G. ROPER *Labor's Titan* 37 The Barrier Empire Loyalists, or 'soolers-on', as George Dale called them, were not slow to attack these 'traitors to King and Country'.

sooner. [See quot. 1945.] An idler, a shirker; applied as a term of abuse to an unco-operative person, or obstructive object, etc. Also *attrib.* as **sooner dog**.

1892 K. LENTZNER *Dict. Slang-Eng. Aust.* 117 *Sooner*, a weak idler, a lazy good-for-nothing. **1936** F. CLUNE *Roaming round Darling* 270 Tongue-tied Joe, a sooner-dog, a Scotch dog, a dog of all nations, a hungry goat. **1945** S.J. BAKER *Austral. Lang.* 73 Outback slang terms for dogs include: *sooner* (i.e. one that would sooner rest than work), etc.

sooty, *a.* Used as a distinguishing epithet in the names of birds: **sooty owl**, either of two brownish-grey owls of the genus *Tyto, T. tenebricosa* of s.e Aust. and montane New Guinea, and *T. multipunctata* of the Atherton region, n.e. Qld; **oystercatcher**, the sooty-black bird *Haematopus fuliginosus* of rocky coasts around Aust. incl. Tas.

1848 J. GOULD *Birds of Aust.* I. Pl. 30, *Strix tenebricosus* . . **Sooty Owl. 1845** J. GOULD *Birds of Aust.* (1848) VI. Pl. 8, *Haemotopus fuliginosus* . . **Sooty Oyster-catcher.**

sorcerer. KORADJI.

1843 W. PRIDDEN *Aust.* 141 A profound respect, almost amounting to veneration, is paid in many districts of Australia to shining stones or pieces of crystal, which they call '*Teyl*'. These are carried in the girdles of men, especially of the sorcerers or *corad-jes*. **1985** I. WHITE et al. *Fighters & Singers* 137 Travelling alone I was liable to attack by a sorcerer who had reputedly been seen. . . I was supposed to know about the dangers of sorcery.

sore, *a.* In the phr. **done (or dressed) up like a sore finger** (or **toe**), dressed with unusual care; overdressed.

1918 *7th Field Artillery Brigade Yandoo* Jan. 92 Hullo Digger, you're done up like a sore finger—where to? **1939** K. TENNANT *Foveaux* 430 You ought to a seen us in the ole days when we 'ad a procession every year—done up like a sore toe with banners and floats. **1962** P. WHITE *Four Plays* (1974) 168 I'm gunna get out of this suit. Dressed up like a sore finger.

sort. [Used elsewhere but recorded earliest in Aust.] A female; esp. one who is young and attractive; a girlfriend.

1933 F. CLUNE *Try Anything Once* 93 Lend me a suit of civvies. I've got to meet a great little sort, and her father has a dead nark on soldiers. **1977** C. KLEIN *Pomegranate Tree* 55 We'd grab the good looking sorts.

sosh. *Hist.* Shortened form of 'socialism'; usu. as ANTI-SOSH.

1912 *Bulletin* (Sydney) 22 Feb. 43/1 The Unionist tiger, full brother to 'Sosh'!

souge, sougee, varr. SOOGEE.

soul-case. [Orig. U.S.: see OEDS *soul, sb.* 25.] In the phr. **to worry (belt, sweat) the soul-case out (of)**, to vex, to drive, to punish. Also **to work the soul-case off.**

1901 F.J. GILLEN *Diary* 15 Apr. (1968) 34 Flies were celebrating some festival all night and worried the very soul cases out of us. **1937** K.S. PRICHARD *Intimate Strangers* 288 Eviction was what I got after clearing two thousand acres of virgin land: sweating my soul case out to grow wheat. **1943** *Coast to Coast 1942* 61 Where the 'ell you been? I been worryin' me soulcase out. **1945** G. CASEY *Downhill is Easier* 146 He used t' belt the soulcase out o' her till I come along. **1962** R. TULLIPAN *March into Morning* 13 Then he got this bright idea of bringin' in orphan kids and working the soulcase off them until they turn eighteen and have to be paid more money.

sounding stick. *Obs.* See quot. 1856.

1856 *Jrnl. Australasia* I. 21 In this locality, too, there is plenty of a light, white wood . . also called 'sounding stick', because a solid, ringing sound can be produced by two round billets being beaten together. **1863** J. BONWICK *Wild White Man* 36 The aborigine procured fire from friction of two pieces of wood, called by some 'Thaal Kalk', or sounding sticks.

sour, *a.* Used as a distinguishing epithet in the names of plants: **sour apple** *obs., emu apple* (a), see EMU *n.*[1] 3; **plum**, any of several plants, esp. *emu apple* (a) and *Owenia venosa* of Qld.

1888 L. BAYER *Muutchaka* 1 To black peller say: get away you kunk Go and die under **sour apple** tree. **1874** LINDLEY & MOORE *Treasury of Bot.* (rev. ed.) 1324 *Owenia venosa* is known by the name of the **Sour Plum** among the colonists. **1903** *Austral. Handbk.* 279 Other orders . . furnish . . large-sized timber, particularly the following: 'Sour Plum' (*Owenia venosa*) [etc.].

soursob. Also **soursobs, soursops.** [Transf. use of Br. dial. *soursops, Rumex acetosa*: see EDD *sour* 2.] Any of several perennial herbs of the genus *Oxalis* (fam. Oxalidaceae), esp. the S. African *O. pes-caprae*, naturalized in all States, a proclaimed noxious weed in Qld., Vic., Tas., and parts of S.A.

1885 *Garden & Field* Sept. 41 Now there's a fellow who wants £500 to tell farmers how to kill the Soursops or oxalis. **1949** *S.A. Dept. Agric. Bull.* no. 406 18 As regards *O. cernua*, the names most commonly applied to the plant are 'Soursob', Soursobs', or 'Soursops', in this country, and 'Bermuda Buttercups' in America.

Soustralian. *Obs.* Alteration of 'South Australian'. Also as *adj.* Similarly **Soustralia.**

1900 *Truth* (Sydney) 28 Jan. 1/4 Patriotic Soustralians who sent away a cargo of flour to Kruger and Co. **1916** *Truth* (Sydney) 22 Oct. 1/6 Mr Crawford Vaughan, Soustralian Premier . . is endeavouring to kid Sydneysiders to vote as he believes the Croweaters will. *Ibid.* 10 Dec. 6/6 (*heading*) A spookist from Soustralia.

south. Freq. with **the.** The southern parts of Australia: cf. NORTH 1.

1905 *Bulletin* (Sydney) 13 July 18/3 Some sugar-growers and their barrackers are telling the South that, if they can't have Kanaka, they will have Chow.   1980 *Sunday Mail* (Brisbane) 28 Sept. 2/5 People are coming up from the south in droves to settle here. Not for the beauty of the City of Brisbane, but for the superbness of the quality of life that surrounds it.

southerly. SOUTHERLY BUSTER.

1896 *Bulletin* (Sydney) 4 July 28/1 Let her rip till a 'southerly' comes and rocks her out.   1984 *Overlander* June 52 Governments .. are so bloody jellygutted they'd be hard pressed to stand up to a southerly.

southerly burster. Obs. [f. *southerly, a.* + *burster* that which bursts.] SOUTHERLY BUSTER. See also BURSTER $n.^2$

1850 *Bell's Life in Sydney* 5 Oct. 2/2 The whistlings of old Eolus in the shape of a southerly burster.   *c* 1906 L. BECKE *Settlers Karossa Creek* 39 There was every indication that within a few hours one of those short, but violent, storms known as 'southerly bursters' would sweep along the coast.

southerly buster. [f. *southerly, a.* + *buster*, prob. Br. dial. form of *burster*: see SOUTHERLY BURSTER.]

1. A sudden, strong, cool wind from the south, affecting the south-eastern coast: see esp. quot. 1852.

1850 B.C. PECK *Recoll. Sydney* 132 The evening of a hot-wind day brings up a 'southerly buster', as we have heard the vulgar call it, very chill indeed, not only by contrast, but in reality, as this wind comes from the southerly region of the Australian Alps, which always have snow on them.   1852 W. HUGHES *Austral. Colonies* 63 The wind by which the hot blast of the interior is followed is popularly known at Sydney as a 'brickfielder', or '*southerly buster*'—(the good people of the colonies are not remarkable for the refinement of their vernacular phraseology).   1982 P. RADLEY *My Blue-Checker Corker* 90 Granfarver Jones once saw a Southerly Buster turn a chook inside out.

2. *fig.*

1874 C. DE BOOS *Congewoi Correspondence* 19 If it hadn't been for Jack Robertson getting up the southerly buster as he did, and blowing the dust of Free Selection into their eyes.

Southerly doctor: see DOCTOR $n.^3$

southern, *a.* Used as a distinguishing epithet in the names of flora and fauna: **southern bluefin (tuna),** the large marine fish *Thunnus maccoyii,* bluish above and silvery below; **blue gum,** any of several trees of the genus *Eucalyptus* (fam. Myrtaceae), esp. *E. globulus* ssp. *bicostata* of N.S.W. and Vic.; **stone plover,** the bird *Burhinus grallarius* (see CURLEW).

1951 T.C. ROUGHLEY *Fish & Fisheries Aust.* 115 There has long been speculation whether the Australian **southern bluefin** tuna is identical with the tunny of Europe and the bluefin tuna (*Thunnus thynnus*) of the Pacific and Atlantic coasts of America... However .. the Australian species is entirely distinct.   1969 C. THIELE *Blue Fin* 2 They were southern blue-fins, the most perfectly shaped fish in the sea... They were thirty pounders, small as far as tuna went.   1919 R.T. BAKER *Hardwoods of Aust.* 8 *E*[*ucalyptus*] *Maideni* .. **Southern Blue Gum,** A Spotted Gum.   1948 P.J. HURLEY *Red Cedar* 21 Seeds of Southern Bluegums (*E. bicostata*) were sent to Italy to soak up surplus water in the malaria-infested Pontine.   1845 J. GOULD *Birds of Aust.* (1848) VI. Pl. 5, *Oedicnemus grallarius.* **Southern Stone Plover.**

Southern Cross.

1. The constellation of *Crux Australis,* four stars of which form a cross.

1842 H. PARKES *Stolen Moments* 98 I've wandered where the Southern Cross Glows o'er th' Antipodes.   1986 *Canberra Times* 16 Mar. 2/8 The proposed flag, representing the Southern Cross in a velvet night sky over a red desert is pure poetry.

2. **a.** *Eureka flag,* see EUREKA 2.

1855 R. CARBONI *Eureka Stockade* 50 There is no flag in old Europe half so beautiful as the 'Southern Cross' of the Ballaarat miners, first hoisted on the old spot, Bakery Hill. The flag is silk, blue ground, with a large silver cross, similar to the one in our southern firmament; no device or arms, but all exceedingly chaste and natural.   1984 S. MACINTYRE *Militant* 179 On one occasion when the union was under attack it was in keeping that Paddy should repeat the Eureka oath: 'We swear by the Southern Cross to stand by each other and fight to defend our rights and liberties.'

b. The Australian flag.

1965 G. MCINNES *Road to Gundagai* 169 The Southern Cross, neatly balled, sailed up the halyard of the newly erected post, and .. broke out and flew bravely over the new campsite of the First Toorak Troop: five stars and the great seven pointed star in the fly, and in one corner the small Union Jack with: 'The broad white diagonal stripe Nearest the pole at the top.'

3. Used allusively, esp. in the phr. **land of the Southern Cross,** to designate Australia.

1873 J. BONWICK *Tasmanian Lily* 86 However common the plague of drink may be in Australia and Tasmania, the infirmity is witnessed in those trained amidst the supposed superior moral and intellectual advantages of Great Britain and Ireland, and not with those born under the Southern Cross.   1943 M. LAMB *Red glows Dawn* 36 Until Darwin was bombed .. no hostile, warring shot had ever reverberated through the land of the Southern Cross.

southerner. Used, esp. by residents of Queensland and the Northern Territory, to designate one normally resident in a southern State.

1878 *Queenslander* (Brisbane) 15 June 332/4 If the freshness of these men's complexions had not pointed them out to me as Southerners, their black hats and extra heavy swags would most assuredly have done so.   1975 X. HERBERT *Poor Fellow my Country* 1012 They were all big fellows, Southerners by the conventional dress of black pants, striped shirts, black patent-leather shoes.

southern lights. [Also used elsewhere.] AURORA AUSTRALIS.

1775 *Philos. Trans. R. Soc. London* LXVIII. 409 Some Southern lights, very rare and motionless.   1971 G. WISEWOULD *Outpost* 154 On occasions during summer one sees the 'southern lights', long after sunset, gleaming pale on the horizon, sometimes green—sometimes green and gold.

South Land. Australia, esp. in the collocation **Great South Land.**

1671 J. OGILBY *America* 654 On the eighth of *Octob.* Tasman stood over to the *South-Land,* near which he was surpris'd by a violent Storm.   1957 F. CLUNE *Fortune Hunters* 138 A new deal for the Australian blacks is coming up fast, and the visit of Albert Namatjira to Sydney proved that public conscience is at last awake to our responsibilities to these ancestral folk of the Great South Land.

souvenir, *v.* [Used elsewhere but recorded earliest in Aust.: see OEDS *v.* 3.] *trans.* To appropriate; to steal; to take as a 'souvenir'. Also *absol.* and as *ppl. a.*

1918 C. GARSTIN *Mud Larks* 18 My batman trod me underfoot at seven next morning. 'Goin' to be blinkin' murder done in this camp presently, Sir,' he announced cheerfully. 'Three officers went to sleep in bivvies larst night, but somebody's souvenired 'em since, an' they're all lyin' hout in the hopen now, Sir.' **1926** *Bulletin* (Sydney) 27 May 22/2, I don't think 'Wang' need worry about the effect of war-souvenired cartridges dumped into municipal incinerators. **1956** S. HOPE *Diggers' Paradise* 83 Early, too, numbers of youngsters show that tendency to 'souvenir' which is the euphonious term for pilfering.

Hence **souvenirer** *n.*

1918 *Aussie: Austral. Soldiers' Mag.* Sept. 3/2 When the recent stunt had passed along over the broken remains of murdered villages, my crowd, the Pioneers (better recognised by the unofficial monicker, 'the Souvenirers'), proceeded to make possies for themself among the jumble.

sowl, var. SOOL.

S.P., *attrib.* and *n.* Racing. [f. the initials of *starting price* the final odds on a horse or greyhound at the time of starting.]

A. Used *attrib.* in Special Comb. **S.P. betting** *vbl. n.,* the placing of a bet at starting price; also *attrib.;* **book,** a ledger in which such bets are recorded; **bookie, bookmaker,** one who as a business accepts bets off the race-course, at starting price; so **bookmaking** *vbl. n.;* **job,** such a bet; **joint,** an establishment at which *S.P. betting* takes place; **man,** *S.P. bookmaker.*

1986 *Publicist* (Sydney) ii. 3/1 His song was unheeded by a crowd of whitefellows, who were congregated at that place for the purpose of engaging in **S.P.** illicit **betting**. **1972** *Bulletin* (Sydney) 13 May 13/1 Police difficulties in closing down SP betting shops on the NSW south coast recall the Chester Hill Fortress nonsense of 1968. **1948** G. MEREDITH *Lawsons* 86 What about racing? Maybe Foley is running an **S.P. book** or something, and Chris won it from him. **1962** J.T. LANG *Great Bust* 335 The war between the law and the **S.P. bookies** was unending. **1956** V. COURTNEY *All I may Tell* 165 Another said that he knew I was in the pay of the **S.P. bookmakers** because our paper had favoured the licensing of betting. **1982** *Bulletin* (Sydney) 24 Aug. 41/1 SP bookmaking is still a multi-million dollar business, according to investigators, even though the TAB was set up in Victoria in 1961 to stamp out the then $324 million a year illegal turnover. **1958** F. HARDY *Four-Legged Lottery* 175 An **SP job** (a horse backed away from the course); or a horse from a non-betting stable that drifts in the market because of pressure of money for other horses. **1954** H.G. LAMOND *Manx Star* 107 I'll turn over a new leaf: there's good money to be made running a sly-grog shop or a **S.P. joint**. **1932** *Truth* (Sydney) 9 Oct. 1/4 The friend stated that he had had a successful bet with the bookmaker and that apparently the **S.P. man** had given him the marked notes with which he afterwards liquidated his debt to the constable.

B. *n.* Abbrev. of *S.P. betting, bookmaker, bookmaking;* also as quasi- *adv.* (see quot. 1949).

1941 *Action Front: Jrnl. 2/2 Field Regiment* Nov. 5 A bit of S.P. on the quiet. **1949** L. GLASSOP *Lucky Palmer* 4 Whenever he could 'wag' it from school on Thursdays he did the call for Ross Harrison, who bet S.P. on a house verandah overlooking the track. **1958** F. HARDY *Four-Legged Lottery* 76 Illegal betting has become a normal part of our society. SPs flourish even in the remotest places. **1964** A. STAPLES *Paddo* 79 Saturday afternoon Tony kept the shop open but didn't sell much; it was the front for the S.P.

Hence **S.P.-ing** *vbl. n.*

1985 M. STEWART *Autobiogr. of my Mother* 172 Queenie had what she called 'SP-ing' at the back of the building. She ran an illegal betting establishment and had a room lined with telephones to take bets.

spag, $n.^1$ [Br. dial. *spag* the house-sparrow: see EDD *spag* and also *spadge, spadger, spadgick.*] A sparrow.

1951 *Bulletin* (Sydney) 17 Jan. 12/2 The spag makes no attempt to attack, but waltzes round in a shocked upright posture... Soon a regular chorus of chirrups is in full swing as the junior members of the speckled tribe add their bit of cheek, and the sparrows retire beaten. **1971** D. IRELAND *Unknown Industr. Prisoner* 130 'Those little birds in the yard?' 'Spags. Little brown sparrows.'

spag, $n.^2$ [See quot. 1966.] An Italian immigrant.

[**1966** S.J. BAKER *Austral. Lang.* (ed. 2) 344 *Spaggie,* an Italian. (Ex spaghetti.)] **1967** V.G.C. NORWOOD *Long Haul* 38 A large party of 'Spags'—a slang Aussie term for spaghetti-eating Italian emigrants. **1983** *Nat. Times* (Sydney) 25 Mar. 25/2 The word spaghetti or 'Spag' is synonymous with Italian. Someone is either a 'Spag' or married to a 'Spag'.

spangled drongo. The bird *Dicrurus hottentottus* of n. and e. Aust. and elsewhere, having glossy black plumage with irridescent blue-green spangles or spots.

1845 J. GOULD *Birds of Aust.* (1848) II. Pl. 82, *Dicrurus bracteatus* .. Spangled Drongo. **1984** M. BLAKERS et al. *Atlas Austral. Birds* 613 The Spangled Drongo ranges from southern Asia to New Guinea and Australia.

Spaniard. *Obs.* Spanish dollar, see SPANISH *a.* 1.

1827 *Monitor* (Sydney) 30 Aug. 623/2 Knowing where I could borrow a few dollars, we sallied out on that pursuit, and very soon had the pleasure of pocketing some Spaniards.

Spanish, *a.* and *n. Hist.*

A. *adj.*

1. In the collocation **Spanish dollar,** the foreign coin most common in the early days of the Australian Colonies, circulating at a value of five shillings sterling.

1791 D. COLLINS *Acct. Eng. Colony N.S.W.* (1798) I. 180 The Spanish dollar was the current coin of the colony. **1838** *Sydney Herald* 5 Sept. 2/3 It appears that these [Mexican] dollars have been brought here by the New Union Bank, and issued at the rate of the Spanish dollar.

2. [Also used elsewhere: see OEDS *a.* 8 *a.* (*c*).] Used of sheep, wool, etc., to designate the merino breed. Also **Spanish merino.**

1799 J. HUNTER Let. to Sir J. Banks 1 June 5, I send you three Specimens of Wool. 1 is that of a Spanish Ram. **1853** S. SIDNEY *Three Colonies* (ed. 2) 65 M'Arthur .. was steadily pursuing his great idea of naturalising the 'noble race', or Spanish merino, on the plains of Australia.

B. *n.* A Spanish dollar, esp. in the phr. **to speak Spanish,** to be in possession of money.

1827 *Monitor* (Sydney) 26 July 539/2 Lupus Long-pocket, the sub-Clerk, to whom is entrusted the care of forwarding the applications, has signified as the cause of their detention, the applicant's ignorance of the 'Spanish Language'. 'He must *speak Spanish* first'; are the words of Lupus... The poor fellow picked up *two words of Spanish* and delivered them, but whether from a want of grace, or, what is more probable, from a want of *fluency in the delivery,* it produced no effect upon the *stoney* heart of Long-pocket. **1832** *Hill's Life N.S.W.* (Sydney) 3 Aug. 2 Not being able to speak *Spanish,* the Bench, of course, sent him to the stocks.

spare, *v.* In the phr. **spare me days,** an exclamation, esp. of exasperation.

1915 C.J. DENNIS *Songs of Sentimental Bloke* 16 The music of the sorft an' barmy breeze... Aw, spare me days! **1959** M. RAYMOND *Smiley roams Road* 157 'Spare me days,' roared Mitchum, coming round to the end of the bar. 'You get out of the pub or I'll stoush you.'

spare-chain, *v. trans.* To haul (a load) along by securing it with a chain: see quot. 1851.

1847 A. HARRIS *Settlers & Convicts* (1953) 109 The obstacles to be overcome in getting the plank dragged out of such a hole (which had to be done by spare-chaining it along the ground, a plank at a time). **1851** J. HENDERSON *Excursions & Adventures N.S.W.* I. 129 He has only to send his team to the brush, and spare-chain these slabs. [*Note*] This is the term applied to dragging anything with bullocks, by means of the extra chain belonging to the dray.

sparrowhawk. [Transf. use of *sparrow-hawk* the hawk *Accipiter nisus* of Britain and elsewhere.] **a.** COLLARED SPARROWHAWK. **b.** Nankeen kestrel, see NANKEEN.
1878 R.B. SMYTH *Aborigines of Vic.* II. 38 White crane .. Tirtgerawan. Sparrow hawk .. *Tootooth gwan*. **1965** *Austral. Encycl.* III. 322 The nankeen kestrel .. is often termed 'sparrow-hawk', but this name gives an erroneous idea of its habits. Its food consists almost entirely of mice, lizards, and large insects.

sparrow-starver. A street-cleaner: see quot. 1965.
1950 'B. JAMES' *Advancement Spencer Button* 49 Loutish youths, tough, vocal, conceited and pugnacious, known to the vulgar as 'sparrow-starvers', plied to and fro with yard-brooms and a kind of tray on wheels, collecting the manure and other refuse. **1965** G. McINNES *Road to Gundagai* 113 His humble but essential job was to clean up the droppings from the big drays and waggons that rumbled up to and from the docks. He and his kind were known, with apposite Australian wit, as 'sparrer starvers'.

spear, *n.*
1. a. An Aboriginal spear: see quots.
1787 *Descr. Botany Bay, on East Side New Holland* 7 Their weapons are spears or lances of different kinds. **1910** J. MATHEW *Two Representative Tribes Qld.* 122 The spears, or *koni*, were from 7 to 10 ft. in length; made of iron-bark saplings and hardened at the point by the application of fire.
b. Special Comb. **spear thrower,** WOOMERA.
1896 B. SPENCER *Rep. Horn Sci. Exped. Central Aust.* IV. 89 *Spear-throwers*—'Amera', one type only is used in the regions visited, viz: a broad leaf-shaped instrument which is not only used for throwing the spear, but serves many useful purposes as a working tool.
2. *fig.* Dismissal, esp. in the phr. **to get the spear,** to be dismissed; to be 'fired'.
1897 *Worker* (Sydney) 11 Sept. 1/1 Poor Billy Mayne has got 'the spear' and Dick his mate is 'shot'! **1962** D. McLEAN *World turned upside Down* 121 Danny got the spear from the job.
3. *transf.* A pipe sunk to tap a shallow aquifer: see quot. 1947. Also *attrib.*
1924 *Inlander* Sept. 49 There the farmer merely drives down 'spears' (hollow pipes, perforated freely for a short distance close to their strong pointed heads) and pumps away to his heart's content. **1947** H. DRAKE-BROCKMAN *On N.-W. Skyline* 21 From the main pipe-line 'spears' are thrust down into the river-bed, going to depths of twenty to forty feet, dependent on where the plantation is situated... The 'spears' are made of galvanised piping, flattened at the end, with an added side opening after the fashion of organ-pipes. **1975** *Groundwater Resources Aust.* (Austral. Water Resources Council) 2 Connolly .. shows that towards the end of 1888 an irrigation system utilising a spear point assembly extracted water from unconsolidated sediments adjacent to Sheep Station Creek.

spear, *v.* [f. SPEAR *n.* 2.] *trans.* To dismiss (someone) from employment; to 'fire'. Freq. as past pple.
1911 'S. RUDD' *Dashwoods* 13 If I was the boss here I would. I'd spear him without warnin'. **1958** *Bulletin* (Sydney) 11 June 19/1 Consider the number of ways an Aussie can be dismissed from his job... He can be sacked, fired, hoisted, speared [etc.].

spear grass. Any of many grasses (fam. Poaceae), esp. of the genera *Stipa, Heteropogon* and *Aristida*, bearing a seed with a pointed husk and twisted awn(s), capable of working its way into soil, clothing, etc.: see quot 1844. See also WIRE-GRASS. Also *attrib.*
1840 *S. Austral. Rec.* (London) 28 Nov. 349 A little examination will point out the difference between kangaroo grass and spear grass. **1844** L. LEICHHARDT *Jrnl. Overland Exped. Aust.* 20 Nov. (1847) 45 Very disagreeable, however, was the abundance of Burr and of a spear-grass (Aristida), which attached themselves to our clothes and blankets, and entered (particularly the latter) into the very skin. **1887** J.H. WRIGHT *Our Victorian Coalfields* 22 Some 13,000 acres of poor land, consisting, for the most part, of spear-grass plains, with stunted gum-trees.

spearo. [f. *spear(-fisherman* + -O.] A spear-fisherman.
1963 B. CROPP *Handbk. for Skindivers* 138 This day will see well over a dozen fast boats lined up on a Sydney beach and dozens of 'spearos' preparing for a keen four-hour contest, while the women and children picnic on the beach and prepare refreshments for their return. **1970** J.S. GUNN in W.S. Ramson *Eng. Transported* 55 Some are trite and could fade away, for example, *spearo*, 'fisherman' [etc.].

spearwood. [See SPEAR *n.* 1 a.] Any of several plants furnishing wood traditionally used for making spears, incl. YARRAN and the small tree *Eucalyptus doratoxylon* (fam. Myrtaceae) of s.w. W.A. Also *attrib.*
1837 G.F. MOORE *Evidences Inland Sea* 14 A hedge of spearwood and sedge marking the course of the winter stream. **1875** J. FORREST *Explorations in Aust.* 66 Thence to Cooroo, over grassy country, with spearwood thickets intervening.

spec, var. SPECK *n.* and *v.*

special, *n. Hist.* GENTLEMAN CONVICT.
1832 J. HENDERSON *Observations Colonies N.S.W. & Van Diemen's Land* 9 The gentlemen convicts, who are denominated specials, were in the habit of being sent to a depôt at Wellington. **1952** J. TUCKER *Ralph Rashleigh* p. vi, Writing a novel takes time, so that I felt he must have been what was called a 'special', that is, an educated convict employed at a special task.

special, *a. Hist.* In special collocations: **special country lot** *Vic.*, a small tract of land suitable for cultivation as opposed to grazing (see quot. 1855); **survey,** a survey of land carried out under certain conditions which varied from Colony to Colony; the land so surveyed.
1842 *Act* (G.B.) 5 & 6 Vict. no. 36 Sect. 11, In respect of any Part not exceeding One Tenth of the whole of the Lands of the Third Class for the First Time offered for Sale .. it shall be lawful for any such Governor .. to name an upset Price higher than the lowest upset Price of Waste Lands in the Colony, and such excepted Lands of the Third Class shall be designated as '**Special Country Lots**'. **1855** E.H. HARGRAVES *Aust. & Goldfields* 198 Grazing lands will be sold by auction in sections, never exceeding 140 acres, or one square mile and .. lands suited for cultivation, or likely to be purchased for small farms, and which will be designated as 'special country lots', will be sold in portions of from 20 to 320 acres. **1838** *S. Austral. Rec.* (London) 13 Jan. 31 He is trying to buy town sections, and has been talking to Mr Fisher about a **special survey**. **1843** *Melbourne Times* 4 Aug. 3/1, I live on the special survey called Alger's Survey.

specimen. *Gold-mining.* See quot. 1869. Also *attrib.*
1869 R.B. SMYTH *Gold Fields & Mineral Districts* 622 *Specimen*, a piece of quartz containing gold which is visible to the naked eye. **1932** I.L. IDRIESS *Prospecting for Gold* 16 If you are in reef or 'specimen' country, keep an eye on any iron or quartz stones you pick from the bottom of the wash.

speck, *n.* Also **spec.**

1. *Gold-mining.* A small fragment of gold; FLY-SPECK 2. Also **speck gold.**

1852 J. BONWICK *Notes of Gold Digger* 12 The head stuff is removed to make way for you to get under, to work at the latent treasure of specs, nuggets and washing stuff. **1930** H. REDCLIFFE *Yellow Cygnet* 208 It was 'speck' gold—an amateur could have told that. **1964** H.P. TRITTON *Time means Tucker* 58 In a week we mastered the jargon of the goldfields and spoke wisely of .. colours, specks, slugs *etc.*

2. The (comparatively small) island of Tasmania; FLY-SPECK 1.

1916 *Bulletin* (Sydney) 8 June 24/4 Over the Speck they seldom split really big trees for posts. **1922** *Bulletin* (Sydney) 6 July 22/2 The Speck's early settlers learned from the blacks.

speck, *v. Mining.* Also **spec.**

1. *intr.* To search (for surface gold or opal).

1888 *Bulletin* (Sydney) 22 Dec. 18/1 He used to go 'a-speckin'' and 'fossickin'' amongst the old mullock heaps. **1948** H. DRAKE-BROCKMAN *Sydney or Bush* 26 Time of Kimberley gold rush. I reckoned to spec a bit up the coast. **1969** E. WALLER *And there's Opal* 116 A couple of tourists specking for bits of potch and opal.

2. a. *trans.* To search (the surface of the ground) for gold or opal.

1921 W.H. PHIPPS *Bush Yarns* 24 Set to work with his dishes, meanwhile urging the natives to 'speck' the ground for gold. **1932** I.L. IDRIESS *Prospecting for Gold* 185 You may get a 'line' of floaters leading right to the reef. You 'speck' those floaters.

b. *trans.* To discover (surface particles of gold or opal).

1926 *Bulletin* (Sydney) 11 Feb. 22/3 A friendly nig, especially if occasionally given a trifle of tea or sugar or part of a tin of 'dog', would bring to the tent of the fossicker small pieces of gold specked by him. **1932** I.L. IDRIESS *Prospecting for Gold* 230 That is how White Cliffs was found, a field that supported three thousand people for many years. A kangaroo shooter there 'specked' potch.

Hence **specked** *ppl. a.,* found on the surface of the ground.

1980 S. THORNE *I've met some Bloody Wags* 73 Occasionally a specker is lucky, but a lot of stones sold as 'specked' opal are in reality 'ratted' opal.

specker, *n.*[1] *Mining.* One who looks for surface deposits of a mineral.

1897 *Bulletin* (Sydney) 10 July 9/3 The Girilambone copper-speckers overdid it last Tuesday. **1980** S. THORNE *I've met some Bloody Wags* 73 After a shower or storm the opal fields are swarming with 'speckers'—hopefuls wandering about, heads down, bums in the air, looking for any gems on the ground.

specker, *n.*[2] Alteration of 'speculator'.

1919 *Smith's Weekly* (Sydney) 5 Apr. 9/3 Recent N.S.W. rains caught produce 'speckers' badly... Lucerne dropped from £13 10s. to £9 per ton. **1966** M. CANNON *Land Boomers* 77 As his profits grew, and with them his taste for gracious living, Larkin decided to imitate the Collins Street 'speckers' by building his own mansion.

specking, *vbl. n. Mining.* The action of searching for surface gold or opal. Also *attrib.*

1894 F. HART *Miner's Handbk.* 30 Here are situated the celebrated 'specking' grounds, over which hundreds of men walked day after day, turning over every stone with a forked stick to see if it might not be a specimen or cover a nugget. **1945** *Walkabout* (Melbourne) Mar. 14 Most of the residents of Lightning Ridge are experts at the art of specking.

spectacled, *a.* Used as a distinguishing epithet in the names of animals: **spectacled flycatcher** (or **monarch**), the predom. grey, orange, and white bird *Monarcha trivirgatus* of rainforest in e. mainland Aust., and elsewhere; **hare-wallaby,** the small wallaby *Lagorchestes conspicillatus* of n. Aust.

1898 E.E. MORRIS *Austral Eng.* 149 **Spectacled F[lycatcher]**—*P[iezorhynchus] nitidus.* **1976** *Reader's Digest Compl. Bk. Austral. Birds* 383 (*caption*) Large black eyepatches earn the spectacled monarch its name. **1894** R. LYDEKKER *Hand-Bk. Marsupialia & Monotremata* 52 **Spectacled Hare-Wallaby.** *Lagorchestes conspicillatus...* General colour coarsely grizzled yellowish-grey; under-parts mingled white and slaty-grey; a well-defined chestnut band round the eye.

speedball. [See quot. 1965.] A rissole.

1965 J.S. GUNN *Terminol. Shearing Industry* ii. 26 *Speed balls,* breakfast mincemeat rolls which are reputed (no doubt by the cook) to make shearers faster. The explanation may lie in the effect on the shearers' bowels. **1978** J. DINGWALL *Sunday too far Away* 40 'Bloody good cook.' . . 'Speed balls. That was his specialty.' . . 'Rissoles.'

speel, var. SPIEL.

speeler, var. SPIELER.

Speewah /'spiwa/. Also **Speewa.** [See quot. 1977.] **a.** An imaginary station or place used as a setting for tall stories of the outback. **b.** *transf.* Such a story. Also *attrib.*

1890 *Truth* (Sydney) 16 Nov. 1/4 Dear Mr *Truth*—I have just returned from 'the Spewah Country', where we have to crawl on our hands and knees to get under the clouds. **1911** *Bulletin* (Sydney) 17 Aug. 14/3 If any snagger boasted of having shorn 32 sheep in the breakfast 'run', there was always someone present to mention that 'Crooked Mick', at Speewah, had done 33 in the same time. **1977** L. BLAKE *Place Names Vic.* 242 Speewa: Locality by Murray River, N.W. of Swan Hill; in outback legends name of mythical sheep station, home of tall tales, where men, their locale, and achievements were all exceptionally big. **1979** *Courier-Mail* (Brisbane) 12 May 1/2 Each must tell a speerwah, or bush yarn, for more than four minutes.

speiler, speler, varr. SPIELER.

spell, *n.* [Br. dial.: see OEDS *sb.*[3] 3 b.] A period of rest from work; a holiday. Also *attrib.*

1831 *Sydney Herald* 12 Sept. 3/2 Taking a *spell* from the labours of the pestle and mortar. **1959** H. LAMOND *Sheep Station* 124 Some of the shearers, and an old rouseabout, got their horses in from the spell paddock.

spell, *v.* [f. prec.]

1. *intr.* To rest.

1841 S. STANGER in G. Mackaness *Fourteen Journeys Blue Mountains* (1950) iii. 67 As they formed altogether a jolly company, and had been a week coming from Sydney, they thought well to 'spell' (as they termed it) another day. **1978** D. STUART *Wedgetail View* 50 Sitting on a slope above the camp, spelling while a gang with shovels cleared away the spoil from their work.

2. *trans.* To cause or allow (an animal, person, etc.) to rest in order to recuperate; to leave (land) unused for a period in order to improve its productivity.

1846 J.L. STOKES *Discoveries in Aust.* II. 42 In order .. to spell the oars, we landed at a point on the east side. **1960** R.S. PORTEOUS *Cattleman* 233 We could do with a drop of rain, and even if we did get rain I'd like to see the bullock paddock spelled for a few months.

Hence **spelled** *ppl. a.,* **spelling** *ppl. a.*

1891 D. FERGUSON *Vicissitudes Bush Life* 47 When you are well **spelled** after your long tramp, I may get the Coni to give you a job at hut keeping. **1903** *Bulletin* (Sydney) 30 May 35/1 It was taken up .. partly for a **spelling** and fattening paddock for his bullocks and partly as a home for his wife.

spell-oh. Also **spello.** [f. SPELL *n.* + -O: see quot. 1862.] A call signalling the beginning of a break from work; the break itself.

1862 G.T. LLOYD *Thirty-Three Yrs. Tas. & Vic.* 125 Four or five times in one day .. was the ever-welcome command, 'Spell O, and sling kettles', responded to with marked satisfaction. **1974** J. GABY *Restless Waterfront* 109 We knew also that the men did arrange their spell-ohs for a billy of tea whilst the work still went on.

Hence **spell-oh** *v. intr.*, to rest.

1898 E. DYSON *Below & on Top* 139 You can spell-oh till you pick up a bit, an' then you can get down to graft.

spider.
1. **a.** A drink usually consisting of brandy mixed with lemonade (but see quots. 1861 and 1872).

1850 *Monthly Almanac* (Adelaide) 7 'Shouting' signifies paying for nine nobblers, four spiders, various glasses. **1861** H. EARLE *Ups & Downs* 283 They are .. up to unlimited 'spiders', or lemonade and sherry. **1872** W.H. THOMES *Bushrangers* 333 We .. made him give us a 'spider', or some brandy and beer mixed.

b. A soft drink to which a serving of ice-cream has been added.

1941 *Coast to Coast* 229 'You've had your drink, so now you've got to buy us all a spider at Smith's.' .. I didn't want to .. sit in Smith's and drink silly coloured muck with icecream floating in it. **1981** J. SAXTON *Something will Come* 159 A spider was a parfait glass filled with soft drink and topped off with a scoop of rainbow ice-cream.

2. *Mining.* A candle-holder having a spike able to be thrust into clay, timber, etc.: see quot. 1982.

1912 *Mercury* (Hobart) 17 Oct. 5/1 The following is the text of a letter found pinned to the timber by a miner's 'Spider' close to the body of J. McCarthy at the 700 ft. level. **1982** M. WALKER *Making Do* 98 They were working underground by candlelight, held on the wall by a spider; it's a piece of twisted iron. It had a candle in the middle of it, they would push that into one of the legs, as they call it, which is a timber prop that held up the stopings.

3. A gig used in a trotting race.

1934 T. WOOD *Cobbers* 18 Watching horses race by electric light is increased by the sight of them pulling gigs. These are called 'spiders'. **1969** *W. Austral.* (Perth) 5 July 32/5 Causing Pyraket to strike and badly buckle the inside wheel of Master Flame's spider.

spider flower. Any of several species of *Grevillea* (see GREVILLEA) having spidery flowers.

1913 F. SULMAN *Pop. Guide Wild Flowers N.S.W.* 10 The well-known Spider Flowers .. are .. marked by a more or less spider-like flower arrangement. **1981** G. CROSS *George & Widda-Woman* 9 We gathered small bunches of flowers for Mum .. spider flowers, waratahs.

spider orchid. Any of several terrestrial orchids of the chiefly Austral. genus *Caladenia* (fam. Orchidaceae) having long, narrowed sepals and petals. Also **spider,** and formerly **spider orchis.**

1867 *Lang. Native Flowers Tas.* 6 Spider Orchis .. danger near. **1978** L. WHITE *Memories of Childhood* 1 All the small orchids; spiders, donkeys, yellows, enamels. **1985** MARIS & BORG *Women of Sun* 64 Delicate spider orchids began to venture forth in spots untouched by grazing.

spiel /spil/, *v. Obs.* Also **speel.** [Var. of Br. dial. and slang *speel* to move fast, esp. to make off: see OEDS *speel,* $v.^2$] *intr.* To gallop.

1892 *Truth* (Sydney) 27 Mar. 1/6, I heard the throaty Hebrew shriek as past the post they spieled. .. If you ask me in strict confidence, I think that sheeny's mad. **1918** J.A. PHILP *Jingles that Jangle* 51 It looked good for him, as in the lead he spieled along.

Hence **spieling** *ppl. a.*

1899 J. BRADSHAW *Quirindi Bank Robbery* 42 We reached Tamworth after walking at a speeling rate just in time for tea.

spieler /'spilə/. Also **speeler, speiler, speler.** [Orig. U.S. and now chiefly Austral.: see OED(S.] One who engages in sharp practice; a swindler, orig. a card sharper (see quot. 1886).

1879 *Truth* (Sydney) 23 Dec. 5/4 Formerly a café keeper .. now a professional 'spieler'. **1880** *Bulletin* (Sydney) 12 June 20/2 The gambling mania has reached Auckland. Michael Gallagher, who keeps a 'sporting' house in that town, has been fined in the Police Court for allowing professional 'speelers' to play in his house. **1886** *Adelaide Observer* 29 May 41/5 A speler is known as a man that can do without working, and who travels from meeting to meeting with a pack of cards or a dice-box in his hand. To offer him work would be to take a liberty quite unwarranted. They are independent men; they have no need to work; they live by their wits, and I dare say make a good living at their calling. **1896** N. GOULD *Town & Bush* 222 The 'speilers' cluster together when the favourite wins, and the first backer of the winner, when he asks for his money, is politely told to wait, as an objection is about to be lodged.

spieling, *vbl. n. Obs.* [f. *spiel* to gamble: see OEDS *v.*] The activity of card-sharping; swindling. Also as *ppl. a.*

[N.Z. **1869** *Auckland Punch* 153, I twigged you on your speeling lay.] **1879** *Truth* (Sydney) 23 Dec. 5/4 A gambling den of the most dangerous character, because the 'spieling' is to a great extent a howling swindle and a pitfall for 'mugs'. **1911** *Truth* (Sydney) 26 Mar. 4/3 The spieling sharks of the betting shops .. unlawfully flourish.

spike-rush. [U.S. *spike rush* any sedge of the genus *Eleocharis* in which the flowers grow in dense spikes.] Any of the chiefly perennial sedges of the genus *Eleocharis* (fam. Cyperaceae) of all States and elsewhere.

1909 F.M. BAILEY *Comprehensive Catal. Qld. Plants* (ed. 2) 591 Heleocharis (Eleocharis) .. Spike Rush. **1985** I. & T. DONALDSON *Seeing First Australs.* 192 The spike-rush, *Eleocharis dulcis* .. whose sweet nutty corms are one of the chief foods of the Anbarra people.

spikey. [See quot. 1951.] Any of several fish, incl. the *long-spined flathead* (see LONG 2).

1906 D.G. STEAD *Fishes of Aust.* 198 The fish is known to the fishermen of Coogee by the .. name of 'Spikey'. .. It is of a light sandy colour, spotted over with small, brilliant, red or vermilion spots. **1951** T.C. ROUGHLEY *Fish & Fisheries Aust.* 138 The long-spined flathead has received its name from the prominence of a preopercular spine on each side of the head; this is very sharp and has earned for the fish the name of 'spikey'.

spill. *Politics.* The vacating of other offices in a cabinet, party, etc., after one important change of office.

1956 J.T. LANG *I Remember* 311 There had to be an annual election of leader. That made it inevitable that some members would intrigue against the leader hoping for a Cabinet spill. **1985** *Austral. Financial Rev.* (Sydney) 26 July 2/2 So suspicious is each of the other and so intense is Mr Howard's desire for the top job that a 'spill' for the leadership initiated by either man is seen by senior Liberals as highly likely.

spin, $n.^1$
1. *Two-up.* The act of tossing the coins in the air.

1919 C.H. THORP *Handful of Ausseys* 247 All set 'n away she goes—a fair spin an' a good 'un; an' it's—'eads. 1971 G. MORGAN *We are borne On* 87 There were thousands of troops scattered around and a big two-up school operated day and night, so I adjourned with my five pounds to the school to try my luck. In my first two spins I lost three pounds.

2. With qualifying word: a (good, bad, rough, etc.) run of luck.

1917 W.V. WRIGHT *Diary* 10 Jan., Out of the line at last, by jove she's been a crook spin this trip. 1939 I.L. IDRIESS *Cyaniding for Gold* 86 Jim Albury and his mate on the Bowman River near Gloucester were suffering a bad spin. 1966 A. HOPGOOD *Private Yuk Objects* Pref., I'm an Australian, mate... That means I can have three meals a day, watch the telly every night, go to the footy or the races.. and generally get a good spin out of life. 1974 D. O'GRADY *Deschooling Kevin Carew* 107 He knew Kevin had had a rough spin since the withdrawal of the Education Department scholarship.

spin, *n.*² Abbrev. of SPINNAKER. Also *attrib.*

1941 *Coast to Coast* 225 'How'd you go at the two-up?' I asked. 'Aw, I got a spin,' said Tom... 'I was holdin' a score but I dropped most of it.' 1975 M.B. ROBERTS *King of Con Men* 69 He would thump the bench.. and bark, 'Fined five pounds'... Throughout the length and breadth of Australia he was known as 'Spin McGee'—'spin' being the slang term for £5.

spin, *v. Two-up.*

1. *trans.* To toss (the coins) into the air so that they revolve. Also *absol.*, and with the result of the toss as obj.

1913 *Bulletin* (Sydney) 30 Jan. 16/1 Binghi is the boss person of a two-up ring... As an expert spinner.. few of the thousands of habitual 'swi-up' players I have seen can spin decently without violently swinging the arm. 1916 *Battery Herald:Jrnl. 14th Field Artillery* 9 Oct. 8 Spinning tails about six times in succession. 1941 E. BAUME *I lived These Yrs.* 122, I have often seen at the two-up schools in Sydney, in the old days, five and six hundred pounds 'spun' for on one turn of the coins.

2. *intr.* With **out**: to lose the right to continue as spinner.

1951 E. LAMBERT *Twenty Thousand Thieves* 234 'It's rainin' heads.' 'Well, what are we waiting for?' 'He'll spin out in a minute. He's done four straight.' 1972 J. O'GRADY *It's your Shout, Mate!* 25 After two more spinners had 'spun out', the keeper announced, 'We've got a guest spinner'.

spinach. [Transf. use of *spinach* the cultivated plant *Spinacia oleracea.*] Wild spinach, see WILD 1.

1770 J. BANKS *Endeavour Jrnl.* (1962) II. 114 Spinage (*Tetragonia cornuta*). 1923 J. ARMOUR *Spell of Inland* 10 We have different varieties of creepers, wild melons, bindaii, spinach, and other herbs that cattle eat.

spine-bash, *n.* [See next.] A rest; a sleep; an act of loafing. Formerly also as **spine drill, hour, job.**

1940 *First Post: Mag. 2/1st Battalion A.I.F.* Sept. 11 The science of *spine drill* has been mastered by four Section. 1945 *Atebrin Advocate: Mag. 2/4 Austral. Armoured Regiment* Jan. 3 You blokes can work if you want to... It's a spine job for me. 1949 *Gremlin Jottings* (Canberra) Nov. 1 An hour when respectable people are still getting some 'spine hours' up. 1976 *Tracks we Travel* 17 Old Arty had struggled awake after his spine bash.

spine-bash, *v. intr.* To rest; to loaf. Freq. as *vbl. n.*

1941 *Argus* (Melbourne) 15 Nov. (Week-End Mag.) 1/4 *Spine-bashing*, having a rest; loafing. 1958 R. ROBINSON *Black-Feller White-Feller* 9 They would rather have stayed in the camp to spine-bash or go down to the swy game.

Hence **spine-basher** *n.*

1945 'MASTER-SARG' *Yank discovers Aust.* 75 'A spine basher'—lazy or heavy sleeper.

spinebill. [See quot. 1909.] Either of two small honeyeaters of the genus *Acanthorhynchus, A. tenuirostris* (see *eastern spinebill* EASTERN 2), and *A. superciliosus* of s.w. W.A.; COBBLER'S AWL. Also **spine-bill(ed) honey-eater.**

1848 J. GOULD *Birds of Aust.* (1848) IV. Pl. 61, *Acanthorhynchus tenuirostris* .. Spine-bill, Colonists of New South Wales. 1887 *Illustr. Austral. News* (Melbourne) 21 Dec. 218/1 The honey-eaters seen were nearly all of Tasmanian origin... Only the New Holland and spine bill honey-eaters resemble the Victorian. 1909 G. SMITH *Naturalist in Tas.* 63 Another peculiar Honey-eater, characterized by its exceedingly long curved bill and its chocolate breast, is the Spine Bill. 1929 A.H. CHISHOLM *Birds & Green Places* 118 Once a spine-billed honeyeater came into the nesting-tree.

spine drill (hour, job): see SPINE-BASH *n.*

spine-tailed, *a.* Used as a distinguishing epithet in the names of birds: **spine-tailed log-runner,** see LOG-RUNNER 2; **swift,** the bird *Hirundapus caudacutus*, which breeds in Asia and migrates southward to e. Aust. in summer (see quot. 1986).

1856 H.B. STONEY *Vic.* 212 Of seven Australian swallows, one, the spine-tailed swift, the largest known member of the family is occasionally seen about Sydney. 1986 *Canberra Times* 22 Jan. 17/2 These are white-throated needle-tails (also known as spine-tailed swifts) slicing through the air at up to 130 km/h as they hunt for insects... The tiny, needle-like protrusions on the tail which give it its common name are barely visible except at very close range. They are really modified feathers and are thought to act as a prop when the bird clings to vertical surfaces.

spinifex. [The plant genus *Spinifex* was named by Swedish naturalist Carl von Linné (Linnaeus) (*Mantissa Plantarum* (1771) II. 163), f. mod. L. *spina* spine + *-fex* maker, f. *facere* to make.]

1. **a.** Any of many tussocky, often spiny, perennial grasses of the genera *Triodia* and *Plectrachne* (both fam. Poaceae), chiefly of arid and semi-arid Aust., as *Triodia basedowii, T. irritans*, and *T. pungens*; PORCUPINE GRASS 1. **b.** The similar *Zygochloa paradoxa* (fam. Poaceae; formerly *Spinifex paradoxus*) of arid and semi-arid Aust. **c.** (Occas.) a prostrate grass of the genus *Spinifex* (fam. Poaceae), occurring on coastal sand dunes in Aust., and elsewhere. **d.** With distinguishing epithet, as **buck, old man:** see under first element. **e.** *ellipt., spinifex country.* Also *attrib.*

1825 B. FIELD *Geogr. Mem. N.S.W.* 285 This part of the country is a universal mass of rocks, heaped one upon the other, and the interstices filled with spinifex, a prickly useless grass, of a powerfully aromatic smell. 1841 G. GREY *Jrnls. Two Exped. N.-W. & W.A.* I. 95 The soil beneath our feet was sandy, and thickly clothed with spinifex (a prickly grass). 1935 I.L. IDRIESS *Man Tracks* 23 They returned.. with news from the spinifex natives of the tracks of a white man. 1958 F.B. VICKERS *Though Poppies Grow* 17 If we'd wanted to be on our own we'd have stayed out in the spinifex.

2. Comb. (chiefly in sense 1 a.): **spinifex country, farm, grass, plain.**

1875 J. FORREST *Explorations in Aust.* 212 Most miserable **spinifex country** all day. 1936 C.T. MADIGAN *Central Aust.* 248 There was nothing else of any value to be seen on the whole field; the leases were very aptly called '**spinifex farms**'. 1863 J. DAVIS *Tracks of McKinlay* 41 The ever-recurring **spinifex grass** indicated its accompanying poor soil. 1891 W.H. TIETKENS *Jrnl. Central Austral. Exploring Exped.* 40 The country opened out into **spinifex plains** with an occasional sandhill.

3. Special Comb.: **spinifex gum,** a resin obtained from spinifex (sense 1 a.), esp. *Triodia pungens,* traditionally used in hafting stone tools.
1898 D.W. CARNEGIE *Spinifex & Sand* 245 Two neat articles were fashioned by stringing together red beans set in spinifex gum.

4. In the names of animals occurring in spinifex country: **spinifex parrot,** either of two parrots, NIGHT PARROT and PRINCESS PARROT; **pigeon,** the predom. brown, crested pigeon *Petrophassa plumifera* of central, n., and n.w. Aust.; *plumed pigeon,* see PLUMED; **rat** (or **wallaby**), a hare-wallaby, esp. *Lagorchestes hirsutus,* formerly widespread in arid and semi-arid Aust.; **snake,** a snake or snake-like lizard occurring in spinifex country.
1917 *Bulletin* (Sydney) 6 Dec. 22/1 Most notable bird voices are those of.. myrlumbing (night or **spinifex parrot**) [etc.]. **1935** G. McIVER *Drover's Odyssey* 175 This desolate tract of country was then the home of the beautiful spinifex parrot... The varied tints and brilliance of its plumage were wonderful. **1898** D.W. CARNEGIE *Spinifex & Sand* 303 The prettiest of all the birds is a little plump, quail-like rock- or **spinifex-pigeon,** a dear little shiny, brown fellow with a tuft on his head. **1895** [**spinifex rat**] *Trans. & Proc. R. Soc. S.A.* (1896) XVI. 240 The Blyth Range, Barrow Range, and Victoria Desert tribes inhabit 'spinifex country' where subsistence is difficult to maintain, and but for the numerously-occurring *Largochestes hirsutus* commonly called 'Spinifex-Wallaby'.. it would probably be impossible for them to live in such desolate districts. **1983** R. STRAHAN *Compl. Bk. Austral. Mammals* 199 The Rufous Hare-Wallaby was once common.. particularly in the spinifex hummock grasslands of the sand plain and sand dune deserts. Aborigines hunted it for food and early explorers commented on the large numbers of 'spinifex rats' flushed from cover. **1955** F.B. VICKERS *Mirage* (1958) 155 A **spinifex snake** slid away.

spinnaker. [Fig. use of *spinnaker* a large sail.] A five-pound note; the sum of five pounds. See also SPIN *n.*^{2}
1898 *Bulletin* (Sydney) 1 Oct. 14/3 A few more W.Q. slang words.. £5 is a ' spinnaker'. **1955** N. PULLIAM *I traveled Lonely Land* 152 I'll bet the first Aussie taker a couple of spinnakers the Snowy Mountains dream come true.

spinner. *Two-up.*
a. The player who tosses the coins.
1911 L. STONE *Jonah* 215 The spinner handed his stake of five shillings to the boxer, who cried, 'Fair go!' **1977** R. BEILBY *Gunner* 180 A two-up game proceeded intermittently, the ring-keeper's calls pealing faintly.
b. In the phr. **come in spinner,** the call which signals to the spinner that all bets have been placed and that it is time to toss the coins.
1943 *Troppo Tribune* (Mataranka) 12 Apr. 2 The old saying 'Come in spinner' is now amended. **1977** R. BEILBY *Gunner* 182 Set inna centre, get set onna side! Come in, spinner!

spiny, *a.* Used as a distinguishing epithet in the names of flora and fauna: **spiny anteater,** ECHIDNA; **-cheeked honeyeater,** the predom. grey-brown honeyeater *Acanthagenys rufogularis* of mainland Aust., having spiny feathers from the bill to the cheek; **emex,** DOUBLE-GEE a.
1827 E. GRIFFITH tr. *Cuvier's Animal Kingdom* III. 263 The Echidnes.. otherwise **Spiny Ant-eaters. 1844** J. GOULD *Birds of Aust.* (1848) IV. Pl. 53, The **Spiny-cheeked Honeyeater** ranges very widely over the interior of Australia. **1921** J. MATTHAMS *Rabbit Pest in Aust.* 255 **Spiny Emex,** three cornered jack, or Cat's Head, *Emex Australis.*

spit, *n.* In the phr. **to go for the big spit:** see BIG 3 d.

spit, *v. trans.* In the phr. **to spit chips.**
a. To feel extreme thirst.
1901 *Bulletin Reciter* 108 While you're spitting chips like thunder.. And the streams of sweat near blind you. **1946** A. MARSHALL *Tell us about Turkey, Jo* 142, I was spitting chips. God, I was dry!
b. To manifest extreme anger.
1947 J. MORRISON *Sailors belong Ships* 189 Old Mick Doyle's with them. He's spitting chips because they're not using sea water. **1968** S. GORE *Holy Smoke* 14 When he comes rushing up—spittin' chips, he's so mad—young Dave only lets fly with one shot outa his ging, and the big bloke's stonkered.

spitfire. The larva of a sawfly, esp. of the genus *Perga,* as *P. dorsalis,* a large dark larva which exudes a sticky greenish fluid when disturbed; SPITTER.
1920 M.N. & A.A. BREWSTER *Life Stories Austral. Insects* 110 Family Tenthredinidae (Sawflies)... The larvae of this group are better known than the adults... They may be seen in clusters on the leaves of *Eucalyptus,* and when disturbed, they turn up their tails and eject a greenish fluid, hence the children call them 'spitfires'. **1984** *Canberra Times* 22 Sept. 11/1 The unpleasant habits of larvae of the steel-blue sawfly, or 'spitfires'... A sticky secretion from their mouths.. was high in eucalyptus oil and caused severe pain if it got into the eyes.

spitter. SPITFIRE.
1944 C. FENNER *Mostly Austral.* 153 They develop into very handsome sawflies... Schoolboys call them 'spitters', from their habit of waving their bodies when disturbed, and at the same time emitting a greenish, strong-smelling fluid from their mouths.

split, *v.*
1. *trans. Hist.* [Used elsewhere but of local significance.] To split (a log of wood) with an axe or similar tool, for use as rails, shingles, slabs, etc.; to split (rails, etc.) from a log. Also *absol.*
1793 D. COLLINS *Acct. Eng. Colony N.S.W.* (1798) I. 334 For splitting paling for fences, and bringing it in from the woods, they charged from one shilling and six-pence to two shillings and six-pence per hundred. **1928** *Bulletin* (Sydney) 14 Mar. 23/1 While splitting in the bush I have several times come across a peculiar fungus.

2. *intr. Obs.* Of cattle: to separate from the main group. Freq. as *vbl. n.*
1848 H.W. HAYGARTH *Recoll. Bush Life* 63 The most frequent and troublesome habit is that of breaking off from the main body, or 'splitting'. **1888** W.T. PYKE *Bush Tales* 34 From original mismanagement they had become so wild, and had acquired so firm a habit of 'splitting', that to muster them was an impossibility.

split, *ppl. a. Hist.* [f. SPLIT *v.* 1.]
1. a. Of timber: that has undergone the process of splitting.
1797 D. COLLINS *Acct. Eng. Colony N.S.W.* (1802) II. 23 The miserable quarters which those gentlemen occupied were originally constructed only of split cabbage trees. **1861** T. McCOMBIE *Austral. Sketches* 123 The first object that attracts attention is the wool shed, a large building of slabs or rough split logs.
b. In the collocation **split stuff,** wood split as required for a particular purpose.
1836 *Cornwall Chron.* (Launceston) 1 Oct. 3 On the estate there are upwards of 70,000 bricks, and about 6,000 of split stuff for fencing.

2. a. Made from wood that has undergone the process of splitting.
1828 *Tasmanian* (Hobart) 11 Apr. 2 Sawn timber of various sorts, and sizes, shingles, split posts [etc.]. **1900**

Bulletin (Sydney) 21 July 15/1, I was .. putting up a line of split-fence on a N.S.W. station.

b. Esp. in the collocations **split paling, rail.**

1833 *Launceston Advertiser* 27 June 2, 1000 **split palings**. **1838** *Southern Austral.* (Adelaide) 17 Nov. 4/2 Thirty Cottages or town lands, to be formed of **split rails** for uprights .. and for rafters, and for walls and roofs.

splitter. *Hist.* [Spec. use of *splitter* one who or that which splits.]

1. One whose occupation is the splitting of rails, shingles, slabs, etc., from logs. Also with qualifying word, as **rail-splitter.**

1826 *Colonial Times* (Hobart) 24 June, To Fencers and Splitters. Wanted Four Men, who will Contract to Put up and complete One Thousand Rods of four-railed Fence, near Cape Portland. **1897** J.D. HENNESSY *New-Chum Farmer* 1 Hire yourself out to a dairyman, take a contract with a rail-splitter, sign articles with a cockatoo selector, but don't touch land without knowing something about it.

2. A tree, the trunk of which will split cleanly.

1959 *Overland* xv. 25 All around were gaunt, bent and cross-grained old iron-barks... He said to me, 'Can you pick a splitter, lad?' **1960** *Bulletin* (Sydney) 16 Mar. 19/2 The paling-splitter worked and lived in noble solitude, and because only one stick in a hundred was a 'splitter' he ranged widely and vetted a lot of trees.

splitting, *ppl. a. Hist.* [f. SPLIT *v.* 1.]

1. Used in the process of splitting timber.

1838 *Austral. Mag.* (Sydney) 137, 2 Sets Splitting Wedges. **1839** *Tegg's Handbk. for Emigrants* 12 Grubbing tools. Splitting tools.

2. Of timber: able to be split.

1841 *Port Phillip Gaz.* 16 June 1 Valuable Sawing and Splitting Timber. **1907** *Bulletin* (Sydney) 10 Jan. 15/2 Given good-splitting ironbarks either of these men would cut 18 'eights' in a day.

spons. *Obs.* Abbrev. of 'spondulicks', money.

c **1879** *Ye Prodigal* (Sydney) 201 Those three happy men .. soon stood within the .. deserted house, mourning .. the departed 'spons' that they had lavished with such an utter contempt of riches upon those run-away husseys. **1916** *Truth* (Sydney) 21 May 12/7 Yes, Ethel she had shopping gone, And being minus spons, Nicked what her giglamps lit upon, A statuette of bronze.

spoof. [Of unknown origin.] Seminal fluid. Also as *v. intr.*, to ejaculate seminal fluid.

1916 *Runic Rhymes: Souvenir H.M.A.T. 'Runic'* July 3 Baa Baa Black hand Have you any oof? Yes sir, Yes sir All that we can spoof. **1981** P. RADLEY *Jack Rivers & Me* 61 The amount of spoof is more important to Eternity than the size of your cock.

Hence **spoofie** *n.*, a sexually attractive young woman.

1973 *Bulletin* (Sydney) 13 Jan. 27/1 'Spunk bubbles' or 'spoofies' the life savers call the nubile teenagers.

sport. [Chiefly Austral.: see OED(S *sb.*[1] 8 e.] A familiar form of address: cf. MATE 4.

1923 G.S. BEEBY *Concerning Ordinary People* 305 All right, sport. No offence meant. **1982** H. KNORR *Private Viewing* 104 Don't get y' knickers in a knot, sport!

spot, *n.* [Spec. use of *spot* a small quantity; in Br. use usu. with *of*: see OED(S *sb.*[1] 7 d.]

1. A drink of alcoholic liquor, not necessarily small.

1922 H. LAWSON *Lett.* (1970) 235 There's no pub here. We can only gather .. and hope for demijohns from Narrandera (we call 'em 'jars' or 'spots'). **1942** L. MANN *Go-Getter* 188 It's a time since I saw you, Chris. What about a spot?

2. The sum of one hundred pounds (or dollars).

1945 S.J. BAKER *Austral. Lang.* 109, £100—*spot*. **1983** HIBBERD & HUTCHINSON *Barracker's Bible* 29 A 'spot' is $100.

spot, *v.* [Back-formation f. U.S. *spot-fire* a fire started by flying sparks at a distance from the main fire.] *intr.* Of a bushfire: to break out in patches ahead of the main fire (see quot. 1983). Also as *vbl. n.*

1978 LUKE & MCARTHUR *Bushfires in Aust.* 102 Spotting distances are abnormally high in some rough-barked eucalypts. **1981** *Bega District News* 27 Nov. 5/6 While Milliner was working at the top of the ridge the fire spotted across the gully and crossed the track. **1983** *Blue Mountains Gaz.* 3 Aug. 7/1 The program will also study the behaviour of bushfires, and the process of 'spotting' where firebrands are blown downwind to start new fires ahead of the main fire.

spotted, *ppl. a.* Used as a distinguishing epithet in the names of flora and fauna: **spotted bower-bird,** the spotted brown bird *Chlamydera maculata* of drier mainland Aust.; **ground-bird** (or **ground-thrush**), *spotted quail-thrush*; **gum,** any of several trees of the genus *Eucalyptus* (fam. Myrtaceae), esp. *E. maculata* of e. mainland Aust. and *E. henryi*, both having a colourful mottled trunk; the wood of the tree; **harrier,** the bird of prey *Circus assimilis*, widespread in mainland Aust. and occurring elsewhere, having blue-grey and chestnut plumage with white spots; **native cat,** *native cat* NATIVE *a.* 6 b.; **nightjar,** the nocturnal *Caprimulgus guttatus* of mainland Aust. (except the e. coastal region) and elsewhere, a mottled brown, grey and black bird with conspicuous white spots on the wing; **pardalote** (or **diamond bird**), the small bird *Pardalotus punctatus* of s.w. W.A. and e. Aust. incl. Tas.; see also *diamond sparrow* DIAMOND *n.*[1]; **quail-thrush,** the ground-dwelling thrush *Cinclosoma punctatum* of s.e Aust. incl. Tas., having quail-like plumage and shape; *spotted ground-bird*; **-sided finch,** *diamond firetail*, see DIAMOND *n.*[1]; **whiting,** the carnivorous marine fish *Sillaginodes punctatus* of s. Aust. incl. Tas., valued as food; KING GEORGE WHITING.

1841 J. GOULD *Birds of Aust.* (1848) IV. Pl. 8, *Chlamydera maculata*. **Spotted Bower-bird. 1840** [**spotted ground-bird**] J. GOULD *Birds of Aust.* (1848) IV. Pl. 4, The Spotted Ground-Thrush gives a decided preference to the summits of low stony hills and rocky gullies, particularly those covered with scrubs and grasses. **1945** C. BARRETT *Austral. Bird Life* 202 Quail-Thrushes or ground-birds (*Cinclosoma*) .. live 'close to the ground'... The spotted ground-bird (*C. punctatum*) inhabits southern Queensland, New South Wales, Victoria, South Australia, and Tasmania. **1824** *Austral.* (Sydney) 21 Oct. 2 He found a great deal of pine and iron bark; she oak, swamp oak, and a kind of **spotted gum**. **1880** *Proc. Linnean Soc. N.S.W.* 452 *E. maculata* .. or 'The Spotted Gum', is a fine tree rising to 100 feet and upwards, and sometimes 80 or 90 feet without a branch. **1898** E.E. MORRIS *Austral Eng.* 193 Harrier .. English bird-name .. assigned .. in Australia to *C[ircus] assimilis* .. called **Spotted Harrier. 1933** C.W. PECK *Austral. Legends* (ed. 2) 225 The movement of .. the **spotted native cat** and the wallaroo. **1896** B. SPENCER *Rep. Horn Sci. Exped. Central Aust.* II. 108 *Eurostopodus guttatus*. **Spotted Nightjar** .. I had hoped of securing .. but was disappointed. **1844** J. GOULD *Birds of Aust.* (1848) II. Pl. 35, *Pardalotus punctatus* .. **Spotted Pardalote** .. *Diamond Bird*, Colonists of New South Wales. **1896** F.G. AFLALO *Sketch Nat. Hist. Aust.* 137 The Spotted Diamond Bird (*Pardalotus punctatus*), known to aboriginals from its peculiar cry as the 'Weedupwee', burrows in the earth. **1965** *Austral. Encycl.* VII. 315 The only species of the group that are at all familiar, even to naturalists, are the **spotted quail-thrush** .. and the chestnut-backed quail-thrush. **1848** J. GOULD *Birds of Aust.* (1848) III. Pl. 86, *Amadina lathami.* **Spotted-sided Finch. 1906** D.G. STEAD *Fishes of Aust.* 112 The **Spotted Whiting** .. may be at once distinguished .. by .. the presence of pretty Trout-like spots all over the upper half of the body.

spout, *n.*
1. *Shearing. Obs.* Used *attrib.* with reference to the practice of washing sheep under falling water: see quot. 1842. Esp. as **spout-washed** *ppl. a.*, **-washing** *vbl. n.*
1842 *Portland Mercury* 14 Sept. 4/4 Latterly a great improvement has been introduced, of washing them [*sc.* sheep] under spouts constructed where the river has a fall, by which the fleece is effectually cleansed with very little hand labour. As, however, nearly all Australian rivers cease flowing in severe droughts, the spout system cannot be put in practice then, nor in various extensive districts in the colony, where chains of ponds supply the place of running brooks. **1847** *Port Phillip Herald* 16 Nov. 3/5 It is a very superior run, and watered by the Lardarch and Werriby (both running streams), giving every facility for spout-washing. **1927** A. CROMBIE *After Sixty Yrs.* 115, I can assure you, Crombie, Learmouth took seven shillings a head off all their spout washed sheep.

2. A hollow stump left on a tree (usu. a gum tree) where a branch has broken off.
1840 J. GOULD *Birds of Aust.* (1848) II. Pl. 2, During the day it [*sc.* the owlet nightjar] resorts to the hollow branches or spouts as they are called. **1902** *Emu* II. 36 The nesting place was in the spout of a gum-tree, about 30 feet from the ground.

spout, *v. Obs. Shearing. trans.* To wash (a sheep) under falling water. Also as *vbl. n.* and *ppl. a.*
1871 *Austral. Town & Country Jrnl.* (Sydney) 4 Feb. 138/3 Immediately spouted by the ordinary process, entirely dispensing with hot water, soap, or soda. *Ibid.*, I then found that the proportion of bright spouted sheep was small. **1873** A. TROLLOPE *Aust. & N.Z.* I. 122 There are various modes of washing—but on the stations which I saw on the Darling Downs the sheep were all 'spouted'... But before .. the spouting there is a preliminary washing... The sheep are passed on, one by one, into the hands of the men at the spouts. At one washpool I saw fourteen spouts at work, with two men at each spout... The sheep goes out of the spouter's hands, not into the water, but on to steep boards, arranged so as to give him every facility for travelling up to the pen which is to receive him.
Hence **spouter** *n.*
1873 [see SPOUT *v.*].

sprag, *v.* [Fig. use of *sprag* to stop (a wheel) by the use of a chock or bar which acts as a brake: see OED *v.* 2.]
1. *trans.* To obstruct (a plan, etc.); to thwart.
1911 *Bulletin* (Sydney) 2 Nov. 14/1 Some of these mean whites dummy leases for Chows... But the Commonwealth has got hold of things, and the oldest inhabitants who spragged the wheels of the Territory will have to alter... Nearly every mining lease in the Territory is being worked by Chows and dummies. **1965** U.R. ELLIS (*title*) Attempt to sprag New State Referendum.
2. To accost truculently; to pester.
1915 'LANCE-CORPORAL COBBER' *Anzac Pilgrim's Progress* (1918) 82 He's no bully, doesn't mag, Doesn't swank around an' sprag, You will never hear him brag Like a Hun. **1979** D.R. STUART *Crank back on Roller* 95 This cove, Pommy, all mo. an' buck teeth, he sprags me an' Joey an' nothin'll do but he's gotta buy us grog.

spread. A distribution or scattering of stock over a wide area, esp. in the phr. **to have** (or **get**) **a spread on** and varr.
1903 *Bulletin* (Sydney) 17 Jan. 16/2 If there was a big spread on the sheep the men could not have sighted and 'cleared' every part of the paddock—the true definition of mustering—in time to count 80,000 sheep. **1904** *Emu* III. 174 They can be seen feeding sometimes as far as the eye can reach, in pairs or small mobs, like a flock of sheep 'on a good spread'. **1931** F.D. DAVISON *Man-Shy* (1962) 85 And don't let them get a spread on! **1936** I.L. IDRIESS *Cattle King* 60 The pikers among them would surely have a spread on by now.

spring, *v.* [Spec. use of *spring* to cause to appear.] *trans.* To discover or come upon (something or someone, usu. a concealed object or someone engaged in an illicit activity); esp. in the phr. **to spring the plant** (see PLANT *n.*[1] 1 b.).
1812, etc. [see PLANT *n.*[1] 1 a.]. **1842** *Geelong Advertiser* 18 Apr. 2/5 Having received certain information and a guide, Mr Le Seouff set out about eight days since to 'spring' an illicit still, which he had been told was in full play in the tea-tree scrub at Dandenong. **1981** B. DICKINS *Gift of Gab* 24 Our science teacher .. sprung me acting the goat and I was bumwallopped.

springboard. *Timber-getting.* [Orig. U.S.: see OED(S 3.] See quot. 1920. Also *attrib.*
1912 L. ESSON *Red Gums* 39 The mountain ashes Round the 'springboard' high. 'Cut the calf!' Splitters laugh At the reel and ruction. **1920** C.W. BRYDE *Chart House to Bush Hut* 103 Terry was great on springboard work. A springboard is a six-inch by one-inch board four feet long, with a horse-shoe bolted on one end point up. You cut a notch two inches deep in a tree, insert the board, and stand on it to chop, the point of the shoe being driven by your weight into the upper edge of the notch and holding firm... I have heard it described as chopping with one foot in the grave and the other on a bit of orange peel.

springer.
1. *Obs.* An improvised fishing-rod; see quot. 1900.
1900 *Bulletin* (Sydney) 21 July 15/1 A springer is a tapering mallee rod, perhaps 10 feet long, pointed at the thick end. **1917** C. THACKERAY *Goliath Joe* 46, I was jest skinnin' a black maggy fer bait fer my 'and-line wen I seen my springer bend.
2. A spring-operated trap.
1909 *Emu* VIII. 220 As a boy I did a good deal of trapping .. and a favourite place to set a 'springer' was just where a wallaby would land after leaping over a gully. **1920** *Bulletin* (Sydney) 8 Apr. 22/1 Cut out poison, springers, dog-traps, fencing-wire nooses, 'figgers o' four', and such-like and sink pit-traps.

sprooker, var. SPRUIKER.

spruik /sprʉk/, *n.* [f. SPRUIK *v.*] A speech; a rant.
1911 *Truth* (Sydney) 3 Dec. 1/4 Why not call Sir Edward's spruik a great speech. **1953** T.A.G. HUNGERFORD *Riverslake* 40, I usually go and have a bit of a spruik to him when I knock off.

spruik /sprʉk/, *v.* [Of unknown origin.] *intr.* To hold forth (in public); to deliver a harangue, esp. to advertise a show, etc.: see quot. 1912. Also *trans.*, to discourse on (a subject).
1902 *Truth* (Sydney) 14 Sept. 5/6 'Lockie the Spruiker' that 'spruiked' for years at the Gaiety door, Has gone out of the 'spruiking' business, and never will 'spruik' any more. **1912** *Bulletin* (Sydney) 4 Apr. 14/4 *Spruik?* I just *could*! And wot was more, I used to *look* me part, A-standin' on them marble steps to give the show a start! And talkin' big, and talkin' fast, and poet-like, and free, About the noble fillums wot there was inside to see! **1982** *Bulletin* (Sydney) 26 Oct. 51/2 MacGregor .. didn't mention it (and the man himself has not been heard spruiking the fact).
Hence **spruiking** *vbl. n.* and *attrib.*
1925 *Bulletin* (Sydney) 16 July 47/2, I was lobbying the licensed victuallers' headquarters in the town for a

spruiking job. **1955** E.O. SCHLUNKE *Man in Silo* 26 'Well, you'd do the spruiking all right,' Birnie admitted grudgingly. Henzel was a great reciter at parties and speaker at all public functions.

spruiker /'sprukə/. Also **sprooker**. A speaker employed to attract custom, esp. to a sideshow; a barker; an eloquent speaker.
1902 [see SPRUIK *v*.]. **1910** W.C. WALL *Sydney Stage Employee's Postal Ann.* 100 Mick was also a 'sprooker' for his own and other shows. **1933** J. MCCARTER *Love's Lunatic* 282 An' now y'll see how me little talks—like th' wireless spruikers say—have been goin'. **1977** C. MCCULLOUGH *Thorn Birds* 93 'Come on, chaps, who'll take a glove?' the spruiker was braying.

spud cocky. [f. *spud* potato + COCKY *n.*²] A potato farmer.
1950 *New Settler in W.A.* (Perth) Mar. 21 My next job was with a 'Spud Cocky' (potato farmer) digging taters for 10s. a week plus 1s. a bag bonus. **1985** P. CAREY *Illywhacker* 228 When some stirrers . . tried to organize a strike against the spud farmers . . I was called a scab. . . It was us scabs who brought in the spuds for those celebrated spud cockies.

spunk. A person sexually attractive to members of the opposite sex. Also *attrib*.
1978 J. ROWE *Warlords* 205, I mean I can always round up a boatload of horny looking young spunks, but there's no guarantees for old gits like us from the amateurs. **1981** *Age* (Melbourne) 21 Aug. 11/4 The show attracts a lot of 'spunk mail' from viewers (i.e. Dear John, you are a real spunk, please send me a photo).

spunky, *n*. and *a*.
A. *n*. SPUNK.
1967 *Kings Cross Whisper* (Sydney) xxxix. 4/5 *Spunky*, young female. **1979** *Nat. Times* (Sydney) 17 Nov. 54/4 When we were surfie chicks they used to drive past yelling sexual insults to us. Now we drive past and yell 'Eh, spunky!'
B. *adj*. Sexually attractive.
1979 CAREY & LETTE *Puberty Blues* 5 Sue and I checked out the guys. They were spunkier at North Cronulla. *Ibid.* 9 Once you made it into the surfie gang, you were a top chick, with a spunky boyfriend. **1984** *Good Weekend* (Sydney) 6 Oct. 28/2 Gynaecologists in Sydney have been known to leave their wives for younger, spunkier patients.

spur-winged plover. [See quot. 1822.] The wading bird *Vanellus miles novaehollandiae*, chiefly of e. and s. Aust. incl. Tas., having predom. olive-brown and white plumage, yellow facial wattles, and a loud call; ALARM BIRD 1. Also **spur-wing plover**.
1822 B. FIELD *Geogr. Mem. N.S.W.* 11 Oct. (1825) 442 A bird is frequent here, called the spur-winged plover. It has a dull yellow lappet-like hood and is armed with a claw of the same colour, on the shoulder of each wing. It is a species of jacana. **1975** X. HERBERT *Poor Fellow my Country* 428 A couple of spur-wing plovers swept up shrilly calling from the earthern tank behind a netting fence.

square, *n*. [From the shape of the bottle in which gin was customarily sold; used elsewhere but recorded earliest in Aust.] Gin. Also as **square cut**, **square face**, **square gin**.
1863 *Frank Gardiner, or Bushranging in 1863* 6 Let's have a taste of old square-cut, there, for the rain has almost drowned me. **1865** *Wallaroo Times* (Kadina) 18 Feb. 3/3, I do believe he's adulterated this water with 'square' or whisky. **1871** *Austral. Town & Country Jrnl.* (Sydney) 4 Mar. 266/2 On receipt of the reward, they immediately purchased 'square gin'. **1940** E. HILL *Great Austral. Loneliness* (ed. 2) 83 Glass after glass of squareface was raised to the luck of the new beauty.

square, *a*. *Obs*. [Spec. use of *square* honourable, upright.] Of a female: respectable.
1892 *Bulletin* (Sydney) 5 Nov. 17/2 An tho', in her entirety, the Crimson Streak 'was there', I grieve to state the Crimson Streak was not a 'square affair'. **1916** *Truth* (Sydney) 29 Oct. 5/6 A prostitute is a prostitute and she seldom cares who knows it, but those 'half square.' girls (as some of your correspondents call them) are the hussies that make the mischief.

square, *v. intr*. With **off**: to set matters right; to settle a difference. Also *trans.*, to conciliate (a person).
1943 *Blitz & Pieces: Transport Weekly 2/101 Austral. Gen. Transport Co.* 8 Mar. 1 The officer . . was merely trying to 'square off', we've heard the story . . before. **1976** *Nature* (London) 19 Feb. 519/2 Squaring off the proprietors of the three national chains of newspapers, whose unquestioning support he [*sc.* Mr Fraser] enjoyed throughout the campaign.

squarehead. A person with no criminal convictions.
1939 K. TENNANT *Foveaux* 312 'Never attack a squarehead' had always been Curly's motto. There was too much danger that a squarehead would top-off to the police in a jam. **1984** *Bulletin* (Sydney) 20 Mar. 47/2 He was a one-off offender, a 'squarehead'.

square-tailed kite. The bird of prey *Lophoictinia isura* of mainland Aust.
1841 J. GOULD *Birds of Aust.* (1848) I. Pl. 22, *Milvus isurus* . . Square-tailed Kite. **1976** *Reader's Digest Compl. Bk. Austral. Birds* 119 Although the square-tailed kite might occur over any forested country, it is reasonably abundant only over sandplain country, particularly in Western Australia.

squarie. Also **squarey**. A young woman; a girl-friend. See SQUARE *a*.
1917 *Flotilla Echo: On Board H.M.A.S.* No. 79 Dec. 8 Goes along to a stationer's shop. . . The 'squarie' behind the counter. **1968** G. DUTTON *Andy* 203 His awe of his mate's squarey, this serious girl, overcame the slight delirium of the Do-What-You-Will atmosphere of Lydford's castle by the mountain.

squat, *v. Hist*. [U.S. *squat* to settle on unoccupied land without legal title: see OED *v*. 9.]
1. *intr*. To occupy a tract of Crown land in order to graze livestock (a practice sanctioned in 1836 by the introduction of a licensing system). Occas. as **squat down**.
1827 P. CUNNINGHAM *Two Yrs. in N.S.W.* II. 162 They have therefore nothing to lose and much to gain by new settlers 'squatting' near their locations. **1895** J.T. RYAN *Reminisc. Aust.* 128 They were the first to squat down on that lovely spot called Kelso.
2. *transf*.
1856 *Jrnl. Australasia* I. 247 They invariably seek to procure land adjoining unsold sections, that their own flocks and herds may 'squat' at will over an extended range.

squatocracy, var. SQUATTOCRACY.

squatocratic, var. SQUATTOCRATIC.

squattage.
1. *Hist*. Those leasing Crown land for grazing purposes, viewed collectively (see SQUATTER 2).
1845 *Standard* (Melbourne) 29 Jan. 3/3 Speaking of Mr Scott, the Parliamentary agent for the 'Squattage', he says that the opposition party in the Legislative Council 'will have now an agent in the House of Commons'. **1847** *Atlas*

SQUATTER

(Sydney) III. 222/2 Aroused the ire of our correspondent and caused him to attack the 'squattage' upon the old principle of the 'fox and the grapes'.

2. *Hist.* The occupation of land in this fashion. Also *attrib.*

1847 *Port Phillip Herald* 8 Apr. (Suppl.), 'Settled districts'.. designates the region of lawful 'squattage'. **1972** W.K. HANCOCK *Discovering Monaro* 6 Let us look quickly at successive maps of Monaro, starting with the map of the Squattage District (called later the Pastoral District) as it was in 1840.

3. A tract of grazing land leased from the Crown; a substantial stock-raising establishment.

1846 *Portland Guardian* 25 Dec. 3/1 Then squattages were unequal to the demand; now the demand is unequal to the supply. **1942** H.H. PECK *Mem. of Stockman* 160 Instead of simply acquiring leaseholds of their squattages as was usual then, they bought the freeholds.

squatter. [U.S. *squatter* one settling on land with no legal title: see OED(S *sb.*[1] 1.]

1. *Obs.* One, esp. an ex-convict, who occupies Crown land without legal title.

1828 *Hobart Town Courier* 14 June 3 The measure gives great satisfaction to the settlers generally, with but few if any exceptions, among whom we may include those called squatters. **1848** W. WESTGARTH *Aust. Felix* 246 A set of men who were to be found upon the borders of every large estate, and who were known by the name of *squatters*. These were ticket-of-leave holders or freed-men, who .. immediately became the nuisance of the district.

2. One who occupies a tract of Crown land in order to graze livestock, having title by either licence or lease.

1837 *S. Austral. Rec.* (London) 11 Apr. 53, I am now, therefore, what is termed here a 'squatter'—that is, to occupy, on a rental of £10 per annum, government land beyond the boundaries of land allotted for location. **1903** E. PALMER *Early Days N. Qld.* 8 The name 'squatter' was given in the early days to the pastoral tenants of the Crown, who rented pasture lands in their natural state.

3. One who grazes livestock on a large scale (without reference to the title by which the land is held); such a person as being of an elevated socio-economic status. Also *attrib.*

1841 G. ARDEN *Recent Information Port Phillip* 27 Tobacco .. has been cultivated by squatters .. in quantities sufficient to supply their ordinary demands for *sheep dressing*. **1976** L. OAKES *Crash Through* 35 The marriage united the Frasers with one of the wealthiest and most prominent squatter families of northern Victoria, the Sandford Beggs.

4. Abbrev. of *squatter pigeon*: see sense 5 below.

1872 C.H. EDEN *My Wife & I in Qld.* 122 On the plains you find different kinds of pigeons, the squatters being most common .. crouching down to the ground quite motionless as you pass. **1948** H.A. LINDSAY *Bushman's Handbk.* 21 There is also the squatter, a big pigeon of the open plains, which makes a loud whistling with its wings as it flies.

5. Special Comb. and collocations: **squatter chair, delight,** an outdoor, reclining chair consisting of a wooden frame from which a length of canvas is suspended and having a leg rest; also **squatter's chair, delight; king,** one who grazes livestock on a more than usually large scale; **pigeon,** any of several pigeons, esp. the ground-dwelling *Geophaps scripta* of Qld. and N.S.W.; see also PARTRIDGE PIGEON.

1880 *Blackwood's Mag.* (Edinburgh) Jan. 59/1 John took possession of a **squatter's chair. 1902** E.B. KENNEDY *Black Police Qld.* 218 Pushing them aside he sat down in one of the 'squatter' chairs and lit his pipe. **1862** R. HENNING *Lett.* (1952) 53 Mr Hedgeland has just been making for the veranda two of the easy-chairs called '**squatter's delights**'.

SQUATTING

They are made of two straight poles, which are leant against the wall of the house ladderwise. These are held together by two cross-bars, and to the bars is nailed a strip of strong canvas, such as we use for wool-bagging, and this forms the seat and back of the chair. The materials are simple enough, but I think it is the most comfortable kind of easy-chair I know. **1878** 'IRONBARK' *Southerly Busters* 84 The **squatter kings** of New South Wales. **1860** 'LADY' *My Experiences in Aust.* 123 The **squatter pigeon** in particular is so little frightened at the approach of man that it seems almost cruel to betray its confidence.

squatterdom. The squatters collectively (see SQUATTER 2 and 3); the practice of leasing Crown land for grazing purposes.

1855 W. HOWITT *Land, Labor & Gold* II. 132 A perpetual squatterdom would be a perpetual disgrace to our science of colonization. **1963** X. HERBERT *Larger than Life* 94 There is now no 'done thing' in the doings of squatterdom half so classy as an 'eagle shoot'.

squatteress. A female squatter; a squatter's wife (see SQUATTER 3).

1878 G. WALCH *Australasia* 18 Tom Talfourd .. had left her a wealthy squatteress, squattess, squattrix, or whatever the proper term may be. **1975** X. HERBERT *Poor Fellow my Country* 681 Somewhat horse-faced young squatteress visiting from the South.

squatterie. *Hist.* SQUATTAGE 3.

1847 *Atlas* (Sydney) III. 62/2 Purchases a dray and bullocks, loads with supplies, and off all start for new Providence squatterie. **1849** *Bell's Life in Sydney* 27 Jan. 3/4 Where'er we go, from North to South, In City, Town, or Squattery.

squatting, *vbl. n. Hist.* [f. SQUAT *v.*]

1. a. The action of occupying Crown land for grazing purposes; the system which allowed this. Also *attrib.*

1836 *Sydney Herald* 14 Apr. 3/4 An article, purporting to be a petition to the government to prevent improper squatting, has been drawn up. **1861** T. M'COMBIE *Austral. Sketches* 119 Not only squatting but even convictism .. have been of use in the early stages of colonisation. **1869** *Colonial Soc.* (Sydney) 18 Feb. 10 In the wild and squatting regions lived a youth, to fortune and to fame unknown. That is he lived up the country.

b. Special Comb. **squatting act,** any of several squatting acts introduced to restrain the unauthorized occupation of Crown land; **district,** an area available for squatting; **interest,** the squatters (see SQUATTER 2 and 3) collectively, esp. as a political force; **land,** *squatting district;* **lease,** an agreement under which Crown land is occupied for grazing purposes; the land so occupied; **licence,** a permit to occupy Crown land for grazing purposes; **question,** the subject of the squatting system as a matter of debate; **regulation,** a rule governing the practice of squatting; **run, station,** an area of Crown land occupied for grazing purposes (see also RUN 2 and STATION 2 a. and 3); **system,** the practice of occupying Crown land for grazing purposes; the allowing of this.

1840 *S. Austral. Rec.* (London) 29 Aug. 132 By the **Squatting Act** it is provided, that no sawyer shall cut in any district without a license. **1857** *Illustr. Jrnl. Australasia* III. 124 Those who came after him were enabled to occupy large tracts at a nominal rent under the provisions of what is termed the Squatting Act. **1841** *Port Phillip Patriot* 16 Aug. 2/6 It was proposed to divide the country into **squatting districts. 1842** *Colonial Observer* (Sydney) 24 Aug. 421/3 It was, in fact, an attempt to try the strength of the '**squatting interest**' against the strength of the government, in the administration of the government domain, and the protection of the aborigines. **1846** *Moreton Bay Courier* 5 Sept. 2/4 The judicious and permanent regulation of the **squatting lands**—will be found in the Constitution. **1859** W. FAIRFAX *Handbk. to Australasia* 195 At present much of it is shut up in the **squatting leases**. **1859** P. JUST *Aust.* 181 No squatting leases will be issued. **1839** *Sydney Standard* 18 Mar. 4/3 Rents should be paid, as the fees for **Squatting Licenses** now are, to the Colonial Treasurer. **1846** *Moreton Bay Courier* 10 Oct. 2/3 The price of land has little to do with the **squatting question,** and any reduction in price could not affect the interests of graziers any more than it would those other classes of colonists. **1844** *Duncan's Weekly Register* 4 May 566/2 A meeting was held at Windsor, for the consideration of the new **squatting regulations. 1848** *Port Phillip Herald* 27 Apr. 2/4 The **Squatting runs** of the Port Phillip district are nearly equal to the surface of Scotland. **1841** *Port Phillip Patriot* 25 Feb. 4/4 Twenty of the principal **squatting stations** are already marked out for selection. **1853** MOSSMAN & BANISTER *Aust. Visited & Revisited* 67 A run or squatting station is composed of a number of these out-stations surrounding the homestead at distances of four or five miles from each other. **1837** *Colonist* (Sydney) 23 Mar. 95/2 The inroad upon his property is so great as to drive him to the **Squatting System,** actually abandoning all idea of improving the land he has purchased so dearly, and going off miles and miles into the interior beyond all social intercourse with his fellow creatures. **1861** C. CAMPBELL *Squatting Question Considered* 4 By the end of 1839, the country was occupied as far as the dividing range, under a general squatting system, which authorised the occupation of any crown lands on payment of a license at the rate of £10 per annum.

2. a. Sheep or cattle raising by squatters (chiefly senses 2 and 3); stockholding. Also *attrib.*

1845 *Port Phillip Gaz.* 4 June 2 Squatting is, by far, the most gigantic interest in Australia. **1873** A. TROLLOPE *Aust. & N.Z.* I. 115 Unless rain came soon squatting affairs would begin to 'look blue'.

b. Comb. **squatting firm, industry, property.**

1879 S.W. SILVER *Austral. Grazier's Guide* 18 While the colonies are full of instances of prosperous **squatting firms,** the number of pastoral or agricultural companies which have survived their initiation may be counted upon one's finger. **1886** J.F. CONIGRAVE *S.A.* 104 The progress of the **squatting industry** can be judged by the following returns of South Australian grown wools sold in the London auctions. **1871** *Austral. Town & Country Jrnl.* (Sydney) 21 June 92/2 Money being again sufficiently plentiful to cause capitalists to look to **squatting properties** as a safe investment.

squatting, *ppl. a.* [f. SQUAT *v.*] Of a person, etc.: that occupies land as a squatter (see SQUATTER 2 and 3); associated with such occupation.

1835 *True Colonist* (Hobart) 31 July 3/1 To scare away such squatting intruders as Mr Bateman, and his gigantic Company. **1921** C.E.W. BEAN *Official Hist. Aust. 1914–18* I. 138 An officer of the citizen forces, an Australian pastoralist coming of an old 'squatting' family.

squattocracy. Also **squatocracy.** The squatters as an interest group; the squatters as a socio-economic group (see SQUATTER 2 and 3).

1843 *Sydney Morning Herald* 6 July 2/7 The proceeds to be derived from the dairy, will set our squatocracy to rights before Christmas. **1983** *Canberra Times* 2 Oct. 8/4 The scrapbook of an artistically inclined daughter of the squattocracy.

Hence **squattocrat** *n.,* a member of the squattocracy.

1910 *Bulletin* (Sydney) 14 Apr. 14/1 The squattocrats never coined more cash in their lives than they have done during the past five years.

squattocratic, *a.* Also **squatocratic.** Of or pertaining to the squattocracy, or to one of its members. Also **squattocratical** *a.*

1843 *Maitland Mercury* 26 Apr. 2/5 The pernicious code was the offspring of *squattocratical* influence. **1891** D. FERGUSON *Vicissitudes Bush Life* 2, I prepared to start for Australia to join a wealthy, 'squatocratic' relative. **1963** X. HERBERT *Larger than Life* 94 It was inevitable that the aeroplane should replace the horse as the squatter's mount for hunting, for the squattocratic 'shoot'.

squaw. *Obs.* [Transf. use of *squaw* a North American Indian woman or wife.]

1. An Aboriginal woman or wife.

1837 E. FRASER *Narr. of Capture* 7 About half an hour after the departure of the savages, I was visited by a very great number of their squaws, accompanied by their children. **1867** 'COLONIST' *Life's Work* 94 You give us tucker . . squaw very bad, tumble down sick; big lot pain, very ill want good tucker.

2. Special Comb. **squaw man,** a white man consorting with an Aboriginal woman.

1911 L.C.E. GEE *Gen. Rep. Tanami Goldfield* 20 The gin helper was not much in evidence. There were not many 'Komboes' or Squaw men. Still, I am sorry to say that it is a 'custom of the country' throughout the Territory.

squeaker.

1. Any of several birds to which a squeaking call is attributed, as the *noisy miner* (see NOISY), WHITEFACE, and (chiefly W.A.) *grey currawong* (see GREY *a.*).

1848 J. GOULD *Birds of Aust.* II. Pl. 45, *Strepera anaphonensis.* Grey Crow-Shrike. . . *Dje-läak,* Aborigines of Western Australia. *Squeaker,* of the Colonists. **1965** *Austral. Encycl.* VIII. 258 Squeaker, a name commonly used in Western Australia for the grey currawong or crow-shrike (*Strepera versicolor*) because one of its notes has been likened to the mewing of a cat or the sound of a small tin trumpet.

2. Any of several small cicadas of the genera *Melampsalta* and *Pauropsalta.*

1907 W.W. FROGGATT *Austral. Insects* 353 Some species [of *Melampsalta,* cicada] are very numerous in early summer, and are known as 'Squeakers' on account of their musical notes. **1965** *Austral. Encycl.* II. 380 Many small species [of cicada] are grouped together in the genera *Melampsalta* and *Pauropsalta* ('squeakers'), some species of which have been recorded as damaging fruit-trees while laying their eggs.

3. BETTONG.

1941 E. TROUGHTON *Furred Animals Aust.* 155 A variety of more or less local popular names have been applied to the animals [sc. Short-nosed Rat-Kangaroos], including Bettongs . . and Squeakers. **1965** *Austral. Encycl.* V. 157 The short-nosed rat-kangaroos . . are grouped in the genus *Bettongia.* . . Once very plentiful, these attractive marsupials were known as 'squeakers' by the whites and 'tungoos' by the aborigines in South Australia.

squib, *n.* [Spec. use of *squib* 'a mean, insignificant or paltry fellow': see OED(S *sb.* 4.] A horse lacking stamina; hence, a spineless person, a coward.

1908 E.S. SORENSON *Squatter's Ward* 122 It's a monty the little squib would let out a yell jest as I was gettin' clear. **1984** *Sun-Herald* (Sydney) 26 Feb. 78/3 It has been said, among other things, that the Golden Slipper is a race for speedy squibs.

squib, *v.* [Prob. Br. dial. *squib* to run away: see EDD *v.*²]

1. *trans.* To evade (a difficulty or responsibility); to shirk through fear or cowardice (freq. with **it** as obj.). Also *intr.*

1918 G. DALE *Industr. Hist. Broken Hill* 170 All the employers had agreed to fight the Union, but had squibbed it at the last moment. **1946** K. TENNANT *Lost Haven* 308 You'll probably squib out of it at the last moment. **1965** R.H. CONQUEST *Horses in Kitchen* 59 A young fellow like you—a bloke who's never been hurt real bad, and who won't squib the challenge horses.

2. *intr.* To fail to act; to back down; to give in. Also with **on**: to betray or let down.

1934 *Red Star* (Perth) 9 Nov. 3/3 (*heading*) Lang candidate squibbing. 1962 *Coast to Coast 1961–62* 83 He could finish on a good wicket in anything. And never squib on a bloke.

squire. A young SNAPPER: see quot. 1969.

1874 *N.S.W. Rep. R. Comm. Fisheries* (1880) 10 The ordinary schnapper, or count fish, implies that all of a certain size are to count as twelve to the dozen; the shoal or school-fish, eighteen or twenty-four to the dozen; and the squire, thirty or thirty-six to the dozen. 1969 J. POLLARD *Austral. & N.Z. Fishing* 712 At about a foot in length they are called squire, and having reached a legally and domestically acceptable size they are a welcome addition to the angler's catch.

squirrel.
1. A gliding possum (see *flying possum* FLYING); (chiefly *Qld.*) GREATER GLIDER. Also *attrib.*

1788 *HRA* (1914) 1st Ser. I. 31 Many trees were seen with holes that had been enlarged by the natives to get at the animal, either the squirrel [etc.]. 1910 J. MATHEW *Two Representative Tribes Qld.* 121 The women made dillie-bags of various patterns and sizes, the material being grass or string of squirrel fur.

2. Special Comb. **squirrel glider,** the gliding possum *Petaurus norfolcensis* of e. mainland Aust., the soft fur of which is greyish above with a dark central stripe, and pale beneath; see also *sugar squirrel* SUGAR 3; formerly also **squirrel flying phalanger.**

c 1880 *Cassell's Nat. Hist.* III. 207 (OED) The Squirrel Flying Phalanger . . *Petaurus sciureus* . . has been called the Squirrel Flying Phalanger by mistake. 1983 R. STRAHAN *Compl. Bk. Austral. Mammals* 140 Almost twice the size of the Sugar Glider, the Squirrel Glider is otherwise similar to it in appearance and gliding ability.

squirt, $n.^1$ A revolver.

1899 J. BRADSHAW *Quirindi Bank Robbery* 36 He covered me with his squirt, and sang out 'Bail up, or may Hall admire me if I don't blow the stuffing out of you in a slantingdicular direction.' 1925 J.E. LIDDLE *Selected Poems* 82 Rifle and shot-gun, squirt and swag.

squirt, $n.^2$ *Shearing. Obs.* Rhyming slang for EXPERT *n.* a.

1912 R.S. TAIT *Scotty Mac* 78 'Git the squirt'. . . 'Wanted, expert,' he yelled. 1915 *Bulletin* (Sydney) 28 Oct. 22/3 The expert who attends all machinery is invariably 'the squirt'.

squiz, *n.* Also **squizz.** [See next.] A look; an inspection.

1913 C.J. DENNIS *Backblock Ballads* 199 *Squiz*, a glance. 1915 —— *Songs of Sentimental Bloke* 15 Jist take a squiz at this, an' tell me can Some square an' honist tom take this to be 'Er own true man? 1973 J. POWERS *Last of Knucklemen* (1974) 38 Take a squizz out that window. Have a look at it.

squiz, *v.* [Br. dial.: see EDD.] *intr.* To look (at). Also *trans.*, to inspect.

1941 S.J. BAKER *Pop. Dict. Austral. Slang* 71 *Squiz*, to look at, inspect. 1979 J. WILLIAMS *White River* 49 The mechanic refuelled and no doubt squizzed the plane's cargo.

stab, *n. Australian National Football.* [Spec. use of *stab* a vigorous thrust.] Used *attrib.* in Special Comb. **stab kick, (a)** a fast, low kick to a team-mate; **(b)** one skilled at so kicking; **pass,** *stab kick* (a); so **stab-passing** *vbl. n.*

1936 E.C.H. TAYLOR et al. *Our Austral. Game Football* 19 **Stab Kick**—This kick is most effective when short passing is necessary. 1964 J. POLLARD *High Mark* 23, I remember how I first gained a clue or two watching Bobby Rose, the neatest, most accurate stab-kick I have ever seen. 1960 *N.T. News* (Darwin) 12 Jan. 8/3 Like lightning it was Tahs again for Vierk to take a **stab pass** and find the big timber. 1982 *Bulletin* (Sydney) 28 Sept. 37/2 Many stab passes failed to reach their targets, and in any case stab passing was impossible on muddy grounds. The drop kick itself was subject to this limitation, and players of the late 1960s no longer had the time to steady before delivering it properly.

stab, *v. Australian National Football.* [f. prec.] *trans.* To execute (a stab pass).

1964 J. POLLARD *High Mark* 23 Once clear, he suddenly steadied a step, and stabbed the pass.

stack, *v. trans.* With **on**: to contrive; to produce. See also BLUE $n.^2$ 4 and TURN *n.* 2.

1965 J. WYNNUM *Jiggin' in Riggin'* 54 'I'm not stacking on any act, believe me,' moaned Stripey. 1979 B. HUMPHRIES *Bazza comes into his Own*, No worries, Ron, you'll stack on a beaut corroborree dance as soon as youse cop this Abbo style music.

stag. [Br. dial.: see OED $sb.^1$ 3.]
1. A beast castrated after reaching maturity; an inferior bullock.

1848 *Adelaide Miscellany* 2 Dec. 280 My bucolic knowledge . . left me in total ignorance of the nice distinction between yearlings, steers, heifers, stags [etc.]. 1932 H. PRIEST *Call of Bush* 206 There were cattle to be mustered and 'stags' (bulls that have been emasculated when full grown, and that by their sheer savageness oust the effective males from the herd) to be 'cut out'.

2. Shortening of *ram stag* (see RAM *n.* 1).

1919 *Bulletin* (Sydney) 11 Dec. 20/2 A Westralian shearer barbered 321 jumbucks in one day. True, he was paid for 321, but he took the overcoats off only 180. A large number of them were stags and rams, which were counted as 'doubles'.

staggering bob. [Br. dial.: see OED *staggering, ppl. a.* 1 d.] A newly-born calf; veal (see also quot. 1978).

1874 C. DE BOOS *Congewoi Correspondence* 157 Well, there wasn't nothing handy afore I'd cooled down, and so master Staggerin Bob got orf that time, and I was saved from makin a fooler myself. 1959 M. DURACK *Kings in Grass Castles* 230 They had been forced to dispose of no less than thirteen hundred new-born calves during the trip. It was a complete waste, for stockmen were oddly squeamish about eating veal or 'staggering Bob' as it was known in the cattle camps. 1978 F. HOWARD *Moleskin Gentry* 23 The serve of instant veal or calves offal, known on the Lachlan as 'staggering Bob' . . was cut from a fresh-killed beast and cooked over a camp fire.

stagger juice. [Used elsewhere but recorded earliest in Aust.: see OED(S *stagger, sb.*^{1} 4.] Alcoholic liquor. Also *attrib.*

1896 *S.A. Parl. Debates* 14 July 141 The beautiful barmaids could only be regarded as the polished fangs of the stagger-juice rattlesnake. 1962 J. WYNNUM *Tar Dust* 82 'These two bowls of punch look exciting'. . . 'Well now, that one . . is our customary Stagger Juice.'

Hence **stagger juicerie** *n.*, a public house.

1899 K. O'MALLEY *Second Message to Sovereign Electors Encounter Bay* 32 They did not see that the Sunday-closing law was observed. The law was violated by stagger juiceries and booseries in an open way.

stagger-weed. The introduced European annual herb *Stachys arvensis* (fam. Lamiaceae), naturalized in temperate Aust.

1903 *Proc. Linnean Soc. N.S.W.* XXVIII. 766 *Stachys arvensis.* . . The common weed known as 'Stagger Weed' on the

staghorn. [See quot. 1852.] An epiphytic fern of the genus *Platycerium* (fam. Polypodiaceae), esp. the commonly cultivated *P. superbum* of Qld., n. N.S.W., and Malaysia. Also **staghorn fern, stag's horn (fern).**

1852 G.C. MUNDY *Our Antipodes* II. 27 On the forks of some of the older timber-trees grew, also, the stag-horn fern, as large as the biggest cabbage, the fronds exactly resembling the palmated antlers of the moose and reindeer. **1867** *Lang. Native Flowers Tas.* 7 Stag's Horn Fern . . I attach myself to you. **1882** *Austral. Handbk.* 392 Three fourths of Australian ferns belong to this colony. Amongst these are the 'Stag's horn' (*Platycerium grande* . .) [etc.]. **1959** *Meanjin* 135 He raises his eyes to the staghorns that droop from the boles of the tall Burdekin plums or follows the flight of a black-and-orange regent-bird.

stain. *Obs.* The stigma of convict ancestry; TAINT. See also BIRTHSTAIN.

1872 'TASMANIAN LADY' *Treasures, Lost & Found* 134 It will be long, long years before the stain of our birth-mark shall wear away; it will break out again and again; it will cling to us as Gehazi's leprosy clung to his accursed and suffering offspring. **1893** S. NEWLAND *Paving Way* 74 Love her! my God, I do love her! but if there is this convict stain, what am I to do?

stand, *n.* The position occupied by a shearer in a shearing shed; a shearing job; the shearer occupying a stand. Also *attrib.*, as (six, etc.)-**stand shed,** a shed having (a specified number of) stands.

1888 *Boomerang* (Brisbane) Mar. 3 His next 'stand', who was a good man with the clippers, challenged him to a brush for a score. **1895** *Worker* (Sydney) 5 Jan. 3/3 He changed his song before very long, For he learned that to obtain a stand He'd have to revoke, at a single stroke, His liberties at the squatter's command. **1913** J. TRURAN *Where Plain Begins* 148 Bradley's was only a 'six-stand' shed; that is, there were six machines, each with its pen for the shorn and unshorn sheep. **1946** F. CLUNE *Try Nothing Twice* 89 There were fifty stands in Kerabury shed, all driven by the traction engine.

Also (ten, etc.)-**stander.**

1978 J. DINGWALL *Sunday too far Away* 17 'How many sheep at this shed of yours?' . . 'Forty thousand. Thereabouts.' . . 'What is it, a ten stander?' . . 'Eight.'

stand, *v. intr.* With **over**: to intimidate or threaten; to extort money from (someone).

1939 K. TENNANT *Foveaux* 173, I just had Thompson in here and he stood over me for three quid. **1967** K. GILES *Death & Mr Prettyman* 58 'You couldn't, but you could stand over—pardon, persecute—me', said Baker, 'but believe me I'm clean. If I can help you get that bloody old bag count me in.'

standover.

a. An intimidatory tactic. Also as **standover tactic.**

1939 K. TENNANT *Foveaux* 180 'Struth, you earn your money on a stand over. **1954** L.H. EVERS *Pattern of Conquest* 198 Don't come the stand-over tactics you used with Charlie.

b. Special Comb. **standover man, merchant,** one who engages in intimidatory tactics.

1939 K. TENNANT *Foveaux* 174 He didn't deserve to be a 'standover man' if he couldn't move quicker. **1962** A. MARSHALL *This is Grass* 60, I guessed he was a stand-over merchant and that he had brought these two men with him like a hunter who goes out with his dogs.

star grass. [Transf. use of *star-grass* any of several grass-like plants with stellate flowers or a stellate arrangement of leaves.] WINDMILL GRASS.

1844 L. LEICHHARDT *Jrnl. Overland Exped. Aust.* 16 Dec. (1847) 77 The chains of water-holes within the scrub are covered with stiff star-grass, having a great number of spikes rising from the top of the stem. **1938** C.T. WHITE *Princ. Bot. Qld. Farmers* 203 Many other grasses go to make up the mixed native pasture . . Oat Grasses, Star Grasses, &c.

star lot. [Spec. use of *star lot* a starred item in a sale catalogue: see OED *sb.*[1] 20 and quot. 1928.] A small parcel of wool bales.

1899 G. JEFFREY *Princ. Australasian Woolclassing* 92 Lots of three bales or under are marked in the catalogue 'star lots', and are sold by themselves after the larger lots are disposed of. **1928** C.E. COWLEY *Classing Clip* 165 The name *star lot* originated from the London method of wool-selling where both large and small parcels are shown, catalogued and sold together, but the small lots are indicated to the buyers by an asterisk being prefixed to the lot number. Thus in course of time, such lots became known as *star lots*. The term has become a generic one in the wool-trade.

Star of Bethlehem. Also **Stars of Bethlehem.** [Transf. use of *Star of Bethlehem* a plant of the genus *Ornithogalum*, esp. *O. umbellatum*, having white star-like flowers.] Any of several plants bearing a star-like flower, incl. the herb *Chamaescilla corymbosa* (fam. Liliaceae) of s. Aust. incl. Tas.; the flower of one of these plants.

1857 D. BUNCE *Australasiatic Reminisc.* 25 On the pasture lands were many of the pretty bulbous plants called Star of Bethlehem by the colonists, but by botanists known as *Anguillaria*, of which two species clothed the pasture. **1967** B.Y. MAIN *Between Wodjil & Tor* 97 Dark purplish-blue, yellow-centred 'stars of Bethlehem' studded the *Callithryx* shrubs fringing the pine grove.

starve, *v.* In the phr. **starve the rats** (or **roan bullock**): see CROW *n.*[1] 3 and LIZARD 2.

1908 *Bulletin* (Sydney) 9 Jan. 14/2 'Starve the rats' and 'snake's head' are two more poetical phrases that the Adelaide lad is godfather of. **1977** F.B. VICKERS *Stranger no Longer* 147, I was surprised to hear a publisher say: 'Starve the roan bullock! You're the first musterer's cook I've ever seen in a bloody homburg.'

starver.

1. An animal which is starving because of a lack of pasture, esp. as caused by a drought.

1902 *Bulletin* (Sydney) 29 Nov. 15/1 'Starvers' are being travelled in thousands. **1946** *Bulletin* (Sydney) 18 Dec. 28/2 Bought a big mob o' starvers at a bob a head an' kept 'em alive till the drought broke.

2. A saveloy.

1941 S.J. BAKER *Pop. Dict. Austral. Slang* 71 *Starver*, a saveloy. **1981** P. RADLEY *Jack Rivers & Me* 154 Indian dicks (thin sausages), thick-dick saveloys (called starvers in the Depression), and much grog.

starving, *ppl. a.* Of stock: suffering from a lack of pasture (see prec.).

1903 *Bulletin* (Sydney) 3 Jan. 17/1 The Victorian railway department allows a free pass for every truck in a starving-stock train, so when cockie has six trucks of 'starving stock' going practically free, he and five of his friends travel 'on the nod'. **1935** N. HUNT *House of David* 119 Rowel has a thousand 'store cattle'. . . He bought them as 'poor' and 'starving' for a pound. He'll sell them for ten or fifteen.

State.

1. Used *attrib.* in Special Comb. to designate financial support given by a government or a project so supported, as **State aid,** financial assistance, now esp. that

STATION 541 **STATION**

given to private schools; **child** (**boy, kid, orphan,** etc.), a ward of the State; **school,** PUBLIC SCHOOL 1; also *attrib.*

1856 *Jrnl. Australasia* I. 246 He is the opponent of **State Aid** to Religion. **1978** G. HALL *River still Flows* 96 Possibly most people concealed the cogency of the Catholic argument, 'One brick in every four of your public schools is paid for by Catholics.' State Aid had come to stay. **1901** *Bulletin* (Sydney) 5 Oct. 36/1 How different are these bright-eyed youngsters from the usual **State-children** of school age! **1905** *Bulletin* (Sydney) 6 July 36/2 Hard by was an undersized dairy farm run by a hungry couple and four hungrier State kids. **1913** *Truth* (Sydney) 6 Apr. 5/4 A young dairyman . . was . . charged with assaulting a State boy. **1917** A.L. BREWER *'Gators' Euchre* 14 One State orphan was asked, long ago: he glanced fearfully in the direction of the farmer who kept him, shook his little head desperately in the negative, and . . ran behind a barn. **1878** *Illustr. Austral. News* (Melbourne) 13 May 74/2 Our artist has depicted a few of the scholars who may be selected out of almost any **State school** in the colony, and has placed them graphically before us. **1985** *Canberra Times* 1 Sept. 8/4 No wonder we 'Micks' used to have slanging matches . . with the Stateschool kids.

2. **a.** The designation which replaced 'colony' after Federation in the names of New South Wales, Queensland, South Australia, Tasmania, Victoria, and Western Australia. Freq. *attrib.*

1891 *Braidwood Dispatch* 1 Apr. 3/1 The Federation Bill was tabled this afternoon. . . Each colony shall hereafter be designated a state. **1983** *Open Road* Apr. 2/1 N.S.W. is burdened with an inadequate road system, yet this financial year will receive back for roads only about 22 per cent of total State and Federal fuel tax revenue collected from N.S.W. motorists.

b. Special Comb. **State Governor,** the principal representative of the sovereign in one of the Australian States (see also GOVERNOR 1); **Premier,** see PREMIER 1; **rights,** the administrative and legislative responsibilities reserved to a State as distinct from the Federal government; also **State's right** and *attrib.*; **State righter,** one who supports the protection of a State's powers.

1900 *Advocate* (Burnie) 24 Aug. 2/4 The question of the status of **state Governors** is being largely discussed throughout the colonies. **1901** *Truth* (Sydney) 9 June 4/7 The highest interests and cherished **States Rights** of the Mother State. **1910** *Huon Times* (Franklin) 19 Feb. 2/2 Some producers argue that it would be another encroachment on State rights. **1944** G. COCKERILL *Scribblers & Statesmen* 105 Lyne was a thorough going Protectionist. . . Further, he was a 'State rights' man, whose support for the Federal movement was only nominal. **1944** G. COCKERILL *Scribblers & Statesmen* 134 Former **'State-righters'** became earnest Federalists.

station. [Spec. use of *station* a place where soldiers are garrisoned, a military post: see OED(S *sb.* 11 (but see also *sb.* 13 a. and d.).]

1. a. *Hist.* An outpost of a colonial government, esp. as established for the employment of convict labour on public works; *convict station,* see CONVICT B. 3; *penal station,* see PENAL.

1816 *Hobart Town Gaz.* 28 Sept., His Excellency . . having been pleased to appoint Assistant Commissary General Broughton to take the Charge of the Commissariat Department at this Station . . he is directed to assume the Duties of his Office. **1872** 'TASMANIAN LADY' *Treasures, Lost & Found* 127 The ruins of a wooden hut, with a tramroad running past it. . . "Tis only an old station. Years ago the Government had a gang at work here.'

b. *transf.* A tract of land recognized as being occupied by Aborigines; a reserve for Aborigines, esp. as established by a religious mission (see also *mission station* MISSION 1) or government agency. Also *attrib.*

1825 B. FIELD *Geogr. Mem. N.S.W.* 57 The principal station of the tribe . . was about two miles higher up the Pumice-stone River. **1841** *Port Phillip Patriot* 16 Sept. 5/2 There is no station reserved for the tribe the prisoner belongs to. **1965** 'E. LINDALL' *Springs of Violence* 39 These are tribal natives. They don't mix with the station crowd.

2. a. A tract of grazing land, usu. having a discernible centre of occupation: see quot. 1822. Also with distinguishing epithet, as **cattle, dairy, grazing, sheep, squatting, stock** (see under first element). See also RUN $n.^2$ 1 a.

1820 *HRA* (1921) 3rd Ser. II. 207 The Herds at each Station are to be Surveyed by a Committee. **1822** J.T. BIGGE *Rep. State Colony N.S.W.* 161 All persons who apply for the temporary occupation of a large tract of land, for the purpose of grazing . . shall employ an overseer, who shall be a free and unconvicted person, and require his constant residence at the principal station. **1982** R. ELLIS *Bush Safari* 96 The ruins of Annandale Station, one of Sir Sidney Kidman's early runs, and the most remote station he ever owned.

b. *Hist.* In the phr. **right of station,** legal entitlement to the use of a tract of grazing land. See also RUN $n.^2$ 1 c.

1839 *Port Phillip Patriot* 24 Apr. 6/3 These cattle and the right of station Mr Bringle sold to Mr Ward Stephens. **1847** *Port Phillip Gaz.* 30 June 3, 8,392 Sheep, with right of Station given in, situate near the Murray River.

c. *Home station,* see HOME *attrib.*^{2} b.

1840 T. SOUTHEY *Treatise on Sheep* 54 What in England is called a *homestead,* or, in Colonial idiom, a *station,* that is, the farm-yard and out-houses for sheep, cattle, etc. together with the other buildings requisite for the accommodation of the colonist's family. **1979** *Quieter Moments* 28 Scores of men and women worked, to raise a station grand. A homestead and a shearing shed where twenty men could stand.

3. An extensive sheep or cattle raising establishment. See also RUN $n.^2$ 2 and under first element as for sense 2 a.

1843 R.D. MURRAY *Summer at Port Phillip* 151 Few in this country are aware of the vast tracts of land sometimes comprehended in the 'station' of a single individual. In one or two instances, they exhibit the dimensions of a small county. **1986** *Centralian Advocate* (Alice Springs) 15 Jan. 12/2 The stations he managed included Undoolya and later the Barron Creek Pastoral Company properties.

4. Comb. in sense 3: **station boss, cattle, cook, dog, hand, holder, homestead, horse, house, life, manager, overseer, owner, paddock, property, stock, work, yard.**

1936 *Bulletin* (Sydney) 1 Apr. 20/3 The **station boss** was liverish, so we were out of sight. But the new woodand-water joey didn't know the signs. **1902** *Bulletin* (Sydney) 7 June 16/3 In Queensland, the cattle-ticks and sequent redwater are obliterating **station cattle.** **1878** *Squatter's Plum* 42 Pity the shameless indifference to which men are reduced by continual begging from stationmanagers and hungry fawning on **station-cooks.** **1872** G.S. BADEN-POWELL *New Homes for Old Country* 337 Young kangaroo . . readily make friends with the **station-dogs.** **1872** 'RESIDENT' *Glimpses Life Vic.* 175 The kitchen, where the **station-hands** were assembled. **1869** *Bushmen, Publicans, & Politics* 4 To demand that they shall be fed by such **station holders** as they may travel among until they get another 'job'. **1894** A.A. MACINNES *Straight as Line* 293 The carefully tended garden plots surrounding the comfortable, roomy **station homesteads.** **1900** R. BRUCE *Benbonuna* (1904) 261, I don't think you will find it all plain sailing, especially if any of the **station horses** have been running about there lately. **1840** *Sydney Herald* 31 Aug. 6/7 We have since heard that the sheep were not above a mile from the **station-house.** **1880** J. BONWICK *Resources Qld.* 31 One need but go to the Darling Downs . . to find **station life** associated with high civilization. **1878 station man-**

ager [see *station cook*]. **1901** *Truth* (Sydney) 16 June 5/7 The Sultan of Turkey is not more jealous of his veiled mistresses than is a Westralian station manager of his stark naked lubras. **1897** *Tocsin* (Melbourne) 9 Dec. 10/2 The hero is a young **station overseer**, who marries the daughter of a shanty-keeper. **1873** A. TROLLOPE *Aust. & N.Z.* I. 96 The station passes .. into the hands probably of some huge **station owner**, who having commenced life as a shepherd or a drover, has now stations of his own. **1906** W.A. HORN *Notes by Nomad* 82 The traveller simply turns his horse into the **station paddock**. **1877** 'CAPRICORNUS' *Land Laws of Future* 6 The Land Board shall then procure .. a return specifying the sales of **station properties**. **1880** *Austral. Town & Country Jrnl.* (Sydney) 14 Feb. 314/4 The **station stock** seldom feed near the road. **1879** *Kelly Gang* 15 The ostensible occupations of the two elder sons have been horse-breaking and farm and **station work**. **1922** W.R. EASTON *Rep. N. Kimberley District W.A.* 1 We were able to make our starting depot at the Homestead, thus having the use of the **station yards** equipment.

5. Special Comb. **station Abo, black, (a)** an Aboriginal employed on a sheep or cattle station; **(b)** an Aboriginal residing at a reserve or mission station; **boy**, an Aboriginal male employed on a sheep or cattle station; **-bred** *a.*, (of an animal), bred on the property; also as quasi-*n.*; **camp**, a place on a station where stock are mustered for a particular purpose; the personnel, etc., so employed; **country**, land chiefly occupied as sheep or cattle stations; **gin**, an Aboriginal woman employed on a sheep or cattle station; **jack** *obs.*, see quot.; **keeper** *obs.*, HUTKEEPER; **keeping** *vbl. n., obs.*, hut keeping, see HUTKEEP; **man**, one employed on, or one who owns, a sheep or cattle station; so **people; ration**, an allowance of provisions made to an employee on a sheep or cattle station (see RATION *n.* 1 a.); **rouseabout**, ROUSEABOUT *a.*; **run, (a)** an air service using the privately-owned landing fields on stations; **(b)** a stretch of grazing land on a station; **store**, the depot on a station from which supplies are dispensed or sold (see STORE 3); *pl.*, the supplies themselves; so **storekeeper**.

1938 *Bulletin* (Sydney) 1 June 21/1 The **station abo**. usually bears a white-fellow nickname. **1955** J. CLEARY *Justin Bayard* 292 He's only a bush myall. Not even a station abo. **1870** E.B. KENNEDY *Four Yrs. in Qld.* 67 Anyone who is really acquainted with the matter .. from having been not only amongst **station** and town **Blacks**, but also for years in the same country with perfectly wild Blacks. **1961** *Bulletin* (Sydney) 14 Oct. 30/2 Down at the camp of the station blacks size didn't matter. **1890** A.J. VOGAN *Black Police* 90 The hunted-thief look one nearly always sees on the face of the average '**station boy**' (squatter's aboriginal servant) is absent. **1882** ARMSTRONG & CAMPBELL *Austral. Sheep Husbandry* 242 Wild Horses .. when taken young .. are no more difficult to break in and handle than are ordinary **station-bred** horses. **1905** *Bulletin* (Sydney) 23 Feb. 16/3 He takes in at 9d. a head, a train-load of horses, mostly young station-breds. **1937** W. HATFIELD *I find Aust.* 149, I looked for a job with a road mob and joined the **station camp** till they were ready to start. **1938** J.F.W. SCHULZ *Destined to Perish* 23 The station camp at the Big Bend is only periodically used by the stockmen. **1884** J. BAKER *Diary & Sketches Journey S.A.* 18 Oct. 15 Left farming district and started for **station country** thro pass in hills. **1895** L. BECKE *Ebbing of Tide* 187 Chow Kum .. giving away so much rations to the **station gins**. **1853** E. MACKENZIE *Emigrant's Guide to Aust.* 112 Let the Sunday share be soaked on the Saturday, and beat it well with a rolling-pen, as this makes it more tender, take a seventh portion of the flour, and work it into a paste; then put the beef into it, boil it, and you will have a very nice pudding, known in the bush as '**station-jack**'. **1850** W. GATES *Recoll. Van Dieman's Land* (1961) II. 39 Each shepherd has in charge one thousand sheep. To each station are three shepherds, and at the hut—or station is another person, styled **station-keeper**, who remains there. **1856** S.C. BREES *How to farm & settle in Aust.* 11 They can then decide between going into quartz-crushing, store-keeping, cultivating, or **station-keeping**, or breeding and fattening cattle. **1872** 'RESIDENT' *Glimpses Life Vic.* 175 The **station-men** .. slunk away to their sleeping apartment. **1948** P.J. HURLEY *Red Cedar* 23 Terrigal, popular surf and seaside resort .. a summer residence for '**station people**' from the inland. **1903** *Bulletin* (Sydney) 30 May 35/1 His wife .. objected to being carried up and down the road .. among **station-rations** and sundries. **1948** B. CRONIN *How runs Road* 31 In Australia, very little more than half a century ago, bishops and **station rouseabouts** rubbed shoulders amicably in box-seat conversation. **1951** G. FARWELL *Outside Track* 176 Normanton is much more in the swing of modern life. To start with, it enjoys two air services a week, in addition to an enterprising '**station run**' that follows the coastline as far north as Mitchell River. **1972** M. GILBERT *Personalities & Stories Early Orbost* 21 The red cattle graze on the grass of the wide station run. **1872** 'RESIDENT' *Glimpses Life Vic.* 169 Six drays accompanied us, loaded with **station stores**. **1889** H. EGBERT *Pretty Cockey* 63 After shearing and woolwashing, Smith was summoned to the Station Store. This establishment was the office as well. **1976** B. SCOTT *Complete Bk. Austral. Folk Lore* 376 Rations were often of the cheapest and poorest quality. Another economy practised by station storekeepers was the supply of what the ration men called 'post and rail' tea, mainly consisting of the stalks and roughest leaves.

steady, *v.* *Droving.* [Spec. use of *steady* to cause to go at a more regular pace.] *trans.* To regulate the progress of (a travelling mob).

1884 'R. BOLDREWOOD' *Old Melbourne Memories* 134 Was there another man 'steadying the lead' on the opposite side, right well mounted also. **1909** *Bulletin* (Sydney) 28 Oct. 13/3 It's not always easy to steady a big mob and make them feed again. .. Of course, they *can* be stopped.

steaka-da-oyst, var. STEAKDAHOYST.

steak and kidney. Rhyming slang for 'Sydney'. (Quot. 1945 refers to an Australian cruiser of that name.)

1905 J. MEREDITH *Learn to talk Old Jack Lang* (1984) 12 No doubt you have wondered how your old *thief and robber* has been doing since you went back to the *steak and kidney*. **1945** *Dit* (Melbourne) Apr. 3 The old 'Steak and kidney' once fought a battle off Singapore.

steakdahoyst. Also **steaka-da-oyst**. [Joc. representation of an Italian pronunc.] A café or restaurant specializing in steak and oyster dishes.

1916 *Truth* (Sydney) 2 July 6/8 This is nothing to the rough estimate of shells the collective oyster-openers at the numerous city steakdahoysts let fall on Saturday nights. **1928** *Bulletin* (Sydney) 4 Apr. 23/2, I earned £3 2s. over the open season whilst the local steaka-da-oysts had to draw their fish supplies from Melbourne.

steam, *n.*

1. *Hist.* Used *attrib.* with reference to the process of separating fat from an animal carcass by the application of steam.

1840 *Port Phillip Gaz.* 30 Nov. 3 Melbourne. *Melting Establishment, the first steam establishment formed in the colonies.* The Proprietors are purchasers of fat Stock or will melt down for the settlers upon Reduced terms. **1849** *Bell's Life in Sydney* 1 Dec. 4/4 The superiority of steam-rendered tallow.

2. In the phr. **like steam**, furiously; with gusto.

1905 H. LAWSON *When I was King* 39 We was draftin' 'em out for the homeward track and sharin' 'em round like steam. **1979** B. HARDY *World owes me Nothing* 102, I hammered at the door like steam and over he came and opened it.

8. Cheap wine; such wine strengthened with methylated spirits; methylated spirits.
1941 S.J. BAKER *Pop. Dict. Austral. Slang* 71 *Steam,* cheap wine, esp. laced with methylated spirits. **1942** *Sun* (Sydney) 26 Aug. 4/8 Bombo has replaced plonk as a term for cheap wine, and less popular, but equally descriptive, is the use of 'steam' for wine. When a man 'flies for the bombo' or 'raises steam', he is on quite a bender. **1970** *Kings Cross Whisper* (Sydney) lxxxiv. 9/3 Those who curl up in the park with a bottle of steam will have to make their own arrangements.

steam, *v. Hist. trans.* To separate fat from (an animal carcass) by the application of steam. Also with **down,** and as *vbl. n.*
1844 *Parramatta Chron.* 22 June 3/1 Mackellar and White's steaming establishment is going on swimmingly, having more than they can manage. Large quantities of tallow are being produced daily, which, with skin and hides, can find a ready market... Messrs. Benjamin and Moses have a large establishment in the course of erection, with steaming-house apparatus, and everything desirable to carry on the rendering system on a very large scale. **1844** *Sydney Morning Herald* 20 Aug. 2/6 We were invited to inspect the steaming down establishment belonging to Mr George Brown, at Dapto. **1851** H. MELVILLE *Present State Aust.* 74 Last year, 120,690 sheep, and 5,545 head of cattle, were steamed, producing 27,725 cwt. of tallow.

steamer. *Obs. Kangaroo steamer,* see KANGAROO *n.* 6.
1820 C. JEFFREYS *Van Dieman's Land* 70 Their meal consisted of the hind-quarters of a kangaroo cut into mincemeat, stewed in its own gravy, with a few rashers of salt pork, this dish is commonly called a steamer. **1903** *Truth* (Sydney) 1 Oct. 17/1 The menu was curried rabbit and 'kangaroo steamer', and I was the only guest who didn't beam upon the 'steamer' with joy.

steel. Used *attrib.* in Special Comb. **steel band,** a hard thin layer of sandstone immediately above an opal-bearing stratum; **mill** *obs.*, a portable wheat-grinder.
1950 *Bull. no. 17* (Bureau Min. Resources, Geol. & Geophys.) 27 In many places the first or upper level is indicated by the presence of a very thin and hard band of siliceous sandstone known as the '**Steel Band**'... Both in the 'Steel Band'.. and in the Opal Dirt, opal may be found. **1826** J. ATKINSON *Acct. Agric. & Grazing N.S.W.* 30 Perhaps the Settler is sufficiently rich or has credit to procure a small **steel mill** and wire sieve for grinding and dressing his wheat into flour.

stepper. *Obs.* [Used elsewhere but recorded earliest in Aust.: see OED(S 2 a.] The treadmill.
1832 *Sydney Herald* 23 Jan. 2/4 Frank Howard, having moistened his clay the previous evening until he was unable to walk, was sentenced to try 'the stepper' for ten days. **1845** *Melbourne Standard* 15 Mar. 2/6 Our justices, in sentencing delinquents to imprisonment and hard labour, seem to be ignorant of the fact that there is no hard labour to which the men can be placed since the 'stepper' is out of order.
Hence **stepping** *vbl. n.* and *attrib.*
1830 *Sydney Monitor* 14 Aug. 2/3 The sentences to the mill vary from seven to twenty-eight days... The stepping hours are in winter from six to twelve, and from one to six. **1832** *Sydney Herald* 27 Feb. 3/2 For which, seven days stepping was prescribed.

sterks, *pl.* Also **sturks.** [Perh. formed from *stercoraceous* pertaining to excrement.] A fit of exasperation or depression, in the phr. **to give** (one) **the sterks.**
1941 S.J. BAKER *Pop. Dict. Austral. Slang* 71 *Sterks, give one the,* to infuriate, annoy, depress. **1972** N. MILES *Opal Fever* 98 'Wouldn't it give you the sturks?' complained Bill.
Hence **sterky** *a.*, frightened.

1944 J. DEVANNY *By Tropic Sea & Jungle* 162 The croc disappears, and there's Ernest, standing up to his waist in the water.. scared as hell, but too game to come out... So my dad goes in. He's a bit sterky too.

sterling. *Hist.*
1. British currency circulating in the Australian colonies. Also **sterling money** and *attrib.*
1806 *Sydney Gaz.* 2 Nov., All Checks and Promissory Notes issued shall by Public Proclamation be drawn payable in Sterling Money. **1828** *Tasmanian* (Hobart) 5 Sept. 2 When you go to the Merchant's Warehouse or Store to buy a bag of Sugar or a chest of Tea, you must pay *Sterling.* **1832** J. BUSBY *Authentic Information N.S.W. & N.Z.* 4 The shop-keepers and dealers in Sydney came to the resolution of abolishing the *currency prices,* and substituting sterling prices in their stead.

2. A non-convict, British-born resident of Australia. Freq. *attrib.*
1825 *Austral.* (Sydney) 1 Sept. 3 The idea originated in the best intentions.. to do honour to the strangers by bringing together all the Australian and Sterling Beauties of the Colony. **1844** Mrs C. MEREDITH *Notes & Sketches N.S.W.* 50 The natives (not the aborigines, but the 'currency', as they are termed, in distinction from the 'sterling', or British-born residents) are often very good-looking when young.

Stewart's Ballarat seedling. A variety of apple: see quot. 1984. Also **Ballarat (seedling), Stewart's (seedling).**
1893 D.A. CRICHTON *Australasian Fruit Culturist* 183 *Stewarts Seedling.*—An excellent Victorian variety, raised in the Ballarat district.. a first-class dessert Apple; also suitable for export. **1917** *Jrnl. Dept. Agric. Vic.* XV. 543 That very fine quality, double purpose, and profitable apple the Stewart's, formerly known as Stewart's Seedling. The tree is a thrifty, good doer, whose rather large fruit ripens late and keeps well. **1984** *Age* (Melbourne) 19 June 27/2 It's a big round apple, green with a dull, pink blush on one side, and in its time it was also known as Ballarat Seedling, Ballarat, Stewart's, and Stewart's Ballarat Seedling. Its names suggest its history. It was first grown in Ballarat and exhibited there by a Mrs Stewart of Soldier's Hill. A nurseryman of Buninyong, Francis Moss, propagated the variety commercially and named it Stewart's Ballarat Seedling in the 1870s. It grew best in Victoria.

stick, *n.*
1. *pl.* Australian National Football. The goal-posts.
1876 T.P. POWER *Footballer* 9 Let us suppose then the fray fairly begun by kicking off the ball toward the adversaries' sticks. **1944** *Fortress Chron.* (Torres Strait Islands) 25 May 1/1 Scored with a.. kick plumb between the sticks.

2. In the phr. **to have had the stick,** *to have had the dick,* see DICK.
1953 T.A.G. HUNGERFORD *Riverslake* 49 When are you bunnies going to wake up that you've had the stick? **1973** D. WOLFE *Brass Kangaroo* 281 Look at this truck now... She's just about had the stick. Just about wore out.

3. Special Comb. **stick-picker,** see quot. 1959; so **-picking** *vbl. n.*
1959 H.P. TRITTON *Time means Tucker* 58 Burning-off dead timber is a hot game... There were 40 men on the job, made up of six axe-men, 30 'stick-pickers'.. whose job was to pack the timber in heaps. **1981** NGABIDJ & SHAW *My Country of Pelican Dreaming* 25 The council also used its two vehicles for contract work.. and 'stick picking' on the Packsaddle Plain to clear future farmlands.

stick, *v.*
1. *trans.* With **up.**
a. *Obs.* To pierce (a piece of meat) with a spit and roast it before a fire: see STICKER-UP 1. Also as *ppl. a.*
1837 S. HACK *Lett.* Nov., Cut from the hindquarters of a

kangaroo and stuck up before the fire to roast, called in colonial phrase 'stick ups'. **1852** Mrs C. Meredith *My Home in Tas.* I. 55 'And gentlemen', as dear old Hardcastle would have said, if he had dined with us in the bush, 'to men that are hungry, stuck-up kangaroo and bacon are very good eating.' Kangaroo is, in fact, very like hare.

b. [Now also used elsewhere: see OED(S $v.^1$ 34 k.] *trans.* Of an (armed) bushranger: to stop by force and rob (a person or persons) on the road; to rob (a building, coach, etc., or the occupants thereof) under threat of violence. See Bail *v.* 2 a.

1843 F. Landon *Exile from Canada* (1960) 218 There are quite a number more bushrangers but they are not so daring, they do not stick folks up at the houses and rob so openly. **1950** G.M. Farwell *Land of Mirage* 171 Many a man who stuck up a gold escort or a Cobb & Co. coach had started out as a mere gully-raker, putting his brand on scrubbers.

c. *trans.* To frustrate the activity of (a person, etc.); to hamper.

[N.Z. **1863** S. Butler *First Yr. Canterbury Settlement* 68 At last we came to a waterfall... This 'stuck us up', as they say here concerning any difficulty.] **1879** *Kelly Gang* 135 We are stuck up; the Kellys are here, and the police are also stuck up. **1904** *Shearer* (Sydney) 6 Aug. 6/5 The union recently 'stuck up' without notice one of the company's colliers.

d. *trans.* To bring (an animal) to bay.

1884 'R. Boldrewood' *Old Melbourne Memories* 24 We knew then that she had 'stuck up' or brought to bay a large forester. **1910** *Huon Times* (Franklin) 24 Aug. 3/3 There were plenty of opossums. The dogs would stick them up in the day time.

e. *intr.* Of an animal: to stand at bay.

1893 E.D. Cleland *White Kangaroo* 55 He was certain the kangaroo would not go far before 'sticking up' and showing fight. This proved to be the case for very soon the 'old man' faced suddenly round, and sitting erect upon his hind legs he showed a bold front to his pursuers.

2. [Used elsewhere but recorded earliest in Aust.] In the phr. **to get stuck into**, to lay into, to make a physical assault on (someone); to attack (a project, meal, etc.) with gusto.

1941 S.J. Baker *Pop. Dict. Austral. Slang* 31 *Get stuck into*, to engage a person in a bout of fisticuffs. To tackle a job with a will. **1985** *Sunday Territorian* (Darwin) 24 Feb. 6/5 He got stuck into the Feds for providing 'little or nothing' for Northern Australian development.

sticker-up.

1. *Obs.* [See Stick *v.* 1 a.] A method of cooking meat out of doors (see quot. 1852); the meat so cooked. Also *attrib.*

1830 *Hobart Town Almanack* 112 Steaks .. which he cooked in the mode called in colonial phrase a sticker up. **1842** *S. Austral. Mag.* Oct. 21 The sticker-up, which, broiled before the flame, Did, with the ash-baked damper, well agree. **1852** Mrs C. Meredith *My Home in Tas.* I. 54 Here I was first initiated into the bush art of 'sticker-up' cookery... The orthodox material here is of course kangaroo, a piece of which is divided nicely into cutlets two or three inches broad and a third of an inch thick. The next requisite is a straight clean stick, about four feet long, sharpened at both ends. On the narrow part of this, for the space of a foot or more, the cutlets are spitted at intervals, and on the end is placed a piece of delicately rosy fat bacon. The strong end of the stick-pit is now stuck fast and erect in the ground, close by the fire, to leeward; care being taken that it does not burn.

2. [f. Stick *v.* 1 b.] One who robs a person under threat of violence.

1855 W. Howitt *Land, Labor & Gold* II. 43 What are called Bendigo Faugh-a-ballahs, the same class of mortals as M'Ivor Stickers-up and Ballarat All-serenes—in plain English, thieves. **1907** C. MacAlister *Old Pioneering Days* 232 Oh! don't you remember old Melbourne, Ben Bolt, When gold nuggets first were found out? When, mid five feet of mud on the wharves and the streets, And all night, 'stickers-up' roamed about.

sticking up, *vbl. n.* [f. Stick *v.* 1 b.] The action of robbing a person or persons under threat of violence. Also *attrib.*

1853 *Guardian* (Hobart) 10 Aug. 3/2 'Sticking up' still continues in Melbourne and on the roads to a fearful extent. **1900** C.H. Chomley *True Story Kelly Gang* 20 Power, a solitary rover .. had terrorised a large part of the colony by his 'sticking-up' exploits, though murder was a crime of which he was never guilty.

stick-nest rat. [See quot. 1941.] Either of the two rats of the genus *Leporillus, L. apicalis* (prob. extinct) and *L. conditor* (of Franklin Is., S.A.), both of which build a dwelling of sticks containing a soft nest or burrow. See also *rabbit rat* Rabbit A 1. Also **stick-nest building rat.**

1923 *Rec. Austral. Museum* XIV. 23 While on a collecting expedition .. at various stations on the Trans-Australian Railway, I secured several specimens of a stick-nest building rat. **1941** E. Troughton *Furred Animals Aust.* 309 Stick-nest Rats. Genus *Leporillus.* .. The rats of this genus were originally known as the 'Native Rabbit' or 'Rabbit-Rat'... They are gregarious creatures, two species being communal house-builders, an unusual habit which provides the present popular name for the genus.

stick-up.

1. [Orig. Austral. but now chiefly U.S.: see OEDS *sb.* 2.] An instance of Sticking-up. Also *attrib.*

1910 H. Lawson *Skyline Riders* 62 Scott that fired at Brummy Hughson, when the 'stick-ups' used to be. **1942** A.L. Haskell *Waltzing Matilda* 111 Brother Jim was prevented from joining through a ten-year sentence, result of his failure as a 'stick-up man' in New South Wales.

2. The place where an animal is held at bay. See Stick *v.* 1 d.

1978 A. Bentley *Introd. Deer Aust.* (ed. 2) 296 As Harry gets near the 'stick-up' he is cautious and only moves when the hounds are barking and stops when they stop.

sticky. Abbrev. of Stickybeak *n.* 1 and 2. Also as *adj.*

1941 S.J. Baker *Pop. Dict. Austral. Slang* 72 Sticky (adj.), curious, inquisitive. **1974** D. Ireland *Burn* 139 Have a gander. Perhaps your mates'd like a bit of a sticky too.

stickybeak, *n.*

1. An inquisitive person; one who 'sticks his (or her) nose into' the affairs of others. Also *attrib.*, and *transf.*

1920 B. Cronin *Timber Wolves* 159 I've told the girls to give out that we've gone fishing, if any sticky-beaks get to asking why we ain't visible no more. **1933** H.B. Raine *Lash End* 200 If that stickybeak pressman hadn't poked his nose into our business, none of this would have happened. **1943** *Bulletin* (Sydney) 29 Dec. 12/1 When two channels about six inches by a yard sprouted out of one side the stickybeak in me prevailed. 'What's this, a dam?' I asked. **1951** *Ibid.* 25 Apr. 12/2 Cows are natural sticky-beaks.

2. An inquisitive look.

1971 *Bulletin* (Sydney) 21 Aug. 14/1 An old Digger type who was just having a bit of a stickybeak gets spun out of the crush.

stickybeak, *v.* [f. prec.] *intr.* To pry; to snoop.

1933 J. Truran *Where Plain Begins* 13 'So you're the bloke that's been robbin' me traps, are yer?' said the man. 'Serves yer right for stickybeakin' where you 'ad no business.' **1978** H. Haenke *Bottom of Birdcage* 47 Who wants stickybeakin' down a sewer? Catch y' death.

Hence **stickybeaking** *vbl n.* and *ppl. a.*
1948 H. Drake-Brockman *Sydney or Bush* 230 Flat-chested old sticky-beaking romancer, that's what she is! **1965** R.H. Conquest *Horses in Kitchen* 103 'Are you satisfied now?' he said grimly to me. 'See what your sticky-beaking has done?'

sticky wattle. The shrub *Acacia howittii* (fam. Mimosaceae) of e. Vic., cultivated as an ornamental. Also **sticky acacia.**
1930 A.J. Ewart *Flora Vic.* 600 *A[cacia] Howittii* .. Sticky Acacia. A viscid shrub. **1985** *Canberra Times* 15 Aug. 11/2 The sticky wattle from Victoria makes a fine rapidly grown screening shrub.

stiff, *a.* [Prob. f. Br. slang *stiff* a penniless person: see OED(S *sb.* 4.]
1. Penniless. Hence, unlucky. Also as *n.*
1898 *Bulletin* (Sydney) 17 Dec. 15/2 Hard-uppishness a shearer confesses when he says he's *stiff*. **1972** J. de Hoog *Skid Row Dossier* 58 A favourite definition of the word stiff: 'a bloke who's got nothin' and never will have nothin'.'
2. Bad, hard, 'tough'; esp. in the collocation **stiff luck** and varr., 'hard lines'.
1900 *Bulletin* (Sydney) 28 Apr. 14/1 Recently read a stiff yarn about an orchid in Cuba which dropped its tendrils at night and drew up and strangled some Yankee sailors. **1972** *Bulletin* (Sydney) 15 July 15/1 Stiff luck there, we made a mistake. **1979** B. Humphries *Bazza comes into his Own*, If you're an English Aborigine wanting to migrate to Oz—it's stiff cheese! **1980** *Westerly* iv. 30 'People always think I am Aboriginal.' 'Stiff shit.'
3. In the phr. **stiff and swagless:** see *swagless* Swag *n.*

Hence **stiffness** *n.*, bad luck.
1918 *Aussie: Austral. Soldiers' Mag.* Dec. p. ii, Cripes! there's stiffness fer yer! We've just finished building this bonzer possie, stove and all, ready for the Winter, and now they go and make an Armistice!

stiffener. [Used elsewhere but recorded earliest in Aust.: see OEDS 3.] A fortifying or reviving alcoholic drink.
1864 J. Armour *Diggings, Bush & Melbourne* 14 They adjourned to the tap-room for 'a stiffener'. **1937** A.W. Upfield *Winds of Evil* 233 'Here, Barry! Have a stiffener,' Lee said kindly, proffering a tin pannikin.

sting. [f. Br. slang *stingo* strong beer.]
1. Strong drink.
1927 K.S. Prichard *Brumby Innes* (1974) 68 Old Jack's been boozin' up a bit. Never touched a woman in all his born days, he says, but he ain't so teetotal about sting. **1978** D. Stuart *Wedgetail View* 39 'Anyway, I'll set up a bit of a sting, eh?' The pair of them .. sat slowly drinking.
2. A drug, spec. one given illegally to a racehorse by injection.
1949 L. Glassop *Lucky Palmer* 36 They're going to give it the sting. They'll hit it with enough dope to win a Melbourne Cup. **1958** F. Hardy *Four-Legged Lottery* 180 A man should only bet when he's got inside information—and if its information from a stable with a jigger or a good sting, all the better.

Hence as *v. trans.*, to administer an illegal drug to (a racehorse).
1978 H.C. Baker *I was Listening* 109 This feller comes to me and wants me to 'sting' one of his horses. I told him, 'Look, there's nothing I can give you that'll make a horse do better than his best. If he's good enough he'll win; if he ain't, he'll lose.'

stingaree /'stɪŋəri, stɪŋə'ri/. Also **stingeree.** [Altered form of *stingray* a fish of the fam. Dasyatidae.] Any of several rays, esp. *Urolophus testaceus*, commonly found on muddy or sandy flats in shallow waters from Qld. southwards to S.A.
1830 R. Dawson *Present State Aust.* 313 There is a common fish in the colony called a stingaree; its tail is pointed, and so sharp that the natives in bathing near a low shore are frequently wounded by it in the feet. **1850** *Britannia* (Hobart) 17 Jan. 3/1 One of the largest Stingerees ever before seen, the monster being nearly eight feet long, and of nearly equal dimensions in breadth.

stinger.
1. An exceptionally hot spell of weather.
1867 *S.A. Parl. Papers* no. 14 69 It would not find a purchaser at a much higher rate than you suggest?—I do not know; I think people have had such a stinger, there would be no buyers except just to put stock on in good seasons. **1942** E. Langley *Pea Pickers* 220 The next day was a stinger; and we had to pick in Greenfeast's dry, starved bean crop.
2. Shortened form of Stinging tree.
1941 H.D.A. Joske *Life to Live* 186 There are also several plants whose touch is extremely painful, the worst of them being the 'stinger'. **1976** E. Worrell *Things that Sting* 47 A group of prickly-barked, pink-berried trees known as Stinging Trees or Stingers.
3. Box jellyfish. Also *attrib.*
1981 *Ecos* xxviii. 21/1 This lake could prove particularly popular for recreation in summer, when marine 'stingers' (box jellyfish) are a hazard on the coast. **1984** *N.T. News* (Darwin) 9 Nov. 32/4 Stinger suits, box jellyfish at Keith Kemps, Knuckey St sports store.

stingeree, var. Stingaree.

stinging bush, stinging-nettle: see Stinging tree.

stinging-ray. A stingray. Also *attrib.*
1804 *Sydney Gaz.* 30 Sept., A ludicrous contest some days since took place, the parties engaged in which were a seine attendant and a *stinging rae-fish*. **1935** A. Francis *Then & Now* 165 The sting-a-ree, or more properly, stinging-ray, is a flat, repulsive-looking fish, four or five feet across, which lies upon the bottom in shallow water. It has a long, whip-like tail, on the under surface of which is an ivory serrated spike six or more inches long, which is a dangerous weapon, as it produces a lacerated poisoned wound.

stinging tree. Any of several trees or shrubs of the genus *Dendrocnide* (fam. Urticaceae) of N.S.W., Qld., and elsewhere, characterized by stinging hairs, esp. on the leaves and small branches; Nettle tree. See also *giant stinging tree* Giant, Gympie. Also **stinging bush, stinging-nettle tree.**
1836 J. Backhouse *Narr. Visit Austral. Colonies* (1843) 431 We measured three Stinging-trees, *Urtica gigas*, eighteen, twenty, and twenty-one feet in circumference. **1878** C.H. Eden *Fortunes of Fletchers* 76 The stinging-nettle tree .. the intensity of whose poison is so violent that the man or horse unlucky enough to be brought into a prolonged contact with its branches is stricken with a numbness resembling paralysis. **1952** T.A.G. Hungerford *Ridge & River* 145 'Bloody stinging-bush,' Wallace swore, sweeping the leaves from his shoulder.

stinkbird. Either of two birds of the genus *Sericornis, S. fuliginosus* of s.e. Aust. incl. Tas., and *S. campestris* of heathland and drier parts of s. mainland Aust.
1883 A.J. Campbell *Nests & Eggs Austral. Birds* p. xxviii, The Striated Calamanthus .. is not without interest. .. The [Tasmanian] Islanders call it by the somewhat uneuphonious name of 'Stink-bird' or 'Stinker', because it emits a gamey scent, and dogs sometimes point at it. **1954** C. Barrett *Wild Life Aust. & New Guinea* 159 We have four field-wrens, the best known being the striated species, which

sportsmen have given an ugly name—'stinkbird'; the little striped songster leaves a strong scent trail, which sporting dogs refuse to follow.

stinkfish. [See quot. 1906.] Any of several marine fish of the fam. Callionymidae, esp. those of the genus *Callionymus*, some of which are poisonous.

1900 *Proc. Linnean Soc. N.S.W.* XXV. 476 Mr D.G. Stead exhibited a specimen and described the effluvium-producing powers of the so-called 'Stink-Fish'. 1906 D.G. STEAD *Fishes of Aust.* 208 One species [of Dragonet] well-known in Port Jackson (because of the offensive smell exhaled from the gill-openings) is the Stink-Fish (*Callionymus curvicornis*).

stinking Roger. [Spec. use of *stinking Roger* any of several evil-smelling plants.] The strongly aromatic, tall, annual, American herb *Tagetes minuta* (fam. Asteraceae), naturalized in e. mainland Aust.

1871 *Austral. Town & Country Jrnl.* (Sydney) 426/2 'What is that tall bright-green feathery looking plant?' That is . . a Chinese medicinal plant, introduced here rashly at a venture, and dubbed by the euphonious epithet of 'Stinking Roger'. 1979 E. SMITH *Saddle in Kitchen* 20 The creek ran out onto a flat, marshy patch that was overgrown with a tall, rank weed we called 'stinking Roger'.

stinkwood. [Spec. use of *stinkwood* a name for any of several plants the wood of which has an unpleasant smell.] Any of several trees or shrubs, esp. *Zieria arborescens* (fam. Rutaceae) of s.e. Aust., the leaves of which smell unpleasant when crushed, and *Jacksonia scoparia* (see DOGWOOD).

1827 *HRA* (1923) 3rd Ser. VI. 267 'Stink Wood' . . I believe has some what the appearance of Elder, with a very disagreeable smell. 1981 G.M. CUNNINGHAM et al. *Plants Western N.S.W.* 399 The wood emits a most offensive odour when burning, hence two of its common names, stinkwood and dogwood.

stipe. [Transf. use of Br. slang *stipe* stipendiary (magistrate); chiefly Austral.] Abbrev. of 'stipendiary racing steward': see quot. 1983.

1902 *Sporting News* (Launceston) 6 Dec. 1/3 Where were the eyes of the stewards and 'stipe' in the first race? 1983 HIBBERD & HUTCHINSON *Barracker's Bible* 197 Stipes, the Stipendiary Stewards, who for their 'stipend' are charged with the enforcement of the Rules of Racing, and a fair crack of the whip for all concerned especially in matters vetinary [sic] and pharmacological.

stir, *v.* [Spec. use of *stir* to move to action: see *stir the possum* POSSUM *n.* 3. Used elsewhere but recorded earliest in Aust.]

a. *intr.* To cause trouble for its own sake.

1969 *Sunday Mail Mag.* (Brisbane) 22 June 11/4 'Groovy people', 'good clothes', anybody who can stir. 1980 E.R. HALL *Can you hear Me?* 128 Throughout the years there were radio members who would 'stir' mainly in an effort to get the 'System' to work for the individual.

b. *trans.* To provoke (someone) into exhibiting exasperation, etc.

1972 L. IRISH *Time of Dolphins* 33 'You know, Mrs Ro, you've got really nice legs.' 'Not all oldies have fat legs.' . . (You're a woman Ama Ro, oh yes, and she's damned well stirring you.) 1978 B. ST. A. SMITH *Spirit beyond Psyche* 180 She . . had often 'stirred' him about his pretty hair, but secretly she had been proud of him.

Also as *n.*

1981 SMOLICZ & SECOMBE *Austral. School through Children's Eyes* 82 We tend to speak the Polish language among ourselves 'for a stir'.

stirrer. [f. prec.; chiefly Austral.] An agitator; a trouble-maker.

1966 *R.A.N. News* (Sydney) 7 Jan. 8 Leg pulling . . is often used, discreetly, to test the quality of a man. The exponents of this art [are] usually called 'stirrers'. 1982 *Bulletin* (Sydney) 6 July 25/2 The preselection contest could come down to a race between a younger activist—'a stirrer in the best traditions of the Senate' . . and a 61-year-old party man.

stirry, *a.* Of an animal: bad-tempered; restive.

1976 S. WELLER *Bastards I have Met* 116 One big brahman bullock had bailed up. He was real stirry—would blow snot and throw dirt even if you looked his way. 1979 J. LINDEMAN *Red Rumps & White Faces* 29 The calves usually ran well; my worst worry was when a big 'stirry micky' attacked me from behind.

stobie pole. *S.A.* [f. the name of J.C. Stobie (1895–1953), engineer.] A pole of steel and concrete carrying electricity lines.

1970 *S. Austral. Electrical Contractor* Dec. 43 Stobie Poles. Much to do about them at present, their safety and their appearance. To me I cannot understand why wiring does not go underground. 1985 *Advertiser* (Adelaide) 4 Jan. 1/6 That blight of the Australian landscape, the stobie pole, has angered S.A. motorists, town planners and conservationists for decades.

stock. [Spec. use of *stock* livestock: see OED(S *sb.*^{1} 63 a. for numerous Comb. of local significance but well attested elsewhere.]

1. Used *attrib.* in Comb. **stock feed, feeding, owner, pen, train, work, yard.**

1890 A. MACKAY *Austral. Agriculturist* (ed. 2) 67 When half a bushel of tares or vetches are sown with the rye, the mixture is excellent for **stock feed,** or making ensilage. 1853 J.R. GODLEY *Extracts Jrnl. Visit N.S.W.* 9 The present governing, or rather legislating, class . . are, to a preponderable extent, men of considerable fortunes derived from **stock-feeding.** 1804 *Sydney Gaz.* 18 Nov., I am . . anxious to propose, the establishment of a subscription fund, to be raised and supported by the **stock owners** in each particular district. 1808 *Sydney Gaz.* 2 Oct., The deceased went with others to rob the **stock pens** of Robert Ritchie. 1903 *Bulletin* (Sydney) 20 Aug. 17/2 They meet the **stock-trains** Nor'ward And the trains from out the West. 1943 H.G. LAMOND *From Tariaro to Ross Roy* 23 The drudgery of **stock-work** . . galls so many white men. 1794 D. COLLINS *Acct. Eng. Colony N.S.W.* (1798) I. 336 All the people employed about the **stockyard.**

2. Special Comb. **stock agent,** one who deals in the buying and selling of stock; **boot** *obs., stockman's boot,* see STOCKMAN 2; **boy,** an Aboriginal male employed to look after stock; **country,** an area in which stock-raising is the principal industry; an area suitable for this; **driver** *obs.,* DROVER 1; **-driving** *vbl. n.,* DROVING 1; **establishment,** a sheep or cattle farm; **horse,** a horse trained to work with stock; **house** *obs.,* a building in which stock is accommodated; **hut** *obs., stockman's hut,* see STOCKMAN 2; **inspector,** an official employed to ensure that regulations concerning stock are complied with; **market** *obs.,* a place where sheep and cattle are sold; trade in sheep and cattle; **master, proprietor** *obs.,* STOCKHOLDER; **property** *obs., stock establishment;* **reserve,** *travelling stock reserve,* see TRAVELLING STOCK 2; **-rider,** STOCKMAN 1; so **-ride** *v. intr.;* **-riding** *vbl. n.* and *attrib.;* **route,** *travelling stock route,* see TRAVELLING STOCK 2; also *attrib.;* **run,** see RUN *n.*^{2} 2; **saddle,** a heavy saddle made for a stock horse; **station** *obs.,* see STATION 2 a. and 3; **water,** water suitable for stock; **woman,** STOCKHOLDER; a woman employed to tend stock.

1819 *Sydney Gaz.* 20 Feb., An action for breach of agreement as **stock agent** for 3 years. 1841 *Geelong Advertiser* 11 Oct. 1/4 Superior Wellington, Clarence, Blucher, and **Stock Boots.** 1935 K.L. SMITH *Sky Pilot Arnhem Land* 106

We cantered along the bush track, following the **stockboy**, who now had a fresh horse. **1847** A. HARRIS *Settlers & Convicts* (1953) 128 The country we passed through to-day was a very fine **stock-country**, beautiful flats of open meadow on river banks, and fine gentle grassy hills. **1836** *Bent's News* (Hobart) 3 Sept. 3 You have among you so many good bush men, with **stock drivers** and pack bullocks at command. **1849** A. HARRIS *Emigrant Family* (1967) 18 Kicking up the clouds of dust that furnishes the stock-driver with one of the principal parts of his professional avocations, that of chewing sand all day. *Ibid.* 20 Having now given the reader a sufficient sketch of the customs of **stock-driving**. **1831** *Sydney Herald* 23 May 3/4 Superintendent and Overseer. Wants a Situation, in an Agricultural or **Stock Establishment**. **1838** D.L. WAUGH *Three Yrs.' Practical Experience N.S.W.* 26 The **stock horses** know this as well as possible. **1801** *HRA* (1915) 1st Ser. III. 11 The want of **stock-houses** for Government cattle has been a great disadvantage to them, and the sheep in particular. **1826** *Colonial Times* (Hobart) 27 May, The same fate attends many other articles which we had prepared, viz . . on the means of preventing sheep stealing and runaways, particularly as connected with the evils attending the remote **stock huts**. **1896** W.H. WILLSHIRE *Land of Dawning* 86 You shall be a **Stock Inspector** to investigate the red-water disease amongst cattle. **1834** *Perth Gaz.* 8 Nov. 387 These increased demands upon the **stock market** . . add to the advantage of the speculations which are afloat for the importation of a quantity of Sydney sheep. **1890** 'R. BOLDREWOOD' *Colonial Reformer* II. 251 A favourable change would take place in the stock-market. **1839** *Port Phillip Gaz.* 27 Nov. 1 Mr Lewis Robertson . . announces to the Gentlemen and **Stockmasters** generally of Australia Felix, that he intends practising his profession as a *veterinary surgeon*. **1829** *Tasmanian Almanack* 95 Fresh meat taken into the Commissariat Stores, for some years, at 6d. per lb. from **Stock-proprietors** only. **1828** *Tasmanian* (Hobart) 26 Sept. 3 Mr Bryant's valuable **stock property** fetched extremely satisfactory prices yesterday. **1897** *Tocsin* (Melbourne) 16 Dec. 5/2 No attempt was made to let them [*sc.* sheep] encroach upon his well-grassed paddocks, which skirted the **stock reserve**. **1844** N.L. KENTISH *Work in Bush Van Diemen's Land* (1846) 13 Messrs Field's cattle are driven occasionally to or from Middlesex Plains by their **stock-riders** in dry summer weather. **1885** MRS C. PRAED *Austral. Life* 126 My brother Jim, on a stock-riding beat, met one of these gentlemen. **1886** P. FLETCHER 'Hints to Immigrants' in P. Fletcher *Qld.* 4 Learn to milk, break in heifers . . stock-ride and slaughter. **1901** *Advocate* (Burnie) 8 June 4/2 The Duke expressed a desire to see a cattle draft, and in 'cutting out' certain animals and clearing them off, very fine stockriding was shown. **1884** W.J. O'DONNELL *Diary Exploring Exped.* 20 From the telegraph line (Northern Territory) we have proved that a good **stock route** can be made to the Ord River. **1960** *N.T. News* (Darwin) 8 Jan. 4/3 The department has built dipping yards and inoculation depots at stock route junctions in the Territory. **1822** *Hobart Town Gaz.* 9 Mar. (Suppl.), On or about the 22d of February last, Three Hundred and Sixty Sheep were stolen from my **Stock Run**. **1887** A. NICOLS *Wild Life & Adventure* 211 Harold settled the **stock-saddle** on its back. **1824** *Sydney Gaz.* 26 Aug., Attacks on the **stock stations** there, putting some of the keepers to cruel deaths. **1882** ARMSTRONG & CAMPBELL *Austral. Sheep Husbandry* 223 Wells yielding . . a constant supply of good **stock water**. **1835** *Colonist* (Sydney) 10 Sept. 291/4 Any person can become a *stockholder* now, without the least ado, and without the least indelicacy, whether *stockman*, or **stockwoman**.

3. In the collocation **stock and station**.

a. Used *attrib.* to designate firms or their employees dealing in farm land, products, and supplies.

1872 *Causes Ruinous Condition Coal Trade N.S.W.* 15 He may . . invest one portion of his means in a coal-mine, another portion . . in a copper-mine, whilst these two may be supplemented by run-holding and stock and station agency. **1981** *Austral. Women's Weekly* (Sydney) 11 Nov. 30/2 The stock and station fellows and the squattocracy were there after a cattle and pig sale.

b. Comb. **stock and station agent**.

1884 G. RANKEN *Dry Country* ii. 2 In my business of stock and station agent, I am . . behind the scenes. **1985** *Bombala Times* 18 July 6/4 Concern was raised over the possibility of vandalism if a phone was installed . . and over whether or not the stock and station agents really wanted one.

stockade. *Hist.* [Transf. use of *stockade* a military fortification.] A structure in which convict gangs working in outlying districts were accommodated. Also **stockade station** and *attrib.*

1832 N.S.W. Mounted Police Troop Order Bk. 10 Dec. I. 49 The Trooper now stationed at the Fish River be removed from thence to the New Stockade on Cox's River where the Iron Gang is working. **1845** *Star* (Sydney) 11 Oct. 4/1 Fitzpatrick, the Stockade prisoner, found guilty . . of the murder of his fellow convict, is ordered for execution. **1850** C.A. KING *Life* 26, I was . . sentenced to fifty lashes, with orders to be sent to a Stockade station.

stockholder. A sheep or cattle farmer.

1804 *Sydney Gaz.* 14 Oct., The great increase of Male Stock . . requires the Price of Animal Food being reduced in proportion thereto; and any Combination or Monopoly, either on the part of the Stockholders or the Butchers, being counteracted. **1930** BILLIS & KENYON *Pastures New* 21 The more lordly landowners, stockholders and graziers usually lived in the town and kept superintendents to look after their stations.

So **stockholding** *vbl. n.*

1844 S. DAVENPORT *Let.* 29 Feb. in *S. Australiana* (1967) Sept. 74 Land may rise or fall as circumstances occur, but it has always value in conjunction with stockholding, both as giving a run and being more or less improved by the stock.

stock-keep, *v. Obs.* [f. STOCK-KEEPER.] *intr.* To own stock; to tend the stock of another. Freq. as *vbl. n.*

1828 *Tasmanian* (Hobart) 24 Oct. 2 You have several branches of business here, that may be followed successfully; but pray how does stock-keeping get on? **1876** *Austral. Town & Country Jrnl.* (Sydney) 9 Sept. 422/1 'What can you do, young man?' 'Well, most things,' answered the Australian with quiet confidence—'Fence, split, milk, drive bullocks, stock-keep, ploughing.'

stock-keeper. *Obs.*

1. STOCKMAN 1.

1795 S. MACARTHUR ONSLOW *Some Early Rec. Macarthurs* (1914) 49 Mr Macarthur has frequently in his employment 30 or 40 people. . . Eight are employed as stock-keepers, in the garden, stables and house. **1905** J. FURPHY *Rigby's Romance* (1946) p. xxi, The station stock-keeper had then been approached.

2. In special collocations: **stock-keeper's boot, hut**, *stockman's boot, stockman's hut*, see STOCKMAN 2.

1828 *Tasmanian Almanack* 45 It will . . be the duty of the master to furnish each servant with two suits of woollen slop clothing, three pair of **stock-keeper's boots**, four shirts, and one cap or hat, per annum. **1821** *Sydney Gaz.* 21 Apr., An information was exhibited against John Fewins, for the wilful murder of George Hancock, on the 9th of August, last, at a **stock-keepers'** [*sic*] **hut** on Jacob's Plains.

stockman. Also **stocksman**. [Used elsewhere but recorded earliest in Aust.]

1. One employed to tend livestock, esp. cattle.

1803 Banks Papers VIII. 124 What was my nonsensical pursuit to the lives of the stockmen and stock. **1853** H.B. JONES *Adventures in Aust.* 112 Bullock drivers and stocksmen, far from medical advice in the interior.

2. In special collocations: **stockman's boot** *obs.*, an (elastic-sided) riding boot; **stockman('s) cut,** a narrow-legged style (of trousers, etc.); also *attrib.*; **stockman's hat,** a broad-brimmed felt hat; **stockman's hut,** a dwelling provided for a stockman; **stockman's saddle** *obs., stock saddle,* see STOCK 2; **stockman's whip** *obs.*, STOCKWHIP 1.

1839 *Port Phillip Gaz.* 25 Dec. 3 **Stockmen's Boots,** and excellent Strong Shoes. **1882** *Bulletin* (Sydney) 5 Aug. 6/3 The 'Plume' Brand Moleskin Trousers White And Printed, In **Stockman's** Or Ordinary **Cut. 1976** K. BROWN *Knock Ten* 66 The girl in her sweaty, greasy, slop-made man's stockman-cut dungarees, man's cotton shirt and old shapeless felt hat. **1950** G. FARWELL *Surf Music* 28 His weathered face under the tall crown of his **stockman's hat** was seamy and shrivelled as a claypan. **1806** *Sydney Gaz.* 30 Nov., Four muskets, taken from his **stockmen's huts** during the night time. **1837** *Colonist* (Sydney) 5 Jan. 3/4, 90 **Stockmans Saddles** at 25s. each. **1864** W.H. THOMES *Gold Hunters' Adventures* 29 With many a sharp crack of the **stockman's whip,** we crossed the stream, and once more pursued our way towards Ballarat.

stockwhip.

1. A whip used in the handling of cattle: see quot. 1845.

1839 J.C. CRAWFORD *Diary* 11 Mar. in *S. Australiana* (1964) Mar. 63 Mr Coutts and I rode at the leading party at full gallop with our stockwhips. **1845** D. MACKENZIE *Emigrant's Guide* 128 Each rider is armed with a stock-whip, the handle of which is only a little more than a foot in length, while the thong is twelve or fourteen feet long.

2. Special Comb. **stockwhip bird,** the bird *Psophodes olivaceus* (see WHIPBIRD.)

1861 'OLD BUSHMAN' *Bush Wanderings* 151 The *Stock-Whip Bird* .. had rather the appearance of the pied wagtail at home .. a grating call-note, something similar to the springing of an old watchman's rattle, but of course not so loud, ending with a sharp smack.

stone, *n.*[1]

1. Used *attrib.* to designate an Aboriginal weapon or implement fashioned from stone.

1835 J. BATMAN *Settlement in Port Phillip* 7 June (1856) 22 The chiefs of the Port Phillip tribes made me a present of three stone tomahawks .. and other weapons of warfare. **1930** C.C. TOWLE *Certain Stone Implements* 10 The coastal tribes did not use any implement similar in any respect to the long flaked knife or the stone spear head.

2. Special Comb. **stone country,** *gibber country,* see GIBBER 2; **fence** *obs.* [U.S. in both senses], **(a)** a drystone wall; **(b)** an alcoholic drink (see quots. 1853 and 1918); **hut,** a dwelling made of blocks of stone.

1927 M.H. ELLIS *Long Lead* 138 In long grass, 'devil devil' and **stone country.(a) 1861** H. EARLE *Ups & Downs* 125 A small track of ground .. had been securely preserved from the intrusive and destructive tread of cattle by means of a '**stone fence**', formed of small pieces of burnt rock.**(b) 1853** F.J. COCKBURN *Lett.* (1856) 3 A glass of sodawater and brandy is termed a '**stone fence**'. **1918** *Bulletin* (Sydney) 1 Aug. (Red Page), In a 'stone fence' ginger-beer mingled with the brandy. **1845** *S. Austral. Odd Fellows' Mag.* Jan. 11 Some men are felling trees, some are building **stone huts.**

3. In the names of flora and fauna: **stone curlew,** CURLEW; **-fish,** [see quot. 1965, and also OED(S *sb.* 20 b.], any of several venomous fish of the fam. Synanceiidae of n. Aust. and elsewhere in the tropics, having dorsal spines capable of inflicting a painful, and potentially fatal, sting; **plover,** CURLEW.

1855 W. HOWITT *Land, Labor & Gold* II. 78 The **stone curlew.** These birds abound all along the creeks and water sides, and during the night make the loudest and most extraordinary cries. **1908** E.J. BANFIELD *Confessions of Beachcomber* 143 Beware of the **stone fish** (*Synanceia horrida*), the death adder of the sea, called also the sea-devil, because of its malice. **1965** *Austral. Encycl.* VIII. 305 Stone-fishes, venomous fishes of the family Synancejidae. Their popular name is explained by their remarkable resemblance when in the water to blocks of eroded rock or weathered coral. **1878** R.B. SMYTH *Aborigines of Vic.* II. 4 **Stone plover** .. *Wooloo-look.* **1901** *Emu* I. 131 The Stone Plover (*Burhinus grallarius*) also lives on the ground.

4. Intensively, in adj. relation to a noun, as **stone end** (or **finish**), the 'limit', the bitter end.

1946 K. TENNANT *Lost Haven* 22 She had kept her temper so far, she shouted, but this was the 'stone finish'. **1950** E.M. ENGLAND *Where Turtles Dance* 181, I can cure Dirk. To go back to Cooranga might be the stone end. We must have him at Wyuna.

stone, *n.*[2]

1. *Gold-mining.* Quartz.

c **1860** 'AURIFERA' *Victorian Miners' Man.* 104 *Stone,* veinstone; quartz. **1966** *Prospectors' Guide* (Vic. Dept. Mines) 120 *Stone,* miner's name for quartz.

2. *Opal-mining.* Opal or opal-bearing material; an opal. In the phr. **to be on stone,** *to be on opal,* see OPAL 2.

1895 *Rep.* (N.S.W. Dept. Mines) 68 A patch of stone was taken about the end of the year which brought £1,200. **1924** T.C. WOLLASTON *Opal* 61 The men were not 'on stone' it seemed, but perhaps I could change the luck?

stonewall, *n. Obs.* [Fig. use of *stone-wall* barrier, prob. infl. by the nickname of Thomas Jonathan ('*Stonewall*') Jackson (1824–63), Confederate general during the American Civil War.] The obstruction of parliamentary business; a strategem used for this.

1875 *VPD* XXII. 1387/2 Wished to ask the honourable member for Geelong West whether the six members sitting beside him (Mr Berry) constituted the 'stone wall' that had been spoken of? Did they constitute the stone wall which was to oppose all progress—to prevent the finances being dealt with and the business of the country carried on? It was like bully Bottom's stone wall. It certainly could not be a very high wall nor a very long wall if it only consisted of six. **1909** W.G. SPENCE *Aust.'s Awakening* 299 The Labor Party put up a stonewall in the Assembly against the proposals.

stonewall, *v. Obs.* [f. prec.]

1. *trans.* To obstruct (a piece of parliamentary business).

1880 *Argus* (Melbourne) 16 Feb. 5/2 Advised the commission to comply with the demand, as otherwise the unsatisfied demanders might stonewall the bill. **1909** W.G. SPENCE *Aust.'s Awakening* 394 They deliberately stonewalled these measures for weeks.

2. *intr.* To engage in the obstruction of parliamentary business.

1880 *Argus* (Melbourne) 12 Feb. 9/5 The Opposition 'stonewalled' a whole night. September 3, sitting up until half-past 10 the following morning, in order to exact a pledge from the Government. **1892** *Truth* (Sydney) 15 May 2/7 Fur ye've just the schoolin' Bailes to be foolin' Wid a foony roolin', Shud he dar' stonewall.

Hence **stonewalling** *vbl. n.* and *attrib.*

1898 *Truth* (Sydney) 2 Oct. 1/5 The stonewalling tactics of the Opposition in N.Z. Parliament against the Old Age Pension Bill were a disgrace. **1919** C.A. BERNAYS *Qld. Politics during Sixty Yrs.* 159 When his party banded together to resist some Government proposal, and set up a stonewall, Higg's stonewalling was inimitable.

stonewaller. *Obs.* One who obstructs parliamentary business.

1904 *Advocate* (Burnie) 15 Nov. 4/3 The artistic stonewaller tries to give some coherence and semblance of relevance to his remarks. **1905** *Shearer* (Sydney) 2 Dec. 4/1 He was journeying [to Melbourne] to help resist the pestiferous 'stonewallers', then active in the Federal Parliament.

stonker, *v.* [Prob. f. *stonk* the stake in a game, esp. of marbles.] *trans.* To kill; to defeat; to outwit.
1918 *7th Field Artillery Brigade Yandoo* Jan. 95 How to stonker your cobber. **1978** T. DAVIES *More Austral. Nicknames* 95 A teacher guaranteed to stonker any student with ideas above his ability.

stonkered, *ppl. a.* [f. prec.] Exhausted; 'finished'; (very) drunk.
1918 *Aussie: Austral. Soldiers' Mag.* Apr. 14/1 Make way for the wounded! Damn the war!.. It's this rotten pack. By Heaven, I'm feeling stonkered! **1978** K. GARVEY *Tales of my Uncle Harry* 44 One Sunday night he produces a couple of bottles of rum, and we gets really stonkered. **1985** P. CAREY *Illywhacker* 150 She ate heartily.. only announcing herself stonkered after scraping clean the large monogrammed plate of steamed pudding.

Also **stonkering** *vbl. n.*, drinking.
1950 N. LINDSAY *Dust or Polish* 103 'Can't you do your stonkering up here...' 'Not me. I like a free leg when I'm out for a proper booze-up.'

stonkie. [f. *stonk* a coloured marble + -Y.] A coloured marble.
1915 N. LINDSAY *N. Lindsay's Bk. II.* 85 'How many marbles had you...' 'Fifty-eight allies 'n two stonkies.' **1957** A. MARSHALL *Aust.* (1981) 74 Marble games seemed to vary in each State. Even the terms used were different. The names we gave to the cheapest marbles were 'shooks' and 'stonkies'.

stony, *a. Obs.* (except in place-names). In the collocation **stony rise:** see quot. 1846.
1846 W. WESTGARTH *Rep. Conditions Austral. Aborigines* 8 To the west and south west of Mount Rouse, there occur extensive tracts of those curious formations termed by the settlers 'stony rises', and consisting of innumerable heaps of fragments of rocks, forming hillocks or ranges, in general not exceeding 20 to 50 feet in height, distributed in endless variety, and traversing every possible direction. **1861** 'OLD BUSHMAN' *Bush Wanderings* 112 The plover of the plains frequents the most desolate open stony rises.

stoom, *v.* [f. STUMER.] *trans.* To break (a person) financially. Chiefly in pass. Also *transf.*, to knock (someone) unconscious; to kill.
1898 *Bulletin* (Sydney) 17 Dec. 15/2 Hard-uppishness a shearer confesses when he says he's .. *stoomed*. **1908** E.S. SORENSON *Quinton's Rouseabout* 119 Garron .. 'as a kick-up with the ole gerl over something—God knows wot—an' she stooms him out—accidental, as yer might say. **1925** —— *Murty Brown* 68 'The scamps!' said Murty sympathetically. 'Might a 'urt yer!' ''Urt me!' Charcoal snorted. 'Might a stoomed me out!'

stoomer, var. STUMER.

stop, *v. trans.* In the phr. **to stop one (a pint,** etc.), to have an alcoholic drink.
1924 LAWRENCE & SKINNER *Boy in Bush* 251 A man whom they knew from the north .. hailed them. 'Come an' stop one on me, maties.' **1942** T. MANN *Go-Getter* 8 But if he should recognise any one, he could scarcely avoid asking: 'Could you stop a pint?'

stoppers, *pl.* Shearing. *Obs.* See quot. 1965.
1895 *Worker* (Sydney) 28 Sept. 4/1 And set to work with my file—Levelled my knockers quickly, and then I rigged them up in style: Put on the stoppers, and shoved them away After the usual test. **1965** J.S. GUNN *Terminol. Shearing Industry* ii. 27 In the days of hand shears stoppers were pieces of material over the closed points of the blades to stop them springing open when not in use. It became a natural transition to say 'put on your stoppers' instead of stop work, stop taking, etc.

store.
1. *Hist.*
a. Abbrev. of *public store* (see PUBLIC *a.* 2).
1789 D. COLLINS *Acct. Eng. Colony N.S.W.* (1798) I. 88 There was a sort of sacredness about our store; and its preservation pure and undefiled was deemed as necessary as the chastity of Caesar's wife. **1822** J.T. BIGGE *Rep. State Colony N.S.W.* 42 On Saturdays the convicts leave their work at ten in summer and eleven in winter, to enable them to attend at the store to draw their rations.

b. *spec.* In the phr. **off** (or **on**) **the store,** (not) in receipt of provisions, etc. from the public store.
1792 D. COLLINS *Acct. Eng. Colony N.S.W.* (1798) I. 208 Some had become settlers; some had left the country; others, to use their own expressions, had taken themselves **off the stores,** that is to say, had declined receiving any farther provisions from the public stores, or doing any public labour. **1832** *HRA* 1st Ser. XVI. 805 He is first of all taken off the Stores, as it is technically called. **1801** *Gen. Orders issued by Governor King* 20 June (1802) 51 A General Muster of all the Male Prisoners, off and **on the Stores**, also Free Men of all descriptions .. on or off the Stores, will be taken at Hawkesbury, Parramatta and Sydney. **1828** L.E. THRELKELD *Statement* 59 The Governor has kindly acceded to my request that four prisoners of the Crown shall be allowed me 'on the stores'.

c. Special Comb. **store receipt,** a receipt specifying the monetary value of produce accepted at a public store: see quot. 1810.
1810 E. BENT *Let.* 9 Mar. 130 When any persons deliver Beef, corn, flour .. into the Stores of the King, they receive for the Quantity delivered in, at a fixed price, which are signed by the Storekeeper, and are called Store Receipts. These are current for their amount, & are considered as good as Paynotes, because they also on every Quarter day are consolidated in like manner by Bills on the Treasury, on being presented to the Commissary.

2. [Orig. U.S.] A shop stocking a wide range of necessary items, as clothing, hardware, provisions, etc., GENERAL STORE; a shop (usu. large and with a number of departments). Also *attrib.*
1825 *Austral.* (Sydney) 19 May 1 William Powditch having himself experienced the great want of a Store, or General Warehouse at Newcastle, for the supply of the Hunter's River Settlers, has determined upon opening a house of that nature immediately, upon his allotment at Newcastle, where he hopes the business will be conducted with such attention, liberality, and undeviating fairness, as to ensure the support of the numerous and respectable body of settlers in that fine district. **1895** *Western Champion* (Barcaldine) 30 July 1/1 As soon as the average Labor member puts on 'store clothes' he begins to despise the working man. **1985** *Austral.* (Sydney) 18 Aug. 1/2 N.S.W. is the only state which allows general and department stores to open at weekends.

3. A depot on a rural property holding supplies for issue or sale to employees: see quot. 1833. Also *attrib.*
1833 J. KING *Information Van Diemen's Land* 15 Almost every person of property is a store-keeper for all kinds of goods; farmers keeping a store from which they supply all who work for them, and if they happen not to have any article that is wanted, they procure it, and charge the consumer a profit upon the colonial price. **1923** *Bulletin* (Sydney) 11 Oct. 24/4 As a rule native races possess good teeth... But put them on 'store' tucker *i.e.*, salmon, rice, sugar, etc., for any length of time, and almost always they develop dental trouble.

storekeep, *v. intr.* To keep a shop. Chiefly as *pres. pple.* and *vbl. n.*

1856 S.C. BREES *How to farm & settle in Aust.* 11 He can then decide between going into quartz-crushing, storekeeping . . or breeding and fattening cattle. **1904** *Bulletin* (Sydney) 11 Feb. 16/2, I was storekeeping at Hoskins Town . . 30 years ago.

storekeeper.

1. *Hist.* A person employed to administer a public store: see STORE 1 a.

1793 J. HUNTER *Hist. Jrnl. Trans. Port Jackson* 308 Great care is to be taken of all the tools; each man taking his axe or hoe to his tent, or delivering them to the store-keeper. **1829** R. DAWSON *Statement* 14 A large tent was pitched as an issuing store, under the management of a brick-layer (who was the *only* storekeeper provided by the committee for a period of *twenty two months*).

2. a. [Orig. U.S.] One who keeps a shop: see STORE 2.

1828 *Hobart Town Courier* 12 July 4 Mr John MacLeod of Elizabeth River, Storekeeper, has executed an Assignment of all his real and personal Estate and Effects. **1985** *Harden-Murrumburrah Express* 30 Sept. 1/1 The publican was peeved because the wake would be not at his hotel but at the 'restaurant' run by storekeeper 'Windy' Regan.

b. In the special collocation **storekeeper's rush,** a gold rush occasioned by a false rumour (see quot. 1869); the rumour itself; also *fig.*

1869 'E. HOWE' *Boy in Bush* 213 We've heard of *storekeeper's rushes* before now, haven't we? . . Those fellows would make out that there was gold in the moon, if people could get there to buy their damaged goods. **1913** *Bulletin* (Sydney) 2 Jan. 15/1 Many 'storekeepers" rushes on the goldfields have been put down to the big bird's fondness for picking up a bright article. In this way a small slug of gold of three or four dwt. has been unloaded in the bush, and that one piece has led to tons of earth being chucked about by eager hunters for more. **1977** J. DOUGHTY *Gold in Blood* 74 It was contemptuously called a 'storekeeper's rush' designed to revive interest in Larkville and bring men to the town.

3. One employed to run a store on a rural property: see STORE 3.

1833 [see STORE 3]. **1843** *Sydney Morning Herald* 2 Oct. 3/1 Men Wanted—A man and his wife, the former as Storekeeper and the latter as Cook . . to proceed to New England. **1926** *Bulletin* (Sydney) 11 Nov. 22/2 The new Pommy knit his brows when the hatter included in his supply order: '2 tins of cocky's delight and a bottle of Mallee marmalade.' How was he to know that treacle and tomato sauce were indicated?

storm bird. [Transf. use of *storm-bird* a bird, the movements or cries of which are supposed to presage a storm.] Any of several birds, esp. the CHANNEL-BILLED CUCKOO.

1904 *Emu* IV. 46 Channelbill (*Scythrops novae-hollandiae*), or 'Storm-Bird' as it is universally called out here, was first heard in 1902. **1981** A.B. FACEY *Fortunate Life* 90 The blue bird was about the size of the peewit too, but had a black head and a very light blue body. This bird was sometimes called a Storm bird on account of it appearing more frequently just before the weather turned stormy.

stoush /staʊʃ/, *n.* Also **stouch.** [Prob. f. Br. dial. *stashie, stushie* an uproar, disturbance, quarrel: see EDD.]

1. a. Fighting; violence; 'punishment'; a brawl or fight; a punch. Also *transf.* and *fig.*, and as **stoush up.**

1893 *Bulletin* (Sydney) 30 Dec. 4/4 The law of New South Wales . . has practically decided that Government by 'stoush' is an allowable process, so the practice of hiring bulky pugilists to attend political meetings and disfigure anybody who isn't in accord with Freetrade principles will doubtless grow and prosper. **1919** *Smith's Weekly* (Sydney) 19 Apr. 18/1 A certain Sydney artist received in an altercation with a brother-brush a hefty stouch on the eye. **1929** 'F. BLAIR' *Digger Sea-Mates* 73 One mob in the joint nearly 'ad a real stoush up over some slurs at a bloke with an outsize in appetites. **1986** *Bulletin* (Sydney) 28 Jan. 22/1 Hayden . . is prepared to take risks, even a stoush with the Left if necessary.

b. In the phr. **to deal out stoush:** see DEAL 2.

2. A war; military service. In the phr. **the Big Stoush,** the war of 1914–18.

1901 *Tocsin* (Melbourne) 29 Aug. 1/1 'In South Africa I'll get my rations and a chance to pick up some boodle by stoush.'—Explanation vouchsafed by one contingenter who is going back. **1945** D. ROBINSON *Pop's Blonde* 79 Bill was an experienced housebreaker, having been 'inside' only three times since the finish of the 'Big Stoush'.

3. Special Comb. **stoush-artist,** an accomplished and habitual fighter (see ARTIST).

1932 J. MCCARTER *Pan's Clan* 133 Stoush-artists from other places . . come the proverbial gutzers in Longreach.

stoush /staʊʃ/, *v.* Also **stouch.** [f. prec.]

a. *trans.* To punch, strike, or thrash (a person). Also *fig.*

1893 J.A. BARRY *Steve Brown's Bunyip* 66 I'll get stoushed over this job yet. Brombee's got it in for me. **1904** *Truth* (Sydney) 15 May 7/2 'In the tenth year of the reign of Governor Macquarie', whom it was expected Bigge came out to 'stouch'. **1925** *Bulletin* (Sydney) 26 Feb. 22/1 We stoushed a cop at Bredbo who'd surprised us after six. **1982** R. HALL *Just Relations* 52 The two branches of Swans having a shot at one another, somebody forever getting stoushed.

b. *intr.* To fight; to struggle.

1909 *Truth* (Sydney) 16 May 12/4 Sisters stouch. Maria and Kate uncoil themselves in University Street. **1965** R.H. CONQUEST *Horses in Kitchen* 47 The fellow who invented Rafferty's Rules was a dinkum innocent compared with some of the gents who stoushed in hobo camps.

Hence **stouser** *n.*, a fighter; **stoushie** *n.*, a soldier; **stoushing** *vbl. n.*, fighting; beating.

1909 *Truth* (Sydney) 28 Feb. 3/8 A **stouser** stoushed. For assaulting Harold Weekly . . a weed of a young fellow named Albert Margetts was fined £2. **1941** *Action Front: Jrnl. 2/2 Field Regiment* Sept. 9 A real good bunch of **stoushies.** **1898** *Worker* (Sydney) 1 Jan. 7/1 The **stoushing** of the coppers by the push in particular.

stove, *v. trans.* To remove (a tree stump) by burning it in the ground: see quot. 1972. Also as *vbl. n.*

1897 L. LINDLEY-COWEN *W. Austral. Settler's Guide* 229 A plan . . has been adopted in South Gippsland, Victoria, for the last seven or eight years, of burning out or stoving trees or stumps, instead of grubbing. . . Other farmers about there told me it was only half the cost of grubbing to stove the stumps. **1972** K. SILLCOCK *Three Lifetimes* 33 'Stoving' . . was done by digging beside the stump and setting a roaring fire in the hole. . . When there was a good body of live coals the fire was covered over with sods of earth which allowed only a limited supply of air to enter. If this was tended every day or two . . the stump would smoulder for days as the fire followed and burned out all the main roots, finally consuming the aerial part of the stump or making it easy to remove to a heap.

straggler. [Spec. use of *straggler* an animal that strays from its habitat or companions.]

a. A stray or unbranded animal.

1846 S. DAVENPORT *Let.* 9 July in *S. Australiana* (1977) Sept. 157 The cattle had arrived in safety, a few stragglers only having escaped on the journey, which will work their way back to the Murray. **1944** *Bulletin* (Sydney) 26 July 12/3 When, years ago, I was backtracking stragglers, night often found me *minus* nap and tucker.

b. *spec.* A sheep which is overlooked when the flock is rounded up for shearing. Also **straggler sheep**.

[N.Z. **1860** G. DUPPA in S.S. Crawford *Sheep & Sheepmen Canterbury* (1949) 46 Complete dipping flock .. deliver stragglers.] **1897** *Worker* (Sydney) 11 Sept. 1/2 The sheep are 'jumbucks', 'woollies' have the fleece still on their back, And 'stragglers' are the last to come along the woolshed track. **1977** F.B. VICKERS *Stranger no Longer* 111 At the finish of the main run of shearing I went back over my tracks with two shearers .. to comb the Murchison .. for any straggler sheep a squatter might want shearing... We all vowed never to go straggler shearing again.

c. Special Comb. **straggler shearing**, see quot. 1898; also **stragglers' shearing**.

1898 *Bulletin* (Sydney) 17 Dec. 15/2 *Stragglers* are the sheep missed in the general shearing. They are mustered afterwards, and shorn at the second or *straggler-shearing*. **1959** H. LAMOND *Sheep Station* 42 Later .. they had a stragglers' shearing of something over thirty-two thousand!

straight, *a.* Used as an intensive in the collocation **straight goer**, an honest person. See also *straight dinkum* DINKUM C b. and c., *straight oil* OIL *n.* 2, and *straight wire* WIRE 1.

1899 *North-Western Advocate* (Devonport) 8 Feb. 2/6 Several years of experience in the produce trade, and is known as a 'straight goer'. **1953** 'CADDIE' *Caddie* 239 The Missus up at the pub told me about you... She recommended you to me; said you were a straight goer.

strain, *n.* The stretch of fencing wire between two strainers.

1930 D. COTTRELL *Earth Battle* 302 Many found the fence gaps and were through. Many more crashed in headlong flight against the uncut strains. **1978** *Jrnl. Agric. W.A.* 71 For ease of working strains of about 2 km. seem best, although up to 7 km. strains are satisfactory using plain wire.

strain, *v.* In the phr. **to strain the potatoes** (or **spuds**): of a male, to urinate.

1965 *Times Lit. Suppl.* (London) 16 Sept. 812/2 Among his many idiosyncrasies a desire to pass water at the most inopportune moments has become increasingly manifest... McKenzie employs a number of colourful and expressive Australianisms to describe this prosaic function; straining the potatoes [etc.]. **1982** P. BURGESS *Money to Burn* 114 Keep Ted's chair for him. He's only gone out to strain the spuds.

strainer. [Ellipt. form of *straining-post*: see OED *straining, vbl. n.* 6.] A strong post against which the wires of a fence are tightened; *fence strainer*, see FENCE *n.*¹ 1 a. Freq. as **strainer post**.

[N.Z. **1880** E.R. CHUDLEIGH *Diary* (1950) 289 Smith undertakes to cart my posts .. 5d. a post, strainers to count as three posts.] **1891** *Truth* (Sydney) 26 Apr. 7/3 Call that a fence! Look! Crooked as a ram's horn. Posts not rammed; strainers not big enough. **1981** *Practical Farm Fencing* 8 The strainer posts we found most effective were the single span using two 2.4 meter strainer posts and up to 3.0 meter stays.

'Stralia. Abbrev. of 'Australia'.

1955 F. LANE *Patrol to Kimberleys* 84 Course, there's only about nine million people in all of 'Stralia. **1973** H. LEWIS *Crow on Barbed Wire Fence* 5 'Like 'Stralia?' 'Very much,' I said and was glad I said it.

stranger.

1. An animal which has strayed from a neighbouring flock or herd. Also *attrib.*

1845 D. MACKENZIE *Emigrant's Guide* 132, I have never attended a muster .. without seeing several stray cattle (or *strangers*, as they are called) among every mob. **1955** J. CLEARY *Justin Bayard* 28 They had changed the brand on the stranger bullocks.

2. *Rock whiting*, see ROCK *n.* 2.

1873 F. DE CASTELNAU *Edible Fishes Vic.* 14 The *Stranger* (*Odax Richardsonii*) .. is very common in all seasons on the market. It is remarkable by its parrot-like beak and its colours, which are sometimes very beautiful. **1969** J. POLLARD *Austral. & N.Z. Fishing* 749 Stranger[:] Fish of the family Neoodaciidae, also known as weedy whiting or rock whiting.

strapped, *a.* Of trousers: having a strip of material inserted down the back of the leg (see quot. 1899, 2).

1895 *Worker* (Sydney) 29 June 4/1 One of those slight, active, little fellows whom we used to see in cabbage-tree hats, Crimean shirts, 'strapped' trousers, and 'lastic sided boots. **1899** *Bulletin* (Sydney) 25 Feb. (Red Page), 'How did that cove Tom's horse do?' asked the man in strapped pants. **1899** H. LAWSON *Autobiogr. & Other Writings* (1972) 39 Stockmen wore strapped trousers... Rip the side and 'tween-leg seams of a pair of pants, take the back out altogether and put a new one in of a different colour .. for riding.

strata, *pl.* [Pl. of *stratum* a layer.] Used *attrib.* to designate a system of registering ownership of strata of air space in multi-storey buildings, esp. in the Comb. **strata title** (see quot. 1971).

1961 *Act* (N.S.W.) no. 17 Sect. 2, 'Strata plan' means a plan which .. shows the whole or any part of the land comprised therein as being divided into two or more strata. **1971** CONRICK & THOMSON *Sale Real Property N.S.W.* 10 The Strata Titles Act enables land to be divided horizontally as well as by the traditional vertical division. It enables a party to hold ownership of a slice of airspace many feet above the ground, as distinct from ownership of the ground itself.

strawberry box. A cardboard container provided in aircraft, ships, etc., as a receptacle for vomit.

[N.Z. **1936** 'R. HYDE' *Passport to Hell* 93 The ship struck heavy weather... Up galley stairs and down corridors, life just one strawberry-box after another.] **1948** *Gremlin Jottings* (Canberra) May 4 Paper bags and cardboard 'strawberry boxes' are in frequent demand and use. **1965** G. MCINNES *Road to Gundagai* 35 All about us they were vomiting into 'strawberry boxes' while we raced up and down deck.

straw hat. A dandy. Also *attrib.* as **straw hat push**, the 'smart set', and **straw hatter**.

1902 *Truth* (Sydney) 30 Mar. 5/3 So-called 'respectably connected' persons of the class euphemistically known as 'the Straw Hat Push'. **1917** *Ibid.* 15 Apr. 9/4 Aspiring flappers and would-be straw-hatters .. are a type I used to bump whilst in the police. **1930** H. REDCLIFFE *Yellow Cygnet* 20 'There ain't much of the 'straw 'at''—a slang phrase for dandy—'about that nipper.'

straw-necked ibis. [From the yellow straw-like neck plumage of the bird.] The predom. black and white wading bird *Threskiornis spinicollis*, chiefly of mainland Aust.

1841 *Port Phillip Patriot* 9 Aug. 4/3 Thousands of straw-necked Ibises (*Ibis spinicollis*), and of other species of the feathered race, were performing their allotted parts. **1979** D. LOCKWOOD *My Old Mates & I* 76 Straw-necked ibis and pied geese came in hundreds to the watered playing fields of Darwin where they might find worms and grubs.

streak. [Used elsewhere but recorded earliest in Aust.: see OEDS *sb.*¹ 4 b.] A tall, thin person.

[**1937** E. PARTRIDGE *Dict. Slang & Unconventional Eng.* 838 *Streak*, a very thin person: mostly Australian and N.Z.]

1941 S.J. BAKER *Pop. Dict. Austral. Slang* 73 Streak, a tall, lean person. 1972 W. WATKINS *Don't wait for Me* 3 Arsey Arkin.. was a goof. A long streak.

strength. [Spec. use of *strength* the demonstrative force of an argument; chiefly Austral. and N.Z.]

1. With **of:** the point or meaning of; the truth about; STRONG 1.

[N.Z. 1906 *N.Z. Truth* (Wellington) 26 Aug. 5 Wants a friend to get the strength of things.] 1908 H. FLETCHER *Dads & Dan* 112 'So yous thinks I'se wore out.. an' past patchin' an' mendin'?' 'That's about ther strength uv it.' 1980 G. DUTTON *Wedge-Tailed Eagle* 93 What's the strength of this Nikolai?.. I mean, what sort of a bloke is he?

2. In the phr. **to get the strength of,** to comprehend; *to get the strong of,* see STRONG 2.

1904 H. FLETCHER *Dads Wayback* 34 About this forchin-tellin' game; it takes er bit o' knowin' ter get ther full strength of it. 1969 *Advertiser* (Adelaide) 12 May 5/4 Get the strength of this: You talk about bankos and trunks.

stretcher. [Transf. use of *stretcher* camp-bed, spec. in a military or hospital context: see OED(S *sb.* 9.] A (folding) bed, made of canvas, hessian, etc., on a frame: see quot. 1857. Also **stretcher-bed.**

1834 N.S.W. Magistrates' Deposition Bk. 29 Oct., I found fault with the Prisoner for using a Stretcher which I kept for the use of my guests—without Leave and gave him Permission to sleep in the Dairy. 1857 J. ASKEW *Voyage Aust. & N.Z.* 145 Here I first became acquainted with a 'stretcher', which is a very convenient kind of bed, made by nailing a piece of canvass to two pieces of wood, about six feet long and three inches square, these rest upon legs made in the form of the letter X, and are fastened at the crossings by an iron bolt, so as to allow them to separate as far as the canvass will permit. 1961 *Bulletin* (Sydney) 14 Oct. 30/2 The camp is an open-air job with stretcher-beds, trucks and refrigerators standing about under the sparse trees.

striated pardalote. The small bird *Pardalotus striatus* of all States, having a black crown sometimes streaked with white.

1844 J. GOULD *Birds of Aust.* (1848) II. Pl. 38 *Pardalotus striatus*.. Striated Pardalote. 1984 E. ROLLS *Celebration of Senses* 77 The little Striated Pardalote beats out its two notes astonishingly loudly.

strife. [Weakened use of *strife* contention, dispute.]

a. Trouble, disgrace, difficulty; conflict.

1931 'BRENT OF BIN BIN' *Back to Bool Bool* 320 Laleen does not want to come back here and make strife amongst her relatives. 1952 C. SIMPSON *Come away, Pearler* 223 You get a fair amount of strife in a place like this, but the pearlers aren't a bad bunch—three or four bad hats—you know. 1985 *Harden-Murrumburrah Express* 3 Oct. 15/4 First born child—I gave you life, Why do you cause me all this strife?

b. Esp. in the phr. **in(to) strife.**

1950 J. MORRISON *Port of Call* 174 It isn't good for a bloke to be on his own when he's in strife. 1986 *Canberra Times* 13 Feb. 1/4, I suggested.. that they complain to people higher up but they believed they would get into strife if they did that.

strike, *v.* [Fanciful varr. of *strike me blind, dumb, lucky,* etc.: see OED(S *strike, v.* 46 c.]

a. Used as a mild oath, esp. in the phr. **strike me blue (dead, fat, handsome, pink, roan).**

1916 'MEN OF ANZAC' *Anzac Bk.* 127 An' then—oh, strike me blue an' pink—Then don't the Turkies swear! 1932 J.J. HARDIE *Cattle Camp* (1944) 188 Strike me flamin' dead! I could write all he knows about cattle on a fly's eye with a lump of charcoal! [1891 strike me fat: 'SMILER' *Wanderings Simple Child* (ed. 3) 19 'Sailor Bill' was accorded the privilege of acting as taster, to see how the cooking was going on... At length the mariner declared that he'd be 'struck fat' if the 'Kake' wasn't just about ripe.] 1895 *Bulletin* (Sydney) 15/4 Lord strike me fat! what yer givin' us? 1955 N. PULLIAM *I traveled Lonely Land* 390 Strike me handsome.. an exclamation like our 'Well, for goodness sake', 'You don't say', etc. 1892 *Truth* (Sydney) 15 May 1/5 Strike me pink if I tell a lie. 1917 *All abaht It* (London) Feb. (1919) 12 Strike me rone.. I had to laugh. 1982 *Overlander* Sept. 27 Strike me roan! It's a heap faster than Sydney's transport.

b. In the phr. **strike a light:** see LIGHT *n.* 2.

c. As **strike (me)!** *ellipt.* of phr. in sense a. above.

1915 C.J. DENNIS *Songs of Sentimental Bloke* 57 O, strike! I could 'a' blubbed before 'em all! But I sat tight. 1954 *Coast to Coast 1953–54* 78 'Strike me', says Time-Table Tommy, 'things has changed all right and no mistake.'

strike camp. *Hist.* A camp formed by striking shearers; *union camp,* see UNION.

1891 *Great Qld. Strike* (United Pastoralists Assoc. Qld.) 14 During the present strike.. 'sundowners' are nowhere to be seen on the stations in Queensland... They are to be found in the strike camps, living on the strike funds. 1982 L. MATHER *First Notes of Drum* 42 Trouble broke out on Meteor Downs... The bushmen struck and formed a strike camp down on the creek, away from the homestead, from whence they could sit the dispute out and picket the shearing shed at the same time.

Strine /straɪn/, *a.* and *n.* [Repr. an alleged Austral. pronunc. of *Australian,* coined by A.A. Morrison (b. 1911) in 1964.]

A. *adj.* Australian.

1964 *Sydney Morning Herald* 19 Dec. 13/6 (*heading*) New light on the Strine language, by Afferbeck Lauder, Professor of Strine Studies, University of Sinny. 1983 *Weekend Austral.* (Sydney) 8 Oct. 3/7 The flowers are 'strine', with arrangements of banksia and bush flora.

B. *n.*

a. An Australian.

1964 *Sydney Morning Herald* 19 Dec. 13/5 Selected translations of everyday words.. will be of interest.. also to overseas vistas and to the many New Strines in our mist. 1965 *Oz* (Sydney) 17 June 1 (*heading*) The Strines they are a-changing.

b. Australian English; a stylized representation of Australian speech characterized by excessive assimilation, elision, metanalysis, etc.

1965 *Sydney Morning Herald* 6 Jan. 1/10 The first advertisement in pure Strine reached our 'classified' department yesterday. It advertised a 'gloria soame' of 14 squares, with amenities. 1983 M. FIELD *Oz Shrink Lit.* 76 Professor Afferbeck Lauder, That intrepid word-hoarder, With the guile of a dingo Shrink-litted our lingo, Made four syllables combine And christened it Strine.

Hence **strined** *ppl. a.,* Australianized.

1974 R. ROBINSON *Give it Bloody Go, Mate!* 74 'Can't you understand bloody English?' Well I thought I could, but when it was 'strined' like this it was a job.

string, *v.*[1] [Spec. use of *string* to move in a string.]

a. *intr.* Of a mob of sheep or cattle: to stretch out in a straggling line; to move as in a file. Also with **off** and **out,** and as *ppl. a.*

1876 J.A. EDWARDS *Gilbert Gogger* 144 A great number of the sheep had moved from off their camping ground, and were stringing away into the darkness of the bush. 1922 J. LEWIS *Fought & Won* 57 Although the cattle were lying down, we thought it well to be on the alert in case any of them should 'string off'. 1933 A.J. COTTON *With Big Herds in Aust.* 82 The two leading men take care not to close them in too much, otherwise they would walk too fast, and what is termed, 'string out'. 1938 BRIGGS & HARRIS *Joysticks &*

STRING 553 STRIPPER

Fiddlesticks 162 There is a circling mob of overlanding cattle, which .. break out into long, stringing flight.
b. *trans.* To cause (sheep or cattle) to move in a line. Also with **off** and **out**.
1920 J.N. MACINTYRE *White Aust.* 142 Two other members of the party .. were some distance away stringing the mob through the narrow gorge. **1950** I. SHACKCLOTH *Call of Kimberleys* 51 Stringing out the sheep to the water-holes occupied long wearysome hours. **1960** R.S. PORTEOUS *Cattleman* 88 They were stringing the cattle off the dinner camp when the policeman rode up.
Hence **string** *n.*, a line of sheep or cattle.
1931 F.D. DAVISON *Man-Shy* (1961) 24 The cattle, in little strings and squads, were grazing their way in towards the waterholes.

string, *v.*² [Spec. use of orig. U.S. slang *string* to fool, deceive: see OED(S *v.* 15.] *trans.* With **on**: to deceive (someone), to 'string along'.
[N.Z. **1881** A. BATHGATE *Waitaruna* 142 A barmaid .. makes herself agreeable to those who frequent the house, and so she 'strings them on' and induces them to spend their money there.] **1888** 'R. BOLDREWOOD' *Robbery under Arms* III. 81 Mr Hamilton waited for about an hour so as to be sure they weren't stringing him on to go into the open to be potted at. *c* **1907** W.C. CHANDLER *Darkest Adelaide* 1, *Don't worry!* On all Private Complaints, *male* and *female*, Consult *free* the Successful Practitioner, *Prof. A. Mills* who will Guarantee a cure in each case he undertakes. No stringing on, but a Speedy Cure always.

stringy.
1. Abbrev. of STRINGYBARK 1. Also *attrib.*
1901 *Bulletin* (Sydney) 7 Dec. 20/3 It was a small, two-roomed, stringy shanty, built near the foot-track. **1945** *Coast to Coast 1944* 144 The low scrub and fringing bloodwoods and stringies melted into the night.
2. *Obs.* Used *attrib.* in the sense of STRINGYBARK 2.
1845 *Star* (Sydney) 25 Oct. 1/2 Then they shouted—'Braveo Billy! You're a right good, proper mark; There's no stringy stuff about you, You're the real iron-bark.'
3. *Obs.* Abbrev. of STRINGYBARK 3.
1871 *Austral. Town & Country Jrnl.* (Sydney) 1 Apr. 389/3 Its [*sic*] not everybody that does care about 'stringy', whether it be the real Tooth's, or Castlemine, or Parramatta, or even the renowned 'wallop' of the Western line... I well remember a governor of Victoria regaling his guests at the Queen's Birth-night ball, with 'Murphy's entire', the stringy of his colony. **1899** 'T. BLUEGUM' *Backblocks' Parson* 172 In the centre of the building was situated a public bar, furnished with strong liquors answering to the euphemisms, 'Stringy', 'Shandy', 'Tanglefoot', etc.

stringybark.
1. [See quot. 1904.] Any of many trees, chiefly of s.e. mainland Aust., of the genus *Eucalyptus* (fam. Myrtaceae) having a characteristically thick, rough, persistent, long-fibred bark; the bark or wood of the tree. Also with distinguishing epithet, as **red, swamp, white, yellow** (see under first element). Also *attrib.*, esp. as **stringybark tree**.
1799 D. COLLINS *Acct. Eng. Colony N.S.W.* (1802) II. 238 The remains of a canoe made of the stringy bark were lying upon the shore. **1904** J.H. MAIDEN *Notes on Commercial Timbers N.S.W.* 10 The term 'Stringybark' is applied to trees having thick, fibrous bark—bark which is comparatively loose in texture, and which (for a Eucalyptus bark) possesses considerable tenacity. **1928** M.E. FULLERTON *Austral. Bush* 108 String-bark (the outer covering of the stringybark-tree) was a great friend to the early-day settler. Of it he built his bush house, roof and walls.
2. Used allusively as an emblem of the unsophisticated, the remote, and the rustic. Freq. *attrib.*, passing into *adj.*

1833 *N.S.W. Mag.* (Sydney) I. 171 The workmanship of which I beg you will not scrutinize, as I am but, to use a colonial expression, '*a stringy-bark carpenter*'. **1845** *Bell's Life in Sydney* 18 Jan. 2/1 The 'stringy bark' cove, sooner than not have a turn-up with this Liverpool 'Achilles', would fight him for 'love'. **1861** H. EARLE *Ups & Downs* 59 She would never have had the bad taste to prefer a stringy bark like me to such a fine-looking, first-class fellow as yourself.
3. Beer, esp. of poor quality.
1848 *Bell's Life in Sydney* 13 May 2/3 The Drunkards' Sheet at the Police-office on Monday numbered forty male and female sacrificants to hard stuff, stringy bark, and gin and bitterness. **1874** *Illustr. Sydney News* 22 Aug. 10/1 Tattoed dames .. hobbled unsteadily to Johnny Ward's for the inevitable pint of 'stringy-bark'.
4. Comb. **stringybark forest, range, slab**.
1837 H. WATSON *Lecture on S.A.* (1838) 19, I rode to the **stringy-bark forest**. **1841** *S. Austral. Mag.* July 9 Our **stringy bark ranges**, which are considered the most barren land we have, would answer excellently [*sc.* as land for vineyards] when cleared. **1838** T. WALKER *Month in Bush Aust.* 6 The offices are .. mostly built of stone or brick .. not made of the uncouth, rough **stringy-bark slabs**, of which such buildings are usually made in the colony.
5. Special Comb. **stringybark beef**, tough beef; **cockatoo, settler**, a farmer of small means; **squatter**, see quot.
1848 *Bell's Life in Sydney* 19 Aug. 2/4 Beating up for recruits among the voters of those shady and sequestered regions so dear to the devotees of blady-grass, pork, and **stringy bark beef**. **1905** A.B. PATERSON *Old Bush Songs* 45 The old cocky, he grew jealous, and he thumped me black and blue, And he drove me off without a rap—the **stringybark cockatoo**. **1836** 'W. R-s' *Fell Tyrant* 46 Poorest of all is the **stringybark settler**. **1862** C. MUNRO *Fern Vale* I. 47 One or two settlers of minor importance, and dignified with the title of '**stringy bark**' or 'cockatoo **squatters**'.

striped honeyeater. The honeyeater *Plectorhyncha lanceolata* of inland e. mainland Aust.
1898 E.E. MORRIS *Austral Eng.* 199 Striped H[oneyeater]—*Plectorhyncha lanceolata*. **1976** *Reader's Digest Compl. Bk. Austral. Birds* 462 The striped honeyeater .. has a generally streaked appearance, with .. long and spiky feathers on the throat and upper breast.

stripey. Pl. **stripeys, stripies**. Any of several (usu. horizontally) striped marine fish, incl. *Latris lineata* (see TRUMPETER *n.*¹ 1), *Microcanthus strigatus* of s.w., n., and e. Aust. and the skipjack tuna, *Katsuwonus pelamis*.
1924 LORD & SCOTT *Synopsis Vertebrate Animals Tas.* 71 The Real or Tasmanian Trumpeter, .. is often referred to as the 'Stripey'. **1978** N. COLEMAN *Austral. Fisherman's Fish Guide* 125 A common resident of tropical coral reefs, the 'stripey' is mostly encountered in schools. **1980** — *Austral. Sea Fishes* 180 Stripeys swim in small, closely compacted schools... These fish are easy to keep in aquaria. **1986** *Canberra Chron.* 29 Jan. 19/2 The stripies are around but mostly staying well out, beyond the Four Mile.

stripper. [Spec. use of *stripper* a machine for stripping.]
1. A machine used to harvest grain: see quot. 1927.
1867 *Official Rec. Intercolonial Exhib. Australasia* 381 The Jurors award *medals* to the Wind Engine and Stripper, and *honourable mention* to Thresher and Smut Machines. **1927** T.S. GROSER *Lure of Golden West* 144 The stripper is an enormous box-like machine, with spiked prongs or teeth projecting in front, which, drawn through the cornfield, pluck the ears from the stalks.
2. Special Comb. **stripper harvester**, a machine which harvests grain and frees it of chaff: see quot. 1979.
1891 *Australasian Ironmonger* Oct. 329 Stripper-harvester

improvements... A revolving screen or separator arranged within the body or housing of a stripper-harvester or winnower, for separating the grain from chaff and unthreshed heads.   **1979** J. BIRMINGHAM et al. *Austral. Pioneer Technol.* 27 James Martin had already tried unsuccessfully to combine the stripper and winnower in one mobile machine. This was achieved by H.V. McKay in 1885, and in 1887 his new 'stripper-harvester' won a government prize for a reaping machine.

stroke. [Spec. use of *stroke* an amount of work: see OED *sb.*[1] 11.]

1. *Gold-mining*. In the phr. **to do a (good, great, fair) stroke,** to mine profitably.

1851 *Empire* (Sydney) 22 Oct. 282/6 The Wallaby is again getting into favour; and Pattison's Point, between the last named spot and the sheep station, has a few on it doing 'a great stroke'.   **1852** *Ibid.* 23 Jan. 602/4 Washing tailings on the rich points is becoming very common, and many do a fair stroke at it.   **1853** R.M. THOMAS *Present State Melbourne* 34 We have occasionally of large nuggets being found, of men doing what is called '*the good stroke*', or '*taking the trick*'—fortunes being made in a very short time.   **1883** G.E. LOYAU *Personal Adventures* 16 Miners who had 'done a stroke', and whose claims were still being worked by their mates, came by.

2. In the collocation **government stroke**: see GOVERNMENT B. 4.

strong.

1. With *of*: STRENGTH 1.

1915 DREW & EVANS *Grafter* 54 'Hello, Grafter!'.. 'What's the strong of this? I thought you were fielding on the Outer?'   **1983** B. DAWE *Over Here, Harv!* 118 H-hey fellers... What's the strong of this—empty glasses? C'mon it's my shout. What're we having?

2. In the phr. **to get the strong of,** *to get the strength of*, see STRENGTH 2.

[N.Z. **1917** *Chrons. N.Z. Exped. Force* 19 Sept. 63 We sees a new stunt goin' on . . 'n we just halts for a second to get the strong of it.]   **1923** C.E. SAYERS *Jumping Double* 50 Until you get the strong of the horse.   **1970** R. BEILBY *No Medals for Aphrodite* 268 'Is that all you're worrying about?' Harry sounded incredulous. 'You know, I'll never get the strong of you.'

strong-billed honeyeater. The honeyeater *Melithreptus validirostris* of Tasmania and adjacent islands.

1845 J. GOULD *Birds of Aust.* (1848) IV. Pl. 70, *Melithreptus validirostris* . . Strong-billed Honey-eater.   **1903** *Emu* II. 207 *Melithreptus validirostris* (Strong-billed Honey-eater)—This powerfully built bird is ever on the move.   **1976** *Reader's Digest Compl. Bk. Austral. Birds* 490 The strong-billed honeyeater finds larval and adult insects by prizing bark off trees with its stout bill.

strongfish. The greyish marine fish *Dactylophora nigricans* of s. Aust.; TILLYWURTI.

1924 LORD & SCOTT *Synopsis Vertebrate Animals Tas.* 70 Butter fish (of Tasmania) .. is known in New South Wales as the Dusky Morwong, and in South Australia as the Strong Fish or Tillywurti.   **1980** N. COLEMAN *Austral. Sea Fishes* 217 Dusky morwong, strongfish . . *Dactylophora nigricans*.

Stuart's bean tree. [f. the name of the explorer John McDouall *Stuart* (1815-1866) + BEAN TREE.] The deciduous tree *Erythrina vespertilio* (fam. Fabaceae) of n. Aust., having a corky bark and red pea-flowers. See also BEAN TREE.

1873 W.C. GOSSE *Rep. & Diary Central & Western Exped.* (1974) 3 Country still sandy, but not so thickly timbered. Noticed some fine specimens of Stuart's bean-tree.   **1955** DEAN & CARELL *Dust for Dancers* 123 The natives call the bean tree Yinendi . . and it is sometimes known among Europeans as Stuart's Bean Tree. Its colourful red berries are not edible.

stubble quail. [See quot. 1846.] The bird *Coturnix pectoralis*, chiefly of s. Aust., having predom. grey-brown plumage with pale and dark streaks.

1846 J. GOULD *Birds of Aust.* (1848) V. Pl. 88, The chief food of this species is grain, seeds and insects, the grain as a matter of course being only procured in cultivated districts; and hence the name of Stubble Quail has been given to it by the colonists of Van Diemen's Land, from the great numbers that visit the fields after the harvest is over.   **1980** *Ecos* xxvi. 29/2 There is a case for postponing the opening of the season for shooting stubble quail in Victoria and South Australia.

stubby.

1. **a.** A short, squat beer bottle, esp. one with a capacity of 375 ml.; the contents of such a bottle. See also *Darwin stubby* DARWIN. Also **stubby bottle.**

1966 J. IGGULDEN *Summer's Tales* 123 Drinking beer from small, cold stubbies.   **1984** *Canberra Times* 11 Apr. 14/9, I killed a gin at Mount Isa in September. I don't feel sorry for them. I carved her up about the neck with a stubby bottle.

b. Special Comb. **stubby cooler, holder,** a casing made of an insulating material, in which a stubby is held while the contents are being drunk.

1984 *Tourist: Ansett Airlines Mag.* Jan. 11 An Oz flag or that even more patriotic emblem, a folding **stubby cooler.**   **1981** *Woman's Day* (Sydney) 9 Sept. 45/3 When we arrived to visit our son and daughter-in-law after a long trip, our son offered his father a stubby bottle of beer and his wife produced a **stubby holder,** saying, 'Here, Dad, put your beer in this.' And that is what he did—literally. Then he yelled, 'How silly can you get! This so-and-so thing has holes in it.'

2. *pl.* The proprietary name of a brand of shorts.

1973 *Austral. Official Jrnl. Patents* (Canberra) 3602, A263,605... Class 25. Goods: outer wear. Stubbies.   **1986** *Bulletin* (Sydney) 22 Apr. 30/1 Men in Stubbies and heavy boots fell about laughing at the notion that a scribe might actually get his soft, white hands dirty.

stub fence. See quot. 1901. Also **stub wall.**

1882 ARMSTRONG & CAMPBELL *Austral. Sheep Husbandry* 179 A stake fence (by some erroneously called stub) may be erected.   **1901** W.G. ACOCKS *Settlers' Synopsis Land Laws N.S.W.* 116 Schedule of classes of fencing usually prescribed by local land boards... A 'drop' or 'stub' fence, not less than four feet in height, composed of saplings or split rails not more than ten feet in length .. held between two posts or uprights of split or barked round timber .. and tied firmly at the tops with wire of not less than No. 8 gauge.   **1911** *Bulletin* (Sydney) 30 Mar. 44/2 Here and there stub walls have been built as partial protection.

stud.

1. An Aboriginal woman as the source of a white man's sexual gratification. Also **stud gin.**

1929 K.S. PRICHARD *Coonardoo* (1961) 46 'No stud gins for mine—no matter what happens,' he swore.   **1981** NGABIDJ & SHAW *My Country of Pelican Dreaming* 45 Billy Weaber helped another bloke put a station there... My sister came with me to be his stud.

2. Special Comb. **stud book** *N.T.*, a nickname for the register of wards of the State.

1960 *N.T. News* (Darwin) 15 Jan. 9/3 Lucky that Bobby Daly Waters' name is not in the Register of Wards—widely known in the Territory as 'The Stud Book'.

stud fence. [f. *stud* a wooden post of any kind.] See quot. 1928.

1918 *Bulletin* (Sydney) 21 Feb. 22/2 The alleged new fence .. is a 'stud fence' in the bush glossary. The studs of course are the rails.   **1928** C.E. COWLEY *Classing Clip* 159

The most satisfactory yards are those built of posts and rails, or what is commonly known as a 'stud' fence; that is, made of saplings—one resting upon the end of the one in the previous panel, and so on.

stud gin: see STUD 1.

stumer /'stjumə, 'stumə/. *Obs.* Also **stoomer**. [Prob. transf. use of Br. slang *stumer* a forged or dishonoured cheque: see OED(S.).] One who is penniless. In the phr. **to come a stumer,** to lose one's money. See also STOOM.
   1898 *Bulletin* (Sydney) 17 Dec. (Red Page), A *stoomer* or *stumer* is a man without money. **1941** S.J. BAKER *Pop. Dict. Austral. Slang* 73 *Stumer*, (in gambling or racing) a bankrupt, a defaulter... *Come a stumer*, to crash financially, esp. in a racing bet.

stump.
   1. A pile supporting a dwelling; esp. in Qld. (see quot. 1959). Also *attrib*.
   1910 *Huon Times* (Franklin) 13 July 4/3 Police found the traces of a man having stood on one of the stumps on which the building is built. **1951** P. MAYES *Austral. Architects Price Bk. & Guide* (ed. 11) 47 Add stump caps (24 Gauge Galv. Iron). **1959** E. DARK *Lantana Lane* 42 In these parts most houses stand up on stumps high enough to provide room beneath the floorboards for innumerable things, including, of course, the family's motor vehicle.
   2. Used *attrib*. in Special Comb. **stump-grubbing** *vbl. n.*, the removal, by manual or mechanical means, of the stumps of felled trees; also *attrib*.; **hole,** the hole left when a stump has been removed, esp. by fire; -**jump** *a.*, used to designate a machine designed to operate on land from which the tree stumps have not been cleared, esp. as **stump-jump plough** (see quot. 1962); also *absol*. as *n.*, and **stump-jumping** *ppl. a.*; -**picking** *vbl. n., stump-grubbing*; also as *pr. pple.*
   1896 *Bulletin* (Sydney) 4 Apr. 25/2, I would prefer a man that knows something about **stump-grubbing**. **1908** *Ibid.* 15 Oct. 15/2 One of the largest stump-grubbing contests on record has just been completed in S. Aus. A new stock route..has been cleared..mostly through dense mallee scrub, for a distance of 150 miles. **1827** P. CUNNINGHAM *Two Yrs. in N.S.W.* II. 174 It is long before grasses grow upon the places out of which stumps have been burnt... But it is astonishing to observe what a height of richness wheat will attain on these spots, every **stump-hole** being easily reckoned in a field of wheat from this great luxuriance alone. **1882** [**stump-jump**] *SAPD* 2nd Sess. 5 Sept. 565 Bonus to Mr R.B. Smith for his invention of the stump-jumping plough, £500. **1886** N. ROBINSON *Stagg of Tarcowie* 14 May (1977) 67, I was ploughing today with the stumpjump, or more properly it should be called a stonejumper because it is very little better than any plough among roots, but a great deal better among stones. **1960** *Bulletin* (Sydney) 8 June 18/2 The stump-jump harrow.. was another asset to mallee-country development. **1962** O. PRYOR *Aust.'s Little Cornwall* 180 Stump-jump ploughs had been invented by R.B. Smith, in 1876, and others, and had shares that were carried on hinged arms which would ride safely over the immovable stumps and then dig themselves into the ground again. **1926** *Bulletin* (Sydney) 25 Feb. 24/1 The dormouse opossum is not as rare as correspondents seem to believe. While in Parilla (S.A.) **stump-picking**, or 'emu-bobbing' as the old hands termed it, I came across several of the little chaps. **1932** J. TRURAN *Green Mallee* 120 Rafe Burtonwood finished his ploughing and stump-picking on Hoffmeyer's wilderness-block.

stump-jumper.
   1. *Stump-jump plough*, see STUMP 2.
   1882 R. SHAPLAND *Stump-Jumping Plough* 2 It cannot be disputed that the principle of the Stump-jumper was in use for many years before Mr Smith, Mr Shapland, or Mr Branson came before the public as inventors. **1902** *Bulletin* (Sydney) 8 Feb. 3/2 Much of the mallee.. was originally cleared and grubbed before the 'stump-jumper' came into use.
   2. *transf.* and *fig.* See quot.
   1985 *Sydney Morning Herald* 7 Dec. 47/3 He now hopes he has added a new definition, 'stump-jumper: a self-made, resilient Australian achiever of vision', to our national identity.

stump lizard. *Obs.* BOBTAIL.
   1861 'OLD BUSHMAN' *Bush Wanderings* 136 If by chance a snake or stump-lizard shows a head, a congregation of miners will soon gather round it. **1896** F.G. AFLALO *Sketch Nat. Hist. Aust.* 178 The Stump Lizard (*Trachysaurus rugosus*) is .. hideous and inoffensive.

stumpy. Abbrev. of STUMPY TAIL.
   1933 *Bulletin* (Sydney) 31 May 21/2 One fox would probably do more harm..than a thousand 'stumpies'. **1967** R. HAWKER *Emu in Fowl Pen* 115 Out in the paddock there were stumpy-tailed lizards... The stumpies were the ones found run over on the main road, where they had not reckoned on passing traffic.

stumpy tail. BOBTAIL. Also **stump** (or **stumpy**)-**tailed lizard.**
   1914 *Emu* XIV. 83 We witnessed a fight between two stump-tailed lizards (*Trachydosaurus rugosus*). **1925** *Bulletin* (Sydney) 18 June 24/1 The lizard is very much like the common stumpy-tail, but its scales are finer and the tail is more pointed. **1934** T. WOOD *Cobbers* 140 The stumpy-tailed lizard hid in shady patches of sand among the roots.

stung, *ppl. a.* [Prob. formed on STING *n.* 1.] Drunk. Also with **up.**
   1913 *Bulletin* (Sydney) 25 Sept. 22/2 Me for 'Inebriated'.... In the number, aptness and variety of its colloquial equivalents I consider it commandeers the pastry. For instance .. ripe, rolling, paralytic, stung [etc.]. **1981** A. WELLER *Day of Dog* 49 Pretty Boy, Doug and Micky drink three bottles of green ginger wine... Afterwards half stung up, they decide to catch a taxi.

sturks, var. STERKS.

Sturt. [f. the name of Charles *Sturt* (1795–1869), explorer.] In special collocations: **Sturt's desert pea,** the annual or perennial herb *Clianthus formosus* (fam. Fabaceae) of sandy soils in arid parts of all States except Vic. and Tas.; the pea-like flower of this plant, usu. bright red with a shiny black boss, the floral emblem of S.A.; *desert pea*, see DESERT; also **Sturt (desert) pea; Sturt's desert rose,** the shrub of arid central Aust. *Gossypium sturtianum* var. *sturtianum* (fam. Malvaceae); the large flower of this plant, usu. mauve and with a dark red basal spot, the floral emblem of the N.T.; *desert rose*, see DESERT; **Sturt's (terrible) rite** *obs.*, subincision (see WHISTLECOCK *a.*).
   1862 C. ASPINALL *Three Yrs. Melbourne* 165 The most beautiful flower which I saw in Australia was the Clianthus Dampiera, or Captain **Sturt's desert pea. 1898** *Bulletin* (Sydney) 26 Nov. 3/2 Oh, the new-made grave-mound, and the scarlet Sturt-pea wreath! **1985** *Woman's Day* (Sydney) 1 July 20/2 Jack helped raise money by selling bunches of Sturt desert peas to transcontinental train passengers. **1904** *Proc. Linnean Soc. N.S.W.* XXIX. 137 *Gossypium sturtii* .. the 'native cotton' or, as it is sometimes called, '**Sturt's desert rose**'. **1895** *Trans. & Proc. R. Soc. S.A.* (1896) 249 All the aborigines of the interior circumcise, and also slit the urethra. [*Note*] This mutilation is by different writers variously alluded to as the 'terrible rite', the 'mika operation' or '**Sturt's rite**'. **1901** *Brisbane Courier* 19 July 7/4 He speaks emphatically of the practice in vogue of performing what is

known as 'Sturt's terrible rite' on the young of both sexes by the elders of the tribe. By this means the increase of the population is most seriously affected, and the prevalence of the practice he largely ascribes to the difficulty they experience in finding food.

stu-vac /'stju-væk/. [f. abbrev. of *stu(dent* + *vac(ation.*] In a university, college, etc.: the period between the end of classes and the beginning of examinations.
1970 E. & D. CAMPBELL *Demonstrator* 29 Did the university get sick of you or is this another of those long stu-vacs?

sub. [Abbrev. of *subterranean clover.*] In the phr. **sub and super,** applied to the sowing of subterranean clover with superphosphate as a means of establishing or improving pasture.
1977 *Ecos* xii. 6/2 Sowing 'sub and super' brought large areas of southern Australia into more-intensive use... Even the 'sub and super' formula didn't work on all land, especially on the more-sandy soils. 1986 *Austral. Garden Jrnl.* Aug. 230 The pastures were soon invaded by weeds, most of them from the Mediterranean and South Africa. Later, the now degraded pastures were made productive by the sub-and-super revolution, using introduced pasture grasses.

sub-artesian, *a.* [Used elsewhere but of local importance.]
1. Of a bore or water in an artesian basin: see quot. 1965.
1927 M. DORNEY *Adventurous Honeymoon* 31 There is much contention about the word 'sub-artesian'. Out in the back country all water that does not rise to the surface is referred to as sub-artesian although, I believe, that any water which, when it is tapped, rises above its original level, is really artesian. 1965 *Austral. Encycl.* I. 262 If the pressure is such that water is forced up above the ground surface the bore is said to be artesian; if the water rises, but to a point below the surface, it is said to be sub-artesian.
2. Comb. **sub-artesian bore, water.**
1926 A.A.B. APSLEY *Amateur Settlers* 132 Examine one of the **sub-artesian bores.** 1925 M. TERRY *Across Unknown Aust.* 135 The **sub-artesian water**.. was all right for drinking purposes.

subbie, var. SUBBY.

sub-bore. Shortened form of *sub-artesian bore* (see SUB-ARTESIAN 2).
1956 B.J. RAYMENT *My Towri* 60 Although I had worked in many wells, I knew very little about sub-bores.

subby. Also **subbie.** [f. *sub(-contractor* + -Y.] A sub-contractor.
1978 *Sun-Herald* (Sydney) 4 June 21/1 Most owner-drivers or subcontractors, as they are known in the business have to overload if they want to make ends meet. For the independent 'subbie' a couple of extra tonnes over the legal limit is often the only thing separating a profitable run from a straight-out loss. 1985 J. SCHULTZ *Steel City Blues* 108 I'm building a house... I've done it all myself—well, I've got in a few subbies.

subterranean orchid: see UNDERGROUND ORCHID.

suburban swagman: see SWAGMAN b.

suck, $n.^1$ [Prob. Br. dial. var. of SOAK.] SOAK.
1857 *Adelaide Times* 2 Nov., Two small land sucks. 1974 J. BYRNE *Duck Hunting Aust. & N.Z.* 36 If the sun is hot, the presence of the seepage water, or 'sucks' as they are called, shows up only as a dampish spot on the sand in daytime.

suck, $n.^2$ In the phr. **fair suck of the sauce bottle:** see FAIR $a.^1$ 3 a.

sucker, *v.:* see SUCKER-BASH.

sucker, *n.* [Spec. use of *sucker* a shoot arising from the base of a plant, esp. from the underground root; a lateral shoot.] Esp. of eucalypts: see quot. 1903.
1903 *Proc. Linnean Soc. N.S.W.* XXVII. 566 The term 'sucker' is strictly confined in botany to young plants formed on underground rootstocks, while in Australia the same term is popularly applied to adventitious growths on various parts of the stem or branches caused chiefly by that particular part of the tree being either cut or bruised. 1973 C.E. GOODE *Stories Strange Places* 127 The Easternstater saw this chap in town one afternoon, and took him home to clear a field of mallee suckers.

sucker-bash, *v. intr.* To cut down suckers or new growth on newly-cleared land: see quots. 1945 and 1981. Freq. as *vbl. n.*, and *ellipt.* as **sucker** (see quot. 1942).
1942 *Bulletin* (Sydney) 1 July 12/4 Sucker bashing is a costly business, especially when the country has to be gone over a couple of times. Box and broad-leaf ironbark are the worst timbers to sucker. 1945 J.A. ALLAN *Men & Manners* 89 The settlers had cut the scrub a foot above the ground, piled the refuse round the stumps, and fired it as the new shoots appeared. Even after that, 'sucker-bashing'.. had still been needed. 1981 L. MCLEAN *Pumpkin Pie* 88 Dad said he might be able to get him a job 'sucker-bashing', a term used [*sic*] to knock new shoots off ring-barked trees.
Hence **sucker-basher** *n.*
1966 C. MCGREGOR *Profile Aust.* 297 They are the 'abos' most Australians know, living in tin humpies next to the town rubbish tip, scrounging drinks around the pub, working as pea-pickers, suckerbashers, ring-barkers and casual labourers.

suckhole. A sycophant. Also as *adj.*, sycophantic.
1943 D. FRIEND *Gunner's Diary* 37 Rank exhibitionism, of course (gipped up with the 'suckhole' motive). *Ibid.* 53 These sub-sections organise themselves to be bound by strong unwritten laws, and abide by them; thus in the troop, such-and-such a tent (*not* any of the six or eight inhabitants individually) is regarded as being good, bad, 'suckholes' or 'loafers', as the tribal dialect translates it.
Hence as *v. intr.*, to toady.
1969 F.B. VICKERS *No Man is Himself* 72, 'I know yous, yous bastard. You'll suckhole to him. Give it to him straight,' he shouted. *Ibid.* 112 I've had this suckholin' to get a job. Me an' Ted have tried hard.

suffer, *v.* In the phr. **to suffer a recovery:** see RECOVERY.

sugar.
1. Used *attrib.* in Comb. which have a local significance but may not be excl. Austral., as **sugar district, experiment station, farm, farmer, -farming, field, land, -lander.**
1880 J. BONWICK *Resources Qld.* 73 The marvellous extent of sugar lands.. places Queensland at a great advantage. 1886 F.A. HAGENAUER *Rep. Aboriginal Mission Ramahyuck, Vic.* 36 The plantations or sugar fields are smaller or larger tracts of the richest land. 1903 *Truth* (Sydney) 6 Dec. 1/7 There is no possibility of plutocratic slave-owners in the sugar districts getting supplies of fresh niggers. 1930 V. PALMER *Passage* (1957) 64 Got a chance to buy into a sugar-farm with his brother. 1938 F. CLUNE *Free & Easy Land* 172 For years Sugarlanders have advocated the production of power alcohol from molasses. 1946 *Bulletin* (Sydney) 10 Apr. 15/2 We were loafing.. past the sugar-

experiment station near Mackay (N.Q.). *c* 1960 C. MACKNESS *Clump Point & District* 29 They also burned coral for lime which they transported by boat to South Johnstone, for sale to sugar-farmers. *Ibid.* 80 The Government had opened it up in 1924 as a sugar farming soldier settlement.

2. Special Comb. **sugar beer**, a beer which is brewed using sugar instead of malt; also *attrib.*; **cocky**, *cane cocky*, see CANE 2; **doodle**, a tumble; a somersault; **mat**, SUGAR BAG 2 a.; **-squeezer**, one who is employed in the processing of sugar cane.

1831 *Sydney Monitor* 17 Sept. 2/2 The **sugar beer** sells as fast as it can be made, whereas the malt beer, *not being so sweet*, is not half so well relished, especially by the native-born. **1924** H.E. RIEMANN *Nor'-West o' West* 111 Billy Pollock was cook and sugar-beer brewer of Mollyanna sheep station. **1909** *Bulletin* (Sydney) 6 May 14/3 That **sugar-cocky**-fellow .. told me I would find a cane knife outside. **1904** L.M.P. ARCHER *Bush Honeymoon* 9 'By George! he'll get a **sugar doodle** out of that van,' says Fred. **1848** *Sydney Daily Advertiser* 1 Sept. 2/4 Obstructing the footway in the narrow part of King-street, by leaving a quantity of **sugar mats** upon it. **1903** *Bulletin* (Sydney) 6 June 16/4 Charles Kingston's visit to this piebald land upset all calculations. The **sugar-squeezers** and the huge C.S.R. monopoly were aghast at his splendid reception.

3. In the names of flora and fauna: **sugar ant**, any of several stingless ants of the genus *Camponotus*, as the common *C. nigriceps*, having an orange thorax and legs and black head; **glider**, the gliding possum *Petaurus breviceps* of n. and e. Aust. incl. Tas., and New Guinea; see also *sugar squirrel*; **grass**, the tufted perennial grass *Eulalia fulva* (fam. Poaceae), palatable to stock, of mainland Aust. and parts of s.e. Asia; **gum**, any of several trees of the fam. Myrtaceae, esp. *Eucalyptus cladocalyx* of s. S.A. incl. Kangaroo Island, widely planted as a windbreak (see quot. 1889); **squirrel**, (or **possum**), any of several arboreal marsupials, esp. the *sugar glider* and the similar, larger *squirrel glider* (see SQUIRREL 2).

1861 'OLD BUSHMAN' *Bush Wanderings* 208 Ants of every variety and size, from the little **sugar-ant** up to the great red soldier-ant. **1941** E. TROUGHTON *Furred Animals Aust.* 95 '**Sugar Glider**' is now adopted as being brief and suitable for popular use, reflecting the captive's love of sugar derived from the blossom-eating habit, as well as the volplaning ability due to the presence of gliding membranes between the limbs. **1889** J.H. MAIDEN *Useful Native Plants Aust.* 106 *Pollinia fulva* .. the '**Sugar Grass**' of colonists, so called on account of its sweetness; it is highly productive, and praised by stockowners. **1888** *Proc. Linnean Soc. N.S.W.* III. 509 *Eucalyptus gunnii*... In Tasmania this is known as 'Cider Gum', and in South-Eastern Australia occasionally as the '**Sugar Gum**'. **1889** J.H. MAIDEN *Useful Native Plants Aust.* 442 *Eucalyptus corynocalyx*.. (Syn., *E. cladocalyx*)... Sometimes called 'Sugar Gum', on account of its sweetish foliage, which attracts cattle and sheep. **1846** *Portland Guardian* 22 Sept. 4/2 At Port Essington opossums [*sic*] and **sugar squirrels** (*Petaurus sciures* [*sic*]) had been very numerous according to Captain Macarthur, but had now almost disappeared. **1919** *Bulletin* (Sydney) 31 July 20/2 South Coast (N.S.W.) sleeper-cutters come upon the big black, or 'magpie', squirrel occasionally in felling tall stringy-bark or box-trees... The fur is .. not nearly so fine as that of the little grey sugar-squirrel. **1921** *Ibid.* 13 Jan. 20/3 The sugar-'possum, being no larger than a mouse, is hard to find.

sugar bag. Also **choogar bag** (only in sense 1). [Spec. use of *sugar bag* a bag for containing sugar.]

1. *Austral. pidgin.* **a.** The honey of the wild bee; its honeycomb or hive. **b.** *transf.* A bee of any kind; the honey of such a bee. See also quot. 1985. Also *attrib.*

1830 R. DAWSON *Present State Aust.* 136 The strange native pointed with his tomahawk to the tree and .. repeated the words, 'Choogar-bag, choogar-bag, choogar-bag!' (sugar-bag) their English expression for honey or anything sweet. **1881** A.C. GRANT *Bush-Life Qld.* I. 67 The regular sharp chop-chop of the tomahawks could be heard here and there, where some of them [*sc.* Aborigines] had discovered a sugar-bag .. on a tree. [*Note*] A nest of honey. **1935** T. RAYMENT *Cluster of Bees* 513 With the advent of the white man, the more comprehensive term, 'Sugar-bag' was used by the blacks for all species of social bees. **1964** B. CRUMP *Gulf* 124 String that had been waterproofed with the black wax from the hives of the small stingless sugar-bag-bees. **1985** B. ROSSER *Dreamtime Nightmares* 69 'She used to get sugarbags.' 'Sugarbags?' 'Honey ants.'

2. a. A bag of fine sacking made for containing sugar; such a bag as used subsequently for a variety of purposes. Also *attrib.*

1850 *Bell's Life in Sydney* 9 Nov. 1/2 Boots, scraps of paper, torn rags, old sugar-bags, and other useless refuse. **1958** *Overland* 12/7 For a pillow, a sugar bag, stuffed with feathers. **1970** M. VODICKA *Track to Rum Jungle* 51 Walks for miles to do her shopping with a sugar bag. **1981** *Austral. Women's Weekly* (Sydney) 26 Aug. 20/3 Tess, who at times has had 12 men on her payroll, remembered when she first came to Triple Chance with her first husband and they slept under sugar bags. They built a sugar bag shanty and things were very tough for the two fossickers.

b. *transf.* See quot.

1978 H.C. BAKER *I was Listening* 70 A 'sugar bag carpenter' suggested a bush-carpenter or tommyhawk carpenter, which were the most disparaging appellations to be flung at a tradesman. An advertisement in the *Sydney Morning Herald* once read: Carpenters wanted. No sugar bag tradesmen need apply.

3. *fig.* One who accepts bribes or 'sweeteners'.

1877 *Vagabond Papers* 3rd Ser. 139 The warder who overlooks these little things, and who will make [*sic*] presents of tobacco, or traffic, is called a 'sugarbag'. I expect I was about the sweetest sugarbag they have had in Pentridge for a long time. **1972** BERMAN & CHILDS *Why isn't she Dead!* 66 If a policeman is called a 'sugarbag' by other police or the underworld he is on the take, the sugar merely sweetens or lightens any offence.

sugar-bagging, *vbl. n.*

1. The collecting of wild honey.

1906 *Bulletin* (Sydney) 10 May 40/1 There was the hunting and shooting and sugar-bagging.

2. *fig.* The practice of carrying provisions in a sugar bag: see SUGAR BAG 2 a. (*attrib.* in quot.).

1979 B. HARDY *World owes me Nothing* 138 There was plenty of scope for them in the 'sugar-bagging' system shearers had to put up with in these closely-settled areas. The men had to travel to work each day, taking their own tucker.

sugaropolis. A name applied to any of a number of towns in Queensland associated with the sugar industry.

1884 *Qld. Handbk. Information* (Burns, Philp & Co.) 31 Mackay is today the Sugaropolis of Queensland. **1962** *Daily Mercury Centenary Story Mackay* 2 Mackay, the sugaropolis of Australia, and the 'Gateway to the Great Barrier Reef' looks forward to another one hundred years of progress.

sugary, *a. Mining.* [Br. dial.: see EDD *a.* 3.] Friable.

1846 F. DUTTON *S.A. & its Mines* 284 A kindly spar is intermingled with copper ore; 'sugary spar' is in considerable quantity. **1982** M. WATTONE *Winning Gold in W.A.* 70, I bent down and picked up a sugary quartz specimen which contained 2 oz. of gold.

sugee, var. SOOGEE.

suicide, *a. N.T.* Of the 'wet' or rainy season: unendurable.

1971 P. BODEKER *Sandgropers' Trail* 11 We close the dry winter season for our six months' fishing because summer

SUJEE

up north is 'the wet', a contrasting period of searing heat and tropical floods, known in the Territory as the 'suicide months'. **1978** M. DOUGLAS *Follow Sun* 167 The locals call it 'suicide month'—November, that unendurable time of the year when the 'wet' begins in Australia's north.

sujee, var. SOOGEE.

sulky, *n.* [Transf. use of *sulky* a light two-wheeled carriage or chaise seated for one person.] A light horse-drawn vehicle used as a conveyance.

1902 *Bulletin* (Sydney) 31 May 14/1 The sulkies are always well-stocked with 'wobble Charlie' (rum), and the gins now spend their time on a steam merry-go-round in the township. **1981** *New Idea* (Melbourne) 3 Oct. 24/2 The sight of Leo and Lenny Bell trundling down the country roads near Ipswich, Q., high in the seat of their 1931 sulky, is one of peace and tranquility reminiscent of a time long past.

sulky, *a. Austral. pidgin.* Angry; unco-operative. In the phr. **to die sulky,** to die out of favour with one's community. Also **sulky fellow.**

1841 G. GREY *Jrnls. Two Exped. N.-W. & W.A.* I. 363 'Mr Grey sulky yu-a-da'; by which he intended to say '.. Mr Grey is not angry with you.' **1845** *Sentinel* (Sydney) 5 Feb. 3/3 Mount Macedon tribe.. all who die sulky left unburied. Goulburn, as Mount Macedon—All who die sulky left unburied. **1969** F.B. VICKERS *No Man is Himself* 8 Tallish and slim, and sulky-fella by the attitude of her, he thought.

sulphur-crested cockatoo. [See quot. 1849.] *White cockatoo* (a), see WHITE *a.*^{2} 1 b.). Also **sulphur-crested white cockatoo.**

1849 C. STURT *Narr. Exped. Central Aust.* II. 35 App. Cacatua Galerita—*Sulphur-crested Cockatoo*. This Cockatoo, the most common in Australia, is snow-white, with the exception of its crest, which is of a bright sulphur. **1945** C. BARRETT *Austral. Bird Life* 73 The sulphur-crested white cockatoo.. ranges over the continent generally, except in the west.

summer. Used *attrib.* in the names of flora and fauna: **summer bird,** any of several birds appearing in an area in summer, esp. the WOOD SWALLOW and the *black-faced cuckoo-shrike* (see BLACK *a.*^{2} 1 b.); **grass,** any of several native or introduced grasses (fam. Poaceae) able to make rapid growth in summer, esp. the naturalized annual *Digitaria sanguinalis* and the similar *D. ciliaris*.

1861 'OLD BUSHMAN' *Bush Wanderings* 135 Another summer migrant to our district was the **Summer-bird,** about the size of the jay at home. **1895** *Argus* (Melbourne) 29 Nov. 6/7 The wood-swallows, known to us old colonists as summer birds, are migratory, making their appearance about September and disappearing about the end of January. **1846** *Sydney Morning Herald* 28 Feb. 2/6 The grass called joint grass, or water or **summer grass.** **1981** G.M. CUNNINGHAM et al. *Plants Western N.S.W.* 86 Summer grass *Digitaria ciliaris...* An annual grass which makes rapid growth during the summer months.

sun-bake, *v. intr.* To sun-bathe. Freq. as *vbl. n.* and *ppl. a.*

1910 *Truth* (Sydney) 9 Oct. 2/8 If those sun baking barrackers really desire to get sun baked in 'the altogether', why do they not repair to Tamarama Bay. **1934** E. STOREY *Eve's Affairs* 28 Outside was gorgeous.. the sort of day I guess nude sun-baking was invented.

Hence **sun-bake** *n.*, **sun-baker** *n.*

1940 *Digger Yarns: Cream of 'Aussiosities'*, We was in support, a nice cushy possie without much excitement. I'd been 'avin' a bit of a **sunbake** all the mornin'. **1949** C.B. MAXWELL *Surf* 41 A **sunbaker** sat up and pushed forward a well-filled pot. 'Have a beer, sergeant!'.

SUNSHINE STATE

sundown, *v.* [Back-formation f. SUNDOWNER.]

a. *intr.* To travel as a sundowner. Freq. as *vbl.n.*

1882 ARMSTRONG & CAMPBELL *Austral. Sheep Husbandry* 245 An undeserving scoundrel, who spends the greater part of his time 'lounging' or 'sundowning'—*i.e.*, spending his time under a shady currajong, or other sleep-inspiring tree. **1946** D. BARR *Warrigal Joe* 68 Sundowning had got into Joe's blood. Though not one of the cadging sort, he liked an easy life, and was as happy as Larry when on the wallaby.

b. *trans.* To importune (someone) for sustenance.

1924 H.E. RIEMANN *Nor'-West o' West* 58 'Hoped to pay me when he struck it rich.'.. 'That wouldn't be Palmer. A bloke with two thousand quid wouldn't sundown you for flour and sugar, that's certain.'

sundowner. An itinerant, ostensibly seeking work, who arrives at a place at the end of the day: see quots. 1886.

1868 *Sydney Punch* 14 Nov. 198 (*heading*) The song of the sundowner. **1886** P. CLARKE *'New Chum' in Aust.*, I have spoken of 'sundowners' before now... The article is of the animal kingdom, genus *homo*, and generally tramps along during the day from station to station seeking work, timing his way so he may reach a station before 'sundown' in time for tea and bed. **1886** R. HENTY *Australiana* 178 These men were mere loafers or 'sundowners'—fellows who didn't want work, but who sponged upon the settler for a night's lodging and supper.

sundries, *pl. Cricket.* [Chiefly Austral.: see OED(S.] The extras, or runs scored otherwise than off the bat.

1867 *Australasian* (Melbourne) 16 Mar. 332/1 With sundries forty-five, the innings closed for the very long score of 111. **1983** K. DUNSTAN *Cricket Dict.* 28 Extras. Or in politer circles, sundries.

sunnies, *pl.* [f. *sun*(*-glasses* + -Y.] A pair of sunglasses.

1981 *Sun-Herald* (Sydney) 11 Jan. 9/2 On his head was a top hat adorned with dark glasses ('sunnies'). **1985** *Health Standard* Nov. 5/1 Sunnies must now be labelled under a new safety standard which places them in three categories.. sunglasses suitable for everyday use [etc.].

sunset.

1. The western part of New South Wales and Queensland; the west. See also *back o' sunset* BACK D., *west of sunset* WEST. Also **sunset country** and *attrib.*

1908 *Bulletin* (Sydney) 7 May 15/2 During my divagations through the Sunset-country stations, I frequently found that the shearers and co. were decently housed, because of the S.A.A. **1910** *Ibid.* 2 June 15/1 I'll never forget.. one sunset track. I had trudged two tuckerless 16-mile stages... Then I struck my hospitable friend. **1916** *Ibid.* 28 Dec. 24/1 In my early days out in the Sunset.. wild cats had distributed themselves many hundreds of miles from any human habitation.

2. Special Comb. **sunset rum,** see quot. 1951.

1951 E. HILL *Territory* 124 When grog was short they made their own.. methylated spirit and kerosene mixed with Worcestershire Sauce and flavoured with ginger and sugar, known to the diggers as Sunset Rum. **1980** R. SHEARS *Gold* 30 Breweries sprang up selling dubious liquors ranging from amber-coloured water to 'sunset-rum'. This was brewed from methylated spirit, kerosene and Worcestershire sauce and flavoured with ginger and sugar.

Sunshine State. A name for Queensland.

1962 'C. ROHAN' *Delinquents* 128 'If you ask me, all Brisbane's full of coppers and all of them bastards,' she said, expressing in one concise sentence the full theory of central government of the sunshine state. **1984** *Bulletin* (Sydney) 12 June 82/1 Small but insistent reminders of being in the Sunshine State. All those middle-aged men in safari suits, long socks and shorts.

super, *n.*[1] [Spec. use of *super*, abbrev. of *superintendent*.] The manager of a rural property (see also quot. 1967).

1849 *Stephen's Adelaide Miscellany* 8 Nov. 81 There are numberless other characters peculiar to the Bush, all of which are generally denoted very graphically by the technical terms that severally represent them, as—the 'flash gentleman'..the 'super's man', 'the crawler' [etc.]. **1967** G. JENKIN *Two Yrs. Bardunyah Station* 66 But for the lowly rouseabout there is no battle—only work and a bit of skylarking when the boss-of-the-board (known usually as the 'Expert' or the 'Super') isn't looking.

super, *n.*[2]
1. Abbrev. of 'superphosphate'. Also *attrib*.

1925 *Bulletin* (Sydney) 20 Aug. 24/3 Has.. 'Jackeroo' noticed the inordinate desire stock.. show for feeding in paddocks which have been top-dressed with superphosphate? It's not the grass they seek, for the 'super' paddock is picked almost bare. **1985** *Canberra Times* 21 Aug. 27/3 'We were really, genuinely, proud of this car, and very happy with it.' That in spite of critical comments from schoolmates who reckoned you had to put a bag of super in the back to make it handle properly.

2. In the phr. **sub and super**: see SUB.

super, *v.*
1. *trans.* Abbrev.of 'superannuate', to pension off.

1978 R.H. CONQUEST *Dusty Distances* 7, I ruined me back workin' as a ganger on the railways so they've super-ed me out on compo.

2. *intr.* To treat soil with superphosphate. (As *vbl. n.* in quot.)

1980 G. ROBINSON *Decades of Duntroon Bastard* 195 Profligate 'supering' with super-phosphate and drainage, had worked wonders.

superb, *a.* Used as a distinguishing epithet in the names of birds and animals: **superb blue** (or **fairy**) **wren**, the small bird *Malurus cyaneus* of s.e. Aust. incl. Tas., the breeding male having light and dark blue plumage; see also *blue wren* BLUE *a.*, *superb warbler*; **lyrebird**, the bird *Menura novaehollandiae* (see LYRE-BIRD 1); BULLAN BULLAN; **parrot**, the bright green parrot *Polytelis swainsonii* of inland s.e. Aust.; also *ellipt.*; **snake**, COPPERHEAD; **warbler**, *blue wren*, see BLUE *a.*

1945 C. BARRETT *Austral. Bird Life* 192 First of the fairywrens to be discovered was.. the **superb blue wren** or superb warbler. **1984** *A.N.U. Reporter* (Canberra) 26 Oct. 5 A female superb Fairy-Wren had just commenced constructing her dome-shaped nest... Her mate, in his contrasting blue and black colours, fed on insects amongst the ivy. [**1801 superb lyre-bird:** J. LATHAM *Gen. Synopsis Birds* Suppl. II. 271 Menura.. Superb M... This singular bird is about the size of a *Hen Pheasant*... The tail.. is of a singular construction.] **1929** A.H. CHISHOLM *Birds & Green Places* 89 In the richly vegetated areas of the east coast of Australia.. along the coast of New South Wales (the superb lyre-bird). **1917** *Bulletin* (Sydney) 7 June 24/4 Another rare parrot is the green leek, or **superb parrot**... The common green, or swift parrot.. is very often styled 'green leek', though the real Simon Pure is a very different bird. **1975** *Bulletin* (Sydney) 22 Feb. 20/2 The more exotic parrots, such as Golden Shoulders and Superbs fetch $10,000 a pair without difficulty. **1902** *Encycl. Brit.* XXV. 795/1 The death adder, the brown, the black, the **superb** and the tiger **snakes** [of Australia]. **1783** J. LATHAM *Gen. Synopsis Birds* II. 502 **Superb W[arbler]** *Motacilla cyanea*.. inhabits *Van Diemen's Land*, the most southern part of *New Holland*.

supplejack. [Spec. use of *supple-jack* any of several climbing or twining shrubs.]

1. Any of several plants having tough, flexible stems, esp. the climber *Flagellaria indica* (fam. Flagellariaceae) of n. Aust. and the vine or tree *Ventilago viminalis* (fam. Rhamnaceae). Also *attrib*.

1788 *HRA* (1914) 1st Ser. I. 21 The trees [on Norfolk Island] are so bound together by a kind of supple-jack that the penetrating into the interior parts of the island was very difficult. **1912** *Emu* XII. 75 The cunnyanna tree (*Ventilago viminalis*..) here is remarkable; when it grows up isolated from other trees &c., it develops into a tree growth, but if it happens to be near anything it can creep on it takes the form of a vine, and climbs all over the tree it touches; it is also known as supplejack. **1920** G. SARGANT *Winding Track* 34 The boys peeped through the cracks in the slabs, while one of them very quietly and slowly riggled a snake-like supplejack stick through a hole in the fire place. **1938** C.T. WHITE *Princ. Bot. Qld. Farmers* 31 *Flagellaria*, a 'Supple Jack' of the coastal 'brushes' or scrubs.

2. *Obs. fig.*

1843 *Colonial Observer* (Sydney) 1 Feb. 785/1 Such admirable *supple-jacks*.. as the would-be member for Illawarra. **1847** G.F. ANGAS *Savage Life & Scenes* I. 174 One of these fellows was a perfect supple-jack: he danced and capered about as though he was filled with quicksilver.

surf, *n.* [Spec. use of *surf.* Of local significance but not always excl. Austral.: see OED(S *sb.*)]

1. The surf as a place of recreation. Also *attrib*.

1908 *Truth* (Sydney) 20 Dec. 5/5 The Manly maidens shoot the surf, or bake their bingies on the shingly shore. **1979** T. ASTLEY *Hunting Wild Pineapple* 148 A large and shambling young man who.. appeared to have no regular employment though his desperate search for work had taken him to every surf-spot on the eastern seaboard.

2. A swim in the surf, esp. with the intention of riding waves; the riding of a wave.

1934 C. MACKNESS *Young Beachcombers* 46 Wish we had brought togs for a surf. **1975** *Westerly* ii. 25 Two aboriginal children go off to Bondi for a surf.

3. Abbrev. of SURFER.

1975 *Nat. Times* (Sydney) 13 Jan. 40/1 If you are a 14-year-old schoolgirl and you have just discovered boys are not the same thing as your brothers, what really sends your heart into turmoil is the sight of a blond, long-haired, blue-eyed, sun-bronzed surf wearing board shorts and bare feet. **1979** *Westerly* ii. 10 We tried to stay clear of the surfs because they razzed us all the time.

4. In the collocation **surf and turf,** a dish in which lobster and beefsteak are served together.

1975 *New Press* (Perth) II. i. 29/3 Girl chose scallops en brochette and I had 'surf n turf' because I was curious to see what I could get for $1 extra. The answer was a lemon, or a quarter of one, sitting beside a shelled cray. It was accompanied by a minute fillet steak.

5. Special Comb. **surf beach,** a beach from which people surf; **board,** a board on which a surfer rides a wave; so **surf-boarding** *vbl. n.*; **carnival,** a competitive display of the skills of a *surf life-saver;* **club,** abbrev. of *surf life-saving club;* **life-saver,** a member of a *surf life-saving club;* also *attrib.*; **life-saving** *vbl. n.,* the action of saving a swimmer from drowning; the organized safeguarding of swimmers in the surf; also *attrib.* in **surf life-saving club,** a voluntary organization formed to safe-guard lives in the surf; the premises of such an organization; **shooter,** SURFER; **ski,** a long, narrow board propelled with a paddle by the rider; so **-skiing** *vbl. n.*; **team,** a team of *surf life-savers*.

1929 *Bulletin* (Sydney) 13 Feb. 20/4 Off and on the Portugese man-o'-war or 'bluebottle' has been making itself a nuisance on Sydney **surf beaches** this summer. **1930** V. PALMER *Passage* (1957) 127 Hughie would take his **surf-**

board and make his way along the sands to Lavinia beach. **1970** J.S. GUNN in W.S. Ramson *Eng. Transported* 60 The young Australians' sport of surfboarding has usually been content to adopt a great deal of established American terminology. **1914** R. STOCK *Pyjama Man* 93 Manly was *en fête*. A **surf carnival** was in progress. **1913** *Newcastle Morning Herald* 31 Dec. 5/4 Such dangers as these have brought into existence the '**surf clubs**', which are life-saving clubs. **1963** V.B. CRANLEY *27,000 Miles through Aust.* 78 We had been invited out to attend the christening of a new lifeboat donated to the local **surf life-savers**. Their performance of swimming and rescue work was really out-standing. **1965** C. JOHNSON *Wild Cat Falling* 42 A brawny surf-lifesaver type passes along the sea front. **1942** M.L. MACPHERSON *I heard Anzacs Singing* 20 The **Surf Life-Saving** Association of Australia was founded in 1907 for the purpose of making the beaches safe for bathing. **1964** *Austral. Surf Life Saving Competition Handbk.* (Surf Life Saving Assoc. Aust.) 22 Signals are an essential part of surf life saving and any lack of knowledge, more particularly of those from the beltman or patient to the beach, may result in tragedy. **1915** *Byron Bay Rec.* 2 Jan. 8 The members of the local **Surf** and **Life-Saving Club** were in evidence. **1930** *Surf: All abaht It* 9 Getting on to a wave .. is one thing. Stopping on is another. It is at this stage, indeed, that the expert **surf-shooter** .. begins to leave the rough-and-ready novice far behind. **1956** *Truth* (Sydney) 1 Jan. 44/4 Two surf boats and a small flotilla of **surf skis** and rubber floats were used to rescue screaming men and women and children struggling for life 200 yds. from the beach. **1956** S. HOPE *Diggers' Paradise* 193 A number of young Sydneysiders have taken to a new thrill which combines surf-skiing and spearfishing. **1964** *Austral. Surf Life Saving Competition Handbk.* (Surf Life Saving Assoc. Aust.) 14 In **surf teams** races, the team which first has all members of the team to finish shall decide placings in the event of a dead-heat.

surf, *v.* [Used elsewhere but recorded earliest in Aust.: see OED(S *v.* 2.]

1. *intr.* Abbrev. of SURF-BATHE and now the preferred term; now esp. to ride waves on a board. See also BODY SURF.

1913 [see *surfing, vbl. n.*]. **1914** *Truth* (Sydney) 13 Dec. 1/7 Most of our women .. have more clobber on them when in surfing than they do in the theatres and on the block. **1981** *Nat. Times* (Sydney) 20 Dec. 27/4 I've been in the club since 1930 .. and I've surfed every day since, except for the war.

2. *trans.* To surf at (a specified place).

1964 *Surfabout* I. vi. 20 Those of you who have not surfed North Narrabeen, make it a must .. when it's a 'big day' and the ride will leave you really stoked. **1981** *Meanjin* 160 He .. had swum the rivers, surfed the whole coast, camped out in all the bush and hunted there.

Hence **surfing** *vbl. n.* and *ppl. a.*

1913 *Bulletin* (Sydney) 6 Mar. 16/2 The pest of 'bluebottles' (Portugese men-of-war), now infesting the N.S.W. surfing resorts. **1914** H.M. VAUGHAN *Australasian Wander-Yr.* 22 Of recent years 'surfing' has come into fashion on the ocean beaches, especially at Manly and Bondi.

surface, *n. Mining. Hist.* Used *attrib.* in Special Comb. **surface digging** *vbl. n.* [also U.S.], the mining of a deposit at or near the surface; (usu. *pl.*) the site of such a deposit; **stuff,** the material excavated in *surface digging*; **washing** *vbl. n.*, the washing of a surface deposit for gold, etc.; the deposit itself; **working** *vbl. n.*, the place at which a surface deposit is being mined.

1853 J. SHERER *Gold Finder Aust.* 56 In reference to the kinds of digging, they consist of two, technically denominated **surface-digging** and hole-digging. **1853** A. MACKAY *Great Gold Field* 10 There have been some surface diggings on some of the slopes and low rises on the creek, which have turned out very well. **1855** W. HOWITT *Land, Labor & Gold* II. 239 Crowds began digging up **surface-stuff**, and carting it down to the gullies. **1851** *Empire* (Sydney) 13 Dec. 464/5 As the surest plan I would recommend **surface washing** to all beginners, at which from one ounce to four ounces a-day can be obtained, according as they possess facilities for carting the stuff to the cradle. **1853** J. SHERER *Gold Finder Aust.* 176 There is some good surface-washing on the side of the hills, at times on the top of them and sometimes on the flats. **1851** *Empire* (Sydney) 13 Sept. 152/1 It is rather thin, but firm in texture, and of a size something less than a threepenny piece; it was found in a **surface workings**.

surface, *v. Mining. Hist. intr.* To mine at or near the surface; to wash a surface deposit for a mineral, esp. gold.

1853 *Illustr. Sydney News* 12 Nov. 43/1 The sinking is from ten to fifteen feet but a great portion of the diggers are still surfacing, waiting for the drier weather.

Hence **surfacer** *n.*

1852 *Moreton Bay Free Press* 21 Dec. 4/3 A number of diggers here are only surfacers, that is, are only searching for gold about a foot or sometimes less from the surface.

surface tank: see TANK *n.*[1] 1.

surfacing, *vbl. n. Mining. Hist.*

1. The mining of a surface deposit; the washing of material from a surface deposit to extract a mineral, esp. gold.

1852 *Tas. Non-State Rec.* 56/1 15 June, Every gulley crossed more or less occupied. Some at surfacing, some digging. **1853** S. SIDNEY *Three Colonies* (ed. 2) 375 Surfacing is as uncertain as sinking. You may wash a whole day and get nothing, or you may happen upon some ounces in a square foot.

2. Material taken from a surface deposit to be washed for gold, etc.

1852 A. ADAMSON *Lett.* 9 May (1901) 25 On Wednesday Joseph and I went out prospecting to Spring Gully; tried about a dozen pans of surfacing, but found nothing. **1890** 'R. BOLDREWOOD' *Miner's Right* 153 It seems they have been mopping up some rich surfacing.

surf-bathe, *v. Obs.* [Also used elsewhere: see OED(S *sb.* 3.] *intr.* To swim in the sea, esp. to ride waves. Freq. as *vbl. n.*

1906 [see *surf-bather, n.*]. **1907** *Truth* (Sydney) 21 Apr. 1/6 The raising of false alarms on the surf-bathing beaches is nothing short of criminal. **1956** S. HOPE *Diggers' Paradise* 37, I had a natural appreciation for the beauty and charm of the Sydney girls, and sometimes lingered in mixed youthful society to surf-bathe.

Also **surf-bather** *n.*

1906 *Truth* (Sydney) 21 Jan. 1/6 Coogee Bay offers exceptional advantages to surf-bathers.

surfer. [Used elsewhere but recorded earliest in Aust.: see OEDS.] One who swims in the surf, esp. one who does so to ride waves, either as a *body surfer* (see BODY SURF) or on a surfboard. Also *attrib.*

1913 W.K. HARRIS *Outback in Aust.* 93 Out of his hide they commenced to manufacture beautiful bags .. and, most novel of all, a 'surfer's companion', a dainty article intended to hold bathing suit and wet towel in a waterproof case. **1984** P. JARRATT *Aussie* 50 Radio stations ran surfer stomps in surf clubs and on promenades and, for a while there, before the Beatles .. it seemed like the reckless hedonism of the surfing lifestyle was simply going to take over.

surfie. Also **surfy.** [f. SURF(ER + -Y.] A surfer, esp. one dedicated to surfboard-riding; one who frequents surfing beaches (see quots. 1964 and 1982). Also *attrib.*

1962 *Austral. Women's Weekly* (Sydney) 24 Oct. (Suppl.) 3/4 *Surfie*, a fond term for a good and keen surfer. **1964**

M. Hilliard *Running through Rain* 176 It was a gang of Surfies—bronzed youths who lived on the beaches in summer, lolling on the sand . . bleaching their hair.   **1970** P. Slater *Eagle for Pidgin* 3 Twitty lot of ghastly giggling females and scurfy surfy males with fibreglass where their brains should be.   **1982** *Bulletin* (Sydney) 19 Oct. 92/3 A 'monosyllabic cretin' . . who speaks two words of English—'Yeah' and 'Man'—streaks his hair with Clairol . . and, worst of all, drinks milk. In other words, a Bondi surfie.

Surfoplane. Also **surfoplane.** [Proprietary name.] An inflatable rubber mat used esp. for riding waves. Also *attrib.*
1934 *Sydney Morning Herald* 2 Apr. 13/8 Dee Why Surf Life-saving Club had the distinction of promoting the last carnival of the season. . . Results . . Surf-o-plane race—J. Watson (Bondi).   **1981** *Nat. Times* (Sydney) 20 Dec. 27/4 The prototype of the rubber surfoplane was a blown-up pillow case.

surfy, var. Surfie.

surround, *v. Obs. trans.* To drink (alcoholic liquor).
1904 *Bulletin* (Sydney) 1 Dec. 40/1 He used to surround a good deal of liquor and then go down to the camp and 'deal it out' to the little woman for spite.   **1907** *Ibid.* 28 Feb. 15/3 Seventeen beer-chewers went into a Winton (Q.) bar the other day, and came out an hour later, having . . surrounded 28 drinks each.

survey, *n.*[1] *Obs.* [Transf. use of *survey* the process of surveying a tract of ground.] A tract of land which has been surveyed.
1840 *S. Austral. Rec.* (London) 6 June 302 Newly arrived emigrants and the South Australian public generally, are invited to examine section 4208, part of Mr Dutton's splendid survey, at Mount Baker.   **1861** 'Old Bushman' *Bush Wanderings* 95 A great country for pigeons is about the Survey, on the coast, forty miles from Melbourne.

survey, *n.*[2] *S.A. Hist.* [A term used by Cornish miners: see EDD.]
1. The letting of work in a mine.
1844 *S. Austral. Register* (Adelaide) 30 Mar. 2/2 A *survey* will be held at the Montacute Copper Mine, this day (Saturday), for letting the various works of the said Mine. Persons desirous of engaging on the said works are requested to be in attendance at from 12 to 1 o'clock.   **1874** *Yorke's Peninsula Advertiser* (Moonta) 10 Feb. 2/4 'Big Survey' took place on Saturday when the number of men assembled in front of the office were computed at no fewer than twelve hundred. There are two kinds of surveys held on the mines, one denominated the little survey and the other the big survey, each taking place at intervals of nine weeks.
2. Special Comb. **survey-day,** the day appointed for the letting of work in a mine.
1848 *S. Austral. Register* (Adelaide) 12 Apr. 3/2 A new lode has been discovered since the last survey day.

sus /sʌs/. *Hist.* Also **suss.** Abbrev. of Sustenance. Also in the phr. **on (the) sus.**
1972 G.C. Bolton *Fine Country to starve In* 99 Many regarded going 'on sus' as the last extremity.   **1978** B. St. A. Smith *Spirit beyond Psyche* 132 His wife, a tiny wisp of a woman, looked after two sons in their twenties, both out of work and doing a bit of state relief work on the roads when compelled to, but mostly living on the 'Suss', the Sustenance allowance, on State Relief.

susso /'sʌsoʊ/. *Hist.* [f. Sus(tenance + -O.]
a. Sustenance. Also in the phr. **on (the) susso.**
1941 S.J. Baker *Pop. Dict. Austral. Slang* 51 *On the susso,* in receipt of unemployed sustenance.   **1984** *N.T. News* (Darwin) 17 Sept. 7/2 During the great depression my father was forced to work for the Susso (sustenance payments or dole) for five days a week—no work—no money.
b. One who is in receipt of Sustenance. Also *attrib.*
1947 V. Palmer *Cyclone* 8 He thinks it puts hair on his chest knocking around with the sussos.   **1986** *Age* (Melbourne) 6 May 39/3 You can see the bluestone rim of the Boulevard built by 'susso' workers in the Depression.

sustenance. *Hist.* Any of several forms of unemployment relief provided, orig. by State governments, during the Depression.
1932 *Act* (Vic.) no. 4079 Sect. 3, 'Sustenance' includes shelter, clothing, and firewood, and references to receiving sustenance include references to obtaining sustenance.   **1978** B. St. A. Smith *Spirit beyond Psyche* 132 Two sons in their twenties, both out of work and doing a bit of state relief work on the roads when compelled to, but mostly living on the 'Suss', the Sustenance allowance.

swag, *n.* [Transf. use of *swag* a thief's plunder or booty: see OED *sb.* 9.]
1. The collection of possessions and daily necessaries carried by one travelling, usu. on foot, in the bush; esp. the blanket-wrapped roll carried, usu. on the back or across the shoulders, by an itinerant worker.
1841 *Sydney Herald* 10 Nov. 2/6 They gave me back my horse, and on him we fastened 'our swags' (for be it known, they scorned to take our dirty linen).   **1981** A.B. Facey *Fortunate Life* 78 She said, 'I didn't know you. Your swag is bigger than you are. Surely you never carried it all the way from Phillip's place.'
2. *spec.* A bed-roll.
1865 J.O. Tucker *Golden Spring* 86 Disengaging myself of the cumbrous weight of blankets that comprised my 'swag'.   **1982** R. Ellis *Bush Safari* 15 Another frugal meal of 'tinned dog', a couple of flats to mend, and straight into our swags.
3. *Obs.* Abbrev. of Swagman a.
1910 'H.H. Richardson' *Getting of Wisdom* 217 Her time was spent . . in taking long, solitary evening walks . . till Mother, haunted by a lively fear of encounters with 'swags' or Chinamen, put her foot down and forbade them.
4. In phr.: **to up swag,** to pack up one's possessions and set out on a journey; **swag up,** carrying a swag.
1873 *Australasian Sketcher* (Melbourne) 1 Nov. 133 (caption) **Up Swag.**   **1919** A. Wright *Game of Chance* 53 Up swag and ho for the Riverina.   **1901** *Bulletin* (Sydney) 12 Oct. 16/1 Woman, with a **swag up,** recently passed through Walgett.
5. Special Comb. **swag carrier,** Swagman a.; **swag-carrying** *vbl. n.* and *ppl. a.*; **cover,** a waterproof cover for a swag; **strap,** a strap with which a swag is held together and secured to the bearer.
1881 [**swag-carrier**] *Adventures of Strollers Otway Ranges* 7 Feeling just a trifle tired at the usual occupation of swag-carrying, we determined to 'make assurance double sure'.   **1896** H. Lawson *While Billy Boils* (1975) 21 A wretchedly forlorn specimen of the swag-carrying clan whom a boundary-rider had found wandering about the adjacent plain.   **1898** *Bulletin* (Sydney) 26 Feb. 14/1 John Godkin, Tas. prospector, well-remembered in connection with the great Godkin mining case, 'lays over' all swag-carriers in the Land of Sleep-a-Lot.   **1902** H. Lawson *Children of Bush* 212 When the ground got a little drier we rigged a bit of shelter from the showers with some sticks and the oil-cloth **swag-covers.**   **1902** *Bulletin* (Sydney) 18 Oct. 15/1 When a **swag-strap** or anything else is lost a chest-inspection is commenced.

Hence **swagless** *a.,* without a swag, esp. in the phr. **stiff and swagless,** without money or possessions (see also Stiff 1); **swaglike** *a.* and *adv.*
[N.Z. **1885** A.H. Burton *Maori at Home,* We horsemen found ourselves **swagless.**]   **1906** *Bulletin* (Sydney) 12 July 17/1 When the nomad is utterly stiff and swagless, he

obtains three or four discarded corn sacks and sews them together. **1890** *Argus* (Melbourne) 2 Aug. 4/2 He strapped the whole lot together **swag-like**. **1926** L.C.E. GEE *Bush Tracks & Gold Fields* 73 The swaglike object in the back part of the boat.

swag, *v.*

1. *intr.* To carry one's swag; to travel as a swagman. Also with **it.**

1859 'EYE WITNESS' *Voyage to Aust.* 21 All parties coming into the colony, with few exceptions, have to swag it for a time. **1908** E.G. MURPHY *Jarrahland Jingles* 16 It was on the old Kalgoorlie track we met him swagging in.

2. a. *trans.* To travel through (the country) or along (a road) as a swagman.

1871 W. EVANS *Diary Welsh Swagman* (1975) 21 At Ballarat I visited Mr Roberts, the photographer, and asked him to take my portrait .. swagging the Bush with my billy-can. **1960** 'A. CARSON' *Rose by any Other Name* 50, I was swagging my way up to the Northern Territory.

b. *fig.* To support (someone).

1896 *Bulletin* (Sydney) 23 May 3/2 Hold up, Billy; I'll stick to you; they've hit you under the belt; If we get the waddle I'll swag you through, if the blazing mountains melt.

Hence **(be-)swagged** *ppl. a.*, **swagging** *vbl. n.*

1881 *Adventures of Strollers Otway Ranges* 6 And what of W-? Robed and **swagged** like B-, coatless, with a slouching black billy-cock hat. **1906** *Bulletin* (Sydney) 24 May 14/1 Be-swagged, unsteadily he strode To pad it to his native land. **1898** *Ibid.* 20 Aug. (Red Page), It's a tedious job—like **swagging.**

swagger. [f. SWAG *n.* or *v.*] SWAGMAN a. Also *attrib.*

1855 *Argus* (Melbourne) 19 Jan. 6/1 We have observed a great influx of swaggers lately—all seemingly bound for Smith's Creek. **1916** *Truth* (Sydney) 21 May 12/7 (*heading*) Australian swagman. Swagger work of art.

swaggie. [f. SWAG *n.*[1] + -Y.]

a. A SWAGMAN or SWAGWOMAN. Also *attrib.*

1891 *Truth* (Sydney) 19 Apr. 7/3 Many a swaggy has to thank Charlie and the missus .. for a bit of tobacco and a feed. **1898** *Bulletin* (Sydney) 9 Apr. 14/1 Female 'swaggies' are becoming comparatively common in South Australia. **1911** *Ibid.* 10 Aug. 14/2 The bike seems to lend an air of business, which lifts a man right out of the swaggie class.

b. *fig.*

1943 'MRS E.F. BOSWORICK' *Amateur* 11 The wise old swaggy moon.

Hence **swaggying** *pres. pple.* and *vbl. n.*, leading the life of a 'swaggie'.

1905 *Bulletin* (Sydney) 2 Feb. 16/4 Swaggying is a varied and reasonably exciting profession in Westralia. **1923** *Smith's Weekly* (Sydney) 16 June 19/5 The next time I go swaggying I'll put an electric fan in my swag.

swagman. Formerly also **swagsman.**

a. One who carries a swag; an itinerant worker, esp. one in search of employment, who carries a swag; a tramp.

1869 W.M. HUGO *Hist. First Bushmen's Club* (1872) 30 Sir—A swagsman, and not ashamed to own it. I have done the 'wallaby' for years past in search of a billet. **1971** *Bulletin* (Sydney) 4 Sept. 42/2 A nameless swagman who, about 80 years ago, jumped into Combo waterhole, sooner or later haunts all Australians.

b. In the collocation **suburban swagman**: see quots.

1902 *Bulletin* (Sydney) 14 June 14/1 A curious institution is the Sydney suburban swagman. He 'works' his 'beat', or 'round', starting from Willoughby, where he lives in a tent or cave. Sometimes he travels what is known as the 'single triangle'—along Lane Cove-road to Hornsby, thence to Parramatta, and thence back, via Sydney, to his base of operations. He is generally in search of . . odd jobs. The 'double triangle' man usually 'works' from Parramatta to Penrith. Thence to Windsor, and back to the 'Bridge Hotel', Parramatta. **1911** *Bulletin* (Sydney) 6 Apr. 14/1 A long, attenuated, ungainly, awkward, suburban swagman was caught robbing the boss's best bulb beds.

swagwoman. A woman who carries a swag.

1894 *Bulletin* (Sydney) 7 Apr. 13/1 The swagwoman is becoming one of the sights of Maoriland. **1980** BRENNAN & WHITE *Keep Billy Boiling* 86 Occasional swagwomen were to be found, usually characters of note such as 'Menindee Mary' and the 'Portia of Pooncarrie'.

swainsona /sweɪn'soʊnə/. Also **swainsonia**. [The plant genus *Swainsona* was named by R.A. Salisbury (*Parad. Lond.* (1806) Pl. 28) after English naturalist Isaac Swainson (1746–1812). The form *Swainsonia* has also been used as a name for the genus.] Any plant of the chiefly Austral. herbaceous genus *Swainsona* (fam. Fabaceae), perennials or annuals, esp. of drier Aust., having pinnate leaves and colourful pea-flowers. See also *Darling pea* DARLING.

1857 W. HOWITT *Tallangetta* I. 23 Interspersed amongst these were large purple vetches, or Swainsonias, of a most delicious vanilla scent. **1931** M. TERRY *Hidden Wealth* 324 On this station were noted two species of swainsona.

Swainson's phascogale. [First applied as the specific epithet *Swainsonii* by the English naturalist G.R. Waterhouse, after William Swainson (1789–1855), naturalist.] The small marsupial *Antechinus* (formerly *Phascogale*) *swainsonii* (fam. Dasyuridae) of Tas. and s.e. Aust., esp. in mountainous areas. Also **Swainson's pouched mouse.**

1894 R. LYDEKKER *Hand-Bk. Marsupialia & Monotremata* 171 Swainson's Pouched Mouse. *Phascologale swainsoni*. . . Fur very long, soft and thick. General colour deep rufous or umber-brown, under-parts dull brownish-grey .. length of head and body about 5 inches; tail of 4 inches. **1968** D. FLEAY *Nightwatchmen* 25 As I sat motionless a bright-eyed Swainson's phascogale (pouched mouse) emerged from a hollow log and ran perkily up and down my trouser leg.

swallow, *v. Obs. trans.* In the phr. **to swallow bobby,** to make a false statement.

1847 A. HARRIS *Settlers & Convicts* (1953) 51 Some of the first 'nobs' in the colony used to 'swallow bobby' (make false affidavits) to an enormous extent. **1970** J.S. GUNN in W.S. Ramson *Eng. Transported* 63 Other imminent or actual losses which seem regrettable to me are .. *square*, 'sober', *swallow bobby*, 'make a false statement to avoid customs duty'.

swallow-catch, *v. intr.* Of a horse: to run a race in fast time. (As *vbl. n.* in quot.)

1904 L.M.P. ARCHER *Bush Honeymoon* 70 'That's a good horse of yours, miss', he said coolly, 'bit of blood? They're doing some *swallow-catching* to-day; you ought to give him a cut—might win a quid or two.'

Hence **swallow-catcher** *n.*

1913 A. PRATT *Wolaroi* 128 Beehive, a noted swallow-catcher, was the first of all the horses to get moving.

swamp, *n.* Used *attrib.* in the names of flora and fauna having a swampy or periodically flooded habitat: **swamp box,** any of several trees, esp. *Lophostemon suaveolens* (fam. Myrtaceae) of n. Aust., which is also known as *swamp mahogany*; **grass,** any of several native or introduced grasses (fam. Poaceae), incl. the American *Echinochloa crus-galli*, naturalized in all States; *water grass*, see WATER; **gum,** any of several trees of the genus

Eucalyptus (fam. Myrtaceae), esp. *E. ovata* of s.e. Aust. incl. Tas., *E. microtheca* (see COOLIBAH), and (*Tas.*) *E. regnans* (see *mountain ash* MOUNTAIN); the wood of the tree; also *attrib.*; **harrier** (or **hawk**), **(a)** *obs., spotted harrier* (see SPOTTED); **(b)** the bird of prey *Circus approximans*; **hen**, the bird *Porphyrio porphyrio* of Aust. and elsewhere, having blue and black plumage with a bright red bill and head shield; BALDCOOT; see also *red bill* RED *a.* 1 b.; **lily**, either of two perennial herbs, the tall, bulbous *Crinum pedunculatum* (fam. Liliaceae) of swampy land in coastal Qld. and N.S.W., bearing fragrant white flowers, and the aquatic *Ottelia ovalifolia* (fam. Hydrocharitaceae) of mainland Aust.; **mahogany**, any of several trees, esp. the rough-barked coastal species *Eucalyptus robusta* (fam. Myrtaceae) of e. Qld. and N.S.W., yielding a durable red timber, and *Lophostemon suaveolens* (see *swamp box*); the wood of the tree; **oak**, any of several trees or shrubs of the fam. Casuarinaceae, esp. *Allocasuarina paludosa* of s.e. Aust. incl. Tas., and *Casuarina glauca* of near-coastal s.e. N.S.W. to s.e. Qld.; the wood of the tree; also **she-oak; parrot** (or **parakeet**), the bird *Pezoporus wallicus* (see *ground parrot* GROUND *n.*[1]); **pheasant**, *pheasant coucal*, see PHEASANT 2; **quail**, *brown quail*, see BROWN *a.* 1; **rat**, a native rodent of the genus *Rattus*, esp. the grey or greyish brown *Rattus lutreolus* of e. Aust. incl. Tas.; **stringybark**, the small tree *Eucalyptus conglomerata* (fam. Myrtaceae) of s.e. Qld.; **tea-tree**, any of several shrubs or trees of the fam. Myrtaceae, as *Melaleuca ericifolia* of s.e. Aust. incl. Tas., and *Leptospermum myrtifolium* of e. mainland Aust.; **wallaby**, the dark-coloured wallaby *Wallabia bicolor* of areas of dense moist undergrowth in e. mainland Aust.
1878 R.B. SMYTH *Aborigines of Vic.* I. 220 The hunter, in places far removed from permanent water, has to draw his supply of that element from the roots of the **swamp-box** and the weir-mallee, which run a few inches below the surface of the earth. **1978** K. MCARTHUR *Pumicestone Passage* 43 Most of the canoe trees so far found from the Noosa River to the Passage shores have been swamp box (*Tristania suaveolens*). **1840** *S. Austral. Rec.* (London) 20 June 333 The cart was upset, nearly killing one of the men, whose life was only preserved by a bunch of **swamp-grass** and sedge, which prevented the load from crushing him to death. **1970** N.T. BURBIDGE *Austral. Grasses* III. 32 The name of Swamp Grass has been used for *E*[*chinochloa*] *walteri* and for related species, and it has, unfortunately, also been attached to other grasses. It is used here pending the discovery of a better name. **1832** *Colonist* (Hobart) 21 Sept. 1/5 For Sale . . a large quantity of excellent **swamp gum** shingles. **1896** B. SPENCER *Rep. Horn Sci. Exped. Central Aust.* I. 13 The lines of the water-courses are marked by belts of gum trees and acacias . . *Eucalyptus microtheca*, the swamp gum [etc.]. **1967** E. HUXLEY *Their Shining Eldorado* 172 The swamp gum or mountain ash—*Eucalyptus regnans*—survives here [*sc.* Florentine Valley, Tas.] probably in greater numbers than anywhere else on earth. **1843** [**swamp harrier**] J. GOULD *Birds of Aust.* (1848) I. Pl. 26, *Circus assimilis* . . Swamp Hawk, of the Colonists. **1986** *Parkwatch* (Vic. Nat. Parks Assoc.) Mar. 13 A swamp harrier soars over the lake-margins. **1833** *Perth Gaz.* 2 Mar. 35 Wild Birds, the . . **swamp hen** Pigeons, &c. &c., have been offered for sale more generally of late, than usual. **1867** *Lang. Native Flowers Tas.* 6 **Swamp Lily** . . Perishable beauty. **1970** BURBIDGE & GRAY *Flora A.C.T.* 16 Shallow pools in woodland habitats of lower elevations; widespread on Australian mainland; introduced in New Zealand. 'Swamp Lily' . . *O*[*ttelia*] *ovalifolia*. **1979** WRIGLEY & FAGG *Austral. Native Plants* 105 *C*[*rinum*] *pedunculatum* . . Swamp lily. Large plant with upright leaves 1 m. long . . Bears open, white flowers on thick stem . . Makes an excellent feature plant. **1817** A. CUNNINGHAM in I. Marriott *Early Explorers Aust.* (1925) 176 *Eucalyptus robusta* (white or **swamp mahogany**). **1909** R. KALESKI *Austral. Settler's Compl. Guide* 37 Swamp mahogany . . so called because its timber has a figure like Honduras mahogany. **1801** *HRA* (1915) 1st Ser. III. 170 There are gum-trees, **swamp-oak**, the tea-tree. **1880** R. ROSE *Austral. Guide: S.A.* 11 What may not be improperly designated the Australian fir tribe (*Casuarinas*), colonials have invested with very singular names. Thus, we find there . . the 'swamp-oak' (*C. paludosa*). **1901** *Proc. Linnean Soc. N.S.W.* XXVI. 687 *C*[*asuarina*] *Cunninghamiana* is, so far as I have been able to observe, purely a fresh water tree, and must not be confused with the Swamp Oak, *C. glauca*, often found near salt water along the coast. **1983** *Canberra Times* 24 Dec. 7/4 A Canberra firm has won a $617,000 contract to plant 500,000 swamp sheoaks at Brisbane's new airport. **1833** [**swamp parrot**] *Trumpeter* (Hobart) 8 Nov. 227 *To Naturalists*. To be sold . . birds, in skins . . Swamp Parroquite. **1844** G.F. ANGAS *Savage Life & Scenes* 30 Apr. (1847) I. 152 Occasional swamp parrots fluttered up from the grass. **1825** B. FIELD *Geogr. Mem. N.S.W.* 46, I shot two **swamp pheasants** (a pretty black bird not unlike the English pheasants in shape). **1849** C. STURT *Narr. Exped. Central Aust.* II. 47 App. Synoïcus Australis— Swamp Quail, or Partridge . . is generally found in marshes, or marshy ground, and frequently in bevies. **1926** A.S. LE SOUEF et al. *Wild Animals Australasia* 118 The **swamp-rat** is found in swampy country all over South Australia. **1978** S. KELLY *Eucalypts* II. 44 **Swamp stringybark** has a very restricted natural distribution, on the flat land near the coast about 60–150 km. north of Brisbane. **1832** J. BACKHOUSE *Narr. Visit Austral. Colonies* (1843) 58 They cross the mouth of the harbour on floats, in the form of a boat, made of bundles of the paper-bark of the **Swamp Tea-tree**. **1906** *Emu* VI. 54 A frail little nest of this species was found . . in a swamp tea-tree (*Melaleuca ericifolia*). **1970** BURBIDGE & GRAY *Flora A.C.T.* 267 Shrub 1–2 metres high . . of forested gullies and high mountain valleys and ridges, commonly near seepage or swamps . . 'Swamp Tea-tree' . . *L*[*eptospermum*] *myrtifolium*. **1896** F.G. AFLALO *Sketch Nat. Hist. Aust.* II. 40 Into the specific descriptions of the rock, swamp, brush, scrub and other **wallabies** I shall not enter.

swamp, *v.*[1] *trans.* To drink, esp. in the phr. **to swamp one's cheque**, to spend one's entire earnings on alcoholic liquor.
1850 *Bell's Life in Sydney* 12 Jan. 2/7 Other members stayed away because they had taken their dinner before the hour of meeting and some, several of whom had been 'swamping it' at Botany on the previous day, had experienced that the water they then and there tested, disagreed with them. **1920** *Smith's Weekly* (Sydney) 28 Aug. 9/4 No traveller likes to be on the road without a bluey of ordinary dimensions. A man might 'swamp his cheque' . . but he won't part with his bundle.

swamp, *v.*[2] [Transf. use of U.S. *swamp* to clear a road: see OED(S *v.* 5.] *intr.* To travel as a SWAMPER (senses a. and b.); to work as an assistant to a bullock driver or other carrier (see quot. 1944); to work casually in this capacity (see quot. 1944). Also *trans.*, to obtain (a lift), and as *vbl. n.*
1897 *Bulletin* (Sydney) 6 Mar. 28/4 We were swamping back from Lake Darlot rush last winter with Billy Mills's camels. **1944** M.J. O'REILLY *Bouyangs & Boomerangs* 6 My duties were to help to load and unload, bring the horses in the morning, to harness up, help to corduroy bad patches on the track, draw water for the horses at the soaks and wells, hobble out the horses at night, put the bells on, etc. These duties were then known as 'Swamping', a very appropriate name, especially after heavy rains, when the waggons would sink to the axle. All this work for the privilege of having one's tucker, tools, and swag carried on the waggon. Fortunately the chap I 'swamped' for was an exceptionally good sort. **1954** T. RONAN *Vision Splendid* 92 This isn't my camp, I'm only swamping a ride.

swamp cancer. [From the popular belief that the disease is associated with swampy land.] A skin disease of horses, in which a growth of granulation tissue occurs as the result of the presence of larvae of a thread-like parasitic worm of the genus *Habronema*.

1880 J.J. JONES *Openings for Emigrants* 21 Horses that suffer from swamp cancer are hurried off to the salt-bush. **1911** *Cwlth. Parl. Papers* III. 5/9 There are three diseases, however, that seem to constitute drawbacks, to horse breeding in this part of the country. These are commonly known as (1) the 'Walk-about' disease, which is generally fatal; (2) the 'Puffs', and (3) the so-called 'Swamp-cancer'.

swamper. [See SWAMP $v.^2$]

a. One who travels on foot but whose baggage is carried on a wagon.

1894 *Bulletin* (Sydney) 28 Apr. 9/3 Teamsters are now arriving with nothing but swags aboard, the 'swamper's' baggage being more remunerative than ordinary loading. **1983** P. ADAM SMITH *When we rode Rails* 70 Some who walked while paying to send their swags ahead on a wagon were called 'swampers'.

b. One who obtains a lift.

1964 H.M. BARKER *Camels & Outback* 14 On this journey one of my three passengers (or 'swampers') would ride ahead on the horse to pick a camp. **1966** T. RONAN *Once there was Bagman* 15 My .. fellow swamper tossed his swag off [the mailman's truck] here; he was home.

swan. [Spec. use of *swan* a large swimming bird of the genus *Cygnus*.] Black swan, see BLACK $a.^2$ 1 b.

1801 M. FLINDERS *Observations Coasts Van Diemen's Land* 8 These swans are black, the wing feathers excepted. **1935** F. CLUNE *Rolling down Lachlan* 196 Here, ibis, ducks, and swans swim in the shade of box-trees mixed with belahs and yarran.

Swan River mahogany. [f. the name of the river in W.A., on which Perth stands.] JARRAH 1.

1847 E.W. LANDOR *Bushman* 396 We have just inspected about two tons of wood brought to this town (Leeds) under the name of Swan River Mahogany. **1974** *Bulletin* (Sydney) 18 May 24/2 The best bauxite tends to be found under the best jarrah—or Swan River mahogany as it was originally known.

swatser /'swɒtsə/. *Obs.* Also **swatzer.** [f. G. *schwarzer* a black (male) person.] An Aboriginal.

1896 *Truth* (Sydney) 7 June 5/5 They are supposed to repeat Her Majesty's monniker three times, and if the 'swatzer' doesn't halt, they can let go. **1898** *Bulletin* (Sydney) 1 Oct. 14/3 A few more W.Q. slang words .. a black-fellow is a 'swatser'.

sweat, *v.* [Joc. use of *sweat* to give (a horse) a run for exercise.]

1. *trans.* To borrow (a horse) without the owner's permission. Also as *vbl. n.*

1869 *Bushmen, Publicans, & Politics* 6 The *sweating* of a horse is a good joke. **1904** L.M.P. ARCHER *Bush Honeymoon* 115 There were a lot of 'travellers' on the river, and if they struck her, they would probably *collar* the pack and *sweat* her for a week or two.

2. To squander (one's own or someone else's earnings).

1882 *Bulletin* (Sydney) 21 Oct. 8/4 He had sweated his cheque at the hotel, and found himself a boosted-up community, with brain on fire, coppers hot, and a throat like the stove-pipe of Gehenna. **1956** R.G. EDWARDS *Overlander Songbk.* 77 We steer up to the girls, that ring themselves with grandeur, And while they sweat our cheques—they swear, they love the overlander.

sweating pen. A holding pen; orig. a covered lean-to shelter in which sheep, sweating from being mustered or driven, were confined while drying out before being moved to the holding pen in the shearing shed: see quot. 1980. See also *holding pen* HOLDING.

1882 ARMSTRONG & CAMPBELL *Austral. Sheep Husbandry* 175 A narrow race is made, which is filled from the sweating, or night pens. **1980** P. FREEMAN *Woolshed* 18 The sheep enter the Kingsvale woolshed on slotted ramps and are directed by gates into 'sweating' pens. The term is an old one, for it recognises that shearers have always refused to shear 'wet' sheep, and that the sheep require time in these pens to cool down preparatory to shearing.

sweep. Pl. **sweep, sweeps.** [Of unknown origin, but see quot. 1857.] Any of several marine fish, usu. of the fam. Scorpidae, esp. those of the genus *Scorpis*, as *S. lineolatus* of s.e. Aust. incl. Tas.

1840 F.D. BENNETT *Narr. Whaling Voyage* I. 23 They were chiefly of the kinds known as .. 'sweeps', and 'rudder-fish', or scad. **1857** J. ASKEW *Voyage Aust. & N.Z.* 229 There is a curious little flat fish, called 'the sweep', of which many are caught. When first taken out of the water it is bright as silver, but in a few seconds it turns as black as a sweep, hence its name. **1980** G. DUTTON *Wedge-Tailed Eagle* 36 We anchored off the rocks .. and caught sweep and parrot-coloured cod.

sweeper. *Shearing.* One who is employed to sweep pieces of wool which fall during shearing or the handling of the fleece from the floor of a shearing shed: see quot. 1918.

1910 C.E.W. BEAN *On Wool Track* 197 The locks are always being swept up by special boys—'sweepers'. **1918** R.H. KNYVETT *Over there with Australs.* 29 The 'sweeper' gathers into a basket the trimmings and odd pieces.

sweepy. *Obs. Shearing.* [f. *sweeper* + -Y.] SWEEPER.

1898 *Bulletin* (Sydney) 20 Sept. 11/4 The 'sweepy', that swept the board.

sweet, $a.^1$ Used as a distinguishing epithet in the names of plants: **sweet bursaria,** see BURSARIA; **plum,** *Burdekin plum,* see BURDEKIN; **tea,** the wiry climbing plant *Smilax glycophylla* (fam. Smilacaceae) of e. N.S.W. and Qld. (see quot. 1790); SARSAPARILLA b.; see also *native sarsaparilla* NATIVE *a.* 6 a.; also **sweet tea plant.**

1874 LINDLEY & MOORE *Treasury of Bot.* (rev. ed.) 1324 *Owenia cerasifera* is called the **Sweet Plum.** **1790** J. WHITE *Jrnl. Voyage N.S.W.* 155 That which we call the **sweet tea** is a creeping kind of vine, running to a great extent along the ground. .. Of this the convicts and soldiers make an infusion which is tolerably pleasant, and serves as no bad succedaneum for tea. **1860** G. BENNETT *Gatherings of Naturalist* 368 The Sarsaparilla, or Sweet Tea-plant of the colonists .. is very common in the vicinity of Sydney, climbing the trees, or trailing along the ground .. forming a mass of green foliage, diversified by the beautiful reddish tinge of the young leaves and clusters of black berries.

sweet, $a.^2$

1. Good; all right; advantageously situated.

1898 *Bulletin* (Sydney) 17 Dec. (Red Page), *Krook* or *kronk* is bad; while *sweet, roujig,* and *not too stinkin'* are good. **1904** *Sporting News* (Launceston) 2 Jan. 3/1 A three year old colt by Pilgrim's Progress from Nellie, was thought to be a sweet thing, but he failed to find his feet. **1978** J. COLBERT *Ranch* 35 Well, all home to the ranch and see if we're sweet with the babbling brook. **1983** A.F. HOWELLS *Against Stream* 1 The job was a bit of a bore, but I'd had worse. And I was pretty sweet with the boss.

2. In phr.

a. she's sweet and varr., 'all is well'.

1942 *Khamseen Kronikle* 10 Sept. 1 Mick blushed pink and shuffled his feet, Twitched his moustache and murmured 'she's sweet'. **1979** *Bronze Swagman Bk. Bush Verse* 82 When yer board me ute, be careful where yer put yer plates-o'-

meat—If yer'll just avoid me dog-traps, mate, I reckon she'll be sweet.

b. to cop it sweet, to accept a set-back with equanimity; to be fortunate.

1964 *Footy Fan* (Melbourne) II. ii. 13 The result was, down went Martyn, and credit to him, he 'copped it sweet' and for the rest of the day both boys played football. **1984** *Sun-Herald* (Sydney) 29 July 60/1 It was surprising that jockey Bruce Compton, rider of Missile runner-up Buena Gold, copped the flag start so sweet.

3. In the special collocation **sweet cop,** an easy task; an enviable situation.

1918 *Kia Ora Coo-ee* Oct. 9/3 Foraging was no sweet cop, let me tell you. **1979** B. HUMPHRIES *Bazza comes into his Own,* 'I got no job and I'm down to me last razoo!' 'No problem, Barry me boy .. how's about I fix youse a nice sweet cop here at Oz House? I can swing you a beaut little lurk.'

sweetlip. Also **sweetlips.** [See quot. 1965.]

1. Any of many thick-lipped fish, esp. those of the fam. Haemulidae (Pomadasyidae) and some members of the fam. Lethrinidae (see EMPEROR), both predom. tropical families.

1928 S.E. NAPIER *On Barrier Reef* 81 'Sweet Lips', a perchlike fish. **1965** *Austral. Encycl.* VIII. 381 Sweetlips, a name applied to several tropical fishes of the genus *Plectorhinchus,* remarkable for their greatly thickened lips. **1980** T.A. ROY *Vengeance of Dolphin* 16 He was carrying by the gills a large sweetlip—a fine eating fish that abounds in the Great Barrier Reef waters.

2. Special Comb. **sweetlip emperor,** the fish *Lethrinus chrysostomus* of coral reefs in Qld.; any of several related fish. Also *ellipt.* as **sweetlip** (see sense 1).

1951 T.C. ROUGHLEY *Fish & Fisheries Aust.* 75 The sweet-lip emperor .. is one of the best eating fish of the Barrier Reef, its flesh being white, flaky, and of delicate flavour.

sweet-lips, *pl. Shearing. Obs.* A pair of hand shears.

1895 *Bulletin* (Sydney) 13 July 23/2 And there isn't any hurry, as it takes you all the day To get the 'sweet-lips' going. **1895** *Worker* (Sydney) 28 Sept. 4/1 In fact they were just what you might call grand, With their blades so straight and long—Regular 'sweet lips', just to my hand; Lively, but not too strong.

Sweet William. [Transf. use of *sweet-william* any of several small European sharks of the fam. Carcharhinidae.] The small shark *Mustelus antarcticus* (see GUMMY 2); the flesh of the shark.

1926 L.C.E. GEE *Bush Tracks & Gold Fields* 101 A couple of small ground sharks, commonly known as 'Sweet Williams'. **1974** T.D. SCOTT et al. *Marine & Freshwater Fishes S.A.* 32 Gummy Shark; Sweet William. *Mustelus antarcticus* .. Marine.

swelling blight. BUNG EYE.

1859 W. BURROWS *Adventures Mounted Trooper* 149 The dust frequently causes them to be affected by what is called 'blight'. This disorder is attended with a peculiar redness of the eyelids, and an irritation causing the eyes to water considerably, accompanied with a smarting sensation. There are .. two kinds of this complaint, commonly known as 'sandy' and 'swelling' blight. **1901** K.L. PARKER in M. Muir *My Bush Bk.* (1982) 116 Sometimes they would only have swelling blight—'bungey eye' colloquially called—from a fly sting which the blacks used to cure by pressing on hot budtha twigs, and the whites with the blue-bag; but more often, the sandy blight—granulation of the eyelids.

swey, swi, varr. SWY.

swiftie. A piece of sharp practice; an act of deception; a trick; esp. in the phr. **to pull a swiftie.**

1945 S.J. BAKER *Austral. Lang.* 265 Swiftie .. will .. be heard in male conversation to describe a joke or trick that is either agreeable or disagreeable. **1978** B. ST. A. SMITH *Spirit beyond Psyche* 209 Since the ole Jim's been out at the Farm an' they've let that stupid electrical contractor inter the factory on maintenance, me work as foreman 'as just about doubled. A man's gotta watch the cow all the way, otherwise he's liable t' pull a swifty, as y' might say.

swift parrot. [See quots. 1840 and 1976.] The predom. green parrot *Lathamus discolor* of e. Aust., which breeds in Tas.; *red-shouldered parakeet,* see RED *a.* 1 b. Also **swift(-flying) lorikeet,** and formerly **swift parakeet.**

1833 *Trumpeter* (Hobart) 8 Nov. 227 *To Naturalists.* To be sold .. birds, in skins .. Swamp Parroquite .. Swift ditto. **1840** J. GOULD *Birds of Aust.* (1848) V. Pl. 47, *Lathamus discolor.* Swift Lorikeet. . . Swift Parrakeet, Colonists of Van Diemen's Land. . . Small flocks of from four to twenty in number are also frequently to be seen passing over the town [of Hobart], chasing each other with the quickness of thought, and uttering at the same time a shrill screaming noise, like the Swift of Europe, whence in all probability has arisen its colonial name. **1945** C. BARRETT *Austral. Bird Life* 76 The swift-flying lorikeet or swift parrot (*Lathamus discolor*) .. is similar to the other small lorikeets in its habits. **1976** *Reader's Digest Compl. Bk. Austral. Birds* 274 Swift parrots live up to their name, for their flight is extremely swift and direct.

swill.

a. The rapid consumption of drinks in public houses at the end of the working day, as occasioned by the (former) six-o'-clock closing regulations. Also *attrib.*

1945 J. HOLMES *Is it Dinkum?* 6 And as its getting on for six, they are drinking now at will, And 'mobs' are flocking to the bars partaking of the 'swill'. **1952** *Newspaper News* (Sydney) 1 Apr. 10/4 Scotch is as hard to get as dry change in an hotel bar at swill time.

b. *spec.* In the collocation **six o'clock swill.**

1955 A. ROSS *Aust.* 55 81 This evening ritual, known amongst Australians as the 'six o'clock swill', is supported by two large and powerful groups: the brewers and the Methodists, 'wowsers' as they are called here. **1984** S. DOWSE *Silver City* 73 It's a funny place. . . The men drink on their own, standing up, as fast as they can, before the pubs shut. The 'six o'clock swill', it's called.

Hence **swiller** *n.*

1964 *Bulletin* (Sydney) 15 Feb. 22/3 Mr Phillips was not a regular swiller for, according to the law, no drinks must be served after 6 p.m.

swimmers, *pl.* A swimming costume.

1967 *Sunday Truth* (Brisbane) 23 July 1/1 Bikini girls at Parliament House .. when a parade of new season's swimmers .. will be on show. **1986** *Sydney Morning Herald* 25 Jan. 1/5 So Darwin's citizens are being invited to bring their swimmers to the town pool for greasy pole games.

swimming togs: see TOGS.

swing, *v.* In phr.

a. to swing the gate, to be the fastest shearer in a shearing shed.

1898 *Bulletin* (Sydney) 1 Oct. 14/3 To 'ring' the shed or shear most sheep is to 'swing the gate'. **1955** STEWART & KEESING *Austral. Bush Ballads* 234, I heard The Flyer ringing Orange Plains and Compadore; He 'swung the gate' at Netley in Eighteen eighty-four, In those days he was a goer, but the happy time has gone; He thought that Howe deserved the belt for his three-twenty-one.

b. to swing Douglas, Kelly, the banjo: see DOUGLAS, KELLY *n.*[2], BANJO 2.

c. to swing the billy: see BILLY *n.*[1] 6.

d. to swing the bag, (of a bookmaker) to take bets at a race meeting.
1962 E. LANE *Mad as Rabbits* 192 Until that momentous decision he used to 'swing the bag' at every race meeting within a fifty-mile radius, and even after he had reformed he didn't dispose of his double-headed penny. 1982 P. ADAM SMITH *Shearers* 308 Jacky was swinging the bag and he didn't want either horse to win.

swing-gate. [Spec. use of *swing-gate* a gate constructed to swing to or shut of itself.] *Drafting gate,* see DRAFTING 2. Also **swinging gate.**
1865 *Argus* (Melbourne) 7 Feb. 6/6 Again, in 1847, I made another invention, known as the swing-gate. 1921 *Bulletin* (Sydney) 8 Sept. 22/4, I have heard many an argument as to who invented the 'swinging-gate' in drafting yards. The consensus of opinion among the old hands awards the honour to Thos. Hungerford, of Walgett.

swipe. Formerly **swipes.** [Spec. use of Br. slang *swipes* poor, weak beer: see OED.] A disparaging term for beer, esp. (formerly) that brewed in an Australian Colony; any beer. Also *attrib.,* and *transf.*
1848 *Satirist & Sporting Chron.* (Sydney) 1 Apr. 2/4 The waiter being called, each gent. ordered his ball or pot of swipes which ever suited his palate. 1851 *Empire* (Sydney) 23 Sept. 183/6 There was an extensive demand for ale and porter, and as you may suppose, these 'swipe' manufacturers vegetated wonderfully on the temperance cause. 1929 W.J. RESIDE *Golden Days* 375, I only went to church one night—because a feed was on, And looked with scornful eye such swipe as lemonade upon.

swizzle-stick. [Transf. use of *swizzle-stick* a stick used for stirring a drink.] A twig from the shrub *Alyxia ruscifolia* (fam. Apocynaceae) of N.T., Qld., and N.S.W.; the shrub itself. Also *attrib.*
1886 H. FINCH-HATTON *Advance Aust.* (rev. ed.) 31 That's nothing short of a swizzle-stick and it grows on a tree that is peculiar to the Mackay district. *c* 1910 W.R. GUILFOYLE *Austral. Plants* 50 *Alyxia ruscifolia..* 'Swizzle-stick Bush' (evergreen shrub, 8 to 10 ft.), f[lowers] white.

sword. *Obs.*
1. An Aboriginal weapon. In quots. 1796 and 1863 the weapon referred to is a boomerang.
1796 'SOCIETY OF GENTLEMEN' *New & Correct Hist. New Holland* 35 They have, besides, long wooden swords, shaped like a sabre, capable of inflicting a mortal wound, and clubs of an immense size. 1863 W.J. WILLS *Successful Exploration Interior Aust.* 330 He was killed by a stroke from what the natives call a sword (an instrument of semicircular form, five to eight feet long, and very formidable). 1878 R.B. SMYTH *Aborigines of Vic.* I. p. xlv, The *Kul-luk* of the Gippsland natives, the *Bittergan* of the north-east coast, and the large sword made by the people of Rockingham Bay, were no doubt in their earlier forms like clubs, but they are to be classed rather with the *Lil-lil* and the *Quriang-an-wun* than with the *Kud-jee-run.*

2. *fig.* A knife; esp. *attrib.* as **sword-swallower** (see quot. 1965); also **sword-swallowing** *vbl. n.*
1941 S.J. BAKER *Pop. Dict. Austral. Slang* 74 *Sword-swallowing,* the practice of eating with one's knife. 1965 J.S. GUNN *Terminol. Shearing Industry* ii. 30 *Sword swallower,* the fellow who uses his knife as a spoon and eats all his food off it. He is particularly resented by shearers, who are rather fastidious where food is concerned when he uses his knife in the butter.

sword-grass. [Transf. use of *sword-grass* any of several plants having sword-shaped leaves, applied more specifically in Aust. to such a plant when its leaves are capable of inflicting lacerations.] Any of several plants having long serrated leaves, esp. a sedge of the genus *Gahnia* (fam. Cyperaceae), as *G. sieberana* of e. mainland Aust. and elsewhere. See also CUTTING GRASS.
1879 *Kelly Gang* 38 The level space.. on the right hand side has a patch of very tall spear or sword-grass, which affords a jungle-like cover. 1979 K.A.W. WILLIAMS *Native Plants Qld.* I. 128 *Gahnia sieberana..* Sword Grass... The long, narrow leaves have small serrations along the edges. This makes them very dangerous to handle... Even accidentally brushing against these 'blades' can cause quite deeply incised wounds.

swottie. Alteration of 'swaddy', soldier.
1944 *Action Front: Jrnl.* 2/2 *Field Regiment* May 7 A 'Swottie' team won the boat race to the consternation of the matelots. 1953 J.E. MACDONNELL *Gimme Boats* 73 One of them AWAS. Living among them swotties—I dunno. You know what they are with a bit of skirt!

swy. Also **swey, swi, zwei.** [a. G. *zwei* two.]
1. **a.** A two-shilling coin.
1941 S.J. BAKER *Pop. Dict. Austral. Slang* 75 *Swy,* the game of two-up. (2) A sentence of two years' gaol. (3) A florin. 1983 *Age* (Melbourne) 15 Dec. 13 (*caption*) Exhibition of used coin of the realm: bank notes, collector's items, swys, deaners, zacs, treys, brass razoos.

b. *transf.* A two-year prison sentence.
1975 *Bulletin* (Sydney) 26 Apr. 44/1 'So the low creeps got me a swy with a one.'.. He was sentenced to two years' imprisonment with a minimum of one year to be served, depending on how the parole board assessed his case at the end of that year.

2. TWO-UP *n.* Also as **swy-up** and *attrib.*
1913 *Bulletin* (Sydney) 30 Jan. 16/1 Few of the thousand of habitual 'swi-up' players I have seen can spin decently without violently swinging the arm. 1944 *Aust. Week-End Bk.* 109 "Zwei?" What is 'zwei'?' asked the policeman... 'Two-up, an *illegal* Australian gambling game,' grinned one of the Aussie provosts. 1967 F. HARDY *Billy Borker yarns Again* 2 Any experienced swy player can pick a butterflied penny from the genuine spinning article.

3. Special Comb. **swy game,** a game of two-up; **school,** a group of persons who have assembled to play two-up.
1946 *Bulletin* (Sydney) 24 July 29/3 The usual **'swi' game** was in progress. 1944 *Aust. Week-End Bk.* 107 The **'zwei' school** behind the canteen always claimed him. 1945 D. ROBINSON *Pop's Blonde* 20 He had spun six heads yesterday, at the 'swey' school in the camp and his pockets were full of piastres.

Sydney. [The name of the capital city of New South Wales.]
1. Used *attrib.* in Special Comb. **Sydney duck** *hist.* [orig. U.S. (see Mathews)], a name given to an Australian immigrant to the Californian goldfields, esp. an ex-convict (see quots.); **-side,** New South Wales, as being on the other side of a natural barrier or border; see also SIDE *n.*[1] 1; the city of Sydney and its environs; also as *adj.;* **-sider,** a non-Aboriginal person native to or resident in (**a**) New South Wales, (**b**) Sydney, (**c**) Australia.
1889 T.W. KNOX *Boy Travellers in Australasia* 296 He then explained that **Sydney ducks** can hardly be said to exist at present, the term having been applied to runaway convicts, ticket-of-leave men, and other waifs and strays. 1889 J.H.L. ZILLMANN *Past & Present Austral. Life* 62 Botany Bay has still an unsavoury odour about it in England and the States; and to this day the name of 'Sydney ducks' is one of general opprobrium in California. 1846 S. DAVENPORT *Let.* 29 Apr. in *S. Australiana* (1977) Sept. 130 The discovery of a large grazing district to the north by Dr Leichhardt may likely lead to the investment of fresh capital on the **Sydney side** in its occupation with stock. 1888 'R. BOLDREWOOD' *Robbery under Arms* (1937) 1 My name's Dick Marston,

Sydney-side native. **1914** *Bulletin* (Sydney) 22 Oct. 13/4 Shearing cut out at Glengarrie .. yesterday. A barber .. who comes from Sydneyside, I think, put up, on the last day, the respectable total of 304. **1865** *Macmillan's Mag.* (London) Jan. 163 The difference of intercolonial tariffs will make as handsome a cause for a very pretty squabble as the devil himself could desire. 'General Peter Lalor crossed the Murray yesterday, and attacked the enemy's earthworks at Three Mile Creek. He was forced to retire with a loss of 400 men. The **Sydney-siders'** loss is considered by him to have been far greater.' How pretty that will read! **1906** *Truth* (Sydney) 5 Aug. 1/5 The St. Kilda team of kickballers arrived in Sydney .. their mission being to popularise what is termed the Australian game of football. Sydneysiders have hitherto resented the purely Melbourne game being called 'the Australian game'. **1917** *Ibid.* 13 May 1/8 The Dominion soldiers look so much nicer than the Sydneysiders .. because they have their uniforms made to order. **1986** *Nat. Times* (Sydney) 10 Jan. 12/2 My Sydney-born friends tell me that aliens can qualify to be called Sydney-siders after 20 years' continuous residence.

2. In the names of flora and fauna: **Sydney blue gum,** the tall, smooth-barked tree *Eucalyptus saligna* (fam. Myrtaceae) of e. N.S.W. and e. Qld.; the wood of the tree; **cedar** *obs.*, the tree *Toona australis* (see CEDAR 1); the wood of the tree; **funnel web (spider),** the spider *Atrax robustus* (see FUNNEL WEB); **rock (oyster),** the oyster *Saccostrea commercialis* (see *rock oyster* ROCK *n.* 2); *Moreton Bay oyster*, see MORETON BAY; also **Sydney oyster; silky (terrier),** *Australian terrier*, see AUSTRALIAN *a.* 4.

1904 J.H. MAIDEN *Notes on Commercial Timbers N.S.W.* 18 **Sydney blue gum** (*Eucalyptus saligna*) .. requires some distinctive designation to prevent its confusion with the pale-coloured blue gum (*Eucalyptus globulus*) of Tasmania and Victoria. **1838** T.H. JAMES *Six Months S.A.* 29 **Sydney cedar** and laths and shingles from Van Diemen's Land in every direction. **1965** *Austral. Encycl.* VIII. 234 As for the **Sydney funnel-web** spider, six human deaths have been recorded for this species since 1927, all in the neighbourhood of Sydney. **1980** R. MASCORD *Spiders of Aust.* 30 The range of *Atrax robustus* is known to extend from Newcastle, New South Wales, to Nowra, New South Wales, and westwards as far as Lithgow-Oberon, so the so-called Sydney Funnel-web does not belong to Sydney alone. **1851** [**Sydney rock**] *Illustr. Austral. Mag.* (Melbourne) May 303 Bread and cheese, potatoes .. and Sydney oysters, raw and stewed .. gave us all a most agreeable repast. **1917** F.J. MILLS *Dinkum Oil* 97 'Oysters' shouted Jensen .. and in a moment we were all sitting round picking the 'Sydney Rocks' from the cliff. **1984** *Bulletin* (Sydney) 18 Dec. 43/3 There were always Sydney oysters—beaut, sweet, small and reasonably inexpensive. **1986** *Ibid.* 4 Feb. 25/2 The Sydney rock oyster (*Crassostrea commercialis*) has been commercially cultivated since 1870. **1915** *Ibid.* 25 Feb. 22/1 For the bark the gull had copied a lively little '**Sydney silky**' terrier kept in the same house. **1953** D. CUSACK *Southern Steel* 301 A small dog—perhaps a Sydney Silky.

3. In the phr. **Sydney or the bush,** all or nothing (see quot. 1980); also used allusively with reference to the extremes of urban and rural life.

1915 DREW & EVANS *Grafter* 43 'Oh, well, Sydney or the bush', I said to myself, 'and I told him all about it.' **1980** B. HORNADGE *Austral. Slanguage* 110 The long-used expression *Sydney or the bush*, meaning 'all or nothing'. Originally it was used in the context of a man who gambled on making a fortune and living a life of ease in the city, with the penalty for failure being the need to seek a more difficult livelihood in the outback.

symph. [Abbrev. of *symphony*.] A symphony; a symphony orchestra.

1892 *Bulletin* (Sydney) 14 May 7/4 The missionary's daughter was About to play the symph. **1965** K. SMITH *OGF* 220 Limbering up for a session with the Sydney Symph.

T

tab, *n.*¹ *Obs.* [Abbrev. of *tabby* a young woman.] A (young) woman.
   1918 *Aussie: Austral. Soldiers' Mag.* Dec. 5/1 Last night I struck a dinkum little tab and route-marched her to Hyde Park.   1932 H. SIMPSON *Boomerang* 276 We pay our tabs .. when we want 'em, and tell 'em to get to hell out of it when we don't.

TAB /tiː eɪ ˈbiː, tæb/, *n.*² Also **T.A.B., tab.** [Acronym f. the initial letters of *Totalizator Agency Board*, the name of a government agency which controls off-course betting.] The Totalizator Agency Board; a branch or agency of this body; a bet placed with it.
   [N.Z. 1953 *Evening Post* (Wellington) 16 Jan., There is ample evidence that the T.A.B. has captured the interest of our teen-agers.]   1961 *Herald* (Melbourne) 8 Mar. 34/1 There will be no radios at T.A.B. agencies.   1964 *Sydney Morning Herald* 20 May 10/2 The TAB has signed a contract to buy a building in Harris Street.   1973 J. POWERS *Last of Knucklemen* (1974) 51 On Saturdays I'll punt. Not big stuff like Pansy. But I got a system worked out that oughtta cover my tabs—for a while at least.

table. *Shearing.* Abbrev. of *wool table* (see WOOL 2). Also *attrib.* as **table hand, man,** one who trims and rolls a shorn fleece.
   1905 *Shearer* (Sydney) 23 Dec. 7/5 They strut and skite round the woolroom and the galley-fire like 'first-battle' grenadiers to the great amusement of the .. two or three educated and travelled 'loppies' .. generally to be found amongst 'table-men'.   1908 W.H. OGILVIE *My Life in Open* 38 In front of the tables stand the 'wool-rollers', men whose business it is to 'skirt' the fleeces.   1928 C.E. COWLEY *Classing Clip* 33 The table-hands know exactly where to find the skirtings, and can thoroughly trim the fleece in the quickest time. If the fleece is badly 'thrown out', that is, not well spread, or broken, or thrown across the table, the table-hands are compelled to devote time to getting the fleece into a more suitable position.

table-drain. A very shallow surface drain.
   1968 *Swag* (Sydney) i. 42 He was standing, mud-bespattered and forlorn, by the roadside, with his vehicle anchored in the table-drain below him.   1978 C. GREEN *Sun is Up* 25 It had been raining for three weeks. . . The thirsty paddocks drank deep, the table drains gurgled.

table-top. A vehicle for the carriage of goods, having a (large) flat tray.
   1898 W. OGILVIE *Fair Girls* (1906) 113 There were side-rail tubs and table-tops, coaches and bullock-drays, Brown with the Barcoo Wonders, and Speed with the dapple greys Who pulled the front of his wagon out.   1980 M. STRINGER *Austral. Horse Drawn Vehicles* 236 The class of waggon, known as the table-top .. is used in New South Wales and Queensland for the purpose of conveying wool and other produce to the railway. It has an immense carrying capacity, the extreme length over the back and front rails being within two inches of 20 ft., and the width outside the frame 7 ft. 1 in.

tacker. [Br. dial. *tacker* a small child, esp. a boy: see EDD *sb.*²] A small boy.
   1942 P. SOMERVILLE *Not only in Stone* 101 Allen were only a little tacker at the time, an' 'e got lost an' went to sleep with daisies all about un.   1980 M. BAIL *Homesickness* (1981) 52 Ms Cathcart bent down before getting in, 'And what's this little tacker's name?' The boy pointed to himself.

TAFE /teɪf/. [Acronym f. the initial letters of *Technical and Further Education.*] A system of tertiary education offering courses mainly in technical and vocational subjects; an institution offering such courses. Also *attrib.*
   1974 *TAFE in Aust.* (Austral. Committee Techn. & Further Educ.) 11 The systems of TAFE are not .. responsible for ensuring the structural mix or balance of the labour force.   1984 *Bulletin* (Sydney) 11 Dec. 34/2 The present TAFE system offering trade courses, and the theoretical side of apprenticeship training.   1985 *Blue Mountains Echo* (Katoomba) 23 Dec. 22/5 The nature of employment is changing .. with more and more young people turning to Technical Colleges because High Schools are not equipping them with the work skills they need. . . TAFE is preferred because of the contents of the courses, but also because it is less authoritarian.

tag-a-long. See quot. 1963. Also *attrib.* as **tag-a-long tart.**
   1956 J.E. WEBB *So much for Sydney* 64 Our Girls are most 'teenagers', and it doesn't matter whether they are socialites, shopgirls or 'tagalong tarts'.   1963 *Bulletin* (Sydney) 23 Nov. 16/3 *Tag-a-long*, a girlfriend (or boyfriend).

tail, *n.*¹
   1. [Transf. use of *tail* the rear end of a marching column: see OED(S *sb.*¹ 4 c.] The rear of a travelling mob of sheep, cattle, etc.
   1849 A. HARRIS *Emigrant Family* (1967) 16 My cattle travel very wild; some of them are off down every gully they see:—you can .. stick to the tail of 'em.   1980 ANSELL & PERCY *To fight Wild* 80 My father taught me to ride when I was about four or five, and my brothers and sisters. That was doing cattle work, pushing up the tail of the mob, that kind of thing, on quiet horses.
   2. A fine strip of hide, etc., at the end of the thong of a whip: see quot. 1859.
   1859 W. BURROWS *Adventures Mounted Trooper* 133 Their 'stock-whips' .. are made of hide, plaited into a heavy thong, from nine to fifteen feet in length, the thickest part being about an inch in diameter, at the end of which is a 'tail' or point of green hide, crowned with a cracker of twisted raw silk.   1919 V. MARSHALL *World of Living Dead* 64 The flogger raised above his head the thick, short-handled 'cat' from which drooped down in murderous array its knotted 'tails' of hide.
   3. A thread or train of particles of mineral, esp. alluvial gold: see quot. 1898.
   [N.Z. 1898 'H' *Grain of Gold* 12 By a peculiar motion of the wrist, Old Grit separated the lighter iron-sand from a smaller quantity of heavier copper pyrites, and draws the last into a long string into the bottom of the dish, called 'the tail'.]   1937 M. TERRY *Sand & Sun* 75 Gold .. should show up in a bright yellow 'tail' behind the iron and such things.   1946 K.S. PRICHARD *Roaring Nineties* 40 Every dish Dinny panned off showed a fat tail of fine gold.

tail, *n.*² *Mining.*
   1. Usu. in *pl.* as *n.*, in *sing.* when *attrib.* Abbrev. of 'tailings', mining refuse.
   1855 *Illustr. Sydney News* 12 May 231/3 Puddling machines are daily getting more numerous on these diggings and form no very inconsiderable means of surfacing and tail-stuff washing; these machines use a great quantity of water in their washing operations and they are on such an account condemned by the diggers.   1939 I.L. IDRIESS *Cyaniding for Gold* 163 Test your 'heads'—the slime as it goes into the mixer. Test for gold, acid, alkalinity, mineral

combinations. Test your 'tails' (finished slime when discharged).

2. Special Comb. **tail race**, a channel through which the waste material from alluvial mining is carried away.

1856 G. WILLMER *Draper in Aust.* 89 Another man was placed at the 'tail race'.. whose business was to throw up on either side of it the dirt and stones which would otherwise have choked up our stream. **1980** J. WRIGHT *Big Hearts & Gold Dust* 146 There'd been a tail-race there many years ago.

tail, $n.^3$ *Two-up.*

1. *pl.* A fall of the coins in which the tails face upwards; a bet that the coins will fall this way.

1911 A. WRIGHT *Gamblers' Gold* (1923) 55 Throwing a coin on to the bag-covered floor, he called: 'Heads a shilling!' 'Tails one!' **1919** A. WRIGHT *Game of Chance* 32 What about some dough? I'm pretty well emptied out. Been having a trot of tails.

2. Comb. **tail-backer, -bettor**.

1922 C. DREW *Rogues & Ruses* 138 'Has he got you going, too?' laughed a **tail backer**. **1946** *Austral. New Writing* 36 **Tail bettors** toss in their money and soon the pound is covered. Again the side bettors 'get set'.

tail, $v.^1$ [See TAIL $n.^1$ 1.] *trans.* To follow, herd, and tend (livestock): see quot. 1905. Also with **out** and **up**.

1843 *Port Phillip Patriot* 11 May 3/2 The cattle.. were left in the yard all night, and tailed in the day. **1905** L. BECKE *Tom Gerrard* 251 'I'll turn the rest over to you to tail.' 'Tail'—a drover or stockman who is set to keep a mob of cattle from straying 'tails' them—i.e., follows at their tails. **1936** C.P. CONIGRAVE *N. Aust.* 118 Many times their only companion being the native boy who tails up the police-horses. **1957** R.S. PORTEOUS *Brigalow* 127 Every day for a week we would drive them out and tail them on good feed. At sundown we would yard them.. run them through the drafting yards before breakfast and then tail them out again for the day.

tail, $v.^2$ *Two-up.* [f. TAIL $n.^3$ 1.] In the phr. **to tail them** (or **'em**), to toss the coins so that they fall with the tail upwards.

1911 A. WRIGHT *Gamblers' Gold* (1923) 58 Tails some money. Any part of a quid tails. I'll lay odds he tails 'em. **1977** R.E. GREGORY *Orig. Austral. Inventions* 117 If they finish the same side up.. the players shout, 'He's headed them,' or 'He's tailed them.'

tail, $v.^3$ *intr.* With **out**: to work as a TAILER-OUT.

1919 C.J. DENNIS *Jim of Hills* 40 An' there he put me tailin' out.

tailer, var. TAILOR.

tailer, $n.^1$ [f. TAIL $v.^1$]

a. An animal which is being herded; an animal at the 'tail' of a mob; a straying animal.

1890 MRS H.P. MARTIN *Under Gum Tree* 15 The two white stockmen being at an out station with a mob of 'tailers', or weaned heifers. **1946** W.E. HARNEY *North of 23°* 11 Then herds go by, the drovers pass, The leaders feed along the route While cunning tailers nip the grass, Linger, then trot when whips are out. **1960** I.L. IDRIESS *Wild North* 194 The pack-team mooched contentedly along... Silent Jim and I brought up the 'tailers'.

b. One who herds livestock; one who rides at the 'tail' of a travelling mob; a horse used for this. Also *transf.* (see quot. 1930).

1895 K. MACKAY *Yellow Wave* 203 Taking out enough quiet horses to act as 'tailers', a dozen men.. made out early in the morning to where the horses 'ran'. Rounding up the 'tailers' in the bottom of one of the ravines.. the party, leaving half a dozen men in charge, rode off in threes. **1904** *Bulletin* (Sydney) 8 Dec. 36/4 There was a sufficient number of them to drive even such a mob as was on that plain. Flankers, leaders and tailers, plenty there. **1920** *Ibid.* 25 Mar. 22/2 The best horsetailer I ever knew was on a large Queensland cattle-run... He bet the cook a pound of tobacco that before leaving the camp he would tell him where every horse was running... We were all borrowing a pipeful of tobacco from the tailer. **1930** HIVES & LUMLEY *Jrnl. of Jackaroo* 21 On our way we collected the milking herd, consisting of ten quiet beasts, and drove them slowly in the direction the approaching cattle would have to go. These would act as 'tailers', and show the way to their wilder companions through the yard gates.

tailer, $n.^2$ TAILER-OUT.

1937 *N.S.W. Parl. Papers* (1938–40) 2nd Sess. VII. 667 The Aborigines Protection Board is running this sawmill... The tailer gets 22s. 6d. a week and the edging jerker £1 a week.

tailer-out. In a saw-mill: the employee responsible for guiding timber as it comes off the saw.

1895 *Bulletin* (Sydney) 3 Aug. 3/2 Few know the song—for the tailer-out, And the benchman swart, and his underlings, And the truckerman, and the trammer stout, Have their souls in the flitch and in wooden things. **1959** M. RAYMOND *Smiley roams Road* 121 You're going to get a job this arvo straight after dinner. You're going to be tailer-out at the little bandsaw.

tailie. *Two-up.* [f. TAIL $n.^3$ 1 + -Y.] One who bets on the coins falling tails upwards; *tail-backer*, see TAIL $n.^3$ 2.

1919 W.H. DOWNING *Digger Dialects* 49 *Tailie*, a man who backs 'tails' in the game of two-up. **1977** R. BEILBY *Gunner* 296 What about a bitta chop from you tailies? Come on, ya've hada good run. What about a sling?

tailing, *vbl. n.*

1. The herding and tending of livestock: see quot. 1848.

1848 H.W. HAYGARTH *Recoll. Bush Life* 56 When cattle are first brought to a new country they are subjected to a process called 'tailing', which consists in watching them with horsemen by day, and driving them into their enclosures every night: they grow very much out of condition under this treatment, but it must be continued as long as they show any inclination to ramble back to their old pastures, and usually lasts from three to five weeks, according to circumstances. **1938** D. BATES *Passing of Aborigines* 53 The long day's tailing made riding very wearisome.

2. The docking of an animal's tail.

[N.Z. **1864** E.R. CHUDLEIGH *Diary* (1950) 130, I tailed about 600 lambs.] **1916** *Bulletin* (Sydney) 6 July 22/3 Five catchers were allotted to each man, who had to do his own tailing and earmarking. **1955** J. MORRISON *Black Cargo* 57 He and Collins, the overseer, did all the knife-work—castrating, ear-marking, and tailing.

3. Special Comb. **tailing yard**, an enclosure into which cattle are herded temporarily: see quot. 1963.

1930 A. GROOM *Merry Christmas* 158 The cattle could be seen moving quietly to the tailing yards. **1963** M. BRITT *Pardon my Boots* 80 This morning, the cattle, which had been mustered the day before and held in the 'tailing-yard' overnight, were to be drafted. The tailing yard was a single large yard used when it was not necessary to take cattle all the way to the station yards, or when they were to be held just for a night.

tailor. Also **tailer, taylor**. [Orig. U.S.: see OED *sb.* 2. See also quot. 1969.] The marine fish *Pomatomus saltator*, a voracious feeder occurring in coastal waters. See also CHOPPER 2. Also **tailorfish**.

1827 *Tasmanian Almanack* 142 Taylor.. 1s. 6d. each.

1847 E.W. LANDOR *Bushman* 393 There are immense quantities of fish upon this coast. The best kind are called tailors, and have a good deal of the mackerel flavour. **1857** J. ASKEW *Voyage Aust. & N.Z.* 228 The harbour abounds with fish, of which the schnapper, jewfish, tailerfish . . are used for food. **1969** J. POLLARD *Austral. & N.Z. Fishing* 793 These [teeth] intermesh so closely when the fish bites that it is able to shear a garfish or a fine nylon line through with one chop. This shearing action of its teeth undoubtedly gave rise to the name of tailor.

tailor-bird. [Transf. use of *tailor-bird* any of several Asiatic birds stitching leaves to form their nests.] *Golden-headed fantail warbler*, see GOLDEN 3.

1854 W. HOWITT *Boy's Adventures* 43 We have never yet seen the nest of the bower bird . . though we have seen one of the tailor bird, suspended from the bough of a tree. **1964** M. SHARLAND *Territory of Birds* 32 *(caption)* The Tailorbird gets its vernacular name from its habit of sewing leaves round its nest, using cobweb for thread.

tailorfish: see TAILOR.

taint. *Obs.* STAIN.

1841 *Port Phillip Patriot* 10 June 4/3 The progeny of the convict immigrants—persons who have always been free, but have a 'taint' in their blood.

Hence **tainted** *ppl. a.*, of convict descent.

1905 *Horlick's Mag.* (London) Feb. 175/1 The bulk of the population, excluding, of course, the tainted element from the penal colonies, was of the best men of the Old Country.

taipan /'taɪpæn/. [a. Wik-Mungkan *dhayban*.] The brownish snake *Oxyuranus scutellatus* of n. and n.e. Aust. and s. New Guinea, the longest Austral. venomous snake.

1933 *Proc. Zool. Soc. London* 858 The name 'taipan', by which O[*xyuranus*] *scutellatus* is known to the aborigines of Cape York Peninsular, is an excellent vernacular name for the species. The natives hold the taipan in great dread, and it appears to have been responsible for many deaths among them. **1980** B. SCOTT *Darkness under Hills* 157 The fangs of the taipan—the huge, warlike brown snake of the scrubs.

take, *v.*

1. *trans.* [Used elsewhere, esp. in U.S., but of local significance: see OED *v.* 90 d. (b) and DAE *v.* 10 a.] With **up:** to acquire (land) from the Crown as owner or as tenant.

1831 J.G. POWELL *Narr. Voyage Swan River* 130 All the good land is already taken up on both sides of the Swan and Canning Rivers. **1981** A.B. FACEY *Fortunate Life* 49 A settler could take up land and settle on it without much or any money.

2. a. In the phr. **to take it out,** to undergo a punishment; esp. to serve a sentence of imprisonment instead of paying a fine.

1838 *Cornwall Chron.* 1 Sept. 3 James Smith was fined 5s. for being drunk, and not paying, he was ordered to take it out in wood [*sc.* to be put in the stocks]. **1943** K. TENNANT *Ride on Stranger* 176 George Benson told her briefly he would see her husband had a lawyer. He would probably get a month at the most and he'd better 'take it out'.

b. *trans.* With **out:** to win (a prize, etc.).

1976 *Austral.* (Sydney) 15 July 2/2 Helen Morse . . takes out the Australian Film Institute's top actress award. **1979** *Advertiser* (Adelaide) 23 July 7/6 *(heading)* Flautist takes out title.

take-all.

1. [Used elsewhere but recorded earliest in Aust.: see OED(S *take-*.] A disease of wheat and other cereals caused by the fungus *Gaeumannomyces graminis*, producing root rot and causing the death of plants. Also *attrib.*

1866 S. *Austral. Register* (Adelaide) 11 May 2/7 The 'takeall', so called, is too well known in Tasmania. . . The farmers there find they can grow peas on land so infected . . and eventually return to wheat. **1984** *Advertiser* (Adelaide) 3 Jan. 15/2 Farmers and scientists are learning how to handle rhizoctonia and take-all diseases.

2. *transf.* A cutworm. Also *attrib.*

1899 *North-Western Advocate* (Devonport) 6 Jan. 2/1 The crops continue to look well, and the present rain will greatly benefit the potatoes and interfere with the peregrinations of the 'take all'. **1928** R.H. CROLL *Open Road Vic.* 102, I have seen these moths in millions on the summit of Mount Bogong itself. . . When one remembers that they are the 'cutworm' or 'take-all-grub' in its winged form.

talent. The underworld; those who frequent it; an organized gang of these.

1879 D. MAYNE *Westerly Busters* 18 The 'talent', the 'fancy', the 'crushers', were there. **1893** D. HEALEY *Cornstalk* 66 The remaining larrikins are all members of organized gangs, called 'pushes' or 'talents'. . . As these . . gangs, the members of which range in age from 15 to 30 years, have feudal quarrels raging between them, a war of extermination is being continuously waged. **1899** *Truth* (Sydney) 15 Jan. 2/4 Three or four of a talent known as the Cow Lane Push.

talking stick. MESSAGE-STICK.

1913 *Bulletin* (Sydney) 31 July 15/2 'How do you know . . that this corroboree is going to take place?' 'Oh, news come roun',' he answered. My mind jumped to 'talking sticks', smoke signals and so on. **1928** R.M. MACDONALD *Opals & Gold* 200 He held aloft a small piece of pointed wood about four inches long; its surface was roughly tarred with shorthand-like marks and some symbols were also burned into the wood. 'It's a talking stick,' he continued.

tallegalane /tə'lɛgəlem/. Also **tallegallan, talleygallan.** [Prob. f. a N.S.W. Aboriginal language.] The fish *Myxus elongatus* (see *sand mullet* SAND).

1879 *Proc. Linnean Soc. N.S.W.* IV. 426 *Myxus elongatus* . . are known among the Sydney fishermen as the 'Sand Mullet' and 'Tallegallan'. **1896** F.G. AFLALO *Sketch Nat. Hist. Aust.* 232 The Sand Mullet or Talleygallan (*Myxus*) . . frequents the rivers, but goes down to the sea each winter. **1965** *Austral. Encycl.* VI. 195 The sand mullet or tallegalane . . of New South Wales is less valuable as a food fish, although it is at times plentiful in the markets.

tall oat grass. The tall, perennial grass *Themeda avenacea* (fam. Poaceae) of mainland Aust. See also OAT GRASS.

1895 F. TURNER *Austral. Grasses* I. 8 Between Nyngan and Bourke I once saw the 'tall oat grass' growing higher than the railway fences. . . The seeds are large, and in appearance somewhat resemble oats. **1981** G.M. CUNNINGHAM et al. *Plants Western N.S.W.* 148 Tall oatgrass *Themeda avenacea* . . resembles kangaroo grass (*T. australis*) but is often taller (to 1.7 m. high).

tallow. *Obs.* Used allusively to designate a squatter (one who has grown 'fat' as a grazier).

1869 *Colonial Soc.* (Sydney) 18 Feb. 11 To tell you the truth, I should enjoy a peep at the tallow-ocracy of Australia. **1902** M. CANNON *That Damned Democrat* (1981) 122 Balfour . . succeeded in getting his fellow Tallow Fats to amend the Education Act.

tallow-wood. [See quot. 1894.] The tall tree *Eucalyptus microcorys* (fam. Myrtaceae) of n.e. N.S.W. and s.e. Qld.; the greasy, strong, durable wood of the tree; (occas.) a similar eucalypt, or its wood.

1884 A. Nilson *Timber Trees N.S.W.* 67 E[*ucalyptus*] *microcorys.*—Tallowwood; Mahogany.—A tall tree, with a persistent furrowed fibrous bark. 1894 G. Scott *N.S.W. Hardwood Timber* 5 Tallow Wood .. is one of our most valuable timbers, and derives its local name from the fact of its being of an oily or rather greasy nature. 1985 *Parks & Wildlife News* Summer 18 Tallowwoods, up to 70 m. in height and 8 m. in girth.

tally. [Spec. use of *tally* a count, a number, the record of this: see OED(S *sb.*^{1} 2 e., and 5 a. and d.]
1. The number of sheep shorn by an individual shearer in a specified period; the record of this; a high number of sheep shorn (see quot. 1897); a call to mark a stage in the counting (see quot. 1886).
1870 *Austral. Town & Country Jrnl.* (Sydney) 29 Oct. 10/3 At five o'clock the bell rings; the day's labour is over; the men wait to see the sheep counted, and to hear their 'tallies'—the sums total of the day's shearing—read aloud. 1886 P. Clarke *'New Chum' in Aust.* 175 As a 'hundred' is called, one of us calls out 'tally', and cuts one notch in a stick. 1897 L. Lindley-Cowen *W. Austral. Settler's Guide* 635 Cuts in the skin are frequent with careless shearers, anxious only to make a tally. 1980 P. Freeman *Woolshed* 20 On completion of shearing, the sheep is dispatched unceremoniously down a sloped ramp into 'counting-out' pens, where the particular shearer's tally of shorn sheep is counted at the welcome 'smoko' and lunch breaks.

2. As **tally-hi.** [f. sense 1 + *hi(gh.*] See quot. 1964. Also *attrib.*
1964 *Sydney Morning Herald* 6 Apr. 2/6 The new 'tally-hi' shearing method .. cuts out some 15 blows (shearing strokes) a sheep and allows shearers to increase their tally by 20 or 30 sheep the first week they use it. This is not the only advantage of the tally-hi system. It is easier on the shearer because he does not have to lift the sheep or strain across it as much as he used to. It is easier on the sheep, reducing rough handling and the number of skin cuts. And it almost eliminates second cuts... 'The basis of the tally-hi system is that you shear down the sheep instead of across its body,' said Kevin Sarre. 1979 Harmsworth & Day *Wool & Mohair* 154 The feature of this *Tally Hi* method, as it is called, is the way that the strokes of the shearing handpiece progress in a rapid and smooth manner from one shearing position to the next.

tally-walka /'tæli-wɔkə/. Also **tally-walker.** [a. Baagandji *daliwalga.*] See quot. 1947, and cf. Anabranch.
1900 *Pastoral Times* (Deniliquin) 10 Mar. 1/7 That proposal embodied water conservation by using the cowls, tally-walkas, billabongs, and branches of rivers. 1947 M. Maclean *Drummond of Far West* 92 Further along the road, we passed a 'tally-walker', which was a new one to us city folk. According to my informant, a billabong is a backwater of a river, or was so until the water receded and left the billabong isolated. He said a tally-walker is much the same thing, but it rejoins the river farther along again, when flowing sufficiently.

tamar, var. Tammar.

tamarind. [Transf. use of *tamarind* the tree *Tamarindus indica* and its fruit.] *Native tamarind,* see Native *a.* 6 a.; the wood of a native tamarind.
1871 *Austral. Town & Country Jrnl.* (Sydney) 18 Mar. 330/4 A sample of the tamarind in this brush used in a bridge. 1902 *Bulletin* (Sydney) 6 Sept. 17/2 Near Hawkwood and Miles the wild lemon and tamarind trees, which have been regarded by bush naturalists as droughtproof, are dying.

tambaroora /tæmbə'rurə/. Also **tamberoora, tambooroora.** [The name of a goldfield north of Bathurst, N.S.W.]
a. A game in which each participant contributes an agreed sum to a pool which is then gambled for, the winner being required to buy drinks for the participants with (some of) the winnings: see quot. 1882.
1882 A.J. Boyd *Old Colonials* 63 It may be that the exciting game of Tambaroora is not familiar to all my readers... Each man of a party throws a shilling, or whatever sum may be mutually agreed upon, into a hat. Dice are then produced, and each man takes three throws. The Nut who throws highest keeps the whole of the subscribed capital, and out of it pays for the drinks of the rest. The advantage of the proceeding lies in this: Where drinks are charged at sixpence, the subscription is double that amount for each... Thus if ten Nuts go in for a Tambaroora, with nobblers at sixpence, the winner pockets five shillings by the transaction. 1895 *Bulletin* (Sydney) 26 Oct. 7/4 Service was being held on a Northern N.S.W. river, in a hall near the hotel. The landlord's little son .. seeing the priest, a great favourite of his, walked in and took a seat by his friend. The collection-box having been passed round, the child waited till the money was poured on the table in front of the clergyman, and then .. whispered— 'Say, shall I run and tell dad you are going to have a tambooroora?' 1900 *Truth* (Sydney) 11 Feb. 7/3 A sort of tamberoora, each one paying a shilling to enter the ring and get all he could.

b. Special Comb. **Tambaroora muster:** see Muster *n.* 5.

tame, *a. Obs.* [Transf. use of *tame,* as applied to an animal; rarely applied elsewhere to a person but cf. *tame Indian,* Mathews *tame, a.* 2.] Of an Aboriginal: not overtly hostile to the colonists. See also Civilized.
1842 *Portland Mercury* 7 Sept. 3/5 Many of the blacks engaged in this outrage had been for a long time domiciled on the station of Messrs Winter Brothers; in fact, scarcely any attack on any station has been made by the natives save under the guidance of a 'tame black'. 1968 W. Hilliard *People in Between* 67 Some 'boys' who were intelligent could be trained and 'tamed'. Carnegie's standard for 'tameness' is interesting. A 'tame' native was one who spoke English! No other requirements necessary!

tamma /'tæmə/. W.A. [Prob. f. a W.A. Aboriginal language.] A vegetation community consisting of low, thick, shrubby growth, the dominant plants incl. *Allocasuarina campestris* and *A. corniculata* (fam. Casuarinaceae) of W.A.; the plants themselves. Also *attrib.*
1905 *Rep. W.A. R. Comm. Immigration* 217, I have cultivated scrub plains—tamma scrub and blackboy country. 1973 R. Erickson et al. *Flowers & Plants W.A.* 190 Another vegetation type is tamma which is also a shrub formation but is less than 2 m. high and is dominated by *Casuarina campestris.*

tammar /'tæmə/. Also **tamar** and formerly **dama, damar, tamma.** [a. Nyungar *damar.*] The greyishbrown wallaby *Macropus eugenii* of s. S.A. and s.w. W.A. (incl. adjacent islands). Also *attrib.,* esp. as **tammar wallaby.**
1847 E.W. Landor *Bushman* 367 Our guides agreed .. to take us to a hill where a curious species of Kangaroo called 'Damar' by them, would be met with. 1903 *Emu* III. 105 This scrub is the home of numerous tamma. 1943 E. Troughton *Furred Animals Aust.* (rev. ed.) 194 The specific name *eugenii* is correctly used for all races of the Dama Pademelon. 1967 E. Huxley *Their Shining Eldorado* 217 The Tammar wallaby, now virtually extinct on the mainland but still to be found on the Abrolhos islands off the coast near Geraldton. 1978 *Ecos* xv. 27 A colony of tammar wallabies turned up in bush near Cleve on the Eyre Peninsula. 1985 *Austral.* (Sydney) 7 Nov. 8/1 Tamar wallaby joeys, ranging in age from 15 to 70 days, are decapitated, some are killed by night, some by day.

tangle. *Obs.* [Abbrev. of U.S. *tanglefoot* strong drink: see Mathews.] Alcoholic liquor.

1879 *Truth* (Sydney) 6 Nov. 8/1 A wicked female .. had imbibed more 'tangle' than she was able to accommodate without personal inconvenience. 1902 *Truth* (Sydney) 19 Oct. 8/1 Discussing club matters in the hotel bar over pints of tangle.

Hence **tangled** *ppl. a.*, drunk.

1899 J. BRADSHAW *Highway Robbery under Arms* (1912) 33 These two men were pannikin overseers, who had got a bit tangled with rum, and were trying the speed of their mokes.

tanglefoot. The deciduous shrub or small tree *Nothofagus gunnii* (fam. Fagaceae) having wiry, tangled branches, and occurring in the mountains of Tas.; *deciduous beech*, see BEECH; (occas.) any of several other plants of similar habit, as *Bauera rubioides* (fam. Saxifragaceae).

1891 W. TILLEY *Wild West of Tas.* 7 Bauera shrub, whose gnarled branches have earned for it the local and expressive name of 'tanglefoot' or 'leg ropes'. 1980 G.R. COCHRANE et al. *Flowers & Plants Vic. & Tas.* 115 The common name, Tanglefoot, serves to emphasise the density of the plant in exposed areas.

tank, *n.*[1] [Anglo-Indian *tank* artificial reservoir f. Gujarati *tankh* or Pg. *tanque* pond: see OED *sb.*[1]]

1. An artificial reservoir; DAM 1, esp. as excavated to provide water for livestock. Also **earth tank, surface tank.**

1791 D. COLLINS *Acct. Eng. Colony N.S.W.* (1798) I. 189 The governor had employed the stone-mason's gang to cut tanks out of the rock, which would be reservoirs for the water large enough to supply the settlement. 1909 *Bulletin* (Sydney) 10 June 13/2 Among the big cockies of Riverina at the present day is a desire to possess the largest surface-tank in the district. 1960 *N.T. News* (Darwin) 4 Mar. 5/3 Tilmouth went to Inverway to build some earth tanks.

2. Comb. **tank-keeper, -sinker, -sinking, town.**

1913 H. LAWSON *Triangles of Life* 234 Mitchell went, with the billy, into the little galvanized iron pumping-engine room, where the **tank-keeper** (an old sailor) was. 1881 W.E. ABBOTT *Notes Journey on Darling* 60 The station-buildings are erected, stock bought, and fences and **tank-sinkers** set to work in all directions. 1890 E.T. TOWNER *Selectors' Guide Barcoo* 15 The other method of conserving water is by **tank sinking.** 1948 G. MEREDITH *Lawsons* I Wongalee is .. an impressive little one-horse town whose few hundred yards of bitumen, straggling at each end into dusty dirt roads, rouse no excess of enthusiasm. The visitor to all such country towns wonders why they don't plant a few trees... The answer is, of course, that they are mostly **tank towns** and trees are thirsty things.

tank, *n.*[2] [Spec. use of *tank* artificial receptacle.]

1. A safe. Also *attrib.*, esp. as **tank man,** a safe-breaker.

[N.Z. 1937 E. PARTRIDGE *Dict. Slang & Unconventional Eng.* 864 *Tank*, .. a safe: New Zealand c. (-1932).] 1950 *Austral. Police Jrnl.* Apr. 119 *Tank*, a safe. 1974 C. PATON *I was Prison Parson.* As a 'tank' man (safe-blower) Harry had seen a lot a gaol. 1981 *Sydney Morning Herald* 2 Mar. 1/7 Dugan claimed that more than 30 years ago a friend had been arrested, convicted and sentenced for a Sydney 'tank' robbery—a safe cracking—which he had not done. Dugan said he knew this because he had done the job himself.

2. Special Comb. **tank-stand,** a structure which supports a tank in which water is stored.

1902 *Pastoralists' Rev.* Feb. 834 An earth tank stand for large stock tanks .. is constructed of earth bound together with logs scarfed into each other, to prevent the earth from spreading.

Tanna. *Obs.* TOMMY TANNA.

1906 *Bulletin* (Sydney) 3 May 14/1 Why does the allegedly humane missionary insist on Tanna squeezing his expansive feet into a No. 8 shoe?

Tanner's curse. [See quot. 1897.] DOUBLE-GEE.

1897 L. LINDLEY-COWEN *W. Austral. Settler's Guide* 541 My [*sc.* Baron von Mueller's] informant is Mr D. Wansborough, who landed at Fremantle in 1831. He, with his wife, came from England under contract with Mr William Tanner. On their way out the ship put in at the Cape of Good Hope, where Mr Tanner obtained the seed. Eighteen months after arrival in Western Australia Mr Wansborough .. sowed a bed with the seed of this 'Cape spinach'... The seed was obtained from Mr Tanner... However, the plant did not prove a very palatable spinach, and soon became a troublesome weed, causing constant annoyance to the workmen, on account of its spinous seeds... It received the name of 'Tanner's curse' throughout the settlement. 1980 J. FITZPATRICK *Bicycle & Bush* 140 It has been called 'doublegee' .. 'Tanner's curse', [etc.].

Tantanoola tiger /tæntənulə'taɪgə/. [f. the name of a town in s.e. S.A.] An animal reportedly seen at Tantanoola *c* 1889; a fabulous animal.

1893 *S. Austral. Advertiser* (Adelaide) 11 May 5/2 The Tantanoola 'tiger' is the 'lion' of the hour (writes the South-Eastern Star). 1911 *Bulletin* (Sydney) 5 Jan. 13/4 He will fight anything from a cockroach to a Tantanoola tiger.

taori, var. TOWRI.

tarantula. [Transf. use of *tarantula* a European spider of the fam. Lycosidae.] HUNTSMAN SPIDER.

1824 J. LYCETT *Views in Aust.* 4 Of poisonous reptiles, the centipede, tarantula, scorpion .. are the most hurtful. 1985 N. KEESING *Just look out Window* 36 The large brown hairy Huntsman spider, usually called 'tarantula' or 'tri-antelope', often enters houses.

tar-boy. *Shearing.* A hand employed chiefly to apply a disinfectant, orig. tar, to a wound accidentally inflicted on a sheep.

1871 *Austral. Town & Country Jrnl.* (Sydney) 21 Jan. 82/2 As a rule, the quickest men shear the best, and call less for the 'tar-boy'. 1979 K. GARVEY *Absolutely Austral.* 19 The tar-boy by fly-strike kept running.

tarpaulin. Abbrev. of *tarpaulin muster* (see MUSTER *n.* 5).

1946 J.H. FAHEY *Slim Sullivan hits Wallaby* 11 'What about a 'tarpaulin' for a new rifle for Slim?' 'Too right .. I'll sport a quid.'

tart. [Prob. abbrev. of *jam tart* (see quot. 1864), itself prob. rhyming slang for 'sweetheart'. Also used pejoratively, as elsewhere: see OED(S *sb.* 2.] A girl-friend or 'sweetheart'; applied generally to a girl or woman but usu. implying admiration.

[1864 J.C. HOTTEN *Dict. Mod. Slang* (ed. 3) 254 *Tart*, a term of approval applied by the London lower orders to a young woman for whom some affection is felt. The expression is not generally employed by the young men, unless the female is in 'her best', with a coloured gown, red or blue shawl, and plenty of ribbons in her bonnet—in fact, made pretty all over, like the jam tarts in the swell bakers' shops.] 1892 *Truth* (Sydney) 1 May 2/7 They were very fond of music, were this baldy and his 'tart'. 1937 A.W. UPFIELD *Mr Jelly's Business* 28 I'm in love with a tart. Her name's Lucy Jelly. She is the loveliest girl within a thousand miles of Burracoppin. Twenty years old she is. Her father is a cocky four miles out. He doesn't seem to mind me courting his daughter, but he doesn't give me a chance to do any courting.

tar tree. [See quot. 1948.] The tree *Semecarpus australiensis* (fam. Anacardiaceae) of n. Aust. and elsewhere.

1938 C.T. WHITE *Princ. Bot. Qld. Farmers* 176 Family Anacardiaceae .. represented in Queensland by seven native species. These include .. the Tar Tree (*Semecarpus australiensis*) [etc.]. **1948** H.A. LINDSAY *Bushman's Handbk.* 142 On the sea-coasts of Queensland, New Guinea and the Indies there grows a large tree with thick foliage... It can be recognized .. by the black, thick, tar-like sap which flows from any wound in the bark. This is the tar-tree whose sap causes bad ulcers.

tart shop. Used allusively of political office, esp. as able to be exploited by its occupants.

[**1904** A. DEAKIN in J.A. la Nauze *A. Deakin* (1965) 378, I do not propose to reply to him except by saying he presents to you as undignified a spectacle as does the ill-bred urchin whom one sees dragged from a tart-shop kicking and screaming as he goes.] **1908** *Truth* (Sydney) 13 Dec. 1/5 The Reid gang reckon they wouldn't occupy the tart shop if they had the chance, yet the envious hungry crowd are flattening their noses against the outside window like a lot of famished school kids. Could Rumpty's push scoff a tart in the shape of a Ministerial portfolio? **1982** *Sydney Morning Herald* 24 Dec. 12/5 Why should retired politicians, whose superannuation is already generously subsidised from the public purse, get free rides as well? The tart shop, it seems, is not just open to the railway unions.

tarwhine /'tawain/. [a. Dharuk *darrawayin* a fish.] The silvery marine fish *Rhabdosargus sarba* of Aust. and elsewhere.

c **1790** W. DAWES Grammatical Forms Lang. N.S.W., *Tar-ra-wine*, a fish. **1983** *Ecos* xxxv. 5/2 Closer investigation .. has now turned up evidence for sex inversion in yellowfin bream, tarwhine, snapper .. all of them important fish in the market-place.

Tasmaniac. A nickname for a non-Aboriginal person native to or resident in Tasmania.

1867 *Sydney Punch* 23 Feb. 101/1 'Fill we tankards to the brim', Thus Tasmaniacs used to cry. **1982** *Bulletin* (Sydney) 16 Nov. 42/2 In Sydney .. they are called Tasmaniacs.

Tasmanian, *a*. and *n*. [f. *Tasmania*, the name of an island lying south of s.e. Aust., and one of the federated States of Australia.]

A. *adj.*

1. Of or pertaining to the island of Tasmania or to its inhabitants.

1824 *Hobart Town Gaz.* 22 Oct., The *Tasmanian Fleece*, in our Gazette of the 9th of July last, we published some interesting Correspondence on the subject of wool exports from Van Diemen's Land. **1986** *Nat. Times* (Sydney) 31 Jan. 4/1 'Having a good day?' asks Tasmanian Premier Robin Gray, pumping the sticky hand of an ice cream-eating voter.

2. In the names of flora and fauna: **Tasmanian barber** *obs.*, the marine fish *Caesioperca rasor* of Tas., Vic., S.A., and s. W.A.; **blackwood,** BLACKWOOD, esp. the wood of the tree; **blue gum,** the tree *Eucalyptus globulus* subsp. *globulus* (fam. Myrtaceae) of Tas. and s. Vic., the floral emblem of Tas.; the wood of the tree; **devil,** the carnivorous marsupial *Sarcophilus harrisii*, a black animal with white markings, mainly carrion-eating but of fierce appearance, now occurring only in Tas.; *bush devil*, see BUSH C. 3; DEVIL 1; *native devil, native hyena* (b), see NATIVE *a*. 6 b.; **lilac,** either of two shrubs or trees of s.e. Aust. of the genus *Prostanthera* (fam. Lamiaceae), *P. lasianthos* (see *Christmas bush* (a), CHRISTMAS) and *P. rotundifolia*, bearing white or lilac flowers; **myrtle,** MYRTLE 1; **native hen,** the plump, brown bird *Gallinula mortierii*, occurring in fields near water throughout Tas., excl. the south-west; see also *native hen* (a), NATIVE *a*. 6 b.; **oak,** the timber of the trees *Eucalyptus obliqua* (see MESSMATE), *E. regnans* (see *mountain ash* MOUNTAIN), and ALPINE ASH; (occas.) one of the trees themselves; **tiger,** the carnivorous marsupial *Thylacinus cynocephalus*, having sandy brown fur with dark brown stripes across the back and rump, now poss. extinct (see quots. 1885 and 1947); HYENA; *marsupial wolf*, see MARSUPIAL 1; *native hyena* (b), *native tiger*, see NATIVE *a*. 6 b.; *Tasmanian wolf*; THYLACINE; TIGER *n*. 1; see also WOLF a.; **trumpeter,** the fish *Latris lineata* (see TRUMPETER $n.^1$ 1); **waratah,** the shrub *Telopea truncata* (see WARATAH 1); **wolf,** *Tasmanian tiger*.

1842 *Tasmanian Jrnl. Nat. Sci.* I. 59 The *Serranus Rasor*, or **Tasmanian Barber,** is a beautiful fish. **1886** *T.H.A.J.* no. 69 6 **Tasmanian blackwood** .. will ever hold its own against all competitors as to quality, cost, and easy means of transit, whilst for furniture and all decorative purposes it is most valuable. **1880** C. PROUD *S.-E. District S.A.* 45 The longitudinal timbers are of jarrah, and the decking of **Tasmanian bluegum. 1857** W. HOWITT *Tallangetta* I. 217 You have seen the **Tasmanian devil**—a furious beast that will devour its own species when wounded. **1892** M. NORTH *Recoll. Happy Life* II. 174 Shrubs of many kinds, that called the **Tasmanian lilac** (*Prostanthera lasianthos*) being the most striking. **1914** H.M. VAUGHAN *Australasian Wander-Yr.* 119, I was delighted with the so-called Tasmanian Lilac. **1833** J. BACKHOUSE *Narr. Visit Austral. Colonies* (1843) 159 The **Tasmanian Myrtle,** *Fagus Cunninghamii*, here forms trees of moderate size. **1936** *Smith's Weekly* (Sydney) Apr. 20/4, I nominate the **Tasmanian native-hen** as the speediest of Australia's waterfowl. **1919** *Huon Times* (Franklin) 24 Oct. 5/1 Immediately opposite was a dining suite in **Tasmanian oak. 1967** E. HUXLEY *Their Shining Eldorado* 174 Stringybark (*E. delegatensis*) sometimes called Tasmanian oak and sometimes called Alpine ash. **1833** J. BACKHOUSE *Narr. Visit Austral. Colonies* (1843) 30 Apr. 144 Great Swan Port. Upon one part of the beach .. and in several places, we saw the foot-prints of the **Tasmanian Tiger. 1885** *Illustr. Austral. News* (Melbourne) 19 Dec. 218/3 The group of the marsupial wolf, or Tasmanian tiger .. is now entirely confined to Tasmania... In the older geological time of the pleistocene period it seems to have existed on the mainland. **1947** Mrs A.H. GARNSEY *Romance Huon River* 32 The Tasmanian Tiger .. is now protected, though thought to be extinct, as it was much hunted. **1906** D.G. STEAD *Fishes of Aust.* 118 The **Tasmanian Trumpeter** (*Latris hecateia*) .. has only been taken so far on the coasts of Tasmania, Victoria and South Australia. **1835** *Hobart Town Almanack* 110 *Telopea Tasmaniana*. **Tasmanian waratah.** .. The beautiful crimson flowering shrub, with dark green rhododendron like leaves, which grows in the upper region of Mount Wellington. It has not yet been successfully cultivated about Hobart-town. **1855** W. HOWITT *Land, Labor & Gold* II. 392 The **Tasmanian wolf,** or hyena, as they call it here .. is a long, smooth-haired animal, of a grayish-brown, with black stripes across its back.

3. In the collocation **Tasmanian bluey,** a woollen outer garment (see BLUEY 3); the material of which such a garment is made.

1910 *Huon Times* (Franklin) 8 June 4/1 A bluish grey blanket overcoat, known as a Tasmanian bluey. **1962** E. LANE *Mad as Rabbits* 63 Mother used to buy Father's .. Tasmanian-bluey coats for winter that way.

B. *n.*

1. A non-Aboriginal person native to or resident in Tasmania.

1833 W.H. BRETON *Excursions* 389 Tasmanians find great fault with those horses that are imported from Sydney. **1969** *Mercury* (Hobart) 15 May 3/5 Mr Reece said he was making the attack because he was a Tasmanian 'and I fight for Tasmania'.

2. A member of one of the Aboriginal peoples of Tasmania; a descendant thereof.

1844 C. Lyon *Narr. & Recoll. Van Dieman's Land* 30 The ensanguined administration of Sir George Arthur, has destroyed a great part of the native foresters, and reduced the number from seventeen-hundred to about sixty, who are cooped up on a small island in Bass Straits, where they are continually dwindling away... The Tasmanians will rest amid the thousand wrecks of innocence, that England delights to crush when it is in her power. **1981** *Canberra Times* 4 Nov. 13/1 The surviving Tasmanians struggle not only with the problems of all Aborigines in south-east Australia but, more, they have had to prove they existed at all.

tasmanite. A sulphur-rich hydrocarbon compound occurring in laminated shales in the Mersey River, n. Tas. Also *attrib.*
1864 A.H. Church *Phil. Mag.* XXVIII. 465 (OED) Tasmanite, a new Mineral of Organic Origin. **1965** *Austral. Encycl.* II. 83 Australia contains extensive deposits of oil-shale, which term is taken to include .. shales that contain free oil (for instance tasmanite-shale) .. in the Permian coal measures of Tasmania.

Tasmanoid, *a.* [f. Tasmanian *n.* 2.]
1. Of, allied to, or resembling the ethnological type of the Aborigines of Tasmania. Cf. Australoid. Also as *n.*
1925 H. Basedow *Austral. Aboriginal* Pl. 3, Supra-orbital, deep notch at root of nose, prognathism (Tasmanoid features), and female beard, Denial Bay tribeswoman. **1952** R.M. & C.H. Berndt *First Australs.* 25 Except for the Tasmanoids .. they represent some conformity of physical type, but much diversity in headshape and stature.
2. *transf.* See quot.
1982 *Bulletin* (Sydney) 16 Nov. 42/1 Oh, but it's called Tasmanoia: it's an island state of mind. There are Tasmanoids everywhere. Even here in Melbourne the Tasmanians stick together.

Tassie, *n.* and *a.* Also **Tassey, Tassy, Tazzie**. [f. *Tas(mania* or Tas(manian *n.* 1 and *a.* + -Y.]
A. *n.*
1. Tasmania.
1892 *Bulletin* (Sydney) 17 Dec. 19/1, I took a turn in New South, and tried Tassy and New Zealand. **1955** N. Pulliam *I traveled Lonely Land* 222 Every state has 'em, of course—except Tazzie, that is. **1981** Q. Wild *Honey Wind* 73 Tassie's pretty, very English.
2. A non-Aboriginal person native to or resident in Tasmania.
1899 *North-Western Advocate* (Devonport) 27 Feb. 3/3 This time the Tassy happened not to win. **1905** A.B. Paterson *Old Bush Songs* 51 Once more the Maorilander and the Tassey will be seen Cooking johnny cakes and jimmies on the plains of Riverine.
B. *adj.* Tasmanian.
1916 *Bulletin* (Sydney) 8 June 24/3 Tassy bushmen .. never spoke of 'carfing' a tree when they meant chopping or sawing it down. **1984** *Ibid.* 25 Sept. 48/1 Tassie blueys—a heavy wool, fireproof, waterproof and bushproof jacket with a leather collar.

Taswegian, *a.* and *n.* [f. Tas(manian *n.* 1 and *a.* + -wegian as in Glaswegian, etc.]
A. *adj.* Tasmanian.
1961 *Bulletin* (Sydney) 24 May 8/1 The bracing Taswegian climate does not encourage Hobart citizenry to move far from their TV-sets. **1979** P. Adams *More Unspeakable Adams* 101 We do not propose to make the same mistake as our Taswegian forebears did with the Abos.
B. *n.* A non-Aboriginal person native to or resident in Tasmania.
1972 W. Watkins *Don't wait for Me* 3 A dumb Tasmanian, called a Taswegian. **1981** A.J. Burke *Pommies & Patriots* 56 The problem was never properly solved by the Victorian Yarra Yabbies, the New South Wales Corn Stalks, the West Australian Sand Gropers, the South Australian Crow Eaters, the Canberra ACTS, the Taswegians or the Queensland Cane cutters.

tats, *pl.* Also **tatts**. [Fig. use of *tats* dice; chiefly Austral.: see OED(S *tat, sb.*^{1}] Teeth; usu. false teeth.
[N.Z. **1906** *N.Z. Truth* (Wellington) 28 July 1 When swift as a flash, she swished a stinging left hook on to his chin and—presto—his whole set of upper front 'tats' fell into his long beer!] **1919** W.H. Downing *Digger Dialects* 49 Tats, teeth. **1943** S.W. Keough *Around Army* 20 There is the classic case of the Western Front bab. who in 18 months had never boiled it once when making the tea. As he used to say to his offsider, 'Let the blankards strain the leaves through their tatts!'

Tatts. Also **Tatt, tatts**. Abbrev. of 'Tattersall's Sweep', the name of a lottery established in 1881 by George Adams (1839–1904), licensee of Tattersall's Hotel, Sydney. Also **Tatt's sweep**.
1896 *Bulletin* (Sydney) 22 Feb. 27/2 Mr Murphy .. had drawn a minor prize in a Tatt. sweep, and he had been 'on a fair bend' for a week. **1897** *Tocsin* (Melbourne) 9 Dec. 9/2 The lucky drawers of starters in 'Tatt's' sweep were all so anxious to have a fair go with their 'neddies' that they laid the individuals named large sums to nothing in the event of a win. **1979** H. Post *Maintain your Rage* 56 The man who has nothing and wins half a million in tatts may burst his best part through happiness.

taurai, tauri, varr. Towri.

tawarang /ˈtæwəræŋ/. *Hist.* Also **tourang, towerang**. [a. Dharuk *dawarraŋ*.] An Aboriginal shield: see quot. 1798.
1790 D. Southwell Corresp. & Papers, *D'tar-warra*, implement used to fend or ward off blows, a weapon of defence. **1798** D. Collins *Acct. Eng. Colony N.S.W.* I. 585 Ta-war-rang .. is about three feet long, is narrow, but has three sides, in one of which is the handle, hollowed by fire. The other sides are rudely carved with curved and waved lines, and it is made use of in dancing, being struck upon for this purpose with a club. **1851** J. Henderson *Excursions & Adventures N.S.W.* II. 150 The *tourang* is another sort of shield, used for causing missiles to glance aside. It is a solid piece of wood from two to three feet long, pointed at the ends, four-sided, with a hole cut through one edge, at the centre, to hold it by, while the opposite edge, or apex, is presented to the threatening spear. It is not used in those parts of the country where the *heelaman* is known. It is commonly carved all over. **1881** E. Davies *Story Earnest Life* 129 The savages were still yelling and beating on their towerangs with waddies.

tawny frogmouth. The frogmouth *Podargus strigoides* of all States, a mottled grey to brown nocturnal bird having a low, soft call; Mopoke *n.* 1 b. See also Podargus. Formerly also **tawny-shouldered podargus**.
1840 J. Gould *Birds of Aust.* (1848) II. Pl. 3, *Podargus humeralis* .. Tawny-shouldered Podargus. **1985** C. Pallin *Bat came to Stay* 2 A pair of tawny frogmouths waited for someone to push food into their gaping beaks.

taylor, var. Tailor.

tea.
1. [Spec. use of *tea* a meal at which tea is served: see OED(S *sb.* 4.] A substantial meal, usu. eaten in the early evening.
1863 *Jrnls. & Rep. Two Voyages Glenelg River* 24 July (1864) 21 For tea there was the usual dish of salt beef, and in addition a side dish of Fricassee à l'alligator, which under the name of stewed cobbler obtained but a qualified

approval. **1984** B. Dixon *Searching for Aboriginal Lang.* 69 In Australia 'tea' is the main meal of the day—a big slap-up feast with lots of meat, two or three vegetables, slices of bread and butter, and then a helping of pudding.

2. a. In the phr. **Tea and Sugar,** the name of a train conveying supplies to settlements along the Trans-Australian Railway. Also **Tea and Sugar train.**

1937 E. Hill *Great Austral. Loneliness* 225 The 'Trans' and its people are a little world sufficient for themselves, a remarkable colony of government servants... With .. week-end dances at Cook, and a weekly shopping orgy on the 'Tea and Sugar' train that brings their water and supplies. **1977** B. Fuller *Nullarbor Lifelines* 39 It is the custom for the 'Tea and Sugar' to draw off onto a side line for the night, a procedure known as 'stabbing'.

b. In the collocation **tea and sugar burglar (bandit, bushranger),** a swagman; a petty thief. Also as **tea and sugar burgling.**

1900 H. Lawson *On Track* 130 Could I explain that I 'jabbed trotters' and was a 'tea-and-sugar burglar' between sheds. They'd think I'd been a tramp and a beggar all the time. **1930** *Aussie* (Sydney) July 27/1 Other ways of referring to the pastime are 'humping your drum'.. and 'tea and sugar burgling'. **1945** T. Ronan *Strangers on Ophir* 52 Every tea-and-sugar bushranger who rats a boundary rider's hut thinks he's another Ned Kelly. **1967** *Kings Cross Whisper* (Sydney) xxxxi. 4/2 *Tea and sugar bandit*, a petty thief. Usually the type of person who is too lazy to work and too frightened to steal large quantities of other peoples' goods.

3. Special Comb. **tea billy,** a billy in which tea is brewed (see Billy $n.^1$ 1); **bucket** *obs.*, *tea billy*; **-dinner** *obs.*, Tea 1.

1889 E. Giles *Aust. twice Traversed* II. 67 While some were unyoking the horses, some were boiling the **tea-billies**. **1903** *Bulletin* (Sydney) 23 May 17/1 O where's the old cooks smilin', the big **tea buckets** bilin'. **1855** W. Howitt *Land, Labor & Gold* I. 126 Our **tea-dinner**, you will admit, is not to be sneezed at.

tea bush. *Obs.* Any of several shrubs: see quot. 1900.

1839 W.H. Leigh *Reconnoitering Voyages* 127 Wild indigo, or a solitary tea bush. **1900** *Proc. Linnean Soc. N.S.W.* XXV. 598 *Eremophila latifolia*.. (Tea Bush, because a beverage fit to drink is said to have been made from the leaves).

teak. [Tranf. use of *teak* the tree *Tectona grandis* of s.e. Asia, and its wood.] Any of several trees yielding a durable timber resembling teak, esp. Crow's ash.

1849 R.J. Mann *Emigrant's Guide Aust.* 75 Good teak and oak for repairing ships are found at the same place [*sc.* Port Essington]. **1965** *Austral. Encycl.* VIII. 445 The Indian teak, *Tectona grandis* (family Verbenaceae), grows in a few gardens in North Queensland, but in Australia the name teak is applied to *Flindersia australis*.

tear. [Spec. use of U.S. *tear* a spree.] In the phr. **on the tear,** engaged in a drinking bout.

1898 *Bulletin* (Sydney) 23 Apr. 14/1 Our doctor and a huge bushman had been 'on the tear' for some days. **1979** *Sporting Globe* (Melbourne) 19 Sept. 2 Chairman of selectors Wes Lofts was detailed to track down Young—but to no avail as the young Carlton player was dining with his parents, who were over from Tasmania. I think Wes thought Michael might have been out on the tear.

tea scrub. *Obs.* Tea tree 1.

1842 *Geelong Advertiser* 28 Feb. 4/1 The country in the vicinity of the township is described as a useless barren track, covered with dense tea scrubs, intersected here and there with salt water marshes, and a few fresh swamps. **1878** R.B. Smyth *Aborigines of Vic.* II. 39 Tea scrub on hummocks.

tea-tree. Also **ti-tree.** [Transf. use of *tea-tree* the shrub yielding tea: see quot. 1843.]

1. Any of many often aromatic trees and shrubs of the fam. Myrtaceae, incl. those of the genus *Melaleuca* (see Melaleuca) and esp. those of the chiefly Austral. genus *Leptospermum*; the wood of the tree; Tea scrub. Also *attrib.*

1790 J. White *Jrnl. Voyage N.S.W.* 229 Tea tree of New South Wales. Melaleuca? [*sic*] trinervia. This is a small shrub, very much branched. **1843** J. Backhouse *Narr. Visit Austral. Colonies* xxxiii, The genera *Leptospermum* and *Melaleuca* are, in the Island [*sc.* Tasmania], indiscriminately called 'Tea-tree', without reference to species. The leaves of some of them have been used as a substitute for tea; but the flavour is too highly aromatic to please the European taste. **1984** *Southern Cross* (Melbourne) 5 Dec. 3/7 The Elwood foreshore area where work is under way on a ti tree area.

2. Comb. **tea-tree bark, brush, bush, creek, flat, scrub, swamp.**

1825 B. Field *Geogr. Mem. N.S.W.* 57 Their huts are built of long slender wattles .. and the whole is covered with **tea-tree** (melaleuca armilliaris) **bark**, in such a manner as to be quite impervious to the rain. **1810** *HRA* (1921) 3rd Ser. I. 774 The Island is .. covered with Thick **Tea Tree Brush**. **1820** C. Jeffreys *Van Dieman's Land* 133 For tea, they drink a decoction of the sassafras and other shrubs, particularly one which they call the **tea-tree bush**. **1845** L. Leichhardt *Jrnl. Overland Exped. Aust.* 18 Sept. (1847) 408 Two **tea-tree creeks** .. contained fresh water in the upper part of their short courses. **1845** C. Hodgkinson *Aust., Port Macquarie to Moreton Bay* 52 We started across a grassy **tea-tree flat**. **1835** *Jrnl. Australasia* (1856) I. 55 A dense **tea-tree scrub**, which we knew to be the surest indication of good water in its neighbourhood. **1827** *HRA* (1922) 3rd Ser. V. 853 Through low meadows with **Tea-tree swamps**.

3. Special Comb. **tea-tree oil,** a volatile essential oil distilled from species of the genus *Melaleuca* (fam. Myrtaceae), esp. from *M. alternifolia* of Qld. and N.S.W.; also *attrib.*

1933 *Bulletin* (Sydney) 12 July 19/2 The distillation of essential oil from *Melaleuca alternifolia* (tea-tree) has become an established N.S.W. industry... Some 40 tea-tree oil preparations are on the market. **1985** P. Carey *Illywhacker* 222 We were on our way up to Darkville where one of Barret's clerks now had a still for making tea-tree oil.

technicolour, *a.* Also **technicolor.** In the collocation **technicolour yawn (chunder, laugh, yodel),** the act of vomiting.

1964 B. Humphries *Nice Night's Entertainment* 77 But when I'd swallowed the last prawn I had a Technicolor yawn And I chundered in the old Pacific sea. **1967** *Kings Cross Whisper* (Sydney) xxxii. 1/2 It will be available in the form of pills which will .. produce a technicolor chunder. **1967** F. Hardy *Billy Borker yarns Again* 63 Calling for Herb, see, that's one of the many euphemisms for vomit, others include .. throw, the whip o' will, the technicolour laugh and, in Queensland, the chuckle. *Ibid.* 66 Each one sang his own theme song between the technicolour yodels.

teddy bear. Rhyming slang for Lair *n.* a.

1953 S.J. Baker *Aust. Speaks* 135 *Teddy bear*, a flashily dressed, exhibitionistic person; by rhyme on *lair*. **1974** Stackpole & Trengove *Not just for Openers* 128 When Parfitt made the catch Greig jumped in the air, and, as he landed, thumped his fist into the pitch... I said to Greig as I walked past, 'You're nothing but a bloody Teddy Bear.' He returned the pleasantries.

telegram. *Obs.* Bush telegraph *n.* 1.

1899 G.E. Boxall *Story Austral. Bushrangers* 230 During the afternoon a number of other persons were brought into 'the camp'. All except one man were allowed to move about freely. This one man was tied, and was spoken to very roughly and uncivilly. The man was supposed to be 'a telegram', and this show of harshness 'a stall'. **1911** A.L. HAYDON *Trooper Police Aust.* 148 He was well served, also, by 'bush telegraphs'... There was reason to believe that the organisation of this service was so thorough that every township had its 'telegram'. Certain it is that throughout a wide extent of country the bushrangers were kept fully posted as to the movements of the police by their many friends.

telegraph, *n.*

1. Abbrev. of BUSH TELEGRAPH *n.* 1.

1864 *Goulburn Herald* 17 Aug. 2/3 These young scoundrels have got their 'telegraphs' in town, and there is not a stir the police can make but it is known. *Ibid.* 12 Oct. 4/5 It would make me look a gamer man to the police and other people as has got a down on me for being a telegraph to you chaps. **1948** F. CLUNE *Wild Colonial Boys* 329 The police were a quarter of a mile away, but they saw him and beckoned. Charters.. galloped away at full speed... 'A telegraph!' yelled Sanderson. 'Follow him, men!'

2. *Obs.* BUSH TELEGRAPH *n.* 2.

1856 *Tumut & Adelong Times* 1 Jan. 2/3 They approached to within one hundred yards of the camp unobserved, and then it was apparent that the 'telegraph' had done its work.

3. Abbrev. of BUSH TELEGRAPH *n.* 3.

1955 F. LANE *Patrol to Kimberleys* 23 News had a way of filtering in by smoke signal, message stick, or by native runner. This mysteriously accurate 'telegraph' spanned the vast and seemingly impenetrable stretches of the Australian outback.

4. *Obs.* A system of communication between prisoners: see quots. Also *attrib.*

1891 'OLD TIME' *Convict Hulk 'Success'* 20 The 'telegraph' was very extensively worked on board these hulks... The 'telegraph' was a system of speaking from one cell to another by means of tapping on the walls, a certain number of taps meaning a particular letter. **1903** *Bulletin* (Sydney) 10 Jan. 33/1 Gentleman Fred knocked.. so loud that 3rd Class Warder Downey.. caught the 'telegraph-operator' red-handed.

telegraph, *v. trans.* Abbrev. of BUSH TELEGRAPH *v.*

1937 M. TERRY *Sand & Sun* 80 We had been observed on the hilltop and the news was being telegraphed through the bush—a mulga wire.

telopea /tə'loʊpiə/. [The plant genus *Telopea* was named by British botanist R. Brown in 1809 (see quot. 1809), f. Gr. τηλο—comb. form of τῆλε afar + ὠπή sight, view, with reference to the conspicuous flowerhead of the plant.] A shrub or tree of the genus *Telopea* (see WARATAH 1).

[**1809** *Trans. Linnean Soc. London* (1811) X. 197 *Telopea* .. Etym. τηλωπας qui e longinquo cernitur, quod de his fruticibus, floribus coccineis speciosis valet.] **1825** B. FIELD *Geogr. Mem. N.S.W.* 422 The shrubs and flowers are beautiful.. telopea the magnificent and thysanotus the lovely. **1929** *Aussie* (Sydney) Nov. 51/1 Ho, let me sing of the crimson telopea—Waratah, that is.

ten. In the phr. **ten, (ten,) two, and a quarter,** a week's ration of food as issued to a hand by an employer on a rural property: see quots. 1867 and 1957, and also EIGHT.

[**1867** 'CLERGYMAN' *Aust. as it Is* 179 The rations for one man are the well-known weekly allowance of 10 lbs. of flour, 10 lbs. of meat, 2 lbs. of sugar, and a quarter of a pound of tea.] **1903** J. FURPHY *Such is Life* 84 He has some hundreds of pounds lent out (without interest or security) though his pay is only fifteen shillings a week—with ten, ten, two, and a quarter. **1957** J. HAWKE *Follow my Dust* 60 The food was reasonable, based on the old formula of Ten-Two-and-a-Quarter. Ten pounds of flour, two of sugar, a quarter of tea, with tomato sauce and unlimited mutton.

Tench. *Obs.* [Shortened form of *penitentiary* a prison.] A name for the convict barracks in Hobart: see quot. 1829. Also *attrib.*

1829 H. WIDOWSON *Present State Van Diemen's Land* 24 At the back.. is the prisoner's [*sic*] barracks, *alias* the Penitentiary, *alias* 'The Tench', by which latter name it is most frequently called by its inmates. **1892** 'P. WARUNG' *Tales Convict System* 37 The sound of a bell came floating on the pellucid atmosphere to the ears of the dense, waiting crowd. 'That ain't the 'Tench clapper yet, surely?' exclaimed a bleary-eyed old ticket-of-leave man.

Hence **Tenchman** *n.*, an inmate, or former inmate, of the 'Tench'.

1869 *Colonial Soc.* (Sydney) 14 Jan. 6 The Model Country Loafer is usually an old lag. His experiences of Van Diemen's Land are large and instinctive in their nature. He tells some peculiar stories of adventures that happened to him when a 'Tenchman.

tender.

1. A representative of the owner of stray cattle sent to attend a *tender muster.*

1945 F. CORK *Tales from Cattle Country* 23 When the muster falls due, the managers of neighbouring stations are notified and each sends a tender—sometimes two—who are responsible for their 'strangers' who have wandered out of bounds. Visiting tenders are given complete charge of the cattle from the stations they represent.

2. Special Comb. **tender muster,** a round-up of all the cattle in a particular district at which owners lay claim to their strayed cattle.

1979 C. STONE *Running Brumbies* 35 For a tender muster, two or more cattle stations get all their men together on one of the stations to muster all the cattle in the area.

teno /'tɛnoʊ/. Abbrev. of 'tenosynovitis'. Freq. *attrib.*

1984 *Canberra Times* 19 Aug. 5/1 Teno has come in from the cold... The problems that repetition-strain injuries create are now being widely accepted by employers. **1986** *Ibid.* 19 Feb. 14/5 (*heading*) $120,000 in 'teno' case.

tent. *Obs.* Used *attrib.* in Special Comb. **tent hut,** a temporary dwelling made of canvas, etc., stretched over a frame; **-keeper,** one who takes care of a tent, etc. (see HUT-KEEPER).

1804 *Sydney Gaz.* 26 Aug., He had created a **tent hut** with a chimney thereon. **1845** C. HODGKINSON *Aust., Port Macquarie to Moreton Bay* 55, I can give credit to my **tent-keeper's** and bullock driver's account.

teraglin /tə'ræglən/. Also **traglin.** [Prob. f. a N.S.W. Aboriginal language.] The marine fish *Atractoscion aequidens* of N.S.W., s. Qld., and S. Africa; TRAG.

1880 *Proc. Linnean Soc. N.S.W.* V. 48 *Otolithus teraglin*... This fish is abundant on our coasts and attains a very considerable size—three or four feet in length. It is known to the fishermen as the 'Teraglin', and I have made that its specific name. **1945** J. DEVANNY *Bird of Paradise* 104 The traglin was dark green with gold around the gills. I have never tasted a more delicious fish than traglin at Byron Bay is the only place I have seen it.

terrace. Abbrev. of 'terrace house'.

1894 *Bulletin* (Sydney) 3 Feb. 13/1 Formerly, the grasping 'trap', hurrying to get rich and own his little terrace, moved heaven and earth to get on to a 'Chow' beat. **1981** B. OAKLEY *Marsupials & Politics* 39 If I find a guy who's stone deaf, partially sighted and without his sense of smell, I'll have a chance to sell your charming little weatherboard terrace.

terrible rite. *Obs.* The Aboriginal practice of subincision (see WHISTLECOCK a.).
 1886 E.M. CURR *Austral. Race* I. 74, I refer to circumcision, which is performed with a jagged flint, and what I have already spoken of as the *terrible rite*. Of the latter, Eyre gives a sufficient description when he says *funditur usque ad uretheram à parte infera penis*. 1928 W. ROBERTSON *Coo-ee Talks* 59 The '*Mai-ing boo-mung* oath' was classed with the Terrible-Rites of initiation; it was used for the specific purpose of sealing the lips of the initiate, who had passed the three stages of the *Bora*.

Territorian. A non-Aboriginal person native to or resident in the Northern Territory.
 1882 W. SOWDEN *N.T. as it Is* 41 The Territorians attempt races between the animated clothes-horses dubbed equines here. 1985 *Bulletin* (Sydney) 28 May 39/3 The Territorians have their own flag and a quaint, old fashioned pride in their regional identity.

Territory.
 1. Abbrev. of 'Northern Territory'. Also *attrib*.
 1882 W. SOWDEN *N.T. as it Is* 150 The country on this run is some of the best in the Territory. 1944 A.S. SMITH *Boys write Home* 203, I even thought it was a bit of a thrill to be wheeling 1500 head of stampeding territory pikers on a black night down the Georgina.
 2. Special Comb. **Territory rig**, *Darwin rig*, see DARWIN.
 1964 A.H. AFFLECK *Wandering Yrs.* 39 It has taken a third of a century and a visit by a down-to-earth member of the Royal Family to make official in those parts the commonsense dress of slacks, shirt and tie known as 'Territory rig'.

the, *dem. adj.* Used with the names of some towns (esp. in n. Aust.) freq. with ellipsis of a secondary element of the name, as **the Alice, Isa, Tennant** (for Alice Springs, Mount Isa, Tennant Creek): see quot. 1979.
 1883 E.M. CURR *Recoll. Squatting Vic.* 165 (*note*) In Australia it is not unusual to prefix the definite article to the names of places; as *the* Moira, *the* Terricks, *the* Wee-waa, &c. 1979 D. LOCKWOOD *My Old Mates & I* 2 My friend said, 'At least you're not short of definite articles.' I knew what he meant. The Isa. The 'Loo. The Tennant. The Alice. The Elliott. The Kath-er-ine. The Daly. The 'Curry. Yet it's strange that I've never heard The Darwin or The Batchelor or The Renner or The Pine Creek. Some names just seem to fit naturally with an article, others are awkward.

thick-billed grass-wren. The small bird *Amytornis textilis* of w. and central Aust., having predom. brown plumage and a stout bill.
 1913 *Emu* XII. Suppl. 79 *Amytornis modesta* . . thick-billed Grass-Wren. 1984 *Age* (Melbourne) 27 Mar. 24/8 Declining are the thick-billed grass-wren and . . the Plains Wanderer (of which the latest reports are that new populations have been discovered).

thickhead. [See quot. 1898.] WHISTLER 1.
 1837 W. SWAINSON *On Nat. Hist. Birds* II. 250 Pachycephala . . Thickhead. 1898 E.E. MORRIS *Austral Eng.* 336 They . . are called *Thickheads*. . . The name is from Greek παχύς, thick, and κεφαλή, the head.

thirds, *pl. Hist.* In the phr. **(up)on (the) thirds,** an agreement between an owner of livestock and a landholder, whereby the stock are pastured and tended by the landholder in return for one third of the profits: see esp. quot. 1834.
 1828 *Hobart Town Gaz.* 29 Nov., Captain Welsh having made Enclosures on his Farm at the Coal River, for the purpose of protecting Cattle, will take Sheep or Cattle on the Thirds on the usual terms. 1834 T.P. BESNARD *Voice from Bush* 11 Apr. (1839) 14 These sheep I have put out to graze, according to the custom of the country, on *thirds*—that is, the person who grazes and takes care of the flock is entitled to one-third of the produce of the wool, and one-third of the lambs that are dropped. 1898 G.J. DE WINTON *Soldiering Fifty Yrs. Ago* 49 'Theirs upon thirds' refers to the terms upon which sheep and cattle were grazed for other parties.

thong. A flat-soled sandal held on the foot by a bifurcated thong passing between the first and second toes.
 1960 *N.T. News* (Darwin) 8 Jan. 2/7 Just Arrived . . ! Thongs Scuffs Plastic Children's shoes. 1973 *Bulletin* (Sydney) 20 Jan. 10/1 Pat Troy of the Australian National University's urban research unit . . usually wears shorts and thongs to work at this time of year.

thornback. [Transf. use of *thornback* the British ray *Raja clavata*.] The marine fish *Raja lemprieri* of Tas., Vic., and S.A., having thorn-like spines on the dorsal surface. Also **thornback skate**.
 1786 *Hist. Narr. Discovery New Holland & N.S.W.* 10 The sea-fish seen here were . . skates, thornbacks, and other fish. 1974 T.D. SCOTT et al. *Marine & Freshwater Fishes S.A.* 57 Thornback skate. *Raja lemprieri* . . colour of disc greyish-black above, edges pinkish, white below.

thornbill. [Transf. use of *thornbill* an American humming-bird.]
 1. Any of the small, plump birds of the genus *Acanthiza* of Aust. incl. Tas., and sub-alpine New Guinea. See also TIT, TOMTIT.
 1900 A.J. CAMPBELL *Nests & Eggs Austral. Birds* 230 (*footnote*) Some recent authors use the term Thornbill a name already applied to a number of Humming Birds—as a vernacular name for the Acanthizas. 1985 MARIS & BORG *Women of Sun* 68 A group of tiny thornbills with pale yellow breasts and green wings flitted about, calling to one another in their sweet, high-pitched voices.
 2. With distinguishing epithet, as **brown, yellow-tailed**: see under first element.

thorny devil. [From the appearance of the lizard.] *Mountain devil* (a), see MOUNTAIN. Also *attrib*.
 1904 *World's News* (Sydney) 9 Apr. 9 Seeing two illustrations of Moloch Horridus . . which were called 'Thorny Devils'. 1985 *New Idea* (Melbourne) 2 Nov. 33 The thorny devil lizard (Moloch horridus) is extremely difficult to keep in captivity—it feeds only on small black ants, and can't live in a humid climate.

three-cornered jack. [f. *three-cornered*, prob. from the three spines of the fruit + *jack*, as used in the pop. names of various plants.] DOUBLE-GEE. Also **three corner jack**.
 1897 J.J. MURIF *From Ocean to Ocean* 74 Three-cornered Jacks are another enemy to the cyclist. 1986 *Austral. Garden Jrnl.* Apr. 142 There is quite an infestation of rabbits and some weed problems, particularly boxthorn and three corner jack.

three-quarter caste, *a.* Of an Aboriginal: having one non-Aboriginal grandparent; (loosely) an Aboriginal of part-white descent. Also as quasi-*n.*
 1900 *Advocate* (Burnie) 27 July 4/2 Joe Governor, a three-quarter caste. Another was . . a full-blood blackfellow. 1970 *Bulletin* (Sydney) 24 Oct. 30/3 Michael Anderson is 19, a three-quarter caste Aboriginal.

three-rail fence. A fence having three wooden rails as its horizontal members. Also **three-railed fence.**
 1837 *Colonist* (Hobart) 11 May 152/2 The purchaser will have the option of renting from fifty to one hundred acres of land . . part of which is now enclosed with a three-railed fence. 1882 A.J. BOYD *Old Colonials* 19 Things have come to

a pretty pass, when a feller's only offered five bob a rod for a three-rail fence, slip panels included!

three-up. *Obs.* A game in which three coins are tossed and bets laid on the fall, the toss being invalid unless the three display the same face on landing. See TWO-UP *n.* Also *attrib.*

1845 *Parramatta Chron.* 15 Mar. 2/1 The charged was .. descanting most learnedly on the evolution and revolutions of 'three up'.. with upturned eye and outstretched body intently watching the fall of some 'Browns'. 1907 C. MACALISTER *Old Pioneering Days* 191 Some of them were, for instance, ardent followers of the 'three up school' and at such a game I discovered a man who had been recommended as a likely buyer.

throat. In the phr. **to have (got) the game** (or **it**) **by the throat,** to have control of a situation.

1947 J. MORRISON *Sailors belong Ships* 15 We're sailors, see? Two sailors. We got the game by the throat. 1960 R. TULLIPAN *Follow Sun* 105 'Think we'll get it done today?' Brady asked... 'Can't miss... We have it by the throat now all right.'

throw, *n.* [Alteration of *froe*: see quot. 1916.] A tool for cleaving staves, etc., from a block of wood, having the handle at right angles to the blade.

1913 H. LAWSON *For Aust.* 14 The crow-bar, pick-axe and the 'throw'—the axe that morticed well. 1916 *Bulletin* (Sydney) 4 May 22/3 'Coolibah'.. mentions the coastal bullocky's 'Flindozy' (for Flindersia), and writes of splitting timber with the paling 'throw'. Always in the bush I have heard it called throw, but lately in a hardware catalogue I saw the word printed 'froe'.

throw, *v.*

1. *trans.* To cast (an animal) to the ground, preparatory to branding, etc. Also *absol.*

1847 A. HARRIS *Settlers & Convicts* (1953) 28 In latter days it has been found that sometimes the beast has been thrown and the branded section of the hide actually flayed off. 1980 ANSELL & PERCY *To fight Wild* 52 It's not as dangerous as throwing off a horse.

2. In the phr. **to throw off,** to engage in provocative banter; with **at,** to chaff or ridicule (someone); *chuck off,* see CHUCK *v.* 1; *sling off,* see SLING *v.* 3. As *n.*, an instance of this.

1812 J.H. VAUX *Mem.* (1819) II. 218 *Throw off,* to talk in a sarcastical strain, so as to convey offensive allusions under the mask of pleasantry, or innocent freedom; but, perhaps, secretly venting that abuse which you would not dare to give in direct terms. 1962 D. CUSACK *Picnic Races* 183 You're like all the townies. Throwing off at the people on the land.

throw-down. A type of small firework: see quot. 1922.

1890 *Truth* (Sydney) 16 Nov. 1/6 The remedy is to carry a supply of the 'throw downs' or detonators, which boys use on Queen's Birthday. 1922 L.M. PYKE *Jack of St. Virgil's* 138 'Throw-downs?'.. 'You know, crackers that go off with a bang when you throw them down.'

throw-in. [f. *to throw in* to add to a bargain.] A stroke of unexpected good fortune.

1871 *Austral. Town & Country Jrnl.* (Sydney) 11 Feb. 186/1 The owner of Sunbeam took his grueling kindly, and I trust when next the two cracks meet he (Mr Henry) may have better luck. Mr Henry is every inch a sporting man, and deserves to have his throw in sometimes. 1976 C.D. MILLS *Hobble Chains & Greenhide* 7 It was really quite a throw-in, for the plant, well yard-broken, raced down the wing and the dust obscured the rails.

throwing stick. a. WOOMERA (see quot. 1770). **b.** BOOMERANG *n.* 1. **c.** A straight stick of wood used as a missile.

1770 J. COOK *Jrnls.* 23 Aug. (1955) I. 396 They throw the Dart with only one hand, in the doing of which they make use of a peice [*sic*] of wood about 3 feet long made thin like the blade of a Cutlass, with a little hook at one end to take hold of the end of the Dart, and at the other end is fix'd a peice of bone about 3 or 4 inches long; the use of this is, I beleive, to keep the dart steady and to make it quit the hand in a proper direction; by the help of these throwing sticks, as we call them, they will hit a Mark at the distance of 40 or 50 Yards. 1980 B. SCOTT *Darkness under Hills* 119 Bororen sang and tapped his throwing sticks together while Benarby danced the story about an elder.

throw-stick. *Obs.*

1. BOOMERANG *n.* 1.

1847 G.F. ANGAS *Savage Life & Scenes* II. 274 Who taught them the use of the *Boomerang*, which is depicted in the tombs of Egypt, and called by Wilkinson the *Throw-stick*?

2. WOOMERA.

1884 W.H.G. KINGSTON *Adventures in Aust.* 62 The throwing or throw-stick, is to serve the purpose of a sling for casting the spear. A heavy flat piece of wood, between two and three feet long, has at one end a slight hollow into which the end of the spear is fitted while at the other is a heavy weight, thus assisting the hunter in the art of throwing the spear. 1892 J. FRASER *Aborigines N.S.W.* 72 Another curiosity of Australian invention is the throw-stick, with which many of the war-spears are impelled from the hand of the owner. This is already known by the name of 'womara', and I think that the use of any other name for it causes confusion.

thrummer. *Obs.* [f. Br. slang *thrum(s*: see OEDS.] A threepenny piece; SCRUM; SCRUMMY.

1898 *Tocsin* (Melbourne) 24 Nov. 5/3 This has been Charity and Show week with us in Ballarat, and we have been making our annual show of charity in the churches by putting a tanner in the plate instead of the usual thrummer. 1944 *Bulletin* (Sydney) 1 Mar. 12/2 Mac stopped dead, the thrummer half out of his pocket.

thrush. [Transf. use of *thrush* the musical bird *Turdus philomelos,* and other birds of the fam. Turdidae or Muscicapidae. The word is used in Aust. for such birds, incl. the naturalized *T. philomelos.*] Any of several birds having a melodious song, esp. those of the genus *Colluricincla* (see *shrike-thrush* SHRIKE) and those known as *ground thrush* (see GROUND *n.*[1]).

1794 G. SHAW *Zool. New Holland* 25 *Turdus Punctatus.* The Spotted-shouldered Thrush... Greyish-brown Thrush dashed with blackish. 1965 *Austral. Encycl.* VIII. 494 Other Australian birds known as thrushes, but more correctly shrike-thrushes, are members of the genus *Colluricincla*.

thumb-piece. [Br. dial.: see OED b.] A piece of bread, with cheese or meat, held between the thumb and the finger.

1885 N.W. SWAN *Couple of Cups Ago* 122 It [*sc.* the public] could eat its thumb-piece on a bit of bread, and go visiting in crimean shirts and lace-ups. 1951 E. HILL *Territory* 293 Breakfast is a thumb-piece and a quart of tea, standing up.

thunder-bird. [See quot. 1827.] Either of two birds of the genus *Pachycephala,* the *golden whistler* (see GOLDEN 3), and the *rufous whistler* (see RUFOUS); RING-COACHMAN.

a 1827 *Trans. Linnean Soc. London* XV. 239 *Pachycephala .. Gutturalis...* 'This species', Mr Caley says, 'is called *Thunder-bird* by the colonists... The natives tell me, that, when it begins to thunder, this bird is very noisy.' 1981 G. CROSS *George & Widda-Woman* 88 The thunderbirds, the silver-eyes, the warblers and the whipbirds in the scrub beneath.

thunder egg. [U.S.: see OEDS *thunder, sb.* 6.] See quot. 1970.

1965 B. JAMES *Collecting Austral. Gemstones* 21 Essentially it is a broken 'thunder-egg' with half the casing of rhyolite remaining. **1970** J.A. TALENT *Minerals, Rock & Gems* 261 *Thunder egg*—a hollow concretion consisting of layers of siliceous material (usually agate) with a lining of siliceous crystals.

thylacine. /ˈθaɪləsin/. [The animal genus *Thylacine* was named by mammalogist C.J. Temminck (*Monogr. de Mammalogie* (1824) I. 23), f. Gr. θύλακ-ος pouch + L. suffix *-inus* of or pertaining to.] Tasmanian tiger, see TASMANIAN *a.* 2.

1838 *Geol. Soc. London* III. 19 In the numbers of the grinders the Phascolothere resembles the Opossum and Thylacine. **1984** *Age* (Melbourne) 18 Aug. 6/1 The Tasmanian tiger, or Thylacine, seems to have expired in 1934 when the last known animal passed away peacefully, behind bars, in the Hobart zoo.

tick.

1. Used *attrib.* and in Comb. with reference to the control or eradication of cattle-infesting ticks.

1898 *Bulletin* (Sydney) 23 July 15/2 T'other day a celestial cart was crossing the bridge that leads into the N.S.W. hamlet. Tick-inspector vociferates: 'Grease your horse, John!' **1956** T. RONAN *Moleskin Midas* 209 He was south of the Quarantine Line with tick-free cattle.

2. Special Comb. **tick fence,** a fence erected to prevent the movement of tick-infested cattle, etc., into a tick-free area; **gate,** an opening in such a fence at which travelling stock are subject to inspection; **line,** an imaginary line marking the boundary of a tick-infested area from which the movement of stock is prohibited.

1906 *Bulletin* (Sydney) 11 Oct. 17/1 A gatekeeper on the **tick fence** (Queensland border) is a State official. **1927** *Bulletin* (Sydney) 15 Dec. 27/1 It wanders from the **tick-gate** where the main road's traffic spills. **1901** *Western Champion* (Barcaldine) 16 July 14/4 He proposed 'That this meeting strongly protests against the interference of traffic in and about Longreach caused by the **tick line** surrounding the town.'

tick bush. (Chiefly *N.S.W.*) A shrub of the genus *Kunzea* (fam. Myrtaceae), esp. the white-flowering *K. ambigua* of N.S.W., Vic., and Tas.

1935 W.W. FROGGATT *Austral. Spiders* 77 *Ixodes holocyclus.* (The Dog or Bush Tick)... The white flowering *Kunzia capitata* is popularly known about Port Jackson as 'Tick Bush', because it is one of the abundant bushes in the locality upon which these ticks abound. **1968** D. IRELAND *Chantic Bird* 24 A few hundred yards away from the house is the ti-tree bush, we called it tick-bush.

ticket, *n.*[1] *Hist.*

1. TICKET OF LEAVE 1. Also *attrib.*

1819 *HRA* (1921) 3rd Ser. II. 539 Specifying those whose Tickets are made for this Settlement. **1866** *Austral. Monthly Mag.* II. 179 When I gets to Hobart Town, what does I see? Lots of coves, well fed, well looked after; some in quod, some ticket coves.

2. In the phr. **ticket of exemption (from Government Labour or Service),** a permit issued to a convict allowing residence with a spouse: see esp. quots. 1831, 1836, and 1837.

1830 *Sydney Monitor* 2 June 3/6 All holders of tickets-of-leave and tickets of exemption are to be mustered once a month by the Magistrates of the respective districts. **1831** *Austral. Almanack* 78 *A Ticket of Exemption from Government Labor* differs from a Ticket of Leave, in conferring no permission for the individual to employ himself for his own benefit or to acquire property, but simply the privilege of residing until the next 31st December, with the person therein named. **1836** J.F. O'CONNELL *Residence Eleven Yrs. New Holland* 47 Convicts are discharged from the factory by three methods—tickets of leave at the expiration of half their time of sentence, tickets of exemption upon the arrival of their husbands in the colony, and tickets of exemption upon the application of a suitor, who must marry, forthwith, the damsel whose liberty he seeks. **1837** *Rep. Select Committee Transportation* 11 Ticket of exemption.. has been discontinued for some years; but a ticket of exemption was given to men where they were assigned to their wives, or where they were allowed to live with their wives. **1849** A. HARRIS *Emigrant Family* (1967) 114 How easily you can get rid of your ticket of exemption from Government service.

3. Comb. in sense 1: **ticket holder, man, woman.**

1845 *Parramatta Chron.* 31 May 4/1 The man.. turned out to be a **ticket-holder** named Connell, lately.. liberated from custody, on a charge of murder, owing to the evidence against him being defective. **1827** *Monitor* (Sydney) 23 Mar. 356 **Ticket men** up the country have a poor life of it under the present regulations. **1847** *Britannia* (Hobart) 17 June 2/5 A **ticket woman,** flashily dressed.

Hence **ticketer** *n.,* one to whom a ticket of leave is granted. Also *transf.*

1844 *Colonial Times* (Hobart) 2 Nov., He was sent for two months on the roads, his Worship observing that there was rather too much of this sort of work now carrying on amongst the ticketers. **1865** 'SPECIAL CORRESPONDENT' *Transportation* 9 Every other man he sees is a 'ticketer'—as the criminal class, whether bond or free, are termed.

ticket, *n.*[2]

1. A document certifying that the bearer is a member of a trade union.

1899 *Bulletin* (Sydney) 19 Aug. 32/1, I want to see his tickets... The 'Rep' opened the book and sorted out a bundle of grimy Union tickets. **1978** H.C. BAKER *I was Listening* 134 He had been in the building trade all his working life and held 'tickets' as a hoist driver, plant-operator, scaffolder, rigger and everything else covered by the Builders' Labourers' Union.

2. A piece of paper impregnated with lysergic acid diethylamide, the hallucinogenic drug LSD: see quot.

1969 *Pix* (Sydney) 19 Apr. 11 It [*sc.* LSD] is sold usually in absorbent paper in a portion of 120 micrograms known as a ticket. When you take a ticket you are on a trip.

3. In the phr. **to have tickets on** (a person or thing), to hold in high esteem; esp. **to have tickets on oneself,** to be conceited.

[N.Z. **1908** W.H. KOEBEL *Anchorage* 140, I don't know whether she's got any tickets on me.] **1918** B. REYNOLDS *Dawn Asper* 5 There is a current slang phrase.. 'She hasn't many tickets on herself!' Now, as far as Dawn Asper was concerned, this was perfectly true—she had *no* tickets on herself! **1948** K.S. PRICHARD *Golden Miles* 29, I had tickets on her once. But she never had an eye for any man but her husband.

ticket of leave. [Spec. use of *ticket of leave* a ticket or document giving leave or permission.]

1. A permit entitling a convict to live and work as a private individual within a stipulated area until the expiration or remission of sentence. Also *attrib.,* and *transf.*

1801 *HRA* (1915) 1st Ser. III. 48 All prisoners whose terms of transportation is [*sic*] not expired and are off the stores, or those with settlers, are to attend at the Secretary's office at Sydney.. to receive their tickets of leave. **1901** *Bulletin* (Sydney) 7 Sept. 14/2 In consideration of good conduct.. he is now on duty as black tracker under a sort of ticket-of-leave. **1921** J.T. SUTCLIFFE *Hist. Trade*

Unionism Aust. 26 The English Government began to send out shiploads of ticket-of-leave men, who were still legally convicts and subject to police supervision.

2. One to whom a ticket of leave is granted.

1826 *Monitor* (Sydney) 1 Sept. 123/3 The other witness.. was reminded by the Magistrate, previous to his deposition, 'that he was a ticket-of-leave'. **1847** *Port Phillip Herald* 15 Apr. 2/6, I did my best for the emancipists and tickets-of-leave.

3. Comb. **ticket of leave class, constable, convict, farmer, holder, lady, man, servant, woman.**

1851 H. MELVILLE *Present State Aust.* 139 The **ticket of leave class** possess about the same privileges in the colony, as the Jews now do in Great Britain. **1837** *Rep. Select Committee Transportation* 119 A **ticket-of-leave constable** was sent down to Sydney in charge of the prisoner. **1849** *Britannia* (Hobart) 24 May 2/6 From the bad characters we have had sent us under the denomination of exiles and **ticket-of-leave convicts**. **1862** G.T. LLOYD *Thirty-Three Yrs. Tas. & Vic.* 21 Numbers of **ticket of leave farmers**.. were arrested. **1835** *Colonist* (Sydney) 2 July 213/2 In the code of Regulations recently published, there is no requisition for the attendance of **ticket-of-leave holders** at public worship on Sabbath. **1840** *Tasmanian Weekly Dispatch* (Hobart) 6 Mar. 7/1 Ann Burton, a **ticket-of-leave lady**. **1807** *Hist. Rec. N.S.W.* (1898) VI. 292 A considerable injury to the colony had crept in: that of **ticket-of-leave men**—men that were taken off the stores, and permitted to work for themselves. **1829** H. WIDOWSON *Present State Van Diemen's Land* 53 **Ticket-of-leave servants**.. will ask the same wages as the free man. **1820** *Sydney Gaz.* 19 Sept., On Wednesday the 27th Instant, for all the Free Women and Female Convicts, including **Tickets of Leave Women**, on or off the Stores.

4. Special Comb. **ticket of leave muster**, a compulsory assembling of convicts holding tickets of leave: see MUSTER *n.* 1.

1837 *Cornwall Chron.* (Launceston) 2 Sept. 2 The Town has been *enlivened* this day with another of this [*sic*] disgraceful exhibitions, arising out of the Ticket-of-leave musters.

Hence **ticket of leaver,** *ticket of leave holder.*

1852 G.C. MUNDY *Our Antipodes* I. 228 The overseer.. may be a hireling convict-emancipist, expiree, or ticket-of-leaver.

ticket of occupation. *Hist.* A permit to pasture stock on a specified area of Crown land: see quot. 1826. See also LICENCE 1. Also **ticket of occupancy.**

1820 *HRA* (1921) 3rd Ser. III. 304 Do you consider that the Person, who has stock but has no Land, and only a Ticket of occupation, is as much entitled to supply meat as the person who has less stock but possesses Land? **1820** *AJCP* 110 C.O. 201/122 fo. 208, Is any & what fee paid on granting these tickets of occupancy? There is a fee of 7s. 6d. **1826** J. ATKINSON *Acct. Agric. & Grazing N.S.W.* 65 This permission, or *ticket of occupation*, as it is termed.. conveys to the stock-owner a right to occupy a tract usually extending two miles in every direction from his stock-yard; always, however, holding himself in readiness to quit at six months notice from the Surveyor-General, should the land be wanted for the purpose of colonization; and also prohibited from cutting down or removing any timber, except what may be required for stock-yards or huts.

tickey. *Obs.* Also **ticky.** Alteration of TICKPENS.

c **1907** W.C. CHANDLER *Darkest Adelaide* 80 They wear an oily, unctuous expression calculated to deceive the most uncompromising cynic extant, they smoodge for 'tickeys', tea and cake, beer and wide, socks and slippers, and everything they can get for nothing. **1908** C.H.S. MATTHEWS *Parson in Austral. Bush* 272 Most of the boys were puttin' down a quid a time and losin' without a word, but there was one bloke only puttin' down a 'ticky' and losin' like the rest, and he was grousin' and grumblin'.

tickie. [f. *tick(inspector* + -Y.] An official responsible for the eradication of ticks.

1981 K. GARVEY *Rhymes of Ratbag* 51 With five hundred woody weaners We came droving from the east Where the pompous tick inspectors Think there's bugs on every beast. And beside a lonely border gate I saw a tickie sit. **1981** A. WILKINSON *Up Country* 86 Lawrie and 'the tickies' roared with laughter.. watching Hannibull.. try as he always does to jump the dip.

tick-jammer. *Shearing.* Also **tick-jamber.** One who operates a wool press.

1897 *Worker* (Sydney) 11 Sept. 1/1 'Tick-jammer' is the chap who puts the wool into the bales. **1898** *Bulletin* (Sydney) 1 Oct. 14/3 In a shearing shed: The boss is the 'finger'.. the wool-pressers 'tickjambers'.

tickpens. *Austral. pidgin. Obs.* Also **tickpen.** [Alteration of 'sixpence'.] Money; SIXPENCE.

1838 J. BACKHOUSE *Narr. Visit Austral. Colonies* (1843) 539 They [*sc.* the Aborigines] quickly recognized us again and began to beg for 'tickpens', as they call sixpences to buy bread with. **1903** *Bulletin* (Sydney) 15 Oct. 17/1 The blackfellow had (sometimes in consideration of 'tickpen').. shifted his quarters.

ticky, var. TICKEY.

tidal wave. *Obs.* See quot. 1895.

1878 'IRONBARK' *Southerly Busters* 203 Swore they should crush those sons of lush Who dealt in 'tidal-waves'. **1895** 'H. GOLDSMITH' *Euancondit* 178 The tidal wave.. turned out to be the largest glass of colonial beer that could be purchased for sixpence.

tier. Chiefly *Tas.* and *S.A.* [Spec. use of *tier* a row, rank.] A usu. forested range of hills or mountains, esp. one of a series; a mountain; in S.A. used with reference to the Mount Lofty Ranges and hence also to the forests located there (see esp. quots. 1849, 1882, and 1897). Freq. in *pl.*

1826 Tas. Colonial Secretary's Office Rec. 1/10 214, I was with my Sheep up in the Tier. **1849** G.B. WILKINSON *Working Man's Handbk. S.A.* 74 The large stringybark tiers or forests supply abundance of straight barrelled trees. **1882** A. TOLMER *Reminisc.* II. 18 The country is nothing but a dense forest of stringy bark, similar to the 'tiers' near Adelaide. **1897** H. HUSSEY *Colonial Life & Christian Experience* 64 There were several places where these marauders could carry on their nefarious practices, and there were suitable hiding-places for them—especially in the 'Tiers' in the Mount Lofty ranges. **1978** D. VAWR *Ratbag Mind* 96 Tasmania is probably the only place in the world where ranges are called 'tiers'.

tiersman. Chiefly *S.A.* One whose occupation is felling timber in the tiers.

1840 *S. Austral. Rec.* (London) 12 Sept. 167 Intemperance.. prevails chiefly among tiersman, splitters, and sawyers. **1978** M. WALKER *Pioneer Crafts Early Aust.* 37 The other major forest craftsmen, the splitters.. were known in England as 'rivers', in the early days of settlement as 'tiersmen'.

tie-wire. A piece of wire used to fasten two objects, or two parts of an object, together.

1927 J. POLLARD *Rose of Bushlands* 141 'Look for holes in the netting and broken tie-wires,' he told her. **1978** D. STUART *Wedgetail View* 13 Their broken boots held together with cunningly contrived twitches of tie-wire.

tiger, *n.*

1. *Tasmanian tiger*, see TASMANIAN *a.* 2 (see esp. quot. 1852). Also **tiger-wolf.**

1805 R. KNOPWOOD *Diary* 18 June (1977) 85 They

informed me that on the 2 of May when they were in the wood, they see a large tiger; that the dog they had with them went nearly up to it, and when the tiger see the men . . it went away. **1852** J. WEST *Hist. of Tas.* I. 322 The Tiger or Hyaena of the colonists (*Thylacinus cynocephalus*) . . is of a tawny or brownish yellow color, with numerous black bands arranged transversely along the back, from the shoulders to the tail; hence the erroneous names tiger and hyaena, given to it by the early settlers. **1865** G.F. ANGAS *Aust.* 76 The *Thylacinus*, or 'tiger-wolf' and the *Sarcophilus*, or 'native devil', are the two largest and most ferocious of all the Australian carnivorous pouched animals.

2. [Spec. use of *tiger* liveried servant, outdoor servant as a groom, etc.: see OED(S *sb.* 6.] One engaged in menial outdoor employment (see quots. 1853 and 1865); a shearer.

1853 H.B. JONES *Adventures in Aust.* 130 We left . . for the bush, respectively mounted on Admiral, Abelard, and Polka, with a young 'tiger' carrying our saddle bags and 'swag'. **1865** G.S. LANG *Aborigines of Aust.* 37 Nearly all the squatters, at some time or other adopt black boys, keeping them as 'tigers' or horse-breakers. **1956** F.B. VICKERS *First Place to Stranger* 135 Those tigers (he meant the shearers) will make you dance.

3. [Used elsewhere but recorded earliest in Aust.] One who has an insatiable appetite for work, etc. (see quots.).

1896 *Bulletin* (Sydney) 24 Oct. (Red Page), His father thought a lot of Henry; he used to call him a tiger for work. **1959** D. HEWETT *Bobbin Up* 79 'He's a real tiger for his tucker,' Linnie said, smiling wanly through her tears. **1965** J. WYNNUM *Jiggin' in Riggin'* 28 'Some people never learn,' moaned Dinger. 'All I can say is you're a tiger for punishment, Stripey.'

4. Alcoholic liquor; one who consumes this with enthusiasm.

1901 *Truth* (Sydney) 26 May 1/7 The people of New South Wales spent £4,744,000 on 'tiger' during the past year. **1978** T. DAVIES *More Austral. Nicknames* 99 *Tiger.* He likes getting tanked.

5. Remote and inaccessible country. Chiefly as **tiger country**.

1945 E. GEORGE *Two at Daly Waters* 89 The territory a hundred and sixty miles west of Daly Waters and thence to the Western Australian coast is . . dreaded by aviators and generally called by them 'tiger country'. **1979** D. LOCKWOOD *My Old Mates & I* 136 Between him and Arnhem Land proper there was no other white man and few who were black. Tiger country, jump-ups, escarpments, heavily timbered, unknown.

6. Special Comb. **tiger cat,** the large, carnivorous marsupial *Dasyurus maculatus* of e. Aust. incl. Tas., having brown fur with white spots on the body and tail; **flathead,** the marine fish *Platycephalus richardsoni*, predom. brown with darker bands or blotches, of s. N.S.W., e. Vic., and e. Tas., an important commercial species; **prawn,** a large prawn of the genus *Penaeus*, esp. *P. monodon* and *P. semisulcatus* of n. Aust. and elsewhere, and *P. esculentus* of n. Aust.; **snake,** either of the two snakes of the genus *Notechis*, both highly venomous, *N. scutatus* of s.e. mainland Aust. and *N. ater* of s.w. and s. Aust. incl. Tas.; also *attrib.*, and *ellipt.* as **tiger.**

1830 T. BETTS *Acct. Colony Van Diemen's Land* 80 Kangaroo and other skins, such as those of the opossum, **tiger cat,** and plattypus . . are exported. **1918** 'J. SCOTT' *How, when & where to catch Fish* 22 There is also the 'outside' flathead, which is rarely, if ever, caught inside, and it is generally known as the '**Tiger Flathead**'. **1893** J.D. OGILBY *Edible Fishes & Crustaceans N.S.W.* 203 (OEDS) This [*sc. Penaeus monodon*] is the '**Tiger Prawn**' of the Sydney fishermen. . . This species is at times common in the Sydney market, but is irregular in its appearance. **1952** W.J. DAKIN *Austral. Seashores* 176 The tiger-prawn is a large northern species that . . has dark vertical bands on its body. It is one of the commercial edible prawns of southern Queensland. **1859** *Bell's Life in Sydney* 3 Dec. 3/2 Procured a black snake and a **tiger snake. 1979** C. THIELE *River Murray Mary* 29 'What's the matter with him?' 'Snakebite. . . Probably over by the woodheap. This is the time for tigers.' **1986** *Mercury* (Hobart) 19 Feb. 16/5 Tiger snake antivenene was released in 1930, marking the beginning of a long CSL program which led to the development of antivenenes against all major Australian venomous snakes and spiders.

tiger, *v. intr.* To toil (see TIGER *n.* 2); to 'rough it'. Freq. as *vbl. n.*

1957 STEWART & KEESING *Old Bush Songs* 257 Your delicate constitution Is not equal unto mine, To stand the constant tigering On the banks of the Condamine. **1973** R. ROBINSON *Drift of Things* 385 He was a well-built young man, and a good worker as I was to find out; but then I had done my share of tigering and I reckoned I could hold my own.

tight little island. England; also *transf.*, Tasmania.

1868 *Sydney Punch* 25 Jan. 70/1 When you get back to the 'tight little island', otherwise known as England, I hope you'll be able to give a satisfactory account of the antipodes. **1919** J.J. KENNEDY *Whale Oil Guards* 31 Tasmania . . had declared war on the Commonwealth, that the Tight Little Island was now a republic.

tike, var. TYKE.

'Tilda. Also **'Tilder.** Shortened form of MATILDA 1.

1899 *Bulletin* (Sydney) 5 Aug. 35/1 I've dossed in such cabooses out-back that old 'Tilda has nearly crawled away from me. **1912** *Ibid.* 8 Aug. 15/1 We dumped our 'Tilders in the bar to take a little rest.

tilly, $n.^1$ [f. MA)TIL(DA 1 + -Y.] MATILDA 1.

[N.Z. **1906** *N.Z. Truth* (Wellington) 24 Feb. 5 After 8 hours with Tilly up, our destination loomed up at last.] **1927** *Bulletin* (Sydney) 23 June 19 With my old soot-coated billy an' my leather-twisted Tilly I can laugh at every collared city swell.

tilly, $n.^2$ [f. U)TIL(ITY + -Y.] UTILITY.

1957 R.S. PORTEOUS *Brigalow* 26 They rarely showed fear of us, even when Carson careered round a mob in the rattling tilly. **1977** V. PRIDDLE *Larry & Jack* 14 'What makes you walk out here in this heat, George? What's wrong with the old 'Tilly'?' 'I never drive the old bus when I know I'm going to have a few grogs.'

tillywurti /tɪli'wɜti/. Chiefly *S.A.* Also **tilliwurty.** [Prob. f. a S.A. Aboriginal language.] STRONGFISH.

1924 LORD & SCOTT *Synopsis Vertebrate Animals Tas.* 70 Butter fish (of Tasmania) . . is known . . in South Australia as the Strong Fish or Tillywurti. **1980** G. DUTTON *Wedge-Tailed Eagle* 35 We went fish-spearing that night and I brought up a ten pound tilliwurty.

tilting the ring. A game played on horseback: see quot. 1980. Also **tilting in the ring.**

1901 *Advocate* (Burnie) 1 Feb. 2/4 An exhibition of tilting the ring was given when four out of six competitors managed to lift the ring once but could not repeat the performance. **1980** C. BARTLETT *Busy Life* 8 They used to play a game of 'tilting in the ring' on the horses. They had six poles round in a circle of about a hundred yards with short pieces of wire protruding from which was hung a wire ring about 2 inches across. They raced round trying to spear the rings with a long bamboo pole as they went by.

timber. Used *attrib.* in Special Comb. **timber getter,** one employed in felling trees for their wood; so **-getting** *vbl. n.* and *ppl. a.*; **jinker,** see JINKER *n.* 1; **licence,** a permit to fell timber on Crown land.

1849 A. HARRIS *Emigrant Family* (1967) 150 The saw and axe of the **timber-getters**. *Ibid*. 85 Many of them keep timber-getting establishments, and supply Sydney with building stuff. **1917** *Bulletin* (Sydney) 4 Jan. 22/4 A few timber-getting families are .. the only dwellers... The piners formerly went nearly 100 miles up the Gordon, disregarding its rapids. **1916** J.B. COOPER *Coo-oo-ee!* 1 Heavy **timber-jinkers** groaned, on their way to the Ironbark Saw mill. **1840** *Port Phillip Gaz.* 24 Oct. 3 **Timber licenses** .. £64.

time. *Obs*. [Spec. use of *time* prescribed or allotted term: see OED(S *sb.* 7 d. Used elsewhere of a sentence of imprisonment but recorded earliest in Aust.] The duration of a sentence of penal servitude.

1790 *HRA* (1914) 1st Ser. I. 154 The answer you gave to the convict who came to tell you his time was expired— 'Would to God my time was expired, too!'—was not calculated to make him satisfied with his situation. **1799** D. COLLINS *Acct. Eng. Colony N.S.W.* (1802) II. 142 A numerous body of the Irish convicts, many of whom had but lately arrived, insisted that 'their times were out'.

time-expired, *a*. *Hist*. [Spec. use of *time-expired* whose term of engagement has expired.]

1. Of an indentured labourer from the Pacific islands (see KANAKA *n*.): whose contracted term has been served.

1894 *Bulletin* (Sydney) 7 July 11/3 Gangs of time-expired N.Q. Kanakas are combining to cut cane by contract. **1970** K. WILLEY *Naked Island* 152 Captain Rogers landed eleven 'time-expired' natives at Wanderer Bay.

2. Of a convict: whose term of sentence has expired.

1929 'OLD STOCKMAN' *Sensational Cattle-Stealing Case* 77 The time-expired men have been let go, and the long-timers have been sent back to Bathurst. **1940** *Bulletin* (Sydney) 10 July 17/1 When I was a nipper many time-expired convicts from Tasmania were to be met with in Victoria.

time on. *Australian National Football*. Time added to the normal playing time at the direction of a field umpire to compensate for an interruption to the game.

1931 J.F. McHALE et al. *Austral. Game of Football* 52 The field umpire shall instruct the time-keepers to add 'Time on'. **1973** B. HOGAN *Follow Game* (rev. ed.) 14 'Time on' or 'added time' is sometimes incorrectly referred to as 'time off'. 'Time on' is added to the time allocated for each quarter and is added during the quarter in which the 'time on' occurs.

time stick. *Obs*. CLAP STICK.

1856 J. BONWICK *W. Buckley* 59 We distinguish .. the tapping of time sticks. **1896** W.A. SQUIRE *Ritual, Myth, & Customs Austral. Aborigines* 14 Amid the sudden hideous uproar of beaten time-sticks, bullroars and maniacal shouts, supposed to prevent the women from noticing the departure.

Timor. [The name of an island off the n.w. coast of Aust., part of which was formerly a Portuguese colony.] Used *attrib.* esp. as **Timor pony**, to designate a small stocky horse of a breed imported from Timor; also *transf.* (see quot. 1916), and *ellipt*.

1828 *Tasmanian* (Hobart) 11 July 3 *Launceston, July 7*. The Timor Ponies were sold here on Saturday last. **1841** *Port Phillip Patriot* 1 July 1/5 A handsome pony gig suitable for a small timor. **1916** J.M. CREED *Recoll. Aust.* 265 Ponies were also brought from the Malay Islands, being called 'Timor', though but a small number came from that island and those not the best.

timothy. [Of unknown origin.] A brothel.

1953 S.J. BAKER *Aust. Speaks* 124 *Timothy*, a brothel. **1982** *N.T. News* (Darwin) 8 May 9/5 There were 17 men in the 'Timothy' when it 'went off'.

tin, *n*.¹

1. Used *attrib*. in Comb. to designate an artefact made from tin-plate, as **tin billy, pot**.

1881 A.C. GRANT *Bush-Life Qld*. II. 231 Here a party of footmen tramped along with their swags rolled up on their backs, and the **tin-billies** in their hands. **1821** *Austral. Mag.* 91 The corpse having been let down into the grave, they proceeded, as is their custom, to place his spears, waddie, booncooring, net, **tin-pot,** and in short, all his worldly riches, by his side.

2. Special Comb.

a. With reference to the mining of the metal: **tin-digger**, a tin-miner; **-diggings**, a place where tin is mined; **rush**, a sudden influx of miners to a site where deposits of tin have been found; the site itself; **-scratcher**, one who mines surface deposits of tin; any tin-miner; so **tin-scratching** *pres. pple.*; **show**, a tin deposit.

1899 R. SEMON *In Austral. Bush* 269 The **tin-diggers**, on leading their aqueduct from a source near the mountain-top to their camp, had cut a passage into the wood. **1899** *Western Champion* (Barcaldine) 7 Feb. 5/3 Late in the seventies two young men .. struck their camp on one of the Queensland **tin diggings**. **1893** *Braidwood Dispatch* 31 May 2/4 The numbers on the **tin rush** are increasing. **1899** *Western Champion* (Barcaldine) 7 Feb. 5/3 After passing through the bark township, now absolutely deserted from a tin rush some miles further down the creek, they made for Tenterfield. **1910** *Bulletin* (Sydney) 28 Apr. 14/1, I met the Baron on a tinfield... One night the **tin-scratchers** asked the Baron to sing. **1918** *Ibid*. 28 Feb. 24/1 You can tell a tin-scratcher wherever you meet him. .. He will be condemning the storekeeper for the high price of tucker .. and the low price of tin. **1954** T. RONAN *Vision Splendid* 113 Marty Boylan was tin-scratching at Hard Rock. **1920** B. CRONIN *Timber Wolves* 28 A bunch of city mining men .. locate a **tin show**.

b. **tin lid**, rhyming slang for 'kid', a child.

1905 J. MEREDITH *Learn to talk Old Jack Lang* (1984) 14 He introduced me to his *cheese and kisses* and four *tin lids*, two *mother's joys* and two *twist and twirls*. **1981** B. DICKINS *Gift of Gab* 2 What are the things of light that made me bawl as a tinlid?

3. *fig*. in the phr. **in the tin**, in a tight spot.

1940 P. KERRY *Cobbers A.I.F*. 13 Then young Johnny swam in slowly, an' 'is face wus one big grin, As he menshuned ter the breakers, 'Whacko, Serg.! Yer in the tin!'

tin, *n*.² [Fig. use of *tin* money, cash.]

1. Luck.

1918 [see TINNY *a.*]. **1945** *Atebrin Advocate: Mag. 2/4 Austral. Armoured Regiment* 24 Feb. 1 But ask Headquarters batsmen 'How is he for tin?'

2. Special Comb. **tin arse (back, bum)**, an usually lucky person; also as **tin-arsed** *a*.

1898 *Bulletin* (Sydney) 4 June (Red Page), And a 'tinback' is a party Who's remarkable for luck. **1941** S.J. BAKER *Pop. Dict. Austral. Slang* 76 *Tin-ar--ed*, unusually lucky. **1955** D. NILAND *Shiralee* 158, I come up with a stone worth five hundred quid... Tin-bum, they call me. **1975** L. RYAN *Shearers* 79 Good on yer, Joe. You always were a tin-arse.

tin-dish.

1. *Gold-mining*. A shallow vessel in which alluvial soil, gravel, etc., is washed to separate out gold. Also *attrib*. See DISH *n*. 1.

1851 *Empire* (Sydney) 6 Aug. 19/4 About twenty men at work at the diggings, all gathering a good harvest, though in sad want of utensils, there being only one cradle on the ground, all the operations being conducted with a tin dish.

1851 *Ibid.* 13 Sept. 151/7 The tents are struck—the tribes of cradlemen, and the tin dish helotry, have dispersed to the neighbouring tiers—bark huts look desolate and the gunyas are deserted.

2. Special Comb. **tin-dish fossicking** *vbl. n.*, the process of washing for gold in a tin-dish; goldmining in a small way (see FOSSICK *v.* 1); **washing** *vbl. n.*, see quot. 1853 (2).

1852 J. BONWICK *Notes of Gold Digger* 8 A good living may be got .. in a little **tin-dish fossicking** in deserted holes. **1853** MRS C. CLACY *Lady's Visit to Gold Diggings* 85 A very fair amount of gold-dust may be obtained in either by the newcomer by tin-dish fossicking in deserted holes. *Ibid.* 64 **Tin-dish-washing** is generally done beside a stream. **1853** J. SHERER *Gold Finder Aust.* 281 The operation which procured .. three guineas' worth of gold is technically called tin-dish washing, and is very simply performed. The pan .. is generally about eighteen inches or more across the top, and three or four inches deep, with sloping sides. Into this vessel, the earth—which is technically called 'dirt'—is thrown .. and immersed in water several times.

Hence **tin-disher** *n.*

1882 W. SOWDEN *N.T. as it Is* 59 Mr Furner—no tin-disher, by the way—dug out a pie-tin full and washed a couple of pennyweights.

tin dog: see DOG *n.*[1] 2 c. and d.

Tingaringy gum /tɪŋgəˈrɪŋgi gʌm/. [f. the name of Mt. *Tingaringy*, n.e. Victoria, where the type specimen was collected in 1887.] The tree *Eucalyptus glaucescens* (fam. Myrtaceae) of scattered mountainous areas in e. Vic. and s.e. N.S.W.

1967 N.A. WAKEFIELD *Naturalist's Diary* 26 There were thickets of the mallee-like Tingaringy Gum. **1981** L. COSTERMANS *Native Trees & Shrubs S.-E. Aust.* 391 Tingaringi [sic] Gum (*E*[*ucalyptus*] *glaucescens*) was originally described as being a 'mallee' or small tree near the East Gippsland/N.S.W. border, but was later discovered as a tall tree near Mt Erica, almost 200 km. westward.

tin hare.
1. [Chiefly Austral.] An electric hare used in grey-hound racing; also allusively, greyhound racing. Also *attrib.*

1927 *Sydney Morning Herald* 12 Sept. 6/3 Mr Beer's remarks re the Sports Ground for tin hare racing are quite illogical. **1932** *NSWPD* 2nd Ser. vol. 131 7906, I have been out to the 'tin hares' myself; it is a poor person's pastime and quite a lot of cash changes hands there.

2. *transf.* A nickname for a train, esp. a rail-motor. Also *attrib.* and as *v. intr.*

1938 F. CLUNE *Free & Easy Land* 190 We tin-hared sixty miles to Ayr on the Burdekin Delta. There is only one class on the tin-hare (rail motor). **1988** *Sydney Morning Herald* 8 Oct. 37/1 It is the last of the 'tin-hare' rail-motors.

tinned dog: see DOG *n.*[1] 2 c.

tinny, *n.* [f. *tin* + *-Y*.] Also **tinnie**.
1. A can of beer; the contents of such a can.

1964 B. HUMPHRIES *Nice Night's Entertainment* (1981) 79 So we all shacked up there with stacks of the old *glein*, a few crates of tinnies, a couple of little snow bunnies and no complications. **1982** *Canberra Chron.* 3 Mar. 5/2 Asked if they would prefer tea or coffee, one member said, 'Nothing, thanks, love. I'll have a tinny.' **1986** *Canberra Times* 15 Feb. 4/4 A tinnie or two may be good for you.

2. A boat with an aluminium hull.

1979 *Herald* (Melbourne) 7 June 35/1 The aluminium 'tinnie' has long been a major force in the Australian boat market for its low initial cost, durability and ease of use. **1984** *N.T. News* (Darwin) 28 Sept. 37/8 Wanted, Tinny, 13 ft. 6 in.—15 ft. Prefer with trailer and no engine. Will pay up to $1500 for right boat.

tinny, *a.* [See TIN *n.*[2]] Lucky. Also as **tinny luck**, exceptional luck.

[N.Z. **1918** *Chrons. N.Z. Exped. Force* 7 June 205 Remarks are heard on the 'tinny' luck.] **1919** W.H. DOWNING *Digger Dialects* 50 *Tinny*, lucky. **1920** —— *To Last Ridge* 47 McAlister had tinny luck. Got a piece on the leg and went off in a stretcher as happy as Larry.

tip, *n.*[1] *Obs.* [Deteriorated use of *tip* a gratuity.] A bribe; also, without article, bribery.

1812 J.H. VAUX *Mem.* (1819) II. 219 *Tip*, to give, pay, or bribe. To *take the tip*, is to receive a bribe in any shape; and they say of a person who is known to be corruptible, that he will *stand the tip*. The *tip* is a term frequently used to signify the money concerned in any dealings or contract existing between parties; synonymous with *the dues*. **1832** *Currency Lad* (Sydney) 6 Oct. 3 The whole fraternity of constables (save the mark!) as lovers of *tip*, purchaseable at any time for a pot of beer, or a king's picture.

Tip, *n.*[2] *Obs.* [Abbrev. of *Tipperary*, the name of a county in Eire.] An Irishman, esp. a gold-miner.

1862 C.R. THATCHER *Canterbury Songster* 19 To rescue him this rowdie Tip unto his mates he hollered. **1892** 'R. BOLDREWOOD' *Nevermore* III. 105, I paid you honest for Number One South, which I stand a good show of losin' if you don't come out and prove your pegs. The Tips are trying the bluff game, and if you don't stand by me I'll be regular jumped and run off the field.

tip, *v.*[1] *Obs.* [f. TIP *n.*[1]] *trans.* To bribe.

1845 S. SIDNEY *Three Colonies* (1853) 162 On his road, with his sheep, looking for a new station, he meets Timmins, an old 'lag', who, by 'tipping' the Clerks at the Crown Land Office, has had his run kept out of the government sales. **1847** A. HARRIS *Settlers & Convicts* (1953) 49 All these except old Dennis were at this very time prisoners of the Crown, but got out of barracks by 'tipping' (bribing) the watchman and constables.

tip, *v.*[2] [Transf. use of *tip* to give a piece of information.] *trans.* To guess.

1955 R. LAWLER *Summer of Seventeenth Doll* (1965) 51 'Until last Saturday I didn't know you had any—de facto wives.' . . 'But I haven't! Ooh, what you mean is my kids? .. I tipped it'd be like that. Yes, kids I got all right. In three states.' **1977** R. BEILBY *Gunner* 301, I tipped who ya was.

tip-dray. A dray so constructed as to tilt in order to release its load: see DRAY 1.

1899 *North-Western Advocate* (Devonport) 30 June 2/4 We have been shown a very useful tip-dray. .. The wheels and undercarriage are of Victorian wood and the body of Tasmanian timber. **1962** E. LANE *Mad as Rabbits* 214 He had bought himself a horse and a tip-dray and settled down to work very soberly for several years for the Council, road-making.

tip-slinger. A racecourse tipster (see also quot. 1962).

1915 A. WRIGHT *Sport from Hollowlog Flat* 16 Tip-slinger Grif came and whispered, 'You're on a cert., she's the only trier.' **1962** J.T. LANG *Great Bust* 335 On the air the tip-slingers like Rufe Naylor sold their wares.

tissue. Chiefly *Tas.* A cigarette paper. Also **tisher**.

[N.Z. **1952** *Here & Now* Jan. 32/2 See if the parole-jumper in Number 8 has got any tissues left.] **1966** H. PORTER *Paper Chase* 202 In Hobart and Tasmania, the collecting of local idiosyncracies of vocabulary and custom .. suddenly seems the most trivial of things to do. I note that tissue is used for cigarette-paper. **1981** D. STUART *I think I'll Live*

122 Have you noticed that the Tasmanians to a man always refer to a cigarette paper as a 'tisher'?

tit. [Transf. use of *tit* a small bird of the fam. Paridae.] A small bird, esp. a THORNBILL or *scrub wren* (see SCRUB *n.* 5).

1901 *Emu* I. 60 The familiar Tits (*Acanthiza chrysorrhoa*) .. often build their bulky nests in conspicuous places. 1948 P.J. HURLEY *Red Cedar* 33 Tits, pardalotes and other small fry often used these ironbarks as a hiding place.

ti-tree, var. TEA-TREE.

tizzy, *a.* [Prob. f. *tizzy* a state of excitement.] Gaudy; showy.

1953 S.J. BAKER *Aust. Speaks* 103 *Tizzy*, an adjective applied to ostentatious or 'flashy' dressing, or dressing with bad taste. 1969 G. JOHNSTON *Clean Straw for Nothing* (1971) 20, I was also going to say I send you lots of presents. Nice things, too. Nothing tizzy.

tizzy, *v.* [f. prec.] *trans.* To titivate (a person); also *transf.* (see quot. 1977). Usu. with **up** and freq. as *ppl. a.*

1960 K. SMITH *Word from Children* 72 According to children mothers get all 'tizzied up' before they go out. 1977 T.A.G. HUNGERFORD *Wong Chu* 86 A lot of places had been tizzied up. 1986 *Canberra Times* 3 Apr. 2/2 Basically, a mob of tizzied-up birds strutting round the place without contributing much to the common good isn't really what battling out a living from the Great Australian Loneliness is about, eh?

tjuringa, var. CHURINGA.

toa /'toʊə/. [a. Diyari prob. *dhuwa.*] An Aboriginal direction-marker: see quot. 1981.

1927 *Bulletin* (Sydney) 27 Oct. 27/2 *Toas* or direction-finders are in use among the abos. in the Lake Eyre district, Centralia. 1981 J. MULVANEY et al. *Aboriginal Aust.* 11 Very interesting examples of native constructions .. are the little-known Aboriginal directional markers from the Lake Eyre region known as 'toas'. Made of an amalgam of gypsum, wood and feathers, they were stuck in the ground on departure from a camp to communicate the destination of a departing group to anyone able to read them.

toad-fish. [Spec. use of *toad-fish* any of several fish of toad-like appearance.] Any of many self-inflating, usu. poisonous and spiny, marine and estuarine fish of the fam. Tetraodontidae.

1801 *HRA* (1915) 1st Ser. III. 171 One he said was killed by natives, the other eat [*sic*] a toad fish. 1984 B. DIXON *Searching for Aboriginal Lang.* 133 Most fishes are *bayi*, but the stone-fish and the toad-fish—which can inflict injury on a person—are specially marked by being *balan*.

toadie, var. TOADY.

toado. [f. TOAD(-FISH + -O.] TOAD-FISH.

1906 D.G. STEAD *Fishes of Aust.* 225 The Toado (*Tetrodon hamiltoni*) .. is sometimes caught on the small-boy's line with a 'fly-hook'. 1976 E. WORRELL *Things that Sting* 52 Toadfish, often called Toadoes, are easily recognised. They have a thickset body without scales, a broad head with wide beak-like chopping teeth and a fan-tail.

toadskin. *Obs.* [Also U.S. for a green banknote.] FROGSKIN.

1924 A.B. PATERSON *Old Bush Songs* (ed 4) 65 With a toadskin in my pocket I borrowed from a friend, Oh, isn't it nice and cosy to be campin' in the bend.

toady. Also **toadie.** [f. TOAD(-FISH + -Y.] TOAD-FISH. Also **toady-fish.**

1935 DAVISON & NICHOLLS *Blue Coast Caravan* 281 A toady-fish .. who, on being approached, blew himself up into the semblance of a football covered with spines. 1939 *Bulletin* (Sydney) 31 May 21/4 Wouldn't doubt that a very small toadie (we call them blowfish in W.A.) will stiffen the poultry-yard.

to and from. Rhyming slang for POM.

1946 R.D. RIVETT *Behind Bamboo* 399 *To-and-from*, a Pommy, i.e. Englishman. 1982 *Weekend Austral. Mag.* (Sydney) 6 Mar. 8/8 As a 'To-and-From', one of the things that baffled me in this Australian leisure lifestyle when I first arrived here many years ago was the esky routine.

toby. [Transf. use of *Toby*, familiar form of the name *Tobias.*]

1. *Shearing.* See quot. 1964.

1957 STEWART & KEESING *Old Bush Songs* 273 I've been shearing on the Goulburn side and down at Douglas Park, Where every day 'twas 'Wool away!' and Toby did his work. 1964 H.P. TRITTON *Time means Tucker* (rev. ed.) 41 Raddle was a stick of blue or yellow ochre, also called 'Toby' which was used to mark badly shorn sheep.

2. A 'willing horse'.

1941 S.J. BAKER *Pop. Dict. Austral. Slang* 77 *Toby*, a man silly of mind and clumsy of hand, but willing to do whatever asked. 1944 A. MARSHALL *These are my People* 155 I'm not much chop on pies, but I'm a toby on puddin's.

toe. Strength; speed.

1889 *Bulletin* (Sydney) 21 Dec. 15/3 But the goat made it clear each time he drew near That he had what the racing men call 'too much toe' for him. 1983 *Sun-Herald* (Sydney) 23 Oct. 73/4 In Lawson and Hogg we have two penetrating fast bowlers who have enough 'toe' to keep any batsman honest.

toe-rag. *Obs.* [Used elsewhere but recorded earliest in Aust.: see OEDS and EDD.]

1. A strip of cloth wrapped round the foot and worn inside a boot, in place of a sock; see also PRINCE ALBERTS. Also *attrib.* as an emblem of poverty or disreputableness.

1865 J.F. MORTLOCK *Experiences of Convict* 80 Stockings being unknown, some luxurious men wrapped round their feet a piece of old shirting, called, in language more expressive than elegant, a 'toe-rag'. 1898 *Truth* (Sydney) 13 Feb. 3/5 In the early days of the colonies, squatters did not usually keep socks in their stores. .. Many wore boots only, and those who wished for other protection, tore off square pieces of old shirts and wrapped them round their feet. These were called 'toe-rags'. .. A common expression with the shearers is, 'Oh, you belong to the toe-rag mob', meaning .. too poor, or mean, to buy socks. 1901 *Ibid.* 18 Aug. 5/3 After a few years of 'battling' in the Chow's baneful brothel, they were cast adrift to swell the ranks of the toe-rag crowd.

2. *transf.* A one-pound note.

1895 *Bulletin* (Sydney) 16 Feb. 21/2 'Toe-rag'—larrikinese for £1-note, from the odour thereof. 1945 S.J. BAKER *Austral. Lang.* 109 *£1* .. toe-rag.

toe-ragger. [f. TOE-RAG 1.]

1. A tramp; a 'down-and-out'.

1891 *Truth* (Sydney) 1 Feb. 6/4 They receive a consideration to ring in the name of every toe-ragger who may degrade the assembly when a boxing match is made. 1966 G.W. TURNER *Eng. Lang. Aust. & N.Z.* 144 The battler seems to have been the poorest itinerant. The toeragger was not much wealthier than the battler.

2. *transf.* One who is sentenced to a short term of imprisonment.

1918 J. MARSHALL *Jail from Within* 45 Christ Orlmighty, some o' you toeraggers (short-timers) take the cake. 1962

D. McLean *World turned upside Down* 114 He's only a 'toe-ragger', that's what they call a short-term prisoner.

toey, *a.*
1. Restive, touchy; ill-at-ease.
1930 *Bulletin* (Sydney) 8 Oct. 35/2 Wise Force was 'toey' before the race, and behaved in alarming fashion on his way to and at the post. **1982** D. Harris *Drovers of Outback* 58, I had an old night horse which seemed to sense trouble and if the cattle were quiet he would get very 'toey'!
2. Fast.
1977 B. Scott *My Uncle Arch* 35 They had a getaway that Roger Bannister would have envied. Real toey, Arch reckoned.

togs, *pl.* A swimming costume. Also **bathing togs, swimming togs.**
1918 *Kia Ora Coo-ee* Apr. 7/1 Some of the Queenslanders are revelling in the opportunity of getting out in this hot weather in their bathing togs! **1930** V. Palmer *Passage* (1957) 72 'You nip in and get my togs.' He was more at ease in his bathing-trunks than in his double-breasted serge suit. **1944** *Aust.: Nat. Jrnl.* Apr. 65 She struts by swimming togs and towel across one arm.

Tojo. [The name of Hideki *Tojo* (1884–1948), Japanese army officer who became chief of staff and military dictator during the war of 1939–45.] A member of the Japanese armed forces; these forces collectively.
1943 J. Binning *Target Area* 22 The monotone of the bombers is easing. Tojo is on his way out and now it is safe to get up. **1985** N. Medcalf *Rifleman* 113 You should have seen those Tojos run!
Hence **Tojo-land** *n.*, Japan; **Tojo-lander** *n.*, a Japanese person.
1943 *Camp Capers: Official Organ 157 Austral. Gen. Transport Co.* Aug. 12 If 'e ever gets to **Tojo-land** the Japs will die of fright. **1942** *Plane Speaking from R.A.A.F.* 8 We'd rather be in Tokio drinking Jappo beer, Throwing all the empties at some **Tojo-lander's** rear.

tom, *n.*[1] Mining.
1. [U.S.: see Mathews.] Abbrev. of Long Tom 1.
1852 A. Mackay *Great Gold Field* (1853) 5, I fell in with a mulatto .. who was working a small 'tom' by himself, with which he had cleared half an ounce up to twelve o'clock that morning. **1980** M. Temple *Goers & Shicers*, It was put in a bucket and washed on a 'tom'—a sloping table about 2 feet wide with side and cross grooves to catch the gold.
2. [Also U.S.] A prop, as of timber: see quot. 1932.
1932 I.L. Idriess *Prospecting for Gold* 237 An odd 'tom' is occasionally put in underground when you strike an exceptionally large patch of opal and have to chamber out a huge section in the opal dirt... A tom is a prop, you jam one end under the roof with the other end resting on the floor. **1977** J. Doughty *Gold in Blood* 90, I wedged in the short 'toms' of timber to support the 'back' (roof) while I lay on my side, squeezed under the overhang.

tom, *n.*[2] Abbrev. of 'tom-tart' (see quot. 1882), a jocular formation on Tart.
[**1882** *Sydney Slang Dict.* 8 *Tom-tart*, Sydney phrase for a girl or sweetheart. N.Z. **1906** *N.Z. Truth* (Wellington) 31 Mar. 6 For he tells you, not being prudy, That our love's a 'Tom' or 'tart', Or a 'clinah' or a 'Judy'.] *c* **1907** W.C. Chandler *Darkest Adelaide* 9 If his 'tom' had even the inkling of an idea that he was not true to her in word and deed there would be merry L to pay. **1951** D. Stivens *Jimmy Brocket* 102 'You did, Darling', one of the little social toms said. She was a nuggety little sheila.

tom, *v.*[1] *Obs.* [U.S.: see Mathews.] *trans.* To wash (auriferous material), using a long tom.

1855 W. Howitt *Land, Labor & Gold* II. 261 When we went up this gully we found the whole of it most carefully dug out and tommed. **1862** J.A. Patterson *Gold Fields Vic.* 12 Wash-dirt had to be carted across the plain to the banks of the river, to be there 'cradled' or 'tommed'.
Hence **tommer** *n.*, one who washes auriferous material using a long tom.
1855 W. Howitt *Land, Labor & Gold* II. 193 It will not pay the cradler or the tommer to put through much rough earth.

tom, *v.*[2] [Of unknown origin.] *trans.* To bounce: see quot. 1976. Also *intr.*
1947 *Coast to Coast 1946* 182 The tractor stormed ahead, filling the bush with its clamour. 'See how the log toms along,' said Blue watching it. **1976** C.D. Mills *Hobble Chains & Greenhide* 29 They were yoked four abreast, and the outside string drew from the outside hub of the front wheel to enable them to swing, or 'tom' the front wheels away from an obstruction.

tom, *v.*[3] [f. Tom *n.*[1] 2.] *trans.* With **up**: to shore.
1979 J. Williams *White River* 57 We'd sailed together once on an Iron boat... Heavy weather in the Bight had set her rolling and locomotive wheels that hadn't been properly tommed up started chasing us around the hold.

tomahawk, *n.* Also **tommyhawk.** [Transf. use of *tomahawk* the axe of the North American Indian.] A hatchet; the stone hatchet of the Aborigines (see quots. 1840 and 1870).
1808 *Sydney Gaz.* 18 Sept., They never burden themselves with any other luggage than a spear or two, and a short club, unless they have been fortunate enough to get possession of a tomahawk. **1840** A. Russell *Tour through Austral. Colonies* 259 The principal tool used is the tomahawk, a piece of flint ground into a wedge shape, having a twig twisted or tied round the head, leaving a handle some inches long, according to the weight or size of the stone or flint required; the whole being much in shape to a hammer. **1870** E.B. Kennedy *Four Yrs. in Qld.* 78 The Aboriginals .. cut out 'possums from a tree or sugar bag (wild honey) by means of a tomahawk of green stone; the handle is formed of a vine, and fixed in its place with gum. **1914** *Bulletin* (Sydney) 17 Sept. 22/2 With a tommyhawk, or, rather, a half-handled 'Douglas', the gum is chipped off.

tomahawk, *v. Shearing.* Also **tommyhawk.** [f. prec.] *trans.* To shear (a sheep) roughly (see esp. quots. 1864 and 1895); to cut (a sheep) during shearing. Also *absol.*, and as *vbl. n.* and *ppl. a.*
1859 H. Kingsley *Recoll. Geoffry Hamlyn* II. 25 The poor sheep got fearfully 'tomahawked' by the new hands. **1864** J. Armour *Diggings, Bush & Melbourne* 17 We had several who shore sixty, a few eighty, and one or two a hundred, but the latter were often brought to task for 'tomahawking', or leaving ridge-and-furrow shear-marks. **1890** *Bulletin* (Sydney) 20 Sept. 11/4 The 'ringer' that shore a hundred as they never were shorn before, And the novice, who toiling bravely, had 'tommy-hawked' half a score. **1895** J. Kirby *Old Times in Bush* 147 The shearer did not care how much wool he left on the sheep, all his look out was, 'the count'... He would not scruple to leave half an inch long ridges of wool on the sheep, so long as he could get paid for the shearing. This kind of shearing was called 'Tom-a-hawking'. **1905** *Shearer* (Sydney) 23 Dec. 7/5, I once had the doubtful pleasure, many years ago, of working in a woolshed along with a 'tomahawking'.. shearer. **1912** J. Bradshaw *Highway Robbery under Arms* (ed. 3) 7 But I'd rather tomahawk every day and shear a flock, For that's the only way I make some tin.

tomahawker. Also **tommyhawker.** A shearer, esp. one who shears roughly.

1901 *Bulletin* (Sydney) 5 Oct. 16/3 Surely .. bushworkers are as worthy of consideration as the 'swaggers', 'tomahawkers', and 'loppies' of N.S.W. **1912** R.S. TAIT *Scotty Mac* 70 He even recognised the Tommyhawker shearing on the board.

tomato sauce. Rhyming slang for 'horse'.
1905 J. MEREDITH *Learn to talk Old Jack Lang* (1984) 13 A *pot and pan* driving a nice high stepping *tomato sauce* in a flash *big an' bulky* pulled up. **1968** J. ALARD *He who shoots Last* 86 'Nice weak tomato sauce ta be puttin' money on,' said the Wrecker.

tommer: see TOM *v.*[1]

tommy-axe. [Shortened form of TOMAHAWK *n.* + *axe.*] A hatchet.
1898 E.E. MORRIS *Austral Eng.* 474 *Tommy-axe*, a popular corruption of the *Tomahawk*. **1965** G. McINNES *Road to Gundagai* 145 He would chop its head off neatly with a tommy-axe.

tommyhawk, var. TOMAHAWK *n.* and *v.*

tommyhawker, var. TOMAHAWKER.

tommy rough. Also **tommy ruff.** [f. *Tommy* + transf. use of *ruff* a small fresh-water fish of the perch fam., having rough scales: see OED *sb.*[1] 2.] The marine fish *Arripis georgianus*, valued as food; HERRING 1 b.; *native herring*, see NATIVE *a.* 6 b.; ROUGHY a.
1886 J.F. CONIGRAVE *S.A.* 166 The popular opinion in favour of the 'snook' and 'tommy rough' is well grounded. **1984** E. ROLLS *Celebration of Senses* 56 South Australians fishing for the little, good-eating Tommy Ruffs.

Tommy Tanna /tɒmi 'tænə/. *Hist.* [f. *Tommy* a personal name + TANNA the name of an island of Vanuatu (formerly the New Hebrides).] A nickname for a Kanaka; usu. used generically.
1903 *Bulletin* (Sydney) 6 Dec. 1/7 It is only now, when there is no possibility of plutocratic slave-owners in the sugar districts getting supplies of fresh niggers to replace the 'returns', that the inhumanity of sending Tommy Tanna home has been discovered. **1974** N. CATO *Brown Sugar* 28 'Tommy Tanna' was a nick-name for a Kanaka, just like 'John Chinaman' or 'Jacky' for an Abo.

Tom Thumb. [Used elsewhere but recorded earliest in Aust.] Rhyming slang for 'rum'.
1905 J. MEREDITH *Learn to talk Old Jack Lang* (1984) 14, I can go into the *rubbity dub* and have a lemonade, breasting the *near and far* with booze hounds drinking *Tom Thumb*. **1967** *Kings Cross Whisper* (Sydney) xli. 4/4 *Tom Thumb*, rum. Also rhyming slang for the drum, give the strong tip, drum a person up; give him the mail.

tomtit. [Transf. use of *tomtit* a bird of the genus *Parus*, and other small birds.] Any of several small birds, often a THORNBILL, and esp. the *yellow-tailed thornbill* (see YELLOW 1).
1883 A.J. CAMPBELL *Nests & Eggs Austral. Birds* p. iv, On the sunny side of prickly acacia hedges we found numerous nests of Tomtits or Yellow-tailed acanthizas. **1981** A.B. FACEY *Fortunate Life* 89 And there was the little brown and grey tom tit.

tongs. *Shearing.* A pair of hand shears.
c **1895** CLARK & WHITELAW *Golden Summers* (1986) 133 When the Cove sez. Sez he, that shearing wont [*sic*] do my man. So I ship my b–y tongs across the dancing board, straddles my crock, & takes to the water like a b–y rat. **1951** G. PIKE *Campfire Tales* (1981) 104 Jacky Howe with the tongs (as shearers in those days referred to the blades).

tonic. [Joc. use of *tonic* a tonic medicine.] Alcoholic liquor.
1944 F. BERKERY *East goes West* 69 It also used to be the delightful practice of some of the 'dags' to journey on this train to Augusta to arrange for supplies of tonic, and to have a blow-out... No liquor was allowed on any of the trains .. but the harder they tried to enforce the rule, the more the grog came in.

tonicked, *ppl. a.* [Joc. use of *tonic, v.* to administer a tonic.] Drunk.
1911 *Bulletin* (Sydney) 12 Oct. 14/2 Who ever hears .. of a man being 'drunk'? .. The staid and dignified citizen will say he is 'intoxicated'... The average boy that he is 'shickered', 'blithered' or 'tonicked'. **1961** F. LEECHMAN *Opal Bk.* 57 But the wicked old lout had been 'tonic'd' as they call it and had wandered about bushed for twenty-four hours.

tonk. [Of unknown origin.]
a. A male who in speech or manner appears to set himself above his fellows (see quot. 1965); a fool.
1941 S.J. BAKER *Pop. Dict. Austral. Slang* 77 *Tonk*, a simpleton or fool .. a dude or fop .. a general term of contempt. **1965** G. McINNES *Road to Gundagai* 92 Just the same you couldn't help noticing that the Grammar boys came from the wealthiest homes, were C of E and Establishment and blessed by the Anglican Bishop and had ivy-covered walls and generally behaved as if they owned the place. They were known to us as *tonks*, which is an onomatopoetic [*sic*] description of what they were.
b. A male homosexual.
[N.Z. **1943** *Penguin New Writing* XVII. 83 The cook got my goat when he started trying to do the same thing. He was a tonk all right, just a real old auntie.] **1964** G. JOHNSTON *My Brother Jack* 115 He'll either pick up a dose, or he'll get her up the duff... Either that or he'll end up a tonk. **1970** *TV Times* (Sydney) 15 July 41/3 There was also a homosexual (who was referred to as a 'tonk'—thereby dating Mr Porter rather badly).

ton-work. *S.A. Mining. Obs.* [f. *ton* a measure of weight + *work*, by analogy with *tut-work*, designating a system of payment by measure of work done: see OED *tut, sb.*[2]] Piece-work.
1846 *S. Austral. Register* (Adelaide) 21 Oct. 3/4 At tut-work, tribute or ton-work the earnings of miners has been considerable. **1971** *AUMLA* xxxvi. 170 Work in the mines fell broadly into two categories, tutwork or ton-work, and work on tribute.

tooart, tooat, var. TUART.

toodlembuck /'tudləmbʌk/. Also **toodle-em-buck.** [Prob. f. *tootle* to walk, wander + *th)em* + *buck* gambling marker.] A gambling game played by children: see quot. 1960.
1959 A.D. MICKLE *After Ball* 75 There was 'Toodle-em-buck'. That was purely a gambling game. **1960** K. SMITH *Word from Children* 155 Another gay, carefree kind of toy, designed to develop the gambling instinct in innocent children, was the Toodlembuck. It consisted of a disc of cardboard mounted on a cotton-reel and slipped over an old wooden meat-skewer. The top of the disc was divided into segments with a horse's name on each, such as 'Spearfelt', 'Carbine', or 'Heroic'. A pointer was fitted to the skewer and the disc was spun roulette-wise while the young bookie yelled, 'Who'll have a go on me old toodlembuck?'

toolache /tu'leɪtʃi/. Also **toolach,** and formerly **too-latchee, dulachie.** [a. Yaralde *dulaj*.] The large wallaby *Macropus greyi*, formerly of s.e. S.A. and adjacent Vic., now prob. extinct. Also *attrib.*
1879 'OLD HAND' *Journey Port Phillip to S.A.* 35 Kangaroos, Kangaroo rats, toolatchee and wallaby were abundant.

1885 *Eng. Illustr. Mag.* (London) X. 398 There were lots of dulachies, which are smaller than a brown kangaroo, and are grey-haired and red-headed. **1890** J.I. WATTS *Family Life S.A.* 182 There was a species [of kangaroo] that I had not seen on this side of the Murray, called by the blacks Toolaches. They are not so large as the common kangaroo, but are remarkably graceful animals. **1926** A.S. LE SOUEF et al. *Wild Animals Australasia* 189 Grey's wallaby, known as the 'toolach', is now very scarce. It is confined, as far as can be ascertained, to a small area of scrub-land inland from the mouth of the Murray River, South Australia. **1984** *Age* (Melbourne) 18 Aug. 6/1 Like many of its fellow victims, the toolache wallaby was too good-looking to live... Such a beautiful creature was doomed by exploitation for its fur.

too right: see RIGHT *a.* 3.

tooroo /ˈturu/, *int.* [Var. of *toodle-oo* 'goodbye' (see OEDS); the form *tooraloo* is used elsewhere but recorded earliest in Aust. (see OEDS).] 'Goodbye'. Also **tooraloo**, and as *n.*
  1916 *Truth* (Sydney) 23 Jan. 10/5 Page said, 'Well, too-ra-loo; I'm getting off here.' 'Hoo-roo, Page,' he replied. **1927** *Bulletin* (Sydney) 14 Apr. 24/2 Does anybody know the derivation of 'tooroo', used out back in the same sense as 'so long' or 'good-bye'? It may be abo. **1983** B. DAWE *Over here, Harv!* 122 The ambulance whanged by again, on its way to the morgue... And the ambulance bell kept yelling a last tooroo.

toot /tʊt/. [Prob. transf. use of Br. dial. *tut* a small seat or hassock: see OED *sb.*¹ 2.] A lavatory.
  1965 J. O'GRADY *Aussie Eng.* 36 A toilet. Also known as a 'dunny', a 'shouse', a 'toot'. **1978** J. ROWE *Warlords* 258 Waldon added over his shoulder, 'Gobind's in the toot. He'll be right out.'

tooth-billed cat bird. [f. *tooth-billed*, referring to the double notch at the tip of the bird's stout black bill + *cat bird* (see CAT A.).] The bird *Scenopoeetes dentirostris* of rainforest in n.e. Qld. Also **tooth-billed bowerbird.**
  1904 *Emu* III. 188, I am sending you a photo. of the finest playground we found of the Tooth-billed Bower-Bird (*Scenopoeus dentirostris*). **1976** *Reader's Digest Compl. Bk. Austral. Birds* 558 Mountain rainforests of north-east Queensland ring continuously with the loud song of male tooth-billed catbirds during the breeding season.

tooth man. A hearty eater.
  1954 *Barbed Wire & Bamboo* (Sydney) Oct. 8 Rex, Trudy and Mrs Hearne admit to having seen some of the best in tooth men. **1967** *Kings Cross Whisper* (Sydney) xli. 4/4 Tooth man, a good eater.

top, *n.* Northern Australia, esp. in the phr. **up top.** See also TOP END 1.
  1951 R. DORIEN *Venturing to Aust.* 181 The occupants liked living 'up top', would not live anywhere else. **1955** N. PULLIAM *I traveled Lonely Land* 221 He.. went on, 'He's good with stock.. and the cattlemen at The Top need him.'
  Hence **up topper** *n.*, one native to or resident in northern Australia.
  1969 J. DINGWELL *One String* 109 Up Toppers called the fresh-water Johnstone crocodile an alligator.

top, *v.* [Spec. use of *top* (usu. with *off* or *up*) to put the finishing touch to a process.]
  1. *trans.* With **off** or **up**: to fatten (livestock) for market. Also *intr.*
  1889 *Illustr. Austral. News* (Melbourne) 2 Sept. 18/1 Time passes on and he increases in size; but being brought in to be 'topped off' in the fattening paddock he shows a bit of the old leaven to the disgust of the sundowner, who spends the night in the sapling instead of in the men's hut. **1890** 'R. BOLDREWOOD' *Squatter's Dream* 50 The sheep were good sheep; they had well-grown fleeces, rather coarse; but that did not matter with fattening sheep; they were large and would make good wethers when topped up. **1923** J. BOWES *Jackaroos* 101 The cattle.. had 'topped up', and were on their way south to a distant market.
  2. [Prob. joc. alteration of *tip off.*] *intr.* With **off:** to divulge information. Also *trans.*, to betray (someone).
  1939 K. TENNANT *Foveaux* 312 There was too much danger that a squarehead would top-off to the police. **1959** D. NILAND *Gold in Streets* 94 I'll think up something and keep in her good books while I'm doing it, the slut, or she'll top me off.

top end.
  1. Freq. with initial capitals. The northern part of the Northern Territory: see quot. 1963. Also *attrib.*
  1933 F.E. BAUME *Tragedy Track* 158 No party ever given in Australia could reach the heights of that which farewelled a bushwoman of bushwomen when she passed through the Alice from the 'top end' on her way to Adelaide. **1943** *Frontier News* Mar. 5/3 Having had it well impressed upon me from Broken Hill onwards that 'this is a man's country, and women are a nuisance', by one Roy—then driving the 'top-end' mail from Broken Hills [*sic*] to Cordillo Downs. **1963** F. FLYNN *Northern Gateway* 72 The Northern Territory may be divided into two parts—'The Centre' and the 'Top End'. The Centre has Alice Springs as its 'capital', or administrative base. In the Top End, Darwin is episcopal headquarters and the home of the Northern Territory's Administrator.
  2. In local use: the Murray River upstream of its junction with the Darling River: see BOTTOM END, esp. quot. 1947. Also *attrib.*
  1947 W. LAWSON *Paddle-Wheels Away* 102 A dozen rivermen, swearing and shouting, erupted into the bar. 'Where are the 'top-end' crawlers? Come and fight, you dingoes.' **1956** [see BOTTOM END].

top-ender.
  1. Freq. with initial capital. One native to or resident in the northern part of the Northern Territory.
  1941 C. BARRETT *Coast of Adventure* 14 The old Top-ender drank beer, which, to the men up there, is more desirable than iced nectar is to gods. **1984** *N.T. News* (Darwin) 21 Dec. 7/5 How many Top Enders must have marvellous memories.
  2. A member of the crew of a Murray River boat.
  1953 [see *bottom-ender* BOTTOM END]. **1976** DRAGE & PAGE *Riverboats & Rivermen* 212 Alec and David were 'top enders' who spent much of their lives in the Darling, Murrumbidgee, and Edwards rivers.

top feed. [f. *top* upper + FEED.] The foliage of bushes and trees, which provides pasture for livestock.
  1931 M. TERRY *Hidden Wealth* 36 The top feed (edible bushes), associated with buck spinifex.. is raising some of the highest priced wool in Australia. **1976** C.D. MILLS *Hobble Chains & Greenhide* 82 In common with all cameloid ruminants 'Humps' are mainly top-feeders and revel in such timbers as gidyea, mulga, blue-bush and cassia... A pet camel that has been 'poddy-reared' is a menace about a homestead. It will reach out and eat anything available.

topknot pigeon. A pigeon having a crest, esp. *Lopholaimus antarcticus* (see FLOCK PIGEON b.), and *Geophaps lophotes* (see *crested pigeon* (a), CRESTED). Also *ellipt.* as **topknot.**
  1841 J. GOULD *Birds of Aust.* (1848) V. Pl. 61, *Lopholaimus antarcticus*.. Top-knot Pigeon of the Colonists of New South Wales. **1875** P.E. WARBURTON *Journey across Western Interior* 169 The Crested Dove, or Top-knot Pigeon of

Warburton (*Ocyphaps Lophotes*) . . being exclusively an inhabitant of the plains of the interior . . can never become an object of general observation. **1932** H. PRIEST *Call of Bush* 116, I had hit a small crested pigeon, locally known as the Topknot, or Crested Bronzewing, which follows the traveller in the river country.

top-notcher. See quots.

1978 M. WALKER *Pioneer Crafts Early Aust.* 36 The top sawyer was the master craftsman, often termed a 'top notcher'. He was responsible for the sharpening and care of the tools and his partner was the general labourer, both around the site and in the pit. **1981** J.P. GABBEDY *Forgotten Pioneers* 16 'I was a top-notcher'. . . He . . went on to explain that he had been a pit-sawer for half of his life, and that the top-notcher was the man who stood on the topside of the log and guided the cut along the chalked (or ash-marked) line.

top-off. [Prob. alteration of *tip-off*.] An informer. Also **top-off man**, etc.

1941 S.J. BAKER *Pop. Dict. Austral. Slang* 77 *Top-off*, a police informer. **1964** K. TENNANT *Summer's Tales* 99 By all accounts he's been top-off man for the cattle thieves ever since he could walk. . . The sergeant told me he'd never catch any of those poddy dodgers out while the kid's in the district. **1968** *Kings Cross Whisper* (Sydney) lv. 11/2 (heading) Australia's most famous top-off galah, Andrew Dobber, M.P., has put his foot in it again.

top-rail.

1. The upper horizontal member of a fence. Also *fig.* and *attrib.*

1898 G. DUNDERDALE *Bk. of Bush* 102, I . . saw the bandicoot sitting on a top-rail, watching me, and dangling her feet to and fro. She wore towzled red hair, a short print frock, and a look of defiance. . . You bandicooted my potatoes last night, and you've left the marks of your dirty feet on the ground. **1930** 'BRENT OF BIN BIN' *Ten Creeks Run* (1952) 1 Among the top-rail critics and advisers were neighbouring squatters and station-hands.

2. See quot. 1921.

1915 V. PALMER *World of Men* (1962) 35 He always was a grip rider. . . No broncho-straps, or monkey-straps or top rails for him. He'd as soon ride without a saddle as not. **1921** G.A. BELL *Under Brigalows* 122 Some of them had rolled up a bundle of twigs in a bit of saddle cloth, and running straps through the 'dees' on the front of the saddle, strapped it across to give a firmer hold to their legs—top rails or kids they called these inventions.

Torrens. [Used elsewhere but recorded earliest in Aust.] The name of Robert *Torrens* (1814–84), first Premier of South Australia, used *attrib.* in Comb. with reference to a simplified method of land-title registration devised by him, and introduced into South Australia in 1858, as **Torrens system, title.**

1863 R.R. TORRENS *Transfer of Land by 'Registration of Title'* 1 Transfer of land by 'registration of title' as now in operation in Australia, under the 'Torrens System'. **1971** CONRICK & THOMSON *Sale Real Property N.S.W.* 55 The vendor's solicitor submits particulars of the title sufficient to enable the purchaser's solicitor to prepare the transfer. For Torrens Title if the contract was well drawn these will be the same as in the description of the property in the contract.

Torres Strait pigeon. [f. the name of the strait between Cape York Peninsula and the s. coast of New Guinea.] The fruit-eating pigeon *Ducula bicolor* of n. Aust., s. New Guinea, and adjacent islands; *nutmeg pigeon*, see NUTMEG 2.

1848 J. GOULD *Birds of Aust.* (1848) V. Pl. 60, This bird [*sc. Carpophaga luctuosa*] is commonly known by the name of Torres Strait Pigeon, from its being so abundant there that few voyagers pass the straits during its breeding-season without seeing it. **1972** K. WILLEY *Tales Big Country* 174 Once he shot one of the Torres Strait pigeons. These glorious birds . . migrate down from the Pacific to nest in small islands of the Barrier Reef.

toss, *v.*

a. [Fig. use of *to toss* (etc.) *in the towel* to admit defeat: see OEDS *towel, sb.* 1 b.] In the phr. **to toss in the towel,** to die.

1937 V. PALMER *Legend for Sanderson* 32 Tossed in the towel. Seventy-four: he'd had a good spin.

b. In the phr. **to toss it in,** to finish; to give up. See also ALLEY 1.

[N.Z. **1952** THOMSON *Deer Shooter* 21 And though a few had stuck it out . . others had decided out of hand that deer-shooting was not for them and had tossed it in.] **1954** *Tobruk to Borneo* (Perth) Feb. 15 They got me Jack. . . You'd better toss it in. **1958** *Bulletin* (Sydney) 11 June 19/1 Consider the number of ways an Aussie can be dismissed from his job. . . He can be sacked, fired, hoisted [etc.]. . . Should he decide to beat the boss to the punch he may . . pull-out, toss it in [etc.].

tote. [Used elsewhere but recorded earliest in Aust.: see OED(S *sb.*^{1} 2.]

1. **a.** Abbrev. of 'totalizator'. Also *attrib.*

1890 *Truth* (Sydney) 9 Nov. 1/5 He backed the horse on nearly every 'tote' in town, and drew altogether about £300. **1970** K.E.C. GRAVES *Third Chance* 17 His fancy ran second—the tote pay-out was more than for the winning ticket.

b. In the collocation **blind tote,** a totalizator which registers but does not indicate to a bettor the details of wagers laid.

1904 *Sporting News* (Launceston) 16 July 1/3 The committee of the Hobart Trotting Club has made an innovation. . . They have now instituted what is known as the 'blind tote' in order that owners who desire to back their horses without letting the public into the 'know' can do so. **1933** S. GRIFFITHS *Rolling Stone on Turf* 35 A rough and ready 'blind tote' had also been installed. . . At this time the 'tote' was illegal in New South Wales; but the contraption was called a 'blind bookmaker', and the sporting police also were suddenly afflicted with defective vision.

2. Special Comb. **tote shop,** an illegal betting establishment.

1894 *Bulletin* (Sydney) 20 Jan. 6/4 If Parliament will pass an act decreeing that the landlord of every gambling den, 'tote'-shop, and house of ill-fame shall be imprisoned . . it will begin to look as if it was reasonably serious in the matter.

tother side.

1. OTHER SIDE 1.

1858 C.R. THATCHER *Colonial Songster* (rev. ed.) 77 He stuck up to a gal named Moggy, A big stout lass from t'other side. **1889** *Bulletin* (Sydney) 5 Oct. 8/2 In the rouse-abouts' hut . . they always spoke of the Cabbage Garden as 'Port Phillip', of the Holy Land as 'tother side.

2. OTHER SIDE 2 b.

1865 'SPECIAL CORRESPONDENT' *Transportation* 33, I found them all eager for information regarding the 'tother side', as they call the eastern colonies. **1963** X. HERBERT *Disturbing Element* 168 To scoot to T'otherside by way of the new Transcontinental Railway.

tothersider.

1. *W.A.* A person from an eastern State; OTHER-SIDER. Also *attrib.*

c **1872** J.C.F. JOHNSON *Over Island* 1 (note) 'Over the Island.' The term used by old bushmen, more especially the 't'other siders', to imply all over the colonies. **1983**

Sydney Morning Herald 7 Feb. 7/3 Kalgoorlie was a huge seat with a big population of radical T'Othersider miners.

2. In Tasmania, a person from the mainland; on the s.e. mainland, a person from Tasmania.

1899 *Mercury* (Hobart) 18 Mar. 3/7, I, a 'Tother-sider', have been a resident of Hobart for the past three years. **1940** *Bulletin* (Sydney) 10 July 17/1 When I was a nipper many time-expired convicts from Tasmania were to be met with in Victoria. These gentry were generally known as 'T'othersiders'.

tourang, var. TAWARANG.

touri, var. TOWRI.

tourist. [Ironic use of *tourist* a holidaymaker.] An Australian soldier posted to a European front during either of the world wars.

1916 *7th Field Artillery Brigade Yandoo* Aug. 19 Who said . . that stew does not agree with five-bob-a-day tourists. **1944** F. BRUNO *Sa-eeda Wog* 1 The first signs of the generation of returned 'blitzkrieg tourists'—swing through the crowd.

tournefortia /tʊənˈfɔtiə/. [Transf. use of *Tournefortia* a plant genus named by Swedish botanist Carl von Linné (Linnaeus) (*Species Plantarum* (1753) 140), after French botanist J.P. de *Tournefort* (1656–1708).] The shrub or small spreading tree *Argusia* (formerly *Tournefortia*) *argentea* (fam. Boraginaceae) of seashores in n. Aust. and elsewhere.

1928 S.E. NAPIER *On Barrier Reef* 85 The tournefortia, a bushy shrub. **1978** N. COLEMAN *Look at Wildlife Great Barrier Reef* 26 Tournefortias are moderately low, widespreading trees.

towel, *v.* [f. Br. slang *towel* to thrash: see OED(S *v.* 2.] *trans.* With **up:** to beat; to thrash. Also *fig.,* and as *vbl. n.*

1919 C. DREW *Doings of Dave* 170 Eileen will give her such a towelling up. **1955** R. LAWLER *Summer of Seventeenth Doll* (1965) 32 Instead of pointin' out that he had a bad back, he puts himself to work by this Dowd—gunna show him up, see. Well, that's just what he shouldna done, the kid towelled him up proper.

towerang, var. TAWARANG.

towie. [f. *tow(-truck* + -Y.] The driver of a tow-truck.

1975 *Bulletin* (Sydney) 6 Sept. 72/3 People in the tow-truck business say that the average time it takes the first 'towie' to get on the crash scene in a built-up area is between two and three minutes. **1984** R. CASWELL *Scales of Justice* 38 Any of you towies got your Authorities signed?

town.

1. [Br. dial. *town* a (small) group of dwellings, a village or hamlet with little or no local organization: see OED *sb.* 3.] A (small) cluster of dwellings and other buildings recognized as a distinct place: see quots.

1818 W. LAWRY in Methodist Missionary Soc. Rec. 9 Oct., My first place of preaching is Parramatta, a charming village (called a Town in New South Wales). **1839** W.H. LEIGH *Reconnoitering Voyages* 149 A kind of hovel called a store . . added to some half-dozen miserable and comfortless-looking sledge huts, is the 'town of Glenelg'. **1977** W.A. WINTER-IRVING *Bush Stories* 17 Kalkadoon is just better than a hamlet, except that nobody living there would know the meaning of the word hamlet. So it's a town; small, remote, away out in the sticks as they say, far away from the railroad.

2. Used *attrib.* in Comb. designating a surveyed tract of land within a town, as **town acre, allotment, land, lot.**

1888 *S. Austral. Rec.* (London) 13 June 66 **Town acres** are in many situations not to be purchased at all. **1812** *HRA* (1916) 1st Ser. VII. 549 He also received a **Town Allotment** in Sydney, which he enclosed for the purpose of converting into a garden. **1837** *Colonist* (Sydney) 16 Mar. 88/1 The settlers . . were anxiously waiting the completion of the survey of the **town lands,** when they might commence building. **1835** R. TORRENS *Colonization of S.A.* 45 The proprietor of **town lots** could neither erect houses in the cheapest way, nor, when erected, dispose of them to advantage.

3. Special Comb. **town bike,** see BIKE 1; **black,** an Aboriginal who lives in a town (see quot. 1870, 1); see also TOWNY 3; **gang** *hist.,* a party of convicts assigned to hard labour on public works in a town; **reserve** *hist.,* land set aside as the site of a town (see quot. 1857).

1870 C.H. ALLEN *Visit to Qld.* 180 The '**town blacks**' are distinguished from those of the wild interior by the smattering of English they have picked up, and by their love of 'seexpences' and tobacco. **1870** E.B. KENNEDY *Four Yrs. in Qld.* 67 Not only amongst station and town Blacks, but also for years in the same country with perfectly wild Blacks. **1796** D. COLLINS *Acct. Eng. Colony N.S.W.* (1798) I. 485 The **town gang** was employed delivering the storeships. **1836** J. BACKHOUSE *Narr. Visit Austral. Colonies* (1843) 392 The **town reserve,** of Muscle Brook, is marked by a small, weatherboard inn. **1857** W. WESTGARTH *Vic. & Austral. Gold Mines* 83 The map of the colony is plentifully studded with little shaded squares, some of which rejoice in a distinct name, while others are as yet under the generic designation of 'town reserves'.

towney, townie, varr. TOWNY.

township.

1. *Hist.* A site reserved for and laid out as a town. Also **township reserve.**

1789 *HRA* (1914) 1st Ser. I. 127 You are . . to lay out townships of a convenient size and extent, in such places as You, in Your discretion, shall judge most proper. **1870** *Sydney Morning Herald* 2 July 5/5 Calling the at present unnamed township reserve, on which the works are situated, 'Gladstone'.

2. Such a site at an early stage of its occupation and development (see quots. 1830 and 1873); a small town (see quot. 1886). Also *attrib.*

1790 *HRA* (1914) 1st Ser. I. 196 The fixing the first settlers in townships will, I fear, prevent that increase of live stock which would be raised in farms at a distance from a great body of people. **1830** R. DAWSON *Present State Aust.* 377 Here is a small township, which as yet resembles a large village rather than a town. **1873** R.P. WHITWORTH *Lost & Found* 25 Jim and I went into the next township, if a congregation of tents and shanties might be called a township. Township now though, for it was embryonic Ararat. **1886** D.M. GANE *N.S.W. & Tas.* 151 To those unacquainted with Australian colloquialisms the word 'township' is misleading. One is reluctant to give to a little hamlet, containing barely a dozen houses, a title which would more properly apply to a town of moderate size. But, nevertheless, of that character are the majority of colonial townships. **1926** 'S. WESTLAW' *White Peril* 103 He looked at first sight quite the usual type of township lounger.

Townsville stylo. [f. the name of a coastal city of n.e. Qld. + *stylo,* abbrev. of *Stylosanthes.*] The annual or perennial herbaceous legume *Stylosanthes humilis* (fam. Fabaceae) of South America, used as a pasture plant in n. Aust. and elsewhere. Also **Townsville lucerne.**

1937 *Jrnl. Council Sci. & Industr. Research* 201 The so-called wild or Townsville lucerne . . was introduced accidentally into north Queensland. **1985** *Nat. Farmer* (Windsor) 5 Sept. 47/2 Many of the species scientists first enthused over have dropped from the scene. Townsville stylo, once the leguminous coloniser of the north, has bitten the dust of disease.

towny. Also **towney, townie.** [f. *town* + -Y. Used elsewhere but recorded earliest in Aust. (see OED(S *towny, sb.* 1 and also *townee, sb.*).]

1. A newly-arrived immigrant (*spec.* one from London).

1825 *Austral.* (Sydney) 29 Sept. 3 At peep of day, several persons .. assembled on a spot of ground suitable enough for witnessing a pulley hauley match between two ladies of the fancy; the one a towny, and the other of currency worth. **1956** A. UPFIELD *Battling Prophet* 19 Ben Wickham had been a newchum, a towny, an outsider lost in a rough man's country.

2. *transf.* A town-dweller, as distinguished from a country-dweller.

1827 P. CUNNINGHAM *Two Yrs. in N.S.W.* II. 245 The English convicts divide themselves into the two great classes of *townies* and *yokels.* **1893** G.E. LANGRIDGE *Side Lights of Labour* 16 A towney will find the hammering along the hard high road too much.

3. *spec.* An urbanized Aboriginal. See also *town black* TOWN 3.

1959 D. LOCKWOOD *Crocodiles & Other People* 169 The sophisticated 'townies' who keep Darwin's army of civil service clerks in heavily starched white shirts and boiled trousers .. are fed during the week on steak stews and rice puddings. **1977** K. COOK *Man Underground* 29 Detribalized outcasts who hang around the mullock heaps picking up a few scraps of missed opal to trade for liquor. . . The favourite method of straightening out a townie.

towri /'taʊri/. Also **taori, taurai, tauri, touri, tyri.** [a. Kamilaroi *dhawuray.*]

1. COUNTRY 2: see quot. 1892.

1872 G.E. LOYAU *Colonial Lyrics* 23 The native tribes had made their 'towri' here. **1888** *Centennial Mag.* (Sydney) 224 They lived where God placed them; they hunted and fished from one side of their 'tauri' to the other. **1892** J. FRASER *Aborigines N.S.W.* 36 It is well-known here that each tribe had its own 'taurai'—territory or huntingground—usually determined by natural boundaries, such as mountain ridges and rivers. **1899** R.H. MATHEWS *Folklore Austral. Aborigines* 15 The chief of a Kamilaroi tribe whose *taori* comprised the district around Kunopia. **1921** G.A. BELL *Under Brigalows* 76 As a rule if blacks from another 'tyri' trespassed they were instantly killed. **1964** J.S. RYAN *Land of Ulitarra* p. xi, The tribes were many more in number and their *touris* (or special territories) were much smaller than in other parts of the Continent.

2. *transf.* A white person's 'stamping ground'.

1873 *Illustr. Sydney News* 5 July 11/1 The stock-keeper, as may be surmised, means one having the care of stock. He is usually found located at a cattle station far out on the Baloore or Barwon; though the 'towri', or portion of country he inhabits, is not restricted to these neighbourhoods. **1893** J.A. BARRY *Steve Brown's Bunyip* 79, I never was on this field before. Down about the Lachlan's my *towri.*

Tozer /'toʊzə/, *v.* and *n. Obs.* [f. the name of Horace *Tozer* (1844–1916), Queensland politician.]

A. *v. trans.* To remove (a person) from office in response to pressure exerted by another.

1896 *Truth* (Sydney) 7 June 1/6 Mr Reid has incurred the gratitude of all etymologists. . . Mr Reid has given us a new word, and in future, when one person is shunted by another in deference to the wishes of an influential third, he need not labour for a phrase to describe his case; he will say, 'I was tozered'. *Tozer:* verb active, to yank off; to slip, to politely shunt when politic. Queensland papers please copy.

B. *n.* A statement which is inaccurate or untrue. Also *attrib.* and as **Tozerism.**

1898 *Truth* (Sydney) 1 May 1/7 News that the heiress to the Figian [sic] throne is *en route* to England husband hunting. . . Now is not that a nice Tozer tale! **1909** W.G. SPENCE *Aust.'s Awakening* 165 Under a cross-examination of Labor members in the House, Tozer became so notorious for the unreliability of his statements that all over Queensland today, when you don't believe a statement, you say, 'That's a Tozer'. **1919** C.A. BERNAYS *Qld. Politics during Sixty Yrs.* 131 He was one of those comprehensive politicians who never allowed himself to be cornered through the absence of a plausible explanation, and just as in modern times in the House of Commons 'terminological inexactitude' was coined as a synonym for something which is supposed not to lead us to Heaven, so a 'Tozerism' was the invention of John Macrossan to distinguish something which might be true but probably was not.

trac. [Shortening of *intractable.*] A refractory prisoner. Also *attrib.*

1967 *Kings Cross Whisper* (Sydney) xli. 4/4 *Trac,* intractible prisoner. **1980** SIMMONDS & GOLLAN *For Simmo* 138, I was three years in the 'trac' section at Grafton after attempting to escape from Goulburn in 1965.

track, *n.*

1. WALLABY TRACK 2 a., esp. in the phr. **on the track.** See also *tucker track* TUCKER *n.*[1] 3.

1869 M. CLARKE *Peripatetic Philosopher* 41 The Wimmera district is noted for the hordes of vagabond 'loafers' that it supports, and has earned for itself the name of 'The Feeding Track'. I remember an old bush ditty, which I have heard sung when I was on the 'Wallaby': Hurrah! hurrah! for the feeding track, I've left the Avoca behind my back, Hurrah! hurrah! for the feeding track Hurrah! hurrah! for the Wimmera. **1977** F.B. VICKERS *Stranger no Longer* 101, I had learned on the track that the unemployed didn't enjoy the privileges of the 'swaggie' of better days who could always 'front up' to the cook and get a sit-down meal.

2. **a.** The route followed by a drover. See also *cattle track* CATTLE 2, *dry track* DRY *a.* 1, ROAD 2.

1880 'ERRO' *Squattermania* 128, I heard you had gone up the track with a mob of cattle. **1978** D. STUART *Wedgetail View* 110 'You've been on the track with horses?' Colin asked. 'I was horsetailer with a mob of cattle from the Gulf down to the top end of New South Wales.'

b. *transf.* and *fig.*

1939 J.G. PATTISON *'Battler's' Tales Early Rockhampton* 7 On the track for the 'Morning Bulletin' for eight years.

3. That part of the Stuart Highway which runs between Darwin and Alice Springs.

1935 R.B. PLOWMAN *Boundary Rider* 207 Another turn-out had started just before him—a family wagonette from 'up the track'. **1984** *N.T. News* (Darwin) 10 Sept. 22/4 Now calling for expressions of interest from performers including those 'down the track'. 'We want to cover the whole of the NT.'

4. *fig.* The course or progress of an event, action, etc.

1945 L. JILLET *Moresby's Few* 13 The real war is much farther along the track now. **1984** *Canberra Times* 29 Apr. 1/4 An Australian Bill of Rights, was 'a long way down the track'.

5. Used *attrib.* in Comb. with reference to the practice during the Depression of the 1930s of issuing dole cards to unemployed itinerants but not allowing them to remain in any one place, as **track bloke, card, dolie, man, rations** *pl.*: see quots. 1941.

1934 *International Labour Rev.* July 37 (note) Travellers' or 'track' rations are an illustration of the change which has accompanied the systematisation of relief. Many who in pre-depression days only occasionally drew 'track' rations from the police now do it as a matter of course, since they have to be registered to be eligible for any relief at all. **1935** K. TENNANT *Tiburon* 167 The travelling unemployed . . occasionally settle in a town but are usually kept on the move in a wide area in search of work where there is no work. They live on track rations, charity or relief work, according to the type of town they find themselves in. **1941** —— *Battlers* 17 Thursday all over the West is dole day, when the track men come in to have their cards stamped at the police-station and get their rations to carry them to the next 'dole town'. *Ibid.* 24 The men with track-cards.. wander the country in search of work, getting their food-orders from declared 'dole stations' in towns fifty or sixty miles apart. **1944** *Bulletin* (Sydney) 27 Sept. 13/2 The police sergeant.. had a reputation for brusqueness to swagmen calling in for track rations. **1948** *Ibid.* 2 June 28/2 I've had enough o' you loafin' track blokes. **1966** E.J. WALLACE *Sydney & Bush* p. i, 'Track dolies'—swaggies or baggies, who had given up their homes to go on the road—were compelled to keep moving to collect their rations. **1978** W. LOWENSTEIN *Weevils in Flour* 1 A track man looks back with pity on the farmer: 'They had it worse.. lumbered with debt, and with a family. We could just pick up and go!'

6. Special Comb. **track mate**, a travelling companion.

1914 *Bulletin* (Sydney) 19 Mar. 24/1 The bloke who waltzes Matilda falls in with a varied assortment of track mates. **1917** *Ibid.* 16 Aug. 22/1 We were camp-mates on the rivers, We were track-mates on the plains. **1981** R. EDWARDS *Yarns & Ballads* 27 And it's told far and wide that stretched out by his side Was his track-mate—the old cockatoo.

track, *v.* [Fig. use of *track* to follow a path, to go, to travel: see OED(S *v.*¹ 3.] In phr.

a. to track with, to keep company with (a person of the opposite sex), to court: see TRAVEL 4.

1910 *Bulletin* (Sydney) 28 Apr. 13/2 He soon became the recognised bloke that Lizzie was 'tracking' with. **1978** D. STUART *Wedgetail View* 76 Maybe some married couple'll move in with a daughter for you to track with.

b. to track square (or **straight**) (with): see quot. 1919.

1919 W.H. DOWNING *Digger Dialects* 50 *Track square*, to pursue an amorous enterprise with honorable intentions. **1981** *Bulletin* (Sydney) 21 Jan. 20/1 'At last', said Dave, 'I think I've met me fate. I'm trackin' straight As fine a sheila as you'd wish to see.'

tracker. [Spec. use of *tracker* one who tracks.] An Aboriginal employed by police to track down missing persons, esp. fugitives from the law; *black tracker*, see BLACK *a.*¹ 6; *native tracker*, see NATIVE *a.* 5; *police tracker*, see POLICE. Also *attrib.*

1826 *HRA* (1919) 1st Ser. XII. 534, I recommend that.. a party of the Black people on this side be taken out as trackers. **1938** X. HERBERT *Capricornia* 364 O'Crimnell took him over to the police-station and set his tracker-boy to work on him.

track-ride, *v. intr.* See quot. 1978 (here as *vbl. n.*). Also as **track rider** *n.*

1959 E. WEBB *Mark of Sun* 58, I made out that he had been a track rider on a station somewhere when he was younger, and that's where he'd picked up his bit of whiteman's lingo. **1978** TEECE & PIKE *Voice of Wilderness* 21 It was necessary to do what was called 'track riding', looking for tracks of cattle that had strayed across the invisible boundary of the station.

traditional owner. An Aboriginal who is a member of a local descent group having certain rights in a tract of land, esp. as recognized under the *Aboriginal Land Rights (Northern Territory) Act 1976*: see quot. 1976. Also *attrib.*

1974 *Cwlth. Parl. Papers* I. no. 69 53, I have no doubt that the Larrakia people were the traditional owners of what is now the whole Darwin area. **1976** *Act* (Cwlth. of Aust.) no. 191 Sect. 3, 'Traditional Aboriginal owner', in relation to land means a local descent group of Aboriginals who—(a) have common spiritual affiliations to a site on the land, being affiliations that place the group under a primary spiritual responsibility for that site and for the land; and (b) are entitled by Aboriginal tradition to forage as of right over that land. **1982** *Sydney Morning Herald* 17 July 1/3 Surrounding his house are the galvanised iron huts and tents of his brothers, sisters, uncles, aunts and cousins and their children—members of.. one of the two traditional owner clans of the region.

trag. Pl. **trag, trags.** Shortened form of TERAGLIN.

1951 T.C. ROUGHLEY *Fish & Fisheries Aust.* 73 Teraglin (Trag, *Atractoscion atelodus*). **1973** *Kings Cross Whisper* (Sydney) xlv. 16/4 A nice haul of snapper, mowies and even a dozen or so trag. **1984** *Sunday Tel.* (Sydney) 5 Aug. 122/6 Tailor and teraglin could also put in an appearance, with the moon beginning to grow larger. One area which usually produces 'trags' is the Coogee ground.

traglin, var. TERAGLIN.

train, *n.* [Cf. *to pull a train* to copulate successively with more than one partner (see OEDS *pull, v.* 11 g.)] See quot. 1976.

1976 *Nat. Times* (Sydney) 29 Nov. 10/1 A National Times team has interviewed a number of people in a small canegrowing community in north Queensland, where a sexual practice called 'the train' occurs... A train might begin at the Saturday night cabaret, as a couple left together. Other men made a yanking motion in the air, like a conductor pulling the cord, and shouted, 'Too-hoot' All Aboard! And they would follow, and as many as 50 men would have sexual intercourse with the woman. **1980** B. HORNADGE *Austral. Slanguage* 191 A different kettle of fish entirely is the *train*, a subtle form of pack rape achieved by peer group pressures.

train, *v.* [f. prec.] *trans.* To subject (a female) to sexual intercourse with a succession of males.

1976 *Nat. Times* (Sydney) 29 Nov. 10/2 (*heading*) How women are trained. If it's not rape what is it? **1983** G. LEWIS *Real Men like Violence* 81 The notorious gang rapes which occurred at Ingham, North Queensland, in 1977 were based on this kind of male bonding. Gang rape there was referred to as 'training' the local girls.

Hence **trainer** *n.*

1976 *Nat. Times* (Sydney) 29 Nov. 13/4 She knew the three men who raped her; they were leading 'trainers'.

tram. In the phr. **to be on the wrong tram,** to be pursuing an unproductive course.

1955 J. MORRISON *Black Cargo* 223 No, son, you're on the wrong tram with me. **1982** *Bulletin* (Sydney) 19 Jan. 27/3 What McMahon will be telling his former parliamentary colleagues is that the Fraser Government is, in his judgement, on the wrong tram economically.

trammie. [f. *tram* + -Y.] The driver or conductor of a tram.

[N.Z. **1912** *N.Z. Truth* (Wellington) 3 Feb. 5 Many there were who refused to believe the 'Trammies' would do such a thing, but.. the conductors and the motormen meant it, and the street cars were gradually deserted.] **1919** C. DREW *Doings of Dave* 160 'Say, trammie.'.. The tram-guard shook his head. **1983** D.J. BAILEY *Holes in Ground* 12 When 400 trammies marched on eight hour day 1911, Badger closed the company recreation room to them.

tramp, *v.* [Fig. use of *tramp* to stamp on: see OED *v.*¹ 2.] *trans.* To dismiss (a person) from employment.

1941 S.J. BAKER *Pop. Dict. Austral. Slang* 78 *Tramped*, dismissed from employment. **1982** M. WATTONE *Winning*

Gold in W.A. 66, I went to the surface and immediately was tramped (sacked).

tram troub. Also **tram trube.** TROUB.

1912 *Truth* (Sydney) 1 Dec. 3/3 (*heading*) Tricky tram troub's tart. **1979** D. MCCARTHY *Fate of O'Loughlin* 144, I looked up and there's the conductor grinning at me..a bloody tram trube.

Hence **tram troubing** *vbl. n.*

1914 *Truth* (Sydney) 18 Oct. 11/4 (*caption*) Blake makes a break. Takes to tram troubing.

transport, *n. Hist.* [Spec. use of *transport* one under sentence of transportation: see OED *sb.* 5.] One sentenced in the British Isles to a term of servitude in a penal colony in Australia.

1803 *Sydney Gaz.* 10 Apr., On Wednesday 10 prisoners who were capitally convicted at the last Criminal Court were respited by His Excellency, on condition of their becoming Transports for Life. **1893** J. DEMARR *Adventures in Aust.* 44 A man who was transported was said to have been 'lagged' and a transport was an old 'lag'.

transport, *v. Hist.* [Spec. use of *transport* to carry into banishment, as a criminal or slave: see OED *v.* 2 c.]

1. *trans.* To deport (a person sentenced in the British Isles) to a penal colony in Australia.

1788 *HRA* (1914) 1st Ser. I. 87 The knowing when the time expires for which the convicts have been transported is very necessary. **1860** 'LADY' *My Experiences in Aust.* 24 This worthy was transported in the early times of the colony, and from conducting himself properly while passing through the usual gradations of a convict's lot, he obtained in due time his ticket-of-leave, and set up as an auctioneer.

2. a. RETRANSPORT.

1811 *Sydney Gaz.* 16 Feb., *James Frazer* was found *Guilty*.. and sentenced to be transported to Newcastle, and kept to hard labour for the term of seven years. **1847** A. MARJORIBANKS *Travels N.S.W.* 105 Banishment from Australia, for the natives and free persons, is now to Norfolk Island, if for the first offence; but doubly convicted felons—that is, prisoners transported from this country convicted of new crimes there, are now all sent to Van Diemen's Land.

b. *transf.* Of an Aboriginal: to remove forcibly.

1835 H. MELVILLE *Hist. Van Diemen's Land* 25 He was transported from New Holland, and was employed in this Colony as a stock-keeper from which situation he was taken to assist in capturing the bushrangers. **1911** ST. C. GRONDONA *Collar & Cuffs* 60 The blacks have all been transported to Frazer, the dingoes are nearly all poisoned, and the fox has not penetrated so far north as this yet, consequently the turkey flourishes.

transportable, *a. Hist.* Attracting a sentence of transportation to a penal colony in Australia. Also *fig.*

1833 *HRA* (1923) 1st Ser. XVII. 306 Persons who had never been convicted of Felonry or any transportable Offence. **1854** G.H. HAYDON *Austral. Emigrant* 91 You shall hear no more of this joke of yours (by the bye, it is a transportable one you know).

transportation. *Hist.* [Spec. use of *transportation* removal or banishment, as of a criminal to a penal settlement: see OED 2 c.]

1. The deportation to a penal colony in Australia of a person sentenced in the British Isles.

1789 W. TENCH *Narr. Exped. Botany Bay* 143 When the term of their transportation shall be expired. **1865** *Glenorchy Murders* 7 He was sentenced to seven years' transportation. Under this sentence he arrived in Tasmania.. on the 31st July, 1852... Soon after his arrival he was assigned to Mr Turnley... While in his assigned service he frequently manifested habits of intemperance.

2. The committal to a penal settlement of a person sentenced in Australia.

1799 *HRA* (1914) 1st Ser. II. 306 Sentenced to fourteen years' transportation to Norfolk Island. **1853** *Illustr. Sydney News* 12 Nov. 43/3 The four soldiers lately convicted at Launceston of an assault of William Henry Nash, have had their sentence of death commuted to transportation for ten years.

3. Comb. in sense 1: **transportation question, system.**

1847 *Britannia & Trades' Advocate* (Hobart) 15 Apr. 2/2 We solicit attention to that most important of all important matters connected with our colonial interests, namely, the **Transportation question.** **1825** B. FIELD *Geogr. Mem. N.S.W.* 458 The evils and expense of the **transportation-system** would certainly be lessened, by placing the convicts more in the service of farming and grazing settlers, out of the reach of the temptations and evil communications of great towns.

transportationist. *Hist.* One who favours the continuance of the convict system. Also **pro-transportationist.** See also ANTI-TRANSPORTATION.

1847 *Abolitionists & Transportationists* p. x, If he were a Transportationist, it would be cutting the throat of his own argument. **1850** *Irish Exile* (Hobart) 21 Dec. 2/3 We can scarcely imagine it possible for a pro-transportationist to be returned for any one district in the island.

transported, *ppl. a. Hist.* [f. TRANSPORT *v.*]

1. Deported as a convict to a penal colony in Australia.

1822 J. DIXON *Narr. Voyage N.S.W. & Van Dieman's Land* 65 There is a.. factory of a very handsome appearance for such transported females as are not taken into the service of those settlers who require female servants. **1871** C.L. MONEY *Knocking about N.Z.* p. vii, The creature sustains life on 'forty pounds a-year and his tucker' at the remote station of a transported friend of the family.

2. In collocations: **transported convict, felon, offender.**

1824 *Australasian Pocket Almanack* 82 In the Grants is contained a proviso, that the grantee, his heirs and assigns, shall.. procure to be assigned to his or their service.. one **transported convict** for every 100 acres of the said land. **1840** *HRA* (1924) 1st Ser. XX. 527 Every **transported Felon** should, during the period of at least two years, receive no indulgence whatever. **1829** *Colonial Times* (Hobart) 28 Nov., Occupiers of House etc., receiving therein any **transported offender** for the purpose of drinking or gambling, without the leave of such offender's employer, to be liable to penalties.

trap, $n.^1$ [Survival of Br. slang *trap* one whose business is to 'trap' offenders: see OED(S $sb.^1$ 6 and quot. 1859.] An officer of the law, esp. a police officer.

1812 J.H. VAUX *Mem.* (1819) 220 *Traps*, police officers, or runners, are properly so called; but it is common to include constables of any description under this title. **1859** W. KELLY *Life in Vic.* I. 185 The police in the diggings went by the name of traps—an obsolete sobriquet at home.

trap, $n.^2$ [Spec. use of *trap* a snare in which animals are caught.] In the phr. **to go round the traps** and varr., to make a tour of inspection. Freq. *fig.*

1933 J. TRURAN *Where Plain Begins* 224 Reuben and his brother were 'going round the traps'. They carried no lantern; as the traps belonged to somebody else, that would have been an unwise procedure. **1965** J. WYNNUM *Jiggin' in Riggin'* 124 So yesterday she made a trip around the traps, throwing out a few hints, is that it? **1965** W. MOXHAM *Follow That Horse* 105 Mrs Goldstone was.. the owner of a string of dress shops... Mrs Goldstone had been away in Queensland going around her traps.

trap-yard. An enclosure into which wild cattle, horses, etc., are driven and confined: see quots. 1880 and 1963. Also **trapping yard.**
   1880 J.B. STEVENSON *Seven Yrs. Austral. Bush* 93 Our first work was to construct a number of trap yards. These are small but high enclosures which we placed upon some of the most frequented tracks, generally concealed near a sudden turn, wings being run out on either side of the track for some distance. When we started a mob of horses we endeavoured to drive them along one of these tracks; and if we succeeded in this we generally managed to yard the greater part of the mob.   **1926** J. POLLARD *Bushland Man* 57 A trapping-yard had to be built at the pool in which to corral the horses, and the mob yarded when they came to drink.   **1963** W.E. HARNEY *To Ayers Rock & Beyond* 48 The wide gate of the fenced-in enclosure was left open, but when the cattle of that part were to be mustered, the gate was shut and the only entry into the place was through a contraption called a 'bayonet' which was built with logs having sharpened ends in the same manner as a fish-trap. Once the cattle went inside the 'trap-yard' they could not get out.

travel, *v.*
   1. *intr. Obs.* Of livestock: to be driven through the country, freq. in search of pasture.
   1849 A. HARRIS *Emigrant Family* (1967) 16 My cattle travel very wild; some of them are off down every gully they see: you can .. stick to the tail of 'em.   **1887** W.S.S. TYRWHITT *New Chum in Qld. Bush* 172 Drovers are wanted to take sheep and cattle to market when fat .. and in bad seasons to take them travelling for grass.
   2. *trans.* To drive (sheep or cattle) through the country, freq. in search of pasture. Also *intr.*
   1870 E.B. KENNEDY *Four Yrs. in Qld.* 148 Travelling the sheep has to be resorted to when the country is short of water and grass.   **1880** J. BONWICK *Resources Qld.* 35 Many are compelled to *travel* with stock when their own feed at home is destroyed by drought.
   3. *transf. intr.* To journey through the country, usu. on foot and freq. in search of work: see TRAVELLER 1. Also *trans.*
   1892 'J. MILLER' *Workingman's Paradise* 105 Live on rations that the squatters serve out to keep men travelling the country so they can get them if they want them.   **1965** R.H. CONQUEST *Horses in Kitchen* 9 In those days a swaggie couldn't draw rations in the same town two weeks running. He had to 'travel for rations'.
   4. *intr.* To keep company (with a person of the opposite sex). Also *trans.*, to court. See TRACK *v.*
   1892 *Bulletin* (Sydney) 5 Nov. 17/2 Tho' Bleeders deemed the square affair's white innocence a myth, She differed much from other girls that Bill had travelled with. *c* **1907** W.C. CHANDLER *Darkest Adelaide* 8 'E was in awful trouble over the female wot 'e was travellin'.

traveller.
   1. One who journeys through the country (in search of work); SWAGMAN a.
   1845 *Bell's Life in Sydney* 22 Nov. 2/1 The publican can pretty well make the distinction between a 'traveller' and a 'pot-wolloper'.   **1965** R.H. CONQUEST *Horses in Kitchen* 45 Queensland during the depression years attracted the maximum number of travellers during the winter months.
   2. In special collocations: **travellers' flour,** flour of inferior quality (see quot. 1895); **hut,** a dwelling provided on a rural property for the accommodation of travellers (see quot. 1892); **sugar,** sugar of inferior quality.
   1895 *Worker* (Sydney) 9 Feb. 4/2 One squatter on that creek charged me 5d. a lb. for flour of the most inferior quality, and alive with weevils. Storekeepers generally term it **'travellers' flour'**.   **1898** *Ibid.* 1 Jan. 7/2 I've known storekeepers who kept special bins labelled 'travellers' flour', 'travellers' sugar' and so on.   **1868** C.W. BROWNE *Overlanding in Aust.* 63 You go up to the **'travellers hut'**, to see if you can get any traveller going through to accompany you.   **1892** 'E. KINGLAKE' *Austral. at Home* 132 The number of 'sundowners', and the frequency of their visits, was the cause of the establishment of what is called the 'travellers' hut'.   **1898 travellers' sugar** [see *travellers' flour*].

traveller's joy. [Transf. use of *traveller's joy* the trailing plant *Clematis vitalba*.] *Old man's beard*, see OLD MAN *n.* 3.
   1881 *Proc. Linnean Soc. N.S.W.* VI. 741 *Clematis microphylla* or 'Traveller's Joy' which covered the bushes with its slender twining branches.   **1985** *Canberra Times* 20 June (Suppl.) 1/5 *Clematis aristata* (traveller's joy or old man's beard) is a feature of the bushland in moist, sheltered gullies of Queensland, N.S.W., Victoria and Tasmania... It bears masses of creamy-white flowers in spring which are followed by fluffy, white seed heads.

travelling, *vbl. n.*
   1. In the senses of TRAVEL. Also *attrib.*
   1880 J.B. STEVENSON *Seven Yrs. Austral. Bush* 57 A mob, in travelling, generally takes the form of a wedge, the strongest and best travelling beasts going ahead.   **1974** D. STUART *Prince of my Country* 108 With the feeling of being hemmed in, caught, 'But I've got nothing, just a travelling swag.'
   2. Special Comb. **travelling ration,** a ration of provisions, a dole (see TRACK *n.* 5); **statement,** a document in which the details of a travelling herd are recorded (see quot. 1920).
   1959 *Overland* xv. 31 Scores of thousands of 'travellers'—who generally called themselves 'bagmen'—were scouring the roads and railway lines in search of **travelling rations**.   **1878** *Act* (N.S.W.) 41 Vict. no. 19 Sect. 5, Every drover in charge of any travelling sheep and every drover in charge of travelling horses or cattle shall be provided at the time of his departure with a **'travelling statement'**.   **1920** J.B. CRAMSIE *Managem. & Diseases Sheep* 36 He should produce, on demand, his permit and travelling statement, duly signed by a Stock Inspector, setting out full particulars of his sheep, brands, marks, owner, destination, etc., to any police officer, J.P., or Stock Inspector.

travelling, *ppl. a.*[1] [f. TRAVEL *v.* 1 and 2.]
   1. Of livestock: being driven through the country.
   1872 G.S. BADEN-POWELL *New Homes for Old Country* 124 Station shepherds, who feed along the road, may be forewarned, and thus save their own flocks getting 'boxed' with the travelling 'lots'.   **1934** 'E.N. SPEER' *Destiny* 242 He was overtaking a travelling mob of sheep, hoping he would reach them before they left the main road for the two-mile wide stock route.
   2. In collocations: **travelling sheep, shepherd, stockman.**
   1864 H. JONES *New Valuations* 24 From 100,000 to 150,000 sheep leave the North annually for the other colonies... The feed, for a mile to a mile and a half in width, is either eaten or destroyed by these **travelling sheep**.   **1860** 'LADY' *My Experiences in Aust.* 126 A **travelling shepherd** or gold-digger would ask permission to boil his quartpot at our fire.   **1835** J. LHOTSKY *Journey from Sydney* 9 Here the **travelling stockmen** remain with their herds for refreshment.

travelling, *ppl. a.*[2] [f. TRAVEL *v.* 3.] Engaged in journeying through the country (in search of work).
   1909 *Bulletin* (Sydney) 26 Aug. 14/4 A swagwoman is not a very common happening, but a few days ago an old travelling lady .. passed through Moree.   **1935** K. TENNANT *Tiburon* 167 The travelling unemployed .. occasionally settle in a town but are usually kept on the move in a wide area in search of work where there is no work.

travelling manager. On a rural property: a relieving manager (see quot. 1954).

1891 *Truth* (Sydney) 15 Feb. 7/2 There is (as in some woolclassing) a sort of archangel, called the 'superintendent' or 'travelling manager', but his face cannot be looked upon by the ordinary whaler who would live. 1954 T. RONAN *Vision Splendid* 100 'This Vincent who's travelling manager is a damned old fule and no cattleman'... Vincent.. was a hard man to place so, as there was nearly always some station manager away on holiday, Vincent acted as a sort of permanent relieving manager for the firm's northern properties.

travelling stock.

1. Livestock being driven through the country. Also *attrib.*

1872 G.S. BADEN-POWELL *New Homes for Old Country* 122 One meets or passes 'travelling stock'—herds of more or less wild 'beasts' and flocks of sheep, each marked with a tar T, to show that they are 'travelling', *i.e.* moving from one place to another. 1932 J. MCCARTER *Pan's Clan* 155 When waterless stages precluded adherence to the travelling stock laws, the mileage was increased.

2. Special Comb. **travelling stock reserve,** an area of Crown land set aside for the overnight accommodation of travelling stock (see quot. 1977); **route,** a strip of Crown land set aside as a right of way for travelling stock (see quots. 1881 and 1977); formerly also **travelling stock road.** See also T.S.R.

1930 A.E. YARRA *Vanishing Horsemen* 151 Charlie had located the probable site of the cattle camp in the daytime, on a **travelling stock reserve.** 1977 T.L. MCKNIGHT *Long Paddock* 25 Another variable in the spatial extent of TSRs involves areas set aside as overnight or holding paddocks. These paddocks, which are located on or adjacent to the stock routes, are normally identified as Travelling Stock Reserves, although in common parlance 'Routes' and 'Reserves' are often interchangeable. 1881 [**travelling stock route**] A.C. CRUTTWELL *Sketches of Aust.* 42 A travelling stock-road is a straight strip of country, a mile broad, left by the Government for the purposes of large and small cattle travelling from one part of the country to another; they are wire fenced on both sides; but, except in this particular, are undistinguishable from the rest of the country they pass through. 1977 T.L. MCKNIGHT *Long Paddock* 1 Travelling Stock Routes are livestock driveways that are designed for the overlanding of stock, mainly cattle and sheep, from one area to another. The actual land occupied by the routes is government owned. The management and administration of the routeways is vested either in regional pastoral associations, in local governing bodies, or in the state department of agriculture. Normally any grazier may utilise the stock routes, providing he abides by the gazetted regulations and pays fees.

trawler. [Fig. use of *trawler* a fishing vessel.] A police vehicle.

1923 *Austral.* (Sydney) Apr. 56 The trorler is a 'nother name for th' p'leece patrol waggin, on account of it grabbin' up everything it comes across. 1977 D. FOSTER *Escape to Reality* 91 A trawler came cruising by.

tray. The flat, open part of a truck on which goods are carried.

1960 'N. SHUTE' *Trustee from Toolroom* 100 The semi-trailer stood by the aircraft with the sausage-like component on the tray swathed in hessian. 1980 P. DAVIS *Australs. on Road* 125 Ford management conceived the idea of producing.. a passenger-type cab, married to an enclosed load tray; it was called the coupé utility.

tray, var. TREY.

tray-bit, var. TREY-BIT.

traymobile. A small table or stand on wheels or castors for use in carrying or serving food, drinks, etc.

1929 *Austral. Woman's Mirror* (Sydney) 26 Nov. 30/2 Many women fail to realise the labor-saving there is in the systematic use of the traymobile—dumb waiter is the old-fashioned name. Chiefly it is employed for carrying food and table furnishings from kitchen to dining-room, but there are several other ways in which it may be made to fulfil its duty of saving a woman's steps. 1977 *Meanjin* 176 The cleaner brought in the cakes and tea on a traymobile.

treacle-trousers, *pl.* A jibe levelled at a person wearing trousers which are too short. Also ellipt. as **treacle.**

1924 F.J. MILLS *Happy Days* 112 There was a space of three inches between the bottom of each leg and the top of each boot... Other boys 'barracked' him about it.. calling him 'treacle-trousers'. 1944 E.H. BURGMANN *Educ. Austral.* 23, I was growing fast, and as a gap between the top of my boots and the bottom of the legs of my trousers appeared slightly greater day by day I was greeted by the cry of 'treacle'.

tree. Used *attrib.* in the names of flora and fauna: **tree-bear** *obs.,* KOALA 1; **fern,** any of many ferns, esp. of the fam. Cyatheaceae, Dicksoniaceae, and Athyriaceae, having a tall woody trunk topped by large fronds; *fern tree,* see FERN 2; **MAN FERN; grub** (or **maggot**) *obs.,* WITCHETTY 2; **-kangaroo,** a tree-dwelling macropodid of the genus *Dendrolagus* of New Guinea and n.e. Qld., the two Austral. species being *D. bennettianus* and *D. lumholtzi* (see BOONGARRY); *climbing kangaroo,* see CLIMBING; also **tree-climbing kangaroo; lizard** *obs.,* GOANNA 1; **lucerne,** either of two introduced plants of the fam. Fabaceae, the s. European shrub *Medicago arborea,* and the shrub or small tree *Chamaecytisus prolifer* of the Canary Islands, an ornamental and fodder plant widely naturalized in s. Aust.; **martin,** the migratory bird *Cecropis nigricans* of Aust. incl. Tas., and nearby parts of the s.w. Pacific, usu. nesting in a hole in the trunk or bough of a tree; see also MARTIN; also **tree swallow; nettle** *obs.,* STINGING TREE.

1889 *Fortnightly Rev.* (London) Mar. 425 Kangaroos or little brown **tree-bears** or troops of parrots and cockatoos bring sound and movement into these vast solitudes. 1832 J. BACKHOUSE *Narr. Visit Austral. Colonies* (1843) 34 In damp places, by the side of the brook, a princely **tree-fern,** *Cybotium Billardieri,* emerged through the surrounding foliage. 1837 [**tree grub**] E. FRASER *Narr. of Capture* 14 To catch large tree-maggots. 1886 R. HENTY *Australiana* 9 He was one of my instructors in the mysteries of.. finding the great white tree grub (an excellent morsel). 1866 *Illustr. Sydney News* 16 Aug. 19/3 There are more than fifty kinds of kangaroos in Australasia—the kangaroo proper.. and the **tree kangaroo** tribe, the last mentioned family being found in New Guinea only. 1909 G. SMITH *Naturalist in Tas.* 132 [In] the damp tropical and sub-tropical region, including New Guinea and the North Queensland coast.. the curious Tree-climbing kangaroo (*Dendrolagus*) may be mentioned. 1846 G.H. HAYDON *Five Yrs. Experience Aust. Felix* 75 The gigantic, or **tree lizard,** attains to the enormous length of two yards. 1910 *Advocate* (Burnie) 6 Jan. 2/7 The planting of sugar gums, currajungs, **tree lucerne.** 1986 *Western Farmer* (Perth) 15 May 15 Mention the name tree lucerne to researchers these days and you are likely to find yourself quickly corrected. The tree legume most farmers would know of as tree lucerne now is being promoted by its native Canary Island name of tagasaste. 1842 J. GOULD *Birds of Aust.* (1848) II. Pl. 14, *Collocalia arborea.* **Tree Martin.** 1964 M. SHARLAND *Territory of Birds* 146 Another small decimator of flies, and always prominent because of its large flocks, is the Tree Martin, which is also called Tree Swallow. 1830 W.J. HOOKER *Bot. Miscellany* I. 254 Two *Eillmans,* or shields, of the wood of *Urtica Gigas,* or the **Tree Nettle,** as light as cork.

treecreeper. [Transf. use of *tree-creeper* any of several birds of the fam. Certhiidae.]
1. Any of the several small birds of the fam. Climacteridae, members of which hunt for insects on tree trunks and branches. See also WOODPECKER 1.
1855 W. HOWITT *Land, Labor & Gold* I. 63 There is a treecreeper, which keeps up a perpetual pee! pee! pee!—never stopping for a moment, apparently, to take breath, as it runs up the loftiest tree from foot to summit, searching all the way for insects. 1976 *Reader's Digest Compl. Bk. Austral. Birds* 452 Treecreepers are small, brown birds with relatively short tails, fairly long bills and large, strong legs and feet.
2. With distinguishing epithet, as **brown, rufous, white-browed, white-throated**: see under first element.

trevally /trə'væli/. Also **trevalli**, etc. [Poss. an alteration of *cavally* horse-mackerel: see OED *sb.* 2.] Any of several marine fish of the fam. Carangidae (many of which are fished commercially), esp. of the genera *Caranx, Usacaranx,* and *Pseudocaranx.*
1871 *Industr. Progress N.S.W.* 791 Morwong, travally, salmon.. may be taken by the line in almost unlimited quantities. 1883 E.P. RAMSAY *Notes on Food Fishes N.S.W.* 20 The white trevally, *Caranx georgianus*.. on the New South Wales coast.. seldom.. weighing over 1½ to 2 lbs., is found on the shores of Queensland of a much greater size. 1897 'OLD HOUSEKEEPER' *Austral. Plain Cookery* 46 *Trevalli and schnapper..* must be cut across, in pieces about half an inch in thickness, or may be filleted.

trewhella jack. Also **trawalla, trewhalla jack.** [Proprietary name.] *Wallaby jack,* see WALLABY 6.
1898 G.W. WALKER *Notes on Aborigines Tas.* 136 With axe, shovels, 'trewhalla' jacks, saws, horse and bullock teams, the settlers gradually cleared the grounds. [1903 *Australasian Hardware* 13 *Timber jack* manufactured by W. Trewhella Trentham, Vic.] 1964 *Overland* xxx. 14 No bulldozers! Axe, monkey-grubber, and trawalla-jack—and fire.

trey /treɪ/. *Hist.* Also **tray.** [Used elsewhere but recorded earliest in Aust.]
1. Abbrev. of TREY-BIT.
1896 *Bulletin* (Sydney) 15 Aug. 3/2 Then the jay what takes the plate around an' snipes the people's 'trays' 'Ud leave his prayers now an' then an' knock us gutter-ways. 1968 J. BEGLEY *Block with One Holer* 4 Tom was saying, 'Bet you a trey'.
2. Special Comb. **tray-trapper**, one who takes up, or is the recipient of, a collection of money.
1905 *Truth* (Sydney) 12 Mar. 2/5 One of Booth's local tray trappers, a lovely Salvarmy lassie, has skipped by the light of the moon. 1959 D. NILAND *Gold in Streets* 106 'I'm surprised at the Father going him in public.'.. 'You know Liz it puts a new light on that tray-trapper for me.'

trey-bit /'treɪ-bɪt/. *Hist.* Also **tray-bit.** [Spec. use of *trey* the number three.] A threepenny piece.
1898 *Bulletin* (Sydney) 1 Oct. 14/3 A few more W.Q. slang words.. 3d... 'traybit' [etc.]. 1963 J. DUFFY *Outsville Pub* 56 If he had a trey bit in his pocket, it was because it had slipped his notice when he turned the lining inside out.

triangle. *Hist.* [Spec. use of *triangle* a tripod, orig. formed of three halberds stuck in the ground and joined at the top, to which soldiers were formerly bound to be flogged. Used elsewhere but recorded earliest in Aust.: see OED 2 l.] A tripod to which a convict (later a prisoner) was bound before being flogged.
1829 *Cornwall Press* (Launceston) 24 Mar. 35/2 The compassion with which we listened to the shrieks of the beings in human shape suffering at the triangle, was only to be equalled by our disgust at their loud and abandoned laughter at being untied. 1929 'OLD STOCKMAN' *Sensational Cattle-Stealing Case* 77 You should see the lock-up and triangles at Nanima... It is all done away with now.

triantelope /traɪ'æntəloʊp/. [Altered form of TARANTULA.] HUNTSMAN SPIDER.
1845 C. GRIFFITH *Present State & Prospects Port Phillip* 128 There is a great variety of spiders, the largest of which is called the tarantula, and by the old hands the *triantelope*. 1976 E. WORRELL *Things that Sting* 33 The rock-dwelling Triantelope is reputed to give a painful bite.

tribal, *a.* Of or pertaining to a traditional Aboriginal community.
1882 W. SOWDEN *N.T. as it Is* 43 On one of those hills were curious stone erections, marking boundaries of natives' tribal territory. 1977 H. TOWSON *Black & White* 15 The Aboriginals went to their tribal grounds during their walk-about.

tribe. A name applied, orig. by the colonists, to a traditional Aboriginal community, and also (see quot. 1845) to a company of Aborigines.
1790 D. COLLINS *Acct. Eng. Colony N.S.W.* (1798) I. 144 The different tribes (for we had thought fit to class them into tribes). 1845 *Port Phillip Gaz.* 13 Sept. 4 A small tribe of strange blacks.. consisting of four men and five lubras.
Hence **tribesman**, an Aboriginal male; **tribespeople**, the members of an Aboriginal community.
1960 *N.T. News* (Darwin) 2 Feb. 1/5 Two of three Centralian aborigines who pulled a 'Houdini style' escape.. have been re-arrested. The natives were reported to be chained and handcuffed after police had seized arms in possession of a group of **tribesmen**. 1980 ANSELL & PERCY *To fight Wild* 125 Soon after when the mission was started at Port Keats, the **tribespeople** moved over there.

trick. [Orig. U.S.: see OED(S *sb.* 6.] See quot. 1916.
1916 V.G. DWYER *Conquering Hal* 120 'Isn't she a trick?'.. 'A—I beg your pardon?' 'A trick, you know. No one's ever dull when Vi's about. She's real good fun—so full of life, you know, and something smart and funny to say about everybody.' 1968 *Sunday Mail* (Brisbane) 10 Mar. 19/1 My wife was mystified when somebody in Brisbane described our daughter Sally, who is nearly five, as a 'trick'.

tricoloured chat. *Crimson chat,* see CRIMSON. Also **tricoloured bush chat** and formerly **epthianura**.
1842 J. GOULD *Birds of Aust.* (1848) III. Pl. 66, *Epthianura tricolor*.. Tri-coloured Epthianura. 1901 *Emu* I. 127 Nests of the.. Tricoloured Chat.. with four eggs. 1904 *Ibid.* IV. 44 Tri-coloured Bush-Chat.. undoubtedly, I think, a migratory bird.

trier. [Spec. use of *trier* one who tries to do something.] A racehorse which is being ridden to win.
1915 A. WRIGHT *Sport from Hollowlog Flat* 16 Tip-slinger Grif came and whispered, 'You're on a cert., she's the only trier.' 1977 W.A. WINTER-IRVING *Bush Stories* 129 At bush meetings, some horses are not exactly triers.

trifecta /traɪ'fɛktə/. [U.S. *trifecta,* f. *tri-* + *per)fecta* a method of betting in which the bettor must pick first and second: see OEDS *perfecta*.]
1. A method of betting in which the bettor must pick the first, second, and third finishers in a race in the correct order.
1968 *Sporting Globe* (Melbourne) 10 July 20/2 Trifecta: (per $1.00 unit): $21.80. 1981 K. GARVEY *Rhymes of Ratbag* 25 'It's super' says the bloke who has a win on the trifecta.

2. *transf.* A run of three 'wins'.

1982 N. KEESING *Lily on Dustbin* 62 A Sydney woman said of a friend's daughter that she had won the daily double but missed out on the trifecta: the young woman in question was having her wedding at the fashionable St Marks, Darling Point, the reception at the Royal Sydney Yacht Squadron, but had missed out on the honeymoon in Fiji. 1984 *Bulletin* (Sydney) 20 Mar. 54/1 The South-West of New South Wales struck the trifecta last week—the Riverina Merino Field Day, the opening of the duck season and a visit by Prime Minister Bob Hawke.

trigger plant. [See quot. 1984.] Any plant of the large, chiefly Austral. genus *Stylidium* (fam. Stylidiaceae); HAIR-TRIGGER. Also **trigger flower.**

1884 W.A. MILLER *Dict. Eng. Names of Plants*, Trigger-plant, *Stylidium graminifolium* and other species. 1965 *Austral. Encycl.* IX. 36 Except for four species that extend to China, Ceylon and India, all of the 122 different trigger-flowers are exclusively Australian. 1984 E. WALLING *On Trail Austral. Wildflowers* 58 The base of the flower is sensitive to touch and when the pollen is ripe a little hammer springs down and dusts an insect .. with pollen. That is why it is called Trigger-plant.

trimmer. [*Transf.* use of *trimmer* 'one who trims or trounces': see OED(S 6.] A person (or thing) outstanding in some respect.

1878 'IRONBARK' *Southerly Busters* 11, I thought thee a regular 'trimmer', I thought thee a generous man. 1965 E. LAMBERT *Long White Night* 135 A schooner of beer would go down like a trimmer after driving twenty miles along dirt roads on a boiling hot day.

triple antigen. [See *triple vaccine* (OEDS *triple, a.* 5).] A vaccine administered, usu. in infancy, as protection against diphtheria, whooping cough, and tetanus.

1953 *Med. Jrnl. Aust.* Nov. II. 742 Triple antigen contains 30 flocculation units of diphtheria toxoid, 10 flocculation units of tetanus toxoid and 20,000 million *H. pertussis* organisms per millilitre. 1986 *Age* (Melbourne) 2 Sept. 21/7 Her final triple antigen injection at the Infant Welfare Centre, for example, was faced with grace and courage .. by me.

triss. Also **trizz.** [Of unknown origin.] A male homosexual.

1953 K. TENNANT *Joyful Condemned* 165 Think I'm going round flapping my mouth to every silly triss that gets shoved in [the cell] with me? 1983 *Bulletin* (Sydney) 14 June 59/3 What on Earth's wrong with terms such as pouf, fag, fairy, dike, trizz, queer or pansy? Why 'gay'?

Hence **trissy** *a.*, homosexual.

1982 *Sydney Morning Herald* 4 Aug. 8/2 This is where Brideshead fails utterly; with the one exception of the scandalously trissy but minor character Anthony Blanche, they are all such dreary people.

trizzie. [Prob. alteration of TREY.] A threepenny piece.

1941 S.J. BAKER *Pop. Dict. Austral. Slang* 78 Trizzie, a 3d. piece. 1966 *Sunday Truth* (Brisbane) 23 Dec. 22/1 When you peppered the Christmas pud. with trey-bits this year we hope you remembered they will be scarcer next Yuletide and unless you hoard some there will be no trizzies at all for .. the 1968 plum-duff.

troll. Abbrev. of 'trollop'.

1963 J. CANTWELL *No Stranger to Flame* 75, I killed her because she was a troll. I'd been doing her for a year. I was ready to marry her. 1966 P. COWAN *Seed* 152 He had had her watched. Like one of his shady clients. Like some suburban troll.

trooper. *Hist.* [Transf. use of *trooper* a cavalry soldier.] A mounted police officer; *police trooper*, see POLICE.

1840 *Sydney Herald* 11 Nov. 2/4 As a trooper of the border police was coming to Sydney to attend a trial .. he apprehended two men on suspicion of their being runaways. 1958 H.D. WILLIAMSON *Sunlit Plain* 179 The trooper had entered and was asking for information about a quarter-wool skin hanging over a wire.

troppo /'trɒpoʊ/, *a.* [f. *trop(ic* + -O.]

a. Mentally disturbed, allegedly as a result of spending too much time (orig. on war service) in the tropics; mad, crazy. Also as *n.*

1941 *Army News* (Darwin) 14 Nov. 6/3 Some can still take life seriously despite the fact that the majority are slightly 'troppo'. 1944 *Fortress Chron.* (Torres Strait Islands) 4 Mar. 1/1 A typical, tropical 'troppo'.

b. Esp. in the phr. **to go troppo,** to become so disturbed.

1943 *Troppo Topics* 11 Jan. 7 Nearly everyone has gone 'troppo'. 1985 *Good Weekend* (Sydney) 12 Oct. 7/2 It was just the culmination of the songs, the musicians and the director all of my choice and really for the first time having a great time and people going troppo for it.

trot.

1. *pl.* [Spec. use of the pl. of *trot* a trotting-race. Used elsewhere but recorded earliest in Aust.: see OEDS *sb.*¹ 2.] A race-meeting at which the programme consists of trotting and pacing races; orig. (see quot. 1890) a series of trotting races in a mixed meeting.

1890 *Australasian* (Melbourne) 22 Mar. 569/5 A goodly number of people assembled at Elsternwick-park on Saturday, and, excepting the trots, which were of a very uninteresting character, the sport was up to the average. 1979 J. WILLIAMS *White River* 4 Grandma said she was taking me to the Trots.

2. An uninterrupted sequence, esp. in a game of chance; a run of good or bad luck.

1911 L. STONE *Jonah* 216 A trot or succession of seven tails followed, and the kip changed hands rapidly. 1985 N. MEDCALF *Rifleman* 160 Those poor buggers are having a tough trot back home.

troub /trʌb/. [Joc. use of *troubadour.*] A tram-conductor; TRAM TROUB. Also *transf.*, a bus conductor.

1910 *Truth* (Sydney) 13 Mar. 1/6 Troubs at times have a lot to put up with. On Thursday, on a Paddington tram, a fat duchess berated a conductor. 1967 *Kings Cross Whisper* (Sydney) lxi. 4/4 Troub, a bus conductor, or conductress. From the two words tram and bus.

trouble. In the phr. **my troubles,** a dismissive exclamation: see quot. 1895.

1895 C. CROWE *Austral. Slang Dict.* 89 My troubles, what do I care. 1947 G. CASEY *Wits are Out* 44 'You better lay off Kitty while the old man's about, or there'll be one more out-of-work motor salesman kicking round the city,' Syd suggested. 'My troubles!' Jerry jeered.

trout. [Transf. use of *trout* a fresh-water fish of the fam. Salmonidae, esp. of the genus *Salmo.* The name is applied also to some naturalized fish of this fam.] Any of several native fish, esp. of the fam. Galaxiidae: see quot. 1965.

1833 J. BACKHOUSE *Narr. Visit Austral. Colonies* (1843) 179 Some of the pools near George Town produce a small speckled fish, which is named Trout, but is far inferior to the Trout of Europe. 1965 *Austral. Encycl.* IX. 50 Some native fishes, such as the jollytails (*Galaxias*) and the Australian salmon or salmon trout (*Arripis*), are often regarded as trout, though they have little resemblance to and no affinities with the Salmonidae.

troy. [Of unknown origin.] A gambling game. Freq. *attrib.* as **troy school.**

1944 J. DEVANNY *By Tropic Sea & Jungle* 27 Tully was full of gambling joints, poker schools, troy schools.   **1961** *Bulletin* (Sydney) 22 Mar. 28/1 Ollie . . had been unsuccessfully trying to live on the game (troy) in Cairns since he'd had his clavicle broken.

trucker. *Mining.* [Spec. use of *trucker* a labourer who uses a truck or trolley.] One employed in a mine to shift ore in a skip or trolley: see quot. 1946.

1882 L.M. WILLIAMS *Diary of Disaster* (1982) 23 We were the only two working in that drive. We had no truckers, but trucked for ourselves.   **1946** W.E. HARNEY *North of 23°* 36, I became a trucker in the Duchess mine, my duties being to push a skip of ore to the flat so that the ore could go to the surface.

truckie. [f. *truck (driver* lorry driver + -Y.] A (long-distance) truck driver.

1958 *Coast to Coast 1957-58* 201 The truckie looked upwards. 'Whaddya want, mate?'   **1981** *Overland* lxxxv. 17 Stop for a feed at the truckie's cafe in Spencer Street.

trugo /'trugoʊ/. *Vic.* [f. *tru(e + go*: see quot. 1982.] A game in which a disc is struck towards a goal with a mallet: see quots.

1979 *Sunday Press* (Melbourne) 2 Dec. 44/2 Trugo has a following of more than 400 players. . . The disc (plastic these days) is placed between the feet, the back is turned to the opposite end of the rink and the disc is hit 28 metres—hopefully between the posts which are almost two metres apart.   **1982** *Weekend Austral. Mag.* (Sydney) 2 Jan. 10/2 There's even a section on that unique Australian sport of trugo, invented at the Newport railway workshops in Melbourne. The game started in the 1920s when a group of workers with little or nothing to do at lunchtime started hitting a round rubber disc with a mallet towards two markers. One worker scored a goal and shouted to his mates: 'Hey that was a true go.' Hence, trugo. There are 12 clubs in Melbourne now, with more than 100 men and 60 women playing in regular competition.

trump. [Fig. use of *trump* a card of a suit which ranks above the others.] A person in authority.

1925 *Bulletin* (Sydney) 9 Apr. 24/1 The station-manager is known as the 'trump'.   **1978** D. STUART *Wedgetail View* 74 From what I hear there'll be quite a show there in a few months' time, an' I think the trump might be just about ready to put on a few extra hands.

trumpeter, *n.*[1] [See quot. 1885.]

1. Any of several fish of the fam. Latridae, esp. *Latris lineata* of coastal waters of s.e. Aust., and New Zealand, and fish of the genus *Latridopsis*. See also TRUMPETER, STRIPEY, *Tasmanian trumpeter* TASMANIAN *a.* 2.

1827 *Tasmanian Almanack* 142 Trumpeter, very large, 2s. ditto.   **1885** *Adelaide Observer* 18 Apr. 29 The fish known to Port Adelaide fishermen as the 'silver fish', and sometimes as the trumpeter (from the peculiar squeaking noise made by them when caught).

2. Special Comb. **trumpeter whiting,** any of several fish of the whiting fam., esp. *Sillago maculata* of n., e., and w. Aust.

1878 *Proc. Linnean Soc. N.S.W.* III. 380 *Sillago Bassensis*. . . Called at Sydney *Trumpeter Whiting*. . . Very common also at Brisbane, where it is the common whiting.   **1965** *Austral. Encycl.* IX. 298 The trumpeter whiting (*S[illago] maculata*) is a northern fish ranging from the tropics southward to Port Jackson.

trumpeter, *n.*[2] *Hist.* A type of fetter: see quot. 1894.

1892 *Bulletin* (Sydney) 2 July 21/4 'I thought he was celled?' 'So he is, sir. No. 5!' 'And ironed?' 'Trumpeters— fifteen's [*sic*]—and wall-cuffs!'   **1894** 'P. WARUNG' *Tales Early Days* 131 A brace of staples apiece driven in, and twenty-pound trumpeters, will hold 'em in, or else my name isn't Wright. [*Note*] Trumpeters, irons which connected the ordinary leg-chains with a bazil riveted around each leg immediately below the knees.

try, *v. Mining.* [Spec. use of *try* to endeavour to ascertain by experiment.] *trans.* To test (soil, gravel, etc.) for the presence of a precious mineral.

1876 'EIGHT YRS.' RESIDENT' *Queen of Colonies* 134 With a pick, shovel, tin dish, and bag as tools, a blanket, billy, and quart-pot as equipment, they swarm over the country 'trying' it. Wherever they come across a 'likely-looking spot' they dig or 'bottom' a hole, take out a dishful of the 'washdirt', if any is found, and try it by washing at the nearest water-hole.   **1902** E.B. KENNEDY *Black Police Qld.* 66, I made up my mind to try a spec., so from Grafton I did wander, And bought a mob of nuggets there to begin as an overlander.

try diver. *Pearling.* An apprentice diver: see quot. 1956.

1913 *Cwlth. Parl. Papers* III. 691 Of the divers licensed, however, there are a number of learners—men known as 'try' divers.   **1956** S. GORE *Overlanding with Annabel* 85 Pearl-divers are not born—they are made. A likely man serves one season as a 'try-diver', during which time he is head-crew of the boat, his assorted duties at sea leaving him only Saturday afternoons free to serve his apprenticeship in the diving dress, at all depths from seven to seventeen fathoms.

try the acid: see ACID.

T.S.R. *Travelling stock route, reserve,* see TRAVELLING STOCK 2.

1897 *Bulletin* (Sydney) 11 Dec. 30/1 We were camped in ridgy country with a homestead fence aback And twenty chains of T.S.R. to shield us from the track.   **1977** T.L. MCKNIGHT *Long Paddock* 2 Now that road transport has become so widespread . . it may be that TSRs are more important as supplemental grazing areas than as accessways to market.

tuan /'tjuən/. [a. Wathawurung *duwan*.] **a.** PHASCOGALE. **b.** *Flying possum,* see FLYING. Formerly also **tuan-tuan.**

1842 H. MCCRAE *Georgiana's Jrnl.* 16 Dec. (1934) 71 'Murray' brought us a live 'tuan-tuan'—a sort of flying squirrel, with extremely soft fur.   **1979** DOUGLAS & HEATHCOTE *Far Cry* 121 The Tuan, or brush-tailed phascogale (pencillata) [*sic*] is a Dasure, like the spotted native cat.

tuart /'tjuat/. Formerly also **tooat, tooart.** [a. Nyungar *duward*.] The medium to tall tree *Eucalyptus gomphocephala* (fam. Myrtaceae) of coastal s.w. W.A.; the strong, hard, yellowish wood of the tree. Also *attrib.*

1836 H.W. BUNBURY *Early Days W.A.* (1930) 71 We now came into a more open country with a good deal of grass growing on a light soil under very large White Gums, called by the natives 'Tooats'.   **1842** 'J.K.C.' *Jrnl. of Voyage* 19 The different varieties of trees hereabouts are the red, white, and flooded gums . . and a few tuarts.   **1869** F. ALGAR *Hand-Bk. Qld.* 13 Those [*sc.* trees] chiefly valuable for ship-building purposes are known by the native names of the Jarrah and Tooart.   **1985** *Austral. Garden Jrnl.* June 127 Tuart trees are indigenous to Western Australia, and have been planted widely throughout the drier rural areas along the southern coast.

tub. *Gold-mining. Obs. Puddling tub,* see PUDDLING 2.

1852 *Argus* (Melbourne) 8 Mar. 2/7 The 'rush' has left little elbow-room for those who are lucky enough in finding places for their tubs and cradles.   **1871** J. BALLANTYNE *Homes & Homesteads* 40 With his 'cradle' he could wash his gravelly soil, or with his 'tub' he could puddle his clayey gatherings.

tube.
1. *Shearing. Obs.* A tubular casing containing the flexible shaft which drives the shears. Also *fig.*
1904 *Shearer* (Sydney) 29 Oct. 4/2 The tubes at Rhodesia are swinging with a will, and the tallies that will be cut at that shed will cause a panic in the opposition camp. **1963** *Sydney Morning Herald* 17 Aug. 11/7 I've shorn in hundreds of sheds with thousands of shearers... Get off the tube (out of the game) while you are young enough.
2. A can (or sometimes a bottle) of beer.
1964 B. HUMPHRIES *Nice Night's Entertainment* (1981) 77 We were on the beach or in the surf club cracking the tubes or demolishing a twelve. **1973** J. POWERS *Last of Knucklemen* (1979) 19 Moments like these are the glory of bein' old. You can just sit back an' suck on your tube an' watch.

tucker, $n.^1$ [f. Br. slang *tuck* to consume (food or drink): see OED $v.^1$ 10.]
1. a. *Obs.* A meal.
1833 *Launceston Advertiser* 24 Oct. 3 They then asked for a 'tucker' (the slang word for a meal), which was supplied. **1846** L.W. MILLER *Notes of Exile Van Dieman's Land* 280 The wardsmen .. got all their hard labour performed by gorging the scoundrel with a '*good tucker*', as it was called.
b. Food. Also *attrib.*
1850 *Monthly Almanac* (Adelaide) 44 So hearing that 'plenty tucker' was their desire, I let them know by signs that I was not the sort of fellow to offer opposition to their very proper request. **1981** D. STUART *I think I'll Live* 86 Yeah, she's a good tucker joint, this Java, be the look of it. Plenty o' fruit, bananas, all that stuff.
c. In the collocation **saddle-pouch tucker:** see quot. 1947.
1947 V.C. HALL *Bad Medicine* 14 Out on the run with the cattle he lives on 'saddle-pooch tucker' of damper and salt beef, and as one of them told me without a smile, 'a couple of tins of jam in case of sickness'.
d. A supply of provisions.
1933 J.M. HARCOURT *Pearlers* 146 We've got to live till the boats come in again at the end of the first tucker.
2. Comb. **tucker bill, pack, time.**
1897 *Worker* (Sydney) 18 Sept. 3/4 The **tucker bill** at Mooloomon amounted to 21s. 2d. per man per week, the prices charged for rations being something dreadful, as the above figures go to show. **1922** 'J. BUSHMAN' *In Musgrave Ranges* 237 His own **tucker-packs** had not been interfered with. **1912** *Bulletin* (Sydney) 1 Aug. 15/2 They're always ready for **tucker-time.**
3. Special Comb. **tucker bag,** a provision bag, esp. as carried by a swagman; **box,** a box for the storing or conveyance of provisions; **cart,** a vehicle for the conveyance of provisions; **shop,** a food shop; a restaurant; **track,** a route followed by itinerant rural workers and other travellers, judged according to the generosity with which provisions are supplied along the way (see WALLABY TRACK 2 a.).
1885 *Bulletin* (Sydney) 5 Sept. 5/3 Is your brain 'on the gutter'—a fanciful 'drunk'? Have your pannings today made the **tucker bag** right? **1897** A.F. PATERSON '*Mid Saltbush & Mallee* 30 'Now, Miss Kerr .. will you .. help me to pack the **tucker box.**' 'Tucker box, what is that?' 'Well, perhaps I ought to say lunch box; for in the bush we do not boast of hamper baskets.' **1905** *Bulletin* (Sydney) 20 Apr. 19/2 **Tucker cart** broke down. **1907** A. MACDONALD *In Land of Pearl & Gold* 110 You should make for Sydney too, Dave... There's some good **tucker-shops** there. **1984** W.W. AMMON et al. *Working Lives* 190 The hotel was a good tucker shop as Mrs Neville was a fine cook. **1896** H. LAWSON *While Billy Boils* (1975) 54 The men get a little more sociable .. and exchange hints as to good **tucker-tracks,** and discuss the strike, and curse the squatter.

tucker, $n.^2$ and *attrib.* [Transf. use of TUCKER $n.^1$]
A. *n.* The means of subsistence, esp. in the phr. **to make tucker.**
1858 *Colonial Mining Jrnl.* Oct. 23/2 They seemed to think that to work for any wages at all, over and above 'tucker' would be considerably to improve their fortunes. **1973** C. AUSTIN *I left my Hat in Andamooka* 60 There are worse ways of living to a ripe old age, even if you only find enough opal to 'make tucker'.
B. *attrib.* Subsistence; yielding only the means of subsistence.
1882 A.J. BOYD *Old Colonials* 142, I spent a week prospecting about, and got good tucker gold. **1929** W.J. RESIDE *Golden Days* 340 Employed at a mere 'tucker' wage.
2. In Comb. designating a mine or mining area, as **tucker claim, diggings, field, ground, show.**
1859 *Colonial Mining Jrnl.* Jan. 76/1 All are not, however, lucky enough to strike even upon a '**tucker' claim,** and shicers are neither few nor far between. **1874** C. DE BOOS *Congewoi Correspondence* 115 There's no mistake about the Treasurer bein a fust-rate fossicker. My word! Why, if he was on a **tucker diggins** I believe he'd fossick good wages in the old drives. **1933** W.L. OWEN *Cossack Gold* 92 When the richest plums had been picked it became a '**tucker-field**' to which the diggers returned to feed on the duff. **1869** R.B. SMYTH *Gold Fields & Mineral Districts* 624 **Tucker Ground,** ground which yields only sufficient gold to provide miners with *tucker*. **1906** E. DYSON *In Roaring Fifties* 99 He didn't believe he'd got a **tucker show,** and sadly advised Mike to shepherd a hole down to the left.
3. Special Comb. **tucker job,** a poorly paid job; **money,** a small sum of money; a pittance.
1905 *Bulletin* (Sydney) 13 Apr. 19/1 If a bootless man happens along, as is sometimes the case in Victoria, he is offered a '**tucker' job;** and a real good-natured cocky has been known to throw in a pair of his own cast-off 'crabs'. **1892** 'MRS A. MACLEOD' *Silent Sea* I. 236 He had gone almost hungry, certainly very dirty, and in very broken boots, once when he was working in a poor patch of country, which did not yield '**tucker' money.**

tucker, $v.^1$ [f. TUCKER $n.^1$ and $n.^2$]
1. a. *intr.* To eat food; to take a meal.
1870 G.P. DEANE *Diary* 10 Feb., They shifted us out of our Mess hut. Tuckering now in the stable shed. **1978** D. STUART *Wedgetail View* 61 A greasy chop an' a hunk o' bread .. an' y' reckoned you were tuckerin' like a lord.
b. *intr.* To subsist.
1925 E. McDONNELL *My Homeland* 24 Loafed about the camp, tuckering mostly on damper and tea.
2. a. *trans.* To supply (a person) with food or provisions. Also *refl.* and *absol.*
1891 E.H. HALLACK *W.A. & Yilgarn Goldfields* 13 'What about tucker, have you any?' I was asked before starting. A reply in the negative caused the obliging Manager to arrange with the driver to take sufficient to 'tucker' me. **1943** *Bulletin* (Sydney) 27 Oct. 12/1 What I can't understand is how the devil he's goin' to keep her. Took him all his time to tucker himself. **1960** M. VIZZERS *She'll do Me!* 20 My best plan would be take a room in a cheap residential, do my own 'tuckering' and start looking for a job, any job.
b. *intr.* With **up:** to acquire a supply of food or provisions.
1915 E.R. MASSON *Untamed Territory* 53 The Japanese .. then return to Darwin, where they hand over their shell, and 'tucker up', as provisioning is called. **1969** J. DINGWELL *One String* 64 'I expect you've come to tucker up,' he asked the geologist presently.

tucker, $v.^2$ [U.S. *tucker* to tire: see Mathews.] *intr.* With **out** or **up:** to tire. Freq. as **tuckered out** (or **up**) *ppl. a.,* exhausted.

TUCKERLESS 599 **TUPONG**

1911 A.L. HAYDON *Trooper Police Aust.* 390 He had been travelling round about a good part of the night and was fairly tuckered out. 1920 A.G. HALES *McGlusky Gold-Seeker* 54 That grey mare .. looks a bit tuckered up to *me*.

tuckerless, *a*. Without food or a means of subsistence.
1910 *Bulletin* (Sydney) 2 June 15/1 I'll never forget .. one sunset track. I had trudged two tuckerless 16-mile stages .. then I struck my hospitable friend, and inquired .. where the Government tank resided. 1937 E. HILL *Great Austral. Loneliness* 82 The rind of the pods .. makes an acrid but nourishing food .. that tides over the tuckerless white man to the next out-camp.

tuckeroo /tʌkə'ru/. [Prob. a. Yagara *dagaru*.] The tree *Cupaniopsis anacardioides* (fam. Sapindaceae) of n. and e. Aust., cultivated as an ornamental.
1889 J.H. MAIDEN *Useful Native Plants Aust.* 410 *Cupania anacardioides* .. 'Brush Deal' and 'Tuckeroo' are Queensland colonial and aboriginal names respectively. 1985 N. & H. NICHOLSON *Austral. Rainforest Plants* 23 Tuckeroo makes a handsome small to medium-sized shade tree for coastal areas.

tuck-out. *Obs.* [Transf. use of *tuck-out* a hearty meal, a 'blow-out': see OED *tuck, sb.*[1] 6.]
1. A beating; a fight.
1832 *Hill's Life N.S.W.* (Sydney) 31 Aug. 3 (Advt.), Bill Dargin was beaten by me; and I think never before or since received such a *tuck-out*. 1847 *Bell's Life in Sydney* 25 Dec. 2/2 A hostile meeting took place this morning .. on the Richmond Bottoms, for what is vulgarly termed a *tuck-out*, not of *bacon and eggs*, or roast beef and plum-pudding, but a reciprocal interchange .. between two very formidable farmers of the locality.
2. *Austral. pidgin.* Food.
1847 [see sense 1]. 1863 J. BONWICK *Wild White Man* 66 The aborigines were .. regaled with 'plenty tuck out'. 1935 F. BIRTLES *Battle Fronts Outback* 80 The piccaninnies, too, had been earning their 'tuckout', digging down into the soft soil at the foot of long creeping vines, for the yam roots.
Hence as *v. trans.*, to eat.
1981 NGABIDJ & SHAW *My Country of Pelican Dreaming* 66 We used also to tuck out goose—that was good food.

tug. [Of unknown origin.] A sharper (but see quots. 1896 and 1898). Also *attrib.*
1896 *Bulletin* (Sydney) 11 Apr. 17/4 Quite a number of bookies are migrating in view of the dull Australian winter tug-catching season. 1898 *Ibid.* 4 June (Red Page), And a sharper is a 'spieler' And a simpleton's a 'tug'. 1933 A. REID *Those were Days* 55 So that chaps could know why a top-notch tug Can work 'his' ramps in a card-room snug.

tula /'tula/. Also **tuhla**. [Poss. a. Luritja dial. of Western Desert *tula*.] An Aboriginal tool used for wood-working: see quot. 1981.
1930 C.C. TOWLE *Certain Stone Implements* 10 The coastal tribes .. did not possess symmetrical types, of which the gouge (or adze, or tuhla) was the most widely distributed. 1981 J. MULVANEY et al. *Aboriginal Aust.* 70 (*caption*) Tula adze, or woodworking chisel, from Barrow Creek, Northern Territory .. exhibits the characteristically curved and stout handle, with stone tip firmly fixed with *Triodia* cement.

tulip oak. [With reference to the grain of the timber which is reminiscent of that of the oak *Quercus* and SILKY OAK.] BOOYONG; the wood of this tree.
1938 C.T. WHITE *Princ. Bot. Qld. Farmers* 212 *Tarrietia* (Booyongs, Tulip Oaks or Stave Woods). 1985 *Austral. Garden Jrnl.* Oct. 17 Do look down at the tulip oak flooring as you walk around the corner.

tulip tree. *Obs.* WARATAH 1. Also **tulip**.
1831 *Acct. Colony Van Diemen's Land* 66 The whole of this country is also interspersed with that magnificent shrub called Warrataw or tulip tree and its beautiful scarlet flowers. 1898 E.E. MORRIS *Austral Eng.* 498 The generic name *Telopea* .. has been corrupted into *Tulip*.

tulipwood. Any of several trees yielding an attractively streaked timber, esp. *Harpullia pendula* (fam. Sapindaceae) of rainforest in n.e. N.S.W. and e. Qld., which is cultivated as an ornamental; the wood of the tree. Also *ellipt.* as **tulip**.
1830 W.J. HOOKER *Bot. Miscellany* I. 239 Extensive brushwoods, the latter exhibiting a profusion of *Yellow Wood*, (*Oxyleya xanthoxyla*) and *Tulip Wood*. 1921 *Smith's Weekly* (Sydney) 1 Jan. 9/3 Saw a walking-stick the other day made from tulip.

tumble down, *v. Austral. pidgin. Obs.*
1. *intr.* To die; to fall down. Also *fig.*
1803 J.G. GRANT *Narr. Voyage N.S.W.* 113 Through Euranabie .. I found the bones were those of a white man that had come in a canoe from the southward, where the ship *tumble down*, the expression he made use of for being wrecked. 1933 R.B. PLOWMAN *Man from Oodnadatta* 195, I have told the blacks that I am going to shoot the moon and that it is going to tumble down (die).
2. *trans.* To kill. (As *vbl. n.* in quot.).
1834 G. BENNETT *Wanderings N.S.W.* I. 131 Unceasingly complained of the 'tumbling down him brother'.

tumble down, *n. Austral. pidgin. Obs.* [f. prec.] Alcoholic liquor.
1827 P. CUNNINGHAM *Two Yrs. in N.S.W.* I. 236 A good jorum of *bull* (washings of a sugar bag) or *tumble down* (grog) at the conclusion of the harvest, sends them all merrily and gaily away. 1843 W. PRIDDEN *Aust.* 143 Tobacco and spirits, which the poor natives call '*tumble-down*', are articles in constant request.

tumbling-tommy. [Alteration of *tumbling tom*: see OED *tumbling*.]
1. A horse-drawn scoop, having a tipping bucket and used esp. for earth-moving. Also *attrib*.
1934 *Bulletin* (Sydney) 9 May 20/2 Drawing .. water for stock from a well .. the bucket came off the 'tumbling-tommy' hook and sank to the bottom. 1981 G. ELLIS *Hey Doc, let's go Fishing* 67 Early in this century a canal was cut from Basalt River to Lolworth to water some intervening country. . . In those days bulldozers and scrapers weren't known and it was a case of Tumbling Tommies, horse-drawn ploughs and wheelbarrows.
2. *transf.* See quot.
1977 B. FULLER *Nullarbor Lifelines* 56 Oddly enough, scoop men were known as 'tumbling tommies' after the small ground-clearing implements they drove.

tunnel. *Surfing.* The hollow curve of a breaking wave; a 'tube'.
1963 J. POLLARD *Austral. Surfrider* 104 There's a story about Mickey Munez, one of the great Hawaiian riders starting into a tube just after taking off on Rincon Point. He disappeared... They reckon he was inside that tunnel for 20 seconds. 1964 B. HUMPHRIES *Nice Night's Entertainment* (1981), When we weren't zipping, cutting and flicking the boards through tunnels and wipe-outs .. we were on the beach or in the surf club.

tupong /'tupoŋ/. [a. Kuupn Kopan Noot *duboŋ*.] The small, chiefly marine fish *Pseudaphritis urvilli* of s.e. Aust. incl. Tas.
1897 *Proc. Linnean Soc. N.S.W.* XXII. 557 Some months ago I received .. three fine specimens of a *Pseudaphritis*

from the fresh waters of Victoria, where it is known to anglers as the 'Tupong'. **1974** L. WEDLICK *Sporting Fish* 17 The tupong is dark blue to purple on the back, and silver on the belly. *Ibid.*, All early articles referred to this fish as marble trout, freshwater flathead or congolli, the last name being the only by which the tupong is known in South Australia.

turkey, *n.*[1] [Transf. use of *turkey* a large gallinaceous bird.]

1. Either of two birds, the *wild turkey* (see WILD 1), and the *brush turkey* (see BRUSH *n.*[1] B. 2); *native turkey*, see NATIVE *a.* 6 b.

1827 *Monitor* (Sydney) 20 Aug. 599/1 Entered a thick shrub, at the foot of Mount Dumuresq [*sic*] .. found several turkies, and a remarkably large pigeon, upwards of three pounds weight. **1973** R. ROBINSON *Drift of Things* 418 The gang at the end of our section told us of the turkeys they shot. They were in mungerai (a succulent plant) country and we were in parakelia country.

2. With other distinguishing epithets, as **plain**, **scrub**: see under first element.

3. *transf.* SWAG *n.* 1; also a packhorse.

1905 *Shearer* (Sydney) 17 June 6/2 If you meet him on the track with your 'turkey coiled' (swag) no introduction is necessary. **1912** 'IRONBARK' *Ironbark Splinters* 6 *Turkey*, bushman's slang for 'swag', a bundle of blankets and clothes. The term is sometimes also applied to a packhorse.

4. In the phr. **head over turkey** and varr., 'head over heels'; also *fig.*, in disarray.

1915 C.J. DENNIS *Songs of Sentimental Bloke* 43 'E swallers lysol, throws a fancy fit, 'Ead over turkey, an' 'is soul 'as flit. **1955** A. MARSHALL *I can jump Puddles* 46 Before I quieten her, I knock Sir Frederick Salisbury, or whatever his name is, head over turkey into a clump of peacocks.

5. Special Comb. **turkey bush,** ELLANGOWAN POISON BUSH; *emu bush* (a), see EMU *n.*[1] 3; also *attrib.*; **nest dam** (or **tank**), a reservoir built in flat country where there is no natural run-off, having high earth walls and so resembling the mound of the brush turkey (see quot. 1974); also *ellipt.* as **turkey nest**.

1899 *Western Champion* (Barcaldine) 15 Aug. 5/1 All the wattle trees and bloodwoods have been killed for miles around... Wonder if it affected the **turkey bush**. **1927** *Bulletin* (Sydney) 14 Apr. 27/2 A large area of country south of the Escape River, Cape York Peninsula, is .. covered by the accursed 'turkey bush' scrub. **1961** [**turkey nest dam**] J.W. JORDAN *Practical Sheep Farming* 66 The finished earth works and embankments form a nest-shaped storage, called a 'turkey-nest'. **1968** D. CAMPBELL *Drought* 104 The grazier on dead flat country .. may require bores or specially constructed 'ring' dams or 'turkey-nest' dams with a system of sprays for a limited crop area. **1974** F. STEVENS *Aborigines in N.T. Cattle Industry* 119 (*note*) A 'turkey-nest' tank is so described because of its appearance. Normally built in plains country, the earth walls of the dam usually rise 20 or 30 feet above the surrounding countryside, holding anywhere up to 20,000 gallons of water.

Turkey, *n.*[2] [The name of the country in s.e. Europe and s.w. Asia.]

1. In Services' speech: a Turkish soldier.

1916 'MEN OF ANZAC' *Anzac Bk.* 127 An' then—oh, strike me blue an' pink—Then don't the Turkies swear! **1974** D. STUART *Prince of my Country* 102 Knock the Turkey out, up through the Balkans an' in through the back door.

2. Special Comb. **turkey lolly,** a confection of spun sugar; *fairy floss*, see FAIRY *n.*[1] 2.

1971 J. HETHERINGTON *Morning was Shining* 45 In those days Turkey Lolly was sold on the Sandringham beach on hot summer afternoons by a tall copper-hued man who wore a turban... He would dip his dark hand into the tub and shovel the filmy confection into funnel-shaped homemade bags.

turn, *n.* [Transf. use of *turn* an item in a variety entertainment.]

1. A party.

1953 T.A.G. HUNGERFORD *Riverslake* 94 The Causeway's all right—a damned sight better than the turns up at the Albert Hall. Anyway, it's a football dance, not just one of those .. turns they slap on for the locals. **1979** B. HUMPHRIES *Bazza comes into his Own*, Jeez, no bastard tipped me the wink this turn was fancy dress!

2. In the phr. **to stack on a turn,** to make a fuss.

1953 T.A.G. HUNGERFORD *Riverslake* 173 'When we got back—stone the crows, I thought she'd shed her blasted skin!' 'You might've told her before.' 'Like hell! She would've just stacked on a turn.' **1981** *Weekend Austral.* (Sydney) 21 Nov. 19/8 For reasons best known to himself, Mr Bjelke-Petersen stacked on a turn and the negotiations broke down.

turn, *v.*

1. *trans. Obs.* With **in**: to return (an assigned convict) to official custody. Also in the phr. **to turn (a convict) in to government.**

1830 R. DAWSON *Present State Aust.* 201, I asked him .. the reason of his having been 'turned in', as they call it, to government. **1843** *Sydney Morning Herald* 26 Sept. 4/5, I went to Mr Sparke's place in search of him, and was told there that he had been turned into Government.

2. *intr. Obs.* With **out**: to become a bushranger.

1862 *Western Post* (Mudgee) 24 Sept. 2/2 He was immediately told by the robber they ought to turn out. **1910** J. CAMERON *Spell of Bush* 131 [The bush] had been his home; for even before he had 'turned out', four walls had never held Michael Moran for long.

3. *trans.* Chiefly *N.T.* [Also U.S.] With **off**: to consign (livestock) to market.

1942 H.H. PECK *Mem. of Stockman* 103 Tatong always turned off many fat bullocks. **1960** *N.T. News* (Darwin) 26 Feb. 3/1 He predicted many stations would switch from breeding fat cattle up to four and five years old and turn off 18 months to two-year-old stores instead.

4. *trans.* With **on**: to provide (refreshments, esp. alcoholic liquor). Freq. in the phr. **to turn it on.**

1941 S.J. BAKER *Pop. Dict. Austral. Slang* 79 *Turn it on*, to provide liquor at a party .. to 'shout' drinks. **1977** B. SCOTT *My Uncle Arch* 109, I thought I'd die laughing at the big dinner the firm turned on. ... All the grog you could drink and baretop gogo dancers.

5. *trans.* To earn (a sum of money).

1960 R. PULLAN *Hardskins* 29 New Australians .. chase all over, looking for bargains, trying to beat you down, anything to turn a quid. **1976** F. MOORHOUSE *Conference-Ville* 106 Just been turning a quid.

turnipwood. Any of several trees the bark or wood of which has a turnip-like smell, as *Dysoxylum muelleri* (see *red bean* RED *a.* 1 a.), and esp. *Akania lucens* (fam. Akaniaceae) of n.e. N.S.W. and s.e. Qld.; the wood of the tree. Formerly also **turnip-tree**.

1871 *Austral. Town & Country Jrnl.* (Sydney) 18 Mar. 330/4 Another peculiar tree is detected by its smell to be the turnip-tree, from its aroma resembling the smell of Swede turnips. **1984** WRIGLEY & FAGG *Austral. Native Plants* (ed. 2) 431 Turnipwood. Small tree to 10 m. .. Has great potential for indoor plant work. Beautiful foliage.

turn-off. Chiefly *N.T.* [f. TURN *v.* 3; also U.S.] The quantity of marketable livestock produced by a rural property or district. Also *attrib.*

1960 *N.T. News* (Darwin) 11 Mar. 7/3 There is sufficient feed throughout the Alice Springs district at present to ensure a good turnoff by the middle of the year. **1968** F. ROSE *Aust. Revisited* 269 *Turn-off cattle*, those cattle marketed from a property or station.

turpentine. [See quot. 1904.]
1. Any of several trees, usu. of the fam. Myrtaceae, esp. the tall *Syncarpia glomulifera* (syn. *S. laurifolia*) of e. N.S.W. and e. Qld., having a thick fibrous bark and yielding a reddish timber valued for its durability in sea water; the wood of the tree. Also *attrib.*, esp. as **turpentine-tree.**

1803 *Sydney Gaz.* 26 June, Timber in this colony includes Turpentine etc. **1904** J.H. MAIDEN *Forest Flora N.S.W.* I. 16 'Turpentine-tree.' It is so-called because of the resinous exudation which flows from between the bark and the wood when the timber is cut into. It is an unfortunate name, as it suggests inflammability, and turpentine is one of the most uninflammable of timbers. . . Turpentine timber has scarcely any odour.

2. Special Comb. **turpentine bush,** any of several often resinous or aromatic shrubs, esp. some species of the genera *Beyeria* (fam. Euphorbiaceae) and *Eremophila* (fam. Myoporaceae) incl. *E. sturtii* of e. mainland Aust. Also *ellipt.* as **turpentine.**

1885 P.R. MEGGY *From Sydney to Silverton* 124 Another feature of the vegetation is the turpentine bush, remarkable for its irritating properties. **1985** *Austral. Financial Rev.* (Sydney) 18 Dec. 25 Noxious and inedible shrubs—like turpentine, punty and hopbush.

turps. [Transf. use of *turps* abbrev. of *turpentine.*] Alcoholic liquor. Esp. in the phr. **on the turps.**

1865 H. KINGSLEY *Hillyars & Burtons* 294 They tossed for a go of turps and a hayband—I ask your ladyship's pardon, that means a glass of gin and a cigar. **1980** S. THORNE *I've met some Bloody Wags* 36 Dan was a good bloke, but a terror on the turps. Once he started on rum—look out!

turquoise wren. The bird *Malurus splendens callainus* of arid central Aust.

1898 E.E. MORRIS *Austral Eng.* Turquoise W[ren]—*Malurus callainus.* **1976** *Reader's Digest Compl. Bk. Austral. Birds* 410 There are three subspecies of splendid wren, which were, until recently, regarded as separate species . . the turquoise wren [etc.].

turrum /'tʌrəm/. [Prob. f. a W.A. Aboriginal language.] Any of several large marine fish of n. Aust., of the fam. Carangidae, valued as game fish, incl. *Carangoides fulvoguttatus* and *Caranx ignobilis.*

1936 T.C. ROUGHLEY *Wonders Great Barrier Reef* 196 The most stubborn fighter of the reef is probably the turrum, a giant trevally which attains a weight of upwards of seventy pounds. **1981** G. ELLIS *Hey Doc, let's go Fishing!* 14 The turrum belongs to the trevally family, but it is a very deep chunky fish with shoulders (if such a description can be used of fish) like a working bullock.

tussock: see TUSSOCK GRASS b.

tussock, *v. Obs.* [f. *tussock*, abbrev. of TUSSOCK GRASS.] *intr.* To clear land of tussock grass. Chiefly as *vbl. n.*

[N.Z. **1866** J. MURRAY *Descr. of Southland* 28 [The intending farmer] will do well to 'tussac' a few acres;—that is chip off with an adze the flax and coarse grass growing on the land.] **1888** *Devon Herald* (La Trobe) 6 Mar. 2/2 We would remind persons interested that tenders invited by Mr G. Atkinson for tussocking on Pig Island, close tomorrow. **1904** *Bulletin* (Sydney) 7 Jan. 16/2 The swagman . . may obtain a little 'tussocking' at a contract price.

tussock grass. a. Any of several tussock-forming plants, usu. perennial grasses of the genus *Poa* (fam. Poaceae), esp. *P. labillardieri* of e. Aust. incl. Tas., and the related *P. sieberana.* **b.** (Freq. *ellipt.* as **tussock**) SERRATED TUSSOCK. Also *attrib.*

1870 J. BONWICK *Last Tasmanians* 243 The Bishop of Tasmania described it in 1854 as 'little more than a succession of sand heaps, covered here and there with tussock and stunted shrubs'. **1871** *Austral. Town & Country Jrnl.* (Sydney) 15 July 34/3 The tussac grass . . grows freely in most places in Australia where the soil is sufficiently rich. **1983** *Warwick Daily News* 14 June 3/1 Stands of apple box . . and tall tussock grassland.

tussy-jumper. [f. TUSS(OCK GRASS + -Y + *jumper.*] One employed as a hand on a rural property.

1967 G. JENKIN *Two Yrs. Bardunyah Station* 6 All the tussy-jumpers there . . Give up a mournful moan. **1975** M. THORNTON *It's Jackaroo's Life* 64 So with tussie jumper Harry and the ute filled up with gas.

twang. [Prob. back-formation f. *Twankay* a variety of green tea.] Opium.

1898 *Bulletin* (Sydney) 1 Oct. 14/3 A few more W.Q. slang words . . opium 'twang', a Chinaman a 'canary' [etc.]. **1961** I.L. IDRIESS *Tracks of Destiny* 94 This Chinaman was a 'runner', carrying smuggled 'twang' (opium) from Port Darwin to his compatriots inland at the Creek.

tweed-capper. *Obs.* A British immigrant.

1912 *Truth* (Sydney) 31 Mar. 5/1 The jimmygrants . . tough tweed-cappers and verdant mugs. **1912** *Bulletin* (Sydney) 15 Aug. 15/2 A newly arrived 'Jimmy Grant' passed a paddock of dead, ring-barked timber. . . 'Crikey!' he howled, 'have all those trees been struck by lightning?' This part (Moombooldool) is thick with tweed-cappers, and the mistakes they invent keep the countryside from ever feeling dull.

tweeds, *pl.* Trousers. Also *transf.*

1954 T.A.G. HUNGERFORD *Sowers of Wind* 117 'I take my coat off every day, and it don't stop the flaming traffic!' 'Try taking your tweeds off, boof-head!' **1969** A. BUZO *Rooted* (1973) 85 Susan was a lovely girl. She never dropped her tweeds for anyone.

twelve apostles, *pl.* Freq. also as *sing.* See APOSTLE. Also **twelve apostle (bird).**

1889 *Proc. Linnean Soc. N.S.W.* IV. 412 *Struthidea cinerea.* . . About Cobbora [N.S.W.] they are known as 'Twelve Apostles', a title shared by *Pomatostomus.* **1930** A. RUSSELL *Sunlit Trails* 53 The babblers are often erroneously called the 'jumpers', a name which should only be applied to the Apostle bird, the 'Twelve Apostle'. . of the bushman. **1963** O. RUHEN *Flockmaster* 93 On a bloodwood tree, a busy family of the Twelve Apostle birds, skipping from twig to twig as though they played some organised game.

twenty-eight. [See quot. 1843.] The parrot *Barnardius zonarius semitorquatus* of s.w. W.A., a predom. green bird with a black head, red bar on forehead, and yellow collar; (esp. *W.A.*) more generally, any subspecies of PORT LINCOLN PARROT. Also **twenty-eight parrot** and formerly **twenty-eight parakeet.**

1843 J. GOULD *Birds of Aust.* (1848) V. Pl. 19, While on the wing . . it often utters a note, which from its resemblance to those words has procured for it the appellation of 'twenty-eight' Parrakeet from the colonists; the last word or note being sometimes repeated five or six times in succession. **1847** *Atlas* (Sydney) III. 111/2 A new and beautiful variety of the parrot tribe is to be seen . . somewhat less in size than that commonly known as the 'twenty-eight'. **1957** J. NAIRN *Out of Back Streets* 172 They watched the green *twenty-eight* parrots, and the gaily coloured *galahs.*

twicer.
1. *Obs.* One who has been convicted of a criminal offence twice.

1856 *Moreton Bay Free Press* 28 Apr. 3/5 He was at once despatched on board a steamer for the Hunter, in company with a female who has by marriage, since, changed her name and by two 'twicers' from Norfolk Island, who were to put the man out of the way and pay themselves.

2. *transf.* [Used elsewhere but recorded earliest in Aust.: see OEDS 3.] One who engages in double-dealing.

1879 *Truth* (Sydney) 24 Oct. 4/4, I .. cannot fail to observe the evil intention lurking beneath that stamps the writer as the *twicer* he is. **1966** D. NILAND *Pairs & Loners* 68 She was no good, anyway; putting over her people like that, the twicer.

twining fringed lily: see FRINGED LILY.

twitch-stick. [f. Br. dial. *twitch* to draw tight: see OED v.¹ 6.] A forked stick used to tighten a securing rope: see quot. 1908.

1901 *Proc. Linnean Soc. N.S.W.* XXVI. 330 *E[ucalytus] viridis*. . . Over the Macquarie and Lachlan country it is the most eastern of all the Mallees, and in approaching its habitat its presence is often indicated by the fact that the straight tough stems of these little trees may be seen on the carrier's wagons, where they are used as 'twitch sticks' to tighten the ropes which fasten the loads. **1908** W.H. OGILVIE *My Life in Open* 50 Powerful ropes—as thick as a man's wrist—are used, and the system by which they are drawn tight is that of 'twitch sticks'. A rope is slung loosely round the second tier of bales and held in position from below by men holding the forked sticks. The teamster then inserts a short, strong twitch stick into the looped slack of the rope, and turning it over and over draws the rope tighter. . . Then he lays the stick level along the rope, and with strong twine binds stick and rope together.

two-bob, *a.* and *n.*

A. *adj.*

1. Cheap; of little consequence.

1944 L. GLASSOP *We were Rats* 144 Bert was more the 'two-bob lair' type. **1984** *Nat. Times* (Sydney) 23 Mar. 31/1 Curtis used to be a two-bob revolutionary, wearing a North Vietnam badge on his school uniform and clutching Martin Sharp's Oz.

2. a. In the phr. **silly** (or **mad**) **as a two-bob watch,** unpredictable; very silly.

1954 P. GLADWIN *Long Beat Home* 72 There now, I clean forgot. I'm getting silly as a two-bob watch. **1985** N. MEDCALF *Rifleman* 112 You're as mad as a two-bob watch!

b. In the phr. **to go off like a two-bob watch:** (of a woman) to be sexually very responsive.

1971 B. HUMPHRIES *Bazza pulls it Off*, I reckon she would have dropped her harolds and gone off like a two bob watch at the first Pom to have a Captain Cook at her bloody norks! **1976** J. JOHNSON *Low Breed* 231 Good fucks these educated birds, they went off like two bob watches!

B. *n.*

1. In the phr. **two-bob-in,** a collection to which subscriber donates two shillings (see BOB-IN).

1934 T. WOOD *Cobbers* 218 Experts who began the day with 'two-bob-in'. This means that everybody put a florin into a hat and the money went to him who caught the first fish: sharks barred. (A well-established custom. On the Day of Judgement all the Australians present will have two-bob-in for the first man who gets past Peter.) **1954** T. RONAN *Vision Splendid* 117 Bridge or poker at night with 'wet' two-bob-ins after every couple of hands.

2. In the phr. **to have two-bob each way,** to arrange one's affairs so that one cannot lose, to 'hedge one's bets'; also **two-bob each way** as *adj. phr.*, uncommitted.

1967 C.W. WILLIAMS *Yellow, Green & Red* 239 Some of the Queensland Trade-Hallers in their 'wishy-washy' 2-bob each way, attitude. **1984** *Age* (Melbourne) 16 July 12/7 Mr Hawke has gone down in my estimation also, he seems to want two bob each way on this one.

two kilometre law. *N.T.* A law prohibiting the consumption of alcoholic liquor out of doors within 2 km. of licensed premises: see quot. 1985.

1982 *Weekend Austral.* (Sydney) 28 Aug. 13/5 It is known throughout the Territory as the two kilometre law, and it is due to come into force at the end of the month. **1985** *Canberra Times* 17 Dec. 11/2 The Northern Territory Government's 'two-kilometre law', established several years ago prohibits Aborigines from drinking in public places, such as the Todd River bed, because it is within two kilometres of licenced liquor outlets.

two ones: see ONES.

two pot screamer: see SCREAMER.

two-rail fence. A fence having two horizontal members. Also **two-railed fence,** and *ellipt.* as **two-rail.**

1840 *Port Phillip Gaz.* 5 Sept. 6 The whole of it is fenced in with a substantial two-rail fence. **1844** *Sydney Morning Herald* 8 Apr. 1/5 Fenced in with a two-railed fence. **1900** H. LAWSON *Over Sliprails* 95 There was .. a thin 'two-rail' (dignified with the adjective 'split-rail'—though rails and posts were mostly of saplings split in halves) running along the frontage.

two-up, *n.* and *attrib.*

A. *n.* A gambling game in which two coins are tossed in the air and bets laid as to whether both will fall heads or tails uppermost; SWY 2. Also **two-up game.**

1884 *Adelaide Observer* 4 Oct. 30/4 Since his arrival the Sergeant has incarcerated one bibulous visitor for mulcting a publican .. and just lately gave another individual a 'Barcoo start' in consequence of an irrepressible predilection for the game known as 'two up'. **1954** J. CLEARY *Climate of Courage* 152 They're just starting a two-up game down at the back of the kitchens.

B. 1. *attrib.*

1886 *Austral. Town & Country Jrnl.* (Sydney) 3 July 23/2 The other class, as described by your contributor 'A. Sullivan', as 'two-up men', should be culled as soon as discovered. **1980** M. WILLIAMS *Dingo!* 13, I got a job being the cockatoo for the two-up players, watching out for coppers.

2. Special Comb. **two-up king,** a successful promoter of two-up games; **kip,** KIP; **ring,** see RING n.² 1; **school,** a group of persons who have assembled to play two-up; the place where such an assemblage is regularly held (see also SCHOOL 3).

c **1930** 'N. GHURKA' *Graft* 12 Henry Stokes, Melbourne's erstwhile **two-up king,** originally rented the premises. **1922** *Sydney Morning Herald* 1 July 17/6 Binghi is an expert with a **two-up kip.** He seems to 'swing' only with his wrist, instead of with his whole arm, and he is able to make the coins spin faster and cleaner than most white men. **1897** *Worker* (Sydney) 18 Dec. 3/4 The town's **'two-up' school** met and duly opened 'biz' in the backyard of 'The Traveller's Rest Hotel'. **1973** D. FOSTER *North South West* 22, I showed her where all the two-up schools and sly grog shops were.

Hence **two-uppian** *a.*, of or pertaining to the game of two-up.

1916 *Truth* (Sydney) 19 Mar. 1/8 The *twouppian* era. I love to look on a scene like this Of wild and careless play.

two-upper. One who plays the game of two-up.

1905 *Truth* (Sydney) 11 June 1/3 The 'two-upper' spins and reaps, yet the Holy Joes don't consider him an ideal citizen. **1955** N. PULLIAM *I traveled Lonely Land* 76 The cockie okays or rejects the credentials of the players—the two-uppers—and you've got to be vouched for 'absolutely' before you can get in.

two ups, in: see UP *n.*

tyke. Also **tike**. [Prob. alteration of *Teague* a nickname for an Irishman, perh. infl. by Br. dial. *tike* churlish fellow (see EDD *sb.*[1] 2).] A Roman Catholic. Also *attrib.*

1902 *Truth* (Sydney) 27 Apr. 8/1 The 'Tike's concerts', was the usual manner among the Wesleyan class of referring to Amy Castles' season here. **1983** P. WHITE *Netherwood* 21 Don't want ter listen to any of yer tyke arguments.

Hence **tykery** *n.*, a Roman Catholic school.

1963 K. COOK *Stormalong* 84 'An old boy of St. Ignatius College, Boroen'... 'That's a tykery, isn't it?'

tyri, var. TOWRI.

Tyson. The name of James *Tyson* (1819–1898), rural land-holder, used allusively as the type of richness, parsimony, or enterprise.

1877 L.T. HERGENHAN *Colonial City* (1972) 387 When the stranger hears that the magnificent and park-like lands through which he drives are the property of 'Scabby Moffatt', 'Hungry-man Tyson', and 'Pig-pig Carter', he is apt to understand why a witty barrister called the squattocracy of the colonies the wealthy lower orders. **1928** A. WRIGHT *Good Recovery* 8 Th'old bloke's as rich as Tyson. **1950** *Coast to Coast 1949–50* 190 No more bunging a job in at a minute's notice and walking off with a billycan and a roll of blankets, as independent as Tyson.

U

uey /'juɪ/. Also **uy, youee**. [f. U(-turn + -Y.] A U-turn. Also *fig.*, and *attrib*.

1973 F. MOORHOUSE *Austral. Stories* 58 Before they'd done the Uey, he'd brushed his hair back, lit a Rothman's and had the window down and his arm in place. 1973 R.D. JONES *Mad Vibe* 28 You describe the quiet sunday when you caught a bus home in sunlight warmth and almost rural day but actually is [*sic*] suspect you of chucking a Uy. 1976 *Bulletin* (Sydney) 28 Feb. 27/3 Ted Heath, like Fraser, began as a professed opponent of big government but was soon 'doing a youee' (U-turn) all over the place. 1983 *Truckin' Life* VI. xi. 70 The turning circle is 15.2 m. (49.8 ft.). Not natural U-ey material but adequate for a six tonner.

ugari /'jugəri/. *Qld*. Also **eugari, yugari**. [a. Yagara *yugari*.] PIPI. Also *attrib*.

1917 *Bulletin* (Sydney) 16 Aug. 22/4 The shell-fish *Donax deltoideus*, commonly called 'ugari' in Southern Queensland, seem gifted with intellect or reasoning powers. 1941 H.D.A. JOSKE *Life to Live* 29, I did learn the art of collecting pippies, which I found later were called in Queensland by their native name of eugaries. 1980 T.A. ROY *Vengeance of Dolphin* 144 There was the inner core ready to eat with the wallaby, the baked fish, big pearl shell oysters in their shells, and yugari shell-fish.

ugly Australian. [Prob. following *ugly American*: see OEDS *ugly, a*. 4 b.] OCKER n. 2. Also *attrib*.

1971 *Bulletin* (Sydney) 8 May 32/1 There was an 'Ugly Australian' parallel during the Cook Bi-Centennial celebrations last year, when attention was paid to Australia's responsibilities in the Pacific. 1980 *Southerly* ii. 146 Our Ugly Australian, our professional Ocker, had boasted he'd brought forty pounds of *proper* food from Hong Kong 'ter see me through'.

Ulysses butterfly. [See quot. 1911.] The large swallowtail butterfly *Papilio ulysses joesa* of n. Qld. and elsewhere, having brilliant metallic blue, black-bordered wings. Also *ellipt*. as **Ulysses**.

1911 E.J. BANFIELD *My Tropic Isle* 106 The great high-flying Ulysses, first observed in Australia on this very island over half a century ago. It was but a passing gleam, for the visiting scientist lamented that it flew so high over the treetops that he failed to obtain the specimen. True to name, the Ulysses still flies high and wide—a lustrous royal blue with black trimmings and dandified tails to his wings that answer the dual purpose of use and ornament. 1985 *Melbourne Winners Weekly* 16 Dec. 4/1 A waterfall tumbles into a little terraced valley so that visitors look down from an aerial walk for a different view of the .. glorious turquois Ulysses butterflies. The Ulysses are being sponsored by Dunk Isle resort, of which they are the emblem.

umbrella. Used *attrib*. in the names of plants having some resemblance to an open umbrella: **umbrella fern**, any of several ferns of the fam. Gleicheniaceae, esp. *Sticherus flabellatus* of e. Aust. and elsewhere; **grass**, any of several grasses (fam. Poaceae), esp. perennials of the pantropical genus *Digitaria*, and *Panicum decompositum* (see *native millet* NATIVE *a*. 6 a.); **tree**, the tree *Schefflera actinophylla* (fam. Araliaceae) of Qld. and N.T., cultivated as an ornamental and an indoor plant; a similar plant (see quot. 1970).

1898 E.E. MORRIS *Austral Eng*. 143 **Umbrella F[ern]**, Tasmanian name for Fan F[ern, *Gleichenia flabellata*.] 1883 E. PALMER *Plants N. Qld*. 10 *Panicum decompositum*... The 'umbrella' grass; grows on all western country with a fine branching seed-head and broad leaves. 1870 E.B. KENNEDY *Four Yrs. in Qld*. 141 The **umbrella-tree**, with its large dark shiny leaves, of which there are usually five growing at the end of each stalk, and surmounted by its crimson flowers, forming brilliant stars, each red spray being fifteen inches long. 1970 W.D. FRANCIS *Austral. Rain-Forest Trees* (ed. 3) 344 *Polyscias murrayi*... Sometimes called Umbrella tree.

ump: see UMPY.

umpty-doo, *a*. Also **humpty-doo**. [Prob. joc. formation on *Humpty-Dumpty*.] **a**. Intoxicated. **b**. Topsy-turvy.

1911 *Bulletin* (Sydney) 12 Oct. 14/2 Who ever hears.. of a man being 'drunk'? .. The words supplied by individual fancy, such as 'skew-whiff', 'umpty-doo', etc., who would undertake to number them? 1955 F. LANE *Patrol to Kimberleys* 105 Still, there are some queer animals in Australia. Take the platypus. That's the humptydoo cove what had all the professors scratchin' their heads when they first saw him.

umpy. Chiefly *Australian National Football*. [f. *ump(ire* + -Y.] An umpire. Also **ump**.

1963 *Footy Fan* (Melbourne) I. vii. 22 That case was summarily dismissed, much to the chagrin of the boundary 'ump' who vowed he would never again report a player. 1981 *Sun-Herald* (Sydney) 18 Jan. 63/2 The ball was going so far down the leg side Howarth must have thought someone had moved the stumps when he saw the umpy's finger go up.

underground mutton: see MUTTON 2.

underground orchid. Either of two completely subterranean saprophytic orchids (fam. Orchidaceae), *Rhizanthella gardneri* of s.w. W.A. and *R. slateri* of e. Aust. Also **subterranean orchid**.

1968 C.A. GARDNER *Wildflowers W.A*. 16 The subterranean orchid .. has a lily-like inflorescence with crowded, dark coloured flowers in the base of its tube. 1985 *Canberra Times* 12 Nov. 1/3 Australia has the only two underground orchids in the world, and there is intense interest in their evolution and biology.

underscrub: see SCRUB *n*. 2 b.

undress, *v*. [Joc. use of *undress* to divest of clothes.] *trans*. To shear (a sheep).

1927 *Bulletin* (Sydney) 20 Jan. 24/2 At Wondong station, in seven and a half hours, 2472 jumbucks were undressed. 1984 W.W. AMMON et al. *Working Lives* 155 In it were five shearers, all full of whisky... They had been knocking down several cheques .. and were heading up to Byro Station .. to 'undress the woollies'.

unfinancial, *a*. Insolvent. See also FINANCIAL.

1891 *Bulletin* (Sydney) 26 Dec. 14/1 The present 'unfinancial' condition of one or two titled Southern citizens is a miserable satire upon the 'handles' they wear. 1935 N. HUNT *House of David* 129 The continuance of the 'bad' year .. had from the first been compelling the 'weak'—unfinancial—men to send their stock regardless of condition or prices to the markets to 'lighten off'.

uni /'juni/. Abbrev. of 'university'. Also *attrib*.

1898 *Bulletin* (Sydney) 17 Dec. (Red Page), The only

UNION UP

classical idioms I have found . . are *rotter*, i.e., an adept in learning anything; and *panem agere*, Sydney Uni. slang for 'doing a loaf'. **1984** *Austral.* (Sydney) 29 Aug. 17/1 (*heading*) Unis look to industry for more funds.

union. *Hist.* [Shortened form of *trade union*.] Used *attrib.* in Special Comb. **union camp**, STRIKE CAMP; **cut**, a shearing job for which the rate of pay is in accord with union scales; **tucker**, food provided for the inhabitants of a strike camp.
1889 *Braidwood Dispatch* 28 Aug. 2/4 Although all approaches to the station are blocked by **union camps**, work is still proceeding under the shed rules. **1899** *Bulletin* (Sydney) 19 Aug. 32/2 The mates again battled out across the whitening plains in search of a '**Union cut**'. **1896** *Worker* (Sydney) 5 Sept. 3/3 Buttabone camp has broken up, and a great number of the members of it, who ate good **Union tucker**, turned dog and went into the Buttabone shed at the reduced price.

Union Jack. [Of unknown origin.] A cicada; formerly applied to the large black and orange *Macrotristria angularis* of e. Aust., and later to the *double drummer* (see DOUBLE *a*. 2).
1895 *Proc. Linnean Soc. N.S.W.* X. 529 Macrouistria [sic] angularis . . ('The Union Jack') . . . This Cicada does not appear about Sydney every year, but during this last season it was comparatively numerous. **1965** *Austral. Encycl.* II. 380 The double drummer (*Thopa saccata*) is a large black and orange insect remarkable for its swollen tympana; it is sometimes known as the Union Jack.

unit. [Spec. use of *unit* accommodation unit in a larger building or group of buildings: see OEDS *sb*. 2 f.] Abbrev. of *home-unit* (see HOME *n*.² 2).
1949 *Sydney Morning Herald* 3 May 11/4 Flatettes, Paddington. 5 fullfurn. units in exc. condition. Beaut home and profits. **1980** *Westerly* iii. 31 After returning to her unit, she switched the electricity off, wrote a note to me and her past lover, walked into the middle of the busy street, and was mown down immediately by a milk truck.

unity ticket. In a (trade-union) election: an alliance of candidates, of differing political or ideological persuasion, united for electoral advantage (see esp. quot. 1980).
1961 *Bulletin* (Sydney) 15 Feb. 11/2 In these days of frequent unity-tickets between the Communist party and A.L.P. members it is unusual to discover that any State A.L.P. branch recognises the position. **1980** *Dict. Austral. Politics* 276 *Unity tickets*, how-to-vote cards issued for trade union elections on which the names of *Communist Party* candidates appeared jointly with those of ALP members.

unlocated, *ppl. a. Hist.*
1. Of land: not allocated to a settler. See LOCATED.
1821 *Sydney Gaz.* 20 Jan., At the back of the Land is an extensive range of hills unlocated, capable of maintaining a numerous herd of cattle, exclusive of the run on the Farm. **1846** *Portland Gaz.* 16 Oct. 3/3 The settlers pushing down the Macintyre have joined issue with those pushing up the Barwin, and there is now no unlocated country betwixt them.
2. In the collocation **unlocated grant** (or **order**), an entitlement to the choice of a specified area of unidentified land (see LOCATE *v*. 1).
1823 *Hobart Town Gaz.* 4 Oct., To be Exchanged for an Unlocated Grant, a Farm of 700 acres. **1840** *Tasmanian Weekly Dispatch* (Hobart) 19 June 2/1 For Sale, an unlocated order for One Thousand and Seventy Acres of Land.

unlock, *v. Hist.* In the phr. **to unlock the land**, to release for occupation by small farmers Crown land already leased as grazing land; also in the imperative, as a political slogan. See also LOCK.

1855 *Ovens & Murray Advertiser* (Beechworth) 3 Mar. (Suppl.) 5/3 *Unlock the lands*—It is gratifying to find that the Government has at length seen the necessity for throwing open the lands in the vicinity of the gold fields for farming and agricultural purposes. . . The Government surveyor, is now employed in laying out farms in the neighbourhood of the Three-mile Creek, which . . will vary in extent from 10 to 50 acres. **1886** 'THIRTY-FIVE YRS. COLONIST' *Hard Times* 5 For upwards of thirty years past, there has always been an outcry to unlock the land.

unmade, *ppl. a.* In the collocation **unmade road**, a vehicular way which has been cleared of vegetation but not formed. See MADE 1.
1857 W. WESTGARTH *Vic. & Austral. Gold Mines* 197 We had now the unmade or bush road to put up with. **1920** *Smith's Weekly* (Sydney) 13 Nov. 17/5, I lived for years on an unmade road, where bullockies passed each day.

unoccupied, *ppl. a.* Of land: not taken up by a settler or settlers.
1803 S. MACARTHUR ONSLOW *Some Early Rec. Macarthurs* (1914) 71 Permission to occupy a sufficient Track of unoccupied Lands to feed his flocks. **1862** C. MUNRO *Fern Vale* I. 4 You say the country is quite unoccupied: will not the natives be dreadfully wild.

unsettled, *ppl. a. Hist.*
a. Orig. used to designate Crown land which was inalienable; (loosely) unpopulated, or very sparsely populated, other than by Aborigines. See SETTLED 1.
1842 *Penny Mag.* (London) Jan. 2/1 Agricultural and pastoral pursuits are carried on in the 'bush', that is in the unsettled parts of the district. **1961** M. KIDDLE *Men of Yesterday* 63 It was impossible to prevent scabbed sheep being moved through unsettled country.
b. *spec.* In collocations: **unsettled district, land**.
1844 *Colonial Times* (Hobart) 23 Jan., In the **unsettled districts**, free persons attached to the Convict Establishments . . are to be supplied by the Contractors with Rations. **1845** *Atlas* (Sydney) I. 241/1 'All went merry as a marriage bell' whilst, in the natural order of things, convict labour was employed in preparing hitherto **unsettled lands** for settlement and sale.

unshingle, *v. Obs.* [f. *shingle* house-tile.] *trans.* To knock a hat from a person. Usu. as *ppl. a.* and *vbl. n.*
1827 *Hobart Town Courier* 10 Nov. 3/2 A man is said to be well shingled when he has a new English hat upon his head, worth 50s. and when the person that remarks it runs up behind him in the evening and carries off his hat, the bare-headed gentleman is said to be *unshingled*. **1857** D. BUNCE *Australasiatic Reminisc.* 58 The system of *unshingling*, or taking a hat from the traveller's head in the darkness of night, during his wanderings through the streets, did not fall to our lot to experience.

up, *n.* In the phr. **in two ups**, 'in two shakes', in a trice.
1934 T. WOOD *Cobbers* 25 He said we'd be there in two ups. **1968** S. GORE *Holy Smoke* 52 They go to the pack straight orf. And in about two ups they're all slingin' their stuff overboard and callin' on their gods 'n' that.

up, *adv.*
a. In the phr. **up the country**, away from a centre of population; into the interior of the country. Also as quasi-*n.*
1805 J. GRANT *Let.* 28 Apr., Cap^n Bishop . . resided upon Prospect-Hill 20 miles up the Country. **1896** H. LAWSON *In Days when World was Wide* 156 You'll admit that Up-the-Country, more especially in drought, Isn't quite the Eldorado that the poets rave about.
b. Also as **up (in, to) (the) bush** (or **mulga**).

1840 A. RUSSELL *Tour through Austral. Colonies* 86 When up in the bush, we met several females employed in chopping wood with axes. 1857 'RETURNED DIGGER' *Six Yrs. in Aust.* 21 Even carters, up the bush, get £2 a week. 1867 'CLERGYMAN' *Aust. as it Is* 272 The merchants of Sydney know well that bad goods, bad everything, are sent up to the bush. 1876 'RESIDENT' *Girl Life in Aust.* 137 Grandpapa had a station up bush. 1968 S. GORE *Holy Smoke* 58 'Man ought to get his head seen to,' he said moodily. 'Stuck up here in the mulga, when he could be earning good money down in the city.'

c. Ellipt. for *up the country*.

1852 J. BONWICK *Notes of Gold Digger* 4 Tools are dearer up than in town. 1965 G. McINNES *Road to Gundagai* 248 Though he might speak *de haut en bas* to a young fellow 'up from town' or to one of his social equals whom he happened to dislike, he was on terms of free and easy yet dignified familiarity with the stockmen and the boundary riders and even with the itinerant shearers.

d. *transf.* With reference to specific locations.

1884 *Austral. Tit-Bits* (Melbourne) 26 June 13/3 Decency is at a discount with certain folks up Shields way. 1980 M. WILLIAMS *Dingo!* 45 Dad sat up the back yard talking to himself.

e. *spec.* In the phr. **up east**, along the coast of W.A., north and east of Broome.

1913 *Cwlth. Parl. Papers* III. 739 Yes, from Broome is .. 80 miles to the 90-mile beach. We used to go up east for eight or nine months at a time. 1940 E. HILL *Great Austral. Loneliness* (ed. 2) 242 You hire an old lugger at Broome for £1 a month .. and set out for where you fancy 'up east'.

up-country, *a., adv.,* and *n.* [Used elsewhere (though rarely in Brit.) but of local significance: see OED(S.)]

A. 1. *adj.* Situated in, belonging or relating to, etc., country which is inland and away from a major centre of population.

1816 [see *up-country settler*, sense 2 below]. 1826 *Austral.* (Sydney) 5 Jan. 2/4 Many Up-country people are in want of assigned servants. 1980 A.S. VEITCH *Run from Morning* 22 I'd hate to count the number of times I've had to sit behind an Austral Felix semi-trailer on an up country road!

2. In collocations: **up-country mail, settler, station, town, township.**

1855 *Bell's Life in Sydney* 12 May 3/2 The whole of the **up-country mails.** 1816 *Hobart Town Gaz.* 7 Sept., The Black Natives of this Colony have for the last few weeks manifested a stronger Hostility towards the **Up-Country Settlers.** 1845 C.J. BAKER *Sydney & Melbourne* 31 Change of air and scene may be obtained by visiting the **up-country station** of some friend. 1896 N. GOULD *Town & Bush* 224 The amateur bookmaker resides in the **up-country town** near which the picnic races take place. 1871 *Austral. Town & Country Jrnl.* (Sydney) 1 Apr. 390/2 The various **up-country townships** in Victoria signalized the day fixed for the marriage of the Princess Louise .. by liberal displays of bunting.

B. *adv.* In or to country which is inland and away from a major centre of population.

1854 MRS C. CLACY *Lights & Shadows* I. 39 It was some one going up country and lost their track. 1882 J. SCHLEMAN *Life in Melbourne* 16 The cry for workmen up country was as earnest when I left as when I landed.

C. *n.* Country which is inland and away from a major centre of population.

1872 G.S. BADEN-POWELL *New Homes for Old Country* 374 The rivers of the up-country .. are mere long chains of water-holes. 1978 G. HALL *River still Flows* 16 We come from up country, we come from out back, The homestead, the hut and the wallaby-track, We come from the land where the riders are made, And we're all of us mates in the Bushman's Brigade.

uphill, *a.* [Transf. use of *uphill* presenting difficulties.] Hard-pressed.

1945 T. RONAN *Strangers on Ophir* 184 Peter'll be a bit uphill getting Luke out of the cooler, won't he? 1978 *Sun-Herald* (Sydney) 15 Jan. 44/3 The Opposition .. will be uphill in persuading the voters to reject this opportunity to have the Council democratically elected.

up-jump. [f. *jumped-up* newly risen in status, arrogant.] An upstart; also as a general term of abuse. Also *attrib.*

1919 W.H. DOWNING *Digger Dialects* 51 *Upjump*, upstart; interloper. 1968 D. O'GRADY *Bottle of Sandwiches* 89 Bloody rotten up-jump never-come-down .. rotten mongrel bloody stinkin' flamin' mongrel bloody bastard.

Hence **up-jumped** *a.*, upstart; disagreeable.

1938 X. HERBERT *Capricornia* (1939) 285 He told Frank that .. he was considered too superior to associate with an up-jumped yeller-feller.

upter, *a.* Also **upta,** and formerly **up to.** [Abbrev. of *up to putty* (see PUTTY).] Bad; hopeless; no good.

1918 C.L. HARTT *Diggerettes* 19 With four hours to go and a booze-inflated headpiece, the outlook was 'up to'. 1919 W.H. DOWNING *Digger Dialects* 52 *Upter*, a corruption of 'Up to Putty'. 1947 J. CLEARY *You can't see round Corners* 167 'How you going?' 'Upta. I've lost on every race so far.'

upya. Alteration of 'up you!', an exclamation of contemptuous rejection.

1941 S.J. BAKER *Pop. Dict. Austral. Slang* 79 *Upya!*, a contemptuous ejaculation. 1955 D. NILAND *Shiralee* 101 No, he said, I won't truckle to you. Upya for the rent.

urger.

1. One who gives (unsolicited) tips at a race meeting; a tipster: see quot. 1958.

1919 V. MARSHALL *World of Living Dead* 69 The truly light-fingered gentry, the racecourse urger (tipslinger), the magsman .. never hesitate to express their contempt for the more roughly inclined of the profession. 1958 F. HARDY *Four-Legged Lottery* 175 That's old 'Don't tell a soul', the urger. He gives you a tip and then persuades you to put a few quid on it for him. Gives a different horse to every victim.

2. *transf.* One who takes advantage of others; a petty racketeer.

1943 *Troppo Tribune* (Mataranka) 25 July 2 Who is the bloke from No. 1 earning the reputation of being an urger? 1983 STURGESS & BIRNBAUER *Journalist who Laughed* 79 Clancy was a free enterprise man. He thought all unionists were urgers.

uro, var. EURO.

useful. A general factotum, esp. in a public house. Formerly also **general useful, generally useful.**

1891 *Bulletin* (Sydney) 4 Apr. 15/1 A 'billiard-marker and generally useful', engaged by a Macalister River .. hotel-keeper .. arose early on the morning after his arrival and proceeded to energetically scrub-brush the billiard-table with hot soap-and-water. 1907 W.R.O. HILL *Forty-Five Yrs. Experience N. Qld.* 30, I had a young fellow named Jack Hoare working for me as a 'general useful'. 1972 *Kings Cross Whisper* (Sydney) cxxxviii. 2/3 Bertram Baits .. for some times was engaged as useful at the pub.

ute /jut/. Also **ut.** Abbrev. of UTILITY.

1943 *Troppo Tribune* (Mataranka) 8 Feb. 4 Drives round in his ute Now isn't that cute? 1944 S. KELLEN *Camp Happy* 11, I drove the 'ut' among narrow, dangerous curves.

utility. A small truck, having a cab and a tray used for carrying light loads: see quot. 1985. Also **utility truck.**

1935 K.L. Smith *Sky Pilot Arnhem Land* 96 In 1931 an old T-model Ford was converted into a utility truck and pressed into service. **1985** *Overlander* Aug. 38 Australia developed the ute. For lore has it that in 1933/34 it produced the world's first utility—a 'coupé utility'—in response to a farmer's wife bewailing the fact that no-one produced a vehicle suitable for work during the week that would double to go to church on Sunday.

uy, var. Uey.

V

vag, *n.* and *a.* [U.S., abbrev. of *vagrant* or *vagrancy*: see OEDS.]

A. *n.*

1. A vagrant.

1888 J. FREEMAN *Lights & Shadows Melbourne Life* 100 A few 'vags' of all ages and both sexes, who have just left the holes and corners where they have passed the night, prowl about the carts and stalls. **1979** M. RUTHERFORD *Departmental* 69 The vag waited but the policeman just walked past him to a car.

2. **a.** Vagrancy, esp. in the phr. **on** (or **under**) **the vag**, on a charge of vagrancy. Also *attrib.*

1877 *Vagabond Ann.* 58 Many young larrikins are brought up 'on the vag'. **1891** *Truth* (Sydney) 10 May 3/3 The young victim of a constable's malevolence was charged 'under the vag.', with having no visible lawful means of support. **1919** V. MARSHALL *World of Living Dead* 12 Three charges agin' me—righteous, vag, an' resisting. **1937** WISBERG & WATERS *Bushman at Large* 87 You'll be up before the beak for an on-the-vag charge.

b. A charge of vagrancy; imprisonment as the result of such a charge.

1896 *Bulletin* (Sydney) 11 Apr. 17/4 A layer and a backer were run in at a Perth (W.A.) rural meeting, though everybody else was betting all day... Under W.A.'s precious law if they again offend they are liable to 12 months 'vag'. **1936** *Red Star* (Perth) 7 Feb. 1/1 Destitute men camping round Kalgoorlie are hunted away on threat of the 'vag'.

B. *adj.* Vagrant.

1963 *N.T. News* (Darwin) 3 Jan. 10/5 They asked me if I was working and I said no .. then the copper said 'you're vag' and they arrested me.

vag, *v.* [U.S.; f. prec.] *trans.* To arrest (a person) for vagrancy. Freq. in *pass.*

1903 *Truth* (Sydney) 22 Feb. 3/2 (heading) Two University Park sirens vagged, and sent to Bieola. **1984** P. READ *Down there with me on Cowra Mission* 57, I walked into town .. and I got vagged... Got ten days out of it.

values, *pl. Mining.* [Also U.S.] Payable quantities of a mineral. In the phr. **to make values**, to yield such quantities. See also MAKE *v.*¹ b.

1911 E.D. CLELAND *W. Austral. Mining Practice* 14 Occasionally values are found along the fault-lines .. but as a general rule, values are not found in appreciable quantity along the fault-lines. **1939** I.L. IDRIESS *Cyaniding for Gold* 184 You may locate such an outcrop. Sink on it, for gossan often 'makes' values at shallow depth. **1948** K.S. PRICHARD *Golden Miles* 93 'I'll get a couple of 'toms' for her, Ted,' Abel exclaimed affably. 'Now y're showin' values she's worth shorin' up.'

Vandemonia. *Hist.* [f. *Van Diem(en's Land*, the name given to Tasmania by its discoverer Abel Tasman in 1642, in honour of Anthony *Van Diemen* (1593–1645), governor of the Dutch East Indies + *demon* + *-ia*.] A name for Tasmania, esp. as a penal colony.

1838 *Cornwall Chron.* (Launceston) 15 Sept. 1 Was Vandemonia formed but to propagate the convict's foul breath? **1903** *Truth* (Sydney) 1 Mar. 1/6 One-sided summings up .. may please the social vampires and political pirates of Vandemonia.

Vandemonian, *n.* and *a. Hist.* Also **Vandiemenian**, **Vandiemonian**. [f. prec.]

A. *n.*

a. A non-Aboriginal person native to or resident in Tasmania. Formerly also **Vandiemener.**

1828 *Hobart Town Courier* 12 July 2 You have frequently expressed yourself interested much in us Van Diemeners. **1832** *Sydney Herald* 9 Apr. 2/3 We perceive that the Vandiemonians are not less in raptures than the Sydneyites. **1839** *Port Phillip Patriot* 24 Apr. 4 Would not a standing committee be useful in our rising Capital? Could we not meet in such a committee, not as Vandemonians, or Sydneyites, but as Australia Felixians?

b. A convict who has served a sentence in Tasmania.

1847 *Port Phillip Herald* 12 Jan. 2/5 The Van Diemonians are, it appears, resolved to go to work at last, as no less than two gross robberies, accompanied by violence, were committed in the town of Melbourne on the night of Friday last. **1865** 'SPECIAL CORRESPONDENT' *Transportation* 55 The free colonies plead that the Vandemonians by whom they have been outraged came, not as escaped convicts, but as men free in one form or another, by pardon or servitude. **1893** S. NEWLAND *Paving Way* 235 'An old lag', 'a Van Diemenian', he was a living reproach to the arbitrary, unjust, and iniquitous laws of his country.

B. *adj.*

a. Of, belonging to, or inhabiting Tasmania.

1832 *Currency Lad* (Sydney) 25 Aug. 2 The unlimited admission of Vandemonian wheat. **1976** B. SCOTT *Complete Bk. Austral. Folk Lore* 15 There were American sealers harvesting the islands in Bass Strait and to the south of New Zealand along with their Currency and Vandiemonian cousins.

b. *spec.* Of or pertaining to Tasmania as a penal colony or to one who has served a sentence of transportation there.

1847 L. FROST *No Place for Nervous Lady* (1984) 175 Nearly all the men about this part are old Vandemonian convicts and a notable set they are, but I trust their days of extortion and impudence are nearly over. **1961** M. KIDDLE *Men of Yesterday* 26 The corrupting processes of the British and Vandiemonian penal systems.

Van Diemen's Lander. *Obs.*

1. An Aboriginal native to Tasmania.

1825 B. FIELD *Geogr. Mem. N.S.W.* 207 The difference between the New Hollander and the Van Diemen's-lander is slight in the skull.

2. A non-Aboriginal person native to or resident in Tasmania.

1888 *Sydney Morning Herald* 24 Jan. (Centennial Suppl.) 2/3 Tasmania runs so smoothly in all its forms that if the people owning it have little interest in the discoverer from whom they received the name, they ought at least to be grateful for their escape from being Dutched 'Van Diemenslanders'.

Vandy, *n.* and *a. Obs.*

A. *n.* Abbrev. of VANDEMONIAN *n.* b.

1858 'A. PENDRAGON' *Queen of South* 80 Tacks, abashed at this attack, ventured, in a low tone, to mutter something about strangers, and 'sticking-up' and 'Vandies'. **1873** W. THOMSON-GREGG *Desperate Character* I. 181 Jones started when he heard the Irishman speak of 'Vandies' .. and .. perceived three rough-looking fellows.

B. *adj.* Abbrev. of VANDEMONIAN *adj.* a.

1896 *Bulletin* (Sydney) 29 Feb. 25/2 Vandy girls are quick!

varando, var. VERANDAH.

varied lorikeet. The lorikeet *Psitteuteles versicolor*, a red-capped bird with green, yellow, and pink plumage, occurring in woodlands and forests of n. Aust.

1842 J. GOULD *Birds of Aust.* (1848) V. Pl. 51, *Trichoglossus versicolor*.. Varied Lorikeet.. *Wē-ro-ole*, Aborigines of Port Essington. **1964** M. SHARLAND *Territory of Birds* 37 The Varied Lorikeet, another bushland inhabitant, was in big flocks.

variegated wren. The small bird *Malurus lamberti lamberti* of the e. slopes of the central part of the Great Dividing Range; more generally, any bird of the widespread species *M. lamberti*; LAMBERT'S WREN. Also **variegated fairy wren**, and formerly **variegated warbler**.

1822 J.W. LEWIN *Nat. Hist. Birds N.S.W.* 15 (*caption*) Variegated Warbler.. inhabits thick brushy woods; frequents the low bushes, creeping close to the ground in search of its food. **1900** A.J. CAMPBELL *Nests & Eggs Austral. Birds* 176 The Variegated Wren is one of the few common birds of Australia of which Gould was unable to find the nest. **1984** M. BLAKERS et al. *Atlas Austral. Birds* 438 The Variegated Fairy-wren includes a high proportion of plant bugs and weevils in its diet.

vegetable John. *Hist.* A Chinese greengrocer.

1922 *Smith's Weekly* (Sydney) 15 July 17/4 My vegetable John told me that at one time he was a heavy opium smoker. **1982** N. KEESING *Lily on Dustbin* 118 The horse of the Chinese 'vegetable John' pulled a distinctive open cart covered by a brown awning.

velvet. Abbrev. of *black velvet* (see BLACK *a.*¹ 6).

1956 T. RONAN *Moleskin Midas* 106 This bitchin' country is going to the dogs. You got to pay so much for a bit of velvet that it'd be nearly as cheap to get married.

verandah, *n.* and *attrib.* Also **veranda** and formerly **varando, viranda**. [Used elsewhere of similar structures but important because of its frequency in Aust.: see OED(S.]

A. *n.*

1. a. An open-sided, roofed structure abutting on one or more faces of a domestic or commercial building, the main purpose of which is the provision of shelter: see quots. 1872 and 1886.

1805 *Sydney Gaz.* 17 Feb., A Varando in front, with a small room at each end. **1811** *Ibid.* 8 June, Government House was ornamented in a superior style of taste and elegance; the Viranda was arched with boughs fancifully dispersed between the colonades. **1872** MRS E. MILLETT *Austral. Parsonage* 55 A verandah, formed by the continuation of the roof itself, until its eaves came to within seven feet of the grounds. **1886** D.M. GANE *N.S.W. & Vic.* 54 The chief peculiarity.. about Australian towns in general is the verandah. Few houses are without this necessary shelter. The shops, too, in the principal thoroughfares, by means of their broad porticoes, afford the pavements a cooling atmosphere. **1943** *Coast to Coast 1942* 82 It had a wide veranda round three sides of it like a squatter's.

b. *spec.* Such a structure abutting a commercial building as a place where business is customarily transacted. Freq. in the phr. **under the verandah**.

1842 *Royal S. Austral. Almanack* p. xxi (Advt.), An extensive Verandah runs round the whole of the Market Place, under which the business can be conveniently transacted in all weathers. **1898** E.E. MORRIS *Austral Eng.* 489 Verandahs.. are an architectural feature.. of most City shops, where they render the broad side-walks an almost continuous arcade. 'Under the Verandah' has acquired the meaning, 'where city men most do congregate'.

2. Such a structure which is either partially or fully enclosed to provide additional living space.

1839 W.H. LEIGH *Reconnoitering Voyages* 120 Thermometer in the evening stood at.. 130° in the verandah. **1981** A.B. FACEY *Fortunate Life* 53 They had only a two-roomed bag hut with a small lean-to verandah built on the north side. I was to sleep in the lean-to.

3. Such a structure which is floored and used as a place for relaxation.

1843 *Teetotal Advocate* (Launceston) 17 July 2/2 One of them kept sentry on the verandah. **1979** *Westerly* ii. 33 On the hospital verandah, he talked of the parrots.

4. With distinguishing epithet, as **back verandah, front verandah, side verandah**.

1849 A. HARRIS *Emigrant Family* (1967) 404 Mary stood a little way from the **back verandah**. **1849** A. HARRIS *Emigrant Family* (1967) 402 Mary and Margaret sat in the **front verandah**. **1916** T. WARLOW *By Mirage & Mulga* 72 McInverness.. lay on a stretcher-bed made up on the **side verandah**.

B. *attrib.*

1. *Obs.* Of a building: having a verandah, as **verandah cottage, house, store**.

1819 *Hobart Town Gaz.* 16 Oct. (Suppl.), Mr W.A. Brodrebb.. has opened an Office at the Veranda House, Elizabeth Street. **1838** *Southern Austral.* (Adelaide) 30 June 2/4 *Verandah Store*, North Terrace, near the bank. *On sale.* **1870** *Sydney Morning Herald* 2 July 3/5 There is a pretty 4-room Verandah Cottage, with cellar.

2. *fig.* Of a person: inclined to direct from afar and to take no active part, 'arm chair': see quot. 1973.

1929 K.S. PRICHARD *Coonardoo* (1961) 195 Yet Hugh Watt slogged on; no verandah manager about him. **1973** H. HOLTHOUSE *S'pose I Die* 34 Paddy was what they called a 'veranda boss'—he did most of his supervising from the house.

3. Comb. **verandah post**.

1825 *Austral.* (Sydney) 21 July 2 These two rushed into the house, seized the overseer, tied his hands behind his back and then to one of the verandah posts.. and then plundered the house.

4. Special Comb. **verandah bed**, a bed in a *verandah room*; **chair**, *squatter chair*, see SQUATTER 5; **room**, a room made out of part or the whole of an enclosed verandah (see *n.* 2).

1950 G.S. CASEY *City of Men* 210 Just before lunch-time he rolled out of his **verandah bed** at his boarding-house. **1886** P. FLETCHER 'Hints to Immigrants' in P. Fletcher *Qld.* 42 Then there is the squatter's or **verandah chair**, which is very comfortable to rest and smoke in, but which takes up too much room to be used indoors. **1848** *Maitland Mercury* 10 May 2/3 About eleven o'clock, he noticed a light in the **verandah room** of Mr Ballard's inn, the door of which room was open, although no-one was in it.

Hence **verandahless** *a.*, lacking a veranda.

1910 *Bulletin* (Sydney) 7 July 44/1 One small, oblong, weather-board, bare, verandah-less 'cottage'.

vermin, *collect*. [Spec. use of *vermin, collect.* animals of a noxious or objectionable kind.] Animals which prey upon crops, etc., esp. rabbits and dingoes. Used *attrib.* and in Comb., esp. as **vermin (proof) fence**.

1905 *Bulletin* (Sydney) 2 Nov. 14/2 Queensland keeps an expensive vermin fence going on the S.A. border. **1970** P. SLATER *Eagle for Pidgin* 51 It looks as if wedgies could come off the vermin list sometime in the near future, anyway. **1972** ANDERSON & BLAKE *J.S. Neilson* 35 Concern with the increasing amount of rural depredation by the plague of rabbits caused the State Government on 2 March to declare that three vermin-proof fences would be erected in the north-west.

Victorian, *n.* and *a.* [f. the name of the State of

Victoria, officially named in 1851 after Queen Victoria, reigned 1837-1901.]

A. *n.* A non-Aboriginal person native to or resident in Victoria.

1850 *Irish Exile* (Hobart) 28 Dec. 7/2 The Port Phillipians—we beg their pardon, the Victorians—have displayed their loyalty. **1986** *Canberra Times* 3 Mar. 1/1 (*heading*) Victorian to direct Office of Status of Women.

B. *adj.* Of or pertaining to the State of Victoria or to its inhabitants.

1855 W. HOWITT *Land, Labor & Gold* II. 246 Reselling it at a truly Victorian profit. **1984** G. BLAINEY *Our Side of Country* 46 The secret ballot was introduced for the first time in the world at the elections of 1856, and in the United States it became known as 'the Victorian ballot'.

Victoria rifle-bird. [f. *Victoria,* first applied as the specific name *Victoriae* by English zoologist J. Gould (see quot. 1849) + RIFLE-BIRD.] The bird *Ptiloris victoriae* of tropical rainforest in n.e. Qld. See also BIRD OF PARADISE 2. Also **Queen Victoria rifle-bird.**

1856 H.B. STONEY *Vic.* 215 The *Ptiloris paradisea,* or rifle bird, is well known to collectors... The smaller one .. has been deemed worthy to be associated with the name of our Queen, and is known as the Victoria rifle-bird. **1980** M. GRANT *Barrier Reef* 161 There were bowerbirds like .. the Prince Albert Rifle Bird and the Queen Victoria Rifle Bird.

vigoro /ˈvɪgərəʊ/. [Prob. formed on *vigour.*] A game played by women, combining elements of baseball and cricket. Also *attrib.*

c **1930** *Laws of Vigoro* 1 The Game 'Vigoro' (a combination of Cricket and Baseball) was invented to give the world a game—simple to interpret, interesting and exciting—which would enable all to became efficient players. **1951** *Ibid.* 4 Mar. (Sports Section) 14/2 N.S.W., 56 and 10-66, beat Queensland, 59 and 62, in the women's interstate vigoro carnival yesterday.

village. *Obs.*

1. A small (rural) settlement. See also TOWNSHIP 2.
1803 J. GRANT *Narr. Voyage N.S.W.* 82 Paramatta .. is a very pretty village. **1882** *Bulletin* (Sydney) 3 June 10/1 The village of Queanbeyan has become a cock-pit.

2. A cluster of Aboriginal dwellings.
1827 P. CUNNINGHAM *Two Yrs. in N.S.W.* I. 134 A stately healthy race, easy to be civilized. Their huts form villages of forty or fifty. **1862** BACKHOUSE & TYLOR *Life & Labours G.W. Walker* 243 The Aborigines had a little village of huts made of bark.

3. Special Comb. **village reserve,** a site reserved for a small rural settlement; **settlement, (a)** VILLAGE 1; **(b)** a government-sponsored co-operative farming community; **settler,** a member of a *village settlement* (b).

1837 *Tegg's N.S.W. Pocket Almanac* 67 On its banks are grants belonging to Messrs Percy Simpson, Tingecombe, and Campbell, also a **village reserve. 1840** *S. Austral. Rec.* (London) 7 Mar. 98 A community has been formed for the purpose of purchasing a special survey of 4,160 acres, 80 acres of which will be laid out in a central situation, as a **village settlement,** and divided into 320 allotments of a quarter of an acre each. **1976** DRAGE & PAGE *Riverboats & Riverman* 12 A scheme started by the South Australian Government to help the unemployed. Over a period of two or three years they sent families up the Murray to establish what they called 'village settlements' at Holder, New Era, Waikerie, Gillen East, Moorook, Kingston-on-Murray, Pyap, and Lyrup. **1894** *Bulletin* (Sydney) 3 Nov. 15/1 The child of a **village settler** at Kardella (Vic.), died of starvation, the other day.

vine scrub. Formerly, any tropical or sub-tropical rainforest; now spec. a seasonally dry forest of this type. Formerly also **vine brush.**

1826 J. ATKINSON *Acct. Agric. & Grazing N.S.W.* 3 Vine brushes are mostly found on the sides and summits of steep mountains near the sea. It is here we may see the vegetable kingdom in its most magnificent form, lofty cedar and turpentine trees of the grandest dimensions, with large vines or parasitical plants of various kinds, thick as a man's leg, twining up to their very tops, catching hold of other trees in all directions, until an immense net-work is formed, impervious to the sun's rays. **1984** K.A.W. WILLIAMS *Native Plants Qld.* II. 224 Native Mulberry .. is a very common plant .. in the dry vine scrubs that grow on lava flows.

violet wood. *Obs.* The violet-scented wood of any of several trees; a tree having such wood.

1847 E.W. LANDOR *Bushman* 395 There is another highly-fragrant wood peculiar to this colony, called by the settlers 'raspberry jam', from its resembling that sweet meat in its scent. A small quantity sent to Tonbridge-Wells, was worked up into boxes, and highly approved of by the cabinet-makers, who gave it the name of 'violet wood'. **1861** F. ALGAR *Handbk. to Colony Qld.* 7 Violet Wood, Silk Oak, Tulip Wood, and Forest Oak .. are plentiful.

viranda, var. VERANDAH.

Vitamizer. Also **vitamizer.** [Proprietary name.] An appliance for blending cooking ingredients or for reducing raw fruit and vegetables to liquid form.

1951 *Austral. Official Jrnl. Patents* (Canberra) 3922 *Vitamizer* 102,530. 16th May, 1950. Food and drink mixing machines. Semak Electrics Pty. Limited. **1969** *Meanjin* 361 From a pocket he produces carrots in a plastic bag. His vitamiser whines. 'Carrot juice. I live on it.'

vulpine opossum. *Obs.* [See quot. 1848.] *Brush-tailed possum,* see BRUSH-TAILED.

1789 A. PHILLIP *Voyage to Botany Bay* 150 (*caption*) Vulpine Opossum. **1848** *Bell's Life in Sydney* 20 May 1/2 The opossum is something like a fox (and thence called the vulpine opossum) but inferior in size.

W

wacker, var. WHACKER.

wacko, var. WHACKO.

waddy /'wɒdi/, *n.*¹ Also **waddi, waddie, wody, woodah**. [a. Dharuk *wadi* a tree, a stick of wood, a wooden weapon (see quots. 1790 in senses 1 a. and b.).]

1. a. An Aboriginal war-club; a piece of wood used as a club. In quot. 1798 the weapon referred to is apparently a boomerang.

1790 D. SOUTHWELL Corresp. & Papers, *Wad-di* or *waddy*, a stick or club. **1798** M. FLINDERS *Voyage Terra Australis* (1814) I. p. cxxxix, He was of a middle age, unarmed, except with a *whaddie*, or wooden scimitar. **1825** *Howe's Weekly Commercial Express* (Sydney) 2 May 3 Her enamoured swain . . sneaking softly behind her, with one blow of his *waddie* stretched her quivering at his feet. **1901** *Bulletin* (Sydney) 5 Oct. 17/1 You must see the native throwing . . to understand what woolanä-throwing is. Unlike the spear, the woolanä cannot be dodged, and escape depends on the manipulation of the shield or woodäh.

b. Chiefly *Austral. pidgin*. A tree; a piece of wood. Also *attrib.* and as *adj.* (see quot. 1856).

c **1790** W. DAWES Grammatical Forms Lang. N.S.W., *Wad-day*, wood (lignum). **1856** W.W. DOBIE *Recoll. Visit Port-Phillip* 93 Borak you ever see black fellow with waddie (wooden) leg. **1884** A.W. HOWITT *On Some Austral. Ceremonies Initiation* 9 The Baiangal are . . correctly speaking, 'Tree-climbers' . . as distinguished from the Katungal, who live on fish . . and are therefore properly spoken of as 'Fishermen'. The whites know them by this name, but speak of the others as 'Waddy men', from the word *waddy*, colonially used for *tree*. **1956** B.J. RAYMENT *My Towri* 96, I can only recall odd words of their language and am not certain about some of them. Yowi, yes; bal, no . . wody, wood [etc.].

2. a. A club or cudgel as used by a person other than an Aboriginal; a piece of wood used as a weapon.

1809 *Sydney Gaz.* 14 May, Several depredations . . attributed to the offenders who have betaken themselves to the woods. . . A man, who resides at Hawkesbury was attacked and severely wounded in the head with a *waddy or club*. **1981** L. MCLEAN *Pumpkin Pie* 79 They could possibly have . . 'jumped the rattler' . . but knew that extra inspectors had been employed to hunt the free riders. . . Most of them carried a piece of wood, called a 'waddy', and would hit anyone unlucky enough to be caught on the train.

b. *fig.* In the phr. **to take up the waddy**, to engage in a vigorous defence (cf. 'to take up the cudgels').

1907 *Bulletin* (Sydney) 7 Feb. 15/1, I beg to take up the waddy of disputation on behalf of 'Crossnibs'.

waddy /'wɒdi/, *n.*² [a. Western Desert *wadi*.] An Aboriginal male.

1935 H.H. FINLAYSON *Red Centre* 68 Over large portions of the interior the aborigine distinguishes himself from the white man by the term 'waddi' and this might perhaps serve as a name for the race. **1963** O. RUHEN *Flockmaster* 58 Some waddy's got himself lost—he's got a woman with him. They're out of tucker . . a bit lucky I came along.

waddy /'wɒdi/, *v.* [f. WADDY *n.*¹]

a. *trans.* To strike, beat, or kill (an animal or person) with a waddy (see WADDY *n.*¹ a.). Also *intr.* and as *vbl. n.*

1833 *Launceston Advertiser* 31 Oct. 3 The spearing and waddying are yet of too recent occurrence to be remembered with indifference by our settlers. **1857** J. BONWICK *Early Days Melbourne* 33 The women gathered roots, and picked out grubs, while the men waddied down birds, netted fish, speared kangaroos, and pulled opossums from their holes. **1914** T.C. WOLLASTON *Spirit of Child* 191 A good many people would succeed better in life if they were periodically *waddied*.

b. *fig.* To importune.

1880 H. KENDALL *Songs from Mountains* 201 Laura's lovers every day In sweet verse embody her. Katie's have a different way, Being frank, they 'waddy' her.

waddy wood. [See WADDY *n.*¹ a.] Any of several trees yielding a hard wood, esp. *Acacia peuce* (fam. Mimosaceae) of s.w. Qld. and N.T., and WHALEBONE TREE; the wood of the tree. Also **waddy tree**, and *attrib.*

1912 *Mod. Dict. Eng. Lang.* 803 *Wad'-dy-wood* . . a Tas. tree yielding a dense, hard, white wood which was used by aborigines for making waddies. **1946** C.T. MADIGAN *Crossing Dead Heart* 35 Near the bore there was a patch of 'waddy' trees, tall, straight trees some fifty feet high, with thin and drooping foliage and seeds in long pods. **1967** M. & M. LEYLAND *Where Dead Men Lie* 133 The moon shone through the chinks in the Waddy wood walls as I listened to the sounds of the others breathing.

wadgula /'waɪdʒələ, 'wɒdʒələ/. *Austral. pidgin*. Also **waigella, waijela**. [Alteration of WHITE FELLOW.] A white person.

1923 A.G. BOLAM *Trans-Austral. Wonderland* 76 'Waijela bool-ga munda?' (Whitefellow dig big earth?). **1969** L. HADOW *Full Cycle* 157 'Hah, ha!' Jimmy Dabchick turned a cartwheel. 'Us all N-Yoongars. What she? Sister Merry Christmas only Waigella!' **1981** A. WELLER *Day of Dog* 7 We'll go and pick up a woman for ya, Dougo. Would ya like a big fat wadgula or a skinny little gin?

wadna /'wɒdnə/. *S.A. Obs.* [a. Gaurna *wadna*.] An Aboriginal hunting weapon: see quots.

1842 *S. Austral. News* (London) 46/2 The larger [skins] have their inner layers shaven off by the katta, kandappi, or wadna. **1860** *Trans. & Proc. R. Soc. Vic.* (1861) 170 The 'wadna' is a kind of weapon about three feet long, with a knee in the middle. It is never used as a weapon for fighting, but only for killing large fish.

wage. Usu. as **wages**.

1. Used *attrib.*, with reference to an amount paid periodically to an employee, in Special Comb. **wage plug, wages man; wages award,** AWARD *n.*; **board**, a body responsible for determining conditions of employment; also *attrib.*; **man**, one who works for a wage.

1918 G. DALE *Industr. Hist. Broken Hill* 206 The **wage-plug** on the surface is keeping in motion the machines of production. **1933** R.D TATE *Doughman* 42 Three or four had been finishing very late—and that was dangerous, the **Wages Award** expressly stating that every carter must be off the premises on the stroke of six. **1909** *Truth* (Sydney) 25 July 1/3 'Are you a married man?' was asked a witness at a **Wages Board**. **1915** M. ATKINSON *Trade Unionism in Aust.* 21 Undoubtedly the most important and significant activity of trade unionism has been in the sphere of the Wages Board system. **1871** *Austral. Town & Country Jrnl.* (Sydney) 21 Jan. 71/1 The cause is the old one of defective timbering, and it is somewhat queer that in both cases it is **wages men** that have been hurt.

2. Chiefly *Mining*. In *pl.*

a. *transf.* A sum sufficient to live on, esp. in the phr. **to make wages**, to earn an adequate living; **to pay wages**, (of a mine, a mineral deposit, etc.) to yield an adequate return.

1853 J.R. GODLEY *Extracts Jrnl. Visit N.S.W.* 19 'Making wages'.. in the mouths of diggers means earning 10s. a day, or £3 a week. **1855** *Ovens & Murray Advertiser* (Beechworth) 27 Jan. 4/2 It requires a great amount of patience and labour to work the claims, which in many instances barely pay wages to the parties working them. **1858** *Colonial Mining Jrnl.* Nov. 44/2 The companies that have bottomed and struck the gutter, are obtaining very fair wages.

b. *Attrib.* passing into *adj.* Modestly profitable.

1871 *Austral. Town & Country Jrnl.* (Sydney) 13 May 591/1 Nine claims are known to be on payable gold, while three or four more can obtain what is called a 'small wages prospect'. **1968** M.T. CLARKE *Spark of Opal* (1973) 54 The yield being enough to cover their overhead expenses—a 'wages' claim.

Wagga /'wɒgə/, *attrib.* and *n.* Also **Wogga, Wogger**. [Abbrev. of *Wagga Wagga* a town in s. N.S.W.: see B. quot. 1913.]

A. *attrib.* In Special Comb. **Wagga blanket, rug**, an improvised covering, usu. of sacking (see esp. quot. 1906); **pot** (**bell**), a cattle bell.

1933 J. TRURAN *Where Plain Begins* 143 He laid his blankets.. covering everything with what bushmen call a '**Wagga blanket**', that is, three or four wheat sacks sewn together, side by side. **1900** H. LAWSON *Over Sliprails* 62 The live cinders from the firebox.. fell in showers on deck. Every now and again a spark would burn through the '**Wagga rug**' of a sleeping shearer, and he'd wake suddenly and get up and curse. **1900** *Bulletin* (Sydney) 21 Apr. 32/2 A cast-off wool-bale is his eider-down, or, as he call [*sic*] it, his 'Wagga-rug'. **1906** *Ibid.* 9 Aug. 17/3 This is the only genuine 'Wagga rug'. Take three wheat or corn sacks and sew them together with a packing-needle and twine, side to side. Nothing more is needed. **1903** J. FURPHY *Such is Life* 19, I swapped her for a new thirty-by-twenty-four wool-rug, and a **Wagga pot**, good for eight or ten mile on a still night. **1981** A. MARSHALL *Aust.* 111 Mennicke of Wagga made a bell sometimes referred to as the 'Wagga Pot Bell'.

B. *n.* Short for *Wagga blanket, rug.*

1904 *Worker* (Sydney) 3/3 The nights of cold and shiver In our Waggas 'neath the fly! **1913** *Bulletin* (Sydney) 27 Nov. 22/2 As for Wagga, it is written on the doors and walls of travelling huts in three States that, in that town, age and dirt and many rents alone can save Matilda from.. the marauder. Hence 'Wagga'.. meaning three or four.. bales sewn together and wrapped around a swag. **1978** S. BALL *Mama's Boarding House* 24 As blankets became threadbare and unattractive they were converted into the ubiquitous wogger. **1979** G. STEWART *Leveller* 20 A bagman was an unemployed person whose only possessions were bags: a water bag, a tucker bag, flour bags washed and sewn together called a Wogga.

waggy. [f. WAG(TAIL + -Y.] WILLY WAGTAIL.

1921 *Bulletin* (Sydney) 17 Nov. 20/3 Only three of our bush birds will attack man in defence of their nest. They are the willy-wagtail, the magpie and the butcher-bird. I think Waggy must be given the palm for downright pluck in view of his size. **1948** *Ibid.* 4 Feb. 29/3 There is a shed built from undressed bush timber where two waggies have nested for three seasons at least.

wagtail. [Transf. use of *wagtail* a small bird of the fam. Motacillidae, having a characteristic wagging tail.] Any of several small birds, usu. fantails of the fam. Muscicapidae, esp. WILLY WAGTAIL.

1831 G.F. MOORE *Diary Ten Yrs.* 4 Nov. (1884) 87 A young wagtail, which has as varied a style of singing as it has varied names, being called, besides the name just stated, razor-grinder, and superb-warbler. **1974** BUCKLEY & HAMILTON *Festival* 71 His eyes darted like a wagtail in search of solidity.

wahbegong, var. WOBBEGONG.

waigella, waijela, varr. WADGULA.

wait-a-while. [Transf. use of *wait-a-bit* or *wait-a-while* any of several S. African thorny plants, incl. various species of *Mimosa*.] Any of several plants which may impede passage with their spiny leaves or prickles, esp. the tangled shrub *Acacia colletioides* (fam. Mimosaceae) of drier s. Aust., the similar *A. nyssophylla*, and LAWYER VINE. Also **wait-a-bit**, and *attrib.*, esp. as **wait-a-while bush**.

1889 J.H. MAIDEN *Useful Native Plants Aust.* 306 *Acacia colletioides*.. 'Wait-a-while' (a delicate allusion to the predicament of a traveller desirous of penetrating a belt of it). **1897** A.F. PATERSON *'Mid Saltbush & Mallee* 31 It is a wonder the trees ever come to maturity, but they sometimes grow in the wait-a-while bushes, then nothing can touch them. **1911** ST. C. GRONDONA *Collar & Cuffs* 70 'Wait-a-bit', so-called from the difficulty experienced by a stockman in pulling a switch.

wait for a death, to: see DEATH.

Wakefield. *Hist.* [f. the name of Edward Gibbon *Wakefield* (1796–1862), author and colonist.] Used *attrib.* esp. in Comb. **Wakefield principle, system, theory**, to designate the application of Wakefield's doctrines of colonization to South Australia and, in a modified form, in other Australian Colonies (see quots.).

1842 *Geelong Advertiser* 9 May 4/1 Government.. is to borrow money on the '**Wakefield principle**', for colonization. **1839** *S. Austral. Rec.* (London) 9 Oct. 248 Comparing the operation of the **Wakefield system** in South Australia with that of the free-grant system in Canada. **1843** *N.S.W. Monthly Mag.* Oct. 619 'Sell the land to the capitalists', cried Wakefield, 'and with the proceeds export labourers to till the land thus sold.' In these few words is comprised the whole of what has somewhat ambitiously been called, 'The **Wakefield Theory** of Colonization'.

Hence **Wakefieldism** *n.*, this set of doctrines; **Wakefieldite** *n.*, WAKEFIELDIAN *n.* (*attrib.* in quot.).

1844 *Atlas* (Sydney) I. 25/2 Socialism, and **Wakefieldism**, and wild doctrines of a kindred nature run rampant. **1849** S. & J. SIDNEY *Emigrant's Jrnl.* 201 The exaggerated pictures of 'the felony of New South Wales', to use a **Wakefieldite** phrase.

Wakefieldian, *a.* and *n. Hist.* [f. WAKEFIELD.]

A. *adj.* Of or pertaining to the doctrines of Wakefield, esp. as these were implemented in South Australia.

1843 *Sydney Morning Herald* 19 Aug. 3/1 He must say from what has taken place in this colony since the introduction of the Wakefieldean system that the free grant system was the true system. **1858** *Illustr. Jrnl. Australasia* IV. 197 The adjoining colony of South Australia was settled on what is termed the Wakefieldian plan of colonization, the leading feature in which was 'a sufficient price'.

B. *n.* A supporter of the doctrine of Wakefield.

1847 *Heads of People* (Sydney) 18 Dec. 68/1 Arguments which have been sneered at, but never answered, by the Wakefieldians.

wake-up. Also **awake-up.**

1. An alert and resourceful person, esp. one who is alert to the possibilities of a situation.

1916 *Rising Sun: On Board 'Themistocles'* 26 Aug. (Suppl.), Now, boys, when you arrive at your destination, be the true

Australian 'wake up'. **1975** L.H. CLARK *Rouseabout Reflections* 100 The game was over, 'Right,' roared Snowie, 'I'm a wake-up now'; Ted pumped his hand, 'You've proved your mettle son.'

2. Passing into *adj.* In the phr. **to be** (or **take**) **a (full) wake-up** (to someone or something), to be (or become) (fully) alert to, or aware of, the intentions of a person or the possibilities of a situation.

1930 *Bulletin* (Sydney) 16 Apr. 58/2 'Cripes you're a full wake-up to that at last, are you?' Snow exclaimed. **1945** D. CUSACK *Shoulder Sky* (1950) 114 No; Ginger wasn't like that. I'm awake-up to that kind. She was just nice and friendly. **1968** W.N. SCOTT *Some People* 119 Now, this cocky was a shrewdie and he took a wake-up to Arch early on and sneaked round and watched what Arch was doing from behind the guava bushes near the dunny.

wal /wɒl/. Abbrev. of WALLOPER.

1944 *Quickmatch: Souvenir Mag. H.M.A.S. 'Quickmatch'* 42 By this time all dinner was eaten and the 'Wals' were asleep again. **1966** *Kings Cross Whisper* (Sydney) July 8/3 Rub shoulders with the socially prominent, the sportsman, the crims and maybe even a wal or two.

waler, var. WHALER *n.*[1]

waler. Also **whaler**. [f. shortened form of *New South) Wale(s + -er.*]

1. A horse bred in Australia, esp. in New South Wales, and imported into India; a light, Australian-bred horse.

1849 J. PATTISON *N.S.W.* 65 The colonial-bred horses, or Walers, as they are called in India. **1919** E. DYSON *Hello, Soldier* 16 There was one pertickler whaler, known aboard ez Marshal Neigh, Whose monkey tricks with Privit Rowe was better than a play.

2. Abbrev. of NEW SOUTH WALER; also, loosely, an Australian. In quot. 1906 the reference is to the New South Wales Government.

1880 J. INGLIS *Our Austral. Cousins* 159 In the matter of awnings and verandahs the 'Walers' had a grand chance for a bright, cheerful .. display. **1906** *Gadfly* (Adelaide) 11 Apr. 5/1 Item No. 7 on the agenda stands in the Wailers' name. **1943** S. BROGDEN *Sudan Contingent* 44 So the New South Welshmen lined up ashore .. trying not to grin as the Tommos found a nickname for them—'Walers'.

walk, *v. Austral. pidgin.*

a. *intr.* With **about:** to travel across country without restriction.

1828 *Sydney Gaz.* 2 Jan., When the executioner had adjusted the rope, and was about to pull the cap over his eyes .. he said, in a tone of deep feeling, which it was impossible to hear without strong emotion, 'Bail more walk about', meaning that his wanderings were all over. **1965** R. OTTLEY *By Sandhills* 38 'Me walk-about'... His voice hissed... 'Bye an' bye, maybe two, t'ree weeks, come back.'

b. *Obs.* Also **to walk all about.**

1847 J.D. LANG *Cooksland* 270 The very prohibition of the Aborigines to 'walk all about', as they express it themselves in their broken English. **1851** H. MELVILLE *Present State Aust.* 114 Squatters take possession of the hunting grounds, the natives to whom they belong have no land to call their own—no country as they term it to 'walk all about'.

walkabout. [f. WALK a.]

1. a. *Austral. pidgin.* One who travels on foot; a swagman or traveller. Also *attrib.*

1872 MRS J. FOOTT *Sketches Life in Bush* 28 We had visitors every day in the shape of travellers, or, as the blacks call them, 'walkabouts'. **1893** S. NEWLAND *Paving Way* 264 'That one stupid walk-about white fellow, bale black fellow', was their comment when spoken to on the subject.

b. *spec. Hist.* A Kanaka whose initial contract has expired and who remains in Australia: see quot. 1899. Also *attrib.* as **walkabout Kanaka.**

1895 *Bulletin* (Sydney) 21 Sept. 16/3 Again the walkabout Kanaka. It is now suggested that restrictive legislation be introduced. **1899** *Progress* (Brisbane) 13 May 1/2 The whites, even in the districts where kanaka labour is most employed, are beginning to find out that the 'walk about' is a nuisance. It appears from our exchanges that the kanaka who has put in one period of service is not compelled to enter into another engagement or go back to his island. He puts a price on his services and hangs about at Kanaka boarding-houses, until there is a scarcity of labour and he can secure full wages.

2. COUNTRY 2.

1899 W.E. ROTH Rep. to Commissioner Police 3 Their walk-about extends on the one hand up the *Eastern* coast of the Peninsula as far as perhaps as the Stewart River. **1935** M. GILMORE *More Recoll.* 34 'The Dead Water' was a .. waterhole at which no black sat, because all the group in whose walk-about it had been were killed out.

3. a. A journey on foot, as undertaken by an Aboriginal in order to live in the traditional manner (esp. one undertaken as a temporary withdrawal from white society). See also PINK-EYE *n.*[2] Also *attrib.*

1910 *Bulletin* (Sydney) 22 Dec. 13/4 Shearing over, black brother was sent off on his walk-about, the squatter supplying him with .. a few garments. **1969** H. HUTT *Ballad of Boot* 7 'What you're looking for', he decided, 'are 'walk-about' aborigines. That is, tribal aborigines who take an annual stroll through the bush living on snakes and roots and—er—wild biscuits and the like.'

b. Quasi-*adv.* in phr. **to go** (or **send walkabout**). Also *transf.* and *fig.*

1927 R.S. BROWNE *Journalist's Memories* 291 Black brother and his spouse, or sister, or mother may 'go walk-about', and live on 'possum. **1956** T. RONAN *Moleskin Midas* 192 Yates .. sent his blacks walkabout. **1974** *Bulletin* (Sydney) 25 May 23/1 He has noticed that maggots 'go walkabout', and after some research he learned that they look for sand or soil in which to develop to their pupae stage.

4. a. *transf.* A period of rest; a holiday.

1908 MRS A. GUNN *We of Never-Never* 218 The day after that was filled in with preparations for a walk-about. **1974** D. IRELAND *Burn* 15 You like Billy the best even though he's gone away on walkabout and Gordon's got brains and working in the city.

b. A straying; a journey; a 'look around'. Also *attrib.*

1926 A.A.B. APSLEY *Amateur Settlers* 114 The bulls go on what the blacks call a 'walk about'. **1983** C. BINGHAM *Beckoning Horizon* 33 How far the goats roamed depended on grass and water. There was also a 'walkabout' time, which could lead to our scouring the country up to 10 miles from the township.

5. See WALKABOUT DISEASE.

walkabout disease.

a. A disease of horses, generally *Kimberley disease* (see KIMBERLEY). Also *ellipt.* as **walkabout.**

1911 *Cwlth. Parl. Papers* III. 519 There are three diseases, however, that seem to constitute drawbacks to horse breeding in this part of the country. These are commonly known as (1) the 'Walk-about' disease, which is generally fatal [etc.]. **1976** C.D. MILLS *Hobble Chains & Greenhide* 1 'Walkabout' and Birdsville had taken heavy toll of our horses.

b. *transf.* and *fig.*

1951 E. HILL *Territory* 260 Wanderlust .. walkabout disease .. call it what you will. They called it 'ridin' around'.

walkabout Kanaka: see WALKABOUT 1 b.

walking man. *Obs.* SWAGMAN a.

1904 *Bulletin* (Sydney) 24 Nov. 18/2 'Any chance iv a job, mister?' said the swaggie. 'Dunno,' replied the man on the fence. 'If you like to tackle clearin' the rocks outer this yer paddock I'll gi' yer fi' bob a day. . . ' The walking man suggested 6s. **1910** *Ibid.* 7 July 13/2 The patience and long-suffering of the Australian walking-man had touching expression in rhyme.

walking-stick palm. [See quot. 1981.] The small palm *Linospadix monostachyus* (fam. Arecaceae) of s.e. Qld. and n.e. N.S.W.

1869 R.T.M. PESCOTT *W.R. Guilfoyle* (1974) 46 *Chamaedon* or walking stick palm is very plentiful. **1981** PUGH & RITCHIE *Guide to Rainforests N.S.W.* 4 Moving back into the forest you will find the smaller Walking Stick Palm, so named because its slender trunk with its knob on the end has been used for walking sticks.

walk-in, walk-out. Used to designate a method of selling a rural property, house, livestock, etc., by which the purchaser agrees to take possession unconditionally. Freq. *attrib.*

1930 *Bulletin* (Sydney) 4 June 20/1 Woolpacks acquired Whoopybilla Downs on walk-in walk-out terms. **1974** W. ROEDIGER *We Survived* 41 Dad finally sold them all to a butcher, walk-in walkout, for a trifling sum.

wallaby /ˈwɒləbi/, *n.* Formerly also with much variety, as **wallaba, wallabee, wallabi, wollaba, wollabi,** and with pl. **wallaby.** [a. Dharuk *walabi*.]
1. a. Any of many smaller marsupials of the fam. Macropodidae (see KANGAROO *n.* 1 a.), of several genera as *Macropus, Wallabia, Lagorchestes, Lagostrophus, Onychogalea, Petrogale, Thylogale,* and *Setonix.* Also *attrib.*
b. With distinguishing epithet, as **agile, Bennett's, black-gloved, brush, hare, nail-tailed, parma, red-necked, rock, scrub, swamp, tammar, whiptail:** see under first element.

1798 D. COLLINS *Acct. Eng. Colony N.S.W.* I. 614 *Wal-li-bah,* black [kangaroo]. **1805** *Sydney Gaz.* 16 June, Then anxious, my eyes each direction pursue, Till the fleet-footed *wallaba* rises to view! **1824** *Sydney Herald* (1831) 4 July 3/1 Pheasants, and the black brush Kangaroo, called Wallaby, were plentiful. **1835** T.B. WILSON *Narr. Voyage round World* 201 The dogs . . caught two *wallabi*. **1844** *Dispatch* (Sydney) 27 Jan. 2/3 We trust a good collection of Kangaroos, Wild-dogs, Oppossums, Wollabi . . and wild Indians, will be got together to welcome the strangers, and we doubt not Zoological gardens on an extensive scale may soon be formed. **1856** *Jrnl. Australasia* I. 112 A porcupine and a wollaba had been caught.

2. a. WALLABY TRACK 2 a., esp. in the phr. **on the wallaby.**

1867 *Austral. Monthly Mag.* (Melbourne) IV. 41, I have just had a row with my people and am off anywhere, on the *wallabee*, to try my luck. **1974** M. TERRY *War of Warramullas* 143 A station cook . . had taken to the wallaby and camped with me in western Queensland.
b. *transf.* and *fig.* The 'circuit'; **on the wallaby,** on the move.

1887 *Bulletin* (Sydney) 19 Nov. 5/1 An obviously inspired paragraph is going the journalistic wallaby—we have even seen it in the Argus and S.M.H. **1973** P. ADAM SMITH *Barcoo Salute* 2 Up to the age of seventy my mother was still 'on the wallaby' even with the frugal means at her disposal. However, to the surprise of everyone who knows her, she has now lived in the same house for four unbroken years, the longest residence in any one place in her life.

3. An itinerant rural worker; SWAGMAN a. Also *attrib.*

1869 M. CLARKE *Peripatetic Philosopher* 41 At the station where I worked for some time (as 'knock-about man') three cooks were kept during the 'wallaby' season—one for the house, one for the men, and one for the travellers. **1956** H. FRAUCA *In New Country* 59 We didn't know his kind existed in Australia any longer, but there he was, a real swagman walking down the road. . . We waved at him but he didn't wave back at us. 'He's probably a 'wallaby',' said Wally.

4. *pl.* The name of the Australian international Rugby Union team; in *sing.*, a member of such a team. Cf. KANGAROO *n.* 3 b. and SOCCEROO.

1908 *Referee* (Sydney) 4 Nov. 9/2 The discussion as to the name by which the team should be called was settled by the 'Daily Mail' wiring to the 'Wallabies', asking them to choose and nominate their sobriquet. They duly chose the name 'Wallabies' at a special meeting. 'Rabbits' has, therefore, been dropped by many papers. **1957** *Sun* (Sydney) 13 Apr. 5/1 If original plans stand the Australian Rugby Union selectors on August 25 will name 30 players to make what is regarded as the best sporting trip available to Australians. *Twenty three* days later they will set off—as the Wallabies—for the United Kingdom on a tour that will take in France, Italy and the USA.

5. Comb. **wallaby hunt, hunting, scalp, skin, stew, trap, trapping.**

1896 *Bulletin* (Sydney) 4 July 28/1 When it was not a bees-nest to chop out it was a **wallaby-hunt,** or an unbranded calf. **1885** D.E. MCCONNELL *Austral. Etiquette* 467 It is impossible to devote space to a full description of the exciting and pleasurable features of kangaroo-hunting, or of that other native sport, **wallaby-hunting,** which latter is pursued in a similar way to kangarooing, though the subject is a tempting one. **1885** *Bulletin* (Sydney) 5 Dec. 10/4 Kangaroo scalps are paid for at the rate of 9d. each. . . **Wallaby scalps** are only worth 4d. **1832** BACKHOUSE & TYLOR *Life & Labours G.W. Walker* 12 Oct. (1862) 104 The natives carried our bush apparatus, consisting of one of our water-proof covers, a **wallaby-skin** coverlet [etc.]. **1938** D. BATES *Passing of Aborigines* 50 Three pairs of laced wallaby-skin shoes. **1895** *Devil in Sydney* 61, I consider a **wallaby stew** one of the greatest delicacies a person can sit down to. **1930** 'BRENT OF BIN BIN' *Ten Creeks Run* (1952) 246 Abracadabra, a mountain-bred horse, had fallen into old Billy Heffernan's **wallaby-traps.** **1906** *Bulletin* (Sydney) 18 Oct. 44/1 Dave goes to look after his private enterprise of **wallaby trapping,** and Dad to the 'cultivation' he has already spent months clearing.

6. Special Comb. **wallaby drive,** an operation in which wallabies are herded, trapped and slaughtered, or otherwise hunted; **jack,** a heavy-duty, lever-action jack used for lifting logs, stumps, etc. (see also FOREST DEVIL, *kangaroo jack* KANGAROO *n.* 6); **net,** a net used by Aborigines to snare wallabies; **rug,** a rug made from wallaby skin; **tail,** the tail of a wallaby as an article of food, esp. *attrib.* as **wallaby-tail soup.**

1882 *Bulletin* (Sydney) 15 July 13/1 A **Wallaby drive** took place in the Bulli Mountains last week. **1906** *Australasian* (Melbourne) 7 July 2/4 The **wallaby jack** is suitable for a great variety of purposes, besides the usual stump grubbing. **1883** E. PALMER *Plants N. Qld.* 18 A tall, shady tree, called Kurrijong. . . Inside bark worked up into strong cord for **wallaby nets** and bags. **1832** BACKHOUSE & TYLOR *Life & Labours G.W. Walker* 12 Oct. (1862) 105 We composed ourselves to rest, making the best use we could of the **wallaby rug.** **1839** W.H. LEIGH *Reconnoitering Voyages* 126 The **wallaba tails** again continually passing round our circle, to enable every one to suit himself. **1979** D. LOCKWOOD *My Old Mates & I* 69 And wallaby tail soup! She has a recipe she could sell for a thousand dollars if enough people were hungry castaways with money to spend.

7. In the names of flora and fauna: **wallaby grass,** any of many perennial grasses, usu. of the genus *Danthonia* (fam. Poaceae) of Aust. and elsewhere, typically fine-leaved tussocky plants valued as winter fodder; **rat** *Tas.,* the long-nosed potoroo *Potorous tridactylus apicalis.*

1889 J.H. MAIDEN *Useful Native Plants Aust.* 82 *Danthonia penicillata* . . '**Wallaby Grass**'. This perennial grass is useful for artificial mixed pasture. **1909** G. SMITH *Naturalist in*

Tas. 85 Besides the Wallabies, there are two similarly shaped animals known as Kangaroo and **Wallaby Rats** (*Bettongia cuniculus* and *tridactylus*), small black creatures about the size of a Hare.

wallaby /'wɒləbi/, *v. Obs.* [f. WALLABY *n.* 2.] *intr.* To journey through the country, to go 'on the wallaby track'.

1885 *Australasian Printers' Keepsake* 26 The white-folk wallaby, in numbers vast, Fill all the valleys where my fathers sprang when Jacky Jacky hurled his boomerang. **1906** *Bulletin* (Sydney) 31st May 40/2 So you wallaby and wander North and South, and East and West.

wallaby track.
1. The path worn by a wallaby.
1846 J.L. STOKES *Discoveries in Aust.* II. 390 In some parts of the tall scrub were wallaby tracks. **1926** A.S. LE SOUEF et al. *Wild Animals Australasia* 189 *M. ualabatus*, known as the black and also as the swamp wallaby, inhabits scrubby damp gullies, through which it has well-marked paths or 'wallaby tracks'.

2. **a.** *transf.* The route followed by one who journeys through the country in search of seasonal work (but see also quot. 1871); esp. in the phr. **on the wallaby track.**
1849 *Stephen's Adelaide Miscellany* 4 Oct. 42 The police themselves are usually well-treated in the bush .. they make a 'round' through the district, and get a meal at every hut, and one man from every said hut (besides those mobs on the 'wallaby track') stops for a night at the police-station in return. **1871** *Illustr. Sydney News* 18 Mar. 154/1 'On the Wallaby track'. This expression designates a peculiar phase of Australian life. It is applied to a class of men who contrive to exist in the bush without a home, and, in a great measure, without work. **1974** *Austral. Folksongs* (Folk Lore Council Aust.) 59 The hills and the plains are well trodden By the men of the wallaby track.

b. A tramp.
1865 *Sydney Punch* 23 Sept. 555/1 The principal animals in the district are wallaby tracks, and the principal birds, Cockatoo settlers.

Hence **wallaby tracker** *n.*
1888 E. FINN *Chron. Early Melbourne* I. 371 The 'wallaby trackers' would, on a certain evening, treat all the blacks that might cross the river.

wallaroo /wɒlə'ru:/. [a. Dharuk *walaru*.] Any of several large, stocky kangaroos of rocky or hilly country, most commonly *Macropus robustus*, esp. the dark, shaggy-haired *M. robustus robustus* of N.S.W. and s. Qld.; HILL KANGAROO. See also EURO, *rock kangaroo* ROCK *n.* 2. Also *attrib.*
1826 J. ATKINSON *Acct. Agric. & Grazing N.S.W.* 24 There is also found far in the interior another variety, called wall-aroos. **1974** *Southerly* ii. 147 I'd like a nice black wallaroo rug for my room.

wall-cuff. *Obs.* A manacle securing a prisoner's wrist to a wall-staple.
1892 *Bulletin* (Sydney) 2 July 21/4 'I thought he was celled?' 'So he is, sir. No. 5!' 'And ironed?' 'Trumpeters—fifteen's [*sic*]—and wall-cuffs!' **1937** W. & T.I. MOORE *Best Austral. One-Act Plays* 262 You can gi'e me double darbies, solitary, wall cuffs, tube-gag, trumpeters. . . I don't give a bugger.

wallom, var. WALLUM.

wallop. [Used elsewhere but recorded earliest in Aust.: see OEDS *sb.* 4 c.] Alcoholic liquor, esp. beer. Also *attrib.*
1871 *Austral. Town & Country Jrnl.* (Sydney) 1 Apr. 389/3 Not everybody .. does care about .. the real Tooth's, or Castlemine, or Parramatta, or even the renowned 'wallop' of the Western line. **1909** *Bulletin* (Sydney) 7 Jan. 39/2 Jigger .. made for Mander's wallop shop.

walloper. [f. *wallop, v.* to beat, belabour.] A policeman; also *transf.* (see quot. 1968).
1945 S.J. BAKER *Austral. Lang.* 137 We also call a policeman a .. walloper. **1968** F. ROSE *Aust. Revisited* 78 'We're from the Attorney General's Department.' The Australian Security Intelligence Organisation was nominally under the control of the Attorney General's Department although answerable only to the Prime Minister. *So that's it: two Security wallopers.*

wallow. *Mining. S.A.* [Poss. f. *wallow* to abound (in wealth, etc.).] A rich deposit of ore.
1914 *Wallaroo & Moonta Mines* 20 These [deposits] formed a series of small 'bonanzas' ('wallows' in local phrase). **1962** O. PRYOR *Aust.'s Little Cornwall* 52 A very rich pocket of ore was known as a 'wallow'. The largest wallow found at Moonta was struck in the Prince Alfred shaft in 1870.

wallum /'wɒləm/. Formerly also **wallom.** [a. Gabi-gabi *walum.*] **a.** The shrub or tree *Banksia aemula* (fam. Proteaceae) of s.e. Qld. and e. N.S.W. **b.** The sandy coastal heathland in which the plant grows; more generally, an area of coastal heath (see quots. 1979 and 1980). Also *attrib.*, esp. as **wallum country.**
1861 J.D. LANG *Qld., Aust.* 122 Good agricultural country, intersected by patches of wallom flats and tea-tree swamps. **1876** 'EIGHT YRS.' RESIDENT' *Queen of Colonies* 104 Patches of most excellent land will be found here and there, usually on the banks of the streams, which will abruptly terminate in that worst of all coast-land 'wallum country', as it is called, from the native name of the shrub which principally grows on it. The soil in this wallum country is of the vilest description, producing scarcely any grass and only a few stunted honeysuckle and gum-trees, besides the never-ending wallum. **1979** K.A.W. WILLIAMS *Native Plants Qld.* I. 70 In many parts of coastal Queensland south of the Tropic of Capricorn, there are areas of forest, woodland and heathland that have developed on acid, sandy soils of sandhills, sand dunes, and on flat or gently undulating sandy country with a high water table. Generally these areas are known as 'Wallum', a name derived from the Aboriginal word for *Banksia aemula*, a conspicuous tree of the habitat. **1980** E. McDONALD *Wildflowers of Wallum* Dustjacket, Nowadays, by popular consent, the term 'Wallum' is not confined to the heathy country on which the Wallum tree grows, but is used to include all parts of the coastal lowlands having low natural fertility but which yet enjoys high rainfall. It embraces a wide variety of habitats.

walnut. [Transf. use of *walnut* a tree of the genus *Juglans.*] Any of several trees, usu. of the fam. Lauraceae, having attractively figured wood supposed to resemble that of the Northern Hemisphere walnut; the wood of the tree. Also *attrib.*, and with distinguishing epithet, as *Queensland walnut* (see QUEENSLAND 2).
1926 *Qld. Agric. Jrnl.* XXV. 437 *Beilschmiedia elliptica* .. Walnut (Fraser Island). **1985** *Age* (Melbourne) 31 Oct. 11/3 There is no evidence that the animals which cannot survive in logged areas move to unlogged areas. People sitting at their blackbean and walnut tables don't think about that.

wambat, var. WOMBAT.

wambenger /'wɒmbɛŋgə/. [Poss. a. Nyungar *wambanaŋ.*] PHASCOGALE 1 a.
1928 *Pop. Names for Marsupials* (Public Library, Museum, & Art Gallery W.A., Museum Leaflet no. 1), *Phascogale penicillata* .. Wambenger. **1970** W.D.L. RIDE *Guide Native*

Mammals Aust. 112 The wambengers are arboreal and appear usually to make their nests in hollows.

wampoo pigeon, var. WOMPOO PIGEON.

wanderer. [See quot. 1926.] The migratory, predom. reddish-brown and black butterfly *Danaus plexippus* of Aust. and elsewhere.

1926 J. POLLARD *Bushland Man* 227, I captured an interesting fellow .. one of the 'wanderers', a fine big fellow with golden-feathered wings, the veins forming a mazy black pattern. It had brushy feet and a downy body... He is well called a wanderer, for he is known in many countries... He has another name 'monarch'. **1986** *Age* (Melbourne) 6 May 36/3 You will see Common Browns floating through your garden and throughout the countryside. Do not confuse this butterfly with the Monarch or Wanderer, a butterfly that is also reasonably common in Victoria. This large and darker orange-brown butterfly has distinctive black wings, veins and margins to the wings. It is an American butterfly that spread to Australia and other parts of the world more than 100 years ago.

Wandjina /'wɒn'dʒinə/. Also **Wondjina**. [a. Ungarinyin *wanjina* (several etymologies have been suggested for this word in Ungarinyin but none is plausible).] A category of spirit people depicted in rock paintings of the Kimberley Ranges in Western Australia: see esp. quot. 1969.

1930 *Oceania* I. 259, I shall describe the paintings of this site... The most striking of these is a large man, about thirteen feet from the sole of his foot to the top of his hair, depicted horizontally along the rock-face. He has eyes and nose but no mouth. His face is partly surrounded by a horse-shoe shaped head-dress. [*Note*] Figures of this kind are called *wondjina* in the language. **1938** A.P. ELKIN *Austral. Aborigines* 179 Each gallery includes at least one painting of a personal being known as Wondjina, associated with the sky, rain, rainbow, the rainbow-serpent, spirit-children and the increase of natural species. **1969** EDWARDS & GUERIN *Aboriginal Bark Paintings* 23 The Wandjinas of the Kimberleys are creative ancestral beings. When first discovered their white bodies and halo-like head-dresses led to some fanciful theories linking them with Christian myths... To the Aborigines, the Wandjinas are not just paintings, but spirits.

wandoo /wɒn'du/. Formerly also **wando**. [a. Nyungar *wandu*.] The tree *Eucalyptus wandoo* (syn. *E. redunca* var. *elata*; fam. Myrtaceae) of s.w. W.A., usu. having a smooth mottled white or grey bark; the very hard, strong, durable wood of the tree. Also *attrib.*

1837 G.F. MOORE *Evidences Inland Sea* 15 The trees are .. Wando (white gum with a rusty tinge). **1893** A.F. CALVERT *W.A. & its Gold Fields* 16 *Eucalyptus redunca* (or Wandoo) the principal white gum-tree of Western Australia, derives its name from the hue of its bark, which on friction imparts a white colour. **1981** J.P. GABBEDY *Forgotten Pioneers* 72, I was one of a busy-bee group .. cutting wandoo poles for our tennis court fence.

wanga-wanga, var. WONGA-WONGA.

wangi, var. WONGI *v.*

wangie, var. WONGI *n.*[1]

wanna /'wɒnə/. Also **wonna, wonnah**. [a. Nyungar (and other w. Austral. languages) *wana*.] An Aboriginal digging-stick. Also *attrib.*

1841 G. GREY *Jrnls. Two Exped. N.-W. & W.A.* II. 320 They came .. slowly forward with their *wan-nas* (a long stick they use for digging up roots) in their hands. **1920** *Smith's Weekly* (Sydney) 25 Sept. 17/4 In the northern parts of West Australia the gins all carry a stick about five feet long and 1½ inches thick (the 'wonnah'), which they use when digging for grubs. **1950** V.E. TURNER *Ooldea* 109 The women carried the babies on their backs and a 'weerah' full of water on their heads, leaving the hands free .. for the inevitable 'wonna', or digging stick. **1962** B.W. LEAKE *Eastern Wheatbelt Wildlife* 57 The women never failed to carry a Wanna stick. One of these would be about five feet long and one and a half inches in diameter, made out of a white gum or jamwood sapling.

wap, var. WOP.

waratah /'wɒrəta/. Formerly also **warata, warratah, warrataw, warrettah**. [a. Dharuk *warrada*.]

1. Any shrub or small tree of the genus *Telopea* (fam. Proteaceae) of s.e. Aust., esp. *T. speciosissima* (the floral emblem of N.S.W.) and (*Tas.*) *T. truncata*; the striking, bright red flower-head of the plant, for which it is often cultivated; TULIP TREE. See also *native tulip* NATIVE *a.* 6 a., TELOPEA.

1788 J. HUNTER *Birds & Flowers N.S.W.* Pl. 62, *Wa-ra-ta*. **1791** J. COBLEY *Sydney Cove* 3 Dec. (1965) 176, I send you a drawing of the War-ret-tah, several plants of which are in the tubs. **1793** J.E. SMITH *Specimen Bot. New Holland* 19 The most magnificent plant which the prolific soil of New Holland affords is, by common consent both of Europeans and Natives, the Waratàh. **1805** Banks Papers 12 Jan. VIII. 172, I have not been able to send any seeds of the Warratah this time; by the natives having burned the woods. **1838** J. MARTIN *Austral. Sketch Bk.* 22 One of his pupils borne down by an immense bundle of *warrataws*, or colonial tulips.

2. Abbrev. of *Waratah Festival*, a celebratory occasion (in quot. *transf.*).

1975 E. GOOLAGONG et al. *Evonne* 189 When would they stop clapping? Not for five minutes, according to the journalists who timed it. It was a regular waratah (party) in the stadium.

3. Special Comb. **Waratah (Spring) Festival,** a carnival formerly held annually in Sydney, usu. in spring.

1956 *Sydney Morning Herald* 12 Sept. 4/4 The city will be dressed with flowers, flags and bunting for Sydney's first Waratah Spring Festival. **1984** P. JARRATT *Aussie* 204 Sydney once had its Waratah Festival in which there was a parade and little else.

warb /wɒb/. Also **waub, worb.** [Prob. f. *warble* the maggot of a warble-fly: see OED *sb.*[2] 3.]

1. An idle, unkempt, or disreputable person: see quot. 1959.

1933 MURDOCH & DRAKE-BROCKMAN *Austral. Short Stories* (1951) 215 We were both of us what, in the back country, are called 'warbs', meaning confirmed and irredeemable loafers. **1959** S.J. BAKER *Drum* II. 155 *Warb*, a low-paid manual worker... A dirty or untidy person... A simpleton or fool. **1984** *Sydney Morning Herald* 4 Feb. 37/2 She picks up an intoxicated person (police call them waubs, slang passed down from they don't know where).

2. An unskilled circus hand.

1945 S.J. BAKER *Austral. Lang.* 249 *Warb*, a circus labourer. **1967** J. YEOMANS *Scarce Australs.* 30 There are four general hands (known in Australian circus slang as worbs).

warbler. [Transf. use of *warbler* any of many small birds of the fam. Sylviidae.]

1. Any of many small birds of several fam., usu. having a melodic call, esp. those of the genus *Gerygone* and other members of the fam. Acanthizidae, and of the fam. Maluridae and Ephthianuridae.

1790 J. WHITE *Jrnl. Voyage N.S.W.* 257 *Motocilla*, or *Warbler*. Motacilla Pusilla... This little bird is about the same size with [*sic*] the Superb Warbler. **1985** *Age* (Melbourne) 9 Sept. 15/5 The Australian wrens, warblers and robins are quite unrelated to their namesakes in the Northern Hemisphere.

2. With distinguishing epithet, as **brown, reed, rock, superb, white-throated:** see under first element.

warbling grass parakeet. BUDGERIGAR. Also **warbling grass parrot.**

1840 J. GOULD *Birds of Aust.* (1848) V. Pl. 44, *Melopsittacus undulatus* . . Warbling Grass-Parakeet. . . Betcherrygah, Natives of Liverpool Plains. **1934** H.G. LAMOND *Aviary on Plains* 8 That's a mob of budgerigars (Warbling Grass-parrots).

warby, *a.* [See WARB.] Of clothes, etc.: shabby, decrepit. Also, unappealing.

1923 *Aussie* (Sydney) 15 Nov. 39 When your overcoat's warby, and turned to bottle-green, And the whole of your outfit's not fit to be seen. **1941** K. TENNANT *Battlers* 207 'Of all the warby ideas', he said . . 'the warbiest is you going on your own.'

warden. *Hist.* Gold warden, see GOLD 3.

1855 *Ovens & Murray Advertiser* (Beechworth) 7 Apr. 3/4 The present expensive staff of commissioners is to be entirely abolished; and the management of each district entrusted to one officer of high rank, and invested with grave authority, called a *warden*, who is to be directly responsible to the Government for his actions. **1938** C.P. CONIGRAVE *Walk-About* 12 Warden Finnerty . . had gone to inspect the new rush.

warragal, warragul, *var.* WARRIGAL.

warran /'wɒrən/. *Obs.* Also **warrein.** [a. Nyungar *warran*.] ADJIGO.

1840 S. *Austral. Rec.* (London) 21 Nov. 324 The warran, or native yam . . always grows in the most fertile tracts. 1863 *Jrnls. & Rep. Two Voyages Glenelg River* 1 Aug. (1864) 27 Edible roots, two species of which we recognised; they are identical with those of Champion Bay (warrein and adjiko).

warratah, warrataw, *var.* WARATAH.

warra-warra /'wɒrə-wɒrə/. *Obs.* [a. Gaurna *warra*.] KORADJI.

1842 S. *Austral. News* (London) 15 Nov. 55/1 Their influence is counteracted by major evolutions, chiefly by the *yammai ama* or *warra-warra* (sorcerers). **1863** J. BONWICK *Wild White Man* 56 These Boylyas, Warrawarras, or doctors can . . carry themselves into the camp of an opposing tribe.

warregal, *var.* WARRIGAL.

warrein, *var.* WARRAN.

warrettah, *var.* WARATAH.

warrigal /'wɒrəgəl/, *n.* and *a.* Formerly also **warragal, warragul, warregal, warrigul, worrogal.** [a. Dharuk *warrigal*.]

A. *n.*

1. DINGO *n.* 1.

c 1790 W. DAWES *Grammatical Forms Lang. N.S.W., Wor-re-gal,* a dog. **1834** G. BENNETT *Wanderings N.S.W.* I. 125 Like a warragul, or native dog. **1851** *Illustr. Austral. Mag.* (Melbourne) Sept. 178 The 'worrogal' finds it is becoming serious . . then he tries to shake his pursuers off. **1867** A.K. COLLINS *Waddy Mundoee* 12 Them Warregals is most owdacious bad about us. They was howling and yelpin' around Crowther's Creek last night. **1874** C. DE BOOS *Congewoi Correspondence* 127 There was the dog, a reglar old man warrigal, with the ends of his red hair turnin' grey.

2. MYALL *n.*¹ 2.

1847 *Port Phillip Herald* 21 Jan. 2/6 On his way to the scrub, one of the Warrigals yabbered to him, which seemed to frighten him. **1863** J. BONWICK *Wild White Man* 80 The Warriguls, or wild blacks, of Gipps Land, dwelt in the rocky fastnesses of the Australian Alps. **1890** A.J. VOGAN *Black Police* 133 Frazer went about for years shooting all and every native he could see, 'station boys', warragals, or town blacks—he was not very particular.

3. The plant *Tetragonia tetragonoides* (fam. Aizoaceae), occurring in Aust. and elsewhere, having fleshy leaves used as a vegetable. In full **warrigal cabbage.**

1861 *Bell's Life in Sydney* 2 Feb. 2/6 The land's first rate, you all must know, It's 'bosh' to say that nought will grow Save cabbage known as 'Warrigal'. **1981** J.A. BAINES *Austral. Plant Genera* 368 *T[etragonia] tetragonioides,* NZ Spinach, Warrigal Cabbage, all States and NZ . . . Early settlers actually cooked it like spinach.

4. A wild or untamed horse. Also *transf.*

1881 *Australasian* (Melbourne) 21 May 647/4 How we ran in 'The Black Warrigal'. **1905** J. FURPHY *Rigby's Romance* (1946) p. xviii, These were warrigals, even as scrub-bred cattle . . . You know the class—long-bodied, clean-flanked, hard-muscled, ardent-eyed, and always in the same advanced-store condition. **1935** G. MCIVER *Drover's Odyssey* 204 When the white stockman could not . . ride a wild horse or 'warrigal' from fear of being thrown, the black would be ordered to mount him.

B. *adj.*

1. MYALL *n.*¹ B. 2 *a.*

1847 *Atlas* (Sydney) III. 21/3 They discovered two Warrigal natives who had been fishing for eels. **1920** C.H. SAYCE *Golden Buckles* 119 Tynan despatched a warragal nigger from the black's camp, to The Cliff telephone station.

2. Wild; untamed. Also *fig.*

1881 *Australasian* (Melbourne) 21 May 647/4 The 'Pet of the Devil' looked awfully grand, Spieling well out on the wing, With four mares without ever a brand, Loping in to the Warrigal spring. **1904** *Truth* (Sydney) 31 July 9/5 The warrigal wowsers of Waine were conspicuous by their absence. These lewd, larrikin louts, who seek fatuously to foster the cause of pure, pious, parson-petted Jack Wayne.

war service home. A house purchased under a scheme providing for assistance to returned services personnel or their dependants: see quot. 1936.

1918 *Act* (Cwlth. of Aust.) no. 43 Sect. 1, This Act may be cited as the *War Service Homes Act* 1918. **1936** E. SCOTT *Aust. during War* in *Official Hist. Aust. 1914–18* XI. 840 Under the War Service Homes Act the persons who were eligible to apply for assistance were returned soldiers or sailors who were married, or about to marry, or who had dependants for whom it was necessary to provide homes; or any soldier's widow, or the mother of a deceased soldier who had been dependant upon him before his enlistment, or who was a widow, or who, if she had a husband, was not supported by him owing to his incapacity.

warty-faced honeyeater. *Regent honeyeater,* see REGENT 2.

1843 J. GOULD *Birds of Aust.* (1848) IV. Pl. 48, *Zanthomyza phrygia* . . Warty-faced Honey-eater. **1976** *Reader's Digest Compl. Bk. Austral. Birds* 467 Regent honeyeater *Xanthomyza phrygia*. . . Other names . . warty-faced honeyeater.

waub, *var.* WARB.

Warwick Farm. [The name of a racecourse in Sydney.] Rhyming slang for 'arm'. Also *ellipt.* as **Warwick.**

1944 *Biscuit Bomber Weekly: Mag. 1st Austral. Air Maintenance Co.* 4 Nov. 2 So I put my Warwick-Farm around her bushel-and-peck and kissed her on the North-and-South. **1962** D. McLean *World turned upside Down* 40, I don't want to get elephants. I just want a drop of dad 'n' mum to loosen up me warwicks.

wash, *n. Obs.* Abbrev. of Wash-pool.
1886 R. Henty *Australiana* 216 There were four of these paddocks between the 'wash' and the shed, and when the sheep arrived at the last paddock, near the shearing shed, it was put into the shed for the night and shorn the next day.

wash, $v.^1$ *Obs. intr.* (in quots.) Sheep-wash. Freq. as *vbl. n.*
1847 *Bell's Life in Sydney* 28 Aug. 3/5, I understand washing and shearing commence at Boyd and Co.'s next month. **1874** R.P. Falla *Knocking About* (1976) 21 Mr G. Rutherford is the only one on the Lower Avoca who will wash this shearing.

wash, $v.^2$ *Gold-mining. intr.* Usu. with **up**. To wash for gold in a sluice-box, etc., esp. after accumulating a quantity of wash-dirt; (of a claim, etc.) to yield gold through this process. Also *trans.*, with **off**, and freq. as **washing-up** *vbl. n.*
1859 *Colonial Mining Jrnl.* Apr. 123/3 The miners are not yet washing up. **1871** *Austral. Town & Country Jrnl.* (Sydney) 28 Jan. 113/1 The Enterprize Company had a splendid washing up last week; the yield was 70 oz. for about a fortnight's crushing. *Ibid.* 8 Apr. 431/2 Very few washings have taken place during the week, but the claims that did wash up yielded up to the average. **1872** 'Demonax' *Mysteries & Miseries* 17 They washed off the first lot, and the result was 12½ oz. of gold. This was left in the washing-off dish.

washaway. [Used elsewhere but chiefly Austral.: see OED.] The removal of earth by flood; the washing away of a portion of a railway line, road, etc., by flood; the hole or channel caused by this.
1893 *Westminster Gaz.* (London) 7 Mar. 8/3 The new railway also suffered severely, and traffic has been interfered with owing to several washaways. **1951** *New Settler in W.A.* (Perth) Feb. 7 We came across a big Chrysler wedged hard in a three-foot deep washaway in the crumbling, red, clayey soil bank of a wide watercourse. **1962** J. Hedge *Trout Fishing N.S.W.* 117 Opposite, on the left, are the shearing sheds. The old crossings to reach 'Koorabri' have now been discarded owing to the river having caused washaways.

washer. A face-cloth.
1951 D. Cusack *Say no to Death* 194 Doreen had given her a washer and a drop of warm water to wash the sleep out of her eyes. **1974** A. Buzo *Coralie Lansdowne says No* 71 I'll get you a cold washer.

washing, *vbl. n. Obs.*
1. Used *attrib.* with reference to the washing of sheep before shearing.
1847 *Bell's Life in Sydney* 24 July 3/1 Upon arriving at the banks of the Campaspie the river was 'up' and the opposite side presented a small pavement where sheep were driven down in the washing season. **1891** H. Nisbet *Colonial Tramp* I. 132 In the way of wool-sheds, sheep-pens, washing-ponds, &c.
2. Special Comb. **washing pen**, Wash-pen; **washing-pool**, Wash-pool.
1847 *Bell's Life in Sydney* 25 Sept. 3/3 In commencing operations for washing, there is frequently considerable difficulty to make the sheep enter the **washing pen**. **1841** *Port Phillip Gaz.* 7 Aug. 1 **Washing pools** of size to wash all sheep in the district.

washing stuff. *Gold-mining. Obs.* Wash-dirt. Also **wash-stuff.**
1852 J. Bonwick *Notes of Gold Digger* 10 Most of that through which you are now digging may prove 'washing stuff'. **1872** 'Resident' *Glimpses Life Vic.* 274 The heaps of washstuff and clay thrown up by the miners.

wash-pen. *Obs.* [f. Wash $v.^1$] An enclosure into which sheep are driven preparatory to being washed. Also *attrib.*
1847 *Maitland Mercury* 29 Sept. 2/5 This gate, during the time the sheep are being driven into the wash-pen, should be closed, that the water may not be seen. **1942** W. Glasson *Our Shepherds* 20 Washing sheep was strenuous work... At the end of the day a rum ration would be distributed among the wash pen workers.

wash-pool. *Obs.* [f. Wash $v.^1$ In Br. use but chiefly Austral.: see OED.] A pool, usu. in a natural watercourse, in which sheep are washed before shearing.
1830 R. Dawson *Present State Aust.* 291 A large party of natives was taken up the country to assist in making a washpool at the river for sheep. **1928** M. Forrest *Reaping Roses* 146 Across the lagoon was the long galvanized iron-roofed wool-shed, and, some miles out, an up-to-date wash-pool for the scouring of the fleeces.

wash stuff: see Washing stuff.

wash-up. *Gold-mining. Washing-up*, see Wash $v.^2$
1880 *Austral. Town & Country Jrnl.* (Sydney) 3 July 30/3 As soon as we had finished the next wash-up, I was to go back to Yatala. **1913** H. Lawson *Triangles of Life* 187 One morning in the New Year after the wash-up (and the claim panned out very well), the four of them went away.

waste, *a. Obs.* [Spec. use of *waste* uncultivated and uninhabited.] Of land: unalienated from, and unimproved by, the Crown; esp. in the collocation **waste land (of the Crown).**
1804 HRA (1921) 3rd Ser. I. 246 Two Acres for every Acre of Waste Land. **1890** 'R. Boldrewood' *Squatter's Dream* 43 He once more sighted the unromantic but priceless waters of the Warroo, and beheld, with the eye of a proprietor, the 'waste lands of the Crown'—most literally deserving that appellation.

watch-box. *Obs.* [Spec. use of *watch-box* a small structure providing shelter for a person on watch.] A movable sleeping compartment provided for the use of a watchman: see quot. 1848.
1826 J. Atkinson *Acct. Agric. & Grazing N.S.W.* 74 The watchman is provided with a moveable watch-box, and usually two or three dogs, and generally keeps up fires all night. **1848** H.W. Haygarth *Recoll. Bush Life* 44 He resigns all charge of them to the watchman, who passes the night alongside the folds in a 'watch-box'. This is simply a sort of wooden frame, covered with hides, or the bark of trees, and standing about a foot from the ground, with an opening on one side large enough to admit a small mattress and blankets.

watch-house. [Survival of *watch-house* a house used by municipal night-watchmen for the temporary custody of persons under arrest: see OED.]
1. A building, now usu. attached to a police station, in which suspected law-breakers are held under temporary arrest.
1810 *Sydney Gaz.* 29 Dec., The District Constable shall every Night place in the Watch-house, at Sun-set, a Constable to be called the *Constable of the Night*. **1978** R. Coleman *Pyjama Girl* 78 At 2 p.m. that day he was taken to the city watchhouse and charged with the murder of his wife.
2. Comb. **watch-house keeper.**
1835 *Colonist* (Sydney) 243/1 The police force at present

consists of fifteen constables .. lock-up keeper, watch-house keeper, and scourger.
Hence **watch-house** *v. trans.*, to confine (someone) in a watch-house.
1829 *Sydney Monitor* 4 July, Had we not been considerate, the man would have been watch-housed.

watchman. *Obs.* [Spec. use of *watchman* a person employed to guard private property.] One who is employed to watch over sheep during the night: see quot. 1848.
1825 B. FIELD *Geogr. Mem. N.S.W.* 445 The settlers' convict-servants (stockmen and sheep watchmen) do little but drone about their filthy turf-huts. **1848** H.W. HAYGARTH *Recoll. Bush Life* 44 For every flock two men are required, the shepherd, and another called the watchman, whose duty consists in taking care of the station, preparing the meals, watching the sheep at night, and shifting the folds every day.

water. Used *attrib.* in the names of flora and fauna: **water bush,** any of several plants, esp. *Myoporum acuminatum* (see *native myrtle* NATIVE *a*. 6 a.), common along inland watercourses, *Adriana hookeri* (fam. Euphorbiaceae) of sandy soils in all mainland States, and (*W.A.*) shrubs of the Austral. genus *Bossiaea* (fam. Fabaceae) incl. *B. aquifolium*; **couch,** either of two perennial grasses (fam. Poaceae) of damp or wet places in Aust. and widespread elsewhere, *Paspalum distichum* of all mainland States and *P. paspalodes* of all States; **dragon** (formerly **iguana**), any of several lizards occurring near water, esp. those of the fam. Agamidae, as *Physignathus lesueurii* of e. mainland Aust; **goanna,** any of several species of goanna (see GOANNA 1) occurring near water, usu. in n. Aust., esp. *Varanus mertensi*; **grass,** *swamp grass,* see SWAMP *n.*; **gum,** any of several trees of the fam. Myrtaceae, esp. *Tristaniopsis laurina* (also called KANOOKA) and the rainforest tree *Syzygium francisii* of n.e. N.S.W. and s.e. Qld.; (formerly) any of several trees of the genus *Eucalyptus* (fam. Myrtaceae) occurring along watercourses (see quots. 1826 and 1834); **-holding frog,** any of several burrowing frogs of drier inland Aust., esp. *Cyclorana platycephalus* of all mainland States exc. Vic.; **mallee,** any of several mallee eucalypts the roots of which are a source of water, as *Eucalyptus dumosa* and *E. oleosa* (fam. Myrtaceae); also *water tree*; **mole** *obs.,* PLATYPUS 1; also *attrib.*; **rat,** the large aquatic rodent *Hydromys chrysogaster*, widespread near water in Aust. and occurring elsewhere, having dense soft fur and webbed hind feet; BEAVER RAT; **tree,** any of many trees yielding water from the roots, or from hollows in the trunk, esp. *water mallee*, some species of *Acacia* (fam. Mimosaceae), *Brachychiton* (fam. Sterculiaceae), and *Hakea* (fam. Proteaceae), as *H. leucoptera* (see NEEDLEWOOD); **vine,** any of several climbing plants, esp. the woody *Cissus hypoglauca* (fam. Vitaceae) of e. Aust.; see also *wild grape* WILD 1.
1893 D. LINDSAY *Jrnl. Elder Sci. Exploring Exped.* 6 The sandhills were covered with the green **water-bush** (*Pollechia Zeylanica*). **1982** ELLIOTT & JONES *Encycl. Austral. Plants* II. 355 *Bossiaea*... A common name in W.A. is water bush, derived from the fact that after rain, water is often retained between the leaves and stems. **1882** *Proc. Linnean Soc. N.S.W.* VII. 312 *Paspalum distichum* or the **Water-Couch**.. has established itself on the banks of our rivers. **1968** N.T. BURBIDGE *Austral. Grasses* II. 152 Water Couch.. grows in shallow water or in lawns and, as its common name indicates, it has a spreading habit with a number of more or less horizontal stems rooting at the nodes. **1899** [**water dragon**] R. SEMON *In Austral. Bush* 183 The water 'guanas (*Physignathus Lesueuri*) are expert swimmers. **1923** *Bulletin* (Sydney) 11 Jan. 24/3, I confess to having frequently mistaken the 'eastern water dragon' (*Physignathus lesueurii*) for the varanus. **1901** *Bulletin* (Sydney) 23 Mar. 14/4 **Water-'goannas'** are very common on Condamine river. **1977** H. BUTLER *In Wild* 17 Here's a Water Goanna, one of the Racehorse Goanna group. This one is totally adapted for water life: in fact most people who see them think they're crocodiles. **1829** *Sydney Monitor* 26 Jan. 1480/1 We were in the midst of bull-rushes and coarse **water-grass**. **1826** J. ATKINSON *Acct. Agric. & Grazing N.S.W.* 14 Flooded or **Water Gum**—is found in low situations. **1834** G. BENNETT *Wanderings N.S.W.* I. 187 A canoe.. had been scooped by Mr Manton's servants from the solid trunk of a 'water gum' tree, (*Eucalyptus sp.*). **1929** W.D. FRANCIS *Austral. Rain-Forest Trees* 286 The name 'Water Gum' originated from the fact that quantities of a watery sap are sometimes contained in a central cavity or pipe of the stem, and it flows out when the trees [*sc. Eugenia francisii*] are being felled. **1938** C.T. WHITE *Princ. Bot. Qld. Farmers* 190 The name 'Water Gum' is one rather loosely used in Queensland for a number of Myrtaceous trees, being applied to species of *Tristania* and *Agonis*. **1896** B. SPENCER *Rep. Horn Sci. Exped. Central Aust.* I. 21 The most interesting animal is the Burrowing or **Water-holding Frog** (*Chiroleptes platycephalus*). As the pool begins to dry up it fills itself out with water, which in some way passes through the walls of the alimentary canal filling up the body cavity and swelling the animal out until it looks like a small orange. **1855** J. BONWICK *Geogr. Aust. & N.Z.* (ed. 3) 202 The red or **water mallee,** from the cut rootlets of which water may be procured. **1975** A.B. & J.W. CRIBB *Wild Food in Aust.* 167 In dry country, the shallow roots of eucalypts have been the main suppliers of emergency water... Best known of these eucalypts are *E*[*ucalyptus*] *dumosa* (.. bull mallee, water mallee..) and *E. oleosa*. **1800** Banks Papers 20 Sept. VII. 100, I send you.. *a cask in which is a* **Water Mole**. **1837** *Lit. News* (Sydney) 21 Oct. 105 In the course of time, we might have become expert 'water-mole' hunters. **1834** G. BENNETT *Wanderings N.S.W.* I. 306 An animal, called '**Water-rat**' by the colonists, and Biddunong by the aborigines, burrowed in the banks. **1895** *Proc. R. Geogr. Soc. Australasia: S.A.* (1899) 72 Several varieties of acacia are referred to by explorers and bushmen as '**water trees**', the roots yielding a fair supply. **1948** H.A. LINDSAY *Bushman's Handbk.* 3 On reaching the crest of the ridge you.. survey the scrub, looking for water-trees.. water mallees, a needlebush.. a banksia. **1965** *Austral. Encycl.* IV. 411 *H*[*akea*] *leucoptera* has been called water-bush and water-tree because aborigines (and probably thirst-stricken explorers) have obtained water from the fleshy roots by digging them up, cutting them into pieces, and placing one end in a slow fire. **1908** *Emu* VII. 203, I saw a female Rifle Bird fly.. down upon a **water vine** (*Vitis hypoglauca*). **1978** R.J. BRITTEN *Around Cassowary Rock* 101 Big heavy water-vines.. hang down out of trees like ship's hawsers.

water-bag. [Spec. use of *water-bag* a bag of skin or leather used for holding or carrying water.] A canvas bag used to carry water whilst travelling: see quot. 1914. See also quot. 1964.
1879 *Illustr. Austral. News* (Melbourne) 22 Jan. 7/3 We found at this camp two riding saddles, two pack saddles, six ten-gallon water-bags; three blankets, some tea and sugar. **1914** C.H.S. MATTHEWS *Bill* 88 A water-bag.. i.e. a canvas bag in which water is carried for drinking purposes. The water percolates through the canvas and evaporates on the outside of the bag, absorbing heat as it does so, and so keeping the water inside the bag beautifully cool. **1964** *N. Austral. Monthly* July 13 A common sight in most homes is a waterbag, suspended from a piece of wire in the shade.

water-burner: see WATER-SCORCHER.

water core. A disease of apples: see quot. 1891. Also as **water-cored** *ppl. a.*
1891 *Braidwood Dispatch* 22 Apr. 2/4 Water-core is easily known by the watery or waxy appearance it gives either the whole or part of an apple. **1930** *Jrnl. Council Sci. & Industr. Research* 177 The fact that water-cored apples are

subject to breakdown is well known... Water core is of two types. The first is developed in immature fruit and involves more or less of the core... The second type develops in maturing fruit and does not involve the tissues within the core line of vasculars.

water frontage: see FRONTAGE 1.

waterhole. [Used elsewhere but of local significance: see OED.]

1. **a.** A depression in which water collects; a pond or pool, which may be of considerable extent.

1817 J. OXLEY *Jrnls. Two Exped. N.S.W.* (1820) 154 At the eighth mile we came upon a small water-hole, which our poor horses soon emptied. **1874** R.P. FALLA *Knocking About* (1976) 5 The length of this magnificent water-hole cannot be less than two miles.

b. An artificial reservoir for the collection or retention of water.

1827 P.P. KING *Narr. Survey Intertropical & Western Coasts* I. 13 Our water-holes .. dug at the edge of the sand, within thirty yards of the vessel. **1843** *Sydney Morning Herald* 24 May 3/6 A large waterhole or dam is now being constructed, which will insure a supply of water during the driest seasons.

c. A cavity in the bed of a watercourse, esp. one that retains water when the main stream dries up: see quot. 1869.

1843 R.D. MURRAY *Summer at Port Phillip* 119 It is rare to find the channel of one of these streams without some portion of its contents remaining in those deep pools of water that occur at greater or less intervals in its course, and in colonial phrase are termed 'water-holes'. **1869** E.C. BOOTH *Another England* 18 In seasons of extreme drought, the river would .. cease to run; but at frequent intervals, reaches of from a few hundred yards to five miles in length were met with and upon the banks, the flocks and herds could drink in the driest season. These reaches (water-holes) is the homely colonial name for them) have, many of them, depths not yet fathomed.

2. *transf.* A public house or bar, esp. one frequented by a coterie; a 'watering hole'.

1968 D. O'GRADY *Bottle of Sandwiches* 191 There was a water-hole on the corner, so we left old Nebby where she was and visited it. 'Hey, mate—no dogs in the bar.' **1983** *Truckin' Life* VII. ii. 25 Billo Mullane .. a few Saturdays back after a prolonged stop-over at the .. water hole on Friday night.

3. Special Comb. **waterhole squatter,** *claypan squatter,* see CLAYPAN 2.

1904 *S. Austral. Public Service Rev.* Dec. 27 We picked out the best way we could .. and in a few miles came to another watering place where another resident of the district, of the waterhole squatter variety, had his headquarters.

water-joey. One who is employed to carry water to supply the needs of a group. See WOOD-AND-WATER JOEY a.

1916 *Bulletin* (Sydney) 14 Dec. 24/4 A young half-caste aborigine .. for a screw of 12 bob a day, is water-joey to the gangs. **1981** D. STUART *I think I'll Live* 235 No water to be drunk except it's boiled first. No one to go to the river 'cept the water joeys.

water-scorcher. An inferior cook. Also **water-burner.**

1916 *All abaht It* (London) Nov. 27 Commotion caused after tea—stretcher seen with our poor water-scorcher aboard. **1982** P. ADAM SMITH *Shearers* 264 They call him the water burner, cookoo, Silly Look, baitlayer, babbling brook.

watersider. WATERSIDE WORKER.

[N.Z. **1914** *Evening Post* (Wellington) 4 Feb. 10 Watersider (signature to letter).] **1937** L. ROSS *W. Lane & Austral. Labor Movt.* 124 The A.L.F. called on the watersiders. The watersiders responded. **1978** *Cattleman* (Rockhampton) Sept. 1/1 (*caption*) Watersiders will load beef.

waterside worker. One who is employed to load and unload a ship's cargo; a wharf-labourer.

1903 *Waterside Workers' Gaz.* Sept. 5/3 Waterside workers have sometimes good grounds for complaining that they do not get their full pay. **1982** LOWENSTEIN & HILLS *Under Hook* 20 Most waterside workers lived close to their jobs— the nature of the industry demanded it.

Watson. [See quot. 1966.] In the phr. **to bet like the Watsons,** to bet heavily.

1949 L. GLASSOP *Lucky Palmer* 163 Bet well? You bet like the Watsons. **1966** S.J. BAKER *Austral. Lang.* (ed. 2) 273 *Watson's, bet like the,* to wager heavily. There were apparently two Watson brothers, but legend disagrees when they operated—it varies from the 1880s to 'about 1910'. They are alleged to have been born at Bendigo, Victoria, and also to have been Sydney hotel-keepers and outback N.S.W. shearers.

wattle. [Transf. use of *wattle, pl.* and *collect. sing.* rods or stakes interlaced with branches in the construction of fences or wattle-and-daub buildings, from the use of the branches of wattles and similar plants for this purpose: see quots. 1790 and 1803.]

1. **a.** Any plant of the largest Austral. plant genus *Acacia* (fam. Mimosaceae), of which there are in Aust. nearly 800 described species, widespread elsewhere, esp. in the Southern Hemisphere; the wood of many of these species. The plants usu. have pale cream to orange-yellow, often fragrant flowers in spikes or globular heads, and vary in growth habit from prostrate shrubs to tall trees. Also *attrib.*

[**1790** W. TENCH *Compl. Acct. Settlement* (1793) 78, 32 houses .. built of wattles plastered with clay.] **1796** D. COLLINS *Acct. Eng. Colony N.S.W.* (1798) I. 556 The fiz-gig is made of the wattle. [**1803** *Sydney Gaz.* 20 Nov., A few pannels of houses built upon the principle of ancient colonial architecture were washed down... The crash of decayed posts and wattles was repeated but fortunately without injury to any of the tenants.] **1823** *Hobart Town Gaz.* 15 Feb. (Suppl.), A woman .. also swore to having seen a pot boiling there, with wattle-tan in it. **1982** R. HALL *Just Relations* 453 The plants themselves tell their own saga, geraniums among grevillea, honeysuckle behind the wattle.

b. With distinguishing epithet, as **black, cedar, coast, Cootamundra, golden, green, pycnantha, sally, sandhill, scrub, silver, willow:** see under first element.

c. Rarely, and usu. with distinguishing epithet, a tree of another genus, as a species of *Albizia* (see ACACIA 2). See also *black wattle* (b), BLACK $a.^2$ 1 a.

1902 J.S. HASSALL *In Old Aust.* 145 The first building ever set up in Australia for the worship of God was erected by the Reverend Richard Johnson... It was built of wattle, not the tree we know by that name, but a sort of Christmas bush, *Callicoma serratifolia.* *c* **1910** W.R. GUILFOYLE *Austral. Plants* 49 *Albizzia lophantha*.. 'Green Crested Wattle'.. (evergreen tree, 20 to 30 ft.) .. W. Aust.

2. The flower of the wattle; also *fig.,* and as the floral emblem of Australia (see also *golden wattle* GOLDEN 3).

1858 W.A. CAWTHORNE *Legend of Kupirri* 28 The cricket chirps beneath the grass, The wodlalla bends beneath the blast; The fragrant wattle scents the air, The yerké skips around his lair. **1891** *Worker* (Brisbane) 16 May 8 We'll make the tyrants feel the sting O' those that they would throttle; They needn't say the fault is ours, If blood should stain the wattle. **1956** J.T. LANG *I Remember* 197 His own epitaph to fit the occasion would have been .. 'I held Australia first, I wrote for her, I fought for her And when at last I lie, Then who to wear the wattle has A better right than I?'

3. In the phrase **up a wattle (tree),** *up a gum tree,* see GUM TREE 2.

1941 *Pow-Wow* (Shepparton) July 3 We think she was well kidded right up the wattle-tree. **1963** *Gumsuckers' Gaz.* (Melbourne) July 2 *Up a gum-tree,* in a quandary (a variant is *up a wattle*).

4. Comb. **a.** In sense 1: **wattle bush, scrub, tree.**

1837 *Tas. Non-State Rec.* 157/1 19 Nov., In this Collony [*sic*] .. though I Could not find a Furze Bush I Could find A **Wattle Bush.** **1853** J. SHERER *Gold Finder Aust.* 227 The robbers .. ordered them to proceed with their cart into an adjacent **Wattle Scrub.** *c* **1810** *Trans. Linnean Soc. London* (1827) XV. 239 This species .. is called *Thunder-bird* by the colonists... It frequents the *green* **wattle-trees** in Parramatta.

b. In sense 2: **wattle ball, bloom, blossom, gold.**

1963 R. STOW *Tourmaline* 24 The single soft **wattle-ball** of the evening star, which does not, alas, belong to me. **1884** D.B.W. SLADEN *Summer Christmas* 14 'Twas Christmaseve, and they sat round Th' hearth filled with **wattle-bloom** still found on stray trees. **1857** J. BONWICK *Early Days Melbourne* 14 **Wattle blossoms** perfumed the country. **1870** A.L. GORDON *Bush Ballads* 9 In the Spring, when the **wattle gold** trembles 'Twixt shadow and shine.

5. Special Comb. **wattle bark,** the bark of any of several species of wattle, some of which are cultivated commercially for the high tannin content of their bark; also *attrib.;* so **wattle-barker** (or **-stripper), wattle-barking** *vbl. n.,* **wattle bark stripping** *vbl. n.;* **extract** [used elsewhere but recorded earliest in Aust.], a concentrated tannin-rich substance produced from wattle bark; **gum,** a gum exuded from the trunk and branches of species of wattle.

1824 *Austral.* (Sydney) 16 Dec. 3 **Wattle-bark,** it is said, has been successfully tried in the sister colony for the purposes of tanning. **1886** J.F. CONIGRAVE *S.A.* 125 Tanning and wattle bark-stripping, wine making, olive oil making, and fruit preserving are occupations particularly adapted to this climate and soil. **1891** J. FENTON *Bush Life Tas.* (1964) 20 Mr Charles Friend had a party of wattle strippers at Port Sorell. **1898** *Tocsin* (Melbourne) 6 Jan. 3/1 A grave slur has been cast on Australian leather, and more especially upon the wattle bark method of tanning by the late action of the War Office authorities. **1898** *Bulletin* (Sydney) 26 Feb. 14/2 Amongst the community of wattle-barkers in the vicinity of Warrayadin, the marriage ceremony is regarded .. as a wasteful and ridiculous business. **1920** *Ibid.* 6 May 20/2 About the toughest of all bushwork, not excepting wattle-barking or log-fencing, is burning. [**1889 wattle extract:** J.H. MAIDEN *Useful Native Plants Aust.* 308 As far back as 1823 a fluid extract of Wattle Bark was shipped to London, fetching then the extraordinary price of £50 per ton, one ton of bark yielding 4 cwt. of extract of tar consistence.] **1927** *Council Sci. & Industr. Research Bull.* no. 32 13 Of more recent origin is the wattle extract industry of South Africa. **1843** *Portland Mercury* 10 May 3/1 The Countess of Durham, the last wool ship of the season, had on board 581 bales of wool .. 2 casks of **wattle gum** [etc.].

6. In the names of insects feeding on the wattle: **wattle goat moth,** any of several cossid moths of the genus *Xyleutes,* esp. the large *X. encalypti* and *X. liturata,* the larvae of which are among the insects called witchetty grubs; **grub,** a grub, prob. a WITCHETTY 2; **pig,** the weevil *Leptopius duponti.*

1885 F. MCCOY *Prodromus Zool. Vic.* I. iii. 47 *Zeuzera (Eudoxyla) Eucalypti* .. the **Wattle Goat-Moth** .. common in the winged state about February, flying in the twilight, in all parts of the colony where Wattle trees abound. **1968** H. FRAUCA *Bk. of Insects* 52 Among the world's most spectacular moths are some native species in the family Cossidae .. one of which is the Wattle Goat Moth... The female of this species has a wingspan of about seven inches and her fur-covered body is larger than a mouse. **1854** W. HOWITT *Boy's Adventures* 301 The women .. hunt for the **wattle grub,** a great luxury of these people. **1907** W.W. FROGGATT *Austral. Insects* 183 *L*[*eptops*] *tribulus,* often called by the Sydney boys the '**Wattle Pig**', feeds on the foliage of the black wattle; it is .. about 1 inch in length.

wattle bird. a. Any of the several birds of the genus *Anthochaera* of s. Aust., large honeyeaters having loud harsh calls, two species of which have conspicuous facial wattles; GILL BIRD. **b.** With distinguishing epithet, as **brush, little, red, yellow:** see under first element.

1819 W.C. WENTWORTH *Statistical, Hist., & Pol. Descr. N.S.W.* 119 The wattle bird .. is about the size of a snipe, and considered a very great delicacy. **1984** SIMPSON & DAY *Birds of Aust.* 329 The large wattlebirds .. use the richest and most dense nectar sources (*Banksia, Eucalyptus*) and aggressively exclude smaller species from these.

Wattle Day. An annual celebration, the date of which varies locally, of the blossoming of the wattle.

1910 *Bulletin* (Sydney) 29 Dec. 14/3 The R.C. mission, near Geraldton (W.A.) .. instituted the are called 'gohanna days', which, in black brother's mind are equivalent to our Empire Day or Wattle Day. **1985** *Canberra Chron.* 21 Aug. 3/1 Today is Wattle Day in the ACT—the middle of the Week of the Wattle, which began on Sunday and will end on Saturday.

wattled bee-eater. *Obs.* WATTLE BIRD.

1788 J. WHITE *Jrnl. Voyage N.S.W.* (1790) 144 The Wattled Bee-eater .. fell in our way... Under the eye, on each side, is a kind of *wattle,* of an orange colour. **1847** J. GOULD *Birds of Aust.* (1848) IV. Pl. 55, *Anthochaera carunculata* .. Wattled Bee-eater .. Wattle Bird of the Colonists.

wax. Used *attrib.* in the names of plants having waxy or glossy fruits or flowers: **wax-cluster** *obs.,* the shrub *Gaultheria hispida* (fam. Ericaceae) of Tas.; **flower,** any of several plants having waxy flowers, esp. species of the genus *Eriostemon* (fam. Rutaceae) occurring in all States but not N.T., and cultivated as ornamentals; also *attrib.;* **-lip (orchid),** either of the two terrestrial orchids of the genus *Glossodia* (fam. Orchidaceae) of s.e. Aust. incl. Tas.

1834 *Hobart Town Almanack* 133 *Gaultheria hispida*—The **wax cluster,** abundant in the middle region of Mount Wellington. *c* **1910** W.R. GUILFOYLE *Austral. Plants* 182 *Gaultheria hispida* .. 'Wax-cluster', or 'White Cluster-berry' (evergreen shrub, 3 to 5 ft.) f[lowers] white. *Ibid.* 158 *Eriostemon obovalis* .. 'Fairy **Wax-flower**' (evergreen shrub, 2 to 3 feet). *Ibid.* 174 *Eupomatia Bennettii* .. 'Wax Flower Bush' .. f[lowers] yellow and dark red. **1931** *Victorian Naturalist* XLVIII. 160 Of orchids, those found were mainly **Waxlips** (*Glossodia*). These were growing in profusion. **1947** T.Y. HARRIS *Wild Flowers Aust.* (rev. ed.) 45 Wax-lip Orchid *Glossodia major.* The solitary purple or blue flowers, on their slender stems, are very lovely.

waxie. [f. *wax* + -Y.] A wax match.

1928 *Bulletin* (Sydney) 29 Feb. 21/2 We were out of matches except for a chip from the head of a waxie found in my 'bumper' pocket. **1959** D. LOCKWOOD *Crocodiles & Other People* 70 'Throw a match into that grass,' Jack yelled. .. Before I could stop him he had struck a waxie and tossed it into the matted tangle beside the track.

wayback, *adv., a.,* and *n.* Also **away back.** [U.S. *wayback:* see OEDS.]

A. *adv.* OUTBACK *adv.*

1899 *Bulletin* (Sydney) 14 Jan. 14/1 Some years ago, when school-mastering way back, had occasion to call on

Mrs Casey. **1903** *Advocate* (Burnie) 10 Feb. 3/4 One of the settlers away back.

B. *adj.* OUTBACK *a.*

1899 *Bulletin* (Sydney) 28 Jan. 14/3 On a N.S.W. wayback selection lives a family containing three male idiots. **1967** *Southerly* iii. 205 This sun-baked, squalid . . wayback establishment.

C. *n.*

1. OUTBACK *n.*

1899 *North-Western Advocate* (Devonport) 21 Apr. 4/2 A man writes from way-back. **1956** *Bulletin* (Sydney) 15 Feb. 12/1 Our carriage was invaded by a couple of half-stonkered ringers from way back who had a good supply of bottled-stuff to help them onward.

2. OUTBACKER *n.*[1]

1903 *Bulletin* (Sydney) 11 Apr. 16/3 He had been a red-headed jackaroo but had evoluted to a perfect 'wayback' and attained management of a small station. **1956** T. RONAN *Moleskin Midas* 165 Of course, I'm only a wayback meself with no schoolin' so I wouldn't know.

waybacker. [f. prec.] OUTBACKER *n.*[1]

1899 *Bulletin* (Sydney) 5 Aug. 35/1 That's the Waybacker's ambition, to get 'paralytic drunk'. **1927** T.S. GROSER *Lure of Golden West* 277 Lightening the lot of the 'way-backer'.

weaner.

1. [Used elsewhere but recorded earliest in Aust.] An animal, usu. a lamb or calf, weaned during the current year. Also *transf.* and *attrib.*

1865 R. HENNING *Lett.* 19 Aug. (1966) 208 He takes the heaviest flock of all, 2,200 weaners. **1895** G. RANKEN *Windabyne* 43 This was the cattle-run proper. Smaller paddocks were made lower down the river for weaners, heifers, and fattening stock. **1980** ANSELL & PERCY *To fight Wild* 84 Came across a couple of weaner buffalo feeding right on the edge of the river.

2. *fig.* One who is young and inept; one who is new to a particular situation.

1892 *Truth* (Sydney) 22 May 1/5 Young Australia has too big a percentage of black sheep amongst its weaners. **1944** C. WILMOT *Tobruk* 43 We overtook a column of prisoners. . . An Australian sergeant hopped on the running-board and said, 'Would you drive us along a bit? I want to head these bloody weaners off down the road to Bardia.'

weaning paddock. An enclosure in which animals being weaned are confined.

1845 D. MACKENZIE *Emigrant's Guide* 120 Without a weaning or heifer paddock, you will be obliged to allow your calves to continue sucking their mothers for a whole year. **1945** E. MITCHELL *Speak to Earth* 149 A morning spent in the first weaning-paddock yard was quite exciting.

weatherboard, *a.* and *n.* [Transf. use of *weatherboard* a series of boards nailed horizontally, with overlapping edges, as an outside covering for walls.]

A. *adj.*

1. Of a building: having external walls covered with overlapping horizontal boards; weatherboarded.

1827 [see *weatherboard hut*]. **1847** *Moreton Bay Courier* 13 Nov. 3/1 We understand that a weatherboard building . . was blown down during the storm on Thursday evening. **1972** ANDERSON & BLAKE *J.S. Neilson* 44 Down near the Well men had built a little weatherboard church.

2. In collocations: **weatherboard cottage, house, hut.**

1837 BACKHOUSE & TYLOR *Life & Labours G.W. Walker* (1862) 277 It already consists of nearly a hundred buildings, chiefly **weather-board cottages,** and a few rude, turf huts. **1847** *Moreton Bay Courier* 11 Sept. 3/2 In addition to these, several **weather-board houses** in various parts of the town are fast approaching towards completion. **1827** P. CUNNINGHAM *Two Yrs. in N.S.W.* I. 163 From hence to the **Weather-board hut,** on King's Table Land, the distance is sixteen miles.

B. *n.* A weatherboarded building, usu. a dwelling. Also *attrib.*

1921 *Bulletin* (Sydney) 14 Apr. 56/3 When Joseph Appleby bought Mon Rèpos, Beach-road Carragool, he went straight to his friend Briggs to get it fully insured. . . 'Against fire, yes,' said Briggs. 'Though the premium is stiff for seaside weatherboards.' **1968** *Bulletin* (Sydney) 31 Aug. 42/3 Out in the older weatherboard suburbs, the three-yearly paint job is still the only defence against the sub-tropical seediness.

weather shed. SHELTER-SHED; now usu. a structure in a school playground.

1889 *Braidwood Dispatch* 17 Aug. 3/5 Residence of 4 rooms with . . weather sheds. **1980** M. WILLIAMS *Dingo!* 25 After school most of the boys in Number Seven home hung around me in the weathershed.

wedding bush. [See quot. 1981.] Any of several white-flowered shrubs of the Austral. genus *Ricinocarpos* (fam. Euphorbiaceae).

1914 E.E. PESCOTT *Native Flowers Vic.* 100 The 'wedding bush' is a free-flowing heath-like bush, covered with masses of white starry flowers, . . botanically known as Ricinocarpus pinifolius. **1981** J.A. BAINES *Austral. Plant Genera* 320 Wedding Bush . . a bushy shrub with white flowers like those traditionally used for weddings.

wedgebill. Either of two conspicuously-crested brown and grey birds of the genus *Psophodes, P. cristatus* of drier e. Aust. and *P. occidentalis* of drier w. Aust.

1841 J. GOULD *Birds of Aust.* (1848) III. Pl. 17, *Sphenostoma cristatum* . . Crested Wedge-bill. **1916** S.A. WHITE *In Far Northwest* 8 The wedgebill, another bird which came under our notice, was smart-looking, with crest and long tail.

wedge-tailed, *a.* Used as a distinguishing epithet in the names of birds: **wedge-tailed eagle,** the large eagle *Aquila audax,* widespread in Aust. incl. Tas., and occurring in s. New Guinea, having dark brown plumage and a wedge-shaped tail; *mountain eagle,* see MOUNTAIN; WEDGIE; see also EAGLE HAWK; also **wedge-tail, wedge-tail(ed) eagle(-hawk); shearwater** (formerly *petrel*), the dark brownish-black sea bird *Puffinus pacificus* of coastal e. and w. Aust., and elsewhere in the Indian and Pacific oceans.

1832 J. BACKHOUSE *Narr. Visit Austral. Colonies* 28 Dec. (1843) 118 Two **Wedge-tailed Eagles,** called in the colony Eagle Hawks, showed a disposition to carry off a small dog. **1896** F.G. AFLALO *Sketch Nat. Hist. Aust.* 143 The Wedge-tailed Eagle *(Aquila audax)* . . is easily approached when gorged from a recent feed. **1912** SPENCER & GILLEN *Across Aust.* 67 However bad the season may be, you are certain to see great wedge-tailed eagle-hawks . . hovering about or perched on trees. **1935** T. RAYMENT *Cluster of Bees* 63 The majesty of the wedge-tail eagle cleaving the air to pick up deftly with its talons the timorous rabbit. **1978** D. STUART *Wedgetail View* 2 The wedgetails would plane in on wide wings to land awkwardly. **1848** [**wedge-tailed shearwater**] J. GOULD *Birds of Aust.* VII. Pl. 58, *Puffinus sphenurus* . . Wedge-tailed Petrel. **1976** *Reader's Digest Compl. Bk. Austral. Birds* 57 Even when the wedge shape of its large tail is not clearly visible, the wedge-tailed shearwater can be distinguished at sea from other similar dark petrels.

wedgie. [f. WEDGE(-TAILED + -Y.] *Wedge-tailed eagle,* see WEDGE-TAILED.

1941 *Bulletin* (Sydney) 26 Mar. 17/2 On several occasions lately I have lost the services of my trapdog through the wedgies chasing him home. **1970** P. SLATER *Eagle for Pidgin* 50 In most countries people go for miles to see an eagle... Anyway scientific studies show only the odd wedgie will take a lamb.

weeai, weeay, varr. WEEI.

weebill. [See quot. 1984.] The smallest Austral. bird, *Smicrornis brevirostris*, an olive-brown to yellowish bird widespread in mainland Aust.
  1931 J. DEVANEY *Earth Kindred* 14 The weebill, hid in his sapling top Whistled as tho' he would never stop. **1984** SIMPSON & DAY *Birds of Aust.* 326 The Weebill .. is thornbill-like but has a small, short bill.

weegie, var. WIDGIE.

weei /'wiaɪ/. Also **weeai, weeay, wei.** [a. Aranda *aweye*.] An Aboriginal boy.
  1886 D. LINDSAY *Exped. across Aust.* (1889) 12 They also promised to bring in a *wei* (small boy) for me next day, in exchange for our dog 'Toby'. **1973** *Bronze Swagman Bk. Bush Verse* (1974) 46 I'm a wee-i in my mia-mia on the Mulligan. **1974** N. PHILLIPSON *As Other Men* 121 A wife could find another buck and weeays could die; tribal groups could be dispossessed. **1976** C.D. MILLS *Hobble Chains & Greenhide* 72 The 'weeais' usually scored knives and mouth organs. A pocket knife was highly prized and carefully guarded.

wee juggler /wi 'dʒʌglə/. Also **weejugla.** [a. Wiradhuri *wijagala*.] MAJOR MITCHELL COCKATOO.
  1898 D.W. CARNEGIE *Spinifex & Sand* 274 Throughout the day, galahs, wee-jugglers .. and an occasional hawk or crow, came to the spring. **1904** *Bulletin* (Sydney) 4 Feb. 17/1 Re age of cockatoos. I know of a 'wee juggler' (pink with yellow crest) that was trapped .. on the Lachlan, in 1884. **1921** *Ibid.* 5 May 22/1 The weejugla, or pink cockatoo .. keeps religiously to itself.

weekender. [Used elsewhere but recorded earliest in Aust.] A holiday house.
  1921 *Bulletin* (Sydney) 14 Apr. 56/3 A man .. bought a week-ender which he confessedly didn't intend to inhabit for more than four months of the year. **1981** B. OAKLEY *Marsupials & Politics* 52 Fifteen years ago we had a nice house in Melbourne, a weekender in the country, friends, parties, restaurants.

weelo /'wiloʊ/. Also **weeloo, weelow.** [a. Nhanta (and other w. Austral. languages) *wirlu*.] CURLEW.
  1845 J. GOULD *Birds of Aust.* (1848) VI. Pl. 5, At night it [sc. the 'Large-billed Plover'] is said to utter a loud scream or cry, resembling the word *Weē-lo*, whence its Aboriginal name: it is somewhat singular that the same name is applied to the *Oedicnemus grallarius* by the natives of Western Australia .. the cry of the two birds being similar. **1904** *Emu* III. 174 *Burhinus grallarius* (Stone Plover, Weeloo) .. pass the day sleeping on the stony ranges. **1962** B.W. LEAKE *Eastern Wheatbelt Wildlife* 89 The curlew or stone plover .. called weelow by aborigines will seek protection for hatching out and rearing its young.

weeping, *ppl. a.* Used as a distinguishing epithet in the names of plants: **weeping fig,** the large, spreading tree *Ficus benjamina* (fam. Moraceae) of n. Qld. and elsewhere, cultivated as an ornamental; **gum,** any of several trees of the genus *Eucalyptus* (fam. Myrtaceae) esp. (*Tas.*) *E. pauciflora* (see *snow gum* SNOW 1); **myall,** the tree *Acacia pendula* (see MYALL *n.*^{2}); **Polly grass,** a grass of the genus *Poa*.
  1890 F.M. BAILEY *Catal. Indigenous & Naturalised Plants Qld.* (ed. 2) 103 **Weeping Fig**—*Ficus Benjaminea*. **1836** J. BACKHOUSE *Narr. Visit Austral. Colonies* (1843) 440 Goulburn Plain is an extensive down .. with thinly scattered trees, such as **Weeping Gum**. **1848** *Maitland Mercury* 6 Dec. 4/3 The road is tolerably well defined, and passes through groves of **weeping myall** (acacia pendula). **1880** J. BONWICK *Resources Qld.* 45 The *Poa brownii* is good in all seasons; the *P. cespitosa* [sic], or **Weeping Polly grass,** though tufty, is sweet and indicates good soil.

weero /'wiroʊ/. [Prob. f. a W.A. Aboriginal language.] COCKATIEL.
  1948 D.L. SERVENTY *Handbk. Birds W.A.* 3 Some aboriginal names .. have passed into use as vernacular names, either locally or generally. Such include .. 'Weero' for the Cockatoo Parrot. **1973** D. STUART *Morning Star, Evening Star* 59 Then after a while, the others, all round the dishes outside. Wagtails and finches .. and weeros once.

weet-weet /'wit-wit/. [a. Wuywurung *wij-wij*.] An Aboriginal weapon and toy: see quot. 1967.
  1878 R.B. SMYTH *Aborigines of Vic.* I. 353 Weet-Weet .. the plaything .. called by the natives of the Yarra *Wi-tch-Wi-tch, We-a-witch, Weet-weet,* or *Wa-voit,* is one of the most extraordinary instruments used by savages. **1967** D.J. MULVANEY *Cricket Walkabout* 65 Blood sports were exceptional, and throwing the 'kangaroo-rat' was no exception. The name is misleading. Normally termed a 'weet-weet', this weapon consisted of a solid wooden or bone knob on a flexible handle about two feet in length. It was normally used for bringing down birds or small animals. After it had been swung rapidly backwards and forwards to gather momentum and flex the weapon, it was skimmed low along the ground with an underarm jerky motion.

wei, var. WEEI.

weight. *Gold-mining.* Abbrev. of 'pennyweight', 20th part of 1 oz. Troy or 1.55 g.
  1890 *Argus* (Melbourne) 9 Aug. 4/6 Tried a crushing and didn't get four weights to the ton. **1948** K.S. PRICHARD *Golden Miles* 27 The majority of workin' miners don't take the game seriously. If they get away with a few 'weights now and then, its only to show they've got the guts.

weir mallee /'wɪə mæli/. *Obs.* [a. Wergaia *wiyar-gajin* water tree + MALLEE 1 a.] The mallee or small tree *Eucalyptus dumosa* of drier s.e. mainland Aust.
  1858 *Trans. Philos. Inst. Vic.* III. 32 The water-yielding Malleè, called the Weir Malleè, was known to the natives long before the arrival of the whites. **1888** *Proc. Linnean Soc. N.S.W.* III. 509 *Eucalyptus dumosa* .. 'Weir-Mallee' of aboriginals.

welcome swallow. [See quot. 1945.] The swallow *Hirundo neoxena* of Aust. and, recently, New Zealand.
  1842 J. GOULD *Birds of Aust.* (1848) II. Pl. 13, *Hirundo neoxena* .. Welcome Swallow. **1945** C. BARRETT *Austral. Bird Life* 166 The welcome swallow (*Hirundo neoxena*) is happily named, for no bird enjoys a larger share of public favour. Welcome wherever it appears, the common swallow nests above shop doorways and windows in suburbia, and beneath verandahs and the eaves of houses.

well-in, *a.* Affluent, well-to-do.
  1845 T. MCCOMBIE *Adventures of Colonist* 241 They had a pretty little farm, and were well in. **1976** D. IRELAND *Glass Canoe* 180 Someone saw her at the trots with some of the trotting men who were really well in, and she was regarded with awe ever after.

Welshie. [f. WELSH(MAN + -Y.] NEW SOUTH WELSHMAN.
  1923 'J. NORTH' *Son of Bush* 115 Tommy ther drover! W'y, 'e wuz a Welshie, not er furriner!

Welshman. NEW SOUTH WELSHMAN.
  1891 H. NISBET *Colonial Tramp* I. 171 On this side of the bridge which crosses the Murray the Echucans are rabid

welter. [Spec. use of Br. dial. *welter* something exceptionally big or heavy of its kind, a 'whopper': see OED *sb.*³ 2.] In the phr. **to make** (something) **a welter, to make a welter of it,** to engage (in an activity) to excess.

1918 *Kia Ora Coo-ee* May 5/2 She was apparently English, and was walking arm in arm with a Tommy. My oath! he was making a welter of it. **1918** A. WRIGHT *Breed holds Good* 10 Frank had gone into town, and .. made the pace a 'welter'.

west, *adv.* Chiefly in N.S.W. and Qld.: west of closely settled districts; beyond the limits of settled, and by implication, civilized districts, esp. in the phr. **west of sunset.** See also SUNSET 1.

1905 *Truth* (Sydney) 19 Nov. 1/6 There is evidently a drought out west of West, even yet, for a Barringus correspondent writes that a wave of rabbits is on them from the West, evidently starved out. **1910** *Bulletin* (Sydney) 7 Apr. 14/1 In a West-o'-Sunset township two station hands argued all night.

western, *a.* Used as a distinguishing epithet in the names of animals: **western black cockatoo,** *red-tailed black cockatoo,* see RED *a.* 1 b.; **bristlebird,** the rare, ground-dwelling, brownish bird *Dasyornis longirostris* of s.w. W.A.; **brown snake,** the venomous snake *Pseudonaja nuchalis* (see *brown snake* BROWN *a.* 1); **grey kangaroo,** the kangaroo *Macropus fuliginosus* of s.w. and central s. Aust.; see also *grey kangaroo* GREY *a.*; also *ellipt.* as **western grey; rosella,** the predom. red, black, and green parrot *Platycercus icterotis* of s.w. W.A.; **whipbird,** the predom. olive-green bird *Psophodes nigrogularis* of coastal heaths and mallee scrubs in parts of s. Aust., lacking the distinctive cracking call of *P. olivaceus* (see WHIPBIRD).

1847 J. GOULD *Birds of Aust.* (1848) V. Pl. 9, *Calyptorhynchus naso* .. **Western Black Cockatoo** .. Red-Tailed Black Cockatoo of the Colonists. [**1945 western bristlebird**: C. BARRETT *Austral. Bird Life* 191 The eastern bristlebird (*D*[*asyornis*] *brachyptera*) inhabits eastern New South Wales. .. The western form (*D. longirostris*) is confined to South-western Australia.] **1983** *Western Farmer* (Perth) 10 Nov. 59/4 A search will start at Twertup on Saturday for the rare western bristle bird. **1967** H. COGGER *Austral. Reptiles* 98 The **Western Brown Snake** is similar in shape, size and habits to the Eastern Brown Snake, but is much more variable in colour. It varies from olive-grey to rich brown above. **1941** E. TROUGHTON *Furred Animals Aust.* 218 **Western** Forester or **Grey Kangaroo** .. *Macropus ocydromus.* .. This rather warmly coloured western member of the great-grey group is generally regarded as a geographical race of the eastern species, *M. major.* **1983** *Mercury* (Hobart) 8 Sept. 16/2 There were about .. 1,800,000 western greys predominantly in South Australia. **1945** C. BARRETT *Austral. Bird Life* 80 The **western rosella** .. (*P*[*latycercus*] *icterotis*) inhabits South-western Australia. **1945** C. BARRETT *Austral. Bird Life* 137 The **western whipbird** (*P*[*sophodes*] *nigrogularis*) had not been met with for many years in South-western Australia .. when it was rediscovered, in Mallee country near the South Australian-Victorian border.

western grey kangaroo: see KANGAROO *n.* 2.

westie, *n.* and *a.* [f. *west(ern suburb* + -Y.]

A. *n.* A resident of one of the western suburbs of Sydney.

1977 *Sea Notes* June-July 10/4 In Sydney, anyone who lives west of *you*, can be broadly dismissed as a 'Parra', or a 'Westie'. The first of these much loved expressions deriving from that satellite city of Sydney's, Parramatta. **1986** *Nat. Times* (Sydney) 10 Jan. 24/1, I met some young people we'd call 'westies' through a self-help organisation and I got on well .. but I would probably be embarrassed to bring them to a club or a party with my school friends.

B. *adj.* Of, pertaining to, or belonging to a resident of a western suburb of Sydney.

1982 *Austral. Women's Weekly* (Sydney) 10 Feb. 108/2 Incidentally, in the patois of the Bondi car park, panel vans are considered 'Westy'—a reference to Sydney's beachless western suburbs. **1986** *Nat. Times* (Sydney) 10 Jan. 24/4, I like wearing stylish, snobby clothes that are not 'westy'.

Westralia. Shortened form of 'Western Australia'.

1893 *Bulletin* (Sydney) 29 July 7/4 A Melb. timber-merchant formed a syndicate .. to prospect Westralia for gold. **1969** L. HADOW *Full Cycle* 123 All well in Westralia stop.

Westralian, *n.* and *a.* [f. prec.]

A. *n.* A non-Aboriginal person native to or resident in Western Australia.

1891 E.H. HALLACK *W.A. & Yilgarn Goldfields* 34 Parting advice to Westralians is—try and inculcate the principles of self-help. **1977** C.T. CASSIDY *Random Thoughts* 1 And gather here Westralians all, By birth, adoption, distant call, In confirmation of that day, When this State started on its way.

Hence **Westralienne** *n.*, a female Westralian.

1956 J.E. WEBB *So much for Sydney* 61 Westraliennes were equally loyal to Agnes Robertson.

B. *adj.* Of or pertaining to Western Australia.

1896 *Worker* (Sydney) 7 Mar. 1/3 What *can* you expect after a diet of 'tinned dog', the great Westralian standby, and when on your cuticle you've got a crust of real Westralian dirt—*not* 'wash' dirt? **1953** *New Settler in W.A.* (Perth) Mar. 39 All the main North-West centres are now served by one or other of the Westralian air services.

westringia /wɛˈstrɪndʒiə/. [The plant genus *Westringia* was named by English botanist J.E. Smith (*Vet. Akad. Handl. Stockh.* (1797) 171) after the Swedish physician J.P. *Westring,* a student of lichens.] Any plant of the genus of shrubs *Westringia* (fam. Lamiaceae) of temperate Aust., having white or bluish flowers and whorled leaves.

1814 R. BROWN *Gen. Remarks Bot. Terra Australis* 33 Westringia and Prostanthera, with the genera nearly related to each of these, are the most worthy of notice among Labiatae, all of them are limited to Terra Australis. **1984** E. WALLING *On Trail Austral. Wildflowers* 51 A Westringia with dainty white flowers spotted with purple and whorled leaves covered with white hairs on the under surface.

wet, *a.* and *n.*

A. *adj.*

1. In the collocation **wet season,** a period of substantial rainfall; a rainy season.

1842 *Austral. & N.Z. Monthly Mag.* 29 The wet season commences with slight showers in April. **1984** B. DIXON *Searching for Aboriginal Lang.* 1 The first big storm of the wet season had just started.

2. Of sheep: having a fleece which is too damp to be shorn. Also as quasi-*adv.*

1894 *Bulletin* (Sydney) 20 Jan. 9/4, I can recall many instances of *some* shearers voting 'wet sheep' while at the hut. **1982** P. ADAM SMITH *Shearers* 228 Before the union was founded, voting 'wet' was one of the few retaliations against the squatter that the men had. .. After the need for retaliation was past, the use of a 'wet' vote was still handy for the odd days off.

3. *fig.* Irritable; exasperated. Freq. in phr. **to get wet.**

1898 *Bulletin* (Sydney) 17 Dec. (Red Page), To *get narked* is to lose your temper; also expressed by *getting dead wet*. **1977** B. SCOTT *My Uncle Arch* 3 Naturally, Grandad was wet as hell. Pushing a pumper home eleven miles on a Friday night didn't make him too happy.

B. *n.* Chiefly *N.T.* Abbrev. of *wet season*.

1908 *Truth* (Sydney) 2 Feb. 12/3 In the dry season they are waiting for the wet. **1984** *N.T. News* (Darwin) 15 Sept. 41/7 Make your trees happy. Fertilize before the wet. Aged chook manure.

whacker. Also **wacker.** [f. *whacky* crazy, odd, peculiar.] A fool; a generalized term of abuse. Also as *adj.*

1966 D. NILAND *Pairs & Loners* 40 'Listen,' he ground out. 'You listen to me: am I among men or curs? What's the grouch against me? If you pack of whackers think you're going to freeze me and my kid out you can think again.' **1981** A. WELLER *Day of Dog* 48 The Boys from Brazil saunter back to their car and glide away... 'Ya want to look out for those wackers. They hate us nigs.'

whacko, *int.* and *a.* Also **wacko.** [f. *whack* a blow + *-o*. Used elsewhere but recorded earliest in Aust.: see OEDS.]

A. *int.* An exclamation of approbation: see quot. 1941. Esp. in the phr. **whacko the diddle oh.**

1937 W. POLLOCK *So this is Aust.* 48, I like you Australia. I am glad I came and have begun to know you. I shall be saying, 'Good-o', 'Too right', and 'Whack-o', with you soon. **1941** S.J. BAKER *Pop. Dict. Austral. Slang* 81 *Whacko,* good! Hurrah! A popular ejaculation. **1967** *Kings Cross Whisper* (Sydney) xliv. 8/1 (*heading*) Super-secret, top-level you-beaut discovery. *Wacko for the CSIRO*. **1971** *Bulletin* (Sydney) 16 Oct. 20/3 Labor might get into power and then whacko the diddle-oh!

B. *adj.* 'Absolutely splendid'. Also in the phr. **whacko the chook (diddle-oh, goose).**

1970 *Kings Cross Whisper* (Sydney) lxxxiv. 5/4 Ample Petrolillium, the all-Aussie you-beaut whacko-the-goose petrol pedlar, tonight admitted it encouraged drunken driving. **1973** L. OAKES *Whitlam PM* 38 In Margaret's words, quoted in Women's Day in July 1972: 'We'd have a whacko time anywhere—whether at the Australia Hotel or the Cafe de Fairfax to have meat pies.' **1977** S. LOCKE ELLIOTT *Water under Bridge* 313 Look, it'll be whacko the diddle-o, I'm not worried. **1981** *Weekend Austral. Mag.* (Sydney) 19 Dec. 7/1 Fifth-generation-Australian Patsy Adam-Smith is a real, fair dinkum, bewdy-bonzer, whacko the chook, little-Aussie-battler if ever there was one.

whale, *n.*

1. [See quot. 1900.] *Murray cod,* see MURRAY 2.

[**1873** see Whale *v.*] **1900** *Tocsin* (Melbourne) 6 Sept. 5/2 The cod being a large fish, is by reason of his size facetiously termed a whale, and his captor a whaler accordingly. **1926** *Aussie* (Sydney) Aug. 50/1 The Murrumbigee whalers were mostly old men, and their 'whales' were Murray cod.

2. In the phr. **a whale in the bay,** a person with money to spend.

1961 W.E. HARNEY *Grief, Gaiety & Aborigines* 20 Everywhere I heard the term.. 'a whale in the bay' and came to realise it meant someone was in town who had money to spend. **1984** *Austral.* (Sydney) 14 Nov. 3/4 Mr Read said he.. had told his staff the only way such a poor horse could possibly win such a race was 'by a ring-in'. 'I knew there had to be some kind of whale in the bay for this kind of activity to go on,' he said.

3. In the phr. **to play the whale,** to vomit.

1968 B. HUMPHRIES *Wonderful World Barry McKenzie,* I'll *chunder* so help me—you know.. *play the whale.* **1974** *Bulletin* (Sydney) 19 Jan. 13/1 Lofty's always getting full and playing the whale.

whale, *v.* [See quot. 1873.]

1. *trans.* To travel along (the banks of a river) as a swagman. Also *fig.,* and as *vbl. n.*

1873 J.C.F. JOHNSON *Christmas on Carringa* 16 Men when on the tramp through the Riverina country often carry a piece of twine and a hook to catch cod or blackfish. This is termed 'Murrumbidgee Whaling'. **1924** E.J. BRADY *Land of Sun* 14 After leaving Newcastle, we smoked and talked with the unrestraint of old bush-mates who had 'whaled' the rivers of prosperity in company and padded the hoof across arid plains of life.

2. *intr.* To travel as a swagman along the banks of a river. Also as *ppl. a.*

1898 *Worker* (Sydney) 2 July 6/1 There are thousands of men tramping the sun-scorched grassless plains of Australia, or whaling up and down the muddy streams (termed 'noble rivers' by the politicians who ride in Pullman cars). **1900** *Tocsin* (Melbourne) 13 Sept. 6/1 In the hour of leaving Wagga we had passed a proper 'whaling sundowner', arrayed in garments of sacking and boots fashioned chiefly from bark.

whalebone tree. [See quot. 1965.] The rainforest tree *Streblus brunonianus* (fam. Moraceae) of e. N.S.W., e. Qld., and New Guinea. See also WADDY WOOD.

1889 J.H. MAIDEN *Useful Native Plants Aust.* 591 *Pseudomorus Brunoniana* .. called 'Whalebone Tree' in Southern New South Wales... Wood light brown, close-grained, hard, and tough. **1965** *Austral. Encycl.* VI. 147 *Pseudomorus* is.. represented in Australia by *P. brunoniana* (white handlewood), which possesses a very springy timber and flexible branches, by virtue of which it is sometimes called whalebone-tree.

whaler, var. WALER.

whaler, $n.^1$ Also **waler.** [See WHALE $n.^1$ and *v.*]

a. A swagman whose route follows the course of a river.

1878 'IRONBARK' *Southerly Busters* 177, I know the Murrumbidgee's bends, Though not a 'whaler' now, And many a score of sheep I've shore For good old Jacky Dow. **1953** H.M. EASTMAN *Mem. of Sheepman* 70 'Walers'.. were a carefree lot.

b. *spec.,* as **Darling, Murray, Murrumbidgee whaler.**

1894 G. BOOTHBY *On Wallaby* 318 The '**Darling whalers**', as they are called: idle, loafing, thieving tramps, somewhat after the fashion of the 'Travellers' in North Queensland, who move up and down the river (up one bank and down the other), from year's end to year's end, doing no work and depending for their existence upon the charity of the unfortunate squatter. **1926** L.C.E. GEE *Bush Tracks & Gold Fields* 69 Those curious people, 'the **Murray whalers**'. **1878** *Squatters' Plum* 15 At length he is advised to take to the bush and crawl from station to station looking for employment, and the adoption of this step gives him a new designation, that of Sun-downer, or **Murrumbidgee Whaler.**

c. In the collocation **whalers' delight:** see quots.

1901 *Bulletin* (Sydney) 14 Sept. 16/4 'Murrumbidgee jam' consists of brown sugar muddled up with cold tea... It is also called Whaler's Delight. **1920** *Ibid.* 24 June 22/3 'Murrumbidgee jam'—brown sugar made into a thick paste by mixing it with cold tea.. was also well known as Whalers' Delight.

whaler, $n.^2$ [See quot. 1969.] Any of several sharks of the fam. Carcharhinidae, esp. the large bronze whaler *Carcharhinus brachyurus* of s. Aust. and elsewhere in temperate seas. Also **whaler shark.**

1882 J.E. TENISON-WOODS *Fish & Fisheries N.S.W.* 92 It is very probable that the majority of our sharks have a very wide range... The following list includes all that are known to occur in our seas.. the Whaler, *Galeocerdo rayneri* [etc.]. **1936** N. CALDWELL *Fangs of Sea* 9 The whaler shark, probably the most numerous of all Australian sharks, has a hide of medium thickness. **1969** J. POLLARD *Austral. & N.Z. Fishing* 686 The name whaler appears to go back to the days of the old whalers at Twofold Bay, on the New South Wales south coast, where they were among the most common species seen around the whales.

whaling station. *Hist.* [Used elsewhere but recorded earliest in Aust.: see OEDS *whaling, vbl. sb.* 2.] A port serving as a base for whalers. See also *fishing station* FISHING.

1833 *Launceston Advertiser* 17 Oct. 3 The brig Socrates is entered at the Custom House for Portland Bay (whaling station). **1977** C. MCCULLOUGH *Thorn Birds* 20 The eleven men . . came out at the whaling station at Hobart.

whampoo pigeon, var. WOMPOO PIGEON.

wharfie. [f. WHARF(-LUMPER or *labourer* + -Y.] WATER-SIDE WORKER.

1911 *Truth* (Sydney) 16 Apr. 5/8 '*Wharfies*' *take a hand*. . . The wharf laborers have good cause to thank 'Truth'. **1983** *Daily Tel.* (Sydney) 26 Feb. 1/2 His wife was the reason the former wharfie, brickie, bridge rigger, and battler got his start in television.

wharf-lumper. [f. *wharf* + *lumper* a labourer employed in loading or unloading cargo.] A wharf-labourer; WATERSIDE WORKER.

1899 *North-Western Advocate* (Devonport) 8 Mar. 2/8 Short strike amongst Hobart wharf lumpers. **1965** N. LINDSAY *Bohemians of Bulletin* 15 The old man's a wharf-lumper.

Also **wharf-lumping** *pres. pple.* and *vbl. n.*

1898 *Worker* (Sydney) 23 Apr. 5/2 If I were asked which was the best for a man to do—go gold-digging or stick to comping—I would say go 'wharf-lumping' or anything else. **1921** *Bulletin* (Sydney) 7 July 20/3 Here are the countries represented in a wharf-lumping gang that lately worked a steamer at Thursday Island: Britain, Russia, Germany, Denmark, Greece, Ceylon, Malay States, South Sea Islands. . . They all get award rates.

wheat. [Spec. use of *wheat* the cereal plant.] Used attrib. in Special Comb. **wheat cocky,** a wheat farmer; see COCKY *n.*²; also *attrib.*; so **wheat cockying** *vbl. n.*; **lumper,** one employed to load or unload sacks of wheat; so **wheat lumping** *pres. pple.* and *vbl. n.*; **paddock,** an enclosure in which wheat is grown; see PADDOCK *n.* 1 a.; also *attrib.*

1908 *Bulletin* (Sydney) 17 Dec. 15/1 The **wheat cockies** upon the Vic. northern plains are singing out that they cannot get enough men to do the harvesting. **1949** G. BERRIE *Morale* 218 What about you, Mac? Going back to wheat cockying? **1971** W.G. HOWCROFT *This Side Rabbit Proof Fence* 68 A bachelor wheat-cocky neighbour arrived one evening in an ancient touring car. **1911** *Bulletin* (Sydney) 16 Feb. 13/3 This man was filling-in time trying to beat out the fire, when a **wheat lumper** carrying a large billycan of beer transpired. **1946** *Bulletin* (Sydney) 2 Jan. 13/2 I'm wheatlumpin' at Cowangie with four other blokes. **1975** R. BEILBY *Brown Land Crying* 179 Now they got this bulk-'andlin', tipped out from the 'arvesters inta a truck an' inta them bins at the railway. No wheat-lumpin' any more. **1846** *Moreton Bay Courier* 12 Dec. 2/4 A short time ago as Robert Tomlinson, a farm servant . . was reaping in the **wheat paddock,** a green snake bit him on the hand. **1879** *Native Tribes S.A.* 99 Jackson was working by himself at the wheat-paddock fence.

wheat-eared Mitchell: see MITCHELL GRASS 2.

wheel, *n.*

1. [Chiefly Austral.: see OEDS *wheel, sb.* 7 b.] In the phr. **to be on** (someone's) **wheel,** to hound, or put pressure on (a person).

1922 C. DREW *Rogues & Ruses* 34 Me and Finger was on their wheels, but by the time we hit the ring Smiles' mount was three to one on. **1969** O. WHITE *Under Iron Rainbow* 118 The inspector's been on my wheel to trace him.

2. In the phr. **silly as a wheel,** very silly.

1952 T.A.G. HUNGERFORD *Ridge & River* 57 Oscar was sound, but silly as a wheel. **1985** J. CLANCHY *Lie of Land* 112 Father Tierney was mad. Cracked as an egg, some boys said, silly as a wheel, mad as a two-bob watch.

wheel, *v.* [Spec. use of *wheel* to turn (a person, animal, or thing) round or aside.]

1. *trans.* To cause (a stampeding mob of cattle, etc.) to turn back or to the side.

1872 G.S. BADEN-POWELL *New Homes for Old Country* 186 People will risk their necks merely to turn or 'wheel' a mob of cattle. **1972** *Bronze Swagman Bk. Bush Verse* (1973) 9 'Twixt the river bank and the myall scrub Where Gold Star wheeled the lead.

2. *transf.* To discountenance (someone).

1912 *Bulletin* (Sydney) 28 Nov. 16/4 One of the fraternity confided to me on the board . . that he 'had peeled 88, and was dragging the chain behind Nugget Smith', but had bet him 'a bottle of sheep dip' that he'd 'wheel him next day'. This being translated means my friend had shorn 88 sheep, which was the lowest tally. The next most meagre barbering was that of the aforesaid Nugget, and my friend had wagered him a bottle of whisky he would disrobe more jumbucks than Nugget on the following day. **1915** *Anzac Rec. Gaz.* (Alexandria, Egypt) 12 Nov. 2/2 He had the good luck to miss being 'wheeled' many a time.

wheelbarrow. *Austral. pidgin. Obs.* A dray.

1848 C. COZENS *Adventures of Guardsman* 127 On perceiving what they termed the 'wheelbarrow' approaching, they set up a simultaneous shout, running to meet us . . readily lending their assistance in unloading the dray. *c* **1879** A. MACPHERSON *Mount Abundance* 14 They knew the words 'white fellow' and 'wheelbarrow' (their corrupt word for *drays*)—words got from some semi-civilised tribes on the Lower Balonne.

wheeler. *Mining.* One employed underground to haul skips or trolleys of ore: see quot. 1962.

1901 *Illawarra Mercury* (Wollongong) 5 Jan. 2/3 The miners' wheelers held another meeting on Saturday last and decided that the wheelers do not return to work unless guaranteed the advance as agreed upon by the joint committee. **1962** O. PRYOR *Aust.'s Little Cornwall* 35 The ore in the underground workings was hauled from chutes to the haulage shaft in wooden barrows, often through levels where the roof was so low that the wheelers had to walk with bent backs.

wheel of fire tree: see FIRE-WHEEL TREE.

Whelan the Wrecker. The trading name of a demolition contractor, applied allusively to a demolitionist or vandal (see quot. 1929).

[**1929** *Melbourne Telephone Directory* May 390/2 Whelan the Wrecker—Sydney rd Cobg N13.] **1940** *Puckapunyal: Official Jrnl. 17th Austral. Infantry Brigade* Apr. 15 Did anyone see anything happen on the last train from Spencer Street . . Whelan the Wrecker was abroad apparently. **1980** *R.A.N. News* (Sydney) 13 June 5 Knocking it down? Send for Whelan the Wrecker.

wherang, var. WIRRANG.

whingeing pom. See quot. 1962. See also POM and POMMY. Also **whingeing pommy.**

1962 MARSHALL & DRYSDALE *Journey among Men* 189 The British national pastime of 'grousing' (to use an English phrase) has given rise in Australia to the derisive expression *wingeing pommy*. **1972** T. KENEALLY *Chant of Jimmie Blacksmith* 17 It'll pass a law to give every single wingein bloody Pommie his fare home to England. Back to the smoke and the sun shining ten days a year and shit in the streets. Yer can have it.

whip, *n.*

1. *pl.* [Br. dial. *whips* 'lashings', an abundance: see OED(S *sb.* 3 c.] An abundance.

1890 *Quiz* (Adelaide) 5 Dec. 6/3 In what Literary Society are the terms, 'That's fair dinkum' and 'Oh, yes, whips' to be heard? **1978** D. STUART *Wedgetail View* 33 Soothes all the gut, good hot tea with whips o' sugar.

2. In the phr. **when the whips are cracking,** 'when the action starts'.

1906 A.B. PATERSON *Outback Marriage* 243 The boco's one eye's worth any horse's two. Me an' the boco will be near the lead when the whips is crackin'. **1977** R. BEILBY *Gunner* 116 I'll be there when the whips're crackin'! I'll keep up with you blokes if I hafta crawl!

3. In the phr. **fair crack of the whip:** see FAIR *a.*¹ 3 a. and b.

4. Special Comb. **whip mark,** used allusively of meat to indicate toughness.

1917 *'Brisbane' R.A.N.: On Board H.M.A.S. 'Brisbane'* I. 26 Look at the whip marks on the beef. **1941** *Men may Smoke* (Sydney) May 6 Pork . . its Buffalo! There's whipmarks on its hide.

whip, *v.* [Transf. use of Br. dial. and colloq. *to whip the cat,* used in various senses: see OED(S *v.* 16 a.] In the phr. **to whip the cat,** to suffer remorse; to complain; to 'cry over spilled milk'.

1847 A. HARRIS *Settlers & Convicts* 349 And now it was my turn to 'whip the cat'. **1926** M. FORREST *Hibiscus Heart* 100 They are pretty disgusting . . but they never realize it when in liquor . . and whipping the cat afterwards doesn't seem to cure them. **1968** S. GORE *Holy Smoke* 56 It's no good whipping the cat if a man's such a dill as to come the double on anyone . . and then gets the mockers put on him.

whipbird. [Shortened form of 'coach(man's) whip bird': see COACHMAN and COACH-WHIP.] Either of two predom. olive-green birds of the genus *Psophodes,* esp. the common *P. olivaceus* of e. mainland Aust., also known as COACHMAN, COACH-WHIP, *stockwhip bird* (see STOCKWHIP 2). See also *western whipbird* WESTERN.

1843 R.D. MURRAY *Summer at Port Phillip* 196 Terms such as the bell-bird and whip-bird denote two little birds that tinkle their bells and crack their whips with a surprising likeness to the original sounds. **1955** V. PALMER *Let Birds Fly* 25 Whipbirds calling from one ferny hillside to another.

Hence **whip-birding** *pres. pple.,* imitating the sound made by a whipbird.

1909 *Bulletin* (Sydney) 26 Aug. 40/2 Some of the youngsters were shouting and whip-birding again, attracting everybody's attention.

whipping side. *Shearing.* [f. *whip, v.* to move (something) vigorously or quickly, with reference to the stroke of the shears.] The last side of the sheep to be shorn.

1899 J. BRADSHAW *Quirindi Bank Robbery* 3 Put me on a shearing floor and it's there I'm game to bet That I'd give to any ringer ten sheep start; When on the whipping side away from them I slide, Just like a bullet or a dart. **1982** *Sydney Morning Herald* 23 Oct. 29/3, I grabbed my boggi and ran her down the whipping side.

whippy. [Of unknown origin.]

1. The base in a kind of hide-and-seek game.

1964 *Bulletin* (Sydney) 22 Aug. 31/3 The Tree was the whippy for hidings, the base for releasings. **1980** C. JAMES *Unreliable Mem.* 34, I noticed a girl using the fence as a whippy. She was leaning against it with her face buried in her folded arms while other girls hid. If some other girl got to the whippy while she was away searching, there would be a cry of 'all in, the whippy's taken'.

2. *transf.* A place in which money is kept; the money in such a place.

1973 *Kings Cross Whisper* (Sydney) cliv. 16/2 I've never yet met a Kiwi who didn't cry poor mouth while he snipped you bone dry and all the time had a secret whippy tucked away somewhere you didn't know about. **1980** *Sun-Herald* (Sydney) 27 Jan. 66/4 Fair dinkum, if a man had enough in the willy, I mean whippy, I'd get myself a charlie . . and shout her seven or so ounces of sheer joy.

whip snake. [See quot. 1893.] Any of several slender, whip-like snakes, esp. of the genus *Demansia* of mainland Aust. and New Guinea, esp. the widespread, venomous *D. psammophis.*

1844 *Duncan's Weekly Register* (Sydney) 16 Nov. 246/1 All the whip snakes are proverbially dangerous and the poison most active and fatal. **1893** J. DEMARR *Adventures in Aust.* 206 A whip-snake is so called, owing to its resemblance in length and thickness to the thong of a whip.

whipstick. [Transf. use of *whip-stick* a pliant stick used as a whip.]

1. a. A form of growth (usu. of mallee eucalypts) characterized by a number of erect, slender stems; a tree of this habit. **b.** An area of vegetation dominated by such trees. Also *attrib.*

1855 *Illustr. Sydney News* 9 June 296/1 A considerable number of diggers have located themselves at the 'whipsticks', with the view of giving the celebrated Scrub . . a thorough prospecting this winter. **1981** L. COSTERMANS *Native Trees & Shrubs S.-E. Aust.* 374 If the aerial parts of the plant are burnt or broken off, new shoots will sprout from the lignotuberous root-stock, usually producing the 'whipstick' type of growth.

2. Comb. **whipstick mallee, scrub.**

1900 *Proc. Linnean Soc. N.S.W.* XXV. 602 *E*[*ucalyptus*] *viridis* . . is known as **Whipstick Mallee** from its erect slender stems. **1853** C.R. READ *What I heard, saw, & Did* 53 Find a track through the **whip stick scrub.**

whiptail wallaby. [See quot. 1941.] The wallaby *Macropus parryi* of e. Qld. and e. N.S.W., light to brownish-grey in colour, having a long, slender, dark-tipped tail; PARRY'S WALLABY; PRETTY FACE. Also **whiptail, whip-tailed wallaby.**

1900 *Bulletin* (Sydney) 7 July 15/1 The white-bellied wallaby, known in Q. as the 'whiptail', is even a better jumper than the 'roo. **1924** *Ibid.* 3 Jan. 22/2 A whip-tail wallaby and a rock wallaby in captivity. **1941** E. TROUGHTON *Furred Animals Aust.* 200 *Wallabia elegans. . . This is . .* generally known as the Whip-tail owing to the great length of the slender tail, which equals that of the combined head and body. **1986** *Sydney Morning Herald* 15 Jan. 5/2 High killing quotas, illegal interstate trade in skins and constant pressure from the shooting industry have put the future of red kangaroos and the whip-tailed wallaby in jeopardy in Queensland.

whirley, whirlie, varr. WURLEY.

whirly. Also **wurley.** [f. *whirl(wind* + -Y.] WILLY WILLY

1. Also **whirly-wind, wind-whirly.**

1894 H. NISBET *Bush Girl's Romance* 9 Only the Wurley caused any discomfort, or an occasional bush-fire made them apprehensive. **1925** *Bulletin* (Sydney) 12 Feb. 24/1 He watched the whirlies lift The sand off the grassless plain. **1974** *Bronze Swagman Bk. Bush Verse* 62 Over went the locust tree, The chooks blew away. Blimey, what a whirly-wind We had that day. **1980** J. WRIGHT *Big Hearts & Gold Dust* 9

whirly-whirly. Also **wurly-wurly.** [Reduplication of WHIRLY, by analogy with WILLY WILLY.] WILLY WILLY 1.
1926 *Bulletin* (Sydney) 25 Feb. 1/1 The 'wurly-wurly' of the native has become the 'willy-willy' of the white. **1972** *Southerly* i. 4 A small whirly-whirly swept down the verandah, lifting dust and lolly papers in a mini-spiral.

whirly-wind: see WHIRLY.

whisperer. A racecourse tipster.
1914 M. CANNON *That Damned Democrat* (1981) 97 His non-productiveness surpasses that of the bookmaker.. and the professional 'whisperer' on racecourses all rolled into one. **1936** A.B. PATERSON *Shearer's Colt* 37 'Did you ever hear of a whisperer?' 'I have', said Fitzroy, 'plenty of 'em. They're fellows who come to you on the racecourse and whisper to you what'll win.'

whistle, *v.* [See WHISTLECOCK a.] *trans.* To perform subincision upon (an Aboriginal male). The examples are *vbl. n.*
1897 W.E. ROTH *Ethnol. Studies* 177 Introcision, otherwise known as 'Sturt's terrible rite', 'whistling', artificial hypospadias, &c., is met with throughout the Boulia, Leichhardt-Selwyn, and Upper Georgina Districts. **1974** *Forum* vii. 37 Some scientists say whistling was a form of population control.

whistlecock. a. In an Aboriginal initiation ritual: the slitting of the underside of the penis in order to make a permanent opening into the urethra; subincision. **b.** An Aboriginal male on whom this operation has been performed. Also **whistle-prick,** and as *v. trans.* See also *Sturt's rite* STURT, TERRIBLE RITE.
1969 A.A. ABBIE *Original Australs.* 147 One Australian name for subincision is *mika* while Curr calls it the 'terrible rite'. Outback whites familiar with Aborigines refer to the condition as 'whistle-cock'. **1970** N.A. BEAGLEY *Up & Down Under* 52 The virile youths were operated on with a piece of sharp stone and made 'whistle cocks'... I asked were they married. 'Oh yes.' 'Any children?' 'No, me whistle cock.' **1974** *Forum* vii. 37 That whistle-prick no good. Just wettem libral's arse. **1985** B. ROSSER *Dreamtime Nightmare* 75 'How do they whistle-cock them?' 'They put a kangaroo bone down the hole [of the penis] then they rip them up with a sharp stone.'

whistler.
1. Any of the small, insectivorous birds of the chiefly Austral. genus *Pachycephala,* typically having a rich, whistled song; THICKHEAD.
1924 LORD & SCOTT *Synopsis Vertebrate Animals Tas.* 207 The whistlers, or 'thickheads', as they are often termed, constitute one of the joys of the Tasmanian bush. **1984** SIMPSON & DAY *Birds of Aust.* 322 Whistlers.. are robust birds with.. distinctive voices—some are among Australia's most beautiful songsters, with variable repertoires of rich, melodic phrases.
2. With distinguishing epithet, as **golden, rufous:** see under first element.
3. See *whistling duck* (b), WHISTLING.

whistling, *ppl. a.* Used as a distinguishing element in the names of fauna: **whistling dick** (esp. *Tas.*), grey thrush, see GREY *a.*; **duck, (a)** either of two ducks of the genus *Dendrocygna* of n. and e. Aust., *D. eytoni* (see *plumed tree duck* PLUMED) and *D. arcuata* of Aust. and elsewhere in the Indo-Pacific region; also **whistling tree duck; (b)** *pink-eared duck,* see PINK *a.*; also **whistle-duck, whistler; eagle** (or **kite**), the dark and light brown bird of prey *Haliastur sphenurus* of Aust. and elsewhere, having a loud whistling call; formerly also **whistling hawk; tree frog,** the frog *Litoria verreauxi* of s.e. mainland Aust.
1848 J. GOULD *Birds of Aust.* II. Pl. 77, *Colluricincla Selbii*.. **Whistling Dick,** of the Colonists of Van Diemen's Land. **1770** J. BANKS *Jrnl.* 8 July (1896) 286 On our passage down we met several flocks of **whistling ducks,** of which we shot some. **1964** M. SHARLAND *Territory of Birds* 105 Here also was a pair of unusual perching ducks, the handsome *Dendrocygna,* commonly called 'Whistler', and in ornithological vernacular 'Plumed Tree Duck'. *Ibid.* 105 A second species, the Whistling Tree Duck, much like it in general appearance, but without the plume-like flank feathers, is more commonly dispersed and occurs on lagoons close to Darwin. **1974** J. BYRNE *Duck Hunting Aust. & N.Z.* 191 The long legs and neck of the Whistle-ducks are quite distinctive on land, and in flight, the legs trail behind the tail and the neck is bent downwards in a characteristic attitude. **1827** [**whistling eagle**] *Trans. Linnean Soc. London* XV. 187 It is called the Whistling Hawk by the settlers. **1849** C. STURT *Narr. Exped. Central Aust.* II. 13 App. *The Whistling Eagle*.. is a dull and stupid bird, and is easily approached. **1984** M. BLAKERS et al. *Atlas Austral. Birds* 96 As with other carrion eaters, the Whistling Kite has probably benefited greatly from agriculture, farming providing carcasses and clearing making them visible. **1969** D. CLYNE *Austral. Frogs* 77 *Hyla verreauxi,* **Whistling Tree Frog.**.. The call is.. long and shrill, rather like a series of whistled notes... Queensland and N.S.W.

white, $n.^1$, $a.^1$ (and *attrib.*), and *adv.* [Spec. use of *white* a person of a race distinguished by a light complexion.]
A. *n.* WHITE MAN 1.
1818 *Hobart Town Gaz.* 26 Dec., The blows and cries of the Blacks, excited to uproar and outrage by the Whites, who take pleasure in the sufferings of their fellow men. **1986** *Centralian Advocate* 15 Jan. 5/2 There are numerous bush foods all over Australia which have been discarded by whites in their attempts to cart England around with them.

B. *adj.* (and *attrib.*)
1. Of British or European descent; of or pertaining to a person of such descent, or to such people collectively.
1835 J. BONWICK *W. Buckley* (1856) 20 The commission of any outrages upon the White Immigrants. **1986** *Canberra Times* 15 Mar. 2/4 White settlement, white cattle and sheep have destroyed many of the traditional food sources.
2. [Used elsewhere but recorded earliest in Aust.: see Mathews *a.* 1.] Of exemplary character. See also WHITE MAN 2.
1856 J. BONWICK *Bushrangers* 94 According to the testimony of his overseer, Connell, he was 'the whitest man on the farm'. **1980** HOLTH & BARNABY *Cattlemen of High Country* 63 In deference to his experience, bushcraft and reputation as a 'white bloke', Wally Ryder has been tacitly acknowledged as Ben's successor as the boss at the big muster. In cattlemen's terms, to be called a 'white bloke' is the greatest praise.
3. Exclusive of non-whites.
1901 *Bulletin* (Sydney) 11 May 14/1 M'Parritch was very strong against the admission of aboriginal children to 'white' schools. **1936** C.P. CONIGRAVE *N. Aust.* 250 Who can say.. Australia may not be called upon to defend her persistence in putting a white fence around her continent.
4. In Comb. and collocations in sense 1 (*n.* and *a.*): **white labour, person, population.**
1899 *Progress* (Brisbane) 29 Apr. 9/1 The return of a **white labour** candidate for such a multi-coloured district as Cairns, is one more indication that the revolt against the rule of the black-labour party will come from the white men who have the misfortune to live in those parts of the colony where the Curse most abounds. **1808** *Sydney Gaz.* 19 June, A boat was upset off Bradley's Head, in which

there were three **white persons** and two natives. **1848** *Port Phillip Mag.* Feb. 88 As to medicine they never knew that such a powerful means of relief existed until the arrival of the **white population**.

5. In Special Comb. and collocations: **white brother**, used ironically to designate a non-Aboriginal Australian male; cf. *black brother* BLACK *a.*[1] 5; **gin, lubra** *Austral. pidgin*, a white woman; see GIN 1, LUBRA 1; **Mary**, see MARY c.; **native**, NATIVE *n.* 2; **settlement**, SETTLEMENT 1 b.; **settler**, SETTLER 1.
1918 *Bulletin* (Sydney) 30 Jan. 16/1 Binghi .. runs risks which would end in serious disablement for **White Brother**. **1843** *Sydney Morning Herald* 19 Sept. 2/7 He rushed past me towards the women, saying—white fellow have black gins, now black fellow have **white gins**. **1843** *Portland Mercury* 20 Dec. 3/2 She stated she had been sent by the owner of the house (**white loubra**). **1830** T.J. MASLEN *Friend of Aust.* 132 There are now .. many **white natives** in Australia. **1849** A. HARRIS *Guide Port Stephens* 71 Those who remain wandering about in the **white settlements** half-civilized. **1840** *S. Austral. Register* (Adelaide) 23 July 8 Surveys carried on by modern **white settlers**.

C. *adv.*

1. Honourably; in the manner of a WHITE MAN 2.
1897 *Worker* (Sydney) 11 Sept. 1/1 A pound a hundred, 'in or out', with rules and tucker fair, He designates as 'working white' and shearing 'on the square'.

2. In the phr. **to live white**, (of an Aboriginal) to live in the manner of white people.
1940 E. HILL *Great Austral. Loneliness* (ed. 2) 273 Since he died, the policeman at Beltana and the Chief Protector of Aborigines in Adelaide have written to me, asking if I would leave the camp and live white again. **1951** — *Territory* 217 The harbour swarmed with crocodiles, for the blacks, 'living white' for a generation, had given up hunting their eggs.

white, *a.*[2] and *n.*[2] [Spec. use of *white* the colour.]

A. *adj.*

1. a. Used as a distinguishing epithet in the names of plants: **white apple**, any of several trees, esp. the tall *Syzygium cormiflorum* (fam. Myrtaceae) of n. Qld., having round white edible fruits, and the similar *S. forte*; **ash**, any of several trees, usu. of the genus *Eucalyptus* (fam. Myrtaceae), esp. *E. fraxinoides* of easternmost Vic. and s.e. N.S.W., having a white smooth upper trunk and strong whitish timber, and *E. oreades* of e. N.S.W. and s.e. Qld.; the wood of the tree; also **white mountain ash; beech**, see BEECH; **box**, any of several trees, usu. of the fam. Myrtaceae, esp. *Eucalyptus albens* of s.e. mainland Aust., yielding a pale, strong timber; the wood of the tree; **cedar**, the deciduous tree *Melia azedarach* var. *australasica* (fam. Meliaceae) of Qld., N.S.W., and New Guinea, widely cultivated, esp. as a street tree, having a furrowed bark and strongly scented, lilac-coloured flowers; the attractively figured wood of the tree; LILAC; also *attrib.*; **cypress pine**, see *white pine*; **gum**, any of many trees of the genus *Eucalyptus* (fam. Myrtaceae) having a smooth, whitish bark; the wood of the tree; also *attrib.*; **honeysuckle**, the tree or shrub of coastal e. Aust. *Banksia integrifolia* (fam. Proteaceae), having leaves which are white underneath; the wood of the tree; **ironbark**, any of several trees of the genus *Eucalyptus* (fam. Myrtaceae), incl. *E. leucoxylon* (see YELLOW GUM 2); **lily** *obs.*, a plant of the genus *Crinum* (fam. Liliaceae), perh. *Darling lily* (see DARLING); **mahogany**, any of several trees of the genus *Eucalyptus* (fam. Myrtaceae), esp. *E. acmenioides* of n.e. N.S.W. and e. Qld., yielding a hard, durable, brown timber; the wood of the tree; **mangrove**, the tree or shrub *Avicennia marina* var. *resinifera* (fam. Verbenaceae), widespread in coastal mainland Aust., having leaves glossy above and whitish below; *grey mangrove*, see GREY *a.*; **mountain ash**, see *white ash*; **oak**, any of several trees yielding a whitish wood, esp. *Lagunaria patersonia* (fam. Malvaceae) of e. Qld., Norfolk Is., and Lord Howe Is.; **pine**, the straight-trunked tree *Callitris glaucophylla* (fam. Cupressaceae) of s. mainland Aust., having aromatic green to grey-green foliage; the close-grained, termite-resistant, fragrant wood of the tree; see also *Murray pine* MURRAY 2, *Murrumbidgee pine* MURRUMBIDGEE A.; also **white cypress (pine); punk**, the white, spongy fruiting body of the bracket fungus *Piptoporus portentosus*; see also PUNK; **sally**, any of several trees, esp. *E. pauciflora* (see *snow gum* SNOW 1); **stringybark**, any of several rough-barked trees of the genus *Eucalyptus* (fam. Myrtaceae) yielding a pale timber, esp. *E. eugenioides* and *E. globoidea* of s.e. mainland Aust.; **waratah**, the shrub or small tree *Agastachys odorata* (fam. Proteaceae) of Tas., bearing spikes of fragrant white flowers.

1852 J. MACGILLIVRAY *Narr. Voyage H.M.S. Rattlesnake* II. 152 Sixty feet high, the straight trunks rising twenty or thirty feet from the ground to the branches... We called it the **white apple**. It is a species of *Eugenia*. **1985** N. & H. NICHOLSON *Austral. Rainforest Plants* 60 Like all the Lillypillies, White Apple makes a handsome tub plant when young. **1898** *Proc. Linnean Soc. N.S.W.* XXIII. 412 *Eucalyptus fraxinoides*, sp. n. .. Because of its resemblance to American Ash it goes under the name of **White Ash**; it also goes under the name of Mountain Ash, a name which, however, should be reserved for *E. Sieberiana*. **1947** W.A.W. DE BEUZEVILLE *Austral. Trees* 166 White Mountain Ash .. is very similar to the Blue Mountain Ash... The timber is .. sought after for construction of propellor blades for aircraft, car body building, etc. **1963** C. BURGESS *Blue Mountain Gums* 41 '*Blue mountain ash*', '*white ash*' or '*smooth-barked mountain ash*' was described by R.T. Baker in 1899 and named *Eucalyptus oreades*... The bark is smooth, white and deciduous in ribbons. **1867** A.K. COLLINS *Waddy Mudoee* 7 On the Condamine .. where the myall flourishes, and the **white box**, and sandal-wood, and pine, spring into glorious life. **1965** *Austral. Encycl.* III. 406 The common names are often derived from the colours of bark, timber or foliage .. white box (*E*[*ucalyptus*] *albens*, having pallid glaucescent foliage). **1808** J.W. LEWIN *Birds New Holland* 9 These birds .. are fond of the berry of the **white cedar** of the colony. **1902** *Emu* II. 101 The Bower-Birds appear to be living almost solely on white cedar berries. **1793** J. HUNTER *Hist. Jrnl. Trans. Port Jackson* 525 The face of the country .. was a poor soil, but finely formed, and covered with the stately **white gum**-tree. **1977** *Ecos* xiv. 21/3 *Eucalyptus alba*, the white gum of northern Australia, Papua New Guinea, and Timor. **1801** *HRA* (1915) 1st Ser. III. 175 The hills are covered with excellent verdure without trees, except in the valleys, and they are chiefly Banksia new, or what is commonly called the **white honeysuckle**. **1843** *Sydney Morning Herald* 6 May 1/7 Building and sawn timber, cut from **white iron bark**. **1909** R. KALESKI *Austral. Settler's Compl. Guide* 32 In the coastal district we find .. white and red ironbark. **1857** D. BUNCE *Australasiatic Reminisc.* 91 In the richest soil .. large groups of the *Crinum*, **white lily**. **1880** *Proc. Linnean Soc. N.S.W.* V. 455 The **White Mahogany** (*E*[*ucalyptus*] *acmenoides*) was regarded by Mr Bentham as a variety of *E. pilularis*, but this cannot be the case. **1888** *Proc. R. Soc. Qld.* (1889) V. 11 *Avicennia officinalis*... Many cattle that would, doubtless, have perished during the recent protracted drought from failure of other fodder, were sustained by browsing on the foliage of the **white mangrove**. **1835** J. BACKHOUSE *Narr. Visit Austral. Colonies* (1843) 258 Scattered on the grassy hills, is *Hibiscus* or *Lagunea* Patersonii, which forms a spreading tree of forty feet in height; it is called here **White Oak**. **1896** *Proc. Linnean Soc. N.S.W.* XXI. 464 *C*[*allitris*] *columellaris* .. '**White Pine**'. **1938** C.T. WHITE *Princ. Bot. Qld. Farmers* 66 Plants which are found growing thickly together, forming at times almost pure stands, are said to be gregarious. Examples in Queensland are .. White Cypress (*Callitris glauca*) [etc.]. **1984** E. ROLLS *Celebration of Senses* 28 A bigger farm on sandy loam scattered with Kurrajongs and White Cypress Pines. **1941** J.H. WILLIS *Victorian Fungi* 62 The name '**White Punk**' has been applied to *Polyporus* eucalyptorum—a large, spongy bracket .. appearing at a considerable height on the boles of eucalypts throughout the State. 1896 *Proc. Linnean Soc. N.S.W.* X. 599 *Eucalyptus coriacea* .. '**White Sally**' is a name in use at Queanbeyan. 1963 C. BURGESS *Blue Mountain Gums* 47 '*Snow gum*' or '*white sally*' was named *Eucalyptus pauciflora* by Sieber and the description published in 1827. 1880 *Proc. Linnean Soc. N.S.W.* V. (1881) 491 *E*[*ucalyptus*] *piperita* .. is sometimes called, especially to the Southward, '**White Stringy Bark**'. *Ibid.* 492 Mr Bentham considered *E*[*ucalyptus*] *eugenioides*, or the White Stringy Bark to be a variety of *E. piperita*. 1932 R.H. ANDERSON *Trees of N.S.W.* 110 *Eucalyptus globoidea*, a species closely related to the white stringybark [*E. eugenioides*] occurs as a small to medium-sized tree. . . The pale, almost white, timber is generally useful. 1903 L. RODWAY *Tasmanian Flora* 307 **Waratah, white:** *Agastachys odorata*.

b. In the names of animals: **white-backed magpie** (formerly **crow-shrike**), a magpie having a white back, as *Gymnorhina tibicen hypoleuca* of Vic., S.A., and Tas., and *G. tibicen dorsalis* of w. Aust.; **-backed swallow,** the black and white bird *Cheramoeca leucosternum* of drier mainland Aust.; *black and white swallow,* see BLACK *a.*² 1 b.; **-bearded honeyeater,** *New Holland honeyeater,* see NEW HOLLAND 2; **-bellied** (or **-breasted**) **sea eagle,** the large, grey and white bird of prey *Haliaeetus leucogaster* of Aust. and elsewhere; **-breasted cormorant,** the black and white bird *Leucocarbo fuscescens* of rocky coasts of s. Aust. incl. Tas.; **-breasted robin,** the small, grey bird *Eopsaltria georgiana* of s.w. W.A., having a whitish breast; formerly also **white-bellied robin, white-breasted flycatcher; -breasted wood swallow,** the dark grey and white bird *Artamus leucorhynchus* of Aust. and the s.w. Pacific; also **white-rumped wood swallow; -browed babbler,** the greyish-brown and white bird *Pomatostomus superciliosus* of s. mainland (exc. easternmost) Aust., having a long white eyebrow; see also HAPPY JACK; **-browed scrub wren,** the small bird *Sericornis frontalis* of e. and s. Aust., having brownish upper parts and a white eyebrow; **-browed treecreeper,** the predom. brown bird *Climacteris affinis* of inland s. Aust., having a white streak above the eye; **-browed wood swallow,** the predom. slaty-grey and chestnut bird *Artamus superciliosus*, having a white stripe above the eye; also **white-eyebrowed wood swallow; -capped noddy,** the sooty black bird *Anous minutus* of n.e. Aust. and elsewhere in the tropics, having a white crown and forehead; **-cheeked honeyeater,** the bird *Phylidonyris nigra* of e. and s.w. Aust.; **cockatoo, (a)** the cockatoo *Cacatua galerita* of n., e., and s.e. Aust. incl. Tas., New Guinea, and New Britain, a predom. white bird with a curving yellow crest and raucous call, popular as a pet; *lemon-crested cockatoo,* see LEMON 1; SULPHUR-CRESTED COCKATOO; *yellow-crested cockatoo,* see YELLOW 1; **(b)** any of several other, predom. white, cockatoos, esp. the *long-billed corella* (see LONG 2); **crane** (or **egret**), the white, long-necked wading bird *Egretta alba*, widespread in Aust. and elsewhere; **cray** *W.A.*, the crustacean *Panulirus cygnus* (see *rock lobster* ROCK *n.* 2), having a pale colour after ecdysis; WHITE *n.*² 2; also **white crayfish; death,** *white pointer;* **eagle** *obs., white goshawk;* **-eared honeyeater,** the predom. olive-grey honeyeater *Lichenostomus leucotis* of s. and e. mainland Aust., having a black face and white ear-patch; **-eye,** *silver-eye,* see SILVER 1; **-eyebrowed wood swallow,** see *white-browed wood swallow;* **-eyed crow,** either of two large black birds of the genus *Corvus, C. coronoides* (see RAVEN) and *C. orru* of Aust. and New Guinea; **-eyed duck,** the duck *Aythya australis* of all States, the mature male having predom. brown plumage and a white eye; PUNKARI; **-faced** (or **-fronted**) **heron,** the predom. grey, white-faced wading bird *Ardea novaehollandiae*, widespread and common in Aust. and occurring elsewhere; *blue crane,* see BLUE *a.*; **-faced storm-petrel,** the migratory *Pelagodroma marina,* a greyish and white sea-bird, breeding on islands of s. Aust. and elsewhere; **-faced xerophila** *obs.*, WHITEFACE; **-fronted chat,** the white, black, and grey bird *Epthianura albifrons* of s. Aust. incl. Tas.; NUN; also **white-fronted bush chat; -fronted falcon** *obs., little falcon,* see LITTLE 2; **-fronted honeyeater,** the honeyeater *Phylidonyris albifrons* of drier mainland Aust.; **-gaped honeyeater,** the greyish honeyeater *Lichenostomus unicolor* of n. Aust.; **goshawk** (or **hawk**), the bird of prey *Accipiter novaehollandiae,* of n. and e. Aust. incl. Tas. and elsewhere, in its white-plumed phase; *white eagle;* **-headed fishing-** (or **fish-**) **eagle,** either of two white-headed birds of prey, the *white-bellied sea eagle* and the *red-backed sea eagle* (see RED-BACKED); **-headed pigeon,** the pigeon *Columba leucomela* of e. Qld. and e. N.S.W., the mature male having a dark body and white head; **-headed sea eagle,** *red-backed sea eagle,* see RED-BACKED; **-headed stilt,** the long-legged, black and white wading bird *Himantopus leucocephalus* of Aust. and elsewhere; **ibis,** the black and white wading bird *Threskiornis molucca* of Aust. and elsewhere; **kangaroo,** an albino kangaroo; **-naped honeyeater,** the olive and white honeyeater *Melithreptus lunatus* of forests in e., s.e., and s.w. mainland Aust., having a black head with a white nape; see also *black cap* BLACK *a.*² 1 b.; **-necked (Pacific) heron,** *Pacific heron,* see PACIFIC; **-plumed honeyeater,** the honeyeater *Lichenostomus penicillatus* of mainland Aust. exc. the n., n.e., and s.w., a predom. olive, yellow, and grey-brown bird with a white tuft behind the ear; **pointer** (or **shark**), the large shark *Carcharodon carcharias* of s. Aust. incl. Tas., and worldwide in temperate and tropical seas; *white death;* **-quilled pygmy goose,** the waterbird *Nettapus coromandelianus* (see *pygmy goose* PYGMY); also **white-quilled goose; -quilled rock pigeon,** the predom. brown pigeon *Petrophassa albipennis* of N.T. and n. W.A.; see also *rock pigeon* ROCK *n.* 2; **-rumped wood swallow,** see *white-breasted wood swallow;* **-shafted fantail,** CRANKY FAN; **-shouldered caterpillar-eater,** *white-winged triller;* **-tailed black cockatoo,** either of two black cockatoos of s.w. W.A. having a broad white band on the tail, *Calyptorhynchus latirostris* and the long-billed black cockatoo, *C. baudinii;* also **white-tailed cockatoo; -tailed kingfisher,** the migratory kingfisher *Tanysiptera sylvia* of rainforest in n. Qld., and New Guinea; **-throated grass-wren,** the bird *Amytornis woodwardi* of Arnhem Land, N.T., having black, brown, and white plumage with a white throat and breast; **-throated honeyeater,** either of two white-throated honeyeaters of n. Aust. and elsewhere, *Conopophila albogularis* and (more often) the black, olive-yellow, and white *Melithreptus albogularis;* **-throated nightjar,** the nocturnal bird *Caprimulgus mystacalis*, having mottled black, grey, and brown plumage with white throat markings, and occurring in e. mainland Aust. and nearer Melanesia; **-throated thickhead,** *golden whistler,* see GOLDEN 3; **-throated treecreeper,** the bird *Cormobates leucophaea* of e. Aust., having dark olive-brown upper parts and a white throat; (occas.) a similar treecreeper; **-throated warbler** (or **flyeater**), the woodland bird *Gerygone olivacea* of n. and e. Aust., having a grey back, white throat, and yellow breast; *bush canary,* see BUSH C. 3; see also *native canary* NATIVE *a.* 6 b.; **-winged chough,** see CHOUGH; **-winged triller,** the migratory bird *Lalage tricolor,* widespread in mainland Aust., the breeding male having a loud chattering song; *white-shouldered caterpillar-eater;* **-winged wren,** the small bird *Malurus leucopterus* of drier mainland Aust., the breeding male having bright blue plumage with white wings.

1844 [**white-backed magpie**] J. GOULD *Birds of Aust.* (1848) II. Pl. 47, *Gymnorhina leuconata* .. White-backed Crow-Shrike. 1986 *Canberra Times* 19 Feb. 21/6 In the wake of last week's column about white-backed and black-backed magpies two people have reported sightings of grey magpies. **1945** C. BARRETT *Austral. Bird Life* 167 Ranging widely over the continent, the **white-backed** or white-breasted **swallow** (*Cheramoeca leucosterna*) is an inland species in the eastern states, but in South and Western Australia also frequents coastal districts. **1902** *Emu* II. 24 Late in January last a nest of the **White-bearded Honeyeater** (*Meliornis novae-hollandiae*) was taken in a briar bush close to a public road, a few miles from Hobart. **1841** J. GOULD *Birds of Aust.* (1848) I. Pl. 3, *Ichthyiaëtus leucogaster*. **White-bellied Sea-eagle. 1968** R. HILL *Bush Quest* 19 In one ancient towering eucalypt I found the nest of a white-breasted sea eagle. **1843** J. GOULD *Birds of Aust.* (1848) VII. Pl. 69, *Phalacrocorax leucogaster* .. **White-breasted Cormorant. 1846** [**white-breasted robin**] J. GOULD *Birds of Aust.* (1848) III. Pl. 13, The White-bellied Robin is a native of Western Australia, but only to be met with in the hilly portions of the country. **1880** 'OLD HAND' *Experiences of Colonist* (ed. 2) ii. 50 The white-breasted flycatcher would hover around, warbling lowly its sweet liquid notes. **1984** M. BLAKERS et al. *Atlas Austral. Birds* 372 The White-breasted Robin feeds on insects collected in sallies from a bare twig or other vantage point. **1842** [**white-breasted wood swallow**] J. GOULD *Birds of Aust.* (1848) II. Pl. 33, *Artamus leucopygialis* .. White-rumped Wood Swallow. **1982** *Reader's Digest Compl. Bk. Austral. Birds* (rev. ed.) 570 The white-breasted wood swallow is seldom found far from fresh or brackish water and is mainly a bird of the tropics. **1898** E.E. MORRIS *Austral Eng.* 13 **White-browed B[abbler]**—P[*omatostomus*] *superciliosus*. **1898** E.E. MORRIS *Austral Eng.* 408 **White-browed S[crub]-W[ren]**.—S[*ericornis*] *frontalis*. **1913** *Emu* XII. Suppl. 84 *Climacteris superciliosa* .. **White-browed Tree-creeper**. .. Range: S. Queensland, New South Wales, Victoria, S., Central, and W. Australia. **1842** [**white-browed wood swallow**] J. GOULD *Birds of Aust.* (1848) II. Pl. 32, *Artamus superciliosus* .. White Eye-browed Wood Swallow. **1984** M. BLAKERS et al. *Atlas Austral. Birds* 632 The White-browed Woodswallow inhabits woodlands. It is usually in large flocks, often in company with the Masked Woodswallow. **1898** E.E. MORRIS *Austral Eng.* 322 **White-capped N[oddy]**—A[*nous*] *leucocapillus*. **1843** J. GOULD *Birds of Aust.* (1848) IV. Pl. 25, The **White-cheeked Honey-eater** is an inhabitant of New South Wales, and certainly proceeds as far to the eastward as Moreton Bay. [**1770 white cockatoo**: J. COOK *Jrnls.* 4 Aug. (1955) I. 367 The Land fowls we met with here .. were .. Cockadores of two sorts the one white and the other brown.] **1788** J. WHITE *Jrnl. Voyage N.S.W.* 22 Apr. (1790) 148 We made a kettle of excellent soup out of a white cockatoo and two crows. **1970** P. SLATER *Eagle for Pidgin* 45 A flock of white cockatoos—corellas I thought .. their pale wings flushed pink as the sun lit them. **1814** M. FLINDERS *Voyage Terra Australis* II. 226 The aquatic birds were blue and **white cranes**, seapies, and sand-larks. **1977** *Ecos* xi. 21/2 Bird experts surprised to find that the white ibis, little egret, and white egret all move between southern Australia and New Guinea. **1958** [**white cray**] *Austral. Jrnl. Marine & Freshwater Research* 538 Towards the end of the period in which whites are caught the colour of the white crayfish tends to deepen and these crayfish are often referred to as 'pinks'. **1985** *West Austral.* (Perth) 21 Nov. 41/1 The 1985 season opened slowly on Friday with the start of the white cray run. White crays are young adults four or five years old. **1948** R.S. CLOSE *Morn of Youth* 62 Our twenty-foot shark .. was still far short of the record **White Death** (.. *Carchardon Albimors*), caught .. off Port Fairy, Victoria. **1840** T.J. BUCKTON *W.A.* 77 The most singular among the rapacious birds is a **White Eagle**. **1822** J. LATHAM *Gen. Hist. Birds* IV. 186 **White-eared Honey-eater** .. common about Port Jackson, Sydney, and Parametta [*sic*], in thick woods, at all seasons. **1843** J. GOULD *Birds of Aust.* (1848) IV. Pl. 81, *Zosterops dorsalis* .. **White-eye**, Colonists of New South Wales. **1845** J. GOULD *Birds of Aust.* (1848) IV. Pl. 18, *Corvus coronoïdes* .. **White-eyed Crow**. **1931** *Bulletin* (Sydney) 1 Apr. 21/4 A sagacious scamp is the Australian raven, known in the bush as the white-eyed crow. **1847** J. GOULD *Birds of Aust.* (1848) VII. Pl. 16 *Nyroca australis* .. **White-eyed Duck**. **1789** [**white-faced heron**] A. PHILLIP *Voyage to Botany Bay* 163 White-Fronted Heron. . . This bird was sent from Port Jackson in New Holland, and as it has not been noticed by any author, we consider it as a new species. **1984** *A.N.U. Reporter* (Canberra) 26 Oct. 5 (*caption*) A White-faced Heron skims over the placid waters of Sullivans Creek. **1845** J. GOULD *Birds of Aust.* (1848) VII. Pl. 61, *Thalassidroma marina* .. **White-faced Storm-Petrel**. **1844** J. GOULD *Birds of Aust.* (1848) III. Pl. 67 *Xerophila leucopsis* .. **White-faced Xerophila**. [**1842 white-fronted chat**: J. GOULD *Birds of Aust.* (1848) III. Pl. 64, *Epthianura albifrons*. White-fronted Epthianura.] **1903** *Emu* II. 163 White-fronted Chat. . . Plentiful all over the plains. **1918** *Bulletin* (Sydney) 14 Feb. (Red Page), *White-fronted Bush-Chat* (Tang, Nun, Tintac) and other members of the genus *Epthianura*. **1841** J. GOULD *Birds of Aust.* (1848) I. Pl. 10, *Falco frontatus* .. **White-fronted Falcon** .. Little Falcon, Colonists of Western Australia. **1822** J. LATHAM *Gen. Hist. Birds* IV. 173 **White-fronted Honey-eater** .. inhabits New South Wales; said to be fond of honey, but will also feed on flies. **1898** E.E. MORRIS *Austral Eng.* 199 **White-gaped H[oneyeater]**—*Stomiopora unicolor*. **1790** [**white goshawk**] J. WHITE *Jrnl. Voyage N.S.W.* 250 The White Hawk. *Falco albus*. .. With black beak, cere and legs yellow. **1981** M. SHARLAND *Tracks of Morning* 78 The white goshawk is a beautiful forest-loving species. **1856** H.B. STONEY *Vic.* 212 The large **white-headed fishing-eagle** of Australia may daily be seen about the harbour. **1926** K. DAHL *In Savage Aust.* 301 Small white-headed fish-eagle (*Haliastur girrenera*). **1898** E.E. MORRIS *Austral Eng.* 156 **White-headed F[ruit]-P[igeon]**—*Columba leucomela*. **1852** J. MACGILLIVRAY *Narr. Voyage H.M.S. Rattlesnake* I. 105 A pair of **white-headed sea-eagles** had established their aërie in a tree. **1841** J. GOULD *Birds of Aust.* (1848) VI. Pl. 24, *Himantopus leucancephalus* .. **White-headed Stilt**. **1842** J. GOULD *Birds of Aust.* (1848) VI. Pl. 49, Straw-necked and **White Ibises** (*Ibis spinicollis* and *Ibis strictipennis*). **1878** R.B. SMYTH *Aborigines of Vic.* I. 250 The **white** and red **kangaroo**, sleeping very fast, have their own way to guard themselves against being surprised. **1822** J. LATHAM *Gen. Hist. Birds* IV. 168 **White-naped Honey-eater**. .. One, supposed to differ in sex, had the band across the nape pale blue, instead of white. **1847** J. GOULD *Birds of Aust.* (1848) VI. Pl. 52 *Ardea pacifica* .. Pacific Heron .. **White-necked Heron** of the Colonists. **1945** C. BARRETT *Austral. Bird Life* 55 The white-necked Pacific heron (*N[otophoyx*] *pacifica*) is a larger bird than the 'blue crane', and comparatively rare. **1845** J. GOULD *Birds of Aust.* (1848) IV. Pl. 43, *Ptilotis penicillatus* .. **White-plumed Honey-eater**. **1881** *Proc. Linnean Soc. N.S.W.* VI. 358 *Carcharodon rondeletii* .. 'The **White Pointer**' of Sydney Fishermen. **1965** *Austral. Encycl.* IX. 297 White shark (*Carcharodon albimors*), one of the most ferocious of marine animals .. being provided with many rows of large triangular teeth, well adapted for tearing flesh. [**1898 white-quilled pygmy goose**: E.E. MORRIS *Austral Eng.* 165 Goose-teal. . . The English name for a very small goose of the genus *Nettapus*. The Australian species are—Green, *Nettapus pulchellus* .. White-quilled, *N. albipennis*.] **1913** *Emu* XII. Suppl. 41 *Nettapus albipennis* .. White-quilled Pigmy-Goose. .. *Range*: Queensland, New South Wales. **1980** C. ALLISON *Hunter's Man. Aust. & N.Z.* 122 The White pygmy or White-quilled goose and the Cape Barren goose. **1913** *Emu* XII. Suppl. 25 *Petrophassa albipennis* .. **White-quilled Rock-Pigeon**. .. *Range*: N.W. Australia. **1840** J. GOULD *Birds of Aust.* (1848) II. Pl. 83, *Rhidipura albiscarpa* .. **White-shafted Fantail**. **1901** *Emu* I. 127 The following day, nests of the **White-shouldered Caterpillar-eater** (*Lalage tricolor*), with young. **1846** J. GOULD *Birds of Aust.* (1848) V. Pl. 13, *Calyptorhynchus baudinii* .. **White-tailed Black Cockatoo** of the Colonists. **1903** *Emu* III. 12 We also secured the eggs of the White-tailed Cockatoo. **1896** F.G. AFLALO *Sketch Nat. Hist. Aust.* 117 The **White-tailed Kingfisher** (*Tanysiptera sylvia*) is found only in the Cape York Peninsula. **1926** *Official Checklist Birds Aust.* (R. Australasian Ornith. Union) p. v, A few long names such as **White-throated Grass-Wren** .. have so far defied efforts for improvement. **1843** J. GOULD *Birds of Aust.* (1848) IV. Pl. 51, *Entomophila albogularis* .. **White-throated Honey-eater**. **1848** *Ibid.* Pl. 74, *Melithreptus albogularis* .. White-throated Honey-eater. **1976** *Reader's Digest Compl. Bk. Austral. Birds* 491 White-throated honeyeaters keep mostly to the upper foliage of trees, where their white throats, black heads and extensive white crescents on the back of their heads contrast conspicuously with the green leaves. **1865** J. GOULD *Handbk. Birds Aust.* I. 96 *Eurostopodus albigularis.* **White-throated nightjar**. . . In the daytime it sleeps on the ground on some dry knoll or open part of the forest, and as twilight approaches sallies forth . . in search of insects. **1902** *Emu* II. 14 Just in this country, too, the **White-throated Thickhead** (*Pachycephala gutturalis*) is found. **1841** J. GOULD *Birds of Aust.* (1848) IV. Pl. 95, From the manner of its [*sc.* the Red-eyebrowed Tree-Creeper's] ascending the trees and keeping almost entirely to the small upright stems of the *Casuarina*, I believed it to be the **White-throated Tree-Creeper** (*Climacteris picumnus*). [**1847** *white-throated warbler:* J. GOULD *Birds of Aust.* (1848) II. Pl. 97, *Gerygone albogularis* . . White-throated Gerygone.] **1900** A.J. CAMPBELL *Nests & Eggs Austral. Birds* 155 *Gerygone albigularis* . . white-throated fly eater. . . From its song . . and partly on account of its yellow breast, it has gained the local name of 'Native Canary'. **1976** *Reader's Digest Compl. Bk. Austral. Birds* 448 Each spring the familiar liquid song of the white-throated warbler heralds the bird's arrival in the southern parts of its range. **1926** *Official Checklist Birds* (R. Australasian Ornith. Union) p. v, Some long formal names such as . . White-shouldered Caterpillar-eater, and Rose-breasted Cockatoo, have been replaced by . . **White-winged Triller,** and Galah respectively. **1841** J. GOULD *Birds of Aust.* (1848) III. Pl. 25, *Malurus leucopterus* . . **White-winged wren.**

2. In special collocations: **white choker** [used elsewhere but recorded earliest in Aust.], a clergyman; also *attrib.*; so **white chokerism** *n.*; **house,** aperient salts; **lady,** a drink, one ingredient of which is methylated spirits; also *attrib.*; **leghorn,** a female player of lawn bowls; also *attrib.*; **money** *Austral. pidgin, obs.*, a silver coin; **wing(er),** one who refuses to join a trade union (see also quot. 1982, 1); also **white wings** and *attrib.*

1851 *Bell's Life in Sydney* 19 Apr. 1/4 Despite the croaking anathemas of pseudo-saints and whinings of **whitechokers.** **1867** *Sydney Punch* 29 June 45/2 The utter extermination of chicanery, charlatanism, white-chokerism, and cant. *c* **1907** W.C. CHANDLER *Darkest Adelaide* 58 'But surely', I said . . 'a child like you should be home instead of accosting men old enough to be your father in the streets.' 'Garn', she said, 'I suppose you are one of those whitechoker blokes who mother told me to dodge.' **1943** S.W. KEOUGH *Around Army* 25 There is still something that the M.O. can try on him—**whitehouse;** the only reason he hasn't ordered it so far is that it doesn't go with Number Nines and oil. **1935** K. TENNANT *Tiburon* 24 The exceptions were two old men in the corner lying stupified over a mixture of '**white lady**'—boiled methylated spirit with a dash of boot-polish and iodine, which they had spent the afternoon concocting. **1940** *Sentry Go* (Keswick) Aug. 29 A White Lady case. Methylated spirit drinker. **1975** L. RYAN *Shearers* 155 **White leghorn:** Breed of fowl. Colloquial term for a woman bowler. **1982** N. KEESING *Lily on Dustbin* 59 Since bowling clubs, and some golf clubs, segregate the sexes, Ladies' Day at the bowling club is 'White Leghorn Day'. **1889** W. MANN *Six Yrs.' Residence* 153 After receiving a few shillings, which they call **white money,** they retired. **1898** *Worker* (Sydney) 30 July 3/3 Men are still scarce in these parts, but those who are here are of a superior class to what we have had during the few seasons since '94, the '**White Wings**' gentry must have received their just deserts—the dirty kick-out. **1911** *Huon Times* (Franklin) 30 Sept. 6/2 He was followed by an assistant from No. 1 establishment, who explained that he was 'a white wing'. **1982** LOWENSTEIN & HILLS *Under Hook* 63 There was some Union members took out a licence before the Union said, 'Okay, we'll go back as a body and take out licences'. These fellers, even though they're not scabs, they're classed as 'white wingers'. Not really accepted. **1982** P. ADAM SMITH *Shearers* 127 Whitely King, secretary of the Pastoralists' Union, unwittingly lent his name to a whole army of men when the 'free' labourers became known as 'White Wings'.

B. *n.*

1. *Australian National Football.* In the phr. **the man in white,** a referee or umpire.

1968 EAGLESON & MCKIE *Terminol. Austral. Nat. Football* ii. 22 *Man in white* . . (a) field umpire . . (b) referee, (c) umpire. **1984** *Sun* (Melbourne) 16 July 68/5 An earlier incident involving Footscray skipper Jim Edmond and Swans defender David Ackerley went unseen by the men in white.

2. *W.A.* **White cray,** see WHITE *a.*^{2} 1 b. Also *attrib.*

1958 *Austral. Jrnl. Marine & Freshwater Research* 542 It . . seems . . that whites are not a species distinct from the reds, but are, in fact, animals in one of the many moult phases in the life history of the crayfish *Panulirus longipes*. . . Some crayfish marked in the white phase have been recaptured as reds, while penned whites have deepened in colour to red after 2 months. **1973** *W. Coast Fisherman* Sept. 3 It is during November and December—the 'white' season— that most fishermen expect to earn enough to tide them over the less productive summer months. They could not survive without the 'whites'.

white, *v.* In the phr. **to white it out,** to serve a gaol sentence.

1885 *Australasian Printers' Keepsake* 25 He caught a month, and had to 'white it out' At diamond-cracking in Castieau's Hotel. **1955** N. PULLIAM *I traveled Lonely Land* 393 *White it out*, serve a jail sentence.

white ant, *n.* [Fig. use of *white ant* termite.]

1. Used of a person's failing sanity or intelligence, as if white ants were the agents of its attrition. Esp. in the phr. **to have white ants,** to be eccentric or 'dotty'.

1908 *Austral. Mag.* (Sydney) Nov. 1250/1 If you show signs of mental weakness you are either balmy, dotty, ratty, or cracked, or you may even have white ants in your attic. **1983** *Weekend Austral. Mag.* (Sydney) 27 Aug. 20/8 Australian slanguage is well stocked with words and phrases to describe those who are a bit slow off the mental mark. . . Suffering from white ants upstairs, to put it succinctly.

2. A saboteur; one who undermines (a political party, policy, etc.).

1969 J. O'GRADY *O'Grady Sez* 54 'Wine . . is the oldest drink known to man.' A white ant from the temperance society said, 'What about water?' **1972** A. CHIPPER *Aussie Swearers Guide* 70 *White ant*, someone who betrays his fellow workers.

white-ant, *v.* [Used elsewhere but recorded earliest in Aust.: see OEDS *v.*] *trans.* **a.** To destroy (a wooden structure) in the manner of white ants. **b.** *fig.* To undermine or sabotage (an enterprise, organization, etc.).

1922 *Daily Mail* (Sydney) 9 Jan. 4/3 Any man who attempts by insidious means to white-ant our White Australian policy should be firmly handled. **1944** *Action Front: Jrnl.* 2/2 *Field Regiment* May 4 Let us build our house upon a rock for it will not then be white-anted.

Hence **white-anted** *ppl. a.*, **white-anter** *n.*, **whiteanting** *vbl. n.* and *attrib.*

1936 F. CLUNE *Roaming round Darling* 205 The piece of the boat is five feet long and is made of soft wood, badly **white-anted.** **1955** N. PULLIAM *I traveled Lonely Land* 393 *White-ant*, to sabotage a labor movement. **White-anter,** one who does so. **1930** H. REDCLIFFE *Yellow Cygnet* 46 He was in no error in regard to the upright character of the young man, and that it would require much 'whiteanting' and the use of insidious and convincing argument to undermine his integrity. **1985** *Bulletin* (Sydney) 11 June 34/3 Hawke and his staff, on an overseas trip . . formed the suspicion that Hayden was doing a white-anting job back in Australia.

white Australia.

1. a. Shortening of *white Australia policy* (see sense 2).
1898 *Tocsin* (Melbourne) 3 Feb. 7/1 'A white Australia is the most sacred article in the creed of every Australian.'—Premier Reid. **1977** R. MACKLIN *Paper Castle* 182 We've got enough on our hands without White Australia rearing its ugly head again, especially now.

b. Australia as a society into which immigration of non-whites is restricted.
1901 PARSONS & HOLTZE *N.T. of S.A.* 8 This is not high class humanitarianism, but it is probably necessary for race preservation, and it will maintain a 'White Australia' in the only sense compatible with the development of its agricultural resources. **1916** *Truth* (Sydney) 22 Oct. 7/8 We want a white Australia, No other shall she be.

c. A white person, considered as representing white Australia (see sense 1 b.).
1913 *Bulletin* (Sydney) 10 Apr. 14/3 White Australia and Black Australia were engaged taking out the bottom wire of the station boundary fence.

2. Special Comb. **white Australia policy,** a policy of restricting immigration into Australia to white people.
1901 *Truth* (Sydney) 10 Mar. 1/4 Barton's white Australia policy will yet secure for him Reid's soubriquet of Yes-No.

white Australian.

1. AUSTRALIAN *n.* 2. Also as *adj.*
1847 A. HARRIS *Settlers & Convicts* (1953) 205, I should suppose there are few races, if indeed there is any race of men, in the habitual enjoyment of such sound health as the white Australians. Most of the young men are of very good stature; a great number extraordinarily so. The most obvious characteristic of the Australian white women is peculiar and striking womanliness; a strongly feminine aspect and a tone of voice; and I think I may add that the same quality runs no less distinctly into their style of thought and general mental character. **1942** T. KELAHER *Digger Hat* 55 We go to spoil another Axis feast—To guard our own good white Australian land.

2. A supporter of a *white Australia policy* (see WHITE AUSTRALIA 2).
1901 *Truth* (Sydney) 1 Sept. 5/7 Being .. a white Australian 'to the backbone and spinal marrow'. **1924** H.E. RIEMANN *Nor'-West o' West* 103 'Welly fine day, Mister Hullicane Joe,' he said in feeble tones. Joe was a keen White Australian. 'That's all right,' he said stiffly.

whitebait. [Transf. use of *whitebait* a small fish used as food.] Any of several fish caught small and eaten whole, as *Lovettia sealii* and the young of the JOLLYTAIL.
1861 E.P. RAMSAY-LAYE *Social Life & Manners* 99 We had caught a famous basketful of a little fish called *whitebait*, from its resemblance to the old country fish of that name. **1974** *Ecos* i. 6/3 At the University of Tasmania Mr M. Cassidy .. has shown that a local fish, *Galaxias* (often known as whitebait or native trout), cannot detect low concentrations of cadmium in streams.

White Elephant. [Spec. use of *white elephant* a burdensome possession.] A name applied metaphorically to the Northern Territory. Also **White Elephant of South Australia.**
1887 MRS D.D. DALY *Digging, Squatting, & Pioneering Life* 209 The Northern Territory .. the 'White Elephant of South Australia'—to use a term very freely used for the Territory in the colonies. **1936** C.T. MADIGAN *Central Aust.* 10 The Northern Territory .. has often been called Australia's 'White Elephant'.

whiteface. Any of the three species of the genus *Aphelocephala* of s. and central mainland Aust., small brownish birds, the most common and widespread being *A. leucopsis*; (formerly) *white-faced xerophila*, see WHITE $a.^2$ 1 b. See also SQUEAKER 1.
1903 *Emu* III. 72 Near Jan Juc, close to the edge of the coastal ranges, the Whiteface (*Xerophila leucopsis*), an inland species, was seen breeding. **1981** M. SHARLAND *Tracks of Morning* 110 Tapping a post may bring from an old knot hole a small, modest looking bird called the whiteface.

white fellow, *n.* and *a.* Austral. pidgin. Also **white fella, white feller.**

A. *n.* A non-Aboriginal person.
1826 R. DAWSON *Private & Confidential* 5 This was not the first time they had seen White 'Fellows' as they call us. **1898** D.W. CARNEGIE *Spinifex & Sand* 284 He knew the words 'white-fella' and 'womany', and had certainly heard of a rifle.

B. *adj.* Non-Aboriginal; alien (to the Aborigines).
1834 G. BENNETT *Wanderings N.S.W.* I. 210, I was accosted by a native black, who asked, whether 'I white feller parson, for me want shilling'; but not being of the clerical profession, I did not consider myself liable to be placed under contribution. **1980** ANSELL & PERCY *To fight Wild* 133 The ranges on the boundary they called High Lonesome. These are all whitefellow names, but they have blackfellow or old-time names for the same places.

whiteheads, *pl.* [See quot. 1956.] Of wheat: diseased or dead plants, affected by root rot such as TAKEALL 1.
1833 *Sydney Monitor* 20 Apr. 3/3 The machine will .. clean 100 bushels of wheat a day, dividing the whiteheads and chaff, and leaving the grain free from dirt. **1956** CALLAGHAN & MILLINGTON *Wheat Industry Aust.* 296 The plants may be killed [by root rot] at a comparatively early stage of growth or they may be killed after heading but before the formation of grain in the ear. These are termed, from their bleached appearance, 'whiteheads' and they constitute a major loss of yield in affected crops.

Whiteley King. [f. the name of John *Whitely King* (1857–1905), president of the Pastoralists' Union of N.S.W., 1890–1902: see quots.] Used *attrib.* and *absol.* to designate an improvised billy-can.
1902 *Bulletin* (Sydney) 1 Feb. 16/2 A billy fashioned from a fruit tin is universally known as a 'Whiteley King', from the secretary of the Pastoralists' Union, who, during the shearing troubles, sent out bands of non-unionists furnished with these impromptu utensils. **1911** *Bulletin* (Sydney) 24 Aug. 14/2 'Ah' .. asks why any old tin used instead of the orthodox billy is called a 'Whiteley King'? During the shearers' strike the 'free' laborers, sent by Whitely and Co., to take the place of the shearers on strike, almost invariably sported an old treacle pot, or some similar makeshift thing, presumably from motives of economy. **1919** *Port Hacking Cough* (Sydney) 11 Jan. 65 Three small puppies played around a time-worn 'Whiteley King' billycan.

white man. [Spec. use of *white man* a man belonging to a race having naturally light-coloured skin or complexion.]

1. A non-Aboriginal inhabitant of Australia, usu. of British or European descent. Also as adj. (in *Austral. pidgin.*).
1833 *Perth Gaz.* 7 Sept. 143 A wish, that 'white man' would go into the bush with them, and 'boo' (shoot) black man. **1981** NGABIDJ & SHAW *My Country of Pelican Dreaming* 9, I had to distinguish between the 'white man way' whereby relationships are described in terms of actual 'blood' ties, and 'blackfeller Law' by which persons become classificatory kin (sometimes referred to as the 'skinning Law').

2. [U.S.: see Mathews 2.] A person of impeccable character. See also WHITE $a.^1$ 2.
[N.Z. **1888** P.W. BARLOW *Kaipara* 192 A 'white man' as a

good fellow is called out here.] **1891** *Truth* (Sydney) 19 Apr. 1/5 Queensland shearers regard Sir Charles Lilley as a white man from his boots to his belltopper. **1978** S. BALL *Muma's Boarding House* 129, I don't like Paddies much but I've seen a lot of Arthur up at the hospital and I can see he's a real white man.

whitewash, *v. Shearing. trans.* To shear (a sheep, esp. a lamb) lightly. Also as *ppl. a.*

1905 *Shearer* (Sydney) 23 Dec. 7/5, I once had the doubtful pleasure, many years ago, of working in a woolshed along with a 'tomahawking' and 'whitewashing' shearer who rejoiced in or groaned under the suggestive 'monniker' of 'More Tar'. **1925** *Bulletin* (Sydney) 21 May 22/2 If a lamb is 'whitewashed' (that is, merely 'topped') at, say, five months old, the fleece 12 months later will be even in length.

whitewash gum. [See quot. 1928.] Any of several trees of the genus *Eucalyptus* (fam. Myrtaceae) having a smooth, whitish bark, incl. GHOST GUM.

1926 A.A.B. APSLEY *Amateur Settlers* 131 Tall white-wash gums. **1928** B. SPENCER *Wanderings in Wild Aust.* 366 Now and again there were a few beautiful white-stemmed, or white-wash, gum-trees. This special kind (*Eucalyptus terminalis*) is especially abundant in this part of the Centre. . . The bush men call them white-wash gums for the simple reason that their trunks and boughs are coated with a fine pure white powder that rubs off.

whitewood. [Transf. use of *whitewood* a tree with light-coloured wood.] Any of many plants yielding a pale wood, esp. the small tree or tall shrub *Atalaya hemiglauca* (fam. Sapindaceae) of drier inland Aust., having waxy grey-green leaves and generally valued as fodder (although the fruits can be poisonous to horses). Also **whitewood tree.**

1826 J. ATKINSON *Acct. Agric. & Grazing N.S.W.* 3 Here are found . . the whitewood or boula tree, with its dark green foliage and smooth bark, resembling the beech of Europe. **1953** H.G. LAMOND *Big Red* 133, I saw ninety-three bodies of dead 'roos under a clump of whitewood trees.

whiting. [Transf. use of *whiting* a European gadoid fish, *Merlangius merlangus*, valued as food.]

1. Any of several marine fish of several fam., esp. of the Indo-Pacific fam. Sillaginidae, valued as food.

1792 *Hist. Rec. N.S.W.* (1893) II. 794 The best fish that are caught are . . flatheads, salmon, whitings. **1974** T.D. SCOTT et al. *Marine & Freshwater Fishes S.A.* 208 Family Sillaginidae. The fishes of this family are known popularly as Whiting. However, they should not be confused with European Whiting, which are members of the family Gadidae. . . Members of the Sillaginidae are restricted to the western Pacific region.

2. With distinguishing epithet, as **King George, rock, sand, spotted, trumpeter:** see under first element.

whombat, whombatt, varr. WOMBAT.

wicked willainy. *Obs.* [Repr. non-standard pronunc. of *wicked villainy.*] The illicit distillation of spirits; such spirits. Also *attrib.*

1844 *Bee of Aust.* (Sydney) 26 Oct. 2/5 It . . will, doubtless, cause the eyes of the honest good man 'wot despises wicked willainy' to be suffused with tears at finding what extensive *plants* there were to *cooper* his fair trade. **1846** *Cumberland Times* (Parramatta) 3 Jan. 2/2 Wicked willainy case.—On Monday Mr Patrick Hayes, out on bail, appeared to answer the charge of working an illicit still upon his premises at the Emu Brewery.

wicket. [Fig. use of *wicket* a cricket pitch. Used elsewhere but recorded earliest in Aust.: see OEDS 3 d.]

In the phrase **to be on a good wicket,** to be in an advantageous or comfortable position.

1910 L. ESSON *Woman Tamer* (1976) 70 We were on a good wicket when Pete says to his bit o' fluff: 'Would you like to see a real solid bracelet, duckie?' **1966** D. NILAND *Pairs & Loners* 46 I'm on a good wicket, making a packet. Everything's fine.

wide, *a.* In the phr. **the wide brown land,** Australia.

1908 *Call* (Sydney) Nov. 7 Her beauty and her terror— The wide brown land for me. **1973** *Austral.* (Sydney) 4 May 11/4 Migrants are staying away in droves from the widest and brownest part of this wide, brown land.

wideawake. A wallaby, perh. a HARE-WALLABY.

1863 J.B. AUSTIN *Mines S.A.* 30 During the journey we saw innumerable Kangaroo rats, 'wideawakes' (a variety of the wallaby) a few Kangaroo and some five turkeys. **1909** LINDSAY & HOLTZE *Territoria* 24 Kangaroo rats, wideawakes, and mountain devils.

wide comb: see COMB 2.

wide working, *vbl. n.* Of a sheep-dog: the controlling of the movement of sheep while remaining at some distance from them. See WORK 2.

1902 *N.S.W. Sheepbreeders Yr. Bk.* 41 The awards shall be by points. The following are the maximum number of points—Under command 30, activity 15, wide working 15, steadiness 15, putting through hurdles, poles and yarding 25, total 100. **1923** *Austral.* (Sydney) June 11 The dog is racing them again. He keeps well out from the woollies. Wide-working is a test of his worth.

Hence **wide worker** *n.*

1977 *Working Dog* (Vic. Dept. Agric., N.E. Region) 12 Some dogs are bred to be wide workers and it can be very difficult, at times impossible, to make these dogs work in close.

widgeon. [Spec. use of *widgeon* a wild duck.] Any of several ducks, esp. *pink-eared duck* (see PINK *a.*).

1840 *Corresp. on Secondary Punishment* (Great Brit. Parl.) 27 Feb. (1841) 32 Called by one of the men who had been at Macquarie Island, where they are in great abundance, a widgeon . . a very pretty bird, delicate eating. **1980** C. ALLISON *Hunter's Man. Aust. & N.Z.* 115 The beautiful Pink-ear is known in some places as the Zebra or Widgeon.

widgery, var. WITCHETTY.

widgie. Also **weegie.** [Of unknown origin.] The female counterpart of a BODGIE *n.*[1] Also *attrib.*

1950 *Sun* (Sydney) 5 July 19/3 There'll be prizes . . for the most colorfully dressed 'bodgy' and 'weegie'. **1951** *Argus* (Melbourne) 11 Dec. 5/3 He had become a member of the 'bodgie-widgie cult', and they had got the idea to go with other 'bodgies' and 'widgies' to Sydney.

wife-starver. A husband who defaults on the payment of maintenance to a wife or ex-wife.

1966 S.J. BAKER *Austral. Lang.* (ed. 2) 155 *Wifestarver*, a prisoner confined under the provisions of the Deserted Wives and Childrens Act, 1901–6. **1976** D. HEWETT *Golden Oldies* (1981) 47 He's left her, alright, run off to Darwin where all the wife-starvers go.

wig, *n. Shearing.* The wool which grows above and around the eyes of a sheep.

1964 R. WARD *Penguin Bk. Austral. Ballads* 228 Two blows to chip away the wig. **1972** G.W. TURNER *Good Austral. Eng.* 61 One thing I did notice about shearing was . . two terms for the one idea . . for example . . topknot/wig.

wig, *v. Shearing. trans.* To clip wool from about the eyes of (a sheep). Freq. as *vbl. n.*
1913 W.K. HARRIS *Outback in Aust.* 151 'Wigging'.. consists of shearing the wool away between the eyes.. to prevent the sheep being blinded by the seeds. **1975** L.A. POCKLEY *Handbk. for Jackeroos* 88 When sheep are shorn around the faces.. they are said to be 'wigged'.

So **wiggings** *pl.*, the pieces of wool so removed.
1958 H.D. WILLIAMSON *Sunlit Plain* 204 Regan bent down to look behind a bale of wiggings. He pulled a skin out by the tail.

wigwam. *Obs.* [Transf. use of *wigwam* the dwelling of the North American Indian.]
1. A name applied by the colonists to an Aboriginal's dwelling (see GUNYAH 1); also *transf.*, a roughly-constructed dwelling occupied by a white person.
1792 W. BLIGH *Voyage to South Sea* 214 The wigwam and turtle shell, were proofs that the natives at times visited this place. **1843** MACARTHUR & THERRY *Election County of Camden* 37, I asked him in what consisted his qualification, and find it to consist of a lease-hold in land on which a few gunyas or wig-wams were erected, and no house worth £200 a-year, I told him—and I think satisfied him—that he was not qualified to be an elector.

2. *fig.* In the phr. **a wigwam for a goose's bridle,** used as a reply to an unwanted question: see quot. 1982.
1960 K. SMITH *Word from Children* 155 In more colourful times, thirty years ago, a stickybeak would be told 'It's a wigwam for a goose's bridle' or, 'The first prize in a mind-your-own-business contest'. **1982** N. KEESING *Lily on Dustbin* 68 'A wigwam for a goose's bridle'.. is one of the most used and widespread of all snubs and put-downs to children in Australia.

Wilcannia shower /wɪlkænjə 'ʃaʊə/. [f. the name of a town in w. N.S.W.] A dust storm.
1903 J. FURPHY *Such is Life* 290 Here was the true key to the Wilcannia shower. **1961** G. FARWELL *Vanishing Australs.* 174 There was the day the *Florence Annie* was bushed in a Darling dust storm—a 'Wilcannia shower', as they used to be called.

wild, *a.*
1. Used as a distinguishing epithet in the names of flora and fauna: **wild banana,** *native banana*, see NATIVE *a.* 6 a.; **carrot,** *native carrot*, see NATIVE *a.* 6 a.; **celery** *obs.*, a herbaceous plant of the genus *Apium* (fam. Apiaceae), esp. *native parsley* (see NATIVE *a.* 6 a.); **cherry,** CHERRY 1; **clematis,** any of several vigorous climbing plants of the genus *Clematis* (fam. Ranunculaceae), incl. *C. microphylla, C. pubescens, C. glycinoides,* and *C. aristata* (see *old man's beard* OLD MAN *n.* 3); **cucumber,** any of several plants bearing a melon-like fruit, esp. naturalized species of the genus *Cucumis* (fam. Cucurbitaceae); **currant,** *native currant*, see NATIVE *a.* 6 a.; **dog,** DINGO *n.* 1; **fig,** any of several plants of the genus *Ficus* (fam. Moraceae); the fruit of the plant; **geranium,** any of several introduced or native plants of the fam. Geraniaceae, esp. the perennial *Pelargonium australe* of all States; **ginger,** any of several plants of the fam. Zingiberaceae, esp. of the genus *Alpinia* of n. Aust. and elsewhere; **goose** *obs.*, **(a)** *Cape Barren goose*, see CAPE BARREN; **(b)** *magpie goose*, see MAGPIE *n.* 2; **grape,** any of several plants bearing a grape-like fruit, incl. the climber *Legnephora moorei* (fam. Menispermaceae) of Qld. and N.S.W., and species of *Cissus* (see *water vine* WATER); the fruit of the plant; **hop** (usu. in *pl.*), *native hop*, see NATIVE *a.* 6 a.; also *attrib.*; **indigo** *obs.*, INDIGO a.; also *attrib.*; **lemon,** any of several trees or shrubs supposed to resemble the lemon, esp. *Canthium oleifolium* (fam. Rubiaceae) of inland Qld. and N.S.W., bearing fragrant white flowers; **lime,** *native cumquat*, see NATIVE *a.* 6 a.; **melon,** any of several plants bearing a melon-like fruit, esp. the naturalized perennial *Citrullus colocynthis* (fam. Cucurbitaceae), the fruit of which has a bitter flesh, and *C. lanatus* (see PIE-MELON); the fruit of the plant; **nutmeg,** NUTMEG 1; also *attrib.*; **onion,** *onion weed* (c), see ONION 1; **orange,** any of several small spiny, small trees or shrubs of the genus *Capparis* (fam. Capparaceae) of mainland Aust., esp. the inland *C. mitchellii*, bearing an edible, rounded fruit with numerous seeds; the fruit of the plant; BUMBLE TREE; *native pomegranate* (a), see NATIVE *a.* 6 a.; see also *native orange* NATIVE *a.* 6 a.; also *attrib.*; **parsley,** the shrub *Lomatia silaifolia* (fam. Proteaceae) of e. N.S.W. and e. Qld.; **parsnip,** any of several herbs of the genus *Trachymene* (fam. Apiaceae) having a pale, fleshy root, esp. *T. anisocarpa* of s. Aust. incl. Tas.; the root of the plant; **passionfruit,** any of several plants, esp. native or introduced tendril-bearing climbers of the genus *Passiflora* (fam. Passifloraceae); **peach,** any of several plants incl. the tree *Terminalia carpentariae* (fam. Combretaceae) of n. Aust.; the wood or fruit of the plant; **pineapple,** any of several species of MACROZAMIA; **plum,** *native plum*, see NATIVE *a.* 6 a.; also *attrib.*; **raspberry,** *native raspberry*, see NATIVE *a.* 6 a.; **rhubarb,** any of several plants incl. the naturalized succulent annual *Rumex vesicarius* (fam. Polygonaceae) of mainland Aust.; **sorghum,** any of several grasses (fam. Poaceae) incl. *Sorghum leiocladum* of e. mainland Aust.; **spinach,** any of several plants used as a green vegetable incl. WARRIGAL *n.* 3 and some plants of the fam. Chenopodiaceae; SPINACH; **tobacco,** any of several plants incl. the naturalized shrub or small tree *Solanum mauritianum* (fam. Solanaceae) of disturbed land in parts of e. Aust., and species of *Nicotiana*, esp. the S. American *N. glauca*, naturalized in mainland Aust. and elsewhere; see also *native tobacco* NATIVE *a.* 6 a.; also *attrib.*; **turkey,** the large, nomadic, often solitary game bird *Ardeotis kori*, of mainland Aust. and New Guinea; *plain turkey* (a), see PLAIN 2; see also TURKEY *n.*[1] 1; **turnip,** any of several plants, usu. naturalized herbs of the fam. Brassicaceae, and esp. the annual *Brassica tournefortii* naturalized in mainland Aust.; **violet,** any of several plants bearing bluish-violet or white flowers, usu. of the genus *Viola* (fam. Violaceae), esp. the perennial herb *V. hederacea* of e. and s.e. Aust.; **yam,** YAM.

1864 J. MORRILL *Sketch of Residence* 228 A **wild banana**, full of black seed, and very little flesh. **1844** *Swan River News* June 47/2 The **wild carrot** is.. an excellent vegetable, and from its root rich wine has been extracted. **1788** *HRA* (1914) 1st Ser. I. 23 The heaths that are free from timber are covered with a variety of the most beautiful flowering shrubs, **wild celery** [etc.]. **1871** 'IOTA' *Kooroona* 60 The beautiful tree to which English settlers have given the name of the **wild cherry**. **1845** *Sydney Morning Herald* 14 Jan. 4/4 Here the scene changes to a brush of cedar.. over which the **wild clematis,** and fifty other specimens of woodland creeper, either hang in festoons.. or playfully arch themselves over the brook in beautiful luxuriance. **1866** *Australasian* (Melbourne) 25 Aug. 665/2 There are a variety of herbs on which stock are found to thrive exceedingly; amongst which may be enumerated.. '**wild cucumber**' and 'carrots'. **1965** P. JONES *Johnny Lost* 52 Weeds grew overnight in the vegetable patch—stickfast and wild cucumber and cobbler's peg. **1803** *Sydney Gaz.* 26 June, After they had eaten their provisions they found nothing to subsist on but **wild-currants** and sweet-tea leaves. **1793** W. TENCH *Compl. Acct. Settlement* 172 The Indians sometimes kill the kanguroo, but their greatest destroyer is the **wild dog,** who feeds on them. **1788** *HRA* (1914) 1st Ser. I. 23 The heaths that are free from timber are covered with a variety of the most beautiful flowering shrubs, wild celery, spinages, samphose, a small **wild fig**. **1839** *S. Austral. Rec.* (London) (1840) 18 July 45 Thousands and tens of thousands of acres of land, fit for the plough and level as a bowling-green, covered with thousands of **wild geraniums** and other flowers. **1870** E.B. KENNEDY *Four Yrs. in Qld.* 142 **Wild ginger** of an excellent quality is found everywhere. **1981** J.A. BAINES *Austral. Plant Genera* 26 *A[lpinia] arundelliana,* Wild Ginger, in E. Aust. **1770** J. COOK *Jrnls.* 4 Aug. (1955) I. 367 Some of our gentlemen .. in the Country heard and saw **wild Geese** in the night. **1882** W. SOWDEN *N.T. as it Is* 36 The croaking of frogs... Plaintively mingle with it the cackling of wild geese. **1852** J. MORGAN *Life & Adventures W. Buckley* 101 We made a lengthy halt at Mangowak where we lived on .. a sort of **wild grape** which grows in great abundance thereabouts. **1947** T.Y. HARRIS *Wild Flowers Aust.* (rev. ed.) 35 Wild grape *Cissus Baudinianus* syn. *Vitis Baudiniana.* In the richer jungle country of the coast of New South Wales this climbing plant is common... The berries are round and black. **1979** K.A.W. WILLIAMS *Native Plants Qld.* I. 170 *Legnephora moorei* Menispermaceae. Wild Grape: A strong, twining climber... The common name could be misleading with regard to the edible qualities of the attractive fruit. It is suspected of being toxic and therefore should be avoided. **1854** W. HOWITT *Boy's Adventures* 5 He .. browses on the acacia trees and the bitter **wild hop** shrub. **1979** B. MARTYN *First Footers S. Gippsland* 14 Pungent smelling wild hops. **1804** *HRA* (1915) 1st Ser. IV. 602, I send some samples of the produce extracted from the **Wild Indigo** Plant of this Country. **1880** J. BONWICK *Resources Qld.* 47 Among poison plants are .. the wild Indigo. **1861** *Sydney Mail* 6 July 3/3 *P[ittosporum] revolutum* .. is locally designated the '**Wild Lemon**' from the colour of its fruit. **1901** K.L. PARKER in M. Muir *My Bush Bk.* (1982) 103 Gaengaen, the olive-foliaged **wild limes**, whose miniature lemon-like fruit is a boon in a thirsty climate, ripening as it does in summer. **1849** J.P. TOWNSEND *Rambles & Observations N.S.W.* 181 On some stations in the district it [*sc.* the feed] is composed of barley grass, wild carrots, and **wild melons.** Of the long runners of the last the cattle are very fond. **1973** W.T. PARSONS *Noxious Weeds Vic.* 139 There can be some confusion between colocynth and wild melon (*Citrullus lanatus*). Wild melon differs in being an annual with a much less robust taproot. **1829** R. MUDIE *Picture of Aust.* 152 On the tropical shores, a species of **wild nutmeg** (*myristica insipida*) is not uncommon, but it is perfectly useless. **1841** G. GREY *Jrnls. Two Exped. N.-W. & W.A.* I. 85 The space between these trees and the cliffs was filled by a dense forest, principally composed of the Pandanus and wild nutmeg trees. **1864** 'E.S.H.' *Narr. Trip Sydney to Peak Downs* 11 Crinum Creek .. is so named from the lilies, which travellers call **wild onions. 1885** P.R. MEGGY *From Sydney to Silverton* 124 **Wild oranges** as bitter as gall .. may be occasionally seen on the plains. **1912** B. SPENCER *Wanderings in Wild Aust.* 12 Nov. (1928) 902, I watched one woman making little dampers .. out of a big lot of wild orange (Capparis) seed that she pounded up on stone. **1947** T.Y. HARRIS *Wild Flowers Aust.* (rev. ed.) 68 **Wild Parsley** *Lomatia silaifolia* .. is a small shrub with deeply-toothed, divided leaves and long, loose spikes of cream flowers. **1805** *Acct. Voyage to establish Colony Port Phillip* 162 Of potable vegetables, wild celery, **wild parsnip**, scurvygrass .. were found in great abundance. **1870** E.B. KENNEDY *Four Yrs. in Qld.* 142 **Wild passionfruit**, bearing red flowers, handsomer than the cultivated ones, creeps in and out of the bushes. **1853** A. KINLOCH *Murray River* 16 The only fruit .. in use amongst the whites is that called the 'quondong'—a species of **wild peach**, which is largely used as a preserve. **1901** J.H. MAIDEN *Plants reputed to be Poisonous* 31 *Macrozamia* spp.—'Zamia palm', 'Burrawang', '**Wild pine-apple**' .. are gregarious plants. **1849** J.P. TOWNSEND *Rambles & Observations N.S.W.* 131 Amongst the trees .. in this district is the gigantic fig-tree. It is produced by a seed deposited by birds, in an undigested state, in the cleft of a gum or of a **wild plum**- tree. **1949** G. FARWELL *Traveller's Tracks* 87 There was a 'forest' of wild plum, at least six inches high, with more exposed roots than branches. **1845** R. HOWITT *Impressions Aust. Felix* 75 The bramble, too, with a red berry instead of a black, called here the **wild raspberry**, yet the fruit neither tasting like the one nor the other. **1878** R.B. SMYTH *Aborigines of Vic.* II. 173 **Wild rhubarb** .. Lanangárangal. **1948** G. FARWELL *Down Argent Street* 92 Red dock (Rumex vesicarium), otherwise known as wild rhubarb. **1895** F. TURNER *Austral. Grasses* 49 In the New England district the '**wild sorghum**', when in flower, is quite a feature in the pastures, and is described as a valuable grass. **1793** J. HUNTER *Hist. Jrnl. Trans. Port Jackson* 63 A convalescent [from scurvy] who had been sent from the hospital to gather **wild spinach** or other greens, was murdered by the natives. **1827** *HRA* (1923) 3rd Ser. VI. 267 An unpleasant smelling viscous plant, called by the Sealers '**Wild Tobacco**'. **1973** R. ERICKSON et al. *Flowers & Plants W.A.* 198 In sheltered spots such as breakaways, delicate herbs are found, e.g. wild tobacco, *Nicotiana* species. **1986** *Your Garden* Jan. 23 *Solanum mauritianum* wild tobacco tree (NSW). **1825** *Howe's Weekly Commercial Express* (Sydney) 1 Aug. 3 Our **wild turkeys** are a species of bustard. **1899** *North-Western Advocate* (Devonport) 5 May 3/5 The land .. was literally covered with **wild turnip** of abnormal growth. **1986** *Trees & Natural Resources* Mar. 2 The annual, Wild Turnip (*Brassica tournefortii*) and Poached Eggs Daisy .. became the dominant plants in the dune grasslands. **1916** *Bulletin* (Sydney) 13 Apr. 24/3 Kosciusko and the Kiandra country, in midspring and early summer .. become matted with .. swamp lilies, the feathery **wild violets**, butter-cups, yams and thousands of unnamed plants. **1770** J. COOK *Jrnls.* 29 June (1955) I. 353 We found some **wild Yamms** or Coccos growing in the swampy grounds.

2. Of an Aboriginal or group of Aborigines, in the collocations **wild Aboriginal, black, blackfellow, fellow** (also *attrib.*), **man, native, nigger, tribe:** used **(a)** by whites, to designate an Aboriginal who is hostile to white society or who lives in a traditional manner and is independent of it; **(b)** by Aborigines, to designate an Aboriginal from another group or tribe.

1848 *Bell's Life in Sydney* 5 Feb. 1/2 The **wild aboriginal** stood on the banks of the brawling current. **1838** *S. Austral. Rec.* (London) (1839) 13 Mar. 159 We have no **wild blacks** nor wild beasts here. **1842** *Portland Mercury* 7 Sept. 2/5 The aboriginal Roger .. still denies that he committed the murder, and says that it was done by other **wild black fellows. 1927** M. DORNEY *Adventurous Honeymoon* 34 Consider themselves a peg or two above the '**wild-feller** myall' who roams the bush and is not employed by the whites. **1935** H. BASEDOW *Knights of Boomerang* 20 Between themselves they had the closest ties of kinship... All outside the clique were 'wild-fellows'. **1867** J. BONWICK *J. Batman* 18 Now comes the interesting entry about the **wild man. 1827** P. CUNNINGHAM *Two Yrs. in N.S.W.* II. 40 You must never strike one of the **wild natives**, unfamiliarized to Europeans, even if you detect them in theft—or they will revenge themselves by taking your *life* some time or other. **1896** W.H. WILLSHIRE *Land of Dawning* 5 We all pretty well know why we carry revolvers on our belts—not only for **wild niggers. 1846** *Portland Guardian* 8 Dec. 3/3 It is hard to surmise what has been their fate, for it is evident that they were with the **wild tribes**, as the remains of their mia mias and capups are still in existence.

3. Of a tract of land, in the collocations **wild bush, country, ground, land, pasture, territory:** unalienated; unimproved. See also WASTE.

1832 *Sydney Monitor* 11 Aug. 2/1 We are Colonists old enough to remember, when Liverpool was the **wild bush**, with a few acres of the trees felled, but not burnt off. **1942** C. BARRETT *From Bush Hut* 7, I 'killed' and scattered my last camp-fire, coming down from **wild country**, the old way of living seemed to go. **1849** S. & J. SIDNEY *Emigrant's Jrnl.* 162, I will begin by describing the operations on taking a bush farm, that is, **wild** government **ground** covered with trees and grass never used before, except for feeding black fellows, kangaroos, cattle, horses and sheep. **1839** *Sydney Standard* 1 Apr. 3/3 An appropriation of the *nett* proceeds of **wild lands**, has been very earnestly recommended. **1839** *S. Austral. Rec.* (London) 10 Apr. 171 It may be expedient to reduce the rent of the **wild pastures. 1840** *Sydney Herald* 19 June (Suppl.) 1/3 The Land Fund, arising from the sale of the **wild territory** of the Colony is to be reserved for immigration.

WILD CAT 637 WILLOW

4. Of a domesticated animal: used to designate one which has strayed and established itself in the wild, and the progeny of such animals, esp. in the collocations **wild buffalo, cattle, herd, horse, mob, pig.**

1841 *Geelong Advertiser* 20 Sept. 4/2 It was in these luxuriant tracts that we started up large numbers of **wild buffaloes** and ponies, all as fat as our cattle at home when driven to market at Christmas time. 1801 *HRA* (1915) 1st Ser. III. 11 Of the **wild cattle**, no other calculation can be made of them than that they are alive and increase fast in numbers. 1806 *HRA* (1915) 1st Ser. V. 675 The **Wild Herds**.. are now the exclusive property of the Crown. 1854 S. SIDNEY *Gallops & Gossips* 40 It was at a spring in this flat that Long Peter, while cutting out some wild honey with a black, had caught sight of the **wild horses.** 1881 A.C. GRANT *Bush-Life Qld.* I. 200 He is a large roan bullock.. that has been missing from the run for the last year or two, and has been seen to-day for the first time in that period. Most probably he has been away in the scrub with a **wild mob.** 1854 F. ELDERSHAW *Aust. as it really Is* 122 Some of the Coast Scrubs are infested with large numbers of **Wild Pigs.**

5. In the collocation **wild colonial boy,** a bushranger (see quot. 1905); a larrikin (see LARRIKIN 2 a.).

c 1881 R.G. EDWARDS *Index Austral. Folk Songs* (1971) (song title), The wild colonial boy. 1905 A.B. PATERSON *Old Bush Songs* 33 'Tis of a wild Colonial boy, Jack Doolan was his name, Of poor but honest parents he was born in Castlemaine. 1984 R.F. BRISSENDEN *Gough & Johnny were Lovers* 21 Oh, so loverly when professors never make a noise; Universities don't like the wild colonial boys.

6. In the adj. phr. **wild and woolly,** 'rough and ready'.

1936 I.L. IDRIESS *Cattle King* 85 Where shall we go now... Well then, say Queensland and the wild and woolly Paroo? 1981 Q. WILD *Honey Wind* 77 Everyone pretends Australia is a wild and woolly country... 'But we've gone the way of the bush... Got too many shire engineers and council inspectors.'

wild cat, n.¹ *Native cat,* see NATIVE *a.* 6 b.

1831 *Acct. Colony Van Diemen's Land* 227 The skins of the opossum, of the wild and tiger cat.. and of several other animals, also fetch a tolerable price in England. 1962 B.W. LEAKE *Eastern Wheatbelt Wildlife* 51 This Wild cat (Dasyurus geoffroyi fortis) was more slender than the domestic cat, but very strong for its size.

wild cat, n.² [U.S. *wild cat* 'a mine of doubtful value or one serving as the basis of fraudulent transactions': see Mathews *n.* 2 b.] An unproductive mine; one falsely represented as productive. Also **wild-cat mine.**

1892 'A.M.' *From Aust. & Japan* 10 His prospects.. struck me about being on a par with those of a Queensland wildcat mine after the directors and promoter-shareholders have succeeded in unloading every share of their scrip on a gullible London public. 1962 O. PRYOR *Aust.'s Little Cornwall* 92 Not all the mining shows outside the original Wallaroo and Moonta leases of the type known in business circles as 'wild cats'.

wilga, var. WILGIE.

wilga /'wɪlgə/. [a. Wiradhuri *wilgarr.*] A shrub or small tree of the genus *Geijera* (fam. Rutaceae), esp. *G. parviflora* of inland e. Aust., having a spreading crown and pendulous foliage; SHEEP BUSH. Also *attrib.*

1887 W.H. SUTTOR *Austral. Stories Retold* 127 Near the hut is a large wilgar tree, the most shapely and beautiful of all trees in that region. 1986 *Sun-Herald* (Sydney) 26 Jan. 7/1 Property owners had begun noticing kurrajongs and wilgas losing their leaves.

wilgie /'wɪlgi/. Chiefly *W.A.* Also **wilga, wilghi, wilgi, wilgy.** [a. Nyungar *wilgi.*] A red ochre used by Aborigines to paint the body on ceremonial occasions.

1836 H.W. BUNBURY *Early Days W.A.* (1930) 83 The Wilghi, which is a preparation of red earth and grease, constitute their favourite ornament and covering. 1840 T.J. BUCKTON *W.A.* 96 Both smear themselves with a pigment they call wilga, which is red, and mixed with grease. 1857 W.S. BRADSHAW *Voyages* 101 The natives are a very dirty race, they take a delight in smearing themselves with grease and wilgie. 1929 W.J. RESIDE *Golden Days* 162 Native ochre, or what the natives call 'wilgi', is the material used for the painting of their bodies. 1970 J. DAVIS *First-Born* 23 He squats on a narrow ledge in the summer shade; A spear and an axe of stone lay at his side: The wilgy, gently moulded, mixed with care and pride.

wilgied, *a.* [f. prec.] Painted with WILGIE.

1840 A. HASLUCK *Portrait with Background* (1955) 192 They dislike Flowers, and will not suffer any one to be placed on their heads... I never knew any but one.. who permitted me at Augusta to place a large piece of the crimson Antirrhinum in his Wilgied Locks. 1863 *Jrnls. & Rep. Two Voyages Glenelg River* 30 July (1864) 24 There is a red ochreous stain upon them [*sc.* Aborigines' canoes] here and there to be detected, but we account for these as having been communicated from the wilgied persons, or they possibly have been designedly covered with wilgi (red ochre).

wilgy, var. WILGIE.

wilja, var. WILTJA.

will, *v.* In the interrogative phr. **wouldn't it?,** see WOULD.

William.

1. Joc. substitution for BILLY *n.*¹ 1.

1902 *Bulletin* (Sydney) 26 Apr. 3/2 The William-cans are loaded at the hostel 'cross the road. 1925 *Bulletin* (Sydney) 19 Mar. 24/2, I left my william-can at home one day.

2. In the phr. **William the Third,** rhyming slang for 'turd'.

1968 *Swag* (Sydney) iv. 26 What a nasty-minded, thoroughly suspicious little William the Third he is. 1979 B. HUMPHRIES *Bazza comes into his Own*, Them robbers always leave a helluva lot of William the Thirds on the carpet when they've done some poor bastard's nice home.

willie wagtail, var. WILLY WAGTAIL.

willing, *a.* [Spec. use of *willing* without reluctance.] Vigorous; aggressive. Freq. in the collocation **willing go,** a vigorous contest.

1899 *Bulletin* (Sydney) 12 Aug. 14/2 Came across two wallabies having such a 'willing go' that they let me come within a dozen yards. 1975 *Bulletin* (Sydney) 26 Apr. 45/3 He was willing (courageous and daring) and would jeopardise his own safety.. so that the bagman (the take man carrying a bag) could get out of the store with the booty.

willow. [Transf. use of *willow* a plant of the genus *Salix*, having long, narrow, pendulous leaves and occurring along watercourses.]

1. Any of several trees or shrubs resembling the willow, incl. species of *Acacia* (fam. Mimosaceae), and *willow myrtle*. Also *attrib.*

1826 J. ATKINSON *Acct. Agric. & Grazing N.S.W.* 4 In willow brushes the ground is more or less covered with the white or woolly gum trees, and underneath thickly covered with what is termed in the Colony willow brush, growing to the height of 2 or 3 feet. **1934** W.A. OSBORNE *Visitor to Aust.* 62 The visitor, therefore, when he hears such terms as . . willow (the indigenous and not the imported), box, hickory, and others must not expect striking resemblances to the originals.

2. Special Comb. **willow myrtle,** the tree or shrub *Agonis flexuosa* (see PEPPERMINT 2); **wattle,** any of several trees or shrubs of the genus *Acacia* (fam. Mimosaceae), usu. having pendulous foliage and occurring along watercourses, esp. *A. salicina* (see COOBA); formerly also **willow-leaved acacia.**

1898 E.E. MORRIS *Austral Eng.* 513 **Willow Myrtle** . . a tree, *Agonis flexuosa* . . native of West Australia, and cultivated for ornament as a greenhouse shrub. **1835** [**willow wattle**] *Hobart Town Almanack* 62 *Acacia saligna?* Willow leaved Acacia. A fragrant flowering species, forming a large shrub. **1981** L. COSTERMANS *Native Trees & Shrubs S.-E. Aust.* 107 Small tree; green leaves thinnish, willowy . . Willow Wattle.

willy, *n.*[1] Abbrev. of WILLY WILLY 1.

1906 *Bulletin* (Sydney) 23 Aug. 16/3 A recent 'willy' unroofed a house on the outskirts of the township. **1977** B. FULLER *Nullarbor Lifelines* 40 There is nothing to break the force of the winds, and they blow very fiercely at times. . . The 'willies' are the terror of all, especially of the boarding house people.

willy, *n.*[2] [Unexplained use of a form of the name William.] The amount of money at one's disposal, esp. for betting; money; a wallet.

1949 L. GLASSOP *Lucky Palmer* 36 Two quid? Break it down. That's me willie. That's all I got. **1977** J. RAMSAY *Cop it Sweet* 96 *Willy*: Supply of betting money; wallet.

willy nilly. [f. *willy-nilly, adv.* whether one likes it or not.] Fanciful alteration of WILLY WILLY 1.

1920 *N.T. Times* (Darwin) 10 Jan. 5/2 The men were Japanese and had been fishing and had secured a good haul when a willy nilly came along and upset the boat. **1955** J. CLEARY *Justin Bayard* 185 A willy-nilly of dust rose up and spun away over the trees.

willy-wag.

1. Abbrev. of WILLY WAGTAIL.

1938 F. BLAKELEY *Hard Liberty* 178 It is almost impossible to hunt if a couple of willy-wags decide to accompany the hunter. **1958** *Bulletin* (Sydney) 24 Sept. 18/3 A jackywinter . . is on equal terms with the willy-wag and not overawed even by a maggie.

2. Rhyming slang for 'swag'.

1905 J. MEREDITH *Learn to talk Old Jack Lang* (1984) 12, I . . finished up in the dead house, broke to the wide. But they left me my *Willy Wag* and gave me a bit of tucker. **1964** D. LOCKWOOD *Up Track* 100 'Well, mate,' George said, 'I'm going to roll out the willy-wag. I'm on watch at three-thirty for two and a half hours.'

willy wagtail. Also **willie wagtail.** [Transf. use of *willy-wagtail* the water wagtail *Motacilla lugubris.*] The black and white bird *Rhipidura leucophrys*, widespread in Aust. and occurring elsewhere, sometimes confused with the RESTLESS FLYCATCHER; *black and white fantail*, see BLACK *a.*[2] 1 b.; SHEPHERD'S COMPANION; WAGGY. See also WAGTAIL.

1885 Mrs C. PRAED *Head Station* II. 151 A brisk little willy-wagtail hopping about on the gravel. **1984** SIMPSON & DAY *Birds of Aust.* 323 The familiar, misnamed Willie Wagtail is a fantail, not a wagtail (Motacillidae); it occurs throughout Australia (except Tasmania).

willy willy /ˈwɪli wɪli/. Chiefly *n.w. Aust.* [a. Yinjibarndi *wili wili.*]

1. A whirlwind: see quot. 1898.

1894 *Age* (Melbourne) 20 Jan. 13/4 The Willy Willy is the name given to these periodical storms by the natives in the north west. **1898** R. RADCLYFFE *Wealth & Wild Cats* 70 'Willie-willies' . . are water-spouts made of sand instead of water. . . They usually begin upon a very small scale . . a dancing column of dust, dung, dead flies, and old paper. Give them time and they will show sport. But the 'williewillie' has no perseverance; he lacks continued effort, and the slightest opposition in the shape of a tin hut or a telegraph pole so destroys his symmetry that he dies of disgust in a small heap of refuse. But with plenty of room he becomes rampant. When he gets over fifty feet high his power is vast.

2. *transf.* and *fig.* Also *attrib.*

1928 J. POLLARD *Bushland Vagabonds* 8 The little black pony Johnny was riding shied nervously as the dust rose about her feet in a tiny willy-willy. **1974** C. THIELE *Albatross Two* 135 Andy ran hands through his willy-willy hair. 'Aren't we poetic this morning?'

3. Comb. **willy-willy season.**

1914 *Pastoral Rev.* 16 Feb. 110 The summer rains already received . . will be followed up during the Willy-Willy season in March.

wiltja /ˈwɪltjə/. Also **wilja.** [a. Western Desert language *wilja.*] An Aboriginal shelter. See also GUNYAH.

1950 V.E. TURNER *Ooldea* 136 There are three kinds of native homes—houses (karrpa), shelter (wilja) and breakwinds (yaw). **1986** *Good Weekend* (Sydney) 26 Apr. 62/3 The local community is building a traditional wiltja (hut).

Wimmera /ˈwɪmərə/. [The name of a region of w. Victoria.] Used *attrib.* in the name of **Wimmera ryegrass,** the Mediterranean annual grass *Lolium rigidum* (fam. Poaceae), widely sown as a pasture grass, and also naturalized and sometimes regarded as a weed. Also **Wimmera rye.**

1920 *Proc. R. Soc. Vic.* XXXII. 199 'Wimmera Rye Grass'. . . This is a new record as a naturalised alien in Victoria. **1966** N.T. BURBIDGE *Austral. Grasses* I. 118 Wimmera Rye . . is one of the most important annual grasses in improved pastures, especially when used in rotation with cereals.

wind-grass. The grass *Aristida contorta* (see *mulga grass* MULGA B. 3).

1845 L. LEICHHARDT *Jrnl. Overland Exped. Aust.* 21 July (1847) 339 This was not covered with the stiff grass, nor the dry wind-grass of the plains north of the Staaten. **1978** D. STUART *Wedgetail View* 57 Spinifex plains, wind-grass plains, mulga country.

Windies, *pl.* [Contraction of *West Indies.* Used elsewhere but recorded earliest in Aust.] A nickname for the West Indian cricket team. Also in *sing.*, a member of this team.

1964 K. MACKAY *Slasher opens Up* 89 This impulsive batting is crowd-pleasing stuff, but should never be recommended. But the 'Windies'—and more power to them—are not meant to be shackled by convention. **1984** P. JARRATT *Aussie* 109 It doesn't matter whether he's a Pommie, Windie or Kiwi, if he hits our Lillee or Lawson over the fence.

windmill grass. [See quot. 1983.] Any of several grasses (fam. Poaceae), usu. bearing a digitate flowerhead; often of the genus *Chloris*, esp. the widespread *C. truncata* of all mainland States; STAR GRASS.

1889 J.H. MAIDEN *Useful Native Plants Aust.* 80 *Chloris truncata* . . 'Windmill Grass' . . is perennial and showy, an excellent summer and autumn grass, of ready growth, and relished by stock. **1983** G.G. ROBINSON *Native Grasses*

Northern Tablelands 11 Windmill grass is easily recognised by its windmill like flower. It forms a dense turf of pale green folded leaves. On the tablelands it is not a highly productive species and its hard leaves are not relished by sheep.

windmill magistrate. *Obs.* See quot. 1869.

1869 J. MARTINEAU *Lett. from Aust.* 134 Lest the term *Windmill Magistrate* should be unintelligible to those who are not fully initiated into the mysteries of colonial democracy, perhaps I should explain that there have been persons aspiring .. to the honour of being magistrates whose early education was not very comprehensive, and who, not being able to sign their names, were in the habit of affixing their mark X instead. The supposed resemblance of this mark to the sails of a windmill suggested the term. **1918** *Bulletin* (Sydney) 1 Aug. (Red Page), During one of the Ministries of Henry Parkes in the 'seventies, that consummate old general smoothed out a somewhat ruffled political situation by a judicious and generous creation of Jay Pees. So generous .. that a number .. could not read or write and signed their names with an X. The resemblance of this monogram to the sails of a windmill suggested the happy appellation of 'windmill magistrates'.

wind-whirly: see WHIRLY.

wine. Used *attrib.* in Special Comb. **wine cask,** see CASK; **dot** [pun on *Wyandotte* a breed of fowl], an habitual drinker of cheap wine; **saloon,** an establishment licensed to sell wine only; **shanty,** SHANTY *n.*[1] a.

1940 *Sentry Go* (Keswick) Dec. 24/2 In an hotel near Adelaide .. a chap, apparently a '**wine-dot**'. **1933** H.B. RAINE *Lash End* 88 She strutted away to the nearest **wine saloon**. **1878** *Squatter's Plum* 16 As a rule, he [*sc.* the station hand with cheque] has not far to go in search of friendly voices. The sly grog-shop or the **wine-shanty** stands on the road-side ready to receive him with open door... At length, partially drugged with the insidious liquor, he consents to trust his cheque in the publican's possession, and 'shouts' at random for all comers.

wing, *n.*[1]

a. A fence, usu. one of a pair, built out from a stock yard and serving to guide or channel stock towards its entrance: see quot. 1888 (2). Also **wing fence.**

1887 K. MACKAY *Stirrup Jingles* 16 Gone is the rush and rattle Of pikers on the rails, When wings were full of cattle, And thongs came down like flails. **1888** 'R. BOLDREWOOD' *Robbery under Arms* (1937) 14 There was a 'wing' ran a good way out through the scrub—there's no better guide to a yard like that. **1888** W.T. PYKE *Bush Tales* 37 Two side fences, called 'wings', are carried out in front of the enclosures, extending to a distance of 10 or 12 roods. These are sufficiently wide at the outer extremities to admit at once the whole herd. **1962** *N.T. News* (Darwin) 4 Jan. 11/4 Council had inspected the existing set-up which has a gap between two wing fences at the Northern end.

b. Special Comb. **wing yard,** a stock yard of this sort; also **winged yard.**

1916 *Bulletin* (Sydney) 13 July 24/1 The whole district turned out to round up kangaroos and yard them. We camped out overnight and started the 'drive' at daybreak into a wing-yard. **1945** F. CORK *Tales from Cattle Country* 34 Well-trained 'coachers' lure the brumbies into a winged yard. The 'coachers' are broken station horses which have been at the game for years.

2. a. The flank of a travelling mob of sheep, cattle, etc. Also *attrib.*

1895 A.B. PATERSON *Man from Snowy River* 6 So Clancy rode to wheel them—he was racing on the wing Where the best and boldest riders take their place. **1913** W.H. OGILVIE *Overlander* 66 The sheep are running a mile a-head, And there, whenever the leaders string, Laggards loiter, or wing-sheep spread, Every kelpie's a king.

b. *transf.* A number of livestock detached from the main body, esp. illicitly.

1943 H.G. LAMOND *From Tariaro to Ross Roy* 33 The sheep were shepherded and enclosed in brush yards at night. If a wing of a flock was lost .. that lost flock would be torn by dingoes. **1966** T. RONAN *Strangers on Ophir* (rev. ed.) 52 Some of those blokes from the Georgina could slip and lift a wing of good butchers' cattle before you knew anything about it.

c. A team or group.

1976 S. WELLER *Bastards I have Met* 76 The bloke looking after it was a real good urger and he's got a wing of young blokes around him giving them the spiel.

wing, *n.*[2] *Obs.* [Of unknown origin.] A penny.

c **1907** W.C. CHANDLER *Darkest Adelaide* 58 What, 'arfa caser, and I have to sling a bob for the room out of it. Only eighteen wing for myself? Can't do it. **1936** W. HATFIELD *Aust. through Windscreen* 2 'I've only one-and-six.' . . 'Tell you what. . . Gimme the eighteen wing and we'll go inside and shout the house.'

winger. [f. WING *n.*[1] 2 a.] A stockman controlling the flank of a travelling mob.

1951 E. HILL *Territory* 293 A ringer riding ahead, wingers on the flank, and the boss drover behind, they string out and move off.

wingman. *Australian National Football.* A player in the wing position.

1931 J.F. MCHALE et al. *Austral. Game of Football* 60 The half-backs on the flanks and the wing men should in most cases play out towards the fence, unless the centre and the half-forward centre are absolutely unguarded, when an easy pass is possible. **1963** L. RICHARDS *Boots & All!* 133 Dixon must be rated as one of the best wingmen Melbourne has ever had.

winking owl. [See quots. 1905 and 1968.] *Barking owl,* see BARKING.

1844 J. GOULD *Birds of Aust.* (1848) I. Pl. 34, *Athene connivens.* Winking Owl. **1905** *Emu* IV. 128 Winking Owl (*Ninox connivens*). . . The .. eyes .. constantly 'winking' (conniving), hence the specific name. **1968** D. FLEAY *Nightwatchmen* 71 Known as the Winking Owl in the official checklist and in various bird books, this strong, golden-eyed bird actually does not blink or wink any more than do other Australian owls.

wipe, *v. trans.* To dismiss, discard, disown (esp. a person).

1941 K. TENNANT *Battlers* 196 Giving her money . . in the casual manner that wiped her from all consideration as a human being. **1975** R. BEILBY *Brown Land Crying* 295 You can wipe that idea, if that's what you're thinking.

wipe-off.

1. A total loss, a 'write-off'.

1945 *Victory Roll* 59 One slip in this work and pilot and aircraft were a 'wipe-off'. **1945** L. JILLETT *Moresby's Few* 96 The Kittyhawk .. was a 'wipe-off'.

2. A 'sure thing'.

1946 *They wrote it Themselves* (W.A.A.A.F.) 18 *It's a wipe-off,* or *I thought I could swing it* both mean *it's in the bag.*

wira, var. WIRRA *n.*[1]

wire.

1. In the phr. **straight wire.**

a. The complete truth; an honest account.

1892 'J. MILLER' *Workingman's Paradise* 104 If I was pretty flush .. I'd waltz right up to him .. to ask the time, and if he came any of his law-de-dah squatter funny business on me I'd give him the straight wire, I promise you. **1955**

N. Pulliam *I traveled Lonely Land* 237 Why I'd even make it for the Olympics . . and that's the straight wire.

b. As adj. phr., honest.

1908 'Fifty-Three Yrs.' Miner' *So Long* 20 Is it another 'fairy' or a 'straight-wire' yarn?

c. As adv. phr., truly; honestly.

1917 P. Austen *Bill-Jim* 27 These 'ighfaluten tikes gives me th' 'ump—Straite wire, I'd like ter douse em in th' pump. **1949** C. Benham *Diver's Luck* 108 Well, Jim, I'm telling you, straight-wire, that I won't get drinking.

2. Special Comb. **wire door,** *fly door,* see Fly $n.^1$ 1; **fake,** *v. intr.*, to make wire clothes pegs, toasting forks, etc.; freq. as *vbl. n.*; so **faker; inspector,** *boundary rider,* see Boundary B. 2; **strainer,** an implement used to tighten the horizontal wires of a fence.

1935 F. Clune *Rolling down Lachlan* 129 The kitchen **wire-door** slapped and re-clapped. **1935** K. Tennant *Tiburon* 29 'What's 'e doing?' '**Wire-fakin'**.' 'He would be... Man's a genius. Make any mortal thing out of wire—clothes-pegs, bottle-cleaners, anything.' **1977** L. Fox *Depression Down Under* 99 Men would go 'wire-faking'. Out of wire they would create toasting forks with long handles, meat holders for open fire grilling, even a strong wire clothes peg. *Ibid.*, The wire-fakers raised a few shillings from their craft. **1905** *Shearer* (Sydney) 4 Feb. 4/2 What do you know of . . 'tick-jammers', or of 'lizards' and '**wire inspectors**'? **1882** Armstrong & Campbell *Austral. Sheep Husbandry* 204 Novel **Wire Strainer**. . . This instrument . . should be made of light iron. . . Three short spikes, or legs, should be fixed behind, so as to give the instrument a grip of the post as soon as the wire is tightened.

wiree /'waɪri/. [See quot. 1965.] *Rufous whistler,* see Rufous.

1921 'J. O'Brien' *Around Boree Log* 15 Did you wonder why the wiree comes to sing his sweetest song? *[Note]* Also known as the Chocolate Wiree (pronounced 'wiry'): a very fine songster, called by ornithologists 'Rufous-breasted Whistler'. **1965** *Austral. Encycl.* IX. 292 The rufous whistler . . proclaims its presence with a song that is remarkably melodious and sprightly. . . Other names based on the bird's calls are 'ee-chong' and 'wiree'.

wire-grass. Any of many perennial grasses, usu. of the genus *Aristida* (fam. Poaceae), having a tufted or tussocky habit and stiff, wiry stems.

1817 J. Oxley *Jrnls. Two Exped. N.S.W.* 1 June (1820) 52, I wish the grass had proved equally good, but there is nothing for them but dead wire-grass (*ira*). **1985** J. Galbraith *Garden in Valley* 9 Dense shrubs and tangles of wiregrass grew on the sheltered slopes.

wireweed. Any of several plants having wiry stems, usu. herbs of the genus *Polygonum* (fam. Polygonaceae), esp. *P. aviculare* of all States, and allied species.

1875 *Papers & Proc. R. Soc. Tas.* (1876) 96 Underneath there is generally a tall and tangled growth of wireweed (*Bauera*) . . with horizontal scrub (*Anodopetalum*). **1985** *Weekly Times* (Melbourne) 7 Aug. 6/4 Brome grass and wireweed were perennial problems on his land. Spraying the year before on ground that was going to be cropped helped to control them.

wirilda /wəˈrɪldə/. [a. Yaralde *wurrulde*.] The shrub or small tree *Acacia retinodes* (fam. Mimosaceae) of S.A., Vic., and Tas., cultivated as an ornamental. Also **wirilda wattle.**

1930 A.J. Ewart *Flora Vic.* 596 *A[cacia] rhetinodes* [*sic*] . . Wirilda. Glabrous shrub or small tree. **1985** E. Coleman *Come back in Wattle Time* 40 *Wirilda wattle* . . flowers practically all the year round—with restraint during the winter.

wirra, var. Wirri.

wirra /'wɪrə/, $n.^1$ Also **wira, wirree, worra.** [Western Desert language *wirra.*] A shallow wooden scoop used by Aborigines as a container and as a digging implement.

1897 K.L. Parker *Austral. Legendary Tales* (ed. 2) 16 Ye have filled your goolays and comebees with fruits, and your wirrees with honey. **1935** H.H. Finlayson *Red Centre* 79 The *wirra* is a shallow wooden dish which functions as a sand scoop. **1936** J.E. Hammond *Western Pioneers* 216 Worra, for digging up roots for food and digging graves etc. **1940** L.E. Sheard *Austral. Youth among Desert Aborigines* (1964) 77 The men then scraped the earth with a 'wira' completely covering the grave.

wirra /'wɪrə/, $n.^2$ [a. Diyari *wirra.*] The plant *Acacia salicina* (see Cooba).

1906 J.H. Maiden *Wattles & Wattle-Barks* (ed. 3) 90 *A[cacia] salicina.* . . Following are some additional aboriginal names . . 'Wirrha', Cooper's Creek, near Lake Eyre. **1941** I.L. Idriess *Great Boomerang* 102 Burned leaves of the wirra (a species of acacia, the leaves of which when burned yield a powder of potash).

Wirra /'wɪrə/, $n.^3$ Abbrev. of 'Wirraway', the name of an Australian modification of the North American NA/6 military aircraft.

1941 *Air Force News* (Melbourne) 15 Nov. 5 All eyes go up as the 'Wirras' dive. **1968** G. Dutton *Andy* 47 Do you think I enjoy pushing a bloody great Wirra into a hangar?

wirrah /'wɪrə/. [Prob. f. a N.S.W. Aboriginal language.] Either of two marine fish of rocky reefs of the genus *Acanthistius, A. ocellatus* of s.e. Aust. and *A. serratus* of s.w. Aust.

1880 *Proc. Linnean Soc. N.S.W.* V. 324 *Plectropoma ocellatum.* . . This is the 'Wirrah' of the aborigines, a common fish, but valueless for food. **1985** *Canberra Chron.* 13 Nov. 19/2 The best catch of fish I saw was a load of wirrahs, catties, eels and ling. Not exactly the most exciting fishing in the world.

wirrang /'wɪræŋ/. Also **wherang, wirring, woorang, worrung.** [a. Wiradhuri *wiraŋ.*] *Rock wallaby,* see Rock *n.* 2.

1833 W.H. Breton *Excursions* 251 Wirrang.—Bittang. Rock kangaroos. **1850** *Australasian Sporting Mag.* 92 The Woorang or Wirring, as it is there called, is the Rock Wallaby. They average about twenty five pounds weight, and would bother a chamois with their pace over a country all but impracticable to human beings. **1855** R. Austin *Jrnl. Interior W.A.* 14 Several worrungs, a small and very beautiful species of kangaroo, about the size of a rabbit, were shot today. **1900** *Bulletin* (Sydney) 21 July 15/1 'Coolawine' and 'wherang' (orthography not guaranteed) for bear and rock-wallaby, are commonly used on some of the coastal rivers.

wirree, var. Wirra $n.^1$

wirri /'wɪri/. *Obs.* Also **wirra.** [a. Gaurna *wirri.*] An Aboriginal weapon, used as a club or missile: see quot. 1860.

1841 C.G. Teichelmann *Aborigines S.A.* 10 His coming they prevent by striking with their *wirri*, the air around the hut in different directions. **1860** *Trans. & Proc. R. Soc. Vic.* (1861) 170 Another weapon, called 'wirra', is made of the stem of young trees, about one and a-half feet long, and barely an inch thick. The thin end, which serves for the handle, is generally notched, while towards the thicker end it is a little bent, somewhat in the shape of a sword. . . This weapon the natives use for killing kangaroo rats and other small animals.

wirring, var. Wirrang.

wise man. *Obs.* KORADJI.

1805 J. TURNBULL *Voyage round World* I. 85 This operation is performed very simply by their curradiges or wise-men. 1857 J. BONWICK *Early Days Melbourne* 38 The doctors, or wise men, are dreaded by the others.

witarna /ˈwɪtanə/. [a. Banggala *widarna*.] An Aboriginal ceremonial object: see quot. 1846 and BULL-ROARER.

1846 C.W. SCHURMANN *Aboriginal Tribes Port Lincoln* 5 The witarna, an oval chip of wood, say eighteen inches long and three or four broad, smooth on both sides and not above half an inch thick. By a long string which passes through a hole at one end, the native swings it round his head through the air, when it gradually, as the string becomes twisted, produces a deep unearthly sound. 1878 R.B. SMYTH *Aborigines of Vic.* I. p. xxiii, In Africa .. the fetich-man blows a kind of whistle made of hollowed mangrove wood, and the sound is probably a signal to those not privileged to keep away; just as the *Witarna* is used for this purpose in Australia.

witchetty /ˈwɪtʃəti/. Also with much variety, as **widgery**, **witchety**, **witjuti**. [Prob. a. Adnyamadhanha *wityu* hooked stick used to extract grubs + *varti* grub.]

1. *Obs.* A hooked stick for obtaining witchetty grubs. Also *attrib.*

1862 W.R.H. JESSOP *Travels & Adventures* II. 214 Besides the yam-stick, which is made of the hardest wood, there is the grub stick, called witchertie, a small hooked twig, which the women carry in the nose, and the men in a fillet round the head: this last is used for extracting the grub from crevices and holes. 1925 H. BASEDOW *Austral. Aboriginal* 125 This implement is from four to six inches long and is usually cut from a small pronged twig... The stick is inserted into the hole occupied by the witchedy grub, hook foremost, and pushed in until the grub is penetrated... The witchedy-hook is known throughout central and southern Australia.

2. *transf.* The large, edible, wood-eating larva or pupa of any of several moths, esp. cossids of the genus *Xyleutes*, and beetles of the fam. Cerambycidae; GRUB; MARGOO; *tree grub*, see TREE; *wood grub*, see WOOD *n.*[1] 3 b. See also BARDIE. Also **witchetty grub** (sometimes *attrib.*).

1891 *Trans. R. Soc. S.A.* XIV. 158 They did, however, eat one 'witchety', the native name of large white grubs, much relished by the blacks as an article of food, which are the larval forms of certain Longicorn beetles and Lepidoptera. 1894 R. LYDEKKER *Hand-Bk. Marsupialia & Monotremata* 191 The Marsupial Mole .. 'was fed on the 'witchetty' (a kind of grub)'. 1897 J.J. MURIF *From Ocean to Ocean* 176 The best bait one can use is a section of widgery (or 'witchery', a grub three or four inches in length, found at the roots of gum trees, and tasting, when slightly roasted, not unlike a hen's egg). 1901 F.J. GILLEN *Diary* 3 May (1968) 63 My old friend Unchalka head of the Udnirringita or Witchetty grub totem to which I have the honour to belong. 1953 *Trans. R. Soc. S.A.* LXXVI. 59 Aborigines with access to *witjuti* grubs usually are healthy and properly nourished.

3. Special Comb. **witchetty bush**, any of several plants of the genus *Acacia* of drier Aust., esp. the shrub or tree *A. kempeana* of all mainland States exc. Vic.

1935 H.H. FINLAYSON *Red Centre* 30 The broad-leafed mulga or witchetty bush, the roots of which harbour a grub beloved by the blacks.

wizard. *Obs.* KORADJI. Also *attrib.*

1884 A.W. HOWITT *On Some Austral. Ceremonies Initiation* 4 The doctors and wizards of some distant tribes .. might .. become acquainted with the leading Wolgal men. 1888 *Proc. Linnean Soc. N.S.W.* III. 422 Mr Froggatt exhibited a fine collection of native weapons and implements... It comprises spears .. coolamons .. wizard-stick used for bewitching enemies.

wobbegong /ˈwɒbigɒŋ/. Also **wahbegong, wobbygong, wobegong.** [Prob. f. a N.S.W. Aboriginal language.] Any of several slow-moving, bottom-dwelling sharks of the fam. Orectolobidae, esp. of the genus *Orectolobus*, commonly found among seaweed-encrusted rocks; *carpet shark*, see CARPET.

1852 G.C. MUNDY *Our Antipodes* I. 392 The most hideous to behold of the shark tribe is the wobegong, or woe-begone, as the fishermen call it. 1874 *N.S.W. Rep. R. Comm. Fisheries* (1880) 19 The wahbegong, of which there are several varieties on this coast, is chiefly nocturnal. 1896 F.G. AFLALO *Sketch Nat. Hist. Aust.* 221 A Tiger Shark (*Galeocerdo*).. lay alongside our steamer off Cairns... The variegated pattern on its back was not unlike that of the Wobbegong or Carpet-Shark of Sydney. 1981 *Bulletin* (Sydney) 9 June 56/2 Wobbygongs have teeth similar in size and shape to those of the grey nurse. Althought much more docile in appearance, wobbygongs or carpet sharks have an aggressive nature. They will bite a diver and frequently take speared fish.

wobbles, *pl.* [See quot. 1897.] An affliction of stock, usu. of cattle, attributed to consumption of the leaves of plants of the fam. Zamiaceae, and characterized by loss of control, and gradual loss of use, of the hindquarters.

1894 *Jrnl. Bureau Agric. W.A.* I. xviii. 225 The disease 'wobbles' is essentially peculiar to zamia districts. 1897 L. LINDLEY-COWEN *W. Austral. Settler's Guide* 587 The macrozamia .. has long been known to possess deleterious properties, due partly to indigestibility, but more from the poisonous constituents that bring on in the animals feeding on them a series of symptoms ending in partial paralysis of their hind quarters. The disease is known by the names 'rickets' and 'wobbles', from the 'wobbling' character of the gait of the animal affected by it.

wobbygong, wobegong, varr. WOBBEGONG.

wodgil /ˈwɒdʒəl/. *W.A.* Also **wodjil.** [Prob. f. a W.A. Aboriginal language.] A vegetation community of tall shrubby growth dominated by plants of the genus *Acacia*, esp. *A. neurophylla*; the wood of the plants. Freq. *attrib.*, esp. as **wodgil scrub**.

1948 J.K. EWERS *For Heroes to live In* 5 The wodgil and wattle scrub had been cleared in the early days to make a horse yard. 1973 R. ERICKSON et al. *Flowers & Plants W.A.* 190 On poor sandy clays there is frequently a tall thicket formation known as wodjil. 1973 C.E. GOODE *Stories Strange Places* 11 About half a mile away, in a dense patch of wodgil scrub ending in a line of breakaways, was suitable stone.

wog, *n.* [Of unknown origin.]

1. A name applied to various insects and grubs, esp. those regarded as predatory or otherwise disagreeable.

1938 *Bulletin* (Sydney) 7 Sept. 20/2 As the water moves slowly down the bays countless root-eating 'wogs' break for cover and an irregular line of starlings perform efficient mopping-up. 1982 J.A. SHARWOOD *Vocab. Austral. Dried Vine Fruits Industry* 32 A grower .. who is *chasing the wogs* is examining his vines closely for signs of insect damage.

2. A microbe or germ, a 'bug'; an illness. Also *attrib.*

1941 S.J. BAKER *Pop. Dict. Austral. Slang* 82 *Wog*, a germ or parasite. 1948 *Bulletin* (Sydney) 11 Feb. 23/3 Alf .. watched them pack and head for the falls on Crow Bend, where, after testing the wog-content, the scientific bloke voted it safe to drink.

wog, *v.* [f. *wog*, a colloq. name for a foreigner.] *trans.* In Services' speech: to buy (goods) from or sell to the local inhabitants.

1940 *Action Front: Jrnl.* 2/2 Field Regiment Oct. 5 Whilst short of cash, he wogged his fountain pen. 1981

D. STUART *I think I'll Live* 103 Some of my blokes have been seeing a few of the locals at night, at a corner of the back fence, an' wogging a bit of gear.

Wogga, Wogger, varr. WAGGA.

wogoit /'woʊɡɔɪt/. [Waray prob. *wogoj.*] *Rock ringtail,* see ROCK *n.* 2. Also *attrib.*
1926 K. DAHL *In Savage Aust.* 203 Upon my questions as to the nature of the 'wogoit', he informed me that the wogoit was a large kind of opossum which spent the days in hollows and crevasses among the rocks, feeding in the trees at night. 1946 D. BARR *Warrigal Joe* 20 Poor country; but worse lay ahead of them—'wogoit' land. It was walk-march for the horses, from the time the outfit left camp.

woilie, var. WOYLIE.

wolf. [Transf. use of *wolf* the large canine *Canis lupus.*] **a.** Any of several carnivorous native quadrupeds, esp. *Thylacinus cyanocephalus* (see *Tasmanian tiger, wolf* TASMANIAN *a.* 2). **b.** DINGO *n.* 1. Also **wolf-dog.**
1770 J. COOK *Jrnls.* 4 Aug. (1955) I. 367 Here are wolves. 1837 E. FRASER *Narr. of Capture* 8 The kangaroos and wolf-dog are the chief quadrupeds. 1898 E.E. MORRIS *Austral Eng.* 514 It [*sc. Thylacinus*] is the largest carnivorous marsupial extant, and is so much like a wolf in appearance that it well deserves its vernacular name of Wolf, though now-a-days it is generally called Tiger.

wollaba, wollabi, varr. WALLABY.

wollamai /'wɒləmaɪ/. [a. Dharuk *walamay.*] The marine fish *Chrysophrys auratus,* a SNAPPER.
1790 D. SOUTHWELL Corresp. & Papers, *Woa-la-mi,* snapper. 1952 *Austral. Museum Mag.* June 310 The Australian aborigines had their names for fishes, of course, and still have in the more remote places, and some of these, even though tribes which invented them have become extinct or have 'lost their tongues', are currently used in everyday speech. I need only mention the following .. Turrum .. Wobbegong, and Wollomai.

Wolseley. *Obs.* [Proprietary name, f. the name of F.Y. Wolseley (1837–1899), inventor.] A Wolseley shearing-machine. Freq. *pl.* for *sing.*
1897 *Bulletin* (Sydney) 20 Feb. 3/2 And Bogan laid his 'Wols'ley' down and knocked that rouser out. 1905 J. MEREDITH *Learn to talk Old Jack Lang* (1984) 13, I can blind Tom Power with wool with the Wolseleys and give Jacky Howe a fifty start.

woma, var. WOMMA *n.*²

wombat /'wɒmbæt/, *n.* and *attrib.* Formerly also with much variety, as **wambat, whombat, whombatt, womat, wombach, womback.** [a. Dharuk *wambad.*]
A. *n.*
1. Any of the several thickset, burrowing, herbivorous marsupials of the fam. Vombatidae of s. and e. Aust. incl. Tas., the commonest and most widespread of which is *Vombatus ursinus.* See also BADGER. Also *attrib.*, and with distinguishing epithet, as **hairy-nosed** (see under first element).
1798 *Hist. Rec. N.S.W.* (1895) III. 821 Different animals, one of which Wilson called a whom-batt, which is an animal about 20 inches high, with short legs and a thick Body forwards, with a large head, round ears, and very small eyes; is very fat. 1798 Banks Papers 5 Aug. XIX. 48 A new animal discovered on an island on the coast of New South Wales .. the Mountain Natives call it Wombach. .. One is female and has the false belly for the security of its young. 1798 D. COLLINS *Acct. Eng. Colony N.S.W.* (1802) II. 99 The mountain natives named this new animal Wom-bat, and said it was good eating; but it was wholly unknown to those who were admitted into the settlement. 1799 *Ibid.* 153 The *Wom-bat* (or, as it is called by the natives of Port Jackson, the *Womback*). 1801 M. FLINDERS *Observations Coasts Van Diemen's Land* 26 The new animal called, Womat, by the natives at the back of Port Jackson, is found in no inconsiderable numbers upon Cape-Barren Island. 1806 *Hist. Rec. N.S.W.* (1898) VI. 66 The native told me that the porcupine ant-eater and the whombat must be common by his frequent seeing their tracks, and our dog catching one of both. 1834 C.O. BOOTH *Jrnl.* 8 Mar. (1981) 172 Massacred a brace of Kangaroo and pair of very fine Badgers (very improperly so named) called Wambats by the Natives. 1982 P. GOLDSWORTHY *Archipelagoes* 43 The old wombat joke—it eats roots and leaves.

2. a. A slow or stupid person. Also *attrib.*
1905 *Bulletin* (Sydney) 3 Aug. 16/2 Murphy was a member of Jackson's road gang, in the wombat country, near where Bill Lyne gets his votes. 1984 *Bulletin* (Sydney) 20 Nov. 33/1 Those who follow Sinclair on his mostly rural election train are known as wombats. They wear ties with yellow wombats on them. They read Phantom comics.

b. Appled *fig.* in allusion to the wombat's ability to burrow.
1917 *Byron Bay Rec.* 7 July 4 In addition to the important work of tunnelling, units under the supervision of officers and n.c.o.'s, thousands of infantrymen, the greater majority of whom were entirely ignorant of underground work, have been transformed into excellent wombats. 1984 *Bulletin* (Sydney) 13 Nov. 32/3 Men known colloquially as 'wombats', says Costigan, illegally transmit prices to an operator outside racetracks by talking into radio devices in their pockets.

B. *attrib.*
1. Of a tract of land: inhabited by wombats.
1824 W. BLAND *Journey of Discovery Port Phillip* 7 Oct. (1831) 2 In the evening pass through Wombat brush. [*Note*] This brush, like most other parts of the country frequented by the animal from which it takes its name, is an excellent light soil. 1913 W.M. ANDERSON *Rhymes of Rouseabout* 6 With the wombat range before us and another league of plain.

2. Of a hole: made by a wombat. Also *fig.*
1845 E.J. EYRE *Jrnls. Exped. Central Aust.* I. 190 There were in places a great many wombat holes. 1945 J. DEVANNY *Bird of Paradise* 134 The first thing should be to cut out all these here State Governments. They're jest wombat holes for grafters to crawl into.

3. Special Comb. **wombat berry,** the climbing plant *Eustrephus latifolius* (fam. Liliaceae) of e. mainland Aust. and elsewhere, bearing a globular orange berry and cultivated as an ornamental.
1880 *Argus* (Melbourne) 12 Jan. 6/7 In the borders many interesting plants are in flower, notably .. the wombat berry (Eustrephus) [etc.].

Hence **wombat** *v.*, to dig or tunnel, like a wombat; also as *vbl. n.*, **wombatty** *a.*, heavily populated by wombats (see quots.).
1852 J. BONWICK *Notes of Gold Digger* 12 The constraint of body in work, the damp, the closeness of the atmosphere, the gloom, the fear of impending rocks, with occasional raps of knuckles and skull against the sides and roof, altogether make this **wombatting** not the most amusing operation in life. 1973 D. WOLFE *Brass Kangaroo* 143 Above the road a bent figure scratched around in the last remnants of the morning mist. 'And that there's old Clarrie trying to wombat the spuds out.' 1908 *Bulletin* (Sydney) 2 July 15/3 It is my ill-fortune to live in what is the **wombattiest** region on earth.

womera, var. WOOMERA.

womera /'wɒmərə/. Also **womerang, woomera,** and with much variety. [a. Dharuk *wumeraŋ* a club, the form prob. infl. by WOOMERA.] An Aboriginal club; an Aboriginal weapon (in quots. 1821, 1832 (1), and 1843, a boomerang). Also **womera-spear.**

1798 D. COLLINS *Acct. Eng. Colony N.S.W.* I. 613 *Wo-murrāng* [in a list of the names of clubs]. **1821** S. LEIGH in Methodist Missionary Soc. Rec. 18 Nov., The Wamareen. This Instrument or Weapon is made of heavy wood and is intended to disperse a Crowd, the skill which they have acquired in throwing it is highly wonderful. **1832** J. HENDERSON *Observations Colonies N.S.W. & Van Diemen's Land* 151 A womroo . . resembles the blade of a sabre, imitated in wood, and deprived of the handle; both ends are however similarly pointed, and the general curve possesses a considerable convexity. It is thrown, with the concave side towards the object, and is made to revolve horizontally. **1832** *Hill's Life N.S.W.* (Sydney) 21 Sept. 4 Unerring his aim when his barbed spear flew, Nor less so, when wamrah, or bomring, he threw To lay the wing'd game at his feet. **1843** C. ROWCROFT *Tales of Colonies* II. 34 Almost before I could take aim at the native, the womera, skimming through the air, returned to the spot from which the native had cast it. **1864** J. ROGERS *New Rush* 46 Next—high in air the womerang-spear he flings. **1928** W. ROBERTSON *Coo-ee Talks* 66 The performers looked terrible as they rushed upon each other with woomera-spears.

womma /'wɒmə/, $n.^1$ [a. Yankunytjatjara dial. of Western Desert *wama.*] *Honey ant*, see HONEY.

1916 S.A. WHITE *In Far Northwest* 120 These are formed by the natives when in search of sugar ants, which they call 'womma'. These ants were described in 1880 by Sir John Lubbock as Camponotus inflatus. **1932** *Bulletin* (Sydney) 13 Jan. 21/2 The sugar-ant provides a choice dainty. Binghi digs down into the nests, being very careful not to damage the 'womma' he is after.

womma /'wɒmə/, $n.^2$ Also **woma.** [a. Diyari *wama.*] The python *Aspidites ramsayi* of arid Aust.

1935 H. BASEDOW *Knights of Boomerang* 75 Rock-pythons attain a length of from fifteen to seventeen feet. In Central Australia the recognised delicacy . . is a large brown variety of the carpet-snake. . . By nature it is sluggish and voracious, and therefore usually well-nourished and fat. . . It is known as 'womma', which means 'fat'. **1967** H. COGGER *Austral. Reptiles* 80 The Woma inhabits the arid centre of Australia, extending outwards into the dry inland of all mainland States except Victoria.

wommara, wommera, var. WOOMERA.

wompoo pigeon /wɒmpu 'pɪdʒən/. Also **wampoo, whampoo pigeon.** [Imitative: see quot. 1976.] The fruit-pigeon *Ptilinopus magnificus* of near-coastal rainforest in n.e. Aust., also occurring in New Guinea; *king pigeon*, see KING $n.^1$ 2; *magnificent fruit pigeon*, see MAGNIFICENT; *painted pigeon*, see PAINTED.

1870 E.B. KENNEDY *Four Yrs. in Qld.* 111 One may find a large one with green back and purple and yellow breast, called the Whompoa, or painted pigeon. **1901** *Truth* (Sydney) 10 Mar. 5/5 Whampoo pigeons, green and rich gold, crowd the showers of ruddy-berries to the ground. **1910** *Emu* X. 207 A pair of the Purple-breasted Fruit Pigeons (*Megaloprepia magnifica*) commonly known as the 'Whampoo', on account of their deep note. **1944** J. DEVANNY *By Tropic Sea & Jungle* 157 The wampoo pigeon's a good beefy bloke, and fine eating too. **1976** *Reader's Digest Compl. Bk. Austral. Birds* 227 (*caption*) The wompoo pigeon—named for its booming, far-carrying call.

wompy, *a.* [Of unknown origin.] Ill. Also as *n.*, something liable to make one ill.

1920 *Bulletin* (Sydney) 24 June 20/2, I have seen seasoned breakers and horsemen . . get very 'wompy' inside after riding two or three willing three-year-olds in quick succession. **1982** P. RADLEY *My Blue-Checker Corker* 47 A guy called Nickie Johnson went on the piss . . with half a gallon of wompy, a toothbrush and a small tin of red paint.

womra, var. WOOMERA.

Wondjina, var. WANDJINA.

wonga, var. WONGI *v.*

wonga: see WONGA-WONGA 1.

wonga /'wɒŋgə/, $n.^1$ [a. Wemba-wemba *waŋgal* reedbed, bulrush.] BULRUSH.

1865 *Trans. Philos. Soc. N.S.W.* 361 In this part of the county where extensive reed beds are of common occurrence, the natives live for several months during the year on 'Typha roots', or Wongal (*Typha Shuttleworthii*). **1965** *Austral. Encycl.* IX. 347 'Wonga' is a Lower Murray aboriginal word conveying the idea of 'quivering motion' or 'suddenly springing up' and was originally applied to *Typha angustifolia*, the reed mace.

wonga /'wɒŋgə/, $n.^2$ [a. Pajamal *waŋga.*] CORROBOREE *n.* 1. Also *attrib.*

1946 W.E. HARNEY *North of 23°* 220 The aboriginals are singing and stamping their feet down in the camp, for they are dancing a wonga, the trade dance of these people. **1955** F. LANE *Patrol to Kimberleys* 8 'The others are in Derby for the big fella wonga—that's the corroboree.' 'Corroboree?' 'That's a native shindig they put on when they get together.' *Ibid.* 133 Later many of Tiger's 'plays' had been pirated by less talented wonga makers.

wongai /'wɒŋgaɪ/. [a. Kala Lagaw Ya *woŋay.*] A tree occurring on the islands of n.e. Aust., bearing an edible fruit, as *Zizyphus jujuba* (fam. Rhamnaceae) and a species of *Terminalia* (fam. Combretaceae); the fruit of these trees. Also *attrib.*, esp. as **wongai tree.**

1904 *Emu* III. 183 The date-like fruit of the terminalia (native 'wongai'). **1968** *Courier-Mail* (Brisbane) 10 July 2/8 Thursday Island . . has an informal charm and friendliness which easily tempts one to bite into the sticky fruit of the wongai tree. If you eat this fruit, legend says, you are bound to return.

wonga-wonga /'wɒŋgə-wɒŋgə/. Also **wanga-wanga.** [a. Dharuk *waŋa waŋa.*]

1. The ground-feeding, grey and white pigeon *Leucosarcia melanoleuca* of e. mainland Aust. Also *attrib.*, esp. as **wonga-wonga pigeon,** and freq. abbrev. as **wonga (pigeon).**

1821 L. MACQUARIE *Jrnls. of Tours* 20 Nov. (1956) 223 Major Morisett has most kindly sent his young friend Lachlan the following very handsome present of pets; vizt. four black swans . . and one wanga-wanga pigeon. **1827** P. CUNNINGHAM *Two Yrs. in N.S.W.* I. 321 We have a large pigeon named the *wanga-wanga*, of the size and appearance of the ringdove. **1868** J. BAIRD *Emigrant's Guide Australasia* 39 The wonga wonga pigeons, each weighing about a pound, were delicious. **1922** R.L. JACK *Northmost Aust.* I. 314 Scrub turkeys, wonga wongas and Torres Strait pigeons were seen. **1935** F. CLUNE *Rolling down Lachlan* 45 They . . caught a wonga pigeon for breakfast. **1984** M. BLAKERS et al. *Atlas Austral. Birds* 238 The Wonga is a ground-feeding pigeon that lives mainly in rainforest and eucalypt forest.

2. Special Comb. **wonga-wonga vine,** the climbing plant *Pandorea pandorana* (fam. Bignoniaceae) of e. Aust. incl. Tas., bearing clusters of showy pale-coloured flowers and cultivated as an ornamental. Also **wonga vine.**

1895 J.H. MAIDEN *Flowering Plants & Ferns N.S.W.* 33 The Wonga Wonga Vine. *Tecoma australis* . . a tall, woody, glabrous climber, with more or less twining branches.

1985 *Canberra Times* 20 June (Suppl.) 4/2 *Pandorea pandorana* (wonga vine) is .. an extremely floriferous, strong-growing climber with a twining habit... The creamy or pale-brown flowers are borne in loose clusters. The throat of the floral tube may be dotted or wholly suffused with colours varying from red to purple or maroon.

wongi /'wɒŋgi/, *n.*[1] *Austral. pidgin.* Also **wangie, wongie, wongy**. [f. WONGI *v.*] A conversation; a chat; also the local idiom (see quot. 1931). Also *attrib.*

1903 *Folklore* (London) XIV. iv. 342 Jack went to have a *wangie* (talk) with the native who gave it. **1929** K.S. PRICHARD *Coonardoo* 243 He .. had seen smoke .. and come in for a bit of sugar and a wongie. **1931** O. WALTERS *Shrapnel Green* 33 The wongi was 'ard to get on to... A shanty was sometimes a caffey. **1945** *Frontier News* June 6/2 Those of us .. who used to pull up, whenever we did meet someone on the track, to boil the billy and have a 'wongy'. **1984** *Sunday Independent* (Perth) 28 Oct. 8/4 Senator Withers plays down his role and dislikes the term 'Peacock's right-hand man'. 'Call me his 'wongi man'—I'm just someone he can have a chat with at the end of the day,' he said with a smile.

wongi /'wɒŋgi/, *n.*[2] [Western Desert language *waŋgayi.*] An Aboriginal from the vicinity of Kalgoorlie, W.A. See also quot. 1981.

1950 K.S. PRICHARD *Winged Seeds* 161 'Bob Brown'd never forgive us if he heard we'd been calling on the wongi and hadn't paid him and his missus a visit,' Dinny chuckled. **1981** A. WELLER *Day of Dog* 61 Charley's woman, a shy dark wongi from Kalgoorlie, comes out and takes the baby... [*Note*] Really the people from Kalgoorlie way, but any full-blood Aboriginal.

wongi /'wɒŋgi/, *v. Austral. pidgin.* Also **wangi, wonga**. [a. *waŋga* to talk, common to most w. Austral. languages.] *intr.* To talk; also *trans.*, to tell.

1872 MRS E. MILLETT *Austral. Parsonage* 79 'I tell him let her *wonga*' (*i.e.* talk)—'morning all right.' **1927** K.S. PRICHARD *Brumby Innes* (1974) 60 You wongie them not to be damn fools, Polly. **1955** F.B. VICKERS *Mirage* (1958) 26 'White fella all time wangi,' Bungil said. **1976** C.D. MILLS *Hobble Chains & Greenhide* 35 We used to 'wongi' in the dialect.

wonguim /'wɒŋgwəm/. [a. Wathawurung and Wuywurung *waŋgim.*] A boomerang which can be made to return to the thrower.

1878 R.B. SMYTH *Aborigines of Vic.* I. 317 The *Wonguim*, the weapon that has a return flight. **1965** A.W. UPFIELD *Lure of Bush* 69 'There are three kinds of boomerang,' he went on. 'The Wonguim, which returns in its flight to the thrower; the Kirras, which does not return; and the very heavy Murrawirrie.'

wongy, var. WONGI *n.*[1]

wonk. [Prob. f. *wonky* unstable, faulty.]

1. A white person; also *transf.* as a generalized term of abuse.

1938 X. HERBERT *Capricornia* 252 He went to the Dagoes and Roughs of second-class and won their friendship by .. telling them how he had been cast out by the Wonks of the saloon. **1951** *Bulletin* (Sydney) 6 June 15/4 'What's a soda?' repeated the big bloke. 'Why a soda's a woolly, o' course. I mean, it's—Well he's a wonk.' The bloke looked more confused than before. 'What, don't you know what a wonk is either?' Hec scowled at him. 'Well, look here, it's a .. a dill, see?'

2. An effeminate or homosexual male.

1945 S.J. BAKER *Austral. Lang.* 123 An effeminate male is a .. gussie, spurge and wonk. **1970** P. WHITE *Vivisector* 213 I'd have to have a chauffeur to drive me about—with a good body—just for show, though. I wouldn't mind if the chauffeur was a wonk.

wonky, *a.* [Spec. use of *wonky*: see prec.] Mad. Also **wonkyite** *n.*, a mad person.

1959 A. UPFIELD *Bony & Mouse* 76 Plenty of wonkyites down at Dryblowers, but not that bad. Take a ride over that way and look-see for yourself. Characters, all of 'em. No, this feller muderin' people isn't that sort of lunatic. **1973** J. GREENWAY *Down among Wild Men* 102 One could let one's tongue slip easily into 'wonky'—bush yabber for 'crazy'.

wonna, var. WANNA.

wood, *n.*[1]

1. *Obs.* Applied to a tract of naturally treed land, and now superseded by BUSH *n.* 1.

1770 J. BANKS *Endeavour Jrnl.* (1962) II. 56 Dr Solander and myself went a little way into the woods and found many plants, but saw nothing like people. **1892** 'MRS A. MACLEOD' *Silent Sea* III. 171 The wide shadowy woods and softly swelling rises that succeeded the boundless horizons and arid monotony of that region exhilarated the spirits like an escape from captivity.

2. *Obs.* In phr. with various verbs of motion, esp. **to take to the woods,** (of a convict) *to take to the bush*, see BUSH *n.* 4 a.

1788 *HRA* (1914) 1st Ser. I. 57 A convict who fled to the woods after committing a robbery, returned after being absent eighteen days. **1818** T.E. WELLS *M. Howe* (1945) 17 He eloped into the Woods and joined twenty-eight felons at that time at large committing depredations. **1827** P. CUNNINGHAM *Two Yrs. in N.S.W.* II. 194 Some .. will occasionally take to the woods, and subsist by plundering the settlers around... This method of robbery is denominated 'bush-ranging'.

3. Special Comb. **a.** In sense 1. (*Obs.*): **wood man, native,** an Aboriginal living in the bush; **ranger,** one who travels through the bush (cf. BUSHRANGER 2).

1798 D. COLLINS *Acct. Eng. Colony N.S.W.* I. 555 The hut of the **woodman** is made of the bark of a single tree. **1800** *Ibid.* (1802) II. 300 With the **wood natives** he had sufficient influence to persuade them that he had once been a black man. **1804** *Sydney Gaz.* 30 Sept., *To Stock-keepers, and* **Wood Rangers,** lost, a Brindled Cow.

b. Used to designate the habitat of animals: **wood adder,** any of several small, harmless lizards of the fam. Gekkonidae, esp. *Diplodactylus vittatus* of s. mainland Aust; **duck,** the perching duck *Chenonetta jubata*, occurring in lightly-wooded country near water in Aust. incl. Tas; MANED GOOSE; **grub,** WITCHETTY 2.

1903 *Bulletin* (Sydney) 9 July 17/1 The '**wood-adder**' of western N.S.W., a lizard about 3½ in. long, dark brown with blue-black markings is reputed to be venomous. **1825** B. FIELD *Geogr. Mem. N.S.W.* 440 Shot a **wood-duck** for breakfast. **1827** P. CUNNINGHAM *Two Yrs. in N.S.W.* I. 345 Our **wood-grub** is a long soft thick worm, much relished by the natives, who have a wonderful tact in knowing what part of the tree to dig into for it.

c. Used to designate the material: **wood-chop,** CHOP *n.*[2]; also as **wood-chop contest;** and *attrib.*; **joey,** one who is responsible for maintaining a supply of firewood; **line,** a railway constructed for the transport of timber; also *attrib.*; **splitter,** SPLITTER 1; also **splitting** *pres. pple.*

1918 *Bulletin* (Sydney) 16 May 48/2 Bill Lucas will chop against a local champion... After the **wood-chop** five rounds between. **1981** J.P. GABBEDY *Forgotten Pioneers* p. xi, All logs for woodchop contests shall be classified by diameter and not by girth or circumference. **1986** *Sunday Examiner* (Launceston) 30 Mar. 33/1 George and David Foster cruised to victory in the Royal Easter Show's woodchop arena. **1963** X. HERBERT *Disturbing Element* 74 That firewood business made Mother angry, when she saw the way Phil and I leapt into it. She yelled at Dad: 'Making **wood-joeys** of my sons!' **1929** W.J. RESIDE *Golden Days* 24 Our return journey on the **wood-line** train. **1979**

J. WILLIAMS *White River* 81 The old woodline, where my grandfather Seagrim had gone in the early 1900's and worked felling wood to keep the boilers hissing steam for the gold mine. **1855** G.H. WATHEN *Golden Colony* 91 We had with us as guide through the forest a **wood-splitter**. **1861** 'OLD BUSHMAN' *Bush Wanderings* 216 On their own resources, living by wood-splitting, shooting, etc.

wood, $n.^2$ [Prob. in fig. allusion to WOODEN or WOODENER.] In the phr. **to have the wood on** (someone), to have an advantage over (someone).
    [N.Z. *c* **1926** 'MIXER' *Transport Workers' Songbk.* 7, I hold the 'wood' on those who work.] **1949** L. GLASSOP *Lucky Palmer* 156 She's got you taped, too, kid. She's got the wood on all of us. **1977** N. MANNING *Us or Them* (1984) 46 We've got the wood on Wilkie and McKenzie. . . I caught them smoking pot in the out-of-bounds area.

woodah, var. WADDY *n.*

wood-and-water joey. [f. *wood-and-water,* in allusion to 'hewers of wood and drawers of water' (*Josh.* ix. 21) + JOEY $n.^2$ 2.]
    a. An unskilled labourer who performs the menial tasks of an establishment; USEFUL.
    1882 *Sydney Mail* 1 Nov. 783/4 Bobby, he don't know a p'leeceman from a wood-an'-water joey. **1978** D. STUART *Wedgetail View* 46 You might consider taking a job here with me, wood-and-water joey, general rouseabout.
    b. *fig.* A servile employee or hanger-on, a 'bum boy'.
    1898 *Truth* (Sydney) 14 Aug. 4/2 You acted as Parkesian wood-and-water joey. **1963** R.H. CONQUEST *Spurs are Rusty Now* 144 'Can't he get his own beer?' I asked. 'How long have you been that old sinner's wood-and-water Joey?'
    Hence **wood-and-water joeying** *vbl. n.*
    1917 A.B. PATERSON in C. Semmler *World of Banjo Paterson* (1967) 254 He was to do a year in the shops, and pick up all the wrinkles, and get a car for the old man. Bit better than wood and water joeying wasn't it?

Woodbine. [Transf. use of *Woodbine* the proprietary name of an English cigarette.] An English person, esp. a soldier. Also *attrib.*
    1919 W.H. DOWNING *Digger Dialects* 54 Woodbine, an English soldier, so called from the name of a cheap brand of cigarette favored by Englishmen. **1937** E. HILL *Water into Gold* 192 Bagtown became 'Woodbine Ave'. . so-called for the number of English settlers in residence.

wooden, *v.* [Formed after *stiffen* to make a corpse of, but cf. WADDY *v.* a.] *trans.* To strike; to knock down; also *fig.,* to stun. Also with **out.**
    [N.Z. **1904** 'G.B. LANCASTER' *Sons o' Men* 252 He'll wooden more of you out if you scare him.] **1905** *Truth* (Sydney) 9 July 1/7 A Perth (W.A.) paper says that 'the proportion of Dagos to the British population is nothing less than alarming and that a secret society exists among the savage scum for woodening-out the white'. **1936** J. DEVANNY *Sugar Heaven* 255 That woodened the organisers properly. They couldn't reply. **1957** J. HAWKE *Follow my Dust* 174 He'll be having the ding-bats in no time. Best thing is to wooden him with a shovel.

woodener. [See prec.] A staggering blow; a knock-out punch. Also *fig.*
    1899 *Bulletin* (Sydney) 2 Sept. 14/3, I gave him a regular woodener on the jaw and stretched him. **1900** *N.T. Times* (Darwin) 19 Jan. 2/7 She . . poured 'a real woodener' of raw three-star brandy into her.

wooden pear. [See quot. 1865.] Any of the several shrubs or small trees of the Austral. genus *Xylomelum* (fam. Proteaceae), of Qld., N.S.W., and s.w. W.A. See also *native pear* NATIVE *a.* 6 a., PEAR 1. Also **woody pear,** and *attrib.*
    1835 J. BACKHOUSE *Narr. Visit Austral. Colonies* (1843) 292 He told us, that the leaves of the Wooden-pear, *Xylomelum pyriforme,* dye wool yellow. **1865** G.F. ANGAS *Aust.* 121 Amongst the anomalies of the Australian vegetable world are the 'wooden pear tree' and the native cherry: the former, which grows near Sydney, has a seed vessel in size and aspect like an ordinary pear, but which consists entirely of hard wood, enclosing a few flat seeds in the centre. **1985** *Blue Mountains Gaz.* (Springwood) 18 Dec. 35/1 Botanical highlights of the walk include the largest stand of woody pears in the Upper Mountains.

woodheap, *n.* A pile or stack of wood, esp. firewood.
    1918 *23rd: Voice of Battalion* 15 Oct. 15 Papa Dear—I hope you're well. . . How's the wood heap. **1979** *N.S.W. Parl. Papers* (1980–81) 3rd Sess. IV. 701, I had to work on the wood heap and carry my swag.

woodheap, *v. trans.* [f. prec.] **a.** To ostracize (a fellow worker). **b.** To require (an itinerant worker, swagman, etc.) to cut firewood in exchange for a meal.
    1932 *Bulletin* (Sydney) 9 Nov. 21/2 A shearer up Armidale way had been 'woodheaped' for refusing to take out his A.W.U. ticket. 'Woodheaping' is about as old as shearing in Australia. In pre-union days it was applied to the man who made himself a general nuisance. . . It consists in expelling the offender from the shearers' mess, with the result that he has to have his meals in solitude, sitting on the woodheap, which lies behind every shed cookhouse. **1957** D. WHITTINGTON *Treasure upon Earth* 90 Mick inquired about the attitude of station owners on the roads leading south. 'No hand-outs. . . They'll woodheap you on Yarranook and Wineba, but the rest'll turn the dogs on you.'

woodpecker.
    1. [See quot. 1965.] TREECREEPER 1; SITTELLA.
    1833 *Trumpeter* (Hobart) 8 Nov. 227 *To Naturalists.* To be sold . . birds, in skins . . Woodpecker, Green Linnet, Goldfinch. **1965** *Austral. Encycl.* IX. 21 Their [*sc.* treecreepers'] habit of pecking at the bark has given them in Australia the name of woodpeckers; but they are not related to the true woodpeckers, which are unaccountably absent from Australia.
    2. [U.S.: see OEDS 3.] A machine-gun.
    1943 A. DAWES *Soldier Superb* 59 The throb of enemy aircraft engines and the cough of enemy 'woodpeckers' always menacing in your ears. **1985** N. MEDCALF *Rifleman* 197 Find that bloody woodpecker. You will not . . attack it! I don't want nine . . men arguing with a heavy machine-gun.

woodser. Abbrev. of JIMMY WOODSERR
    1942 *Bulletin* (Sydney) 23 Sept. 12/2 He was too well known to risk going to the bar for a 'woodser'. **1976** S. WELLER *Bastards I have Met* 21 Of course we enjoy our beer too. But this is only secondary. If it wasn't you'd see a lot more blokes drinking 'woodsers'.

wood swallow. A bird of the genus *Artamus,* chiefly of mainland Aust. See also *blue martin* (b), BLUE *a.,* *summer bird* SUMMER. Also with distinguishing epithet, as **black-faced, little, masked, white-breasted, white-browed** (see under first element).
    1827 *Trans. Linnean Soc. London* XV. 211 Artamus . . Albovittatus . . called *Wood Swallow,* as we find in Mr Caley's notes. **1984** SIMPSON & DAY *Birds of Aust.* 340 Woodswallows' movements are in response to the availability of their main food item, namely, flying insects.

woody pear: see WOODEN PEAR.

wool.

1. In the imperative phr. **wool away!** the call of a shearer to a picker-up, requesting the clearing away of the fleece just shorn.

1879 S.W. Silver *Austral. Grazier's Guide* 55 The fleece is thrown upon the shed-floor, the words 'Wool away!' are shouted, and another sheep caught. **1982** *Sydney Morning Herald* 23 Oct. 29/4 There are cries of .. Wool Away! when the fleece piles up around the shearers' feet and the picker-up is busy elsewhere.

2. Special Comb. **wool barber,** a shearer; **bin,** any of several boxes or compartments into which a wool classer directs graded fleeces; **blind** *a.*, (of a sheep) having wool growing over the eyes; also as *n.*; hence **blindness** *n.*; **book,** see quot. 1979; **cheque,** the amount received from the sale of a season's wool by a sheep-farmer or by the sheep-farmers of a district, etc., collectively; **-classer,** one who grades fleeces; **classing** *vbl. n.*, the grading of fleeces; also as *pres. pple.*; **clip,** the annual wool production of a sheep-farmer, or of sheep-farmers of a district, etc., collectively; **dray** *obs.*, a wagon in which wool is carried; see Dray 1; **hawk,** a shearer; **hook,** a hook used to manoeuvre a bale of wool; **house** *obs.*, a building for the storage or processing of wool, esp. when shearing is done out of doors; **king,** a large-scale sheep-farmer; **man,** a sheep-farmer; **press,** a machine which compresses bales of wool; **presser,** one who operates a *wool press*; **pressing** *vbl. n.*, the compressing of wool bales in a *wool press*; **roller,** see quot. 1979; so **rolling** *vbl. n.* and *attrib.*; **room,** that part of a wool shed in which the shorn fleeces are processed and packed; **scour,** a shed where wool is washed; **screw** *obs.*, *wool press*; **season,** the period during which sheep are shorn and the wool marketed; **shed,** *shearing shed*, see Shearing B. 3; also *attrib.* as **wool shed dance,** a dance held in a wool shed, esp. an annual dance held to celebrate the end of shearing; **sorter** *obs.*, *wool-classer*; **store,** a warehouse in which wool is stored; **table,** the table on which a shorn fleece is processed; **team,** a team of draught animals used to pull a vehicle carrying wool; **track,** the route by which consignments of wool are conveyed to a port; **wash,** *wool scour*.

1962 T. Ronan *Deep of Sky* 58 They're short of shearers... Old Beadsman has picked up enough to beat anything that those **wool-barbers** will own. **1879** S.W. Silver *Austral. Grazier's Guide* 54 The fleece is spread out by the wool-roller, preparatory to being folded up and tossed into a **wool-bin**. **1914** *Pastoral Rev.* 16 Mar. 242 Treatment of **wool-blind** sheep (wigging) is also very desirable. **1935** R.B. Plowman *Boundary Rider* 158 The sheep had been run in so that they could be gone over for wool blindness, and for blowfly damage. **1982** J. Morrison *North Wind* 197 In addition the sheep were wet from the showers during the day. With a fading light it was going to be about ten times worse than pushing a mob of wool-blinds up the ramp of a shearing shed. **1961** *Bulletin* (Sydney) 15 Mar. 40/3 The admirable first type says: 'I'll leave the preparation of the clip to you.'... You show him the lines, and except for an occasional look in the **wool-book**.. you scarcely see him. **1979** Harmsworth & Day *Wool & Mohair* 177 The wool book is the official record of all bales pressed in the wool shed and in it are recorded the full details concerning the contents of the bales, their weight and number. **1930** A.E. Yarra *Vanishing Horsemen* 20 There isn't enough left from the **wool cheque** to pay the income tax people. **1951** G. Farwell *Outside Track* 14 Our wool cheque for 1950–51 was over £600,000,000. **1879** S.W. Silver *Austral. Grazier's Guide* 78 The process of culling is generally performed by the aid of an experienced **'wool-classer'**. **1847** *Port Phillip Gaz.* 8 Nov. 3 He has commenced the business of Wool Sorting, **Classing,** Packing, and Purchasing and selling Wool on Commission. **1899** G. Jeffrey *Princ. Australasian Woolclassing* 41 In Australia the term 'Woolclassing' is applied to the work carried on at the station at shearing time, when the wool is being prepared for market. **1844** Macarthur Papers LXII. 215 It now becomes my duty to inform you that the whole of my private Property in New South Wales, with the exception of the **Wool Clip** of the approaching season, has been sold. **1937** *Publicist* (Sydney) vii. 10/2 Yorkshire's mills consume less than a quarter of the Australian wool clip. **1835** *Cornwall Chron.* (Launceston) 21 Feb. 3 *Tarpaulings* [sic] for covering of **wool drays**. **1916** *Bulletin* (Sydney) 20 July 26/2 Among western **wool-hawks** the 'bindie-eye' ranks first of things that are forever accursed. It is a spidery vegetable that spreads over the sheepfolds and sheds innumerable spiny burrs into the jumbuck's overcoat. **1908** W.H. Ogilvie *My Life in Open* 45 All handling of wool bales is done with **wool hooks**. **1827** P. Cunningham *Two Yrs. in N.S.W.* I. 273 The fleeces are rolled and carried to the **wool-house,** being sorted according to their qualities into different binns, and weights being placed above them to press them down. **1839** *Port Phillip Patriot* 3 Apr. 3 The actual murderers [of aborigines] appear to have been set on and supported by some of the **Wool Kings** of New South Wales. **1850** *Irish Exile* (Hobart) 17 Aug. 4/3 *Bankers!* merchants, lawyers, **woolmen**—all of them. **1829** *Hobart Town Almanack* 141 **Wool presses** on the different farms of the interior are also becoming more common every day. **1846** C.P. Hodgson *Reminisc. Aust.* 107 A man being on the alert to pick up the fleeces as soon as they are clipt, conveys them to the woolsorter, who arranges them according to their quality; after that they are handed over to the **wool-presser** and by him to the bale. **1848** S. & J. Sidney *Emigrant's Jrnl.* 66 **Wool-pressing** is done by the bale. **1879** S.W. Silver *Austral. Grazier's Guide* 54 The fleece is spread out by the **wool-roller,** preparatory to being folded up and tossed into a wool-bin. **1882** Armstrong & Campbell *Austral. Sheep Husbandry* 174 The T shed.. is built as though it were two buildings—the one forming the cross of the T being used as a shearing board, sheep and sweating pens. This part of the building, and as much of the other as may be required for wool-classing, wool-rolling, etc., is built upon blocks. **1928** C.E. Cowley *Classing Clip* 32 It can be 'thrown out' on the wool-rolling table. **1979** Harmsworth & Day *Wool & Mohair* 159 The men employed as wool rollers remove all faulty portions and roll the fleece into a compact bundle so that the bulk quality of the fleece is exposed to the classer's view. **1836** J. Backhouse *Narr. Visit Austral. Colonies* (1843) 441 We.. returned to Goulburn, after having a meeting with about forty persons, in the **wool-room,** at Rossiville. **1896** T. Heney *Girl at Birrell's* 68 Then there were the people wanting work in the **wool-scour,** the shearing-sheds, mustering-yard, shearers' hut and kitchen. **1827** P. Cunningham *Two Yrs. in N.S.W.* (ed. 2) II. 82 Wooden **wool-screw** (warranted) £15. **1841** *Geelong Advertiser* 8 May 2/5 Ere the return of another **wool season** our bay will be crowded with a fleet of merchantmen. **1835** J. Backhouse *Narr. Visit Austral. Colonies* (1843) 318 At Myami, a Sydney merchant, has erected some good, wooden buildings.. prisoners' huts, a large **wool-shed,** etc. Most of them are weatherboard, of the Pine of this neighbourhood. **1965** L. Walker *Other Girl* 190 The annual **woolshed dance** is always pandemonium. **1805** S. Macarthur Onslow *Some Early Rec. Macarthurs* (1914) 113 A person who came with Mr McArthur said to be a professed **Wool-sorter**. **1840** *Port Phillip Gaz.* 13 June 1 Extensive **Wool Stores** at Williams Town are now completed, and ready for the reception of Wool. (N.Z.) **1865** M.A. Barker *Let.* 1 Dec. in *Station Life N.Z.* (1870) 32 We next inspected the **wool tables,** to which two boys were incessantly bringing armfuls of rolled-up fleeces.] **1879** S.W. Silver *Austral. Grazier's Guide* 40 Hogget fleeces.. make a very respectable show on the wool-table. **1836** *Cornwall Chron.* (Launceston) 31 Dec. 2 A great number of **wool teams** are on the road to Sydney. **1903** J. Furphy *Such is Life* 248 These **wool-tracks,** that knew him so well, will know him no more again for ever. **1900** H. Lawson *On Track* 131 The engine drivers at the shed or **wool-wash**.

Woolloomooloo /wʊləməˈluː/, *attrib.* and *n.* [Transf. use of the name of a wharf-side suburb in Sydney.]

A. *attrib.*

1. Rough, uncultivated; thug-like.
1891 *Truth* (Sydney) 3 May 4/5 One prisoner is confined in No. 3 yard—a 'Queen's pleasure man'—and who is now perfectly sane, could tell you how he was pummelled by two Woolloomooloo bummers placed in charge of him. **1967** *Kings Cross Whisper* (Sydney) xliii. 11/3 *Woolloomooloo upper-cut*, a strategic boot in the groin.

2. Applied to one who affects the manner of the type specified: see quots. 1900 and 1984.
1900 *Truth* (Sydney) 28 Jan. 5/5 Other men .. could not tell a brigalow scrub from a dog-leg fence .. and .. ride a horse like a tailor, 'Woolloomooloo bushmen' in short. **1984** V. DARROCH *On Coast* 42 *Woolloomooloo Yank*, a name applied to any seaman (or shore worker) of Australian origin who adopted an American accent—usually after his first short visit to the U.S.A.

B. *n.* A fight.
1981 P. RADLEY *Jack Rivers & Me* 95 Tony roared... 'Oh, my aching heart, what a name,' Connie said and then she roared like Tony. Nance put a stop to their private woolloomooloo.

woolly, *n.* and *a.*

A. *n.*

1. [Used elsewhere but recorded earliest in Aust.] A sheep, esp. one which is ready for shearing. Also *attrib.*
1897 *Worker* (Sydney) 11 Sept. 1/2 The sheep are 'jumbucks', 'woollies' have the fleece still on their back. **1909** *Bulletin* (Sydney) 28 Oct. 13/3 Only newchums and woollystockmen (i.e., sheep-men) use the whip as a plaything.

2. *transf.* A sheep-farmer.
1961 *Bulletin* (Sydney) 15 Mar. 40/1 There are many types of guessers. The ideal is the big-bull boy covered in competence, confidence, doctor's white coat and cook's white trousers. Many cockies are quite unimpressed with such sartorial ostentation; but one woollie maintains: 'You can get more out of the rousies if you lair up.'

B. *adj.*

1. In the collocation **woolly back** (or **coat**), a sheep.
1915 *Bulletin* (Sydney) 2 Sept. 26/4 A vegetable much abused in parts of Westralia is commonly known as 'blind grass'... The woolly-coats, as a rule, won't tackle it. **1977** F.B. VICKERS *Stranger no Longer* 107 We shore 42,000 sheep at Bindimia in that year—2,000 more woolly backs than in the previous year.

2. Oriented towards sheep-farming.
1942 *Bulletin* (Sydney) 23 Sept. 13/2 A hundred years ago Australia was more woolly than it has ever been since. In N.S.W. the whole country was arranged for the convenience of the woolgrower.

woolly bull. A one-piece garment worn under a flying suit. Also *attrib.*
1949 A. SCHOLES *Fourteen Men* 10 Tons of equipment, from 'woolly-bull' zipper flying suits to pre-fab huts .. had been accumulating at the Tottenham Air Force Depôt in Melbourne's western suburbs. **1969** J. PEARCE *Look Mum I'm Flying* 12 The next day we were issued with flying clothing. The inner suit called a Woolly Bull.

woolly bush. Any of several plants of the genus *Adenanthos* (fam. Proteaceae) having silky hairs on the leaves, esp. the shrubs *A. sericeus* and *A. cygnorum* of s.w. W.A.
1897 L. LINDLEY-COWEN *W. Austral. Settler's Guide* 182 The wooly bush has a characteristic which is worthy of note; it carries a fibre which would make a good rope. **1978** R. ERICKSON et al. *Flowers & Plants W.A.* 15 A shrubby member of the *Banksia* family, *Proteaceae*, is the Common Woollybush, *Adenanthos cygnorum*... This is a grey-green bush covered with soft, hairy leaves.

woollybutt. [See quot. 1965.] Any of several trees of the genus *Eucalyptus* (fam. Myrtaceae) having a rough bark on part or all of the trunk, esp. *E. longifolia* of e. N.S.W. and *E. miniata* of n. Aust.; the wood of these trees; WOOLLY GUM. Also *attrib.*, and formerly **woollybutted gum.**
1836 J. BACKHOUSE *Narr. Visit Austral. Colonies* (1843) 445 One called here, the Woolly-butted Gum, seems identical with the Black-butted Gum of Tasmania. **1958** *Bulletin* (Sydney) 26 Nov. 19/2, I noticed two strange-looking bits of woollybutt-wood. **1965** *Austral. Encycl.* IX. 369 Woollybutt, the standardized name in the timber trade for *Eucalyptus longifolia*... The name refers to the thick fibrous bark, present only on the lower part of the trunk. Three other eucalypts .. are also known by this name.

woolly gum. *Obs.* WOOLLYBUTT.
1826 J. ATKINSON *Acct. Agric. & Grazing N.S.W.* 4 In willow brushes the ground is more or less covered with the white or woolly gum trees. **1902** *Proc. Linnean Soc. N.S.W.* XXVI. 556 *E[ucalyptus] Stuartiana*.. is perhaps the 'Woolly Gum' of Berrima.

woolly kangaroo. *Obs.* A sheep. See also quot. 1829.
1829 R. MUDIE *Picture of Aust.* 168 In the interior a kangaroo has been met with, with fur so long and soft, as to get the name of the woolly kangaroo. **1903** *Truth* (Sydney) 4 Jan. 8/1 The white man quarrelled with the black-fellows about their gins, and the latter naturally retaliated by stealing the 'woolly kangaroos'.

woomera, *var.* WOMERA.

woomera /'wʊmərə/. Also **womera, wommara, wommera, womra, womra,** etc. [a. Dharuk *wamara*.] An Aboriginal implement used to propel a spear (see quot. 1963); *spear-thrower*, see SPEAR *n.* 1 b.; THROWING STICK a.
1793 J. HUNTER *Hist. Jrnl. Trans. Port Jackson* 410 *Womar*, a throwing-stick. **1798** D. COLLINS *Acct. Eng. Colony N.S.W.* I. 584 The wo-mer-ra, or throwing-stick, is .. about three feet long, with a hook at one end (and a shell at the other, secured by gum), to receive which there is a small hole at the head of the spear. **1846** C.W. SCHÜRMANN *Aboriginal Tribes Port Lincoln* 3 The catch of the wommara is hooked, in throwing the spear. **1853** I. CHAMBERLAYNE *Austral. Captive* 145 All the editor knows of the *womra* is, that it is normally employed in launching the spear at a distant object. **1963** D. ATTENBOROUGH *Quest under Capricorn* 73 He also owned a few spears and a wommera or spear-thrower, a long slat of wood shaped into a handle at one end and fitted with a spike at the other. **1984** B. DIXON *Searching for Aboriginal Lang.* 79 A party of hunters crept stealthily up, spears at the ready in their woomeras, to let loose an attack once they were close enough.

Woop Woop /'wʊp wʊp/. [Jocular formation, prob. infl. by the use of reduplication in Aboriginal languages to indicate plurality or intensity; but see also WOPWOP.]

1. (The type of) a remote and supposedly backward rural town or district. Also (with **the** and without initial capitals) **woop-woops,** remote country. See also BULLAMAKANKA, OODNAGALAHBI.
1918 N.P.H. NEAL *Back to Bush* 32, I once went to church in Woop-woop. **1950** J. MORRISON *Port of Call* 241 'He's got to go to Mordialloc first to get spruced up. He ain't in the race.' 'That's what comes of living out in the woopwoops.'

2. An inhabitant of such a place. Also **woop.**
1936 M. FRANKLIN *All that Swagger* 472 Adrienne was no blob or woop-woop. **1939** FRANKLIN & CUSACK *Pioneers on Parade* 73 'The Mitchell, what's that?' asked Willie. 'Don't be such a woop,' said Prim. 'It's a library.'

woorang, var. WIRRANG.

wop. *Obs.* Also **wap.** [A coinage of popular journalism and unrelated to *wop* a southern European.] A 'whore'; used as a term of generalized abuse. Also **wopster.**
1899 *Truth* (Sydney) 5 Feb. 14/3 The peculiar notions of Mrs Grundy [sc. *The Sydney Morning Herald*], who, since her settlement in New South Wales, has gone from bad to worse until she has at last come to be derided and despised as the degraded, despicable sort of social 'wop' of the worst kind that she really is. **1909** *Ibid.* 20 June 5/2 As a newspaper proprietor, he could confidently claim to have done more for the material and moral welfare of the People than all *the wowsers of Wellington* and their wopsters put together. **1910** *Ibid.* 4 Dec. 7/1 Without the wanging and whangdoodling of waps and Wowsers, or the discordant ding-dong din of cracked church and chapel bullock bells.

wop-wop. *Obs.* [Perh. f. Br. dial. *wap* (or *wop*) to wrap, to make a careless bundle of anything: see EDD *v.*[1] 1.] ROUSEABOUT *n.* a.
1900 *Bulletin* (Sydney) 18 Aug. 14/3 The shearer terms the rouseabout variously a 'loppy'.. 'wop-wop' [etc.]. **1915** *Ibid.* 28 Oct. 22/3 A shed-hand is a 'rousie'.. or 'wop-wop'.

worb, var. WARB.

word, *n.* [Ellipt. form of *upon my word* assuredly, certainly: see OED(S *word, sb.* 15. In Br. use *my word* is an ejaculation of surprise.] In the phr. **my word,** an expression of emphatic agreement or endorsement; 'indeed'; 'my oath' (see OATH).
1857 *Illustr. Jrnl. Australasia* II. 179 'Surely the report of a pistol would bring some of you to my assistance.' 'My word!' cried the stockman, 'you may safely say it would bring me.' **1967** G. JENKIN *Two Yrs. Bardunyah Station* 4 'Would you care for a cuppa tea mate?' I said, 'My word I would!'

word, *v. trans.* To speak to or tell; to accost. Also to rebuke.
1905 *Bulletin* (Sydney) 19 Nov. 5/1 A woman standing at the door 'worded' them, and asked them if they were not going to 'set 'em up'. **1919** V. MARSHALL *World of Living Dead* 22 There is the chance to 'word' a mate whom maybe one never sees elsewhere. **1968** S. GORE *Holy Smoke* 28 Y' look as if you'd been dragged though a barb-wire fence backwards! Come on, and while you're gettin' tizzed up I'll word yer Mum to slaughter a fatted calf. **1973** J. MURRAY *Larrikins* 117 The 'donahs' would grimace and giggle, and the boys would 'word 'em'.

work, *v.*

1. *Hist.* In the phr. **to work in chains** (or **irons**).
a. Of a convict: to wear fetters while engaged in hard labour.
1790 D. COLLINS *Acct. Eng. Colony N.S.W.* (1798) I. 111 These were the people who were ordered by the justices to work in irons. **1843** C. ROWCROFT *Tales of Colonies* (1858) 219 You must know that the different gangs that work in chains are watched by overseers, who have their eyes constantly on them.
b. To cause (a convict) to labour in fetters. Chiefly in *pass.*
1807 W. PATERSON Let. to Sir J. Banks 13 Nov. 4 The most worthless characters might be worked in Irons as a punishment. **1844** *Sydney Morning Herald* 3 Feb. 2/5 A man of the name of Miers, a prisoner of the crown, residing with his wife has been sentenced to be worked in irons for twelve months for purchasing stolen goods.
2. *trans.* To herd (sheep, cattle, etc.). Also *transf.*, to accommodate (stock) and as *vbl. n.* See also WIDE WORKING.
1880 J.B. STEVENSON *Seven Yrs. Austral. Bush* 115 A cattle yard capable of working a moderate herd of cattle usually covers about two acres, and is constructed of posts and rails. **1890** 'R. BOLDREWOOD' *Squatter's Dream* 140 The collie 'Help', then, as he grew up, showed great hereditary aptitude for every kind of knowledge connected with the 'working' of sheep. **1960** E. O'CONNER *Irish Man* 210 He and Paula and Dalgliesh mustered near the homestead, and worked cattle in the yards close to the house.
3. In the phr. **to work back,** to work overtime.
1926 'S. WESTLAW' *Mystery of Lombardy Chambers* 10 Ralph Harding was 'working back'. Business at present was pretty brisk; and besides, he was keen to get on. **1986** *Poets' Lunch* (A.N.U. Staff Centre) 10 You mean you haven't met Cherisse? She's working back tonight.

worker. [Survival of Br. *worker* draught animal: see OED 2 d.] A draught bullock or horse.
1847 *Bell's Life in Sydney* 20 Mar. 3/1 Seed any workers this morning? I'se a missed two.. both on 'em was hobbled. **1959** H. LAMOND *Sheep Station* 74 Those sheep were let go in the horse-paddock—an area large enough to necessitate workers being hobbled and belled at night so they could be easily got next morning.

workers' compensation. a. Used *attrib.* to designate legislation which provides for the compensation of an employee who sustains an injury in the course of employment (see quot. 1906). **b.** A payment or series of payments made under this legislation (also *attrib.*).
1902 *Act* (W.A.) 1 & 2 Edw. no. 5 Sect. 1 (1), The short title of this Act is the Workers' Compensation Act, 1902. **1906** J.W. BLAIR et al. *Workers' Compensation Act* p. xxxi, By 'The Workers' Compensation Act of 1905' an entirely new principle was introduced. By this Act the worker is given a right to compensation from his employer for accidental injuries sustained in the course of the employment. **1961** *Sydney Morning Herald* 4 Aug. 7/1 A male nurse who was injured while playing with the Callan Park Staff Soccer Club when off duty was entitled to workers' compensation. **1985** *West Austral.* (Perth) 12 June 10/4 Men in the WA workforce make four times as many workers' compensation claims each year as women, according to the TLC.

working, *ppl. a.* In special collocations: **working bee,** a gathering of volunteers to perform a (communal) task; **bullock, (a)** WORKER; **(b)** a hard-working person; a 'willing horse'; **gang** *hist.*, GANG; **mate,** see MATE 1 a.; **overseer** *obs.*, a person employed on a rural property both to work and to supervise the work of others.
1908 *Bulletin* (Sydney) 12 Mar. 15/1 The **Working Bee** of alleged farmers.. made a goodly stretch of the Prospect Road. **(a) 1805** *Sydney Gaz.* 24 Feb., The Stock consists of 2 **Working Bullocks. (b) 1874** C. DE BOOS *Congewoi Correspondence* 168 It's because they're such reglar stickers that they say a feller's a reglar **workin bullock** when he does all he knows for his master or anybody else. **1790** D. COLLINS *Acct. Eng. Colony N.S.W.* (1798) I. 101 The **working gangs** being now so much reduced by the late embarkation, the hoy was employed in bringing the timber. **1833** *Launceston Advertiser* 4 July 2 Wanted, on a small Farm near Town, a **Working Overseer.**

working man's block. *Obs.* See quots. 1891 and 1901. Also *attrib.*, and as **working man's homestead block.**
1886 N. ROBINSON *Stagg of Tarcowie* 16 Apr. (1977) 65 He has one of the working man's blocks up the creek towards O'Grady's. **1890** *Quiz* (Adelaide) 4 July 2/1 Mr Cotton stuck to the working men's blocks system until it became an accomplished fact. **1891** J. HUGHES *Aust. Revisited* 129

Working men's homestead blocks, not exceeding twenty acres .. may be leased by auction at an upset price of sixpence per acre. **1901** *Austral. Handbk.* 95 Every person who does not own land within the Colony .. who is the head of a family, or a male who has attained the age of 18 years, shall be entitled to obtain a lease of lands *set apart for Working Men's Blocks.*

worra, var. WIRRA *n.*[1]

worrogal, var. WARRIGAL.

worrung, var. WIRRANG.

worry. In phr.
 a. **no worries:** see No *a.* 2.
 b. **my worries,** *my troubles,* see TROUBLE.
 1949 A. MARSHALL *How Beautiful are thy Feet* 50 'My worries,' said Correll, contemptuously gesturing, 'She's got nothing on me.' **1963** A. UPFIELD *Madman's Bend* 96 'It's going to be another fine day, isn't it?' 'My worries if it's fine or wet.'

would. [Ellipt. for *wouldn't it (make you sick,* etc.).]
 a. In the interrogative phr. **wouldn't it,** an exclamation of dismay, exasperation, or disgust.
 1940 *Wouldn't It: Souvenir Mag. H.M.T. 'Orcades'* 7 Feb., In this brief foreward to *'Wouldn't It'* .. one is tempted first to speculate on the origin of the name. A catch phrase .. obviously expressive of disgust. More often than not .. at the actions or orders of higher authority. Be that as it may *'Wouldn't It'* in common with so many equally succinct expressions coined by the old A.I.F. has apparently come to stay. **1972** J. O'GRADY *It's your Shout, Mate!* 14 The barmaid's sigh was greatly exaggerated. She said to the audience, 'Wouldn't it? It's just not my day.'
 b. Similarly in the phr. **wouldn't it rip (root, rotate) you.**
 1941 *Somers Sun* 24 July 1 Wouldn't it rip yer? **1945** S.J. BAKER *Austral. Lang.* 152 *(note)* The authentic digger form is *Wouldn't it root you!* A regimental paper 'Wiry' (1941) took its name from the first letters of the words in this phrase. **1961** L. GLASSOP *We were Rats* (ed. 3) 117 Well woulden it rotate ya?

wowse /waʊz/, *v.* [Back-formation f. WOWSER *n.* 2.] *intr.* To preach; to behave puritanically. Also as *vbl. n.*
 1906 *Truth* (Sydney) 24 June 1/7 Now then, ye wowsers—rise up and wowse violently. **1983** *Nat. Times* (Sydney) 8 July 20/4 You bunch of wowsing do-gooders, I suggest you ring Keith Van der Linden, who is the company secretary, to register your complaint.

wowser /'waʊzə/, *n.* and *a.* [Prob. f. Br. dial. *wow* to howl or bark as a dog; to whine, grumble, make complaint (see EDD *v.*[1]); claimed by John Norton (*c* 1858–1916), editor of the Sydney *Truth* (1891–1916), as his coinage: see quot. 1910 (2) at sense 2 of the *n.*, but also quots. 1879 and 1910 (3) at senses 1 a. and 2 respectively.]
 A. *n.*
 1. *Obs.*
 a. A person who is obnoxious or annoying to the community or who is in some way disruptive. Also *transf.* [The final word of quot. 1879 is unlikely to be 'whores', which is used freely elsewhere in the text.]
 [**1879** *Truth* (Sydney) 20 Nov. 5/1 Now she may be seen on Sydney streets—varying between a state of idiotic drunk and beastly drunk—generally in company with a very seedy and disreputable looking being of the masculine order... Who shall say our editor (who is so heavy on the Prostitution question) is wrong when he states that some women are born w–s?] **1899** *Ibid.* 8 Oct. 5/6 The Parraween push. A partisan protest. Willoughby 'wowsers' worried. The 'talent' get a 'turn'. **1904** *Ibid.* 31 July 9/5 The warrigal wowsers of Waine were conspicuous by their absence. These lewd, larrikin louts, who seek fatuously to foster the cause of pure, pious, parson-petted Jack Wayne.
 b. As a generalized term of abuse.
 1899 *Truth* (Sydney) 26 Nov. 6/3 O is the ordeal of facing a mauser, P is the Paddington Popinjay wowser. Q are the qualms which made some heroes queer, R and the reasons (?) they'd not volunteer. **1915** B. GAMMAGE *Broken Yrs.* (1974) 87 The *right* type of Australian is a real firm fellow and can't be beaten *anywhere,* that *does not* include the street corner wowsers of the towns but chiefly the country lads.
 2. One who is publically censorious of others and the pleasures they seek; one whose own behaviour is puritanical or prudish. (Now the general use.)
 1900 *Truth* (Sydney) 8 Apr. 7/1 That old Y.M.C.A. wowser, whose journalistic virtue is of such transparent purity that it could not be suffered to endure more wear and tear without a knighthood. **1910** *Ibid.* 13 Feb. 1/8 Whose hand is cold, and limp, and dank, And breath most strange, and weird, and rank, A sort of human septic tank? The Wowser. *Ibid.* 8 May 1/5 Therefore, 'Palmam qui meruit ferat'—the motto of Lord Nelson. Let it be the motto of John Norton in the circumstances of this case, and for the purposes of establishing his claim to immortal glory as the inventor of the word Wowser. *Ibid.* 15 May 5/6 In the ordinary parlance of the proletariat, it [*sc.* wowser] signifies a 'bald-headed, bad-breathed, bible-banging bummer, who ought to be banged with a bowser, which is a wig for a wire-whiskered wowser'... There is no doubt you have enlarged the scope of, and popularised, the expression; but you have not in the least detracted from its original meaning... Of course, a false sense of public decency forbids the publication of the derivation and true meaning... From 'Subscriber and Constant Reader of 'Truth' who actually pays for the paper, and never forgets to 'rouse on' the agent when it is not delivered.' **1975** *Bulletin* (Sydney) 18 Jan. 6/1 But members of this odd body of wowsers want the right to *force* their opinions on to others.
 B. *adj.* (and *attrib.*) Of or pertaining to a wowser (see sense 2 above); (repressively) puritanical.
 1913 *Bulletin* (Sydney) 11 Dec. 3/2 The primitive, pre-Wowser days, when Life, with hard knocks and rubs Was gradually and silently shaping in her fecund processes. **1957** F. CLUNE *Fortune Hunters* 28 Instead of buying a drink at the side-door of the closed bar, we raided our own emergency desert-crossing supplies, and drank damnation to Tom Playford's wowser laws.
 Hence **wowseress, wowserette, wowserine** *n.,* a female wowser.
 1910 *Bulletin* (Sydney) 22 Dec. 13/4 The female is rather dingy-looking and might be a **Wowseress. 1911** *Truth* (Sydney) 29 Jan. 1/6 The **wowserette**.. kept quiet on the subject of mixed bathing. **1917** *Bulletin* (Sydney) 22 Nov. 3/2 And now My Little **Wowserine** is tenant of my heart. (Excuse me while I make attempt a ruling right to get: Should she be 'Little Wowserine' or 'Little Wowserette'?).

wowserdom. Wowsers collectively: see WOWSER *n.* 2.
 1906 *Truth* (Sydney) 28 Oct. 5/5 Never before had Wowserdom received such a shock in its respectability weskit. **1984** *Bulletin* (Sydney) 17 Apr. 47/1 As a veteran student of wowserdom, I will watch his progress with devoted interest.

wowserish, *a.* Puritanical or prudish.
 1906 *Truth* (Sydney) 20 May 5/8 As long as they are not Wesleyan wowserish, pragmatically Puritanical, and noxiously Nonconformist-Conscience-like. **1983** *Age* (Melbourne) 3 Dec. 11/2 Coming hard on the heels of the casino inquiry, which also recommended in the negative, the Government's decision on poker machines may give it a puritanical or wowserish image.

wowserism.

a. An act or utterance characteristic of a wowser: see WOWSER n. 2.

1904 *Truth* (Sydney) 3 Jan. 5 (*heading*) Wonders and 'wowserisms' of the week. **1975** *Bulletin* (Sydney) 19 Apr. 21/1 Not all the Rev Saunders' arguments against the club licence are wowserisms. He draws attention to the part booze plays in the road toll.

b. The behaviour or beliefs of such a person; puritanism.

1906 *Truth* (Sydney) 28 Oct. 10/4 An anti-Puritan league fights wowserism. **1984** *Canberra Times* 11 July 5/4 The liquor poll is a curious survivor from the turn-of-the-century days when the country was in the grip of wowserism.

wowseristic, a. Puritanical; prudish: see WOWSER n. 2.

1907 *Truth* (Sydney) 17 Mar. 6/6 Chain prayers. The latest production. A lamentable wowseristic exhibition. **1951** D. STIVENS *Jimmy Brockett* 207, I kept thinking of the beaut times I used to have with Jack Harper when we were good cobbers—that was before he went all respectable and wowseristic on me.

wowserly, adv. In the manner of a wowser: see WOWSER n. 2.

1907 *Truth* (Sydney) 20 Jan. 1/4 Mem. for 'wowserly' females—'A woman can be serious without being sour.' **1963** X. HERBERT *Disturbing Element* 164 Even we, reared in the wowserly tradition of Phil the Fluter, always had a flagon or two.

wowsery, a. Characteristic of a wowser: see WOWSER n. 2.

1912 *Truth* (Sydney) 11 Aug. 8/5 Three petitions .. all of which were slightly wowsery in their tone. **1960** *Westerly* ii. 31 Probably some woman flying off the handle, about her near-inebriate spouse to a wowsery neighbour.

wowsey, a. Obs. [f. WOWSE + -Y.]

a. Sanctimonious.

1909 *Truth* (Sydney) 17 Oct. 1/6 Has it ever struck you lately Mister Norton, to be shure, That a smock-faced wowsey sperrit Hangs around about each dore?

b. Disorderly; disruptive.

1911 *Bulletin* (Sydney) 7 May 8/2 William Whitfield wollops the wowsey wasters... William James Whitfield summoned Hugh Sebbens for riotous behavior and assault on the 9th April last, the last named retaliating with a 'poultice' for assault.

woylie /'wɔɪli/. W.A. Also woilie. [a. Nyungar walyu.]

The small marsupial *Bettongia penicillata* (see BETTONG).

1928 *Pop. Names for Marsupials* (Public Library, Museum, & Art Gallery W.A., Museum Leaflet no. 1), *Bettongia penicillata* .. Woilie. **1985** *West Austral.* (Perth) 6 Nov. 54/2 The long-term health of some W.A. woodlands could depend on a small fungus-loving marsupial, the rare and endangered woylie. Sometimes called the bettong or the rat kangaroo, it is thought to be the main agent in spreading underground fungi that speed up plant regeneration after fires.

wrap n. and v., var. RAP n. and v.

wrapped, ppl. a. [Blend of wrapped 'deeply interested, centred or absorbed, in a person or thing' (see OED 4) and rapt entranced, enraptured (see OED 1).] Overjoyed; with in, engrossed in; infatuated by. Also rapt.

1963 'C. ROHAN' *Down by Dockside* 212 She gave me a quid now and then. I never stood over her for it. She's wrapped in me, see. **1971** D. WILLIAMSON *Don's Party* (1973) 53 *Don*: How did she take it? *Susan*: I don't think she was wrapped. **1986** *Centralian Advocate* (Alice Springs) 2 May 1/1 The newly-chosen minister has declared he was 'rapt' with his new portfolio.

wren. [Transf. use of wren the small passerine bird *Troglodytes troglodytes* of Europe, and other related birds.] Any of many small, ground-frequenting, insectivorous birds, usu. having an upright tail, esp. those of the genus *Malurus* (see *fairy wren* FAIRY n.[1] 1) and others of the fam. Maluridae. Also with other distinguishing epithets, as **black-backed, blue, emu, Lambert's, purple-backed, purple-crowned, red-winged, scrub, superb blue, turquoise, variegated, white-winged**: see under first element.

1833 *Trumpeter* (Hobart) 8 Nov. 227 *To Naturalists*. To be sold .. birds, in skins .. House Robin .. Wren. **1985** *Age* (Melbourne) 9 Sept. 15/5 The Australian wrens, warblers and robins are quite unrelated to their namesakes in the Northern Hemisphere.

wriggle. In the phr. to get a wriggle on, to move with expedition; to 'get a move on'.

1911 ST. C. GRONDONA *Collar & Cuffs* 11 After the fire on 'Macara' station the sheep had to get a 'wriggle on' pretty quickly, as nearly the whole reserved paddocks suffered from the fire. **1962** MARSHALL & DRYSDALE *Journey among Men* 70 Ray .. clung like a possum to the rigging... The kid in the rigging exhorted the gunman not to waste time, to get a wriggle on, to wake up.

wriggler. A snake.

1927 *Bulletin* (Sydney) 3 Nov. 24/2 A handsome little wriggler is the red-naped or scarlet-spotted snake (*Pseudelaps diadema*). **1972** W. WATKINS *Wayward Gang* 144 'Let's go in here and get the wriggler.' 'The men will be home soon.' 'Bugger the men... The snake will have gone by then.'

wrought, var. RORT n.

wroughter, var. RORTER.

wurley, var. WHIRLY.

wurley /'wɜli/. Pl. wurlies. Also whirley, whirlie, wurlie, and formerly with much variety. [a. Gaurna (and related languages) warli.]

1. The temporary shelter of an Aboriginal; an Aboriginal dwelling (see quots. 1854, 1871, and 1975). See also GUNYAH 1.

1839 *Port Phillip Patriot* 10 June 6/1 The Governor has made good wurleys for them [*sc.* Aborigines] to sleep in when the nights are cold. **1854** W. SHAW *Land of Promise* 209 They live in what are termed 'whirleys', which are fragile erections made of rushes or bark, disposed in a conical shape, and about the size of an oven. **1863** J. DAVIS *Tracks of McKinlay* 231 A 'whirlie', or temporary shelter of the wandering natives. **1871** 'IOTA' *Kooroona* 188 When they arrive at a spot where they choose to 'sit down', for that is the literal meaning of the expression they use in place of the English word, 'camp', they break down a few small trees, lay them on the ground in a circle, a foot or at most two feet high, leaving a wide opening on one side, and there they sit, doing nothing, when tired of walking about. These small enclosures of boughs they call wurleys. **1975** *Bulletin* (Sydney) 16 Aug. 22/2 Also in sight are the wurlies made of corrugated iron, canvas sacks and rugs. These are occupied by the Aborigines and cost nothing.

2. *transf.* Any temporary shelter.

1840 *S. Austral. Rec.* (London) 28 Mar. 143 What would you think in England of leaving a good bed and warm fireside, and going into the forest by some water hole, and making a break wind (or werlie) formed of boughs, to protect you from the wind and wet. [*Note* House or shelter in the native language.] **1980** M. DUGAN *Early Dreaming* 25 You stood one sheaf up like a tentpole, held it there, and laid other sheaves against it until you had a wurlie or wigwam of hay.

wurly-wurly, var. WHIRLY-WHIRLY.

wurrung /'wʊrʊŋ/. [a. Nyungar *waraŋ*.] The nail-tailed wallaby *Onychogalea lunata* having a crescentic white shoulder marking, now presumed extinct; *crescent nail-tailed wallaby*, see NAIL-TAILED WALLABY.

1875 J. FORREST *Explorations in Aust.* 225 Shot a wurrung on our way. **1962** B.W. LEAKE *Eastern Wheatbelt Wildlife* 46 To procure Wurrungs for food, the aborigines used to light a fire and smoke them out.

X

xanthorrhoea /zænθɒˈriːə/. [The plant genus *Xanthorrhoea* was named by English botanist J.E. Smith (*Trans. Linn. Soc. London* (1798) IV. 219), f. Gr. ξανθός yellow + ῥοία flowing, referring to the yellow resin exuded by the type species, *X. resinosa*.] Any plant of the genus *Xanthorrhoea* (fam. Xanthorrhoeaceae) of all States, varying in form from herb-like plants to small trees, many species bearing a tall flowering spike rising from the crown of grass-like leaves. See also GRASS-TREE 1. Also *attrib.*, esp. as **xanthorrhoea resin**.

1814 R. BROWN *Gen. Remarks Bot. Terra Australis* 44 Xanthorrhoea .. is in habit one of the most remarkable genera of Terra Australis. **1955** *Austral. Jrnl. Chem.* 263 The complex mixture of aromatic compounds found in Xanthorrhoea resins.

X-ray. Used *attrib.* to designate a style of Aboriginal painting which originated in Western Arnhem Land and which is characterized by the depiction of internal as well as external organs of the subject: see quot. 1978.

1943 *Primitive Art Exhib. Catal.* (Nat. Gallery & Nat. Museum Vic.) 2 Some of them .. are likely to appeal more strongly to the European than the 'X-ray' paintings from the Northern Territory of Australia, with their representations of the spine, ribs and inner organs. **1978** R. EDWARDS *Aboriginal Art in Aust.* 42 The famous X-ray paintings have their home in the west. In them, the artist portrays not only the external features of the animal, human or spirit being he is painting, but also the spinal column, heart, lungs and other internal organs. It is a conventional way of showing that there is more to a living thing than external appearances.

Y

-y, *suffix*. Also **-ey**, **-ie**. [Orig. used to form pet names and familiar diminutives and now widespread as elsewhere in informal English, esp. as a mark of familiarity.] Added as a final syllable to: **(a)** discrete, usu. monosyllabic, forms (but see e.g. BULLOCKY *n.* 2 and 3), as BLOCKIE, BLUEY, BROOMIE, BROWNIE *n.*[1] and *n.*[2], BUSHY *n.*, CHALKIE, CREAMY, DOLEY, GREENIE, GUMMY, HEADY, JACKY *n.*[1] and *n.*[4], KIPPY, LITTLEY, MATEY, RINGIE, ROANY, ROUGHIE, SCALIE, SCHOOLIE *n.*[2], SCRUMMY, SHARPIE, SHORNIE, SHREWDIE, STONKIE, SWAGGIE, TAILIE, TINNY *n.*, TRAMMIE, TOWNY, UEY, WAXIE, YOUNGIE, ETC.; **(b)** shortened forms of words or collocations, as AUSSIE *n.*, BARBIE, BIKIE, BLOWEY *n.*[1] and *n.*[2], BODGIE *n.*[1], BOMMIE, BOSIE, BRICKIE, BRUMMY *n.*, BUDGIE, BULLY, BUNDY *n.*[3], CARBY, CHEWY, CHRISSY, COCKY *n.*[1] and *n.*[2], COLDIE, CONNIE, COSSIE, DECKIE, FOOTY, FOXIE, FRESHY, GROUPIE, GUVVIE, HALFIE, HIDEY, HODDIE, HOSTIE, HOTTIE, JEWIE, JUMMY, KINDY, KINGIE, KOOKY, LIMEY, LIPPY, LOBBY, LOWIE, MOSSIE, MOWIE, MUDDIE, NEWIE, NOGGY, OCKY, OSSIE, POKIE, POMMY, POSSIE, PREZZIE, ROUGHY, ROUSIE, SALTIE, SCHOOLIE *n.*[1], SICKIE, SLUSHY *n.*[2], SMOOY, SUBBY, SUNNIES, SURFIE, SWEEPY, TASSIE *n.*, TICKIE, TILLY *n.*[1] and *n.*[2], TOADY, TOWIE, TRUCKIE, UMPY, WAGGY, WEDGIE, WELSHIE, WESTIE *n.*, WHARFIE, WHIRLY, YACHTIE, etc. For forms previously used elsewhere, see BLACKIE, COVIE, MAGGIE, POLLY, SLUSHY *n.*[1], etc.

yaahoo, var. YAHOO *n.*[1]

yabber /'jæbə/, *n.* Also **yabba**. [f. YABBER *v.*]
1. Talk; conversation; discussion; language. See also *paper yabber* PAPER. ALSO **yabber yabber**.
1855 R. CARBONI *Eureka Stockade* 5 There was .. a great waste of yabber-yabber about the diggers not being represented in the Legislative Council. **1966** D. NILAND *Pairs & Loners* 80 After a couple of hours yabber and taking it easy we were good cobbers.
2. Special Comb. **yabber stick**, MESSAGE-STICK.
1893 *Trans. & Proc. R. Soc. S.A.* 243, I have, in travelling over the district, often carried 'Yabber-sticks' for the natives.

yabber /'jæbə/, *v.* Orig. Austral. pidgin. Also **yabba**. [Prob. f. an Aboriginal language.]
1. *intr.* To talk; to converse. Also **yabber yabber**.
1841 *Port Phillip Patriot* 7 Jan. 2/3 A black named Winberry said he commanded the party. They pointed their guns at them. Deighton at last got out, and called upon Winberry to protect them. Winberry said he was no good, 'he' (meaning Deighton), 'too much yabber to master'. **1857** K. CORNWALLIS *Yarra Yarra* 5 Oh! I rejoice to think on Quilla Quah, The fairest virgin that o'er Mookerwaa Danced to the war-song of a naked throng, Or yabba yabbaad o'er old Burrendong.
2. *trans.* To say; to ask.
1847 *Port Phillip Herald* 25 Feb. (Suppl.), Bobby cried out to Mr Beveridge, 'what for you yabber me cram jumbuck?' *anglice*, 'why did you charge me with stealing your sheep?' **1859** W. BURROWS *Adventures Mounted Trooper* 83 The missionaries yabber plenty daily bread and trippenny pieces.

yabbering, *vbl. n.* [f. YABBER *v.*] Talking; conversing. Also as *ppl. a.*
1847 *Maitland Mercury* 16 Oct. 2/5 When .. within a few rods' distance of Five Dock, such a piercing cry of misery was raised, that Captain Morris at once stopped the steamer; and no sooner was this done than there was a tremendous 'yabbering' heard, the only distinguishable sounds amongst which however were 'Missa Boyd'. **1968** D. O'GRADY *Bottle of Sandwiches* 211 Eventually we ignored the yabbering, jabbering and pointing people.

yabby /'jæbi/, *n.* Also **yabbie**. [a. Wemba-wemba *yabij*.]
1. Any of several fresh-water crayfish (usu. of the genus *Cherax*) valued as food, esp. the common *C. destructor*, native to s.e. Aust.; LOBBY. Also *attrib*.
1894 *Argus* (Melbourne) 6 Oct. 11/2 In the case of the small crayfish, called 'Yabbies' by the blacks in New South Wales, these may be found all over Australia, I think, both in large and small lagoons. **1935** J.K. EWERS *Fire on Wind* 62, I keep a good table here. .. Parrot pie, braised wallaby, yabbi mayonaise. **1962** J. HEDGE *Trout Fishing N.S.W.* 97 The Little Pied Cormorant is highly beneficial because of its intensive feeding on the destructive Yabby. **1977** P. ADAMS *Unspeakable Adams* 71 My epic is called *Claws* and it stars that most awesome of Antipodean creatures, the *Cherax*, otherwise known as the yabbie.
2. Chiefly *Qld.* NIPPER *n.*[1]
1952 W.J. DAKIN *Austral. Seashores* 199 This [*sc. Callianassa .. australiensis*] is the species that is popularly known in northern New South Wales and Queensland as the yabby. **1968** W.N. SCOTT *Some People* 132 The point is, as any Queensland fisherman can tell you, that a yabby is a sort of saltwater crayfish with claws, that looks as though someone has stepped on it.
3. *transf.* A wicket-keeper.
1983 HIBBERD & HUTCHINSON *Barracker's Bible* 235 Yabbie .. wicket keeper: from the curious stance and gauntlets of the pudgy breed.

yabby /'jæbi/, *v.* [f. prec.] *intr.* To fish for yabbies. Chiefly as *pres. pple.* and *vbl. n.*
1934 *Bulletin* (Sydney) 24 Oct. 21/2 Here's a sport for those who .. forget their bait when yabbying. **1962** E. LANE *Mad as Rabbits* 161 The glorious summer-time sport of yabbying.

yacca, var. YAKKA, YAKKER.

yacca /'jækə/. Chiefly *S.A.* Also **yacka**. [Prob. a. S.A. Aboriginal language.]
1. GRASS-TREE 1 a. Also *attrib.*
1890 *Oldest Coursing Club in Aust., being Hist. Narracoorte Club* 16 The soil excellent and dotted over in places somewhat thickly with clumps of yacca grass. **1979** DOUGLAS & HEATHCOTE *Far Cry* 4 There was no green pasture .. or even English weeds among the yackas and stunted gumtrees.
2. Special Comb. **yacca gum**, *grass-tree gum*, see GRASS-TREE 1 c.
1908 M. VIVIENNE *Sunny S.A.* 405 A large trade is being done with Germany in valuable 'yacca gum'.

yachtie. [f. *yacht(sman* + -Y.] A yachting enthusiast.
[N.Z. **1943** *Amer. Speech* XVIII. 88 Yachty.] **1951** L. D'ALPUGET *Let's go Sailing* 39 Any 'yachtie' who has crewed in a trans-Tasman can command a place in just about whatever boating company he chooses. **1984** *Weekend Austral. Mag.* (Sydney) 21 Apr. 20/1 Club members still faced levies to pay for the privilege of defending the Cup .. despite rumblings from some disaffected yachties.

yacka, var. YACCA, YAKKA.

yackai /'jækaɪ/, *n.* and *int.* Also with much variety (see quots.) [a. Wiradhuri (and many other languages) *yagaay*.] A call used by an Aboriginal to command attention or express emotion. Cf. COOEE *n.* and *v.*

1903 H. BASEDOW *Jrnl. Govt. N.-W. Exped.* 16 May (1914) 104 We had not proceeded far when we heard the 'yackai' or 'coo-ee' of the tribe. **1964** *N. Austral. Monthly* Oct. 22 At the creek at Weipa we yelled a loud 'yakai' and lots of natives came down from the mission. **1967** R. DONALDSON et al. *Cane!* 34 A hundred *yack-ies* and *cooees* rang out over the corn. **1977** V. PRIDDLE *Larry & Jack* 70 In no time his brother Jack and three other searchers appeared and gave a 'Yakki' of delight when they saw Larry had the little girl.

Hence **yackai** *v. intr.*, to utter such a call; also as *vbl. n.*

1903 H. BASEDOW *Jrnl. Govt. N.-W. Exped.* 20 May (1914) 109 We can hear voices and the 'yackaiing' of the dusky folk in the neighbouring hills to-night. **1925** M. TERRY *Across Unknown Aust.* 126 In the North one hears them yackai-ing, laughing.

yacker, var. YAKKA, YAKKER.

yacker. Also **yakker.** [Var. of *yatter* idle talk, incessant chatter: see OEDS.] Talk; chatter.

1882 *Sydney Slang Dict.* 9 *Yacker*, talk. **1973** P. WHITE *Eye of Storm* 306 She wished it had been a hospital, when she could have produced a chart, handed over .. and swept off without further yakker.

yacker, var. YAKKA, YAKKER.

yahoo /ja'hu/, *n.*[1] *Obs.* Also **yaahoo, yahor.** [Perh. a. N.S.W. Aboriginal (poss. Dharuk) *yahoo* catbird, owl. See also quot. 1844.] **a.** A name given by Aborigines to an evil spirit (cf. BUGEEN). **b.** *transf.* A monster or 'hairy man' (see quots. 1847 and 1937).

1835 J. HOLMAN *Travels* IV. 480 The natives are greatly terrified by the sight of a person in a mask calling him 'devil' or *Yah-hoo*, which signifies evil spirit. **1844** MRS C. MEREDITH *Notes & Sketches N.S.W.* 94 The name Devil-devil is of course borrowed from our vocabulary... That of Yahoo, being used to express a bad spirit or 'Bugaboo', was common also with the aborigines of Van Diemen's Land, and is as likely to be a coincidence with, as a loan from, Dean Swift. **1847** *Moreton Bay Courier* 6 Feb. 4/3 In this locality it is called *Yaa-hoo*, and is described as having much resemblance in form to the human figure, but with frightful features. **1856** G. WILLMER *Draper in Aust.* 227 The evil spirit they term 'Yahor', (devil, devil) of whom they live in great terror. **1937** *Mankind* June 91 In the Mudgee district .. a scrubby place was reputed to be the abode of a 'Yahu', and a resident in the Maitland district told me a 'Yahu' was reputed to live in a thick scrub there. Each said he was a big hairy man.

yahoo /ja'hu/, *n.*[2] [Imitative (see quot. 1931): but see also prec.] *Grey-crowned babbler*, see GREY *a.*

1928 R.H. CROLL *Open Road Vic.* 49 Forceful note of the 'yah-hoo' or catbird. **1931** N.W. CAYLEY *What Bird is That?* 124 Grey-crowned Babbler *Pomatostomus temporalis* .. also called .. Yahoo [etc.]... Many of its calls are difficult to describe, but the loud 'Ya-hoo, Ya-hoo' is a very familiar call.

yahor, var. YAHOO *n.*[1]

yakka /'jækə/. Also **yacca, yacka, yacker, yakker.** [f. YAKKER.] Work; strenuous labour; esp. in the phr. **hard yakka.**

1888 *Boomerang* (Brisbane) 14 Jan. 13 The Brisbane wharf labourers are so accustomed to hard yacker that they can't be happy for a single day without it. **1905** *Shearer* (Sydney) 19 Aug. 8/3 If for 'yakker' you're a demon You can do *their* share as well! **1942** *Khamseen Kronikle* 27 Aug. 2 We didn't like the .. beer, the yacka or the oranges. **1942** L. MANN *Go-Getter* 12 Relief was, in a way, like work in the army. You did the job and had nothing much to think about. Even on this hot day Chris would rather have been doing such yacca than delivering bills. **1986** *Nat. Times* (Sydney) 21 Feb. 16/3 Child care remains women's responsibility... There's no evidence that men are taking part in the hard yakka.

yakker, var. YACKER.

yakker /'jækə/, *v.* Also **yacca, yacker.** [a. Yagara *yaga*.] *intr.* To work; to labour.

1847 J.D. LANG *Cooksland* 123 'What for Commandant yacca paper?' What is the gentleman working at the paper for? **1926** *Bulletin* (Sydney) 24 June 22/2, I was yakkering on Brooklyn station, Windellama Creek (N.S.W.). **1934** *Ibid.* 10 Jan. 20/1 'Do we have to yacker this afternoon?' asked one of the hands.

yalka, var. YELKA.

yam. [Transf. use of *yam* the starchy, tuberous root of *Dioscorea* species.] Any of several plants having an edible tuberous root, incl. MURNONG, and species of the genus *Dioscorea* (fam. Dioscoreaceae) and of other families; the tuber of these plants; *native yam*, see NATIVE *a.* 6 a.; *wild yam*, see WILD 1. Also *attrib.*

1770 J. BANKS *Endeavour Jrnl.* (1962) II. 127 The only vegetables we saw them use were Yams of 2 sorts, the one long and like a finger the other round and coverd with stringy roots, both sorts very small but sweet. **1845** L. LEICHHARDT *Jrnl. Overland Exped. Aust.* 9 May (1847) 249 They threw some yam-roots over to us, the plant of which we were not able to ascertain.

yammagi /'jæmədʒi/. *W.A.* Also **yamagee, yamagi, yamidgee, yammagee, yammogee.** [a. Watjari *yamaji*.] A generic term for an Aboriginal; an Aboriginal male.

1925 J.E. LIDDLE *Selected Poems* 89 They talked of 'Yammogees' and 'Jinns'. **1926** *Bulletin* (Sydney) 14 Oct. 24/2 A pot-bellied old yammagi came along to the outcamp one evening, accompanied by several gins. **1937** E. MORROW *Law Provides* 145 You know 'em yamagi called Spider? **1965** R. STOW *Merry-Go-Round* 186 'What's yamidgees?' said the boy. 'Boongs. Noogs. Coloured folk.' **1976** B. BENNETT *New Country* 42 That's her, over there. Holding court with the local yammagees. **1983** G.E.P. WELLARD *Bushlore* 55, I was standing outside the humpy discussing the days work with three of the Yamagee musterers. I use the word 'Yamagee' because that is the name they call themselves in that district. They never say 'Blackman' or 'Aborigine', it is always 'Yamagee'.

yam-stick. DIGGING STICK.

1846 F. DUTTON *S.A. & its Mines* 330 His 'gin' will ply the 'yamstick', and dig from the soil the same miserable subsistence as heretofore. **1969** A.A. ABBIE *Original Australs.* 75 Women are the main collectors of vegetable food. They always carry a fairly long 'digging-stick'... In the north where yams are the chief objective the stick is usually called a 'yam stick'.

yan /jæn/, *v. Austral. pidgin. Obs.* [a. Aboriginal *yan-* (common to most languages).] *intr.* To go; to move.

1839 T.L. MITCHELL *Three Exped. Eastern Aust.* (rev. ed.) II. 71 And then he yan (i.e goes) away! **1882** A.J. BOYD *Old Colonials* 16 He shouted to them to 'yan' (clear out).

yanaman, var. YARRAMAN.

yandy /'jændi/, *n.* Also **yandi, yandie**. [a. Yinjibarndi *yandi*.] A shallow (wooden) dish used to separate seeds, etc., from refuse or particles of a mineral from alluvial material: see quot. 1914. Also **yandy-dish**.

1903 *Folklore* (London) XIV. iv. 349 The only other acquisition we have made is a 'Yandie', the native cradle or basket made out of a piece of bark.   1914 *Register* (Adelaide) 30 July 8/7 Moolyella has been a very rich tinfield. . . There are a number of aborigines in the locality, and the whites employ the gins to 'yandie' their tin—i.e., to clean it—which is done on a piece of wood hollowed out after the fashion of a butcher's tray, and described by natives as a 'yandie'. . . This contrivance is jugged [*sic*] by a peculiar motion of the wrist that impels the dirt in one direction while the tin goes the other. Only the gins do it.   1956 *Bulletin* (Sydney) 13 June 12/3 After the natives had gathered what pods they could off the trees they got to work on the fallen seeds with yandi-dishes.   1962 *Texas Q.* 45 The women used a long, shallow, oval wooden dish called a yandy to separate grain from husks.

yandy /'jændi/, *v.* [f. prec.] *trans.* To separate (seeds, etc., or a mineral) from the surrounding refuse by shaking the raw material in a yandy: see esp. quots. 1914, 1933, and 1956. Also *absol.* and as *vbl. n.*

1914 [see YANDY *n.*].   1919 *Bulletin* (Sydney) 22 May 22/4 At Moolyella, in the nor'-west of West, yandying lead is the chief industry of the tribes, who make a good thing out of it.   1933 C. FENNER *Bunyips & Billabongs* 158 When a gin has collected a coolamon (shallow wooden vessel) full of seed she has also a good deal of sand, dust, grass and leaves. But by shaking and twisting the coolamon in a particularly skilful way an almost perfect separation is made. This art of separation is called 'yandying'.   1956 *Bulletin* (Sydney) 13 June 12/3 A gin who's a good hand at yandying can separate white-ant eggs from dirt.   1984 W.W. AMMON et al. *Working Lives* 63 Duster pulled in on his way back to his tin show at Nullagine where he had these young gins yandying for him.

Hence **yandier** *n.*, one who yandies.

1954 I.L. IDRIESS *Nor'-Westers* 165 A noted yandier, Mary Ann, had . . yandied a whole bag of stream tin.

yang yang, *n.* [Of unknown origin.] A cicada.

1926 L.C.E. GEE *Bush Tracks & Gold Fields* 93 And then, out of the branches of this tree, the yang yangs sing—I don't know what their proper name is (Cicada, I think).

yang-yang, *a.* [Of unknown origin.] Of a horse: spirited.

1976 C.D. MILLS *Hobble Chains & Greenhide* 149 If any of the storybook Romeos had tried any of those tricks on some of the 'yang-yang-yowadas' we had, they'd have been in strife.   1982 P. ADAM SMITH *Shearers* 366 Those 'yang-yang' horses which were always left in the camp for some new chum stockman to ride do not exist.

Yankee. Used *attrib.* in Special Comb. **Yankee grab,** a game of chance played with dice, resembling craps; **grubbing** *vbl. n.*, see quot. 1914; also **grubbed** *ppl. a.*; **shout,** an occasion the expenses of which are shared by the participants.

1879 'NEW CHUM' *Ramble in Launceston* 53 The golden youth from the shops are here playing '**Yankee grab**' for shillings' [*sic*] till daylight dawns.   1914 *Pastoral Rev.* 15 Apr. 335 **Yankee grubbing** means the preparation of timbered land for cropping by grubbing all the small timber and cutting the large trees down just under the surface of the soil, so that stump-jump machinery can be used.   1980 O. RUHEN *Bullock Teams* 230, I always disliked having an onlooker when I was tree-pulling. We would often snag a 'Yankee-grubbed' stump—that is, a sapling cut just above the ground.   1945 S.J. BAKER *Austral. Lang.* 171 We have many versions of the shout, such as the *American shout*, **Yankee shout** (we also call it a *Yank* or *Yankee*), *Scotch shout*, etc.

Yank-happy, *a.* Of an Australian woman: favouring the company of an American serviceman.

1948 *Full-Times Gaz.* (Rockhampton) 13 Jan. 3 Most of our girls have gone Yank happy.   1968 G. DUTTON *Andy* 110 The Americans, with their retinue of Yank-happy sheilas and Australian racketeers.

Yan Yean /jæn 'jin/. [The name of a reservoir supplying water to Melbourne.] Tap-water. Also as quasi-*adj.*, 'as water is to wine'.

1868 *Australasian* (Melbourne) 25 Jan. 113/3 It might be thought that an occasional sprinkling of Yan Yean scattered upon him by a careless or lively city Aquarius would not cause him much chagrin.   1972 J. HIBBERD *Stretch of Imagination* (1973) 18 Must have an 1876 Château Carbonnieux with the basted salamander, anything else would be unspeakably yan yean, eh Jeremy?

Hence **Yan Yean** *v. trans.*, to douse with water, to quench (in quot. *fig.*).

1885 *Austral. Tit-Bits* (Melbourne) 26 Feb. 11/1 One day they have had to fan the patriotic flame, and the next to Yan Yean it.

yapunyah /jə'pʌnjə/. [a. Gunya *yapan*ʸ.] Either of two trees of the genus *Eucalyptus* (fam. Myrtaceae), *E. ochrophloia* occurring along watercourses and seasonally inundated land in s.w. Qld. and n.w. N.S.W., and *E. thozetiana* of Qld. and N.T.; the wood of these trees; LAPUNYAH b; NAPUNYAH. Also **yapunyah-tree**.

1878 'IRONBARK' *Southerly Busters* 144 The tall yapunyah's shadow Rests upon the stockman's grave. [*Note*] A species of Eucalyptus which flourishes on the Paroo and in the west of Queensland.   1942 F. CLUNE *Last of Austral. Explorers* 99 They reached the Paroo River, a chain of waterholes, fringed by yapunyah-trees.

yard, *n.*

1. [Spec. use of *yard* an enclosure for poultry or cattle adjacent to a farm building: see OED *sb.*¹ 2.] An enclosure, sometimes makeshift and (formerly) movable, in which sheep, cattle, etc., are confined for a particular purpose. Also *attrib.*

1810 *Sydney Gaz.* 8 Dec., Grazing Farm—on which there is . . Dairy &c and good Yards well adapted for Horned Cattle or Sheep.   1955 *Bulletin* (Sydney) 18 May 13/1 The camp shifted into gidgee country for a yard-building job.

2. [Also Br. dial. and U.S.: see OED(S *sb.*¹ 3.] The enclosed area surrounding a house; a domestic garden. See also BACK YARD 1.

1848 *Teetotal Advocate* (Launceston) 31 July 3/5 A four-roomed Cottage, with Garden or Yard behind.   1982 N. KEESING *Lily on Dustbin* 77 The traditional Australian dream is to own a home with a garden which is called a 'yard'.

yard, *v.* [Also U.S.: see OED *v.*¹ 1.]

1. *trans.* To confine (livestock) in an enclosure, either overnight or for a particular purpose. Also *absol.* and as *ppl. a.*

1821 *Regulations respecting Assigned Convict Servants* 30 June 15 It is not deemed eligible in this island to yard the flocks at night.   1888 T.V. FOOTE *My Weird Wooing* 152 Shoot the scouring parties of police like yarded bullocks.   1960 *Centralian Advocate* (Alice Springs) 15 Jan. 4/4 If two butchers yard on the same day they have to box the cattle to water them, because the receiving yard is the only yard serviced with water.

2. *trans.* To round up and confine (wild cattle, pigs, etc.). Also with **up**.

1867 'COLONIST' *Life's Work* 47 They're a mob of the wildest cattle we ever yarded.   1891 T. BATEMAN *Valley Council* p. iii, We . . yarded-up brumbies or scrubbers from the back districts.

3. a. *trans.* To secure (kangaroos, rabbits, etc.), preparatory to their slaughter.

1886 R. HENTY *Australiana* 224 Mr Moffat set out at once to round up the kangaroos, it being arranged that when sufficient had been yarded a signal would be given. **1926** *Smith's Weekly* (Sydney) 22 May 19/7 The largest number of rabbits caught in one drive was 14,700 yarded years ago at Coonamble (N.S.W.) by an assorted crowd of bushmen and townspeople.

b. *transf.* Also with **up.**

1930 V. PALMER *Passage* (1957) 184 The killers .. would yard a whale up like dingoes would a stray sheep. **1951** J. DEVANNY *Travels N. Qld.* 45 Only once did I see sharks engaged in what fishermen call 'yarding' their prey.

4. *transf.* and *fig.*

1892 *Bulletin* (Sydney) 31 Dec. 9/2 Yard-up, in one enclosed space, all the present Australian members of Parliament. **1963** M. BRITT *Pardon my Boots* 52 Jack had only brought him out of retirement for me to ride. 'You could yard a fly in a bottle on him,' he said, lovingly adjusting the bridle.

yarder.

1. One responsible for the yarding of animals, esp. of sheep prior to shearing. Also **yarder-up.**

1888 *Illustr. Austral. News* (Melbourne) 28 Nov. 194/3 Suddenly we come upon three individuals, whistling, shouting and yelling their level best—or their level worst. These are the 'yarders' who keep the shearers supplied from sunrise to sunset with a continual and incessant stream of living animals. **1899** *Bulletin* (Sydney) 1 Apr. 14/2 The real 'cobbler' was kept in the pen, perhaps all day, as the yarder-up used him as a decoy-sheep.

2. *transf.* A horse used in yarding stock.

1927 K.S. PRICHARD *Bid me to Love* (1974) 6 My yarder's got out of the paddock. You might keep an eye out for him over your way.

yarding, *vbl. n.* [f. YARD *v.* 1.] The confining of animals in an enclosure; the animals so confined. Also with **up.**

1889 *Illustr. Austral. News* (Melbourne) 1 May 74/2 Then comes the excitement of yarding, the cracking of the stockwhips, and the shouting of the men, and finally, the most important of all, the drafting of the herd for both fats and stores. **1963** M. BRITT *Pardon my Boots* 70 Jack rode over and told me that they were going to start yarding up, and that I had better ride away a bit to be out of the rumpus.

yarn, *n.* [See YARN *v.*] A chat, a discussion.

1852 F.R. GODFREY *Extracts Old Jrnls.* 11 Aug. (1926) 137, I had a long 'yarn' with Pearson and Augusta about my affairs. **1986** *Sydney Morning Herald* 12 Apr. 1/2 He says he doesn't really want to do any sort of interview, but it doesn't take long to see that deep down, the man likes a good yarn.

yarn, *v.* [Transf. use of *yarn* to tell a tale. Used elsewhere but recorded earliest in Aust.: see OED(S *v.* 1.] *intr.* To talk; to chat. Also as *vbl. n.*

1847 A. HARRIS *Settlers & Convicts* (1953) 90 As R– and his acquaintance 'yarned', I took up one of the books. **1896** M. CLARKE *Austral. Tales* 7 By 'yarning', dear reader, I don't mean mere trivial conversation, but hard, solid talk.

yarra /'jærə/, *n. Obs.* [Prob. a. Wiradhuri *yara*.] A name given to any of several trees occurring near watercourses, perh. chiefly *Eucalyptus camaldulensis* (see RED GUM 1): see quot. 1889. Also *attrib.*

1834 G. BENNETT *Wanderings N.S.W.* I. 251 Magnificent water gum-trees, (Dad'ha and Yarra of the aborigines). **1889** J.H. MAIDEN *Useful Native Plants Aust.* 511 'Yarrah', according to Dr Woolls, is a name applied by the aboriginals to almost any tree. **1893** D. LINDSAY *Jrnl. Elder Sci. Exploring Exped.* 163 There are several beefwood or 'yarra' trees growing around the well.

yarra /'jærə/, *a.* [f. the name of a psychiatric hospital at *Yarra* Bend, Victoria.] Insane; stupid. Also as *n.*

1943 S.J. BAKER *Pop. Dict. Austral. Slang* (ed. 3) 89 *Yarra* .. stupid, crazy. **1967** *Kings Cross Whisper* (Sydney) xliii. 11/3 *Yarra*, a stupid person. **1980** *Sydney Morning Herald* 20 Oct. 26/7 Kingston Town is a good horse .. but in my opinion he would not have lived with Phar Lap. I know a lot of people will say I'm 'Yarra'; but that's my belief.

Yarra-banker /jærə-'bæŋkə/. [f. the name of the *Yarra* River, upon which Melbourne stands.] **a.** *Obs.* A vagrant (see quot. 1895). **b.** A soap-box orator. See also DOMAIN. Also *attrib.*

1895 C. CROWE *Austral. Slang Dict.* 98 *Yarra bankers,* vagrants living on the banks of the Yarra. **1897** *Bulletin* (Sydney) 18 Sept. 20/2 Yarrabanker Fleming indulged in some pretty plain speaking.

Hence **Yarra-banking** *ppl. a.*, 'tub-thumping'.

1905 W. MOORE *City Sketches* 46 The genteel cadger, known professionally as the suburban swagman, frequents other haunts than those of his Yarra-banking brother.

yarraman /'jærəmən/. Chiefly *Austral. pidgin.* Pl. **yarraman(s), yarramen.** Also **yanaman.** [Prob. a. Aboriginal *yiraman*, f. *yira-* teeth: see quot. 1984.] A horse.

1842 *Legends of Aust.* Mar. 49 'Got it coat, yarraman, and musket, just like it soger.' (Meaning that they were equipped with horses, fire-arms, &c., and drest like the mounted police.) **1876** F. NAPIER *Notes Voyage N.S.W. to N. Coast* 40 They told us that they had seen the captain on a 'yanaman' (horse). **1882** A.J. BOYD *Old Colonials* 69 Well, then there's seventeen yarramen—call 'em thirty pounds a head. **1923** J. BOWES *Jackaroos* 67 'Lot of pfellers go longa here.' 'How many yarramans?' **1984** B. DIXON *Searching for Aboriginal Lang.* 72 In fact, *yarraman* 'horse' comes originally from a language just south of Sydney where it may have meant 'long teeth'. It was adopted into the peculiar pidgin that early settlers used in communicating with Aborigines. When the first white men came into Queensland, they used the word *yarraman* 'horse', thinking that they were speaking '*the* Aboriginal language'. The Aborigines imagined they were being taught an English word.

yarran /'jærən/. Also **yarren.** [a. Kamilaroi (and related languages) *yarraan*.] The small to medium tree *Acacia omalophylla* (*A. homalophylla*) (fam. Mimosaceæ) of inland N.S.W., Qld., and n. Vic., having a rough bark and smooth foliage; the dark brown, durable wood of the tree. Also *attrib.*

1882 ARMSTRONG & CAMPBELL *Austral. Sheep Husbandry* 196 Dry yarren makes the best fence. **1959** C.V. LAWLOR *All This Humbug* 14 They sat round a fire of dead yarran wood.

yartz /jatz/. [Coinage of Barry Humphries (b. 1934), entertainer and writer: see quot. 1978.] Fanciful alteration of 'the arts'.

1978 B. HUMPHRIES *Nice Night's Entertainment* (1981) 183 This pome is dedicated to something Australians hold very precious beginning with Y—'the Yartz'. **1984** *Age* (Melbourne) 5 May 3/4 (*heading*) Horne looks forward to the end of the yartz.

yate /jeɪt/. Formerly **yeit.** [Perh. f. a W.A. Aboriginal language.] Any of several trees of the genus *Eucalyptus* (fam. Myrtaceae) of s. W.A., esp. the rough-barked *E. cornuta*, yielding a remarkably hard, strong timber; the wood of the tree. Also **yate tree,** and *attrib.*

1833 *Jrnls. Several Exped. W.A.* 142 A plain of sandy soil, and white gum and yeit trees. **1965** A.R. BARRETT *Hist. War Service Land Settlement Scheme W.A.* 23 The Jerramungup Station Area was practically all Yate (*Euc. occidentalis*) country, a large proportion of which had been ringbarked. **1983** *Newsletter* (Soc. for Growing Austral. Plants, Canberra Region) June 20 The first eucalypt to be collected in Western Australia, the Yate.

yaw, var. YU.

yeelaman, yelaman, varr. HIELEMAN.

yelka /ˈjɛlkə/. Also **yalka, yulka**. [a. Aranda *yalge*.] Any of several sedges of the genus *Cyperus* (fam. Cyperaceae) yielding an edible tuber; the tuber itself. Also *attrib.*

1896 B. SPENCER *Rep. Horn Sci. Exped. Central Aust.* IV. 60 *Cyperus rotundus*. In almost every camp we saw large quantities of the tunicated tubers of this plant, which are generally called 'Erriákura' or 'Irriakura' by the Arunta natives. In some parts however the term 'Yelka', 'Yelki' or 'Yilka' is used, and this is the name by which it is generally known amongst the whites. **1936** C. CHEWINGS *Back in Stone Age* 2 If seeds require roasting . . or yelka-bulbs peeling, they are placed in this tray. **1980** R. DAVIDSON *Tracks* 137 For me there were yalka (like tiny onions) to be dug up and roasted in the coals. **1985** *Austral. Plants* June 127 *Cyperus bulbosus*. . . Widely known as 'Yulka' in central Australia, this sedge grows up to 40 cm. high. . . The edible part is the small tuber. It can be eaten raw or lightly roasted.

yellow, *a.* Also **yeller** (only sense 4).

1. Used as a distinguishing epithet in the names of flora and fauna: **yellow-bellied glider,** the gliding possum *Petaurus australis* of e. mainland Aust., having a greyish-brown back and yellow to white belly; formerly also **yellow-bellied flying phalanger;** also *attrib.*; **-bellied** (or **-breasted**) **shrike-tit,** *shrike-tit,* see SHRIKE; **-billed kingfisher,** the kingfisher *Syma torotoro* of Cape York Peninsula (n. Qld.) and New Guinea; **-billed** (or **-legged**) **spoonbill,** the spoonbill *Platalea flavipes* of all States, having white plumage and a yellow bill; **bloodwood,** any of several trees of e. Qld. and e. N.S.W. of the genus *Eucalyptus* (fam. Myrtaceae) having rough, tesselated, sometimes yellow bark, as *E. eximia* of N.S.W.; **bob,** *yellow robin*; **box,** any of several trees of the genus *Eucalyptus* (fam. Myrtaceae), esp. *E. melliodora* of s.e. mainland Aust.; the wood of the tree; also *attrib.*; **-crested (white) cockatoo,** the cockatoo *Cacatua galerita* (see *white cockatoo* WHITE *a.*[2] 1 b.); **-eye mullet,** the marine and estuarine fish *Aldrichetta forsteri* of s. Aust. and New Zealand, having a slender body and yellow eye; also *ellipt*. as **yellow-eye; -faced honeyeater,** the predom. grey-brown honeyeater *Lichenostomus chrysops* of e. Aust., having a broad yellow stripe, bordered by black, through the eye; **-footed rock wallaby,** the rock wallaby *Petrogale xanthopus* of S.A., w. N.S.W., and s.w. Qld.; **hammer,** *yellow robin*; **honeyeater,** the greenish-yellow honeyeater *Lichenostomus flavus* of n. Qld.; **jacket** (or **jack**), any of several trees, usu. of the genus *Eucalyptus* (fam. Myrtaceae) having at times a yellowish trunk or bark, incl. *E. similis* and *E. peltata* subsp. *peltata* of Qld., and *E. lirata* of the n. Kimberley region, W.A.; **monday** (also **munday, mundy**), the cicada *Cyclochila australasiae* of s.e. Aust., when yellow; see also GREENGROCER; **oriole,** the yellowish-green bird *Oriolus flavocinctus* of n. Aust. and elsewhere, having a loud, melodious call; **parrot,** see *yellow rosella*; **-plumed honeyeater,** the predom. olive-brown and grey honeyeater *Lichenostomus ornatus* of s. mainland Aust., having a yellow neck plume; **robin,** either of two small, predom. greyish birds of mainland Aust. having a partly or wholly yellow underside, **(a)** the eastern *Eopsaltria australis* (also **yellow-breasted robin**), **(b)** the western *E. griseogularis*; *yellow bob, hammer;* **rosella,** the parrot *Platycercus elegans flaveolus* of the Murray-Murrumbidgee Rivers region of inland s.e. Aust.; *Murray smoker*, see MURRAY 2; also **yellow parrot; -spotted honeyeater,** the dark olive-green honeyeater *Meliphaga notata* of rainforest in n.e. Qld., having a rounded yellow ear patch; **stringybark,** any of several rough-barked trees of the genus *Eucalyptus* (fam. Myrtaceae), esp. *E. muellerana* of e. Vic. and s.e. N.S.W.; the wood of the tree; **-tailed black cockatoo,** the black cockatoo *Calyptorhynchus funereus* of s.e. Aust. incl. Tas., having a broad yellow band on the tail; also **yellow-tailed cockatoo; -tailed** (or **-rumped**) **thornbill,** the small, predom. olive-grey and buff bird *Acanthiza chrysorrhoa* of all States; see also TOMTIT; also **yellow-rumped tit; -throat,** see *yellow-throated scrub wren;* **-throated miner,** the predom. grey-brown bird *Manorina flavigula* of mainland Aust., having yellow and black markings on the head and throat; **-throated scrub wren,** the small bird *Sericornis citreogularis* of forested parts of e. mainland Aust., having brown, black, and yellow plumage with a bright yellow throat; also **yellow-throat; -tufted honeyeater,** the predom. dark olive to olive-yellow honeyeater *Lichenostomus melanops* of s.e. mainland Aust.; **walnut,** the tall rainforest tree *Beilschmiedia bancroftii* (fam. Lauraceae) of n.e. Qld.; the wood or fruit of the tree; **wattle bird,** the brown and white streaked bird *Anthochaera paradoxa* of Tas., the largest Austral. honeyeater, having long orange-yellow facial wattles; **weebill,** the yellowish northern form, *Smicrornis brevirostris flavescens*, of the WEEBILL; **-wing,** *New Holland honeyeater,* see NEW HOLLAND 2; also **yellow-wings.**

1860 [**yellow-bellied glider**] G. BENNETT *Gatherings of Naturalist* 150 The Long-Tailed Flying Opossum, or Flying Squirrel of the colonists (*Belideus flaviventris*) is widely distributed. . . It is also known as the Yellow-bellied Flying Phalanger. **1973** S. & K. BREEDEN *Wildlife Eastern Aust.* 123 The Yellow-bellied Glider's progress through the forests can be followed by sound—nearly every glide is accompanied by his wild call. **1986** *Sydney Morning Herald* 22 Feb. 11/1 Populations of yellow-bellied glider possums, one of Australia's most spectacular, colorful, and vocal, tree-dwelling marsupials. **1918** *Bulletin* (Sydney) 14 Feb. (Red Page), **Yellow-bellied Shrike-Tit** (Yellow-Hammer, Crested Tit). **1929** A.H. CHISHOLM *Birds & Green Places* 132 The yellow-breasted shrike-tit has been heard, in New South Wales, to utter 'one curious note, something between the miewing and spitting of a cat'. **1898** E.E. MORRIS *Austral Eng.* 248 **Yellow-billed K[ingfisher]**— *Syma flavirostris*. **1842** [**yellow-billed spoonbill**] J. GOULD *Birds of Aust.* (1848) VI. Pl. 49, *Platalea flavipes* . . Yellow-legged Spoonbill. **1984** M. BLAKERS et al. *Atlas Austral. Birds* 67 The Yellow-billed Spoonbill is typically an inland bird. **1880** *Proc. Linnean Soc. N.S.W.* V. 467 *E*[*ucalyptus*] *eximia* . . the 'Smooth-barked', '**Yellow**', or 'Mountain **Bloodwood**'. **1926** *Qld. Agric. Jrnl.* XXV. 439 Eucalyptus trachyphloia, White, Yellow or . . Bastard Bloodwood. **1909** A.E. MACK *Bush Calendar* 68 Then a **yellow-bob** came to visit us. **1877** F. VON MUELLER *Introd. Bot. Teachings* 15 The Honey-Eucalypt (*Eucalyptus melliodora*) . . passes by the very unapt vernacular name **Yellow Box**-tree, though no portion of it is yellow, not even its wood, and though the latter resembles the real boxwood in no way whatever. **1952** E. WALLING *Austral. Roadside* 21 The prevalence of the Yellow Box . . is a sign of good sheep country. **1852** W. HUGHES *Austral. Colonies* 82 The **yellow-crested** white **cockatoo** is very numerous, and is a great pest to the farmer. **1984** B. DIXON *Searching for Aboriginal Lang.* 122, I sat and had lunch on the sandy river shore, to the annoyance of a yellow-crested cockatoo who insistently proclaimed from the top branch of a tea-tree that this was *his* territory. **1906** D.G. STEAD *Fishes of Aust.* 79 The **Yellow-eye Mullet** . . is distributed right round the southern half of Australia. **1983** *Canberra Chron.* 28 Sept. 19/1 He also took some good mullet to about 900 gm., which I presume were big yelloweye. **1846** J. GOULD *Birds of Aust.* (1848) IV. Pl. 45, *Ptilotis chrysops.* **Yellow-faced Honey-eater. 1894** R. LYDEKKER *Hand-Bk. Marsupialia & Monotremata* 47 **Yellow-footed Rock-wallaby.** *Petrogale xanthopus.* . . Fur long, soft, and silky. General colour grey, white beneath. . . Tail ringed above and on the sides with dark brown and pale yellow. **1876** *Observer Miscellany* (Adelaide) 8 Apr. 257/2 **Yellow-hammers** are everywhere, and very tame. **1845** J. GOULD *Birds of Aust.* (1848) IV. Pl. 42, *Ptilotis flava* . . **Yellow Honey-eater. 1882** ARMSTRONG & CAMPBELL *Austral. Sheep Husbandry* 231 The trees found to die most quickly after being operated upon are box, peppermint, and '**yellow-jacket**'. **1943** *Coast to Coast 1942* 14, I tied the horse to a yellow jack and crept towards the river. **1984** D.J. BOLAND et al. *Forest Trees Aust.* (rev. ed.) 239 Two species, viz. the yellow jackets (*E[ucalyptus] lirata* and *E. similis*), have a yellow fibrous bark somewhat like yellow bloodwoods. **1895** *Proc. Linnean Soc. N.S.W.* X. 529 *Cyclochila Australasiae* . . ('The Green Monday'). . . This is our commonest Sydney Cicada. . . There is a yellow variety of this species, which is popularly called the '**Yellow Monday**'. **1905** *Bulletin* (Sydney) 16 Feb. 16/2 Where the locusts . . ? The trees in the parks are unscaled by eager imps, seeking on the brittle bough the 'floury baker' and the 'yellow munday'. **1951** CUSACK & JAMES *Come in Spinner* 163 She uncurled her fingers and showed the jewelled head of a cicada. 'He's a Yellow Mundy.' **1945** C. BARRETT *Austral. Bird Life* 137 The **yellow oriole** (*Oriolus flavocinctus*) frequents palm scrubs and the mangroves. **1898** E.E. MORRIS *Austral Eng.* 199 **Yellow-plumed H[oney-eater]**—*P[tilotis] ornata.* **1827** *Trans. Linnean Soc. London* XV. 242 [*Pachycephala*] . . Australis. . . 'This bird', Mr Caley says, 'is called **yellow Robin** by the colonists. It is an inhabitant of brushes.' **1843** J. GOULD *Birds of Aust.* (1848) III. Pl. 11, *Eöpsaltria australis.* Yellow-breasted Robin. . . Yellow Robin, Colonists of New South Wales. **1981** G. CROSS *George & Widda-Woman* 88 He taught her how to spot at a distance the yellow robins. **1849** [**yellow rosella**] *Adelaide Miscellany* 20 Sept. 25 The bright yellow parrot of the Murray was flitting from tree to tree. **1969** J.M. FORSHAW *Austral. Parrots* 185 The yellow rosella . . a riparian species closely associated with the Murray, Murrumbidgee and Lachlan Rivers. **1869** J. GOULD *Birds of Aust.* Suppl. Pl. 41, *Ptilotis notata* . . **Yellow-spotted Honey-eater.** . . This species of Ptilotis is a native of the Cape-York peninsula, where appears to be tolerably common. **1904** J.H. MAIDEN *Notes on Commercial Timbers N.S.W.* 12 *Blackbutt* (*Eucalyptus pilularis*) . . is a strong, durable, thoroughly safe and well-tried timber. . . There is a variety of it (var. *Muelleriana* . .), which sometimes goes under the name of '**yellow stringybark**'. **1837** J. BACKHOUSE *Narr. Visit Austral. Colonies* (1843) 505 There are also **Yellow-tailed** and Red-tailed **Black Cockatoos**. **1985** P. CAREY *Illywhacker* 493 The day he brought the yellow-tailed cockatoo down from the tree at Bendigo School. **1898** [**yellow-tailed thornbill**] E.E. MORRIS *Austral Eng.* 470 Yellow-rumped T[it]—*Geobasileus chrysorrhoea.* **1933** *Bulletin* (Sydney) 5 Apr. 27/1 The yellow-tailed thornbill constructs a double nest, the lower cavity being lined with feathers and containing the eggs. **1976** *Reader's Digest Compl. Bk. Austral. Birds* 440 A bright yellow rump distinguishes the yellow-rumped thornbill from all other thornbills. **1848** J. GOULD *Birds of Aust.* VI. Pl. 79, *Myzantha flavigula* . . **Yellow-throated Miner. 1898** E.E. MORRIS *Austral Eng.* 408 **Yellow-throated S[crub]-W[ren]**—*S[ericornis] citreogularis.* **1965** *Austral. Encycl.* VIII. 48 The yellow-throat is further distinguished by the possession of a most spirited and melodious song, which frequently extends into admirable mimicry of the notes of other birds. **1844** J. GOULD *Birds of Aust.* (1848) IV. Pl. 37, The **Yellow-tufted Honey-eater** is abundant in New South Wales, inhabiting at one season or other every portion of the country. **1926** *Qld. Agric. Jrnl.* XXV. 435 *Cryptocarya Bancroftii* **Yellow Walnut** (Atherton), Canary Ash. **1951** W.D. FRANCIS *Austral. Rain-Forest Trees* (rev. ed.) 403 *Beilschmiedia bancroftii* . . Yellow Walnut . . wood yellow, often with darker streaks. **1903** *Emu* II. 208 *Acanthochaera* [*sic*] *inauris* (**Yellow Wattle-bird**)—one pair noted feeding on a flowering blue gum tree. **1945** C. BARRETT *Austral. Bird Life* 187 The **yellow weebill** (*S[micrornis] flavescens*) is found in Central and North-western Australia, the Northern Territory and North Queensland. **1908** *Emu* VIII. 41 The white-bearded Honey-eater (*Meliornis novaehollandiae*), often called the '**Yellow-wing**' is to be seen flitting in the thick bushes. **1918** *Bulletin* (Sydney) 14 Feb. (Red Page), *Honey-Birds* generally, especially the . . *White-bearded Honey-eater* (Yellow-wings).

2. *Obs.*

a. Used of convicts (see also CANARY 1 a.) with reference to the colour of their clothing: see quot. 1826. Esp. in the collocation **yellow jacket.**

[**1826** Tas. Colonial Secretary's Office Rec. 1/34 133, I should recommend Yellow Jackets and Trowsers as being the most conspicuous. . . For the Goals [*sic*] I recommend a Party dress of Jackets and Trowsers, one half of which should be yellow—and the other half Black.] **1837** P. ADAM SMITH *When we rode Rails* (1983) 13 She was carried along the track on a kind of sedan chair, made of kangaroo skins spread over boards attached to two poles. These, she said, were 'strapped to two yellow men' (the convicts who wore sulphur coloured uniforms marked with the broad arrow). **1843** C. ROWCROFT *Tales of Colonies* (1858) 386 It was a road-gang of yellow-jackets going to work.

b. In the collocation **yellow frigate,** a hulk used for the accommodation of convicts: see quot. 1859.

1859 W. BURROWS *Adventures Mounted Trooper* 171 After he had been for some time in fine, airy lodgings in the 'yellow frigates', as the hulks are called from their being painted yellow, he fancied he should like to get out. **1891** 'OLD TIME' *Convict Hulk 'Success'* 20 The convicts on board the 'yellow frigates' had a dull time of it.

3. [Used elsewhere but of local significance.] Having a yellowish complexion or skin, esp. in the collocations **yellow agony,** the Chinese in Australia; a member of this community; also *attrib.*; **peril,** immigration from Asian countries to Australia; the Asiatic peoples collectively; an Asiatic person.

1879 *Illustr. Austral. News* (Melbourne) 22 Jan. 18/2 Although a satisfactory settlement has been arrived at between the Sydney seamen and their employers as to the introduction of Chinese sailors, the agitation relative to the '**yellow agony**' question has by no means subsided. **1908** *Bulletin* (Sydney) 10 July 14/3 The honor of introducing the yellow agony into Queensland rests with Arthur Hodgson of Eden Vale. A batch of Chinkies was landed at the station to do the shepherding. **1905** *Nat. Rev.* (London) 542 It was while he was a resident in South Australia and Victoria, and a Minister of the Crown in the latter State, that Professor C.H. Pearson . . wrote his book containing the earliest sufficient prophecy of the '**Yellow Peril**'. **1929** P.R. STEPHENSEN *Bushwhackers* 44 As Willy Ah Foo was the only Yellow Peril left in our district, pressure was put upon him to clear out.

4. Usu. **yeller.** Of mixed Aboriginal and white parentage, esp. in the collocation **yellow fellow.** Also *fig.* (see quot. 1965).

1913 W.K. HARRIS *Outback in Aust.* 115 We asked how they got on before the advent of the white man. The reply was not quite unexpected: 'Plenty tucker, no yeller-fellers' (half-castes). **1965** M. PATCHETT *Last Warrior* 253 They are in towns now learning the white men's ways, becoming 'yellow boys'. **1975** X. HERBERT *Poor Fellow my Country* 52 Now, I'm using the term Black Velvet not simply to apply to fullblood women, but any of obvious Aboriginal strain, 'yeller girls', or 'creamy pieces', as they're called, half and quarter.

yellowbelly. [f. the pale, sometimes yellow, underside of the fish.] *Golden perch,* see GOLDEN 3.

1880 *Proc. Linnean Soc. N.S.W.* (1881) 354 *Ctenolates ambiguus* . . the *'Golden Perch'* and *'Yellow belly'* of the Colonists. **1985** *Trees & Natural Resources* Dec. 29 They landed a Yellowbelly that fed five adults for breakfast.

yellow fever. *Obs. Gold fever,* see GOLD 3.
   1849 *Argus* (Melbourne) 3 Aug. 4/2 The 'yellow' fever is very prevalent, many persons sacrificing their little all to hasten to the 'diggings'.   1897 A.F. CALVERT *My Fourth Tour W.A.* 15 The air in Perth is full of the yellow fever. Its germs, in the shape of talk of reefs, leases, claims, yields, trial crushings, camels, syndicates, stocks, and company flotations, are as thick as a London fog.

yellow gum.
   1. *Obs.* [See quot. 1834.] **a.** The yellow resin exuded by *Xanthorrhoea resinosa* (fam. Xanthorrhoeaceae), and allied species, used in medicines and as an adhesive. See also *grass-tree gum* GRASS-TREE 1 c. **b.** Any of these plants, occurring in e. Aust. Also *attrib.,* esp. as **yellow gum tree.**
   1770 J. BANKS *Jrnl.* 23 May (1896) 271 The plant yielding the yellow gum, of which, though we saw vast numbers, we did not see any that showed signs of gum.   1834 G. BENNETT *Wanderings N.S.W.* I. 62 It is named '*grass tree*' by the colonists for its long pendent grassy foliage, and '*yellow gum tree*' from secreting a quantity of yellowish gum.   1886 F. COWAN *Aust.* 16 The grass-tree . . Yellow-gum: a monstrous aborescent [*sic*] Rush . . of divers uses . . from dyeing silk to making an illuminating gas.
   2. [From the colour of the bark or wood.] Any of several trees of the genus *Eucalyptus* (fam. Myrtaceae) esp. *E. leucoxylon* of s.e. mainland Aust., having a mottled, sometimes yellow, smooth bark. See also *white ironbark* WHITE *a.*² 1 a.
   1848 T.L. MITCHELL *Jrnl. Exped. Tropical Aust.* 107 We this day passed a small group of trees of the yellow gum, a species of eucalyptus growing only on the poor sandy soil near Botany Bay.   1981 A.B. & J.W. CRIBB *Useful Wild Plants Aust.* 28 The yellow gum, *E*[*ucalyptus*] *leucoxylon,* of western Victoria and southern ranges of South Australia.

yellowtail. [Spec. use of *yellowtail* a name for various fish.] Any of several fish having a yellow caudal fin, esp. *Trachurus novaezelandiae* of estuaries and coastal waters, which is commonly used as bait, and *Seriola lalandi* (see KINGFISH).
   1839 *Tasmanian* (Hobart) 26 Apr. 133/3 The fish was of the description called yellow tail or trumpeter.   1951 *Bulletin* (Sydney) 14 Mar. 12/1 He took small yellowtail and 'old wives' off the hook and flung them contemptuously into his sugarbag.

yellow-wood.
   1. Any of several trees, esp. some species of the genus *Flindersia* (fam. Rutaceae), *Ristantia pachysperma* (fam. Myrtaceae) of lowland rainforest in n. Qld., and *Acronychia oblongifolia* (fam. Rutaceae) of e. Vic., N.S.W., and Qld.; the yellowish wood. Also *attrib.*
   1791 P.G. KING in *Extracts Lett. Arthur Phillip* 10 Jan. 17 The live oak, yellow wood, black wood, and beech, are all of a close grain, and are a durable wood.   1848 *Portland Gaz.* 8 Apr. 4/4 The yellow-wood tree is the same as the fustic of South America—the low price of £4 per ton in the London market precludes the prospect of its ever being exported.
   2. With distinguishing epithet: **deep** (or **dark**) **yellow-wood,** the rainforest tree *Rhodosphaera rhodanthema* (fam. Anacardiaceae) of Qld. and n.e. N.S.W., having a very scaly bark; the wood of the tree; **light yellow-wood,** any of several species of yellow-wood yielding a pale, yellowish timber; the wood itself.
   1880 J. BONWICK *Resources Qld.* 82 **Dark Yellow Wood,** a *Rhus*, with a scaly bark and red flower, is eagerly sought after by sawyers for furniture use.   1965 *Austral. Encycl.* IX. 527 The name deep yellow-wood is often applied to the tulip satinwood, *Rhodosphaera rhodanthema*.   1880 J. BONWICK *Resources Qld.* 81 The **Light-yellow Wood** is *Flindersia*, as useful as cedar, with excellent dyeing properties, and capable of good polish.

yeo, var. YOE.

yike. [Of unknown origin.] A quarrel; a fight. Also as *v. intr.*
   1940 *Mod. Standard Eng. Dict.* (Odhams Press, rev. ed.) *Yike, v.,* to fight.   1984 *Business Rev. Weekly* (Sydney) 7 Jan. 18/1 We have had a couple of small yikes, mainly on things like contract prices.

yodel, *v. intr.* To vomit.
   1965 J. WYNNUM *Jiggin' in Riggin'* 45 'Can you yodel?' grinned Cal. 'I understand that's a definite aid to sales.' 'Only in a bucket,' chortled Stripey. 'Six meals Muldoon the troops call him. Three down and three up. The most seasick sailor in the service.'   1971 B. HUMPHRIES *Bazza pulls it Off,* What bastard yodelled all over the Migrant Information Desk?

yoe /joʊ/. Also **yeo, yowe,** and diminutive **yowie.** [Br. dial. form of *ewe*: see OED *yeo* and *yowie,* OED(S *yow(e)*.] A ewe.
   1900 H. LAWSON *Verses Pop. & Humorous* 171 He thought that he'd be fined all right—he couldn't turn the 'yoe'.   1903 J. FURPHY *Such is Life* 233 Ole hon t'we gits a holt of 'em fellers' mongreals!—bin leavin' three o' hour gates hopen; an' the yowes an' weaners is boxed.   1904 J. FARRELL *My Sundowner* 73 I've been a sinner and I've stown the young of Your yowies.   1965 L. HAYLEN *Big Red* 100 The sweat of agony on their brows at 'spells', the deep gash in the bare-bellied 'yeo', the strident call for 'Tar!'

yohi /'joʊwaɪ/, *adv. Austral. pidgin.* Also **ooah, oowa, yoi, youai, yowhi, yowi.** [a. Yagara (and many other languages) *yaway*.] An affirmative reply, 'yes'.
   1859 H. KINGSLEY *Recoll. Geoffry Hamlyn* II. 215 'Yowi; but mine want it big one flying doe.' [*Note*] Yowi means eyes . . more of a Moreton Bay word.   1881 A.C. GRANT *Bush-Life Qld.* I. 236 'You patter (eat) potchum?' 'Yohi' (yes) said John, rather doubtfully, for he is not sure how his stomach will agree with the strange meat.   1889 *Centennial Mag.* (Sydney) 775 'Youai,' said Pompey, pleased at this proof of the truthfulness of his tale.   1926 M. FORREST *Hibiscus Heart* 188 'You after honey, Tim?' . . 'Yowhi,' Tim grinned.   1936 A. RUSSELL *Gone Nomad* 34 The big chief smiled, politely inscrutable. 'Oo-ah' (yes) he said.   1949 C. FENTON *Flying Doctor* 32 Yo-I boss, him Florina all right.   1965 F.G.G. ROSE *Wind of Change* 157, I asked him . . to which he answered with a smile '*Ooowa!*' (Yes!).

yoke, *v.* [Elsewhere constr. without *up.*] *trans.* With **up:** to put a yoke on (draught animals).
   1848 T.L. MITCHELL *Jrnl. Exped. Tropical Aust.* 107 The cattle were yoked up early and we travelled on over fine grassy plains.   1900 L. HENSLOWE *Ann.* 70 The horses not put to, or 'yoked up' as a colonial would express it.

yonnie /'jɒni/. Also **yonny.** [Poss. f. a Vic. Aboriginal language.] A small stone; a pebble.
   1941 S.J. BAKER *Pop. Dict. Austral. Slang* 84 *Yonnie,* a small stone; a pebble.   1979 *Age* (Melbourne) 2 July 9/8 You should have included 'brinny' and 'yonny' as synonyms for 'stone'.

yoolahng /'juːlæŋ/. Also **yoolang.** [a. Dharuk *yulaŋ.*] An Aboriginal ceremony during which a youth is initiated into manhood; the place where such ceremonies take place.
   1829 R. MUDIE *Picture of Aust.* 260 The first part of the ceremony consists in preparing the proper arena for the future operations, which is an oval of about twenty-seven feet by eighteen, cleared from grass and roots, and called the yoolahng.   1847 G.F. ANGAS *Savage Life & Scenes* II. 217

An open space, called Yoolang, had been cleared for the purpose.

York gum. [f. the name of a town e. of Perth in W.A.: see quot. 1889.] The tree *Eucalyptus loxophleba* (fam. Myrtaceae) of s.w. W.A., varying in form from a rough-barked tree to a smooth-barked mallee; the wood of the tree. Also *attrib*. Quot. 1837 may refer to a different tree, the TUART.
  1837 G.F. MOORE *Evidences Inland Sea* 15 The trees are .. Toart (the York gum).   1855 R. AUSTIN *Jrnl. Interior W.A.* 6 The jam and York gum forests growing on brown gravelly loam around the outcrop of the granite.   1889 J.H. MAIDEN *Useful Native Plants Aust.* 448 *E*[*ucalyptus*] *loxophleba* is known by the aboriginal name of 'Yandee', but usually to the colonists of Western Australia as 'York Gum', as it is very abundant near the town of York.

York road poison. [See quot. 1926.] The shrub *Gastrolobium calycinum* (fam. Fabaceae) of s.w. W.A., which is poisonous to stock. Also *ellipt.* as **York road,** and *attrib.*
  1865 'SPECIAL CORRESPONDENT' *Transportation* 14 The York-road plant, a low bushy scrub, with narrow fresh green leaves, and a light-coloured stem. After a bush fire this is the first plant to spring up.   1897 L. LINDLEY-COWEN *W. Austral. Settler's Guide* 578 The well-known 'York road' occurs as a small shrub.   1926 *Poison Plants W.A.* (W.A. Dept. Agric.) 32 The name York Road Poison was given to it because of the heavy losses of stock from eating it along the York Road between Guildford and York [*sc.* W.A.] from 1854 onwards.

youai, var. YOHI.

youee, var. UEY.

young, *a.* In special collocations: **young Australia,** the youth of Australia collectively; recently colonized Australia; **country,** applied to Australia as having only a short history since European settlement.
  1848 *Sydney Morning Herald* 29 Jan. 3/1 We have Young France and Young England in Europe, and it is very obvious that we shall soon have **Young Australia.**   1929 P.R. STEPHENSEN *Bushwhackers* 42 The *Bulletin* and the *Worker* used to come out in those days with front-page cartoons indicating the Yellow Peril peering over the Great Wall at Young Australia, with horrible, sly grimaces.   1876 G.H. REID *Essay on N.S.W.* 81 It would be absurd to expect manufacturers in a **young country** under a policy of free trade, to appear .. imposing.

youngie. [f. *young* + -Y.] A young woman; a young person. Also *attrib.*
  1965 *Oz* (Sydney) xxiii. 8 So I figured that we'd have 250 fiddlies left for turps and a bit of youngie jumping.   1971 *Bulletin* (Sydney) 17 Apr. 19/2 *Kids, just,* first launched as 'youngies', Youth Power has now become a conventional wisdom.

youngon, youngun, var. YUNGAN.

youse, *pers. pron.* and *possessive pron.* Also **yous.** [Prob. orig. in Irish English: see EDD (which cites Irish, U.S., and Austral. examples), OED *yez* and OEDS *yous*. In predom. sub-standard use in Aust.]
  A. *pers. pron.*
  1. Used when addressing more than one person; you (*pl.*).
  1902 *Bulletin* (Sydney) May 642/2 The men persuaded us to try our luck with them, at least for a time. 'Yous can leave us when you like, if it doesn't pay.'   1984 P. READ *Down there with me on Cowra Mission* 23 Dad said we gotta keep away from youse.

  2. Used when addressing one person; you (*sing.*).
  1885 E. NEVILL *Gleanings with Meanings* 3 As he staggered along the footpath, he met a gentleman, whom he thus accosted, 'Plaise, sor, can yiz be afther tellin me which is the other soide ave the sthreet?'   1976 HURST & CAMERON *In Collaboration* 39 Listen Harry, if youse were an out of work streaker no one'd lend you a pair of strides.

  B. *possessive pron.* Your.
  1979 B. HUMPHRIES *Bazza comes into his Own*, Keep youse eyes peeled.   1983 E. JOLLEY *Mr Scobie's Riddle* 122 'Aw come on. Get all of youse things off,' she said.

yow. [Of unknown origin.] In the phr. **to keep yow,** *to keep nit*, see NIT 2.
  1942 E. LANGLEY *Pea Pickers* 283 You keep yow .. and whistle .. if anyone comes along.   1965 G. MCINNES *Road to Gundagai* 206 Molly kept a look out ('kept yow', as we used to say).

Yowah nut /'jaʊə nʌt/. [f. the name of an opal field w. of Cunnamulla in s. Qld.] An ironstone nodule (see quot. 1972), occas. having a core of precious opal.
  1932 I.L. IDRIESS *Prospecting for Gold* 249 Inside an occasional boulder is a 'kernel' of opal, hence 'kernel opal'. The 'Yowah nuts', in the Eulo district, are famous. These 'nuts' are ironstone packed like pebbles and the kernels when produced gems fit for a queen's purse.   1972 S.N. BAWDEN *Austral. Gemstones* 68 Yowah Nut is the name given to almond-shaped nodules of ironstone on the opal fields at Yowah in south-western Queensland.

yowe, yowie, varr. YOE.

yowhi, yowi, varr. YOHI.

yowie /'jaʊi/. [a. Yuwaalaraay *yuwi* dream spirit.] An ape-like monster supposed to inhabit parts of eastern Australia: see quot. 1980 (1). Also *attrib.* and *transf.*
  1975 *Bulletin* (Sydney) 17 May 20/1 The monster—the 'Yowie'—currently causing trouble in the central-west of N.S.W.   1980 M. MCADOO *If only I'd Listened* ('George Nott'), 'E'd be about six foot easy tall, broad, an' a sort of brownish fur lookin' stuff all over 'im, an' standing up like a man... We didn't know what the name of it was then, but .. a lot of people've been seein' them around the eastern parts, an' they're known as the 'Yowie'.   1980 *Austral. Infantry* Dec. 10 Current equipment includes .. Denison smock or 'Yowie Suit'.   1982 ROBSON & BARNES *Dare to be Different* 31 The city fathers met and agreed to build a yowie. You know .. a yeti .. an abominable snowman.

yu /juː/. Also **yaw.** [a. Western Desert language *yuu*.] An Aboriginal shelter, *spec.* BREAKWIND 1.
  1950 V.E. TURNER *Ooldea* 136 There are three kinds of native homes—houses (karrpa), shelter (wilja) and breakwinds (yaw).   1979 M. HEPPELL *Black Reality* 144 The two traditional shelters of an Aboriginal camp are the *yu* (windbreak) and the *wiltja* (literally, shade). As their names imply, one is protection from the wind, the other is protection from the heat of the sun.

yugari, var. UGARI.

yulka, var. YELKA.

yungan /'jʌŋgən/. *Obs.* Also **youngon, youngun, yungun.** [a. Yagara (and neighbouring languages) *yaŋan*.] A dugong. See also MANATEE.
  1836 J. BACKHOUSE *Narr. Visit Austral. Colonies* (1843) 368 The Blacks .. value the flesh of another cetaceous animal, called here Youngon, the Dugong of India, *Halicore Dugong*.   1841 *Sydney Herald* 5 May 2/5 Should any of the tribes on the sea coast have been so fortunate as to catch a sea-hog—called *youngun*—which sometimes is the size of a young bullock, intelligence of the event is immediately sent along

the coast. **1847** J.D. LANG *Cooksland* 97 But the fish, or rather sea-monster, peculiar to Moreton Bay, and the East coast to the northward, is a species of sea-cow or manatee, called by the black natives *yungan*. **1852** J. MACGILLIVRAY *Narr. Voyage H.M.S. Rattlesnake* I. 48 The Australian dugong (*Halicore Australis*) which is the object of a regular fishery .. on account of its valuable oil .. and is harpooned by the natives, who know it under the name of *Yung-un*.

Z

zac. Also **sac, zack**. [Prob. f. Scot. dial. *saxpence*.]
1. A sixpence. Also *transf*., a trifling sum of money.
1898 *Bulletin* (Sydney) 1 Oct. 14/3, 6d. a 'zack'. 1908 *Truth* (Sydney) 8 Nov. 1/7 'Wanted, respectable person, all duties, wages 2s. 6d. per week!' Ye gods! respectability at two and a sac per week.
2. A prison sentence of six years or six months.
1919 V. MARSHALL *World of Living Dead* 84 Done the zac I got fer cattle duffin' up Gilgandra way, A zac's hard labour—wot I had ter do. 1971 J. MCNEIL *Chocolate Frog* (1973) 20 *Tosser*: How long are yer doin'? *Kevin*: Six months .. down at the Petty Sessions. . . *Shirker*: . . Why'd yer *get* the zac?

Zambuk /'zæmbʌk/. Also **Zambuck**. [The proprietary name of an antiseptic ointment.] A member of the St John's Ambulance Brigade, esp. such a person in attendance at a sporting event.
[1902 *Truth* (Sydney) 21 Dec. 7/4 *Zam-buk*. Name carries no meaning. The ointment carries a blessing. 1918 N.Z. *Chrons. N.Z.E.F.* 21 June 221 The tenderfoot and Zambuk, Working madly in the trenches.] 1941 S.J. BAKER *Pop. Dict. Austral. Slang* 91 *Zambuck*, a first-aid man in attendance at a sporting contest. 1948 R. RAVEN-HART *Canoe in Aust.* 145 Play struck me as very clean, but accidents are frequent, and ambulance men, 'Zambuks' in Australian slang, are often busy.

zamia /'zeɪmɪə/. [Transf. use of the plant genus name *Zamia*, under which Austral. species of *Macrozamia* were formerly classified.] A cycad, esp. of the genus *Macrozamia* (see MACROZAMIA). Also *attrib.*, esp. as **zamia palm**.
1838 J. BACKHOUSE *Narr. Visit Austral. Colonies* (1843) 541 In some places between Perth and Guildford the Zamias are very fine their trunks, which are always blackened by fire, being six or eight feet in circumference, and as much in height, and surmounted by fine crests, of stiff pinnate palm-like leaves four feet long or more. . . In this part the natives bury or macerate the nuts, till the rinds become half decomposed, in which state they eat the rind, ejecting the kernel; in N.S. Wales, they pound and macerate the kernels and then roast and eat, the rough paste. 1984 *Austral. Plants* Dec. 15 *Macrozamia riedlei* is commonly called the 'Zamia palm' by West Australians.

zebra. Used *attrib.* in the names of animals: **zebra duck**, *pink-eared duck*, see PINK *a*.; also *ellipt*. as **zebra**; **finch**, the small bird *Taeniopygia guttata* widespread in much of mainland Aust., having black and white tail bars, the mature male having a chestnut ear patch; *chestnut-eared finch*, see CHESTNUT *a*.; **fish**, any of several marine fish, usu. of s. Aust., esp. *Melambaphes zebra* and *Enoplosus armatus* (see OLD WIFE); **parrot** *obs*., BUDGERIGAR; also **zebra parakeet**.
1955 S. OSBORNE *Duck Shooting Aust.* 11 They have most peculiar brown and white striped markings on their breast, and an inconspicuous pink marking near the ear; hence the name Zebra or pink-eared **duck**. 1966 P. COWAN *Seed* 141 Grey teal, Zebras, Black duck. Get some really good sport here. 1936 C.T. MADIGAN *Central Aust.* 103 Flocks of the most typical bird of Central Australia, the pretty little zebra **finch**, with its husky chirp. 1771 *Philos. Trans. R. Soc. London* LXI. 247 It is called by the Commodore the Zebra **fish**. 1860 G. BENNETT *Gatherings of Naturalist* 228 A very delicate and beautiful little Parrot . . is the Canary or Zebra **Parrot**. 1896 F.G. AFLALO *Sketch Nat. Hist. Aust.* 125 Grass Parrakeets .. feed .. mostly on the ground .. and almost the only one in evidence at the stores of London dealers is the favourite little warbling Bujerigar (*Melopsittacus undulatus*), or, as it is variously called, the 'Zebra Parrakeet' .. 'Shell Parrot', etc.

ziff. [Of unknown origin.] A beard; also *transf.*, an old man, a 'grey-beard'.
1917 *Stretcher* (Melbourne) Mar. 9 Z is for 'Ziff' which appears on the lip To call it a 'mo' would give one the pip. 1961 C. MCKAY *This is Life* 141 This brought the 'ziffs' into the picture—ancient white-bearded directors who should make way for young men.
Hence **(be-)ziffed** *a*., bearded.
1973 *Southerly* i. 7 Other foreigners in Ellie's court are from a nearby cell of the B.B.C., multi-lingual translators from the Foreign News Service, all with crystalline English accents . . and be-ziffed as wisdom-saturated Mamelukes. 1978 R.J. BRITTEN *Around Cassowary Rock* 53 The adventures of Long John Silver, Blackbeard, Bully Hayes and Mutiny on the Bounty all rolled up and thrown together in one big black-ziffed personage by the name of Glub.

zigzag.
1. *Hist*. A type of railway line designed for very steep gradients, having the track laid in the form of one or more Zs with reversing points where the line doubles back to enable a train to reverse its direction.
1871 *Austral. Town & Country Jrnl.* (Sydney) 13 May 590/3 The difficulties are comparatively removed now that railways and zig-zags carry us in comfort over what was at one time the worst parts of the road. 1935 A. RAYMENT *Romance of Railway* 27 Mr Whitton's great engineering feat of the two Zig Zags; the lesser, known as the Lapstone Zig Zag on the eastern approach and the Great Zig Zag near Lithgow.
2. Special Comb. **zigzag fence**, see quot. 1890. Also *ellipt*., as **zigzag**.
1882 ARMSTRONG & CAMPBELL *Austral. Sheep Husbandry* 194 Zig-Zag Fence. This fence resembles the chock and log in its formation, but differs from it in having no chocks. 1890 A. MACKAY *Austral. Agriculturist* (ed. 2) 32 Zigzag Fence .. is made by embedding the butt end of one tree in a notch cut for the purpose in the top end of another, laying them along the ground in a zigzag form, so that each log intersects the entire line at an angle of forty-five degrees. When the logs have been piled up to the desired height, cross-logs and a heavy top-rail are then put up . . so as to bind the whole. 1978 M. WALKER *Pioneer Crafts Early Aust.* 28 In the Wimmera about 1863–4, another type was termed 'zig-zag', being made up from five pine or buloke logs nine feet (2.7 m.) long each with a V-shaped indentation, top and bottom, allowing the logs to be seated securely one to the other.

zwei, var. SWY.

zygomaturus /zaɪgoʊməˈtjurəs/. [The animal genus *Zygomaturus* was named by W.S. Macleay (1792–1865), Trustee of the Australian Museum: see quot. 1857.] A large extinct marsupial of the Austral. genus *Zygomaturus*.
1857 *Sydney Morning Herald* 9 Sept. 2/6 Another characteristic of this new quadruped, which may be called Zygomaturus, is the great distance of the zygomaturic arch from the temporal bone. 1986 *Sydney Morning Herald* 15 Jan. 24/4 The Victoria Cave was first explored in 1969. 'So far we have discovered 78 different species from frogs to the Zygomaturus, which is a very large quadruped marsupial, about as large as a bull.